CIVIL AIRCRAFT AND GLIDER

REGISTERS

OF THE

UNITED KINGDOM & IRELAND

2002

CIVIL AIRCRAFT AND GLIDER REGISTERS OF UNITED KINGDOM AND IRELAND 2002

Thirty Eighth Year of Publication - Compiled & Edited by Barrie Womersley

CONTENTS PAGES

Published by: Air-Britain (Historians) Limited
Sales Department: 41 Penshurst Road, Leigh, Tonbridge, Kent TN11 8HL
Membership Enquiries: (UK) 1 Rose Cottages, 179 Penn Road, Hazlemere, Bucks HP15 7NE
Web-site: http://www.air-britain.com Sales e-mail: mike@absales.demon.co.uk

Front Cover: Lindstrand LBL-31A balloon lifting off at Chateau d'Oex 20.1.01 (Peter Bish)

Rear Cover: Chrislea CH.3 Super Ace departing from Wroughton's Great Vintage Flying Weekend on 12.5.01 (Dave Partington)
Auster 5 G-BXKX was a visitor to Air-Britain's Fly-In at North Weald 25.8.01 (Chris Chatfield)
Schleicher Ka 6CR BTM/BGA1222 "211" seen in the July sunshine at Aston Down (Dave Partington)

ISBN 0 85130 324 2 ISSN 0264-5270

Printed by Bell and Bain Ltd, Glasgow

INTRODUCTION AND EDITORIAL

Welcome to the 38th annual Civil Aircraft & Glider Registers of the United Kingdom & Ireland.

The year 2001 was a significant one in that two new series were introduced. Finally, the Civil Aviation Authority (CAA) introduced the G-Cxxx series properly, and within the normal sequence of events, whilst the British Gliding Association (*BGA) Trigraph system moved into the KAA set of letters. The CAA has also gone on-line and many members are now making use of their web-site facility. For the first time access can be made on a daily basis to inspect full details of individual aircraft and also download brief lists covering both new and cancelled registrations. All this some days before the information appears in the UK Register section of "Air-Britain News". Nonetheless, both "News" and this annual Register will continue to record the complete and accurate picture behind this basic information and thereby expand the historic source in the fullness of time.

Following on from my comments last year about the CAA's registration system we continue to record numerous entries where aircraft have lapsed Certificates of Airworthiness including some many years out of date. The fact that the aircraft themselves retain their Certificates of Registration and remain current on the Register complicates matters. As part of a continuing review we have noted those aircraft, where there have not been any reports of recent sightings, by use of the term "current status unknown". This term is also used for those aircraft which have been formally cancelled by the CAA from the official Register but which have remained in this register, as denoted by an asterisk, for the very reason that they have been observed in recent years. In this case I am conscious that there has been a considerable accumulation of elderly entries without any recent justification and a number of members have pointed this out. Therefore, unless any fresh information is received during this year it is proposed to remove those aircraft that are formally cancelled and for which there has been no sighting since the end of 1999. I hope all this will stimulate members to research the latest situation and report back either to me or to Air-Britain News' "Round and About" section. Of course, this guiding principle will not apply to those civil aircraft held in Museums or private collections although I am aware that a number of historic entries have been retained where aircraft have long been removed from the CAA Register, sold abroad to overseas collections, but remain displayed in their original "G-xxxx" markings. Ideally, these could be listed separately.

There are a number of presentational changes again this year. There has been some re-alignment of the text and whilst doing this I have formatted all supporting notes in italics. In this context as British Airways continue to remove their varied World tail schemes there is no longer a need to refer to "Union Flag" tail-schemes because they are now the norm. Throughout the book type descriptions continue to be enhanced. The list of airfield frequencies has now been removed and placed within the new base index that is including for the first time in this year's UK Quick Reference book. I have also established separate indices for the UK & Irish registers. Finally, I have introduced two new sub-sections. There are now listings of both "B Conditions" identities and ICAO registrations, both past and current. I hope this will serve to amplify the Previous Identities columns.

I must single out a few people for specific mention. Once again Colin Smith has provided us with a significant amount of new, and correcting information relating to type designations and previous identities of Piper aircraft. Our microlight specialist, Barry Taylor, has also supplied a considerable quantity of new historical detail going back to the early 1980s. In both cases there is a good deal of fresh and amended information and this is underlined. In the glider area you will note that Phil Butler is now expanding the information in the British Glider Association register to cover full C of A dates. Bernard Martin has again ensured that the facts, especially relating to probable bases, are correct and then providing a master list to work on. Peter Hornfeck has overseen the Irish Section again this year. Paul Hewins has also worked hard to bring the non-UK section up to date and to point out the numerous elderly entries in the UK register. Finally, Mike Cain continues to monitor and report the Southend area each month without fail. Gentlemen, my thanks to you all.

The CAA's annual UK statistical information is again included. In 2001 the culling of non-effective microlights abated somewhat and attention turned to removing numerous Hot Air & Minimum Lift Balloons from the Register. As a result of this action and a general turndown in the airline economy the overall trend flattened and the Register grew by a single aircraft over the previous year! I am grateful to the CAA for providing me with similar registration data for the years 1985 to 2000 and this is reproduced below. It makes interesting reading when placed with the summary data for 2001. I will leave readers to draw their own conclusions.

Many thanks to this year's contributors and to the continued support from the regular stalwarts. For this edition I would like to thank the following correspondents [as always in alphabetic order}: Dave Almey/Skycraft web site, Michael Austen, Ron Bartlett/Autogyro Quarterly, Rob Barlex, Steve Barnes, Jeff Bell, Blackpool Spotters, D Bougourd/Channel Isles Aviation News, Richard Bowater, Jim Brazier, Peter Budden, Chris Busby, Phil Butler, Ian Burnett, Mike Cain, Paul Carr, Russell Carter, Richard Cawsey, Chris Chatfield, Barry Clay, Dennis Clement, Mark Collington, Howard Curtis, Terry Dann, Mike Draper, Phil Dunnington, Ken Ede, Malcolm Fillmore, Bill Fisher, Ray Fitton, Peter Gerhardt, Jennifer Gradidge, Dave Haines, Paul Hewins, Nigel Hitchman, Peter Hornfeck, Paul Hughes, Pete Hughes, Mark Jones, Phil & Nigel Kemp, Bob Kent,, Kevin Latham, Bernard Martin, Neil McKinnon, Terry Mitchell, Tony Morris, Alistair Ness, Dave Partington, Dave Peel, Tony Pither, Nigel Ponsford, Geoff Potts, Robin Sauvery, Don Schofield, Trevor Sexton, Mark Shortman, Graham Slack, Colin M Smith, Tony Smith, Martyn Steggalls, Keith Tayles, Barrie V Taylor, John Tietjen, Henk Wadman, Rod Webb, Pete Webber, Steve Wells, David Wise and, finally, to Angela for her tolerance!

Thanks are also due to those who send in relevant reports and material direct to our monthly "Air-Britain News" sub-editors and, in particular to Graham Slack, Co-ordinating Editor for supplying essential updates throughout the year. Many thanks again to Alan Johnson, editor of A-BN's "United Kingdom Register" section, for supplying the official Civil Aviation Authority data and to the CAA in London for their assistance.

All official UK registration information is published by the CAA and includes the issue and status of each Certificate of Airworthiness. Both Registration & Ownership data is correct to 31st January 2002. Glider information is current to 30th January 2002.

Comments and further information for the 2003 edition should reach me no later than 15th January 2003, please.

FEBRUARY 2002

BARRIE WOMERSLEY
19 The Pastures, Westwood
Bradford-on-Avon
Wiltshire BA15 2BH
email: brw936@netscapeonline.co.uk

USERS' GUIDE

There are a number of purposes to this annual volume. The primary one is to list all aircraft on the current civil aircraft registers, giving full details of types and previous identities, registered ownership and/or operator, probable home base and certification of airworthiness status. This information reproduces, expands upon and amplifies the official country registers. However, we go well beyond that; included are all other known, but no longer currently registered, UK and Irish aircraft noted in a reasonably identifiable condition and which are displayed or on/for rebuild. Some of these are held for instructional, fire or spares use. The majority of these are in located in the UK and Ireland but a few are resident abroad. In addition we detail the extensive numbers of foreign registered aircraft now located in both the UK and Ireland, some of which may aspire to G- & EI- registrations in due course. Finally, we include a comprehensive listing of all gliders in use throughout the area in order to present an all-inclusive guide of the civil aviation scene.

Secondly on a more technical level, we cater for the aviation specialist and historian who wishes to know more about a particular aircraft by providing detailed information such as non-standard engine power and reasons for that aircraft's non-airworthy state, if applicable and where known. It has been the policy for some years to record engine details in the text, for example the modification of an airframe to receive a non standard engine has to be approved by the CAA and is then recorded in their Register .We also record this change. When microlights first arrived in 1981 there was little standardisation and, consequently, we recorded all engine information. Now that the majority of microlight/SLAs are commercially produced, either in whole or kit form, engine fitment has become more standard to type but not in all cases. A similar situation exists for BMAA and PFA approved types. An initial attempt has been made in year's edition to remove engine model information where we judge this to be superfluous. This will continue next year.

A guide to the main text is as follows:

Registration (Regn) Registrations are set out in alphabetic order. Aircraft no longer currently registered are marked with an asterisk (*). A few aircraft, either real or static reproductions are identified in fictitious UK civil marks for display purposes and are shown in the Index. Those marks which have been re-issued or re-allotted, particularly either if the first holder or allottee did not use the marks or they were not allocated at the time, are shown with the suffix (2) after the registration.

Type We adopt the official type description as set down by the manufacturer or designer. Where there is doubt, reference is made to the relevant issue of "Jane's All the Worlds Aircraft", "Airlife's World Aircraft" and the annual "World Directory of Leisure Aviation". Indication is given if the manufacturer is a successor company or a licence builder - although not always if it is merely a sub-contractor. Under this column, we show engine types in parenthesis if the engine is non-standard, for all PFA & BMAA approved SLA types and for those vintage and classic aircraft where engines can vary. Additional explanatory notes show details of any unrepaired accidents and comments on the airframe's identity and where the true position is at variance with the official records.

Constructors' Number (C/N) This is the often referred to as the Manufacturers' Serial Number and is generally quoted in the official registers. Some aircraft have more than one c/n, for example PFA and BMAA approved types can have the home-builders' own reference number as well as an official sequential number allotted by these organisations plus, on occasion, a manufacturers' plan or kit number. All are shown where known. Those homebuilds and microlights which have been registered without a c/n are identified by the CAA using owners' initials following by "01". These numbers are replaced if the correct c/n is identified. Although manufacturers often identify weightshift microlights with separate c/ns for the Trike unit and for the Wing respectively the CAA usually only records the latter c/n. For example, manufacturers Hornet, Mainair and Medway issue a composite c/n comprising both units. Both c/ns are identified, if known, with the c/n for the Trike unit preceding that for the Wing.

Previous Identities (P/I) These are set out in reverse order with the most recent identity first. Those registrations shown in parenthesis were allotted but believed never officially used. The nationality of foreign military serials is indicated only where it may not be apparent. Manufacturers' test marks, also known as "B Conditions" identities are given where known.

Registration Date (Date) This is the date of the original registration for those particular marks even where subsequently removed and restored.

Owner/Operator This is the registered owner for current aircraft as recorded in CAA records. Where the operator is known to be different this is shown in parenthesis. Included under this column are details of the latest reported status, for example if the C of A is not current or the aircraft is known to be under repair plus details of any names and, in particular, any military colour schemes and marks worn. Some aircraft are shown as temporary un-registered ("Temp unregd"); this is where the CAA has not received an application from a new owner following a sale. Usually the CAA gives a period of discretion and if no

response is received the Certificate is cancelled and the aircraft is not permitted to fly. Such action usually stimulates the new owner to produce the relevant documentation.

Probable Base The information in this column is not guaranteed: there is no official information. Reports by members and other readers who visit airfields and strips are perused to compile this column. Aircraft change base frequently. Balloons are generally shown as being based at the owner's registered address. When the location is uncertain the owner's hometown is shown in parenthesis except in the case of balloons. Readers are reminded that the identification of a base, particularly if it is a private strip, is not an invitation to visit and in a number of cases visiting is actively discouraged because of previous abuses. We recognise the need for privacy in this area and consequently not all information held is published.

C of A Expiry Information is taken from the monthly and annual details published by the CAA. The expiry date indicates the currency of the aircraft's Certificate and details of the suffix letters applied are set out below. Where a C of A has expired or lapsed and an aircraft has been reported since that date further details are shown.

UK CERTIFICATES OF AIRWORTHINESS (C OF A) STATUS

The coding after the date of expiry indicates the C of A category. No code letter indicates a private category C of A of one or three year duration.

Others are: -

A	Aerial Work: Normally indicating crop-spraying or banner towing/aerial advertising.
E	Exemption: Applicable only to microlights not subject to permit to fly status, no new issues are being made.
F	Ferry: normally issued for two months, and commonly for overseas sale, or an unlicensed aircraft being flown to another airfield for overhaul.
NE	Non-Expiring: Hot-Air balloons were, until recently, usually certified as such. The suffix in parenthesis indicates whether it is an Aerial Work, Private or Transport certificate. Non-Expiring exemptions were also given a few years ago to certain early microlights. These are being progressively upgraded. Any without a date should be considered to have lapsed. A few other N/E certificates are used for exports.
P	Permit to Fly: Introduced in 1950 covering homebuilders, microlights and vintage aircraft - normally issued for one year.
PF	Permit to Fly (Ferry): Issued for one specific flight only - the aircraft need not be of a type that normally operates under a permit to fly.
P	Permit to Fly (Test): Issued for varying periods of one, two or three months for test purposes leading usually to the issue of a full one year permit to fly. Only a few now seem to be issued.
S	Special: Mainly lapsed now and replaced by permits to fly but sometimes still used for manufacturers trials aircraft, particularly for overseas demonstration.
T	Transport (Passenger): Issued to any aircraft operated for hire or reward, usually for either one or three years duration.
TC	Transport (Cargo): As above, but aircraft restricted to carrying cargo for hire or reward. Few aircraft fall into this category, and
X	Export: Issued for limited period solely to facilitate delivery overseas.

GLOSSARY of TERMS and ABBREVIATIONS

AA	Automobile Association
AB	Aktiebolaget (1)
AAC	Army Air Corps
AAIU	Aircraft Accident Investigation Unit
AERONCA	Aeronautical Corpn of America
AESL	Aero Engine Services Ltd
AIRCO	Aircraft Manufacturing Co
ALAT	Aviation Légère de l'Armée de Terre
AMD-BA	Avions Marcel Dassault-Breguet & Aviation
ANEC	Air Navigation & Engineering Co
ANG	Air National Guard
APSS	Aviation Preservation Society of Scotland
ASS	Air Signals School
AVIA	Azionara Vercellese Ind.Areo
A/c	Aircraft
Aka	also known as
Assn	Association
BA	British Aircraft Manufacturing Co Ltd
BAC	British Aircraft Company
BAC	British Aircraft Corporation
BAT	British Aerial Transport Co Ltd
BoBMF	Battle of Britain Memorial Flight
BMAA	British Microlight Aircraft Association
BV	Besloten Vennootschap (2)
CAARP	Coopérative des Ateliers a Aeronautiques de la Région Parisienne
CAF	Candian Air Force
CASA	Construcciones Aeronáuticas SA
CC	County Council
CCF	Canadian Car & Foundry
CEA	Centre Est Aviation
CZAL	Ceskoslovenske Zavody Automobilove a Letecke
Coln	Collection
Corpn	Corporation
C	circa
C of A	Certificate of Airworthiness
C of R	Certificate of Registration
cf/f	Cleared for first flight (PFA clearance)
c/s	Colour scheme
DBF	Destroyed by fire
DOSAAF	Dobrovol'noe Obshchestvo Sodeistviya Armii, Aviasii i Flotu
EMBRAER	Empresa Brasileira de Aeronautica SA
Eng	Engineering
EoN	Elliotts of Newbury Ltd
ERCO	Engineering & Research Corporation
ETPS	Empire Test Pilots' School
Ets.	Etablissement
FAA	Fleet Air Arm
FTS	Flying Training School
FB	Free Balloon
FTS	Flying Training School
f/c	Flying Club
f/f	First flight
fsm	Full Scale Model
GAF	Government Aircraft Factory
GC	Gliding Club
GmbH	Gesellschaft mit beschrankter Haftung (3)
HAFB	(Hot-Air) Free Balloon
IAR	Industria Aeronautica Romania
IAV	Intreprindere deAvione
ICA	Intreprinderea de Constructii Aeronautice
ICAO	International Civil Aviation Organisation
III	Initiziative Industriali Italian
IMCO	Intermountain Manufacturing Co
IWM	Imperial War Museum
Intl	International
JAA	Joint Aviation Authorities
JAR	Joint Aviation Regulations
JEFTS	Joint Elementary Flying Training School
KG	Kommanditgesellschaft (4)
KK	Kabushiki Kaisha (5)
LAK	Litovskaya Aviatsyonnaya Konstruktsiya
LET	Letecky Narodny Podnik
LLC	Limited Liability Corporation (6)
LVG	Luft-Verkehrs Gesellschaft
Lsg	Leasing
Ltd	Limited (7)
MBB	Messerschmitt-Bölkow-Blohm
MLB	Minimum Lift Balloon
MPA	Man Powered Aircraft
NV	Naamloze Vennootschap (8)
Nk	Not known
Ntu	Not taken up
n/w	nose-wheel
OGMA	Oficinas Gerais de Material Aeronautico
Op	Operated by
PFA	Popular Flying Association
PIK	Polytecknikkojen Ilmailukerho
PLC	Public Limited Company (9)
PRC	Peoples' Republic of China
PT	Pesawat Terbang (10)
PWFU	Permanently WFU
PZL	Panstwowe Zaklady Lotnicze (State Aviation Works)
qv	which see
R	Reservation
RAF	Royal Aircraft Factory
RAF	Royal Air Force
RAFC	RAF College

RCAF	Royal Candian Air Force
Rep	Reproduction
RFC	Royal Flying Corps
RN	Royal Navy
RNAS	Royal Naval Air Service
RSAF	Royal Saudi Air Force
RTS	Reduced to spares
SA	Société Anonyme (11)
SA	Sociedad Anónima (12)
SA	Spoika Akeyjna (13)
SAAC	Society of Amateur Aircraft Constructors
SAI	Skandinavsk Aero Industri
SAN	Société Aeronautique Normande
SAR	Search and Rescue
SIPA	Société Industrielle pour l'Aéronautique
SNCAC	Société Nationale de Constructions Aéronautiques du Centre
SNCAN	Société Nationale de Constructions Aéronautiques du Nord
SOCATA	Société de Construction d'Avions de Tourisme et d'Affaires
SRL	Société Anonyme à Responsabilité Limitée (14)
SpA	Societa per Azioni (15)
SPP	Strojirny Prvni Petiletky
SEAE	School of Electrical & Aeronautical Engineering
Srs.	Series
SS	Special Shape
SZD	Szybowcowy Zaklad Dowswiadczalny
TAD	Technical Aid & Demonstrator
TBA	To be advised
TEAM	Tennessee Engineering & Manufacturing
TWU	Tactical Weapons Unit
t/a	trading as
tr	Trustee
t/s	tail scheme
t/w	tail-wheel
UAS	University Air Squadron
USAAC	United States Army Air Corps
VW	Volkswagen
WACO	Weaver Aircraft Corpn
WFU	Withdrawn from Use

<u>Company Constitution Notes</u>

(1)	Sweden	Joint Stock
(2)	Netherlands	Private
(3)	Germany	Private Limited
(4)	Germany	Limited Partnership
(5)	Japan	
(6)	USA	Limited Partnership
(7)	UK	Private Limited
(8)	Belgium/Netherlands	
(9)	UK	Public Limited
(10)	Indonesia	
(11)	France/Romania	Public Limited
(12)	Spain	Public Limited
(13)	Poland	
(14)	Italy	Public Limited Company
(15)	Italy	Public Limited Company

AIRCRAFT ON THE UNITED KINGDOM REGISTER OF CIVIL AIRCRAFT AS AT 1 JANUARY 2002 [2001]

SUMMARY

CLASS		CERTIFICATION STATUS							TOTAL
		TC(P)	TC(C)	AW	PTE	SPEC	PERMIT	NOT CURRENTLY CERTIFICATED	
1.	HEAVIER THAN AIR AIRCRAFT								
1.1	AEROPLANES								
1.1.1	MAX. WEIGHT EXCEEDING 5700 KG	974 [919]	7 [10]	20 [22]	20 [26]		27 [30]	133 [78]	1181 [1085]
1.1.2	MAX. WEIGHT EXCEEDING 2730 KG BUT NOT EXCEEDING 5700 KG	149 [144]		9 [8]	48 [54]		71 [75]	101 [90]	378 [371]
1.1.3	MAX. WEIGHT NOT EXCEEDING 2730 KG	2229 [2154]		18 [19]	2571 [2594]	3 [2]	1398 [1319]	1991 [2163]	8210 [8251]
1.1.4	MICROLIGHTS INC SLA						2161 [2029]	1360 [1426]	3521 [3462]
1.2	ROTORCRAFT								
1.2.1	HELICOPTERS	749 [703]			154 [165]		32 [23]	155 [166]	1090 [1057]
1.2.2	GYROPLANES						64 [57]	178 [176]	242 [233]
1.3	GLIDERS							1 [1]]	1 [1]
1.4	HANG GLIDERS (INCL FLPH)							10 [7]	10 [7]
2.	LIGHTER THAN AIR AIRCRAFT								
2.1	AIRSHIPS								
2.1.1	GAS FILLED AIRSHIPS	1 [0]		-				3 [3]	4 [4]
2.1.2	HOT AIR AIRSHIPS			12 [11]				12 [19]	24 [30]
2.2	FREE BALLOONS								
2.2.1	GAS FILLED BALLOONS			1 [3]	0 [1]			10 [8]	11 [12]
2.2.2	HOT AIR BALLOONS	153 [210]		479 [515]	27 [36]			1017 [1044]	1676 [1806]
2.2.3	GAS/HOT AIR BALLOONS			0 [1]				7 [10]	7 [11]
2.2.4	MINIMUM LIFT BALLOONS							118 [150]	118 [150]
TOTALS		4255 [4130]	7 [10]	539 [579]	2820 [2876]	3 [3]	3753 [3533]	5096 [5341]	16473 [16472]

NOTES

1) Includes aeroplanes, which are, classified as Self-Launching Motor Gliders (SLMG)

2) The criteria for classifying an aircraft as a Microlight are specified in British Civil Airworthiness Requirements (Section S). Originally this was 390kg limit but changed in 1999 with the introduction of the temporary category Small Light Aeroplane (SLA) with a maximum permitted gross weight of 450kg. A revised definition of the Microlight category @ 450kg comes into force 1st April 2002.

3) A glider may fly unregistered on any flight within the United Kingdom when not used for public transport or Aerial work.

4) FLPH = Foot Launched Powered Hang-Glider.

5) Certification Status:

a)	TC(P) = Transport (Passenger)	2730 kg	b)	TC(C) = Transport (Cargo)	2730 to 5700 kg
c)	AW = Aerial Work	5700 kg	d)	PTE =Private	
e)	SPEC= Special		f)	PERMIT =Permit to Fly	

g) NCC =Not currently certificated, that is aircraft awaiting certification, certification expired or withdrawn, or not subject to certification.

Data produced by CAA Aircraft Registration Section, Kingsway, London WC2

UK REGISTERED AIRCRAFT AS AT 1ST JANUARY EACH YEAR

ALL WEIGHTS

AIRCRAFT CLASS	1985	1986	1987	1988	1989	1990	1991	1992	1993	1994	1995	1996	1997	1998	1999	2000	2001	2002
AIRSHIP	31	35	34	38	46	53	50	51	54	47	47	40	40	40	40	42	33	28
BALLOON	525	608	702	821	966	1146	1302	1437	1499	1505	1586	1650	1730	1727	1693	1757	1829	1694
BALLOON (MLB)	504	500	504	497	246	245	243	245	245	163	172	171	168	169	150	150	150	118
FIXED WING	6365	6688	6777	7024	7539	7975	8361	8460	8548	8604	8644	8667	8784	8940	9191	9284	9436	9769
FIXED WING (SLMG)	136	156	178	183	192	195	208	213	237	233	238	238	244	254	262	267	271	Note 1
GLIDER	13	14	13	7	7	6	6	9	9	9	8	8	8	7	7	7	1	1
GYROPLANE	116	121	130	134	161	202	228	210	218	229	246	257	261	261	265	244	233	242
HANG-GLIDER	0	0	0	0	0	0	0	0	0	0	0	0	0	0	0	1	7	10
HELICOPTER	520	571	587	601	703	842	912	902	876	832	828	838	859	906	980	1013	1057	1090
MICROLIGHT	1574	1900	2299	2628	3011	3290	3030	3167	3314	3299	3225	3163	3183	3259	3378	3410	3261	3521
SMALL LIGHT AEROPLANE	0	0	0	0	0	3	9	15	16	19	20	22	25	30	46	117	194	Note 2
TOTAL	9784	10593	11224	11993	12871	13957	14349	14709	15016	14940	15014	15058	15302	15593	16012	16292	16472	16473

Note 1: Included in FIXED WING entry

Note 2: Included in MICROLIGHT entry

Data produced by CAA Aircraft Registration Section, Kingsway, London WC2

SECTION 1

PART 1 – FIRST PERMANENT UNITED KINGDOM REGISTER

The Air Board was formed in May 1916 and established the Civil Aerial Transport Committee (CATC) a year later. The CATC's primary brief was to report on the measures necessary to develop aviation for civil and commercial purposes. Meantime the Air Force Bill received the Royal Assent in November 1917 leading to the creation of the Air Council and Air Ministry. Although the Armistice was negotiated in November 1918 official restrictions on civil flying were not lifted as, technically, a state of war continued until the signing of the Peace Treaty in July 1919.

There were no international regulations controlling the registration of civil aircraft within the United Kingdom at the end of the First World War. Consequently the Air Ministry's Civil Air Department specified a system of temporary registration marks in May 1919. This ran until July 1919. Two registers were established for (i) military aircraft sold for civil purposes and already bearing Service serials - they would be allocated their serials as registration marks with the Service ring markings obliterated and (ii) new aircraft and those built from spares - they were allocated marks in a special Service sequence commencing at K100. Subsequently, a number of these aircraft were re-allocated registrations in the first Permanent United Kingdom Register of Civil Aircraft which replaced the two Temporary Registers. This was inaugurated on 31st July 1919 and ran until 29th July 1928 when the registration G-EBZZ had been issued. With the growth of international civil aviation new regulations commenced on 1st January 1929 - see below.

Meantime the civil use of Airships and Balloons came under the supplementary air traffic regulations of the Air Navigation Act 1911-1919. A separate Lighter-than-Air Register (G-FAAA-FAAZ) was established until the end of 1928 when the Director-General of Civil Aviation decided to terminate it and authorise that all airships and balloons would be registered in the new sequence of registration marks commencing at G-AAAA. The fresh series of registrations was introduced retrospectively from 30th July 1928 - see SECTION 1, Part 2.

Regn	Type	C/n	P/I	Date	Owner/operator	Probable Base	CA Expy

G-EAAA – G-EAZZ

Regn	Type	C/n	P/I	Date	Owner/operator	Probable Base	CA Expy
G-EACN*	BAT FK.23 Bantam 1	FK23/15	K-123	29. 5.19	Aviodome/Early Birds Foundation		
	(ABC Wasp)		F1654			Lelystad, The Netherlands	
					(NTU - No CofA issued: on rebuild 1992)		
G-EACQ*	Avro 534 Baby	534/1	VH-UCQ	29. 5.19	Queensland Cultural Centre		
			G-AUCQ/G-EACQ/K-131			Brisbane, Australia	
	(Sold Australia 6.21 & regd G-AUCQ 12.7.21: cancelled 7.21: to VH-UCQ 10.30) (On display as "G-EACQ")						
G-EAML*	Airco DH.6	-	C9449	8. 9.19	South African Air Force Museum		
						Pretoria, South Africa	18. 9.20
	(Cancelled 19.9.19: to South Africa &.components only preserved as "G-EAML": current status unknown)						
G-EAOU*	Vickers FB.27A Vimy IV	-	(A5-1)	23.10.19	Sir Ross & Sir Keith Smith War Memorial		
			G-EAOU/F8630			Adelaide, Australia	31.10.20
	(Cancelled 1920: on display Airport Museum as "G-EAOU"- also see SECTION 8, Part 4						
G-EAQM*	Airco DH.9	-	F1278	31.12.19	Australian War Memorial		
	(AS Puma)					Canberra, Australia	1. 1.21
	(NTU & to Australia 1920: cancelled 8.1.20: on display as "G-EAQM")						
G-EASD	Avro 504L floatplane	E.5	S-AHAA	26. 3.20	AJD Engineering Ltd	Moat Farm, Milden	
	(Le Clerget 130hp)		S-AAP/G-EASD/(RAF)		*(Stored pending rebuild 8.93: current status unknown)*		

G-EBAA – G-EBZZ

Regn	Type	C/n	P/I	Date	Owner/operator	Probable Base	CA Expy
G-EBHX	de Havilland DH.53 Humming Bird	98	No.8	22. 9.23	The Shuttleworth Trust	Old Warden	11. 7.02P
	(ABC Scorpion II)		(Lympne 1923)		*"L'Oiseau-Mouche"*		
G-EBIA	R.A.F. SE-5A	654/2404	F904	26. 9.23	The Shuttleworth Trust	Old Warden	31. 5.02P
	(Wolseley Viper 200hp)		"D7000"/G-EBIA/F904		*(As "F904/H" in 56 Sqdn RFC c/s)*		
G-EBIB*	R.A.F. SE.5A	687/2404	F938	26. 9.23	The Science Museum (Flight Gallery)		
	(Regd with c/n 688/2404)					South Kensington, London SW7	8. 8.35
					(WFU & cancelled 1.12.46) (On display as "F937")		
G-EBIC*	R.A.F. SE.5A	688/2404	"B4563"	26. 9.23	RAF Museum	Hendon	3. 9.30
	(Wolseley Viper 200hp)		9208M/G-EBIC/F937		*(WFU 9.30: cancelled 31.12.38) (On display as "F938")*		
	(Regd with c/n 687/2404)						
G-EBIR	de Havilland DH.51	102	VP-KAA	22. 1.24	The Shuttleworth Trust	Old Warden	31. 5.02P
	(ADC Renault 120hp)		G-KAA/G-EBIR		*"Miss Kenya"*		
G-EBJE*	Avro 504K	927		7.24	RAF Museum	Hendon	29. 9.34
	(Includes components of Avro 548A G-EBKN ex E449: allocated 9205M 1994: as "E449")						
G-EBJG*	Parnall Pixie III	-	No.17/18	?. 9.24	Midland Air Museum	Coventry	2.10.36
			(Lympne 1924)		*(Components only for long term rebuild 4.96)*		
G-EBJO	ANEC II	2	No.7	17. 7.24	The Shuttleworth Trust	Old Warden	30.11.35
			(Lympne 1924)		*(Rebuild nearing completion 12.00)*		

G-EBKY	Sopwith Pup	w/o 3004/14	"N5180"	27. 3.25	The Shuttleworth Trust	Old Warden	9. 5.02P
	(Le Rhone 80hp) (ex Sopwith Dove)		"N5184"/G-EBKY		(As "N6181" in 3 Sqdn RNAS c/s) "Happy"		
G-EBLV	de Havilland DH.60 Moth	188		22. 6.25	BAE Systems (Operations) Ltd	Old Warden	21. 6.02P
	(ADC Cirrus III)				(On loan to The Shuttleworth Trust)		
G-EBMB*	Hawker Cygnet I	1	No.14	29. 7.25	RAF Museum	Hendon	30.11.61
	(Bristol Cherub III)		(Lympne 1924)		(Cancelled 30.11.61)		
G-EBNV	English Electric S.1 Wren	4	(BAPC11)	9. 4.26	The Shuttleworth Trust	Old Warden	23.6.87P*
	(ABC 398cc)		G-EBNV				
	(Composite aircraft · principally c/n 3 rebuilt 1955/56: as "No.4": no marks carried: noted 5.01)						
G-EBOV*	Avro 581E Avian	5116	No 9	7. 7.26	Queensland Cultural Centre		
			(Lympne 1926)			Brisbane, Australia	30. 1.29
	(Originally regd as Avro 581, to 581A in 1927 & modified to 581E: cancelled 14.1.30 as sold in Australia)						
G-EBQP	de Havilland DH.53 Humming Bird	114	J7326	?. 4.27	M.C.Russell	Audley End	
					(Stored 12.01: will use wings ex Martin Monoplane G-AEYY & carry "J7326")		
G-EBWD	de Havilland DH.60X Moth	552		2. 3.28	The Shuttleworth Trust	Old Warden	24. 4.02P
	(ADC Hermes 2)						
G-EBXU	de Havilland DH.60X Moth	627		2. 5.28	D.E.Cooper-Maguire	Goodwood	17. 4.02P
	(DH Gipsy II)						
G-EBYY*	Avro 617 Cierva C.8L Mk.2	-		21. 6.28	Musee de l'Air et de l'Espace		
	(AS Lynx 180hp)					Le Bourget, Paris	13. 7.29
G-EBZM*	Avro 594A Avian IIIA	R3/CN/160		7.28	The Aeroplane Collection	Manchester	20. 1.38
	(ADC Cirrus) (Fitted with parts from G-ABEE)				(On loan to Museum of Science & Industry)		

PART 2 – SECOND PERMANENT UNITED KINGDOM REGISTER

The transition to a second series of registrations, commencing from G-AAAA onwards, was made with effect from 30th July 1928. Registrations were usually allocated in alphabetical sequence until the late 1970s although there have been numerous sporadic exceptions to this rule throughout the period. The G-AAAA-AZZZ series were all allocated by July 1972 and a new series G-BAAA onwards was used in the same month: this series became exhausted in June 2001. Notwithstanding this, and commencing in 1974, many registrations were issued ahead of the natural alphabetical sequence and came from all of the forthcoming G-Bxxx to G-Zxxx series, examples being Concorde G-BSST (5.68), Accountant G-BTEL (8.57) and Harrier G-VSTO (6.71).

All the advance G-Bxxx registrations have been now subsumed within the proper sequence and the new G-Cxxx series came into use, formally, in June 2001. However, some G-Cxxx registration series, namely G-CAAA to G-CAXP was allocated to Canada from April 1920 until January 1929 whilst G-CYAA to G-CYZZ and G-CYUA to G-CYZZ were allocated to Canadian military aircraft from June 1920 until 1931. Consequently, with the onset of the new series, the Civil Aviation Authority will not be allocating any further registrations from the G-CAxx range. Nine advance registrations, which were issued between December 1977 and March 1999, remain. None of these was ever allocated previously, although two of them were reserved in 1928.

In addition, a number of special registration series were allocated as follows:
 a) G-N81AC and G-N94AA to N94AE, specific alpha-numeric marks, were used for British Airways' Concordes in 1979 & 1980,
 b) G-FYAA-FYZZ were dedicated for minimum lift balloons from January 1982 until 1997, and
 c) G-MBAA-MBZZ, G-MGAA-MGZZ, G-MJAA-MJZZ, G-MMAA-MNZZ, G-MTAA-MTZZ & G-MYAA-MZZZ were dedicated for microlight aircraft from 1981 to 1998 until the CAA decided to allocate new registrations from the current series.

Regn	Type	C/n	P/I	Date	Owner/operator	Probable Base	CA Expy

G-AAAA – G-AAZZ

G-AAAH*	de Havilland DH.60G Moth	804		30. 8.28	The Science Museum (Flight Gallery)		
					"Jason"	South Kensington, London SW.7	23.12.30
	(Two reproductions both depicted as "G-AAAH" are in existence · see SECTION 4, Part 1 & SECTION 8 (ii) for details)						
G-AACD*	de Havilland DH.60M Moth	340		16.10.28	(St.Ives, Huntingdon)		8. 4.38
	(DH Gipsy I)				(Crashed Fen Ditton, Cambridge 24.6.37, rebuilt but stored 1989: current status unknown)		
G-AACN*	Handley Page HP.39 Gugnunc	1	K1908	2.11.28	Science Museum Air Transport Coln & Storage Facility		
			G-AACN		(Cancellation details not known) Wroughton		19. 9.30
G-AADR(2)	Moth Corporation DH.60GM Moth	138	NC939M	2. 6.86	H.F.Moffatt	Woodlow Farm, Bosbury	16. 8.02P
	(DH Gipsy I)						
G-AAEG	de Havilland DH.60G Moth	1027	D-EUPI	4. 2.29	I.B.Grace	(Ada, MI, USA)	
			D-1599/G-AAEG		(New owner 1.02)		
G-AAHI	de Havilland DH.60G Moth	1082		25. 5.29	N.J.W.Reid	Lee-on-Solent	30. 6.02P
	(DH Gipsy I)				(Original fuselage use in 1953 rebuild of G-AAWO)		
G-AAHY	de Havilland DH.60M Moth	1362	HB-AFI	10. 5.29	D.J.Elliott	Thruxton	13. 8.02P
	(DH Gipsy I)		(CH-480)/G-AAHY		(Brooklands Flying Club c/s)		
G-AAIN	Parnall Elf II	2 & J.6		11. 6.29	The Shuttleworth Trust	Old Warden	8. 7.02P
	(ADC Hermes 2)						
G-AALP*	Surrey Flying Services AL-1	AL-1		29. 8.29	Arden Family Trust (Stored 1.98)		
						Thorns Cross Farm, Caudleigh	17. 5.40
G-AALY	de Havilland DH.60G Moth	1175	F-AJKM	9. 9.29	K M Fresson	Hill Farm, Durley	
	(DH Gipsy I)		G-AALY		(Composite: on rebuild from components 2000)

G-AAMX(2)*	Moth Corporation DH.60GM Moth	125	NC926M	11. 9.86	RAF Museum	RAF Cosford	7. 5.94P
	(DH Gipsy II)				*(Cancelled 19.8.95 as WFU)*		
G-AAMY(2)	Moth Corporation DH.60GMW Moth	86	N585M	2. 5.80	Totalsure Ltd		
	(Wright Gipsy L320)		NC585M			Seppe-Hoeven, The Netherlands	23. 6.02P
G-AANF(2)*	Moth Corporation DH.60GMW Moth	49	N298M	3. 2.87	C.Smith	Mandeville, New Zealand	17. 4.90P
	(Wright Gipsy 1)		N237K/NC237K		*(Damaged near Popham 8.8.89: on rebuild 2.91)*		
G-AANG(2)	Bleriot Type XI	14	BAPC3	29.11.81	The Shuttleworth Trust	Old Warden	
	(Anzani 25hp) *(1910 original)*				*(No external marks: noted 5.01)*		
G-AANH(2)	Deperdussin Monoplane	43	BAPC4	29.10.81	The Shuttleworth Trust	Old Warden	14. 5.83P
	(Anzani Y 35hp) *(Possibly c/n 143)*				*(No external marks: noted 5.01)*		
G-AANI(2)	Blackburn 1912 Monoplane	725	BAPC5	29.10.81	The Shuttleworth Trust	Old Warden	14. 6.02P
	(Gnome 683 50hp)		No.9		*(No external marks)*		
G-AANJ(2)	Luft-Verkehrs Gesellschaft C.VI	4503	9239M	29.10.81	The Shuttleworth Trust	Old Warden	12. 5.02P
	(Benz 230hp)		C7198/18/"1594"/C7198/18		*(As "7198/18" in German Air Force c/s)*		
	(Composite aircraft including parts from LVG 1594: captured 1916/17 and allotted RFC serial "XG7")						
G-AANL(2)	de Havilland DH.60M Moth	1446	OY-DEH	26. 6.87	P.L.Allwork *(National Flying Services titles)*		
	(DH Gipsy II) *(Composite rebuild)*		RDAF S-357/S-107			Roughay Farm, Bishops Waltham	29. 6.00P
G-AANM(2)	Bristol F.2b	"67626"	BAPC166	16. 7.87	Aero Vintage Ltd	Old Warden	
	(RR Falcon)				*(Noted 5.01 as "D7889")*		
G-AANO(2)	Moth Corporation DH.60GMW Moth	165	N590N	3. 3.88	A.W. & M.E.Jenkins	(Comberton, Cambridge)	
			NC590N		*(Composite rebuild 11.91: current status unknown)*		
G-AANV(2)	Morane Saulnier Moth 60M	13	HB-OBU	8. 3.84	R A Seeley	Longwood Farm, Southampton	30. 9.02P
	(DH Gipsy I)		CH-349/F-AJNY				
G-AAOK(2)	Curtiss-Wright Travel Air CW-12Q		N370N	18.11.81	Shipping & Airlines Ltd		
	(Warner Scarab 145)	12Q-2026	NC370N/NC352M			Rushett Farm, Chessington	18. 1.84P
					(Damaged in gales Rijeka, Yugoslavia 21.10.83: on rebuild 5.01)		
G-AAOR(2)	de Havilland DH.60G Moth	1075	EC-AAO	15. 4.85	V.S.E.Norman	Rendcomb	20. 5.02P
	(DH Gipsy I) *(C/n uncertain: probably a composite)*						
G-AAPZ	Desoutter I	D.25		?. ?.31	The Shuttleworth Trust	Old Warden	12. 4.01P
	(ADC Hermes)				*(National Flying Services titles)*		
G-AAUP	Klemm L 25-1a	145		19. 2.30	Janice I.Cooper t/a Newbury Aeroplane Co		
	(Salmson AD9)				*"Clementine"*	Denford Manor, Hungerford	21.11.84P
					(On rebuild 10.01)		
G-AAWO	de Havilland DH.60G Moth	1235		2. 5.30	N.J.W.Reid & L.A.Fenwick	Lee-on-Solent	10. 2.02P
	(DH Gipsy I)				*(1953 rebuild substituted original fuselage of G-AAHI)*		
G-AAXK*	Klemm L 25-1a	182		?. 5.30	C.C.Russell-Vick	Orpington	29.11.60
					(Damaged White Waltham 3.62: fuselage stored 3.00)		
G-AAYX	Southern Martlet	202		14. 5.30	The Shuttleworth Trust	Old Warden	7. 5.02P
	(AS Genet Major 1A)						
G-AAZG	de Havilland DH.60G Moth	1253	EC-AAE	23. 5.30	J.A.Pothecary	Old Sarum	
			Spanish AF EM-??? (Code 30-94)/EC-MMA/M-CMMA/MW-133/G-AAZG				
G-AAZP	de Havilland DH.80A Puss Moth	2047	HL537	4. 6.30	R.P.Williams	Denford Manor, Hungerford	29. 5.03
	(DH Gipsy Major)		G-AAZP/SU-AAC/G-AAZP		*"British Heritage"*		

G-ABAA – G-ABZZ

G-ABAA*	Avro 504K	-	9244M	11. 9.30	RAF Museum	Manchester	11. 4.39
			"H2311"/G-ABAA		*(Cancelled 1939?) (On loan to Museum of Science & Industry)*		
G-ABAG	de Havilland DH.60G Moth	1259		23. 6.30	The Shuttleworth Trust	Old Warden	2. 5.02P
	(DH Gipsy I)						
G-ABBB*	Bristol 105A Bulldog IIA	7446	"K2227"	12. 6.30	RAF Museum	Hendon	
			G-ABBB/R-11/G-ABBB		*(As "K2227")*		
G-ABDX	de Havilland DH.60G Moth	1294	HB-UAS	22. 8.30	M.D.Souch	Hill Farm, Durley	28. 7.99P
	(DH Gipsy I)		G-ABDX				
G-ABEV(2)	de Havilland DH.60G Moth	1823	N4203E	10. 3.77	S.L.G.Darch	East Chinnock, Yeovil	9.10.97P
	(DH Gipsy I)		G-ABEV(2)/HB-OKI/CH-217		*(Noted Chilbolton 10.01)*		
G-ABLM*	Cierva C.24	710		22. 4.31	De Havilland Heritage Museum		
	(DH Gipsy III)		*(Cancellation details not known)*		*(On loan from Science Museum)*	London Colney	16. 1.35
G-ABLS	de Havilland DH.80A Puss Moth	2164		7. 5.31	R.C.F.Bailey	(Ledbury)	24. 9.02P
	(DH Gipsy Major)						
G-ABMR*	Hawker Hart	H.H-1	"J9933"	28. 5.31	RAF Museum	Hendon	11. 6.57
			G-ABMR		*(As "J9941" in 57 Sqn c/s)*		
G-ABNT	Civilian CAC.1 Coupe	0.2.3		10. 9.31	Shipping & Airlines Ltd	Biggin Hill	16. 9.02P
	(AS Genet Major 1A) *(C/n also quoted as 0.3)*						
G-ABNX	Robinson Redwing 2	9		2. 7.31	J.A.Pothecary	Old Sarum	9. 5.01P
G-ABOI*	Wheeler Slymph	AHW.1		17. 7.31	A.H.Wheeler	Coventry	
			(Cancellation details not known)		*(Dismantled components on loan to Midland Air Museum)*		
G-ABOX(2)	Sopwith Pup	-	N5195	12. 9.84	C.M.D. & A.P.St.Cyrien	AAC Middle Wallop	22. 4.93P
	(Le Rhone 80hp)				*(On loan to Museum of Army Flying) (As "N5195")*		
G-ABSD	de Havilland DH.60G Moth	1883	A7-96	21.11.31	M.E.Vaisey	(Hemel Hempstead)	
			VH-UTN/G-ABSD				
			(On rebuild following import from USA in 1985 as basket case: identity unconfirmed)				

G-ABTC*	Comper CLA.7 Swift	S.32/1		1. 1.32	P.Channon *"Spirit of Butler"*	Lelant	18. 7.84P
	(Pobjoy Niagara)				*(Stored 11.93: cancelled 22.2.99 by CAA) (Current status unknown)*		
G-ABUS	Comper CLA.7 Swift	S.32/4		27. 2.32	R.C.F.Bailey	(Ledbury)	19. 6.79P
	(Pobjoy Niagara 3)				*(On rebuild 1989: current status unknown)*		
G-ABVE	Arrow Active 2	2		19. 3.32	J.D.Penrose	Old Warden	1. 5.02P
	(DH Gipsy III)				*(On loan to The Shuttleworth Trust)*		
G-ABWP	Spartan Arrow 1	78		?. 4.32	R.E.Blain	Redhill	19. 7.01P
	(Cirrus Hermes 2)						
G-ABXL	Granger Archaeopteryx	3A		3. 6.32	The Shuttleworth Trust	Old Warden	22. 9.82P
	(Cherub III)						
G-ABYA	de Havilland DH.60G Moth	1906		?. 7.32	D A Hay & J.F.Moore	Biggin Hill	21. 5.73
	(DH Gipsy I)				*(Crashed Biggin Hill 21.5.72: stored 2.95: new owners 1.02)*		
G-ABYN*	Spartan Three-Seater II	102	EI-ABU	?. 8.32	Julie D Souch	Mandeville, New Zealand	
			G-ABYN		*(On rebuild by Croydon Aviation Co 1995: cancelled 31.3.99 by CAA)*		
G-ABZB(2)	de Havilland DH.60G III Moth Major		SE-AEL	11. 9.80	R.Earl & B.Morris	Folley Farm, Berks	15. 8.02P
	(DH Gipsy Major 1C)	5138	OY-DAK				

G-ACAA – G-ACZZ

G-ACAA(2)	Bristol F.2b	- 7434	F4516	25.10.91	Patina Ltd	Duxford	25. 4.01P
	(RR Falcon)				*(Op The Fighter Collection) (As "D8084/S")*		
	(Restored as original but rebuilt from various components)						
G-ACBH*	Blackburn B.2	4700/3	2895M	1.12.32	R.Coles	Temple Farm, West Hanningfield	27.11.41
			G-ACBH		t/a Coles Auto Supplies		
	(Thought to be composite with G-ADFO [5920/2] written off in 1940: crashed near Brough 16.3.40: fuselage impressed 17.2.42 as 2895M but as "G-ACBH" when used by 692 ATC Sqdn, Brentwood Institute, Essex from 2.42 until c.1945: fuselage stored 1.96 for possible refurbishment: current status unknown)						
G-ACCB	de Havilland DH.83 Fox Moth	4042		24. 1.33	E.A.Gautrey	(Nuneaton)	20. 7.57
					(Crashed off Southport 25.9.56 & on rebuild 10.95: current status unknown)		
G-ACDA	de Havilland DH.82A Tiger Moth	3175	BB724	6. 2.33	B.D.Hughes	Denford Manor, Hungerford	26. 6.82
			G-ACDA				
	(Crashed & burned out near Cirencester 27.6.79 - fuselage reported stored 10.01)						
G-ACDC	de Havilland DH.82A Tiger Moth	3177	BB726	6. 2.33	The Tiger Club (1990) Ltd	Headcorn	15. 4.02T
	(Composite airframe)		G-ACDC				
G-ACDI	de Havilland DH.82A Tiger Moth	3182	BB742	6. 2.33	J.A.Pothecary	Old Sarum	
	(Composite rebuild)		G-ACDI		*(On rebuild 10.99)*		
G-ACDJ	de Havilland DH.82A Tiger Moth	3183	BB729	6. 2.33	de Havilland School of Flying Ltd		
			G-ACDJ			White Waltham	16. 8.04T
G-ACEJ	de Havilland DH.83 Fox Moth	4069		21. 4.33	Janice I.Cooper	Rendcomb	14. 8.04
					t/a Newbury Aeroplane Co *(Scottish Motor Traction titles)*		
G-ACET	de Havilland DH.84 Dragon	6021	2779M	21. 4.33	M.D.Souch	(Hedge End, Southampton)	
			AW171/G-ACET		*(On rebuild 1.00: composite based on original wings)*		
G-ACGR*	Percival Gull Four IIA	D.29		11. 5.33	Musee Royal de l'Armee Brussels, Belgium		20. 6.35
	(DH Gipsy Major I)				*(Crashed Waterloo, Belgium 12.34: cancelled 12.34)*		
G-ACGT*	Avro 594B Avian IIIA	R3/CN/171	EI-AAB	?. 5.33	Not known	(Leeds)	21. 7.39
					(Cancellation details not known) (On rebuild 4.00)		
G-ACGZ	de Havilland DH.60G III Moth Major		VT-AFW	30. 5.33	N.H.Lemon	(Maidenhead)	
		5030	G-ACGZ		*(Restored 28.9.99: on rebuild 2000)*		
G-ACIT	de Havilland DH.84 Dragon 1	6039		24. 7.33	Science Museum Air Transport Coln & Storage Facility		
					"Aberdeen"	Wroughton	25. 5.74
					(Highland Airways titles)		
G-ACLL	de Havilland DH.85 Leopard Moth		AW165	16. 1.34	D.C.M. & V.M.Stiles	Jurby, IoM	6.12.95P
		7028	G-ACLL		*(Stored 10.96)*		
G-ACMA	de Havilland DH.85 Leopard Moth	7042	BD148	14. 3.34	S.J.Filhol	Headcorn	3. 2.94P
			G-ACMA		*(Stored 2.95: current status unknown)*		
G-ACMD(2)	de Havilland DH.82A Tiger Moth	3195	N182DH	20. 1.88	M.J.Bonnick	Rectory Farm, Abbotsley	27. 5.02
			EC-AGB/Sp AF 33-5				
G-ACMN	de Havilland DH.85 Leopard Moth	7050	X9381	?. 4.34	Carolyn S.Grace	Duxford	25. 7.03
			G-ACMN				
G-ACNS	de Havilland DH.60G III Moth Major		ZS-???	?. 3.34	R.I.& D.Souch	Hill Farm, Durley	5. 3.40
		5068			*(Restored 19.5.00) (On rebuild 12.01)*		
G-ACOJ(2)	de Havilland DH.85 Leopard Moth	7035	F-AMXP	5. 6.87	A.J.Norman	Rendcomb	3. 9.04
	(Composite with wings from HB-OXO)				t/a Norman Aeroplane Trust		
G-ACSP	de Havilland DH.88 Comet	1994	CS-AAJ	21. 8.34	K.Fern & T.M.Jones	(Stoke-on-Trent)	
			G-ACSP/E-1		*(On rebuild 2000 based on some original components)*		
G-ACSS	de Havilland DH.88 Comet	1996	K5084	4. 9.34	The Shuttleworth Trust	Old Warden	2. 6.94P
	(DH Gipsy Queen 2)		G-ACSS		*"Grosvenor House/34"*		
					(Last flown Hatfield 1993, on overhaul to fly in 2002)		
	(i) Two static reps exist with identities BAPC216 & BAPC257 - see SECTION 4)						
	(ii) A flying rep was built 1993 by Repeat Aircraft, Riverside, CA, USA for T J Wathen & regd N88XD c/n T7)						
G-ACTF	Comper CLA.7 Swift	S.32/9	VT-ADO	24. 5.34	The Shuttleworth Trust	Old Warden	29. 4.99P
	(Pobjoy Niagara 2)				*"The Scarlet Angel"*		

G-ACUS(2) de Havilland DH.85 Leopard Moth 7082 HB-OXA 17.11.77 R.A.& V.A.Gammons RAF Henlow 8.11.02
(Composite incl parts ex HB-OXO c/n 7045) (G-ACUS)
G-ACUU* Avro 671 Cierva C.30A Autogiro 726 (G-AIXE) 26. 6.34 Imperial War Museum - Skyfame Collection
(AS Civet) HM580/G-ACUU *(As "HM580/KX-K")* Duxford 30. 4.60
(WFU 4.60: cancelled 14.11.88 as WFU)
G-ACUX* Short S.16 Scion 1 S.776 VH-UUP 26. 6.34 Ulster Folk & Transport Museum
G-ACUX *(Cancelled 7.81) (As "VH-UUP")* Holywood, Belfast
G-ACVA* Kay Gyroplane 33/1 1002 26. 6.34 Glasgow Museum of Transport East Fortune
(Pobjoy R 75hp) *(Cancelled 9.58) (On loan to Museum of Flight)*
G-ACWM* Avro 671 Cierva C.30A Autogiro 715 (G-AHMK) 24. 7.34 E.D.ap Rees Weston-super-Mare 13. 7.40
AP506/G-ACWM t/a The Helicopter Museum
(Final cancellation details not known)
G-ACWP* Avro 671 Cierva C.30A Autogiro 728 AP507 24. 7.34 The Science Museum (Flight Gallery)
G-ACWP South Kensington, London SW7 6. 3.41
(As "AP507/KX-P" in 529 Sqn c/s) (Final cancellation details not known)
G-ACXB(2) de Havilland DH.60G III Moth Major EC-ABY 24. 1.89 D.F.Hodgkinson (Gravesend)
5098 EC-BAX/Sp AF 30-53/EC-YAY *(On rebuild 2000)*
G-ACXE British Klemm L 25c1 Swallow 21 29.10.34 J.G.Wakeford (Bexhill-on-Sea) 7. 4.40
(On rebuild since 1989 using components to re-draw plans and produce a substantially "new-build" airframe. Progress continuing 10.01 with some mainspar build sub-contracted to Denford Manor)
G-ACYK* Spartan Cruiser III 101 2. 5.35 National Museums of Scotland/Museum of Flight
(Crashed Largs, Ayrshire 14.1.38 & remains recovered 7.73) East Fortune 2. 5.38
G-ACZE de Havilland DH.89A Dragon Rapide G-AJGS 20.11.34 Wessex Aviation & Transport Ltd
6264 G-ACZE/Z7266/G-ACZE *(Stored 9.00)* Haverfordwest 18. 3.95

G-ADAA – G-ADZZ

G-ADAH* de Havilland DH.89 Dragon Rapide 30. 1.35 The Aeroplane Collection Manchester 9. 6.47
6278 *"Pioneer" (Allied Airways (Gandar Dower) titles)*
(WFU 1969: on loan to Museum of Science & Industry)
G-ADEV(2) Avro 504K R3/LE/61400 G-ACNB 18. 4.84 The Shuttleworth Trust Old Warden 24. 4.02P
(Le Rhone 110hp) "E3404" *(As "H5199")*
(P/i not confirmed but, if correct, full p/i is 3118M/BK892/G-ADEV/H5199)
G-ADFV* Blackburn B.2 5920/8 2893M 3. 4.35 Not known (St.Ives, Huntingdon) 26. 6.41
G-ADFV
(To 574 ATC Sqdn Caterham School, Surrey as 2893M on 17.2.42: cut up in 1950, rear fuselage preserved: reconstruction commenced in 1967: forward fuselage for rebuild 3.00)
G-ADGP Miles M.2L Hawk Speed Six 160 G-ADGP 20. 5.35 R.A.Mills Booker 7. 5.02P
G-ADGT de Havilland DH.82A Tiger Moth 3338 BB697 23. 5.35 D.R. & M.Wood *(Current status unknown)*
G-ADGT Fowle Hall Farm, Paddock Wood, Kent 18. 8.97
G-ADGV de Havilland DH.82A Tiger Moth 3340 (D-E) 23. 5.35 K.J. & P.J.Whitehead
G-ADGV/(G-BACW)/BB694/G-ADGV Whitchurch Hill, Reading 10. 6.02
G-ADHD(2) de Havilland DH.60G III Moth Major EC-... 17. 2.88 M.E.Vaisey Henlow
5105 Sp AF 34-5/EC-W32 *(Rebuild of ex Spanish components acquired from USA)*
G-ADIA de Havilland DH.82A Tiger Moth 3368 BB747 13. 8.35 S.J. Beaty Wold Lodge, Finedon 20. 5.02
G-ADIA
G-ADJJ de Havilland DH.82A Tiger Moth 3386 BB819 29. 8.35 J.M.Preston Great Eversden 20. 3.75
G-ADJJ *(Stored 4.95: noted 11.01)*
G-ADKC de Havilland DH.87B Hornet Moth 8064 X9445 27. 3.36 A.J.Davy Redhill 20.12.04
G-ADKC
G-ADKK de Havilland DH.87B Hornet Moth 8033 W5749 9.11.35 R M & D R Lee Kemble 10. 8.03
G-ADKL de Havilland DH.87B Hornet Moth 8035 F-BCJO ?.11.35 P.R.& M.J.F.Gould *(Noted 5.01)*
G-ADKL/W5750/G-ADKL Coulommiers, Seine-et-Marne, France 29. 5.95
G-ADKM de Havilland DH.87B Hornet Moth 8037 W5751 12.11.35 L.V.Mayhead Hill Farm, Durley 6. 7.01
G-ADKM
G-ADLY de Havilland DH.87B Hornet Moth 8020 W9388 5.10.35 Totalsure Ltd
G-ADLY Seppe-Hoeven, The Netherlands 24. 5.04
G-ADMT de Havilland DH.87B Hornet Moth 8093 8. 5.36 P.A.D.Swoffer *"Curlew"* Popham 19. 5.04
G-ADMW* Miles M.2H Hawk Major 177 DG590 30. 7.35 RAF Museum Reserve Collection & Restoration Centre
8379M/G-ADMW NK 30. 7.65
(Cancelled 16.9.86 by CAA) (Noted M6/Stafford 11.01)
G-ADND de Havilland DH.87B Hornet Moth 8097 W9385 4. 8.36 The Shuttleworth Trust Old Warden 8. 8.02P
G-ADND *(As "W9385/YG-L/3" in 502 Sqn c/s)*
G-ADNE de Havilland DH.87B Hornet Moth 8089 X9325 10. 3.36 G-ADNE Ltd Lee-on-Solent 25. 4.03
G-ADNE *"Ariadne"*
G-ADNL Miles M.5 Sparrowhawk 239 12. 8.35 A.G.Dunkerley (Bristol) 13. 5.58S
(On rebuild 6.00 from components discarded from the reconstruction in 1953 as M.77 Sparrowjet)
G-ADNZ(2) de Havilland DH.82A Tiger Moth 85614 6948M 10.10.74 D.C.Wall Swanton Morley 1. 8.03
DE673 *(As "DE673")*
G-ADOT* de Havilland DH.87B Hornet Moth 8027 X9326 ?.11.35 De Havilland Heritage Museum
G-ADOT *(WFU 15.10.59)* London Colney 15.10.59
G-ADPC de Havilland DH.82A Tiger Moth 3393 BB852 24. 9.35 D J Marshall Charity Farm, Baxterley 2. 8.03
G-ADPC

G-ADPJ	BAC Drone 2 (Douglas Sprite)	7		21. 8.35	N.H.Ponsford	(Selby)	17. 5.55
					(Crashed Leicester 3.4.55: on rebuild 12.99 using parts from G-AEJR c/n 22)		
G-ADPS	BA Swallow 2 (Pobjoy Cataract 2)	410		4. 9.35	J.F.Hopkins	Watchford Farm, Yarcombe	31. 5.02P
G-ADRA(2)	Pietenpol Air Camper (Continental A65)	PFA 1514		10. 4.78	A.J.Mason *"Edna May"*	Hinton-in-the-Hedges	11. 4.02P
G-ADRH(2)	de Havilland DH.87A Hornet Moth	8038	(ZK-ANR) G-ADRH/F-AQBY/HB-OBE	6. 8.82	R G Grocott *(On rebuild 2000)*	Mandeville, New Zealand	
G-ADRR(2)	Aeronca C.3	A.734	N17423 NC17423	6. 9.88	S.J.Rudkin *(Stored 1992: wings @ Skycraft/Spalding 11.01)*	Roughay Farm, Bishops Waltham	
G-ADUR	de Havilland DH.87B Hornet Moth	8085		10. 3.36	R.A.Seeley	Spanhoe	1. 8.04
G-ADWJ	de Havilland DH.82A Tiger Moth	3450	BB803 G-ADWJ	9.12.35	C.Adams *(Under restoration 3.97: CofR @ 3.01)*	(Madley)	
G-ADWO*	de Havilland DH.82A Tiger Moth	3455	BB807 G-ADWO	9.12.35	Hall of Aviation	Southampton	
	(After restoration @ 3.51 a/c overhauled using fuselage of BB860 (ex G-ADXT): damaged on landing Christchurch 31.7.58 and wfu: cancelled 15.9.58 as destroyed: fuselage/parts ex G-AOAC & parts ex G-AOJJ used in composite rebuild 1987/90: completed to static condition 1990 as "BB807")						
G-ADWT	Miles M.2W Hawk Trainer	215	CF-NXT G-ADWT/NF750/G-ADWT	18.11.35	R.Earl & B.Morris *(On rebuild 10.01)*	Denford Manor, Hungerford	15 .6.62
G-ADXS*	Mignet HM.14 Pou-Du-Ciel (Scott Squirrel A2S)	CLS.1		18.11.35	(PFA Cambridge Strut) *"The Fleeing Fly" (On rebuild 7.96: current status unknown) (Cancellation details not known)*	Cambridge	1.12.36
G-ADXT*	de Havilland DH.82A Tiger Moth *(Mainly a rebuild of components)*	3436		9.12.35	J.R.Hanauer	Goodwood	18. 7.03T
					(Forced landed & overturned Fishbourne 22.6.01: cancelled 7.12.01 by CAA)		
G-ADYS	Aeronca C.3 (Aeronca E113C)	A.600		?. 1.36	Janice I Cooper *(London Air Park Flying Club titles)*	Rendcomb	3.10.02P

G-AEAA – G-AEZZ

G-AEBB	Mignet HM.14 Pou-Du-Ciel	KWO.1		24. 1.36	The Shuttleworth Trust *(Noted 5.01)*	Old Warden	31. 5.39
G-AEBJ	Blackburn B.2 (DH Gipsy Major)	6300/8		4. 2.36	BAE Systems (Operations) Ltd	Warton	20. 6.03
G-AEDB	BAC Drone 2 (Cherub III)	13		18. 3.36	P.L.Kirk & R E Nerou	Hucknall	26. 5.87P
	(Registered as BGA2731 31.3.81: composite with wings of G-AEJH & tail end of G-AEEN: noted 7.01)						
G-AEDU(2)	de Havilland DH.90A Dragonfly	7526	N190DH G-AEDU/ZS-CTR/CR-AAB	4. 6.79	A.J.Norman t/a Norman Aeroplane Trust	Langham	18. 7.02
G-AEEG	Miles M.3A Falcon Major	216	SE-AFN Fv913/SE-AFN/G-AEEG/U-20	14. 3.36	P.R.Holloway	Old Warden	18. 6.04
G-AEEH*	Mignet HM.14 Pou-Du-Ciel	EGD.1		13. 3.36	Cosford Aerospace Museum *(WFU on 15.5.38: cancelled 8.46 in census)*	RAF Cosford	15. 5.38
G-AEFG*	Mignet HM.14 Pou-Du-Ciel (Scott Flying Squirrel)	JN.1	BAPC75	27. 3.36	N.H.Ponsford	(Selby)	31. 3.38
	(Cancelled in 31.3.38 census: rebuilt using 65% of original incl engine: on rebuild 1.00)						
G-AEFT	Aeronca C.3 (JAP J.99)	A.610		17. 4.36	N.C.Chittenden	Kineton	1. 8.02P
	(Rebuilt in 1976 with major parts of G-AETG (qv) & carries c/n AB.110 thereof)						
G-AEGV*	Mignet HM.14 Pou-Du-Ciel	EMAC.1		22. 4.36	Midland Air Museum	Coventry	26. 5.37
					(WFU on 26.5.37: cancelled in 12.37: rebuild with some original components)		
G-AEHM*	Mignet HM.14 Pou-Du-Ciel (ABC Scorpion 35 hp)	HJD.1		30. 4.36	Science Museum Air Transport Coln & Storage Facility *(Cancelled in 3.39 in census) "Blue Finch"*	Wroughton	
G-AEJZ*	Mignet HM.14 Pou-Du-Ciel	TLC.1	BAPC120	9. 6.36	Bomber County Aviation Museum *(Cancelled 31.12.38 in census)*	Hemswell	
G-AEKR*	Mignet HM.14 Pou-Du-Ciel	CAC.1		26. 6.36	Museum & Art Gallery	Doncaster	22. 6.37
	(WFU & cancelled 31.7.38: stored Doncaster 1938 -1960: damaged by fire RAF Finningley 4.9.70: rebuilt Claybourn Co with c/n CAC.1 using original engine & some original components: allocated BAPC121)						
G-AEKV*	Kronfeld (BAC) Drone de luxe	30		13. 1.37	M.L.Beach *(Allocated BGA.2510 5.79) (Cancelled as WFU 14.1.99)*	Brooklands Museum	6.10.60P
G-AEKW*	Miles M.12 Mohawk	298	HM503 G-AEKW/"G-AEKN"	14. 7.36	RAF Museum Reserve Collection & Repair Centre	RAF Wyton	1. 3.50
					(Crashed Spain 1.1.50: on rebuild by Skysport Engineering @ Hatch 2001)		
G-AELO	de Havilland DH.87B Hornet Moth	8105	AW118 G-AELO	30. 7.36	M.J.Miller	Little Gransden	9. 5.03
G-AEML	de Havilland DH.89 Dragon Rapide	6337	X9450 G-AEML	1. 9.36	Amanda Investments Ltd *"Proteus"*	Rendcomb	22. 5.02
G-AEMY*	Mignet HM.14 Pou-Du-Ciel	NMB.1		25. 8.36	N.Ponsford *(Cancelled 31.7.37: small parts stored 12.99)*	(Selby)	
G-AENP(2)	Hawker Afghan Hind (Kestrel V)	41H/81902	(BAPC78) R.Afghan AF	29.10.81	The Shuttleworth Trust *(As "K5414 "in 15 Sqdn c/s)*	Old Warden	6. 5.02P
G-AEOA	de Havilland DH.80A Puss Moth (DH Gipsy Major)	2184	ES921 G-AEOA/YU-PAX/UN-PAX	1.10.36	A. & P.A.Wood t/a P & A Wood *(Current status unknown)*	Audley End	27. 6.95P
G-AEOF(2)	Rearwin 8500 Sportster (Le Blond 5DF 85hp)	462	N15863 NC15863	1.12.81	Shipping & Airlines Ltd	Biggin Hill	5.10.01P

G-AEPH	Bristol F.2b	7575	D8096	13.11.36	The Shuttleworth Trust	Old Warden	5. 9.02P
	(RR Falcon 3)		G-AEPH/D8096		*(As "D8096")*		
	(Original c/n 3746 & rebuilt c.1931)						
G-AERV*	Miles M.11A Whitney Straight	307	EM999	30.12.36	Not known		
			G-AERV		Upper Ballinderry, Lisburn, Co.Antrim		9. 4.66
			(Cancelled 7.9.81 by CAA:.on rebuild 4.96: current status unknown)				
G-AESB(2)	Aeronca C.3	A.638	N15742	5. 8.88	R.J.M.Turnbull		
			NC15742			Rydinghurst Farm, Cranleigh	
					(On rebuild 1997: current status unknown)		
G-AESE	de Havilland DH.87B Hornet Moth	8108	W5775	13. 1.37	J.G.Green	White Ox Mead, Bath	4.10.01
			G-AESE		*"Sheena"*		
G-AESZ	Chilton DW.1	DW.1/1		?. 1.37	R.E.Nerou	Rendcomb	4. 3.53
	(Carden Ford 32hp)						
	(Rebuild completed mid 2001 using some parts of original a/c badly damaged in forced landing near Felixstowe 24.5.53)						
G-AETA*	Caudron G.III	7487	OO-ELA	29. 1.37	RAF Museum	Hendon	
	(Anzani 90hp)		O-BELA		*(Sold to RAF 1972: as "(N)3066" in RNAS c/s)*		
	(Also reported as either c/n 5019 or 5021: allotted "9203M" 1994)						
G-AETG*	Aeronca 100	AB.110		?. 2.37	(B R Cox)		
						(Brickhouse Farm, Frogland Cross)	9. 4.68
	(Crashed Booker 7.4.69: cancelled 29.2.72 as destroyed: major parts to G-AEFT in 1976: for rebuild with parts from G-AEWV 4.96 (qv))						
G-AEUJ	Miles M.11A Whitney Straight	313		19. 2.37	R.E.Mitchell	RAF Cosford	4. 6.70
					(Stored 6.92: current status unknown)		
G-AEVS	Aeronca 100	AB.114		3.37	A.M.Lindsay & N.H.Ponsford	Breighton	12. 8.02P
	(JAP J.99)				*(Composite including parts of original G-AEXD)*		
G-AEWV*	Aeronca 100	AB.117		3.37	(B R Cox)		
						(Brickhouse Farm, Frogland Cross)	
			(Crashed Dunstable 6.64: cancelled 1967 as WFU: frame stored 1998)				
G-AEXD	Aeronca 100	AB.124		1. 4.37	M A & R W Mills		
	(JAP J.99)					(Brickhouse Farm, Frogland Cross)	20. 4.70P
	(Mostly comprises parts of G-AESP after rebuild in 1958: stored by B R Cox 1998: current status unknown)						
G-AEXF	Percival P.6 Mew Gull	E.22	ZS-AHM	18. 5.37	J.D.Penrose	Old Warden	10. 6.02P
	(Rebuilt with c/n PFA 013-10020)						
G-AEXT	Dart Kitten II	123		?. 4.37	A.J.Hartfield	Marsh Hill Farm, Aylesbury	27. 6.02P
	(JAP J.99)						
G-AEXZ	Piper J-2 Cub	997		5. 2.38	J.R. & Mrs M.Dowson	(Leicester)	2.11.78S
	(Continental A75)				*(On rebuild 3.00)*		
G-AEYY*	Martin Monoplane	1	G-AAJK	6. 7.37	R.W.E.Lake, A.D.Raby & D.W.Brabham		
					t/a Martin Monoplane Syndicate	Hitchin	3.11.39
		(See G-EBQP: on long term rebuild 4.92: cancelled 3.6.98 by CAA) (Current status unknown)					
G-AEZF*	Short S.16 Scion 2	PA.1008	M-5	18. 6.37	R.Jackson/Acebell Aviation Ltd	Redhill	5. 5.54
			G-AEZF		*(On rebuild 6.00)*		
G-AEZJ	Percival P.10 Vega Gull	K.65	SE-ALA	2. 7.37	R.A.J.Spurrell	White Waltham	10. 6.04
			D-IXWD/PH-ATH/G-AEZJ				
G-AEZX(2)	Bücker Bü.133C Jungmeister	1018	N5A	10. 5.88	A.J.E.Ditheridge	Moat Farm, Milden	27. 7.00P
			PP-TDP		*(As "LG+03" in Luftwaffe c/s)*		

G-AFAA – G-AFZZ

G-AFAX	BA Eagle 2	138	VH-ACN	26.10.37	J.G.Green	White Ox Mead, Bath	4. 8.00
	(DH Gipsy Major)		G-AFAX				
G-AFBS*	Miles M.14A Hawk Trainer 3	539	(G-AKKU)	17. 9.37	Imperial War Museum	Duxford	25. 2.63
			BB661/G-AFBS		*(Cancelled 22.12.95 by CAA) (On rebuild 2000 - bare fuselage)*		
G-AFCL	BA L.25c Swallow II	462		3.11.37	M.Mordue & C.P.Bloxham	(Southam)	11. 6.02P
	(Pobjoy Niagara 3)						
G-AFDO(2)	Piper J-3C-65 Cub	2593	N21697	7. 6.88	R.Wald	Hill Farm, Durley	27. 7.99P
	(Frame No.2633)		NC21697		*"Butter Cub" (On rebuild 12.01)*		
G-AFEL(2)	Monocoupe 90A	A.782	N19432	7. 6.82	M.Rieser	(Germany)	3. 9.02P
	(Lambert R266)		NC19432				
G-AFFD	Percival P.16A Q-Six	Q.21	(G-AIEY)	12. 2.38	B.D.Greenwood	Sywell	31. 8.56
			X9407/G-AFFD		*(On rebuild - fuselage @ Ronaldsway 12.01)*		
G-AFFH	Piper J-2 Cub	1166	EC-ALA	26. 3.38	M.J.Honeychurch	(Pewsey)	29. 8.53
	(Continental A40)		G-AFFH		*(On rebuild 10.01)*		
G-AFGC	BA L.25c Swallow II	467	BK893	4. 4.38	G E.Arden	Thorns Cross Farm, Chudleigh	20. 3.51
	(Pobjoy Niagara 3)		G-AFGC		*(Stored 1.98: current status unknown)*		
G-AFGD*	BA L.25c Swallow II	469	BK897	4. 4.38	A.T.Williams, B.Arden, C.A.Cook, J.Hughes & M.Barmby		
	(Pobjoy Cataract 3)		G-AFGD		t/a South Wales Swallow Group	Shobdon	9. 4.01P
					(Cancelled 6.4.01 by CAA)		
G-AFGE	BA L.25c Swallow II	470	BK894	4. 4.38	G.R.French	Benson's Farm, Laindon	27. 7.98P
	(Pobjoy Niagara 2)		G-AFGE		*"Maggie" (Stored 8.01)*		
G-AFGH	Chilton DW.1	DW.1/2		20. 3.38	M.L. & G.L.Joseph *(On rebuild 10.01)*		
	(Lycoming O-145-A2) *(To be re-engined with Carden-Ford)*					Denford Manor, Hungerford	7. 7.83P

G-AFGI	Chilton DW.1	DW.1/3		30. 3.38	J.E. & K.A.A. McDonald	White Waltham	18. 6.02P
	(Walter Mikron 2)						
G-AFGM(2)	Piper J-4A Cub Coupe	4-943	N26895	30.12.81	P.H.Wilkinson	Carlisle	9.11.99P
			NC26895		*(Noted 1.02)*		
G-AFGZ	de Havilland DH.82A Tiger Moth	3700	G-AMHI	9. 5.38	M.R.Paul & P.A.Shaw	Lee-on-Solent	16. 3.03
			BB759/G-AFGZ				
G-AFHA(2)	Mosscraft MA.1	MA.1/2		27. 2.67	C.V.Butler	(Allesley, Coventry)	
					(Small components only stored)		
G-AFHC*	BA L.25c Swallow II	486		17. 5.38	Arden Family Trust		
	(Cirrus Minor)	*(Cancellation details not known) (Stored 1.98)*				Thorns Cross Farm, Chudleigh	20. 3.51
G-AFIN	Chrislea LC.1 Airguard	LC.1	BAPC203	7. 7.38	N H Wright	Queach Farm, Bury St Edmunds	
			(On rebuild 12.01 using original wings, tailplane & metal fittings)				
G-AFIR	Luton LA-4 Minor	JSS.2		7. 7.38	A.J.Mason	(Aylesbury)	30. 7.71
	(JAP J-99)				*(Damaged near Cobham 14.3.71 & on rebuild 2000)*		
G-AFIU*	Parker CA-4 Parasol	CA-4		19.10.82	S P Connatty	Barton	
	(Luton Minor variant with reserved marks from 1938)				*(Cancelled 31.3.99 by CAA) (Stored 2.00)*		
G-AFJA	Taylor-Watkinson Dingbat	DB.100		2. 8.38	K.Woolley	(Berkswell, Coventry)	23. 6.75
	(Carden-Ford 32hp)				*(Damaged Headcorn 19.5.75 and partially rebuilt: stored 12.01)*		
G-AFJB	Foster-Wikner GM.1 Wicko	5	DR613	15. 8.38	J.Dibble	Hill Farm, Durley	12. 7.63
	(DH Gipsy Major 1)		G-AFJB		*(On rebuild 12.01)*		
G-AFJR*	Tipsy Trainer 1	2		20. 8.38	Musee Royal de L'Armee	Brussels	10. 9.64
	(Converted to Belfair)	*(Cancelled 12.4.89 as TWFU) (Stored 1992 for static rebuild with remains of G-AFRV)*					
G-AFJU*	Miles M.17 Monarch	789	X9306	25. 8.38	Aircraft Preservation Society of Scotland		
			G-AFJU			East Fortune	18. 5.64
			(Final cancellation details not known) (On loan to Museum of Flight)				
G-AFJV(2)	Mosscraft MA.2	MA.2/2		27. 2.67	C.V.Butler	(Allesley, Coventry)	
					(Small components only stored)		
G-AFLW*	Miles M.17 Monarch	792		2.11.38	N.I.Dalziel	White Waltham	30. 7.98
					(Cancelled 3.5.01 by CAA)		
G-AFNG	de Havilland DH.94 Moth Minor	94014	AW112	2. 5.39	D.Saunders	Connemore	21.10.98P
			G-AFNG		t/a The Gullwing Trust		
G-AFNI	de Havilland DH.94 Moth Minor	94035	W7972	11. 5.39	J.Jennings	(Royston)	26. 5.67
			G-AFNI		*(On rebuild 12.99: current status unknown)*		
G-AFOB	de Havilland DH.94 Moth Minor	94018	X5117	16. 5.39	Wessex Aviation & Transport Ltd		
			G-AFOB		*(Stored 6.96: current status unknown)*	Chalmington	11. 5.93P
G-AFOJ	de Havilland DH.94 Moth Minor	9407	E-1	21. 7.39	R.M.Long *"Bugs 2"*	London Colney	27. 8.69P
	(Cabin)		E-0236/G-AFOJ		*(On loan to De Havilland Heritage Museum)*		
G-AFPN	de Havilland DH.94 Moth Minor	94044	X9297	23. 5.39	J.W. & A.R.Davy	Redhill	9. 5.02
	(Now regd with c/n 94016)		G-AFPN				
G-AFRZ	Miles M.17 Monarch	793	G-AIDE	24. 3.39	R.E.Mitchell	RAF Cosford	29. 6.70
			W6463/G-AFRZ		*(Stored 6.92: current status unknown)*		
G-AFSC	Tipsy Trainer 1	11		15. 7.39	D.M.Forshaw	Panshanger	6. 6.02P
	(Walter Mikron 2)						
G-AFSV	Chilton DW.1A	DW.1A/1		5. 4.39	R.E.Nerou	(Coventry)	12. 7.72
	(Train 45hp)				*(On rebuild 12.93: current status unknown)*		
G-AFSW*	Chilton DW.2	DW.2/1		6. 4.39	R.I.Souch	(Hedge End, Southampton)	
	(Not completed originally: fuselage box in poor condition: stored 1.00: current status unknown						
G-AFTA	Hawker Tomtit	30380	K1786	26. 4.39	The Shuttleworth Trust	Old Warden	31. 8.02P
	(Mongoose 3C)		G-AFTA/K1786		*(As "K1786")*		
G-AFTN*	Taylorcraft Plus C2	102	HL535	2. 5.39	Leicestershire County Council Museums		
			G-AFTN		*(Cancelled 13.1.99 by CAA)*	Coalville	1.11.57
G-AFUP(2)	Luscombe 8A Master	1246	N25370	7. 6.88	R.Dispain	Chilbolton	12. 3.97P
	(Continental A65)		NC25370		*(Restored 5.01)*		
G-AFVE(2)	de Havilland DH.82A Tiger Moth	83720	T7230	1. 2.78	W.N.Gibson	Booker	30. 4.04T
					t/a Tigerfly *(As "T7230")*		
G-AFVN	Tipsy Trainer 1	12		15. 7.39	D.F.Lingard	Fenland	30. 8.01P
	(Walter Mikron 2)						
G-AFWH(2)	Piper J-4A Cub Coupe	4-1341	N33093	14. 1.82	C.W.Stearn & R.D.W.Norton	Southery	2. 7.01P
	(Continental A65)		NC33093		*(Stored mid 2001)*		
G-AFWI	de Havilland DH.82A Tiger Moth	82187	BB814	19. 7.39	E.Newbigin		
			G-AFWI		Brown Shutters Farm, Norton St Philips, Somerset		12. 8.03
G-AFWT	Tipsy Trainer 1	13		1. 8.39	J.M.Lovell	Chilbolton	1. 3.02P
	(Walter Mikron 2)						
G-AFYD(2)	Luscombe 8AF Silvaire	1044	N25120	29. 7.75	J.D.Iliffe	Oaksey Park	14. 9.03
	(Continental C90)		NC25120				
G-AFYO(2)	Stinson HW-75 Model 105	7039	F-BGQP	25. 4.77	R.N.Wright		
	(Continental C90)		NC22586		Red House Farm, Gedney Marsh, Holbeach		8. 5.02P
			(Probably ex Fr.Mil with identity "22586")				
G-AFZA(2)	Piper J-4A Cub Coupe	4-873	N26198	27. 6.84	M Robinson	Eggesford	2.12.02P
	(Continental A65)		NC26198		t/a G-AFZA Group		
G-AFZE*	Heath Parasol	PA.1		25. 8.39	Estate of K.C.D.St.Cyrien	Horley, Surrey	10. 5.64P
	(Bristol Cherub III)		*(Stored 11.93) (Cancelled 11.6.96 by CAA) (Current status unknown)*				
G-AFZK(2)	Luscombe 8A Master	1042	N25118	24.10.88	M.G.Byrnes	Walkeridge Farm, Overton	29. 5.97P
	(Continental A65)		NC25118		*(Current status unknown)*		

G-AFZL(2)	Porterfield CP-50 (Continental A50)	581	N25401 NC25401	18. 3.82	P.G.Lucas & S.H.Sharpe t/a The Skinny Bird Flyers	White Waltham	29. 5.02P
G-AFZN(2)	Luscombe 8A Master (Continental A65)	1186	N25279 NC25279	5.10.81	A.L.Young	Henstridge	2.12.02P

G-AGAA – G-AGZZ

G-AGAT(2)	Piper J-3F-50 Cub (Franklin 4AC-150)	4062	N26126 NC26126	17. 7.87	O.T.Taylor & C.J.Marshall	(Newark)	30. 4.02P
G-AGBN*	General Aircraft GAL.42 Cygnet 2	111	ES915 G-AGBN	4.10.40	National Museums of Scotland/Museum of Flight *(Cancelled 15.11.88 as WFU)*	East Fortune	28.11.80P
G-AGEG(2)	de Havilland DH.82A Tiger Moth	82710	N9146 D-EDIL/R.Neth AF A-32/PH-UFK/A-32/R4769	16. 8.82	A.J.Norman t/a Norman Aeroplane Trust	Rendcomb	15. 5.04
G-AGFT(2)	Avia FL.3 (CNA D4S)	176	I-TOLB MM.....	21. 8.84	K.Joynson & K.Cracknell *(As "W7" in Italian Co-Belligerent AF c/s)*	(Yeadon)	4.12.02P
G-AGHB(2)*	Hawker Sea Fury FB.XI	41H-636336	CF-CHB RAN WH589/WH589	9. 5.74	(Charleston Aviation Services)	(Colchester)	
	(Damaged landing Munster, West Germany 24.6.79: cancelled 9.9.81 as WFU: (i) some parts to USA & incorporated into rebuild of N4434P as "WH589": (ii) other parts on rebuild 3.94 using major sections of wreck plus original centre section of TF956, rear fuselage of R.Neth Navy 10-14, ex 6-14/VX715 & parts from G-FURY/WJ244)						
G-AGHY(2)	de Havilland DH.82A Tiger Moth	82292	N9181	17. 2.88	P.Groves	Stubbington	
			(On rebuild from ex Rollason airframe/components) (Current status unknown)				
G-AGIV(2)	Piper J-3C-65 Cub (L-4J-PI) *(Frame No.12506)*	12676	OO-AFI OO-GBA/44-80380	13. 8.82	P.C. & F.M.Gill	Waits Farm, Belchamp Walter	2.10.02P
G-AGJG	de Havilland DH.89A Dragon Rapide	6517	X7344	25.10.43	M.J. & D.J.T.Miller *(On rebuild 2001)*	Duxford	15.11.74
G-AGLK	Taylorcraft Auster 5D	1137	RT475	25. 8.44	C R Harris	Rochester	13. 4.04
G-AGMI(2)	Luscombe 8A Master (Continental A65)	1569	N28827 NC28827	15.11.88	P.R.Bush	RAF Kinloss	9. 4.02P
G-AGNJ(2)	de Havilland DH.82A Tiger Moth *(Built DH Australia)*	660	VP-YOJ ZS-BGF/SAAF 2366	21. 2.89	B.P., A.J. & P.J.Borsberry *(On rebuild 6.95)*	Kidmore End, Reading	
G-AGNV*	Avro 685 York C.1	1223	"MW100" "LV633"/G-AGNV/TS798	20. 8.45	RAF Museum *(WFU on 9.10.64:.as "TS798")*	RAF Cosford	6. 3.65
G-AGOH	Auster V J/1 Autocrat	1442		19. 4.45	Leicestershire County Council Museums *(On loan to Newark Air Museum)*	Winthorpe	24. 8.95
G-AGOS*	Reid & Sigrist RS.4 Desford Trainer	3	VZ728 G-AGOS	?. 5.45	Leicester Museum of Science & Industry *(As "Bobsleigh" "VZ728": WFU 9.11.81: stored 4.96)*	Coalville	28.11.80P
G-AGOY	Miles M.48 Messenger 3	4690	EI-AGE G-AGOY/HB-EIP/G-AGOY/U-0247	5. 6.45	P.A.Brook *(On rebuild 4.92: to carry "U-0247")*	West Chiltington, Pulborough	25.11.53
G-AGPG*	Avro 652A Anson 19 Srs.2	1212		15. 6.45	The Aeroplane Collection	Hooton Park	13. 2.71
	(Originally regd as Anson XII, to Anson XIX 1.47 & to 19 Srs.2 5.52) *(CofA expired 13.2.71: WFU Southend: cancelled 5.11.75) (Stored 10.00 - for restoration to display standard)*						
G-AGPK(2)	de Havilland DH.82A Tiger Moth	86566	N657DH F-BGDN/Fr AF/PG657	27.10.88	Delta Aviation Ltd.	Sywell/White Waltham	21.12.01T
G-AGRU*	Vickers V.657 Viking 1	112	VP-TAX G-AGRU	8. 5.46	British Airways plc *(WFU 9.63) "Vagrant" (BEA c/s)*	Brooklands	9. 1.64
G-AGRW*	Vickers V.639 Viking 1	115		8. 5.46	Not known *(WFU 8.64)*	Vienna-Schwechat , Austria	9. 7.68
G-AGSH	de Havilland DH.89A Dragon Rapide 6	6884	EI-AJO G-AGSH/NR808	25. 7.45	Techair London Ltd *"Jemma Meeson" (BEA c/s)*	Bournemouth	11. 7.04
G-AGTM	de Havilland DH.89A Dragon Rapide 6	6746	JY-ACL OD-ABP/G-AGTM/NF875	19. 9.45	Aviation Heritage Ltd	Coventry	11. 5.03T
G-AGTO	Auster V J/1 Autocrat	1822		2.10.45	M.J.Barnett & D.J.T.Miller	Duxford	22. 2.03
G-AGTT	Auster V J/1 Autocrat	1826		2.10.45	R.Farrer *(Stored 12.97) (Current status unknown)*	(Bromham, Bedford)	11. 2.93
G-AGVG	Auster V J/1 Autocrat (Lycoming O-360-A2A + modified tail surfaces)	1858		7.12.45	S.J.Riddington	Leicester	15. 6.03
G-AGVN	Auster V J/1 Autocrat	1873	EI-CKC G-AGVN	18. 1.46	G.H.Farrar	Abbeyshrule, Co Longford	21. 4.02
G-AGVV(2)	Piper J-3C-65 Cub (L-4H-PI)	11163	F-BCZK Fr.AF/43-29872	19. 2.81	M.Molina-Ruano	(Malaga, Spain)	2. 9.02P
G-AGWE*	Avro 19 Srs.2	1286	TX201	28.12.45	Valiant Air Command Museum *(Stored 6.94)*	Tico, Florida, USA	5. 3.73
G-AGXN	Auster J/1N Alpha	1963		22. 1.46	Gentleman's Aerial Touring Carriage Syndicate Ltd	Popham	14. 4.02
G-AGXU	Auster J/1N Alpha	1969		24. 1.46	B.H.Austen	Oaksey Park	25. 4.03
G-AGXV	Auster V J/1 Autocrat	1970		1. 2.46	B.S.Dowsett *"Pamela IV"*	Little Gransden	7. 9.03
G-AGYD	Auster J/1N Alpha	1985		4. 2.46	P.R.Hodson	(Norwich)	24.11.90
			(Damaged near Felthorpe 25.11.90: on rebuild 4.94: current status unknown)				
G-AGYH	Auster J/1N Alpha	1989		4. 2.46	W.R.V.Marklew *(Current status unknown)*	(Barrow-in-Furness)	10.10.72S

G-AGYK	Auster V J/1 Autocrat	2002		4. 2.46	M.C.Hayes	Shobdon	25. 6.04
					t/a Autocraft Syndicate		
G-AGYT	Auster J/1N Alpha	1862		18. 1.46	P.J.Barrett	(Lightwater, Surrey)	27. 2.91
					(On overhaul 6.94: current status unknown)		
G-AGYU	de Havilland DH.82A Tiger Moth	85265	DE208	10. 1.46	P.L.Jones *(As "DE208")*	Ronaldsway	11. 8.04
G-AGYY(2)	Ryan ST3KR (PT-21-RY)	1167	N56792	15. 6.83	J.J.van Egmond t/a Nostalgic Flying		
	(Kinner R56)		41-1942		*(As "27" in USAAC c/s)*	Hoogeveen, The Netherlands	19. 7.02P
G-AGZZ(2)	de Havilland DH.82A Tiger Moth		N3862	14. 5.82	G.C.P.Shea-Simonds	France Farm, Upavon	23. 4.04
	(Built DH Australia)	T256 & 926	VH-BTU/VH-RNM/VH-BMY/A17-503				

G-AHAA – G-AHZZ

G-AHAG	de Havilland DH.89A Dragon Rapide	6926	RL944	31. 1.46	Pelham Ltd	Membury	15. 7.73
					(On rebuild 10.01)		
G-AHAL	Auster J/1N Alpha	1870		31. 1.46	Wickenby Flying Club Ltd	Wickenby	7. 6.04T
G-AHAM	Auster V J/1 Autocrat	1885		21. 1.46	C.P.L.Jenkins	Rush Green	24.10.02
G-AHAN(2)	de Havilland DH.82A Tiger Moth	86553	N90406	31. 5.85	Tiger Associates Ltd	White Waltham	1. 6.04T
			F-BGDG/Fr.AF/PG644				
G-AHAP	Auster V J/1 Autocrat	1887		8. 2.46	F J.Bellamy	Haverfordwest	20. 2.91P
	(Rover V-8 conversion)				*(Noted 9.00)*		
G-AHAR*	Auster V J/1 Autocrat	1888	F-BGRZ	7. 2.46	W.P.Miller	Mavis Enderby	
	(Frame No.TAY347E/EGA304)				*(Fuselage frame for rebuild 8.98)*		
G-AHAT*	Auster J/1N Alpha	1849	(HB-EOK)	11. 2.46	Dumfries & Galloway Aviation Museum		
			(Crashed 31.8.74: cancelled 7.7.75 as WFU) (Fuselage frame only)			Dumfries	6. 2.75
G-AHAU	Auster V J/1-160 Autocrat	1850	(HB-EOL)	11. 2.46	A.C.Webber	Andreas, IoM	13. 4.03
	(Lycoming O-320-A) (Built-up fin/fuselage fillet)						
G-AHAV*	Auster V J/1 Autocrat	1863	(HB-EOM)	13. 2.46	C.J.Freeman	Headcorn	21. 6.75
					(Cancelled 22.2.99 by CAA) (Fuselage stored 4.00)		
G-AHBL	de Havilland DH.87B Hornet Moth	8135	P6786	6. 2.46	H.D.Labouchere	Blue Tile Farm, Langham	9. 5.03
			CF-BFN				
G-AHBM	de Havilland DH.87B Hornet Moth	8126	P6785	6. 2.46	P.A. & E.P.Gliddon	Redhill	21. 6.02
			CF-BFJ/(CF-BFO)/CF-BFJ				
G-AHCK*	Auster J/1N Alpha	1973		25. 3.46	Not known	Mavis Enderby	7. 5.94T
			(Damaged Ingoldmells 14.9.91 stored 5.93: cancelled 22.4.94 by CAA)				
G-AHCL	Auster J/1N Alpha	1977	G-OJVC	13. 5.46	Electronic Precision Ltd	RAF Mona	10.10.91
			G-AHCL		*(On rebuild 8.92 with Lycoming 0-320: current status unknown)*		
G-AHCR	Gould-Taylorcraft Plus D Special	211	LB352	15. 4.46	D.E.H.Balmford & D.R.Shepherd	Dunkeswell	2. 9.02P
	(Continental C90)				t/a Wagtail Flying Group		
G-AHEC(2)	Luscombe 8A Silvaire	3428	N72001	28.10.88	P.G.Baxter	Hill Farm, Nayland	22. 5.02P
	(Continental A65)		NC72001				
G-AHED*	de Havilland DH.89A Dragon Rapide 6	6944	RL962	27. 2.46	RAF Museum Reserve Collection & Repair Centre		
					(WFU & cancelled 3.3.69) (In store 1.00)	RAF Wyton	17. 4.68
G-AHGD	de Havilland DH.89A Dragon Rapide	6862	NR786	1. 4.46	R.Jones t/a Southern Sailplanes	Membury	20. 9.92
			(Destroyed near Audley End 30.6.91: components for possible rebuild 8.97)				
G-AHGW	Taylorcraft Plus D	222	LB375	2. 9.46	C.V.Butler	Shenington	3. 5.96P
					(Op Military Auster Flight) (As "LB375")		
G-AHGZ	Taylorcraft Plus D	214	LB367	24. 4.46	M.Pocock *(As "LB367")*	Duxford	13.10.02
					(To Stephen White mid 2001)		
G-AHHH	Auster 5 J/1N Alpha	2011	F-BAVR	11. 5.46	H.A.Jones	Brampton	2. 8.02P
			G-AHHH				
G-AHHP*	Auster 5 J/1N Alpha	2019	G-SIME	11. 5.46	M.J.Bonnick	NK	8. 3.86
			G-AHHP				
			(Damaged in mid-1980s: on rebuild 1992: cancelled 22.2.99 by CAA) (Current status unknown)				
G-AHHT	Auster 5 J/1N Alpha	2022		11. 5.46	A.C.Barber & N.J.Hudson t/a Southdowns Auster Group		
						Durleighmarsh Farm, Rogate, Petersfield	7. 5.01
G-AHHU*	Auster 5 J/1N Alpha	2023		11. 5.46	Not Known	(Southampton)	12. 6.63
			(Crashed Soria, Spain 10.6.63 & on rebuild 12.91: current status unknown)				
G-AHIP(2)	Piper J-3C-65 Cub (L-4H-PI)	12122	OO-GEJ(2)	3. 7.85	A.R.M.Cot-Croft	Hounslow Farm, Dunmow	15.10 02P
	(Frame No.11950)		OO-ALY/44-79826		*(Official c/n is 12008: see G-AJAD)*		
G-AHIZ	de Havilland DH.82A Tiger Moth	86533	PG624	23. 4.46	CFG Flying Ltd	Cambridge	1. 6.03T
	(Regd with Fuselage No.4610)						
G-AHKX	Avro 19 Srs.2	1333		18. 5.46	BAE Systems (Operations) Ltd	Woodford	14.10.02P
					(First post-restoration flight on 8.3.01)		
G-AHKY*	Miles M.18 Srs.2	4426	HM545	26. 4.46	National Museums of Scotland/Museum of Flight		
			U-0224/U-8		*(Cancelled 19.3.92 as WFU)*	East Fortune	20. 9.89P
G-AHLK	Taylorcraft E Auster III	700	NJ889	1. 5.46	E.T.Brackenbury	Leicester	21. 9.97
					(On rebuild 1.02)		
G-AHLT	de Havilland DH.82A Tiger Moth	82247	N9128	2. 5.46	K.J.Jarvis	Seppe, The Netherlands	1. 6.03
G-AHMM	de Havilland DH.82A Tiger Moth	86072	EM870	8. 5.46	M D Souch	Hill Farm, Durley	24 .2.55
			(Crashed near Newport Pagnell on 10.7.54: restored 1.01 & on rebuild)				
G-AHMN*	de Havilland DH.82A Tiger Moth	82223	N6985	8. 5.46	Museum of Army Flying	AAC Middle Wallop	27. 5.02P
			(Damaged landing Middle Wallop 30.5.00: cancelled 14.9.00 by CAA) (As "N6985")				

G-AHNR(2)	Taylorcraft BC-12D	7204	N43545	15.11.88	P.E.Hinkley	Downland Farm, Redhill	2. 6.02P
	(Continental A65)		NC43545				
G-AHOO(2)	de Havilland DH.82A Tiger Moth	86150	6940M	6. 6.85	J.T. & A.D.Milsom		
	(Regd with c/n 86149)		EM967			Little Farm, Hampstead Marshall	10. 8.03
G-AHPZ	de Havilland DH.82A Tiger Moth	83794	EI-AFJ	22. 5.46	N.J.Wareing	Goodwood	5. 1.50
			G-AHPZ/T7280		*(Noted 8.01)*		
G-AHRI*	de Havilland DH.104 Dove 1B	04008	4X-ARI	11. 7.46	Newark Air Museum	Winthorpe	
			G-AHRI		*(Cancelled 18.5.72 as WFU)*		
G-AHRO(2)	Cessna 140	8069	N89065	25. 1.82	R.H.Screen	RAF Bicester	20. 7.03
			NC89065				
G-AHSA	Avro 621 Tutor	-	K3215	21. 6.46	The Shuttleworth Trust	Old Warden	1. 5.02P
	(Lynx IVM)		G-AHSA/K3215		*(As "K3215")*		
G-AHSD	Taylorcraft Plus D	182	LB323	1. 7.46	A.L.Hall-Carpenter	(Thetford)	10. 9.62
					(On rebuild 8.95)		
G-AHSO	Auster 5 J/1N Alpha	2123		8. 8.46	W.P.Miller	Mavis Enderby	6. 4.95T
					(On rebuild 8.98)		
G-AHSP	Auster V J/1 Autocrat	2134	F-BGRO	8. 8.46	R.M.Weeks	Earls Colne	27. 9.03
			G-AHSP				
G-AHSS	Auster J/1N Alpha	2136		8. 8.46	A.M.Roche	Swanton Morley	6. 7.03
G-AHST*	Auster J/1N Alpha	2137		8. 8.46	A.C.Frost	Standalone Farm, Meppershall	3. 7.03
					(Cancelled 24.7.01 by CAA)		
G-AHTE	Percival P.44 Proctor 5	Ae58		26. 6.46	D.K.Tregilgas	Hill Farm, Nayland	10. 3.61
					(On rebuild 7.99)		
G-AHTW*	Airspeed AS.40 Oxford 1	3083	V3388	6. 6.46	Imperial War Museum - Skyfame Collection		
					(Cancelled 3.4.89 by CAA) (As "V3388")	Duxford	15.12.60
G-AHUF(2)	de Havilland DH.82A Tiger Moth	86221	A2123	26. 2.85	First County Finance (UK) Ltd		
			NL750		*(As "T7997") (See G-AOBH)*	Lee-on-Solent	10.12.99
G-AHUG	Taylorcraft Plus D	153	LB282	5. 6.46	D.Nieman	(Thame)	12. 7.70
G-AHUI(2)*	Miles M.38 Messenger 2A	6335		19. 7.46	Royal Berkshire Aviation Society	Woodley	4. 9.60
	(WFU 9.60: fuselage stored off-site 11.93 - to go The Aeroplane Collection, Manchester for restoration 2001)						
G-AHUJ*	Miles M.14A Hawk Trainer 3	1900	R1914	6. 6.46	Sir W J D Roberts	Strathallan	9. 7.98P
					t/a Strathallan Aircraft Collection		
					(Cancelled 19.11.99 as WFU) (Noted 12.99 as "R1914")		
G-AHUN(2)*	Temco Globe GC-1B Swift	3536	EC-AJK	24. 7.86	R.J.Hamlett	Kings Farm, Thurrock	4. 8.95P
	(Lycoming IO-360-A1D)		OO-KAY/NC77764				
					(Damaged Urchfont 4.8.92: on rebuild 25.9.99: cancelled 31.8.00 by CAA)		
G-AHUV	de Havilland DH.82A Tiger Moth	3894	N6593	24. 6.46	J.D.Gordon	Blair Atholl	10. 7.00
G-AHVU	de Havilland DH.82A Tiger Moth	84728	T6313	14. 8.46	R.A.L.Hubbard *(As "T6313")*	Meon	17. 3.03
G-AHVV	de Havilland DH.82A Tiger Moth	86123	EM929	24. 6.46	B.M.Pullen	Thruxton	18. 1.03
G-AHWJ	Taylorcraft Plus D	165	LB294	20. 6.46	M.D.Pitcher *(On rebuild 5.01)*	(Ferndown)	30. 6.71
G-AHWO*	Percival P.44 Proctor 5	Ae72	(EI-ALY)	22. 7.46	P.Bedford	Celbridge, Co.Kildare	11. 3.61
			G-AHWO		*(Crashed Collinstown, Dublin 5.5.59 & stored 4.96)*		
G-AHXE	Taylorcraft Plus D	171	LB312	9. 7.46	Jenny M.C.Pothecary	AAC Netheravon	17. 7.02P
					(As "LB312")		

G-AIAA – G-AIZZ

G-AIBE*	Fairey Fulmar 2	F.3707	N1854	29. 7.46	Fleet Air Arm Museum	RNAS Yeovilton	6. 7.59
			G-AIBE/N1854		*(As "N1854")*		
G-AIBH	Auster 5 J/1N Alpha	2113		19. 8.46	M.J.Bonnick	Standalone Farm, Meppershall	17. 7 02P
G-AIBM	Auster V J/1 Autocrat	2148		2. 9.46	D.G.Greatrex	Thatcham	9.11.04
G-AIBR	Auster V J/1 Autocrat	2151		2. 9.46	K.L.Clarke	(Horncastle)	24. 7.02T
G-AIBW	Auster J/1N Alpha	2158		2. 9.46	W.B.Bateson *(Stored 12.01)*	Blackpool	4. 5.97T
G-AIBX	Auster V J/1 Autocrat	2159		2. 9.46	B.H.Beeston	Panshanger	29.11.02
					t/a The Wasp Flying Group		
G-AIBY	Auster V J/1 Autocrat	2160		2. 9.46	D.Morris *(Stored 6.97)*	Sherburn in Elmet	13. 4.81
G-AICX(2)	Luscombe 8A Silvaire	2568	N71141	27. 1.88	R.V.Smith	Henstridge	24. 6.02P
	(Continental A65)		NC71141		*"Easy Grace"*		
G-AIDL	de Havilland DH.89A Dragon Rapide 6	6968	TX310	23. 8.46	Atlantic Air Transport Ltd	Coventry	13. 6.02T
					(Air Caernarfon c/s)		
G-AIDS	de Havilland DH.82A Tiger Moth	84546	T6055	22. 8.46	K.D.Pogmore & T.Dann		
					"The Sorcerer"	Benson's Farm, Laindon	24. 7.03
G-AIEK	Miles M.38 Messenger 2A	6339	U-9	27. 8.46	J.Buckingham	New Farm, Felton, Bristol	29. 8.03
					(As "RG333" in 2 TAF Comm Sqn c/s)		
G-AIFZ	Auster J/1N Alpha	2182		2.11.46	M.D.Anstey	Rushett Manor, Chessington	20. 8.01
G-AIGD	Auster V J/1 Autocrat	2186		2.11.46	R.B.Webber	Trenchard Farm, Eggesford	6. 7.00P
	(Officially regd incorrectly as J/1N Alpha)						
G-AIGF	Auster J/1N Alpha	2188		5.11.46	A.R.C.Mathie	(Southampton)	19. 5.85
					(Last reported 12.96: CofR @ 3.01)		
G-AIGP*	Auster V J/1 Autocrat	2165		12.10.46	W.P.Miller	Mavis Enderby	19. 6.72
	(Lycoming O-320)				*(Cancelled 30.10.73 as WFU) (On rebuild 8.98)*		

G-AIGR*	Auster J/1N Alpha	2172		12.10.46	C.J. & D.J.Baker	Carr Farm, Newark	25. 4.88T
	(Rebuilt 1953 with spare fuselage no.TAY/R/308G: damaged Cranfield 3.86: cancelled 20.1.96 by CAA)				*(Derelict frame stored 4.98)*		
G-AIGU*	Auster J/1N Alpha	2180		12.10.46	Not known *(Cancelled 1.7.92 as TWFU) (On rebuild 3.96)*	(Selby)	5. 9.74S
G-AIIH	Piper J-3C-65 Cub (L-4H-PI)	11945	44-79649	14. 9.46	J.A.de Salis	Oxford	15.11.01P
G-AIJI*	Auster J/1N Alpha	2307		15. 4.47	C.J.Baker	Carr Farm, Newark	30. 4.76
					(Damaged 12.1.75: cancelled 12.3.75 as WFU) (Frame only for spares use 4.98)		
G-AIJK*	Auster V J/4	2067		13.11.46	Leicester Museum of Science & Industry *(On rebuild off-site 2.00)*	Coalville	24. 8.68
G-AIJM	Auster V J/4	2069	EI-BEU G-AIJM	13.11.46	N.Huxtable *"Priscilla"* *(Damaged near Tring 5.1.97: stored pending overhaul/repairs)*	Cheddington	28. 3.97
G-AIJS*	Auster V J/4	2074		13.11.46	R.W.Brown *(Cancelled 1.9.81 as WFU) (Stored 5.96)*	Clothall Farm, Clothall Common	14.12.71
G-AIJT	Auster V J/4 Srs.100 (Continental O-200-A)	2075		13.11.46	J.L.Thorogood t/a The Aberdeen Auster Flying Group	Whiterashes	5. 4.02
G-AIJZ*	Auster V J/1 Autocrat	2195		5.11.46	A.A.Marshall *(Crashed Kingsland, Hereford 25.10.70 & frame stored 11.95)*	(Derby)	17. 6.71
G-AIKE	Taylorcraft J Auster 5 *(Frame No.TAY 2450)*	1097	NJ728	15.11.46	C.J.Baker *(Crashed Luton 1.9.65 & dismantled 4.98)*	Carr Farm, Newark	3. 2.66
G-AIKR*	Airspeed AS.65 Consul	4338	PK286	25. 9.46	National Aviation Museum *(As "G-AIKR")*	Ottawa, Ontario, Canada	14. 5.65
G-AILL*	Miles M.38 Messenger 2A	6341		14.11.46	Miles Aircraft Collection	Woodley	11. 4.73
					(Cancelled 30.3.89 as WFU) (Major components stored off-site 3.96)		
G-AIPR	Auster V J/4	2084		9. 1.47	R.W. & Mrs M.A.Mills t/a The MPM Flying Group	Church Farm, North Moreton	27. 5.00P
G-AIPV	Auster V J/1 Autocrat	2203		9. 1.47	W.P.Miller *"Buttercup"*	Mavis Enderby	8.12.01
G-AIRC	Auster V J/1 Autocrat	2215		13. 1.47	A.Noble	Perth	14. 1.04
G-AIRI*	de Havilland DH.82A Tiger Moth	3761	N5488	22.10.46	E.R.Goodwin *(Cancelled 3.4.89 as WFU) (Stored 10.01)*	Little Gransden	9.11.81
G-AIRK	de Havilland DH.82A Tiger Moth	82336	N9241	22.10.46	R.C.Teverson, R.W.Marshall & C.E.McKinney	Waits Farm, Belchamp Walter	5. 7.04
G-AISA	Tipsy B Srs.1	17		24. 4.47	A.A.M.& C.W.N.Huke	RAF Shawbury	19.10.01P
G-AISC	Tipsy B Srs.1	19		24. 4.47	D.R.Shepherd t/a Wagtail Flying Group *(Stored 1.02)*	Cumbernauld	23. 5.79P
G-AISS(2)	Piper J-3C-65 Cub (L-4H-PI) *(Frame No.11904)*	12077	D-ECAV SL-AAA/44-79781	3. 9.85	K.W.Wood & F.Watson *(Noted 6.00)*	Insch	25. 6.97P
G-AIST	Supermarine 300 Spitfire IA *(Built Westland Aircraft)*	WASP/20/2	AR213	25.10.46	Sheringham Aviation UK Ltd *(As "AR213/PR-D" in 609 Sqdn c/s)*	Booker	26. 3.02P
	(Also has c/n HA1 63/5 139 - Heston Aircraft Company issued c/n)						
G-AISU*	Supermarine 349 Spitfire LF.VB	CBAF.1061	AB910	25.10.46	Battle of Britain Memorial Flight *"President Roosevelt"* *(As "AB910/ZD-C" in 222 Sqn)*	RAF Coningsby	
G-AISX	Piper J-3C-85 Cub (L-4H-PI) *(Frame No.11489) (Rebuilt with ex Spanish airframe)*	11663	43-30372	28.10.46	A M Turney t/a Cubfly	Booker	21. 5.02P
G-AITB*	Airspeed AS.40 Oxford 1	-	MP425	1.11.46	RAF Museum *(As "MP425" in 1536 BATF c/s)*	Hendon	24. 5.61
G-AITF*	Airspeed AS.40 Oxford 1	-	ED290	1.11.46	SAAF Museum *(As "G-AITF": on rebuild to flying condition 3.96)*	Port Elizabeth, S.Africa	8. 6.60
G-AIUA	Miles M.14A Hawk Trainer 3	2035	T9768	11.11.46	R.Trickett	(King's Lynn)	13. 7.67P
	(Crashed Roborough 26.9.65: fuselage stored by 1995 for long term rebuild: original centre section used in rebuild of G-AKPF: wings fitted in the 1960's came from G-ANWO: on rebuild 9.00)						
G-AIUL*	de Havilland DH.89A Dragon Rapide 6	6837	NR749	8.11.46	I.Jones *(Cancelled 6.4.73 as WFU) (Fuselage noted 2.00)*	Ley Farm, Chirk	29. 9.67
G-AIVG*	Vickers V.610 Viking 1B	220		18.11.46	Musée National de l'Automobile	Mulhouse, France	12. 2.54
					(Crashed Le Bourget 12.8.53 & airframe stored 4.01)		
G-AIXA	Taylorcraft Plus D	134	LB264	13. 1.47	G.L.Brown *(Noted 11.01)*	Spanhoe	21. 2.02P
G-AIXJ	de Havilland DH.82A Tiger Moth *(Probably composite airframe rebuilt by Newbury Aeroplane Co 1991)*	85434	DE426	28.11.46	D.Green	Goodwood	13. 8.03
G-AIXN	Automobilove Zavody Mraz M.1C Sokol	112	OK-BHA	22. 4.47	A.J.Wood	Breighton	31. 1.02P
G-AIYG(2)	SNCAN Stampe SV-4B (DH Gipsy Major)	21	OO-CKZ F-BCKZ/Fr Mil	31. 8.89	L.Casteleyn	Antwerp-Deurne, Belgium	7. 6.03
G-AIYR	de Havilland DH.89A Dragon Rapide	6676	HG691	11.12.46	Fairmont Investments Ltd *"Classic Lady"* *(Op Classic Wings)*	Clacton/Duxford	29. 4.02T
G-AIYS	de Havilland DH.85 Leopard Moth	7089	YI-ABI SU-ABM	16.12.46	R.A.& V.A. Gammons	(Letchworth)	16. 4.04
G-AIZE*	Fairchild F.24W-41A Argus II (UC-61A-FA)	565	N9996F G-AIZE/43-14601	18.12.46	RAF Museum *(WFU & cancelled 6.4.73) (As "FS628")*	RAF Cosford	6. 8.66
G-AIZG*	Supermarine VS.236 Walrus 1	6S/21840	EI-ACC IAC N-18/L2301	20.12.46	Fleet Air Arm Museum *(Cancelled 1963).(As "L2301")*	RNAS Yeovilton	
G-AIZU	Auster V J/1 Autocrat	2228		31. 1.47	C.J. & J.G.B.Morley	Popham	19. 6.03
G-AIZY	Auster V J/1 Autocrat	2233		31. 1.47	B.J.Richards	(Portskewett, Gwent)	20. 9.78S
					(Damaged Portskewett 8.89: on rebuild at Brunel Technical College, Ashley Down, Bristol 6.91)		

G-AJAA – G-AJZZ

G-AJAC* Auster J/1N Alpha 2236 4. 2.47 N.J.Mortimore & H.A.Bridgman
Watchford Farm, Yarcombe 8. 3.79
(Crashed 14.5.78 & on rebuild 6.94: cancelled 28.1.99 as WFU)

G-AJAD(2) Piper J-3C-65 Cub (L-4H-PI) 12008 OO-GEJ(1) 26. 6.84 N.A.Rooney Leicester 11.10.01P
(Frame No.11835) (Regd with c/n 11700) 44-79712
(Airframe has original fuselage of OO-GEJ discarded in a rebuild in 1970s: OO-GEJ was rebuilt using Frame No.11950 (c/n 12122) ex OO-ALY/44-79826 and is now G-AHIP: OO-ALY was then rebuilt from c/n 11700 ex OO-TON/43-30409)

G-AJAE Auster J/1N Alpha 2237 4. 2.47 A.C.Ladd Romney Street Farm, Sevenoaks 5. 7.03

G-AJAJ Auster J/1N Alpha 2243 4. 2.47 R.B.Lawrence Trenchard Farm, Eggsford 18. 4.94
(Noted 6.01)

G-AJAM Auster V J/2 Arrow 2371 8. 2.47 D.A.Porter Griffins Farm, Temple Bruer 14. 6.02P

G-AJAP(2) Luscombe 8A Silvaire 2305 N45778 26. 1.89 R J Thomas Hamilton Farm, Bilsington 1. 8.02P
(Continental A65) NC45778

G-AJAS Auster J/1N Alpha 2319 14. 3.47 C.J.Baker Carr Farm, Newark 11. 4.90
(On rebuild 4.98)

G-AJBJ* de Havilland DH.89A Dragon Rapide NF894 20. 1.47 John Pierce Aviation Ltd Ley Farm, Chirk 14 .9.61T
6765 *(Under rebuild 9.00) (Cancelled 16.12.91 by CAA)*

G-AJCL(2)*de Havilland DH.89A Dragon Rapide NF851 7. 9.48 (John Pierce Aviation Ltd)
6722 Ley Farm, Chirk
(WFU Shobdon 11.1.71 &:broken up: cancelled 24.5.71: noted 9.99)

G-AJCP(2) Rollason-Druine D.31 Turbulent 9. 2.59 B.R.Pearson Eaglescott 4. 9.78S
(Ardem 4C02) PFA 512 t/a Turbulent Group *(Stored 10.95)*

G-AJDW* Auster V J/1 Autocrat 2320 14. 3.47 D.R.Hunt Mavis Enderby 17.11.77
(Cancelled 20.11.96 by CAA) (Being restored to Husky configuration 8.98 with wings of G-AVOD)

G-AJDY* Auster V J/1 Autocrat 2322 14. 3.47 (R Farrer) (Bromham, Bedford) 9. 7.71
(Cancelled 13.1.99 by CAA) (Stored for rebuild with possible fuselage frame from G-ASEE)

G-AJEB* Auster J/1N Alpha 2325 14. 3.47 The Aeroplane Collection Manchester 27. 3.69
(Cancelled 9.6.81 as WFU) (On loan to Museum of Science & Industry)

G-AJEE* Auster V J/1 Autocrat 2309 14. 3.47 A.R.Carillo De Albornoz Ronaldsway 10. 7.89
(Stored 8.92: cancelled 1.9.00 by CAA)

G-AJEH Auster J/1N Alpha 2312 14. 3.47 J.T.Powell-Tuck (Pontypool) 28. 5.90
(Current status unknown)

G-AJEI Auster J/1N Alpha 2313 14. 3.47 W.P.Miller Mavis Enderby 13. 8.94T
(i) Composite, rebuilt 1976 with fuselage of F-BFUT c/n 3357: stored 9.98)
(ii) Original fuselage stored by Crofton Aeroplane Services, Stubbington 1.95)

G-AJEM* Auster V J/1 Autocrat 2317 F-BFPB 14. 3.47 K.A.Jones Haverfordwest 18. 2.72
G-AJEM *(Cancelled 1.9.00 by CAA: noted as unofficial "G-GINO" 4.01)*

G-AJES(2) Piper J-3C-65 Cub (L-4H-PI) 11776 OO-ACB 21. 9.84 G.W.Jarvis Shifnal 24. 7.02P
(Frame No.11602) 43-30485 *(As "330485/44/C" in USAAC c/s)*

G-AJGJ Taylorcraft J Auster 5 1147 RT486 31. 1.47 D.Gotts & E.J.Downing Pauncefoot 19. 7.03
t/a Auster RT486 Flying Group *(As "RT486/PF-A")*

G-AJHJ* Taylorcraft J Auster 5 1067 NJ676 10. 2.47 Arden Family Trust
(WFU 6.49: stored 1.98) Thorns Cross Farm, Chudleigh 27. 6.49

G-AJHS de Havilland DH.82A Tiger Moth 82121 N6866 12. 2.47 J.M.Voeten & H.Van Der Paauw *(Op Vliegend Museum)*
Seppe, The Netherlands 18. 6.03

G-AJHU de Havilland DH.82A Tiger Moth 83900 T7471 12. 2.47 G.Valenti (Parma, Italy) 23. 8.98T
(Noted as "T7471" 8.00: sold to Patrick Siegwald, Orbigny, Indre et-Loire, France 2001 and on rebuild)

G-AJIH Auster V J/1 Autocrat 2318 2. 4.47 A.H.Diver Newtownards, Co.of Down 19.11.94
(Stored 3.01)

G-AJIS Auster J/1N Alpha 2336 30. 4.47 J.D.Smith & J.M.Hodgson t/a Husthwaite Auster Group
Baxby Manor, Husthwaite 25. 5.03

G-AJIT Auster V J/1 Kingsland 2337 30. 4.47 A.J.Kay Netherthorpe 14. 6.02P
(Continental O-200-A) t/a G-AJIT Group

G-AJIU Auster V J/1 Autocrat 2338 30. 4.47 M.D.Greenhalgh Netherthorpe 20. 6.03

G-AJIW Auster J/1N Alpha 2340 30. 4.47 Truman Aviation Ltd Nottingham 16.10.82
(On rebuild 7.99)

G-AJJS(2) Cessna 120 13047 8R-GBO 7. 1.87 R.W.Marchant, I.D.Ranger & S.C.Parsons
(Continental O-200-A) VP-GBO/VP-TBO/N1106M/YV-T-CTA/NC2786N t/a Robhurst Flying Group
(Thought rebuilt 1994 with new imported airframe) Headcorn 8. 5.02P

G-AJJT(2) Cessna 120 12881 N2621N 27. 1.88 J.S.Robson
(Continental C85) NC2621N Franklyns Field, Chewton Mendip 27.11.02P

G-AJJU(2) Luscombe 8E Silvaire 2295 N45768 10. 1.89 L.C.Moon White Waltham 20. 8.02P
(Continental C85) NC45768

G-AJKB(2) Luscombe 8E Silvaire 3058 N71631 4. 1.89 A.F.Hall & S.P.Collins Tibenham 23. 8.99P
(Continental C85) NC71631 *(Noted 7.01)*

G-AJOA de Havilland DH.82A Tiger Moth 83167 T5424 29. 4.47 F.P.Le Coyte *(As "T5424")*
Lotmead Farm, Wanborough, Swindon 22. 5.03

G-AJOC* Miles M.38 Messenger 2A 6370 23. 4.47 Ulster Folk & Transport Museum
Holywood, Belfast 18. 5.72

G-AJOE Miles M.38 Messenger 2A 6367 28. 4.47 P.W.Bishop Kemble 18.10.04

G-AJON(2) Aeronca 7AC Champion 7AC-2633 OO-TWH 3. 1.86 A.Biggs & J.L.Broad Shenington 30. 6.02P
t/a Oscar November 92 Syndicate

G-AJOZ* Fairchild F.24W-41A Argus 1 347 FK338 21. 4.47 Yorkshire Air Museum Elvington 15.12.63
(Ranger UC-61-FA) 42-32142
(Crashed Rennes, France 16.8.62 & cancelled) (For restoration 10.00)

G-AJPI Fairchild F.24R-46A Argus 3 851 HB614 26. 4.47 T.H.Bishop Horsford, Norwich 30. 1.04
(UC-61A-FA) 43-14887 *(As "314887" in USAAF c/s)*

G-AJPZ* Auster V J/1 Autocrat 2348 F-BFPE 12. 5.47 W.Hamblen (Stoke-on-Trent) 14. 6.85
G-AJPZ
(Damaged in gales Thruxton 2.3.84: cancelled 18.11.88 as WFU) (On rebuild 1999: wings noted Abbots Bromley 8.00)

G-AJRB Auster V J/1 Autocrat 2350 12. 5.47 R.H.Ford c/o Fordair Aviation Ltd & B.Brooks
Sywell 8. 3.04

G-AJRC Auster V J/1 Autocrat 2601 12. 5.47 M Barker Willy Howe Farm, Wold Newton 14. 7.02

G-AJRE Auster V J/1 Autocrat 2603 12. 5.47 R.R.Harris Crowfield 8. 8.02

G-AJRH* Auster J/1N Alpha 2606 12. 5.47 Leicestershire County Council Museums
Charnwood Museum, Loughborough 5. 6.69
(Cancelled 18.1.99 by CAA)

G-AJRS Miles M.14A Hawk Trainer 3 1750 P6382 30. 4.47 The Shuttleworth Trust Old Warden 21. 7.01P
G-AJDR/G-AJRS/P6382 *(As "P6382/C" in 16 EFTS c/s)*
(Composite aircraft which flew as "G-AJDR" 1.54/3.71)

G-AJSN* Fairchild F.24W-41A Argus 2 849 HB612 8. 5.47 V.Trimble Banbridge, Co.Down 9. 5.69T
43-14885
(Damaged Cork 10.6.67: cancelled 12.3.73 as WFU) (Stored 2.95: current status unknown)

G-AJTW de Havilland DH.82A Tiger Moth 82203 N6965 21. 5.47 J.A.Barker *(As "N6965/FL-J")* Tibenham 9. 9.00
(Crashed landing Raydon near Ipswich 7.6.99 & extensively damaged)

G-AJUD* Auster V J/1 Autocrat 2614 5. 6.47 C.L.Sawyer (Bromham, Bedford) 18. 5.74
(On rebuild 12.97: cancelled 31.3.99 by CAA) (Noted for sale 2000)

G-AJUE Auster V J/1 Autocrat 2616 5. 6.47 P.H.B.Cole Lavington, Devizes 31.10.02

G-AJUL Auster J/1N Alpha 2624 18. 6.47 M.J.Crees Halstead, Essex 11. 9.81
(On rebuild 12.90)

G-AJVE de Havilland DH.82A Tiger Moth 85814 DE943 28. 5.47 R.A.Gammons RAF Henlow 10. 6.03
(Composite 1981 rebuild including substantial parts of G-APGL c/n 86460/NM140)

G-AJVH* Fairey Swordfish II - LS326 28. 5.47 RN Historic Flight RNAS Yeovilton
(Restored to RN & cancelled 30.4.59) (As "LS326/L2" in 836 Sqdn c/s)

G-AJVT* Taylorcraft J Auster 5 1495 TJ478 4. 6.47 S.Craggs
Lane House Farm, Burneston, Bedale 25. 8.70
(Frame/wings stored 5.86: cancelled 3.4.89 as WFU) (Current status unknown)

G-AJWB Miles M.38 Messenger 2A 6699 17. 6.47 G.E.J.Spooner Earls Colne 11. 5.68
(F/f @ Hatch 19.12.01 after rebuild)

G-AJXC* Taylorcraft J Auster 5 1409 TJ343 11. 6.47 J.Graves Scotland Farm, Hook 2. 8.82
(Damaged Hook in gales 16.10.87: cancelled 3.4.89 by CAA) (Stored 9.94: fuselage noted 5.00)

G-AJXV Taylorcraft G Auster 4 1065 F-BEEJ 8. 9.47 Barbara A.Farries Carr Farm, Newark 27. 2.03
G-AJXV/NJ695 *(As "NJ695")*

G-AJXY Taylorcraft G Auster 4 792 MT243 4. 5.48 D.A.Hall (Melton Mowbray) 10.11.70
(On rebuild 1993: new owner 7.00)

G-AJYB Auster J/1N Alpha 847 MS974 3. 2.49 P.J.Shotbolt
Ingthorpe Farm, Great Casterton, Lincs 25. 7.02

G-AKAA – G-AKZZ

G-AKAT Miles M.14A Hawk Trainer 3 2005 F-AZOR 2. 7.47 J.D.Haslam Breighton 27. 7.02P
G-AKAT/T9738 *(As "T9738")*

G-AKAZ(2) Piper J-3C-65 Cub AN.1 & 8499 F-BFYL 19. 4.82 Frazerblades Ltd Duxford 26. 7.02P
(L-4A-PI) *(Frame No.8616)* Fr Mil/42-36375 *(As "57-H" in 83rd FS/78th FG USAAF c/s)*

G-AKBO Miles M.38 Messenger 2A 6378 15. 7.47 R.W.Littledale Turweston 3. 8.03
t/a Bravo Oscar Syndicate

G-AKDK* Miles M.65 Gemini 1A 6469 22. 8.47 Danmarks Flyvemuseum
Kongelunden, Billund, Denmark 27. 3.70
(Cancelled 5.11.73 as WFU) (For rebuild with parts from G-AJWA c/n 6290: stored 2000)

G-AKDN de Havilland DHC.1A Chipmunk 10 11 14. 8.47 P.S.Derry Bagby 17. 5.03

G-AKDW de Havilland DH.89A Dragon Rapide F-BCDB 25. 8.47 De Havilland Aircraft Museum Trust Ltd
6897 G-AKDW/YI-ABD/NR833 *"City of Winchester"* London Colney 8. 5.59
(On rebuild 4.00)

G-AKEK* Miles M.65 Gemini 3A 6483 8. 9.47 M.Vaisey & T.Moore Rotary Farm, Hatch 22. 9.72
t/a Gemini Wanderers
(Cancelled 20.11.74 as WFU) (On long term rebuild 12.94) (Current status unknown)

G-AKEL* Miles M.65 Gemini 1A 6484 8. 9.47 Ulster Folk & Transport Museum
(Cancelled 30.5.84 as WFU) (Components only 4.96: for rebuild with G-AKGE) Holywood, Belfast 29. 4.72

G-AKEZ Miles M.38 Messenger 2A 6707 27. 8.47 P.G.Lee *(Noted on rebuild 10.01)*
Fanners Farm, Great Waltham, Essex 15.11.68

G-AKGD* Miles M.65 Gemini 1A 6492 11. 9.47 The Miles Aircraft Collection Woodley 14.11.66
(Cancelled 22.11.73 as WFU) (Parts only stored off-site 2.00)

G-AKGE* Miles M.65 Gemini 3C 6488 EI-ALM 18.10.47 Ulster Folk & Transport Museum
G-AKGE *(Cancelled 30.5.84: stored 4.96)* Holywood, Belfast 7. 6.74
G-AKHP Miles M.65 Gemini 1A 6519 3.10.47 P.A.Brook Shoreham 11. 6.03
G-AKHW* Miles M.65 Gemini 1A 6524 ZK-KHW 21.10.47 (S Smith) (Dairy Flat, New Zealand)
(Shipped to New Zealand 16.5.91 & cancelled 9.12.94: noted 2.00 as "G-AKHW")
G-AKHZ* Miles M.65 Gemini 7 6527 21.10.47 The Miles Aircraft Collection Woodley 8. 1.64
(Composite airframe with parts from G-ALMU, G-ALUG & G-AMME: on rebuild 5.01)
G-AKIB(2) Piper J-3C-90 Cub 12311 OO-RAY 18. 4.84 M.C.Bennett Bodmin 16. 8.02P
(L-4H-PI) *(Frame No.12139)* 44-80015 *(As "480015/M/44" in USAAC c/s)*
G-AKIF de Havilland DH.89A Dragon Rapide LN-BEZ 24. 9.47 Airborne Taxi Services Ltd (London SW1) 19. 8.03T
6838 G-AKIF/NR750
G-AKIN Miles M.38 Messenger 2A 6728 19. 9.47 R.Spiller & Sons Ltd Sywell 3. 5.02
G-AKIS* Miles M.38 Messenger 2A 6725 19. 9.47 Koninklijk Legermuseum/Musée Royal de L'Armee
(Cancelled 24.2.70 as WFU) (Stored as "G-AKIS") Brussels 5. 8.70
G-AKIU Percival P.44 Proctor 5 Ae129 20. 2.48 Air Atlantique Ltd Coventry 24. 1.65
(Current status unknown)
G-AKKB Miles M.65 Gemini 1A 6537 28.10.47 J.Buckingham New Farm, Felton, Bristol 19. 9.98
(Air Total c/s)
G-AKKH Miles M.65 Gemini 1A 6479 OO-CDO 23. 7.48 J.S.Allison RAF Halton 13.11.03T
G-AKKR* Miles M.14A Hawk Trainer 3 1995 "T9967" 23. 6.48 RAF Museum AAC Middle Wallop 10. 4.65
(May be T9967 [2160] from 1943 rebuild) 8378M/G-AKKR/T9708 *(On loan to Museum of Army Flying as "T9707")*
G-AKKY* Miles M.14A Hawk Trainer 3 2078 T9841 23. 6.48 Royal Berkshire Aviation Society Woodley 6.11.64
(WFU 11.60 & cancelled 12.4.73 as WFU) (Allocated BAPC44 to reflect rebuild status from various parts) (As "L6906")
G-AKLW* Short SA.6 Sealand 1 SH.1571 (USA) 26.11.47 Ulster Folk & Transport Museum Belfast
R Saudi AF/SU-AHY/G-AKLW *(Sold abroad 8.51: stored 3.01)*
G-AKOE de Havilland DH.89A Dragon Rapide 4 X7484 3.12.47 J.E.Pierce Ley Farm, Chirk 25. 7.82
6601 *(British Airways c/s: stored 9.99)*
G-AKOW* Taylorcraft J Auster 5 1579 PH-NAD(2) 23.12.47 Museum of Army Flying AAC Middle Wallop 26. 6.82
PH-NEG/G-AKOW/TJ569 *(Cancelled 5.8.87 as WFU) (As "TJ569")*
(Regd as c/n TJ569A after rebuild in Holland)
G-AKPF Miles M.14A Hawk Trainer 3 2228 V1075 27. 1.48 P.R.Holloway Old Warden 8. 4.02P
(As "V1075" in RAF c/s)
(i) Rebuilt 1955 as composite with centre-section from G-AIUA, fuselage from G-ANLT, wings from G-AHYL.
(ii) Rebuilt 1970/80 with about 10% of fuselage from G-AKPF: tail unit also from G-ANLT)
G-AKRA(2) Piper J-3C-65 Cub 11255 I-FIVI 15. 6.84 W.R.Savin (Cambridge)
(L-4H-PI) *(Frame No.11080)* 43-29964 *(On rebuild 9.00)*
G-AKRP de Havilland DH.89A Dragon Rapide 4 CN-TTO 26. 1.48 R.H.Ford Sywell 26. 6.03
6940 (F-DAFS)/G-AKRP/RL958 c/o Fordaire Aviation Ltd
G-AKSY Taylorcraft J Auster 5D 1567 F-BGOO 10. 2.48 A.Brier Breighton 22. 3.04
G-AKSY/TJ534 *(As "TJ534")*
G-AKSZ Taylorcraft J Auster 5C 1503 F-BGPQ 10. 2.48 A.R.C.Mathie Crowfield 9. 5.02
(DH Gipsy Major 1) *(Has large fin & rudder)* G-AKSZ/TJ457
G-AKTH(2) Piper J-3C-65 Cub (L-4J-PI) 13211 OO-AGL 14. 7.86 G.J.Harry, The Viscount Goschen
(Frame No.13041) PH-UCR/45-4471 Eaglescott 14. 4.02P
(Regd with incorrect c/n 13047)
G-AKTI(2) Luscombe 8A Silvaire 4101 N1374K 27. 5.87 M.W.Olliver Old Sarum 20. 4.01P
(Continental A65) NC1374K
G-AKTK(2) Aeronca 11AC Chief 11AC-1017 N9379E 13. 3.89 R.W.Marshall, G.C.Jones & R Lloyd
(Continental A65) NC9379E Waits Farm, Belchamp Walter 5. 8.02P
G-AKTM(2)*Luscombe 8F Silvaire 90 6174 C-GGMZ 2. 6.88 (Hampshire Light Plane Services)
N1547B Chilbolton
(Crashed landing Sandford Hall, near Oswestry 21.9.97: cancelled as 12.1.98 destroyed: cabin noted 5.98)
G-AKTN(2) Luscombe 8A Silvaire 3540 N77813 22. 7.88 D.Taylor (Canvey Island) 21. 9.01P
(Continental A65) NC77813
G-AKTO(2) Aeronca 7BCM Champion 7AC-940 N8515X 19. 5.88 D.C.Murray Lee-on-Solent 29. 3.02P
(Continental A75) N82311/NC82311
(Modified from 7AC standard 8.50)
G-AKTP(2) Piper PA-17 Vagabond 17-82 N4683H 24. 6.88 G.Campbell Old Sarum 21. 6.02P
(Continental C85) NC4683H t/a G-AKTP Flying Group
G-AKTR(2) Aeronca 7AC Champion 7AC-3017 N58312 19. 6.89 C.Fielder New Farm, Felton 27. 7.96P
NC58312 *"Eddie"*
G-AKTS(2) Cessna 120 11875 N77434 26. 5.88 W.Fairney Kemble 17. 6.02P
NC77434 *"Southern Belle"*
G-AKTT(2) Luscombe 8A Silvaire 3279 N71852 21. 7.88 S.J.Charters (Leeds) 23. 6.92P
(Continental A65) NC71852 *(Crashed 6.7.91: stored 1.96) (Current status unknown)*
G-AKUE(2) de Havilland DH.82A Tiger Moth P.68 ZS-FZL 12. 2.86 D.F.Hodgkinson White Waltham 4. 4.04T
(Built OGMA) CR-AGM/FAP
G-AKUF(2) Luscombe 8F Silvaire 4794 N2067K 1. 8.88 E.J.Lloyd Caterham 7. 8.02P
(Continental C90) NC2067K
G-AKUG(2) Luscombe 8A Silvaire 3689 N77962 21. 7.88 P Groves Lee-on-Solent 15. 1.02P
(Continental A65) NC77962 t/a G-AKUG Group
G-AKUH(2) Luscombe 8E Silvaire 4644 N1917K 24.10.88 I.M.Bower Leicester 18.10.02P
(Continental O-200-A) NC1917K *"Lucy Too"*

G-AKUI(2)	Luscombe 8E Silvaire	2464	N45937	24.10.88	D.A.Sims	(Stoke-on-Trent)	17. 1.90P
	(Continental O-200-A)		NC45937				
G-AKUJ(2)	Luscombe 8E Silvaire	5282	N2555K	4. 8.88	R.C.Green	Coventry	8.11.02P
	(Continental C85)		NC2555K				
G-AKUK(2)	Luscombe 8A Silvaire	5793	N1166B	28.10.88	N.B.Brown	Leckhampstead Farm, Newbury	21. 6.02P
	(Continental A65)		NC1166B		t/a Leckhampstead Flying Group		
G-AKUL(2)	Luscombe 8A Silvaire	4189	N1462K	9. 2.89	E.A.Taylor	Southend	21. 5.90P
	(Continental A65)		NC1462K		*(Noted 1.02)*		
G-AKUM(2)	Luscombe 8F Silvaire	6452	N2025B	17. 2.88	D A Young	North Weald	30. 9.02P
	(Continental C90)						
G-AKUN(2)	Piper J-3C-85 Cub	6914	N38304	13. 1.89	W.R.Savin	Cold Harbour Farm, Willingham	29. 4.02P
			NC38304				
G-AKUO(2)	Aeronca 11AC Chief	11AC-1376	N9730E	16. 1.89	L.W.Richardson	Denham	12. 9.02P
			NC9730E				
G-AKUP(2)	Luscombe 8E Silvaire	5501	N2774K	9. 5.89	D.A.Young	(Enfield)	
	(Lycoming O-320)		NC2774K		*(Stored 3.97/: current status unknown)*		
G-AKUR(2)	Cessna 140	13819	N1647V	26. 1.89	J.Greenaway & C.A.Davis	Popham	21. 9.95
			NC1647V				
G-AKUW	Chrislea CH.3 Srs.2 Super Ace	105		8. 3.48	J & S Rickett	(Louth)	15. 5.02P
G-AKVF	Chrislea CH.3 Srs.2 Super Ace	114	AP-ADT	8. 3.48	B.Metters		
			G-AKVF			Bourne Park, Hurstbourne Tarrant	6.11.01P
G-AKVM(2)	Cessna 120	13431	N3173N	10. 1.89	N.Wise & S.Walker		
			NC3173N			Croft-on-Tees, Darlington	23. 5.02P
G-AKVN(2)	Aeronca 11AC Chief	11AC-469	N3742B	13. 1.89	C.E.Ellis	Priory Farm, Tibenham	3. 4.02P
			NC3742B		t/a Breckland Aeronca Group		
G-AKVO(2)	Taylorcraft BC-12D	9845	N44045	10. 1.89	R.J.Whybrow & M.J.Steward t/a Albion Flyers		
	(Continental A65)		NC44045			Priory Farm, Tibenham	8. 3.02P
G-AKVP(2)	Luscombe 8A Silvaire	5549	N2822K	21. 7.48	J M Edis	Charity Farm, Baxterley	4.11.02P
	(Continental A65)		NC2822K				
G-AKVR	Chrislea CH3 Srs.4 Skyjeep	125	VH-OLD	8. 3.48	N.D.Needham	Old Manor Farm, Anwick	
			VH-RCD/VH-BRP/G-AKVR		*(New owner 3.01)*		
G-AKVZ	Miles M.38 Messenger 4B	6352	RH427	25. 6.48	Shipping & Airlines Ltd	Biggin Hill	4.10.03
G-AKWS	Auster 5A-160	1237	RT610	1. 4.48	Fast Aerospace Ltd	Crowfield	4. 6.03
	(Lycoming O-320)				*(As "RT610")*		
G-AKWT*	Taylorcraft J Auster 5	998	MT360	1. 4.48	C.J.Baker	Carr Farm, Newark	22. 7.49
					(Crashed Nottingham 7.8.48: derelict frame stored 4.98)		
G-AKXP	Taylorcraft J Auster 5	1017	NJ633	13. 4.48	M.Pocock	Hedge End, Southampton	19.12.70
	(Crashed St.Mary's, Isles of Scilly 9.4.70: on long term rebuild 6.95: current status unknown)						
G-AKXS	de Havilland DH.82A Tiger Moth	83512	T7105	13. 4.48	P.A.Colman		
						Luxters Farm, Hambleden, Henley-on-Thames	21. 3.03
G-AKZN*	Percival P.34A Proctor 3	K.386	Z7197	24. 5.48	RAF Museum	Hendon	29.11.63
			(8380M)		*(As "Z7197")*		

G-ALAA – G-ALZZ

G-ALAH*	Miles M.38 Messenger 4A	-	RH377	28. 5.48	Not known	Sabadell, Barcelona, Spain	18. 4.65
					(WFU 18.4.65: stored as "G-ALAH" 3.95: noted 11.01)		
G-ALAX*	de Havilland DH.89A Dragon Rapide		RL948	27. 5.48	Durney Collection/D.Johnson	(Andover)	8. 3.67
		6930					
	(Fuselage stored 1994 with components from G-AFRK, G-AHGC, G-AHJS & G-ASRJ: current status unknown))						
G-ALBD	de Havilland DH.82A Tiger Moth	84130	T7748	27. 5.48	C.H.Schoonbeek		
						Midden Zeeland, The Netherlands	31.10.81
	(Damaged Leopoldsburg, Belgium 24.5.81: noted 5.00 with Gyrocopter Aviation being rebuilt for static display)						
G-ALBJ	Taylorcraft J Auster 5	1831	TW501	3. 6.48	P.N.Elkington	Bloxholm, Sleaford	23. 8.03
G-ALBK	Taylorcraft J Auster 5	1273	RT644	3. 6.48	S.J.Wright & Co (Farmers) Ltd	(Lincoln)	17. 4.03
G-ALBN*	Bristol 173 Mk.1	12871	7648M	22. 7.48	Bristol Aero Collection	Kemble	
			XF785		*(To RAF as XF785 in 1953 & cancelled)*		
G-ALCK*	Percival P.34A Proctor 3	H.536	LZ766	18. 6.48	Imperial War Museum - Skyfame Collection		
					(As "LZ766")	Duxford	19. 6.63
G-ALCU*	de Havilland DH.104 Dove 2B	04022	VT-CEH	3. 8.48	Midland Air Museum	Coventry	16. 3.73
					(Cancelled 8.9.78 as WFU)		
G-ALDG*	Handley Page HP.81 Hermes IV	HP.81/8		27.10.49	Duxford Aviation Society	Duxford	9. 1.63
					(BOAC c/s) "Horsa" (WFU 9.62: fuselage only)		
G-ALEH(2)	Piper PA-17 Vagabond	17-87	N4689H	17. 8.81	A.D.Pearce	White Waltham	28. 3.02P
	(Continental A65)		NC4689H				
G-ALFA	Taylorcraft J Auster 5	1236	RT607	20.10.48	S.P.Barrett	Leicester	14. 9.04
					t/a Golf Alfa Auster Group		
	(P/i uncertain as c/n 1236 considered sold as HB-EOC 4.48: reported as c/n 826 (MS958) but doubtful)						
G-ALFT*	de Havilland DH.104 Dove 6	04233		14.12.48	Air Atlantique Ltd	Caernarfon	13. 6.73
					(Cancelled 11.2.77 as WFU) (Under restoration 12.99)		
G-ALFU*	de Havilland DH.104 Dove 6	04234		14.12.48	Duxford Aviation Society	Duxford	4. 6.71
					(Cancelled 14.11.72 as WFU)		

G-ALGA(2)	Piper PA-15 Vagabond (Lycoming O-145)	15-348	N4575H NC4575H	3.12.86	G.A.Brady	Enstone	14. 5.02P
G-ALIJ(2)	Piper PA-17 Vagabond (Continental A65)	17-166	N4866H	13. 2.87	A.S.Cowan t/a Popham Flying Group G-ALIJ	Popham	19. 3.02P
G-ALIW(2)	de Havilland DH.82A Tiger Moth	82901	N27WB ZK-ATI/NZ899/R5006	17. 8.81	D.I.M.Geddes & F.R.Curry t/a Provost Flying Group	Shoreham	14. 8.03
G-ALJF	Percival P.34A Proctor 3	K.427	Z7252	3. 3.49	J.F.Moore	Biggin Hill	8. 7.04
G-ALJL*	de Havilland DH.82A Tiger Moth	84726	T6311	7. 3.49	Not known	(Southampton)	28. 9.50
					(Cancellation details not known) (On long term rebuild from components 8.00)		
G-ALNA	de Havilland DH.82A Tiger Moth	85061	T6774	11. 4.49	R.J.Doughton *(Brooklands Aviation c/s)*	Vendee Air Park, France	11.11.01T
G-ALND	de Havilland DH.82A Tiger Moth	82308	N9191	12. 4.49	J.T.Powell-Tuck	Abergavenny	11. 4.82
					(Crashed Panshanger 8.3.81 & on rebuild 3.96: as "N9191" in RN c/s)		
G-ALNV*	Taylorcraft J Auster 5	1216	RT578	21. 4.49	C.J.Baker *(Frame stored 4.98)*	Carr Farm, Newark	4. 7.50
G-ALOD(2)	Cessna 140	14691	N2440V	14.10.83	J.R.Stainer	Whitehall Farm, Benington	11. 1.05
G-ALRI	de Havilland DH.82A Tiger Moth	83350	ZK-BAB G-ALRI/T5672	2. 5.51	Wessex Aviation & Transport Ltd	Chalmington	19. 8.94
					(As "T5672" in RAF c/s: noted 6.96: current status unknown)		
G-ALRX*	Bristol 175 Britannia Srs.101	12874	(WB473) (VX447)	25. 6.51	Bristol Aero Collection	Kemble	
					(DBR landing Littleton-upon-Severn 4.2.54: fuselage as instructional airframe: now nose only)		
G-ALSX*	Bristol 171 Sycamore 3	12892	G-48/1 G-ALSX/VR-TBS/G-ALSX	17.11.50	E.D.ap Rees t/a The Helicopter Museum	Weston-super-Mare	24. 9.65
G-ALTO(2)	Cessna 140 (Continental C85)	14253	N2040V	19. 1.82	J.M.Edis	Charity Farm, Baxterley	3. 7.04
G-ALTW*	de Havilland DH.82A Tiger Moth	84177	T7799	13. 6.49	A.Mangham	Denford Manor, Hungerford	8. 6.70
					(Crashed Panshanger 5.11.69: cancelled 7.9.81 by CAA) (Tailplane & wings stored 10.01)		
G-ALUC	de Havilland DH.82A Tiger Moth	83094	R5219	28. 6.49	D.R. & Mrs M.Wood	Fowle Hall Farm, Paddock Wood, Kent	7.11.04
G-ALVP*	de Havilland DH.82A Tiger Moth	82711	R4770	26. 9.49	V.& R.Wheele *(Stored for rebuild 2002)*	(Nottingham)	15. 2.61
G-ALWB	de Havilland DHC.1 Chipmunk 22A	C1/0100	OE-ABC G-ALWB	28.12.49	D J Neville & P A Dear-Neville	(Royston)	18. 5.03
G-ALWC*	Douglas C-47A-25DK Dakota 4	13590	(F-GBOL) KG723/42-93654	10. 1.50	Ailes Anciennes Toulouse	Toulouse-Blagnac	6. 2.83A
					(Cancelled 3.4.89 by CAA) (Open storage 6.95: current status unknown))		
G-ALWF*	Vickers V.701 Viscount	5		2. 1.50	Duxford Aviation Society *(BEA c/s) "RMA Sir John Franklin" (Cancelled 18.4.72 as WFU)*	Duxford	16. 4.72
G-ALWS	de Havilland DH.82A Tiger Moth *(Regd with c/n 82413)*	82415	N9328	24. 1.50	A.P.Beynon *(On rebuild 8.00)*	Welshpool	
G-ALWW	de Havilland DH.82A Tiger Moth	86366	NL923	24. 1.50	D.E.Findon t/a Stratford-upon-Avon Tiger Moth Group	Bidford	11. 3.03
G-ALXT*	de Havilland DH.89A Dragon Rapide	6736	4R-AAI CY-AAI/G-ALXT/NF865	24. 1.50	Science Museum Air Transport Coln & Storage Facility *(Railway Air Service titles) "Star of Scotia"*	Wroughton	
G-ALXZ	Taylorcraft J Auster 5-150 (Lycoming O-320) (Frame No.TAY24070)	1082	D-EGOF PH-NER/G-ALXZ/NJ689	1. 2.50	M.F.Cuming	Sackville Farm, Riseley	12. 7.03
G-ALYB*	Taylorcraft J Auster 5	1173	RT520	3. 2.50	South Yorkshire Aviation Museum		
					(Cancelled 29.2.84 by CAA) (On rebuild 2001)	Home Farm, Firbeck	26. 5.63
G-ALYG	Taylorcraft J Auster 5D	835	MS968	14. 3.50	A.L.Young	Henstridge	19. 1.70
					(Regd with incorrect identity MT968: frame stored 3.00: for rebuild as Auster 5)		
G-ALYW(2)*	de Havilland DH.106 Comet 1	06009	(G-ALYV)	18. 9.51	RAF Exhibition Unit	RAF St.Athan	14. 6.54
					(BU 6.55: fuselage converted to "Nimrod" exhibition airframe as "XV238") (Current status unknown)		
G-ALZE*	Britten-Norman BN-1F	1		16. 3.50	Hall of Aviation *(Cancelled 8.6.89 as WFU)*	Southampton	
G-ALZO(2)*	Airspeed AS.57 Ambassador 2	5226	RJordAF-108 G-ALZO/(G-AMAD)	5. 4.50	Duxford Aviation Society *(Cancelled 10.9.81 as WFU) (On rebuild 5.00)*	Duxford	14. 5.71

G-AMAA – G-AMZZ

G-AMAU*	Hawker Hurricane IIc *(12,780th & final Hurricane built)*	-	PZ865	1. 5.50	Battle of Britain Mememorial Flight	RAF Coningsby	
					(Transferred to Military Marks on 19.12.72:.as "PZ865/Q" in RAFSEAC c/s)		
G-AMAW	Luton LA-4 Minor (Bristol Cherub 3) *(AKA as Swalesong SA.I)*	JRC.1 & SA.I		29. 4.50	R.H.Coates *(Stored 12.01)*	Breighton	6. 8.88P
G-AMBB	de Havilland DH.82A Tiger Moth	85070	T6801	1. 5.50	J.Eagles	Oaksey Park	
	(Composite rebuild - parts to "G-MAZY" ? - see SECTION 9, Part 2(i): on rebuild 6.95)						
G-AMCA	Douglas C-47B-30DK Dakota 3	16218/32966	KN487 44-76634	1. 6.50	Atlantic Air Transport Ltd *(Partially dismantled 1.02)*	Coventry	10.12.00A
G-AMCK	de Havilland DH.82A Tiger Moth	84641	N65N C-GBBF/SLN-05/D-EGXY/HB-UAC/G-AMCK/T6193	15. 6.50	Avia Special Ltd	Leicester	15. 3.04T

G-AMCM de Havilland DH.82A Tiger Moth 85295 DE249 14.12.50 A K & J.I Cooper
(Regd with c/n "89259") Denford Manor, Hungerford 28. 5.56
(Crashed near Somerton 25.9.55: rear fuselage frame on restoration 10.01 but not original G-AMCM!)
G-AMDA* Avro 652A Anson 1 N4877 20. 7.50 Imperial War Museum - Skyfame Collection
(Cancelled 9.9.81 by CAA) (On rebuild 2000: as "N4877") Duxford 14.12.62
G-AMEN(2) Piper PA-18 Super Cub 95 18-1998 (G-BJTR) 29.12.81 A.Lovejoy & W.Cook Popham 26. 7.02P
(L-18C-PI) *(Frame No.18-1963)* MM52-2398 "EI.71"/I-EIAM/MM52-2398/52-2398 t/a Sierra Golf Flying Group
(Italian rebuild c/n OMA.71-08)
G-AMHF de Havilland DH.82A Tiger Moth 83026 R5144 6. 2.51 Wavendon Social Housing Ltd Sywell 14. 9.03
(Rebuilt with components from G-BABA c/n 86584 ex F-BGDT/PG687)
G-AMHJ Douglas C-47A-25DK Dakota 6 13468 SU-AZI 6. 2.51 Atlantic Air Transport Ltd Coventry 5.12.00A
G-AMHJ/ZS-BRW/KG651/42-108962 *(Partially dismantled 1.02)*
G-AMIU de Havilland DH.82A Tiger Moth 83228 T5495 9. 4.51 M D Souch (Hill Farm, Durley) 9. 9.71
(Crashed Booker 15.10.69: frame reported on restoration Denford Manor 10.01: now departed for completion)
G-AMIV* de Havilland DH.82A Tiger Moth 83105 R5246 9. 4.51 Not known NK
(WFU 12.11.65 & cancelled as WFU 15.6.73) (Stored on rebuild 2002)
G-AMKL* Auster B.4 2983 XA177 3. 7.51 Not known Carr Farm, Newark
G-AMKL/G-25-2
(Cancelled 24.9.58) (On rebuild with new fuselage & some original components 4.98)
G-AMKU Auster 5 J/1B Aiglet 2721 ST-ABD 10. 7.51 P.G.Lipman Romney Street Farm, Sevenoaks 5. 7.03
SN-ABD/G-AMKU
G-AMLZ* Percival P.50 Prince 6E P.46 (VR-TBN) 23.11.51 Air Atlantique Ltd Caernarfon 18. 6.71
G-AMLZ *(Cancelled 9.10.84 as WFU) (Under restoration 12.99)*
G-AMMS Auster J/5K Aiglet Trainer 2745 11.10.51 A.J.Large Trenchard Farm, Eggsford 19.10.98
(Noted 6.01)
G-AMNN de Havilland DH.82A Tiger Moth 86457 NM137 24.12.51 M.Thrower *"Spirit of Pashley"* Shoreham 20. 7.03T
t/a Northbrook College of Aeronautical Engineering
(Composite from unidentified airframe: the original G-AMNN may have been absorbed into G-BPAJ)
G-AMOG(2)* Vickers V.701 Viscount 7 (G-AMNZ) 23. 5.52 RAF Museum RAF Cosford 14. 6.77
(Cancelled 17.5.76 as WFU) (BEA c/s) "RMA Robert Falcon Scott"
G-AMPG(2) Piper PA-12 Super Cruiser 12-985 N2647M 25. 3.85 R.Simpson Preston Court, Ledbury 16. 4.02P
(Hoerner wing-tips) NC2647
G-AMPI(2) SNCAN Stampe SV-4C 213 N6RA 13. 2.84 T.W.Harris Booker 14. 6.03
F-BCFX
G-AMPO* Douglas C-47B-30DK Dakota 3 LN-RTO 25. 2.52 (Royal Air Force) RAF Lyneham 29. 3.97A
(Regd as c/n 16438/33186) 16437/33185 G-AMPO/KN566/44-76853 *(Cancelled 18.10.01 as wfu) (Gate Guardian)*
G-AMPP* Douglas C-47B Dakota 3 15272/26717 XF756 4. 3.52 *(Euro-Disney)* (Paris, France) 7. 2.71
G-AMPP/KK136/43-49456
(Cancelled 7.2.71) (As "G-AMSU" in Dan-Air c/s)) (Current status unknown)
G-AMPY Douglas C-47B-15DK Dakota 3 (EI-BKJ) 8. 3.52 Atlantic Air Transport Ltd Coventry 5. 1.02A
15124/26569 G-AMPY/N15751/G-AMPY/TF-FIO/G-AMPY/JY-ABE/G-AMPY/KK116/43-49308
(Op Atlantic Airlines)
G-AMPZ Douglas C-47B-30DK Dakota 4 EI-BDT 8. 3.52 Air Service Berlin CFH GmbH
16124/32872 G-AMPZ/TF-AIV/G-41-3-66/PH-RIC/G-AMPZ/OD-AEQ/G-AMPZ/KN442/44-76540
Berlin Templehof 29. 4.04T
G-AMRA Douglas C-47B-15DK Dakota 6 XE280 8. 3.52 Atlantic Air Transport Ltd Coventry 13. 7.02T
15290/26735 G-AMRA/KK151/43-49474
G-AMRF Auster J/5F Aiglet Trainer 2716 VT-DHA 20. 3.52 A.I.Topps East Midlands 2. 1.04
G-AMRF
G-AMRK Gloster Gladiator 1 - L8032 16. 5.52 The Shuttleworth Trust Old Warden 1. 8.02P
(Bristol Mercury XXX) "K8032"/G-AMRK/L8032 *(As "423-Port/427-Starboard" in R.Nor AF c/s)*
G-AMSG SIPA 903 77 OO-VBL 25.11.81 S.W.Markham Valentine Farm, Odiham 1. 5.02P
F-BGHB
G-AMSM* Douglas C-47B-20-DK Dakota KN274 28. 4.52 Brenzett Aeronautical Museum Trust
15764/27209 43-49948 Brenzett
(Ground-looped on take-off Lydd 17.8.78: cancelled 11.9.78 as WFU) (Nose displayed)
G-AMSN* Douglas C-47B-35DK Dakota 4 N3455 28. 4.52 Aces High Ltd North Weald 3. 1.68
16631/33379 G-AMSN/EI-BSI/SU-BFZ/G-AMSN/KN673/44-77047
(Stored North Weald 6.98: cancelled 25.1.00 as WFU)
G-AMSV Douglas C-47B-25DK Dakota 3 (F-BSGV) 15. 5.52 Atlantic Air Transport Ltd Inverness 10. 7.02A
16072/32820 G-AMSV/KN397/44-76488 *(Op Atlantic Airlines)*
G-AMTA Auster J/5F Aiglet Trainer 2780 24. 5.52 N.H.J.Cottrell Headcorn 3. 8.03
G-AMTF de Havilland DH.82A Tiger Moth 84207 ZK-AVE 11. 6.52 M.Lageirse & P.Winters *(As "T-7842")*
G-AMTF/T7842 (St. Martens-Leerne, Belgium) 19. 7.04
G-AMTK de Havilland DH.82A Tiger Moth 3982 N6709 18. 6.52 S.W.McKay & M.E.Vaisey (Berkhamsted) 27. 5.66
(Stored 12.99: CofR @ 3.01)
G-AMTM Auster V J/1 Autocrat 3101 G-AJUJ 3. 7.52 R.J.Stobo
(Auster rebuild - originally c/n 2622) Oaklands Farm, Stonesfield, Oxon 27. 6.02P
G-AMTV de Havilland DH.82A Tiger Moth 3858 OO-SOE 5. 8.52 Medalbest Ltd Old Sarum 16. 1.04
G-AMTV/N6545
G-AMUF de Havilland DHC.1 Chipmunk 21 2. 9.52 Redhill Tailwheel Flying Club Ltd
C1/0832 Redhill 24. 1.02
G-AMUI Auster J/5F Aiglet Trainer 2790 29. 8.52 Deborah Hatelie (Liverpool) 15. 2.66T
(On rebuild 7.93)

G-AMVD	Taylorcraft J Auster 5	1565	F-BGTF	6.10.52	M.Hammond	Hardwick	14. 5.04
			G-AMVD/TJ565		*(As "TJ565")*		
G-AMVP	Tipsy Junior	J.111	OO-ULA	23.10.52	A.R.Wershat	Sandown	22. 6.94P
	(Walter Mikron 2)				*(Damaged Wroughton 4.7.93: under repair 1.00)*		
G-AMVS	de Havilland DH.82A Tiger Moth	82784	OO-SOJ	12.11.52	J.T.Powell-Tuck	(Pontypool)	21.12.53
			G-AMVS/R4852		*(On rebuild 8.92: current status unknown)*		
G-AMYD	Auster J/5L Aiglet Trainer	2773		13. 2.53	G.H.Maskell		
						Duckend Farm, Wilstead, Bedford	3. 9.04
G-AMYJ*	Douglas C-47B-25DK Dakota 6		SU-AZF	23. 2.53	(Yorkshire Air Museum)	Elvington	4. 4.97A
		15968/32716	G-AMYJ/XF747/G-AMYJ/KN353/44-76384		*(Cancelled 12.12.01 as wfu)*		
G-AMYL(2)	Piper PA-17 Vagabond	17-30	N4613H	24. 4.87	P.J.Penn-Sayer t/a The Fun Airplane Co		
	(Continental C75)		NC4613H			Scaynes Hill, Haywards Heath	20. 5.89P
					"Yankee Lady" (Stored 9.97: current status unknown)		
G-AMZI	Auster J/5F Aiglet Trainer	3104		4. 5.53	J.F.Moore	Rexden, Rye	9. 1.04
G-AMZT	Auster J/5F Aiglet Trainer	3107		28. 5.53	D.Hyde, J.W.Saull & J.C.Hutchinson		
						Standalone Farm, Meppershall	25. 5.04
G-AMZU	Auster J/5F Aiglet Trainer	3108		28. 5.53	J.A.Longworth, A.R.M. & C.B.A.Eagle		
					t/a Flying Flicks	Booker	11. 9.02

G-ANAA – G-ANZZ

G-ANAF	Douglas C-47B-35DK Dakota 3		N170GP	17. 6.53	Atlantic Air Transport Ltd	Coventry	27. 2.02A
		16688/33436	G-ANAF/KP220/44-77104		*(Op Thales for radar & electronic trials)*		
G-ANAP*	de Havilland DH.104 Dove 6	04433		17. 7.53	Brunel Technical College	Bristol	
					(Cancelled 31.8.73 as WFU) (To fire dump by 1.99)		
G-ANCF*	Bristol 175 Britannia 308F	12922	5Y-AZP	3. 1.58	R.Hargreaves	Kemble	12. 1.81T
			G-ANCF/LV-GJB/LV-PPJ/(G-ANCF)/G-14-1/G-18-4/(N6597C)/G-ANCF				
					t/a Britannia Aircraft Preservation Trust		
			(WFU 12.12.81 & broken up: cancelled 21.2.84 as WFU) (Fuselage stored 6.97)				
G-ANCS	de Havilland DH.82A Tiger Moth	82824	R4907	12. 9.53	C.E.Edwards & E.A.Higgins	Rush Green	8. 5.02
G-ANCX	de Havilland DH.82A Tiger Moth	83719	T7229	15. 9.53	D.R.Wood	Fowle Hall Farm, Paddock Wood	28. 7.02
G-ANDE	de Havilland DH.82A Tiger Moth	85957	EM726	23. 9.53	Montrose Aviation Ltd	Redhill	4. 4.03T
G-ANDM	de Havilland DH.82A Tiger Moth	3946	EI-AGP	23. 9.53	N.J.Stagg	Bristol	14. 8.03
			G-ANDM/EI-AGP/G-ANDM/(G-ANDI)/N6642				
G-ANDP	de Havilland DH.82A Tiger Moth	82868	D-EBEC	22. 9.53	A.H.Diver	Newtownards, Co.of Down	20. 7.01
			N9920F/G-ANDP/R4960				
G-ANEH	de Havilland DH.82A Tiger Moth	82067	N6797	29. 9.53	G.J.Wells *(As "N6797")*	(Booker)	24. 7.04
G-ANEL	de Havilland DH.82A Tiger Moth	82333	N9238	1.10.53	R A G Lucas	(Godalming)	17. 6.02
G-ANEM	de Havilland DH.82A Tiger Moth	82943	EI-AGN	1.10.53	P.J.Benest	Hamstead Marshall	16. 7.02
			G-ANEM/R5042				
G-ANEN	de Havilland DH.82A Tiger Moth	85418	OO-ACG	2.10.53	A.J.D.Douglas-Hamilton	Goodwood	13. 4.02
			G-ANEN/DE410				
G-ANEW	de Havilland DH.82A Tiger Moth	86458	NM138	6.10.53	A.L.Young *(Frame stored 9.01)*	Henstridge	18. 6.62T
G-ANEZ	de Havilland DH.82A Tiger Moth	84218	T7849	20.10.53	C.D.J.Bland	Sandown	14. 6.02P
G-ANFC	de Havilland DH.82A Tiger Moth	85385	DE363	13.10.53	J.E.Pierce	Welshpool	9.10.03T
G-ANFH*	Westland WS.55 Whirlwind 1	WA.15		27.10.53	E.D.ap Rees	Weston-super-Mare	17. 7.71
					t/a The Helicopter Museum *(Cancelled 2.9.77 as WFU)*		
G-ANFI	de Havilland DH.82A Tiger Moth	85577	DE623	16.10.53	G.P.Graham *(As "DE623")*	Shobdon	2. 2.03
	(Another Tiger Moth "DE623", alias D-EDON, is displayed @ Auto und Technik Museum, Sinsheim, Germany)						
G-ANFL	de Havilland DH.82A Tiger Moth	84617	T6169	22.10.53	R.P.Whitby	Swanton Morley	13. 6.04
					t/a IDA Flying Group		
G-ANFM	de Havilland DH.82A Tiger Moth	83604	T5888	22.10.53	L.S.Mitton, A.J.Coker & N.H.Lemon		
					t/a Reading Flying Group	White Waltham	15. 8.04
G-ANFP	de Havilland DH.82A Tiger Moth	82530	N9503	28.10.53	G D Horn	(Fordingbridge)	1. 7.63
					(Frame only 1.00)		
G-ANFU*	Taylorcraft J Auster 5	1748	TW385	31.10.53	J.Stelling	Newcastle	17. 2.71
					t/a Newcastle Vehicle Museum		
	(Cancelled 3.8.76 as WFU) (On rebuild with frame from un-identified Auster 6 5.93: to be "NJ719" with starboard wing ex G-AKPH)						
G-ANFV	de Havilland DH.82A Tiger Moth	85904	DF155	1.12.53	R.A.L.Falconer		
					(As "DF155")	Shempston Farm, Lossiemouth	4. 2.01
G-ANFW*	de Havilland DH.82A Tiger Moth	85660	DE730	5.11.53	Malta Aviation Museum	Ta'Qali, Malta	21. 7.01
	(Built Morris Motors: regd with Fuselage No.3737)				*(Cancelled 10.3.00 by CAA)*		
G-ANFY*	de Havilland DH.82A Tiger Moth	86349	NL906	13.11.53	B.Knock	(Ashford, Kent)	25. 5.68
	(Converted to Thruxton Jackaroo 11.57)				*(Cancelled 22.2.73 as WFU) (Airframe stored 1.96)*		
G-ANGK(2)	Cessna 140A	15396	N9675A	10. 3.89	G.A.Copeland	Popham	12. 8.04
G-ANHK	de Havilland DH.82A Tiger Moth	82442	F-BHIM	4.12.53	J.D.Iliffe	Hampstead Norreys	19. 3.03
			G-ANHK/N9372				
G-ANHR	Taylorcraft J Auster 5	759	MT192	5.12.53	C.G.Winch	Rushett Farm, Chessington	20. 7.86
					(Dismantled & stored 5.01)		
G-ANHS	Taylorcraft G Auster 4	737	MT197	5.12.53	R.G.Tomlinson	Spanhoe	22. 8.04
					t/a Tango Uniform Group		

G-ANHU	Taylorcraft G Auster 4	799	EC-AXR	5.12.53	D.J.Baker	Carr Farm, Newark	22.10.66
			G-ANHU/MT255		*(Dismantled 4.98)*		
G-ANHW*	Taylorcraft J Auster 5D	1396	TJ320	5.12.53	C.J.Baker	Carr Farm, Newark	9. 3.70
			(Damaged Carlton Manor, Newark 1970 & WFU 15.12.71) (Derelict fuselage 4.98)				
G-ANHX	Taylorcraft J Auster 5D	2064	TW519	5.12.53	D.J.Baker	Carr Farm, Newark	2.11.73
					(Crashed 28.3.70: dismantled 4.98)		
G-ANIE	Taylorcraft J Auster 5	1809	TW467	5.12.53	S.J.Partridge	Bassingbourn	20.10.02
					(Op Military Auster Flight) (As "TW467/ROD-F" in 664 Sqn c/s)		
G-ANIJ	Taylorcraft J Auster 5D	1680	TJ672	5.12.53	M.Pocock	Kemble	5. 5.71
					t/a Military Auster Flight		
					(As "TJ672" in 657 Sqdn c/s: noted 12.00)		
G-ANIS*	Taylorcraft J Auster 5	1429	TJ375	5.12.53	R.W.Hall	Longford, Co.Longford	19. 9.76
					t/a Halls Autospares		
				(Cancelled 8.10.81 by CAA) (Stored 6.97: current status unknown)			
G-ANJA	de Havilland DH.82A Tiger Moth	82459	N9389	7.12.53	P.Aukland *(As "N9389")*	Seething	15. 2.02
G-ANJD	de Havilland DH.82A Tiger Moth	84652	T6226	8.12.53	A.C.Ladd	Romney Street Farm, Sevenoaks	7. 8.03
G-ANJK*	de Havilland DH.82A Tiger Moth	84557	T6066	12.12.53	Not known	Rhos-Y-Gilwen Farm, Rhos Hill	12. 5.85
				(Stored 5.94) (Cancelled 1.3.96 by CAA) (Current status unknown)			
G-ANJV*	Westland WS-55 Whirlwind 3	WA.24	VR-BET	14.12.53	E.D.ap Rees	Weston-super-Mare	
			G-ANJV		t/a The Helicopter Museum		
G-ANKK	de Havilland DH.82A Tiger Moth	83590	T5854	24.12.53	P A.Cambridge	Charity Farm, Baxterley	20. 6.04
					t/a Halfpenny Green Tiger Group *(As "T5854")*		
G-ANKT	de Havilland DH.82A Tiger Moth	85087	T6818	24.12.53	The Shuttleworth Trust	Old Warden	16. 8.02P
					(As "T6818")		
G-ANKV*	de Havilland DH.82A Tiger Moth	84166	T7793	30.12.53	Westmead Business Group	Croydon Airport	
	(Not converted & cancelled 9.56: provenance uncertain: as "T7793" in RAF c/s at Terminal Building)						
G-ANKZ	de Havilland DH.82A Tiger Moth	3803	(N)	30.12.53	D.W.Graham	Biggin Hill	15. 4.99
			F-BHIO/G-ANKZ/N6466		*(As "N6466")*		
G-ANLD	de Havilland DH.82A Tiger Moth	85990	OO-DPA	30.12.53	K.Peters	Rushett Manor, Chessington	7.12.02
			G-ANLD/EM773		*(Crashed Old Warden 23.6.01 & substantially damaged)*		
G-ANLH	de Havilland DH.82A Tiger Moth	86546	N3744F	4. 1.54	T R Green	Sywell	16. 5.03T
	(Fuselage No. MCO/de Havilland DH.4623)		OO-EVO/G-ANLH/PG637				
G-ANLS	de Havilland DH.82A Tiger Moth	85862	DF113	7. 1.54	P.A.Gliddon	Great Fryup, Egton, Whitby	29. 6.03
G-ANLU	Taylorcraft J Auster 5	1780	TW448	8. 1.54	B.H.Hargrave	(Southampton)	8. 8.68
					(Stored 1.95: current CofR @ 3.01)		
G-ANLW	Westland WS.51 Srs.2 Widgeon	WA/H/133	"MD497"	23. 3.54	Sloane Helicopters Ltd	Sywell	27. 5.81A
			G-ANLW		*(Stored 9.99: current CofR @ 3.01)*		
G-ANMO	de Havilland DH.82A Tiger Moth	3255	F-BHIU	22. 1.54	E. & K.M.Lay	White Waltham	17. 8.03
			G-ANMO/K4259		*(As "K4259/71")*		
G-ANMV	de Havilland DH.82A Tiger Moth	83745	F-BHAZ	22. 1.54	B.P.Sanders t/a Tigerfly	Booker	26. 6.01T
			G-ANMV/T7404		*(As "T7404/04") (Damaged and stored dismantled 7.01)*		
G-ANMY	de Havilland DH.82A Tiger Moth	85466	OO-SOL	22. 1.54	R.Earl & B.Morris	White Waltham	3. 9.04
			"OO-SOC"/G-ANMY/DE470		*(As "DE470/16" in RAF c/s)*		
G-ANNB	de Havilland DH.82A Tiger Moth	84233	N6037	22. 1.54	G.M.Bradley	(Rothesay)	12. 6.58
			D-EGYN/G-ANNB/T6037		*(On rebuild 4.92: current status unknown)*		
G-ANNE(2)	de Havilland DH.82A Tiger Moth	"83814"		15. 4.94	C.R.Hardiman	Shobdon	30. 5.58
	(G-ANNE(1) ex T7418, sold as OO-CCI/90-CCI/9Q-CCI)				*(Composite airframe: on rebuild 11.98)*		
G-ANNG	de Havilland DH.82A Tiger Moth	85504	DE524	22. 1.54	P.F.Walter	Farnborough	18. 5.01
G-ANNI	de Havilland DH.82A Tiger Moth	85162	T6953	22. 1.54	A.R.Brett *(As "T6953)*	Little Gransden	6. 9.03
G-ANNK	de Havilland DH.82A Tiger Moth	83804	F-BFDO	22. 1.54	Patricia J.Wilcox	(Cranfield)	25. 9.87
			G-ANNK/T7290		*(On rebuild 5.92: current status unknown)*		
G-ANOD	de Havilland DH.82A Tiger Moth	84588	T6121	16. 2.54	Penelope G.Grafton	Kidmore End, Reading	7. 2.60
			(Composite rebuild: on long term rebuild 6.94: current status unknown)				
G-ANOH	de Havilland DH.82A Tiger Moth	86040	EM838	22. 2.54	N.Parkhouse	Redhill	14. 9.02T
G-ANOK*	SAAB 91C Safir	91311	SE-CAH	22. 4.54	A.F.Galt & Co Ltd	(Yarrow Ford)	5. 2.73
					(Cancelled 15.10.81 by CAA) (Stored 6.00)		
G-ANOM	de Havilland DH.82A Tiger Moth	82086	N6837	2. 3.54	A.L.Creer	(Bristol)	3. 5.62T
					(Crashed Fairoaks 17.12.61: on rebuild 6.00)		
G-ANON	de Havilland DH.82A Tiger Moth	84270	T7909	4. 3.54	R.C.Hields	Gloucestershire	23. 2.03T
					t/a Hields Aviation *(Op Tiger Airways as "T7909")*		
G-ANOO	de Havilland DH.82A Tiger Moth	85409	DE401	11. 3.54	R.K.Packman	Compton Abbas	12. 9.02
G-ANOR	de Havilland DH.82A Tiger Moth	85635	DE694	4. 3.54	R.Clifford	Rayne Hall Farm, Rayne	8. 5.04
					(As "T6991": see G-ACDA)		
G-ANOV*	de Havilland DH.104 Dove 6	04445	G-5-16	11. 3.54	National Museums of Scotland/Museum of Flight		
		(Cancelled 6.7.81 as WFU) (Civil Aviation Authority c/s)				East Fortune	31. 5.75
G-ANPC*	de Havilland DH.82A Tiger Moth	82858	R4950	19. 3.54	Irish Aviation Museum		
		(Crashed near Loch Leven 2.1.67: stored 4.96)				Castlemoate House, Dublin	2. 9.67
G-ANPE	de Havilland DH.82A Tiger Moth	83738	G-IESH	27. 3.54	I.E.S.Hudleston	Crowfield	23.11.02
			G-ANPE/F-BHAT/G-ANPE/T7397				
G-ANPK	de Havilland DH.82A Tiger Moth	3571	L6936	5. 4.54	A.D.Hodgkinson	Dunkirk Farm, Canterbury	10. 7.97T
			(Damaged Jaywick Sands, Clacton 18.8.96: stored 1.97: new owner 11.99)				
G-ANPP*	Percival P.34 Proctor III	H.264	HM354	8. 4.54	P Jeffery	(Cutlers Green, Essex)	5. 5.69
					(Cancelled 3.4.89 by CAA) (Stored 2000)		
G-ANRF	de Havilland DH.82A Tiger Moth	83748	T5850	24. 5.54	C.D.Cyster	Glenrothes	24. 8.04

G-ANRM	de Havilland DH.82A Tiger Moth	85861	DF112	8. 6.54	Fairmont Investments Ltd *(As "DF112")*	Clacton/Duxford	28. 7.04T
G-ANRN	de Havilland DH.82A Tiger Moth	83133	T5368	24. 5.54	J.J.V.Elwes	Rush Green	26. 4.04
G-ANRP	Taylorcraft J Auster 5	1789	TW439	21. 5.54	I.C.Naylor & P.G.Wood *(As "TW439")*	Bagby	16.12.02
G-ANRX*	de Havilland DH.82A Tiger Moth	3863	N6550	25. 5.54	De Havilland Heritage Museum *"Border City"* *(WFU 20.6.61)*	London Colney	20. 6.61
G-ANSM	de Havilland DH.82A Tiger Moth	82909	R5014	3. 6.54	R.M.Kimbell	Sywell	17. 8.03
G-ANTE	de Havilland DH.82A Tiger Moth	84891	T6562	20. 9.54	P Reading *(As "T6562")*	Sywell/White Waltham	7. 4.02T
G-ANTK*	Avro 685 York C1		MW232	23. 7.54	Duxford Aviation Society	Duxford	29.10.64T
	(Dan Air titles) (WFU Lasham 30.4.64: on rebuild 2000)						
G-ANUO*	de Havilland DH.114 Heron 2D	14062		27. 9.54	Westmead Business Centre	Croydon Airport	12. 9.86T
	(Cancelled 9.8.96 as WFU) (As "G-AOXL" in Morton Air Services titles)						
G-ANUW*	de Havilland DH.104 Dove 6	04458		16. 5.55	G Yates (Jet Aviation Preservation Group)		
	(Cancelled 5.6.96 as WFU) (Noted 9.99)					Long Marston	22. 7.81
G-ANWB	de Havilland DHC.1 Chipmunk 21	C1/0987	G-5-17	15. 2.55	G.Briggs	Blackpool	17.12.04T
G-ANWO	Miles M.14A Hawk Trainer 3	718	L8262	31.12.58	A.G.Dunkerley	West Chiltington, Pulborough	18. 4.63
	(Most unlikely anything of G-ANWO remains: wings went to G-AIUA in the 1960s and the fuselage remains comprised very little of substance: nonetheless valid CofR 4.01)						
G-ANWX*	Auster J/5L Aiglet Trainer	3131		25.11.54	D.Hodgkinson *"Shepherd's Delight"*	Canterbury	2. 5.94
	(Damaged Nayland 1.8.93: cancelled 24.9.93 as WFU) (On rebuild 9.96: current status unknown)						
G-ANXB*	de Havilland DH.114 Heron 1B	14048	G-5-14	3.12.54	Newark Air Museum	Winthorpe	25. 3.79
	(Cancelled 2.11.81 as PWFU) (BEA Scottish Airways titles) "Sir James Young Simpson"						
G-ANXC	Auster J/5R Alpine	3135	5Y-UBD VP-UBD/G-ANXC/(AP-AHG)/G-ANXC	4.12.54	R.B.Webber t/a Alpine Group	Trenchard Farm, Eggesford	2. 8.98
G-ANXR	Percival P.31C Proctor 4	H.803	RM221	14.12.54	L.H.Oakins *(As "RM221")*	Biggin Hill	14.12.03
G-ANZT	Thruxton Jackaroo	84176	T7798	4. 3.55	D.J.Neville & P.J.Dear	Rush Green	14. 8.02
G-ANZU	de Havilland DH.82A Tiger Moth	3583	L6938	9. 3.55	P.A.Jackson *(Stored 1994)*	Brookfield Farm, Great Stukeley	17. 3.91
G-ANZZ	de Havilland DH.82A Tiger Moth	85834	DE974	14. 3.55	J.I.B.Bennett & P.P.Amershi *(Current CofR 3.01)*	(Hatfield)	28. 2.69T

G-AOAA – G-AOZZ

G-AOAA	de Havilland DH.82A Tiger Moth	85908	DF159	14. 3.55	R.C.P.Brookhouse *(Damaged Redhill 4.6.89: under restoration 2002)*	Thruxton	8.12.91T
G-AOBG*	Somers-Kendall SK-1	1		30. 3.55	A.J.E.Smith	Breighton	26. 6.58
	(WFU after engine turbine failure 11.7.57: stored 12.01)						
G-AOBH	de Havilland DH.82A Tiger Moth	84350	T7997	31. 3.55	P.Nutley	Thruxton	25. 5.03
	(Regd with c/n 83818 ex T7439: as "NL750" which belongs to G-AHUF now marked "T7997": both a/c regd to same owner)						
G-AOBO	de Havilland DH.82A Tiger Moth	3810	N6473	23. 4.55	J.S. & J.V.Shaw *(On rebuild 10.97: current status unknown)*	Cubert, Newquay	28. 8.69T
G-AOBU	Hunting Percival P.84 Jet Provost T.1	P84/6	XM129 G-AOBU/G-42-1	2. 5.55	T.J.Manna t/a Kennet Aviation *(As "XD693/Z-Q" in 2 FTS c/s)*	Cranfield	18. 2.02P
G-AOBV*	Auster J/5P Autocar	3171		9. 5.55	Not known	(Cheshunt)	7. 4.71T
	(Cancelled 14.11.91 by CAA) (Stored 10.97: current status unknown)						
G-AOBX	de Havilland DH.82A Tiger Moth	83653	T7187	26. 4.55	S.Bohill-Smith t/a David Ross Flying Group	Uffley Common, Odiham	5.11.02
G-AOCP(2)*	Taylorcraft J Auster 5	1800	TW462	25. 5.56	C.J.Baker	Carr Farm, Newark	22. 6.68
	(WFU 22.6.68: fuselage stored 4.98: current status unkrown)						
G-AOCR(2)	Taylorcraft J Auster 5D	1060	EI-AJS G-AOCR/NJ673	25. 5.56	G.J.McDill *(As "NJ673")*	Park Farm, Eaton Bray	8. 9.01
G-AOCU(2)	Taylorcraft J Auster 5	986	MT349	8. 6.56	S.J.Ball *(On rebuild 1.02)*	Leicester	22. 2.04
G-AODA*	Westland WS.55 Whirlwind Srs.3	WA/113	9Y-TDA EP-HAC/G-AODA	13. 5.55	The Helicopter Museum *(Bristow Helicopters c/s) "Dorado"* *(Cancelled 23.9.93 by CAA)*	Weston-super-Mare	23. 8.91A
G-AODT	de Havilland DH.82A Tiger Moth	83109	R5250	4. 8.55	R.A.Harrowven	Tibenham	30. 4.01
G-AOEH	Aeronca 7AC Champion (Continental A65)	7AC-2144	N79854 OO-TWF	8. 9.55	R.A. & S.P.Smith	Crowfield	21. 2.02P
G-AOEI	de Havilland DH.82A Tiger Moth	82196	N6946	14. 9.55	CFG Flying Ltd	Cambridge	11. 7.02T
	(Regd with fuselage no.MCO/DH3409 which should correspond to ex DE298 [85332]: a/c is probably composite airframe)						
G-AOEL*	de Havilland DH.82A Tiger Moth	82537	N9510	27. 9.55	National Museums of Scotland/Museum of Flight *(WFU 18.7.72)*	East Fortune	18. 7.72
G-AOES	de Havilland DH.82A Tiger Moth	84547	T6056	6.10.55	K.A.& A.J.Broomfield	Charity Farm, Baxterley	15. 6.02
G-AOET	de Havilland DH.82A Tiger Moth	85650	DE720	7.10.55	Techair London Ltd	Oaklands Farm, East Tytherley	1.11.02
G-AOEX	Thruxton Jackaroo	86483	NM175	10.10.55	A.T.Christian *(On rebuild 10.01)*	Walkeridge Farm, Overton	3. 2.68T

G-AOFE de Havilland DHC.1 Chipmunk 22A WB702 13. 9.56 W.J.Quinn (Goodwood) 8.10.04
C1/0150 *(As "WB702")*

G-AOFJ(2)* Auster Alpha 5 3401 3.10.56 R.Drew Perth 20. 9.79
(Cancelled 3.4.89 by CAA) (Stored dismantled 11.00)

G-AOFM Auster J/5P Autocar 3178 16. 6.55 S J Cooper *(New owner 1.02)* (Lincoln) 22.10.00

G-AOFS Auster J/5L Aiglet Trainer 3143 EI-ALN 28.10.55 P.N.A.Whitehead Leicester 26. 4.04
G-AOFS

G-AOGA* Miles M.75 Aries 1 75/1007 EI-ANB 9.11.55 The Irish Aviation Museum
G-AOGA Castlemoate House, Dublin 10.10.69
(Cancelled 30.5.84: stored 4.96: current status unknown)

G-AOGE* Percival P.34A Proctor 3 H.210 BV651 24.11.55 N.I.Dalziel Biggin Hill 21. 5.84
(Stored 8.97: cancelled 19.1.99 by CAA)

G-AOGI de Havilland DH.82A Tiger Moth 85922 (N) 14.12.55 W.J.Taylor Ingoldmells 23. 8.91
OO-SOA/G-AOGI/DF186 t/a Lincs Aerial Spraying Co *(Stored 10.92)*

G-AOGR de Havilland DH.82A Tiger Moth 84566 XL714 20. 1.56 M.I.Edwards Swanton Morley 16. 9.96T
G-AOGR/T6099 *(As "XL714": stored 5.01)*

G-AOGV Auster J/5R Alpine 3302 2. 2.56 R.E.Heading *(Stored 12.97: current status unknown)*
Walnut Tree Farm, Thorney, Whittlesey 17. 7.72

G-AOHL* Vickers V.802 Viscount 161 2. 1.56 London-Southend Airport Co Ltd Southend 11. 4.80T
(WFU 6.2.81 as cabin services trainer: cancelled 27.3.81: spares 1992: derelict @ 1.94: Fire Service trainer 1.02)

G-AOHY* de Havilland DH.82A Tiger Moth 3850 N6537 23. 2.56 M.Somerton-Rayner AAC Middle Wallop 20. 8.60
t/a AAC Reserve Collection Trust
(On rebuild 9.00: cancelled 5.3.01 as temporarily wfu)

G-AOHZ Auster J/5P Autocar 3252 28. 2.56 A.D.Hodgkinson Dunkirk, Canterbury 25. 9.03

G-AOIL de Havilland DH.82A Tiger Moth 83673 XL716 20. 8.56 J.W.Lawless Lee-on-Solent 17. 9.02
G-AOIL/T7363

G-AOIM de Havilland DH.82A Tiger Moth 83536 T7109 27. 8.56 D.A.Hardiman Shobdon 8. 4.04

G-AOIR Thruxton Jackaroo 82882 R4972 13. 1.56 L.H.Smith & I.M.Oliver
Charity Farm, Baxterley 18. 3.02

G-AOIS de Havilland DH.82A Tiger Moth 83034 R5172 13. 1.56 J.K.Ellwood Sherburn in Elmet 10. 7.04

G-AOIY Auster J/5V-160 Autocar 3199 1. 3.56 J.B.Nicholson Watchford Farm, Yarcombe 26. 8.90
(Lycoming O-320) *(On rebuild 9.00: current status unknown)*

G-AOJD* Vickers V.802 Viscount 153 (G-AOHD) 2. 1.56 Jersey Airport Fire Service Jersey 13. 6.77T
(Cancelled 7.5.76 as WFU) (Used by Fire Service: extant 9.99)

G-AOJH de Havilland DH.83C Fox Moth FM.42 AP-ABO 29. 3.56 A.J.Norman Rendcomb 17.10.02
t/a Norman Aeroplane Trust

G-AOJJ de Havilland DH.82A Tiger Moth 85877 DF128 5. 4.56 E.& K.M.Lay White Waltham 26. 7.03
(As "DF128/RCO-U")
(Swung on take-off Goodwood 8.7.01, stuck parked aircraft, somersaulted and came to rest inverted:
extensively damaged with wings and tail broken off: new owners 10.01)

G-AOJK de Havilland DH.82A Tiger Moth 82813 R4896 5. 4.56 D.E.Guck & P.W.Crispe
Hinton-in-the Hedges 18. 8.02

G-AOJR de Havilland DHC.1 Chipmunk 22 SE-BBS 9. 4.56 G J G-H Caubergs & N Marien
C1/0205 OY-DFB/D-EGIM/G-AOJR/D-EGIM/G-AOJR/WB756 Grimbergen, Belgium 28. 7.02

G-AOJT* de Havilland DH.106 Comet 1XB 06020 F-BGNX 11. 5.56 De Havilland Heritage Museum
London Colney 5. 7.56
(Fuselage only as "F-BGNX" in Air France c/s)

G-AOJZ* de Havilland DHC.1 Chipmunk 21 "G-ASTD" 16.4.56 Air Service Training Ltd Perth 13.11.66
C1/0181 G-AOJZ/WB732 *(Crashed near Perth 31.5.66: instructional airframe 12.95)*

G-AOKH* Percival P.40 Prentice 1 PAC/212 VS251 11. 4.56 J.F.Moore Biggin Hill 2. 8.73
(Cancelled 17.6.92 by CAA) (Stored 12.00)

G-AOKL Percival P.40 Prentice 1 PAC/208 VS610 13. 4.56 The Shuttleworth Trust Old Warden 20. 9.96
(As "VS610/K-L": under restoration 5.01)

G-AOKO* Percival P.40 Prentice 1 PAC/234 VS621 13. 4.56 Atlantic Air Transport Ltd Doncaster 23.10.72
(Cancelled 9.10.84 as WFU) (On loan to South Yorkshire Aviation Museum)

G-AOKZ* Percival P.40 Prentice 1 PAC/238 VS623 20. 4.56 Midland Air Museum *(As "VS623")* Coventry

G-AOLK Percival P.40 Prentice 1 PAC/225 VS618 25. 4.56 A.Hilton *(Noted 8.01)* Southend 3.12.98

G-AOLU Percival P.40 Prentice 1 EI-ASP 25. 4.56 N.J.Butler (Montrose) 14. 6.04
(Regd with c/n 5830/3) B3/1A/PAC/283 G-AOLU/VS356 t/a Montrose Air Station Museum *(As "VS356")*

G-AORB(2) Cessna 170B 20767 OO-SIZ 13. 2.84 A.R.Thompson Hawley Farm, Tadley 2. 3.03
N2615D t/a Hawley Farm Group

G-AORG de Havilland DH.114 Heron 2 14101 XR441 1. 5.56 Duchess of Brittany (Jersey) Ltd Jersey 23. 4.02
(Built as Sea Heron C.1) G-AORG/G-5-16 *(Jersey Airlines c/s) "Duchess of Brittany"*

G-AORW de Havilland DHC.1 Chipmunk 22A WB682 28. 5.56 Bushfire Investments Ltd Booker 3.11.02
C1/0130 *"Kate"*

G-AOSF de Havilland DHC.1 Chipmunk 22 D-EIIZ 25. 6.56 D.Mercer Porta Westfalica, Germany 25.10.02
C1/0023 G-AOSF/HB-TUA/G-AOSF/WB571 *(As "WB571/34")*

G-AOSK de Havilland DHC.1 Chipmunk 22 A WB726 26. 6.56 E.J.Leigh Audley End 23.11.02
C1/0178 *(As "WB726/E" in Cambridge UAS c/s)*

G-AOSO de Havilland DHC.1 Chipmunk 22 WD288 26. 6.56 The Earl of Suffolk & Berkshire & J.Hoerner
C1/0227 *(As "WD288")* Charlton Park, Malmesbury 19.10.03

G-AOSU de Havilland DHC.1 Chipmunk 22 WB766 28. 6.56 T.Holloway Easterton 28. 6.03
(Lycoming O-360) C1/0217 t/a RAFGSA *(Op Fulmar Gliding Club)*

G-AOSY	de Havilland DHC.1 Chipmunk 22	C1/0037	WB585	29. 6.56	B.A.Webster t/a WFG Chipmunk Group *(As "WB585/M)*	Seething	14. 6.02
G-AOTD	de Havilland DHC.1 Chipmunk 22	C1/0040	WB588	30. 6.56	S.Piech *(As "WB588/D" in Oxford UAS c/s)*	Old Sarum	4.10.03
G-AOTF	de Havilland DHC.1 Chipmunk 23 (Lycoming O-360)	C1/0015	WB563	2. 7.56	T.Holloway t/a RAFGSA	Bicester	17. 10.04
G-AOTI*	de Havilland DH.114 Heron 2D	14107	G-5-19	25. 7.56	De Havilland Heritage Museum *(Cancelled 17.10.95 as WFU)*	London Colney	24. 6.87T
G-AOTK	Druine D.53 Turbi (Walter Mikron 3)	1 & PFA 230		1.11.56	T.J.Adams	Whitehall Farm, Benington	9.12.01P
G-AOTR	de Havilland DHC.1 Chipmunk 22	C1/0045	HB-TUH D-EGOG/G-AOTR/WB604	12. 7.56	M.R.Woodgate	Belfast	30. 3.03
G-AOTY	de Havilland DHC.1 Chipmunk 22A	C1/0522	WG472	12. 7.56	A.A.Hodgson *(As "WG472" in RAF c/s)*	(Abergele)	22. 1.04T
G-AOUJ*	Fairey Ultralight Helicopter	F.9424	XJ928	1. 8.56	E.D.ap Rees t/a The Helicopter Museum *(WFU: to Cotswold Aircraft Restoration Group 11.99)*	RAF Innsworth	29. 3.59
G-AOUO	de Havilland DHC.1 Chipmunk 22 (Lycoming O-360)	C1/0179	WB730	10. 8.56	T.Holloway t/a RAFGSA	RAF Cosford	16. 3.03
G-AOUP	de Havilland DHC.1 Chipmunk 22	C1/0180	WB731	10. 8.56	A.R.Harding	(Newton Green, Sudbury)	24.10.02
G-AOUR*	de Havilland DH.82A Tiger Moth	86341	NL898	14. 8.56	Ulster Folk & Transport Museum *(Crashed Newtownards 6.6.65: stored 4.96)*	Holywood, Belfast	19.11.66
G-AOVF*	Bristol 175 Britannia 312F	13237	9Q-CAZ G-AOVF	13. 2.57	RAF Museum *(Cancelled 21.11.84 as WFU) (BOAC titles)*	RAF Cosford	
G-AOVS*	Bristol 175 Britannia 312F	13430	(G-BRAC)	28. 2.58	(Redcoat Airlines) *(Broken up 10.79: fuselage for Fire Service use 3.00)*	Luton	31 .7.79T
G-AOVT*	Bristol 175 Britannia 312	13427		23. 6.58	Duxford Aviation Society *(Cancelled 21.9.81 as WFU)* (Monarch titles)	Duxford	11. 3.75T
G-AOVW	Taylorcraft J Auster 5	894	MT119	16.11.59	B.Marriott	Ropsley Heath Farm, Grantham	1.10.03
G-AOXG*	de Havilland DH.82A Tiger Moth	83805	XL717 T7291	3.10.56	Fleet Air Arm Museum *(Sold as XL717 10.56 & cancelled) (As "G-ABUL")*	RNAS Yeovilton	
G-AOXN	de Havilland DH.82A Tiger Moth	85958	EM727	31.10.56	S.L.G.Darch	East Chinnock, Yeovil	21.12.01
G-AOZE*	Westland-Sikorsky WS-51/2 Widgeon	WA/H/141	5N-ABW G-AOZE	11. 1.57	E.D.ap Rees t/a The Helicopter Museum	Weston-super-Mare	
G-AOZH	de Havilland DH.82A Tiger Moth	86449	NM129	18. 1.57	M.H.Blois-Brooke *(As "K2572")*	Redhill	28. 9.02T
G-AOZL	Auster J/5Q Alpine	3202		5. 2.57	R.M.Weeks *(On rebuild 3.00)*	Leicester	28. 5.88
G-AOZP	de Havilland DHC.1 Chipmunk 22A	C1/0183	WB734	14. 2.57	H.Darlington	High Easter	24. 3.02

G-APAA – G-APZZ

G-APAF	Auster Alpha 5	3404	G-CMAL G-APAF	25. 3.57	J J J Mostyn *(As "TW511")*	Henstridge	22. 7.02
G-APAH	Auster Alpha 5	3402		29. 3.57	T.J.Goodwin	Hill Farm, Nayland	5. 4.04
G-APAL	de Havilland DH.82A Tiger Moth	82102	N6847	3. 4.57	Avia Special Ltd *(As "N6847")*	Barton	9. 7.03T
G-APAM	de Havilland DH.82A Tiger Moth	3874	N6580	3. 4.57	R.P.Williams t/a Myth Group *"Myth"*	Denford Manor, Hungerford	8. 7.04
G-APAO	de Havilland DH.82A Tiger Moth	82845	R4922	3. 4.57	Fairmont Investments Ltd *(Op Classic Wings)*	Duxford	10. 8.02T
G-APAP	de Havilland DH.82A Tiger Moth	83018	R5136	3. 4.57	J.Romain *(As "R5136")*	Duxford	30. 4.04
G-APAS*	de Havilland DH.106 Comet 1A	06022	8351M XM823/G-APAS/G-5-23/F-BGNZ	23. 5.57	RAF Museum *(BOAC c/s)*	RAF Cosford	
G-APBE	Auster Alpha 5	3403		7. 5.57	A.M.Edwards	Swanton Morley	6.12.04
G-APBI	de Havilland DH.82A Tiger Moth	86097	EM903	16. 5.57	A.Wood *(Damaged Audley End 7.7.80: on rebuild 12.90: current status unknown)*	Halstead, Essex	19. 4.82
G-APBO	Druine D.53 Turbi (Continental C75)	PFA 229		3. 6.57	R.C.Hibberd	(Devizes)	13. 5.02P
G-APBW	Auster Alpha 5A	3405		23. 5.57	N.Huxtable	Cheddington, Bucks	1. 6.03
G-APCB	Auster J/5Q Alpine	3204		5. 6.57	A.A.Beswick & I.A.Freeman	Thruxton	7. 3 04
G-APCC	de Havilland DH.82A Tiger Moth	86549	PG640	11. 6.57	L.J.Rice	Bishopstrow Farm, Warminster	25. 5.03
G-APDB*	de Havilland DH.106 Comet 4	6403	9M-AOB G-APDB	2. 5.57	Duxford Aviation Society *(Cancelled 18.2.74 as WFU) (Dan-Air c/s)*	Duxford	7.10.74
G-APDF*	de Havilland DH.106 Comet 4	6407		2. 2.57	Not known *(To RAE as XV814 3.67 & cancelled: nose only 3.00)*	(Chipping Campden)	
G-APEK*	Vickers V.953C Vanguard Merchantman	714		9. 9.57	Europe Aero Service *(Stored 6.95: cancelled 7.11.96 as WFU) (Current status unknown)*	Perpignan	16.12.89F
G-APEP*	Vickers V.953C Vanguard Merchantman	719		9. 9.57	Brooklands Museum *"Superb"* *(Cancelled 28.2.97 as WFU) (Hunting Cargo Airlines titles)*	Brooklands	1.10.98T
G-APES*	Vickers V.953C Vanguard Merchantman	721		9. 9.57	East Midlands Aeropark *(Cancelled 28.2.97 as WFU) "Swiftsure" (Nose only)*	East Midlands	2.10.95T
G-APFA	Druine D.52 Turbi (Continental A65)	PFA 232		5. 2.57	F.J.Keitch	Smiths Farm, Brixham	22. 9.92P

G-APFG*	Boeing 707-436	17708	N5094K	7. 8.59	Phoenix Aviation	Bruntingthorpe	24. 5.81T
					(WFU 11.80: nose only 4.00)		
G-APFJ*	Boeing 707-436	17711		7. 8.59	RAF Museum	RAF Cosford	16. 2.82T
					(WFU on 12.6.81) (British Airtours titles)		
G-APFU	de Havilland DH.82A Tiger Moth	86081	EM879	28. 8.57	Leisure Assets Ltd	Goodwood	11. 4.03T
G-APGL	de Havilland DH.82A Tiger Moth	86460	NM140	6. 9.57	K.A.Broomfield	Charity Farm, Baxterley	
					(Not previously converted: on rebuild 3.97: see G-AJVE)		
G-APHV*	Avro 652A Anson C.19 Srs.2	-	VM360	19. 9.57	National Museums of Scotland/Museum of Flight		
					(Cancelled 21.1.82 as PWFU) (As "VM360")	East Fortune	15. 6.73
G-APIE	Tipsy Belfair (Walter Mikron 2)	535	(OO-TIE)	22.10.57	D.Beale	Witchford	15. 4.02P
G-APIH	de Havilland DH.82A Tiger Moth	82981	N111DH OY-DGJ/D-EMEX/G-APIH/R5086	25.10.57	K.Stewering	Borken-Gemen, Germany	23. 3.03
G-APIK	Auster Alpha	3375		11.11.57	T P Hancock t/a G-APIK Flying Group	Leicester	14.12.02
G-APIM*	Vickers V.806 Viscount	412		19.11.57	Brooklands Museum	Brooklands	19. 7.88T
					(British Air Ferries titles) "Viscount Stephen Piercey"		
G-APIT*	Percival P.40 Prentice T.1	PAC/016	VR192	28.11.57	Second World War Aircraft Preservation Society		
					(Cancelled 8.11.79 as WFU) (As "VR192")	Lasham	7. 9.67
G-APIU*	Percival P.40 Prentice T.1	PAC/024	VR200	28.11.57	Atlantic Air Transport Ltd	Coventry	23. 3.67
					(Derelict 1972 & cancelled 9.10.84 as WFU) (Spares use 5.96)		
G-APIY*	Percival P.40 Prentice T.1	PAC/075	VR249	28.11.57	Newark Air Museum	Winthorpe	18. 3.67
					(WFU 18.3.67 & cancelled 19.4.73) (As "VR249/FA-EL" in RAFC c/s)		
G-APIZ	Rollason-Druine D.31 Turbulent (VW 1600)	PFA 478		22.11.57	E J I Musty *"Witch Lady"*	White Waltham	29.10.02P
G-APJB	Percival P.40 Prentice T.1	PAC/086	VR259	28.11.57	Atlantic Air Transport Ltd *(As "VR259/M" in 2 ASS c/s)*	Coventry	3. 7.02T
G-APJJ(2)*	Fairey Ultralight Helicopter	F.9428		4.12.57	Midland Air Museum *(Cancelled 2.3.73 as WFU)*	Coventry	1. 4.59
G-APJO	de Havilland DH.82A Tiger Moth	86446	NM126	23.12.57	D.R. & Mrs M.Wood	Tunbridge Wells	27. 3.59T
	(C/n quoted as "17712": crashed Ross-on-Wye 5.8.58: on rebuild & may include components from G-APJR)						
G-APJZ	Auster Alpha	3382	5N-ACY (VR-NDR)/G-APJZ	3. 1.58	P.G.Lipman *(Damaged Thornicombe 10.11.75: on rebuild 12.97)*	Romney Street Farm, Sevenoaks	15. 7.77
G-APKH	de Havilland DH.85 Leopard Moth	PPS.85/1/DH7131		23. 1.58	A R Tarleton	Konstanz, Germany	14. 8.02P
	(Composite rebuild of c/n 7002 [G-ACGS/PH-ALM/G-ACGS] & c/n 7040 [G-ACLZ/AW121/G-ACLZ] - mainly the latter)						
G-APKM*	Auster Alpha	3385		27. 1.58	D.E.A.Huggins	(Meriden, Coventry)	9. 1.89
					(Stored 4.90: cancelled 9.10.91 as TWFU) (Current status unknown)		
G-APKN	Auster Alpha	3387		27. 1.58	P.R.Hodson t/a The Felthorpe Auster Group	Felthorpe	9. 8.02
G-APLG*	Auster J/5L Aiglet Trainer	3148		4. 3.58	Solway Aviation Museum *(Cancelled 11.2.99 by CAA)*	Carlisle	26.10.68
G-APLK*	Miles M.100 Student 2	100/1008		11. 3.58	See G-MIOO		
G-APLO	de Havilland DHC.1 Chipmunk 22A	C1/0144	EI-AHU WB696	1. 5.58	Lindholme Aircraft Ltd *(As "WD379/K" in Cambridge UAS c/s)*	Jersey	2.11.03T
G-APLU	de Havilland DH.82A Tiger Moth	85094	VR-AAY F-OBKK/G-APLU/T6825	2. 4.58	R.A.Bishop & M.E.Vaisey	Rush Green	14. 8.04
G-APMB*	de Havilland DH.106 Comet 4B	6422		15. 4.58	Gatwick Handling Ltd	Gatwick	18. 5.79
					(Cancelled 19.1.79 as WFU) (Ground Trainer airframe 9.00)		
G-APMH	Auster J/1U Workmaster	3502	F-OBOA G-APMH	15. 4.58	J.L.Thorogood	Insch	19. 5.04
G-APML*	Douglas C-47B-1DK Dakota 6	14175/25620	KJ836 43-48359	17. 3.58	Dak Holdings Ltd	Redhill	27. 7.84T
	(Fuselage sold mid 1998 to a new owner who had it cut into two pieces: front section was transported to Kuwait: the rear fuselage went to Redhill in 11.99 for Aceball Aviation to be refurbished at Westmeads Business Group's Terminal Building, Croydon Airport: cancelled 20.3.01 as wfu)						
G-APMX	de Havilland DH.82A Tiger Moth	85645	DE715	9. 5.58	M.A.Broughton	Popham	21.10.02
G-APMY*	Piper PA-23-160 Apache	23-1258	EI-AJT	15. 5.58	W.Fern	Home Farm, Firbeck	1.11.81
					(WFU 1.11.81: on loan to South Yorkshire Aviation Museum)		
G-APNJ*	Cessna 310	35335	EI-AJY N3635D	2. 6.58	Northbrook College *(Cancelled 5.12.83 as WFU) (Instructional Airframe)*	Shoreham	28.11.74
G-APNS	Garland-Bianchi Linnet (Continental C90)	001		17. 6.58	P.M.Busaidy	Scaynes Hill, Haywards Heath	6.10.78S
					(Stored 6.95) (Valid CoR 4.01) (Current status unknown)		
G-APNT	Bellamy Currie Wot (Continental PC60) *(Regd with c/n P.6.399)*	HAC/3		18. 6.58	B.J.Dunford *"Airymouse"*	Long Wood, Morestead	14. 6.02P
G-APNZ	Rollason-Druine D.31 Turbulent (Ardem 4C02)	PFA 482		17. 4.58	J.Knight *(Damaged River Rother near Iden 3.9.95: on rebuild)*	Hailsham	13.12.95P
G-APOD*	Tipsy Belfair (Walter Mikron 2)	536	(OO-TIF)	16. 7.58	L.F.Potts *(Under restoration 6.00: cancelled 6.9.00 by CAA)*	(Bannockburn)	23. 8.88P
G-APOI	Saunders-Roe Skeeter Srs.8	S2/5081		29. 7.58	B.Chamberlain	Otley, Ipswich	2. 8.00P
G-APOL*	Druine D.31 Turbulent (Ardem 4C02)	PFA 439		31. 7.58	A.Gregori & S.Tinker	Charterhall	18. 6.94P
					(Damaged Charterhall 24.7.93: stored 6.00: cancelled 13.9.00 as wfu)		
G-APPA	de Havilland DHC.1 Chipmunk 22	C1/0792	N5073E G-APPA/WP917	11. 9.58	D.M.Squires *(On rebuild 7.97) (Current status unknown)*	Wellesbourne Mountford	14. 7.85

G-APPL	Percival P.40 Prentice 1	PAC/013	VR189	7.10.58	Susan J.Saggers	Biggin Hill	1.10.03
G-APPM	de Havilland DHC.1 Chipmunk 22	C1/0159	WB711	14.10.58	Freston Aviation Ltd *(As "WB711")*	Crowfield	22. 7.02
G-APPN	de Havilland DH.82A Tiger Moth 83839		T7328	17.10.58	E.G.Waite-Roberts	Longwood, Southampton	18. 4.04
	(Crashed Mendlesham 14.7.64: rebuilt 2000/01 as "T7328": believed to be same aircraft as G-DHTM (qv))						
G-APRF	Auster Alpha 5	3412	VR-LAF G-APRF	8.12.58	W.B.Bateson *(Stored 12.01)*	Blackpool	14.11.00
G-APRJ	Avro 694 Lincoln B.2	-	RF342 G-36-3/G-29-1/G-APRJ/RF342	29.12.58	D.Copley	Sandtoft	
	(Confirmed most parts present dismantled and in open storage 2001: fuselage still bearing "G-29-1" & wings "RF342")						
G-APRL*	Armstrong-Whitworth 650 Argosy Srs.101	AW.6652	N890U N602Z/N6507R/G-APRL	2. 1.59	Midland Air Museum "Edna" *(Cancelled 19.11.87 as WFU) (Elan titles)*	Coventry	23. 3.87T
G-APRR	CZL Super Aero 45 Srs.04	04-014	OK-KFQ	5. 1.59	R.H.Jowett	Ronaldsway	26. 9.03
G-APRS	Scottish Aviation Twin Pioneer 3	561	G-BCWF XT610/G-APRS/(PI-C430)	9. 1.59	Bravo Aviation Ltd *(Op Atlantic Air Transport Ltd)* *(In "ETPS" c/s)*	Coventry	15. 7.02T
G-APRT	Taylor JT.1 Monoplane (Ardem 4C02)	PFA 537		15. 1.59	D.A.Slater	Rushett Farm, Chessington	21. 5.02P
G-APSA	Douglas DC-6A	45497	4W-ABQ HZ-ADA/G-APSA/CF-MCK	12. 2.59	Atlantic Air Transport Ltd *(Op Air Atlantique)*	Coventry	11. 4.02T
G-APSO*	de Havilland DH.104 Dove 5	04505	(N1046T) G-APSO	16. 2.59	Cormack (Aircraft Services) Ltd *(To Devonair)*	Kemble	8. 7.78T
	(Wings fitted to G-BWWC: forward part of fuselage fitted with stub wings & used as engine test-bed by 4.00) *(Cancelled 2.5.01 as wfu)*						
G-APSR	Auster J/1U Workmaster	3499	OO-HXA G-APSR/VP-JCD/G-APSR/(F-OBHR)	22. 4.59	D & K Aero Services Ltd *(Op P.De Liens)*	Namur-Temploux, Belgium	30. 9.02A
G-APSY*	Bensen B-7Mc	JH/001 & 2		25. 2.59	J.Howell *(Cancelled 13.4.73 as WFU) (Current status unknown)*	Copthorne, Sussex	
G-APSZ*	Cessna 172	46472	N6372E	21. 5.59	Not known	Ronaldsway	4. 6.84
	(Damaged Barton 2.3.84: cancelled 8.1.8 :as TWFU) (Stored 6.96: current status unknown)						
G-APTP	Piper PA-22-150 Tri-Pacer *(Modified to PA-20 Pacer configuration)*	22-5009	EI-AJN	20. 3.59	Comunica Industries International Ltd	Roughay Farm, Bishops Waltham	1. 5.03
G-APTR	Auster Alpha	3392		15. 4.59	C.J. & D.J.Baker *(Complete 4.98) (Current status unknown)*	Carr Farm, Newark	11. 4.87
G-APTU	Auster Alpha 5	3413		20. 4.59	A.J. & J.M.Davis t/a G-APTU Flying Group *(On rebuild 3.00)*	Leicester	8. 6.98
G-APTW*	Westland WS-51/2 Widgeon	WA/H/150		27. 4.59	North East Aircraft Museum *(Cancelled 24.8.77 as WFU)*	Sunderland	26. 9.75
G-APTY	Beechcraft G35 Bonanza	D-4789	EI-AJG	4. 6.59	G.E.Brennand	Blackpool	23. 3.03
G-APTZ	Rollason-Druine D.31 Turbulent (VW 1600)	PFA 508		18. 3.59	Tiger Club (1990) Ltd	Headcorn	15. 5.02P
G-APUD*	Bensen B-7Mc	1		11. 5.59	The Aeroplane Collection *(Cancelled 27.2.70 as WFU) (On loan to Museum of Science & Industry)*	Manchester	27. 9.60
G-APUE	Orlican L-40 Meta-Sokol	150708	OK-NMB	2. 6.59	S.E. & M.J.Aherne	Top Farm, Croydon	13. 5.03
G-APUK*	Auster V J/1 Autocrat	1843	5N-ADW VR-NDJ/G-APUK/D-EGEG/SE-ARA	16. 6.59	P.L.Morley *(Cancelled 3.4.89 by CAA) (Stored 1995) (Current status unknown)*	(Yateley)	8.10.75
G-APUP*	Sopwith Pup rep (Le Rhone)	B.5292 & PFA 1582	9213M N5182	13. 2.59	RAF Museum *(Cancelled 4.10.84 by CAA) (As "N5182")*	Hendon	28. 6.78
G-APUR	Piper PA-22-160 Tri-Pacer	22-6711		3. 7.59	L F Miller	Kildare	20. 8.04
G-APUW	Auster J/5V Srs.160 Autocar	3273		23. 6.59	E.A.J.Hibbard	Hill Farm, Nayland	18.12.03
G-APUY	Druine D.31 Turbulent (VW 1300)	PFA 509		24. 6.59	C.Jones *(Stored 2.00)*	Barton	10. 6.86P
G-APUZ	Piper PA-24-250 Comanche	24-1094	N6000P	3. 7.59	Tatenhill Aviation	Tatenhill	23. 1.02
G-APVF	Putzer Elster B (Continental O-200-A)	006	D-EEQX 97+04/D-EJUH	29.12.83	A.& E.A.Wiseman *(As "97+04" in Luftwaffe c/s)*	Breighton	27. 2.02P
G-APVG	Auster J/5L Aiglet Trainer	3306	(ZK-BQW)	10. 7.59	R.Farrer	Cranfield	20. 3.00
G-APVN	Druine D.31 Turbulent (VW 1600)	PFA 511		24. 7.59	R.Sherwin *(Stored 3.97: current status unknown)*	Swanborough Farm, Lewes	24. 6.94P
G-APVS	Cessna 170B	26156	N2512C	7. 8.59	N.Simpson *"Stormin' Norman"*	East Kirkby	23. 6.03
G-APVU	Orlican L-40 Meta-Sokol	150706	OK-NMI	21. 8.59	S.A. & M.J.Aherne *(Damaged Manchester 12.9.78: on rebuild 1993)*	(St.Albans)	27. 6.79
G-APVV*	Mooney M.20A	1474	N8164E	30. 7.59	Newark Air Museum	Winthorpe	19. 9.81
	(Crashed at Barton 11.1.81: cancelled 3.4.89 by CAA) (Stored 4.97)						
G-APVZ	Rollason-Druine D.31 Turbulent (Ardem 4C02)	PFA 545		23. 7.59	I.D.Daniels	Maypole Farm, Chislet	20. 8.01P
G-APWA*	Handley Page HPR.7 Dart Herald 100	149	PP-SDM G-APWA/PP-SDM/PP-ASV/G-APWA	28. 9.59	Museum of Berkshire Aviation/The Herald Society *(BEA titles)* *(Cancelled 29.1.87 as WFU)*	Woodley	6. 4.82T
G-APWJ*	Handley Page HPR.7 Dart Herald 201	158		28. 9.59	Duxford Aviation Society *(Cancelled 10.7.85 as WFU) (Air UK titles)*	Duxford	21.12.85
G-APWL	EoN AP.10 460 Srs.1A	EoN/S/001	BGA.1172 G-APWL/RAFGSA.268/G-APWL	2. 9.59	D.G.Andrew *(Valid CofR 4.01)*	Eaglescott	
G-APWN*	Westland WS-55 Whirlwind 3	WA.298	VR-BER G-APWN/5N-AGI/G-APWN	8. 9.59	Midland Air Museum *"Skerries"* *(Cancelled 25.6.81 as WFU).(Bristow Helicopters c/s)*	Coventry	17. 5.78

G-APWP	Druine D.31 Turbulent	PFA 497		14. 9.59	C.F.Rogers	(Wheathamstead)	27. 6.67
					(Current status unknown)		
G-APWY*	Piaggio P.166	362		16.12.59	Science Museum Air Transport Coln & Storage Facility		
					(Cancelled 20.10.00 by CAA)	Wroughton	14. 3.81
G-APWZ	Lancashire Aircraft EP-9 Prospector	42		5.11.59	G.B.Pearce t/a Prospector Flying Group	Washington, West Sussex	5. 7.04
G-APXJ	Piper PA-24-250 Comanche	24-291	VR-NDA N10F	11.12.59	T.Wildsmith	Gamston	15.11.02
G-APXR	Piper PA-22-160 Tri-Pacer	22-7172	N10F	29. 1.60	A.Troughton	Belfast	2.12.04
G-APXT	Piper PA-22-150 Tri-Pacer	22-3854	N4545A	16. 2.60	A E Cuttler	(Wokingham)	5. 7.87T
	(Damaged Southend 26.12.85 & on rebuild to PA-20 Pacer configuration: new owner 12.01)						
G-APXU	Piper PA-22-150 Tri-Pacer	22-474	N1723A	10. 2.60	The Scottish Aero Club Ltd	Perth	20. 2.85
					"The Cloth Bomber" (Rebuild nearing completion 11.00)		
G-APXW*	Lancashire Aircraft EP-9 Prospector	43		22.12.59	Museum of Army Flying	AAC Middle Wallop	22. 5.76
			(Cancelled 20.5.82: composite rebuild ex G-APWZ & others: as "XM819" - Army c/s)				
G-APXX*	de Havilland DHA.3 Drover 2	5014	VH-EAS VH-EAZ	15.12.59	Second World War Aircraft Preservation Society	Lasham	
					(Not converted: cancelled 26.11.73 as WFU) (As "VH-FDT")		
G-APXY	Cessna 150	17711	N7911E	15. 1.60	The Merlin Flying Club Ltd	Hucknall	24. 3.02T
G-APXZ*	Knight Twister	3KT-001 & PFA 1307		7. 1.60	N.H.Ponsford	Breighton	
			(Cancelled 26.3.73: identity unconfirmed: incomplete frame stored 4.96)				
G-APYB	Tipsy T.66 Nipper 3 (VW 1834) *(Built Avions Fairey SA)*	T66/S/39		28. 1.60	B.O.Smith *(On rebuild 1.02)*	Yearby	12. 6.96P
G-APYD*	de Havilland DH.105 Comet 4B	6438	SX-DAL G-APYD	21. 1.60	Science Museum Air Transport Coln & Storage Facility		
					(Cancelled 23.11.79 as WFU) (Dan-Air titles)	Wroughton	3. 8.79T
G-APYG	de Havilland DHC.1 Chipmunk 22	C1/0060	OH-HCB WB619	11.11.60	E.J.I.Musty & P.A.Colman	White Waltham	5. 7.04
G-APYI	Piper PA-22-135 Tri-Pacer	22-2218	N8031C	8. 2.60	B.T. & J.Cullen	Ballyboy, Co.Meath	16. 8.03
	(Modified to PA-20 Pacer configuration)						
G-APYN	Piper PA-22-160 Tri-Pacer	22-6797	N2804Z	24. 2.60	S.J.Raw	Morgansfield, Fishburn	21. 6.02
G-APYT	Champion 7FC Tri-Traveler	7FC-387		9. 5.60	B.J.Anning	Watchford Farm, Yarcombe	16. 9.02P
G-APYU*	Champion 7FC Tri-Traveler	7FC-388		12. 5.60	R.W.Brown	Clothall Farm, Clothall Common	6. 8.72
			(Crashed Old Warden 23.4.72: cancelled 3.4.89 by CAA) (Stored 5.96)				
G-APZJ	Piper PA-18-150 Super Cub	18-7233	N10F	29. 1.60	R.Jones t/a Southern Sailplanes	Aston Down	15. 5.03
	(Rebuilt 1986 after accident 12.6.83 using un-identified new fuselage frame: original frame open store Membury 1989)						
G-APZL	Piper PA-22-160 Tri-Pacer	22-7054	EI-ALF N10F	27. 1.60	B.Robins	Dunkeswell	14. 5.99
G-APZR*	Cessna 150	17861	N6461T	31. 3.60	Avtech Ltd	Biggin Hill	4. 4.81
			(Damaged Biggin Hill 14.1.81: front fuselage used as engine test-bed: noted 12.00)				
G-APZX	Piper PA-22-150 Tri-Pacer	22-5181	N7420D	28. 4.60	Applied Signs Ltd	Tatenhill	20. 6.03
	(Modified to PA-20 Pacer configuration)						

G-ARAA – G-ARZZ

G-ARAD	Phoenix Luton LA-5A Major	PAL/1204 & PFA 836		29. 4.60	D.J.Bone & P.L.Jobes		
			(Completed but not flown: stored 3.94)			Lennox Plunton, Borgue	
G-ARAI	Piper PA-22-160 Tri-Pacer	22-7421	N10F	17. 5.60	J.Mann	(Cheshunt)	14.11.04
G-ARAN	Piper PA-18-150 Super Cub	18-7307	N10F	28. 4.60	A.P.Docherty	Redhill	8. 6.04
G-ARAO	Piper PA-18 Super Cub 95	18-7327	N10F	17. 5.60	R.G.Manton *(As "607327/L/09" in USAAC c/s)*	Denham	2. 4.01
G-ARAP*	Champion 7EC Traveler	7FC-394		12. 9.60	J.McGonagal	(Londonderry)	26. 6.82P
			(Damaged Eglinton 22. 9.81: on rebuild 12.92) (Current status unknown)				
G-ARAS	Champion 7FC Tri-Traveler	7FC-396		12. 9.60	G.J.Taylor t/a Alpha Sierra Flying Group	(Lichfield)	22. 6.01P
G-ARAT	Cessna 180C	50827	N9327T	18. 5.60	C.Buck *(Noted 7.01)*	Swanton Morley	14. 6.04
G-ARAU*	Cessna 150	17894	N6494T	29. 4.60	Colton Aviation Ltd	Little Staughton	14. 9.84T
					(Cancelled 3.4.89 by CAA) (Stored unmarked 9.96)		
G-ARAW	Cessna 182C Skylane	52843	N8943T	18. 5.60	R.P.Beck, G.& R.L.McLean t/a Ximango UK	Rufforth	1. 6.02T
G-ARAX	Piper PA-22-150 Tri-Pacer	22-3830	N4523A	22. 4.60	J.J.Bywater	Old Sarum	14. 4.02
G-ARAY*	Avro 748 Srs.1A/200	1535	OY-DFV G-11/G-ARAY/PI-C784/G-ARAY/VP-LIO/G-ARAY/PP-VJQ/G-ARAY/YV-C-AMC/G-ARAY	21. 4.60	Not known	(Lasham)	16. 6.90T
	(WFU 17.10.89: broken up 5.92: cancelled 2.11.95 as WFU) (Fuselage to Hampshire Fire Service 12.95: nose section in Air Salvage International yard adjoining Hillside Nurseries 11.01)						
G-ARAZ	de Havilland DH.82A Tiger Moth	82867	R4959	25. 3.60	D.A.Porter *(As "R4959/59" in RAF c/s)*	Griffins Farm, Temple Bruer	28. 5.04
G-ARBE	de Havilland DH.104 Dove 8	04517		6. 5.60	M.Whale & M.W.A.Lunn	Kemble	3.10.02
G-ARBG	Tipsy T.66 Nipper 2 (VW 1834 Acro) *(Built Avions Fairey SA)*	ABAC.1 & 57		11. 5.60	J.Horovitz & J.McLeod	Felthorpe	17. 8.84P
					(Damaged Felthorpe 6.5.84: on rebuild 5.91)		
G-ARBM	Auster 5 J/1B Aiglet	2792	EI-AMO G-ARBM/VP-SZZ/VP-KKR	8. 6.60	A.D.Hodgkinson	Dunkirk Farm, Canterbury	6. 6.03

G-ARBN* Piper PA-23-160 Apache 23-1385 EI-AKI 1. 6.60 Busy Bee Aviation Ltd Sibson 25. 8.86T
N3421P
(Damaged Sibson 8.86: cancelled 5.1.89 as WFU) (Fuselage stored unmarked 10.01)
G-ARBO Piper PA-24-250 Comanche 24-2117 N10F 15. 6.60 Arrow Aviation Services Ltd Exeter 27. 5.84
(Force landed Morecambe Bay 27.4.83: new owner 6.01)
G-ARBP Tipsy T.66S Nipper 2 54 7. 6.60 F.W.Kirk Seighford 21. 6.02P
(VW 1834) *(Built Avions Fairey SA)*
G-ARBS Piper PA-22-160 Tri-Pacer 22-6858 N2868Z 24. 8.60 S.D.Rowell Valley Farm, Winwick 2.12.01
(Modified to PA-20 Pacer configuration) *"Greta"*
G-ARBV Piper PA-22-160 Tri-Pacer 22-5836 N8633D 29. 6.60 D.J.Sheen Oaksey Park 19. 7.03
(Rebuilt 1983/84 using fuselage of G-ARDP c/n 22-4254) t/a Oaksey Pacers
G-ARBZ Rollason-Druine D.31 Turbulent 6. 5.60 G Richards & R Bishop Headcorn 15.10.99P
(Ardem 4C02) PFA 553 *(Damaged East Mersea, Essex 17.7.99: remains noted 10.99)*
G-ARCC Piper PA-22-150 Tri-Pacer 22-4006 N4853A 23. 6.60 A.S.Cowan Popham 23. 5.03
t/a Popham Flying Group G-ARCC
G-ARCF Piper PA-22-150 Tri-Pacer 22-4563 N5902D 28. 6.60 M.J.Speakman North Coates 20. 5.02
G-ARCI* Cessna 310D 39266 N6966T 21.10.60 Not known Blackpool 25. 4.84
(Damaged Sandtoft 22.8.86: cancelled 3.1.89 by CAA) (Open store 12.01)
G-ARCS Auster D.6 Srs.180 3703 4. 7.60 E.A.Matty Shobdon 3. 9.03
G-ARCT Piper PA-18 Super Cub 95 18-7375 EI-AVE 6. 7.60 C.F.O'Neil (Belfast) 21. 4.86
G-ARCT/N10F *(Damaged Mullaghmore 29.3.87: stored 1996)*
G-ARCV Cessna 175A Skylark 17556757 N8057T 7.11.60 R.Francis & C.Campbell Sandtoft 6. 7.02
(Continental O-300D)
G-ARCW Piper PA-23 Apache 23-796 N2187P 7. 7.60 F W Ellis Water Leisure Park, Skegness 17. 4.04
(Mod to PA-23-160 standard)
G-ARCX* Gloster Meteor NF.14 AW.2163 WM261 8. 9.60 National Museums of Scotland/Museum of Flight
(Built Armstrong-Whitworth Aircraft) *(WFU 2.69: cancelled 25.10.73 as WFU)* East Fortune 20. 2.69S
G-ARDB Piper PA-24-250 Comanche 24-2166 PH-RON 15. 8.60 P.Crook Andrewsfield 7. 6.04
G-ARDB/N7019P
G-ARDD Scintex CP.301C-1 Emeraude 549 4. 7.60 G.E.Livings RAF Halton 26. 7.02P
(Rebuilt EMK Aeroplanes with c/n EMK.004)
G-ARDE* de Havilland DH.104 Dove 6 04469 I-TONY 15.11.60 T.E.Evans Wellesbourne Mountford 25. 8.91
"Sir Geoffrey de Havilland" (Stored 6.98: cancelled 30.5.01 by CAA)
G-ARDG* Lancashire Aircraft EP-9 Prospector 2 14. 7.60 G.Pearce/Museum of Army Flying
47 Durrington, W.Sussex
(Cancelled 28.5.82 as WFU) (Stored 7.93 with parts from G-APWZ & G-APXW)
G-ARDJ Auster D.6 Srs.180 3704 15. 7.60 R.E.Neal Leicester 7. 7.88T
t/a RN Aviation (Leicester Airport)
(Damaged near Leicester 30.5.86: dismantled 1.02)
G-ARDO Wassmer Jodel D.112J 146 F-PBTE 22. 8.60 W.R.Prescott Kilkeel, Co.Down 25. 3.02P
(Built Ets Couesnon) F-BBTE/F-WBTE *(Composite with fuselage of G-AYEO c/n 684 ex F-BIGG)*
G-ARDS Piper PA-22-150 Caribbean 22-7154 N3214Z 4. 9.60 A.C.Donaldson & C.I.Lavery
Newtownards, Co.of Down 31. 3.01
G-ARDT Piper PA-22-160 Tri-Pacer 22-6210 N9158D 15. 9.60 M.Henderson Cheyene Farm, Stonehaven 29. 6.02
G-ARDV Piper PA-22-160 Tri-Pacer 22-7487 EI-APA 28. 7.60 R.W. Christie (Ballymena, Co.Antrim) 2. 1.99
G-ARDV/N10F *(Damaged Ballymena 10.7.98: current status unknown)*
G-ARDX* Auster 6A Tugmaster 1905 TW524 2. 8.60 A.A.Marshall
(Damaged Lasham 1.1.64: frame stored 3.96) Yeatsall Farm, Abbots Bromley 29. 8.64A
G-ARDY Tipsy T.66 Nipper 2 55 10. 8.60 D.Best Enstone 12.12.00P
(Martlet VW) *(Built Avions Fairey SA)*
G-ARDZ* SAN Jodel D.140A Mousquetaire 49 10.11.60 M.J.Wright Cherry Tree Farm, Monewden 29.11.91
(Cancelled 26.2.99 by CAA) (Noted 5.00)
G-AREA* de Havilland DH.104 Dove 8 04520 3. 8.60 De Havilland Heritage Museum
(Cancelled 19.9.00 by CAA) London Colney 18. 9.87
G-AREH de Havilland DH.82A Tiger Moth 85287 (G-APYV) 4. 7.60 N.K.Geddes (Bridge of Weir) 19. 4.66T
6746M/DE241 *(On long-term rebuild 6.00)*
G-AREI Taylorcraft Auster III 518 9M-ALB 14.12.60 P.J.Stock "Akyab" (Petersfield) 21. 4.03
VR-RBM/VR-SCJ/MT438 *(Op Military Auster Flight) (As "MT438" in SEAC c/s)*
G-AREL Piper PA-22-150 Caribbean 22-7284 N3344Z 14. 9.60 H.H.Cousins t/a Fenland Aerosvcs Fenland 22. 8.98
G-AREO Piper PA-18-150 Super Cub 18-7407 N10F 24. 8.60 Crown Service Gliding Club Farnborough 17. 9.04
G-ARET Piper PA-22-160 Tri-Pacer 22-7590 N10F 2. 9.60 I.S.Runnalls Church Farm, North Moreton 20. 5.83T
(On rebuild 5.99)
G-AREV Piper PA-22-160 Tri-Pacer 22-6540 N9628D 25.10.60 D.J.Ash *"Smart Cat"* Barton 2. 1.04
G-AREX Aeronca 15AC Sedan 15AC-61 CF-FNM 12. 9.60 R.J.M.Turnbull & P.Lowndes
Rydinghurst Farm, Cranleigh 4.10.04
G-AREZ Rollason-Druine D.31 Turbulent 22. 9.60 J.St.Clair-Quentin (Ledbury) 19. 9.84P
(Ardem 4C02) PFA 561 *(Stored 10.97: Valid CofR @ 3.01)*
G-ARFB Piper PA-22-150 Caribbean 22-7518 N3625Z 8. 9.60 R.Burgun Derby 28. 2.03
G-ARFD Piper PA-22-160 Tri-Pacer 22-7565 N3667Z 8. 9.60 J.R.Dunnett Poplar Hall Farm, Elmsett 31. 5.04
G-ARFG Cessna 175AX Skylark 56505 N7005E 15.11.60 P.K.Blair Stapleford 28. 1.04T
(Rebuilt to Cessna 172 standard 1988) t/a Foxtrot Golf Group
G-ARFH Piper PA-24-250 Comanche 24-2240 N7087P 13.10.60 A.B.W.Taylor Great Massingham 25. 1.04
G-ARFI Cessna 150A 15059100 N41836 1. 2.61 J.H.Fisher Haverfordwest 19. 7.03
G-ARFI/N7000X

G-ARFL	Cessna 175B Skylark	17556868	N8168T	2. 2.61	D.J.Mason	Denham	7. 3.03
G-ARFO	Cessna 150A	15059174	N7074X	23. 3.61	Breakthrough Aviation Ltd	Leicester	25. 4.03T
G-ARFT	SAN Jodel DR.1050 Ambassadeur	170		27.10.60	R.Shaw	(Sowerby Bridge)	13.10.84
					(Damaged Prestwick 15.6.84: current status unknown)		
G-ARFV	Tipsy T.66 Nipper 2	44		5.10.60	C.J.Pidler	(Wellington)	29.11.01P
	(Built Avions Fairey SA) (VW 1834)						
G-ARGB*	Auster 6A	2593	VF635	12.10.60	C.J.Baker	Carr Farm, Newark	21. 6.74
					(Dismantled fuselage stored 4.98)		
G-ARGG	de Havilland DHC.1 Chipmunk 22	C1/0247	WD305	19.10.60	B.Hook	Coventry	21. 4.96
					(As "WD305": stored w/o engine 5.00)		
G-ARGI(1)*	Auster 6A	2299	VF530	8.12.60	Not known	(Yorkshire)	4. 7.76
					(Bare frame noted 4.98: current status unknown)		
G-ARGO	Piper PA-22-108 Colt	22-8034		18. 1.61	D R Smith	Sleap	27. 6.02
G-ARGV	Piper PA-18-150 Super Cub	18-7559	N10F	20.12.60	Wolds Gliding Club Ltd	Pocklington	15. 3.02
	(Lycoming O-360-A4)						
G-ARGY	Piper PA-22-160 Tri-Pacer	22-7620	G-JEST	20.12.60	G.K.Hare	Fenland	7.12.02
	(Modified to PA-20 configuration)		G-ARGY/N10F				
G-ARGZ	Rollason-Druine D.31 Turbulent	PFA 562		7.11.60	The Tiger Club (1990) Ltd	Headcorn	4.10.02P
	(VW 1600)						
G-ARHB	Forney F-1A Aircoupe	5733		17. 4.61	A.V.Rash & D.R.Wickes t/a Aircoupe Hotel Bravo	Earls Colne	7.11.02
G-ARHC	Forney F-1A Aircoupe	5734		26. 5.61	A.P.Gardner	Little Gransden	21. 6.04
G-ARHF*	Forney F-1A Aircoupe	5737		26. 5.61	(R Ford)	Sywell	10. 5.94
					(Cancelled 10.11.95 by CAA) (On rebuild 8.01)		
G-ARHI	Piper PA-24-180 Comanche	24-2260	N7299P	20.12.60	D.D.Smith	Norwich	27. 7.03
			N10F				
G-ARHL*	Piper PA-23-250 Aztec	27-402		3. 3.61	C.J.Freeman	Headcorn	23.11.79
					(On overhaul 4.00: cancelled 15.3.01 as wfu)		
G-ARHM	Auster 6A	2515	VF557	5. 1.61	D.F.Hodgkinson	(Gravesend)	9.12.01
G-ARHN	Piper PA-22-150 Caribbean	22-7514	N3622Z	10. 1.61	J.R.Lawrence	Nether Huntlywood Farm, Gordon	5. 3.03
	(Rebuilt with parts of G-ATXB - DBR 26.8.74)						
G-ARHP	Piper PA-22-160 Tri-Pacer	22-7549	N3652Z	10. 1.61	R.N.Morgan	Boones Farm, High Garrett, Braintree	22. 5.03
G-ARHR	Piper PA-22-150 Caribbean	22-7576	N3707Z	10. 1.61	A.R.Wyatt	Fowlmere	22.10.04
G-ARHU	Piper PA-22-160 Tri-Pacer	22-7602	N3726Z	10. 1.61	M.S.Bird *(New owner 1.02)*	(Salisbury)	10.12.98
G-ARHW	de Havilland DH.104 Dove 8	04512		10. 1.61	Pacelink Ltd	Fairoaks	14. 3.02T
G-ARHX*	de Havilland DH.104 Dove 8	04513		11. 1.61	South Yorkshire Aviation Museum *(WFU 8.9.78)*	Doncaster	8. 9.78
G-ARHZ	Rollason-Druine D.62A Condor	PFA 247 & RAE/602		13.12.60	T.J.Goodwin	Hill Farm, Nayland	26. 7.95P
	(Continental O-200-A)				*(Damaged Damyns Hall, Upminster 4.9.94)*		
G-ARID	Cessna 172B Skyhawk	48209	N7709X	2. 2.61	L.M.Edwards	Sleap	25. 6.03
G-ARIF	Ord-Hume O-H 7 Minor Coupe	O-H 7 & PAL/1401		22. 8.60	N.H.Ponsford	Wigan	
	(Modified Luton LA-4C Minor)				*(Stored incomplete 3.96)*		
G-ARIH	Auster 6A	2463	TW591	23. 1.61	R.Tarder & J.J.Fisher t/a India Hotel Group	Yeatsall Farm, Abbots Bromley	14. 6.04
			(As "TW591" in 664 (AOP) Sqdn c/s)				
G-ARIK	Piper PA-22-150 Caribbean	22-7570	N3701Z	26. 1.61	C.J.Berry	Booker	3. 5.03
G-ARIL	Piper PA-22-150 Caribbean	22-7574	N3705Z	26. 1.61	T.I.Carlin	City of Derry	21.12.01
G-ARIM	Druine D.31 Turbulent	PFA 510		27. 2.61	R M.White *(Current status unknown)*	(Chapel/High Kype Farm), Strathaven	
G-ARIN*	Piper PA-24-250 Comanche	24-1182	N6084P	10. 2.61	Not known	(Bruntingthorpe)	
	(Crashed near Bodmin 20.5.90 on take-off: cancelled 29.8.90 as WFU) (Fuselage noted in scrapyard compound outside airfield 11.01)						
G-ARJB	de Havilland DH.104 Dove 8	04518		29. 9.60	M.Whale & M.W.A.Lunn	Kemble	10.12.73T
					"Exporter" (Stored 12.00)		
G-ARJE	Piper PA-22-108 Colt	22-8184		29. 3.61	C.I.Fray	(Disley)	29. 4.73
					(On rebuild 1993: new owner 10.00)		
G-ARJF	Piper PA-22-108 Colt	22-8199		23. 3.61	A.M.Noble	Pepperbox, Salisbury	17. 4.03
G-ARJH	Piper PA-22-108 Colt	22-8249		29. 3.61	A.Vine	Goodwood	10. 9.03
G-ARJR*	Piper PA-23-160 Apache G	23-1966	N4447P	1. 3.61	Oxford Air Training School	Oxford	24.10.78
					(DBR Little Berkhampstead 22.7.78: instructional airframe 5.95)		
G-ARJS	Piper PA-23-160 Apache G	23-1977	N10F	3. 3.61	Bencray Ltd	Blackpool	12.11.03T
					(Op Blackpool & Fylde Aero Club)		
G-ARJT	Piper PA-23-160 Apache G	23-1981	N10F	3. 3.61	J.A.Cole	Netherthorpe	29. 1.01T
G-ARJU	Piper PA-23-160 Apache G	23-1984	N10F	3. 3.61	G.R.Manley	Biggin Hill	5. 3.03T
G-ARJV	Piper PA-23-160 Apache G	23-1985	N10F	3. 3.61	Metham Aviation Ltd	Blackbushe	11.11.01
G-ARJZ*	Rollason-Druine D.31 Turbulent	PFA 564		8. 2.61	C.J.Tilson	Great Massingham	4. 9.95P
	(VW 1700)				*(Stored 2.99: cancelled 11.9.00 by CAA)*		
G-ARKG	Auster J/5G Cirrus Autocar	3061	AP-AHJ	22. 2.61	G.C.Milborrow	Spanhoe	8. 8.04
			VP-KKN				
G-ARKJ	Beechcraft N35 Bonanza	D-6736		5. 5.61	P.A.Brook	Shoreham	2. 6.01
G-ARKK	Piper PA-22-108 Colt	22-8290		12. 4.61	The Rochford Hundred Flying Group Ltd	Southend	7.11.03
G-ARKM	Piper PA-22-108 Colt	22-8313		12. 4.61	D.Dytch & J.Moffat	Perth	1.12.04T
G-ARKN	Piper PA-22-108 Colt	22-8327		9. 5.61	T.D.Fuller	(Swadlincote)	21. 7.02

G-ARKP	Piper PA-22-108 Colt	22-8364		19. 5.61	C.J.& J.Freeman	Headcorn	20.12.04T
G-ARKS	Piper PA-22-108 Colt	22-8422		7. 6.61	R.A.Nesbitt-Dufort		
	(Lycoming O-320)					Bradleys Lawn, Heathfield	28.11.04
G-ARLG	Auster D.4/108	3606		4. 4.61	R.D.Helliar-Symons t/a Auster D4 Group		
						Bourne Park, Hurstbourne Tarrant	14. 5.02P
G-ARLK	Piper PA-24-250 Comanche	24-2433	EI-ALW	25. 5.61	Gibad Aviation Ltd	Stapleford	2. 4.02
			G-ARLK/N10F				
G-ARLO*	Beagle A.61 Terrier 1	2500	TW642	11. 4.61	S.C.Challis	Hedge End, Southampton	3.11.79
					t/a British Classic Aircraft Restorations		
			(Damaged off Shoreham 10.7.79: stored 3.96 for rebuild as Auster AOP.6)				
G-ARLP	Beagle A.61 Terrier 1	3724(1)	VX123	11. 4.61	D.R.Whitby	(Fakenham)	31.10.91
					t/a Gemini Flying Group		
	(Official c/n of 2573/VF631 became G-ARLM(2)/G-ASDK: damaged Truleigh Farm, Edburton 4.8.91: on rebuild 2000)						
G-ARLR	Beagle A.61 Terrier 2	3721 & B.601	VW996	11. 4.61	M. Palfreman	Bagby	9. 9.01
G-ARLU(2)*	Cessna 172B	48502	N8002X	14. 6.61	Irish Air Corps	Baldonnel	6.10.78
			(Damaged 30.10.77: cancelled 6.8.80 as WFU) (Instructional airframe 8.93)				
G-ARLX	SAN Jodel D.140B Mousquetaire II	66		12. 4.61	M.J.Dunkerly	(Ouessant, France)	30. 5.04T
G-ARLZ	Rollason-Druine D.31A Turbulent			7. 4.61	Little Bear Ltd	Exeter	18. 7.02P
	(Ardem 4C02)	RAE/578					
G-ARMA	Piper PA-23-160 Apache G	23-1967	N4448P	8. 5.61	C J Hopewell *(Noted 10.01)*	Sibson	22. 7.77
G-ARMB	de Havilland DHC.1 Chipmunk 22A		WB660	26. 4.61	G.E.J.Spooner*(As "WB660")*	Old Buckenham	20. 5.02
			C1/0099				
G-ARMC	de Havilland DHC.1 Chipmunk 22A		WB703	26. 4.61	J.T.H.Henderson	White Waltham	7. 6.02
		C1/0151			*(As "WB703" in RAF c/s)*		
G-ARMD	de Havilland DHC.1 Chipmunk 22A		WD297	26. 4.61	D M Squires	Wellesbourne Mountford	5. 6.76
		C1/0237			*(Valid CofR 3.01)*		
G-ARMF	de Havilland DHC.1 Chipmunk 22A		WG322	26. 4.61	D.M.Squires	(Wellesbourne Mountford)	12.10.98
		C1/0394			*(Damaged 1996) (As "WZ868": stored 2001)*		
G-ARMG	de Havilland DHC.1 Chipmunk 22A		WK558	26. 4.61	D.K.Keays	Bidford	1. 3.04
		C1/0575			t/a The MG Group		
G-ARML	Cessna 175B Skylark	17556995	N8295T	12. 7.61	R.W.Boote	RAF Lyneham	31. 3.02
G-ARMN	Cessna 175B Skylark	17556994	N8294T	18. 8.61	G.A.Nash	Lower Wasing Farm, Brimpton	22. 5.02
G-ARMO	Cessna 172B Skyhawk	48560	N8060X	12. 6.61	G.M.Jones	Little Staughton	21. 3.02
G-ARMR	Cessna 172B Skyhawk	48566	N8066X	12. 6.61	Sunsaver Ltd	Barton	16. 8.03
G-ARMX*	Avro 748 Srs.1A/101	1538	VP-LVN	28. 4.61	Manchester Airport Fire Training Services		
			G-ARMX			Manchester	18. 3.84T
			(Cancelled 21.10.92: fuselage on fire dump 4.97) (Current status unknown)				
G-ARMZ	Rollason-Druine D.31 Turbulent			2. 5.61	J.Mickleburgh & D.Clark	Headcorn	25. 1.02P
	(VW 1500)	PFA 565					
G-ARNA*	Mooney M.20B Mark 21	1806		26. 6.61	Not known	Casablanca-Anfa, Morocco	14. 8.81
			(Cancelled 16.12.91 as WFU) (Stored 3.94) (Current status unknown)				
G-ARNB	Auster J/5G Cirrus Autocar	3169	AP-AHL	18. 5.61	R.F.Tolhurst	Lenham, Maidstone	19. 2.77
			VP-KNL		*(Possibly on rebuild 1995: current status unknown)*		
G-ARND	Piper PA-22-108 Colt	22-8484		6. 6.61	E.J.Clarke	Seighford	4. 8.99
G-ARNE	Piper PA-22-108 Colt	22-8502		15. 6.61	T.D.L.Bowden	Knettishall	7. 6.04
	(Lycoming O-320)						
G-ARNG	Piper PA-22-108 Colt	22-8547		26. 6.61	F.B.Rothera	(Ashford, Kent)	10. 1.04
	(Lycoming O-320)						
G-ARNH*	Piper PA-22-108 Colt	22-8558		5. 9.61	Fenland & West Norfolk Aero Club Preservation Socy		
						West Walton, Wisbech	20. 3.73
		(Crashed 1.9.72: cancelled 24.5.73 as WFU) (Fuselage on rebuild 4.96: current status unknown)					
G-ARNI	Piper PA-22-108 Colt	22-8575		26. 7.61	B.A.Drury	Rochester	15. 6.98T
G-ARNJ	Piper PA-22-108 Colt	22-8587		3. 8.61	R.A.Keech	Woodvale	18. 1.03
G-ARNK	Piper PA-22-108 Colt	22-8622		5. 9.61	N.G. & A.N.M.McDonald	RAF Coltishall	5.11.04
	(Reported as converted to PA-20 configuration with Lycoming O-320 as "Super Colt" although CAA records identify as "modified" whilst retaining Lycoming O-235)						
G-ARNL	Piper PA-22-108 Colt	22-8625		3. 8.61	Miss J.A.Dodsworth	White Waltham	19. 9.03
G-ARNN	Globe GC-1B Swift	1272	VP-YMJ	11. 5.61	K.E.Sword	(Leicester)	11. 7.74
			VP-RDA/ZS-BMX/NC3279K		*(Crashed Hucknall 1.9.73: current status unknown)*		
G-ARNO*	Beagle A.61 Terrier 1	3722	VX113	8. 5.61	R.Webber	Trenchard Farm, Eggesford	19. 6.81
					(Cancelled 17.12.91 as WFU) (Frame noted 11.01)		
G-ARNP	Beagle A.109 Airedale	B.503		10. 5.61	S.T. & M.Isbister	North Weald	5. 4.03
	(Original c/n A109-P1)						
G-ARNY	SAN Jodel D.117	595	F-BHXQ	13. 6.61	P.Jenkins	Inverness	9. 4.02P
G-ARNZ	Rollason-Druine D.31 Turbulent			28. 6.61	The Tiger Club (1990) Ltd	Headcorn	4.11.02P
	(VW 1600)	PFA 579					
G-AROA	Cessna 172B Skyhawk	48628	N8128X	19. 9.61	D.E.Partridge	Rayne Hall Farm, Rayne	29. 8.03T
					t/a The D & P Group		
G-AROC	Cessna 175BX Skylark	1756997	G-OTOW	2.10.61	A.J.Symms	High Ham, Yeovil	3. 2.03
	(Modified to 172 configuration)		G-AROC/N8297T				
G-AROJ*	Beagle A.109 Airedale	B.508	HB-EUC	17. 5.61	C.J.Baker	Carr Farm, Newark	8. 1.76
			G-AROJ		*(Dismantled 4.98)*		
G-ARON	Piper PA-22-108 Colt	22-8822		23.11.61	R.W.Curtis	(Warminster)	5. 7.01
G-AROO	Forney F.1A Aircoupe	5750	N25B	3.11.61	W.J.McMeekan	Newtownards, Co.of Down	21.11.04

G-AROW	SAN Jodel D.140B Mousquetaire II	71		13. 9.61	Mousquetaire Ltd	Redhill	3. 4.03
G-AROY	Boeing-Stearman A75N1(PT-17) Kaydet		N56418	6. 6.61	W.A.Jordan	Spanhoe	17. 9.03
	(Pratt & Witney R985)	75-4775	42-16612				
G-ARPH*	de Havilland DH.121 Trident 1C	2108		13. 4.61	RAF Museum	RAF Cosford	8. 9.82T
					(WFU 26.3.82: British Airways titles)		
G-ARPK*	de Havilland DH.121 Trident 1C	2111		13. 4.61	Manchester Airport Fire Service		
						Manchester	17. 5.82T
					(WFU 24.5.82) (To Fire School: on fire dump 9.99)		
G-ARPL*	de Havilland DH.121 Trident 1C	2112		13. 4.61	Not known	Glasgow	13. 8.84T
				(WFU 24.5.82) (Cockpit section on fire training ground 12.01)			
G-ARPO(2)*	de Havilland DH.121 Trident 1C	2116	(G-ARPP)	23. 3.64	International Fire Training Centre		
				(WFU 12.12.83) (To Fire School: extant 3.00)		Teesside	12. 1.86T
G-ARPP(2)*	de Havilland DH.121 Trident 1C	2117	(G-ARPR)	23. 3.64	Glasgow Airport Ltd	Glasgow	16. 2.86T
					(WFU 2.83 & cancelled) (For Training use 12.01)		
G-ARPZ(2)*	de Havilland DH.121 Trident 1C	2128		23. 3.64	British Airways Aircraft Recovery Unit		
						Dunsfold	26. 1.86T
	(WFU 7.4.83 & cancelled) (Used as escape systems test airframe- airframe parts for Trident Preservation Society 3.00)						
G-ARRD	SAN Jodel DR.1051 Ambassadeur	274		20. 7.61	C.M.Fitton	Watchford Farm, Yarcombe	30.11.02P
G-ARRE	SAN Jodel DR.1050 Ambassadeur	275		20. 7.61	A.Luty & M.P.Edwards	Barton	21. 4.02
G-ARRG*	Cessna 175B Skylark	17556999	N8299T	5.10.61	Not known	Little Staughton	4. 5.73
		(Damaged Great Yarmouth 3.11.70: cancelled 7.12.70 as destroyed) (Fuselage stored unmarked 9.00)					
G-ARRI	Cessna 175B Skylark	17557001	N8301T	5.10.61	R.D.Fowden	Stapleford	2. 5.04
G-ARRL	Auster 5 J/1N Alpha	2115	VP-KFK	13. 6.61	G.N.Smith & C.Webb	Headcorn	1. 7.99
			VP-KPF/VP-KFK/VP-UAK				
G-ARRM*	Beagle B.206X	B.001		23. 6.61	Bristol Aero Collection	Kemble	23.12.64
	(Originally regd as Beagle B.2 Srs.1 [B2/1010]: re-designated 9.61) (WFU 1965?)						
G-ARRO	Beagle A.109 Airedale	B.507	EI-AYL(2)	16. 6.61	M.& S.W.Isbister	Spanhoe	17. 1.74
	(Originally regd with c/n A.109-P5)		G-ARRO/(EI-AVP)/G-ARRO *(Stored 4.01)*				
G-ARRS	Menavia Piel CP.301A Emeraude	226	F-BIMA	29. 6.61	Julia P.Drake & N.W.Cawley	Sturgate	26. 6.02P
					t/a ARSSY Aviation		
G-ARRT	Wallis WA-116/Mc	2		28. 6.61	K.H.Wallis	Reymerston Hall, Norfolk	26. 5.83P
	(McCulloch 4318A) *(Orig regd as a Wallis Gyroplane then became WA-116/Mc) (Noted 8.01)*						
G-ARRX	Auster 6A	2281	VF512	4. 7.61	J.E.D.Mackie *"Peggy Too"*	Popham	7. 6.03
					(As "VF512/PF-M" in 43 OTU c/s)		
G-ARRY	SAN Jodel D.140B Mousquetaire II	72		13. 9.61	Fictionview Ltd	(Lichfield)	11.11.04
G-ARRZ	Rollason-Druine D.31 Turbulent			21. 8.61	C.I.Jefferson *"Tarzan"*	Hingham, Norfolk	21.12.90P
	(Ardem 4C02)	PFA 580	*(Damaged Horley, Surrey 21.7.90: on rebuild 9.97: current status unknown)*				
G-ARSB(2)*	Cessna 150A	15059337	N7237X	25. 9.61	Not known	Little Staughton	10. 6.88
					(Cancelled 1.8.94 by CAA) (Fuselage stored 2.00)		
G-ARSG	Roe Triplane Type IV rep	HAC.1	(BAPC1)	29.10.81	The Shuttleworth Trust	Old Warden	8. 8.02P
	(ADC Cirrus III) *(Also c/n TRI.1)*				*(No external marks)*		
G-ARSL	Beagle A.61 Terrier 2	2539	VF581	13. 7.61	D.J.Colclough	Trenchard Farm, Eggsford	10. 9.03
					(As "VF581")		
G-ARSU	Piper PA-22-108 Colt	22-8835	EI-AMI	23.11.61	D.P.Owen	Thruxton	11. 6.03
			G-ARSU				
G-ARSW	Piper PA-22-108 Colt	22-8858		23.11.61	A.Barrow	(Bolton)	30. 1.97
G-ARSX	Piper PA-22-160 Tri-Pacer	22-6712	N2907Z	8. 8.61	S.Hutchinson	Rathfriland, Co.Down	19. 5.02
	(Lycoming O-320)		*(Forced landed 5m S Portadown 6.7.0: believed damaged beyond repair)*				
G-ARTH	Piper PA-12 Super Cruiser	12-3278	EI-ADO	22. 9.61	R.I.Souch & B.J.Dunford		
					(Stored 12.01)	Hill Farm, Durley	21. 4.95P
G-ARTJ*	Bensen B.8M Gyrocopter	7		22. 9.61	M A Stewart	(Cupar)	
	(VW 1600) *(Originally regd with c/n 8-104-100)*		*(Cancelled 6.6.75 as WFU) (Stored 6.00: current status unknown)*				
G-ARTL	de Havilland DH.82A Tiger Moth		"T7281"	22. 9.61	F G Clacherty	Great Fryup, Egton, Whitby	25. 5.03
	(P/i is doubtful- if correct th c/n is 83795)				*(As "T7281" in RAF c/s)*		
G-ARTM*	Beagle A.61 Terrier 1	3723	WE536	9.10.61	C.J.Baker	Carr Farm, Newark	13.11.71
		(Crashed Priory Farm, Turvey, Beds 28.5.70: cancelled 12.9.73 as WFU) (On rebuild 4.98)					
G-ARTY*	Cessna 150B	15059482	N7382X	23. 2.62	Not known	Popham	6.10.68
				(Cancelled 4.12.68 as WFU) (Noted 8.96: current status unknown)			
G-ARTZ(2)	McCandless M.4	M4/1		24.10.61	W.R.Partridge *(Noted 10.00)*	St.Merryn	13.10.69P
	(VW 1500) *(Two Gyrocopters may have worn these marks - the prototype M.2 (650cc Triumph) is on display & un-marked at the Ulster Folk & Transport Museum, Belfast)*						
G-ARUG	Auster J/5G Cirrus Autocar	3272		2. 1.62	D.P.H.Hulme	Biggin Hill	18. 4.03
G-ARUI	Beagle A.61 Terrier 1	2529	VF571	9. 3.62	T.W.J.Dann	Southend	28.10.01
G-ARUL	LeVier Cosmic Wind	103	N22C	28.11.61	P.G.Kynsey	Duxford	4. 7.02P
	(Continental O-200-A) *(Rebuilt 1973 as c/n PFA 1511)*				*"Ballerina"*		
	(Contains little of original as fuselage, wings & data plate for original held elsewhere)						
G-ARUO*	Piper PA-24-180 Comanche	24-2427	N7251P	16. 1.62	J.B.W.Dore	(Bruntingthorpe)	22. 8.00
		(Cancelled 18.7.00 by CAA) (Fuselage noted in scrapyard compound outside airfield 11.01)					
G-ARUR*	Piper PA-28-160 Cherokee	28-133		16. 1.62	M.Jarrett	Crowland	12.10.92
		(Damaged in forced landing near Redhill on 14.9.92: cancelled 27.11.92 as destroyed) (Fuselage stored 6.00)					
G-ARUV	Piel CP.301 Emeraude Srs.1	PFA 700		2. 2.62	P.O'Fee	(Chippenham)	22. 4.02P
	(Continental C90)				*"Emma"*		
G-ARUY	Auster J/1N Alpha	3394		2. 2.62	D Burnham	Andrewsfield	7. 7.02
G-ARUZ	Cessna 175C Skylark	17557080	N8380T	23. 2.62	S.R.Page & M.Lowe	Cardiff	25. 3.03

					t/a Cardiff Skylark Group		
G-ARVM(2)*	Vickers VC-10 Srs.1101	815	(G-ARVJ)	16. 1.63	RAF Museum	RAF Cosford	5. 8.80
					(WFU 22.10.79) (British Airways titles)		
G-ARVN(2)*	Servotec Rotorcraft Grasshopper 1	1		16. 2.63	E.D.ap Rees	Weston-super-Mare	18. 5.63
					t/a The Helicopter Museum		
	(Two airframes identified as G-ARVN: the other stored by J.Wilkie at Blackpool) (Cancelled 14.3.77 as WFU)						
G-ARVO	Piper PA-18 Super Cub 95	18-7252	D-ENFI	18. 1.83	Northamptonshire School of Flying Ltd.		
			N3376Z			Sywell	20.11.04T
G-ARVT	Piper PA-28-160 Cherokee	28-379		21. 3.62	Red Rose Aviation Ltd	Liverpool	11. 4.04
G-ARVU	Piper PA-28-160 Cherokee	28-410	PH-ONY	30. 3.62	Barton Mudwing Ltd	Barton	2. 5.04
			G-ARVU				
G-ARVV	Piper PA-28-160 Cherokee	28-451		11. 7.62	G.E.Hopkins	Shobdon	10. 4.04
G-ARVZ	Rollason-Druine D.62B Condor	RAE/606		6.12.61	R.N.Wilkinson	RAF Shawbury	8. 5.02P
G-ARWB	de Havilland DHC.1 Chipmunk 22A		WK611	2. 1.62	P.G.Alston	Thruxton	29. 6.02
		C1/0621			t/a Thruxton Chipmunk Flying Group *(As "WK611")*		
G-ARWH*	Cessna 172C Skyhawk	49166	N1466Y	18. 4.62	Not known		
						Stoneacre Farm, Farthing Corner	28. 4.86
					(Cancelled 29.11.88 as WFU) (Stored for spares 5.99)		
G-ARWO	Cessna 172C Skyhawk	49187	N1487Y	10. 4.62	J.J.Sheeran	(Naas, Co.Kildare)	20. 3.03
G-ARWR	Cessna 172C Skyhawk	49172	N1472Y	13. 4.62	M.McCann	Insch	26. 7.04
					t/a Devanha Flying Group		
G-ARWS	Cessna 175C Skylark	17557102	N8502X	12. 4.62	B.A.I.Torrington	Swansea	28. 8.04
G-ARXB	Beagle A.109 Airedale	B.509	EI-BBK	5. 2.62	M.Isbister	Spanhoe	9. 9.76
	(Originally regd with c/n A.109-2)		G-ARXB/EI-ATE/G-ARXB		*(Stored awaiting rebuild 12.01)*		
G-ARXC*	Beagle A.109 Airedale	B.510	EI-ATD	9. 4.62	C.J.Baker	Carr Farm, Newark	27. 6.76
	(Originally regd with c/n A.109-3)		G-ARXC		*(Cancelled 12.4.89 as WFU) (Fuselage on rebuild 4.98)*		
G-ARXD	Beagle A.109 Airedale	B.511		9. 4.62	D.Howden	Lumphanan	13. 6.86
					(Under restoration 6.00)		
G-ARXG	Piper PA-24-250 Comanche	24-3154	N10F	21. 2.62	R.F.Corstin	Fairoaks	13. 6.02
					t/a Fairoaks Comanche		
G-ARXH	Bell 47G	40	N120B	13. 2.62	A.B.Searle	Cranfield	6. 7.90
			NC120B		*(Noted 7.00)*		
G-ARXN*	Tipsy T.66 Nipper 2	77		3. 7.62	I.Wood & C.E.Pickton	Hucknall	19. 8.80P
	(VW 1800) *(Built Cobelavia)*				*(Cancelled 12.4.89 by CAA) (Stored 5.96)*		
G-ARXP	Phoenix Luton LA-4A Minor			23. 2.62	E.Evans	Benson's Farm, Laindon	17.10.95P
	(Walter Mikron 3)	PAL/1119 & PFA 816			*(Wings stored 8.01: fuselage elsewhere)*		
G-ARXT	SAN Jodel DR.1050 Ambassadeur	355		14. 3.62	M.F.Coy	Wellesbourne Mountford	13.11.04
					t/a CJM Flying Group		
G-ARXU	Auster 6A	2295	VF526	5. 3.62	E.C.Tait & M.Pocock	AAC Netheravon	12. 9.02
					(As "VF526/T" in Army c/s)		
G-ARXW	Morane MS.885 Super Rallye	100		30. 3.62	A.F.Danton & A.Kennedy		
						Dunnamanagh, Londonderry	4. 5.04
G-ARYB*	de Havilland DH.125 Srs.1	25002		1. 3.62	Midland Air Museum	Coventry	22. 1.68
					(Cancelled 4.3.69)		
G-ARYC*	de Havilland DH.125 Srs.1	25003		1. 3.62	De Havilland Heritage Museum		
						London Colney	1. 8.73
					(WFU Hatfield 1.8.73: cancelled 31.3.76 as WFU) (On rebuild 2.00)		
G-ARYD*	Auster AOP.6	-	WJ358	8. 3.62	Museum of Army Flying	AAC Middle Wallop	
					(Conversion abandoned 9.63: cancelled 5.8.87 as WFU) (As "WJ358")		
G-ARYF	Piper PA-23-250 Aztec B	27-2065	N10F	11. 4.62	I.J.T.Branson	Biggin Hill	18. 6.99
G-ARYH	Piper PA-22-160 Tri-Pacer	22-7039	N3102Z	9. 3.62	C.Watt	Crosland Moor	12. 5.02
G-ARYI	Cessna 172C	49260	N1560Y	13. 7.62	Joyce Rhodes	Blackbushe	10. 8.03T
G-ARYK	Cessna 172C	49288	N1588Y	13. 7.62	G.W.Goodban	Lydd	30. 9.03T
G-ARYR	Piper PA-28-160 Cherokee B	28-770		12. 7.62	R.P.Synge & C.S.Wilkinson	Turweston	4. 5.03
					t/a GARYR Flying Group		
G-ARYS	Cessna 172C Skyhawk	49291	N1591Y	13. 7.62	D.J.Squires, C.J & J.Hill	Coventry	31. 8.03
G-ARYV	Piper PA-24-250 Comanche	24-2516	N7337P	17. 4.62	A.G.Wintle & D.C.Hanss	Elstree	10. 6.02
G-ARYZ*	Beagle A.109 Airedale	B.512		9. 4.62	S.Barker t/a Rutland Aviation	Spanhoe	26. 2.01
					(Cancelled 31.10.01 by CAA)		
G-ARZB	Beagle-Wallis WA-116 Srs.1 Agile		XR943	18. 4.62	K.H.Wallis	Reymerston Hall, Norfolk	29. 6.93P
	(McCulloch 4318A)	B.203	G-ARZB		*"Little Nellie" (Noted 8.01)*		
	(Flown with serial XR943 for Service evaluation during 1962 although never cancelled from the UK Register: flown in 1966 for James Bond film "You Only Live Twice")						
G-ARZE*	Cessna 172C	49388	N1688Y	22. 6.62	Black Knight Parachute Centre		
						Bank End Farm, Cockerham	16. 3.77
					(Damaged beyond repair Brawdy 11.9.76 & cancelled) (Training airframe 2.00)		
G-ARZM*	Rollason-Druine D.31 Turbulent			23. 3.62	Not known	Headcorn	
		PFA/581					
					(Damaged Boughton Monchelsea, Kent 23.6.91: cancelled 4.2.99 as PWFU) (Residue stored 10.99)		
G-ARZN	Beechcraft N.35 Bonanza	D-6795	N215DM	23. 5.62	D.W.Mickleburgh	(Oakham)	5. 9.04
G-ARZS	Beagle A.109 Airedale	B.515	EI-BAL	11. 5.62	M.& S.W.Isbister	Spanhoe	23. 5.75
			G-ARZS		*(Stored 4.01)*		
G-ARZW	Phoenix Currie Wot	1 & HAC/5		25. 5.62	B.R.Pearson	Eaglescott	7. 1.89P
	(Walter Mikron 3)				*(Damaged near Headcorn 12.2.88: on rebuild 10.99 as Pfalz D.VII scale rep)*		

G-ASAA – G-ASZZ

G-ASAA Phoenix Luton LA-4A Minor O-H/4 19. 4.62 M.J.Aubrey (Kington, Hereford) 7. 6.01P
(JAP J.99)

G-ASAI Beagle A.109 Airedale B.516 26. 6.62 K.R.Howden (Lumphanan) 20. 5.77S
(On rebuild 6.00)

G-ASAJ Beagle A.61 Terrier 2 B.605 WE569 26. 6.62 R.Skingley Bassingbourn 19. 8.01
(Initially allocated c/n 3732) t/a G-ASAJ Flying Group *(As Auster T.7 "WE569")*
(Op Military Auster Flight)

G-ASAK Beagle A.61 Terrier 2 B.604 WE591 26. 6.62 J.H.Oakins Persan-Beaumont, France 8. 6.02
(As "WE591/Y")

G-ASAL(2) Scottish Aviation Bulldog Srs.120/124 BH120/239 (G-BBHF) G-31-17 5. 9.73 Pioneer Flying Co Ltd Prestwick 7. 6.02P

G-ASAM* Rollason-Druine D.31 Turbulent PFA/595 25. 4.62 Not known Headcorn
(Damaged Coxheath, Kent 23.6.91: cancelled 4.2.99 as PWFU) (Stored 10.99)

G-ASAN* Beagle A.61 Terrier 2 B.608 VX928 26. 6.62 R.J.Bentley Haverfordwest 28. 6.96
(On rebuild 4.97: cancelled 12.9.00 by CAA: current status unknown)

G-ASAT Morane MS.880B Rallye Club 178 21. 6.62 M.Cutovic Croft Farm, Defford 2.11.03

G-ASAU Morane MS.880B Rallye Club 179 21. 6.62 D.M.Dawson Blackpool 10. 9.03

G-ASAX Beagle A.61 Terrier 2 B.609 TW533 12. 6.62 P.G.Morris Cheyene Farm, Stonehaven 1. 9.96
(Converted from Auster 6 c/n 1911) *"The Jacobite Air Force" (Under restoration 6.00)*

G-ASAZ Hiller UH-12E-4 2070 N5372V 18. 6.62 R.C.Hields Sherburn-in-Elmet 18.12.97T
t/a Hields Aviation *(Stored 2.00)*

G-ASBA Phoenix Currie Wot AE.1 & PFA 3005 16. 8.62 C.C.& J.M.Lovell Chilbolton 30. 4.02P
(Continental C90)

G-ASBH Beagle A.109 Airedale B.519 26. 6.62 D.T.Smollett
Bratton Clovelly, Okehampton 19. 2.99

G-ASBU* Beagle A.61 Terrier 2 3733(1) & B.613 WE570 12. 7.62 P G Morris Cheyene Farm, Stonehaven 5. 7.82
(Damaged Netherley 12.8.80: cancelled 16.10.85 as WFU) (Stored for spares 6.00)

G-ASBY Beagle A.109 Airedale B.523 23. 7.62 R.K.Wilson (St Ives, Huntingdon) 22. 3.80
(Stored 3.98)

G-ASCC Beagle E.3 Mk.11 B.701 (G-25-12) XP254 23. 7.62 P.T.Bolton South Lodge Farm, Widmerpool 1. 7.02P
(As "XP254")

G-ASCD* Beagle A.61 Terrier 2 B.615 PH-SFT G-ASCD/VW993 23. 7.62 Yorkshire Air Museum Elvington 26. 9.71
(Cancelled as WFU 5.10.89: under restoration 10.00)

G-ASCJ* Piper PA-24-250 Comanche 24-2368 5N-AEB N7197P 2. 8.62 Not known (Bruntingthorpe)
(DBR landing Bournemouth 10.9.86: cancelled 8.1.87 as WFU) (Fuselage in scrapyard compound outside airfield 11.01)

G-ASCM Isaacs Fury II PFA 2002/1B & 1 1. 8.62 E.C.& P.King Kemble 24.10.02P
(Lycoming O-290) *(As "K2050" in pre-war RAF c/s: new owners 6.01)*
(Built J O Isaacs: PFA c/n = Builder's membership no.?)

G-ASCT* Bensen B.7Mc DC.3 14. 8.62 The Helicopter Museum Weston-super-Mare 11.11.66P
(Built D.Campbell) (McCulloch 4318E) *(WFU & stored dismantled 8.97: current status unknown)*

G-ASCU Piper PA-18A-150 Super Cub 18-6797 VP-JBL 31. 8.62 Farm Aviation Services Ltd
Hinton-in-the-Hedges 13. 9.02

G-ASCZ Menavia Piel CP.301A Emeraude 233 F-BIMG 1.10.62 P.Johnson Goodwood 20.11.02P

G-ASDA* Beechcraft 65-80 Queen Air LD-64 2.10.62 Biggin Hill Airport Fire Service
Biggin Hill 8.11.79
(Cancelled 31.1.89 by CAA) (Front section only) (Current status unknown)

G-ASDB* Rollason-Druine D.31 Turbulent 23. 8.62 C.I.Jefferson Hingham, Norfolk 11. 9.68P
(Ardem 4C02) PFA 1600 *(Crashed Shoreham 11.8.68: components stored 9.97: current status unknown)*

G-ASDF* Edwards Helicopter NAFE.1 17.10.62 J.Parkin RAF Innsworth
(Modified Adams-Wilson Hobbycopter) t/a Computair Consultants
(Orig regd as Edwards Gyrocopter: based upon Bensen B.8M c/n 9 regd as G-ARUN to the same initial owner [N.A.F.Edwards, Gillingham, Kent]: cancelled 3.10.63 as PWFU: on long term rebuild 10.99: current status unknown)

G-ASDK Beagle A.61 Terrier 2 B.702 G-ARLM(2) G-ARLP(1)/VF631 26.10.62 S.C.M.Jackson Shenington 5. 8.99
(Converted from Auster AOP.6 c/n 2573)

G-ASDL Beagle A.61 Terrier 2 B.703 G-ARLN(2) WE558 26.10.62 C.E.Mason Marsh Hill Farm, Aylesbury 30. 5.03
(Also c/ns 3727(1) & B.632(1))

G-ASDO* Beechcraft 95-A55 Baron TC-401 5.11.62 RAF Northolt Fire Service RAF Northolt 16. 4.83
(Cancelled 27.1.89 as WFU) (Current status unknown)

G-ASDY Beagle-Wallis WA-116/F B.205 XR944 (G-ARZC(1)) 9.11.62 K.H.Wallis Reymerston Hall, Norfolk 28.10.97P
(Franklin 2A-120-B) *(Noted 8.01)*
(Regd with c/n B.204 as Beagle-Wallis WA.116 Srs 1 & powered by McCulloch 4318A: fitted with 990cc Hillman Imp engine 1965 (then known as WA.119): re-engined 1971 with 60hp 2-cylinder Franklin 2A-120-A & re-designated)

G-ASEA Phoenix Luton LA-4A Minor PAL/1154 14.11.62 J.Bradstock (Bath) 16. 8.89P
(JAP J.99) *(Stored 10.00)*
(Regd with c/n PFA 1154: c/n also quoted as PFA 1319 which corresponds to EAA Biplane G-AYFY)

G-ASEB Phoenix Luton LA-4A Minor PAL/1149 26.11.62 S.R.P.Harper Walkeridge Farm, Hannington 29.10.82P
(Lycoming O-145) *(Under restoration 10.01)*

G-ASEE* Auster Alpha 3359 I-AGRI 1. 2.63 R.Harper Spanhoe 1. 6.74S
(Damaged RAE Bedford 9.2.74: cancelled by CAA 29.11.89. stored 8.92: fuselage frame to rebuild G-AJDY?)
(Current status unknown)

G-ASEF*	Auster 6A	-	VW985	17.12.62	Not known	Bicester	19.12.66
			(Damaged Bicester 1966: cancelled 13.1.67: stored 11.92) (Current status unknown)				
G-ASEG	Beagle A.61 Terrier 1	2506	VF548	17.12.62	M.J.Kirk	Haverfordwest	16. 7.98
			(Very little remained by 4.01 and may well be absorbed into rebuild of G-ASAN qv)				
G-ASEO	Piper PA-24-250 Comanche	24-3367	(G-ASDX) N10F	23. 1.63	M.Scott t/a Pixies Day Nursery	Southampton	18.10.03
G-ASEP	Piper PA-23-235 Apache	27-541		28. 1.63	Air Warren Ltd	Denham	10. 7.02
G-ASER*	Piper PA-23-250 Aztec B	27-2283	N10F	28. 1.63	Not known	(Smeeth, Kent)	17. 8.74
			(Crashed Nigg Bay, Aberdeen 14.9.72: cancelled 24.11.72 as WFU) (Noted 12.99)				
G-ASEU	Rollason-Druine D.62A Condor	RAE/607		12. 2.63	W.M.Grant	Inverness	4. 5.02P
G-ASFA	Cessna 172D Skyhawk	17250182	N2582U	21. 2.63	D.Halfpenny	Maypole Farm,Chislet	18. 6.04
G-ASFD*	LET L-200A Morava	170808	OK-PHH	26. 2.63	M.Emery *(Stored 7.95: cancelled 12.9.00 by CAA)*	Guildford	12. 7.84T
G-ASFK	Auster J/5G Cirrus Autocar	3276		7. 3.63	T.D.G.Lancaster	Poplar Hall Farm, Elmsett	24. 5.03
G-ASFL	Piper PA-28-180 Cherokee B	28-1170		7. 3.63	J.Simpson & D.Kennedy	Lee-on-Solent	2. 1.04
G-ASFR	Bölkow Bö.208C Junior	522	D-EGMO	12. 3.63	S.T.Dauncey *(Stored 1.02)*	Yearby	29. 3.90P
G-ASFX	Druine D.31 Turbulent (VW 1600)	PFA 513		18. 3.63	E.F.Clapham & W.B.S.Dobie	Oldbury-on-Severn	16. 8.02P
G-ASGC*	Vickers Super VC-10 Srs.1151	853		11. 4.63	Duxford Aviation Society *(WFU 15.4.80) (BOAC-Cunard titles)*	Duxford	20. 4.80
G-ASHD*	Brantly B.2A	314		2. 4.63	The Helicopter Museum	Weston-super-Mare	5. 6.67
			(Crashed off Brightlingsea, Essex 19.2.67: components stored 5.97)				
G-ASHH	Piper PA-23-250 Aztec	27-63	N455SL N4557P	25. 3.63	C.Fordham & L.Barr	Leicester	29. 8.03
G-ASHS	SNCAN Stampe SV-4C (DH Gipsy Major)	265	F-BCFN	23. 4.63	M & B Tools Ltd	Liverpool	6. 2.05T
			(Orig.fuselage for rebuild of G-AWEF 1980: rebuilt 1984 with fuselage of G-AZIR c/n 452 ex F-BCXR)				
G-ASHT	Rollason-Druine D.31 Turbulent (VW 1600)	PFA 1610		23. 4.63	C.W.N.Huke	RAF Shawbury	19.12.02P
G-ASHU	Piper PA-15 Vagabond (Rotax 912UL)	15-46	N4164H NC4164H	1. 5.63	G.J.Romanes & T.J.Ventham *"Calybe"*	Little Bredy	15. 8.02P
G-ASHV*	Piper PA-23-250 Aztec B	27-2347	N10F	1. 5.63	Alderney Airport Fire Service *(Cancelled 20.6.88 as WFU) (On fire dump 12.01)*	Alderney	22. 7.85T
G-ASHX	Piper PA-28-180 Cherokee B	28-1266	N7382W	3. 5.63	Powertheme Ltd	Barton	29. 4.02
G-ASIB	Reims Cessna F172D Skyhawk *(Wichita c/n 17250091)*	F172-0006	F-WLIR	9. 5.63	R.G.Jones & D.A.Smart t/a G-ASIB Flying Group	Hawarden	18. 4.04
G-ASII	Piper PA-28-180 Cherokee B	28-1264		21. 5.63	T.R.Hart & R.W.S.Matthews	Exeter	13. 6.04
G-ASIJ	Piper PA-28-180 Cherokee B	28-1333	N7445W	21. 5.63	G.R.Moore t/a G-ASIJ Group	Andrewsfield	1. 3.04T
G-ASIL	Piper PA-28-180 Cherokee B	28-1350	N7461W	21. 5.63	J.Dickenson & C.D.Powell	Leicester	8.11.04
G-ASIP*	Auster 6A	2549	VF608	22. 5.63	Cotswold Aircraft Restoration Group *(Damaged Nympsfield 7.5.73: stored 8.98)*	(Kemble)	19. 7.73
G-ASIT	Cessna 180	32567	N7670A	24. 5.63	A. & P.A.Wood	Audley End	8.12.00
G-ASIY	Piper PA-25-235 Pawnee	25-2446		30. 5.63	T.Holloway t/a RAFGSA	Bicester	18. 1.05
G-ASJL	Beechcraft H35 Bonanza	D-5132	N5582D	14. 6.63	D.G.Lewendon	Gloucestershire	14. 6.02
G-ASJO	Beechcraft 23 Musketeer	M-518		18. 6.63	K A Boon t/a G-ASJO Syndicate	Bembridge	12. 2.01
G-ASJV	Supermarine 361 Spitfire LF.IXB	CBAF.IX.552	OO-ARA Belgian AF SM-41/Fokker B-13/R Neth H-68/H-105/MH434	3. 7.63	Merlin Aviation Ltd	Duxford	3 5.02P
			(Op The Old Flying Machine Co) (As "MH434/ZD-B" in 316 Sqdn c/s)				
G-ASJY	Gardan GY-80-160 Horizon	13		9. 7.63	P.D.Bradbury & S.M.Derbyshire	Bagby	24. 3.02
G-ASJZ	SAN Jodel D.117A	826	F-BITD	5. 7.63	W.J.Siertsema Church Farm, North Moreton		19. 6.02P
G-ASKC*	de Havilland DH.98 Mosquito TT.35		TA719	8. 7.63	Imperial War Museum - Skyfame Collection *(Crashed on 27.7.64: as "TA719")*	Duxford	18. 1.64S
G-ASKJ*	Beagle A.61 Terrier 1	3730	(EI-AMC) VX926	16. 7.63	C.C.Irvine	Gamlingay	7. 2.85
			(On rebuild 1.96 in T.7 configuration as "VX926" in 664 Sqdn c/s: cancelled 7.8.00 by CAA)				
G-ASKK*	Handley Page HPR.7 Dart Herald 211	161	PP-ASU G-ASKK/PI-C910/CF-MCK	17. 7.63	City of Norwich Aviation Museum *(Cancelled 29.4.85 as WFU)*	Norwich	19. 5.85T
G-ASKL	SAN Jodel 150 Mascaret	27		18. 7.63	J.M.Graty	Nuthampstead	11. 7.02P
G-ASKP	de Havilland DH.82A Tiger Moth	3889	N6588	22. 7.63	The Tiger Club (1990) Ltd	Headcorn	4. 3.03T
G-ASKT	Piper PA-28-180 Cherokee B	28-1410	N7497W	24. 7.63	A.A.Mattacks	Biggin Hill	10. 9.02
G-ASKV	Piper PA-25-235 Pawnee	25-2272	9Q-CHV G-ASKV/ST-ACW/G-ASKV/ST-ACF/G-ASKV/N6700Z	31. 7.63	Southdown Gliding Club Ltd	Parham Park	22. 3.02
G-ASLK	Piper PA-25-235 Pawnee	25-2370	9Q-CFK G-ASLK/ST-ADT/G-ASLK/N6801Z/N10F	20. 8.63	Bristol Gliding Club (Pty) Ltd	Nympsfield	20. 2.03
G-ASLL*	Cessna 336 Skymaster	336-0074	N1774Z	23. 8.63	Not known	Farley Farm, Winchester	6. 1.74
			(Cancelled 6.12.77 as WFU) (Fuselage cabin stored 3.92) (Current status unknown)				
G-ASLP*	Bensen B.7	11		3. 9.63	R Light & T Smith *(Cancelled 4.9.73 as WFU) (Stored 12.00)*	Stockport	
G-ASLV	Piper PA-28-235 Cherokee	28-10048		11. 9.63	I.L.Harding t/a Sackville Flying Group	Sackville Farm, Riseley	10. 2.05
G-ASLX	Menavia Piel CP.301A Emeraude	292	F-BISV	12. 9.63	P White	(Fethard, Co.Tipperary)	16. 1.03P
G-ASMA	Piper PA-30 Twin Comanche *(Modified to PA-39 C/R status)*	30-143	N10F	17. 9.63	A.J.Mew & M.F.Oliver t/a Mike Alpha Group *"Double Trouble"*	White Waltham	5. 1.03

G-ASMC*	Hunting-Percival P.56 Provost T.1	PAC/F/417	XF908	19. 9.63	Not known	Moenchengladbach, Germany	14. 2.72S
					(Stored 5.86: cancelled 22.11.91 by CAA) (Current status unknown)		
G-ASME	Bensen B.8M (Arrow GT500R)	12		24. 9.63	R.M.Harris & R.T.Bennett	(Nottingham)	9. 7.02P
G-ASMF	Beechcraft D95A Travel Air	TD-565		26. 9.63	M.J.A.Hornblower	Southend	3.10.02T
G-ASMJ	Reims Cessna F172E *(Wichita c/n 17250534)*	F172-0029		25.10.63	A.J.G.Crawshaw	Sherburn in Elmet	20. 5.04T
G-ASML	Phoenix Luton LA-4A Minor (VW 1600)	PAL/1148 & PFA 802		28.10.63	B.A.Schussler t/a West Kesteven Flyers *(Stored 11.01)*	(Spalding)	20.12.99P
G-ASMM	Rollason-Druine D.31 Turbulent (Ardem 4C02)	PFA 1611		31.10.63	W.J. Browning *"Mouche Miel"*	Redhill	4.11.02P
G-ASMO*	Piper PA-23-160 Apache G	23-1995	5N-AAU 5N-ADB/N4473P	30.10.63	Not known	Wallington Green	14. 7.99T
	(WFU Bournemouth 2.9.81: cancelled 17.11.82) (Stored behind "Surrey Guns" shop @ junction of A237/A212: noted 3.00)						
G-ASMS	Cessna 150A	15059204	N7104X	18.11.63	P.P.Connor	Barton	8. 2.04
G-ASMT	Fairtravel Linnet 2	004		20.11.63	A.F.Cashin	Maypole Farm, Chislet	25. 9.01P
G-ASMU*	Cessna 150D	15060252	N4252U	26.11.63	Not known	(Moss-Side, Manchester)	3.11.85T
	(Damaged in gales Barton 13.2.89: on rebuild 1991: cancelled 17.12.93 by CAA) (Current status unknown)						
G-ASMV*	Scintex CP.1310-C3 Super Emeraude	919		22.11.63	P.F.D.Waltham *(Stored 10.97: cancelled 8.8.00 by CAA)*	Leicester	7.11.94
G-ASMW	Cessna 150D	15060247	N4247U	26.11.63	Aviation Business Centres Ltd	Humberside	4. 7.04T
G-ASMY*	Piper PA-23-160 Apache H	23-2032	N4309Y	3.12.63	R.D. & E.Forster *(Stored 10.01) (Cancelled 13.12.01 by CAA)*	Beccles	25.11.95T
G-ASMZ	Beagle A.61 Terrier 2 *(Conversion of Auster AOP.10 c/n 2285)*	B.629	G-35-11 VF516	4.12.63	B.Andrews *(As "VF516")*	Trenchard Farm, Eggsford	30. 3.03
G-ASNB	Auster 6A Tugmaster	3725(2)	VX118	6.12.63	C J Harrison *(As "VX118")*	Bidford	14. 1.02T
G-ASNC	Beagle D.5/180 Husky	3678		9.12.63	Peterborough & Spalding Gliding Club Ltd	Crowland	13.11.03
G-ASND	Piper PA-23-250 Aztec	27-134	N4800P	10.12.63	J.R.Grange	Alderney	6. 7.03T
G-ASNG*	de Havilland DH.104 Dove 6	04485	(EI-BJW) G-ASNG/HB-LFF/G-ASNG/HB-LFF/G-ASNG/PH-IOM	16.12.63	Not known *(Cancelled 7.11.80) (On fire dump as "G-ASNG" 8.93)*	Waterford, Co.Waterford	18.11.80P
G-ASNI	Scintex CP.1310-C3 Super Emeraude	925		20.12.63	D.Chapman	(Louth)	22.12.02
G-ASNK	Cessna 205	205-0400	N8400Z	27.12.63	Justgold Ltd *(Op Blackpool Air Centre)*	Blackpool	10. 1.03T
G-ASNN*	Cessna 182F Skylane	18255012	N3612U	27.12.63	Manchester Free-Fall Parachute Club	Tilstock	3. 5.85
	(Damaged near Whitchurch, Shropshire 5.1.85: cancelled 13.6.85 as destroyed) (Used as para-trainer 5.97)						
G-ASNW	Reims Cessna F172E *(Wichita c/n 17250613)*	F172-0031		13. 1.64	B.M.Tremain t/a G-ASNW Group	Draycott Farm, Chiseldon	8. 5.04
G-ASNY*	Campbell-Bensen B.8M (McCulloch 4318A)	RCA/203		15. 1.64	R Light & T.Smith *(Cancelled 17.12.91 as WFU) (On rebuild 2.99)*	Stockport	16. 3.70P
G-ASOC	Auster 6A Tugmaster	2544	VF603	21. 1.64	R.J.McCarthy t/a Auster 6 Group	Haverfordwest	18. 5.02
G-ASOH	Beechcraft 95-B55A Baron	TC-656		31. 1.64	G.S.Goodsir t/a GMD Group	Biggin Hill	14. 6.04
G-ASOI	Beagle A.61 Terrier 2	B.627	G-35-11 WJ404	31. 1.64	N.K. & C.M.Geddes t/a Ranfurly Flying Group	South Barnbeth Farm, Bridge of Weir	19. 6.98
G-ASOK	Reims Cessna F172E	F172-0057		31. 1.64	D.W.Disney	Derby	6. 9.02
G-ASOL*	Bell 47D-1	4	N146B	31. 1.64	The Helicopter Museum *(Cancelled 5.12.83 as WFU) (Stored 8.97)*	Weston-super-Mare	6. 9.71
G-ASOM	Beagle A.61 Terrier 2	B.622	G-JETS G-ASOM/G-35-11/VF505	3. 2.64	D.Humphries	Biggin Hill	15. 3.02
G-ASON*	Piper PA-30-160 Twin Comanche	30-312	(N7273Y)	4. 2.64	Not known *(Cancelled 9.7.92 by CAA) (Stored WFU 1.00)*	Elstree	30.11.91
G-ASOX*	Cessna 205A	205-0556	N4856U	13. 2.64	A.Turnbull *(On rebuild 1.99: cancelled 15.8.00 by CAA)*	Bournemouth	1. 8.92
G-ASPF	Jodel-Wassmer D.120 Paris-Nice	02	F-BFNP	26. 2.64	T.J.Bates	Dairy House Farm, Worleston	19. 6.02P
G-ASPI	Reims Cessna F172E	F172-0050		26. 2.64	J.Henderson	Blackbushe	18. 4.03
G-ASPK	Piper PA-28-140 Cherokee	28-20051		28. 2.64	Westward Airways (Lands End) Ltd	St.Just	30. 3.02T
G-ASPP	Bristol Boxkite rep (Continental O-200-B)	BOX.1 & BM.7279	(BAPC2)	29.10.81	The Shuttleworth Trust *"No.12A" (No external registration) (Noted 5.01)*	Old Warden	2. 5.99P
G-ASPS	Piper J-3C-65 Cub Special *(Frame No.21971)*	22809	N3571N NC3571N	2. 3.64	A.J.Chalkley	Rhoshirwaun, Pwllheli	30. 5.02P
G-ASPU	Druine D.31 Turbulent (VW 1500)	PFA 1623		4. 3.64	M.W.Bodger	Sleap	3. 1.02P
G-ASPV(2)	de Havilland DH.82A Tiger Moth	84167	T7794	5. 3.64	B.S.Charters	Benson's Farm, Laindon	31. 8.97
	(P/I obscure - original G-ASPV sold Norway 7.75 & rebuilt as LN-MAX) (Stored 8.01)						
G-ASRB	Rollason-Druine D.62B Condor	RAE/608		11. 3.64	T.J.McRae & H.C.Palmer	Shoreham	1.11.98
G-ASRC	Rollason-Druine D.62C Condor	RAE/609		11. 3.64	C.R.Isbell	Andrewsfield	7. 5.02P
G-ASRI*	Piper PA-23-250 Aztec B	27-2352	N5287Y	24. 3.64	Witney Technical College	Witney	30. 8.87A
					(Cancelled 19.11.87 as WFU: instructional airframe 1.96)		
G-ASRK	Beagle A.109 Airedale	B.538		26. 3.64	Bio Pathica Ltd.	(London EC4)	2. 6.04

G-ASRO	Piper PA-30 Twin Comanche	30-395	N10F	31. 3.64	D.W.Blake t/a Five Star Flying Group	Gloucestershire	27. 5.02
G-ASRR	Cessna 182G Skylane	18255135	(G-CBIL) EI-ATF/G-ASRR/N3735U	2. 4.64	P.Ragg	(Schwaz, Austria)	5. 7.02
G-ASRT	SAN Jodel 150 Mascaret	45		6. 4.64	P.Turton *(Current status unknown)*	Welshpool	3. 6.94P
G-ASRW	Piper PA-28-180 Cherokee B	28-1606	N11C	21. 4.64	Alliance Aerolink Ltd	Andrewsfield	10. 7.03T
G-ASSB*	Piper PA-30 Twin Comanche	30-432	N10F	22. 4.64	Brooklands Technical College	Weybridge	11. 3.93T
					(Cancelled 25.8.92 as WFU) (Instructional airframe 2.00)		
G-ASSE*	Piper PA-22-108 Colt	22-9832	N5961Z	28. 4.64	A.Ingold t/a G-ASSE Flying Group *(Cancelled 14.8.01 as wfu)*	(Birmingham)	12. 6.00
G-ASSF	Cessna 182G Skylane	18255593	N2493R	5. 5.64	B.W.Wells	Baxterley	5. 3.01
G-ASSM*	Hawker Siddeley HS.125 Srs.1/522	25010	5N-AMK G-ASSM	5. 5.64	The Science Museum (Flight Gallery) *(Cancellation details not known)*	South Kensington, London SW7	
G-ASSP	Piper PA-30 Twin Comanche	30-458	N10F	7. 5.64	P.H.Tavener	Redhill	9. 8.03
G-ASSS	Cessna 172E	17251467	N5567T	7. 5.64	D.H.N.Squires & P.R.March	Filton	27. 5.03
G-ASST	Cessna 150D	15060630	N5930T	7. 5.64	F.R.H.Parker	Pear Tree Farm, Marsh Gibbon, Bicester	1 .8.04
G-ASSV	Kensinger KF (Continental C85)	02	N23S	11. 5.64	C.I.Jefferson *(Crashed Wolverhampton 2.7.69: on rebuild 5.98)*	Deopham Green	30. 7.69P
G-ASSW	Piper PA-28-140 Cherokee	28-20055	N11C	11. 5.64	G S Stone	Biggin Hill	9. 7.04
G-ASSY	Druine D.31 Turbulent (VW 1500)	PFA 586		12. 5.64	D.Silsbury *(Noted 5.93: current status unknown)*	Dunkeswell	20. 4.84P
G-ASTA	Druine D.31 Turbulent (Ardem 4C02)	152	F-PJGH	12. 5.64	P.A.Cooke	RAF Brize Norton	13.11.97P
G-ASTG	Nord 1002 Pingouin II	183	F-BGKI Fr.AF 183	21. 5.64	L.M.Walton *(On rebuild - in primer fuselage & unmarked.10.01)*	Duxford	26.10.73S
G-ASTI	Auster 6A Tugmaster	3745	WJ359	27. 5.64	C.J.Harrison	Oxford	12. 7.03
G-ASTH*	Mooney M.20C	2701	N6906U	22. 5.64	Not known	Sausmarez Park, Guernsey	
					(Crashed Dinard, France 16.11.66 & cancelled: stored 4.90)		
G-ASTL*	Fairey Firefly 1	F.5607	SE-BRD Z2033	1. 6.64	Fleet Air Arm Museum *(WFU 3.2.82: as "Z2033/275/N" in 1771 Sqn RN c/s)*	RNAS Yeovilton	
G-ASTP*	Hiller UH-12C	1045	N9750C	4. 6.64	The Helicopter Museum *(Cancelled 24.1.90 by CAA) (Under restoration 8.98)*	Weston-super-Mare	3. 7.82
G-ASUA*	Nord 1002 Pingouin	248	F-BFDY	23. 6.64	L.M.Walton	Long Sutton, Kings Lynn	28. 7.65
		(Crashed Elstree 30.7.64: in store) (Cancellation details not known) (Current status unknown)					
G-ASUB	Mooney M.20E Super 21	397	N7158U	24. 6.64	S.C.Coulbeck	North Coates	10. 4.04
G-ASUD	Piper PA-28-180 Cherokee B	28-1654	N7673W	29. 6.64	S.J.Rogers & M.N.Petchey	Andrewsfield	28.11.03
G-ASUE	Cessna 150D	15060718	N6018T	30. 6.64	D.Huckle *(Stored 6.94: restored 9.00)*	West Thurrock	1. 8.90
G-ASUG*	Beechcraft E18S-9700	BA-111	N575C N555CB/N24R	3. 7.64	National Museums of Scotland/Museum of Flight *(WFU 12.5.75) (Loganair titles)*	East Fortune	23. 7.75
G-ASUH*	Reims Cessna F172E	F172-0070		6. 7.64	Not known	Clacton	14. 4.78
			(Cancelled 22.3.89 as WFU) (Fuselage in open store 7.95) (Current status unknown)				
G-ASUI	Beagle A.61 Terrier 2 *(Conversion of Auster AOP.10 c/n 2570)*	B.641	VF628	6. 7.64	R.J.Bentley	(Nenagh, Co Tipperary)	19. 1.03
G-ASUP	Reims Cessna F172E	F172-0071		22. 7.64	P.T. & L.E.Trivett t/a G-ASUP Air	Cardiff	14. 6.03
G-ASUR	Dornier Do.28A-1	3051	D-IBOM	28. 7.64	P R Dyson	Thruxton	22. 5.03
G-ASUS	Jurca MJ.2E Tempete (Continental O-200-A)	PFA 2001		28. 7.64	D.G.Jones	Coventry	3. 8.02P
G-ASVG	Rousseau Piel CP.301B Emeraude	109	F-BILV	7. 8.64	K.S.Woodard *"Emma II"*	(Tibenham)	24. 5.02P
G-ASVM	Reims Cessna F172E	F172-0077		11. 8.64	R Seckington	(Fareham)	27. 1.03
G-ASVN	Cessna 206 Super Skywagon	206-0275	N5275U	12. 8.64	D.& L.Johnston	(Kerrville, TX, USA)	21. 2.03
G-ASVO*	Handley Page HPR.7 Dart Herald 214	185	PP-SDG G-ASVO/G-8-3	13. 8.64	Dart Group plc	Shoreham	14. 1.00T
		(WFU after collision Hurn 8.4.97: cancelled 25.9.01 by CAA) (Cockpit @ The Archive Visitor Centre)					
G-ASVP	Piper PA-25-235 Pawnee	25-2978	N10F	17. 8.64	Aquila Gliding Club Ltd	Hinton-in-the-Hedges	13. 4.02
G-ASVZ	Piper PA-28-140 Cherokee	28-20357	N11C	24. 8.64	J.S. Garvey	Tatenhill	19. 7.03
G-ASWB*	Beagle A.109 Airedale	B.543		25. 8.64	A.E.F.Bryant *(Cancelled 10.6.98 by CAA) (Open storage 8.00)*	Antwerp-Deurne	27. 6.97
G-ASWF*	Beagle A.109 Airedale	B.537		26. 8.64	Not known *(Cancelled 3.2.89 by CAA) (Dismantled 4.98)*	Carr Farm, Newark	27. 4.83
G-ASWJ*	Beagle B.206 Srs.1	B.009	8449M G-ASWJ	9. 9.64	Midland Air Museum *(Cancelled 9.9.75 as WFU) (On loan to Brunel Technical College)*	Ashley Down, Bristol	30. 1.75
G-ASWL	Reims Cessna F172F	F172-0087		10. 9.64	J.A.Clegg	Swansea	10. 6.04
G-ASWN	Bensen B.8M	14		15. 9.64	D.R.Shepherd *(Partially built 12.00*	(Prestwick)	
G-ASWP*	Beechcraft A23 Musketeer II	M-587		22. 9.64	J.Holden & G.Benet	(Hastings)	27. 4.95
			(Damaged Sedlescombe 5.3.94: cancelled 17.8.00 by CAA: current status unknown)				

G-ASWW	Piper PA-30 Twin Comanche	30-556	N7531Y	1.10.64	R.Jenkins t/a RJ Motors	Bournemouth	10. 6.03
			N10F				
G-ASWX	Piper PA-28-180 Cherokee C	28-1932	N11C	1.10.64	A.F.Dadds	Biggin Hill	16. 4.03
G-ASXC	SIPA 903	8	F-BEYK	6.10.64	M.K.Dartford & M.Cookson	Andrewsfield	21.11.01P
	(Continental C90)						
G-ASXD	Brantly B.2B	435		7.10.64	Lousada plc		
						Crawley Park, Husborne Crawley, Bedford	28. 9.99
G-ASXF*	Brantly 305	1014		7.10.64	Not known *(Cancelled 24.5.82) (Stored 3.00)*		
						Amen Corner, Binfield, Bracknell	16 .2.79
G-ASXI	Tipsy T.66 Nipper 3	56	VH-CGH	13.10.64	B.Dixon	Bagby	4. 4.02P
	(Built Avions Fairey SA) (Jabiru 2200A)		OO-KOC/(VH-CGC)				
G-ASXJ	Phoenix Luton LA-4A Minor	PFA 801		14.10.64	M.R.Sallows	Damyns Hall, Upminster	28. 4.02P
	(Lycoming O-145)				*"Pride & Joy"*		
G-ASXR	Cessna 210 Centurion	57532	5Y-KPW	16.10.64	A.Schofield	Barton	3. 1.93
			VP-KPW/N6532X		*(Dismantled 5.01)*		
G-ASXS	SAN Jodel DR.1050 Ambassadeur	133	F-BJNG	19.10.64	R.A.Hunter	Finmere	2. 8.03
G-ASXU	Jodel Wassmer D.120A Paris-Nice	196	F-BKAG	19.10.64	M.G.Porter	Croft Farm, Defford	12. 3.02P
					t/a The Jodel Group Defford		
G-ASXX*	Avro 683 Lancaster B.VII	-	(8375M)	22.10.64	F.Panton/Lincolnshire Aviation Heritage Centre		
			WU-15 Fr.Navy/NX611/		*(Cancelled 16.2.79 as WFU)*	East Kirkby	
	("NX611/LE-C"/630 Sqdn c/s "City of Sheffield"/starboard & "NX611/DX-C"/57 Sqdn c/s "Just Jane"/port)						
G-ASXY	SAN Jodel D.117A	914	F-BIVA	27.10.64	P.A., R.A.Davies & D.G.Claxton	Cardiff	8. 1.02P
G-ASXZ	Cessna 182G Skylane	18255738	N3238S	28.10.64	Last Refuge Ltd		
						Trenchard Farm, Eggesford	20. 7.03
G-ASYD*	British Aircraft Corporation One-Eleven 475AM	BAC.053		9.11.64	Brooklands Museum	Brooklands	13. 7.94
	(Originally regd as Srs.400AM: converted to prototype Srs.500 1967: to Srs.475EM 1970) (Cancelled 25.7.94 as WFU)						
G-ASYG	Beagle A.61 Terrier 2	B.637	VX927	3.11.64	G.Rea *(On rebuild 1.95)*	Turweston	19. 2.70T
G-ASYJ	Beechcraft D95A Travel Air	TD-595	N8675Q	6.11.64	Crosby Aviation (Jersey) Ltd	Jersey	31.10.04
G-ASYN*	Beagle A.61 Terrier 2	B.634	VF519	16.11.64	A.A.Marshall	(Derby)	28. 3.76
	(Converted from Auster 6 c/n 2288)				*(Damaged Netherthorpe 2.1.76: stored 2.96)*		
G-ASYP	Cessna 150E	15060794	N6094T	23.11.64	A.C.Melmore	RAF Henlow	10.10.03
					t/a Henlow Flying Group		
G-ASZB	Cessna 150E	15061113	N3013J	16.12.64	R.J.Scott	Blackbushe	19. 4.04
G-ASZD	Bölkow Bö.208A2 Junior	563	D-ENKI	16.12.64	M.J.Ayres	Full Sutton	11.10.01P
G-ASZE	Beagle A.61 Terrier 2	B.636	VF552	17.12.64	P.J.Moore	Lee-on-Solent	9. 8.02
	(Conversion of Auster 6 c/n 2510)						
G-ASZR	Fairtravel Linnet 2	005		5. 1.65	R.Palmer & D.Scott		
						Swanborough Farm, Lewes	9. 8.02P
G-ASZS	Gardan GY-80-160 Horizon	70		6. 1.65	L.R.Burton	Wellesbourne Mountford	25.11.04
					t/a ZS Group		
G-ASZU	Cessna 150E	15061152	N3052J	13. 1.65	T.H.Milburn	Blackbushe	8. 4.02
G-ASZV	Tipsy T.66 Nipper 2	45	5N-ADE	14. 1.65	J.M.Gough	(Sale)	23. 5.90P
	(VW 1835) *(Built Avions Fairey SA)*		5N-ADY/VR-NDD		*(Stored 9.97: new owner 5.01)*		
G-ASZX	Beagle A.61 Terrier 1	3742	(SE-ELO)	18. 1.65	R.B.Webber	Exeter	11. 9.03
			WJ368				

G-ATAA – G-ATZZ

G-ATAA*	Piper PA-28-180 Cherokee C	28-2055	(OO-...)	20. 1.65	Not known	Southend	16. 5.87
			G-ATAA/(CN-...)/G-ATAA/N11C				
	(Damaged near Melan, France: 12.9.86: cancelled 24.11.86 by CAA) (Wreck stored dismantled 1.02)						
G-ATAF	Reims Cessna F172F	F172-0135		25. 1.65	P.J.Thirtle	Humberside	23. 5.04T
G-ATAG	CEA Jodel DR.1050 Ambassadeur	226	F-BKGG	25. 1.65	T.M.Dawes-Gamble	Oxford	4.10.02
G-ATAH*	Cessna 336 Skymaster	336-0007	N1707Z	26. 1.65	Not known	Farley Farm, Winchester	5.12.76
	(Cancelled 25.7.96 by CAA) (Open storage 3.92: current status unknown)						
G-ATAS	Piper PA-28-180 Cherokee C	28-2137	N11C	4. 2.65	R Osborn t/a Atlas Group	Andrewsfield	17. 8.03
G-ATAU	Rollason-Druine D.62B Condor	RAE/610		10. 2.65	M.A.Peare	Siege Cross Farm, Thatcham	16.11.02
					t/a Golf Alpha Uniform Group		
G-ATAT*	Cessna 150E	15061141	N3041J	9. 2.65	Not Known	Shobdon	29. 7.85
					(Cancelled 15.8.85 by CAA) (Stored for rebuild 5.98)		
G-ATAU	Rollason-Druine D.62B Condor	RAE/610		10. 2.65	M.A.Peare	White Waltham	16.11.02
					t/a Golf Alpha Uniform Group		
G-ATAV	Rollason-Druine D.62C Condor	RAE/611		10. 2.65	R.W.H.Watson *(Stored 6.00)*	Kilkerran	6. 8.94
G-ATBG	Nord 1002 Pingouin II	121	F-BGVX	24. 2.65	T.W.Harris	Booker	3.10.01P
			F-OTAN-5/Fr.Mil		*(As "NJ+C11" in Luftwaffe c/s)*		
G-ATBH	CZL Aero 145	172015		24. 2.65	P.D.Aviram	Kingston-upon-Thames	26.10.81
					(On rebuild 1997: current status unknown)		
G-ATBI	Beechcraft A23 Musketeer II	M-696		26. 2.65	A.C.Dent	Enstone	2. 6.03
					t/a Three Musketeers Flying Group		
G-ATBJ	Sikorsky S-61N	61-269	N10043	12. 3.65	CHC Scotia Ltd	Aberdeen	2. 6.03T
	(P/I not confirmed)						

G-ATBL	de Havilland DH.60G Moth	1917	HB-OBA	2. 3.65	J.M.Greenland		
	(DH Gipsy I)		CH-353			Blackacre Farm, Holt, Wilts	23. 7.02P
G-ATBP	Alpavia Fournier RF3	59		11. 3.65	D.McNicholl	Inverness	19.10.02
G-ATBS	Druine D.31 Turbulent	PFA 1620		16. 3.65	D.R.Keene & J.A.Lear	Wigtown	3. 1.01P
	(VW 1500)				*"Fly Baby Fly"*		
G-ATBU	Beagle A.61 Terrier 2	B.635	VF611	17. 3.65	D.M.Snape	Hucknall	2. 6.02
	(Conversion of Auster 6 c/n 2552)				t/a K9 Flying Group		
G-ATBW	Tipsy T.66 Nipper 2	52	OO-MAG	19. 3.65	S.Bloomfield & C.Firth	Stapleford	24. 9.01P
	(VW 1834 Acro) *(Built Cobelavia)*				t/a Stapleford Nipper Group		
G-ATBX	Piper PA-20-135 Pacer	20-904	VP-KRX	19. 3.65	G.D. & P.M.Thomson		
			VR-TCH/VP-KKE			Standalone Farm, Meppershall	11 .5.02
G-ATBZ*	Westland Wessex 60 Srs.1	WA/461	G-17-4	22. 3.65	The Helicopter Museum	Weston-super-Mare	5.12.81
			G-ATBZ		*(Cancelled 23.11.82 as TWFU)*		
G-ATCC	Beagle A.109 Airedale	B.542		25. 3.65	J.R.Bowden	Headcorn	13.10.01
G-ATCD	Beagle D.5/180 Husky	3683		25. 3.65	D.J.O'Gorman	Enstone	12. 3.03
G-ATCE	Cessna U206 Super Skywagon	U206-0380	N2180F	25. 3.65	Pathcircle Ltd	Langar	25. 5.02
					t/a British Parachute Schools		
G-ATCJ	Phoenix Luton LA-4A Minor			5. 4.65	P.R.Diffey	Top Farm, Royston	8. 6.01P
	(VW 1600)	PAL/1163 & PFA 812					
					(Force landed Moggerhanger, Beds 10.11.01: damage to wing, propeller, cowling and undercarriage)		
G-ATCL	Victa Airtourer 100	93		5. 4.65	A.D.Goodall	Cardiff	13. 6.02
G-ATCN*	Phoenix Luton LA-4A Minor	PAL/1118		7. 4.65	J.C.Gates & C.Neilson *(Cancelled 6.6.01 by CAA)*		
	(Lycoming O-145)					Comarques Farm, Thorpe-Le-Soken	26. 6.98P
G-ATCU	Cessna 337 Super Skymaster	3370133	N2233X	22. 4.65	The Committee for Aerial Photography,		
					University of Cambridge	Cambridge	25. 4.02A
G-ATCX	Cessna 182H Skylane	18255848	N3448S	26. 4.65	K.J.Fisher	St.Merryn	23. 8.03
					(Note: fuselage of cancelled G-OLSC is also marked as "G-ATCX")		
G-ATDA	Piper PA-28-160 Cherokee	28-206	EI-AME	27. 4.65	J.Gosling	Shobdon	27. 9.02
			(G-ARUV)		t/a Portway Aviation		
G-ATDB	SNCAN 1101 Noralpha	186	F-OTAN-6	27. 4.65	J.W.Hardie	(Skelmorlie, Largs)	22.11.78S
			Fr.Mil		*(On rebuild 6.00)*		
					(A Nord 1101 was reported Barton @ 8.96 as "F-OTAN-6" but believed to be G-BAYV)		
G-ATDD*	Beagle B.206 Srs.1	B.013	(VH-...)	27. 4.65	Bristol Aero Collection	Kemble	
	(Orig regd @ B.206R - to Srs.1 1966)		G-ATDD		*(U/c collapsed Sherburn 6.73: cancelled 9.4.74 as PWFU) (Nose only)*		
G-ATDN	Beagle A.61 Terrier 2	B.638	TW641	7. 5.65	Susan J.Saggers	Biggin Hill	8. 7.04T
	(Conversion of Auster 6 c/n 2499)				*(As "TW641")*		
G-ATDO	Bölkow Bö.208C Junior	576	D-EGZU	10. 5.65	P.Thompson	(Huddersfield)	29. 3.02P
G-ATEF	Cessna 150E	15061378	N3978U	25. 5.65	A.J.White & B.M.Scott	Blackbushe	8.11.02
					t/a Swans Aviation		
G-ATEM	Piper PA-28-180 Cherokee C	28-2329	N11C	26. 5.65	Chiltern Valley Aviation Ltd	Bovingdon	11. 4.04
G-ATEP*	EAA Biplane	PFA 1301		28. 5.65	E.L.Martin,	Sausmarez Park, Guernsey	18. 6.73
	(Continental C75)				*(Cancelled 14.7.86 by CAA) (Frame stored 12.01)*		
G-ATES*	Piper PA-32-260 Cherokee Six	32-20		31. 5.65	Stirling Parachute Centre *(Ceased operations 2000)*		
						(Easter Poldar Farm, Thornhill)	11. 6.83
	(Crashed near Kinglassie 8.2.81: cancelled 22.10.84 as WFU)				*(Used as para-trainer 6.00: current status unknown)*		
G-ATEV	CEA Jodel DR.1050 Ambassadeur	18	F-BJHL	31. 5.65	J.C.Carter & J.L.Altrip	(Cambridge)	13. 8.71
					(On rebuild 9.00)		
G-ATEW	Piper PA-30 Twin Comanche	30-719	N7640Y	3. 6.65	Air Northumbria (Woolsington) Ltd		
						Newcastle	26. 7.04
G-ATEX	Victa Airtourer 100	110	(VH-MTU)	3. 6.65	A K Smart	(Sunbury-on-Thames)	12.10.02
					t/a Halton Victa Group		
G-ATEZ	Piper PA-28-140 Cherokee	28-21044	N11C	8. 6.65	EFI Aviation Ltd	Norwich	18. 5.03T
G-ATFD	CEA Jodel DR.1050 Ambassadeur	311	F-BKIM	14. 6.65	V.Usher	Wickenby	21. 2.04
G-ATFF	Piper PA-23-250 Aztec C	27-2898	N5769Y	16. 6.65	Neatspin Ltd	Tatenhill	13. 8.01
G-ATFG*	Brantly B.2B	448		16. 6.65	Aircraft Preservation Society of Scotland		
	(Composite with parts from G-ASLO/G-AXSR)					East Fortune	25. 3.85
					(Cancelled 25.9.87 as WFU) (On loan to Museum of Flight)		
G-ATFM	Sikorsky S-61N Mk.II	61-270	CF-OKY	21. 6.65	Veritair Ltd		
	(USA P/I not confirmed)		N10052			Mount Pleasant, Falkland Islands	1.10.03T
G-ATFR	Piper PA-25 Pawnee	25-135	OY-ADJ	28. 6.65	Borders (Milfield) Gliding Club Ltd		
			N10F			Milfield	29. 5.03
G-ATFV*	Agusta-Bell 47J-2A Ranger	2093	9J-ACX	1. 7.65	Not known	Ley Farm, Chirk	8. 8.92T
			G-ATFV/MM80417		*(Cancelled 22.12.92 by CAA) (Stored 9.00)*		
G-ATFW	Phoenix Luton LA-4A Minor	PFA 811		2. 7.65	P.A.Rose	(Walney)	2.12.97P
	(Lycoming O-145)						
G-ATFX*	Reims Cessna F172G	F172-0196		8. 7.65	Not known	Croydon Whitgift Centre	12. 2.92
					(Damaged Booker 25.1.90: cancelled 22.3.91 by CAA) (Displayed 3.00)		
G-ATFY	Reims Cessna F172G	F172-0199		8. 7.65	H.Cowan	Abbeyshrule, Co.Longford	25. 5.01
G-ATGE	SAN Jodel DR.1050 Ambassadeur	114	F-BJJF	9. 7.65	L.S.& K.L.Johnson	Lodge Farm, Clacton	14. 2.04
G-ATGN*	Thorn K-800 Coal Gas Balloon	2		12. 7.65	British Balloon Museum & Library	Newbury	
					"Eccles" (Cancelled 23.6.81 as WFU)		
G-ATGO	Reims Cessna F172G	F172-0181		12. 7.65	JP Aviation Ltd	Stapleford	19. 7.04
G-ATGY	Gardan GY-80-160 Horizon	121		20. 7.65	P.W.Gibberson	Wellesbourne Mountford	1. 3.03

G-ATGZ Griffiths GH-4 Gyroplane G.1 20. 7.65 R.W.J.Cripps (Shardlow, Derby)
(Stored 7.91: current status unknown)
G-ATHA* Piper PA-23-235 Apache 27-610 N4326Y 21. 7.65 Brunel Technical College
Ashley Down, Bristol 7. 6.86
(Cancelled 7.6.86 as WFU) (Instructional airframe 6.91) (Current status unknown)
G-ATHD de Havilland DHC.1 Chipmunk 22 WP971 26. 7.65 O.L.Cubitt & K.P.A.Lewis Denham 30. 6.03
C1/0837 G-ATHD/WP971 t/a Spartan Flying Group *(As "WP971")*
G-ATHI* Piper PA-28-180 Cherokee C 28-2545 N11C 2. 8.65 Dublin Institute of Technology
Bolton St, Dublin 26.10.74
(Crashed Castlebar, Co.Mayo 9.5.74: cancelled 8.7.74: instructional airframe 5.92) (Current status unknown)
G-ATHK Aeronca 7AC Champion 7AC-971 N82339 2. 8.65 T.P.McDonald, T.Crawley & E.Walker
(Continental A75) NC82339 Crosland Moor 10. 5.02P
G-ATHM Wallis WA-116/F 402 & 211 4R-ACK 3. 8.65 Wallis Autogyros Ltd
G-ATHM *(Noted 8.01)* Reymerston Hall, Norfolk 23. 5.93P
(Originally McCulloch engine but fitted with 60hp Franklin in 1974)
G-ATHN* SNCAN 1101 Noralpha 84 F-BFUZ 5. 8.65 E.L.Martin St.Peter Port, Guernsey 27. 6.75S
Fr.Mil *(Cancelled 16.12.91 by CAA) (Stored 12.01 in container)*
G-ATHR Piper PA-28-180 Cherokee C 28-2343 EI-AOT 11. 8.65 Britannia Airways Ltd Luton 10. 8.04T
N11C
G-ATHT Victa Airtourer 115 120 16. 8.65 D.A.Beese Gloucestershire 23.12.02
G-ATHU Beagle A.61 Terrier 1 AUS/127/FM 7435M 16. 8.65 J.A.L.Irwin Park Farm, Eaton Bray 24. 9.04
WE539
G-ATHV Cessna 150F 15062019 N8719S 16. 8.65 S.Greenwood Sherburn in Elmet 2. 2.03
t/a Cessna Hotel Victor Group
G-ATHX* SAN Jodel DR.100A Ambassadeur 74 F-OBMM 17. 8.65 W.R.Prescott Kilkeel, Co.Down 2. 6.99
t/a Mourne Flying Club *(Cancelled 14.8.01 by CAA)*
G-ATHZ* Cessna 150F 15061586 (EI-AOP) 20. 8.65 E. & R.D.Forster Beccles 27.3.98T
N6286R *(Noted 10.01) (Cancelled 13.12.01 by CAA)*
G-ATIA Piper PA-24-260 Comanche 24-4049 N8650P 20. 8.65 L.A.Brown Leicester 22.10.04
N10F t/a The India Alpha Partnership
G-ATIC CEA Jodel DR.1050 Ambassadeur 6 F-BJCJ 23. 8.65 R.E.Major (St.Agnes, Cornwall) 1. 6.81
(On overhaul 1993: current status unknown)
G-ATID* Cessna 337 Super Skymaster 3370239 N6239F 24. 8.65 Not known Stapleford 6. 1.97
(Temp unregd 7.7.97: stored 5.98: current status unknown)
G-ATIE* Cessna 150F 15061591 N6291R 24. 8.65 Staffordshire Sports Skydiving Club
(Crashed near Shobdon 28.7.79: fuselage as para-trainer 4.97) Chetwynd, Shropshire 7 .9.81
G-ATIG* Handley Page HPR.7 Dart Herald 214 PP-SDI 25. 8.65 Nordic Oil Services Ltd Norwich 14.10.97T
177 G-ATIG *(Cancelled 29.10.96 as WFU: stored 5.00: current status unknown)*
G-ATIN SAN Jodel D.117 437 F-BHNV 8. 9.65 G.G.Simpson Muirhouses Farm, Errol 18. 4.96P
(On rebuild 6.00)
G-ATIR AIA Stampe SV-4C 1047 F-BNMC 9. 9.65 Austin Trueman Ltd (St Albans) 29. 6.03
G-ATIR/F-BMKQ/Aeronavale/F-BCDM/Aeronavale
G-ATIS Piper PA-28-160 Cherokee C 28-2713 N11C 9. 9.65 R.M.Jenner & J.H.Peploe
Lower Upham Farm, Chiseldon 10. 2.03
G-ATIZ SAN Jodel D.117 636 F-BIBR 15. 9.65 D.K.Shipton Deenethorpe 17. 6.02P
G-ATJA SAN Jodel DR.1050 Ambassadeur 378 F-BKHL 15. 9.65 D.A.Head & G.W.Cunningham RAF Bicester 13. 1.03
t/a Bicester Flying Group
G-ATJC Victa Airtourer 100 125 16. 9.65 Aviation West Ltd Cumbernauld 14.12.03T
G-ATJF* Piper PA-28-140 Cherokee 28-21283 20. 9.65 Not known Sabadell, Spain 16. 6.82
(Crashed Corcubion, Spain 29.8.79: fuselage stored 3.89) (Current status unknown)
G-ATJG Piper PA-28-140 Cherokee 28-21299 20. 9.65 C.A.McGee North Weald 21.10.02T
G-ATJL Piper PA-24-260 Comanche 24-4203 N8752P 23. 9.65 M.J.Berry & T.R.Quinn Blackbushe 20. 5.03
N10F
G-ATJM Fokker DR.1 Triplane rep 002 N78001 23. 9.65 R.J.Lamplough North Weald 10. 9.93P
(Siemens SH-14A-165) EI-APY/G-ATJM *(As "152/17": noted 12.00)*
G-ATJN Dormois Jodel D.119 863 F-PINZ 23. 9.65 Advanced Power Systems Ltd Crosland Moor 27. 5.02P
G-ATJR* Piper PA-E23-250 Aztec C 27-3033 N5881Y 30. 9.65 Not known Manchester 23. 7.95
(Cancelled 21.3.96 as WFU) (Stored 11.98)
G-ATJT Gardan GY-80-160 Horizon 108 4.10.65 N.Huxtable Cheddington 23. 5.02
G-ATJV Piper PA-32-260 Cherokee Six 32-103 TF-GOS 7.10.65 Wingglider Ltd Hibaldstow 15. 2.04A
G-ATJV/N11C
G-ATKF Cessna 150F 15062386 N3586L 20.10.65 J P A Freeman Headcorn 4. 9.03T
G-ATKG* Hiller UH-12B 496 103 Thai AF 21.10.65 Not known Eshott 28.11.69
(Cancelled 21.1.80) (Noted dumped 11.01)
G-ATKH Phoenix Luton LA-4A Minor PFA 809 25.10.65 H.E.Jenner Brenchley, Kent 24. 6.92P
(Lycoming O-145) *(Stored 1.96)*
G-ATKI Piper J-3C-65 Cub 17545 N70536 25.10.65 J.P.Conlan (Macroom, Co.Cork) 18. 3.02P
(Continental A75) NC70536
G-ATKT Reims Cessna F172G F172-0206 9.11.65 P.J.Megson Goodwood 13. 2.02
G-ATKU* Reims Cessna F172G F172-0232 9.11.65 Holdcroft Aviation Services Ltd Popham 31. 1.95T
(On rebuild 1.97: cancelled 1.9.00 as wfu)
G-ATKX SAN Jodel D.140C Mousquetaire III 19.11.65 A.J.White & G.A.Piper Redhill 23. 5.04T
163 *(Op Acebell Aviation)*

G-ATKZ	Tipsy T.66 Nipper 2 (VW 1834) *(Built Cobelavia)*	72		24.11.65	J.W.Macleod	Felthorpe	29. 4.02P
G-ATLA	Cessna 182J Skylane	18256923	N2823F	24.11.65	J W & J T Whicher	(York)	26.10 02
G-ATLB	SAN Jodel DR.1050M Excellence	78	F-BIVG	29.11.65	B.Lumb t/a La Petit Oiseau Syndicate	Breighton	24. 8.02
G-ATLH*	Fewsdale Tigercraft Gyroplane	F.T5		6.12.65	Not known *(Cancelled 10.2.82 as WFU: stored 12.00)*	(Stockport)	
G-ATLM	Reims Cessna F172G	F172-0252		6.12.65	Airfotos Ltd	Newcastle	3. 3.03T
G-ATLP	Bensen B.8M (McCulloch 4318F)	17		9.12.65	R.F.G.Moyle	(Penryn)	19. 5.97P
G-ATLT	Cessna U206A Super Skywagon	U206-0523	N4823F	13.12.65	A.I.M & A.J. Guest	Dunkeswell	6. 6.02T
G-ATLV	Jodel Wassmer D.120 Paris-Nice	224	F-BKNQ	15.12.65	L.S.Thorne	Shenstone Hall Farm, Shenstone	8. 7.02P
G-ATMC	Reims Cessna F150F *(Wichita c/n 15062849)*	F150-0020		28.12.65	G.H. Farrah & D.Cunnane	Abbeyshrule, Co Longford	1. 7.04
G-ATMH	Beagle D.5/180 Husky	3684		3. 1.66	Dorset Gliding Club Ltd	Gallows Hill, Bovington	18. 7.03
G-ATMI*	Hawker Siddeley HS.748 Srs.2A/225	1592	VP-LIU G-ATMI/VP-LIU/G-ATMI/VP-LIU/G-ATMI/VP-LIU/G-ATMI	4. 1.66	Emerald Airways Ltd *(Cancelled 30.7.01 as wfu) (Fuselage on fire dump 12.01)*	Blackpool	18. 5.00T
G-ATMJ	Hawker Siddeley HS.748 Srs.2A/225	1593	VP-LAJ G-ATMJ/6Y-JFJ/G-ATMJ	4. 1.66	Emerald Airways Ltd	Liverpool	7. 9.03T
G-ATML	Reims Cessna F150F *(Wichita c/n 15062722)*	F150-0014		6. 1.66	G.I.Smith	Eddsfield	4.10.04
G-ATMM	Reims Cessna F150F *(Wichita c/n 15062775)*	F150-0016		6. 1.66	Skytrax Aviation Ltd	(Atherstone)	18. 4.04T
G-ATMN(2)*	Reims Cessna F150F *(Wichita c/n 15063526)*	F150-0060	(G-ATNE)	6. 1.66	Not known *(Ditched off Isle of Grain 11.5.84: salvaged & cancelled 22.8.85 as destroyed) (Stored 5.98)*	Shobdon	
G-ATMT	Piper PA-30 Twin Comanche	30-439	XW938 G-ATMT/N7385Y	10. 1.66	Montagu-Smith & Co Ltd	Hinton-in-the Hedges	11. 7.02
G-ATMU	Piper PA-23-160 Apache G	23-2000	N4478P	11. 1.66	P.K.Martin & R.W.Harris *(Stored dismantled 10.01)*	Sibson	14. 4.90T
G-ATMW	Piper PA-28-140 Cherokee	28-21486		11. 1.66	Bencray Ltd *(Op Blackpool & Fylde Aero Club)*	Blackpool	15. 3.04T
G-ATMY	Cessna 150F	15062642	SE-ETD N8542G	13. 1.66	A.Dobson	(Newark)	15. 9.03
G-ATNB	Piper PA-28-180 Cherokee C	28-3057	N11C	20. 1.66	M A Tidmarsh t/r Bravo-180 Group	(Burton-on-Trent)	31. 3.03
G-ATNE	Reims Cessna F150F *(Wichita c/n 15063252)*	F150-0042		20. 1.66	A.D.Revill	Leicester	14.12.03
G-ATNL	Reims Cessna F150F *(Wichita c/n 15063652)*	F150-0066		25. 1.66	G.A.Lauf t/a G-ATNL Flying Group	Lower Upham Farm, Chiseldon	4. 7.02
G-ATNV	Piper PA-24-260 Comanche	24-4350	N8896P	28. 1.66	B.S.Reynolds	Bourne	14.11.04
G-ATOA	Piper PA-23-160 Apache G	23-1954	N4437P	31. 1.66	Oscar Alpha Ltd	Stapleford	13. 6.03
G-ATOD	Reims Cessna F150F *(Wichita c/n 15062342)*	F150-0003		1. 2.66	J.H.A.Boyns, E.Watson & G.Bold	St.Just	6. 9.02
G-ATOE	Reims Cessna F150F *(Wichita c/n 15063096)*	F150-0031		1. 2.66	J.A.Richardson	Enniskillen, Co.Fermanagh/Popham	25. 8.04
G-ATOH	Rollason-Druine D.62B Condor	RAE/612		3. 2.66	J Cooke t/a Three Spires Flying Group	(Lichfield)	14. 6.02P
G-ATOI	Piper PA-28-140 Cherokee	28-21556	N11C	3. 2.66	R.W.Nash	RAF Brize Norton	27. 5.02
G-ATOJ	Piper PA-28-140 Cherokee	28-21584	N11C	3. 2.66	A Flight Aviation Ltd *(Op Prestwick Flying Club)*	Prestwick	29. 8.03T
G-ATOK	Piper PA-28-140 Cherokee	28-21612	N11C	3. 2.66	G.T.S.Done & P.R.Harrison t/a ILC Flying Group	White Waltham	8. 3.04
G-ATOL	Piper PA-28-140 Cherokee	28-21626	N11C	3. 2.66	L.J.Nation & G.Alford t/a G-ATOL Flying Group	Cardiff	23. 1.98
G-ATOM	Piper PA-28-140 Cherokee	28-21640	N11C	3. 2.66	A Flight Aviation Ltd *(Op Prestwick Flying Club)*	Prestwick	27. 8.04T
G-ATON	Piper PA-28-140 Cherokee	28-21654	N11C	3. 2.66	R.G.Walters	Shobdon	18. 9.04
G-ATOO	Piper PA-28-140 Cherokee	28-21668	N11C	3. 2.66	Wayauto Ltd *(Wrecked fuselage noted 12.01)*	Blackpool	24. 9.84
G-ATOP	Piper PA-28-140 Cherokee	28-21682	N11C	3. 2.66	P.R.Coombs t/a The Aero 80 Flying Group	Compton Abbas	16. 5.02
G-ATOR	Piper PA-28-140 Cherokee	28-21696	N11C	3. 2.66	D.Palmer t/a Aligator Group	Shobdon	22. 6.03
G-ATOT	Piper PA-28-180 Cherokee C	28-3061	N11C	3. 2.66	Totair Ltd *"Totty"*	Shipdham	22. 6.03T
G-ATOU	Mooney M.20E Super 21	961	N5946Q	3. 2.66	A.C.Mate t/a M20 Flying Group	Sherburn in Elmet	28. 5.03
G-ATOY*	Piper PA-24-260 Comanche B *(Crashed near Elstree 6.3.79: fuselage only)*	24-4346	N8893P	7. 2.66	National Museums of Scotland/Museum of Flight *"Myth Too"*	East Fortune	
G-ATOZ	Bensen B.8M (Rotax 503)	18		7. 2.66	N.C.White & W.Stark *(Substantially rebuilt in 1986, original airframe now stored Wimborne)*	Sorbie Farm, Kingsmuir	18. 7.00P

G-ATPD	Hawker Siddeley HS.125 Srs.1B/522		5N-AGU	11. 2.66	Wessex Air (Holdings) Ltd	Bournemouth	14.10.98T
		25085	G-ATPD		*(WFU 1997 - for spares 7.01: valid CofR 3.01)*		
G-ATPN	Piper PA-28-140 Cherokee	28-21899	N11C	18. 2.66	R.W.Harris, M.F.Hatt, P.E.Preston & A.Jahanfar		
					(Op Southend Flying Club)	Southend	24. 3.02T
G-ATPT	Cessna 182J Skylane	18257056	N2956F	22. 2.66	G.B.Scholes t/a Papa Tango Group	Elstree	11. 8.04
G-ATPV	Barritault JB.01 Minicab	01	F-PJKA	22. 2.66	C.F.O'Niell	Newtownards, Co.of Down	28. 4.99P
	(Continental C90) *(Rebuild of GY-20 F-PHUC c/n A.155)*						
G-ATRG	Piper PA-18-150 Super Cub	18-7764	5B-CAB	1. 3.66	Lasham Gliding Society Ltd	Lasham	31. 5.04
	(Lycoming O-360-A4)		N4985Z				
G-ATRI	Bölkow Bö.208C Junior	602	D-ECGY	3. 3.66	S.Alexander	Bidford	22. 4.01
					t/a Interesting Aircraft Co		
G-ATRK	Reims Cessna F150F	F150-0049	(G-ATNC)	4. 3.66	G.G. & J.G.Armstrong	Wigtown	19. 8.02
	(Wichita c/n 15063381)				t/a Armstrong Aviation		
G-ATRM	Reims Cessna F150F	F150-0053	(G-ATNJ)	4. 3.66	J.Redfearn	Morgansfield, Fishburn	29.11.00T
	(Wichita c/n 15063454)						
G-ATRO	Piper PA-28-140 Cherokee	28-21871	N11C	4. 3.66	J.S.Jewell & H.A.Aldous	Ludham	20. 7.03
G-ATRP*	Piper PA-28-140 Cherokee	28-21885	N11C	4. 3.66	JRB Aviation Ltd	Southend	20. 9.84
					(Damaged Boughton Monchelsea 16.10.81: cancelled 10.11.86 as WFU) (Wreck stored 1.02)		
G-ATRR	Piper PA-28-140 Cherokee	28-21892	N11C	4. 3.66	Marham Investments Ltd	Ronaldsway	1.11.03T
					(Op Manx Flyers Aero Club)		
G-ATRW	Piper PA-32-260 Cherokee Six	32-360	N11C	8. 3.66	Moxley & Frankl Ltd & J.Pringle	Seething	31. 7.04
G-ATRX	Piper PA-32-260 Cherokee Six	32-390	N11C	8. 3.66	Central Aviation Ltd	Nottingham	4.10.04T
G-ATSI	Bölkow Bö.208C Junior	605	D-EFNU	14. 3.66	M.R.Reynolds & R.S.Jordan	Shipdham	15. 2.03
					t/a G-ATSI Group		
G-ATSL	Reims Cessna F172G	F172-0260		16. 3.66	L.McMullin	Belfast	28. 8.04
G-ATSM	Cessna 337A Super Skymaster	337-0434	N5334S	23. 3.66	I.J. & H.R.Jones	Thruxton	10. 7.97T
					t/a Landscape & Ground Maintenance		
G-ATSR	Beechcraft M35 Bonanza	D-6236	EI-ALL	29. 3.66	D.G.Lewendon	Gloucestershire	28. 9.01
G-ATSX	Bölkow Bö.208C Junior	608	D-EJUC	7. 4.66	R.J.Campbell & M.H.Goley		
						Westbury-sub-Mendip	1. 7.02
G-ATSY	Wassmer WA.41 Super Baladou IV	117		12. 4.66	R.L.& K.P.McLean	Rufforth	23.11.91
					t/a McLean Aviation *(Spares use for G-ATZS 5.01)*		
G-ATSZ	Piper PA-30 Twin Comanche B	30-1002	EI-BPS	13. 4.66	Sierra Zulu Aviation Ltd	Cambridge	6. 6.02
			G-ATSZ/(AN-...)/G-ATSZ/(EI-BBS)/G-ATSZ/N7912Y				
G-ATTB	Wallis WA-116/F	214		19. 4.66	D.A.Wallis	Reymerston Hall, Norfolk	18. 5.98P
	(Franklin 2A) *(Rebuild of WA-116 G-ARZC(2)/XR944 c/n 205)*				*(As "XR944") (Noted 8.01)*		
	(Orig regd as Wallis WA.116 Srs 1 with McCulloch engine: fitted with Franklin 2A 1981 and renamed WA-116/F: reverted to serial XR944 for Service participation)						
G-ATTD	Cessna 182J Skylane	18257229	N3129F	19. 4.66	M.Brennan, M.A.Griggs & P.J.Ackerley		
						Blackpool	30. 4.01
G-ATTF	Piper PA-28-140 Cherokee	28-21939	N11C	25. 4.66	D.H.Fear	Bembridge	10. 6.00
G-ATTI	Piper PA-28-140 Cherokee	28-21951	N11C	24. 4.66	R.H.Rathbone	Sywell	26. 9 04T
					t/a G-ATTI Flying Group		
G-ATTK	Piper PA-28-140 Cherokee	28-21959	N11C	25. 4.66	D.J.E.Fairburn	Southend	3. 5.04
					t/a The G-ATTK Flying Group		
G-ATTM	CEA Jodel DR.250 Srs.160	65		26. 4.66	R.W.Tomkinson	Seletar, Singapore	15.12.01
G-ATTN*	Piccard HAFB (62,000 cu ft)			27. 4.66	The Science Museum *"The Red Dragon"*		
		15 & 1352	*(Envelope/basket stored 6.94)*			South Kensington, London SW7	
G-ATTR	Bölkow Bö.208C Junior	612	D-EHEH	28. 4.66	S.Luck	Audley End	1.10.03
G-ATTV	Piper PA-28-140 Cherokee	28-21991	N11C	2. 5.66	N.E.Leech t/a G-ATTV Group	Andrewsfield	19.11.01
G-ATTX	Piper PA-28-180 Cherokee C	28-3390	PH-VDP	2. 5.66	IPAC Aviation Ltd	Earls Colne	25. 1.03
			(G-ATTX)/N11C				
G-ATUB	Piper PA-28-140 Cherokee	28-21971	N11C	2. 5.66	R.H.Partington & M.J.Porter	Wombleton	18. 3.02
G-ATUD	Piper PA-28-140 Cherokee	28-21979	N11C	2. 5.66	J.J.Ferguson	(Bideford)	24. 8.03T
G-ATUF	Reims Cessna F150F	F150-0040		4. 5.66	D.P.Williams	Hill Farm, Nayland	27. 4.02
	(Wichita c/n 15063229)				*"Honeysuckle"*		
G-ATUG	Rollason-Druine D.62B Condor	RAE/614		4. 5.66	R.Crosby	Watchford Farm, Yarcombe	26. 6.02P
G-ATUH	Tipsy T.66 Nipper 1	6	OO-NIF	4. 5.66	M.D.Barnard & C.Voelger	RAF Henlow	29. 1.02P
	(VW 1600) *(Built Avions Fairey SA)*						
G-ATUI	Bölkow Bö.208C Junior	611	D-EHEF	4. 5.66	A.W.Wakefield	Stapleford	29. 6.02
G-ATUL	Piper PA-28-180 Cherokee C	28-3033	N9007J	6. 5.66	Kirkland Ltd	Ronaldsway	21. 6.02
G-ATVF	de Havilland DHC.1 Chipmunk 22		WD327	25. 5.66	T.M.Holloway	RAF Syerston	9. 5.04
	(Lycoming AEIO-360)	C1/0265			t/a RAFGSA *(Op Four Counties Gliding Club)*		
G-ATVK	Piper PA-28-140 Cherokee	28-22006	N11C	27. 5.66	J.K.Beauchamp	(London SW11)	11.12.04T
G-ATVL*	Piper PA-28-140 Cherokee	28-22013	N11C	27. 5.66	White Waltham Airfield Ltd	White Waltham	8. 9.00T
					(Cancelled 22.11.01 as destroyed) (For fire practice 11.01)		
G-ATVO	Piper PA-28-140 Cherokee	28-22020	N11C	27. 5.66	G.R.Bright	Little Gransden	13. 2.03T
G-ATVP*	Vickers FB.5 Gunbus rep			31. 5.66	RAF Museum	Hendon	6. 5.69P
	(Gnome Monosoupape 100 hp)	VAFA-01 & FB.5			*(Cancelled 27.2.69 as WFU) (As "2345/"Bombay(2)" in RFC c/s)*		
G-ATVS	Piper PA-28-180 Cherokee C	28-3041	N9014J	1. 6.66	S.M. Patterson	Sandown	26.10.03T
					(Noted 6.01)		
G-ATVW	Rollason-Druine D.62B Condor	RAE/615		7. 6.66	J.P.Coulter & J.Chidley	Nuthampstead	24. 5.04
					t/a Alpha One Flying Group		

G-ATVX	Bölkow Bö.208C Junior	615	D-EHER	9. 6.66	D.E.Thomas & R.G.Morris	Swansea	30.10.02P
					t/a D & G Aviation		
G-ATWA	SAN Jodel DR.1050 Ambassadeur	296	F-BKHA	10. 6.66	P.J.Charnell, J.D.Atkinson, H.R.Browning & C.Clarke		
						Popham	13.12.02
G-ATWB	SAN Jodel D.117	423	F-BHNH	10. 6.66	C.R.Isbell	Andrewsfield	26. 7.02P
					t/a Andrewsfield Whiskey Bravo Group		
G-ATWE*	GEMS MS.892A Rallye Commodore 150			13. 6.66	D.I.Murray	(Newport, Gwent)	15. 2.82
		10634	*(Damaged near Taunton 29.3.81) (Cancelled 17.2.99 by CAA) (Stored 10.01)*				
G-ATWJ	Reims Cessna F172F	F172-0095	EI-ANS	21. 6.66	C.J. & J.Freeman	Headcorn	21. 5.04T
					t/a Weald Air Services		
G-ATWR*	Piper PA-30 Twin Comanche B	30-1134	N8025Y	30. 6.66	Not known	Wickenby	22.12.94T
	(Damaged Crosland Moor 14.9.93: stored 8.94: cancelled 18.4.95 as TWFU) (Current status unknown)						
G-ATWS*	Phoenix Luton LA-4A Minor			30. 6.66	Not known	(Tain)	26. 3.69P
		PAL/1195 & PFA 818	*(Cancelled 8.2.82: on rebuild 4.97: current status unknown)*				
G-ATXA	Piper PA-22-150 Tri-Pacer	22-3730	N4403A	8. 7.66	S.Hildrop	Top Farm, Croydon	17. 5.04
	(Modified to PA-20 Super Pacer configuration)						
G-ATXD	Piper PA-30 Twin Comanche B	30-1166	N8053Y	12. 7.66	LGH Aviation Ltd	Fairoaks	26. 4.03T
G-ATXJ*	Handley Page HP.137 Jetstream 300			15. 7.66	Cardiff-Wales Airport Fire Service		
		200	*(Mod to Jetstream 41 mock-up & display unit)*			Cardiff	8. 2.71
					(Cancelled 11.4.72)		
G-ATXM	Piper PA-28-180 Cherokee C	28-2759	N8809J	19. 7.66	M.J.Stack	Stapleford	12.10.02
					t/a G-ATXM Flying Group		
G-ATXN	Mitchell-Procter Kittiwake 1			19. 7.66	R.G.Day	Biggin Hill	14. 3.01P
	(Lycoming O-290)	1 & PFA 1306					
G-ATXO	SIPA 903	41	F-BGAP	19. 7.66	S.A. & D.C.Whitehead	Eaglescott	22. 7.02P
					"La Pirouette"		
G-ATXR*	Abingdon Gas Balloon HAFB	A.F.B.1		22. 7.66	British Balloon Museum & Library	Newbury	1. 9.76
					(Cancelled 14.7.86 by CAA) (Basket only)		
G-ATXX*	McCandless M.4 Gyrocopter	M4/3		27. 7.66	Ulster Folk & Transport Museum	Belfast	
	(VW 1600)				*(Cancelled 9.9.70 as WFU)*		
G-ATXZ	Bölkow Bö.208C Junior	624	D-ELNE	28. 7.66	M.R.Kaye t/a G-ATXZ Group	Tatenhill	23. 5.02P
					(Remains noted 2001)		
G-ATYM	Reims Cessna F150G	F150-0074		15. 8.66	J.F.Perry	Rochester	28. 9.92
					t/a J.F.Perry & Co *(Stored 6.00)*		
G-ATYS	Piper PA-28-180 Cherokee C	28-3296	N9226J	19. 8.66	E.Baker	Headcorn	24. 5.03
					t/a G-ATYS Flying Group		
G-ATZK	Piper PA-28-180 Cherokee C	28-3128	N9090J	21. 9.66	B.H. & E.F.Austen	Oaksey Park	21.10.02T
			(D-EFUN)/N9090J		t/a Zulu Kilo Group		
G-ATZM	Piper J-3C-90 Cub Special	20868	N2092M	26. 9.66	R.W.Davison	Holywell	25. 9.02P
	(Frame No.21310)		NC2092M				
G-ATZS	Wassmer WA.41 Super Baladou IV	128		30. 9.66	Temporal Songs Ltd & Anti Climb Guards Ltd		
						Rufforth	28.11.02
G-ATZY	Reims Cessna F150G	F150-0135		14.10.66	Fraggle Leasing Ltd	Edinburgh	1. 7.00T

G-AVAA – G-AVZZ

G-AVAR	Reims Cessna F150G	F150-0122		27.10.66	J.A.Rees	Haverfordwest	25. 9.04T
G-AVAU	Piper PA-30 Twin Comanche B	30-1328	N8230Y	8.11.66	Enrico Ermano Ltd	Fairoaks	19. 5.02
			N10F				
G-AVAW	Rollason-Druine D.62C Condor	RAE/617		10.11.66	S.Banyard	Swanton Morley	25. 5.03
					t/a Condor Aircraft Group		
G-AVAX	Piper PA-28-180 Cherokee C	28-3798	N11C	11.11.66	J.J.Parkes	Wolverhampton	30. 5.02
G-AVBG	Piper PA-28-180 Cherokee C	28-3801	N11C	11.11.66	R.A.Cayless & R.D.B.Severn	White Waltham	9. 4.03
					t/a G-AVBG Flying Group		
G-AVBH	Piper PA-28-180 Cherokee C	28-3802	N11C	11.11.66	T.R.Smith (Agricultural Machinery) Ltd		
						New Lane Farm, North Elmham	18. 5.03
G-AVBS	Piper PA-28-180 Cherokee C	28-3938	N11C	14.11.66	A.G.Arthur	Perranporth	1. 7.04T
G-AVBT	Piper PA-28-180 Cherokee C	28-3945	N11C	14.11.66	J.F.Mitchell	Shoreham	26. 4.01T
G-AVCC*	Reims Cessna F172H	F172-0365		28.11.66	Bedford College	Bedford	6.11.88
			(Damaged 31.12.87: cancelled 8.3.88 as destroyed) (Instructional airframe 6.99)				
G-AVCM	Piper PA-24-260 Comanche B	24-4520	N9054P	5.12.66	Airbase Aircraft Ltd	Stapleford	16. 6.02
G-AVCN	Britten-Norman BN-2A-8 Islander	3	N290VL	6.12.66	Airstream International Group Ltd		
	(Originally regd as BN-2)		F-OGHG/G-AVCN			Bembridge	5.11.76T
	(For restoration to flying condition 2001 by Britten-Norman Aircraft Preservation Society (BNAPS): G-AVCN [f/f 24.4.67] is the oldest surviving production example)						
G-AVCS*	Beagle A.61 Terrier 1	-	WJ363	12.12.66	J.May	Ballynahinch	28. 6.82
	(Damaged Finmere 18.10.81: cancelled 3.4.89 by CAA) (On rebuild 11.95) (Current status unknown)						
G-AVCT*	Reims Cessna F150G	F150-0128		12.12.66	Not known	(Compton Abbas)	
					(Cancelled 1.5.98 as WFU) (On rebuild 12.97)		
G-AVCV	Cessna 182J Skylane	18257492	N3492F	15.12.66	The University of Manchester Institute		
					of Science & Technology	Woodford	22. 2.04
G-AVCX	Piper PA-30 Twin Comanche B	30-1302	N8185Y	16.12.66	J H West	(Exeter)	12. 8.03

G-AVCY* Piper PA-30 Twin Comanche B 30-1367 N8241Y 16.12.66 Not known (Bruntingthorpe)
(Crashed on take-off Cardiff 9.3.91: cancelled 17.7.91 as WFU) (Fuselage noted in scrapyard compound outside 11.01)
G-AVDA Cessna 182K Skylane 18257959 N2759Q 16.12.66 F.W.Ellis & M.C.Burnett
Water Leisure Park, Skegness 17. 6.01
G-AVDB* Cessna 310L 310L0079 N2279F 20.12.66 Not known Coventry 8. 7.79
(WFU Perth 8.7.79: cancelled 6.8.79) (Noted 1999: port wing @ Perth 1.00)
G-AVDF* Beagle B.121 Pup Srs.100 B.121-001 28.12.66 D Collings
Bourne Park, Hurstbourne Tarrant 22. 5.68
(Originally regd as B.121C c/n B.151, became B.121 Srs.100 2.69) (WFU Shoreham 22.5.68) (Stored 10.01)
G-AVDG Wallis WA-116 Srs.1 Agile 215 28.12.66 K.H.Wallis Reymerston Hall, Norfolk 23. 5.92P
(Stored 8.01)
(Variously powered by McCulloch: Fuji 440, Norton twin-rotor Wankel & now Rotax 532)
G-AVDR* Beechcraft 65-B80 Queen Air LD-339 A40-CR 5. 1.67 Brunel Technical College
(Originally regd with c/n LD-333) G-AVDR Ashley Down, Bristol 30. 6.86T
(Cancelled 18.5.90 as WFU) (Instructional airframe 5.91) (Current status unknown)
G-AVDS* Beechcraft 65-B80 Queen Air LD-337 A40-CS 5. 1.67 Brunel Technical College Filton 26. 8.77
G-AVDS *(Cancelled 1.3.89 as WFU) (Dumped 9.01 as "G-A")*
G-AVDT Aeronca 7AC Champion 7AC-6932 N3594E 5. 1.67 D.Cheney & G.Moore (Newry, Co.Armagh) 10. 7.90P
NC3594E *(Current status unknown)*
G-AVDV Piper PA-22-150 Tri-Pacer 22-3752 N4423A 5. 1.67 Suzanne C.Brooks
(Modifed to PA-20 Super Pacer configuration) Wellcross Grange, Slinfold 23.10.03
G-AVDY Phoenix Luton LA-4A Minor 10. 1.67 M.Stoney Stapleford 9. 8.00P
(Lycoming O-145) PAL/1183 & PFA 808 *(Damaged landing Stapleford 18.12.99: stored 12.01)*
G-AVEC Reims Cessna F172H F172-0405 13. 1.67 W.H.Ekin (Engineering) Co Ltd Aberdeen 11. 5.02
G-AVEF SAN Jodel 150 Mascaret 16 F-BLDK 19. 1.67 Heavy Install Ltd Headcorn 16. 6.02T
G-AVEH SIAI-Marchetti S.205-20R 346 20. 1.67 M.Jarrett, K.Fear, R.L.F.Darby & A D F Flintoff
t/a EH Aviation Crowland 30. 3.03
G-AVEM Reims Cessna F150G F150-0198 23. 1.67 T.D.& J.A.Warren Goodwood 24. 3.02
G-AVEN Reims Cessna F150G F150-0202 23. 1.67 N.J. Richardson Southampton 3. 9.01
t/a 150 Flying Group
G-AVER Reims Cessna F150G F150-0206 23. 1.67 LAC (Enterprises) Ltd Barton 17. 8.01
t/a Lancashire Aero Club
G-AVEU Wassmer WA.41 Super Baladou IV 136 27. 1.67 H & S Roberts Enstone 10.12.01
G-AVEX Rollason-Druine D.62B Condor RAE/616 31. 1.67 J.Riley & M.Mordue Hinton-in-the-Hedges 21. 2.02P
G-AVEY Phoenix Currie Super Wot 31. 1.67 B.J.Anning Watchford Farm, Yarcombe 14. 8.02P
(Pobjoy "R") SE.100 & PFA 3006
G-AVEZ* Handley Page HPR.7 Dart Herald 210 PP-ASW 31. 1.67 Norwich Airport Fire Service Norwich 5. 1.81
169 G-AVEZ/HB-AAH
(WFU 5.1.81 & cancelled 4.1.83) (For rescue training: on fire dump 2.99)
G-AVFB* Hawker Siddeley HS.121 Trident 2E 5B-DAC 1. 2.67 Duxford Aviation Society Duxford 30. 9.82
2141 G-AVFB *(WFU 27.3.82 & cancelled 9.7.82) (BEA c/s)*
G-AVFE* Hawker Siddeley HS.121 Trident 2E 1. 2.67 Belfast Airport Fire Service Belfast 6. 5.85T
2144 *(WFU 20.3.85) (Noted 5.00)*
G-AVFG* Hawker Siddeley HS.121 Trident 2E 1. 2.67 British Airports Authority Heathrow 2. 7.85T
2146
(WFU 5.85 & used for ground training & fire service: cancelled 19.1.89 as WFU) (Used as aircrash set for TV documentary & fuselage cut into three pieces 3.00: some fuselage parts to Trident Preservation Society)
G-AVFH* Hawker Siddeley HS.121 Trident 2E 1. 2.67 De Havilland Heritage Museum
2147 *(WFU 24.10.81 & cancelled 12.5.82: for'd fuselage only)* London Colney 18. 5.83T
G-AVFJ* Hawker Siddeley HS.121 Trident 2E 1. 2.67 International Fire Training Centre
2149 *(WFU 6.82: cancelled 9.7.82) (Front fuselage extant 3.00)* Teesside 18. 9.83T
G-AVFK* Hawker Siddeley HS.121 Trident 2E 1. 2.67 Royal Air Force RAF Lyneham 15. 8.83T
2150 *(WFU 31.12.81 & cancelled 12.5.82) (For Rescue training 1.00)*
G-AVFM* Hawker Siddeley HS.121 Trident 2E 1. 2.67 Brunel Technical College Bristol 2. 6.84T
2152 *(WFU 30.3.83) (Instructional airframe 10.99)*
G-AVFP Piper PA-28-140 Cherokee 28-22652 N11C 1. 2.67 Rebecca L.Howells Barton 14. 7.02
G-AVFR Piper PA-28-140 Cherokee 28-22747 N11C 1. 2.67 J.B.Edgar & J.E.Brown t/a VFR Flying Group
Newtownards, Co.of Down 6. 4.02
G-AVFU Piper PA-32-300 Cherokee Six N11C 1. 2.67 M.J.Hoodless Castlerock, Co Londonderry 30. 4.03T
32-40182
G-AVFX Piper PA-28-140 Cherokee 28-22757 N11C 1. 2.67 R.A.Irwin Thruxton 26. 7.04
t/a Wessex Flyers Group
G-AVFZ Piper PA-28-140 Cherokee 28-22767 N11C 1. 2.67 C.M.Toyne Yeovil 25. 9.04
t/a G-AVFZ Flying Group
G-AVGA Piper PA-24-260 Comanche B 24-4489 N9027P 31. 1.67 M.D.Crooks, J.R.Butterworth & V.R.Dennay
t/a Conram Aviation Group *"C'est Si Bon"* White Waltham 19. 1.03
G-AVGC Piper PA-28-140 Cherokee 28-22777 N11C 31. 1.67 A.P.H.Hay Popham 7. 5.04
G-AVGD Piper PA-28-140 Cherokee 28-22782 N11C 31. 1.67 M.Tyler-Bennett Sywell 25. 8.02T
G-AVGE Piper PA-28-140 Cherokee 28-22787 N11C 31. 1.67 A.J.Cutler Bournemouth 11. 4.04T
G-AVGG* Piper PA-28-140 Cherokee 28-22797 N11C 31. 1.67 Yorkshire Light Aircraft Ltd Duxford 3. 7.71
(Crashed Papplewick, Notts 10.8.70: cancelled 16.3.73 as WFU) (Wrecked cabin only 9.00)
G-AVGH* Piper PA-28-140 Cherokee 28-22802 N11C 31. 1.67 Not known Cardiff 5.12.91T
(Cancelled 19.2.92 as WFU) (Wreck stored 1.97)

G-AVGI	Piper PA-28-140 Cherokee	28-22822	N11C	31. 1.67	D.G.Smith & C.D.Barden t/a Golf India Group	Liverpool	16.12.04
G-AVGJ*	SAN Jodel DR.1050 Ambassadeur	265	F-BJYJ	31. 1.67	Not known	Enstone	22. 4.85
	(WFU with glue failure 1985: on rebuild off-site 6.95) (Current status unknown)						
G-AVGK	Piper PA-28-180 Cherokee C	28-3639	N9516J	2. 2.67	N.K.Lamping & S.B.Smith t/a Golf Kilo Flying Group	Liverpool	14.10.02T
G-AVGU	Reims Cessna F150G	F150-0199		8. 2.67	Coulson Flying Services Ltd	Little Staughton	13. 2.04T
G-AVGY	Cessna 182K Skylane	18258112	N3112Q	17. 2.67	R.M.C.Sears & R.N.Howgego	Stoke Ferry	28. 3.03
	(Ran into ditch landing Maney, Cambs 2.4.00: damage to fuselage, wing and propeller)						
G-AVGZ	CEA Jodel DR.1050 Sicile	341	F-BKPR	14. 2.67	D.C.Webb *(Stored 10.00)*	Bagby	13. 7.97
G-AVHH	Reims Cessna F172H	F172-0337		20. 2.67	Avon Aviation Ltd t/a The Bristol & Wessex Aeroplane Club	Bristol	10. 2.02T
G-AVHL	SAN Jodel DR.105A Ambassadeur	90	F-BIVY	23. 2.67	J.R.Tonkin	(Norwich)	17. 8.03
G-AVHM	Reims Cessna F150G	F150-0181		24. 2.67	M.Murphy t/a M & N Flying Group	(Epsom)	30.11.01T
	(Rebuilt 1997 with fuselage from G-ATRL [F150-0050]: old fuselage dumped Shoreham 12.99)						
G-AVHN*	Reims Cessna F150G	F150-0182		24. 2.67	Not known	Shobdon	
	(Damaged 28.1.85: used as instructional airframe: cancelled 5.8.94 as destroyed: noted 3.96)						
G-AVHT*	Beagle E.3 (Auster AOP.9M) (Lycoming O-360)	-	WZ711	1. 3.67	M.Somerton-Raynor *(Cancelled 10.4.01 by CAA: stored 2000) (As "WZ711")*	AAC Middle Wallop	29. 4.01
G-AVHY	Sportavia Fournier RF4D	4009		10. 3.67	I K G Mitchell	Halesland	16. 1.02P
G-AVIA	Reims Cessna F150G	F150-0184		10. 3.67	Cheshire Air Training Services Ltd	Liverpool	21.11.03T
G-AVIB	Reims Cessna F150G	F150-0180		10. 3.67	Edinburgh Air Centre Ltd *(Op Highland Flying Club)*	Inverness	22. 8.03T
G-AVIC	Reims Cessna F172H	F172-0320	N17011	10. 3.67	Leeside Flying Ltd	Cork, Co.Cork	9. 5.04
G-AVID	Cessna 182K	18257734	N2534Q	10. 3.67	Jaguar Aviation Ltd *(Op Fife Parachute Centre)*	Eroll	18. 4.03
G-AVII	Agusta-Bell 206B JetRanger II	8011		10. 3.67	Bristow Helicopters Ltd *"Brighton Belle"*	North Denes	4. 1.04T
G-AVIL	Alon A.2 Aircoupe	A.5	N5471E	14. 3.67	D.J.Hulks *(As "VX147" in RAF c/s)*	Headcorn	16. 8.04
G-AVIN	SOCATA MS.880B Rallye Club	884		14. 3.67	P.Bradley	Compton Abbas	25. 5.02
G-AVIP	Brantly B.2B	471		14. 3.67	N.J.R.Minchin	Hill Top Farm, Hambledon	18.10.01
G-AVIS	Reims Cessna F172H	F172-0413		14. 3.67	J P A Freeman	Headcorn	17. 9.01T
G-AVIT	Reims Cessna F150G	F150-0217		14. 3.67	S.Vint t/a Invicta Flyers	Manston	26. 9.04
G-AVIZ	Scheibe SF-25A Motorfalke	4552	(D-KOFY)	21. 3.67	T.J.Wiltshire t/a Splisby Gliding Trust	Spilsby	19. 9.91
G-AVJE	Reims Cessna F150G	F150-0219		29. 3.67	T.F.Fisher t/a G-AVJE Syndicate	Hinton-in-the-Hedges	24. 5.04
G-AVJF	Reims Cessna F172H	F172-0393		31. 3.67	J.A. & G.M.Rees	Haverfordwest	1. 1.04T
G-AVJH*	Druine D.62 Condor (Continental O-200-A)	PFA 603		31. 3.67	(R Chapman)	East Grinstead	4.11.83P
	(Crashed Nefyn, Gwynedd 31.7.83: cancelled 5.1.89) (As spares 4.00 for rebuild of G-AXGU qv)						
G-AVJI*	Reims Cessna F172H	F172-0442		31. 3.67	(Northbrook College)	Shoreham	29. 9.98
	(Damaged Croft Farm, Defford 28.10.95: to College as instructional airframe)						
G-AVJJ	Piper PA-30 Twin Comanche B	30-1420	N8285Y	7. 4.67	A.H.Manser	Gloucestershire	30. 7.04T
G-AVJK	SAN Jodel DR.1050M Excellence *(Orig built as DR.1051)*	453	F-BLJH	7. 4.67	M.H.Wylde	Husbands Bosworth	20. 7.02
G-AVJO	Fokker E.III rep (Continental C85) *(Regd as c/n PPS/FOK/6)*	PPS/FOK/1 & PPS/REP/6		12. 4.67	Bianchi Aviation Film Services Ltd *(Op "Blue Max" Movie Aircraft Collection) (As "E.III 422/15" in German c/s)*	Booker	29. 6.01P
G-AVJV	Wallis WA-117 Srs.1 (RR Continental O-200-B)	K/402/X		12. 4.67	K.H.Wallis	Reymerston Hall, Norfolk	21. 4.89P
	(Used major components of G-ATCV c/n 301) (Stored 8.01)						
G-AVJW	Wallis WA-118/M Meteorite (Meteor Alfa 1)	K/502/X		12. 4.67	K.H.Wallis	Reymerston Hall, Norfolk	21. 4.83P
	(Orig regd as Wallis WA.118 Srs 2: used major components of G-ATPW c/n 401) (Stored 8.01)						
G-AVKB	Brochet MB.50 Pipistrelle (Walter Mikron 3)	02	F-PFAL	17. 4.67	W.B.Cooper	Walkeridge Farm, Hants	30.10.96P
G-AVKD	Sportavia Fournier RF4D	4024		19. 4.67	R.E.Cross t/a Lasham RF4 Group	Lasham	30. 5.02P
G-AVKE*	Gadfly HDW-1 (Continental IO-340A)	HDW-1		19. 4.67	E.D.ap Rees t/a The Helicopter Museum *(Cancelled 12.10.81 as WFU)*	Weston-super-Mare	
G-AVKG	Reims Cessna F172H	F172-0345		21. 4.67	Aerogroup 98 Ltd	Ronaldsway	10.10.03
	(Rebuilt with fuselage of G-AVDC c/n F172-0382 in 1986)						
G-AVKI	Slingsby Nipper T.66 RA.45 Srs.3 (Ardem 4C02) *(Tipsy c/n 31)*	S.102/1586		24. 4.67	J.M.Greenway	(Wolverhampton)	7. 8.91P
G-AVKK	Slingsby Nipper T.66 RA.45 Srs.3 (Ardem 4C02) *(Tipsy c/n 74)*	S.104/1588	EI-BJH G-AVKK	24. 4.67	C.Watson	Newtownards, Co.of Down	6. 4.02P
G-AVKL	Piper PA-30 Twin Comanche B	30-1418	OY-DHL G-AVKL/N8284Y	25. 4.67	Bravo Aviation Ltd	Jersey	8. 6.02
G-AVKM*	Rollason-Druine D.62B Condor	RAE/620		26. 4.67	M Hobson	(Cruden Bay, Peterhead)	30. 6.82
	(Damaged in gales Wilkieston Farm, Cupar, Angus 2/3.3.82) (Stored 6.00: current status unknown)						
G-AVKN	Cessna 401	401-0082	(N3282Q)	26. 4.67	Law Leasing Ltd	Rochester	22. 5.02
G-AVKP	Beagle A.109 Airedale	B.540	SE-EGA	26. 4.67	D.R.Williams	Peplow	26. 9.03
G-AVKR	Bölkow Bö.208C Junior	648	D-EGRA	28. 4.67	A.C.Dufton & S.F.Jeffery *(Fuselage noted 7.01)*	Bournemouth	10.10.04

G-AVKT*	Tipsy Nipper T.66 Srs.3	70	OO-HEL	1. 5.67	Not known	Yearby	
	(Built Cobelavia)		OO-DEL				
	(Crashed Constable Burton, Paull, Yorks 19.9.72: cancelled 14.2.73 as destroyed) (Frame noted 1.02)						
G-AVLB	Piper PA-28-140 Cherokee	28-23158	N11C	8. 5.67	M.Wilson	Little Gransden	2.12.03
G-AVLC	Piper PA-28-140 Cherokee	28-23178	N11C	8. 5.67	NE Wales Institute of Higher Education	Welshpool	25. 9.98
G-AVLD	Piper PA-28-140 Cherokee	28-23193	N11C	8. 5.67	S.H.A.Petter t/a The West London Strut Flying Group	White Waltham	30. 5.03
G-AVLE	Piper PA-28-140 Cherokee	28-23223	N11C	8. 5.67	G.E.Wright t/a Video Security Services	South Lodge Farm, Widnerpool	22.12.04
G-AVLF	Piper PA-28-140 Cherokee	28-23268	N11C	8. 5.67	G.H.Hughesdon	White Waltham	18. 2.04T
G-AVLG	Piper PA-28-140 Cherokee	28-23358	N11C	8. 5.67	R.Friedlander & D.C.Raymond	Grateley, Andover	23. 8.03
G-AVLH	Piper PA-28-140 Cherokee	28-23368	N11C	8. 5.67	M.B.Rothschild	North Weald	18. 8.00
G-AVLI	Piper PA-28-140 Cherokee	28-23388	N11C	8. 5.67	Lima India Aviation Ltd	Southend	1. 4.01
G-AVLJ	Piper PA-28-140 Cherokee	28-23393	9H-AAZ G-AVLJ/N11C	8. 5.67	Cherokee Aviation Holdings Jersey Ltd	(Jersey)	1. 8.02T
G-AVLM	Beagle B.121 Pup 2	B121-003		8. 5.67	T.M. & D.A.Jones *(On rebuild 8.99: current status unknown)*	Derby	29. 4.69S
G-AVLN	Beagle B.121 Pup 2	B121-004		8. 5.67	A.P.Marks	Sywell	9. 7.04S
G-AVLO	Bölkow Bö.208C Junior	650	D-EGUC	8. 5.67	P.J.Swain	Sandford Hall, Knockin	8. 6.02P
G-AVLR	Piper PA-28-140 Cherokee	28-23288	N11C	9. 5.67	S.W.Slade t/a Group 140	Cambridge	11. 4.04
G-AVLT	Piper PA-28-140 Cherokee	28-23328	G-KELC G-AVLT/N11C	9. 5.67	L I Bailey	(Daventry)	20. 9.04T
G-AVLW	Sportavia Fournier RF4D	4025		9. 5.67	J.C.A.C.da Silva	Damyns Hall, Upminster	1. 2.01
G-AVLY	Jodel Wassmer D.120A Paris-Nice	331		11. 5.67	N.V. de Candole	Boarsbarrow Farm, Bridport	3. 5.02P
G-AVMA	SOCATA GY-80-180 Horizon	196		12. 5.67	B.R.Hildick	Shenstone Hall Farm, Shenstone	3. 4.04
G-AVMB	Rollason-Druine D.62B Condor	RAE/621		12. 5.67	L.J.Dray *"Spirit of Silver City"*	Watchford Farm, Yarcombe	1. 9.02P
G-AVMD	Cessna 150G	15065504	N2404J	16. 5.67	T.A.White t/a Bagby Aviation	Bagby	16. 8.04
G-AVMF	Reims Cessna F150G	F150-0203		17. 5.67	J.F.Marsh	Newton Green, Sudbury	21. 7.03
G-AVMH	British Aircraft Corporation One-Eleven 510ED	BAC.136		11. 5.67	European Aviation Ltd *(Stored 7.01)*	Bournemouth	9. 2.01T
G-AVMI	British Aircraft Corporation One-Eleven 510ED	BAC.137		11. 5.67	European Aviation Ltd *(Stored 7.01)*	Bournemouth	25. 1.01T
G-AVMJ*	British Aircraft Corporation One-Eleven 510ED	BAC.138		11. 5.67	European Aviation Ltd *(WFU 6.94: cancelled 11.5.01 by CAA) (Used as cabin trainer 5.01)*	Bournemouth	17.11.94T
G-AVMK	British Aircraft Corporation One-Eleven 510ED	BAC.139		11. 5.67	European Aviation Ltd *(Stored 7.01)*	Bournemouth	8. 8.00T
G-AVMN	British Aircraft Corporation One-Eleven 510ED	BAC.142		11. 5.67	European Aviation Ltd *(AB Airlines c/s) (To Aviation Museum 5.01)*	Bournemouth	21. 6.00T
G-AVMO*	British Aircraft Corporation One-Eleven 510ED	BAC.143		11. 5.67	RAF Museum *(Cancelled 12.7.93 as WFU) (British Airways titles) "Lothian Region"*	RAF Cosford	3. 2.95T
G-AVMP	British Aircraft Corporation One-Eleven 510ED	BAC.144		11. 5.67	European Aviation Ltd *"The Madrid Express" (Stored 5.01)*	Bournemouth	6. 4.01T
G-AVMS	British Aircraft Corporation One-Eleven 510ED	BAC.146		11. 5.67	European Aviation Ltd *"The London Express" (Stored 5.01)*	Bournemouth	26. 2.01T
G-AVMT	British Aircraft Corporation One-Eleven 510ED	BAC.147		11. 5.67	European Aviation Ltd *(European Minardi F1 titles) (Op Minardi F1 team)*	Bournemouth	5.12.03T
G-AVMU*	British Aircraft Corporation One-Eleven 510ED	BAC.148		11. 5.67	Duxford Aviation Society *(Cancelled 12.7.93 as WFU) (British Airways titles) "County of Dorset"*	Duxford	8. 1.95T
G-AVMW	British Aircraft Corporation One-Eleven 510ED	BAC.150		11. 5.67	European Aviation Ltd *(Scrapped by 23.1.02)*	Bournemouth	4.10.00T
G-AVMY	British Aircraft Corporation One-Eleven 510ED	BAC.152		11. 5.67	European Aviation Ltd *(Stored 5.01)*	Bournemouth	28. 6.01T
G-AVMZ	British Aircraft Corporation One-Eleven 510ED	BAC.153	(5N-OSA)/G-AVMZ	11. 5.67	European Aviation Ltd *(Stored 5.01)*	Bournemouth	17.10.02T
G-AVNC	Reims Cessna F150G	F150-0200		18. 5.67	J.Turner	Enstone	24. 5.04
G-AVNE*	Westland Wessex 60 Srs.1	WA/561	G-17-3 G-AVNE/5N-AJL/G-AVNE/9M-ASS/VH-BHC/PK-HBQ/G-AVNE/(G-AVMC)	15. 5.67	The Helicopter Museum *(Cancelled 23.11.82 as TWFU) (As "G-17-3")*	Weston-super-Mare	7. 2.83
G-AVNN	Piper PA-28-180 Cherokee C	28-4049	N11C	26. 5.67	J.Acres t/a G-AVNN Flying Group	Trenchard Farm, Eggesford	21. 3.03
G-AVNO	Piper PA-28-180 Cherokee C	28-4105	N11C	26. 5.67	Allister Flight Ltd	Southend	11.10.04T
G-AVNP*	Piper PA-28-180 Cherokee C	28-4113	N11C	26. 5.67	R W Harris, P E Preston, M F Hatt & M Jahanfar *(Op Southend Flying Club)*	Southend	25.10.04T
	(Force landed near Nayland 28.4.01 & cancelled 27.11.01 as destroyed: wreck noted 12.01)						
G-AVNR	Piper PA-28-180 Cherokee C	28-4121	N11C	26. 5.67	R.R.Livingstone	Biggin Hill	25.10.04T
G-AVNS	Piper PA-28-180 Cherokee C	28-4129	N11C	26. 5.67	E.Alexander	Andrewsfield	13. 7.03T
G-AVNU	Piper PA-28-180 Cherokee C	28-4153	N11C	26. 5.67	O.Durrani	Lydd	11. 2.04T
G-AVNW	Piper PA-28-180 Cherokee C	28-4210	N11C	26. 5.67	Len Smith's School & Sports Ltd	Fairoaks	6. 7.03T
G-AVNX	Sportavia Fournier RF4D	4026		26. 5.67	J.A.Hallam & A.Duerden	AAC Dishforth	5. 2.02P

G-AVNZ	Sportavia Fournier RF4D	4030		26. 5.67	V.S.E.Norman	Rendcomb	9. 7.01
G-AVOA	SAN Jodel DR.1050 Ambassadeur	195	F-BJYY	31. 5.67	D.A.Willies	Anwick	5. 9.03
G-AVOC	CEA Jodel DR.221 Dauphin	67		2. 6.67	T.Q.Loveday	Nuthampstead	27. 1.02
G-AVOD*	Beagle D.5/180 Husky	3688		6. 6.67	W.P.Miller	Mavis Enderby	31. 7.92T
	(Crashed Crosland Moor 31.7.92: cancelled 8.9.92: wings donated to J/1 G-AJDW 9.98: on rebuild 1999)						
G-AVOH	Rollason-Druine D.62B Condor	RAE/622		6. 6.67	Halegreen Associates Ltd	Hinton-in-the-Hedges	1.10.99T
G-AVOM	CEA Jodel DR.221 Dauphin	65		6. 6.67	M.A.T.Mountford	Maypole Farm, Chislet	21. 8.03
G-AVOO	Piper PA-18-150 Super Cub (Lycoming O-360-A4)	18-8511	N10F	7. 6.67	London Gliding Club Pty Ltd "Terry Mac"	Dunstable	27. 3.03
G-AVOZ	Piper PA-28-180 Cherokee C	28-3711	N9574J	13. 6.67	P.Hoskins & R.Flavell t/a Oscar Zulu Flying Group	Booker	30. 5.04
G-AVPC	Druine D.31 Turbulent (VW 1500)	PFA 544		15. 6.67	S.A.Sharp	Wigtown	28. 9.99P
G-AVPD	Jodel D.9 Bebe (VW 1500)	521/MAC.1/PFA 927		15. 6.67	S.W.McKay *(Stored 12.99: CofR @ 3.01)*	(Berkhamsted)	6. 6.75S
G-AVPH	Reims Cessna F150G	F150-0197		20. 6.67	Zero 9 Flight Academy *(Fuselage noted 3.00)*	Beccles	9. 4.86T
G-AVPI	Reims Cessna F172H	F172-0409		20. 6.67	R.W.Cope	Netherthorpe	30. 5.03
G-AVPJ	de Havilland DH.82A Tiger Moth	86326	NL879	20. 6.67	Catherine C.Silk	Bericote Farm, Blackdown, Leamington Spa	13. 8.04
G-AVPK*	SOCATA MS.892A Rallye Commodore 150	10736		20. 6.67	B.A.Bridgewater	Shelsley Beauchamp, Worcester	10. 1.92
	(Stored 8.92: cancelled 13.4.99 by CAA) (Current status unknown)						
G-AVPM	SAN Jodel D.117	593	F-BHXO	20. 6.67	J.C.Haynes	Breighton	10. 6.02P
G-AVPN*	Handley Page HPR.7 Dart Herald 213	176	I-TIVB G-AVPN/D-BIBI/(HB-AAK)	22. 6.67	Yorkshire Air Museum	Elvington	14.12.99T
	(Cancelled 8.12.97 as WFU) (Channel Express c/s)						
G-AVPO	Hindustan HAL-26 Pushpak (Continental C90)	PK-127	9M-AOZ VT-DWL	31. 3.83	J.A.Coutts & W.G. Mitchell-Hudson	Cherry Tree Farm, Monewden	28. 7.99P
G-AVPS	Piper PA-30 Twin Comanche B	30-1548	N8393Y	27. 6.67	J.M.Bisco	Farley Farm, Winchester	9. 8.02
G-AVPV	Piper PA-28-180 Cherokee C	28-2705	9J-RBP N11C	27. 6.67	K.A.Passmore	Rayne Hall Farm, Rayne	8. 3.03
G-AVPY	Piper PA-25-235 Pawnee C	25-4330	N4636Y N10F	7. 7.67	Farm Aviation Services Ltd	(Enstone)	14.10.77
	(Crashed Lower Radbourne Farm, Ladbroke, Warwicks 25.6.76: current status unknown: valid CofR 4.01)						
G-AVRK	Piper PA-28-180 Cherokee C	28-4041	N11C	11. 7.67	J.Gama	Tatenhill	9. 3.03
G-AVRP	Piper PA-28-140 Cherokee	28-23153	N11C	14. 7.67	R J Guest t/a Trent-199	Tatenhill	6. 6.03
G-AVRS	SOCATA GY-80-180 Horizon	224		14. 7.67	Air Venturas Ltd	Bagby	7. 8.00
	(Damaged landing Throstle Nest Farm, Cleveland 12.9.99)						
G-AVRU	Piper PA-28-180 Cherokee C	28-4025	N11C	17. 7.67	D.J.Rowell t/a G-AVRU Partnership	Clacton	22. 3.02
G-AVRW	Barritault JB-01 Minicab (Continental C90)	OH-1549 & PFA 1800		18. 7.67	D.J.Smith t/a Kestrel Flying Group	Hucknall	28. 8.02P
G-AVRY	Piper PA-28-180 Cherokee C	28-4089	N11C	24. 7.67	Brigfast Ltd	Popham	6. 4.03
G-AVRZ	Piper PA-28-180 Cherokee C	28-4137	N11C	24. 7.67	Mantavia Group Ltd	Guernsey	27.10.02
G-AVSA	Piper PA-28-180 Cherokee C	28-4184	N11C	24. 7.67	D.J.Royle & W.Beaty t/a G-AVSA Flying Group	Barton	5. 5.02
G-AVSB	Piper PA-28-180 Cherokee C	28-4191	N11C	24. 7.67	D.L.Macdonald	Denham	2. 5.02
G-AVSC	Piper PA-28-180 Cherokee C	28-4193	N11C	24. 7.67	MSC019 Ltd	White Waltham	26. 4.03T
G-AVSD	Piper PA-28-180 Cherokee C	28-4195	N11C	24. 7.67	Landmate Ltd	Haverfordwest	18. 5.04
G-AVSE*	Piper PA-28-180 Cherokee C	28-4196	N11C	24. 7.67	G.Cotrulia *(Cancelled 18.5.99 by CAA) (Noted 5.00)*	Kildare	30. 4.00T
G-AVSF	Piper PA-28-180 Cherokee C	28-4197	N11C	24. 7.67	S.E.Pick & D.A.Rham t/a Monday Club	Blackbushe	6. 4.03
G-AVSI	Piper PA-28-140 Cherokee	28-23148	N11C	24. 7.67	C.M.Royle t/a G-AVSI Flying Group	White Waltham	29. 2.04
G-AVSP	Piper PA-28-180 Cherokee C	28-3952	N11C (PJ-ACT)	8. 8.67	Airways Flight Training (Exeter) Ltd	Exeter	4. 1.04T
G-AVSR	Beagle D.5/180 Husky	3689		8. 8.67	A.L.Young	Henstridge	19.10.02A
G-AVSZ	Agusta-Bell 206B JetRanger II	8032	VH-BEQ PK-HBZ/VR-BCR/PK-HBD/VR-BCR/G-AVSZ	8. 8.67	Burman Aviation Ltd	Newcastle/Cranfield	16. 6.99T
G-AVTL*	Brighton Ax7-65 HAFB *(Originally regd as Hot-Air Group ¼ Free Balloon c/n 1)*	01		17. 8.67	(Cameron Balloons Ltd) *"Bristol Belle" (Envelope only)*	Bristol	
	(Retired from active flying & stored: cancelled 11.9.81 as WFU) (Current status unknown)						
G-AVTP	Reims Cessna F172H	F172-0458		17. 8.67	A.S.Watkins & M.J.Green, t/a Tango Papa Group	White Waltham	11. 7.04
G-AVTT	Ercoupe 415D (Continental C85)	4399	SE-BFZ NC3774H	21. 8.67	Wright Farm Eggs Ltd *(Stored 6.00)*	Cherry Tree Farm, Monewden	20. 1.86
G-AVTV	SOCATA MS.893A Rallye Commodore 180	10725		24. 8.67	D.B.& M.E.Meeks	Seighford	6. 8.03
G-AVUD	Piper PA-30 Twin Comanche B	30-1515	N8422Y N9???N	5. 9.67	P.M.Fox t/a FM Aviation	Biggin Hill	11. 7.04
G-AVUG	Reims Cessna F150H	F150-0234		11. 9.67	R.K.Moody & V.J.Larkin t/a Skyways Flying Group	Netherthorpe	9. 6.02

G-AVUH	Reims Cessna F150H	F150-0244		11. 9.67	C.M.Chinn	North Coates	6. 8.04
G-AVUO	Phoenix Luton LA.4A Minor	PAL/1313		21. 9.67	M.E.Vaisey	(Hemel Hempstead)	
	(Initially not completed: parts used in construction of G-AXKH - possible long-term build project)						
G-AVUS	Piper PA-28-140 Cherokee	28-24065	(G-AVUT) N11C	25. 9.67	D.J.Hunter	Norwich	6.12.04T
G-AVUT	Piper PA-28-140 Cherokee	28-24085	(G-AVUU) N11C	25. 9.67	Bencray Ltd *(Op Blackpool & Fylde Aero Club)*	Blackpool	17. 5.04T
G-AVUU	Piper PA-28-140 Cherokee	28-24100	(G-AVUS) N11C	25. 9.67	R.W.Harris, A.Jahanfar, P.E.Preston & M.F.Hatt *(Op Southend Flying Club)*	Southend	11. 5.03T
G-AVUZ	Piper PA-32-300 Cherokee Six	32-40302	N11C	29. 9.67	Ceesix Ltd	Jersey	23. 4.03
G-AVVC	Reims Cessna F172H	F172-0443		29. 9.67	A.Turnbull	(Bedlington)	21.10.01T
G-AVVF*	de Havilland DH.104 Dove 8	04541		2.10.67	Not known	Gloucestershire	11. 2.88
					(Cancelled 26.6.91 as WFU) (Wreck on fire dump 4.01)		
G-AVVJ	SOCATA MS.893A Rallye Commodore 180	10752		6.10.67	M.Powell	Tibenham	28. 7.02
G-AVVL	Reims Cessna F150H (Wilksch Airmotive WAM-120)	F150-0257		6.10.67	N.E.Sams *"Samurai"* t/a International Aerospace Engineering	Cranfield	11. 3.89T
G-AVVO*	Avro 652A Anson C.19 Srs.2	34219	VL348	6.10.67	Newark Air Museum	Winthorpe	
					(Cancelled 16.9.72 by CAA) (As "VL348")		
G-AVVW*	Reims Cessna F150H	F150-0258		19.10.67	Brunel Technical College	Ashley Down, Bristol	31. 5.82
					(Cancelled 4.6.82 as WFU) (Instructional airframe 6.91) (Current status unknown)		
G-AVWA	Piper PA-28-140 Cherokee	28-23660	N11C	19.10.67	SFG Ltd	Shipdham	19.12.02T
G-AVWD	Piper PA-28-140 Cherokee	28-23700	N11C	19.10.67	C.Bentley & B.Marlowe t/a Evelyn Air	Leeds-Bradford	30. 9.04T
G-AVWE*	Piper PA-28-140 Cherokee	28-23720	N11C	19.10.67	Not known	Blackpool	22. 4.82T
					(WFU & cancelled 8.6.89 by CAA) (Fuselage noted 3.00: current status unknown)		
G-AVWG	Piper PA-28-140 Cherokee	28-23760	N11C	19.10.67	Bencray Ltd	Blackpool	11. 8.91T
	(Damaged Tal y Fan, Conwy, Gwynedd 11.12.88: components used to rebuild G-BBEF in 1998/99 (qv)): wings only 12.01)						
G-AVWI	Piper PA-28-140 Cherokee	28-23800	N11C	19.10.67	Mrs.L.M.Middleton	Cranfield	17. 2.03
G-AVWJ	Piper PA-28-140 Cherokee	28-23940	N11C	19.10.67	A.M.Harrhy	Sandown	29. 7.04
G-AVWL	Piper PA-28-140 Cherokee	28-24000	N11C	19.10.67	B.W.Griffiths & R.Fraser-Duthie t/a Bobev Aviation	Coventry	4.10 04
G-AVWM	Piper PA-28-140 Cherokee	28-24005		19.10.67	A.Jahanfar, P.E.Preston, M.F.Hatt & R.W.Harris *(Op Southend Flying Club)*	Southend	18. 6.04T
G-AVWN	Piper PA-28R-180 Cherokee Arrow	28R-30170	N11C	19.10.67	Vawn Air Ltd	Jersey	10. 4.02
G-AVWO	Piper PA-28R-180 Cherokee Arrow	28R-30205	N11C	19.10.67	R.G.Tweddle	White Waltham	15.11.03
G-AVWR	Piper PA-28R-180 Cherokee Arrow	28R-30242	N11C	19.10.67	S.J.French, G.A.Rogers, C.A.Bailey & R.J.Doughton	Dunkeswell	31. 8.03
G-AVWT	Piper PA-28R-180 Cherokee Arrow	28R-30362	N11C	19.10.67	Cloudbase Aviation Ltd	Barton	21. 5.03
G-AVWU	Piper PA-28R-180 Cherokee Arrow	28R-30380	N11C	19.10.67	Arrow Flyers Ltd	Booker	18. 5.01
G-AVWV	Piper PA-28R-180 Cherokee Arrow	28R-30404	N11C	19.10.67	R.V.Thornton & R.Barron t/a Strathtay Flying Group	Perth	18. 6.02
G-AVWY	Sportavia Fournier RF4D	4031		26.10.67	P Turner	Halesland	1. 7.02P
G-AVXA	Piper PA-25-235 Pawnee C *(Re-built using new frame)*	25-4244	N4576Y	26.10.67	South Wales Gliding Club Ltd	Usk	5. 4.03
G-AVXB*	Bensen B.8 Gyrocopter	PCL-1	G-ARTN	26.10.67	Not known	(Kingsbridge)	23. 6.87P
	(Rebuild of Campbell-Bensen B.7Mc G-ARTN [DC/61/008 & then 8]: designated "Lovegrove PL.1 Gyrocopter" 6.80: cancelled by CAA 4.12.90: stored 10.98)						
G-AVXC	Slingsby Nipper T.66 RA.45 Srs.3 (Ardem 4C02)	S.108/1605		26.10.67	D.S.T.Eggleton	Waits Farm, Belchamp Walter	3. 5.02P
G-AVXD	Slingsby Nipper T.66 RA.45 Srs.3 (VW 1834 Acro)	S.109/1606		26.10.67	R.L.Fraser t/a Tayside Nipper Group	Dundee	29.10.02P
G-AVXF	Piper PA-28R-180 Cherokee Arrow	28R-30044	N11C	26.10.67	J.A.Lunness t/a JDR Arrow Group	Top Farm, Croydon	25. 6.04
G-AVXI*	Hawker Siddeley HS.748 Srs.2A/238	1623		2.11.67	Not known	NK	30. 8.98T
					(Cancelled 24.10.01 by CAA: fuselage departed Southend on low-loader 11.01)		
G-AVXJ	Hawker Siddeley HS.748 Srs.2A/238	1624		2.11.67	Emerald Airways Ltd *(External storage 11.01)*	Exeter	22. 8.98T
G-AVXW	Rollason-Druine D.62B Condor	RAE/625		3.11.67	A.J.Cooper	Rochester	30. 9.01
G-AVXY	Auster AOP.9 *(Regd with c/n AUS/120)*	B5/10-120	XK417	7.11.67	E.Wright t/a Auster Nine Group *(As "XK417" in Army c/s)*	South Lodge Farm, Widmerpool	9. 7.00P
G-AVYE*	Hawker Siddeley HS.121 Trident 1E-140	2139		13.11.67	British Aerospace plc	Hatfield	13. 7.82
					(WFU 24.4.81: cancelled 19.5.81) (Fuselage noted 9.99)		
G-AVYK	Beagle A.61 Terrier 3	B.642	WJ357	20.11.67	J.P.Roland *(Stored 6.00)*	Eggington	28. 8.93
G-AVYL	Piper PA-28-180 Cherokee D	28-4622	N11C	24.11.67	N.E.Binner	Full Sutton	23. 5.02
G-AVYM	Piper PA-28-180 Cherokee D	28-4638	N11C	24.11.67	Carlisle Aviation (1985) Ltd	Carlisle	14. 5.04T
G-AVYP	Piper PA-28-140 Cherokee	28-24211	N11C	24.11.67	K.Hobbs t/a Aldergrove Flight Training Centre	Belfast	14. 2.04T

G-AVYR	Piper PA-28-140 Cherokee	28-24226	N11C	24.11.67	DR Flying Club Ltd	Gloucestershire	18. 6.03
G-AVYS	Piper PA-28R-180 Cherokee Arrow	28R-30456	N11C	24.11.67	A.M.Playford	Poplar Hall Farm, Elmsett	2. 2.03
G-AVYT	Piper PA-28R-180 Cherokee Arrow	28R-30472	N11C	24.11.67	J.R.Tindale	Blackpool	7. 6.03
G-AVYV	Jodel Wassmer D.120A Paris-Nice	252	F-BMAM	27.11.67	A.J.Sephton *(Stored 4.96)*	Brickhouse Farm, Frogland Cross	30. 8.93P
G-AVZB*	LET Z-37 Cmelak	04-08	OK-WKQ	30.11.67	Science Museum Air Transport Coln & Storage Facility *(Cancelled 21.12.88 as WFU)*	Wroughton	5. 4.84A
G-AVZI	Bölkow Bö.208C Junior	673	D-EGZF	19.12.67	C.F.Rogers *(Stored @ home 10.00)*	(Wheathampstead)	24. 7.76
G-AVZN	Beagle B.121 Pup 1	B121-006		19.12.67	D J Mounter t/a Shipdham Aviators Flying Group	Shipdham	16. 8.04
G-AVZP	Beagle B.121 Pup 1	B121-008		19.12.67	T.A.White	Bagby	21. 6.04
G-AVZR	Piper PA-28-180 Cherokee C	28-4114	N4779L	19.12.67	Lincoln Aero Club Ltd	Sturgate	4. 5.03T
G-AVZU	Reims Cessna F150H	F150-0283		29.12.67	R.D. & E.Forster *(Op Norfolk & Norwich Aero Club)*	Beccles	1.12.02T
G-AVZV	Reims Cessna F172H	F172-0511		29.12.67	E.L. & D.S.Lightbown	Crosland Moor	3.12.03
G-AVZW	EAA Model P Biplane (Lycoming O-290)	PFA 1314		29.12.67	R.G.Maidment & G.R.Edmondson	(Goodwood)	19. 9.02P
G-AVZX	SOCATA MS.880B Rallye Club	1165		29.12.67	J.Nugent	(Glengeary, Co.Dublin)	19.11.02

G-AWAA – G-AWZZ

G-AWAA*	SOCATA MS.880B Rallye Club	1174		29.12.67	(P.A.Cairns) *(Stored 10.95: cancelled 4.3.99 by CAA) (Noted 8.01)*	NK	4. 8.91
G-AWAC	SOCATA GY-80-180 Horizon	234		29.12.67	Gardan Party Ltd *"Le Fantome"*	Popham	11. 6.04
G-AWAH	Beechcraft D55 Baron	TE-540		1. 1.68	B.J.S.Grey	Duxford	2. 7.03
G-AWAJ	Beechcraft D55 Baron	TE-536		1. 1.68	Standard Hose Ltd	Blackpool	19. 6.04
G-AWAT	Rollason-Druine D.62B Condor	RAE/627		8. 1.68	Tamwood Ltd	Shoreham	16. 7.04
G-AWAU*	Vickers FB.27A Vimy rep	VAFA-02	"H651"	8. 1.68	RAF Museum *"Triple First"* *(Cancelled 19.7.73 as WFU) (As "F8614")*	Hendon	4. 8.69
G-AWAV*	Reims Cessna F150F *(Wichita c/n 15062476)*	F150-0007	OY-DKL	5. 1.68	Not known *(Damaged Ipswich 10.10.83: noted 5.98)*	Shobdon	
G-AWAW*	Reims Cessna F150F *(Wichita c/n 15063167)*	F150-0037	OY-DKJ	5. 1.68	The Science Museum (Flight Laboratory) *(Cancelled 16.5.90 as WFU)*	South Kensington, London SW7	8. 6.92T
G-AWAX	Cessna 150D *(Tail-wheel conversion)*	15060153	OY-TRJ N4153U	5. 1.68	H.H.Cousins	Fenland	14. 8.04
G-AWAZ	Piper PA-28R-180 Cherokee Arrow	28R-30512	N11C	8. 1.68	R.Z.Staniszewski	Barton	28. 7.02
G-AWBA	Piper PA-28R-180 Cherokee Arrow	28R-30528	N11C	8. 1.68	A.Taplin & G.A.Dunster t/a March Flying Group	Stapleford	16. 2.03
G-AWBB	Piper PA-28R-180 Cherokee Arrow	28R-30552	N11C	8. 1.68	M.D.Parker & J.Lowe	Bourn	24. 6.02
G-AWBC	Piper PA-28R-180 Cherokee Arrow	28R-30572	N11C	8. 1.68	Anglo Aviation (UK) Ltd	Bournemouth	28.12.03
G-AWBE	Piper PA-28-140 Cherokee	28-24266	N11C	8. 1.68	B.E.Boyle	Shenington	28. 6.02
G-AWBG	Piper PA-28-140 Cherokee	28-24286	N11C	8. 1.68	Westward Airways (Lands End) Ltd	St.Just	26. 4.04T
G-AWBH	Piper PA-28-140 Cherokee	28-24306	N11C	8. 1.68	Proofgolden Ltd t/a Mainstreet Aviation	Newcastle	16.10.01T
G-AWBJ	Sportavia Fournier RF4D	4055		12. 1.68	J.M.Adams	RAF Syerston	6. 4.02P
G-AWBM	Druine D.31A Turbulent (VW 1700)	PFA 1647		17. 1.68	A.D.Pratt	North Coates	20. 7.95P
G-AWBN	Piper PA-30 Twin Comanche B	30-1472	N8517Y	18. 1.68	Stourfield Investments Ltd	Jersey	2.12.02
G-AWBS	Piper PA-28-140 Cherokee	28-24331	N11C	22. 1.68	M.A.English & T.M.Brown	Little Snoring	25.11.01
G-AWBT*	Piper PA-30 Twin Comanche B	30-1668	N8508Y	22. 1.68	Cranfield University	Cranfield	25. 3.89
	(Damaged Humberside 10.3.88: cancelled 15.7.88 as WFU) (Instructional airframe 6.00)						
G-AWBU	Morane-Saulnier Type N Rep (Continental C90-8F)	PPS/REP/7		22. 1.68	Bianchi Aviation Film Services Ltd *(As "MS824" in French AF c/s)* *(Op "Blue Max" Movie Aircraft Collection)*	Booker	29. 6.01P
G-AWBW*	Reims Cessna F172H	F172-0486		22. 1.68	Brunel Technical College	Ashley Down, Bristol	15. 5.75
	(Crashed Compton Abbas 20.5.73: cancelled 23.5.74 as WFU) (Instructional airframe 6.91) (Current status unknown)						
G-AWBX	Reims Cessna F150H	F150-0286		22. 1.68	J.Meddings	Tatenhill	20.12.02
G-AWCK*	Reims Cessna F150H	F150-0278		25. 1.68	Not Known *(Crashed Baginton 30.9.75: noted 5.98)*	Shobdon	
G-AWCM	Reims Cessna F150H	F150-0281		25. 1.68	R.Garbett	Wolverhampton	14. 8.99T
G-AWCN	Reims FR172E Rocket	FR17200020		25. 1.68	Y.F.Herdman	Stapleford	4. 7.04
G-AWCO*	Reims Cessna F150H	F150-0338		29. 1.68	Not known	Biggin Hill	29. 8.75
	(Cancelled 14.10.86 by CAA) (Wreck in open storage 2.95) (Current status unknown)						
G-AWCP	Reims Cessna F150H *(Tail-wheel conversion)*	F150-0354		29. 1.68	C.E.Mason	Shobdon	12. 2.03

G-AWCR*	Piccard Ax6 HAFB	6204		29. 1.68	British Balloon Museum & Library Newbury		
					"London Pride 1" (Cancelled 24.5.78 as WFU)		
G-AWDA	Slingsby Nipper T.66 RA.45 Srs.3			7. 2.68	J.A.Cheesbrough	(Ottringham)	16. 5.02P
	(VW Acro 1834)	S.117/1624					
G-AWDO	Druine D.31 Turbulent	PFA 1649		21. 2.68	R.N.Crosland	Deanland, Hailsham	8. 5.02P
	(VW 1600)						
G-AWDP	Piper PA-28-180 Cherokee D	28-4870	N11C	21. 2.68	B.H. & P.M.Illston	Norwich	7.12.01T
					(Op Norwich School of Flying)		
G-AWDR	Reims FR172E Rocket	FR17200004		21. 2.68	B.A.Wallace	Nuthampstead	9. 4.04
G-AWDU	Brantly B.2B	481		23. 2.68	B.M.Freeman	(Stourport-on-Severn)	22. 7.01
G-AWDW	Campbell-Bensen CB.8MS	DS.1330		26. 2.68	M.R.Langton	(Taplow)	7.10.71P
	(McC.4318C)				*(Stored 12.00)*		
G-AWEF	SNCAN Stampe SV-4C	549	F-BDCT	29. 3.68	The Tiger Club (1990) Ltd	Headcorn	19.12.04T
	(DH Gipsy Major)						
G-AWEI	Rollason-Druine D.62B Condor	RAE/628		6. 3.68	J.M.C.Coyle *(Stored 6.01)*		
						Roughay Farm, Bishops Waltham	10.11.98T
G-AWEL	Sportavia Fournier RF4D	4077		7. 3.68	A.B.Clymo	Wolverhampton	14.11.02P
G-AWEM	Sportavia Fournier RF4D	4078		7. 3.68	B.J.Griffin	Wickenby	11. 6.02P
G-AWEN*	SAN Jodel DR.1050 Ambassadeur	67	F-BIVD	8. 3.68	(Skycraft Ltd)	(Spalding)	8.11.85
			(Crashed Crosland Moor 11.8.83: cancelled 28.11.91 by CAA) (Stored 11.01)				
G-AWEO*	Reims Cessna F150H	F150-0342		11. 3.68	Not known	Shobdon	30. 9.90T
			(Damaged Coventry 22.11.89: cancelled 30.1.90 as destroyed) (On rebuild 3.96)				
G-AWEP	Barritault JB-01 Minicab	PFA 1801		12. 3.68	A.Louth	(Boston)	20.11.02P
	(Continental C90)						
G-AWES	Cessna 150H	15068626	N22933	20. 3.68	P.Montgomery-Stuart	Leicester	5. 8.84
			(Damaged in gale @ Glenrothes 2.10.81: on rebuild 1.97: current status unknown)				
G-AWET	Piper PA-28-180 Cherokee D	28-4871	N11C	21. 3.68	Broadland Flying Group Ltd	Old Buckenham	25. 5.03
G-AWEV	Piper PA-28-140 Cherokee	28-24460	N11C	21. 3.68	Norflight Ltd	Ludham	6. 1.01
G-AWEX	Piper PA-28-140 Cherokee	28-24472	N11C	21. 3.68	N.D. Wyndow	Coventry	10. 5.04
					t/a Sir W.G.Armstrong-Whitworth Flying Group		
G-AWEZ	Piper PA-28R-180 Cherokee Arrow		N11C	21. 3.68	T.R.Leighton, R.G.E.Simpson & D.A.C.Clissett		
		28R-30592				Stapleford	7.12.02
G-AWFB	Piper PA-28R-180 Cherokee Arrow		N11C	21. 3.68	J.C.Luke	Filton	19.11.01
		28R-30689					
G-AWFC	Piper PA-28R-180 Cherokee Arrow		N11C	21. 3.68	B.J.Hines	White Waltham	23. 8.04
		28R-30670					
G-AWFD	Piper PA-28R-180 Cherokee Arrow		N11C	21. 3.68	D.J.Hill	Cambridge	19. 5.02
		28R-30669					
G-AWFF	Reims Cessna F150H	F150-0280		25. 3.68	West Wales Airport Ltd	Gloucestershire	19. 9.02T
G-AWFH*	Reims Cessna F150H	F150-0274		25. 3.68	Cheshire Fire Brigade Training School		
						Winsford	17.12.81
	(Crashed Swanton Morley 16.12.79: fitted with tail from G-AWTX: demonstrator 12.93) (Current status unknown)						
G-AWFJ	Piper PA-28R-180 Cherokee Arrow		N11C	26. 3.68	Parplon Ltd	Barton	7. 5.02
		28R-30688					
G-AWFN	Rollason-Druine D.62B Condor	RAE/629		27. 3.68	R.James	Shobdon	17. 6.02P
G-AWFO	Rollason-Druine D.62B Condor	RAE/630		27. 3.68	R.E.Major	Porthtowan, Cornwall	5.11.02P
G-AWFP	Rollason-Druine D.62B Condor	RAE/631		27. 3.68	D.J.Taylor	Blackbushe	22. 5.04
					t/a Blackbushe Flying Club		
G-AWFR	Druine D.31 Turbulent			27. 3.68	J.R.Froud	(Edenbridge, Kent)	
		SU.001 & PFA 1652			*(Under construction 2000)*		
G-AWFT	Jodel D.9 Bebe	PFA 932		29. 3.68	W.H.Cole	Spilsted Farm, Sedlescombe	22. 7.69P
	(VW 1200)				*(Stored 8.94: noted 5.01)*		
G-AWFW	SAN Jodel D.117	599	PH-VRE	2. 4.68	C.J.Rodwell	(Keighley)	30. 8.02P
			F-BHXU				
G-AWFZ	Beechcraft 19A Musketeer Sport		N2811B	3. 4.68	K A W Ashcroft	(St Neots)	12. 5.94
		MB-323			*(Current status unknown)*		
G-AWGD	Reims Cessna F172H	F172-0503		5. 4.68	R.P.Vincent	Shoreham	18. 7.03T
G-AWGK	Reims Cessna F150H	F150-0347		8. 4.68	G.E.Allen	(Lincoln)	1. 5.04
G-AWGM*	Mitchell Kittiwake II	002 & PFA 1329		9. 4.68	M.K.Field	Astley, Shrewsbury	13.10.86P
	(Continental O-240-A)	*(Damaged Halton 18.1.86: open store 9.95: cancelled 4.3.99 by CAA) (Current status unknown)*					
G-AWGN	Sportavia Fournier RF4D	4084		9. 4.68	R.H.Ashforth	Gloucestershire	9. 6.02P
					t/a The Gloster Aero Group		
G-AWGR	Reims Cessna F172H	F172-0484		9. 4.68	Pauline A.Hallam	Barton	27. 5.04
G-AWGY*	Reims Cessna F150H	F150-0306		11. 4.68	Not known	Shobdon	10..4.82
			(Crashed landing Dunkeswell 9.4.82 & cancelled) (Noted 3.96: current status unknown)				
G-AWGZ	Taylor JT.1 Monoplane			17. 4.68	R.L.Sambell	Stoke Golding	21. 6.93P
	(Ardem 4C02)	M.1 & PFA 1406			*(Damaged Sleap 14.7.92: current status unknown)*		
G-AWHX	Rollason Beta B.2	RAE/04	(G-ATEE)	17. 4.68	S.G.Jones *"Vertigo"*	Membury	14. 6.87P
					(On rebuild 10.01)		
G-AWHY	Falconar F-11-3	PFA 1322	G-BDPB	17. 4.68	B.E.Smith	Wellcross Grange, Slinford	21. 5.02P
	(Continental C90)		(G-AWHY)				
G-AWIF*	Brookland Mosquito	3 & LC.1		17. 4.68	Not known	St.Merryn	7. 1.82P
					(Cancelled 30.5.84 as WFU) (Stored 8.01)		

G-AWII	Supermarine 349 Spitfire LF.Vc		AR501	25. 4.68	The Shuttleworth Trust	Old Warden	15. 5.02P
	(Built Westland Aircraft) WASP/20/223				*(As "AR501/NN-A" in 310 Sqn c/s)*		
G-AWIJ*	Supermarine 329 Spitfire IIA	CBAF.14	P7350	25. 4.68	Battle of Britain Memorial Flight	RAF Coningsby	
					(Returned to RAF & cancelled 29.2.84 to MOD) (As "P7350/BA-Y" in 277 Sqdn c/s)		
G-AWIP	Phoenix Luton LA-4A Minor			30. 4.68	J.Houghton	(North Ferriby)	8. 5.89P
	(Continental A65)	PAL/1308 & PFA 830			*(Damaged near Holme-on-Spalding Moor 20.7.88: stored 2000)*		
G-AWIR	Bushby-Long Midget Mustang	PFA 1315		30. 4.68	K.E.Sword	Leicester	6. 3.90P
	(Continental O-200-A)				*(On overhaul 1991: current status unknown)*		
G-AWIT	Piper PA-28-180 Cherokee D	28-4987	N11C	30. 4.68	Cherry Orchard Aparthotel Ltd	Ronaldsway	16. 6.02T
					(Op Manx Flyers Aero Club)		
G-AWIV	Airmark TSR.3	PFA 1325		30. 4.68	F.R.Hutchings	St. Just	17. 6.02P
	(Continental PC60)				*"Stor"*		
G-AWIW	SNCAN Stampe SV-4B	532	F-BDCC	2. 5.68	R.E.Mitchell	RAF Cosford	6. 5.73
					(On rebuild 8.99)		
G-AWJE	Slingsby Nipper T.66 RA.45 Srs.3			8. 5.68	T.S.Mosedale	Barton	30. 8.01P
	(VW 1834)	S.121/1628					
G-AWJF*	Slingsby Nipper T.66 RA.45 Srs.3			8. 5.68	S.Maric	(Glasgow)	7. 6.88P
		S.122/1629			*(Cancelled 17.9.91 by CAA) (Stored 6.00)*		
G-AWJV*	de Havilland DH.98 Mosquito TT.35		TA634	21. 5.68	De Havilland Heritage Museum	London Colney	
					(Cancelled 19.10.70 as WFU) (As "TA634/8K-K" in 571 Sqdn c/s)		
G-AWJX	Moravan Zlin Z.526 Trener Master			22. 5.68	Aerobatics International Ltd *(Stored 5.01)*		
		1049				Rushett Manor, Chessington	29. 5.85A
G-AWJY	Moravan Zlin Z.526 Trener Master			22. 5.68	M.Gainza	White Waltham	26. 4.03
		1050					
G-AWKD	Piper PA-17 Vagabond	17-192	F-BFMZ	27. 5.68	A.T. & Mrs.M.R.Dowie	Scotland Farm, Hook	12. 9.02P
	(Continental A65)		N4892H				
G-AWKM	Beagle B.121 Pup 1	B121-017		11. 6.68	D.M.G.Jenkins		
						Bourne Park, Hurstbourne Tarrant	29. 6.84
					(Damaged Swansea 7.91: stored less wings 10.01)		
G-AWKO	Beagle B.121 Pup 1	B121-019		11. 6.68	E.C.Felix	Elstree	7. 6.04T
G-AWKP*	CEA Jodel DR.253 Regent	130		14. 6.68	Blackpool Air Centre	Blackpool	
					(Forced landed SE Waterford on 8.6.98: cancelled 13.10.98 by CAA) (Fuselage noted 12.01)		
G-AWKT	SOCATA MS.880B Rallye Club	1235		17. 6.68	A.Ringland & P.Keating	Enniskellen	5. 3.03
G-AWKX*	Beechcraft A65 Queen Air	LC-303		21. 6.68	Northbrook College	Shoreham	25.10.89T
					(Cancelled 19.12.90 as WFU) (Instructional airframe 8.97)		
G-AWLA	Reims Cessna F150H	F150-0269	N13175	27. 6.68	T.A.White t/a Bagby Aviation	Bagby	28. 6.04T
G-AWLF	Reims Cessna F172H	F172-0536		27. 6.68	Gannet Aviation Ltd	City of Derry	6 .7.03
G-AWLG	SIPA 903	82	F-BGHG	27. 6.68	S.W.Markham	Valentine Farm, Odiham	22. 8.79P
					(Stored 1997: current status unknown)		
G-AWLI	Piper PA-22-150 Tri-Pacer	22-5083	N7256D	1. 7.68	J.S.Lewery *"Little Peach"*	Shoreham	15. 8.02
G-AWLJ*	Reims Cessna F150H	F150-0328		3. 7.68	Not known	Shobdon	
					(Crashed landing Tillingham 20.11.84: cancelled 3.8.94 by CAA) (Remains noted 4.97)		
G-AWLM*	Campbell-Bensen B.8MS	CA/311	EI-ATE	8. 7.68	Not known	Haslemere, Surrey	20. 3.80P
	(McCulloch 4318A)		G-AWLM		*(Cancelled 16.12.91 by CAA) (Stored 1992: current status unknown)*		
G-AWLO	Boeing Stearman E75 (PT-13D) Kaydet		5Y-KRR	9. 7.68	N.D.Pickard	Little Gransden	7.10.01
	(P&W R985)	75-5563	VP-KRR/42-17400				
G-AWLP	Mooney M.20F Executive 21	680200		9. 7.68	I.C.Lomax	Ottringham	7. 7.00
G-AWLR	Slingsby Nipper T.66 RA.45 Srs.3			9. 7.68	T.D.Reid	Newtownards, Co.of Down	6. 7.01P
		S.125/1662					
G-AWLS	Slingsby Nipper T.66 RA.45 Srs.3			9. 7.68	G.A.Dunster & B.Gallagher		
		S.126/1663				(Loughton, Essex)	25. 3.88P
					(Damaged Stapleford 14.1.88: on rebuild 1995: current status unknown)		
G-AWLX*	Auster 5 J/2 Arrow	2378	F-BGJQ	10. 7.68	W.J.Taylor	RAF West Raynham	23. 4.70
			OO-ABZ		*(Cancelled 14.4.73: on rebuild 11.93: current status unknown)*		
G-AWLZ	Sportavia Fournier RF4D	4099		12. 7.68	J.H.Taylor	Nympsfield	31. 1.02P
					t/a Nympsfield RF4 Group		
G-AWMD	Jodel D.11	PFA 904		19. 7.68	D.A.Barr-Hamilton	Shobdon	23. 4.02P
	(Continental C90)				*"Moby Dick"*		
G-AWMF	Piper PA-18-150 Super Cub	18-8674	N4356Z	23. 7.68	Booker Gliding Club Ltd	Booker	26. 8.03
	(Lycoming O-360-A4)						
G-AWMI	AESL Airtourer T.2 (115)	505		24. 7.68	M.Furse	Cardiff	10. 5.04
G-AWMN	Phoenix Luton LA-4A Minor	PFA 827		30. 7.68	B.J.Douglas	Kildare	26. 7.02P
	(VW 1800)						
G-AWMP	Reims Cessna F172H	F172-0488		31. 7.68	R.J.D.Blois	Yoxford, Saxmundham	23.12.02
G-AWMR	Druine D.31 Turbulent	43 & PFA 1661		1. 8.68	M.J.Bond	RAF Kinloss	23.10.01P
	(VW 1390)				*"Demelza"*		
G-AWMT	Reims Cessna F150H	F150-0360		1. 8.68	M.Paisley	(Bangor)	24. 6.00
G-AWMZ*	Reims Cessna F172H Skyhawk	F172-0554		2. 8.68	Not known	Cark	
					(Hit ground near Bootle 18.1.76: cancelled 1.9.81 as WFU) (Used as para-training aid 10.97)		
G-AWNT	Britten-Norman BN-2A Islander	32		2. 8.68	Sterling Helicopters Ltd	Norwich	6. 6.04A
G-AWOA	SOCATA MS.880B Rallye Club	1258		2. 8.68	J.A.Rimmer	RAF Mona	20.10.02

G-AWOE	Aero Commander 680E	753-41	N3844C	5. 8.68	J.M.Houlder	Elstree	19 3.03
					t/a Elstree Flying Club		
G-AWOF	Piper PA-15 Vagabond	15-227	F-BETF	6. 8.68	C.M.Hicks	Barton	21. 5.02P
	(Continental C90)						
G-AWOH	Piper PA-17 Vagabond	17-191	F-BFMY	6. 8.68	W.M.Haley, D.Ridley & R.H.Ryle		
	(Continental C90)		N4891H		t/a The High Flatts Flying Group		
						High Flatts Farm, Chester-le-Street	18. 7.02P
G-AWOK*	Sussex Gas (Free) Balloon	SARD.1		7. 8.68	British Balloon Museum & Library	Newbury	
					"Sardinia" (Withdrawn 1970: cancelled 29.2.84 as WFU)		
G-AWOT	Reims Cessna F150H	F150-0389		14. 8.68	A.J.Hurran		
						Bourne Park, Hurstbourne Tarrant	28. 1.04T
G-AWOU	Cessna 170B	25829	VQ-ZJA	16. 8.68	S.Billington	(Macclesfield)	27. 5.01
			ZS-CKY/CR-ADU/N3185A				
G-AWOX*	Westland Wessex 60 Srs.1	WA/686	G-17-2	28. 8.68	Paintball Adventure West	Bristol	13. 1.83
			G-AWOX/5N-AJO/G-AWOX/9Y-TFB/G-AWOX/VH-BHE(3)/G-AWOX/VR-BCV/G-AWOX/G-17-1				
					(Cancelled 23.11.82 as TWFU) (Extant 2.00)		
G-AWPH	Percival P.56 Provost T.1	PAC/F/003	WV420	6. 9.68	J.A.D.Bradshaw	Three Mile Cross, Reading	28. 6.02P
G-AWPJ	Reims Cessna F150H	F150-0376		9. 9.68	W.J.Greenfield	Humberside	24. 4.02T
					(Op Humberside Flying Club)		
G-AWPN	Shield Xyla	2 & PFA 1320		13. 9.68	K.R.Snell	Deanland, Hailsham	23. 6.02P
	(Continental A65)						
G-AWPP	Reims Cessna F150H	F150-0348		13. 9.68	Coulson Flying Services Ltd	Cranfield	22. 7.01T
G-AWPS	Piper PA-28-140 Cherokee	28-20196	5N-AEK	16. 9.68	A.R.Matthews	Sittles Farm, Alrewas	19.11.03
G-AWPU	Reims Cessna F150J	F150-0411		18. 9.68	LAC (Enterprises) Ltd	Barton	29.11.03T
					t/a Lancashire Aero Club		
G-AWPW	Piper PA-12 Super Cruiser	12-3947	N78572	23. 9.68	AK Leasing (Jersey) Ltd	Jersey	5. 4.04
			NC78572				
G-AWPY	Campbell-Bensen B.8M	CA/314		20. 9.68	J.Jordan	Melrose Farm, Melbourne	
					(Current status unknown)		
G-AWPZ	Andreasson BA-4B	1	SE-XBS	24. 9.68	J.M.Vening	Goodwood	3. 5.02P
G-AWRK	Reims Cessna F150J	F150-0410		8.10.68	Systemroute Ltd	Shoreham	23. 7.03T
G-AWRP*	Cierva Rotorcraft CR.LTH.1 Grasshopper III	GB.1		14.10.68	The Helicopter Museum	Weston-super-Mare	12. 5.72P
					(Cancelled 5.12.83 as WFU)		
G-AWRS*	Avro 652A Anson C.19 Srs.2	"33785"	TX213	14.10.68	North East Aircraft Museum	Sunderland	10. 8.73
					(WFU 5.2.73 & cancelled 30.5.84 as PWFU)		
G-AWRY	Hunting-Percival P.56 Provost T.1	PAC/F/339	XF836	29.10.81	Sylmar Aviation & Services Ltd		
			8043M		*(As "XF836")*	Lower Wasing Farm, Brimpton	22. 8.88P
				(Damaged near Newbury 28.7.87: on rebuild 6.94: current status unknown)			
G-AWSA*	Avro 652A Anson C.19/2	"293483"	(N5054)	21.10.68	Norfolk & Suffolk Aviation Museum		
			G-AWSA/VL349			Flixton	
				(Cancelled 18.8.69 as sold in USA: not delivered: as "VL349")			
G-AWSD*	Reims Cessna F150J	F150-0406		21.10.68	Not known	Sibson	
			(Damaged by storm Denham 16.10.87: cancelled 8.4.92 as WFU) (Stored 5.98)				
G-AWSH	Moravan Zlin Z.526 Trener Master	1052	OK-XRH	23.11.68	Aerobatics International Ltd		
			G-AWSH			White Waltham	23.12.04T
G-AWSL	Piper PA-28-180 Cherokee D	28-4907	N11C	30.10.68	Fascia Services Ltd		
						King's Farm, Thurrock	14.11.03
G-AWSM	Piper PA-28-235 Cherokee C	28-11125	N11C	30.10.68	N.A.Wright	(London SW20)	19. 4.04T
					t/a Aviation Projects		
G-AWSN	Rollason-Druine D.62B Condor	RAE/632		31.10.68	M.K.A.Blyth	Little Gransden	27. 8.02P
	(RR Continental O-200A)						
G-AWSP	Rollason-Druine D.62B Condor	RAE/634		31.10.68	R.Q. & A.S.Bond	Enstone	23. 1.95
	(RR Continental O-200A)				*(Stored 4.00)*		
G-AWSS	Rollason-Druine D.62B Condor	RAE/636		31.10.68	N.J. & D.Butler	(Fordoun)	19.10.94P
	(RR Continental O-200A)				*(Stored 3.98: current status unknown)*		
G-AWST	Rollason-Druine D.62B Condor	RAE/637		31.10.68	P.L.Clements	Beeches Farm, South Scarle	31. 5.02P
	(RR Continental O-200A)						
G-AWSV*	Saro Skeeter AOP.12	S2/5107	XM553	31.10.68	Major M.Somerton-Rayner *(As "XM553")*		
				(Cancelled 23.5.95 as TWFU)		AAC Middle Wallop	22. 2.95P
G-AWSW	Beagle D.5/180 Husky	3690	XW635	4.11.68	C.Tyers	Spanhoe	18. 5.01T
			G-AWSW		t/a Windmill Aviation *(As "XW635")*		
G-AWTJ	Reims Cessna F150J	F150-0419		8.11.68	D.G.Williams	Headcorn	8.12.04T
G-AWTL	Piper PA-28-180 Cherokee D	28-5068	N11C	12.11.68	E.Alexander	Andrewsfield	23. 7.04T
G-AWTS	Beechcraft 19A Musketeer Sport	MB-412	OO-BGN	14.11.68	J.Holden & G.Benet	Lydd	15. 8.02T
			G-AWTS/N2763B				
G-AWTV	Beechcraft 19A Musketeer Sport	MB-424	N2770B	14.11.68	J.Whittaker	(Market Drayton)	11.10.03
				(Crashed near Tilstock 10.11.00 & substantially damaged)			
G-AWTX*	Reims Cessna F150J	F150-0404		18.11.68	R.D. & E.Forster	Beccles	25. 6.95T
					(Noted 11.00) (Cancelled 13.12.01 by CAA)		
G-AWUA*	Cessna P206D Super Skylane	P206-0550	N8750Z	21.11.68	Not known	Blackpool	4.12.87
		(Damaged Thruxton 16.10.87: cancelled 11.8.88 as destroyed) (Wreck stored 12.01)					
G-AWUB	Gardan GY-201 Minicab	A.205	F-PERX	22.11.68	R.A.Hand	RAF Barkston Heath	23.10.80P
					(Noted complete 11.01)		

G-AWUE	SAN Jodel DR.1050 Ambassadeur	299	F-BKHE	22.11.68	K.W. & F.M.Wood	Insch	17.10.87
					(On rebuild 4.97: current status unknown)		
G-AWUG	Reims Cessna F150H	F150-0299		25.11.68	Fraggle Leasing Ltd	Edinburgh	31. 1.03T
					(Op Edinburgh Air Centre)		
G-AWUH*	Reims Cessna F150H	F150-0307		25.11.68	Not known	Farley Farm, Winchester	16. 7.94T
			(Cancelled 8.7.97 as WFU) (Fuselage stored 6.99) (Current status unknown)				
G-AWUJ	Reims Cessna F150H	F150-0332		25.11.68	S.R.Hughes	Netherthorpe	14. 2.03
G-AWUK*	Reims Cessna F150H	F150-0344		25.11.68	Not known	Oaksey Park	3. 9.73
		(Crashed Shoreham 4.9.71: cancelled 13.4.73 as WFU) (Stored 4.95) (Current status unknown)					
G-AWUL	Reims Cessna F150H	F150-0346		25.11.68	C.A. & L.P.Green	Drayton St.Leonard	20. 5.02
G-AWUN	Reims Cessna F150H	F150-0377		25.11.68	D.Dean	Sturgate	12.11.01
G-AWUO	Reims Cessna F150H	F150-0380		25.11.68	S.Stevens	Popham	22. 5.04
					t/a SAS Flying Group		
G-AWUT	Reims Cessna F150J	F150-0405		25.11.68	S.J.Black	Sherburn in Elmet	19.10.03
G-AWUU	Reims Cessna F150J	F150-0408	EI-BRA	25.11.68	A.L.Grey	Armshold Farm, Kingston, Cambs	15. 6.97
			G-AWUU				
G-AWUX	Reims Cessna F172H	F172-0577		25.11.68	D.K.& K.Brian, A.M.Martin & C.Kelly		
						St.Just	25. 4.04
G-AWUZ	Reims Cessna F172H	F172-0587		25.11.68	I.R.Judge	Shoreham	27.10.04
					t/a G-BUJU Flying Group		
G-AWVA	Reims Cessna F172H	F172-0597		25.11.68	Barton Air Ltd	Barton	29 6.03
G-AWVB	SAN Jodel D.117	604	F-BIBA	26.11.68	H.Davies	Swansea	31. 5.02P
G-AWVC	Beagle B.121 Pup 1	B121-026	(OE-CUP)	27.11.68	J.H.Marshall & J.J.West	Sturgate	17. 7.04
G-AWVE	CEA Jodel DR.1050/M1 Sicile Record	612	F-BMPQ	27.11.68	E.A.Taylor	Southend	18. 5.00
G-AWVF	Hunting-Percival P.56 Provost T.1	PAC/F/375	XF877	28.11.68	Hunter Wing Ltd	Sandown	19. 7.02P
					(As "XF877/J-X")		
G-AWVG	AESL Airtourer T2 (115)	513	OO-WIC	29.11.68	C.J.Scholfield	Top Farm, Croydon	9. 7.04
			G-AWVG				
G-AWVN	Aeronca 7AC Champion	7AC-6005	N2426E	4.12.68	P.K.Brown	Rush Green	19. 2.02P
			NC2426E		t/a Champ Flying Group		
G-AWVZ	Jodel D.112	898	F-PKVL	12.12.68	D.C.Stokes	Dunkeswell	16. 7.02P
G-AWWE	Beagle B.121 Pup 2	B121-032	G-35-032	12.12.68	J.N.Randle	Coventry	10. 5.02
G-AWWI	SAN Jodel D.117	728	F-BIDU	13.12.68	W.J.Evans	Rhigos	1. 6.02P
G-AWWM	Gardan GY-201 Minicab	A.195	F-BFOQ	1. 1.69	P J Brayshaw *(Current status unknown)*		
						Haddock Stone Farm, Markington	10.12.92P
G-AWWN	SAN Jodel DR.1050 Sicile	398	F-BLJA	8. 1.69	R.A.J.Hurst	Nuthampstead	18. 6.04
G-AWWO	CEA Jodel DR.1050 Sicile	552	F-BLOI	8. 1.69	A.R.Grimshaw & J.Hodcroft	Barton	15. 5.03
					t/a The Whiskey Oscar Group		
G-AWWP	Aerosport Woody Pusher Mk.3	WA/163 & PFA 1323		7. 1.69	M.S.& Mrs R.D.Bird	Pepperbox, Salisbury	
					(Stored 6.93)		
G-AWWT	Druine D.31 Turbulent	PFA 1653		15. 1.69	E.L.Phillips	Andrewsfield	23. 4.97P
	(VW 1600)				*(Damaged Andrewsfield 7.10.96: current status unknown)*		
G-AWWU	Reims FR172F Rocket	FR17200111		15. 1.69	Westward Airways (Lands End) Ltd	St.Just	16. 3.03T
G-AWWW	Cessna 401	401-0294	N8446F	19.12.68	Treble Whiskey Aviation Ltd	Blackpool	17. 6.02T
					(Op Westair Flying Services)		
G-AWXR	Piper PA-28-180 Cherokee D	28-5171	N11C	24. 1.69	Aero Club de Portugal	(Lisbon, Portugal)	14. 4.04
G-AWXS	Piper PA-28-180 Cherokee D	28-5283	N11C	24. 1.69	J.A.Hardiman	Shobdon	3. 3.03T
G-AWXZ	SNCAN Stampe SV-4C	360	F-BHMZ	30. 1.69	Bianchi Aviation Film Services Ltd		
			Fr.Mil/F-BCOI			Booker	10. 6.02A
					(Op "Blue Max" Movie Aircraft Collection)		
G-AWYB	Reims FR172F Rocket	FR17200075		30. 1.69	C.W.Larkin	Sandown	27. 8.04
G-AWYJ	Beagle B.121 Pup 2	B121-038	G-35-038	10. 2.69	H.C.Taylor	Popham	27. 4.02
G-AWYL	CEA Jodel DR.253B Regent	143		11. 2.69	K.Gillam	Radley, Hungerford	19. 4.03
G-AWYO	Beagle B.121 Pup 1	B121-041	G-35-041	11. 2.69	B.R.C.Wild	Popham	5.12.02
G-AWYV	British Aircraft Corporation One-Eleven 501EX	BAC.178		11. 2.69	European Aviation Ltd	Bournemouth	24. 6.04T
G-AWYX	SOCATA MS.880B Rallye Club	1311		11. 2.69	Marjorie J.Edwards	Henstridge	27. 6.86
					(Open storage 4.98)		
G-AWYY*	Slingsby T.57 Sopwith Camel F.1 rep	1701	"C1701"	14. 2.69	Fleet Air Arm Museum	RNAS Yeovilton	1. 9.85P
	(Clerget)		N1917H/G-AWYY		*(Cancelled 25.11.91 as WFU) (As "B6401")*		
G-AWZI*	Hawker Siddeley HS.121 Trident 3B Srs.101	2310		14. 1.69	Surrey Fire & Rescue Service HQ	Reigate	5. 8.85T
		(WFU 1.5.85: broken up 6.87: cancelled 9.7.87 as destroyed) (Fuselage used as Instructional Airframe 12.98)					
G-AWZJ*	Hawker Siddeley HS.121 Trident 3B Srs.101	2311		14. 1.69	Dumfries & Galloway Aviation Museum		
						Dumfries	12. 9.86T
					(Cancelled 7.3.86 as WFU: forward fuselage only)		
G-AWZK*	Hawker Siddeley HS.121 Trident 3B Srs.101	2312		14. 1.69	Trident Preservation Society	Heathrow	14.10.86T
					(BEA "Quarter Union Jack" c/s)		
		(WFU 1.11.85 & cancelled as WFU 29.5.90: op British Airways Service Delivery Unit: instructional airframe 12.01)					
G-AWZM*	Hawker Siddeley HS.121 Trident 3B Srs.101	2314		14. 1.69	Science Museum Air Transport Coln & Storage Facility		
						Wroughton	13.12.85T
					(WFU 13.12.85 & cancelled 18.3.86 as WFU) (British Airways titles)		

G-AWZO*	Hawker Siddeley HS.121 Trident 3B Srs.101	2316		14. 1.69	De Havilland Heritage Museum	Hatfield	13. 2.86T
	(WFU 31.12.85 & cancelled 27.5.86 as WFU: stored 2.01)						
G-AWZP*	Hawker Siddeley HS.121 Trident 3B Srs.101	2317		14. 1.69	Museum of Science & Industry	Manchester	14. 3.86T
	(WFU 13.12.85 & broken up 6.86: cancelled 27.6.86 as destroyed) (Nose section preserved)						
G-AWZR*	Hawker Siddeley HS.121 Trident 3B Srs.101	2318		14. 1.69	International Fire Training Centre *(WFU 27.9.85 & cancelled 26.3.86 as WFU) (noted 3.00)*	Teesside	9. 4.86T
G-AWZS*	Hawker Siddeley HS.121 Trident 3B Srs.101	2319		14. 1.69	International Fire Training Centre *(WFU 5.12.85 & cancelled 18.3.86 as WFU: noted 3.00)*	Teesside	9. 9.86T
G-AWZU*	Hawker Siddeley HS.121 Trident 3B Srs.101	2321		14. 1.69	British Airways Authority	Stansted	3. 7.86T
	(Cancelled 18.3.86 as WFU) (Used for training 3.00)						
G-AWZX*	Hawker Siddeley HS.121 Trident 3B Srs.101	2324		14. 1.69	Gatwick Handling Ltd	Gatwick	30. 4.84T
	(Cancelled 29.11.84 as WFU) (Ground Trainer airframe 9.99)						

G-AXAA – G-AXZZ

G-AXAB	Piper PA-28-140 Cherokee	28-20238	EI-AOA N6206W	17. 2.69	Bencray Ltd *(Op Blackpool & Fylde Aero Club)*	Blackpool	25. 6.04T
G-AXAN	de Havilland DH.82A Tiger Moth *(Official c/n EM720-85)*	85951	F-BDMM Fr.AF/EM720	21. 2.69	M.E.Carrell *(As "EM720")*	Little Gransden	17. 3.99
G-AXAS	Wallis WA-116-T/Mc (McCulloch 4318A 72hp)	217		25. 2.69	K.H.Wallis *(Noted 8.01)*	Reymerston Hall, Norfolk	15. 6.99P
	(Orig regd as Wallis WA-116-T two-seater tandem version: used major components from G-AVDH c/n 216)						
G-AXAT	SAN Jodel D.117A	836	F-BITJ	26. 2.69	P.S.Wilkinson	Insch	23. 1.02P
G-AXAU	Piper PA-30 Twin Comanche C	30-1753	N8613Y	25. 2.69	Bartcourt Ltd *(Stored 2.96: current status unknown)*	Bournemouth	8. 3.86T
G-AXBF	Beagle D.5/180 Husky	3691	OE-DEW	17.10.84	C.M.Barnes	Garden Piece, Basingstoke	8. 8.03
G-AXBG	Bensen B.8M	RC.1		12. 3.69	R.Curtis	(Bury St.Edmunds)	
G-AXBH	Reims Cessna F172H	F172-0571		12. 3.69	D.F.Ranger	Popham	20. 3.03T
G-AXBJ	Reims Cessna F172H	F172-0573		12. 3.69	T.P.Hancock t/a BJ Flying Group	Leicester	25. 1.04
G-AXBU*	Reims FR172F Rocket	FR17200073		12. 3.69	M.Hobson	(Cruden Bay, Peterhead)	23. 8.75
	(Crashed near Priestland, Darvel 13.10.74: cancelled 12.79) (Stored 6.00: current status unknown)						
G-AXBW	de Havilland DH.82A Tiger Moth	83595	6854M T5879	12. 3.69	Hunter Wing Ltd *(As "T5879/RUC-W")*	Frensham	5. 4.04
G-AXBZ	de Havilland DH.82A Tiger Moth	86552	F-BGDF Fr.AF/PG643	14. 3.69	D.H.McWhir	Newtownards, Co.of Down	6. 9.01
G-AXCA	Piper PA-28R-200 Cherokee Arrow	28R-35053	N11C	18. 3.69	R.A.Symmonds	Southend	26. 3.03
G-AXCG	SAN Jodel D.117	510	PH-VRA F-BHXI	19. 3.69	C.A.White t/a The Charlie Golf Group	Andrewsfield	20. 6.02P
G-AXCI*	Bensen B.8M	CEW.1		20. 3.69	Not known	(Lichfield)	
	(Cancelled 7.2.74 as WFU) (Stored 9.93: current status unknown)						
G-AXCL	SOCATA MS.880B Rallye Club	1321		25. 3.69	P.P.Loucas	Seething	9. 7.00
G-AXCM	SOCATA MS.880B Rallye Club	1322		25. 3.69	D.C.Maniford	Croft Farm, Defford	18.12.04
G-AXCN*	SOCATA MS.880B Rallye Club	1328		25. 3.69	J.E.Compton	Kemble	24. 7.87
	(Damaged Thruxton 16.10.87: on rebuild 1992: wrecked fuselage 5.99 & cancelled 16.10.99 as WFU)						
G-AXCX	Beagle B.121 Pup 2	B121-046	G-35-046	31. 3.69	L.A.Pink *(Stored 6.99: current status unknown)*	Farley Farm, Winchester	10. 7.94
G-AXCY	SAN Jodel D.117A	499	F-BHXB	31. 3.69	R.D.P.Cadle	Long Marston	31. 5.02P
G-AXCZ	SNCAN Stampe SV-4C	186	ZS-VFW G-AXCZ/F-BCFG	31. 3.69	J.Price *(Stored 1.02)*	Trenchard Farm, Eggesford	10. 7.83
G-AXDC	Piper PA-23-250 Aztec D	27-4169	N6829Y	8. 4.69	N.J.Lilley	Bodmin	24. 8.98T
G-AXDI	Reims Cessna F172H	F172-0574		14. 4.69	M.F. & J.R.Leusby t/a Jeanair	Rochester	29.12.02
G-AXDK	CEA DR.315 Petit Prince	378		16. 4.69	M.R.Weatherhead & T.J.Thomas t/a Delta Kilo Flying Group	Sywell	6. 5.02
G-AXDM	Hawker Siddeley HS.125 Srs.400B	25194		17. 4.69	GEC - Marconi Avionics (Holdings) Ltd *(Op BAE Systems)*	Edinburgh	7. 6.02
G-AXDN*	British Aircraft Corporation-Aérospatiale Concorde	13522 & 01		16. 4.69	Duxford Aviation Society *(Cancelled 10.11.86 as WFU)*	Duxford	30. 9.77
G-AXDV	Beagle B.121 Pup 1	B121-049		18. 4.69	T.A.White	Bagby	28. 6.04
G-AXDW	Beagle B.121 Pup 1	B121-053		18. 4.69	I.Beaty, P.J.Abbott & J.R.A.Stevens t/a Cranfield Delta Whiskey Group	Cranfield	28. 1.02
G-AXDY*	Falconar F-11	PFA 906		21. 4.69	R.A.Yates	Sibsey	
	(Incorporated redundant parts ex Jodel D.112 G-AYBR: cancelled 26.9.84 as TWFU) (Fuselage stored 9.91: current status unknown)						
G-AXED	Piper PA-25-235 Pawnee B	25-3586	OH-PIM OH-CPY/N7540Z	24. 4.69	Wolds Gliding Club Ltd	Pocklington	11. 3.03
G-AXEH*	Beagle B.125 Bulldog 1	B.125-001		25. 4.69	National Museums of Scotland/Museum of Flight *(Cancelled 15.1.77 as WFU)*	East Fortune	15. 1.77
G-AXEI*	Ward P.45 Gnome	P.45		25. 4.69	A.J.E.Smith & N.H.Ponsford *(Cancelled 30.5.84 as WFU) (Noted 12.01)*	Breighton	

G-AXEO	Scheibe SF-25B Falke	4645	D-KEBC	1. 5.69	The Borders (Milfield) Gliding Club Ltd		
						Millfield	30. 4.04
G-AXEV	Beagle B.121 Pup 2	B121-070		6. 5.69	D.S.Russell & J.Powell-Tuck		
						Gloucestershire	21. 5.03
G-AXFM*	Cierva Rotorcraft CR.LTH.1 Grasshopper III			19. 5.69	The Helicopter Museum	Weston-super-Mare	
		GB.2	*(Completed as Ground-Running Rig: cancelled 5.12.83 as WFU) (Stored 3.96)*				
G-AXFN	Jodel D.119	980	F-PHBU	19. 5.69	D.M.Jackson & P.A.Munster	Netherthorpe	17. 7.02P
					t/a Fox November Group		
G-AXGA*	Piper PA-18 Super Cub 95	18-2047	PH-NLE	22. 5.69	R.A.Yates	Sibsey	1. 8.89
	(L-18C-PI) *(Frame No.18-2059)*		(PH-CUB)/R.Neth.AF R-51/8A-51/52-2447				
			(Damaged Felthorpe 26.12.86: cancelled 29.5.87 as WFU) (Frame stored 8.00)				
G-AXGC*	SOCATA MS.880B Rallye Club	1349		23. 5.69	P.A.Crawford & M.C.Bennett	Elstree	12. 5.88
					(Stored 9.95: cancelled 21.9.00 as wfu)		
G-AXGE	SOCATA MS.880B Rallye Club	1353		23. 5.69	R.P.Loxton	(Bridport)	25. 9.04
G-AXGG	Reims Cessna F150J	F150-0440		28. 5.69	U.Schluter	Little Staughton	17. 8.03
G-AXGP	Piper J-3C-90 Cub (L-4J-PI)	12544	F-BGPS	2. 6.69	W.K.Butler	Whittles Farm, Mapledurham	9. 8.02P
	(Frame No.12374)		F-BDTM/44-80248	*(Quoted as c/n 9542 ex 43-28251)*			
G-AXGR	Phoenix Luton LA-4A Minor	PAL/1125		2. 6.69	B A Schlussler	Fenland	22. 7.02P
	(JAP J.99)						
G-AXGS	Rollason-Druine D.62B Condor	RAE/638		3. 6.69	P.A.Kirkham	Wellcross Grange, Slinfold	1. 7.02P
					t/a G-AXGS Condor Group		
G-AXGU*	Rollason-Druine D.62B Condor	RAE/640		3. 6.69	(R Chapman)	East Grinstead	22. 5.76
			(Crashed near Godalming, Surrey 31.3.75: cancelled 8.3.88 as WFU) (Stored 4.00)				
G-AXGV	Rollason-Druine D.62B Condor	RAE/641		3. 6.69	S.B.Robson	Watchford Farm, Yarcombe	18. 4.02P
G-AXGZ	Rollason-Druine D.62B Condor	RAE/643		3. 6.69	A J Cooper	Rochester	7. 5.02P
G-AXHA	Cessna 337A Super Skymaster	3370484	(EI-ATH)	5. 6.69	G.R.E.Evans	Little Staughton	30. 8.02
			N5384S				
G-AXHC	SNCAN Stampe SV-4C	293	F-BCFU	6. 6.69	D.L.Webley	Cranwell	26. 4.03
G-AXHE*	Britten-Norman BN-2A Islander	86	4X-AYV	6. 6.69	The Scottish Parachute Club	Strathallan	15. 4.94
			G-AXHE				
		(Crashed Cark 5.2.94: cancelled 31.3.94 as WFU) (Rear fuselage for para-training 6.00)					
G-AXHO	Beagle B.121 Pup 2	B121-077		9. 6.69	L.H.Grundy	Brock Farm, Billericay	24. 5.04
G-AXHP	Piper J-3C-65 Cub (L-4J-PI)	12932	F-BETT	9. 6.69	Witham (Specialist) Vehicles Ltd		
	(Frame No.12762)		NC74121/44-80636			(Grantham)	9. 8.02P
	(Regd with c/n "AF36506" which is a USAAC contract number: as "480636 A-58" in US Army c/s)						
G-AXHR	Piper J-3C-65 Cub (L-4H-PI)	10892	F-BETI	9. 6.69	K.B.Raven & E.Cundy	Hill Farm, Nayland	18. 7.02P
			43-29601		t/a G-AXHR Cub Group *(As "329601/D-44" in US Army c/s)*		
G-AXHS	SOCATA MS.880B Rallye Club	1357		9. 6.69	B. & A.Swales	Bagby	29. 5.03
G-AXHT	SOCATA MS.880B Rallye Club	1358		9. 6.69	J.M.Hedges	Elstree	19. 4.04
G-AXHV	SAN Jodel D.117A	695	F-BIDF	9. 6.69	J.S.Ponsford	Hucknall	1. 5.02P
					t/a Derwent Flying Group		
G-AXIA	Beagle B.121 Pup 1	B121-078		17. 6.69	N.J.Mines & K.Fernandez	Kemble	7. 5.04T
G-AXIE	Beagle B.121 Pup 2	B121-087		17. 6.69	G.McD.Moir	Derby	7. 6.04
G-AXIF	Beagle B.121 Pup 2	B121-088	(SE-FGV)	17. 6.69	J.A.Holmes & S.A.Self	RAF Brize Norton	16. 9.02T
					"Susie II"		
G-AXIG	Scottish Aviation Bulldog Srs.100/104			24. 6.69	A.A.Douglas-Hamilton		
		BH120/002				Archerfield Estate, Dirleton	25. 4.02
G-AXIO	Piper PA-28-140 Cherokee B	28-25764	N11C	26. 6.69	White Waltham Airfield Ltd	White Waltham	18. 1.02T
					(Op West London Aero Services)		
G-AXIR	Piper PA-28-140 Cherokee B	28-25795	N11C	26. 6.69	A.G.Birch	Weston Zoyland	10. 5.04
G-AXIW	Scheibe SF-25B Falke	4657	(D-KABJ)	3. 7.69	M.B.Hill	Nympsfield	20. 9.02
G-AXIX	AESL Airtourer T4 (150)	A.527		3. 7.69	J.C.Wood	Bidford	1 .3.04
G-AXIY*	Bird Gyrocopter	GB.001		3. 7.69	R Light & T Smith	Stockport	
					(Cancelled 9.8.91) (Complete - awaiting restoration 2.99)		
G-AXJB	Omega 84 HAFB	04		9. 7.69	Semajan Ltd	Romsey, Hants	20. 8.73S
	(Initially flown as G-AXDT)				t/a Southern Balloon Group *"Jester"*		
G-AXJH	Beagle B.121 Pup 2	B121-089		11. 7.69	D.Collings	Popham	2. 5.04
					t/a The Henry Flying Group		
G-AXJI	Beagle B.121 Pup 2	B121-090		11. 7.69	D.R.Vale	Derby	12. 8.02
G-AXJJ	Beagle B.121 Pup 2	B121-091		11. 7.69	M.L.,T.M.,D.A.& P.M.Jones	Derby	24. 8.03T
G-AXJO	Beagle B.121 Pup 2	B121-094		11. 7.69	J.A.D.Bradshaw	Three Mile Cross, Reading	9. 8.03
					"Joey"		
G-AXJR	Scheibe SF-25B Falke	4652	D-KICD	14. 7.69	R.I.Hey	Nympsfield	16. 5.03
					t/a The Falke Syndicate		
G-AXJV	Piper PA-28-140 Cherokee B	28-25572	N11C	14. 7.69	ATC (Lasham) Ltd	Lasham	7. 6.04T
G-AXJX	Piper PA-28-140 Cherokee B	28-25990	N11C	14. 7.69	Patrolwatch Ltd	Barton	2.10.04
G-AXKH	Phoenix Luton LA-4A Minor			21. 7.69	M.E.Vaisey	(Hemel Hempstead)	18. 4.84P
	(VW 1600)	PAL/1316 & PFA 823			*(Current status unknown)*		
G-AXKO	Westland-Bell 47G-4A	WA/720	G-17-5	22. 7.69	G.P.Hinkley	Channons Hall, Tibenham	27. 1.03
G-AXKS*	Westland-Bell 47G-4A	WA/723	G-17-8	22. 7.69	Museum of Army Flying	AAC Middle Wallop	21. 9.82
					(Cancelled 22.4.82 as WFU) (As "G-AXKS")		
G-AXKW	Westland-Bell 47G-4A	WA/727	G-17-12	22. 7.69	Eyre Spier Associates Ltd		
						Richmond, N.Yorks	8. 8.02T

G-AXKX	Westland-Bell 47G-4A	WA/728	G-17-13	22. 7.69	Copley Farms Ltd		
						Copley Hill Farm, Babraham	3. 6.04
G-AXKY	Westland-Bell 47G-4A	WA/729	G-17-14	22. 7.69	G.A.Knight & G.M.Vowles	Gamston	1. 8.02
G-AXLG	Cessna 310K	310K0204	N3804X	25. 7.69	Smiths (Harlow) Aerospace Ltd	Willingale	16. 7.04
G-AXLI	Slingsby Nipper T.66 RA.45 Srs.3			25. 7.69	K.R.H.Wingate	Halwell, Totnes	28. 4.02P
		S.131/1707					
G-AXLS	SAN Jodel DR.105A Ambassadeur	86	F-BIVR	31. 7.69	J.C.M.Robb	Popham	15. 3.04
					t/a Axle Flying Club		
G-AXLZ	Piper PA-18 Super Cub 95	18-2052	PH-NLB	31. 7.69	R.J.Quantrell	Low Farm, South Walsham	23. 4.00
	(L-18C-PI) *(Frame No.18-2065)*		R.Neth.AF R-45/8A-45/52-2452				
					(Damaged Low Farm 14.8.97: current status unknown)		
G-AXMA	Piper PA-24-180 Comanche	24-3467	N8214P	5. 8.69	J.D.Bingham	Gamston	18. 6.04
G-AXMD*	Omega O-20 HAFB	06		7. 8.69	British Balloon Museum & Library	Newbury	
	(Acquired second envelope c/n 07 but not known which one BBML holds) "Nimble" (Cancelled 7.12.89 as WFU)						
G-AXMN	Auster J/5B Autocar	2962	F-BGPN	14. 8.69	C.D.Wilkinson	Trenchard Farm, Eggesford	30. 6.04
G-AXMT	Dornier Bücker Bü.133C Jungmeister		N133SJ	19. 8.69	R.A.Fleming	Breighton	25. 1.02P
		46	G-AXMT/HB-MIY/U-99		*(As "U-99")*		
G-AXMW	Beagle B.121 Pup 1	B121-101		19. 8.69	DJP Engineering (Knebworth) Ltd		
						Cambridge	3. 5.04
G-AXMX	Beagle B.121 Pup 2	B121-103	VH-UPT	19. 8.69	Susan A.Jones	Derby	5.10.03T
			G-AXMX/G-35-103				
G-AXNJ	Jodel Wassmer D.120 Paris-Nice	52	F-BHYO	29. 8.69	D.I.Vernon t/a Clive Flying Group	Sleap	4.11.02P
G-AXNL	Beagle B.121 Pup 1	B121-113		3. 9.69	CAVOK Ltd	Barton	7. 4.04T
G-AXNM	Beagle B.121 Pup 1	B121-114		3. 9.69	F.E.Green *"Bertie"*		
						Bourne Park, Hurstbourne Tarrant	17.10.02
G-AXNN	Beagle B.121 Pup 2	B121-104		3. 9.69	Gabrielle Aviation Ltd	Compton Abbas	13. 8.03
					"Gabrielle"		
G-AXNP	Beagle B.121 Pup 2	B121-106		3. 9.69	J.W.Ellis	Ashcroft Farm, Winsford	1. 7.02
G-AXNR	Beagle B.121 Pup 2	B121-108		3. 9.69	J R Clegg	Raby's Farm, Great Stukeley	17. 2.02
					t/a November Romeo Group		
G-AXNS	Beagle B.121 Pup 2	B121-110		3. 9.69	D Beckwith & D Long	Gamston	8. 7.04
					t/a Derwent Aero Group		
G-AXNW	SNCAN Stampe SV-4C	381	F-BFZX	11. 9.69	Carolyn S.Grace		
			Fr.Mil			Blooms Farm, Sible Hedingham	4. 5.02
G-AXNX	Cessna 182M	18259322	N70606	16. 9.69	D.B.Harper	Biggin Hill	15. 7.02T
G-AXNZ	Pitts S-1C Special	EB.1 & PFA 1383		16. 9.69	W.A.Jordan	(Sandy)	30. 8.91P
	(Lycoming IO-360) *(Quoted c/n EB.2)*				*(Stored 12.97)*		
G-AXOH	SOCATA MS.894A Rallye Minerva 220		D-EAGU	17. 9.69	Bristol Cars Ltd	White Waltham	24. 5.03
		11062					
G-AXOJ	Beagle B.121 Pup 2	B121-109	G-35-109	24. 9.69	T.J.Martin	Rochester	27. 3.04
					t/a Pup Flying Group		
G-AXOM*	Penn-Smith Gyroplane	DJPS.1		26. 9.69	Stondon Transport Museum		
	(VW 1600)				*(Cancelled 11.10.74 as WFU)*	Lower Stondon, Beds	24. 2.71P
G-AXOR	Piper PA-28-180 Cherokee D	28-5453	N11C	30. 9.69	Oscar Romeo Aviation Ltd	Redhill	1. 4.02
G-AXOS	SOCATA MS.894A Rallye Minerva 220			3.10.69	A.V.Hurley	RAF Henlow	14. 5.03
		11079			t/a Henlow Thunderbolts		
G-AXOT	SOCATA MS.893A Rallye Commodore 180			3.10.69	P.Evans & J.C.Graves	Doncaster	26. 3.03
		11433					
G-AXOZ	Beagle B.121 Pup 1	B121-115	N70290	7.10.69	R.J.Ogborn	Hawarden	12. 9.03
			G-AXOZ/G-35-115				
G-AXPA	Beagle B.121 Pup 1	B121-116	D-EATL	7.10.69	D.G.Lewendon	Manor Farm, Glatton	4.11.87
			G-AXPA/G-35-116		*(On rebuild 10.01)*		
G-AXPB	Beagle B.121 Pup 1	B121-117	G-35-117	7.10.69	M.J.K.Seary & R.T.Austin	Leicester	11.11.01
G-AXPC	Beagle B.121 Pup 1	B121-119	PH-VRS	7.10.69	T.A.White	Bagby	30. 8.03
			G-AXPC				
G-AXPF	Reims Cessna F150K	F15000543		14.10.69	D.R.Marks	Hinton-in-the-Hedges	22. 4.02
G-AXPG	Mignet HM.293	PFA 1333		14.10.69	W.H.Cole	Spilsted Farm, Sedlescombe	20. 1.77P
	(VW 1300)				*(Noted 5.01)*		
G-AXPM	Beagle B.121 Pup 1	B121-122	G-35-122	20.10.69	R.G.Hayes	North Weald	20. 4.02
G-AXPN	Beagle B.121 Pup 2	B121-123	G-35-123	20.10.69	D.M.Bell	Top Farm, Croydon	12. 2.02
					t/a The Pup Club		
G-AXPZ	Campbell Cricket	CA/320		3.11.69	W.R.Partridge	St.Merryn	27. 4.99P
	(Rotax 582)				*(Noted 10.00)*		
G-AXRC	Campbell Cricket	CA/323		3.11.69	R.T.Jakeway	(Grantham)	18. 5.78S
	(VW 1600)		*(Damaged Wittering 22.10.77: stored Tattershall Thorpe 7.91: new owner 4.01)*				
G-AXRK*	Practavia Pilot Sprite 115			4.11.69	M.Oliver	Crowborough	
		15 & PFA 1381	*(Cancelled 26.7.91 by CAA) (Under construction 7.95) (Current status unknown)*				
G-AXRP	SNCAN Stampe SV.4A	554	F-BDCZ	7.11.69	C C Manning	Rotary Farm, Hatch	5. 6.76
	(Originally registered as SV.4C (Renault 4P): damaged Gransden 19.10.74: restored 2.85 as SV-4A G-BLOL with c/n SS-SV-R1: NTU and restored 9.94 as G-AXRP but stored as "G-BLOL" 10.99: on rebuild with DH Gipsy Major 2 @ 2.01)						
G-AXRR	Auster AOP.9	AUS.178 & B5/10/178	XR241	7.11.69	R.J.Burgess	Duxford	16. 9.02P
			G-AXRR/XR241		*(As "XR241" in Army yellow c/s)*		

G-AXRT	Reims Cessna FA150K Aerobat *(Tail-wheel conversion)*	FA15000018		12.11.69	C.C.Walley	Elstree	25. 1.03T
G-AXRU*	Reims Cessna FA150K Aerobat	FA15000020		12.11.69	Arrival Enterprises Ltd *(Cancelled 2.3.99 by CAA) (Noted 4.01)*	Haverfordwest	10.12.87
G-AXSC	Beagle B.121 Pup 1	B121-138	G-35-138	13.11.69	R.J.MacCarthy	Denham	6. 3.04
G-AXSD	Beagle B.121 Pup 1	B121-139	G-35-139	13.11.69	T.A.White t/a Bagby Aviation	Bagby	2. 9.01
G-AXSF	Nash Petrel (Lycoming O-360)	PFA 1516 & P.003		17.11.69	Nash Aircraft Ltd *(Stored 10.95: current status unknown)*	Lasham	? .4.94P
	(This second allocation of PFA 1516 has no connection with G-BACA)						
G-AXSG	Piper PA-28-180 Cherokee E	28-5605	N11C	17.11.69	Admiral Property Ltd	Old Buckenham	21. 2.02
G-AXSI	Reims Cessna F172H	F17200687	G-SNIP G-AXSI	19.11.69	A.J.G.Davis t/a St.Marys Flying Group	St.Mary's, Isles of Scilly	23. 7.04
G-AXSM	CEA Jodel DR.1051 Sicile	512	F-BLRH	20.11.69	T.R.G.Barnby & M.S.Regendanz *(New owners 6.01)*	Headcorn	3.10.98
G-AXSR	Brantly B.2B	474	G-ROOF G-AXSR/N2237U	24.11.69	A.Murzyn	West End Farm, Stevington, Bedford	6. 7.01
G-AXSW	Reims Cessna FA150K Aerobat	FA15000003		25.11.69	R.Mitchell	(Chalfont St.Giles)	2. 3.04
G-AXSZ	Piper PA-28-140 Cherokee B	28-26188	N11C	26.11.69	R.Gibson & B.Collins t/a The White Wings Flying Group	White Waltham	24. 4.03
G-AXTA	Piper PA-28-140 Cherokee B	28-26301	N11C	26.11.69	P.J.Farrell t/a G-AXTA Aircraft Group	Shoreham	25. 5.04
G-AXTC	Piper PA-28-140 Cherokee B	28-26265	N11C	26.11.69	W.J.Knott t/a G-AXTC Group	Beeches Farm, South Scarle	8. 4.02
G-AXTJ	Piper PA-28-140 Cherokee B	28-26241	N11C	26.11.69	K.Patel	Elstree	13. 2.04T
G-AXTL	Piper PA-28-140 Cherokee B	28-26247	N11C	26.11.69	Pegasus Aviation (Midlands) Ltd	Tatenhill	6.11.04
G-AXTO	Piper PA-24-260 Comanche C	24-4900	N9449P N9705N	28.11.69	Jean L.Richardson *"Betsy Baby"*	Turweston	23. 7.03
G-AXTP	Piper PA-28-180 Cherokee C	28-3791	OH-PID	1.12.69	C.W.R.Moore	Elstree	10. 1.04
G-AXTZ*	Beagle B.121 Pup 1	B121-148	G-35-148	4.12.69	R.S. & A.D.Kent	NK	14. 2.76
	(Crashed Andrewsfield 30.3.75: on rebuild 10.96: cancelled 2.3.99 by CAA) (Current status unknown)						
G-AXUA	Beagle B.121 Pup 1	B121-150	G-35-150	4.12.69	P.Wood	Bourn	12. 6.03
G-AXUB	Britten-Norman BN-2A Islander	121	5N-AIJ G-AXUB/N859JA/G-51-47	4.12.69	Headcorn Parachute Club Ltd	Headcorn	15. 5.02
G-AXUC	Piper PA-12 Super Cruiser	12-621	5Y-KFR VP-KFR/ZS-BIN	5.12.69	J.J.Bunton	Maypole Farm, Chislet	28.10.01
G-AXUE*	CEA Jodel DR.105A Ambassadeur	59	F-BKFX F-OBFX	9.12.69	L Lewis *(Crashed Bagby on 11.6.89 & cancelled 23.4.90 as WFU) (Stored for rebuild 1.02)*	(Redcar)	
G-AXUF	Reims Cessna FA150K Aerobat	FA15000043		9.12.69	W.B.Bateson	Blackpool	10. 1.03T
G-AXUM*	Handley Page 137 Jetstream 1	245		12.12.69	(IGF - Sodetag Training School) *(Cancelled 20.1.99 as PWFU) (Noted 6.01)*	Toussous-le-Noble, France	
G-AXUK	SAN Jodel DR.1050 Ambassadeur	292	F-BJYU	11.12.69	G.J. Keegan t/a Downland Flying Group (2KI)	(Lewes)	23. 8.03
G-AXUY*	SAN Jodel DR.100A Ambassadeur	51	F-BIZI	18.12.69	J.J.Mott/162 Sqdn ATC	Stockport	3.11.78
	(Crashed Ash House Farm, Winsford 3.9.78: instructional airframe 1.96)						
G-AXVB	Reims Cessna F172H	F17200703		22.12.69	R.& J.Turner	Charlton Park, Malmesbury	26. 5.04
G-AXVK	Campbell Cricket	CA/327		1. 1.70	P.C.Lovegrove *(Stored 12.00)*	(Didcot)	8. 3.89P
G-AXVM	Campbell Cricket (VW 1834)	CA/329		1. 1.70	D.M.Organ	Stoke Orchard, Cheltenham	18. 5.01P
G-AXVN	McCandless M.4 Gyroplane (VW 1700)	M4/6		5. 1.70	W.R.Partridge *(Stored 8.96: current status unknown)*	St.Merryn	
G-AXVU*	Omega 84 HAFB	09		7. 1.70	British Balloon Museum & Library "Henry VIII" *(Cancelled 22.8.89 as WFU)*	Newbury	28. 4.77S
G-AXWA	Auster AOP.9	B5/10/133	XN437	13. 1.70	M.L. & C.M.Edwards *(Noted 2.00 as "XN437")*	North Weald	
G-AXWF*	Reims Cessna F172H	F17200697		16. 1.70	Not known	Starling's Green, Clavering	22. 5.85T
	(Damaged Clacton 26/27.11.83: cancelled 3.4.89 by CAA) (Stored 7.95) (Current status unknown)						
G-AXWT	Jodel D.11 (Continental C90)	PFA 911		26. 1.70	R.C.Owen	Danehill	2. 6.00P
G-AXWV	CEA DR.253 Regent	104	F-OCKL	2. 2.70	R Friedlander & D C Ray	(Andover)	26.11.04
G-AXWZ	Piper PA-28R-200 Cherokee Arrow	28R-35605	N11C	3. 2.70	P.Walkley	Pittrichie Farm, Whiterashes	15. 9.02P
G-AXXC	Rousseau Piel CP.301B Emeraude	117	F-BJAT	4. 2.70	L.F.Clayton	Wellesbourne Mountford	15. 1.02P
G-AXXP*	Bradshaw HAB-76 (Ax7) HAFB	RB.001		20. 2.70	British Balloon Museum & Library *"Ignis Volens" (WFU 2.77: cancelled 9.9.81)*	Newbury	
G-AXXV	de Havilland DH.82A Tiger Moth	85852	F-BGJI Fr.AF/DE992	24. 2.70	C.N.Wookey *(As "DE992")*	France Farm, Upavon	17. 6.04
G-AXXW	SAN Jodel D.117	632	F-BIBN	26. 2.70	D.F.Chamberlain & J.M.Walsh	Haverfordwest	23. 8.02P

G-AXYK	Taylor JT.1 Monoplane PFA 1409 (VW 1500)		2. 3.70	D.J.Hulks & R.W.Davies Little Robhurst Farm, Woodchurch 9. 9.00P
G-AXYU	Jodel D.9 Bebe 547 (VW 1600)	EI-BVE G-AXYU	5. 3.70	P.Turton & H.C.Peake-Jones Ash House Farm, Winsford 13. 9.01P
G-AXYZ	WHE Airbuggy 1005 (VW 1600) *(Originally regd as McCandless M.4 Gyroplane)*		10. 3.70	B.Gunn (Melbourne) 22.12.92P
G-AXZA*	WHE Airbuggy 1006 (VW 1700) *(Originally regd as McCandless M.4 Gyroplane)*		10. 3.70	C Verlaan (Lelystad, The Netherlands) 15. 8.96P *(Cancelled 19.9.00 by CAA) (Current status unknown)*
G-AXZD	Piper PA-28-180 Cherokee E 28-5609	N11C	12. 3.70	G.M.Whitmore High Cross, Ware 15.10.04
G-AXZF	Piper PA-28-180 Cherokee E 28-5688	N11C	12. 3.70	E.P.C. & W.R.Rabson Compton Abbas 23. 7.04T *(Op Carill Aviation)*
G-AXZK	Britten-Norman BN-2A-26 Islander 153	V2-LAD VP-LAD/G-AXZK/G-51-153	12. 3.70	P.Johnson Hinton-in-the Hedges 14. 2.02
G-AXZM	Slingsby Nipper T.66 RA.45 Srs.3A (VW 1600) PFA 1378 *(Slingsby kit c/n S.133/1709)*		16. 3.70	G.R.Harlow Newcastle 24. 8.89P *(Damaged near Eshott 21.8.89: possible rebuild 5.90: current status unknown)*
G-AXZO	Cessna 180 31137	N3639C	17. 3.70	J.C.King t/a Bourne Park Flyers *(On rebuild 10.01)* Bourne Park, Hurstbourne Tarrant 8.12.99
G-AXZP	Piper PA-E23-250 Aztec D 27-4464	N13819	17. 3.70	D.Barnett Bristol 22. 8.04T t/a Aztec Flying Group G-AXZP
G-AXZT	SAN Jodel D.117A 607	F-BIBD	17. 3.70	N.Batty Bagby 30. 4.02P
G-AXZU	Cessna 182N Skylane 18260104	N92233	19. 3.70	C D Williams Goodwood 31. 3.02

G-AYAA – G-AYZZ

G-AYAB	Piper PA-28-180 Cherokee E 28-5804	N11C	24. 3.70	Films Ltd Fairoaks 16. 8.03
G-AYAC	Piper PA-28R-200 Cherokee Arrow 28R-35606	N11C	24. 3.70	G.A.J.Smith-Bosanquet Knettishall 23. 4.04 t/a The Fersfield Flying Group
G-AYAJ*	Cameron O-84 HAFB 11		31. 3.70	British Balloon Museum & Library Newbury *"Flaming Pearl" (Cancelled 1.2.90 as WFU)*
G-AYAL*	Omega 56 HAFB 10		2. 4.70	British Balloon Museum & Library Newbury 25. 8.76 *"Nimble II" (Cancelled 18.10.84 by CAA)*
G-AYAN	Slingsby Cadet III 003 & PFA 1385 (VW 1600)	BGA1224 RAFGSA.223	6. 4.70	D.C.Pattison "Thermal Hopper" Brunton 20. 8.02P *(Converted from T.31B [Frame No.SSK/FF776])*
G-AYAR	Piper PA-28-180 Cherokee E 28-5797	N11C	8. 4.70	Seawing Flying Club Ltd & A.Jahanfar Southend 28. 1 02T
G-AYAT	Piper PA-28-180 Cherokee E 28-5801	N11C	8. 4.70	A.J.Foyster & J.B.R.Elliot Ludham 18. 3.04T t/a G-AYAT Flying Group
G-AYAW	Piper PA-28-180 Cherokee E 28-5805	N11C	14. 4.70	R.C.Pendle & M.J.Rose Blackbushe 5. 5.02T
G-AYBD	Reims Cessna F150K F15000583		7. 4.70	Premiair Engineering Ltd Shoreham 12. 9.04T
G-AYBG	Scheibe SF-25B Falke 4696	(D-KECJ)	13. 4.70	H.H.T.Wolf Gallows Hill, Bovington 4. 4.97 *(Stored 5.98: new owner 6.01)*
G-AYBO	Piper PA-23-250 Aztec D 27-4510	N13874	15. 4.70	Twinguard Aviation Ltd Denham 28. 3.03
G-AYBP	Jodel D.112 1131	F-PMEK	16. 4.70	G.J.Langston Bidford 30.10.02P
G-AYBR	Wassmer Jodel D.112 1259	F-BMIG	16. 4.70	R.T.Mosforth Netherthorpe 30.10.02P
G-AYCC	Campbell Cricket CA/336 (Rotax 582)		20. 4.70	D.J.M.Charity Hinton-in-the-Hedges 17.12.01P
G-AYCE	Scintex CP.301C1 Emeraude 530	F-BJFH	20. 4.70	S.D.Glover Plymouth 5. 9.02P
G-AYCF	Reims Cessna FA150K Aerobat FA15000055		22. 4.70	E.J.Atkins Thruxton 8. 6.03
G-AYCG	SNCAN Stampe SV-4C 59	F-BOHF F-BBAE/Fr.Mil	24. 4.70	Nancy Bignall White Waltham 6. 6.04
G-AYCJ	Cessna TP206D Turbo Super Skylane *(Regd with c/n T206-0552)* P206-0552	N8752Z	27. 4.70	White Knuckle Airways Ltd Leeds-Bradford 30. 4.03
G-AYCK	AIA Stampe SV-4C 1139 (DH Gipsy Major)	G-BUNT G-AYCK/F-BANE	28. 4.70	J.F.Graham Jersey 12. 9.04
G-AYCN	Piper J-3C-65 Cub "13365" *(Frame No.not known: c/n quoted became PH-UCM in 11.46 & p/i is doubtful) (Stored 4.91: current status unknown)*	F-BCPO	28. 4.70	W.R. & B.M.Young Furze Hill Farm, Rosemarket, Milford Haven 27. 1.89P
G-AYCO	CEA DR.360 Chevalier 362	F-BRFI	29. 4.70	P.L.Buckley (Colchester) 30.10.03 t/a Charlie Oscar Club
G-AYCP	Jodel D.112 67	F-BGKO	30. 4.70	D.J.Nunn St.Just 28. 6.02P
G-AYCT	Reims Cessna F172H F17200724		1. 5.70	Haimoss Ltd & D.C.Scouller Old Sarum 8.12.04T *(Op Old Sarum Flying Club)*
G-AYDG	SOCATA MS.894A Rallye Minerva 220 11620		7. 5.70	Hunt and Partners Ltd Lower Wasing Farm, Brimpton 25. 5.03T
G-AYDI	de Havilland DH.82A Tiger Moth 85910	F-BDOE Fr.AF/DF174	7. 5.70	R.B. & E.W.Woods & J.D.M.Barr (Thatcham) 10. 1.03
G-AYDR	SNCAN Stampe SV-4C 307	F-BCLG	13. 5.70	A.J.McLuskie Bishopstrow Farm, Warminster 27. 3.75 *(Damaged 16.6.73: on rebuild 8.93: current status unknown)*
G-AYDW*	Beagle A.61 Terrier 2 B.646 *(Conversion of Auster 6 c/n 1936)*	G-ARLM(1) TW568	20. 5.70	Stick & Rudder Associates NK 1. 7.73 *(Cancelled 1.7.85 by CAA: on rebuild 5.97: current status unknown)*

G-AYDX	Beagle A.61 Terrier 2	B.647	VX121	20. 5.70	R.A.Kirby	Spanhoe	12. 1.03
G-AYDY	Phoenix Luton LA-4A Minor			21. 5.70	T.Littlefair	Lymington, Hants	15. 8.97P
	(VW 1600)	PAL/1302 & PFA 817			*(On rebuild 3.00)*		
G-AYDZ	CEA Jodel DR.200	01	F-BLKV	21. 5.70	M.W.Albery	Hucknall	29. 3.02
	(Lycoming O-235)		F-WLKV		t/a Zero One Group		
G-AYEB	Wassmer Jodel D.112	586	F-BIQR	26. 5.70	C.H.G.Baulf	RAF Wattisham	26. 7.02P
G-AYEC	Menavia Piel CP.301A Emeraude	249	F-BIMV	26. 5.70	J.J.Shepherd *"Antoinette"*	Netherthorpe	17. 3.02P
					t/a Red Wing Flying Group		
G-AYED	Piper PA-24-260 Comanche C	24-4923	N9417P	28. 5.70	J.V.Hutchinson	(Frangy, France)	7.11.02
G-AYEE	Piper PA-28-180 Cherokee E	28-5813	N11C	28. 5.70	Halegreen Associates Ltd		
						Hinton-in-the-Hedges	16. 6.02T
G-AYEF	Piper PA-28-180 Cherokee E	28-5815	N11C	28. 5.70	J.C.Rideout & A.L.Beaumont	Barton	1.12.01
					t/a G-AYEF Group		
G-AYEG	Falconar F-9	PFA 1321		29. 5.70	A L Smith	Sackville Farm, Riseley	16. 7.02P
	(VW 1600)						
G-AYEH	SAN Jodel DR.1050 Ambassadeur	455	F-BLJB	8. 6.70	J.W.Scott	Wellesbourne Mountford	18. 8.02
					t/a John Scott Jodel Group *"Jemima"*		
G-AYEI*	Piper PA-31 Turbo Navajo	31-631	N6730L	29. 5.70	Not known	Southend	11. 5.89
					(Cancelled 5.6.92 as WFU: hulk on fire dump 1.02)		
G-AYEJ	SAN Jodel DR.1050 Ambassadeur	253	F-BJYG	1. 6.70	J.M.Newbold	Enstone	7. 1.04
G-AYEN	Piper J-3C-65 Cub (L-4H-PI)	12184	F-BGQD	4. 6.70	P.J.Warde & C.F.Morris		
	(Frame No.12012)		(F-BGQA)/Fr.AF/44-79888			Grove Farm, Raveningham	27. 6.02P
	(Official identity is c/n 9696/43-835 but fuselages probably exchanged with F-BGQA on conversion in 1952/53)						
G-AYET*	SOCATA MS.892A Rallye Commodore 150		F-BNBR	8. 6.70	Not known	NK	15. 9.96
		10565					
	(Cancelled 22.10.96 by CAA: stored 3.97: wreck noted London Docklands in TV series 1998/99: current status unknown)						
G-AYEV	SAN Jodel DR.1050 Ambassadeur	179	F-BERH	10. 6.70	L.G.Evans	Redhill	10. 2.03
			F-OBTH/F-OBRH				
G-AYEW	CEA Jodel DR.1050 Sicile	443	F-BLMJ	11. 6.70	J.M.Gale & J.R.Hope		
						Westacott Farm, Crediton	16.11.03
G-AYEY*	Reims Cessna F150K	F15000553		15. 6.70	W.J.Moyse	Bournemouth	15.10.99T
					(Damaged near Exbury 24.6.88: stored 8.95: cancelled 2.3.99 by CAA: current status unknown)		
G-AYFA*	Scottish Aviation Twin Pioneer Mk.3		G-31-15	15. 6.70	Solway Aviation Museum	Carlisle	24. 5.82
	(Originally regd as a CC.2)	538	XM285		*(Cancelled 16.5.91 as WFU: nose only)*		
G-AYFC	Rollason-Druine D.62B Condor	RAE/644		19. 6.70	A.R.Chadwick	Breighton	26.12.02P
G-AYFD	Rollason-Druine D.62B Condor	RAE/645		19. 6.70	B.G.Manning	Little Down Farm, Milson	3. 7.04
G-AYFE	Rollason-Druine D.62C Condor	RAE/646		19. 6.70	D.I.H.Johnstone & W.T.Barnard	Strathaven	6.12.01
G-AYFF	Rollason-Druine D.62B Condor	RAE/647		19. 6.70	D.Ellis	Park Farm, Eaton Bray	9. 7.02P
					t/a Condor Syndicate		
G-AYFG	Rollason-Druine D.62C Condor	RAE/648		19. 6.70	C Jobling & A J Mackay		
						St Ghislain, Belgium	28.10 02
G-AYFP	SAN Jodel D.140 Mousquetaire	18	F-BMSI	24. 6.70	A.R.Wood	Audley End	23. 5.02
			F-OBLH/F-WNDO				
G-AYFV	Crosby Andreasson Super BA.4B			26. 6.70	A.R.C.Mathie	RAF Coltishall	5. 7.95P
	(Lycoming IO-320)	002 & PFA 1359			*(Current status unknown)*		
G-AYGA	SAN Jodel D.117	436	F-BHNU	30. 6.70	R.L.E.Horrell	Oxenhope	10. 4.02P
G-AYGB*	Cessna 310Q	310Q0111	N7611Q	2. 7.70	Perth College	Perth	23.10.87T
					(Cancelled 23.6.94 by CAA: instructional airframe 6.00)		
G-AYGC	Reims Cessna F150K	F15000556		2. 7.70	P Maher	Barton	21. 5.04
					t/a Alpha Aviation Group		
G-AYGD	CEA Jodel DR.1050 Sicile	515	F-BLRE	3. 7.70	D.Street	Netherthorpe	9.12.04
					t/a G-AYGD Flying Group		
					(Damaged Grove Farm, Retford 24.6.99: current status unknown)		
G-AYGE	SNCAN Stampe SV-4C	242	F-BCGM	6. 7.70	I.,L.J. & S.Proudfoot	Duxford	4. 6.03
G-AYGG	Jodel Wassmer D.120 Paris-Nice	184	F-BJPH	10. 7.70	J.M.Dean	Stoneacre Farm, Farthing Corner	5. 4.02P
G-AYGX	Reims FR172G Rocket	FR17200208		15. 7.70	D.Waterhouse	Barton	13. 8.03
					t/a Reims Rocket Group		
G-AYHA	American AA-1 Yankee Clipper		N6196L	21. 7.70	E.C.Felix	Elstree	4. 3.02
		AA1-0396					
G-AYHX	SAN Jodel D.117A	903	F-BIVE	23. 7.70	L.J.E.Goldfinch	Old Sarum	2. 5.02P
G-AYHY	Sportavia Fournier RF4D	4156		24. 7.70	P.J. & S.M.Wells	Booker	3. 8.03
G-AYIA	Hughes 369HS (500)	99-0120S		29. 7.70	G.D.E.Bilton	Sywell	16. 7.88
					(Damaged S.France 1.6.88: stored for spares 8.97: current status unknown)		
G-AYIG	Piper PA-28-140 Cherokee C	28-26878	N11C	31. 7.70	Biggles Ltd	Booker	26.11.02T
G-AYII	Piper PA-28R-200 Cherokee Arrow		N11C	4. 8.70	P.W.J. & P.A.S.Gove	Exeter	22. 3.03
		28R-35736					
G-AYIJ	SNCAN Stampe SV-4B	376	F-BCOM	4. 8.70	T.C.Beadle	Spilsted Farm, Sedlescombe	16. 6.03
G-AYIM	Hawker Siddeley HS.748 Srs.2A/270		G-11-687	11. 8.70	Emerald Airways Ltd	Liverpool	21.12.04T
		1687	CS-TAG/G-AYIM/G-11-5				
G-AYIT	de Havilland DH.82A Tiger Moth	86343	F-BGEZ	20. 8.70	S.R.Pollitt & H.M.Eassie t/a Ulster Tiger Group		
			Fr.AF/NL896			Newtownards, Co.of Down	15.11.04
G-AYJA	SAN Jodel DR.1050 Ambassadeur	150	F-BJJJ	8. 9.70	G.Connell	Navan, Co.Meath	2. 6.02
G-AYJB	SNCAN Stampe SV-4C	560	F-BDDF	8. 9.70	F.J.M. & J.P.Esson	Bere Farm, Warnford	26. 5.01
					"Odette"		

G-AYJD	Alpavia Fournier RF3	11	F-BLXA	8. 9.70	E.Shouler	Beeches Farm, South Scarle	6. 8.02P
G-AYJP	Piper PA-28-140 Cherokee C	28-26403	N11C	15. 9.70	RAF Brize Norton Flying Club Ltd		
						RAF Brize Norton	9. 5.04T
G-AYJR	Piper PA-28-140 Cherokee C	28-26694	N11C	15. 9.70	RAF Brize Norton Flying Club Ltd		
						RAF Brize Norton	8. 1.04T
G-AYJW	Reims FR172G Rocket	FR17200225		17. 9.70	N.D.Wyndow	Coventry	27. 7.03T
					t/a Sir W.G. Armstrong-Whitworth Flying Group		
G-AYJY	Isaacs Fury II	PFA 1373		23. 9.70	M.F.Newman	Swanton Morley	1.10.02P
	(RR Continental C90)						
G-AYKA*	Beechcraft 95-B55A Baron	TC-523	HB-GEW	30. 9.70	Northbrook College	Shoreham	15. 9.91
			G-AYKA/D-IKUN/N8683M				
			(Damaged Elstree 18. 6.89: cancelled 28.2.90 by CAA: instructional airframe 8.99)				
G-AYKD	SAN Jodel DR.1050 Ambassadeur	351	F-BKHR	30. 9.70	B F Hill	(Tamworth)	20. 6.03
G-AYKJ	SAN Jodel D.117A	730	F-BIDX	6.10.70	J.M.Alexander	Lichfield	20. 6.02P
G-AYKK	SAN Jodel D.117	378	F-BHGM	6.10.70	D.M.Whitham	Crosland Moor	22. 5.85S
					(On rebuild 11.99: current status unknown)		
G-AYKL	Reims Cessna F150L	F15000676		6.10.70	M.A.Judge	Netherthorpe	19.12.02T
					t/a Aero Group 78		
G-AYKS	Leopoldoff L.7 Colibri	125	F-PCZX	8.10.70	W.B.Cooper	Walkeridge Farm, Overton	11.11.02P
	(Continental A65)		F-APZQ				
G-AYKT	SAN Jodel D.117	507	F-BGYY	9.10.70	D.I.Walker	Lower Upham Farm, Chisledon	1. 8.02P
			F-OAYY				
G-AYKW	Piper PA-28-140 Cherokee C	28-26931	N11C	12.10.70	B.A.Mills	Bourn	18.11.02T
G-AYKX	Piper PA-28-140 Cherokee C	28-26933	N11C	12.10.70	B.Malpas	Woodford	9. 1.04
					t/a Robin Flying Group		
G-AYKZ	SAI KZ-VIII	202	HB-EPB	13.10.70	R.E.Mitchell	RAF Cosford	17. 7.81P
	(DH Gipsy Major 7)		OY-ACB		*(Stored 3.95: current status unknown)*		
G-AYLA	AESL Airtourer T2 (115)	524		12.10.70	D.S.P.Disney	Bristol	2. 7.01
G-AYLC	CEA Jodel DR.1051 Sicile	536	F-BLZG	12.10.70	E.W.B.Trollope		
	(Lycoming O-235)					Wing Farm, Longbridge Deverill	3. 9.02P
G-AYLF	CEA Jodel DR.1051 Sicile	547	F-BLZQ	14.10.70	L.Daglish	(Harpenden)	18. 7.01
					t/a Sicile Flying Group		
G-AYLL	CEA Jodel DR.1050 Ambassadeur	11	F-BJHK	27.10.70	C.Joly	Lee-on-Solent	18. 5.01
G-AYLP	American AA-1 Yankee	AA1-0445	EI-AVV	21.10.70	D.Nairn & E.Y.Hawkins	Henstridge	10. 2.02
			G-AYLP				
G-AYLV	Wassmer Jodel D.120 Paris-Nice	300	F-BNCG	27.10.70	M.R.Henham	(London N2)	13. 9.83P
					(Current status unknown)		
G-AYLZ	SPP CZL Super Aero 45 Srs.04	06-014	9M-AOF	2.11.70	M.J.Cobb	(East Grinstead)	11. 6.76
			F-BILP *(Damaged Andrewsfield 2.1.76: stored 1997: current status unknown)*				
G-AYME	Sportavia Fournier RF5	5089		6.11.70	R.D.Goodger	Laddingford	26. 6.02P
G-AYMF*	AESL Airtourer T6/24	B.557		10.11.70	Not known	St.Just	20. 1.73
			(Crashed near St.Just 9.6.72: wreck stored 4.96: current status unknown)				
G-AYMK	Piper PA-28-140 Cherokee C	28-26772	N11C	17.11.70	M.Wright	Newcastle	8.10.04
			(PT-DPU)		t/a The Piper Flying Group		
G-AYMO	Piper PA-23-250 Turbo Aztec C		5Y-ACX	18.11.70	R.Stephenson	Southend	4. 4.04
		27-2995	N5845Y/(N5844Y)				
G-AYMP*	Phoenix Currie Wot Special	PFA 3014		18.11.70	H.F.Moffatt	Woodlow Farm, Bosbury	4.10.94P
	(Walter Mikron 3)				*(Cancelled 19.9.00 by CAA)*		
G-AYMR	Lederlin 380L Ladybug			19.11.70	P.Brayshaw	(Harrogate)	
	(Continental C90) EAA/55189 & PFA 1513			*(Last reported under construction 1992: current status unknown)*			
G-AYMU	Wassmer Jodel D.112	1015	F-BJPB	23.11.70	M.R.Baker	Bradleys Lawn, Heathfield	5. 6.92P
			(Damaged Hailsham, E.Sussex 7.1.92: on rebuild Eastbourne 7.92: current status unknown				
G-AYMV	Western 20 HAFB	002		23.11.70	G.F.Turnbull	Clyro, Hereford	
					"Tinkerbelle"		
G-AYMW	Bell 206B JetRanger II	587	EI-BJR	25.11.70	PLM Dollar Group Ltd	Cumbernauld	21. 4.04T
			G-AYMW				
G-AYNA	Phoenix Currie Wot	PFA 3016		25.11.70	D.Silsbury	Dunkeswell	5. 7.02P
	(Continental A65)						
G-AYND	Cessna 310Q	310Q0110	N7610Q	2.12.70	Source Group Ltd	Bournemouth	25. 6.04T
G-AYNF	Piper PA-28-140 Cherokee C	28-26778	N11C	3.12.70	W.S.Bath, M.H.Jones & G.H.Round		
			(PT-DPV)		t/a BW Aviation	Wellesbourne Mountford	25. 7.03T
G-AYNJ	Piper PA-28-140 Cherokee C	28-26810	N11C	3.12.70	R.H.Ribbons	Swansea	16. 5.03T
G-AYNN	Cessna 185B Skywagon	185-0518	8R-GCC	11.12.70	Bencray Ltd	Blackpool	26.12.03T
			VP-GCC/N2518Z		*(Op Blackpool & Fylde Aero Club)*		
G-AYOW	Cessna 182N Skylane	18260481	N8941G	6. 1.71	D.W.Parfrey	Coventry	3. 5.04
G-AYOY	Sikorsky S-61N	61-476		7. 1.71	CHC Scotia Ltd	Sumburgh	21. 4.03T
G-AYOZ	Reims Cessna FA150L Aerobat			7. 1.71	S.A.Hughes	Andrewsfield	12.12.03
		FA15000085					
G-AYPE	MBB Bö.209 Monsun 160RV	123	D-EFJA	11. 1.71	Papa Echo Ltd	Biggin Hill	9.11.03
					"Buswells Spirit"		
G-AYPG	Reims Cessna F177RG Cardinal			11. 1.71	D.P.McDermott	Haverfordwest	20.12.01
	(Wichita c/n 17700102)	F177RG0007					
G-AYPH	Reims Cessna F177RG Cardinal			11. 1.71	M.R. & K.E.Slack	Cambridge	19. 4.04
	(Wichita c/n 17700146)	F177RG0018					

G-AYPI	Reims Cessna F177RG Cardinal			11. 1.71	Cardinal Aviation Ltd	Guernsey	20. 4.03
	(Wichita c/n 17700177)	F177RG0025			*(Ditched 1m off Guernsey 29.10.01)*		
G-AYPJ	Piper PA-28-180 Cherokee E	28-5821	N11C	12. 1.71	Mona Aviation Ltd	RAF Mona	1.10.04T
					(Op Mona Flying Club)		
G-AYPM	Piper PA-18 Super Cub 95	18-1373	ALAT	13. 1.71	R.Horner	Trenchard Farm, Eggesford	28. 6.02P
	(L-18C-PI) *(Frame No.18-1282)*		18-1373/51-15373				
G-AYPO	Piper PA-18 Super Cub 95	18-1615	ALAT	13. 1.71	A.W.Knowles	Bodmin	22. 6.03
	(L-18C-PI) (RR Continental O-200-A)		18-1615/51-15615				
	(Rebuilt 1984 using OO-TSJ c/n 18-1398 (Frame No.18-1325) & ex (LN-TSJ)/OO-HMH/51-15398)						
G-AYPP*	Piper PA-18 Super Cub 95	18-1626	ALAT	13. 1.71	R.W.Sage	Priory Farm, Tibenham	31. 8.85
	(L-18C-PI)		18-1626/51-15626		t/a Blackbarn Aviation		
	(Crashed Stoke St.Mary, Norfolk 29.12.83: cancelled 30.7.84 by CAA: stored 8.97: current status unknown)						
G-AYPR	Piper PA-18 Super Cub 95	18-1631	ALAT	13. 1.71	D.G.Holman & J.E.Burrell	Leicester	27.11.03T
	(L-18C-PI)		18-1631/51-15631				
G-AYPS	Piper PA-18 Super Cub 95	18-2092	ALAT	13. 1.71	R.J.Hamlett, L.G & D.C.Callow		
	(L-18C-PI)		18-2092/52-2492			Andrewsfield	22. 5.02P
G-AYPT	Piper PA-18 Super Cub 95	18-1533	(D-EALX)	13. 1.71	B.L.Proctor & T.F.Lyddon	Dunkeswell	11. 5.02
	(L-18C-PI) (RR Continental O-200-A) *(Frame No.18-1508)*		ALAT 18-1533/51-15533				
G-AYPU	Piper PA-28R-200 Cherokee Arrow B	28R-7135005	N11C	13. 1.71	Monalto Investments Ltd	Jersey	14. 3.02
G-AYPV	Piper PA-28-140 Cherokee D	28-7125039	N11C	13. 1.71	Ashley Gardner Flying Club Ltd	Ronaldsway	6. 9.04T
G-AYPZ	Campbell Cricket	CA/343		13. 1.71	A.Melody	Uxbridge	20. 8.87P
	(VW 1600)				*(Current status unknown)*		
G-AYRF	Reims Cessna F150L	F15000665		14. 1.71	D.T.A.Rees	Haverfordwest	25.11.00T
					(Crashed Upper Welson Farm, Haverfordwest 13.3.99)		
G-AYRG	Reims Cessna F172K	F17200761		14. 1.71	Comed Aviation Ltd	Blackpool	26. 7.00T
G-AYRH	GEMS MS.892A Rallye Commodore 150	10558	F-BNBX	14. 1.71	J.D.Watt	Damyns Hall, Upminster	13. 1.03
G-AYRI	Piper PA-28R-200 Cherokee Arrow B	28R-7135004	N11C	15. 1.71	A.E.Thompson & Delta Motor Co (Windsor) Sales Ltd	White Waltham	25. 7.02
G-AYRK*	Cessna 150J	15070856	5N-AII	19. 1.71	Not known	Shobdon	25. 4.76
			N61170	*(Cancelled 3.4.89 by CAA: noted 5.98: current status unknown)*			
G-AYRM	Piper PA-28-140 Cherokee D	28-7125049	N11C	19. 1.71	M.J.Saggers	Biggin Hill	7. 8.03T
G-AYRO	Reims Cessna FA150L Aerobat	FA1500102		21. 1.71	F.E.Baldwin	Hinton-in-the-Hedges	21. 5.04T
					t/a Fat Boys Flying Club		
G-AYRP*	Reims Cessna FA150L Aerobat	FA1500101		21. 1.71	Not known	Sibson	
	(Overturned landing Andrewsfield 2.8.87: cancelled 28.11.89 as WFU: stored 3.98: current status unknown)						
G-AYRS	Jodel Wassmer D.120A Paris-Nice	255	F-BMAV	22. 1.71	L.R.H.D'Eath	(Diss)	8. 5.02P
G-AYRT	Reims Cessna F172K	F17200777		22. 1.71	P.E.Crees	Shobdon	8. 4.04
G-AYRU	Britten-Norman BN-2A-6 Islander	181	G-51-181	22. 1.71	G. Burton	AAC Netheravon	10. 3.00A
			OH-BNA/G-51-181		t/a Army Parachute Association *(New owner 10.01)*		
G-AYSA	Piper PA-23-250 Aztec C	27-3799	N6509Y	1. 2.71	R.F. Kuester-Johansson	(Northampton)	2. 6.02T
G-AYSB	Piper PA-30 Twin Comanche C	30-1916	N8760Y	1. 2.71	C.P.Heptonstall	Sturgate	2. 3.03
G-AYSD	Slingsby T.61A Falke	1726		4. 2.71	P.W.Hextall	Tatenhill	29. 4.94
					(Stored 1.95: current status unknown)		
G-AYSH	Taylor JT.1 Monoplane	PFA 1413		10. 2.71	C.J.Lodge	Hill Farm, Nayland	13. 5.02P
	(VW 1600)						
G-AYSJ	Dornier Bücker Bü.133C Jungmeister	-	D-EHVP	12. 2.71	Patina Ltd	Duxford	15. 3.02P
			G-AYSJ/HB-MIW/Swiss AF U-91		*(As "LG+01" in Luftwaffe c/s)*		
					(Op The Fighter Collection)		
G-AYSK	Phoenix Luton LA-4A Minor	PFA 832		17. 2.71	S.R.Smith	Barton	23. 1.02P
	(Continental A65)				t/a Luton Minor Group		
G-AYSX	Reims Cessna F177RG Cardinal			17. 2.71	A.P.R.Dean	Hawarden	16. 5.02
	(Wichita c/n 17700175)	F177RG0024					
G-AYSY	Reims Cessna F177RG Cardinal			17. 2.71	Horizon Flyers Ltd	Denham	31. 7.03
	(Wichita c/n 17700180)	F177RG0026					
G-AYTA*	SOCATA MS.880B Rallye Club	1789		19. 2.71	The Aeroplane Collection	Manchester	7.11.88
					(Cancelled 12.5.93 as wfu: to Museum of Science & Industry)		
G-AYTR	Menavia Piel CP.301A Emeraude	229	F-BIMD	3. 3.71	G.N.Hopcraft	Croft Farm, Defford	11. 6.02P
G-AYTT	Phoenix PM-3 Duet	PFA 841		4. 3.71	H.E.Jenner	Rochester	31. 8.02P
	(Continental C90) *(Regd as Luton Minor III)*						
G-AYTV	Jurca MJ.2D Tempete	PFA 2002		10. 3.71	C W Kirk	Swanborough Farm, Lewes	21. 2.02P
	(Continental C90)				t/a Shoestring Flying Group		
G-AYUA	Auster AOP.9	B5/10-119	7855M	12. 3.71	P.T.Bolton	South Lodge Farm, Widmerpool	
			XK416		*(As "XK416": noted 12.96: current status unknown)*		
G-AYUB	CEA Jodel DR.253B Regent	185		15. 3.71	D.J.Clark	Sywell	14. 9.02
G-AYUH	Piper PA-28-180 Cherokee F	28-7105042	N11C	17. 3.71	C.S.Sidle	Sherburn in Elmet	21. 3.02
G-AYUI*	Piper PA-28-180 Cherokee F	28-7105043	N8557	17. 3.71	Ansair Aviation Ltd	Andrewsfield	5.11.93T
			G-AYUI/N11C		*(Cancelled 27.10.98 by CAA: dismantled & hangared 12.01)*		

G-AYUJ	Evans VP-1 (VW 1776)	PFA 1538		17. 3.71	T.N.Howard *"Unforgettable Juliet"*	Woodvale	28. 2.97P
					(Damaged Ainsdale Beach, Southport 16.6.96: current status unknown		
G-AYUM	Slingsby T.61A Falke	1730		19. 3.71	N A Stone & M H Simms	Swanton Morley	10. 6.02
G-AYUN	Slingsby T.61A Falke	1731		19. 3.71	C.W.Vigar & R.J.Watts	Rattlesden	15. 5.03
G-AYUP	Slingsby T.61A Falke	1735	XW983 G-AYUP	19. 3.71	P.R.Williams *(Stored 2.97: current status unknown)*	Bicester	15. 7.96
G-AYUR	Slingsby T.61A Falke	1736		19. 3.71	R.Hannigan & R.Lingard	Strubby	4.11.01
G-AYUS	Taylor JT.1 Monoplane (VW 1600)	PFA 1412		19. 3.71	R.R.McKinnon	Old Sarum	8.10.93P
					(Damaged Coombe Down, Salisbury 3.11.92: current status unknown)		
G-AYUT	SAN Jodel DR.1050 Ambassadeur	479	F-BLJZ	22. 3.71	D.M.Whitham	Crosland Moor	29. 9.01
G-AYUV	Reims Cessna F172H	F17200752		26. 3.71	Justgold Ltd *(Stored 12.01)*	Blackpool	11. 3.00T
G-AYVA*	Cameron O-84 HAFB	17		30. 3.71	Balloon Preservation Group *"April Fool" (Cancelled 19.5.93 by CAA)*	Alfriston	6. 9.76S
G-AYVO	Wallis WA-120 Srs.1 (RR Continental O-240-B @ 130hp)	K/602/X		6. 4.71	K.H.Wallis *(Stored 8.01)*	Reymerston Hall, Norfolk	31.12.75P
G-AYVP	Aerosport Woody Pusher	181 & PFA 1344		6. 4.71	J.R.Wraight *(Stored incomplete: current status unknown)*	Chatham	
G-AYVT*	Brochet MB.84	9	F-BGLI	13. 4.71	R.A.Yates	Sibsey	20. 7.77
					(Damaged 28.6.77: cancelled 3.9.81 as WFU: fuselage & wings stored 8.00)		
G-AYWA*	Avro 19 Srs.2	1361	OO-VIT OO-DFA/OO-CFA	14. 4.71	(Air Atlantic Historic Flight) *(Cancelled 22.8.73 as PWFU: on long term restoration 4.00)*	Coventry	
G-AYWD	Cessna 182N Skylane	18260468	N8928G	15. 4.71	S.I.Zorb t/a Wild Dreams Group	Leicester	4.11.02T
G-AYWE	Piper PA-28-140 Cherokee C	28-26826	N5910U	16. 4.71	Intelcomm (UK) Ltd	Denham	31. 3.02
G-AYWH	SAN Jodel D.117A	844	F-BIVO	16. 4.71	D.Kynaston & J.Deakin	Cambridge	23. 7.02P
G-AYWM	AESL Airtourer T5 (Super 150)	A.534		16. 4.71	H.E.Collett t/a The Star Flying Group	Gloucestershire	24. 5.03
G-AYWT	AIA Stampe SV-4C (DH Gipsy Major 10)	1111	F-BLEY F-BAGL	21. 4.71	Dawn Patrol Flight Training Ltd	Dunkeswell	25. 1.03T
G-AYWY*	Piper PA-23-250 Aztec D	27-4069	EI-ATI N6735Y	22. 4.71	Dublin College of Technology	Dublin	21. 5.77
	(Crashed Castlebridge, Wexford 15.10.75: cancelled 26.3.76 as destroyed: instructional airframe 5.92: current status unknown)						
G-AYXP	SAN Jodel D.117A	693	F-BIDD	27. 4.71	G.N.Davies	Vowchurch, Hereford	30. 5.02P
G-AYXS	SIAI-Marchetti S.205-18R	4-165	OY-DNG	28. 4.71	T.Montague-Moore	Denham	26. 6.04
G-AYXT*	Westland WS-55 Whirlwind HAS.7 (Srs.2)	WA/167	XK940	28. 4.71	The Helicopter Museum *(Cancelled 8.8.00 by CAA) (As "XK940")*	Weston-super-Mare	4. 2.99P
G-AYXU	Champion 7KCAB Citabria	232-70	N7587F	28. 4.71	E.T.& P.A.Wild	(Loughborough)	21. 5.04
G-AYXW	Evans VP-1 (Ardem 4C02)	PFA 1544		30. 4.71	M.Howe	North Coates	15. 8.01P
G-AYYL	Slingsby T.61A Falke	1738		10. 5.71	C.Wood	(Aylesbury)	2. 6.83
					(Gale damage Manston 15.12.82: on rebuild 7.90: current status unknown)		
G-AYYO	CEA Jodel DR.1050/M1 Sicile Record	622	EI-BAI G-AYYO/F-BMPZ	11. 5.71	D.J.M.White t/a Bustard Jodel Group	Boscombe Down	6. 5.02
G-AYYT	CEA Jodel DR.1050/M1 Sicile Record	587	F-BMGU	13. 5.71	C.J.Turner & S.D.Kent t/a Echo November Flight	Garston Farm, Marshfield	22. 6.02
G-AYYU	Beechcraft C23 Musketeer Custom	M-1353		14. 5.71	M.A.Webb t/a The Beech Group	Sturgate	3. 5.04
G-AYYX	SOCATA MS.880B Rallye Club	1812		18. 5.71	J.G.MacDonald	Morgansfield, Fishburn	23. 1.02
G-AYZE	Piper PA-39 Twin Comanche C/R	39-92	N8934Y	20. 5.71	J.E.Balmer	Gloucestershire	29. 8.03
G-AYZI	SNCAN Stampe SV-4C	15	(EI-) G-AYZI/F-BBAA/Fr mil	24. 5.71	W.H.Smout *(On rebuild 6.98: current status unknown)*	Spanhoe	28. 7.95
G-AYZJ*	Westland WS-55 Whirlwind HAS.7 *(Also c/n WAG/34)*	WA/263	XM685	24. 5.71	Newark Air Museum *(Cancelled as WFU 29.12.80: as "XM685/PO-513")*	Winthorpe	
G-AYZK	CEA Jodel DR.1050/M1 Sicile Record	590	F-BMGY	24. 5.71	R.L.Sambell & D.G.Hesketh	Stoke Golding	18. 7.03
G-AYZS	Rollason-Druine D.62B Condor	RAE/650		4. 6.71	M.N.Thrush	Manor Farm, Inglesham	4.11.02P
G-AYZU	Slingsby T.61A Falke	1740		4. 6.71	R.G.Garner t/a The Falcon Gliding Group	Wellesbourne Mountford	10. 6.04
G-AYZW	Slingsby T.61A Falke	1743		4. 6.71	R.S.Jones & J.McGouldrick t/a Portmoak Falke Syndicate	Portmoak	10. 4.04

G-AZAA – G-AZZZ

G-AZAB	Piper PA-30 Twin Comanche B	30-1475	5H-MNM 5Y-AGB	8. 6.71	Bickertons Aerodromes Ltd	Denham	19. 8.04
G-AZAJ	Piper PA-28R-200 Cherokee Arrow	28R-7135116	N11C	18. 6.71	J.C.McHugh & P.Woulfe	Stapleford	22. 6.03
G-AZAU*	Cierva Rotorcraft Grasshopper III	GB.3		21. 6.71	The Helicopter Museum *(Incomplete: cancelled 5.12.83 as WFU: stored 3.96)*	Weston-super-Mare	
G-AZAW	Gardan GY-80-160 Horizon	104	F-BMUL	24. 6.71	T.Brown	Maypole Farm, Chislet	11. 2.02

G-AZAZ*	Bensen B-8M	RNEC.1		2. 7.71	Fleet Air Arm Museum	RNAS Yeovilton	
					(Cancelled 19.9.75 as WFU)		
G-AZBA	Tipsy T.66 Nipper Srs.3B	PFA 1390		30. 6.71	L.A. Brown	Swansea	4. 6.02P
	(VW 1834) *(Slingsby-built kit)*						
G-AZBB	MBB Bo 209 Monsun 160FV	137	D-EFJO	1. 7.71	G.N.Richardson t/a GN Richardson Motors		
						Shelsley Beauchamp, Worcester	9. 7.04
G-AZBE	AESL Airtourer T5 (Super 150)	A.535		5. 7.71	R.G.Vincent	Gloucestershire	15.12.02
					t/a BE Flying Group		
G-AZBH*	Cameron O-84 HAFB	23		8. 7.71	British Balloon Museum & Library	Newbury	10. 5.81
					"Serendipity" (Cancelled 30.8.85 as WFU)		
G-AZBI	SAN Jodel 150 Mascaret	43	F-BMFB	12. 7.71	F.M.Ward	AAC Dishforth	8. 2.02P
G-AZBL	Jodel D.9 Bebe	PFA 938		12. 7.71	J.Hill	(Dudley)	15.10.85P
	(VW 1500)				*(On rebuild 1993 ?: current status unknown)*		
G-AZBN	Noorduyn AT-16-ND Harvard IIB		PH-HON	13. 7.71	Swaygate Ltd	Goodwood	12. 7.01P
		14A-1431	R.Neth.AF B-97/FT391/43-13132 *(As "FT391")*				
G-AZBT*	Western O-65 HAFB	005		15. 7.71	D Harries	Brighton	9. 4.76S
					"Hermes" (Cancelled 19.5.93 by CAA: stored 7.98)		
G-AZBU	Auster AOP.9	AUS.183	7862M	15. 7.71	E.Wright	North Coates	4. 5.02P
			XR246		t/a Auster Nine Group *(As "XR246" in RAE c/s)*		
G-AZBY*	Westland Wessex 60 Srs.1	WA 740	G-17-5	21. 7.71	Not known	Honey Crook Farm, Redhill	14.12.82
	(Possibly former G-AWOX)		G-AZBY/5N-ALR/G-AZBY		*(Cancelled 23.11.82 as TWFU: on rebuild 8.98)*		
					(As "EM-16" in USMC c/s)		
G-AZCB	SNCAN Stampe SV-4C	140	F-BBCR	21. 7.71	M.L.Martin	Redhill	30. 4.96
	(DH Gipsy Major 1C)						
G-AZCE	Pitts S.1C Special	373.H & PFA 1527		26. 7.71	R J Oulton	(Chepstow)	18. 6.76S
	(Lycoming O-235)		*(Crashed Eastbach Farm 2.9.75) (Valid CofR 4.01) (Current status unknown)*				
G-AZCI*	Cessna 320A Skyknight	320A0021	CF-PKY	29. 7.71	Not known	Kano, Nigeria	29. 6.83A
			N3021R				
		(Cancelled 16.12.91 by CAA: stored in wrecked condition 1999?) (Current status unknown)					
G-AZCK	Beagle B.121 Pup 2	B121-153		30. 7.71	D.R.Newell	Newtownards, Co.of Down	7. 5.04
G-AZCL	Beagle B.121 Pup 2	B121-154		30. 7.71	J.J.Watts & D.Fletcher	Old Sarum	8. 7.04T
G-AZCN	Beagle B.121 Pup 2	B121-156	HB-NAY	30. 7.71	D.M.Callaghan & I.C.Haywood	Derby	20. 6.04
			G-AZCN				
G-AZCP	Beagle B.121 Pup 1	B121-158	(D-EKWA)	30. 7.71	T.J.Watson	Elstree	18. 7.04
			G-AZCP				
G-AZCT	Beagle B.121 Pup 1	B121-161		30. 7.71	J.Coleman	Sywell	28. 7.02T
G-AZCU	Beagle B.121 Pup 1	B121-162		30. 7.71	A.A.Harris	Shobdon	5. 8.04
G-AZCV	Beagle B.121 Pup 2	B121-163	HB-NAR	30. 7.71	N.R.W.Long	Compton Abbas	20. 7.02
			G-AZCV		*("Great Circle Design" titles)*		
G-AZCY	Beagle B.121 Pup 2	B121-166	HB-NAW	30. 7.71	D.J. Deas	Bentwaters	15.11.01T
			G-AZCY		*(Carries Swiss Cross on fin)*		
G-AZCZ	Beagle B.121 Pup 2	B121-167		30. 7.71	L. & J.M.Northover	Cardiff	9. 7.04T
G-AZDA	Beagle B.121 Pup 1	B121-168		30. 7.71	B.D.Deubelbeiss	Luton	10. 1.03
G-AZDD	MBB Bö.209 Monsun 150FF	143	D-EBJC	3. 8.71	J D Hall & D Lawrence	Biggin Hill	28. 6.04
					t/a Double Delta Flying Group		
G-AZDE	Piper PA-28R-200 Cherokee Arrow		N11C	3. 8.71	C.Wilson	Elstree	15. 9.02
		28R-7135141			*(Flyteam Aviation titles)*		
G-AZDF(2)*	Cameron O-84 HAFB	24		18. 8.71	K L C M Busemeyer	Aachen, Germany	9. 5.88A
					"Hanniball" (Cancelled 22.4.98 as WFU: extant 2000)		
G-AZDG	Beagle B.121 Pup 2	B121-145	(G-BLYM)	17. 6.85	J.R.Heaps	Elstree	14. 3.04
			HB-NAM/(VH-EPT)/G-35-145 *(DHL c/s)*				
G-AZDJ	Piper PA-32-300 Cherokee Six D		OY-AJK	23. 8.71	Delta Juliet Ltd	Cardiff	19. 4.03T
		32-7140068	G-AZDJ/N5273S				
G-AZDK	Beechcraft 95-B55 Baron	TC-1406		23. 8.71	C.C.Forrester	Meppershall	10. 4.04
G-AZDX	Piper PA-28-180 Cherokee F		N11C	25. 8.71	M.Cowan	Hundon, Suffolk	4. 2.02
		28-7105186					
G-AZDY	de Havilland DH.82A Tiger Moth	86559	F-BGDJ	25. 8.71	J.B.Mills	(Cambridge)	18. 8.97
			Fr.AF/PG650		*(Current status unknown)*		
G-AZDZ*	Cessna 172K Skyhawk	17258501	5N-AIH	25. 8.71	Home Office Fire & Emergency Training Centre		
			N1647C/N84508			Moreton-in-Marsh	25. 2.83
			(Damaged Delapre GC, Northants 19.9.81 & used for fire training 8.98)				
G-AZEE	Morane MS.880B Rallye Club	74	F-BKKA	1. 9.71	J.Shelton	Water Leisure Park, Skegness	27. 9.98
	(Composite incl fuselage of G-AZNJ c/n 5375 in 1980: original fuselage stored South Scarle 9.94: for rebuild 6.01)						
G-AZEF	Jodel Wassmer D.120 Paris-Nice	321	F-BNZS	1. 9.71	D.A.Palmer	Bidford	14. 8.01P
G-AZEG	Piper PA-28-140 Cherokee D		N11C	1. 9.71	The Ashley Gardner Flying Club Ltd		
		28-7125530				Ronaldsway	3. 7.04T
G-AZER*	Cameron O-42 HAFB	26		9. 9.71	Not known *"Shy-Tot"*	NK	15. 5.81A
			(Cancelled 25.3.92 by CAA: noted inflated 9.93) (Current status unknown)				
G-AZEU	Beagle B.121 Pup 2	B121-130	VH-EPL	15. 9.71	G.M.Moir	Derby	15. 2.03
			G-35-130				
G-AZEV	Beagle B.121 Pup 2	B121-131	VH-EPM	15. 9.71	C.J.Partridge	Blackbushe	23. 8.02
			G-35-131				
G-AZEW	Beagle B.121 Pup 2	B121-132	VH-EPN	15. 9.71	K.Cameron	Headcorn	18. 5.03
			G-35-132				

G-AZEY	Beagle B.121 Pup 2	B121-136	HB-NAK G-AZEY/VH-EPP/G-35-136	15. 9.71	M.E.Reynolds	Goodwood	5.12.03
G-AZFA	Beagle B.121 Pup 2	B121-143	VH-EPR G-35-143	15. 9.71	J.Smith	Sandown	22. 7.04
G-AZFC	Piper PA-28-140 Cherokee D	28-7125486	N11C	16. 9.71	M.L.Hannah	Blackbushe	27. 7.02
G-AZFF	Wassmer Jodel D.112	1175	F-BLFI	17. 9.71	D.J.Laughlin	Mullaghmore, Co.Sligo	24. 5.02P
G-AZFI	Piper PA-28R-200 Cherokee Arrow B	28R-7135160	N11C	21. 9.71	GAZFI Ltd	Sherburn in Elmet	6. 4.04
G-AZFM	Piper PA-28R-200 Cherokee Arrow B	28R-7135218	N11C	24. 9.71	P.J.Jenness	(Ringwood)	1. 8 04
G-AZFR	Cessna 401B	401B0121	N7981Q	30. 9.71	R E Wragg	Blackpool	7. 9.02T
G-AZGA	Jodel Wassmer D.120 Paris-Nice	144	F-BIXV	30. 9.71	A.F.Vizoso	RAF Halton	1. 8.02P
G-AZGC*	SNCAN Stampe SV-4C	120	F-BCGE	4.10.71	V.Lindsay	Kidmore End, Reading	22. 2.91
	(As "No.120" in French A/F c/s) (Damaged Folly Farm, Hungerford 28.5.90: stored 6.95: cancelled 19.9.00 by CAA)						
G-AZGE	SNCAN Stampe SV-4C	576	F-BDDV	6.10.71	M.R.L.Astor *(Stored 3.97: current status unknown)*	East Hatley, Tadlow	15. 8.94
G-AZGF	Beagle B.121 Pup 2	B121-076	PH-KUF G-35-076	6.10.71	K.Singh	Barton	2. 5.98
G-AZGI	SOCATA MS.880B Rallye Club	1896		7.10.71	B.McIntyre	Mullaghmore, Co.Sligo	12.11.01
G-AZGL	SOCATA MS.894A Rallye Minerva 220	11929		7.10.71	The Cambridge Aero Club Ltd	Cambridge	7. 9.02T
G-AZGY	Rousseau CP.301B Emeraude	122	F-BRAA	12.10.71	C.J.R.Gray	(Wrexham)	21. 5.02P
G-AZGZ	de Havilland DH.82A Tiger Moth	86489	F-BGCF Fr.AF/NM181	13.10.71	R.J.King *(As "NM181")*	Rush Green	16. 3.02
G-AZHB	Robin HR.100/200B Royal	118		14.10.71	C. & P.P.Scarlett	Headcorn	6. 8.03
G-AZHC	Wassmer Jodel D.112	585	F-BIQQ	18.10.71	D.H.Wilson t/a Aerodel Flying Group	Netherthorpe	9. 8.02P
G-AZHD	Slingsby T.61A Falke	1753		18.10.71	Nicola J.Orchard-Armitage	(Deal)	3. 8.03
G-AZHE*	Slingsby T.61B Falke	1755	N61TB G-AZHE	18.10.71	M.R.Shelton	Tatenhill	
	(Damaged 17.6.88 & on rebuild - cancelled 14.3.99 by CAA) (Current status unknown)						
G-AZHH	K & S SA.102.5 Cavalier (Lycoming O-290)	PFA 1393		20.10.71	D.W.Buckle	Morton Carr Farm, Nunthorpe	20. 1.00P
G-AZHI	AESL Airtourer T5 (Super 150)	A.540		20.10.71	Flying Grasshoppers Ltd	Headcorn	9. 5.03T
G-AZHJ*	Scottish Aviation Twin Pioneer 3	577	G-31-16 XP295	20.10.71	Air Atlantique Ltd *(Cancelled 23.7.97 as TWFU: stored 7.97: current status unknown)*	Coventry	23. 8.90S
G-AZHK	Robin HR.100/200B Royal	113	G-ILEG G-AZHK	22.10.71	D.J.Sage	(Reigate)	19. 5.02
G-AZHR	Piccard Ax6 HAFB	617	N17US	27.10.71	C.Fisher t/a Halcyon Balloon Group *"Happiness"*	Sheffield	
G-AZHT	AESL Airtourer T3	525		29.10.71	Aviation West Ltd *(Damaged Glenforsa, Mull 29.4.88: stored 6.00)*	(Glasgow)	29. 1.89T
G-AZHU	Phoenix Luton LA-4A Minor (VW 1834)	PFA 839		1.11.71	W.Cawrey	Netherthorpe	31. 5.02P
G-AZIB	SOCATA ST-10 Diplomate	141		4.11.71	W.B.Bateson	Blackpool	21.12.03
G-AZID	Reims Cessna FA150L Aerobat	FA15000083	N9447	8.11.71	Aerobat Ltd	Wolverhampton	18.11.02T
G-AZII	SAN Jodel D.117A	848	F-BNDO F-OBFO	12.11.71	P J Brayshaw	Haddock Stone Farm, Markington	11. 4.01P
G-AZIJ	Robin DR.360 Chevalier	634		15.11.71	K.J.Fleming	Coventry	4. 6.03
G-AZIK	Piper PA-34-200 Seneca	34-7250018	N2392T	15.11.71	Walkbury Aviation Ltd	Sibson	25. 3.02T
G-AZIL	Slingsby T.61A Falke	1756		16.11.71	D.W.Savage	Arbroath	19.11.02
G-AZIP	Cameron O-65 HAFB	29		24.11.71	P.G.Dunnington *"Dante"* t/a Dante Balloon Group *(Non-airworthy - stored 2.97)*	Hungerford	5. 5.81A
G-AZJC	Sportavia Fournier RF5	5108		30.11.71	W.S.V.Stoney	(Arezzo, Italy)	1. 5.03P
G-AZJE	Barritault JB.01 Minicab (Continental C90)	JBE.1 & PFA 1806		1.12.71	J.B.Evans *(Stored 1.98: current status unknown)*	Ventnor, IOW	7. 7.82P
G-AZJI*	Western O-65 HAFB	007		2.12.71	British Balloon Museum & Library *"Peek-A-Boo" (Cancelled 19.5.93 by CAA) (Active 4.99)*	Newbury	NE(A)
G-AZJN	Robin DR.300/140 Major	642		6.12.71	Wright Farm Eggs Ltd	Cherry Tree Farm, Monewden	3. 6.02
G-AZJV	Reims Cessna F172L	F17200810		8.12.71	J.A. & A.J.Boyd	Cardiff	13. 2.03
G-AZJY	Reims Cessna FRA150L Aerobat	FRA15000126		8.12.71	R.P.Smith	Barton	7. 6.04
G-AZKC	SOCATA MS.880B Rallye Club	1914		8.12.71	L.J.Martin	Sandown	2. 7.03
G-AZKE	SOCATA MS.880B Rallye Club	1950		8.12.71	D.A.Thompson & S.H.Little	Trier, Luxembourg	3. 2.03
	(LX-SDT reserved 8.00 but suspended because of costs of UK Export CofA & Luxembourg Registry problems)						
G-AZKK	Cameron O-56 HAFB	32		13.12.71	P.J.Green & C.Bosley t/a Gemini Balloon Group *"Gemini"*	Newbury	NE(A)
G-AZKN*	Robin Jodel HR.100/200B Royal	122		20.12.71	Not known	Hinton-in-the-Hedges	6.12.96
	(Damaged in force-landing near Long Watton, Leics 1.9.95: cancelled 31.5.96 as WFU: dismantled wreck stored 10.01)						

G-AZKO	Reims Cessna F337F Super Skymaster			20.12.71	P.W. Crispe	Wellesbourne Mountford	10. 8.03
	(Wichita c/n 33701380)	F33700041			*"Bird Dog"*		
G-AZKP	SAN Jodel D.117	419	F-BHND	20.12.71	B.N.Stevens	North Connel, Oban	11. 4.02P
G-AZKR	Piper PA-24-180 Comanche	24-2192	N7044P	23.12.71	J.Van Der Kwast	(Chelmsford)	21. 6.04
G-AZKS	American AA-1A Trainer	0334	N6134L	23.12.71	M.D.Henson	Coventry	23. 8.03
G-AZKV*	Reims Cessna FRA150L Aerobat			23.12.71	B.Flay & T.C.Hocking	Bodmin	21.10.93T
		FRA15000127	*(Damaged Redlake, Lostwithiel 15.9.91: cancelled 30.10.91 as destroyed:*				
	small parts & wings stored 8.96: current status unknown)						
G-AZKW	Reims Cessna F172L	F17200836		23.12.71	J.C.C.Wright	Hinton-in-the-Hedges	21. 6.02T
G-AZKZ	Reims Cessna F172L	F17200814		23.12.71	R.D. & E.Forster	Beccles	14. 8.04T
					(Op Norfolk Flying Club)		
G-AZLE	Boeing-Stearman E75 (N2S-5) Kaydet		CF-XRD	29.12.71	A.E.Poulsom	Manor Farm, Tongham	28. 5.04
	(Continental W670)	75-8543	N5619N/Bu43449		t/a Air Farm Flyers *(As "2"in US Army c/s)*		
G-AZLF	Jodel Wassmer D.120 Paris-Nice	230	F-BLFL	30.12.71	M.S.C.Ball	Garston Farm, Marshfield	16.11.02P
G-AZLH	Reims Cessna F150L	F15000757		31.12.71	Coulson Flying Services Ltd	Cranfield	30.11.03T
G-AZLJ*	Britten-Norman BN-2A mk.III-1 Trislander		G-OREG	31.12.71	(Mike Collett/Atlantic Group)	Coventry	2. 2.00T
		319	SX-CBN/G-OREG/G-OAVW/G-AZLJ/G-51-319				
					(Cancelled as 1.3.01 temp wfu) (Used for spares)		
G-AZLL*	Reims Cessna FRA150L Aerobat			31.12.71	Rankart Ltd	Hinton-in-the-Hedges	19.11.01T
		F1500135	*(Crashed Turweston 4.2.99 & destroyed: cancelled 21.7.99: wreck noted 10.01)*				
G-AZLM*	Reims Cessna F172L	F17200842		31.12.71	Norfolk & Suffolk Aviation Musm	Flixton	16. 7.93T
	(Crashed Badminton 23.3.91: cancelled 15.4.91 as destroyed: fuselage stored 9.97: current status unknown)						
G-AZLN	Piper PA-28-180 Cherokee F		N11C	3. 1.72	Liteflite Ltd	Oxford	5. 3.04
		28-7105210					
G-AZLO*	Reims Cessna F337F Super Skymaster			4. 1.72	Not known	Bourn	22. 4.82
	(Wichita c/n 33701347)	F33700029	*(WFU 4.82: cancelled 4.12.86 by CAA: unmarked rear-fuselage stored 1.01)*				
G-AZLP*	Vickers V.813 Viscount	346	(ZS-SBT)	4. 1.72	International Fire Training Centre		
			ZS-CDT		*(Cancelled 19.12.86 as WFU: fuselage only 3.00)*	Teesside	3. 4.82T
G-AZLS*	Vickers V.813 Viscount	348	(ZS-SBV)	4. 1.72	International Fire Training Centre		
			ZS-CDV		*(Cancelled 19.12.86 as WFU: noted 3.00)*	Teesside	9. 6.83T
G-AZLV	Cessna 172K	17257908	4X-ALM	10. 1.72	B.L.F.Karthaus	Newcastle	8. 4.04
			N79138				
G-AZLY	Reims Cessna F150L	F15000771		10. 1.72	Cleveland Flying School Ltd	Teesside	5.12.02T
G-AZLZ	Reims Cessna F150L	F15000772		10. 1.72	A.G.Martlew	Haverfordwest	16. 7.00
G-AZMC	Slingsby T.61A Falke	1757		12. 1.72	Essex Gliding Club Ltd	Challock	22. 9.86
					(Sold - stored 8.90: current status unknown)		
G-AZMD	Slingsby T.61C Falke	1758		12. 1.72	R.A.Rice	Wellesbourne Mountford	1. 6.04
G-AZMF	British Aircraft Corporation One-Eleven 530FX			14. 1.72	European Aviation Ltd	Bournemouth	22. 1.04T
		BAC.240	7Q-YKJ/G-AZMF/PT-TYY/G-AZMF *(Op European VIP First) "The European Express"*				
G-AZMJ	American AA-5 Traveler	0019		27. 1.72	R.T.Love	St.Merryn	1. 5.04
G-AZMN*	AESL Airtourer T5 (Super 150)	A.550		28. 1.72	Not known	Oaksey Park	7. 5.89
			(Crashed near Glasgow 23.6.87: cancelled 14.9.88 by CAA: stored 5.00)				
G-AZMX*	Piper PA-28-140 Cherokee	28-24777	SE-FLL	7. 2.72	North East Wales Institute, Dee-side College		
			LN-LMK			Connah's Quay	9. 1.82
			(Cancelled: as instructional airframe 3.96: current status unknown)				
G-AZMZ	SOCATA MS.893A Rallye Commodore 180			8. 2.72	Patricia J.Wilcox	Lyveden	10. 5.03
		11927					
G-AZNC*	Vickers V.813 Viscount	352	(ZS-SBZ)	8. 2.72	(Airport Fire Services)	Teesside	18. 5.83T
			ZS-CDZ *(WFU2.82: cancelled 27.10.88 as WFU: non-destructive training 3.00)*				
G-AZNK	SNCAN Stampe SV-4A	290	F-BKXF	15. 2.72	P.D.Jackson & R.A.G.Lucas	Redhill	20. 5.04
	(DH Gipsy Major 10)		F-BCGZ		*"Globird"*		
G-AZNL	Piper PA-28R-200 Cherokee Arrow II		N11C	16. 2.72	B.P.Liversidge	Earls Colne	8. 8.02T
		28R-7235006					
G-AZNO	Cessna 182P Skylane	18261005	N7365Q	18. 2.72	T & K.Andrewes	Brunton	3. 5.03
G-AZNT	Cameron O-84 HAFB	34		21. 2.72	N.Tasker *"Oberon"*	Bristol	5. 6.85
G-AZOA	MBB Bö.209 Monsun 150FF	183	D-EAAY	21. 2.72	M.W.Hurst	Seighford	14. 6.04
G-AZOB	MBB Bö.209 Monsun 150FF	184	D-EAAZ	21. 2.72	G.N.Richardson		
						Shelsley Beauchamp, Worcester	9. 7.84
			(Crashed Droitwich 21.8.83: stored 8.92: current status unknown)				
G-AZOE	AESL Airtourer T2 (115)	528		21. 2.72	B.J.Edmondson & J.K.Smithson	Newcastle	15. 8.03
					t/a G-AZOE 607 Group		
G-AZOF	AESL Airtourer T5 (Super 150)	A.549		21. 2.72	R.J.W.Bayliff & A.C.Hart	Kirknewton	17. 2.04
					t/a Cirrus Flying Group		
G-AZOG	Piper PA-28R-200 Cherokee Arrow II		N11C	21. 2.72	Atromin Ltd	Southend	8. 8.04
		28R-7235009			t/a Southend Flying Club		
G-AZOL	Piper PA-34-200 Seneca	34-7250075	N4348T	28. 2.72	D.I.Barnes	Stapleford	28. 6.03
G-AZOO	Western O-65 HAFB	015		1. 3.72	Semajan Ltd *"Carousel"*	Newbury	6. 6.77S
					(On loan to British Balloon Museum & Library)		
G-AZOR	MBB Bö.105DB	S.20	EC-DOE	1. 3.72	Bond Air Services	Boreham	31. 5.02T
			G-AZOR/D-HDAC		*(Op Essex Air Ambulance)*		
G-AZOS	Jurca MJ.5-H1 Sirocco 001 & PFA 2206			1. 3.72	N.M.Robbins	Hill Farm, Nayland	18. 3.02P
	(Lycoming O-320)						
G-AZOT	Piper PA-34-200 Seneca	34-7250073	N4340T	3. 3.72	Alliance Aerolink Ltd	(Harlow)	13. 9.03T

G-AZOU SAN Jodel DR.1050 Sicile 354 F-BJYX 7. 3.72 D.Elliott & D.Holl t/a Horsham Flying Group
Wellcross Grange, Slinfold 1. 6.02

G-AZOZ Reims Cessna FRA150L Aerobat FRA15000136 7. 3.72 Seawing Flying Club Ltd Southend 14. 7.02T
"The Wizard of Oz"

G-AZPA Piper PA-25-235 Pawnee C 25-5223 N8797L N9???N 7. 3.72 Black Mountains Gliding Club Ltd
Talgarth 1. 5.04

G-AZPC Slingsby T.61C Falke 1767 7. 3.72 The Surrey Hills Gliding Club Ltd Kenley 31. 7.04

G-AZPF Sportavia Fournier RF5 5001 D-KOLT 10. 3.72 R.Pye Blackpool 19. 7.02P

G-AZPH* Craft-Pitts S.1S Special S1S-001-C (Lycoming IO-360) N11CB 13. 3.72 The Science Museum (Flight Gallery)
South Kensington, London SW7 4. 9.91P
(Ground-looped landing Little Snoring 10.5.91: cancelled as WFU 8.1.97)

G-AZPV Phoenix-Luton LA-4A Minor PFA 833 (Lycoming O-145) 14. 3.72 J.R.Faulkner (Brize Norton) 18. 9.97P
(Stored 3.01)

G-AZPX Western O-31 HAFB 011 20. 3.72 B.L.King Coulsdon
t/a Eugena Rex Balloon Group *"Eugena Rex"*

G-AZRA MBB Bö.209 Monsun 150FF 192 D-EAIH 21. 3.72 Alpha Flying Ltd Booker 3. 5.04

G-AZRD Cessna 401B 401B0218 N7999Q 22. 3.72 G.Hatton Blackpool 6. 4.03T
t/a Romeo Delta Group

G-AZRG* Piper PA-23-250 Aztec D 27-4386 N6536Y 23. 3.72 Woodgate Aviation (IOM) Ltd Ronaldsway 8. 7.93T
(Cancelled 19.10.93 as WFU: on fire dump 7.99)

G-AZRH Piper PA-28-140 Cherokee D 28-7125585 N11C 23. 3.72 H.B.Carter Jersey 24. 2.02
t/a Trust Flying Group

G-AZRI Payne HAFB (56,500 cu.ft) GFP.1 21. 3.72 C.A.Butter & J.J.T.Cooke *"Shoestring"*
t/a Aardvark Balloon Co Newbury/Southall

G-AZRK Sportavia Fournier RF5 5112 23. 3.72 A.B.Clymo & J.F.Rogers Shenington 3. 7.02P

G-AZRL Piper PA-18 Super Cub 95 18-1331 (L-18C-PI) *(Frame No.18-1213)* OO-SBR OO-HML/ALAT 18-1331/51-15331 23. 3.72 M.G.Fountain Leicester 16.10.04

G-AZRM Sportavia Fournier RF5 5111 (VW 1834) 24. 3.72 A.R.Dearden & R.Speer
Upper Broyle Farm, Ringmer 7. 3.01P

G-AZRN Cameron O-84 HAFB 28 28. 3.72 C.J.Desmet Brussels, Belgium 4. 7.81A
(New owner 5.01)

G-AZRP AESL Airtourer T2 (115) 529 28. 3.72 B.F.Strawford Shobdon 19. 8.04

G-AZRR Cessna 310Q 310Q0490 N9923F 28. 3.72 Routarrow Ltd Seething 23. 4.04

G-AZRS Piper PA-22-150 Tri-Pacer 22-5141 XT-AAH F-OCGZ/ALAT 22-5141/"FMKAC"/N10F 28. 3.72 R.H.Hulls Trenchard Farm, Eggesford 5. 9.03
"Sandpiper"

G-AZRV* Piper PA-28R-200 Cherokee Arrow B 28R-7135191 N2309T 4. 4.72 Not known Compton Abbas
(Crashed on take-off Compton Abbas 30.12.00: cancelled 20.6.01 as destroyed: fuselage & port wing dumped 8.01)

G-AZRX* Gardan GY-80-160 Horizon 14 F-BLIJ 4. 4.72 Adventure Island Pleasure Ground
Marine Parade, Southend-on-Sea 20. 2.92
(Damaged Sandtoft 14.8.91: cancelled 21.10.91 by CAA: on display in Crazy Golf Course, Seafront 1.01)

G-AZRZ Cessna U206F Stationair U20601803 N9603G 4. 4.72 M.R.Browne & R.G.Wood t/a Hinton Skydiving Centre
Hinton-in-the-Hedges 26. 5.03

G-AZSA Stampe et Renard SV-4B 1203 *(Official c/n is 64)* V-61 Belgian AF 5. 4.72 J.K.Faulkner Biggin Hill 31. 7.04P

G-AZSC Noorduyn AT-16-ND Harvard IIB 14A-1363 PH-SKK B-19 R.Neth AF/FT323/43-13064 *(As "43/SC" in USAAF c/s)* 7. 4.72 Machine Music Ltd North Weald 2.10.02P

G-AZSD Slingsby T.29B Motor Tutor RGB 01/72 & PFA 1574 7. 4.72 R.G.Boyton Halstead, Essex
t/a Essex Aviation
(Rebuild of Slingsby c/n 561) *(Current status unknown: valid CofR 3.01)*

G-AZSF Piper PA-28R-200 Cherokee Arrow II 28R-7235048 N11C 10. 4.72 W.T.Northorpe Coventry 5. 8.02
t/a Flight Simulation Air Park

G-AZSP* Cameron O-84 HAFB 43 18. 4.72 British Balloon Museum & Library Newbury 22. 3.82
"Esso" (Cancelled 11.1.82 as WFU)

G-AZSW Beagle B.121 Pup 1 B121-140 PH-VRT G-35-140 24. 4.72 J.R.Parry Caernarfon 4.11.02

G-AZSZ Piper PA-23-250 Aztec D 27-4194 N6851Y 25. 4.72 Industrial Cladding Systems Ltd Kemble 2. 6.01T

G-AZTA MBB Bö.209 Monsun 150FF 190 D-EAIF 25. 4.72 A.Brinkley & D.Morris Top Farm, Croydon 20. 9.04T
t/a Just Plane

G-AZTD* Piper PA-32-300 Cherokee Six D 32-7140001 N8611N 26. 4.72 Presshouse Publications Ltd Enstone 16. 8.98T
(Cancelled 11.4.01 by CAA: noted 7.01)

G-AZTF Reims Cessna F177RG Cardinal F177RG0054 28. 4.72 D.A.Wiggins Denham 13. 8.04

G-AZTK Reims Cessna F172F F17200116 PH-CON OO-SIR 27. 4.72 S.O'Ceallaigh (Cork) 20.10.00

G-AZTN* AESL Airtourer T2 (115) A.531 28. 4.72 Not known St.Just 24. 6.78
(Crashed Puriton, Somerset 27.6.77: cancelled 30.3.83 as WFU: wreck stored 9.95: current status unknown)

G-AZTR* SNCAN Stampe SV-4C 596 F-BDEQ 28. 4.72 P.G.Palumbo Booker 15. 7.94
(Stored "Blue Max" Movie Aircraft Collection 3.96: cancelled 10.10.00 by CAA)

G-AZTS Reims Cessna F172L F17200866 28. 4.72 C.E.Stringer Bagby 17.12.03T

G-AZTV Stolp SA.500 Starlet (Continental C90) SSM.2 & PFA 1584 19. 5.72 G.G.Rowland (Christchurch) 19.11.92
(Damaged Manor Farm, Grateley, Hants 4.7.92: current status unknown)

G-AZTW Reims Cessna F177RG Cardinal F177RG0043 28. 4.72 I.M.Richmond Panshanger 15. 6.03

G-AZUM Reims Cessna F172L F17200863 11. 5.72 L.R.Sullivan Fowlmere 18.12.03
t/a Fowlmere Flyers

G-AZUP Cameron O-65 HAFB 36 11. 5.72 R.S.Bailey & A.B.Simpson *"Eight of Hearts"*
Aylesbury/Hemel Hempstead 23.10.77S

G-AZUT SOCATA MS.893A Rallye Commodore 180 10963 VH-TCH 12. 5.72 J.Palethorpe Blakedown, Kidderminster 9.11.02
t/a Rallye Flying Group

G-AZUV* Cameron O-65 HAFB 41 12. 5.72 British Balloon Museum & Library Newbury 23. 6.83
"Icarus" (Damaged & WFU Rendharn Green, Suffolk: cancelled 6.1.82)

G-AZUX* Western O-56 HAFB 017 15. 5.72 D.M.Sandford *"Slow Djinn"* Knutsford
(Cancelled 10.10.01 by CAA)

G-AZUY Cessna 310L 310L0012 SE-FEC 15. 5.72 W.B.Bateson Blackpool 1.12.99
LN-LMH/N2212F

G-AZUZ Reims Cessna FRA150L Aerobat FRA15000146 16. 5.72 D.J.Parker Netherthorpe 16.12.03

G-AZVA MBB Bö.209 Monsun 150FF 177 (D-EAAQ) 16. 5.72 P.J.Fahie Old Sarum 8. 9.03

G-AZVB MBB Bö.209 Monsun 150FF 178 (D-EAAS) 16. 5.72 M.H.James & D.Shrimpton Compton Abbas 14. 6.03

G-AZVF SOCATA MS.894A Rallye Minerva 220 11999 (F-OCSR) 16. 5.72 F.A.Cavacuiti & G.Hammond
t/a Minerva Flying Group Upfield Farm, Usk 9. 3.02

G-AZVG American AA-5 Traveler AA5-0075 16. 5.72 Whelan Building & Development Ltd
(Luton) 25. 8.02

G-AZVH SOCATA MS.894A Rallye Minerva 220 12017 16. 5.72 P.L.Jubb Poplar Hall Farm, Elmsett 17. 6.01

G-AZVI SOCATA MS.892A Rallye Commodore 150 12039 16. 5.72 H.R.Dyas & V.S.Bryan Shobdon 12. 8.04
t/a Shobdon Flying Group

G-AZVJ Piper PA-34-200 Seneca 34-7250125 N4529T 16. 5.72 Andrews Professional Colour Laboratories Ltd
Lydd 21. 8.03A

G-AZVL Jodel D.119 794 F-BILB 19. 5.72 P.T.East Stapleford 8.12.04P
(Built Ets Valladeau) t/a Forest Flying Group

G-AZVM Hughes 369HS (500C) 61-0326S N9091F 19. 5.72 GTS Engineering (Coventry) Ltd Coventry 6. 9.03

G-AZVP Reims Cessna F177RG Cardinal F177RG0057 22. 5.72 Cardinal Flyers Ltd Denham 25. 6.04

G-AZVT* Cameron O-84 HAFB 40 30. 5.72 Jenny Robinson London SE5 2. 6.78
"Jules Verne" (Extant 2.97: cancelled 4.8.98 by CAA)

G-AZWB Piper PA-28-140 Cherokee E 28-7225244 N11C 5. 6.72 B.N.Rides & L.Connor Kemble 19.12.03

G-AZWD Piper PA-28-140 Cherokee E 28-7225298 N11C 6. 6.72 C.B.Mellor Southampton 6. 5.02T
t/a BM Aviation

G-AZWE Piper PA-28-140 Cherokee E 28-7225303 N11C 6. 6.72 P.M.Tucker Dunkeswell 18. 3.02T
t/a G-AZWE Flying Group

G-AZWF SAN Jodel DR.1050 Ambassadeur 130 F-BJJT 7. 6.72 J A D Reedie Inverness 5.12.04
(Composite including fuselage of DR.1050M F-BLJX c/n 492) t/a Cawdor Flying Group

G-AZWS Piper PA-28R-180 Cherokee Arrow 28R-30749 N4993J 8. 6.72 G.S.Blair & I.Parkinson Eshott 2. 5.03
t/a Arrow 88 Flying Group

G-AZWT Westland Lysander IIIA Y1536 RCAF 1582 9. 6.72 The Shuttleworth Trust Old Warden 6. 8.02P
V9552 *(As "V9367/MA-B" of 161 Sqdn)*

G-AZWY Piper PA-24-260 Comanche C 24-4806 N9310P 16. 6.72 Keymer, Son & Co Ltd Biggin Hill 24. 4.03

G-AZXA Beechcraft 95-C55 Baron TE-72 SE-EKZ 19. 6.72 Cobham Leasing Ltd Bournemouth 3. 5.02A

G-AZXB Cameron O-65 HAFB 48 20. 6.72 R.J.Mitchener & P.F.Smart Andover 6. 5.81A
t/a Balloon Collection *"London Pride II"*

G-AZXC Reims Cessna F150L F15000793 20. 6.72 D.C.Bonsall Netherthorpe 28. 4.03T

G-AZXD Reims Cessna F172L F17200878 20. 6.72 Birdlake Ltd Birmingham 26. 6.03T
(Op Birdlake Aviation)

G-AZXG* Piper PA-23-250 Aztec D 27-4328 N6963Y 23. 6.72 Cranfield University Cranfield 18. 9.94
(Crashed Little Snoring 25.10.91: cancelled 6.5.93 by CAA: instructional airframe 6.00)

G-AZYA Gardan GY-80-160 Horizon 57 F-BLPT 7. 7.72 T.Twelvetree & M.L.Moore Old Sarum 9. 8.03

G-AZYB* Bell 47H-1 1538 LN-OQG 4. 7.72 E.D.ap Rees Weston-super-Mare 8. 9.84
SE-HBE/OO-SHW t/a The Helicopter Museum
(Crashed St.Mary Bourne, Thruxton 21.4.84: cancelled 22.4.85 as destroyed: cockpit on rebuild 2.00)

G-AZYD GEMS MS.893A Rallye Commodore 180 10645 F-BNSE 30. 6.72 P.Storey Husbands Bosworth 8. 8.02
t/a Storey Aviation Services

G-AZYM Cessna 310Q 310Q0507 N218Y 6. 7.72 C.Matthews & G.J.Tickton Guernsey 16. 3.03P
G-AZYM/N5893M/N4592L

G-AZYS Scintex CP.301C-1 Emeraude 568 F-BJAY 7. 7.72 C.G.Ferguson & D.Drew (Nottingham) 10. 5.02P

G-AZYU Piper PA-23-250 Aztec E 27-4601 N13983 13. 7.72 L.J.Martin Redhill/Sandown 16. 5.04

G-AZYY Slingsby T.61A Falke 1770 12. 7.72 J.A.Towers Yearby 22. 3.02

G-AZYZ Wassmer WA.51A Pacific 30 F-OCSE 14. 7.72 C.R.Buxton (Gourvillette, France) 28. 6.04

G-AZZG* Cessna 188 Agwagon 230 188-0279 OY-AHT 12. 7.72 N.C.Kensington (Bridge of Cally) 1. 5.81A
N8029V *(On rebuild 6.00: cancelled 21.9.00 by CAA)*

G-AZZH Practavia Pilot Sprite 115 PFA 1532 13. 7.72 A.Moore *(Stored 8.01)* (Dagenham)

G-AZZO Piper PA-28-140 Cherokee 28-22887 N4471J 18. 7.72 R.J.Hind Stapleford 6. 8.03

G-AZZR Reims Cessna F150L F15000690 LN-LJX 24. 7.72 M.W.Smith t/a G-AZZR Flying Group Exeter 20. 7.04T

G-AZZV Reims Cessna F172L F15000883 18. 7.72 D.J.Hockings Rochester 7. 7.02T

G-AZZZ de Havilland DH.82A Tiger Moth 86311 F-BGJE 27. 7.72 S.W.McKay Blue Tile Farm, Langham 21.12.04
Fr.AF/NL864

G-BAAA – G-BAZZ

G-BAAD	Evans Super VP-1	PFA 1540		27. 7.72	K.Wigglesworth	Breighton	29.10.02P
	(VW 1600)				t/a Breighton VP-1 Group		
G-BAAF	Manning-Flanders MF.1 rep	PPS/REP/8		27. 7.72	Bianchi Aviation Film Services Ltd		
	(Continental C75)				*(No external marks)*	Booker	6. 8.96P
					(Op "Blue Max" Movie Aircraft Collection)		
G-BAAI	SOCATA MS.893A Rallye Commodore 180	10705	F-BOVG	31. 7.72	R.D.Taylor	Thruxton	11. 9.00
G-BAAL	Cessna 172A	47678	PH-KAP D-ELGU/N9878T	31. 7.72	M.J.McRobert	Headcorn	20. 5.04T
G-BAAT	Cessna 182P Skylane	18260835	N399JF G-BAAT/N9295G	10. 8.72	Melrose Pigs Ltd	Melrose Farm, Melbourne	21. 5.03
G-BAAU	Enstrom F-28A-UK	092		10. 8.72	G.Firbank	(Macclesfield)	6. 5.02T
G-BAAW	Jodel D.119	366	F-BHMY	11. 8.72	P J Newson	Cherry Tree Farm, Monewden	1. 4.02P
	(Continental O-200-A) *(Built Ets Valladeau)*				t/a Alpha Whiskey Flying Group		
G-BABB	Reims Cessna F150L	F15000830		15. 8.72	Seawing Flying Club Ltd	Southend	6. 7.03T
G-BABC	Reims Cessna F150L	F15000831		15. 8.72	Fordaire Aviation Ltd	Sywell	17. 9.03T
G-BABD	Reims Cessna FRA150L Aerobat	FRA1500153		3. 8.72	K.F.Mason & D.Featherby	Norwich	18. 2.04T
					t/a Anglia Flight		
G-BABE	Taylor JT.2 Titch	PEB/01 & PFA 1394		3. 8.72	M.Bonsall	Netherthorpe	7. 5.98P
	(Continental O-200-A)				*(New owner 4.01)*		
G-BABG	Piper PA-28-180 Cherokee C	28-2031	PH-APU N7978W	15. 8.72	C.E.Dodge	Bristol	9.11.03
					t/a Mendip Flying Group		
G-BABH	Reims Cessna F150L	F15000820	EI-CCZ G-BABH	15. 8.72	Tindon Ltd	Little Snoring	1. 4.04T
G-BABK	Piper PA-34-200 Seneca	34-7250219	PH-DMN G-BABK/N5203T	18. 8.72	D.F.J.Flashman	Biggin Hill	24. 9.01
G-BACB	Piper PA-34-200 Seneca	34-7250251	N5354T	25. 8.72	Halegreen Associates Ltd & G-BACB Ltd	Oxford	24. 6.02T
G-BACC	Reims Cessna FRA150L Aerobat	FRA1500157		16. 8.72	C.M. & J.H.Cooper	Cranfield	13.12.04
G-BACE	Sportavia Fournier RF5	5102	(PT-DVZ) D-KCID	25. 8.72	R.W.K.Stead	Perranporth	27.11.04
					t/a Clockwork Mouse Flying Group *"The Clockwork Mouse"*		
G-BACJ	Jodel Wassmer D.120 Paris-Nice	315	F-BNZC	1. 9.72	J.M.Allan	Newcastle	15. 3.02P
					t/a Wearside Flying Association		
G-BACL	SAN Jodel 150 Mascaret	31	F-BSTY CN-TYY	4. 9.72	G.R.French	Benson's Farm, Laindon	8. 9.01
G-BACN	Reims Cessna FRA150L Aerobat	FRA1500161		4. 9.72	Cornwall Flying Club Ltd	Plymouth	14. 6.03T
G-BACO	Reims Cessna FRA150L Aerobat	FRA1500163		4. 9.72	M.M.Pepper	Sibson	14. 5.04
G-BACP	Reims Cessna F150L Aerobat (Built as FRA150L)	FRA1500164		4. 9.72	Vectair Aviation 1995 Ltd	Goodwood	14. 5.04T
G-BADC	Rollason-Luton Beta B.2A	JJF.1 & PFA/1384		7. 9.72	D.H.Greenwood	Barton	31. 1.85P
					(On overhaul 5.95: new owner 10.00)		
	(CAA quote c/n as PFA 002-10140 as originally allocated to Beta G-BETA, cancelled 3.2.87 by CAA. The two Betas are closely related. John Kinch started construction of Beta project 002-10140 in 1974 and registered it as G-BETA in 1977 as soon as the regn. was available 'in sequence'. Meantime in 1976 he had acquired from Tom Storey & Steve Thompson Beta G-BADC (PFA 1384) which was nearer completion than his own project. G-BADC was completed first with G-BETA to follow. This did not happen & G-BETA was duly cancelled. G-BADC has since had a long history of rebuild & restoration: the quoted c/n now suggests it incorporates large parts of the unfinished G-BETA)						
G-BADH	Slingsby T.61A Falke	1774		6. 9.72	D.W.Smart	Gallows Hill, Bovington	31. 3.02
					t/a Falke Flying Group		
G-BADI	Piper PA-23-250 Aztec D	27-4235	N6885Y	5. 9.72	West London Aero Services Ltd	North Weald	29.10.92T
	(Fuselage noted 12.00 as "G-BABF" but repainted as fictitious "G-ESKY" Air Ambulance titles 8.01: valid CofR 3.01)						
G-BADJ	Piper PA-E23-250 Aztec E	27-4841	N14279	11. 9.72	C.Papadakis	Oxford	21.12.01T
G-BADM	Rollason-Druine D.62B Condor	AE/653 & PFA 049-11442		8. 9.72	M.Harris & J.StJ.Mehta	Yeldon Farm, Nutley	18. 6.01P
G-BADV*	Brochet MB.50 Pipistrelle	78	F-PBRJ	13. 9.72	H.F.Moffatt	Woodlow Farm, Bosbury	9. 5.79P
	(Salmson AD9B)				*(WFU & cancelled 3.4.89 by CAA: on rebuild: current status unknown)*		
G-BADW	Aerotek Pitts S-2A Special	2035		21. 9.72	R.E.Mitchell	RAF Cosford	16. 9.95T
G-BADZ	Aerotek Pitts S-2A Special	2038		21. 9.72	A.F.D.Kingdon	Blackpool	5. 6.00T
G-BAEB	Robin DR.400/160 Knight	733		19. 9.72	P.D.W.King	Lydd	21. 3.04T
G-BAEC	Robin HR.100/210 Royal	145	EI-BDG G-BAEC	15. 9.72	Datacorp Enterprises Pty Ltd	Denham	6. 4.03
G-BAEE	CEA Jodel DR.1050/M1 Sicile Record	579	F-BMGN	29. 9.72	R.Little	Shoreham	19. 6.03
G-BAEM	Robin DR.400/125 Petit Prince	728		25. 9.72	M.A.Webb	Denham	31. 5.03
G-BAEN	Robin DR.400/180 Regent	736		25. 9.72	European Soaring Club Ltd	Le Blanc, France	8.10.03

G-BAEO	Reims Cessna F172M	F17200911		14. 9.72	L.W.Scattergood *(Re-built with original fuselage & remains of G-YTWO: noted 1.01)*	Breighton	
G-BAEP	Reims Cessna F150L Aerobat *(Built as FRA150L)*	FRA1500170		14. 9.72	A.M.Lynn t/a Busy Bee	Fenland	17. 5.04T
G-BAER	LeVier Cosmic Wind (Continental O-200-A)	106 & PFA 1571		14. 9.72	R.S.Voice "Filly"	Rushett Manor, Chessington	17.12.01P
G-BAET	Piper J-3C-65 Cub (L-4H-PI) *(Frame No.11430)*	11605	OO-AJI 43-30314	26. 9.72	C.J.Rees	Valley Farm, Winwick	21. 5.02P
G-BAEU	Reims Cessna F150L	F15000873		26. 9.72	L.W.Scattergood	Humberside	30. 1.04T
G-BAEV	Reims Cessna FRA150L Aerobat	FRA1500173		27. 9.72	Richardson Technology Ltd	Sibson	.6 3.04
G-BAEW*	Reims Cessna F172M	F17200914	N12798	27. 9.72	Westley Aircraft *(Damaged near Sywell 12.11.93: fuselage stored 7.97)*	(Cranfield)	9. 4.94T
G-BAEY	Reims Cessna F172M	F17200915		28. 9.72	Skytrax Aviation Ltd	Sibson	9. 3.03T
G-BAEZ	Reims Cessna FRA150L Aerobat	FRA1500169		28. 9.72	Donair Flying Club Ltd	East Midlands	19. 6.03T
G-BAFA	American AA-5 Traveler	AA5-0201	N6136A	6.10.72	C.F.Mackley	Sleap	31. 8.01
G-BAFG	de Havilland DH.82A Tiger Moth	85995	F-BGEL Fr.AF/EM778	13.10.72	J.E. & P.E.Shaw	Nottingham	18. 8.02
G-BAFH*	Evans VP-1	PFA 1579		5.10.72	Not known *(Permit expired 14.7.87 & cancelled 4.12.96: open stored 8.99)*	Thruxton	
G-BAFL	Cessna 182P Skylane	18261469	N21180	15. 8.72	M.A.Pruden	Standalone Farm, Meppershall	23. 7.01
G-BAFP	Robin DR.400/160 Knight	735		19.10.72	T.A.Pugh t/a Breidden Flying Group	Pool Quay, Breidden	22. 2.01
G-BAFT	Piper PA-18-150 Super Cub	18-5340	(D-E...) ALAT 18-5340/N10F	3. 8.72	T.J.Wilkinson	Sackville Farm, Riseley	2. 5.03
G-BAFU	Piper PA-28-140 Cherokee	28-20759	PH-NLS	11.10.72	D.Matthews	Humberside	19. 4.03T
G-BAFV	Piper PA-18 Super Cub 95 (L-18C-PI) *(Frame No.18-2055)*	18-2045	PH-WJK R.Neth AF R-40/8A-40/52-2445	24.10.72	T.F. & S.J.Thorpe	Coldharbour Farm, Willingham	1.10.04
G-BAFW	Piper PA-28-140 Cherokee	28-21050	PH-NLT	24.10.72	S.S.Delwarte	Shoreham	6. 4.03
G-BAFX	Robin DR.400/140 Earl	739		30.10.72	K.R.Gough	Clutton Hill Farm, Clutton	4. 5.04
G-BAGB	SIAI-Marchetti SF.260	1-07	LN-BIV	20.10.72	British Midland Airways Ltd	East Midlands	27. 4.03
G-BAGC	Robin DR.400/140 Earl	737		13.10.72	W.P.Nutt	(Scarborough)	15. 6.02
G-BAGF	Jodel D.92 Bebe	59	F-PHFC	13.11.72	E.Evans *(Wings stored 8.01: fuselage elsewhere)*	Benson's Farm, Laindon	
G-BAGG(2)	Piper PA-32-300 Cherokee Six	32-7340186	N9562N	7.12.73	S.A.Fell & N.J.Falla t/a G-BAGG Group	Guernsey	16. 2.04
G-BAGI*	Cameron O-31 HAFB	56		25.10.72	D.C.Boxall *"Vital Spark"* *(Cancelled 10.10.01 by CAA)*	Bristol	19. 9.76S
G-BAGL	Westland SA.341G Gazelle 1	1067		26.10.72	Foremans Aviation Ltd	(Beverley)	30. 8.03T
G-BAGN	Reims Cessna F177RG Cardinal	F177RG0068		24.10.72	R.W.J.Andrews	Wolverhampton	2. 8.04
G-BAGO	Cessna 421B Golden Eagle	421B0356	N7613Q	24.10.72	M.S.Choksey	Coventry	15.10.03
G-BAGR	Robin DR.400/140 Petit Prince	753		30.10.72	F.C.Aris & J.D.Last	Caernarfon	11. 4.04
G-BAGS	Robin DR.400/100 2+2	760		30.10.72	M Whale & M M A Lunn	Kemble	16. 1.03T
G-BAGT	Helio H.295 Super Courier	1288	CR-LJG	31.10.72	B.J.C.Woodall Ltd	Rushett Manor, Chessington	11.11.04
G-BAGV	Cessna U206F Stationair	U20601867	N9667G	31.10.72	K.Brady t/a The Scottish Parachute Club	Strathallan	14. 5.04
G-BAGX	Piper PA-28-140 Cherokee	28-23633	N3574K	30.10.72	J.R.Clayton t/a The Golf X-Ray Group	Conington	20.10.02T
G-BAGY	Cameron O-84 HAFB	54		17.10.72	P.G.Dunnington *"Beatrice" (Stored 2.97: current status unknown)*	Hungerford	16. 6.81A
G-BAHD	Cessna 182P Skylane	18261501	N21228	25.10.72	G.G.Ferriman t/a Lambley Flying Group	Jericho Farm, Lambley	13. 2.04
G-BAHE	Piper PA-28-140 Cherokee C	28-26494	N5696U	30.10.72	A.O.Jones & M W Kilvert *(Stored 5.96: new owner 10.00)*	Welshpool	8. 6.95
G-BAHF	Piper PA-28-140 Flite Liner	28-7125215	N431FL	30.10.72	BJ Services (Midlands) Ltd	Coventry	27. 6.04T
G-BAHG	Piper PA-24-260 Comanche B	24-4306	5Y-AFX N8831P	2.11.72	D.G.Sheppard	Earls Colne	31. 8.03
G-BAHH	Wallis WA-121/Mc (Wallis modified McCulloch)	K/701/X		7.11.72	K.H.Wallis *(Noted 8.01)*	Reymerston Hall, Norfolk	27. 5.98P
G-BAHI	Reims Cessna F150H	F150-0330	PH-EHA	6.11.72	I.S.McLeod	Elstree	19.11.01
G-BAHJ	Piper PA-24-250 Comanche	24-1863	PH-RED N6735P	6.11.72	K.Cooper	Wolverhampton	21. 8.04
G-BAHL	Robin DR.400/160 Knight	704	F-OCSR	8.11.72	M.D.Hinge & L.A.Maynard	Old Sarum	10. 4.03T
G-BAHO	Beechcraft C23 Sundowner	M-1456		7.11.72	P.H.White & J.A.L.Staig	Bournemouth	22.11.02
G-BAHP	Volmer VJ.22 Sportsman (Continental C90)	PFA 1313		9.11.72	G.K.Holloway t/a Seaplane Group *(Stored 6.00)*	Aboyne	18.10.93P
G-BAHS	Piper PA-28R-200 Cherokee Arrow II	28R-7335017	N15147	9.11.72	A.R.N.Morris	Shobdon	20. 6.03
G-BAHX	Cessna 182P Skylane	18261588	N21363	16.11.72	A.P.Stone t/a Dupost Group	Blackpool	15. 8.03

G-BAIG	Piper PA-34-200 Seneca	34-7250243	OY-BSU	21.11.72	Mid-Anglia Flying Centre Ltd	Cambridge	27. 9.03T
			G-BAIG/N5257T		t/a Mid-Anglia School of Flying		
G-BAIH	Piper PA-28R-200 Cherokee Arrow II	28R-7335011	N11C	21.11.72	M.G.West	King's Farm, Thurrock	22. 6.04
G-BAII	Reims Cessna FRA150L Aerobat	FRA1500178		22.11.72	Cornwall Flying Club Ltd	Bodmin	14. 6.03T
					(Force landed Hendra Farm, Bodmin 9.9.01 & severely damaged)		
G-BAIK	Reims Cessna F150L	F15000903		22.11.72	Wickenby Aviation Ltd	Wickenby	9. 4.03T
					(Op Lincoln Flight Centre)		
G-BAIL*	Reims FR172J Rocket	FR17200370		22.11.72	R.H.Blair	Farley Farm, Winchester	7. 7.00
	(Damaged landing Farley Farm, Winchester 6.3.99: cancelled 6.7.99 by CAA wreck acquired by Bournemouth College)						
G-BAIN	Reims Cessna FRA150L Aerobat	FRA1500177		23.11.72	S.J.Windle	Bodmin	25. 7.04T
G-BAIP	Reims Cessna F150L	F15000898		13.11.72	G. & S.A.Jones	Linley Hill, Leven	28. 9.97T
					(Damaged Linley Hill 30.5.95: current status unknown)		
G-BAIR*	Thunder Ax7-77 HAFB	003		27.11.72	S.Faithfull *"Jumping Jack"*	NK	NE(A)
					(Cancelled 26.2.90 by CAA: current status unknown)		
G-BAIS	Reims Cessna F177RG Cardinal	F177RG0069		13.11.72	R.M.Graham & E.P.Howard	Seething	22. 8.02
					t/a Cardinal Syndicate		
G-BAIW	Reims Cessna F172M	F17200928		14.11.72	W.J.Greenfield	Humberside	10. 1.04T
G-BAIX	Reims Cessna F172M	F17200931		14.11.72	R.A.Nichols	Elstree	22.12.02
G-BAIZ	Slingsby T.61A Falke	1776		27.11.72	G.C.Rumsey & R.G.Sangster t/a Falke Syndicate	Hinton-in-the-Hedges	21. 5.03
G-BAJA	Reims Cessna F177RG Cardinal	F177RG0078		29.11.72	Don Ward Productions Ltd	Rochester	17. 1.03
G-BAJB	Reims Cessna F177RG Cardinal	F177RG0080		29.11.72	C.M.Bain	Inverness	29. 8.03
G-BAJC	Evans VP-1 Srs.2 (VW 1834)	PFA 1548		30.11.72	S.J.Greer	Dunkeswell	22. 3.99P
					(Damaged landing Bovingdon 4.3.99: stored 11.01)		
G-BAJE	Cessna 177 Cardinal	17700812	N29322	30.11.72	H.Snelson	Nottingham	3.10.03
G-BAJN	American AA-5 Traveler	AA5-0259		29.11.72	K.Bell & J.C.Robinson	Blackpool	16. 5.03
					t/a Janacrew Flying Group		
G-BAJO	American AA-5 Traveler	AA5-0260		29.11.72	P.J.Kelsall	Blackpool	30. 5.04
					t/a G-BAJO Flying Group		
G-BAJR	Piper PA-28-180 Challenger	28-7305008	N11C	1.12.72	D.P.Bannister & D.T.Given		
					t/a Chosen Flew Flying Group	Newtownards, Co.of Down	5. 4.03
G-BAJY	Robin DR.400/180 Regent	758		4.12.72	J.H.Fenwick	Wickenby	28. 8.04
					t/a Rolincs Aviation		
G-BAJZ	Robin DR.400/125 Petit Prince	759		4.12.72	Weald Air Services Ltd	Headcorn	27. 7.03T
G-BAKD	Piper PA-34-200 Seneca	34-7350013	N1378T	28.11.72	Andrews Professional Colour Laboratories Ltd		
					(Op Foto Flite)	Headcorn	7. 5.04A
G-BAKH	Piper PA-28-140 Cherokee F	28-7325014	N11C	12.12.72	Marham Investments Ltd	Belfast	6. 9.03T
					(Op Ulster Flying Club)		
G-BAKJ	Piper PA-30 Twin Comanche B	30-1232	TJ-AAI	13.12.72	G.D.Colover, R.Jones & N. O'Connor		
			TJ-ADH/N8122Y			Elstree	3. 5.03T
G-BAKM	Robin DR.400/140 Earl	755		15.12.72	D.V.Pieri	Carlisle	5. 2.04
G-BAKN	SNCAN Stampe SV-4C	348	F-BCOY	15.12.72	M.Holloway	(Chard)	13. 6.02
G-BAKO*	Cameron O-84 HAFB	57		18.12.72	Balloon Preservation Group	Kirdford	12. 7.76S
					"Pied Piper" (Cancelled 19.5.93 by CAA)		
G-BAKR	SAN Jodel D.117	814	F-BIOV	27.12.72	R.W.Brown	Stoneacre Farm, Farthing Corner	7.11.02P
G-BAKV	Piper PA-18-150 Super Cub	18-8993	N9???N	22.12.72	A.J.B.Shaw, Western Air (Thruxton) Ltd & F.Taylor	Thruxton	15. 8.04T
G-BAKW	Beagle B.121 Pup 2	B121-175		15.12.72	H.Beavan	White Waltham	21. 6.03
G-BAKY	Slingsby T.61C Falke	1777		20.12.72	T.J.Wiltshire	Spilsby	7. 8.98
G-BALD	Cameron O-84 HAFB	58		2. 1.73	C.A.Gould	Ipswich	2. 7.78S
					t/a Inter-Varsity Balloon Club *"Puffin"*		
					(WFU after severe damage 25.6.78: basket to G-PUFF: current CofR)		
G-BALF	Robin DR.400/140 Earl	772		5. 1.73	G.& D.A.Wasey	Kemble	5. 7.03
G-BALG	Robin DR.400/180 Regent	771		5. 1.73	R.Jones	Aston Down	5. 8.04
					t/a Southern Sailplanes		
G-BALH	Robin DR.400/140B Earl	766		5. 1.73	C.Johnson	Fenland	21. 6.04
					t/a G-BALH Flying Group		
G-BALI	Robin DR.400 2 + 2	764		5. 1.73	A.Brinkley	Standalone Farm, Meppershall	3. 9.88
					(On rebuild 3.96)		
G-BALJ	Robin DR.400/180 Regent	767		5. 1.73	D.A.Batt & D.de Lacey-Rowe	Fridd Farm, Bethersden, Kent	31. 5.03
G-BALK*	SNCAN Stampe SV-4C	387	F-BBAN	3. 1.73	J.Thorogood	Insch	
			Fr.Mil				
			(No UK CofA or Permit issued: cancelled 4.12.96 by CAA: fuselage only 6.00)				
G-BALN	Cessna T310Q	310Q0684	N7980Q	8. 1.73	O'Brien Properties Ltd	Shoreham	1. 5.00T
G-BALY	Practavia Pilot Sprite 150	PFA 05-10009		10. 1.73	A.L.Young t/a Aly Aviation	(Henstridge)	
					(Project part completed and stored 8.95: current status unknown)		
G-BALZ	Bell 212	30542	EC-GCR	10. 1.73	Bristow Helicopters Ltd	Aberdeen	5.10.03T
			EC-931/G-BALZ/9Y-TIL/G-BALZ/VR-BIB/N8069A/G-BALZ/N99040/G-BALZ/EI-AWK/G-BALZ/VR-BEK/N2961W				

G-BAMB	Slingsby T.61C Falke	1778		9. 1.73	C Kaminski	Eaglescott	2.10.03
					t/a G-BAMB Syndicate		
G-BAMC	Reims Cessna F150L	F15000892		12. 1.73	Systems & Research Ltd	Caernarfon	18. 7.02T
G-BAMF	MBB Bö.105DB	S.36	D-HDAM	10. 1.73	Bond Air Services	Sullom Voe	20. 6.03T
					(Op Sullom Voe Harbour Trust)		
G-BAMG*	Avions Lobet Ganagobie	PFA 1336		11. 1.73	Not known	Yearby	
	(Cancelled by CAA 5.8.91: complete 4.97 but unflown: dismantled but complete 1.02)						
G-BAMJ	Cessna 182P	18261650	N21469	10. 1.73	A.E.Kedros	Enstone	29. 5.03
G-BAMK*	Cameron D-96 Hot-Air Airship	72		11. 1.73	British Balloon Museum & Library	Newbury	24. 4.90A
					"Isibidbi" *(Cancelled 16.8.00 by CAA)*		
G-BAML	Bell 206B JetRanger II	36	N7844S	5. 1.73	Heliscott Ltd	Walton Wood, Pontefract	1. 6.03T
G-BAMM	Piper PA-28-235 Cherokee	28-10642	SE-EOA	16. 1.73	T.R.Astell	Goodwood	9. 8.01
G-BAMR	Piper PA-16 Clipper	16-392	F-BFMS	12. 1.73	H.Royce	Bradleys Lawn, Heathfield	21. 8.04
	(Lycoming O-290)		CU-P339				
G-BAMS	Robin DR.400/160 Knight	774		15. 1.73	G-BAMS Ltd	Biggin Hill	31. 5.03T
G-BAMT*	Robin DR.400/160 Knight	775		15. 1.73	Southern Sailplanes	Membury	15. 5.79
	(Crashed Cudham 8.1.78: wreck stored 1.92: current status unknown)						
G-BAMU	Robin DR.400/160 Knight	778		15. 1.73	J.W.L.Otty	Sywell	9. 7.03
					t/a The Alternative Flying Group		
G-BAMV	Robin DR.400/180 Regent	777		15. 1.73	K.Jones & E.A.Anderson	Booker	3. 5.03
G-BAMY	Piper PA-28R-200 Cherokee Arrow II	28R-7335015	N11C	9. 1.73	G.R.Gilbert	Birmingham	29. 3.04
					t/a G-BAMY Group		
G-BANA	CEA Jodel DR.221 Dauphin	73	F-BOZR	22. 1.73	G.T.Pryor	Seething	21.10.02
G-BANB	Robin DR.400/180 Regent	776		22. 1.73	D.R.L.Jones	Kemble	15. 3.03T
G-BANC	Gardan GY-201 Minicab	A.203	F-PCZV	22. 1.73	J.T.S.Lewis & J.E.Williams		
	(Continental C90)		F-BCZV			Brickhouse Farm, Frogland Cross	31. 5.02P
G-BAND*	Cameron O-84 HAFB	52		22. 1.73	Balloon Preservation Group	Southampton	
					"Clover" *(Cancelled 17.4.98 as WFU)*		
G-BANF	Phoenix Luton LA-4A Minor	PFA 838		22. 1.73	W.J.McCollum	Coagh, Co.Londonderry	5. 6.92P
	(Continental A65)				*(Damaged Mullaghmore 27.6.92: noted 11.01)*		
G-BANU	Jodel Wassmer D.120 Paris-Nice	247	F-BLNZ	31. 1.73	W.M. & C.H.Kilner	(Rutland Water)	23. 7.02P
G-BANV	Phoenix Currie Wot	PFA 3010		25. 1.73	K.Knight	(Malvern)	26. 6.84P
	(Lycoming O-290)				*(Damaged near Leek, Staffs 15.9.83: current status unknown)*		
G-BANW	CAARP CP.1330 Super Emeraude	941	PH-VRF	30. 1.73	P.S.Milner	Scotland Farm, Hook	28. 6.02P
	(Lycoming O-235-C1)						
G-BANX	Reims Cessna F172M	F17200941		31. 1.73	Oakfleet 2000 Ltd	Biggin Hill	6. 8.03T
G-BANY*	Glos-Air Airtourer 115	A533		31. 1.73	Not known	St.Just	25. 3.77
	(Crashed near Wick 10.8.75: cancelled 30.3.83 as WFU: fuselage stored 8.96: current status unknown)						
G-BAOB	Reims Cessna F172M	F17200949		2. 2.73	M.Nicoll, D.Williams-Gardner & R.H.Taylor		
						Andrewsfield	22. 4.04T
G-BAOG	SOCATA MS.880B Rallye Club	2249		6. 2.73	J.Luck	Rochester	31. 1.03T
G-BAOH	SOCATA MS.880B Rallye Club	2250		6. 2.73	A.P.Swain	Haverfordwest	28. 7.01
G-BAOJ	SOCATA MS.880B Rallye Club	2252		6. 2.73	R.E.Jones	Emlyns Field, Rhuallt	13. 8.01
G-BAOM	SOCATA MS.880B Rallye Club	2255		6. 2.73	P.J.D.Feehan	Exeter	17. 4.03
G-BAOP	Reims Cessna FRA150L Aerobat	FRA1500190		5. 2.73	S.A.Boyall	Norwich	11. 4.02
G-BAOS	Reims Cessna F172M	F17200946		6. 2.73	Wingtask 1995 Ltd	Seething	14. 8.03T
G-BAOU	Grumman-American AA-5 Traveler	AA5-0298		8. 2.73	R.C.Mark	Shobdon	18. 9.04
G-BAOW*	Cameron O-65 HAFB	59		6. 2.73	Balloon Preservation Group	Southampton	9. 5.74S
					"Winslow Boy" *(Cancelled 15.10.01 by CAA)*		
G-BAPB	de Havilland DHC-1 Chipmunk 22A	C1/0001	WB549	26. 2.73	G.V.Bunyan	Bidford	31. 5.98
G-BAPF*	Vickers V.814 Viscount	338	SE-FOY	12. 2.73	Home Office Fire & Emergency Training Centre		
			G-BAPF/D-ANUN			Moreton-in-Marsh	13. 6.90T
	(Cancelled 17.6.92 by CAA: instructional airframe 8.98)						
G-BAPH*	Reims Cessna FRA150L Aerobat	FRA1500194		8. 2.73	South Yorkshire Aviation Museum		
						Home Farm, Firbeck	26. 7.82
	(Damaged Bodmin 12.7.81: used for spares: cancelled 21.1.87 by CAA: rear fuselage displayed)						
G-BAPI	Reims Cessna FRA150L Aerobat	FRA1500195		8. 2.73	Industrial Supplies (Peterborough) Ltd		
						Sibson	6. 3.04
G-BAPJ	Reims Cessna FRA150L Aerobat	FRA1500196		8. 2.73	M.D.Page	Manston	10. 6.02
G-BAPL	Piper PA-23-250 Turbo Aztec E	27-7304966	N14377	12. 2.73	Donington Aviation Ltd	East Midlands	27. 8.01T
G-BAPM*	Fuji FA.200-160 Aero Subaru	FA-200-172		13. 2.73	Not known	Farley Farm, Winchester	
					(Cancelled 6.11.98 by CAA: wreck noted 6.99)		
G-BAPR	Jodel D.11	5295 & PFA 914		14. 2.73	J.P.Liber & J.F.M.Bartlett	Kemble	17. 4.02P
	(Continental PC60)						
G-BAPS*	Campbell Cougar Gyroplane	CA/6000		14. 2.73	A.M.W.Curzon-Howe-Herrick		
	(Continental O-240-A)					Weston-super-Mare	20. 5.74S
	(Cancelled 21.1.87 by CAA:.on loan to The Helicopter Museum)						
G-BAPV	Robin DR.400/160 Knight	742	F-OCSR	19. 2.73	J.D. & M.Millne	Newcastle	22. 8.03
					(Stored 9.97)		

G-BAPW	Piper PA-28R-180 Cherokee Arrow	28R-30697	5Y-AIR N4951J	21. 2.73	P.S.Farren & I.W.Lindsey t/a Papa Whisky Flying Group	Denham	7.12.03
G-BAPX	Robin DR.400/160 Knight	789		21. 2.73	M.Stanton t/a G-BAPX Group	Sywell	11. 6.03
G-BAPY	Robin HR.100/210 Royal	153		21. 2.73	D.M.Hansell	Old Buckenham	7. 7.01
G-BARC	Reims FR172J Rocket	FR17200356	(D-EEDK)	5. 3.73	C.H.Porter t/a Severn Valley Aviation Group	Croft Farm, Defford	10. 4.04
G-BARD*	Cessna 337C Super Skymaster	3370857	SE-FBU N2557S	1. 3.73	Not known	North Coates	9. 1.97
	(Damaged North Coates 12.6.94: cancelled 7.2.96 as WFU: current status unknown)						
G-BARF	Wassmer Jodel D.112	1019	F-BJPF	5. 3.73	J.J.Penney	Neath	21. 1.01P
G-BARG	Cessna E310Q	310Q0712	N8237Q	2. 3.73	Tibus Aviation Ltd	Blackbushe	8.12.02T
G-BARH	Beechcraft C23 Sundowner	M-1473		2. 3.73	J.R.Pybus	Sherburn in Elmet	4. 2.01
G-BARI*	Beechcraft C23 Sundowner	M-1475		2. 3.73	Not known	Bushey	15. 7.75
	(Crashed near Coventry 23.4.75: cancelled 5.8.75 as destroyed: wreck displayed in car-breaker's yard 5.95: current status unknown)						
G-BARN	Taylor JT.2 Titch (Continental C90)	PFA 060-11136		5. 3.73	R.G.W.Newton *(On rebuild: current status unknown)*	(Seaford)	2.10.92P
G-BARP	Bell 206B JetRanger II	967	N18092	5. 3.73	South Western Electricity plc	Bristol	9. 5.03T
G-BARS	de Havilland DHC-1 Chipmunk 22	C1/0557	WK520	26. 2.73	J.Beattie *(As "1377" in Portuguese AF c/s)*	RNAS Yeovilton	3. 8.02
G-BARV	Cessna 310Q	310Q-0774		7. 3.73	Old England Watches Ltd	Elstree	9. 8.04
G-BARZ	Scheibe SF-28A Tandem Falke	5724	(D-KAUK)	8. 3.73	K.Kiely	AAC Dishforth	1.12.02
G-BASG*	Grumman-American AA-5 Traveler	AA5-0320	N5420L	12. 3.73	(Skycraft Ltd)	(Spalding)	20. 1.00
	(Damaged Isle of Rothsay 3.9.00: PWFU 6.12.00: fuselage for sale/repairable 11.01)						
G-BASH	Grumman-American AA-5 Traveler	AA5-0319	EI-AWV G-BASH/N5419L	12. 3.73	G.Jenkins t/a BASH Flying Group	Popham	9. 9.02T
G-BASJ	Piper PA-28-180 Cherokee Challenger	28-7305136	N11C	13. 3.73	T.J.McElwee t/a Challenger Flying Group	Filton	7.12.03T
G-BASL	Piper PA-28-140 Cherokee F	28-7325195	N11C	13. 3.73	Justgold Ltd	Blackpool	2. 8.04T
G-BASM	Piper PA-34-200 Seneca	34-7350120	N16272	13. 3.73	M.Gipps & J.R.Whetlor	Denham	19.11.01
G-BASN	Beechcraft C23 Sundowner	M-1476		13. 3.73	M.F.Fisher	Tatenhill	6.11.04
G-BASO	Lake LA-4-180 Amphibian	358	N2025L	16. 3.73	C.J.A.Macaulay	Popham	24. 6.02
G-BASP	Beagle B.121 Pup 1	B121-149	SE-FOC G-35-149	14. 3.73	B.J.Coutts	Sywell	19. 7.04
G-BAST*	Cameron O-84 HAFB	70		15. 3.73	Balloon Preservation Group *"Honey" (Cancelled 19.5.93 by CAA)*	Kirdford	2. 5.84A
G-BASU*	Piper PA-31-350 Navajo Chieftain	31-7305023	N7693L	15. 3.73	Not known	Exeter	3.11.87T
	(Damaged Dounreay 12.5.87: cancelled 24.7.89 as destroyed: fuselage on fire dump 11.93: current status unknown)						
G-BASX	Piper PA-34-200 Seneca	34-7350123	N15781	16. 3.73	Air Consul SL	(Seville, Spain)	22. 9.02T
G-BATC	MBB Bö.105DB	S.45	D-HDAW	9. 3.73	Bond Air Services	East Midlands	22. 6.02T
	(Originally regd as Bö.105D: rebuilt using new MBB pod 1989 c/n NK)						
G-BATD*	Cessna U206F Stationair	U20602014	N60204	12. 3.73	British Parachute School	Langar	13. 7.79
	(Crashed Shobdon 5.4.80: cancelled 19.6.80 as destroyed: used as para-trainer: current status unknown)						
G-BATJ	Jodel D.119 (Continental C90) *(Built Ecole Technique Aeronautique)*	287	F-PIIQ	21. 3.73	D.J. & K.S.Thomas	Fenland	24. 6.02P
G-BATN	Piper PA-23-250 Aztec E	27-7304987	N14391	26. 3.73	Marshall of Cambridge Aerospace Ltd	Cambridge	9. 1.03T
G-BATR	Piper PA-34-200 Seneca	34-7250290	9H-ABH G-BATR/LN-BDT	23. 3.73	A.S.Bamrah t/a Falcon Flying Services	Biggin Hill	30. 3.02T
G-BATV	Piper PA-28-180 Cherokee F	28-7105022	N5168S	26. 3.73	J.N.Rudsdale t/a The Scoreby Flying Group	Sherburn in Elmet	8.11.02
G-BATW	Piper PA-28-140 Cherokee Flite Liner	28-7225587	N742FL	26. 3.73	M.Butterworth & K Simons t/a Tango Whiskey Flying Partnership	Earls Colne	10.12.02
G-BAUC	Piper PA-25-235 Pawnee C	25-5243	N8761L	26. 3.73	Southdown Gliding Club Ltd	Parham Park	29. 5.03
G-BAUH	Dormois Jodel D.112	870	F-BILO	29. 3.73	G.A. & D.Shepherd t/a G-BAUH Flying Group	Seething	19.10.01P
G-BAUI*	Piper PA-23-250 Aztec D	27-4335	LN-RTS	29. 3.73	Brunel Technical College	Bristol	5.12.88T
	(Cancelled 26.1.89 by CAA) (Stored 12.98: current status unknown)						
G-BAUJ	Piper PA-23-250 Aztec E	27-7304986	N14390	29. 3.73	S.Bramwell *(Stored 7.97: current status unknown)*	Cranfield	25. 7.94T
G-BAUR*	Fokker F.27 Friendship 200	10225	PH-FEP 9V-BAP/9M-AMI/(VR-RCZ)/PH-FEP	5. 4.73	Jersey European Airways (UK) Ltd	Exeter	5. 4.96T
	(Cancelled 25.1.96 as WFU: stored 2.96: fuselage only 10.99)						
G-BAUW	Piper PA-23-250 Aztec E	27-4814	N14253	9. 4.73	R.E.Myson	Jersey/Hardings Farm, Ingatestone	22. 7.03
G-BAVA*	Piper PA-18-150 Super Cub	18-5391	D-EFKC ALAT 18-5391/N10F	10. 4.73	Not known	Membury	
	(Crashed Newtownards 20.11.77: cancelled 19.4.83 as WFU: frame noted 1.92: current status unknown)						
G-BAVB	Reims Cessna F172M	F17200965		10. 4.73	C.P.Course	Church Farm, Wellingborough	27. 2.02T
G-BAVH	de Havilland DHC-1 Chipmunk 22 (Lycoming 350hp)	C1/0841	WP975	10. 4.73	D.C.Murray t/a Portsmouth Naval Gliding Club	Lee-on-Solent	24. 3.96

G-BAVL	Piper PA-23-250 Aztec E	27-4671	N14063	10. 4.73	S.P. & A.V.Chilcott	Teesside	12. 6.04T
G-BAVO	Boeing-Stearman A75N-1 Kaydet	-	4X-AIH	13. 4.73	M.Shaw	Old Buckenham	28. 6.04T
	(Continental W670)				*(As "26" in US Army c/s)*		
	(Regd with c/n "3250-1405" which is a part number: original identity unknown)						
G-BAVR	Grumman-American AA-5 Traveler	AA5-0348		12. 4.73	G.E.Murray	Haverfordwest	25. 9.04
G-BAVS*	Grumman-American AA-5 Traveler	AA5-0349		12. 4.73	Not known	Bournemouth	8.11.94
					(Stored 7.93: cancelled 31.10.96 by CAA: current status unknown)		
G-BAVU*	Cameron A-105 HAFB	66		11. 4.73	British Balloon Museum & Library	Newbury	5.10.84A
					(Cancelled 6.12.01 by CAA)		
G-BAVZ	Piper PA-23-250 Aztec E	27-7305045	N40241	18. 4.73	Cheshire Flying Services Ltd t/a Ravenair	Liverpool	12. 3.04T
G-BAWG	Piper PA-28R-200 Cherokee Arrow II	28R-7335133	N11C	18. 4.73	Solent Air Ltd	Goodwood	1. 3.04
G-BAWI*	Enstrom F-28A-UK	120		9. 4.73	Lodge Road Flying Services	Tattershall Thorpe	10. 4.94T
					(Crashed Bosworth Hall 26.6.92: cancelled 17.8.92 by CAA: stored 10.92: current status unknown)		
G-BAWK	Piper PA-28-140 Cherokee Cruiser	28-7325243		24. 4.73	Newcastle-upon-Tyne Aero Club Ltd	Newcastle	3. 8.04T
G-BAWR	Robin HR.100/210 Royal	156		27. 4.73	T.Taylor	Thruxton	8. 6.00
G-BAWW*	Thunder Ax7-77 HAFB	004	(PH-AWW) G-BAWW	30. 4.73	S.Faithfull *"Taurus"*	NK	11. 5.84A
					(Cancelled 2.4.92 by CAA) (Current status unknown)		
G-BAXE	Hughes 269A-1	113-0313	N8931F	2. 5.73	Reeve Newfields Ltd	Sywell	21.12.93S
					(Frame only noted 11.01)		
G-BAXF*	Cameron O-77 HAFB	74		3. 5.73	British Balloon Museum & Library *"Granna"* *(Cancelled 5.9.95 by CAA)*	Newbury	NE(A)
G-BAXJ	Piper PA-32-300 Cherokee Six B	32-40763	N1362Z (N59RG)/N1362Z/G-BAXJ/4X-ANY/N5224S	8. 5.73	A.G.Knight t/a Airlaunch	Old Buckenham	14. 6.03
G-BAXK*	Thunder Ax7-77 HAFB	005		9. 5.73	A.R.Snook *"Jack O'Newbury"*	Newbury	2. 7.91A
					(Cancelled 7.9.01 as wfu)		
G-BAXS	Bell 47G-5	7908	5B-CFB G-BAXS/N4098G	11. 5.73	R.M.Kemp t/a RK Helicopters	Fairoaks	14.12.03T
G-BAXU	Reims Cessna F150L	F15000959		14. 5.73	M.A.Wilson	RAF Mona	11. 4.04
G-BAXV	Reims Cessna F150L	F15000966		14. 5.73	G. & S.A.Jones	Sandtoft	17. 5.04T
G-BAXY	Reims Cessna F172M	F17200905	N10636	15. 5.73	Eaglesoar Ltd	Humberside	9.10.04T
G-BAXZ	Piper PA-28-140 Cherokee C	28-26760	PH-NLX N11C	15. 5.73	D.Norris & H.Martin t/a G-BAXZ Syndicate	Turweston	8. 3.04T
G-BAYC*	Cameron O-65 HAFB	68	(HB-BOU) G-BAYC	17. 5.73	Not known	NK	
					(Cancelled 15.5.98 as WFU) (Noted 2000)		
G-BAYL*	SNCAN Nord 1203 Norecrin VI	161	F-BEQV	18. 5.73	J.E.Pierce	Ley Farm, Chirk	
					(Cancelled 14.11.91 by CAA: fuselage only stored outside 9.00)		
G-BAYO	Cessna 150L	15074435	N19471	18. 5.73	J A, G M, D T A & J A Rees t/a Messrs Rees of Poyston West	Haverfordwest	27. 6.04T
G-BAYP	Cessna 150L	15074017	N18651	18. 5.73	D.I.Thomas t/a Yankee Papa Flying Group	Denham	6. 4.02T
G-BAYR	Robin HR.100/210 Royal	164		18. 5.73	Linda A.Christie	Stapleford	23. 5.03
G-BAYV*	SNCAN 1101 Noralpha	193	F-BLTN Fr.AF	22. 5.73	P.Smith	Eccleston, Leyland	2. 8.75
					(Crashed Longbridge Deverill 23.2.74: cancelled 28.4.83 as WFU)		
					(Loaned to Bygone Times Antique Warehouse & displayed as "F-OTAN-6": see G-ATDB)		
G-BAZC	Robin DR.400-160 Knight	824		29. 5.73	R.Jones t/a Southern Sailplanes	Membury	24. 6.88
					(Damaged Crosland Moor 21.5.88: stored 10.01)		
G-BAZJ*	Handley Page HPR.7 Dart Herald 209	183	4X-AHR G-8-1	30. 5.73	Guernsey Airport Fire Service	Guernsey	24.11.84T
					(Cancelled 4.1.85 as WFU: open storage 12.01)		
G-BAZM	Jodel D.11 (Continental O-200-A) *(Identified as "D.113")*	PAL/1416 & PFA 915		31. 5.73	A.F.Simpson *"L'Oiseau Jaime"*	Watchford Farm, Yarcombe	16. 7.02P
G-BAZS	Reims Cessna F150L	F15000954		1. 6.73	L.W.Scattergood	Humberside	22. 5.03T
G-BAZT	Reims Cessna F172M	F17200996		1. 6.73	Exeter Flying Club Ltd	Exeter	22. 5.03T
G-BAZU	Piper PA-28R-200 Cherokee Arrow	28R-7135151	EI-AVH N11C	6. 6.73	S.C.Simmons	White Waltham	17.12.04

G-BBAA – G-BBZZ

G-BBAK	SOCATA MS.894A Rallye Minerva 220	12080	(D-ENMK)	6. 6.73	J.E.Selman	(Ardagh, Co.Limerick)	8. 8.98
G-BBAW	Robin HR.100/210 Royal	167		12. 6.73	J.R.Williams	Goodwood	1.10.03
G-BBAX	Robin DR.400/140 Earl	835		12. 6.73	G.J.Bissex & P.H.Garbutt	New Farm, Felton	21.11.03
G-BBAY	Robin DR.400/140 Earl	841		12. 6.73	D.S.Brown & V.H.R. Gray t/a Rothwell Group	Rothwell Lodge Farm, Kettering	31. 1.02
G-BBAZ*	Hiller UH-12E	2165	EC-DOR G-BBAZ/N31707/CAF112276/RCAF10276	13. 6.73	Not known	Gamlingay	23. 5.91
					(Cancelled 29.5.96 by CAA: stored for restoration 2.00)		

G-BBBB	Taylor JT.1 Monoplane			4. 6.73	S.A.MacConnacher	(Northampton)	
	(VW 1600)	SAM/01 & PFA 1422			*(Current status unknown)*		
G-BBBC	Reims Cessna F150L	F15000864	N10635	14. 6.73	A.A.Gardner	Humberside	15.12.01T
G-BBBI	Grumman-American AA-5 Traveler			15. 6.73	J.C.McCaig	West Freugh	20.12.02
		AA5-0392					
G-BBBK	Piper PA-28-140 Cherokee	28-22572	SE-EYF	18. 6.73	Bencray Ltd	Blackpool	8. 8.04
					(Op Blackpool & Fylde Aero Club)		
G-BBBL*	Cessna 337B Super Skymaster	3370555	EI-AVF	19. 6.73	P.R.Moss	Farley Farm, Winchester	12. 2.77
			5H-MNL/N5455S				
				(Cancelled 21.1.87 by CAA: stored 3.92: current status unknown)			
G-BBBN	Piper PA-28-180 Cherokee Challenger		N11C	20. 6.73	Estuary Aviation Ltd	Southend	16. 1.03T
		28-7305365					
G-BBBO	SIPA 903	67	F-BGBQ	16. 1.74	G.K.Brothwood & P.R.Tonks	Liverpool	6. 6.02P
					t/a Mersey SIPA Group		
G-BBBW	Clutton FRED Srs.2	DLW.1 & PFA 1551		26. 6.73	M.Palfreman	Bagby	5. 4.01P
	(VW 1834)						
G-BBBX	Cessna 310L	310L0134	OY-EGW	28. 6.73	Atlantic Air Transport Ltd		
			N3284X			Jersey/Coventry	23.10.02
G-BBBY	Piper PA-28-140 Cherokee Cruiser		N9501N	28. 6.73	D.T.Wright & D.L.Holland	(Swinderby)	5. 5.03
		28-7325533			t/a G-BBBY Syndicate		
G-BBCA	Bell 206B JetRanger II	1101	N18091	29. 6.73	Heliflight (UK) Ltd	Wolverhampton	17.10.04T
G-BBCB	Western O-65 HAFB	018		29. 6.73	G.M.Bulmer *"Cee Bee"*	Hereford	19. 5.76S
G-BBCC	Piper PA-23-250 Aztec D	27-4317	N6953Y	29. 6.73	Richard Nash Cars Ltd	Norwich	11. 4.04T
G-BBCF*	Reims Cessna FRA150L Aerobat			3. 7.73	Air Service Training Ltd	Perth	6. 3.86T
		FRA1500209					
		(Damaged near Harrogate 8.9.84: cancelled 31.7.89 as WFU: noted 8.99: current status unknown)					
G-BBCH	Robin DR.400 2 + 2	850		4. 7.73	A.J.& S.P.Smith	(Oxford)	19. 3.04T
G-BBCI	Cessna 150H	15069282	N50409	4. 7.73	A L & F Alam	Elstree	9. 8.03T
G-BBCK	Cameron O-77 HAFB	76		4. 7.73	W R Teasdale	Maidenhead	15. 6.89S
G-BBCN	Robin HR.100/210 Royal	168		11. 7.73	S.J.Goodburn	Gloucestershire	6. 9.03
					t/a Gloucestershire Flying Club		
G-BBCP*	Thunder Ax6-56 HAFB	007		11. 7.73	J.M.Robinson	(Oxfordshire)	10. 7.81A
					"Jack Frost" (Cancelled.29.10.01 as wfu & stored)		
G-BBCS	Robin DR.400/140B Earl	851		12. 7.73	J.C.Harvey	Spilsted Farm, Sedlescombe	12. 5.04
					t/a Westfield Flying Group		
G-BBCW	Piper PA-23-250 Aztec E	27-4806	N14251	17. 7.73	Jack Tighe Holdings Ltd	Sturgate	20.10.00T
					(Op Eastern Air Executive)		
G-BBCY	Phoenix Luton LA-4A Minor	PFA 825		17. 7.73	G.I.Ciupka	(St. Albans)	13. 6.02P
	(VW 1600)						
G-BBCZ	Grumman-American AA-5 Traveler			18. 7.73	Southern Flight Centre Ltd	Shoreham	29. 4.04T
		AA5-0382					
G-BBDB*	Piper PA-28-180 Cherokee Challenger		N11C	18. 7.73	Not known	Newtownards, Co.of Down	7. 6.85
		28-7305361		*(Cancelled 31.7.89 as WFU) (Wreck stored 4.96: current status unknown)*			
G-BBDC	Piper PA-28-140 Cherokee Cruiser		N11C	18. 7.73	P.A.Gray & B.Scragg	Andrewsfield	26. 4.04
		28-7325437			t/a G-BBDC Group		
G-BBDE	Piper PA-28R-200 Cherokee Arrow II		(EI-)	18. 7.73	R.L.Coleman & A.E.Stevens	Panshanger	9. 9.02
		28R-7335250	G-BBDE/N11C				
G-BBDG*	British Aircraft Corporation-Aérospatiale Concorde 100			7. 8.73	British Airways plc	Filton	1. 3.82P
		13523 & 100-002			*(Cancelled 12.81 as WFU: stored for spares 9.01)*		
G-BBDH	Reims Cessna F172M	F17200990		19. 7.73	J.C.Holland	(Hungerford)	18. 5.02
G-BBDJ*	Thunder Ax7-65 HAFB	006		20. 7.73	Balloon Preservation Group	Southampton	
					"Jack Tar" (Cancelled 11.5.93 by CAA)		
G-BBDL	Grumman-American AA-5 Traveler			18. 7.73	W B Bateson	Blackpool	4. 2.02
		AA5-0406					
G-BBDM	Grumman-American AA-5 Traveler			18. 7.73	P.J.Marchant	Rush Green	1.10.04
		AA5-0407					
G-BBDO	Piper PA-23-250 Aztec E	27-7305120	N40361	24. 7.73	J W Anstee	Filton	24. 5.03T
					t/a G-BBDO Flying Group		
G-BBDP	Robin DR.400/160 Knight	853		25. 7.73	Robin Lance Aviation Associates Ltd		
						Rochester	11. 9.04
G-BBDS	Piper PA-31-310 Turbo Navajo B		N97RJ	26. 7.73	Elham Valley Aviation Ltd.	Lydd	8. 8.97T
		31-7300956	G-SKKB/G-BBDS/N7565L				
G-BBDT	Cessna 150H	15068839	N23272	26. 7.73	C.I.Beilby	Sherburn in Elmet	19. 3.03
					t/a Delta Tango Group		
G-BBDV	SIPA 903	7/21	F-BEYY	30. 7.73	W.McAndrew	Sackville Farm, Riseley	11. 6.02P
	(Continental C90) *(Originally ex F-BEYJ c/n 7 but rebuilt in 1978 from F-BEYY c/n 21)*						
G-BBEA	Phoenix Luton LA-4A Minor	PFA 843		30. 7.73	R Q T Newns	White Waltham	29. 4.02P
	(VW 1600)				t/a Luton Group		
G-BBEB	Piper PA-28R-200 Cherokee Arrow II		N9514N	31. 7.73	R.D.W.Rippingale	Anvil Farm, Hungerford	22. 2.04
		28R-7335292					
G-BBEC	Piper PA-28-180 Cherokee Challenger		N11C	30. 7.73	J.B.Conway	Ronaldsway	31. 5.04T
		28-7305478					
G-BBED	SOCATA MS.894A Rallye Minerva 220			30. 7.73	C.A.Shelley	Alcester	13. 9.87T
		12097			t/a Vista Products *(Stored 9.95: current status unknown)*		

G-BBEF	Piper PA-28-140 Cherokee Cruiser	28-7325527	N9500N	31. 7.73	Comed Aviation Ltd *(Rebuilt using components from damaged G-AVWG by 4.99)*	Blackpool	20.10.01T
G-BBEL	Piper PA-28R-180 Cherokee Arrow	28R-30877	SE-FDX	6. 8.73	S.J.Weaving & K.S.Kalsi	Conington	26. 4.04T
G-BBEN	Bellanca 7GCBC Citabria	496-73	(D-EAUT) N36416	7. 8.73	C.A.G.Schofield	Harpsden, Henley-on-Thames	10. 5.02
G-BBEO	Reims Cessna FRA150L Aerobat	FRA1500205		3. 8.73	AIRX Ltd	Inverness	7. 6.01T
G-BBEV	Piper PA-28-140 Cherokee D	28-7125340	LN-MTM	8. 8.73	Comed Aviation Ltd	Blackpool	9. 9.01T
G-BBEW*	Piper PA-23-250 Aztec E	27-7305075	EI-BYK G-BBEW/N40262	9. 8.73	Mano et Mano Ltd *(Damaged landing Phoenix Farm, Lower Upham 20.4.99: cancelled 16.8.99 by CAA: current status unknown)*	(New Malden)	2.11.02T
G-BBEX	Cessna 185A Skywagon	185-0491	EI-CMC G-BBEX/4X-ALD/N99992/N1691Z	7. 8.73	V.M.McCarthy	Kildare	2.11.02T
G-BBEY	Piper PA-23-250 Aztec E	27-7305160	LN-FOE G-BBEY/N40396	8. 8.73	M.Hall	Blackpool	29. 1.01T
G-BBFC*	Grumman-American AA-1B Trainer	AA1B-0245	(N9945L)	14. 8.73	Not known *(Damaged Perranporth 9.6.96: temp unregd 14.10.96: on rebuild 1.00)*	Bournemouth	25.12.96
G-BBFD	Piper PA-28R-200 Cherokee Arrow II	28R-7335342	N9517N	8. 8.73	CR Aviation Ltd	White Waltham	17. 4.04T
G-BBFL	SRCM Gardan GY-201 Minicab (Continental A65)	21	F-BHCQ	17. 8.73	D.Silsbury Roughay Farm, *(Damaged Bere Alston, Devon 9.6.93: on rebuild 12.01)*	Bishops Waltham	21. 9.93P
G-BBFS*	Van Den Bemden K-460 (Gas) Free Balloon	VDB-16	OO-BGX	10. 8.73	British Balloon Museum & Library *"Le Tomate" (Cancelled 19.5.93 by CAA)*	Newbury	
G-BBFV	Piper PA-32-260 Cherokee Six	32-778	5Y-ADF	13. 8.73	A.G.Knight t/a Airlaunch	Old Buckenham	26. 2.03
G-BBGB	Piper PA-E23-250 Aztec E	27-7305004	N40206	16. 8.73	Cheshire Flying Services Ltd t/a Ravenair	Liverpool	21. 2.03T
G-BBGC	SOCATA MS.893E Rallye 180GT	12215	F-BUCV	16. 8.73	P M Nolan	Kilkenny, Co.Kilkenny	7. 6.04
G-BBGE*	Piper PA-23-250 Aztec D	27-4373	N6137Y	20. 8.73	Not known *(Cancelled 2.9.91 by CAA: stored 9.96: current status unknown)*	Bournemouth	17. 8.92T
G-BBGI	Fuji FA.200-160 Aero Subaru	228		21. 8.73	M.S.Bird	Pepperbox, Salisbury	17. 9.98
G-BBGL	Oldfield Baby Lakes (Continental C90)	7223-B412-B & PFA 1593		22. 8.73	F.Ball	Fenland	21. 3.02P
G-BBGR	Cameron O-65 HAFB	85		20. 8.73	M.L. & L.P.Willoughby *"Jabberwock"*	Reading	26. 5.81A
G-BBGX	Cessna 182P Skylane	18262350	N58861	30. 8.73	D.I.Sutton t/a GX Group	Denham	2. 5.04T
G-BBGZ*	Cambridge Hot-Air Ballooning Association HAFB (42,000 cu.ft)	CHABA 42		31. 8.73	British Balloon Museum & Library *"Phlogiston" (Cancelled 27.12.01 as wfu)*	Newbury	
G-BBHE	Enstrom F-28A	153	EI-BSD G-BBHE	3. 9.73	Clarke Aviation Ltd	Waterford, Co.Waterford	21.11.04
G-BBHF	Piper PA-23-250 Aztec E	27-7305166	N40453	5. 9.73	G.J.Williams	Sherburn in Elmet	25. 5.02T
G-BBHI	Cessna 177RG Cardinal RG	177RG0225	5Y-ANX N1825Q	7. 9.73	T.G.W.Bunce	Belfast	26. 9.03
G-BBHJ	Piper J-3C-85 Cub *(Frame No.16037)*	16378	OO-GEC	7. 9.73	J.Stanbridge & R.V.Miller t/a Wellcross Flying Group	Wellcross Grange, Slinfold	4. 6.02P
G-BBHK	Noorduyn AT-16-ND Harvard IIB	14-787	PH-PPS (PH-HTC)/R.Neth AF B-158/FH153/42-12540	7. 9.73	R.F.Warner t/a Bob Warner Aviation *(As "FH153") (Noted 9.01)*	Derby	7. 5.86
G-BBHL	Sikorsky S-61N Mk.II	61-712	N4032S	7. 9.73	Bristow Helicopters Ltd *(Op H.M.Coastguard) "Glamis"*	Stornoway	4.12.04T
G-BBHM	Sikorsky S-61N Mk.II	61-713	8Q-HUM G-BBHM/N4033S	7. 9.73	Bristow Helicopters Ltd *"Braemar" (Stored unmarked from mid 2001)*	Redhill	1.11.01T
G-BBHX*	SOCATA MS.893E Rallye 180GT	12211		7. 9.73	Not known *(Cancelled 28.4.95 as destroyed: wreck in open store 5.96: current status unknown)*	Bidford	7. 4.96
G-BBHY	Piper PA-28-180 Cherokee Challenger	28-7305474	EI-BBS G-BBHY/N9508N	7. 9.73	Air Operations Ltd	Guernsey	8. 6.02
G-BBIA	Piper PA-28R-200 Cherokee Arrow II	28R-7335287	N11C	7. 9.73	G.H.Kilby	Stapleford	11. 1.04
G-BBIF	Piper PA-23-250 Aztec E	27-7305234	N9736N	10. 9.73	D M Davies *"Flying Miss Daisie"*	Tatenhill	25. 9.04T
G-BBIH	Enstrom F-28A-UK	026	N4875	12. 9.73	Stephenson Marine Co Ltd	Goodwood	28. 6.02T
G-BBII	Fiat G.46-3B	44	I-AEHU MM52801	13. 9.73	R.P.W.Steele t/a Godshill Aviation *(In Italian markings)*	Sandown	3. 4.02P
G-BBIL	Piper PA-28-140 Cherokee	28-22567	SE-FAR N4219J	13. 9.73	M.C.Addison & J.T.Fairbrass t/a India Lima Flying Group	Andrewsfield	22. 5.04
G-BBIO	Robin HR.100/210 Royal	178		14. 9.73	R.A.King	Headcorn	29.10.00
G-BBIX	Piper PA-28-140 Cherokee E	28-7225442	LN-AEN	17. 9.73	Sterling Aviation Ltd	Elstree	28. 1.02T
G-BBJD*	Cessna 172M	17261374	N20537	17. 9.73	Not known *(Crashed Sywell 30.6.78: fuselage as para-trainer 9.95: current status unknown*	Oaksey Park	18. 1.80
G-BBJI	Isaacs Spitfire (Continental O-200-A)	2 & PFA 027-10055		18. 9.73	T.E.W.Terrell *(As "RN218/N")*	(Atherstone)	23. 7.02P

G-BBJU	Robin DR.400/140 Earl	874		19. 9.73	J.C.Lister t/a Victor Sierra Aero Club	Valley Farm, Winwick	25. 5.04
G-BBJV	Reims Cessna F177RG Cardinal RG	F177RG0098		20. 9.73	3GRCOMM Ltd	(Hereford)	11. 4.03
G-BBJX	Reims Cessna F150L	F15001017		20. 9.73	L.W.Scattergood	Sherburn-in-Elmet	5. 8.02T
G-BBJY	Reims Cessna F172M Skyhawk II	F17201075		20. 9.73	J.Lucketti	Fenland	17. 6.02
G-BBJZ	Reims Cessna F172M Skyhawk II	F17201035		20. 9.73	J.K.Green t/a Burks Green & Partners	Gamston	28. 2.04T
G-BBKA	Reims Cessna F150L	F15001029		20. 9.73	W.M.Wilson & R.Campbell	(Doncaster)	20. 7.03T
G-BBKB	Reims Cessna F150L	F15001030		20. 9.73	Justgold Ltd t/a Blackpool Air Centre	Blackpool	10. 1.03T
G-BBKE	Reims Cessna F150L	F15001026		20. 9.73	J.D.Woodward	Westbury-sub-Mendip	8. 8.04T
G-BBKF	Reims Cessna FRA150L Aerobat	FRA1500222		20. 9.73	D.W.Mickleburgh *(Stored 6.95: current status unknown)*	Compton Abbas	13. 6.91T
G-BBKG	Reims FR172J Rocket	FR17200465		20. 9.73	R.Wright	Twycross/Coventry	1. 3.04
G-BBKI	Reims Cessna F172M Skyhawk II	F17201069		20. 9.73	C.W. & S.A.Burman	East Winch	20.12.04
G-BBKL	Menavia Piel CP.301A Emeraude	237	F-BIMK	21. 9.73	R.K.Griggs t/a Piel G-BBKL	Perth	13. 6.02P
G-BBKR	Scheibe SF-24A Motorspatz	4018	D-KECA	24. 9.73	P.I.Morgans	Furze Hill Farm, Rosemarket, Milford Haven	30. 3.79S
G-BBKU	Reims Cessna FRA150L Aerobat	FRA1500214		26. 9.73	T.Hartley & R.J.Stainer t/a Penguin Group	Bodmin	19. 6.04T
G-BBKX	Piper PA-28-180 Cherokee Challenger	28-7305581	N9550N	26. 9.73	RAE Aero Club Ltd	Farnborough	11.10.04T
G-BBKY	Reims Cessna F150L	F15000991		26. 9.73	Telesonic Ltd	Barton	7. 1.04
G-BBKZ	Cessna 172M	17261495	N20694	27. 9.73	R.S.Thomson t/a KZ Flying Group	Exeter	26. 4.03T
G-BBLH	Piper J-3C-65 Cub (L-4B-PI) *(Frame No.9838) (Regd with c/n 10549)*	10006	F-BFQY Fr.Mil/43-1145	24. 9.73	Shipping & Airlines Ltd *(As "31145/26/G" in 183rd Field Battalion US Army c/s)*	Biggin Hill	4. 2.02T
G-BBLL*	Cameron O-84 HAFB	84		2.10.73	British Balloon Museum & Library *"Boadicea" (Cancelled 19.5.93 by CAA)*	Newbury	25. 5.81A
G-BBLM	SOCATA Rallye 100S	2392		3.10.73	Oakmast Systems Ltd	Wolverhampton	19.12.04
G-BBLS	Grumman-American AA-5 Traveler	AA5-0440	EI-AYM G-BBLS	8.10.73	A.D.Grant	Perth	28. 3.02
G-BBLU	Piper PA-34-200 Seneca	34-7350271	N55984	8.10.73	A.S.Bamrah t/a Falcon Flying Services	Biggin Hill	3. 4.00T
G-BBMB	Robin DR.400/180 Regent	848	5Y-ASB	27. 9.73	I.James t/a Regent Flying Group	King's Farm, Thurrock	13. 5.04
G-BBMH	EAA Sport Biplane Model P.1 (Continental C90-14F)	PFA 1348		11.10.73	I.S.Parker	Damyns Hall, Billericay	31. 1.02P
G-BBMJ	Piper PA-23-250 Aztec E	27-7305150	N40387	12.10.73	Tindon Ltd	Little Snoring	21. 9.02T
G-BBMN	de Havilland DHC-1 Chipmunk 22	C1/0300	WD359	12.10.73	R.Steiner	North Weald	4. 4.04
G-BBMO	de Havilland DHC-1 Chipmunk 22	C1/0550	WK514	12.10.73	D.M.Squires	Wellesbourne Mountford	10. 6.04
G-BBMR	de Havilland DHC-1 Chipmunk 22	C1/0213	WB763	12.10.73	P J Wood *(New owner 1.02)*	(Twyford, Bucks)	
G-BBMT	de Havilland DHC-1 Chipmunk 22	C1/0712	WP831	12.10.73	J.Evans & D.Withers	Graveley	26. 4.02
G-BBMV	de Havilland DHC-1 Chipmunk 22	C1/0432	WG348	12.10.73	P.J.Morgan (Aviation) Ltd *(As "WG348")*	Sywell	9. 4.03
G-BBMW	de Havilland DHC-1 Chipmunk 22	C1/0641	WK628	12.10.73	J.A.Challen & B.J.Pook t/a Mike Whiskey Group *(As "WK628")*	Shoreham	15.12.04
G-BBMX	de Havilland DHC-1 Chipmunk 22	C1/0800	WP924	12.10.73	K.A.Doornbos	Teuge, The Netherlands	12. 5.02
G-BBMZ	de Havilland DHC-1 Chipmunk 22	C1/0563	WK548	12.10.73	P.C.G.Wyld t/a The Wycombe Gliding School Syndicate	Booker	21. 9.03
G-BBNA	de Havilland DHC-1 Chipmunk 22 (Lycoming O-360)	C1/0491	WG417	12.10.73	Coventry Gliding Club Ltd *"Carrie"*	Husbands Bosworth	22. 6.03
G-BBNC*	de Havilland DHC-1 Chipmunk T.10	C1/0682	WP790	12.10.73	De Havilland Heritage Museum *(Used for spares: cancelled 23.9.74 as WFU) (As "WP790/T")*	London Colney	
G-BBND	de Havilland DHC-1 Chipmunk 22	C1/0225	WD286	12.10.73	W.Norton & D.Fradley t/a Bernoulli Syndicate *(As "WD286/J")*	Top Farm, Croydon	19. 4.03
G-BBNG	Bell 206B JetRanger II	134	VH-BHX G-BBNG/VR-BEY/G-BBNG/PK-HBO/N6268N	16.10.73	MB Air Ltd *(Op Eagle Helicopters)*	Winchester Farm, Ouston	9. 5.02T
G-BBNH	Piper PA-34-200 Seneca	34-7350339	N56492	16.10.73	M.G.D.Baverstock	Bournemouth	15. 2.04
G-BBNI	Piper PA-34-200 Seneca	34-7350312	N56286	16.10.73	Noisy Moose Ltd	(London W5)	26. 3.04T
G-BBNJ	Reims Cessna F150L	F15001038		16.10.73	Sherburn Aero Club Ltd	Sherburn in Elmet	27.10.02T
G-BBNV	Fuji FA.200-160 Aero Subaru	232		23.10.73	Caseright Ltd	Hinton-in-the-Hedges	25. 4.99
G-BBNX	Reims Cessna FRA150L Aerobat (Continental O-200-A)	FRA1500219		23.10.73	General Airline Ltd t/a European Flyers *(Ceased trading 10.01)*	Blackbushe	17. 6.04T

G-BBNY*	Reims Cessna FRA150L Aerobat	FRA1500223		23.10.73	Air Tows Ltd	White Waltham	2. 8.87T
	(Damaged Blackbushe 8.6.86: cancelled 3.6.93 as destroyed: wreck in open storage 9.96: current status unknown)						
G-BBNZ	Reims Cessna F172M Skyhawk II	F17201054		23.10.73	R.E.Nunn	Maypole Farm, Chislet	24. 5.03
G-BBOA	Reims Cessna F172M Skyhawk II	F17201066		23.10.73	J.D.& A.M.Black	Clacton	15. 6.02
G-BBOC	Cameron O-77 HAFB	86		24.10.73	J.A.B.Gray *"Bacchus"* t/a Bacchus Balloons	Cirencester	6. 1.90A
G-BBOD	Thunder 0.5 HAFB MLB	013		24.10.73	B.R. & M.Boyle *"Little Titch"* *(On loan to British Balloon Museum & Library)*	Newbury	
G-BBOE	Robin HR.200/100	26		24.10.73	R.J.Powell	(Wickham, Hants)	7. 7.02
	(Offered for sale by tender 10.01 by GAB Robins Aviation Ltd on behalf of owner in "as is" condition following being badly damaged on striking hedge & concrete post landing Wells Cross Farm, Horsham 24.6.01: dismantled and recovered to owner)						
G-BBOH	AJEP Pitts S-1S Special (Lycoming IO-360)	AJEP-PS1-S-1 & PFA 1570		25.10.73	Techair London Ltd	Popham	8. 9.97P
G-BBOL	Piper PA-18-150 Super Cub	18-7561	D-EMFE N3821Z	26.10.73	Lakes Gliding Club Ltd	Walney Island	17. 9.99
G-BBOO	Thunder Ax6-56 HAFB	012		24.10.73	K.Meehan *"Tiger Jack"*	Much Wenlock, Shropshire	22. 9.96A
G-BBOR	Bell 206B JetRanger II	1197	(SE-) G-BBOR	30.10.73	M.J.Easey	Town Farm, Hoxne, Eye	8. 7.02T
G-BBOX	Thunder Ax7-77 HAFB	011		24.10.73	R.C.Weyda *"Rocinante"* *(On loan to British Balloon Museum & Library)*	Newbury	23.12.82A
G-BBOY*	Thunder Ax6-56A HAFB	001		24.10.73	Not known	(The Netherlands)	5.10.83
	"Eric of Titchfield" (Cancelled 23.6.98 by CAA) (Current status unknown)						
G-BBPN	Enstrom F-28A-UK	166		30.10.73	Smarta Systems Ltd	(Pencader)	8. 8.03T
G-BBPO	Enstrom F-28A	176		30.10.73	Wilco (Helicopters) Ltd	Shoreham	8. 6.03T
G-BBPS	SAN Jodel D.117	597	F-BHXS	30.10.73	A.Appleby	Burtenshaw Farm, Barcombe	26. 5.01P
G-BBPW	Robin HR.100/210 Royal	176		7.11.73	S.D.Cole *(Damaged Kemble 24.8.98: airframe noted 9.99)*	Kemble	13. 4.97
G-BBPX	Piper PA-34-200 Seneca	34-7250262	N1202T	7.11.73	Richel Investments Ltd	Guernsey	15. 9.01
G-BBPY	Piper PA-28-180 Challenger	28-7305590	N9554N	8.11.73	Sunsaver Ltd	Barton	29. 7.02
G-BBRA	Piper PA-23-250 Aztec E	27-7305197	N40479	12.11.73	R.C.Lough	Stapleford	7. 5.03
G-BBRB	de Havilland DH.82A Tiger Moth	85934	OO-EVB Belgian AF T-8/ETA-8/DF198	21.11.73	R.Barham	(Biggin Hill)	
	(Damaged Biggin Hill 16.1.87: sold for long-term rebuild - current status unknown)						
G-BBRC	Fuji FA.200-180 Aero Subaru	235		8.11.73	G-BBRC Ltd	Blackbushe	31. 7.02T
G-BBRI	Bell 47G-5A	25158	N18092	8.11.73	Alan Mann Helicopters Ltd	Fairoaks	28. 7.02T
	(Composite following several major rebuilds)						
G-BBRN	Mitchell-Procter Kittiwake I (Continental O-200-A)	02 & PFA 1352	XW784	20.11.73	R.D.Dobree-Carey *(As "XW784/VL")*	Henstridge	25.11.02P
G-BBRV	de Havilland DHC-1 Chipmunk 22	C1/0284	WD347	13.11.73	J A Keen & H M Farrelly *(As "WD347" in RAF grey & orange dayglo stripes)*	Liverpool	17. 2.03T
G-BBRX	SIAI-Marchetti S.205-18F	342	LN-VYH OO-HAQ	13.11.73	R.C. & A.K.West	Popham	21.12.04
G-BBRY*	Cessna 210	57091	5Y-KRZ VP-KRZ/N7391E	15.11.73	Not known	Enstone	13. 4.79
	(Crashed Chessington 2.4.78: used for spares: cancelled 5.12.83 as destroyed: in open storage unmarked 9.99)						
G-BBRZ	Grumman-American AA-5 Traveler	AA5-0471	(EI-AYV) G-BBRZ	15.11.73	C.P.Osborne *(Noted 8.01)*	Mullaghmore, Co.Sligo	30. 4.99
G-BBSA	Grumman-American AA-5 Traveler	AA5-0472		15.11.73	Usworth 84 Flying Associates Ltd	Newcastle	31. 1.02
G-BBSB	Beechcraft C23 Sundowner 180	M-1516		15.11.73	Amalmay Ltd t/a Sundowner Group	Blackpool	31. 7.02T
G-BBSC*	Beechcraft B24R Sierra 200	MC-217		15.11.73	I.Millar & G.H.Emerson t/a The Beechcombers Flying Group	Belfast	3. 6.99
	(Cancelled 27.7.01 by CAA) (Noted in wrecked condition 10.01)						
G-BBSM	Piper PA-32-300 Cherokee Six	32-7440005	N9577N	14.11.73	MT Management Ltd	Ronaldsway	21. 8.03T
G-BBSS	de Havilland DHC-1 Chipmunk 22 (Lycoming)	C1/0520	WG470	21.11.73	Coventry Gliding Club Ltd	Husbands Bosworth	1. 4.04
G-BBSW	Pietenpol Air Camper	PFA 1506		21.11.73	J.K.S.Wills	(London SE3)	
G-BBTB	Reims Cessna FRA150L Aerobat	FRA1500224		26.11.73	BBC Air Ltd *(Op Abbas Air)*	Compton Abbas	2.11.02T
G-BBTG	Reims Cessna F172M Skyhawk II	F17201097		26.11.73	R.W. & V.P.J.Simpson t/a Tango Golf Flying Group	Redhill	15. 5.02
G-BBTH	Reims Cessna F172M Skyhawk II	F17201089		26.11.73	K.Kwok-Kin Lee	Newtownards, Co.of Down	3. 8.02
G-BBTJ	Piper PA-23-250 Aztec E	27-7305131	N40369	27.11.73	Cooper Aerial Surveys Ltd	Sandtoft	8. 4.04T

G-BBTK	Reims Cessna FRA150L Aerobat	FRA1500230		27.11.73	Cleveland Flying School Ltd	Teesside	17.10.99T
G-BBTL	Piper PA-23-250 Aztec C	27-3816	N6525Y	29.11.73	Air Navigation & Trading Co Ltd *(Wreck stored 3.00)*	Blackpool	14. 8.89T
G-BBTS	Beechcraft V35B Bonanza	D-9551	N3051W	29.11.73	Sarah Wenham t/a Eastern Air	Cannes-Mandelieu	5. 6.03
G-BBTT*	Reims Cessna F150L Commuter	F15001055		30.11.73	Not known *(Crashed Newtownards 9.3.75: cancelled 6.1.84 as WFU: stored 2.01)*	Newtownards, Co.of Down	12. 3.76
G-BBTU*	SOCATA ST-10 Diplomate	140	F-BTIO	18.12.73	Not known *(Cancelled 13.9.90 by CAA: wreck stored 3.94: current status unknown)*	Coventry	14. 4.88
G-BBTX	Beechcraft C23 Sundowner 180	M-1524	5N-AGJ G-BBTX	29.11.73	K.Harding *(U/c collapsed landing Blackbushe 27.2.01: wreck sold for instrumentation: airframe for storage in local barn for spares use 5.01)*	Wellesbourne Mountford	8. 6.01
G-BBTY	Beechcraft C23 Sundowner 180	M-1525		29.11.73	A.W.Roderick & W.Price	Cardiff	6. 7.04
G-BBTZ	Reims Cessna F150L	F15001063		30.11.73	Marham Investments Ltd *(Op Cumbernauld Flying School)*	Cumbernauld	22. 6.03T
G-BBUE	Grumman-American AA-5 Traveler	0479		6.12.73	Hebog (Mon) Cyf	Caernarfon	10. 3.00
G-BBUF	Grumman-American AA-5 Traveler	0480		6.12.73	W.McLaren *(Op Tayside Aviation)*	Perth	22.12.02T
G-BBUG	Piper PA-16 Clipper	16-29	F-BFMC	6.12.73	J.Dolan	Enniskillen, Co.Fermanagh	19. 7.02
G-BBUJ	Cessna 421B Golden Eagle	421B0335	OY-RYD	7.12.73	Coolflourish Ltd.	(Mansfield)	18. 5.00
G-BBUT	Western O-65 HAFB	020		11.12.73	G.F.Turnbull "Christabelle II"	Clyro, Hereford	23. 4.97A
G-BBUU	Piper J-3C-75 Cub (L-4A-PI) *(Frame No.10354)*	10529	F-BBSQ F-OAEZ/Fr.AF/43-29238	14. 1.74	O.J.J.Rogers	Hulcote Farm, Salford, Beds	5. 8.02P
G-BBVA	Sikorsky S-61N Mk.II	61-718		12. 2.74	Bristow Helicopters Ltd *(Op H M Coastguard) "Vega"*	Lee-on-Solent	24. 2.03T
G-BBVF*	Scottish Aviation Twin Pioneer 3	558	7978M XM961	17.12.73	National Museums of Scotland/Museum of Flight *(Cancelled 8.8.83)*	East Fortune	14. 5.82
G-BBVG*	Piper PA-23-250 Aztec C	27-2610	ET-AEB 5Y-AAT/N5514Y	20.12.73	Colton Aviation Ltd *(Cancelled 10.2.89 as WFU: stored 11.00)*	Gamston	10. 9.88T
G-BBVJ	Beechcraft B24R Sierra 200	MC-230		21.12.73	T.Keely	Gamston	7. 6.03
G-BBVO	Isaacs Fury II (Lycoming O-320)	PFA 011-10091		20.12.73	J Moore *(As Hawker Nimrod "S1579/571" of 408 Flight FAA, HMS Glorious)*	(Great Yarmouth)	20. 6.02P
G-BBVP*	Westland-Bell 47G-3B1 *(Line No.WAS/177)*	WA/580	401 S.YemenAF /XT401	3. 1.74	Not known *(Cancelled 26.3.93 as WFU: stored 5.93: current status unknown)*	Barton	3. 6.93T
G-BBWN*	de Havilland DHC-1 Chipmunk 22	C1/0913	WZ876	11. 1.74	P Wood *(Damaged Thorpe Salvin, Netherthorpe 25.2.96: dismantled for spares: cancelled 13.3.96 as destroyed: noted as "WZ876" 11.99: current status unknown)*	Twyford, Bucks	
G-BBWZ	Grumman-American AA-1B Tr 2	AA1B-0334		14. 1.74	Teleco Trading Ltd	Popham	20. 8.03T
G-BBXB	Reims Cessna FRA150L Aerobat	FRA1500236		16. 1.74	D.M.Fenton	Breighton	12. 7.98T
G-BBXH	Reims FR172F Rocket	FR1720113	SE-FKG	21. 1.74	D.Ridley	(Chester-le-Street)	8.11.03
G-BBXJ*	Handley Page HPR.7 Dart Herald 203	196	I-TIVI	18. 1.74	(Jersey Airport Fire Service) *(Crashed Jersey 24.12.74: fuselage to Fire Service: extant 12.96)*	Jersey	30. 5.75T
G-BBXK	Piper PA-34-200 Seneca	34-7450056	N54366	21. 1.74	J.A.Rees	Haverfordwest	15. 3.02T
G-BBXL	Cessna 310Q II	310Q1076	EI-CLX G-BBXL/(N1223G)	21. 1.74	Appleton Aviation Ltd	Full Sutton	23. 7.04T
G-BBXO	Enstrom F-28A-UK	181		29. 1.74	Stephenson Marine Co Ltd	Goodwood	29. 9.01T
G-BBXS	Piper J-3C-65 Cub (L-4H-PI) (Continental C90) *(Frame No.12042)* *(Officially regd as c/n "9865")*	12214	N9865F G-ALMA/44-79918	25. 1.74	M.J.Butler *(Noted 11.01)*	Spanhoe	14. 9.00P
G-BBXU*	Beechcraft B24R Sierra 200	MC-238		30. 1.74	J.Coggins *(Stored 11.95: cancelled 13.12.96 by CAA: current status unknown)*	Coventry	18.11.93T
G-BBXY	Bellanca 7GCBC Citabria	614-74	N57639	1. 2.74	R.R.L.Windus	Truleigh Manor Farm, Edburton	12. 6.99
G-BBXZ	Evans VP-1 (VW 1600)	PFA 1562		31. 1.74	R.W.Burrows *(Stored 5.99: current status unknown)*	Swanton Morley	8. 3.96P
G-BBYB	Piper PA-18 Super Cub 95 (L-18C-PI) *(Frame No.18-1628)*	18-1627	PH-TMA (D-ENCH)/ALAT 18-1627/51-15627	4. 2.74	The Tiger Club (1990) Ltd	Headcorn	17. 7.04T
G-BBYH	Cessna 182P	18262814	N52744	6. 2.74	Croftmarsh Ltd	Poplar Farm, Croft, Skegness	1.12.02
G-BBYL*	Cameron O-77 HAFB	89		8. 2.74	R.Warner *"Phoenix"* *(Cancelled 19.5.93 by CAA: noted 2.97)*	NK	19. 6.77S
G-BBYM*	Handley Page HP.137 Jetstream 200	243	G-AYWR G-8-13	13. 2.74	RAF Museum *(Cancelled 7.6.00 as wfu)*	RAF Cosford	20. 9.98A
G-BBYO*	Britten-Norman BN-2A Mk.III-1 Trislander	362	ZS-KMH G-BBYO/G-BBWR	27. 2.74	Aurigny Air Services Ltd *(WFU 2.92: noted 12.01: possible rebuild with fuselage of c/n 1072/N3267J)*	Guernsey	1. 5.92T
G-BBYP	Piper PA-28-140 Cherokee F	28-7425158	N9620N	19. 2.74	Jersey Aircraft Maintenance Ltd	Jersey	6. 7.03T

G-BBYR*	Cameron O-65 HAFB	97		14. 2.74	Balloon Preservation Group *"Phoenix" (Cancelled 30.1.87 by CAA)*	Kirdford	15. 7.81
G-BBYS	Cessna 182P Skylane	18261520	5Y-ATE N21256	14. 2.74	I.M.Jones	Gamston	1. 5.03
G-BBYU*	Cameron O-56 HAFB	96		19. 2.74	British Balloon Museum & Library *"Chieftain" (Cancelled 9.8.89 as WFU)*	Newbury	28. 2.82A
G-BBZF	Piper PA-28-140 Cherokee F	28-7425195	N9501N	19. 2.74	J T Mirley	Wolverhampton	23. 6.03
G-BBZH	Piper PA-28R-200 Cherokee Arrow II	28R-7435102	N9608N	22. 2.74	M.J.Sandry t/a Zulu Hotel Club	Exeter	4. 6.04
G-BBZJ	Piper PA-34-200-2 Seneca	34-7450088	N40880	26. 2.74	General Airline Ltd t/a European Flyers *(Ceased trading 10.01)*	(Blackbushe)	11. 8.03T
G-BBZN	Fuji FA.200-180 Aero Subaru	230		26. 2.74	J.Westwood & P.D.Wedd	Cambridge	10. 4.03T
G-BBZO	Fuji FA.200-160 Aero Subaru	238		26. 2.74	L.A.N.King & M.J.Herlihy t/a G-BBZO Group	Redhill	1. 7.02
G-BBZS*	Enstrom F-28A-UK	192		27. 2.74	Not known *(Damaged near Tyldesley 29.4.89: stored 6.93: cancelled 29.5.96 as WFU: current status unknown)*	Goodwood	30. 9.89T
G-BBZV	Piper PA-28R-200 Cherokee Arrow II	28R-7435105	N9609N	11. 3.74	P.B.Mellor	Cambridge	2. 9.02T

G-BCAA – G-BCZZ

G-BCAC*	SOCATA MS.894A Rallye Minerva 220	12099		4. 3.74	Not known Clarence Way, Westpoint Enterprise Park *(Damaged Sandown 6.5.90: displayed 1994 @ Kamikazee Ken's Kitchens: cancelled 18.1.95 as WFU: current status unknown)*	Trafford Park	7.12.90
G-BCAH	de Havilland DHC-1 Chipmunk 22	C1/0372	WG316	6. 5.74	Southern Flight Centre Ltd *(As "WG316")*	Rochester	7. 6.02T
G-BCAN*	Thunder Ax7-77 HAFB	015		5. 3.74	D.D.Owen *"Beacon"* *(Cancelled 27.9.01 by CAA)*	Wotton-under-Edge	7. 8.88A
G-BCAP*	Cameron O-56 HAFB	92		5. 3.74	Balloon Preservation Group *"Honey Child" (Cancelled 30.3.93 as WFU)*	Lancing	NE(A)
G-BCAR*	Thunder Ax7-77 HAFB	019		5. 3.74	British Balloon Museum & Library *"Marie Antoinette" (Cancelled 2.4.92 by CAA)*	Newbury	NE(A)
G-BCAS*	Thunder Ax7-77 HAFB	018		5. 3.74	Balloon Preservation Group *"Drifter" (Cancelled 30.11.01 by CAA)*	Southampton	9. 4.91A
G-BCAZ	Piper PA-12 Super Cruiser	12-2312	5Y-KGK VP-KGK/ZS-BYJ/ZS-BPH	12. 3.74	A.D.Williams	Rhos-y-Gilwen Farm, Rhos Hill	10. 8.01
G-BCBG	Piper PA-23-250 Aztec E	27-7305224	VP-BBN VR-BBN/(VR-BDM)/G-BCBG/N40494	13. 3.74	M.J.L Batt	Booker	8.11.04
G-BCBH	Fairchild 24R-46A Argus III (UC-61K-FA)	975	(VH-AAQ) G-BCBH/ZS-AXH/HB737/43-15011	13. 3.74	Dreamticket Promotions Ltd	Rochester	28. 6.03
G-BCBJ	Piper PA-25-235 Pawnee C	25-2380/R		18. 3.74	Deeside Gliding Club (Aberdeenshire) Ltd *(Rebuild of c/n 25-2380/G-ASLA/N6802Z, quoting c/n 25-5544 the new fuselage of G-ASLA !)*	Aboyne	2. 9.04
G-BCBL	Fairchild 24R-46A Argus III (UC-61K-FA)	989	OO-EKE D-EKEQ/HB-AEC/HB751/43-15025	19. 3.74	F.J.Cox *(As "HB751")*	Eaglescott	31. 3.96
G-BCBM	Piper PA-23-250 Aztec C	27-3006	N5854Y	19. 3.74	Hatton & Westerman Trawlers	Blackpool	12. 5.01
G-BCBR	AJEP/Wittman W.8 Tailwind (Continental O-200-A)	TW3-380		20. 3.74	D.P.Jones	Top Farm, Croydon	1. 7.02P
G-BCBX	Reims Cessna F150L	F15001001	F-BUEO	25. 3.74	J.Kelly *(Stored 10.02)*	Belfast	19. 2.95T
G-BCBZ	Cessna 337C Super Skymaster (Robertson STOL conversion)	3370942	SE-FKB N2642S	28. 3.74	J.J.Zwetsloot	Bourn	18. 2.02
G-BCCB*	Robin HR.200/100 Club	29		2. 4.74	M.J.Ellis *(Damaged by gales 25.01.90: stored 8.90: cancelled 2.3.99 by CAA: current status unknown)*	Old Sarum	12. 6.89
G-BCCC	Reims Cessna F150L	F15001041		8. 4.74	R D Billins	Denham	25. 4.04T
G-BCCD	Reims Cessna F172M Skyhawk II	F17201144		8. 4.74	R.M.Austin t/a Austin Aviation	Rochester	28. 6.04T
G-BCCE	Piper PA-23-250 Aztec E	27-7405282	N40544	3. 4.74	Golf Charlie Echo Ltd	Shoreham	1. 8.02T
G-BCCF	Piper PA-28-180 Cherokee Archer	28-7405069	N9632N	3. 4.74	Topcat Aviation Ltd	Liverpool	27. 6.03
G-BCCG	Thunder Ax7-65 HAFB	020		4. 4.74	N.H.Ponsford t/a Rango Balloon & Kite Co *"Zephyr" (Active 1999)*	Leeds	7.11.83A
G-BCCH*	Thunder Ax6-56A HAFB	024	G-BCCH	4. 4.74	Balloon Preservation Group *"Wrangler" (Cancelled 15.11.82 as sold Belgium but NTU)*	Kirdford	
G-BCCJ	Grumman-American AA-5 Traveler	AA5-0546		8. 4.74	T.Needham	Dunkeswell	18. 6.03
G-BCCK	Grumman-American AA-5 Traveler	AA5-0547		8. 4.74	Prospect Air Ltd	Manchester	14. 9.02
G-BCCR	Piel CP.301A Emeraude (Continental O-200-A)	PFA 712		8. 4.74	J.H. & C.J.Waterman	Armshold Farm, Kingston, Cambs	22. 2.02P
G-BCCX	de Havilland DHC-1 Chipmunk 22 (Lycoming O-360)	C1/0531	WG481	17. 4.74	T.Holloway t/a RAFGSA *(Op Clevelands Gliding Club)*	AAC Dishforth	28. 3.03
G-BCCY	Robin HR.200/100 Club	37		18. 4.74	Charlie Yankee Ltd	Filton	30. 6.02

G-BCDJ	Piper PA-28-140 Cherokee	28-24276	PH-NLV	29. 4.74	B.F.Graham	Filton	26. 5.04T
			N1841J		t/a Bristol Aero Club		
G-BCDK(2)	Partenavia P.68B	32	A6-ALN	4. 7.75	Flyteam Aviation Ltd	Elstree	26. 4.02T
			G-BCDK				
G-BCDL	Cameron O-42 HAFB	115		24. 4.74	D.P. & Mrs B.O.Turner *"Chums"*	Bath	13. 7.83A
G-BCDN*	Fokker F.27 Friendship 200	10201	PH-OGA	29. 4.74	Air UK Ltd	Norwich	19. 7.96T
			JA8615/(LV-PMR)/PH-FDP				
				(Cancelled 28.1.98 as WFU: used as apprentice trainer 5.99)			
G-BCDO*	Fokker F.27 Friendship 200	10234	PH-OGB	29. 4.74	Air UK Ltd	Norwich	20. 6.91T
			JA8621/PH-FEZ		*"Friendship Lord Butler"*		
		(Damaged Amsterdam 19.7.90: cancelled 27.1.95 as PWFU: Technical College airframe 10.96)					
G-BCDY	Reims Cessna FRA150L Aerobat	FRA1500237		7. 5.74	W Bayman & C Draycott	Compton Abbas	11. 7.03T
G-BCEA	Sikorsky S-61N Mk.II	61-721		7. 6.74	Veritair Ltd	Mount Pleasant, Falkland Islands	13. 7.03T
G-BCEB	Sikorsky S-61N Mk.II	61-454	N4023S	2.10.74	Veritair Ltd	Penzance	16.12.02T
					"The Isles of Scilly"		
G-BCEC	Reims Cessna F172M Skyhawk II	F17201082		7. 5.74	Trim Flying Club Ltd.	(Trim, Co.Meath)	9. 7.03T
G-BCEE	Grumman-American AA-5 Traveler	AA5-0571		7. 5.74	N.F.Harrison	Stapleford	15. 5.03
G-BCEF	Grumman-American AA-5 Traveler	AA5-0572		7. 5.74	J.Fitzpatrick	(Urrugne, France)	1. 7.00
					(New owner 10.01)		
G-BCEN	Fairey Britten-Norman BN-2A-26 Islander	403	4X-AYG	6. 5.74	Atlantic Air Transport Ltd	Manston	7.11.03A
			SX-BFB/4X-AYG/N90JA/G-BCEN		*(Op HM Coastguard)*		
G-BCEO	Grumman-American AA-5 Traveler	AA5-0575		7. 5.74	D.G.I.Wheldon	Teesside	25.11.02
					t/a Echo Oscar Flying Group		
G-BCEP	Grumman-American AA-5 Traveler	AA5-0576		7. 5.74	G.Edelmann	Blackbushe	8. 6.03
G-BCER	CAB GY-201 Minicab	8	F-BGJP	8. 5.74	D.Beaumont	West Freugh	2. 4.02P
G-BCEU*	Cameron O-42 HAFB	111		9. 5.74	Not known *"Harlequin"*	NK	
					(Cancelled 19.5.93 by CAA: noted Ashton Court 8.99)		
G-BCEX	Piper PA-23-250 Aztec E	27-7305024	N40225	13. 5.74	Western Air (Thruxton) Ltd	Thruxton	23. 6.02T
G-BCEY	de Havilland DHC-1 Chipmunk 22	C1/0515	WG465	14. 5.74	T.C.B.Dehn & C.A.Robey	White Waltham	14. 1.02
					t/a Gopher Flying Group *(As "WG465" in RAF c/s)*		
G-BCEZ	Cameron O-84 HAFB	107		13. 5.74	P.F.Smart & R.J.Mitchener	Romsey/Andover	20. 7.82A
					t/a Balloon Collection *"Stars & Bars"*		
G-BCFD*	West Ax3-15 HAFB	JW.1		16. 5.74	British Balloon Museum & Library	Newbury	
					"Hellfire" (Cancelled 30.1.87 by CAA)		
G-BCFF	Fuji FA.200-160 Aero Subaru	237		21. 5.74	G.W.Brown & M.R.Gibbons	Popham	2.12.03
G-BCFN	Cameron O-65 HAFB	109		23. 5.74	W.G.Johnston & H.M.Savage	Edinburgh	15. 5.77S
					"Fireball" (Noted 6.00)		
G-BCFO	Piper PA-18-150 Super Cub	18-5335	(D-EIOZ)	29. 5.74	D.C.Murray	Lee-on-Solent	11. 4.04
			ALAT 18-5335/N10F		t/a Portsmouth Naval Gliding Club		
G-BCFR	Reims Cessna FRA150L Aerobat	FRA1500244		30. 5.74	Bulldog Aviation Ltd & Motorhoods Colchester Ltd		
					(Op Essex Flying School)	Earls Colne	13.12.02T
G-BCFU	Thunder Ax6-56 HAFB	027	EI-BAF	17. 5.74	Zebedee Balloon Service Ltd	Hungerford	
			(G-BCFU)		*"Smithwicks" (Restored & noted 1.00)*		
G-BCFW	SAAB 91D Safir	91-437	PH-RLZ	29. 5.74	D.R.Williams	Peplow	22. 7.03
G-BCFY	Phoenix Luton LA-4A Minor	PAL/1301 & PFA/824		29. 5.74	G.Capes	(Brough)	17. 1 92P
					(Stored Sywell 8.92: new owner 10.00)		
G-BCGA*	Piper PA-34-200 Seneca	34-7450166	N41975	4. 6.74	Not known	Ronaldsway	15. 7.78
			(Crashed Waddington 18.12.77: wreck stored 4.91: current status unknown)				
G-BCGB	Bensen B.8 (Rotax 503)	PCL.14		3. 6.74	J.W.Birkett	(Bursledon)	5. 7.01P
					(Flies from Chilbolton)		
G-BCGC	de Havilland DHC-1 Chipmunk 22	C1/0776	WP903	13. 3.74	J C Wright	(Potters Bar)	26. 7.04T
					(As "WP903" in Queen's Flight c/s)		
G-BCGH	SNCAN NC.854S	122	F-BAFG	10. 6.74	T.J.N.H.Palmer	Hill Farm, Nayland	28. 5.01P
					t/a Nord Flying Group		
G-BCGI	Piper PA-28-140 Cherokee Cruiser	28-7425283	N9573N	10. 6.74	J.C.,T.,T. & H.R.Dodd	Panshanger	8. 6.03T
G-BCGJ	Piper PA-28-140 Cherokee Cruiser	28-7425286	N9574N	10. 6.74	BCT Aircraft Leasing Ltd	Filton	1. 8.03T
					(Op Bristol Aero Club)		
G-BCGL	Jodel D.112 *(Built Ets Valladeu)*	668	F-BIGL	24. 4.74	T.J.Maynard	Kemble	29. 6.01P
G-BCGM	Jodel Wassmer D.120 Paris-Nice	50	F-BHQM	15. 7.74	M.H.D.Soltau	Croft Farm, Defford	20.12.00P
			F-BHYM				
G-BCGN	Piper PA-28-140 Cherokee F	28-7425323	N9595N	10. 6.74	Golf November Ltd	Oxford	4. 8.02
G-BCGP*	Gazebo Ax6-65 HAFB	1		13. 6.74	British Balloon Museum & Library	Newbury	
					"Aries" (Cancelled 18.12.79 as WFU)		
G-BCGS	Piper PA-28R-200 Cherokee Arrow II	28R-7235133	N4893T	13. 6.74	S.Rayne	Cambridge	17. 2.03
					t/a Arrow Aviation Group		
G-BCGT	Piper PA-28-140 Cherokee	28-24504	N6779J	17. 6.74	L.Maikowski	Shoreham	16. 7.03T

G-BCGW	Jodel D.11			14. 6.74	G.H.& M.D.Chittenden	Highwood Hall	30. 1.85P
	(Lycoming O-290) CC.001 & EAA/61554 & PFA 912				*(Stored)*		
G-BCHK	Reims Cessna F172H	F17200716	9H-AAD	19. 6.74	D Darby	(Cowbridge)	23.11.03
G-BCHL	de Havilland DHC-1 Chipmunk 22A		WP788	20. 6.74	Shropshire Soaring Ltd	Sleap	18.10.04
		C1/0680			*(As "WP788")*		
G-BCHM	Westland SA.341G Gazelle 1	1168	G-17-20	14. 6.74	Stratton Motor Co (Norfolk) Ltd		
					(Stored 8.01)	(Long Stratton)	23. 8.99
G-BCHP	Scintex CP.1310-C3 Super Emeraude		G-JOSI	24. 6.74	G.Hughes & A.G.Just	Earls Colne	6. 8.02P
		902	G-BCHP/F-BJVQ				
G-BCHT	Schleicher ASK 16	16021	(BGA1996)	25. 6.74	D.E.Cadisch & K.A.Lilleywhite	Dunstable	31. 5.04
			D-KAMY		t/a Dunstable K16 Group		
G-BCHV*	de Havilland DHC-1 Chipmunk 22		WP807	27. 6.74	N.F.Charles	Old Manor Farm, Anwick	20. 6.98
		C1/0703			*(Cancelled 29.6.99 by CAA: current status unknown)*		
G-BCHX	Scheibe SF-23A Sperling	2013	D-EGIZ	28. 6.74	R.L.McLean	Rufforth	29. 6.83P
					t/a DG Powered Sailplanes *(Damaged 7.8.82: frame stored 9.01)*		
G-BCID	Piper PA-34-200 Seneca	34-7250303	N1381T	3. 7.74	Shenley Farms (Aviation) Ltd	Headcorn	27. 7.01T
G-BCIE*	Piper PA-28-151 Cherokee Warrior		N9588N	3. 7.74	(Perth College)	Perth	19.12.99T
		28-7415405					
	(Extensively damaged Perth 27.5.99: cancelled 15.9.99 as destroyed: wreck for static rebuild 2.00)						
G-BCIH	de Havilland DHC-1 Chipmunk 22		WD363	3. 7.74	J.M.Hosey	North Weald	19. 6.99
		C1/0304			*(As "WD363")*		
G-BCIJ	Grumman-American AA-5 Traveler		N6143A	3. 7.74	D.G.Page	Elstree	7. 6.03
		AA5-0603			t/a Arrow Association		
G-BCIK	Grumman-American AA-5 Traveler		N6144A	3. 7.74	Trent Aviation Ltd	Tatenhill	28. 5.03
		AA5-0604			*(Reported in wrecked condition outside hangar 8.00)*		
G-BCIL*	Grumman-American AA-1B Trainer	0378	N6168A	5. 7.74	M.Hobson	(Cruden Bay, Peterhead)	2.10.88
		AA1B-0378	*(Crashed Auchnagatt, Aberdeen 14.6.86: cancelled 24.11.86 as WFU: stored 6.00)*				
G-BCIN	Thunder Ax7-77 HAFB	030		5. 7.74	R A, P M G.& N T M Vale	Kidderminster	5. 5.84A
					t/a Isambard Kingdom Brunel Balloon Group		
G-BCIR	Piper PA-28-151 Cherokee Warrior		N9587N	9. 7.74	P.J.Brennan	Southend	16.10.03
		28-7415401					
G-BCIW*	de Havilland DHC-1 Chipmunk 22		(PH-...)	8. 7.74	M.L.Biggs	Sandtoft	11. 7.94
		C1/0899	G-BCIW/WZ868		*(As "WZ868/H" in Cambridge UAS c/s)*		
	(Damaged Hulcote Farm, Beds 26.11.91: cancelled 18.3.92 as destroyed: rear fuselage stored 9.98: other parts used in rebuild of replacment a/c G-ARMF which also carries "WZ868/H").						
G-BCJH*	Mooney M.20F Executive 21	670126	N9549M	11. 7.74	P.J.Bossard	Bourn	30. 6.91
					(Cancelled 26.9.00 by CAA) (Open store 11.01)		
G-BCJM	Piper PA-28-140 Cherokee F		N9592N	17. 7.74	Topcat Aviation Ltd	Manchester	10.11.02T
		28-7425321			*(Op Manchester School of Flying)*		
G-BCJN	Piper PA-28-140 Cherokee Cruiser		N9618N	17. 7.74	Topcat Aviation Ltd	Barton	15. 8.02T
		28-7425350					
G-BCJO	Piper PA-28R-200 Cherokee Arrow II		N9640N	17. 7.74	R.Ross	Pittrichie Farm, Whiterashes	9. 7.03
		28R-7435272					
G-BCJP	Piper PA-28-140 Cherokee	28-24187	N1766J	15. 8.74	D.J. & D.Pitman	Bournemouth	11. 4.04
					t/a Omletair Flying Group		
G-BCKF*	K & S SA.102.5 Cavalier			29. 7.74	K Fairness c/o R Collin	(Eyemouth)	
		71055 & PFA 1594			*(No Permit issued &.cancelled 8.7.91 by CAA) (Stored 2001)*		
G-BCKN	de Havilland DHC-1 Chipmunk 22		WP811	5. 8.74	T.Holloway	RAF Cranwell	16. 2.04
	(Lycoming O-360)	C1/0707			t/a RAFGSA *(Op Cranwell Gliding Club)*		
G-BCKS	Fuji FA.200-180AO Aero Subaru			2. 8.74	Kestrel Aviation Ltd	Thruxton	30. 4.01T
		FA200-250					
G-BCKT	Fuji FA.200-180 Aero Subaru			2. 8.74	P Chilcott	Shoreham	20. 5.02
		FA200-251			t/a Kilo Tango Group		
G-BCKU	Reims Cessna FRA150L Aerobat			1. 8.74	Stapleford Flying Club Ltd	Stapleford	24.10.04T
		FRA1500256					
G-BCKV	Reims Cessna FRA150L Aerobat			1. 8.74	Cleveland Flying School Ltd	Teesside	6. 1.03T
		FRA1500251					
G-BCLC	Sikorsky S-61N Mk.II	61-737		9. 1.75	Bristow Helicopters Ltd	Sumburgh	12. 1.03T
					(Op HM Coast Guard) "Craigievar"		
G-BCLD	Sikorsky S-61N Mk.II	61-739		4. 2.75	Bristow Helicopters Ltd	Aberdeen	2. 2.03T
					"Slains"		
G-BCLI	Grumman-American AA-5 Traveler			12. 8.74	Pioneer Aviation Ltd	Elstree	13. 9.03T
		AA5-0643					
G-BCLL	Piper PA-28-180 Cherokee C	28-2400	SE-EON	13. 8.74	J.Nash & D.F.Amos	Popham	23.10.04
					t/a G-BCLL Group		
G-BCLS	Cessna 170B	20946	N8094A	23. 8.74	N Simpson	(Lincoln)	27. 1.83
					(Stored 7.99: new owner 12.01)		
G-BCLT	SOCATA MS.894A Rallye Minerva 220		EI-BBW	1. 8.74	K.M.Hood	Bristol	3. 6.02
		12003	G-BCLT/F-BTRL		t/a Rallye Group		
G-BCLU	SAN Jodel D.117	506	F-BHXG	28. 8.74	N.A.Wallace	Knettishall	22. 9.02P
G-BCLV*	Bede BD-5A	4885 & PFA 014-10074		28. 8.74	R A Gardiner	(Bridge of Weir)	
			(Not completed & unfinished frame stored: cancelled 31.7.89 as WFU) (Noted 6.00)				
G-BCLW	Grumman-American AA-1B Tr2	AA1B-0463		29. 8.74	J R Faulkner	(Oakham)	27. 7.02T

G-BCMD	Piper PA-18 Super Cub 95	18-2055	OO-SPF	4. 9.74	P.Stephenson	Clacton	4. 2.02
	(L-18C-PI) *(Frame No. 18-2071)*		R.Neth AF R-70/52-2455				
G-BCMF*	Levi Go-Plane RL.6 Srs.1	EAA.3678		5. 9.74	R.Levi	Newport, IoW	
			(Damaged Bembridge 16.11.74: cancelled 5.12.83 by CAA) (Stored 12.95)				
G-BCMJ*	K & S SA.102.5 Cavalier MJ.1 & PFA 1546			9. 9.74	R.G.Sykes	Cranfield	8. 8.85P
	(Continental O-200-A) *(Tail-wheel conversion)*		*(On rebuild 7.94: cancelled 2.3.99 by CAA: current status unknown)*				
G-BCMT	Isaacs Fury II	PFA 1522		9. 9.74	M.H.Turner	(Brixham)	
	(Continental O-200-A)						
G-BCNC	Gardan GY-201 Minicab	A.202	F-BICF	9. 9.74	J.R.Wraight	(Chatham)	
G-BCNP	Cameron O-77 HAFB	117		16. 9.74	P.Spellward *"Blue Fret"*	Bristol	28. 7.00A
G-BCNR*	Thunder Ax7-77A HAFB	028		13. 9.74	R.Warner *"Howdy"*	Cranfield	15. 5.81A
G-BCNX	Piper J-3C-65 Cub (L-4H-PI)	11168	F-BEGM	17. 9.74	K.J.Lord	Cherry Tree Farm, Monewden	23. 5.02P
	(Frame No.10993)		Fr AF/43-29877		t/a The Grasshopper Flying Group		
					(As "540" in USAF c/s)		
G-BCNZ	Fuji FA-200-160 Aero Subaru	257		16. 9.74	J.Bruton & A.Lincoln	Barton	8. 2.99
					t/a G-BCNZ Fuji Group		
G-BCOB	Piper J-3C-65 Cub (L-4H-PI)	10696	F-BCPV	19. 9.74	R.W. & Mrs.J.Marjoram		
	(Frame No.10521)		43-29405			Low Farm, South Walsham	24. 5.02P
					(As "329405/A/23" in USAAC c/s)		
G-BCOI	de Havilland DHC-1 Chipmunk 22	C1/0759	WP870	24. 9.74	D.S.McGregor	Rayne Hall Farm, Rayne	13. 8.04
G-BCOJ	Cameron O-56 HAFB	124		25. 9.74	T.J.Knott & M.J.Webber	Rickmansworth	12. 7.87A
					t/a Phoenix Balloon Group *"Red Squirrel"*		
G-BCOL	Reims Cessna F172M Skyhawk II	F17201233		25. 9.74	A.H.Creaser	Old Manor Farm, Anwick	25. 5.03T
G-BCOM	Piper J-3C-90 Cub (L-4A-PI)	10478	F-BDTP	27. 9.74	D.S.Clarke & N.P.Cook *"Dougal"*	Shoreham	8. 7.02P
	(Frame No.10303)		F-BFQP/OO-ADI/43-29187		t/a Dougal Flying Group		
	(Officially regd as c/n 12040 which is correct identity of G-BGPD: fuselages probably exchanged in France)						
G-BCOO	de Havilland DHC-1 Chipmunk 22	C1/0209	WB760	10.10.74	T.G.Fielding & M.S.Morton	Blackpool	10.11.03
G-BCOP*	Piper PA-28R-200-2 Cherokee Arrow	28R-7435296		8.10.74	(Skycraft Ltd)	(Spalding)	26. 2.01
					(Cancelled 6.11.00 as destroyed: spares 11.01)		
G-BCOR	SOCATA Rallye 100ST	2544	F-OCZK	7. 1.75	P.R.W.Goslin, P.Nichamin & I.M.Speight	Henstridge	27. 9.04
G-BCOU	de Havilland DHC-1 Chipmunk 22	C1/0559	WK522	10.10.74	P.J.Loweth *"Thunderbird 5"*	(Billericay)	30. 3.95
					(As "WK522" in RAF c/s: current status unknown)		
G-BCOX	Bede BD-5A	HJC.4523		10.10.74	H.J.Cox & B.L.Robinson	Chivenor	27.11.95P
					(Noted 7.99)		
G-BCOY	de Havilland DHC-1 Chipmunk 22		WB762	10.10.74	Coventry Gliding Club Ltd		
	(Lycoming O-360)	C1/0212				Husbands Bosworth	23. 1.03
G-BCPD	CAB GY-201 Minicab	18	F-BGKN	24.10.74	P.R.Cozens	Hinton-in-the-Hedges	14. 7.02P
G-BCPG	Piper PA-28R-200 Cherokee Arrow	28R-35705	N4985S	16.10.74	A.G.Antoniades	Barton	24. 6.04
					t/a Roses Flying Group		
G-BCPH	Piper J-3C-65 Cub (L-4H-PI)	11225	F-BCZA	13.12.74	M.J.Janaway	Siege Cross Farm, Thatcham	2. 4.04P
	(Frame No.11050)		Fr.AF/43-29934				
			(As "329934/B/72" in 25th AOP French Armoured Divn of US 3rd Army c/s)				
G-BCPJ	Piper J-3C-65 Cub (L-4J-PI)	13206	F-BDTJ	5.11.74	S.Hollingsworth	Popham	17. 4.02P
	(Frame No.13036)		45-4466		t/a Piper Cub Group		
G-BCPK	Reims Cessna F172M Skyhawk II	F17201194	(D-ELOB)	21.10.74	D.C.C.Handley	Sywell	12. 1.01T
G-BCPN	Grumman-American AA-5 Traveler	AA5-0665	N6155A	21.10.74	G.K.Todd	Full Sutton	25.10.03
G-BCPU	de Havilland DHC-1 Chipmunk 22	C1/0839	WP973	24.10.74	P.Waller	Booker	3. 3.02
G-BCRB	Reims Cessna F172M Skyhawk II	F17201259		29.10.74	D.E.Lamb	Fenland	7. 5.04
G-BCRE*	Cameron O-77 HAFB	128		30.10.74	Balloon Preservation Group	Aylesbury	6.10.83A
					"Snapdragon" (Cancelled 19.5.93 by CAA)		
G-BCRI	Cameron O-65 HAFB	135		5.11.74	V.J.Thorne *"Joseph"*	Bristol	26. 8.81A
G-BCRK	K & S SA.102.5 Cavalier	PFA 01-10049		5.11.74	P.G.R.Brown	Trenchard Farm, Eggsford	14. 7.00P
	(Lycoming O-235)						
G-BCRL	Piper PA-28-151 Cherokee Warrior	28-7415689	N9564N	5.11.74	BCRL Ltd	Humberside	21. 6.03T
G-BCRP	Piper PA-E23-250 Aztec E	27-7305082	N40269	7.11.74	Airlong Charter Ltd	Norwich	27. 9.03T
					(Op Skydrift Ltd)		
G-BCRR	Grumman-American AA-5B Tiger	AA5B-0006		7.11.74	N.A.Whatling	Deenethorpe	5.12.03
G-BCRT	Reims Cessna F150M	F15001164		18.11.74	G.Matthews	Sywell	24. 3.01T
					t/a Blue Max Flying Group		
G-BCRX	de Havilland DHC-1 Chipmunk 22	C1/0232	WD292	22.11.74	Tuplin Ltd	White Waltham	1. 8.03
					(As "WD292" in RAF c/s)		
G-BCSA	de Havilland DHC-1 Chipmunk 22		WP799	25.11.74	T.Holloway	RAF Bicester	14. 2.03
	(Lycoming O-360)	C1/0691			t/a RAFGSA		

G-BCSL	de Havilland DHC-1 Chipmunk 22		WG474	26.11.74	Jalawain Ltd	Barton	30. 3.02
		C1/0524			t/a Barton Chipmunk Flyers		
G-BCSM	Bellanca 8GCBC Scout	108-74		14. 7.99	The Furness Gliding Club Pty Ltd	Walney	30. 4.04
					t/a Lakes Gliding Club Ltd		
G-BCST	SOCATA MS.893A Rallye Commodore 180		F-BPQD	18.11.74	Patricia J.Wilcox	Spanhoe	5.12.03
		10748					
G-BCSX	Thunder Ax7-77 HAFB	031		2.12.74	C.Wolstenholme *"Woophski"*	Macclesfield	5. 7.86A
G-BCSY	Taylor JT.2 Titch	PFA 1504		5.12.74	I.L.Harding	Sackville Farm, Riseley	
	(VW 1600)	*(Construction abandoned at advanced state: stored 3.97: current status unknown)*					
G-BCTF	Piper PA-28-151 Cherokee Warrior		N9585N	11.12.74	E.Reed	Teesside	2. 9.02T
		28-7515033			t/a The St.George Flying Club		
	(Rebuilt 1989/90 using major components from G-BFXZ)						
G-BCTI	Schleicher ASK 16	16029	D-KIWA	23.12.74	A.J.Southard	Hinton-in-the-Hedges	24. 7.04
					t/a Tango India Syndicate		
G-BCTJ	Cessna 310Q II	310Q1072	N1219G	23.12.74	D.Pearce & P.Golding	Biggin Hill	14. 7.02T
					t/a TJ Flying Group		
G-BCTK	Reims FR172J Rocket	FR17200546		23.12.74	R.T.Love	Bodmin	13. 3.03
G-BCTT	Evans VP-1	PFA 1543		24.12.74	M.J.Watson	Knettishall	25. 6.99P
	(VW 1600)						
G-BCTU*	Reims Cessna FRA150M Aerobat			30.12.74	J.A.Rees	Haverfordwest	24. 3.02T
		FRA1500268			t/a Haverfordwest School of Flying		
					(Cancelled 17.1.00 as WFU)		
G-BCTW*	Reims Cessna F150M	F15001170		2. 1.75	Wickenby Aviation Ltd	Wickenby	20.12.91T
		(Damaged Strangford Lough 12.4.89: cancelled 20.6.89 as WFU: stored 2.93: current status unknown)					
G-BCUB	Piper J-3C-65 Cub (L-4J-PI)	13370	F-BFBU	13.12.74	A.L.Brown & G.Attwell	Bourn	13. 6.01P
	(Lippert Reed conversion)		45-4630				
	(Officially regd wit c/n 13186 now known to be G-BDOL (qv): airframes possibly switched during conversion in UK)						
G-BCUF	Reims Cessna F172M Skyhawk II			3. 1.75	John L.R.James & Co Ltd		
		F17201279				Clough Farm, Croft, Skegness	19. 7.03
G-BCUH	Reims Cessna F150M	F15001195		7. 1.75	M.G.Montgomerie	Elstree	10. 1.04T
					t/a G-BCUH Group		
G-BCUJ	Reims Cessna F150M	F15001176		9. 1.75	BCT Aircraft Leasing Ltd	Full Sutton	13.12.01T
G-BCUL	SOCATA Rallye 100ST	2545	F-OCZL	27. 1.75	C.A.Ussher & Fountain Estates Ltd	Bagby	8. 5.00
G-BCUO	Scottish Aviation Bulldog Srs.120/122		G-107	9. 1.75	Cranfield University	Cranfield	27. 4.04T
		BH120/371	Ghana AF/G-BCUO				
G-BCUS	Scottish Aviation Bulldog Srs.120/122		G-109	9. 1.75	S.J. & J.J.Ollier	Tatenhill	29. 4.02
		BH120/373	Ghana AF/G-BCUS				
G-BCUV	Scottish Aviation Bulldog Srs.120/122		G-112	9. 1.75	Dolphin Property (Management) Ltd		
		BH120/376	Ghana AF/G-BCUV			Old Sarum	17. 5.03T
	(As "CB733" in RAF c/s - pseudo serial for Sir Christopher Benson (CB) and, allegedly, his date of birth (7.33))						
G-BCUW	Reims Cessna F177RG Cardinal RG		SE-GKL	10. 1.75	S.J.Westley	(Bedford)	12. 5.00T
		F177RG0119					
G-BCUY	Reims Cessna FRA150M Aerobat			14. 1.75	J.C.Carpenter	Clipgate Farm, Denton	8. 3.04
		FRA1500269					
G-BCVB	Piper PA-17 Vagabond	17-190	F-BFMT	22. 1.75	A.T.Nowak	Popham	5. 7.02P
	(Continental A65)		N4890H				
G-BCVC	SOCATA Rallye 100ST	2548	F-OCZO	16. 1.75	N.R Vine	Popham	25. 1.05
G-BCVE*	Evans VP-2	V2-1015 & PFA 7210		16. 1.75	North Western PFA Strut	Barton	
					(Cancelled 9.6.93 as TWFU) (Noted 5.01)		
G-BCVF	Practavia Pilot Sprite 115			27. 1.75	D.G.Hammersley	Tatenhill	17. 6.02P
	(Continental C125)	GBC.1 & PFA 1362					
G-BCVG	Reims Cessna FRA150L Aerobat		(I-AFAD)	16. 1.75	I.G.Cooper	Compton Abbas	19.12.03
		FRA1500245			t/a G-BCVG Flying Group		
G-BCVH	Reims Cessna FRA150L Aerobat			16. 1.75	Multiflight Ltd	Leeds-Bradford	20.10.02T
		FRA1500258					
G-BCVJ	Reims Cessna F172M Skyhawk II			16. 1.75	Rothland Ltd	RAF Woodvale	13.12.03
		F17201305					
G-BCVY	Piper PA-34-200T Seneca II		N32447	28. 1.75	Oxford Aviation Services Ltd	Oxford	16. 3.03T
		34-7570022					
G-BCWB	Cessna 182P Skylane II	18263566	N5848J	29. 1.75	Whisky Bravo Ltd	Kemble	17.12.01T
G-BCWH	Practavia Pilot Sprite 115	PFA 1366		3. 2.75	R.Tasker	Blackpool	24. 6.02P
	(Continental 0-240-A)						
G-BCWK	Alpavia Fournier RF3	24	F-BMDD	7. 2.75	T.J.Hartwell & D.R.Wilkinson	Thurleigh	13. 8.02P
G-BCXB	SOCATA Rallye 100ST	2546	F-OCZM	7. 2.75	A.Smails	Morgansfield, Fishburn	15. 3.04
G-BCXE	Robin DR.400 2+2	1015		19. 2.75	Weald Air Services Ltd	Headcorn	3. 8.02T
G-BCXJ	Piper J-3C-65 Cub (L-4J-PI)	13048	F-BFFH	21. 2.75	B.Walsh	Old Sarum	15. 8.02P
	(Frame No.12878)		OO-SWA/44-80752		t/a Old Sarum Piper Cub Syndicate		
					(As "480752/E-39" in USAAC c/s)		
G-BCXN	de Havilland DHC-1 Chipmunk 22		WP800	7. 3.75	G.M.Turner	RAF Halton	7. 5.03
		C1/0692			*(As "WP800/2" in Southampton UAS c/s)*		
G-BCXO*	MBB Bö.105D	S.80	D-HDCE	27. 2.75	Lands End Theme Park	Lands End	23. 5.94T
		(Cancelled 4.3.92 as WFU: original pod replaced & rebuilt as a display piece as "G-CDBS")					
G-BCXZ*	Cameron O-56 HAFB	154		4. 3.75	Not known *"Olive"*	NK	NE(A)
					(Cancelled 19.5.93 by CAA)		

G-BCYH	DAW Privateer Mk.3 Motor Glider	BGA.1158	10. 3.75	D.B.Limbert	Crosland Moor	17. 6.02P
	(VW 1600) 2 & PFA 1568	RAFGSA.264/XA297				
	(Regd as Cadet III and is a converted Slingsby T.31B c/n 839: marked incorrectly as "RAFGSA.246")					
G-BCYJ	de Havilland DHC-1 Chipmunk 22	WG307	12. 3.75	R.A.L.Falconer		
	C1/0360			*(As "WG307")* Shempston Farm, Lossiemouth		19.12.02
G-BCYK*	Avro (Canada) CF-100 Canuck Mk.IV -	18393	18. 3.75	Imperial War Museum	Duxford	
		RCAF		*(Cancelled 15.9.81 as WFU) (As "18393" in RCAF c/s)*		
G-BCYM	de Havilland DHC-1 Chipmunk 22	WK577	13. 3.75	C.H.Nicholls	Kemble	6. 9.03
	C1/0598			t/a G-BCYM Group		
G-BCYR	Reims Cessna F172M Skyhawk II		20. 3.75	J. & L.Donne	Inverness	4.12.04T
	F17201288			t/a Donne Enterprise *(Op Highland Flying Club)*		
G-BCZH	de Havilland DHC-1 Chipmunk 22	WK622	19. 3.75	A.C.Byrne	Botany Bay, Horsford, Norwich	31. 7.87
	C1/0635					
	(As "WK622" in RAF c/s: crashed Pentney, Norfolk 6.9.87: stored 8.93: current status unknown)					
G-BCZI	Thunder Ax7-77 HAFB 037		24. 3.75	R.G.Griffin & R.Blackwell	Newbury	16. 3.86A
				t/a North Hampshire Balloon Group *"Motorway"*		
G-BCZM	Reims Cessna F172M Skyhawk II		3. 4.75	Cornwall Flying Club Ltd	Bodmin	2. 1.04T
	F17201350					
G-BCZN	Reims Cessna F150M F15001149		27. 3.75	Mona Aviation Ltd	RAF Mona	10.12.03T
G-BCZO	Cameron O-77 HAFB 158		27. 3.75	W.O.T.Holmes *"Leo"*	Shrewsbury	11.10.86A

G-BDAA – G-BDZZ

G-BDAC*	Cameron O-77 HAFB 146		2. 4.75	Not known *"Chocolate Ripple"*	NK	NE(A)
				(Cancelled 14.11.95 by CAA)		
G-BDAD	Taylor JT.1 Monoplane PFA 1453		2. 4.75	J.Gunson t/a G-BDAD Group	(Preston)	3. 4.92P
	(VW 1700)			*(Damaged Blackpool 21.7.91: current status unknown)*		
G-BDAG	Taylor JT.1 Monoplane PFA 1430		1. 4.75	T.K.Gough	(Worcester)	20. 5.00P
	(VW 1600)			*"Biggles Too"*		
G-BDAH*	Evans VP-1 PFA 7007		2. 4.75	G.H.J.Geurts	Cranfield	26. 5.99
	(VW 1600)			*(Cancelled 12.4.00 as temporarily wfu)*		
G-BDAI	Reims Cessna FRA150M Aerobat		21. 4.75	A.Sharma	Popham	25. 7.04T
	FRA1500266					
G-BDAK	Rockwell Commander 112A 252	N1252J	10. 4.75	R.A.Denton	Sherburn-in-Elmet	31. 8.03
G-BDAL	Rockwell Shrike Commander 500S 3226	N57134	25. 4.75	Xjet Ltd	Farnborough	5. 9.04
G-BDAM	Noorduyn AT-16-ND Harvard IIB 14-726	LN-MAA	10. 4.75	Silver Victory BVBA		
		Fv16047/FE992/42-12479			(Brasschaat, Belgium)	6. 9.02P
				(As "FE992/K-T" in 5(P)AFU c/s)		
G-BDAO	SIPA 91 2	F-BEPT	10. 4.75	J.E.Mead	(Cowbridge)	1. 8.00P
	(Continental C85)					
G-BDAP	AJEP/Wittman TW.8 Tailwind		9. 4.75	J.Whiting	Bagby	22. 8.02P
	(Continental O-200-A) 0387 & PFA 3507					
G-BDAR	Evans VP-1 Srs.2		10. 4.75	R.B.Valler	(Waterlooville)	20. 7.84P
	(VW 1600) PFA 1537 & PFA 062-10461			*(Current status unknown) (Valid CofR 4.01)*		
G-BDAX*	Piper PA-23-250 Aztec C 27-3494	5B-CAO	15. 4.75	Barry Technical College		
		N6399Y/N10F			Cardiff Airport Industrial Park	12.11.93
		(Cancelled 13.3.92 as WFU) (Stored 11.95: current status unknown)				
G-BDAY	Thunder Ax5-42A HAFB 042		8. 4.75	T.M.Donnelly *"Meconium"*	Doncaster	16. 1.93A
G-BDBD	Wittman W.8 Tailwind 133	N1198S	25. 4.75	S.D.Arnold & T.Douglas		
	(Continental O-200-A)			t/a Tailwind Taildragger Group		
					Wellesbourne Mountford	28. 6.02P
G-BDBF	Clutton FRED Srs.II PFA 1528		15. 4.75	J.M.Brightwell & A.J.Wright	Hucknall	18. 3.98P
	(VW 1600)			*(Noted 7.01)*		
G-BDBH	Bellanca 7GCBC Citabria 758-74	OE-AOL	15. 4.75	C.J.Gray	Buttermilk Farm, Easton Maudit	1. 2.04
G-BDBI	Cameron O-77 HAFB 162		15. 4.75	C Jones	Reading	11. 7.87A
				"Funny Money" (New owner 12.01)		
G-BDBJ	Cessna 182P Skylane II 18263646	N4644K	18. 4.75	H.C.Wilson	Great Ashfield, Suffolk	30. 1.03
G-BDBS*	Short SD.3-30 UTT SH.1935 & SH.3001	G-14-3001	21. 4.75	Ulster Aviation Heritage *(Cancelled 1.7.93 as WFU)*		
	(Airframe originally laid down as SC.7 Skyvan c/n SH.1935)				Langford Lodge, Belfast	28. 9.92S
G-BDBU	Reims Cessna F150M F15001174		30. 4.75	R.Edgar	Prestwick	6. 7.03
G-BDBV	Aero Jodel D.11A V.3	D-EGIB	23. 4.75	G.G.Long	Seething	31.10.02P
	(Continental C90)			t/a Seething Jodel Group		
G-BDBZ*	Westland WS.55 Whirlwind 2 (HAR.10)	XJ398	23. 4.75	Yorkshire Air Museum	Elvington	
	(Regd with c/n WA.386) WA/62	(XD768)				
G-BDCC	de Havilland DHC-1 Chipmunk 22	WD321	25. 4.75	Coventry Gliding Club Ltd		
	(Lycoming O-360 C1/0258				Husbands Bosworth	24. 3.02
G-BDCD	Piper J-3C-65 Cub (L-4J-PI) 12429	OO-AVS	28. 4.75	Suzanne C.Brook		
	(Continental C90) *(Frame No.12257)*	44-80133			Wellcross Grange, Slinfold	22. 7.00P
				(As "480133/B/44" in US Army c/s)		
G-BDCE	Reims Cessna F172H F17200704	PH-EHB	5. 5.75	Copperplane Ltd	Bournemouth	26. 4.01T
				(Damaged in gales Bournemouth 3.1.99: fuselage stored 5.00)		
G-BDCI	Scanor Piel CP.301C Emeraude 503	F-BIRC	25. 4.75	D.L.Sentance		
					Rothwell Lodge Farm, Kettering	22.11.02P

G-BDCL	Grumman-American AA-5 Traveler	AA5-0773	EI-CCI G-BDCL/EI-BGV/G-BDCL/N1373R	5. 5.75	J.Crowe *(Stored w/o wings 5.00)*	Coventry	29.11.93T
G-BDCO	Beagle B.121 Pup 1	B121-171		6. 5.75	R.J.Page & M.H.Simms *(New owner 4.01)*	(Haywards Heath)	28. 7.97
G-BDCU*	Cameron O-77 HAFB	126		11. 6.75	Not known *(Cancelled 4.8.98 by CAA: extant 2000)*	NK	20. 2.86
G-BDDD	de Havilland DHC-1 Chipmunk 22	C1/0326	WD387	16. 5.75	RAE Aero Club Ltd	Farnborough	16. 8.02T
G-BDDF	Jodel Wassmer D.120 Paris-Nice	97	F-BIKZ	20. 5.75	A.J.Hobbs	(Norwich)	17. 8.02P
G-BDDG	Dormois Jodel D.112	855	F-BILM	20. 5.75	J Pool & D.G.Palmer	Sturgate	9. 8.02P
G-BDDS	Piper PA-25-260 Pawnee C	25-4757	CS-AIU N10F	22. 5.75	T.J.Price t/a Vale of Neath Gliding Club	Rhigos	21. 4.02
G-BDDT	Piper PA-25-235 Pawnee C	25-5324	CS-AIX N8820L	22. 5.75	W.J.& A.E.Taylor t/a Pawneee Aviation *(Noted 12.01)*	East Winch	8. 7.99A
G-BDDX*	Whittaker MW2B Excalibur (VW 1500)	001 & PFA 041-10106		28. 5.75	Flambards Village Theme Park *(WFU 1976)*	Helston	
G-BDDZ	Menavia Piel CP.301A Emeraude	253	F-BIMZ	30. 5.75	E.C.Mort *(Damaged Cranwell North 3.6.84: on rebuild 1.01)*	(Warrington)	20. 6.84P
G-BDEC	SOCATA Rallye 100ST	2552	F-OCZS	28. 5.75	M.Mulhall	Kilkenny, Co.Kilkenny	10. 8.03
G-BDEF	Piper PA-34-200T Seneca II	34-7570150	N33695	2. 6.75	Anglo American Automotive Ltd	Bournemouth	24. 5.02T
G-BDEH	Jodel Wassmer D.120A Paris-Nice	239	F-BLNE	2. 6.75	M.D.Nichol t/a EH Group	Oaksey Park	23. 8.02P
G-BDEI	Jodel D.9 Bebe (VW 1600)	585 & PFA 936		2. 6.75	R.Q.T.Newns t/a The Noddy Group *"Noddy"*	White Waltham	9.12.02P
G-BDEU	de Havilland DHC-1 Chipmunk 22	C1/0704	WP808	17. 6.75	A.Taylor *(As "WP808")*	Manor Farm, Binham	28. 1.02
G-BDEX	Reims Cessna FRA150M Aerobat	FRA1500279		12. 6.75	R.A.Powell	Lower Wasing Farm, Brimpton	11. 5.03T
G-BDEY	Piper J-3C-65 Cub (L-4J-PI) *(Frame No.12366)*	12538	OO-AAT OO-GAC/44-80242	17. 6.75	W.J. & Mrs.J.Morecraft t/a Ducksworth Flying Club *(Fuselage noted Sibsey 7.01)*	Highfield Farm, Empingham	22. 4.02P
G-BDEZ	Piper J-3C-65 Cub (L-4J-PI) *(Frame No.12211)*	12383	OO-SOC OO-EPI/44-80087	17. 6.75	R.J.M.Turnbull	Rydinghurst Farm, Cranleigh	10. 6.02P
G-BDFB	Phoenix Currie Wot (Walter Mikron III)	PFA 3008		20. 6.75	J.Jennings	Fenland	9. 6.02P
G-BDFG*	Cameron O-65 HAFB	179		24. 6.75	N.A.Robertson *"Golly II" (Cancelled 21.10.01 as wfu & stored)*	Combe Hay Manor, Bath	16. 4.88A
G-BDFH	Auster AOP.9 *(Frame No.AUS 177 FM)*	B5/10/176	XR240	24. 6.75	R.O.Holden *(As "XR240")*	Booker	20. 9.02P
G-BDFJ	Reims Cessna F150M	F15001182		25. 6.75	Cassandra J.Hopewell	Sibson	13. 7.02T
G-BDFR	Fuji FA.200-160 Aero Subaru	FA200-262		7. 7.75	A.Houghton t/a Fugi Group	Blackpool	1.11.04
G-BDFS	Fuji FA.200-160 Aero Subaru	FA200-263		7. 7.75	B.Lawrence	Goodwood	24. 9.00T
G-BDFU*	PMPS Dragonfly MPA Mk.1	01	*(Cancelled 12.83 as WFU)*	14. 7.75	R.J.Hardy & R.Churcher *(On loan to National Museums of Scotland/Museum of Flight)*	East Fortune	
G-BDFW	Rockwell Commander 112A	308	N1308J	18. 6.75	M.E.& E.G.Reynolds	Blackbushe	22.11.04
G-BDFX	Taylorcraft J Auster 5	2060	F-BGXG TW517	9. 7.75	J.Eagles *(Damaged Oaksey Park 10.10.93: on rebuild 4.00)*	Kemble	3. 6.94T
G-BDFY	Grumman-American AA-5 Traveler	AA5-0806		10. 7.75	R.L.Bagnall & J.Wishart t/a Grumman Group *(Op Edinburgh Flying Club)*	Edinburgh	22. 8.03
G-BDFZ	Reims Cessna F150M	F15001184	(D-EIWB) (F-BXIH)	14. 7.75	L.W.Scattergood	Sherburn in Elmet	17. 5.03T
G-BDGB	Barritault JB-01 Minicab (Continental PC-60)	PFA 1819		23. 6.75	D.G.Burden	Armshold Farm, Kingston, Cambs	12. 6.01P
G-BDGH	Thunder Ax7-77 HAFB	049		16. 7.75	R.J.Mitchener & P.F.Smart t/a Balloon Collection *"London Pride III"*	Andover	NE(A)
G-BDGM	Piper PA-28-151 Cherokee Warrior	28-7415165	N41307	30. 7.75	Comed Aviation	Blackpool	23. 1.04T
G-BDGO	Thunder Ax7-77 HAFB	048		16. 7.75	Justerini & Brooks Ltd *"J & B"* *(Op Balloon Preservation Group)*	Kirdford	2. 2.82A
G-BDGP*	Cameron V-65 HAFB	658	(N.....) G-BDGP	2. 9.80	A.Mayes & V.Lawton t/a Warwick Balloons *"Ladbroke Motor Group"* *(Cancelled 10.10.01 by CAA)*	Leamington Spa	17.11.96A
G-BDGY	Piper PA-28-140 Cherokee	28-23613	N3536K	5. 8.75	S.J.Willcox	Compton Abbas	2. 9.02T
G-BDHK	Piper J-3C-65 Cub (L-4A-PI) *(Frame No.9068)* *(Official c/n quoted as "261" with p/i 42-36414 but this corresponds to c/n 8538/N75366)*	8969	F-PHFZ 42-38400	24. 7.75	A.Liddiard *(As "329417" in USAAC c/s)*	Eastbach Farm, Coleford	9. 9.02P
G-BDIE	Rockwell Commander 112A	342	N1342J	14. 8.75	R.J.Adams	RAF Brize Norton	10. 7.04T
G-BDIG	Cessna 182P Skylane II *(Reims-assembled with c/n F18200020)*	18263938	N9877E	26. 8.75	P.B.Barrett & A R Bruce t/a Air Group 6	Sturgate	13. 7.02
G-BDIH	SAN Jodel D.117 *(Regd with incorrect c/n 817)*	812	F-BIOT	22. 8.75	N.D.H.Stokes *(Damaged Rydinghurst Farm, Cranleigh 9.12.84: on rebuild: current status unknown)*	(Bath)	4. 7.85P

G-BDIJ	Sikorsky S-61N Mk.II	61-751	9M-AYF	3.10.75	Bristow Helicopters Ltd	Lee-on-Solent	31. 5.04T
	(SAR conversion)		G-BDIJ		*(Op H M Coastguard) "Crathes"*		
G-BDIX*	de Havilland DH.106 Comet 4C	6471	XR399	1. 9.75	National Museums of Scotland/Museum of Flight		
					(Dan-Air titles)	East Fortune	11.10.81T
					(Cancelled 2.9.91 by CAA)		
G-BDJB*	Taylor JT.1 Monoplane Srs.2			2. 9.75	J.F.Barber	Benfleet	19. 1.79S
		JB.JT.1 001 & PFA 1428					
	(On rebuild with VW 1835 engine after accident Andrewsfield 25.5.78: cancelled 2.3.99 by CAA: current status unknown)						
G-BDJC	AJEP/Wittman W.8 Tailwind			29. 8.75	M.A. Hales	(Gainsborough)	20. 6.01P
	(Continental O-200-A) 387AW & PFA 3508						
G-BDJD	Jodel D.112	PFA 910		3. 9.75	J.E.Preston	(Ottringham)	29. 6.02P
	(Continental A65)				*"Marianne"*		
G-BDJF	Bensen B.8MV	RPW.1 & PFA G/01-1075		4. 9.75	R.P.White	(Haslemere)	
G-BDJG	Phoenix Luton LA-4A Minor	PFA 828		3. 9.75	S.C.Barry	White Waltham	9. 6.02P
	(VW 1835)				t/a Very Slow Flying Club		
G-BDJP	Piper J-3C-65 Cub Special	22992	OO-SKZ	11.12.75	Holdcroft Aviation Services Ltd		
	(Continental C90) *(Frame No.21017)*		PH-NCV/NC3908K			Hinton-in-the-Hedges	18. 5.03T
G-BDJR	SNCAN NC.858S	2	F-BFIY	30. 9.75	R.F.M.Marson *(On rebuild 9.00)*	(Fleet)	23. 5.92P
G-BDKB*	SOCATA Rallye 150ST	2631		30. 9.75	N.C.Anderson	(North Devon)	4. 6.82
					(Damaged Coleraine 5.7.81: cancelled 18.2.99 by CAA) (On rebuild 2.00)		
G-BDKC	Cessna A185F Skywagon	185-02569	N1854R	30. 9.75	Bridge of Tilt Co Ltd	Blair Atholl	23. 4.01
G-BDKD	Enstrom F-28A	319		30. 9.75	M A Crook & A E Wright	(Warrington)	16.12.01
G-BDKH	Menavia Piel CP.301A Emeraude	241	F-BIMN	15.10.75	P.N.Marshall	Insch	11. 6.01P
G-BDKJ	K & S SA.102.5 Cavalier			14.10.75	D.A.Garner	(Swansea)	5. 6.95P
	(Continental O-240-A) 72207 & PFA 1589				*(Damaged Gloucestershire 14.9.97: current status unknown)*		
G-BDKM	SIPA 903	98	F-BGHX	17.11.75	S.W.Markham	Valentine Farm, Odiham	30. 4.02P
G-BDKU	Taylor JT.1 Monoplane	PFA 1456		22.10.75	B.N.Stevens & A.J.L.Eves,		
	(VW 1500) *(Possibly incorporates PFA 055-10301)*					St Mary's, Scilly Isles	10. 9.01P
G-BDKW	Rockwell Commander 112	106	N1277J	3.11.75	Orwell Flying Ltd		
			ZS-MIB/N1106J			Poplar Hall Farm, Elmsett	16. 7.03T
G-BDLO	Grumman-American AA-5A Cheetah		N6154A	3.11.75	S. & J.Dolan	Elstree	19. 7.04T
		AA5A-0026					
G-BDLS	Grumman-American AA-1B Tr.2		N6153A	3.11.75	C.R.Tilley	Shobdon	28.10.04
		AA1B-0564					
G-BDLT	Rockwell Commander 112A	363	N1363J	4.11.75	D.L.Churchward	Popham	18. 5.02
G-BDLY	K & S SA.102.5 Cavalier			14.11.75	P.R.Stevens	Thruxton	27. 7.99P
	(Lycoming O-290)	PFA 01-10011					
G-BDMM*	Jodel D.11	PFA 901		5.11.75	P.N.Marshall	(Aboyne)	
					(Cancelled 27.1.97 by CAA) (Stored but removed late 2000: current status unknown)		
G-BDMO*	Thunder Ax7-77 HAFB	053	(EC-)	25.11.75	Balloon Preservation Group	Kirdford	
			G-BDMO		*"Flash Harry" (Cancelled 8.3.95 as WFU)*		
G-BDMS	Piper J-3C-65 Cub (L-4J-PI)	13049	F-BEGZ	4.11.75	A.T.H.Martin	Old Sarum	10. 5.02P
			44-80753		*(As "FR886" in RAF c/s)*		
G-BDMW	SAN Jodel DR.100A Ambassadeur	79	F-BIVM	2.12.75	R.O.F.Harper	Yew Tree Farm, Lymm Dam	12. 8.02
					t/a G-BDMW Flying Group		
G-BDNC	Taylor JT.1 Monoplane	PFA 1454		8.12.75	D.W.Mathie	(Diss)	6. 3.02P
	(Walter Mikron III)						
G-BDNG	Taylor JT.1 Monoplane	PFA 1405		12.12.75	S.B.Churchill	Eastbach Farm, Coleford	15. 8.02P
	(VW 1834)				*"The Red Sparrow"*		
G-BDNO	Taylor JT.1 Monoplane	PFA 1431		15.12.75	S.D.Glover	Bodmin	2. 5.96P
	(VW 1600)				*(Hangared dismantled 6.01)*		
G-BDNR*	Reims Cessna FRA150M Aerobat			18.12.75	Busy Bee Aviation Ltd	Sibson	26. 7.92T
		FRA1500284			*(Damaged Liverpool 22.1.92: cancelled 14.10.96 by CAA) (Stored 9.99)*		
G-BDNT	Jodel D.92	397	F-PINL	2. 1.76	R.F.Morton	Kemble	20.12.02P
	(VW 1600)						
G-BDNU	Reims Cessna F172M Skyhawk II			2. 1.76	J. & K.G.McVicar	Elstree	31. 3.03T
		F17201405					
G-BDNW	Grumman-American AA-1B Trainer			8. 1.76	P.Mitchell	Humberside	16. 4.03
		AA1B-0588					
G-BDNX	Grumman-American AA-1B Trainer			8. 1.76	R.M.North	Kimbolton	23. 8.04
		AA1B-0590					
G-BDNZ*	Cameron O-77 HAFB	203		8. 1.76	I.L.McHale	Sutton, Surrey	28. 7.81A
					"Winston Churchill"		
G-BDOC	Sikorsky S-61N Mk.II	61-765		20. 3.76	Bristow Helicopters Ltd	Sumburgh	28.12.04T
	(SAR conversion)				*(Op H M Coastguard) "Tolquhoun"*		
G-BDOD	Reims Cessna F150M	F15001266		20. 1.76	D.M.Moreau	(Wickham)	2. 7.03
G-BDOE	Reims FR172J Rocket	FR1720559		20. 1.76	D. & P.A.Sansome		
						Little Chase Farm, Kenilworth	5. 1.03
G-BDOG	Scottish Aviation Bulldog Srs.200			18.12.75	D.C.Bonsall	Netherthorpe	27. 6.02P
		BH200/381			*(Phoenix Flying Group c/s)*		
G-BDOL	Piper J-3C-65 Cub (L-4J-PI)	13186	F-BCPC	18.12.75	L.R.Balthazor	Lee-on-Solent	15. 3.02P
	(Frame No.13016)		45-4446				
	(Officially c/n 13370 but holds genuine c/n and USAAC plates relating to c/n 13370/ex 45-4630 now G-BCUB: airframes possibly switched during conversion in UK)						

G-BDON	Thunder Ax7-77A HAFB	063		17.12.75	M.J.Smith *"Fred"*	York	24. 6.94A
G-BDOT	Britten-Norman BN-2A mk.III-2 Trislander		ZK-SFF	21. 1.76	Atlantic Bridge Aviation Ltd	Lydd	3.12.00T
		1025	N900TA/N903GD/N3850K/VH-BPB/G-BDOT		*(Op Sky Trek Airways)*		
G-BDOW	Reims Cessna FRA150M Aerobat			26. 1.76	Boldlake Ltd	(Holywell)	3. 4.04T
		FRA1500296					
G-BDPA	Piper PA-28-151 Cherokee Warrior		N9630N	26. 1.76	D.R.Allard	Gloucestershire	6.11.03
		28-7615033			t/a G-BDPA Flying Group		
G-BDPJ	Piper PA-25-235 Pawnee B	25-3665	PH-VBF	2. 2.76	T.M.Holloway	Bicester	19.12.03
	(Lycoming O-540A1B5-@ 250hp)		SE-EPZ		t/a RAFGSA		
G-BDPK	Cameron O-56 HAFB	191		4. 2.76	N.H.Ponsford & A.M.Lindsay	Leeds	29.12.88A
					t/a Rango Balloon & Kite Co		
G-BDRD	Reims Cessna FRA150M Aerobat			9. 2.76	I.P.Diment	Perth	27. 6.03T
		FRA1500289					
G-BDRG	Taylor JT.2 Titch	PFA 060-10295		19.12.78	D.R.Gray	(Wilmslow)	
G-BDRJ	de Havilland DHC-1 Chipmunk 22		WP857	19. 2.76	J.C.Schooling	Elstree	4. 7.02
		C1/0742			*(As "WP857/24")*		
G-BDRK	Cameron O-65 HAFB	205		12. 2.76	D.L.Smith *"Smirk"*	Eling Hill, Newbury	20. 6.86A
G-BDRL*	Stits SA-3A Playboy	P-689	N730GF	12. 2.76	O.C.Bradley	Mullaghmore, Co.Sligo	17. 6.98P
	(Continental C85)				*(Cancelled 11.5.01 by CAA) (Stored 8.01)*		
G-BDSA*	Clutton-Tabenor FRED Srs.II		EI-BFS	23. 2.76	W D M Turtle	Rich Hill, Co.Armagh	5. 7.79P
		LAS.1803 & PFA 029-10141	G-BDSA		*(Cancelled by CAA 29.9.00: current status unknown)*		
G-BDSB	Piper PA-28-181 Cherokee Archer II		N8221C	23. 2.76	Testfair Ltd	Fairoaks	19. 7.04
		28-7690107					
G-BDSE	Cameron O-77 HAFB	210		27. 2.76	British Airways plc	Worplesdon	31. 3.90A
					"Concorde"		
G-BDSF	Cameron O-56 HAFB	209		1. 3.76	J.H.Greensides *"Itzuma"*	Hull	24. 5.93A
G-BDSH	Piper PA-28-140 Cherokee Cruiser		N9638N	1. 3.76	D.Jones	Nottingham	26. 8.02
		28-7625063			t/a The Wright Brothers Flying Group		
G-BDSK	Cameron O-65 HAFB	166		3. 3.76	Semajan Ltd	Romsey	5. 9.02A
					t/a Southern Balloon Group *"Carousel II"*		
G-BDSL	Reims Cessna F150M	F15001306		5. 3.76	D.C.Bonsall	Netherthorpe	24. 6.04T
G-BDSM	Slingsby T.31 Motor Cadet III			5. 3.76	N.F.James	Husbands Bosworth	22. 5.02P
		PFA 042-10507					
G-BDTB	Evans VP-1 Srs.2	PFA 7009		15. 3.76	J.A.Hanslip	Fenland	16.10.02P
	(VW 1834)						
G-BDTL	Evans VP-1	PFA 7012		17. 3.76	A.K.Lang	(Stoke-sub-Hamdon, Somerset)	5. 9.85P
	(VW 1600)				*(Stored 5.98: current status unknown)*		
G-BDTN	Fairey Britten-Norman BN-2A Mk III-2 Trislander			16. 3.76	Aurigny Air Services Ltd	Guernsey	10. 6.98T
		1026	S7-AAN/VQ-SAN/G-BDTN		*(Stored 12.01)*		
G-BDTO	Fairey Britten-Norman BN-2A Mk.III-2 Trislander			16. 3.76	Aurigny Air Services Ltd	Guernsey	31. 3.02T
		1027	G-RBSI/G-OTSB/G-BDTO/8P-ASC/G-BDTO/(C-GYOX)/G-BDTO				
					"Nessie" (Merrill Lynch titles)		
G-BDTT*	Bede BD-5	3795 & PFA 014-10084		17. 3.76	Martini's Night-Club	Barrow-in-Furness	
			(Not completed: cancelled 2.2.87 by CAA: noted 5.97: current status unknown)				
G-BDTU	Van Den Bemden Omega III (Gas) Free Balloon (20,000 cu.ft)						
		VDB-35 & AFB.4		16. 3.76	R.G.Turnbull *"Omega III"*	Clyro, Hereford	4. 8.99A
G-BDTV	Mooney M.20F Executive	22-1307	N6934V	16. 3.76	S.Redfearn	Gamston	15. 6.03
G-BDTW*	Cassutt Racer IIIM	PFA 034-10102		18. 3.76	R.Mohlenkamp	Damme, Germany	1.11.99P
	(Continental C90)				*"The Thunder Box" (Cancelled 21.1.00 as WFU)*		
G-BDTX	Reims Cessna F150M	F15001275		19. 3.76	S.L.Lefley & F.W.Ellis		
						Water Leisure Park, Skegness	7. 6.03T
G-BDUI	Cameron V-56 HAFB	218		19. 3.76	D.C.Johnson *"True Brit"*	Farnham	6. 7.91A
G-BDUL	Evans VP-1	PFA 1557		25. 3.76	C.K.Brown	(Helston)	23. 4.02P
	(VW 1834)						
G-BDUM	Reims Cessna F150M	F15001301	F-BXZB	29. 3.76	B.P.Thorogood	Andrewsfield	3. 4.03
G-BDUN	Piper PA-34-200T Seneca II		(EI-BLR)	29. 3.76	Air Medical Ltd	Oxford	27. 2.04T
		34-7570163	G-BDUN/SE-GIA				
G-BDUO	Reims Cessna F150M Commuter			29. 3.76	C.B.Mellor	Popham	25. 4.04T
		F15001304			t/a BM Aviation		
G-BDUY	Robin DR.400/140B Major	1120		5. 4.76	J.G.Anderson		
						Ardiffery Mains Farm, Hatton	20. 1.03
G-BDUX*	Slingsby T.21B "1146" & PFA 042-10163			29. 3.76	Not known	Cranfield	23. 2.84P
	(Based on T.31)		*(WFU Southend & cancelled 7.1.85 as WFU) (Stored 7.90: current status unknown)*				
G-BDUZ	Cameron V-56 HAFB	213		30. 3.76	P.J.Bish	Hungerford	19. 2.00A
					t/a Zebedee Balloon Service *"Hot Lips"*		
G-BDVA	Piper PA-17 Vagabond	17-206	CN-TVY	23. 4.76	I.M.Callier	Liss	7. 8.02P
	(Continental C90)		F-BFFE				
G-BDVB	Piper PA-15 Vagabond	15-229	F-BHHE	23. 4.76	B.P.Gardner	Whittles Farm, Mapledurham	5. 6.02P
	(Continental C90)		SL-AAY/F-BETG				
G-BDVC	Piper PA-17 Vagabond	17-140	F-BFBL	29. 9.76	A.R.Caveen	Sandford Hall, Knockin	9. 9.02P
	(Continental C90)						
G-BDWA	SOCATA Rallye 150ST	2695		20. 4.76	J.T.Wilson	Bann Foot, Lough Neagh	7. 6.01
G-BDWE	Flaglor Sky Scooter			12. 4.76	D.R.Leggett	Fenland	17. 4.01P
	(VW 1600) KF-S-66 & DWE-01 & PFA 1332				t/a Fenland Strut Flying Group		

G-BDWH	SOCATA Rallye 150ST	2697		20. 4.76	M.A.Jones		
					Upper Harford Farm, Bourton-on-the-Water		10. 4.02
G-BDWJ	Replica Plans SE-5A	PFA 020-10034	"C1904"	27. 4.76	D.W.Linney	(Langport)	18. 7.02P
	(Continental C90)		"F8010"		*(As "F8010/Z" in RFC c/s)*		
G-BDWL	Piper PA-25-235 Pawnee B	25-3575	PH-IPO	4. 5.76	Peterborough & Spalding Gliding Club Ltd		
			N7531Z			Crowland	31. 7.03
G-BDWM	Bonsall DB-1 Mustang	PFA 073-10200		3. 5.76	D.C.Bonsall	Netherthorpe	15. 6.98P
	(Lycoming IO-360)				*(As "FB226/MT-A" in RAF c/s) (Noted 3.00)*		
G-BDWO	Howes Ax6 HAFB	RBH.2		5. 5.76	R.B. & Mrs C.Howes	Keysoe, Bedford	
	(Complete and extant 11.88 but never certified)				*"Griffin"*		
G-BDWP	Piper PA-32R-300 Cherokee Lance	32R-7680176	N8784E	7. 5.76	W.M.Brown & B.J.Wood	Coventry	26.10.03
G-BDWX	Jodel Wassmer D.120A Paris-Nice	311	F-BNHT	13. 5.76	R.P.Rochester	Wombleton	19. 9.02P
G-BDWY	Piper PA-28-140 Cherokee E	28-7225378	PH-NSC N11C	14. 5.76	Comed Aviation Ltd	Blackpool	7. 3.03T
G-BDXA	Boeing 747-236B	21238	N1790B	18. 3.77	Snapdragon Ltd.	(Hamilton, Bermuda)	26. 7.02T
G-BDXB	Boeing 747-236B	21239	N8280V	13. 1.77	Snapdragon Ltd	(Hamilton, Bermuda)	15. 6.02T
G-BDXC	Boeing 747-236B	21240		18. 3.77	British Airways plc	Cardiff	21. 6.02T
					(For disposal as spares 12.01)		
G-BDXE	Boeing 747-236B	21350		23. 2.78	European Skybus Ltd	Bournemouth	4. 4.03T
					(Op European Aviation Air Charter)		
G-BDXF	Boeing 747-236B	21351		23. 3.78	British Airways plc	Cardiff	30. 4.03T
					(Stored 1.02)		
G-BDXG	Boeing 747-236B	21536		16. 6.78	British Airways plc	Bournemouth	30. 6.03T
					(For European Aviation Air Charter 2002)		
G-BDXH	Boeing 747-236B	21635		23. 2.79	European Skybus Ltd	Bournemouth	2. 5.04T
					(Op European Aviation Air Charter)		
G-BDXI	Boeing 747-236B	21830		21. 2.80	British Airways plc	Cardiff	13. 3.04T
					"City of Cambridge" (Stored 1.02)		
G-BDXJ	Boeing 747-236B	21831	N1792B	2. 5.80	British Airways plc	Cardiff	7. 5.01T
					"City of Birmingham" (Stored 1.02)		
G-BDXK	Boeing 747-236B	22303		29. 4.83	British Airways plc	Cardiff	13. 6.03T
					(Stored 1.02)		
G-BDXL	Boeing 747-236B	22305	N8280V	9. 1.84	British Airways plc	Cardiff	7.11.03T
					"City of Westminster" (Stored 1.02)		
G-BDXN	Boeing 747-236M	23735	N6046P	17. 3.87	British Airways plc	Cardiff	12. 4.03T
					"City of Stoke-on-Trent" (Stored 12.01)		
G-BDXO	Boeing 747-236B	23799	N6055X	22. 4.87	British Airways plc	Cardiff	14. 5.03T
					(Stored 12.01)		
G-BDXX	SNCAN NC.858S	110	F-BEZQ	17. 5.76	M.Gaffney & K.Davis	North Weald	3. 7.96P
					(On rebuild 12.00)		
G-BDYD	Rockwell Commander 114	14014	N1914J	21. 5.76	M.B.Durkin	(Shifnal)	11. 9.03
G-BDYF	Cessna 421C Golden Eagle II	421C0055	N98468	24. 5.76	Widehawk Aviation t/a Hawkair	Cambridge	3. 7.01T
G-BDYG*	Percival P.56 Provost T.1	PAC/F/056	7696M	25. 5.76	National Museums of Scotland/Museum of Flight		
			WV493			East Fortune	28.11.80P
					(Cancelled 4.11.91 by CAA) (As "WV493/29/A-P")		
G-BDYH	Cameron V-56 HAFB	233		24. 5.76	B.J.Godding *"Novocastrian"*	Didcot	25.11.90A
G-BDZA	Scheibe SF-25E Super Falke	4320	(D-KECW)	1. 6.76	D.C.Mason	Crowland	3.10.04
					t/a Hereward Flying Group		
G-BDZC	Reims Cessna F150M	F15001316		1. 6.76	A.M.Lynn	Sibson	21. 7.02T
G-BDZD	Reims Cessna F172M Skyhawk II	F17201478		1. 6.76	JNJ Aviation Ltd	Hinton-in-the-Hedges	20. 9.03T
G-BDZU	Cessna 421C Golden Eagle II	421C0094	N98791	14. 6.76	R.Richardson	East Midlands	27. 4.03T
					t/a Eagle Flying Group		

G-BEAA – G-BEZZ

G-BEAB	CEA Jodel DR.1051 Sicile	228	F-BKGH	18. 8.76	R.C.Hibberd	Draycott Farm, Chiseldon	9. 3.03
G-BEAC	Piper PA-28-140 Cherokee	28-21963	4X-AND	4. 6.76	C.E.Stringer	Bagby	4. 6.03T
					t/a Clipwing Flying Group		
G-BEAD*	Westland WG.13 Lynx	WA.00.001	XW835	15. 6.76	Army Air Corps, 9 Regiment AAC	Dishforth	
					(Cancelled 15.7.83: stored 8.93)		
G-BEAG	Piper PA-34-200T Seneca II	34-7670204	N9395K	18. 6.76	Oxford Aviation Services Ltd	Oxford	22.10.03T
G-BEAH	Auster V J/2 Arrow	2366	F-BFUV	28. 6.76	J.G.Parish t/a Bedwell Hey Flying Group		
	(Continental C85)		F-BFVV/OO-ABS		Bedwell Hey Farm, Little Thetford, Ely		2. 4.02P
G-BEBC*	Westland WS-55 Whirlwind HAR.10		8463M	25. 6.76	City of Norwich Aviation Museum	Norwich	
	(Line No. WAJ/30)	WA/371	XP355		*(As "XP355/A")*		
G-BEBE	Grumman-American AA-5A Cheetah	AA5A-0154		28. 6.76	Bills Aviation Ltd	Biggin Hill	26.10.02T
G-BEBG	WSK-PZL SZD-45A Ogar	B-655		29. 6.76	D.W.Coultrip	Hinton-in-the-Hedges	23. 9.02
					t/a The Ogar Syndicate		

G-BEBI	Reims Cessna F172M Skyhawk II	F17201461		28. 6.76	K.Tomlin t/a Hatfield Flying Club	Elstree	6. 2.03T
G-BEBN	Cessna 177B Cardinal	17701631	4X-CEW N34031	1. 7.76	E.J.Lamb	Earls Colne	22. 3.03
G-BEBO	Turner Special TSW.2 (Lycoming O-290)	PFA 046-10127		30. 6.76	E.Newsham	Breighton	4.11.02P
G-BEBS	Andreasson BA-4B (Continental O-200-A)	HA/01 & PFA 038-10157		7. 7.76	N.J.W.Reid	Lee-on-Solent	11. 7.02P
G-BEBT	Andreasson BA-4B (Lycoming O-235)	HA/02 & PFA 038-10158		7. 7.76	M.Swanborough	Breighton	7. 6.02P
G-BEBU	Rockwell Commander 112A	272	N1272J	8. 7.76	Cardiff Wales Aviation Services Ltd	Cardiff	19. 4.04T
G-BEBZ	Piper PA-28-151 Cherokee Warrior	28-7615328	N6193J	14. 7.76	Goodwood Road Racing Co Ltd	Goodwood	19. 4.03T
G-BECA	SOCATA Rallye 100ST	2751		14. 7.76	M.A.Neale & P.A.Brain t/a Bredon Flying Group	Bidford	30. 6.03
G-BECB	SOCATA Rallye 100ST	2783		14. 7.76	A.J.Trible	Henscott Farm, Holsworthy	12. 2.01
G-BECC	SOCATA Rallye 150ST	2748		14. 7.76	D.T.Price	Cardiff	15. 5.00
G-BECE*	Aerospace Developments AD-500 Airship	1214/1		14. 7.76	Airship Heritage Trust/Airship & Balloon Museum *(Damaged Cardington 9.3.79: gondola stored 1.00)*	Cardington	1. 4.79P
G-BECF	Scheibe SF-25A Motorfalke	4555	OO-WIZ (D-KARA)	14. 7.76	North County Ltd	(Middleton)	1. 3.94P
G-BECK	Cameron V-56 HAFB	136		27. 7.76	H. & D.J.Farrar "Joyride"	Seacroft, Leeds	21. 3.00A
G-BECN	Piper J-3C-65 Cub (L-4J-PI)	12776	F-BCPS HB-OCI(1)/44-80480	27. 7.76	G Denney *(As "80480/44/E" in US Army c/s)*	Earls Colne	30. 8.02
G-BECS	Thunder Ax6-56A HAFB	074		4. 8.76	A.Sieger	Munster, Germany	19. 5.02A
G-BECT	CASA I-131E Jungmann	"3974"	E3B-338	3. 8.76	G.M.S.Scott t/a Alpha 57 Group *(As "A-57" in Swiss AF c/s)*	Headcorn	5. 6.02P
G-BECW	CASA I-131E Jungmann *(Incorporating parts of G-BECY ex E3B-459)*	2037	E3B-423	3. 8.76	R.G.Meredith *(As "A-10" in Swiss AF c/s)*	Denham	4.11.02P
G-BECZ	Mudry/CAARP CAP.10B	68	F-BXHK	26. 7.76	Avia Special Ltd	White Waltham	18. 3.04T
G-BEDA*	CASA I-131E Jungmann Srs.2000	2099	E3B-504	3. 8.76	M.G.Kates & D.J.Berry t/a DA Group *(Cancelled 2.11.01 by CAA)*	Sheffield Park, Haywards Heath	2. 4.00P
G-BEDB*	SNCAN 1203 Norecrin II	117	F-BEOB	5. 8.76	J.E.Pierce *(Cancelled 14.11.91 by CAA) (Stored 9.00)*	Ley Farm, Chirk	11. 6.80P
G-BEDD	SAN Jodel D.117A	915	F-BITY	3. 8.76	P.B.Duhig	Fenland	29. 9.00P
G-BEDF	Boeing B-17G-105-VE Flying Fortress	8693	N17TE F-BGSR/44-85784	5. 8.76	B-17 Preservation Ltd *(As "124485/DF-A" in USAAC c/s)* *"Sally B"(Pt)/Memphis Belle(Stbd)"*	Duxford	21. 5.02P
G-BEDG	Rockwell Commander 112A	482	N1219J	5. 8.76	P.J.Lawton	Blackbushe	13.12.02
G-BEDJ	Piper J-3C-65 Cub (L-4J-PI) *(Frame No.12720)*	12890	F-BDTC 44-80594	5. 8.76	R.Earl *(As "44-805942 in USAAC c/s) (Stored 10.01)*	Denford Manor, Hungerford	8.10.96P
G-BEDK*	Hiller UH-12E	2300	XS706	5. 8.76	Alpha Aerotech Ltd *(Pod in open store 1.96: cancelled 6.3.99 by CAA)*	Chilbolton	14. 6.85T
G-BEDP	BN-2A mk.III-2 Trislander	1039	ZK-SFG N902TA/N1FY/N401JA/G-BEDP	17. 8.76	Atlantic Bridge Aviation Ltd *(Op Sky Trek Airways)*	Lydd	12.10.00
G-BEDV*	Vickers V.668 Varsity T.1	-	WJ945	26. 7.76	Duxford Aviation Society *(As "WJ945/21")*	Duxford	15.10.87P
G-BEEE*	Thunder Ax6-56A HAFB	070		20. 8.76	British Balloon Museum & Library *"Avia" (Cancelled 19.5.93 by CAA)*	Newbury	11. 5.84A
G-BEEG	Fairey Britten-Norman BN-2A-26 Islander	550	(C-GYUH) G-BEEG	25. 8.76	North West Parachute Centre Ltd	Cark	30. 3.04T
G-BEEH	Cameron V-56 HAFB	250		24. 8.76	Sade Balloons Ltd "Tywi"	Coulsdon, Surrey	26. 5.01A
G-BEEI*	Cameron N-77 HAFB	249		24. 8.76	Not known *(Cancelled 4.8.98 by CAA: extant 2000)*	(The Wirral)	11. 3.90
G-BEEP	Thunder Ax5-42 HAFB	086		20. 8.76	B.C.Faithfull *"Also Kenneth"*	Wagenberg, The Netherlands	11. 5.84A
G-BEER	Isaacs Fury II (Lycoming O-235)	PFA 1588		31. 8.76	D.Crowhurst *(As "K2075" in RAF c/s)*	Sywell	2. 5.02P
G-BEEU	Piper PA-28-140 Cherokee F	28-7325247	PH-NSE N11C	9. 9.76	H & E Merkado	Panshanger	6. 3.03T
G-BEEV*	Piper PA-28-140 Cherokee F *(Damaged Rayne 16.4.91: cancelled 25.6.91 by CAA: stored 5.97: current status unknown)*	28-7325229	PH-NSG N11C	29. 9.76	Not known	Panshanger	28. 3.93
G-BEEX*	de Havilland DH.106 Comet 4C *(Not converted & broken up Lasham 8.77: cancelled 19.5.83: nose section held 11.01)*	6458	SU-ALM	10. 9.76	North East Aircraft Museum	Sunderland	
G-BEFA	Piper PA-28-151 Cherokee Warrior	28-7615416	N6978J	8. 9.76	M.A.Verran t/a Verran Freight	Booker	6. 4.03
G-BEFF	Piper PA-28-140 Cherokee F	28-7325228	PH-NSF N11C	27. 9.76	H.Howard	Panshanger	19. 5.03

G-BEFO Fairey Britten-Norman BN-2A mk.III-2 Trislander 27. 9.76 Keen Leasing Ltd Belfast 28.11.02T
1041 5H-AZP/G-BEFO/G-SARN/F-BYCJ/V2-LMB/VP-LMB/G-BEFO
(Op Woodgate Executive Air Services)

G-BEFV* Evans VP-2 5.10.76 Not known Mickleton, Long Marston
(Continental A65) V2-2390, YA-3 & PFA 063-10203 *(Stored incomplete 8.93: current status unknown)*

G-BEGG Scheibe SF-25E Super Falke 4326 (D-KDFB) 15.10.76 R.Culley & A.Collett
t/a G-BEGG Flying Group Hall Farm, Turweston 17. 5.03

G-BEHH Piper PA-32R-300 Cherokee Lance N6172J 29.10.76 SMK Engineers Ltd Sherburn in Elmet 5. 9.03
32R-7680323

G-BEHM* Taylor JT.1 Monoplane PFA 1420 29.10.76 Not known (Bedfordshire)
(VW 1700) *(Modified as Wildfire PDH.001: complete 1990 but C of A problems: on rebuild 11.95: current status unknown)*

G-BEHU Piper PA-34-200T Seneca II N6175J 3.11.76 Pirin Aeronautical Ltd Stapleford 4. 3.02T
34-7670265

G-BEHV Reims Cessna F172N Skyhawk II 3.11.76 Fraggle Leasing Ltd Edinburgh 13. 4.01T
F17201541 *(Op Edinburgh Air Centre)*

G-BEHX Evans VP-2 V2-2338 & PFA 7222 8.11.76 G.S.Adams Stewartstown, Co.Tyrone 22. 1.90P
(VW 1834) *"Ulster Flyer" (Stored 11.01)*

G-BEIA Reims Cessna FRA150M Aerobat 8.11.76 Halegreen Associates Ltd
FRA1500317 Hinton-in-the-Hedges 27.10.03T

G-BEIF Cameron O-65 HAFB 259 17.11.76 C Vening *"Solitaire"* Kirdford 25. 3.90A
(Op Balloon Preservation Group)

G-BEIG Reims Cessna F150M F15001361 18.11.76 T.J.Chapman (Beccles) 14. 1.02T

G-BEII Piper PA-25-235 Pawnee D 25-7656059 N54918 16.11.76 Burn Gliding Club Ltd Burn 7. 4.02T

G-BEIL SOCATA Rallye 150T 2653 F-BXDL 1.12.76 J.I.Oakes & R.A.Harris
t/a The Rallye Flying Group Hill Farm, Nayland 2. 4.04

G-BEIP Piper PA-28-181 Cherokee Archer II N6628F 22.11.76 S.Pope Barton 16. 9.04
28-7790158

G-BEIS Evans VP-1 PFA 7029 25.11.76 P.J.Hunt Thruxton 16. 7.90P
(VW 1600) *(Stored 2.99)*

G-BEJB Thunder Ax6-56A HAFB 096 31.12.76 Justerini & Brooks Ltd Kirdford 21. 5.87A
(Flies with second canopy: first one destroyed by fire Latimer 4.9.77) "Baby J & B" (Op Balloon Preservation Group)

G-BEJD Avro 748 Srs.1/105 1543 LV-HHE 17.12.76 Emerald Airways Ltd Liverpool 29. 3.03T
LV-PUF *(Reed Aviation titles) "Sisyphus"*

G-BEJK Cameron S-31 HAFB 256 1.12.76 N.H.Ponsford & A.Lindsay Leeds 16. 2.92A
t/a Rango Balloon & Kite Co *"L'Essence" (or "Esso")*

G-BEJL Sikorsky S-61N mk.II 61-224 EI-BPK 30.12.76 Scotia Helicopter Services Ltd Longside 30. 9.98
G-BEJL/N4606G *(Stored 2001)*

G-BEJV Piper PA-34-200T Seneca II N7657F 31.12.76 Oxford Aviation Services Ltd Oxford 12. 4.03T
34-7770062

G-BEKL Bede BD-4E-150 151 & BD4E/2 (G-AYKB) 11. 1.77 A.J.Harpley (Hawes, N.Yorks) 14.10.80P
(Lycoming O-320) *(On rebuild Bladon-on-Tyne 5.93: current status unknown)*

G-BEKM Evans VP-1 PFA 7025 12. 1.77 G.J.McDill Park Farm, Eaton Bray 23. 3.95P
(VW 1834) *(Stored 7.98: current status unknown)*

G-BEKN Reims Cessna FRA150M Aerobat 12. 1.77 RFC (Bourn) Ltd Bourn 8.10.89T
FRA1500318 *(Open store w/o engines 11.01)*

G-BEKO Reims Cessna F182Q Skylane 12. 1.77 G.J. & F.J.Leese Old Buckenham 11. 6.03
F18200037

G-BEKR Rand Robinson KR-2 14. 1.77 A.N.Purchase
(VW 1834) EAA/102591 & PFA 0129-11046 *(Current status unknown)* (Woodlands Park, Maidenhead) 20. 8.88P

G-BELF Fairey Britten-Norman BN-2A-26 Islander D-IBRA 13. 1.77 The Black Knights Parachute Centre Ltd
(Built IRMA) 823 G-BELF *(Abandoned 10.01)* Cumbernauld 12. 3.01

G-BELP Piper PA-28-151 Cherokee Warrior N9543N 18. 1.77 Aerohire Ltd Wolverhampton 2. 8.04T
28-7715219

G-BELT Reims Cessna F150J F150-0409X 26. 1.77 Multiflight Ltd Leeds-Bradford 22. 8.04T
(Mainly rebuild of G-AWUV & parts of G-ATND)

G-BELX* Cameron V-56 HAFB 261 31. 1.77 V. & A.M.Dyer *"Topsy Taffy"* Launceston 15. 8.93A
(Cancelled 15.10.01 by CAA)

G-BEMB Reims Cessna F172M Skyhawk II 27. 1.77 Stocklaunch Ltd Goodwood 23. 4.04T
F17201487

G-BEMM Slingsby Cadet III 1247 BGA942 27. 1.77 B.J.Douglas Newtownards, Co.of Down 1. 2.02P
(VW 1600) *(Converted from T.31B)* RAFGSA 289/BGA942

G-BEMU Thunder Ax5-42 HAFB 097 9. 2.77 M.A.Hall *"Chrysophylax"* Stoneleigh 16. 1.99A

G-BEMW Piper PA-28-181 Cherokee Archer II N9566N 9. 2.77 Touch & Go Ltd White Waltham 10. 9.03
28-7790243

G-BEMY Reims Cessna FRA150M Aerobat 9. 2.77 A J Roper & P A L Baker Rochester 12.11.04T
FRA1500315

G-BEND Cameron V-56 HAFB 260 14. 2.77 P.J.Bish Hungerford 1. 1.94A
t/a Dante Balloon Group *"Le Billet"*

G-BENF* Cessna T210L Turbo Centurion II N732AE 17. 2.77 Not known Cherry Tree Farm, Monewden 24. 5.82
21061356 D-EIPY/N732AE
(Crashed Ipswich 29.5.81: cancelled 25.3.85 as destroyed: wreck in open storage 6.00)

G-BENJ Rockwell Commander 112B 522 N1391J 7. 3.77 E.J.Percival Blackbushe 3. 8.03

G-BENK Reims Cessna F172M Skyhawk II 2. 3.77 Graham Churchill Plant Ltd Turweston 4. 6.03
F17201509

G-BENL* Piper PA-25-235 Pawnee D 25-7656038 N54893 1. 3.77 W.J. & A.E.Taylor RAF West Raynham 14.11.85
(Crashed Sutton Bank 10.7.85: cancelled 17.12.90 as WFU) (Stored 2.96: current status unknown)

G-BENN Cameron V-56 HAFB 278 4. 3.77 S.J.Hollingsworth & M.K.Bellamy *(New owners 10.01)*
"English Rose" Bleasby, Notts 15. 3.87A

G-BEOD* Cessna 180 32092 OO-SPZ 14. 3.77 I.Addy (Ivychurch, Kent) 6. 9.91
D-EDAH/SL-AAT/N3294D
(Damaged Errol, Perthshire 29.6.89: cancelled 6.12.89 by CAA) (Stored 3.97: current status unknown)

G-BEOE Reims Cessna FRA150M Aerobat 21. 3.77 W.J.Henderson Carlisle 11. 7.03T
FRA1500322 t/a Air Images

G-BEOH Piper PA-28R-201T Turbo Cherokee Arrow III N1905H 11. 3.77 J.J.Evendon Blackbushe 6. 7.04
28R-7703038 t/a G-BEOH Group

G-BEOI Piper PA-18-150 Super Cub 18-7709028 N54976 11. 3.77 Southdown Gliding Club Ltd Parham Park 17.12.04
(Lycoming O-360-A4)

G-BEOK Reims Cessna F150M F15001366 14. 3.77 D.C.Bonsall Netherthorpe 11. 5.03T

G-BEOL Short SC.7 Skyvan 3 Var.100 SH.1954 ZS-OIO 16. 3.77 Invicta Aviation Ltd Manston 28. 2.02T
JA8803(2)/G-BEOL/G-14-122

G-BEOX* Lockheed 414 Hudson IIIA 414-6464 VH-AGJ 25. 3.77 RAF Museum RAF Hendon
(A-29A-LO) VH-SMM/R.Australian AF A16-199/FH174/41-36975 *(As "A16-199/SF-R")*
(Cancelled 22.12.81 as WFU

G-BEOY Reims Cessna FRA150L Aerobat F-BTFS 30. 3.77 R.W.Denny Crowfield 23. 2.02T
FRA1500150 *(Op Crowfield Flying Club)*

G-BEOZ* AW.650 Argosy 101 6660 N895U 28. 3.77 East Midlands Aeropark East Midlands 28. 5.86T
N6502R/G-1-7 *(Cancelled 19.11.87 as WFU) "Fat Albert" (Elan c/s)*

G-BEPC SNCAN Stampe SV-4C 64 F-BFUM 17.10.77 Dawn Patrol Flight Training Ltd
F-BFZM/Fr.Mil Dunkeswell 24. 3.01T

G-BEPF SNCAN Stampe SV-4C 424 F-BCVD 30. 3.77 L.J.Rice *(Stored 5.00)* Chilbolton

G-BEPN* Piper PA-25-235 Pawnee D 25-7656022 N54877 7. 4.77 Not known (Shobdon) 6. 4.79
(Crashed near Cirencester 11.2.78: frame in store 3.96: current status unknown)

G-BEPO* Cameron N-77 HAFB 279 1. 4.77 British Balloon Museum & Library Newbury
"Sungas" (Cancelled 14.5.98 as WFU)

G-BEPS Short SC.5 Belfast C.1 SH.1822 G-52-13 6. 4.77 Heavylift Aviation Holdings Ltd Southend 31. 8.02T
XR368 *(Wfu & stored for spares 1.02)*

G-BEPV Fokker S.11.1 Instructor 6274 PH-ANK 13. 4.77 L.C.MacKnight Elstree 15. 4.93P
174 Dutch Navy 174/E-31 Dutch AF *(Frame stored 10.01)*

G-BEPY Rockwell Commander 112B 524 N1399J 20. 4.77 S.A.Pigden t/a G-BEPY Group Blackbushe 28. 6.04

G-BERA SOCATA Rallye 150ST 2821 F-ODEX 13. 4.77 P.J.Bloore & J.M.Biles (Evesham) 10. 8.03T

G-BERC SOCATA Rallye 150ST 2858 13. 4.77 R S Jones Welshpool 14. 3.02
t/a The Severn Valley Aero Group

G-BERD Thunder Ax6-56A HAFB 106 25. 4.77 P.M.Gaines "Goldfinger" Stockton-on-Tees 19. 5.01A

G-BERI Rockwell Commander 114 14234 N4909W 6. 5.77 K.B.Harper Blackbushe 12. 5.03

G-BERN Saffery S.330 MLB 4 19. 4.77 B.Martin *"Beeze I"* Somersham, Cambs
(Stored 12.01)

G-BERT Cameron V-56 HAFB 273 19. 4.77 Semajan Ltd Romsey 5. 9.02A
"Bert" t/a Southern Balloon Group

G-BERW Rockwell Commander 114 14214 N4884W 6. 5.77 Romeo Whisky Ltd Old Buckenham 5. 5.04

G-BERY Grumman-American AA-1B Trainer 0193 N9693L 27.10.77 R.H.J.Levi Stapleford 20. 6.04

G-BESY* British Aircraft Corporation BAC.167 Strikemaster Mk.80A Imperial War Museum Duxford
(Officially regd as Mk.88) PS.364 G-27-299 26. 4.77 *(Cancelled 7.77) (As "1133" in Saudi c/s)*
Saudi AF 1133/G-27-299

G-BETD Robin HR.200/100 Club 20 PH-SRL 28. 4.77 W.A.Stewart North Connel, Oban 18. 2.02

G-BETE Rollason Beta B.2A PFA 02-10169 26. 4.77 T.M.Jones Derby
(Incorporates parts from PFA 01304: under construction 8.99)

G-BETF* Cameron Champion 35SS HAFB 280 17. 5.77 British Balloon Museum & Library Newbury 6. 4.84A
(Champion Spark Plug shape) *"Champion" (Cancelled 24.1.92 as WFU)*

G-BETG Cessna 180K Skywagon 180-52873 N64146 17. 5.77 A.J.Norman Rendcomb 11. 6.03
t/a Norman Aeroplane Trust

G-BETH* Thunder Ax6-56A HAFB 113 27. 5.77 British Balloon Museum & Library Newbury 31. 5.78S
"Debenhams" (Cancelled 11.5.93 as WFU)

G-BETL Piper PA-25-235 Pawnee D 25-7656016 N54874 27. 5.77 Cambridge Gliding Club Ltd
Gransden Lodge 11.12.03

G-BETM Piper PA-25-235 Pawnee D 25-7656066 N54927 5. 5.77 Yorkshire Gliding Club (Pty) Ltd
Sutton Bank 9. 4.04

G-BETO MS.885 Super Rallye 34 F-BKED 18. 5.77 A.J. & A.Hawley Farley Farm, Winchester 11.12.04
t/a G-BETO Group

G-BETP* Cameron O-65 HAFB 286 3. 5.77 J.R.Rix & Sons Ltd *"Rix"* Hull 12. 6.88A
(Cancelled 2.11.01 as wfu & stored)

G-BETT Piper PA-34-200 Seneca 34-7250011 EI-BCD 20. 6.77 D.F.J.Flashman Biggin Hill 28. 7.99A
PH-AVM/N1978T

G-BETW Rand Robinson KR-2 PFA 129-10251 26. 4.77 S.C.Solley Clipgate Farm, Denton
(C/n previously quoted as KR-2/TAW.1 & first registered to T A Wiffen with c/n KR-2/TAW-1 but no PFA project number. PFA project no.10251 allocated to Mr Wiffen as a VP-1 type [c/n 62-10251]. Possibly VP-1 project abandoned in favour of KR-2. Project no.10251 appears to have remained with Mr.Wiffen as a KR-2 before passing on to Mr.Solley)

G-BEUA Piper PA-18-150 Super Cub 18-8212 D-ECSY 21. 6.77 London Gliding Club Pty Ltd Dunstable 27. 2.03
(Lycoming O-360-A4) N4146Z

G-BEUD	Robin HR.100/285 Tiara	534	F-BXRC	8. 6.77	E.A. & L.M.C.Payton	Cranfield	11. 8.02
G-BEUI	Piper J-3C-65 Cub (L-4H-PI) *(Frame No.12002) (Regd as ex 43-29245)*	12174	F-BFEC F-OAJF/Fr.AF/44-79878	19. 5.77	B.W.Webb t/a G-BEUI Group	(Canterbury)	25. 2.02P
G-BEUK	Fuji FA.200-160 Aero Subaru	284		24. 5.77	C.B.Mellor t/a BM Aviation *(Damaged Glebe Farm, Stockton, Wilts 8.1.99: current status unknown)*	Southampton	2.11.00T
G-BEUM	Taylor JT.1 Monoplane (VW 1700)	PFA 1438		8. 6.77	J.M.Burgess *(Noted 8.01)*	St Just	1. 8.02P
G-BEUN	Cassutt Racer IIIM (Continental C90)	PFA 034-10241		20. 2.78	R.McNulty *(Noted 11.01)*	Bourn	7. 7.97P
G-BEUP	Robin DR.400/180 Regent	1228		19. 5.77	Legal Week Ltd t/a Samuels Aviation	Biggin Hill	4. 5.04
G-BEUU	Piper PA-18 Super Cub 95 (L-18C-PI) *(Frame No.should be 18-1523)*	18-1551	F-BOUU ALAT 18-1551/51-15551	27. 6.77	F.Sharples	Sandown	11. 6.02P
G-BEUX	Reims Cessna F172N	F17201596		30. 5.77	Multiflight Ltd	Leeds-Bradford	16.11.03T
G-BEUY	Cameron N-31 HAFB	283		31. 5.77	M.L.& L.P.Willoughby *"Little Red"*	Reading	17.10.90A
G-BEVB	SOCATA Rallye 150ST	2860		2. 6.77	N.R.Haines	RAF Hullavington	22. 7.01
G-BEVC	SOCATA Rallye 150ST	2861		2. 6.77	B.W.Walpole	Swanton Morley	6. 7.03
G-BEVG	Piper PA-34-200T Seneca II	34-7570060	VQ-SAM N32854	31. 5.77	C.Deith	(Harrogate)	22. 6.02T
G-BEVI(3)*	Thunder Ax7-77A HAFB	125		30. 5.77	British Balloon Museum & Library *"Prime Bang" (Cancelled 8.1.92 as WFU)*	Newbury	NE(A)
G-BEVO	Sportavia Fournier RF5	5107	5N-AIX D-KAAZ	27. 6.77	T.Barlow *(Stored 12.97: current status unknown)*	Barton	20. 8.96P
G-BEVP*	Evans VP-2 (VW 2074) *(Damaged Truleigh Manor Farm, Edburton 13.6.92: cancelled 24.8.94 by CAA: on rebuild 10.95: current status unknown)*	ISW/7207/1 & PFA 7207		9. 6.77	G.Moscrop & R.C.Crowley	Netherthorpe	22. 9.80P
G-BEVR	Fairey Britten-Norman BN-2A Mk.III-2 Trislander	1056	6Y-JQE/G-BEVR/XA-THE(2)/G-BEVR	10. 6.77	Cormack (Aircraft Services) Ltd *(On rebuild 6.00)*	Cumbernauld	6. 7.82S
G-BEVS	Taylor JT.1 Monoplane (VW 1835)	PFA 1429		8. 6.77	D.Hunter	Kemble	22. 7.02P
G-BEVT	Fairey Britten-Norman BN-2A Mk.III-2 Trislander	1057		10. 6.77	Aurigny Air Services Ltd *(Islands Insurance titles)*	Guernsey	15.11.03T
G-BEVV	Fairey Britten-Norman BN.2A Mk.111-2 Trislander	1059	6Y-JQK/G-BNZD/G-BEVV	10. 6.77	Cormack (Aero Club Services) Ltd *(To BN Group 2.00)* *(Fuse. stored @ "6Y-JQK" 1.02)*	Bembridge	
G-BEVW	SOCATA Rallye 150ST	2928		2. 6.77	P.G.A.Sumner	Town Farm, Woolaston	27. 3.03
G-BEWN	de Havilland DH.82A Tiger Moth *(Built DH Australia -rebuild c/n T305)*	952	VH-WAL *RAAF A17-529*	16. 6.77	H.D.Labouchere	Blue Tile Farm, Langham	18. 7.03
G-BEWO	Moravan Zlin Z.326 Trener Master	915	CS-ALU	23.11.77	P.A.Colman	Luxters Farm, Hambleden	2. 7.03
G-BEWP*	Reims Cessna F150M	F15001426		13. 6.77	Perth College *(Crashed Aboyne 4.10.83: cancelled 5.12.83 as destroyed: instructional use 6.00)*	Perth	12. 8.85
G-BEWR	Reims Cessna F172N Skyhawk II	F17201613		13. 6.77	Cheshire Air Training Services Ltd	Liverpool	3. 5.04T
G-BEWX	Piper PA-28R-201 Cherokee Arrow III	28R-7737070	N5723V	23. 6.77	A.Vickers	North Weald	23. 5.03
G-BEWY	Bell 206B JetRanger II	348	G-CULL EI-BXQ/G-BEWY/9Y-TDF	27. 6.77	Polo Aviation Ltd	Bristol	13. 5.04T
G-BEXN	Grumman-American AA-1C Lynx	AA1C-0045	N6147A	7. 9.77	D.M.Lockley	Plockton	6. 4.03
G-BEXO	Piper PA-<u>23</u> Apache	23-213	OO-APH N1176P	4. 7.77	G.R.Moore & A.K.Hulme	Rayne Hall Farm, Rayne	13. 8.03
G-BEXW	Piper PA-28-181 Cherokee Archer II	28-7790521	N38122	11. 7.77	T.R.Kingsley	Norwich	23. 3.03T
G-BEXX	Cameron V-56 HAFB	274		29. 6.77	K.A.Schlussler *"Rupert of Rutland"*	Bourne	2. 7.86A
G-BEXZ	Cameron N-56 HAFB	294		7. 7.77	D.C.Eager & G.C.Clark *"Valor"*	Bracknell/Worcester	13. 4.97A
G-BEYA	Enstrom 280C Shark	1104		15. 8.77	Hovercam Ltd	Goodwood	11. 2.04T
G-BEYB*	Fairey Flycatcher rep (PW R985)	WA/3		11. 7.77	Fleet Air Arm Museum *(Cancelled 12.7.96 as WFU) (As "S1287/5" in 405 Flight FAA c/s)*	RNAS Yeovilton	4. 7.96P
G-BEYF*	Handley Page HPR.7 Dart Herald 401	175	FM1022	13. 7.77	Dart Group plc *(Cancelled 18.11.99 as WFU) (To Bournemouth Aviation Museum 1999)*	Bournemouth	11. 3.01T
G-BEYL	Piper PA-28-180 Cherokee Archer	28-7405098	PH-SDW N9518N	6. 9.77	J. & N.Baker t/a Yankee Lima Group	Compton Abbas	28. 3.04
G-BEYN*	Evans VP-2	V2-3167 & PFA 063-10271		1. 8.77	H P Vox & T Rayner *(Cancelled 2.9.91 by CAA) (Incomplete airframe stored in hangar roof 6.00)*	East Fortune	
G-BEYO	Piper PA-28-140 Cherokee Cruiser	28-7725215	N9648N	14. 7.77	W.B.Bateson	Blackpool	30. 5.04T
G-BEYT	Piper PA-28-140 Cherokee	28-20330	D-EBWO N6280W	19. 7.77	B.A.Mills *(Noted 10.01)*	Bourne	
G-BEYV	Cessna T210M Turbo Centurion II	210-61583	N732KX	19. 7.77	P.J.W. & N.Austen t/a Austen Aviation	Guernsey	13. 4.04T
G-BEYW	Taylor JT.1 Monoplane (VW 1834)	RJS.100 & PFA 055-10279		22. 7.77	R.A.Abrahams *"Red Hot"*	Barton	17. 4.02P

G-BEYZ	CEA Jodel DR.1050/M1 Sicile Record	588	F-BMGV	22. 7.77	M.L.Balding	Biggin Hill	4. 6.03
G-BEZA	Moravan Zlin Z.226T Trener 6	370	HA-TRL G-BEZA/D-EMUD/OK-MUA	24. 1.78	L.Bezak	(Sittingbourne)	
G-BEZC	Grumman-American AA-5 Traveler	AA5-0493	F-BUYN (N7193L)	29. 7.77	T.V.Montgomery	Elstree	25. 7.04
G-BEZE	Rutan VariEze (Continental O-200-A)	PFA 074-10207		26. 7.77	H.C.MacKinnon *(Current status unknown)*	(Alton)	2. 6.92P
G-BEZF	Grumman-American AA-5 Traveler	AA5-0538	F-BVJP	29. 7.77	RAF College Flying Club Ltd	RAF Cranwell	17.12.04T
G-BEZG	Grumman-American AA-5 Traveler	AA5-0561	F-BVRJ	29. 7.77	M.D.R.Harling	Andrewsfield	31. 5.02
G-BEZH	Grumman-American AA-5 Traveler	AA5-0566	F-BVRK N9566L	29. 7.77	L. & S.M.Sims	Fenland	25. 2.01
G-BEZI	Grumman-American AA-5 Traveler	AA5-0567	F-BVRL N9567L	29. 7.77	Heather Matthews t/a The BEZI Flying Group	Cranfield	6. 3.04
G-BEZK(2)	Reims Cessna F172H	F172-0462	D-EBUD D-ENHC/SLN-07/N20462	17. 8.77	C.F.Strowger	Beccles	18. 7.02
G-BEZL	Piper PA-31 Navajo C	31-7712054	SE-GPA	1. 8.77	A.Jahanfar *(Op JRB Aviation)*	Southend	29. 6.03T
G-BEZO	Reims Cessna F172M Skyhawk II	F17201392		24. 8.77	Gloucestershire Flying Services Ltd	Gloucestershire	1. 4.04T
G-BEZP	Piper PA-32-300 Cherokee Six	32-7740087	N38572	19. 8.77	Falcon Styles Ltd	Booker	3. 4.04
G-BEZR	Reims Cessna F172M Skyhawk II	F17201395		24. 8.77	Kirmington Aviation Ltd	Sandown	8. 5.04T
G-BEZS*	Reims FR172J Rocket	FR1720562	(I-CCAJ)	11. 8.77	Not known	Bourn	22. 9.79
					(Damaged near Stapleford 15.6.79: front fuselage stored 11.01)		
G-BEZV	Reims Cessna F172M Skyhawk II	F17201474	(I-CCAY)	24. 8.77	A.T.Wilson t/a Insch Flying Group	Insch	21. 4.04
G-BEZY	Rutan VariEze (Continental PC60)	1167 & PFA 074-10225		26. 7.77	I.J.Pountney	(Malvern)	18. 5.96P
G-BEZZ	Jodel D.112 *(Built Passot Aviation)*	397	F-BHMC	12. 8.77	M.J.Coles t/a G-BEZZ Jodel Group	Barton	10. 7.02P

G-BFAA – G-BFZZ

G-BFAA	SOCATA GY-80-160 Horizon	78	F-BLVY	20.10.77	Mary Poppins Ltd *(Current status unknown)*	(Stoke-on-Trent)	18.11.90
G-BFAB*	Cameron N-56 HAFB	297		15. 8.77	A.Gibson *"Phonogram"*	Newbury	NE(A)
					(On loan to British Balloon Museum & Library) (Cancelled 21.4.92 by CAA)		
G-BFAF	Aeronca 7BCM Champion (L-16A-AE)	7BCM-11	N797US N2552B/47-797	15. 8.77	D.C.W.Harper *(As "7797" in US Army c/s)*	Finmere	30. 8.01P
G-BFAH	Phoenix Currie Wot	PFA 3017		22. 8.77	R.W.Clarke	(Cheadle)	
	(Continental O-200A) *(Regd as c/n PFA 058-11376 but mistaken with PFA 101-11376, a Sopwith Pup rep by same owner/builder: being built as Replica SE-5A and to be in RFC c/s)*						
G-BFAI	Rockwell Commander 114	14304	N4984W	17. 8.77	G.Gore-Brown t/a Alpha India Flying Group	Sherburn-in-Elmet	21.10.02
G-BFAK	GEMS MS.892A Rallye Commodore 150	10595	F-BNNJ	9. 8.77	J.R.Hammett	(Wokingham)	19. 4.04
G-BFAM*	Piper PA-31P Pressurised Navajo	31P-39	SE-GLV OH-PNF	1. 9.77	Middle East Business Club Ltd	(Guernsey)	
					(Cancelled - to G-SASK 30.10.97 but noted as "G-BFAM" on repair Biggin Hill 12.00)		
G-BFAP	SIAI-Marchetti S.205-20R	4-213	I-ALEN	1. 9.77	A.O'Broin	Raby's Farm, Great Stukeley	11. 6.03
G-BFAS	Evans VP-1 Srs.2 (VW 1834)	PFA 7033		15. 8.77	A.I.Sutherland	Fearn	13. 3.02P
G-BFAW	de Havilland DHC-1 Chipmunk 22	C1/0733	8342M WP848	31. 8.77	R.V.Bowles	Husbands Bosworth	23.10.03
G-BFAX	de Havilland DHC-1 Chipmunk 22	C1/0496	8394M WG422	31. 8.77	A.C.Kerr *(As "WG422")*	Strathaven	28. 4.02
G-BFBA	SAN Jodel DR.100A Ambassadeur	88	F-BIVU	12. 9.77	W.H.Sherlock	Drayton Manor, Drayton St.Leonard	7.10.02
G-BFBB	Piper PA-23-250 Aztec E	27-7405294	SE-GBI	1. 9.77	Air Training Services Ltd	Booker	16. 6.04T
G-BFBC	Taylor JT.1 Monoplane (VW 1600)	PFA 055-10280		5. 9.77	G Heins *(Under construction 2.93: new owner 1.02)*	(Rochdale)	
G-BFBE	Robin HR.200/100	12	PH-SRK	9. 9.77	A.C.Pearson	Denham	23. 3.02
G-BFBF	Piper PA-28-140 Cherokee F	28-7325240	EI-BMG G-BFBF/PH-SRF	9. 9.77	Marham Investments Ltd *(Op Woodgate Executive Air Services)*	Belfast	30. 9.01T
G-BFBM	Saffery S.330 MLB	7		1. 9.77	B.Martin *"Beeze II"* *(Stored 12.01)*	Somersham, Cambs	
G-BFBR	Piper PA-28-161 Cherokee Warrior II	28-7716277	N38845	15. 9.77	Lowery Holdings Ltd	Fairoaks	13. 2.04T
G-BFBU	Partenavia P.68B	24	SE-FTM	25. 1.78	Premiair Charter Ltd	Bournmouth	24. 4.03T

G-BFBY	Piper J-3C-65 Cub (L-4H-PI)	10998	F-BDTG 43-29707	29. 9.77	U.Schuhmacher	Hahn, Germany	7. 9.01P
G-BFCT	Cessna TU206F Turbo Stationair II	U20603202	(LN-TVF) N8341Q	15. 9.77	Cecil Aviation Ltd	Cambridge	26. 1.01
G-BFCZ	Sopwith Camel F.1 rep (Clerget 9B)	WA/2		12.10.77	Brooklands Museum Trust Ltd *(As "B7270")*	Brooklands	23. 2.89P
G-BFDC	de Havilland DHC-1 Chipmunk 22	C1/0525	7989M WG475	15.11.77	N.F.O'Neill	Newtownards, Co.of Down	12. 6.03
G-BFDE*	Sopwith Tabloid Scout rep (Continental PC.60)	168 & PFA 067-10186		22. 9.77	RAF Museum *(Cancelled 8.12.86 as WFU) (As "168" in RNAS c/s)*	Hendon	4. 6.83P
G-BFDF	SOCATA Rallye 235E	12834	F-GAKT	6.10.77	M.A.Wratten	Bourne Park, Hurstbourne Tarrant	21. 2.02
G-BFDI	Piper PA-28-181 Cherokee Archer II	28-7790382	N2205Q	5.10.77	Truman Aviation Ltd	Nottingham	1.10.04T
G-BFDK	Piper PA-28-161 Warrior II	28-7816010	N40061	23. 9.77	R.D.H.Cole t/a Priory Garage	Enstone	9. 5.04T
G-BFDL	Piper J-3C-65 Cub (L-4J-PI) (Continental O-200-A) *(Frame No.13107)*	13277	HB-OIF 45-4537	30.11.77	S.Beresford & G.S.Claybourn *(As "454537/04-J" in US Army c/s)*	Walton Wood	7. 4.02P
G-BFDO	Piper PA-28R-201T Turbo Cherokee Arrow III	28R-7703212	N38396	3.10.77	A.J.Gow	Denham	22. 9.02
G-BFDV*	Westland WG.13 Lynx HC.28 *(Originally regd as "Lynx 02F")*	WA/028	TAD.013 Qatar AF 1/G-17-20	3.10.77	SEAE Princess Marina College, Arborfield *(Cancelled 6.78: now instructional airframe as "QP-30")*		
G-BFDZ	Taylor JT.1 Monoplane (VW 1600)	PFA 055-10185		5.10.77	G.J.Clare	(Bath)	23. 9.99P
G-BFEB	SAN Jodel 150 Mascaret	34	F-BMJR OO-LDY/F-BLDX	14.10.77	A.W.Russell t/a Jodel Syndicate	Portmoak	12. 6.02P
G-BFEF	Agusta-Bell 47G-3B1	1541	XT132	11.10.77	R.C.Hields	Sherburn-in-Elmet	17. 6.02T
G-BFEH	SAN Jodel D.117A	828	F-BITG	5.10.77	J.A.Crabb *(New owner 12.01)*	Dunkeswell	30. 9.94P
G-BFEK	Reims Cessna F152 II	F152201442		11.10.77	Gloucestershire Flying Services Ltd	Gloucestershire	20. 2.04T
G-BFER	Bell 212	30835	N18099	7.11.77	Bristow Helicopters Ltd	(Kazakhstan)	27.11.02T
G-BFEV	Piper PA-25-235 Pawnee D	25-7756060	N82547	20.10.77	Trent Valley Aerotowing Club Ltd	Kirton-in-Lindsey	18. 4.04
G-BFEW	Piper PA-25-235 Pawnee D	25-7756062	N82553	20.10.77	Cornish Gliding & Flying Club Ltd	Perranporth	25. 3.04
G-BFFB*	Evans VP-2	V2-2289 & PFA 063-10159		27.10.77	Not known *(Cancelled 2.9.91 by CAA) (Stored 7.98: current status unknown)*	Park Farm, Eaton Bray	
G-BFFC	Reims Cessna F152 II	F15201451		27.10.77	Multiflight Ltd	Leeds-Bradford	15.11.04T
G-BFFE	Reims Cessna F152 II	F15201454		27.10.77	A.J.Hastings *(Damaged 13.3.97: on rebuild 5.01)*	Edinburgh	19. 4.98T
G-BFFJ	Sikorsky S-61N Mk.II	61-777	N6231	17. 1.78	Veritair Ltd *"Tresco"*	Penzance	22. 3.03T
G-BFFP	Piper PA-18-150 Super Cub (Lycoming O-360-A4) *(Frame No.18-8402)*	18-8187	PH-OTC N10F	9.11.77	Booker Gliding Club Ltd	Booker	7. 5.04
G-BFFT	Cameron V-56 HAFB	360		7.11.77	R.I.McKean Kerr & D.C.Boxall t/a The Red Section Balloon Group *"Red Leader"*	Bristol	21. 7.01A
G-BFFW	Reims Cessna F152 II	F15201447		14.11.77	Tayside Aviation Ltd	Dundee	12. 6.04T
G-BFFY	Reims Cessna F150M	F15001376		14.11.77	G.A.Rodmell	Linley Hill, Beverley	26. 3.04T
G-BFFZ	Reims Cessna FR172K Hawk XPII	FR17200603	F-WZDU	14.11.77	E.Francis	Compton Abbas	15. 6.03T
G-BFGD	Reims Cessna F172N Skyhawk II	F17201545	F-WZDT	14.11.77	J.T.Armstrong	Fairoaks	4.10.04T
G-BFGG	Reims Cessna FRA150M Aerobat	FRA1500321	F-WZDS	14.11.77	Cornwall Flying Club Ltd	Plymouth	5. 4.04T
G-BFGH	Reims Cessna F337G Skymaster II (Wichita c/n 33701754)	F33700081		14.11.77	T.Perkins	Bagby	5. 7.02
G-BFGK	SAN Jodel D.117	644	F-BIBT	27. 6.78	B.F.J.Hope	Stoneacre Farm, Farthing Corner	19 6.02P
G-BFGL	Reims Cessna FA152 Aerobat	FA1520339		14.11.77	Multiflight Ltd	Leeds-Bradford	10. 5.04T
G-BFGO*	Fuji FA.200-160 Aero Subaru *(Damaged Rush Green 18.8.93: stored 7.96: cancelled 31.10.00 by CAA: current status unknown)*	219	PH-KDB	25.11.77	R.J.Everett	Cranfield	23. 8.92
G-BFGS	SOCATA MS.893E Rallye 180GT	12571	F-BXYK Fr.AF 12571 FSCAZ/"41-AZ"	31. 8.76	Chiltern Flyers Ltd	Park Farm, Eaton Bray	15. 9.03
G-BFGW	Reims Cessna F150H	F150-0370	PH-TGO	24.11.77	C.E.Stringer	Humberside	19.10.95T
G-BFGX	Reims Cessna FRA150M Aerobat	FRA1500328	F-BUDX	28.11.77	Active Services Ltd	Kirknewton	27. 8.04T
G-BFGZ	Reims Cessna FRA150M Aerobat	FRA1500329		28.11.77	C.M.Barnes	Garden Piece, Basingstoke	10. 3.03T
G-BFHH	de Havilland DH.82A Tiger Moth	85933	F-BDOH Fr.AF/DF197	25.11.77	P.Harrison & M.J.Gambrell	Swanborough Farm, Lewes	22.10.03
G-BFHI	Piper J-3C-65 Cub (L-4J-PI)	12532	F-BFBT 44-80236	25.11.77	N Glass & A J Richardson	Bann Foot, Lough Neagh	26. 1.00P
G-BFHP	Champion 7GCAA Citabria	114	HB-UAX	8.12.77	A.M.Read	(Milton Keynes)	30. 9.02T
G-BFHR	CEA Jodel DR.220 2 + 2	30	F-BOCX	1.12.77	J.E.Sweetman	Bourne Park, Hurstbourne Tarrant	19. 6.03

G-BFHT	Reims Cessna F152 II	F15201441		7.12.77	Westward Airways (Lands End) Ltd	St.Just	14. 5.04T
G-BFHU	Reims Cessna F152 II	F15201461		7.12.77	D.J.Cooke	Hawarden	11.10.04T
G-BFHV	Reims Cessna F152 II	F15201470		21.12.77	A.S.Bamrah t/a Falcon Flying Services	(Blackbushe)	22.11.04T
G-BFHX	Evans VP-1 (VW 1600)	PFA 062-10283		2.12.77	A.D.Bohanna & D.I.Trussler	Compton Abbas	7. 4.99P
G-BFIB	Piper PA-31 Turbo Navajo	31-684	LN-NPE OY-DVH/LN-RTJ	21.12.77	Richard Hannon Ltd	Thruxton	26.12.03T
G-BFID	Taylor JT.2 Titch Mk.III (Continental O-200-A)	PFA 060-10311		13.12.77	N.A.Scully *(Damaged Breighton 31.5.99)*	Griffins Farm, Temple Bruer	23. 8.99P
G-BFIE	Reims Cessna FRA150M Aerobat	FRA1500331		12. 1.78	G-BFIE Ltd	(Herne Bay)	14.12.03T
G-BFIG	Reims Cessna FR172K Hawk XPII	FR17200615		12. 1.78	Tenair Ltd	Barton	2. 1.04
G-BFIJ	Grumman-American AA-5A Cheetah	AA5A-0486	N6160A	1. 3.78	T.H.& M.G.Weetman	West Freugh/Prestwick	23. 1.04
G-BFIN	Grumman-American AA-5A Cheetah	AA5A-0520	N6145A	22. 3.78	I.W.Lewis t/a G-BFIN Flying Group	Wellesbourne Mountford	21. 1.02
G-BFIP*	Wallbro Monoplane rep (McCulloch/Wallis)	WA-1		16.12.77	K.H.Wallis *(No external marks: cancelled 28.3.01 as temporarily wfu) (On loan to Norfolk & Suffolk Museum)*	Flixton, Suffolk	22. 4.82P
G-BFIT*	Thunder Ax6-56Z HAFB	136		20.12.77	J A G Tyson *"Folly"* *(Cancelled 4.8.98) (Stored 2001)*	Torphins	3. 5.91
G-BFIU	Reims Cessna FR172K Hawk XP	FR17200591	N96098	12. 1.78	B.M.Jobling	Hinton-in-the-Hedges	18. 5.03
G-BFIV	Reims Cessna F177RG Cardinal RG II	F177RG0161	N96106	12. 1.78	Kingfishair Ltd	Blackbushe	27. 5.02
G-BFIX	Thunder Ax7-77A HAFB	133		9.12.77	R.Owen *"Animal Magic"*	Wigan	23. 1.79S
G-BFIY	Reims Cessna F150M	F15001381	OE-CMT	11. 1.78	R J Scott	(Bracknell)	23. 6.02T
G-BFJJ	Evans VP-1 (VW 1800)	PFA 062-10273		30.12.77	Marion J.Collins	Farley Farm, Winchester	23. 6.96P
G-BFJR	Reims Cessna F337G Skymaster II (Wichita c/n 33701761)	F33700082	N46297 (N53658)	4. 1.78	Mannix Aviation	East Midlands	11. 2.02
G-BFJZ	Robin DR.400/140B Major	1290		20. 1.78	Weald Air Services Ltd	Headcorn	26. 8.04T
G-BFKB	Reims Cessna F172N Skyhawk II	F17201601	PH-AXO	16. 1.78	R.L.Clarke & D.Tench t/a Shropshire Flying Group	(Crewe)	2. 3.03T
G-BFKC	Rand Robinson KR 2	KKC.5 & PFA 0129-10809		20. 1.78	L.H.S.Stephens & I.S.Hewitt	(Littleover, Derby)	
G-BFKF	Reims Cessna FA152 Aerobat	FA1520337		26. 1.78	Aerolease Ltd	Conington	27. 4.04T
G-BFKG*	Reims Cessna F152 II	F15201463		26. 1.78	Not known *(Damaged Luton 11.11.89: cancelled 16.3.92 as WFU: wreck stored 8.97: current status unknown)*	Biggin Hill	25.11.90T
G-BFKH	Reims Cessna F152 II	F15201464		26. 1.78	TG Aviation Ltd *(Op Thanet Flying Club)*	Manston	26. 3.04T
G-BFKL	Cameron N-56 HAFB	369		23. 1.78	Merrythought Ltd	Telford	17. 7.92A
G-BFKY	Piper PA-34-200 Seneca	34-7350318	PH-NAZ N56332	22. 2.78	SLH Construction Ltd	Biggin Hill	24. 9.01T
G-BFLH	Piper PA-34-200T Seneca II	34-7870065	N2126M	16. 2.78	Air Medical Ltd	Oxford	8. 6.03T
G-BFLI	Piper PA-28R-201T Turbo Arrow III	28R-7803134	N2582M	16. 2.78	J.K.Chudzicki *"Spirit of Rita May"*	Elstree	11. 6.04
G-BFLM*	Cessna 150M	15076352	N3017V	15. 6.78	Cornwall Flying Club Ltd *(Crashed near Bodmin 14.1.97: cancelled 12.2.97 as WFU: open store 7.97: current status unknown)*	Bodmin	16.11.96T
G-BFLP*	Amethyst Ax6-56 HAFB	001		20. 2.78	K.J.Hendry *"Amethyst"* *(Cancelled 22.11.01 as wfu &.stored)*	Gillingham, Kent	
G-BFLU	Reims Cessna F152 II	F15201433		15. 2.78	Bravo Aviation Ltd *(Op Air Alpha/Dalcross Flying Club)*	Inverness	17. 5.04T
G-BFLX	Grumman-American AA-5A Cheetah	AA5A-0524	N6147A	14. 3.78	G Force Two Ltd	Blackbushe	23.11.04
G-BFLZ	Beechcraft 95-A55 Baron	TC-220	PH-ILE HB-GOV	16. 3.78	K.A.Graham t/a Caterite Food Service	Carlisle	23. 8.04
G-BFME*	Cameron V-56 HAFB	371		17. 2.78	A.Mayes & V.Lawton t/a Warwick Balloons *"Avon Lad"* *(Cancelled 10.10.01 by CAA)*	Leamington Spa	29. 1.88A
G-BFMF*	Cassutt Racer IIIM (Continental C90)	PFA 034-10147		17. 2.78	Not known *(Stored 8.95: cancelled 27.1.99 by CAA) (Current status unknown)*	(Shaftesbury)	24. 5.91P
G-BFMG	Piper PA-28-161 Cherokee Warrior II	28-7716160	N3506Q	11. 5.78	Stardial Ltd	Fairoaks	16. 9.02T
G-BFMH	Cessna 177B Cardinal	17702034	N34836	18. 4.78	Span Aviation Ltd	Newcastle	16. 5.02T
G-BFMK	Reims Cessna FA152 Aerobat	FA1520344		6. 3.78	RAF Halton Aeroplane Club Ltd	RAF Halton	23. 2.02T
G-BFMM	Piper PA-28-181 Archer II	28-7890127	N47735	28. 2.78	K.Hobbs t/a Aldergrove Flight Training Centre	Belfast	4.10.04T
G-BFMR	Piper PA-20 Pacer 125	20-130	N7025K	20. 2.78	J.Knight	Headcorn	14. 2.03
G-BFMX	Reims Cessna F172N Skyhawk II	F17201732		24. 8.78	Broomco (406) Ltd	Farley Farm, Winchester	1. 8.03

G-BFMZ	Payne Ax6-62 HAFB	GFP.2		1. 3.78	E.G.Woolnough *(Active 8.99)*	Halesworth, Suffolk	
G-BFNG	Wassmer Jodel D.112	1321	F-BNHI	6. 3.78	M.T.Taylor	Griffins Farm, Temple Bruer	5. 9.02P
G-BFNI	Piper PA-28-161 Warrior II	28-7816215	N9505N	8. 3.78	P.Elliott	Biggin Hill	26. 7.02
G-BFNJ	Piper PA-28-161 Warrior II	28-7816281	N9520N	8. 3.78	Fleetlands Flying Association Ltd	Lee-on-Solent	6. 6.04T
G-BFNK	Piper PA-28-161 Warrior II	28-7816282	N9527N	8. 3.78	Oxford Aviation Services Ltd	Oxford	9. 1.03T
G-BFNU*	Britten-Norman BN-2B-21 Islander *(Built IRMA)*	877		16. 3.78	Isles of Scilly Skybus Ltd *(Cancelled 28.1.94 as WFU) (Stored 10.00)*	St.Just	18. 8.89T
G-BFOD	Reims Cessna F182Q Skylane II	F18200068		23. 3.78	G.N.Clarke	Alderney	6. 6.04
G-BFOE	Reims Cessna F152 II	F15201475		23. 3.78	Redhill Air Services Ltd	Redhill	19.12.02T
G-BFOF	Reims Cessna F152 II	F15201448		9. 3.78	Gloucestershire Flying Services Ltd	Gloucestershire	21. 6.02T
G-BFOG	Cessna 150M	15076223	N66706	13. 3.78	BBC Air Ltd	Compton Abbas	24. 4.04T
G-BFOJ	American AA-1 Yankee	AA1-0395	OH-AYB (LN-KAJ)/(N6195L)	4. 4.78	A.J.Morton & N.W.Thomas	Bournemouth	14.10.02
G-BFOM	Piper PA-31-325 Navajo C/R	31-7512017	EI-DMI G-BFOM/HB-LHH/N59933	17. 3.78	Ashton Air Services Ltd	(Evesham)	1. 2.02T
G-BFOP	Jodel Wassmer D.120 Paris-Nice	32	F-BHTX	23. 3.78	R.J.Wesley & G.D.Western *"Jean"*	Sampsons Hall, Kersey	16. 4.02P
G-BFOS	Thunder Ax6-56A HAFB	147		20. 3.78	N.T.Petty *"Milton Keynes"*	Sudbury, Suffolk	25.11.93A
G-BFOU	Taylor JT.1 Monoplane	PFA 055-10333		17. 3.78	G.Bee	(Stockton-on-Tees)	
G-BFOV	Reims Cessna F172N Skyhawk II	F17201675		18. 5.78	D.J.Walker	Shoreham	18.10.02
G-BFOZ*	Thunder Ax6-56 Plug HAFB	144		20. 3.78	British Balloon Museum & Library *"Motorway" (Cancelled 16.4.92 by CAA)*	Newbury	
G-BFPA	Scheibe SF-25B Falke	46179	D-KAGM	29. 3.78	N.Meiklejohn & J.Steel	Falgunzeon	13. 9.98
G-BFPB	Grumman-American AA-5B Tiger	AA5B-0706		7. 4.78	Stesco Ltd	Elstree	1. 9.02
G-BFPH	Reims Cessna F172K	F17200802	PH-VHN	23. 3.78	M.Pollard t/a Linc-Air Flying Group	Sturgate	13. 6.02
G-BFPM	Reims Cessna F172M Skyhawk II	F17201384	PH-MIO	13. 4.78	Sigma Corporation Ltd	Wickenby	22.12.02T
G-BFPO	Rockwell Commander 112B	530	N1412J	10. 5.78	J.G.Hale Ltd	Shoreham	9.11.03
G-BFPP	Bell 47J-2 Ranger	2851	F-BJAN TR-LKD/F-OCBU	23. 5.78	M.R.Masters	Phoenix Farm, Lower Upham	11.11.99
G-BFPS	Piper PA-25-235 Pawnee D	25-7856013	N82598	4. 4.78	Kent Gliding Club Ltd	Challock	10. 2.03
G-BFRA*	Rockwell Commander 114	14292	N4972W	28. 3.78	Ischia Investments Ltd *(Cancelled 15.2.00 by CAA)*	Cascais, Portugal	24.10.00
G-BFRD	Bowers FlyBaby 1A	PFA 016-10300		27. 1.78	R.A.Phillips *(Under construction 6.00)*	(Elgin)	
G-BFRF	Taylor JT.1 Monoplane (VW 1500)	PFA 055-10330		7. 4.78	E.R.Bailey	(Hockley, Essex)	
G-BFRI	Sikorsky S-61N Mk.II	61-809		26. 5.78	Bristow Helicopters Ltd *(As "001" with UN titles)*	Aberdeen	14. 6.04T
G-BFRL*	Reims Cessna F152 II	F15201490		11. 4.78	Bristol & Wessex Flying Club Ltd *(Damaged 24.8.92: cancelled 14.3.97 by CAA: stored 1.99: current status unknown)*	Bristol	
G-BFRR	Reims Cessna FRA150M Aerobat	FRA1500326	LN-ALO	19. 4.78	S.Cosgrove t/a Romeo Romeo Flying Group	Tatenhill	27. 7.03
G-BFRS	Reims Cessna F172N Skyhawk II	F17201555	LN-ALP	19. 4.78	Poplar Models Ltd	Poplar Hall Farm, Elmsett	2. 5.03T
G-BFRV	Reims Cessna FA152 Aerobat	FA1520345		17. 4.78	Solo Services Ltd	Shoreham	22. 9.02T
G-BFRX*	Piper PA-25-235 Pawnee D	25-7405787	SE-GDZ	23. 5.78	Yorkshire Gliding Club (Pty) Ltd *(Damaged Sutton Bank 27.3.94: cancelled 3.6.94 as destroyed) (Spares use 1.95) (Current status unknown)*	Sutton Bank	28. 2.96
G-BFRY	Piper PA-25-260 Pawnee D	25-7405789	SE-GIB	23. 5.78	Yorkshire Gliding Club (Pty) Ltd	Sutton Bank	15. 6.03
G-BFSA	Reims Cessna F182Q Skylane II	F18200074	F-WZDG	17. 4.78	Clark Masts Teksam Ltd	Zwartberg/Sandown	28. 9.02
G-BFSB	Reims Cessna F152 II	F15201506		20. 4.78	M.R.Shelton t/a Tatenhill Aviation *(Landed short of runway Tatenhill 28.10.01 and undercarriage severely damaged)*	Tatenhill	17. 2.03T
G-BFSC	Piper PA-25-235 Pawnee D	25-7656068	N82302	2. 6.78	M.A.Pruden	(Bedford)	14. 6.04A
G-BFSD	Piper PA-25-235 Pawnee D	25-7656084	N82338	2. 6.78	Deeside Gliding Club (Aberdeenshire) Ltd	Aboyne	8.11.01
G-BFSR	Reims Cessna F150J	F150-0504	OH-CBN	7. 7.78	S.Bourne	Crowfield	21. 6.04T
G-BFSS	Reims FR172G Rocket	FR17200167	OH-CDY	7. 7.78	J.R.,S.J.Goddard & F.West t/a Minerva Services	Grateley, Andover	6 4.03
G-BFSY	Piper PA-28-181 Cherokee Archer II	28-7890200	N9503N	19. 4.78	A.S.Domone t/a Downland Aviation	Goodwood	24. 5.02

G-BFTC	Piper PA-28R-201T Turbo Arrow III		N3868M	19. 4.78	M.J.Milns	Sherburn in Elmet	22. 6.03
		28R-7803197					
G-BFTF	Grumman-American AA-5B Tiger			7. 9.78	F.C.Burrow Ltd	Sherburn in Elmet	31. 5.03
		AA5B-0879					
G-BFTG	Grumman-American AA-5B Tiger			15. 5.78	D.Hepburn & G.R.Montgomery	Perth	29. 9.02
		AA5B-0777					
G-BFTH	Reims Cessna F172N Skyhawk II			3. 5.78	J.Birkett	Wickenby	12. 9.02T
		F17201671					
G-BFTT	Cessna 421C Golden Eagle II		N6789C	3. 5.78	P & B Metal Components Ltd	Manston	15. 5.02T
		421C-0462			*(Op TG Aviation)*		
G-BFTX	Reims Cessna F172N Skyhawk II			2. 5.78	S.& R.J.Casey	Manston	28. 3.03
		F17201715			t/a G-BFTX Group		
G-BFTZ*	SOCATA MS.880B Rallye Club	1269	F-BPAX	2. 6.78	The Aeroplane Collection Ltd	Winthorpe	19. 9.81
				(Cancelled by CAA 14.11.91) (On loan to Newark Air Museum)			
G-BFUB	Piper PA-32RT-300 Lance II		N9509C	18. 5.78	Jolida Holdings Ltd	Jersey	3. 4.02
		32R-7885052					
G-BFUD	Scheibe SF-25E Super Falke	4313	D-KLDC	19. 5.78	P.A.Lewis	Walney Island	13.12.04
					t/a The Lakes Libelle Syndicate		
G-BFUF*	Piper PA-30 Twin Comanche	30-363	F-OCZF	19. 5.78	Not known	Wilson, Nairobi	
			5R-MCA/N7361Y				
	(Cancelled 12.3.79 on sale to Kenya as 5Y-III?: dismantled & stored 9.92 as "G-BFUF": current status unknown)						
G-BFUG	Cameron N-77 HAFB	394		15. 5.78	Cornwall Ballooning Adventures Ltd		
						Newquay	19. 4.99A
G-BFVF	Piper PA-38-112 Tomahawk	38-78A0055	N9691N	1. 6.78	Goodair Leasing Ltd	Cardiff	18. 8.02T
G-BFVG	Piper PA-28-181 Cherokee Archer II		N31746	1. 6.78	M.S.Cornah	Blackpool	22. 6.02
		28-7890408	N9558N		t/a G-BFVG Flying Group		
G-BFVH	Airco DH.2 rep	WA4	"5964"	1. 6.78	M.J.Kirk	Haverfordwest	23. 7.86P
	(Kinner B54 125 hp) *(Flew 12.7.00 after two-year rebuild at Withybush: as "5964") (See SECTION 4 also)*						
G-BFVM*	Westland-Bell 47G-3B1	WA393	XT234	14. 6.78	Not known	Coventry	20.11.87T
	(Line No. WAP/96)				*(Stored 5.96: current status unknown)*		
G-BFVP	Piper PA-23-250 Aztec F	27-7854096	N63966	6. 7.78	Sub Marine Services Ltd.	(Falmouth)	24. 7.02
G-BFVS	Grumman-American AA-5B Tiger	0784	N28736	11. 8.78	S.W.Biroth & T.Chapman	Denham	8.11.03
G-BFVU	Cessna 150L Commuter	15074684	N75189	10. 8.78	Deer Hill Aviation Ltd	RAF St.Mawgan	12. 7.03T
					(Op Celtic West)		
G-BFWB	Piper PA-28-161 Cherokee Warrior II		N31752	22. 6.78	Mid-Anglia Flight Centre Ltd	Cambridge	17. 7.02T
		28-7816584			t/a Mid-Anglia School of Flying		
G-BFWD	Phoenix Currie Wot	PFA 3009		22. 6.78	F.R.Donaldson	Goodwood	6.10.96P
	(Walter Mikron 3)						
G-BFWE	Piper PA-23-250 Aztec E	27-4583	9M-AQT	13. 7.78	Air Navigation & Trading Co Ltd		
			9V-BDI/N13968			Blackpool	15. 2.03T
G-BFWK*	Piper PA-28-161 Warrior II		N9589N	23. 6.78	Marham Investments Ltd	Belfast	8.12.99T
		28-7816610		*(Cancelled 26.5.98 as WFU) (Wrecked fuselage stored 10.01)*			
G-BFWL*	Reims Cessna F150L	F15000971	PH-KDC	4.10.78	P.Maher	Barton	27. 3.00
					t/a G-BFWL Flying Group		
				(Cancelled 21.2.00 as WFU: fuselage noted behind hangar 11.01)			
G-BFXF	Andreasson BA.4B			10. 7.78	A.Brown	Sherburn-in-Elmet	
		AAB-001 & PFA 038-10351			*(Noted 5.01)*		
G-BFXG	Druine D.31 Turbulent	PFA 1663		10. 7.78	E.J.I.Musty & M.J.Whatley	White Waltham	
					(Partially complete 6.00)		
G-BFXK	Piper PA-28-140 Cherokee F		PH-NSK	1. 8.78	I.Simpson	Carlisle	24. 5.03
		28-7325387					
G-BFXL*	Albatros D.Va rep	0034	D-EGKO	24. 8.78	Fleet Air Arm Museum	RNAS Yeovilton	5.11.91P
	(Ranger 6-440-C5) *(Built Williams Flugzeugbau)*				*(Cancelled 10.3.97 as WFU: as "D5397/17" in German c/s)*		
G-BFXR	Wassmer Jodel D.112	247	F-BFTM	27. 7.78	J.M.Pearson & S.J.Haigh	Crosland Moor	24.11.02P
G-BFXS	Rockwell Commander 114	14271	N4949W	3. 8.78	G.L.Owens	Conington	22. 8.02
G-BFXW	Gulfstream AA-5B Tiger	AA5B-0940		21. 2.79	Campsol Ltd	Leeds-Bradford	19. 6.03
G-BFXX	Gulfstream AA-5B Tiger	AA5B-0917		3.10.78	W.R.Gibson	Stapleford	22.11.03
G-BFYA	MBB Bö.105DB	S.321	D-HJET	31.10.78	Sterling Helicopters Ltd	Norwich	12. 5.03T
					(Op Norfolk Police)		
G-BFYC	Piper PA-32RT-300 Lance II		N36645	31. 7.78	A.A.Barnes	Biggin Hill	24. 4.03
		32R-7885200			t/a Cyril Silver & Ptnrs		
G-BFYI	Westland-Bell 47G-3B1	WA/326	XT167	24. 1.79	B.Walker & Co (Dursley) Ltd	Nympsfield	28. 6.03
	(Line No.WAN/17)						
G-BFYK	Cameron V-77 HAFB	433	EI-BAY	16. 8.78	Louise E.Jones	Worcester	31.12.99A
			G-BFYK				
G-BFYL	Evans VP-2	PFA 063-10146		15. 8.78	W.C.Brown	(Camberley)	17.12.98P
	(VW 1834)						
G-BFYO*	SPAD XIII rep	0035	D-EOWM	16.11.78	American Air Museum	Duxford	21. 6.82P
	(Lycoming AIO-360) *(Built Williams Flugzeugbau)*						
			(Cancelled 14.10.86 as WFU) (As "1/4513" in 3rd Escadrille French AF c/s)				
G-BFYP	Wombat Gyrocopter	AJP.1		7. 7.78	A.J.Philpotts	St.Merryn	
	(Originally regd to unbuilt Philpotts/Bensen B.7 with same c/n: - built Wombat 1995)						
G-BFZA	Alpavia Fournier RF3	5	F-BLEL	14. 9.78	T.J.Hartwell	Sackville Farm, Riseley	
G-BFZB	Piper J-3C-65 Cub (L-4J-PI)	13019	D-ECEL	21. 9.78	N.Rawlinson	Derby	9. 4.88P

	(Continental C85) *(Frame No.12849)*		HB-OSP/44-80723		*(On rebuild 9.01)*		
G-BFZD	Reims Cessna FR182 Skylane RG II	FR18200010		9.10.78	R B Lewis t/a R B Lewis & Co	Sleap	1. 2.03
G-BFZH	Piper PA-28R-200 Cherokee Arrow	28R-35307	OY-BDB	25.10.78	W.E.Lowe	Turweston	25. 9.03
G-BFZM	Rockwell Commander 112TC-A	13191	N4661W	9.10.78	J A Hart & R.J.Lamplough	Filton	29. 8.03
G-BFZN	Reims Cessna FA152 Aerobat	FA1520348		20.10.78	A.S.Bamrah t/a Falcon Flying Services	Biggin Hill	29.11.81T
					(Crashed Narborough, Leics 4.10.80: on rebuild 2.95: current status unknown)		
G-BFZO	Gulfstream AA-5A Cheetah	AA5A-0697		1.11.78	P.Young t/a Coleraine Landscape Services	City of Derry	12. 5.03
G-BFZT	Reims Cessna FA152 Aerobat	FA1520356		4. 7.79	Pooler-LMT Ltd	Sleap	14.11.03T
G-BFZU	Reims Cessna FA152 Aerobat	FA1520355		29. 6.79	Redhill Air Services Ltd	Redhill	10. 2.02T
G-BFZV	Reims Cessna F172M	F17201093	SE-FZR	2.11.78	R.Thomas	AAC Middle Wallop	16. 3.03T

G-BGAA – G-BGZZ

G-BGAA	Cessna 152 II	15281894	N67529	18. 7.78	PJC (Leasing) Ltd	Stapleford	24. 6.04T
G-BGAB	Reims Cessna F152 II	F1521531		13.10.78	TG Aviation Ltd *(Op Thanet Flying Club)*	Manston	7. 4.03T
G-BGAD*	Reims Cessna F152 II	F1521532		13.10.78	Not known	Belfast	
					(DBR in a landing accident Newtownards 5.7.01 & cancelled 17.8.01 as destroyed) (Noted as wreck 10.01)		
G-BGAE	Reims Cessna F152 II	F1521540		8.11.78	Aerolease Ltd	Conington	30. 4.03T
G-BGAF	Reims Cessna FA152 Aerobat	FA1520349		13.10.78	M.F.Hatt, P.E.Preston, R.W.Harris, A.Jahanfar & D.S.Woolf *(Op Southend Flying Club)*	Southend	16. 8.03T
G-BGAG	Reims Cessna F172N Skyhawk II	F17201754	"G-KING"	13.10.78	A.S.Bamrah t/a Falcon Flying Services	Rochester	11. 5.02T
G-BGAH*	Clutton Fred Srs.II	PFA 029-10324		15. 2.78	Not known	Hethersett, Wymondham	
					(Cancelled 2.9.91 by CAA) (Under construction 8.97: current status unknown)		
G-BGAJ	Reims Cessna F182Q Skylane II	F18200096		13.10.78	Ground Airport Services Ltd	Guernsey	4. 5.03
G-BGAS*	Colting Ax8-105A HAFB	001		27. 6.78	British Balloon Museum & Library	Newbury	
					(Destroyed Flims, Switzerland 20.9.80 & cancelled) (Basket only)		
G-BGAX	Piper PA-28-140 Cherokee F	28-7325409	PH-NSH	20.10.78	C.D.Brack	Breighton	17. 6.02
G-BGAZ	Cameron V-77 HAFB *(New envelope ?)*	439		20.10.78	C.J.Madigan & D.H.McGibbon *"Silicon Chip/Robocop"*	Bristol	4. 8.01A
G-BGBA	Robin R.2100A Club	133	F-OCBJ	2. 5.78	D.Faulkner	Headcorn	24. 5.03
G-BGBE	SAN Jodel DR.1050 Ambassadeur	260	F-BJYT	29.11.78	J.A. & B.Mawby	Gravely	6. 9.01
G-BGBF	Druine D.31A Turbulent (VW 1600)	PFA 1658		24.10.78	R.S.Jordan	Shipdham	25.11.02P
G-BGBG	Piper PA-28-181 Archer II	28-7990012	N39730	2.11.78	Harlow Printing Ltd	Newcastle	24. 5.03
G-BGBI	Reims Cessna F150L	F15000688	PH-LUA	28.11.78	A.S.Bamrah t/a Falcon Flying Services	Rochester	5. 4.03T
G-BGBN	Piper PA-38-112 Tomahawk	38-78A0511	N9657N	29.11.78	Bonus Aviation Ltd	Cranfield	7. 8.03T
G-BGBR	Reims Cessna F172N Skyhawk II	F17201772		8.11.78	A.S.Bamrah t/a Falcon Flying Services *(Op Willowair Flying Club)*	Southend	16. 2.04T
G-BGBU*	Auster AOP.9	B5/10/131	XN435	8.11.78	P.Neilson	(Egham)	
					(Cancelled 1.10.90 by CAA) (On rebuild 1992: current status unknown)		
G-BGBW	Piper PA-38-112 Tomahawk	38-78A0670	N9710N	8.11.78	Truman Aviation Ltd	Nottingham	10. 7.03T
G-BGBY	Piper PA-38-112 Tomahawk	38-78A0711	N9689N	8.11.78	Cheshire Flying Services Ltd	Liverpool	6. 2.04T
G-BGBZ	Rockwell Commander 114	14423	N5878N	9.10.78	R.S.Fenwick	Rochester	9. 8.04
G-BGCG*	Douglas C-47A-85DL Dakota	20002	N5595T G-BGCG/Sp.AF T3-27/N49V/NC50322/43-15536	28.11.78	Datran Holdings Ltd	Rotary Farm, Hatch	8. 8.80P
					(Cancelled 3.4.89 by CAA) (Stored 8.95: current status unknown)		
G-BGCM	Gulfstream AA-5A Cheetah	AA5A-0835		23. 3.79	G. & S.A.Jones	Linley Hill, Beverley	13. 9.04T
G-BGCO	Piper PA-44-180 Seminole	44-7995128	N2103D	20.12.78	J.R.Henderson *(Op BAE Systems (Operations) Ltd)*	Warton	21. 8.03
G-BGCY	Taylor JT.1 Monoplane (VW 1600)	PFA 055-10370		23.11.78	J.C.Metcalf	Spanhoe	30. 4.02P
G-BGEA	Reims Cessna F150M	F15001396	OY-BJK	22. 3.79	Mrs C.J.Hopewell	Sibson	28. 6.03T
G-BGED	Cessna U206F Stationair	U20602279	LN-BGQ N1911U	12.12.78	Chapman Aviation Ltd *"Sky Diva"*	Tilstock	11. 4.03
G-BGEE	Evans VP-1 (VW 1679)	PFA 062-10287		27.11.78	R E Holmes	(Ely)	16. 5.95P
					(On rebuild 9.00: wings @ Priory Farm, Tibenham 8.97)		
G-BGEF*	Wassmer Jodel D.112	1309	F-BMYL	7.12.78	Not known	North Coates	12. 9.96P
					(Damaged North Coates 8.10.95: cancelled 29.1.96 by CAA: stored 6.96: current status unknown)		
G-BGEH	Monnett Sonerai II (VW 2234)	209 & PFA 015-10254		1.12.78	D.& V.T.Hubbard	(Basingstoke)	16. 8.96P
G-BGEI	Oldfield Baby Lakes (Continental A65) *(Fuselage of PFA 01576 incorporated during construction)*	PFA 010-10016		1.12.78	A.R.Robinson	Tatenhill	20.11.02P

G-BGEK	Piper PA-38-112 Tomahawk	38-78A0575	N9662N	13.12.78	Cheshire Flying Services Ltd t/a Ravenair	Liverpool	16. 4.03T
G-BGEW	SNCAN NC.854S (Continental A65)	63	F-BFSJ	13.12.78	Tavair Ltd	Holywell	11. 6.02P
G-BGEX*	Brookland Mosquito Mk.2 (VW 1800)	JB.1		13.12.78	Not known *(Cancelled 28.2.95 by CAA) (Stored 9.97: current status unknown)*	Horsford, Norwich	14. 8.81P
G-BGFC	Evans VP-2 (VW 1834)	V2-1278 & PFA 063-10441		15.12.78	S.W.C.Hollins	Llandegla	29. 9.93P
G-BGFF	Clutton FRED Srs.II (VW 1834)	PFA 029-10261		18.12.78	I.Daniels	Popham	2. 7.02P
G-BGFG	Gulfstream AA-5A Cheetah	AA5A-0687	N6158A	25. 1.79	Plane Talking Ltd	Blackbushe	30. 5.03T
G-BGFH	Reims Cessna F182Q Skylane II *(Rebuilt with fuselage of G-EMMA [F18200099] 1994/95: original fuselage scrapped)*	F18200105		18. 1.79	Rayviation Ltd	(Driffield)	20. 4.04T
G-BGFI	Gulfstream AA-5A Cheetah	AA5A-0733	N6142A	5. 3.79	I.J.Hay & A.Nayyar t/a GFI Group	Biggin Hill	25.10.03
G-BGFJ	Jodel D.9 Bebe (VW 1600)	PFA 1324		11.12.78	M.D.Mold	Watchford Farm, Yarcombe	25.11.02P
G-BGFK*	Evans VP-1	PFA 062-10343		20.12.78	I.N.M.Cameron *(Cancelled 7.4.99 by CAA) (Stored 7.01)*	Wathstones Farm, Newby Wiske	
G-BGFT	Piper PA-34-200T Seneca II	34-7870218	N9714C	17. 1.79	Oxford Aviation Services Ltd *(Made wheels-up landing Coventry 30.5.01: damage to underside & both propellers)*	Oxford	15. 8.03T
G-BGFX	Reims Cessna F152 II	F15201555		28.12.78	A.S.Bamrah t/a Falcon Flying Services *(Spares use 2.95)*	Biggin Hill	23. 6.91T
G-BGGA	Bellanca 7GCBC Citabria 150S	1104-79		5. 2.79	L.A.King	North Connel, Oban	24. 1.04
G-BGGB	Bellanca 7GCBC Citabria 150S	1105-79		7. 2.79	G.H.N.Chamberlain	Rattlesden	2.12.01
G-BGGC	Bellanca 7GCBC Citabria 150S	1106-79		5. 2.79	R.P.Ashfield & J.M.Stone	Gorwell Farm, Littlebredy, Dorset	21. 9.03
G-BGGD	Bellanca 8GCBC Scout	284-78		5. 2.79	Bristol & Gloucestershire Gliding Club Ltd	Nympsfield	22. 6.04
G-BGGE	Piper PA-38-112 Tomahawk	38-79A0161	N9673N	10. 1.79	Truman Aviation Ltd	Nottingham	25. 6.03T
G-BGGF	Piper PA-38-112 Tomahawk	38-79A0162	N9674N	10. 1.79	Truman Aviation Ltd *(Stored 7.99)*	Nottingham	15.10.94T
G-BGGG	Piper PA-38-112 Tomahawk	38-79A0163	N9675N	10. 1.79	Teesside Flight Centre Ltd	Teesside	28. 6.04T
G-BGGI	Piper PA-38-112 Tomahawk	38-79A0165	N9675N	10. 1.79	Truman Aviation Ltd	Nottingham	6. 3.04T
G-BGGL	Piper PA-38-112 Tomahawk	38-79A0169	N9696N	10. 1.79	Grunwick Processing Laboratories Ltd *(Op Bonus Aviation)*	Cranfield	27. 6.03T
G-BGGM	Piper PA-38-112 Tomahawk	38-79A0170	N9698N	10. 1.79	Grunwick Processing Laboratories Ltd *(Op Bonus Aviation)*	Cranfield	16.11.03T
G-BGGN	Piper PA-38-112 Tomahawk	38-79A0171	N9706N	10. 1.79	Domeastral Ltd	Pansahnger	31. 8.03T
G-BGGO	Reims Cessna F152 II	F15201569		8. 3.79	East Midlands Flying School Ltd	East Midlands	13. 7.03T
G-BGGP	Reims Cessna F152 II	F15201580		8. 3.79	East Midlands Flying School Ltd	East Midlands	12.10.03T
G-BGGU	Wallis WA-116 RR (Subaru EA61)	702		28.12.78	K.H.Wallis *(Noted 8.01)*	Reymerston Hall, Norfolk	
G-BGGV	Wallis WA-120 Srs.2	703		28.12.78	K.H.Wallis *(Not completed: valid CofR 4.01)*	Reymerston Hall, Norfolk	
G-BGGW	Wallis WA-122 RR (RR Continental O-240-A)	704		28.12.78	K.H.Wallis *(Noted 8.01)*	Reymerston Hall, Norfolk	24. 4.98P
G-BGHE	Convair L-13A-CO		N1132V 47-346	4. 8.80	J.M.Davis *(On long-term rebuild: current status unknown)*	Wichita, USA	
G-BGHF*	Westland WG.30 Srs 100-60	WA.001.P		4. 1.79	The Helicopter Museum *(Cancelled as WFU 29.3.89)*	Weston-super-Mare	1. 8.86S
G-BGHI	Reims Cessna F152 II	F15201560		15. 1.79	V.R.McCready	(Sutton)	18. 5.03T
G-BGHJ	Reims Cessna F172N Skyhawk II	F17201777	EI-BVF G-BGHJ	15. 1.79	M.D.N.Fisher t/a F & H (Aircraft & Castle Aviation Ltd *(Op Almat Flying Club)*	Coventry	26. 7.04T
G-BGHM	Robin R.1180T Aiglon	227		19. 2.79	H.Price	Blackpool	5.11.03
G-BGHP	Beechcraft 76 Duchess	ME-190	N60132	16. 1.79	Magenta Ltd *(Op Airways Flight Training)*	Exeter	22. 4.03T
G-BGHS	Cameron N-31 HAFB	501		15. 1.79	W.R.Teasdale "Baby Champion" *(On loan to British Balloon Museum & Library)*	Newbury	17. 1.00A
G-BGHT	Falconar F-12 (Lycoming O-290)	PFA 022-10040		17. 1.79	C.R.Coates	Sneaton Thorpe, Whitby	
G-BGHU	North American T-6G-NF Texan	182-729	FAP1707 Fr.AF 115042/51-15042	22. 1.79	C.E.Bellhouse *(As "115042/TA-042" in USAF c/s) "Carly"*	Headcorn	6.12.01P
G-BGHV	Cameron V-77 HAFB	483		12. 1.79	E.Davies t/a Adeilad Claddings *"Adclad"*	Penlan Farm, Llanwrda	28. 5.00A
G-BGHW*	Thunder Ax8-90 HAFB	175		30. 1.79	W G Johnston *(Cancelled 19.5.93 by CAA) (Stored 2001)*	Edinburgh	
G-BGHY	Taylor JT.1 Monoplane (VW 1600)	PFA 1455		12. 1.79	R.A.Hand *"Shy Talk"*	RAF Barkston Heath	27. 6.02P

G-BGHZ	Clutton FRED Srs.II	PFA 029-10445		12. 1.79	A.Smith	(Swansea)	
					(Under construction Birmingham 1999)		
G-BGIB	Cessna 152 II	152-82161	N68169	3. 7.79	Redhill Air Services Ltd	Redhill	24. 2.04T
G-BGID	Westland-Bell 47G-3B1	WA/340	XT181	28. 2.79	A.Tasker	Coney Park, Leeds	10. 5.02
	(Line No. WAN/31)						
G-BGIG	Piper PA-38-112 Tomahawk	38-78A0773	N2607A	23. 1.79	Air Claire Ltd	Glasgow	8. 4.04T
					(Op Glasgow Flying Club)		
G-BGIO	Montgomerie-Bensen B.8MR			11. 1.79	R.M.Savage	Carlisle	23. 7.02P
	(Rotax 503)	GJ.1 & PFA G/01-1259			t/a Great Orton Group		
G-BGIP	Colt 56A HAFB	038		2. 2.79	R.D.Allen & M.Walker *"The Snake"*	Bristol	21. 6.94A
G-BGIU	Reims Cessna F172H	F172-0620	PH-VIT	26. 2.79	D W Clifton & M Ruggieri t/a Skyhawk Flying Group		
						Standalone Farm, Meppershall	8. 7.04
G-BGIX	Helio H.295 Super Courier	1467	(G-BGAO)	17.10.79	Caroline M.Lee		
			N68861			Fanners Farm, Great Waltham, Essex	23.11.01
G-BGIY	Reims Cessna F172N Skyhawk II			31. 1.79	Air Claire Ltd	Glasgow	12. 8.03T
		F17201824			*(Op Glasgow Flying Club)*		
G-BGJB	Piper PA-44-180 Seminole	44-7995112	G-ISFT	1. 2.79	Magenta Ltd	Exeter	22.10.03T
			EI-CHF/G-BGJB/N3046B				
G-BGJU	Cameron V-65 HAFB	499		5. 2.79	Janet A.Folkes *"Spoils"*	Loughborough	4. 4.93A
G-BGKC	SOCATA Rallye 110ST	3262		25. 4.79	J.H.Cranmer & T.A.Timms	Bidford	8. 9.99
G-BGKJ*	MBB Bö.105D	S.128	D-HDDV	20. 4.79	Bond Helicopters Ltd	Bourn	19. 4.88T
	(Ditched near Mossbank, Shetland Isles 25.4.89: used as demonstration airframe 7.93: cancelled as WFU 29.6.94)						
	(Current status unknown)						
G-BGKO	Gardan GY-20 Minicab	PFA 1827		14. 2.79	R.B.Webber	Trenchard Farm, Eggesford	
					(Stored incomplete 6.01)		
G-BGKS	Piper PA-28-161 Warrior II		N9562N	12. 2.79	Marham Investments Ltd	Belfast	6. 4.03T
		28-7916221			*(Op Woodgate Executive Air Services)*		
G-BGKT	Auster AOP.9	B5/10/137	XN441	28.12.78	E.Wright	South Lodge Farm, Widmerpool	4 .4.02P
	(C/n possibly B5/10/139 ?)				t/a Auster Nine Group *(As "XN441" in RAF c/s)*		
G-BGKU	Piper PA-28R-201 Arrow III		N31585	8. 3.79	Aerolease Ltd.	Conington	4. 2.04T
		28R-7837237					
G-BGKV	Piper PA-28R-201 Cherokee Arrow III		N44985	21. 5.79	R.Haverson & R.G.Watson	Shipdham	2. 3.04
		28R-7737156					
G-BGKY	Piper PA-38-112 Tomahawk	38-78A0737	N9732N	2. 3.79	Top Cat Aviation Ltd	Manchester	7. 7.03T
G-BGKZ	Auster J/5F Aiglet Trainer	2776	F-BGKZ	15.12.78	Deborah Hatelie	(Liverpool)	25. 2.95
					(Damaged near Nayland 30.1.93)		
G-BGLA	Piper PA-38-112 Tomahawk	38-78A0741	N9699N	9. 3.79	B.H. & P.M.Illston	Hardwick	24. 8.03T
					t/a Norwich School of Flying		
G-BGLB*	Bede BD.5B	3796 & PFA 014-10085		2. 3.79	Science Museum Air Transport Coln & Storage Facility		
	(Hirth 230R)				*(Cancelled 21.11.91 by CAA)*	Wroughton	4. 8.81P
G-BGLF	Evans VP-1 Srs.2	PFA 062-10388		28. 2.79	J.B.McNab	Dunkeswell	1. 8.00P
	(VW 1834)						
G-BGLG	Cessna 152 II	15282092	N67909	11. 4.79	L.W.Scattergood	Breighton	1. 7.04T
G-BGLK*	Monnett Sonerai IIL	PFA 015-10304		24. 2.78	N.M.Smorthit	RAF Linton-on-Ouse	31. 8.89P
	(VW 1783)			*(Stored 10.92: cancelled 6.3.99 by CAA: current status unknown)*			
G-BGLN	Reims Cessna FA152 Aerobat	FA1520354		8. 3.79	Bflying Ltd	Bournemouth	24. 8.03T
					(Op Bournemouth Flying Club)		
G-BGLO	Reims Cessna F172N Skyhawk II			8. 3.79	A.H.Slaughter	Southend	10.12.03
		F17201900					
G-BGLS	Oldfield Super Baby Lakes			11.12.78	J.F.Dowe	(Ipswich)	18. 6.88P
	(Lycoming O-235)	PFA 010-10237			*(Current status unknown)*		
G-BGLW	Piper PA-34-200 Seneca	34-7250132	(G-BFPF)	2. 6.78	London Executive Aviation Ltd	Stapleford	28. 8.03T
			OY-BDZ/SE-FYS				
G-BGLZ	Stits SA-3A Playboy	71-100	N9996	19. 6.79	S.A.Cooke	Mitchell's Farm, Wilburton	1. 1.02P
	(Continental C90)				t/a Stitts Playboy (Fenland) Flying Group		
					(Damaged landing Fenland 1.9.01)		
G-BGME*	SIPA 903	96	G-BCML	1. 1.81	M.Emery & C.A.Suckling	Guildford	17. 6.94P
			"G-BCHU"/F-BGHU				
				(Stored 1995: cancelled 15.11.00 by CAA: current status unknown)			
G-BGMJ	CAB GY-201 Minicab	12	F-BGMJ	19. 6.78	S.L. & A.W.Wakefield, J.F.Hawkins & N.Birchall		
						Sibson	20. 8.02P
G-BGMN	Hawker Siddeley HS.748 Srs.2A/347		PK-OCH	9. 3.79	Emerald Airways Ltd	Liverpool	19.11.04T
		1766	G-BGMN/9Y-TGH/G-BGMN/9Y-TGH				
G-BGMO	Hawker Siddeley HS.748 Srs.2A/347		ZK-MCB	9. 3.79	Emerald Airways Ltd	Liverpool	22. 4.02T
		1767	G-BGMO/9Y-TGI/V2-LDB/9Y-TGI/(G-BGMO)				
G-BGMP	Reims Cessna F172G	F172-0240	PH-BNV	26. 3.79	R.W.Collings	Hinton-in-the-Hedges	5. 7.04
G-BGMR	Barritault JB-01 Minicab			12. 3.79	R.A.M.Smith	White Waltham	3. 5.02P
	(Continental C90)	PFA 056-10153			t/a Mike Romeo Flying Group		
G-BGMS	Taylor JT.2 Titch			20.10.78	M.A.J.Spice	(Middlewich, Cheshire)	
		MS.1 & PFA 060-10400					
G-BGMT	SOCATA Rallye 235E	13126		14. 9.78	C.G.Wheeler	Morgansfield, Fishburn	26.12.03
G-BGMU	Westland-Bell 47G-3B1	WA/514	XT807	14. 5.79	V.L.J. & V.English		
	(Line No. WAP/83)					Whittlesey, Peterborough	16.11.03

G-BGMV Scheibe SF-25B Falke 4648 D-KEBG 15. 5.79 C.A.Bloom & A.P Twort Shoreham 16.11.01
G-BGND Reims Cessna F172N Skyhawk II PH-AYI 3. 3.78 A.J.M.Freeman Andrewsfield 19. 8.02
F17201576 (F-GAQA)
G-BGNH* Short SD.3-30 Var.200 SH.3035 N331L 22. 3.79 Newcastle Airport Fire Service
G-BGNH Newcastle 22. 9.79
(To spares 5.92: cancelled 11.11.92 as WFU: fuselage extant 3.98 in all green finish: current status unknown)
G-BGNS* Reims Cessna F172N Skyhawk II 23.10.79 F & H (Aircraft) Ltd Tattershall Thorpe 6. 1.89T
F17201901
(Damaged Shoreham 16.10.87: cancelled 11.4.88 as WFU: wreck stored 10.92: current status unknown)
G-BGNT Reims Cessna F152 II F15201644 23.10.79 Aerolease Ltd Conington 1. 3.04T
G-BGNV Gulfstream GA-7 Cougar GA7-0078 N790GA 20. 4.79 G.J.Bissex Filton 6.12.03T
G-BGOD Colt 77A HAFB 040 4. 4.79 C. & M.D.Steuer London NW1 18. 6.97A
"Harvey Wallbanger"
G-BGOG Piper PA-28-161 Warrior II N9639N 8. 6.79 W.D.Moore Cranfield 31.10.03
28-7916350
G-BGOI Cameron O-56 HAFB 526 4. 4.79 S.Ellis *"Skymaster"* Bristol 13. 5.87A
(Active 2001)
G-BGOL Piper PA-28R-201T Turbo Arrow III N36705 11. 4.79 Valley Flying Co Ltd
28R-7803335 Valley Farm, Stafford 14. 5.03
G-BGON Gulfstream GA-7 Cougar GA7-0095 N9527Z 24. 4.79 J.P.E.Walsh Elstree 13. 8.03T
t/a Walsh Aviation *(Op Cabair)*
G-BGOO* Colt Flame 56SS HAFB 039 27. 4.79 British Balloon Museum & Library Newbury NE(A)
("Smiling Flame") *"Mr Gas" (Cancelled 19.5.93 by CAA)*
G-BGOR North American AT-6D-NT Harvard III FAP1508 28. 3.79 M.L.Sargeant Goudhurst 20. 5.02
(Reported as c/n 88-14880) 88-14863 SAAF7504/EX935/41-33908 *(As "14863/TA-863" in USAAF c/s)*
G-BGPA Cessna 182Q Skylane II 18266538 C-GYBW 11. 7.79 J.J. & J.Walsh Bodmin 22. 4.04
(N94935) t/a Papa Alpha Group
G-BGPB CCF Harvard 4 CCF4-538 FAP1747 4. 4.79 J.Romain Duxford 22. 3.03
(T-6J-CCF Texan) West German AF BF+050/WGAF AA+050/53-4619 *(Op Aircraft Restoration Co)*
(As "1747" in Portuguese AF c/s)
G-BGPD Piper J-3C-65 Cub (L-4H-PI) 12040 F-BFQP 18. 4.79 P.D.Whiteman Marsh Hill Farm, Aylesbury 18. 4.02P
(Frame No.11867) F-BDTP/44-79744
(Officially regd as c/n 10478 which is ex 43-29187/OO-ADI/F-BFQP: G-BGPD is ex 44-79744/F-BDTP: presumably fuselages exchanged in France - see G-BCOM) *(As "479744/49/M" in 92nd Armoured FA Btn, US 9th Army c/s)*
G-BGPF* Thunder Ax6-56Z HAFB 206 13. 7.79 P.J.Bish *"Pepsi"* Newbury 27. 6.82A
(On loan to British Balloon Museum & Library
(Cancelled 21.11.89 as WFU)
G-BGPH Gulfstream AA-5B Tiger AA5B-1248 (G-BGRU) 14. 8.79 Shipping & Airlines Ltd Biggin Hill 30. 9.01T
G-BGPI Plumb BGP.1 Biplane PFA 083-10359 26. 6.78 B.G.Plumb Hinton-in-the-Hedges 15.10.02P
(Continental O-200A)
G-BGPJ Piper PA-28-161 Warrior II N9602N 24. 4.79 West Lancs Warrior Co Ltd Woodvale 24. 6.03
28-7916288
G-BGPL Piper PA-28-161 Warrior II N9603N 20. 4.79 TG Aviation Ltd Manston 12. 6.03T
28-7916289 *(Op Thanet Flying Club)*
G-BGPM* Evans VP-2 PFA 063-10335 17. 4.79 M.G.Reilly (Basingstoke) 29. 4.86P
(VW 2075) *(Open storage Old Sarum 9.91: cancelled 4.10.00 by CAA: current status unknown)*
G-BGPN Piper PA-18-150 Super Cub 18-7909044 N9750N 12. 4.79 D.McHugh & A.R.Darke (Beaconsfield) 7. 3.92T
(Damaged Nayland 27.1.90: on rebuild 5.93: current status unknown)
G-BGPU Piper PA-28-140 Cherokee F PH-GNT 25. 4.79 Air Navigation & Trading Co Ltd
28-7325282 Blackpool 17. 8.03T
G-BGPZ Morane MS.890A Rallye Commodore 145 F-BLBD 3. 5.79 A.S.Cowan Popham 28. 1.02
10284 t/a Popham Flying Group G-BGPZ
G-BGRC Piper PA-28-140 Cherokee B 28-26208 SE-FHF 12. 6.79 Tecair Aviation Ltd & G.F.Haigh
N5501U Swanton Morley 26.10.97T
G-BGRE Beechcraft 200 Super King Air BB-568 8. 5.79 Martin-Baker (Engineering) Ltd Chalgrove 23.10.02T
G-BGRG Beechcraft 76 Duchess ME-233 8. 5.79 S.J.Skilton Bournemouth 24. 2.02T
t/a Aviation Rentals *(Op Professional Air Training)*
G-BGRH Robin DR.400 2+2 1411 21. 5.79 C.R.Beard Grassthorpe Grange 5. 4.04
G-BGRI CEA Jodel DR.1050 Sicile 540 F-BLZJ 27. 4.79 R.T.Gunn & J.R.Redhead Breighton 14.12.03
G-BGRL Piper PA-38-112 Tomahawk 38-79A0917 N9725N 25. 4.79 G.G.Mepham Goodwood 18. 5.03T
G-BGRM Piper PA-38-112 Tomahawk 38-79A1067 N9673N 1. 8.79 D.E.Bamber Goodwood 30. 5.03T
G-BGRN* Piper PA-38-112 Tomahawk 38-79A0897 N9684N 25. 4.79 Goodwood Road Racing Co Ltd Goodwood 12. 2.00T
(Donated to Fire Section 5.01 minus outer wings: cancelled 30.8.01 as wfu)
G-BGRO Reims Cessna F172M Skyhawk II PH-KAB 4. 5.79 A.N.Pirie RAF Leuchars 14.12.03T
F17201129 t/a Cammo Aviation *(Op Leuchars Flying Club)*
G-BGRR Piper PA-38-112 Tomahawk 38-78A0336 OO-FLT 8. 5.79 Goodair Leasing Ltd Cardiff 23. 8.02T
N9685N
G-BGRS Thunder Ax7-77Z HAFB 203 21. 5.79 P.M.Gaines Stockton-on-Tees 19. 8.95A
"Hassall Homes" (Sole owner 10.01)
G-BGRT Steen Skybolt RCT.001 & PFA 064-10171 12. 9.78 J.H.Kimber & O.Meier
(Lycoming O-360) Damyns Hall, Upminster 24.12.03P
G-BGRX Piper PA-38-112 Tomahawk 38-79A0609 N9662N 11. 5.79 Bonus Aviation Ltd Cranfield 31.10.03T
G-BGSA SOCATA MS.892E Rallye 150GT 12838 F-GAKC 29. 5.79 D.H.Tonkin Bodmin 14. 6.04
G-BGSG Piper PA-44-180 Seminole 44-7995004 N36538 21. 5.79 Shemburn Ltd Weston, Co.Kildare 8.10.04T

G-BGSH	Piper PA-38-112 Tomahawk	38-79A0562	N9719N	11. 5.79	Scotia Safari Ltd *(Op Carlisle Flight Centre)*	Carlisle	1. 9.02T
G-BGSI	Piper PA-38-112 Tomahawk	38-79A0564	N9720N	18. 5.79	Cheshire Flying Services Ltd t/a Ravenair *(Had accident and for spares use by 8.01 apparently)*	Liverpool	29. 9.03T
G-BGSJ	Piper J-3C-65 Cub (L-4A-PI) *(Frame No.8917)*	8781	F-BGXJ Fr.AF/42-36657	21. 5.79	A.J.Higgins	(Lanport)	24 9.02P
G-BGSN	Enstrom F-28C-UK-2	472-2	G-OIGS G-BGSN	11. 5.79	Tindon Ltd	Little Snoring	27. 8.98
G-BGST*	Thunder Ax7-65 Bolt HAFB	217		14. 5.79	J.L.Bond *"Black Fred"* *(Cancelled 7.12.01 by CAA) (Stored 2002)*	Billingshurst	23. 3.91A
G-BGSV	Reims Cessna F172N Skyhawk II	F17201830		1. 8.79	Southwell Air Services Ltd	Linley Hill, Leven	24. 1.04
G-BGSW	Beechcraft F33 Bonanza	CD-1253	OH-BDD	30. 5.79	C.Wood	Wellesbourne Mountford	28. 4.02T
G-BGSY	Gulfstream GA-7 Cougar	GA7-0096		4. 6.79	Plane Talking Ltd	Biggin Hill	29. 4.02T
G-BGTC	Auster AOP.9	AUS/168	XP282	12.10.79	P.T.Bolton *(As "XP282") (Damaged Widmerpool 2.10.96: current status unknown)*	South Lodge Farm, Widmerpool	9. 6.97P
G-BGTF	Piper PA-44-180 Seminole	44-7995287	N2131Y	20. 6.79	NG Trustees & Nominees Ltd	Jersey	26. 4.03
G-BGTG	Piper PA-23-250 Aztec F	27-7954061	N2454M	23. 5.79	Keen Leasing (IOM) Ltd	Belfast	21.10.03T
G-BGTI	Piper J-3C-65 Cub (L-4J-PI) (Rotax 582) *(Frame No.12770)*	12940	F-BFFL 44-80644	17. 5.79	A.P.Broad	Brandy Wharf, Waddingham	28. 8.02P
G-BGTJ	Piper PA-28-180 Cherokee Archer	28-7405083	OY-BIO SE-GAH	3. 7.79	Serendipity Aviation Ltd	Gloucestershire	17.12.03
G-BGTP*	Robin HR.100/210 Safari	188	(G-BGTN) F-BVCP	25. 6.79	J.C.Parker *(Cancelled 25.1.00 as WFU)*	Thruxton	18. 1.01
G-BGTT	Cessna 310R II	310R1641	N1AN (N2635D)	13. 7.79	Aviation Beauport Ltd	Jersey	29. 5.04T
	(Made emergency landing Bournemouth 6.6.01: damage to starboard wing tip, propeller & undercarriage)						
G-BGTX	SAN Jodel D.117	698	F-BIDI	22. 6.79	C.Adams & H F Young t/a Madley Flying Group (Cisavia) *(Crashed Gaydon 6.01 and moved to Sibsey for repair by 7.01)*	Shobdon	4.11.02P
G-BGUB(2)	Piper PA-32-300 Six	32-7940252	N2387U	29.11.79	A.J.Diplock	Biggin Hill	27. 2.04
G-BGUY	Cameron V-56 HAFB	441		27. 9.78	J.L.Guy *"Good Guy"*	Skipton	13.10.95A
G-BGVB	CEA DR.315 Petit Prince	308	F-BPOP	20. 7.79	P.J.Leggo	Leicester	25. 7.02
G-BGVE	Scintex CP.1310-C3 Super Emeraude	931	F-BMJE	8. 6.79	R.T.L.Arkell t/a Victor Echo Group *"Mon Papillon"*	Little Battleflats Farm, Ellistown, Coalville	15.10.02P
G-BGVH	Beechcraft 76 Duchess	ME-260		8. 6.79	W.J. & J.C.M.Golden t/a Valco Marketing	Bowerchalke, Salisbury	8. 7.04
G-BGVK	Piper PA-28-161 Cherokee Warrior II	28-7816400	PH-WPT G-BGVK/N6244C	13. 6.79	K.R.Holland	Coventry	29. 5.04
G-BGVL*	Piper PA-38-112 Tomahawk	38-78A0263	N9963T	13. 6.79	NK	(Shipdham)	5. 2.95T
	(Crashed Priory Farm, Tibenham 16.7.93: cancelled 5.7.95 as WFU: spares for G-BPHI) (Current status unknown)						
G-BGVN	Piper PA-28RT-201 Arrow IV	28R-7918168	N2846U	22. 6.79	C.Smith & S.Carrington	Fairoaks	15.11.03
G-BGVS	Reims Cessna F172M	F17200992	PH-HVS (PH-LUK)	3. 5.79	J.W.Tulloch t/a Kirkwall Flying Club	Kirkwall	14.12.03T
G-BGVV	Gulfstream AA-5A Cheetah	AA5A-0750		27. 6.79	A.H.McVicar	Prestwick	28. 5.04T
G-BGVW	Gulfstream AA-5A Cheetah	AA5A-0774		21. 6.79	Computech Aviation Ltd	Biggin Hill	23. 8.03T
G-BGVY	Gulfstream AA-5B Tiger	AA5B-1080	(G-BGVU) (F-GBOO)	21. 8.79	R.J.C.Neal-Smith	Old Sarum	4.10.03
G-BGVZ	Piper PA-28-181 Archer II	28-7990528	N2886A	12. 7.79	W.Walsh & S.R.Mitchell	Liverpool	3. 7.03T
G-BGWC	Robin DR.400/180 Regent	1420		26. 6.79	P.R.Deacon	Frinsted	29. 5.04T
G-BGWH*	Piper PA-18-150 Super Cub	18-7605	ST-ABR G-ARSR/N10F	18. 6.79	V.D.Speck	Clacton	14. 6.93T
	(Damaged Clacton 7.7.92: stored 10.99: cancelled 17.5.01 by CAA: current status unknown)						
G-BGWJ	Sikorsky S-61N Mk.II	61-819		20. 8.79	Bristow Helicopters Ltd *"Monadh Mor"*	Faeroe Isles	4. 6.04T
G-BGWK	Sikorsky S-61N Mk.II	61-820	N1346C G-BGWK	10. 9.79	Bristow Helicopters Ltd *"Dunrobin"*	Aberdeen	28.11.02T
G-BGWM	Piper PA-28-181 Archer II	28-7990458	N2817Y	29. 6.79	Thames Valley Flying Club Ltd	Turweston	10. 5.03T
G-BGWN	Piper PA-38-112 Tomahawk	38-79A0918	N9693N	2. 7.79	Teesside Flight Centre Ltd	Teesside	25. 3.02T
G-BGWO	Jodel D.112 *(Built Ets Valladeau)*	227	F-BHGQ	22. 6.79	R.C.Williams t/a G-BGWO Group	Breighton	4. 6.02P
G-BGWR	Cessna U206A Super Skywagon	U206-0653	G-DISC G-BGWR/PH-OTD/N4953F	6. 7.79	The Parachute Centre Ltd	Tilstock	25. 1.04
G-BGWS	Enstrom 280C Shark	1050		8.11.76	R.L.Heath t/a Whisky Sierra Helicopters	Goodwood	6. 2.04T
G-BGWU	Piper PA-38-112 Tomahawk	38-79A0788	N9703N	2. 7.79	J.S. & L.M.Markey	Draycott Farm, Chiseldon	1. 2.04
G-BGWV	Aeronca 7AC Champion	7AC-4082	OO-GRI OO-TWR	23. 8.79	J.A.Webb t/a RFC Flying Group *(Damaged Popham 8.6.86: current status unknown)*	(Alton)	10.10.86P
G-BGWW	Piper PA-23-250 Turbo Aztec E	27-4587	OO-ABH N13971	15. 6.79	Kathleen Hobbs t/a Aldergrove Flight Training Centre	Belfast	28. 9.01T
G-BGWY	Thunder Ax6-56Z HAFB	229		23. 8.79	P.J.Eley	Braintree	19. 8.95A

G-BGWZ*	Eclipse Super Eagle	ESE.007		29. 6.79	Fleet Air Arm Museum	RNAS Yeovilton	
					(Cancelled 5.12.83 as WFU)		
G-BGXA	Piper J-3C-65 Cub (L-4H-PI)	10762	F-BGXA	1. 3.78	E.C. & P.King	Kemble	29.11.02P
	(Frame No.10587 - regd with c/n 11170)		Fr.AF/43-29471		*(As "329471/F/44" in USAAC c/s)*		
G-BGXB	Piper PA-38-112 Tomahawk	38-79A1007	N9728N	2. 7.79	Signtest Ltd	Cardiff	16. 8.04T
G-BGXC	SOCATA TB-10 Tobago	35		19.10.79	D.H.Courtley	Alderney	12. 8.04
G-BGXD	SOCATA TB-10 Tobago	39		19.10.79	D.F.P.Finan	Teesside	31. 5.04T
G-BGXJ	Partenavia P.68B	189		6. 9.79	Cecil Aviation Ltd	Cambridge	3.10.02
G-BGXN	Piper PA-38-112 Tomahawk	38-79A0898	N9708N	5. 7.79	Panshanger School of Flying Ltd		24. 8.91T
	(Damaged 1991: stored for rebuild 4.98: scrapped and all remains gone by 10.01: valid CofR 4.01)						
G-BGXO	Piper PA-38-112 Tomahawk	38-79A0982	N9703N	5. 7.79	Goodwood Road Racing Co Ltd	Goodwood	12. 2.02T
G-BGXR	Robin HR.200/100	53	F-BVYH	1.10.79	M. Miles t/a Exray Group	Southampton	27.11.01
G-BGXS	Piper PA-28-236 Dakota	28-7911198	N2836Z	12. 7.79	Bawtry Road Service Station Ltd	Gamston	23. 3.01T
G-BGXT	SOCATA TB-10 Tobago	40		3.10.79	D.A.H.Morris	Wolverhampton	30. 9.04
G-BGYN	Piper PA-18-150 Super Cub	18-7709137	N62747	19. 7.79	B.J.Dunford	Long Wood, Morestead	26. 4.01
G-BGYR	Hawker Siddeley HS.125 Srs.F600B		G-5-11	3.12.79	BAE Systems (Operations) Ltd	Warton	10.10.02
		256045	EC-CQT/G-5-18				
G-BGYT	Embraer EMB-110P1 Bandeirante		N104VA	11.10.79	Keenair Charter Ltd	Blackpool	12. 1.02T
		110.234	G-BGYT/PT-SAA		*(Keenair c/s)*		
G-BGZF	Piper PA-38-112 Tomahawk	38-79A1015	N9700N	26. 7.79	Metropolitan Services Ltd	Hawarden	15. 2.04T
G-BGZJ*	Piper PA-38-112 Tomahawk	38-79A0999	N9665N	7. 9.79	Midland Aircraft Maintenance Ltd		
						Bourne Park, Hurstbourne Tarrant	14. 6.92T
	(Damaged Cambridge 5.8.90: cancelled 25.2.97 by CAA: stored for spares 10.01)						
G-BGZL	Eiri PIK.20E	20218		21. 8.79	F.Casolari	(Castellarano, Italy)	9. 8.04
G-BGZO*	SEEMS MS.880B Rallye Club	378	F-BKZO	24.10.79	Not known	(Shoreham)	9. 4.92
	(Damaged East Meon, Petersfield 3.5.89: stored 12.92: cancelled 3.2.95 by CAA: current status unknown)						
G-BGZW	Piper PA-38-112 Tomahawk	38-79A1068	N9674N	1. 8.79	Cheshire Flying Services Ltd t/a Ravenair	Manchester	11.12.04T
G-BGZY	Jodel Wassmer D.120 Paris-Nice	118	F-BIQU	17. 8.79	M.Hale	(La Trinite Sur Mer, France)	7. 6.02P
G-BGZZ	Thunder Ax6-56 Bolt HAFB	220		10. 8.79	J M.Eaton & K A Wilmore *(New owners 12.01)*		
						Milton-under-Wychwood	16. 7.94A

G-BHAA – G-BHZZ

G-BHAA	Cessna 152 II	15281330	N49809	12. 2.79	Herefordshire Aero Club Ltd	Shobdon	16. 3.03T
G-BHAC	Cessna A152 Aerobat	A1520776	N7595B	12. 2.79	Herefordshire Aero Club Ltd	Shobdon	17. 4.03T
G-BHAD	Cessna A152 Aerobat	A1520807	N7390L	12. 2.79	Shropshire Aero Club Ltd	Sleap	11. 4.03T
					(Substantially damaged Tatenhill 16.6.00)		
G-BHAI	Reims Cessna F152 II	F15201625	(D-EJAY)	14. 8.79	Fraggle Leasing Ltd	Edinburgh	14.10.01T
G-BHAJ	Robin DR.400/160 Major 80	1430		22. 8.79	Rowantask Ltd	Rochester	15. 3.04T
G-BHAM*	Thunder Ax6-56 Bolt HAFB	251		28. 1.80	D.M. & K.R.Sandford	Stockport	7. 4.86A
					"Levitation" (Cancelled 4.12.01 by CAA) (Stored 2002)		
G-BHAR	Westland-Bell 47G-3B1	WA/353	XT194	7. 8.79	J.Bird & R.Cove	Cranfield	16.11.03
	(Line No.WAN/44)						
G-BHAT*	Thunder Ax7-77 Bolt HAFB	250		28. 1.80	Balloon Preservation Group	Kirdford	6. 2.83A
					"Witter" (Cancelled 29.4.93 as WFU)		
G-BHAV	Reims Cessna F152 II	F15201633		15. 8.79	T.M. & M.L.Jones t/a Derby Aero Club	Derby	13. 8.01T
G-BHAW	Reims Cessna F172N Skyhawk II			15. 8.79	E.Alexander	(Braintree)	19. 6.04T
		F17201858					
G-BHAX	Enstrom F-28C-2-UK	486-2	N5689N	22.10.79	J.L.Ferguson	South Wirral	21. 3.02
G-BHAY	Piper PA-28RT-201 Arrow IV		N2910N	17. 8.79	Alpha Yankee Ltd	Newcastle	26. 3.04
		28R-7918213					
G-BHBA	Campbell Cricket	SMI/1		15. 8.79	G.J.Layzell	Quedgeley, Glos	13. 9.02P
	(Rotax 503)						
G-BHBB*	Colting 77A HAFB	77A-012	EI-BFG	14. 9.79	Not known	NK	
					(Cancelled 19.5.93 by CAA: tethered 5.99)		
G-BHBE	Westland-Bell 47G-3B1	WA/422	XT510	29.10.79	T.R.Smith (Agricultural Machinery) Ltd		
	(Soloy conversion) (Line No.WAP/136)					Dereham	21.12.01
G-BHBF	Sikorsky S-76A II Plus	760022	N4247S	9.11.79	Bristow Helicopters Ltd	North Denes	2. 1.04T
					"Spirit of Paris"		
G-BHBG	Piper PA-32R-300 Cherokee Lance		N408RC	18. 9.79	L.T.Halpin	Leicester	4. 6.00T
		32R-7780515	N9590N				
G-BHBI	Mooney M.20J (201)	24-0842	N4764H	24. 9.79	A.M.McGlone t/a G-BHBI Group	Biggin Hill	10. 4.03
G-BHBT	Marquart MA-5 Charger	PFA 068-10190		3. 9.79	R.G. & C.J.Maidment	Jackals Farm, Sussex	6..9.02P
G-BHBZ	Partenavia P.68B Victor	191		10. 9.79	P.C.Hamer & P.C.W.Landau	Sturgate	31. 3.02
G-BHCA*	Fokker D.VIII rep			7. 3.80	Not known	St Just	
		HA/01 & PFA 082-10358			*(As "124" in German A/F c/s)*		
	(Destroyed near White Waltham 21.8.81: cancelled 4.2.87 by CAA: wreck noted 7.01)						
G-BHCC	Cessna 172M Skyhawk II	17266711	(G-BGLY)	26.10.79	Langtry Flying Group Ltd	Bournemouth	16. 6.02T
			N80713				
G-BHCE	SAN Jodel D.117A	381	F-BHME	1.10.79	D.M.Parsons t/a Parwebb Flying Group *(Stored unmarked 4.01)*	Gloucestershire	27. 2.85P

G-BHCM	Reims Cessna F172H	F172-0468	SE-FBD	25. 9.79	J. Dominic	Denham	24. 4.04
G-BHCP	Reims Cessna F152 II	F15201640		31.10.79	D.Copley	Sandtoft	12.10.98T
G-BHCX*	Reims Cessna F152 II	F15201642		24. 9.79	Not known	Biggin Hill	
		(Damaged in storms on 16.10.87: cancelled 27.6.94 as destroyed: wreck noted unmarked 4.01)					
G-BHCZ	Piper PA-38-112 Tomahawk	38-78A0321	N214MD	26. 9.79	Jennifer E.Abbott	Goodwood	2.10.03
G-BHDD	Vickers V.668 Varsity T.1		WL626	18.10.79	G.Vale *(As "WL626/P": to Aeropark)*	East Midlands	
G-BHDE	SOCATA TB-10 Tobago	58		2. 1.80	Alpha-Alpha Ltd	Liverpool	8. 3.04
	(Went off end of runway landing Caernarfon 16.7.01: struck barbed-wire fence, damaging both wings & propeller)						
G-BHDK*	Boeing TB-29A-45-BN Superfortress	11225	44-61748	27. 9.79	Imperial War Museum *(As "461748/Y" in USAF c/s) "Hawg Wild"*	Duxford	
G-BHDM	Reims Cessna F152 II	F15201684		15.10.79	Tayside Aviation Ltd	Dundee	19. 4.04T
G-BHDP	Reims Cessna F182Q Skylane	F18200131		15.10.79	Zone Travel Ltd	Turweston	21.12.02
G-BHDR	Reims Cessna F152 II	F15201680		15.10.79	Tayside Aviation Ltd	Dundee	5. 7.04T
G-BHDS	Reims Cessna F152 II	F15201682		15.10.79	Tayside Aviation Ltd	Dundee	8. 7.02T
G-BHDU	Reims Cessna F152 II	F15201681		15.10.79	A.S.Bamrah t/a Falcon Flying Services	Biggin Hill	29. 5.04T
G-BHDV	Cameron V-77 HAFB	585		1. 2.80	P.Glydon *"Dormouse"*	Barnt Green, Birmingham	16. 6.02A
G-BHDW	Reims Cessna F152 II	F15201652		15.10.79	Tayside Aviation Ltd	Dundee	30. 5.04T
G-BHDX	Reims Cessna F172N Skyhawk II	F17201889		5.10.79	J.Mitchell t/a Skyhawk DX Group	Newtownards, Co.of Down	28. 6.04
G-BHDZ	Reims Cessna F172N Skyhawk II	F17201911		3.12.79	Arrow Flying Ltd.	Denham	15. 5.04T
G-BHEC	Reims Cessna F152 II	F15201676		3.12.79	Stapleford Flying Club Ltd	Stapleford	19. 7.04T
G-BHED	Reims Cessna FA152 Aerobat	FA1520359		3.12.79	TG Aviation Ltd *(Op Thanet Flying Club)*	Manston	1. 5.04T
G-BHEG	SAN Jodel 150 Mascaret	46	PH-ULS OO-SET	3. 7.80	D.M.Griffiths	RAF Mona	25. 6.02P
G-BHEH*	Cessna 310G	310G-0016	N1720 N8916Z	14. 4.80	Not known *(Cancelled 24.8.00 as wfu: fuselage on fire dump 4.01)*	Shoreham	9.12.96
G-BHEK	Scintex CP.1315-C3 Super Emeraude	923	F-BJMU	11.10.79	D.B.Winstanley	Barton	9.11.00P
G-BHEL	SAN Jodel D.117	735	F-BIOA	8.10.79	N.Wright & C.M.Kettlewell	Queach Farm, Bury St.Edmunds	22. 1.02P
G-BHEM	Bensen B.8MV (Rotax 503)	EK.14 & PFA G/01-1016		8.10.79	G.C.Kerr	(Great Orton)	5.10.00P
G-BHEN	Reims Cessna FA152 Aerobat	FA1520363		3. 1.80	Leicestershire Aero Club Ltd	Leicester	3.12.01T
G-BHER	SOCATA TB-10 Tobago	60	4X-AKK G-BHER	19.10.79	Air Touring Ltd	Gloucestershire	20. 7.03T
G-BHEU	Thunder Ax7-65 Srs.1 HAFB	238		16.10.79	D.G.Such *"Polomoche"*	Birmingham	18. 5.02A
G-BHEV	Piper PA-28R-200 Cherokee Arrow II	28R-7435159	PH-BOY N41244	23.10.79	P.Hardy t/a 7-Up Group	Nottingham	12. 4.03T
G-BHEX	Colt 56A HAFB	056		15.10.79	A.S.Dear, R.B.Green & W.S.Templeton *"Superwasp"* t/a Hale Hot-Air Balloon Group	Fordingbridge	11.11.98A
G-BHEZ	SAN Jodel 150 Mascaret	22	F-BLDO	31. 1.80	A.Shorter t/a Air Yorkshire Group	Sherburn in Elmet	20. 6.02P
G-BHFC	Reims Cessna F152 II	1436		7. 4.78	TG Aviation Ltd *(Op Thanet Flying Club)*	Manston	1. 8.02T
G-BHFE	Piper PA-44-180 Seminole	44-7995324	ADAF 005 G-BHFE/N2383U	22.10.79	Grunwick Ltd *(Op Bonus Aviation)*	Cranfield	24. 1.03T
G-BHFF	Dormois Jodel D.112	322	F-BEKJ	19.10.79	P.A.Dowell	Garston Farm, Marshfield	28. 3.02P
	(Force landed 4 nm W Marlborough 1.9.01 due to engine failure: damage to port undercarriage, port wing & engine)						
G-BHFG	SNCAN Stampe SV-4C	45	F-BJDN Fr.Mil	31.10.79	Stormswift Ltd	Gloucestershire	7.10.01T
G-BHFH	Piper PA-34-200T Seneca II	34-7970482	N8075Q	23.10.79	G-WATS Aviation Ltd	Wolverhampton	14. 2.04T
G-BHFI	Reims Cessna F152 II	1685		22.10.79	R.Bilson & D.Turner t/a BAe Warton Flying Club	Blackpool	8. 4.04T
G-BHFJ	Piper PA-28RT-201T Turbo Arrow IV	28R-7931298	N8072R	22.10.79	J.K.Beauchamp	White Waltham	30. 9.04
G-BHFK	Piper PA-28-151 Cherokee Warrior	28-7615088	N8325C	12.12.79	Ilkeston Car Sales Ltd	Jericho Farm, Lambley	25. 3.04
G-BHFR	Eiri PIK-20E Srs.1	20228	(D-KHJR) G-BHFR	8.11.79	J.T.Morgan *"FR"*	Husbands Bosworth	5. 8.01
G-BHFS	Robin DR.400/180 Regent	1304		7. 3.78	C.J.Moss	Shoreham	4.11.02
G-BHGC	Piper PA-18-150 Super Cub	18-8793	PH-NKH N4447Z	3. 4.79	Vectis Gliding Club Ltd	Sandown	28. 2.03
G-BHGF	Cameron V-56 HAFB	574		5.11.79	P.Spellward *"Biggles"*	Bristol	29. 8.00A
G-BHGJ	Jodel Wassmer D.120 Paris-Nice	336	F-BOYB	15. 1.80	Q.M.B.Oswell	RAF Halton	12. 4.02P
G-BHGK	Sikorsky S-76A II Plus	760049	N1545Y	27. 3.80	Scotia Helicopter Services Ltd	North Denes	8. 5.03T

G-BHGO	Piper PA-32-260 Cherokee Six	32-7800007	PH-BGP N9656C	16.11.79	DDCS Ltd *(Op Cherokee Six Group)*	Newcastle	30. 9.04
	(Damaged in hangar fire on 5.2.01, to Leeds by road 16.03.01 - not yet returned 12.01)						
G-BHGP	SOCATA TB-10 Tobago	100		17. 1.80	D.Suleyman	Stapleford	12. 5.02
G-BHGX*	Colt 56B HAFB	057		22.11.79	M.N.Dixon *"Prospect"* *(Cancelled 6.11.01 as wfu & stored)*	Bicester	22. 7.90A
G-BHGY	Piper PA-28R-200-2 Cherokee Arrow II	28R-7435086	PH-NSL N57365	23.11.79	V.Humphries	Nottingham	5. 8.04
G-BHHB	Cameron V-77 HAFB	170		26.11.79	R.M.Powell *"Pax"*	Stockbridge	20. 6.02T
G-BHHE	CEA Jodel DR.1051/M1 Sicile Record	628	F-BMZC	26. 4.80	P.Bridges	Hamilton Farm, Kent	6.12.04
G-BHHG	Reims Cessna F152 II	F15201725		4. 3.80	TG Aviation Ltd *(Op Thanet Flying Club)*	Manston	5. 7.04T
G-BHHH	Thunder Ax7-65 Bolt HAFB	245		5.12.79	C.A.Hendley (Essex) Ltd *"Christmas"*	Loughton	27. 9.87A
G-BHHK	Cameron N-77 HAFB	547		5.12.79	I.S.Bridge *"Shadowfax II"*	Shrewsbury	7.12.87A
G-BHHN	Cameron V-77 HAFB	549		29.11.79	P.Gooch t/a The Itchen Valley Balloon Group *"Valley Crusader"*	Alresford, Hants	5. 5.02A
G-BHHX	Jodel D.112 *(Built Ets Valladeau)*	223	F-BFAJ	19. 2.80	B.P.Harrison t/a Hotel X-Ray F/Group	Dunkeswell	11.12.02P
G-BHHZ	Rotorway Scorpion 133 (Rotorway 133)	MSI.1195		12.12.79	L.W. & O.Underwood *(Stored 12.94: current status unknown)*	Stoneacre Farm, Farthing Corner	23. 9.81P
G-BHIB	Reims Cessna F182Q Skylane II	F18200134		18.12.79	S.N.Chater & B.Payne	Sherburn-in-Elmet	16. 4.03
G-BHIC	Reims Cessna F182Q Skylane II	F18200135		18.12.79	W W, J B & D S Alton t/a W.F.Alton & Son	Sherburn-in-Elmet	16. 6.02
G-BHIG	Colt 31A Air Chair HAFB	060	SE-... G-BHIG	12.12.79	P.A.Lindstrand *(Op S.Ericsson)*	Upplands Vasby, Sweden	13. 3.00A
G-BHIH	Reims Cessna F172N Skyhawk II	F17201945		3. 1.80	M.A.Wilkinson	Spanhoe	15. 8.04
G-BHII	Cameron V-77 HAFB	548		10.12.79	R.V.Brown *"Tosca"*	Maidenhead	2. 9.96A
G-BHIK	Adam RA.14 Loisirs (Continental A65)	11-bis	F-PHLK	6. 2.80	L.Lewis *(Damaged near Lancaster 17.4.85: stored 1.02)*	(Redcar)	20. 8.85P
G-BHIN*	Reims Cessna F152 II	F15201715		28. 1.80	P.Skinner *(Noted wrecked 6.99: cancelled as WFU 4.11.99)*	Derby	7. 7.98T
G-BHIR	Piper PA-28R-200 Cherokee Arrow	28R-35614	SE-FHP	21. 2.80	Factorcore Ltd *(Op Manchester School of Flying)*	Woodford	6.12.04T
G-BHIS	Thunder Ax7-65 Bolt HAFB	254		26.11.79	J.R.Wilson t/a The Hedgehoppers Balloon Group *"Yo-Yo"*	Didcot	21. 3.96A
G-BHIT	SOCATA TB-9 Tampico	63		7.12.79	C.J.P.Webster	Biggin Hill	31. 1.01T
G-BHIY	Reims Cessna F150K	F15000627	F-BRXR	18.12.79	G.J.Ball	Old Sarum	17. 4.04
G-BHJA	Cessna A152 Aerobat	A1520835	N4954A	11. 3.80	Cornwall Flying Club Ltd	Bodmin	9. 4.92T
	(Damaged Bodmin 21.7.90: stored 5.98: current status unknown)						
G-BHJB	Cessna A152 Aerobat	A1520856	N4662A	11. 3.80	Flight Ltd	Netherthorpe	13. 4.02T
G-BHJF	SOCATA TB-10 Tobago	83		2. 1.80	P.Crutchfield t/a Flying Fox Group	Blackbushe	26. 9.03
G-BHJI	Mooney M.20J (201)	24-0925	N3753H	11. 2.80	G Harding *(New owner 12.01)*	(Worksop)	19.12.98
G-BHJK	Maule M-5-235C Lunar Rocket	7296C	N56359	25. 2.80	T.P.Spurge	Great Oakley	23. 2.02
G-BHJN	Sportavia Fournier RF4D	4021	F-BORH	3. 1.80	G.E.Reeman & G.R.Beers t/a RF4 Flying Group	Enstone	19. 9.02P
G-BHJO	Piper PA-28-161 Cherokee Warrior II	28-7816213	OO-FLD N9507N/N6034H	4. 1.80	J.G.Chree, K.J.Utting & A.Sangster t/a The Brackla Flying Group	Inverness	12. 5.04
G-BHJS	Partenavia P.68B	172	I-KLUB	28.12.79	J.J.Watts & D.Fletcher	Bournemouth	1. 7.04T
G-BHJU	Robin DR.400 2+2	1288	D-ECDK	9. 1.80	J.Barlow & P.Crow t/a Ageless Aeronauts	Lydd	29. 5.04
G-BHKE	Bensen B.8MS	VW.1 & PFA G/01-1009		7. 1.80	N.B.Gray	(Great Orton)	
G-BHKH	Cameron O-65 HAFB	592		7. 1.80	D.G.Body t/a Mid-Bucks Farmers Balloon Group *"Daisy"*	Leighton Buzzard	11. 8.96A
G-BHKJ	Cessna 421C Golden Eagle III *(Robertson STOL conversion)*	421C0848	(N26596)	25. 1.80	Totaljet Ltd	Blackpool	10. 9.04T
G-BHKN*	Colt 14A Cloudhopper HAFB *(Officially regd as Colt 12A)*	068		17. 1.80	British Balloon Museum & Library *"Green Ice 2" (Cancelled 5.12.89 as WFU)*	Newbury	
G-BHKR*	Colt 14A Cloudhopper HAFB *(Officially regd as Colt 12A)*	071		17. 1.80	British Balloon Museum & Library *"Green Ice 5" (Cancelled 5.12.89 as WFU)*	Newbury	
G-BHKT	Wassmer Jodel D.112	1265	F-BMIQ	10. 1.80	K.A.Stewart & G.Oldfield t/a The Evans Flying Group	Croft Farm, Darlington	19.10.01P
G-BHKV*	Gulfstream AA-5A Cheetah	AA5A-0894	N27465	31. 1.80	Not known	Biggin Hill	24. 4.95T
	(Damaged Deanland 11.6.94: cancelled 14.9.94 by CAA) (On rebuild 9.94: current status unknown)						
G-BHLE	Robin DR.400/180 Regent	1466		25. 1.80	B.D.Greenwood	Ronaldsway	16. 5.04
G-BHLH	Robin DR.400/180 Regent	1320	F-GBIG	11. 2.80	P.E.Davis	Netherthorpe	1. 7.04
G-BHLJ	Saffery-Rigg S.200 Skyliner MLB	IAR/01		23. 1.80	I.A.Rigg *"Skyliner"*	Manchester	

G-BHLT	de Havilland DH.82A Tiger Moth	84997	ZS-DGA	9. 6.80	P.J. & A.J.Borsberry		
	(Regd as c/n "911")		SAAF2272/T6697			Kidmore End, Reading	26. 2.90
					(On rebuild 8.90: current status unknown)		
G-BHLU	Alpavia Fournier RF3	79	F-BMTN	14. 4.80	Skyview Systems Ltd	(Sudbury)	12.11.01P
G-BHLW	Cessna 120	10210	N73005	24. 3.80	L.W.Scattergood	Sherburn in Elmet	12. 9.02P
	(Continental C85)		NC73005		*"Sky Ranger"*		
G-BHLX	Grumman-American AA-5B Tiger	AA5B-0573	OY-GAR	1. 2.80	M.D.McPherson	Cranfield	28. 6.04T
G-BHMA	SIPA 903	61	OO-FAE	13. 3.80	H.J.Taggart	Ballymoney, Co.Antrim	18. 5.98P
			F-BGBK				
G-BHMG	Reims Cessna FA152 Aerobat	FA1520368		10. 6.80	R.D.Smith	Popham	19. 4.02
G-BHMH*	Reims Cessna FA152 Aerobat	FA1520367		16. 5.80	Not known	Biggin Hill	
			(Damaged Hale Farm, Chiddingstone 22.9.86: cancelled 9.8.89 as WFU: noted 4.01)				
G-BHMI	Reims Cessna F172N Skyhawk II	F17202036	G-WADE	6. 8.80	GMI Aviation Ltd	Blackpool	9. 3.02T
			G-BHMI				
G-BHMJ	Avenger T.200-2112 MLB	002		29. 1.80	R.Light *"Lord Anthony I"*	Stockport	
G-BHMK	Avenger T.200-2112 MLB	003		29. 1.80	P.Kinder *"Lord Anthony II"*	Stockport	
G-BHMR	Stinson 108-3 Station Wagon	108-4352	F-BABO	12. 2.80	D.G.French	Sandown	23.11.90
			F-DABO/NC6352M		*(Stored 6.01)*		
G-BHMT	Evans VP-1	PFA 062-10473		18. 2.80	P.E.J.Sturgeon	Chestnut Farm, Tipps End	14. 6.01P
	(VW 1834)						
G-BHMY	Fokker F.27 Friendship 200	10196	F-GBDK	6. 5.80	(City of Norwich Aviation Museum)		
			(F-GBRV)/PK-PFS/JA8606/PH-FDL			Norwich	22. 5.99T
			(Cancelled 4.10.95 as WFU) (Donated by KLM (UK) Ltd 8.00, less engines)				
G-BHNA	Reims Cessna F152 II	F15201683		12. 2.80	Sheffield Aero Club Ltd	Sturgate	19.12.03T
G-BHNC	Cameron O-65 HAFB	588		7. 2.80	D. & C.Bareford	Kidderminster	5. 3.94A
					"Hot N'Cold"		
G-BHND	Cameron N-65 HAFB	582		7. 2.80	S.M.Wellband	Frome	24. 6.89A
G-BHNG*	Piper PA-23-250 Aztec E	27-7405432	N54125	13. 5.80	Riverside Metals Ltd		
	(Crashed Shoreham 19.12.81: cancelled by CAA 12.12.86:*.fuselage stored 3.97)*					Cradle Hill, Seaford	11. 8.83T
G-BHNK	Jodel Wassmer D.120A Paris-Nice	243	F-BLNK	26. 3.80	D.A.Bates	St.Marys, Isles of Scilly	12. 3.02P
					t/a G-BHNK Flying Group		
G-BHNL	Wassmer Jodel D.112	1206	F-BLNL	30. 1.80	J.C.Mansell	Watchford Farm, Yarcombe	15.10.02P
G-BHNO	Piper PA-28-181 Archer II	28-8090211	N81413	7. 2.80	Airfluid Hydraulics & Pneumatics (Wolverhampton) Ltd		
						Sleap	28. 6.04
G-BHNP	Eiri PIK-20E Srs.1	20253		29. 2.80	D.A.Sutton *"NP"*	Sackville Farm, Riseley	26. 5.02
G-BHNV	Westland-Bell 47G-3B1	WA/700	F-GHNM	11. 3.80	Leyline Helicopters Ltd	(Billingham)	28. 5.89T
	(Line No.WAT/222)		G-BHNV/XW180				
G-BHNX	SAN Jodel D.117	493	F-BHNX	7. 9.78	A.J.Chalkley	(Pwllheli)	12. 1.87P
					(On rebuild 4.91: current status unknown)		
G-BHOA	Robin DR.400/160 Major 80	1478		27. 1.80	M.L.Sargeant	Goudhurst	1. 9.02
G-BHOH	Sikorsky S-61N Mk.II	61-827		25. 4.80	Bristow Helicopters Ltd	Aberdeen	20. 5.02T
					"Ben Avon"		
G-BHOJ	Colt 14A Cloudhopper HAFB	080		27. 2.80	J.A.Folkes	Oswestry	
	(Re-registered as Colt 12A 10.00)						
G-BHOL	CEA Jodel DR.1050 Ambassadeur	35	F-BJQL	6. 2.80	J.E.Sharkey *"Nicolette"*	Inverness	12.11.04
G-BHOM	Piper PA-18 Super Cub 95	18-1391	OO-PIU	7. 3.80	J.R.Hannen & A.W.Kennedy t/a Oscar Mike Flying Group		
	(L-18C-PI) *(Frame No.18-1272)*		OO-HMT/ALAT 51-15391			Whitehall Farm, Benington	2. 4.02P
G-BHOO	Livesey-Purves Thunder Ax7-65 HAFB	001		26. 2.80	D.Livesey & J.M.Purves	Crayke, York	
					"Scraps"		
G-BHOR	Piper PA-28-161 Warrior II	28-8016331	N82162	12. 6.80	A.J.Harewood	Biggin Hill	26. 6.04
					t/a Oscar Romeo Flying Group		
G-BHOT	Cameron V-65 HAFB	777		15. 9.81	J.A.Baker	Marsh Benham	8. 8.99A
					t/a The Dante Balloon Group *"Le Billet Doux"*		
G-BHOZ	SOCATA TB-9 Tampico	84		11. 3.80	A.N.Hendley	Blackbushe	15. 5.04
G-BHPK	Piper J-3C-65 Cub (L-4A-PI)	8979	F-BEPK	26. 2.80	L.B.Smith	Priory Farm, Tibenham	15. 3.02P
			Fr.Mil/42-38410		t/a L4 Group *(As "236800/44/A" in USAAF c/s)*		
	(Frame No.9098: official c/n is 12161/44-79865 which is F-BFYU)						
G-BHPL	CASA I-131E Jungmann	1058	E3B-350	17. 7.80	R.G.Gray	North Weald	1. 8.02P
					(As "E3B-350/05-97" in Spanish AF c/s)		
G-BHPM	Piper PA-18 Super Cub 95	18-1501	F-BOUR	10. 4.80	P.I.Morgans *(Stored 5.95: current status unknown)*		
	(L-18C-PI) *(Frame No.18-1469)*		ALAT 51-15501			Furze Hill Farm, Rosemarket, Milford Haven	
G-BHPN	Colt 14A Cloudhopper HAFB	081	(SE-)	6. 3.80	Lindstrand Balloons Ltd		
			G-BHPN		*(Op S.Ericsson)*	Upplands Vasby, Sweden	13. 3.00A
G-BHPS	Jodel Wassmer D.120A Paris-Nice	148	F-BIXI	11. 6.80	T.J.Price	Rhigos	21. 6.02P
G-BHPY	Cessna 152 II	15282983	N46009	26. 3.80	Halegreen Associates Ltd		
						Hinton-in-the-Hedges	27. 9.04T
G-BHPZ	Cessna 172N Skyhawk II	17272017	N6411E	26. 3.80	O'Brien Properties Ltd	Shoreham	4.10.02T
G-BHRB	Reims Cessna F152 II	F15201707		20. 3.80	LAC (Enterprises) Ltd	Barton	27. 1.02T
					t/a Lancashire Aero Club		
G-BHRC	Piper PA-28-161 Warrior II	28-7916430	N9527N	3. 4.80	Sherwood Flying Club Ltd	Nottingham	25. 2.04T
G-BHRH	Reims Cessna FA150K Aerobat	FA1500056	PH-ECB	24. 3.80	Merlin Flying Club Ltd	Hucknall	17. 6.02T
			D-ECBL/(D-EKKW)				

G-BHRM	Reims Cessna F152 II	F15201718	F-GCHR	8. 4.80	Aerohire Ltd	Wellesbourne Mountford	27. 9.02T
G-BHRN	Reims Cessna F152 II	F15201728	F-GCHV	8. 4.80	Fraggle Leasing Ltd	Edinburgh	27. 7.02T
G-BHRO	Rockwell Commander 112A	364	N1364J	20. 3.80	John Raymond Transport Ltd	Cardiff	17. 8.04
G-BHRP	Piper PA-44-180 Seminole	44-8095021	N81602	1. 4.80	M.S.Farmers	Leicester	5. 3.04T
G-BHRR	Menavia Piel CP.301A Emeraude	270	F-BISK	28. 3.80	T.W.Offen	Spilsted Farm, Sedlescombe	28. 5.87P
					(Stored 5.01)		
G-BHRW	CEA Jodel DR.221 Dauphin	93	F-BPCP	10. 7.80	M.F.Filer & D.H.Williams	Dunkeswell	13. 4.02
G-BHRY	Colt 56A HAFB	030		2. 4.80	A.S.Davidson	Burton-on-Trent	29. 4.95A
					"Turkish Delight"		
G-BHSA	Cessna 152 II	15283693	(N4889B)	1. 5.80	D.Copley	Sandtoft	11. 4.98T
					(Noted hangared 7.01 in bare metal)		
G-BHSB	Cessna 172N Skyhawk II	17272977	(N1225F)	25. 6.80	ABK Aviation Services Ltd	Leeds-Bradford	3. 1.02T
G-BHSD	Scheibe SF-25E Super Falke	4357	D-KDGG	21. 7.80	Lasham Gliding Society Ltd	Lasham	1. 2.02
G-BHSE	Rockwell Commander 114	14161	N4831W	15. 5.80	604 Squadron Flying Group Ltd	Booker	7. 5.02
			AN-BRL/(N4831W)				
G-BHSL*	CASA I-131E Jungmann	1117	E3B-236	18. 6.80	Not known	Gloucestershire	19. 7.96P
			Spanish AF				
			(Damaged on take off Cranfield on 6.7.96. stored dismantled 4.01)				
G-BHSN	Cameron N-56 HAFB	595		10. 4.80	I.Bentley	Bath	12. 7.02A
G-BHSP	Thunder Ax7-77Z HAFB	272		15. 4.80	G.A.Fisher	Guildford	23. 2.94A
	(Originally built as D-TRIER c/n 221)				t/a Out-Of-The-Blue *"Chicago"*		
G-BHSS	Pitts S-1C Special	C.1461M	N1704	19. 9.80	S.P.A.Hill	Long Marston	10.12.02P
	(Lycoming O-320)						
G-BHSY	CEA Jodel DR.1050 Sicile	546	F-BLZO	6. 5.80	T.R.Allebone	Easton Maudit	10.10.04
G-BHTA	Piper PA-28-236 Dakota	28-8011102	N8197H	22. 4.80	Dakota Ltd	Jersey	23. 9.04
G-BHTC	CEA Jodel DR.1051/M1 Sicile Record	581	F-BMGR	1. 5.80	G.Clark	Garston Farm, Marshfield	20.12.04
G-BHTD	Cessna T188C AGhusky	T188-03338T	(G-BGTN)	18. 4.80	ADS (Aerial) Ltd	(Benfleet)	26. 6.83A
			N2033J				
	(Probably exported/destroyed in Sudan/Egypt area: current status unknown valid CofR 3.01)						
G-BHTG	Thunder Ax6-56 Bolt HAFB	273		18. 4.80	F.R. & Mrs S.H.MacDonald		
					"Halcyon"	Newdigate, Surrey	18.12.91A
G-BHUB*	Douglas C-47A-85DL Dakota	19975	"G-AGIV"	30. 4.80	Imperial War Museum/American Air Museum		
			Sp.AF T3-29/N51V/N9985F/SE-BBH/43-15509			Duxford	
					(Cancelled 19.10.81 as WFU) (As "315509/W7-S" in USAAF c/s)		
G-BHUE	SAN Jodel DR.1050 Ambassadeur	185	F-BERM	21. 4.80	M.J.Harris	(Worcester)	19.10.92
			F-OBRM				
G-BHUG	Cessna 172N Skyhawk II	17272985	N1283F	24. 6.80	F.G.Baulch	Dunkeswell	14. 9.01T
					t/a FGT Aircraft Hire		
G-BHUI	Cessna 152 II	15283144	N46932	27. 5.80	Galair International Ltd		
						Wellesbourne Mountford	16.12.04T
G-BHUJ	Cessna 172N Skyhawk II	17271932	N5752E	27. 5.80	Flightline Ltd	Southend	8. 4.02T
G-BHUM	de Havilland DH.82A Tiger Moth	85453	VT-DGA	9. 6.80	S.G.Towers	Beckwithshaw, Harrogate	9.12.02
			VT-DDN/RIAF/SAAF 4622/DE457				
G-BHUP*	Reims Cessna F152 II	F15201773		2. 5.80	Not known	Stapleford	9.10.89T
		(Damaged near Barton 17.5.89: cancelled 15.2.95 by CAA) (Stored 5.98: current status unknown)					
G-BHUR	Thunder Ax3 Mini Sky Chariot HAFB	277		9. 5.80	B.F.G.Ribbans *"Ben Hur"*	Newbury	31. 8.90A
					(On loan to British Balloon Museum & Library)		
G-BHUU	Piper PA-25-260 Pawnee	25-8056035	N2440Q	28. 5.80	Booker Gliding Club Ltd	Booker	2.11.03
G-BHVB	Piper PA-28-161 Warrior II	28-8016260	N9638N	16. 5.80	Caine Aviation Ltd	Wolverhampton	30. 7.04T
G-BHVF	SAN Jodel 150A Mascaret	11	F-BLDF	28.10.80	J.D.Walton	Swanborough Farm, Lewes	12.11.02P
G-BHVP	Cessna 182Q Skylane II	18267071	N97374	15.12.80	R.J.W.Wood	Gregory Farm, Mirfield	20. 9.04T
G-BHVR	Cessna 172N Skyhawk II	17270196	N738SG	27. 5.80	M.G.Montgomerie	Elstree	7. 6.03T
					t/a G-BHVR Group		
G-BHVV	Piper J-3C-65 Cub (L-4A-PI)	8953	F-BGXF	27. 6.80	I.J.M.Donnelly	Aboyne	3. 7.85P
	(Frame No.9048)		Fr Mil/42-38384		*(Stored 6.00) (New owner 10.01)*		
	(Regd with c/n 10291/43-1430 which was F-BEGF: frames probably exchanged in 1953 rebuild)						
G-BHWA	Reims Cessna F152 II	F15201775		28. 3.80	M.Housley & J.H.Mills	Wickenby	2. 6.04T
					t/a Lincoln Aviation		
G-BHWB	Reims Cessna F152 II	F15201776	(G-BHWA)	14. 4.80	M.Housley & J.H.Mills	Wickenby	20. 8.04T
					t/a Lincoln Aviation		
G-BHWH	Weedhopper JC-24A	0074		23. 4.80	G.A.Clephane	Basingstoke	30.11.86E
	(Fuji-Robin EC-34-PM) *(Modified to JC-24C)*				*"Dream Machine" (As "Bu.126603" in US Navy c/s)*		
G-BHWK	SOCATA MS.880B Rallye Club	870	F-BONK	27. 8.80	L.L.Gayther	Shobdon	16.12.04
G-BHWY	Piper PA-28R-200-2 Cherokee Arrow II	28R-7435059	N56904	17. 6.80	P.R.Gould & R.B.Cheek	Sandown	8. 4.02
					t/a Kilo Foxtrot Flying Group		
G-BHWZ	Piper PA-28-181 Cherokee Archer II	28-7890299	N3379M	8. 4.80	M A Abbott	Bournemouth	3. 7.04T
G-BHXA	Scottish Aviation Bulldog Srs.120/1210	BH120/407	Botswana DF	9. 6.80	Air Plan Flight Equipment Ltd	Barton	25..7.03T
			OD1/G-BHXA				
G-BHXD	Jodel Wassmer D.120 Paris-Nice	258	F-BMIA	3. 7.80	P.H.C.Hall	Manor Farm, Inglesham	31. 8.01P
G-BHXJ*	Nord 1203-2 Norecrin II	103	F-BEMX	23.10.80	Camp Hill Ltd	(Kirklington, Bedale)	
					(For rebuild 1.99: current status unknown)		

G-BHXK	Piper PA-28-140 Cherokee	28-21106	VR-HGB	14. 7.80	J.Moreland t/a GXK Flying Group		
			9V-BAJ/(9M-AOM)			Bourne Park, Hurstbourne Tarrant	1. 6.03
G-BHXL	Evans VP-2	PFA 063-10520		17. 6.80	R.S.Wharton	(Cardiff)	
	(VW 1834)						
G-BHXN*	Van's RV-3			9. 6.80	Not known	Bourn	
		EAA/105098 & PFA 099-10518			*(Cancelled 2.9.91 by CAA: on rebuild 4.99)*		
G-BHXS	Jodel Wassmer D.120 Paris-Nice	133	F-BIXS	27. 8.80	I.R.Willis	Dundee	16.10.02P
G-BHXT*	Thunder Ax6-56Z HAFB	281		2. 7.80	Not known *"Blue Eagle"*	(Wigan)	NE(A)
					(Cancelled 19.5.93 by CAA: noted 2.97)		
G-BHXY	Piper J-3C-65 Cub (L-4H-PI)	11905	D-EAXY	1. 7.80	F.W.Rogers *"Heather"*	Dunkeswell	16.10.02P
	(Frame No.11733)		F-BFQX/44-79609		*(As "479609/PR-L4" in USAAC c/s)*		
G-BHYA	Cessna R182 Skylane RG II	R18200532	N1717R	10. 7.80	Card Tech Ltd	Denham	9. 3.02
G-BHYC	Cessna 172 RG Cutlass II	172RG0404	(N4868V)	24. 6.80	IB Aeroplanes Ltd.	City of Derry	28. 3.02
G-BHYD	Cessna R172K Hawk XP II	R1722734	N736RS	11.12.80	Sylmar Aviation & Services Ltd		
						Lower Wasing Farm, Brimpton	16. 9.02
G-BHYE	Piper PA-34-200T Seneca II		N8225U	27. 6.80	Oxford Aviation Services Ltd	Oxford	10. 6.04T
		34-8070233					
G-BHYF	Piper PA-34-200T Seneca II		N8225V	27. 6.80	Oxford Aviation Services Ltd	Oxford	25.11.02T
		34-8070234					
G-BHYG	Piper PA-34-200T Seneca II		N8225X	30. 6.80	Oxford Aviation Services Ltd	Oxford	9.10.04T
		34-8070235					
G-BHYI	SNCAN Stampe SV-4A	18	F-BAAF	11. 7.80	P.Chamberlain	White Waltham	22.10.03
			Fr.Mil				
G-BHYO	Cameron N-77 HAFB	659		30. 6.80	Adventure Balloon Co Ltd	London W3	8. 5.97A
G-BHYP	Reims Cessna F172M Skyhawk II		OY-BFR	30. 6.80	Avior Ltd	Oxford	16. 6.02T
		F17201108					
G-BHYR	Reims Cessna F172M	F17200922	OY-DZH	30. 6.80	S.D.Undrill	Stapleford	23. 6.99
			SE-FZH/(OH-CFQ)		t/a G-BHYR Group		
G-BHYS*	Piper PA-28-181 Archer II	28-8090319	N8218Y	30. 6.80	Not known	Biggin Hill	22. 8.86T
	(Damaged Biggin Hill 7.12.85: cancelled 24.6.86 as WFU: wreck in open storage 8.97: current status unknown)						
G-BHYV	Evans VP-1	LC.2 & PFA 01569		2. 7.80	L.Chiappi	(Blackburn)	
	(VW 1600)				*(Flown 5.89: stored Blackpool 8.90 - current status unknown)*		
G-BHYX	Cessna 152 II	15281832	N67434	4. 7.80	Stapleford Flying Club Ltd	Stapleford	31. 3.02T
G-BHZE	Piper PA-28-181 Cherokee Archer II		OO-FLR	4.11.80	Zegruppe Ltd	White Waltham	12.12.02T
		28-7890291	(OO-HÇM)/N3053M				
G-BHZH	Reims Cessna F152 II	F15201786		25. 7.80	Plymouth School of Flying Ltd	Plymouth	24. 9.04T
G-BHZK	Grumman-American AA-5B Tiger		N28670	8. 9.80	R.G.Seth-Smith	Elstree	23. 5.02
		AA5B-0743			t/a Zulu Kilo Group		
G-BHZO	Gulfstream AA-5A Cheetah	AA5A-0692	N26750	21. 7.80	A.H.McVicar	Prestwick	23.12.04T
					(Op Prestwick Flight Centre)		
G-BHZR	Scottish Aviation Bulldog Srs.120/1210		OD4	23. 7.80	R Burgess	Haverfordwest	29. 6.03
		BH120/410	Botswana DF/G-BHZR				
G-BHZS	Scottish Aviation Bulldog Srs.120/1210		OD5	23. 7.80	Air Plan Flight Equipment Ltd	Barton	8. 2.99T
		BH120/411	Botswana DF/G-BHZS				
G-BHZT	Scottish Aviation Bulldog Srs.120/1210		OD6	23. 7.80	D.M.Curties	Kemble	18. 2.02T
		BH120/412	Botswana DF/G-BHZT				
G-BHZU	Piper J-3C-65 Cub (L-4B-PI)	9775	F-BETO	17. 7.80	J.K.Tomkinson		
	(Continental O-200-A)		(F-BFKH)/43-914			Brook Farm, Boylestone, Derbyshire	29. 4.02P
	(Regd with Frame No.9606 fitted to F-BETO in 1961 rebuild replacing c/n 13164 ex 45-4424)						
G-BHZV	Jodel Wassmer D.120A Paris-Nice	278	F-BMON	23. 7.80	K.J.Scott		
						Stoneacre Farm, Farthing Corner	26. 6.00P
G-BHZX	Thunder Ax7-69A HAFB	288		25. 7.80	R.J. & H.M.Beattie	Aylesbury	10. 6.94A
					"After Eight"		

G-BIAA – G-BIZZ

G-BIAC	SOCATA Rallye 235E Gabier	13323		17. 7.80	A.Pound	Oakley	18. 6.02T
G-BIAH	Wassmer Jodel D.112	1218	F-BMAH	20. 8.80	D.Mitchell	Muirhouses Farm, Errol	22. 5.02P
G-BIAI	Wallingford WMB.2 Windtracker MLB			1. 7.80	I.Chadwick	Horsham	
		008			t/a Unicorn Group *"Amanda I"*		
G-BIAK	SOCATA TB-10 Tobago	150		17. 7.80	Westmead Business Group Ltd	Biggin Hill	13. 8.03
G-BIAP	Piper PA-16 Clipper	16-732	F-BBGM	25. 6.80	P.J.Bish	Draycott Farm, Chisledon	19. 3.04
	(Frame No.16-733)		F-OAGS				
G-BIAR	Rigg Skyliner II MLB	AKC-59 & IAR/02		9. 7.80	I.A.Rigg	Manchester	
G-BIAU*	Sopwith Pup rep	EMK/002		4. 1.83	Fleet Air Arm Museum	RNAS Yeovilton	13. 9.89P
	(Le Rhone 80hp)				*(Cancelled 10.3.97 as WFU) (As "N6452" in RNAS c/s)*		
G-BIAX	Taylor JT.2 Titch	GFR-1 & PFA 3228		30. 7.80	J.T.Everest	Popham	26. 7.02P
	(Continental O-200)				*(Stored at owner's home during Winter)*		
G-BIAY	Grumman-American AA-5 Traveler		OY-GAD	26. 8.80	S.Martin	Southend	28. 7.02
		AA5-0423	N7123L				
G-BIAZ*	Cameron AT-165 (Helium/Hot-Air) Free Balloon			7. 2.78	British Balloon Museum & Library	Newbury	31.10.78
	(Used for 1978 Atlantic attempt)	400			*"Zanussi"*		
	(Hot Air envelope destroyed Trubenbuch, Austria 14.1.80: inner helium cell envelope held: cancelled 27.5.80)						

G-BIBA	SOCATA TB-9 Tampico	149		17. 7.80	TB Aviation Ltd	Denham	14. 7.00
G-BIBB	Mooney M.20C Mark 21	2803	OH-MOD	22. 7.80	P.M. Breton	Oaksey Park	2.12.01
G-BIBJ	Enstrom 280C-UK-2 Shark	1187		13. 8.80	Tindon Ltd	Little Snoring	30.11.01
G-BIBN	Reims Cessna FA150K Aerobat	FA1500078	F-BSHN	29.10.80	B.V.Mayo	Maypole Farm, Chislet	22.11.01
G-BIBO	Cameron V-65 HAFB	667		7. 8.80	I.Harris *"Diadem"*	Devizes	30. 6.89A
G-BIBS	Cameron P-20 HAFB	671		14. 8.80	Cameron Balloons Ltd	Bristol	
G-BIBT	Gulfstream AA-5B Tiger	AA5B-1047	N4518V	8. 9.80	Vizor Tempered Glass Ltd	(Port Talbot)	12. 7.04
G-BIBW	Reims Cessna F172N Skyhawk II	F17201756		13.10.78	P.T.Fellows & J.C.Waller	Rochester	28. 2.02
G-BIBX	Wallingford WMB.2 Windtracker MLB	9		18. 8.80	I.A.Rigg *"Bumble"*	Manchester	
G-BICD	Taylorcraft J Auster 5	735	F-BFXH MT166	20. 8.80	R.T.Parsons	Beeches Farm, South Scarle	3. 8.02P
G-BICE	North American AT-6C-1NT Harvard IIA	88-9755	FAP1545	3. 9.80	C.M.L.Edwards	Cherry Tree Farm, Monewden	30. 3.00P
			SAAF 7084/EX302/41-33275 *(As "41-33275/CE" in US Army c/s)*				
G-BICG	Reims Cessna F152 II	F15201796		3. 9.80	A.S.Bamrah t/a Falcon Flying Services	Biggin Hill	24. 3.02T
G-BICJ	Monnett Sonerai II			22. 8.80	I.Parr	(Berwick-on-Tweed)	20.10.90P
	(VW 1834) 726 & PFA 015-10531				*(On rebuild 1997)*		
G-BICM	Colt 56A HAFB	095		1. 9.80	W.S.Templeton & R.B.Green t/a The Avon Advertiser Balloon Club *"Ladybird"*	Fordingbridge	6. 7.00A
G-BICP	Robin DR.360 Chevalier	610	F-BSPH	2.10.80	A.E.Smith	Breighton	13. 5.02
G-BICR	Jodel Wassmer D.120A Paris-Nice	135	F-BIXR	5. 9.80	G.L.Perry t/a Beehive Flying Group	White Waltham	23. 5.02P
G-BICS	Robin R.2100A Club	128	F-GBAC	4.12.80	I.Young	Sandown	18. 5.03
G-BICT*	Evans VP-1	PFA 062-10455		12. 8.80	A.C.Combe & D.L.Tribe	RAF Upavon	20. 2.97P
	(Volkswagen 1600)	*(Damaged near Evesham 4.8.96: cancelled 30.4.01 as wfu) (Fuselage only noted 5.01)*					
G-BICU	Cameron V-56 HAFB	680		9. 9.80	S.D.Bather *"Nobby"*	Melksham	7. 5.01A
G-BICW	Piper PA-28-161 Warrior II	28-7916309	N2091U	8.10.80	D.Gellhorn	Blackbushe	15. 2.03
G-BICX	Maule M-5-235C Lunar Rocket	7287C	(G-MAUL(1)) N56352	2. 2.81	A.T.Jeans & J.F.Clarkson	Compton Chamberlayne, Salisbury	1. 7.02
G-BICY	Piper PA-23-160 Apache	23-1640	PH-ACL	26. 9.80	A.M.Lynn	Netherthorpe	9. 7.01T
			N4010P/(PH-ACL)/N4010P/N10F *(Op Busy Bee)*				
G-BIDD	Evans VP-1	PFA 062-10974		27.10.78	Jane Hodgkinson	Thruxton	2.12.00P
	(VW 1600) *(Initially regd with c/n PFA 062-10167 and combined with both projects)*						
G-BIDF	Reims Cessna F172P Skyhawk II	F17202045	(PH-JPO)	18. 9.80	E.Alexander	King's Farm, Thurrock	6. 6.03T
G-BIDG	SAN Jodel 150A Mascaret	08	F-BLDG	11. 9.80	D.R.Gray	Barton	26. 6.02P
G-BIDH	Cessna 152 II	15280546	G-DONA G-BIDH/N25234	12. 9.80	C.Clark-Monks	(Richmond)	23. 6.02T
G-BIDI	Piper PA-28R-201 Arrow III	28R-7837135	N3759M	11.11.80	Ambrit Ltd	Elstree	9. 5.02
G-BIDJ	Piper PA-18A-150 Super Cub	18-6007	PH-MAY N7798D	22. 9.80	Flight Solutions Ltd	Panshanger	13. 7.03T
	(Frame No.18-6089)						
G-BIDK	Piper PA-18-150 Super Cub	"18-6591"	PH-MAI	22. 9.80	J.& M.A.McCullough		
	(L-21A-PI)		R.Neth AF R-211/51-15679/N7194K			Newtownards, Co.of Down	19. 8.01
	(This is a composite aircraft - PH-MAI was originally c/n 18-6591 (Frame No.18-6714) ex LN-TVB/N9285D but was rebuilt in 1976 using Frame No.18-503 (c/n 18-565) and ex R.Neth AF R-211 as shown)						
G-BIDO*	Piel CP.301A Emeraude	327	F-POIO	25. 3.81	A.R.Plumb *(Stored 5.00: cancelled 21.5.01 by CAA)*	Hill Farm, Nayland	24. 6.97P
G-BIDU	Cameron V-77 HAFB	660		8. 1.81	E.Eleazor *"Margaret"*	Windermere, Cumbria	26. 8.87A
G-BIDV*	Colt 17A Cloudhopper HAFB	789		29. 1.79	British Balloon Museum & Library *"Smirnoff" (Cancelled 20.5.93 by CAA)*	Newbury	NE(A)
	(Originally was Colt 14A c/n 034)						
G-BIDW*	Sopwith "1 ½" Strutter rep	WA/5	"9382"	24. 9.80	RAF Museum	Hendon	29.12.80P
	(Le Clerget)				*(Cancelled 4.2.87 by CAA) (As "A8226" in 45 Sqn RFC c/s)*		
G-BIDX	Dormois Jodel D.112	876	F-BIQY	19. 9.80	P.Turton & H.C.Peake-Jones	Ash House Farm, Winsford	23.10.01P
G-BIEF	Cameron V-77 HAFB	679		25. 9.80	D.S.Bush *"Daedalus"*	Hertingfordbury, Herts	6. 3.94A
G-BIEJ	Sikorsky S-76A II Plus	760097		21.10.80	Bristow Helicopters Ltd *"Glenlossie"*	North Denes	21. 2.01T
G-BIEN*	Jodel Wassmer D.120A Paris-Nice	218	F-BKNK	3. 6.81	R.J.Baker *"The Lady Savage"*	Andrewsfield	14. 4.00P
		(Cancelled 21.2.01 by CAA: stored after dispute over ownership & hangarage fees 12.01)					
G-BIEO	Wassmer Jodel D.112	1296	F-BMOK	19. 3.82	S.C.Solley t/a Clipgate Flyers	Clipgate Farm, Denton	6. 8.01P
G-BIES	Maule M-5-235C Lunar Rocket	7334C	N56394	24. 7.81	W.Procter t/a William Procter Farms	Stowes Farm, Tillingham	25. 3.03
G-BIET	Cameron O-77 HAFB	674		30. 9.80	G.M.Westley *"Archimedes"*	London SW15	11. 1.02A
G-BIEY	Piper PA-28-151 Cherokee Warrior	28-7715213	PH-KDH OO-HCB/N9540N	10.11.80	A.S.Bamrah t/a Falcon Flying Services	Southend	15. 2.04T
G-BIFA	Cessna 310R II	310R1606	N36868	29. 1.81	J.S.Lee	Denham	17. 9.03
G-BIFB	Piper PA-28-150 Cherokee C	28-1968	4X-AEC	6.10.80	N.A.Ayub *(Withdrawn from use 5.01)*	Biggin Hill	12.12.98T

G-BIFN	Bensen B.8MR	KW.1 & PFA G/01-1010		7.10.80	B.Gunn	(North Ferriby)	
G-BIFO	Evans VP-1 (VW 1834)	PFA 062-10411		29. 9.80	R.Broadhead	Bagby	11. 9.02P
G-BIFY	Reims Cessna F150L	F15000829	PH-CEZ	9.10.80	B.W.Davis t/a Astra Associates	Panshanger	21. 8.02T
G-BIFZ	Partenavia P.68C	229		24. 6.81	Eli Sud SRL	(Salerno, Italy)	22.12.02T
G-BIGF*	Thunder Ax7-77 Bolt HAFB	295		20.10.80	M.D.Steuer & C A.Allen	Monmouth	6. 9.91A
	"Low Rider" (Cancelled 6.11.01 as wfu: current status unknown)						
G-BIGJ	Reims Cessna F172M	F17200936	PH-SKT	2.12.80	V.D.Speck	Clacton	5. 8.02T
G-BIGK	Taylorcraft BC-12D (Continental A65)	8302	N96002 NC96002	29.10.80	N.P.St.J.Ramsay	Bentwaters	14.10.02P
G-BIGL	Cameron O-65 HAFB	690		22.10.80	P.L.Mossman *"Biggles"*	Bristol	28. 5.00A
G-BIGP	Bensen B.8M (McCulloch)	PFA G/01-1005		14.10.80	R.H.S.Cooper	Cross Houses, Shrewsbury	20.10.97P
G-BIGR	Avenger T.200-2122 MLB	004		6.10.80	R.Light	Stockport	
G-BIGT*	Colt 77A HAFB	078		28. 2.80	British Balloon Museum *"Big T"*	Newbury	20. 2.83A
	(Damaged Belton Hall, Grantham 23.8.81: cancelled 4.2.87 by CAA & stored)						
G-BIGU	Bensen B8MR	JRM.1 & G/01-1032		5.11.80	C.G.Ponsford	(Maldon)	
	(Roaded into Margaretting for flying - noted 9.01)						
G-BIGY*	Cameron V-65 HAFB	655		4. 9.80	Not known	Hungerford	
	"Gemma" (Cancelled 3.6.98 by CAA: extant 2000)						
G-BIGZ	Scheibe SF-25B Falke	46142	D-KCAI	22.12.80	R.F.Smith & C.R.Sproson t/a G-BIGZ Syndicate	Saltby	22. 7.02
G-BIHD	Robin DR.400/160 Major 80	1510		29.10.80	A.J.Fieldman	King's Farm, Thurrock	4. 2.04
G-BIHE*	Reims Cessna FA152 Aerobat	FA1520373		6.11.80	Walkbury Aviation Ltd	Spanhoe	5. 3.99T
	(Damaged near Sheerness 10.3.99: cancelled as destroyed 21.7.99: substantial parts stored 10.01)						
G-BIHF	Replica Plans SE.5A (Continental O-200-A) *(Plans No.079275)*	PFA 020-10548		27.10.80	S.H.O'Connell *"Lady Di"* *(As "F-943" in 92 Sqdn RFC c/s)*	White Waltham	5. 1.01P
G-BIHG	Piper PA-28-140 Cherokee	28-24376	OO-JAR N6686J	25.11.80	C.McGee & C.Staniszewski t/a Madley Flying Group	Shobdon	7. 6.02T
G-BIHI	Cessna 172M Skyhawk II	17266854	(G-BIHA) N1125U	18.11.80	L.R.Haunch t/a Fenland Flying School	Fenland	5. 5.02T
G-BIHN*	Airship Industries Skyship 500	1214/02		2.11.80	Airship Heritage Trust/Airship & Balloon Museum	Cardington	1. 4.79P
	(Destroyed San Francisco, CA, USA filming "A View To A Kill" 1985: cancelled 31.1.91 by CAA: gondola stored 1.00)						
G-BIHO	de Havilland DHC.6 Twin Otter 310	738	A6-ADB G-BIHO	9. 1.81	Isles of Scilly Skybus Ltd	St.Just	18. 4.03T
G-BIHP	Van Den Bemden 1000m3 Gas Free Balloon	VDB-38	OO-VBA	19.12.80	J.J.Harris *"Belgica"*	London SW6	3. 5.01
	(C/n quoted as "18" on Belgian CofR: believed rebuilt with 600m3 canopy c/n VDB-47)						
G-BIHT	Piper PA-17 Vagabond (Continental A65)	17-41	N138N N8N/N4626H/NC4626H	9. 1.81	W.E.Willets	Bewdley	15. 5.01P
G-BIHU	Saffery S.200 MLB	25		5.11.80	B.L.King	Coulsdon	
G-BIHX	Bensen B.8MR (Rotax 503)	PFA G/01-1003		12.11.80	P.P.Willmott	North Coates	10. 7.02P
G-BIIA	Alpavia Fournier RF3	51	F-BMTA	14.11.80	P.K.Jenkins *(Noted 1.02)*	Croft Farm, Defford	16. 7.87P
G-BIIB	Reims Cessna F172M Skyhawk II	F17201110	PH-GRE	18.11.80	Civil Service Flying Club (Biggin Hill) Ltd	Biggin Hill	24. 4.03T
	(Heavy landing Biggin Hill 26.6.01: substantial damage to nosewheel, propeller and engine)						
G-BIID	Piper PA-18 Super Cub 95 (L-18C-PI) *(Frame No.18-1558)*	18-1606	OO-LPA OO-HMK/ALAT 18-1606/51-15606	5. 1.81	D.A.Lacey	Cumbernauld	9. 7.02P
G-BIIE	Reims Cessna F172P Skyhawk II	F17202051		31.12.80	Sterling Helicopters Ltd	Norwich	4. 3.02T
G-BIIF*	Sportavia Fournier RF4D	4047	G-BVET F-BOXG	25.11.80	Not known	Biggin Hill	18. 3.93A
	(Cancelled 24.9.92 by CAA: stored 5.99: current status unknown)						
G-BIIG	Thunder AX6-56Z HAFB	307		26.11.80	A.Spindler	(Cleish)	19. 8.01A
G-BIIK	SOCATA MS.883 Rallye 115	1552	F-BSAP	28.11.80	K.M.Bowen	Upfield Farm, Whitson	22.10.01
G-BIIL	Thunder Ax6-56 Bolt HAFB	306		12.11.80	M Reader *(New owner 12.01)*	Selby	1. 6.84A
G-BIIP	Pilatus Britten-Norman BN-2B-27 Islander	2103	6Y-JQJ 6Y-JKJ/N411JA/G-BIIP	1.12.80	Hebridean Air Services Ltd *"County of Westmoreland"*	Cumbernauld	21. 1.02T
G-BIIT	Piper PA-28-161 Warrior II	28-8116052	N82744	1.12.80	Tayside Aviation Ltd	Dundee	23. 3.02T
G-BIIV	Piper PA-28-181 Archer II	28-7990028	N20875	19.12.80	E.Bensoussan	(Paris, France)	21. 8.03T
G-BIIZ	Great Lakes 2T-1A Sport Trainer (Warner Super Scarab 165D-5)	57	N603K NC603K	1. 4.81	Circa 42 Ltd	(Colchester)	4. 2.99P
	(Damaged Upper Harford, Glos 8.8.98: current status unknown)						
G-BIJB	Piper PA-18-150 Super Cub	18-8009001	N23923 <u>N2573H</u>	18. 8.80	Essex Gliding Club Ltd	North Weald	3. 4.04
G-BIJD	Bölkow Bö.208C Junior	636	PH-KAE (PH-DYM)/OO-SIS/(D-EGFA)	9.12.80	C.G.Stone	Biggin Hill	1.10.04
G-BIJE	Piper J-3C-65 Cub (L-4A-PI) *(Frame No.8504)*	8367	F-BIGN Fr.AF/42-15248	5. 5.81	R.L.Hayward & A.G.Scott *(On rebuild 4.91: current status unknown)*	Cardiff	
G-BIJS	Phoenix Luton LA-4A Minor (VW 1600)	PAL/1348 & PFA 835		18. 5.78	I.J.Smith	Brook Farm, Boylestone	14.11.95P

G-BIJU	Menavia Piel CP.301A Emeraude	221	G-BHTX	10. 6.80	A.G.Bailey	Stapleford	23. 5.02P
			F-BIJU		t/a Eastern Taildraggers Flying Group		
G-BIJV	Reims Cessna F152 II	F15201813		22.12.80	A.S.Bamrah	Biggin Hill	4. 3.02T
					t/a Falcon Flying Services		
G-BIJW	Reims Cessna F152 II	F15201820		22.12.80	A.S.Bamrah	(Blackbushe)	24. 2.02T
					t/a Falcon Flying Services		
G-BIJX	Reims Cessna F152 II	F15201829		29.12.80	A.S.Bamrah	Goodwood	3. 6.02T
					t/a Falcon Flying Services		
G-BIKB	Boeing 757-236	22173		25. 1.83	European Air Transport NV/SA		
						Brussels, Belgium	26. 1.03T
G-BIKC	Boeing 757-236	22174		31. 1.83	Barclays Mercantile Business Finance Ltd		
						(Basingstoke)	9. 2.03T
G-BIKD	Boeing 757-236	22175		10. 3.83	European Air Transport NV/SA		
						Brussels, Belgium	14. 3.03T
G-BIKE	Piper PA-28R-200 Cherokee Arrow II		OY-DVT	18. 4.80	R.V.Webb Ltd	Elstree	7.10.04
		28R-7335173	N55047				
G-BIKF(2)	Boeing 757-236	22177	(G-BIKG)	28. 4.83	British Airways plc	Heathrow	28. 4.03T
					(Wanula Dreaming t/s) (For disposal 4.02)		
G-BIKG(2)	Boeing 757-236	22178	(G-BIKH)	26. 8.83	DHL Holdings (UK) Ltd	(Hounslow)	26. 8.03T
	(For freigher conversion 8.01)						
G-BIKJ(2)	Boeing 757-236	22181	(G-BIKK)	9. 1.84	DHL Holdings (UK) Ltd	(Hounslow)	11. 1.04T
G-BIKK(2)	Boeing 757-236	22182	(G-BIKL)	1. 2.84	Barclays Mercantile Business Finance Ltd		
						(Basingstoke)	1. 2.04T
G-BIKL(2)	Boeing 757-236	22183	(G-BIKM)	29. 2.84	European Air Transport NV/SA		
						Brussels, Belgium	28. 2.04T
G-BIKM(2)	Boeing 757-236	22184	N8293V	21. 3.84	British Airways plc	Heathrow	22. 3.04T
			(G-BIKN)		*"Glamis Castle"*		
G-BIKN(2)	Boeing 757-236	22186	(G-BIKP)	23. 1.85	British Airways plc	Lasham	24. 1.02T
					(Rendezvous t/s) (Stored 1.02)		
G-BIKO(2)	Boeing 757-236	22187	(G-BIKR)	14. 2.85	British Airways plc	Heathrow	18. 2.02T
					(Benyhone Tartan t/s) (For disposal 1.02)		
G-BIKP(2)	Boeing 757-236	22188	(G-BIKS)	11. 3.85	DHL Holdings (UK) Ltd	(Hounslow)	14. 3.02T
G-BIKR(2)	Boeing 757-236	22189	(G-BIKT)	29. 3.85	British Airways plc	Heathrow	2. 4.02T
					(For disposal 12.01)		
G-BIKS(2)	Boeing 757-236	22190	(G-BIKU)	31. 5.85	British Airways plc	Heathrow	2. 6.02T
G-BIKT(2)	Boeing 757-236	23398		1.11.85	British Airways plc	Heathrow	3.11.02T
					(Crossing Borders t/s)		
G-BIKU(2)	Boeing 757-236	23399		7.11.85	Barclays Mercantile Business Finance Ltd		
						(Basingstoke)	7.11.02T
G-BIKV	Boeing 757-236	23400		9.12.85	DHL Holdings (UK) Ltd	(Hounslow)	11.12.02T
G-BIKW	Boeing 757-236	23492		7. 3.86	British Airways plc	Heathrow	9. 3.02T
					(Stored 11.01)		
G-BIKX	Boeing 757-236	23493		14. 3.86	British Airways plc	Lasham	16. 3.02T
					(Delftblue Daybreak t/s) (Stored 1.02)		
G-BIKY	Boeing 757-236	23533		28. 3.86	British Airways plc	Heathrow	31. 3.02T
					(Primavara t/s) (For disposal 10.02)		
G-BIKZ	Boeing 757-236	23532		15. 5.86	Barclays Mercantile Business Finance Ltd		
						(Basingstoke)	15. 5.02T
G-BILA*	Dalotel-Michel DM-165L Viking	01	F-PPZE	5. 2.81	Not known	(Bristol)	14. 9.83P
	(WFU Lower Upham 1983: cancelled 31.10.85 as WFU: for rebuild 1994: current status unknown)						
G-BILB	Wallingford WMB-2 Windtracker MLB	14		22. 1.81	B.L.King	Coulsdon	
G-BILE	Scruggs BL-2B MLB	81231		13. 3.81	P.D.Ridout	Botley	
G-BILG	Scruggs BL-2B MLB	81232		13. 3.81	P.D.Ridout	Botley	
G-BILI	Piper J-3C-65 Cub (L-4J-PI)	13207	F-BDTB	14. 1.81	S.C.Wilson & J A Goodridge	White Waltham	12. 6.02P
	(Frame No.13044)		45-4467		t/a G-BILI Flying Group		
					(As "454467/J/44" in US Army c/s)		
G-BILJ	Reims Cessna FA152 Aerobat	FA1520376		31.12.80	Bflying Ltd	Bournemouth	7. 6.02T
					(Op Bournemouth Flying Club)		
G-BILL	Piper PA-25-235 Pawnee D	25-7856028	N9174T	3. 1.79	A E & W.J.Taylor	East Winch	28. 6.03A
	(Lycoming O-540-G2A5 @ 260hp)				t/a Pawnee Aviation		
G-BILR	Cessna 152 II	15284822	N4822P	19. 3.81	Shropshire Aero Club Ltd	Sleap	8. 5.02T
G-BILS	Cessna 152 II	15284857	N4954P	3. 6.81	Keen Leasing (IOM) Ltd		
						Newtownards, Co.of Down	5. 7.02T
G-BILU	Cessna 172 RG Cutlass II	172RG0564	N5540V	29. 1.81	R.M.English & Sons Ltd	Full Sutton	6. 7.03T
G-BILZ	Taylor JT.1 Monoplane	PFA 055-10244		15.12.80	A.Petherbridge	Sibsey	29. 2.91P
	(VW 1600) *(Regd as c/n PFA 055-10124)*				*(Damaged Ingoldmells 10.6.90: stored 8.00)*		
G-BIMK	Tiger T.200 Srs.1 MLB	7/MKB-01		22.12.80	M.K.Baron	Stockport	
G-BIMM	Piper PA-18-150 Super Cub	18-3868	PH-VHO	8. 1.81	Fairmont Investments Ltd	Clacton	6. 8.04T
	(L-21B-PI) *(Frame No.18-3881)*		R.Neth AF R-178/54-2468				
	(Swung on landing Clacton 9.10.01 and went through boundary hedge: damage to struts, undercarriage & propeller)						
G-BIMN	Steen Skybolt	PFA 064-10329		31.12.80	D.Watt	Conington	6. 8.02P
	(Lycoming IO-360)						
G-BIMO	SNCAN Stampe SV-4C	394	F-BADG	5. 3.81	R.A.Robert	Goodwood/Pulborough	17. 3.02
	(DH Gipsy Major 10)		Fr.Mil		*(As "394" in French AF c/s)*		

G-BIMT	Reims Cessna FA152 Aerobat	FA1520361	N8062L	9. 1.81	Gloucestershire Flying Services Ltd	Gloucestershire	26. 5.02T
G-BIMU	Sikorsky S-61N Mk II	61-752	N8511Z	9. 1.81	Bristow Helicopters Ltd	Stornoway	23.10.02T
	(SAR conversion)		VH-CRU/N4042S		*(Op HM Coastguard) "Stac Pollaidh"*		
G-BIMX	Rutan VariEze	PFA 074-10544		6. 1.81	D.G.Crew	Biggin Hill	8. 5.02P
	(Continental O-200-A)						
G-BIMZ	Beechcraft 76 Duchess	ME-169	N6021K	20. 3.81	Firfax Systems Ltd	Gloucestershire	15.12.02
G-BING	Reims Cessna F172P Skyhawk II	F17202084		12. 1.81	M.P.Dolan	City of Derry	16. 4.02
G-BINL	Scruggs BL-2B MLB	81216		5. 2.81	P.D.Ridout	Botley	
G-BINM	Scruggs BL-2B MLB	81217		5. 2.81	P.D.Ridout	Botley	
G-BINR	Unicorn UE-1A MLB	81004		20. 1.81	I.Chadwick	Horsham	
					t/a Unicorn Group *"Lady Diana"*		
G-BINS	Unicorn UE-2A MLB	80002		22.12.80	I.Chadwick	Horsham	
					t/a Unicorn Group *"Caroline"*		
G-BINT	Unicorn UE-1A MLB	80001		22.12.80	D.E.Bint	(Downham Market)	
G-BINX	Scruggs BL-2B MLB	81219		5. 2.81	P.D.Ridout	Botley	
G-BINY	Oriental Air-Bag MLB	OAB-001		22. 1.81	J.L.Morton	Wokingham	
G-BIOA	Hughes 369D (500)	120-0880D	OO-HFS	9. 2.81	AH Helicopter Services Ltd	Newton Abbot	8. 5.03T
			LX-HLE/OO-HFS/G-BIOA				
G-BIOB	Reims Cessna F172P Skyhawk II	F17202042		23. 1.81	Aerofilms Ltd	Luton	3. 4.02T
G-BIOC	Reims Cessna F150L	F15000848	F-BUEC	3. 2.81	D.J.Gage & G.Burns	Prestwick	3. 8.02T
					t/a Southside Flyers		
G-BIOI	SAN Jodel DR.1050/M Excellence	477	F-BLJQ	21. 1.81	R.Pidcock	Fenland	28. 5.02P
G-BIOJ	Rockwell Commander 112TC-A	13192	N4662W	22. 1.82	A.T.Dalby	Sywell	13.12.02
G-BIOK	Reims Cessna F152 II	F15201810		2. 2.81	Tayside Aviation Ltd	Dundee	15. 4.02T
G-BIOM	Reims Cessna F152 II	F15201815		5. 2.81	A.S.Bamrah	Headcorn	25. 4.02T
					t/a Falcon Flying Services		
G-BIOR	SOCATA MS.880B Rallye Club	1229	OO-SAF	3. 2.81	R.L. & K.P.McLean	Rufforth	26. 9.02
	(Composite rebuild with components from G-AZGJ)				t/a McLean Aviation		
G-BIOU	SAN Jodel D.117A	813	F-BIOU	9. 8.78	M.D.Howlett	Ilmer, Bucks	23. 5.02P
					t/a Dubious Group		
G-BIOW	Slingsby T.67A	1988		26. 2.81	A.B.Slinger	Sherburn in Elmet	31. 3.03
					t/a Slingsby T67A Group		
G-BIPA	Grumman-American AA-5B Tiger	AA5B-0200	OY-GAM	24. 3.81	J.Campbell	Walney Island	15. 6.02
G-BIPH	Scruggs BL-2B MLB	81224		10. 2.81	C.M.Dewsnap	Camberley	
G-BIPI	Everett Gyroplane	001		30. 4.81	C A Reeves	Apperley, Glos	19. 6.01P
	(VW 1834)						
G-BIPN	Alpavia Fournier RF3	35	F-BMDN	26. 2.81	J.C.R.Rogers & I.F.Fairhead	Cranwell	20.12.02P
G-BIPO	Mudry/CAARP CAP.20LS-200	03	F-GAUB	5. 3.81	M.C.Sandford	White Waltham	14. 1.02S
G-BIPT	Wassmer Jodel D.112	1254	F-BMIB	11. 3.81	C.R.Davies	Allensmore, Hereford	7. 9.99P
G-BIPV	Gulfstream AA-5B Tiger	AA5B-0981	N28266	10. 3.81	Airtime Aviation Ltd.	Bournemouth	13. 5.02T
G-BIPW	Avenger T200-2112 MLB	10		24. 2.81	B.L.King	Coulsdon	
G-BIPY	Montgomerie-Bensen B.8MR			25. 2.81	C.G.Ponsford	(Maldon)	13.10.95P
	(Rotax 532)	AJW.01 & PFA G/01-1007					
G-BIRB*	SOCATA MS.880B Rallye 100T	2460	F-BVAQ	30. 3.81	(Hawick ATC Squadron)	Carlisle	16. 6.90
					(Cancelled 13.7.92 by CAA) (Stored 9.97: current status unknown)		
G-BIRD	Pitts S-1D Special	707-H & PFA 1596		3.11.77	P Metcalfe	(Stockton-on-Tees)	22. 1.03P
	(Lycoming IO-360)						
G-BIRE	Colt Bottle 56SS HAFB	323		4. 3.81	K.R.Gafney *"Satzenbrau"*	Bracknell	10. 1.84A
	(Satzenbrau Bottle)						
G-BIRH	Piper PA-18-150 Super Cub	18-3853	PH-LET	19. 3.81	Aquila Gliding Club Ltd		
	(L-21B-PI) (Lycoming O-360-A4)		R Neth AF R-163/54-2453			Hinton-in-the-Hedges	10. 6.02
	(Frame No.18-3857)				*(As "R-163" in R.Neth AF c/s)*		
G-BIRI	CASA I-131E Jungmann	1074	E3B-113	14. 4.81	M.G. & J.R.Jefferies	Little Gransden	27. 9.01P
					(Stored 9.96: current status unknown)		
G-BIRL	Avenger T200-2112 MLB	008		10. 3.81	R.Light	Stockport	
G-BIRP	Ridout Arena Mk.17 Skyship MLB	01		13. 3.81	Annette S.Viel	Botley	
G-BIRS	Cessna 182P Skylane	18261436	G-BBBS	10. 3.81	Auto Corporation Ltd	Hawarden	19. 4.04T
			N21131				
G-BIRT	Robin R.1180TD Aiglon	276		25. 3.81	W.D'A.Hall	White Waltham	29. 9.02
G-BIRW*	Morane-Saulnier MS.505 Criquet	<u>695/28</u>	OO-FIS	10. 4.81	National Museums of Scotland/Museum of Flight		
			F-BDQS/<u>French AF 695</u>		*(As "FI+S" in Luftwaffe c/s)*	East Fortune	3. 6.83P
					(Cancelled 15.11.88 as WFU)		
G-BIRY	Cameron V-77 HAFB	715		12. 3.81	P.& H.Mann *"Magic Carpet"*	Luton	15. 5.99A
G-BIRZ	Zenair CH.250-100			10. 3.81	L.D.Johnston	Perth	5. 8.02P
	(Lycoming O-290-G)	2-454 & PFA 024-10459					
G-BISG	Clutton FRED Srs.III			13. 3.81	T.Littlefair	Lymington	29.10.86P
	(VW 1600)	RAC 01-224 & PFA 029-10675			*"Fuzz Bee" (New owner 10.00)*		
G-BISH	Cameron V-65 HAFB	707		16. 3.81	P.J.Bish & C.Hall	Hungerford	26. 7.02A
					t/a Zebedee Balloon Service *"Tsaritsa"*		

G-BISJ	Cessna 340A II	340A0497	OO-LFK	10. 4.81	Midland Airline Transport Services Ltd		
			N6328X			Birmingham	13. 7.02T
G-BISL	Scruggs BL-2B MLB	81233		13. 3.81	P.D.Ridout	Botley	
G-BISM	Scruggs BL-2B MLB	81234		13. 3.81	P.D.Ridout	Botley	
G-BISS	Scruggs BL-2C MLB	81235		13. 3.81	P.D.Ridout	Botley	
G-BIST	Scruggs BL-2C MLB	81236		13. 3.81	P.D.Ridout	Botley	
G-BISW*	Cameron O-65 HAFB	713		18. 3.81	N H Ponsford	Leeds	6 .8.88
					(Cancelled 5.6.98 by CAA) (Noted 4.99)		
G-BISX	Colt 56A HAFB	324		18. 3.81	C.D.Steel	St Boswells	18. 8.99A
G-BISZ	Sikorsky S-76A II Plus	760156		19. 3.81	Bristow Helicopters Ltd	Redhill	23.10.04T
G-BITA	Piper PA-18-150 Super Cub	18-8109037	N82585	24. 3.81	D.J.Gilmour	North Weald	7. 7.02
					t/a Intrepid Aviation Co		
G-BITE	SOCATA TB-10 Tobago	193		7. 5.81	M.A.Smith & R.J.Bristow	Fairoaks	4.10.02
G-BITF	Reims Cessna F152 II	F15201822		27. 3.81	Tayside Aviation Ltd	Dundee	18. 6.03T
G-BITH	Reims Cessna F152 II	F15201825		27. 3.81	Tayside Aviation Ltd	Dundee	31. 8.03T
G-BITK	Clutton FRED Srs.II	PFA 029-10369		23. 3.81	D.J.Wood	(Dover)	
	(VW 1500)						
G-BITM	Reims Cessna F172P Skyhawk II			13. 4.81	Dreamtrade Ltd	Barton	12. 8.02T
		F17202046					
G-BITO	Wassmer Jodel D.112D	1200	F-BIUO	20. 3.81	A.Dunbar	Barton	5. 9.02P
G-BITS	Drayton B-56 HAFB	MJB-01/81		16. 3.81	M.J.Betts *"Hedger"*	Drayton, Norwich	
					t/a Eastern Region, British Balloon & Airship Club		
G-BITW*	Short SD.3-30 Var.100	SH.3070	G-EASI	26. 3.81	Air Salvage International	Alton	9. 6.98T
			(G-BITW)/G-14-3070				
	(WFU Coventry 7.97 & broken up 7.99: cancelled 20.7.99 as WFU: remains 11.01 @ scrap-yard)						
G-BITY	Bell FD.31T Flying Dodo MLB	2604		25. 3.81	A.J.Bell	Luton	
G-BIUL*	Cameron Bellows 60 SS HAFB	703		27. 3.81	British Balloon Museum & Library	Newbury	12..5.91
	(Expansion Joint shape)				*(Cancelled 26.6.98 by CAA)*		
G-BIUM	Reims Cessna F152 II	F15201807		3. 4.81	Sheffield Aero Club Ltd	Netherthorpe	31. 1.03T
G-BIUO*	Rockwell Commander 112A	281	OY-PRH	30. 3.81	Not known	Bristol	28.10.84
			N1281J				
	(Collided with Cirrus BGA.2138 Longdon 12.5.84: cancelled 10.1.89 as destroyed: wreck dumped 9.00)						
G-BIUP	SNCAN NC.854S	54	(G-AMPE)	4. 6.81	D.F.Hurn	Popham	4. 7.02P
			G-BIUP/F-BFSC		t/a BIUP Flying Group		
G-BIUV	Hawker Siddeley HS.748 Srs.2A/266LFD		5W-FAN	11. 5.81	Emerald Airways Ltd	Liverpool	16. 6.02T
		1701	G-AYYH/G-11-8		*"City of Liverpool"*		
G-BIUW	Piper PA-28-161 Warrior II		N9506N	14. 4.81	D.R.Staley	Sturgate	27. 6.02
		28-8116128					
G-BIUY	Piper PA-28-181 Archer II	28-8190133	N8318X	3. 4.81	J.S.Devlin & Z.Islam	Shoreham	27.11.01T
G-BIVA	Robin R.2112	137	F-GBAZ	6. 5.81	P.A.Richardson	Conington	4. 8.02
G-BIVB	Wassmer Jodel D.112	1009	(G-BIVC)	18. 9.81	M.J.Hayman	Watchford Farm, Yarcombe	22. 8.02P
			F-BJII				
G-BIVC	Wassmer Jodel D.112	1219	F-BMAI	1. 6.81	M.J.Barnby		
	(Continental A65)					Brickhouse Farm, Frogland Cross	13. 7.00P
G-BIVF	Scintex CP.301C3 Emeraude	594	F-BJVN	4.11.81	R.J.Moore	Sywell	3.12.02P
G-BIVK	Bensen B.8V	PFA G/01-1008		10. 4.81	K.Balch	Henstridge	10. 7.01P
	(VW 1834) *(Regd as B.8M)*				*"Skyrider"*		
G-BIVL*	Bensen B.8M	PFA G/01-1011		10. 4.81	Not known	St.Merryn	29. 4.87P
	(McCulloch)				*(Noted 6.96: cancelled 3.4.97 by CAA)*		
G-BIVV	Gulfstream AA-5A Cheetah	AA5A-0857	N26979	26. 5.81	R.Afia	Denham	18. 7.02T
					t/a Robert Afia Consulting Engineer		
G-BIWA	Stevendon Skyreacher MLB	102		8. 6.81	S.D.Barnes	Botley	
G-BIWB	Scruggs RS.5000 MLB	81541		8. 6.81	P.D.Ridout	Botley	
G-BIWC	Scruggs RS.5000 MLB	81546		26. 6.81	P.D.Ridout *"Waterloo"*	Botley	
G-BIWF	Ridout Warren Windcatcher MLB	WW.013		3. 7.81	P.D.Ridout	Botley	
G-BIWG	Ridout Zelenski Mk.2 MLB	Z.401		3. 7.81	P.D.Ridout	Botley	
	(Regd with c/n 2401)						
G-BIWJ	Unicorn UE-1A MLB	81014		14. 7.81	B.L.King	Coulsdon	
G-BIWK	Cameron V-65 HAFB	719		22. 4.81	I.R.Williams & R.G.Bickerdike		
					"Double Fantasy"	Bedford/Huntingdon	30. 3.99A
G-BIWL	Piper PA-32-301 Saratoga	32-8106056	N83684	23. 4.81	A.R.Ward	Southend	28. 6.02
G-BIWN	Wassmer Jodel D.112	1314	F-BNCN	5. 6.81	C.R.Coates	Sneaton Thorpe, Whitby	8.10.02P
G-BIWR	Mooney M.20F Executive	22-1339	N6972V	1. 6.81	A.C.Brink	Bourn	19.10.03
G-BIWU	Cameron V-65 HAFB	717		15. 5.81	L.P. Hooper *"Bumble Bee"*	Bristol	3.12.98A
G-BIWW	American AA-5 Traveler	AA5-0263	OY-AYV	2 .6.81	B.M.R. & K.R.Sheppard	Deenethorpe	8. 8.02
					t/a B & K Aviation *(Op Sandra's Flying Group)*	*"Kit-Kat"*	
G-BIWY*	Westland WG-30-100	901		30. 4.81	The Helicopter Museum	Weston-super Mare	30. 3.86T
					(Cancelled 29.1.87 as WFU)		
G-BIXA	SOCATA TB-9 Tampico	205		7. 5.81	W.& K.J.C.Maxwell	Perth	2. 9.02
G-BIXB	SOCATA TB-9 Tampico	208		7. 5.81	L.B.W.& F.H.Hancock	Kemble	7. 3.03T
G-BIXH	Reims Cessna F152 II	F15201840		30. 4.81	The Cambridge Aero Club Ltd	Cambridge	28. 2.03T
G-BIXI	Cessna 172 RG Cutlass II	172RG0861	N7533B	7. 7.81	J.F.P.Lewis	Sandown, IoW	10. 6.02
					t/a X India Group		

G-BIXL	North American P-51D-20NA Mustang	122-38675	IDF/AF2343 Fv.26116/44-72216	3. 7.81	R.J.Lamplough *"Miss L"*	North Weald	19. 6.02P
	(As "472216/HO-M" in 487th Fighter Sqn/352nd Fighter Group c/s)						
G-BIXN	Boeing-Stearman A75N1 (PT-17-BW) Kaydet (Continental W670)	75-2248	N51132 41-8689	15. 6.81	V.S.E.Norman *(As "FJ777" in RCAF c/s)*	Rendcomb	3. 8.96
G-BIXV	Bell 212	30870	N16931	27. 5.81	Bristow Helicopters Ltd	(Kazakhstan)	22. 7.02T
G-BIXW	Colt 56B HAFB	348		18. 5.81	N.A.P.Bates *"Spam"*	Tunbridge Wells	17. 8.97A
G-BIXX	Pearson Srs.II MLB	00327		8. 5.81	D.Pearson	Solihull	
G-BIXZ	Grob G-109	6019	D-KGRO	14. 5.81	D.L.Nind & I.Allum	Booker/Enstone	10. 6.04
G-BIYI	Cameron V-65 HAFB	722		21. 5.81	P.F.Smart t/a The Sarnia Balloon Group *"Penny"*	Basingstoke	16. 4.97A
G-BIYJ	Piper PA-18 Super Cub 95 (L-18C-PI)	18-1000	MM51-15303 I-EIST/MM51-15303/51-15303	5. 6.81	S.Russel	Wilkieston Farm, Peat Inn	30. 5.02P
G-BIYK	Isaacs Fury II (Continental C90)	PFA 011-10418		20. 5.81	C.W.Wilkins	(Peterborough)	8. 2.02P
G-BIYP	Piper PA-20 Pacer 125	20-802	CN-TYP F-DACJ/OO-ADP	25. 5.83	A.W.Hoy & S.W.M.Johnson	(Farnham)	8. 7.02
G-BIYR	Piper PA-18-150 Super Cub (L-21B-PI) *(Frame No. 18-3843)*	18-3841	(G-BIYB) PH-GER/ R.Neth AF R-151/5G-96/54-2441	26. 5.81	B.H.& M.J.Fairclough t/a The Delta Foxtrot Flying Group *(As "R-151" in R.Neth AF c/s)*	Watchford Farm, Yarcombe	1. 6.04
G-BIYT	Colt 17A Cloudhopper HAFB	344		13. 7.81	J-M Francois	Salles-Courbatiers, France	7. 9.02A
G-BIYU	Fokker S.11-1 Instructor	6206	(PH-HOM) R.Neth AF E-15	13. 5.81	C.Briggs *(As "E-15" in R.Neth AF c/s)*	Bagby	24.10.01P
G-BIYW	Wassmer Jodel D.112	1209	F-BLNR	26. 5.81	K.Balaam t/a Pollard/Balaam/Bye Flying Group	Poplar Hall Farm, Elmsett	5. 8.02P
G-BIYX	Piper PA-28-140 Cherokee Cruiser	28-7625064	OY-BLD	19. 6.81	W.B.Bateson *(Stored 12.01)*	Blackpool	19.12.96T
G-BIYY	Piper PA-18 Super Cub 95 (L-18C-PI) *(Frame No.18-1914)*	18-1979	MM52-2379 I-EIGA/MM52-2379/52-2379	2. 6.81	A.E. & W.J.Taylor	Fenland	23. 2.02T
G-BIZB*	Agusta-Bell 206B-3 JetRanger III	8611		10. 6.81	Not known	Corfu, Greece	
	(Crashed Corfu, Greece 28.6.89 filming: cancelled 2.10.89 as destroyed) (Used as fire training aid)						
G-BIZE	SOCATA TB-9 Tampico	209	9H-ABJ G-BIZE	15. 6.81	C.Fordham	Bourn	29. 7.02
G-BIZF	Reims Cessna F172P Skyhawk II	F17202070		16. 6.81	R.S.Bentley	Cambridge	31. 5.03
G-BIZG	Reims Cessna F152 II	F15201873		16. 6.81	M.A.Judge t/a Aero Group 78	Old Sarum	31. 5.03T
G-BIZI	Robin DR.400 2+2	1543		29. 5.81	BIZI Club Ltd	Standalone Farm, Meppershall	18. 4.03T
G-BIZK	Nord 3202B1	78	N2255E ALAT	22.11.85	A.I.Milne *(All-yellow French AF c/s)*	Little Snoring	30.10.02P
G-BIZM	Nord 3202B	91	N2256K ALAT	22.11.85	Magnificent Obsessions Ltd	Humberside	31.10.00P
G-BIZO	Piper PA-28R-200 Cherokee Arrow II	28R-7535339	OY-DLH N1578X	16. 6.81	Bizo Air Ltd	Clutton Hill Farm, Clutton	1. 2.03
G-BIZR	SOCATA TB-9 Tampico	210	G-BSEC G-BIZR	15. 6.81	R M A Kedzlie & E S Murphy tr Fenland Flying Group	Fenland	19. 7.04
G-BIZT*	Bensen B.8M (VW 1835)	PFA G/01-1015		10. 6.81	J.Ferguson *(Cancelled 3.4.97 by CAA) (Stored 6.00)*	Kilkerran	12. 8.88P
G-BIZU	Thunder Ax6-56Z HAFB	358		15. 6.81	M.J.Loades *"Greenall Whitley"*	Southampton	9. 6.01A
G-BIZV	Piper PA-18 Super Cub 95 (L-18C-PI)	18-2001	EI-74 I-EIDE/MM522401/52-2401	12. 6.81	S.J.Pugh & R.L.Wademan *(As "18-2001" in US Army c/s)*	Oxenhope	27. 6.02P
G-BIZW	Champion 7GCBC Citabria	0157	D-EGPD	16. 7.81	J.C.Read t/a G.Read & Sons	North Reston	30. 8.04
G-BIZY	Wassmer Jodel D.112	1120	F-BKJL	13. 7.81	W.Tunley t/a Wayland Tunley & Associates	Hinton-in-the-Hedges	20. 5.02P

G-BJAA – G-BJZZ

G-BJAD	Clutton FRED Srs.2	CA.1 & PFA 029-10586		11. 6.81	Newark (Nottinghamshire & Lincolnshire) Air Museum Ltd	Newark	
G-BJAE	Lavadoux Starck AS.80 Holiday (Continental A65)	04	F-PGGA F-WGGA	17. 6.81	D.J. & Mrs S.A.E.Phillips *(Damaged Woburn 17.8.91: current status unknown)*	(Leamington Spa)	8. 8.92P
G-BJAF	Piper J-3C-65 Cub (L-4A-PI) *(Frame No.8540)*	8437	D-EJAF HB-OAD/42-15318	23. 6.81	P.J.Cottle	Craysmarsh Farm, Melksham	3. 7.02P
G-BJAG	Piper PA-28-181 Archer II	28-7990353	PH-LDB (PH-BEG)/(OO-FLM)/N2244W	23. 6.81	J.F.Clark	Conington	19. 6.02
G-BJAJ	Gulfstream AA-5B Tiger	AA5B-1177	N4532V	2. 7.81	A.H.McVicar *(Op Prestwick Flight Centre)*	Prestwick	17. 5.03T
G-BJAL	CASA I-131E Jungmann *(Spanish AF serial no. conflicts with G-BUCC)*	1028	E3B-114	11. 9.78	I.C.Underwood & S.B.J.Chandler	Breighton	29. 6.02P

Regn	Type	C/n	Previous identity	Regd	Owner (operator)	Probable base	CofA expiry
G-BJAO	Montgomerie-Bensen B.8MR			28. 8.81	A.P.Lay	Henstridge	2. 4.01P
	(Rotax 582) GLS-01 & PFA G/01-1001 *(Regd with c/n GL5-01)*						
G-BJAP	de Havilland DH.82A Tiger Moth			15. 6.81	K.Knight	Shobdon	24. 7.02P
	(Composite rebuild) 0482 & PFA 157-12897				*(As "K2587" in pre-war 32 Sqn/CFS c/s)*		
G-BJAS	Rango NA-9 MLB	TL-19		22. 6.81	A.Lindsay	Twickenham	
G-BJAV	Gardan GY-80-160 Horizon	28	OO-AJP	8. 9.81	P.L.Lovegrove	(Ferndown)	26.10.03
			F-BLVB				
G-BJAW	Cameron V-65 HAFB	745		19. 6.81	G.A.McCarthy *"Breezin"*	Shepton Mallet	16. 4.86A
G-BJAY	Piper J-3C-65 Cub (L-4H-PI)	12086	F-BFBN	1.11.78	D W Finlay	(Ely)	18. 7.02P
	(Frame No.11914)		OO-EAC/44-79790		*(On overhaul @ Booker 11.01)*		
G-BJBK	Piper PA-18 Super Cub 95	18-1431	F-BOME	21. 8.81	M.S.Bird	Pepperbox, Salisbury	30. 5.02P
	(L-18C-PI) (Continental O-200-A)		ALAT/51-15431				
	(Frame No.18-1370)						
G-BJBM	Monnett Sonerai I			2. 7.81	T.F.Harrison	(Wolverhampton)	9. 1.97P
	(VW 2074) MEA-117 & PFA 015-10022				t/a Sonerai G-BJBM Group *(New owner 1.02)*		
G-BJBO	CEA Jodel DR.250/160 Capitaine	40	F-BNJG	24. 8.81	R.C.Thornton	Oaksey Park	1. 8.03
					t/a Wiltshire Flying Group		
G-BJBW	Piper PA-28-161 Warrior II		N2913Z	22. 7.81	T.G.Phillips, C.Greenland & J.Page		
		28-8116280			t/a 152 Group	Popham	11. 1.03
G-BJBX	Piper PA-28-161 Warrior II		N8414H	17. 7.81	Haimoss Ltd	Old Sarum	15. 3.03T
		28-8116269			*(Op Old Sarum Flying Club)*		
G-BJBY*	Piper PA-28-161 Warrior II		N8415L	20. 7.81	Haimoss Ltd	Old Sarum	10.12.99T
		28-8116270	*(Damaged Old Sarum 23.11.97: cancelled 3.3.98 as WFU) (Fuselage noted 8.01)*				
G-BJCA	Piper PA-28-161 Warrior II		N2846D	30. 7.81	QBS Trading Co Ltd	Plymouth	17. 2.03T
		28-7916473					
G-BJCF	Scintex CP.1310-C3 Super Emeraude		F-BMJH	19.11.81	K.M.Hodson & C.G.H.Gurney		
		936				Manor Farm, Binham	15. 7.02P
G-BJCI	Piper PA-18-150 Super Cub	18-6658	N9388D	10. 9.81	The Borders (Milfield) Aero-Tow Club Ltd		
	(Lycoming O-360-A4)					Milfield	10. 7.03
G-BJCW	Piper PA-32R-301 Saratoga SP		N2866U	6. 8.81	Golf Charlie Whisky Ltd	Fairoaks	20. 5.02
		32R-8113094					
G-BJDE	Reims Cessna F172M	F17200984	OO-MSS	25. 8.81	S.P.Heathfield	Cranfield	31. 8.03
			D-EGBR		t/a Cranfield Aircraft Partnership		
G-BJDF	SOCATA MS.880B Rallye 100T	3000	F-GAKP	21. 9.81	A.J.Wilkinson t/a G-BJDF Group		
						Coldharbour Farm, Willingham	28. 2.03
G-BJDI	Reims Cessna FR182 Skylane RG		N8062H	7. 8.81	P.R.Piggin	Leicester	3. 4.03
		FR18200046					
G-BJDJ	British Aerospace HS.125 Srs.700B		G-RCDI	27. 7.81	Falcon Jet Centre Ltd	Farnborough	8.10.02T
		257142	G-BJDJ/G-5-12				
G-BJDK	Ridout European E.157 MLB	S.2		17. 8.81	E.Osborn	Southampton	
					t/a Aeroprint Tours		
G-BJDO	Gulfstream AA-5A Cheetah	AA5A-0823	N26936	3. 8.81	J.J.Woodhouse	(Fleet)	11. 4.03T
					t/a Flying Services		
G-BJDT	SOCATA TB-9 Tampico	227		21. 8.81	M J Foggo	(Isleworth)	22. 5.03T
G-BJDW	Reims Cessna F172M Skyhawk II		PH-JBE	10. 8.81	J.Rae	Earls Colne	16.12.02T
		F17201417					
G-BJEI	Piper PA-18 Super Cub 95	18-1988	EI-66	27. 7.81	H.J.Cox	Wendover Farm, Sheepwash	10. 5.02P
	(L-18C-PI) *(Frame No.18-1938)*		I-EILO/MM522388/52-2388				
G-BJEL	SNCAN NC.854S	113	F-BEZT	7. 8.81	N.F. & S.G.Hunter	Wolvesnewton, Chepstow	5. 9.02P
G-BJEV	Aeronca 11AC Chief	11AC-270	N85897	12. 8.81	R.F.Willcox *(As "E/897" in US Navy c/s)*		
			NC85897			Eastbach Farm, English Bicknor	28. 1.02P
G-BJEX	Bölkow Bö.208C Junior	690	F-BRHY	27. 8.81	G.D.H.Crawford	(Henley-on-Thames)	28. 1.88
			D-EEAM		*(Current status unknown)*		
G-BJFB	Eaves Dodo Mk.1A MLB	DD.5		27. 8.81	S.D.Loveridge	Southampton	
					t/a Aeroprint Photographics		
G-BJFC	Ridout European E.8 MLB	S.1		17. 8.81	P.D.Ridout	Botley	
G-BJFE	Piper PA-18 Super Cub 95	18-2022	EI-91	17. 8.81	P.H.Wilmot-Allistone	Kemble	8. 4.02P
	(L-18C-PI)		I-EISU/MM522422/52-2422				
G-BJFL	Sikorsky S-76A II Plus	760056	N106BH	28. 8.81	Bristow Helicopters Ltd	Aberdeen	17. 9.02T
			N1546T/(G-BHRK)		*"Glenmoray"*		
G-BJFM	Jodel Wassmer D.120 Paris-Nice	227	F-BLFM	8.10.81	J.V.George & P.A.Smith	Popham	29.11.02P
G-BJGE*	Thunder Ax3 Sky Chariot HAFB	367		21. 8.81	R.Warner	Cranfield	
G-BJGK	Cameron V-77 HAFB	696		3. 9.81	T.J.Orchard, N.J.Glover & S.R.Godfrey		
					"Dollar"	Reading	21. 7.01A
G-BJGM	Unicorn UE-1A MLB	81015		21. 8.81	D.Eaves & P.D.Ridout	Southampton	
					"Capricorn"		
G-BJGX	Sikorsky S-76A II Plus	760026	N103BH	4. 9.81	Bristow Helicopters Ltd	North Denes	8.10.03T
			N4251S		*"Glenelgin"*		
G-BJGY	Reims Cessna F172P Skyhawk II			13.10.81	Kit Martin (Historic Houses Rescue) Ltd		
		F17202128				Gunton Hall, Somerton, Norfolk	13. 4.03
G-BJHB	Mooney M.20J (201)	24-1190	N1145G	23.12.81	Zitair Flying Club Ltd	Booker	23 5.02T
G-BJHK	EAA Acro-Sport 1	PFA 072-10470		20. 3.80	M.R.Holden		
	(Lycoming IO-360)					Stoneacre Farm, Farthing Corner	7. 6.02P

G-BJHT*	Thunder Ax7-65 Bolt HAFB	368		27. 8.81	A.H. & L.Symonds "Aura"	Chelmsford	
					(Cancelled 1.2.00 as WFU)		
G-BJHV*	Voisin Scale rep	MPS-1		1. 9.81	M.P.Sayer	Brooklands	
					(Cancelled 4.7.91 by CAA: on loan to Museum)		
G-BJIA	Allport Aerostatics YUO-1A-1-DA MLB	01		2. 9.81	D.J.Allport	Bourne, Lincs	
G-BJIC	Eaves Dodo 1A MLB	DD.3		4. 9.81	P.D.Ridout	Botley	
G-BJID	Osprey Lizzieliner 1B MLB	AKC.28		4. 9.81	P.D.Ridout	Botley	
G-BJIG	Slingsby T.67A	1992		16. 9.81	D.Lacy	White Waltham	15. 4.04
					t/a G-BJIG Slingsby Syndicate		
G-BJIR	Cessna 550 Citation II	550-0296	N6888C	17. 9.81	Gator Aviation Ltd	Jersey	17. 1.03T
					(Op Aviation Beauport Ltd)		
G-BJIV	Piper PA-18-150 Super Cub	18-8262	N5972Z	17. 9.81	Yorkshire Gliding Club (Pty) Ltd		
	(Lycoming 0-360-A4)					Sutton Bank	30. 7.03
G-BJKF	SOCATA TB-9 Tampico	240		30. 9.81	P.C.Churcher	Denham	8. 4.04
					t/a Venue Solutions		
G-BJKW	Wills Aera 2	A3JKW		1. 3.78	J.K.S.Wills	London SE3	
G-BJKX*	Reims Cessna F152 II	F15201881		22. 9.81	Not known	Abbeyshrule, Co.Longford	1. 7.91T
		(Crashed near Letterkenny 24.9.88: cancelled 19.1.89 as WFU: wreck stored 4.96: current status unknown)					
G-BJKY	Reims Cessna F152 II	F15201886		22. 9.81	Manx Aero Marine Management Ltd		
					(Op Westair Flying Services)	Blackpool	14.10.04T
G-BJLB	SNCAN NC.854S	58	(OO-MVM)	5.11.81	N.F.Hunter	Wolvesnewton, Chepstow	30. 6.83P
			F-BFSG				
			(Crashed near Newport,Gwent 29.7.84: stored 8.90: current status unknown)				
G-BJLC	Monnett Sonerai IIL			18. 9.81	A.R.Ansell *"Elsie"*	AAC Netheravon	11. 5.98P
	(VW 1835) 942L & PFA 015-10634				*(Noted 6.01)*		
G-BJLF	Unicorn UE-1C MLB	81018		21. 9.81	I.Chadwick t/a Unicorn Group	Horsham	
G-BJLG	Unicorn UE-1B MLB	81017		21. 9.81	I.Chadwick t/a Unicorn Group	Horsham	
G-BJLH	Piper PA-18 Super Cub 95	18-1541	F-BOUM	26.10.81	Felthorpe Flying Group Ltd	Felthorpe	13. 6.02P
	(L-18C-PI) *(Frame No.18-1513)*		ALAT 51-15541		*(As "K-33 44" in US Army c/s)*		
G-BJLO	Piper PA-31 Turbo Navajo B	31-815	F-BTQG	23.10.81	RJ Aviation Ltd	Fairoaks	23.12.01
			(F-BTDV)				
G-BJLX	Cremer Cracker MLB	15.711 PAC		24. 9.81	P.W.May	Wilmslow	
G-BJLY	Cremer Cracker MLB	15.709 PAC		24. 9.81	P.Cannon	Luton	
G-BJML	Cessna 120	10766	N76349	5.10.81	D.F.Lawlor	Inverness	1. 8.01P
	(Continental C90)		NC76349				
G-BJMO	Taylor JT.1 Monoplane	PFA 055-10612		30. 9.81	R.C.Mark	(Ludlow)	
G-BJMR	Cessna 310R II	310R1624	N2631Z	16. 7.79	J.M.Robinson	Rufforth	29. 2.04
G-BJMW	Thunder Ax8-105 Srs.2 HAFB	369		14.10.81	G.M.Westley	London SW15	11. 1.02A
G-BJMX	Ridout Jarre JR-3 MLB	81601		6.10.81	P.D.Ridout	Botley	
G-BJMZ	Ridout European EA-8A MLB	S.5		6.10.81	P.D.Ridout	Botley	
G-BJNA	Ridout Arena Mk.117P MLB	202		6.10.81	P.D.Ridout	Botley	
G-BJNB*	WAR Vought F-4U Corsair rep			13.10.81	Not known	Beeches Farm, South Scarle	
		PFA 118-10711		*(No Permit to Fly issued: cancelled 8.11.89 by CAA: on build 3.00)*			
G-BJND	Chown Osprey Mk.1E MLB	AKC.53		7.10.81	A.Billington & D.Whitmore	Liverpool	
G-BJNF	Reims Cessna F152 II	F15201882		21.10.81	Exeter Flying Club Ltd	Exeter	10. 2.03T
G-BJNG	Slingsby T.67AM	1993		16.10.81	D.F.Hodgkinson	(Gravesend)	23. 7.01T
G-BJNH	Chown Osprey Mk.1E MLB	AKC.57		8.10.81	D.A.Kirk	Manchester	
G-BJNN	Piper PA-38-112 Tomahawk	38-80A0064	N9684N	15.10.81	Scotia Safari Ltd	Carlisle	25. 8.00T
G-BJNY	Aeronca 11CC Super Chief	11CC-264	CN-TYZ	28.10.81	P.I.& D.M.Morgans *(Stored 4.91)*		
			F-OAEE		Furze Hill Farm, Rosemarket, Milford Haven		9. 8.90P
G-BJNZ	Piper PA-23-250 Aztec F	27-7954099	G-FANZ	5.10.81	Bonus Aviation Ltd	Cranfield	3. 8.01T
			N6905A/C-GTJG				
G-BJOA	Piper PA-28-181 Archer II	28-8290048	N8453H	29.10.81	Channel Islands Aero Services Ltd	Jersey	21. 1.02T
					(Op Jersey Aero Club)		
G-BJOB	SAN Jodel D.140C Mousquetaire III		F-BMBD	2.11.81	T.W.M.Beck & M.J.Smith		
		118				Monks Gate, Horsham	20. 6.03
G-BJOE	Jodel Wassmer D.120A Paris-Nice	177	F-BJIU	12.11.81	J.F.Govan	East Fortune	5. 7.02P
					t/a Forth Flying Group		
G-BJOP	Pilatus Britten-Norman BN-2B-26 Islander			29.10.81	Loganair Ltd	Kirkwall	5. 9.02T
		2132			*(Colum t/s)*		
G-BJOT	SAN Jodel D.117	688	F-BJCO	12.11.81	R, J & Z Meares-Davies	(Stafford)	19. 9.02P
			CN-TVH/F-DABU				
G-BJOV	Reims Cessna F150K	F15000558	PH-VSD	4. 2.82	J.A.Boyd	(Maidstone)	19. 7.03
G-BJPI	Bede BD-5G	1 & PFA 014-10218		30.10.81	M.D.McQueen	(Beckenham, Kent)	
	(Hirth 230R)						
G-BJPL	Chown Osprey Mk.4A MLB	AKC-39		13.10.81	M.Vincent	Jersey	
G-BJRA	Chown Osprey Mk.4B MLB	AKC.87		23.10.81	E.Osborn	Southampton	
G-BJRG	Chown Osprey Mk.4B MLB	AKC.95		26.10.81	A.de Gruchy	Jersey	
G-BJRH	Rango NA-36/Ax3 MLB	NHP-23		4.11.81	N.H.Ponsford	Leeds	
					t/a Rango Balloon & Kite Co		
G-BJRP	Cremer Cracker MLB	15.712 PAC		29.10.81	M.D.Williams	Dunstable	
G-BJRR	Cremer Cracker MLB	15.715 PAC		29.10.81	M.D.Williams	Houghton Regis	
G-BJRV	Cremer Cracker MLB	15.713 PAC		29.10.81	M.D.Williams	Dunstable	

G-BJSS	Allport YUO-1B-1-DA Neolithic Invader Superballoon Srs.2/20 MLB						
		01-8101002		9.11.81	D.J.Allport	Bourne, Lincs	
G-BJST	CCF Harvard 4	CCF4-...	MM53795	21.12.81	Tuplin Holdings Ltd	Little Gransden	
			SC-66		*(On rebuild 4.99: new owner 8.00)*		
G-BJSU*	Bensen B-8M	PFA G/01-1026		11.11.81	J.D.Newlyn	River, Dover	
			(No Permit to Fly issued: cancelled 24.1.96 by CAA: stored in garden 5.00)				
G-BJSV	Piper PA-28-161 Warrior II		PH-VZL	25.11.81	Airways Flight Training (Exeter) Ltd		
		28-8016229	(OO-HLM)/N35787			Exeter	9. 9.03T
G-BJSW	Thunder Ax7-65Z HAFB	378		16.11.81	Sandicliffe Garage Ltd	Stapleford, Notts	3.11.01A
					"Sandicliffe Ford"		
G-BJSZ*	Piper J-3C-65 Cub (L-4H-PI)	12047	D-EHID	20.11.81	H.Gilbert	Enstone	14. 6.94P
	(Regd with c/n 11874)		(D-ECAX)/(D-EKAB)/PH-NBP/44-79751				
				(Stored 6.95: cancelled 9.10.00 by CAA: current status unknown			
G-BJTB	Cessna A150M Aerobat	A1500627	(G-BIVN)	28.10.82	V.D.Speck	Clacton	21. 7.02T
			N9818J				
G-BJTF	Kirk Skyrider Mk.1 MLB	KSR-01		18.11.81	D.A.Kirk	Manchester	
G-BJTN	Chown Osprey Mk.4B MLB	ASC-112		23.11.81	M.Vincent	Jersey	
G-BJTO	Piper J-3C-65 Cub (L-4H-PI)	11527	F-BEGK	1.12.81	K.R.Nunn	Fritton Decoy, Great Yarmouth	27. 3.02P
	(Frame No.11352)		OO-AAL/43-30236				
G-BJTP	Piper PA-18 Super Cub 95	18-999	EI-51	26.11.81	J.T.Parkins *"Sittin'Duck"*	Bidford	20.10.002
	(L-18C-PI)		I-EICO/MM5115302/51-15302 *(As "115302/TP" in VMO-6 Sqn, US Marines c/s)*				
G-BJTY	Chown Osprey Mk.4B MLB	ASC-115		23.11.81	A.E.de Gruchy	Jersey	
G-BJUB	Wild BVS Special 01 MLB	VS/PW01		25.11.81	P.G.Wild	Beverley	
G-BJUC	Robinson R22HP	0228		13. 1.82	A.J.& J.F.Thomasson	Blackpool	15.10.03T
					t/a HeliServices		
G-BJUD	Robin DR.400/180R Remorqueur	870	PH-SRM	27.11.81	Lasham Gliding Society Ltd	Lasham	5. 1.03
	(Rebuilt using new fuselage: original scrapped Membury 11.88)						
G-BJUE	Chown Osprey Mk.4B MLB	ASC-114		23.11.81	M.Vincent	Jersey	
G-BJUG*	Socata TB-9 Tampico	248		30.12.81	Not known	Biggin Hill	
			(Crashed Oaksey Park 16.9.96: cancelled 1.10.96 as WFU: fuselage stored 4.01)				
G-BJUR	Piper PA-38-112 Tomahawk	38-79A0915	N9722N	5. 2.82	Truman Aviation Ltd	Nottingham	23.11.03T
					(Op Nottingham School of Flying)		
G-BJUS	Piper PA-38-112 Tomahawk	38-80A0065	N9690N	10.12.81	Panshanger School of Flying Ltd		
						High Cross, Ware	21. 9.03T
G-BJUU	Chown Osprey Mk.4B MLB	ASC-113		23.11.81	M.Vincent	Jersey	
G-BJUV	Cameron V-20 HAFB	792		9.12.81	P.Spellward *"Busy Bee"*	Bristol	
G-BJUY	Colt Ax7-77A HAFB	384	EI-BDE	15.12.81	Balloon Sports HB	Partille, Sweden	
	(Special Golf Ball shape) (Rebuild of Colting Ax7-77A c/n 77A-003) (Op P.Lesser)						
G-BJVB	Cremer Cremcorn Ax1-4 MLB	82029		11.12.81	P.A.Cremer	Camberley	
G-BJVC	Evans VP-2	PFA 063-10599		17. 2.82	C.J.Morris	(Andover)	19. 6.91P
	(VW 1911)				*(Current status unknown)*		
G-BJVF*	Thunder Ax3 Maxi Sky Chariot HAFB			15.12.81	A.G.R.Calder	California, USA	6.10.91A
	(C/n duplicates G-SPOP)	187			*(Cancelled 23.11.01 as wfu: current status unknown)*		
G-BJVH	Reims Cessna F182Q Skylane	F18200106	D-EJMO	21.12.81	R.J.D.Cuming	Wolverhampton	31. 8.03
			PH-AXU(2)				
G-BJVJ	Reims Cessna F152 II	F15201906		6. 1.82	The Cambridge Aero Club Ltd	Cambridge	31. 5.04T
G-BJVK	Grob G-109	6074		11. 3.82	B.A.Kimberley	(Banbury)	22. 5.92
					(Current status unknown)		
G-BJVM	Cessna 172N Skyhawk II	17269374	N737FA	14.12.81	I.C.Maclennan	Swanton Morley	1. 8.03T
G-BJVS	Scintex CP.1310-C3 Super Emeraude		F-BJVS	5. 1.79	A.P.Milton	(Sidmouth)	8.10.02P
		903			t/a BJVS Group		
G-BJVT	Reims Cessna F152 II	F15201904		12. 1.82	The Cambridge Aero Club Ltd	Cambridge	7.12.03T
G-BJVU	Thunder Ax6-56 Bolt HAFB	397		31.12.81	G.V.Beckwith *"Cooper"*	York	26. 4.91A
G-BJVV	Robin R.1180TD Aiglon	279		5.11.81	Medway Flying Group Ltd	Rochester	18. 6.03T
G-BJVX	Sikorsky S-76A II Plus	760100	N108BH	15. 1.82	Bristow Helicopters Ltd	North Denes	23. 3.03T
			N1548G				
G-BJWC*	Saro Skeeter AOP.10	S2/3070	7840M	30.11.82	D.A.George	Sywell	
			XK482 *(Op Sloane Helicopters Ltd) (Cancelled 23.2.94 by CAA: stored 3.00)*				
G-BJWH	Reims Cessna F152 II	F15201919		7. 5.82	Plane Talking Ltd	Blackbushe	7. 9.03T
G-BJWI	Reims Cessna F172P Skyhawk II			14. 5.82	Bflying Ltd	Bournemouth	28. 8.04T
		F17202172			*(Op Bournemouth Flying Club)*		
G-BJWJ	Cameron V-65 HAFB	802		25. 1.82	R.G.Turnbull & S.G.Farse *"Gawain"*		
						Glasbury, Hereford	24.11.00A
G-BJWO	Fairey Britten-Norman BN-2A-26 Islander		4X-AYR	16. 2.82	Peterborough Parachute Centre Ltd	Sibson	11. 2.02
		334	SX-BBX/4X-AYR/G-BAXC				
G-BJWT	Wittman W.10 Tailwind	PFA 031-10688		5. 1.82	J.F.Bakewell	Hucknall	29. 8.02P
	(Lycoming O-290-G)				t/a Tailwind Group		
G-BJWV	Colt 17A Cloudhopper HAFB	391		22. 1.82	D.T.Meyes *"Bryant Homes"*	Leamington Spa	26. 3.97A
G-BJWW	Reims Cessna F172P Skyhawk II		(D-EFTV)	1. 2.82	Manx Aero Marine Management Ltd		
		F17202148			*(Op Westair Flying Services)*	Blackpool	17. 9.03T
G-BJWX	Piper PA-18 Super Cub 95	18-1985	EI-64	23. 2.82	R.A.G.Lucas	Redhill	21.12.01P
	(L-18C-PI) (Continental O-200-A)		I-EIME/MM522385/52-2385		t/a G-BJWX Syndicate		

G-BJWY*	Sikorsky S-55 (HRS-2) Whirlwind HAR.21	55???	A2576 WV198/Bu.130191	25. 1.82	D.Charles *(On loan to Solway Aviation Society) (As "WV198/K") (Cancelled 23.2.94 by CAA)*	Carlisle	
G-BJWZ	Piper PA-18 Super Cub 95 (L-18C-PI) *(Frame No.18-1262)*	18-1361	OO-HMO ALAT 18-1361/51-15361	18. 1.82	R.C.Dean t/a G-BJWZ Syndicate	Redhill	26.11.01P
G-BJXA	Slingsby T.67A	1994		8. 2.82	Comed Aviation Ltd	Blackpool	5. 4.01T
G-BJXB	Slingsby T.67A	1995		8. 2.82	XRay Bravo Ltd	Barton	16. 9.04
G-BJXK	Sportavia Fournier RF5	5054	D-KINB	3. 2.82	E.Fitzgerald & J.T.Phillips t/a G-BJXK Syndicate	Usk	12. 3.04
G-BJXP	Colt 56B HAFB	393		29. 3.82	H.J.Anderson *"Bart"*	Oswestry	9. 9.00A
G-BJXR*	Auster AOP.9	184	XR267	2. 2.82	A.Southern & R.J.Rudhall t/a Cotswold Aircraft Restoration Group *(On rebuild: cancelled 12.4.99 by CAA)*	(Gloucester)	
G-BJXX	Piper PA-23-250 Aztec E	27-4692	F-BTCM N14094	7. 4.82	V.Bojovic	(Biggin Hill)	23. 6.01
G-BJXZ	Cessna 172N Skyhawk II	17273039	PH-CAA N1949F	24. 3.82	T.M.Jones *(Op Derby Aero Club)*	Derby	8.11.04T
G-BJYD	Reims Cessna F152 II	F15201915		25. 3.82	Cleveland Flying School Ltd	Teesside	21. 9.03T
G-BJYF	Colt 56A HAFB	401		1. 3.82	H.Dos Santos *"Fanta"*	Caxton, Cambs	8. 6.02A
G-BJYG	Piper PA-28-161 Warrior II	28-8216053	N8458B	4. 3.82	S.R.Mitchell	(Prescot)	20. 6.03T
G-BJYK	Jodel Wassmer D.120A Paris-Nice	185	(G-BJWK) F-BJPK	11. 5.82	T.Fox & D.A.Thorpe	Crowland	9. 6.02P
G-BJYN	Piper PA-38-112 Tomahawk	38-79A1076	G-BJTE N24310	12. 3.82	Panshanger School of Flying Ltd	High Cross, Ware	6. 3.00T
G-BJZA	Cameron N-65 HAFB	820		4. 3.82	A.D.Pinner *"Digby"*	Northampton	3. 6.97A
G-BJZB	Evans VP-2 (VW 1834)	PFA 063-10633		10. 3.82	G.A.Shaw	Breighton	9. 7.01P
G-BJZC*	Thunder Ax7-65Z HAFB	416		5. 3.82	Balloon Preservation Group *"Greenpeace Trinity" (Cancelled 8.7.98 as WFU)*	Kirdford	17. 6.94A
G-BJZF	de Havilland DH.82A Tiger Moth *(Built Norfolk Aerial Spraying Ltd from spares)*	NAS-100		8. 3.82	R.Blasi	White Waltham	21. 6.02P
G-BJZN	Slingsby T.67A	1997		31. 3.82	A.R.T.Marsland	Breighton	20. 8.04
G-BJZR	Colt 42A HAFB	402		18. 3.82	A.F.Selby t/a Selfish Balloon Group *"Selfish"*	Loughborough	24. 7.02A
G-BJZX	Grob G-109	6109	(D-KGRO)	3. 9.82	Oxfordshire Sport Flying Ltd *(Wrecked fuselage noted 12.01)*	Blackpool	4. 9.00

G-BKAA – G-BKZZ

G-BKAB*	ICA IS-28M2A *(Crashed Rattlesden 19.5.84: cancelled 25.3.85 as PWFU: forward fuselage to G-BMOM: rest for scrap 5.01)*	23A		19. 3.82	Skycraft Ltd	(Spalding)	20. 5.85
G-BKAE	Jodel Wassmer D.120 Paris-Nice	200	F-BKCE	5. 5.82	M.P.Wakem	Barton	2. 9.02P
G-BKAF	Clutton FRED Srs.II (VW 1835)	PFA 029-10337		23. 3.82	J.M.Robinson	(Achill Island, Co.Mayo)	30. 5.97P
G-BKAM	Slingsby T.67M Firefly 160	1999		26. 4.82	A.J.Daley	Wellcross Grange, Slinfold	26. 7.02
G-BKAO	Wassmer Jodel D.112	249	F-BFTO	22. 3.82	R.Broadhead	Bagby	4. 5.02P
G-BKAS	Piper PA-38-112 Tomahawk	38-79A1075	N24291	16. 4.82	E.Reed t/a The St.George Flying Club	Teesside	27. 6.02T
G-BKAY	Rockwell Commander 114	14411	SE-GSN	28. 9.81	D.L.Bunning t/a The Rockwell Group	Dunkeswell	16. 5.04
G-BKAZ	Cessna 152 II	15282832	N89705	27. 4.82	L.W.Scattergood	Breighton	27. 4.03A
G-BKBB	Hawker Fury rep (RR Kestrel 5)	WA/6	OO-HFU OO-XFU/G-BKBB	2. 4.82	Brandish Holdings Ltd *(As "K1930" in 43 Sqn c/s) (Flew 17.1.01)*	Wevelgem, Belgium	
G-BKBD	Thunder Ax3 Maxi Sky Chariot HAFB	418		5. 4.82	M.J.Casson	Kendal	
G-BKBF	SOCATA MS.894A Rallye Minerva 220	11622	F-BSKZ	8. 9.82	K A Hale & L C Clark	Draycott Farm, Chisledon	15. 8.04
G-BKBH*	Hawker Siddeley HS.125 Srs.600B	256052	5N-DNL G-5-698/5N-DNL/5N-NBC/G-5-698/G-BKBH/G-5-698/TR-LAU/G-BKBH/G-BDJE/G-5-11	1. 4.82	Beamalong Ltd *(Cancelled 15.7.99 by CAA: noted fire dump 9.00)*	Southampton	
G-BKBN	SOCATA TB-10 Tobago	287		4. 6.82	D.S.& W.A.Newby t/a David Newby Associates	Bodmin	31. 7.04
G-BKBO	Colt 17A Cloudhopper HAFB	342		1. 9.82	J.Armstrong, M.A.Ashworth & H.Davey *"Captain Courageous"*	Newquay	23. 1.00A
G-BKBP	Bellanca 7GCBC Scout	465-73	N8693	1. 6.82	M.G. & J.R.Jefferies t/a H.G.Jefferies & Son *(Damaged Graveley, Herts 23.5.93: stored 9.95: new owner 10.00)*	Little Gransden	8. 5.95T
G-BKBR(2)*	Cameron Chateau 84SS HAFB *(Forbes "Chateau de Balleroy" shape)*	743		11. 5.82	Forbes Europe Inc *(Cancelled 29.4.93 as WFU) (Stored 6.93) (Current status unknown)*	Balleroy, Normandy	NE(A)
G-BKBS	Bensen B.8MV	PFA G/01-1027		14. 4.82	C R Gordon	Carlisle	6. 8.02P
G-BKBV	SOCATA TB-10 Tobago	288	F-BNGO	4. 6.82	The Studio People Ltd	Sleap	3. 2.03

G-BKBW	SOCATA TB-10 Tobago	289		4. 6.82	P.J.Bramhall & D.F.Woodhouse t/a Merlin Aviation	Bristol	1. 5.04
G-BKCC	Piper PA-28-180 Cherokee Archer	28-7405099	OY-BGY	13. 5.82	Aeros Leasing Ltd	Gloucestershire	6. 9.04T
G-BKCE	Reims Cessna F172P Skyhawk II	F17202135	N9687R	26. 4.82	M.O.Loxton	Leysdown-on-Sea, Sheppey	15. 5.03T
G-BKCI	Brugger MB.2 Colibri (VW 1600)	PFA 043-10692		22. 4.82	E.R.Newall *"Bugsy"*	Breighton	
G-BKCJ	Oldfield Baby Lakes (Continental O-200-A)	PFA 010-10714		12. 5.82	S.V.Roberts	Sleap	26. 1.99P
G-BKCL	Piper PA-30 Twin Comanche C	30-1982	G-AXSP N8824Y	12. 1.81	Yorkair Ltd	Full Sutton	26. 1.00T
G-BKCN	Phoenix Currie Wot (Continental A65)	PFA 3018		27. 4.82	N.A.A.Pogmore	Benson's Farm, Laindon	7. 9.01P
G-BKCR	SOCATA TB-9 Tampico	297		6. 5.82	A.Whitehouse *(Fuselage noted 9.00: current status unknown)*	Haverfordwest	3. 8.98T
G-BKCV	EAA Acro Sport II (Lycoming O-360)	430 & PFA 072A-10776		5. 5.82	T.N.Jinks	Charity Farm, Baxterley	27. 9.01P
G-BKCW	Jodel D.120A Paris-Nice *(Built Societe Wassmer)*	285	(G-BKCP) F-BMYF	1. 6.82	M.K.McGreavey t/a Dundee Flying Group	Perth	21. 2.02P
G-BKCX	Mudry/CAARP CAP-10B	149		28. 7.82	R.Ingleton	Popham	19. 8.04
G-BKCY*	Piper PA-38-112 Tomahawk II	38-81A0027	OO-XKU N25629	22. 5.82	Wellesbourne Aviation Ltd *(Stored 12.97: cancelled 30.6.00 as wfu: current status unknown)*	Welshpool	7.11.94T
G-BKCZ	Jodel D.120A Paris-Nice *(Built Société Wassmer)*	207	F-BKCZ	23. 4.82	M.R.Baker *(On rebuild 5.00)*	Popham	
G-BKDC	Monnett Sonerai IIL (VW 1834)	876 & PFA 015-10597		2. 7.82	K.J.Towell *(Damaged Breighton 7.8.90: current status unknown)*	(Guildford)	18. 6.90P
G-BKDH	Robin DR.400/120 Dauphin 80	1582	PH-CAB	25. 5.82	Dauphin Flying Group Ltd	Draycott Farm, Chisledon	6.12.04T
G-BKDI	Robin DR.400/120 Dauphin 80	1583	PH-CAD	25. 5.82	The Cotswold Aero Club Ltd	Shoreham	7. 5.04T
G-BKDJ	Robin DR.400/120 Dauphin 80	1584	PH-CAC	25. 5.82	I.H.Taylor	(Doncaster)	28. 4.04
G-BKDK	Thunder Ax7-77Z HAFB	428		21. 6.82	A.J.Byrne *"Cider Riser"*	Thatcham	17. 9.95A
G-BKDP	Clutton FRED Srs.III	PFA 029-10650		24. 5.82	M.Whittaker	(Wolverhampton)	
G-BKDR	Pitts S-1S Special (Lycoming IO-360)	PFA 009-10654		14. 6.82	T.J.Reeve	(Bury St. Edmunds)	2. 5.02P
G-BKDT*	RAF SE.5A rep	278 & PFA 080-10325		26. 5.82	Yorkshire Air Museum *(No CofA or Permit issued: cancelled 11.7.91 by CAA: under restoration 10.00)*	Elvington	
G-BKDX	SAN Jodel DR.1050 Ambassadeur	55	F-BITX	1. 6.82	T.V.Thorp & G.J.Slater t/a DX Group *(Fuselage noted but wings at Siege Cross Farm, Thatcham 10.01)*	Clench Common	10. 9.99
G-BKEK	Piper PA-32-300 Cherokee Six	32-7540091	OY-TOP	30. 6.82	P.H.Maynard	Turweston	9. 5.04T
G-BKEP	Reims Cessna F172M Skyhawk II	F17201095	OY-BFJ	8. 7.82	S.W.Watkins t/a G-BKEP Group	Trecorras Farm, Llangarron	8.10.04
G-BKER	Replica Plans SE.5A (Continental O-200A)	PFA 020-10641		15. 6.82	N.K.Geddes *(As "F5447/N")*	South Barnbeth Farm, Bridge of Weir	11. 7.02P
G-BKES*	Cameron Bottle 57 SS HAFB *(Robinsons Barley Water Bottle)*	846		25. 6.82	British Balloon Museum & Library *"Robinsons Barley Water" (Cancelled 1.5.90 by CAA)*	Newbury	NE(A)
G-BKET	Piper PA-18 Super Cub 95 (L-18C-PI)	18-1990	EI-67 I-EIBI/MM522390/52-2390	17. 6.82	H.M.MacKenzie	Inverness	22.11.00P
G-BKEU	Taylor JT.1 Monoplane (VW 1600)	PFA 055-10553		18. 6.82	R.J.Whybrow & J.M.Springham	Knettishall	20. 7.95P
G-BKEV	Reims Cessna F172M Skyhawk	F17201443	PH-WLH OO-CNE	8. 7.82	A.G.Measey t/a Echo Victor Group	(Countesthorpe)	8. 3.04T
G-BKEW	Bell 206B-3 JetRanger III	3010	D-HDAD	8. 7.82	N.R.Foster t/a Foster Associates	Biggin Hill	17. 7.03
G-BKEY	Clutton FRED Srs.III (VW 1600)	PFA 029-10208		27. 5.82	G.S.Taylor *(Current status unknown)*	(Bewdley,Worcs)	
G-BKFA*	Monnett Sonerai IIL	PFA 015-10524		21. 6.82	Not known *(Cancelled 12.4.99 by CAA) (Not completed & stored awaiting rebuild)*	Roughay Farm, Bishops Waltham	
G-BKFC	Reims Cessna F152 II	F15201443	OO-AWB	1. 9.82	Sulby Aerial Surveys Ltd	Sibbertoft, Husbands Bosworth	11.11.04T
G-BKFI	Evans VP-1 Srs.2 (VW 1834)	PFA 062-10491		24. 6.82	P.L.Naylor *(New owner 10.01)*	(Durham)	2. 8.02P
G-BKFK	Isaacs Fury II (Lycoming O-290-D)	PFA 011-10038		25. 6.82	G.C.Jones *"Cia Cia San" (Persian AF c/s)*	Waits Farm, Belchamp Walter	27. 8.02P
G-BKFL	Aerosport Scamp	PFA 117-10814		17. 8.82	J.Sherwood *(Noted 2.01)*	Breighton	
G-BKFM	QAC Quickie 1 (Rotax 503)	PFA 094-10570		28. 6.82	G.E.Meakin *(Damaged on take off Cranfield 4.7.98: new owner 7.01)*	(Ruddington)	29. 6.98P
G-BKFN	Bell 214ST Super Transport	28109	LZ-CAW G-BKFN/VH-BEE/VH-LHT/G-BKFN	16. 8.82	Bristow Helicopters Ltd *"Loch Broome"*	Aberdeen	24.10.04T
G-BKFR	Scintex CP.301C Emeraude	519	F-BUUR F-BJFF	30. 6.82	J.J.Beall	Perth	27. 8.02P

G-BKFW	Percival P.56 Provost T.1	PAC/F/303	XF597	21. 9.82	Sylmar Aviation & Services Ltd		
						Lower Wasing Farm, Brimpton	19. 7.02P
					(As "XF597/AH" in RAF College c/s)		
G-BKFZ	Piper PA-28R-200 Cherokee Arrow II		OY-BLE	17. 8.82	R.S.Watt	Shacklewell Lodge, Empingham	14.11.03
		28R-7635127			t/a Shacklewell Flying Group		
G-BKGA	SOCATA MS.892E Rallye 150GT	13287	F-GBXJ	15. 7.82	W.Fairney	Wadswick Manor Farm, Corsham	3. 8.03
					t/a BJJ Aviation		
G-BKGB	Jodel Wassmer D.120 Paris-Nice	267	F-BMOB	21. 6.82	B.A. Ridgway	Rhigos	21. 2.02P
G-BKGC	Maule M-6-235C Super Rocket	7413C	N56465	23. 7.82	D.W.Pennell	Gloucestershire	4. 6.03
G-BKGD*	Westland WG.30 Srs.100	002	(G-BKBJ)	15. 7.82	Westland Helicopters Ltd	Yeovil	6. 7.93T
					(Cancelled 15.4.93 as WFU: stored 3.93: current status unknown		
G-BKGL	Beechcraft D18S (3TM)	CA-164	CF-QPD	14. 7.82	Propshop Ltd & T.Darrah	Duxford	1.11.04
	(Beech c/n A-764)		RCAF 5193/1564		*(As "1164" in 1942 USAAC c/s)*		
G-BKGM	Beechcraft 3NM (D18S)	CA-203	N5063N	14. 7.82	A.E.Hutton	North Weald	25. 6.03
	(Beech c/n A-853)		G-BKGM/CF-SUQ/RCAF 2324		*(Op Harvard Formation Team)*		
					(As "HB275" in RAF/SEAC c/s)		
G-BKGR	Cameron O-65 HAFB	864		6. 8.82	K.Kidner & L.E.More	Newton Abbot	8. 5.93P
					(Amended CofR 12.01)		
G-BKGT	SOCATA Rallye 110ST Galopin	3361		23. 7.82	A.G.Morgan	Wellesbourne Mountford	28.11.03
					t/a Long Marston Flying Group		
G-BKGW	Reims Cessna F152 II	F15201878	N9071N	11. 8.82	Leicestershire Aero Club Ltd	Leicester	18. 6.04T
G-BKHD	Oldfield Baby Lakes 8133-F-802B & PFA 010-10718			25. 8.82	P.J.Tanulak	Sleap	11. 4.96P
	(Continental O-200-A)				*(Damaged Shrewsbury 22.10.95: current status unknown)*		
G-BKHG	Piper J-3C-65 Cub (L-4H-PI)	12062	F-BCPT	13. 9.82	K.G.Wakefield *"Puddle Jumper"*		
			NC79807/44-79766			Brickhouse Farm, Frogland Cross	30. 4.02P
					(As "479766/D-63" in HQ 9th Army, USAAC c/s)		
G-BKHJ	Cessna 182P Skylane II	18264129	PH-CAT	25. 8.82	Augur Films Ltd	Swanton Morley	14. 7.02
	(Reims c/n F18200040)		D-EATV/N6223F				
G-BKHR	Luton LA-4A Minor	PFA 051-10228		24. 8.82	C.B.Buscombe & R.Goldsworthy	Bodmin	6. 3.02P
	(VW 1834)						
G-BKHW	Stoddard-Hamilton Glasair IIRG			27.8.82	G.R.W.Monksfield, D.Callabritto & S.T.Ballard		
	(Lycoming O-320)	357 & PFA 149-11312				Stapleford	6. 6.02P
G-BKHY	Taylor JT.1 Monoplane	PFA 1416		8. 9.82	B.C.J.O'Neill	Damyns Hall, Upminster	11. 6.02P
	(VW 1600)						
G-BKHZ	Reims Cessna F172P Skyhawk II		D-EJOK	15.10.82	L.R.Leader	Clacton	8.10.04
		F17202169					
G-BKIA	SOCATA TB-10 Tobago	322		25. 8.82	M.F.McGinn	Prestwick	24. 8.04T
G-BKIB	SOCATA TB-9 Tampico	323		25. 8.82	G.A.Vickers	Hawarden	22.10.01T
G-BKIE*	Short SD.3-30 Var.100	SH.3005	G-SLUG	15. 9.82	CAA Fire Training Centre	Teesside	22. 8.93T
			G-METP/G-METO/G-BKIE/C-GTAS/G-14-3005				
					(Cancelled 16.9.97 as WFU: noted in poor condition 4.99)		
G-BKIF	Fournier RF6B-100	3	F-GADR	8.10.82	D.J.Taylor & J.T.Flint	Kimbolton	20. 9.03
G-BKII	Reims Cessna F172M Skyhawk II		PH-PLO	8.10.82	M.S.Knight	Goodwood	20. 2.04T
		F17201370	(D-EGIA)		t/a Sealand Aerial Photography		
G-BKIJ	Reims Cessna F172M	F17200920	PH-TGZ	15.10.82	V.D.Speck	Clacton/Duxford	2. 9.00T
G-BKIK*	Cameron DG-19 Helium Airship	776		23. 8.82	Balloon Preservation Group	Farnborough	4. 9.88A
	(Rotax 400)				*(Cancelled 5.9.00 as wfu)*		
					(On loan to Farnborough Air Sciences Trust: stored)		
G-BKIN	Alon A-2A Aircoupe	B-253	N5453F	24. 9.82	D.W.Vernon	Blackpool	8.10.00
G-BKIR	SAN Jodel D.117	737	F-BIOC	30. 9.82	R.Shaw & D.M.Hardaker		
						Birds Edge, Penistone	28. 8.92P
					(On rebuild 3.96: current status unknown)		
G-BKIS	SOCATA TB-10 Tobago	329		22. 9.82	R.A.Irwin	Thruxton	9. 6.02
					t/a Wessex Flyers Group		
G-BKIT	SOCATA TB-9 Tampico	330		22. 9.82	D.N.Garlick, P.D.Foreman, P.Johnson & R.A.Hawkins		
						Southend	14. 6.04
G-BKIU*	Colt 17A Cloudhopper HAFB	420		29. 9.92	Not known *"Just One"*	NK	
					(Cancelled 15.5.98 by CAA) (Noted 1999)		
G-BKIV*	Colt 21A Cloudhopper HAFB	447		29. 9.82	Not known	NK	NE(A)
					(Cancelled 21.11.89 by CAA) (Noted 2.97)		
G-BKIX*	Cameron V-31 Air Chair HAFB	863	(G-BKGJ)	23. 9.82	Not known "Every Penny"	NK	21. 9.95
					(Cancelled 4.8.98 by CAA) (Noted 1999)		
G-BKIY*	Thunder Ax3 Sky Chariot HAFB	464		7.10.82	Balloon Preservation Group	Kirdford	
					"Michaelangelo" (Cancelled 15.11.01 as wfu)		
G-BKJB	Piper PA-18-135 Super Cub	18-574	PH-GAI	1. 8.83	Haimoss Ltd	Old Sarum	6. 9.04T
	(L-21A-PI) *(Frame No.18-522)*		R Neth AF R-204/51-15657/N1003A				
G-BKJF	SOCATA MS.880B Rallye 100T	2300	F-BULF	16.12.82	Journeyman Aviation Ltd	Sywell	12. 7.04
G-BKJS	Jodel Wassmer D.120A Paris-Nice	191	F-BJPS	4.10.82	J.H.Leigh	Clipgate, Denton	23. 7.02P
					t/a Clipgate Flying Group		
G-BKJT*	Cameron O-65 HAFB	148	EI-BAN	2.11.82	Not known	(Lancashire/Cheshire)	
					(Cancelled 19.5.93 by CAA) (Noted active 2000)		
G-BKJW	Piper PA-23-250 Aztec E	27-4716	N14153	3.11.78	Alan Williams Entertainments Ltd		
						Southend	25. 5.02

G-BKKI*	Westland WG.30 Srs.100	003		1.11.82	Westland Helicopters Ltd *(Cancelled 8.1.91 as WFU) (Stored 6.91)*	Yeovil	28. 6.85P
G-BKKN	Cessna 182R Skylane II	18267801	N6218N	30.11.82	R.A.Marven t/a Marvagraphic	Coleman Green, Herts	30. 4.04
G-BKKO	Cessna 182R Skylane II	18267852	N4907H	30.11.82	B & G Jebson Ltd	Crosland Moor	21. 3.02
G-BKKZ	Pitts S-1S Special	PFA 09-10525	(G-BIVW)	10.11.82	J.A.Coutts	(Harleston)	15. 6.02P
G-BKLJ*	Westland Scout Srs.1	F.9618	5X-UUX G-17-2	6. 7.83	R.Dagless	East Dereham	
	(Not converted & believed to R.Windley as spares for G-BMIR: cancelled 7.2.91 by CAA) (Stored as "5X-UUX" in poor condition 6.93: current status unknown)						
G-BKLO	Reims Cessna F172M Skyhawk II	F17201380	PH-BET D-EFMS	22. 3.83	Stapleford Flying Club Ltd	Stapleford	11. 6.04T
G-BKLP	Reims Cessna F172N Skyhawk II	F17201809	PH-BYL	22. 3.83	M.J.Jones	Cranfield	8. 7.04T
G-BKLS*	Aérospatiale SA.341G Gazelle 1	1445	G-TURP G-BKLS/N17MT/N14MT/N49549	11. 1.83	Apollo Helicopters Ltd	Charlwood, Surrey	2.12.91T
	(Damaged Stanford-le-Hope 9.9.91 as G-TURP: restored as G-BKLS 5.11.91 & on rebuild using fuselage ex N341BB [1421]: current status unknown: original fuselage to Gatwick Aviation Museum as "G-TURP")						
G-BKMA	Mooney M.20J (201)	24-1316	N1170N	13.12.82	C.A.White t/a Foxtrot Whisky Aviation	Cambridge	1. 5.04
G-BKMB	Mooney M.20J (201)	24-1307	N1168P	15.12.82	W.A.Cook, B.Pearson & P.Turnbull	Sherburn in Elmet	3.12.04
G-BKMG	Handley Page O/400 rep	TPG-1		8.12.82	M.G.King t/a The Paralyser Group *(Under construction 1993: current status unknown)*	(Wroxham, Norwich)	
G-BKMI	Supermarine 359 Spitfire HF.VIIIc	6S/583793	A58-671 MV154	23.12.82	The Aerial Museum (North Weald) Ltd *(As "MT928/ZX-M" in 145 Sqn c/s)*	Filton	4. 7.02P
G-BKMR*	Thunder Ax3 Maxi Sky Chariot HAFB	497		12. 1.83	British Balloon Museum & Library *"The Weasel" (Cancelled 23.4.98 as WFU)*	Newbury	
G-BKMT	Piper PA-32R-301 Saratoga SP	32R-8213013	N8005Z	4. 2.83	P.R. & B.N.Lewis t/a Severn Valley Aviation Group	Shobdon	9. 4.04
G-BKMW*	Short SD.3-30 Sherpa Var.100	SH.3094	G-14-3094	13.12.82	Ulster Folk & Transport Museum	Belfast	14. 9.90
	(Broken up 3.96 Belfast City: cancelled 14.11.96 as WFUO (Cockpit section only).						
G-BKMX	Short SD.3-60 Var.100	SH.3608	G-14-3608	13.12.82	BAC Leasing Ltd *(Op BAC Express titles) "City of Bristol"*	Exeter	15. 3.02T
G-BKNA	Cessna 421	421-0097	F-BUYB HB-LDZ/N4097L	28. 1.83	Launchapart Ltd *(Damaged Penbridge, Hereford 3.8.97)*	Barton	13. 8.97
G-BKNB	Cameron V-42 HAFB	887		10. 1.83	D.N.Close	Andover	17. 7.97A
G-BKNI	Gardan GY-80-160D Horizon	249	F-BRJN	28. 1.83	A.Hartigan t/a Blue Horizon Flying Group *"Blue Lady"*	Bourn	13. 5.02
G-BKNO	Monnett Sonerai IIL (VW 1834)	792 & PFA 015-10528		11. 3.83	S.Hardy	(Hemel Hempstead)	15. 6.99P
G-BKNP	Cameron V-77 HAFB	874		22.12.82	I.Lilja *"Winnie The Pooh"*	Kvanum, Sweden	17. 2.02A
G-BKNZ	Menavia Piel CP.301A Emeraude	296	F-BISZ	21. 1.83	C.J.Bellworthy	Finmere	17. 4.02P
G-BKOA	SOCATA MS.893E Rallye 180GT	12432	F-BOFB F-ODAT/F-BVAT	2. 3.83	P.Howick	Bodmin	31.10.02
G-BKOB	Moravan Zlin Z.326 Trener Master	757	F-BKOB	28. 9.81	W.G.V.Hall *(Damaged on take off Old Sarum 12.3.00: on rebuild 11.01)*	Old Sarum	17. 5.02
G-BKOT	Wassmer WA.81 Piranha	813	F-GAIP	17. 2.87	Barbara N.Rolfe *(Stored 9.01)*	Little Gransden	
G-BKOU	Hunting P.84 Jet Provost T.3	PAC/W/13901	XN637	17. 2.83	Seagull Formation Ltd *(As "XN637/03" in TWU/79 Sqn markings)*	North Weald	21. 8.02P
G-BKOW*	Colt 77A HAFB	505		6. 9.84	Balloon Preservation Group *"Lady Di" (Elle titles) (Cancelled 29.4.97 as WFU)*	Kirdford	14. 2.88A
G-BKPA	Hoffmann H-36 Dimona	3522		16. 6.83	A.Mayhew	Rochester	4. 6.02
G-BKPB	Aerosport Scamp (VW 1834)	PFA 117-10736		23. 2.83	B.R.Thompson	Leicester	27.11.02P
G-BKPC	Cessna A185F AGcarryall	185-03809	N4599E	10. 7.80	The Black Knights Parachute Centre Ltd	Bank End Farm, Cockerham	11.10.04
G-BKPD	Viking Dragonfly 302 & (Revmaster 2100D)	PFA 139-10897		11. 3.83	E.P.Browne & G.J.Sargent *(Damaged Cambridge 17.7.99)*	Cambridge	20. 1.00P
G-BKPE	CEA Jodel DR.250/160 Capitaine	35	F-BNJD	18. 3.83	J.S. & J.D.Lewer	Dunkeswell	16.12.04
G-BKPG*	Luscombe P3 Rattler Strike	003		7. 3.83	Not known	Tatenhill	
	(Cancelled 31.7.91 by CAA) (Stored 5.95: current status unknown)						
G-BKPK	Everett Gyroplane (VW 1834)	005		19. 4.83	J.C.McHugh *(Stored Sproughton 12.95: current status unknown)*	(Stapleford Abbotts)	23. 3.93P
G-BKPN	Cameron N-77 HAFB	923		9. 3.83	R.H.Sanderson *"Do It All"*	Nuneaton	21. 5.87A
G-BKPS	Grumman-American AA-5B Tiger	AA5B-0007	OO-SAS OO-HAO/(OO-WAY)/N1507R	7. 3.83	A.E.T.Clarke	Manston	1.10.03
G-BKPX	Jodel Wassmer D.120A Paris-Nice	240	F-BLNG	19. 1.84	N.H.Martin	Skipwith, Selby	12. 2.00P
G-BKPY	SAAB 91B/2 Safir	91321	56321 R NorAF "UA-B"	23. 3.83	Newark Air Museum Ltd *(As "321" in R.NorAF c/s)*	Winthorpe	
G-BKPZ	Pitts S-1T Special (Lycoming AEIO-360)	PFA 09-10852		4. 3.83	Mary A.Frost	Downland Farm, Redhill	2. 7.02P

G-BKRA	North American T-6G-NH Texan	188-90	MM53664	19. 8.83	Transport Command Ltd	Shoreham	25. 6.03T
			RM-9/51-15227		*(As "51-15227/10" in US Navy c/s)*		
G-BKRB*	Cessna 172N Skyhawk II	17272969	EI-BKR	23. 3.83	Not known	Clacton	15. 5.89
			G-BHKZ/N1207F				
			(Cancelled 20.4.88 as WFU: wreck stored 7.95: current status unknown)				
G-BKRD*	Cessna 320E Skyknight	320E0101	D-IACB	24. 3.83	Home Office Fire & Emergency Training Centre		
			HB-LDN/N2201Q			Moreton-in-Marsh	30. 9.93
			(Crashed Lille, France 5.11.90: cancelled 6.4.92 as destroyed: for fire service use 8.98)				
G-BKRF	Piper PA-18 Super Cub 95	18-1525	F-BOUI	7.11.83	K.M.Bishop	Croft Farm, Defford	29. 9.98P
	(L-18C-PI) *(Frame No.18-1502)*		ALAT/51-15525				
G-BKRG*	Beechcraft C-45G-BH	AF-222	N75WB	5. 5.83	Aces High Ltd	Bruntingthorpe	
	(Regd as C-45H)		N9072Z/51-11665				
			(Cancelled 27.4.98 as WFU: stored as spares source G-BKRN 1.00 qv)				
G-BKRH	Brugger MB.2 Colibri			15. 3.83	M.R.Benwell	Hinton-in-the-Hedges	2. 8.02P
	(VW 1835) 142 & PFA 043-10150						
G-BKRK	SNCAN Stampe SV-4C	57	Fr.Navy	30. 3.83	J.R.Bisset	Insch	28. 6.98
					t/a Strathgadie Stampe Group		
G-BKRL*	Chichester-Miles Leopard	001		21. 3.83	Chichester-Miles Consultants Ltd		
	(Noel Penny 301)				*(Cancelled 25.1.99 as WFU: stored 10.01)*	(Old Sarum)	14.12.91P
G-BKRN	Beechcraft D.18S	A-675	CF-DTN	14. 4.83	A.A.Marshall & P.L.Turland		
			RCAF A675/RCAF 1500		*(Stored 1.00)*	Bruntingthorpe	26. 6.83P
	(Official c/n is CA-75 suggesting Canadian rebuild)						
G-BKRS	Cameron V-56 HAFB	908		23. 3.83	D.N. & L.J.Close *"Bonkers"*	Andover	17. 7.97A
G-BKRU*	Ensign Crossley Racer	PFA 131-10797		30. 3.83	M.S.Crossley	Redhill	24. 1.90P
	(Continental C90)				*(Stored 9.90: cancelled 2.3.99 by CAA: current status unknown)*		
G-BKRZ	Dragon 77 HAFB	001		11. 4.83	J.R.Barber *"Rupert"*	Newbury	5. 3.94A
					(On loan to British Balloon Museum & Library)		
G-BKSB	Cessna T310Q II	310Q0914	VR-CEM	22. 4.83	D.H.& P.M.Smith	Bagby	4. 5.03
			G-BKSB/HB-LMO/OE-FYL/(N69680)		t/a G.H.Smith & Son		
G-BKSC*	Saro Skeeter AOP.12	S2/7157	XN351	23. 5.83	R.A.L.Falconer	(Ipswich)	8.11.84P
	(Official c/n S2/7076 but may be component identity)						
			(As "XN351": on overhaul 10.96: cancelled 11.10.00 by CAA: current status unknown)				
G-BKSD	Colt 56A HAFB	361		11. 4.83	M.J.Casson *"Entwhistle Green"*	Kendal	2. 6.96A
G-BKSE	QAC Quickie 1	PFA 094-10748		6. 4.83	M.D.Burns	(Bridge of Weir)	8. 5.89P
	(Onan B48M) *(Regd with c/n PFA 094-10784)*				*(Stored 6.00: current status unknown)*		
G-BKSH*	Colt 21A Cloudhopper HAFB	510		16. 5.83	Not known *"Mekon*	NK	
					(Cancelled 12.5.98 by CAA: extant 2000)		
G-BKSP	Schleicher ASK 14	14028	D-KOMO	25. 5.83	J.H.Bryson	Bellarena	16. 5.03
G-BKSS	SAN Jodel 150 Mascaret	48	F-BMFC	14. 9.83	D.H.Wilson-Spratt	Ronaldsway	
					(Noted 8.00)		
G-BKST	Rutan VariEze	12718-001		20. 4.83	R.Towle	(Hexham)	
G-BKSX	SNCAN Stampe SV-4C	61	F-BBAF	16. 5.83	C.A.Bailey & J.A.Carr		
			Fr.Mil			Trenchard Farm, Eggesford	15. 6.89
					(Stored 8.90: current status unknown)		
G-BKTA	Piper PA-18 Super Cub 95	18-3223	OO-HBA	10. 5.83	M.J.Dyson & M.T.Clark	Fradley	8. 7.02P
	(L-18C-PI) *(Frame No.18-3246)*		Belg AF OL-L49/L-149/53-4823				
G-BKTH	Hawker Sea Hurricane IB	CCF/41H/4013	Z7015	24. 5.83	The Shuttleworth Trust	Old Warden	3. 5.01P
	(Built CCF)				*(As "Z7015/7-L" in 880 Sqdn, RN c/s)*		
G-BKTM	PZL SZD-45A Ogar	B-656		31. 5.83	Repclif Chemical Services Ltd	Sleap	13. 6.03
G-BKTR	Cameron V-77 HAFB	951		6. 6.83	A.Palmer *"Diddlybopper"*	Tonbridge	1. 6.02A
G-BKTV	Reims Cessna F152 II	F15201450	OY-BJB	8. 8.83	A.Jahanfar	Southend	28. 7.02T
					(Op Seawing Flying Club)		
G-BKTZ	Slingsby T.67M Firefly	2004	G-SFTV	26. 8.83	T.D.Reid	Blackpool	18. 8.02
					(Fuselage noted 12.01)		
G-BKUE	SOCATA TB-9 Tampico	369	F-BNGX	31. 5.83	Pool Aviation (NW) Ltd	Blackpool	6. 2.03T
G-BKUJ*	Thunder Ax6-56 Srs.1 HAFB	520		17. 6.83	R.J.Bent *"Edward Bear"*	Torquay	28. 9.88A
					(Cancelled 10.10.01 by CAA)		
G-BKUR	Menavia Piel CP.301A Emeraude	280	(G-BKBX)	19.10.83	R.Wells	Peterlee	21. 6.02P
			F-BMLX/F-OBLY				
G-BKUS*	Bensen B.8M	PFA G/01-1045		7. 7.83	A.Charles	Newbury	21. 6.88P
					(Cancelled 11.10.00 by CAA: current status unknown)		
G-BKUT*	Morane-Saulnier MS.880B Rallye Club	376	F-BKZT	22. 7.83	Not known	(West Scotland)	
			(Crashed Nayes Coppice Farm, Havant 16.2.92: cancelled 7.4.92 by CAA)				
					(Instructional use 6.00: current status unknown)		
G-BKUU	Thunder Ax7-77 Srs.1 HAFB	522		3. 8.83	M.A.Mould *"Tanglefoot"*	Winchester	23. 4.02A
G-BKVA	SOCATA Rallye 180T Galerien	3274	SE-GFS	30. 6.83	J.M.Airey	Saltby	7. 6.04T
			F-GBXA		t/a Buckminster Gliding Club Syndicate		
G-BKVB	SOCATA Rallye 110ST Galopin	3258	OO-PIP	22. 6.83	A. & K.Bishop	(Swansea)	16.12.01
G-BKVC	SOCATA TB-9 Tampico	372	F-BNGQ	4. 7.83	H.P.Aubin-Parvu	Biggin Hill	11. 2.02
G-BKVE	Rutan VariEze	PFA 074-10236	G-EZLT	5. 7.83	K.Cox	(Alton)	3. 9.99P
	(Continental O-200-A)		*(Force landed Waltham near Canterbury 11.4.99: current status unknown)*				
G-BKVF	Clutton FRED Srs.III	PFA 029-10791		29. 7.83	J.M.Brightwell & A.J.Wright	(Derby)	
G-BKVG	Scheibe SF-25E Super Falke	4362	(D-KNAE)	25. 8.83	G-BKVG Ltd	North Hill	4. 6.02

G-BKVK	Auster AOP.9	AUS/10/2	WZ662	8. 8.83	J.D.Butcher	AAC Netheravon	29. 9.00P
					(Op Military Auster Flight) (As "WZ662" in Army c/s)		
G-BKVL	Robin DR.400/160 Major	1625		26. 7.83	M.R.Shelton	Tatenhill	22. 7.02T
					t/a Tatenhill Aviation		
G-BKVM	Piper PA-18-150 Super Cub	18-849	PH-KAZ	26. 8.83	D.G.Caffrey	North Coates	3.10.02
	(L-21A-PI) *(Frame No.18-824)*		RNeth AF R-214/51-15684		*(As "115684/VM" in US Army c/s)*		
					"Spirit of Goxhill"		
G-BKVO	Pietenpol Air Camper	PFA 047-10799		8. 8.83	M.C.Hayes	(Woonton, Hereford)	25. 5.99P
	(Continental A65)				*(New owner 6.01)*		
G-BKVP	Pitts S-1D Special	002 & PFA 09-10800		19. 8.83	S.W.Doyle	Leicester	19. 5.02P
	(Lycoming IO-360)						
G-BKVS	Campbell Cricket	PFA G/01-1047		11. 8.83	K.Hughes	(Amlwch)	27. 9.02P
	(VW 1834)						
G-BKVT	Piper PA-23-250 Aztec F	27-7754002	G-HARV	6. 2.84	BKS Surveys Ltd.	Belfast	3. 4.03T
			N62760				
G-BKVW	Airtour AH-56 HAFB	AH.003		27. 6.84	L.D. & H.Vaughan *"Lunardi"*	Tring	
G-BKVX	Airtour AH-56C HAFB	AH.002		27. 6.84	P.Aldridge	Halesworth, Suffolk	
					"Featherspin" or *"Liebling"* ?		
G-BKVY	Airtour B-31 HAFB	AH.001		9. 8.83	M.Davies	Callington, Cornwall	15. 8.01A
					"Day Dream"		
G-BKWD	Taylor JT.2 Titch	PFA 060-10232		17. 8.83	E.H.Booker	Valley Farm, Winwick	11. 6.02P
	(Continental PC60) *(Originally regd as c/n PFA 060-10143: presumed absorbed into both projects)*						
G-BKWR	Cameron V-65 HAFB	970		26. 8.83	K.J.Foster	Coleshill, Birmingham	9. 7.00A
					"White Spirit"		
G-BKWW	Cameron O-77 HAFB	984		13. 9.83	A.M.Marten *"Kouros"*	Woking	18. 1.89A
G-BKWY	Reims Cessna F152T	F15201940		22. 9.83	The Cambridge Aero Club Ltd	Cambridge	5. 9.02T
G-BKXA	Robin R.2100	114	F-GAOS	24.11.83	M.Wilson	Little Gransden	22.10.99
					(New owner 8.01)		
G-BKXD	Aérospatiale SA.365N Dauphin 2	6088	F-WMHD	7. 9.83	Scotia Helicopter Services Ltd	Blackpool	8.12.04T
G-BKXF	Piper PA-28R-200 Cherokee Arrow II	28R-7335351	OY-DZN	10.11.83	P.L.Brunton	Caernarfon	22. 6.02T
			N56092				
G-BKXM	Colt 17A Cloudhopper HAFB	531		3.10.83	R.G.Turnbull	Glasbury, Hereford	16. 2.01A
G-BKXN	ICA IS-28M2A	48		24.10.83	D.C.Wellard	(Cheltenham)	3. 5.03
G-BKXO	Rutan LongEz	PFA 074A-10580		24.10.83	D.F.P.Finan	Teesside	27. 6.00P
	(Continental O-200-A)				*(Stored 12.01)*		
G-BKXP	Auster AOP.6	2830	A-14	12.10.83	B.J.Ellis	Thruxton	
	(Frame No.TAY841BJ)		Belg AF/VT987		*(On rebuild 7.91: new owner 12.01)*		
G-BKXR	Druine D.31A Turbulent	303	OY-AMW	1.11.83	M.B.Hill	Draycott Farm, Chiseldon	20.11.02P
	(VW 1700)						
G-BKXX*	Cameron V-65 HAFB	1000	(OO-)	1. 9.83	L.J.H.Decabooter & L.P.Neirynck *"Hot Mille"*		
			G-BKXX			St.Niklaas/Ostend, Belgium	24. 7.99A
					(Cancelled 28.11.01 as wfu)		
G-BKXY*	Westland WG.30 Srs.100	013	N113WG	2.11.83	Westland Helicopters Ltd	Yeovil	
			G-BKXY/N113WG/G-BKXY		*(Cancelled 11.8.88 as WFU) (Dumped 12.99)*		
					(Chicago Airlink titles)		
G-BKZB	Cameron V-77 HAFB	995		11.11.83	K.B.Chapple	Didcot	6. 7.01A
G-BKZE	Aérospatiale AS332L Super Puma	2102	F-WKQE	30. 9.83	Scotia Helicopter Services Ltd	Aberdeen	13. 3.03T
G-BKZF	Cameron V-56 HAFB	246	F-BXUK	14.11.83	A.D.Brice *"Xplorer"*	Cowbridge	18. 3.97A
G-BKZG	Aérospatiale AS332L Super Puma	2106	HB-ZBT	30. 9.83	Scotia Helicopter Services Ltd	Aberdeen	25. 8.02T
	(Additional p/i UN417 not confirmed)		G-BKZG				
G-BKZH	Aérospatiale AS332L Super Puma	2107		30. 9.83	Scotia Helicopter Services Ltd	Aberdeen	4. 4.03T
	(Rolled over on take-off from offshore drilling vessel 'West Navion' 10.11.01, 50 m west of Shetland)						
G-BKZI	Bell 206A JetRanger	118	(5B-CGC/'D?)	7.12.83	Dolphin Property (Management) Ltd		
			G-BKZI/N6238N			Thruxton	19. 9.04T
G-BKZM	Isaacs Fury II	PFA 011-10742		27. 9.83	B.Jones	Haverfordwest	1.10.90P
	(Continental O-200-A)				*(As "K2060": stored 8.96: current status unknown)*		
G-BKZT	Clutton FRED Srs.II	PFA 029-10715		20.10.83	U.Chakravorty	(Margate)	2. 7.02P
	(VW 1834)						
G-BKZV	Bede BD-4	380	ZS-UAB	31. 8.84	G.I.J.Thomson	Little Snoring	20. 8.02P
	(Lycoming O-320)						

G-BLAA – G-BLZZ

G-BLAA	Sportavia Fournier RF5	5011	D-KIHI	3.10.83	A.D.Wren	Southend	11. 9.99
	(Destroyed by fire when YS-11 9U-BHP, parked adjacent to G-BLAA's canvas hangar, caught fire on 3.11.01)						
G-BLAC	Reims Cessna FA152 Aerobat	FA1520370		25. 3.80	D.C.C.Handley	Bourn	26. 7.04T
G-BLAD	Thunder Ax7-77 Srs.1 HAFB	485		7.12.83	P.J.Bish *"Big Lad"*	Hungerford	15.10.92A
					(Stolen from Hungerford 5.8.92: current status unknown)		
G-BLAF	Stolp SA.900 V-Star	PFA 106-10651		13. 9.83	P.R.Skeels	Lymm Dam	18.10.02P
	(Continental O-200-A)						
G-BLAG	Pitts S-1D Special	PFA 09-10195		1.12.83	P.M.Ambrose	Popham	12. 4.02P
	(Lycoming AEIO-360)						
G-BLAH	Thunder Ax7-77 Srs.1 HAFB	526		3.10.83	T.M.Donnelly *"Blah"*	Doncaster	19. 8.01A

G-BLAI	Monnett Sonerai IIL *(Regd with c/n PFA 015-10584)*	PFA 015-10583		6.12.83	T.Simpson *(Noted 12.01)*	Breighton	12. 1.99P
G-BLAM	CEA DR.360 Chevalier	345	F-BRCM	6. 2.84	D.J.Durell	Maypole Farm, Chislet	8. 8.02
G-BLAT	SAN Jodel 150 Mascaret	56	F-BNID	30. 1.84	D.J.Dulborough & A.J.Court	Popham	11. 6.02P
G-BLAX	Reims Cessna FA152 Aerobat	FA1520385		11.10.83	Bflying Ltd *(Op Bournemouth Flying Club)*	Bournemouth	11. 5.02T
G-BLCA	Bell 206B-3 JetRanger III	3443	N20982	1.12.83	RMH Stainless Ltd *(Op Central Helicopters)*	Orgreave Gorse Farm, Lichfield	27. 5.02T
G-BLCG	SOCATA TB-10 Tobago	61	G-BHES	17. 3.80	P.Hickey & M.E.Woodroffe t/a Charlie Golf Flying Group	Shoreham	15. 7.04
G-BLCH	Colt 56D HAFB	392		14.11.83	Balloon Flights Club Ltd *"Geronimo"*	Leicester	
G-BLCI	EAA AcroSport P	P-10A	N6AS	29. 2.84	M.R.Holden *"Bluebottle"* *(Damaged Farthing Corner late 1996: current status unknown)*	Stoneacre Farm, Farthing Corner	16. 6.97P
G-BLCM	SOCATA TB-9 Tampico	194	OO-TCT (OO-TBC)	2.12.83	Repclif Chemical Services Ltd *(Op Liverpool Flying School)*	Liverpool	29. 5.02T
G-BLCT	CEA Jodel DR.220 2+2	23	F-BOCQ	22.12.83	C.J.Snell t/a Christopher Robin Flying Group	Shoreham	21. 7.02
G-BLCU	Scheibe SF-25B Falke	4699	D-KECC	30.12.83	C.F.Sellers	Rufforth	19. 7.02
G-BLCV	Hoffmann H-36 Dimona	36113	EI-CJO G-BLCV	21. 3.84	R.L.Braithwaite	Rufforth	14. 6.02
G-BLCW	Evans VP-1 (VW 1600)	PFA 062-10835		19.12.83	M.Flint *"Le Plank"*	Fenland	24. 6.02P
G-BLCY	Thunder Ax7-65Z HAFB	487		13. 1.84	C.M.George *"Warsteiner"*	Brixton, Plymouth	26. 2.99A
G-BLDB	Taylor JT.1 Monoplane (VW 1600)	PFA 055-10506		28.12.83	C.J.Bush	Great Oakley, Harwich	15. 5.02P
G-BLDD	WAG-Aero CUBy AcroTrainer (Lycoming O-320)	PFA 108-10653		29.12.83	J.Harper	(Evesham)	14. 3.01P
G-BLDG	Piper PA-25-260 Pawnee C	25-4501	SE-FLB LN-VYM	9. 1.84	Ouse Gliding Club Ltd	Rufforth	20. 6.02
G-BLDK	Robinson R22	0139	C-GSGU	17. 1.84	Helicentre Ltd	Blackpool	28. 6.02T
G-BLDL*	Cameron Truck 56 SS HAFB	990		10. 1.84	Balloon Preservation Group *"Europa" (Cancelled as WFU 21.10.96)*	Kirdford	NE(A)
G-BLDN	Rand-Robinson KR-2	PFA 129-10913		12. 1.84	S.C.Solley *(Rebuilt, overhauled 2000 & noted 4.01)*	Mavis Enderby	14. 6.02P
G-BLDV	Pilatus Britten-Norman BN-2B-26 Islander	2179	D-INEY G-BLDV	13. 1.84	Loganair Ltd *(Benyhone Tartan t/s)*	Kirkwall	18. 7.02T
G-BLEJ	Piper PA-28-161 Cherokee Warrior II	28-7816257	N2194M	8. 2.84	Eglinton Flying Club Ltd	City of Derry	29. 3.02T
G-BLEP	Cameron V-65 HAFB	1022		7. 2.84	D.Chapman t/a The Ground Hogs *"Manor Marquees"*	Maidstone	10. 9.96A
G-BLES	Stolp SA.750 Acroduster Too (Lycoming O-360)	197 & PFA 089-10428		8.12.83	G.N.Davies	Enstone	9. 9.02P
G-BLET	Thunder Ax7-77 Srs.1 HAFB	539		16. 2.84	Servatruc Ltd *"Servatruc"*	Nottingham	15. 8.97A
G-BLEW	Reims Cessna F182Q Skylane II	F18200039	F-GAQD	21. 6.78	Seager Publishing Ltd	Kemble	3. 9.03
G-BLEZ	Aérospatiale SA.365N Dauphin 2	6131		24. 1.84	CHC Scotia Ltd *(Op First Aim Medevac)*	(Forties Oil Field)	27. 8.02T
G-BLFI	Piper PA-28-181 Archer II	28-8490034	N4333Z	22. 2.84	Bonus Aviation Ltd	Cranfield	27. 7.03T
G-BLFW	Grumman-American AA-5 Traveler	AA5-0786	OO-GLW	22. 2.84	D.C.A.Milne t/a Grumman Club	Draycott Farm, Chiseldon	2. 9.02
G-BLFY	Cameron V-77 HAFB	1030		16. 3.84	A.N.F.Pertwee *"Groupie"*	Frinton-on-Sea	5. 4.92A
G-BLFZ	Piper PA-31 Navajo C	31-7912106	PH-RWS (PH-ASV)/N3538W	21. 3.84	London Executive Aviation Ltd	Stapleford	10. 7.02T
G-BLGB*	Short SD.3-60 Var.100	SH.3641	G-14-3641	24. 2.84	British Regional Airlines Ltd *(Damaged Stornoway 9.2.98: cancelled 19.11.98 as PWFU: hulk remains dumped 6.01)*	Lasham	31. 3.98T
G-BLGH	Robin DR.300/180R Remorqueur	570	D-EAFL	10. 4.84	Booker Gliding Club Ltd	Booker	2. 3.03
G-BLGO	Bensen B.8MV (VW 1834)	RB-01		18. 6.84	F.Vernon *(Stored 5.98: current status unknown)*	St.Merryn	15. 5.87P
G-BLGR	Bell 47G-4A	7501	N3236G HC-ASQ/N1186W	2. 5.84	H., J.R. & H.C.Wake & S.P.Broughton & Co Ltd t/a Courteenhall Farms	Courteenhall, Northampton	24. 6.02
G-BLGS	SOCATA Rallye 180T	3206		7. 7.78	A.Waters t/a London Light Aircraft	Dunstable	21. 5.99
G-BLGT	Piper PA-18 Super Cub 95 (L-18C-PI) *(Frame No.18-1399)*	18-1445	D-EAGT D-EOCC/ALAT 51-15445	1. 6.84	Liddell Aircraft Ltd	Bournemouth	23. 5.02P
G-BLGV	Bell 206B JetRanger II	982	5B-JSB C-FDYL/CF-DYL	2. 5.84	Heliflight (UK) Ltd	Wolverhampton	22. 5.02T
G-BLGX*	Thunder Ax7-65 HAFB	551		16. 4.84	"The 45" *(Cancelled 19.5.93 by CAA) (Noted active 9.94) (Stored 2001)*	Uttoxeter	NE(A)
G-BLHH	CEA DR.315 Petit Prince	324	F-BPRH	3. 7.84	Central Certification Service Ltd	Tower Farm, Woolaston	6. 6.03

G-BLHI	Colt 17A Cloudhopper HAFB	506		8. 9.86	Janet A.Folkes *"Hopping Mad"*	Loughborough	24.11.01A
G-BLHJ	Reims Cessna F172P Skyhawk II	F17202182		26. 3.84	Fraggle Leasing Ltd *(Op Edinburgh Air Centre)*	Edinburgh	8.12.02T
G-BLHK	Colt 105A HAFB	576		19. 6.84	A.S.Dear, R.B.Green & W.S.Templeton t/a Hale Hot-Air Balloon Group *"Gloworm"*	Fordingbridge	12. 7.97A
G-BLHL*	Menavia CP.301A Emeraude	275	F-BLHL F-OBLM	2. 3.78	Home Office Fire & Emergency Training Centre *(Crashed Slinfold 4.8.81 & for fire service use 8.98)*	Moreton-in-Marsh	27. 5.81P
G-BLHM(2)	Piper PA-18 Super Cub 95 (L-18C-PI) *(Frame No.18-3088)*	18-3120	LX-AIM D-EOAB/Belg AF OL-L46/L-46/53-4720	23. 7.84	A.G.Edwards	(Llandegla)	8. 8.02P
G-BLHN	Robin HR.100/285 Tiara	539	F-GABF	20. 2.78	N.A.Onions	Stapleford	17. 8.03
G-BLHR	Gulfstream GA-7 Cougar	GA7-0109	OO-RTI (OO-HRC)/N751G	12. 4.84	T.E.Westley	Fowlmere	9.12.02T
G-BLHS	Bellanca 7ECA Citabria 115	1342-80	OO-RTQ	12. 4.84	N.J.F.Campbell	Inverness	29. 4.02
G-BLHW	Varga 2150A Kachina	VAC161-80		17. 7.84	W.D.Garlick t/a Kachina Hotel Whiskey Group	Damyns Hall, Upminster	10. 5.03
G-BLID	DH.112 Venom FB.50 (FB.1) *(Built F + W)*	815	J-1605	13. 7.84	P.G.Vallance Ltd *(Gatwick Aviation Museum: as "J-1605" in Swiss AF c/s)*	Charlwood, Surrey	
G-BLIH	Piper PA-18-135 Super Cub (L-21B-PI) *(Frame No.18-3827)*	18-3828	(PH-KNG) R Neth AF R-138/(PH-KNG)/(PH-GRC)/R-138/54-2428	12.11.84	I.R.F.Hammond	Stubbington	
G-BLIK	Wallis WA-116/F/S (Franklin 2A-120)	K-218X		30. 4.84	K.H.Wallis *(Noted 8.01)*	Reymerston Hall, Norfolk	24. 4.98P
G-BLIO*	Cameron R-42 Gas/HAFB	1015		17. 4.84	British Balloon Museum & Library *(Cancelled 24.1.90 as destroyed)*	Newbury	17. 5.84P
G-BLIP*	Cameron N-77 HAFB	1031		17. 4.84	Balloon Preservation Group *"Systems 80" (Cancelled 23.6.98 as WFU)*	Kirdford	26. 3.94A
G-BLIT	Thorp T-18CW (Lycoming O-320)	PFA 076-10550		24. 4.84	A.P.Tyrwhitt-Drake	Fairoaks	6.11.02P
G-BLIW	Percival P.56 Provost T.53	PAC/F/125	IAC.177	12. 6.85	D.Mould & J.De Uphaugh t/a Provost Flying Group *(As "177" in Irish Air Corps c/s)*	Shoreham	2. 9.00P
G-BLIX	Saro Skeeter AOP.12	S2/5094	PH-HOF (PH-SRE)/XL809	3. 5.84	K.M.Scholes *(As "XL809"in Army c/s)*	Wilden	13. 9.02P
G-BLIY	SOCATA MS.892A Rallye Commodore 150	11639	F-BSCX	9. 5.84	A.J.Brasher & K.R.Haynes	Church Farm, North Moreton	27. 7.03
G-BLJD	Glaser-Dirks DG-400	4-85		15. 6.84	M.I.Gee	Rufforth	29. 5.03
G-BLJF	Cameron O-65 HAFB	1041		14. 5.84	M.D.& C.E.C.Hammond *"Fat Lady"*	Burgess Hill	16. 8.00A
G-BLJH	Cameron N-77 HAFB	1047		14. 5.84	K A Kent *"Daydream"* *(Op Balloon Preservation Group)*	Lancing	27. 6.89A
G-BLJM	Beechcraft 95-B55 Baron	TC-1997	SE-GRT	3. 3.78	R.A.Perrot	Guernsey	22. 8.03
G-BLJO	Reims Cessna F152 II	F15201627	OY-BNB	21. 6.84	Redhill School of Flying Ltd t/a Redhill Flying Club	Blackbushe	3.10.04T
G-BLKA*	de Havilland DH.112 Venom FB.54 (FB.4) *(Built F + W)* *(Regd with c/n 431)*	960	(G-VENM) J-1790 Sw AF	13. 7.84	De Havilland Aviation Ltd *(As "WR410/N" in 6 Sqdn RAF c/s)* *(Dismantled/stored 5.99: cancelled 13.10.00 by CAA)*	Swansea	14. 7.95P
G-BLKJ*	Thunder Ax7-65 HAFB	580		18. 7.84	Balloon Preservation Group Museum *"Up & Coming"* *(Cancelled 22.5.97 as PWFU)*	Lancing	3. 2.96A
G-BLKK	Evans VP-1 (VW 1834)	PFA 062-10642		15. 6.84	N.Wright	Queach Farm, Bury St Edmunds	27. 6.02P
G-BLKM	CEA Jodel DR.1051 Sicile	519	F-BLRO	26. 6.84	T.C.Humphreys	Goodwood	27. 6.03
G-BLKP	British Aerospace Jetstream Srs.3102	634	(G-BLEX) G-31-634	9. 7.84	BAE Systems (Corporate Air Travel) Ltd	Warton	19. 4.02T
G-BLKU*	Colt Flame 56SS HAFB	572		17. 7.84	British Balloon Museum & Library *"Mr.Wonderful II" (Cancelled 1.5.92 as WFU)*	Newbury	NE(A)
G-BLKY	Beechcraft 58 Baron	TH-1440		22. 8.84	J.C.Hall	Guernsey	28. 6.03
G-BLKZ	Pilatus P.2-05	600-45	U-125 A-125	30. 7.84	R.W.Hinton *(As "A-125" in Swiss AF c/s)*	Duxford	24. 1.01P
G-BLLA	Bensen B.8M (VW 1834)	PFA G/01-1055		27. 6.84	K.T.Donaghey	Henstridge	26. 7.02P
G-BLLB	Bensen B.8MR (Rotax 532)	PFA G/01A-1059		4. 9.84	D.H.Moss	Chilbolton	14. 6.01P
G-BLLD	Cameron O-77 HAFB	1060		16. 7.84	G.Birchall	Ormskirk	18. 7.01A
G-BLLF*	Westland WG.30 Srs.100	015	N115WG (G-BLLF)/N115WG	22. 4.85	Westland Helicopters Ltd *(Cancelled 11.8.88 as WFU) (Dumped 12.99)* *(Chicago Airlink titles)*	Yeovil	
G-BLLH	CEA Jodel DR.220A/B 2+2	131	F-BROM	17. 7.84	M.D.Hughes	Pauncefoot, Romsey	18. 6.03
G-BLLM	Piper PA-23-250 Aztec E	27-4619	G-BBNM OY-POR/G-BBNM/N14001	18. 1.84	C & M Thomas t/a Ammanford Trade Sales	Cardiff	21. 8.98
G-BLLN	Piper PA-18 Super Cub 95 (Continental O-200A) (L-18C-PI) *(Frame No.18-3380)*	18-3447	D-ECLN 96+23/PY+901/QZ+011/AC+507/AS+508/54-747	27. 6.84	P.L.Pilch & C.G.Fisher	(Wadhurst)	25. 1.04T

G-BLLO*	PA-18-95 Super Cub	18-3099	D-EAUB	11. 7.84	D.G. & M.G.Margetts	Sleap	12.10.96P
	(L-18C-PI) *(Frame No 18-3058)*		Belgium AF OL-L25/L-25/53-4699				
					(Cancelled 15.11.00 by CAA) (Dismantled 12.01)		
G-BLLP	Slingsby T.67B Firefly	2008		19. 7.84	Cleveland Flying School Ltd	Bagby	4.12.00T
G-BLLR	Slingsby T.67C Firefly	2011		19. 7.84	R.L.Brinklow	Gloucestershire	28.11.04T
	(Lycoming 0-320) (Regd as "T.67B (mod)")				*(Op Cotswold Aero Club) (www.cotswoldaeroclub.co.uk titles)*		
G-BLLS	Slingsby T.67B Firefly	2013		19. 7.84	Western Air (Thruxton) Ltd	Thruxton	17. 2.03T
G-BLLV	Slingsby T.67C Firefly	2015		3. 9.84	R.L.Brinklow	Wellesbourne Mountford	10.11.00T
					(Fuselage dumped 11.01)		
G-BLLW	Colt 56B HAFB	578		11. 9.84	G.Fordyce, R.Wickens & S.A.Sawyer	Olney	20. 4.02A
					"Angel Clare"		
G-BLLZ	Rutan LongEz	PFA 074A-10830		16. 7.84	R.S.Stoddart-Stones	Henstridge	22. 6.94P
	(Lycoming 0-235)						
G-BLMA	Moravan Zlin Z.526A Trener Master	922	F-BORS	23. 7.84	G.P.Northcott	Redhill	24. 6.01
G-BLMC*	Avro 698 Vulcan B.2A	-	XM575	R	East Midlands Aeropark	East Midlands	
	(Reservation @ 8.84, for proposed ferry flight to Bruntingthorpe, not taken up) (As "XM575")						
G-BLME	Robinson R22HP	0032	N90261	16. 4.85	Heli Air Ltd	Liverpool	15. 9.02T
G-BLMG	Grob G-109B	6322		27. 9.84	R.W.Littledale	Enstone	1.11.02
					t/a Mike Golf Syndicate		
G-BLMI	Piper PA-18 Super Cub 95	18-2066	D-ENWI	5. 6.84	R.Gibson	White Waltham	31. 5.87P
	(L-18C-PI) *(Frame No.18-2086)*		R Neth AF R-55/52-2466		t/a G-BLMI Flying Group *(As "R-55") (Noted 12.01)*		
G-BLMN	Rutan LongEz	PFA 074A-10643		3. 7.84	S.E.Bowers	Thruxton	15. 5.02P
	(Lycoming 0-235) *(Regd as c/n PFA 074A-10648)*				t/a G-BLMN Flying Group		
G-BLMP	Piper PA-17 Vagabond	17-193	F-BFMR	15. 5.84	M.Austin	Longwood, Southampton	29. 6.02P
	(Continental A65)		N4893H				
G-BLMR	Piper PA-18-150 Super Cub	18-2057	PH-NLD	29. 5.84	Transport Command Ltd	Shoreham	9. 6.02T
	(L-18C-PI) *(Frame No.18-2070)* (Lycoming 0-320)		R Neth AF R-72/52-2457		t/a Flying Services		
G-BLMT	Piper PA-18-135 Super Cub	18-2706	D-ELGH	12. 9.84	I.S.Runnalls	Church Farm, North Moreton	22. 8.02
	(Frame No.18-2724)		N8558C				
G-BLMW	Nipper T.66 RA45 Mk.IIIB			31. 8.84	S.L.Millar	Crowland	19. 7.02P
	(Ardem 10)	PFA 025-11020					
G-BLMZ	Colt 105A HAFB	404		24. 9.84	Mandy D.Dickinson *"Zulu"*	Bristol	28. 3.97A
G-BLNJ	Pilatus Britten-Norman BN-2B-26 Islander	2189		3. 9.84	Loganair Ltd	Kirkwall	3.12.02T
					(Martha Masanabo/Ndebele t/s)		
G-BLNO	Clutton FRED Srs.III	PFA 029-10559		17.10.84	L.W.Smith	(Sale, Cheshire)	
G-BLNW	Pilatus Britten-Norman BN-2B-26 Islander	2197		3. 9.84	Loganair Ltd	Glasgow	21.12.02T
					"Chatham Historic Dockyard"		
G-BLOB	Colt 31A Air Chair HAFB	599		11. 9.84	Jacques W.Soukup Enterprises Ltd	South Dakota, USA	5. 6.91A
G-BLOL					*See entry for G-AXRP*		
G-BLOR	Piper PA-30 Twin Comanche	30-59	HB-LAE	19. 7.85	R.L.C.Appleton	Sheepwash	22. 4.02T
			N7097Y/N10F				
G-BLOS	Cessna 185A Skywagon	185-0359	LN-BDS	17. 9.84	Elizabeth Brun	Great Massingham	24. 4.03
			N4159Y				
G-BLOT	Colt 56B HAFB	424		11. 9.84	H.J.Anderson *"Pathfinder"*	Oswestry	17. 7.96A
G-BLOV	Thunder Ax5-42 Srs.1 HAFB	590		11. 9.84	A.G.R.Calder	London SE16	17.10.01A
					"Puff The Magic Dragon"		
G-BLPA	Piper J-3C-65 Cub	11327	OO-AJL	27. 9.84	A.C.Frost	Rectory Farm, Abbotsley	15. 8.02P
	(L-4H-PI) *(Frame No.11152)*		OO-JOE/43-30036				
G-BLPB	Turner TSW Hot Two Wot	PFA 046-10606		19.10.84	I.R.Hannah	Redhill	10. 5.02P
	(Lycoming 0-320-A)						
G-BLPE	Piper PA-18 Super Cub 95	18-3084	D-ECBE	28. 9.84	A.A.Haig-Thomas	Clacton	17. 6.02P
	(L-18C-PI) (Continental 0-200-A) *(Also quoted as 18-3083)*		Belg Army L-10/53-4684				
G-BLPF	Reims FR172G Rocket	FR17200187	N4594Q	29. 1.85	G.E.McFarlane	Prestwick	2. 5.03T
			D-EEFL				
G-BLPG	Auster J/1N Alpha	3395	G-AZIH	21. 5.82	D.Taylor	Clacton	18. 3.04
					(As "16693" in RCAF c/s)		
G-BLPH*	Reims Cessna FRA150L Aerobat	FRA1500239	EI-BHH	19. 9.84	G.K. & T.G.Solomon t/a The New Aerobat Group	Kittyhawk Farm, Deanland	25. 6.00
			PH-ASH		*(Cancelled 25.8.00 as temp wfu)*		
G-BLPI	Slingsby T.67B Firefly	2016		24. 9.84	RAF Wyton Flying Club Ltd	RAF Wyton	30. 7.03T
G-BLPP	Cameron V-77 HAFB	432		19. 9.78	L.P.Purfield *"Merlin"*	Leicester	30. 4.94A
G-BLRA	British Aerospace BAe 146 Srs.100	E1017	N117TR	3.10.84	BAE Systems (Operations) Ltd	Woodford	15.10.03T
			N462AP/CP-2249/N462AP/G-BLRA/G-5-02				
G-BLRC	Piper PA-18-135 Super Cub	18-3602	OO-DKC	27.11.84	A.J.McBurnie	Poplar Hall Farm, Elmsett	20.12.03
	(L-21B-PI) *(Frame No.18-3790)*		PH-DKC/R Neth R-112/54-2402				
G-BLRD	MBB Bö.209 Monsun 150FV	101	D-EBOA	15.10.84	T.G.Lloyd	Kemble	16. 8.04
			(OE-AHM)				
G-BLRF	Slingsby T.67C Firefly	2014		30.11.84	R.C.Nicholls	Wellesbourne Mountford	10. 1.03T
G-BLRG	Slingsby T.67B Firefly	2020		30.11.84	R.L.Brinklow *(Wreck 4.00)*	Turweston	17. 7.00T
G-BLRJ	CEA Jodel DR.1051 Sicile	502	F-BLRJ	8. 2.78	M.P.Hallam	Jackrells Farm, Horsham	17. 7.00
G-BLRL	Scintex CP-301C1 Emeraude	552	(G-BLNP)	5.11.84	N.Thorne	Breighton	8.10.02P
			F-BJFT				

G-BLRM	Glaser-Dirks DG-400	4-107		5. 2.85	J.A.& W.S.Y.Stephen	Aboyne	19. 4.03
G-BLRN	de Havilland DH.104 Dove 8	04266	N531WB	30.10.84	J.F.M.Bleeker	Lelystad, The Netherlands	13. 3.96
			G-BLRN/WB531		*(To Pionier Hangaar Collection: as "WB531" in RAF c/s)*		
G-BLRW	Cameron Elephant 77SS HAFB	1074		14.12.84	Forbes Europe Inc	Balleroy, Normandy	1.10.00A
					"Great Sky Elephant"		
G-BLRY	Aérospatiale AS332L Super Puma	2111	LN-ONA	5. 2.85	Bristow Helicopters Ltd	Aberdeen	17. 6.02T
			G-BLRY/LN-ONA/G-BLRY/P2-PHP/VR-BIJ/G-BLRY/C-GQGL/G-BLRY				
G-BLSD*	de Havilland DH.112 Venom FB.54	928	N203DM	20. 5.85	R.J.Lamplough	North Weald	
	(Built F + W)		G-BLSD/J-1758		*(Cancelled 5.6.96 as WFU)*		
				(Open storage	*less booms and tail 5.01 as "J-1758 in Swiss AF c/s)*		
G-BLSF	Gulfstream AA-5A Cheetah	AA5A-0802	G-BGCK	21. 2.83	J.P.E.Walsh	Elstree	15. 6.03T
					t/a Walsh Aviation *(Op London School of Flying)*		
G-BLSH*	Cameron V-77 HAFB	1085		7.12.84	Balloon Preservation Group	Kirdford	14. 1.95A
					"Compass Rose" (Cancelled 30.3.98 as WFU)		
G-BLSK*	Colt 77A HAFB	617		29.11.84	R.D.MacKenzie	Gerrards Cross	22. 5.96A
					(Cancelled 5.7.00 by CAA)		
G-BLSM	British Aerospace BAe 125 Srs.700B	NA0346 & 257208	G-5-19	18.10.84	Dravidian Air Services Ltd	Heathrow	19.11.02
			(G-BLMJ)/N710BR				
G-BLST	Cessna 421C Golden Eagle III	421C0623	N88638	29.11.78	Cecil Aviation Ltd	Cambridge	20.11.02T
G-BLTA	Colt 77A Coil HAFB	525		8. 6.84	K.A.Schlussler	Bourne, Lincs	7. 8.91A
					"James Sadler"		
G-BLTC	Druine D.31A Turbulent	PFA 048-10964		18.12.84	G.P.Smith & A.W.Burton		
	(VW 1600)					Little Down Farm, Milson	8. 5.02P
G-BLTF	Robinson R22 A lpha	0428	N8526A	10. 1.85	Brian Seedle Helicopters Ltd	Blackpool	5. 4.04T
G-BLTK	Rockwell Commander 112TC-A	13106	SE-GSD	11.12.84	B.Rogalewski	Denham	26. 5.03
G-BLTM	Robin HR.200/100 Club	96	F-GAEC	21.11.84	J.S.Swale t/a Barton Robin Group	Barton	30. 7.03
G-BLTN	Thunder Ax7-65 HAFB	621		4. 1.85	J.A.Liddle *"Frederica"*	Reading	3. 9.88A
G-BLTP	British Aerospace BAe 125 Srs.700B	NA0347 & 257210	G-5-18	18.10.84	Dravidian Air Services Ltd	Heathrow	15. 1.02
			(G-BLMK)/N710BQ				
G-BLTR	Sportavia-Putzer Scheibe SF-25B Falke	4823	D-KHEC	23. 1.85	V.Mallon	RAF Bruggen	1. 4.94
G-BLTS	Rutan LongEz	PFA 074A-10741		14. 1.85	R.W.Cutler	(Thorverton, Exeter)	
G-BLTT	Slingsby T.67B Firefly	2023		16. 1.85	C.W.Ward	Cardiff	5. 8.00T
G-BLTU	Slingsby T.67B Firefly	2024		16. 1.85	RAF Wyton Flying Club Ltd	RAF Wyton	21. 9.03T
G-BLTV	Slingsby T.67B Firefly	2025		16. 1.85	R.L.Brinklow	Hinton-in-the-Hedges	9. 3.02T
G-BLTW	Slingsby T.67B Firefly	2026		16. 1.85	R.L.Brinklow	Turweston	14.10.02T
G-BLTY	Westland WG.30 Srs.160	019	VT-EKG	14. 1.85	D.Brem-Wilson	(Bromley)	
			G-17-9/G-BLTY/G-17-19				
G-BLUE*	Colting Ax7-77A HAFB	77A-011		2. 5.78	Balloon Preservation Group	Southampton	20. 9.99A
	(Regd as Colt 77A c/n 11)				*"Bluebird" (Cancelled 30.11.01 by CAA)*		
G-BLUI	Thunder Ax7-65 HAFB	553		22. 2.85	Susan Johnson	Blackpool	31. 7.00A
					"Rhubarb & Custard"		
G-BLUK*	Bond Sky Dancer	85/1		16. 1.85	J.Owen	Spilsted Farm, Sedlescombe	
		(Under construction 8.93 - wings noted 8.94: cancelled 15.4.99 by CAA: current status unknown)					
G-BLUL	CEA Jodel DR.1050/M1 Sicile Record	601	F-BMPJ	7. 3.85	J.Owen	Spilsted Farm, Sedlescombe	24.10.91
					(On overhaul 11.01)		
G-BLUM	Aérospatiale SA.365N Dauphin 2	6101		21. 1.85	Scotia Helicopter Services Ltd	Blackpool	14. 4.02T
G-BLUN	Aérospatiale SA.365N Dauphin 2	6114	PH-SSS	21. 1.85	Scotia Helicopter Services Ltd	Blackpool	5. 3.02T
			G-BLUN				
G-BLUV	Grob G-109B	6336		1. 2.85	R.J.Buckels & S.K.Durso	North Weald	16. 2.02
					t/a The 109 Flying Group		
G-BLUX	Slingsby T.67M-200 Firefly	2027	G-7-145	31. 1.85	R.L.Brinklow	Hinton-in-the-Hedges	8. 8.04T
			G-BLUX/G-7-113		t/a Richard Brinklow Aviation		
G-BLUZ	de Havilland DH.82B Queen Bee	1435 & SAL.150	LF858	9. 4.85	C.I.Knowles & J.Flynn	RAF Henlow	24. 5.02P
					t/a The Bee Keepers Group *(As "LF858")*		
G-BLVA	Airtour AH-31 HAFB	AH.004		12. 2.86	A.van Wyk	London SE12	
G-BLVB	Airtour AH-56 HAFB	AH.005		12. 2.86	R.W.Guild	Vilharino do Bairo, Portugal	
					"Bluejay"		
G-BLVI	Slingsby T.67M Firefly II	2017	(PH-KIF)	1. 2.85	Babcock Rosyth Defence Ltd		
			G-BLVI		t/a Hunting Contract Services *(Op JEFTS)*		
						RAF Barkston Heath	24. 1.03T
G-BLVK	Mudry/CAARP CAP-10B	141	JY-GSR	11. 3.85	E.K.Coventry	Childerditch	8. 5.03
G-BLVL	Piper PA-28-161 Warrior II	28-8416109	N43677	11. 2.85	Marair (Jersey) Ltd	Jersey	15. 5.03
G-BLVN*	Cameron N-77 HAFB	1098		4. 2.85	Servo & Electronic Sales Ltd	Lydd	9. 4.96A
					"Connect One" (Cancelled 18.9.01 as wfu)		
G-BLVS	Cessna 150M Commuter	15076869	EI-BLS	19. 2.85	Tindon Ltd	Conington	30. 7.03T
			N45356				
G-BLVW	Reims Cessna F172H	F172-0422	D-ENQU	16. 5.85	R & D Holloway Ltd	Stapleford	10. 7.00
G-BLWB*	Thunder Ax6-56 Srs.1 HAFB	645		22. 2.85	G.J.Bell *"Porky"*	Wokingham	10.11.99A
					(Cancelled 28.11.01 as wfu)		
G-BLWD	Piper PA-34-200T Seneca II	34-8070334	ZS-KKV	14. 3.85	Acre 123 Ltd.	Biggin Hill	6. 5.02T
			ZS-XAT/N8253E				

G-BLWE	Colt 90A HAFB	648		5. 3.85	Huntair Ltd	Aachen, Germany	11. 5.00A
					"Rair Computers"		
G-BLWF	Robin HR.100/210 Safari	183	F-BUSR	8. 3.85	Starguide Ltd	Stapleford	7. 6.03
G-BLWH	Fournier RF6B-100	7	F-GADF	3. 4.85	I.R.March	Booker	5. 9.03
G-BLWM*	Bristol M.1C rep	PFA 112-10892	"C4912"	12. 3.85	RAF Museum	Hendon	12. 8.87P
	(110 hp Gnome)				*(Cancelled 12.5.88 by CAA) (As "C4994" in RFC c/s)*		
G-BLWP	Piper PA-38-112 Tomahawk	38-78A0367	OY-BTW	7. 6.85	J.C.,T.,T. &, H.R Dodd	Panshanger	8. 3.04T
G-BLWT	Evans VP-1 Srs.2	PFA 062-10639		27. 3.85	J.S.Peplow	(Ledbury)	8. 7.02P
	(VW 1834)						
G-BLWV	Reims Cessna F152 II	F15201843	EI-BIN	25. 2.85	Redhill Aviation Ltd	Redhill	1. 6.03T
					t/a Redhill Flying Club		
G-BLWW*	Aerocar Mini-Imp Model C			1. 3.85	M.K.Field	Sleap	4. 6.87P
	(Continental O-200-A)	PFA 136-10880			t/a The Brize Group		
					(Cancelled 13.10.00 by CAA: noted 10.00)		
G-BLWX*	Cameron N-56 HAFB	1096		15. 2.85	Not Known	NK-	NE(A)
	(Sold RP-C1483 9.94: ntu? & cancelled 13.9.94: noted Ashton Court, Bristol 8.95 as "G-BLWX") (Current status unknown)						
G-BLWY	Robin R.2160D	176	F-GCUV	15. 4.85	K.D.Boardman	Perth	23.10.03
			SE-GXE				
G-BLXA	SOCATA TB-20 Trinidad	284	SE-IMO	11. 4.85	Tango Bravo Aviation Ltd	Blackbushe	14. 6.03
			F-ODOH				
G-BLXF*	Cameron V-77 HAFB	1144		2. 4.85	P.Lawman *"Candytwist III"*	Northampton	2. 4.97A
					(Cancelled 29.10.01 as wfu & stored for possible rebuild)		
G-BLXG	Colt 21A Cloudhopper HAFB	605		2. 5.85	A.Walker	Richmond, Surrey	6. 5.98A
					"Britannia Park"		
G-BLXH	Alpavia Fournier RF3	39	F-BMDQ	25. 3.85	A.Rawicz-Szczerbo	Eaglescott	2. 7.02P
G-BLXI	Scintex CP.1310-C3 Super Emeraude	937	F-BMJI	1. 4.85	R.Howard	Grove Moor Farm, Grassthorpe	11. 4.02P
G-BLXO	SAN Jodel 150 Mascaret	10	F-BLDB	9. 5.85	P.R.Powell	Allensmore, Hereford	17. 7.02P
G-BLXP	Piper PA-28R-200 Cherokee Arrow II	28R-7235200	N5226T	29. 7.85	M.B.Hamlett	Le Plessis-Belleville, France	20. 6.02
G-BLXR	Aérospatiale AS332L Super Puma	2154		14. 5.85	Bristow Helicopters Ltd	Aberdeen	1. 7.03T
					"Cromarty"		
G-BLYD	SOCATA TB-20 Trinidad	518		1. 5.85	Yankee Delta Corporation Ltd	Redhill	4. 4.04
G-BLYE	SOCATA TB-10 Tobago	521		1. 5.85	G.Hatton	Blackpool/Carlisle	6. 4.04T
G-BLYK	Piper PA-34-220T Seneca III	34-8433083	N4371J	30. 5.85	Oxford Aviation Services Ltd	Gloucestershire	31.10.03T
G-BLYP	Robin R.3000/120	109		15. 5.85	Weald Air Services Ltd	Headcorn	5. 5.01T
G-BLYT	Airtour AH-77 HAFB	AH.008		7. 7.87	I.J.Taylor & R.C Kincaid	Bristol	9. 8.02A
					"Signal 2"		
G-BLZA	Scheibe SF-25B Falke	4684	D-KBAJ	22. 5.85	T.A.Lacey	RAF Halton	21. 9.03
					t/a Chiltern Gliding Club		
G-BLZB*	Cameron N-65 HAFB	1164		21. 5.85	Balloon Preservation Group	Kirdford	25. 4.90A
					"Pro-Sport" (Cancelled 22.11.01 as wfu)		
G-BLZE	Reims Cessna F152 II	F15201579	G-CSSC	3. 5.85	Redhill Aviation Ltd	Redhill	12. 4.04T
			PH-AYF(2)		t/a Redhill Flying Club		
G-BLZF	Thunder Ax7-77 HAFB	660		3. 6.85	H.M.Savage *"Hector"*	Edinburgh	20. 8.00A
G-BLZH	Reims Cessna F152 II	F15201965		21. 6.85	Plane Talking Ltd	Blackbushe	3. 5.04T
G-BLZN	Bell 206B JetRanger II	314	ZS-HMV	12. 7.85	Hughes Helicopter Co Ltd	Biggin Hill	9. 7.04T
			C-GWDH/N1408W		t/a Biggin Hill Helicopters		
G-BLZP	Reims Cessna F152 II	F15201959		10. 7.85	East Midlands Flying School Ltd	East Midlands	16.11.03T
G-BLZS	Cameron O-77 HAFB	479		22. 5.85	M.M.Cobbold *"Rainbow Brite"*	Plymouth	28. 8.00A
					(Henry Africa's Hothouse Restaurant titles)		
G-BLZT	Short SD.3-60 Var.100	SH.3676	G-14-3676	18. 6.85	BAC Express Airlines Ltd	Exeter	29. 8.01T
					(Stored 11.01)		

G-BMAA – G-BMZZ

G-BMAD	Cameron V-77 HAFB	1166		10. 6.85	M.A.Stelling *"Nautilus"*	Bedford	29. 9.99A
G-BMAL	Sikorsky S-76A II Plus	760120	F-WZSA	27.11.80	Scotia Helicopter Services Ltd	North Denes	9. 5.04T
			G-BMAL		*(Tail boom struck ground North Denes 12.7.01 & damaged)*		
G-BMAO	Taylor JT.1 Monoplane	PFA 1411		29. 7.85	S.J.Alston	Hinton-in-the-Hedges	4. 7.01P
G-BMAV	Aérospatiale AS350B Ecureuil	1089		1. 6.79	PLM Dollar Croup Ltd	Inverness	4. 8.00T
G-BMAX	Clutton FRED Srs.II	PFA 029-10322		20.12.78	D.A.Arkley	(Chelmsford)	24. 8.99P
	(VW 1834)						
G-BMAY	Piper PA-18-135 Super Cub	18-3925	OO-LWB	3. 7.85	R.W.Davies	Little Robhurst Farm, Woodchurch	15.11.04T
	(L-21B-PI) *(Frame No.18-3961)*		"EI-229"/I-EIJZ/MM542525/54-2525				
G-BMBB	Reims Cessna F150L	F15001136	OO-LWM	2. 8.85	LBA Aviation Ltd	Leeds-Bradford	15.11.02T
			PH-GAA				
G-BMBJ	Schempp-Hirth Janus CM	20/209	(G-BLZL)	9. 9.85	T.M.Holloway t/a RAFGSA	Cambridge	20. 3.04
G-BMBS	Colt 105A HAFB	704		18. 7.85	H.G.Davies	Cheltenham	27. 8.91A

G-BMBW	Bensen B.8MR	MV-001 & PFA G/01-1064		27. 8.85	M.E.Vahdat	Uxbridge	30. 6.93P
	(Rotax 503)						
G-BMBZ	Scheibe SF-25E Super Falke	4322	D-KEFQ	17. 7.85	Cornish Gliding & Flying Club Ltd		
						Perranporth	11.10.03
G-BMCC	Thunder Ax7-77 HAFB	705		12. 7.85	A.K. & C.M.Russell	Stafford	23. 2.99A
					"Charlie Charlie"		
G-BMCD	Cameron V-65 HAFB	1234		26. 6.85	M.C.Drye *"My Second Fantasy"*	Winkfield	11. 6.02A
G-BMCG	Grob G-109B	6362	(EAF673)	25. 7.85	Lagerholm Finnimport Ltd	Booker	26. 7.04
G-BMCI	Reims Cessna F172H	F17200683	OO-WID	19. 8.85	A.B.Davis	Edinburgh	13.11.04T
					(Op Edinburgh Flying Club)		
G-BMCK*	Cameron O-77 HAFB	1180		9. 7.85	D.L.Smith *"Touchy"*	Newbury	20.10.92A
				t/a Smith Smart	Partnership *(Cancelled 6.12.01 as wfu) (Stored 2002)*		
G-BMCN	Reims Cessna F152 II	F15201471	D-ELDM	7. 8.85	Lincoln Aero Club Ltd	Sturgate	24.11.04T
G-BMCS	Piper PA-22-135 Tri-Pacer	22-1969	5Y-KMH	6. 9.85	P.R.Deacon	Rochester	15. 7.01
			VP-KMH/ZS-DJI				
G-BMCV	Reims Cessna F152 II	F15201963		2.10.85	Leicestershire Aero Club Ltd	Leicester	9. 4.04T
G-BMCW	Aérospatiale AS332L Super Puma	2161	F-WYMG	4.10.85	Bristow Helicopters Ltd	Aberdeen	7.11.02T
			G-BMCW		*"Monifieth"*		
G-BMCX	Aérospatiale AS332L Super Puma	2164		7.10.85	Bristow Helicopters Ltd	Aberdeen	14.11.04T
					"Lossiemouth"		
G-BMDB	Replica Plans SE.5A	PFA 020-10931		12. 8.85	D.Biggs	Boscombe Down	27. 5.02P
	(Continental O-200-A)				*(As "F235/B" in RFC c/s)*		
G-BMDC	Piper PA-32-301 Saratoga	32-8006075	OO-PAC	13. 8.85	J.D.M.Tickell	Fairoaks	5.10.03T
			OO-HKK/N8242A		t/a MacLaren Aviation		
G-BMDD*	Slingsby T.29 Motor Tutor			8. 8.85	A.R.Worters	(Dunoon)	7.10.88P
	(VW 1834)	PFA 042-11070			*(On rebuild 6.00: cancelled 13.10.00 by CAA: current status unknown)*		
G-BMDE	Pietenpol Air Camper	PFA 047-10989		12. 8.85	P.B.Childs	New Farm, Felton	3. 1.02P
	(Continental O-200-A)						
G-BMDJ	Price Ax7-77S HAFB	TPB.1 & 003		1. 8.85	R.A.Benham	Burton-on-Trent	
					"Wings of Phoenix" (New owner 10.01)		
G-BMDK	Piper PA-34-220T Seneca III		ZS-LOS	16. 9.85	Air Medical Ltd	Oxford	24.11.04T
		34-8133155	N84209/N9553N				
G-BMDP	Partenavia P.64B Oscar 200	08	HB-EPQ	20. 8.85	S.T.G.Lloyd	(Blackwood)	25. 5.04
G-BMDS	Jodel Wassmer D.120 Paris-Nice	281	F-BMOS	12. 8.85	J.V.Thompson	Breighton	1.10.02P
G-BMEA	Piper PA-18 Super Cub 95	18-3204	(D-ECZF)	27. 8.85	C.L.Towell	Ranksborough Farm, Langham	15.10.02P
	(L-18C-PI)		Belg AF OL-L07/L-130/53-4804				
	(Frame No. reported as 18-3206 [c/n 18-3194 ex OL-L20/L-120/53-4794]: c/n 18-3204 has Frame No.18-3216)						
G-BMEB	Rotorway Scorpion 145	2896	VR-HJB	10.12.85	P.Trainor	(Newry, Co.Armagh)	
G-BMEE	Cameron O-105 HAFB	1189		4. 9.85	A.G.R.Calder	Los Angeles, USA	8.10.89A
G-BMEG	SOCATA TB-10 Tobago	530		23.10.85	G.H.N. & R.V.Chamberlain t/a Chamberlain Leasing		
						Great Yeldham, Essex	17.11.04
G-BMEH	Jodel 150 Special Super Mascaret			15. 8.85	R.J.& C.J.Lewis	Garston Farm, Marshfield	20. 5.02P
	(Lycoming O-235)	PFA 151-11047	*(Rebuild of incomplete SAN Jodel 150 Mascaret c/n 62)*				
G-BMET	Taylor JT.1 Monoplane	PFA 1465		4. 9.85	M.K.A.Blyth	Little Gransden	7.11.02P
	(VW 1600)						
G-BMEU	Isaacs Fury II	PFA 011-10179		11. 9.85	G.R.G.Smith	Hints Farm, Coreley, Ludlow	
	(Salmson 90hp)				*(90% complete 6.99: current status unknown)*		
G-BMEV	Piper PA-32RT-300T Turbo Lance II		OO-CHB	30. 4.86	Arrow Aviation Ltd	Jersey	14.12.04
		32R-7887056	G-BMEV/ZS-KFK/N36591				
G-BMEX	Cessna A150K Aerobat	A1500169	N8469M	18. 9.85	N.A.M.Brain & C.Butler	Netherthorpe	21. 4.02
G-BMEZ*	Cameron DP-70 Hot-Air Airship	1130		18. 9.85	British Balloon Museum & Library	Newbury	4. 5.89A
	(Originally regd as a D-50 model)				*(Sold as EC-FUS: cancelled 20.6.91) (Envelope only)*		
G-BMFD	Piper PA-23-250 Aztec F	27-7954080	G-BGYY	6. 9.79	Gold Air International Ltd	Cambridge	5. 2.04T
			N6834A/N9741N				
G-BMFG	Dornier Do.27A-1	27-1003-342	FAP 3460	23. 9.85	R.F.Warner	(Broughton, Norfolk)	
			AC+955		t/a Sigma Services		
					(On rebuild 2.99: current status unknown)		
G-BMFI	PZL SZD-45A Ogar	B-657		23. 9.85	S.L.Morrey	Andreas, IoM	25. 4.02
G-BMFL	Rand Robinson KR-2	PFA 129-11050		24. 9.85	E.W.B.Comber & M.F.Leusby	(Huntingdon)	
G-BMFN	QAC Quickie Tri-Q 200			27. 9.85	A.H.Hartog	Thruxton	1. 5.02P
	(Continental O-200-A) EMK-017 & PFA 094A1-11062						
G-BMFP	Piper PA-28-161 Warrior II		N3032L	1.11.85	T.J.Froggatt & C.A.Lennard	Blackbushe	8. 7.04
		28-7916243			t/a Bravo Mike Fox Papa Group		
G-BMFU	Cameron N-90 HAFB	628		1.10.85	J.J.Rudoni	Rugeley, Staffs	30. 9.01T
G-BMFY	Grob G-109B	6401		8.10.85	P.J.Shearer	Kirkwall	3. 7.04
G-BMFZ	Reims Cessna F152 II	F15201953		3.12.85	Cornwall Flying Club Ltd	Bodmin	30. 1.04T
					(Crashed 1 mile north Topsham 2.5.01)		
G-BMGB	Piper PA-28R-200 Cherokee Arrow II		N15864	8.11.85	A.L.Ings	Kemble	16. 8.04
		28R-7335099			t/a Malmesbury Specialist Cars		
G-BMGC*	Fairey Swordfish II	--	G-BMGC	23.10.85	RN Historic Flight	RNAS Yeovilton	
	(Built Blackburn Aircraft)		RCN W5856/RN W5856		*"City of Leeds" (As "W5856/A2A" in 810 Sqn c/s)*		
					(Cancelled 2.9.91 by CAA)		
G-BMGG	Cessna 152 II	15279592	OO-ADB	10.10.85	A S Bamrah	Biggin Hill	24.10.03T
			PH-ADB/D-EHUG/F-GBLM/N757AT		t/a Falcon Flying Services		

G-BMGR	Grob G-109B	6396		27.11.85	D.S.Hawes & M.Clarke t/a BMGR Group	Lasham	9. 2.04
G-BMHA	Rutan LongEz	PFA 074A-10973		18.10.85	S.F.Elvins	(Bristol)	
G-BMHC	Cessna U206F Stationair II	U20603427	N10TB G-BMHC/N8571Q	17.11.76	Fairmont Investments Ltd	Duxford/Clacton	22. 8.97T
G-BMHJ	Thunder Ax7-65 Srs.1 HAFB	743		2. 1.86	M.G.Robinson *"Kittylog"*	Great Milton, Oxon	19. 5.92A
G-BMHL	Wittman W.8 Tailwind (Continental O-200-A)	PFA 031-10503		28.11.85	T V Thorp	(Burbage, Marlborough)	18.12.02P
G-BMHS	Reims Cessna F172M	F17200964	PH-WAB	7. 4.86	R.A.Hall t/a Tango Xray Flying Group	Rayne Hall Farm, Rayne	21. 7.04
G-BMHT	Piper PA-28RT-201T Turbo Arrow IV	28R-8231010	ZS-LCJ N8462Y	18.11.85	White Aviation Ltd	Leeds-Bradford	22. 4.04T
G-BMID	Jodel Wassmer D.120 Paris-Nice	259	F-BMID	18. 8.81	P.E.S.Latham t/a G-BMID F/Group	RAF Shawbury	27. 4.02P
G-BMIG	Cessna 172N Skyhawk II	17272376	ZS-KGI (N48630)	13. 5.86	Walkbury Aviation Ltd	Sibson	21. 6.04T
G-BMIM	Rutan LongEz (Lycoming O-235)	8102/160	OY-CMT OY-8102	12.12.85	R.M.Smith	Biggin Hill	1. 8.02P
G-BMIO	Stoddard-Hamilton Glasair IIRG	PFA 149-11016		25.11.85	J.M.Ayres & S.C.Ellerton *(Noted 3.01)*	Kemble	3.10.02P
G-BMIP	Wassmer Jodel D.112	1264	F-BMIP	7.12.78	M.T.Kinch t/a The Inglesham Flying Group	Manor Farm, Inglesham	11. 9.02P
G-BMIR(2)*	Westland Wasp HAS.1	F.9670	XT788	24. 1.86	Park Aviation Supply	Little Glovers Farm, Charlwood, Surrey	
					(Cancelled 22.12.95 by CAA) (Stored as "XT788" 7.00)		
G-BMIS	Monnett Sonerai II (Revmaster R2100DQ)	755 & PFA 015A-10813	VR-HIS	26. 2.87	B.A.Bower *(Stored 2000)*	Middle Wyke, St Mary Bourne	26.10.89P
G-BMIV	Piper PA-28R-201T Turbo Cherokee Arrow III	28R-7703154	ZS-JZW N5816V	7. 1.86	Firmbeam Ltd	Booker	22. 5.04
G-BMIW	Piper PA-28-181 Archer II	28-8190093	ZS-KTJ N8301J	6.12.85	Oldbus Ltd	Shoreham	14. 5.04T
G-BMIY	Oldfield Baby Lakes (Continental O-200-A)	PFA 010-10194	G-NOME	3.12.85	J.B.Scott *(Stored 12.01)*	Blackpool	27. 8.87P
G-BMJA	Piper PA-32R-301 Saratoga SP	32R-8113019	ZS-KTH N8309E	23.12.85	H Merkado	Panshanger	22. 7.02T
G-BMJB*	Cessna 152 II	15280030	N757VD	3. 2.86	Bobbington Air Training School Ltd *(Cancelled 12.6.00 as wfu)*	Wolverhampton	21. 3.01T
G-BMJC	Cessna 152 II	15284989	N623AP	3. 2.86	The Cambridge Aero Club Ltd	Cambridge	22. 7.04T
G-BMJD	Cessna 152 II	15279755	N757HP	21.11.85	Donair Flying Club Ltd	Tatenhill	5. 7.04T
G-BMJG*	Piper PA-28R-200 Cherokee Arrow	28R-35046	ZS-TNS ZS-FYC/N9345N	23.12.85	Western Air (Thruxton) Ltd	Blackpool	4. 2.99T
			(Damaged Thruxton 11.10.98: cancelled 15.4.99 by CAA) (Fuselage noted 12.01)				
G-BMJL	Rockwell Commander 114	14006	A2-JRI ZS-JRI/N1906J	8. 1.86	Wardair Ltd.	Goodwood	10. 7.03T
G-BMJM	Evans VP-1 (VW 1834)	PFA 062-10763		21.11.85	M.J.Veary	Sywell	25. 6.01P
G-BMJN	Cameron O-65 HAFB	1212		6.12.85	P.M.Traviss *"F'red"*	Yarm	4. 5.02A
G-BMJO	Piper PA-34-220T Seneca III	34-8533036	N6919K N9565N	5.12.85	Oxford Aviation Services Ltd	Gloucestershire	9. 5.04T
G-BMJR	Cessna T337H Turbo Skymaster II	33701895	G-NOVA N1259S	10. 7.84	Eastcote Services Ltd	Cranfield	12. 7.02
G-BMJS	Thunder Ax7-77 HAFB	754		3.12.85	S.E.Burton	Northampton	7. 4.96A
G-BMJT	Beechcraft 76 Duchess	ME-376	ZS-KMI N3718W	4.12.85	Mike Osborne Properties Ltd	Ronaldsway	30. 3.04
G-BMJW*	North American AT-6D-NT Harvard III	88-15963	EZ259 SAAF7631/EZ259/42-84182	28.11.85	B.Fenton	Wakefield	
	(Composite with rear fuselage of KF487)		*(Cancelled 2.9.91 by CAA: fuselage on rebuild 2.96: current status unknown)*				
G-BMJX	Wallis WA-116/X Srs.1 (Limbach L-2000)	K/219/X		31.12.85	K.H.Wallis *(Stored 8.01)*	Reymerston Hall, Norfolk	1. 4.89P
G-BMJY	SPP Yakovlev C.18A	NK	(France) Egypt AF 627	21. 1.86	R.J.Lamplough *(As "07" (yellow) in Russian AF c/s)*	North Weald	27.11.01P
G-BMJZ	Cameron N-90 HAFB	1219		16.12.85	P.Spellward *"Uvistat"* t/a Bristol University Hot-Air Ballooning Society	Bristol	31. 3.94A
G-BMKB	Piper PA-18-135 Super Cub (L-21B-PI) *(Frame No.18-3818)*	18-3817	OO-DKB PH-DKB/(PH-GRP)/R Neth AF R-127/54-2417	11.12.85	Cubair Flight Training Ltd	Redhill	21. 2.03T
G-BMKC	Piper J-3C-65 Cub (L-4H-PI) (Continental C90) *(Frame No.10970)*	11145	F-BFBA 43-29854	2. 1.86	J.W.Salter *(As "329854/R/44" in USAAC 533rd BS/381st Bomb Group c/s)* *"Little Rockette Jnr"*	(Holywood, Co of Down)	11.10.02P
G-BMKD	Beechcraft C90A King Air	LJ-1069	N223CG N67516	30.12.85	A.E.Bristow	Fairoaks	13. 4.03
G-BMKF	CEA Jodel DR.221 Dauphin	96	F-BPCS	3. 2.86	L., S.T.Gilbert & L.M.Radcliffe	Enstone	6. 8.03
G-BMKG	Piper PA-38-112 Tomahawk II	38-82A0050	ZS-LGC N91544	3. 2.86	APB Leasing Ltd	Welshpool	13. 8.04T

G-BMKI	Colt 21A Cloudhopper HAFB	753		30.12.85	A.C.Booth	Bristol	25. 7.02A
G-BMKJ	Cameron V-77 HAFB	1235		2. 1.86	R.C.Thursby	Barry	2. 5.00A
G-BMKK	Piper PA-28R-200 Cherokee Arrow II		ZS-JNY	16. 1.86	Comed Aviation Ltd	Blackpool	5. 1.01T
		28R-7535265	N9537N				
G-BMKP	Cameron V-77 HAFB	724	(G-BMFX)	10. 1.86	R.Bayly *"And Baby Makes 10"*	Bristol	7. 8.93A
G-BMKR	Piper PA-28-161 Warrior II		G-BGKR	14. 6.84	D.R.Shrosbee	Goodwood	6. 6.03
		28-7916220	N9561N		t/a Field Flying Group		
G-BMKW	Cameron V-77 HAFB	608		29. 1.86	A.C.Garnett *"Aorangi"*	Guildford	21. 9.00A
G-BMKX*	Cameron Elephant 77SS HAFB	1196		6. 2.86	Balloon Preservation Group	Kirdford	19. 2.89A
					"Benjamin I" (Cancelled 21.10.96 as WFU)		
G-BMKY	Cameron O-65 HAFB	1246		4. 3.86	Ann R.Rich *"Orion"*	Hyde	13. 4.02A
G-BMLB	Jodel Wassmer D.120A Paris-Nice	295	F-BNCI	20. 1.86	W.O.Brown	Seighford	1.10.02P
G-BMLC	Short SD.3-60 Var.100	SH.3688	SE-LDA	18. 2.86	Aurigny Air Services Ltd	Guernsey	24 .5.02T
			G-BMLC/G-14-3688				
G-BMLJ	Cameron N-77 HAFB	1263		7. 3.86	C.J.Dunkley	Aylesbury	13. 4.01A
					t/a Wendover Trailers *"Mr Funshine"*		
G-BMLK	Grob G-109B	6424		24. 2.86	J.J.Mawson t/a Brams Syndicate	Rufforth	29. 5.04
G-BMLL	Grob G-109B	6420		13. 3.86	C.Rupasinha	Denham	24. 7.04
					t/a G-BMLL Flying Group		
G-BMLM	Beechcraft 95-58 Baron	TH-405	N111LM	2. 7.79	N.J.Webb	Cranfield	12.10.02
			G-BMLM/F-GEPV/3D-ADF/ZS-LOZ/G-BMLM/G-BBJF				
G-BMLS	Piper PA-28R-201 Cherokee Arrow III		N47496	11. 2.86	R.M.Shorter	Booker	24. 4.02T
		28R-7737167					
G-BMLT	Pietenpol Air Camper	PFA 047-10949		28. 1.86	W.E.R.Jenkins		
	(Continental C90)					Waits Farm, Belchamp Walter	20. 5.02P
G-BMLU*	Colt 90A HAFB	786		10. 4.86	L.J.Goldsmith *"Firebird"*	Biggin Hill	6. 3.97A
					(Cancelled 10.10.01 by CAA)		
G-BMLW	Cameron O-77 HAFB	813		6. 2.86	M.L. & L.P.Willoughby *"Stelrad"*	Reading	7. 8.95A
G-BMLX	Reims Cessna F150L	F15000700	PH-VOV	21. 3.86	J P A Freeman	Headcorn	20.12.04T
G-BMMC	Cessna 310Q	310Q0041	YU-BGY	11. 2.86	I T Cooper	Gloucestershire	30. 3.02
			N7541Q				
G-BMMD	Rand Robinson KR-2	PFA 129-10817		7. 2.86	D.J.Howell	Panshanger	14. 6.01P
	(VW 1834 Acro)						
G-BMMF	Clutton FRED Srs.II	PFA 029-10296		20. 2.86	E.C.King	Kemble	6. 4.99P
	(VW 1834)				*"Thankyou Girl"*		
G-BMMI	Pazmany PL-4A	PFA 017-10149		6. 2.86	L.J.Greenhough	Bodmin	30. 5.04P
	(Continental PC 60)						
G-BMMK	Cessna 182P Skylane II	18264117	OO-AVU	24. 3.86	G.G.Weston	Denham	23. 8.04T
	(Reims-assembled c/n F18200038)		N6129F				
G-BMML	Piper PA-38-112 Tomahawk	38-80A0079	PH-TMG	2. 4.86	J.C.& C.H.Strong	(Wantage)	19. 5.04T
			OO-HKD/N9662N				
G-BMMM	Cessna 152 II	15284793	N4652P	10. 9.86	A.S.Bamrah	Biggin Hill	20.10.04T
					t/a Falcon Flying Services		
G-BMMP	Grob G-109B	6432		27. 6.86	E.W.Reynolds	Tatenhill	24. 5.02
G-BMMU*	Thunder Ax7-77 HAFB	719		4. 3.86	Nicola Metcalfe *"Pansy"*	Didcot	11. 8.97A
					(Cancelled 21.9.01 by CAA)		
G-BMMV	ICA IS-28M2A	57		10. 3.86	F.R.Temple-Brown	Henstridge	24. 8.03
G-BMMW	Thunder Ax7-77 HAFB	782		10. 3.86	P.A.George *"Ethos"*	Princes Risborough	3. 6.96A
					(Sports Council titles)		
G-BMMY	Thunder Ax7-77 HAFB	716		11. 3.86	S.M.Wade & Sheila E.Hadley	Salisbury	29. 7.02A
					"Winco"		
G-BMNL	Piper PA-28R-200 Cherokee Arrow II		N32280	17. 9.86	Elston Ltd	Elstree	30. 5.02
		28R-7535040	(N18MW)/N32280		t/a Arrow Flying Group		
G-BMNP*	Piper PA-38-112 Tomahawk II		N23352	24. 3.86	APB Leasing Ltd	Welshpool	27. 6.98T
		38-81A0133		*(Dismantled/stored 8.99: cancelled 19.10.99 as destroyed) (Noted 8.00)*			
G-BMNV	SNCAN Stampe SV-4C	108	F-BBNI	14. 3.86	Wessex Aviation & Transport Ltd		
	(Lycoming IO-360)					Chalmington	8. 6.94P
G-BMNX	Colt 56A HAFB	790		14. 4.86	C.N.Marshall *"Rosie"*	Tonbridge	28. 7.00A
G-BMOE	Piper PA-28R-200 Cherokee Arrow II		PH-PCB	20. 5.86	E.P.C.Rabson	Compton Abbas	22.11.02T
		28R-7635226	OO-HAS/N9221K				
G-BMOF	Cessna U206G Stationair II	U20603658	N7427N	17. 4.86	D.M.Penny	Movenis, Co.Londonderry	12. 4.03
					t/a Wild Geese Skydiving Centre		
G-BMOG	Thunder Ax7-77 HAFB	793		2. 4.86	R.M.Boswell	Bawburgh, Norwich	28. 8.95A
					(Amended CofR 12.01)		
G-BMOH	Cameron N-77 HAFB	1270		2. 4.86	P.J.Marshall & M.A.Clarke	Ruislip	20. 8.91A
					"Ellen Gee"		
G-BMOI	Partenavia P.68B	103	I-EEVA	4. 4.86	Simmette Ltd	Exeter	6.11.04
G-BMOJ*	Cameron V-56 HAFB	1275		4. 4.86	S.R.Bridge	Grantham	27. 7.89A
					(Cancelled 6.11.01 as wfu: current status unknown)		
G-BMOK	ARV1 Super 2	011		14. 4.86	R.E.Griffiths	Stoke, Kent	17. 8.03
G-BMOM	ICA IS-28M2A	50		30. 6.86	R.M.Cust	Sandtoft	5. 9.04
	(Rebuilt 2001 with forward fuselage of G-BKAB)						
G-BMOO*	Clutton FRED Srs.II	PFA 029-10770		11. 4.86	N.Purllant	(Leicester)	8. 8.91P
	(Continental A65)				*(Cancelled 22.2.99 by CAA: current status unknown)*		

G-BMOT	Bensen B.8M	PFA G/01-1066		17. 4.86	Austin Trueman Ltd	(St. Albans)	13. 8.01P
	(VW 1834)						
G-BMOV	Cameron O-105 HAFB	1307		11. 4.86	Cheryl Gillott *"Up & Down"*	Stroud	1. 7.99A
G-BMPC	Piper PA-28-181 Cherokee Archer II		LN-NAT	23. 4.86	C.J. & R.J.Barnes	East Midlands	6. 2.02T
		28-7790436					
G-BMPD	Cameron V-65 HAFB	1200		4. 6.86	D.E. & J.M.Hartland	Matlock	12. 8.01A
					"Second Dawn"		
G-BMPF*	Optica OA.7 Optica	010		14. 4.86	FLS Aerospace (Light Aircraft) Ltd		
						Bournemouth	14. 1.93T
					(Cancelled 2.9.91 by CAA: stored 11.95: current status unknown)		
G-BMPL	Optica OA.7 Optica	016		14. 4.86	Sunhawk Ltd *(Noted 7.00)*	Farnborough	2. 8.97T
G-BMPP	Cameron N-77 HAFB	1303		15. 4.86	N.A.Apsey *"Tuppence"*	High Wycombe	14. 5.93A
G-BMPR	Piper PA-28R-201 Arrow III		ZS-LMF	22. 4.86	B.Edwards	Full Sutton	10. 5.02
		28R-7837175	N417GH				
G-BMPS	Strojnik S-2A	045		18. 4.86	G.J.Green	(Matlock)	
G-BMPY	de Havilland DH.82A Tiger Moth	"82619"	ZS-CNR	25. 4.86	S.M.F.Eisenstein	Sandford Hall, Knockin	16.11.01
			SAAF??				
G-BMRA	Boeing 757-236	23710		2. 3.87	British Airways plc	Heathrow	3.12.02T
					(Paithani t/s) (For disposal 1.02)		
G-BMRB	Boeing 757-236	23975		25. 9.87	British Airways plc	Heathrow	29. 9.03T
G-BMRC	Boeing 757-236	24072	(N)	2.12.87	British Airways plc	Heathrow	26. 1.04T
			G-BMRC		*(British Olympic Association t/s) (For disposal 12.01)*		
G-BMRD	Boeing 757-236	24073	(N)	2.12.87	British Airways plc	Heathrow	3. 3.04T
			G-BMRD		*(Chelsea Rose t/s) (For disposal 1.02)*		
G-BMRE	Boeing 757-236	24074	(N)	2.12.87	British Airways plc	Heathrow	28. 3.04T
G-BMRF	Boeing 757-236	24101		13. 5.88	Barclays Mercantile Business Finance Ltd		
					(To USA for freighter conversion 11.01)	(Basingstoke)	17. 5.04T
G-BMRG	Boeing 757-236	24102		31. 5.88	British Airways plc	Heathrow	2. 6.04T
					(Rendezvous t/s) (For disposal 12.01)		
G-BMRH	Boeing 757-236	24266		21. 2.89	British Airways plc	Heathrow	28. 2.02T
					(Nalanji Dreaming t/s) (For disposal 4.02)		
G-BMRI	Boeing 757-236	24267		17. 2.89	British Airways plc	Heathrow	23. 2.02T
					(Blomsterang/Flower Field t/s) (For disposal 3.02)		
G-BMRJ	Boeing 757-236	24268		6. 3.89	British Airways plc	Heathrow	13. 3.02T
					(Grand Union t/s) (For disposal 1.02)		
G-BMSA	Stinson HW-75 Model 105	7040	G-BCUM	26. 3.86	M.A.Thomas	Barton	16. 9.02P
	(Continental O-200-A)		F-BGQO/NC21189		t/a The Stinson Group *"Iron Eagle"*		
G-BMSB	Supermarine 509 Spitfire XI		G-ASOZ	3. 5.78	M.S.Bayliss	Coventry	12. 3.99P
	(Regd as c/n 6S/R/749433)	CBAF.7722	IAC158/G-15-171/MJ627		*(As "MJ627/9G-P" in 441 Sqn c/s)*		
					(Damaged Coventry 25.4.98: current status unknown)		
G-BMSC	Evans VP-2	V2-482MSC & PFA 063-10785		25. 8.82	S.Whitehead	(Melton Mowbray)	8.10.99P
	(VW 1834)				*(New owner 12.01)*		
G-BMSD	Piper PA-28-181 Cherokee Archer II		EC-CVH	2. 7.86	H Merkado	Panshanger	20. 9.04T
		28-7690070	N9646N				
G-BMSE	Valentin Taifun 17E	1082	D-KHVA(17)	20. 5.86	A.J.Nurse	Kemble	19. 7.02
G-BMSF	Piper PA-38-112 Tomahawk	38-78A0524	N4277E	9. 2.79	B.Catlow	Crosland Moor	30. 6.99
G-BMSG	SAAB 32A Lansen	32028	Fv.32028	22. 7.86	J.E.Wilkie	Cranfield	
					(Open storage 6.00)		
G-BMSL	Clutton FRED Srs.III	PFA 029-11142		19. 5.86	A.C.Coombe	Long Marston	4. 7.01P
	(VW 1834)						
G-BMST*	Cameron N-31 HAFB	1317		4. 6.86	Balloon Preservation Group *"B&Q"*	Lancing	NE(A)
					(Cancelled 1.5.92 as WFU: badly damaged & for spares 12.01)		
G-BMSU	Cessna 152 II	15279421	N714TN	29. 8.86	S.Waite t/a G-BMSU Group	Sandtoft	27.10.02T
G-BMTA	Cessna 152 II	15282864	N89776	27. 8.86	Alarmond Ltd	Prestwick	22. 2.02T
					(Op Prestwick Flight Centre)		
G-BMTB	Cessna 152 II	15280672	N25457	19. 8.86	Sky Leisure Aviation (Charters) Ltd		
						Shoreham	16. 7.03T
G-BMTJ	Cessna 152 II	15285010	N6389P	19. 6.86	The Pilot Centre Ltd	Denham	14. 6.04T
G-BMTN	Cameron O-77 HAFB	1305		4. 6.86	Industrial Services (MH) Ltd	Bristol	1. 6.97A
					t/a Flete Rental *"Fletie"*		
G-BMTO	Piper PA-38-112 Tomahawk II		N25679	28.11.86	A.S.Bamrah	Biggin Hill	10. 8.02T
		38-81A0051			t/a Falcon Flying Services		
G-BMTP*	Piper PA-38-112 Tomahawk	38-79A0034	N2392B	14. 8.86	Not known	Jersey	26. 4.93T
					(Damaged Alderney 1.9.92: cancelled 7.3.96 by CAA: stored 12.96: current status unknown)		
G-BMTR	Piper PA-28-161 Warrior II		N83179	19. 6.86	Aeroshow Ltd	Gloucestershire	23. 9.01T
		28-8116119					
G-BMTS	Cessna 172N Skyhawk II	17270606	N739KP	17. 7.86	A.S.Bamrah	(Blackbushe)	23. 8.04T
					t/a Falcon Flying Services		
G-BMTU	Pitts S-1E Special	PFA 009-10801		4. 6.86	Aerodynamics Ltd	Gloucestershire	22. 5.02P
	(Lycoming O-360)						
G-BMTX	Cameron V-77 HAFB	733		19. 6.86	J.A.Langley *"Boondoggle"*	Stroud	15. 7.01A
					(Buses For Bristol titles)		
G-BMUD	Cessna 182P Skylane	18261786	OY-DVS	6.11.81	Mescal E.Taylor	Netherthorpe	31. 7.03T
			N78847		*(www.newbridge.com titles)*		

G-BMUG	Rutan LongEz	PFA 074A-10987		17. 6.86	P.Richardson & J.Shanley		
	(Lycoming O-235)					Croft Farm, Teesside	24. 6.02P
G-BMUJ	Colt Drachenfisch SS HAFB	835		3. 6.86	Virgin Airship & Balloon Co Ltd	Telford	27. 7.91A
	(Futuristic shape)				*"Drachenfisch"*		
G-BMUK	Colt UFO SS HAFB	836		3. 6.86	Virgin Airship & Balloon Co Ltd	Telford	26. 4.95A
	(Futuristic shape)				*"UFO/Dream Station"*		
G-BMUL	Colt Kindermond SS HAFB	837		3. 6.86	Virgin Airship & Balloon Co Ltd	Telford	26. 9.91A
	(Futuristic shape)				*"Kindermond/Childrens' Moon"*		
G-BMUO	Cessna A152 Aerobat	A1520788	4X-ALJ	4. 6.86	Sky Leisure Aviation (Charters) Ltd		
			N7328L			Redhill	30. 8.04T
G-BMUT	Piper PA-34-200T Seneca II		EC-CUH	23. 1.87	High Flyers Aviation Ltd	Newcastle	4. 7.02T
		34-7570320	N3935X				
G-BMUU	Thunder Ax7-77 HAFB	827		1. 8.86	G.Anorewartha *"Fiesta"*	Kings Lynn	29.10.98A
G-BMUZ	Piper PA-28-161 Warrior II		EC-DMA	24. 7.86	Newcastle-upon-Tyne Aero Club Ltd		
		28-8016329	N9559N			Newcastle	14. 2.02T
G-BMVA	Scheibe SF-25B Falke	46223	RAFGGA.512	28. 7.86	M.L.Jackson	Bidford	18. 1.02
			D-KAEN				
G-BMVB	Reims Cessna F152 II	F15201974		10. 9.86	LAC (Enterprises) Ltd	Barton	10. 2.00T
					t/a Lancashire Aero Club		
G-BMVG	QAC Quickie Q-1	PFA 094-10749		11. 6.86	P.M.Wright	Coventry	1. 1.02P
	(Rotax 503)						
G-BMVI	Cameron O-105 HAFB	1326		19. 6.86	M.L.Gabb *"Securicor"*	Alcester	7. 7.95A
					t/a Heart of England Balloons		
G-BMVJ	Cessna 172N Skyhawk II	17272232	N9347E	27. 6.86	Green Aviation Associates Ltd		
						Leeds-Bradford	25. 2.02T
G-BMVL	Piper PA-38-112 Tomahawk	38-79A0033	N2391B	5. 9.86	Airways Aero Associations Ltd	Booker	20.12.04T
					(Op British Airways Flying Club) (Blue Poole t/s)		
G-BMVM	Piper PA-38-112 Tomahawk	38-79A0025	N2359B	5. 9.86	Airways Aero Associations Ltd	Booker	4. 3.04T
					(Op British Airways Flying Club) (Waves of the City t/s)		
G-BMVO*	Cameron N-77 HAFB	1309		23. 6.86	Warners Motors (Leasing) Ltd	Gloucester	3. 5.97A
					"Warners" (Cancelled 6.11.01 as wfu: current status unknown)		
G-BMVS*	Cameron Benihana 70SS HAFB	1252		27.10.86	Shellrise Ltd *"Rocky"*	Miami, USA	NE(A)
	(Chef's Hat)				*(Cancelled by CAA 19.5.93) (Current status unknown)*		
G-BMVT	Thunder Ax7-77A HAFB	102	SE-ZYY	15. 7.86	M.L. & L.P.Willoughby	Reading	
					"Trygg Hansa"		
G-BMVU	Monnett Moni	PFA 142-10948		14. 8.86	N.J.Cowley	Old Sarum	20. 9.99P
	(KEF-107)						
G-BMVW	Cameron O-65 HAFB	1331		27. 6.86	S.P.Richards *"Olau Ferries"*	Cranbrook	15. 8.91A
G-BMWA	Hughes 269C	14-0271	N8998F	1. 7.86	EBG Helicopters Ltd	Redhill	16.11.02T
G-BMWE	ARV1 Super 2	012		1. 7.86	R.J.N.Noble	Farnborough	16. 1.00
G-BMWF	ARV1 Super 2	013		1. 7.86	N.R.Beale Deppers Bridge, Leamington Spa		2. 4.90T
	(Rotax 914 Turbo)				*(Under construction 7.96: current status unknown)*		
G-BMWM	ARV1 Super 2	020		30. 3.87	T.C.Robson	(Thetford)	8. 5.02P
	(Hewland AE75)						
G-BMWN	Cameron Temple 80SS HAFB	1211		9. 7.86	Forbes Europe Inc	Balleroy, Normandy	17. 6.96A
					"Temple"		
G-BMWR	Rockwell Commander 112A	365	N1365J	23. 9.86	M. & J.Edwards	Blackbushe	6. 5.02
G-BMWU	Cameron N-42 HAFB	1346		22.12.88	I Chadwick *"Baby Helix"*	Partridge Green	
					(Op Balloon Preservation Group)		
G-BMWV	Putzer Elster B	024	D-EEKB	5. 8.86	E.A.J.Hibbard	Hill Farm, Nayland	
			97+14/D-EBGI		*(Noted 5.00)*		
G-BMXA	Cessna 152 II	15280125	N757ZC	14. 7.86	E.Alexander	Andrewsfield	28. 9.02T
G-BMXB	Cessna 152 II	15280996	N48840	14. 7.86	H.Daines Electronics Ltd.	(Beccles)	21. 3.93T
G-BMXC	Cessna 152 II	15280416	N24858	14. 7.86	Devon School of Flying Ltd.	Dunkeswell	7. 1.02T
G-BMXD	Fokker F.27 Friendship 500	10417	TF-FLR	6.10.86	BAC Express Airlines Ltd	Gatwick	12.12.04T
			HL5210/(HL5206)/PH-FOR		*"Scottish Trader"*		
G-BMXJ	Reims Cessna F150L	F15000853	F-BUBA	18. 7.86	R.Harman	Tatenhill	20. 6.03
					t/a Arrow Aircraft Group		
G-BMXL	Piper PA-38-112 Tomahawk	38-80A0018	N25060	4. 9.86	Airways Aero Associations Ltd	Booker	17. 6.02T
					(Op British Airways Flying Club) (Benyhone Tartan t/s)		
G-BMXX	Cessna 152 II	15284953	N5469P	10. 9.86	Aerohire Ltd	Wolverhampton	1. 9.02T
G-BMYA*	Colt 56A HAFB	864		13. 8.86	British Balloon Museum & Library	Newbury	2.12.92A
					"British Gas" (Cancelled 29.4.97 as WFU)		
G-BMYC	SOCATA TB-10 Tobago	696		1. 9.86	Elizabeth A. Grady	Old Buckenham	29. 4.02T
G-BMYD	Beechcraft A36 Bonanza	E-2350		28.11.86	Seabeam Partners Ltd	Coventry	21. 3.02
G-BMYF	Bensen B.8M	PE-01		18. 8.86	G.Callaghan	Rich Hill, Co.Armagh	
G-BMYG	Reims Cessna FA152 Aerobat	FA1520365	OO-JCA	23.10.86	Tayside Aviation Ltd	Dundee	13. 6.02T
			(OO-JCC)/PH-AXG				
G-BMYI	Grumman-American AA-5 Traveler		EI-BJF	1. 9.86	W.C. & S.C.Westran	Shoreham	24. 5.02T
		AA5-0568	F-BVRM/N9568L				
G-BMYJ	Cameron V-65 HAFB	726		8. 9.86	J.R.Christopher & U.Feierabend	Ulverston	17. 7.01A
					"Skylark II"		
G-BMYN	Colt 77A HAFB	873		2. 9.86	F.R.Batersby & J.Jones	Manchester	3. 1.02A
					t/a Spectacles Balloon Group *"Spectacles"*		

G-BMYP	Fairey Gannet AEW.3	F.9461	8610M XL502	16. 9.86	D.Copley	Sandtoft	29. 9.89P
					(As "XL502" in 849 Sqdn/"B" Flight RN c/s: external storage 7.01)		
G-BMYS	Thunder Ax7-77Z HAFB	887		3.11.86	J.E.Weidema t/a Pinkel Balloons	Baambrugge, The Netherlands	1. 6.01A
G-BMYU	Jodel Wassmer D.120 Paris-Nice	289	F-BMYU	23. 6.78	N.P.Chitty	Drayton St.Leonard	1. 8.02P
G-BMZA	Air Command 503 Modac (Rotax 503) *(Probably c/n 0389)*	0589		11. 2.87	R.W.Husband	Blackbrook Farm, Sheffield	17.12.01P
					(Stolen from owner at this location on or about 6.9.01 c/w trailer)		
G-BMZB	Cameron N-77 HAFB	1370		30.10.86	D.C.Eager *"Dreamland"*	Bracknell	30. 4.95A
G-BMZE	SOCATA TB-9 Tampico	708		5.12.86	R.F.Keene	Turweston	3. 8.02T
G-BMZF*	WSK-Mielec LIM-2 (MiG-15bis)	1B-01420	1420 Polish AF	18.12.86	Fleet Air Arm Museum	RNAS Yeovilton	
					(Cancelled 23.2.90 as WFU) (As "01420" in North Korean c/s)		
G-BMZG*	QAC Quickie Q2 (Revmaster 2100D)	PFA 094A-10919		1.10.86	R.Dann *(Cancelled 28.11.01 by CAA)*	Haverfordwest	20. 9.00P
G-BMZN	Everett Gyroplane 1 (VW 1835)	008		13.11.86	K.Ashford	(Walsall)	2.12.02P
G-BMZP	Everett Gyroplane 1 (VW 1835)	010		14.11.86	M.N.Morris-Jones	Wing Farm, Longbridge Deverill	10. 4.02P
G-BMZS	Everett Gyroplane 1 (VW 1835)	012		13.11.86	L.W.Cload	St.Merryn	4.11.02P
G-BMZW	Bensen B.8MR (Rotax 532)	PFA G/01-1021		16.10.86	P.D.Widdicombe	Huntingdon, York	25. 8.99P
G-BMZX	Wolf W-11 Boredom Fighter (Continental A65) *(Represents a Spad rep)*	PFA 146-11042		31.10.86	A.R.Meakin & S.W.Watkins *(As "146-11042/7" in AEF France 94th Aero Sqdn c/s)*	Trecorras Farm, Llangarron	26. 5.95P

G-BNAA – G-BNZZ

G-BNAD	Rand Robinson KR-2 (VW 1834)	PFA 129-11077		10.11.86	P.J.Brookman *(Stored 7.90: current status unknown)*	(Ottringham)	27. 2.90P
G-BNAG	Colt 105A HAFB	906		31.10.86	R.W.Batchelor	Thame	19.12.89A
G-BNAH*	Colt Paper Bag SS HAFB	865		12.11.86	Not known *(Cancelled 4.8.98 by CAA) (Noted active USA 10.98)*	(USA)	14..6.86
G-BNAI	Wolf W-11 Boredom Fighter (Continental A65) *(Represents Spad rep)*	PFA 146-11083		31.10.86	P.J.D.Gronow *(As "146-11083/5" in AEF France 94th Aero Sqdn c/s)*	Haverfordwest	2. 1.02P
G-BNAJ	Cessna 152 II	15282527	C-GZWF (N69173)	3.11.86	Galair Ltd *(Op Surrey & Kent Flying Club)*	Biggin Hill	17. 4.02T
G-BNAN	Cameron V-65 HAFB	1333		28.10.86	Anne M.Lindsay & N.H.Ponsford t/a Rango Balloon & Kite Co *"Actually"*	Leeds	7. 7.01A
G-BNAO*	Colt AS-105 Hot Air Airship	897		28.10.86	Heather Flight Ltd *(Cancelled 9.10.00 by CAA)*	London SE16	20.10.90A
G-BNAR	Taylor JT.1 Monoplane (VW 1600)	PFA 055-10569		14.11.86	C.J.Smith *(Current status unknown)*	(Blackfield, Southampton)	28.12.90P
G-BNAU	Cameron V-65 HAFB	1395		13.11.86	Cherry L.E.Lewis	Colwyn Bay	14. 7.02A
G-BNAW	Cameron V-65 HAFB	1366		24.10.86	A. & P.A.Walker *"Hippo-Thermia" (HMS Recruitment titles)*	Richmond, Surrey	25. 6.95A
G-BNBL	Thunder Ax7-77 HAFB	910		7. 1.87	D.G.Such	Redditch	18. 5.02A
G-BNBP*	Colt Snowflake SS HAFB	913		21.11.86	D.Partridge/Air 2 Air Balloons Ltd	Bristol	
					(Cancelled 19.7.90 as WFU: stored 8.95: current status unknown)		
G-BNBU	Bensen B.8MV	PFA G/01-1070		1.12.86	B.A.Lyford	St Merren	
G-BNBV	Thunder Ax7-77 HAFB	915		2.12.86	Jennifer M.Robinson *"Layla"*	Milton-under-Wychwood	29.11.01A
G-BNBW	Thunder Ax7-77 HAFB	914		11.12.86	I.S. & S.W.Watthews *"Mutley"*	Grange-over-Sands	9. 9.99A
G-BNBY	Beechcraft 95-B55A Baron	TC-1347	G-AXXR	14. 2.83	J.Butler	(Lisle Sur Tarn, France)	2. 6.04
G-BNBZ	LET L-200D Morava	171329	D-GGDC EI-AOY/(D-GLIN)/EI-AOY/OK-SHB	16.12.86	C.A.Suckling	Rushett Manor, Chessington	15. 5.00
G-BNCB	Cameron V-77 HAFB	1401		2.12.86	C.W.Brown *(New owner 10.01)*	Melton Mowbray	11. 5.02A
G-BNCC	Thunder Ax7-77 HAFB	924		11.12.86	Celia J.Burnhope *"Charlie"*	(USA)	9.10.99A
G-BNCE*	Grumman G159 Gulfstream I	9	N436M N436/N436M/N43M/(N709G)	7. 4.87	Dundee Airport Fire Service	Dundee	9. 4.92T
					(WFU 10.91 due to corrosion & cannibalised: cancelled 4.5.93 as WFU) (Fuselage in use 2001)		
G-BNCH	Cameron V-77 HAFB	1398		11.12.86	N.F.Mulliner t/a Royal Engineers Balloon Club *"Sapper II"*	Chatham	19. 6.92A
G-BNCJ	Cameron V-77 HAFB	815		16.12.86	D.Scott *"Sunshine Desserts"*	Melksham	6. 1.02A
G-BNCK*	Cameron V-77 HAFB	1420		7. 1.87	G.Randall *(Cancelled 19.4.00 as wfu)*	Bielefeld, Germany	9.11.91A
G-BNCN	Glaser-Dirks DG-400	4-198		22. 1.87	A.C.E.Vongontard *"421"*	Portmoak	31. 3.02
G-BNCO	Piper PA-38-112 Tomahawk	38-79A0472	N2482F	8. 1.87	Diane K.Walker	(Oakham, Leics)	25.11.04T

G-BNCR	Piper PA-28-161 Warrior II		G-PDMT	10.12.86	Airways Aero Associations Ltd	Booker	2. 5.02T
		28-8016111	ZS-LGW/N8103D		*(Op British Airways Flying Club) (Chelsea Rose t/s)*		
G-BNCS	Cessna 180	30022	OO-SPA	7. 1.87	C.Elwell Transport Ltd	Tatenhill	17. 2.95
			D-ENUX/N2822A				
G-BNCU	Thunder Ax7-77 HAFB	928		7. 1.87	P.Mann *"Skylark"*	Luton	14. 7.00A
G-BNCX*	Hawker Hunter T.7	41H/695454	XL621	9. 1.87	(J Hallett)	Brooklands	28. 3.87P
					(Cancelled 1.3.93 as WFU: on loan to Museum as "XL621")		
G-BNCZ	Rutan LongEz	PFA 074A-10723		8. 1.87	P.A.Ellway	Sherburn in Elmet	4.10.94P
	(Lycoming O-235)				*"Atlas..T" (Dismantled 2.00)*		
G-BNDG	Wallis WA-201/R Srs.1	K/220/X		22. 1.87	K.H.Wallis	Reymerston Hall, Norfolk	3. 3.88P
	(2 x Rotax 64hp)				*(Stored 8.01)*		
G-BNDN	Cameron V-77 HAFB	1443		8. 1.87	J.A.Smith	Bristol	22.10.93A
G-BNDO	Cessna 152 II	15284574	N5387M	11. 2.87	Simair Ltd	Andrewsfield	20. 8.02T
					(Op Essex School of Flying)		
G-BNDP	Brugger MB.2 Colibri	PFA 043-10956		8. 1.87	J.P.Kynaston	Burcott	17. 8.01P
	(VW 1834)						
G-BNDR	SOCATA TB-10 Tobago	740		12. 2.87	P.F.Rothwell	(Alderley Edge)	28. 2.03T
G-BNDT	Brugger MB.2 Colibri	PFA 043-10981		8. 1.87	H.Haigh	Bagby	10. 7.02P
	(VW 1834)				t/a Colibri Flying Group		
G-BNDV	Cameron N-77 HAFB	1427		25. 2.87	R.E.Jones	Lytham St.Annes	9. 5.93A
					"English Lake Hotels"		
G-BNDW	de Havilland DH.82A Tiger Moth	3942	N6638	10.12.86	N.D.Welch	Shobdon	
					(Components stored 3.96: current status unknown)		
G-BNDY	Cessna 425 Conquest I	425-0236	N1262T	2. 6.87	Standard Aviation Ltd	Newcastle	14.10.02
G-BNED	Piper PA-22-135 Tri-Pacer	22-1640	OO-JEF	26. 1.87	P.Storey	Sywell	
			N3385A				
G-BNEE	Piper PA-28R-201 Arrow III		N630DJ	28. 1.87	Britannic Management (Aviation) Ltd		
		28R-7837084	N9518N			Turweston	8. 8.03
G-BNEI	Piper PA-34-200T Seneca II		N3058K	12. 6.87	P.J.Morrison	North Weald	24. 5.03
		34-7870429	VQ-LBC/N9646N				
G-BNEK	Piper PA-38-112 Tomahawk II		N9096A	28. 1.87	APB Leasing Ltd	Welshpool	17. 5.00T
		38-82A0081					
G-BNEL	Piper PA-28-161 Warrior II		N2246U	27. 4.87	S.C.Westran	Shoreham	14. 9.02T
		28-7916314					
G-BNEN	Piper PA-34-200T Seneca II		N8232V	18. 2.87	Warwickshire Aerocentre Ltd	Birmingham	20. 3.02T
		34-8070262					
G-BNEO	Cameron V-77 HAFB	1408		9. 2.87	J.G.O'Connell *"Rowtate"*	Braintree	2.11.00
G-BNES	Cameron V-77 HAFB	1426		19. 2.87	G.Wells	Congleton	7. 1.99A
					t/a Northern Counties Photographers		
G-BNET	Cameron O-84 HAFB	1368		22. 1.87	C.& A.I.Gibson	Stockport	19. 5.02A
G-BNEV	Viking Dragonfly	PFA 139-10935		28.11.86	N.W.Eyre	(Kirkbymoorside)	
	(VW 1834)				*(Nearing completion 6.92: current status unknown)*		
G-BNEX	Cameron O-120 HAFB	1414		3. 4.87	The Balloon Club Ltd	Bristol	6. 5.90A
					t/a Bristol Balloons *"Sue Sheppard Employment Agency"*		
G-BNFG	Cameron O-77 HAFB	1416		5. 3.87	Capital Balloon Club Ltd	London NW1	13. 1.94A
					"Dolores"		
G-BNFI	Cessna 150J	15069417	N50588	8. 1.87	T.D.Aitken	Lower Wasing Farm, Brimpton	1. 5.03
G-BNFK	Cameron Egg 89SS HAFB	1436		20. 2.87	Forbes Europe Inc	Balleroy, Normandy	15. 7.02A
	(Faberge Rosebud Egg shape)				*"Faberge Easter Egg"*		
G-BNFM	Colt 21A Cloudhopper HAFB	668		5. 3.87	M.E.Dworski	Vermenton, France	24. 7.01A
G-BNFN	Cameron N-105 HAFB	1442		13. 3.87	P.Glydon	Barnt Green, Birmingham	17. 6.97T
G-BNFO	Cameron V-77 HAFB	816		5. 3.87	J.King & T.Ellenrieder	Bristol	10. 3.01A
					t/a Fox Group *"Funshine"*		
G-BNFP	Cameron O-84 HAFB	1474		29. 4.87	B.F.G.Ribbans *"Dragonfly"*	Woodbridge	29.12.01A
G-BNFR	Cessna 152 II	15282035	N67817	8. 4.87	Eastern Executive Air Charter Ltd		
					(Op Seawing Flying Club)	Southend	25. 4.03T
G-BNFS	Cessna 152 II	15283899	N5545B	10. 4.87	C & S Aviation Ltd	Wolverhampton	9. 7.02T
G-BNFV	Robin DR400/120 Dauphin 80	1767		4. 3.87	J.P.A.Freeman	Headcorn	15. 7.02T
G-BNGE	Auster AOP.6	1925	7704M	18. 3.87	M.Pocock	AAC Middle Wallop	6. 5.02P
			TW536		*(Op Military Auster Flight) (As "TW536/TS-V" in 657 AOP Sqn c/s)*		
G-BNGJ	Cameron V-77 HAFB	1487		18. 3.87	Lathams Ltd *"Latham Timber"*	High Wycombe	18.10.01A
G-BNGN	Cameron N-77 HAFB	817		3. 4.87	Catherine B.Leeder *"Falcon"*	Diss	29. 8.01A
G-BNGO	Thunder Ax7-77 HAFB	971		26. 3.87	J.S.Finlan	Hamilton, New Zealand	6. 4.02A
					t/a The G-BNGO Group *"Thunderbird" (Philips titles)*		
G-BNGP	Colt 77A HAFB	1033		30. 3.87	Cornwall Ballooning Adventures Ltd		
					"Headland Hotel II"	Newquay	1. 8.99A
G-BNGR	Piper PA-38-112 Tomahawk	38-79A0479	N2492F	26. 3.87	Teesside Flight Centre Ltd	Teesside	1. 8.03T
G-BNGS	Piper PA-38-112 Tomahawk	38-78A0701	N2463A	26. 3.87	Teesside Flight Centre Ltd	Teesside	
					(Noted as not assembled 12.01)		
G-BNGT	Piper PA-28-181 Archer II	28-8590036	N149AV	29. 4.87	J.H.Berry	Edinburgh	18. 5.02T
			N9559N		t/a Berry Air *(Op Edinburgh Flying Club)*		
G-BNGV	ARV1 Super 2	021		4. 6.87	N.A.Onions	Manor Farm, Glatton	6. 3.03
G-BNGW	ARV1 Super 2	022		4. 6.87	Southern Gas Turbines Ltd	Manston	8. 7.90T
					(Stored 6.94: current status unknown)		

G-BNGY	ARV1 Super 2	019	(G-BMWL)	9. 6.87	M.T.Manwaring	RAF Halton	28.11.04
G-BNHB	ARV1 Super 2	026		13. 7.87	J.K.Davies	Green Farm, Chester	24. 7.04
G-BNHE*	ARV1 Super 2	029		14. 8.87	L.J.Joyce	Dunkeswell	7. 8.99
					(Wrecked 5.00: cancelled 7.8.01 by CAA)		
G-BNHG	Piper PA-38-112 Tomahawk II	38-82A0030	N91435	23. 3.87	D.A.Whitmore	Norwich	31. 5.03T
G-BNHI	Cameron V-77 HAFB	1249		26. 3.87	C.J.Nicholls	Warwick	10. 6.02A
					"Fun-Der-Bird"		
G-BNHJ	Cessna 152 II	15281249	N49418	4. 6.87	The Pilot Centre Ltd	Denham	1.12.02T
G-BNHK	Cessna 152 II	15285355	N80161	30. 3.87	General Airline Ltd	(North Weald)	7. 6.03T
					(Ceased trading 10.01)		
G-BNHL*	Colt Beer Glass 90SS HAFB	1042		24 .3.87	Balloon Preservation Group	Kirdford	4. 3.97A
					"Gatzweiler Alt" (Cancelled 22.6.98 as WFU)		
G-BNHN*	Colt Ariel Bottle SS HAFB	1045		30. 3.87	British Balloon Museum & Library	Newbury	NE(A)
					"Ariel" (Cancelled 24.1.92 as WFU)		
G-BNHO*	Thunder Ax7-77 HAFB	1057		30. 3.87	M.J.Forster *"Bloody Mary"*	Newcastle	16. 7.97A
					(Cancelled 15.11.01 by CAA & stored)		
G-BNHT	Alpavia Fournier RF3	80	(D-KITX)	13. 4.87	D.G.Hey	Little Gransden	29. 3.02P
			G-BNHT/F-BMTO		t/a G-BNHT Group		
G-BNID	Cessna 152 II	15284931	N5378P	24. 4.87	M.J.Ireland	Wellesbourne Mountford	21. 5.01T
G-BNIE*	Cameron O-160 HAFB	1450		5. 5.87	D.K.Fish	Bedford	20. 7.95T
					(Cancelled 9.10.01 as wfu)		
G-BNIF	Cameron O-56 HAFB	1464		15. 4.87	D.V.Fowler *"Nifty"*	Cranbrook, Kent	19. 5.00A
G-BNII	Cameron N-90 HAFB	1497		15. 4.87	S.Saunders	Farnham	16. 8.01
					t/a Topless Balloon Group		
G-BNIJ	SOCATA TB-10 Tobago	758		27. 4.87	R.E.Price	East Midlands	16. 8.04
G-BNIK	Robin HR200/120 Club	43	LX-AIK	15. 4.87	A.W.Eldridge	Leicester	17. 5.03
			LX-PAA				
G-BNIM	Piper PA-38-112 Tomahawk	38-78A0148	N9631T	18. 6.87	Aurs Aviation Ltd	Glasgow	30. 3.03T
					(Op Glasgow Flying Club)		
G-BNIN	Cameron V-77 HAFB	1079	G-RRSG(1)	15. 4.87	M.K.Grigson	Shoreham	10. 6.02A
			(G-BLRO)		t/a Cloud Nine Balloon Group *"Cloud Nine"*		
G-BNIO	Luscombe 8AC Silvaire	2120	N45593	15. 4.87	G.G.Pugh	Stapleford	13.11.01P
	(Continental A75)		NC45593				
G-BNIP	Luscombe 8A Silvaire	3547	N77820	15. 4.87	D.R.C.Hunter & S.Maric	Cumbernauld	10. 2.93P
	(Continental A65)		NC77820		*(Stored 2001)*		
G-BNIU	Cameron O-77 HAFB	1499		28. 4.87	MC VH SA	Brussels, Belgium	3. 4.00A
G-BNIV	Cessna 152 II	15284866	N4972P	24. 4.87	Aerohire Ltd	Wolverhampton	17. 8.03T
					(Op Halfpenny Green Flight Centre)		
G-BNIW	Boeing-Stearman A75N1 (PT-17) Kaydet		N49291	22. 4.87	R.C.Goold	East Midlands	17. 4.04
	(P&W R985)	75-1526	41-7967				
G-BNIZ	Fokker F.27 Friendship 600F	10405	OY-SRA	1. 6.87	Dart Group plc	Bournemouth	3.11.03T
			G-BNIZ/9Q-CLQ/PH-FOD		t/a Channel Express		
G-BNJA	WAG-Aero Wag-a-Bond	PFA 137-10886		3. 4.87	B.E.Maggs	Clutton Hill Farm, Clutton	20. 8.02P
	(Continental O-200-A)						
G-BNJB	Cessna 152 II	15284865	N4970P	27. 4.87	Aerolease Ltd	Conington	20. 7.03T
G-BNJC	Cessna 152 II	15283588	N4705B	27. 4.87	Stapleford Flying Club Ltd	Stapleford	26. 8.02T
G-BNJD	Cessna 152 II	15282044	N67833	27. 4.87	Fraggle Leasing Ltd	Aberdeen	24. 5.03T
G-BNJF	Piper PA-32RT-300 Lance II	32R-7885098	N31539	8. 6.78	PFB Aviation Ltd	Jersey	2.12.02T
G-BNJG	Cameron O-77 HAFB	1502		9. 5.89	A.M.Figiel	High Wycombe	4. 4.97
G-BNJH	Cessna 152 II	15285401	C-GORA	21. 7.87	J.McAuley	Prestwick	5. 9.03T
			(N93101)		*(Op Prestwick Flight Centre)*		
G-BNJJ*	Cessna 152 II	15283625	N4767B	22. 6.87	Home Office Fire & Emergency Training Centre	Moreton-in-Marsh	14. 7.90T
			(Damaged Cranfield 18.5.88: cancelled 3.2.95 by CAA) (Fire service use 8.98)				
G-BNJK*	Hawker Siddeley HS.748 Srs.2A	1594	C-GEPI	5. 5.87	Macavia International Ltd		
			HP-432			Chateauroux, France	NE(X)
	(Converted MacAvia 748 Turbine Tanker water-bomber: stored 6.95: cancelled 29.2.96 by CAA) (Current status unknown)						
G-BNJL	Bensen B.8MR	PFA G/01-1020		30. 4.87	J.M.Cox	(Windsor)	29. 3.02P
	(Rotax 532)						
G-BNJM	Piper PA-28-161 Warrior II	28-8216078	N8015V	27. 5.87	Teesside Flight Centre Ltd	Biggin Hill	4. 6.90T
					(Damaged Middleton, Cumbria 18.5.89: fusealge only 5.01)		
G-BNJO	QAC Quickie Q2	2217	N17LM	6.10.87	J.D.McKay	Crowfield	14. 5.93P
	(Revmaster 2100D)						
G-BNJR	Piper PA-28RT-201T Turbo Arrow IV	28R-8031104	N8212U	8. 5.87	D.Crocker	Blackbushe	5. 8.02
G-BNJT	Piper PA-28-161 Warrior II	28-8116184	N8360T	11. 6.87	B.J.Newman, B.C.Williams, T.Kermode & M.Jones		
					t/a Chester Flying Group	Hawarden	8.11.02T
G-BNJU	Cameron Bust 80SS HAFB	1324		13. 5.87	Ballon Team Bonn GmbH & Co KG		
					"Ludwig von Beethoven"	Meckenheim, Germany	21. 1.00A
G-BNJV*	Cessna 152 II	15283840	N5333B	13. 5.87	Not known	Biggin Hill	29. 6.93T
	(Crashed Stoneacre Farm, Bredhurst 8.3.92: Cancelled 31.3.92 as destroyed) (Stored 2.95: current status unknown)						

G-BNJZ	Cassutt Racer IIIM	PFA 034-11228		14. 5.87	A.P.Meredith & Jill R.Burry		
	(Continental O-200-A)					Hilden-le-Noble, Hants	21. 6.99P
G-BNKC	Cessna 152 II	15281036	N48894	26. 5.87	Herefordshire Aero Club Ltd	Shobdon	31. 8.02T
G-BNKD	Cessna 172N Skyhawk II	17272329	N4681D	19. 5.87	Bristol Flying Centre Ltd	Bristol	17.10.03T
G-BNKE	Cessna 172N Skyhawk II	17273886	N6534J	20. 5.87	T.Jackson	Manchester	18. 4.03T
					t/a Kilo Echo Flying Group		
G-BNKF*	Colt AS-56 Hot-Air Airship	899		20. 5.87	Formtrack Ltd	Tucson, Arizona	14. 9.88A
					(Cancelled 20.10.00 by CAA)		
G-BNKH	Piper PA-38-112 Tomahawk II		N25874	14. 5.87	Goodwood Road Racing Co Ltd	Goodwood	5. 7.02T
		38-81A0078					
G-BNKI	Cessna 152 II	15281765	N67337	19. 5.87	RAF Halton Aeroplane Club Ltd	RAF Halton	6. 7.02T
G-BNKP	Cessna 152 II	15281286	N49460	18. 5.87	Fairmont Investments Ltd	Clacton	21. 8.03T
G-BNKR	Cessna 152 II	15281284	N49458	18. 5.87	Keen Leasing (IOM) Ltd		
						Newtownards, Co.of Down	10. 7.02T
G-BNKS	Cessna 152 II	15283186	N47202	18. 5.87	Shropshire Aero Club Ltd	Sleap	9. 5.02T
G-BNKT	Cameron O-77 HAFB	1356		13. 2.87	British Airways plc *"Katie II"*	Gatwick	29.12.01A
G-BNKV	Cessna 152 II	15283079	N46604	18. 5.87	S.C.Westran	Shoreham	26. 9.02T
G-BNLA	Boeing 747-436	23908	N60665	30. 6.89	British Airways plc	Gatwick	29. 6.02T
					(Op Nigerian Airways)		
G-BNLB	Boeing 747-436	23909		31. 7.89	British Airways plc	Gatwick	31. 7.02T
G-BNLC	Boeing 747-436	23910		21. 7.89	British Airways plc *(Colum t/s)*	Gatwick	26. 7.02T
G-BNLD	Boeing 747-436	23911	N6018N	5. 9.89	British Airways plc	Heathrow	5. 9.02T
					(Delftblue Daybreak t/s)		
G-BNLE	Boeing 747-436	24047		14.11.89	British Airways plc	Heathrow	16.11.02T
G-BNLF	Boeing 747-436	24048		23. 2.90	British Airways plc	Heathrow	11.10.02T
G-BNLG	Boeing 747-436	24049		23. 2.90	British Airways plc	Heathrow	1.10.02T
					(Whale Rider t/s)		
G-BNLI	Boeing 747-436	24051		19. 4.90	British Airways plc	Heathrow	20. 4.03T
					(Op British Asia Airways) (Benyhone Tartan t/s)		
G-BNLJ	Boeing 747-436	24052	N60668	23. 5.90	British Airways plc	Gatwick	24. 5.03T
					(Ndebele Martha t/s)		
G-BNLK	Boeing 747-436	24053	N6009F	25. 5.90	British Airways plc	Heathrow	28. 5.03T
					(Water Dreaming t/s)		
G-BNLL	Boeing 747-436	24054		13. 6.90	British Airways plc	Heathrow	13. 6.03T
					(Chelsea Rose t/s)		
G-BNLM	Boeing 747-436	24055	N6009F	28. 6.90	British Airways plc	Gatwick	27. 6.03T
					(Ndebele Martha t/s)		
G-BNLN	Boeing 747-436	24056		26. 7.90	British Airways plc	Heathrow	26. 7.03T
					(Nalanji Dreaming t/s)		
G-BNLO	Boeing 747-436	24057		25.10.90	British Airways plc	Heathrow	24.10.03T
G-BNLP	Boeing 747-436	24058		17.12.90	British Airways plc	Gatwick	10. 9.03T
G-BNLR	Boeing 747-436	24447	N6005C	15. 1.91	British Airways plc	Heathrow	16. 1.04T
					(Rendezvous t/s)		
G-BNLS	Boeing 747-436	24629		13. 3.91	British Airways plc	Heathrow	12. 3.04T
					(Wanula Dreaming t/s)		
G-BNLT	Boeing 747-436	24630		19. 3.91	British Airways plc	Gatwick	14.11.03T
					(Koguty Lowickie t/s)		
G-BNLU	Boeing 747-436	25406		28. 1.92	British Airways plc	Heathrow	27. 1.02T
					"City of Bangor"		
G-BNLV	Boeing 747-436	25427		20. 2.92	British Airways plc	Gatwick	19. 2.02T
					(Waves of the City t/s)		
G-BNLW	Boeing 747-436	25432		4. 3.92	British Airways plc	Heathrow	4. 3.02T
					"City of Norwich"		
G-BNLX(2)	Boeing 747-436	25435		1. 4.92	British Airways plc	Heathrow	2. 4.02T
G-BNLY(3)	Boeing 747-436	27090	N60659	10. 2.93	British Airways plc	Heathrow	9. 2.03T
G-BNLZ(3)	Boeing 747-436	27091		4. 3.93	British Airways plc	Heathrow	3. 3.03T
					(Animals & Trees t/s)		
G-BNMA	Cameron O-77 HAFB	830		15.12.87	A.Wilkes & N.Woodham	Bristol	22. 7.01A
					"Finian		
G-BNMB	Piper PA-28-151 Cherokee Warrior		N6826J	6.10.87	Britannia Airways Ltd	Liverpool	26. 1.03T
		28-7615369			*(Op Britannia Airways Flying Club)*		
G-BNMC	Cessna 152 II	15282564	N69218	29. 5.87	M.L.Jones *(Op Derby Aero Club)*	Derby	10. 8.03T
G-BNMD	Cessna 152 II	15283786	N5170B	28. 5.87	T.M.Jones *(Op Derby Aero Club)*	Derby	28. 7.01T
G-BNME	Cessna 152 II	15284888	N5159P	25. 9.87	Northamptonshire School of Flying Ltd		
						Sywell	16.12.02T
G-BNMF	Cessna 152T	15285563	N93858	21. 7.87	Aerohire Ltd	Wolverhampton	22. 8.03T
					(Op Midland Flight Centre)		
G-BNMG	Cameron O-77 HAFB	1500		27. 5.87	J.H.Turner	Bridgnorth	25. 8.01A
G-BNMH	Pietenpol Air Camper	NH-1-001		2. 6.87	N.M.Hitchman	(Stoke Gifford)	
G-BNMI	Colt Black Knight HAFB	1096		1. 6.87	Virgin Airship & Balloon Co.Ltd	Telford	26. 9.91A
G-BNMK	Dornier Do.27A-1	271	OE-DGO	14. 8.87	G.Mackie	Belfast	
			56+04/BD+397/BA+399		*(Noted 10.01)*		
G-BNML	Rand Robinson KR-2	PFA 129-11240		23. 6.87	R.F.Cresswell	(Alfreton)	17. 8.00P
	(VW 1834)						

G-BNMO	Cessna R182 Skylane RG II	R18200956	N738RK	3. 7.87	Kenrye Developments Ltd	Trim	26. 4.03
G-BNMT	Short SD.3-60 Var.100	SH.3723	N160DD G-BNMT/G-14-3723	18. 6.87	Loganair Ltd *(Koguty Lowickie t/s)*	Glasgow	15.10.01T
					(Crashed into Firth of Forth near Granton harbour 27.2.01 on take-off from Edinburgh)		
G-BNMU	Short SD.3-60 Var.100	SH.3724	N161DD G-BNMU/G-14-3724	18. 6.87	Loganair Ltd *(Colum t/s)*	Glasgow	22.11.02T
G-BNMX	Thunder Ax7-77 HAFB	1003		15. 6.87	S.A.D.Beard	Cheltenham	8. 7.02A
G-BNNA	Stolp SA.300 Starduster Too (Lycoming O-360)	1462	N8SD	29. 6.87	D.S.Milne	Banchory	11. 7.02P
G-BNNC*	Cameron N-77 HAFB	1523		16. 6.87	T McCoy *(Cancelled 2.6.98 as WFU: stored 2000)*	Bath	9.10.96
G-BNNE	Cameron N-77 HAFB	1413		15. 6.87	Balloon Flights International Ltd *(Noted active 9.01)*	Bath	
G-BNNI	Boeing 727-276	20950	VH-TBK	10.12.86	Couga Leasing *(Open store 1.02)*	Southend	17. 3.02T
G-BNNL*	Boeing 737-4Q8	24070		26. 1.89	National Jet Italia SpA *(Cancelled 30.11.01 by CAA) (Stored 1.02)*	Lasham	30. 1.02T
G-BNNO	Piper PA-28-161 Warrior II	28-8116099	N8307X	15. 6.87	Tindon Ltd	Norwich	5. 8.02T
G-BNNR	Cessna 152 II	15285146	N40SX N40SU/N6121Q	15. 6.87	Sussex Flying Club Ltd	Shoreham	13.10.02T
G-BNNS	Piper PA-28-161 Warrior II	28-8116061	N8283C	26. 6.87	M.J.Allen & R.Inskip t/a Warrior Aircraft Syndicate	Fowlmere	21. 5.02
G-BNNT	Piper PA-28-151 Cherokee Warrior	28-7615056	N7624C	12. 6.87	S.T.Gilbert & D.J.Kirkwood	Hinton-in-the-Hedges	1. 7.04T
G-BNNU	Piper PA-38-112 Tomahawk II	38-81A0037	N25650	12. 6.87	Edinburgh Flying Club Ltd	Edinburgh	11.11.02T
G-BNNX	Piper PA-28R-201T Turbo Cherokee Arrow III	28R-7703009	N9005F	14. 7.87	J.G.Freeden	Sherburn-in-Elmet	10.11.02T
G-BNNY	Piper PA-28-161 Warrior II	28-8016084	N8092M	1. 9.87	A.S.Bamrah t/a Falcon Flying Services *(Op Southern Air)*	Biggin Hill	14.12.02T
G-BNNZ	Piper PA-28-161 Warrior II	28-8016177	N8135Y	24. 7.87	A S Bamrah t/a Falcon Flying Services	Biggin Hill	20.10.02T
G-BNOB	Wittman W.8 Tailwind (Continental.PC60)	258/DH1 & PFA 3502		13. 7.87	M.Robson-Robinson *"Imogen"*	(Abbots Bromley)	14. 5.02P
G-BNOE	Piper PA-28-161 Warrior II	2816013	N9121X N9568N	26. 6.87	Sherburn Aero Club Ltd	Sherburn in Elmet	12. 2.04T
G-BNOF	Piper PA-28-161 Warrior II	2816014	N9122B	26. 6.87	Tayside Aviation Ltd	Dundee	29. 3.04T
G-BNOG	Piper PA-28-161 Warrior II	2816015	N9122D	26. 6.87	BAE Systems Flight Training (UK) Ltd	Jerez, Cadiz, Spain	5. 7.01T
G-BNOH	Piper PA-28-161 Warrior II	2816016	N9122L	26. 6.87	Sherburn Aero Club Ltd	Sherburn in Elmet	25. 1.04T
G-BNOI	Piper PA-28-161 Warrior II	2816017	N9122N	26. 6.87	BAE Systems Flight Training (UK) Ltd	Jerez, Cadiz, Spain	2.11.02T
G-BNOJ	Piper PA-28-161 Warrior II	2816018	N9122R	26. 6.87	R.D.Turner & W.M.Brown t/a BAE (Warton) Flying Club	Blackpool	13. 7.03T
G-BNOK	Piper PA-28-161 Warrior II	2816019	N9122U	26. 6.87	BAE Systems Flight Training (UK) Ltd	Jerez, Cadiz, Spain	19. 5.01T
G-BNOL	Piper PA-28-161 Warrior II	2816023		26. 6.87	BAE Systems Flight Training (UK) Ltd	Jerez, Cadiz, Spain	17. 5.01T
G-BNOM	Piper PA-28-161 Warrior II	2816024		26. 6.87	Sherburn Aero Club Ltd	Sherburn in Elmet	14. 2.04T
G-BNON	Piper PA-28-161 Warrior II	2816025		26. 6.87	Tayside Aviation Ltd	Dundee	8. 3.04T
G-BNOO	Piper PA-28-161 Warrior II	2816026		26. 6.87	BAE Systems Flight Training (UK) Ltd	Jerez, Cadiz, Spain	16. 8.02T
G-BNOP	Piper PA-28-161 Warrior II	2816027		26. 6.87	R.D.Turner & F.J.Smith t/a BAE (Warton) Flying Club	Blackpool	29. 7.02T
G-BNOR	Piper PA-28-161 Warrior II	2816028		26. 6.87	BAE Systems Flight Training (UK) Ltd	Jerez, Cadiz, Spain	7. 9.02T
G-BNOS	Piper PA-28-161 Warrior II	2816029		26. 6.87	BAE Systems Flight Training (UK) Ltd	Jerez, Cadiz, Spain	28. 2.03T
G-BNOT	Piper PA-28-161 Warrior II	2816030		26. 6.87	BAE Systems Flight Training (UK) Ltd	Jerez, Cadiz, Spain	24. 6.01T
G-BNOU	Piper PA-28-161 Warrior II	2816031		26. 6.87	BAE Systems Flight Training (UK) Ltd	Jerez, Cadiz, Spain	11.11.02T
G-BNOV	Piper PA-28-161 Warrior II	2816032		26. 6.87	BAE Systems Flight Training (UK) Ltd	Jerez, Cadiz, Spain	18. 6.03T
G-BNOW	Piper PA-28-161 Warrior II	2816033		26. 6.87	BAE Systems Flight Training (UK) Ltd	Jerez, Cadiz, Spain	30. 8.02T
G-BNOX	Cessna R182 Skylane RG II	R18201026	N756AW	24. 6.87	G.T.Grimward	Denham	2. 4.03
G-BNOZ	Cessna 152 II	15281625	EI-CCP G-BNOZ/N65570	22. 6.87	Halfpenny Green Flight Centre Ltd	Wolverhampton	17. 2.02T
G-BNPE	Cameron N-77 HAFB	1519	(G-BNPX)	25. 8.87	Zebedee Balloon Service Ltd *(New owner 4.01)*	Hungerford	22. 3.02A
G-BNPF	Slingsby T.31M Cadet III (Stark Stamo MS.1400A) *(Contains wings from XE791 which became OO-ZDQ)*	826 & PFA 042-11122	XA284	3.11.87	S.Luck, P.Norman & D.R.Winder *"Noddy"*	Audley End	10. 8.00P

G-BNPH	Hunting-Percival P.66 Pembroke C.1 *(Regd with c/n "PAC66/027")* P66/41	WV740	30. 6.87	M.J.Willing *(As "WV740" in 60 Sqn RAF c/s)*	Jersey	5. 5.02P
G-BNPI	Colt 21A Cloudhopper HAFB 1038		23. 6.87	Virgin Airship & Balloon Co Ltd *"Virgin Cloudhopper"*	Telford	7. 8.95A
G-BNPL	Piper PA-38-112 Tomahawk 38-79A0524	N2420G	28. 7.87	Modern Air (UK) Ltd	Fowlmere	30. 1.03T
G-BNPM	Piper PA-38-112 Tomahawk 38-79A0374	N2561D	28. 7.87	Papa Mike Aviation Ltd *(Op Bonus Aviation)*	Blackbushe	10. 5.02T
G-BNPO	Piper PA-28-181 <u>Cherokee</u> Archer II 28-7890123	N47720	28. 7.87	Bonus Aviation Ltd	Cranfield	15. 6.03T
G-BNPU*	Hunting-Percival P.66 Pembroke C.1 *(Regd with c/n "K66/089")* P66/87	XL929	30. 6.87	Museum of D-Day Aviation *(Cancelled 11.8.88 as WFU) (As "XL929")*	Shoreham	17. 5.88P
G-BNPV	Bowers Fly Baby 1B PFA 016-11120 (Continental C90) *(Orig. regd & built as Fly Baby 1A - converted to <u>1B</u> [bi-plane configuration] in 1990s)*		2. 7.87	J.G.Day & R.Gauld-Galliers	Rushett Manor, Chessington	7.11.02P
G-BNPY	Cessna 152 II 15280249	N24388	30. 6.87	J.C.Birdsall t/a Traffic Management Services	Gamston	19.12.02T
G-BNPZ	Cessna 152 II 15285134	N6109Q	30. 6.87	C & S Aviation Ltd	Wolverhampton	17.10.02T
G-BNRA	SOCATA TB-10 Tobago 772		15. 7.87	M.Walshe t/a Double D Airgroup *"Triple One"*	Nottingham	8. 5.03
G-BNRG	Piper PA-28-161 Warrior II 28-8116217	N83810	7. 7.87	RAF Brize Norton Flying Club Ltd	RAF Brize Norton	26. 3.03T
G-BNRI	Cessna U206G Stationair II U20604024	N756ED	28. 7.87	Bob Crowe Aircraft Sales Ltd	Cranfield	24. 4.03T
G-BNRK	Cessna 152 II 15284659	N6297M	29. 7.87	Redhill Aviation Ltd t/a Redhill Flying Club	Redhill	6. 2.03T
G-BNRL	Cessna 152 II 15284250	N5084L	13. 7.87	Walkbury Aviation Ltd	Sibson	25. 4.03T
G-BNRP	Piper PA-28-181 <u>Cherokee</u> Archer II 28-7790528	N984BT	25.11.87	Bonus Aviation Ltd	Cranfield	25. 5.03T
G-BNRR	Cessna 172P Skyhawk II 17274013	N5213K	13. 7.87	PHA Aviation Ltd	Elstree	15.12.02T
G-BNRX	Piper PA-34-200T Seneca II 34-7970336	N2898A	25.11.87	Truman Aviation Ltd	Nottingham	8. 3.03T
G-BNRY	Cessna 182Q Skylane II 18265629	N735RR	20. 7.87	Reefly Ltd	Booker	30. 5.03T
G-BNSG	Piper PA-28R-201 Arrow III 28R-7837205	N9516C	30. 7.87	Armada Aviation Ltd	Redhill	26. 7.03
G-BNSI	Cessna 152 II 15284853	N4945P	6. 8.87	Sky Leisure Aviation (Charters) Ltd	Shoreham	3.11.02T
G-BNSL	Piper PA-38-112 Tomahawk II 38-81A0086	N25956	21. 7.87	APB Leasing Ltd	Welshpool	1. 5.03T
G-BNSM	Cessna 152 II 15285342	N68948	23. 7.87	Cornwall Flying Club Ltd	Bodmin	26. 7.03T
G-BNSN	Cessna 152 II 15285776	N94738	21. 7.87	The Pilot Centre Ltd	Denham	8. 5.03T
G-BNSO	Slingsby T.67M Firefly II 2021		20. 8.87	Babcock Rosyth Defence Ltd t/a Hunting Contract Services *(Op JEFTS)*	RAF Barkston Heath	17. 2.03T
G-BNSP	Slingsby T.67M Firefly II 2044		20. 8.87	Babcock Rosyth Defence Ltd t/a Hunting Contract Services *(Op JEFTS)*	RAF Barkston Heath	15. 2.03T
G-BNSR	Slingsby T.67M Firefly II 2047		20. 8.87	Babcock Rosyth Defence Ltd t/a Hunting Contract Services *(Op JEFTS)*	RAF Barkston Heath	15. 5.03T
G-BNST	Cessna 172N Skyhawk II 17273661	N4670J	21. 9.87	J.Revill t/a CSG Bodyshop	Netherthorpe	16. 4.03T
G-BNSU	Cessna 152 II 15281245	N49410	2.12.87	A.R.Brown t/a Channel Aviation Ltd *(Op Rural Flying Corps)*	Bourn	31. 8.03T
G-BNSV	Cessna 152 II 15284531	N5322M	4.12.87	A.R.Brown t/a Channel Aviation Ltd *(New CofR 6.01)*	Bourn	12. 7.97T
G-BNSY	Piper PA-28-161 Warrior II 28-8016017	N4512M	18. 8.87	Carill Aviation Ltd	Southampton	12. 3.03T
G-BNSZ	Piper PA-28-161 Warrior II 28-8116315	N8433B	20. 8.87	Carill Aviation Ltd	Compton Abbas	2.12.02T
G-BNTC	Piper PA-28RT-201T Turbo Arrow IV 28R-8131081	N83428	4.11.87	M.F.Lassan	Wolverhampton	14. 6.02T
G-BNTD	Piper PA-28-161 Cherokee Warrior II 28-7716235	N38490 N9539N	5. 8.87	A.M.& F.Alam	Elstree	28.10.02T
G-BNTP	Cessna 172N Skyhawk II 172-72030	N6531E	4. 9.87	Westnet Ltd	Barton	30. 1.03
G-BNTS	Piper PA-28RT-201T Turbo Arrow IV 28R-8131024	N8296R	6. 8.87	Nasaire Ltd	Liverpool	11. 2.03
G-BNTT	Beechcraft 76 Duchess ME-228	N54SB	8.10.87	S.J.Skilton t/a Aviation Rentals *(Op Professional Air Training)*	Bournemouth	22. 5.03T
G-BNTW	Cameron V-77 HAFB 1574		13. 8.87	P.Goss *"Cecilia"*	Alton	6.11.99A
G-BNTZ	Cameron N-77 HAFB 1518		27. 8.87	P.M.Watkins t/a Balloon Team	Chippenham	20. 5.00A
G-BNUC	Cameron O-77 HAFB 1575		18. 8.87	T.J.Bucknall *"Bridges Van Hire II"*	Hawarden	
G-BNUI	Rutan VariEze PFA 074-10960 (Continental O-200-A)		12. 8.87	I.T.Kennedy & K.H.McConnell	Belfast	10.12.01P
G-BNUL	Cessna 152 II 152-84486	N4852M	2.10.87	Exeter Air Training School Ltd	Exeter	3. 5.03T

G-BNUN	Beechcraft 58PA Baron	TJ-256	N6732Y	19. 8.87	British Midland Airways Ltd		
						East Midlands	16. 5.02T
G-BNUO	Beechcraft 76 Duchess	ME-250	N6635Y	29. 9.87	G.A.F.Tilley	Bournemouth	27. 5.02T
G-BNUS	Cessna 152 II	15282166	N68179	26. 8.87	Stapleford Flying Club Ltd	Stapleford	6. 7.03T
G-BNUT	Cessna 152 II	15279458	N714VC	26. 8.87	Stapleford Flying Club Ltd	Stapleford	1. 6.03T
G-BNUV	Piper PA-23-250 Aztec F	27-7854038	N97BB	2.10.87	L.J.Martin	Sandown/Redhill	9. 1.03
			N63894				
G-BNUX	Hoffmann H.36 Dimona	36236		26. 8.87	G.Hill	Saltby	13. 6.03
					t/a Buckminster Dimona Syndicate		
G-BNUY	Piper PA-38-112 Tomahawk II		N26006	10. 9.87	Cardiff-Wales Aviation Services Ltd		
		38-81A0093				Cardiff	17. 8.03T
G-BNVB	Grumman-American AA-5A Cheetah		N26843	28. 8.87	V.R.Coultan	Turweston	23. 2.03T
		AA5A-0758			t/a Grumman Group		
	(Regd as such but plate indicates <u>*Gulfstream*</u>*-American production)*						
G-BNVD	Piper PA-38-112 Tomahawk	38-79A0055	N2421B	16.11.87	D.A.Whitmore	Turweston	19. 6.03T
G-BNVE	Piper PA-28-181 Archer II	28-8490046	N4338D	28. 8.87	S.Parrish	Fowlmere	24.11.02T
					t/a Steve Parrish Racing		
G-BNVT	Piper PA-28R-201T Turbo Cherokee Arrow III			26. 1.88	T.Yeung	Glasgow	12.11.03T
		28R-7703157	N5863V		t/a Victor Tango Group *(Op Glasgow Flying Club)*		
G-BNVZ	Beechcraft 95-B55 Baron	TC-2042	N17720	25. 9.87	W.J.Forrest	White Waltham	14. 6.04
G-BNWA	Boeing 767-336ER	24333	N6009F	19. 4.90	British Airways plc	Heathrow	24. 4.03T
					(Delftblue Daybreak t/s)		
G-BNWB	Boeing 767-336ER	24334	N6046P	2. 2.90	British Airways plc	Heathrow	12. 2.03T
					(Chelsea Rose t/s) (Stored 1.02)		
G-BNWC	Boeing 767-336ER	24335		2. 2.90	British Airways plc	Heathrow	21. 2.03T
					(Rendezvous t/s) (Stored 1.02)		
G-BNWD	Boeing 767-336ER	24336	N6018N	2. 2.90	British Airways plc	Heathrow	29.11.02T
					(Ndebele Emmly t/s) (Stored 1.02)		
G-BNWH	Boeing 767-336ER	24340	N6005C	31.10.90	British Airways plc	Heathrow	30.10.03T
G-BNWI	Boeing 767-336ER	24341		18.12.90	British Airways plc	Gatwick	17.12.03T
G-BNWM	Boeing 767-336ER	25204		24. 6.91	British Airways plc	Manchester	24. 6.04T
G-BNWN	Boeing 767-336ER	25444		30.10.91	British Airways plc	Heathrow	29.10.04T
G-BNWO	Boeing 767-336ER	25442		2. 3.92	British Airways plc	Gatwick	1. 3.02T
					"City of Barcelona"		
G-BNWR	Boeing 767-336ER	25732		20. 3.92	British Airways plc	Gatwick	19. 3.02T
G-BNWS	Boeing 767-336ER	25826	N6018N	19. 2.93	British Airways plc	Heathrow	18. 2.03T
G-BNWT	Boeing 767-336ER	25828		8. 2.93	British Airways plc	Birmingham	29.11.02T
					(Benyhone Tartan t/s) (Stored 10.01)		
G-BNWU	Boeing 767-336ER	25829		16. 3.93	British Airways plc	Gatwick	15. 3.03T
					(Blomstrang t/s)		
G-BNWV	Boeing 767-336ER	27140		29. 4.93	British Airways plc *(Colum t/s)*	Heathrow	28. 4.03T
G-BNWW	Boeing 767-336ER	25831		3. 2.94	British Airways plc	Birmingham	2. 2.03T
					(Stored 1.02) (For Quantas 3.02)		
G-BNWX	Boeing 767-336ER	25832		1. 3.94	British Airways plc	Cambridge	28. 2.03T
					(Stored 1.02)		
G-BNWY	Boeing 767-336ER	25834	N5005C	22. 4.96	British Airways plc	Birmingham	21. 4.02T
					(Stored 1.02) (For Quantas 3.02)		
G-BNWZ	Boeing 767-336ER	25733		25. 2.97	British Airways plc	Heathrow	24. 2.03T
G-BNXC	Cessna 152 II	15285429	N93171	24. 9.87	N.D.Wyndow	Coventry	8. 3.04T
					t/a Sir W.G.Armstrong-Whitworth Flying Group		
G-BNXD	Cessna 172N Skyhawk II	17272692	N6285D	25. 9.87	Hedcray Co Ltd	Southend	9. 5.04T
					t/a Direct Helicopters *(Op Southend School of Flying)*		
G-BNXE	Piper PA-28-161 Warrior II		N8262D	24. 9.87	M.S.Brown	Coventry	23.12.02
		28-8116034			t/a Rugby Autobody Repairs		
G-BNXI	Robin DR.400/180R Remorqueur	1021	SE-FNI	13.10.87	London Gliding Club Pty Ltd	Dunstable	8. 2.03
G-BNXK	Nott/Cameron/Airship Industries ULD/3 Explorer Rozier HAFB						
		7 & 1110	(G-BLJN)	23. 9.87	J.R.P.Nott	London NW3	
	(Hot-air envelope in Twain Harte, California, USA 12.97 - helium inner envelope stored Bristol 1995)						
G-BNXL	Glaser-Dirks DG-400	4-216		2.10.87	J.McLaughlin	Rufforth	14. 4.03
					t/a G-BNXL Group		
G-BNXM	Piper PA-18 Super Cub 95	18-4019	MM54-2619	23.11.87	R.Thorp	Gipsy Wood	3. 9.02P
	(Continental O-200-A) (L-21B-PI)		EI-276/I-EIVC/MM54-2619/54-2619		t/a G-BNXM Group		
	(Italian Frame rebuild No.0006)						
G-BNXR	Cameron O-84 HAFB	1515		23. 9.87	J.A.B.Gray *"Bacchus II"*	Cirencester	8. 5.01T
G-BNXT	Piper PA-28-161 Cherokee Warrior II		N4047Q	23. 9.87	A.S.Bamrah	Biggin Hill	27.10.02T
		28-7716168			t/a Falcon Flying Services *(Op Euroflyers)*		
G-BNXU	Piper PA-28-161 Warrior II		N2082C	23. 9.87	D.J.G.Carphin & R.E.Woolsey		
		28-7916129			t/a Friendly Warrior Group	Newtownards, Co.of Down	3. 2.03
G-BNXV	Piper PA-38-112 Tomahawk	38-79A0826	N2399N	10.12.87	E.Reed	Blackpool	5.10.01T
					t/a The St.George Flying Club		
G-BNXX	SOCATA TB-20 Trinidad	664	N20GZ	15. 9.87	D.M.Carr	Wellesbourne Mountford	12. 5.03
G-BNXZ	Thunder Ax7-77 HAFB	1105		13.10.87	W.S.Templeton, R.B.Green & A.S.Dear *"Dragonfly"*		
					t/a Hale Hot-Air Balloon Group	Fordingbridge	6. 7.00A

G-BNYB	Piper PA-28-201T Turbo Dakota	28-7921040	N2856A N9533N	27. 1.88	Rosetta Milestone Ltd	Blackbushe	11. 2.04T
G-BNYD	Bell 206B JetRanger II	1911	N3254P C-GTWM/N49712	1.10.87	Sterling Helicopters Ltd	Norwich	3.11.02T
G-BNYI	Short SD.3-60 Var.100	SH.3731	N360CC G-BNYI/G-14-3731	12.10.87	Lynrise Aircraft Financing Ltd *(Op Loganair) "Chathm Historic Dockyard"*	Glasgow	10. 5.02T
G-BNYK	Piper PA-38-112 Tomahawk II	38-82A0059	N2376V	23.10.87	APB Leasing Ltd	Welshpool	17. 5.02T
G-BNYL	Cessna 152 II	15280671	N25454	6.10.87	V.J.Freeman	Headcorn	9.11.03T
G-BNYM	Cessna 172N Skyhawk II	17273854	N6089J	13.11.87	D.J.Skinner t/a Kestrel Syndicate	AAC Netheravon	16. 4.03
G-BNYN	Cessna 152 II	15285433	N93185	2.10.87	Redhill Aviation Ltd	Blackbushe	17. 2.03T
G-BNYO	Beechcraft 76 Duchess	ME-78	N2010P	28.10.87	R.E.Wragg t/a Harding Wragg	Blackpool	5. 7.04T
G-BNYP	Piper PA-28-181 Archer II	28-8490027	N4330K	19.10.87	R.D.Cooper *(Op Sandra's Flying Group)*	Cranfield	13. 3.03T
G-BNYV	Piper PA-38-112 Tomahawk	38-78A0073	N9364T	13.11.87	Goodair Leasing Ltd	Cardiff	2. 5.03T
G-BNYX	Denney Kitfox mk.1 (Rotax 532)	PFA 172-11285		28.10.87	R.W.Husband *(Stored 3.96: current status unknown)*	Birds Edge, Penistone	14. 3.95P
G-BNYZ	SNCAN Stampe SV-4E (Lycoming O-360)	200	F-BFZR Fr Mil	10.12.87	M.J.Heudebourck & D.E.Starkey	White Waltham	5.10.03
G-BNZB	Piper PA-28-161 Warrior II	28-7916521	N2900U	18.11.87	EFG Flying Services Ltd	Biggin Hill	24. 1.03T
G-BNZC	de Havilland DHC-1 Chipmunk 22	C1/0778	G-ROYS 7438M/WP905	11.11.87	The Shuttleworth Trust *(As "18013" in RCAF c/s)*	Old Warden	27. 9.03
G-BNZG*	Piper PA-28RT-201T Turbo Arrow IV	28R-8031132	N82376	23.11.87	Brightday Ltd *(Cancelled 12.12.01 by CAA)*	Sleap	18. 3.02
G-BNZJ*	Colt 21A Cloudhopper HAFB	1150		27.10.87	N.Charbonnier *(Cancelled 10.10.01 by CAA)*	Aosta, Italy	31. 8.96A
G-BNZK	Thunder Ax7-77 HAFB	1104		10.11.87	T.D.Marsden *"Shropshire Lass"*	Grimsby	28. 5.97A
G-BNZL	Rotorway Scorpion 133	2839		2.11.87	J.R.Wraight *(Complete but stored 5.95: current status unknown*	Stoneacre Farm, Farthing Corner	
G-BNZM	Cessna T210N Turbo Centurion II	21063640	N4828C	9.11.87	A.J.M.Freeman	North Weald	13. 3.03
G-BNZO	Rotorway Executive (Rotorway RW162)	RW152/3535		9.11.87	D.Collins & R.Ayres *"Bonzo"*	Street Farm, Takeley	4. 1.02P
G-BNZR	Clutton FRED Srs.II (VW 1834)	PFA 029-10727		10.11.87	R.M.Waugh	Newtownards, Co.of Down	25. 5.99P
G-BNZV	Piper PA-25-235 Pawnee D	25-7405649	C-GSKU N9548P	22. 2.88	Northumbria Gliding Club Ltd	Currock Hill	27. 4.03
G-BNZZ	Piper PA-28-161 Warrior II	28-8216184	N8253Z	17.11.87	Zooom Aviation Ltd	Denham	8. 3.03T

G-BOAA – G-BOZZ

G-BOAA	British Aircraft Corporation-Aérospatiale Concorde 102	100-006	G-N94AA/G-BOAA	3. 4.74	British Airways plc	Heathrow	24. 2.01T
G-BOAB	British Aircraft Corporation-Aérospatiale Concorde 102	100-008	G-N94AB/G-BOAB	3. 4.74	British Airways plc	Heathrow	19. 9.01T
G-BOAC	British Aircraft Corporation-Aérospatiale Concorde 102	100-004	G-N81AC/G-BOAC	3. 4.74	British Airways plc	Heathrow	11. 2.01T
G-BOAD	British Aircraft Corporation-Aérospatiale Concorde 102	100-010	G-N94AD/G-BOAD	9. 5.75	British Airways plc	Heathrow	3.12.04T
G-BOAE	British Aircraft Corporation-Aérospatiale Concorde 102	100-012	G-N94AE/G-BOAE	9. 5.75	British Airways plc	Heathrow	18. 7.02T
G-BOAF	British Aircraft Corporation-Aérospatiale Concorde 102	100-016	G-N94AF/G-BFKX	12. 6.80	British Airways plc	Heathrow	11. 6.04T
G-BOAG	British Aircraft Corporation-Aérospatiale Concorde 102	100-014	G-BFKW	9. 2.81	British Airways plc	Heathrow	3. 4.02T
G-BOAH	Piper PA-28-161 Warrior II	28-8416030	N43401 N9554N	21. 1.88	N.Singh & H.Kaur	Prestwick	19. 3.03T
G-BOAI	Cessna 152 II	15279830	C-GSJH N757LS	8. 1.88	Galair Ltd	Biggin Hill	22. 5.03T
G-BOAL	Cameron V-65 HAFB	1600		5.11.87	A.Lindsay *"No Name Balloon"*	Twickenham	7. 7.02A
G-BOAM	Robinson R22 Beta	0717		10.12.87	Plane Talking Ltd	Elstree	21.12.02T
G-BOAO	Thunder Ax7-77 HAFB	1162		2.12.87	D.V.Fowler	Cranbrook, Kent	16. 6.97A
G-BOAS	Air Command 503 Commander (Rotax 503)	0388 & PFA G/04-1094		3.12.87	R.Robinson	(Leighton Buzzard)	
G-BOAU	Cameron V-77 HAFB	1606		10.12.87	G.T.Barstow *"Flying Colours/Duster I"*	Llandrindod Wells	9.12.96A
G-BOBA	Piper PA-28R-201 Arrow III	28R-7837232	N31249	4. 1.88	Atlantic Air Transport Ltd t/a Atlantic Flight Training	Coventry	4. 7.03T

G-BOBB	Cameron O-120 HAFB	1609		24.11.87	Over The Rainbow Balloon Flights Ltd	Mansfield	17. 4.02A
G-BOBD*	Cameron O-160 HAFB	1594		22.12.87	J.Spindler *"Jill"*	Cleish	6. 9.95T
					(Cancelled 25.10.01 by CAA)		
G-BOBF*	Brugger MB.2 Colibri	PFA 043-11172		10.12.87	R.Bennett	Sproughton, Ipswich	
	(Not completed & sold to a new owner in 1997: cancelled 6.3.99 by CAA: current status unknown)						
G-BOBG*	Jodel D.150	PFA 151-11222		18.12.87	L Lewis	(Redcar)	
					(No Permit to Fly issued & cancelled 29.12.95 by CAA) (Stored 1.02)		
G-BOBH	Airtour AH-77B HAFB	009		2.12.87	J. & K.Francis *"Gloworm"*	Southampton	29. 6.02A
G-BOBJ*	Piper PA-38-112 Tomahawk	38-80A0021	N25096 N9656N	4. 1.88	Skycraft Ltd	(Spalding)	9. 8.03T
					(Cancelled 21.9.01 as wfu: for spares 11.01)		
G-BOBK*	Piper PA-38-112 Tomahawk	38-79A0503	N2352G	4. 1.88	(Skycraft Ltd)	(Spalding)	23. 3.00T
					(Cancelled 23.5.01 as wfu: for spares 11.01)		
G-BOBL	Piper PA-38-112 Tomahawk II	38-81A0140	N91335	4. 1.88	Cardiff Wales Aviation Services Ltd	Cardiff	28. 9.03T
G-BOBR	Cameron N-77 HAFB	1623		10.12.87	C.Bradley & M.Morris	Llanymynech, Powys	4. 5.00A
					(Loganair titles)		
G-BOBS*	QAC Quickie Q2 (Revmaster 2100)	PFA 094A-10840		27. 9.82	M.A.Hales	RAF Brize Norton	22.12.92P
					(Wreck stored 4.95: cancelled 18.3.99 by CAA: current status unknown)		
G-BOBT	Stolp SA.300 Starduster Too (Lycoming O-360)	CJ-01	N690CM	15.12.87	S.C.Lever t/a G-BOBT Group	White Waltham	28. 6.02P
G-BOBU	Colt 90A HAFB	900		15.12.87	Prescott Hot Air Balloons Ltd	Cheltenham	26. 9.00A
G-BOBV	Reims Cessna F150M	F15001415	EI-BCV	14.12.87	Sheffield Aero Club Ltd	Netherthorpe	6. 4.03T
G-BOBY	Monnett Sonerai II (VW 2233)	PFA 015-10223		26.10.78	R.G.Hallam	Netherthorpe	8.11.82P
					(Damaged near Barton 31.10.82: stored 9.96: current status unknown)		
G-BOBZ	Piper PA-28-181 Archer II	28-8090257	N81671	21.12.87	Trustcomms International Ltd	Goodwood	9. 3.98T
G-BOCB*	Hawker Siddeley HS.125 Srs.1B/522	25106	G-OMCA G-DJMJ/G-AWUF/5N-ALY/G-AWUF/HZ-BIN	14. 9.87	Not known	NK	16.10.90T
	(WFU @ Luton 1994 for spares: cancelled 22.2.95 as WFU) (Instructional airframe @ Barry Technical College: disposed but nose section saved by local collector 2.01)						
G-BOCC	Piper PA-38-112 Tomahawk	38-79A0362	N2540D	14.12.87	J.M.Green	Goodwood	1. 1.04T
G-BOCF	Colt 77A HAFB	1178		4. 1.88	Lindstrand Balloons Ltd	Oswestry	25. 7.94T
					(Stored 9.95: current status unknown)		
G-BOCG	Piper PA-34-200T Seneca II	34-7870359	N36759	30.12.87	Oxford Aviation Services Ltd	Oxford	5.12.03T
G-BOCI	Cessna 140A (Continental C90)	15497	N5366C	17.11.87	J.B.Bonnell *"Whitey"*	Thruxton	30. 9.02
G-BOCK	Sopwith Triplane rep (Clerget Rotary 9B 130 hp)	153 & NAW-1		26. 1.88	The Shuttleworth Trust	Old Warden	31. 7.02P
					(As "N6290" in RNAS 8 Sqdn c/s) "Dixie II"		
G-BOCL	Slingsby T.67C Firefly	2035		5. 1.88	Richard Brinklow Aviation Ltd	Shoreham	31. 8.03T
G-BOCM	Slingsby T.67C Firefly	2036		5. 1.88	Richard Brinklow Aviation Ltd	Hinton-in-the Hedges	15. 6.03T
G-BOCN	Robinson R22 Beta	0726	N.... G-BOCN	8. 1.88	Cookie Boy Consultants Ltd	Denham	1. 2.03T
G-BOCP	Piper PA-34-220T Seneca III	3433089		17.12.87	BAE Systems Flight Training (UK) Ltd	Jerez, Cadiz, Spain	13. 6.04T
G-BOCR	Piper PA-34-220T Seneca III	3433111		26. 2.88	BAE Systems Flight Training (UK) Ltd	Jerez, Cadiz, Spain	10.12.04T
G-BOCS	Piper PA-34-220T Seneca III	3433112		26. 2.88	BAE Systems Flight Training (UK) Ltd	Jerez, Cadiz, Spain	24. 9.01T
G-BOCT	Piper PA-34-220T Seneca III	3433113		26. 2.88	BAE Systems Flight Training (UK) Ltd	Jerez, Cadiz, Spain	1.11.03T
G-BOCU	Piper PA-34-220T Seneca III	3433114		26. 2.88	BAE Systems Flight Training (UK) Ltd	Jerez, Cadiz, Spain	20. 9.04T
G-BOCV	Piper PA-34-220T Seneca III	3433115		26. 2.88	BAE Systems Flight Training (UK) Ltd	Jerez, Cadiz, Spain	11. 3.02T
G-BOCW	Piper PA-34-220T Seneca III	3433120	N9612N	25. 8.88	BAE Systems Flight Training (UK) Ltd	Jerez, Cadiz, Spain	30.11.01T
G-BOCX	Piper PA-34-220T Seneca III	3433121	N9613N	29. 9.88	BAE Systems Flight Training (UK) Ltd	Jerez, Cadiz, Spain	31. 5.02T
G-BOCY	Piper PA-34-220T Seneca III	3433122	N9614N	29. 9.88	BAE Systems Flight Training (UK) Ltd	Jerez, Cadiz, Spain	3.12.01T
G-BODA	Piper PA-28-161 Warrior II	2816037	N9601N	19. 1.88	Oxford Aviation Services Ltd	Oxford	7. 5.03T
G-BODB	Piper PA-28-161 Warrior II	2816042	N9606N	23. 2.88	Oxford Aviation Services Ltd	Oxford	28. 9.03T
G-BODC	Piper PA-28-161 Warrior II	2816041	N9605N	23. 2.88	Oxford Aviation Services Ltd	Oxford	12. 4.03T
G-BODD	Piper PA-28-161 Warrior II	2816040	N9604N	23. 2.88	Oxford Aviation Services Ltd	Oxford	24. 8.03T
G-BODE	Piper PA-28-161 Warrior II	2816039	N9603N	23. 2.88	Oxford Aviation Services Ltd	Oxford	22. 6.03T
G-BODF	Piper PA-28-161 Warrior II	2816038	N9602N	19. 1.88	Oxford Aviation Services Ltd	Oxford	15. 6.03T
G-BODG*	Slingsby Cadet III *(Conversion of T.31B c/n 706)*	PFA 042-11310	WT911	9. 6.88	H.P.Vox	East Fortune	
					(Op East Fortune Flying Group) *(Cancelled 15.4.99 by CAA) (Stored incomplete 6.00)*		
G-BODH	Slingsby Cadet III	PFA 042-10108	BGA.474	5. 1.88	M.M.Bain	East Fortune	13. 8.02P
	(VW 1834) *(If p/i is correct then converted ex T.8 Tutor c/n MHL/RT.13 ex G-ALNK/BGA.474) "Fochinell"*						

G-BODI	Stoddard-Hamilton SH-3R Glasair III *(Built Jackson Barr Ltd)* EMK-030 & 3088	(HB-) G-BODI	14. 4.89	G.M.Howard	(Coppet, Switzerland)	21.11.02P
G-BODM	Piper PA-28-180 Cherokee Challenger 28-7305519	N56016	2. 2.88	R.Emery	Clutton Hill Farm, Clutton	14. 9.02T
G-BODO	Cessna 152 II 15282404	N68923	29. 1.88	Annie R.Sarson	Popham	29. 5.03
G-BODP	Piper PA-38-112 Tomahawk II 38-81A0010	N25616	5. 1.88	D.A.Whitmore	Turweston	17.12.03T
G-BODR	Piper PA-28-161 Warrior II 28-8116318	N8436B	5. 1.88	Airways Aero Associations Ltd *(Op British Airways Flying Club) (Waves & Cranes t/s)*	Booker	2. 9.03T
G-BODS	Piper PA-38-112 Tomahawk 38-79A0410	N2379F	3. 2.88	M.R.Cavinder	(Hilton, Hunts)	11. 9.04T
G-BODT	Jodel D.18 173 & PFA 169-11290 (Rotax 912UL)		14. 1.88	L.D.McPhillips t/a Jodel G-BODT Syndicate	Portmoak	22. 5.02P
G-BODU	Scheibe SF.25C-2000 Falke 44434	D-KIAA	19. 1.88	J P English t/a Monica English Memorial Trust	Rufforth	9. 5.03
G-BODX	Beechcraft 76 Duchess ME-309	N67094	26. 2.88	S.J.Skilton t/a Aviation Rentals *(Op Professional Air Training)*	Bournemouth	16. 8.03T
G-BODY	Cessna 310R II 310R1503	N4897A	17.12.87	Atlantic Air Transport Ltd	Coventry	23. 2.03T
G-BODZ	Robinson R22 Beta 0729		8. 1.88	Langley Construction Ltd	Nottingham	21. 4.04
G-BOEE	Piper PA-28-181 Cherokee Archer II 28-7690359	N6168J	20. 1.88	T.B.Parmenter	Lodge Farm, St.Osyth, Clacton	13. 6.03
G-BOEH	Robin DR.340 Major 434	F-BRVN	4. 1.88	G.Bowles t/a Piper Flyers Group	Bradleys Lawn, Heathfield	14. 6.04
G-BOEK	Cameron V-77 HAFB 1658		25. 1.88	A.J.E.Jones *"Secret One"*	Bristol	7. 8.97A
G-BOEM	Aerotek Pitts S-2A Special 2255 (Lycoming AEIO-360)	N31525	17. 2.88	Margaret Murphy	Spanhoe	21. 7.01
G-BOEN	Cessna 172M Skyhawk 17261325	N20482	12. 2.88	H.B.Davies	Elstree	27. 6.03T
G-BOER	Piper PA-28-161 Warrior II 28-8116094	N83030	21. 1.88	M. & W.Fraser-Urquhart	Blackpool	18. 4.03
G-BOET	Piper PA-28RT-201 Arrow IV 28R-8018020	G-IBEC G-BOET/N8116V	28. 1.88	B.C.Chambers	Jersey	4. 8.03
G-BOEW	Robinson R22 Beta 0750		27. 1.88	Plane Talking Ltd	Cranfield	21. 3.03T
G-BOEX	Robinson R22 Beta 0751		27. 1.88	Plane Talking Ltd	Elstree	12. 3.03T
G-BOEZ	Robinson R22 Beta 0753		27. 1.88	Plane Talking Ltd	Elstree	15. 3.03T
G-BOFC	Beechcraft 76 Duchess ME-217	N6628M	28. 1.88	Magenta Ltd *(Op Airways Flight Training)*	Exeter	9. 3.03T
G-BOFD	Cessna U206G Stationair II U20604181	N756LS	27. 1.88	D.M.Penny *(Op Wild Geese Parachute Centre)*	Cark	16. 8.03
G-BOFE	Piper PA-34-200T Seneca II 34-7870381	N39493	22. 2.88	Alstons Upholstery Ltd	Poplar Hall Farm, Elmsett	8. 8.03T
G-BOFF	Cameron N-77 HAFB 1666		26. 1.88	R.C.Corcoran	Bristol	14. 7.02A
G-BOFL	Cessna 152 II 15284101	N5457H	28. 1.88	Gem Rewinds Ltd	Coventry	27. 3.03T
G-BOFM	Cessna 152 II 15284730	N6445M	28. 1.88	Gem Rewinds Ltd	Coventry	14. 6.03T
G-BOFO*	Ultimate Aircraft 10 Dash 200 (Lycoming HIO-360) 10-200-004 & PFA 180-11319	(HB-) G-BOFO	15. 2.88	M.Werdmuller *(Cancelled 12.6.00 as wfu) (Current status unknown)*	(Felton, Bristol)	16. 6.92P
G-BOFW	Cessna A150M Aerobat A1500612	N9803J	15. 2.88	D.F.Donovan	Elstree	12.10.03T
G-BOFX	Cessna A150M Aerobat A1500678	N9869J	15. 2.88	K.Hobbs t/a Aldergrove Flight Training Centre	Belfast	27.11.00T
G-BOFY	Piper PA-28-140 Cherokee Cruiser 28-7425374	N43521	3. 2.88	BCT Aircraft Leasing Ltd	Exeter	30. 4.04T
G-BOFZ	Piper PA-28-161 Cherokee Warrior II 28-7816255	N2189M	10. 2.88	R.W.Harris *(Op Willowair Flying Club)*	Southend	19. 1.02T
G-BOGC	Cessna 152 II 15284550	N5346M	8. 2.88	Keen Leasing (IOM) Ltd	(Castletown, IoM)	29. 8.04T
G-BOGG	Cessna 152 II 15282960	N45956	15. 2.88	The Royal Artillery Aero Club Ltd	AAC Middle Wallop	26. 9.03T
G-BOGI	Robin DR.400/180 Regent 1821		15. 2.88	A.L.M.Shepherd	Rochester	23. 5.03T
G-BOGK	ARV Super 2 K.006 & PFA 152-11138 (Hewland AE75)		10. 2.88	D.R.Trouse t/a Suffolk Super Two Group	Cherry Tree Farm, Monewden	1. 5.02P
G-BOGM	Piper PA-28RT-201T Turbo Arrow IV 28R-8031077	N8173C	10. 2.88	R.J.Pearce t/a RJP Aviation	Wolverhampton	9.11.03T
G-BOGO	Piper PA-32R-301T Saratoga SP 32R-8029064	N8165W	6. 4.88	A.S.Doman	Biggin Hill	26. 7.03T
G-BOGP	Cameron V-77 HAFB 896		30. 3.88	T.Gunn *"Dire Straits"*	Crowborough	10. 7.00A
G-BOGR*	Colt 180A HAFB 1183		11. 5.88	British Balloon Museum & Library *"Britannia" (Cancelled 28.4.97 as WFU)*	Newbury	13. 3.92T
G-BOGT*	Colt 77A HAFB 1212		21. 3.88	Balloon Preservation Group *"British Gas" (Cancelled 9.5.97 as WFU)*	Kirdford	2.12.94A
G-BOGV*	Air Command 532 Elite (Rotax 532) 0399 & PFA G/04-1102		10. 3.88	G.M.Hobman *(Cancelled 1.2.00 as WFU)*	Heworth, York	10. 1.91P
G-BOGY	Cameron V-77 HAFB 1650		15. 2.88	R.A.Preston *"Bella"*	Bristol	7.10.01A
G-BOHA	Piper PA-28-161 Cherokee Warrior II 28-7816352	N3526M	16. 3.88	T.F.& M.I.Hall	Shoreham	12. 6.03T
G-BOHD	Colt 77A HAFB 1214		4. 3.88	D.B.Court *"Bluebird"*	Ormskirk	5. 8.02A
G-BOHF	Thunder Ax8-84 HAFB 1197		8. 4.88	J.A.Harris	Sturminster Newton	19. 9.94A

G-BOHG	Air Command 532 Elite			10. 3.88	T.E.McDonald	Melrose Farm, Melbourne	4. 6.91P
	(Rotax 532)	0402 & PFA G/04-1122					
G-BOHH	Cessna 172N Skyhawk II	17273906	N131FR	19. 2.88	T.Scott	Gamston	23. 5.04T
			N7333J				
G-BOHI	Cessna 152 II	15281241	N49406	29. 2.88	V.D.Speck	Clacton	16. 7.03T
G-BOHJ	Cessna 152 II	15280558	N25259	29. 2.88	A.G.Knight t/a Airlaunch	Old Buckenham	10. 2.02T
G-BOHL	Cameron A-120 HAFB	1701		11. 3.88	T.J.Bucknall	Hawarden	3. 2.98
					"Son of City of Bath"		
G-BOHM	Piper PA-28-180 Cherokee Challenger		N55000	18. 2.88	B F Keogh & R A Scott		
		28-7305287				Lockmead Farm, South Marston	23. 4.03
G-BOHN*	Piper PA-38-112 Tomahawk II		N23593	19. 2.88	Not known	(Pathhead)	19. 6.94T
		38-81A0151					
	(Crashed Cardiff 13.8.93: cancelled 1.11.95 as WFU) (Fuselage stored 6.00: current status unknown)						
G-BOHO	Piper PA-28-161 Warrior II		N747RH	25. 2.88	G.J.Craig & D.L.H.Barrel	Cambridge	3. 9.03T
		28-8016196	N9560N		t/a Egressus Flying Group		
G-BOHR	Piper PA-28-151 Cherokee Warrior		C-GNFE	29. 2.88	M C Wilson	Top Farm, Croydon	13. 4.04
		28-7515245					
G-BOHS	Piper PA-38-112 Tomahawk	38-79A0988	N2418P	26. 2.88	A.S.Bamrah	Biggin Hill	1. 4.04T
					t/a Falcon Flying Services		
G-BOHT	Piper PA-38-112 Tomahawk	38-79A1079	N25304	14. 4.88	E.Reed	Teesside	11. 9.03T
			C-GAYW/N24052		t/a The St.George Flying Club		
G-BOHU	Piper PA-38-112 Tomahawk	38-80A0031	N25093	26. 2.88	D.A.Whitmore	Turweston	1. 5.03T
G-BOHV	Wittman W.8 Tailwind			3. 3.88	R.A.Povall	Yearby	10. 9.02P
	(Continental O-200-A)	621 & PFA 031-11151					
G-BOHW	Van's RV-4	PFA 0181-11309		16. 6.88	P.J.Robins	Deenethorpe	20. 8.02P
	(Lycoming O-320)						
G-BOHX	Piper PA-44-180 Seminole	44-7995008	N36814	9. 3.88	Airpart Supply Ltd	Oxford	6. 8.03T
G-BOIA	Cessna 180K Skywagon II	18053121	N2895K	3. 3.88	R.E., P.E.R., J.E.R. & R.J.W.Styles		
					t/a Old Warden Flying & Parachute Group	Rush Green	10. 1.04
G-BOIB	Wittman W.10 Tailwind	PFA 031-10551		3. 3.88	R.F.Bradshaw	Valley Farm, Winwick	25. 9.01P
G-BOIC	Piper PA-28R-201T Turbo Arrow III		N2336M	7. 4.88	M.J.Pearson	Stapleford	12. 7.03
		28R-7803123					
G-BOID	Bellanca 7ECA Citabria	1092-75	N8676V	3. 3.88	D.Mallinson	Birds Edge, Penistone	14. 3.04
G-BOIG	Piper PA-28-161 Warrior II		N4390B	1. 3.88	D.Vallance-Pell	Gamston	5. 9.03
		28-8516027	N9519N				
G-BOIJ	Thunder Ax7-77 Srs.1 HAFB	964		11. 3.88	K.Dodman	Stowmarket	12.10.02A
G-BOIK	Air Command 503 Commander			8. 3.88	F.G.Shepherd	Alston, Cumbria	22. 1.90P
	(Rotax 503)	0420 & PFA G/04-1087	*(Officially regd as c/n PFA G/04-1090)*				
G-BOIL	Cessna 172N Skyhawk II	17271301	N23FL	2. 3.88	Upperstack Ltd	Barton	15. 6.03T
			N23ER/(N2494E)				
G-BOIN	Bellanca 7ECA Citabria	1190-77	N4160Y	7. 3.88	M.A.N.Newall	Bagby	27. 6.04T
G-BOIO	Cessna 152 II	15280260	N24445	7. 3.88	AV Aviation Ltd	Perth	7. 8.04T
					(Op Tayside Aviation)		
G-BOIP	Cessna 152 II	15283444	N49264	7. 3.88	Stapleford Flying Club Ltd	Stapleford	26. 5.91T
					(Damaged Uckington 11.1.90: stored 5.98: current status unknown)		
G-BOIR	Cessna 152 II	15283272	N48041	7. 3.88	Shropshire Aero Club Ltd	Sleap	13. 6.03T
G-BOIT	SOCATA TB-10 Tobago	810		10. 3.88	Buckland Newton Hire Ltd	Henstridge	21.11.04T
G-BOIU	SOCATA TB-10 Tobago	811		10. 3.88	R & B Aviation Ltd	Guernsey	20. 4.04
G-BOIV	Cessna 150M Commuter	15078620	N704HH	30. 3.88	J.B.Green	Seething	25.11.03
G-BOIW	Cessna 152 II	15282845	N89731	6. 4.88	F M D S C Fernandes	(Cascais, Portugal)	15.10.03T
G-BOIX	Cessna 172N Skyhawk II	17271206	C-GMMX	9. 3.88	JR Flying Ltd	Bournemouth	6. 2.04T
			N2253E				
G-BOIY	Cessna 172N Skyhawk II	17267738	N73901	9. 3.88	White Aviation Ltd	Leeds-Bradford	27. 7.03T
G-BOIZ	Piper PA-34-200T Seneca II		N81081	25. 2.88	R.W.Tebby	Bristol	17. 8.03T
		34-8070014			t/a S.F.Tebby & Son *(Op Bristol Flying Centre)*		
G-BOJB	Cameron V-77 HAFB	1615		11. 3.88	R.M.Trotter	Bristol	29. 7.02A
G-BOJD	Cameron N-77 HAFB	1653		11. 3.88	L.H.Ellis *"Bluebird"*	Marlow	13. 7.02
G-BOJF*	Air Command 532 Elite Two Seat	0425		11. 3.88	C Verlaan	Waits Farm, Belchamp Walter	4. 6.91P
	(Built Skyrider Aviation) (Rotax 532)		*(Cancelled 20.10.00 by CAA: airframe stored: current status unknown)*				
G-BOJI	Piper PA-28RT-201 Arrow IV		N2919X	31. 3.88	T.A.Stoate & K.D.Head	Blackbushe	7. 5.03
		28R-7918221			t/a Arrow Two Group		
G-BOJK	Piper PA-34-220T Seneca III	3433020	G-BRUF	11. 3.88	Redhill Aviation Ltd	Blackbushe	11. 4.03T
			N9113D		t/a Redhill Flying Club		
G-BOJM	Piper PA-28-181 Archer II	28-8090244	N8155L	21. 3.88	Fernborough Ltd	Humberside	12. 5.03
G-BOJR	Cessna 172P Skyhawk II	17275574	N64539	22. 4.88	Exeter Flying Club Ltd	Exeter	8. 5.03T
G-BOJS	Cessna 172P Skyhawk II	17274582	N52699	29. 3.88	I.S.H.Paul	Denham	25. 5.03T
G-BOJU	Cameron N-77 HAFB	1718		21. 3.88	M.A.Scholes *"GB Transport"*	London SE25	7. 9.97A
G-BOJW	Piper PA-28-161 Cherokee Warrior II		N1668H	28. 3.88	Brewhamfield Farm Ltd	(Wantage)	5.12.03T
		28-7716038					
G-BOJZ	Piper PA-28-161 Warrior II		N2113J	28. 3.88	A.S.Bamrah	Rochester	2. 4.04T
		28-7916223			t/a Falcon Flying Services		
G-BOKA	Piper PA-28-201T Turbo Dakota		N2860S	15. 3.88	CBG Aviation Ltd	Fairoaks	14. 5.03
		28-7921076					

G-BOKB	Piper PA-28-161 Warrior II	28-8216077	N8013Y	29. 3.88	Premiair Engineering Ltd	Shoreham	31. 7.03T
G-BOKD	Bell 206B-3 JetRanger III	3654	G-ISKY G-PSCI/G-BOKD/N3171A	30. 8.01	Sterling Helicopters Ltd	Norwich	13. 4.03T
G-BOKF	Air Command 532 Elite (Rotax 532)	0404 & PFA G/04-1101		28. 3.88	D.Beevers	Melrose Farm, Melbourne	22. 9.99P
G-BOKH	Whittaker MW7 (Rotax 532) *(Regd as PFA 171-11231)*	PFA 171-11281	(G-MTWT)	21. 3.88	I.D.Evans	Thame	1. 7.96P
G-BOKJ*	Whittaker MW7 (Rotax 532)	PFA 171-11283	(G-MTWV)	21. 3.88	M.R.Payne *(Cancelled 17.5.01 as wfu) (Parts noted 12.01)*	Wing Farm, Longbridge Deverill	4. 6.97P
G-BOKK*	Piper PA-28-161 Warrior II	28-8116300	N8427L	6. 4.88	Not known *(Damaged Hamgreen, Redditch 18.5.95: cancelled 8.9.95 as WFU: wreck noted 12.01)*	Blackpool	7. 6.97T
G-BOKL	Piper PA-28-161 Warrior II	2816044	N9607N	24. 3.88	BAE Systems Flight Training (UK) Ltd	Jerez, Cadiz, Spain	27. 7.03T
G-BOKM	Piper PA-28-161 Warrior II	2816045	N9608N	24. 3.88	BAE Systems Flight Training (UK) Ltd	Jerez, Cadiz, Spain	12.11.02T
G-BOKN	Piper PA-28-161 Warrior II	2816046	N9609N	24. 3.88	BAE Systems Flight Training (UK) Ltd	Jerez, Cadiz, Spain	7.11.02T
G-BOKO	Piper PA-28-161 Warrior II	2816049	N9610N	24. 3.88	BAE Systems Flight Training (UK) Ltd	Jerez, Cadiz, Spain	22.12.02T
G-BOKP	Piper PA-28-161 Warrior II	2816050	N9611N	24. 3.88	BAE Systems Flight Training (UK) Ltd	Jerez, Cadiz, Spain	18. 6.03T
G-BOKR	Piper PA-28-161 Warrior II	2816051		24. 3.88	BAE Systems Flight Training (UK) Ltd	Jerez, Cadiz, Spain	22. 4.01T
G-BOKS	Piper PA-28-161 Warrior II	2816052		24. 3.88	BAE Systems Flight Training (UK) Ltd	Jerez, Cadiz, Spain	30. 3.03T
G-BOKT	Piper PA-28-161 Warrior II	2816053		24. 3.88	BAE Systems Flight Training (UK) Ltd	Jerez, Cadiz, Spain	28. 5.04T
G-BOKU	Piper PA-28-161 Warrior II	2816054		24. 3.88	BAE Systems Flight Training (UK) Ltd	Jerez, Cadiz, Spain	21.11.02T
G-BOKX	Piper PA-28-161 Cherokee Warrior II	28-7816680	N39709	28. 3.88	Shenley Farms (Aviation) Ltd	Headcorn	21. 9.03T
G-BOKY	Cessna 152 II	15285298	N67409	6. 4.88	D.F.F.Poore	Bournemouth	17. 6.04T
G-BOLB	Taylorcraft BC-12-65 (Continental A65)	3165	N36211 NC36211	17. 5.88	F J Pacewicz & R.J.Rhys-Williams *"Spirit of California"*	Eastbach Farm, English Bicknor	10. 7.98P
G-BOLC	Fournier RF6B-100	1	F-BVKS	28. 3.88	W.H.Hendy	Dunkeswell	26.12.03
G-BOLD	Piper PA-38-112 Tomahawk	38-78A0180	N9740T	8. 7.88	B.R.Pearson t/a G-BOLD Group *(Stored 9.00)*	Eaglescott	21. 1.96T
G-BOLE	Piper PA-38-112 Tomahawk	38-78A0475	N2506E	13. 7.88	J.& G.Stevenson	Nottingham	28. 5.04
G-BOLF	Piper PA-38-112 Tomahawk	38-79A0375	N583P YV-583P/YV-133E/YV-1696P/N9666N	13. 7.88	Teesside Flight Centre Ltd	Teesside	19. 7.04T
G-BOLG	Bellanca 7KCAB Citabria	517-75	N8706V	25.11.88	B.R.Pearson t/a Aerotug	Eaglescott	22. 5.04
G-BOLI	Cessna 172P Skyhawk II	17275484	N63794	30. 3.88	W White t/a BOLI Flying Club	Denham	11. 7.03T
G-BOLL	Lake LA-4-200 Skimmer	295	(F-GRMX) G-BOLL/EI-ANR/N1133L	4. 5.88	M.C.Holmes	City of Derry	14. 6.03
G-BOLN	Colt 21A Cloudhopper HAFB	1226		4. 5.88	G.Everett	Maidstone	28. 5.02A
G-BOLO	Bell 206B JetRanger II	1522	N59409	2.11.87	Hargreaves Leasing Ltd *(Op Blades Helicopters)*	Goodwood	2. 3.03T
G-BOLP	Colt 21A Cloudhopper HAFB	1227		4. 5.88	J.E.Rose	Abingdon	1. 5.02A
G-BOLR	Colt 21A Cloudhopper HAFB	1228		3. 5.88	C.J.Sanger-Davies	Uttoxeter	7. 8.95A
G-BOLS	Clutton FRED Srs.II	PFA 029-10676		6. 4.88	I.F.Vaughan *"The Ruptured Uck"*	(Melton Mowbray)	
G-BOLT	Rockwell Commander 114	14428	N5883N	16.10.78	H. Gafsen	Elstree	4. 7.04T
G-BOLU	Robin R.3000/120	106	F-GFAO SE-IMS	14. 4.88	I.W.Goodger t/a Classair	Biggin Hill	18. 7.03T
G-BOLV	Cessna 152 II	15280492	N24983	8. 4.88	A.S.Bamrah t/a Falcon Flying Services	Biggin Hill	20.12.02T
G-BOLW	Cessna 152 II	15280589	N25316	9. 6.88	JRB Aviation Ltd *(Op Seawing Flying Club)*	Southend	30. 8.03T
G-BOLX	Cessna 172N Skyhawk II	17269099	N734TK	8. 4.88	R.J.Burrough	Lydd	20.11.03
G-BOLY	Cessna 172N Skyhawk II	17269004	N734PJ	31. 3.88	D.A.T.Skidmore	Andrewsfield	16.10.00T
G-BOLZ	Rand Robinson KR-2 (VW 1834)	PFA 129-10866		6. 4.88	B.Normington	Coventry	24. 7.02P
G-BOMB	Cassutt Racer IIIM (Continental O-200-A)	PFA 034-10386		18.12.78	S.Adams *"Blind Panic"* *(Damaged Weston Park, Telford 22.6.97: current status unknown)*	RAF Weston-on-the-Green	23. 5.98P
G-BOMG	Pilatus Britten Norman BN-2B-26 Islander	2205	D-IBNF G-BOMG	6. 4.88	B-N Group Ltd	Bembridge	12. 9.02T
G-BOMN	Cessna 150F	15063089	N6489F	25. 4.89	D.G.Williams	Shoreham	28. 8.03T
G-BOMO	Piper PA-38-112 Tomahawk II	38-81A0161	N91324	8. 4.88	APB Leasing Ltd	Welshpool	17. 6.04T

G-BOMP	Piper PA-28-181 Cherokee Archer II	28-7790249	N8482F	8. 4.88	SRC Contractors Ltd & D Carter	Elstree	12. 2.04T
G-BOMS	Cessna 172N Skyhawk II	17269448	N737JG	11. 4.88	Almat Flying Club Ltd & Penchant Ltd	Coventry	25.10.04T
G-BOMT	Cessna 172N Skyhawk II	17270396	N739AU	12. 7.88	R.A.Witchell	Andrewsfield	6. 5.04T
G-BOMU	Piper PA-28-181 Cherokee Archer II	28-7790318	N1631H	8. 4.88	J.Sawyer & P.R.Kinge t/a RJ Aviation	Blackbushe	19. 7.03T
G-BOMY	Piper PA-28-161 Warrior II	28-8216049	N8457S	28. 6.88	D.Knight t/a Southern Care Maintenance	Headcorn	17. 1.04T
G-BOMZ	Piper PA-38-112 Tomahawk	38-78A0635	N2315A	30. 6.88	I.C.Barlow & G.W.G.Young t/a BOMZ Aviation	Booker	25. 4.03T
G-BONC	Piper PA-28RT-201 Arrow IV	28R-7918007	C-GXYX N3069K	13. 5.88	Finglow Ltd	Fowlmere	7. 7.03T
G-BONE	Pilatus P.2-06	600-62	Sw.AF U-142/U-113	8. 7.81	G.B.E.Pearce	Shoreham	14. 8.02P
G-BONK*	Colt 180A HAFB	1167		14.12.87	Balloon Preservation Group *"Bonkette" (Cancelled 28.11.01 as wfu)*	Kirdford	2.11.94T
G-BONO	Cessna 172N Skyhawk II	17270299	C-GSMF N738WS	11. 5.88	Mer-Air Aviation Ltd	Denham	24. 9.03T
G-BONP	CFM Streak Shadow (Rotax 582)	108, SS-01P & PFA 161A-11344		4. 5.88	T.J.Palmer	Prestwick	11. 9.02P
G-BONR	Cessna 172N Skyhawk II	17268164	C-GYGK (N733BH)	18. 4.88	D.I.Claik	Biggin Hill	24. 8.03
G-BONS	Cessna 172N Skyhawk II	17268345	C-GIUF	18. 4.88	M.G.Montgomerie t/a G-BONS Group	Elstree	31. 8.03
G-BONT	Slingsby T.67M Firefly II	2054		3. 5.88	Babcock Rosyth Defence Ltd t/a Hunting Contract Services *(Op JEFTS)*	RAF Barkston Heath	26. 9.03T
G-BONU	Slingsby T.67B Firefly	2037		3. 5.88	R.L.Brinklow	Hinton-in-the-Hedges	29. 6.00T
G-BONV*	Colt 17A Cloudhopper HAFB	1238		3. 5.88	Balloon Preservation Group *"Bryant Group" (Cancelled 22.11.01 as wfu)*	Kirdford	1. 4.93A
G-BONW	Cessna 152 II	15280401	OY-CPL N24825	15. 4.88	Lincoln Aero Club Ltd	Sturgate	17. 8.03T
G-BONY	Denney Kitfox mk.1 (Rotax 532)	166 & PFA 172-11351	*(Inscribed as "mk.2")*	11. 5.88	M.J.Walker	Enstone	8. 6.02P
G-BONZ	Beechcraft V35B Bonanza	D-10282	N6661D	6. 4.88	P.M.Coulten	Boughton, Norfolk	1. 8.03
G-BOOB	Cameron N-65 HAFB	515		12.11.79	J.Rumming *"Cracker"*	Swindon	8. 4.90A
G-BOOC	Piper PA-18-150 Super Cub	18-8279	SE-EPC	29. 4.88	R.R. & S.A.Marriott	Meon	23. 8.03
G-BOOD	Slingsby T.31M Motor Tutor (Fuji-Robin EC-44-2PM)	PFA 042-11264	*(Wings ex XE810 c/n 923)*	4. 5.88	K.A.Hale	Clench Common	21.12.02P
G-BOOE	Gulfstream GA-7 Cougar	GA7-0093	N718G	7. 6.88	N.Gardner	Southampton	31. 7.03T
G-BOOF	Piper PA-28-181 Cherokee Archer II	28-7890084	N47510	16. 6.88	H Merkado	Panshanger	19.10.03T
G-BOOG	Piper PA-28RT-201T Turbo Arrow IV	28R-8331036	N4303K	6. 5.88	Simair Ltd	Andrewsfield	14. 1.02
G-BOOH	Jodel D.112 *(Built Ets Valladeau)*	481	F-BHVK	16. 5.88	J.A.Crabb	Dunkeswell	3. 6.02P
G-BOOI	Cessna 152 II	15280751	N25590	22. 8.88	Stapleford Flying Club Ltd	Stapleford	23. 4.04T
G-BOOJ	Air Command 532 Elite II (Rotax 532)	PB206 & PFA G/04-1098		4. 5.88	Roger Savage Gyroplanes Ltd	Kingsmuir Sorbie	6.12.91P
G-BOOL	Cessna 172N Skyhawk II	17272486	C-GJSY N5271D	27. 4.88	Surrey & Kent Flying Club Ltd	Biggin Hill	16.12.03T
G-BOON*	Piper PA-32RT-300 Lance II	32R-7885253	N361DB	25. 4.88	Not known	Andrewsfield	28. 5.00T
	(Damaged landing Connemara 10.10.97: cancelled 3.3.98 by CAA: wreck noted 12.01)						
G-BOOP*	Cameron N-90 HAFB	1702	(G-BOMX)	11. 5.88	Balloon Preservation Group *"Betty Boop" (Unipart titles) (Cancelled 31.10.95 by CAA)*	Aylesbury	28. 9.95A
G-BOOV	Aérospatiale AS355F2 Twin Squirrel	5374		3. 5.88	Merseyside Police Authority Air Support Group	Liverpool	2.10.03T
G-BOOW	Aerosport Scamp (VW 1834)	PFA 117-10709		10. 5.88	I.E.Bloys	Fenland	17. 8.02P
G-BOOX	Rutan LongEz (Lycoming O-235)	PFA 074A-10844		3. 5.88	I.R.Wilde	Deenethorpe	7. 3.02P
G-BOOZ	Cameron N-77 HAFB *(New home built envelope c 6.98)*	904	(G-BKSJ)	21. 6.83	J.E.F.Kettlety *"Bluebell"*	Chippenham	
G-BOPA	Piper PA-28-181 Archer II	28-8490024	N43299	28. 4.88	J H & L F Strutt	Denham	4. 8.03
G-BOPC	Piper PA-28-161 Warrior II	28-8216006	N2124X	6. 5.88	Aeros Ltd	Gloucestershire	19. 7.03T
G-BOPD	Bede BD-4 (Lycoming O-320)	632	N632DH	25. 5.88	S.T.Dauncey	Yearby	16. 6.02P
G-BOPG	Cessna 182Q Skylane II	18266689	N95962	6. 5.88	G.Wimlett	Blackpool	20. 3.04T
G-BOPH	Cessna TR182 Turbo Skylane RG II	R18201031	N756BJ	11. 5.88	Grandsam Investments Ltd	Cambridge	31. 5.03T
G-BOPO	FLS OA.7 Optica 301	021	EC-FVM EC-435/G-BOPO	17. 5.88	Sunhawk Ltd	Jersey	27. 5.96T

G-BOPR	FLS OA.7 Optica 301	023		17. 5.88	Sunhawk Ltd.	Jersey	
G-BOPT	Grob G-115	8046		10. 5.88	LAC (Enterprises) Ltd t/a Lancashire Aero Club	Barton	7.12.03T
G-BOPU	Grob G-115	8059		10. 5.88	LAC (Enterprises) Ltd t/a Lancashire Aero Club	Barton	18. 7.03T
G-BOPV	Piper PA-34-200T Seneca II	34-8070265	N82323	7. 6.88	G.J.Powell	Biggin Hill	11. 7.03T
G-BOPX	Cessna A152 Aerobat	A1520932	N761BK	11. 5.88	Aerohire Ltd *(Stored 10.01 less wings)*	Bourne Park, Hurstbourne Tarrant	24. 1.98T
G-BORA*	Colt 77A HAFB	1233		19. 5.88	Balloon Preservation Group *"Carla" (Cancelled 17.9.98 as WFU)*	Kirdford	24. 8.94A
G-BORB	Cameron V-77 HAFB	1348		24. 8.88	M.H.Wolff	Liskeard	7. 7.02A
G-BORD	Thunder Ax7-77 HAFB	1164		26. 5.88	D.D.Owen *"Marvin"*	Wotton-under-Edge	11.12.99A
G-BORE	Colt 77A HAFB	642		24. 5.88	J.D.Medcalf & C.Wilson t/a Little Secret Hot Air Balloon Group *"My Little Secret"*	Enfield	22. 7.01A
G-BORG	Campbell Cricket (Rotax 503)	PFA G/03-1085		8. 6.88	G.Davison & H.Hayes *(Noted 1.02)*	Carlisle	11. 2.02P
G-BORH	Piper PA-34-200T Seneca II	34-8070352	N8261V	7. 6.88	Aerolease Ltd	Conington	31. 1.04T
G-BORI	Cessna 152 II	15281672	N66936	8. 6.88	Staryear Ltd	Barton	16.10.03T
G-BORJ	Cessna 152 II	15282649	N89148	27. 5.88	Pool Aviation (NW) Ltd	Blackpool	19.12.03T
G-BORK	Piper PA-28-161 Warrior II	28-8116095	N83036	13. 6.88	A.W.Collett	Turweston	29.11.03T
G-BORL	Piper PA-28-161 Cherokee Warrior II	28-7816256	N2190M	28. 9.88	Westair Flying School Ltd	Blackpool	8. 1.04T
G-BORM*	Hawker Siddeley HS.748 Srs.2B/217	1670	RP-C1043 V2-LAA/VP-LAA/9Y-TDH	29. 7.88	Not known *(WFU - to Fire Service: cancelled 18.6.92 by CAA) (Noted 10.00)*	Exeter	
G-BORN	Cameron N-77 HAFB	1777		13. 5.88	I.Chadwick *"Ian"*	Partridge Green, W.Sussex	10. 6.02A
G-BORO	Cessna 152 II	15283767	N5130B	27. 5.88	M.R.Shelton t/a Tatenhill Aviation	Tatenhill	8. 2.04T
G-BORR	Thunder AX8-90 HAFB	1256		13. 6.88	W.J.Harris	Cheltenham	17. 8.01A
G-BORS	Piper PA-28-181 Archer II	28-8090156	N8127C	31. 5.88	B.K.Ambrose t/a G-BORS Flying Group	Cambridge	29. 6.03T
G-BORT	Colt 77A HAFB	1255		7. 6.88	J.Triquet	St. Gemmes-Le-Robert, France	10. 9.01A
G-BORV	Bell 206B JetRanger II	2202	C-GVTY N16763	8. 6.88	C.A.Rosenberg	Abergavenny	5. 5.02T
G-BORW	Cessna 172P Skyhawk II	17274301	N51357	23. 8.88	Briter Aviation Ltd	Coventry	26. 7.04T
G-BORY	Cessna 150L	15072292	N6792G	27. 5.88	D.G.Bell & S.J.Green	Derby	19. 9.02T
G-BOSB	Thunder Ax7-77 HAFB *(Regd as c/n 581 but built as c/n 1199)*	1199		7. 6.88	M.Gallagher	Consett	17. 9.99A
G-BOSD	Piper PA-34-200T Seneca II	34-7570085	N33086	7. 6.88	Barnes Olson Aeroleasing Ltd *(Op Bristol Flying Centre)*	Bristol	11. 8.04T
G-BOSE	Piper PA-28-181 Archer II	28-8590007	N143AV	17. 5.88	C.A.W.Godfrey	(London W4)	23. 5.03T
G-BOSF*	Colt 69A HAFB	1271		23. 6.88	Virgin Airship & Balloon Co Ltd *"Lloyds Bank" (Cancelled 8.11.01 as wfu & stored)*	Telford	28. 1.93A
G-BOSG*	Colt 17A Cloudhopper HAFB	1272		23. 6.88	Virgin Airship & Balloon Co Ltd *"Lloyds Bank Cloudhopper" (Cancelled 8.11.01 as wfu & stored)*	Telford	22. 5.89A
G-BOSJ	Nord 3400	124	N9048P ALAT "MOO"	26. 5.88	A.I.Milne *(As "124" in Fr.AF c/s)* *(Damaged Fenland 12.6.94: stored 9.97: current status unknown)*	Little Snoring	1.11.94P
G-BOSM	CEA Jodel DR.253B Regent	168	F-BSBH	24. 5.88	S.H.Gibson t/a Sierra Mike (Ware) Group	High Cross, Ware	11.12.04
G-BOSN	Aérospatiale AS355F1 Twin Squirrel	5266	N2109L 5N-AYL/G-BOSN/5N-AYL	22. 8.88	L.Smith t/a Helicopter Services	Booker	20. 2.03T
G-BOSO	Cessna A152 Aerobat	A1520975	N761PD	25. 5.88	J.S.Develin & Z.Islam	Blackbushe	20. 8.04T
G-BOSR	Piper PA-28-140 Cherokee	28-22092	N7464R	26. 5.88	C R.Guggenheim t/a Sierra-Romeo Group	Farley Farm, Winchester	27. 6.03T
G-BOSU	Piper PA-28-140 Cherokee Cruiser	28-7325449	N55635	19. 7.88	R.A.Sands	Oxford	8. 6.04
G-BOSV*	Cameron V-77 HAFB	1320		17. 6.88	K.H.Greenaway *"Joyride II" (Cancelled 7.11.01 as wfu & stored)*	Market Harborough	7. 6.97A
G-BOTB*	Cessna 152 II	15285733	N94571	7. 6.88	Stapleford Flying Club Ltd *(Cancelled 17.11.00 by CAA: current status unknown)*	Stapleford	18. 9.00T
G-BOTD	Cameron O-105 HAFB	1611		6. 6.88	P.J.Beglan	Belves, France	8. 8.02A
G-BOTE*	Thunder Ax8-90 HAFB	555		14. 6.88	Balloon Preservation Group *"Barge Fox" (Cancelled 12.12.95 as WFU)*	Kirdford	16. 2.95T
G-BOTF	Piper PA-28-151 Cherokee Warrior	28-7515436	C-GGIF	8. 6.88	D.S.Woolf t/a G-BOTF Group *(Op Southend Flying Club)*	Southend	4.10.03T
G-BOTG	Cessna 152 II	15283035	N46343	9. 6.88	Donington Aviation Ltd	East Midlands	27. 9.03T
G-BOTH	Cessna 182Q Skylane II	18267558	N202PS N114SP/N5172N	9. 6.88	A.C.Hinton-Lever t/a G-BOTH Group	Barton	28. 3.04

G-BOTI	Piper PA-28-151 Cherokee Warrior		C-GNFF	9. 6.88	A.J.Bamrah	Southend	29. 8.03T
	(Convd to Srs.161 status)	28-7515251			t/a Falcon Flying Services *(Op Seawing Flying Club)*		
G-BOTK	Cameron O-105 HAFB	1765		9. 6.88	F.R. & V.L.Higgins	Bath	12. 7.96T
					"Champagne Rides"		
G-BOTL*	Colt 42A SS HAFB	466		23.11.82	British Balloon Museum & Library	Newbury	
					"Bottle" (Cancelled 21.11.89 as WFU)		
G-BOTM	Bell 206B-3 JetRanger III	3881	N31940	9. 6.88	David McLean Homes Ltd	Cambridge	8. 8.03
G-BOTN	Piper PA-28-161 Warrior II	28-7916261	N2173N	9. 6.88	Premiair Engineering Ltd	Southend	25. 1.04T
G-BOTO	Bellanca 7ECA Citabria	939-73	N57398	9. 6.88	A.K.Hulme	Rayne Hall Farm, Rayne	7. 1.04
					t/a G-BOTO Group		
G-BOTP	Cessna 150J	15070736	N61017	2. 8.88	R.F.Finnis & C.P.Williams	Thruxton	20. 5.04
G-BOTU	Piper J-3C-65 Cub	19045	N98803	8. 7.88	T.L.Giles	Hill Farm, Nayland	20. 6.02P
	(Continental A75)		NC98803				
G-BOTV	Piper PA-32RT-300 Lance II	32R-7885153	N36039	7. 6.88	Robin Lance Aviation Associates Ltd	Rochester	7. 7.02
G-BOTW	Cameron V-77 HAFB	1761		14. 6.88	M.R.Jeynes	(Worcester)	10. 6.02A
G-BOTZ	Bensen B.8MR	PFA G/01-1086		17. 6.88	C.Jones	(East Kilbride)	9.12.00P
	(Rotax 532)				*(Flies from Strathaven)*		
G-BOUD	Piper PA-38-112 Tomahawk II	38-82A0017	N91365	26. 7.88	A.J.Wiggins	(Longhope, Glos)	25. 3.01T
G-BOUE	Cessna 172N Skyhawk II	17273235	N6535F	8. 8.88	Aviation Access Ltd	Leeds-Bradford	22. 2.04T
G-BOUF	Cessna 172N Skyhawk II	17271900	N5605E	24. 6.88	M.I. & B.P.Sneap	Ripley, Derby	5. 7.04T
					t/a Amber Valley Aviation		
G-BOUJ	Cessna 150M Commuter	15076373	N3058V	25. 8.88	R.D.Billins	Cranfield	11. 1.03T
G-BOUK	Piper PA-34-200T Seneca II	34-7570124	N33476	31. 8.88	C.J. & R.J.Barnes	East Midlands	28. 7.02T
G-BOUL	Piper PA-34-200T Seneca II	34-7670157	N8936C	28. 6.88	Oxford Aviation Services Ltd	Oxford	5. 4.04T
G-BOUM	Piper PA-34-200T Seneca II	34-7670136	N8401C	3. 8.88	Oxford Aviation Services Ltd	Oxford	19. 8.04T
G-BOUN*	Rand Robinson KR-2	PFA 129-10945		23. 6.88	W.J.Allan	Charterhall	27. 7.99P
	(VW 1834)				*(Cancelled 25.10.01 by CAA)*		
G-BOUP	Piper PA-28-161 Warrior II	2816059	N9139X	12. 7.88	Oxford Aviation Services Ltd	Oxford	10. 2.03T
G-BOUR	Piper PA-28-161 Warrior II	2816060	N9139Z	12. 7.88	Oxford Aviation Services Ltd	Oxford	14.10.03T
G-BOUT	Zenair Colomban MC-12 Cri-Cri	12-0135	N120JN	14. 6.88	C.K.Farley	Southampton	
G-BOUU	Everett Autogyro	015		R	A.Everett	Sproughton, Ipswich	
					(Stored 5.97: current status unknown)		
G-BOUV	Montgomerie-Bensen B.8MR	PFA G/01-1092		23. 6.88	G.C.Kerr	(Great Orton)	16.10.01P
	(Rotax 532)						
G-BOUX	Everett Autogyro	016		R	A.Everett	Sproughton, Ipswich	
					(Stored 7.94: current status unknown)		
G-BOUZ	Cessna 150G	15065606	N2606J	15. 6.88	Atlantic Bridge Aviation Ltd	Lydd	16. 3.04T
G-BOVB	Piper PA-15 Vagabond	15-180	N4396H	23. 6.88	P.Laycock & J R Pike	Twineham	14. 5.02P
	(Lycoming O-145)		NC4396H		t/a Oscar Flying Group		
G-BOVG*	Reims Cessna F172H	F172-0627	OO-ANN	2. 8.88	No.1476 Squadron, ATC	Rayleigh, Essex	14. 9.91
			D-ELTR				
			(Damaged Southend 1991: cancelled 26.9.95 as WFU: instructional airframe 1.01)				
G-BOVK	Piper PA-28-161 Warrior II	28-8516061	N69168	7. 9.88	Auto Corporation Ltd	Hawarden	14. 5.04T
G-BOVR	Robinson R22HP	0176	N9069D	28. 6.88	J.O'Brien	(Gorey, Co.Wexford)	19. 8.00T
G-BOVS	Cessna 150M Commuter	15078663	N704KC	21. 7.88	Blue Skies Aviation Ltd	Exeter	21.12.03T
G-BOVT	Cessna 150M Commuter	15078032	N8962U	1.12.88	C.J.Hopewell	Fenland	15. 4.04T
G-BOVU	Stoddard-Hamilton Glasair III	3090		16. 9.88	B.R.Chaplin	Deenethorpe	6. 3.02P
	(Lycoming IO-540)						
G-BOVV	Cameron V-77 HAFB	1724		26. 9.88	P.Glydon *(Active 8.00)*	Birmingham	17. 9.92T
G-BOVW	Colt 69A HAFB	1286		13. 7.88	V.Hyland	Nottingham	6. 4.94A
					"Enderby-Hyland Painting"		
G-BOVX	Hughes 269C	38-0673	N58170	12. 7.88	P.E.Tornberg	Sywell	25. 9.04T
G-BOWB	Cameron V-77 HAFB	1767		13. 7.88	R.C.Stone *"Richard's Rainbow"*	Reading	16. 7.01A
G-BOWC*	Cessna 150J	15070458	N60626	24.10.88	Not known	NK	
	(Force landed near Barton 10.7.94: cancelled 16.9.94 as WFU: wore fictitious marks "G-AMAF" & used by Missionary Aviation Fellowship in 1997-99 for fund-raising events: current status unknown)						
G-BOWD	Reims Cessna F337G Skymaster	F33700084	N337BC	8. 7.88	Badgehurst Ltd	Southend	4. 4.01T
	(Wichita c/n 33701791)		G-BLSB/EI-BET/D-INAI/(N53697)				
G-BOWE	Piper PA-34-200T Seneca II	34-7870405	N39668	14. 7.88	Oxford Aviation Services Ltd	Oxford	1. 7.04T
G-BOWK*	Cameron N-90 HAFB	1764		1. 8.88	S.R.Bridge *"Burley Stables"*	Grantham	
					(Cancelled 8.11.01 as wfu: current status unknown)		
G-BOWL	Cameron V-77 HAFB	1780		26. 7.88	P.G. & G.R.Hall *"Matrix"*	Chard	12. 5.00A
G-BOWM	Cameron V-56 HAFB	1781		26. 7.88	C.G.Caldecott & G.Pitt	Newcastle-under-Lyme	30. 7.00A

G-BOWN	Piper PA-12 Super Cruiser	12-1912	N3661N	26. 7.88	R.W.Bucknell	Andrewsfield	26. 2.00T
	(Lycoming 0-235)		NC3661N				
G-BOWO	Cessna R182 Skylane RG II	R18200146	(G-BOTR)	20. 7.88	P.C.Lever	Membury	12.11.04
			N2301C				
G-BOWP	Jodel Wassmer D.120A Paris-Nice	319	F-BNZM	26. 7.88	H.W.Machell	Old Sarum	2. 2.01P
	(Continental 0-200-A)						
G-BOWU	Cameron 0-84 HAFB	1779		1. 8.88	C.F.Pooley & D.C.Ball	Gloucester	7. 8.01A
					t/a St.Elmos Fire Syndicate *"Elmo"*		
G-BOWV	Cameron V-65 HAFB	1800		24. 8.88	R.A.Harris *"Sigmund"*	Axminster	14. 5.02A
G-BOWY	Piper PA-28RT-201T Turbo Arrow IV		N404EL	8. 8.88	A.Davies	Blackbushe	17. 8.03T
		28R-8131114	N83648				
G-BOWZ	Bensen B.80V	PFA G/01-1060		27. 7.88	M D Cole	Carlisle	31. 7.98P
	(Rotax 532)				*(Noted 1.02)*		
G-BOXA	Piper PA-28-161 Warrior II	2816075	N9149Q	1.11.88	Channel Islands Aero Services Ltd	Jersey	8. 1.04T
					t/a Jersey Aero Club		
G-BOXB	Piper PA-28-161 Warrior II	2816064	N9142H	12. 8.88	Channel Islands Aero Services Ltd	Jersey	6. 2.03T
					t/a Jersey Aero Club		
G-BOXC	Piper PA-28-161 Warrior II	2816063	N9142D	12. 8.88	Channel Islands Aero Services Ltd	Jersey	15. 5.03T
					t/a Jersey Aero Club		
G-BOXG	Cameron 0-77 HAFB	1792		26. 8.88	R.A.Wicks	Norwich	14. 7.02A
G-BOXH	Pitts S-1S Special	MP4	N8LA	29. 7.88	D.Medrek & M.Turkington		
	(Lycoming 0-360)					Wevelgem, Belgium	1. 8.02P
G-BOXJ	Piper J-3C-65 Cub (L-4H-PI)	12193	OO-ADJ	1. 8.88	J.D.Tseliki	Shoreham	20. 3.91P
	(Continental C90) *(Frame No.12021)*		44-79897				
G-BOXR	Grumman American GA-7 Cougar		N772GA	19.10.88	Plane Talking Ltd	Biggin Hill	11. 9.03T
		GA7-0059					
G-BOXT	Hughes 269C	104-0367	SE-HMR	1. 8.88	Jetscape Leisure Ltd	Gloucestershire	15. 6.03T
			PH-JOH/D-HBOL				
G-BOXU	Grumman-American AA-5B Tiger		N1526R	28. 7.88	G.C.Baker	Welshpool	15. 5.04
		AA5B-0026			t/a Marcher Aviation Group		
G-BOXV	Pitts S-1S Special	7-0433	N27822	8. 8.88	G.R.Clark	Yeatsall Farm, Abbots Bromley	12. 6.02P
	(Lycoming 0-360)						
G-BOXW	Cassutt Racer IIIM	PFA 034-11317		11. 8.88	D.I.Johnson	(Leigh-on-Sea)	
G-BOXX*	Robinson R22 Beta	0815	N2640D	15. 6.88	Plane Talking Ltd	Redhill	26. 7.03T
					(Cancelled 24.7.01 by CAA)		
G-BOXY	Piper PA-28-181 Archer II	28-7990175	N3073D	29. 7.88	Sheffield Aero Club Ltd	Netherthorpe	11. 4.04T
G-BOYB	Cessna A152 Aerobat	A1520928	N761AW	29. 7.88	Northamptonshire School of Flying Ltd		
						Sywell	14.12.03T
G-BOYC	Robinson R22 Beta	0837		22. 8.88	M.D.Thorpe	Coney Park, Leeds	9. 8.04T
					t/a Yorkshire Helicopters		
G-BOYF	Sikorsky S-76B	760343		15. 9.88	Darley Stud Management Co Ltd	Cambridge	24.11.02T
					(Op Air Hanson)		
G-BOYH	Piper PA-28-151 Cherokee Warrior		N8795F	8. 8.88	Superpause Ltd	White Waltham	26. 4.04T
	(Convd to Srs.161 status)	28-7715290			*(Op West London Aero Club)*		
G-BOYI	Piper PA-28-161 Warrior II		N9032K	8. 8.88	S.J.Harris & A.Ware	Welshpool	3. 4.04
		28-7816183			t/a G-BOYI Group		
G-BOYL	Cessna 152 II	15284379	N6232L	11. 8.88	Aerohire Ltd	Wolvehampton	26. 2.01T
G-BOYM	Cameron 0-84 HAFB	1796		25. 8.88	M.P.Ryan *"Frontline"*	Newbury	
G-BOYO*	Cameron V-20 HAFB	1843		27. 9.88	J.M.Willard	Burgess Hill, W.Sussex	
					(Cancelled 18.10.01 by CAA)		
G-BOYP	Cessna 172N Skyhawk II	17270349	N738YU	22. 8.88	Guildtons Ltd	North Weald	3. 5.04
G-BOYS	Cameron N-77 HAFB	1759		16. 6.88	J King	Bristol	2.12.94T
G-BOYU	Cessna A150L Aerobat	A1500497	N8121L	31. 8.88	Upperstack Ltd	Barton	1.10.03T
G-BOYV	Piper PA-28R-201T Turbo Cherokee Arrow III		N1143H	1. 9.88	Arrow Air Ltd	Wellesbourne Mountford	21. 3.04T
		28R-7703014					
G-BOYX	Robinson R22 Beta	0862	N90813	25. 8.88	R.Towle	Hexham	28. 9.91T
					(Damaged Teesside 18.7.90: current status unknown)		
G-BOYY*	Cameron A-105 HAFB	1786		22. 8.88	Hoyers (UK) Ltd *"Hoyer"*	Huddersfield	20. 4.97A
					(Cancelled 28.11.01 as wfu)		
G-BOZI	Piper PA-28-161 Warrior II		(G-BOSZ)	14. 7.88	Aerolease Ltd	Conington	25.11.03T
		28-8116120	N8318A				
G-BOZK	Aérospatiale AS332L Super Puma	2179	F-WQED(1)	5. 8.88	CHC Scotia Ltd	Aberdeen	8. 7.03T
			LN-OMQ/G-BOZK/F-GINN				
G-BOZN	Cameron N-77 HAFB	1807		1. 9.88	Calarel Developments Ltd		
					"Calarel Developments"	Chipping Campden	17. 9.02A
G-BOZO	Gulfstream AA-5B Tiger	AA5B-1282	N4536Q	12. 8.88	Caslon Ltd	Elstree	14.12.03T
G-BOZR	Cessna 152 II	15284614	N6083M	7. 9.88	Gem Rewinds Ltd	Coventry	18.12.00T
G-BOZS	Pitts S-1C Special	221-H	N10EZ	31. 8.88	T.A.S.Rayner	Perth	24. 7.02P
	(Lycoming 0-320-A2B)						
G-BOZU	Aero Dynamics Sparrow Hawk Mk II			12.12.88	R.V.Phillimore	(Bexhill-on-Sea)	
		PFA 184-11371					
G-BOZV	Robin DR.340 Major	416	F-BRTS	9. 8.88	C.J.Turner & S.D.Kent	(Bristol)	21.12.03
G-BOZW	Bensen B.8MR	PFA G/01-1096		1. 9.88	M.E.Wills	Lytchett Matravers	1. 8.02P
	(Rotax 532)						

G-BOZY	Cameron RTW-120 HAFB	1770		1. 9.88	Magical Adventures Ltd	Chirk	21. 4.97A
G-BOZZ	Gulfstream AA-5B Tiger	AA5B-1155	N4530N	22. 8.88	A.W.Matthews	Southampton	1.11.03
					t/a Solent Tiger Group		

G-BPAA – G-BPZZ

G-BPAA	Akro Advanced AA-001 & PFA 200-11528			26. 8.88	Acro Engines & Airframes Ltd	Yearby	26. 6.02P
	(VW Acro VW 2100)						
G-BPAB	Cessna 150M Commuter	15077244	N63335	21. 9.88	M.J.Diggins	Rayne Hall Farm, Rayne	7. 8.04
G-BPAC	Piper PA-28-161 Cherokee Warrior II		N2567Q	21. 9.88	G.G.Pratt	High Cross	11. 4.04
		28-7716112					
G-BPAD*	Piper PA-34-200T Seneca II		N21208	23. 8.88	Home Office Fire & Emergency Training Centre		
		34-7870431				Moreton-in-Marsh	9. 4.95T
		(Damaged Bowland, Lancs 15.7.92: cancelled 20.2.97 as destroyed) (Fire service use 8.98)					
G-BPAF	Piper PA-28-161 Cherokee Warrior II		N3199Q	6. 9.88	RAF Brize Norton Flying Club Ltd		
		28-7716142				RAF Brize Norton	30. 5.03T
G-BPAH	Colt 69A HAFB	512		2. 6.83	Justerini & Brooks Ltd *"Phil"*	(Kirdford)	15. 8.88A
					(Op Balloon Preservation Group)		
G-BPAI	Bell 47G-3B-1	6528	N8588F	9. 9.88	LRC Leisure Ltd	Barton	29. 3.01
					(Op Manchester Helicopter Centre)		
G-BPAJ	de Havilland DH.82A Tiger Moth	83472	G-AOIX	5.11.80	P.A.Jackson	Raby's Farm, Great Stukeley	15. 6.03
	(Composite with "real" G-AMNN ? qv)		T7087				
G-BPAL	de Havilland DHC-1 Chipmunk 22		G-BCYE	29.10.86	K.F. & P.Tomsett	Popham	3. 8.03
		C1/0437	WG350		*(As "WG350")*		
G-BPAO*	Air Command 503 Commander			8. 9.88	Not known	Croft Farm, Defford	8. 8.91P
		0424 & G 04-1097			*(Cancelled 23.2.99 as PWFU) (Noted 1.02)*		
G-BPAS	SOCATA TB-20 Trinidad	283	A2-ADR	9.11.88	Syndicate Clerical Services Ltd	Exeter	1. 3.04T
			F-GDBO				
G-BPAU	Piper PA-28-161 Warrior II		N3063H	3.11.88	Lapwing Flying Group Ltd	Denham	4. 4.04T
		28-7916218					
G-BPAV	Clutton FRED Srs.II	PFA 029-10274		21.11.78	P.A.Valentine	(Uxbridge)	
	(VW 1600)				*(Under construction 1990: current status unknown)*		
G-BPAW	Cessna 150M Commuter	15077923	N8348U	5. 9.88	P.D.Sims	(Farnham)	18.10.04
G-BPAX	Cessna 150M Commuter	15077401	N63571	5. 9.88	W.E.Rodwell & N.J.Smith	Shoreham	22. 5.04
					t/a The Dirty Dozen		
G-BPAY	Piper PA-28-181 Archer II	28-8090191	N3568X	12. 9.88	Leicestershire Aero Club Ltd	Leicester	10. 4.04T
G-BPBA*	Bensen B.80MR	PFA G/01-1036		5. 9.88	M.E.Green	Crewe	17. 9.90P
	(Rotax 532)			*(Noted 7.93) (Cancelled by CAA 10.2.97) (Current status unknown)*			
G-BPBB*	Evans VP-2	PFA 063-11261		2. 9.88	P.J.Manifold	Priory Farm, Tibenham	9. 6.97P
	(Arrow GT500)				*(Cancelled 3.10.01 by CAA)*		
G-BPBG	Cessna 152 II	15284941	N5418P	16. 9.88	Tatenhill Aviation Ltd	Tatenhill	18. 7.04T
G-BPBJ	Cessna 152 II	15283639	N4793B	9. 9.88	W.Shaw & P.G.Haines		
						Whaley Farm, New York, Lincs	28. 1.04
G-BPBK	Cessna 152 II	15283417	N49095	9. 9.88	N.D.Wyndow	Coventry	23. 1.04T
					t/a Sir W.G.Armstrong-Whitworth Flying Group		
G-BPBM	Piper PA-28-161 Warrior II		N3050N	12. 9.88	Halfpenny Green Flight Centre Ltd		
		28-7916272				Wolverhampton	18. 1.04T
G-BPBO	Piper PA-28RT-201T Turbo Arrow IV		N8431H	28. 9.88	Tile Holdings Ltd	Sandtoft	6. 6.04
		28R-8131195					
G-BPBP	Brugger MB.2 Colibri mk.II			6. 2.78	D.A.Preston	(Ulverston)	5. 2.02P
	(VW 1600)	PFA 043-10246					
G-BPBU	Cameron V-77 HAFB	1844		23. 9.88	M.C.Gibbons & J.E.Kite *"Sky Maid"*	Bristol	16. 6.02A
					t/a G-BPBU Skymaid Balloon *(Keep Music Live titles)*		
G-BPBV	Cameron V-77 HAFB	1821		21. 9.88	S.J.Farrant *"Sugar Plumb"*	(Godalmimg)	
G-BPBW	Cameron O-105 HAFB	1841		14.10.88	R.J.Mansfield	Huddersfield	15. 9.96A
					"October Gold"		
G-BPBY	Cameron V-77 HAFB	1818	(G-BPCS)	9.12.88	Louise Hutley *"Brewster's Toy"*	Guildford	15. 8.97A
G-BPBZ	Thunder Ax7-77 HAFB	1258		10.10.88	A.W.J.Weston	Ross-on-Wye	
G-BPCA	Pilatus Britten-Norman BN-2B-26 Islander		G-BLNX	28. 1.88	Loganair Ltd	Kirkwall	16. 2.02T
		2198			*"Chatham Historic Dockyard"*		
G-BPCE*	Stolp SA.300 Starduster Too	36	N8HM	26. 9.88	Not known	Sabadell, Barcelona, Spain	14. 2.89P
	(Continental O-470-M)			*(Cancelled 1.12.89 by CAA: stored 2.92: current status unknown)*			
G-BPCF	Piper J-3C-65 Cub	4532	N140DC	12. 5.89	T.I.Williams	Shoreham	5. 7.02P
	(Continental O-200-A)		N28033/NC28033				
	(Lippert Reed clipped-wing conversion - S/No.SA811SW)						
G-BPCG	Colt AS-80 Mk.II Hot-Air Airship			14.10.88	N.Charbonnier	Aosta, Italy	10.10.96A
		1300			*"Greensport/Napapijri"*		
G-BPCI	Cessna R172K Hawk XP II	R1722360	N9976V	3. 1.89	P.A.Warner & E.S.Scotchbrook		
						Lower Wasing Farm, Brimpton	24. 5.02
G-BPCJ*	Cessna 150J	15070797	N61096	26. 9.88	Solihull College Engineering Dept		
						Blossomfield Rd, Solihull	3. 8.92T
	(Damaged Compton Abbas 25.1.90: cancelled 4.7.90 by CAA) (Instructional airframe 3.95: current status unknown)						

G-BPCK	Piper PA-28-161 Warrior II	28-8016279	N8529N C-GMEI/N9519N	26. 9.88	W.G.Booth	Compton Abbas	20. 8.04T
G-BPCL	Scottish Aviation Bulldog Srs.120/128	BH120/393	HKG-6 G-31-19	20. 9.88	Isohigh Ltd t/a 121 Group *(As "HKG-6" in Hong Kong DF c/s)*	North Weald	12. 7.04T
G-BPCM	Rotorway Executive (Rotorway RW152)	E.3293	N979WP	21. 9.88	R.J.Turner t/a Aircare Group *(Stored 7.96: current status unknown)*	Weavers Loft, Wem	25.11.91P
G-BPCR	Mooney M.20K (231)	25-0532	N98433	23. 9.88	T. & R.Harris *"Over The Moony"*	Biggin Hill	15.11.04
G-BPCV	Montgomerie-Bensen B-8MR	PFA G/01-1088		11.10.88	O.J.Blackbourn *(Current status unknown)*	(Penzance)	25. 7.91P
G-BPCX	Piper PA-28-236 Dakota	28-8211004	N8441S	25.10.88	G.E.J.Spooner	Andrewsfield	27. 6.04T
G-BPDF	Cameron V-77 HAFB	1806		6.10.88	The Ballooning Business Ltd *"Burning Ambition"*	Northampton	31. 7.00T
G-BPDG	Cameron V-77 HAFB	1839		21.10.88	D.F.H.Smith *"Pretty Damn Good"*	Burnley	4. 9.00A
G-BPDJ	Chris Tena Mini Coupe (VW 1835)	275	N13877	4.10.88	J.J.Morrissey *(Stored 10.01)*	Popham	
G-BPDK*	Sorrell SNS-7 Hyperbipe (Lycoming IO-360)	242	N85BL	6.10.88	A.J.Cable *(Cancelled 17.2.99 by CAA: on rebuild 4.99: current status unknown)*	Barton	23. 6.95P
G-BPDM	CASA I-131E Jungmann	2058	E3B-369	24.10.88	J.D.Haslam *(As "E3B-369/781-32" in Spanish AF c/s)*	(Northallerton)	22. 6.96P
G-BPDT	Piper PA-28-161 Warrior II	28-8416004	N4317Z	22.12.88	Channel Islands Aero Services Ltd t/a Jersey Aero Club	Jersey	18.12.04T
G-BPDU	Piper PA-28-161 Cherokee Warrior II	28-7716195	N5672V	30. 9.88	Shoreham Flight Centre Ltd	Shoreham	14. 7.02T
G-BPDV	Pitts S-1S Special (Lycoming O-360)	27P	N330VE	15. 9.88	J.Vize	Sywell	17. 6.02P
G-BPDY	Westland-Bell 47G-3B1 *(Line No.WAN/48)*	WA/356	OY-HCO SE-HIF/XT197	10.10.88	M.O.Simpson & A.C.Lindner t/a Howden Helicopters	Howden	3. 8.01T
G-BPEC	Boeing 757-236ER	24882		6.11.90	British Airways plc *(Waves & Cranes t/s)*	Gatwick	12.11.03T
G-BPED	Boeing 757-236	25059		30. 4.91	British Airways plc *(Koguty Lowickie t/s)*	Heathrow	29. 4.04T
G-BPEE	Boeing 757-236ER	25060		3. 5.91	British Airways plc	Gatwick	2. 5.04T
G-BPEF	Boeing 757-236ER	24120	G-BOHC EC-ELA/EC-516/G-BOHC/EC-ELA/EC-202/G-BOHC	18. 5.92	British Airways plc	Gatwick	17. 5.02T
G-BPEI	Boeing 757-236	25806	(G-BMRK)	9. 3.94	British Airways plc *"Chatham Historic Dockyard"*	Heathrow	8.12.02T
G-BPEJ	Boeing 757-236	25807	(G-BMRL)	22. 4.94	British Airways plc	Heathrow	24. 4.03T
G-BPEK	Boeing 757-236	25808	(G-BMRM)	17. 3.95	British Airways plc	Heathrow	16. 3.04T
G-BPEL	Piper PA 28-151 Cherokee Warrior	28-7415172	C-FEYM	10.10.88	R.W.Harris & A.Jahanfar *(Dismantled wreck stored 1.02)*	Southend	8. 2.92T
G-BPEM	Cessna 150K	15071707	N6207G	24.10.88	R.Strong & R.G.Lindsey	Netherthorpe	17. 6.04
G-BPEO	Cessna 152 II	15283775	C-GQVO (N5147B)	10.10.88	Seawing Flying Club Ltd & Eastern Executive Air Charter Ltd	Southend	1. 7.01T
G-BPES	Piper PA 38-112 Tomahawk II	38-81A0064	N25728	2.11.88	Sherwood Flying Club Ltd	Nottingham	5. 1.04T
G-BPEZ	Colt 77A HAFB	1324		14.10.88	J.E.F.Kettlety & W.J.Honey	Chippenham/Bristol	6. 6.01A
G-BPFB	Colt 77A HAFB	1334		26.10.88	S.Ingram	Oldham	9. 6.02A
G-BPFC	Mooney M.20C Ranger	20-1243	N3606H	21.10.88	D.P.Wring	Dunkeswell	1. 3.02
G-BPFD	Jodel D.112	312	F-PHJT	3.11.88	K.Manley	Swanborough Farm, Lewes	9. 4.02P
G-BPFH	Piper PA-28-161 Warrior II	28-8116201	N83723	3.11.88	Muriel H.Kleiser *(Op Edinburgh Flying Club)*	Edinburgh	4.12.03T
G-BPFI	Piper PA 28-181 Archer II	28-8090113	N8103G	5. 1.89	F.Teagle	Perranporth	12. 7.04
G-BPFJ*	Cameron Can 90SS HAFB *(Budweiser Beer Can shape)*	1834		14.11.88	Balloon Preservation Group *"Budweiser Can" (Cancelled 9.5.97 as WFU)*	Kirdford	10.12.93A
G-BPFL	Davis DA-2A (Continental O-200-A)	051	N72RJ	27.10.88	B.W.Griffiths	Coventry	18. 1.03P
G-BPFM	Aeronca 7AC Champion	7AC-4751	N1193E NC1193E	13.10.88	Linda A.Borrill	Netherthorpe	16. 4.02P
G-BPFN	Short SD.3-60 Var.100	SH.3747	N747HH N747SA/G-BPFN/G-14-3747 *(Benyhone Tartan t/s)*	2.11.88	Loganair Ltd.	Glasgow	28. 8.02T
G-BPFX*	Colt 21A Cloudhopper HAFB	1348		7.11.88	Balloon Preservation Group Museum *"Budweiser Hopper"* *(Cancelled 23.12.98 as WFU)*	Lancing	
G-BPFZ	Cessna 152 II	15285741	N94594	27.10.88	C.J.Ward	Wellesbourne Mountford	3. 8.01T
G-BPGB*	Cessna 150J	15069722	N51042	2.11.88	Magnificent Obsessions Ltd *(Stored 10.92: cancelled 23.10.00 by CAA: current status unknown)*	(Grimsby)	1. 3.92T
G-BPGC	Air Command 532 Elite (Rotax 532)	0440 & PFA G/04-1108		11.10.88	G.A.Speich *(Active 8.01)*	Beausdale, Kenilworth	1. 8.91P
G-BPGD	Cameron V-65 HAFB *(New envelope c 8.01 c/n 4969)*	2000		9. 9.88	Gone With The Wind Ltd *"Silver Lining"*	Bristol	4.12.99A
G-BPGE	Cessna U206C Super Skywagon	U2061013	N29017	7.11.88	K.Brady t/a The Scottish Parachute Club	Strathallan	14. 5.04

G-BPGF	Thunder Ax7-77 HAFB	1355		22.11.88	M.Schiavo *"Dovetail"*	Manchester	25. 8.95A
G-BPGH	EAA Acrosport II	422	N12JE	14.11.88	G.M.Bradley	Crowfield	11. 9.02P
	(Continental IO-346)						
G-BPGK	Aeronca 7AC Champion	7AC-7187	N4409E	7. 2.89	D.A.Crompton	(Stoke-on-Trent)	22. 2.02P
	(Continental A65)						
G-BPGM	Cessna 152 II	15284932	N5380P	14.11.88	Fraggle Leasing Ltd	Edinburgh	18. 2.02T
G-BPGT	Colt AS-80 Mk.II HA Airship	1248	(I-)	14.11.88	P.Porati	Milan, Italy	20. 7.00A
			G-BPGT				
G-BPGU	Piper PA-28-181 Archer II	28-8490025	N4330B	26.10.88	G.Underwood	Nottingham	30. 1.04
G-BPGV	Robinson R22 Beta	0887		3.11.88	Leinster Warehousing & Distribution Ltd		
						(Dublin)	21.11.03T
G-BPGX	SOCATA TB-9 Tampico Club	884		4.11.88	D.A.Lee	Denham	13. 2.03T
G-BPGY	Cessna 150H	15067325	N6525S	24. 1.89	Premiair Engineering Ltd	Southend	2.12.02T
G-BPGZ	Cessna 150G	15064912	N3612J	14.11.88	J.B.Scott	Blackpool	17. 5.04
G-BPHB	Piper PA-28-161 Warrior II	2816069	N9148G	14.11.88	M.J.Wade	(Buckingham)	22. 2.04T
G-BPHD	Cameron N-42 HAFB	1863		21. 2.89	P.J.Marshall & M.A.Clarke	Ruislip	9. 6.02A
					"Ellen Gee II"		
G-BPHE	Piper PA-28-161 Warrior II		N2911D	28.12.88	APB Leasing Ltd	Welshpool	26. 3.04T
		28-7916536					
G-BPHG	Robin DR.400/180 Regent	1887		29.11.88	K.J. & M.B.White		
						Homefield Farm, Crowhurst, Lingfield	6. 6.04
G-BPHH	Cameron V-77 HAFB	1840		2.12.88	C.D.Aindow *"Office Angels"*	London SW18	2. 9.00A
G-BPHI	Piper PA-38-112 Tomahawk	38-79A0002	N2535T	22.11.88	J.S.Devlin & Z.Islam	Hurstbourne Tarrant	12. 7.04T
					(Reported in wrecked condition 9.00)		
G-BPHJ	Cameron V-77 HAFB	1881		23.11.88	C.W.Brown *"Twiggy"*	Nottingham	11. 5.02A
G-BPHK	Whittaker MW7	PFA 171-11389		24.11.88	P.J.D.Kerr	(Bridgwater)	25.10.02P
G-BPHL	Piper PA-28-161 Warrior II		N555PY	2.12.88	Teesside Flight Centre Ltd	Teesside	19. 7.04T
		28-7916315	N2247U				
G-BPHO	Taylorcraft BC-12D	8497	N96197	10. 1.89	A.A.Alderdice *"Spirit of Missouri"*		
			NC96197			Woodview, Armagh, Co.Armagh	17. 9.01P
G-BPHP	Taylorcraft BC-12-65	2799	N33948	12.12.88	D.C.Stephens	Llangarron	2.11.99P
	(Continental A65)		NC33948		*"Spirit of Mississippi"*		
			(Crashed on landing Wellesbourne Mountford 11.4.99: current status unknown)				
G-BPHR	DH 82A Tiger Moth	45	N48DH	3. 1.89	N.Parry *(As "A17-48" in RAAF c/s)*		
	(Built de Havilland Aircraft Pty Ltd)		VH-BLX/A17-48			Lotmead Farm, Wanborough, Swindon	11.10.01
G-BPHT	Cessna 152 II	15282401	N961LP	5.12.88	Evensport Ltd	(Rayleigh)	16. 8.01T
G-BPHU	Thunder Ax7-77 HAFB	1365		19.12.88	R.P.Waite	St.Helens	11. 8.00A
G-BPHV*	Colt Montgolfiere SS HAFB	1281	F-GGFK	9.12.88	Not known	NK	
			F-GFLZ				
	(Cancelled 5.10.90 as sold to France: noted 8.98 as "G-BPHV" in UK: current status unknown)						
G-BPHW	Cessna 140	11035	N76595	13. 1.89	M.Day	White Waltham	17. 6.02
	(Continental C85)		NC76595				
G-BPHX	Cessna 140	12488	N2252N	2.12.88	M.McChesney	Enniskillen, Co.Fermanagh	23. 5.93
	(Continental C85)		NC2252N		*(Stored 2.93: re-regd to same owner 10.00)*		
G-BPHZ	Morane-Saulnier MS.505 Criquet	53/7	F-BJQC	17. 4.89	G.A.Warner	Duxford	26. 4.99P
			Fr Mil		t/a The Aircraft Restoration Co		
					(As "TA+RC" in I/JG54 Luftwaffe c/s)		
G-BPID	Piper PA-28-161 Warrior II		N2137V	16. 3.89	T W Pullin	(Barrow-in-Furness)	24. 5.04T
		28-7916325					
G-BPIF	Bensen-Parsons Two Place Gyrocopter			19.12.88	B.J.L.P.de Saar	Shipdham	28. 3.96P
	(Rotax 532)	UK-01					
G-BPIH	Rand Robinson KR-2			19.12.88	J.R.Rowley & T.E.Masters	(Birmingham)	
		8023 & PFA 129-11436					
G-BPII	Denney Kitfox	213 & PFA 172-11496		15.12.88	P.Etherington	(Hucknall)	3. 2.02P
	(IAME KFM 112)				t/a G-BPII Group		
G-BPIJ	Brantly B.2B	465	N2293U	23. 3.89	R.B.Payne	Willand, Cullompton	13. 7.98
G-BPIK	Piper PA-38-112 Tomahawk II		N3947M	2.12.88	Metropolitan Services Ltd	Hawarden	12. 7.03T
		38-82A0028	ZP-EAP/N91423				
G-BPIL	Cessna 310B	35620	N620GS	16.11.89	A.L.Brown & R.A.Parsons	Bourn	28. 4.00T
			OO-SEF/N5420A		*"Fast Lady"*		
G-BPIN	Glaser-Dirks DG-400	4-242		14.12.88	J.N.Stevenson	Lasham	11. 4.04
G-BPIO	Reims Cessna F.152 II	F15201556	PH-VSO	23. 1.89	I.D.McClelland	Biggin Hill	12. 9.04T
			PH-AXS				
G-BPIP	Slingsby T.31 Cadet III			14.11.88	J.H.Beard	Bodmin	27. 9.96P
	(VW 1600)	PFA 042-10771					
G-BPIR	Scheibe SF-25E Super Falke	4332	N25SF	15.12.88	K.E.Ballington		
			(D-KDFX)			Yeatsall Farm, Abbots Bromley	5. 4.04
G-BPIT	Robinson R22 Beta	0907	N80011	22.12.88	NA Air Ltd	Hawarden	27. 6.02T
G-BPIU	Piper PA-28-161 Warrior II		N3028T	28.12.88	P.G.Doble & P.G.Stewart	Fairoaks	28. 3.04
		28-7916303					
G-BPIV	Bristol 149 Blenheim IV	-	"Z5722"	15 2.89	G.A.Warner	Duxford	19. 6.02P
			RCAF 10201		t/a The Aircraft Restoration Co *(As "R3281/UX-N")*		
	(Built Fairchild Aircraft Ltd as Bollingbroke IVT)				*"Spirit of Britain First"*		
G-BPIZ	Gulfstream AA-5B Tiger	AA5B-1154	N4530L	14. 2.89	N.R.F.McNally	Shoreham	21. 8.04

G-BPJB	Schweizer Hughes 269C	S.1331	N75065	7.11.88	Elborne Holdings Ltd	Cascais, Portugal	24.10.02
G-BPJD	SOCATA Rallye 110ST	3253	OY-CAV	22.12.88	J.G.Murphy	Morgansfield, Fishburn	21. 6.04
					t/a G-BPJD Rallye Group		
G-BPJE	Cameron A-105 HAFB	1864		8.11.88	J.S.Eckersley	Henley-on-Thames	11. 5.02A
					"Burley Stables"		
G-BPJF*	Piper PA-38-112 Tomahawk	38-78A0021	N9312T	5. 4.89	S McNulty	Coventry	4.10.98
					(Crashed on take-off at Derby 20.6.98: cancelled 2.10.98 by CAA) (For rescue training 5.00)		
G-BPJG	Piper PA-18-150 Super Cub	18-8350	SE-EZG	4. 1.89	M.W.Stein	Oaksey Park	8. 8.04
			N4172Z				
G-BPJH	Piper PA-18 Super Cub 95	18-1980	EI-59	24. 5.83	P.J.Heron	City of Derry	31. 1.02P
	(L-18C-PI)		I-EICA/MM522380/52-2380				
G-BPJK	Colt 77A HAFB	1362		22.12.88	Saran UK Ltd	Cheltenham	7. 7.01A
G-BPJL	Cessna 152 II	15281296	N49473	28.12.88	Eastern Executive Air Charter Ltd		
					(Op Seawing Flying Club)	Southend	10. 7.04T
G-BPJO	Piper PA-28-161 Cadet	2841014	N9153Z	15.12.88	Plane Talking Ltd	Denham	20.12.04T
					(Op Denham School of Flying)		
G-BPJP	Piper PA-28-161 Cadet	2841015	N9154K	22.12.88	S.J.Skilton	Bournemouth	27. 6.04T
					t/a Aviation Rentals		
G-BPJR	Piper PA-28-161 Cadet	2841024	N9154X	17. 1.89	J.P.E.Walsh t/a Walsh Aviation	Denham	21.12.04T
G-BPJT*	Piper PA-28-161 Cadet	2841031	N9156X	6. 1.89	Home Office Fire & Emergency Training Centre		
						Moreton-in-Marsh	17. 2.95T
					(Crashed Oxford 12.7.92: cancelled 31.10.94 as destroyed) (Fire service use 8.98)		
G-BPJU	Piper PA-28-161 Cadet	2841032	N9156Z	11. 1.89	S.J.Skilton	Bournemouth	1. 4.04T
					t/a Aviation Rentals		
G-BPJV	Taylorcraft F-21	F-1005	N2004L	12. 1.89	P.Glennon t/a TC Flying Group	Booker	17. 6.02P
G-BPJW	Cessna A150K Aerobat	A1500127	C-FAJX	4. 1.89	G & S.A.Jones	Linley Hill, Leven	4. 6.03T
			CF-AJX/N8427M				
G-BPKF	Grob G-115	8075		3. 1.89	R.V.Morgan & J.F.W.Steventon		
					t/a Steventon Morgan Aviation	Compton Abbas	14. 4.04
G-BPKK	Denney Kitfox mk.1			19.12.88	D.Moffat	Lochview House, Limerigg	11.10.02P
	(Rotax 532)	264 & PFA 172-11411					
G-BPKM	Piper PA-28-161 Warrior II		PH-CKO	6. 1.89	M.J.Greasby	RAF Halton	12. 7.04T
		28-7916341	N2140X/N9630N				
G-BPKN*	Colt AS-80 Mk.II Hot-Air Airship			11. 1.89	British Balloon Museum & Library	Newbury	14. 3.91A
		1297			*"Fuji" (Cancelled 7.1.91 by CAA)*		
G-BPKO	Cessna 140	8936	N89891	12. 1.89	M.J.Patrick	(Pulborough)	18. 5.03
			NC89891				
G-BPKR	Piper PA-28-151 Cherokee Warrior		N4341X	13. 3.89	Aeroshow Ltd	Filton	5. 4.04T
		28-7515446					
G-BPLF	Cameron V-77 HAFB	1903		16. 1.89	I.R.Warrington & R.A.Macmillan	Stamford	5. 6.01A
					"Star Attraction"		
G-BPLH	CEA Jodel DR.1051 Sicile	401	F-BLAE	27. 2.89	D.W.Tovey	Dunkeswell	24.11.01
	(Potez 4E20A)						
G-BPLM	AIA Stampe SV-4C	1004	F-BHET	8. 2.89	C.J.Jesson	Headcorn	19. 8.01T
			Fr.Mil/F-BDKC				
G-BPLR	Pilatus Britten-Norman BN-2B-26 Islander		JA5298	20. 1.89	Hebridean Air Services Ltd	Liverpool	12.12.02T
		2209	G-BPLR		*(Op Keenair)*		
G-BPLV	Cameron V-77 HAFB	1822		23. 1.89	MC VH SA	Brussels, Belgium	1. 2.00A
G-BPLY	Christen Pitts S-2B Special	5149		25. 1.89	J.D.Haslam	Teesside	20. 6.04
	(Lycoming AEIO-540)						
G-BPLZ	Hughes 369HS	91-0342S	N126CM	15. 2.89	Pyramid Helicopters Ltd	Wolverhampton	18. 6.04
G-BPMB	Maule M-5-235C Lunar Rocket	7284C	N5635T	13. 8.79	Earth Products Ltd	Sherburn-in-Elmet	23. 1.04
G-BPME	Cessna 152 II	15285585	N94021	24. 1.89	Eastern Executive Air Charter Ltd		
					(Op Seawing Flying Club) Hill Farm,	Nayland	5. 8.04T
G-BPMF	Piper PA-28-151 Cherokee Warrior		C-GOXL	2. 2.89	L. & A.Hill	Blackpool	2. 5.04
		28-7515050					
G-BPMH	Schempp-Hirth Nimbus 3DM	7/23		20. 3.89	R.Jones *"60"*	Lasham	10.10.04
	(Regd as c/n 07)				t/a Southern Sailplanes		
G-BPML	Cessna 172M Skyhawk II	17267102	N1435U	17.11.89	N.A.Bilton & P.R.Bennett	(Norwich)	29. 5.03T
G-BPMM	Champion 7ECA Citabria	7ECA-498	N5132T	22. 3.89	J.Murray	(Ballymoney, Co.Antrim)	25. 2.97P
G-BPMR	Piper PA-28-161 Warrior II		N4373S	25. 1.89	B.McIntyre	Gloucestershire	17. 5.04T
		28-8416119	N9620N				
G-BPMU	Nord 3202B	70	(G-BIZJ)	26. 1.89	A.I.Milne	Little Snoring	19.10.90P
			N22546/ALAT "AIX"		*(Stored 9.97: current status unknown)*		
G-BPMW	QAC Quickie Q2	PFA 094A-10790	G-OICI	13. 3.89	P.M.Wright	Enstone	17. 8.91P
	(Revmaster R2100DQ)		G-OGKN				
			(Damaged near Basingstoke 16.2.91: on repair 9.00: current status unknown)				
G-BPMX	ARV1 Super 2	K.005 & PFA 152-11128		30. 1.89	T.P.Toth	Enstone	20. 8.02P
	(Hewland AE75)						
G-BPNA	Cessna 150L	15073042	N1742Q	10. 2.89	BBC Air Ltd *(Op Abbas Air)*	Compton Abbas	30. 3.03T
G-BPND	Boeing 727-2D3	21021	OK-EGK	18.12.87	Couga Leasing *"Katie"*	Bournemouth	10. 4.01T
			N500AV/G-BPND/PH-AHZ/N500AV/HI-452/JY-ADV *(Sabre Airways titles)*				
G-BPNI	Robinson R22 Beta	0948		6. 2.89	Heliflight (UK) Ltd	Wolverhampton	8. 4.01T

G-BPNL	QAC Quickie Q2 (Revmaster 2100D)	PFA 094A-11014		6. 2.89	J R Jensen *(Damaged Swansea 30.4.95: wreck stored 3.99: current status unknown)*	Longbridge Deverill	16. 1.96P
G-BPNN	Montgomerie-Bensen B.8MR	MV-003		3. 2.89	M.E.Vahdat	(Uxbridge)	
G-BPNO	Moravan Zlin Z.526 Trener Master	930	F-BPNO	18. 2.86	J.A.S.Baldry & S.T.Logan	RAF Cranwell	17. 6.03
G-BPNT	British Aerospace BAe 146 Srs.300	E3126		4. 1.89	Flightline Ltd *(Swissair Express titles) (Stored 10.01)*	Southend	31. 5.02T
G-BPNU	Thunder Ax7-77 HAFB	1011		9. 2.89	M.J.Barnes *"Firefly"*	Ivybridge	15. 1.02T
G-BPOA*	Gloster Meteor T.7	-	WF877	16. 3.89	Not known *(Cancelled 5.6.96 as WFU) (Stored 8.99 as "WF877")*	Kemble	
G-BPOB	Tallmantz Sopwith Camel F.1 rep (Warner Scarab 165)	TM-10	N8997	14. 3.89	Bianchi Aviation Film Services Ltd *(Op "Blue Max" Movie Aircraft Collection) (As "B2458/R" in RFC c/s)*	Booker	2. 9.02P
G-BPOL	Pietenpol Air Camper	PFA 047-10941		16. 2.89	G.W.Postance	(Burgess Hill, Sussex)	
G-BPOM	Piper PA-28-161 Warrior II	28-8416118	N4373Q N9619N	15. 2.89	APB Leasing Ltd	Norwich	13. 5.01T
G-BPON	Piper PA-34-200T Seneca II	34-7570040	N675ES N32644	13. 2.89	Aeros Leasing Ltd	Gloucestershire	15. 6.04T
G-BPOO	Montgomerie-Bensen B.8MR	MV-002 & PFA G/01A-1109		3. 2.89	M.E.Vahdat *(Not constructed)*	(Uxbridge)	
G-BPOS	Cessna 150M	15075905	N66187	21. 2.89	K.J.Goggins	Bourn	29.12.02T
G-BPOT	Piper PA-28-181 Cherokee Archer II	28-7790267	N8807F	7. 2.89	F A Yeates t/a Icarus Flying Group	Rochester	17.12.04
G-BPOU	Luscombe 8A Silvaire (Continental A65)	4159	N1432K NC1432K	14. 2.89	M.J.Negus & R.Hardley	Stoneacre Farm, Farthing Corner	4.11.02P
G-BPOV	Cameron Magazine 90SS HAFB *(Forbes Magazine shape)*	1890		10. 3.89	Forbes Europe Inc *"Forbes Capitalist Tool"*	Balleroy, Normandy	5. 7.01A
G-BPPA	Cameron O-65 HAFB	1930		15. 2.89	Rix Petroleum Ltd *"Rix Petroleum"*	Hull	24. 8.02A
G-BPPD	Piper PA-38-112 Tomahawk	38-79A0457	N2456F	15. 2.89	S.Snodgrass & M.A.Wood t/a AS Belting Products	Kemble	26. 9.04T
G-BPPE	Piper PA-38-112 Tomahawk	38-79A0189	N2445C	15. 2.89	D.J.Woodnutt	Norwich	5. 9.04T
G-BPPF	Piper PA-38-112 Tomahawk	38-79A0578	N2329K	15. 2.89	D.J.Bellamy t/a Bristol Strut Flying Group	Bristol	5.12.04
G-BPPJ	Cameron A-180 HAFB	1924		2. 3.89	Heather R.Evans	Ross-on-Wye	12. 3.01T
G-BPPK	Piper PA-28-151 Cherokee Warrior	28-7615054	N7592C	10. 3.89	UK Technical Consultants Ltd	(Turweston)	30. 6.02T
G-BPPL	Enstrom F-28A	251	HB-XER	15. 2.89	M & P Food Products Ltd t/a Coventry Helicopters	Coventry	9. 5.98T
G-BPPM	Beechcraft B200 Super King Air	BB-1044	N7061T C-GJJT/N815CE/(N815CF)/N815CE/N62895	16. 2.89	Gama Aviation Ltd *(Op Bond Air Services)*	Aberdeen	17.10.04T
G-BPPO	Luscombe 8A Silvaire (Continental A65)	2541	N3519M N71114/NC71114	15. 2.89	I.K.Ratcliffe *(Noted 10.01)*	Deanland	28. 6.02P
G-BPPP	Cameron V-77 HAFB	1700		29. 2.88	P.F.Smart t/a The Sarnia Balloon Group *"Thruppence"*	Basingstoke	28. 6.97A
G-BPPR*	Air Command 532 Elite	0434 & PFA G/04-1105		22. 2.89	T.D.Inch *(Cancelled 10.3.99 by CAA: used as Gyro-glider 2000)*	Swansea	14. 5.91P
G-BPPS	Mudry/CAARP CAP.21	9	F-GDTD	3. 5.85	N.B.Gray & L.Van Vuuren	Teesside	14. 3.04S
G-BPPU	Air Command 532 Elite (Rotax 532)	0438 & PFA G/04-1120		22. 2.89	J.Hough	Alresford, Hants	18.10.91P
G-BPPY	Hughes 269B (300)	20-0448	N9554F	10. 3.89	A.Harvey & R.C.S.Timbrell	Whimple, Exeter	29.10.99
G-BPPZ	Taylorcraft BC-12D (Continental C85)	7988	N28286 NC28286	22. 3.89	J.Gordon & M.Hart t/a Zulu Warriors Flying Group	Charterhall	20. 9.02P
G-BPRA	Aeronca 11AC Chief	11AC-1344	N9702E NC9702E	22. 3.89	R.M.C.Hunter	Wellcross Grange, Slinfold	16. 7.02P
G-BPRC	Cameron Elephant 77SS HAFB	1871		21. 2.89	A.Schneider *"Elefant Benjamin"*	Borken, Germany	29. 4.02A
G-BPRD	Pitts S-1C Special (Lycoming O-360)	ZZ.1	N10ZZ	21. 2.89	Shiela M.Trickey	St Just	15. 5.01P
G-BPRI	Aérospatiale AS355F1 Twin Squirrel	5181	G-TVPA G-BPRI/N364E	22. 2.89	Quay Contracts Ltd	(Portsmouth)	9. 9.02T
G-BPRJ	Aérospatiale AS355F1 Twin Squirrel	5201	N368E	22. 2.89	PLM Dollar Group Ltd	Cumbernauld	14.12.04T
G-BPRL	Aérospatiale AS355F1 Twin Squirrel	5154	N362E	22. 2.89	Gas & Air Ltd *(Op Virgin Helicopters)*	Booker	19. 4.03T
G-BPRM	Reims Cessna F172L	F17200825	G-AZKG	20. 4.88	M.R.H.Wishart	Tingwall	19. 4.01
G-BPRN	Piper PA-28-161 Warrior II	28-8116109	N83112	6. 3.89	Air Navigation & Trading Co Ltd	Blackpool	2. 8.04T
G-BPRP*	Cessna 150E	15061269	N3569J	10. 3.89	P.A.Griffin *(Cancelled 22.10.99 as wfu) (Remains noted 12.99: current status unknown)*	Shoreham	23 5.98T
G-BPRR	Rand Robinson KR-2	PFA 129-11105		1. 3.89	A.M.Witt *(Under construction 6.01)*	Barton	
G-BPRS	Air Command 532 Elite	0432		14. 4.89	B.K.Snoxall *(Believed damaged: cancelled 3.3.99 by CAA: current status unknown)*	(Whitchurch, Hants)	

G-BPRX	Aeronca 11AC Chief	11AC-94	N86288	3. 3.89	D.J.Dumolo & C.R.Barnes	(Selby)	23. 8.99P
	(Continental A75)		NC86288		*(On rebuild 12.01)*		
G-BPRY	Piper PA-28-161 Warrior II		N4373Y	2. 3.89	R.C.White	East Midlands	21. 6.04T
		28-8416120	N9621N		t/a White Wings Aviation		
G-BPSH	Cameron V-77 HAFB	1837		21. 2.89	P.G.Hossack *"Coconut Ice"*	Pewsey	5. 4.97T
G-BPSI	Thunder Ax10-160 HAFB	1420		10. 3.89	M.E.White	Dublin	24. 6.02T
G-BPSJ	Thunder Ax6-56 HAFB	1479		13. 3.89	Capricorn Balloons Ltd	Loughborough	4. 4.99A
G-BPSK	Montgomerie-Bensen B.8M			15. 3.89	P.T.Ambrozik	(Great Orton)	25.11.99P
	(Rotax 532)	PFA G/01-1100			*(Current status unknown)*		
G-BPSL	Cessna 177 Cardinal	17701138	N659SR	3. 3.89	N.P.Bendle t/a G-BPSL Group	Dunkeswell	14.11.04
G-BPSO	Cameron N-90 HAFB	1959		10. 3.89	J.Oberprieler	Mauern, Germany	1. 7.02A
G-BPSP	Cameron Ship 90SS HAFB	1848		10. 3.89	Forbes Europe Inc	Balleroy, Normandy	17. 6.94
	(Columbus "Santa Maria" shape)				*"Santa Maria"*		
G-BPSR	Cameron V-77 HAFB	1962		10. 3.89	K.J.A.Maxwell *"Norma Jean"*	Haywards Heath	22. 8.01T
G-BPSS	Cameron A-120 HAFB	1947		27. 2.89	T.J.Parker	Burnham-on-Crouch	9. 5.02T
					t/a Anglian Countryside Balloons		
G-BPTA	Stinson 108-2 Station Wagon	108-3429	N429C	22. 3.89	M.L.Ryan	Garston Farm, Marshfield	1.10.04
	(Franklin 6A4)		NC429C				
G-BPTD	Cameron V-77 HAFB	2001		14. 3.89	J.Lippett	South Petherton, Somerset	11. 8.01A
					"Visions 2001"		
G-BPTE	Piper PA-28-181 Cherokee Archer II		N8553E	9. 3.89	J.S.Develin & Z.Islam	Redhill	9. 8.04T
		28-7690178					
G-BPTF	Cessna 152 II	15281979	N67715	9. 3.89	A.S.Bamrah	Shoreham	20. 8.04T
					t/a Falcon Flying Services		
G-BPTG	Rockwell Commander 112TC	13067	N4577W	31. 3.89	Marita A.Watteau	Shoreham	25.10.03
G-BPTH*	Air Command 532 Elite	01	N532KR	25. 4.89	R.Wheeler		
						North Green Farm, Reymerston, Norfolk	
		(Damaged 1991 - parts only remain 1992: cancelled 16.4.99 by CAA: current status unknown)					
G-BPTI	SOCATA TB-20 Trinidad	414	N41BM	21. 4.89	N.Davis	Blackbushe	3. 7.04
G-BPTL	Cessna 172N Skyhawk II	17268652	N733YJ	22. 3.89	Cleveland Flying School Ltd	Teesside	3.12.01T
G-BPTO	Zenair CH-200-AA	2-563	EI-BKP	22. 3.89	Barbara Philips	Ledbury/Gloucestershire	8. 9.91P
	(Lycoming O-320)				*(Damaged Aldersfield, Worcs 27.5.91)*		
G-BPTS	CASA I-131E Jungmann	NK	E3B-153	23. 5.89	Aerobatic Displays Ltd	Duxford	19.12.02P
			"781-75"		*(Op The Old Flying Machine Co)*		
					(As "E3B-153/781-75" in Spanish AF c/s)		
G-BPTU	Cessna 152 II	15282955	N45946	22. 3.89	A.M.Alam	Elstree	23. 6.02T
G-BPTV	Bensen B.8	PFA G/01-1058		30. 3.89	C.Munro	(Colne)	
G-BPTX	Cameron O-120 HAFB	1972		29. 3.89	S.J.Colin & A.S.Pinder	Maidstone	14. 5.97T
					t/a Skybus Ballooning		
G-BPTZ	Robinson R22 Beta	0958		22. 3.89	J. Lucketti	Barton	16. 11.98
G-BPUA	EAA Sport Biplane	SAAC-02	EI-BBF	30. 3.89	Skyview Systems Ltd	(Sudbury)	30. 3.02P
	(Lycoming O-235)						
G-BPUB	Cameron V-31 Air Chair HAFB	1114		15. 3.89	M.T.Evans	Bath	3. 6.94A
G-BPUC	QAC Quickie Q.235	2583	N250CE	22. 3.89	S.R.Harvey	Enstone	31. 5.02P
	(Lycoming O-235)				*(Noted 7.01)*		
G-BPUD*	Ryan PT-22-RY (ST3KR)	1265	N53189	22. 3.89	Not known		
			41-15236		Bericote Farm, Blackdown, Leamington Spa		
	(Damaged in forced landing Great Ryburgh, Norfolk 8.11.92: cancelled 3.3.99 as destroyed) (For spares use 11.01)						
G-BPUE	Air Command 532 Elite			29. 3.89	A.H.Brent	Brough	11. 9.91P
	(Rotax 532) 0441 & PFA G/04-1136						
G-BPUF	Thunder Ax6-56Z HAFB	270	(G-BHRL)	30. 4.80	R.C. & M.A.Trimble	Henley-on-Thames	10. 2.90A
					"Buf Puf"		
G-BPUG	Air Command 532 Elite			29. 3.89	T.A.Holmes	Melrose Farm, Melbourne	18. 4.91P
	(Rotax 532) 0401 & PFA G/04-1157				*(Possibly moved to Spain by 2000: current status unknown)*		
G-BPUJ	Cameron N-90 HAFB	1977		17. 4.89	D.Grimshaw	Preston	4. 6.01T
G-BPUL	Piper PA-18A-150 Super Cub	18-2517	OO-LUL	12. 4.89	C.D.Duthy-James	(Presteigne)	15. 6.02
	(L-18C-PI)		PH-NEV				
	(Frame No now thought to be in 18-25xx series: therefore all previously published p/is fall)						
G-BPUM	Cessna R182 Skylane RG II	R18200915	N738DZ	2. 5.89	R.C.Chapman	Marley Hall, Ledbury	30. 4.04
G-BPUP	Whittaker MW7	PFA 171-11473		2. 8.89	J.H.Bèard	(Buckfastleigh, Devon)	
G-BPUR	Piper J-3L-65 Cub	4708	N30228	14. 6.89	H.A.D.Monro	(Hastings)	
	(Frame No.4764)		NC30228		*(On rebuild 2000)*		
G-BPUS*	Rans S-9	PFA 196-11487		7. 4.89	T.A.Wright *(Cancelled 22.11.01 by CAA)*		
	(Rotax 532)					Blackspring Farm, Castle Bytham	21. 4.00P
G-BPUU	Cessna 140	13722	N4251N	31. 3.89	Sherburn Aero Club Ltd	Sherburn in Elmet	28.11.02T
			NC4251N				
G-BPUW	Colt 90A HAFB	1436		12. 4.89	Huntair Ltd	London SE16	17. 7.02A
G-BPUX	Cessna 150J Commuter	15070619	N60851	25. 4.89	BCT Aero Club Leasing Ltd	(Chesterfield)	13. 2.97
G-BPVA	Cessna 172F Skyhawk	17252286	N8386U	13. 4.89	J.Pilkington & P.Makin	Barton	13. 7.03
					t/a South Lancashire Flyers Group		
G-BPVC*	Cameron V-77 HAFB	1302		7. 4.89	J.B.R.Elliot	Great Yarmouth	18. 9.97A
					(Cancelled 18.10.01 by CAA)		
G-BPVE	Bleriot XI 1909 rep	1	N1197	20. 6.89	Bianchi Aviation Film Services Ltd		
	(Built R.D.Henry, Texas 1967)				*(Op "Blue Max" Movie Aircraft Collection) (As "1197")*	Booker	29. 6.01P

G-BPVH	Piper Cub J-3 Prospector (Continental C85)	178C	CF-DRY	7. 4.89	D.E.Cooper-Maguire	Findon, Worthing	18. 8.02P
G-BPVI	Piper PA-32R-301 Saratoga SP	3213021	N91685	24. 4.89	M.T.Coppen	Goodwood	16. 7.01
G-BPVK	Varga 2150A Kachina	VAC85-77	N4626V	4. 5.89	H.W.Hall	Southend	12.12.02P
G-BPVM	Cameron V-77 HAFB	1970		4. 4.89	N.F.Mulliner t/a Royal Engineers Balloon Club *"Viscount"*	Chatham	6. 9.97A
G-BPVN	Piper PA-32R-301T Turbo Saratoga SP	32R-8029073	N8178W	14. 4.89	Y.Leysen	Goodwood	23. 8.04T
G-BPVO	Cassutt Racer IIIM (Continental O-200-A)	DG.1	N19DD	13. 4.89	A.J.Brown *"VooDoo"*	Old Buckenham	22. 9.98P
G-BPVP	Aerotek Pitts S-2B Special	5000	N5302M	13. 4.89	R P Millinship *(Damaged Clacton 19.6.92: on rebuild 5.93: new owner 12.01)*	Leicester	17. 5.95
G-BPVU	Thunder Ax7-77 HAFB	965		12. 4.89	B.J.Hammond	Chelmsford	28. 3.02T
G-BPVW	CASA I-131E Jungmann	2133	E3B-559	17. 5.89	C. & J.W.Labeij	(Pulborough)	26. 7.02P
G-BPVY	Cessna 172D Skyhawk	17250568	N2968U	20. 4.89	O.Scott-Tomlin	Denham	11. 6.02
G-BPVZ	Luscombe 8E Silvaire (Continental C85)	5565	N2838K NC2838K	9. 5.89	W.E.Gillham & P.Ryman	Croft Farm, Darlington	31. 5.02P
G-BPWA	Piper PA-28-161 Cherokee Warrior II	28-7816074	N47450	7. 4.89	Proudpixie Productions Ltd	(London NW10)	15. 5.04T
G-BPWB	Sikorsky S-61N	61822	EI-BHO G-BPWB/EI-BHO	4. 5.89	Bristow Helicopters Ltd *(Op HM Coastguard) "Portland Castle"*	Portland	10. 7.04T
G-BPWC	Cameron V-77 HAFB	1986		12. 4.89	H.B.Roberts "Hot Flush"	Bristol	29. 5.02T
G-BPWD	Cessna 120 (Continental O-240-E)	10026	N72839 NC72839	14. 4.89	M.W.Albery tr Peregrine Flying Group	Hucknall	27. 8.02P
G-BPWE	Piper PA-28-161 Warrior II	28-8116143	N8330P	2. 5.89	RPR Associates Ltd	Swansea	22. 6.02T
G-BPWG	Cessna 150M	15076707	(G-BPTK) N45029	10. 4.89	W.R.Spicer & I.D.Carling	Nanbeck Farm, Wilsford, Grantham	20. 8.04
G-BPWI	Bell 206B-3 JetRanger III	3087	9M-BSR VH-HXZ/ZK-HXX/XC-PFH	14. 4.89	M.J Coates t/a Warren Aviation	Goodwood	21. 8.04T
G-BPWK	Sportavia Fournier RF5B Sperber	51036	N56JM (D-KEAR)	17. 4.89	S.L.Reed	Usk	20. 8.02P
G-BPWL	Piper PA-25-235 Pawnee	25-2304	N6690Z G-BPWL/N6690Z	14. 4.89	Tecair Aviation Ltd	Shipdham	19. 4.03
G-BPWM	Cessna 150L	15072820	N1520Q	17. 4.89	M.E.Creasey	Crowfield	11.11.02
G-BPWN	Cessna 150L	15074325	N19308	17. 4.89	International Aerospace Engineering Ltd	Top Farm, Croydon	12. 9.02T
G-BPWP	Rutan LongEz (Continental O-240)	PFA 074A-11132		17. 4.89	J.F.O'Hara & A.J.Voyle	Denham	27. 6.02P
G-BPWR	Cessna R172K Hawk XPII	R1722953	N758AZ	21. 4.89	A.M.Skelton	Humberside	7.10.04
G-BPWS	Cessna 172P Skyhawk II	17274306	N51387	21. 4.89	Chartstone Ltd	Redhill	2. 8.04T
G-BPWT*	Cameron DG-19 Helium Airship	1772		18. 4.89	Airspace Outdoor Advertising Ltd *(Cancelled 23.10.00 by CAA)*	Southampton	3. 7.90A
G-BPWV*	Colt 56A HAFB	1444		21. 4.89	Not known *"Coopers Exeter"* *(Cancelled 4.8.98 by CAA) (Noted 2000)*	Newbury	
G-BPWW*	Focke-Wulf Piaggio FWP.149D *(Force landed near Lydd 17.5.98: cancelled 10.6.99) (Fuselage noted 7.99: current status unknown)*	087	OO-FDF D-EFDF/(D-EBDF)/West German AF 90+69/SC+332/AS+496	12. 6.89	J S Holborn t/a G-BPWW Group	Standalone Farm, Meppershall	23..4.01
G-BPXA	Piper PA-28-181 Archer II	28-8390064	N4305T	12. 5.89	D.Howdle & D.L.Heighington t/a Cherokee Flying Group	Netherthorpe	4. 6.04
G-BPXB	Glaser-Dirks DG-400	4-248		2. 5.89	G.C.Westgate t/a Guy Westgate & Syndicate Partners	Parham Park	25. 7.02
G-BPXE	Enstrom 280C Shark	1089	N379KH C-GMLH/N660H	21. 4.89	A.Healy	Littlehampden, Bucks	4. 1.02
G-BPXF	Cameron V-65 HAFB	2003		21. 4.89	D.Pascall *"Gwei-Lo"*	Croydon	
G-BPXH	Colt 17A Cloudhopper HAFB	667	OO-BWG	21. 4.89	Sport Promotion SRL	Belbo, Italy	8. 9.00A
G-BPXJ	Piper PA-28RT-201T Turbo Arrow IV	28R-8231023	N8061U	21. 4.89	K.M.Hollamby	Biggin Hill	7. 7.01
G-BPXX	Piper PA-34-200T Seneca II	34-7970069	N923SM N9556N	21. 4.89	E.C.& S.G.D.Clark t/a Laden Project Management Services	Biggin Hill	24. 7.04T
G-BPXY	Aeronca 11AC Chief	11AC-S-50	N3842E	10. 4.89	J.H.Tetley	Sherburn-in-Elmet	30. 8.02P
G-BPYI	Cameron O-77 HAFB	1988		9. 5.89	N.J.Logue	Pembroke Dock	25. 7.02A
G-BPYJ	Wittman W.8 Tailwind (Continental PC60)	PFA 031-11028		12. 5.89	J.Dixon	Bagby	19.10.00P
G-BPYK	Thunder Ax7-77 HAFB	1166		15. 5.89	A.R.Swinnerton *"Yorick"*	London EC2	29. 5.93
G-BPYL	Hughes 369D	100-0796D	N65AM G-BPYL/HB-XKT	10. 5.89	Morcorp (BVI) Ltd	Wolverhampton	8. 7.04T
G-BPYN	Piper J-3C-65 Cub (L-4H-PI)	11422	F-BFYN HB-OFN/43-30131	14. 3.79	D.W.Stubbs t/a The Aquila Group	White Waltham	7. 8.02P
G-BPYO	Piper PA-28-181 Archer II	2890114	SE-KIH	22. 5.89	Sherburn Aero Club Ltd	Sherburn in Elmet	29. 7.04T
G-BPYR	Piper PA-31 Navajo C	31-7812032	G-ECMA N27493	15. 5.89	Multi Ltd *(Op Adam Construction)*	Sturgate	28.11.01T
G-BPYS	Cameron O-77 HAFB	2008		9. 5.89	D.J.Goldsmith *"Aqualisa II"*	Edenbridge	14.12.99A
G-BPYT	Cameron V-77 HAFB	1984		9. 5.89	M.H.Redman	Sturminster Newton	

G-BPYV	Cameron V-77 HAFB	1992		17. 5.89	R.J.Shortall	Bath	13. 5.02A
					(Spa Vehicle Electrics titles)		
G-BPYY	Cameron A-180 HAFB	2013		11. 5.89	G.D.Fitzpatrick	Thame	28. 6.96T
G-BPYZ	Thunder Ax7-77 HAFB	1521		11. 5.89	J.E.Astall *"Axis"*	Hinton St.George	7. 7.96A
					(Stolen Crewkerne, Somerset 23.10.97: current status unknown)		
G-BPZA	Luscombe 8A Silvaire	4326	N1599K	18. 4.89	P J Kirkpatrick	Top Farm, Croydon	4. 7.02P
	(Continental A65)		NC1599K				
G-BPZB	Cessna 120	8898	N89853	25. 5.89	C. & M.A.Grime	Headcorn	18. 6.02P
	(Continental C90)		NC89853				
G-BPZC	Luscombe 8A Silvaire	4322	N1595K	6. 6.89	C C Lovell	(Winchester)	5. 7.90P
	(Continental A65)		NC1595K				
	(Damaged by gales Cranfield 25.1.90: used for spares 10.96) (Valid CofR 4.01: current status unknown)						
G-BPZD	SNCAN NC.858S	97	F-BEZD	26. 1.79	S.J.Gaveston, G.Richards & M.S.Regendanz		
	(Continental C90) *(Built as NC.854S with Continental C65)*					Headcorn	14. 5.02P
G-BPZE	Luscombe 8E Silvaire	3904	N1177K	6. 6.89	B.A.Webster	Seething	8.11.01P
	(Continental C85)		NC1177K		t/a WFG Luscombe Associates		
G-BPZI	Christen Eagle II	T.0001	N48BB	22. 5.89	R.J.Allan & A.J.Maxwell	Barton	18. 4.02P
	(Lycoming IO-360)				*"Thunder Eagle"*		
G-BPZK	Cameron O-120 HAFB	1982		7. 4.89	D.L.Smith *"Hot Stuff"*	Newbury	12. 5.97T
G-BPZM	Piper PA-28RT-201 Arrow IV		G-ROYW	12. 5.89	Airways Flight Training (Exeter) Ltd		
		28R-7918238	G-CRTI/SE-ICY			Exeter	9.10.04T
G-BPZP	Robin DR.400/180R Remorqueur	1471	D-EFZP	4. 5.89	Lasham Gliding Society Ltd	Lasham	23. 5.04
G-BPZS	Colt 105A HAFB	1312		25. 5.89	Magical Adventures Ltd	Chirk	2. 8.01A
					"Chamonix"		
G-BPZU	Scheibe SF-25C-2000 Falke	44471	D-KIAV	21. 7.89	D.A.Hatfield	Parham Park	12. 8.04
					t/a G-BPZU Group		
G-BPZY	Pitts S-1C Special	RN-1	N1159	15. 5.89	J.S.Mitchell	White Waltham	24. 5.02P
	(Lycoming O-320)						
G-BPZZ	Thunder Ax8-105 HAFB	1441		25. 5.89	Capricorn Balloons Ltd	Loughborough	27. 3.00T

G-BRAA – G-BRZZ

G-BRAF	Supermarine 394 Spitfire FR.XVIIIe	6S/663052	HS877 Indian AF/SM969	29.12.78	Wizzard Investments Ltd. *(As "SM969/D-A" ?)*	North Weald	23. 9.93P
G-BRAJ	Cameron V-77 HAFB	1876		25. 5.89	A.W.J.& C.Weston	Ross-on-Wye	
G-BRAK	Cessna 172N Skyhawk II	17273795	C-GBPN (N5438J)	23. 6.88	Rangecycle Ltd t/a Masonair *(Fuselage noted 6.01)*	Bodmin	14. 2.04T
G-BRAM*	Mikoyan MiG-21PF	NK	503 Hungarian AF	22. 5.89	Bournemouth Aviation Museum *(Cancelled 16.4.99 by CAA) (As "503" in Russian AF c/s)*	Bournemouth	
G-BRAR	Aeronca 7AC Champion	7AC-6564	N2978E NC2978E	14. 6.89	C.D.Ward	Wombleton	8.10.02P
G-BRAW	Pitts S-1C Special (Lycoming O-290)	52544	N24DB	24. 5.89	P.G.Bond & P.B.Hunter	Felthorpe	13. 6.02P
G-BRAX	Payne Knight Twister 85B (Continental O-200-A)	203	N979	24. 5.89	R.Earl	White Waltham	29. 9.93P
G-BRBA	Piper PA-28-161 Warrior II	28-7916109	N2090B	25. 5.89	R.Clarke & S.H.Pearce	Wolverhampton	29.11.04T
G-BRBB	Piper PA-28-161 Warrior II	28-8116030	N8260W	28. 6.89	Aeros Leasing Ltd	Gloucestershire	24.10.04T
G-BRBC	North American T-6G Texan *(Reported as c/n 182-155 ex 51-14469)*	182-156	MM54099 RR-56/51-14470	4. 9.92	A.P.Murphy *(On rebuild Audley End 9.90 - current status unknown)*	(Chigwell)	
G-BRBD	Piper PA-28-151 Cherokee Warrior	28-7415315	N41702	28. 6.89	W.E.Rispin t/a Bravo Delta Group *"Shaftesbury Belle"*	Compton Abbas	22. 3.02
G-BRBE	Piper PA-28-161 Warrior II	28-7916437	N2815D	13. 6.89	Solo Services Ltd *(Op Sussex Flying Club)*	Shoreham	17.12.01T
G-BRBG	Piper PA-28-180 Cherokee Archer	28-7505248	N3927X	12. 6.89	Ken MacDonald & Co	Stornoway	22. 8.04
G-BRBH	Cessna 150H	15069283	N50410	13. 6.89	J.Maffia	Panshanger	7. 8.04T
G-BRBI	Cessna 172N Skyhawk II	17269613	N737RJ	7. 7.89	M.D.Harcourt-Brown t/a G-BRBI Flying Group	Popham	3. 9.04
G-BRBJ	Cessna 172M Skyhawk II	17267492	N73476	26. 5.89	L.C.Macknight	Elstree	12. 1.02
G-BRBK	Robin DR.400/180 Regent	1915		31. 5.89	R.Kemp	Thruxton	17.10.04
G-BRBL	Robin DR.400/180 Regent	1920		5. 7.89	C.A.Marren	Upavon	6. 3.04
G-BRBM	Robin DR.400/180 Regent	1921		5. 7.89	R.W.Davies	Little Robhurst Farm, Woodchurch	24. 1.02
G-BRBN	Pitts S-1S Special (Lycoming O-360)	G.3	N81BG	14. 7.89	D.R.Evans	Gloucestershire	14. 6.02P
G-BRBO	Cameron V-77 HAFB	1877		30. 5.89	M B Murphy *"Patches"*	Cheltenham	10. 6.021
G-BRBP	Cessna 152 II	15284915	N5324P	14. 6.89	Staverton Flying Services Ltd	Gloucestershire	24. 7.04T
G-BRBS	Bensen B.8M (Rotax 503)	PFA G/01-1039		30. 5.89	K.T.MacFarlane *(Under construction 6.00)*	(Kilmacolm, Renfrew)	
G-BRBT	Trotter Ax3-20 HAFB	RMT-001		13. 6.89	R.M.Trotter	Bristol	
G-BRBU*	Colt 17A Cloudhopper HAFB	1506		12. 6.89	Virgin Airship & Balloon Co Ltd *"National Theatre" (Cancelled 8.11.01 as wfu & stored)*	Telford	29. 5.90A
G-BRBW	Piper PA-28-140 Cherokee Cruiser	28-7425153	N40737	3. 7.89	R.W.Langley t/a Cherokee Cruiser Aircraft Group	Shoreham	1.11.04
G-BRBX	Piper PA-28-181 Cherokee Archer II	28-7690185	N8674E	20. 7.89	M.J.Ireland t/a Archer Air	Leicester	18. 2.02T
G-BRBY	Robinson R22 Beta	1027		15. 6.89	D Brown	Cumbernauld	26. 7.04T
G-BRCA	Jodel D.112 *(Built Ets Valladeau)*	1203	F-BLIU	11. 7.89	R.C.Jordan	Turweston	3. 4.02P
G-BRCD	Cessna A152 Aerobat	A1520796	N7377L	8. 6.89	D.E.Simmons t/a Charlie Delta Group	Shoreham	30. 8.04
G-BRCE	Pitts S-1C Special (Lycoming O-290)	1001	N4611G	22. 6.89	R.D.Rogers *(Op Skylark Aerobatic Co)*	Hulcote Farm, Salford, Beds	25.11.97P
G-BRCF	Montgomerie-Bensen B.8MR (Rotax 532)	PFA G/01A-1131		12. 6.89	J.S.Walton	Mold	30.10.91P
G-BRCG	Grob G-109	6077	N64BG D-KGRO	15. 6.89	I.R.Taylor	(Sutton Coldfield)	15. 1.04
G-BRCI	Pitts S-1C Special (Lycoming O-320)	4668	N351S	6. 7.89	G.L.A.Vandormael	Wevelgem, Belgium	18. 3.04P
G-BRCJ	Cameron H-20 HAFB	2028		13. 6.89	P.de Cock	Waasmunster, Belgium	18. 3.02A
G-BRCM	Cessna 172L Skyhawk	17259960	N38600	19. 6.89	S.G.E.Plessis & D.C.C.Handley *(Op Osprey Flying Club)*	Cranfield	22. 7.02T
G-BRCO*	Cameron H-20 HAFB	2030		19. 6.89	M.Davies *"Shell Unleaded" (Cancelled 27.11.01 by CAA)*	Callington, Cornwall	17. 6.97A
G-BRCT	Denney Kitfox mk.2 (Rotax 582)	396 & PFA 172-11521		23. 6.89	M.L.Roberts	Bodmin	1. 1.02P
G-BRCV	Aeronca 7AC Champion (Continental A65)	7AC-282	N81661 NC81661	19. 9.89	J.M.Gale	Westacott Farm, Crediton	25. 6.02P

G-BRCW	Aeronca 11BC Chief	11AC-366	N85954	16.10.89	R.B.McComish	Bow, Totnes	4. 6.02P
	(Continental C85)		NC85954				
	(Registered p/i & c/n match but correct p/i is N85964 c/n 11AC-386)						
G-BRDB	Zenair CH-701 STOL	PFA 187-11412		11. 7.89	D.L.Bowtell	(Ware)	
G-BRDC	Thunder Ax7-77 HAFB	1547		26. 6.89	P.J.Bish & C.Kunert	Hungerford	18. 1.00A
					t/a Zebedee Balloon Service *"Purple Rising"*		
G-BRDD	Mudry CAP.10B	224		3. 8.88	R.D.Dickson	Coal Aston/Gamston	14.12.03
G-BRDE	Thunder Ax7-77 HAFB	1538		22. 6.89	C.C.Brash *"Veronica"*	Maidenhead	24. 7.96A
G-BRDF	Piper PA-28-161 Cherokee Warrior II		N1139Q	26. 6.89	White Waltham Airfield Ltd	White Waltham	19. 5.02T
		28-7716085			*(Op West London Aero Services)*		
G-BRDG	Piper PA-28-161 Cherokee Warrior II		N44934	26. 6.89	White Waltham Airfield Ltd	White Waltham	10.12.01T
		28-7816047			*(Op West London Aero Services)*		
G-BRDJ	Luscombe 8A Silvaire	3411	N71984	28. 6.89	J.D.Parker		
	(Continental A65)		NC71984			Franklyn's Field, Chewton Mendip	29.11.02P
G-BRDM	Piper PA-28-161 Cherokee Warrior II		N8464F	26. 6.89	White Waltham Airfield Ltd	White Waltham	4.12.04T
		28-7716004			*(Op West London Aero Services)*		
G-BRDN	SOCATA MS.880B Rallye Club	1212	OY-DTV	14. 7.89	B.J.D.Peatfield	Redhill	27. 4.02
G-BRDO	Cessna 177B Cardinal II	17702166	N35030	13. 7.89	I.Jane & A.Lidster,	Teesside	21.12.01
					t/a Cardinal Aviation		
G-BRDP	Colt Jumbo SS HAFB	1526		3. 7.89	Virgin Airship & Balloon Co Ltd		
						Florida, USA	3. 8.94A
G-BRDT	Cameron DP-70 Hot-Air Airship	2029		3. 7.89	Tim Balloon Promotion Airships Ltd		
	(1 x Konig SD 570)					Bristol	23.10.01A
G-BRDV*	Supermarine Spitfire Prototype rep			3. 7.89	Replica Spitfire Ltd	(Sandown)	18. 2.95P
	(Jaguar V-12 350hp) HD36/001 & PFA 130-10796				*(As "K5054" in RAF c/s)*		
			(Cancelled as wfu 19.5.00 & believed acquired by Hall of Aviation, Southampton)				
G-BRDW	Piper PA-24-180 Comanche	24-1733	N6612P	12. 3.90	I.P.Gibson	Southampton	19.12.02
G-BREA	Bensen B.8MR	PFA G/01-1006		6. 7.89	T.J.Deane	Henstridge	24.10.00P
	(Rotax 503)						
G-BREB	Piper J-3C-65 Cub	7705	N41094	3. 7.89	L.W.& O.Usherwood	Rochester	21. 8.02P
			NC41094				
G-BREE	Whittaker MW7	PFA 171-11497		22. 6.89	G.Hawkins	Newton Peverill	24. 7.01P
	(Rotax 503)						
G-BREH	Cameron V-65 HAFB	2049		7. 7.89	S.E. & V.D.Hurst *"Promise"*	Mansfield	7. 6.01A
G-BREM*	Air Command 532 Elite			20. 7.89	T.W.Freeman	Wimpole Royston	25. 3.91P
	(Rotax 532)	0614 & PFA G/04-1139		*(Stored 7.91: cancelled 16.11.01 by CAA: current status unknown)*			
G-BRER	Aeronca 7AC Champion	7AC-6758	N3157E	12. 7.89	I.Sinnett	Bodmin	8. 7.02P
	(Continental A65)		NC3157E		t/a Rabbit Flight		
G-BREU	Montgomerie-Bensen B.8			20. 7.89	J.S.Firth	Sherburn-in-Elmet	31. 5.02P
	(Rotax 582)	PFA G/01A-1137					
G-BREY	Taylorcraft BC-12D	7299	N43640	14. 7.89	R.J.Pitts	Leicester	5. 6.02P
			NC43640		t/a BREY Group		
G-BRFB	Rutan LongEz	PFA 074A-10646		14. 7.89	R.Young	Perth	3. 7.02P
	(Lycoming O-290)						
G-BRFE	Cameron V-77 HAFB	1835		20. 7.89	D.L.C.Nelmes	Bristol	30. 7.02A
					t/a Esmerelda Balloon Syndicate *"Esmerelda"*		
G-BRFH*	Colt 90A HAFB	1543		14. 7.89	Polydron International Ltd	Kemble	14. 3.97A
					"Polydron" (Cancelled 9.11.01 as wfu & stored)		
G-BRFI	Aeronca 7DC Champion	7AC-4609	N1058E	1. 8.89	A.C.Lines	Leicester	19. 2.91P
	(Continental C85)		NC1058E		*(Damaged 1990: on rebuild 4.96)*		
G-BRFJ	Aeronca 11AC Chief	11AC-796	N9163E	28. 7.89	J.M.Mooney	Lochview House, Limerigg	11. 9.02P
	(Continental A65)		NC9163E		*(Dismantled 7.01)*		
G-BRFL	Piper PA-38-112 Tomahawk	38-79A0431	N2416F	17. 8.89	Teesside Flight Centre Ltd	Teesside	13. 8.02T
G-BRFM	Piper PA-28-161 Warrior II		N2234P	17.10.89	Atlantic Air Transport Ltd	Coventry	15.12.01T
		28-7916279					
G-BRFN	Piper PA-38-112 Tomahawk	38-79A0397	N2326F	23.10.89	Light Aircraft Leasing (UK) Ltd	Norwich	10.12.03T
G-BRFO	Cameron V-77 HAFB	2025		6. 7.89	N.J.Bland	Oxford	31. 7.00A
					t/a Hedgehoppers Balloon Group *"Lurcher"*		
G-BRFR*	Cameron N-105 HAFB	2042		14. 7.89	Balloon Preservation Group	Kirdford	6.12.93A
				"Rover" (Cancelled 9.5.97 as WFU) (Badly damaged, spares use only)			
G-BRFW	Montgomerie-Bensen B.8 Two-Seat			20. 7.89	A.J.Barker	(Dundee)	9. 4.02P
	(Rotax 582)	PFA G/01-1073					
G-BRFX	Pazmany PL-4A	PFA 017-10079		14. 7.89	D.E.Hills	(Ipswich)	
	(VW 1700)						
G-BRGD	Cameron O-84 HAFB	2043		20. 7.89	J.R.H. & M.A.Ashworth	Newquay	
G-BRGE	Cameron N-90 HAFB	2047		20. 7.89	Oakfield Farm Products Ltd *"Oakfield Farm Products"*		
						Broadway, Worcester	15.12.99A
G-BRGF	Luscombe 8E Silvaire	5475	N23FP	20. 7.89	N.Surman	RAF Henlow	11. 5.02P
	(Continental C85)		N944BL/N2748K/NC2748K		t/a Luscombe Flying Group		
G-BRGG	Luscombe 8A Silvaire	3795	N1068K	20. 7.89	M.A.Lamprell	Popham	22. 8.02P
	(Continental A65)		NC1068K				
G-BRGI	Piper PA-28-180 Cherokee E	28-5827	N77VG	24. 7.89	Golf India Aviation Ltd	Redhill	31. 3.02
			N11VG				

G-BRGN	British Aerospace Jetstream Srs.3102	637	G-BLHC G-31-637	20. 3.87	BAE Systems (Corporate Air Travel) Ltd	Warton	16. 5.02T
G-BRGO	Air Command 532 Elite (Rotax 532)	0615 & PFA G/04-1149		7. 8.89	A.McCredie *(Airframe noted 5.00)*	Kingsmuir Sorbie	13. 2.91P
G-BRGP*	Colt Flying Stork SS HAFB	1409		25. 7.89	Not known *"Great Eggspectations"*	(USA)	NE(A)
	(Cancelled 10.3.95 by CAA: noted Albuquerque, New Mexico, USA 10.00)						
G-BRGT	Piper PA-32-260 Cherokee Six	32-658	N3744W	7.11.89	P.Cowley	East Midlands	28. 6.02
G-BRGW	Barritault JB-01 Minicab (Continental O-200-A)	PFA 1823		13.11.78	R.G.White	Hildon-le-Noble, Hants	18. 6.02P
G-BRGX	Rotorway Executive (Rotorway RW 152D)	3597		3. 8.89	D.W.J.Lee	South Burlingham, Norwich	8. 6.00P
G-BRHA	Piper PA-32RT-300 Lance II	32R-7985076	N2093P	27. 7.89	D.J.Chatterton & P.MacKinnon t/a Lance G-BRHA Group	Earls Colne/Southend	29.11.04
G-BRHB	Boeing-Stearman B75N1 (N2S-3) Kaydet	75-6508 AC	EC-AID N67955/Bu.05334	10. 8.89	P R Bennett & R Sage *(New owners 12.01)*	Priory Farm, Tibenham	
G-BRHC*	Cameron V-77 HAFB	1842		3. 8.89	Golf Centres Balloons Ltd *"Green Dragon"* *(Cancelled 8.11.01 as wfu: current status unknown)*	Gargonza, Italy	30. 8.94T
G-BRHG	Colt 90A HAFB	1568		11. 9.89	Bath University Students Union *"Badgerline"*	Bath	9. 8.02A
G-BRHL	Montgomerie-Bensen B.8MR (Rotax 503)	PFA G/01A-1123		7. 8.89	R.M.Savage & T.M.Jones	Carlisle	23. 7.02P
G-BRHO	Piper PA-34-200 Seneca	34-7350037	N15222	20. 9.89	D.A.Lewis	Luton	5. 9.04
G-BRHP	Aeronca O-58B Defender (Continental A65)	058B-8533	N58JR N46536/43-1923	2. 8.89	C.J.Willis *(As "3-1923" in US Army c/s)*	RAF Giola dell Colle, Italy	22. 2.01P
	(If US Army serial is correct, type should be L-3C-AE Grasshopper)						
G-BRHR	Piper PA-38-112 Tomahawk	38-79A0969	N2377P	21. 8.89	J.Davies	Hawarden	28. 9.04T
G-BRHT	Piper PA-38-112 Tomahawk	38-79A0199	N2474C	4. 8.89	Auto Corporation Ltd	Hawarden	9. 8.04T
G-BRHW	de Havilland DH.82A Tiger Moth	85612	7Q-YMY VP-YMY/ZS-DLB/SAAF 4606/DE671	26. 7.89	P.J. & A.J.Borsberry *(On rebuild 6.95*	Kidmore End, Reading	
G-BRHX	Luscombe 8E Silvaire (Continental C90)	5114	N176M N2387K/NC2387K	8. 8.89	J.Lakin	Eaglescott	1. 8.02P
G-BRHY	Luscombe 8E Silvaire (Continental C85)	5138	N2411K NC2411K	8. 8.89	D.Lofts & A.R.W.Taylor	Sleap	29. 4.02P
G-BRHZ*	Stephens Akro Z (Lycoming IO-360) *(Aka "Astro 235")*	A-235	N35EJ	20.12.89	T.A.Shears *(Cancelled 22.5.01 by CAA) (Stored dismantled in hangar 10 01)*	Membury	16. 4.98P
G-BRIA	Cessna 310L	310L0010	N2210F	4. 8.89	B.J.Tucker & R.C.Pugsley	Kemble	15.10.01T
G-BRID*	Cessna U206A Super Skywagon	U2060574	N4874F	7. 5.87	British Skysports	Grindale	20. 5.93
	(Cancelled 4.10.93 as WFU: used as para-trainer 1.96: current status unknown)						
G-BRIE	Cameron N-77 HAFB	2076		8. 8.89	S.F.Redman	Sturminster Newton	24. 6.02A
G-BRIF	Boeing 767-204ER	24736	(PH-AHM) G-BRIF	10. 3.90	Britannia Airways Ltd *"Lord Horatio Nelson"*	Luton	18.11.02T
G-BRIG	Boeing 767-204ER	24757	(PH-AHN) G-BRIG	10. 4.90	Britannia Airways Ltd *"Eglantyne Jebb"*	Luton	17. 4.03T
G-BRIH	Taylorcraft BC-12D (Continental A75)	7421	N43762 NC43762	24. 8.89	A.D.Duke	Leicester	11. 9.02P
G-BRII	Zenair CH-600 Zodiac	PFA 162-11392		18. 8.89	A.C.Bowdrey *(Under build 2000)*	(Hemel Hempstead)	
G-BRIJ	Taylorcraft F-19	F-119	N3863T	23. 8.89	K.E.Ballington	Yeatsall Farm, Abbots Bromley	12. 6.01P
G-BRIK	Nipper T.66S RA45 Srs.3B (VW 1834)	PFA 025-10174 *(Rebuild of G-AVKH)*		26. 4.77	P.R.Bentley *(Fuselage away on rebuild 11.01)*	Roughay Farm, Bishops Waltham	1. 8.02P
G-BRIL	Piper J-5A Cub Cruiser (Continental A75)	5-572	N35183 NC35183	2. 8.89	P.L.Jobes	Spilhall Farm, Co.Durham	19.12.02P
G-BRIM*	Cameron O-160 HAFB	1856		10. 8.89	Golf Centres Balloons Ltd *(Cancelled 8.11.01 as wfu: current status unknown)*	Bridport	11. 8.93T
G-BRIO	Turner Super T-40A (Continental O-200-A) *(Regd incorrectly as PFA 104-10736)*	PFA 104-10636		7. 8.89	R.W.L.Breckell t/a BRIO Flyers	(Liverpool)	15. 8.02P
G-BRIR	Cameron V-56 HAFB	2056		17. 8.89	H.G.Davies & C.Dowd *"Spirit of Century" (Skyviews Windows titles)*	Cheltenham	6. 9.97A
G-BRIS	Steen Skybolt (Lycoming IO-360)	01	N870MC	30. 8.89	Little Bear Ltd	Exeter	3. 1.02P
G-BRIV	SOCATA TB-9 Tampico Club	939		24. 8.89	P.M.Harrison	Wickenby	10. 2.03T
G-BRIY	Taylorcraft DF-65 (Continental A65) *(Built as TG-6 glider)*	6183	N59687 NC59687/42-58678	1. 2.90	S R Potts *(As "42-58678/IY" in L-2A USAAC c/s) (New owner 1.02)*	(Morpeth)	10. 7.98P
G-BRJA	Luscombe 8A Silvaire (Continental A65)	3744	N1017K NC1017K	12. 9.89	A.D.Keen	Dunkeswell	17. 4.02P
G-BRJB	Zenair CH-600 Zodiac	6-1283 & PFA 162-11573		2. 8.89	D.J.Hunter *(On build 7.95: current status unknown)*	Priory Farm, Tibbenham	
G-BRJC	Cessna 120 (Continental C85)	12077	N1833N NC1833N	21. 8.89	One Twenty Flyers Ltd	Nottingham	21. 3.02P
G-BRJK	Luscombe 8A Silvaire (Continental A65)	4205	N1478K NC1478K	21. 8.89	C.J.L.Peat & M.Richardson	Popham	11. 4.02P

G-BRJL	Piper PA-15 Vagabond (Continental C85)	15-157	N4370H NC4370H	21. 8.89	C.P.Ware & A R Williams	Garston Farm, Marshfield	8. 7.02P
G-BRJN	Pitts S-1C Special (Lycoming O-320)	1-MA	N6A	23. 8.89	W.Chapel	Sherburn-in-Elmet	16.11.01P
G-BRJR	Piper PA-38-112 Tomahawk	38-79A0144	N2598B	31. 8.89	Chester Aviation Ltd	Hawarden	31. 3.02T
G-BRJT	Cessna 150H	15068426	N44SS N22649	31. 8.89	B.J.Christopher & R.J.C.Borchardt t/a Pink Panther Flying Group	Kemble	30. 8.04T
G-BRJV	Piper PA-28-161 Cadet	2841167	N9185G	24. 8.89	Newcastle upon Tyne Aero Club Ltd	Newcastle	4.12.01T
G-BRJW	Bellanca 7GCBC Citabria 150S	1200-80	OO-LPG	7. 4.82	F.A.L.Castleden & A.J.Sillis	Horham	24. 8.03
G-BRJY	Rand-Robinson KR-2 (Revmaster 2100D)	PFA 129-11308		22. 8.89	R.E.Taylor *(Under restoration 6.00)*	(Bonar Bridge)	23. 5.96P
G-BRKA*	Luscombe 8F Silvaire (Continental C90)	5084	N2357K NC2357K	13. 3.89	H.Savage-Jones *(Cancelled 20.4.99 as destroyed: on rebuild 8.01)*	Bodmin	1. 8.99P
G-BRKC	Auster V J/1 Autocrat	2749	F-BFYT	31. 8.89	J.W.Conlon	High Easter	18. 9.02P
G-BRKD*	Piaggio P.149D	306	D-EAMS 92+10/AC+457/AS+457	15. 9.89	P.E.H.Scott *(Cancelled 28.5.99 by CAA: noted 9.00)*	Standalone Farm, Meppershall	5.11.92
G-BRKH	Piper PA-28-236 Dakota	28-7911003	N21444	30. 8.89	Dateworld Ltd	(Romsey)	28.12.04
G-BRKL	Cameron H-34 HAFB	2075		29. 8.89	P.L.Harrison	Rushden, Northampton	18. 3.01A
G-BRKN	Robinson R22 Mariner	0578M	N2454M	5. 9.89	Sloane Helicopters Ltd *(Wreck stored 5.01)*	Sywell	9. 6.99
G-BRKO	Oldfield Baby Great Lakes	CMK.1	N8GL	18. 1.90	R.Trickett	(Downham Market)	9. 1.02P
G-BRKR	Cessna 182R Skylane II	18268468	N9896E	2. 6.89	A.R.D.Brooker	Springfield Farm, Ettington	27. 1.05
G-BRKW	Cameron V-77 HAFB	2093		1. 9.89	T.J.Parker	Burnham-on-Crouch	29.12.01
G-BRKX	Air Command 532 Elite (Rotax 532)	0619 & PFA G/04-1150		8. 9.89	K.Davis	Alfreton, Derbyshire	10.12.90P
G-BRKY	Viking Dragonfly mk II (VW 2180)	PFA 139-11117		7. 9.89	G.D.Price *(Stored 3.97: current status unknown)*	Deanland,.Hailsham	8. 6.94P
G-BRLB	Air Command 532 Elite	0622		4. 9.89	F.G.Shepherd *(Valid CofR 3.00: current status unknown)*	(Great Orton)	
G-BRLF	Campbell Cricket (Rotax 503)	PFA G/03-1077		6. 9.89	D.Wood	Holbeach	1.12.00P
G-BRLG	Piper PA-28RT-201T Turbo Arrow IV	28R-8431027	N4379P N9600N	12. 9.89	C.G.Westwood	RAF Shawbury	11. 1.02
G-BRLH*	Air Command 532 Elite	0623 & PFA G/04-1148		12. 9.89	Childs Garages (Sherborne) Ltd *(Stored 4.96: cancelled 26.1.99 by CAA: current status unknown)*	Henstridge	28.12.90P
G-BRLI	Piper J-5A Cub Cruiser (Lycoming O-290)	5-822	N35951 NC35951	23. 8.89	Little Bear Ltd	Exeter	16. 6.02P
G-BRLK*	Air Command 532 Elite	0618 & PFA G/04-1155		7. 9.89	G.L.Hunt *(Used for spares 1998: cancelled 10.3.99 by CAA: current status unknown)*	Ripley, Derbyshire	1. 1.91P
G-BRLL	Cameron A-105 HAFB	2032		7. 9.89	A.J.Street *(Chris Evans Ltd titles)*	Exeter	27.11.01T
G-BRLO	Piper PA-38-112 Tomahawk	38-78A0621	N2397K N9680N	26.10.89	A.H.McVicar *(Noted 11.01)*	Carlisle	25. 2.04T
G-BRLP	Piper PA-38-112 Tomahawk	38-78A0011	N9301T	4.10.89	P D Brooks	Inverness	5. 4.04T
G-BRLR	Cessna 150G	15064822	N4772X	4.10.89	D.Carr & M.R.Muter	Newcastle	10. 5.04
G-BRLS	Thunder Ax7-77 HAFB	1603		29. 9.89	Elizabeth C.Meek	Oswestry	5. 8.01A
G-BRLT	Colt 77A HAFB	1588		12. 9.89	D.Bareford *"Pro-Sport"*	Kidderminster	10. 6.02A
G-BRLV	CCF Harvard 4	CCF4-194	N90448 RCAF 20403	14. 9.89	Extraviation Ltd *"Texan Belle" (As "93542/LTA-542" in 6148th TCS USAF c/s)*	North Weald	7.11.02P
G-BRLX*	Cameron N-77 HAFB	2095		13. 9.89	Balloon Preservation Group *"National Power" (Cancelled 23.10.01 by CAA)*	Kirdford	1. 6.96A
G-BRMA*	Westland WS-51 Dragonfly HR.5	WA/H/50	WG719	15. 6.78	E.D.ap Rees t/a The Helicopter Museum *(Cancelled 30.3.89 as WFU) (As "WG719")*	Weston-super-Mare	
G-BRMB*	Bristol 192 Belvedere HC.1	13347	7997M XG452	15. 6.78	E.D.ap Rees t/a The Helicopter Museum *(Cancelled 3.7.96 as WFU) (As "XG452")*	Weston-super-Mare	
G-BRME	Piper PA-28-181 Cherokee Archer II	28-7790105	OY-BTA	14. 9.89	Keen Leasing Ltd	Belfast	21. 4.02T
G-BRMG	Supermarine 384 Seafire F.XVI	FLWA.25488	A2055 SX336	19. 9.89	T.J.Manna *(Sold 12.01) (As "SX336")*	Cranfield	
G-BRMI	Cameron V-65 HAFB	2104		14. 9.89	M.Davies *"Sapphire"*	Callington, Cornwall	25. 8.01A
G-BRMJ*	Piper PA-38-112 Tomahawk	38-79A0784	N2316N	15. 9.89	Aerohire Ltd *(Op Wellesbourne Aviation) (Cancelled 24.10.00 by CAA)*	Wellesbourne Mountford	25. 4.96T
G-BRML	Piper PA-38-112 Tomahawk	38-79A1017	N2510P	3.10.89	P.H.Rogers	Wolverhampton	3. 6.02T
G-BRMS	Piper PA-28RT-201 Arrow IV	28R-8118004	N82708	25. 9.89	Fleetbridge Ltd	White Waltham	22. 6.02
G-BRMT	Cameron V-31 Air Chair HAFB	2038		31. 8.89	T.C.Hinton	Tunbridge Wells	
G-BRMU	Cameron V-77 HAFB	2109		19. 9.89	K.J. & G.R Ibbotson	Gloucester	

G-BRMV	Cameron O-77 HAFB	2103		25. 9.89	P.D.Griffiths *"Viscount"*	Southampton	29. 6.02A
G-BRMW	Whittaker MW7	PFA 171-11395		25. 9.89	N.Crisp	Sittles Farm, Alrewas	15.11.01P
	(Rotax 532)						
G-BRNC	Cessna 150M Commuter	15078833	N704SG	29. 9.89	D.C.Bonsall	Netherthorpe	9. 9.02T
G-BRND	Cessna 152 II	15283776	N5148B	7.11.89	T.M. & M.L.Jones	Derby	28. 3.02T
					(Op Derby Aero Club)		
G-BRNE	Cessna 152 II	15284248	N5082L	4.10.89	Redhill Air Services Ltd	Shoreham	2. 3.03T
					(Op Sky Leisure)		
G-BRNJ	Piper PA-38-112 Tomahawk	38-79A0415	N2395F	22. 9.89	Cardiff Wales Aviation Services Ltd		
						Cardiff	4.11.02T
G-BRNK	Cessna 152 II	15280479	N24969	22. 9.89	Sheffield Aero Club Ltd	Netherthorpe	18. 2.02T
G-BRNM	Chichester-Miles Leopard	002		17.10.89	Chichester-Miles Consultants Ltd		
						Bournemouth	
G-BRNN	Cessna 152 II	15284735	N6452M	22. 9.89	Sheffield Aero Club Ltd	Netherthorpe	23.12.01T
G-BRNT	Robin DR.400/180 Regent	1935		3.10.89	M.J.Cowham	Top Farm, Croydon	20.12.01
G-BRNU	Robin DR.400/180 Regent	1937		31.10.89	November Uniform Travel Syndicate Ltd		
						White Waltham	19. 5.02
G-BRNV	Piper PA-28-181 Cherokee Archer II		N2537Q	7.12.89	B.S.Hobbs	Goodwood	10. 3.02
		28-7790402					
G-BRNW	Cameron V-77 HAFB	2138		2.10.89	N.Robertson & G.Smith	Truro/Bristol	9. 8.02A
					"Mr Blue Sky"		
G-BRNX	Piper PA-22-150 Tri-Pacer	22-2945	N2610P	3.10.89	C.A.Robbins	(Royston)	19.12.02
G-BRNZ	Piper PA-32-300 Cherokee Six B		N4229R	7. 2.90	L.I.Bailey	(Daventry)	4. 6.02T
		32-40594			t/a Longfellow Flying Group		
G-BROB	Cameron V-77 HAFB	2073		29. 8.89	R.W.Richardson	Cardiff	18. 3.01A
G-BROE	Cameron N-65 HAFB	2098		5.10.89	R.H.Sanderson *"Lancia Dedra"*	Nuneaton	3. 8.97A
G-BROG	Cameron V-65 HAFB	2121		6. 9.89	R.Kunert *"The Dodger"*	Wokingham	13. 1.02A
G-BROH	Cameron O-90 HAFB	2120		6.10.89	P A.Wenlock *"Linde"*	Stretton, Staffs	1. 8.99T
G-BROI	CFM Streak Shadow			16.11.89	G.W.Rowbotham	Wymeswold	18. 7.00P
	(Rotax 532) K.115-SA & PFA 161-11586						
G-BROJ*	Colt 31A HAFB	1468		6.10.89	Virgin Airship & Balloon Co Ltd	Telford	23. 9.92A
					"Fly Virgin" (Cancelled 8.11.01 as wfu & stored)		
G-BROL	Colt AS-80 Mk.II Hot-Air Airship			6.10.89	Ballonwerbung Hamburg GmbH		
	(Rotax 462)	1578				Hamburg, Germany	21. 6.02A
G-BROM*	ICA IS-28M2A	04A		5.12.77	Not known	Cuatro Vientos, Spain	18. 8.87
			(Cancelled 24.2.92 by CAA: open storage/derelict 4.95: current status unknown)				
G-BROO*	Luscombe 8E Silvaire	6154	N75297	28. 9.89	(P Bush)	RAF Kinloss	30. 9.93P
	(Cont PC.60)		N1527B/NC1527B				
					(Damaged landing Enstone 19.6.93: wreck purchased 10.01 for rebuild)		
G-BROP	Van's RV-4	3	N19AT	25.10.89	K.E.Armstrong		
	(Lycoming O-360)					Armshold Farm, Kingston, Cambs	22. 8.02P
G-BROR	Piper J-3C-65 Cub	10885	F-BHMQ	7.12.89	J.H.Bailey & A.P.J.Wiseman	Sturgate	25. 6.02P
	(L-4H-PI)		43-29594		t/a White Hart Flying Group		
G-BROX	Robinson R22 Beta	1127	N8061V	13.10.89	P.Malone & R.Hill	(Richmond, Surrey)	9.11.04T
					t/a Richmond Helicopters		
G-BROY	Cameron O-90 HAFB	2173		6. 9.89	T.G.S.Dixon	Bromsgrove	27. 9.02A
					"Dixon Furnace Division"		
G-BROZ	Piper PA-18-150 Super Cub	18-6754	HB-ORC	20. 9.89	P.G.Kynsey	Rushett Manor, Chessington	7. 3.02T
			N9572D				
G-BRPE	Cessna 120	13326	N3068N	11.10.89	J.M.Fowler	Nottingham	4. 9.01P
	(Continental C85)		NC3068N				
G-BRPF	Cessna 120	9902	N72723	11.10.89	D.Sharp	Breighton	19. 5.02P
	(Continental C85)		NC72723				
G-BRPG	Cessna 120	9882	N72703	11.10.89	I.C.Lomax	Ottringham	29. 8.94P
	(Continental C85)		NC72703				
G-BRPH	Cessna 120	12137	N1893N	11.10.89	J.A.Cook	Pent Farm, Postling, Kent	1. 8.02P
	(Continental C85)		NC1893N				
G-BRPJ	Cameron N-90 HAFB	2071		11. 9.89	Paul Johnson	Consett	10. 3.99T
					t/a Cloud Nine Balloon Co *"Presto"*		
G-BRPK	Piper PA-28-140 Cherokee Cruiser		N15449	17.11.89	J.P.A.Gomes	Cascais, Portugal	17. 6.02
		28-7325070					
G-BRPL	Piper PA-28-140 Cherokee Cruiser		N15771	13.10.89	Comed Aviation Ltd	Blackpool	10. 8.02T
		28-7325160					
G-BRPM	Nipper T.66 Srs.3B	PFA 025-11038		4. 3.85	T.C.Horner	(Barrhead)	
					(Under construction 6.00)		
G-BRPO	Enstrom 280C Shark	1092	N636H	13.10.89	C.M.Evans & J.W.Blaylock	(Boston)	24. 5.02
G-BRPP	Brookland Hornet	DC-1		16.10.89	B.J.L.P.& W.J.A.L.de Saar		
	(VW 1776)				*(For rebuild 2000)*	(Great Yarmouth)	19. 8.93P
G-BRPR	Aeronca L-3C Defender	058B-8823	N49880	17.10.89	C.S.Tolchard	Earls Colne	20. 6.02P
	(Continental A65)		43-1952		*(As "31952" in US Army c/s)*		
G-BRPS	Cessna 177B Cardinal	17702101	N34935	23.10.89	R.C.Tebbett	Shobdon	12. 1.02
G-BRPT	Rans S-10 Sakota	PFA 194-11554		18.10.89	B.G.Morris	Dunkeswell	17. 6.00P
	(Rotax 532)						

G-BRPU	Beechcraft 76 Duchess	ME-140	N6007Z	17.10.89	Leeds Flying School Ltd	Leeds-Bradford	4.10.04T
G-BRPV	Cessna 152 II	15285228	N6311Q	6.11.89	GEM Rewinds Ltd	Coventry	7. 2.02T
G-BRPX	Taylorcraft BC-12D	6462	N39208	12.12.89	R.A.C.Lees	Leicester	11. 9.02P
	(Continental A65)		NC39208		t/a The BRPX Group		
G-BRPY	Piper PA-15 Vagabond	15-141	N4356H	23.10.89	D.J.Palmer	Popham	13. 6.02P
	(Continental C85)		NC4356H				
G-BRPZ	Luscombe 8A Silvaire	911	N22089	13.12.89	S.L. & J.P.Waring		
	(Continental A65)		NC22089			Shacklewell Lodge, Empingham	30. 5.02P
G-BRRA	Supermarine 361 Spitfire LF.IXc		SM.29	10.10.89	Historic Flying Ltd	Duxford	13. 9.02P
	(Regd as c/n CBAF.8185)	CBAF.IX.1875	Belg AF/R.Neth AF H.59/H.119/Fokker B-1/MK912				
					(As "MK912/SH-L" of 350 (Belgian) Squadron)		
G-BRRB*	Luscombe 8E Silvaire	2611	N71184	23.10.89	G.Crocker	(Southampton)	14. 5.00P
	(Continental C85)		NC71184		*(Cancelled 13.9.01 by CAA)*		
G-BRRD	Scheibe SF-25B Falke	4811	D-KBAT	30.10.89	R.M.Murray	Hinton-in-the-Hedges	9. 5.04
					t/a The G-BRRD Syndicate		
G-BRRF	Cameron O-77 HAFB	2101		24.10.89	D.G.Body	Leighton Buzzard	25. 3.00T
					t/a Mid-Bucks Farmers Balloon Group *"Daisy Chain"*		
G-BRRG	Glaser-Dirks DG-500M	5E7-M5		7.11.89	D.C.Chaplin *"492"*	Sutton Bank	16.10.03
					t/a Glider Syndicate		
G-BRRJ	Piper PA-28RT-201T Turbo Arrow IV		N4353T	27.11.89	M.Stower	Elstree	6. 7.02
		28R-8431021					
G-BRRK	Cessna 182Q Skylane II	18266160	N759PW	30.10.89	Werewolf Aviation Ltd	Elstree	7. 5.02
G-BRRL	Piper PA-18 Super Cub 95	<u>18-1615</u>	<u>G-AYPO(1)</u>	17. 9.90	A.J.White	Whitehall Farm, Benington	
	(L-18C-PI)		<u>ALAT 18-1615/51-15615</u>		t/a Acebell G-BRRL Syndicate		
	<u>(Regd using paperwork of wrecked D-EMKE [18-2050])</u>				*(On rebuild 4.93: current status unknown)*		
G-BRRN	Piper PA-28-161 Warrior II		N84533	30.10.89	Spinseal Ltd	Cranfield	22. 1.02T
		28-8216043					
G-BRRO	Cameron N-77 HAFB	2142		30.10.89	B.Birch	Bath	7. 9.02A
					"Newbury Building Society II"		
G-BRRR	Cameron V-77 HAFB	2070		13.10.89	L.M.Heal & A.P.Wilcox	Chippenham	16. 6.02A
					"Breezy"		
G-BRRS	Pitts S-1S Special	TM-1	N18TM	1.11.89	R.C.Atkinson	Ranksborough Farm, Langham	25. 6.93P
	(Lycoming O-360)				*(Stored 5.95: current status unknown)*		
G-BRRU	Colt 90A HAFB	1591		1.11.89	Reach For The Sky Ltd	Guildford	24. 7.02T
G-BRRW	Cameron O-77 HAFB	2125		7.11.89	D.V.Fowler *"Mobiloon"*	Cranbrook	26. 6.01T
G-BRRY	Robinson R22 Beta	1193		14.11.89	P.W.Vellacott	Thruxton	11.12.01T
G-BRSA(2)	Cameron N-56 HAFB	2113		8.11.89	C.Wilkinson	Newcastle	17.10.92A
G-BRSC(2)	Rans S-10 Sakota	0589.051		8.11.89	P.Wilkinson	Blackpool	12. 8.97P
	(Rotax 532)				*(Stored 12.01)*		
G-BRSE(2)	Piper PA-28-161 Warrior II		N8163R	5.12.89	Aerohire Ltd	Wolverhampton	24. 2.02T
		28-8016276					
G-BRSF(2)*	Supermarine 361 Spitfire HF.IXc		5632	22.11.89	J.Peace	(Exeter)	
			SAAF/RR232		*(Cancelled 23.6.94 by CAA) (As "RR232": on rebuild 10.01)*		
	(Composite incl tail/parts ex Mk.VIII/JF629 from W.Australia & wings ex Mk.XIV/R.Thai AF U14-6/93/RAF RM873)						
G-BRSG(2)	Piper PA-28-161 Cadet	2841285	N92011	23.11.89	J.Appleton	Denham	4. 1.05T
					t/a Holmes Rentals *(Op Denham School of Flying)*		
G-BRSH(2)	CASA I-131E Jungmann	2156	E3B-540	29.11.89	L.Ness	(Nannestad, Norway)	9. 5.02P
	(C/n also reported as <u>2140</u>: Spanish AF serial conflicts with F-AZGG) (As "781-25" in Spanish AF c/s)						
G-BRSJ(2)	Piper PA-38-112 Tomahawk II		N25664	29.12.89	APB Leasing Ltd	Welshpool	25. 3.02T
		38-81A0044					
G-BRSK	Boeing-Stearman B75N1 (N2S-3) Kaydet		N5565N	15.11.89	C.R.Lawrence	(Wymondham)	20. 1.97
	(Continental W670)	75-1180	Bu.3403		t/a Wymondham Engineering *(On rebuild 12.01)*		
G-BRSN	Rand Robinson KR-2	PFA 129-11178		10.11.89	K.W.Darby	(Teignmouth)	
	(VW 1834)						
G-BRSO	CFM Streak Shadow			16.11.89	D.J.Smith	Old Sarum	5.12.01P
	(Rotax 618) K.133-SA & PFA 161A-11601						
G-BRSP	Air Command 532 Elite			13.11.89	G.M. Hobman	(York)	10. 1.92P
	(Rotax 532) 0626 & PFA G/04-1158						
G-BRSW	Luscombe 8AC Silvaire	3249	N71822	15.11.89	P.H.Needham	Fenland	25. 6.02P
	(Continental A75)		NC71822		t/a Bloody Mary Aviation *"Bloody Mary"*		
G-BRSX	Piper PA-15 Vagabond	15-117	N4334H	27.10.89	C.Milne-Fowler	Craysmarsh Farm, Melksham	6. 6.02P
	(Continental A65)		NC4334H				
G-BRSY	Hatz CB-1	6	N2257J	15.11.89	J.P.Barrett	Breighton	19. 9.02P
	(Lycoming O-290-D)				t/a G.A.Barrett & Son		
G-BRTD	Cessna 152 II	15280023	N757UW	11. 1.90	T.G.Phillips, C.Greenland & J.Page		
					t/a 152 Group	Booker	21. 6.02
G-BRTH	Cameron A-180 HAFB	2016		21.11.89	The Ballooning Business Ltd	Northampton	27. 7.02T
	(Replacement envelope c/n 3199 fitted 1994)				*"Burning Ambition II"*		
G-BRTJ	Cessna 150F	15061749	N8149S	22.11.89	Avon Aviation Ltd	Bristol	24. 5.03T
G-BRTK	Boeing-Stearman E75 (PT-13D) Kaydet		N16716	29.11.89	Eastern Stearman Ltd	Rendcomb	24. 4.93
	(Continental W670)	75-5949	42-17786/Bu.38728				
	(CAA CofR is current but reported as donating parts to N52485 [75-4494] @ 12.01 - <u>see Section 5</u>)						
G-BRTL	MD Helicopters Hughes 369E	0356E	(F-GHLF)	5. 1.90	Crewhall Ltd	Leatherhead	31. 3.02

G-BRTM	Piper PA-28-161 Warrior II	28-8416083	N4334L	12.12.89	Oxford Aviation Services Ltd	Oxford	15. 2.02T
G-BRTN	Beechcraft 58 Baron	TH-1400	N58VF N6763U	29.11.89	Colneway Ltd	Guernsey	28. 1.02
G-BRTP	Cessna 152 II	15281275	N49448	28.11.89	M.R.Shelton t/a Tatenhill Aviation	Tatenhill	29. 7.02T
G-BRTT	Schweizer Hughes 269C	S.1411		29.11.89	Technical Exponents Ltd	Bennetts Field, Middlesex	27. 5.02T
G-BRTV	Cameron O-77 HAFB	2182		1.12.89	Carole Vening *"Solitaire II"*	Littlehampton	3. 3.01A
G-BRTW	Glaser-Dirks DG-400	4-259		22.12.89	I.J.Carruthers	(Great Orton)	4. 2.02
G-BRTX	Piper PA-28-151 Cherokee Warrior	28-7615085	N8307C	27.12.89	J.Phelan & D.G.Scott t/a Spectrum Flying Group	Belfast	19. 4.04T
G-BRTZ	Slingsby Cadet III (VW 1600)	PFA 042-10545		24. 1.90	R.R.Walters *(Stored 2001)*	(Midden-Zeeland, The Netherlands)	14. 3.97P
G-BRUA	Cessna 152 II	15281212	N49267	11. 1.90	BBC Air Ltd *(Op Abbas Air)*	Compton Abbas	12. 9.02T
G-BRUB	Piper PA-28-161 Warrior II	28-8116177	N8351Y	27.12.89	Flytrek Ltd	Compton Abbas	12. 1.03
G-BRUD	Piper PA-28-181 Archer II	28-8390010	N8300S	9. 2.90	Wilkins & Wilkins (Special Auctions) Ltd t/a Henlow Flying Club	RAF Henlow	18. 3.02T
G-BRUG	Luscombe 8E Silvaire (Continental C85)	4462	N1735K NC1735K	15.12.89	P.A.Cain & N.W.Barratt	Compton Abbas	21. 3.02P
G-BRUH	Colt 105A HAFB	1650		15.12.89	D.C.Chipping	Evora, Portugal	29. 7.93T
G-BRUI	Piper PA-44-180 Seminole	44-7995150	N2230E G-BRUI/N2230E	15.12.89	M.R.Shelton t/a Tatenhill Aviation	Tatenhill	28. 8.02T
G-BRUJ	Boeing-Stearman A75N1 (PT-17) Kaydet (Continental R670)	75-4299	N55557 42-16136	6. 4.90	M.Walker *(As "16136/205" in USN c/s)*	Liverpool	16. 7.04T
G-BRUM	Cessna A152 Aerobat	A1520870	N4693A	12. 3.86	Aerohire Ltd	Wolverhampton	6. 9.04T
G-BRUN	Cessna 120 (Continental C85)	9294	G-BRDH N72127/NC72127	29. 8.89	O.C.Brun	Great Massingham	10. 1.02P
G-BRUO	Taylor JT.1 Monoplane (VW 1600)	PFA 055-10859		15.12.89	P.M.Beresford	Crosland Moor	8. 2.02P
G-BRUU	EAA Biplane Model P1 (Lycoming O-360)	1	N41MW N4775G	22.12.89	E.C.Murgatroyd	Sackville Lodge, Riseley	17. 6.98P
G-BRUV	Cameron V-77 HAFB	2100		16. 8.89	T.W. & R.F.Benbrook *"biGBRUVver"*	Romford	27. 9.01A
G-BRUX	Piper PA-44-180 Seminole	44-7995151	N2245E	8. 3.79	Hambrair Ltd	Nottingham	13.12.03
G-BRVB	Stolp SA.300 Starduster Too (Lycoming O-360)	409	N33MH	21.12.89	M.N.Petchey & S.Turner	Andrewsfield	27. 6.02P
G-BRVC	Cameron N-180 HAFB	2180		15.12.89	The Balloon Club Ltd	Bristol	18. 7.01T
G-BRVE	Beechcraft D17S Traveller (UC-43-BH)	6701	N1193V NC1193V/Bu.32874/FT475/44-67724/(Bu.23689)	12. 3.90	P.A.Teichman	(London NW2)	25. 2.02
G-BRVF	Colt 77A HAFB	1651		19.12.89	The Ballooning Business Ltd	Northampton	18. 5.02T
G-BRVG	North American SNJ-7C Texan	88-17676	N830X N4134A/Bu.90678/(42-85895)	24. 1.90	D.J.Gilmour t/a Intrepid Aviation Co *(As "27" in VS-932 Sqn, USN c/s)*	Goodwood	6. 6.02
G-BRVH	Smyth Model S Sidewinder (Lycoming O-290)	PFA 092-11251		19.12.89	I.C.White	Glenrothes	10. 5.02P
G-BRVI	Robinson R22 Beta	1240		27.12.89	P.M.Whitaker	Ilkley	12. 4.02
G-BRVJ	Slingsby Cadet III (VW 1600) *(Modified ex T.31B)*	701 & PFA 42-11382	(BGA3360) WT906	24. 1.90	B.Outhwaite	Breighton	22. 5.02P
G-BRVL	Pitts S-1C Special (Lycoming IO-320)	559H	N2NW	10. 1.90	M.F.Pocock	RAF Mona	10. 6.02P
G-BRVN	Thunder Ax7-77 HAFB	1614		28.12.89	D.L.Beckwith	Northampton	25. 6.02A
G-BRVO	Aérospatiale AS350B Ecureuil	2315		3. 1.90	Gama Leasing Ltd.	Sandhurst, Kent	24. 4.02T
G-BRVR	Barnett Rotorcraft J4B-2	216-2		20. 2.90	M.Richardson t/a Ilkeston Contractors	Ilkeston	
G-BRVS	Barnett Rotorcraft J4B-2	210-2		20. 2.90	M.Richardson t/a Ilkeston Contractors	Ilkeston	
G-BRVT	Christen Pitts S-2B Special (Lycoming AEIO-540)	5189		6. 4.90	A.Caramella & R.Woollard *"The Tart"*	Biggin Hill	14. 1.03T
G-BRVU	Colt 77A HAFB	1652		4. 1.90	J.K.Woods *"Concorde Watches"*	Chatham	25. 6.02A
G-BRVX*	Cameron A-210 HAFB	2194		9. 1.90	Not known *(Cancelled 3.6.98 as WFU: noted 1999: current status unknown)*	NK	
G-BRVY	Thunder Ax8-90 HAFB	1676		9. 1.90	G.E. & J.V.Morris *"Golden Gem"*	Cheltenham	9. 7.02A
G-BRVZ	SAN Jodel D.117	433	F-BHNR	22.12.89	J.G.Patton	South Lodge Farm, Widmerpool	19. 6.02P
G-BRWA	Aeronca 7AC Champion	7AC-351	N81730 NC81730	20. 3.90	D.D.Smith & J.R.Edwards	Scotland Farm, Hook	2.10.02P
G-BRWC*	Cessna 152 II	15281918	TF-GMT N67569	19. 1.90	T.Hayselden (Doncaster) Ltd *(Damaged Sandtoft 29.8.90: original fuse.in open store Derby 3.98) (Rebuilt using cockpit/front fuse of G-BITG 6.96 to become G-ODAC: cancelled 16.2.99 as wfu: cockpit @ Firbeck 8.99)*	Sandtoft	15. 5.93T

G-BRWD	Robinson R22 Beta	1231	N8064U	15. 1.90	Matrix Aviation Ltd	Loddon, Norfolk	12. 5.02
G-BRWF	Thunder Ax7-77 HAFB	1200		15. 1.90	D.R.& C.L.Firkins	Tewkesbury	24. 9.01A
G-BRWO	Piper PA-28-140 Cherokee Cruiser	28-7325548	N55985	11. 1.90	Spitfire Aviation Ltd	Bournemouth	17.11.02T
G-BRWP	CFM Streak Shadow (Rotax 532)	K.122 & PFA 161A-11596		17. 1.90	R.Biffin *(New owner 5.01)*	Kirknewton	16. 8.02P
G-BRWR	Aeronca 11AC Chief (Continental A65)	11AC-1319	N9676E	17. 1.90	A.W.Crutcher	Cardiff	2. 7.02P
G-BRWT	Scheibe SF-25C-2000 Falke	44480	D-KIAY	11. 1.90	Booker Gliding Club Ltd	Booker	8. 4.02
G-BRWU	Phoenix Luton LA-4A Minor (JAP J.99)) *(Officially regd as PFA 1141: correct PFA No.not known)*	PAL/1141		18. 1.90	R.B.Webber & P.K.Pike	Trenchard Farm, Eggesford	3. 7.01P
G-BRWV	Brugger MB.2 Colibri (VW 1834)	PFA 043-11027		18. 1.90	R.W.Chatterton	(Grantham)	13. 6.02P
G-BRWX	Cessna 172P Skyhawk II	17274729	N53363	17. 1.90	D.A.Abels	Oaksey Park	26.10.02T
G-BRWY*	Cameron H-34 HAFB	2214		17. 1.90	E.Krafft *(Cancelled 6.11.01 by CAA: current status unknown)*	Annweiler, Germany	17. 4.94A
G-BRWZ	Cameron Macaw 90SS HAFB	2206		29. 1.90	Forbes Europe Inc "Capitalist Tool"	Balleroy, Normandy	3. 9.00
G-BRXA	Cameron O-120 HAFB	2217		19. 1.90	Gone With The Wind Ltd & R.J.Mansfield	Bowness-on-Windermere/Huddersfield	19. 2.01T
G-BRXB	Thunder Ax7-77 HAFB	1631		18. 1.90	H.Peel	Worcester	22. 7.02A
G-BRXC	Piper PA-28-161 Warrior II	28-8416043	N4339X N9563N	19. 2.90	Oxford Aviation Services Ltd	Oxford	24. 3.02T
G-BRXD	Piper PA-28-181 Archer II	28-8290126	D-EHWN N9690N/N8203E	19. 2.90	D.D.Stone	Wellesbourne Mountford	29. 3.03
G-BRXE	Taylorcraft BC-12D (Continental A65)	9459	N95059 NC95059	25. 1.90	Wendy J.Durrad "Flying Fishes"	Eastbach Farm, Coleford	28. 9.02P
G-BRXF	Aeronca 11AC Chief (Continental A65)	11AC-1033	N9396E NC9396E	25. 1.90	C.G.Nice t/a Aeronca Flying Group	Andrewsfield	22. 6.02P
G-BRXG	Aeronca 7AC Champion (Continental A65)	7AC-3910	N85178 NC85178	1. 3.90	J.D.Webb t/a X-Ray Golf Flying Group	Hill Farm, Nayland	13. 8.02P
G-BRXH	Cessna 120 (Continental C85)	10462	N76068 NC76068	25. 1.90	A.C.Garside t/a BRXH Group	Headcorn	1. 4.02P
G-BRXL	Aeronca 11AC Chief (Continental A65)	11AC-1629	N3254E NC3254E	31. 1.90	G.Taylor *"Fat Bullet" (As "42-78044" in US Army L-3F c/s)*	Hawarden	22. 9.99P
G-BRXN	Montgomerie-Bensen B.8MR (Rotax 532)	PFA G/01-1160		31. 1.90	G.Robertson	Sorbie Farm, Kingsmuir	13. 9.00P
G-BRXO	Piper PA-34-200T Seneca II	34-7970149	N111ED N9618N	12. 4.90	Aviation Services Ltd	Toussus-le-Noble, France	31. 7.02
G-BRXP	SNCAN Stampe SV-4C (Lycoming)	678	N33528 F-BGGU/FrAF 678/(F-BDNX) *(Fuselage noted 3.00)*	2. 2.90	T.Brown	Maypole Farm, Chislet	
G-BRXS	Howard Special T-Minus (Lycoming O-290) *(Modified Taylorcraft BC)*	REC-1	N2278C	14. 2.90	A.Shuttleworth	Barton	11.11.02P
G-BRXU	Aérospatiale AS332L Super Puma	2092	VH-BHV G-BRXU/HC-BMZ/C-GSLO	6. 3.90	Bristow Helicopters Ltd "Crail"	Aberdeen	11. 9.04T
G-BRXV	Robinson R22 Beta	1246		7. 2.90	J.W.F. & S.M.Tuke t/a Tukair Aircraft Charter	Headcorn	31. 5.02T
G-BRXW	Piper PA-24-260 Comanche	24-4069	N8621P	16. 2.90	P.A.Jenkins t/a Oak Group	Coventry	18. 1.03
G-BRXY	Pietenpol Air Camper (Continental C90)	PFA 047-11416		7. 2.90	P.S.Ganczakowski	Great Eversden	3. 6.02P
G-BRYI	de Havilland DHC.8-311A	256	C-GEOA	26. 3.91	Brymon Airways Ltd *"Northumberland/Drigantes" (Chelsea Rose t/s)*	Bristol	27. 3.03T
G-BRYJ	de Havilland DHC.8-311A	319	C-GEOA	27. 3.92	Brymon Airways Ltd *"Somerset/Gwlad-yr-Haff"*	Bristol	2. 4.03T
G-BRYM	de Havilland DHC.8-311A	305	N433AW C-GDFT	25. 3.96	Brymon Airways Ltd	Bristol	24. 3.02T
G-BRYO	de Havilland DHC.8-311A	311	N434AW C-GEVP	26. 4.96	Brymon Airways Ltd *"Harveys"*	Bristol	25. 4.02T
G-BRYP	de Havilland DHC.8-311A	315	N435AW C-GFCF	22. 4.96	Brymon Airways Ltd	Bristol	26. 5.02T
G-BRYS	de Havilland DHC.8-311A	296	PH-SDG D-BKIS/C-GFQL	23. 4.97	Brymon Airways Ltd	Bristol	4. 5.03T
G-BRYT	de Havilland DHC.8-311A	334	D-BKIR C-GFEN	11. 3.97	Brymon Airways Ltd *(Colour Down the Side t/s)*	Bristol	25. 3.03T
G-BRYU	de Havilland DHC.8-311A (Q300)	458	(9M-PGA) C-GFEN	4. 4.98	Brymon Airways Ltd *(Benyhone Tartan t/s)*	Bristol	3. 4.04T
G-BRYV	de Havilland DHC.8-311A (Q300)	462	(9M-PGD) C-GFHZ	10. 4.98	Brymon Airways Ltd *(Colum t/s)*	Bristol	9. 4.04T
G-BRYW	de Havilland DHC.8-311A (Q300)	474	(9M-PG.) C-GDIU	26. 5.98	Brymon Airways Ltd *(Koguty Lowickie t/s)*	Bristol	24. 5.04T
G-BRYX	de Havilland DHC-8-311A (Q300)	508	C-GDOE	25. 9.98	Brymon Airways Ltd.	Plymouth	27. 9.04T
G-BRYY	de Havilland DHC-8-311A (Q300)	519	C-FDHD	11.12.98	Brymon Airways Ltd. *(Rendezvous t/s)*	Plymouth	10.12.04T

G-BRYZ	de Havilland DHC-8-311A (Q300)	464	C-FCSG	16.10.98	Brymon Airways Ltd	Plymouth	15.10.04T
G-BRZA	Cameron O-77 HAFB	2231		7. 2.90	L. & R.J.Mold *"Breezy"*	High Wycombe	12. 2.01A
G-BRZB	Cameron A-105 HAFB	2212		7. 2.90	Cornwall Ballooning Adventures Ltd		
					"Headland Hotel"	Newquay	13. 3.00A
G-BRZC*	Cameron N-90 HAFB	2227		8. 2.90	British Balloon Museum & Library	Newbury	2.12.92A
					"Unipart II" (Cancelled 29.4.97 as WFU)		
G-BRZD	HAPI Cygnet SF-2A	PFA 182-11443		8. 2.90	C.I.Coghill	(Farnham)	15. 3.02P
	(VW 2078)						
G-BRZE	Thunder Ax7-77 HAFB	1633		8. 2.90	G.V.Beckwith & F.Schoeder *"Jenlain"*	York	31. 8.97A
G-BRZG	Enstrom F-28A	169	N9053	8. 2.90	Metropolitan Services Ltd	Hawarden	7. 4.03
G-BRZI	Cameron N-180 HAFB	2215		8. 2.90	C.E.Wood	Witham	24. 2.00T
					t/a Eastern Balloon Rides		
G-BRZK	Stinson 108-2 Voyager	108-2846	N9846K	17. 4.90	P.C.G.Wyld	Booker	13. 2.03
			NC9846K		t/a Voyager G-BRZK Syndicate		
G-BRZL*	Pitts S-1D Special	01	N899RN	26. 2.90	R.T.Cardwell	Challock	2. 8.96P
	(Lycoming O-360)				*(Noted on rebuild 5.00: cancelled 25.10.00 by CAA)*		
G-BRZO	Jodel D.18	PFA 169-11275		14. 2.90	J.D.Anson	(Liskeard)	
G-BRZS	Cessna 172P Skyhawk II	17275004	N54585	2.10.90	H.Hargreaves & P.F.Hughes	Blackpool	24. 2.03
					t/a G-BHYP Flying Group		
G-BRZT	Cameron V-77 HAFB	2241		21. 2.90	Beverley Drawbridge	Cranbrook, Kent	19. 2.01A
					"Hoopla"		
G-BRZU*	Colt Flying Cheese SS HAFB	1544		26. 2.90	N.Charbonnier	Aosta, Italy	25. 9.97A
					"Grana Padano" (Cancelled 25.9.97 as wfu)		
G-BRZV	Colt Flying Apple SS HAFB	1662		26. 2.90	Obst Vom Bodensee Marketing Gbr		
						Tettnang-Siggenweiler, Germany	14. 9.97A
G-BRZW	Rans S-10 Sakota			21. 2.90	D.L.Davies	Emlyn's Field, Rhuallt	6. 8.98P
	(Rotax 532) 0789.058 & PFA 194-11932						
G-BRZX	Pitts S-1S Special	711-H	N272H	22. 2.90	J.L.Dixon	Sherburn-in-Elmet	21. 4.02P
	(Lycoming O-320)						
G-BRZZ	CFM Streak Shadow K.135 & PFA 161A-11628			22. 2.90	T.Mooney	Sumburgh	3. 9.02P
	(Rotax 532) *(C/n duplicates Renegade Spirit G-MWDM)*				t/a Shetland Flying Group		

G-BSAA – G-BSZZ

G-BSAI	Stoddard-Hamilton Glasair III	3102		31. 1.90	K.J. & P.J.Whitehead	Booker	3. 9.02P
G-BSAJ	CASA I-131E Jungmann	2209	E3B-209	23. 1.90	P.G.Kynsey	Headcorn	7. 5.02P
G-BSAK	Colt 21A Sky Chariot HAFB	1696		26. 2.90	K.Meehan	Much Wenlock	24. 7.99A
					t/a Northern Flights		
G-BSAS	Cameron V-65 HAFB	2191		27. 2.90	J.R.Barber	King's Lynn	5. 8.01A
G-BSAV	Thunder Ax7-77 HAFB	1555		26. 2.90	E.A., H.A.Evans, I.G. & C.A.Lloyd		
					"Burnt Savings"	Chesterfield	11. 5.02A
G-BSAW	Piper PA-28-161 Warrior II		N8203C	27. 2.90	Carill Aviation Ltd	Southampton	12. 7.02T
		28-8216152	YV-2265P/N8203C				
G-BSAZ	Denney Kitfox mk.2		(G-BRVW)	5. 3.90	A.J.Lloyd, D.M.Garrett & J.T.Lane		
	(Rotax 582)	602 & PFA 172-11664				(Bromyard)	26. 6.97P
G-BSBA	Piper PA-28-161 Warrior II		N2574U	1. 3.90	London Transport Flying Club Ltd		
		28-8016041				Fairoaks	15. 5.03T
G-BSBG	CCF Harvard 4 (T-6J-CCF Texan)	1753	Moz.PLAF	5. 3.90	A.P.St.John	Liverpool	26. 7.02P
		CCF4-483	FAP 1753/BF+053/AA+053/52-8562 *(As "20310/310" in RCAF c/s)*				
G-BSBI	Cameron O-77 HAFB	2245		6. 3.90	D.M.Billing	Uckfield	29.12.01A
					"Calibre"		
G-BSBK*	Colt 105A HAFB	1319		6. 3.90	Zebra Ballooning Ltd	Maidstone	12. 6.97T
					(Cancelled 18.10.01 by CAA)		
G-BSBM*	Cameron N-77 HAFB	2229		8. 3.90	Balloon Preservation Group	Kirdford	21.11.96A
					"Nuclear Electric 1" (Cancelled 15.7.98 as WFU)		
G-BSBN	Thunder Ax7-77 HAFB	1531		6. 3.90	B.Pawson *"Venus"*	Cambridge	9.12.93A
G-BSBP	Jodel D.18	PFA 169-11613		15. 1.90	R.T.Pratt	(Crickhowell)	
	(Revmaster R2100)						
G-BSBR	Cameron V-77 HAFB	2247		26. 2.90	R.P.Wade *"Honey"*	Wigan	12.10.02A
G-BSBT	Piper J-3C-65 Cub	17712	N70694	9. 3.90	R.W.H.Watson	Grimmet Farm, Maybole	11. 2.02P
			NC70694				
G-BSBV	Rans S-10 Sakota			9. 3.90	R.G.Cameron	Muirhouses Farm, Errol	20. 7.00P
	(Rotax 532) 1089.064 & PFA 194-11769						
G-BSBW	Bell 206B-3 JetRanger III	3664	N43EA	12. 3.90	D.T.Sharpe	Sherburn in Elmet	8. 7.02T
			N6498V/9Y-THC				
G-BSBX	Montgomerie-Bensen B.8MR			12. 3.90	R.J.Roan	(Peterborough)	26. 5.93P
	(Rotax 503)	PFA G/01A-1135					
G-BSBZ	Cessna 150M	15077093	N63086	29. 3.90	D.T.Given	Newtownards, Co.of Down	13. 6.99T
					t/a DTG Aviation		
G-BSCA	Cameron N-90 HAFB	2237		12. 3.90	P.J.Marshall & M.A.Clarke	Ruislip	9. 6.02A
					"The Graduate"		

G-BSCB	Air Command 532 Elite			16. 3.90	P.H.Smith	Nottingham	18. 9.97P
	(Rotax 532)	0627 & PFA G/04-1172					
G-BSCC	Colt 105A HAFB	1006		15. 3.90	Capricorn Balloons Ltd	Loughborough	4. 3.01T
G-BSCE	Robinson R22 Beta	1245		15. 3.90	H.Sugden	Humberside	14. 3.02T
G-BSCF	Thunder Ax7-77 HAFB	1537		14. 3.90	V.P.Gardiner	Stoke-on-Trent	15. 8.01A
					"Charlie Farley"		
G-BSCG	Denney Kitfox mk.2	PFA 172-11620		23. 4.90	N.L.Beever	Sibsey	30.10.01P
	(Rotax 582)						
G-BSCH	Denney Kitfox mk.2			16. 3.90	M.P.M.Read	(Annan)	4. 1.99P
	(Rotax 582)	510 & PFA 172-11621					
G-BSCI	Colt 77A HAFB	1683		16. 3.90	J.L. & S.Wrigglesworth *"Brody"*	Ilminster	12. 6.00A
G-BSCK	Cameron H-24 HAFB	2263		16. 3.90	J.D.Shapland *"Monacle"*	Wadebridge	11. 6.95A
G-BSCL	Robinson R22 Beta	1249		28. 3.90	Flightworks Sales & Leasing Ltd	Booker	11. 8.02T
G-BSCM	Denney Kitfox mk.2			28. 3.90	S.A.Hewitt	Sheepcote Farm	1. 1.02P
	(Rotax 582)	638 & PFA 172-11745					
G-BSCN	SOCATA TB-20 Trinidad	1070	D-EGTC	27. 3.90	B.W.Dye	Biggin Hill	1. 6.02
			G-BSCN				
G-BSCO	Thunder Ax7-77 HAFB	1635		6. 3.90	F.J.Whalley *"Bluebell"*	Cleish	8. 9.02A
G-BSCP	Cessna 152 II	15283289	N48135	20. 3.90	Moray Flying Club (1990) Ltd	RAF Kinloss	13.10.02T
G-BSCR*	Cessna 172M Skyhawk II	17262182	N12693	20. 3.90	London Link Flying Ltd	Elstree	16. 1.00T
			(Crashed Clacton 19.6.99: cancelled 21.10.99 as WFU: wreck noted 6.00)				
G-BSCS	Piper PA-28-181 Cherokee Archer II	28-7890064	N47392	3. 4.90	Wingtask 1995 Ltd	Seething	30. 5.02T
G-BSCV	Piper PA-28-161 Cherokee Warrior II	28-7816135	C-GQXW	22. 3.90	S.E.Burton	Earls Colne	18.10.02
					t/a Southwood Flying Group		
G-BSCW	Taylorcraft BC-65	1798	N24461	22. 3.90	S.Leach	(Honiton)	30. 6.02P
			NC24461				
G-BSCX	Thunder Ax8-105 HAFB	1748		21. 3.90	Balloon Flights Club Ltd	Leicester	14. 7.99T
					"Balloon Flights"		
G-BSCY	Piper PA-28-151 Cherokee Warrior		C-GOBE	22. 3.90	A.S.Bamrah	Lydd	1. 8.02T
	(Cnvtd to Srs.161 status)	28-7515046			t/a Falcon Flying Services		
G-BSCZ	Cessna 152 II	15282199	N68226	22. 3.90	Eastern Executive Air Charter Ltd		
					(Operated Seawing Flying Club)	Southend	6. 7.03T
G-BSDA	Taylorcraft BC-12D	7316	N43657	15.11.90	D.G.Edwards	Shoreham	8.10.01P
	(Continental A75)		NC43657				
G-BSDB	Pitts S-1C Special	01	(N1867)	22. 3.90	J.T.Mielech	(Frankfurt, Germany)	31. 5.99P
	(Lycoming O-320)		N77R		*(New owner 5.01)*		
G-BSDD	Denney Kitfox mk.2			28. 3.90	J.Windmill	Priory Farm, Tibenham	21. 6.96P
	(Rotax 582)	639 & PFA 172-11797					
G-BSDH	Robin DR.400/180 Regent	1980		18. 4.90	R.L.Brucciani	Leicester	16. 5.02
G-BSDI	Corben Junior Ace Model E	3961	N91706	28. 3.90	T.K.Pullen & A.J.Staplehurst	Eaglescott	23.10.02P
	(Continental A75)						
G-BSDJ	Piper J-4E Cub Coupe	4-1456	N35975	13. 2.91	B.M.Jackson	(Thame)	29. 1.02P
	(Continental C85)		NC35975				
G-BSDK	Piper J-5A Cub Cruiser	5-175	N30337	28. 3.90	S.Haughton & I.S.Hodge		
	(Continental A75)		NC30337			Field Farm, Great Missenden	19. 4.02P
G-BSDL	SOCATA TB-10 Tobago	156		7.10.80	P.Middleton & G.Corbin	Sherburn in Elmet	14. 6.03
					t/a Delta Lima Group		
G-BSDN	Piper PA-34-200T Seneca II	34-7970335	N2893A	2. 4.90	McCormick Consulting Ltd	Manchester	20. 6.02T
G-BSDO	Cessna 152 II	15281657	N65894	23. 5.90	L.W.Scattergood	Sherburn-in-Elmet	13. 7.03T
G-BSDP	Cessna 152 II	15280268	N24468	11. 6.90	I.S.H.Paul	Denham	27. 7.03T
					(Op The Pilot Centre)		
G-BSDS	Boeing-Stearman E75 (PT-13A) Kaydet		N57852	6. 4.90	A.Basso	Biel, Switzerland	13. 5.03
	(Continental W670)	75-118	38-470		*(As "118" in US Army c/s)*		
G-BSDV	Colt 31A HAFB	1722		30. 3.90	C.D.Monk	Bath	27. 6.96A
					(Active 2001)		
G-BSDW	Cessna 182P Skylane II	18264688	N9125M	9. 4.90	Glanwith Ltd	Panshanger	30. 5.02T
G-BSDX	Cameron V-77 HAFB	2050		30. 3.90	D.K.Fish	Bedford	
	(Canopy fitted to G-SNOW and rebuilt with G-SNOW's original canopy)						
G-BSDZ	Enstrom 280FX	2051	OO-MHV	3. 4.90	Avalon Group Ltd	Hawarden	3. 1.02
			(OO-JMH)/G-ODSC/G-BSDZ				
G-BSED	Piper PA-22-160 Tri-Pacer	22-6377	N9404D	7. 6.90	B.W.Haston	Cheyene Farm, Stonehaven	5. 9.03
	(Hoerner wing-tips: tail-wheel conversion)						
G-BSEE	Rans S-9	PFA 196-11635		2. 3.90	P.M.Semler		
	(Rotax 532)					Buttermilk Farm, Easton Maudit	26.11.01P
G-BSEF	Piper PA-28-180 Cherokee C	28-1846	N7831W	18. 4.90	I.D.Wakeling		
						Franklyns Field, Chewton Mendip	4.11.02
G-BSEG	Ken Brock KB-2	PFA G/01-1106		3. 4.90	S.J.M.Ledingham	Carlisle	27. 6.01P
	(Rotax 582) (C/n possibly PFA G/06-1106)						
G-BSEJ	Cessna 150M Commuter	15076261	N66767	4. 5.90	I.Shackleton	Wolverhampton	15. 9.02T
G-BSEK	Robinson R22	0027	N45AD	10. 4.90	Helicentre Ltd	Blackpool	28. 4.02T
			N90193				

G-BSEL	Slingsby T.61G Super Falke	1986		31. 3.80	T.Holloway	RAF Keevil	23. 5.04
					t/a RAFGSA *(Op Bannerdown Gliding Club)*		
G-BSEP	Cessna 172	46555	N6455E	12. 4.90	A.P Wall, R.J.Tyson & R.J Watts	Biggin Hill	19. 8.02
G-BSER	Piper PA-28-160 Cherokee B	28-790	N5665W	19. 4.90	Yorkair Ltd	Sandtoft	17. 7.03T
G-BSET	Beagle B.206 Basset CC.1	B.006	XS765	3.12.86	Lawgra (No.386) Ltd	Cranfield	28. 7.98
					t/a International Aerospace Engineering		
					(As "XS765" in RAF Transport Command c/s)		
G-BSEU	Piper PA-28-181 Cherokee Archer II	28-7890108	N47639	1. 5.90	Euro Aviation 91 Ltd	Blackbushe	23. 6.02
G-BSEV	Cameron O-77 HAFB	2271		20. 4.90	The Ballooning Business Ltd	Northampton	12. 5.00A
G-BSEY	Beechcraft A36 Bonanza	E-1873	N1809F	17. 5.90	K.Phillips Ltd	Coventry	24. 8.02
G-BSFA	Aero Designs Pulsar *(Tri-cycle u/c)* (Rotax 582)	176 & PFA 202-11754		18. 4.90	S.A.Gill	(Maidenhead)	7. 7.02P
					(Flies from White Waltham)		
G-BSFB	CASA I-131E Jungmann Srs.2000	2053	E3B-449	27. 4.90	C.D.Beal	Andrewsfield	17.12.01P
					(As "S5+B06" in Luftwaffe c/s)		
G-BSFD	Piper J-3C-65 Cub	16037	N88419 NC88419	25. 5.90	AJD Engineering Ltd	Milden	19.10.01P
G-BSFE	Piper PA-38-112 Tomahawk II	38-82A0033	N91452	26. 4.90	Mopps (UK) Ltd	Perth	19. 3.03T
G-BSFF	Robin DR.400/180R Remorqueur	1295	D-ELMM	20. 4.90	Lasham Gliding Society Ltd	Lasham	11. 7.02
G-BSFK	Piper PA-28-161 Warrior II	28-8516062	N6918D	1. 5.90	Oxford Aviation Services Ltd	Oxford	16. 6.02T
G-BSFP	Cessna 152T	15285548	N93764	9. 5.90	Walkbury Aviation Ltd	Sibson	5. 8.02T
G-BSFR	Cessna 152 II	15282268	N68341	9. 5.90	Galair Ltd	Biggin Hill	10. 7.02T
G-BSFU*	Sud SE.313B Alouette II	1645	XR385	30. 5.90	Not known	Coventry	
		(No UK CofA issued: cancelled 2.2.93 by CAA: stored 7.97: current status unknown)					
G-BSFV	Woods Woody Pusher (Continental C85)	201	N16WP	30. 4.90	M.J.Wells	Watchford Farm, Yarcombe	3. 5.02P
					"Woody's Pusher"		
G-BSFW	Piper PA-15 Vagabond (Continental A65)	15-273	N4484H NC4484H	26. 4.90	J.R.Kimberley	Bounds Farm, Ardleigh	18.12.02P
G-BSFX	Denney Kitfox mk.2 (Rotax 582)	506 & PFA 172-11723		23. 4.90	T.A.Crone	Croft Farm, Defford	2. 9.02P
					(Noted 1.02)		
G-BSFY	Denney Kitfox mk.2 (Rotax 582)	PFA 172-11632		16. 3.90	C.I.Bates	Long Marston	17. 4.02P
G-BSGB	Gaertner Ax4 Skyranger HAFB	SR.0001		30. 3.90	B.Gaertner	Oxford	
G-BSGC*	Piper PA-18 Super Cub 95 (L-18C-PI)	18-3227	OO-HBC OL-L53/L-153/53-4827	22. 3.90	G.Churchill	(Towcester)	
			(On overhaul Norfolk 1996: cancelled 15.5.99 as WFU: current status unknown)				
G-BSGD	Piper PA-28-180 Cherokee E	28-5691	N3463R	4. 5.90	R.J.Cleverley	Draycott Farm, Chiseldon	6. 6.03
G-BSGF	Robinson R22 Beta	1383		1. 5.90	Hecray Co Ltd	Southend	24. 6.02T
					t/a Direct Helicopters		
G-BSGG	Denney Kitfox mk.2 (Jabiru 2200A)	PFA 172-11666		1. 5.90	C.G.Richardson	Fulbeck, Lincs	9. 5.02P
G-BSGH	Airtour AH-56B HAFB	014		1. 5.90	A.R.Hardwick	Shefford	
					"Battle of Britain"		
G-BSGJ	Monnett Sonerai II (VW 1835)	300	N34WH	1. 5.90	G.A.Brady	Enstone	6. 9.91P
G-BSGK	Piper PA-34-200T Seneca II	34-7870331	N36450	22. 5.90	R.Hope, M.J.Martin & B.W.Powell	Manston	17.11.02
					t/a GK Aviation		
G-BSGL	Piper PA-28-161 Warrior II	28-8116041	N82690	10. 5.90	Keywest Air Charter Ltd	Liverpool	8. 8.02T
					(Op Liverpool Flying School) "Liverbird V"		
G-BSGP	Cameron N-65 HAFB	2293		1. 5.90	G.J.Bell	Wokingham	16.12.02A
G-BSGR*	Boeing-Stearman E75 (PT-17) Kaydet	75-4721	N75864 EC-ATY/N55050/42-16558	19. 6.90	A.G.Dunkerley	Kemble	
			(Cancelled 10.3.99 by CAA: noted unmarked 12.00)				
	(Reported as c/n 75-6714 ex N66870/Bu.07110)						
G-BSGS	Rans S-10 Sakota (Rotax 532)	1289.076 & PFA 194-11724		9. 5.90	M.R.Parr	(Holmbrook, Cumbria)	17. 7.02P
					(Damaged Coventry late 1.93: current status unknown)		
G-BSGT	Cessna 210N Turbo Centurion II *(Reims-assembled c/n F2100020)*	21063361	LX-ATL D-EOGB/N5308A	21. 5.90	B.J.Sharpe	Booker	17. 3.03
G-BSGV*	Rotorway Executive (RW 152)	3823		8. 5.90	Not known	Chirk	14. 7.92P
					(Cancelled by CAA 7.4.95: stored 5.95: current status unknown)		
G-BSGY	Thunder Ax7-77 HAFB *(Envelope ex G-BROA c/n 1535)*	1760		18. 7.90	P.B.Kenington	Winterbourne, Bristol	15. 5.00A
					"Bugsy"		
G-BSHA	Piper PA-34-200T Seneca II	34-7670216	N9707K	2. 5.90	Justgold Ltd	Blackpool	24. 7.99T
G-BSHC	Colt 69A HAFB	1668		8. 5.90	Magical Adventures Ltd	Chirk	12.10.98A
G-BSHD	Colt 69A HAFB	1736		8. 5.90	D.B.Court *"Jester"*	Ormskirk	14. 7.02A
G-BSHH	Luscombe 8E Silvaire (Continental C85)	3981	N1254K NC1254K	11. 5.90	G.M.Wightman	Coventry	21. 9.01P
G-BSHI	Luscombe 8DF Silvaire Trainer (Continental C90)	1821	N39060 NC39060	11. 5.90	Catcott Garage Ltd	Dunkeswell	14. 8.01P

G-BSHK	Denney Kitfox mk.2			11. 5.90	D.Doyle & C.Aherne	Kildare	5. 7.02P
	(Rotax 532)	449 & PFA 172-11752					
G-BSHO	Cameron V-77 HAFB	2313		16. 5.90	D J Duckworth & C Stewart	Chesham	23. 8.01A
					"Peugeot/Talbot"		
G-BSHR	Reims Cessna F172N Skyhawk II		G-BFGE	23.10.84	Deep Cleavage Ltd	Exeter	24. 4.03T
		F17201616					
G-BSHS	Colt 105A HAFB	1674	(D-OCAT)	16. 5.90	I.Novosad	Planegg, Germany	9. 9.01A
			G-BSHS				
G-BSHT	Cameron V-77 HAFB	2321		30. 5.90	E.C.Moore *"Buckshot II"*	Great Missenden	24. 5.01T
G-BSHV	Piper PA-18-135 Super Cub	18-3123	OO-GDG	5. 7.90	G.T Fisher	Northside, Thorney	20. 5.04
	(L-18C-PI)		Belgian Army L-49/53-4723				
G-BSHX	Enstrom F-28A	155	N9605	16. 5.90	Stephenson Aviation Ltd	Goodwood	
					(Stored 4.96: current status unknown)		
G-BSHY	EAA Acrosport 1	PFA 072-10928		17. 4.90	R.J.Hodder	Eastfield Farm, Manby	14. 6.02P
	(Lycoming O-290)						
G-BSHZ	Enstrom F-28F	427	N51702	16. 5.90	G.Birchmore	(Tiverton)	25. 3.00
G-BSIC*	Cameron V-77 HAFB	2322		17. 5.90	C.Wilcock	Rickmansworth	5. 5.01A
					(Cancelled 19.6.01 by CAA)		
G-BSIF	Denney Kitfox mk.2			5. 7.90	P.Annable	(Belper)	21. 3.02P
	(Rotax 582)	563 & PFA 172-11889					
G-BSIG	Colt 21A Cloudhopper HAFB	1322		18. 5.90	E.C. & A.J.Moore	Great Missenden	31. 3.01A
G-BSIH	Rutan LongEz	1200-1 & PFA 074A-11492		31. 5.90	W.S.Allen	(Cheltenham)	
G-BSII	Piper PA-34-200T Seneca II		N8253N	16. 5.90	T Belso	Top Farm, Croydon	4. 8.02
		34-8070336					
G-BSIJ	Cameron V-77 HAFB	2164		23. 5.90	A.S.Jones	Wolverhampton	14. 8.02A
G-BSIK	Denney Kitfox mk.1	51		5. 6.90	S.P.Collins	Hill Farm, Nayland	31. 1.01P
G-BSIM	Piper PA-28-181 Archer II		N9092Y	22. 5.90	Bobbington Air Training School Ltd		
		28-8690017				Wolverhampton	25. 8.02T
G-BSIN	Robinson R22 Beta	1379	N4015H	25. 5.90	Griffin Helicopters Ltd	(Dunmow)	6.10.02T
G-BSIO	Cameron Furness House 56SS HAFB	2310		25. 5.90	R.E.Jones *"Pinkie"*	Lytham St.Annes	9. 6.02A
G-BSIU	Colt 90A HAFB	1774		25. 5.90	S.Travaglia	Firenze, Italy	20.11.01A
G-BSIY	Schleicher ASK14	14005	5Y-AID	4. 6.90	E.V.Goodwin	(Huntingdon)	20.10.96
			D-KOIC		t/a Winwick Flying Group		
G-BSIZ	Piper PA-28-181 Archer II	28-7990377	N2162Y	25. 5.90	A.M.L.Maxwell	Alderney	20. 6.02
G-BSJB	Bensen B.8	PFA G/01-1080		5. 6.90	J.W.Limbrick	(Bewdley)	
G-BSJU	Cessna 150M	15076430	N3230V	14. 6.90	A.C.Williamson	Crowfield	4. 4.04T
					(Op Crowfield Flying Club)		
G-BSJW	Everett Gyroplane Srs.2	020		6. 6.90	R.Sarwan	(Beccles)	25.10.91P
	(Rotax 532)						
G-BSJX	Piper PA-28-161 Warrior II		N8036N	30. 5.90	D.A.Shields & L.C.Brekkeflat	Denham	22. 7.02T
		28-8216084					
G-BSJZ	Cessna 150J	15070485	N60661	7. 5.91	BCT Aircraft Leasing Ltd	Denham	1. 3.01T
G-BSKA	Cessna 150M	15076137	N66588	31. 7.90	H.Daines Electronics Ltd	(Beccles)	16. 3.03T
G-BSKC*	Piper PA-38-112 Tomahawk	38-79A0748	OY-PJB	27. 7.90	J.Marioni	Panshanger	24. 1.97T
			N748RM/C-GRQI				
	(Damaged near Tewin 2.6.96: stored 9.97: cancelled 22.11.01 as wfu: current status unknown)						
G-BSKD	Cameron V-77 HAFB	2336		4. 6.90	M.J.Gunston *"Skulduggery"*	Camberley	1. 7.01A
G-BSKE	Cameron O-84 HAFB	1604	ZS-HYD	4. 6.90	B.W.Smith	Wisborough Green, W.Sussex	20. 7.01A
			G-BSKE		t/a The Blunt Arrows Balloon Team		
G-BSKG	Maule MX-7-180 Star Rocket	11072C		7. 6.90	J.R.Surbey	Blockmoor Farm, Barway, Ely	6. 2.03
G-BSKI	Thunder Ax8-90 HAFB	1623		18. 5.90	P.G.Ward	Camberley	17.10.01A
					t/a G-BSKI Balloon Group *"Ski Maiden"*		
G-BSKK	Piper PA-38-112 Tomahawk	38-79A0671	N2525K	11. 6.90	A.S.Bamrah	Biggin Hill	20.11.02T
					t/a Falcon Flying Services		
G-BSKL	Piper PA-38-112 Tomahawk	38-78A0509	N4252E	11. 6.90	A.S.Bamrah	Birmingham	20.11.02T
					t/a Falcon Flying Services *(Op Warwickshire Aero Centre)*		
G-BSKO	Maule MXT-7-180 Star Rocket	14008C		7. 6.90	M.A.Ashmole	Perth	12. 5.03
G-BSKP	Supermarine 379 Spitfire F.XIVe		SG-31	27. 6.90	Historic Flying Ltd	Duxford	
		6S/663417	Belg AF/RN201		*(As "RN201/SG-13")*		
G-BSKU	Cameron O-84 HAFB	2330		8. 6.90	Alfred Bagnall & Sons (West) Ltd		
					"Bagnalls II"	Bristol	7. 6.02A
G-BSKW	Piper PA-28-181 Archer II	2890138	N91940	1. 6.90	Shropshire Aero Club Ltd	Sleap	9. 4.03T
G-BSLA	Robin DR.400/180 Regent	1997		22. 6.90	A.B.McCoig	Rochester	24. 6.02
					t/a Robin Lima Alpha Group		
G-BSLE	Piper PA-28-161 Warrior II		N8260L	25. 6.90	Oxford Aviation Services Ltd	Oxford	6. 9.02T
		28-8116028					
G-BSLH	CASA I-131E Jungmann Srs.2000	2222	E3B-622	27. 7.90	P.Warden	Biel, Switzerland	20. 8.02P
	(Despite quoted c/n & p/i this is a new-build aircraft by Bücker Prado SL, Albacete, Spain who have acquired the rights and drawings from CASA)						
G-BSLI	Cameron V-77 HAFB	2115		15. 6.90	J.D.C. & F.E.Bevan	Market Drayton	30. 7.00T
					"Blackbird"		
G-BSLK	Piper PA-28-161 Warrior II		N20849	15. 6.90	R.A.Rose	Wellesbourne Mountford	6. 4.03T
		28-7916018					

G-BSLM	Piper PA-28-160 Cherokee	28-308	N5262W	22. 6.90	A S Thorogate & K Richards t/a Old Sarum Cherokee Group	Old Sarum	6. 3.03
G-BSLT	Piper PA-28-161 Warrior II	28-8016303	N81817	19. 6.90	APB Leasing Ltd	Welshpool	25. 1.03T
G-BSLU	Piper PA-28-140 Cherokee	28-24733	OY-PJL OH-PJL/SE-FFA	19. 6.90	D.J.Budden Ltd	Shobdon	22. 9.02
G-BSLV	Enstrom 280FX	2054	D-HHAS G-BSLV	26. 6.90	K Ward	(Wrexham)	10. 7.03T
G-BSLW	Bellanca 7ECA Citabria	431-66	N9696S	16. 7.90	D.W.Mann t/a Shoreham Citabria Group	Shoreham	6. 9.03
G-BSLX	WAR Focke-Wulf 190 rep	24	N698WW	19. 6.90	D.Featherby t/a FW190 Gruppe *(As "1+4" in Luftwaffe c/s)*	Norwich	2. 8.02P
G-BSMB	Cessna U206E Super Skywagon	U20601659	N9459G C-GUUW/N9459G	25. 6.90	London Parachute School Ltd	Gloucestershire	9. 3.03
G-BSMD	SNCAN 1101 Noralpha	139	F-GDPQ F-YEEE/F-YCZK/CAN-11/Fr.Mil	26. 6.90	R.J.Lamplough *(Stored 12.00: as "+14" in Luftwaffe c/s)*	North Weald	4. 5.96P
G-BSME	Bölkow Bö.208C Junior	596	D-ECGA	25. 6.90	D.J.Hampson	Fenland	17. 5.03
G-BSMG	Montgomerie-Bensen B.8M (Rotax 532)	PFA G/01-1170		22. 6.90	A.C.Timperley	(Aberfeldy)	16. 7.97P
G-BSMK	Cameron O-84 HAFB	2328		26. 6.90	D.F.Maine & D.M.Newton t/a G-BSMK Shareholders	Redditch	10. 6.02A
G-BSML	Schweizer Hughes 269C (300C)	S.1462	PH-HUH N134DM	10.10.90	K.P.Foster & B.I.Winsor	Bodmin	3. 4.03
G-BSMM	Colt 31A Sky Chariot HAFB	1779		27. 6.90	D.V.Fowler	Cranbrook, Kent	1. 6.01A
G-BSMN	CFM Streak Shadow (Rotax 582)	K.137-SA & PFA 161A-11656		26. 6.90	P.J.Porter	(Wincanton)	16. 9.02P
G-BSMO	Denney Kitfox (Rotax 582)	PFA 172-11773		16. 7.90	R.H.Taylor t/a Kitfox Group	Seething	17. 7.01P
G-BSMS	Cameron V-77 HAFB	2356		26. 6.90	Sade Balloons Ltd *"Sadie"*	Coulsdon	1. 6.02A
G-BSMT	Rans S-10 Sakota (Rotax 532)	1289.077 & PFA 194-11793		29. 6.90	P.J.Barker	(South Croydon)	19.10.99P
G-BSMU	Rans S-6 Coyote II	1089.090 & PFA 204-11732	G-MWJE	27. 6.90	G.C.Hutchinson	(Bedale)	12.11.01P
G-BSMV	Piper PA-17 Vagabond (Continental C85)	17-94	N4696H NC4696H	29. 6.90	A.Cheriton *"Sophie"*	Wellesbourne Mountford	11. 1.01P
G-BSMX	Bensen B.8MR	PFA G/01-1171		3. 7.90	J.S.E.R.McGregor	(Birmingham)	
G-BSND	Air Command 532 Elite	PFA G/04-1180		16. 7.90	K.Brogden & W.B.Lumb	(Heywood, Manchester)	
G-BSNE	Luscombe 8E Silvaire (Continental C85)	5757	N1130B NC1130B	2.11.90	N.Reynolds & C.Watts	(Guildford)	11. 7.02P
G-BSNF	Piper J-3C-65 Cub (Continental O-200-A) *(Frame No.<u>3116</u>)* *(Lippert Reed conversion)*	3070	N23317 NC23317	17. 8.90	D.A.Hammant	Bere Farm, Warnford, Southampton	17. 9.02P
G-BSNG	Cessna 172N Skyhawk II	17270192	N738SB	19. 7.90	A.J. & P.C.MacDonald	Edinburgh	12.10.02T
G-BSNJ	Cameron N-90 HAFB	2335		6. 7.90	D.P.H.Smith	(France)	15. 5.02A
G-BSNL	Bensen B.8MR (Rotax 532)	PFA G/01-1181		16. 7.90	A.C.Breane	(Balleybofey, Co.Donegal)	20. 7.97P
G-BSNN	Rans S-10 Sakota (Rotax 532)	PFA 194-11846		31. 7.90	O. & S.D.Barnard *(Noted 1.02)*	Leicester	27. 6.00P
G-BSNO*	Denney Kitfox	PFA 172-11813		29. 6.90	Not known *(Damaged Sweethope Farm, Kelso 9.7.97: cancelled 18.11.97 as destroyed: stored 2001)*	East Fortune	
G-BSNP	Piper PA-28R-201T Turbo <u>Cherokee</u> Arrow III	28R-7703236	N38537	18. 7.90	D.F.K.Singleton	(Teck, Germany)	14. 9.02
G-BSNR	British Aerospace BAe 146 Srs.300	E3165	EC-FGT EC-807/G-6-165/G-BSNR/N886DV/G-BSNR/(N886DV)/G-6-165	13. 7.90	KLM UK Ltd *(Op Buzz)*	Stansted	20.11.03T
G-BSNT	Luscombe 8A Master (Continental A65)	1679	N37018 NC37018	16. 7.90	A.L.Nightingale *"Beryl" (Noted 9.00)*	RAF Mona	1. 1.02P
G-BSNU	Colt 105A HAFB	1811		23. 7.90	Sun Life Assurance Society plc *"Sun Life"*	Bristol	2. 2.97A
G-BSNV	Boeing 737-4Q8	25168		5. 2.92	British Airways (European Operations at Gatwick) Ltd	Gatwick	18. 2.02T
G-BSNW	Boeing 737-4Q8	25169		12. 3.92	British Airways (European Operations at Gatwick) Ltd	Gatwick	19. 3.02T
G-BSNX	Piper PA-28-181 Archer II	28-7990311	N3028S	19. 7.90	Halfpenny Green Flight Centre Ltd	Wolverhampton	19. 8.02T
G-BSNY	Bensen B.8M (Arrow GT500R)	PFA G/01-1176		16. 7.90	H.McCartney	Newtownards, Co.of Down	6. 9.01P
G-BSNZ	Cameron O-105 HAFB	2364		16. 7.90	Zebedee Balloon Service Ltd	Hungerford	21. 9.02A
G-BSOE	Luscombe 8A Silvaire *(C/n would indicate Model 8E)*	4331	N1604K NC1604K	22. 8.90	S.B.Marsden *(Stored dismantled as "N1604K" 4.00)*	Sturgate	
G-BSOF	Colt 25A Sky Chariot Mk.II HAFB	1820		27. 7.90	L P Cooper	Bristol	22. 7.00A
G-BSOG	Cessna 172M Skyhawk II	17263636	N1508V	16. 7.90	B.Chapman & A.R.Budden	Goodwood	12.12.02

G-BSOI	Aérospatiale AS332L Super Puma	2063	C-GSLE G-BSOI/C-GSLE	21. 9.90	CHC Scotia Ltd	Aberdeen	28. 3.03T
G-BSOJ	Thunder Ax7-77 HAFB	1818	JA-... G-BSOJ	31. 7.90	R.J.S.Jones	Stourbridge	3. 1.02A
G-BSOK	Piper PA-28-161 Cherokee Warrior II	28-7816191	N9749K	19. 7.90	Aeroshow Ltd	Gloucestershire	20. 1.03T
G-BSOM	Glaser-Dirks DG-400	4-126	LN-GMC D-KGDG	12. 7.90	M.J.Watson *"403"* t/a G-BSOM Group	Rufforth	4. 4.03
G-BSON	Green S-25 HAFB	001		7. 6.90	J.J.Green	Newbury	
G-BSOO	Cessna 172F	17252431	N8531U	19. 7.90	P.W.Lawrence t/a Double Oscar Flying Group	Seething	28.10.02
G-BSOR	CFM Streak Shadow (Rotax 532)	K.131-SA & PFA 161A-11602		23.10.89	J.P.Sorenson	Cranfield	21. 1.02P
G-BSOT	Piper PA-38-112 Tomahawk II	38-81A0053	N25682	23. 7.90	APB Leasing Ltd	Welshpool	22. 7.04
	(Veered off runway landing Welshpool 6.9.01: damage to engine cowling, undercarriage & both wings)						
G-BSOU	Piper PA-38-112 Tomahawk II	38-81A0130	N23373	23. 7.90	Mopps (UK) Ltd	Perth	10. 9.00T
G-BSOX	Luscombe 8AE Silvaire (Continental C85)	2318	N45791 NC45791	7. 8.90	R.S.Lanary *"Bobby Sox"*	Compton Abbas	19. 5.02P
G-BSOY	Piper PA-34-220T Seneca III	3433155	OY-CEU	1. 8.90	BAE Systems Flight Training (UK) Ltd *(Noted w/o BAE titles 11.00)*	(Perth)	8. 4.04T
G-BSOZ	Piper PA-28-161 Warrior II	28-7916080	N30220	14. 8.90	The Moray Flying Club 1990	RAF Kinloss	28.12.02T
G-BSPA	QAC Quickie Q.2 (Revmaster R2100DQ)	2227	N227T	16. 8.90	G.V.Mckirdy & B.K.Glover	Enstone	21. 8.01P
G-BSPB	Thunder Ax8-84 HAFB	1803		24. 7.90	Nigs Pertwee Ltd	Frinton-on-Sea	22. 9.00T
G-BSPC*	SAN Jodel D.140C Mousquetaire III	150	F-BMFN	2.11.81	Not known	Headcorn	31.10.85
	(Cancelled 15.8.94 by CAA: on overhaul 9.97: derelict remains noted 10.00)						
G-BSPE	Reims Cessna F172P Skyhawk II	F17202073		31.12.80	A.M.J.Clark	(Northallerton)	8. 6.02
G-BSPF*	Cessna T303 Crusader	T30300100	OY-SVH N3116C	31. 7.90	K P Gibben t/a G-BSPF Crusader Group	Blackpool	
	(Crashed Burton Joyce, Notts 16.7.98: cancelled 25.8.98 as WFU: wreck noted 12.01)						
G-BSPG	Piper PA-34-200T Seneca II	34-8070168	N8176S	8. 8.90	D.P.Hughes	Elstree	4.11.02
G-BSPI	Piper PA-28-161 Warrior II	28-8116025	N8258V	26. 7.90	Oxford Aviation Services Ltd	Oxford	9. 4.04T
G-BSPJ	Bensen B.8	PFA G/01-1061		3. 8.90	C.M.Jones *(Noted 1.02)*	Carlisle	
G-BSPK	Cessna 195A (Jacobs R-755-9)	7691	N1079D	14. 8.90	A.G. & D.L.Bompas	Biggin Hill	25. 4.03
G-BSPL	CFM Streak Shadow (Rotax 582)	K.140-SA		26. 7.90	MEL (Aviation Oxygen) Ltd	Northrepps	1. 9.00P
G-BSPM	Piper PA-28-161 Warrior II	28-8116046	N82679	27. 7.90	White Waltham Airfield Ltd *(Op West London Aero Services)*	White Waltham	11.10.03T
G-BSPN	Piper PA-28R-201T Turbo Cherokee Arrow III	28R-7703171	N5965V	31. 7.90	V.E.H.Taylor	(Carmarthen)	10. 1.03
G-BSPW*	Avid Speed Wing (Rotax 582)	PFA 189-11840		17. 7.90	M J Sewell *(Cancelled 20.9.00 by CAA) (Stored 12.01)*	Blackpool	27. 5.94P
G-BSPX	Neico Lancair 320	521-320-259FB & PFA 191-11865		31. 7.90	C.H.Skelt	(Reigate)	
G-BSRH	Pitts S-1C Special (Lycoming O-360)	LS-2	N4111	7. 8.90	M.R.Janney	Redhill	31. 8.02P
G-BSRI	Neico Lancair 235 (Lycoming O-235) *(Tri-cycle u/c)*	PFA 191-11467		9. 8.90	G.Lewis	Liverpool	1. 8.02P
G-BSRJ	Colt AA-1050 Gas FB	1782		20. 8.90	Trezpark Ltd *"White Fang"*	Colorado, USA	25. 9.02A
G-BSRK	ARV1 Super 2 (Hewland AE75)	K.007	ZK-FSQ	8. 8.90	D.M.Blair	(Holywell)	1. 6.02P
G-BSRL	Campbell Cricket Mk.4 rep	PFA G/03-1325		8. 8.90	I.Rosewall	Henstridge	17. 4.02P
	(Regd as, and rebuilt from, Everett Gyroplane Srs.2 c/n 0022 - converted by Peter Lovegrove)						
G-BSRP	Rotorway Executive (Rotorway RW 152)	3824		15. 8.90	R.J.Baker	Hawarden	8. 8.02P
G-BSRR	Cessna 182Q Skylane II	18266915	N96961	25. 7.90	Select Management Services Ltd	Egelsbach, Germany	10. 7.03
G-BSRT	Denney Kitfox mk.2 (Rotax 582)	742 & PFA 172-11873		9. 8.90	A.J.Lloyd	Little Down Farm, Milson	16. 7.02P
G-BSRX	CFM Streak Shadow (Rotax 618)	K.148-SA & PFA 206-11870		15. 8.90	P.Williams	Netherthorpe	22. 5.02P
G-BSRZ	Air Command 532 Elite Two-Seat	PFA G/05-1188		15. 8.90	A.S.G.Crabb	(Buxton)	
G-BSSA	Luscombe 8E Silvaire (Continental C85)	4176	N1449K NC1449K	15. 8.90	Luscombe Aircraft Ltd	White Waltham	29. 4.02P

G-BSSB	Cessna 150L Commuter	15074147	N19076	15. 8.90	D.T.A.Rees	Haverfordwest	14. 6.03T
G-BSSC	Piper PA-28-161 Warrior II		N81993	15. 8.90	Oxford Aviation Services Ltd		
		28-8216176	N9529N/N8234B			Gloucestershire	9. 2.03T
G-BSSE	Piper PA-28-140 Cherokee Cruiser		N33440	22.10.90	Comed Aviation Ltd	Blackpool	27. 5.02T
		28-7525192					
G-BSSF	Denney Kitfox mk.2			15. 8.90	S.G.Moores	Manston	20.11.02P
	(Rotax 582)	738 & PFA 172-11796					
G-BSSI	Rans S-6 Coyote II		(G-MWJA)	17. 8.90	J.Currell	(Bangor, Belfast)	16.11.99P
	(Rotax 582)	0190.112 & PFA 204-11782			*(New owner 9.01)*		
G-BSSK	QAC Quickie Q.200	PFA 094A-11354		5. 9.90	D.G.Greatrex	Enstone	23. 9.99P
	(Continental O-200-A)						
G-BSSO	Cameron O-90 HAFB	2255		23. 7.90	R.R. & J.E.Hatton *"Just So"*	Bristol	16. 1.02A
G-BSSP	Robin DR.400/180R Remorqueur	2015		24. 9.90	Soaring (Oxford) Ltd	RAF Syerston	8. 1.03
					(Op Air Cadets Gliding School)		
G-BSST*	British Aircraft Corporation-Sud Concorde SST			6. 5.68	The Science Museum	RNAS Yeovilton	31.10.74P
		13520 & 002			*(WFU 4.3.76 & cancelled 21.1.87 as WFU)*		
G-BSSV	CFM Streak Shadow			21. 8.90	R.W.Payne	Langtoft	5. 5.98P
	(Rotax 532)	K.129-SA & PFA 206-11657					
G-BSSW	Piper PA-28-161 Cherokee Warrior II		N47850	29. 8.90	R.L.Hayward	Filton	8. 7.02T
		28-7816143			*(Op Bristol Flying Club)*		
G-BSSX	Piper PA-28-161 Warrior II	2816056	N9141H	11. 9.90	Airways Aero Associations Ltd	Booker	11.11.02T
					(Op British Airways Flying Club)		
G-BSTC	Aeronca 11AC Chief	11AC-1660	N3289E	15.10.90	J Armstrong & D Lamb	(Crook)	26. 6.93P
	(Continental A65)		NC3289E	*(Damaged Henstridge 18.4.93: on rebuild 12.95: new owners 1.02)*			
G-BSTE	Aérospatiale AS355F2 Twin Squirrel			29. 8.90	Hygrade Foods Ltd	Biggin Hill	10. 8.03
		5453					
G-BSTH	Piper PA-25-235 Pawnee C	25-5009	N8599L	25. 9.90	Scottish Gliding Union Ltd	Portmoak	15. 3.03
G-BSTI	Piper J-3C-65 Cub	19144	N6007H	31. 8.90	I.Fraser & G.L.Nunn	Knettishall	3. 2.01P
	(Continental C85) *(Frame No.19073)*		NC6007H				
G-BSTK	Thunder Ax8-90 HAFB	1838		17. 9.90	M.Williams	Wadhurst, E.Sussex	4. 5.95A
G-BSTL	Rand Robinson KR-2	PFA 129-11863		6. 9.90	C.S.Hales	Shenington	27. 6.02P
					(May incorporate G-BYLP qv)		
G-BSTM	Cessna 172L Skyhawk	17260143	N4243Q	25. 9.90	A.H.Windle t/a G-BSTM Group	Cambridge	1. 3.03
G-BSTO	Cessna 152 II	15282133	N68005	4. 9.90	Plymouth School of Flying Ltd	Plymouth	5.12.02T
G-BSTP	Cessna 152 II	15282925	N89953	4. 9.90	Cobham Leasing Ltd	Bournemouth	4.11.02T
G-BSTR	Grumman-American AA-5 Traveler		OO-ALR	8.10.90	James Allan (Aviation & Engineering) Ltd		
		AA5-0688	OO-HAN/(OO-WAZ)			Sorbie Farm, Kingsmuir	4.12.02
G-BSTT	Rans S-6 Coyote II			5. 9.90	D.G.Palmer	Fetterangus	2.12.02P
	(Rotax 582)	0190.115 & PFA 204-11880					
G-BSTV	Piper PA-32-300 Cherokee Six		N4069R	13. 9.90	B.C.Hudson	Popham	
		32-40378			*(Open store 7.00)*		
G-BSTX	Luscombe 8A Silvaire	3301	EI-CDZ	10. 9.90	G.R.Nicholson	(Newry, Co.Armagh)	29.11.02P
			G-BSTX/N71874/NC71874				
G-BSTY	Thunder Ax8-90 HAFB	394		12. 9.90	M.V.Farrant	Billingshurst	24. 6.01A
					t/a Shere Balloon Group *"Beastie"*		
G-BSTZ	Piper PA-28-140 Cherokee Cruiser		N1674H	10.10.90	Air Navigation & Trading Co Ltd		
		28-7725153				Blackpool	18.11.02T
G-BSUA	Rans S-6 Coyote II	PFA 204-11910		29.10.90	A.J.Todd		
	(Rotax 582)					Abbey Warren Farm, Bucknall, Lincoln	17. 7.02P
G-BSUB	Colt 77A HAFB	1801		30.10.90	R.R.J.Wilson & M.P.Hill	Bristol	16. 6.02A
G-BSUD	Luscombe 8A Master	1745	N37084	14. 9.90	I.G.Harrison	Derby	18.12.02P
	(Continental A65)		NC37084				
G-BSUE	Cessna U206G Stationair II	U20604334	N756TB	6. 9.90	R D Masters	Andrewsfield	7. 3.04
					(Noted for rebuild 12.01 following landing damage)		
G-BSUF	Piper PA-32RT-300 Lance II		N32PL	17. 9.90	S.T.Laffin	Blackbushe	21. 8.03
		32R-7885240	ZP-PJQ/N9641N				
G-BSUH*	Cessna 140	8092	N89088	15.10.90	Not known	Abbeyshrule, Co.Longford	2. 5.94
	(Continental C85)		NC89088				
			(Damaged Gowran Grange 6.93: cancelled 28.4.95 by CAA: airframe stored 5.00)				
G-BSUJ	Brugger MB.2 Colibri	PFA 043-10726		17. 9.90	M.A.Farrelly	(Liverpool)	
G-BSUK	Colt 77A HAFB	1374		21. 9.90	A.J.Moore	Northwood, Middlesex	2. 8.94A
G-BSUO	Scheibe SF-25C-2000 Falke	44501	D-KIOK	6.12.90	British Gliding Association Ltd	Bicester	22. 6.03
G-BSUR	Rotorway Executive 90	5003		21. 9.90	Psion Manufacturing Ltd *(Current status unknown)*		
	(Rotorway RI 162)					(Ballynacarrigy, Co.Westmeath)	1.12.93P
G-BSUT	Rans S-6-ESA Coyote II			2.10.90	J.Bell	Barton	20.12.01P
	(Rotax 582)	0990.138 & PFA 204-11897					
G-BSUU	Colt 180A HAFB	1851		17. 9.90	Balloon School (International) Ltd	Bath	18. 2.01T
					t/a British School of Ballooning		
					(Op Heritage Balloons) (VW/Audi titles)		
G-BSUV	Cameron O-77 HAFB	2407		26. 9.90	R.Moss	Banchory	8. 9.02A
G-BSUW	Piper PA-34-200T Seneca II		N2360M	26. 9.90	TG Aviation Ltd	Manston	20.12.02T
		34-7870081			*(Op Thanet Flying Club)*		

G-BSUX	Carlson Sparrow II	PFA 209-11794		5.10.90	J.Stephenson	Wombleton	20. 5.02P
	(Rotax 532)						
G-BSUZ	Denney Kitfox mk.3			10. 9.90	M.J.Clark	Sedgwick	3. 9.02P
	(Rotax 582)	745 & PFA 172-11875					
G-BSVB	Piper PA-28-181 Archer II	2890098	N9155S	10. 9.90	Datewold Ltd	Bournemouth	16. 1.03T
G-BSVE	Binder CP.301S Smaragd	113	HB-SED	27. 9.90	R.E.Perry	Halesland	21.11.02P
					t/a Smaragd Flying Group		
G-BSVG	Piper PA-28-161 Warrior II		C-GZAV	2.10.90	Airways Aero Associations Ltd	Booker	22.12.02T
		28-8516013			*(Op British Airways Flying Club) (Colum t/s)*		
G-BSVH	Piper J-3C-65 Cub	15360	N87702	2.10.90	A.R.Meakin	Eastbach Farm, Coleford	13. 8.01P
	(Continental A75) *(Frame No.15003)*		NC87702				
G-BSVI	Piper PA-16 Clipper	16-186	N5379H	7.11.90	I.R.Blakemore	Old Sarum	30. 6.01
					"Spirit of St.Petersburg"		
G-BSVK	Denney Kitfox mk.2	PFA 172-11731		2.10.90	C.M.Looney	(Leatherhead)	5. 4.94P
	(Rotax 582)						
G-BSVM	Piper PA-28-161 Warrior II		N8351N	7.11.90	EFG Flying Services Ltd	Biggin Hill	2. 2.03T
		28-8116173					
G-BSVN	Thorp T-18	107	N4881	17. 9.90	J.H.Kirkham	Barton	18. 6.02P
	(Lycoming O-290)						
G-BSVP	Piper PA-23-250 Aztec F	27-7754115	N63787	9. 2.78	Time Electronics Ltd	Lydd	24. 6.02
G-BSVR	Schweizer Hughes 269C (300C)	S.1236	OO-JWW	14.11.90	Martinair Ltd	Sherburn in Elmet	4. 6.04
			D-HLEB				
G-BSVS	Robin DR.400/100 Cadet	2017		22.10.90	D.M.Chalmers	Upper Harford	22. 3.03
G-BSVV	Piper PA-38-112 Tomahawk	38-79A0723	N2492L	3.10.90	H & E Merkado	Panshanger	10. 6.03T
G-BSVW	Piper PA-38-112 Tomahawk	38-79A0149	N2606B	9.11.90	Goodair Leasing Ltd	Cardiff	25. 4.04T
G-BSVX	Piper PA-38-112 Tomahawk	38-79A0950	N2336P	10. 1.91	Cristal Air Ltd.	Rochester	14. 5.03T
G-BSVZ	Pietenpol Air Camper	1008	N3265	6.11.90	G.F.M.Garner	(Wootton Rivers)	6. 9.93P
	(Regd as a Pietenpol/Challis Chaffinch)				*(On rebuild 2000)*		
G-BSWB	Rans S-10 Sakota			8.10.90	F.A.Hewitt	Garston Farm, Marshfield	15. 5.02P
	(Rotax 532)	0489.046 & PFA 194-11560					
G-BSWC	Boeing-Stearman E75 (PT-13D) Kaydet		N17112	16.11.90	R.J.Thwaites	(Apperley, Glos)	11. 9.03T
	(Lycoming R-680)	75-5560	N5021V/42-17397		*(As "112" in US Army c/s)*		
G-BSWF	Piper PA-16 Clipper	16-475	N5865H	12.10.90	T.M.Storey	Redhill	4. 2.02
	(Lycoming O-320)						
G-BSWG	Piper PA-17 Vagabond	15-99	N4316H	8.10.90	P.E.J.Sturgeon		
	(Continental A65-8)		NC4316H			Queach Farm, Bury St Edmunds	24.10.02P
G-BSWH	Cessna 152 II	15281365	N49861	15.10.90	Airspeed Aviation Ltd	Derby	14. 3.02T
G-BSWI*	Rans S-10 Sakota	PFA 194-11872		16.10.90	J.M.Mooney	(Shotts, Lanark)	11. 6.94P
	(Rotax 532)	*(Damaged Braehead 26.10.93: cancelled 1.2.00 as temporarily WFU: current status unknown)*					
G-BSWL	Slingsby T.61F Venture T.2	1974	EI-CCQ	15.10.90	K.Richards	Talgarth	11. 3.04
			G-BSWL/ZA655				
G-BSWM	Slingsby T.61F Venture T.2	1965	ZA629	12.10.90	L.J.McKelvie	Bellarena	26. 3.03
					t/a The Venture Gliding Group		
G-BSWR	Pilatus Britten-Norman BN-2T Turbine Islander			22.10.90	Police Authority for Northern Ireland		
		2245			*(Op Royal Ulster Constabulary)*	Belfast	2. 3.04T
G-BSWV	Cameron N-77 HAFB	2369		22.10.90	S.Charlish	Leicester	19. 2.01A
					"Leicester Mercury"		
G-BSWX	Cameron V-90 HAFB	2401		22.10.90	B.J.Burrows *"Beeswax"*	Bristol	29. 6.01A
G-BSWY	Cameron N-77 HAFB	2428		12.10.90	M.R.Nanda	Nottingham	19. 6.02A
					t/a Nottingham Balloon Club		
G-BSWZ	Cameron A-180 HAFB	2419	C-FGWZ	22.10.90	G.C.Ludlow	Kirdford	19. 7.99T
			G-BSWZ		*"Keep Britain Farming" (Op Balloon Preservation Group)*		
G-BSXA	Piper PA-28-161 Warrior II		N4373Z	11.12.90	A.S.Bamrah	Biggin Hill	2. 8.03T
		28-8416121	N9622N		t/a Falcon Flying Services		
G-BSXB	Piper PA-28-161 Warrior II		N4374D	4.12.90	Aeros Leasing Ltd	Gloucestershire	13. 4.03T
		28-8416125	N9626N				
G-BSXC	Piper PA-28-161 Warrior II		N4374F	4.12.90	L.T.Halpin	Clutton Hill Farm, Clutton	2. 9.04T
		28-8416126	N9627N				
G-BSXD	Soko P-2 Kraguj	030	30146	22.10.90	L.C.MacKnight	Elstree	22. 4.99P
			Yugoslav Army		*(As "30146" in Yugoslav Army c/s)*		
G-BSXI	Mooney M.20E Chapparal	700056	N6766V	31.10.90	A.N.Pain	Southend	4. 5.03
G-BSXM	Cameron V-77 HAFB	2446		5.11.90	C.A.Oxby *"Oxby"*	Doncaster	15. 1.02A
G-BSXN	Robinson R22 Beta	1611		14.11.90	J.G.Gray	Berwick-upon-Tweed	9. 2.03
G-BSXS	Piper PA-28-181 Archer II	28-7990151	N3055C	26.11.90	Jaxx Landing Ltd	Swansea	9.12.02T
G-BSXT	Piper J-5A Cub Cruiser	5-498	N33409	8.11.90	M.G. & K.J.Thompson		
	(Continental C85)		NC33409			Belle Vue Farm, Yarnscombe	26. 7.02P
G-BSXX	Whittaker MW7	PFA 171-11469		16.10.90	H.J.Stanley	(Abingdon)	
G-BSXZ	British Aerospace BAe 146 Srs.300		G-NJIB	14.11.90	Flightline Ltd	Southend	11. 4.04T
		E3174	B-1776/G-BSXZ/G-6-174				
G-BSYA	Jodel D.18	PFA 169-11316		7.11.90	S.Harrison	Eshott	26. 6.02P
	(VW 1834)						
G-BSYB	Cameron N-120 HAFB	2406		7.11.90	M.Buono	Siena, Italy	15. 6.02A

G-BSYC	Piper PA-32R-300 Lance	32R-7780159	N7745T N1435H	2. 4.91	M.N.Pinches	Wolverhampton	8. 5.03
G-BSYD	Cameron A-180 HAFB	2426		18.10.90	A.A.Brown t/a Balloon Company *"Discovery"*	Guildford	20. 9.02T
G-BSYF	Luscombe 8A Silvaire	3455	N72028 NC72028	12.11.90	Atlantic Connexions Ltd t/a Atlantic Aviation *(Noted 9.01)*	Little Gransden	
G-BSYG	Piper PA-12 Super Cruiser (Lycoming O-235)	12-2106	N3228M NC3228M	12.11.90	E.R.Newall t/a Fat Cub Group	Breighton	15. 7.02P
G-BSYH	Luscombe 8A Silvaire (Continental A65)	2842	N71415 NC71415	13.11.90	N.R.Osborne	Insch	28.11.02P
G-BSYI	Aérospatiale AS355F1 Twin Squirrel	5197	M-MJI	14.11.90	Lynton Aviation Ltd t/a Signature Aircraft Charter	Denham	28.11.02T
G-BSYK*	Piper PA-38-112 Tomahawk II	38-81A0143	N23449	30. 1.91	Flychoice Ltd *(No CofA issued: cancelled 10.3.99 by CAA: stored 5.01)*	Wolverhampton	
G-BSYL*	Piper PA-38-112 Tomahawk II	38-81A0172	N91333	23. 1.91	Flychoice Ltd *(No CofA issued: cancelled 10.3.99 by CAA: stored 5.01)*	Wolverhampton	
G-BSYM*	Piper PA-38-112 Tomahawk II	38-82A0072	N2507V	30. 1.91	Flychoice Ltd *(Damaged 27.7.94: noted 5.00: cancelled 26.10.00 by CAA)*	Wellesbourne Mountford	4. 9.94T
G-BSYO	Piper J-3C-65 Cub (L-4B-PI) (Continental O-200-A) *(Frame No.12639)* *(Officially regd as c/n 10244 which is HB-OVG ex 43-1383/F-BFYF)*	12809	(G-BSMJ) (G-BRHE)/EC-AIY/HB-ODO/HB-OUA/44-80513	19. 2.91	C.R.Reynolds & J.D.Fuller *(Force landed & overturned 1 mile NW Cranfield 23.6.00 due to engine failure)*	Pent Farm, Postling, Kent	12. 3.02P
G-BSYU	Robin DR.400/180 Regent	2027		26.11.90	K.J.J.Jarman & P.D.Smoothy	Hinton-in-the-Hedges	11. 4.03
G-BSYV	Cessna 150M	15078371	N9423U	16.11.90	L.R.Haunch t/a Fenland Flying School	Fenland	16. 3.03T
G-BSYW*	Cessna 150M	15078446	N9498U	16.11.90	J Cropper *(Cancelled 19.4.01 by CAA)*	Barton	25. 3.00
G-BSYZ	Piper PA-28-161 Warrior II	28-8516051	N6908H	22.11.90	S.W.Cowie t/a Yankee Zulu Group *(Op Glasgow Flying Club)*	Glasgow	26. 9.03T
G-BSZB	Stolp SA.300 Starduster Too (Lycoming O-360)	545	N5495M	3.12.90	D.T.Gethin	Haverfordwest	24. 6.02P
G-BSZC	Beechcraft C-45H-BH Expeditor *(Originally built as AT-7 42-2490 c/n 4166: re-manufactured 4.52)*	AF-258	N9541Z 51-11701	14.12.90	A.A.Hodgson *"Southern Comfort" (As "AF258/51-11701A" in USAF c/s)*	Bryngwyn Bach	1. 6.03
G-BSZD	Robin DR.400/180 Regent	2029		21.11.90	R.J.Hitchman & M.Rowland	Draycott Farm, Chiseldon	4. 4.03
G-BSZF	CEA Jodel DR.250/160 Capitaine	32	F-BNJB	29.11.90	J.B.Randle	Piltdown, E.Sussex	24. 4.03
G-BSZG	Stolp SA.100 Starduster (Lycoming O-320)	101	N70P	27.11.90	D.F.Chapman *(Noted 4.01)*	Headcorn	4. 7.00P
G-BSZH	Thunder Ax7-77 HAFB	1848		27.11.90	K.E.Viney & L.J.Weston *"Her Outdoors"*	Olney	29.11.01T
G-BSZI	Cessna 152 II	15285856	N95139	17.12.90	Eglinton Flying Club Ltd	City of Derry	27. 2.03T
G-BSZJ	Piper PA-28-181 Archer II	28-8190216	N8373Z	6.12.90	R.D.Fuller & M.L.A.Pudney	St Lawrence, Bradwell-on-Sea	3. 5.03
G-BSZM	Montgomerie-Bensen B.8MR (Rotax 582)	PFA G/01-1193		30.11.90	A.McCredie	Carlisle	6. 9.02P
G-BSZN	Bücker Bü.133D-1 Jungmeister (Siemens Bramo SH14A) *(Built Bitz)*	2002	N8103 D-ECAY(1)	30.11.90	A.J.Norman t/a Norman Aeroplane Trust	Cambridge	21.10.01P
G-BSZO	Cessna 152 II	15280221	N24334	30.11.90	Hecray Co Ltd t/a Direct Helicopters *(Op Southend School of Flying)*	Southend	17.12.04T
G-BSZS	Robinson R22 Beta	1235	N8058J	13.12.90	A.Liddiard t/a Bladerunner Helicopters	Shobdon	3. 4.03T
G-BSZT	Piper PA-28-161 Warrior II	28-8116027	N8260D	31.12.90	Jade Air plc	Shoreham	8. 4.03T
G-BSZU	Cessna 150F	15063481	N6881F	3.12.90	M.J.Tarrant	Old Sarum	19.12.00T
G-BSZV	Cessna 150F	15062304	N3504L	3.12.90	Kirmington Aviation Ltd	Sandown, IoW	17. 7.03T
G-BSZW	Cessna 152 II	15281072	N48958	3.12.90	Haimoss Ltd	Old Sarum	6.12.03T
G-BSZY*	Cameron A-180 HAFB	2479		3. 1.91	K.H.Benning *(Cancelled 18.10.01 by CAA)*	Telgte, Germany	2. 1.96A

G-BTAA – G-BTZZ

G-BTAB	British Aerospace BAe.125 Srs.800B	258088	G-5-563 G-BOOA/(ZK-RHP)/G-5-563	12. 7.88	Aravco Ltd	Farnborough	6. 5.02T
G-BTAG	Cameron O-77 HAFB	2454		12.11.90	R.A.Shapland *"Tag-Along"*	Petworth	13. 1.02A
G-BTAH	Bensen B.8M (Arrow GT500R)	PFA G/07-1196		13.12.90	C.J.Toner *(Noted 5.00)*	Abbeysrule	31. 8.98P
G-BTAK	EAA Acrosport 2 (Lycoming O-320)	1-468	N440X	27.12.90	P.G.Harrison *"The Duck"*	Sywell	15. 3.02P
G-BTAL	Reims Cessna F.152 II	F15201444		7. 4.78	TG Aviation Ltd *(Op Thanet Flying Club)*	Manston	16. 3.03T

G-BTAN	Thunder Ax7-65Z HAFB	517		4. 5.83	A.S.Newnham	Southampton	2. 8.00A
G-BTAP	Piper PA-38-112 Tomahawk	38-78A0141	N9603T	8. 1.91	Western Air (Thruxton) Ltd	Thruxton	20. 7.03T
G-BTAR	Piper PA-38-112 Tomahawk	38-79A0383	N2584D	13. 2.91	Aerohire Ltd	Blackpool	12. 3.00T
					(Damaged Liverpool 19.6.98: on rebuild 12.01)		
G-BTAS	Piper PA-38-112 Tomahawk	38-79A0545	F-GTAS	21. 2.91	Goodair Leasing Ltd	Cardiff	13. 6.03T
			G-BTAS/N2492G				
G-BTAT	Denney Kitfox mk.2			6.11.90	J M Keane	(Brighton)	22. 4.02P
	(Rotax 582)	689 & PFA 172-11832					
G-BTAU	Thunder Ax7-77 HAFB	1429		13.12.90	S.& G.Gebauer	Lippstadt, Germany	17. 4.02A
G-BTAW	Piper PA-28-161 Warrior II		N9259T	14.12.90	A.J.Wiggins	Gloucestershire	16. 5.03T
		28-8616031			*(Op Gloucester & Cheltenham Flying School)*		
G-BTAZ	Evans VP-2	PFA 063-11474		13.12.90	G.S.Poulter	Norwich	
					(Noted complete 6.00)		
G-BTBA	Robinson R22 Beta	1717		18. 3.91	Heliflight (UK) Ltd	Wolverhampton	30. 4.03
G-BTBB	Thunder Ax8-105 Srs.2 HAFB	1871		23.11.90	W.J.Brogan	(Steiermark, Austria)	3. 3.98T
G-BTBC	Piper PA-28-161 Warrior II		N28755	19.12.90	M.J.L.MacDonald	Wellesbourne Mountford	21. 4.03T
		28-7916414			*(Op Wellesbourne Aviation)*		
G-BTBF	Fisher FP.202 Super Koala		(G-MWOZ)	24.12.90	E.A.Taylor	(Southend)	
		SK.067 & PFA 158-11954			*(Under construction 1.02)*		
G-BTBG	Denney Kitfox mk.2	PFA 172-11845		18.12.90	P D Brookes	Long Marston	2. 1.03P
G-BTBH	Ryan ST3KR (PT-22-RY)	2063	N854	18. 2.91	A.T.Hooper & C.C.Silk t/a Ryan Group		
	(Kinner R56)		N50993/41-20854		Bericote Farm, Blackdown, Leamington Spa		9.12.02P
					(As "854" in US Army c/s)		
G-BTBI	WAR P-47 Thunderbolt rep	0054	N47DL	8. 1.91	E.C.Murgatroyd	Sackville Farm, Riseley	8. 9.98P
	(Continental O-200-A) *(Marked as "Project No.52685A")*				*(As "85" in USAF c/s) "Lil Jug"*		
					(Crashed on take off Carlisle 26.4.99: current status unknown)		
G-BTBJ	Cessna 190	16046	N4461C	2.10.91	P.Camus	(Dijon, France)	21. 8.03
	(Orig regd as Cessna 195B) (Re-designated 6.01 fitted with Jacobs Aircraft & Engines R-755-B2)						
G-BTBL	Montgomerie-Bensen B.8MR Merlin			21.12.90	N.H.Collins	Cork Farm, Streethay	2. 9.01P
	(Rotax 532)	PFA G/01A-1183			t/a AES Radionic Surveillance Systems		
					(Lost power on take-off Roddidge, Alrewas 27. 4.01 & incurred substantial damage)		
G-BTBN	Denney Kitfox mk.2			31.12.90	R.C.Bowley	Croft Farm, Defford	1. 8.02P
	(Rotax 582)	686 & PFA 172-11859					
G-BTBP	Cameron N-90 HAFB	2464		21.12.90	Julia B.Turnau	Pianella, Italy	21. 6.00A
					t/a Chianti Balloon Club		
G-BTBR	Cameron DP-80 Hot-Air Airship	2344		21.12.90	Cameron Balloons Ltd	Bristol	3.12.97A
G-BTBU	Piper PA-18-150 Super Cub	18-7509010	N9665P	3. 1.91	A.J.White t/a G-BTBU Syndicate	Redhill	24. 7.03
G-BTBV	Cessna 140	12727	N2474N	2. 4.91	M.S.Johnson	Enstone	6. 8.03
	(Continental C85)		NC2474N				
G-BTBW	Cessna 120	14220	N2009V	24. 1.91	Melanie J.Willies		
	(Continental C90)		NC2009V			Standalone Farm, Meppershall	25. 7.04
G-BTBX	Piper J-3C-65 Cub	6334	N35367	29. 1.91	J.B.Hargrave & D.T.C.Collins	RAF Henlow	3.10.03
			NC35367		t/a Henlow Taildraggers		
G-BTBY	Piper PA-17 Vagabond	17-195	N4894H	4. 1.91	G.J.Smith	Clipgate Farm, Denton	1. 5.02P
	(Continental C85)						
G-BTCA	Piper PA-32R-300 Lance	32R-7780381	N5941V	10. 1.91	P.Taylor	Wolverhampton	26. 5.03
					t/a Lance Group		
G-BTCB	Air Command 582 Sport			9. 1.91	G.Scurrah	Millom	
		0634 & PFA G/04-1198			*(Nearing completion 5.95: current status unknown)*		
G-BTCC	Grumman F6F-5K Hellcat	A-11286	(N10CN)	31.12.90	Patina Ltd	Duxford	6. 7.02P
			N100T/FN80142/Bu.80141		*(Op The Fighter Collection)*		
	(Composite with centre section from F6F-3 Bu.08831 c/n A-218)				*(As "Bu.40467/19" in VF-6 Sqn US Navy c/s)*		
G-BTCD	North American P-51D-25NA Mustang		N51JJ	11. 1.91	Pelham Ltd	Duxford	2. 5.02P
		122-39608	N6340T/RCAF 9568/44-73149		*(Op The Old Flying Machine Co) "Candyman"/Moose"*		
					(As "463221/E2-Z" in 362nd FS/357th FG USAAF c/s)		
G-BTCE	Cessna 152 II	15281376	N49876	10. 1.91	S.T.Gilbert	Enstone	11. 4.04T
	(Tail-wheel conversion)						
G-BTCH	Luscombe 8E Silvaire	6403	N1976B	11. 2.91	J.Grewcock & R.C.Carroll	Popham	13. 9.02P
	(Continental C85)		NC1976B				
G-BTCI	Piper PA-17 Vagabond	17-136	N4839H	11. 1.91	T.R.Whittome	Inverness	5. 7.02P
	(Continental A65)		NC4839H				
G-BTCJ	Luscombe 8AE Silvaire	1869	N41908	16. 1.91	Mrs J.M.Lovell	Chilbolton	28. 5.02P
	(Continental O-200A)		NC41908				
G-BTCM	Cameron N-90 HAFB	1306	(G-BMPW)	8. 5.86	Zebedee Balloon Service Ltd	Hungerford	10.10.00A
G-BTCR	Rans S-10 Sakota	PFA 194-11877		11. 1.91	B.J.Hewitt	Newtownards, Co.of Down	11. 1.02P
	(Rotax 532)						
G-BTCS	Colt 90A HAFB	1895		11. 1.91	R.C.Stone	Reading	16. 7.01A
					"Rosie Rags" (Variety Club of GB titles)		
G-BTCW	Cameron A-180 HAFB	2458		17. 1.91	P.Clark t/a Bristol Balloons	Bristol	21. 7.00T
G-BTCZ	Cameron Chateau 84SS HAFB	2246		18. 1.91	Forbes Europe Inc	Balleroy, Normandy	7. 7.02
					"Chateau II"		

G-BTDA	Slingsby T.61F Venture T.2	1870	XZ550	17. 4.91	T.Holloway t/a RAFGSA *(Op Anglia Gliding Club)*	RAF Wattisham	29. 5.03
G-BTDC	Denney Kitfox mk.2	405 & PFA 172-11483		11. 1.91	O.Smith	(Crook)	
G-BTDD	CFM Streak Shadow (Rotax 582)	K.127-SA & PFA 161A-11622		14. 1.91	N.D.Ewer	Plaistows, St Albans	1. 9.01P
G-BTDE	Cessna C-165 Airmaster	551	N21911 NC21911	18. 1.91	G.S.Moss	Popham	11.10.03
G-BTDF	Luscombe 8AF Silvaire (Continental C90)	2205	N45678 NC45678	17. 4.91	R.Harrison t/a Delta Foxtrot Group *(Current status unknown)*	(Sunderland)	19. 8.93P
G-BTDN	Denney Kitfox mk.2	688 & PFA 172-11826		22. 1.91	S.D.Arnold t/a Foxy Flyers Group	Long Marston	17. 6.02P
G-BTDP	Grumman TBM-3R Avenger	3381	N3966A Bu.53319	5. 2.91	A.Haig-Thomas *(As "53319/RB-319" in USN c/s)*	North Weald	18. 5.02P
G-BTDR	Aero Designs Pulsar (Rotax 582)	PFA 202-11962		24. 1.91	M.Jordan	North Weald	14. 6.02P
G-BTDS	Colt 77A HAFB	1897		29. 1.91	CP Witter Ltd *"Witters II"*	Chester	28. 3.02A
G-BTDT	CASA I-131E Jungmann Srs.2000	2131	E3B-505	5. 2.91	T.A.Reed *(Noted 9.00)*	Watchford Farm, Yarcombe	22. 5.02P
G-BTDV	Piper PA-28-161 Cherokee Warrior II	28-7816355	N3548M	25. 2.91	Southern Flight Centre Ltd	Shoreham	18. 6.04T
G-BTDW	Cessna 152 II	15279864	N757NC	25. 2.91	J.A.Blenkharn	Carlisle	18.10.03T
G-BTDX	Piper PA-18-150 Super Cub	18-7809098	N62595	28. 1.91	A.D. Hammond t/a Hammond Aviation	Waits Farm, Belchamp Walter	15. 3.04T
G-BTDZ	CASA I-131E Jungmann Srs.2000	2104	E3B-524	5. 2.91	R.J.Pickin & I.M.White	Headcorn	29. 5.02P
G-BTEA	Cameron N-105 HAFB	284		31. 5.77	M.W.A.Shemilt *"Big Red"*	Henley-on-Thames	8. 5.99A
G-BTEE	Cameron O-120 HAFB	2499		24. 1.91	W.H. & J.P.Morgan *"Y Ddraig Goch/The Red Dragon"*	Swansea	17. 5.02T
G-BTEF*	Pitts S-1 Special (Lycoming IO-360)	515H	N88PR	19. 2.91	C.Davidson t/a Northwest Aerobatics *(Cancelled 29.10.01 by CAA) (Stored 12.01)*	Blackpool	28.10.97P
G-BTEI*	Everett Campbell Cricket Gyroplane Srs.3	023		31. 1.91	R A Jarvis *(Damaged landing nr Great Orton 15.8.95: stored 2001) (Cancelled 23.5.01 by CAA)*	Sorbie Farm, Kingsmuir	21.12.98P
G-BTEK	SOCATA TB-20 Trinidad	1240		4. 2.91	M Northwood	Enstone	19. 8.02
G-BTEL	CFM Streak Shadow (Rotax 618)	K.125-SA & PFA 206-11667		31. 1.91	J.E.Eatwell	Boscombe Down	30. 8.01P
G-BTES	Cessna 150H	15068371	N22575	29. 4.91	R.A.Forward	Spilsted Farm, Sedlescombe	19. 6.04
G-BTET	Piper J-3C-65 Cub	18296	N98141 NC98141	5. 2.91	R.M.Jones	Blackpool	24. 5.02P
G-BTEU	Aérospatiale SA.365N2 Dauphin 2	6392		11. 2.91	CHC Scotia Ltd	Humberside	1. 4.01T
G-BTEW	Cessna 120 (Continental C90)	10238	CF-ELE	29. 4.91	Kay F.Mason	Norwich	28. 6.04
G-BTEX	Piper PA-28-140 Cherokee	28-23773	CF-XXL N3907K	24. 4.91	McAully Flying Group Ltd	Little Snoring	11. 4.04T
G-BTFA	Denney Kitfox mk.2 (Rotax 503)	566 & PFA 172-11520		13. 2.91	K.R.Peek *(Damaged North Moreton 18.6.97: current status unknown)*	Church Farm, North Moreton	6.10.94P
G-BTFC	Reims Cessna F.152 II	F15201668		23. 5.79	Tayside Aviation Ltd	Dundee	29. 3.04T
G-BTFD*	Colt AS-105 mk.II Hot-Air Airship	1856		13. 2.91	Media Fantasy Aviation UK Ltd *(No CofA issued: cancelled 26.10.00 by CAA)*	London SE16	
G-BTFE	Parsons Gyroplane Model 1 (Rotax 582) *(Tandem Trainer)*	38		13. 2.91	J.R.Goldspink	Haverfordwest	27.10.01P
G-BTFF	Cessna T310R II	310R0718	N1363G	25. 2.91	Clear Prop Ltd	Blackbushe	29. 5.03
G-BTFG	Boeing-Stearman A75N1 (N2S-4) Kaydet (Continental W670)	75-3441	N4467N Bu.30010	20. 2.91	D.S.Milne *(As "441" in USN c/s)*	Dundee	6. 4.02
G-BTFJ	Piper PA-15 Vagabond (Lycoming O-145)	15-159	N4373H NC4373H	13. 2.91	C.W.Thirtle & R.J.Court t/a Vagabond FJ Flying Group	Old Sarum	8. 6.02P
G-BTFK	Taylorcraft BC-12D (Continental A65)	10540	N599SB N5240M	13. 2.91	M.Gibson	(Raheen, Co.Limerick)	16. 2.00P
G-BTFL	Aeronca 11AC Chief	11AC-1727	N3403E NC3403E	18. 2.91	J.G.Vaughan t/a BTFL Group	Eastbach Farm, Coleford	26.11.02P
G-BTFM	Cameron O-105 HAFB	2623		12. 8.91	P.Forster & J.Trehern t/a Edinburgh University Hot-Air Balloon Club	Edinburgh	18. 8.99A
G-BTFO	Piper PA-28-161 Cherokee Warrior II	28-7816580	N31728	12. 3.91	Flyfar Ltd	Blackpool	22. 5.03
G-BTFP	Piper PA-38-112 Tomahawk	38-78A0340	N6201A	17. 4.91	Teesside Flight Centre Ltd *(Stored 12.01)*	Teesside	6. 8.00T
G-BTFS	Cessna A150M Aerobat	A1500719	N20331	20. 2.91	P.A.James	Redhill	1. 5.03T
G-BTFT	Beechcraft 58 Baron	TH-979	N2036W	14. 3.91	Fastwing Air Charter Ltd	Thruxton	8. 4.04T
G-BTFU	Cameron N-90 HAFB	2391		28. 2.91	J.J.Rudoni & A.C.K.Rawson t/a Wickers World Hot Air Balloon Co *"Maltesers II"*	Stafford	30. 9.01A
G-BTFV	Whittaker MW7 (Rotax 532)	PFA 171-11722		8. 2.91	S.J.Luck	Tower Farm, Wollaston	29.11.01P

G-BTFW	Montgomerie-Bensen B.8MR			20. 2.91	J.R.J.Read	(North Cotes, Grimsby)	9. 8.96P
	(Rotax 532)	PFA G/01A-1141					
G-BTFX	Bell 206B JetRanger II	1648	N400MH	20. 2.91	J.Selwyn Smith (Shepley) Ltd		
			N90219			Shepley, Huddersfield	1. 5.03T
G-BTFY	Bell 206B JetRanger II	1714	(ZS-)	20. 2.91	Hughes Helicopter Co. Ltd.	Biggin Hill	29. 5.04T
			G-BTFY/N49590		t/a Biggin Hill Helicopters		
G-BTGA	Boeing-Stearman A75N1 (PT-17) Kaydet		N65501	21. 2.91	Classic Aviation Ltd	Duxford	6. 7.01
	(P+W R985)	75-3132	41-25625		*(Shipped to New Zealand by 1.02)*		
G-BTGD	Rand Robinson KR-2	PFA 129-11150		22. 2.91	A.M.Chester	Turweston	20.12.01P
	(VW 1915)				*(Noted 6.01)*		
G-BTGG	Rans S-10 Sakota	PFA 194-11944		20. 2.91	A.R.Cameron	Oaksey Park	22. 6.96P
	(Rotax 582)						
G-BTGH	Cessna 152 II	15281048	N48919	2. 4.91	C & S Aviation Ltd	Wolverhampton	9. 4.04T
G-BTGI	Rearwin 175 Skyranger	1517	N32308	26. 2.91	A.H.Hunt		
	(Continental A75)		NC32308			Lower Botrea Farm, Newbridge, Penzance	27. 6.01P
G-BTGJ	Smith DSA-1 Miniplane	NM.II	N1471	25. 3.91	G.J.Knowles	Little Gransden	20. 5.94P
	(Continental C90)				*(Stored 4.99: current status unknown)*		
G-BTGL	Avid Speed Wing	PFA 189-11885		27. 2.91	A.F.Vizoso	RAF Halton	1. 8.02P
G-BTGM	Aeronca 7AC Champion	7AC-3665	N84943	11. 3.91	G.P.Gregg	Spanhoe	27. 2.01P
	(Continental A65)		NC84943				
G-BTGN	Cessna 310R II	310R1541	N5331C	3. 4.91	Alarmond Ltd	Edinburgh	27. 1.01T
					t/a Turnhouse Flying Club		
G-BTGO	Piper PA-28-140 Cherokee D		N1998T	20. 2.91	Halegreen Associates Ltd		
		28-7125613				Hinton-in-the-Hedges	13. 7.03T
G-BTGP	Cessna 150M Commuter	15078921	N704WA	28. 2.91	Billins Air Services Ltd	Cranfield	16. 5.03T
					(Op City Air)		
G-BTGR	Cessna 152 II	15284447	N6581L	28. 2.91	A.J.Gomes	Shoreham	26. 7.02T
					(Op Sky Leisure Aviation)		
					(Substantially damaged landing near Shoreham 7.10.99)		
G-BTGS(2)	Stolp SA.300 Starduster Too		G-AYMA	30. 9.87	G.N.Elliott	(Steyning)	19. 7.02P
	(Lycoming O-320)	EAA/50553 & PFA 035-10076			t/a Mr.G.N.Elliott & Partners		
G-BTGT	CFM Streak Shadow		(G-MWPY)	1. 3.91	G.D.Bailey	Popham	23. 7.02P
	(Rotax 582)	K.164-SA & PFA 206-11964			*(New owner 8.01)*		
G-BTGU	Piper PA-34-220T Seneca III		N999PW	1. 3.91	Carill Aviation Ltd	Southampton	30. 5.03T
		34-8233106	N8160V				
G-BTGV	Piper PA-34-200T Seneca II		N3004H	26. 3.91	Roper & Wreaks Ltd	Shobdon	3. 8.03T
		34-7970077					
G-BTGW	Cessna 152 II	15279812	N757KY	5. 3.91	Stapleford Flying Club Ltd	Stapleford	10. 8.03T
G-BTGX	Cessna 152 II	15284950	N5462P	5. 3.91	Stapleford Flying Club Ltd	Stapleford	24. 8.03T
G-BTGY	Piper PA-28-161 Warrior II		N209FT	5. 3.91	Stapleford Flying Club Ltd	Stapleford	23. 6.03T
		28-8216199	N9574N				
G-BTGZ	Piper PA-28-181 Cherokee Archer II		N47956	8. 4.91	Allzones Travel Ltd	Biggin Hill	17. 9.03T
		28-7890160					
G-BTHA	Cessna 182P	18263420	N2932P	22. 3.91	T.P.Hall	Liverpool	21. 8.03
					t/a Hotel Alpha Flying Group		
G-BTHD	Yakovlev Yak-3U	170101	(France)	7. 3.91	Patina Ltd	Duxford	
	(Conversion of LET Yak C.11)		EAF.533		*(Op The Fighter Collection) (On restoration 6.01)*		
G-BTHE	Cessna 150L	15075340	N11348	7. 3.91	J.H.Loose & F.P.White	Burn	8. 6.03T
					t/a Humberside Police Flying Club		
G-BTHF	Cameron V-90 HAFB	2543		7. 3.91	N.J. & S.J.Langley	Bristol	22. 5.02T
G-BTHH	CEA Jodel DR.100A Ambassadeur	5	F-BJCH	28. 2.91	H.R.Leefe	Bourg-en-Bresse, France	1. 9.02
G-BTHI	Robinson R22 Beta	1732		26. 3.91	M.D.Thorpe	Coney Park, Leeds	27. 7.03T
					t/a Yorkshire Helicopters		
G-BTHJ	Evans VP-2	PFA 063-10901		14. 3.91	C.J.Moseley	Bournemouth	
					(Under construction 8.92: current status unknown)		
G-BTHK	Thunder Ax7-77 HAFB	1906		11. 3.91	M.J.Chandler	Cranbrook	29. 8.99A
G-BTHM	Thunder Ax8-105 HAFB	1925		11. 3.91	J.K.Woods	Chatham	20. 6.02A
G-BTHN	Murphy Renegade 912			12. 3.91	F.A.Purvis	Eshott	19. 4.00P
	(Rotax 912)	384 & PFA 188-12005			*"Spirit of England II"*		
G-BTHP	Thorp T.211	101		13. 6.91	M.J.Newton	Barton	27.11.04P
G-BTHR	SOCATA TB-10 Tobago	1296		13. 3.91	P, A, A & J McRae	White Waltham	25. 3.02
G-BTHU	Avid Flyer	PFA 189-11427		14. 3.91	R.C.Bowley	(Earls Croome, Worcester)	
	(Rotax 532)	*(Damaged Field Head Farm, Denholme, Bradford 7.6.92: on rebuild 5.95: current status unknown)*					
G-BTHV	MBB Bö.105DBS-4	S.855	D-HMBV	20. 3.91	Bond Air Services Ltd	Aberdeen	12. 5.03T
			G-BTHV/D-HFHM				
G-BTHW	Beechcraft F33C Bonanza	CJ-130	PH-BNA	18. 3.91	Robin Lance Aviation Associates Ltd		
			N23787			Rochester	20. 8.03
G-BTHX	Colt 105A HAFB	1939		18. 3.91	R.Ollier	Northwich, Cheshire	14. 2.02A
G-BTHY	Bell 206B-3 JetRanger III	2290	N6606M	20. 3.91	Sterling Helicopters Ltd	Norwich	19. 5.03T
			VH-BIQ/ZK-HBQ/DQ-FEN/ZK-HLU				
G-BTHZ	Cameron V-56 HAFB	486	OO-BBC	20. 3.91	C.N.Marshall	Nairobi, Kenya	
					(Noted as "OO-BBC" 9.95)		

G-BTID	Piper PA-28-161 Warrior II	N82647	25. 6.91	Plymouth School of Flying Ltd	Plymouth	24. 5.03T
	28-8116036					
G-BTIE	SOCATA TB-10 Tobago 187		30. 3.81	I.M.D.Weston	Blackbushe	18. 1.03T
G-BTIF	Denney Kitfox mk.3		27. 2.91	D.A.Murchie	(Blackwaterfoot, Arran)	10. 8.01P
	(Rotax 582) 684 & PFA 172-11862					
G-BTIG	Montgomerie-Bensen B.8MR		21. 3.91	K.Jarvis	Carlisle	15. 5.02P
	(Rotax 532) PFA G/01-1093					
G-BTII	Gulfstream AA-5B Tiger AA5B-1256	N4560S	5. 6.91	B.D.Greenwood	Ronaldsway	13. 5.02
G-BTIJ	Luscombe 8E Silvaire 5194	N2467K	3. 4.91	S.J.Hornsby	Compton Abbas	16. 9.02P
	(Continental C85)	NC2467K				
G-BTIK	Cessna 152 II 15282993	N46068	26. 3.91	P.R.Edwards & E.Alexander	Andrewsfield	25. 5.02T
G-BTIL	Piper PA-38-112 Tomahawk 38-80A0004	N24730	26. 3.91	B.J.Pearson	Eaglescott	
				(Fuselage noted 10.00 with Fresca titles)		
G-BTIM	Piper PA-28-161 Cadet 2841159	N9185D	24. 8.89	M.J.Joslin	Redhill	25.10.04T
		(SE-KIO)		t/a JMS Janitorial Supplies		
G-BTIN*	Cessna 150C 15059905	N7805Z	26. 3.91	Alarmond Ltd	(Edinburgh)	17. 4.00
				t/a Turnhouse Flying Club		
	(Damaged in gales Edinburgh 12.98 but roaded out)			*(Cancelled 10.5.01 as wfu) (Current status unknown)*		
G-BTIO	SNCAN Stampe SV-4C 303	N73NS	28. 3.91	M.D. & C.F.Garratt	(Bushey, Watford)	11. 5.02
		F-BCLC				
G-BTIR	Denney Kitfox mk.2 PFA 172-11952		26. 3.91	R.B.Wilson	(Kendal)	5.10.02P
	(Hewland AE75)					
G-BTIS	Aérospatiale AS355F1 Twin Squirrel	G-TALI	10. 4.91	J.P.E.Walsh	Elstree	9. 6.04T
	5261			t/a Walsh Aviation *(Op Cabair Helicopters)*		
G-BTIU	SOCATA MS.892A Rallye Commodore 150	F-BPQS	7. 5.91	W.H.Cole	Spilsted Farm, Sedlescombe	30. 6.01
	10914					
G-BTIV	Piper PA-28-161 Warrior II	N82697	10. 5.91	B.R.Pearson	Eaglescott	6. 7.03T
	28-8116044			t/a Warrior Group		
G-BTIW*	CEA Jodel DR.1050/M1 Sicile Record	F-BMPV	28. 6.91	Not known	Crosland Moor	4. 7.94
	618					
	(Damaged Westbury-sub-Mendip 1.7.94: cancelled 5.9.94 as destroyed: stored 9.96: current status unknown)					
G-BTIX	Cameron V-77 HAFB 2087		27. 3.91	D.J.Cook *"Sky's The Limit"*	Norwich	23. 9.99T
G-BTIZ	Cameron A-105 HAFB 2546		11. 3.91	Wendy A.Board	Penshurst	8. 7.02A
				t/a Glen Board Promotions		
G-BTJA	Luscombe 8E Silvaire 5037	N2310K	4. 4.91	M.W.Rudkin	Woodford	17. 6.02P
	(Continental C85)	NC2310K				
G-BTJB	Luscombe 8E Silvaire 6194	G-BTJA	4. 4.91	M.Loxton	Leysdown-on-Sea, Sheppey	13. 8.01P
	(Continental C85)	N1567B/NC1567B				
	(Carried identity of "G-BTJA" in error during UK certification process)					
G-BTJC	Luscombe 8F Silvaire 6589	N2162B	4. 4.91	Alison M.Noble	Thruxton	18.10.99P
	(Lycoming O-290)	*(Damged Glebe Farm, Stockton, Warminster 31.7.99: current status unknown)*				
G-BTJD	Thunder Ax8-90 Srs.2 HAFB 1865		28. 3.91	R.E.Vinten	Wellingborough	5. 5.02A
G-BTJF	Thunder Ax10-180 Srs.2 HAFB 1952		28. 3.91	Airborne Adventures Ltd	Skipton	4. 5.01T
				"Yorkshire Lad"		
G-BTJH	Cameron O-77 HAFB 2559		3. 4.91	H.& F.Stringer *"Oriel"*	Scarborough	3. 4.00T
G-BTJK	Piper PA-38-112 Tomahawk 38-79A0838	N2427N	3. 4.91	Western Air (Thruxton) Ltd	Thruxton	6. 9.03T
G-BTJL	Piper PA-38-112 Tomahawk 38-79A0863	N2477N	3. 4.91	J.S.Develin & Z.Islam	Shoreham	22. 8.04T
G-BTJN	Montgomerie-Bensen B.8MR		3. 4.91	A.Hamilton	Stonehouse	9.12.00P
	(Rotax 532) PFA G/01-1194			*(Flies from Strathaven)*		
G-BTJS	Montgomerie-Bensen B.8MR		8. 4.91	T.C. & P.K.Jackson		
	(Rotax 532) PFA G/01-1083				Melrose Farm, Melbourne	18.10.00P
G-BTJU	Cameron V-90 HAFB 2554		8. 4.91	C.W.Jones (Floorings) Ltd	Bristol	9. 8.02A
G-BTJX	Rans S-10 Sakota PFA 194-12014		9. 4.91	W.C.Dobson	Beeches Farm, South Scarle	22. 3.01P
	(Rotax 582)					
G-BTKA	Piper J-5A Cub Cruiser 5-954	N38403	11. 4.91	Janet M.Lister	Valley Farm, Winwick	9. 5.02P
		NC38403				
G-BTKB	Murphy Renegade 912		11. 4.91	G.S.Blundell	Perth	17. 7.02P
	(Rotax 912) 376 & PFA 188-11876			*"Spirit of Kinross"*		
G-BTKD	Denney Kitfox mk.4		15. 4.91	J.F.White	Walkerburn Farm, Peebles	21. 5.02P
	(Rotax 582) 853 & PFA 172-11941	*(Denney c/n conflicts with N653CP)*		*(Op Border Aviation Ltd)*		
G-BTKG	Avid Flyer PFA 189-12037		16. 4.91	I.Holt	(Reading)	15. 8.02P
	(Rotax 582)					
G-BTKL	MBB Bö.105DB-4 S.422	D-HDMU	2. 5.91	Veritair Ltd	Wolverhampton	2. 3.03T
		Swedish Army/D-HDMU		*(Op Central Counties Police Air Operations Unit)*		
G-BTKP	CFM Streak Shadow		24. 4.91	G.D.Martin	(Cambridge)	20. 8.02P
	(Rotax 582) K.174 & PFA 206-12036					
G-BTKT	Piper PA-28-161 Warrior II	N429FT	9. 5.91	Eastern Executive Air Charter Ltd & E.Alexander		
	28-8216218	N9606N		t/a General Aero Services		
					King's Farm, Thurrock	14. 7.97T
		(Damaged near Shoreham 8.8.95: fuselage only 9.99: current status unknown)				
G-BTKV	Piper PA-22-160 Tri-Pacer 22-7157	N3216Z	25. 4.91	R.A.Moore	Newtownards, Co.of Down	1. 8.04
G-BTKW	Cameron O-105 HAFB 2566		25. 4.91	P.Spellward	Bristol	9. 3.01A

G-BTKX	Piper PA-28-181 Cherokee Archer II	28-7890146	N47866	14. 5.91	R.M.Pannell	Eaglescott	30. 4.03
G-BTKZ	Cameron V-77 HAFB	2573		26. 4.91	S.P.Richards *"Lancaster Jaguar"*	Cranbrook	7. 6.97T
G-BTLB	Wassmer WA.52 Europa	42	F-BTLB	17. 4.89	M.D.O'Brien	Shoreham	14. 6.04
G-BTLE	Piper PA-31-350 Navajo Chieftain	31-7405428	D-IBPL N54288	20.10.77	Boal Air Services (UK) Ltd	Rotterdam, The Netherlands	10. 9.03
G-BTLG	Piper PA-28R-200 Cherokee Arrow	28R-35811	N5045S	29. 4.91	W.B.Bateson	Blackpool	15. 3.04
G-BTLL*	Pilatus P.3-03	323-5	A-806	18. 4.91	Not known *(As "A-806" in Swiss AF c/s: stored 10.00)*	Headcorn	23. 6.94P
G-BTLM	Piper PA-22-160 *(Tail-wheel conversion)*	22-6162	N9025D	16. 5.91	A.C.& M.D.N.Fisher	Fenland	12.10.03
G-BTLP	Grumman-American AA-1C Lynx	AA1C-0109	N9732U	13. 5.91	Partlease Ltd	Stapleford	23. 1.04
G-BTMA	Cessna 172N Skyhawk II	17273711	N5136J	2. 5.91	East of England Flying Group Ltd	North Weald	20. 9.03T
G-BTMH	Colt 90A HAFB	1963		14. 5.91	European Balloon Corporation	Espinette, Belgium	19. 8.01A
G-BTMJ	Maule MX-7-180 Star Rocket	11073C		11. 6.91	C.M.McGill	White Waltham	4. 9.04
G-BTMK	Cessna R172K Hawk XP II	R1722787	N736TZ	10. 6.91	S.P. & A.C.Barker	East Midlands	12.12.03T
G-BTML*	Cameron Rupert Bear 90SS HAFB	2533		16. 5.91	Balloon Preservation Group *"Rupert The Bear" (Cancelled 29.4.97 as WFU)*	Kirdford	31.12.94A
G-BTMO	Colt 69A HAFB	2004		20. 5.91	Cameron Balloons Ltd t/a Thunder & Colt	Bristol	
G-BTMP	Everett Campbell Cricket (Rotax 532)	024 & PFA G/03-1226		20. 5.91	P.W.McLaughlin	Henstridge	24.10.02P
G-BTMR	Cessna 172M Skyhawk II	17264985	N64047	20. 5.91	Linley Aviation Ltd	(Hornsea)	15. 6.03T
G-BTMS	Avid Speed Wing	908 & PFA 189-12023	(CS-) G-BTMS	24. 4.91	F.Sayyah *(Flies from Redhill)*	(Crawley)	19. 2.02P
G-BTMT	Denney Kitfox mk.1 (Rotax 532)	66		10. 5.91	M.D.Burns t/a Skulk Flying Group	Cumbernauld	24. 9.02P
G-BTMV	Everett Gyroplane Srs.2	025		21. 5.91	L.Armes	Basildon	
G-BTMW	Zenair CH-701 STOL (Rotax 582)	PFA 187-11808		21. 5.91	L.Lewis *(Stored 1.02)*	Yearby	9. 4.96P
G-BTMX	Denney Kitfox mk.3 (Rotax 582)	916 & PFA 172-12079		13. 5.91	P.B.Lowry	Deanland	24. 9.01P
G-BTNA	Robinson R22 Beta	1800	N40820	23. 5.91	Heli Charter Ltd	Manston	24.11.01T
G-BTNB	Robinson R22 Beta	1802	N23006	30. 5.91	Kuki Helicopter Ltd	Gamston	24. 7.03T
G-BTNC	Aérospatiale SA.365N2 Dauphin 2	6409		21. 6.91	CHC Scotia Ltd	Humberside	9.10.04T
G-BTND	Piper PA-38-112 Tomahawk	38-78A0155	N9671T	23. 5.91	R.B.Turner	Gloucestershire	8.12.01T
G-BTNE	Piper PA-28-161 Warrior II	28-8116212	N8379H	22. 7.91	D.Rowe	Wellesbourne Mountford	21. 6.04T
G-BTNI	British Aerospace ATP	2038	EC-GSE EC-GKJ/G-OEDI/G-BTNI/(N238JX)/G-BTNI/TC-THU/G-BTNI/(G-SLAM)	29. 5.91	Trident Aviation Leasing Services (Jersey) Ltd	Woodford	
G-BTNL	Thunder AX10-180 HAFB	2006	(OO-ntu) G-BTNL	29. 5.91	M.P.A.Sevrin	Court St.Etienne, Belgium	29 .7.01T
G-BTNN	Colt 21A Cloudhopper HAFB	2018		3. 6.91	Cameron Balloons Ltd	Bristol	9. 6.92A
G-BTNO	Aeronca 7AC Champion	7AC-3132	N84441 NC84441	31. 5.91	D.B.Evans & A.McGarrell t/a November Oscar Group	Netherthorpe	10. 7.02P
G-BTNP	Avid Commuter (Rotax 582)	PFA 189-11988		31. 5.91	N.Evans *(Damaged Swardeston, Norfolk 25.6.92: stored 8.97: current status unknown)*	Silfield, Wymondham	23. 6.92P
G-BTNR	Denney Kitfox mk.3 (Rotax 582)	921 & PFA 172-12035		31. 5.91	H.Thompson	(Tenbury Wells)	21. 6.02P
G-BTNS	WSK PZL-104 Wilga 80	CF.20890883	N71695	22. 7.91	D.Rowland	Shoreham	25. 6.04A
G-BTNT	Piper PA-28-151 Cherokee Warrior	28-7615401	N6929J	31. 5.91	Britannia Airways Ltd *(Op Britannia Airways Flying Club)*	Luton	24.11.03T
G-BTNV	Piper PA-28-161 Cherokee Warrior II	28-7816590	N31878	20. 6.91	D.E.Peet	(Claygate)	17. 7.03
G-BTNW	Rans S-6-ESA Coyote II (Rotax 582)	0391.171 & PFA 204-12077		3. 6.91	B.Read *(Rans' kit c/n incorrect as this became G-MWUM: possibly 0391.174)*	Ince Blundell	14. 6.02P
G-BTOA*	Mong Sport MS-2 (Continental C85)	FHC-1	N1067Z	3. 6.91	G.Gilding *(Cancelled 26.10.00 by CAA) (On rebuild 8.01)*	Swanton Morley	28. 9.94P
G-BTOC	Robinson R22 Beta	1801	N23004	10. 6.91	N.Parkhouse	Chelwood Gate, W.Sussex	19. 6.03T
G-BTOD	Piper PA-38-112 Tomahawk	38-78A0675	N2421A	7. 6.91	S.M.P & D.A.Adams	Gamston	18.10.03T
G-BTOG	de Havilland DH.82A Tiger Moth	86500	F-BGCJ Fr.AF/NM192	5. 9.91	P.T.Szluha *(Stored as "F-BGCJ" 4.99)*	Audley End	
G-BTOI	Cameron N-77 HAFB	2588		20. 6.91	The Nestle Co Ltd *"Rowntree/Nestle"*	Croydon	29. 6.95A
G-BTOL	Denney Kitfox mk.3 (Rotax 582)	919 & PFA 172-12052		26. 6.91	P.J.Gibbs	(Truro)	9. 5.02P

G-BTOM*	Piper PA-38-112 Tomahawk	38-78A0763	N9679N	15. 1.79	Lorch Airways Ltd	Norwich	10. 4.94T
	(Crashed Alderney 26.9.92: cancelled 26.10.92 as WFU: stored 10.97: current status unknown)						
G-BTON	Piper PA-28-140 Cherokee Cruiser	28-7425343	N43193	15. 7.91	S.G.Woodsford	Earls Colne	19. 7.04T
G-BTOO	Pitts S-1C Special	5215-24A	N37H	12. 6.91	G.H.Matthews *(On overhaul 5.92: current status unknown)*	Sandown	
G-BTOP	Cameron V-77 HAFB	2484		14. 6.91	J.J.Winter *"Big Top"*	Cardiff	
G-BTOS	Cessna 140 (Continental C85)	8353	N89325 NC89325	7. 6.91	J.L.Kaiser *(Current status unknown)*	Nancy-Essey, France	1. 7.99
G-BTOT	Piper PA-15 Vagabond (Lycoming O-145)	15-60	N4176H NC4176H	22. 5.91	M.S.Rogerson t/a Vagabond Flying Group	Ferryhill	26.10.01P
G-BTOU	Cameron O-120 HAFB	2606		2. 7.91	R.M.Horn	Hatfield Peverel	13. 7.01T
G-BTOW	SOCATA Rallye 180T Galerien	3360	F-BNGZ	9.11.82	Cambridge Gliding Club Ltd	Gransden Lodge	11. 4.04
G-BTOZ	Thunder Ax9-120 Srs.2 HAFB	2008		28. 6.91	H.G.Davies	Cheltenham	5. 9.01T
G-BTPA	British Aerospace ATP	2007	EC-HGC G-BTPA/EC-GYE/G-BTPA/(N377AE)	19. 8.88	Capital Bank Leasing 12 Ltd	Woodford	18.11.98T
G-BTPB	Cameron N-105 HAFB	1536		6. 7.87	C.N.Rawnson t/a Test Valley Balloon Group *"Phone Book"*	Stockbridge	21. 9.96A
G-BTPC	British Aerospace ATP	2010	EC-HGB G-BTPC/EC-GYF/G-BTPC/G-11-10/(N380AE)	1. 9.88	Capital Bank Leasing 1 Ltd	Woodford	29.12.98T
G-BTPD	British Aerospace ATP	2011	EC-HGD G-BTPC/EC-GYR/G-BTPD/(N381AE)	1. 9.88	Seaforth Marime (JARL) Ltd & Flexify Ltd t/a NWS2	Woodford	6. 2.99T
G-BTPF	British Aerospace ATP	2013	EC-HCY G-BTPF/G-11-013/G-BTPF/(N383AE)	2. 9.88	Capital Bank Leasing 5 Ltd	Woodford	17. 4.99T
G-BTPG	British Aerospace ATP	2014	EC-HEH G-BTPG/(N384AE)	2. 9.88	Capital Bank Leasing 5 Ltd	Woodford	22. 5.99T
G-BTPH	British Aerospace ATP	2015	EC-HFM G-BTPH/(N385AE)	2. 9.88	Capital Bank Leasing 6 Ltd *(Noted 2.02)*	Southend	11. 6.99T
G-BTPJ	British Aerospace ATP	2016	EC-HFR G-BTPJ/(N386AE)	2. 9.88	Capital Bank Leasing 7 Ltd.	Woodford	9. 7.99T
G-BTPK	British Aerospace ATP	2041	EC-GSG EC-GLC/G-BTPK/G-11-041	3.10.91	Trident Aviation Leasing Services (Jersey) Ltd	Woodford	
G-BTPL	British Aerospace ATP	2042	EC-HES G-BTPL/EC-GLH/G-BTPL/G-11-042	3.10.91	Trident Aviation Leasing Services (Jersey) Ltd	Woodford	21.11.95T
G-BTPM	British Aerospace ATP	2043	EC-GSH EC-GNI/G-BTPM	19.11.91	Trident Aviation Leasing Services (Jersey) Ltd	Woodford	
G-BTPN	British Aerospace ATP	2044	EC-GSI EC-GNJ/G-BTPN/G-11-044	19.11.91	Trident Aviation Leasing Services (Jersey) Ltd	Woodford	
G-BTPT	Cameron N-77 HAFB	2575		10. 6.91	Derbyshire Building Society	Derby	15.12.01A
G-BTPV*	Colt 90A HAFB	1956		14. 6.91	Balloon Preservation Group *"Mondial" (Cancelled 25.3.99 as PWFU)*	Kirdford	1. 8.97A
G-BTPX	Thunder Ax8-90 HAFB	1873		18. 6.91	E.Cordall	Chichester	19. 6.02
G-BTPZ	Isaacs Fury II	PFA 011-11927		1. 7.91	M.A.Farrelly *(As "85" in Portuguese AF c/s)*	Ormskirk	
G-BTRB	Colt Mickey Mouse SS HAFB	1959		4. 7.91	Benedikt Haggeney GmbH "Calibre"	Ennigerloh, Germany	17 .7.02A
G-BTRC	Avid Speed Wing (BMW R100)	913 & PFA 189-12076		2. 7.91	Grangecote Ltd	Goodwood	17.12.01P
	(Engine lost power after touch & go Trueleigh Farm, Brighton 22.6.01: substantially damaged in following landing)						
G-BTRE	Reims Cessna F172H	F17200657	N10657	3. 7.91	M.L.J.Warwick	Stapleford	18.10.04T
G-BTRF	Aero Designs Pulsar (Rotax 582)	PFA 202-12051		4. 7.91	C.Smith	Spilsted Farm, Sedlescombe	19.10.02P
G-BTRG	Aeronca 65C Super Chief (Continental A65)	C4149	N22466 NC22466	4. 7.91	H.J.Cox	Lukes Farm, Sheepwash	31. 8.01P
G-BTRH	Aeronca 7AC Champion (Continental A65)	7AC-2895	N84204 NC84204	4. 7.91	J.Horan	(Abbeyfeale, Co.Kerry)	15. 5.02P
G-BTRI	Aeronca 11CC Super Chief (Continental C85)	11CC-246	N4540E NC4540E	4. 7.91	P.A.Wensak	Bounds Farm, Ardleigh	17. 7.02P
G-BTRK	Piper PA-28-161 Warrior II	28-8216206	N297FT N9594N	8. 7.91	Stapleford Flying Club Ltd	Stapleford	26.10.03T
G-BTRL	Cameron N-105 HAFB	2622		5. 7.91	J.Lippett *"Harrods"*	South Petherton, Somerset	11. 8.01A
G-BTRN	Thunder AX9-120 S2 HAFB	1983		11. 7.91	P.B.D.Bird	Bristol	21. 6.02T
G-BTRO	Thunder Ax8-90 HAFB	1872		11. 7.91	Capital Balloon Club Ltd	London NW1	1. 5.02A
G-BTRP	MD Helicopters Hughes 369E (500E)	0475E	N1607D	11. 7.91	P.C.Shann & P.C.Shann Management & Research Ltd	Fulford, York	15. 4.01
G-BTRR	Thunder Ax7-77 HAFB	1905		12. 7.91	Sheila M.Roberts	Skipton	26. 8.96A
G-BTRS	Piper PA-28-161 Warrior II	28-8116004	N8248V	12. 7.91	K.D.Taylor & D.Provost t/a Airwise Flying Group	Barton	16.12.01
G-BTRT	Piper PA-28R-200 Cherokee Arrow II	28R-7535270	N1189X	24. 7.91	C.E.Yates	Barton	22. 1.04
G-BTRU	Robin DR.400/180 Regent	2089		12. 7.91	R & M Engineering Ltd	Easterton	30. 1.04

G-BTRW	Slingsby T.61F Venture T.2	1968	ZA632	5. 7.91	G.B.Monslow t/a The Falke Syndicate	Long Marston	3.12.03
G-BTRY	Piper PA-28-161 Warrior II	28-8116190	N8363L	18. 7.91	Oxford Aviation Services Ltd	Oxford	6.12.04T
G-BTRZ	Jodel D.18 (VW 1834)	148 & PFA 169-11271		16. 7.91	R.M.Johnson & R.Collin	Midlem Farm, Midlem	12. 9.02P
G-BTSB	Corben Baby Ace D (Continental A65)	JC-1	N3599	16. 7.91	J.A.MacLeod	Stornoway	17. 4.02P
G-BTSC	Evans VP-2 (Arrow GT500)	PFA 063-10342		20.10.78	G.B.O'Neill *(Stored 6.00)*	(Upwood, Cambs)	13. 2.96P
G-BTSJ	Piper PA-28-161 Cherokee Warrior II	28-7816473	N9417C	23. 7.91	Plymouth School of Flying Ltd	Plymouth	11. 1.04T
G-BTSL	Cameron Glass 70SS HAFB *(Tennent's Lager Glass shape)*	1627		27. 1.88	M.R.Humphrey & J.R.Clifton *"Tennent's Glass"*	Brackley	25. 4.90A
G-BTSM	Cessna 180A	32678	P2-DEQ VH-DEQ/VH-DEC/N7781A	9. 7.91	C.Couston t/a Sierra Mike Group	Church Farm, North Moreton	12. 4.02
G-BTSN	Cessna 150G	15065106	N3806J	30. 8.91	N.A.Bilton	Priory Farm, Tibenham	23. 3.02
G-BTSP	Piper J-3C-65 Cub	7647	N41013 NC41013	30. 8.91	J.A.Walshe & A.Corcoran	Strandhill, Sligo	31. 8.01P
G-BTSR	Aeronca 11AC Chief (Continental A65)	11AC-785	N9152E NC9152E	30. 8.91	R.D.& E.G.N.Morris	Perth	17. 4.02P
G-BTST	Bensen B.8M	002VS		23. 7.91	V.Scott	Shipdham	
G-BTSV	Denney Kitfox mk.3 (Rotax 582)	PFA 172-11920		24. 7.91	M.G.Dovey	Popham	5. 6.02P
G-BTSW	Colt AS-105GD Hot-Air Airship	1999		24. 7.91	Gefa-Flug GmbH *(Adler Modemarkt titles)*	Aachen, Germany	17. 4.02A
G-BTSY*	English Electric Lightning F.6	95207	XR724	25. 7.91	B.J.Pover t/a Lightning Association *(As "XR724")* *(No Permit issued: cancelled 26.5.92 as TWFU: stored 8.00)*	Binbrook	
G-BTSZ	Cessna 177A Cardinal	17701198	N30332	30. 7.91	K.D.Harvey	Cranfield	27. 6.03T
G-BTTB	Cameron V-90 HAFB	2624		22. 7.91	N.F.Mulliner t/a Royal Engineers Balloon Club *"Sapper IV"*	Chatham	19. 6.02A
G-BTTD	Montgomerie-Bensen B.8MR (Rotax 582)	PFA G/01-1204		31. 7.91	K.B.Gutridge	Carlisle	22. 7.02P
G-BTTE	Cessna 150L	15075558	N11602	31. 7.91	W.E.Rodwell	Shoreham	19. 7.04T
G-BTTK	Thunder Ax8-105 HAFB	2036		9. 8.91	Tempowish Ltd	Frinton-on-Sea	11. 6.02A
G-BTTL	Cameron V-90 HAFB	2649		12. 8.91	A.J.Baird *"Hyde Farm Dairy"*	Cheltenham	10. 8.02A
G-BTTO	British Aerospace ATP	2033	EC-HNA EC-GJU/G-BTTO/G-OEDE/G-BTTO/TC-THV/G-BTTO/S2-ACZ/G-11-033	16. 8.91	Trident Aviation Leasing Services (Jersey) Ltd	Woodford	
G-BTTP	British Aerospace BAe 146 Srs.300	E3203	G-6-203	20. 8.91	KLM UK Ltd *(Op Buzz)*	Stansted	11.11.03T
G-BTTR	Aerotek Pitts S-2A Special (Lycoming IO-360)	2208	N38MP	16. 8.91	P.Shaw	Breighton	22. 3.04
G-BTTS	Colt 77A HAFB	1861		16. 8.91	J.A.Lomas t/a Rutland Balloon Club	Melton Mowbray	12. 7.01A
G-BTTW	Thunder Ax7-77 HAFB	2016		27. 8.91	J.Kenny	Athlone, Co.Roscommon	5. 9.02A
G-BTTY	Denney Kitfox mk.2	PFA 172-11823		29. 7.91	K.J.Fleming	(Liverpool)	
G-BTTZ	Slingsby T.61F Venture T.2	1961	ZA625	30. 7.91	M.W.Olliver	Old Sarum	3. 9.03
G-BTUA	Slingsby T.61F Venture T.2	1985	ZA666	20. 8.91	C.Edmunds t/a Shenington Gliding Club	Shenington	17. 6.04
G-BTUB	LET Yakovlev C.11 *(Identity of 039 quoted)*	172623	(France) Egyptian AF 543	29. 8.91	M.G. & J.R.Jefferies *(Soviet AF c/s without serial)*	Little Gransden	17. 6.02P
G-BTUC*	Embraer EMB-312 Tucano	312-007	G-14-007 PP-ZTC	19. 6.86	Ulster Aviation Heritage *(Cancelled 20.12.96 as WFU)*	Langford Lodge	11. 9.93
G-BTUE	British Aerospace ATP	2039	EC-GSF EC-GKI/G-OEDH/(G-OGVA)/G-OEDH/G-BTUE/TC-THT/G-11-039/G-BTUE/G-11-039	5. 9.91	Trident Aviation Leasing Services (Jersey) Ltd	Woodford	
G-BTUG	SOCATA Rallye 180T	3208		10. 7.78	Herefordshire Gliding Club Ltd	Shobdon	16. 4.03
G-BTUH	Cameron N-65 HAFB	1452		28. 8.91	B.J.Godding	Didcot	
G-BTUJ	Thunder Ax9-120 HAFB	2022		30. 8.91	ECM Construction Ltd	Great Missenden	20. 5.02T
G-BTUK	Aerotek Pitts S-2A Special (Lycoming AEIO-360)	2260	N5300J	2. 9.91	S.H.Elkington	Wickenby	24.10.03T
G-BTUL	Aerotek Pitts S-2A Special (Lycoming AEIO-360)	2200	N900RS	2. 9.91	J.M.Adams	Tatenhill	26. 2.04
G-BTUM	Piper J-3C-65 Cub (Continental C85) *(Frame No.19586)*	19516	N6335H NC6335H	6. 9.91	I.M.Mackay t/a G-BTUM Syndicate *"Jingle-Belle"*	White Waltham	13. 6.02P
G-BTUR	Piper PA-18 Super Cub 95 (Continental C90) (L-18C-PI) *(Frame No.18-3218)*	18-3205	OO-LVM Belg AF OL-L08/L-131/53-4805	11. 9.91	Liddell Aircraft Ltd	Bournemouth	25. 3.02T
G-BTUS	Whittaker MW7 (Rotax 503)	PFA 171-11999		5. 9.91	J.D.Webb	(Hereford)	9. 6.98P
G-BTUU	Cameron O-120 HAFB	2669		16. 9.91	J.L.Guy	Skipton	29.10.99T

G-BTUV	Aeronca 65TAC Defender	C.1661TA	N36816	12. 9.91	M.B.Hamlett & R.E.Coates		
			NC36816			(Lagny de Sec, France)	
					(Partially rebuilt 1.00: new owners 9.01)		
G-BTUW	Piper PA-28-151 Cherokee Warrior		N54458	12. 9.91	T.S.Kemp	Enstone	12. 7.04T
		28-7415066					
G-BTUX	Aérospatiale SA.365N2 Dauphin 2	6424		12. 9.91	CHC Scotia Ltd	Humberside	1. 2.02T
G-BTUZ	American General AG-5B Tiger	10075	N11939	3.10.91	Grocontinental Ltd	Sleap	26. 2.03
G-BTVA	Thunder Ax7-77 HAFB	2009		16. 9.91	A.H.Symonds *"Bertie Bassett"*	Chelmsford	29. 6.02A
G-BTVB	Everett Gyroplane Srs.3	026		24. 9.91	J.Pumford	Henstridge	18. 4.02P
	(Rotax 532)						
G-BTVC	Denney Kitfox mk.2	PFA 172-11784		23. 9.91	P.Mitchell	Long Marston	5. 9.02P
	(Rotax 582)				*"Zebedee"*		
G-BTVE	Hawker Demon I	-	2292M	18. 9.91	Demon Displays Ltd	Rotary Farm, Hatch	
	(Kestrel V)		K8203		*(On rebuild 10.99: as "K8203" in 64 Sqn c/s)*		
	(Composite of ex IAC Hector - front & K8203 - rear)						
G-BTVF	Rotorway Executive 90	5058		13. 9.91	E.P.Sadler	(Market Drayton)	
G-BTVG*	Cessna 140	12350	N2114N	30. 8.91	V C Gover	Inverness	15. 4.99
	(Continental O-200-A)		NC2114N		*(Cancelled 18.5.01 by CAA) (Stored 2001)*		
G-BTVH*	Colt 77A HAFB	1027	G-ZADT	24. 9.91	D.N. & L.J.Close	Andover	19. 8.97A
			G-ZBCA		*(Cancelled 18.10.01 by CAA)*		
G-BTVO	British Aerospace BAe 146 Srs.300		G-NJID	18. 9.91	Flightline Ltd	Southend	18.10.03T
		E3205	B-1777/G-BTVO/G-6-205				
G-BTVR	Piper PA-28-140 Cherokee Cruiser		N4328X	16. 9.91	Full Sutton Flying Centre Ltd		
		28-7625012				Full Sutton	9. 4.04T
G-BTVU	Robinson R22 Beta	1937		26. 9.91	B.Enzo	Bologna, Italy	17. 3.03
G-BTVV	Reims Cessna F337G Skymaster		PH-RPD	25. 9.91	C. Keane,	(Saggart, Co.Dublin)	12. 1.03T
	(Wichita c/n 33701476)	F33700058	N1876M				
G-BTVW	Cessna 152 II	15279631	N757CK	23. 9.91	Halegreen Associates Ltd		
						Hinton-in-the-Hedges	14. 1.01T
G-BTVX	Cessna 152 II	15283375	N48786	23. 9.91	J.C.Birdsall	Gamston	2. 8.04T
					t/a Trafic Management Services		
G-BTWB*	Denney Kitfox mk.3		(G-BTTM)	21. 8.91	J.E.Tootell	East Fortune	
		920 & PFA 172-12278			*(Cancelled 14.3.99 by CAA) (Under construction 8.01)*		
G-BTWC	Slingsby T.61F Venture T.2	1975	ZA656	23. 9.91	T.M.Holloway	Upavon	4. 1.02
					t/a RAFGSA		
G-BTWD	Slingsby T.61F Venture T.2	1976	ZA657	23. 9.91	Ouse Gliding Club Ltd	Rufforth	26. 3.04
					t/a York Gliding Centre		
G-BTWE	Slingsby T.61F Venture T.2	1980	ZA661	23. 9.91	T.M.Holloway t/a RAFGSA	RAF Syerston	13. 3.04
					(Op Four Counties Gliding Club)		
G-BTWF	de Havilland DHC-1 Chipmunk 22		WK549	30. 9.91	J.A. & V.G.Simms	Breighton	24. 4.04
		C1/0564			*(As "WK549")*		
G-BTWI	EAA Acrosport I	230	N10JW	2.10.91	C.N.Carter	Charterhall	1. 2.02P
	(Lycoming O-290)				t/a WI Group		
G-BTWJ	Cameron V-77 HAFB	2670		3.10.91	S.J. & J.A.Bellaby	Nottingham	11. 5.02A
					"Windy Jack"		
G-BTWL	Wag-Aero CUBy Acro Sport Trainer			3.10.91	I.M.Ashpole	Llangarron	25. 9.02P
	(Lycoming O-235)	PFA 108-10893					
G-BTWM	Cameron V-77 HAFB	2163		4.10.91	R.C.Franklin *"Aerolus"*	Chesham	31. 3.01A
G-BTWN	Maule MXT-7-180 Star Rocket	14025C		7.10.91	C.T.Rolls	Redhill	11. 7.04
G-BTWR	Bell P-63A-7BE Kingcobra	33-397	N52113	7.10.91	Patina Ltd *"Trust Me"*	Duxford	29. 5.02P
			NX52113/42-69097		*(Op B.J.S.Grey/The Fighter Collection)*		
	(Official c/n 33-37: also quoted as 296A-5-3)		*(As "269097" in USAAF c/s) (Crashed Biggin Hill 3.6.01 & destroyed)*				
G-BTWU	Piper PA-22-135 Tri-Pacer	22-2135	N3320B	10.10.91	Prestige Air (Engineers) Ltd		
					(Noted as "N3320B" 7.99)	Haverfordwest	
G-BTWV	Cameron O-90 HAFB	2675		10.10.91	S.F.Hancke	Sunbury-on-Thames	30. 6.01A
G-BTWX	SOCATA TB-9 Tampico Club	1401		14.10.91	D.Weston	Bourn	20. 9.03T
					t/a British Car Rentals		
G-BTWY	Aero Designs Pulsar	PFA 202-12040		15.10.91	M.Stevenson	Pepperbox, Salisbury	6. 8.02P
	(Rotax 582) *(Tail-wheel u/c)*						
G-BTWZ	Rans S-10 Sakota	PFA 194-12117		15.10.91	D.G.Hey	Little Gransden	
					(Under construction 3.97: current status unknown)		
G-BTXB	Colt 77A HAFB	2072		16.10.91	A Derbyshire	Telford	1. 8.99T
					"Shellgas" (New owner 11.01)		
G-BTXD	Rans S-6-ESA Coyote II *(Tail-wheel u/c)*			22.10.91	M.Isterling	Insch	14. 6.02P
	(Rotax 582) 0591.191 & PFA 204-12104						
G-BTXF	Cameron V-90 HAFB	2692		2.10.91	G.Thompson	Ambleside	24. 1.96T
G-BTXG	British Aerospace Jetstream Srs.3102		SE-FVP	23.10.91	Highland Airways Ltd	Inverness	9. .7.03T
		719	G-BTXG/OK-REJ/G-BTXG/OY-EEC/G-BTXG/N418MX/G-31-719				
G-BTXH	Colt AS-56 Hot-Air Airship	2078		23.10.91	L.Kiefer	March-Flugstetten, Germany	26. 3.93A
G-BTXI	Noorduyn AT-16-ND Harvard IIB	14-429	Fv.16105	25.10.91	Patina Ltd	Duxford	22. 8.02P
			RCAF FE695/FE695/42-892		*(Op The Fighter Collection: as "FE695/94")*		
G-BTXK	Thunder Ax7-65 HAFB	1910	ZS-HYP	28.10.91	T.M.Dawson	Woodford Green	5.12.96
			G-BTXK				

G-BTXM*	Colt 21A Cloudhopper HAFB	2082		29.10.91	Virgin Airship & Balloon Co Ltd	Telford	22. 8.97A
					"Virgin Megastore Hopper" (Cancelled 13.11.01 as wfu: stored)		
G-BTXS	Cameron O-120 HAFB	2141		16.10.91	Semajan Ltd	Romsey	16. 6.02A
					t/a Southern Balloon Group		
G-BTXT	Maule MXT-7-180 Star Rocket	14027C		7.10.91	H.Balfour-Paul	Inverness	4. 1.04
G-BTXV	Cameron A-210 HAFB	2703		30.10.91	The Ballooning Business Ltd	Northampton	27. 3.99T
					"Burning Ambition III"		
G-BTXW	Cameron V-77 HAFB	2717		31.10.91	P.C.Waterhouse	Wadhurst, E.Sussex	29. 8.99A
					"Scott's Whisky"		
G-BTXX	Bellanca 8KCAB Decathlon	595-80	OY-CYC	1.10.91	M.R.Shelton	Tatenhill	4. 3.04T
			SE-IEP/N5063G		t/a Tatenhill Aviation		
G-BTXZ	Zenair CH.250	PFA 113-12170		24.10.91	I.Parris & P.W.J.Hull		
	(Lycoming O-290)					Hinton-in-the-Hedges	31.10.02P
G-BTYC	Cessna 150L	15075767	N66002	4.11.91	Polestar Aviation Ltd	Jersey	5. 3.02T
G-BTYE	Cameron A-180 HAFB	2704		5.11.91	K.J.A.Maxwell & D.S.Messmer *"Rolling Rock"*		
						Haywards Heath	26. 3.00T
G-BTYF	Thunder Ax10-180 Srs.2 HAFB	2086		7.11.91	P.Glydon	Barnt Green, Birmingham	5. 4.01T
G-BTYH	Pottier P.80S	PFA 160-11121		11.11.91	R.Pickett	Tatenhill	3. 9.02P
	(VW 1834)						
G-BTYI	Piper PA-28-181 Archer II	28-8190078	N8287T	15.11.91	C.E.Wright	Fenland	28. 2.04
G-BTYK	Cessna 310R II	310R0138	N200VC	21.11.91	Revere Aviation Ltd	Jersey	12. 7.03
			N5018J				
G-BTYT*	Cessna 152 II	15280455	N24931	25.11.91	M.J.Green	Southend	20. 3.99T
					(Cancelled 19.9.00 by CAA) (Noted w/o engine 1.02)		
G-BTYW	Cessna 120	11725	N77283	27.11.91	C.J.Parker	Shacklewell Farm, Wittering	1.10.04
	(Continental C85)		NC77283		t/a G-BTYW Group		
G-BTYY	Curtiss Robin C-2	475	N348K	8.10.91	R.R.L.Windus		
	(Continental W-670)		NC348K			Truleigh Manor Farm, Edburton	1. 9.97P
G-BTYZ	Colt 210A HAFB	2083		17.10.91	T.M.Donnelly	Doncaster	2.12.01T
G-BTZA	Beechcraft F33A Bonanza	CE-957	PH-BNT	22.11.91	H.Mendelssohn	Kirknewton	13. 4.04
					t/a G-BTZA Group		
G-BTZB	Yakovlev Yak-50	801810	DOSAAF 77	27.11.91	J.S.& J.S.Allison	Duxford	2. 2.02P
					(As "69" in Soviet AF c/s)		
G-BTZD	Yakovlev Yak-1 Srs.1	8188	1342	10.12.91	Historic Aircraft Collection Ltd		
	(C/n stamped on engine bearers)		(Soviet AF)			Audley End	
			(Salvaged from lake in N.Russia mid 1991 after forced landing c.1942: stored 3.96)				
G-BTZE	LET Yakovlev C.11	171312	(France)	11. 2.92	Bianchi Aviation Film Services Ltd		
			Egypt AF/OK-JIK			Booker	
					(Op "Blue Max" Movie Aircraft Collection)		
G-BTZG	British Aerospace ATP	2046	PK-MTV	11.12.91	Trident Aviation Leasing Services (Jersey) Ltd		
			(PK-MAA)/G-BTZG		*(Stored 12.01)*	Woodford	
G-BTZH	British Aeropsace ATP	2047	PK-MTW	11.12.91	Trident Aviation Leasing Services (Jersey) Ltd		
			(PK-MAC)/G-BTZH		*(Stored 12.01)*	Woodford	
G-BTZK	British Aerospace ATP	2050	PK-MTZ	11.12.91	Trident Aviation Leasing Services (Jersey) Ltd		
			G-BTZK/(PK-MAF)/G-BTZK		*(Stored 12.01)*	Woodford	
G-BTZL	Oldfield Baby Lakes	8506-M-28B	N2288B	12.12.91	K.P.Rusling	Little Gransden	3. 7.02P
	(Continental C85)						
G-BTZO	SOCATA TB-20 Trinidad	1409		18.12.91	M.R.Munn	(Leighton Buzzard)	2. 4.04
G-BTZP	SOCATA TB-9 Tampico Club	1421		18.12.91	M.W.Orr	(Banbury)	21. 8.04T
G-BTZR	Colt 77B HAFB	2087		18.12.91	P.J.Fell *"Bullet"*	Maidenhead	15.12.01A
G-BTZS	Colt 77B HAFB	2088		18.12.91	P.T.R.Ollivere *"Petal"*	Sutton	20. 6.02A
G-BTZU	Cameron Concept 60 HAFB	2734		20.12.91	A.C.Rackham	Keswick	28. 1.96A
G-BTZV	Cameron V-77 HAFB	2410		20.12.91	A.W.Sumner *"Vulcan"*	Newark	8. 9.01A
G-BTZX	Piper J-3C-65 Cub	18871	N98648	27. 2.92	D.A.Woodhams & J.T.Coulthard	Bidford	4.12.01P
			NC98648				
G-BTZY	Colt 56A HAFB	2084		17.10.91	T.M.Donnelly	Doncaster	13.10.94A
G-BTZZ	CFM Streak Shadow			23.12.91	D.R.Stennett	Mendlesham	2. 8.01P
	(Rotax 582) K.169-SA & PFA 206-12155						

G-BUAA – G-BUZZ

G-BUAA	Corben Baby Ace D	561	N516DH	19.11.91	M.W.Chamberlain	(Magor)	16. 5.02P
	(Continental A65)						
G-BUAB	Aeronca 11AC Chief	11AC-1759	N3458E	17. 1.92	J.Reed	Craysmarsh Farm, Melksham	10. 6.02P
	(Continental A65)		NC3458E				
G-BUAC	Slingsby Cadet III	PFA 042-12059	(ex??)	17. 1.92	D.A.Wilson	Brunton	4.10.94P
	(VW 1200) *(Original identity unknown, possibly home-built: stored 2.00)*						
G-BUAF	Cameron N-77 HAFB	2746		2. 1.92	T.H.Wadden	Ringwood	17. 3.01
	(Rebuilt from 5N-ATT)				*"Ariston"*		
G-BUAG	Jodel D.18	PFA 169-11651		3. 1.92	A.L.Silcox	Bodmin	16. 8.99P
	(VW 1834)						

G-BUAI	Everett Gyroplane Srs.3 (Rotax 532)	030		6. 1.92	C.G.Brown & D.H.Kirton t/a Pop-Corn Group	(Hinckley)	3. 4.02P
G-BUAJ	Cameron N-90 HAFB	2735		7. 1.92	J.R. & S.J.Huggins *"Chunnel Plant Hire"*	Dover	31. 5.01A
G-BUAM	Cameron V-77 HAFB	2470		10. 1.92	N.Florence *"J & E Page Flowers"*	London SW11	21.10.01T
G-BUAN	Cessna 172N Skyhawk II	17270290	N738WH	23.12.91	R.J.Cawdell	Booker	2. 9.04T
G-BUAO	Luscombe 8A Silvaire (Continental A65)	4089	N1362K NC1362K	15. 1.92	D.Sweeney & G.R.Thomas	Kemble	21. 6.02P
G-BUAR	Supermarine 358 Seafire LF.IIIc (Built Westland)	--	PP972- Aeronavale/PP972	21. 1.92	Wizzard Investments Ltd *(Op David Arnold/Flying A Services: as "PP972")*	Earls Colne	
G-BUAT	Thunder Ax9-120 HAFB	2093		24. 1.92	J.Fenton *"Calor"*	Preston	17. 3.00T
G-BUAU*	Cameron A-180 HAFB	2744		17. 1.92	C.J.Sandell t/a Out of this World Balloons *(Cancelled by CAA 18.10.01)*	Sevenoaks	22. 3.96T
G-BUAW	Pitts S-1C Special (Lycoming O-320)	1921-77	N29DH	27. 1.92	D.G.Crawley	Liverpool	1.12.00P
G-BUAX	Rans S-10 Sakota (Rotax 582)	PFA 194-11848		28. 1.92	S.P.Wakeham & N.Parsons *(New owners 9.01)*	RAF St.Mawgan	12. 7.99P
G-BUAY	Cameron A-210 HAFB	2751		28. 1.92	Virgin Balloon Flights Ltd	London SE16	3. 5.96T
G-BUBA	Piper PA-18S-150 Super Cub	18-7909047	N6BL N83522	17. 1.92	Liddell Aircraft Ltd *(Op Solent Flight Training)*	Bournemouth	4. 6.04T
G-BUBC	QAC Quickie Tri-Q 200 (Continental O-200-A)	PFA 094-11909		3. 2.92	D.J.Clarke	Sturgate	24. 1.02P
G-BUBL*	Thunder Ax8-105 HAFB	1147		10.12.87	British Balloon Museum & Library *"Mercier/l'Espit D'Adventure" (Cancelled 16.6.98 as WFU)*	Newbury	
G-BUBN	Pilatus Britten-Norman BN-2B-26 Islander	2270		14. 2.92	Isles of Scilly Skybus Ltd	St.Just	18. 2.03T
G-BUBR	Cameron A-250 HAFB	2779		5. 2.92	Balloon Flights International Ltd *(Bath Building Society titles) "BIBS I"*	Bath	2. 9.01T
G-BUBS	Lindstrand LBL-77B HAFB *(Possibly a new envelope c 9.95?)*	144		10.10.94	Beaulah J.Bower *"Bubbles Balloon"*	Middle Wyke Farm, St.Mary Bourne, Andover	10. 9.00A
G-BUBT	Stoddard-Hamilton IIS RG Glasair (Lycoming IO-320)	2026 & PFA 149-11633		6. 2.92	M.D.Evans	Dunkeswell	7. 8.02P
G-BUBU	Piper PA-34-220T Seneca III	34-8233060	N8043B	9. 7.87	Brinor (Holdings) Ltd	Poplar Hall Farm, Elmsett	3. 8.03
G-BUBW	Robinson R22 Beta	2048		7. 2.92	Forth Helicopter Services Ltd	Edinburgh	6. 9.04T
G-BUBY	Thunder Ax8-105 Srs.2 HAFB	2115		3. 2.92	T.M.Donnelly *"Jorvik Viking Centre"*	Doncaster	12. 6.02T
G-BUCA	Cessna A150K Aerobat	A1500220	N5920J	14. 6.89	D.Featherby t/a BUCA Group	Norwich	3. 3.02T
G-BUCB	Cameron H-34 HAFB	2777		11. 2.92	A.S.Jones	Wolverhampton	14. 8.02A
G-BUCC	CASA I-131E Jungmann *(Spanish AF serial conflicts with G-BJAL)*	1109	G-BUEM G-BUCC/E3B-114	11. 9.78	P.L.Gaze *(As "BU+CC" in Luftwaffe c/s)*	Goodwood	2. 7.02P
G-BUCG	Schleicher ASW 20L (Konig SD430)	20396	BGA.3140 I-FEEL	19. 2.92	W.B.Andrews *"344"*	Booker	3. 8.03
G-BUCH	Stinson V-77 (AT-19) Reliant	77-381	N9570H FB531(RN)	21. 2.92	Pullmerit Ltd	White Waltham	7. 9.02
G-BUCI*	Auster AOP.9	B5/10/150	XP242	10. 2.92	M.Somerton-Rayner t/a Historic Aircraft Flight Reserve Collection (As "XP242" in Army Air Corps c/s: *cancelled 5.3.01 as temporarily wfu)*	AAC Middle Wallop	19. 5.00P
G-BUCJ	de Havilland DHC.2 Beaver AL.1	1442	XP772	23. 3.92	Propshop Ltd & G.Warner t/a British Aerial Museum *(As "XP772" in Army c/s)*	Duxford	
G-BUCK	CASA I-131E Jungmann Srs.1000	1113	E3B-322	11. 9.78	R.A.Cayless & J.G.Brander t/a Jungmann Flying Group *(As "BU+CK" in Luftwaffe c/s)*	White Waltham	20. 7.99P
G-BUCM	Hawker Sea Fury FB.11	-	VX653	26. 2.92	Patina Ltd *(Op The Fighter Collection as "VX653")*	Duxford	
G-BUCO	Pietenpol Air Camper (Continental C90)	PFA 047-11829		10. 2.92	A.James	Siege Cross Farm, Thatcham	1. 8.02P
G-BUCS	Cessna 150F	15062368	N3568L	25. 8.89	Atlantic Bridge Aviation Ltd	Lydd	1. 4.04T
G-BUCT	Cessna 150L	15075326	N11320	14. 6.89	Atlantic Bridge Aviation Ltd	Lydd	5.11.03T
G-BUDA	Slingsby T.61F Venture T.2	1963	ZA627	18. 2.92	T.M.Holloway t/a RAFGSA	RAF Halton	26. 6.04
G-BUDB	Slingsby T.61F Venture T.2	1964	ZA628	18. 2.92	T.M.Holloway t/a RAFGSA	Bicester	5. 9.04
G-BUDC	Slingsby T.61F Venture T.2	1971	ZA652	18. 2.92	I.P.Litchfield t/a T.61 Group	Enstone	30. 8.02
G-BUDE	Piper PA-22-135 Tri-Pacer *(Tail-wheel conversion)*	22-980	N1144C	9. 4.92	B.A.Bower	(Andover)	1. 2.04
G-BUDF	Rand-Robinson KR-2 (HAPI Magnum 75)	PFA 129-11155		26. 2.92	E.C.King	Kemble	30. 8.01P
G-BUDI	Aero Designs Pulsar (Rotax 582)	PFA 202-12185		25. 2.92	R.W.L.Oliver	Popham	28. 2.01P
G-BUDK	Thunder Ax7-77 HAFB	2076		2. 3.92	W.Evans	Wrexham	1. 7.02A
G-BUDL	Taylorcraft E Auster III *(Regd with Frame No.TAY 5810)*	458	PH-POL 8A-2/R Neth AF R-17/NX534	5. 3.92	M.Pocock *(As "NX534")* *(On rebuild 6.98 for Military Auster Flight)*	AAC Middle Wallop	

G-BUDN	Cameron Shoe 90SS HAFB *(Converse Allstar Trainers shape)*	2761		6. 3.92	Magical Adventures Ltd *"Converse Allstar Boot"*	Chirk	1. 8.00A
G-BUDO	PZL-110 Koliber 150	03900045	(D-EIVT)	12. 3.92	A.S.Vine	Haverfordwest	27. 7.02
G-BUDR	Denney Kitfox Mk.3 (Rotax 582)	1086 & PFA 172-12107		16. 3.92	N.J.P.Mayled	Dunkeswell	17. 8.02P
G-BUDS	Rand Robinson KR-2	PFA 129-10937		31.12.85	D.W.Munday *(Noted unmarked nearing completion 9.01)*	Popham	
G-BUDT	Slingsby T.61F Venture T.2	1883	XZ563	30. 3.92	R.V.Andrews t/a G-BUDT Group	Eaglescott	10. 7.04
G-BUDU	Cameron V-77 HAFB	2447		16. 3.92	T.M.G.Amery	Faux Court, Llandeilo, Dyfed	28. 5.00A
G-BUDW	Brugger MB.2 Colibri (VW 1600)	PFA 43-10644	G-GODS	19. 3.92	J.M.Hoblyn *(Crashed Taunton Racecourse 13.8.00: dismantled 9.00)*	Watchford Farm, Yarcombe	3.10.00P
G-BUEC	Van's RV-6 (Lycoming O-360)	21015 & PFA 181C-11884		17. 3.92	R.D.Harper	High Ham, Langport	27. 7.02P
G-BUED	Slingsby T.61F Venture T.2	1979	ZA660	12. 3.92	D.J.Wood t/a SE Kent Civil Service Flying Club	Waldershare Park	4. 7.04
G-BUEE	Cameron A-210 HAFB	2803		20. 3.92	The Balloon Club Ltd t/a Bristol Balloons *"Wookey Hole Caves"*	Bristol	21. 7.00T
G-BUEF	Cessna 152 II	15280862	N25928	17. 3.92	A.L.Brown t/a Channel Aviation	Bourn	12.11.98T
G-BUEG	Cessna 152 II	15280347	N24736	17. 3.92	Plymouth School of Flying Ltd	Plymouth	9.11.01T
G-BUEI	Thunder Ax8-105 HAFB	2172		23. 3.92	Elinore French Ltd t/a Imagination Balloon Flights	Morpeth	30. 3.01A
G-BUEK	Slingsby T.61F Venture T.2	1879	XZ559	30. 3.92	Norfolk Gliding Club Ltd	Tibenham	14.11.04
G-BUEL*	Colt Bottle II SS HAFB *(Korbel California Champagne Bottle shape)*	2141		26. 3.92	Not known *"Korbel Brut"* *(Cancelled 30.7.98 by CAA) (Noted 2000)*	USA	
G-BUEN	VPM M.14 Scout (Arrow GT1000R)	VPM14-UK101		19. 3.92	F.G.Shepherd *(Noted 11.01)*	Carlisle	4.12.96P
G-BUEP	Maule MXT-7-180 Star Rocket	14023C		24. 3.92	G.M.Bunn	Goodwood	1. 5.04
G-BUET*	Colt Flying Drinks Can SS HAFB *(Budweiser Can shape)*	2162		30. 3.92	Balloon Preservation Group *"Bud King of Beers" (Cancelled 29.4.97 as WFU)*	Kirdford	10.12.93A
G-BUEU*	Colt 21A Cloudhopper HAFB *(Budweiser Can shape)*	2163		30. 3.92	Balloon Preservation Group *"Bud King of Beers" (Cancelled 29.4.97 as WFU)*	Kirdford	2.12.94A
G-BUEV	Cameron O-77 HAFB	2810	EI-CFW G-BUEV	31. 3.92	R.R.McCormack	Belfast	29. 6.02A
G-BUEW	Rans S-6 Coyote II	D-190111 & PFA 204-12021	G-MWYF (EI-CEL)	1. 4.92	M.F.Hadley *(New owner 1.02)*	Margaretting, Essex	
G-BUEX	Schweizer Hughes 269C (300C)	S.1412	G-HFLR	14. 4.92	Group 2 Aviation Ltd	(Market Rasen)	5. 6.02T
G-BUEZ*	Hawker Hunter F.6A *(Built Armstrong-Whitworth Aircraft)*	S4U-3275	8736M XF375	3. 4.92	The Old Flying Machine (Air Museum) *(Cancelled 28.8.01 as wfu) (Stored 12.01)*	Duxford	
G-BUFA	Cameron R-77 Gas/HAFB	2712		19. 3.92	Noble Adventures Ltd *(Stored 1996: current status unknown)*	(The Netherlands)	10. 6.93A
G-BUFC	Cameron R-77 Gas/HAFB	2823		19. 3.92	Noble Adventures Ltd *(Stored 1996: current status unknown)*	(The Netherlands)	23. 6.93A
G-BUFE	Cameron R-77 Gas/HAFB	2825		19. 3.92	Noble Adventures Ltd *(Stored 1996: current status unknown)*	(The Netherlands)	21. 6.93A
G-BUFG	Slingsby T.61F Venture T.2	1977	ZA658	3. 4.92	Halegreen Associates Ltd	Hinton-in-the-Hedges	16. 8.04
G-BUFH	Piper PA-28-161 Warrior II	28-8416076	N43520	15. 4.92	M.P.Rainford & J.E.Slee t/a The Tiger Leisure Group	Blackpool	3. 6.04T
G-BUFJ	Cameron V-90 HAFB	2809		7. 4.92	S.P.Richards	Cranbrook	30. 5.00T
G-BUFK	Cassutt Racer IIIM	PFA 034-11069		7. 4.92	D.I.H.Johnstone & W.T.Barnard *(Under construction 6.00)*	(Lanark)	
G-BUFN	Slingsby T.61F Venture T.2	1967	ZA631	8. 4.92	S.C.Foggin t/a BUFN Group	Sandhill Farm, Shrivenham	3.10.04
G-BUFO	Cameron UFO 70SS HAFB *(Flying Saucer shape)*	1929		10. 3.89	Virgin Airship & Balloon Co Ltd *"UFO"*	Telford	26. 4.97A
G-BUFR	Slingsby T.61F Venture T.2 (Rollason RS Mk.2)	1880	XZ560	9. 4.92	East Sussex Gliding Club Ltd	Ringmer	3. 6.04
G-BUFT	Cameron O-120 HAFB	2814		9. 4.92	N.D.Hicks	Alton	24. 9.01T
G-BUFV	Avid Speed Wing Mk.4	PFA 189-12192		15. 4.92	M.& B.Gribbin	(Antrim, Co.Antrim)	19. 6.02P
G-BUFX	Cameron N-90 HAFB	2835		22. 4.92	Kerridge Computer Co Ltd *"Kerridge II"*	Newbury	5. 7.02A
G-BUFY	Piper PA-28-161 Warrior II	28-8016211	N130CT N8TS/N3571K	14. 4.92	Bickertons Aerodromes Ltd *(Op The Pilots Centre)*	Denham	30. 6.04T
G-BUGB	Stolp SA.750 Acroduster Too (Lycoming O-360-A1D)	PFA 089-11942		22. 4.92	R.M.Chaplin	Rochester	27. 8.02P
G-BUGD	Cameron V-77 HAFB	2195		23. 4.92	P.Haslett	Arcy sur Cure, France	24. 7.01A
G-BUGE	Bellanca 7GCAA Citabria	339-77	N4165Y	23. 4.92	P.White	(Fethard, Co.Tipperary)	13. 9.04T
G-BUGG	Cessna 150F	15062479	N8379G	24. 3.92	C.P.J.Taylor & D.M.Forshaw	Panshanger	13. 5.02
G-BUGH*	Rans S-10 Sakota (Rotax 582)	0790.110 & PFA 194-11899		24. 4.92	D.T.Smith *(Cancelled 3.8.01 by CAA)*	Bagby	31. 8.99P
G-BUGI	Evans VP-2 (Continental A65-8)	PFA 7201		16. 4.92	D.G.Gibson *(Noted 3.01)*	Cardiff	25.11.02P
G-BUGJ	Robin DR.400/180 Regent	2137		28. 4.92	W.M.Patterson	(Manorcunningham)	19. 7.04

G-BUGL	Slingsby T.61F Venture T.2	1966	ZA630	29. 4.92	J.Edwards & B.L.Owen t/a VMG Group	Tibenham	1. 6.04
G-BUGM	CFM Streak Shadow (Rotax 582)	K.176-SA & PFA 206-12069		29. 4.92	D.Penn-Smith t/a The Shadow Group	Sywell	29. 6.02P
G-BUGN*	Colt 210A HAFB	2193		1. 5.92	R.W.Batchelor *(Cancelled 29.11.01 as wfu)*	Thame	31. 7.99T
G-BUGO	Colt 56B HAFB	2143		18. 5.92	Escuela de Aerostacion Mica	Valencia, Spain	19. 7.00A
G-BUGP	Cameron V-77 HAFB	2278	OO-BEE	10. 3.92	R. Churcher	Canterbury	14. 7.02A
G-BUGS	Cameron V-77 HAFB	2482		14. 4.92	T J Orchard t/a A Load of Hot Air *"Bugs Bunny"*	Booker	14. 9.01T
G-BUGT	Slingsby T.61F Venture T.2	1871	XZ551	22. 4.92	R.W.Hornsey	Rufforth	5. 8.02
G-BUGV	Slingsby T.61F Venture T.2	1884	XZ564	28. 4.92	Oxfordshire Sportflying Ltd	Enstone	28. 6.01
G-BUGW	Slingsby T.61F Venture T.2	1962	ZA626	22. 4.92	Halegreen Associates Ltd	Hinton-in-the-Hedges	16. 8.04
G-BUGX*	SOCATA MS.880B Rallye Club	2957	OO-FLO	24. 4.92	R.W.H.Watson *(Fuselage stored 4.99: cancelled 24.8.01 by CAA)*	(Spalding)	9. 9.99
G-BUGY	Cameron V-90 HAFB	2800		9. 4.92	I.J.Culley t/a Dante Balloon Group *"Florance"*	Hungerford	26. 7.02A
G-BUGZ	Slingsby T.61F Venture T.2	1981	ZA662	22. 4.92	R.W.Spiller t/a Dishforth Flying Group	AAC Dishforth	24. 5.02
G-BUHA	Slingsby T.61F Venture T.2	1970	ZA634	29. 4.92	G.A.Rodwell t/a G-BUHA Group *(As "ZA634/C")*	Rufforth	19. 7.02
G-BUHJ	Boeing 737-4Q8	25164		19. 3.93	British Airways (European Operations at Gatwick) Ltd	Gatwick	18. 3.03T
G-BUHK	Boeing 737-4Q8	26289		14. 6.93	British Airways (European Operations at Gatwick) Ltd	Gatwick	13. 6.03T
G-BUHL	Boeing 737-4S3	25134	9M-MLH N1799B/(G-BSRB)	22. 3.93	GB Airways Ltd *(Wings t/s)*	Gatwick	6. 4.03T
G-BUHM	Cameron V-77 HAFB	2481		7. 5.92	L.A.Watts *"Blue Horizon"*	Pangbourne, Reading	5. 7.01A
G-BUHO	Cessna 140 (Continental C90)	14402	N2173V	1. 5.92	W.B.Bateson	Blackpool	19.11.04T
G-BUHR	Slingsby T.61F Venture T.2	1874	XZ554	8. 5.92	S J Wright t/a Denbeigh Falke Group	Lleweni Parc	27. 4.02
G-BUHS	Stoddard-Hamilton Glasair I TD (Lycoming O-360)	149	C-GYMB	8. 5.92	E.J.Spalding	Inverness	6. 9.00P
G-BUHU	Cameron N-105 HAFB	2785		13. 5.92	Unipart Group Ltd t/a Unipart Balloon Club *"Land Rover"*	Cowley, Oxford	21.11.96A
G-BUHY	Cameron A-210 HAFB	2858		14. 5.92	Adventure Balloon Co Ltd	London W7	21. 9.99T
G-BUHZ	Cessna 120	14950	N3676V	1. 5.92	J.Redfarn	(Ely)	12.11.01P
G-BUIC	Denney Kitfox mk.2	PFA 172-11802		1. 5.92	C.R.Northrop & B.M.Chilvers	(Huntingdon/Wisbech)	
G-BUIE	Cameron N-90 HAFB	2863		22. 5.92	Flying Pictures Ltd *"Unipart III"*	Fairoaks	24. 1.01A
G-BUIF	Piper PA-28-161 Warrior II	28-7916406	N28375	29. 5.92	Newcastle upon Tyne Aero Club Ltd	Newcastle	8. 9.04T
G-BUIG	Campbell Cricket (Rotax 532)	PFA G/03-1173		27. 5.92	T.A.Holmes	Melrose Farm, Melbourne	9. 6.97P
G-BUIH	Slingsby T.61F Venture T.2	1876	XZ556	29. 5.92	Yorkshire Gliding Club (Pty) Ltd	Sutton Bank	8. 6.04
G-BUIJ	Piper PA-28-161 Warrior II	28-8116210	N83784	3. 6.92	Tradecliff Ltd	Blackbushe	9. 7.04
G-BUIK	Piper PA-28-161 Warrior II	28-7916469	N2845P	2. 6.92	A.S.Bamrah t/a Falcon Flying Services	Shoreham	23. 8.04T
G-BUIL	CFM Streak Shadow (Rotax 582)	K.182-SA & PFA 206-12121		8. 5.92	P.N.Bevan & L.M.Poor *"Mr Bounce"*	Perth	6.11.01P
G-BUIN	Thunder Ax7-77 HAFB	1882		5. 6.92	P C Johnson	Gloucester	20. 9.02A
G-BUIO	British Aerospace Jetstream Srs.3202	835	OH-JAB G-BUIO/C-GZRT/G-31-835	1. 9.92	Air Kilroe Ltd *(Op Eastern Airways)*	Humberside	26. 4.02T
G-BUIP	Denney Kitfox mk.2 (Rotax 582)	710 & PFA 172-11874		8. 6.92	Avcomm Developments Ltd	Enstone	1. 8.02P
G-BUIR	Avid Speed Wing Mk.4	PFA 189-12213		9. 6.92	K.N.Pollard *(Damaged near Gainsborough 26.1.97: on rebuild 5.97: current status unknown)*	Sturgate	29. 4.97P
G-BUIU	Cameron V-90 HAFB	2641		11. 6.92	H.Micketeit	Bielefeld, Germany	13. 3.02A
G-BUIZ*	Cameron N-90 HAFB	2850		12. 6.92	Balloon Preservation Group *"Hutchinson Telecom" (Cancelled 19.10.00 as wfu)*	Kirdford	7. 8.95A
G-BUJA	Slingsby T.61F Venture T.2	1972	ZA653	22. 5.92	T.M.Holloway t/a RAFGSA *(Op Wrekin Gliding Club)*	RAF Cosford	8. 7.01
G-BUJB	Slingsby T.61F Venture T.2	1978	ZA659	21. 5.92	O.F.Vaughan & D.A.Fall t/a Falke Syndicate	Shobdon	11. 7.04
G-BUJE	Cessna 177B Cardinal	17701920	N34646	10. 6.92	J.Flux t/a FG93 Group	Old Sarum	5. 5.04

G-BUJH	Colt 77B HAFB	2207		23. 6.92	R.P.Cross & R.Stanley	Luton/Harpenden	22. 7.01A
G-BUJI	Slingsby T.61F Venture T.2	1882	XZ562	22. 5.92	Solent Venture Syndicate Ltd		
						Lee-on-Solent	28. 5.04
G-BUJJ*	Avid Speed Wing	213	N614JD	20.10.92	P.A.Ellis	Popham	21. 6.00P
					(Cancelled 29.8.00 by CAA)		
G-BUJK	Montgomerie-Bensen B.8MR Merlin			25. 6.92	K.J.Robinson	(Oxford)	16. 4.02P
	(Rotax 582)	PFA G/01-1211					
G-BUJL	Aero Designs Pulsar	PFA 202-11892		16. 6.92	J.J.Lynch	(Dunstable)	
G-BUJM	Cessna 120	11784	N77343	19. 6.92	B.R.Johnstone	RNAS Yeovilton	28.10.02
	(Continental C85)		NC77343		t/a Cessna 120 Flying Group		
G-BUJN	Cessna 172N Skyhawk II	17272713	N6315D	19. 6.92	Aerohire Ltd	Wolverhampton	30.11.95T
G-BUJO	Piper PA-28-161 Cherokee Warrior II	28-7716077	N1014Q	19. 6.92	Anglo American Airmotive Ltd	Jersey	24. 3.03T
G-BUJP	Piper PA-28-161 Warrior II	28-7916047	N21624	19. 6.92	White Waltham Airfield Ltd	White Waltham	27. 6.02T
G-BUJR	Cameron A-180 HAFB	2821		22. 6.92	W.I.Hooker & C.Parker	Nottingham	16.10.00T
G-BUJV	Avid Speed Wing Mk.4	PFA 189-12250		3. 7.92	C.Thomas	(Tamworth)	28. 7.94P
					(Damaged Caernarfon 13.8.93: current status unknown)		
G-BUJW	Thunder Ax8-90 Srs.2 HAFB	2208		6. 7.92	R.T.Fagan	Bath	6. 8.95T
G-BUJX	Slingsby T.61F Venture T.2	1873	XZ553	7. 7.92	J.R.Chichester-Constable		
						Burton Constable, Hull	19. 7.02
G-BUJY	de Havilland DH.82A Tiger Moth	"OU/04/1967"		1. 7.92	P.Winters	(Mechelen, Belgium)	
	(Provenance unknown)				*(Dismantled & stored 10.00)*		
G-BUJZ	Rotorway Executive 90	5119		9. 7.92	M.P.Swoboda	Street Farm, Takeley	9.10.02P
	(Rotorway RI 162)						
G-BUKA	Fairchild SA.227AC Metro III	AC-706B	ZK-NSQ	24. 8.88	Atlantic Air Transport Ltd	Coventry	11. 6.03T
			N27185/G-BUKA/N27185		*(Atlantic Airlines c/s)*		
G-BUKB	Rans S-10 Sakota	PFA 194-12078		13. 7.92	M.K.Blatch	RAF Keevil	28. 8.02P
	(Rotax 582)						
G-BUKC*	Cameron A-180 HAFB	2870		3. 7.92	Balloon Preservation Group	Malpas	
					"Cloud Nine" (Cancelled 11.10.99 as WFU)		
G-BUKF	Denney Kitfox mk.4	PFA 172A-12247		2. 6.92	A.G.V.McClintock	East Fortune	6.12.01P
	(Rotax 582)				t/a Kilo Foxtrot Group		
G-BUKH	Druine D.31 Turbulent	PFA 048-11419		14. 8.92	P.M.Newman		
	(VW 1600)					Stoneacre Farm, Farthing Corner	8. 4.02P
G-BUKI	Thunder Ax7-77 HAFB	2239		8. 7.92	Virgin Airship & Balloon Co Ltd	Telford	9. 7.01T
G-BUKJ	British Aerospace ATP	2052	EC-HCO	5. 8.92	Trident Aviation Leasing Services (Jersey) Ltd		
			G-BUKJ/EC-GLD/G-OEDF/G-BUKJ/TC-THZ/G-BUKJ			Woodford	
G-BUKK	Dornier Bücker Bü.133D Jungmeister	27	N44DD	15.11.89	E.J.F.McEntee	Kirdford, Billingshurst	10.10.02P
			HB-MKG/Sw AF U-80		*(As "U-80" in Swiss AF c/s)*		
G-BUKN	Piper PA-15 Vagabond	15-215	N4427H	15. 7.92	B.F. & M.A.Goddard	(Southampton)	
			NC4427H		*(New owners 4.01)*		
G-BUKP	Denney Kitfox mk.2	PFA 172-12301		22. 7.92	S.Moreton	Shenstone	1. 7.02P
	(Rotax 582)						
G-BUKR	SOCATA MS.880B Rallye 100T	2923	LN-BIY	27. 7.92	G.R.Russell	Bridport	14.11.02
					t/a G-BUKR Flying Group		
G-BUKS	Colt 77B HAFB	2241		6. 7.92	R.& M.Bairstow	Middlewich, Cheshire	5. 7.02A
G-BUKT	Luscombe 8E Silvaire	2197	N45670	30. 7.92	M.G.Talbot & J.N.Wilshaw		
	(Continental C85)		NC45670			Sherburn in Elmet	13.11.02P
G-BUKU	Luscombe 8E Silvaire	4720	N1993K	30. 7.92	F.G.Miskelly	Thruxton	12.11.02P
	(Continental C85)		NC1993K				
G-BUKV	Colt AS-105 Mk.II Hot-Air Airship	2212	ZS-HYO	3. 8.92	A.Ockelmann	Buchholz, Germany	17. 4.02A
			G-BUKV		t/a Ballon Reisen		
G-BUKX	Piper PA-28-161 Cherokee Warrior II	28-7816674	N231PA	5. 8.92	LNP Ltd	Exeter	12.12.04T
G-BUKZ	Evans VP-2	PFA 063-10761		5. 8.92	P.R.Farnell *(Extant 5.00)*	Wombleton	
G-BULB	Thunder Ax7-77 HAFB	1968		3. 7.92	Richard Nash Cars Ltd	Norwich	7. 4.02A
G-BULC	Avid Flyer Mk.4	PFA 189-12202		6. 7.92	C.Nice	Popham	3. 7.02P
	(Rotax 582)						
G-BULD	Cameron N-105 HAFB	2136		6. 8.92	C.L.Jenkins	Bristol	17. 2.01T
G-BULE*	Price TPB.2 HAFB	004		10. 8.92	A.G.R.Calder	London NW1	
					(Cancelled 23.11.01 as wfu)		
G-BULF	Colt 77A HAFB	2043		10. 8.92	P.Goss & T.C.Davies	Christchurch	20. 4.02A
G-BULG	Van's RV-4	JRV4-1	C-FELJ	28. 7.92	M.J.Aldridge	Priory Farm, Tibenham	20. 5.02P
	(Lycoming O-320)						
G-BULH	Cessna 172N Skyhawk II	17269869	N738CJ	2. 7.92	Touchdown Properties Ltd	Blackpool	9. 9.02T
G-BULJ	CFM Streak Shadow			10. 8.92	C.C.Brown	Lubenham	1. 8.02P
	(Rotax 582)	K.191-SA & PFA 206-12199					
G-BULK	Thunder Ax9-120 Srs.2 HAFB	2237		3. 7.92	S.J.Colin & A.S.Pinder	Maidstone	12. 6.02T
					t/a Skybus Ballooning		
G-BULL	Scottish Aviation Bulldog Srs.120/128	BH120/392	HKG-5	20. 9.88	Solo Leisure Ltd	Old Sarum	23. 9.04T
			G-31-18		*(As "HKG-5" in Hong Kong c/s)*		

G-BULM	Aero Designs Pulsar	PFA 202-12010		11. 8.92	J.Lloyd	(Wokingham)	1. 5.02P
	(Rotax 582) (Tri-cycle u/c)						
G-BULN	Colt 210A HAFB	2265		13. 8.92	H.G.Davies	Cheltenham	29. 7.02T
G-BULO	Luscombe 8A Silvaire	4216	N1489K	13. 8.92	A.F.S.Caldecourt	Popham	8. 2.02P
	(Continental A65)		NC1489K				
G-BULR	Piper PA-28-140 Cherokee B	28-25230	HB-OHP	8. 7.92	R & H Wale (General Woodworks) Ltd		
			N7320F		*"Margaret Ann"*	Little Gransden	15.10.01T
G-BULT	Campbell Cricket	PFA G/03-1213		20. 8.92	A.T.Pocklington	(Bishops Stortford)	
					(Test flown @ Henstridge 23.9.00)		
G-BULW*	Rans S-10 Sakota	PFA 194-11663		18. 8.92	J.L.M. van Hoesel		
						Lelystad, The Netherlands	
					(To PH-RNS 98R. cancelled 17.4.98: noted as "G-BULW" 6.01)		
G-BULY	Avid Flyer	PFA 189-12309		12. 8.92	D.R.Piercy	Newton Peverill	23. 7.02P
	(Rotax 582)				*"Lady Irene"*		
G-BULZ	Denney Kitfox mk.2	PFA 172-11546		31. 7.92	T.G.F.Trenchard	Newton Peverill	30.10.02P
	(Rotax 582)						
G-BUMP	Piper PA-28-181 Cherokee Archer II		PH-MVA	17. 1.79	Marham Investments Ltd	Ronaldsway	20.11.03T
		28-7790437	OO-HCH/N3105Q		*(Op Manx Flyers Aero Club)*		
G-BUNB	Slingsby T.61F Venture T.2	1969	ZA633	25. 8.92	T.M.Holloway	RAF Cranwell	14.12.01
					t/a RAFGSA *(Op Cranwell Gliding Club)*		
G-BUNC	PZL-104 Wilga 35A	129444	SP-TWP	2. 9.92	Fast Aerospace Ltd	Hill Farm, Nayland	8. 6.02
G-BUND	Piper PA-28RT-201T Turbo Arrow IV		N8219V	18. 7.88	Jenrick Ltd & A.Somerville	Blackbushe	20. 8.04
		28R-8031107					
G-BUNG	Cameron N-77 HAFB	2905		2. 9.92	A.Kaye	Wellingborough	29.12.01A
					t/a The Bungle Balloon Group *"Bungle" (Aspen titles)*		
G-BUNH	Piper PA-28RT-201T Turbo Arrow IV		N8255H	26. 8.92	Jennifer A.Blenkharn	Carlisle	30.11.01T
		28R-8031166			t/a JB Consultants (Aviation)		
G-BUNI	Cameron Bunny 90SS HAFB	2897		23. 9.92	Virgin Airship & Balloon Co Ltd	Telford	29.10.99A
	(Cadburys Caramel Bunny shape)						
G-BUNJ	K & S SA.102-5 Cavalier	PFA 01-10058		10. 9.92	J.A.Smith	Great Massingham	
					(Nearing completion 9.97: current status unknown)		
G-BUNM	Denney Kitfox mk.3	PFA 172-12111		15. 9.92	P.N.Akass	Inverness	16.11.00P
	(Rotax 582) *(Floatplane)*				*(Overturned landing Beauly Firth 28.8.01 as wheel element of landing gear not retracted)*		
G-BUNO	Neico Lancair 320	PFA 191-12332		11. 9.92	J.Softley *(On build 2000)*	(Newbury)	
G-BUNS	Reims Cessna F150K	F15000648	F-BSIL	28. 8.92	R.W.H.Cole	Spilsted Farm, Sedlescombe	
					t/a Cole Aviation *(Stored 11.01)*		
G-BUNV	Thunder Ax7-77 HAFB	1967		23. 9.92	J.A.Lister *"Skylark"*	Aldershot	12. 8.02A
G-BUNZ	Thunder Ax10-180 Srs.2 HAFB	2271		7. 9.92	T.M.Donnelly	Doncaster	26. 4.00T
G-BUOA	Whittaker MW6-S Srs.A Fatboy Flyer			25. 9.92	R.Blackburn	(Raphoe, Co.Donegal)	5.11.02P
	(Rotax 582)	PFA 164-11959					
G-BUOB	CFM Streak Shadow			29. 9.92	A.M.Simmons	Belle Vue Farm, Yarnscombe	16. 7.02P
	(Rotax 582)	K.186-SA & PFA 206-12156					
G-BUOC	Cameron A-210 HAFB	2924		5.10.92	C.& J.Bailey	Bristol	11. 3.01T
					t/a Bailey Balloons		
G-BUOD	Replica Plans SE.5A	PFA 20-10474		5.10.92	M.D.Waldron	Kemble	8. 4.02P
	(Continental C90)				*(As "B595/W" in 56 Sqdn, RFC c/s)*		
G-BUOE	Cameron V-90 HAFB	2938		6.10.92	B. & J.Smallwood	Chippenham	22. 4.02A
					t/a Dusters & Co *"Flying Colours 2"*		
G-BUOF	Druine D.62B Condor	PFA 049-11236		6.10.92	R.P.Loxton	Loxton Farm, Sherbourne	29. 3.02P
	(Continental O-200-A)						
G-BUOI	Piper PA-20-135 Pacer (mod)	20-571	OY-ALS	18. 9.92	R.A.L.Hubbard	Meon	15. 5.02
	(Lycoming O-320) *(Hoerner wing-tips)*		D-EHEN/N7750K		t/a Foley Farm Flying Group		
G-BUOJ	Cessna 172N Skyhawk II	17271701	N5064E	8.10.92	EFG Flying Services Ltd	Biggin Hill	12. 7.04T
G-BUOK	Rans S-6-116 Coyote II			9.10.92	M.Morris		
	(Rotax 912UL)	0692.314 & PFA 204A-12317				Fieldhead Farm, Denholme, Bradford	9. 8.02P
G-BUOL	Denney Kitfox mk.3	PFA 172-12142		12.10.92	J.G.D.Barbour		
	(Rotax 582)					Sheriff Hall, Balgone, Berwick	14. 6.02P
G-BUON	Avid Aerobat	PFA 189-12160		13.10.92	N.T.Hawkins	(Mold)	6.11.01P
	(Rotax 582)						
G-BUOR	CASA I-131E Jungmann Srs.2000	2134	N89542	21.10.92	M.I.M.Schermer Voest *(On rebuild 2001)*		
			EC-336/E3B-508			(Lelystad, The Netherlands)	13.11.95P
G-BUOS	Supermarine 394 Spitfire FR.XVIIIe		HS687	19.10.92	Historic Flying Ltd	Duxford	21. 8.02P
	(Regd as c/n 6S/676224)	6S/672224	Ind AF/SM845		*(Op Aircraft Restoration Company) (As "SM845")*		
G-BUOW	Aero Designs Pulsar XP	PFA 202-12206		22.10.92	T.J.Hartwell	Sackville Lodge, Riseley	8. 6.95P
	(Rotax 912)				*(New owner 7.01)*		
G-BUOX	Cameron V-77 HAFB	2925		23.10.92	R.M.Pursey & C.M.Richardson		
					"High Flyer"	Newbury/Oxford	14. 5.00A
G-BUOZ	Thunder Ax10-180 HAFB	1962	(SX-)	29.10.92	Zebedee Balloon Service Ltd	Hungerford	31. 3.01T
			G-BUOZ				
G-BUPA	Rutan LongEz	750	N72SD	22. 9.92	G.J.Banfield	Gloucestershire	5. 6.02P
	(Lycoming O-235)						
G-BUPB	Stolp SA.300 Starduster Too	RH.100	N8035E	3.11.92	J.R.Edwards	Popham	7. 8.01P
	(Lycoming IO-360)				t/a Starduster PB Group		

G-BUPC	Rollason Beta B2 (Continental C90)	PFA 02-12369		29.10.92	C.A.Rolph	Liverpool	3. 6.02P
G-BUPF	Bensen B.8MR (Rotax 532)	PFA G/01-1209		5.11.92	P.W.Hewitt-Dean	(Wootton Bassett)	1. 8.02P
G-BUPG	Cessna 180J Skywagon	18052490	N52086	15.10.92	T.P.A.Norman	Rendcomb	17.10.02
G-BUPI	Cameron V-77 HAFB	1778	G-BOUC	28. 7.88	Sally A.Masey *"Bristol United Press"* *(Western Daily Press/Evening Post titles)*	Bristol	30. 4.00A
G-BUPJ	Sportavia Fournier RF4D	4119	N7752	10.11.92	M.R.Shelton	Tatenhill	
G-BUPM	VPM M-16 Tandem Trainer (Rotax 914)	VPM16-UK-102		16.10.92	Roger Savage Gyroplanes Ltd	Carlisle	2. 4.02P
G-BUPO*	Moravan Zlin Z.526F Trener Master	1267	YR-OAZ YR-ZAO	23.11.92	P.J.Behr & F.Mendelssohn *(Cancelled 2.10.00 as wfu: current status unknown)*	(Sarreguemines/Strasbourg, France)	31. 1.96
G-BUPP	Cameron V-42 HAFB	2789		21. 7.92	L.J.Schoeman	Basildon	28. 3.02A
G-BUPR	Jodel D.18 (Limbach L2000)	PFA 169-11289		23.11.92	R.W.Burrows	Priory Farm, Tibenham	1. 5.02P
G-BUPS	ATR 42-300	109	DQ-FEP F-WWEF	16.12.92	Titan Airways Ltd	Stansted	5. 6.02T
G-BUPT	Cameron O-105 HAFB	2960		25.11.92	P.M.Simpson t/a Chiltern Balloons	Hemel Hempstead	4. 3.01T
G-BUPU	Thunder Ax7-77 HAFB	2305		25.11.92	R.C.Barkworth & D.G.Maguire *"Puzzle"*	(USA)	26. 3.01A
G-BUPV	Great Lakes 2T-1A Sport Trainer (Gladden Kinner R55)	126	N865K NC865K	26.11.92	R.J.Fray	Sibson	28. 6.02P
G-BUPW	Denney Kitfox mk.3 (Rotax 912)	PFA 172-12281		22.10.92	G.M.Park t/a Forfoxake Flyers	(Lochwinnoch)	10. 7.02P
G-BURD	Reims Cessna F172N Skyhawk II	F17201677	PH-AXI	26. 4.78	M.O.Loxton *(Island Aviation - Historic Air Tours titles)*	Leysdown-on-Sea, Sheppey	26.11.02T
G-BURE	Jodel D.9 Bebe	PFA 944		30.11.92	Lucy J.Kingsford *(Noted 3.00)*	Headcorn	
G-BURF	Rand Robinson KR-2 (VW 1834)	PFA 129-11345		30.11.92	P.J.H.Moorhouse & B.L.Hewart	(Stockport)	
G-BURG	Colt 77A HAFB	2042		12. 1.93	S.T.Humphreys *"Lily"*	Great Missenden	13. 6.01A
G-BURH	Cessna 150E	15061225	EI-AOO G-BURH/EI-AOO/N2125J	2.12.92	C.A.Davis & R F H Roberts t/a BURH Flying Group	Popham	6.11.02
G-BURI	Enstrom F-28C	433	N51743	11.12.92	R.L.Heath t/a India Helicopters Group	Goodwood	31. 3.02
G-BURL	Colt 105A HAFB	2297		18.11.92	J.E.Rose	Abingdon	12. 1.02T
G-BURM	English Electric Canberra TT.18 *(Built Handley Page Ltd)*	-	WJ680	11.12.92	Mitchell Aircraft Ltd *(As "WJ680/CT" in 100 Sqdn c/s)* *(Sold to Temora Aviation Museum, Canberra, Australia and due to be flown out 1.02)*	Bournemouth	2.12.02P
G-BURN	Cameron O-120 HAFB	2793		18. 2.92	Innovation Ballooning Ltd *"Innovations II"*	Bath	18. 7.02T
G-BURP	Rotorway Executive 90 (Rotorway RI 162)	5116		8.10.92	N.K.Newman *(Stored 7.99)*	Sywell	13. 9.96P
G-BURR*	Auster AOP.9	-	7851M WZ706	28. 9.92	R.P.D.Folkes *(Op Military Auster Flight as "WZ706)* *(Cancelled 18.3.99 by CAA) (Current status unknown)*	AAC Middle Wallop	
G-BURS	Sikorsky S-76A II Plus	760040	(HP-) G-BURS/G-OHTL	4. 5.89	Lynton Aviation Ltd t/a Signature Aircraft Charter	Blackbushe	25.10.02T
G-BURT	Piper PA-28-161 Cherokee Warrior II	28-7716105	N2459Q	10. 6.81	J.D.F.Fendick	Tibenham	2. 6.02
G-BURU	British Aerospace Jetstream Srs.3202 *(Originally regd as Srs.3206)*	974	F-GMVH G-BURU/(F-OHFT)/G-31-974	14. 1.93	Trident Aviation Leasing Services (Ireland) Ltd	(Dublin)	
G-BURZ	Hawker Nimrod II	41H-59890	K3661	22.12.91	Historic Aircraft Collection Ltd *(On rebuild 8.95: current status unknown)*	St.Leonards-on-Sea	
G-BUSB	Airbus A320-111 *(Originally flown as G-BRSA)*	0006	(G-BRAA) F-WWDD	30. 3.88	British Airways plc *(Koguty Lowickie t/s)*	Heathrow	19. 4.04T
G-BUSC	Airbus A320-111	0008	(G-BRAB) F-WWDE	26. 5.88	British Airways plc	Heathrow	1. 6.04T
G-BUSD	Airbus A320-111	0011	(G-BRAC) F-WWDF	21. 7.88	British Airways plc *"Isle of Mull"*	Heathrow	21. 7.04T
G-BUSE	Airbus A320-111	0017	F-WWDG	1.12.88	British Airways plc	Heathrow	30.11.04T
G-BUSF	Airbus A320-111	0018	F-WWDH	26. 5.89	British Airways plc	Heathrow	25. 5.02T
G-BUSG	Airbus A320-211	0039	F-WWDM	30. 5.89	British Airways plc	Heathrow	30. 5.02T
G-BUSH	Airbus A320-211	0042	F-WWDT	19. 6.89	British Airways plc	Heathrow	18. 6.02T
G-BUSI	Airbus A320-211	0103	F-WWDB	23. 3.90	British Airways plc *(Grand Union t/s)*	Heathrow	21. 3.03T
G-BUSJ	Airbus A320-211	0109	F-WWIC	6. 8.90	British Airways plc *(Water Dreaming t/s)*	Heathrow	5. 8.03T
G-BUSK	Airbus A320-211	0120	F-WWIN	12.10.90	British Airways plc	Heathrow	11.10.03T
G-BUSN	Rotorway Executive 90 (Rotorway RI 162)	5141		6. 1.93	J.A.McGinley	(Dublin)	10. 5.01P

G-BUSR	Aero Designs Pulsar	PFA 202-12356		15.12.92	S.S.Bateman & R.A.Watts	Cheddington	21. 6.02P
	(Rotax 582) *(Tail-wheel u/c)*						
G-BUSS	Cameron Bus 90SS HAFB	1685		11. 3.88	Magical Adventures Ltd	Chirk	31. 1.96A
					"National Express"		
G-BUST	Neico Lancair IV	LIV-114A		23.10.92	C.C.Butt	Hawarden	
					(Stored incomplete 2.99: current status unknown)		
G-BUSV	Colt 105A HAFB	2324		12. 1.93	M.N.J.Kirby	Northwich, Cheshire	26. 1.95
G-BUSW	Rockwell Commander 114	14079	N4749W	18. 1.93	P.A.Nesbitt	(Bohemia, NY, USA)	
G-BUSY	Thunder Ax6-56A HAFB	111		20. 6.77	M.E.Hooker *"Busy Bodies"*	Whitchurch	27. 4.86A
G-BUSZ	Avid Speed Wing Mk.4	PFA 189-12280		20. 1.93	T.J.Allan	Drayton St.Leonard	30. 4.02P
G-BUTA	CASA I-131E Jungmann Srs.2000	1101/A	E3B-336	20. 1.93	A.G.Dunkerley	Breighton	8. 2.02P
	(Correct c/n not known)						
G-BUTB	CFM Streak Shadow			20. 1.93	S.Vestuti	Swansea	11. 4.02P
	(Hirth 2706 R05) K.190 & PFA 206-12243						
G-BUTD	Van's RV-6	PFA 181-12152		21. 1.93	N.W.Beadle	Benson's Farm, Laindon	26. 7.02P
	(Lycoming O-320)						
G-BUTE	Anderson EA-1 Kingfisher Amphibian		G-BRCK	15. 8.91	T.Crawford	Cumbernauld	15.10.99P
	(Lycoming O-235)	PFA 132-10798					
G-BUTF	Aeronca 11AC Chief	11AC-1578	N3231E	21. 1.93	N.J.Mortimore	Watchford Farm, Yarcombe	12. 9.02P
			NC3231E				
G-BUTG	Zenair CH-601HD Zodiac	PFA 162-12225		22. 1.93	J.M.Palmer	Coldharbour Farm, Willingham	12. 5.02P
	(Continental C90)						
G-BUTH	CEA Jodel DR.220 2+2	6	F-BNVK	10. 2.93	A.A.M. & C.W.N.Huke	RAF Shawbury	6. 6.03
G-BUTJ	Cameron O-77 HAFB	2991		25. 1.93	A.J.A. & P.A.Bubb	Guildford	29. 6.02A
					"Purple Haze"		
G-BUTK*	Murphy Rebel	PFA 232-12091		25. 1.93	L.D.Johnston	(Spalding)	29. 5.02P
	(Rotax 912-UL)				*(Cancelled 31.7.01 as wfu: for sale 11.01)*		
G-BUTL	Piper PA-24-250 Comanche	24-2352	G-ARLB	4. 4.84	D.Heater	Blackbushe	28. 7.02
			N10F				
G-BUTM	Rans S-6-116 Coyote II *(Tailwheel u/c)*			22. 1.93	N.D.White	(Northampton)	2. 7.02
	(Rotax 912UL)	PFA 204A-12414			t/a G-BUTM Group		
G-BUTT*	Reims Cessna FA150K Aerobat	FA1500029	G-AXSJ	18. 8.86	C.R.Guggenheim	Bournemouth	24.10.99T
	(Blown over in gales 1.99 & fuselage stored 5.00: cancelled 4.10.01 by CAA: current status unknown)						
G-BUTW	British Aerospace Jetstream Srs.3202		F-GMVI	23. 2.93	Trident Aviation Leasing Services (Ireland) Ltd		
	(Originally regd as Srs.3206)	975	G-BUTW/(F-OHFU)/G-31-975			(Dublin)	
G-BUTX	Bücker Bü.133C Jungmeister		E1-4	3. 2.93	A.J.E.Smith *(Op Real Aeroplane Company)*		
	(Warner Super Scarab)		Sp AF ES.1-4/35-4			Leeward Air Ranch, Florida, USA	23.10.02P
	(Possibly c/n 1010 or a CASA built I-133L)						
G-BUTY	Brugger MB.2 Colibri	PFA 043-12387		30.11.92	R.M.Lawday	(Milford, Derby)	
G-BUTZ	Piper PA-28-180 Cherokee C	28-3107	G-DARL	23. 4.93	A.J. & J.M.Davis	Sywell	13. 7.03T
			4R-ARL/4R-ONE/SE-EYD				
G-BUUA	Slingsby T.67M Firefly II	2111		17. 3.93	Babcock Rosyth Defence Ltd		
					t/a Hunting Contract Services		
						AAC Middle Wallop	23. 8.02T
G-BUUB	Slingsby T.67M Firefly II	2112		17. 3.93	Babcock Rosyth Defence Ltd		
					t/a Hunting Contract Services		
						AAC Middle Wallop	1. 6.02T
G-BUUC	Slingsby T.67M Firefly II	2113		17. 3.93	Babcock Rosyth Defence Ltd		
					t/a Hunting Contract Services		
						AAC Middle Wallop	14. 8.02T
G-BUUD	Slingsby T.67M Firefly II	2114		17. 3.93	Babcock Rosyth Defence Ltd		
					t/a Hunting Contract Services *(Op JEFTS)*		
						RAF Barkston Heath	31. 8.02T
G-BUUE	Slingsby T.67M Firefly II	2115		17. 3.93	Babcock Rosyth Defence Ltd		
					t/a Hunting Contract Services *(Op JEFTS)*		
						RAF Barkston Heath	29. 9.02T
G-BUUF	Slingsby T.67M Firefly II	2116		17. 3.93	Babcock Rosyth Defence Ltd		
					t/a Hunting Contract Services *(Op JEFTS)*		
						RAF Barkston Heath	26.10.02T
G-BUUG	Slingsby T.67M Firefly II	2117		17. 3.93	Babcock Rosyth Defence Ltd		
					t/a Hunting Contract Services *(Op JEFTS)*		
						RAF Barkston Heath	19. 7.02T
G-BUUI	Slingsby T.67M Firefly II	2119		17. 3.93	Babcock Rosyth Defence Ltd		
					t/a Hunting Contract Services *(Op JEFTS)*		
						RAF Barkston Heath	18.11.02T
G-BUUJ	Slingsby T.67M Firefly II	2120		17. 3.93	Babcock Rosyth Defence Ltd		
					t/a Hunting Contract Services		
						AAC Middle Wallop	20. 8.02T
G-BUUK	Slingsby T.67M Firefly II	2121		17. 3.93	Babcock Rosyth Defence Ltd		
					t/a Hunting Contract Services *(Op JEFTS)*		
						RAF Barkston Heath	16. 1.03T

G-BUUL	Slingsby T.67M Firefly II	2122		17. 3.93	Babcock Rosyth Defence Ltd t/a Hunting Contract Services *(Op JEFTS)*	RAF Barkston Heath	16. 1.03T
G-BUUM	Piper PA-28RT-201 Arrow IV	28R-7918090	N2145X	14. 1.93	J.Phelan & D.G.Scott t/a Bluebird Flying Group	Belfast	3. 4.02
G-BUUN	Lindstrand LBL-105A HAFB	015		9. 2.93	Flying Pictures Ltd *"British Gas"*	Fairoaks	11. 3.02A
G-BUUO	Cameron N-90 HAFB	2994		9. 2.93	M.P.Rich t/a Gone Ballooning Group	Bristol	16. 6.02A
G-BUUP	British Aerospace ATP	2008	G-MANU G-BUUP/CS-TGA/G-11-8/(N378AE)	18. 2.93	Trident Aviation Leasing Services (Jersey) Ltd	Woodford	24. 3.03T
G-BUUR	British Aerospace ATP	2024	EC-GUX G-OEDJ/G-BUUR/CS-TGC/G-BUUR/CS-TGC/G-11-024	18. 2.93	Trident Aviation Leasing Services (Jersey) Ltd	Woodford	14. 8.98T
G-BUUS*	Skyraider Gyrocopter (Arrow GT500)	P.01		9. 2.93	Sycamore Aviation Ltd *(Cancelled 13.4.99 as WFU: stored 2000)*	Healinks Farm, Clitheroe	11. 5.95P
G-BUUT	Interavia 70TA HAFB	04509-92		21. 1.93	Aero Vintage Ltd	Rye	
G-BUUU*	Cameron Bottle 77SS HAFB *(Bells Whisky Bottle shape)*	2980		11. 2.93	(British Balloon Museum & Library) *"Bells Whisky"* *(Cancelled 22.10.01 by CAA)*	Newbury	4. 3.94A
G-BUUX	Piper PA-28-180 Cherokee D	28-5128	OY-BCW	17. 2.93	M.A.Judge t/a Aero Group 78	Netherthorpe	22. 9.02T
G-BUUZ	British Aerospace Jetstream Srs.3202 *(Originally regd as Srs.3206)*	976	F-GMVJ G-BUUZ/(F-OHFV)/G-31-976	10. 3.93	Trident Aviation Leasing Services (Ireland) Ltd	(Dublin)	
G-BUVA	Piper PA-22-135 Tri-Pacer	22-1301	N8626C	12. 2.93	K.W.Thomas t/a Oaksey VA Group	Oaksey Park	18. 4.03
G-BUVB*	Colt 77A HAFB	2041		22. 2.93	T.L.Regan *(Cancelled 17.9.01 by CAA)*	Newcastle	23. 3.94A
G-BUVC	British Aerospace Jetstream Srs.3202	970	F-GMVP F-GLPY/G-BUVC/F-GLPY/(F-OHFS)/G-BUVC/G-31-970	10. 3.93	Air Kilroe Ltd	Manchester	5. 3.04T
G-BUVD	British Aerospace Jetstream Srs.3202	977	F-GMVK G-BUVD/(F-OHFR)/(F-OHFW)/G-31-977	10. 3.93	Air Kilroe Ltd	Manchester	26. 4.04T
G-BUVE	Colt 77B HAFB	2376		8. 3.93	G.D.Philpot *"Trident"*	Hemel Hempstead	2. 9.01A
G-BUVG	Cameron N-56 HAFB	3012		8. 3.93	Cameron Balloons Ltd	Bristol	10. 8.00A
G-BUVK*	Cameron A-210 HAFB	2996		8. 3.93	Balloon Preservation Group *"Burgundy Blaze" (Cancelled 2.12.98 as WFU)*	Lancing	18. 8.97T
G-BUVL	Fisher Super Koala (Jabiru 2200)	PFA 228-11399		3. 3.93	A.D.Malcolm *"Spirit of Throwley"*	Park Farm, Throwley, Faversham	24. 6.02P
G-BUVM	CEA Jodel DR.250/160 Capitaine	54	OO-NJR F-BNJR	11. 3.93	G.G.Milton	Kimbolton	29.11.02
G-BUVN	CASA I-131E-2000 Jungmann	2092	EC-333 E3B-487	12. 3.93	W.Van Egmond *(As "BI-005" in R.Neth AF c/s)*	Hoogeveen, The Netherlands	27. 7.02P
G-BUVO	Reims Cessna F182P Skylane II	F18200022	G-WTFA PH-VDH/D-EJCL	10. 3.93	D.W.Wall t/a BUVO Group	Southend	1. 6.02
G-BUVP	CASA I-131E-2000 Jungmann Srs.2000 *(Regd with c/n 2155)*	2139	EC-338 E3B-539	12. 3.93	M.I.M.Schermer Voest	Lelystad, The Netherlands	14. 9.98P
G-BUVR	Christen A-1 Husky	1162		12. 3.93	A.E.Poulsom	Manor Farm, Tongham	26. 4.02
G-BUVS	Colt 77A HAFB	2381		12. 3.93	S.J.Chatfield	(Guildford)	20. 2.01A
G-BUVT	Colt 77A HAFB	2382		12. 3.93	N.A.Carr	Leicester	24. 2.02A
G-BUVW	Cameron N-90 HAFB	3020		19. 3.93	Bristol Balloon Fiestas Ltd	Bristol	7. 2.01A
G-BUVX	CFM Streak Shadow SA (Rotax 582)	K.214SA & PFA 206-12410		22. 3.93	G.K.R.Linney	Latch Farm, Kirknewton	1. 4.02P
G-BUVZ	Thunder Ax10-180 Srs.2 HAFB	2380		24. 3.93	A.Van Wyk	Caxton, Cambs	7. 4.01T
G-BUWE	Replica Plans SE.5A (Continental C90)	PFA 020-11816		25. 3.93	P.N.Davis & H.Wilebore t/a Taildragger Classics *(As "C9533/M" in RFC c/s)*	Leicester	30. 5.02P
G-BUWF	Cameron N-105 HAFB	3036		26. 3.93	R.E.Jones *"British Aerospace II"*	Lytham St.Annes	27. 1.02T
G-BUWH	Parsons Two-Place Gyroplane (Rotax 532)	PFA G/08-1215		1. 4.93	R.V.Brunskill	Melrose Farm, Melbourne	22. 8.95P
G-BUWI	Lindstrand LBL-77A HAFB	023		5. 4.93	Capital Balloon Club Ltd *"Throw Up"*	London NW1	6. 4.02T
G-BUWJ	Pitts S-1C Special (Lycoming O-320)	2002	N110R	25. 3.93	J.I.Greenshields	Dunkeswell	20. 9.02P
G-BUWK	Rans S-6-116 Coyote II (Rotax 912)	PFA 204A-12448		7. 4.93	R.Warriner	Bradleys Lawn, Heathfield	8. 6.02P
G-BUWM	British Aerospace ATP	2009	CS-TGB G-BUWM/CS-TGB/G-11-9	19. 4.93	BAE Systems (Operations) Ltd *(Stored 12.01)*	Woodford	
G-BUWR	CFM Streak Shadow (Rotax 582)	K.177-SA & PFA 206-12068		26. 4.93	T.Harvey	Grove Farm, Raveningham	21. 5.02P
G-BUWS	Denney Kitfox mk.2	PFA 172-11831		26. 4.93	J.E.Brewis	(Castletown, IoM)	
G-BUWT	Rand Robinson KR-2	PFA 129-10952		5. 4.93	Cynthia M.Coombe	(Greenford, Middx)	
G-BUWU	Cameron V-77 HAFB	3053		27. 4.93	G.Thompson	Ashford, Kent	5. 9.01A
G-BUWY	Cameron V-77 HAFB	2961		27. 4.93	P.A.Sachs *"Pixel"*	West Byfleet	30. 7.00A
G-BUWZ	Robin HR.200/120B	254		22. 4.93	A.Cox	Lydd	27. 1.00

G-BUXA*	Colt 210A HAFB	2400		28. 4.93	Balloon Preservation Group *"Buxam" (Cancelled 20.12.01 as wfu)*	Kirdford	7. 4.99T
G-BUXB	Sikorsky S-76A	760086	(F-GSJG) G-BUXB/VR-CCZ/N399BB/N39RP	11. 6.93	Lynton Aviation Ltd t/a Signature Aircraft Charter	Blackbushe	16. 8.02T
G-BUXC	CFM Streak Shadow (Rotax 582)	K.188 & PFA 206-12177		20. 4.93	J.P.Mimnagh	(Wirral)	11. 2.02P
G-BUXD	Maule MXT-7-160 Star Rocket *(Tri-cycle u/c)*	17001C	N9231R	4. 5.93	S.Baigent	Jersey	12. 9.02
G-BUXI	Steen Skybolt (Lycoming IO-360)	PFA 064-10755		16. 3.93	M.Frankland	Caernarfon	9. 8.02P
G-BUXJ	Slingsby T.61F Venture T.2	1878	XZ558	6. 5.93	D.Mihailovic t/a Venture Motor Glider Club	RAF Halton	17. 6.02
G-BUXK	Pietenpol Aircamper (Continental C90)	PFA 047-11901		12. 5.93	B.P.Hogan	Sywell	14. 7.01P
G-BUXL	Taylor JT.1 Monoplane	PFA 055-11819		12. 5.93	M.W.Elliott	(Derby)	
G-BUXM	QAC Quickie Tri-Q (Revmaster 2100D)	2343	N4435Y	23. 2.93	A.J.Ross & D.Ramwell *(Stored 10.97: current status unknown)*	Tatenhill	10. 8.95P
G-BUXN	Beechcraft C23 Sundowner	M-1752	N9256S	13. 5.93	C.J.Addis t/a Private Pilots Syndicate	Bournemouth	16. 9.02
G-BUXO	Pober P-9 Pixie	PFA 105-10647		17. 5.93	J.Mangiapane t/a P-9 Flying Group *(Nearing completion 2000)*	(Matlock)	
G-BUXR	Cameron A-250 HAFB	3056		13. 5.93	D.S.King t/a Celebration Balloon Flights	Nottingham	7. 5.01T
G-BUXS	MBB Bö.105DBS-4 *(Originally c/n S.41: rebuilt 1993)*	S.913	G-PASA G-BGWP/F-ODMZ/G-BGWP/HB-XFD/N153BB/D-HDAS	19. 5.93	Bond Air Services *"Irn Bru"*	Glasgow City Heliport	25. 5.04T
G-BUXT	Dornier 228-202K	8065	D-CBOL TC-FBM/D-CBOL	24. 5.93	Air Wales Ltd	Cardiff	26. 5.04T
G-BUXU	Beechcraft D17S (GB-2) Traveler	4823	N9113H Bu 33024	20. 5.93	S.J.Ellis *(Noted 9.99)*	Bryngwyn Bach	
G-BUXV	Piper PA-22-160 Tri-Pacer *(Super Pacer Tail-wheel conversion)*	22-6685	N9769D	20. 5.93	T.McManus & W.Connor t/a Bogavia Two	Weston, Dublin	11.10.03
G-BUXW	Thunder Ax8-90 Srs.2 HAFB	2405		25. 5.93	J.M.Percival *"Silver Lady"*	Burton-on-the-Wolds	19. 6.02A
G-BUXX	Piper PA-17 Vagabond (Continental A75)	17-28	N4611H NC4611H	31. 3.93	R.H.Hunt	Old Sarum	16. 5.02P
G-BUXY	Piper PA-25-235 Pawnee	25-2705	C-GZCR N6959Z	18. 3.93	Bath, Wilts & North Dorset Gliding Club Ltd	Kingston Deverill	30. 1.04
G-BUYB	Aero Designs Pulsar (Rotax 582) *(Tail-wheel u/c)*	PFA 202-12193		28. 5.93	A.P.Fenn	Shobdon	20.12.01P
G-BUYC	Cameron Concept 80 HAFB	3095		28. 5.93	P.J.Dorward	Witney	20. 7.94
G-BUYD	Thunder Ax8-90 HAFB	2422		28. 5.93	Anglia Balloon School Ltd t/a Anglia Balloons *"Air UK"*	Norwich	26.12.01A
G-BUYE	Aeronca 7AC Champion (Continental A65)	7AC-4327	N85584 NC85584	30. 4.93	R.Mazey *(On rebuild 9.00)*	(Bristol)	16.11.96P
G-BUYF	American Aircraft Falcon XP (Rotax 503)	600179	N512AA	13. 5.93	D.S.Bremner t/a G-BUYF Syndicate	Barton	1. 1.02P
G-BUYG*	Colt Flying Gin Bottle 12 SS HAFB *(Gordon's Gin Bottle shape)*	2331		28. 5.93	United Distillers plc *"Gordon's Gin" (Cancelled 7.11.01 by CAA: current status unknown)*	(Spain)	20. 5.96
G-BUYI*	Thunder Ax7-77 HAFB	1266		20. 6.88	Chelmsford Management Ltd *"Elevation" (Cancelled 9.11.01 as wfu: current status unknown)*	Chelmsford	18. 7.99A
G-BUYJ	Lindstrand LBL-105A HAFB	039		1. 6.93	D.K.Fish	Bedford	6.10.00T
G-BUYK	Denney Kitfox mk.4 (Rotax 912UL)	PFA 172A-12214		1. 6.93	A.W.Shellis	Otherton, Cannock	25. 9.01P
G-BUYL	Rotary Air Force RAF 2000 *(Rebuilt by Newtonair using parts from G-TXSE)*	H2-92-361	C-FPFN	2. 6.93	Newtonair Gyroplanes Ltd *(Flew 11.00)*	Dunkeswell	21. 2.02P
G-BUYN	Cameron O-84 HAFB	1214	OE-KZG	4. 6.93	Reach For The Sky Ltd	(Guildford)	16.12.01A
G-BUYO	Colt 77A HAFB	2398		4. 6.93	S.F.Burden	Noordwijk, The Netherlands	1. 6.00A
G-BUYR	Mooney M.20C Mark 21	2650	N1369W	7. 6.93	Charmaine R.Weldon	Haverfordwest	15. 9.00
G-BUYS	Robin DR.400/180 Regent	2197		21. 6.93	F.A.Spear	Nuthampstead	7. 4.02
G-BUYT*	Ken Brock KB-2 (Rotax 582)	PFA G/06-1214		7. 6.93	Janet E.Harris *(Cancelled 16.10.00 by CAA)*	(Ashby-De-La-Zouch)	6. 2.95P
G-BUYU	Bowers Fly Baby 1A (Continental A65)	PFA 016-12222		7. 6.93	J.A.Nugent	Haverfordwest	18. 7.02P
G-BUYY	Piper PA-28-180 Cherokee B	28-1028	C-FXDP CF-XDP/N7214W	18. 3.93	A.J.Hedges & C.E.Yates t/a G-BUYY Group	Bristol	25. 4.02T
G-BUZA	Denney Kitfox mk.3 (Rotax 582)	1178 & PFA 172-12547		10. 6.93	J.Thomas	(St. Neots)	2. 4.02P
G-BUZB	Aero Designs Pulsar XP (Rotax 912) *(Tail-wheel u/c)*	PFA 202-12312		14. 6.93	S.M.Lancashire	Lymm Dam	21. 5.02P
G-BUZC	Everett Gyroplane Srs.3A	034		14. 7.93	M.P.Lhermette *(Damaged 7.94: stored Sproughton 12.95: current status unknown)*	(Faversham)	
G-BUZD	Aérospatiale AS332L Super Puma	2069	C-GSLJ N189EH/C-GSLJ/HC-BNB/C-GSLJ/PT-HRN/C-GSLJ	11. 2.93	CHC Scotia Ltd	Aberdeen	14.12.02T

G-BUZE	Avid Speed Wing	PFA 189-12047		16. 6.93	J.M.Fforde	(Talgarth)	21. 3.02P
G-BUZF	Colt 77B HAFB	1993		16. 6.93	A.E.Austin	Naseby	18. 5.02A
G-BUZG	Zenair CH.601HD Zodiac	PFA 162-12457		17. 6.93	N.C.White	Sorbie Farm, Kingsmuir	17. 6.02P
	(Continental O-200-A)						
G-BUZH	Star-Lite SL-1	119	N4HC	17. 6.93	C.A.McDowall	Farley Farm, Winchester	8. 9.00P
	(Rotax 447) *(Built H M Cottle)*				*(Noted in container 9.00 - fuselage only)*		
G-BUZJ	Lindstrand LBL 105A HAFB	038		17. 6.93	Eastgate Motor Co Ltd	Bristol	13. 9.02A
					t/a Eastgate Mazda *(Damaged nr Lulsgate mid 2000)*		
G-BUZK	Cameron V-77 HAFB	2962		17. 6.93	J.T.Wilkinson	Calne	16. 6.02A
G-BUZL	VPM M-16 Tandem Trainer	VPM16-UK-105		18. 6.93	R.M.Savage	Carlisle	12. 3.02P
	(Rotax 914)				t/a Roger Savage (Photography)		
G-BUZM	Avid Speed Wing mk.3	PFA 189-12179		30. 4.93	R.McLuckie & O.G.Jones	RAF Mona	27. 7.00P
	(Jabiru 2200)				*(Damaged nosewheel and propeller taxying Caernarfon 13.5.01)*		
G-BUZN	Cessna 172H	17256056	N2856L	24. 6.93	H.Jones	Barton	26.10.02
G-BUZO	Pietenpol Aircamper	PFA 047-12408		28. 6.93	D.A.Jones	(Maidenhead)	
	(Salmson AD9)						
G-BUZR	Lindstrand LBL-77A HAFB	044		29. 6.93	Lindstrand Balloons Ltd	Oswestry	11. 1.00A
G-BUZS	Colt Flying Pig SS HAFB	2415		2. 7.93	Banco Bilbao Vizcaya	(Spain)	20. 5.96A
G-BUZT	Kolb Twinstar Mk.3	PFA 205-12367		1. 7.93	A.C.Goadby	(Sudbury)	
G-BUZV	Ken Brock KB-2	PFA G/06-1152		1. 7.93	K.Hughes	(Amlwch, Gwynedd)	
G-BUZY	Cameron A-250 HAFB	2936		29. 4.93	P.J.D.Kerr	Bridgwater	31. 5.02T
G-BUZZ	Agusta-Bell 206B JetRanger II	8178	F-GAMS	13. 4.78	European Skytime Ltd	Gloucestershire	19. 6.02T
			HB-XGI/OE-DXF				

G-BVAA – G-BVZZ

G-BVAA	Avid Speed Wing Mk.4	PFA 189-12166		10. 6.93	D.T.Searchfield	Popham	5. 9.01P
G-BVAB	Zenair CH.601HDS Zodiac			26. 5.93	T.J.Smith	(Ellesmere)	22. 5.02T
	(Rotax 912UL)	PFA 162-12475					
G-BVAC	Zenair CH.601HD Zodiac	PFA 162-12504		1. 6.93	A.G.Cozens	Goodwood	6. 9.02P
	(Rotax 912UL)						
G-BVAF	Piper J-3C-65 Cub	4645	OO-UBU	14. 6.93	N.M.Hitchman	Garston Farm, Marshfield	18. 6.02P
	(Continental C85)		N28199/NC28199				
G-BVAG	Lindstrand LBL-90A HAFB	022		7. 7.93	R.Tillson & P.Ellis	Ilkeston	11. 5.02A
					t/a Firefly Balloon Team *"Gee Tee"*		
G-BVAH	Denney Kitfox mk.3	PFA 172-12031		22.10.91	D.A.Lord	Shoreham	6.11.02P
	(Rotax 912)						
G-BVAI	PZL-110 Koliber 150	03900040	OY-CYJ	7. 7.93	A.R.Howard	Gamston	15. 6.03
G-BVAM	Evans VP-1	PFA 062-12132		7. 7.93	R.F.Selby	(Littlehampton)	
G-BVAN	SOCATA MS.892E Rallye 150GT	12376	F-BVAN	21.11.88	K.Taylor	(Driffield)	17. 5.04T
G-BVAO	Colt 25A Sky Chariot HAFB	2024		9. 7.93	Janice M.Frazer	Hexham, Northumberland	22. 5.02A
G-BVAW	Staaken Z-1 Flitzer	PFA 223-12058		12. 7.93	D.J.Evans & L.R.Williams *(As "D692")*		
	(VW 1834)					(Merthyr Tydfil)	29. 6.99P
G-BVAX	Colt 77A HAFB	1213		30. 3.88	P.H.Porter *"Vax"*	Tenbury Wells	5. 8.95A
G-BVAY	Rutan VariEze	RS.8673/345	N5MS	3. 9.93	D.A.Young	(Sunderland)	11.11.02P
G-BVAZ	Montgomerie-Bensen B.8MR			12. 7.93	R.M.Savage	Carlisle	3. 4.02P
		PFA G/01-1190			t/a Great Orton Group		
G-BVBD	Vertical Aviation Technologies S-52-3		N4643S	21. 7.93	J.Windmill	Ilkeston	
		52014	Bu.125521		*(Stored 10.95: current status unknown)*		
G-BVBF*	Piper PA-28-151 Cherokee Warrior		N31JM	22. 7.93	R.K.Spence	Cardiff	
		28-7515206	N32633	*(Cancelled 18.3.99 by CAA: noted 11.99: current status unknown)*			
G-BVBG	Piper PA-32R-300 Cherokee Lance		N19BP	22. 7.93	R.K.Spence	Cardiff	7. 1.01T
		32R-7680151					
G-BVBJ*	Colt Flying Coffee Jar 1 SS HAFB			27. 7.93	Balloon Preservation Group	Kirdford	21.11.96A
	(Maxwell House Jar)	2427			*"Maxwell House 1" (Cancelled 29.4.97 as WFU)*		
G-BVBK*	Colt Flying Coffee Jar 2 SS HAFB			27. 7.93	Balloon Preservation Group	Malpas	14. 2.97A
	(Maxwell House Jar)	2428			*"Maxwell House 2" (Cancelled 29.4.97 as WFU)*		
G-BVBN	Cameron A-210 HAFB	2904		2. 8.93	M.L. & S.M.Gabb	Alcester	10.10.01T
					t/a Heart of England Balloons		
G-BVBO	Vertical Aviation Technologies S-52-3		N9329R	4. 8.93	M.Richardson	Ilkeston	
		52046	Bu.128616		t/a Ilkeston Contractors		
					(Stored 10.95: current status unknown)		
G-BVBP	Avro 683 Lancaster B.10		KB994	4. 8.93	D Copley	North Weald	
	(Built Victory Aircraft, Canada as B.X)		RCAF		*(Forward fuselage only hangared 8.01)*		
G-BVBR	Avid Speed Wing	PFA 189-12085		3. 8.93	N J Garbett	(Grantham)	16. 4.02P
G-BVBS	Cameron N-77 HAFB	3128		4. 8.93	Marley Building Materials Ltd	Birmingham	7. 5.02A
G-BVBT	de Havilland DHC-1 Chipmunk 22		WK511	4. 8.93	T Curtis-Taylor & J H Slade	(Royston)	11. 5.03
		C1/0547			*(As "WK511/901" in RN c/s)*		
G-BVBU	Cameron V-77 HAFB	3076	(OO-BYS)	5. 8.93	J.Manclark	Haddington	26. 7.97A
					(Op Alba Ballooning)		
G-BVBV	Avid Speed Wing	PFA 189-12187		4. 8.93	L.W.M.Summers	Sandown	19. 5.02P

G-BVBX*	Cameron N-90M HAFB	3102		10. 8.93	British Balloon Museum & Library	Newbury	27. 9.95A
					"Mercury" (Cancelled 10.2.97 as temporary WFU)		
G-BVCA	Cameron N-105 HAFB	3129		11. 8.93	Unipart Group Ltd	Cowley	25. 6.00A
					t/a Unipart Balloon Club *"Unipart 4"*		
G-BVCB	Rans S-10 Sakota	PFA 194-11882		11. 8.93	M.D.T.Barley	Cambridge	27. 9.02P
	(Rotax 912-UL)						
G-BVCC	Monnett Sonerai 2LT	PFA 015-10547		12. 8.93	J.Eggleston	(Northallerton)	
G-BVCG	Van's RV-6	PFA 181-11783		17. 8.93	C.J.F.Flint	Sleap	28. 5.02P
	(Lycoming O-320)						
G-BVCJ	Agusta A109A II	7265	G-CLRL	23. 8.93	Castle Air Charters Ltd	Liskeard	5. 3.03T
			G-EJCB				
G-BVCL	Rans S-6-116 Coyote II	PFA 204A-12551		25. 8.93	R J Powell	(Fareham)	9. 2.02P
	(Rotax 912UL)						
G-BVCM	Cessna 525 CitationJet	525-0022	N1329N	2. 5.94	Kwik Fit plc	Edinburgh	22. 5.03
G-BVCN*	Colt 56A HAFB	2445		25. 8.93	N.R.Mason	Llandudno	8. 9.94A
					(Cancelled 22.10.01 by CAA)		
G-BVCO	Clutton Fred Srs.2	PFA 029-10947		25. 8.93	I.W.Bremner	(Dornoch, Sutherland)	25. 6.02P
G-BVCP	Piper CP.1 Metisse	PFA 253-12512		24. 6.93	C.W.R.Piper	Hinton-in-the-Hedges	14. 8.02P
	(Revmaster 2200)						
G-BVCS	Aeronca 7AC Champion	7AC-1346	N69BD	1. 9.93	P.C.Isbell	Cherry Tree Farm, Monewden	26.11.02P
	(Continental A65)		N82702/NC82702				
G-BVCT	Denney Kitfox mk.4-1200			27. 8.93	A.F.Reid	Comber, Co of Down	14. 6.02P
	(Rotax 912UL)	1761 & PFA 172A-12456					
G-BVCY	Cameron H-24 HAFB	3136		3. 9.93	Bryant Group plc	Solihull	19. 1.02A
G-BVDB	Thunder AX7-77 HAFB	2364	G-ORDY	6. 9.93	M.J.Smith & J.Towler	York	17.10.99A
G-BVDC	Van's RV-3	PFA 099-12218		12. 7.93	J.A.A.Schofield	(Henley-on-Thames)	27. 5.00P
	(Lycoming O-235)						
G-BVDD	Colt 69A HAFB	2170		6. 9.93	R.M.Cambridge & D.Harrison-Morris		
					"Delta Dawn Fantasia"	Oswestry	31. 8.02P
G-BVDE	Taylor JT-1 Monoplane	PFA 055-11278		6. 9.93	S.G.Hammond	(Rushden)	31. 1.02P
	(VW 1834)						
G-BVDF*	Cameron Doll 105SS HAFB	3112		7. 9.93	Cameron Balloons Ltd	(Germany)	3.11.94A
					(Cancelled 19.9.01 as wfu)		
G-BVDH	Piper PA-28RT-201 Arrow IV		N2176L	13. 9.93	Goodair Leasing Ltd	Cardiff	18. 4.03T
		28R-7918030					
G-BVDI	Van's RV-4	2058	N55GJ	13. 9.93	D.F.Brown	Perth	7. 3.01P
	(Lycoming O-320)						
G-BVDJ	Campbell Cricket	PFA G/03-1189		13. 9.93	Shirley Jennings	St Merren	1. 6.01P
	(Rotax 582)						
G-BVDM	Cameron Concept 60 HAFB	3141		15. 9.93	M.P.Young	Dover	31. 5.01A
G-BVDN	Piper PA-34-220T Seneca III		G-IGHA	16. 9.93	Convergence Aviation Ltd	Jersey	12. 8.04T
		34-8133185	G-IPUT/N8424D				
G-BVDO	Lindstrand LBL-105A HAFB	055		16. 9.93	J.Burlinson	Aston Clinton	5. 4.01T
					"West Lodge Hotel II"		
G-BVDP	Sequoia F8L Falco	PFA 100-10879		17. 9.93	T.G.Painter	(Felixstowe)	
G-BVDR	Cameron O-77 HAFB	2452		21. 9.93	T.Duggan	Selby	7. 9.01T
G-BVDS	Lindstrand LBL-69A HAFB	102		23. 9.93	Lindstrand Balloons Ltd	Oswestry	26. 6.01A
G-BVDT	CFM Streak Shadow SA-1			23. 9.93	H.J.Bennet	North Connel, Oban	2. 5.01P
	(Rotax 582)	K.223 & PFA 206-12462					
G-BVDW	Thunder Ax8-90 HAFB	2507		30. 9.93	S.C.Vora *"Cosmic"*	Oadby	6. 6.02
G-BVDX	Cameron V-90 HAFB	3159	OO-BMY	30. 9.93	R.K.Scott	Yeovil	14. 5.02A
			G-BVDX				
G-BVDY	Cameron Concept 60 HAFB	3167		30. 9.93	K.A. & G.N.Connolly	Monmouth	23. 3.96A
G-BVDZ	Taylorcraft BC-12D	9043	N96743	21. 1.94	P.N.W.England	(Hove)	
			NC96743				
G-BVEA	Nostalgair N.3 Pup		G-MWEA	7. 6.93	N.Lynch	Breighton	20. 8.02P
	(Mosler MM-CB35)	01-GB & PFA 212-11837					
G-BVEF	ATR 42-300	331	F-GKNF	24. 3.94	GPA-ATR Ltd	Exeter	23. 3.03T
			F-WWLP		*(Stored 11.01)*		
G-BVEH	Wassmer Jodel D.112	1294	F-BMOH	29.10.93	M.L.Copland	Breighton	8. 3.01P
G-BVEJ	Cameron V-90 HAFB	3169		5.10.93	J.D.A.Snields & A.R.Craze	Battle	1. 6.02T
G-BVEK	Cameron Concept 80 HAFB	3133		5.10.93	A.D.Malcolm	Devizes	17. 3.01A
G-BVEL*	Evans VP-1 Srs.2	PFA 062-11983		6.10.93	M.J. & S.J.Quinn	(Kilmacolm)	
					(Cancelled 22.3.99 by CAA: under construction 6.00)		
G-BVEN	Cameron Concept 80 HAFB	3164		6.10.93	Hildon Associates Ltd	Stockbridge	10. 6.02T
G-BVEP	Luscombe 8A Master	1468	N28707	8.10.93	B.H.Austen	Oaksey Park	21.10.02
			NC28707				
G-BVER	de Havilland DHC.2 Beaver 1	1648	G-BTDM	13. 8.91	Seaflite Ltd	Lochearnhead	23. 4.95T
			XV268		*(New owner 11.01) (As "XV268" in AAC c/s)*		
G-BVES	Cessna 340A II	340A0077	N1378G	8. 9.93	K.P.Gibbin & I.M.Worthington	Nottingham	9.12.02T
G-BVEU	Cameron O-105 HAFB	3145		12.10.93	H.C.Wright	Kelfield, York	8. 2.02T
G-BVEV	Piper PA-34-200 Seneca	34-7250316	N1428T	8.10.93	R.W.Harris, M.F.Hatt & JRB Aviation Ltd		
			HB-LLN/D-GHSG/N1428T		*(Op Southend Flying Club)*	Southend	9. 8.03T

G-BVEW	Lindstrand LBL-150A HAFB	057		14.10.93	A.Van Wyk	Cambridge	15. 8.02T
G-BVEY	Denney Kitfox mk.4-1200			14.10.93	J.H.H.Turner	(Houston)	24. 5.02P
	(Rotax 582)	PFA 172A-12527					
G-BVEZ	Hunting-Percival P.84 Jet Provost T.3A		XM479	13.10.93	Newcastle Jet Provost Co Ltd	Newcastle	27. 8.02P
		PAC/W/9287			*(As "XM479/54" in RAF c/s)*		
G-BVFA	Rans S-10 Sakota	PFA 194-12298		7. 9.93	J.Holme	Old Sarum	20. 8.02P
	(Rotax 582)						
G-BVFB	Cameron N-31 HAFB	3175		20.10.93	Bath City Council *"Bath Heritage"*	Bath	13. 5.02A
G-BVFF	Cameron V-77 HAFB	3161		26.10.93	I.R.Warrington	Stamford	12. 1.02A
G-BVFM	Rans S-6-116 Coyote II			2.11.93	J.Gorman	(Banstead)	23. 5.02P
	(Rotax 912UL) 0793.522 & PFA 204A-12579						
G-BVFO	Avid Speed Wing	PFA 189-12053		9. 9.93	P.Chisman	Enstone	20. 4.02P
G-BVFP	Cameron V-90 HAFB	3179		2.11.93	C.Duppa-Miller	Warwick	16. 2.02A
G-BVFR	CFM Streak Shadow			3.11.93	R.W.Chatterton		
	(Rotax 582) K.237-SA & PFA 206-12567					Griffins Farm, Temple Bruer	6. 3.02P
G-BVFS	Slingsby T.31M Cadet III	PFA 042-11387	ex RAF?	3.11.93	V.M.Crabb	(Southend)	
	(Arrow) *(Converted to Motor Tutor)*				*(Stored dismantled 1.02 but not confirmed)*		
G-BVFT	Maule M-5-235C Lunar Rocket	7183C	N6180M	5.11.93	Pagodaplan Ltd	Bodmin	6. 6.03T
					t/a Avon Air Services		
G-BVFU	Cameron Sphere 105SS HAFB	3137		18.11.93	Stichting Phoenix		
						Amsterdam, The Netherlands	27. 5.02A
G-BVFY	Colt 210A HAFB	2493	DQ-BVF	30. 9.93	T.J.Bucknall	Malpas	
			G-BVFY		*"Scotair" (Op Balloon Preservation Group)*		
G-BVFZ	Maule M-5-180C Lunar Rocket	8082C	N5664D	21. 2.94	C.N.White		
						Franklyns Field, Chewton Mendip	7. 3.03
G-BVGA	Bell 206B-3 JetRanger III	2922	N54AJ	11.11.93	J.L Leonard	Shoreham	30. 1.03T
			VH-SBC		t/a Findon Air Services		
G-BVGB	Thunder Ax8-105 Srs.2 HAFB	2408		11.11.93	M.E.Dunstan-Sewell	Bristol	26. 3.02A
G-BVGE	Westland WS-55 Whirlwind HAR.10		8732M	18.11.93	J.F.Kelly	(Mullingar, Co.Westmeath)	18. 9.02P
		WA/100	XJ729		*(As "XJ729" in RAF Rescue c/s)*		
G-BVGF	Europa Aviation Europa			18.11.93	A.Graham & G.G.Beal	Brunton	23.10.02P
	(Rotax 912UL)	34 & PFA 247-12565					
G-BVGG	Lindstrand LBL-69A HAFB	011		30.11.93	Lindstrand Balloons Ltd	Oswestry	6. 4.01A
G-BVGH	Hawker Hunter T.7	HABL 004328	XL573	26.11.93	DAT Enterprises Ltd	North Weald	10. 7.02P
	(Centre fuselage no.is confirmed as HABL 003360)				*(As "XL573")*		
G-BVGI	Pereira Osprey 2	PFA 070-10536		29.11.93	A.A.Knight	North Connel, Oban	7. 5.01P
	(Lycoming O-320)						
G-BVGJ	Cameron Concept 80 HAFB	3099		7.12.93	D.T.Watkins *"Pizza Express"*	Hexham	23. 4.00A
G-BVGO	Denney Kitfox mk.4-1200			15.11.93	A.Morgan	(Ilkeston)	8. 9.00P
	(Rotax 582)	PFA 172A-12362					
G-BVGR	Royal Aircraft Factory BE.2E		A1325	8.12.93	Aero Vintage Ltd	Rotary Farm, Hatch	
	(RAF 1e) *(Built 1917)*	"133/A1325"	133/37 R Nor AF		*(On rebuild 8.95: current status unknown)*		
G-BVGS	Robinson R22 Beta	2389	N2363S	9.12.93	Bristol & Wessex Helicopters Ltd	Bristol	25. 7.03T
G-BVGT	Crofton Auster V J/1A Special			19.11.93	P.N.Birch	(North Walsham)	16. 8.02P
	(Blackburn Cirrus 2)	PFA 00-220	*(Rebuild of unregd Auster J/1 Autocrat frame used as engine test rig)*				
G-BVGW	Luscombe 8A Silvaire	4823	N2096K	18.11.93	L.A.Groves	Lee-on-Solent	26. 9.02P
			NC2096K				
G-BVGY	Luscombe 8E Silvaire	4754	N2027K	18.11.93	Tracey Groves	(Fareham)	
			NC2027K				
G-BVGZ	Fokker DR.1 Triplane rep			20.12.93	P.N.Davis & H.Wilebore	Leicester	29. 3.02P
	(Lycoming AIO-360) VHB-10 & PFA 238-12654				t/a Taildragger Classics *(German AF c/s)*		
G-BVHC	Grob G-115D-2 Heron	82005	D-EARG	14.12.93	VT Aerospace Ltd	Plymouth	30. 3.03T
					(Op Royal Navy)		
G-BVHD	Grob G-115D-2 Heron	82006	D-EARJ	14.12.93	VT Aerospace Ltd	Plymouth	5. 6.03T
					(Op Royal Navy)		
G-BVHE	Grob G-115D-2 Heron	82008	D-EARQ	14.12.93	VT Aerospace Ltd	Plymouth	27. 3.03T
					(Op Royal Navy)		
G-BVHF	Grob G-115D-2 Heron	82011	D-EARV	14.12.93	VT Aerospace Ltd	Plymouth	18. 5.03T
					(Op Royal Navy)		
G-BVHG	Grob G-115D-2 Heron	82012	D-EARX	14.12.93	VT Aerospace Ltd	Plymouth	8. 5.03T
					(Op Royal Navy)		
G-BVHI	Rans S-10 Sakota	PFA 194-12608		20.12.93	P.D.Rowley	Popham	2. 6.99P
	(Rotax 582)						
G-BVHK	Cameron V-77 HAFB	3209		23.12.93	Ann R.Rich *"Intel Inside"*	Hyde	7. 9.02
G-BVHM	Piper PA-38-112 Tomahawk	38-79A0313	G-DCAN	14.11.91	A.J.Gomes	Shoreham	17. 7.02T
			N2490D		*(Op Sky Leisure Aviation)*		
G-BVHL	Nicollier HN.700 Menestrel II			24.12.93	W.Goldsmith	(Boldon Colliery)	
		PFA 217-12614					
G-BVHO	Cameron V-90 HAFB	3158		29.12.93	N.W.B.Bews	Tenbury Wells	17. 7.00
G-BVHP	Colt 42A HAFB	2533		31.12.93	Danny Bertels Ballooning BVBA		
						Wommelgem, Belgium	27. 7.02
G-BVHR	Cameron V-90 HAFB	3174		5. 1.94	G.P.Walton	Bagshot	14. 7.02T

G-BVHS	Murphy Rebel 050 & PFA 232-12180		5. 1.94	J.R.Malpass	(Coal Aston)	8. 5.02P
	(Lycoming O-235)					
G-BVHT	Avid Speed Wing Mk.4 PFA 189-12226		28.10.93	R.S.Holt	Long Marston	15. 6.02P
G-BVHU*	Colt Flying Bottle 13 SS HAFB 2499		6. 1.94	Bias International Ltd *(Cancelled 22.10.01 by CAA)*		
				"Kaiser"	Rio De Janeiro, Brazil	19. 2.95A
G-BVHV	Cameron N-105 HAFB 3215		6. 1.94	Flying Pictures Ltd *"Rover"*	Fairoaks	14.12.98A
G-BVHX*	Pilatus Britten-Norman BN-2T-4R Defender 4000		21. 1.94	Britten-Norman Ltd	Bembridge	
	4003			*(Stored 8.99: cancelled 5.4.00 as wfu)*		
G-BVHY	Pilatus Britten-Norman BN-2T-4R Defender 4000		21. 1.94	B N Group	Bembridge	
	4004			*(Stored 11.00)*		
G-BVIA	Rand Robinson KR-2 PFA 129-11004		14. 1.94	K.Atkinson	(Ulverston)	
G-BVIC	English Electric Canberra B.2/B.6	XH568	25.10.93	Classic Aviation Projects Ltd *(As "XH568")*		
	71105				Bruntingthorpe	30. 1.97P
	(C/n relates to nose section ex WG788 from 1970 rebuild: XH568 has c/n 71399) (Stored 9.97: current status unknown)					
G-BVID	Lindstrand LBL Lozenge SS HAFB 064		17. 1.94	Respatex International Ltd		
					Chesham, Bucks	4. 6.00A
G-BVIE	Piper PA-18 Super Cub 95 18-1549	G-CLIK	26. 1.94	J.C.Best *"C'est La Vie"*	Andrewsfield	18. 4.02P
	(Continental O-200-A) (L-18C-PI)	(G-BLMB)/D-EDRB/ALAT 18-1549/51-15549 t/a C'est La Vie Group				
	(Frame No.18-1521)					
G-BVIF	Montgomerie-Bensen B.8MR		26. 1.94	R.M. & D.Mann	(Brodick, Arran)	21. 8.95P
	(Rotax 582) PFA G/01A-1228			*(Noted 4.00)*		
G-BVIG	Cameron A-250 HAFB 3213		26. 1.94	Balloon Flights International Ltd	Bath	2. 9.01T
				(Bath Building Society titles) "BIBS II"		
G-BVIH	Piper PA-28-161 Warrior II	G-GFCE	26.10.93	Ocean Developments Ltd	Redhill	23. 1.00T
	28-7916191	G-BNJP/N2212G				
G-BVIK	Maule MXT-7-180 Star Rocket 14056C		31. 1.94	D S Simpson	Graveley	17. 8.03
				tr Graveley Flying Group		
G-BVIL	Maule MXT-7-180 Star Rocket 14059C		31. 1.94	K. & S.C.Knight	Shobdon	5. 7.03
G-BVIM	Cameron N-77 HAFB 2222		2. 2.94	The Ballooning Business Ltd	Northampton	14. 7.00T
				"NAPS"		
G-BVIN	Rans S-6-ESA Coyote II PFA 204-12533		25.10.93	T.J.Wilkinson		
	(Rotax 503)				Sackville Lodge Farm, Riseley	5. 7.02P
G-BVIO*	Colt Flying Drinks Can SS HAFB 2538		4. 2.94	Balloon Preservation Group	Kirdford	9. 6.00A
	(Budweiser Can shape)			*"Budweiser" (Cancelled 6.11.01 as wfu)*		
G-BVIR	Lindstrand LBL-69A HAFB 079		2. 2.94	Aerial Promotions Ltd *"Vauxhall"*	Cannock	25. 5.01A
G-BVIS	Brugger MB.2 Colibri PFA 043-10666		2. 2.94	B.H.Shaw	Spanhoe	9.12.02P
G-BVIT	Campbell Cricket PFA G/03-1229		4. 2.94	D.R.Owen	(Blackburn)	24. 7.97P
	(Rotax 582)			*(Sold 3.01)*		
G-BVIV	Avid Speed Wing PFA 189-12034		25.10.93	M.Burton	(Malpas)	17. 3.00P
G-BVIW	Piper PA-18-150 Super Cub 18-8277	SE-EPD	4. 2.94	T W M Beck	Monks Gate, Horsham	28. 6.03T
G-BVIX	Lindstrand LBL-180A HAFB 082		8. 2.94	European Balloon Display Co Ltd		
				"Drifter"	Great Missenden	31. 3.01T
G-BVIZ	Europa Aviation Europa		24. 1.94	T.J.Punter & P.G.Jeffers	Booker	17. 3.02P
	(Rotax 912UL) 52 & PFA 247-12601					
G-BVJA	Fokker F.28 Mk.100 11489	PH-EZE	22. 4.94	British Midland Airways Ltd		
	(Fokker 100)			*(Op bmi Regional)*	East Midlands	24. 4.03T
G-BVJB	Fokker F.28 Mk.100 11488	PH-EZD	7. 7.94	British Midland Airways Ltd		
	(Fokker 100)			*(Op bmi Regional)*	East Midlands	6. 7.03T
G-BVJC	Fokker F.28 Mk.100 11497	PH-EZJ	2.12.94	British Midland Airways Ltd		
	(Fokker 100)			*(Op bmi Regional)*	East Midlands	1.12.03T
G-BVJD	Fokker F.28 Mk.100 11503	PH-EZO	14.12.94	British Midland Airways Ltd		
	(Fokker 100)			*(Op bmi Regional)*	East Midlands	13.12.03T
G-BVJE	Aérospatiale AS350B1 Ecureuil 1991	SE-HRS	3. 2.94	PLM Dollar Group Ltd	Inverness	24. 2.03T
G-BVJF	Montgomerie-Bensen B.8MR		18. 2.94	D.M.F.Harvey	(Yate, Bristol)	
	PFA G/01-1082					
G-BVJG	Cyclone AX3/K	G-69-14	15. 2.94	T.D.Reid	Tandragee, Co.Armagh	8.12.02P
	(Rotax 582) C.3123187 & PFA 245-12663	(G-MYOP)				
G-BVJH	Aero Designs Pulsar PFA 202-12196		22. 2.94	J.P.Kynaston	(Luton)	21. 3.01P
	(Rotax 582)					
G-BVJK	Glaser-Dirks DG-800A 8-24-A21		30. 3.94	B.A.Eastwell	Ringmer	21. 8.03
G-BVJN	Europa Aviation Europa *(Tri-cycle u/c)*		2. 3.94	A.C.Beaumont	White Waltham	11.10.02P
	(Rotax 912UL) 66 & PFA 247-12666			t/a JN Europa Group *"Better by Redesign"*		
G-BVJP	ATR 42-300 371	F-WWLN	7. 4.94	Gill Aviation Ltd	Dinard, France	6. 4.03T
				(Stored 10.01)		
G-BVJT	Reims Cessna F406 Caravan II		2. 2.94	P Madent & M Evans	Farnborough	29. 3.03
	F406-0073			t/a Nor Leasing		
G-BVJU	Evans VP-1 PFA 062-10691		10. 3.94	Barbara A.Schlussler	(Bourne)	
G-BVJX	Marquart MA.5 Charger PFA 068-11239		12. 1.94	M.L.Martin	Redhill	1. 7.21P
	(Lycoming O-360)					
G-BVJZ	Piper PA-28-161 Cherokee Warrior II	N2088M	22. 3.94	A.R.Fowkes	Denham	24. 7.03T
	28-7816248					
G-BVKA	Boeing 737-59D 24694	SE-DNA	15. 2.94	British Midland Airways Ltd		
		(SE-DLA)		*"Vauxhall"*	East Midlands	28. 2.03T

G-BVKB	Boeing 737-59D	27268	SE-DNM	24. 3.94	British Midland Airways Ltd	East Midlands	11. 4.03T
G-BVKC	Boeing 737-59D	24695	SE-DNB (SE-DLB)	5. 5.94	British Midland Airways Ltd	East Midlands	15. 5.03T
G-BVKD	Boeing 737-59D	26421	SE-DNK	25.11.94	British Midland Airways Ltd	East Midlands	15.12.03T
G-BVKF	Europa Aviation Europa *(Tri-cycle u/c)* (Rotax 912UL)	50 & PFA 247-12638		11. 3.94	T.R.Sinclair	Lamb Holm Farm, Orkney	1. 6.02P
G-BVKG	Colt Flying Hot Dog SS HAFB	2571		15. 3.94	Longbreak Ltd	Greenwood, MS, USA	23. 4.00A
G-BVKH	Thunder Ax-8-90 HAFB	2574		15. 3.94	R.B.Gruzelier	Salisbury	26. 7.02
G-BVKJ	Bensen B.8M (Arrow GT500R)	PFA G/01-1221		17. 3.94	A.G.Foster	Grimsby	27. 8.99P
G-BVKK	Slingsby T.61F Venture T.2	1984	ZA665	22. 2.94	K.E.Ballington	Saltby	13. 9.01
G-BVKL	Cameron A-180 HAFB	3255		17. 3.94	W.I. & C.Hooker	Nottingham	1. 4.01T
G-BVKM	Rutan VariEze (Continental O-200-A)	1933	N7137G	5. 4.94	J.P.G.Lindquist	(Mulhouse, Switzerland)	13. 8.02P
G-BVKR	Sikorsky S-76A	760115	734 RJordAF	4. 3.94	Bristow Helicopters Ltd	Aberdeen	8.12.03T
G-BVKU	Slingsby T.61F Venture T.2	1877	XZ557	22. 3.94	S.P.Wareham t/a G-BVKU Syndicate	Kingston Deverill	6.12.04
G-BVKV*	Cameron N-90 HAFB	3236		24. 3.94	Pringle of Scotland Ltd *(Cancelled 24.9.01 as wfu)*	Hawick	3. 2.97A
G-BVKX	Colt 14A Cloudhopper HAFB	2580		28. 3.94	H.C.J.Williams	Bristol	
G-BVKZ	Thunder Ax9-120 HAFB	2547		23. 3.94	D.J.Head	Newbury	25. 7.00T
G-BVLC	Cameron N-42 HAFB	3256		28. 3.94	Cameron Balloons Ltd	Bristol	26. 7.02A
G-BVLD	Campbell Cricket (Arrow GT500)	PFA G/01A-1163		29. 3.94	C.Berry	(Swansea)	7. 9.01P
G-BVLE	McCandless M.4	PFA G/10-1232		29. 3.94	H.Walls *(Under construction 11.01)*	Victoria Bridge, Strabane	
G-BVLF	CFM Starstreak Shadow SS-D	K.250-SSD		4. 3.94	B.R.Johnson *(Current status unknown)*	(Farnham)	
G-BVLG	Aérospatiale AS355F1 Twin Squirrel	5011	N57745	31. 3.94	PLM Dollar Group Ltd	Inverness	6. 4.03T
G-BVLH	Europa Aviation Europa	PFA 247-12491		30. 3.94	D.Barraclough	Brunton	2. 8.02P
G-BVLI	Cameron V-77 HAFB	5568	N9544G	30. 3.94	Janet Lewis-Richardson	Waiheke, New Zealand	6. 4.02A
G-BVLK	Rearwin 8125 Cloudster	803	N25403 NC25403	6. 4.94	M.C.Hiscock *(On rebuild 2.96: current status unknown)*	Titchfield, Hants	
G-BVLL	Lindstrand LBL-210A HAFB	101		9. 3.94	Aerial Promotions Ltd	Cannock	30. 7.02T
G-BVLP	Piper PA-38-112 Tomahawk II	38-82A0002	N91355	8. 4.94	Turweston Aero Club Ltd	Turweston	14. 5.03T
G-BVLR	Van's RV-4 (Lycoming O320-E2A s/n 46482-27A)	PFA 181-12306		13. 4.94	S.D.Arnold & S.J.Moodey t/a RV4 Group *(Under construction 7.99)*	(Coventry)	
G-BVLS	Thunder Ax8-90 Srs.2 HAFB	2577		13. 4.94	J.R.Henderson	Stratford-upon-Avon	11. 6.02A
G-BVLT	Bellanca 7GCBC Citabria 150S	1103-79	SE-GHV	6. 4.94	M.D.Hinge	Old Sarum	26. 8.02T
G-BVLU	Druine D.31 Turbulent	PFA 1604		18. 4.94	C.D.Bancroft	Litte Down Farm, Milson	5.11.02P
G-BVLV	Europa Aviation Europa *(Mono-wheel u/c)* (Rotax 912UL)	39 & PFA 247-12585		10. 3.94	J.T.Naylor t/a Euro 39 Group	Bidford	18. 4.02P
G-BVLW	Avid Hauler Mk.4 (Hirth F30)	PFA 189-12577		24. 3.94	D.M.Johnstone	Shobdon	28. 9.02P
G-BVLX	Slingsby T.61F Venture T.2	1973	ZA654	19. 4.94	T.M.Holloway t/a RAFGSA *(Op Fulmar Gliding Club)*	Easterton	11. 3.04
G-BVLZ	Lindstrand LBL-120A HAFB	063		4. 3.94	Balloon Flights Club Ltd	Kings Norton, Leicester	12.10.02T
G-BVMA	Beechcraft 200 Super King Air	BB-797	G-VPLC N84B	22. 7.93	Manhattan Air Ltd	Blackbushe	21.10.04T
G-BVMB	Hawker Hunter T.7A *(Regd with c/n 41H/695334)*	41H/695347	XL613	26. 4.94	Hunter Aviation Ltd *(Sold to South Africa 6.01 but retains CofR @ 12.01)*	Exeter	5. 4.02P
G-BVMC	Robinson R44 Astro	0060		15. 4.94	E.Wooton	Sywell	13. 7.03T
G-BVMD	Luscombe 8E Silvaire	5265	9Q-CGB KAT-?/VP-YRB/ZS-BWC/NC2538K	15. 4.94	G.M.Scott	Top Farm, Croydon	24. 5.02P
G-BVMF	Cameron V-77 HAFB	3195		22. 4.94	P.A.Meecham	Milton-Under-Wychwood	31. 7.02A
G-BVMG*	Bensen B.80V Gyrocopter	PFA G/01-1056		25. 4.94	Not known *(Cancelled by CAA 11.12.00 - no PtoF issued: noted complete 7.01)*	Lochview House, Limerigg	
G-BVMH	Wag-Aero Sport Trainer (Continental C90-8)	PFA 108-12647		28. 4.94	R.A.Durance *(As "624/D-39" in US Army c/s)*	(Wellingore)	12. 6.02P
G-BVMI	Piper PA-18-150 Super Cub *(Frame No.18-4613)*	18-4649	D-EIAC (PH-WDP)/D-EIAC/D-EKAF/N10F	6. 4.94	S.Sampson	Bagby	7. 3.04
	(Officially regd with c/n 18-8482 ex OH-PIN/N4262Z but rebuilt from D-EIAC [18-4649] after crash 15.8.95)						
G-BVMJ	Cameron Eagle 95SS HAFB	3262		28. 4.94	R.D.Sargeant	Maidenhead	1. 6.01A
G-BVML	Lindstrand LBL-210A HAFB	094		29. 4.94	Ballooning Adventures Ltd	Hexham	30. 5.02T
G-BVMM	Robin HR.200/100 Club	41	F-BVMM	18. 8.80	R.H.Ashforth	Gloucestershire	30. 7.04

G-BVMN	Ken Brock KB-2	PFA G/06-1218		29. 4.94	S.McCullagh	Chilbolton	4. 7.01P
	(Rotax 582)						
G-BVMR	Cameron V-90 HAFB	3269		28. 3.94	I.R.Comley *"Midnight Rainbow"*	Gloucester	19. 5.04A
G-BVMU	Aerostar Yakovlev Yak-52	9211809	YR-013	11. 5.94	A.L.Hall-Carpenter	Shipdham	29. 8.02P
	(Official c/n is 9411809)				*(As "09" in DOSAAF c/s)*		
G-BVMZ	Robin HR.100/210 Safari	198	F-BVMZ	20. 3.85	Chiltern Handbags (London) Ltd		
						North Weald	16. 7.01
G-BVNG	de Havilland DH.60G III Moth Major	NK	EC-AFK	17. 5.94	J.A.Pothecary	Old Sarum	
			EE1-81/30-81		*(On rebuild 2.96: current status unknown)*		
G-BVNI	Taylor JT.2 Titch	PFA 060-11107		20. 5.94	T.V.Adamson *(Noted 7.01)*	Rufforth	
G-BVNL	Rockwell Commander 114	14118	I-ECCE	13. 5.94	S.J.Healey & R.Lockyer	Birmingham	5. 7.03
			N4789W				
G-BVNM	Boeing 737-4S3	24163	G-BPKA	31. 3.92	British Airways plc	Gatwick	31. 3.02T
			9M-MJJ/G-BPKA				
G-BVNN	Boeing 737-4S3	24164	G-BPKB	18. 3.92	British Airways plc	Gatwick	18. 3.02T
			9M-MLA/G-BPKB				
G-BVNO	Boeing 737-4S3	24167	G-BPKE	18. 3.92	British Airways plc	Gatwick	14. 4.02T
			9M-MLB/G-BPKE		*(Benyhone Tartan t/s)*		
G-BVNR	Cameron N-105 HAFB	3288		24. 5.94	Liquigas SpA	Milan, Italy	21. 6.00A
	(New envelope 1.01 c/n 4994)						
G-BVNS	Piper PA-28-181 Cherokee Archer II		N6163J	13. 4.94	Scottish Airways Flyers (Prestwick) Ltd		
		28-7690358				Prestwick	11. 8.03T
G-BVNU	FLS Aerospace Sprint Club	004		25. 5.94	Sunhawk Ltd	North Weald	17.10.98T
G-BVNY	Rans S-7 Courier	PFA 218-11951		24. 5.94	G.Doyle & P.Morris		
	(Rotax 582)					(Athlone, Co.Westmeath)	15. 2.02P
G-BVOA	Piper PA-28-181 Archer II	28-7990145	N2132C	31. 5.94	M.J. & R.J.Millen	Rochester	20. 7.03T
					t/a Millen Aviation Services *(Cable Consult Ltd titles*		
G-BVOB	Fokker F.27 Friendship 500	10366	PH-FMN	5. 7.94	BAC Express Airlines Ltd.	Exeter	6.10.03T
			PT-LZM/F-BPNA/PH-FMN		*"Euro Trader"*		
G-BVOC	Cameron V-90 HAFB	3291		8. 6.94	Sally A.Masey *"Scoop"*	Bristol	4. 8.01A
					(Bristol Evening Post/Western Daily Press titles)		
G-BVOH	Campbell Cricket	PFA G/03-1220		14. 6.94	G.A.Speich	Beausale, Warwick	10. 5.02P
	(Rotax 532)						
G-BVOI	Rans S-6-116 Coyote II	PFA 204A-12712		14. 6.94	A.P.Bacon	Wick	31. 5.02P
	(Rotax 582)						
G-BVOK	Aerostar Yakovlev Yak-52	9111505	RA-9111505	14. 6.94	D.J.Gilmour	Goodwood	4. 4.02P
			DOSAAF55		t/a Intrepid Aviation Co *(As "55" in DOSAAF c/s)*		
G-BVON	Lindstrand LBL-105A HAFB	001	N532LB	16. 6.94	P.A.Lindstrand	Dallas, Texas, USA	5. 6.01
			G-BVON		*"Phoenix"*		
G-BVOO	Lindstrand LBL-105A HAFB	123		16. 6.94	T.G.Church	Blackburn	18. 1.01T
G-BVOP	Cameron N-90 HAFB	3317		21. 6.94	Cambury Ltd	Stockton-on-Tees	19. 2.01T
					t/a Mr.Lazenbys		
G-BVOR	CFM Streak Shadow			31. 3.94	K.Fowler	(Basingstoke)	20. 6.02P
	(Rotax 582)	K.238-SA & PFA 206-12695					
G-BVOS	Europa Aviation Europa	PFA 247-12562		11. 4.94	D.A.Young	Brunton	21. 1.02P
					t/a Durham Europa Group		
G-BVOU	Hawker Siddeley HS.748 Srs.2A/270		CS-TAH	21. 6.94	Emerald Airways Ltd	Exeter	30. 7.04T
		1721	G-11-6		*(Lynx titles)*		
G-BVOV	Hawker Siddeley HS.748 Srs.2A/372		CS-TAO	21. 6.94	Emerald Airways Ltd	Liverpool	11. 5.04T
		1777	G-11-4				
G-BVOW	Europa Aviation Europa *(Mono-wheel u/c)*			27. 6.94	M.W.Cater	Husbands Bosworth	12. 6.02P
	(Rotax 912UL)	84 & PFA 247-12679			t/a Europa Syndicate		
G-BVOX	Taylorcraft F-22	2208	N221UK	20. 5.94	Jones Samuel Ltd	Leicester	22. 6.03
G-BVOY	Rotorway Executive 90	5238		17. 6.94	Southern Helicopters Ltd		
	(Rotorway RI 162)					Street Farm, Takeley	
G-BVOZ	Colt 56A HAFB	2595		21. 6.94	Balloon School (International) Ltd		
					t/a British School of Ballooning	Petworth	27. 2.02A
G-BVPA	Thunder Ax8-105 Srs.2 HAFB	2600		24. 6.94	J.Fenton	Preston	30.12.02T
					t/a Firefly Balloon Promotions		
G-BVPD	CASA I-131E Jungmann	2086	F-AZNG	12. 7.94	D.Bruton	Abbeyshrule, Co.Longford	16. 1.02P
			E3B-482				
G-BVPK	Cameron O-90 HAFB	3313		1. 7.94	D.V.Fowler	Cranbrook	30. 6.02T
G-BVPL	Zenair CH.601HD Zodiac	PFA 162-12693		4. 7.94	A.F.Walters	Elstree	6. 8.02P
	(Continental O-200-A)						
G-BVPM	Evans VP-2 Coupe	V2-1016 & PFA 7205		6.11.78	P.Marigold	(Locking, Weston super Mare)	31. 5.94P
	(Continental A65)				*(Stored 7.95: current status unknown)*		
G-BVPN	Piper J-3C-65 Cub	6917	G-TAFY	6. 7.94	C.Willoughby	Turweston	19. 7.02P
			N31073/N38207/N38307/NC38307				
	(Regd as c/n 5298 but has Frame No.7002 which was N38207: probably used in rebuild of N31073 in early 1970s)						
G-BVPP	Folland Gnat T.1	FL.536	8620M	22. 4.94	T.J.Manna	Cranfield	12.12.02P
			XP534		t/a Kennet Aviation *(As "XR993" in Red Arrows c/s)*		
G-BVPR	Robinson R22 Beta	1612	G-KNIT	17. 6.94	E.Bailey	Spoonley/Gloucestershire	4. 2.03T
G-BVPS	Jodel D.112	PFA 917		6. 7.94	P.J.Sharp	(Harpenden)	

G-BVPU*	Cameron A-140 HAFB	3296		12. 7.94	Cameron Balloons Ltd	(Canada)	22. 7.97A
					(Cancelled 10.10.01 by CAA)		
G-BVPV	Lindstrand LBL-77B HAFB	119		13. 7.94	A.R.Greensides	Burton Pidsea, Hull	8. 9.01A
G-BVPW	Rans S-6-116 Coyote II *(Tri-cycle u/c)*			12. 7.94	J.G.Beesley	Halwell, Totnes	19.10.02P
	(Rotax 582) 029H.587 & PFA 204A-12737						
G-BVPX	Bensen B8 Tyro Gyro mk.II			13. 7.94	A.W.Harvey	Henstridge	9. 5.02P
	(Modified P Lovegrove) PCL125 & PFA G/011-1237						
G-BVPY	CFM Streak Shadow			14. 6.94	R.J.Mitchell	(Scalloway, Shetland)	10. 5.02P
	(Rotax 582)	K.204 & PFA 206-12375			*(Flies from Tingwall)*		
G-BVRA	Europa Aviation Europa	PFA 247-12635		25. 7.94	N.E.Stokes	(Ellesmere)	24.10.02P
	(Rotax 912-UL)						
G-BVRH	Taylorcraft BL-65	1657	N23929	15. 7.94	M.J.Smith	(Henfield)	25. 7.03
			G-BVRH/N24322/NC24322				
G-BVRI	Thunder Ax6-56 HAFB	2622		2. 8.94	A.Van Wyk	Caxton, Cambs	13. 9.01A
G-BVRK	Rans S-6-ESA Coyote II	1193.566	G-MYPK	14. 7.94	J.Secular	(Beckenham)	
G-BVRL	Lindstrand LBL-21A HAFB	130		3. 8.94	A.M.Holly	Berkeley	18. 9.02A
					t/a Exclusive Ballooning		
G-BVRR	Lindstrand LBL-77A HAFB	133		9. 8.94	G.C.Elson	Ronda, Spain	23. 6.03A
					t/a Lindstrand Balloon School		
G-BVRU	Lindstrand LBL-105A HAFB	131		15. 8.94	Flying Pictures Ltd	Fairoaks	11. 3.02A
G-BVRV	Van's RV-4	793	N144TH	23. 6.94	A.Troughton	Armagh Field, Woodview	29. 9.00P
	(Lycoming AEIO-320)						
G-BVRY	Cyclone AX3K C3013085 & PFA 245-12471			18. 8.94	A.N.Bowerman	(Dorking)	2. 3.99P
	(Rotax 582)						
G-BVRZ*	Piper PA-18 Super Cub 95	18-3442	SE-ITP	22.11.94	R.G.Warwick	Kilrea, Co.Londonderry	25. 5.01
	(Regd with Frame No.18-3381)		LN-LJG/D-EDCM/96+19/QW+901/QZ+001/AC+507/AS+506/54-752				
			(Damaged on take off Kilrea 30.7.98: cancelled 12.7.01 by CAA: current status unknown)				
G-BVSB	TEAM mini-MAX 91A	PFA 186-12241		1. 7.94	D.G.Palmer	Fetterangus	2.12.02P
	(Rotax 503)						
G-BVSD	Sud SE.3130 Alouette II	1897	V-54	8. 9.94	M.J.Cuttell	Gloucestershire	12. 4.02
			Swiss AF		*(As "V-54" in Swiss AF c/s)*		
G-BVSF	Aero Designs Pulsar	PFA 202-12071		1. 7.94	S.N. & R.J.Freestone	Deanland	20. 5.02P
	(Rotax 582) *(Tri-cycle u/c)*						
G-BVSJ	Pilatus Britten-Norman BN-2T Islander			31. 1.95	B-N Group Ltd	Bembridge	
		2286					
G-BVSL*	Pilatus Britten-Norman BN-2B-26 Islander			31. 1.95	Britten-Norman Ltd	Bembridge	
		2288			*(Cancelled 12.10.00 as temporarily wfu)*		
G-BVSM	Rotary Air Force RAF 2000	EW-42		24. 8.94	S Ram *(New owner 12.01)*	(Lowestoft)	24. 1.97P
G-BVSN	Avid Speed Wing	PFA 189-12088		24. 8.94	A.S.Markey	Old Sarum	30. 9.02P
G-BVSO	Cameron A-120 HAFB	3339		25. 8.94	J.F.Till	York	28. 7.02T
G-BVSP	Hunting P.84 Jet Provost T.3A		XM370	31. 8.94	H.G.Hodges & Son Ltd	Long Marston	5. 8.01P
		PAC/W/6327					
G-BVSS	Jodel 150 Mascaret			22. 8.94	A.P.Burns	RAF Woodvale	19. 5.02P
		118 & PFA 151-11878					
G-BVST	Jodel 150 Mascaret			11. 8.94	A.Shipp	Full Sutton	24. 9.02P
	(Continental O-200-A) 130 & PFA 235-12198						
G-BVSV*	Cameron C-80 HAFB	3194		5. 9.94	Cameron Balloons Ltd	Beirut, Lebanon	1. 9.95A
					(Cancelled 19.9.01 as wfu: current status unknown)		
G-BVSW*	Cameron C-80 HAFB	3210		5. 9.94	Cameron Balloons Ltd	Beirut, Lebanon	1. 9.95A
					(Cancelled 19.9.01 as wfu: current status unknown)		
G-BVSX	TEAM mini-MAX 91A	PFA 186-12463		9. 9.94	G.N.Smith	Headcorn	5. 7.02P
	(Mosler MM CB-35)						
G-BVSY	Thunder Ax9-120 HAFB	2631		16. 8.94	G.R.Elson	Ronda, Spain	15. 2.00T
					t/a Lindstrand Balloon School		
G-BVSZ	Pitts S-1E(S) Special	PFA 09-11235		9. 9.94	R.C.F.Bailey	(Swinmore Farm, Ledbury)	10.11.02P
	(Lycoming AEIO-360)						
G-BVTA	Tri-R Kis	PFA 239-12450		26. 8.94	P.J.Webb	Dunkeswell	8.10.02P
G-BVTC	British Aircraft Corporation BAC.145 Jet Provost T.5A			7. 9.94	Global Aviation Ltd	Humberside	12. 2.02P
		EEP/JP/997	XW333		*(As "XW333")*		
G-BVTD	CFM Streak Shadow SA			14. 9.94	M.Walton	Old Sarum	12. 4.04P
	(Rotax 582) K.159-SA & PFA 206-11972						
G-BVTE	Fokker F.28 Mk.070	11538	PH-EZX	13. 4.95	British Midland Airways Ltd		
	(Fokker 70)				*(Op bmi Regional)*	East Midlands	12. 4.04T
G-BVTF	Fokker F.28 Mk.070	11539	PH-EZZ	24. 5.95	British Midland Airways Ltd		
	(Fokker 70)		PH-EZA		*(Op bmi Regional)*	East Midlands	23. 5.04T
G-BVTG	Fokker F.28 Mk.070	11551	PH-EZK	1. 9.95	British Midland Airways Ltd		
	(Fokker 70)				*(Op bmi Regional)*	East Midlands	31. 8.04T
G-BVTJ	ATR 72-202	342	F-WWEV	7.12.94	CityFlyer Express Ltd	Gatwick	6.12.04T
			F-GKOI/F-WWLX		*(Waves & Cranes t/s)*		
G-BVTK	ATR 72-202	357	F-WWEW	21.10.94	CityFlyer Express Ltd	Gatwick	20.10.01T
			F-GKOJ		*(Chelsea Rose t/s)*		
G-BVTL	Colt 31A Air Chair HAFB	2572		5. 7.94	A.Lindsay	Twickenham	15. 5.97

G-BVTM	Reims Cessna F152 II	F15201827	G-WACS	31. 8.94	RAF Halton Aeroplane Club Ltd	RAF Halton	29. 8.04T
			D-EFGZ				
G-BVTN	Cameron N-90 HAFB	3361		16. 9.94	P.Zulehner	Peterskirchen, Austria	27. 9.02A
G-BVTO	Piper PA-28-151 Cherokee Warrior		G-SEWL	19. 9.94	A.S.Bamrah	Lydd	7. 2.04T
		28-7415253	D-EDOS/N9550N		t/a Falcon Flying Services		
G-BVTV	Rotorway Executive 90	5243		16. 9.94	H.G.Orchin	Street Farm, Takeley	16.12.02P
	(Rotorway RI 162)						
G-BVTW	Aero Designs Pulsar	PFA 202-12172		14. 9.94	J.D.Webb	(Hereford)	
G-BVTX	de Havilland DHC-1 Chipmunk 22A		WP809	2. 8.94	M.W.Cater	Husbands Bosworth	11.11.04
		C1/0705			t/a TX Flying Group *(As "WP809/Z78" in RN c/s)*		
G-BVUA	Cameron O-105 HAFB	3369		27. 9.94	D.C.Eager	Bracknell	28. 5.00A
G-BVUC	Colt 56A HAFB	2608	G-639*	30. 9.94	Cameron Balloons Ltd	Bristol	19. 9.01A
	("B" Conditions markings carried as such 9.94)*				t/a Thunder & Colt		
G-BVUG	Betts TB.1	PFA 265-12770		3.10.94	William Tomkins Ltd	Spanhoe	20. 5.02P
	(Modified AIA Stampe SV.4C c/n 1045 ex G-BEUS/F-BKFK/F-DAFK/Fr.Mil)						
G-BVUH	Thunder Ax6-65B HAFB	243	JA-A0075	3.10.94	N.C.A.Crawley	Great Yarmouth	
G-BVUI	Lindstrand LBL-25A Cloudhopper HAFB			5.10.94	J.W.Hole	Much Wenlock	12. 4.01A
		148					
G-BVUJ	Ken Brock KB-2	PFA G/06-1244		10.10.94	R.J.Hutchinson	Kemble	17. 5.99P
	(Rotax 503)						
G-BVUK	Cameron V-77 HAFB	3372		11.10.94	H.G.Griffiths & W.A.Steel	Reading	12. 8.02A
G-BVUM	Rans S-6-116 Coyote II	PFA 204A-12685		11.10.94	M.A.Abbott	Newbigging Farm, Montrose	9. 8.02P
	(Rotax 582)						
G-BVUN	Van's RV-4	3363UK & PFA 181-12488		11.10.94	A.E.Kay		
	(Lycoming O-360)					Parsons Farm, Waterperry Common, Oakley	7. 6.02P
G-BVUO	Cameron R-150 Gas/HAFB	3365		13.10.94	M.Sevrin	Court St.Etienne, Belgium	21.12.95A
G-BVUT	Evans VP-1 Srs.2	PFA 62-12092		24.10.94	P.J.Weston	Pepperbox, Salisbury	29. 9.99P
	(VW 1600)				*(Damaged on take off Pepperbox 13.3.99: current status unknown)*		
G-BVUU	Cameron C-80 HAFB	3383		11.10.94	T.M.C.McCoy	Bath	27. 9.02T
					(Op Ascent Balloons) "Ascent"		
G-BVUV	Europa Aviation Europa			23. 9.94	R.J.Mills	Gamston	19. 3.02P
	(Rotax 912-UL)	141 & PFA 247-12762					
G-BVUZ	Cessna 120	11334	Z-YGH	20. 9.94	N.O.Anderson	(Trumpington, Cambridge)	
			VP-YGH/VP-NAM/VP-YGH				
G-BVVA	Aerostar Yakovlev Yak-52	877610	LY-ANN	24.10.94	T.W.Freeman	Litle Gransden	15. 7.02P
			DOSAAF 52				
	(Holds c/n plate 889109 & marked as ex "LY-AMV")						
G-BVVB	Carlson Sparrow II	PFA 209-11809		26. 9.94	L.M.McCullen	North Connel, Oban	21. 3.02P
	(Rotax 532)						
G-BVVC	Hawker Hunter F.6A	S4/U/3362	8685M	28.10.94	P.Hellier	Exeter	16.10.02P
	(Built Armstrong-Whitworth Aircraft)		XF516		*(As "XF516/19" of 234 Sqn)*		
G-BVVE	Wassmer Jodel D.112	1070	F-BKAJ	28.10.94	G.W.Jarvis	Shifnal	5. 4.02P
G-BVVG	Nanchang CJ-6A (Yak 18)	2751219	(F-....)	10.10.94	G.Beda	Breighton	23. 8.02P
			G-BVVG/Chinese PLAAF				
G-BVVH	Europa Aviation Europa	PFA 247-12505		31.10.94	T.G.Hoult	Gamston	27. 8.02P
G-BVVI	Hawker Audax I		2015M	3.11.94	Aero Vintage Ltd	St.Leonards-on-Sea	
	(Built Avro)		K5600		*(On rebuild 8.95: current status unknown)*		
G-BVVK	de Havilland DHC.6-310 Twin Otter		LN-BEZ	21.12.94	Loganair Ltd	Glasgow	12. 1.02T
		666			*"Chatham Historic Dockyard"*		
G-BVVL	EAA Acrosport 2	PFA 072A-10887		11.11.94	G.A.Breen	(Algarve, Portugal)	2. 7.02P
	(Lycoming O-360)						
G-BVVM	Zenair CH.601HD Zodiac	PFA 162-12539		3.10.94	A.Rooker	Bourn	9. 5.02P
	(Rotax 912UL)						
G-BVVN	Brugger MB.2 Colibri	PFA 043-10979		12.10.94	N.F.Andrews	Emlyns Field, Rhuallt	11. 9.02P
	(VW 1834)						
G-BVVP	Europa Aviation Europa			20. 9.94	I Mansey	(Salisbury)	9.12.02P
	(Rotax 912UL)	88 & PFA 247-12697					
G-BVVR	Stits SA-3A Playboy	P-736	N4620S	14.11.94	I.T.James	Enstone	14. 3.02P
	(Continental A65)						
G-BVVS	Van's RV-4	PFA 181-12324		15.11.94	E.C. & N.S.C.English	North Weald	1. 8.02P
	(Lycoming O-320)						
G-BVVT	Colt 240A HAFB	2682		17.11.94	R.W.Keron	Dereham	19. 6.01T
G-BVVU	Lindstrand LBL Four SS HAFB	155	HB-QAP	18.11.94	Magical Adventures Ltd	Chirk	6.12.01P
			G-BVVU				
G-BVVW	IAV-Bacau Yakovlev Yak-52	844605	RA-01361	16.11.94	J.E.Blackman	Andrewsfield	22.11.02P
	(C/n plate shows c/n 833519)		DOSAAF15/DOSAAF95				
G-BVVX	Yakovlev Yak-18A	NK	307	11.11.94	J.M. & E.M.Wicks		
			Russian AF			Boones Farm, High Garrett, Braintree	
					(On rebuild 10.96: current status unknown)		
G-BVVZ	Corby CJ-1 Starlet	PFA 134-12293		9.11.94	P.V.Flack	Fairoaks	18. 4.02P
	(VW 1834)						
G-BVWA	SOCATA MS.880B Rallye 100T	2747	F-GACD	29.11.94	G.K.Brunwin	Kemble	14. 4.01
G-BVWB	Thunder Ax8-90 Srs.2 HAFB	3000		2.12.94	S.C.Clayton	Shrewsbury	19. 7.00

G-BVWC	English Electric Canberra B.2	71399	WK163	2.12.94	Classic Aviation Projects Ltd	Coventry	29. 5.01P
	(C/n relates to nose section originally fitted to XH568)				*(As "WK163") (Acquired by Mike Collett/Atlantic Group)*		
G-BVWE	Cameron C-80 HAFB	3414		6.12.94	D.G.Body	Leighton Buzzard	18. 6.01T
					t/a Mid-Bucks Farmers Balloon Group		
G-BVWH*	Cameron N-90 Lightbulb SS HAFB	3404		8.12.94	Balloon Preservation Group	Kirdford	2. 9.98A
					"Phillips Light Bulb" (Cancelled 17.12.01 as wfu)		
G-BVWI*	Cameron Light Bulb 65SS HAFB	3405		8.12.94	Balloon Preservation Group	Kirdford	2. 6.97A
					"Phillips Energy Saver" (Cancelled 17.12.01 as wfu)		
G-BVWK*	Air & Space 18-A Gyroplane	18-14	SE-HID	19.12.94	Whisky Mike (Aviation) Ltd		
			N6108S			(Kinnettles, Forfar)	
					(Cancelled 18.10.00 as temporarily wfu)		
G-BVWL*	Air & Space 18-A Gyroplane	18-63	SE-HIE	19.12.94	Whisky Mike (Aviation) Ltd		
			N90588/N6152S			(Kinnettles, Forfar)	
					(Cancelled 18.10.00 as temporarily wfu)		
G-BVWM	Europa Aviation Europa	PFA 247-12620		14.12.94	A.Aubeelack	White Waltham	8. 8.02P
					t/a Europa Syndicate		
G-BVWP	de Havilland DHC-1 Chipmunk 22		WP856	19.12.94	T.W.M.Beck	Monks Gate, Horsham	24. 5.04
		C1/0741			*(As "WP856/904" in RN c/s)*		
G-BVWW	Lindstrand LBL-90A HAFB	169		28.12.94	Drawflight Ltd *"Double Whiskey"*	Hastings	11. 6.02A
G-BVWX	VPM M-16 Tandem Trainer	VPM16-UK-111		3. 1.95	M.L.Smith	Popham	17. 6.02P
	(Arrow GT1000R)						
G-BVWY	Porterfield CP.65	720	N27223	23.11.94	B.Morris	Oaksey Park	24. 7.02P
	(Continental A65)		NC27223				
G-BVWZ	Piper PA-32-301 Saratoga	3206055	I-TASP	3. 1.95	N.N.Kenny	(Lymm)	3.12.03
			N9184N				
G-BVXA	Cameron N-105 HAFB	3441		4. 1.95	R.E.Jones	Lytham St.Annes	27. 1.02T
					(Ribby Hall titles)		
G-BVXB	Cameron V-77 HAFB	3442		4. 1.95	J.A.Lawton *"Pat McLean"*	Godalming	25. 4.01A
G-BVXC	English Electric Canberra B(I).8		WT333	9. 1.95	Classic Aviation Projects Ltd *(As "WT333")*		
		6649			*(Current status unknown)*	Bruntingthorpe	
G-BVXD	Cameron O-84 HAFB	3432		5. 1.95	N.J.Langley *"Prudential"*	Bristol	12. 1.02A
G-BVXE	Steen Skybolt	PFA 064-11123	G-LISA	5. 1.95	J.Buglass	Sleap	17.12.01P
	(Lycoming IO-360)						
G-BVXF	Cameron O-120 HAFB	3400		21. 9.94	Gone With The Wind Ltd		
						Carryduff, Co.Down	29. 6.02T
G-BVXG	Lindstrand LBL-90A HAFB	110		5. 1.95	G.C.Elson	Ronda, Spain	8. 9.02A
					t/a Lindstrand Balloon School		
G-BVXJ	Bücker Bü.133 Jungmeister	NK	E1-9	11. 1.95	J.D.Haslam	Newby Wiske	15. 8.02P
	(Built CASA)		ES1-9/35-9				
			(First post-restoration flight in 9.00: as "ES-9/G-BVXJ" in Spanish Air Force c/s)				
G-BVXK	Aerostar Yakovlev Yak-52	9111306	RA-44508(1)	12. 1.95	E.Gavazzi	White Waltham	5. 7.02P
			DOSAAF 26		*(As "26" in DOSAAF c/s)*		
G-BVXM	Aérospatiale AS350B Ecureuil	2013	I-AUDI	10. 1.95	The Berkeley Leisure Group Ltd	Sparkford	4. 3.04T
			I-CIOC				
G-BVXR	de Havilland DH.104 Devon C.2	04436	XA880	13. 1.95	M.Whale & M.W.A.Lunn	Kemble	
					(As "XA880" in RAE c/s: stored 12.00)		
G-BVXS	Taylorcraft BC-12D	9284	N96984	27. 1.95	Janet M.Allison	Swanton Morley	21. 8.02P
	(Continental A65)		NC96984		*"Obsession"*		
G-BVXW	Short SC.7 Skyvan 3A-100	SH.1889	LX-DEF	15.11.95	Babcock Rosyth Defence Ltd		
			PA-52 Arg.Coast Guard/G-14-61		t/a Hunting Contract Services		
						Weston-on-the-Green	30. 1.02T
G-BVYA	Airbus A320-231	354	F-WQAY	7. 4.95	JMC Airlines Ltd	Manchester	20. 1.04T
			(N301SA)/F-WWDZ				
G-BVYB	Airbus A320-231	357	F-WQAZ	20. 4.95	JMC Airlines Ltd	Manchester	19. 4.04T
			(N302SA)/F-WWBH				
G-BVYC	Airbus A320-231	411	F-WWQB	26. 4.95	JMC Airlines Ltd	Manchester	25. 4.04T
			(N303SA)/F-WWDX				
G-BVYF	Piper PA-31-350 Navajo Chieftain		G-SAVE	8. 2.95	J.A., G.M, D.T.A. & J.A.Rees		
		31-7952102	N3518T		t/a Messrs Rees of Poynston West		
						Haverfordwest	23. 1.03T
G-BVYG	Robin DR.300/180R	611	F-BSQB	9. 1.95	Ulster Gliding Club Ltd	Bellarena	9. 4.02
			F-BSPI				
G-BVYK	TEAM mini-MAX 91A	PFA 186-12598		13. 2.95	S.B.Churchill	Eastbach Farm, Coleford	4. 8.98P
	(Rotax 447)						
G-BVYM	Robin DR.300/180R	656	F-BTBL	9.12.94	London Gliding Club Pty Ltd	Dunstable	19. 7.04
G-BVYO	Robin R.2160	288		11. 1.95	S.J. Skilton	Bournemouth	15. 4.04T
					t/a Aviation Rentals		
G-BVYP	Piper PA-25-235 Pawnee B	25-3481	N7475D	13. 2.95	Bidford Airfield Ltd	Bidford	16. 3.04
			OY-CLT/N7475Z				
G-BVYR	Cameron A-250 HAFB	3411		2. 2.95	Voyager Balloons Ltd	Cambridge	15. 8.02T
G-BVYT	QAC Quickie Q-2	2443	N3797S	18. 1.95	C.A.McGee	Enstone	2. 9.00P
	(Revmaster R2100D)						
G-BVYU	Cameron A-140 HAFB	3544		17. 2.95	A J Nunns *"Blue Belle"*	Oswestry	4. 4.02T

G-BVYX	Avid Speed Wing Mk.4	PFA 189-12370		16. 2.95	G.J.Keen	Andrewsfield	15. 2.02P
G-BVYY	Pietenpol Aircamper	PFA 047-12559		20. 2.95	J.R.Orchard	Wolverhampton	28. 6.98P
G-BVYZ	Stemme S-10V	14-011	D-KGDD	6. 3.95	L.Gubbay & S.Sagar	Denham	7. 7.01
G-BVZD	Tri-R Kis (Canadian Air Motive CAM.100) *(Tri-cycle u/c)*	PFA 239-12416		21. 2.95	D.R.Morgan	Old Sarum	18. 6.02P
G-BVZE	Boeing 737-59D	26422	SE-DNL	7. 3.95	British Midland Airways Ltd	East Midlands	22. 3.04T
G-BVZG	Boeing 737-5Q8	25160	SE-DNF	12. 4.95	British Midland Airways Ltd	East Midlands	1. 5.04T
G-BVZH	Boeing 737-5Q8	25166	SE-DNG	25. 4.95	British Midland Airways Ltd	East Midlands	26. 5.04T
G-BVZI	Boeing 737-5Q8	25167	SE-DNH	15. 5.95	British Midland Airways Ltd *(Star Alliance c/s)*	East Midlands	11. 6.04T
G-BVZJ	Rand Robinson KR-2 (Revmaster)	PFA 129-11049		21. 2.95	J.P.McConnell-Wood *(Damaged landing Phoenix Farm 15.7.98: current status unknown)*	Phoenix Farm, Hants	
G-BVZM	Cessna 210M Centurion II	21061674	OO-CNJ N732PV	28. 2.95	J.J.M.Feeney	Elstree	25. 3.04
G-BVZN	Cameron C-80 HAFB	3546		28. 2.95	Sally J.Langley t/a Sky Fly Balloons *"Taywood Homes"*	Bristol	22. 5.02A
G-BVZO	Rans S-6-116 Coyote II (Rotax 582)	0494.606 & PFA 204A-12710		1. 3.95	P.Atkinson	Sandtoft	23. 7.01P
G-BVZR	Zenair CH.601HD (Rotax 912UL)	PFA 162-12417		2. 3.95	J.D.White	Nottingham	18.10.02P
G-BVZT	Lindstrand LBL-90A HAFB	183		9. 3.95	F.W.Farnsworth Ltd t/a Pork Farms Bowyers	Nottingham	24. 7.02A
G-BVZV	Rans S-6-116 Coyote II (Rotax 582)	PFA 204A-12832		16. 2.95	A.G.Cameron & W.G.Dunn	(Winkleigh)	16. 5.02P
G-BVZX	Cameron H-34 HAFB	3564		15. 3.95	Julia B.Turnau t/a Chianti Balloon Club	Siena, Italy	21. 6.96A
G-BVZZ	de Havilland DHC-1 Chipmunk 22	C1/0687	WP795	5. 1.95	D.C.Murray t/a Portsmouth Naval Gliding Club *(As "WP795/901" in RN c/s)*	Lee-on-Solent	14. 6.04

G-BWAA – G-BWZZ

G-BWAA	Cameron N-133 HAFB	3471		9. 3.95	C.& J.Bailey t/a Bailey Balloons	Bristol	26. 4.01T
G-BWAB	Jodel D.140 Mousquetaire	PFA 251-12469		25. 1.95	W.A.Braim	(Driffield)	29.10.02P
G-BWAC	Waco YKS-7 (Jacobs R-755)	4693	N50RA N2896D/NC50	19. 8.92	D.N.Peters	Little Gransden	19.10.04
G-BWAD	Rotary Air Force RAF 2000 *(Two-seat trainer)*	147 & PFA G/13-1254		27. 2.95	Newtonair Gyroplanes Ltd *(Op A Melody)*	Henstridge	16. 4.02P
G-BWAE	Rotary Air Force RAF 2000	PFA G/13-1252		27. 2.95	D.P.Kearns	(Lichfield)	23. 7.02P
G-BWAF	Hawker Hunter F.6A *(Built Armstrong-Whitworth Aircraft)*	S4/U/3393	8831M XG160	24. 2.95	RV Aviation Ltd *(Noted 11.01 in natural metal finish)*	Bournemouth	
G-BWAG	Cameron O-120 HAFB	3478		3. 2.95	P.M.Skinner	Maidstone	14. 7.02T
G-BWAH	Montgomerie-Bensen B.8MR	PFA G/01-1208		16. 3.95	J.B.Allan	(Stanford-le-Hope)	
G-BWAI	CFM Streak Shadow SA (Rotax 582)	K.235SA & PFA 206-12556		21. 3.95	N.J.Mines	Kemble	9. 5.01P
G-BWAJ	Cameron V-77 HAFB	3579		22. 3.95	R.S. & S.H.Ham *"Robsel"*	Axbridge, Somerset	9. 8.01A
G-BWAN*	Cameron N-77 HAFB	3499		24. 3.95	Balloon Preservation Group *"National Power" (Cancelled 6.11.01 as wfu)*	Kirdford	16. 8.97A
G-BWAO	Cameron C-80 HAFB	3436		24. 3.95	Virgin Airship & Balloon Co Ltd *"One 2 One"*	Telford	24. 7.02T
G-BWAP	Clutton FRED Srs.3	PFA 029-10959		24. 3.95	G.A.Shepherd	Seething	
G-BWAR	Denney Kitfox mk.3 (Rotax 582)	PFA 172-12432		16. 3.95	I.Wightman	Croft Farm, Defford	29. 8.02P
G-BWAT	Pietenpol Aircamper (Continental C90)	PFA 047-11594		15. 3.95	P.W.Aitchison	(Llandrindod Wells)	28. 7.02P
G-BWAU	Cameron V-90 HAFB	3569		27. 3.95	K.M. & A.M.F.Hall	London N10	16. 9.01A
G-BWAV	Schweizer Hughes 269C (300C)	S.1204	SE-JAY LN-OTS/OY-HDW/N41S	28. 2.95	B.Maggs t/a Helihire	(Guildford)	29. 7.04T
G-BWAW	Lindstrand LBL-77A HAFB	207		28. 3.95	D.Bareford *(Seton Healthcare titles)*	Kidderminster	10. 6.02A
G-BWBA	Cameron V-65 HAFB	3456		27. 2.95	P.G.Dunnington t/a Dante Balloon Group *(British Airways titles)*	Hungerford	19. 8.02A
G-BWBB	Lindstrand LBL-14A HAFB	222		3. 4.95	Oxford Promotions (UK) Ltd *(Op F Prell)*	Kentucky, USA	

G-BWBC	Cameron N-90AS HAFB	3574		12. 6.95	Wetterauer Montgolfieren EV *"Zeppelin"*	Budingen, Germany	28. 3.02A
G-BWBE	Colt Flying Ice Cream Cone SS HAFB	3560		3. 4.95	Benedikt Haggeney GmbH	Ennigerloh, Germany	20. 2.02A
G-BWBF	Colt Flying Ice Cream Cone SS HAFB	3561		3. 4.95	Benedikt Haggeney GmbH	Ennigerloh, Germany	21. 2.02A
G-BWBG	Cvjetkovic CA-65 Skyfly	PFA 1566		6. 4.95	T.White & M.C.Fawkes	Charity Farm, Baxterley	
G-BWBH	Thunder Fork Lift Truck 90SS HAFB	3472		6. 4.95	Jungheinrich AG	Hamburg, Germany	18. 4.01A
G-BWBI	Taylorcraft F-22A	2207	N22UK	3. 4.95	P.J.Wallace	Eshott	10. 3.02
G-BWBJ	Colt 21A HAFB	3532		6. 4.95	U.Schneider	Giessen, Germany	8. 7.00A
G-BWBO	Lindstrand LBL-77A HAFB	157		10. 4.95	T.J.Orchard, N.J.Glover & S.R.Godfrey *(New owners 1.02)*	Aylesbury	30. 5.97A
G-BWBT	Lindstrand LBL-90A HAFB	184		3. 4.95	British Telecommunications plc	Newbury	10. 4.02A
G-BWBV*	Colt Piggy Bank SS HAFB	3535		19. 4.95	Iduna-Bausparkasse AG *(Cancelled 16.11.01 as wfu) (Preserved)*	(The Netherlands)	5. 4.01A
G-BWBY	Schleicher ASH26E	26076		30. 8.95	J.S.Wand	Aston Down	14.11.04
G-BWBZ	ARV1 Super 2 (Mid-West AE.100R)	PFA 152-12802		10. 3.95	J.N.C.Shields & D.J.Millar	Newtownards, Co.of Down	11. 5.02P
G-BWCA	CFM Streak Shadow (Rotax 582)	K.160 & PFA 206-11985		19. 4.95	S.Woolmington	(Colchester)	1. 8.02P
G-BWCC	Van Den Bemden 460m3 (Gas) Free Balloon	"022" *(C/n may be a corruption of Dutch CofR 622)*	PH-BOX	5. 4.95	R.W.Batchelor *"Prof A.Piccard"* t/a Piccard Balloon Group	Thame	
G-BWCG	Lindstrand LBL-42A HAFB	223		25. 4.95	Oxford Promotions (UK) Ltd *(Op F Prell)*	Kentucky, USA	10. 1.97A
G-BWCK	Everett Gyroplane Srs.3 (Rotax 582)	036		26. 4.95	A.C.S.M.Hart	Farley Farm, Winchester	13. 2.02P
G-BWCO	Dornier Do.28D-2 Skyservant	4337	EI-CJU (N5TK)/5N-AOH/D-ILIF	19. 6.95	Wingglider Ltd *(Stored 8.00)*	Hibaldstow	19. 5.99A
G-BWCS	British Aircraft Corporation BAC.145 Jet Provost T.Mk.5	EEP/JP/957	XW293	28. 4.95	R.E.Todd *(As "XW293/Z")*	Sandtoft	15. 3.02P
G-BWCT	Tipsy T.66 Nipper Srs.1 *(Built Avions Fairey SA)*	11	"OO-NIC" PH-MEC/D-EMEC/OO-NIC	27. 4.95	J.S.Hemmings & C.R.Steer	(Rye/Bexhill-on-Sea)	
G-BWCV	Europa Aviation Europa (NSI EA-81/100)	<u>41</u> & PFA 247-12591		4. 5.95	G.V.McKirdy *(Damaged Coxwold 31.10.97: on rebuild 9.00: new owner 6.01)*	Enstone	14. 4.98P
G-BWCW	Barnett Rotorcraft J4B (Lycoming)	PFA G/14-1256		5. 5.95	S.H.Kirkby *(Noted 11.00)*	Sunny Down, Stockbridge	
G-BWCY	Murphy Rebel (Lycoming O-235)	PFA 232-12135		15. 5.95	A.Konieczek	St.Michaels	2. 8.01P
G-BWCZ	Revolution Helicopters Mini-500 (Rotax 582)	0010		1. 5.95	D.Nieman	(Thame)	
G-BWDA	ATR 72-202	444	F-WWEQ	29. 6.95	Gill Aviation Ltd *(Stored 10.01)*	Dinard, France	28. 6.04T
G-BWDB	ATR 72-202	449	F-WWEE	14. 6.95	Gill Aviation Ltd *(Stored 10.01)*	Dinard, France	13. 6.04T
G-BWDE	Piper PA-31P Pressurised Navajo	31P-7400193	G-HWKN HB-LIR/D-IAIR/N7304L	12. 5.95	Tomkat Aviation Ltd *(Stored 10.97)*	Shoreham	18.12.96T
G-BWDF	WSK PZL-104 Wilga 35A	21950955		17. 5.95	Shivair Ltd *(Last noted dismantled 5.01 Rushett Farm, Chessington)*	(London SW7)	30.11.98
G-BWDH	Cameron N-105 HAFB	3549		22. 5.95	Bridges Van Hire Ltd	Awsworth, Nottingham	11. 6.01T
G-BWDM	Lindstrand LBL-120A HAFB	263		26. 5.95	G.D. & L.Fitzpatrick	Thame	14. 2.02T
G-BWDO	Sikorsky S-76B	760356	VR-CPN N9HM	2. 6.95	Haughey Air Ltd	(Newry, Co.Armagh)	8. 6.02T
G-BWDP	Europa Aviation Europa (Rotax 912UL) *(Suffered fire refuelling 14.5.00 - severe damage deforming fuselage: new owner 5.01 - & new fuselage/kit no??)*	62 & PFA 247-12637		7. 6.95	W.Hueltz	(Bonn, Germany)	9. 8.02P
G-BWDR	Hunting-Percival P.84 Jet Provost T.3A	PAC/W/6603	XM376	6. 6.95	W.O.Bayazid *(As "XM376/27")*	Humberside	24.10.02P
G-BWDS	Hunting P.84 Jet Provost T.Mk.3A *(C/n incomplete ?)*	'PAC/W/932'	XM424 N77506-ntu?	6. 6.95	J.Sinclair *(As "XM424")*	North Weald	23. 5.01P
G-BWDT	Piper PA-34-220T Seneca <u>III</u>	34-8233045	PH-TWI G-BKHS/N8472H	21. 9.88	H.R.Chambers	Redhill	16. 8.03
G-BWDU	Cameron V-90 HAFB	3143		19. 6.95	C.J.Jenkins & M.Stone t/a Bath & West Security *"Stella Tortoise"*	Bath	16. 6.02A
G-BWDV	Schweizer Hughes 269C	S.1712	N86G	16. 6.95	Oxford Aviation Services Ltd	Oxford	3. 9.04T
G-BWDX	Europa Aviation Europa (Rotax 912UL)	<u>56</u> & PFA 247-12603		13. 6.95	J.B.Crane	Fenland	22. 5.02P
G-BWDZ	Sky 105-24 HAFB	002		13. 6.95	Skyride Balloons Ltd	King's Lynn	26. 5.02T
G-BWEA	Lindstrand LBL-120A HAFB	252		14. 6.95	S.R.Seager *(Parrott & Coales titles)*	Aylesbury	8. 7.00T

G-BWEB	British Aircraft Corporation BAC.145 Jet Provost T.5A	EEP/JP/1044	XW422	19. 6.95	D.W.N.Johnson	North Weald	29. 5.02P
					(Transair Pilot Shop titles)		
G-BWEC	Cassutt-Colson Variant	PFA 034-10444		20.12.78	N.R.Thomson & M.P.J.Hill	Sywell	11. 9.91P
					(On overhaul 5.98: current status unknown)		
G-BWED	Thunder Ax7-77 HAFB	3575		20. 6.95	J.Tod	London WC2	20. 6.96
G-BWEE	Cameron V-42 HAFB	3480		8. 3.95	Aeromantics Ltd	Bristol	
G-BWEF	SNCAN Stampe SV-4C	208	G-BOVL	13. 5.93	A.J.White	Redhill	7. 3.04
	(DH Gipsy Major 10)		N20SV/F-BHES/F-BBLC		t/a Acebell BWEF Syndicate		
G-BWEG	Europa Aviation Europa			4. 4.95	B.A.Selmes & R.J.Marsh	Dunkeswell	9. 5.02P
	(Rotax 912UL)	53 & PFA 247-12600			t/a Wessex Europa Group		
G-BWEH	HOAC DV-20 Katana	20123		19. 6.95	Lowlog Ltd.	Elstree/Cranfield	19. 7.04T
G-BWEL	Sky 200-24 HAFB	003		27. 6.95	M.W.A.Shemilt	Henley-on-Thames	10. 5.01T
					t/a H-O-T Air Balloons		
G-BWEM	Supermarine 358 Seafire L.III	--	IAC.157	28. 6.95	C.J.Warrilow & S.W.Atkins	(Exeter)	
			RX168		*(On rebuild 10.01)*		
G-BWEN	Macair Merlin GT			20. 6.95	B.W.Davies *(Stored 11.01)*		
	(Subaru EA81)	050194 & PFA 208A-12859				Lower Mountpleasant, Chatteris	7.12.95P
G-BWEO	Lindstrand LBL-14M HAFB	285		23. 6.95	Lindstrand Balloons Ltd	Oswestry	19. 5.00A
G-BWEP*	Lindstrand LBL-77M HAFB	286		23. 6.95	Lindstrand Balloons Ltd	Oswestry	19. 5.00A
					(Cancelled 17.5.00 as wfu)		
G-BWER	Lindstrand LBL-14M HAFB	287		23. 6.95	Lindstrand Balloons Ltd	Oswestry	4.11.97A
G-BWEU	Reims Cessna F152 II	F15201894	EI-BNC	15. 6.95	Flight Ltd	Netherthorpe	2. 9.04T
			N9097Y				
G-BWEV	Cessna 152 II	15283182	EI-BVU	28. 6.95	Haimoss Ltd	Old Sarum	10.10.04T
			N47184				
G-BWEW	Cameron N-105 HAFB	3637		30. 6.95	Unipart Group Ltd	Cowley, Oxon	17. 1.00A
					t/a Unipart Balloon Club *(Unipart titles) "Unipart 5"*		
G-BWEY	Bensen B.8	PFA G/01-1197		3. 7.95	F.G.Shepherd	Alston, Cumbria	
G-BWEZ	Piper J-3C-85 Cub	6021	N29050	3. 7.95	J.G.McTaggart	Cumbernauld	19. 7.02P
			NC29050		t/a PJ L4 Group *(As "FR887" in silver c/s)*		
G-BWFD	HOAC DV-20 Katana	20127		5. 7.95	Cumbernauld Flying School Ltd	Cumbernauld	30. 7.04T
G-BWFE	HOAC DV-20 Katana	20129		5. 7.95	Airways Ltd	(Buxton)	23. 7.04T
G-BWFG	Robin HR.200/120	293		20. 7.95	Atlantic Air Transport Ltd	Coventry	20. 1.02T
G-BWFH	Europa Aviation Europa	PFA 247-12842		14. 7.95	B.L.Wratten	Kemble	29. 6.04T
	(Rotax 912-UL)						
G-BWFI	HOAC DV-20 Katana	20128		17. 7.95	Lowlog Ltd	Elstree/Cranfield	12. 8.04T
G-BWFJ	Evans VP-1	PFA 062-10349		1. 9.78	P.A.West	Old Sarum	27. 1.93P
	(VW 1600)				*(Stored 5.94: current status unknown)*		
G-BWFK*	Lindstrand LBL-77A HAFB	289		17. 7.95	Virgin Airship & Balloon Co Ltd	Telford	24. 8.00A
					"Orange" *(Cancelled 2.3.01 as wfu)*		
G-BWFM	Yakovlev Yak-50	781208	NX5224R	19. 7.95	Classic Aviation Ltd	Little Gransden	5. 4.01P
			DDR-WQX/DM-WQX		*(Op The Old Flying Machine Co)*		
G-BWFN	HAPI Cygnet SF-2A	PFA 182-11335		19. 7.95	T.Crawford	Cumbernauld	
					(Under construction 1.02)		
G-BWFO	Colomban MC-15 Cri-Cri	PFA 133-11253		19. 7.95	O.G.Jones	(Llanbedr)	
	(JPX PUL-212)						
G-BWFP	IAV-Bacau Yakovlev Yak-52	855503	RA-44501(1)	20. 7.95	M.C.Lee	Liverpool	6.12.01P
			DOSAAF 43				
	(C/n plate shows c/n 855606 ex DOSAAF 61 (blue) - possibly composite)						
G-BWFR	Hawker Hunter F.58	41H-697398	J-4031	24. 7.95	The Old Flying Machine Air Museum Co Ltd		
					(As "J-4031")	Scampton	3. 8.99P
G-BWFS	Hawker Hunter F.58	41H-697425	J-4058	24. 7.95	The Old Flying Machine Air Museum Co Ltd		
					(As "J-4058")	Scampton	5. 7.99P
G-BWFT	Hawker Hunter T.8M	41H-695332	XL602	24. 7.95	B.R.Pearson t/a T8M Group	Exeter	23. 7.99P
					(As "XL602")		
G-BWFV	HOAC DV-20 Katana	20132		26. 7.95	Plane Talking Ltd	Elstree	29. 8.04T
G-BWFX	Europa Aviation Europa			26. 7.95	A.D.Stewart	Rayne Hall Farm, Rayne	21. 2.02P
	(Rotax 912UL)	38 & PFA 247-12586					
G-BWFY	Aérospatiale AS350B1 Ecureuil	1963	N518R	31. 7.95	PLM Dollar Group Ltd	Inverness	21. 7.04T
G-BWFZ	Murphy Rebel	PFA 232-12536	G-SAVS	19. 7.95	I.E.Spencer	St Michaels	13. 5.02P
	(Lycoming O-235-L2C) *(Made forced landing Pilling Sands, Morecambe Bay & struck a ditch 8.9.01: damage to undercarriage, fuselage floor, windscreen, struts & propeller)*						
G-BWGA*	Lindstrand LBL-105A HAFB	295		2. 8.95	Balloon Preservation Group	Kirdford	24. 3.97A
					"Asda" (Cancelled 14.5.99 as WFU)		
G-BWGF	British Aircraft Corporation BAC.145 Jet Provost T.5A	EEP/JP/989	XW325	10. 8.95	J.W.Cullen	Blackpool	27. 7.02P
					t/a Specialscope Jet Provost Group *(As "XW325/E")*		
G-BWGG	Max Holste MH.1521C1 Broussard	20	F-GGKG	10. 7.95	M.J.Burnett Jnr. & R.B.Maalouf	Rednall	21. 8.03
			F-WGKG/Fr mil		*(As "315-SQ" in ALAT c/s)*		
G-BWGH	Europa Aviation Europa	PFA 247-12589		23. 8.95	M.H.B.Heathman	Exeter	2. 4.02P
	(Rotax 912-UL) *(Tri-cycle u/c)*				t/a Golf Hotel Group		
	(While en route Jersey/Exeter 13.10.01 engine failed & forcelanded Sark: tail broken off, u/c nose damage)						

G-BWGJ	Chilton DW.1A	PFA 225-12615		11. 8.95	T.J.Harrison	Lower Upham, Hants	
	(Lycoming O-145-A2)				*(Complete 5.00)*		
G-BWGK	Hawker Hunter GA.11	HABL-003032	XE689	15. 8.95	B.R.Pearson t/a GA11 Group	Exeter	11. 7.01P
	(Centre fuselage no.confirmed as 41HR HABL 003032)				*(As "XE689/864/VL")*		
G-BWGL	Hawker Hunter T.8C	HABL-003086	XF357	15. 8.95	Old Flying Machine Co	Duxford	20. 6.02P
	(Regd with c/n 41H-695946)				*(As T.Mk.7 prototype "XJ615")*		
G-BWGM	Hawker Hunter T.8C	HABL-003008	XE665	15. 8.95	B.J.Pover t/a The Admirals Barge	Exeter	24. 6.98P
	(Regd with c/n 41H-695940)				*(As "XE665/876/VL")*		
G-BWGN	Hawker Hunter T.8C	41H-670689	WT722	15. 8.95	B.J.Pearson t/a T8C Group	Exeter	3. 9.97P
					(As "WT722/878/VL")		
G-BWGO	Slingsby T.67M-200 Firefly	2048	SE-LBC	15. 8.95	R.Gray	Fairoaks	31. 3.02
G-BWGP	Cameron C-80 HAFB	3631		17. 8.95	D.J.Groombridge	Bristol	6. 9.02A
					"London Camera Exchange"		
G-BWGR	North American TB-25N-NC Mitchell	108-34200	N9494Z 44-30925	18. 8.95	D Copley	Sandtoft	
					(Noted as "151632/N9494Z" 4.01)		
	(Official c/n is 108-30925 - a corruption of USAAF serial)						
G-BWGS	British Aircraft Corporation BAC.145 Jet Provost T.5A	EEP/JP/974	XW310	18. 8.95	Katharina K.Gerstorfer	North Weald	23. 8.01P
					(As "XW310/37")		
G-BWGT	Hunting-Percival P.84 Jet Provost T.4	PAC/W/21624	8991M XR679	21. 8.95	R.E.Todd	Sandtoft	30. 5.02P
					(Op The Jet Provost Club)		
	(Reported as c/n PAC/W/19992)						
G-BWGU	Cessna 150F	15062962	EI-CDU N8862G	18. 8.95	Goodair Leasing Ltd	Hill Farm, Nayland	31. 5.04
G-BWGX	Cameron N-42 HAFB	3633		21. 8.95	Newbury Building Society	Newbury	19. 1.00A
G-BWGY	HOAC DV-20 Katana	20134		22. 8.95	Plane Talking Ltd	Elstree	12.10.04T
G-BWGZ	HOAC DV-20 Katana	20135		22. 8.95	Diamond Aircraft Industries GmbH	Gamston	12.10.01T
G-BWHA*	Hawker Hurricane IIB	41H/G5/21232	Z5053 (Soviet AF)/Z5053	23. 8.95	Historic Flying Ltd	(Audley End)	
	(Regd with c/n 41H-G3121232)				*(As "Z5252/GO-B")*		
				(On rebuild 8.95: cancelled 2.8.01 by CAA: current status unknown)			
G-BWHB	Cameron O-65 HAFB	2759		24. 8.95	G.Aimo	Mondovi, Italy	14. 6.02A
G-BWHC	Cameron N-77 HAFB	3647		25. 8.95	R.B.Craik	Northampton	25. 6.02A
G-BWHD	Lindstrand LBL-31A HAFB	292		29. 8.95	J.C.E.Price	Portadown	12. 1.01A
					t/a Army Air Corps Balloon Club		
G-BWHF	Piper PA-31-325 Navajo C/R	31-7612076	F-GECA D-IBIS/N59862	7. 9.95	Awyr Cymru Cyf	Shobdon	31.10.02T
G-BWHG	Cameron N-65 HAFB	3619		7. 9.95	M.Stefanini & F.B.Alaoui	Florence, Italy	4. 9.02A
G-BWHH	Piper PA-18-135 Super Cub	18-3605	PH-KNA	9. 8.95	JME Ltd	Felthorpe	18. 2.02
	(L-21B-PI) *(Frame No.18-3789)*		R.Neth AF R-115/54-2405		*(As "44" in US Army c/s)*		
G-BWHI	de Havilland DHC-1 Chipmunk 22A	C1/0637	WK624	8. 9.95	N.E.M.Clare	Duxford	9. 9.01T
					(As "WK624/M")		
	(It is possible the bulk of WK624/M was used in the rebuild of G-AOSY at Duxford during 1998/99)						
G-BWHK	Rans S-6-116 Coyote II *(Tri-cycle u/c)*			15. 9.95	M.Knowles		
	(Rotax 582) 0695.834 & PFA 204A-12908					Lane Green Farm, Six Ashes, Bridgnorth	30. 4.02P
G-BWHM	Sky 140-24 HAFB	006		18. 9.95	C.J.S.Limon	London NW1	21. 9.02T
G-BWHP	CASA I-131E Jungmann	2109	E3B-513	18. 8.95	J.F.Hopkins	Watchford Farm, Yarcombe	16. 7.02P
					(As "S4+A07" in Luftwaffe c/s)		
G-BWHR	Tipsy Nipper T.66 Srs.1	PFA 025-12843	(OO-KAM) OO-69	19. 9.95	L.R.Marnef	(Koningshooikt, Belgium)	
	(Composite homebuild of original Fairey built c/n 29 & 71)						
G-BWHS	Rotary Air Force RAF.2000			25. 9.95	J M Cox	(Windsor)	20.12.01P
	(Subaru EA82)	PFA G/13-1253					
G-BWHT	Everett Campbell Cricket	046		27. 9.95	D.Brown	(Newton Stewart)	
G-BWHU	Westland Scout AH.1	F.9517	XR595	27. 9.95	N.J.F.Boston	Oreston, Plymouth	27. 1.02P
					(As "XR595/M" in Army c/s)		
G-BWHV	Denney Kitfox mk.2	PFA 172-11857		28. 9.95	A.C.Dove	(Ashtead)	13. 3.02P
G-BWHW	Cameron A-180 HAFB	3634		29. 9.95	Societe Bombard SARL	Meursanges, France	10.10.02A
G-BWHY	Robinson R22	0098	N90366	24. 3.87	Finnigan-Wood Ltd	Blackpool	9. 6.02T
G-BWIA	Rans S-10 Sakota	PFA 194-12044		15. 9.95	P.A.Beck	Cambridge	24. 9.01P
	(Rotax 582)						
G-BWIB	Scottish Aviation Bulldog Srs.120/122	BH120/227	G-103 Ghana AF	10.10.95	D.J.T.John	Leicester	8. 5.04T
					t/a Aerofab Restorations *(As "XX514")*		
G-BWID	Druine D.31 Turbulent	201	F-PHFR	16.10.95	A.M.Turney	(Tring)	16. 1.02P
	(VW 1200)						
G-BWII	Cessna 150G	15065308	N4008J (G-BSKB)/N4008J	22. 9.95	J.D.G.Hicks	Beeches Farm, South Scarle	10. 2.02
G-BWIJ*	Europa Aviation Europa	PFA 247-12513		19.10.95	R.Lloyd	Gloucestershire	
					(Noted 9.99: cancelled 2.11.00 by CAA: current status unknown)		
G-BWIK	de Havilland DH.82A Tiger Moth	86417	7015M NL985	20.10.95	B.J.Ellis	Little Gransden	
					(On rebuild as "NL985": current status unknown)		
G-BWIL	Rans S-10 Sakota		G-WIEN	4.10.95	J.C.Longmore	Netherthorpe	29. 1.02P
	(Rotax 582) 1089.065 & PFA 194-11770						

G-BWIP	Cameron N-90 HAFB	3668		20.10.95	Noble Adventures Ltd *(Noted Ashton Court 8.99)*	Bristol	27.10.96A
G-BWIR	Dornier 328-100	3023	D-CDXF N328DA/D-CDHH	18.10.95	Suckling Airways (Norwich) Ltd t/a Scot Airways	Cambridge	19.10.02T
G-BWIT	QAC Quickie 1 (Rotax 503)	484	N4482Z	21. 9.95	D.E., M.S. & I.E.Johnson *(Damaged near Coventry 12.10.97: current status unknown)*	Coventry	31.10.00P
G-BWIU	Hawker Hunter F.58 *(Reported as c/n 41H/694926)*	41H-691770	J-4021	26.10.95	Classic Aviation Ltd *(As "XG232" in RAF c/s)*	Scampton	24. 2.99P
G-BWIV	Europa Aviation Europa (Rotax 912UL)	210 & PFA 247-12871		27.10.95	T.G.Ledbury	White Waltham	9. 9.99P
G-BWIW	Sky 180-24 HAFB	008		1.11.95	J.A.Cooper	Ivybridge	16. 7.01T
G-BWIX	Sky 120-24 HAFB	009		31.10.95	J.M.Percival *"Mayfly III"*	Loughborough	25. 6.01
G-BWJG	Mooney M.20J (201MSE)	24-3319	N1083P	7.11.95	Samic Ltd	Elstree	4. 2.02
G-BWJH	Europa Aviation Europa (Rotax 912UL)	7 & PFA 247-12643		10.11.95	D.P.Cripps & P.J.Rudling	Enstone	20. 9.02P
G-BWJI	Cameron V-90 HAFB	3727		13.11.95	Calarel Developments Ltd	Chipping Camden	17. 9.02A
G-BWJK*	Rotorway Executive (Rotorway RW 152)	CWT.1	G-OKIT	24.10.95	B.Singh *(No PtoF issued: cancelled 29.8.01 by CAA)*	(Huddersfield)	
G-BWJM	Bristol M.1C rep *(Built Northern Aeroplane Workshops)*	NAW-2		23.11.95	The Shuttleworth Trust *(As "C4918" in 72 Sqn c/s)*	Old Warden	7. 5.02P
G-BWJN	Montgomerie-Bensen B.8MR (Rotax 582)	PFA G/01-1262		16.11.95	M.Johnston	Carlisle	8. 9.01P
G-BWJP	Cessna 172C	17249424	N1824Y	21.11.95	T.W.R.Case *(New owner 8.01)*	(Sidmouth)	
G-BWJR*	Sky 120-24 HAFB	007		22.11.95	W.J.Brogan *"Filzmooser" (Cancelled 22.10.01 by CAA)*	Steiermark, Austria	21.12.96
G-BWJT	Yakovlev Yak-50	812003	RA-01385 DOSAAF50	23.11.95	D Bonucchi *"www.YAKUK.Co.Uk"*	(Watford)	31.12.02P
G-BWJW	Westland Scout AH.1	F.9705	XV130	29.11.95	C.L.Holdsworth *(As "XV130/R" in 666 Sqdn c/s)*	Redhill	18.12.01P
G-BWJY	de Havilland DHC-1 Chipmunk 22	C1/0519	WG469	5.12.95	K.J.Thompson *(As "WG469")*	Newtownards, Co.of Down	23. 5.03
G-BWKB	Hawker Hunter F.58	41H-697448	J-4081	12.10.95	Classic Aviation Ltd *(Current status unknown)*	Scampton	
G-BWKD	Cameron O-120 HAFB	3773		8.12.95	K.E. & L.J.Viney *"Rainbow"*	Olney, Bucks	29.11.01T
G-BWKE	Cameron AS-105GD Hot Air Airship	3685		8.12.95	W.Arnold	Kassel, Germany	4. 2.02A
G-BWKF	Cameron N-105 HAFB	3736		8.12.95	R.M.M.Botti	Grosseto, Italy	7.12.01A
G-BWKG	Europa Aviation Europa	PFA 247-12451		28.11.95	T.C.Jackson	Gamston	30. 4.02P
G-BWKJ	Rans S-7 Courier (Verner SVS1400)	PFA 218-12918		14.12.95	R.W.Skelton *"Festina Lente/Nihl Timeo"*	Portadown, Co.Armagh	14.10.02P
G-BWKK	Auster AOP.9	AUS.166 & B5/10/165	XP279	30. 7.79	C.A.Davis & D.R.White *(As "XP279" in Army c/s)*	Popham	1. 8.96P
G-BWKR	Sky 90-24 HAFB	014		18.12.95	Beverley Drawbridge	Cranbrook	17. 2.02T
G-BWKT	Stephens Akro Lazer	PFA 123-11421		19.12.95	P.D.Begley	Sywell	15. 3.02P
G-BWKU	Cameron A-250 HAFB	3730		21.12.95	Balloon School (International) Ltd t/a British School of Ballooning	Petworth	23. 7.02T
G-BWKV	Cameron V-77 HAFB	3780		27.12.95	Poppies (UK) Ltd	Wootton Fitzpaine, Dorset	5. 3.02A
G-BWKW	Thunder Ax8-90 HAFB	3770		28.12.95	Venice Simplon Orient Express Ltd *"Road to Mandalay"*	Frinton-on-Sea	9. 1.97A
G-BWKX	Cameron A-250 HAFB	3731		2. 1.96	Balloon School (International) Ltd t/a Hot Airlines	Petworth	23. 7.02T
G-BWKZ	Lindstrand LBL-77A HAFB	340		21.12.95	J.H.Dobson	Reading	5. 3.02T
G-BWLA	Lindstrand LBL-69A HAFB	339		3. 1.96	Virgin Airship & Balloon Co Ltd	Telford	26. 4.00A
G-BWLD	Cameron O-120 HAFB	3774	(I-....)	16. 1.96	D & P Pedri & C.Nicolodi	(Villa Lagarina, Italy)	3.12.00A
G-BWLF	Cessna 404 Titan II	404-0414	G-BNXS HKG-4/(N8799K)	26.10.94	P.Maden & M Evans t/a Nor Leasing	Farnborough	19. 3.03
G-BWLJ	Taylorcraft DCO-65	04331	C-GUSA	16. 1.96	C.Evans	Hill Farm, Nayland	18.12.02P
G-BWLL	Murphy Rebel (Lycoming O-235)	PFA 232-12499		22. 1.96	F.W.Parker	Richmond, N.Yorks	16. 7.02P
G-BWLM	Sky 65-24 HAFB	015		24. 1.96	W.J.Brogan t/a Dachstein Tauern Balloons KG *"Innsbruck"*	Steiermark, Austria	5. 2.97
G-BWLN	Cameron O-84 HAFB	3737		24. 1.96	Reggiana Riduttori SRL	S.Polo d'Enza, Italy	11. 6.02A
G-BWLP	HOAC DV-20 Katana	20141	OE-UDV	6. 2.96	Plane Talking Ltd	Elstree	12.11.03T
G-BWLR	Max Holste MH.1521C1 Broussard	185	F-GGKJ F-WGKJ/French AF	25. 1.96	Chicory Crops Ltd *(As "185/44-CA" in French AF c/s)*	Sywell	16. 3.03
G-BWLS	HOAC DV-20 Katana 100	20142	OE-UHK	6. 2.96	M. Reed t/a Shadow Aviation	Elstree	19. 7.03T
G-BWLT	HOAC DV-20 Katana	20149		6. 2.96	Plane Talking Ltd	Elstree	12.11.03T
G-BWLV	HOAC DV-20 Katana	20151		6. 2.96	Plane Talking Ltd	Elstree	16. 6.02T
G-BWLW	Avid Speed Wing Mk.4	PFA 189-12763		26. 1.96	P.C. & Susan A.Creswick	Weston Zoyland	

G-BWLX	Westland Scout AH.1	F.9709	XV134	29.12.95	R.E.Dagless *(As "XV134" in AAC c/s)*	Yaxham, Dereham	4. 7.02P
G-BWLY	Rotorway Executive (Rotorway RI 162)	5142		11. 1.93	P.W. & I.P.Bewley	Ley Farm, Chirk	17.10.02P
G-BWLZ	Wombat Gyrocopter	PFA G/09-1255		28.12.95	M.R.Harrisson *(Stored 3.98: new owner 10.00)*	Guernsey	
G-BWMA	Colt 105A HAFB	1853		31.10.90	C.C.Duppa-Miller	Warwick	14.12.02A
G-BWMB	Jodel D.119	77-1492	F-BGMA	17. 2.78	C.Hughes	Finmere	19. 5.02P
	(Original F-BGMA c/n 77 became F-PHQH and was rebuilt as a Larrieu JL.2: this is presumed to be a rebuild using some components of c/n 77 plus new build c/n 1492)						
G-BWMC	Cessna 182P Skylane II	18263117	N5462J G-BWMC/OO-RGM/(OO-RAN)/F-BVOU/N7333N	30. 1.96	P.F.N.Burrow & E.N.Skinner t/a Eggesford Eagles Flying Group	Trenchard Farm, Eggesford	11. 7.03
G-BWMD	Enstrom 480	5013		5. 2.96	Lamindene Ltd	Goodwood	8. 7.02T
G-BWMF	Gloster Meteor T.7	G5/356460	7917M WA591	15.12.95	M.Jones t/a Meteor Flight *(On rebuild 3.96)*	Yatesbury	
G-BWMG	Aérospatiale AS332L Super Puma	2046	OY-HMG	1. 2.96	Bristow Helicopters Ltd *"Catterline"*	Aberdeen	24. 6.03T
G-BWMH	Lindstrand LBL-77B HAFB	152		7. 2.96	J.W.Hole	Much Wenlock	17. 7.99A
G-BWMI	Piper PA-28RT-201T Turbo Arrow IV	28R-8031131	F-GCTG N82482/N9571N	31. 1.96	Oxford Aviation Services Ltd	Oxford	7.11.02
G-BWMJ	Nieuport Scout 17/23 rep (Warner Scarab 165)	PFA 121-12351		8. 2.96	R.Gauld-Galliers & Lisa J.Day *(As "B3459/2" in RFC c/s)*	Popham	27. 7.01P
G-BWMK	de Havilland DH.82A Tiger Moth	84483	T8191	9. 2.96	Schneider Trophy Ltd *(Noted as "T8191" 8.90)*	Welshpool	
G-BWML	Cameron A-275 HAFB	3725		12. 2.96	A.J.Street *(Exeter Balloons titles)*	Exeter	17. 8.01T
G-BWMN	Rans S-7 Courier (Rotax 912UL)	PFA 218-12446		14. 2.96	G.J.Knee & G.Keyser	Turweston	23. 3.02P
G-BWMO	Oldfield Baby Lakes (Continental C85)	JAL.3	G-CIII N11JL	14. 2.96	P.J.Tanulak	Sleap	17. 2.02P
G-BWMS	de Havilland DH.82A Tiger Moth	82712	OO-EVJ T-29/R4771	14. 2.96	Foundation Early Birds *(Current status unknown)*	(Nederhorst, The Netherlands)	
G-BWMU	Cameron Monster Truck 105SS HAFB	3607		20. 2.96	Magical Adventures Ltd *"Skycrusher"*	Chirk	2. 8.01A
G-BWMV	Colt AS-105 mk.II Hot Air Airship	3775		22. 2.96	D.Stuber	Bad Krenznach, Germany	10. 7.02A
G-BWMX	de Havilland DHC-1 Chipmunk 22	C1/0481	WG407	19. 2.96	K.S.Kelso t/a 407th Flying Group *(As "WG407/67")*	Top Farm, Croydon	2. 4.02
G-BWMY	Cameron Bradford & Bingley 90SS HAFB	3808		23. 2.96	Magical Adventures Ltd	Chirk	20. 4.00A
G-BWNB	Cessna 152 II	15280051	N757WA	23. 8.96	Galair International Ltd	Wolverhampton	30. 9.02T
G-BWNC	Cessna 152 II	15284415	N6487L	23. 8.96	Galair International Ltd	Wellesbourne Mountford	24.11.02T
G-BWND	Cessna 152 II	15285905	N95493	23. 8.96	Galair International Ltd, M.R.Galiffe & G.Davis	Wellesbourne Mountford	21. 9.02T
G-BWNH	Cameron A-375 HAFB	3553		28. 2.96	Noble Adventures Ltd *(Amended CofR 12.01)*	Bristol	12. 5.97A
G-BWNI	Piper PA-24-180 Comanche	24-136	N5123P	15. 2.96	T.D.Cooper & D.F.Hurn	Popham	6. 7.02
G-BWNJ	Hughes 269C	86-0528	N42LW N27RD/N7458F	29. 2.96	L.R.Fenwick	Long Fosse House, Beelsby, Grimsby	12. 6.02
G-BWNK	de Havilland DHC-1 Chipmunk 22	C1/0317	WD390	4. 3.96	B.Whitworth *(As "WD390")*	Breighton	6. 4.03
G-BWNM	Piper PA-28R-180 Cherokee Arrow	28R-30435	N934BD	5. 3.96	D.Houghton	Croft Farm, Defford	28. 9.02
G-BWNO	Cameron O-90 HAFB	3716		5. 3.96	M.A.Pratt & T Knight	Hertford	28..7.02A
G-BWNP	Cameron Club-90 SS HAFB (Club Orange Soft Drink Can shape)	1717	EI-BVQ	6. 3.96	C.J.Davies & P.Spellward	Hope Valley	2. 5.00
G-BWNR	Piper PA-38-112 Tomahawk	38-78A0449	N2361E	6. 3.96	APB Leasing Ltd	Sleap	6. 5.02T
G-BWNS	Cameron O-90 HAFB	3842		6. 3.96	Smithair Ltd. *(Self Assessment Tax titles) "Hector"*	Billingshurst	15. 8.02T
G-BWNT	de Havilland DHC-1 Chipmunk 22	C1/0772	WP901	7. 3.96	R.A.Stafford t/a Three Point Aviation *(As "WP901")*	East Midlands	24. 5.03T
G-BWNU	Piper PA-38-112 Tomahawk	38-78A0334	N9294T	8. 3.96	Rosemary E.Best t/a G-BWNU Group	Kemble	9. 9.02
G-BWNX	Thunder Ax10-180 Srs.2 HAFB	2352	G-OWBC	2. 1.96	MJN Balloon Management Ltd	Longleat, Warminster	2. 4.01T
G-BWNY	Aeromot AMT-200 Super Ximango	200-055		11. 6.96	H.G.Nicklin	Rufforth	31. 5.02
G-BWNZ	Agusta A109C	7654		3. 4.96	Anglo Beef Processors Ltd	Shrewsbury	13. 4.02T
G-BWOA	Sky 105-24 HAFB	027		13. 3.96	Akhter Group Holdings plc	Harlow	11. 7.02A
G-BWOB	Luscombe 8F Silvaire	6179	N1552B NC1552B	14. 3.96	P.J.Tanulak & H.T.Law	(Shrewsbury)	

G-BWOD	IAV-Bacau Yakovlev Yak-52	833810	LY-ALY	14. 3.96	Insurefast Ltd	Sywell	17. 5.02P
			DOSAAF 139		*(As "DOSAAF 139")*		
G-BWOE	Yakovlev Yak-3U	1701231	(G-BUXZ)	14. 3.96	R.G.Hanna	Duxford	
	(Converted from LET Yak C.11)		NX11SN/(France)/Egyptian AF		*(Op The Old Flying Machine Co)*		
					(On long-term restoration 12.01)		
G-BWOF	British Aircraft Corporation BAC.145 Jet Provost T.5	EEP/JP/955	XW291	18. 3.96	Techair London Ltd	Bournemouth	29. 3.02P
G-BWOK	Lindstrand LBL-105G HAFB	370		19. 3.96	Lindstrand Balloons Ltd	Oswestry	31. 8.01A
G-BWOL*	Hawker Sea Fury FB.11	ES.3617 & 61631	D-CACY(2)	18. 3.96	The Old Flying Machine (Air Museum)	Catfield, Norfolk	
			G-9-66/WG599				
	(On restoration for K Weeks 2.00: cancelled 4.1.01 by CAA: current status unknown)						
G-BWOM	Cessna 550 Citation II	550-0671	N671EA	22. 3.96	Ferron Trading Ltd	Jersey	18. 4.04
			9M-TAA/(N6761L)		*(Op Aviation Beauport Ltd)*		
G-BWON	Europa Aviation Europa			29. 1.96	G.T.Birks	Oaksey Park	26. 7.02P
	(Rotax 912UL)	112 & PFA 247-12720					
G-BWOR	Piper PA-18-135 Super Cub	18-2547	OO-WIS	21. 3.96	C.D.Baird	Roughay Farm, Bishops Waltham	23. 7.99
	(L-18C)		OO-HMF/ALAT/52-6229		*(On rebuild 11.01)*		
G-BWOT	Hunting P.84 Jet Provost T.3A		XN459	25. 3.96	Red Pelicans Formation Ltd	North Weald	15. 3.02P
	(Reported as c/n PAC/W/949267)	PAC/W/10138			*(As "XN459" in all-red Red Pelicans c/s)*		
G-BWOU	Hawker Hunter F.58A	HABL.003067	J-4105	26. 3.96	The Old Flying Machine (Air Museum) Co Ltd		
			G-9-315/A2565/XF303		*(As "105")*	Scampton	20. 1.99P
	(Regd with c/n 41H-003067 ex XF306/7776M/G-9-402 which became J-4133:- G-BWOU may be a composite)						
G-BWOV	Enstrom F-28A	222	N690BR	26. 3.96	A.P.Goddard	(Southampton)	16. 5.03T
			G-BWOV/F-BVRG				
G-BWOW	Cameron N-105 HAFB	3805		31. 1.96	S.J.Colin & A.S.Pinder	Maidstone	30. 5.02T
					t/a Skybus Ballooning *"Skybus"*		
G-BWOX	de Havilland DHC-1 Chipmunk 22	C1/0728	WP844	27. 3.96	J.St Clair-Quentin	Spanhoe	10. 7.00
					(As "WP844")		
G-BWOY	Sky 31-24 HAFB	029		28. 3.96	C.Wolstenholme	Bristol	5. 4.97A
					(New owner 11.01)		
G-BWOZ	CFM Streak Shadow SA			1. 4.96	N.P.Harding	Plaistows Farm, St Albans	4.11.02P
	(Rotax 582)	K.154SA & PFA 206-12988					
G-BWPA	Cameron A-340 HAFB	3714		29. 3.96	A.A.Brown	Guildford	7. 4.01T
G-BWPB	Cameron V-77 HAFB	3866		1. 4.96	R.H. & N.K.Calvert	Bristol	25. 6.02A
					t/a The Fair Weather Friends Ballooning Co		
G-BWPC	Cameron V-77 HAFB	3867		1. 4.96	Helen Vaughan *"Olive"*	Tring	15. 6.01A
G-BWPE	Murphy Renegade Spirit UK	PFA 188-12791		2. 4.96	G.Wilson	(Solihull)	
G-BWPF	Sky 120-24 HAFB	028		3. 4.96	H. & R.T.Revel *"Whisper"*	High Wycombe	28. 8.01T
G-BWPG*	Robin HR.200/120B	299		15. 4.96	Air Alba Ltd	Inverness	7. 7.99T
	(Damaged off Cromarty Gap, Nigg Bay 29.10.97: cancelled 26.1.98 as destroyed: fuselage stored 6.98: current status unknown)						
G-BWPH	Piper PA-28-181 Cherokee Archer II	28-7790311	N1408H	4. 4.96	H & E Merkado	Panshanger	1. 5.02T
G-BWPJ	Steen Skybolt	PFA 064-12854		9. 4.96	W.R.Penaluna	St Just	28. 8.02P
	(Continental IO-346)						
G-BWPL*	Airtour AH-56 HAFB	011	G-OAFC	19. 3.96	Balloon Preservation Group	Wokingham	
					"Paul J Donnellan" (As "G-OAFC" qv) (Cancelled 17.9.01 as wfu)		
G-BWPM*	Pilatus Britten-Norman BN-2T-4R Defender 4000	4007		24. 4.96	Britten-Norman Ltd	Bembridge	
					(Cancelled 19.10.00 as temporarily wfu)		
G-BWPP	Sky 105-24 HAFB	031		9. 4.96	P.F.Smart	Basingstoke	17. 7.00A
					t/a The Sarnia Balloon Group *"Fourpence"*		
G-BWPR	Pilatus Britten-Norman BN-2T-4S Defender 4000	4010		24. 4.96	B-N Group Ltd	Bembridge	
G-BWPS	CFM Streak Shadow SA			9. 2.96	P.M.E.D.McNair-Wilson	Old Sarum	4. 8.02P
	(Rotax 618)	K.275SA & PFA 206-12954					
G-BWPT	Cameron N-90 HAFB	3838		5. 3.96	G.Burrows	Sheffield	1. 5.00A
G-BWPU	Pilatus Britten-Norman BN-2T-4S Defender 4000	4011		24. 4.96	B-N Group Ltd	Bembridge	
G-BWPV*	Pilatus Britten-Norman BN-2T-4S Defender 4000	4012		24. 4.96	Britten-Norman Ltd	Bembridge	
					(Cancelled 19.10.00 as temporarily wfu)		
G-BWPW*	Pilatus Britten-Norman BN-2T-4S Defender 4000	4013		24. 4.96	Britten-Norman Ltd	Bembridge	
					(Cancelled 19.10.00 as temporarily wfu)		
G-BWPX*	Pilatus Britten-Norman BN-2T-4S Defender 4000	4014		24. 4.96	Britten-Norman Ltd	Bembridge	
					(Cancelled 19.10.00 as temporarily wfu)		
G-BWPY	HOAC DV-20 Katana 100	20158	OE-UDV	10. 6.96	S.Phillips	(Amersham)	14. 6.04T
					t/a SAS Flight Services		
G-BWPZ	Cameron N-105 HAFB	3889		19. 4.96	Flying Pictures Ltd *"Jaguar"*	Fairoaks	17. 4.02A
G-BWRA	Sopwith LC-1T Triplane rep		G-PENY	19. 4.96	S.M.Truscott & J.M.Hoblyn *(As "N500" in RNAS c/s)*		
	(Warner Scarab 165)	PFA 021-10035				Watchford Farm, Yarcombe/RNAS Yeovilton	10.11.02P
G-BWRC	Avid Hauler Mk.4	PFA 189-12979		22. 2.96	B.Williams	Chilsfold Farm, Crawley	11. 6.02P
	(Hirth F30)						
G-BWRM	Colt 105A HAFB	3734		23. 4.96	N.Charbonnier	Aosta, Italy	21. 1.02A

G-BWRO	Europa Aviation Europa (Rotax 912UL)	196 & PFA 247-12849		22. 4.96	J.G.M.McDiarmid *(Noted 8.01)*	Bodmin	29. 5.02P
G-BWRP	Beechcraft 58 Baron	TH-1737	VR-BVB N3217H	23. 4.96	Astra Aviation Ltd	Guernsey	27. 5.02
G-BWRR	Cessna 182Q Skylane II	18266660	N95861	29. 3.94	D.O.Halle	East Midlands	15. 8.03T
G-BWRS	SNCAN Stampe SV-4C	437	(N) F-BCVQ	24. 4.96	G.P.J.M.Valvekens	(Diest, Belgium)	
G-BWRT	Cameron Concept-60 HAFB	3078	EI-BYP	22.10.96	W.R.Teasdale	Maidenhead	
G-BWRV	Lindstrand LBL-90A HAFB	371		23. 4.96	Flying Pictures Ltd *"Audi"*	Fairoaks	24. 2.01A
G-BWRW	Sky 220-24 HAFB	032		23. 4.96	Sky Trek Ballooning Ltd	Longfield, Kent	30. 5.02T
G-BWRY	Cameron N-105 HAFB	3817		24. 4.96	G.Aimo *"Ferodo"*	Mondovi, Italy	14. 6.02A
G-BWRZ	Lindstrand LBL-105A HAFB	383		26. 4.96	Flying Pictures Ltd *"Rover"*	Fairoaks	17. 3.02A
G-BWSB	Lindstrand LBL-105A HAFB	384		26. 4.96	Flying Pictures Ltd *"MG"*	Fairoaks	17. 3.02A
G-BWSC	Piper PA-38-112 Tomahawk II	38-81A0125	N23203	29. 4.96	APB Leasing Ltd	Welshpool	15. 7.02T
G-BWSD	Campbell Cricket	PFA G/03-1216		3. 5.96	R.F.G.Moyle	(Penryn)	
G-BWSG	British Aircraft Corporation BAC.145 Jet Provost T.5	EEP/JP/988	XW324	13. 5.96	R.M.Kay *(As "XW324" in 6FTS c/s)*	Jersey	15. 3.02P
G-BWSH	Hunting P.84 Jet Provost T.3A	PAC/W/10159	XN498	13. 5.96	Global Aviation Ltd	Humberside	9. 7.02P
G-BWSI	K & S SA.102.5 Cavalier (Lycoming O-235)	PFA 01-10624		18. 4.84	B.W.Shaw	Wathstow Farm, Newby Wiske	9. 5.01P
G-BWSJ	Denney Kitfox mk.3 (Rotax 582)	PFA 172-12204		15. 5.96	J.M.Miller	Beccles	2. 2.02P
G-BWSK	Enstrom 280FX	2016	ZK-HIR JA7724	16. 5.96	M.A. & M.Gradwell	Barton	2. 8.02
G-BWSL	Sky 77-24 HAFB	004		16. 5.96	The Balloon Co Ltd	Cheltenham	15. 1.02A
G-BWSN	Denney Kitfox mk.3 (Rotax 582)	PFA 172-12141		16. 5.96	W.J.Forrest	Siege Cross Farm, Thatcham	4. 9.02P
G-BWSO	Cameron Apple Sainsbury 90SS HAFB	3915		17. 5.96	Flying Pictures Ltd *"Sainsbury's Apple"*	Fairoaks	11. 6.02A
G-BWSP	Cameron Carrots Sainsbury 80SS HAFB	3914		17. 5.96	Flying Pictures Ltd *"Sainsbury's Carrots"*	Fairoaks	5. 7.02A
G-BWST	Sky 200-24 HAFB	036		20. 5.96	S.A.Townley t/a Sky High Leisure	Wrexham	15. 8.02T
G-BWSU	Cameron N-105 HAFB	3848		20. 5.96	A.M.Marten *"Wonder Bra"*	London SW1	23. 9.99A
G-BWSV	IAV-Bacau Yakovlev Yak-52	877601	DOSAAF 43	20. 5.96	P.Traynor	Wellesbourne Mountford	20.11.02P
G-BWSX	Piper PA-28-236 Dakota	28-7911130	C-FLMJ N2169V	28. 5.96	C. & C.Bowie	Dunkeswell	7. 7.02
G-BWSY	British Aerospace BAe 125 Srs.800B	258201	G-OCCI G-5-699	28. 5.96	BAE Systems (Operations) Ltd	Filton/Warton	26. 8.03
G-BWSZ	Montgomerie-Bensen B.8MR (Rotax 582)	PFA G/01-1268		14. 5.96	D.Cawkwell	Goole	6. 1.98P
G-BWTA	HOAC DV-20 Katana	20159	OE-UDV	10. 6.96	Diamond Aircraft Industries GmbH *(Op Cotswold Aviation Services)*	Gloucestershire	14.10.02T
G-BWTB	Lindstrand LBL-105A HAFB	374		29. 5.96	Servatruc Ltd	Nottingham	14. 5.00A
G-BWTC	Moravan Zlin Z.242L	0697		2. 8.96	Oxford Aviation Services Ltd	Oxford	17.11.02T
G-BWTD	Moravan Zlin Z.242L	0698		2. 8.96	Oxford Aviation Services Ltd	Oxford	18. 9.02T
G-BWTE	Cameron O-140 HAFB	3885		30. 5.96	R.J. & A.J.Mansfield	Windermere	19. 2.01T
G-BWTF	Lindstrand Bear SS HAFB	375		3. 6.96	Free Enterprise Balloons Ltd *"Mr Biddle"*	East Leroy, MI, USA	25. 3.01A
G-BWTG	de Havilland DHC-1 Chipmunk 22	C1/0119	WB671	4. 6.96	P M M de Graaf t/a Chipmunk 4 Ever Foundation *(As "WB671/910")*	Teuge, The Netherlands	2. 8.03
G-BWTH	Robinson R22 Beta	1767	HB-XYD N4052R	5. 6.96	L.Smith t/a Helicopter Services	Booker	17. 6.02T
G-BWTJ	Cameron V-77 HAFB	3917		7. 6.96	A.J.Montgomery	Yeovil	29. 6.01A
G-BWTK	Rotary Air Force RAF 2000 GTX-SE	PFA G/13-1264		7. 6.96	Terrafirma Services Ltd	Lamberhurst Farm, Faversham	24. 6.02P
G-BWTN	Lindstrand LBL-90A HAFB	357		12. 6.96	Clarks Drainage Ltd	Oakham	12. 7.01A
G-BWTO	de Havilland DHC-1 Chipmunk 22	C1/0852	WP984	5. 6.96	A.C.Eltis & P.L.Reilly *(As "WP984/H")*	(Fen Drayton)	21. 6.04
G-BWTR	Slingsby T.61F Venture T.2	1881	XZ561	12. 6.96	P.R.Williams	(Brackley)	
G-BWTU	Lindstrand LBL-77A HAFB	376		17. 6.96	Virgin Airship & Balloon Co Ltd *"Land Rover"*	Telford	14. 1.02A
G-BWTW	Mooney M.20C	20-1188	EI-CHI N6955V	5. 6.96	R.C.Volkers	Henstridge	18.11.02
G-BWUA	Campbell Cricket	PFA G/03-1248		17. 6.96	R.T.Lancaster	Ash, Hants	
G-BWUB	Piper PA-18S-135 Super Cub (L-21C) *(Regd with c/n 18-3786)*	18-3986	N786CS G-BWUB/SX-AHB/EI-263/I-EIUO/MM54-2586/54-2586 *(On rebuild 2001)*	13. 6.96	Caledonian Seaplanes Ltd	Dunkeswell	23. 6.01T
G-BWUE	Hispano HA-1112-M1L *(Reported as c/n 172: C4K-155 was c/n 223)*	223	N9938 G-AWHK/C4K-102	14. 6.96	R.A.Fleming *(On rebuild 12.01)*	Breighton	
G-BWUF	WSK PZL-Mielec Lim-5 (MiG-17F)	1C-1211	1211 (Polish AF)	14. 6.96	Classic Aviation Ltd *(Op The Flying Machine Co) (As "1211" in Korean c/s)*	Duxford	

G-BWUH	Piper PA-28-181 Archer III	2843048	N9272E (G-BWUH)	30. 8.96	J E Thorne	(Ashford)	7.10.02
G-BWUJ	Rotorway Executive 162F (Rotorway RW.162F)	6153		2. 7.96	Southern Helicopters Ltd	Street Farm, Takeley	29.10.02P
G-BWUK	Sky 160-24 HAFB	043		2. 7.96	Spotlight Group Ltd	Axbridge	2. 8.02T
G-BWUL	Noorduyn AT-16 Harvard IIB	14A-1415	N16NA G-BWUL/FT375/43-13116	4. 7.96	Aereo Servizi Bresciana SRL	(Montichiari, Italy)	13.10.97
G-BWUM	Sky 105-24 HAFB	038		5. 7.96	P.Stern & F.Kirchberger *"Wanninger"*	Regen/Lam, Germany	22. 7.02
G-BWUN	de Havilland DHC-1 Chipmunk 22	C1/0253	WD310	5. 7.96	T.Henderson *(As "WD310")*	Upper Broyle Farm, Ringmer	10. 1.03
G-BWUP	Europa Aviation Europa (NSI EA81/100)	PFA 247-12703		3. 7.96	T.J.Harrison	Shenington	20. 1.02P
G-BWUR	Thunder Ax10-210 Srs.2 HAFB	3910		11. 7.96	T.J.Bucknall *"Kinetic"* *(Op Balloon Preservation Group)*	Malpas	7. 4.01T
G-BWUS	Sky 65-24 HAFB	040		16. 7.96	N.A.P.Bates	Tunbridge Wells	25. 5.02A
G-BWUT	de Havilland DHC-1 Chipmunk 22	C1/0918	WZ879	4. 6.96	Aero Vintage Ltd *(As "WZ879/73")*	(Rye)	22. 3.03
G-BWUU	Cameron N-90 HAFB	3954		17. 7.96	South Western Electricity plc	Bristol	27. 6.01A
G-BWUV	de Havilland DHC-1 Chipmunk 22A	C1/0655	WK640	18. 7.96	P.Ray *(As "WK640/C")*	Wombleton	16. 8.03
G-BWUW	British Aircraft Corporation BAC.145 Jet Provost T.5A	EEP/JP/1045	XW423	18. 7.96	Tindon Ltd *(As "XW423/14")*	(Little Snoring)	14. 2.02P
G-BWUZ	Campbell Cricket (Rotax 582)	PFA G/03-1267		24. 6.96	M.A.Concannon	Henstridge	20. 3.02P
G-BWVB	Pietenpol Aircamper (Continental O-200-A)	PFA 047-11777		24. 7.96	M.J.Whatley	White Waltham	1.11.02P
G-BWVC	Jodel D.18	PFA 169-11331		29. 7.96	R.W.J. Cripps	(Spondon, Derby)	
G-BWVH	Robinson R44 Astro	0072	SX-HDE (D-HBBT)	10. 9.96	Glenwood Transport Ltd	(Naas, Co.Kildare)	30. 9.02T
G-BWVI	Stern ST.80 Balade (VW 1834)	PFA 166-11190		7. 8.96	M.P.Wakem	Barton	1. 7.02P
G-BWVL	Cessna 150M	15077229	N50NA N63286	13. 8.96	A.H.Shaw	Gloucestershire	18. 1.03T
G-BWVM	Colt AA-1050 Gas FB	3806		14. 8.96	B.B.Baxter Ltd.	London SE16	29. 7.01A
G-BWVN	Whittaker MW7	PFA 171-11839		19. 8.96	R.K.Willcox	(Bristol)	
G-BWVR	IAV-Bacau Yakovlev Yak-52	878202	LY-AKQ DOSAAF 134	27. 8.96	J.H. Askew *"52"*	Barton	24. 7.02P
G-BWVS	Europa Aviation Europa (Rotax 912-UL)	PFA 247-12686		28. 8.96	D.R.Bishop	Kemble	9. 4.02P
G-BWVT	de Havilland DHA.82A Tiger Moth *(Built DH Australia)*	1039	N1350 VH-SNZ/A17-604/VH-AIN/A17-604	27. 8.96	R.Jewitt *(On rebuild 2000)*	(Horley)	
G-BWVU	Cameron O-90 HAFB	3204		28. 8.96	J.Atkinson	Dorchester	26. 1.99A
G-BWVV	Jodel D.18 (VW 1834)	PFA 169-12699		29. 8.96	P.Cooper	Sherburn in Elmet	22.11.02P
G-BWVY	de Havilland DHC-1 Chipmunk 22	C1/0766	WP896	3. 9.96	P.W.Portelli *(As "WP896/M")*	Audley End	17. 6.04
G-BWVZ	de Havilland DHC-1 Chipmunk 22	C1/0614	WK590	16. 7.96	D.Campion *(As "WK590/69")*	Grimbergen, Belgium	18.10.02
G-BWWA	Ultravia Pelican Club GS (Rotax 912-UL)	PFA 165-12242		6. 9.96	T.J.Franklin & D.S.Simpson	(Hitchin)	21. 5.02P
G-BWWB	Europa Aviation Europa (Rotax 912-UL)	PFA 247-12670		9. 9.96	M.G.Dolphin *"The Wheelbarrow"*	RAF Syerston	21. 2.02P
G-BWWC	de Havilland DH.104 Dove 7 *(Wings from G-APSO fitted early 2000)*	04498	XM223	14. 6.96	Air Atlantique Ltd *(As "XM223")*	Coventry	
G-BWWE	Lindstrand LBL-90A HAFB	410		11. 9.96	B.J.Newman	Rushden, Northants	18. 3.01T
G-BWWF	Cessna 185A Skywagon	185-0240	N4893K G-BWWF/9J-MCK/5Y-BBG/ET-ACI/N4040Y	13. 9.96	S M Craig Harvey	Hinton-in-the-Hedges	15.10.03
G-BWWG	SOCATA Rallye 235E Gabier	13121	EI-BIF HB-EYT/N344RA	23.10.96	J.McEleney	City of Derry	18. 5.03
G-BWWH	Yakovlev Yak-50	853010	LY-ABL LY-XNI/DOSAAF	16. 9.96	De Cadenet Motor Racing Ltd *"853010"*	Little Gransden	17. 5.02P
G-BWWI	Aérospatiale AS332L Super Puma	2040	OY-HMF (G-TIGT)	11. 9.96	Bristow Helicopters Ltd *"Johnshaven"*	Aberdeen	8.11.02T
G-BWWJ	Hughes 269C (300C)	113-0256	G-BMYZ N8996F	25. 2.87	Dave Nieman Toys Ltd *(Current status unknown)*	Milton Common, Oxon	28.10.96
G-BWWK	Hawker Nimrod I (RR Kestrel)	41H-43617	S1581	13. 9.96	Historic Aircraft Collection Ltd (Jersey) *(As "S1581/573" of 802 Sqdn)*	Duxford	16. 5.02P
G-BWWL	Colt Flying Egg SS HAFB	1813	JA-A0513	19. 9.96	Magical Adventures Ltd	(USA)	2. 8.01
G-BWWN	Isaacs Fury II (Lycoming O-235-H2C)	PFA 011-10957		23. 9.96	R.I.Warman *(As "K8303/D")*	Priory Farm, Tibenham	13 .6.02P
G-BWWP	Rans S-6-116 Coyote II (Rotax 582)	PFA 204A-12648		2.10.96	S.A.Beddus	Cherry Tree Farm, Monewden	20. 8.99P

G-BWWS	Rotary Air Force RAF 2000 GTX-SE	PFA G/13-1277		7.10.96	R.I.Grant	(Bristol)	1. 2.01P
G-BWWT	Dornier 328-110	3022	D-CDXO VT-VIG/D-CDHG	12.11.96	Suckling Airways (Luton) Ltd t/a Scot Airways	Cambridge	12.11.02T
G-BWWU	Piper PA-22-150 Tri-Pacer *(Hoerner wing-tips: tail-wheel conversion)*	22-5002	N7139D	9.10.96	Aerocars Ltd	Lower Upham	26. 5.02
G-BWWW	British Aerospace Jetstream Srs.3102	614	G-31-614	18. 7.83	BAE Systems (Operations) Ltd	Warton	9. 2.01A
G-BWWX	Yakovlev Yak-50	853003	LY-AOI DOSAAF	11.10.96	J.L.Pfundt	Hilversum, The Netherlands	25. 2.02P
G-BWWY	Lindstrand LBL-105A HAFB	411		14.10.96	M.J.Smith	Westow, York	28. 7.02T
G-BWWZ	Denney Kitfox mk.3 (Rotax 912)	PFA 172-13054		15.10.96	A.I.Eskander	Barton	20..6.02P
G-BWXA	Slingsby T.67M-260 Firefly	2236		19. 3.96	Babcock Rosyth Defence Ltd t/a Hunting Contract Services *(Op JEFTS)*	RAF Barkston Heath	27. 6.02T
G-BWXB	Slingsby T.67M-260 Firefly	2237		19. 3.96	Babcock Rosyth Defence Ltd t/a Hunting Contract Services *(Op JEFTS)*	RAF Barkston Heath	17. 7.02T
G-BWXC	Slingsby T.67M-260 Firefly	2238		19. 3.96	Babcock Rosyth Defence Ltd t/a Hunting Contract Services *(Op JEFTS)*	RAF Barkston Heath	1. 8.02T
G-BWXD	Slingsby T.67M-260 Firefly	2239		19. 3.96	Babcock Rosyth Defence Ltd t/a Hunting Contract Services *(Op JEFTS)*	RAF Barkston Heath	15. 8.02T
G-BWXE	Slingsby T.67M-260 Firefly	2240		19. 3.96	Babcock Rosyth Defence Ltd t/a Hunting Contract Services *(Op JEFTS)*	RAF Barkston Heath	28. 8.02T
G-BWXF	Slingsby T.67M-260 Firefly	2241		19. 3.96	Babcock Rosyth Defence Ltd t/a Hunting Contract Services *(Op JEFTS)*	RAF Barkston Heath	5. 9.02T
G-BWXG	Slingsby T.67M-260 Firefly	2242		19. 3.96	Babcock Rosyth Defence Ltd t/a Hunting Contract Services *(Op JEFTS)*	RAF Barkston Heath	23. 9.02T
G-BWXH	Slingsby T.67M-260 Firefly	2243		19. 3.96	Babcock Rosyth Defence Ltd t/a Hunting Contract Services *(Op JEFTS)*	RAF Barkston Heath	20.10.02T
G-BWXI	Slingsby T.67M-260 Firefly	2244		19. 3.96	Babcock Rosyth Defence Ltd t/a Hunting Contract Services *(Op JEFTS)*	RAF Barkston Heath	7.10.02T
G-BWXJ	Slingsby T.67M-260 Firefly	2245		19. 3.96	Babcock Rosyth Defence Ltd t/a Hunting Contract Services *(Op JEFTS)*	RAF Barkston Heath	28.10.02T
G-BWXK	Slingsby T.67M-260 Firefly	2246		19. 3.96	Babcock Rosyth Defence Ltd t/a Hunting Contract Services *(Op JEFTS)*	RAF Barkston Heath	5.11.02T
G-BWXL	Slingsby T.67M-260 Firefly	2247		19. 3.96	Babcock Rosyth Defence Ltd t/a Hunting Contract Services *(Op JEFTS)*	RAF Barkston Heath	20.11.02T
G-BWXM	Slingsby T.67M-260 Firefly	2248		19. 3.96	Babcock Rosyth Defence Ltd t/a Hunting Contract Services *(Op JEFTS)*	RAF Barkston Heath	26.11.02T
G-BWXN	Slingsby T.67M-260 Firefly	2249		19. 3.96	Babcock Rosyth Defence Ltd t/a Hunting Contract Services *(Op JEFTS)*	RAF Barkston Heath	4.12.02T
G-BWXO	Slingsby T.67M-260 Firefly	2250		19. 3.96	Babcock Rosyth Defence Ltd t/a Hunting Contract Services *(Op JEFTS)*	RAF Barkston Heath	21.12.02T
G-BWXP	Slingsby T.67M-260 Firefly	2251		19. 3.96	Babcock Rosyth Defence Ltd t/a Hunting Contract Services *(Op JEFTS)*	RAF Barkston Heath	8. 1.03T
G-BWXR	Slingsby T.67M-260 Firefly	2252		19. 3.96	Babcock Rosyth Defence Ltd t/a Hunting Contract Services *(Op JEFTS)*	RAF Barkston Heath	13. 1.03T
G-BWXS	Slingsby T.67M-260 Firefly	2253		19. 3.96	Babcock Rosyth Defence Ltd t/a Hunting Contract Services *(Op JEFTS) "6"*	RAF Barkston Heath	29. 1.03T
G-BWXT	Slingsby T.67M-260 Firefly	2254		19. 3.96	Babcock Rosyth Defence Ltd t/a Hunting Contract Services *(Op JEFTS)*	RAF Barkston Heath	5. 2.03T
G-BWXU	Slingsby T.67M-260 Firefly	2255		19. 3.96	Babcock Rosyth Defence Ltd t/a Hunting Contract Services *(Op JEFTS)*	RAF Barkston Heath	11. 2.03T

G-BWXV	Slingsby T.67M-260 Firefly	2256		19. 3.96	Babcock Rosyth Defence Ltd t/a Hunting Contract Services *(Op JEFTS)*	RAF Barkston Heath	20. 2.03T
G-BWXW	Slingsby T.67M-260 Firefly	2257		19. 3.96	Babcock Rosyth Defence Ltd t/a Hunting Contract Services *(Op JEFTS)*	RAF Barkston Heath	27. 2.03T
G-BWXX	Slingsby T.67M-260 Firefly	2258		19. 3.96	Babcock Rosyth Defence Ltd t/a Hunting Contract Services *(Op JEFTS)*	RAF Barkston Heath	11. 3.03T
G-BWXY	Slingsby T.67M-260 Firefly	2259		19. 3.96	Babcock Rosyth Defence Ltd t/a Hunting Contract Services *(Op JEFTS)*	RAF Barkston Heath	13. 3.03T
G-BWXZ	Slingsby T.67M-260 Firefly	2260		19. 3.96	Babcock Rosyth Defence Ltd t/a Hunting Contract Services *(Op JEFTS)*	RAF Barkston Heath	26. 3.03T
G-BWYB	Piper PA-28-160 Cherokee	28-263	N6374A G-BWYB/6Y-JLO/6Y-JCH/VP-JCH	16. 9.96	I.M.Latiff	Little Staughton	9..8.03
G-BWYC	Cameron N-90 HAFB	3994		17.10.96	Cameron Balloons Ltd	Bristol	14. 9.02A
G-BWYD	Europa Aviation Europa (Rotax 912-UL)	PFA 247-12621		28. 8.96	H.J.Bendiksen	Biggin Hill	28. 8.02P
G-BWYE	Cessna 310R II	310R1654	F-GBPE (N26369)	6. 9.96	Air Charter Scotland Ltd	Edinburgh	8.12.02T
G-BWYG	Cessna 310R II	310R1580	F-GBMY (N1820E)	28.10.96	R.F.Jones t/a Kissair Aviation	(London SE10)	20.11.03T
G-BWYH	Cessna 310R II	310R1640	F-GBPC N2634Y	28.10.96	Air Charter Scotland Ltd	Edinburgh	4. 6.03T
G-BWYI	Denney Kitfox mk.3 (Rotax 912)	PFA 172-12143		30.10.96	J.Adamson	Beeches Farm, South Scarle	30. 3.02P
G-BWYK	Yakovlev Yak-50	812004	RA-01386 DOSAAF 51	9. 8.96	Titan Airways Ltd	North Weald	14. 1.03P
G-BWYM	HOAC DV-20 Katana	20067	D-EWAU	27. 1.97	Plane Talking Ltd	Elstree	18. 6.03T
G-BWYN	Cameron O-77 HAFB	1162	G-ODER	13.11.96	W.H.Morgan *"Hobo"*	Swansea	29. 4.01A
G-BWYO	Sequoia Falco F.8L (Lycoming O-320-E2A)	PFA 100-10920		7.11.96	N.G.Abbott & J.Copeland	Flamstone Park, Bishopstone	29. 4.02P
	(Bounced landing Flamstone Park 14.7.01 & struck oil-seed rape crop: rear fuselage broke off aft of cockpit canopy)						
G-BWYP	Sky 56-24 HAFB	053		8.11.96	S.A.Townley t/a Sky High Leisure	Wrexham	9.11.01A
G-BWYR	Rans S-6-116 Coyote II (Rotax 912-UL)	PFA 204A-13058		8.11.96	R.C.Burden	Bagby	23. 8.02P
G-BWYS	Cameron O-120 HAFB	3997		30. 9.96	J.M.Stables t/a Aire Valley Balloons	Knaresborough	10. 6.02T
G-BWYU	Sky 120-24 HAFB	052		13.11.96	D.J.Tofton	Warboys	26. 5.02A
G-BWYZ*	Pilatus Britten-Norman BN-2B-20 Islander	2300		2.12.96	Britten-Norman Ltd *(Cancelled 19.10.00 as temporarily wfu)*	Bembridge	
G-BWZA	Europa Aviation Europa (Rotax 912-UL)	63 & PFA 247-12626		1.11.96	M.C.Costin	Sywell	13. 7.02P
G-BWZD	Avid Flyer Mk.4	PFA 189-12453		29.11.96	B.Moore	(Keady, Co.Armagh)	
G-BWZF*	Pilatus Britten-Norman BN-2B-20 Islander	2301		12.12.96	Britten-Norman Ltd *(Cancelled 19.10.00 as temporarily wfu)*	Bembridge	
G-BWZG	Robin R.2160	311	F-WZZZ	6.11.96	Sherburn Aero Club Ltd	Sherburn in Elmet	17. 5.03T
G-BWZI	Agusta A109A II	7269	OH-HAD N109AK	29.11.96	P.W.Harris t/a Pendley Farm	Pendley Farm, Aldbury, Tring	5. 3.03T
G-BWZJ	Cameron A-250 HAFB	4021		2.12.96	Balloon School (International) Ltd t/a Balloon Club of Great Britain	Petworth	23 7.02T
G-BWZK	Cameron A-210 HAFB	4020		2.12.96	Balloon School (International) Ltd t/a Balloon Club of Great Britain	Petworth	24. 7.02T
G-BWZP	Cameron Home Special 105SS HAFB	4051		6.12.96	Flying Pictures Ltd *"Barclays Mortgages"*	Fairoaks	10. 4.02A
G-BWZT	Europa Aviation Europa (Rotax 912-UL) *(Mono-wheel u/c)*	PFA 247-12727		9.12.96	A.M.Smyth t/a G-BWZT Group	Crowfield	16. 9.02P
G-BWZU	Lindstrand LBL-90B HAFB	418		12.12.96	K.D.Pierce	Cranbrook, Kent	19. 8.01
G-BWZW	Bell 206B-3 JetRanger III	12	G-CTEK N7812S	26.11.96	R & M International Engineering Ltd	Dereham	15. 6.98T
G-BWZX	Aérospatiale AS332L Super Puma	2120	F-WQDX G-BWZX/F-WQDX/5V-MCD/5V-TAH/LN-OLE	12.12.96	Bristow Helicopters Ltd *"Muchalls"*	Aberdeen	5. 5.04T
G-BWZY	Hughes 269A	95-0378	G-FSDT N269CH/N1336D/64-18066	4.12.96	Katharine B.Elliott	Redhill	19. 6.04
G-BWZZ	Hunting Percival P.84 Jet Provost T.3A	PAC/W/9278	XM470	5. 9.96	R.G.Schreiber & J.P.Trevor	Hawarden	30. 9.01P

G-BXAA – G-BXZZ

G-BXAB	Piper PA-28-161 Warrior II	28-8416054	G-BTGK N4344C	7.10.96	TG Aviation Ltd	Manston	25. 4.03T
G-BXAC	Rotary Air Force RAF 2000 GTX-SE	PFA G/13-1279		21.11.96	D.C.Fairbrass	Fyfield	31. 5.02P
G-BXAD	Cameron Thunder Ax11-225 Srs.2 HAFB	4052		18.12.96	M E White	Dublin	21. 6.02T
G-BXAF	Pitts S-1D Special (Lycoming O-360)	PFA 09-12258		6.12.96	N.J.Watson	(Tattershall)	2. 5.02P
G-BXAH	Piel CP.301A Emeraude (Continental C90)	AB.422	D-EBAH	29.10.96	G.E.Valler	(Stafford)	6. 7.02P
G-BXAI	Cameron Colt 120A HAFB	4056		20.12.96	E.F. & R.F.Casswell	Maidstone	9. 6.00T
G-BXAJ	Lindstrand LBL-14A HAFB	425		23.12.96	Oscair Project AB	Taby, Sweden	
G-BXAK	IAV-Bacau Yakovlev Yak-52	811508	LY-ASC DOSAAF	23.12.96	J.G.McTaggart *(New owner 4.01)*	Cumbernauld	23. 4.02P
G-BXAL	Cameron Bertie Bassett 90SS HAFB	4034		13. 1.97	Trebor Bassett Ltd *"Bertie Bassett" (Op Balloon Preservation Group)*	Kirdford	27. 1.02A
G-BXAM	Cameron N-90 HAFB	4035		13. 1.97	Trebor Bassett Ltd *"Bertie Junior"*	Howden, Yorks	19. 4.02A
G-BXAN	Scheibe SF-25C Falke 1700	44299	D-KDGQ	13. 1.97	E.R.Boyle t/a C Falke Syndicate	Winthorpe	15.10.03
G-BXAO	Jabiru Jabiru SK (Jabiru 2200A)	PFA 274-13066		14. 1.97	P.J.Thompson	(Gaerwen)	23. 4.99P
					(Damaged Ledicot near Shobdon 3.5.98: current status unknown)		
G-BXAR	British Aerospace Avro 146-RJ100	E3298	G-6-298	27. 3.97	CityFlyer Express Ltd *(Delftblue Daybreak t/s)*	Gatwick	29. 3.03T
G-BXAS	British Aerospace Avro 146-RJ100	E3301	G-6-301	23. 4.97	CityFlyer Express Ltd *(Animals & Trees t/s)*	Gatwick	29. 4.03T
G-BXAU	Pitts S-1 Special (Lycoming O-320)	GHG.9	N9GG	22. 1.97	P J Tomlinson	Gloucestershire	6. 6.02P
G-BXAV	Aerostar Yakovlev Yak-52	9111608	RA-01325 DOSAAF 73	24. 1.97	Skytrace (UK) Ltd t/a G-BXAV Group *(As "DOSAAF 72")*	Wolverhampton	21. 2.02P
G-BXAX*	Cameron N-77 HAFB	2010		25. 5.89	Balloon Preservation Group *"Citroen" (Cancelled 31.1.02 as wfu)*	Kirdford	21.11.96A
G-BXAY	Bell 206B-3 JetRanger III	3946	N85EA N521RC/N3210D	24. 1.97	Viewdart Ltd	Conington	30. 7.03T
G-BXBA	Cameron A-210 HAFB	4072		10. 1.97	Reach For The Sky Ltd	Guildford	4. 6.02T
G-BXBB	Piper PA-20-135 Pacer *(Mod 150hp)*	20-959	EC-AOZ N1133C	24. 1.97	M.E.R.Coghlan *(On rebuild: current status unknown)*	Thornicombe, Dorset	
G-BXBC	Anderson EA-1 Kingfisher Amphibian	PFA 132-11302		28. 1.97	S.Bisham	Swanbister Farm, Orphir, Kirkwall	
G-BXBD	CASA I-131 Jungmann	1052	E3B-317	28. 1.97	P.B.Childs & B.L.Robinson	Kemble	
	(P/i uncertain as Jungmann "E3B-317" displayed Musee de Jean Tinguely, Basel, Switzerland: noted 1.02)						
G-BXBG	Cameron A-275 HAFB	4023		28. 1.97	M.L.Gabb	Alcester	10.10.01T
G-BXBH	Hunting Percival P.84 Jet Provost T.3A	PAC/W/9241	XM365	29. 1.97	G-BXBH Provost Ltd *(As "XM365")*	Little Snoring	31. 8.01P
G-BXBI	Hunting Percival P.84 Jet Provost T.3A	PAC/W/11799	XN510	29. 1.97	Global Aviation Ltd	(Binbrook)	
G-BXBK	Mudry/CAARP CAP.10B	17	N170RC French AF "307-SO"	30. 1.97	S.Skipworth	White Waltham	31. 7.03
G-BXBL	Lindstrand LBL-240A HAFB	317		31. 1.97	J.Fenton t/a Firefly Balloon Promotions	Preston	8.11.00T
G-BXBM	Cameron O-105 HAFB	3990		31. 1.97	P.Spellward *"Open University"* t/a Bristol University Hot Air Ballooning Society	Bristol	16. 2.02A
G-BXBN	Rans S-6-116 Coyote II (Rotax 582)	PFA 204A-13062		31. 1.97	A.G.Foster	North Coates	17. 5.01P
					(Crashed on approach mid 2001 and noted dismantled in hangar 7.01)		
G-BXBP	Denney Kitfox mk.2	PFA 172-12149		3. 2.97	G.S.Adams	Enniskillen, Co.Fermanagh	5.11.02P
G-BXBR	Cameron A-120 HAFB	1983	SE-ZDY	4. 2.97	M.G.Barlow	Skipton	
G-BXBT	Aérospatiale AS355F1 Twin Squirrel	5262	G-TMMC G-JLCO	11. 2.97	McAlpine Helicopters Ltd	Oxford	28. 9.04T
G-BXBU	Mudry/CAARP CAP.10B	103	N173RC French AF	11. 2.97	J.F.Cosgrave & H.R.Pearson	Denham	24. 6.03
G-BXBY	Cameron A-105 HAFB	4077		13. 2.97	S.P.Watkins *(Op D Littlewood) "Roman Baths"*	Bath	13. 5.02T
G-BXBZ	WSK PZL-104 Wilga 80 *(C/n quoted officially as CF21930941)*	CF21910941	EC-GDA ZK-PZQ	13. 2.97	P.G.Marks	Husbands Bosworth	25. 6.03
G-BXCA	Hapi Cygnet SF-2A (Rotax 912-UL)	PFA 182-12921		22. 1.97	J N Harley	Popham	5. 9.02P
G-BXCC	Piper PA-28-201T Turbo Dakota	28-7921068	D-EKBM N2855A	19. 2.97	Greer Aviation Ltd	Kirknewton	25. 7.03T
G-BXCD	TEAM mini-MAX 91A	PFA 186-12393		18. 2.97	R.Davies	South Cerney	26.10.02P

G-BXCG	CEA Jodel DR.250/160 Capitaine 60 & PFA 299-13146	D-EHGG	22. 5.97	J.M.Scott t/a G-BXCG Group	Cambridge	25. 8.02P
G-BXCH	Europa Aviation Europa (Rotax 912UL) 186 & PFA 247-12980		19. 2.97	D.M.Stevens	Haverfordwest	24. 5.02P
G-BXCJ	Campbell Cricket PFA G/03-1177 (Rotax 532)		24. 2.97	J.R.Cooper *(Damaged near Swansea 26.9.99: current status unknown)*	Swansea	11. 7.02P
G-BXCK	Cameron Douglas-Lurpak Butterman 110SS HAFB 4076		25. 2.97	Flying Pictures Ltd *"Douglas-Lurpak Butter"*	Fairoaks	8.10.02A
G-BXCL	Montgomerie Bensen B.8MR (Rotax 582) PFA G/01-1287		26. 2.97	A.D.Gordon	Blair Atholl	27. 9.02P
G-BXCM	Lindstrand LBL-150A HAFB 443		26. 2.97	A M Holly t/a Exclusive Ballooning	Berkeley	29. 4.00T
G-BXCN	Sky 105-24 HAFB 047		27. 2.97	Capricorn Balloons Ltd	Loughborough	16. 3.98T
G-BXCO	Colt 120A HAFB 4086		3. 3.97	G.C.Ludlow	Hythe, Kent	15. 6.01T
G-BXCP	de Havilland DHC-1 Chipmunk 22 C1/0744	WP859	27. 2.97	S.Conlan *(As "WP859")*	Kildare	15. 6.01
G-BXCS	Cameron N-90 HAFB 4122		4. 3.97	Flying Pictures Ltd *"Lurpak"*	Fairoaks	9. 5.02A
G-BXCT	de Havilland DHC-1 Chipmunk 22 C1/0145	WB697	3. 3.97	Wickenby Aviation Ltd *(As "WB697")*	Wickenby	2. 5.03T
G-BXCU	Rans S-6-116 Coyote II PFA 204A-13105 (Rotax 912UL)		6. 3.97	M.R.McNeil	Breighton	22. 6.02P
G-BXCV	de Havilland DHC-1 Chipmunk 22 C1/0807	WP929	3. 3.97	Ocean Flight Holdings Ltd *(As "WP929/F")*	Duxford	22.10.03T
G-BXCW	Denney Kitfox mk.3 PFA 172-12619		6. 3.97	M.J.Blanchard	(Swanage)	
G-BXDA	de Havilland DHC-1 Chipmunk 22 C1/0747	WP860	7. 3.97	S.R.Cleary *(As "WP860/6")*	Cumbernauld	17. 6.03
G-BXDB	Cessna U206F Stationair U20602233	G-BMNZ F-BVJT/N1519U	18.12.96	Tindon Ltd	Little Snoring	6. 8.04T
G-BXDD	Rotary Air Force RAF 2000 GTX-SE PFA G/13-1284		9. 1.97	R.M.Savage t/a Roger Savage (Photography)	Carlisle	4. 7.00P
G-BXDE	Rotary Air Force RAF 2000 GTX-SE PFA G/13-1280		14. 1.97	A.McRedie	Carlisle	23. 1.02P
G-BXDF	Beechcraft 95-B55 Baron TC-2011	SE-IXG OY-ASB	7. 3.97	Chesh-Air Ltd	Liverpool	17. 1.03T
G-BXDG	de Havilland DHC-1 Chipmunk 22 C1/0644	WK630	7. 3.97	R.E.Dagless	Swanton Morley	16. 8.04
G-BXDH	de Havilland DHC-1 Chipmunk 22 C1/0270	WD331	10. 3.97	Victory Workwear Ltd *(As "WD331")*	Kemble	21. 1.01
G-BXDI	de Havilland DHC-1 Chipmunk 22 C1/0312	WD373	10. 3.97	J.R.Gore *(As "WD373/12" in RAF c/s)*	Gloucestershire	31.10.03
G-BXDL	Hunting Percival P.84 Jet Provost T.3A PAC/W/9286	8983M XM478	18. 3.97	Seagull Formation Ltd *(As "XM478")*	Bournemouth	15. 3.02P
G-BXDM	de Havilland DHC-1 Chipmunk 22 C1/0723	WP840	28. 2.97	The RAF Halton Aeroplane Club Ltd (As "WP840/9")	RAF Halton	25. 6.03T
G-BXDN	de Havilland DHC-1 Chipmunk 22 C1/0618	WK609	18. 3.97	W.D.Lowe & L.A.Edwards *(As "WK609/93")*	Booker	1.11.03
G-BXDO	Rutan Cozy PFA 159-12032 (Lycoming O-235-C2C)		21. 3.97	C.R.Blackburn	(Kirk Michael, IoM)	18.12.02P
G-BXDP	de Havilland DHC-1 Chipmunk 22 C1/0659	WK642	27. 2.97	J.S.J.Valentine & J.P.Conlan *(As "WK642")*	Kildare	11. 9.03
G-BXDR	Lindstrand LBL-77A HAFB 441		25. 3.97	British Telecommunications plc *"Bright Future"*	(Thatcham, Berks)	12. 3.01A
G-BXDS	Bell 206B-3 JetRanger III 2734	G-OVBJ G-BXDS/OY-HDK/N661PS	19. 2.98	Sterling Helicopters Ltd	Norwich	24. 7.03T
G-BXDT	Robin HR.200/120B 315		25. 3.97	Multiflight Ltd	Leeds-Bradford	3. 6.03T
G-BXDU	Aero Designs Pulsar PFA 202-11991		25. 3.97	M.P.Board	(London E4)	
G-BXDV	Sky 105-24 HAFB 049		26. 3.97	J.Skinner	Maidstone	5. 7.01
G-BXDW	Sky 120-24 HAFB 059		26. 3.97	M. & S.M.Sarti *"Sky-Q-West"*	Fowey	21. 3.01T
G-BXDY	Europa Aviation Europa PFA 247-12914 (Rotax 912UL) *(Mono-wheel u/c)*		27. 3.97	D.G. & S.Watts *"The Rocketeer"*	Rochester	1. 2.02P
G-BXDZ*	Lindstrand LBL-105A HAFB 437		4. 4.97	M.A.Webb *(Cancelled 2.3.00 by CAA)*	Yarcombe	14. 4.99A
G-BXEA	Rotary Air Force RAF 2000 GTX-SE PFA G/13-1270		2. 4.97	R.Firth	Netherthorpe	19. 1.02P
G-BXEB	Rotary Air Force RAF 2000 GTX-SE PFA G/13-1285		2. 4.97	Penny Hydraulics Ltd	Netherthorpe	19. 1.02P
G-BXEC	de Havilland DHC-1 Chipmunk 22 C1/0647	WK633	3. 4.97	M.F.Watts t/a M.A.D.Flying Group *(As "WK633/B")*	Gamston	27. 4.03
G-BXEE	Enstrom 280C Shark 1117	OH-HAN N336AT	9. 4.97	S.T.Raby	Grange Farm, Woodwalton	28. 6.04
G-BXEF	Europa Aviation Europa PFA 247-12790		7. 4.97	C. & W.P.Busuttil-Reynaud	(Emsworth, Hants)	

G-BXEJ	VPM M16 Tandem Trainer	D-9302	D-MIFF	8. 4.97	N.H.Collins	Cork Farm, Streethay	15.10.01P
	(Arrow GT 1000)				t/a AES Radionic Surveillance Systems		
G-BXEN	Cameron N-105 HAFB	4090		11. 4.97	G.Aimo	Mondovi, Italy	14. 6.02A
G-BXEP	Lindstrand LBL-14M HAFB	460		14. 4.97	Lindstrand Balloons Ltd	Oswestry	19. 5.00A
G-BXER	Piper PA-46-350P Malibu Mirage	4636110		21. 7.97	Glasdon Group Ltd	Blackpool	3. 9.03
G-BXES	Hunting Percival P.66 Pembroke C.1		N4234C	14. 4.97	Atlantic Air Transport Ltd	Coventry	8. 8.01P
	(Regd with c/n PAC/W/3032)	P66/101	9042M/XL954		*(As "XL954")*		
G-BXET	Piper PA-38-112 Tomahawk	38-80A0028	N25089	14. 4.97	APB Leasing Ltd	Welshpool	10. 8.03T
G-BXEX	Piper PA-28-181 Cherokee Archer II	28-7790463	N3562Q	16. 4.97	R.Mayle	Biggin Hill	12. 5.03T
G-BXEY	Colt AS-105GD Hot-Air Airship	3936		15. 4.97	D.Mayer	Neidenstein, Germany	10. 9.02A
G-BXEZ	Cessna 182P Skylane II	18264344	OH-CHJ	16. 4.97	Forhawk Ltd	Bodmin	6. 1.03T
	(Reims assembled c/n F18200054)		N1479M				
G-BXFB	Pitts S-1 Special	9543	N77ZZ	16. 4.97	D.Dobson	Deenethorpe	3. 1.02P
	(Lycoming O-360-A4A)						
G-BXFC	Jodel D.18	PFA 169-11322		17. 4.97	B.S.Godbold	Little Gransden	24. 7.02P
G-BXFD	Enstrom 280C Shark	1084	N88MD	18. 4.97	R.Collenette	Bournemouth	25. 7.03T
			N632H				
G-BXFE	Mudry/CAARP CAP.10B	135	N175RC	18. 4.97	Avion Aerobatic Ltd	(London N1)	26. 3.04T
			French AF				
G-BXFG	Europa Aviation Europa	PFA 247-12500		21. 4.97	A.Rawicz-Szczerbo	Eaglescott	8..4.02P
	(Rotax 912-UL)						
G-BXFI	Hawker Hunter T.7	41H-670815	WV372	24. 4.97	Fox-One Ltd	Kemble	13. 9.02P
					(As "WV372/R" of 2 Sqn)		
G-BXFK	CFM Streak Shadow K.206 &	PFA 206-12329		24. 4.97	D.Adcock	Old Buckenham	11.10.01P
	(Rotax 582) *(Four-bladed propellor)*						
G-BXFN	Cameron Colt 77A HAFB	4145		25. 4.97	Cameron Balloons Ltd	Bristol	26. 8.01A
G-BXFP	British Aircraft Corporation BAC.167 Strikemaster mk.87						
		EEP/JP/2873 & PS.165	OJ5	29. 4.97	C.J.& S.M.Thompson	North Weald	27. 7.01P
		(or PS.171?)	Botswana DF/Kenyan AF 602/G-27-192		*(As "NZ6361" in RNZAF c/s)*		
G-BXFU	British Aircraft Corporation BAC.167 Strikemaster mk.83						
		EEP/JP/???? & PS.158	OJ1	29. 4.97	Global Aviation Ltd	Humberside	6. 8.02P
			Botswana DF/ZG805/Kuwait AF 110/G-27-151		*(As "OJ-1")*		
G-BXFV	British Aircraft Corporation BAC.167 Strikemaster mk.83						
		EEP/JP/???? & PS.173	OJ8	29. 4.97	Global Aviation Ltd	Humberside	19. 6.02P
			Botswana DF/ZG811/Kuwait AF 119/G-27-188		*(As "OJ-8")*		
G-BXFY	Cameron Bierkrug-90 SS HAFB	4133	D-OIBP	29. 4.97	Ballooning Bavaria	Ruhstorf, Germany	27. 2.02A
			G-BXFY				
G-BXFZ*	Sky 65-24 HAFB	065		22. 4.97	Aerial Promotions Ltd	Cannock	14. 5.99A
		(Stolen & recovered in damaged state 4.99: cancelled 2.11.01: current status unknown)					
G-BXGA	Eurocopter AS 350B2 Ecureuil	2493	OO-RCH	30. 4.97	PLM Dollar Group Ltd.	Inverness	27. 8.03T
			OO-XCH/F-WZFX				
G-BXGC	Cameron N-105 HAFB	4137		6. 5.97	Cliveden Ltd	Bath	16. 5.02T
					"The Royal Crescent Hotel" (Op Ascent Balloons)		
G-BXGD	Sky 90-24 HAFB	067		6. 5.97	Servo & Electronic Sales Ltd	Lydd	11. 6.02T
G-BXGE	Cessna 152 II	15282700	N89283	8. 5.97	APB Leasing Ltd	Tatenhill	16. 7.00T
					(Noted 9.01 less wings)		
G-BXGG	Europa Aviation Europa	PFA 247-12803		29. 4.97	C.J.H & P.A.J.Richardson	(Tiverton)	23. 9.02P
	(Rotax 912-UL)						
G-BXGH	Diamond DA-20-A1 Katana	10151		20. 5.97	Diamond Aircraft Industries GmbH		
					(Op Cumbernauld School of Flying)	Cumbernauld	21. 6.04T
G-BXGK	Lindstrand LBL-203M HAFB	468		12. 5.97	Lindstrand Balloons Ltd	Oswestry	
G-BXGL	de Havilland DHC-1 Chipmunk 22	C1/0924	WZ884	12. 5.97	Airways Aero Associations Ltd	Booker	26.10.03T
					(Op British Airways Flying Club) (BOAC c/s)		
G-BXGM	de Havilland DHC-1 Chipmunk 22	C1/0806	WP928	9. 5.97	M.A.Petrie	Shoreham	28.10.03
					(As "WP928/D")		
G-BXGO	de Havilland DHC-1 Chipmunk 22	C1/0097	WB654	13. 5.97	A.Judd	Booker	26.10.03
					t/a Trees Group *(As "WB654/U")*		
G-BXGP	de Havilland DHC-1 Chipmunk 22	C1/0927	WZ882	12. 5.97	J.Pote	Eaglescott	20. 8.04T
					t/a Eaglescott Chipmunk Group *(As "WZ882/K")*		
G-BXGS	Rotary Air Force RAF 2000 GTX-SE	PFA G/13-1290		14. 5.97	C.R.Gordon	(Cupar)	21.12.01P
G-BXGT	III Sky Arrow 650T	PFA 298-13085		7. 5.97	Sky Arrow (Kits) UK Ltd	Old Sarum	29. 6.02P
	(Rotax 912-UL)						
G-BXGV	Cessna 172R Skyhawk II	17280240	N9300F	7. 1.98	Billingshurst Holdings Ltd	White Waltham	8. 2.04T
G-BXGW	Robin HR.200/120B	317		16. 5.97	Multiflight Ltd	Leeds-Bradford	3.10.03T
					(Op Multiflight Flying Club)		
G-BXGX	de Havilland DHC-1 Chipmunk 22	C1/0609	WK586	19. 5.97	Interflight (Air Charter) Ltd	Blackbushe	24.10.03
					(As "WK586")		
G-BXGY	Cameron V-65 HAFB	4125		18. 4.97	Gone With The Wind Ltd	Hungerford	13. 1.02A
G-BXGZ	Stemme S-10V	14-023	D-KSTE	18. 8.97	D.Tucker & K.Lloyd *"S10"*	Aston Down	10. 1.04
			EC-GGD/D-KGDF		*(Noted 5.01)*		

G-BXHA	de Havilland DHC-1 Chipmunk 22	C1/0801	WP925	20. 5.97	F.A.de Munck & C.S.Huijers *(As "WP925/C" in Army c/s)*	(Seppe, The Netherlands)	28. 8.03
G-BXHD	Beechcraft 76 Duchess	ME-284	OY-ARM N223JC	22. 5.97	S.J.Skilton t/a Aviation Rentals *(Op Professional Air Training)*	Bournemouth	7. 8.03T
G-BXHE	Lindstrand LBL-105A HAFB	459		23. 5.97	Independent Insurance Co Ltd	London EC3	11. 3.01T
G-BXHF	de Havilland DHC-1 Chipmunk 22	C1/0808	WP930	28. 5.97	R.Beresford *(As "WP930/J")*	Redhill	23. 5.04
G-BXHH	Grumman-American AA-5A Cheetah	AA5A-0105	N9705U	3. 6.97	M.G.Greenslade t/a Oaklands Flying	Biggin Hill	6. 6.03T
G-BXHJ	Hapi Cygnet SF-2A (VW 1835)	PFA 182-12159		29. 5.97	I.J.Smith	Brook Farm, Boylestone, Derby	
G-BXHL	Sky 77-24 HAFB	055		29. 5.97	R.K.Gyselynck *"Harlequin"*	Port Erin, IoM	5. 6.02
G-BXHM*	Lindstrand LBL-25A Cloudhopper HAFB	466		30. 5.97	Balloon Preservation Group *"Bud Ice/Michelob" (Cancelled 6.11.01 as wfu)*	Kirdford	7. 5.00A
G-BXHN*	Lindstrand Budweiser Can SS HAFB	465		30. 5.97	Balloon Preservation Group *"Budweiser Can" (Cancelled 6.11.01 as wfu)*	Kirdford	8. 3.01A
G-BXHO	Lindstrand Telewest Sphere SS HAFB			30. 5.97	Flying Pictures Ltd *"Telewest"*	Fairoaks	21. 3.01A
G-BXHP	Lindstrand LBL-105A HAFB	458		30. 5.97	Flying Pictures Ltd *"Britannia"*	Fairoaks	5. 7.02A
G-BXHR	Stemme S-10V	14-030		23. 7.97	J.H.Rutherford	Teesside	11. 9.03
G-BXHU	Campbell Cricket mk.6 (Rotax 503) *(Officially regd with c/n PFA G/16-1293)*	PFA G/16-1292		3. 6.97	P.J.Began *(Noted 11.01)*	Carlisle	31. 5.02P
G-BXHY	Europa Aviation Europa (Rotax 912-UL) *(Mono-wheel u/c)*	PFA 247-12514		6. 6.97	A.L.Thorne & B.Lewis t/a Jupiter Flying Group	White Waltham	19. 2.02P
G-BXHZ	Supermarine 361 Spitfire HF.IX	CBAF.10164	SAAF??? SM520	9. 6.97	A.G.Dunkerley *(On rebuild in Oxfordshire 6.97: current status unknown)*	(Bury)	
G-BXIA	de Havilland DHC-1 Chipmunk 22	C1/0056	WB615	9. 6.97	W.Askew, G.Bullock & C.Duckett t/a Dales Aviation *(As "WB615/E") (Stored 12.01)*	Blackpool	16. 3.01T
G-BXIC	Cameron A-275 HAFB	4162		9. 6.97	A.J.Street	Exeter	21. 2.02T
G-BXID	IAV-Bacau Yakovlev Yak-52	888802	LY-ALG DOSAAF 74	10. 6.97	E.S.Ewen	Kemble	25. 2.02P
G-BXIE	Cameron Colt 77B HAFB	4181		11. 6.97	The Aerial Display Co Ltd *(Michelin titles)*	Looe	19. 7.01A
G-BXIF	Piper PA-28-181 Cherokee Archer II	28-7690404	PH-SWM OO-HAY/N6827J	12. 6.97	Piper Flight Ltd	RAF Brize Norton	9. 7.03T
G-BXIG	Zenair CH-701 STOL (Rotax 912-UL)	PFA 187-12065		16. 6.97	A.J.Perry	Goodwood	20. 5.02P
G-BXIH	Sky 200-24 HAFB	076		16. 6.97	G.C.Ludlow	Hythe	13. 8.02P
G-BXII	Europa Aviation Europa	PFA 247-12812		30. 4.97	D.A.McFadyean	(Alvechurch, Birmingham)	
G-BXIJ	Europa Aviation Europa (Rotax 912UL) *(Mono-wheel u/c)*	PFA 247-12698		16. 6.97	D.G. & E.A.Bligh *"Bligh's Ballistic"*	(Nairn)	16.5.01P
G-BXIM	de Havilland DHC-1 Chipmunk 22	C1/0548	WK512	13. 5.97	P.R.Joshua & A.B.Ascroft *(As "WK512/A/ARMY")*	RAF Brize Norton	2. 7.03
G-BXIO	SAN Jodel DR.1050M Excellance	493	F-BNIO	16. 5.97	D.N.K. & M.A.Symon	Perth	3. 7.04
G-BXIT	Zebedee V-31 HAFB	Z1/3999		8. 5.97	P.J.Bish t/a Zebedee Balloon Service	Hungerford	
G-BXIV	Agusta A109A	7135	F-GERU HB-XOK/D-HFZF	13. 6.97	Heli-Tele Ltd	North Weald	22.10.04T
G-BXIW	Sky 105-24 HAFB	073		24. 6.97	L.A.Watts	Pangbourne, Reading	8. 5.02
G-BXIX	VPM M-16 Tandem Trainer (Arrow GT1000R)	PFA G/12-1292		13. 6.97	D.Beevers	Pocklington	12. 7.00P
G-BXIY	Blake Bluetit (Gnat 32hp)	01	BAPC37	26. 6.97	J.Bryant *(Pre-war composite from Spartans G-AAGN/G-AAJB & Avro 504K: on rebuild 10.01)*	North Weald	
G-BXIZ*	Lindstrand LBL-31A HAFB	476		3. 7.97	Hyundai Car (UK) Ltd *(Cancelled 7.1.00 as wfu)*	High Wycombe	24. 7.00A
G-BXJA	Cessna 402B	402B0356	N5753M XA-RFK/N5753M	17. 7.97	Air Charter Scotland Ltd	Edinburgh	23. 1.04T
G-BXJB	IAV-Bacau Yakovlev Yak-52	877403	LY-ABR DOSAAF 15	30. 6.97	A.M.Playford, D.J.Young & N. Willson *"15"*	Poplar Hall Farm, Elmsett	16. 5.02P
G-BXJC	Cameron A-210 HAFB	4191		2. 7.97	Balloon School (International) Ltd t/a British School of Ballooning	Petworth	23. 7.02T
G-BXJD	Piper PA-28-180 Cherokee C	28-4215	OY-BBZ	27. 6.97	BCT Aircraft Leasing Ltd *(Op Bristol Flying Club)*	Filton	14.11.03T
G-BXJG	Lindstrand LBL-105B HAFB	478		11. 7.97	C.E.Wood	Witham	27. 6.02T
G-BXJH	Cameron N-42 HAFB	4194		15. 7.97	Flying Pictures Ltd *"Unipart"*	Fairoaks	22. 9.01A
G-BXJI	Tri-R Kis	PFA 239-12573		2. 7.97	R.M.Wakeford *(F/f 21.10.00: damaged during take-off early 4.01 losing undercarriage & under repair)*	Cumbernauld	
G-BXJJ	Piper PA-28-161 Cadet	2841200	G-GFCC N9189N	26. 6.97	Plane Talking Ltd *(Op Denham School of Flying)*	Denham	13.12.04T
G-BXJM	Cessna 152 II	15282380	OO-HOQ F-GHOQ/N68797	15. 7.97	E.Alexander	Andrewsfield	20. 8.03T
G-BXJO	Cameron O-90 HAFB	4190		16. 7.97	W.I. & C.Hooker	Nottingham	26. 6.01T

G-BXJP	Cameron C-80 HAFB	4171		17. 7.97	AR Cobaleno Pasta Fresca SRL	Perugia, Italy	16. 7.00A
G-BXJS	Schempp-Hirth Janus CM	35/265	OH-819	7. 7.97	R.A.Hall t/a Janus Syndicate	Enstone	17. 8.03
G-BXJT	Sky 90-24 HAFB	072		18. 7.97	J.G. O'Connell	Braintree	25. 1.02A
G-BXJU*	Sky 90-24 HAFB	077		18. 7.97	Sky Operations Ltd	Thailand	24. 7.98A
					(Castrol titles) (Cancelled 26.6.01 by CAA)		
G-BXJV	Dimona DA-20-A1 Katana	10152		23. 7.97	Tayside Aviation Ltd	Dundee	30. 7.03T
G-BXJW	Dimona DA-20-A1 Katana	10211	(OE-) N811CH	23. 7.97	Tayside Aviation Ltd	Dundee	15. 8.03T
G-BXJY	Van's RV-6 PFA 181-12447 (Lycoming O-320-D3G)			23. 7.97	D.J.Sharland	Popham	5. 5.02P
G-BXJZ	Cameron C-60 HAFB	4168		23. 7.97	R.S.Mohr	Chippenham	20. 3.01A
G-BXKA	Airbus A320-214	714	N714AW G-BXKA/F-WWIX	24.11.97	JMC Airlines Ltd *(Op Ryan International)*	Manchester	23.11.02T
G-BXKB	Airbus A320-214	716	N716AW G-BXKB/F-WWIZ	10.12.97	JMC Airlines Ltd	Manchester	5. 5.02T
G-BXKC	Airbus A320-214	730	F-WWBQ	15.12.97	JMC Airlines Ltd	Manchester	14.12.03T
G-BXKD	Airbus A320-214	735	F-WWBV	17.12.97	JMC Airlines Ltd	Manchester	25.11.03T
G-BXKF	Hawker Hunter T.7 *(Regd with c/n 41H-003315)*	HABL-003314	8676M XL577	28. 7.97	R.F.Harvey	Kemble	
G-BXKH	Cameron Colt Sparkasse Box 90SS HAFB	4161		4. 8.97	Westfalisch-Lippischer Sparkassen und Giroverband *"Spardueschen"*	Münster, Germany	16. 8.01A
G-BXKJ	Cameron A-275 HAFB	4215		4. 8.97	Ballooning Network Ltd	Bristol	18. 8.01T
G-BXKL	Bell 206B-3 JetRanger III	3006	N5735Y	8.10.97	Swattons Aviation Ltd	Thruxton	18.11.03T
G-BXKM	Rotary Air Force RAF 2000 GTX-SE	PFA G/13-1291		5. 8.97	J.R.Huggins	Lamberhurst Farm, Faversham	3. 9.01P
G-BXKO	Sky 65-24 HAFB	083		11. 8.97	J-M.Reck	Evette-Salbert, France	9. 3.02
G-BXKU	Cameron Colt AS-120 mk.II HA Airship	4165		15. 8.97	D.C.Chipping	Evora, Portugal	19. 4.01A
G-BXKW	Slingsby T.67M-200 Firefly	2061	VR-HZS HKG-13/G-7-129	15. 8.97	W.R.Tandy *(As "HKG-13")*	(Hong Kong, PRC)	1. 5.04T
G-BXKX	Taylorcraft J Auster 5	803	D-EMXA HB-EOK/MS938	19. 8.97	A.L.Jubb	Rochester	21. 5.04
G-BXLA	Robinson R22 Beta	1368	SE-HVX N4014G	12. 8.97	Fast Helicopters Ltd	Thruxton	27. 9.03T
G-BXLC	Sky 120-24 HAFB	085		20. 8.97	A.F.Selby	Loughborough	5.10.99A
G-BXLF	Lindstrand LBL-90A HAFB	487		3. 9.97	R. & J.Moffatt t/a Variohm Components *"Variohm"*	Towcester	8. 9.01A
G-BXLG	Cameron C-80 HAFB	4250		5. 3.98	D. & L.S.Litchfield *"Borne Again"*	Reading	15. 8.02A
G-BXLI	Bell 206B-3 JetRanger III	4041	N206JR G-JODY	8. 9.97	Williams Grand Prix Engineering Ltd	Wantage	19.11.03T
G-BXLK	Europa Aviation Europa PFA 247-12613 (Rotax 912-UL)			11. 9.97	R.G.Fairall	Redhill	23. 2.02P
G-BXLN	Sportavia Fournier RF4D	4022	F-BORK	15. 9.97	E.H.Booker	(Peterborough)	27. 2.03
G-BXLO	Hunting Percival P.84 Jet Provost T.4	PAC/W/19986	9032M XR673	14. 8.97	HCR Aviation Ltd	North Weald	30.11.01P
G-BXLP	Sky 90-24 HAFB	084		18. 9.97	G.B.Lescott	Oxford	14. 1.02A
G-BXLR	PZL-110 Koliber 160A *(Regd with c/n 04970077)*	04980077	SP-WGF(2)	10. 6.98	PZL International Aviation Marketing & Sales plc	Leicester	31.10.04T
G-BXLS	PZL-110 Koliber 160A *(Regd with c/n 04970078)*	04980078	SP-WGG	23. 6.98	P.A.Rickells	Gamston	23. 9.04
G-BXLT	SOCATA TB-200 Tobago XL	1457	F-GRBB EC-FNX/EC-234/F-GLFP	28. 4.97	R.M.Shears	Blackbushe	25. 5.03
G-BXLV	Enstrom F-28F	733	1711 Thai Government/KASET	11. 9.97	Solent Projects Ltd	Southampton	16. 2.01T
G-BXLW	Enstrom F-28F	734	1712 Thai Government/KASET	11. 9.97	M & P Food Products Ltd	Coventry	
G-BXLY	Piper PA-28-151 Cherokee Warrior	28-7715220	G-WATZ N7641F	19. 9.97	Auto Corporation Ltd	Hawarden	16. 7.04T
G-BXLZ	Europa Aviation Europa PFA 247-12815 (NSI EA81/100)			24. 6.97	A.R.Round	Breighton	31.10.01P
G-BXMF	Cassutt Racer IIIM	PFA 034-13003		19. 9.97	J.F.Bakewell *(Noted 7.01)*	Hucknall	
G-BXMG	Rotary Air Force RAF 2000 GTX	H2-92-3-59	PH-TEN	18. 8.97	R.Paolone	(Kenilworth)	
G-BXMH	Beechcraft 76 Duchess	ME-168	F-GDMO N6021Y	19. 9.97	R.Clarke	Wolverhampton	25. 2.04T
G-BXML	Mooney M.20A	1594	OY-AIZ	26. 9.97	G.Kay	Crosland Moor	25. 1.02
G-BXMM	Cameron A-180 HAFB	4252		28.10.97	Flying Pictures Ltd *"Unipart"*	Fairoaks	3.11.00A
G-BXMN*	de Havilland DH.82A Tiger Moth	86243	N82RD N8353/ZS-IGJ/CR-AGL/FAP/NL772	2.10.97	Linda V.Handley *(As "NL772")*	Higher Barn Farm, Houghton	27. 7.02

(Damaged landing Springwood, Blackburn 25.5.99: cancelled 13.11.99 as Destroyed: wreck @ Welshpool 8.00)

G-BXMU	WSK PZL-104 Wilga 80	CF20890880	EC-GMH	9.10.97	D.J.S.McClean	City of Derry	27. 7.02
			ZK-PZP/SP-FWP		t/a G-BXMU Group		
G-BXMV	Scheibe SF-25C Falke 1700	44223	D-KDFV	7. 8.97	J.B.Marett	Sandhill Farm, Shrivenham	23. 5.04
					t/a Falcon Flying Group		
G-BXMW	Cameron A-275 HAFB	4247		19. 2.98	Ballooning Network Ltd	Bristol	4. 8.02T
					(Bath Building Society titles) "BIBS III"		
G-BXMX	Phoenix Currie Wot	PFA 058-13055		23. 9.97	M.J.Hayman	(Totnes)	
G-BXMY	Hughes 269C	74-0328	N9599F	20.10.97	DS Air Ltd	(Horsham)	7.12.03T
G-BXMZ	Diamond DA-20-A1 Katana	10236		4.12.97	Tayside Aviation Ltd	Dundee	12. 2.04T
G-BXNA*	Avid Flyer	118	N5531J	10.10.97	Isobel Brooks	Sywell	
				(No PtoF issued: cancelled 25.5.01 by CAA) (Noted 11.01)			
G-BXNC	Europa Aviation Europa	PFA 247-12970		13.10.97	J.K.Cantwell	(Ashton-under-Lyne)	
					"The Magic Leprechaun"		
G-BXND	Cameron Thomas The Tank Engine 110SS HAFB	4254	(JA-A0935)	2. 2.98	Virgin Airship & Balloon Co Ltd	Telford	25. 6.02A
G-BXNG	Beechcraft 58 Baron	TH-874	N18747	13.10.97	Bonanza Flying Club Ltd	Booker	4.11.03
G-BXNH	Piper PA-28-161 Cherokee Warrior II	28-7816314	N2828M	22.10.97	CC Management Associates Ltd	Redhill	7.12.03T
G-BXNL	Cameron A-120 HAFB	4241		3. 3.98	R.G.Griffin *"Kenett Centre"*	Newbury	16. 2.02T
					t/a Newbury Balloons & Land Securities Properties Ltd		
G-BXNM	Cameron A-210 HAFB	4245		12.12.97	N.D.Hicks t/a Horizon Ballooning	Alton	22.11.01T
G-BXNN	de Havilland DHC-1 Chipmunk 22	C1/0849	WP983	4. 8.97	J.N.Robinson	Old Sarum	27. 7.04
					(As "WP983/B" in RAF c/s)		
G-BXNS	Bell 206B-3 JetRanger III	2385	N16822	3.11.97	Sterling Helicopters Ltd	Norwich	19.12.03T
G-BXNT	Bell 206B-3 JetRanger III	2398	N94CA	11.11.97	Sterling Helicopters Ltd	Norwich	3.12.03T
			N123AL				
G-BXNU	Jabiru Jabiru SK	PFA 274-13218		31.10.97	J.Smith	(Downham Market)	14. 7.01P
	(Jabiru 2200A)		*(Crashed 7.00 and written off: fuselage converted into static exhibition)*				
G-BXNV	Cameron Colt AS-105 GD Hot-Air Airship	4231		19. 2.98	The Sleeping Society	Edegem, Belgium	16. 6.02A
G-BXNX	Lindstrand LBL-210A HAFB	318		3.11.97	Jane H.Cuthbert	Sevenoaks	22. 1.02T
					t/a Spirit of Adventure		
G-BXNZ	Hawker Hunter F.58	41H-697433	J-4066	7.11.97	Classic Aviation Ltd	RAF Scampton	
	(Regd with c/n 41H-28364)				*(Stored 1999: current status unknown*		
G-BXOA	Robinson R22 Beta	1614	N41132	10.11.97	MG Group Ltd	Sywell	25. 1.04
			JA7832				
G-BXOB	Europa Aviation Europa	PFA 247-12892		6.11.97	S.J.Willett	(Maidstone)	
G-BXOC	Evans VP-2	PFA 063-10305		29. 9.97	H.J. & E.M.Cox	(Bideford)	
G-BXOF	Diamond DA-20-A1 Katana	10256		4.12.97	Diamond Aircraft UK Ltd	Cumbernauld	30. 1.04T
					(Op Cumbernauld School of Flying)		
G-BXOI	Cessna 172R Skyhawk II	17280145	N9990F	17.11.97	J.S.& J.Q.Malcolm	Wolverhampton	2. 2.04T
G-BXOJ	Piper PA-28-161 Warrior III	2842010	N9265G	15.12.97	Plane Talking Ltd	Elstree	15.12.00T
G-BXOM	Isaacs Spitfire	PFA 027-12768		25.11.97	J.H.Betton	(Ammanford)	
G-BXON	Auster AOP.9	AUS/10/60	WZ729	1.12.97	C.J. & D.J.Baker	Carr Farm, Newark	
					(On rebuild 4.98: current status unknown)		
G-BXOO	Grumman-American AA-5A Cheetah	AA5A-0674	N26721	10.12.97	ENS-Entire Network Solutions Ltd	Blackbushe	15.12.03T
G-BXOR	Robin HR.200/120B	321		1.12.97	Multiflight Ltd	Leeds-Bradford	5. 3.04T
G-BXOS	Cameron A-200 HAFB	4286		19. 2.98	Airborne Balloon Management Ltd	Beltring, Kent	20. 6.02T
G-BXOT	Cameron C-70 HAFB	4200		21.10.97	Gone With The Wind Ltd	Bristol	6. 1.02A
					(Op Dante Balloon Group)		
G-BXOU	CEA Jodel DR.360 Chevalier	312	F-BPOU	6.10.97	S.H. & J.A.Williams	Blackpool	11. 2.04
G-BXOV	Cameron Colt 105A HAFB	4227		12.12.97	The Aerial Display Co Ltd	Looe	15.11.00A
					(Michelin titles)		
G-BXOW	Cameron Colt 105A HAFB	4228		9. 1.98	The Aerial Display Co Ltd	Looe	16. 1.02A
					(Michelin titles)		
G-BXOX	Grumman American AA-5A Cheetah	AA5A-0694	F-GBDS	27. 2.98	A.J.Radford	Tattenhill	11. 4.04T
G-BXOY	QAC Quickie Q.235	PFA 94-12183		17.11.97	C.C.Clapham	North Weald	23. 7.02P
	(Originally regd as "Q.200")						
G-BXOZ	Piper PA-28-181 Cherokee Archer II	28-7790173	N6927F	14.10.97	Spritetone Ltd	White Waltham	15. 2.04T
G-BXPB	Diamond DA-20-A1 Katana	10257		4.12.97	Diamond Aircraft UK Ltd	Kirknewton	21. 1.04T
					(Op J Bain)		
G-BXPC	Diamond DA-20-A1 Katana	10258		4.12.97	Cubair Flight Training Ltd	Redhill	30. 1.04T
G-BXPD	Diamond DA-20-A1 Katana	10259		4.12.97	Cubair Flight Training Ltd	Redhill	5. 3.04T
G-BXPE	Diamond DA-20-A1 Katana	10263		4.12.97	Tayside Aviation Ltd	Dundee	5. 3.04T
G-BXPF	Venture Thorp T.211	105	N6524Y	8.12.97	AD Aviation Ltd	Carlisle	1. 4.04T
G-BXPH	Sky 220-24 HAFB	096		4.12.97	J.Nolte	Aachen, Germany	1. 4.00
G-BXPI	Van's RV-4	PFA 181-12426		2. 1.98	Cavendish Aviation Ltd	Gamston	31. 8.01P
	(Lycoming O-360-A1A)						

G-BXPK	Cameron A-250 HAFB	4226		2. 2.98	Richard Nash Cars Ltd	Norwich	8. 7.02T
					(Express Logo titles)		
G-BXPL	Piper PA-28-140 Cherokee	28-24560	N7224J	10.12.97	C.R.Guggenheim	Bournemouth	21. 3.04T
G-BXPM	Beechcraft 58 Baron	TH-1677	N207ZM	10.10.97	Foyle Flyers Ltd	City of Derry	21. 2.04
G-BXPO	Venture Thorp T.211	104	N6524Q	10.12.97	AD Aviation Ltd	Teesside	29. 3.04T
G-BXPP	Sky 90-24 HAFB	092		17.12.97	Adam Associates Ltd	Thatcham, Berks	11. 6.01A
					"Niceday"		
G-BXPR	Cameron Colt Can 110SS HAFB	4218		2. 2.98	FRB Fleishwarenfabrik Rostock-Bramow		
						Rostock, Germany	20. 2.02A
G-BXPS	Piper PA-23-250 Aztec C	27-3498	G-AYLY	10.12.90	Wendy A.Moore	Redhill	16.10.97T
			N6258Y				
G-BXPT	Ultramagic H-77 HADB	77-140		22.12.97	G.D.O.Bartram	Ordino, Andorra	22. 6.02A
G-BXPV	Piper PA-34-220T Seneca III	3448035	A7-FCH	24.12.97	Oxford Aviation Services Ltd		
			N9198X			Gloucestershire	7. 2.04T
G-BXPW	Piper PA-34-220T Seneca III	3448034	A7-FCG	9. 2.98	Oxford Aviation Services Ltd		
			N9171R			Gloucestershire	3. 4.04T
G-BXPY	Robinson R44 Astro	0154	OY-HFV	22.12.97	O.Desmet & B.Mornie	Amougies, Belgium	25. 1.04
G-BXRA	Mudry/CAARP CAP.10B	3	03 FrAF	12.12.97	P.A.Soper	Fenland	17. 8.04
			F-TFVR				
G-BXRB	Mudry/CAARP CAP.10B	100	100 FrAF	12.12.97	T.T.Duhig	Spilsted Farm, Sedlescombe	9. 7.04
G-BXRC	Mudry/CAARP CAP.10B	134	134 FrAF	12.12.97	I.F.Scott t/a Group Alpha	Fenland	9. 2.02
G-BXRD	Enstrom 280FX	2012	PH-JVM	22.12.97	S.G.Oliphant-Hope	Shoreham	8. 2.04
			N213M		t/a Eastern Atlantic Helicopters		
G-BXRF	Scintex CP.1310-C3 Super Emeraude		OO-NSF	9. 1.98	D.T.Gethin	Swansea	28..2.03
		935	F-BMJG				
G-BXRG	Piper PA-28-181 Archer II	28-7990036	PH-LEC	29. 1.98	Alderney Flying Training Ltd	Alderney	1. 3.04T
			N21173				
G-BXRH	Cessna 185A Skywagon	185-0413	HB-CRX	10.12.97	R.E.M.Holmes	Ronaldsway	4. 6.04
	(Hoerner wing-tips)		N1613Z				
G-BXRK*	Robinson R22 Beta	1341	N341MB	20. 1.98	Moy Motorsport Ltd	Sywell	5. 2.01T
					(Cancelled 26.6.01 by CAA)		
G-BXRM	Cameron A-210 HAFB	4237		23. 4.98	W. & C.Hooker	(Nottingham)	28. 4.01T
G-BXRN*	Reims Cessna F.152 II	F15201440	G-RICH	27. 1.98	Exeter Flying Club Ltd	Exeter	21. 9.01T
			OO-FTC		*(Cancelled 21.11.00 as wfu)*		
G-BXRO	Cessna U.206G Stationair II		OH-ULK	9. 2.98	M.Penny	Moyenis, Co.Londonderry	17. 4.01
		U20604217	N756NE				
G-BXRP	Schweizer Hughes 269C	S.1334	OH-HSP	27. 1.98	C.W.Larner	Haverfordwest	21. 3.04T
			N7506U				
G-BXRR	Westland Scout AH.1	F.9740	XW612	28. 1.98	T.K.Phillips	Thruxton	7. 2.02P
G-BXRS	Westland Scout AH.1	F.9741	XW613	28. 1.98	R.P.Coplestone	Thruxton	
					(As "XW613/T": noted 9.00)		
G-BXRT	Robin DR.400/180	2382		23. 2.98	R.A.Ford	White Waltham	26. 4.04
G-BXRV	Van's RV-4	PFA 181-12482		12. 1.98	B.J.Oke	Gloucestershire	
					t/a Cleeve Flying Group *(Fuselage noted 4.01)*		
G-BXRY	Bell 206B JetRanger II	208	N4054G	19. 3.98	John Mann International Ltd	(Sleaford)	6. 8.04T
G-BXRZ	Rans S-6-116 Coyote II	PFA 204A-13195		3. 2.98	C.M.White	Perth	19. 2.02A
G-BXSA	Cameron PM-80 HAFB	4297		11. 3.98	Flying Pictures Ltd	(Dubai)	2. 6.00A
	(Coca Cola bottle)						
G-BXSC	Cameron C-80 HAFB	4251		12.12.97	S.J.Coates	Barton-le-Clay, Bedford	12.10.01A
					"Keepsake"		
G-BXSD	Cessna 172R Skyhawk II	17280310	N431ES	12. 3.98	K.K.Freeman	Bodmin	29. 3.04
G-BXSE	Cessna 172R Skyhawk II	17280352	N9321F	19. 5.98	MK Aero Support Ltd	Bristol	12. 7.04T
					(Op Bristol & Wessex Flying Club)		
G-BXSG	Robinson R22 Beta-II	2789		3. 2.98	R.M.Goodenough	Wotton-under-Edge	1. 3.04T
G-BXSH	Glaser-Dirks DG-800B	8-121-B50		5. 2.98	D.S.MaKay	Hinton-in-the-Hedges	4. 6.01
G-BXSI	Jabiru Jabiru SK	PFA 274-13204		5. 2.98	M.H.Molyneux	Wickenby	8. 5.02P
	(Jabiru 2200A)						
G-BXSJ	Cameron C-80 HAFB	4330		24. 3.98	Balloon School (International) Ltd		
					t/a British School of Ballooning	Petworth	24. 7.02T
G-BXSL	Westland Scout AH.1	F.9762	XW799	17. 2.98	B.J.Green	(Marlborough)	19. 8.02P
G-BXSM	Cessna 172R Skyhawk II	17280320	N432ES	10. 3.98	East Midlands Flying School Ltd		
						East Midlands	11. 4.04T
			(Made heavy landing East Midlands 23.6.01: damage to engine cowling & firewall)				
G-BXSO	Lindstrand LBL-105A HAFB	114	HB-BBJ	18. 2.98	Lindstrand Balloons Ltd	Oswestry	23. 7.02A
G-BXSP	Grob G-109B	6335	D-KNEA	25. 3.98	I.M.Donnelly	Aboyne	7. 4.04
G-BXSR	Reims Cessna F172N	F17202003	PH-SPY	6. 2.98	S.A.Parkes	King's Farm, Thurrock	21. 4.04T
			D-EITH				
G-BXST	Piper PA-25-235 Pawnee C	25-4952	PH-BAT	9. 2.98	P.Channon	Porthtowan	5. 5.02A
	(Frame No.25-4971)		N8532L				
G-BXSU	TEAM mini-MAX 91A	PFA 186-12357	G-MYGL	20. 2.98	M.R.Overall	(Wethersfield)	4. 4.02P
	(Rotax 503)						
G-BXSX	Cameron V-77 HAFB	4329		6. 4.98	D.R.Medcalf	(Bromsgrove)	22. 7.02A
G-BXSY	Robinson R22 Beta-II	2778		27. 1.98	N.M.G.Pearson	Bristol	5. 2.04T

G-BXTB	Cessna 152 II	15282516	OH-CMS N69151	25. 2.98	Haimoss Ltd	Old Sarum	25. 4.04T
G-BXTC	Taylor JT.1 Monoplane	PFA 055-13142		25. 2.98	R.Holden-Rushworth	(Devizes)	
G-BXTD	Europa Aviation Europa	PFA 247-12772		26. 2.98	P.R.Anderson	Hucknall	14. 6.02P
G-BXTE	Cameron A-275 HAFB	4028		30. 3.98	Adventure Balloon Co Ltd	Hook	1.11.01T
G-BXTF	Cameron N-105SS HAFB	4304		2. 4.98	Flying Pictures Ltd *"Sainsbury's Strawberry"*	Fairoaks	17. 3.02A
G-BXTG	Cameron N-42 HAFB	4305		2. 4.98	Flying Pictures Ltd *"Sainsbury"*	Fairoaks	26. 7.01A
G-BXTH	Westland SA.314D Gazelle HT.3	1120	XW866	13. 3.98	Flightline Ltd *(As "E" in RAF c/s: stored 1.02)*	Southend	
G-BXTI	Pitts S-1S Special	NP-1	ZS-VZX N96MM	9. 3.98	A.B.Treherne-Pollock	White Waltham	5. 6.02P
G-BXTJ	Cameron N-77 HAFB	4332		6. 4.98	J M Albury *(Chubb titles)*	Cirencester	8. 3.02A
G-BXTK	Dornier Do.28D-2	4080	D-IDBB 58+05 German AF	15. 5.98	R.Ebke	(Porta Westfalica, Germany)	
G-BXTL	Schweizer 269C-1	0075		13. 3.98	Oxford Aviation Services Ltd	Oxford	2. 4.04T
G-BXTN	ATR 72-202	483	F-WWEV	24.10.97	CityFlyer Express Ltd *(Whale Rider t/s)*	Gatwick	23.10.03T
G-BXTO	Hindustan HAL-26 Pushpak (Continental C90-8F)	PK-128	9V-BAI VT-DWM	12. 2.98	A.M.Pepper t/a Pushpak Flying Group	(Stone)	1..2.02P
G-BXTP	Diamond DA-20-A1 Katana	10306	N636DA	10. 3.98	Diamond Aircraft UK Ltd *(Op Cotswold Flying Club)*	Gloucestershire	23. 4.04T
G-BXTR	Diamond DA-20-A1 Katana	10307	N607DA	10. 3.98	Diamond Aircraft UK Ltd	Norwich	23. 4.04T
G-BXTS	Diamond DA-20-A1 Katana	10308	N638DA	10. 3.98	Avon Aviation Ltd	Bristol	21. 5.04T
G-BXTT	Grumman-American AA-5B Tiger	AA5B-0749	F-GBDH	27. 2.98	P.Curley & R.Bailes-Brown t/a G-BXTT Group	Tatenhill	14. 3.04
G-BXTU	Robinson R22 Beta-II	2790		3. 3.98	TDR Aviation Ltd	(Craigavon, Co.Armagh)	7. 4.04T
G-BXTV	Cope Bug	BUG.2		12. 3.98	B.R.Cope	(Bewdley)	
G-BXTW	Piper PA-28-181 Archer III	2843137	N41279 (G-BXTW)/N41279	26. 5.98	J.N.Davison t/a Davison Plant Hire	Wolverhampton/Compton Abbas	17. 6.04
G-BXTY	Piper PA-28-161 Cadet	2841179	PH-LED	11. 3.98	Bflying Ltd *(Op Bournemouth Flying Club)*	Bournemouth	27. 6.04T
	(Swung during touch & go Bournemouth 23.9.01: nose u/c broke off with damage to main u/c, engine and propeller)						
G-BXTZ	Piper PA-28-161 Cadet	2841181	PH-LEE	11. 3.98	Bflying Ltd *(Op Bournemouth Flying Club)*	Bournemouth	25. 3.04T
G-BXUA	Campbell Cricket Mk.5	PFA G/03-1272		12. 3.98	R.N.Bodley	Henstridge	10 .5.02P
G-BXUB	Lindstrand Syrup Bottle SS HAFB	508		30. 4.98	Free Enterprise Balloons Ltd *"Mrs Butterworth"*	Mason, Wi. USA	25. 3.01A
G-BXUC	Robinson R22 Beta	0908	OY-HFB	17. 3.98	R.C.Hields t/a Hields Aviation	Sherburn-in-Elmet	29. 3.04T
G-BXUE	Sky 240-24 HAFB	098		30. 4.98	G.M.Houston t/a Scotair Balloons	Lesmahagow	7. 4.01T
G-BXUF	Agusta-Bell 206B JetRanger II	8633	EC-DUS OE-DXE	12. 5.98	SJ Contracting Services Ltd	Oxford	26. 7.04T
G-BXUG	Lindstrand Baby Bel SS HAFB	512		14. 5.98	Virgin Airship & Balloon Co Ltd *"Mr Cool"*	Telford	13. 4.01A
G-BXUH	Lindstrand LBL-31A HAFB	513		2. 6.98	Virgin Airship & Balloon Co Ltd *"Baby-Bel"*	Telford	12. 4.01A
G-BXUI	Glaser-Dirks DG-800B	8-105-B39	BGA.4382 D-KKLC	12. 5.98	J.Le Coyte	Rufforth	28. 5.04P
G-BXUK	Robinson R44 Astro	0093	D-HIFF	19. 6.95	G.Elliott t/a Hertfordshire Helicopters	(Luton)	26. 6.04T
G-BXUL	Vought (Goodyear) FG-1D Corsair *(Officially regd as c/n P32823)* *(P/i of Bu.88439 quoted)*	3205	N55JP "NZ5611"/NZ5648/Bu.88391	25. 3.98	The Old Flying Machine (Air Museum) Co *(As "NZ5648" in RNZAF c/s)*	Duxford	14. 7.02P
G-BXUM	Europa Aviation Europa (Rotax 912-UL)	PFA 247-12611		19. 3.98	D.Bosomworth	Popham	18. 5.02P
G-BXUO	Lindstrand LBL-105A HAFB	520		27. 3.98	Lindstrand Balloons Ltd	Oswestry	8. 5.01A
G-BXUP	Schweizer Hughes 269C	S.1317	SE-HTB	30. 3.98	J.N.Crewdson	(Dorking)	6. 4.01T
G-BXUS	Sky 65-24 HAFB	111		6. 4.98	K.Coate-Bond	Basingstoke	2. 7.02A
G-BXUU	Cameron V-65 HAFB	4362		23. 4.98	D.I.Gray-Fisk *"Aeolus"*	Burnham	11. 6.00A
G-BXUW	Cameron Colt 90A HAFB	4317		23. 4.98	Zycomm Electronics Ltd	Ripley	11. 5.02A
G-BXUX	Brandli Cherry BX-2 (Continental C90-12F)	PFA 179-12571		4. 4.98	M.F.Fountain	Manston	11.10.02P
G-BXUY	Cessna 310Q	310Q0231	N137SA D-IHMT/N7731Q	16. 4.98	D.A.De Horne Rowntree	Kemble	23. 4.04
G-BXUZ	Cessna 152 II	15282810	N89638	14. 4.98	Stapleford Flying Club Ltd	Stapleford	2.11.03T
G-BXVA	SOCATA TB-200 Tobago XL	1325	F-GJXL F-WJXL	15. 4.98	H.R.Palser	Cardiff	28. 6.04
G-BXVB	Cessna 152 II	15282584	N69250	15. 4.98	PJC (Leasing) Ltd	Stapleford	25. 9.04T
G-BXVC	Piper PA-28RT-201T Turbo Arrow IV	28R-7931113	D-ELIV N2152V	20. 4.98	J.S.Develin & I.Zahurul	Redhill	28. 6.01T

G-BXVD	CFM Streak Shadow SA			1. 4.98	Rotech Frabrication Ltd		
	(Rotax 912) K.301SA & PFA 206-13304					Pittrichie Farm , Whiterashes	24. 8.01P
G-BXVE	Lindstrand LBL-330A HAFB	492		6. 5.98	Adventure Balloon Co Ltd	London W7	24. 7.02T
G-BXVF	Thunder Ax11-250 Srs.2 HAFB	4371		22. 5.98	T.J.Parker	Burnham-on-Crouch	9. 5.02T
					t/a Anglian Countryside Balloons		
G-BXVG	Sky 77-24 HAFB	99		28. 5.98	M.Wolf	Wallingford	20. 7.02
G-BXVH	Sky 25-16 HAFB	120		23. 4.98	Flying Pictures Ltd	Fairoaks	14. 3.00A
					"Encylopedia Britannica"		
G-BXVI	Supermarine 361 Spitfire LF.XVIe		6944M	27.12.84	Wizzard Investments Ltd	North Weald	
		CBAF.IX.4644	"RF114"/RW386		*(On rebuild 4.89: current status unknown)*		
G-BXVJ	Cameron O-120 HAFB	2201	PH-VVJ	12. 3.98	MJN Balloon Management Ltd		
			G-IMAX			Longleat, Warminster	6. 4.01T
G-BXVK	Robin HR.200/120B	326		1. 7.98	Northamptonshire School of Flying Ltd		
						Sywell	23. 6.04T
G-BXVL	Sky 180-24 HAFB	113		16. 6.98	S.Stanley t/a Purple Balloons	Sudbury	21. 6.02T
G-BXVM	Van's RV-6A	PFA 181-13103		26. 2.98	J.G.Small	RAF Woodvale	21..6.02P
G-BXVN*	Sky 105-24 HAFB	115		17. 9.98	L.V.D. Avyle,	Wachtebetie, Belgium	
					t/a Skydance *(Cancelled 23.10.00 by CAA - no CofA issued)*		
G-BXVO	Van's RV-6A	PFA 181-12575		28. 4.98	P.J.Hynes & M.E.Holden	Sleap	24..8.02P
	(Lycoming O-320-D1A)						
G-BXVP	Sky 31-24 HAFB	056		28. 4.98	L.Greaves	Doulting, Somerset	2.10.02A
G-BXVR	Sky 90-24 HAFB	061		20. 7.98	P.Hegarty	Magherafelt, Co.Londonderry	30. 8.02
G-BXVS	Brugger Colibri MB.2	PFA 043-11948		5. 5.98	G.T.Snoddon	Newtownards, Co.of Down	18. 4.02
	(VW 1834)						
G-BXVT	Cameron O-77 HAFB	1444	PH-MKB	30. 7.98	R.P.Wade	Wigan	
G-BXVU	Piper PA-28-161 Cherokee Warrior II		N47372	5. 5.98	Gordon Air Ltd	Lydd	17. 7.04T
		28-7816063					
G-BXVV	Cameron V-90 HAFB	4369		5. 5.98	Floating Sensations Ltd	Thatcham	14. 6.02A
G-BXVW	Colt Piggy Bank SS HAFB	4366		2. 7.98	G.Binder	Sonnerbuhl, Germany	8. 6.02A
G-BXVX	Rutan Cozy	PFA 159-12680		6. 5.98	G.E.Murray	Swansea	30. 5.02P
	(Lycoming O-320-E2A)						
G-BXVY	Cessna 152	15279808	N757KU	11. 5.98	Stapleford Flying Club Ltd	Stapleford	13.11.04T
G-BXVZ	WSK-PZL Mielec TS-11 Iskra	3H-1625	SP-DOF	27. 3.98	J.Ziubrzynski	Shoreham	
			Polish AF?/SP-DOF		*(Noted 2000)*		
G-BXWA	Beechcraft 76 Duchess	ME-232	OY-CYM	8. 4.98	Plymouth School of Flying Ltd	Plymouth	23. 6.04T
			(SE-IUY)/D-GBTD				
G-BXWB	Robin HR.100/200B Royale	08	HB-EMT	29. 4.98	W.A.Brunwin	Oaksey Park	25. 7.04T
G-BXWC	Cessna 152	15283640	N4794B	11. 5.98	PJC (Leasing) Ltd	Stapleford	12. 7.04T
G-BXWD	Agusta A109A-II	7266	N565RJ	14. 5.98	Castle Air Charters Ltd	Liskeard	
			I-URIA/D-HEMZ/N109BD				
G-BXWE	Fokker F.28 Mk.0100	11327	PH-CFE	6. 7.98	British Midland Airways Ltd *(Op bmi Regional)*		
	(Fokker 100)		F-GJAO/PH-CFE/PH-EZL/(G-FIOX)/PH-EZL			East Midlands	30. 8.04T
G-BXWF	Fokker F.28 Mk.0100	11328	PH-CFF	13. 7.98	British Midland Airways Ltd *(Op bmi Regional)*		
	(Fokker 100)		F-GKLX/PH-CFF/PH-EZM/(G-FIOY)/PH-EZM			East Midlands	31. 8.04T
G-BXWG	Sky 120-24 HAFB	114		28. 5.98	Airbourne Adventures Ltd	Skipton	23. 4.02T
G-BXWH	Denney Kitfox mk.4-1200 Sportster			4. 3.98	B.J.Finch	Croft Farm, Defford	23. 5.02P
		PFA 172A-12343					
G-BXWI(2)	Cameron N-120 HAFB	4395		12. 6.98	Flying Pictures Ltd	Fairoaks	30. 7.02A
	(Rebuilt 1999)				*(Energis titles)*		
G-BXWK	Rans S-6-ESA Coyote II *(Tri-cycle u/c)*			19. 5.98	R.J.Teal	(Harrogate)	13.11.02P
	(Rotax 582) 0298.1020 & PFA 204-13317						
G-BXWL	Sky 90-24 HAFB	117		20. 7.98	I.S.Bridge	Shrewsbury	28.12.01A
					t/a The Shropshire Hills Balloon Company		
G-BXWO	Piper PA-28-181 Archer II	28-8190311	D-ENHA(2)	22. 5.98	J.S.Develin & Z.Islam	Shoreham	23. 7.04T
			N8431C				
G-BXWP	Piper PA-32-300 Cherokee Six		N8143D	26. 5.98	J.B.Tucker & D.J.Royle	Barton	27. 7.04
		32-7340088	G-BXWP/OE-DRR/N16452		t/a Alliance Aviation		
G-BXWR	CFM Streak Shadow SA		G-MZMI	22. 5.98	M.A.Hayward	Bodmin	16. 1.02P
	(Rotax 912) K.289-SA & PFA 206-13205						
G-BXWT	Van's RV-6	PFA 181-12639		19. 7.96	R.C.Owen	(Haywards Heath)	26. 7.02P
G-BXWU	FLS Aerospace Sprint 160	003	G-70-503	5. 6.98	Sunhawk Ltd *(Noted 4.00)*	North Weald	
G-BXWV	FLS Aerospace Sprint 160	005	G-70-505	5. 6.98	Sunhawk Ltd *(Noted 4.00)*	North Weald	
G-BXWX	Sky 25-16 HAFB	082		29. 5.98	Zebedee Balloon Service Ltd	Hungerford	14. 3.00A
G-BXWY	Cameron A-105 HAFB	4410		12. 6.98	Richard Nash Cars Ltd	Norwich	8. 7.02A
G-BXXC	Scheibe SF-25C Falke 1700	44151	D-KEFA(2)	3. 6.98	K.E.Ballington	(Burton-on-Trent)	24. 5.02
G-BXXD	Cessna 172R Skyhawk	17280068	N9739F	15. 6.98	Oxford Aviation Services Ltd	Oxford	30. 6.01T
G-BXXE	Rand Robinson KR-2S	PFA 129-10927		8. 6.98	N.Rawlinson	(Leek)	
					(Under construction 5.99)		
G-BXXG	Cameron N-105 HAFB	3662		19. 6.98	Allen Owen Ltd	Wotton-under-Edge	5. 1.01A
G-BXXH	Hatz CB-1	PFA 143-12445		9. 6.98	R.D.Shingler	Forest Farm, Welshpool	
G-BXXI	Grob G-109B	6400	F-CAQR	9. 6.98	M.N.Martin	Lyveden	23.10.04
			F-WAQR				
G-BXXJ	Colt Flying Yacht SS HAFB	1797	JA-A0515	10. 6.98	Magical Adventures Ltd	Chirk	7. 9.01A

G-BXXK	Reims Cessna F172N	F17201806	D-EOPP	15. 6.98	E.Alexander	Andrewsfield	22. 8.04T
G-BXXL	Cameron N-105 HAFB	4408		16. 7.98	Flying Pictures Ltd	Fairoaks	17. 8.01A
					(Blue Peter titles)		
G-BXXN	Robinson R22 Beta	0720	N720HH	16. 6.98	Murray Galloway Ltd	Booker	5. 7.04T
G-BXXO	Lindstrand LBL-90B HAFB	534		6. 7.98	K.Temple *(New owner 11.01)*	Diss	7. 9.00A
G-BXXP	Sky 77-24 HAFB	124		20. 7.98	C.J.James	Wincanton	14. 5.02A
G-BXXR	Lovegrove AV-8 Gyroplane			29. 6.98	P.C.Lovegrove	Didcot	
		PFA G/15-1263	*(Registered as Lovegrove BGL Four Runner c/n PFA G/15-1273)*				
G-BXXS	Sky 105-24 HAFB	116		30. 7.98	L.D.& H.Vaughan	Tring	3. 8.00A
					(Eyewitness Guides titles)		
G-BXXT	Beechcraft 76 Duchess	ME-212	(N212BE)	17. 7.98	S.J.Skilton	Southampton	21. 7.04T
		F-GBOZ			t/a Aviation Rentals *(Op Solent Flight Training)*		
G-BXXU	Colt 31A HAFB	4427		21. 8.98	Sade Balloons Ltd	Coulsdon	1. 6.02
G-BXXW	Enstrom F-28F	771	G-SCOX	2. 7.98	G.Kidger	(Worksop)	22.10.04
			N330SA/G-BXXW/JA7823				
G-BXXZ	CFM Starstreak Shadow SA-II			19. 5.98	A.V. & B.T.Orchard	RAF Mona	29.10.02P
	(Rotax 618)	K.211 & PFA 206-13171					
G-BXYC	Schweizer 269C	S.1716	D-HFDZ	8. 7.98	Foremans Aviation Ltd	(Beverley)	20. 8.04T
G-BXYD	Eurocopter EC 120B	1006		7. 7.98	Airmac Ltd	(Carluke)	13.12.04T
G-BXYE	Scintex CP.301-C1 Emeraude	559	F-BTEO	8. 7.98	D.T.Gethin	Swansea	
			F-PTEO/F-WTEO/F-BJFV				
G-BXYF	Colt AS-105 GD Airship	4433		7. 8.98	LN Flying Ltd	Frinton-on-Sea	16. 9.02A
G-BXYG	Cessna 310D	39089	HB-LSF	14. 8.98	Equitus SARL	(Bailleul, France)	7.12.01T
			F-GEJT/3A-MCA/F-BBOT/F-OBOT/(N6789T)				
G-BXYH	Cameron N-105 HAFB	4441		7. 8.98	Virgin Airship & Balloon Co Ltd	Telford	1.10.01A
					(Fairy titles)		
G-BXYI	Cameron H-34 HAFB	4442		7. 8.98	Virgin Airship & Balloon Co.Ltd	Telford	17.10.01A
					(Fairy Liquid titles)		
G-BXYJ	SAN Jodel DR.1050 Ambassadeur	143	F-BJNA	28. 7.98	R.Manning	Netherthorpe	21.10.04
G-BXYK	Robinson R22 Beta	1579	N4037B	27. 7.98	D.N.Whittlestone	(Oxenhope)	19. 8.01T
G-BXYL	Cameron A-275 HAFB	4450		22. 7.98	Ballooning Network Ltd	Bristol	14. 7.02T
G-BXYM	Piper PA-28-235 Cherokee B	28-10858	SE-FAM	18. 8.98	Ashurst Aviation Ltd	Shoreham	22.12.04T
G-BXYN	Van's RV-6	PFA 181-13265		29. 7.98	J.A.Tooley & R.M.Austin	(Thatcham)	
G-BXYO	Piper PA-28RT-201 Arrow IV		PH-SDD	18. 8.98	Oxford Aviation Services Ltd	Oxford	1.12.04T
		28R-8018046	N8164M				
G-BXYP	Piper PA-28RT-201 Arrow IV		PH-SBO	18. 8.98	Oxford Aviation Services Ltd	Oxford	6.11.04T
		28R-8018050	N8168H				
G-BXYR	Piper PA-28RT-201 Arrow IV		PH-SDA	3. 8.98	Oxford Aviation Services Ltd	Oxford	26.11.04T
		28R-8018101	N8251B				
G-BXYS	Piper PA-28RT-201 Arrow IV		PH-SBS	3. 8.98	Oxford Aviation Services Ltd	Oxford	23. 4.04T
		28R-7918145	N29561				
G-BXYT	Piper PA-28RT-201 Arrow IV		PH-SBN	3. 8.98	Oxford Aviation Services Ltd	Oxford	9. 9.04T
		28R-7918198	(PH-SBM)/OO-HLA/N2878W				
G-BXYV	ATR 72-202	322	B-22708	12.10.98	Gill Aviation Ltd *(Stored 10.01)*		
			F-WWEQ			Maastricht, The Netherlands	15.10.01T
G-BXYX	Van's RV-6	22293	N2399C	31. 7.98	A G Palmer	Wellesbourne Mountford	7.12.01P
	(Lycoming O-320-E2D)						
G-BXYY	Reims FR172E Rocket	FR17200016	OY-AHO	20. 4.98	Haimoss Ltd	Old Sarum	13. 6.04T
			F-WLIP				
G-BXZA	Piper PA-38-112 Tomahawk	38-79A0864	N2480N	6. 8.98	P.D.Brooks	Inverness	30.10.04T
G-BXZB	Nanchang CJ-6A	2632019	Chin AF	18. 9.98	Wingglider Ltd	Hibaldstow	31. 5.02P
					(As "2632019")		
G-BXZD	Westland SA.314C Gazelle HT.2	1174	XW895	25. 8.98	Middleton Miniature Mouldings Ltd		
						Teesside	23. 1.02P
G-BXZE	Westland SA.314D Gazelle HT.3	1228	XW910	25. 8.98	Leisure Park Management Ltd	Goodwood	7. 6.02P
	(Control lost on take off Hickstead Showground, West Sussex 3.9.01: damage to fenestron, tail boom, fin and skids)						
G-BXZF	Lindstrand LBL-90A HAFB	575		8. 1.99	L.Van Den Avyle	Cascais, Portugal	7. 1.00A
G-BXZG	Cameron A-210 HAFB	4424		21. 8.98	Societe Bombard SARL	Beaume, France	10.10.02A
G-BXZH	Cameron A-210 HAFB	4423		21. 8.98	Societe Bombard SARL	Beaume, France	10.10.02A
G-BXZI	Lindstrand LBL-90A HAFB	543		14. 8.98	S.Stanley t/a Purple Balloons	Sudbury	21. 6.02A
G-BXZK	MD Helicopters Explorer	900-00057	N9238T	27. 8.98	Dorset Police Air Support Unit	Winfrith	1. 2.02T
			G-76-057				
G-BXZM	Cessna 182S	18280310	N2683L	8.10.98	Oxford Aviation Services Ltd	Oxford	8.10.01T
G-BXZN	Advanced Technologies Firebird CH1 ATI			25. 8.98	Intora-Firebird plc	Southend	
		00002	N8186E		*(Stored 1.02)*		
G-BXZO	Pietenpol Air Camper	PFA 047-12818		10. 7.98	P.J.Cooke	(Uckfield)	14. 7.02P
G-BXZS	Sikorsky S-76A II Plus	760287	N190AL	14. 9.98	Bristow Helicopters Ltd.	Redhill	3. 5.02T
			N190AE/N153AE/N7265A				
G-BXZT	MS.880B Rallye Club	1733	OO-EDG	2. 9.98	K.P. Snipe	Draycott Farm, Chiseldon	11.12.02
			D-EBDG/F-BSVL				
G-BXZU	Micro Aviation Bantam B22 S	98-015	ZK-JJL	21. 9.98	M.R.M.Welch	Swanborough Farm, Lewes	8. 5.02P
	(Rotax 582)						

G-BXZV	CFM Streak Shadow (Rotax 912-UL) K.293SA & PFA 206-13357 *(Orig regd as Streak Shadow Srs SA: new designation 8.01: kit c/n unchanged)*			18. 9.98	CFM Aircraft Ltd. *(Noted 5.00)*	Framlingham	30. 7.02P
G-BXZY	CFM Streak Shadow DD (Rotax 582)	296-DD		21. 9.98	P.A.James t/a Cloudbase Aviation G-BXZY	Redhill	16.12.02P
G-BXZZ	Sky 160-24 HAFB	109		14. 7.98	S.J.Colin & A.S.Pinder t/a Skybus Ballooning	Maidstone	30. 5.02T

G-BYAA – G-BYZZ

G-BYAA	Boeing 767-204ER	25058	PH-AHM G-BYAA/N60659	23. 4.91	Britannia Airways Ltd *"Sir Matt Busby CBE"*	Luton	13.11.02T
G-BYAB	Boeing 767-204ER	25139	(PH-AHN) G-BYAB	11. 6.91	Britannia Airways Ltd *"Brian Johnston CBE"*	Luton	26. 3.02T
G-BYAD	Boeing 757-204ER	26963		6. 5.92	Britannia Airways Ltd	Luton	22. 2.02T
G-BYAE	Boeing 757-204ER	26964		12. 5.92	Britannia Airways Ltd	Luton	26. 4.04T
G-BYAF	Boeing 757-204ER	26266		13. 1.93	Britannia Airways Ltd	Luton	19. 1.03T
G-BYAH	Boeing 757-204ER	26966		5. 2.93	Britannia Airways Ltd	Luton	10. 2.03T
G-BYAI	Boeing 757-204	26967		1. 3.93	Britannia Airways Ltd	Luton	4. 3.03T
G-BYAJ	Boeing 757-204ER	25623		4. 3.93	Britannia Airways Ltd	Luton	23. 1.02T
G-BYAK	Boeing 757-204	26267		6. 4.93	Britannia Airways Ltd	Luton	13. 4.03T
G-BYAL	Boeing 757-204	25626		13. 5.93	Britannia Airways Ltd	Luton	18. 5.03T
G-BYAN	Boeing 757-204	27219		26. 1.94	Britannia Airways Ltd	Luton	14. 2.04T
G-BYAO	Boeing 757-204	27235		3. 2.94	Britannia Airways Ltd	Luton	2. 2.03T
G-BYAP	Boeing 757-204	27236		15. 2.94	Britannia Airways Ltd	Luton	14. 2.03T
G-BYAR	Boeing 757-204	27237		1. 3.94	Britannia Airways Ltd	Luton	28. 2.03T
G-BYAS	Boeing 757-204	27238		9. 3.94	Britannia Airways Ltd	Luton	31. 1.02T
G-BYAT	Boeing 757-204	27208		21. 3.94	Britannia Airways Ltd	Luton	24. 3.04T
G-BYAU	Boeing 757-204	27220		18. 5.94	Britannia Airways Ltd	Luton	17. 5.03T
G-BYAV	Taylor JT.1 Monoplane (VW 1600)	PFA 055-11010		27. 8.98	T Adams	Little Gransden	4.10.01P
G-BYAW	Boeing 757-204	27234		3. 4.95	Britannia Airways Ltd *"Eric Morecambe OBE"*	Luton	2. 4.04T
G-BYAX	Boeing 757-204	28834		24. 2.99	Britannia Airways Ltd	Luton	28. 2.02T
G-BYAY	Boeing 757-204	28836		13. 4.99	Britannia Airways Ltd	Luton	12. 4.02T
G-BYAZ	CFM Streak Shadcw SA (Rotax 582) K.244 & PFA 206-12656			1. 9.98	A.G.Wright	(Camberley)	23. 2.02P
G-BYBA	Agusta-Bell 206B-3 JetRanger III	8596	G-BHXV G-OWJM/G-BHXV	31. 3.98	R.Forests Ltd	White Waltham	8. 8.02T
G-BYBC	Agusta-Bell 206B JetRanger II	8567	G-BTWW EI-BJV/G-BTWW	31. 3.98	Proofgolden Ltd t/a Mainstreet Aviation	(Durham)	28. 6.03T
G-BYBD	Reims Cessna F172H	F172-0487	G-OBHX G-AWMU	6. 7.98	R Ross	Pittrichie Farm, Whiterashes	23. 6.02T
G-BYBE	Wassmer Jodel D.120A Paris-Nice	269	OO-FDP	24. 7.98	R.J.Page	Swanton Morley	27. 1.02
G-BYBF	Robin R.2160i	329		1.10.98	D.J.R.Lloyd-Evans	Compton Abbas	10. 3.02T
G-BYBH	Piper PA-34-200T Seneca II	34-8070078	N119SA (G-BYBH)/N4023K/N3567B	9. 6.00	Goldspear (UK) Ltd	White Waltham	
G-BYBI	Bell 206B-3 JetRanger III	3668	ZS-RGP N5757M	19.10.98	Winkburn Air Ltd	Elstree	19. 7.02T
G-BYBJ	Medway Hybred 44XLR	MR156/135		22. 1.99	M Gardner	Rochester	25. 4.01P
G-BYBK	Murphy Rebel (Lycoming O-235-L2C) *(Built L A Dyer)*	260R	N95LD	19. 8.98	D.Webb	Shobdon	11. 1.02P
G-BYBL	Gardan GY-80 Horizon 160D	127	F-BMUY	25. 9.98	P.T.Harmsworth	Exeter	21.11.03
G-BYBM	Jabiru Jabiru SK (Jabiru 2200A)	PFA 274-13377		18. 9.98	P.J.Hatton	(Okehampton)	5. 9.02P
G-BYBN	Cameron N-77 HAFB	3082	N6004M	30. 9.98	M.G.& R.D.Howard	Bristol	5. 3.01A
G-BYBO	Medway EclipseR (Jabiru 2200A)	155/134		14. 9.98	R.Skene	Rochester	16. 3.01P
G-BYBP	Cessna A185F	18503804	OO-DCD F-GDCD/F-ODIA/N4593E	15.10.98	G.M.S.Scott	Headcorn	4. 2 02
G-BYBR	Rans S-6-116 Coyote II (Rotax 912-UL)	PFA 204A-13081		10. 7.98	J.B.Robinson	Blackpool	20. 8.02P
G-BYBS	Sky 80-16 HAFB	136		27.10.98	K.B.Chapple	Didcot	12. 8.02
G-BYBU	Murphy Renegade Spirit UK (Rotax 582)	PFA 188-13229		12.10.98	L.C.Cook *"Wayward Spirit"*	Sywell	30. 5.02P
G-BYBV	Mainair Rapier (Rotax 503-2V)	1183-1198-7-W986		20.10.98	M.W.Robson	York	1.11.02P
G-BYBW	TEAM mini-MAX (Rotax 447)	PFA 186-12120		19.10.98	N.E.Johnson	Kettering	22.11.00P
G-BYBX	Slingsby T.67M-260 Firefly	2261		21.10.98	Slingsby Aviation Ltd	Kirkbymoorside	
G-BYBY	Thorp T-18C Tiger	492	N77KK	17. 7.98	L.J.Joyce *(Cf/f 20.8.99)*	Liverpool	3.10.02P

G-BYBZ	Jabiru Jabiru SK (Jabiru 2200A)	PFA 274-13290		7. 9.98	A.W.Harris	Coventry	9. 6.02P
G-BYCA	Piper PA-28-140 Cherokee D	28-7125223	PH-VRZ N11C	24. 9.98	I.J.Sixsmith	(Haywards Heath)	16.11.01T
G-BYCB	Sky 21-16 HAFB	142		28.10.98	Zebedee Balloon Service Ltd	Hungerford	
G-BYCD	Cessna 140 (Continental O-200-A)	13744	N4273N NC4273N	28. 9.98	G.P.James	Fenland	7. 4.02
G-BYCE	Robinson R44 Astro	0520		12.10.98	Walters Plant Hire Ltd	(Aberdare)	30.10.04T
G-BYCF	Robinson R22 Beta-II	2866		12.10.98	Teleology Ltd	(Todmorden)	9.12.04T
G-BYCJ	CFM Shadow DD (Rotax 582)	K.294-DD & PFA 161-13258		14.10.98	J.W.E.Pearson	Plaistows Farm, St Albans	30.11.02P
G-BYCL	Raj Hamsa X'Air 582 (1)	331 & BMAA/HB/088		15.10.98	D.O'Keefe, M.J.Sullivan & A.Nottage	London Colney	28. 6.02P
G-BYCM	Rans S-6-ES Coyote II (Rotax 503 DCDI)	PFA 204-13315		15. 9.98	E.W.McMullan *(Noted 8.01)*	Dunnyvadden, Co.Antrim	7.11.00P
G-BYCN	Rans S-6-ES Coyote I (Rotax 582-48)	PFA 204-13314		15. 9.98	J.K.& R.L.Dunseath	Mullaghmore, Co.Sligo	15. 3.02P
G-BYCO*	Rans S-6-ES Coyote II *(Struck ground in practice forced landing Limavady 23.8.01 & cancelled 3.1.02 as wfu) (Wreck noted 9.01)*	PFA 204-13318		17. 9.98	T J Croskery	City of Derry	8. 5.02P
G-BYCP	Beechcraft B200 Super King Air	BB-966	F-GDCS	15.10.98	Comex Services Ltd	Blackbushe	17.11.01
G-BYCS	CEA Jodel DR.1051 Sicile	201	F-BJUJ	28.10.98	Fire Defence plc	Trenchard Farm, Eggesford	13. 2.02
G-BYCT	Aero L-29A Delfin	395142	ES-YLH Estonian AF/Soviet AF	29.10.98	M.Beesley	Manston	10. 5.02P
G-BYCU	Robinson R22 Beta	1094	G-OCGJ	3.11.98	K.S.& S.A.Faria	Redhill	15. 9.04T
G-BYCV	Murphy Maverick (Rotax 503)	PFA 259-12925		24. 9.98	J.M.Swash	Otherton, Cannock	30. 9.02P
G-BYCX	Westland Wasp HAS.Mk.1	F.9754 & WA-B-Z3	ZK-HOX 92 SA Navy	9.11.98	B.H.Austen *"92"* t/a Austen Associates	Thruxton	30. 4.02P
G-BYCY	III Sky Arrow 650T (Rotax 912-UL)	PFA 298-13332		10.11.98	K.A.Daniels	Gloucestershire	10. 5.02P
G-BYCZ	Jabiru Jabiru SK (Jabiru 2200A)	PFA 274-13388		16.10.98	R.Scroby	(Leicester)	22. 2.01P
G-BYDA	McDonnell Douglas DC-10-30	46990	OY-CNO XA-SYE/F-GGMZ/C-GFHX/9V-SDA	25. 3.99	Airtours International Airways Ltd	Manchester	29. 3.02T
G-BYDB	Grob G-115B	8025	VH-JVL D-EFCG	26 3.99	J.B.Baker	Tatenhill	12. 4.02
G-BYDD	Mooney M.20J	24-0847	D-EIWM	19.10.98	A.D.E.Eade	(Salisbury)	22. 2.02T
G-BYDE	Supermarine 361 Spitfire IX	--	Sov AF PT879	11.11.98	A.H.Soper	(Romford)	
G-BYDF	Sikorsky S-76A	760364	JA6615	9. 1.98	Brecqhou Development Ltd	Guernsey	8. 7.04T
G-BYDG	Beechcraft C24R Sierra	MC-627	OY-AZL	9.11.98	Professional Air Training Ltd	Bournemouth	19. 4.02T
G-BYDI	Cameron A-210 HAFB	4495		4. 2.99	N.J.Appleton t/a First Flight *(Park Furnishers titles)*	Bristol	16. 2.02T
G-BYDJ	Colt 120A HAFB	3527		17.11.98	D.K.Hempleman-Adams	Box, Wilts	19. 6.02A
G-BYDK	Stampe SV-4C (P/i quoted officially as F-BCXV which was c/n 298)	55	F-BCXY	20.11.98	Bianchi Aviation Film Services Ltd	Booker	
G-BYDL	Hawker Hurricane IIB	-	Sov AF Z5207	17.11.98	Retro Track & Air (UK) Ltd *(New owner 12.01)*	(Dursley)	
G-BYDM	Pegasus Quantum 15-912	7488		18.11.98	B.J.Fallows	(Ammanford)	14.12.01P
G-BYDN	Fokker F.28 Mk.0100 *(Fokker 100)*	11329	N130ML SE-DUF/PH-CFG/PH-EZV/(G-FIOZ)/PH-EZV	4. 6.99	Gill Aviation Ltd *(Stored 10.01)*	Woensdrecht, The Netherlands	3. 6.02T
G-BYDO	Fokker F.28 Mk.0100 *(Fokker 100)*	11323	N131ML SE-DUB/PH-CFA/(PH-LNP)/PH-EZC/(G-FIOT)/PH-EZC	17. 3.99	Gill Aviation Ltd *(Stored 10.01)*	Woensdrecht, The Netherlands	25. 3.02T
G-BYDP	Fokker F.28 Mk.0100 *(Fokker 100)*	11321	F-WQJA N132ML/SE-DUA/PH-RRC/G-FIOS/PH-EZA	18. 2.99	Gill Aviation Ltd *(Stored 10.01)*	Eindhoven, The Netherlands	10. 3.02T
G-BYDR	North American B-25D-30NC Mitchell II *(C/n 100-23644 reported)*	100-20644	N88972 CF-OGQ KL161 RCAF/43-3318	22. 3.99	Patina Ltd *(Op B J S Grey/The Fighter Collection)* *(As "VO-B" in 98 Sqdn RAF c/s) "Grumpy"*	Duxford	25. 5.02P
G-BYDS	Messerschmitt Bf109E-3	1342	Luft'ffe	24.11.98	Alpine Deer Group Ltd *(On rebuild 11.99 for American Flying Heritage Collection, Seattle, Washington)*	Not known	
G-BYDT	Cameron N-90 HAFB	4499		28. 1.99	N.J.Langley	Bristol	22. 5.02A
G-BYDU*	Cameron Cart SS HAFB	4500		28. 1.99	Virgin Airship & Balloon Co Ltd *(Tesco titles) (Cancelled 13.3.01 by CAA)*	Telford	29.11.00A
G-BYDV	Van's RV-6 (Lycoming O-320-D1F)	PFA 181-13264		3.12.98	R G Andrews	Killarney Co.Kerry	8. 6.02P
G-BYDW	Rotary Air Force RAF 2000 GTX-SE	PFA G/13-1302		4.12.98	R G Turck	Rayne Hall Farm, Rayne	21. 9.01P

G-BYDX	American General AG-5B Tiger	10051	N374SA	25. 3.99	A.J.Watson	Southampton	19. 4.02
			G-BYDX/F-GKBH/N1191Y		t/a Bibit Group		
G-BYDY	Beech 58 Baron	TH-1852	C-GBWF	10.11.98	J.F.Britten	Blackbushe	16.12.04
G-BYDZ	Pegasus Quantum 15-912	7493		22.12.98	W.McCormack	Broomhill Farm, West Calder	15. 9 02P
G-BYEA	Cessna 172P	17275464	PH-ILL	7.10.98	Plane Talking Ltd	Redhill	19.10.04T
			N63661				
G-BYEB	Cessna 172P	17274634	PH-ILM	7.10.98	Plane Talking Ltd	Elstree	18.10.04T
			N52917				
G-BYEC	Glaser-Dirks DG-800B	8-102-B36	D-KSDG	13.11.98	P.R.Redshaw	Rufforth	23.11.01
G-BYEE	Mooney M.20K (231)	25-0282	N231JZ	20. 7.88	R.J.Baker & W.Woods	Coventry	10. 4.04
					t/a Double Echo Flying Group		
G-BYEF*	Lockheed L.188CF Electra	2006	EI-CHX	14.12.98	Dart Group plc	Bournemouth	
			SE-IVR/N853U/PH-LLC				
	(Stored in Hunting Cargo c/s as "EI-CHX" 1.01: cancelled 5.7.01 as wfu: current status unknown)						
G-BYEH	CEA DR.250/160 Capitaine	15	OO-SOL	6.10.98	E.J.Horsfall	Blackpool	25. 8.02
			F-BMZL				
G-BYEI	Cameron 90SS Chick	4519		1. 4.99	Virgin Airship & Balloon Co Ltd	Telford	5.10.00A
					(Bic SoftFeel titles)		
G-BYEJ	Scheibe SF-28A Tandem Falke	5713	OE-9070	18.12.98	D.Shrimpton	RAF Keevil	14. 3.02
			(D-KDAM)				
G-BYEK	Stoddard-Hamilton GlaStar	PFA 295-13087		14. 9.98	G.M.New	Breighton	1. 7.02P
G-BYEL	Van's RV-6	PFA 181-12560		7. 1.99	D.Millar	Bidford	10. 6.02P
G-BYEM	Cessna R182 Skylane RG II	R18200822	N494	8. 1.99	Wycombe Air Centre Ltd	Booker	28. 1.02T
			D-ELVI/N737FT				
G-BYEO	Zenair CH.601HDS Zodiac *(Tail-wheel u/c)* (Rotax 912-UL)	PFA 162-13345		11. 1.99	M.J.Diggins	White Waltham	21. 6.02P
					t/a Cloudbase Flying Group		
G-BYEP	Lindstrand LBL 90B HAFB	560		20.11.98	D.G Macguire	Pulborough	26. 3.01A
G-BYER	Cameron C-80 HAFB	4513		19.11.98	Cameron Balloons Ltd *"E2"*	Bristol	14. 2.01A
G-BYES	Cessna 172P	17274514	PH-ILN	7.10.98	Plane Talking Ltd	Elstree	24.10.04T
			N172TP/N52424				
G-BYET	Cessna 172P	17275122	PH-ILP	7.10.98	Plane Talking Ltd	Redhill	15.10.04T
			N55158				
G-BYEU	Pegasus Quantum 15	7495		28. 1.99	T.C.Brown	Mill Farm, Shifnal	2. 3.02P
G-BYEW	Pegasus Quantum 15-912	7499		15. 1.99	P.M.Coppola	East Fortune	15. 2.02P
G-BYEX	Sky 120-24 HAFB	135		21. 1.99	Ballongflyg Upp and Ner AB	Stockholm, Sweden	19. 2.02A
G-BYEY	Lindstrand LBL-21 Silver Dream	577		15. 1.99	Oscair Project Ltd	Taby, Sweden	
G-BYEZ	Dyn'Aéro MCR-01 Ban-bi (Rotax 912)	47 & PFA 301-13185		25.11.98	J.P.Davies	Leicester	28. 6.02P
G-BYFA	Reims Cessna F152 II	F15201968	G-WACA	19.11.98	A.J.Gomes	Biggin Hill	5. 5.96
G-BYFB	Cameron N-105 HAFB	4532		15. 1.99	Cameron Balloons Ltd	Bristol	11. 2.00A
G-BYFC	Jabiru Jabiru SK (Jabiru 2200A)	PFA 274-13344		5. 2.99	A.C.N.Freeman	Booker	7. 6.02P
G-BYFD	Grob G-115A	8100	EI-CCN	15. 1.99	D.Lewis	(Basingstoke)	24. 5.03T
			G-BSGE				
G-BYFE	Pegasus Quantum 15-912	7496		21. 6.99	N.C.Hurry	Knapthorpe Lodge, Caunton	13. 2.02P
					t/a G-BYFE Flying Group		
G-BYFF	Pegasus Quantum 15-912	7500		1. 2.99	D.Young	Kemble	8. 2.02P
					t/a Kemble Flying Club		
G-BYFG	Europa Aviation Europa XS	PFA 247-13407		22. 1.99	P R Brodie	(Guildford)	
G-BYFH	Bede BD-5B	665		22. 1.99	G M J Monaghan	(Bury St Edmunds)	
G-BYFI	CFM Starstreak Shadow SA	PFA 206-13300		11. 2.99	D.G.Cook	Leiston	
G-BYFJ	Cameron N-105 HAFB	4545		4. 3.99	R.R.McCormack	Carryduff, Belfast	19. 4.01A
G-BYFK	Cameron Printer-105 SS HAFB	4522		4. 3.99	Flying Pictures Ltd	Fairoaks	8. 4.02A
					(Samsung Printers titles)		
G-BYFL	Diamond HK 36 TTS	36623		5. 2.99	C.N.J.Squibb	RNAS Culdrose	14. 6.02
					t/a Seahawk Gliding Club		
G-BYFM	Jodel DR.1050-M1 Sicile Record rep (Continental O-200-A)	PFA 304-13237		26. 2.99	P.M.Standen & A.J.Roxburgh	Barton	5. 6.02P
G-BYFN	Thruster T600N (Rotax 503-2V)	9029-T600N-030		8. 2.99	J.S.Manning	(Abuferia, Portugal)	30. 6.01P
G-BYFP	Piper PA-28-181 Archer III	2843238	N4137N	5. 7.99	B.Badley	Andrewsfield	5. 7.02T
			G-BYFP/N41270				
G-BYFR	Piper PA-32R-301 Saratoga IIHP	3246133	N4135P	13. 4.99	Buckleton Ltd	(Jersey)	8. 7.04T
			G-BYFR/N9515N				
G-BYFS*	Airbus A320-231	0230	(D-AFRO(2))	27. 3.99	Airtours International Airways	Manchester	
			A40-MA/N230RX/SX-BSJ/N230RX/F-WWDI				
			(Sold as D-AFRO(2) & cancelled 14.4.99) (For restoration 2002)				
G-BYFT	Pietenpol Aircamper	PFA 047-13057		22.12.98	M W Elliott	(Tamworth)	

G-BYFU	Lindstrand LBL-105B HAFB	594		9. 3.99	Balloons Lindstrand France	Curcay Sur Dive, France	4. 3.02A
G-BYFV	TEAM mini-MAX 91	PFA 186-13431		5. 2.99	W.E.Gillham *(Under construction 2.00)*	Croft Farm, Darlington	
G-BYFX	Colt 77A HAFB	4547		4. 3.99	Flying Pictures Ltd *(Agfa titles)*	Fairoaks	19. 1.01A
G-BYFY	Avions Mudry CAP.10B	263	F-GKKD	9. 3.99	R.W.H.Cole t/a Cole Aviation *(Noted 11.01)*	Spilsted Farm, Sedlescombe	
G-BYGA	Boeing 747-436	28855		15.12.98	British Airways plc *(Chelsea Rose t/s)*	Heathrow	13.12.04T
G-BYGB	Boeing 747-436	28856		17. 1.99	British Airways plc *(Colum t/s)*	Heathrow	16. 1.02T
G-BYGC	Boeing 747-436	25823		19. 1.99	British Airways plc *(Chelsea Rose t/s)*	Heathrow	18. 1.02T
G-BYGD	Boeing 747-436	28857		26. 1.99	British Airways plc *(Rendezvous t/s)*	Heathrow	25. 1.02T
G-BYGE	Boeing 747-436	28858		5. 2.99	British Airways plc *(Rendezvous t/s)*	Heathrow	4. 2.02T
G-BYGF	Boeing 747-436	25824		17. 2.99	British Airways plc *(Chelsea Rose t/s)*	Heathrow	16. 2.02T
G-BYGG	Boeing 747-436	28859		29. 4.99	British Airways plc *(Rendezvous t/s)*	Heathrow	28. 4.02T
G-BYHC	Cameron Z-90 HAFB	4555		16. 3.99	A.M. Holly t/a Exclusive Ballooning	Bristol	25. 3.02T
G-BYHD	Robinson R22 Beta	1455	N900AB	22. 3.99	C.G.P.Holden	Gamston	17. 3.02T
G-BYHE	Robinson R22 Beta	2023	N82128 LV-VAB	14. 1.99	L Smith t/a Helicopter Services	Booker	7. 2.02T
G-BYHG	Dornier 328-100	3098	D-CDAE	7. 4.99	Suckling Aviation (Cambridge) Ltd t/a Scot Airways	Cambridge	6. 4.02T
G-BYHH	Piper PA-28-161 Warrior <u>III</u>	2842050	N4126Z <u>G-BYHH/N9527N</u>	15. 6.99	Stapleford Flying Club Ltd	Stapleford	17. 6.02T
G-BYHI	Piper PA-28-161 Warrior II	28-8116084	SE-IDP	4. 1.99	Haimoss Ltd	Old Sarum	10. 2.02T
G-BYHJ	Piper PA-28R-201 Arrow	2844020	N41675 G-BYHJ/N41675	25. 2.00	Bflying Ltd *(Op Bournemouth Flying Club)*	Bournemouth	10. 4.03T
G-BYHK	Piper PA-28-181 Archer II	2843240	N4128V (G-BYHK)/N9519N	20. 5.99	Southnet Ltd	(Douglas, IoM)	20. 5.02T
G-BYHL	de Havilland DHC-1 Chipmunk 22	C1/0361	WG308	15. 3.99	M.R.& I.D.Higgins	Gamston	18. 6.03
G-BYHM	British Aerospace BAe 125 Srs.800B	258233	VP-BTM VR-BTM/(VR-BQH)/F-WQCD/D-CAVW/G-5-770	12. 2.99	Corporate Aircraft Leasing Ltd	Jersey	23. 2.02
G-BYHN	Mainair Blade 912	1191-0399-7-W994		9. 4.99	R.Stone	(Stoke-on-Trent)	24. 2.02P
G-BYHO	Mainair Blade 912	1197-0599-7-W1000		16. 3.99	P.J.Morton	(St.Michaels)	22. 3.02P
G-BYHP	CEA DR.253B Regent	161	OO-CSK	29. 3.99	D.A.Hood	Sywell	25. 8.02P
G-BYHR	Pegasus Quantum 15-912	7518		6. 4.99	I.D.Chantler	Long Acre Farm, Sandy	6. 4.02P
G-BYHS	Mainair Blade 912	1187-0299-7-W990		11. 3.99	D.A.Bolton	Barton	26. 4.02P
G-BYHT	Robin DR.400-180R Remorqueur	811	HB-EUU	9. 4.99	M.Recht	Aboyne	5. 7.02
G-BYHU	Cameron N-105 HAFB	4567		30. 4.99	Freeup Ltd *(Iveco Ford Truck titles)*	Bristol	22. 5.02A
G-BYHV	Raj Hamsa X'Air 582 (1)	361 & BMAA/HB/090		25. 3.99	S.N.J.Huxtable	(Highbridge)	16.10.01P
G-BYHW	Cameron A-160	2848	D-OWEH	25. 3.99	R H Etherington	Siena, Italy	4. 9.02A
G-BYHX	Cameron A-250 HAFB	4565		16. 4.99	Global Ballooning Ltd	Uckfield	28. 3.02T
G-BYHY	Cameron V-77	4493		22. 3.99	P Spellward	Bristol	19. 5.02A
G-BYHZ	Sky 160-24	140		13. 5.99	Skyride Balloons Ltd	King's Lynn	9. 8.02T
G-BYIA	Jabiru Jabiru SK (Jabiru 2200A)	PFA 274-13436		10. 2.99	G.M.Geary	Morgansfield, Fishburn	11. 5.02P
G-BYIB	Rans S-6-ES Coyote II (Rotax 582-48)	PFA 204-13387		26. 3.99	G A Clayton	(Chesterfield)	20. 9.02P
G-BYIC	Cessna U.206G Turbo Stationair	U20605476	OY-NUA N113RS/N3RS/N6398U	27. 4.99	D.M.Penney	Peterlee	29. 7.02
G-BYID	Rans S-6-ES Coyote II (Rotax 582-48)	PFA 204-13348		11. 5.99	D.J.Brotherhood	Tollerton	24. 9.02P
G-BYIE	Robinson R22 Beta-II	2933		22. 4.99	J.W.Ramsbottom t/a Jepar Rotorcraft	Blackpool	27. 4.02T
G-BYIF	Jabiru Jabiru UL (Jabiru 2200A)	PFA 274A-13364		26. 3.99	J.A.Moss	Priory Farm, Tibenham	21. 6.02P
G-BYIG	Murphy Renegade Spirit <u>UK</u> (Rotax 582)	PFA 188-12519		26. 2.99	J.Hatswell	(Menton, France)	4.10.02P
G-BYII	TEAM mini-MAX	PFA 186-11820		22. 1.99	J S R Moodie	Rovie Farm, Rogart	
G-BYIJ	CASA I-131E Jungmann	2110	E3B-514	16. 7.90	P.R.Teager & R.N.Crosland	Spilsted Farm, Sedlescombe	29. 5.02P
G-BYIK	Europa Aviation Europa (Rotax 912-UL)	PFA 247-12771		2. 2.99	P.M.Davis	Oxford	30. 8.02P

G-BYIL	Cameron N-105 HAFB	4591		29. 4.99	Oakfield Farm Products Ltd	Broadway	10. 6.02A
G-BYIM	Jabiru Jabiru UL (Jabiru 2200A)	PFA 274A-13397		22.12.98	W J Dale	Langar	21. 3.02P
G-BYIN	Rotary Air Force RAF 2000 GTX-SE	PFA G/13-1305		19. 1.99	J.R.Legge	(Rossendale)	12.10.02P
G-BYIO	Colt 105A HAFB	4601		30. 4.99	N.Charbonnier *(Lindt titles)*	Aosta, Italy	21. 1.02A
G-BYIP	Aerotek Pitts S-2A (Lycoming AE10-360-A1E)	2244	N109WA TC-ECN	23. 2.99	D.P.Heather-Hayes	Perth	14. 9.02T
G-BYIR	Aerotek Pitts S-1S Special (Lycoming AE10-360-B4A)	1-0063	N103WA TC-ECP	23. 2.99	Hampshire Aeroplane Co.Ltd	Sancreed	14. 9.02
G-BYIS	Pegasus Quantum 15-912	7508		25. 2.99	A.J.Ridell	Knapthorpe Lodge, Caunton	18. 3.02P
G-BYIT	Robin DR.500/200i President *(Registered as DR.400/500)*	0010		27. 1.99	P.R.Liddle	Rochester	23. 5.02
G-BYIU	Cameron V-90 HAFB	4552		6. 4.99	H.Micketeit	Bielefeld, Germany	29. 3.01A
G-BYIV	Cameron PM-80 HAFB *(Coca Cola bottle)*	4595		14. 5.99	A.Schneider	Borken, Germany	17. 4.02A
G-BYIW	Cameron PM-80 HAFB *(Coca Cola bottle)*	4596		14. 5.99	A.Schneider	Borken, Germany	13.10.00A
G-BYIX	Cameron PM-80 HAFB *(Coca Cola bottle)*	4597		14. 5.99	A.Schneider	Borken, Germany	17. 4.02A
G-BYIY	Lindstrand LBL-105B	601		26. 3.99	J.H.Dobson	Reading	16.12.01A
G-BYIZ	Pegasus Quantum 15-912	7504		8. 2.99	J.D.Gray	Eshott	24. 2.02P
G-BYJA	Rotary Air Force RAF 2000 GTX-SE	PFA G/13-1297		6. 4.99	B.Errington-Weddle *(Damaged rolling-over late Summer 2001)*	Henstridge	18. 7.02P
G-BYJB	Mainair Blade 912	1192-0499-7-W995		6. 4.99	J.H.Bradbury	Arclid Green, Sandbach	11. 4.02P
G-BYJC	Cameron N-90 HAFB	4562		30. 4.99	D.E.Bentley Ltd	Sheffield	16. 6.02A
G-BYJD	Jabiru Jabiru UL (Jabiru 2200A)	PFA 274-13376		16. 4.99	M.W.Knights	Hinddeston	21. 5.02P
G-BYJE	TEAM mini-MAX 91	PFA 186-12327		6. 4.99	A.W.Austin	(Cheltenham)	
G-BYJF	Thorp T.211	107	N2545C	20. 5.99	AD Aviation Ltd	Liverpool	25. 7.02
G-BYJG	Lindstrand LBL 77A HAFB	600		16. 4.99	Lindstrand Balloons Ltd	Oswestry	7. 5.01A
G-BYJH	Grob G.109B	6512	D-KFRI	19. 5.99	J.D.Scott	Cambridge	20. 5.02
G-BYJI	Europa Aviation Europa (Rotax 912UL)	004 & PFA 247-13010	G-ODTI	19. 4.99	P S Jones	Wolverhampton	22. 7.02P
G-BYJJ	Cameron C-80 HAFB	4436	SX-MAX	20. 4.99	Proxim Franchising SRL	Milan, Italy	7.12.01A
G-BYJK	Pegasus Quantum 15-912	7524		7. 5.99	B S Smy	East Fortune	16. 5.02P
G-BYJL	Aero Designs Pulsar	PFA 202-13311		20. 4.99	F.A.H.Ashmead	Gore Farm, New Milton	4..7.02P
G-BYJM	Cyclone AX2000 (Rotax 582-48)	7523		25. 5.99	A.R.Hood t/a Caunton Ax2000 Syndicate	Knapthorpe Lodge, Caunton	20. 5.02P
G-BYJN	Lindstrand LBL-105A HAFB	605		30. 4.99	B.Meeson	Pwllheli	29. 4.00A
G-BYJO	Rans S-6-ES Coyote II (Rotax 582-48) *(Tail-wheel u/c)*	PFA 204-13338		4. 3.99	G.Ferguson	King's Lynn	22. 4.02P
G-BYJP	Aerotek Pitts S-1S Special (Lycoming AE10-360-B4A)	1-0064	N105WA TC-ECR	16. 3.99	T.Riddle t/a Eaglescott Pitts Group	Eaglescott	14. 9.02
G-BYJR	Lindstrand LBL-77B HAFB	608		30. 4.99	C.D.Duthy-James	Presteigne	10. 5.02A
G-BYJS	SOCATA TB-20 Trinidad	1875	F-OIGE	15. 1.99	J K Sharkey	Denham	25. 1.02
G-BYJT	Zenair CH.601HD Zodiac (Rotax 912S)	PFA 162-13130		4. 5.99	J.D.T.Tannock	Nottingham	5. 3.02P
G-BYJU	Raj Hamsa X'Air 582	429		6. 5.99	C.W.Payne	Croft Farm, Defford	20. 4.02P
G-BYJV	Cameron A-210 HAFB	4612		4. 6.99	Societe Bombard SRL	Beaune, France	10.10.02P
G-BYJW	Cameron Sphere 105SS HAFB	4585		15. 6.99	Forbes Europe Inc	Far Hills, NJ, USA	30. 6.01A
G-BYJX	Cameron C-70 HAFB	4580		30. 4.99	B.Perona	Torino, Italy	25. 4.00A
G-BYJZ	Lindstrand LBL 105A HAFB	609		27. 5.99	M.A..Webb	Chard	26. 7.02A
G-BYKA	Lindstrand LBL-69A HAFB	612		7. 5.99	Aerial Promotions Ltd *(Vauxhall titles)*	Cannock	30. 7.02A
G-BYKB	Rockwell Commander 114	14121	SE-GSM N4801W	18. 5.99	A.Walton	(March)	27. 5.02P
G-BYKC	Mainair Blade 912 (Rotax 912-UL)	1196-0599-7-W999		7. 5.99	D.Gabott	Ince Blundell	30. 5.02P
G-BYKD	Mainair Blade 912 (Rotax 912-UL)	1198-0599-7-W1001		7. 5.99	D.C.Boyle	(Chorley)	21. 6.02P
G-BYKE	Rans S-6-ESA Coyote II	PFA 204-13327		22. 1.99	C.Townsend	Kemble	4. 3.02P
G-BYKF	Enstrom F-28F	725	JA7684	19. 5.99	Battle Helicopters Ltd	(Battle)	22.12.02T
G-BYKG	Pietenpol Aircamper	PFA 047-12827		17. 3.99	K.B.Hodge *(Nearing completion 2000)*	(Mold)	
G-BYKI	Cameron N-105 HAFB	4635		4. 6.99	Flying Pictures Ltd	Navan, Co.Meath	29. 7.02A
G-BYKJ	Westland Scout AH.Mk.1 *(Pod build no.F8-6043)*	F.9696	XV121	6. 8.99	B.H.Austen t/a Austen Associates	Oaksey Park	18. 9.02P
G-BYKK	Robinson R44 Astro	0572		4. 3.99	Banner Helicopters Ltd	(Heywood)	18. 3.02T
G-BYKL	Piper PA-28-181 Archer II	28-8090162	HB-PFB N8129Y	15. 7.99	Alliance Aerolink Ltd	Norwich	18. 7.02T

Regn	Type	C/n	Previous identity	Regd	Owner/operator	Base	CofA
G-BYKM	Piper PA-34-220T Seneca III	34-8133177	HB-LMV	22. 6.99	Oxford Aviation Services Ltd	Gloucestershire	21.10.02T
G-BYKN	Piper PA-28-161 Warrior II	28-7916307	HB-PDO N2838C/N9613N	22. 6.99	Oxford Aviation Services Ltd	Oxford	1. 8.02T
G-BYKO	Piper PA-28-161 Warrior II	28-8516063	HB-PKA F-GECN/N6920C	22. 6.99	Oxford Aviation Services Ltd	Gloucestershire	1. 8.02T
G-BYKP	Piper PA-28R-201T Turbo Arrow IV	28R-7931029	HB-PDB N3010G	22. 6.99	Oxford Aviation Services Ltd	Oxford	24.11.02T
G-BYKR	Piper PA-28-161 Warrior II	2816061	HB-PLM	22. 6.99	Oxford Aviation Services Ltd	Oxford	25. 7.02T
G-BYKS	Leopoldoff L.6 Colibri	129	N10LC F-BGIT/F-WGIT	19. 4.99	I.M.Callier *(On restoration 10.01)*	(Basingstoke)	
G-BYKT	Pegasus Quantum 15-912	7529		28. 5.99	D.A.Bannister & N.J.Howarth	Deenethorpe	26. 5.02P
G-BYKU	BFC Quad City Challenger II	PFA 177A-13252	*(BFC-supplied kit as distinct from Quad City version)*	25. 5.99	K.W.Seedhouse	Walsall	
G-BYKV	Avro 504K rep	0015		27. 5.99	Hawker Restorations Ltd	Milden	
G-BYKW	Lindstrand LBL 77B HAFB	620		22. 6.99	P-J.Fuseau	(Chanteloup, France)	3. 7.02A
G-BYKX	Cameron N-90 HAFB	4657		10. 8.99	G.Davis *"Knowledgepool"*	Reading	24. 7.00A
G-BYKY	Jabiru Jabiru SK (Jabiru 2200A)	PFA 274-13385		6. 5.99	N.C.Cowell	Tatenhill	30. 8.02P
G-BYKZ	Sky 140-24 HAFB	147		25. 2.99	D.J.Head	Newbury	2. 2.00T
G-BYLA	Clutton-Tabenor FRED Srs.3	PFA 029-10775		11. 5.99	R.Holden-Rushworth	(Devizes)	
G-BYLB	de Havilland DH.82A Tiger Moth	83286	T5595	24. 5.99	P.W. Payne	(Kingston-Upon-Thames)	
G-BYLC	Pegasus Quantum 15-912	7528		25. 6.99	T.Marriott	Derby	10. 8.02P
G-BYLD	Pietenpol Aircamper	PFA 047-13392		27. 4.99	S.Bryan	(Banbury)	
G-BYLE	Piper PA-38-112 Tomahawk II	38-82A0031	N91437	18. 6.99	Surrey & Kent Flying Club Ltd	Biggin Hill	6. 3.03T
G-BYLF	Zenair CH.601HDS Zodiac	PFA 162-13179		3. 6.99	M.Thomas	(Cowbridge)	
G-BYLG	Robin HR.200/120B	336		20. 7.99	Building and Commercial Ltd	Gloucestershire	1. 8.02T
G-BYLH	Robin HR.200/120B	335		9. 7.99	Multiflight Ltd	Leeds-Bradford	19. 7.02T
G-BYLI	NOVA Vertex 22	14319		9. 4.99	M.N.Maclean	(Dundee)	
G-BYLJ	Letov LK-2M Sluka	PFA 263-13464		9. 6.99	N.E.Stokes *(Noted 4.00)*	Dunkeswell	
G-BYLK	Mainair Blade	1201-0699-7-W1004		9. 6.99	Hummingbird Microlight Flight Training Ltd	(Norwich)	25. 7.02P
G-BYLL	Sequoia Falco F.8L (Lycoming O-320-A3C)	PFA 100-10843		6.12.85	N.J.Langrick	Breighton	6. 3.02P
G-BYLM	Piper PA-46-350P Malibu Mirage	4636217		30. 7.99	Polestar Holdings Ltd	Alderney	5. 8.02T
G-BYLN	Raj Hamsa X'Air 532 (1)	430 & BMAA/HB/096		7. 7.99	R.Gillespie & S.P.McGirr	(Killygordon, Co.Donegal)	
G-BYLO	Tipsy Nipper T.66 Srs.1 (Built Avions Fairey SA)	04	OO-NIA	27. 4.99	M.J.A.Trudgill	RAF Henlow	18. 2.02P
G-BYLP	Rand Robinson KR-2	PFA 129-11431		19. 4.99	C.S.Hales (See G-BSTL)	(Walsall)	
G-BYLR	Cessna 404 Titan	404-0046	OH-CDC SE-GZH/N5428G	14. 6.99	Air Charter Scotland Ltd	Edinburgh	19. 6.03T
G-BYLS	Bede BD-4 (Lycoming O-320-E2F)	PFA 037-11288		13.12.90	G.H.Bayliss	Shobdon	17. 6.02P
G-BYLT	Raj Hamsa X'Air 582 (1)	411 & BMAA/HB/095		8. 6.99	T.W.Phipps & B.G.Simons	Craymarsh Farm, Melksham	26. 6.02P
G-BYLU	Cameron A-140 HAFB	4566		22. 6.99	Cameron Balloons Ltd	Bristol	20. 6.00A
G-BYLV	Thunder Ax8-105 S2 HAFB	4061		6. 7.99	Wind Line SRL	Iesolo, Italy	3.10.02A
G-BYLW	Lindstrand LBL 77A HAFB	615		11. 6.99	Associazione Gran Premio Italiano	Perugia, Italy	10. 6.00A
G-BYLX	Lindstrand LBL 105A HAFB	614		11. 6.99	Italiana Aeronavi	Cervignano, Italy	5. 5.02A
G-BYLY	Cameron V-77 HAFB	3375	G-ULIA(2)	16. 7.97	R.Bayly (See G-ULIA)	Bristol	21. 7.01A
G-BYLZ	Rutan Cozy	PFA 159-12464		21. 5.99	E.R.Allen	(Billingshurst)	
G-BYMA	British Aerospace Jetstream Srs.3202	840	(G-OESU) OH-JAE/N840JX/C-GSCS/G-31-840/N332QK/G-31-840	28. 7.99	Air Kilroe Ltd *(Op Eastern Airways)*	Humberside	1. 9.02T
G-BYMB	Diamond Katana DA.20-C1	C0051		9. 7.99	S.C.Brown t/a Enstone Flying Club	Enstone	15. 5.03T
G-BYMC	Piper PA-38-112 Tomahawk II	38-82A0034	N91457	18. 6.99	B W Gomez *(Force landed nr Alsager, Staffs 23.11.01 due to engine failure)*	Coventry	10..5.03T
G-BYMD	Piper PA-38-112 Tomahawk II	38-82A0009	N91342	18. 6.99	Surrey & Kent Flying Club Ltd	Biggin Hill	19. 8.02T
G-BYME	Gardan GY-80 Horizon 180	207	F-BPAA	24. 5.99	Air Venturas Ltd	Teesside	9. 9.02
G-BYMF	Pegasus Quantum 15-912	7540		9. 7.99	G.R.Stockdale	Rufforth	16. 7.01P
G-BYMG	Cameron A-210 HAFB	4631		17. 9.99	P.Johnson t/a Cloud Nine Balloon Co	Consett	31. 5.02T
G-BYMH	Cessna 152	15284980	N6127P	15. 7.99	PJC (Leasing) Ltd	Stapleford	20. 7.02T
G-BYMI	Pegasus Quantum 15	7533		9. 7.99	N.C.Grayson	Rufforth	13. 7.02P
G-BYMJ	Cessna 152	15285564	N93865	16. 7.99	PJC (Leasing) Ltd	Stapleford	15.11.02T

G-BYMK	Dornier 328-100	3062	LN-ASK D-CDXE	9. 6.99	Suckling Aviation (Cambridge) Ltd t/a Scot Airways	Cambridge	8. 6.04T
G-BYML	Dornier 328-100	3069	D-CDUL LN-ASL/D-CDXT(2)	27. 7.99	Suckling Aviation (Cambridge) Ltd t/a Scot Airways	Cambridge	14. 8.04T
G-BYMM	Raj Hamsa X'Air 582 (1)	417 & BMAA/HB/093		29. 4.99	R.W.F Boarder	Oakley	28. 4.02P
G-BYMN	Rans S-6-ESA Coyote II Rotax 582-48)	PFA 204-13477		16. 6.99	H.Smith	Morgansfield, Fishburn	16.10.02P
G-BYMO	Campbell Cricket	PFA G/03-1266		16. 7.99	D.G.Hill	(Stockton-on-Tees)	6. 3.02P
G-BYMP	Campbell Cricket Mk 1	PFA G/03-1265		16. 6.99	J.J.Fitzgerald	(Newtownards, Co.of Down)	
G-BYMR	Raj Hamsa X'Air 582 (1)	432 & BMAA/HB/094		18. 6.99	W.M/McMinn	(Craigavon)	2.11.02P
G-BYMT	Pegasus Quantum 15-912	7549		16. 7.99	S.A.Owen	Latch Farm, Kirknewton	30. 7.02P
G-BYMU	Rans S-6-ES Coyote II	PFA 204-13424		25. 6.99	I.R.Russell & G.Frogley *(Bounced on landing Barton 25.7.01 and nose u/c collapsed)*	(Northampton)	24..5.02P
G-BYMV	Rans S-6-ES Coyote II	PFA 204-13444		25. 6.99	G.A.Squires	(Wakefield)	25..7.02P
G-BYMW	Boland 52-12 HAFB	001		25. 6.99	C.Jones	Reading	
G-BYMX	Cameron A-105 HAFB	4629		16. 7.99	H.Reis	Aachen, Germany	7.10.02A
G-BYMY	Cameron N-90 HAFB	4653		19. 7.99	Cameron Balloons Ltd	Bristol	1. 9.02A
G-BYNA	Reims Cessna F172H	F172-0626	OO-VDW PH-VDW/(G-AWTH)/F-WLIT	15. 1.99	Heliview Ltd	Blackbushe	4. 3.02T
G-BYND	Pegasus Quantum 15 (Rotax 582-40)	7546		16. 7.99	M.C.Kerr	Clench Common	14. 9.02P
G-BYNE	Pilatus PC-6/B2-H4 Turbo Porter	631	HB-FLW C-FRAV/N631SA/N62148/HS-.../N62148/XW-PFC/XW-PDK/HB-FCR	10. 8.99	D.M.Penny	Le Luc, Cennes, France	1.10.02
G-BYNF	North American NA-64 Yale I	64-2171	N55904 3349 RCAF	10. 1.00	R.S.Van Dijk *(Dismantled & stored 3.00 as "3349")*	Duxford	
G-BYNH	Rotorway Executive 162F (Rotorway RI 162F)	6323		5. 7.99	R.C.Mackenzie	(Saffron Walden)	7. 7.00P
G-BYNI	Rotorway Executive 90 (Rotorway RI 162)	5216		16. 7.99	M.Bunn *(Noted 11.01)*	Street Farm, Takeley	
G-BYNJ	Cameron N-77 HAFB	4661		26. 7.99	A. Giovanni *(Primagaz titles)*	Mondovi, Italy	14. 6.02A
G-BYNK	Robin HR.200/160	338		28. 7.99	M.& K.A.Whittaker	(Henley-on-Thames)	30. 9.02T
G-BYNL	Jabiru Jabiru SK	PFA 274-13328		20. 7.99	R.C.Daykin	Tatenhill	25. 2.02P
G-BYNM	Mainair Blade 912 (Jabiru 2200A)	1204-0799-7-W1007		20. 7.99	M.W.Holmes	(Ilkeston)	27. 7.02P
G-BYNN	Cameron V-90 HAFB	4643		16. 7.99	M.K.Grigson *"Cloud Nine"*	(Shoreham)	10. 6.02
G-BYNO	Pegasus Quantum 15-912	7556		5. 8.99	R.J.Newsham & G.J.Slater	Clench Common	17. 8.02P
G-BYNP	Rans S-6-ES Coyote II	PFA 204-13414		22. 7.99	R.J. Lines	(Scunthorpe)	30. 5.02P
G-BYNR	Jabiru Jabiru UL (Jabiru 2200A)	0129	EI-MAT	23. 7.99	A.Parker	Rufforth	26. 9.02P
G-BYNS	Jabiru Jabiru SK	PFA 274-13235		23. 7.99	D.K.Lawry	(Diss)	
G-BYNT	Raj Hamsa X'Air V2(1) (Victor V2)	457 & BMAA/HB/107		20. 7.99	G.R.Wallis	Lower Mountpleasant, Chatteris	13.12.02P
G-BYNU	Cameron Thunder AX7-77 HAFB	3520		29. 7.99	Aerial Promotions Ltd	Cannock	30. 7.02A
G-BYNV	Sky 105-24 HAFB	165		11. 8.99	Par Rovelli Construzioni SRL	Mazzini, Italy	5. 5.02
G-BYNW	Cameron H-34 HAFB	4666		27. 7.99	Flying Pictures Ltd *(Energis titles)*	Fairoaks	30. 7.02A
G-BYNX	Cameron RX-105 HAFB	4656		26. 7.99	Cameron Balloons Ltd	London	1.11.00A
G-BYNY	Beechcraft 76 Duchess	ME-247	N247ME OE-FES/N6635H	4. 8.99	Magenta Ltd	Exeter	13. 9.02T
G-BYOA	Slingsby T.67M-260 Firefly	2262		8. 6.99	Babcock Rosyth Defence Ltd t/a Hunting Contract Services *(Op JEFTS)*	RAF Barkston Heath	23. 9.02T
G-BYOB	Slingsby T.67M-260 Firefly	2263		8. 6.99	Babcock Rosyth Defence Ltd t/a Hunting Contract Services *(Op JEFTS)*	RAF Church Fenton	6.10.02T
G-BYOD	Slingsby T.67C Firefly	2265		13. 6.00	Slingsby Aviation Ltd	Kirkbymoorside	
G-BYOF	Robin R.2160I	337		29. 7.99	Mistral Aviation Ltd.	Shoreham	9.12.04T
G-BYOG	Pegasus Quantum 15-912	7555		15. 9.99	A.Foote & M.Fizelle	Redlands, Swindon	22.10.02P
G-BYOH	Raj Hamsa X'Air 582 (1)	443 & BMAA/HB/101		23. 7.99	P.H.J.Kent	Davidstowe Moor	3.11.01P
G-BYOI	Sky 80-16 HAFB	163		5. 8.99	I.S.& S.W.Watthews	Cark-in-Cartmel	14. 7.02
G-BYOJ	Raj Hamsa X'Air 582 (1)	458 & BMAA/HB/108		23. 7.99	R.R.Hadley	Dunkeswell	28. 2.02P
G-BYOK	Cameron V-90 HAFB	3726		9. 8.99	D.S.Wilson	Norwich	8..7.02A
G-BYOM	Sikorsky S-76C	760464	G-IJCB	25. 8.99	Starspeed Ltd	Blackbushe	26. 3.02T
G-BYON	Mainair Blade (Rotax 503-2V)	1199-0599-7-W1002		4. 8.99	S.Mills & G.M.Hobman	(North Ferriby)	19.10.02P
G-BYOO	CFM Streak Shadow SA (Rotax 912-UL)	K.270 & PFA 206-12806		6. 8.99	C.I.Chegwen	Otherton, Cannock	20.10.00P

G-BYOR	Raj Hamsa X'Air 582 (2) (3-blade Ivoprop)	472 & BMAA/HB/117		11. 8.99	A.R.Walker	Doncaster	1..7.02P
G-BYOS	Mainair Blade 912 (Rotax 912-UL)	1209-0899-7-W1012		6. 8.99	D.Smith t/a Baxby Airsports Club	Baxby Manor, Husthwaite	15. 8.02P
G-BYOT	Rans S-6-ES Coyote II	PFA 204-13363		29. 7.99	H.F.Blakeman	Arclid Green, Sandbach	6. 9.02P
G-BYOU	Rans S-6-ES Coyote II (Rotax 582-48)	PFA 204-13460		1. 6.99	R.Germany	Knapthorpe Lodge, Caunton	10.10.02P
G-BYOV	Pegasus Quantum 15-912	7554		17. 8.99	K.W.A.Ballinger	(Wokingham)	17. 8.02P
G-BYOW	Mainair Blade (Rotax 582-2V)	1207-0899-7-W1010		9. 8.99	N.Forster	East Fortune	3.11.01P
G-BYOX	Cameron Z-90 HAFB	4672		31. 8.99	Virgin Airship & Balloon Co.Ltd	Telford	19.10.01A
G-BYOY	Canadair T-33AN Silver Star 3	T33-231	N36TH N333DV/N134AT/N10018/N134AT/RCAF 21231	8. 2.00	K.K.Gerstorfer *(On rebuild 12.00)*	North Weald	
G-BYOZ	Mainair Rapier (Rotax 503-2V)	1208-0899-7-W1011		12. 8.99	M.Morgan	Arclid Green, Sandbach	6. 9.00P
G-BYPA	Aérospatiale AS355F2 Twin Squirrel	5348	G-NWPI F-GMAO	20. 8.99	Aeromega Aviation Ltd	Stapleford	28. 3.03T
G-BYPB	Pegasus Quantum 15-912	7566		3. 9.99	S.Graham *(Noted 12.01)*	Clench Common	14. 5.02P
G-BYPC	Lindstrand LBL AS2 Gas *("Super 2" - Superpressure)*	634		17. 8.99	Lindstrand Balloons Ltd	Plano, Texas, USA	
G-BYPD	Cameron A-105 HAFB	4680		6. 1.00	Headland Hotel Co Ltd	Newquay	10. 1.02A
G-BYPE	Gardan GY-80 Horizon 160	180	F-BNYD	10. 8.99	H.I.Smith & P.R.Hendry-Smith	Little Snoring	4.11.02
G-BYPF	Thruster T600N (Rotax 582UL)	9089-T600N-034		17. 8.99	G.E.Hillyer-Jones	Shobdon	3.10.02P
G-BYPG	Thruster T600N (Rotax 582UL)	9089-T600N-035		17. 8.99	A.Stanford	Dunkeswell	22. 3.02P
G-BYPH	Thruster T600N (Rotax 582UL) *(Officially regd with c/n as 9099-T600N-036)*	9089-T600N-036		17. 8.99	A.H.Wooley	(Nuthall, Notts)	29. 4.02P
G-BYPJ	Pegasus Quantum 15-912	7565		17. 9.99	P.J.Manders	Great Bromley	21. 9.02P
G-BYPL	Pegasus Quantum 15-912	7558		9. 9.99	K.J.Hard	Sutton Meadows	9. 9.02P
G-BYPM	Europa Aviation Europa XS	PFA 247-13418		16.12.98	P.Mileham	(Saffron Walden)	
G-BYPN	SOCATA MS.880B Rallye Club	2043	F-BTPN	23. 7.99	R.& T.C.Edwards	Sturgate	19. 4.03
G-BYPO	Raj Hamsa X'Air 582 (1)	439 & BMAA/HB/111		25. 8.99	A Costello & D W Willis	Tarn Farm, Cockerham	24. 7.02P
G-BYPP	Medway Rebel SS	168/146		25.10.99	J.L. Gowens	(Maidstone)	17. 3.01P
G-BYPR	Zenair CH.601HD Zodiac (Lycoming O-235)	PFA 162-12816		25. 8.99	D.Clark	Portmoak	4. 2.02P
G-BYPT	Rans S-6-ES Coyote II (Jabiru 2200)	PFA 204-13508		27. 8.99	G.R & J.A.Pritchard	Newhouse Farm, Hardwicke	2.11.02P
G-BYPU	Piper PA-32R-301 Saratoga II HP	3246150	N4160K G-BYPU/N9518N	2.12.99	Thornfield Enterprises Ltd	Guernsey	1.12.02T
G-BYPW	Raj Hamsa X'Air 582 (3)	441 & BMAA/HB/113		1. 9.99	P.A.Mercer	St.Michaels	
G-BYPY	Ryan ST3-KR	1001	F-AZEV N18926	5.10.99	P.B.Rice *(As "001")*	Breighton	15. 3.02P
G-BYPZ	Rans S-6-116 Super 6 *(Tri-cycle u/c)* (Rotax 912-UL)	0299.13045 & PFA 204A-13448		14. 7.99	P.G.Hayward	Swanton Morley	19. 6.01P
G-BYRA	British Aerospace Jetstream Srs.3202	845	OH-JAG N845JX/N845AE/G-31-845	26.10.99	Air Kilroe Ltd *(Op Eastern Airways)*	Humberside	21.11.02T
G-BYRC	Westland Wessex HC.Mk.2	WA539	XT671	23. 9.99	D.Brem-Wilson	Honey Crock Farm, Redhill	
G-BYRE*	Rans S-10 Sakota	PFA 194-11729		23. 7.91	R J & M B Trickey *(Cancelled 8.5.99 by CAA) (Under construction 6.00).*	(Ythanbank)	
G-BYRF	Cameron N-77 HAFB	4692		20. 9.99	AAA Entertainments Ltd	Richmond, Surrey	15 .9.00A
G-BYRG	Rans S-6-ES Coyote II (Rotax 582-48)	PFA 204-13518		9. 9.99	W.H.Mills	Haverfordwest	18. 2.02P
G-BYRH	Medway Hybred 44XLR (Rotax 503)	MR165/143		25.10.99	M.R.Holland	(Pontyclun)	29. 1.02P
G-BYRJ	Pegasus Quantum 15-912	7548		24. 9.99	D A Chamberlain	Long Marston	27 .9.02P
G-BYRK	Cameron V-42 HAFB	4662		14. 7.99	Gone With The Wind Ltd	Twain-Harte, Ca, USA	22..8.00A
G-BYRM	British Aerospace Jetstream Srs.3202	847	OH-JAF N847JX/N847AE/N332QN/G-31-847	16.12.99	Air Kilroe Ltd *(Op Eastern Airways)*	Humberside	18. 1.02T
G-BYRO	Mainair Blade (Rotax 582-2V)	1210-0899-7-W1013		20. 8.99	P.W.F.Coleman	Corn Wood Farm, Adversane	13 10.02P
G-BYRP	Mainair Blade 912 (Rotax 912-UL)	1075-1295-7-W877		15. 9.99	M.P.Middleton	(Llandrindod Wells)	24. 7.02P
G-BYRR	Mainair Blade 912 (Rotax 912-UL)	1211-0999-7-W1015		17. 8.99	G.R.Sharples	(Harrow)	2 .6.02P
G-BYRS	Rans S-6-ES Coyote II	PFA 204-13425		17. 9.99	R.Beniston	Rufforth	23. 5.02P
G-BYRT	Beechcraft F33A Bonanza	CE-971	ZS-LFB N18384	1. 9.99	A Barham & G Austen	North Weald	14.10.02T

G-BYRU	Pegasus Quantum 15-912	7574		24. 9.99	M.A.McClelland t/a Sarum QTM912 Group	Old Sarum	27 .9.02P
G-BYRV	Raj Hamsa X'Air 582 (1)	367 & BMAA/HB/106		10. 9.99	A.Hipkin	Pound Green, Buttonoak, Kidderminster	4.11.02P
G-BYRX	Westland Scout AH.Mk.1	F.9640	XT634	5.10.99	Historic Helicopters Ltd *(As "XT634")*	Thruxton	1.10.02P
G-BYRY	Slingsby T.67M-200 Firefly	2042	B-HZQ VR-HZQ/HKG-11	28. 9.99	D.S.Balman & W.R.Tandy *(As "HKG-11")*	Kirbymoorside	21. 3.03T
G-BYRZ	Lindstrand LBL 77M HAFB *(Reported to be rebuilt of G-BXDX)*	643		28. 9.99	Challenge Transatlantique *"Conseil Régional de Lorraine"*	Netz, France	5.12.00A
G-BYSA	Europa Aviation Europa XS	PFA 247-13199		23. 8.99	B.Allsop	Gamston	6..4.02P
G-BYSE	Agusta-Bell 206B JetRanger II	8553	G-BFND	3.11.81	Alspath Properties Ltd	(Stratford-upon-Avon)	14. 7.02T
G-BYSF	Jabiru Jabiru UL	PFA 274A-13356		5.10.99	S.J.Marshall	Sittles Farm, Alrewas	7.11.02P
G-BYSG	Robin HR.200/120B	339		22.11.99	Anglian Flight Centres Ltd	Earls Colne	9.12.02T
G-BYSI	PZL-110 Koliber 160A	04990081	SP-WGI	21. 1.00	J.& D.F.Evans	Gamston	15. 3.03
G-BYSJ	de Havilland DHC-1 Chipmunk 22	C1/0021	SE-BON WB569	12.10.99	Silver Victory BVB *(As "WB569")*	Antwerp-Deurne, Belgium	17. 8.03T
G-BYSK	Cameron A-275 HAFB	4699		23. 2.00	Balloon School (International) Ltd *"BSB"*	Petworth	23. 7.02T
G-BYSL*	Cameron O-56 HAFB	1269		10. 4.86	S.M.M.Askey *(Cancelled 19.9.01 as wfu)*	Tring	22. 8.96A
G-BYSM	Cameron A-210 HAFB	4698		12. 4.00	Balloon School (International) Ltd *(Op Heritage Balloons) "Bath Heritage"*	Bath	23. 7.02P
G-BYSN	Rans S-6-ES Coyote II (Rotax 582-48)	PFA 204-13459		19.10.99	A.L.& A.R.Roberts	(Coningsby)	20. 2.02P
G-BYSP	Piper PA-28-181 Archer II	28-8590047	D-EAUL N6909D	12.10.99	Aerohire Ltd	Wolverhampton	16.11.02T
G-BYSR	Pegasus Quantum 15-912	7560		7. 3.00	J.Lane & P.R.Thomas	Clench Common	19. 3.01P
G-BYSS	Medway Rebel SS Two Stroke International (2SI)	167/145		25.10.99	C.R.Stevens	(Ashford)	10 .6.02P
G-BYSV	Cameron N-120 HAFB	4704		15.10.99	Cameron Balloons Ltd	Bristol	3. 3.01T
G-BYSW	Enstrom 280FX Shark	2026	I-LUST N88CV	19. 9.00	D A Marks	(Bedford)	2.11.03
G-BYSX	Pegasus Quantum 15-912	7586		23.11.99	R.H.Braithwaite t/a RAF Microlight Flying Association	RAF Wyton	14.11.02P
G-BYSY	Raj Hamsa X'Air 582 (1)	448 & BMAA/HB/109		21.10.99	J.M.Davidson	(Tewkesbury)	2..5.02P
G-BYTA	Kolb Twinstar Mk.3 (Rotax 582)	PFA 205-13240		2. 9.99	R.E.Gray	(Oxted)	5. 7.02P
G-BYTB	SOCATA TB-20 Trinidad	2002	F-OILE	18. 5.00	Jeff Brown Ltd	(Weston-super-Mare)	7 6.03P
G-BYTC	Pegasus Quantum Q2 Sport 15-912	7571		25.10.99	J.Hood	Eshott	25.10.02P
G-BYTD	Robinson R22 Beta-II	3003		25.10.99	Ace Air Flights Ltd	(Blackrock, Co.Dublin)	4.11.02T
G-BYTE	Robinson R22 Beta	1250		18. 4.90	Burman Aviation Ltd	Cranfield	17. 6.02T
G-BYTG	Glaser-Dirks DG-400	4-211	D-KBBP	18.11.99	P.R.Williams & B.Sebestik	(Brackley)	23. 2.03
G-BYTI	Piper PA-24-250 Comanche	24-3489	D-ELOP N8297P/N10F	9.11.99	P.Marsden t/a G-BYTI Syndicate	Netherthorpe	27. 3.03
G-BYTJ	Cameron Concept-80 HAFB	4703		19.11.99	M.White *"Rapido"*	Cirencester	7. 9.02A
G-BYTK	Jabiru Jabiru UL	PFA 274A-13465		8.11.99	K.A.Fagan & S.R.Pike	Booker	28..3.02P
G-BYTL	Mainair Blade 912	1224-0999-7-W1017		19.10.99	M.E.Keefe	St. Michaels	17.10.02P
G-BYTM	Dyn'Aéro MCR-01 Ban-bi	PFA 301-13440		1.10.99	I.Lang	Gloucestershire	20. 8.02P
G-BYTN	de Havilland DH.82A Tiger Moth	3993	7014M N6720	18.11.99	B.D.Hughes *(On rebuild 10.01: wings @ Denford Manor, Hungerford)*	(Rotary Farm, Hatch)	
G-BYTO	ATR 72-212	472	G-OILA F-WWEJ	17.11.99	Cityflyer Express Ltd	Gatwick	27. 3.02T
G-BYTP	ATR 72-212	473	G-OILB F-WWEG	30. 4.99	CityFlyer Express Ltd *(Colum t/s)*	Gatwick	29. 5.02T
G-BYTR	Raj Hamsa X'Air 582 (1)	460 & BMAA/HB/105		5.10.99	A.P.Roberts & R.Dunn	Dunkeswell	28. 8.02P
G-BYTS	Montgomerie Bensen B.8MR (Rotax 912)	MGM-2		22. 9.99	M.G.Mee	Carlisle	25. 6.02P
G-BYTT	Raj Hamsa X'Air 582 (4)	402 & BMAA/HB/100		22. 9.99	J.L.Pearson	(Roundwood, Co.Wicklow)	25..7.02P
G-BYTU	Mainair Blade 912 (Rotax 912)	1225-1099-7-W1018		26.11.99	L.Chesworth	(Malpas)	22.12.01P
G-BYTV	Jabiru Jabiru UL	PFA 274A-13454		3.11.99	E.Bentley	Morgansfield, Fishburn	9. 4.02P
G-BYTW	Cameron O-90 HAFB	4747		11. 4.00	Sade Balloons Ltd	London EC2	1. 6.02A
G-BYTX	Whittaker MW6-S Fat Boy Flyer (Rotax 532)	PFA 164-12819		2.12.99	J.K.Ewing	(Poole)	12.11.01P
G-BYTY	Dornier 328-100	3104	D-CDXJ 5N-BRI	2.12.99	Sucking Airways (Cambridge) Ltd t/a Scot Airways	Cambridge	8.12.02T

G-BYTZ	Raj Hamsa X'Air 582 <u>(6)</u>	486 & BMAA/HB/120		26.10.99	K.C.Millar	(Dromara, Co.of Down)	26. 2.02P
G-BYUA	Grob G.115E Tutor	82086E	D-EUKB	22. 7.99	VT Aerospace Ltd	RAF Wyton	5. 8.02T
					(Op Cambridge/London UAS)		
G-BYUB	Grob G.115E Tutor	82087E		22. 7.99	VT Aerospace Ltd	RAF St.Athan	5. 8.02T
					(Op University of Wales UAS)		
G-BYUC	Grob G.115E Tutor	82088E		22. 7.99	VT Aerospace Ltd	RAF Woodvale	5. 8.02T
					(Op Liverpool/Manchester UAS) (Code "UC")		
G-BYUD	Grob G.115E Tutor	82089E		22. 7.99	VT Aerospace Ltd	RAF Leeming	5. 8.02T
					(Op Northrumbrian UAS)		
G-BYUE	Grob G.115E Tutor	82090E		12. 8.99	VT Aerospace Ltd	RAF Cranwell	30. 8.02T
					(Op CFS/East Midlands UAS)		
		(Bounced on landing Cranwell 25.9.01, damaging propeller, nose u/c, engine bearers & fuselage)					
G-BYUF	Grob G.115E Tutor	82091E		12. 8.99	VT Aerospace Ltd	RAF Wyton	30..8.02T
					(Op Cambridge/London UAS)		
G-BYUG	Grob G.115E Tutor	82092E		22. 9.99	VT Aerospace Ltd	Glasgow	27 .9.02T
					(Op Universities of Glasgow & Strathclyde AS)		
G-BYUH	Grob G.115E Tutor	82093E		22. 9.99	VT Aerospace Ltd	RAF Colerne	27 .9.02T
					(Op Bristol UAS)		
G-BYUI	Grob G.115E Tutor	82094E		24. 9.99	VT Aerospace Ltd	RAF Woodvale	27 .9.02T
					(Op Liverpool/Manchester UAS) (Code "UI")		
G-BYUJ	Grob G.115E Tutor	82095E		24. 9.99	VT Aerospace Ltd	RAF Leeming	27 .9.02T
					(Op Northrumbrian UAS)		
G-BYUK	Grob G.115E Tutor	82096E		18.10.99	VT Aerospace Ltd	RAF Wyton	28.10.02T
					(Op Cambridge/London UAS)		
G-BYUL	Grob G.115E Tutor	82097E		18.10.99	VT Aerospace Ltd	RAF Wyton	28.10.02T
					(Op Cambridge/London UAS)		
G-BYUM	Grob G.115E Tutor	82098E		18.10.99	VT Aerospace Ltd	Boscombe Down	28.10.02T
					(Op Southampton UAS)		
G-BYUN	Grob G.115E Tutor	82099E		18.10.99	VT Aerospace Ltd	RAF Wyton	28.10.02T
					(Op Cambridge/London UAS)		
G-BYUO	Grob G.115E Tutor	82100E		19.11.99	VT Aerospace Ltd	RAF Wyton	28.11.02T
					(Op Cambridge/London UAS)		
G-BYUP	Grob G.115E Tutor	82101E		19.11.99	VT Aerospace Ltd	RAF Benson	28.11.02T
					(Op Oxford UAS)		
G-BYUR	Grob G.115E Tutor	82102E		19.11.99	VT Aerospace Ltd	RAF Leuchars	28.11.02T
					(Op Aberdeen, Dundee & St.Andrews UAS)		
G-BYUS	Grob G.115E Tutor	82103E		19.11.99	VT Aerospace Ltd	RAF Benson	28.11.02T
					(Op Oxford UAS)		
G-BYUT	Grob G.115E Tutor	82104E		7.12.99	VT Aerospace Ltd	RAF Benson	14.12.02T
					(Op Oxford UAS)		
G-BYUU	Grob G.115E Tutor	82105E		7.12.99	VT Aerospace Ltd	Glasgow	14.12.02T
					(Op Universities of Glasgow & Strathclyde AS)		
G-BYUV	Grob G.115E Tutor	82106E		7.12.99	VT Aerospace Ltd	RAF Benson	14.12.02T
					(Op Oxford UAS)		
G-BYUW	Grob G.115E Tutor	82107E		7.12.99	VT Aerospace Ltd	RAF Leuchars	14.12.02T
					(Op Aberdeen, Dundee & St.Andrews UAS)		
G-BYUX	Grob G.115E Tutor	82108E		18. 1.00	VT Aerospace Ltd	RAF Woodvale	31. 1.02T
					(Op Liverpool/Manchester UAS) (Code "UX")		
G-BYUY	Grob G.115E Tutor	82109E		18. 1.00	VT Aerospace Ltd	RAF Leuchars	31. 1.02T
					(Op Aberdeen, Dundee & St.Andrews UAS)		
G-BYUZ	Grob G.115E Tutor	82110E		18. 1.00	VT Aerospace Ltd	RAF Woodvale	31. 1.02T
					(Op Liverpool/Manchester UAS) (Code "UZ")		
G-BYVA	Grob G.115E Tutor	82111E		18. 1.00	VT Aerospace Ltd	RAF Cranwell	31. 1.02T
					(Op CFS/East Midlands UAS)		
G-BYVB	Grob G.115E Tutor	82112E		17. 2.00	VT Aerospace Ltd	Glasgow	28. 2.03T
					(Op Universities of Glasgow & Strathclyde AS)		
G-BYVC	Grob G.115E Tutor	82113E		17. 2.00	VT Aerospace Ltd	RAF Colerne	2. 3.03T
					(Op Bristol UAS)		
G-BYVD	Grob G.115E Tutor	82114E		17. 2.00	VT Aerospace Ltd	RAF Wyton	2. 3.03T
					(Op Cambridge/London UAS)		
G-BYVE	Grob G.115E Tutor	82115E		17. 2.00	VT Aerospace Ltd	Boscombe Down	2. 4.03T
					(Op Southampton UAS)		
G-BYVF	Grob G.115E Tutor	82116E		22. 2.00	VT Aerospace Ltd	Glasgow	28. 2.03T
					(Op Universities of Glasgow & Strathclyde AS)		
G-BYVG	Grob G.115E Tutor	82117E		22. 3.00	VT Aerospace Ltd	RAF Church Fenton	2. 4.03T
					(Op Yorkshire UAS)		
G-BYVH	Grob G.115E Tutor	82118E		22. 3.00	VT Aerospace Ltd	RAF Leuchars	4. 4.03T
					(Op Aberdeen, Dundee & St.Andrews UAS)		
G-BYVI	Grob G.115E Tutor	82119E		22. 3.00	VT Aerospace Ltd	RAF Leuchars	4. 4.03T
					(Op Aberdeen, Dundee & St.Andrews UAS)		
G-BYVJ	Grob G.115E Tutor	82120E		14. 4.00	VT Aerospace Ltd	RAF Wyton	25. 4.03T
					(Op Cambridge/London UAS)		

G-BYVK	Grob G.115E Tutor	82121E	14..4.00	VT Aerospace Ltd *(Op Aberdeen, Dundee & St.Andrews UAS)*	RAF Leuchars	25. 4.03T
G-BYVL	Grob G.115E Tutor	82122E	14. 4.00	VT Aerospace Ltd *(Op University of Wales UAS)*	RAF St.Athan	26. 4.03T
G-BYVM	Grob G.115E Tutor	82123E	14. 4.00	VT Aerospace Ltd *(Op Aberdeen, Dundee & St.Andrews UAS)*	RAF Leuchars	26. 4.03T
G-BYVN	Grob G.115E Tutor	82124E	18. 5.00	VT Aerospace Ltd *(Op Bristol UAS)*	RAF Colerne	31. 5.03T
G-BYVO	Grob G.115E Tutor	82125E	18. 5.00	VT Aerospace Ltd *(Op Birmingham UAS)*	RAF Cosford	31. 5.03T
G-BYVP	Grob G.115E Tutor	82126E	18. 5.00	VT Aerospace Ltd *(Op CFS))*	RAF Cranwell	31. 5.03T
G-BYVR	Grob G.115E Tutor	82127E	18. 5.00	VT Aerospace Ltd *(Op Oxford UAS)*	RAF Benson	31. 5.03T
G-BYVS	Grob G.115E Tutor	82128E	20. 6.00	VT Aerospace Ltd *(Op Cambridge/London UAS)*	RAF Wyton	29. 6.03T
G-BYVT	Grob G.115E Tutor	82129E	20. 6.00	VT Aerospace Ltd *(Op Cambridge/London UAS)*	RAF Wyton	29. 6.03T
G-BYVU	Grob G.115E Tutor	82130E	20. 6.00	VT Aerospace Ltd *(Op Oxford UAS)*	RAF Benson	29. 6.03T
G-BYVV	Grob G.115E Tutor	82131E	20. 6.00	VT Aerospace Ltd *(Op Yorkshire UAS)*	RAF Church Fenton	29 .6.03T
G-BYVW	Grob G.115E Tutor	82132E	21. 7.00	VT Aerospace Ltd *(Op Yorkshire UAS)*	RAF Church Fenton	6. 8.03T
G-BYVX	Grob G.115E Tutor	82133E	21. 7.00	VT Aerospace Ltd *(Op Southampton UAS)*	Boscombe Down	6. 8.03T
G-BYVY	Grob G.115E Tutor	82134E	21. 7.00	VT Aerospace Ltd *(Op Yorkshire UAS)*	RAF Church Fenton	6. 8.03T
G-BYVZ	Grob G.115E Tutor	82135E	21. 7.00	VT Aerospace Ltd *(Op Yorkshire UAS)*	RAF Church Fenton	6. 8.03T
G-BYWA	Grob G.115E Tutor	82136E	21. 8.00	VT Aerospace Ltd *(Op University of Wales UAS)*	RAF St.Athan	30 .8.03T
G-BYWB	Grob G.115E Tutor	82137E	21. 8.00	VT Aerospace Ltd *(Op Bristol UAS)*	RAF Colerne	30 .8.03T
G-BYWC	Grob G.115E Tutor	82138E	18. 9.00	VT Aerospace Ltd *(Op Bristol UAS)*	RAF Colerne	27 .9.03T
G-BYWD	Grob G.115E Tutor	82139E	18. 9.00	VT Aerospace Ltd *(Op Liverpool/Manchester UAS) (Code "WD")*	RAF Woodvale	27. 9.03T
G-BYWE	Grob G.115E Tutor	82140E	18. 9.00	VT Aerospace Ltd *(Op Bristol UAS)*	RAF Colerne	27 .9.03T
G-BYWF	Grob G.115E Tutor	82141E	18. 9.00	VT Aerospace Ltd *(Op CFS/East Midlands UAS)*	RAF Cranwell	27 .9.03T
G-BYWG	Grob G.115E Tutor	82142E	13.10.00	VT Aerospace Ltd *(Op Bristol UAS)*	RAF Colerne	29.10.03T
G-BYWH	Grob G.115E Tutor	82143E	13.10.00	VT Aerospace Ltd *(Op Northrumbrian UAS)*	RAF Leeming	29.10.03T
G-BYWI	Grob G.115E Tutor	82144E	13.10.00	VT Aerospace Ltd *(Op Bristol UAS)*	RAF Colerne	29.10.03T
G-BYWJ	Grob G.115E Tutor	82145E	13.10.00	VT Aerospace Ltd *(Op Liverpool/Manchester UAS) (Code "WJ")*	RAF Woodvale	29.10.03T
G-BYWK	Grob G.115E Tutor	82146E	17.11.00	VT Aerospace Ltd *(Op CFS/East Midlands UAS)*	RAF Cranwell	28.11.03T
G-BYWL	Grob G.115E Tutor	82147E	17.11.00	VT Aerospace Ltd *(Op Liverpool/Manchester UAS) (Code "WL")*	RAF Woodvale	28.11.03T
G-BYWM	Grob G.115E Tutor	82148E	17.11.00	VT Aerospace Ltd *(Op CFS/East Midlands UAS)*	RAF Cranwell	28.11.03T
G-BYWN	Grob G.115E Tutor	82149E	17.11.00	VT Aerospace Ltd *(Op Liverpool/Manchester UAS) (Code "WN")*	RAF Woodvale	28.11.03T
G-BYWO	Grob G.115E Tutor	82150E	7.12.00	VT Aerospace Ltd *(Op Birmingham UAS)*	RAF Cosford	14. 1.04T
G-BYWP	Grob G.115E Tutor	82151E	7.12.00	VT Aerospace Ltd *(Op Yorkshire UAS)*	RAF Church Fenton	14. 1.04T
G-BYWR	Grob G.115E Tutor	82152E	7.12.00	VT Aerospace Ltd *(Op Cambridge/London UAS)*	RAF Wyton	28. 1.04T
G-BYWS	Grob G.115E Tutor	82153E	7.12.00	VT Aerospace Ltd *(Op Northrumbrian UAS)*	RAF Leeming	16. 1.04T
G-BYWT	Grob G.115E Tutor	82154E	12.12.00	VT Aerospace Ltd *(Op Northrumbrian UAS)*	RAF Leeming	16. 1.04T
G-BYWU	Grob G.115E Tutor	82155E	19. 1.01	VT Aerospace Ltd *(Op Cambridge/London UAS)*	RAF Wyton	28. 1.04T
G-BYWV	Grob G.115E Tutor	82156E	19. 1.01	VT Aerospace Ltd *(Op Birmingham UAS)*	RAF Cosford	28. 1.04T

G-BYWW	Grob G.115E Tutor	82157E		19. 1.01	VT Aerospace Ltd *(Op CFS/East Midlands UAS)*	RAF Cranwell	28. 1.04T
G-BYWX	Grob G.115E Tutor	82158E		14. 2.01	VT Aerospace Ltd *(Op Cambridge/London UAS)*	RAF Wyton	25. 2.04T
G-BYWY	Grob G.115E Tutor	82159E		14. 2.01	VT Aerospace Ltd *(Op CFS/East Midlands UAS)*	RAF Cranwell	25. 2.04T
G-BYWZ	Grob G.115E Tutor	82160E		14. 2.01	VT Aerospace Ltd *(Op CFS/East Midlands UAS) (Code "WZ")*	RAF Cranwell	4. 3.04T
G-BYXA	Grob G.115E Tutor	82161E		14. 2.01	VT Aerospace Ltd *(Op Liverpool/Manchester UAS) (Code "XA")*	RAF Woodvale	4. 3.04T
G-BYXB	Grob G.115E Tutor	82162E		19. 3.01	VT Aerospace Ltd *(Op Southampton UAS)*	Boscombe Down	1. 4.04T
G-BYXC	Grob G.115E Tutor	82163E		19. 3.01	VT Aerospace Ltd *(Op CFS/East Midlands UAS)*	RAF Cranwell	1. 4.04T
G-BYXD	Grob G.115E Tutor	82164E		19. 3.01	VT Aerospace Ltd *(Op CFS/East Midlands UAS)*	RAF Cranwell	1. 4.04T
G-BYXE	Grob G.115E Tutor	82165E		19. 3.01	VT Aerospace Ltd *(Op Yorkshire UAS)*	RAF Church Fenton	1. 4.04T
G-BYXF	Grob G.115E Tutor	82166E		12. 4.01	VT Aerospace Ltd *(Op Birmingham UAS)*	RAF Cosford	25. 4.04T
G-BYXG	Grob G.115E Tutor	82167E		12. 4.01	VT Aerospace Ltd *(Op Birmingham UAS)*	RAF Cosford	25. 4.04T
G-BYXH	Grob G.115E Tutor	82168E		12. 4.01	VT Aerospace Ltd *(Op Cambridge/London UAS)*	RAF Wyton	29. 4.04T
G-BYXI	Grob G.115E Tutor	82169E		12. 4.01	VT Aerospace Ltd *(Op Liverpool/Manchester UAS)*	RAF Woodvale	29. 4.04T
G-BYXJ	Grob G.115E Tutor	82170E		16. 5.01	VT Aerospace Ltd *(Op Southampton UAS)*	Boscombe Down	28. 5.04T
G-BYXK	Grob G.115E Tutor	82171E		16. 5.01	VT Aerospace Ltd *(Op University of Wales UAS)*	RAF St.Athan	28. 5.04T
G-BYXL	Grob G.115E Tutor	82172E		16. 5.01	VT Aerospace Ltd *(Op Birmingham UAS)*	RAF Cosford	28. 5.04T
G-BYXM	Grob G.115E Tutor	82173E		16. 5.01	VT Aerospace Ltd *(Op Southampton UAS)*	Boscombe Down	28. 5.04T
G-BYXN	Grob G.115E Tutor	82174E		8. 6.01	VT Aerospace Ltd *(Op Southampton UAS)*	Boscombe Down	11. 6.04T
G-BYXO	Grob G.115E Tutor	82175E		8. 6.01	VT Aerospace Ltd *(Op Birmingham UAS)*	RAF Cosford	11. 6.04T
G-BYXP	Grob G.115E Tutor	82176E		8. 6.01	VT Aerospace Ltd *(Op Cambridge/London UAS)*	RAF Wyton	11. 6.04T
G-BYXR	Grob G.115E Tutor	82177E		8. 6.01	VT Aerospace Ltd *(Op Oxford UAS)*	RAF Bensen	11. 6.04T
G-BYXS	Grob G.115E Tutor	82178E		18. 7.01	VT Aerospace Ltd *(Op Oxford UAS)*	RAF Bensen	29. 7.04T
G-BYXT	Grob G.115E Tutor	82179E		18. 7.01	VT Aerospace Ltd *(Op CFS/East Midlands UAS)*	RAF Cranwell	29. 7.04T
G-BYXU	Piper PA-28-161 Cherokee Warrior II	28-7716097	EI-BXU G-BNUP/N2282Q	8. 1.99	F.P.McGovern & F.O'Sullivan	Waterford, Co.Waterford	11. 3.02
G-BYXV	Medway EclipseR (Jabiru) *(C/n not confirmed)*	162/140		25.10.99	K.Swann	(Rochester)	25. 5.02P
G-BYXW	Medway EclipseR (Two Stroke International [2SI]) *(Officially registered as c/n 166/144)*	166/147		25.10.99	J.Swann	(Rochester)	22. 5.02P
G-BYXX	Grob G.115E Tutor	82180E		18. 7.01	VT Aerospace Ltd *(Op Liverpool/Manchester UAS)*	RAF Woodvale	29. 7.04T
G-BYXY	Grob G.115E Tutor	82181E		18. 7.01	VT Aerospace Ltd *(Op Northrumbrian UAS)*	RAF Leeming	29. 7.04T
G-BYXZ	Grob G.115E Tutor	82182E		15. 8.01	VT Aerospace Ltd *(Op CFS)*	RAF Cranwell	17. 9.04T
G-BYYA	Grob G.115E Tutor	82183E		15. 8.01	VT Aerospace Ltd *(Op CFS)*	RAF Cranwell	23. 9.04T
G-BYYB	Grob G.115E Tutor	82184E		15. 8.01	VT Aerospace Ltd *(Op CFS)*	RAF Cranwell	17. 9.04T
G-BYYC	Hapi Cygnet SF-2A	PFA 182-12311		25.11.99	C.D.Hughes & G.H.Smith	Shenstone	7. 5.02P
G-BYYD	Cameron A-250 HAFB	4712		31. 3.00	C & J.M.Bailey	Bristol	13..3.01T
G-BYYE	Lindstrand LBL 77A HAFB	151		25.11.99	D.J.Cook	Norwich	25. 6.02A
G-BYYF	Boeing 737-229C	21738	OO-SDR	11. 1.00	European Aviation Air Charter Ltd	Bournemouth	28. 2.04T
G-BYYG	Slingsby T.67C Firefly	2101	PH-SGI	30.11.99	B Dixon & S E Marples	Newcastle	12. 1.03T
G-BYYH	Aérospatiale AS350B Ecureuil	1594	SE-JDU LN-OTO	8. 2.00	RCR Aviation Ltd	Thruxton	18..9.03T
G-BYYI	British Aerospace Jetstream Srs.3107	620	VH-JSW G-31-620	1. 3.00	Vale Aviation Ltd	(London SW1)	

G-BYYJ	Lindstrand LBL 25A Cloudhopper HAFB	651		10.12.99	A.M.Barton	Coulsdon	19. 2.02A
G-BYYK	Boeing 737-229C	20916	OO-SDK	11. 1.00	European Aviation Air Charter Ltd	Bournemouth	
G-BYYL	Jabiru Jabiru UL	PFA 274A-13480		10.12.99	C.Jackson	Ince Blundell	7. 5.02P
G-BYYM	Raj Hamsa X'Air 582 (1)	476 & BMAA/HB/119		21.10.99	D.J.McCall & B.Pilling	Dunkeswell	1. 8.02P
G-BYYN	Pegasus Quantum 15-912	7601		6. 1.00	E.Clarke	Tarn Farm, Cockerham	3. 1.01P
G-BYYO	Piper PA-28R-201 Arrow II	2837061	(N182ND) N9249C/G-BYYO/N9249C	11. 2.00	Stapleford Flying Club Ltd	Stapleford	26..4.03T
G-BYYP	Pegasus Quantum 15 (Rotax 582-40)	7603		11. 2.00	D.A.Linsey-Bloom	Kingston Seymour	1. 2.02P
G-BYYR	Raj Hamsa X'Air 582 (1)	453 & BMAA/HB/115		23.12.99	T D Bawden	Weston Zoyland	
G-BYYT	Jabiru Jabiru UL	PFA 274A-13452		18.11.99	T.D.Saveker	(Truro)	9. 5.02P
G-BYYW	de Havilland DHC-1 Chipmunk T.20 *(Built OGMA)*	57	CS-DAR 1367 Portuguese AF	22 .2.00	R.Farrer *(Stored 2000)*	(Bedford)	
G-BYYX	TEAM mini-MAX 91	PFA 186-13410		6. 1.00	P.L.Turner	(Darlington)	
G-BYYY	Pegasus Quantum 15-912	7564		8.12.99	C.J.Finnigan	Knapthorpe Lodge, Caunton	29.12.01P
G-BYYZ	Staaken Z-21A Flitzer	PFA 223-13324		12.11.99	A.E.Morris	Fairoaks	27. 6.02P
G-BYZA	Aérospatiale AS355F2 Twin Squirrel	5518	JA6784 F-OHNK	20.12.99	Aeromega Aviation Ltd	Stapleford	17. 4.03T
G-BYZB*	Mainair Blade (Rotax 582-2V)	1229-1299-7-W1022		14. 1.00	O.Grati *(Cancelled 22.1.02 by CAA)*	(Annesley, Notts)	16. 1.02P
G-BYZD	Tri-R Kis Cruiser	PFA 302-13156		22.11.99	R.T.Clegg *(Almost complete 4.01)*	Netherthorpe	
G-BYZE	Aérospatiale AS350B2 Ecureuil	2773	F-OGVR	8. 2.00	V.H.L.Ellis	Booker	14. 3.03T
G-BYZF	Raj Hamsa X'Air 582 (1) (Simonini)	461 & BMAA/HB/110	*(BMAA records show as '503 (1))*	7. 1.00	R P Davies	(Harrogate)	
G-BYZG	Cameron A-275 HAFB	4706		23. 2.00	Horizon Ballooning Ltd	Alton	29. 5.02T
G-BYZJ	Boeing 737-3Q8	24962	G-COLE PP-VOX	11. 1.00	British Midland Airways Ltd *(Star Alliance c/s)*	East Midlands	20.11.04T
G-BYZL	Cameron GP-65 HAFB	4494		6. 4.00	P.Thibo	(Junglinster, Luxemburg)	14..6.02A
G-BYZM	Piper PA-28-161 Warrior II	28-8116317	HB-PNK N8436A	4. 2.00	Goodair Leasing Ltd	Cardiff	11. 5.03T
G-BYZO	Rans S-6-ES Coyote II	PFA 204-13560		14. 1.00	A.J.Boulton	Roddidge, Fradley	23. 5.02P
G-BYZP	Robinson R22 Beta-II	3018		9.12.99	P.Young t/a Coleraine Landscape Services	(Ballymoney, Coleraine)	22.12.02T
G-BYZR	III Sky Arrow 650TC	C001	D-ENGF I-TREI	24. 1.00	G.H.Jackson & R.Moncrieff	Derby	12. 4.03P
G-BYZS	Jabiru Jabiru UL-450 (Jabiru 2200A)	PFA 274A-13489		25. 1.00	N.Fielding	Ince Blundell	31. 5.02P
G-BYZT	Nova Vertex 26	13345		21. 1.00	M.N.Maclean	(Dundee)	
G-BYZU	Pegasus Quantum 15 (Rotax 582-40)	7613		15. 2.00	N I Clifton	East Fortune	16. 2.01P
G-BYZV	Sky 90-24 HAFB	174		15. 8.00	P.Farmer	Wadhurst	19. 1.01
G-BYZW	Raj Hamsa X'Air 582 (2)	499 & BMAA/HB/129		19. 1.00	H.C.Lowther	Kirkbride	17 .6.02P
G-BYZX	Cameron R-90 HAFB	4751		31. 3.00	D.K.Hempleman-Adams *"Britannic Challenge"* *(Used for flight Spitsbergen/North Pole/Spitsbergen 28.5/1.6/3.6.00)*	Corsham	
G-BYZY	Pietenpol Aircamper	PFA 047-12190		2.12.99	D.N.Hanchet	White Waltham	
G-BYZZ	Robinson R22 Beta-II	3000		1.12.99	Astra Helicopters Ltd.	Bristol	3. 2.03T

G-BZAA – G-BZZZ

G-BZAA	Mainair Blade 912 (Rotax 462)	1142-0198-7-W945		22.11.99	C.Bodill & R.Locke	(Nottingham)	22.11.00P
G-BZAB	Mainair Rapier (Rotax 503-2V)	1228-1299-7-W1021		23.12.99	G.Verity	(Northwich)	5 .1.02P
G-BZAD	Cessna 152	15279563	N303MA N714ZN	22. 3.00	Cristal Air Ltd	(Heathfield)	6.11.04T
G-BZAE	Cessna 152	15281300	N49480	22. 3.00	Jaxx Landing Ltd	Swansea	4 .5.03T
G-BZAF	Raj Hamsa X'Air 582 (1)	503 & BMAA/HB/130		18. 1.00	Y.A.Evans	Rufforth	5.10.02P
G-BZAG	Lindstrand LBL 105A HAFB	542		29..2.00	R L Mold	High Wycombe	21. 2.01T
G-BZAH	Cessna 208B Caravan I	208B0811	N5196U	28. 2.00	G Burton t/a Army Parachute Association	AAC Netheravon	13. 4.03A
G-BZAI	Pegasus Quantum 15	7614		9. 2.00	D.Paget	Dunkeswell	9. 5.02P
G-BZAJ	PZL-110 Koliber 160A	04990082	SP-WGK	10. 2.00	PZL International Aviation Marketing & Sales plc	North Weald	16. 7.03T

G-BZAK	Raj Hamsa X'Air 582 (9) 477 & BMAA/HB/114		20. 1.00	R.J.Ripley	(Oakley, Beds)	5.11.02P
G-BZAL	Mainair Blade 912 1205-0799-7-W1008 (Rotax 912-UL)		27. 1.00	K.Worthington	Tarn Farm, Cockerham	27. 1.01P
G-BZAM	Europa Aviation Europa PFA 247-12969		6.12.99	D.Corbett *(Under construction 8.00)*	Shobdon	
G-BZAO	Rans S-12XL PFA 307-13394		1. 2.00	M.L.Robinson	Kirkbride	
G-BZAP	Jabiru Jabiru UL-450 PFA 274A-13479		13.12.99	S.Derwin *(Noted 11.01)*	Morgansfield, Fishburn	26. 6.02P
G-BZAR	Denney Kitfox mk.4-1200 Speedster (Rotax 912UL) PFA 172B-12529	G-LEZJ	17. 2.00	C.E.Brookes	Derby	30. 8.02P
G-BZAS	Isaacs Fury II PFA 011-10837 (CAM100)		10. 2.00	H.A.Brunt & H.Frick *"Spirit of Dunsfold" (As "K5673") (See SECTION 4 also)*	Bournemouth	
G-BZAT	British Aerospace Avro 146-RJ100 E3320	G-6-320	18.11.97	CityFlyer Express Ltd *(Waves of the City t/s)*	Gatwick	8. 1.04T
G-BZAU	British Aerospace Avro 146-RJ100 E3328		25. 4.98	CityFlyer Express Ltd *(Colum t/s)*	Gatwick	11. 6.04T
G-BZAV	British Aerospace Avro 146-RJ100 E3331		19. 5.98	CityFlyer Express Ltd *(Chelsea Rose t/s)*	Gatwick	23. 7.04T
G-BZAW	British Aerospace Avro 146-RJ100 E3354		11. 6.99	CityFlyer Express Ltd	Gatwick	15. 7.02T
G-BZAX	British Aerospace Avro 146-RJ100 E3356		9. 7.99	CityFlyer Express Ltd	Gatwick	16. 8.02T
G-BZAY	British Aerospace Avro 146-RJ100 E3368		15. 2.00	Cityflyer Express Ltd	Gatwick	27..3.03T
G-BZAZ	British Aerospace Avro 146-RJ100 E3369		15. 2.00	Cityflyer Express Ltd	Gatwick	13. 4.03T
G-BZBC	Rans S-6-ES Coyote II *(Tri-cycle u/c)* 0499-1314 & PFA 204-13525		2. 2.00	A.J.Baldwin	(Ripley)	16. 3.02P
G-BZBE	Cameron A-210 HAFB 4708		9. 5.00	W.I.& C.Hooker t/a Dragon Balloon Co	Nottingham	4. 4.01T
G-BZBF	Cessna 172M 17262258 (Lycoming O-360)	N126SA G-BZBF/9H-ACV/N12785	20.12.99	M.D.N Fisher t/a F & H Aircraft	Fenland	9. 8.03T
G-BZBG	Thruster T.600N 0100-T600N-040 (Rotax 582-UL)		26. 1.00	Mainair Microlight School Ltd	Barton	1..2.02P
G-BZBH	Thunder Ax7-65 Bolt HAFB 173		28.11.78	R.B. & G.Craik *"Serendipity II"*	Northampton	28. 4.02A
G-BZBI	Cameron V-77 HAFB 4740		4. 4.00	B.Smallwood *"Flying Colours"*	Chippenham	22. 4.02A
G-BZBJ	Lindstrand LBL-77A HAFB 646		29. 2.00	The Cancer Research Campaign	London NW1	13. 2.01A
G-BZBL	Lindstrand LBL-120A HAFB 676		23. 2.00	Flying Pictures Ltd *(betinternet.com titles)*	Fairoaks	17. 4.02A
G-BZBM	Cameron A-315 HAFB 4741		7. 4.00	Listers of Coventry (Motors) Ltd	Alcester, Warks	7..5.02T
G-BZBN	Thunder AX9-120 S2 4786		21. 2.00	K Willie	Maldegem, Belgium	27. 2.02A
G-BZBO	Stoddard-Hamilton Glasair III 3032		21. 2.00	M B Hamlett	Lagny de Sec, France	
G-BZBP	Raj Hamsa X'Air 582 (1) 470 & BMAA/HB/131		29. 2.00	D F Hughes	(London SE9)	
G-BZBR	Pegasus Quantum 15-912 7631		26. 5.00	N.C.Stevenson	Weston Zoyland	28. 9.02P
G-BZBS	Piper PA-28-161 Warrior III 2842080	N4180H G-BZBS/N9529N	10. 5.00	S.J.Skilton t/a Aviation Rentals *(Op Solent Flight Training)*	Southampton	9 .5.03T
G-BZBT	Cameron Hopper H-34 HAFB 4730		18. 5.00	British Telecommunications plc	Thatcham	10. 4.02T
G-BZBU	Robinson R22 0131	OH-HLB SE-HOH	23. 5.00	J.N.A.Cawoood	(Skipton)	28. 6.03T
G-BZBW	Rotorway Executive 162F 6415 (Rotorway RI 162F)		23. 2.00	M Gardiner	(Crewkerne)	
G-BZBX	Rans S-6-ES Coyote II PFA 204-13501		26. 1.00	R.Johnstone	Otherton, Cannock	10. 5.02P
G-BZBZ	Jodel D.9 Bebe 519 (VW 1600) *(Built Etienne de Schrevel, Gent 1970-77)*	OO-48	29. 2.00	S Marom *(Noted 8.01)*	Whitehall Farm, Benington	
G-BZDA	Piper PA-28-161 Warrior III 2842087	N41814 G-BZDA/N41814	29. 6.00	S.J.Skilton t/a Aviation Rentals	Bournemouth	29. 6.03T
G-BZDB	Thruster T600T 0030-T600T-041 (Rotax 582)		7. 3.00	Thruster Air Services Ltd *"Snoopy"* *(Sold M Jones, Wing Farm, Longbridge Deverill 2.02)*	Ginge Farm, Wantage	
G-BZDC	Mainair Blade 1232-0100-7-W1025		13. 3.00	L.J.Dickinson	Old Sarum	14. 3.02P
G-BZDD	Mainair Blade 912 1238-0200-7-W1031 (Rotax 912-UL)		21. 1.00	T.Williams t/a Barton Blade Group	Barton	24. 1.02P
G-BZDE	Lindstrand LBL 210A HAFB 665		6. 3.00	Toucan Travel Ltd	Basingstoke	31.10.01T
G-BZDF	CFM Streak Shadow SA (Rotax 582) K.241 & PFA 206-12609		7. 3.00	J.W.Beckett	(Bromsgrove)	15. 6.01P
G-BZDH	Piper PA-28R-200 Cherokee Arrow II 28R-7235028	HB-OHH N4390T	8. 3.00	E.Alexander	Andrewsfield	4. 6.03T
G-BZDI	Aero L-39C Albatros 031822	ES-ZLB Sov AF	7. 6.00	M.Gainza & E.Gavazzi	North Weald	

G-BZDJ	Cameron Z-105 HAFB	4832		27. 6.00	BWS Security Systems Ltd *(BWS titles)*	Bath	6. 6.02A
G-BZDK	Raj Hamsa X'Air 582 (2)	447 & BMAA/HB/124		8. 2.00	B.Park	(Redruth)	11.10.02P
G-BZDL	Pegasus Quantum 15-912	7629		18. 4.00	D.M.Holman	(Northwich)	24. 5.02P
G-BZDM	Stoddard-Hamilton GlaStar	PFA 295-13283		13. 3.00	F.G.Miskelly	(London SW6)	23..7.02P
G-BZDN	Cameron N-105 HAFB	2840	D-OABB D-Saxonia (2)	26. 4.00	J.D.& K.Griffiths	Bingham	
G-BZDP	Scottish Aviation.Bulldog Srs.120/121	BH120/244	XX551	31. 3.00	D.M.Squires *(As "XX551/E")*	Wellesbourne Mountford	8. 7.04
G-BZDR	Tri-R Kis	9403		8. 3.00	T.J.Johnson *(Noted 7.01)*	(Norwood Lodge, Weeley Heath)	
G-BZDS	Pegasus Quantum 15-912	7633		17. 4.00	J.M.Hardstaff	Rufforth	17. 4.02P
G-BZDT	Maule MXT-7-180 Star Rocket	14099C		11. 8.00	D.J.Brook	Deanland, Hailsham	23 .8.03
G-BZDU	de Havilland DHC-1 Chipmunk 22	C1/0714	WP833	31. 3.00	M.R.Clark	Glenrothes	6. 7.03
G-BZDX	Cameron Colt Sugarbox-90 SS HAFB	4814		17. 5.00	Stratos Ballooning GmbH & Co KG	Ennigerloh, Germany	7. 6.02A
G-BZDY	Cameron Colt Sugarbox-90 SS HAFB	4815		22. 5.00	Stratos Ballooning GmbH & Co KG	Ennigerloh, Germany	7. 6.02A
G-BZDZ	Jabiru Jabiru SP	232	ZU-BVB	14. 5.01	R.M.Whiteside	(Haywards Heath)	
G-BZEA	Cessna A152	A1520824	N7606L	13. 3.00	Sky Leisure Aviation (Charters) Ltd	Redhill	23. 1.04T
G-BZEB	Cessna 152	15282772	N89532	31. 1.00	Sky Leisure Aviation (Charters) Ltd	Shoreham	24. 9.03T
G-BZEC	Cessna 152	15284475	N4655M	21. 1.00	Sky Leisure Aviation (Charters) Ltd	Redhill	
G-BZED	Pegasus Quantum 15-912	7600		17. 3.00	M.P.Wimsey	(Louth)	21. 3.02P
G-BZEE	Agusta-Bell 206B JetRanger II	8554	G-OJCB	22 .2.00	Yateley Helicopters Ltd	Blackbushe	18.10.03T
G-BZEG	Mainair Blade	1239-0200-7-W1032		3. 3.00	Mainair Microlight School Ltd	Ince Blundell	8. 3.02P
G-BZEH	Piper PA-28-235 Cherokee B	28-10838	9M-ARW RP-C704/PI-C704/N9182W	31. 3.00	A.D.Wood *(Noted 6.01)*	Spanhoe	3. 5.04
G-BZEI	Agusta A109E Power	11056		8. 6.00	JJB Sports plc	(Wigan)	11. 6.03T
G-BZEJ	Raj Hamsa X'Air 582 (7)	500 & BMAA/HB/134		31. 3.00	H.Hall	(Willenhall)	
G-BZEK	Cameron C-70 HAFB	4860		30. 5.00	Ballooning 50 Degrees Nord	Fouhren, Luxembourg	28. 5.02A
G-BZEL	Mainair Blade (Rotax 582)	1245-0300-7-W1038		27. 3.00	M.W.Bush	(Ilfracombe)	17..4.02P
G-BZEN	Jabiru Jabiru UL-450	PFA 274-13272		4. 4.00	B.W.Stockil	Rufforth	13. 2.02P
G-BZEP	Scottish Aviation Bulldog Srs.120/121	BH120/257	XX561	4. 4.00	I.D.McClelland	Biggin Hill	
G-BZER	Raj Hamsa X'Air R100 (1) (BMW R100)	526 & BMAA/HB/133		22. 3.00	N.P.Lloyd & H.Lloyd-Jones	(Wrexham)	
G-BZES	Rotorway Exececutive 90	6191	G-LUFF	25. 4.00	Southern Helicopters Ltd *(Noted 11.01)*	Street Farm, Takeley	
G-BZET	Robin HR.200/120B	345	F-GTZG	9. 5.00	Anglian Flight Centres Ltd	Earls Colne	21. 5.03T
G-BZEU	Raj Hamsa X'Air 582 <u>(8)</u>	518 & BMAA/HB/140		20. 4.00	B.P.Percy	Lower Mount Pleasant, Chatteris	25. 9.01P
G-BZEV	Vahdat Semicopter 1 Gyroplane	002		10.10.00	M.E.Vahdat	(Uxbridge)	
G-BZEW	Rans S-6-ES Coyote II *(Tri-cycle u/c)* (Rotax 582-48)	0998.1268.0199.ES & PFA 204-13450		5. 4.00	J.E.Gattrell & A.R.Trace	Sittles Farm, Alrewas	5. 9.02P
G-BZEX	Raj Hamsa X'Air R100 (2) (BMW R100)	530 & BMAA/HB/135		5. 4.00	J.M.McCullough & R.T.Henry	(Castlewellan)	
G-BZEY	Cameron N-90 HAFB	4829		15. 5.00	The Ballooning Business Ltd *(Wrangler Footwear titles)*	Northampton	29. 5.02T
G-BZEZ	CFM Streak Shadow DD	PFA 161-13503		1 .2.00	G.J. Pearce	(Horsham)	27. 2.02P
G-BZFB	Robin R2112A Alpha	175	EI-BIU	7. 4.00	M.R.Brown	Bidford	26. 6.03
G-BZFC	Pegasus Quantum 15 (Rotax 582)	7640		14. 4.00	G.Brown	East Fortune	29. 6.02P
G-BZFD	Cameron N-90 HAFB	2725	OO-BFD	24. 5.00	David Hathaway Transport Ltd	Bristol	
G-BZFF	Raj Hamsa X'Air 582 (2)	521 & BMAA/HB/137		6. 4.00	A.L.H.Seed t/a G-BZFF Flying Group	Tarn Farm, Cockerham	12. 6.02P
G-BZFG	Sky 105 HAFB	4842		27. 4.00	Virgin Airship & Balloon Co Ltd *(Benadryl Allergy Relief titles)*	Telford	17. 4.02P
G-BZFH	Pegasus Quantum 15-912	7660		15. 5.00	J.S.Hamilton t/a Kent Scout Microlights	(Edenbridge)	20. 5.02P
G-BZFI	Jabiru Jabiru UL	PFA 274A-13497		27. 3.00	A.W.J.Findlay t/a Group Family	Sywell	2. 4.02P
G-BZFJ	Westland <u>SA.314C</u> Gazelle HT.2	1098	XW861	9. 5.00	European Marine Ltd	Goodwood	17. 6.02P

(Pod no is WA107) (Assuming p/i is correct c/n should be <u>1102</u>: XW861's reported c/n is thought to be 1096 which corresponds to G-BBHV. Based on owner's registration application CAA show c/n as 1098 which translates to G-BBHW)

G-BZFK	TEAM mini-MAX PFA 186-12060		17. 4.00	H.P.Brooks	(Haywards Heath)	28. 8.02P
	(Rotax 447)					
G-BZFN	Scottish Aviation Bulldog Srs.120/121	XX667	18. 4.00	Towerdrive Ltd	(Ashbourne)	7.10.04
	BH120/325					
G-BZFO	Mainair Blade 1235-0100-7-W1028		29. 3.00	J.E.Walendowski	Crosland Moor	1. 5.02P
	(Rotax 503)					
G-BZFP	de Havilland DHC-6-310 Twin Otter	C-GGNF	11. 8.00	Loganair Ltd	Glasgow	13. 8.02T
	696	N712PV/N696WJ/F-ODUH/TR-LZN/C-GKIQ *"Chatham Historic Dockyard"*				
G-BZFR	Extra EA.300/L 203		26. 6.00	Powerhunt Ltd	Biggin Hill	17. 7.03T
	(Official c/n outside normal EA300L c/n batch at present: possibly ex D-EDGE with published c/n 03?)					
G-BZFS	Mainair Blade 912 1243-0300-7-W1036		23. 3.00	S.P.Stone & F.A.Stephens		
					Baxby Manor, Husthwaite	12. 4.02P
G-BZFT	Murphy Rebel PFA 232-13224		7. 4.00	N.A.Evans	(Cullumpton)	1. 7.02P
G-BZFU	Lindstand LBL HS-110 HA Airship 671		25. 4.00	PNB Entreprenad AB	Malmo, Sweden	16. 6.02A
G-BZFV	Zenair CH.601UL Zodiac		14. 4.00	T.R.Sinclair & T.Clyde		
	(Rotax 912S) PFA 162A-13547				Lamb Holm Farm, Orkney	18. 1.02P
G-BZGA	de Havilland DHC-1 Chipmunk 22	WK585	31. 3.00	Propshop Ltd	Duxford	30. 4.04T
	C1/0608			*(As "WK585)*		
G-BZGB	de Havilland DHC-1 Chipmunk 22	WZ872	31. 3.00	Chipmunk Aviation Ltd	Newcastle	6. 7.03
	C1/0905					
G-BZGC	Aérospatiale AS355F1 Twin Squirrel	G-CCAO	26. 3.99	McAlpine Helicopters Ltd	Warton	21.11.02T
	5077	G-SETA/G-NEAS/G-CMMM/G-BNBJ/C-GLKH *(Police c/s)*				
G-BZGD	Piper PA-18-150 Super Cub 18-8109049	N90943	15. 5.00	M.G.& S.J.White	Compton Abbas	4. 7.03T
				t/a Proline Aviation		
G-BZGE	Medway EclipseR 159/139		6. 5.99	J.A.McGill	Rochester	30. 6.02P
	(Jabiru 2200A) *(Contains original sailwing of G-MZGE)*					
G-BZGF	Rans S-6-ES Coyote II *(Tri-cycle u/c)*		25. 4.00	D.F.Castle	London Colney	13. 7.02P
	0899.1334 & PFA 204-13594 *(Bounced on landing London Colney 22.7.01 with fuselage & propeller damage)*					
G-BZGH	Reims Cessna F172N Skyhawk II	EI-BGH	1.12.98	D.Behan	(Dublin)	11. 3.02
	F17201789			t/a Golf Hotel Group		
G-BZGI	Ultramagic M-145 HAFB 145/12		9. 6.00	European Balloon Co Ltd	Great Missenden	13. 7.02T
G-BZGJ	Thunder AX10-180 S2 HAFB 3956	LN-CBT	8. 5.00	M.Wady t/a Merlin Balloons	Hamstreet	30. 5.02T
G-BZGK	North American OV-10B Bronco 338-17	9932	9. 6.00	Invicta Aviation Ltd	Duxford	
		Luftwaffe/D-9561/Bu 158308 *(Op Aircraft Restoration Co)*				
G-BZGL	North American OV-10B Bronco 338-11	9926	9. 6.00	Invicta Aviation Ltd	Duxford	
		Luftwaffe/D-9555/Bu 158302 *(Op Aircraft Restoration Co)*				
G-BZGM	Mainair Blade 912 1247-0400-7-W1040		14. 4.00	P.Ryder	St Michaels	1. 5.02P
G-BZGN	Raj Hamsa X'Air 582 (2)		3. 5.00	C.S.Warr & P.A.Pilkington	North Coates	27.10.02P
	445 & BMAA/HB/128					
G-BZGO	Robinson R44 Astro 0757		14. 4.00	P.Durkin	Blackpool	14. 5.02P
G-BZGP	Thruster T600N 0400-T600N-043		25. 4.00	M.L.Smith	Ginge Farm, Wantage	29. 8.02P
				(Noted damaged 12.01)		
G-BZGR	Rans S-6-ES Coyote II *(Tri-cyle u/c)*		3. 5.00	J.M.Benton	Long Marston	23. 7.02P
	(Jabiru 2200) 0999.1338.ES & PFA 204-13595					
	(Swung on landing Hardwick 7.5.01 & collided with hedge: damage to cockpit, undercarriage & port wing)					
G-BZGS	Mainair Blade 912 1242-0300-7-W1035		10. 5.00	S.C.Reeve	Ashbourne	14.11.02P
	(Rotax 912)					
G-BZGT	Jabiru Jabiru UL-450 PFA 274A-13539		4. 5.00	P.H.Ronfell	(Chorley)	
G-BZGU	Raj Hamsa X'Air 582 (4) BMAA/HB/138		4. 5.00	C.Kiernan	(Mostrim, Co.Longford)	8.10.02P
G-BZGV	Lindstand LBL 77A HAFB 695		9. 5.00	J.H.Dryden	Okehampton	22. 7.02A
G-BZGW	Mainair Blade 1246-0400-7-W1039		5. 5.00	C.S.M.Hallam	Barton	9. 5.01P
	(Rotax 903)					
G-BZGX	Raj Hamsa X'Air 202 (1)		2. 6.00	A.Crowe	(Ballyclare, Co.Antrim)	
	400 & BMAA/HB/099			*(Under construction 8.01)*		
G-BZGY	Dyn'Aéro CR100C 21	F-TGCI	7. 6.00	D.Hayes	Spilsted Farm, Sedlescombe	4. 2.02P
G-BZGZ	Pegasus Quantum 15-912 7674		7. 6.00	W.H.J.Knowles	Weston Zoyland	2. 8.01P
G-BZHA	Boeing 767-336ER 29230	N60668	22. 5.98	British Airways plc	Heathrow	21. 5.04T
				(Wings t/s)		
G-BZHB	Boeing 767-336ER 29231		30. 5.98	British Airways plc	Heathrow	29. 5.04T
				(Delftblue Daybreak t/s)		
G-BZHC	Boeing 767-336ER 29232		29. 6.98	British Airways plc	Heathrow	28. 6.04T
				(Waves & Cranes t/s)		
G-BZHE	Cessna 152 15281303	D-EAOC	20. 4.00	Two Seven Aviation Ltd	Norwich	22. 6.03T
		N49484				
G-BZHF	Cessna 152 15283986	D-EMJA	20. 4.00	Two Seven Aviation Ltd	Norwich	11. 7.03T
		N4858H				
G-BZHG	Tecnam P92-EM Echo PFA 318-13606		24. 5.00	M.Rudd	Henstridge	2.12.02P
	(Jabiru 2200A)					
G-BZHH	Eurocopter EC 120B 1112		28. 6.00	Airtrol Ltd	(London SW1)	31. 8.03T
G-BZHI	Enstrom F-28A-UK 281	G-BPOZ	14.12.99	Tindon Ltd	Litle Snoring	20. 6.02
		N246Q				
G-BZHJ	Raj Hamsa X'Air 582 (10)		10. 5.00	T Harrison-Smith	Chase Farm, Billericay	20.11.02P
	482 & BMAA/HB/126					

G-BZHK	Piper PA-28-181 Archer III	2843347	N41647	14. 7.00	Premiair Engineering Ltd	Shoreham	13. 7.03T
			N9519N				
G-BZHL	Noorduyn AT-16 Harvard IIB	14A-1158	FT118	6. 6.00	R.H.Cooper & S.Swallow	(Stow, Lincs)	
	(Built Noorduyn, Canada0		43-12859		*(Stored 1.02)*		
	(Officially quoted FT118 matches as above rather with quoted USAAF serial '43-12959')						
G-BZHN	Pegasus Quantum 15-912	7677		20. 6.00	P.L.Cummings	Eaglescott	14. 6.02P
					t/a Eaglescott Microlights		
G-BZHO	Pegasus Quantum 15	7658		19. 5.00	N.D.Meer	Roddige	15. 5.02P
	(Rotax 582)						
G-BZHP	Quad City Challenger II			11. 5.00	F.Payne	Plaistows Farm, St Albans	
	(Rotax 582) CH2-0995-CW-1398 & PFA 177-13153 *(CW denotes "clipwing" although a/c has standard wing configuration)*						
G-BZHR	Jabiru Jabiru UL-450	PFA 274A-13493		16. 5.00	G.W.Rowbotham	(Loughborough)	5. 8.02P
G-BZHS	Europa Aviation Europa	PFA 247-12865		16. 5.00	P.Waugh	(Llangollen)	
G-BZHT	Piper PA-18A-150 Super Cub	18-5886	ZK-BTF	25. 5.00	B.Walker & Co (Dursley) Ltd		
						Gloucestershire	
G-BZHU	Wag-Aero CUBy Sport Trainer	AACA/351	ZK-MPH	25. 5.00	B.Walker & Co (Dursley) Ltd		
						Gloucestershire	28. 8.01P
G-BZHV	Piper PA-28-181 Archer III	2843382	N41848	17.10.00	Anglo American Airmotive Ltd	Bournemouth	19.10.03T
			G-BZHV/N41848				
G-BZHW	Piper PA-28-181 Archer III	2843409	N4184D	16. 2.01	Anglo American Airmotive Ltd	Bournemouth	22. 2.04T
			G-BZHW/N4184D				
G-BZHX	Thunder AX11-250 S2 HAFB	4880		21. 6.00	T.H.Wilson *"Slim Your Bin"*	Diss	11. 6.02T
G-BZHY	Mainair Blade 912	1250-0500-7-W1043		7. 6.00	M.Morris	Tarn Farm, Cockerham	29. 5.02P
	(Rotax 912-UL)						
G-BZIA	Raj Hamsa X'Air 700 (1)			1. 6.00	A.V.I.Hudson	Priory Farm, Tibenham	23. 9.02P
		475 & BMAA/HB/116					
G-BZIB	Denney Kitfox mk.3	PFA 172-11898		4. 5.00	S.L.Symons	(Kettering)	
G-BZIC	Lindstand LBL Sun SS HAFB	702		8. 6.00	Ballongaventyr 1 Skane AB	Lund, Sweden	20. 6.02A
G-BZID	Montgomerie-Bensen B8MR			31. 5.00	A.Gault	Moss Side Farm, Carluke	
		PFA G/01-1315 *(Air Command Elite G-BOGW cannabalised to produce G-BZID)*					
G-BZIF	Dornier 328-100	3053	F-GNBS	20. 6.00	Suckling Airways (Cambridge) Ltd		
			D-CDXU		t/a Scot Airways	Cambridge	12. 7.04T
G-BZIG	Thruster T600N	0400-T600N-042		25. 4.00	Ultra Air Ltd	Leicester	8. 5.02P
	(Rotax 582 UL)						
G-BZIH*	Lindstrand LBL 31A HAFB	700		7. 6.00	Balloon Preservation Group	Kirdford	11. 6.01A
					"Budweiser" (Cancelled 6.11.01 as wfu)		
G-BZII	Extra EA.300/L	119		13. 9.00	J.A.Carr	Guernsey	18. 9.03T
G-BZIJ	Robin DR.500/200i President	0023		9. 3.00	Rob Airways Ltd	Guernsey	13. 4.03
	(Registered as DR.400/500 but c/n plate denotes type as DR.500/200)						
G-BZIK	Cameron A-250 HAFB	4890		27. 6.00	Breckland Balloons Ltd	Dereham	8. 7.02T
G-BZIL	Cameron Colt 120A HAFB	4876		7. 7.00	S.R.Seager	Aylesbury	27. 6.01T
					t/a Champagne Flights *(Parrott & Coales titles)*		
G-BZIM	Pegasus Quantum 15-912	7678		20. 6.00	H.J.W.Munckton	(Farnham)	17. 8.02P
G-BZIN	Robinson R44 Raven	0776		23. 6.00	Helicentre Ltd	Blackpool	12. 7.03T
G-BZIP	Montgomerie-Bensen B.8MR			11. 5.00	S.J.Boxall	(Sheffield)	12. 6.02P
		PFA G/01A-1319					
G-BZIR	Mainair Blade 912	1251-0600-7-W1044		4. 7.00	D.M.Law	(Chiseldon)	10. 7.01P
	(Rotax 912-UL)						
G-BZIS	Raj Hamsa X'Air 582 (2)			12. 6.00	J.Way & R.Bonnett	(Ramsgate)	12.11.012
		520 & BMAA/HB/142			t/a X'Air Group		
G-BZIT	Beechcraft 95-B55 Baron	TC-564	HB-GBS	12. 6.00	Pye Consulting Group Ltd	Blackpool	8. 1.04T
			I-ALGE/HB-GBS/N6845Q				
G-BZIV	Jabiru Jabiru UL	PFA 274A-13587		20. 6.00	V.R.Leggott	Coldharbour Farm, Willingham	30. 8.02P
G-BZIW	Pegasus Quantum 15-912	7681		17. 7.00	J.M.Hodgson	Baxby Manor, Husthwaite	22. 8.02P
G-BZIX	Cameron N-90 HAFB	4867		3. 8.00	Infostrada SpA	Milan, Italy	25. 6.01A
G-BZIY	Raj Hamsa X'Air 582 (2)	BMAA/HB/141		19. 6.00	I.K.Hogg	(Kirkbride)	17. 9.01P
G-BZIZ	Ultramagic H-31 HAFB	31/02		12. 6.00	G.D.O.Bartram	(Andorra la Vella)	24.10.01A
G-BZJA	Cameron Fire-90 SS HAFB	4757		5. 5.00	J M Albury	Cirencester	8. 3.02A
	(Chubb Fire Extinguisher shape)				*(Chubb titles*		
G-BZJB	Aerostar Yakovlev Yak-52	811601	ZU-YAK	18. 9.00	A.D.Heath	(Crewe)	17.10.02P
G-BZJC	Thruster T600N	0070-T600N-044		21. 6.00	Thruster Air Services Ltd	Sandown	8. 4.02P
	(Actually a Thruster Sprint)				*(Op Solent Microlights)*		
G-BZJD	Thruster T600T	0070-T600T-045		21. 6.00	Heart Of The Ocean Ltd	(Sark)	
G-BZJE	Piper PA-46-350P Malibu Mirage		N4137K	15. 9.00	Palace Aviation Ltd	Blackbushe	28. 9.03T
		4636311					
G-BZJF	Pegasus Quantum 15	7696		21. 7.00	A.M.Dalgetty	Perth	20. 7.02P
	(Rotax 582-40)						
G-BZJG	Cameron A-400 HAFB	4715		3. 7.00	Cameron Balloons Ltd	Ontario, Canada	7. 7.01A
G-BZJH	Cameron Z-90 HAFB	4920		10. 7.00	Cameron Balloons Ltd	Italy	15. 6.02A
G-BZJI	Nova X-Large 37	18946		28. 6.00	M.N. Maclean	(Dundee)	
G-BZJJ	Robinson R22 Beta	3081		12. 6.00	Helicentre Ltd	Blackpool	29. 6.03T
G-BZJK	Robinson R22 Beta	3090		20. 6.00	Helicentre Ltd	Blackpool	12. 7.03T

G-BZJL	Mainair Blade 912S 1252-0600-7-W1046 (Rotax 912 ULS)		4. 7.00	D.N.Powell	(Bootle)	3. 7.01P
G-BZJM	VPM M16 Tandem Trainer PFA G/12-1301		19. 6.00	J.Musil	(Cottingham)	
G-BZJN	Mainair Blade 912 1254-0600-7-W1048 (Rotax 912-UL)		13. 7.00	R.M.Pickwick	(Chelmsford)	10. 7.02P
G-BZJO	Pegasus Quantum 15 7699		6. 9.00	J.D.Doran	(Mullingar, Co.Westmeath)	5. 9.02P
G-BZJP	Zenair CH.701UL PFA 187-13579		30. 6.00	D.Jerwood	Upfield Farm, Whitson	24. 5.02P
G-BZJR	Montgomerie-Bensen B.8MR PFA G/01-1320		11. 7.00	N.H.Collins t/a AES Radionic Surveillance Systems	Sittles Farm, Alrewas	
G-BZJS	Taylor JT.2 Titch PFA 060-13622		12. 7.00	R.W.Clarke *(Wings & tail noted 10.01: construction abandoned (temporarily?))*	(Warminster)	
G-BZJU	Cameron A-200 HAFB 4810		30. 6.00	Leeds Castle Enterprises Ltd	Leeds Castle, Kent	22. 6.02T
G-BZJV	CASA 1-131E Jungmann Srs.1000 1075	E3B-367 Spanish AF	31. 7.00	J.A.Sykes	Stretton	15.11.02P
G-BZJW	Cessna 150F 15062054	OO-WIH OO-SIH/N8754S	27. 6.01	R.J.Scott	(Binfield)	
G-BZJX	Ultramagic N-250 HAFB 250/12		4. 7.00	M.W.A.Shemilt t/a Hot Air Balloons	Blackbushe	1. 8.01T
G-BZJY	Lindstrand LBL 69A HAFB 715		28. 6.00	J.J.C.Bernardin	Curcay-sur-Dive, France	3..7.02A
G-BZJZ	Pegasus Quantum 15 7697		2. 8.00	S.Baker	Long Marston	25. 7.01P
G-BZKB	Reims Cessna F172N Skyhawk II F17201914	CS-AQW (G-BOJJ(1))/CS-AQW	3. 7.00	Stapleford Flying Club Ltd	Stapleford	10. 8.03T
G-BZKC	Raj Hamsa X'Air 532 (2) 502 & BMAA/HB/144		12. 7.00	P.J.Cheyney *(Noted 11.01)*	Sywell	
G-BZKD	Stolp SA.300 Starduster Too 1	N70DM	3. 7.00	P.& C.Edmunds *(Noted 7.01)*	Enstone	
G-BZKE	Lindstrand LBL 77B HAFB 708		17. 7.00	P.M.Harrison	(Oswestry)	2. 8.01A
G-BZKF	Rans S-6-ES Coyote II PFA 204-13610		17. 7.00	A.W.Hodder	(Sleaford)	27.11.02P
G-BZKG	Extreme/Silex E761 01A		17. 7.00	R.M.Hardy	(Baldock)	
G-BZKH	Flylight Airsports Doodle Bug/Target DB023		17. 7.00	B.Tempest	(Halifax)	
G-BZKI	Flylight Airsports Doodle Bug/Target DB063		17. 7.00	S.Bond	(Huddersfield)	
G-BZKJ	Flylight Airsports Doodle Bug/Target DB067		17. 7.00	Flylight Airsports Ltd	Sywell	
G-BZKK	Cameron V-56 HAFB 396		2. 8.78	P.J.Green & C.Bosley t/a Gemini Balloon Group *"Gemini II"*	Newbury	13. 8.96A
G-BZKL	Piper PA-28R-201 <u>Cherokee</u> Arrow III 28R-7737152	D-EFFZ N40000	20. 7.00	Van Diemen International Racing Service Ltd	Old Buckenham	30. 8.03
G-BZKN	Campbell Cricket Mk.4 PFA G/03-1304		20. 7.00	C.G. Hooghkirk	(Great Yarmouth)	
G-BZKO	Rans S-6-ES Coyote II PFA 204-13564 *(Struck barbed-wire fence landing Bodmin 1.8.01, damaging nose undercarriage & fuselage)*		20. 7.00	J.A.R. Hartley	Long Marston	21.11.02P
G-BZKP	Boeing 737-229C 20915	OO-SDJ	26. 7.00	European Aviation Air Charter Ltd	Bournemouth	
G-BZKR	Cameron Colt Sugarbox-90 SS HAFB 4922		4. 8.00	Stratos Ballooning GmbH & Co KG	Enningerloh, Germany	8. 8.01A
G-BZKS	Ercoupe 415CD 4834	EI-CIH OO-AIA/(PH-NDO)/N94723/NC94723	22. 8.00	M.D.& W.R.Horler	Haverfordwest	
G-BZKT	Cyclone Pegasus Quantum 15 7711 (Rotax 582)		23. 8.00	K.J.Reynolds	Rochester	21. 8.01P
G-BZKU	Cameron Z-105 HAFB 4931		21. 7.00	Cameron Balloons Ltd	Bristol	31. 8.01P
G-BZKV	Cameron Sky 90-24 HAFB 4857		5. 9.00	Omega Selection Services Ltd	Stonehouse	9. 8.02Q
G-BZKW	Ultramagic M-77 HAFB 77-179		25. 7.00	T.G.Church	Blackburn	8. 8.01T
G-BZKX	Cameron V-90 HAFB 4505		19. 7.00	Cameron Balloons Ltd	Dalien, PRC	26. 7.01A
G-BZKY	Focke-Wulf FW.189-A1 2100 *(Built Aero-Avia)*	V7+1H Luftwaffe	9. 8.00	M T Pearce-Ware *(Restoration being undertaken in UK & Germany)*	(Worthing)	
G-BZKZ	Lindstrand LBL 25A Cloudhopper HAFB 721		14. 8.00	Lindstrand Balloons Ltd	Oswestry	6. 9.01A
G-BZLA	Aérospatiale SA.341G Gazelle 1 1392	N2TV N49534	31. 7.00	Highfield Developments (Yorkshire) Ltd	(Tadcaster)	14.10.04T
G-BZLB	Scottish Aviation Bulldog Srs.120/121 BH120/331	XX685	15. 8.00	L.Bax *(Noted 10.01)*	Bourne Park, Hurstbourne Tarrant	
G-BZLC	PZL-110 Koliber 160A 04980084	SP-WGL	13. 9.00	PZL International Aviation Marketing & Sales plc	North Weald	
G-BZLD	Raj Hamsa X'Air 582 (2) 608 & BMAA/HB/145		3. 8.00	C.Blackburn	(Ballybofey, Co.Donegal)	28. 2.02P
G-BZLE	Rans S-6-ES Coyote II PFA 204-13608		12. 7.00	W.S.Long	Mayfield Farm, Stevenson	18. 9.02P
G-BZLF	CFM Shadow CD <u>K.236</u> & BMAA/HB/053		31. 7.00	D.W.Stacey	(St. Albans)	
G-BZLG	Robin HR.200/120B 353		7. 7.00	G.S.McNaughton *(Op Prestwick Flying Club)*	Prestwick	19.10.03T
G-BZLH	Piper PA-28-161 Warrior II 28-8316075	N43069	23. 8.00	S.J.Skilton t/a Aviation Rentals	Bournemouth	30. 8.03T

G-BZLI	SOCATA TB-21 Tobago TC	500	F-GENI	29. 9.00	K.B.Hallam	(Woking)	2.10.03
G-BZLJ	Cameron N-90 HAFB	2348	LX-BAG	4. 8.00	Gone With The Wind Ltd	Bath	17. 8.01A
			LX-MTC				
G-BZLK	Slingsby T.31M Motor Tutor			2. 8.00	I.P.Manley	(Chichester)	
		PFA 042-13629	*(Formerly T.31B BGA2976/EVA ex WT873 [683])*				
	(Owner's website www.ivannn.flyer.co.uk/t31m.htm intends to record the conversion to powered status)						
G-BZLL	Pegasus Quantum 15-912	7693		9. 8.00	J.J.Smith	Long Marston	7. 8.02P
G-BZLM	Mainair Blade	1257-0800-7-W1051		8. 8.00	K.Bull	(London E7)	8. 8.01P
G-BZLO	Denney Kitfox mk.2	PFA 172-13630		8. 8.00	M.W.Hanley	(Truro)	
G-BZLP	Robinson R44 Raven	0814		17. 7.00	Scotia Helicopters Ltd	Cumbernauld	14. 8.03P
G-BZLS	Cameron Sky 77-24 HAFB	4858		17. 8.00	D.W. Young	(Stenhousemuir)	8. 9.02A
G-BZLT	Raj Hamsa X'Air 582 (1)			10. 8.00	G.Millar	Moygashel, Co.Tyrone	24. 6.02P
		486 & BMAA/HB/125					
G-BZLU	Lindstrand LBL 90A HAFB	719		9. 8.00	A.E.Lusty	Bourne	10. 8.02A
G-BZLV	Jabiru Jabiru UL-450	PFA 274A-13537		15. 8.00	G.Dalton	Bodmin	6. 8.02P
G-BZLX	Pegasus Quantum 15-912	7714		30. 8.00	J.McCormack	Broomhill Farm, West Calder	22. 8.01P
G-BZLY	Grob G.109B	6242	D-KLMG	24. 8.00	M.Yolson	Egelsbach, Germany	14.11.02
			G-BZLY/OE-9230				
G-BZLZ	Pegasus Quantum 15-912	7721		13. 9.00	A.R.Way	Dunkeswell	27. 9.02P
G-BZMB	Piper PA-28R-201 Arrow III		HB-PBY	20. 4.00	D.S.Seex	King's Farm,Thurrock	19. 6.03T
		28R-7837144	N3963M				
G-BZMC	Jabiru Jabiru UL	PFA 274A-13593		18. 8.00	J.R.Banks	(Douglas, IoM)	2. 9.02P
G-BZMD	Scottish Aviation Bulldog Srs.120/121		XX554	18. 8.00	J.Cooper	(Moreton-in-Marsh)	13.11.04
		BH120/247					
G-BZME	Scottish Aviation Bulldog Srs.120/121		XX698	18. 8.00	B.Whitworth	Breighton	2. 9.04
		BH120/347			*(As "XX698")*		
G-BZMF	Rutan LongEZ	PFA 074-10698		30. 8.00	R.A.Gardiner & A.McLaughlin		
						Cumbernauld	
G-BZMG	Robinson R44 Raven	0815		16. 8.00	Ramsgill Aviation Ltd	Sherburn-in-Elmet	14. 9.03T
G-BZMH	Scottish Aviation Bulldog Srs.120/121		XX692	21. 8.00	M.E.J.Hingley & Co.Ltd		
		BH120/341				Wellesbourne Mountford	17.10.04
G-BZMI	Pegasus Quantum 15-912	7716		22. 9.00	T.W.Thiele	Newnham, Baldock	11.10.02P
G-BZMJ	Rans S-6-ES Coyote II	PFA 204-13631		31. 8.00	J.Seddon, F.J.Lloyd t/a Heskin Flying Group		
						Tarn Farm, Cockerham	13. 6.02P
G-BZML	Scottish Aviation Bulldog Srs.120/121		XX693	1. 9.00	I.D.Anderson	(Nayland)	14.11.04
		BH120/342					
G-BZMM	Robin DR.400/180R Remorquer	918	OE-KIR	17. 7.00	N.A.C.Norman	Feshiebridge	5.10.03
			D-EAWR				
G-BZMO	Robinson R22 Beta	1219	N24282	31. 7.00	Sloane Helicopters Ltd	Sywell	4. 9.03T
			JA7814/N8056H				
G-BZMR	Raj Hamsa X'Air 582 (2)			11. 9.00	M.Grime	(Darwen)	
		480 & BMAA/HB/149					
G-BZMS	Mainair Blade	1256-0700-7-W1050		2. 8.00	A.J.Tyler	Beccles	4. 9.02P
	(Rotax 582)						
G-BZMT	Piper PA-28-161 Warrior III	2842107	N4147D	29.11.00	S J Skilton	Wellesbourne Mountford	28.11.03T
			G-BZMT/N9519N/N4147D		t/a Aviation Rentals		
G-BZMV	Cameron Concept-80 HAFB	4930		26. 9.00	Latteria Soresinese Soc Coop ARL		
						Soresina, Italy	22. 4.02P
G-BZMW	Pegasus Quantum 15-912	7720		26. 9.00	J.I. Greenshields	Dunkeswell	3.10.02P
G-BZMX	Cameron Z-90 HAFB	4942		1. 9.00	Cameron Balloons Ltd	Bristol	18. 9.01A
G-BZMY	SPP Yakovlev Yak C-11	171314	F-AZSF	4.10.00	E.G.Gavazzi *"11"*	North Weald	17. 1.02P
			Egyptian AF				
G-BZMZ	CFM Streak Shadow			13. 9.00	J.F.F.Fouche	(London EC1)	
		K265-CD & BMAA/HB/051					
G-BZNA	Lindstrand LBL 90A HAFB	732		21. 9.00	Lindstrand Balloons Ltd	Abuja, Nigeria	28. 9.01A
G-BZNB	Pegasus Quantum 15	7739		10.11.00	R.C.Whittall	Weston Zoyland	9.11.02P
G-BZNC	Pegasus Quantum 15-912	7736		25.10.00	D.E.Wall	Long Marston	2.11.01P
G-BZND	Sopwith Pup rep	PFA 101-11815		27. 9.00	B.F.Goddard	(Southampton)	
G-BZNE	Beechcraft B300 Super King Air		N4486V	17.10.00	G.Davies	Blackbushe	16.11.03
	(Aka "King Air 350")	FL-286					
G-BZNF	Cameron Colt 120A HAFB	4866		13.11.00	N. Charbonnier	Aosta, Italy	21. 1.02A
G-BZNG	Raj Hamsa Jabiru (1)			4.10.00	G.L.Craig	Newtownards, Co.of Down	
		571 & BMAA/HB/147			*(Noted 8.01)*		
	(Officially regd as X'Air 700 (1) but completed as above)						
G-BZNH	Rans S-6-ES Coyote II *(Tricycle u/c)*			18.10.00	R.E.Quine & R.W.Cooper	Jurby, IoM	14. 1.02P
		0899.1333 &.PFA 204-13660					
G-BZNI	Bell 206B JetRanger II	2142	G-ODIG	4.10.00	Trimax Ltd	(Margate)	3. 1.04T
			G-NEEP/N777FW/N3CR				
G-BZNJ	Rans S-6-ES Coyote II	PFA 204-13640		23.10.00	S.P.Read & M.H.Wise	(Langport)	19. 4.02P
	(Tailwheel u/c)						
G-BZNK	Morane Saulnier MS.315E D2	354	F-BCNY	2.11.00	R.H.Cooper & S.Swallow	(Stow, Lincs)	
			French AF		*(Work continuing 11.01)*		

G-BZNM	Pegasus Quantum 15 (Rotax 582)	7754		20.11.00	M.Tomlinson	(Burton-on-Trent)	19.11.02P
G-BZNN	Beechcraft 76 Duchess	ME-343	N6133P F-GHSU/N6722L	25.10.00	S.J.Skilton t/a Aviation Rentals	Bournemouth	14.12.03T
G-BZNO	Ercoupe 415C	2118	N99495	9.11.00	D.K.Tregilgas	(Hedge End, Southampton)	
G-BZNP	Thruster T600N-450 (Rotax 582)	0100-T600N-047		27.10.00	R.S.O'Carroll	(Craigavon, Co.Armagh)	3.12.02P
G-BZNR	British Aerospace BAe 125 Srs.800B	258180	G-XRMC G-5-675	30.10.00	RMC Group Services Ltd	Farnborough	11.12.04T
G-BZNS	Mainair Blade	1263-1000-7-W1057		23.11.00	M.K.B.Molyneux	(Nantwich)	11. 2.02P
G-BZNT	Aero L-29 Delfin	893019	ES-YLG Estonian AF/Soviet AF	3.11.00	Jet Centre Sales Ltd	North Weald	
G-BZNU	Cameron A-300 HAFB	4960		29.11.00	D.K.Hempleman-Adams	Corsham	27.11.01A
G-BZNV	Lindstrand LBL 31A HAFB	741		12.12.00	G.R. Down	Gillingham	14. 1.02A
G-BZNW	Isaacs Fury II	PFA 011-13042		10.11.00	J.E.D.Rogerson	(Ferryhill)	
	(Officially quoted c/n is incorrect: PFA project 13042 relates to 206-13042/Streak Shadow G-SNEV. Project 13402 is recorded as an Isaacs Fury II and, therefore, G-BZNW should be 011-13402)						
G-BZNX	SOCATA MS.880B Rallye Club	2113	F-BTVX	17.11.00	R.E.Knapton	Turweston	30. 1.04
G-BZNY	Europa Aviation Europa XS	PFA 247-13355		14.11.00	A.K.Middlemas	(Bingley)	
G-BZNZ	Lindstrand LBL Cake SS HAFB	747		21.12.00	Oxford Promotions (UK) Ltd *(Op F Prell)*	Kentucky, USA	3. 1.02A
G-BZOB	Slepcev Storch	PFA 316-13592		21.11.00	J.E.& A.Ashby	(Papworth Everard)	
G-BZOC	Pegasus Quantum 15-912	7753		29.11.00	S.J.Doyle	(Liverpool)	28.11.02P
G-BZOD	Pegasus Quantum 15-912	7763		18.12.00	N.F.Mackenzie	East Fortune	28. 3.02P
G-BZOE	Pegasus Quantum 15 (Rotax 582)	7723		14. 9.00	W.E.Richards	Redlands, Swindon	2.10.01P
G-BZOF	Montgomerie-Bensen B.8MR	MGM3/SJML1		7.11.00	S.J.M.Ledingham	Carlisle	2. 8.02P
G-BZOG	Dornier 328-100	3088	D-CDXN(5) F-GNPR	19.12.00	Suckling Airways (Cambridge) Ltd t/a Scot Airways	Cambridge	20.12.02T
G-BZOH	Cameron Bull-110 SS HAFB	4983		12. 1.01	Ballon Team Bonn GmbH & Co KG	Meckenheim, Germany	21. 1.02A
G-BZOI	Nicollier HN.700 Menestrel II	PFA 217-12604		27.10.00	S.J.McCollum	Newtownards, Co.of Down	22. 5.02P
G-BZOL	Robin R.3000/140	124	F-GEKZ	20.12.00	Building and Commercial Ltd	Gloucestershire	6. 3.04T
G-BZOM	Rotorway Exec 162F	6243	N767SG	27. 3.01	J.A.Jackson	(Shrewsbury)	
G-BZON	Scottish Aviation Bulldog Srs.120/121	BH120/214	XX528	19.12.00	Towerdrive Ltd *(As "XX528/D")*	Carlisle	8. 7.04
G-BZOO	Pegasus Quantum 15-912	7702		15. 8.00	C.R.Ashley	Sittles Farm, Alrewas	18.10.02P
G-BZOP	Robinson R44	0958		11. 1.01	20:20 Logistics Ltd	(Stoke-on-Trent)	28. 1.04T
G-BZOR	TEAM mini-Max 91	PFA 186-13312		9. 8.00	A.Watt	Incsh	13. 5.02P
G-BZOS	Westland SA.314C Gazelle HT.2	1173	XW894	15.12.00	South West Aviation Services Ltd	(Truro)	22.10.02P
G-BZOT	Westland SA.314C Gazelle HT.2	1216	XW907	15.12.00	South West Aviation Services Ltd	(Truro)	3.12.02P
G-BZOU	Pegasus Quantum 15-912	7768		22. 3.01	A.J.Gordon	(Aylesbury)	21. 3.02P
G-BZOV	Pegasus Quantum 15-912	7769		22. 3.01	D.Turner	(Bicester)	21. 3.02P
G-BZOW	Whittaker MW7	PFA 171-13118		15.12.00	G.W.Peacock	(Doncaster)	
G-BZOX	Cameron Colt 90B HAFB	10000		8. 2.01	D.J.Head	Newbury	13. 2.02P
G-BZOZ	Van's RV-6	PFA 181-12455		14. 9.00	V.Edmundson	(Blackburn)	
G-BZPA	Mainair Blade 912S	1264-1100-7-W1058		13.12.00	J.McGoldrick	Newtownards, Co.of Down	28. 1.02P
G-BZPB	Hawker Hunter GA.Mk.11	41H-670758	WV256	15. 1.01	B.R.Pearson	Exeter	17. 7.02P
	(As "WB188" Hunter prototype in its first form /duck-egg green c/s)						
G-BZPC	Hawker Hunter GA.Mk.11	HABL-003061	XF300	15. 1.01	B.R.Pearson	Exeter	
	(As "WB188" Hunter prototype in its second form/all-red c/s)						
G-BZPD	Cameron V-65 HAFB	4700		10.11.00	Gone With The Wind Ltd	Bristol	
G-BZPE	Lindstrand LBL 310A HAFB	746		16. 2.01	A.J.Street	Exeter	18. 3.02T
G-BZPF	Scheibe SF-24B Motorspatz 1	4028	PH-971 OE-9005/D-KECO)	19. 1.01	D.Shrimpton	(RAF Keevil)	
G-BZPG	Beechcraft C24R Sierra	MC-556	N23840	27. 3.01	S.J.Skilton t/a Aviation Rentals	Bournemouth	30. 4.04T
G-BZPH	Van's RV-4	PFA 181-12867		6. 9.00	A.G.Truman t/a G-BZPH RV-4 Group	Kemble	24.11.02P
G-BZPI	SOCATA TB-20 Trindad	1814	SX-ATT	20.12.00	P.W.Huntley	Fairoaks	28. 1.04T
G-BZPJ	Beechcraft 76 Duchess	ME-227	N6630Z	2. 3.01	S.J.Skilton t/a Aviation Rentals	Bournemouth	19. 3.04T
G-BZPK	Cameron C-80 HAFB	4183		23. 2.01	Horizon Ballooning Ltd	Alton	5. 2.02T
G-BZPL	Robinson R44	0948		10. 1.01	M.K.Shaw	(Lowestoft)	5. 2.04T
G-BZPM	Cessna 172S Skyhawk	172S8561	N72760	11. 1.01	TDR Aviation Ltd	(Craigavon, Co.Armagh)	4. 3.04T
G-BZPN	Mainair Blade 912S	1268-0101-7-W1062		25. 1.01	M Lovelidge	(London E5)	25. 1.02P
G-BZPP	Westand Wasp HAS.Mk.1	F9675	XT793	15. 1.01	G.P.Hinkley	(Ipswich)	
G-BZPR	Ultramagic N-210 HAFB	210/14		16. 1.01	European Balloon Display Co Ltd	Great Missenden	21. 2.02T

G-BZPS	Scottish Aviation Bulldog Srs.120/121	BH120/316	XX658	8. 1.01	D.M.Squires *(Noted 5.01)*	Wellesbourne Mountford	
G-BZPT	Ultramagic N-210 HAFB	210/15		16. 1.01	European Balloon Display Co. Ltd	Great Missenden	
G-BZPU	Cameron V-77 HAFB	5433	N20726	2. 5.01	J.Vonka	New Malden	
G-BZPV	Lindstrand LBL 90B HAFB	<u>727</u>		17. 1.01	D.P.Hopkins *(Lakeside Lodge titles)*	Pidley, Huntingdon	16. 1.02A
G-BZPW	Cameron V-77 HAFB	6245		2. 2.01	J.Vonka	New Malden	17. 6.02A
G-BZPX	Ultramagic S-105 HAFB	105/78		12. 2.01	G.M.Houston t/a Scotair Balloons	Lesmahagow	21. 2.02T
G-BZPY	Ultramagic H-31 HAFB	31/03		12. 2.01	G.M.Houston t/a Scotair Balloons	Lesmahagow	11. 2.02A
G-BZPZ	Mainair Blade	1265-1200-7-W1059		23. 1.01	M C W Robertson	(Leek, Staffs)	13. 3.02P
G-BZRA	Rans S-6-ES Coyote II	PFA 204-13683		16. 1.01	A.W.Fish	(Telford)	28. 3.02P
G-BZRB	Mainair Blade	1270-0201-7-W1064		7. 3.01	S.B.Brady	(Stoke-on-Trent)	7. 3.02P
G-BZRC	de Havilland DH.115 Vampire T.Mk.11	15143	WZ584	26. 3.01	D.Copley *(Dismantled & unconverted as "WZ584/K" 4.01)*	Sandtoft	
G-BZRD	de Havilland DH.115 Vampire T.Mk.11	15687	XH313	27. 3.01	D.Copley *(Dismantled & unconverted as "XH313/E" 4.01)*	Sandtoft	
G-BZRE	Percival P.56 Provost T.Mk.1	PAC/F/234	7688M WW421	15. 5.01	D.Copley *(Dismantled & unconverted as "WW421" 4.01)*	Sandtoft	
G-BZRF	Percival P.56 Provost T.Mk.1	PAC/F/062	7698M WV499	15. 5.01	D.Copley *(Dismantled & unconverted as "WV499" 4.01)*	Sandtoft	
G-BZRG	Hunt Wing/Avon	<u>Plans No.0009090</u> & BMAA/HB/154		16. 1.01	W.G.Reynolds *(Frame only completed by 7.01)*	(Cromer)	
G-BZRH	Hawker Hunter GA.11	HABL-<u>003097</u>	XF368	26. 1.01	M A B Head *(Sold in South Africa 6.01)*	(Cape Town, SA)	10. 5.02P
G-BZRI	Hawker Hunter T.8B	41H-695343	9186M "XF967"/XL609	30. 1.01	M A B Head *(Sold in South Africa 6.01)*	(Cape Town, SA)	10. 5.02P
	(C/n officially amended from HABL-003122 @ 2.01 but believed this relates solely to two-seat nose section grafted on to airframe '003122 during conversion from F.Mk.4 to T.Mk.7B)						
G-BZRJ	Pegasus Quantum 15-912	7783		5. 2.01	R.W.Goddin	Newnham, Baldock	25. 4.02P
G-BZRN	Robinson R44	0971		1. 2.01	Toriamos Ltd	(Naas, Co.Kildare)	15.11.04T
G-BZRM	Eurocopter EC 135 T1	0149		10. 8.01	Eurocopter Deutschland GmbH	(Donauworth, Germany)	15. 2.04T
G-BZRO	Piper PA-30 Twin Comanche C	30-1923	SE-IYL D-GATI/I-KATI/N8767Y	2. 3.01	Comanche Hire Ltd	Gloucestershire	21. 5.04T
G-BZRP	Pegasus Quantum 15-912	7758		24. 1.01	R H Braithwaite t/a RAF Microlight Flying Association	RAF Cosford	30. 1.02P
G-BZRR	Pegasus Quantum 15-912	7727		4.10.00	R.E.Welch t/a Syndicate Romeo Romeo	(Southwell)	8.10.02P
G-BZRS	Eurocopter EC 135T1	0166		22. 3.01	Bond Air Services Ltd	Aberdeen	8. 4.04T
G-BZRU	Cameron V-90 HAFB	10053		1. 5.01	Close Invoice Finance Ltd	Newbury	31. 7.02A
G-BZRV	Van's RV-6	PFA 181A-13573		12.10.00	E.Hicks & N.M.Hitchman	(Bristol)	
G-BZRW	Mainair Blade 912S	1266-0101-7-W1060		6. 2.01	N.D.Kube	(Groby, Leics.)	19. 2.02P
G-BZRX	Ultramagic M-105 HAFB	105/80		3. 5.01	Specialist Recruitment Group plc	Huntingdon	23. 8.02A
G-BZRY	Rans S-6-ES Coyote II	PFA 204-13666		1. 2.01	S.Forman	Norwich	30. 7.02P
G-BZRZ	Thunder AX11-250 S2 HAFB	10013		11.10.01	T.J.Bucknall t/a Cheshire Balloon Flights	Chester	1. 4.02T
G-BZSA	Pegasus Quantum 15	7784		25. 1.01	Cyclone Airsports Ltd t/a Pegasus Aviation	Manton	2.12.02P
G-BZSB	Pitts S-1S Special	PFA 009-13697		2. 2.01	A.D.Ingold	(Harlow)	
G-BZSC	Sopwith Camel F.1 rep *(Built Northern Aeroplane Workshops)*	NAW-3		15. 1.01	The Shuttleworth Trust	Old Warden	
G-BZSD	Piper PA-46-350P Mailbu Mirage	4636168	N838DB	14. 2.01	Harpin Ltd	(Nun Monkton, York)	13. 2.04T
G-BZSE	Hawker Hunter T.Mk.7	41H-670788	9096M WV322	6. 2.01	Towerdrive Ltd	Kemble	
	(Officially regd as T.Mk.8B with c/n 41H-670792, that is the same c/n as G-FFOX qv: the airframes of WV318 & WV322 became interchanged during service. G-FFOX is c/n 41H-670792 & ex WV318 but now has the centre fuselage from WV322 whilst G-BZSE's c/n plate has been altered to read HABL/R/41H-670792 as per G-FFOX & now has the centre fuselage from WV318!)						
G-BZSF	Hawker Hunter T.Mk.8B	HABL-003150	9237M XF995	6. 2.01	Towerdrive Ltd	(Ashbourne)	
G-BZSG	Pegasus Quantum 15-912	7766		22. 2.01	K.J.Gay	(Bangor, Co.of Down)	21. 2.02P
G-BZSH	Ultramagic H-77 HAFB	77/191		12. 4.01	J.L.Hutsby *(Tethered 5.01)*	Oxhill, Warwicks	13. 6.02A
G-BZSI	Pegasus Quantum 15	7787		12. 3.01	B.& K.Yoxall	Rufforth	11. 3.02P
G-BZSL	Sky 25-16 HAFB	138		31. 1.01	Zebedee Balloon Service Ltd	Hungerford	12. 3.02A
G-BZSM	Pegasus Quantum 15	7788		23. 2.01	S.J.Mawman *(Noted 9.01)*	Knapthorpe Lodge, Caunton	15..3.02P

G-BZSP	Stemme S.10	10-14	HB-2217 D-KDNE	10. 5.01	A.Flewelling, & L.Bleaken *"626"*	Aston Down	22. 8.04
G-BZSR	Hawker Hunter T.Mk.7	41H-693832	A2617 XL601	15. 2.01	Stick & Rudder Aviation Ltd	(Meetkerke, Belgium)	
G-BZSS	Pegasus Quantum 15-912	7770		6. 2.01	T.R.Marsh	Brown Shutters Farm, Norton St Philips, Somerset	20. 2.02P
G-BZST	Jabiru Jabiru UL	PFA 274A-13616		13. 2.01	G.Hammond	Headcorn	4. 9.02T
G-BZSU	Cameron A-315 HAFB	10009		13. 6.01	Ballooning Network Ltd *(Bath Investment & Building Society titles)*	Bristol	15. 5.02T
G-BZSV	Aherne Barracuda	631		20. 2.01	M.J.Aherne	(St. Albans)	
G-BZSX	Pegasus Quantum 15-912	7789		23. 2.01	J.B.Greenwood	Rufforth	22. 2.02P
G-BZSY	SNCAN Stampe SV-4A	677	N12426 F-BGGT/French AF	12. 3.01	G P J M Valvekens	Diest, Belgium	
G-BZSZ	Jabiru Jabiru UL	PFA 274A-13432		16. 2.01	M.C.J.Ludlow	(Ashford)	29. 7.02P
G-BZTA	Robinson R44	0968		20. 2.01	Ash Aviation Ltd	Headcorn	7. 3 04T
G-BZTB	Airbus A310-204	424	HS-TIC F-WWCM	8. 3.01	Cabot Aviation Ltd	(Hassocks)	
G-BZTC	TEAM mini-MAX 91	PFA 186-13336		23. 1.01	G G Clayton	(Looe)	11.12.02P
G-BZTD	Thruster T600T 450 JAB	0021-T600T-049		22. 2.01	B O & B C McCartan	(Banbridge, Belfast)	
G-BZTE	Cameron A-275 HAFB	10028		26. 6.01	Richard Nash Cars Ltd	(Norwich)	6. 3.02T
G-BZTF	IDA Bacau Yakovlev Yak-52	866703	LY-AKE DOSAAF	28. 2.01	M.S.Davy	Beccles	18. 4.02P
G-BZTG	Piper PA-34-220T Seneca V	3449126	EC-HGK N4141N	4. 4.01	L.R.Chiswell	Alderney	16. 4.04T
G-BZTH	Europa Aviation Europa	PFA 247-12494		21.12.00	T J Houlihan *(Noted 5.01)*	Kemble	
G-BZTI	Europa Aviation Europa XS	PFA 247-13172		30. 3.01	W.Hoolachan	Kemble	12. 9.02P
G-BZTJ	CASA Bü.133C Jungmeister	41	ES1-41 Spanish AF	7. 3.01	R.A.Seeley	Denham	
G-BZTK	Cameron V-90 HAFB	10083		6. 3.01	Cameron Balloons Ltd	Bristol	28. 6.02A
G-BZTL	Cameron Colt Flying Ice Cream Cone SS HAFB	10008		16. 5.01	Stratos Ballooning GmbH & Co KG	Ennigerloh, Germany	15. 5.02A
G-BZTM	Mainair Blade	1273-0201-7-W1068		12. 2.01	L.Hogan	East Fortune	12. 3.02P
G-BZTN	Europa Aviation Europa XS	PFA 247-13715		16. 3.01	W.Pringle & J.Dewberry	(Worksop)	
G-BZTO	Lindstrand LBL 150A HAFB	772		10. 4.01	A.M.Holly	Bristol	18. 9.02T
G-BZTP	Piper PA-46-500TP Malibu Meridian	4697050	N53308	15. 6.01	Sunseeker Sales (UK) Ltd	Bournemouth	20 .6.04T
G-BZTR	Mainair Blade	1276-0301-7-W1071		8. 3.01	A.Rees & M.Liptrot	Carlisle	25. 3.02P
G-BZTS	Cameron Bertie Bassett-90 SS HAFB	10050		3. 5.01	Trebor Bassett Ltd	Rickmansworth	2. 5.02A
G-BZTT	Cameron A-275 HAFB	4953		28. 8.01	Spotlight Group Ltd	Axbridge	29. 8.02T
G-BZTU	Mainair Blade 912	1272-0201-7-W1066		8. 2.01	A J Tyler t/a Cloudscape Microlights	Beccles	21. 3.02P
G-BZTV	Mainair Blade 912S	1278-0301-7-W1073		2. 4.01	S.Dornan	(Forth, Lanark)	4 4 02P
G-BZTW	Hunt Wing/Avon	Plans No.9906092 & BMAA/HB/136		17. 1.01	T.S.Walker	(Sandbach)	
G-BZTX	Mainair Blade 912	1267-0101-7-W1061		9. 2.01	K.A.Ingham	(Wilmslow)	15. 2.02P
G-BZTY	Jabiru Jabiru UL	PFA 274A-13533		1. 3.01	R.P.Lewis	(Kings Lynn)	19. 7.02P
G-BZTZ	MD Helicopters MD 600N	RN056	N70412	15. 5.01	Helicorp Ltd	(Stone)	15 .7.04T
G-BZUB	Mainair Blade	1274-0201-7-W1069		27. 3.01	A.J.Lindsay	Newtownards, Co.of Down	13. 6.02P
G-BZUC	Pegasus Quantum 15-912	7796		10. 4.01	G.Breen	(Lagos, Algarve, Portugal)	10. 4 02P
G-BZUD	Lindstrand LBL 105A HAFB	780		27. 3.01	P.N.Rhodes	(Oswestry)	26. 3.02A
G-BZUE	Pegasus Quantum 15	7800		23. 4.01	D.J.& M.E.Walcroft	(Great Missenden)	7. 5.02P
G-BZUF	Mainair Rapier	1277-0301-7-W1072		27. 3.01	S.J.Perry	(Sandbach)	1. 7.02P
G-BZUG	Tiger Cub RL7A XP Sherwood Ranger	PFA 237-13040		23. 3.01	S.P.Sharp	(Crowborough)	
G-BZUH	Rans S-6-ES Coyote II	PFA 204-13716		26. 3.01	G.M.Prowling	(Rothwell)	9. 7.02P
G-BZUI	Pegasus Quantum 15-912	7798		8. 5.01	R. Clark	(Leeds)	21.10.02P
G-BZUK	Lindstrand LBL 31A HAFB	776		7. 3.01	G.R.J.Luckett	Fort Collins, Co, USA	12. 3.02A
G-BZUL	Jabiru Jabiru UL	PFA 274A-13678		28. 3.01	P.Hawkins	(Shipley)	
G-BZUM	Mainair Blade 912	1271-0201-7-W1065		13. 3.01	R.B.Milton	(London E2)	21. 3.02P
G-BZUN	Mainair Blade 912	1279-0301-7-W1074		18. 4.01	E.Paxton & A Jones	Ince Blundell	22. 4.02P
G-BZUO	Cameron A-340HL HAFB	4952		18. 5.01	T.J.Parker t/a Anglian Countryside Balloons	Burnham-on-Crouch	7. 5.02T
G-BZUP	Raj Hamsa X'Air 582 (5)	BMAA/HB/164		24. 4.01	A.A.J.Lappin	Newtownards, Co.of Down	
G-BZUU	Cameron O-90 HAFB	10058		14. 6.01	D.C.Ball & C.F.Pooley	London SE1	3. 6.02A
G-BZUV	Cameron H-24 HAFB	2665	LX-JLW	27. 4.01	J.N.Race	Lewes	18. 5.02A
G-BZUX	Pegasus Quantum 15	7819		22. 5.01	K.M.MacRae, J.D.& C.A.Capewell	East Fortune	29. 4.02P

G-BZUY	Van's RV-6	PFA 181A-13471		23. 5.01	D.M.Gale & K.F.Crumplin	Henstridge	
					(Noted 1.02)		
G-BZUZ	Hunt Avon-Blade R100(1)	BMAA/HB/162		9. 2.01	J.A.Hunt	(Abergavenny)	22. 5.02P
	(BMW R100) *(Mainair sailwing c/n W1067)*						
G-BZVA	Zenair CH.701UL	PFA 187-13635		21. 3.01	M.W.Taylor	Insch	
G-BZVB	Reims FR172H Rocket	FR17200327	G-BLMX	29. 8.00	Tindon Ltd	Little Snoring	13.11.03T
			PH-RPC				
G-BZVC	Mickleburgh L107	PFA 256-12549		21. 3.01	D.R.Mickleburgh	(Milton Keynes)	
					(Exhibited incomplete at 1996 PFA Rally)		
G-BZVD	Cameron Colt Forklift-105 SS HAFB			15. 6.01	Stratos Ballooning GmbH & Co KG		
		10084			*"JungHeinrich"*	Ennigerloh, Germany	25. 6.02A
G-BZVE	Cameron N-133 HAFB	10092		20. 6.01	Flying Pictures Ltd	Fairoaks	15. 5.02A
G-BZVF	Cessna 182T Skylane	T18208009	N109LP	12. 6.01	R. Macaire	Crowfield	8. 7.04T
					t/a Denston Hall Estate		
G-BZVG	Eurocopter AS 350B3 Ecureuil	3368	F-WQOR	5. 3.01	Finlay (Holdings) Ltd		
						(Augher, Co.Tyrone)	
G-BZVH	Raj Hamsa X'Air 582 (1)			20. 4.01	B.& D.Bergin	Enniskillen, Co.Fermanagh	
		561 & BMAA/HB/160 *(Build started as X'Air R100) (Noted 11.01)*					
G-BZVI	Nova Vertex 24 Hang Glider	13379		24. 5.01	M.N.Maclean	(Dundee)	
G-BZVJ	Pegasus Quantum 15	7821		12. 6.01	W.T.Davis	Perth	11. 6.02P
G-BZVK	Raj Hamsa X'Air 582 (2)			22. 2.01	K.P.Taylor	Whitehall Farm, Benington	
		592 & BMAA/HB/152			*(Noted 8.01)*		
G-BZVM	Rans S-6-ES Coyote II	PFA 204-13705		1. 3.01	N.N.Ducker	(Ashbourne)	21. 6.02P
G-BZVN	Van's RV-6	PFA 181-13188		25. 4.01	J.A.Booth	Gamston	7. 8.02P
G-BZVO	Cessna TR182 Turbo Skylane RG		D-EPOL	3. 4.01	Swiftair Ltd	Elstree	
		R18200990	N739CX				
G-BZVP	Robinson R44 Raven	0929		17. 4.01	Heli Air Ltd	(Carluke)	2. 5.04T
G-BZVR	Raj Hamsa X'Air 582 (8)			13. 3.01	R.P.Sims	Davidstowe Moor	10. 9.02P
		566 & BMAA/HB/146			*(Noted 11.01)*		
G-BZVS	CASA 1-131E Jungmann Srs.2000	2013	D-EHEP(2)	3. 5.01	W.R.M.Beesley	Breighton/Lambley	12. 7.02P
	(Avco Lycoming-180hp)		D-EDEE/Spanish AF E3B-409				
G-BZVT	III Sky Arrow 650TC	PFA 298-13333		23. 3.01	R.W.Seabrook & R.N.Wright	(Lewes)	
G-BZVU	Cameron Z-105 HAFB	10078		9. 8.01	Prudential Investment Managers Ltd		
						Bristol	16. 7.02A
G-BZVV	Pegasus Quantum 15-912	7793		12. 3.01	A.Featherstone & D.C.Mott		
						Knapthorpe Lodge, Caunton	18. 3.02P
G-BZVW	Ilyushin Il-2	1870710	Sov AF	16. 5.01	S.Swallow & R.H.Cooper	(Stowe, Lincs)	
G-BZVX	Ilyushin Il-2	1878576	Sov.AF	16. 5.01	S.Swallow & R.H.Cooper	(Stowe, Lincs)	
G-BZVZ	Eurocopter AS355N Twin Squirrel	5691		24. 4.01	Ilona Ltd.	(Greece)	14. 6.04
					(Based on board MV Ilona)		
G-BZWB	Mainair Blade 912	1284-0507-7-W1079		26. 4.01	Mainair Sports Ltd	Barton	2. 5.02P
G-BZWC	Raj Hamsa X'Air Falcon 912 (1)			9. 5.01	G.A.J.Salter	(Taunton)	
		587 & BMAA/HB/157					
G-BZWF	Colt AS-120 Mk.II HA Airship	10095	(HS-...)	2. 5.01	D.C.Chipping	Bangkok, Thailand	20. 6.02A
			G-BZWF				
G-BZWG	Piper PA-28-140 Cherokee Cruiser		N9656K	17. 5.01	H & E Merkado	Panshanger	12. 7.04T
		28-7625188					
G-BZWH	Cessna 152	15281339	N49819	17. 5.01	J & H Aviation Services Ltd	Panshanger	14. 6.04T
G-BZWI	Medway EclipseR	170/148		3. 5.01	R.A.Keene	Over Farm, Gloucester	12. 9.02P
G-BZWJ	CFM Streak Shadow SA	PFA 206-13553		8. 5.01	T.A.Morgan	(Carshalton)	
G-BZWK	Jabiru Jabiru SK	PFA 274-13292		8. 5.01	R.Thompson *(Noted 10.01)*	Redhill	
G-BZWM	Solar Wings Pegasus XL-Q	7792		18. 5.01	D.T.Evans	(Hereford)	17. 5.02P
G-BZWN	Van's RV-8	PFA 303-13692		14. 5.01	A.J.Symms & R.D.Harper	(Langport)	
G-BZWR	Mainair Rapier	1275-0301-7-W1070		7. 3.01	W.E.Ross	(Lancaster)	18. 6.02P
G-BZWS	Pegasus Quantum 15-912	7813		26. 4.01	Cyclone Airsports Ltd	Manton	3. 5.02P
					t/a Pegasus Aviation		
G-BZWT	Technam P92-EM Echo	PFA 318-13681		17. 5.01	R.F.Cooper	(Aylesbury)	
G-BZWU	Pegasus Quantum 15-912	7831		19. 7.01	P.C.Hogg	(Broxbourne)	5. 8.02P
G-BZWV	Steen Skybolt	PFA 064-10751		30. 5.01	P.D.& K.Begley	(Milton Keynes)	
G-BZWX	Whittaker MW5-D Sorcerer			1. 6.01	P.G.Depper	(Kidderminster)	
		PFA 163-13599					
G-BZWY	CFM Streak Shadow SA	PFA 206-13601		31. 5.01	B.Cartwright	(Craigavon)	
G-BZWZ	Van's RV-6	PFA 181A-13419		26. 4.01	J.Shanley	(Middlesbrough)	
G-BZXA	Raj Hamsa X'Air V2 (1)			31. 5.01	D.W.Mullin	Hawarden	
		560 & BMAA/HB/148			*(Noted 12.01)*		
G-BZXB	Van's RV-6	PFA 181A-13625		4. 6.01	B.J.King-Smith & D.J.Akerman	Goodwood	
G-BZXC	Scottish Aviation Bulldog Srs.120/121		XX612	8. 6.01	G.Jones	(New Malden)	
		BH120/260					
G-BZXD	Rotorway Exec 162F	6494		5. 6.01	P.G.King	(Gravesend)	
G-BZXE	de Havilland DHC-1 Chipmunk 22		WP839	5. 6.01	K.Moore	Blackpool	
		C1/0722					
G-BZXG	Dyn'Aéro MCR-01 ULC	PFA 301B-13815		26.10.01	L.J. Scott	Cambridge	
					t/a G-BZXG Group		

G-BZXH	Jodel D.150 Mascaret *(Built M.Busmey)*	149	F-PBUS	22. 6.01	E.J.Horsfall	Blackpool	
G-BZXI	Nova Philou 26 Hang Glider	11207		16. 5.01	M.N.Maclean	(Dundee)	
G-BZXJ	Schweizer 269C-1	0128		20. 6.01	Helicentre Ltd	Liverpool	22. 7.04T
G-BZXK	Robin HR.200/120B	286	F-GNNV	12. 6.01	S.J. Skilton t/a Aviation Rentals	Bournemouth	15. 7.04T
G-BZXL	Whittaker MW5-D Sorcerer	PFA 163-13738		7. 6.01	K.Wright	(Douglas, IoM)	
G-BZXM	Mainair Blade 912	1283-0501-7-W1078		20. 4.01	P.Harper	St.Michaels	24. 4 02P
G-BZXN	Jabiru Jabiru UL-450	PFA 274A-13747		7. 6.01	A.R.Silvester	(Milton Keynes)	28.11.02P
G-BZXO	Cameron Z-105 HAFB	10125		27. 6.01	Virgin Airship & Balloon Co Ltd *(Innogy titles)*	Telford	28. 6.02A
G-BZXP	Air Creation Kiss 400-582(1)	UK001/A00056-0054 & BMAA/HB/169		14. 6.01	P.M.Dewhurst	Sywell	24.10.02P
G-BZXR	Cameron N-90 HAFB	10124		3. 9.01	Derbyshire Building Society	Belper	21. 8.02A
G-BZXS	Scottish Aviation Bulldog Srs.120/121	BH120/296	XX631	21. 6.01	K.J.Thompson *(Noted 11.01)*	Newtownards, Co.of Down	
G-BZXT	Mainair Blade 912	1286-0501-7-W1081		25. 5.01	S.R.Vinsun t/a Barton 912 Flyers	Barton	5. 6.02P
G-BZXU	Solar Wings Pegasus XL-R	SW-WA-1568	EI-CHT	6. 7.01	E.Spain	Monasterevin, Co.Kildare	
G-BZXV	Pegasus Quantum 15-912	7828		28. 6.01	S.Laws	Rufforth	21. 6.02P
G-BZXW	VPM M16 Tandem Trainer (Rotax 912S)	PFA G/12-1249	G-NANA	30. 4.01	S.J.Tyler	(Carlisle)	31. 8.00P
G-BZXX	Pegasus Quantum 15-912	7812		20. 4.01	R.R.Nichol	Carlisle	24. 4 02P
G-BZXY	Robinson R44 Raven	1027		12. 6.01	Extraviation Ltd	Booker	2. 7.04T
G-BZXZ	Scottish Aviation Bulldog Srs.120/121	BH120/294	XX629	21. 6.01	Air & Ground Aviation Ltd *(Noted 9.01)*	Sleap	11. 9.04T
G-BZYA	Rans S-6-ES Coyote II	PFA 204-13529		12. 6.01	D.J.Clack	(West Malling)	
G-BZYB	Westland SA.314D Gazelle HT.3	1272	XX382	14. 6.01	Aerocars Ltd	(Hungerford)	
G-BZYC	Westland SA.314B Gazelle AH.1	1208	XW903	14. 6.01	Aerocars Ltd	(Hungerford)	
G-BZYD	Westland SA.314B Gazelle AH.1 *(C/n 165? quoted also)*	1648	XZ329	14. 6.01	Aerocars Ltd	(Hungerford)	
G-BZYE	Robinson R22 Beta	3231		15. 6.01	Plane Talking Ltd	Elstree	2. 7.04T
G-BZYG	Glaser-Dirks DG-500MB	5E-220-B15		25. 9.01	R.C.Bromwich	(Blandford Forum)	15.11.04
G-BZYI	Nova Phocus 123 Hang Glider	9748		8. 6.01	M.N.Maclean	(Dundee)	
G-BZYK	Jabiru Jabiru UL	PFA 274A-13227		21. 6.01	A.S.Forbes *(Noted 10.01)*	Kingston Seymour	
G-BZYL	Rans S-6-ES Coyote II	PFA 204-13718		22. 6.01	J.D.Harris *(Noted 10.01)*	Kingston Seymour	
G-BZYM	Raj Hamsa X'Air 700 (1A)	649 & BMAA/HB/172		21. 6.01	G.Fleck	(Troon)	
G-BZYN	Pegasus Quantum 15-912	7835		15. 8.01	K.Roberts	(Caernarfon)	14. 8.02P
G-BZYO	Colt 210A HAFB	3523	D-OSPM	19. 7.01	P.M.Forster *(Op Alba Ballooning)*	Edinburgh	
G-BZYP	British Aerospace Jetstream Srs.3200	978	F-GMVL F-OHFX/G-31-978	1. 8.01	Trident Aviation Leasing Services (Ireland) Ltd	(Dublin)	
G-BZYR	Cameron N-31 HAFB	10137		6. 8.01	Virgin Balloon & Airship Co Ltd *(Benadryl titles)*	Telford	12. 8.02A
G-BZYS	Micro Aviation Bantam B22S	94-001	ZK-JDO	12. 7.01	D.L.Howell	(Gillingham, Kent)	12. 9.02P
G-BZYT	Interavia 80TA	0430992		6. 7.01	N.G.Cranham	(Nottingham)	
G-BZYU	Whittaker MW6 Merlin	PFA 164-13647		2. 7.01	K.J.Cole	Over Farm, Gloucester	
G-BZYV	Noble Hardman Snowbird Mk.V 582(1)	BMAA/HB/175		5. 7.01	S.Jones	(Tregaron)	
G-BZYW	Cameron N-90 HAFB	10134		6. 8.01	C.& J.M.Bailey t/a Bailey Balloons	Bristol	5. 8.02T
G-BZYX	Raj Hamsa X'Air 700 (1A)	653 & BMAA/HB/173		15. 6.01	A.G.Marsh	(Inverkip)	
G-BZYY	Cameron N-90 HAFB	10130		30. 8.01	Mason Zimbler Ltd (Oracle titles)	Bristol	16. 7.02A
G-BZYZ	Robin R.2120U	370		27. 6.01	S.J.Skilton t/a Aviation Rentals	Wellesbourne Mountford	29. 7.04T
G-BZZA	Boeing 737-3L9	26441	D-ADBA OY-MAL	17.11.99	KLM UK Ltd *(Op Buzz)*	Stansted	16. 1.03T
G-BZZB	Boeing 737-3L9	25125	D-ADBG OY-MMW/PP-SOR/OY-MMW	17.11.99	KLM UK Ltd *(Op Buzz)*	Stansted	17. 1.03T
G-BZZD	Reims Cessna F172M Skyhawk II	F17201436	G-BDPF	14. 4.98	R.H.M.Richardson-Bunbury	Bodmin	5. 8.02T

G-CAAA – G-CZZZ

G-CAHA	Piper PA-34-200T Seneca II	34-7770010	N23PL SE-GPY/(D-IIIC)/SE-GPY	7. 7.98	H & R.Marshall	Sandtoft	30. 7.01T
G-CAIN	CFM Shadow CD (Rotax 503)	062	G-MTKU	26. 1.99	S.K.Starling	(Wymondham)	28.11.01P
G-CALL	Piper PA-23-250 Aztec F	27-7754061	N62826	21.12.77	Woodgate Aviation (IOM) Ltd	Ronaldsway	29. 5.04T
G-CAMB	Aérospatiale AS355F2 Twin Squirrel	5416	N813LP	17.12.96	Cambridge & Essex Air Support Consortium	RAF Wyton	3. 5.03T
G-CAMM	Hawker Cygnet rep (Mosler MM-CB35)	PFA 77-10245	(G-ERDB)	30. 5.91	D.M.Cashmore *(On loan to The Shuttleworth Collection)*	Old Warden	18. 7.02P
G-CAMP	Cameron N-105 HAFB	4546		24. 3.99	R D Parry t/a Hong Kong Balloon & Airship Club	Hong Kong, PRC	4. 5.02A
G-CAMR	BFC Quad City Challenger II	PFA 177-12569 *(As a BFC Kit the should cary PFA/177A type prefix)*		26. 3.99	P R A Walker	Ringwood	
G-CAPI	Mudry/CAARP CAP.10B	76	G-BEXR	16. 3.99	I.Valentine	Newtownards	20. 8.03
G-CAPX	Avions Mudry CAP.10B	280		21. 9.98	H J Pessall	Leicester	21.12.01T
G-CBAB	Scottish Aviation Bulldog Srs.120/121	BH120/235	XX543	14. 6.01	Propshop Ltd *(As "XX543/F")*	Duxford	
G-CBAC	Short SD.3-60 Var.200	SH.3675	B-3608 G-BLYH/G-14-3675	20.10.95	BAC Leasing Ltd *(Stored 3.98: current status unknown)*	Baiyun, Guangzhou, China	19.11.95F
G-CBAD	Mainair Blade 912	1287-0601-7-W1082		8. 6.01	D.Sykes	Rufforth	21. 6.02P
G-CBAE							
G-CBAF	Neico Lancair 320	PFA 191-13567		11. 6.01	R.W.Fairless	(Portsmouth)	
G-CBAG	Rotary Air Force RAF 2000 GTX-SE	PFA G/13-1296		15. 6.01	G.R.French	Rayne Hall Farm, Rayne	
G-CBAH	Raj Hamsa X'Air 582 (5)	640 & BMAA/HB/174		4. 7.01	D.N.B.Hearn	(Ventnor)	
G-CBAI	Flight Design CT2K (Rotax 912S)	01-02-04-07	G-69-52	4. 7.01	Cyclone Airsports Ltd *(Noted 12.01)*	Sywell	
G-CBAJ	de Havilland DHC-1 Chipmunk 22	C1/0276	WD335	11. 7.01	J.Lamb	(Solihull)	
G-CBAK	Robinson R44 Clipper	1089		2. 8.01	Swift Frame Ltd	(Norwich)	1. 8.04T
G-CBAL	Piper PA-28-161 Warrior II	28-8116087	LN-MAD N83007	25. 3.94	Britannia Airways Ltd	Filton	13. 4.03T
G-CBAN	Scottish Aviation Bulldog Srs.120/121	BH120/334	XX668	26. 7.01	C.J.D.Howcroft & C.Hilliker	RAF Colerne	4.10.04T
G-CBAO							
G-CBAP	Zenair CH.601UL	PFA 162A-13656		12. 7.01	L.J.Lowry	(Huntingdon)	25.11.02P
G-CBAR	Stoddard-Hamilton GlaStar	PFA 295-13133		18. 5.01	C.M.Barnes *(Under construction 10.01)*	(Tadley)	
G-CBAS	Rans S-6-ES Coyote II	PFA 204-13688		4. 7.01	S.R.Green	(Bristol)	
G-CBAT	Cameron Z-90 HAFB	10099		1. 6.01	British Telecommunications plc *(Ignise titles)*	Thatcham	3. 6.02A
G-CBAU	Rand Robinson KR-2	PFA 129-12789		11. 7.01	B.Normington	(Leamington Spa)	
G-CBAV	Raj Hamsa X'Air V2 (2)	399 & BMAA/HB/127		7. 9.01	D.W.Stamp & G.J.Lampitt	(Kidderminster)	
G-CBAW							
G-CBAX	Tecnam P92-EM Echo	PFA 318-13698		26. 6.01	R.P.Reeves	Dunkeswell	3.10.02P
G-CBAY	Pegasus Quantum 15-912	7829		4. 6.01	P.R.Jones	Felthorpe	4. 6.02P
G-CBAZ	Rans S-6-ES Coyote II	PFA 204-13596		12. 7.01	G.V.Willder	(Poynton)	11. 9.02P
G-CBBA	Robin DR.400/180	2505		27. 7.01	A.P.Loch	North Weald	15. 8.04
G-CBBB	Pegasus Quantum 15-912	7827		22. 6.01	Light Flight Ltd	Knapthorpe Lodge, Caunton	21. 6.02P
G-CBBC	Scottish Aviation Bulldog Srs.120/121	BH120/201	XX515	8. 6.01	Bulldog Support Ltd	Wellesbourne Mountford	15.11.04T
G-CBBD	Pegasus Quantum 15-912	7842		20. 8.01	T.D.Grieve	(Hamilton)	19. 8.02P
G-CBBF	Beechcraft 76 Duchess	ME-352	OY-BED EI-BHS	23. 7.01	Liddell Aircraft Ltd	Bournemouth	6.11.04T
G-CBBG	Mainair Blade	1291-0601-7-W1086		23. 7.01	P.J.Donoghue	Warrington	
G-CBBH	Raj Hamsa X'Air V2 (1)	435 & BMAA/HB/143.		19. 7.01	W.G.Colyer *(Build started as X'Air 2706)*	(Tonbridge)	
G-CBBI							
G-CBBL	Scottish Aviation Bulldog Srs.120/121	BH120/243	XX550	8. 8.01	I.R.Bates *(As "XX550/2")*	Fenland	16.10.04
G-CBBM	ICP MXP-740 Savannah J(1) (Jabiru 2200)	BMAA/HB/176		10. 8.01	P.J.Wilson & S.Whittaker t/a Sandtoft Ultralights Partnership *(Noted 12.01)*	Sandtoft	
G-CBBN	Pegasus Quantum 15-912	7844		9. 8.01	C.D.Hogbourne	(Stotfold)	27. 8.02P
G-CBBO	Whittaker MW5-D Sorcerer	PFA 163-13443		23. 7.01	P.J.Gripton	(Sutton-on-the-Forest)	
G-CBBP	Pegasus Quantum 15-912	7843		31. 7.01	V.Causey & F.G.Green	Knapthorpe Lodge, Caunton	30. 7.02P

G-CBBR	Scottish Aviation Bulldog Srs.120/121 BH120/290	XX625	8. 8.01	Elite Consultancy Corporation Ltd	(Spalding)	
G-CBBS	Scottish Aviation Bulldog Srs.120/121 BH120/343	XX694	8. 8.01	Elite Consultancy Corporation Ltd	(Spalding)	
G-CBBT	Scottish Aviation Bulldog Srs.120/121 BH120/344	XX695	8. 8.01	Elite Consultancy Corporation Ltd	(Spalding)	
G-CBBU	Scottish Aviation Bulldog Srs.120/121 BH120/360	XX711	6. 8.01	Elite Consultancy Corporation Ltd	(Spalding)	
G-CBBV	Westland SA.341G Gazelle HT.3 1750	XZ940	28. 8.01	Elite Consultancy Corporation Ltd	Redhill	
G-CBBW	Scottish Aviation Bulldog Srs.120/121 BH120/277	XX619	1. 8.01	S.E.Robottom-Scott *(As "XX619/T")*	Coventry	17.10.04T
G-CBBX	Lindstrand LBL 69A HAFB 805		2. 8.01	J.L.F.Garcia	Guadalajara, Spain	5. 8.02A
G-CBBY	Westland SA.341G Gazelle HT.2 1078	XW856	29.10.01	South West Aviation Services Ltd	(Truro)	
G-CBBZ	Pegasus Quantum 15-912 7840		14. 8.01	A.J.Irving	(St.Albans)	13 .8.02P
G-CBCA	Piper PA-32R-301T Saratoga II TC 3257244	N5338S	4.10.01	Branksome Aircraft Leasing Ltd	Bournemouth	9.10.04T
G-CBCB	Scottish Aviation Bulldog Srs.120/121 BH120/223	XX537	25. 9.01	The General Aviation Trading Co Ltd *(As "XX537/C")*	Southend	28.11.04T
G-CBCC						
G-CBCD	Pegasus Quantum 15 7845		6. 8.01	I.A.Lumley	(Penrith)	6..8.02P
G-CBCE	CASA 1-131E Jungmann rep PFA 242-13171		7. 8.01	E.B.Toulson *(In pre-WW2 Swiss AF dark green/red c/s)*	Breighton	
G-CBCF	Pegasus Quantum 15-912 7846		23. 8.01	D.Seiler	Rufforth	22. 8.02P
G-CBCH	Zenair CH.701UL PFA 187-13568		8. 8.01	L.G.Millen	(Sittingbourne)	
G-CBCI	Raj Hamsa X'Air 582 (2) 659 & BMAA/HB/180 *(Officially regd with c/n BMAA/HB/150)*		9. 8.01	P.A.Gilford	(Penrith)	
G-CBCJ	Rotary Air Force RAF 2000 GTX-SE PFA G/13-1331		13. 8.01	J.P.Comerford	(Fareham)	
G-CBCK	Nipper T.66 RA45 Srs.3 PFA 025-11051 (Jabiru 2200A) *(Fairey c/n 30)*	G-TEDZ	14. 8.01	N.M.Bloom	(Hemel Hempstead)	28. 7.00P
G-CBCL	Stoddard-Hamilton GlaStar PFA 295-13089		5. 9.97	C.F.M.Norman	(Somerton)	
G-CBCM	Raj Hamsa X'Air 700 (1A) 656 & BMAA/HB/177		23. 7.01	A.Hipkin	(Stourbridge)	
G-CBCO	Scottish Aviation Bulldog Srs.120/121 BH120/238	XX546	9. 8.01	P.Stephenson	(Clacton-on-Sea)	
G-CBCP	Van's RV-6A PFA 181A-13643		6. 8.01	A.M.Smith t/a G-CBCP Group	(Woodbridge)	
G-CBCR	Scottish Aviation Bulldog Srs.120/121 BH120/351	XX702	5. 9.01	S.C.Smith *(As "XX702/P")*	Fenland	
G-CBCS	British Aerospace Jetstream Srs.3200 842	SE-LHA N842JX/N842AE/G-31-842/N332QL/G-31-842	27. 9.01	Air Kilroe Ltd t/a Eastern Airways	Humberside	4.10.04T
G-CBCT	Scottish Aviation Bulldog Srs.120/121 BH120/322	XX664	23. 8.01	T.Brun *(Noted 9.01)*	Sleap	
G-CBCU	Hawker Siddeley Harrier GR.3 712229 *(Officially quoted c/n FL/41H-0250295 is forward fuselage no)*	ZD668	9.11.01	Y.Dumortier	(Enghien, Belgium)	
G-CBCV	Scottish Aviation Bulldog Srs.120/121 BH120/348	XX699	30. 8.01	Cheshire Aviators Ltd	(Wrexham)	
G-CBCW	Cameron N-90 HAFB 10159		4. 9.01	Flying Pictures Ltd	Fairoaks	30. 8.02A
G-CBCX	Pegasus Quantum 15 7848		10. 9.01	D.V.Lawrence	(Stourbridge)	9. 9.02P
G-CBCY	Beech C24R Musketeer Super R MC-491	N881RS PH-HLA	26. 9.01	Liddell Aircraft Ltd. *(Noted 11.01 as "N881RS")*	Bournemouth	
G-CBCZ	CFM Streak Shadow SLA PFA 206-13586		13. 9.01	J.A.Hambleton	(Market Drayton)	
G-CBDA	British Aerospace Jetstream Srs.3217.. 986	JA8590 G-31-986	30.10.01	Global Aviation Ltd t/a Eastern Airways *(Op Air Kilroe)*	Humberside	
G-CBDC	Thruster T600N 450 Jab 0071-T600N-054		12. 7.01	D.Clarke t/a David Clarke Microlight Aircraft	Swanton Morley	13. 7.02P
G-CBDD	Mainair Blade 1293-0701-7 & W1088		1. 8.01	R.E.Dugmore	(Northwich)	
G-CBDF	Bell 206B-3 JetRanger III 947	N211KR JA9119/N58064	14. 9.01	R & M International Engineering Ltd	North Creake	
G-CBDG	Zenair CH.601HD PFA 162-13375		3. 9.01	R.E.Lasnier	(Moreton, Wirral)	
G-CBDH	Flight Design CT2K 01.07.02.17 *(Pegasus c/n 7849)*		4.10.01	J.Hosier	Kemble	18.10.02P
G-CBDI	Denney Kitfox Mk.2 PFA 172-11888		4. 9.01	J.G.D.Barbour	Balgone, Berwick	
G-CBDJ	Flight Design CT2K 7850		11.10.01	P.J.Walker	(Lincoln)	12.10.02P
G-CBDK	Scottish Aviation Bulldog Srs.120/121 BH120/259	XX611	26. 9.01	J.N.Randle	Coventry	
G-CBDL	Mainair Blade 1292-0701-7 & W1087		1. 8.01	D.Lightwood	(Macclesfield)	14.11.02P
G-CBDM	Tecnam P92-EM Echo PFA 318-13756		11. 7.01	C.J.Willy & J.J.Cozens	(South Petherton)	
G-CBDN	Mainair Blade 1297-0801-7 & W1092		20. 9.01	P.N.Gibson	(Diss)	
G-CBDO	Raj Hamsa X'Air 582(1) 583 & BMAA/HB/170		12.11.01	R.T.Henry	(Castlewellan, Co of Down)	26. 9.02P
G-CBDP	Mainair Blade 912 1295-0801-7 & W1090		17. 8.01	D.S.Parker	Carlisle	16. 8.02P

G-CBDR	Agusta A109A-II	7413	TC-HIK D-HAAY/JA9906	13. 9.01	Castle Air Charters Ltd	Liskeard	
G-CBDS	Scottish Aviation Bulldog Srs.120/121	BH120/356	XX707	27. 7.01	H R M Tyrell	(Shrewsbury)	6.12.04T
G-CBDT	Zenair CH.601HD	PFA 162-12474		17. 9.01	D.G.Watt	(Kirkby Stephen)	
G-CBDU	Quad City Challenger II	PFA 177-13000		14. 9.01	Hiscox Cases Ltd *(Noted 11.01)*	Otherton, Cannock	
G-CBDV	Raj Hamsa X'Air 582	616 & BMAA/HB/161		6. 8.01	D.J.Prothero *(Noted 11.01)*	Davidstow Moor	
G-CBDW	Raj Hamsa X'Air Jabiru (1)	575 & BMAA/HB/150		18. 9.01	P.R.& V.C.Reynolds *(Noted 11.01)*	Latch Farm, Kirknewton	
G-CBDX	Pegasus Quantum 15	7857		11.10.01	C.C.Beck	(Croydon)	15.10.02P
G-CBDY	Raj Hamsa X'Air V2 (2)	588 & BMAA/HB/155		26. 9.01	D.Mahajan *(Complete 10.01)*	Lower Mount Pleasant, Chatteris	
G-CBDZ	Pegasus Quantum 15-912	7852		11. 9.01	C.I.D.H.Garrison	(Old Weston)	10. 9.02P
G-CBEA							
G-CBEB	Air Creation Kiss 400-582(1)	UK/FL003/135 & BMAA/HB/184		3.10.01	P.R.J.& A.R.R.Williams	(Bristol)	
G-CBEC	Cameron Z-105 HAFB	10105		16.10.01	A.L.Ballarino	Piedimonte Matese, Italy	3.10.02A
G-CBED	Cameron Z-90 HAFB	10121		15.10.01	John Aimo Balloons SAS	Mondovi, Italy	17.10.02A
G-CBEE	Piper PA-28R-200 Cherokee Arrow II	28R-7635055	N4479X	5.10.01	IHC Aviation Ltd	Biggin Hill	15.11.04T
G-CBEF	Scottish Aviation Bulldog Srs.120/121	BH120/286	XX621	3.10.01	M.A.Wilkinson	Sywell	
G-CBEG	Robinson R44 Raven	1124		28. 9.01	Heli Air Ltd *(Op Select Helicopters)*	(Kintore)	11.10.04T
G-CBEH	Scottish Aviation Bulldog Srs.120/121	BH120/207	XX521	28. 9.01	R.E.Dagless	(Dereham)	
G-CBEI							
G-CBEJ	Colt 120A HAFB	10181		11.10.01	Cameron Balloons Ltd	Bristol	15.10.02A
G-CBEK	Scottish Aviation Bulldog Srs.120/121	BH120/349	XX700	26. 9.01	S.Landregan	Blackbushe	15.11.04T
G-CBEL	Hawker Iraqi Fury FB.Mk.11	37579	N36SF Iraqi AF 315	6. 8.01	J.A.D.Bradshaw	Kemble	30.10.02P
G-CBEM	Mainair Blade	1294-0801-7 & W1089		17. 8.01	M.Earp	(Macclesfield)	14.11.02P
G-CBEN	Pegasus Quantum 15-912	7855		8.10.01	B.J.Syson *(Noted 11.01)*	Kemble	22.10.02P
G-CBEO							
G-CBEP	British Aerospace Jetstream 3206	980	F-GMVN G-31-980	23.11.01	Trident Aviation Leasing Services (Ireland) Ltd	(Dublin)	
G-CBER							
G-CBES	Europa Aviation Europa	PFA 247-12691		27. 9.01	M R Hexley	(Penmaenmawr)	
G-CBET	Mainair Blade 912S	1296-0801-7 & W1091		6. 9.01	R.Neale	(Chelmsford)	6. 9.02P
G-CBEU	Pegasus Quantum 15-912	7869		16.10.01	C.Lee	(Luton)	15.10.02P
G-CBEV	Pegasus Quantum 15-912	7854		16.10.01	B.J.Syson	(Luton)	15.10.02P
G-CBEW	Flight Design CT2K	7868		19.10.01	M.Clare	(Gayton, Northants)	16.11.02P
G-CBEX	Flight Design CT2K	7867		29.10.01	B.W.T.Rood	Sywell	14.11.02P
G-CBEY	Cameron C-80 HAFB	10190		31.10.01	D.V.Fowler	(Cranbrook)	17.10.02A
G-CBEZ							
G-CBFA	Diamond DA-40 Star	40063		25.10.01	Diamond Aircraft UK Ltd	Gamston	
G-CBFB							
G-CBFC	Diamond DA-40 Star	40062		22.10.01	Diamond Aircraft UK Ltd	Gamston	
G-CBFD	Westland SA.341C Gazelle HT.2	1158	XW887	24.10.10	Aerocars Ltd	(Hungerford)	
G-CBFE	Raj Hamsa X'Air V2 (1)	636 & BMAA/HB/186		19.10.01	S. Whittle & M.L.Powell	(Wigan)	
G-CBFD							
G-CBFE							
G-CBFF	Cameron O-120 HAFB	10167		20.11.01	T.M.C.McCoy	Bath	4.11.02T
G-CBFG	Cameron Thunder AX8-105 S2 HAFB	10187		13.11.01	Master Ad (UK) Ltd	Bangkok, Thailand	28.10.02A
G-CBFH	Cameron Thunder AX8-105 S2 HAFB	10188		13.11.01	Master Ad (UK) Ltd	Bangkok, Thailand	28.10.02A
G-CBFI	Piper PA-18-150 Super Cub	18-6279	SE-FDY LN-HHA/SE-CTA/N8675D	5.10.01	L.F.Appelbeck	East Winch	
G-CBFJ	Robinson R44 Raven	1131		7.11.01	Heli Air Ltd *(Op Select Helicopters)*	(Kintore)	8.11.04T
G-CBFK	Murphy Rebel	PFA 232-13340		13. 9.01	D.Webb *(Noted 1.02)*	Bidford	
G-CBFL	British Aerospace BAe.146 Srs.200	E2055	SE-DRF N697AA/N145AC/G-5-055/N145AC/G-5-055	25.10.01	BAE Systems (Operations) Ltd	Woodford	
G-CBFM	SOCATA TB-21 Trinidad GT	710	PH-BLM D-EFAK(4)	2. 1.02	Execflight Ltd	(Dartford)	
G-CBFN							
G-CBFO	Cessna 172S Skyhawk	172S8929	N3520A	22.10.01	Halegreen Associates Ltd	Hinton-in-the Hedges	29.10.04T

G-CBFP	Scottish Aviation Bulldog Srs.120/121 BH120/306	XX636	29.10.01	I.D.McClelland	Biggin Hill	
G-CBFR						
G-CBFS	Beechcraft 200 Super King Air BB-487	G-PLAT N8PY/N198SC/PT-OYR/N40QN/VH-NIC/N40QN/N400N/N243KA	6.11.01	Bevair Services Ltd	Southend	6. 5.02T
G-CBFT	Raj Hamsa X'Air 582(5) BMAA/HB/190		6.11.01	T.Collins	(Chard)	
G-CBFU	Scottish Aviation Bulldog Srs.120/121 BH120/293	XX628	12.11.01	J.R.& S.J.Huggins	Lamberhurst Farm., Faversham	
G-CBFV	Comco Ikarus C42 PFA 322-13774		5.11.01	P.A.D.Chubb	(Norwich)	
G-CBFW	Bensen B8 Gyrocopter PFA G/01-1312		6.11.01	B.F.Pearson	(Newark)	
G-CBFX	Rans S-6-ES Coyote II PFA 204-13820 (Rotax 582)		8.11.01	Sport Air (UK) Ltd *(Noted 12.01)*	Felixkirk	
G-CBFY	Cameron Z-250 HAFB 10023		9.11.01	Cameron Balloons Ltd	Bristol	
G-CBFZ	Jabiru Jabiru UL-450 PFA 274-13617		8.11.01	A.H.King	(Orpington)	
G-CBGA	PZL-110 Koliber 160A 04010086	SP-WGM	14.11.01	PZL International Aviation Marketing & Sales plc	North Weald	
G-CBGB	Zenair CH.601UL PFA 162A-13819		12.11.01	R.Germany	(Newark)	
G-CBGC	SOCATA TB-10 Tobago 1584	VH-YHB	21. 9.01	Air Touring Ltd	Biggin Hill	15.11.04T
G-CBGD	Zenair CH.701UL PFA 187-13785		13.11.01	I.S. Walsh	(Ivybridge)	
G-CBGE	Tecnam P92-EM Echo PFA 318-13680		9.11.01	T.C. Robson	(Thetford)	
G-CBGF	Piper PA-31 Navajo 310 31-749	F-BTCP N7227L	2. 1 02	S J Skilton t/a Aviation Rentals	Bournemouth	
G-CBGG	Pegasus Quantum 15 7874		27.11.01	A.R.Cundill	(Wells)	2.12.02P
G-CBGH	Teverson Bisport PFA 267-12784		7.11.01	R.C.Teverson	(Sudbury)	
G-CBGI	CFM Streak Shadow PFA 206-13559		30.10.01	M.W.W.Clotworthy	(Bath)	
G-CBGJ	Aeroprakt A22 Foxbat PFA 317-13803		14.11.01	W.R.Davis-Smith	(Tarporley)	
G-CBGG						
G-CBGH						
G-CBGI						
G-CBGJ						
G-CBGK	Hawker Siddeley.Harrier GR.Mk.3 41H-712218	9220M XZ995 *(Forward fuselage no.FL/41H-0150252)*	13.12.01	Y.Dumortier	(Enghien, Belgium)	
G-CBGL	Max Holste MH.1521M Broussard 19	F-BMJO F-BNEN/Fr AF	3.12.01	A.I.Milne t/a Broussard Flying Group	Little Snoring	
G-CBGM	Mainair Blade 912 1299-1001-7 & W1094		30.10.01	J.R.Pearce	Chilbolton	5.12.02P
G-CBGN	Van's RV-4 PFA 181-12443		16.10.01	G.A.Nash	(Stroud, Glos)	
G-CBGO	Murphy Maverick 430 PFA 259-13470		24.10.01	C.R.Ellis & E.A.Wrathall	(Chapel-en-le-Frith)	
G-CBGP	Comco Ikarus C42 FB UK PFA 322-13741		22.11.01	A.R.Lloyd	(Hannington)	
G-CBGR	Jabiru Jabiru UL PFA 274A-13682		21.11.01	K.R.Emery	(Cannock)	
G-CBGS						
G-CBGT	Mainair Blade 912 1300-1001-7 & W1095		30.10.01	J.A.Cresswell	(Chellaston)	5.12.02P
G-CBGU	Thruster T600N 450 Jab 0121-T600N-055		21.11.01	Thruster Air Services Ltd	Long Marston	6.12.02P
G-CBGV	Thruster T600N 450 Jab 0121-T600N-056		21.11.01	Thruster Air Services Ltd *(On build 12.01)*	Ginge Farm, Wantage	
G-CBGW	Thruster T600N 450 Jab 0121-T600N-058		21.11.01	Thruster Air Services Ltd *(On build 12.01)*	Ginge Farm, Wantage	
G-CBGX	Scottish Aviation Bulldog Srs.120/121 BH120/287	XX622	26.11.01	R.B.Black	(Guildford)	
G-CBGY						
G-CBGZ	Westland SA.341C Gazelle HT.2 1923	ZB646	30.10.01	D.Weatherhead Ltd	(Knebworth)	
G-CBHA	SOCATA TB-10 Tobago 1583	VH-YHA	6.11.01	Air Touring Ltd	Biggin Hill	
G-CBHB	Raj Hamsa X'Air Jabiru(1) BMAA/HB/189		22.11.01	Marine Power Scotland Ltd	(Troon)	
G-CBHC	Rotary Air Force RAF 2000 GTX-SE PFA G/13-1326		22.11.01	A.J.Thomas	(Sutton Coldfield)	
G-CBHD						
G-CBHE	Slingsby T.67M-200 Firefly 2050	SE-LBE LN-TFE/G-7-125	28.12.01	R Swann *(Noted 6.01)*	Bournemouth	
G-CBHF						
G-CBHG	Mainair Blade 912S 1298-1001-7-W1093		12.12.01	J.A.Horn	Peterlee	17.10.02P
G-CBHH						
G-CBHI	Europa Aviation Europa XS PFA 247-13245		31.10.01	B.Price	(Southampton)	
G-CBHJ	Mainair Blade 912 1305-1201-7 & W1100		28. 1.02	B.C.Jones	(Altrincham)	
G-CBHK	Pegasus Quantum 15 (HKS) 7871		6.12.01	Cyclone Airsports Ltd t/a Pegasus Aviation	Manton, Marlborough	
G-CBHL	Eurocopter AS350B2 Ecureuil 2673	C-GKHS JA6123	28. 1.02	Bishop Avionics Ltd	(Reading)	
G-CBHM	Mainair Blade 912 1301-1100-7/W1096		3.12.01	Mainair Sports Ltd	Barton	2.12.02P

G-CBHN	Pegasus Quantum 15-912	7872		6.12.01	Cyclone Airsports Ltd t/a Pegasus Aviation	Manton, Marlborough	
G-CBHO	Gloster Gladiator II	-	N5719 *(P/i not confirmed)*	11.12.01	Retro Track & Air (UK) Ltd	(Dursley)	
G-CBHP	Corby CJ-1 Starlet	PFA 134-12498		12.12.01	J.D.Muldowney	(Braintree)	
G-CBHR	Stephens Akro Z *(Built H Selvey)*	Q056	VH-IAC	31.12.01	D T Karbery	Barton	
G-CBHS	Eurocopter EC 120B	1253		11.12.01	McAlpine Helicopters Ltd	Oxford	
G-CBHT	Dassault Falcon 900EX	48	G-GPWH F-WWFP	3. 1.02	TAG Aviation (UK) Ltd	Farnborough	23.11.02T
G-CBHU	Tiger Cub RL5A Sherwood Ranger	PFA 237-12477		12.12.01	M.J.Gooch	(Tarvin)	
G-CBHV	Raj Hamsa X'Air 582(5)	BMAA/HB/139		12.12.01	J.D.Buchanan	Coldharbour Farm, Willingham	
G-CBHW	Cameron Z-105 HAFB	10217		16. 1.02	Bristol Chamber of Commerce, Industry and Shipping	Bristol	8. 1.03A
G-CBHX	Cameron V-77 HAFB	3950		19.12.01	N.A.Apsey	Hazlemere	
G-CBHY	Pegasus Quantum 15-912	7859		7. 1.02	M.W.Abbott	(Feltham)	6. 1.03P
G-CBHZ	Rotary Air Force RAF 2000 GTX-SE	PFA G/13-1321		2. 1.02	M P Donnelly	(Thurso)	
G-CBIA							
G-CBIB	Flight Design CT2K *(Regd with Pegasus c/n)*	7878		21. 1.02	J.A.Moss	(Harleston)	
G-CBIC	Raj Hamsa X'Air V2(2)	608 & BMAA/HB/156		2. 1.02	J T Blackburn & D R Sutton	(Halifax)	
G-CBID	Scottish Aviation Bulldog Srs.120/121	BH120/242	XX549	14.12.01	D.A.Steven	(Wokingham)	
G-CBIE	Flight Design CT2K *(Regd with Pegasus c/n)*	7879		10. 1.02	S.J.Page	(Wells)	17. 1.03P
G-CBIF	Jabiru Jabiru UL-450	PFA 274A-13789		3. 1.02	J A Iszard	(Woodbridge)	
G-CBIG	Mainair Blade 912	1303-1101-7-W1098		29.11.01	J.H.Bradbury	(Sandbach)	1.12.02P
G-CBIH	Cameron Z-31 HAFB	10243		4. 1.02	Cameron Balloons Ltd	Bristol	
G-CBII	Raj Hamsa X'Air 582(2)	676 & BMAA/HB/185		7. 1.02	A.Worthington	(Chorley)	
G-CBIJ	Comco Ikarus C42	PFA 322-13720		3. 1.02	A Jones	Newark	
G-CBIK	Rotorway Exec 162F	6112		9. 1.02	J.Hodson	(Ashbourne)	
G-CBIL	Cessna 182K Skylane	18257804	(G-BFZZ) D-ENGO/N2604Q	9.10.78	E Bannister & J R C Spooner	East Midlands	3. 2.03T
G-CBIM	Lindstrand LBL 90A HAFB	817		28. 1.02	R.K.Parsons	South Petherton	14. 1.03A
G-CBIN	TEAM mini-MAX 91	PFA 186-13111		7. 1.02	D.E.Steade	(Kempsey, Worcs)	
G-CBIO	Thruster T600N 450 Jab	0022-T600N-062		7. 1.02	Thruster Air Services Ltd	Ginge Farm, Wantage	
G-CBIP	Thruster T600N 450 Jab	0022-T600N-060		7. 1.02	Thruster Air Services Ltd	Ginge Farm, Wantage	
G-CBIR	Thruster T600N 450 Jab	0022-T600N-061		7. 1.02	Thruster Air Services Ltd	Ginge Farm, Wantage	
G-CBIS	Raj Hamsa X'Air 582(2)	708 & BMAA/HB/199		15. 1.02	P.T.W.T.Derges	(Littleover)	
G-CBIT	Rotary Air Force RAF 2000 GTX-SE	PFA G/13-1340		27.11.01	Terrafirma Services Ltd	Lamberhurst Farm, Faversham	
G-CBIU							
G-CBIV	Best Off Skyranger 912(1)	BMAA/HB/201		25. 1.02	P.M.Dewhurst & S.N.Bond	(Banbury)	
G-CBIW	Lindstrand LBL 310A HAFB	821		24. 1.02	C.E.Wood	Witham	
G-CBIX	Zenair CH.601UL	PFA 162A-13765		24.12.01	M F Cottam	(Lincoln)	
G-CBIY	Evektor-Aerotechnik EV-97 Eurostar	PFA 315-13846		23. 1.02	E.M.Middleton	(Hereford)	
G-CBIZ	Pegasus Quantum 15-912	7870		6.12.01	P.A.Bass	Sywell	9.12.02P
G-CBJA	Air Creation Kiss 400-582(1) *(Other c/ns = Kit No FL006/Sailwing A01192-1194/Trike T01101) & BMAA/HB/195)*	BMAA/HB/195		11.12.01	C W Lark	(Dursley)	
G-CBJB							
G-CBJC							
G-CBJD	Stoddard-Hamilton Glastar	PFA 295-13853		23. 1.02	K.F.Farey	(Bourne End, Bucks)	
G-CBJE	Rotary Air Force RAF 2000 GTX-SE	PFA G/13-1342		23. 1.02	K.F.Farey	(Bourne End, Bucks)	
G-CBJF	Eurocopter EC 120B	1257		25. 1.02	McAlpine Helicopters Ltd	Oxford	
G-CBJG							
G-CBJH	Aeroprakt A22 Foxbat	PFA 317-13847		30. 1.02	H.Smith	(Spennymoor)	
G-CBJI							
G-CBJJ	Scottish Aviation Bulldog Srs.120/121	BH120/211	XX525	3.12.01	Elite Consultancy Corporation Ltd	(Spalding)	

G-CBJK	Scottish Aviation Bulldog Srs.120/121 BH120/362	XX713	3.12.01	Elite Consultancy Corporation Ltd Norwich	
G-CBJL					
G-CBJM	Jabiru Jabiru SP-470 PFA 274B-13769		11.12.01	A T Moyce (Donaghadee, Co.of Down)	
G-CBJN	Rotary Air Force RAF 2000 GTX-SE PFA G/13-1335		30. 1.02	R.Hall (Truro)	
G-CBJO	Pegasus Quantum 15-912 7861		10.12.01	J E Borill (Fort William)	9.12.02P
G-CBJP	Zenair CH.601UL PFA 162A-13590		31. 1.02	R.E.Peirse (Royston)	
G-CBJR	Evektor-Aerotechnik EV-97 Eurostar PFA 315-13845		31. 1.02	B.J.Crockett (Hereford)	
G-CBJS					
G-CBJT	Mainair Blade 1302-1101-7-W1097		12.12.01	B.Hunter & K.D.Taylor (Bridlington)	17.12.02P
G-CBJU					
G-CBJV					
G-CBJW					
G-CBJX					
G-CBJY					
G-CBJZ					
G-CBKA					
G-CBKB	Bucker Bu.181C Bestmann 121	F-PCRL F-BCRU	28. 1.02	W.R.& G.D.Snadden (Alexandria)	
G-CBKC					
G-CBKD					
G-CBKE					
G-CBKF	Easy Raider J2.2(1) BMAA/HB/202		24. 1.02	R.J.Creasey (London NW1)	
G-CBKG					
G-CBKH					
G-CBKI					
G-CBKJ					
G-CBKK					
G-CBKL					
G-CBKM	Mainair Blade 912 1310-0102-7 & W1105		21. 1.02	N.Purdy (Sutton-in-Ashfield)	
G-CBKN					
G-CBKO					
G-CBKP					
G-CBKR					
G-CBKS	Air Creation Kiss 400-582(1) FL007 & BMAA/HB/197		28. 1.02	S.Kilpin (Hackleton, Northants)	
G-CBKT					
G-CBKU					
G-CBKV					
G-CBKW					
G-CBKX					
G-CBKY					
G-CBKZ					
G-CBLA					
G-CBLB					
G-CBLC					
G-CBLD					
G-CBLE					
G-CBLF					
G-CBLG					
G-CBLH					
G-CBLI					
G-CBLJ					
G-CBLK					
G-CBLL					
G-CBLM					
G-CBLN					
G-CBLO					
G-CBLP					
G-CBLR					
G-CBLS					
G-CBLT					
G-CBLU					
G-CBLV					
G-CBLW					
G-CBLX					
G-CBLY					
G-CBLZ					
G-CBMA					
G-CBMB					
G-CBMC					

G-CBMD							
G-CBME							
G-CBMF							
G-CBMG							
G-CBMH							
G-CBMI							
G-CBMJ							
G-CBMK							
G-CBML							
G-CBMM							
G-CBMN							
G-CBMO							
G-CBMP							
G-CBMR							
G-CBMS							
G-CBMT							
G-CBMU							
G-CBMV							
G-CBMW							
G-CBKX							
G-CBMY							
G-CBMZ							
G-CBNA							
G-CBNB	Eurocopter EC 120B	1040		8. 6.99	Arenberg Consultadoria E Servicos LDA	(Madeira, Portugal)	29. 6.02
G-CBNC							
G-CBND							
G-CBNE							
G-CBNF							
G-CBNG							
G-CBNH							
G-CBNI							
G-CBNJ							
G-CBNK							
G-CBNL							
G-CBNM							
G-CBNN							
G-CBNO							
G-CBNP							
G-CBNR							
G-CBNS							
G-CBNT							
G-CBNU							
G-CBNV							
G-CBNW							
G-CBNX							
G-CBNY							
G-CBNZ							
G-CBOA							
G-CBOB	Piper PA-34-220T Seneca V	3449091	N9ZB (G-CBOB)/N61HB/N9500N	6. 9.01	Blackbrook Nominee 30 Ltd	(Holsworthy)	13. 9.04T
G-CBOC							
G-CBOD							
G-CBOE							
G-CBOF							
G-CBOG							
G-CBOH							
G-CBOI							
G-CBOJ							
G-CBOK							
G-CBOL							
G-CBOM							
G-CBON							
G-CBOO							
G-CBOP							
G-CBOR	Reims Cessna F172N Skyhawk II	F17201656	PH-BOR PH-AXG(1)	28. 5.87	Pauline Seville	Barton	24. 5.03T
G-CBOS							
G-CBOT							
G-CBOU							
G-CBOV							
G-CBOW							
G-CBOX							
G-CBOY							

G-CBOZ
G-CBPA
G-CBPB
G-CBPC
G-CBPD
G-CBPE
G-CBPF
G-CBPG
G-CBPH
G-CBPI
G-CBPJ
G-CBPK
G-CBPL
G-CBPM
G-CBPN
G-CBPO
G-CBPP
G-CBPR
G-CBPS
G-CBPT
G-CBPU
G-CBPV
G-CBPW
G-CBPX
G-CBPY
G-CBPZ
G-CBRA
G-CBRB
G-CBRC
G-CBRD
G-CBRE
G-CBRF
G-CBRG
G-CBRH
G-CBRI
G-CBRJ
G-CBRK
G-CBRL
G-CBRM
G-CBRN
G-CBRO
G-CBRP
G-CBRR
G-CBRS
G-CBRT
G-CBRU
G-CBRV
G-CBRW
G-CBRX
G-CBRY
G-CBRZ
G-CBSA
G-CBSB
G-CBSC
G-CBSD
G-CBSE
G-CBSF
G-CBSG
G-CBSH
G-CBSI
G-CBSJ
G-CBSK
G-CBSL
G-CBSM
G-CBSN
G-CBSO
G-CBSP
G-CBSR
G-CBSS
G-CBST
G-CBSU
G-CBSV
G-CBSW
G-CBSX

G-CBSY							
G-CBSZ							
G-CBTA							
G-CBTB							
G-CBTC							
G-CBTD							
G-CBTE							
G-CBTF							
G-CBTG							
G-CBTH							
G-CBTI							
G-CBTJ							
G-CBTK							
G-CBTL							
G-CBTM							
G-CBTN							
G-CBTO							
G-CBTP							
G-CBTR							
G-CBTS							
G-CBTT							
G-CBTU							
G-CBTV							
G-CBTW							
G-CBTX							
G-CBTY							
G-CBTZ							
G-CBUA							
G-CBUB							
G-CBUC							
G-CBUD							
G-CBUE							
G-CBUF							
G-CBUG	Tecnam P92-EM Echo	PFA 318-13662		20. 6.01	R.C.Mincik *(Noted 11.01)*	Bournemouth	
G-CCAR	Cameron N-77 HAFB	464		5.12.78	D.P.Turner *"Mitsubishi Cars"*	Bath	19. 7.02A
	(Rebuilt 8.1980 with envelope c/n 670: in 1989 with c/n 2108 & again in 1992 with c/n 2658)						
G-CCAT	Gulfstream AA-5A Cheetah	AA5A-0893	G-OAJH	16. 1.92	Plane Talking Ltd	Cranfield	30.10.02T
			G-KILT/G-BJFA/N27169				
G-CCAU	Eurocopter EC 135T-1	0040	G-79-01	30. 6.98	West Mercia Constabulary	Wolverhampton	21. 7.04T
G-CCCC	Cessna 172H	17255822	SE-ELU	9. 2.79	Springbank Aviation Ltd		
			N2622L			(Castletown, IoM)	1. 5.04T
G-CCCP	IAV-Bacau Yakovlev Yak-52	899404	LY-AKV	30.11.93	R.J.N.Howarth	North Weald	1. 5.02P
			DOSAAF16 (Yellow)				
G-CCIX*	Supermarine 361 Spitfire LF.IXe		G-BIXP	9. 4.85	K.Weeks	Booker	
	(C/n is Firewall No.)	CBAF.IX.558	IDFAF2046/Czech AF/TE517		*(Cancelled 6.1.93 as TWFU)*		
					(As "TE517": stored pending rebuild 3.00)		
G-CCLY	Bell 206B-3 JetRanger III	3594	G-TILT	26. 4.95	Ciceley Ltd	Samlesbury	30.10.04
			G-BRJO/N2295Z				
G-CCMV	Chance Vought FG-1D Corsair	3660	N448AG	21.11.00	P.J.Morgan	Duxford	3. 5.02P
	(Built Goodyear Aircraft Corpn)		N4717C/Bu.92399		*(Op Aircraft Restoration Company)*		
					(As "92399/17" in US Navy c/s)		
G-CCOA	Scottish Aviation Bulldog Srs.120/122		G-111	4. 9.96	Cranfield University	Cranfield	13. 3.03T
		BH120/375	Ghana AF/G-BCUU				
			(Crashed on take-off Cranfield 22.8.01 causing damage to the landing gear & rear of a/c)				
G-CCOZ	Monnett Sonerai II			31. 5.78	P.R.Cozens	Hinton-in-the-Hedges	21. 6.00P
	(VW 1900)	0197 & PFA 015-10107					
G-CCSC	Cameron N-77 HAFB	4282		16. 1.98	C.J.Royden *"Coherent"*	Stroud	7. 1.99A
G-CCST	Piper PA-32R-301 Saratoga II HP		N4180T	14. 2.01	Dorset Aircraft Leasing Ltd	Bournemouth	22. 2.04T
		3246182					
G-CCUB	Piper J-3C-65 Cub	2362A	N33528	2. 4.81	Cormack (Aircraft Services) Ltd	Rothesay	
			NC33528/NX33528		*(On rebuild 2001)*		
G-CCVV*	Supermarine 379 Spitfire FR.XIVe		IAF"42"	18. 5.88	K.Weeks	Catfield, Norfolk	
		6S/649186	MV262		*(Cancelled 6.1.93 as TWFU) (On rebuild 12.99 as "MV262")*		
G-CDAV	Piper PA-34-220T Seneca V	3449033	N9284Q	27.11.97	Neric Ltd	Fowlmere	27.12.03T
			G-CDAV/N9284Q				
G-CDBS	MBB Bö.105DBS-4	S.738	D-HDRZ	29. 9.89	Bond Air Services	St.Mawgan	8.11.02T
	(See G-BCXO)		VH-MBK/N970MB/D-HDRZ		*(Op Cornwall Air Ambulance)*		
G-CDET	Culver LCA Cadet	129	N29261	10.11.86	H.B.Fox	Booker	11.11.02P
	(Continental O-200-A)		NC29261		*(As "29261" in USAAF c/s)*		
G-CDGA	Taylor JT.1 Monoplane			28.12.78	R.M.Larimore	(Spondon, Derby)	
		6020/1 & PFA 055-10382					
G-CDON	Piper PA-28-161 Warrior II		N8254D	24. 5.88	East Midlands Flying School Ltd		
		28-8216185				East Midlands	17. 5.03T
G-CDPY	Europa Aviation Europa	PFA 247-13029		8. 3.00	A.Burrill	(Reading)	

G-CDRU	CASA I-131E Jungmann	2321	EC-DRU	19. 1.90	P.Cunniff	White Waltham	30. 6.02P
			E3B-530		*"Yen a Bon"*		
G-CDUO	Boeing 757-236	24792	SE-DUO	R	Britannia Airways	Luton	
			G-BRJI/SX-BBZ/G-BRJI/SX-BBZ/G-BRJI/EC-FMQ/EC-786/EC-EVC/EC-446/G-BRJI				
G-CDUP	Boeing 757-236	24793	SE-DUP	R	Britannia Airways	Luton	
			G-OOOT/G-BRJJ/EC-490/G-BRJJ				
G-CEAA	Airbus A300B2-1C	062	F-WQGQ	2. 7.98	European Aviation Ltd	Bournemouth	
			F-BUAI		*(Open store 7.01)*		
G-CEAB	Airbus A300B2-1C	027	F-WQGS	15.11.99	European Aviation Ltd	Bournemouth	
			F-BUAH/F-WLGC/F-WLGB		*(Open store 7.01)*		
G-CEAC	Boeing 737-229	20911	OO-SDE	11. 6.99	European Aviation Air Charter Ltd		
			C-GNDX/OO-SDE/C-GNDX/OO-SDE			Bournemouth	25. 8.02T
					(Op Palmair European)		
G-CEAD	Boeing 737-229	21137	OO-SDM	11.10.99	European Aviation Air Charter Ltd		
						Bournemouth	16.11.02T
G-CEAE	Boeing 737-229	20912	OO-SDF	25. 1.00	European Aviation Air Charter Ltd		
						Bournemouth	28. 2.03T
G-CEAF	Boeing 737-229	20910	G-BYRI	13. 1.00	European Aviation Air Charter Ltd		
			OO-SDD/EC-EEG/OO-SDD			Bournemouth	3. 4.03T
G-CEAG	Boeing 737-229	21136	OO-SDL	6. 6.00	European Aviation Air Charter Ltd		
			(OO-SDM)			Bournemouth	14. 6.03T
G-CEAH	Boeing 737-229	21135	OO-SDG	1. 8.00	European Aviation Air Charter Ltd		
						Bournemouth	14.11.03T
G-CEAI	Boeing 737-229	21176	OO-SDN	7. 3.01	European Aviation Air Charter Ltd		
			9M-MBP/OO-SDN/N8277V			Bournemouth	28. 9.04T
G-CEAJ	Boeing 737-229	21177	OO-SDO	5.12.00	European Aviation Air Charter Ltd		
						Bournemouth	22. 4.04T
G-CEAL	Short SD.3-60 Var.100	SH.3761	N161CN	11. 9.95	BAC Express Airlines Ltd	Exeter	12. 1.03T
			N161SB/G-BPXO				
G-CEAS*	Handley Page HPR.7 Dart Herald 214	186	G-BEBB	31. 1.86	Dart Group plc	Bournemouth	4. 6.99T
			PP-SDH		*(Cancelled 23.6.97 as WFU: stored 7.97: current status unknown)*		
G-CEGA	Piper PA-34-200T Seneca II	34-8070367	N8272B	30.12.80	Oxford Aviation Services Ltd	Oxford	22 .8.02T
G-CEGP	Beechcraft 200 Super King Air	BB-726	G-BXMA	14. 5.01	Cega Aviation Ltd	Goodwood	7. 8.03T
			(N58AJ)/G-BXMA/N622JA/N522JA/N222JD				
G-CEGR	Beechcraft 200 Super King Air	BB-351	N68CP	23. 7.97	Cega Aviation Ltd	Goodwood	18. 8.03T
			N351FW/N6666C/N6666K				
G-CEJA	Cameron V-77 HAFB	2469	G-BTOF	17. 6.91	L. & C.Gray	Farnborough	4. 6.02A
G-CERT	Mooney M.20K (252TSE)	25-1134		5.10.87	K.A.Hemming	Fowlmere	24. 2.03
G-CEXA	Fokker F.27 Friendship 500RF	10503	N703A	19. 1.96	Dart Group plc	Bournemouth	24. 3.02TC
			PH-EXK		t/a Channel Express		
G-CEXB	Fokker F.27 Friendship 500RF	10550	N743A	15.11.95	Dart Group plc	Bournemouth	30. 1.02TC
			PH-EXF		t/a Channel Express *(Parcel force titles)*		
G-CEXD	Fokker F.27 Friendship 600	10351	PH-KFE	18. 2.97	Dart Group plc	Bournemouth	18. 2.03TC
			HB-AAX/PH-FLX		t/a Channel Express		
G-CEXE	Fokker F.27 Friendship 500	10654	SU-GAF	2. 4.97	Dart Group plc	Bournemouth	14. 5.03TC
			PH-EXJ		t/a Channel Express		
G-CEXF	Fokker F.27 Friendship 500	10660	SU-GAE	2. 4.97	Dart Group plc	Bournemouth	30. 6.03TC
			PH-EXC		t/a Channel Express		
G-CEXG	Fokker F.27 Friendship 500	10459	G-JEAP	13.11.00	Dart Group plc	Bournemouth	15. 6.04T
			9Q-CBI/OY-APF/9Q-CBI/PH-RUA/VH-EWR/F-BYAH/OY-APF/PH-EXD				
	(For conversion to 'Super Friendship' standard 11.00)				t/a Channel Express		
G-CEXH	Airbus A300B4-203F	117	D-ASAZ	30. 3.98	Dart Group plc	Liege	1. 4.04T
			N14966/N966C/F-OGTB/9V-STA/F-WZER		t/a Channel Express		
G-CEXI	Airbus A300B4-203	121	D-ASAA	3. 9.98	Dart Group plc	Liege	3. 9.04T
			N15967/N967C/F-OGTC/9V-STB/F-WZEK		t/a Channel Express		
G-CEXJ	Airbus A300B4-203F	147	N300FV	17. 3.00	Channel Express (Air Services) Ltd		
			F-WQIP/9M-MHD/F-WZMA			Bournemouth	19. 3.03T
G-CEXP*	Handley Page HPR.7 Dart Herald 209	195	I-ZERC	29.10.87	BAA plc	Gatwick	7.11.96T
			G-BFRJ/4X-AHO		*(WFU 8.3.96: cancelled 22.3.96 by CAA)*		
					(Displayed South Terminal)		
G-CEXS	Lockheed L.188CF Electra	1091	N5539	14. 4.92	Dart Group plc	Bournemouth	15. 4.02T
			N171PS/N971HA/N171PS		t/a Channel Express		
G-CFAA	BAE Systems Avro 146-RJ100	E3373		9. 5.00	Cityflyer Express Ltd	Gatwick	15. 6.03T
G-CFAB	BAE Systems Avro 146-RJ100	E3377		23. 8.00	Cityflyer Express Ltd	Gatwick	28.11.03T
G-CFAC	BAE Systems Avro 146-RJ100	E3379		23. 8.00	Cityflyer Express Ltd	Gatwick	14.12.03T
G-CFAD	BAE Systems Avro 146-RJ100	E3380		23. 8.00	Cityflyer Express Ltd	Gatwick	24. 1.04T
G-CFAE	BAE Systems Avro 146-RJ100	E3381		12. 1.01	Cityflyer Express Ltd	Gatwick	22. 2.02T
G-CFAF	BAE Systems Avro 146-RJ100	E3382		15. 1.01	Cityflyer Express Ltd	Gatwick	22. 3.04T
G-CFAH	BAE Systems Avro 146-RJ100	E3384		15. 1.01	Cityflyer Express Ltd	Gatwick	5. 6 04T
G-CFBI	Colt 56A HAFB	570		11. 7.84	G.A.Fisher	Guildford	24. 7.91A
					t/a Out-of-the-Blue *"Air O"*		
G-CFLY*	Cessna 172F	17252635	PH-SNO	25. 8.78	Not known	Blackpool	13. 7.95
			N8731U		*(Cancelled 5.6.95 by CAA: stored 8.00)*		

G-CFME	SOCATA TB-10 Tobago	1795	F-GNHU	15. 4.98	Charles Funke Associates Ltd	Goodwood	12. 6.04T
G-CFRA	Cessna 560XL Citation Excel	560-5183	N5090V	5. 9.01	Cirrus Aviation Holding Ltd		
						(Douglas, IoM)	5 .9.02T
G-CGHM	Piper PA-28-140 Cruiser	28-7425143	PH-NSM N9614N	25. 4.79	I.J.Sixsmith	(Haywards Heath)	15.10.03T
G-CGOD	Cameron N-77 HAFB	2647		5. 9.91	G.P.Lane *"Neptune"*	Waltham Abbey	7. 9.01A
G-CHAA	Cameron O-90 HAFB	2471		24.10.91	P.Farmer	Wadhurst	23. 8.00T
G-CHAM	Cameron Pot 90SS HAFB *(Chambourcy Pot shape)*	2912		29. 9.92	B.J.Reeves & C.Walker t/a High Exposure Balloons *"Yogpot"*	Brighouse	29. 6.02A
G-CHAP	Robinson R44 Astro	0326		9. 4.97	Brierley Lifting Tackle Co Ltd		
						Wolverhampton	4. 5.03T
G-CHAR	Grob G-109B	6435		21. 5.86	T.Holloway t/a RAFGSA	RAF Bicester	11. 5.02
G-CHAS	Piper PA-28-181 Archer II	28-8090325	N82228	18. 3.91	C.H.Elliott	Stapleford	29. 5.03
G-CHAV	Europa Aviation Europa (Subaru) *(Tail-wheel u/c)*	PFA 247-12769		28.12.94	M.B.Stoner t/a Chavenage Flying Group	Chavenage, Wilts	5.11.02P
G-CHCD	Sikorsky S-76A II Plus	760101	OY-HEZ G-CHCD/G-CBJB/N288SP/C-GIMN/YV-326C	16. 1.98	CHC Scotia Ltd	North Denes	28.11.04T
G-CHCE	Sikorsky S-76A II Plus	760036	G-BOND N4931Y	20. 4.01	CHC Scotia Ltd	North Denes	5. 3.03T
G-CHCF	Eurocopter AS332L2 Super Puma	2567		30.11.01	CHC Scotia Ltd	Aberdeen	
G-CHEB	Europa Aviation Europa (NSI EA-81/100)	263 & PFA 247-12967		16. 9.96	C.H.P.Bell	Brunton	29.10.01P
G-CHEL	Colt 77B HAFB	4823		18. 5.00	Chelsea Financial Services plc		
						Cirencester	29. 5.02P
G-CHEM	Piper PA-34-200T Seneca II	34-8170032	N8292Y	26. 8.87	London Executive Aviation Ltd		
						Stapleford	2. 2.03T
G-CHER	Piper PA-38-112 Tomahawk II	38-82A0004	G-BVBL N91339	19.12.00	Aerohire Ltd	Cardiff	23. 3.03T
G-CHET	Europa Aviation Europa Turbo XS *(Tri-cycle u/c)* (Rotax 914)	376 & PFA 247-13277		12. 2.98	H.P.Chetwynd-Talbot	Wombleton	19. 4.02P
G-CHEZ	Pilatus Britten-Norman BN-2B-20 Islander	2234	9M-TAM G-BSAG	30. 4.01	The Cheshire Police Authority	Liverpool	25. 5.02T
G-CHIK	Reims Cessna F152 II	F15201628	G-BHAZ (D-EHLE)	19.10.81	Stapleford Flying Club Ltd	Stapleford	14.11.03T
G-CHIP	Piper PA-28-181 Archer II	28-8290095	N81337	22. 2.82	C.M.Hough	Fairoaks	26. 4.03
G-CHIS	Robinson R22 Beta	1740		5. 4.91	I.R.Chisholm t/a Bradmore Helicopter Leasing	Costock	8. 8.03T
G-CHIX	Robin DR.400/500	0036	F-GXGD F-WQPN	29.11.01	P.A.& R.Stephens	(Malton)	
G-CHKL*	Cameron Kookaburra 120SS HAFB	3733		8.11.95	Eagle Ltd *(Cancelled 30.3.01 by CAA)*	Canowindra, Australia	21. 3.01A
G-CHKN	Air Creation Kiss 400-582(1)	UK/FL002/134 & BMAA/HB/183		18. 9.01	I.Tomkins *(Noted 11.01)*	Sywell	
G-CHLT	Stemme S-10	10-30	D-KGCD	3. 7.91	J.Abbess	Tibenham	3.12.03
G-CHMP	Bellanca 7ACA Champ	62-72	N68556	21.12.92	I.J.Langley *(Stored 10.92: current status unknown)*	Bidford	
G-CHNX	Lockheed L.188AF Electra	1068	EI-CHO (G-CHNX)/N5535	1.11.94	Dart Group plc *(Op Channel Express) (Withdrawn from use 11.01)*	Bournemouth	31.10.01T
G-CHOK	Cameron V-77 HAFB	1752		25. 5.88	Amanda J.Moore *"S'il Vous Plais"*	Great Missenden	31. 3.01A
G-CHOP	Westland-Bell 47G-3B1 *(Line No.WAN/79)*	WA/380	XT221	19.12.78	Dolphin Property (Management) Ltd		
						Old Sarum	27 2.03T
G-CHPY	de Havilland DHC.1 Chipmunk 22	C1/0093	WB652	7. 3.97	JGH Computer Services Ltd	Cardiff	15.10.01T
G-CHSU	Eurocopter EC 135 T1	0079		4. 2.99	Thames Valley Police Authority *(Op Chiltern Air Support Unit)*	RAF Benson	12..4.02T
G-CHTA	Grumman-American AA-5A Cheetah	AA5A-0631	G-BFRC	3. 3.86	Quickspin Ltd *(Op Biggin Hill School of Flying)*	Biggin Hill	23. 2.03T
G-CHTG	Rotorway Executive 90 (Rotorway RI 162)	5118	G-BVAJ	19.11.99	G.Cooper	Street Farm, Takeley	5.12.01P
G-CHTT*	Varga 2150A Kachina	VAC162-80		7. 9.84	H.W.Hall	Southend	6. 9.87
	(Damaged near Hatherleigh, Devon 27.4.86: cancelled 9.8.94 by CAA: wreck stored dismantled 1.02)						
G-CHUB*	Colt Cylinder Two N-51 HAFB *(Fire Extinguisher shape)*	1720		11. 4.90	British Balloon Museum & Library *"Chubb Fire Extinguisher" (Cancelled 12.12.01 as wfu)*	Newbury	19.12.95A
G-CHUG	Europa Aviation Europa	PFA 247-12960		29. 7.96	C A Pratt	(Stoke-on-Trent)	
G-CHUK	Cameron O-77 HAFB	2773		6. 3.92	L.C.Taylor	Burton-on-Trent	5. 4.93A
G-CHUM	Robinson R44 Raven	0839		2. 8.00	Vitapage Ltd	Elstree	7. 9.03T
G-CHYL	Robinson R22 Beta	1197		28.11.89	Caroline M.Gough-Cooper *(Op Bournemouth Helicopters)*	Bournemouth	10. 1.02
G-CHZN	Robinson R22 Beta	0884	G-GHZM G-FENI	9. 4.99	Cloudbase Ltd	Shobdon	4..3.02T
G-CIAO	III Sky Arrow 650-T (Rotax 912-UL)	PFA 298-13095		23. 7.97	G Arscott	Popham	11.11.02P

G-CIAS	Pilatus Britten-Norman BN-2B-21 Islander	2162	HC-BNS G-BKJM	1. 5.91	Channel Island Air Search Ltd	Guernsey	11. 3.03
G-CICI	Cameron R-15 Gas/HAFB	673	(N) G-CICI/(G-BIHP)	11.11.80	Ballooning Endeavours Ltd	NK	5. 6.91P
G-CIDD	Bellanca 7ECA Citabria	1002-74	N86577	29.11.00	A.& P.West	(Calne)	4.10.04
G-CIFR	Piper PA-28-181 Cherokee Archer II	28-7790208	PH-MIT OO-HBB/N7654F	18. 6.97	Aeroshow Ltd	Cardiff	30. 8.03T
G-CIGY	Westland-Bell 47G-3B1	WA/350	G-BGXP XT191	26.10.98	R.A.Perrot	Guernsey	16. 7.03
G-CIPI*	AJEP Wittman W.8 Tailwind (Continental O-200-A)	AJEP/2 & PFA 1363	G-AYDU	22. 7.87	N.R.Hurley *(Wreck stored 3.00: cancelled 8.8.01 by CAA)*	Cannes, France	15. 6.99P
G-CITA*	Bellanca 7KCAB Citabria	543-75	N14091 G-CITA/N53785/SE-KUI/N53785 *(Cancelled 24.8.99 by CAA)* *(Fuselage last noted Southend 1.01: now removed & current status unknown)*	2. 2.96	J.R.K.Pardoe	NK	21. 3.99T
G-CITI	Cessna 501 Citation I	501-0084	VP-CDM VR-CDM/G-CITI/(N11JC)/(N463CJ)/N3160M	21. 9.87	Euro Executive Jet Ltd	Southampton	19. 9.01T
G-CITY	Piper PA-31-350 Navajo Chieftain	31-7852136	N27741	12. 9.78	Woodgate Aviation (IOM) Ltd	Ronaldsway	5.11.03T
G-CITZ	Bell 206B JetRanger II	1997	G-BRTB N9936K	19. 2.99	Euro Executive Jet Ltd	Thruxton	11. 4.02T
G-CIVA	Boeing 747-436	27092		19. 3.93	British Airways plc *(Op British Asia Airways) (Chelsea Rose t/s)*	Heathrow	18. 3.03T
G-CIVB	Boeing 747-436	25811	(G-BNLY)	15. 2.94	British Airways plc *(Op British Asia Airways) (Chelsea Rose t/s)*	Heathrow	14. 2.04T
G-CIVC	Boeing 747-436	25812	(G-BNLZ)	26. 2.94	British Airways plc *(Delftblue Daybreak t/s)*	Heathrow	25. 2.03T
G-CIVD	Boeing 747-436	27349		14.12.94	British Airways plc *(Waves of the City t/s)*	Gatwick	3. 8.03T
G-CIVE	Boeing 747-436	27350		20.12.94	British Airways plc	Heathrow	22. 8.03T
G-CIVF	Boeing 747-436	25434	(G-BNLY)	29. 3.95	British Airways plc *"City of St Albans"*	Gatwick	20. 9.03T
G-CIVG	Boeing 747-436	25813	N6009F	20. 4.95	British Airways plc *"City of Wells"*	Heathrow	18. 4.04T
G-CIVH	Boeing 747-436	25809		23. 4.96	British Airways plc *"City of Hereford"*	Gatwick	22. 4.02T
G-CIVI	Boeing 747-436	25814		2. 5.96	British Airways plc *"City of Gloucester"*	Gatwick	1. 5.02T
G-CIVJ	Boeing 747-436	25817		11. 2.97	British Airways plc	Heathrow	10. 9.02T
G-CIVK	Boeing 747-436	25818		28. 2.97	British Airways plc	Heathrow	30. 8.02T
G-CIVL	Boeing 747-436	27478		28. 3.97	British Airways plc	Heathrow	26.11.02T
G-CIVM	Boeing 747-436	28700		5. 6.97	British Airways plc *(Waves & Cranes t/s)*	Heathrow	4. 6.03T
G-CIVN	Boeing 747-436	28848		29. 9.97	British Airways plc *(Delftblue Daybreak t/s)*	Gatwick	28. 9.03T
G-CIVO	Boeing 747-436	28849	N6046P	5.12.97	British Airways plc *(Benthone Tartan t/s)*	Heathrow	4.12.03T
G-CIVP	Boeing 747-436	25850		17. 2.98	British Airways plc *(Colum t/s)*	Heathrow	16. 2.04T
G-CIVR	Boeing 747-436	25820		2. 3.98	British Airways plc *(Waves & Cranes t/s)*	Gatwick	21. 2.04T
G-CIVS	Boeing 747-436	28851		13. 3.98	British Airways plc *(Whale Rider t/s)*	Heathrow	12. 3.01T
G-CIVT	Boeing 747-436	25821	(G-CIVN)	20. 3.98	British Airways plc *(Delftblue Daybreak t/s)*	Heathrow	9.11.03T
G-CIVU	Boeing 747-436	25810	(G-CIVO)	24. 4.98	British Airways plc *(Wings t/s)*	Heathrow	23. 4.04T
G-CIVV	Boeing 747-436	25819	N6009F (G-CIVP)	23. 5.98	British Airways plc *(Rendezvous t/s)*	Heathrow	10. 4.04T
G-CIVW	Boeing 747-436	25822	(G-CIVR)	15. 5.98	British Airways plc	Heathrow	14. 5.04T
G-CIVX	Boeing 747-436	28852		3. 9.98	British Airways plc	Heathrow	2. 9.04T
G-CIVY	Boeing 747-436	28853		29. 9.98	British Airways plc *(Whale Rider t/s)*	Heathrow	28. 9.04T
G-CIVZ	Boeing 747-436	28854		31.10.98	British Airways plc *(Benyhone Tartan t/s)*	Heathrow	30.10.04T
G-CJBC	Piper PA-28-180 Cherokee D	28-5470	OY-BDE	28.11.80	J.B.Cave	Wolverhampton	5. 8.02
G-CJCI	Pilatus P.2-06	600-63	U-143	30. 7.84	J.Briscoe & P.G.Bond t/a Pilatus P2 Flying Group *(As "CC+43"" in Luftwaffe c/s in Arado Ar.96B guise)*	Norwich	29. 6.01P
G-CJIM*	Taylor JT.1 Monoplane	PFA 1419	*(Under construction 7.95: cancelled 24.3.99 by CAA: current status unknown)*	28.12.78	J.Crawford	Farnborough	
G-CJUD	Denney Kitfox mk.3 (Rotax 582)	847 & PFA 172-11939		17. 1.91	D.M.Garrett *"Dougal"*	(Defford)	31. 5.02P
G-CKCK	Enstrom 280FX Shark	2071	OO-PVL	5. 5.95	Farmax Ltd *(Noted 11.01)*	Bournemouth	14. 5.98T
G-CLAC	Piper PA-28-161 Warrior II	28-8116241	N8396U	18. 5.87	M.J.Steadman	Blackbushe	3.11.02

G-CLAS	Short SD.3-60 Var.200	SH.3635	EI-BEK G-BLED/G-14-3635	28. 7.93	BAC Express Airlines Ltd *"City of Cardiff"*	Exeter	20. 7.02T
G-CLAX	Jurca MJ.5 Sirocco	PFA 2204	G-AWKB	22. 4.99	G.D.Claxton	(Pontyclun)	
G-CLEA	Piper PA-28-161 Warrior II	28-7916081	N30296	28. 8.80	R.J.Harrison & A.R.Carpenter	Oaksey Park	30.11.01
G-CLEE	Rans S-6-ES Coyote II	PFA 204-13670		29. 6.01	R.Holt	Mill Farm, Shifnal	26. 9.02P
G-CLEM	Bölkow Bö.208A-2 Junior	561	G-ASWE D-EFHE	22. 9.81	J.J.Donely & A.D.P.Thompson t/a Bölkow Group	Coventry	31. 5.02P
G-CLEO	Zenair CH.601HD Zodiac	PFA 162-13500		9. 8.99	K.M.Bowen	Goldcliff	
G-CLHA	British Aerospace BAe 146 Srs.200	E2024	G-DEBC N166US/N348PS	29. 3.00	Business Midland Regional Ltd *(Op BMI Commuter)*	Aberdeen	22. 5.02T
G-CLHB	British Aerospace BAe 146 Srs.200	E2036	G-GNTZ HB-IXB/N175US/N355PS	31. 3.00	Business Midland Regional Ltd *(Op BMI Commuter)*	Aberdeen	25.11.03T
G-CLHC	British Aerospace BAe 146 Srs.200	E2088	G-MANS G-CHSR/G-5-088	22. 5.00	Business Midland Regional Ltd *(Op BMI Commuter)*	Aberdeen	25. 4.03T
G-CLHD	British Aerospace BAe 146 Srs.200	E2023	G-DEBF N165US/N347PS	2. 5.00	Business Midland Regional Ltd *(Op BMI Commuter)*	Aberdeen	26. 9.02T
G-CLHE	British Aerospace BAe 146 Srs.200	E2045	OY-RCA G-DEBH/N185US/N362PS	29. 9.00	Business Midland Regional Ltd *(Op BMI Commuter)*	Aberdeen	28. 9.03T
G-CLIC	Cameron A-105 HAFB *(New envelope c/n 3395 @ 4.95)*	2557		18. 4.91	R.S.Mohr *"Clic Trust"*	Corsham	30. 4.01A
G-CLIP	Eurocopter AS 355N Twin Squirrel	5580		25.11.94	Charterstyle Ltd	Blackbushe	11. 4.04T
G-CLKE	Robinson R44 Astro	0185	G-HREH D-HREH	22. 9.98	J.Clarke t/a Clarke Business	(Burnley)	10. 9.03T
G-CLOE	Sky 90-24 HAFB	019		11. 3.96	C.J.Sandell *"Headfirst"*	Sevenoaks	17. 7.01T
G-CLOS	Piper PA-34-200T Seneca II	34-7870361	HB-LKE N36783	17. 6.86	P.S.Kirby	Coventry	3.10.04
G-CLOW	Beechcraft 200 Super King Air	BB-821	N821RC TC-DBY/N144TM/F-GDCB	2.11.99	Clowes Estates Ltd	(Ashbourne)	7.11.02T
G-CLRK	Sky 77-24 HAFB	101		3. 3.98	William Clark & Son (Parkgate) Ltd	(Dumfries)	2.12.99A
G-CLUB	Reims Cessna FRA150M Aerobat	FRA15000347	OO-AWZ F-WZAZ/(F-WZDZ)	10. 2.83	D.C.C.Handley	Cranfield	13. 5.02T
G-CLUE	Piper PA-34-200T Seneca II	34-7970502	N8089Z	15. 9.92	Kilo Aviation Ltd	(Northwich)	25. 1.02T
G-CLUX	Reims Cessna F172N Skyhawk II	F17201996	PH-AYG(3)	1. 5.80	J.G.Jackman & K.M.Drewitt t/a J & K Aviation	Hawarden	20. 8.04T
G-CMED	SOCATA TB-9 Tampico	1867	F-GSZK	19. 3.01	S.C.Brown t/a Enstone Flying Club	Enstone	28. 3.04T
G-CMGC	Piper PA-25-235 Pawnee D	25-7756042	G-BFEX N82525	19.11.91	Midland Gliding Club Ltd	Long Mynd	19. 4.04
G-CNAB	Jabiru Jabiru UL	PFA 274-13651		27. 9.00	W.A.Brighouse	(Whitby)	26. 9.02P
G-CNDY	Robinson R22 Beta-II	2677	G-BXEW	15. 5.97	Testgate Ltd	Goodwood	8. 6.03T
G-COAI	Cranfield A.1-400 Eagle	001	G-BCIT	1. 6.98	Cranfield University *(Noted 7.99: current status unknown)*	Cranfield	
G-COCO	Reims Cessna F172M Skyhawk II	F17201373	PH-SMO OO-ADI	27.10.80	P.C.Sheard & R.C.Larder	North Reston, Louth	25. 2.02
G-CODE	Bell 206B-3 JetRanger III	3850	N222DM N84TC	27. 8.96	B.Wronski	Gloucestershire	7.12.02
G-COEZ	Airbus A320-231	0179	OY-CNH F-WWIS	10. 2.97	Airtours International Airways Ltd	Manchester	11. 2.03T
G-COIN	Bell 206B JetRanger II	897	EI-AWA	11. 3.85	C.Sarno	Cranfield	6. 7.03
G-COLA	Beechcraft F33C Bonanza	CJ-137	G-BUAZ PH-BNH	31. 3.92	J R C Spooner & P M Scarratt	East Midlands	22.11.04
G-COLH	Piper PA-28-140 Cherokee	28-23143	G-AVRT N11C	13.10.00	J.G.O'Brien	(Brentwood)	10. 2.02
G-COLL	Enstrom 280C-UK-2 Shark	1223		17. 8.81	S.P.Giddings	(Newport Pagnell)	11. 1.01
G-COLR*	Colt 69A HAFB	780		8. 4.86	Balloon Preservation Group *"Bubble" (Cancelled 21.5.93 as WFU)*	Kirdford	N/E(A)
G-COMB	Piper PA-30 Twin Comanche B	30-1362	G-AVBL N8236Y	14. 9.84	J.T.Bateson	Blackpool	27.11.04
G-COMP*	Cameron N-90 HAFB	1564		24. 9.87	Balloon Preservation Group *"Computercentre 1" (Cancelled 18.12.01 by CAA)*	Kirdford	20. 5.97A
G-CONB	Robin DR.400/180 Regent	2176	G-BUPX	14. 4.93	C.C. & C.Blakey t/a Winchcombe Farm	Redhill	24. 2.02T
G-CONC	Cameron N-90 HAFB	2139		13.11.89	British Airways plc "Concorde"	Heathrow	22. 9.02T
G-CONI*	Lockheed 749A-79 Constellation	2553	N7777G (N173X)/N7777G/TI-1045P/PH-LDT/PH-TET	12. 5.82	Science Museum Air Transport Coln & Storage Facility *(Cancelled 13.6.84 as WFU) (As "N7777G" in TWA c/s)*	Wroughton	
G-CONL	SOCATA TB-10 Tobago	173	F-GCOR	22.12.98	J.M.Huntington	(Leeds)	14. 3.02
G-CONV	Convair CV-440-54	484	CS-TML N357SA/N28KE/N28KA/N4402	19. 7.01	Atlantic Air Transport Ltd	Coventry	

G-COOP*	Cameron N-31 HAFB	382		2. 3.78	Balloon Preservation Group Museum *"Co-op"*		
					(Cancelled 22.10.01 by CAA)	Kirdford	13. 5.87A
G-COOT	Taylor Coot A	EE-1A		16. 9.81	P.M.Napp	(Newcastle upon Tyne)	
G-COPS	Piper J-3C-65 Cub	11911	F-BFYC	17. 7.79	R.W.Sproat & C.E.Simpson		
	(L-4H-PI) *(Frame No.11739)*		Fr.AF/44-79615			Lennox Plunton Farm, Borgue	19.12.02P
	(Regd as c/n 36-817 which is a USAAC Contract No)						
G-COPT	Aérospatiale AS350B Ecureuil	2168	9M-FSA	25. 2.98	Owenlars Ltd	(Odiham)	10. 4.04T
			9V-BOR				
G-CORB	SOCATA TB-20 Trinidad	1178	F-GKUX	12. 4.99	G.D.Corbin	Old Sarum	21. 4.02
G-CORD	Slingsby Nipper T.66 RA.45 Srs.3		G-AVTB	21. 3.88	A.V.Lamprell	Charity Farm, Baxterley	8. 3.02P
	(Rebuild from S.105/1565)	S.129/1676					
G-CORN	Bell 206B-3 JetRanger III	3035	G-BHTR	4. 6.99	John A.Wells Ltd	Costock	12. 4.04T
			N18098				
G-CORP	British Aerospace ATP	2037	G-BTNK	2. 3.98	BAE Systems (Operations) Ltd	Warton	28. 3.03T
			N860AW/G-BTNK/G-11-037				
G-CORT	Agusta-Bell 206B-3 JetRanger III			21. 6.96	Helicopter Training & Hire Ltd	Belfast	28. 7.02T
		8739					
G-COSY	Lindstrand LBL-56A HAFB	017		18. 2.93	D.D.Owen	Wotton-under-Edge	10.12.99A
G-COTT	Cameron Flying Cottage 60SS HAFB	687	"G-HOUS"	13. 2.81	M.R.Nanda	Nottingham	15.12.98A
					t/a Nottingham Hot-Air Balloon Club *"Cottage"*		
G-COUP	Ercoupe 415C	1903	N99280	27. 5.93	S.M.Gerrard *"Jenny Lin"*	Bembridge	17. 7.99
	(Continental C75)		NC99280		*(Under rebuild 3.01)*		
G-COVE	Jabiru Jabiru UL	PFA 274A-13409		23. 7.99	A.A.Rowson	Lleweni Parc	17.10.00P
	(Jabiru 2200A)						
G-COWS	ARV Super 2	K.009 & PFA 152-11182	(G-BONB)	27. 5.88	T.C.Harrold	Felthorpe	1. 6.01P
	(Hewland AE75)						
G-COZI	Rutan Cozy III	PFA 159-12162		19. 7.93	D.G.Machin	Lydd	20. 7.02P
	(Lycoming O-320)						
G-CPCD	CEA Jodel DR-221 Dauphin	81	F-BPCD	11.12.90	P.J.Taylor	Enstone	10. 4.04
G-CPDA	de Havilland DH.106 Comet 4C	6473	XS235	10. 8.00	C.Walton Ltd	Bruntingthorpe	
G-CPEL	Boeing 757-236	24398	N602DF	24. 8.92	British Airways plc	Heathrow	26.10.02T
			EC-EOL/EC-597/G-BRJE/EC-EOL/EC-278/G-BRJE		*(Animals & Trees t/s)*		
G-CPEM	Boeing 757-236	28665		28. 3.97	British Airways plc	Heathrow	27. 3.03T
G-CPEN	Boeing 757-236	28666		23. 4.97	British Airways plc	Heathrow	22. 4.03T
G-CPEO	Boeing 757-236	28667		11. 7.97	British Airways plc	Heathrow	10. 7.03T
G-CPEP	Boeing 757-2Y0	25268	C-GTSU	16. 4.97	British Airways plc	Luton	9. 7.03T
			EI-CLP/N400KL/XA-TAE		*(Sold 10.01)*		
G-CPER	Boeing 757-236	29113		29.12.97	British Airways plc	Gatwick	28.12.03T
G-CPES	Boeing 757-236	29114		17. 3.98	British Airways plc	Heathrow	16. 3.04T
G-CPET	Boeing 757-236	29115		12. 5.98	British Airways plc	Heathrow	11. 5.04T
G-CPEU	Boeing 757-236	29941		1. 5.99	British Airways plc	Heathrow	30. 4.02T
					(Rendezvous t/s)		
G-CPEV	Boeing 757-236	29943	(G-CPEW)	11. 6.99	British Airways plc	Heathrow	10 .6.02T
					(Rendezvous t/s)		
G-CPFC	Reims Cessna F152 II	F15201430		1.12.77	Willowair Flying Club (1996) Ltd		
						Southend	12. 7.04T
G-CPMK	de Havilland DHC.1 Chipmunk 22		WZ847	28. 6.96	Towerdrive Ltd	Sleap	19. 9.02
		C1/0866			*(As "WZ847")*		
G-CPMS	SOCATA TB-20 Trinidad	1607	F-GNHA	7. 4.98	Charlotte Park Management Services Ltd		
						Goodwood	1. 5.04T
G-CPOL	Aérospatiale AS355F1 Twin Squirrel		N5775T	30.11.95	Thames Valley Police Authority	Luton	30. 1.02T
		5007	C-GJJB/N5775T		*(Op Chiltern Air Support Unit)*		
G-CPSF	Cameron N-90 HAFB	3747	G-OISK	21. 4.99	S.A.Simington & J.D.Rigden	Norwich	12. 7.01A
G-CPTM	Piper PA-28-151 Cherokee Warrior		G-BTOE	9. 7.91	T.J.Mackay & C.M.Pollett	Woodford	14. 2.04T
		28-7715012	N4264F				
G-CPTS	Agusta-Bell 206B JetRanger II	8556		1. 6.78	A.R.B.Aspinall	Skipton	27. 6.03
G-CPXC	CAP Aviation CAP.10C	301		11.12.01	Cole Aviation Ltd		
						Spilsted Farm, Sedlescombe	
G-CRAK*	Cameron N-77 HAFB	2291		7. 6.90	Mobile Windscreens Ltd	Stafford	14. 7.97A
					"Mobile Windscreens" (Cancelled 20.11.01 as wfu by CAA: stored)		
G-CRAY	Robinson R22 Beta	0919		12. 1.89	W.H.Grimshaw	Barton	7. 4.98
G-CRES	Denney Kitfox mk.2	PFA 172-11574		7. 6.90	K.M.James	Higher Barn Farm, Houghton	3. 9.02P
	(Rotax 912)						
G-CREW	Piper PA-46-350P Malibu Mirage		N41865	20.10.00	Longslow Dairy Ltd	Seething	22.10.03
		4636309					
G-CRIC	Colomban MC.15 Cri-Cri	PFA 133-10915		22. 7.83	R.S.Stoddart-Stones	(Caterham)	5. 5.99P
	(JPX PUL.212)						
G-CRIL	Rockwell Commander 112B	521	N1388J	22. 6.79	J.W.Reynolds	Cardiff	1.10.03
					t/a Rockwell Aviation Group		
G-CRIS	Taylor JT.1 Monoplane	PFA 055-10318		5. 6.79	C.R.Steer	Spilsted Farm, Sedlescombe	
					(Bare fuselage noted 5.01)		
G-CROL	Maule MXT-7-180 Star Rocket	14032C	N9232F	24.11.93	N.G.P.Evans	Oaksey Park	4. 3.04
G-CROW	Robinson R44 Raven	0754		19. 4.00	Longmoore Ltd	(Godalming)	18. 5.03T

G-CROY	Europa Aviation Europa	PFA 247-12896		7. 2.97	A.Croy	Kirkwall	22. 7.02P
	(Rotax 912-UL)						
G-CRPH	Airbus A320-231	0424	F-WQBB	10. 4.95	Airtours International Airways Ltd		
			F-WWIV		*(My Travel titles)*	Manchester	14. 4.04T
G-CRUM	Westland Scout AH.1	F.9712	XV137	17. 3.98	Crummock Development Ltd	Bonnyrigg	25. 7.01P
	(Pod No.F8-6151)				*(As "XV137")*		
G-CRUZ	Cessna T303 Crusader	T30300004	N9336T	7.12.90	Bank Farm Ltd	Bank Farm, Benwick, Cambs	21. 6.03T
G-CSBM	Reims Cessna F150M	F15201359	PH-AYC	24. 5.78	Halegreen Associates Ltd		
						Hinton-in-the-Hedges	6.12.03T
G-CSCS	Reims Cessna F172N Skyhawk II		PH-MEM	28.11.86	Cheryl Sullivan	Stapleford	10. 6.02T
		F17201707	(PH-WEB)/N9899A				
G-CSDJ	Jabiru Jabiru UL	PFA 274A-13337		23. 3.99	D W, J Johnston, C.D & S.Slater	Kemble	24. 4.02P
	(Jabiru 2200A)						
G-CSFC	Cessna 150L	15075360	(G-BFLX)	21. 3.78	I.G.McDonald	RNAS Culdrose	6. 3.02
			N11370		t/a Foxtrot Charlie Flying Group		
G-CSFT*	Piper PA-23-250 Aztec B	27-4521	G-AYKU	20. 9.84	Aces High Ltd	North Weald	3.12.94T
			N13885		*(Cancelled 5.6.96 as WFU) (Fuselage noted 9.01)*		
G-CSIX	Piper PA-32-300 Cherokee Six		ZS-OMX	15. 6.01	G.A.Ponsford	Goodwood	19 .7.04
		32-7840030	Z-WJM/VP-WJM/HB-PCX/ZS-KBR/N9857K				
G-CSMK	Evektor-Aerotechnik EV-97 Eurostar			4.12.01	Cosmik Aviation Ltd	(Southam)	
		PFA 315-13813					
G-CSNA	Cessna 421C Golden Eagle III		(D-IOSS)	11. 6.79	Air Montgomery Ltd	Leeds-Bradford	18. 8.02T
		421C0677	N26522				
G-CSPJ	Hughes 369HS	55-0745S	G-BXJF	24. 7.97	The Hughes Helicopter Co Ltd	Biggin Hill	12. 9.03T
			N99KS/N9KS				
G-CTCL	SOCATA TB-10 Tobago	1107	G-BSIV	16. 7.90	MRS Ltd	Fairoaks	30. 9.02
G-CTCT	Flight Design CT 2K	00-04-04-94	G-69-51	26. 6.00	Cyclone Airsports Ltd t/a Pegasus Aviation		
	(Rotax 912 ULS)					(Manton, Marlborough)	
G-CTEC	Stoddard-Hamilton Glastar			9.11.99	B.N.C.Mogg	Bibberne Farm, Stalbridge	
		PFA 295-13260					
G-CTEL	Cameron N-90 HAFB	3933		27. 8.96	D.Triggse	Alresford	5. 5.02A
G-CTFF	Cessna T206H Turbo Stationair		N24309	29.10.01	Oxford Aviation Services Ltd	Oxford	4.11.04T
		T20608150					
G-CTGR	Cameron N-77 HAFB	1775	G-CCDI	28. 8.97	T.G.Read	Knutsford	14. 7.02T
					(Charles Church titles)		
G-CTIX	Supermarine 509 Spitfire T.IX	---	N462JC	9. 4.85	A.A.Hodgson	Caernarfon	23. 4.02P
	(Major rebuild from parts pre 1994)		G-CTIX/IDFAF 2067/0607/MM4100/PT462 *(As PT462/SW-A")*				
G-CTKL	Noorduyn Harvard IIB	07-30	(G-BKWZ)	22.11.83	M.R.Simpson	(Aberdeen, Hong Kong, PRC)	16. 3.02P
	(C/n quoted as "76-80")		MM54137/RCAF3064		*(As "5413769" in US Navy c/s ?)*		
G-CTOY	Denney Kitfox mk.3			14.10.91	B.McNeilly	Newtownards, Co.of Down	10. 5.93P
	(Rotax 582)	1176 & PFA 172-12150			*(Current status unknown)*		
G-CTPW	Bell 206B-3 JetRanger III	4374	(N9145B)	30.11.95	S.J.Skilton	Bournemouth	19. 2.02T
					t/a Aviation Rentals		
G-CTWW	Piper PA-34-200T Seneca II		G-ROYZ	21. 7.93	Seneca Consortium Ltd	Welshpool	19. 1.03
		34-7970191	G-GALE/N3052X				
G-CUBB	Piper PA-18-150 Super Cub	18-3111	PH-WAM	5.12.78	Bidford Airfield Ltd	Bidford	18. 4.01
	(Lycoming O-360-C2) (L-18C-PI)		Belgian AF OL-L37/53-4711				
	(Frame No.18-3009)						
G-CUBI	Piper PA-18-125 Super Cub	18-3181	PH-GAV	26. 2.79	G.T.Fisher	(Thorney)	4.11.94T
	(L-18C-PI)		PH-VCV/R.Neth AF R-83/Belgian AF L-107/53-4781				
	(Official c/n 18-559 related to PH-GAV prior to 1970 rebuild when it incorporated Frame No.18-3170 from PH-VCV: current status unknown)						
G-CUBJ	Piper PA-18-150 Super Cub	18-2036	PH-MBF	15.12.82	R.A.Fleming	Kemble	19.10.03
	(L-18C-PI) *(Frame No.18-2035)*		PH-NLF/R.Neth AF R-43/8A-43/52-2436 *(As "CDG" in French Army c/s)*				
	(Regd with c/n 18-5395 following 1974 rebuild of PH-NLF which acquired data plate from, and took the identity of, PH-MBF - note also that G-SUPA carries this c/n)						
G-CUBP	Piper PA-18-150 Super Cub	18-8482	N1136Z	8. 8.96	P.Grenet	Shotteswell	24. 8.02
	(Frame No.18-8725)		G-BVMI/OH-PIN/N4262Z				
	(Regd with c/n 18-8823 the "official" identity of N1136Z/D-EIAC. This was rebuilt 1984/85 with Frame No.18-4613 from D-EKAF. This frame fitted to G-BVMI following accident on 15.8.95: repaired frame of G-BVMI has become G-CUBP)						
G-CUBS	Piper J-3C-65 Cub	"17792"	G-BHPT	26.10.01	S.M.Rolfe	Willington, Beds	12. 5.96P
	(Frame No.17792)		F-BSGQ/LX-AIH/N70688/NC70688		t/a Sunbeam Aviation		
	(Quoted p/i is suspect - possibly c/n 18105 ex NC71076/N71076: current status unknown)						
G-CUBY	Piper J-3C-65 Cub	16317	G-BTZW	2. 3.95	Claudine A.Bloom	Shoreham	24. 6.02P
	(Rebuilt with new fuselage 1996/97)		N88689/NC88689				
G-CUCU	Colt 180A HAFB	3869		22. 4.96	G.M.N. & S.Spencer	Watford	14. 7.02T
G-CUPN	Piper PA-46-350P Malibu Mirage			11. 2.98	K.Fletcher	Coventry	25. 4.04
		4636144			t/a Airpark		
G-CURE*	Colt 77A HAFB	1424		3. 7.89	Balloon Preservation Group	Kirdford	21.11.96A
	(Standard with tablet blisters)				*"Alka Seltzer 3" (Cancelled 29.4.97 as WFU)*		
G-CURR	Cessna 172R Skyhawk II	17280143	G-BXOH	27. 5.98	JS Aviation Ltd	Booker	9. 4.04T
			N9989F				
G-CURV	Avid Speed Wing	PFA 189-12169		28. 3.00	K.S.Kelso	(Baldock)	
G-CUTE	Dyn'Aéro MCR-01 Ban-bi	PFA 301-13511		7. 9.99	E.G.Shimmin	Cambridge	20.12.02P

G-CUTY	Europa Aviation Europa	PFA 247-12910		20. 8.96	D.J. & M.Watson	(Selby)	
G-CVBF	Cameron A-210 HAFB	3588		2. 6.95	Virgin Balloon Flights Ltd	Bath	15. 8.01T
G-CVIX	de Havilland DH.110 Sea Vixen D.3 *(Regd as FAW.2 with c/n 10132)*	10125	XP924	26. 2.96	De Havilland Aviation Ltd *(As "XP924")*	Bournemouth	17. 4.02P
G-CVPM	VPM M-16 Tandem Trainer (Arrow GT1000R)	VPM16-UK-110		26. 3.98	C.S.Teuber	(Hannover, Germany)	24. 5.02P
G-CVYD	Airbus A320-231	0393	B-HYO VR-HYO/F-WWIR	24. 2.98	JMC Airlines Ltd	Manchester	25. 1.04T
G-CVYE	Airbus A320-231	0394	B-HYP VR-HYP/F-WWBB	23. 3.98	JMC Airlines Ltd	Manchester	24. 1.04T
G-CVYG	Airbus A320-231	0443	B-HYT VR-HYT/F-WWBV	10.11.98	JMC Airlines Ltd	Manchester	30.11.04T
G-CWAG	Sequoia Falco F.8L (Lycoming O-320)	PFA 100-10895		11. 5.92	I.R.Court & W.Jones	Leicester	3.12.02P
G-CWBM	Phoenix Currie Wot (Continental C85)	PFA 3020	G-BTVP	28. 3.94	K.M.Fresson	Longwood, Southampton	25. 9.02P
G-CWFA	Piper PA-38-112 Tomahawk	38-78A0120	G-BTGC N9507T	17. 8.99	Cardiff-Wales Flying Club Ltd.	Cardiff	7. 9.01T
G-CWFB	Piper PA-38-112 Tomahawk	38-78A0623	G-OAAL N4471E	13. 1.00	Cardiff Wales Aviation Services Ltd	Cardiff	16.12.03T
G-CWFC	Piper PA-38-112 Tomawhawk	38-79A0047	G-BRTA N2407B	12. 6.00	Cardiff Wales Flying Club Ltd	Cardiff	27. 7.03T
G-CWFD	Piper PA-38-112 Tomahawk	38-79A0038	G-BSVY N2396B	10. 8.00	Cardiff Wales Flying Club Ltd	Cardiff	22.10.03T
G-CWFE	Piper PA-38-112 Tomahawk	38-80A0020	G-BPBR N25082/N9652N	29.11.01	Cardiff Wales Flying Club Ltd	Cardiff	30. 6.01T
G-CWFY	Cessna 152 II	15284639	G-OAMY N6214M	13. 1.00	Cardiff Wales Aviation Services Ltd	Cardiff	14.11.03T
G-CWFZ	Piper PA-28-151 Cherokee Warrior	28-7715131	G-CPCH G-BRGJ/(G-BPGP)/N5425F	27.10.99	Cardiff Wales Flying Club Ltd	Cardiff	6. 6.03T
G-CWIZ	Aérospatiale AS350B Ecureuil	1847	CS-HDF G-DJEM/G-ZBAC/G-SEBI/G-BMCU	18.10.95	PLM Dollar Group Ltd	Inverness	6. 4.02T
G-CWOT	Phoenix Currie Wot (Walter Mikron 2)	PFA 3019		31. 1.78	J.Beirne t/a G-CWOT Group *"Jonah"*	Boleybeg, Ballymore, Co.Westmeath	9. 1.02P
G-CXCX	Cameron N-90 HAFB *(Replacement envelope c/n 3332)*	1242		14. 3.86	Cathay Pacific Airways (London) Ltd *"Cathay Pacific IV"*	Swindon	10. 7.02A
G-CXHK	Cameron N-77 HAFB	4978		22. 2.01	Cathay Pacific Airways (London) Ltd	London SW1	16. 1.02A
G-CYGI*	Hapi Cygnet SF-2A	PFA 182-12084		17.12.93	B.Brown *(Cancelled 8.5.99 by CAA: noted 9.99: current status unknown)*	Kemble	
G-CYLS	Cessna T303 Crusader	T30300005	N20736 G-BKXI/N303CC/(N9355T)	20.12.90	Gledhill Water Storage Ltd	Blackpool	29. 3.03
G-CYMA	Gulfstream GA-7 Cougar	GA7-0083	G-BKOM N794GA	15. 8.83	Cyma Petroleum (UK) Ltd	Elstree	13. 6.04
G-CZAG	Sky 90-24 HAFB	171		5.10.99	S.McCarthy	Rothersthorpe	22. 5.02
G-CZAR	Cessna 560 Citation V	560-0046	(N26656)	29.11.89	Chauffair Ltd	Farnborough	6. 3.02T
G-CZCZ	Mudry/CAARP CAP.10B	54	OE-AYY F-WZCG/HB-SAK/F-BUDT	28. 7.94	P.R.Moorhead & M.Farmer	Garston Farm, Marshfield	21. 8.03

G-DAAA – G-DZZZ

G-DAAC	Canadair CL604 Challenger	5424	N604CR C-GLWX	30. 3.00	1427 Ltd *(Op Northern Executive Aviation)*	Manchester	31 12.03T
G-DAAH	Piper PA-28RT-201T Turbo Arrow IV	28R-7931104	N3026U	27. 4.79	R.Peplow	Wolverhampton	24. 5.03
G-DAAM	Robinson R22 Beta	2043		3. 6.92	Hecray Co Ltd t/a Direct Helicopters	Southend	10. 7.04T
G-DABS	Robinson R22 Beta	3083		15. 5.00	B.Seymour	(Middlesbrough)	1. 6.03
G-DACA	Percival P.57 Sea Prince T.1	P57/12	WF118	6. 5.80	P.G.Vallance Ltd *(Gatwick Aviation Museum as "WF118")*	Charlwood, Surrey	17. 7.81P
G-DACC	Cessna 401B	401B-0112	N77GR N4488A/G-AYOU/N7972Q	1. 9.86	Niglon Ltd	Coventry	9. 9.01
G-DACF	Cessna 152 II	152-81724	G-BURY N67285	13. 6.97	T.M. & M.L.Jones t/a Derby Aero Club	Derby	17. 8.03T
G-DACS	Short SD.3-30 Var.100	SH.3089	C-GLAL N330CA/G-BKDM/G-14-3089	6. 7.98	Air Cavrel Ltd *(Open store 1.02)*	Southend	9..8.01T
G-DADS	Hughes 369HS	22-0369S	N888SS N9101F	11. 6.90	Executive Aviation Services Ltd	Gloucestershire	2. 8.02T
G-DAEX	Dassault Falcon 900EX	78	F-WWFR	22. 2.01	Triair (Bermuda) Ltd	Farnborough	22. 2.02T
G-DAFY	Beechcraft 58 Baron	TH-1591	N5684C	6.10.93	P.R.Earp	Gloucestershire	5.12.04
G-DAIR	Luscombe 8A Master (Diesel Air 100hp)	1474	G-BURK N28713/NC28713	3.10.97	D.F.Soul	Standalone Farm, Meppershall	19.10.99P
G-DAIV	Ultramagic H-77 HAFB	77/184		2.11.00	D.Harrison-Morris	Ellesmere	

G-DAJB	Boeing 757-2T7ER	23770		26. 2.87	Monarch Airlines Ltd	Luton	13. 5.02T
G-DAJC	Boeing 767-31KER	27206		15. 4.94	Airtours International Airways Ltd		
						Manchester	14. 4.03T
G-DAKK	Douglas C-47A-35DL Skytrain	9798	(G-OFON)	26. 7.94	General Technics Ltd	Bournemouth	23. 5.02T
			F-GEOM/Fr Navy 36/OK-WZB/OK-WDU/42-23936 *(Op South Coast Airways)*				
G-DAKO	Piper PA-28-236 Dakota	28-7911187	PH-ARW	29. 7.99	Methods Application Ltd	(London WC2)	26. 8.02T
			(PH-MFB)/D-EECG/PH-ARW/OO-HCX/N29718				
G-DAMY	Europa Aviation Europa			21.10.94	M.J.Ashby-Arnold	RAF Leeming	18. 6.02P
	(Rotax 912-UL)	105 & PFA 247-12781					
G-DAND	SOCATA TB-10 Tobago	72		5.12.79	Whitemoor Engineering Co Ltd	Coventry	20. 9.04
G-DANT	Rockwell Commander 114	14298	N4978W	9. 7.96	D.P.Tierney	Biggin Hill	17. 7.02
G-DANY	Jabiru Jabiru UL	PFA 274A-13588		28.12.00	D.A.Crosbie	(Sudbury)	
G-DANZ	Eurocopter AS 355N Twin Squirrel	5658		14. 9.98	Frewton Ltd	Oxford	9. 2.02T
G-DAPH	Cessna 180K Skywagon II	18053016	N2620K	29. 1.92	M.R.L.Astor	East Hatley, Tadlow	18. 2.02
G-DARA	Piper PA-34-220T Seneca III		PH-TCT	8.11.88	Sys (Scaffolding Contractors) Ltd		
		34-8333060	N83JR/N4297J/N9632N			Gamston	11. 4.04
G-DARK	CFM Shadow DD	PFA 161-13308		13. 7.00	P.M.Dewhurst	Sywell	20..8.02P
G-DASH	Rockwell Commander 112A	237	G-BDAJ	31. 3.87	D.& M.Nelson	Bourn	26. 3.03
			N1237J				
G-DASI	Short SD.3-60 Var.100	SH.3606	G-14-3606	14. 2.83	Aerotek Aviation Engineering Ltd		
			G-BKKW		*(Dismantled 2000)*	(Poole)	21. 3.01T
G-DAST	Jodel DR.1050-M1	PFA 304-13351		27. 6.00	D.J.& K.S.Thomas *(Noted 11.01)*	(Spalding)	
G-DASU	Cameron V-77 HAFB	2300		6. 4.90	D. & L.S.Litchfield *"Borne Free"*	Reading	11. 8.97A
G-DATE	Agusta A109C	7633	G-RNLD	30. 3.00	Datel Direct Ltd	Stone	25. 7.02
			I-ANAG				
G-DATG	Reims Cessna F182P Skylane	F18200013	D-EATG	8.11.01	Hangar 8 Aviation Services Ltd	Oxford	
G-DAVD	Reims Cessna FR172K Hawk XP		D-EFJT	23.12.99	D M Driver	Elstree	23.12.02T
		FR17200632	(PH-ADL)/PH-AXO				
G-DAVE	Jodel D.112	667	F-BICH	16. 8.78	D.A.Porter	Griffins Farm, Temple Bruer	11. 3.02P
	(Built Ets Valladeau)						
G-DAVO	Gulfstream AA-5B Tiger	AA5B-1226	G-GAGA	5. 1.96	Kadala Aviation Ltd	Elstree	12. 2.04T
			G-BGPG/(G-BGRW)				
G-DAVT	Schleicher ASH26E	26090		24. 4.96	D.A.Triplett	Sleap	10. 5.02
G-DAYI	Europa Aviation Europa	PFA 247-13027		19. 8.96	A.F.Day	(West Wickham)	
G-DAYS	Europa Aviation Europa			9. 5.95	D.J.Bowie	Sleap	21. 7.02P
	(Rotax 912-UL)	177 & PFA 247-12810					
G-DAYZ	Pietenpol Aircamper	PFA 047-12342		22. 6.01	J.G.Cronk	(Chichester)	
G-DBAL*	Hawker Siddeley HS.125 Srs.3B	25117	G-BSAA	20. 7.84	Southampton Airport Fire Services		
			5N-AKT/5N-AET			Southampton	16. 6.92
			(Cancelled 16.4.93 as WFU:.on fire dump 11.95: current status unknown)				
G-DBDB	VPM M16 Tandem Trainer	PFA 0G/12-1239		19.10.99	D.R.Bolsover	(Lossiemouth)	28. 5.02P
G-DBHH	Agusta-Bell 206B JetRanger II	8111	G-AWVO	24. 5.96	UK Helicopter Charter Ltd	Rochester	22. 6.04T
			VH-BHI/PK-HCA/G-AWVO/9Y-TDN/PK-HBG/G-AWVO				
G-DBYE	Mooney M.20M	27-0098	N91462	24. 3.98	A.J.Thomas	Cranfield	5. 4.04
G-DCAV	Piper PA-32R-301 Saratoga IIHP		N92864	8. 5.97	S.Dixon-Smith	Fowlmere	15 .5.03
		3246075	G-DCAV		t/a Lyons Aviation		
G-DCDB	Bell 407	53137	C-FCDB	19.10.99	Paycourt Ltd	Knocksedan	19.10.02T
			N7238A				
G-DCEA	Piper PA-34-200T Seneca II		N3567D	13. 2.91	Bristol Flying Centre Ltd	Bristol	12. 7.03T
		34-8070079					
G-DCKK	Reims Cessna F172N Skyhawk II		PH-GRT	19. 5.80	J.Maffia	Panshanger	24. 4.04T
		F17201589	PH-AXA				
G-DCOM	Robinson R44 Clipper	0780		2. 6.00	Burlington Publishing Ltd	Manston	5. 7.03T
G-DCPA	MBB BK-117C-1C	7511	D-HECU	16.12.97	Devon & Cornwall Constabulary	Exeter	16. 6.02T
			D-HXXL/G-LFBA/D-HECU/D-HMBF				
G-DCSE	Robinson R44 Astro	0659		23. 9.99	DCS Europe plc	Gloucestershire	28. 9.02T
G-DCXL	SAN Jodel D.140C Mousquetaire III		F-BKSM	27. 5.88	C.F.Mugford	Little Gransden	16. 3.03
		101			t/a X-Ray Lima Group		
G-DDAY	Piper PA-28R-201T Turbo Arrow III		G-BPDO	24.11.88	K.E.Hogg	Tatenhill	15. 4.04
		28R-7703112	N3496Q		t/a G-DDAY Group		
G-DDMV	North American T-6G-NF Texan	168-313	N3240N	30. 4.90	E.A.Morgan	(Sywell)	3. 2.03
			Haitian AF 3209/49-3209 *(As "493209" in Californian ANG c/s) (Sold 11.01)*				
G-DDOG	Scottish Aviation Bulldog Srs.120/121		XX524	18. 6.01	Gamit Ltd	North Weald	
		BH120/210			*(Noted 7.01)*		
G-DEAN	Solar Wings Pegasus XL-Q		G-MVJV	30.11.98	D.C.P.Cardey & G.D.Tannahill	Hereford	10. 9.01P
	(Rotax 462)	SW-TE-0117 & SW-WQ-0123					
G-DEBE	British Aerospace BAe 146 Srs.200		N163US	5. 8.96	Cityjet Ltd	Dublin	6. 8.02T
		E2022	N346PS				
G-DEBR	Europa Aviation Europa	PFA 247-12922		31. 1.01	A J Calvert & C T Smallwood		
						(Buxton/Ripley)	
G-DECK	Cessna T210N Turbo Centurion		N958MK	29. 2.00	R.J.Howard	Sherburn-in-Elmet	16. 3.03
		21064017	D-ERDK/N4834Y				
G-DEER	Robinson R22 Beta-II	2827		17. 7.98	Mightgreat Ltd	(Godalming)	28. 7.04T

G-DEFK	British Aerospace BAe 146 Srs.200	E2012	G-DEBK C-FHAV/N601AW	22.10.99	Flightline Ltd *"Skoda Auto Business Sales"*	Southend	25. 4.02T
G-DEFL	British Aerospace BAe 146 Srs.200	E2014	G-DEBL C-FHAX/N602AW	22.10.99	Flightline Ltd	Aberdeen	28. 1.02T
G-DEFM	British Aerospace BAe 146 Srs.200	E2016	G-DEBM C-FHAZ	22.10.99	Flightline Ltd	Southend	16 .3.02T
G-DELF	Aero L-29A Delfin	194555	ES-YLM Soviet AF 12 (Red)	28. 8.97	B.R.Green *"12"*	Manston	26. 9.01P
G-DELT	Robinson R22 Beta	0898		11.11.88	J.Moodie t/a Jim Moodie Racing	(Hamilton)	15. 4.02T
G-DEMH	Reims Cessna F172M Skyhawk II (Lycoming O-360)	F17201137	G-BFLO PH-DMF/(EI-AYO)	18.11.91	M.Hammond	Crowfield/Hardwick	14. 6.04
G-DENA	Reims Cessna F150G	F150-0204	G-AVEO EI-BOI/G-AVEO	14.12.95	W.M.Wilson & R.Campbell	Sandtoft	20. 1.02T
G-DENB	Reims Cessna F150G	F150-0136	G-ATZZ	14.12.95	Skytrax Aviation Ltd	Spanhoe	11. 6.03T
G-DENC	Reims Cessna F150G	F150-0107	G-AVAP	14.12.95	M Dovey	Top Farm, Croydon	31.10.02T
G-DEND	Reims Cessna F150M	F15001201	G-WAFC G-BDFI/(OH-CGD)	6. 6.97	Deer Hill Aviation Ltd	Exeter	30. 9.04T
G-DENE	Piper PA-28-140 Cherokee	28-21710	G-ATOS N11C	5. 2.98	Avon Aviation Ltd t/a The Bristol and Wessex Aeroplane Club	Bristol	17. 6.02T
G-DENH	Piper PA-28-161 Warrior II	28-8216202	G-BTNH N253FT/N9577N	14. 4.97	Plane Talking Ltd	Blackbushe	8. 3.04T
G-DENI	Piper PA-32-300 Cherokee Six	32-7340006	G-BAIA N11C	7.12.95	A.Bendkowski	Rochester	29. 5.04T
G-DENN	Bell 206B-3 JetRanger III	4409	N75486	10. 6.96	Abbey Flight Ltd	Fairoaks	22. 7.02
G-DENR	Reims Cessna F172N Skyhawk II	F17201839	G-BGNR	30. 4.97	Den Air Aviation Ltd t/a Aviators Flight Center *(Noted w/o engine 1.02)*	Southend	22.10.00T
G-DENS	Binder CP.301S Smaragd *(Also carries c/n AB.429 denoting completion as Amateur Build)*	121	D-ENSA	20.11.85	G.E.Roe & I.S.Leader	Garston Farm, Marshfield	3. 9.02P
G-DENT	Cameron N-145 HAFB	4135		8. 4.97	Deproco UK Ltd	Dorking	6.11.01A
G-DENZ	Piper PA-44-180 Seminole	44-7995327	G-INDE G-BHNM/N8077X	3. 7.97	W.J.Greenfield	Humberside	31. 3.02T
G-DERB	Robinson R22 Beta	1005	G-BPYH	28. 6.95	S Thompson	(Leamington Spa)	3. 7.04T
G-DERV	Cameron Truck 56SS HAFB	1719		21. 3.88	J.M.Percival *"Shell UK Truck"*	Loughborough	22. 2.00A
G-DESS	Mooney M.20J (201)	24-1272	N11598	20.10.87	W.E.Newnes	Birmingham	22. 3.03
G-DEST	Mooney M.20J	24-3429		6.11.98	Allegro Aviation Ltd	(Guernsey)	12. 1.05
G-DESY	Cessna A152 Aerobat	A1520805	G-BNJE N7386L	20.10.97	Westair Flying Services Ltd	Blackpool	19. 4.03T
G-DEVS	Piper PA-28-180 Cherokee B	28-830	G-BGVJ D-ENPI/N7066W	5. 3.85	B.J.Hoptroff & J.M.Whiteley t/a 180 Group	Blackbushe	9. 1.02
G-DEWS	Grob G.109B	6504	D-KLEM	13. 3.00	R.G.Trute	Dunkeswell	17. 5.03
G-DEXP	ARV1 Super 2 (Hewland AE75)	003 & PFA 152-11154		24. 4.85	W.G.McKinnon	Perth	20. 4.02P
G-DEXY	Beechcraft E90 King Air	LW-136	N750DC N30CW/N84GA/N328TB/TR-LTT	6. 4.89	Specsavers Aviation Ltd	Guernsey	15. 3.02
G-DEZC	British Aerospace HS.125 Srs.700B	257070	G-BWCR G-5-604/HB-VGG/G-5-604/HB-VGG	28. 5.96	Bunbury Aviation Ltd	Guernsey	17. 7.02
G-DFLY	Piper PA-38-112 Tomahawk	38-79A0450	N9655N	15. 2.79	P.M.Raggett	(London SE9)	13. 6.03
G-DGCL	Glaser-Dirks DG-800B	8-185-B109		27. 3.00	C.J.Lowrie	Parham Park	19. 4.03
G-DGDG	Glaser-Dirks DG-400-17	4-27		25. 3.83	M.Clarke t/a DG-400 Flying Group	Lasham	28. 5.04
G-DGIV	Glaser Dirks DG-800B	8-145-B69		27.11.98	W.R.McNair	(Holywood, Co.of Down)	23.11.04
G-DGLM	Glaser Dirks DG-400	4-48	D-KMDH	2.12.99	L J McKelvie	(Lisburn, Co.of Down)	14.12.02
G-DGWW	Rand Robinson KR-2 (Hapi Magnum 75)	PFA 129-11044		7. 3.91	W.Wilson	Liverpool	27. 7.02P
G-DHCB	de Havilland DHC.2 Beaver 1 Floatplane	1450	G-BTDL XP779	20. 6.91	Seaflite Ltd *(Stored 2001)*	(Louchearnhead)	16. 9.97T
G-DHCC	de Havilland DHC.1 Chipmunk 22	C1/0393	WG321	28. 5.97	Eureka Aviation NV *(As "WG321")*	Antwerp, Belgium	21. 9.03
G-DHCI	de Havilland DHC.1 Chipmunk 22	C1/0884	G-BBSE WZ858	12. 7.89	Felthorpe Flying Group Ltd	Felthorpe	13.11.03
G-DHDV	de Havilland DH.104 Dove 8	04205	VP981	26.10.98	Air Atlantique Ltd	Coventry	12. 8.01T
G-DHJH	Airbus A321-211	1238	D-AVZL	7. 6.00	Airtours International Airways Ltd	Manchester	6. 6.03T
G-DHLB	Cameron N-90 HAFB	3261		20. 4.94	B.A.Bower	Seaton	28.10.96A
G-DHLI*	Colt World 90SS HAFB	2603		2. 6.94	Balloon Preservation Group *"DHL World" (Cancelled 9.4.99 as WFU)*	Kirdford	17.12.98A
G-DHLZ*	Colt 31A Air Chair HAFB	2604		2. 6.94	Balloon Preservation Group *"DHL Parcel" (Cancelled 9.4.99 as WFU)*	Kirdford	23. 7.99A
G-DHSS	de Havilland DH.112 Venom FB.50 (FB.1) *(Built F + W)*	836	J-1626	26. 3.99	D J L Wood *(As "WR360" in white RAF c/s)*	Bournemouth	19.10.01P
G-DHTM	de Havilland DH.82A Tiger Moth	PFA 157-11095		6. 1.86	E.G.Waite-Roberts *(Believed parts consumed within rebuild of G-APPN qv)*	(Basingstoke)	

G-DHTT	de Havilland DH.112 Venom FB.50 (FB.1) *(Built F + W)*	821	(G-BMOC) J-1611	17.10.96	D.J.Lindsay Wood *(Op Source Classic Jet Flight)* *(Noted 7.01 as "WR421" in all-red c/s)*	Bournemouth	17. 7.99P
G-DHUU	de Havilland DH.112 Venom FB.50 (FB.1) *(Built F + W)*	749	(G-BMOD) J-1539	26. 2.96	D.J.Lindsay Wood *(Op Source Classic Jet Flight) (As "WR410" in 6 Sqdn RAF c/s)*	Bournemouth	24. 5.02P
G-DHVV	de Havilland DH.115 Vampire T.55 *(Built F + W)* *(Reported as built with c/n 974)*	55092	U-1214	5. 9.91	Lindsay Wood Promotions Ltd *(Op Source Classic Jet Flight) (As "XE897" in 54 Sqdn RAF c/s)*	Bournemouth	5. 6.01P
G-DHWW	de Havilland DH.115 Vampire T.55 *(Built F + W)*	979	U-1219	5. 9.91	Lindsay Wood Promotions Ltd *(Op Source Classic Jet Flight) (As "XG775" in RN FOFT Yeovilton c/s)*	Bournemouth	24. 4.01P
G-DHXX	de Havilland DH.100 Vampire FB.6 *(Built F + W)*	682	J-1173	5. 9.91	Lindsay Wood Promotions Ltd *(Op Source Classic Jet Flight) (As "VT871" in 54 Sqdn RAF c/s)*	Bournemouth	14. 8.02P
G-DHYY	de Havilland DH.115 Vampire T.11	15112	WZ553	17. 3.95	Lindsay Wood Promotions Ltd *(Stored 3.96 as "WZ553/40")*	Bruntingthorpe	
G-DHZF	de Havilland DH.82A Tiger Moth	82309	G-BSTJ OO-MEH/OO-GEB/OO-MOR/RNeth AF A-13/PH-UFB/A-13/N9192	7. 7.99	M.R.Parker *(As "N9192" in RAF c/s)*	Sywell	14. 8.02
G-DHZZ	de Havilland DH.115 Vampire T.55 *(Built F + W)*	990	U-1230	5. 9.91	Lindsay Wood Promotions Ltd *(Op Source Classic Jet Flight) (As "WZ589" in 54 Sqdn RAF c/s)*	Bournemouth	18. 7.02P
G-DIAL	Cameron N-90 HAFB	1851		7.11.88	A.J.Street *"London"*	Exeter	11. 5.00A
G-DIAT	Piper PA-28-140 Cherokee Cruiser	28-7425322	G-BCGK N9594N	19. 7.89	The RAF Benevolent Fund Enterprises Ltd *(Op Disabled Flyers Group/Bristol & Wessex Aeroplane Club)*	Bristol	22. 2.04T
G-DICE	Enstrom F-28F	787	D-HANA	8.11.96	Dice Aviation Services Ltd	Goodwood	20.12.02T
G-DICK	Thunder Ax6-56Z HAFB	159		6. 7.78	R.D.Sargeant *"Dandag"*	(Switzerland)	31. 5.01A
G-DIET*	Lindstrand Drinks Can SS HAFB *(Diet Pepsi Can)*	220		1. 5.95	Pepsi Cola Overseas Ltd *(Cancelled 21.9.99 by CAA: current status unknown)*	Des Moines, IA, USA	19. 4.00A
G-DIGI	Piper PA-32-300 Cherokee Six	32-7940224	D-EIES N2947M	13.10.98	D.Stokes t/a Security UN Ltd Group	Stapleford	19.11.04T
G-DIKY	Murphy Rebel	PFA 232-13182		13. 2.98	R.J.P.Herivel	Alderney	
G-DIMB	Boeing 767-31KER	28865		28. 4.97	Airtours International Airways Ltd	Manchester	27. 4.03T
G-DIME	Rockwell Commander 114	14123	N49829	9. 3.88	H.B.Richardson	Badminton	9. 9.04
G-DINA	Gulfstream AA-5B Tiger	AA5B-1218	N4555Y	27. 2.81	J.Gosling & N.R.J.Mifflin t/a Portway Aviation	Shobdon	6. 5.02
G-DING	Colt 77A HAFB	1862		28. 6.91	G.J.Bell *"Dingbat"*	Albuquerque, NM, USA	25. 4.02A
G-DINK	Lindstrand Bulb SS HAFB	785		28. 6.01	Dinkelacker-Schwaben Brau AG	Stuttgart, Germany	22. 7.02A
G-DINO	Pegasus Quantum 15 (Rotax 582)	7225	G-MGMT	15.12.98	G.Van Der Gaag	Lower Mountpleasant, Chatteris	28. 7.02P
G-DINT	Bristol 156 Beaufighter IF	STAN B1 184604	3858M X7688	17. 6.91	T.E.Moore *(On rebuild from various ex Australian components 10.99)*	Rotary Farm, Hatch	
G-DIPI	Cameron Tub 80SS HAFB	1745		6. 5.88	R.A.Preston *"KP Choc Dips Tub"*	Bristol	11.12.98A
G-DIPS*	Taylor JT.1 Monoplane (VW 1500)	PFA 055-10320		19.12.78	B.J.Halls *(Cancelled 31.3.99 by CAA: fuselage stored 8.00)*	Sibsey	
G-DIRK	Glaser-Dirks DG-400	4-124	D-KEKT	18. 9.86	C.J.Lowrie	Rufforth	29. 1.02
G-DISK	Piper PA-24-250 Comanche	24-1197	G-APZG EI-AKW/N10F	9. 8.89	G.A.Burtenshaw t/a G-DIRK Syndicate	Guernsey	30. 5.03
G-DISO	SAN Jodel 150 Mascaret	24	9Q-CPK OO-APK/F-BLDT	16.12.86	P.F.Craven & J.H.Shearer	Cumbernauld	30. 5.02P
G-DIVA	Cessna R172K Hawk XPII	R1723071	N758FX	10. 2.86	Bob Crowe Aircraft Sales Ltd	Cranfield	3.10.04T
G-DIWY	Piper PA-32-300 Cherokee Six	32-40731	OY-DLW D-EHMW/N8931N	26.11.91	IFS Chemicals Ltd	East Winch	6. 6.04
G-DIXY	Piper PA-28-181 Archer III	2843195	N41284 G-DIXY/N41284	10.12.98	L J & T J Francis t/a Dixyair	Fowlmere	16.12.04T
G-DIZO	Jodel Wassmer D.120A Paris-Nice	326	G-EMKM F-BOBG	30. 5.91	D. & E.Aldersea	Breighton	17. 1.02P
G-DIZY	Piper PA-28R-201T Turbo Cherokee Arrow III	28R-7703401	N47570	13.10.88	Calverton Flying Club Ltd	Cranfield	11. 4.04T
G-DIZZ	Hughes 369HE	89-0105E	N9029F	19. 2.97	H.J.Pelham	Cleeves Farm, Salisbury	19. 6.03
G-DJAE	Cessna 500 Citation I	500-0339	G-JEAN N300EC/N707US/G-JEAN/(N5339J)	3.11.98	Source Group Ltd	Bournemouth	27. 3.02T
G-DJAR	Airbus A320-231	0164	OY-CNE (D-ACSL)/OY-CNE/F-WWIE	18. 3.97	Airtours International Airways Ltd	Manchester	17. 3.03T
G-DJAY	Jabiru Jabiru UL-450	PFA 274A-13633		8. 8.00	D.J.Pearce	(Reading)	13 .5.02P
G-DJCR	Varga 2150A Kachina	VAC 155-80	EI-CFK G-BLWG/OO-HTD/N8360J	11. 4.96	D.J.C.Robertson	Perth	30. 4.99
G-DJEA	Cessna 421C Golden Eagle II	421C0654	TC-AAA N37379/(N24BS)/N37379	16. 4.98	Bettany Aircraft Holdings Ltd	Jersey	11.10.01
G-DJHB	Beechcraft A23-19 Musketeer Sport III	MB-200	G-AZZE LN-TVH	6. 8.82	W.B.Murray t/a Nayland Aiglet Group	Hill Farm, Nayland	15. 7.02
G-DJJA	Piper PA-28-181 Archer II	28-8490014	N4326D	14. 9.87	B.Cheese & S.M.Price t/a Choice Aircraft *(Op Modern Air)*	Fowlmere	18.12.02T

G-DJNH	Denney Kitfox mk.3 (Rotax 582)	772 & PFA 172-11896		20. 9.90	D.J.N.Hall	Downwood, Dorset	29. 5.01P
G-DKDP	Grob G-109	6100	(G-BMBD) D-KAMS	9. 7.85	D.W. & J.E.Page	Tibenham	28.11.03
G-DKGF*	Viking Dragonfly mk.1 (VW 1834)	PFA 0139-10898		16.10.86	P.C.Dowbor *(Stored 9.00: cancelled 29.3.01 by CAA: dumped less engine 7.01)*	Enstone	
G-DLCB	Europa Aviation Europa (Rotax 912-UL)	46 & PFA 247-12652		16.11.95	D.J.Lockett & C.R.C.Bowen	Knockbain Farm, Dingwall	8. 5.02P
G-DLDL	Robinson R22 Beta	1971		2. 1.92	Blue Oak Developments Ltd	(Thetford)	5. 4.04T
G-DLFN	Aero L-29 Delfin	294872	ES-YLE Estonian AF/Soviet AF	28. 5.98	T.W.Freeman & N.Gooderham	Southend	26.11.01P
G-DLOM	SOCATA TB-20 Trinidad	1102	N2823Y	13.12.90	J.N.A.Adderley	Rochester	12. 7.04
G-DLTR	Piper PA-28-180 Cherokee E	28-5803	G-AYAV N11C	15. 3.96	BCT Aircraft Leasing Ltd *(Op Bristol & Wessex Aero Club)*	Bristol	18. 7.02T
G-DMAC	Jabiru Jabiru UL (Jabiru 2200A)	PFA 274-13321		15.10.98	C.J.Pratt	Goodwood	16. 7.02P
G-DMAH	SOCATA TB-20 Trinidad GT	2039	F-OILY	2. 4.01	D.M.A.Hutchinson	Gamston	9. 4.04T
G-DMCA	McDonnell Douglas DC-10-30	48266	N3016Z	12. 3.96	Monarch Airlines Ltd *(Stored 1.02)*	Manchester	11. 3.02T
G-DMCD	Robinson R22 Beta	1201	G-OOLI G-DMCD	14.11.89	R.W.Pomphrett	Denham	10.12.01T
G-DMCS	Piper PA-28R-200 Cherokee Arrow II	28R-7635284	G-CPAC PH-SMW/OO-HAU/N75220	29. 5.84	W.G.Ashton & J Bingley t/a Arrow Associates	(Wokingham)	19. 4.02T
G-DMCT	Flight Design CT2K	01-04-02-12		10. 7.01	D.McCormack	Broomhill Farm, West Calder	18. 7.02P
G-DMSS	Westland SA.341D Gazelle HT.3	1089	XW858	13. 7.01	MSS Holdings Ltd *(As "XW858")*	Blackpool	
G-DMWW	CFM Shadow DD (Rotax 582)	304-DD		12.10.98	Microlight Sport Aviation Ltd	Lower Mountpleasant, Chatteris	25. 5.02P
G-DNCN	Agusta-Bell 206A Jet Ranger	8185	9H-AAJ Libyan Arab Rep.AF 8185/5A-BAM	21.11.97	J.J.Woodhouse t/a Flying Services	Sandown	16. 1.04T
G-DNCS	Piper PA-28R-201T Turbo Arrow III	28R-7803024	N47841	3. 1.89	BC Arrow Ltd.	Barton	11. 4.04
G-DNGR	Colt 31A HAFB	10162		18.10.01	G.J.Bell	Wokingham	30. 9.02A
G-DNLB	MBB Bö.105DBS-4 *(Rebuilt with new pod S.850 1992)*	S.60/850	G-BUDP G-BTBD/VH-LCS/VH-HRM/G-BCDH/EC-DUO/G-BCDH/D-HDBK	10. 4.92	Bond Air Services *(Op Northern Lighthouse Board)*	(Stromness)	23. 4.04T
G-DNOP	Piper PA-46-350P Malibu Mirage	4636303	N4174A	26. 7.00	Campbell Aviation Ltd	Denham	3..8.03T
G-DNVT	Gulfstream Gulfstream IV	1078	(G-BPJM) N17589	29. 9.89	Shell Aircraft Ltd	Rotterdam, The Netherlands	28. 9.03T
G-DOBN	Cessna 402B II	402B1243	N24PL N4604G	25. 4.96	Fraggle Leasing Ltd *(Op Ediinburgh Air Centre)*	Edinburgh	27. 6.03T
G-DOCA	Boeing 737-436	25267		21.10.91	British Airways plc *(Benyhone Tartan t/s)*	Heathrow	20.12.03T
G-DOCB	Boeing 737-436	25304		16.10.91	British Airways plc *(Wings t/s)*	Gatwick	15. 2.04T
G-DOCD	Boeing 737-436	25349		6.11.91	British Airways plc *(Animals & Trees t/s)*	Heathrow	6. 5.04T
G-DOCE	Boeing 737-436	25350		20.11.91	British Airways plc *(Blomsterang t/s)*	Heathrow	6. 8.04T
G-DOCF	Boeing 737-436	25407		9.12.91	British Airways plc *(Koguty Lowickie t/s)*	Heathrow	9. 7.04T
G-DOCG	Boeing 737-436	25408		16.12.91	British Airways plc *(Chelsea Rose t/s)*	Gatwick	15. 8.04T
G-DOCH	Boeing 737-436	25428		19.12.91	British Airways plc *(Grand Union t/s)*	Heathrow	18. 8.04T
G-DOCI	Boeing 737-436	25839		8. 1.92	British Airways plc	Gatwick	7. 1.05T
G-DOCJ	Boeing 737-436	25840		15. 1.92	British Airways plc *(Sold to Comair 2002 as ZS-OTG)*	Gatwick	14. 1.05T
G-DOCK	Boeing 737-436	25841		25. 2.92	British Airways plc *(Sold to Comair 2002 as ZS-OTI)*	Heathrow	24. 2.02T
G-DOCL	Boeing 737-436	25842		2. 3.92	British Airways plc *(Ndebele Martha t/s)*	Heathrow	1. 3.02T
G-DOCM	Boeing 737-436	25843		19. 3.92	British Airways plc *(Rendezvous t/s)*	Gatwick	18. 3.02T
G-DOCN	Boeing 737-436	25848		21.10.92	British Airways plc	Gatwick	20.10.02T
G-DOCO	Boeing 737-436	25849		26.10.92	British Airways plc *(Sold to Comair 2002 as ZS-OTJ?)*	Gatwick	25.10.02T
G-DOCP	Boeing 737-436	25850		2.11.92	British Airways plc	Gatwick	1.11.02T
G-DOCR	Boeing 737-436	25851		6.11.92	British Airways plc *(Waves of the City t/s)*	Gatwick	5.11.02T
G-DOCS	Boeing 737-436	25852		1.12.92	British Airways plc	Gatwick	30.11.02T
G-DOCT	Boeing 737-436	25853		22.12.92	British Airways plc *(Crossing Borders t/s)*	Gatwick	23.12.02T
G-DOCU	Boeing 737-436	25854		18. 1.93	British Airways plc *(Ndebele Martha t/s)*	Heathrow	19. 1.03T

G-DOCV	Boeing 737-436	25855		25. 1.93	British Airways plc *(Benyhone Tartan t/s*	Heathrow	24. 1.03T
G-DOCW	Boeing 737-436	25856		2. 2.93	British Airways plc *(Rendezvous t/s)*	Heathrow	3. 2.03T
G-DOCX	Boeing 737-436	25857		29. 3.93	British Airways plc *(Colum t/s)*	Gatwick	28. 3.03T
G-DOCY	Boeing 737-436	25844	OO-LTQ G-BVBY/TC-ALS/G-BVBY/(G-DOCY)	17.10.96	British Airways plc	Heathrow	17.10.02T
G-DOCZ	Boeing 737-436	25858	EC-FXJ EC-657/G-BVBZ/(G-DOCZ)	12.12.94	British Airways plc	Heathrow	11. 1.04T
G-DODB	Robinson R22 Beta	0911	N8005R	3. 5.96	Exmoor Helicopters Ltd	Withiel Farm, Minehead	29. 7.02T
G-DODD	Reims Cessna F172P Skyhawk II	F17202175		5.10.82	K.Watts	Denham	4.10.98
G-DODI	Piper PA-46-350P Malibu Mirage	4636019		26.10.95	CAVOK SRL	(Milan)	22. 2.04T
G-DODR	Robinson R22 Beta	1325	N80721	5. 6.96	Exmoor Helicopters Ltd	Withiel Farm, Minehead	25. 7.04T
G-DOEA	Gulfstream AA-5A Cheetah	AA5A-0895	G-RJMI N27170	30. 4.96	Plane Talking Ltd *(Op Cabair Aerospace Education Sevice)* *(Duke of Edinburgh Award & BAE c/s)*	Elstree	28. 7.03T
G-DOFY	Bell 206B-3 JetRanger III	3637	N2283F	26. 8.87	Cinnamond Ltd *(Op Cabair Helicopters)*	Elstree	8. 6.02T
G-DOGG	Scottish Aviation Bulldog Srs.120/121	BH120/308	XX638	3.10.01	P.Sengupta	(Guildford)	
G-DOGZ	Rogerson Horizon 1 *(Marked as "Fisher Super Koala")*	PFA 241-13129		10. 8.98	J.E.D.Rogerson	Morgansfield, Fishburn	19. 9.02P
G-DOIT	Aérospatiale AS350B2 Ecureuil	1902	F-GMAZ LN-OTA/SE-JAC/LN-OBD/(F-GHYU)/LN-OBD/SE-JAC/HB-XPH	10.10.01	C.C.Blakey	Redhill	22.11.04T
G-DOLY	Cessna T303 Crusader	T30300107	N303MK G-BJZK/(N3645C)	20. 7.94	R.M.Jones	Blackpool	14. 9.03
G-DOME	Piper PA-28-161 Warrior III	2842062	N4160V	12. 1.00	Wakelite Ltd *(Op Denham School of Flying)*	Denham	16. 1.03T
G-DONG	Sky 105-24 HAFB	011	G-BWKP	5. 2.97	G.J.Bell *"Ting A Ling"*	Albuquerque, NM, USA	15.10.01A
G-DONI	Gulfstream AA-5B Tiger	AA5B-1029	G-BLLT OO-RTG/(OO-HRS)	20. 7.95	N.J.Bond	(Tiverton)	7.12.03
G-DONS	Piper PA-28RT-201T Turbo Arrow IV	28R-8131077	N8336L	22. 4.88	D.J.Murphy t/a Arrow One Group	Blackbushe	8.10.03
G-DONZ	Europa Aviation Europa	PFA 247-12545		1. 6.94	D.J.Smith & D.McNicholl *(On build 2000)*	Knockbain Fram, Dingwall	
G-DOOZ	Aérospatiale AS355F2 Twin Squirrel	5367	G-BNSX	13. 5.88	Lynton Aviation Ltd t/a Signature Aircraft Charter	Blackbushe	4. 4.03T
G-DORB	Bell 206B-3 JetRanger III	3955	SE-HTI TC-HBN	15. 8.90	Dorbcrest Homes Ltd	Wrightington, Wigan	28.11.02
G-DORN	Dornier EKW C-3605	332	HB-RBJ SwissAF C-552	15. 5.98	R.G.Gray *(As "C-552")*	Bournemouth	11.11.02P
G-DOVE	Cessna 182Q Skylane II	18266724	N96446	26. 6.80	Carel Investments Ltd	(Alderney)	24. 7.04
G-DOWN	Colt 31A Air Chair HAFB	1570		3. 8.89	M.Williams *"Up & Down"*	Wadhurst, Sussex	8. 6.00A
G-DPPH	Agusta A109E Power	11053	G-BYMS	17.11.99	Dyfed-Powys Police Authority *(Op Heddlu Dyfed Powys Police)*	Carmarthen	9.12.02T
G-DPSP	McDonnell Douglas DC-10-10	46646	OY-CNS SE-DHS/N913WA	12. 9.00	Airtours International Airways Ltd	Manchester	26.10.03T
G-DPST	Phillips ST-2 Speedtwin	PFA 207-12674		10. 5.96	Speedtwin Developments Ltd	Upper Cae Garw Farm, Trelleck, Monmouth	
G-DPUK	Mooney M.20K (231)	25-0631	G-BNZS N1154A	2. 4.98	K.A.Horne	Gamston	12 4.03
G-DRAG	Cessna 152 II *(Tail-wheel conversion)*	15283188	G-REME G-DRAG/G-BRNF/N47217	27. 4.90	L.A.Maynard & M.E.Scouller *(Op Old Sarum Flying Club)*	Old Sarum	5. 8.02T
G-DRAM	Reims FR172F Rocket *(Floatplane)*	FR17200102	OH-CNS	18. 9.98	T.A.Crumpton t/a Clyde River Rats	(Lochearnhead)	4. 2.02T
G-DRAW	Colt 77A HAFB	1830		31. 8.90	C.Wolstenholme	Oswestry	29. 6.02A
G-DRAY	Taylor JT-1 Monoplane	PFA 1452		13. 7.78	L.J.Dray	(Sidmouth)	
G-DRBG	Cessna 172M Skyhawk	17265263	G-MUIL N64486	18. 1.95	Wilkins & Wilkins (Special Auctions) t/a Henlow Flying Club Ltd	RAF Henlow	13. 5.04T
G-DREX	Cameron Saturn 110SS HAFB	4217		28.10.97	LRC Products Ltd	Broxbourne, Herts	3.11.99A
G-DREY	Cessna 172R Skyhawk	17280781	N23726	16.11.99	C.J.& J.M.Wardill	Booker	24.11.02T
G-DRGN	Cameron N-105 HAFB	2024		13. 6.91	W.I.Hooker & C.Parker	Nottingham	4. 7.01T
G-DRGS	Cessna 182S	18280375	N2389X	17.11.98	Walter Scott and Partners Ltd	Edinburgh	14.12.01
G-DRHL	Eurocopter AS 350B2 Ecureuil	3032		12. 1.98	Lytonworth Ltd	Wellesbourne Mountford	29. 4.04T
G-DRKJ	Schweizer Hughes 269C (300C)	S.1172	G-BPPW N3624J	19.10.00	D.R.Kenyon t/a Aviation Bureau	Shoreham	27. 9.04T
G-DRMM	Europa Aviation Europa	PFA 247-13201		27. 7.98	M.W.Mason	(Nantwich)	
G-DRNT	Sikorsky S-76A II Plus	760201	N93WW N3WQ/N3WL/N3121G	5. 4.90	CHC Scotia Ltd *(See SECTION 9. Part 2 (ii) also)*	North Denes	1. 5.03T

G-DROP	Cessna U206C Super Skywagon	U2061230	G-UKNO	7. 8.87	Peterborough Parachute Centre Ltd	Sibson	2. 3.03
			G-BAMN/4X-ALL/N71943				
G-DRSV	Robin DR.315X Petit Prince	624	F-ZWRS	7. 6.90	R.S.Voice	Rushett Manor, Chessington	6.12.01P
	(Regd with c/n PFA 0210-11765 following major rebuild)						
G-DRUM	Thruster TST Mk.1	8068-TST-081	G-MVBR	12. 1.99	C.C.Mercer	Saltash	3. 3.01P
	(Rotax 503)				*(Wings stored Longbridge Deverill 12.01)*		
G-DRYI	Cameron N-77 HAFB	2046		7. 8.89	C.A.Butter *"Barbour"*	Marsh Benham	4. 6.94A
G-DRYS	Cameron N-90 HAFB	3377		1.12.95	C.A.Butter	Marsh Benham	20. 4.02A
G-DRZF	CEA DR.360 Chevalier	451	F-BRZF	4. 9.91	Mavis R.Parker	Sywell	6.12.03
G-DSFT	Piper PA-28R-200 Cherokee Arrow II		G-LFSE	22.11.00	Plane Talking Ltd	Elstree	7. 4.02T
		28R-7335157	G-BAXT/N11C				
G-DSGC	Piper PA-25-260 Pawnee C	25-4890	OY-BDA	3. 5.95	Devon & Somerset Gliding Club Ltd		
						North Hill	14. 8.01
G-DSID	Piper PA-34-220T Seneca	3447001		21. 7.95	R.Howton	Biggin Hill	4. 9.04
G-DSLL	Pegasus Quantum 15-912	7836		5. 7.01	D.Luke	Kemble	4. 7.02P
G-DSPI	Robinson R44 Astro	0661	G-DPSI	25.10.99	D.S.Phelps	(Alresford)	4.11.02T
G-DTCP	Piper PA-32R-300 <u>Lance</u>	32R-7780255	G-TEEM	26. 1.93	C.J.Mewis & T.I.Mason	Kemble	22. 4.04
			N2604Q		t/a Plane Hire		
G-DTOO*	Piper PA-38-112 Tomahawk	38-79A0312	N9713N	15. 2.79	Not known	Panshanger	29. 7.94T
		(Damaged Seething 9.7.94: cancelled 31.1.95 as WFU:fuselage stored 9.00: current status unknown)					
G-DUDE	Van's RV-8	PFA 303-13246		16. 7.99	W.M.Hodgkins	(Stadhampton)	
G-DUDS	CASA I-131E Jungmann	2108	D-EHDS	27. 6.90	B R Cox	(Bristol)	3. 6.00P
	(Enma Tigre G-1V-B)		E3B-512				
G-DUDZ	Robin DR.400/180 <u>Regent</u>	2367	G-BXNK	3.12.97	D.H.Pattison	Lower Upham Farm, Chiseldon	26.11.03
G-DUET	Wood Duet	D.001		19.12.78	C.Wood	(Aston Clinton)	
	(Thought to be modified Brugger Colibri c/n PFA 043-10468)						
G-DUGI	Lindstrand LBL 90A HAFB	562		16. 8.99	D.J.Cook	Norwich	25. 6.02A
G-DUKK	Extra EA.300/L	125	D-EXAC	27.11.00	R.A.& K.M.Roberts	Goodwood	14.12.03
					t/a Puddleduck Plane Partnership		
G-DUNG	Sky 65-24 HAFB	125		20. 7.98	G.J.Bell	Albuquerque, NM, USA	15.10.01A
G-DUNN	Zenair CH.200	AD-1 & PFA 024-10450		5.10.78	A.Dunn	(Lancing)	
	(Lycoming O-320)				t/a Chevalier Flying Group		
					(Under construction 1988: current status unknown)		
G-DURO	Europa Aviation Europa	PFA 247-12554		15.11.93	D.J.Sagar	Bidford	2 .4.02P
	(Rotax 912-UL)						
G-DURX	Colt 77A HAFB	1522		25. 5.89	V.Trimble	Henley-on-Thames	26. 6.02A
					(Durex/Avanti titles)		
G-DUSK	de Havilland DH.115 Vampire T.Mk.11		XE856	1. 2.99	R.M.A.Robinson & R.Horsfield	RAF Henlow	
		15596			*(On rebuild 10.99: current status unknown)*		
G-DUST	Stolp SA.300 Starduster Too	JP-2	N233JP	28. 4.88	J.V.George	(Winchester)	22. 5.90P
	(Lycoming O-360)		*(Damaged in collision with G-AKTM Badminton 16.7.89: on rebuild 2001)*				
G-DUVL	Reims Cessna F172N Skyhawk II		G-BFMU(1)	16. 8.78	A.J.Simpson	White Waltham	26. 6.02
		F17201723					
G-DVON	de Havilland DH.104 Devon C.2/2		(G-BLPD)	26.10.84	C.L.Thatcher	Kemble	29. 5.96
		04201	VP955		t/a The 955 Preservation Group *(As "VP955": stored 12.00)*		
G-DWIA	Chilton DW.1A	PFA 225-12256		25. 1.93	D.Elliott	(Horsham)	
G-DWIB	Chilton DW.1B	PFA 225-12374		22.12.93	J.Jennings	(Bedford)	
G-DWMS	Jabiru Jabiru UL-450			21. 6.00	D.H.S.Williams	Sutton Meadows, Ely	
		0266 & PFA 274A-13491			*(Under construction 5.01)*		
G-DWPH	Ultramagic M-77 HAFB	77/109		17. 3.95	Jennifer M.Robinson	Chipping Norton	21. 6.01
					t/a Ultramagic UK *"Miguel"*		
G-DYNE	Cessna 414 Chancellor	414-0070	N8170Q	4. 8.87	Commair Aviation Ltd	Nottingham	3. 9.02
					t/a Commodore International		
G-DYNG	Colt 105A HAFB	1721	G-HSHS	9. 2.98	M.J.Gunston *"High Society"*	Camberley	16.10.01A
G-DYOU*	Piper PA-38-112 Tomahawk	38-78A0436	N9737N	19.10.78	Not known	Booker	3. 3.94T
			(Damaged Booker 23.7.92: cancelled 24.5.95 as WFU: hulk dumped 11.01)				

G-EAAA – G-EZZZ (see SECTION 1, PART 1 for details of original 1919 to 1928 registrations)

G-EAGA(2)	Sopwith Dove rep	"3004/1"	(G-BLOO)	22.11.89	A.Wood	Old Warden	16. 5.01P
	(Le Rhone 80hp)				*(On loan to The Shuttleworth Collection)*		
	(Orig Dove G-EAGA, c/n 3004/1, exported to Australia & in use as K-157, by 11.12.19. Remains of unregistered Dove, thought to have been K-157, which crashed Essendon, Victoria 9.3.30 brought to UK circa 1987/88 & rebuilt as G-BLOO)						
G-EAVX(2)	Sopwith Pup	PFA 101-10523	B1807	16. 1.87	K.A.M.Baker	(Winscombe, Somerset)	
	(Claimed as rebuild of original a/c written-off Hendon 21.7.21 & cancelled: to carry "B1807/A7" in RFC c/s: current status uncertain)						
G-EBJI(2)	Hawker Cygnet rep	PFA 077-10240		9. 8.77	C.J.Essex	(Coventry)	
					(Under construction 7.99: current status unknown)		
G-EBZN(2)	de Havilland DH.60X Moth	608	VP-NAA	28.10.88	Jane Hodgkinson	(Gravesend)	
	(Cirrus I)		VP-YAA/ZS-AAP/G-UAAP				
			(On rebuild from original components: current status unknown)				
G-ECAB	Curtiss JN-4D	1917	N2525	28. 5.99	V.S.E.Norman	Rendcomb	
	(Curtiss OX-5)						

G-ECAH	Fokker F.27 Friendship Mk.500	10669	G-JEAH	14. 4.00	Euroceltic Airways Ltd	Exeter	14. 2.03T
			VH-EWY/PH-EXL		*(Op BAC Express)*		
G-ECAN	de Havilland DH.84 Dragon	2048	VH-DHX	11. 1.01	A.J. Norman	Chilbolton	
			VH-AQU/RAAF A34-59		t/a Norman Aeroplane Trust *(On rebuild 10.01)*		
	(Built de Havilland Aircraft Pty Ltd, Bankstown, Australia)						
G-ECAS	Boeing 737-36N	28554		16.12.96	British Midland Airways Ltd		
						East Midlands	19.12.02T
G-ECAT	Fokker F.27 Friendship Mk.500	10672	G-JEAI	14. 4.00	Euroceltic Airways Ltd	Exeter	16.12.02T
			VH-EWZ/PH-EXS		*(Op BAC Express)*		
G-ECBH	Reims Cessna F150K	F15000577	D-ECBH	16. 5.85	G.Harber	Haverfordwest	26. 8.02T
					t/a ECBH Flying Group		
G-ECCC	Extra EA.300/L	126	D-EDGE	19. 2.01	Extraviation Ltd	North Weald	13. 3.04T
G-ECDX	de Havilland DH.71 Tiger Moth rep			1.11.94	M.D.Souch & N.Parkhouse		
	(DH Gipsy I)	SP.7			*(Under build 2001)*	Hill Farm, Durley	
G-ECGC	Reims Cessna F172N Skyhawk II			10.10.79	Euroair Flying Club Ltd	Cranfield	26. 7.04T
		F17201850					
G-ECGO	Bölkow Bö.208C Junior	599	D-ECGO	24. 8.89	A Flight Aviation Ltd	Prestwick	30. 3.03T
					(Op Prestwick Flying Club)		
G-ECHO	Enstrom 280C-UK-2 Shark	1017	G-LONS	28. 5.82	A.L.Pattinson	Oaksey Park	1. 6.03
			G-BDIB		t/a ALP Electrical (Maidenhead)		
G-ECJM	Piper PA-28R-201T Turbo Arrow III		G-FESL	25. 9.90	Regishire Ltd	Southampton	4. 3.04
		28R-7803178	G-BNRN/N321EC/N3561M				
G-ECKE	Avro 504K rep	0014		6.10.93	Propshop Ltd	Duxford	25. 4.02P
	(Warner Scarab SS-50 145hp) *(Built AJD Engineering Ltd)*				*(As "D8781" in RFC c/s)*		
G-ECLI	Schweizer 269C	S 1784	N69A	16. 7.99	Eclipse (UK) Ltd	(Taunton)	22. 8.02
G-ECOS	Aérospatiale AS355F1 Twin Squirrel		G-DOLR	24. 9.92	Multiflight Ltd	Leeds-Bradford	20.11.03T
		5300	G-BPVB/OH-HAJ/D-HEHN		*(Op Northern Helicopters (Leeds) Ltd)*		
G-ECOX	Grega GN.1 Air Camper			5.12.78	H.C.Cox	(Bristol)	
		WLAW.1 & PFA 047-10356			*(Under construction 2001)*		
G-ECVB	Pietenpol Aircamper	PFA 047-13014		20. 4.00	K.S.Matcham	(Southampton)	
G-ECZZ	Eurocopter EC 120B	1053		15.10.99	Kensington & Chelsea Aviation Ltd		
						Redhill	21.10.02T
G-EDAV	Scottish Aviation Bulldog Srs.120/121		XX534	8. 8.01	Edwalton Aviation Ltd	(Nottingham)	
		BH120/220					
G-EDEN	SOCATA TB-10 Tobago	66		8. 1.80	N.G.Pistol, J.R.Priest, G.W.Bevan & A.K.Hilton		
						Elstree	17. 4.02
G-EDFS	Pietenpol Aircamper	PFA 047-13206		24. 3.98	D.F.Slaughter	(Redhill)	
G-EDGE	Jodel 150 Mascaret			14. 9.88	A.D.Edge	(Derby)	
	(Continental O-200-A) 111 & PFA 151-11223				*(Under construction 2000)*		
G-EDGI	Piper PA-28-161 Warrior	28-7916565	D-EBGI	19. 1.99	R.A.Forster	Cardiff	14..2.02
			N2941R				
G-EDMC	Pegasus Quantum 15-912	7513		11. 3.99	E.McCallum	Eshott	15. 3.02P
G-EDNA	Piper PA-38-112 Tomahawk	38-78A0364	OY-BRG	4. 9.84	D.J.Clucas	Woodford	7.12.02T
G-EDRV	Van's RV-6A	PFA 181A-13451		20. 8.99	E.A.Yates	(Harlow)	
G-EDTO	Reims FR172F Rocket	FR17200090	D-EDTQ	21. 3.01	N.G.Hopkinson	Fenland	29. 4.04
G-EDVL	Piper PA-28R-200 Cherokee Arrow II		G-BXIN	30. 6.97	J.S.Develin & Z.Islam	Shoreham	24. 5.03T
		28R-7235245	D-EDVL/N1243T		*(Op Sky Leisure)*		
G-EECO	Lindstrand LBL 25A Cloudhopper HAFB			1. 2.00	P.A.Bubb & A.J.Allen	Guildford	7. 5.02A
		668					
G-EEGL	Christen Eagle II	AES/01/0353	5Y-EGL	14.12.90	A.J.Wilson	Deenethorpe	11. 7.02P
	(Lycoming AEIO-360)						
G-EEJE	Piper PA-31 Navajo B	31-825	OH-PNG	18. 5.01	Geeje Ltd	(Fadmoor, York)	6. 8.04T
G-EELS	Cessna 208B Caravan I	208B0619		3. 3.97	Glass Eels Ltd	Gloucestershire	26. 7.03T
G-EENA	Piper PA-32R-301 Saratoga SP		C-GBBU	3.10.97	Gamit Ltd	Andrewsfield	20. 6.04
		32R-8013011					
G-EENI	Europa Aviation Europa	PFA 247-12831		28. 7.98	M.P.Grimshaw	(London W5)	
G-EENY	Gulfstream GA-7 Cougar	GA7-0094	N721G	21. 6.79	J.P.E.Walsh	Cranfield	20. 7.03T
					t/a Walsh Aviation *(Op Cabair)*		
G-EERH	Ruschmeyer R90-230RG	003	D-EERH	5. 4.01	D.Sadler *(Noted 5.01)*	Perth	2. 5.04
G-EERV	Van's RV-6	PFA 181-13381	G-NESI	13. 9.01	C.B.Stirling	(Romford)	
G-EESA	Europa Aviation Europa *(Mono-wheel u/c)*		G-HIIL	9. 4.96	C.B.Stirling	Damyns Hall	3. 6.02P
	(NSI EA-81/100)	25 & PFA 247-12535					
G-EESE*	Cessna U206G Stationair	U20603883	OO-DMA	28. 2.85	Not known	Movenis, Co.Londonderry	1. 4.91
			N7344C				
	(Crashed Magilligan, Co.Londonderry 31.12.88: cancelled 17.7.90 as destroyed: fuselage noted 9.01)						
G-EEST	British Aerospace Jetstream Srs.3102		SE-LGM	16. 8.00	Eastern Airways (Europe) Ltd	Humberside	23.10.02T
		781	OY-SVY/C-FASJ/G-31-781				
G-EEUP	SNCAN Stampe SV-4C	451	F-BCXQ	1. 9.78	A.M.Wajih	Redhill	11.10.02
G-EEZS	Cessna 182P Skylane	18261338	D-EEZS	8.11.99	C.M.Jones	Shoreham	13. 1.03
			N63054/D-EEZS/(N20981)				
G-EFGH	Robinson R22 Beta	1487	G-ROGG	3. 5.01	Foxtrot Golf Helicopters Ltd	Edinburgh	16. 9.02T
G-EFIR	Piper PA-28-181 Archer II	28-8090275	D-EFIR	5. 5.99	Leicestershire Aero Club Ltd	Leicester	8. 6.02T
			N8179R				
G-EFRY	Avid Aerobat	PFA 189-12096		22. 3.93	P.A.Boyden	(Dunsfold)	14. 2.02P

G-EFSM	Slingsby T.67M-260 Firefly	2072	G-BPLK	16. 7.92	Pooler-LMT Ltd	Sleap	3.11.02T
G-EFTE	Bölkow Bö.207	218	D-EFTE	4. 1.90	L.J. & A.A.Rice		
						Bishopstrow Farm, Warminster	22. 6.02
G-EGAL	Christen Eagle II	0042-86	SE-XMU	11. 3.96	J H Penfold	Swanborough Farm, Lewes	29. 4.02P
	(Lycoming AEIO-360)						
G-EGEE	Cessna 310Q	310Q0040	G-AZVY	14.11.83	Excel Automation Ltd	Exeter	19. 7.03T
			SE-FKV/N7540Q				
G-EGEG	Cessna 172R Skyhawk	17280894	N7262H	4. 7.00	C.D.Lever	Elstree	6. 7.03
G-EGGS	Robin DR.400/180 Regent	1443		15.11.79	R.Foot	Lasham	17. 7.04
G-EGHB	Ercoupe 415D	1876	N3414G	1. 9.95	P.G.Vallance	Rochester	13. 7.01
	(Continental O-200-A)		N99253/NC99253				
G-EGHH	Hawker Hunter F.58	41H-697450	J-4083	4. 7.95	G.R Lacey *(As "J-4083")*	(Kemble)	
G-EGHR	SOCATA TB-20 Trinidad	795	F-GGIQ	19.12.97	B.M.Prescott	Goodwood	14. 3.04T
G-EGJA	SOCATA TB-20 Trinidad	1101	N2807D	13.12.90	D.A.Williamson	Alderney	14.12.03
G-EGLD	Piper PA-28-161 Cadet	2841283	N92007	23.11.89	J.Appleton	Denham	6. 1.02T
					t/a Holmes Rentals *(Op Denham School of Flying)*		
G-EGLE	Christen Eagle II	F.0053		30. 3.81	R.L.Mitcham, P.J.Meaton, S.R.Flack & I.Dinermann		
	(Lycoming AEIO-360) *(Built Airmore Aviation)*					Elstree	27. 8.02P
G-EGLS	Piper PA-28-181 Archer III	2843348	N4187C	5. 6.00	D.J.Cooke	Old Sarum	5. 6.03
G-EGLT	Cessna 310R II	310R1874	G-BHTV	9. 9.93	Aviation Beauport Ltd	Jersey	21.12.01T
			N1EU/(N3206M)				
G-EGNR	Piper PA-38-112 Tomahawk	38-79A0233	OY-VIG	6.10.97	Metropolitan Services Ltd	Hawarden	8. 2.04T
			SE-KNI/N2570C				
G-EGTR	Piper PA-28-161 Cadet	2841281	G-BRSI	25. 4.98	Plane Talking Ltd	Elstree	17. 1.02T
			N92001				
G-EGUL	Christen Eagle II	Argence 0001	G-FRYS	19. 1.93	I.S.Smith	Coventry	25. 6.02P
	(Lycoming AEIO-360) *(Built Argence EA)*		N66EA		t/a G-EGUL Flying Group		
G-EGUY	Sky 220-24 HAFB	103		24. 4.98	J.L.Guy	(Skipton)	4. 5.01T
					t/a Black Sheep Balloons		
G-EHBJ	CASA I-131E Jungmann 2000	2150	E3B-550	19. 7.90	E.P.Howard	Priory Farm, Tibenham	6. 8.02P
G-EHGF	Piper PA-28-181 Archer II	28-7790188	D-EHGF	23.10.00	E.Stokes & J.Lamb	Barton	20. 2.04T
			N9534N		t/a Pegasus Flying Group		
G-EHIL*	EH Industries EH-101	50003		9. 7.87	The Helicopter Museum	Weston-super-Mare	
	(Airframe No.PP3)				*(To MoD as ZH647 1993: cancelled 28.4.99 as WFU)*		
G-EHLX	Piper PA-28-181 Archer II	28-8090317	D-EHLX	5.11.99	I.R.Carver, R.J.Barber & B.Cook		
			N8218S		t/a Carver-Barber-Cook	Seething	13. 1.03
G-EHMJ	Beechcraft S35 Bonanza	D-7879	D-EHMJ	12. 1.99	A.L.Burton & A.J.Daley	Gamston	18. 2.02
G-EHMM	Robin DR.400/180R Remorqueur	867	D-EHMM(1)	10.12.84	Booker Gliding Club Ltd	Booker	1. 4.03
G-EHMS	MD Helicopters Explorer	900-00068	N3212K	12. 7.00	Virgin HEMS (London) Ltd	Denham	11.10.03T
G-EHUP	Aérospatiale SA.341G Gazelle 1	1407	F-GIJR	3.10.97	M W Helicopters Ltd	Stapleford	11. 1.04T
			N869GT/N869/N49523				
G-EHXP	Rockwell Commander 112	227	D-EHXP	27. 1.00	H.Hashimi	Teesside	3. 2.03T
			N1227J				
G-EIBM	Robinson R22 Beta	1993	G-BUCL	25. 3.94	XL Aviation Ltd *(Op HJS Helicopters)*		
						Lower Baads Farm, Peterculter	5. 3.04T
G-EIII	Extra EA.300	057	G-HIII	4.12.00	D Dobson	Deenethorpe	16 .8.03T
	(Lycoming AEIO-540-L1B5)		D-ETYD				
G-EIIR*	Cameron N-77 HAFB	358		16.11.77	D.V.Howard *"Silver Jubilee"*	Bath	14. 5.93A
					(Cancelled 23.10.01 by CAA)		
G-EIKY	Europa Aviation Europa			27. 9.94	J.D.Milbank	Insch	7. 6.02P
	(Rotax 912-UL)	<u>54</u> & PFA 247-12634					
G-EIRE	Cessna T182T Turbo Skylane	T18208049	N3500U	24. 7.01	J.Byrne	Lower Wasing Farm, Brimpton	31. 7.04T
G-EISO	SOCATA MS.892A Rallye Commodore 150		D-EISO	23. 1.01	A Head	Bicester	24. 5.04T
		10563	F-BNSO				
G-EITE	Luscombe 8A Silvaire	3407	N71980	27. 7.88	S R H Martin	(Chesham)	19 12.02P
G-EIWT	Reims Cessna FR182 Skylane RG		D-EIWT	28. 1.86	P.P.D.Howard-Johnston	Glenrothes	10. 4.04T
		FR18200052	OO-BLI				
G-EJEL	Cessna 550 Citation II	550-0643	N747CR	19.12.01	A.J.& E.A.Elliott	(Huddersfield)	
			N643MC/PT-ODW/N13091/(N1259S)				
G-EJGO	Zlin Z.226 Trener 6HE Spezial	199	D-EJGO	7. 8.85	Aerotation Ltd	Rochester	15. 4.01
			OK-MHB				
G-EJMG	Reims Cessna F150H	F150-0301	D-EJMG	27. 4.98	T.A.White	Teesside	14.11.04T
					t/a Bagby Aviation		
G-EJOC	Aérospatiale AS350B Ecureuil	1465	G-GEDS	21.12.94	E.& S.Vandyk	(Newbury)	8. 7.02T
			G-HMAN/G-SKIM/G-BIVP		t/a Leisure & Retail Helicopters		
G-EKKL	Piper PA-28-161 Warrior 11		D-EKKL	24. 3.99	Premiair Engineering Ltd	Shoreham	5. 4.02T
		28-8416087	N43588				
G-EKKO	Robinson R44 Raven	0821		18. 7.00	MC Air Ltd	(Solihull)	3..8.03T
	(Tail skid struck ground landing Wellesbourne Mountford 2.9.01: broke up with tail boom & rotors detached)						
G-EKMN	Zlin Z.242L	0652	SE-KMN	15. 5.01	R.C.Poolman	Gloucestershire	21. 6.04T
					(F/f in UK marks 14.6.01)		
G-EKOS	Reims Cessna FR182 Skylane RG		D-EKOS	15. 7.98	S.Charlton	Sherburn-in-Elmet	12. 9.04
		FR18200017					

G-ELBC	Piper PA-34-200 Seneca	34-7350021	G-BANS N15110	4. 4.91	Stapleford Flying Club Ltd *(Op LBC Radio @ "London Lookout")*	Stapleford	27.12.03T
G-ELEE	Cameron Z-105 HAFB	4882		11. 7.00	D.Eliot	Aberdeen	26. 9.02A
G-ELEN	Robin DR.400/180	2363		16. 9.97	N.R. & E.Foster	Cannes, France	30.11.03T
G-ELIE	Cessna 182S Skylane	18280741	N23754	9. 8.00	V.J.R.Baring	Gloucestershire	23. 8.03T
G-ELIT	Bell 206L LongRanger	45091	SE-HTK N2652	28. 7.99	Aeroturbine Ltd	Milton Keynes	25. 8.02T
G-ELIZ	Denney Kitfox mk.2 (Rotax 582)	717 & PFA 172-11835		19. 7.90	A.J.Ellis t/a Tiger Helicopters *(Damaged Brighstone, IoW 10.5.93: current status unknown)*	Sandown	5.11.93P
G-ELKA	Christen Eagle II (Lycoming AEIO-360)	0001	N121DJ	18.10.94	D.Aitken & Skydance Aviation Ltd *"Ping Pong"*	Perth	14. 8.01P
G-ELKS	Avid Speed Wing Mk.4 (Jabiru 2200A)	PFA 189-13109		6. 1.98	H.S.Elkins	Garston Farm, Marshfield	9. 7.02P
G-ELLA	Piper PA-32R-301 Saratoga IIHP	3246050	N9279Q G-ELLA	13. 8.96	C.C.W.Hart	White Waltham	23.11.02
G-ELLE	Cameron N-90 HAFB	4498		11. 1.99	N.D.Eliot	(London SW19)	23. 9.02A
G-ELLI	Bell 206B-3 JetRanger III	4231	D-HMOF	24. 6.97	RA Fleming Ltd	Brandon Hall, Leeds	6. 7.03T
G-ELMH	North American AT-6D-NT Harvard III	88-16336	FAP1662 EZ341/42-84555	22. 7.92	M.Hammond *"Fools Rush-In"* *(As "42-84555/EP-H" in USAAC c/s)*	Hardwick	25. 5.02P
G-ELZN	Piper PA-28-161 Warrior II	28-8416078	D-ELZN N9579N	20. 7.99	Northamptonshire School of Flying Ltd	Sywell	31. 8.02T
G-ELZY	Piper PA-28-161 Warrior II	28-8616027	D-ELZY N9095Z/(N163AV)/N9641N	13. 4.99	Goodwood Road Racing School Ltd	Goodwood	23. 5.02T
G-EMAS	Eurocopter EC 135 T1	0107		6. 7.99	East Midlands Air Support Unit	Sibbertoft	7.10.02T
G-EMAX	Piper PA-31-350 Navajo Chieftain	31-7952029	N276CT SE-KKP/54202 Swedish Navy/SE-KKP/LN-PAI	8.12.98	AM & T Aviation Ltd *(Op Air Mercia)*	Bristol	15.12.01T
G-EMAZ	Piper PA-28-181 Archer II	28-8290088	N8073W G-EMAZ/N8073W	26. 4.90	E.J.Stanley	RAF Woodvale	18.10.02T
G-EMBA	Embraer EMB-145EU	145.016	PT-SYM	17. 7.97	British Regional Airlines Ltd *(Colum t/s)*	East Midlands	14. 8.03T
G-EMBB	Embraer EMB-145EU	145.021	PT-SYR	27. 8.97	British Regional Airlines Ltd *(Bauhaus t/s)*	East Midlands	1. 9.03T
G-EMBC	Embraer EMB-145EU	145.024	PT-SYU	1.10.97	British Regional Airlines Ltd *(Koguty Lowickie t/s)*	East Midlands	8.10.03T
G-EMBD	Embraer EMB-145EU	145.039		7. 1.98	British Regional Airlines Ltd *(Animals & Trees t/s)*	East Midlands	11. 1.04T
G-EMBE	Embraer EMB-145EU	145.042		3. 2.98	British Regional Airlines Ltd *(Waves of the City t/s)*	East Midlands	2. 2.04T
G-EMBF	Embraer EMB-145EU	145.088		10.11.98	British Regional Airlines Ltd *(Grand Union t/s)*	Ronaldsway	9.11.04T
G-EMBG	Embraer EMB-145EU	145.094		18.11.98	British Regional Airlines Ltd *(Water Dreaming t/s)*	Ronaldsway	17.11.01T
G-EMBH	Embraer EMB-145EU	145.107		20. 1.99	British Regional Airlines Ltd *(Blomsterang t/s)*	Birmingham	19. 1.05T
G-EMBI	Embraer EMB-145EU	145.126		23. 4.99	British Regional Airlines Ltd *(Paitahni t/s)*	Manchester	22. 4.02T
G-EMBJ	Embraer EMB-145EU	145.134		24. 5.99	British Regional Airlines Ltd *(Youm-Al-Suq t/s)*	Manchester	26. 5.02T
G-EMBK	Embraer EMB-145EU	145.167		26. 8.99	British Regional Airlines Ltd *(Benyhone Tartan t/s)*	Manchester	25. 8.02T
G-EMBL	Embraer EMB-145EU	145.177		4.10.99	British Regional Airlines Ltd	Manchester	3.10.02T
G-EMBM	Embraer EMB-145EU	145.196		22.11.99	British Regional Airlines Ltd	Manchester	21.11.02T
G-EMBN	Embraer EMB-145EU	145.201		13. 1.00	British Regional Airlines Ltd	Manchester	12 .1.03T
G-EMBO	Embraer EMB-145EU	145.219		14. 3.00	British Regional Airlines Ltd	Manchester	13. 3.03T
G-EMBP	Embraer EMB-145EU	145.300		25. 8.00	British Regional Airlines Ltd	Manchester	24. 8.03T
G-EMBS	Embraer EMB-145EU	145.357		20.12.00	British Regional Airlines Ltd	Manchester	19.12.03T
G-EMBT	Embraer EMB-145EU	145.404		22. 3.01	British Regional Airlines Ltd	Manchester	21. 3.04T
G-EMBU	Embraer EMB-145EU	145.458	PT-SVD	22. 6.01	British Regional Airlines Ltd	Manchester	21. 6.04T
G-EMBV	Embraer EMB-145EU	145.482	PT-SXB	12. 9.01	British Regional Airlines Ltd	Manchester	11. 9.04T
G-EMBW	Embraer EMB-145EU	145.546	PT-SZJ	19.12.01	British Regional Airlines Ltd	Southampton	
G-EMBX	Embraer EMB-145EU	145....		R	British Regional Airlines Ltd *(For delivery 2.02)*	Manchester	
G-EMBY	Embraer EMB-145EU	145....		R	British Regional Airlines Ltd *(For delivery 7.02)*	Manchester	
G-EMCM	Eurocopter EC 120B	1160		20.11.00	C.R.W.Morrell	(London SW7)	28. 2.04
G-EMER	Piper PA-34-200 Seneca	34-7350002	N3081T	29. 7.91	Haimoss Ltd *(Op Old Sarum Flying Club)*	Old Sarum	26. 2.04T
G-EMHH	Aérospatiale AS355F2 Twin Squirrel	5169	G-BYKH SX-HNP/VR-CCM/N57967	3. 8.99	Hancocks Holdings Ltd	Costock	26. 7.02T
G-EMIN	Europa Aviation Europa (Rotax 912-UL)	83 & PFA 247-12673		1. 3.94	S.A.Lamb	Rochester	3. 6.02P

G-EMJA	CASA I-131E-2000 Jungmann (Enma Tigre G-IV-B) 013 & PFA 242-12340 *(Composite from Spanish spares imported in 1991)*		(Span.AF)	2. 9.94	P.J.Brand	High Cross, Ware	20. 5.02P
G-EMLY	Pegasus Quantum 15 (Rotax 582-40)	7531		30. 6.99	A.R.White	(Farnham)	27. 6.02P
G-EMMS	Piper PA-38-112 Tomahawk	38-78A0526	OO-TKT N4414E	14. 9.79	Cheshire Flying Services Ltd t/a Ravenair	Liverpool	12.11.03T
G-EMMY	Rutan VariEze (Lycoming O-235)	577 & PFA 074-10222		21. 8.78	M.J.Tooze	Biggin Hill	3. 6.02P
G-EMNI*	Phillips ST.1 Speedtwin Mk.2	006 & PFA 207-12880		25. 5.95	A.J.Clarry *(Cancelled 17.10.01 as wfu: no PtoF issued)*	(Pewsey, Wilts)	
G-EMSI	Europa Aviation Europa	PFA 247-12817		24. 1.95	P.W.L.Thomas	(York)	
G-EMSY	de Havilland DH.82A Tiger Moth *(Rebuilt with parts from OO-MOT)*	83666	G-ASPZ D-EDUM/T7356	27. 6.91	B.E.Micklewright *(Stored minus wings 11.01)*	Bourne Park, Hurstbourne Tarrant	24.10.03
G-ENCE	Partenavia P.68B	141	G-OROY G-BFSU	1. 6.84	J.J.H.& A.E.Hanna t/a Bicton Aviation	(Budleigh Salterton)	28. 9.03
G-ENEE	CFM Streak Shadow	PFA 206-13628		14. 8.00	T.Green	Wombleton	19.12.01P
G-ENGO	Steen Skybolt	PFA 064-13429		15.11.00	C.Docherty	(Mount Pleasant, Falklands)	
G-ENIE	Nipper T.66 Srs.IIIB (VW 1800)	PFA 025-10214		17. 3.78	E.J.Clarke	Seighford	11. 6.02P
G-ENII	Reims Cessna F172M Skyhawk II	F17201352	PH-WAG (D-EDQM)	18. 1.79	J.Howley	Blackbushe	4.11.02T
G-ENNI	Robin R.3000/180	128	F-GGJA	5.10.99	F.R.Traynor	Wellesbourne Mountford	2.11.02T
G-ENNK	Cessna 172S Skyhawk	172S8538	N72729	15. 9.00	AK Enterprises Ltd	(London N8)	1.11.03T
G-ENNY	Cameron V-77 HAFB	1399		1.12.86	B.G.Jones *"Crocks of Frome"*	Devizes	16. 5.99A
G-ENOA	Reims Cessna F172F	F172-0138	G-ASZW	2. 9.81	M.K.Acors	King's Farm, Thurrock	17.10.03
G-ENRE	Jabiru Jabiru UL-450	PFA 274A-13755		28. 6.01	J.C.Harris	(London SE26)	4.11.02
G-ENRI	Lindstrand LBL-105A HAFB	294		4. 8.95	P.G.Hall *(Henry Numatic Vacuum Cleaners titles)*	Chard	14. 5.02T
G-ENRY	Cameron N-105 HAFB	2096		26. 9.89	P.G. & G.R.Hall *"Henry"*	Chard	7. 7.94T
G-ENSI	Beechcraft F33A Bonanza	CE-699	D-ENSI	17. 3.78	J.M.Eskes	Elstree	19. 5.02
G-ENTT	Reims Cessna F152 II	F15201750	G-BHHI (PH-CBA)	9.11.93	Plane Talking Ltd	Elstree	31. 3.02T
G-ENTW	Reims Cessna F152 II	F15201479	G-BFLK	21. 1.93	Firecrest Aviation Ltd, W.Bagnall & M.Pevan	Elstree	15. 8.04T
G-ENUS	Cameron N-90 HAFB	1914		18. 1.89	Wye Valley Aviation Ltd *"Guinness"*	Ross-on-Wye	9. 6.00T
G-ENVY	Mainair Blade (Rotax 912-UL)	1260-1000-7-W1054		20.12.00	D A Pollitt & P Millership	(Bolton)	11.12.01P
G-EOFM	Reims Cessna F172N Skyhawk	F17201988	D-EOFM	2.11.01	20th Air Training Group Ltd	(Dunsany, Co.Meath)	
G-EOFS	Europa Aviation Europa (Rotax 914-UL) *(Tri-cycle u/c)*	PFA 247-13033		22. 7.98	G.T.Leedham	Gunby Lea Farm, Overseal	24. 9.02P
G-EOFW	Pegasus Quantum Q2 Sport 15-912	7582		15.10.99	G.C.Weighell	Long Marston	14.10.02P
G-EOHL	Cessna 182L Skylane	18259279	D-EOHL N70505	4. 3.99	G.B.Dale & M.C.Terris	Enniskillen, Co.Fermanagh	24. 3.02
G-EOIN	Zenair CH.701UL (Verner SVS1400)	PFA 187-13490		19.11.99	D.G.Palmer	Fetterangus	20. 6.02P
G-EOLD	Piper PA-28-161 Warrior II	28-8516030	D-EOLD N4390F/N9531N	31. 3.00	Goodwood Road Racing Co Ltd	Goodwood	25. 5.03T
G-EOMA	Airbus A330-243	265	F-WWKU	26. 4.99	Monarch Airlines Ltd	Luton	25. 4.02T
G-EORG	Piper PA-38-112 Tomahawk *(Rebuilt with new fuselage: old one stored 9.96)*	38-78A0427	N9734N	18. 9.78	Airways Aero Associations Ltd *(Op British Airways Flying Club) (Whale Rider t/s)*	Booker	14. 7.03T
G-EORJ	Europa Aviation Europa	PFA 247-13139		23. 7.99	P.E.George	(Sutton Coldfield)	
G-EPAR	Robinson R22 Beta-II	2781		26. 2.98	J.W.Ramsbottom t/a Jepar Rotorcraft *(Crashed on landing Blackpool 22.12.99 & severely damaged: pod stored 12.01)*	Blackpool	26. 2.01T
G-EPDI	Cameron N-77 HAFB	370		25. 1.78	R.Moss *"Pegasus"*	Banchory	29. 6.91A
G-EPED	Piper PA-31-350 Chieftain	31-8252040	G-BMCJ N121CF/N41060	22. 3.95	Pedley Furniture International Ltd	Duxford	17. 4.03T
G-EPFR*	Airbus A320-231	0437	D-AAMS (D-AFRO(1))/G-EFPR/C-FTDF/G-EPFR/G-BVJV/N437RX/G-BVJV/C-FWDQ/G-BVJV/N437RX/F-WWDM	18.11.97	Airtours International Airways Ltd *(Sold as D-AAMS & cancelled 27.3.00) (For restoration 2002)*	Manchester	
G-EPOL	Aérospatiale AS355F1 Twin Squirrel	5302	G-SASU G-BSSM/G-BMTC/G-BKUK	13. 1.98	Cambridge and Essex Air Support Unit	Boreham	11.11.02T
G-EPOX	Aero Designs Pulsar XP	PFA 202-12355		27. 4.94	K.F.Farey	(Bourne End)	11. 9.02P
G-EPTR	Piper PA-28R-200 Cherokee Arrow II	28R-7235090	D-EPTR OH-PTR/(SE-KVF)/N4558T	26. 5.98	T.I.Moore	Kirknewton	13. 8.04T
G-ERAD	Beechcraft C90A King Air	LJ-1565	N213NC	18. 7.01	G.R.Kinally t/a GKL Management Services Ltd	(Cranleigh)	25. 7.04
G-ERBL	Robinson R22 Beta-II	2711		26. 6.97	G.V.Maloney	Biggin Hill	27. 7.03T
G-ERCO	Ercoupe 415D (Continental C85)	3210	N2585H NC2585H	7. 4.93	A.R. & M.V.Tapp	Maypole Farm, Chislet	15. 8.02
G-ERDS	de Havilland DH.82A Tiger Moth	85028	ZS-BCU SAAF 2267/T6741	27. 7.94	W.A.Gerdes	Lee-on-Solent	8. 7.04

G-ERIC	Rockwell Commander 112TC	13010	SE-GSA	26. 9.78	Atomchoice Ltd	Cranfield	11. 5.03
G-ERIK	Cameron N-77 HAFB	1753		18. 5.88	T.M.Donnelly *"Norsewind"*	Doncaster	24. 2.00A
G-ERIS	Hughes 369D (500D)	11-0871D	G-PJMD	1. 3.96	R.J.Howard	Leeds	12. 8.01
	(Modified to 500E standard)		G-BMJV/N1110S				
G-ERIX	Boeing-Stearman E75 (PT-13D) Kaydet		N5055V	9. 3.88	Flight Incentives NV	Antwerp, Belgium	3.12.00
	(P&W R985)	75-5093	42-16930		*(As "985" in US Navy c/s)*		
G-ERJA	Embraer EMB-145EP	145.229		25. 2.00	Brymon Airways Ltd	Bristol	24. 2.03T
G-ERJB	Embraer EMB-145EP	145.237	PT-SIC	13. 3.00	Brymon Airways Ltd	Bristol	12. 3.03T
G-ERJC	Embraer EMB-145EP	145.253		25. 4.00	Brymon Airways Ltd	Bristol	25. 4.03T
G-ERJD	Embraer EMB-145EP	145.290		20. 7.00	Brymon Airways Ltd	Bristol	19. 7.03T
G-ERJE	Embraer EMB-145EP	145.315	PT-SMG	15. 9.00	Brymon Airways Ltd	Bristol	14. 9.03T
G-ERJF	Embraer EMB-145EP	145.325		24.10.00	Brymon Airways Ltd	Bristol	23.10.03T
G-ERJG	Embraer EMB-145EP	145.394		8. 3.01	Brymon Airways Ltd	Bristol	7. 3.04T
G-ERMO	ARV Super 2	018	G-BMWK	7. 1.87	T.Pond	(Sutton-in-Ashfield)	19. 5.02
	(Hewland AE75)						
G-ERMS	Thunder AS-33 Hot Air Airship	A.1		28.11.78	B.R. & M.Boyle *"Microbe"*	Newbury	
					(On loan to British Balloon Museum & Library)		
G-ERNI	Piper PA-28-181 Archer II	28-8090146	G-OSSY	9.10.91	D.C.& M.A.Greenaway	Biggin Hill	8. 3.04
			N81215				
G-ERRY	Grumman-American AA-5B Tiger		G-BFMJ	20. 3.84	M.D.Savage & A.F.K.Horne	Shobdon	10. 5.02
		AA5B-0725			*t/a Gemini Aviation*		
G-ESAM	MBB Bö.105DBS-4	S.138/911	G-BUIB	7.12.00	Bond Air Services Ltd	Borehamwood	24. 6.02T
			G-BDYZ/D-HDEF		*(Op Essex Air Ambulance)*		
	(Original a/c remanufactured with new pod c/n S.911 in 1992)						
G-ESFT	Piper PA-28-161 Warrior II		G-ENNA	16. 5.97	Plane Talking Ltd	Elstree	21. 4.03T
		28-7916060	N22065				
G-ESKU*	Piper PA-23-250 Aztec C	27-3823	G-AWIY	11. 4.96	Gold Air International Ltd	NK	16. 7.98
			N6599Y				
		(Stored 12.00: cancelled 23.7.01 as wfu: on fire dump Biggin Hill but removed off site 26.5.01)					
G-ESKY	Piper PA-23-250 Aztec D	27-4172	G-BBNN	24.11.95	Systems & Research Ltd	(Haywards Heath)	5. 6.03T
			N6832Y				
	(Note: The fuselage at North Weald marked "Air Ambulance" and "G-ESKY" is that of G-BADI q.v)						
G-ESSX	Piper PA-28-161 Warrior II		G-BHYY	30. 7.82	S.Harcourt	Cardiff	16. 1.97T
		28-8016261	N9639N		t/a Courtenay Enterprises *(Noted 3.01)*		
G-ESTA	Cessna 550 Citation II	550-0127	G-GAUL	24. 6.98	Executive Aviation Services Ltd		
			N550TJ/(N29TG)/N29TC/N2631N			Gloucestershire	17. 8.02T
G-ESTE	Gulfstream AA-5A Cheetah	AA5A-0780	G-GHNC	28. 4.87	Plane Talking Ltd	Elstree	8.12.04T
			N26877		*(Op Cabair Flying School)*		
G-ESTR	Van's RV-6	PFA 181A-13638		11. 9.00	R.M.Johnson	Midlem Farm, Midlem	
G-ESUS	Rotorway Executive 162F	6169		7.10.96	J.Tickner	Street Farm, Takeley	29. 7.02P
	(Rotorway RI 162F)						
G-ETAV	Piper PA-32-300 Cherokee Six D		G-MCAR	12. 2.01	Erintech Ltd	RAF Henlow	9. 8.02T
		32-7140008	G-LADA/G-AYWK/N8616N				
G-ETBY	Piper PA-32-260 Cherokee Six	32-211	G-AWCY	13. 7.89	K.Richards-Green & R.Fordham	Enstone	31. 5.02
	(Rebuilt with spare Frame No.32-858S)		N3365W		t/a G-ETBY Group		
G-ETCW	Stoddard-Hamilton GlaStar	5627		12.12.01	P.G.Hayward	(North Walsham)	
G-ETDA	Piper PA-28-161 Warrior II		N84051	9. 3.88	T.Griffiths	Oaksey Park	13. 4.03
		28-8116256					
G-ETDC	Cessna 172P Skyhawk II	17274690	N53133	4. 5.88	Osprey Air Services Ltd	RAF Kinloss	20. 7.03T
					(Op Moray Flying Club)		
G-ETFT	Colt Financial Times SS HAFB	1792	G-BSGZ	11. 1.91	Financial Times Ltd	Kirdford	14.10.00A
					(Op Balloon Preservation Group) "Financial Times II"		
G-ETHU	Eurocopter EC 135T1	0198		17. 1.02	McAlpine Helicopters Ltd	Oxford	
G-ETHY	Cessna 208B Caravan	20800293	N1295M	19.10.98	N.A.Moore	Movenis, Co.Londonderry	2. 4.03T
			G-ETHY				
G-ETIN	Robinson R22 Beta	0853	N9081D	7. 9.88	Forestdale Hotels Ltd	Burley	24. 9.03T
G-ETIV	Robin DR.400/180	2454		12. 7.00	J.Macgilvray	North Connel, Oban	6. 8.03T
G-ETME	Nord 1002 Pingouin	274	N108J	18. 4.00	S.H.O'Connell & J.N.Pittock		
	(Renault 6Q)		F-BFRV/French AF 274		t/a 108 Flying Group	White Waltham	20. 7.03
					(As "10/KG+EM" in WW2 Luftwaffe North Africa c/s)		
G-EUGN	Robinson R44 Raven	0822		19. 7.00	Twinlite Developments Ltd		
						(Castleknock, Dublin)	13. 8.03T
G-EUOA	Airbus A319-131	1513	D-AVYE	15. 6.01	British Airways plc	Heathrow	14. 6.04T
G-EUOB	Airbus A319-131	1529	D-AVWH	4. 7.01	British Airways plc	Heathrow	3. 7.04T
G-EUOC	Airbus A319-131	1537	D-AVYP	16. 7.01	British Airways plc	Heathrow	15. 7.04T
G-EUOD	Airbus A319-131	1558	D-AVYJ	16. 8.01	British Airways plc	Heathrow	15. 8.04T
G-EUOE	Airbus A319-131	1574	D-AVWF	5. 9.01	British Airways plc	Heathrow	4. 9.04T
G-EUOF	Airbus A319-131	1590	D-AVYW	23.10.01	British Airways plc	Heathrow	22.10.04T
G-EUOG	Airbus A319-131	1594	D-AVWU	23.10.01	British Airways plc	Heathrow	22.10.04T
G-EUOH	Airbus A319-131	1604	D-AVYM	14.12.01	British Airways plc	Heathrow	13.12.04T
G-EUOI	Airbus A319-131	1606	D-AVYN	13.11.01	British Airways plc	Heathrow	12.11.04T
G-EUOJ	Airbus A319-...			R	British Airways plc	Heathrow	
					(For delivery 4.03)		
G-EUOK	Airbus A320-...			R	British Airways plc		

G-EUOL	Airbus A320-...			R	British Airways plc		
G-EUOM	Airbus A320-...			R	British Airways plc		
G-EUON	Airbus A320-...			R	British Airways plc		
G-EUOO	Airbus A320-...			R	British Airways plc		
G-EUOP	Airbus A320-...			R	British Airways plc		
G-EUOR	Airbus A320-...			R	British Airways plc		
G-EUOS	Airbus A320-...			R	British Airways plc		
G-EUOT	Airbus A320-...			R	British Airways plc		
G-EUOU	Airbus A320-...			R	British Airways plc		
G-EUOV	Airbus A320-...			R	British Airways plc		
G-EUOW	Airbus A320-...			R	British Airways plc		
G-EUOX	Airbus A320-...			R	British Airways plc		
G-EUOY	Airbus A320-...			R	British Airways plc		
G-EUOZ	Airbus A320-...			R	British Airways plc		
G-EUPA	Airbus A319-131	1082	D-AVYK	6.10.99	British Airways plc	Birmingham	5.10.02T
G-EUPB	Airbus A319-131	1115	D-AVYT	9.11.99	British Airways plc	Heathrow	8.11.02T
G-EUPC	Airbus A319-131	1118	D-AVYU	12.11.99	British Airways plc	Heathrow	11.11.02T
G-EUPD	Airbus A319-131	1142	D-AVWG	10.12.99	British Airways plc	Birmingham	9.12.02T
G-EUPE	Airbus A319-131	1193	D-AVYT	27. 3.00	British Airways plc	Birmingham	26. 3.03T
G-EUPF	Airbus A319-131	1197	D-AVWS	30. 3.00	British Airways plc	Birmingham	29. 3.03T
G-EUPG	Airbus A319-131	1222	D-AVYG	25. 5.00	British Airways plc	Heathrow	24. 5.03T
G-EUPH	Airbus A319-131	1225	D-AVYK	23. 5.00	British Airways plc	Birmingham	22. 5.03T
G-EUPJ	Airbus A319-131	1232	D-AVYJ	30. 5.00	British Airways plc	Heathrow	29..5.03T
G-EUPK	Airbus A319-131	1236	D-AVYO	30. 5.00	British Airways plc	Birmingham	29. 5.03T
G-EUPL	Airbus A319-131	1239	D-AVYP	8. 6.00	British Airways plc	Heathrow	7. 6.03T
G-EUPM	Airbus A319-131	1258	D-AVYR	30. 6.00	British Airways plc	Heathrow	29. 6.03T
G-EUPN	Airbus A319-131	1261	D-AVWA	10. 7.00	British Airways plc	Heathrow	9..7.03T
G-EUPO	Airbus A319-131	1279	D-AVYU	1. 8.00	British Airways plc	Heathrow	31. 7.03T
G-EUPP	Airbus A319-131	1295	D-AVWU	14. 8.00	British Airways plc	Heathrow	13. 8.03T
G-EUPR	Airbus A319-131	1329	D-AVYH	9.10.00	British Airways plc	Heathrow	8.10.03T
G-EUPS	Airbus A319-131	1338	D-AVYM	23.10.00	British Airways plc	Birmingham	22.10.03T
G-EUPT	Airbus A319-131	1380	D-AVWH	5.12.00	British Airways plc	Heathrow	4.12.03T
G-EUPU	Airbus A319-131	1384	D-AVWP	14.12.00	British Airways plc	Heathrow	13.12.03T
G-EUPV	Airbus A319-131	1423		13. 2.01	British Airways plc	Heathrow	12. 2.04T
G-EUPW	Airbus A319-131	1440	D-AVYP	6. 3.01	British Airways plc	Heathrow	5. 3.04T
G-EUPX	Airbus A319-131	1445	D-AVWB	14.12.01	British Airways plc	Heathrow	
G-EUPY	Airbus A319-131	1466	D-AVYK	12. 4.01	British Airways plc	Heathrow	11. 4.04T
G-EUPZ	Airbus A319-131	1510	D-AVYY	7. 6.01	British Airways plc	Heathrow	6. 6.04T
G-EURA	Agusta-Bell 47J-2 Ranger	2061	G-ASNV	21. 7.83	L.Goddard	Thornicombe, Dorset	21. 1.04
G-EURX	Europa Aviation Europa XS T-G	PFA 247-13661		15.12.00	C C Napier	Newtownards, Co.of Down	
G-EUUA	Airbus A320-232	1661	F-WWIH	31. 1.02	British Airways plc	Heathrow	
G-EUUB	Airbus A320-232	1689	F-WWBE	R	British Airways plc	*(For delivery 2.02)*	
G-EUUC	Airbus A320-232	1696	F-WWIO	R	British Airways plc	*(For delivery 2.02)*	
G-EUUD	Airbus A320-232			R	British Airways plc	*(For delivery 5.02)*	
G-EUUE	Airbus A320-232			R	British Airways plc	*(For delivery 6.02)*	
G-EUUF	Airbus A320-232			R	British Airways plc	*(For delivery 7.02)*	
G-EUUG	Airbus A320-232			R	British Airways plc	*(For delivery 9.02)*	
G-EUUH	Airbus A320-232			R	British Airways plc	*(For delivery 10.02)*	
G-EUUI	Airbus A320-232			R	British Airways plc	*(For delivery 11.02)*	
G-EUUJ	Airbus A320-232			R	British Airways plc	*(For delivery 12.02)*	
G-EUUK	Airbus A320-232			R	British Airways plc		
G-EUUL	Airbus A320-232			R	British Airways plc		
G-EUUM	Airbus A320-232			R	British Airways plc		
G-EUUN	Airbus A320-232			R	British Airways plc		
G-EUUO	Airbus A320-232			R	British Airways plc		
G-EUUP	Airbus A320-232			R	British Airways plc		
G-EUUR	Airbus A320-232			R	British Airways plc		
G-EUUS	Airbus A320-232			R	British Airways plc		
G-EUUT	Airbus A320-232			R	British Airways plc		
G-EUUU	Airbus A320-232			R	British Airways plc		
G-EUUV	Airbus A320-232			R	British Airways plc		
G-EVES	Dassault Falcon 900B	165	F-WWFD	13.11.97	Northern Executive Aviation Ltd	Manchester/Jersey	12.11.03T
G-EVET	Cameron Concept 80 HAFB	3703		30.10.95	K.J.Foster	Coleshill, Birmingham	16. 4.02A
G-EVEY	Thruster T600N 450 Jab	0121-T600N-057		22.11.01	K J Crompton	(Bangor, Belfast)	16.12.02P
G-EWAN	Protech PT-2C-160 Prostar (Lycoming O-320-B2B)	PFA 249-12425		23. 6.93	C.G.Shaw	Truleigh Manor Farm, Edburton	20.10.01P
G-EWBC	Jabiru Jabiru SK	PFA 274-13457		3.11.00	E.W.B.Comber	Fenland	9. 7.02P
G-EWFN	SOCATA TB-20 Trinidad	1009	G-BRTY	22. 1.90	Trinidair Ltd	Filton	21. 4.02T
G-EWIZ	Pitts S-2SE Special (Lycoming AEIO-540)	S.18	VH-EHQ	12.11.82	S.J.Carver	Netherthorpe	20.10.01P

G-EWUD*	Reims Cessna F172F	F172-0137	(G-ESSO)	26. 5.87	Not known	Wickenby	12.12.93
			G-EWUD/G-ATBK				
			(Damaged Dee Estuary near West Kirby 14.8.92: stored 2.93: current status unknown)				
G-EXEA	Extra EA.300/L	082		9. 3.99	J.A.Carr	Guernsey	30. 3.02
	(Lycoming AEIO-540-L1B5)						
G-EXEC	Piper PA-34-200 Seneca	34-7450072	(G-EXXC)	11. 5.78	Sky Air Travel Ltd	Stapleford	13. 3.03T
			OY-BGU				
G-EXEK	Agusta A109A II	7393	G-SLNE	19. 6.00	Knightway Aviation Ltd		
			G-EEVS/G-OTSL			Ladyswood House, Sherston, Wilts	3 .7.03T
G-EXEX	Cessna 404 Titan II	404-0037	SE-GZF	3. 5.79	Atlantic Air Transport Ltd	Inverness	29. 7.03A
			(N5418G)		*(Op Dept of Transport)*		
G-EXIT	SOCATA MS.893E Rallye 180GT	12979	F-GARX	22. 9.78	M.A.Baldwin	(Canterbury)	31. 5.04
G-EXPD	Stemme S.10-VT	11-063		5. 7.01	Global Gliding Expeditions Ltd		
						(Builth Wells)	30. 8.04
G-EXPL	American Champion 7GCBC Citabria			9. 5.96	E.J.F.McEntee	Goodwood	24.11.02
		1220-96					
G-EXPR	Colt 90A HAFB	1064		17. 8.87	D.P.Hopkins	Pidley, Huntingdon	22. 4.01A
					t/a Lakeside Lodge Golf Centre		
G-EXPS	Short SD.3-60-100	SH.3661	TC-AOA	11. 5.99	BAC Express Airlines Ltd	Jersey	27 .5.02T
			G-BLRT/SE-KRV/G-BLRT/G-14-3661 *"City of Exeter"*				
G-EXTR	Extra EA.260	004	D-EDID	10. 8.92	Diana M.Britten	Fairoaks	7. 4.02P
	(Lycoming AEIO-540)				*(Morse titles)*		
G-EYAS	Denney Kitfox mk.2	PFA 172-11858		3. 3.93	K.Hamnett	Long Marston	15. 2.02P
	(Rotax 582)						
G-EYCO	Robin DR.400/180 Regent	1949		12. 3.90	Cherokee G-AVYL Flying Group Ltd	Perth	25. 4.02
G-EYES	Cessna 402C II	402C0008	SE-IRU	16. 7.90	Atlantic Air Promotions Ltd	Inverness	15. 8.02T
			G-BLCE/N4648N		*(Op Environmental Agency)*		
G-EYET	Robinson R44 Astro	0052	G-JPAD	30.11.98	Warwickshire Flight Training Centre Ltd		
						Coventry	18. 5.03T
G-EYLE	Bell 206L-1 LongRanger II	45232	G-OCRP	20.11.01	Eyles Construction Ltd	(Ramsgate)	10. 8.03T
			V4-AAB/G-OCRP/G-BWCU/N2758A/C-FPET/N2758A/JA9234/N27545/JA9234				
G-EYNL	MBB Bö.105DBS-5	S.382	LN-OTJ	19. 8.96	Sterling Helicopters Ltd	Norwich	5.12.02T
			D-HDLR/EC-DSO/D-HDLR				
G-EYOR	Van's RV-6	PFA <u>181A</u>-13259		15.10.99	S.I.Fraser	Henstridge	14. 1.03P
G-EYRE	Bell 206L-1 LongRanger II	45229	G-STVI	12.11.90	Hideroute Ltd	Stapleford	13. 7.03T
			N60MA/N5091K				
G-EZEL	Westland SA.341G Gazelle 1	1073	(F-GIVQ)	1.12.00	W R Pitcher/Regal Group UK	Leatherhead	13. 9.75
			I-ATOM/F-BXPG/G-BAZL				
G-EZJA	Boeing 737-73V	30235		13.10.00	EasyJet Airline Co Ltd	Luton	12.10.03T
G-EZJB	Boeing 737-73V	30236	N1787B	22.11.00	EasyJet Airline Co Ltd	Luton	21.11.03T
G-EZJC	Boeing 737-73V	30237		15.12.00	EasyJet Airline Co Ltd	Luton	13.12.03T
G-EZJD	Boeing 737-73V	30242		13. 7.01	EasyJet Airline Co Ltd	Luton	12. 7.04T
G-EZJE	Boeing 737-73V	30238		10. 8.01	EasyJet Airline Co Ltd	Luton	9. 8.04T
G-EZJF	Boeing 737-73V	30243		15. 8.01	EasyJet Airline Co Ltd	Luton	14. 8.04T
G-EZJG	Boeing 737-73V	30239		28. 9.01	EasyJet Airline Co Ltd	Luton	27. 9.04T
G-EZJH	Boeing 737-73V	30240		15.10.01	EasyJet Airline Co Ltd	Luton	14.10.04T
G-EZJI	Boeing 737-73V	30241		R	EasyJet Airline Co Ltd	Luton	
G-EZJJ	Boeing 737-73V	30245		30. 1.02	EasyJet Airline Co Lt.	Luton	
G-EZJK	Boeing 737-73V	30247		R	EasyJet Airline Co Ltd	Luton	
G-EZJL	Boeing 737-73V	30241		20.12.01	EasyJet Airline Co Ltd	Luton	
G-EZOS	Rutan VariEze	002 & PFA 074-10221		10. 7.78	C.Moffat	Blackbushe	18.10.02P
	(Continental O-200-A)						
G-EZYB	Boeing 737-3M8	24020	N797BB	17.10.96	EasyJet Airline Co Ltd	Luton	20.10.02T
			I-TEAA/OO-LTA/(OO-BTA)				
G-EZYC	Boeing 737-3Y0	24462	G-BWJA	28. 5.97	EasyJet Airline Co Ltd	Luton	4. 4.02T
			EC-FJR/EC-897/G-TEAA/EI-BZQ/(N116WA)/EI-BZQ/EC-ENS/EC-244/N5573K				
G-EZYD	Boeing 737-3M8	24022	N798BB	5. 2.97	EasyJet Airline Co Ltd	Luton	10. 2.03T
			I-TEAE/OO-LTC/(OO-BTC)				
G-EZYF	Boeing 737-375	23708	D-AGEX	3.11.97	EasyJet Airline Co Ltd	Luton	9.11.03T
			(G-EZYC)/4L-AAA/PT-TEC/(C-GZPW)				
G-EZYG	Boeing 737-33V	29331	N1768B	19. 8.98	EasyJet Airline Co Ltd	Luton	18. 8.04T
G-EZYH	Boeing 737-33V	29332		17. 9.98	EasyJet Airline Co Ltd	Luton	17. 9.04T
G-EZYI	Boeing 737-33V	29333	N1787B	24.11.98	EasyJet Airline Co Ltd	Luton	22.11.04T
G-EZYJ	Boeing 737-33V	29334		18.12.98	EasyJet Airline Co Ltd	Luton	17.12.04T
G-EZYK	Boeing 737-33V	29335		31. 1.99	EasyJet Airline Co.Ltd	Luton	30. 1.02T
G-EZYL	Boeing 737-33V	29336	N1787B	12. 3.99	EasyJet Airline Co Ltd	Luton	11. 3.02T
G-EZYO	Boeing 737-33V	29339		23. 8.99	EasyJet Airline Co.Ltd	Luton	22. 8.02T
G-EZYP	Boeing 737-33V	29340		17. 9.99	EasyJet Airline Co Ltd	Luton	16 .9.02T
G-EZYR	Boeing 737-33V	29341	N1787B	20.10.99	EasyJet Airline Co.Ltd	Luton	18.10.02T
G-EZYT	Boeing 737-3Q8	26307	HB-IIE	28. 6.00	EasyJet Airline Co Ltd	Luton	27. 6.03T
			N721LF/(HB-IIE)				
G-EZYU	Piper PA-34-200-2 Seneca	34-7450110	G-BCDB	4. 7.01	P.A.S.Dyke	Elstree	30. 7.01T
			N41346				

G-FAAA – G-FZZZ

G-FABB	Cameron V-77 HAFB	822	LX-FAB	13.12.89	P.Trumper	Ashford, Kent	31. 5.02T
G-FABI	Robinson R44 Astro	0325		25. 4.97	J.Froggatt Ltd.	(Dukinfield)	27. 4.03T
G-FABM	Beechcraft 95B55A Baron	TC-2259	G-JOND G-BMVC/N66456	22. 2.91	F.B.Miles *(Damaged Guernsey 27.3.99: current status unknown)*	Gloucestershire	17. 8.04
G-FAGN	Robinson R22 Beta	0615	(N2566W)	28.11.86	C.R.Weldon	Dublin	25. 5.96
G-FALC	Aeromere F.8L Falco 3	224	G-AROT	19. 2.81	P.J.Jones	Oxford	28. 6.04
G-FAME	CFM Starstreak Shadow SA-II (Jabiru 2200) K.273SA & PFA 206A-12973			23. 5.96	T.J.Palmer *(Flies from Prestwick & Oban)*	(Symington)	28.11.02P
G-FAMH	Zenair ZH.701 Stol (Jabiru 2200A)	PFA 187-13301		26. 6.98	F.E.Telling	Popham	25.11.02P
G-FANC	Temco Fairchild 24R-46	R46-347	N77647 NC77647	16.10.89	A.T.Fines	Felthorpe	26. 5.03T
G-FANL	Cessna R172K Hawk XPII	R1722873	N736XQ	7. 6.79	J.A.Rees	Haverfordwest	2. 7.03T
G-FANN*	Hawker Siddeley HS.125 Srs.600B	256019	HZ-AA1 G-BARR	13. 2.89	British Airways Aircraft Recovery Unit *(No CofA issued: cancelled 29.3.93 as WFU: on fire dump 3.00 as "HZ-AA1")*	Dunsfold	
G-FARM	SOCATA Rallye 235E	12832	F-GARF	10.10.78	Bristol Cars Ltd	White Waltham	27. 6.04
G-FARO	Star-Lite SL-1 (Rotax 447)	PFA 175-11359		19. 6.89	M.K.Faro *(Noted 11.01)*	Henstridge	16. 4.98P
G-FARR	SAN Jodel 150 Mascaret	58	F-BNIN	21. 7.81	G.H.Farr	Dairy House Farm, Worleston	19. 5.01P
G-FATB	Commander Aircraft Commander 114B	14624	N6037Y	3. 7.96	James D.Peace & Co	(Kirkwall)	11. 8.02
G-FAYE	Reims Cessna F150M	F15001252	PH-VSK	24. 1.80	Cheshire Air Training Services Ltd	Liverpool	5. 7.04T
G-FBAT	Aeroprakt A22 Foxbat	PFA 317-13591		16. 5.00	D.G.Ashcroft	Otherton, Cannock	
G-FBIX	de Havilland DH.100 Vampire FB.9	22100	7705M WL505	24. 7.91	D.G.Jones *(As "WL505": on rebuild 1.01)*	(St Mary Hill, Bridgend)	
G-FBMW	Cameron N-90 HAFB	3019		23. 4.93	K-J.Schwer	Erbach-Donaurieden, Germany	29. 7.02A
G-FBPI	ANEC IV Missel Thrush	PFA 312-13417		19. 1.99	R.Trickett.	(King's Lynn)	
G-FBRN	Piper PA-28-181 Archer II	28-8290166	D-ERBN N82628	3. 8.98	Herefordshire Aero Club Ltd	Shobdon	26. 9.04T
G-FBWH	Piper PA-28R-180 Cherokee Arrow	28R-30368	SE-FCV	23. 8.78	F.T.Short	Whaley Farm, New York, Lincs	2. 4.04
G-FCAL	Cessna 441 Conquest II	441-0293	C-FMHD N88723	19. 3.96	Cobham Leasing Ltd *(Op FR Aviation) (Noted damaged 12.01)*	Teesside	17.10.03T
G-FCDB	Cessna 550 Citation Bravo	550-0985	N5269J	10. 9.01	Eurojet Aviation Ltd	Belfast	9. 9.02T
G-FCLA	Boeing 757-28A	27621	N1789B	26. 2.97	JMC Airlines Ltd	Manchester	25. 2.03T
G-FCLB	Boeing 757-28A	28164	N751NA G-FCLB	25. 3.97	JMC Airlines Ltd	Manchester	29. 4.04T
G-FCLC	Boeing 757-28A	28166		9. 5.97	JMC Airlines Ltd	Manchester	8. 5.03T
G-FCLD	Boeing 757-25F	28718		25. 4.97	JMC Airlines Ltd	Manchèster	24. 4.03T
G-FCLE	Boeing 757-28A	28171		24. 5.98	JMC Airlines Ltd	Manchester	23. 5.04T
G-FCLF	Boeing 757-28A	28835		24. 3.99	JMC Airlines Ltd	Manchester	22. 3.02T
G-FCLG	Boeing 757-28A	24367	N701LF EI-CLM/N381LF/N240LA/C-GTSK/C-GNXI/G-GAWB	18.12.98	JMC Airlines Ltd	Manchester	2..4.02T
G-FCLH	Boeing 757-28A	26274	N751LF EI-CLU/N161LF	17. 2.99	JMC Airlines Ltd	Manchester	12. 5.02T
G-FCLI	Boeing 757-28A	26275	N651LF EI-CLV/N151LF	17. 3.99	JMC Airlines Ltd	Manchester	1. 6.02T
G-FCLJ	Boeing 757-2Y0	26160	N160GE EI-CJX/N3519M/N1786B/(B-2830)	26. 4.99	JMC Airlines Ltd *(Apple Vacations titles - Apple t/s)*	Manchester	25 .4.02T
G-FCLK	Boeing 757-2Y0	26161	N161GE EI-CJY/N3521N	6. 4.99	JMC Airlines Ltd	Manchester	5. 4.02T
G-FCSP	Robin DR.400/180 Regent	2022		24.10.90	F.C.Smith t/a FCS Photochemicals	Biggin Hill	22. 2.03
G-FEBE	Cessna 340A II	340A-0345	N405LS (N37320)	12. 7.88	C.Dugard Ltd & E.C.Dugard	Shoreham	20. 6.04
G-FEBY	Robinson R22 Beta	3179		23. 4.01	Astra Helicopters Ltd	Bristol	25. 4.04T
G-FEDA	Eurocopter EC 120B Colibri	1129	F-WQOD	2. 8.00	Federal Aviation Ltd	(Bury St.Edmunds)	22 .8.03T
G-FEFE	Scheibe SF-25B Falke	46126	EI-BVZ D-KADB	11. 4.94	D.G.Roberts t/a G-FEFE Syndicate	Aston Down	1.11.02
G-FELL	Europa Aviation Europa	PFA 247-13208		17. 3.98	R.Barton	(Milton Keynes)	
G-FELT	Cameron N-77 HAFB	1174		19. 7.85	Allan Industries Ltd *"Fuzzy Felt"*	Chinnor	13. 6.01A
G-FEZZ	Agusta Bell 206B JetRanger II	8317	SU-YAD YU-HAT	16. 9.98	L.Smith t/a Helicopter Services	Booker	4.10.04T
G-FFAB	Cameron N-105 HAFB	4067		20. 2.97	The Andrew Brownsword Collection	Bath	8. 6.02A
G-FFEN	Reims Cessna F150M	F15001204	PH-VGL	25. 8.78	R.J.Everett	Hill Farm, Nayland	19. 3.03T
G-FFFT	Lindstand LBL 31A HAFB	705		30. 5.00	The Aerial Display Co Ltd *(FT titles)*	Looe	7..5.01A

G-FFOX	Hawker Hunter T.7B *(Composite including components of WV322- see G-BZSE)*	41H-670788	WV318	10. 1.96	Delta Engineering Aviation Ltd *(As "WV318" in all-black c/s)*	Kemble	14. 5.02P
G-FFRA	Dassault Falcon 20DC	132	N902FR (N23FR)/(N149FE)/N2FE/N560L/N4348F/F-WMKG	28. 5.92	Cobham Leasing Ltd	Bournemouth	20.10.02A
G-FFRI	Aérospatiale AS355F1 Twin Squirrel	5120	G-GLOW G-PAPA/G-CNET/G-MCAH	15. 4.93	ATC Trading Ltd	Lasham	5. 5.03T
G-FFTI	SOCATA TB-20 Trinidad	1065		23. 2.90	Romsure Ltd	Standalone Farm, Meppershall	9. 6.02T
G-FFTT	Lindstrand LBL Newspaper SS HAFB	673		10. 7.00	The Aerial Display Co Ltd *(FT titles)*	Looe	4. 7.01A
G-FFUN	Pegasus Quantum 15	6655	G-MYMD	9. 6.99	J.B.Hobbs	Long Acre Farm, Sandy	12.12.02P
G-FFWD	Cessna 310R II	310R0579	G-TVKE G-EURO/N87468	20. 2.90	Keef & Co Ltd	Booker	19. 3.04
G-FGID	Vought FG-1D Corsair *(Built Goodyear Aircraft Corporation)*	3111	N8297 N9154Z/Bu.88297	1.11.91	Patina Ltd *(Op The Fighter Collection)* *(As "KD345/A-130" in 1850 Sqn RN c/s)*	Duxford	19. 3.02P
G-FHAJ	Airbus A320-231	0444	D-ACAF N444RX/TC-ONF/N444RX/F-WWBY	14.11.01	Airtours International Airways Ltd	Manchester	15.11.04T
G-FHAS	Scheibe SF-25E Super Falke	4359	(D-KOOG)	14. 5.81	Burn Gliding Club Ltd	Burn	23.11.02
G-FIAT	Piper PA-28-140 Cherokee F	28-7425162	G-BBYW N9622N	19. 7.89	The RAF Benevolent Fund Enterprises Ltd *(Op Disabled Flyers Group)*	Hinton-in-the-Hedges	20. 7.02T
G-FIBS	Aérospatiale AS350BA Ecureuil	2074	JA9732	14. 6.94	Pristheath Ltd	Denham	8. 8.03T
G-FIFE	Reims Cessna FA152 Aerobat	FA15200351	G-BFYN	15. 2.95	Tayside Aviation Ltd	Glenrothes	3. 2.03T
G-FIFI	SOCATA TB-20 Trinidad	688	G-BMWS	16. 1.87	F.A.Saker	Denham	15. 7.02
G-FIGA	Cessna 152 II	15284644	N6243M	3. 6.87	Aerohire Ltd *(Op Midland Flight Centre)*	Wolverhampton	23. 3.03T
G-FIGB	Cessna 152 II	15285925	N95561	16.11.87	Aerohire Ltd	Wellesbourne Mountford	12. 2.00T
G-FIJJ	Reims Cessna F177RG Cardinal *(Wichita c/n 17700194)*	F177RG0031	G-AZFP	29. 4.99	Middleton Miniature Mouldings Ltd	Teesside	15. 6.03
G-FIJR	Lockheed L.188PF Electra	1138	(EI-HCF) G-FIJR/C-FIJR/CF-IJR/N134US	12. 9.91	Atlantic Air Transport Ltd	Liverpool	12. 9.04T
G-FIJV	Lockheed L.188C Electra	1129	EI-HCE G-FIJV/C-FIJV/CF-IJV/N7143C	29. 8.91	Atlantic Air Transport Ltd *(Atlantic Airlines titles)*	Coventry	27. 9.01T
G-FILE	Piper PA-34-200T Seneca II	34-8070108	N8140Z	23. 7.87	Barnes Olson Aeroleasing Ltd	Bristol	23.11.02T
G-FILL	Piper PA-31 Navajo C	31-7912069	OO-EJM N3521C	28. 6.96	P.V.Naylor-Leyland	Deenethorpe	23. 8.02
G-FINA	Reims Cessna F150L	F15000826	G-BIFT PH-CEW	12.10.93	D.Norris	Finmere	15. 8.02T
G-FIND	Reims Cessna F406 Caravan II	F406-0045	OY-PEU 5Y-LAN/G-FIND/PH-ALV/F-WZDT	16. 8.90	Atlantic Air Transport Ltd	Coventry	4. 5.03T
G-FIRM	Cessna 550 Citation Bravo	550-0940	N5263S	29. 9.00	Marshall of Cambridge Aerospace Ltd	Cambridge	2.10.04T
G-FIRS	Robinson R22 Beta-II	2807		15. 4.98	M. & S.Chantler	(Crewe)	13. 5.04
G-FIRZ	Murphy Renegade Spirit UK	PFA 188-13494		10.12.99	D M Wood	(Banbury)	14.11.02P
G-FISH	Cessna 310R II	310R1845	N2740Y	8. 5.81	Air Charter Scotland Ltd	Edinburgh	28.10.02T
G-FISK*	Pazmany PL-4A (VW 1834)	PFA 017-10129		14.12.88	K.S.Woodard *(Stored 6.00: cancelled 8.11.00 by CAA)*	Little Snoring	11. 4.96P
G-FITZ	Cessna 335	335-0044	G-RIND N2710L	20. 4.95	D.S.Hodgetts	Wolverhampton	20. 1.02
G-FIZU	Lockheed L.188CF Electra	2014	EI-CHY G-FIZU/SE-IZU/(N857ST)/N857U/PH-LLG	6. 4.93	Atlantic Air Transport *(Stored 12.01))*	Coventry	3. 1.05T
G-FIZY	Europa Aviation Europa XS	PFA 247-13291	G-DDSC	16.12.99	G.Holland	(Bath)	
G-FIZZ	Piper PA-28-161 <u>Cherokee</u> Warrior II	28-7816301	N2721M	1.12.78	Tecair Aviation Ltd	Shipdham	19.10.03T
G-FJCE	Thruster T600T (Rotax 912-UL)	9120-T600T-032		25.11.98	F Cameron	(Craigavon, Co Armagh)	
G-FJET	Cessna 550 Citation II	550-0419	G-DCFR G-WYLX/VH-JVS/G-JETD/N1217N	7. 7.97	London Executive Aviation Ltd	London City	17. 1.02T
G-FJMS	Partenavia P.68B	113	G-SVHA OY-AJH	7. 9.92	F.J.M.Sanders *(Op Bonus Aviation)*	Cranfield	13. 6.02T
G-FKNH	Piper PA-15 Vagabond (Continental C85)	15-291	CF-KNH N4517H/NC4517H	19. 3.97	M.J.Mothershaw	Hawarden	15. 5.03
G-FLAG	Colt 77A HAFB	2000		20. 9.90	B.A.Williams	Maidstone	10. 6.97T
G-FLAK	Beechcraft E55 Baron	TE-1128	N4771M	26. 9.89	D.Clark *"Red Baron"*	Shipdham	29. 7.02T
G-FLAV	Piper PA-28-161 Warrior II	28-8016283	N8171X	7. 4.94	S.W.Parker t/a The Crew Flying Group	Leicester	23. 5.03
G-FLCA	Fleet 80 Canuck	068	CS-ACQ CF-DQP	18. 7.90	E.C.Taylor *(On rebuild 3.01)*	(Balsall Common)	
G-FLCT	Hallam Fleche	PFA 309-13389		21.10.98	R G Hallam	(Macclesfield)	

G-FLEA	SOCATA TB-10 Tobago	235	PH-TTP	31. 7.81	J.J.Berry	Shoreham	26. 7.02
			G-FLEA				
G-FLEW	Lindstrand LBL-90A HAFB	586		21. 1.99	Lindstrand Balloons Ltd	Oswestry	3. 5.02A
G-FLII	Grumman-American GA-7 Cougar		G-GRAC	18.12.91	Plane Talking Ltd	Elstree	23.10.04T
		GA7-0003	C-GRAC/(N1367R)/N730GA *(Op Capital Radio "Flying Eye")*				
G-FLIK	Pitts S-1S Special	PFA 09-10513		7. 1.81	R.P.Millinship	Leicester	22. 5.02P
	(Lycoming O-320)						
G-FLIP	Reims Cessna FA152 Aerobat		G-BOES	29.12.80	Walkbury Aviation Ltd	Sibson	9. 5.03T
		FA15200375	G-FLIP				
G-FLIT	Rotorway Executive 162F	6324		22.12.98	R.F.Rhodes.	(Maldon)	7.11.02P
	(Rotorway RI 162F)						
G-FLIZ	Staaken Z-21 Flitzer			24. 3.97	M.A.Wood Shempston Farm, Lossiemouth		
		006 & PFA 223-13115			*(As "D-694")*		
G-FLJA	Piper PA-32-260 Cherokee Six	32-219	G-AVTJ	6.12.00	F L Avery	Dunkeswell	20.11.01T
	(Rebuilt using spare Frame No.32-860S)		N3373W				
G-FLKE	Scheibe SF-25C Falke	44673		5.10.01	Faulkes Flying Foundation Ltd	Lasham	18.10.04
G-FLKS	Scheibe SF-25C Falke	44662	D-KIEQ	16.10.00	Faulkes Flying Foundation Ltd		
						Dunstable Downs	19.10.03
G-FLOA	Cameron O-120 HAFB	4006		4.10.96	Floating Sensations Ltd	Thatcham	20. 9.02T
G-FLOR	Europa Aviation Europa	PFA 247-12793		11.11.98	A.F.C.Van Eldik	Pent Farm, Kent	1.10.02P
	(Rotax 912-UL)	*(U/c not locked down & thus retracted on landing at base 13.10.01: damage to engine & propeller)*					
G-FLOX	Europa Aviation Europa	PFA 247-12732		28. 6.95	T.W.Eaton	Redhill	5. 7.02P
	(Jabiru 2200A)				t/a DPT Group		
G-FLPI	Rockwell Commander 112A	205	SE-FLP	16. 3.79	H.J.Freeman	Newcastle	22. 3.03T
			(N1205J)				
G-FLSI	FLS Sprint 160	001		20. 8.93	Sunhawk Ltd	North Weald	
G-FLTA	British Aerospace BAe 146 Srs.200		N189US	25. 2.98	Flightline Ltd	Aberdeen	26. 2.04T
		E2048	N365PS				
G-FLTG	Cameron A-140 HAFB	4506		3.11.00	Floating Sensations Ltd	Thatcham	9.11.01T
G-FLTY	Embraer EMB-110P1 Bandeirante		G-ZUSS	28. 8.92	Keenair Charter Ltd	Blackpool	12. 7.01T
		110.215	G-REGA/N711NH/PT-GMH				
G-FLTZ	Beechcraft 58 Baron	TH-1154	G-PSVS	21. 9.93	Stesco Ltd (Flightline Ltd)		
			N5824T/YV-266P			Southend/Guernsey	16. 8.04
G-FLUF	Lindstrand Bunny SS HAFB	002		7. 4.93	Lindstrand Balloons Ltd	(Oswestry)	
					(Not built: current CofR 3.01))		
G-FLVU	Cessna 501 Citation I	501-0178	N83ND	11. 6.98	Neonopal Ltd	Hawarden	23. 6.04T
			N4246A/LV-PML/N67749				
G-FLYA	Mooney M.20J (201SE)	24-3124		8. 6.89	BRF Aviation Ltd	Full Sutton	3.12.01
G-FLYE	Cameron A-210 HAFB	4216		12.12.97	N J Appleton	Bristol	22. 7.02T
G-FLYI	Piper PA-34-200 Seneca	34-7250144	G-BHVO	1. 9.81	S Papi & R Ruiz	Southend	29. 6.03T
			SE-FYY		t/a G-FLYI Group *(Op Willowair Flying Club)*		
G-FLYN	Reims Cessna F406 Caravan II		OY-PEZ	15.12.00	ILS Air Ltd	(Ely)	21. 6.03T
		F406-0048	D-ILIB/S9-IHB/HP-1236/N6589C/(PH-ALR)/F-WZDX *(Op Link Airlines)*				
G-FLYP	Beagle B.206 Srs 2	B.058	N40CJ	15.10.98	Key Publishing Ltd	Cranfield	29. 4.02T
			N97JH/G-AVHO/VQ-LAY/G-AVHO				
G-FLYS	Robinson R44 Astro	0347		5. 6.97	Newmarket Plant Hire Ltd	Cambridge	21. 6.03T
G-FLYT	Europa Aviation Europa			15. 5.95	K.F.& R.Richardson		
	(NSI EA-81/100)	57 & PFA 247-12653				Wellesbourne Mountford	6. 5.00P
G-FLYY	British Aircraft Corporation BAC.167 Strikemaster mk.80A						
		EEP/JP/163	1112	3. 9.01	B.T.Barber	City of Derry	
			R.Saudi AF/G-27-31				
G-FLZR	Staaken Z-21 Flitzer	PFA 223-13219		21. 9.01	J.F.Govan	East Linton	
G-FMAM	Piper PA-28-151 Cherokee Warrior		G-BBXV	7. 6.90	P B Anderson	Southend	25.11.02T
		28-7415056	N9603N		t/a Lima Tango Flying Group		
G-FMKA	Diamond HK36 TC Super Dimona	36.672		26. 4.00	A.Bailey	Enstone	11. 6.03
G-FMSG	Reims Cessna FA150K Aerobat		G-POTS	4. 1.95	G.Owen	Humberside	9.11.03T
		FA15000081	G-AYUY				
G-FNLD	Cessna 172N Skyhawk II	17270596	(G-BOUG)	3. 8.88	D.Wright & R.C.Laming	Fenland	26. 2.04
			N739KD		t/a Papa Hotel Flying Group		
G-FNLY	Reims Cessna F172M	F17200910	G-WACX	20. 3.89	C.F.Dukes	Exeter	9. 8.03T
			G-BAEX				
G-FODI	Robinson R44 Astro	0513		21. 9.98	Sanna Industries Ltd	Leicester	18.12.04T
G-FOGG	Cameron N-90 HAFB	1365		21.11.86	J.P.E.Money-Kyrle	Chippenham	25..9.96A
					"Phileas Fogg"		
G-FOGY	Robinson R22 Beta	1020	N62991	5. 7.99	P.Turvey	(Brackley)	12. 7.02T
			F-GGAI				
G-FOLD	Avid Speed Wing	PFA 189-12041		30.10.92	S.J.Higgins	(Deeside)	2. 6.01P
G-FOLI	Robinson R22 Beta-II	2813		25. 4.98	K.Duckworth	Wolverhampton	7. 6.04
G-FOLY	Aerotek Pitts S-2A Special	2213	N31477	26. 7.89	A.A.Laing	Perth	24. 2.02
	(Lycoming AEIO-360)						
G-FOPP	Neico Lancair 320	PFA 191-12319		14. 8.92	Airsport (UK) Ltd	Cranfield	19. 6.02P
	(Lycoming IO-320)						

G-FORC	SNCAN Stampe SV-4C	665	(G-BLTJ)	6. 6.85	I.A.Marsh	Little Gransden	24. 5.03
			F-BDNJ				
G-FORD	SNCAN Stampe SV-4C	129	F-BBNS	7. 2.78	P.H.Meeson	Chilbolton	31. 7.98
	(DH Gipsy Major 10)		*(Damaged East Tytherley 16.7.96: stored for re-build 6.99: curent status unknown)*				
G-FORR	Piper PA-28-181 Archer III	2843336	N4160Z	20. 4.00	B.& A.E.Galt	Dundee	19..4.03T
			G-FORR/N4160Z		t/a Buchanan Partnership		
G-FORS	Slingsby T.67C Firefly	2082	PH-SGD	17.11.99	V.R.Coultan, M.J.Golding, E.P.Dablin & M.Glazer		
			(PH-SBD)		t/a Open Skies Partnership	Turweston	1.12.02T
G-FOSY	SOCATA MS.880B Rallye Club	1304	G-AXAK	7.12.00	A.G.Foster	North Coates	17. 5.04
G-FOTO	Piper PA-E23-250 Aztec F	27-7654089	G-BJDH	27. 2.79	Aerofilms Ltd	Cranfield	10. 3.03A
			G-BDXV/N62614				
G-FOWL	Colt 90A HAFB	1198		11. 3.88	N.A.Fishlock	Cheltenham	10. 8.02A
					t/a G-FOWL Ballooning Group *"Chicken"*		
G-FOWS	Cameron N-105 HAFB	3995		11.12.96	Fowlers of Bristol Ltd	Bristol	27.11.01A
					(Fowlers Motorcycles titles)		
G-FOXA	Piper PA-28-161 Cadet	2841240	N9192B	17.11.89	Leicestershire Aero Club Ltd	Leicester	13. 5.02T
G-FOXC	Denney Kitfox mk.3			8. 1.91	G.Hawkins	(Wareham)	10. 9.01P
	(Rotax 582)	773 & PFA 172-11900			*"Foxe Lady"*		
G-FOXD	Denney Kitfox	PFA 172-11618		22.11.89	M.Hanley	Deenethorpe	21. 8.02P
	(Rotax 582)						
G-FOXE	Denney Kitfox mk.2			1. 8.90	K.M.Pinkard	(Chester)	31. 5.95P
	(Rotax 582)	740 & PFA 172-11994			*(Damaged Stewartby Lake, Beds 3.7.94: current status unknown)*		
G-FOXF	Denney Kitfox mk.4	PFA 172-12399		24. 3.00	M.S.Goodwin	(Erskine)	5. 9.02P
G-FOXG	Denney Kitfox mk.2			15. 8.90	A.C.Newman	Romney Street Farm, Sevenoaks	11.12.02P
	(Rotax 532)	452 & PFA 172-11886			t/a Kitfox Group		
G-FOXI	Denney Kitfox mk.2	PFA 172-11508		21. 9.89	B.Johns	Combrook, Stratford-upon-Avon	21. 8.02P
	(Rotax 532)						
G-FOXM	Bell 206B JetRanger II	1514	G-STAK	5. 2.93	R.P.Maydon	Oxford	26. 1.03T
			G-BNIS/N35HF/N135VG		t/a Milton Keynes City Air		
					(Op CSE Helicopters - Fox FM Radio)		
G-FOXS	Denney Kitfox mk.2			15. 8.90	S.P.Watkins & C.C.Rea	Sheepcote	3. 1.02P
	(Rotax 582)	465 & PFA 172-11571					
G-FOXZ	Denney Kitfox	PFA 172-11834		4.12.90	S.C.Goozee	(Wimborne)	19.10.98
G-FPIG	Piper PA-28-151 Cherokee Warrior		G-BSSR	22. 3.00	Flying Pig Aviation Ltd	Biggin Hill	14. 3.03
		28-7615001	N1190X				
G-FPLA	Beechcraft B200 Super King Air		N31WL	3.12.97	FR Aviation Ltd	Teesside	9. 3.04T
		BB-944	HB-GHZ/HL5260/N1824V		*(Op Flight Precision)*		
G-FPLB	Beechcraft B200 Super King Air		N739MG	3.12.97	FR Aviation Ltd	Teesside	11. 1.04T
		BB-1048	N223MD/9Y-TGY		*(Op Flight Precision)*		
G-FPLC	Cessna 441 Conquest II	441-0207	G-FRAX	14. 1.98	FR Aviation Ltd	Teesside	29. 3.03T
			G-BMTZ/N27280		*(Op Flight Precision)*		
G-FPLD	Beechcraft 200 Super King Air		N43CE	2.11.01	Cobham Leasing Ltd	Teesside	19.11.04T
		BB-1433	N43AJ/C-CMEV/C-CMEH/N8043K		*(Op Flight Precision)*		
G-FRAE	Dassault Falcon 20E	280/503	N910FR	23. 9.87	Aviation Defence Services		
			I-EDIS/F-WPXK			Arles Nimes Carmargue, France	19. 1.03A
G-FRAF	Dassault Falcon 20E	295/500	N911FR	1. 9.87	Cobham Leasing Ltd	Bournemouth	18.10.02A
			I-EDIM/F-WRQQ		*(Op FR Aviation)*		
G-FRAG	Piper PA-32-300 Six	32-7940284	N3566L	21. 1.80	T.A.Houghton	(Longfield)	21. 5.04
G-FRAH	Dassault Falcon 20DC	223	G-60-01	31. 5.90	Cobham Leasing Ltd	Teesside	7.10.02A
			N900FR/(N904FR)/N22FE/N4407F/F-WPUX		*(Op FR Aviation)*		
G-FRAI	Dassault Falcon 20E	270	N901FR	17.10.90	Cobham Leasing Ltd	Teesside	18. 4.03A
			N37FE/N4435F/F-WPUZ		*(Op FR Aviation)*		
G-FRAJ	Dassault Falcon 20DC	20	N903FR	30. 4.91	Cobham Leasing Ltd	Bournemouth	12.12.02A
			(N25FR)/N5FE/(N146FE)/N5FE/N367GA/N367/N842F/F-WMKJ		*(Op FR Aviation)*		
G-FRAK	Dassault Falcon 20DC	213	N905FR	9.10.91	Cobham Leasing Ltd	Bournemouth	13. 4.03A
			N32FE/N4390F/F-WJMM		*(Op FR Aviation)*		
G-FRAL	Dassault Falcon 20DC	151	N904FR	17. 3.93	Cobham Leasing Ltd	Teesside	22.12.02A
			(N24FR)/N3FE/(N148FE)/N3FE/N810PA/N810F/N4360F/F-WMKI		*(Op FR Aviation)*		
G-FRAM	Dassault Falcon 20DC	224	N907FR	13. 5.93	Cobham Leasing Ltd	Bournemouth	26. 5.02A
			N23FE/N4408F/F-WPUY		*(Op FR Aviation)*		
G-FRAN	Piper J-3C-65 Cub (L-4J-PI)	12617	G-BIXY	14. 7.86	I.Dole	Rayne Hall Farm, Rayne	19. 4.02P
	Continental C90) *(Frame No.12447)*		F-BDTZ/44-80321		t/a Essex L-4 Group *(As "480321/H-44" in USAAC c/s)*		
G-FRAO	Dassault Falcon 20DC	214	N906FR	23.10.92	Cobham Leasing Ltd	Bournemouth	28. 1.03A
			N33FE/N4400F/F-WNGO		*(Op FR Aviation)*		
G-FRAP	Dassault Falcon 20DC	207	N908FR	12. 7.93	Cobham Leasing Ltd	Bournemouth	19.10.02A
			N27FE/N4395F/F-WMKF		*(Op FR Aviation)*		
G-FRAR	Dassault Falcon 20DC	209	N909FR	2.12.93	Cobham Leasing Ltd	Bournemouth	15. 2.03A
			N28FE/N4396F/F-WLCX		*(Op FR Aviation)*		
G-FRAS	Dassault Falcon 20C	82/418	CAF117501	31. 7.90	Cobham Leasing Ltd	Bournemouth	1.12.02A
			20501/F-WJMM		*(Op FR Aviation)*		
G-FRAT	Dassault Falcon 20C	87/424	CAF117502	31. 7.90	Cobham Leasing Ltd	Teesside	21. 2.03A
			20502/F-WJMJ		*(Op FR Aviation)*		
G-FRAU	Dassault Falcon 20C	97/422	CAF117504	31. 7.90	Cobham Leasing Ltd	Teesside	15.12.02A
			20504/F-WJMJ		*(Op FR Aviation)*		

G-FRAW	Dassault Falcon 20C	114/420	CAF117507	31. 7.90	Cobham Leasing Ltd	Bournemouth	9. 4.02A
			20507/F-WJMM		*(Op FR Aviation)*		
G-FRAY	Cassutt Racer IIIM	PFA 034-11211		24.10.90	C.I.Fray	(Macclesfield)	
G-FRAZ	Cessna 441 Conquest II	441-0035	SE-GYC	14. 9.87	Cobham Leasing Ltd	Bournemouth	24. 9.02A
			(N36965)		*(Op FR Aviation)*		
G-FRBA	Dassault Falcon 20C	178/459	OH-FFA	16. 7.96	FR Finances Ltd	Bournemouth	16 .5.03A
			F-WPXF		*(Op FR Aviation)*		
G-FRBY	Beechcraft E55 Baron	TE-868	N78PS	23. 9.94	FR Finances Ltd	Bournemouth	30. 5.04T
			N77PS		*(Op FR Aviation)*		
G-FRCE*	Folland Gnat T.1	FL.598	8604M	28.11.89	Not known	Cranfield	17. 4.95P
			XS104		*(Cancelled 25.2.00 by CAA: in open storage 6.00)*		
G-FRED*	Clutton Fred Srs.II	PFA 029-10339		18. 5.78	Not known	Priory Farm, Tibenham	
					(Cancelled 2.9.91 by CAA: incomplete and stored 4.96: current status unknown)		
G-FRGN	Piper PA-28-236 Dakota	2811046	N9244N	8. 2.96	Fregon Aviation Ltd	Enstone	5. 3.02T
G-FRJB*	Britten SA-1 Sheriff	0001		18. 5.81	East Midlands Aeropark	East Midlands	
					(Not completed: cancelled by CAA 6.2.87: unfinished airframe on display without marks)		
G-FROH	Eurocopter AS 350B2 Ecureuil	9024		16. 5.00	Specialist Helicopters Ltd	(Munlochcy, Inverness)	18. 5.03T
G-FRST	Piper PA-44-180T Turbo Seminole	44-8207020	N8236B	5.11.82	D.B.Ryder & Co Ltd	(Welwyn Garden City)	18. 8.04
			N9615N				
G-FRYI	Beechcraft 200 Super King Air	BB-210	G-OAVX	15. 3.96	London Executive Aviation Ltd	Stapleford	26. 3.02T
			G-IBCA/G-BMCA/N5657N				
G-FSFT	Piper PA-44-180 Seminole	44-7995190	EI-CCO	12.10.98	M.J.Love	(Southampton)	12.10.04T
			N2135G		*(Op SFT Europe: ceased operations 12.01)*		
G-FSHA	Denney Kitfox Mk.2	PFA 172-11906		20. 9.99	P.P.Trangmar	(Hailsham)	
G-FTAX	Cessna 421C Golden Eagle II	421C0308	N8363G	23. 8.84	Gold Air International Ltd	Cambridge	16. 5.01T
			G-BFFM/N8363G				
G-FTFT*	Colt Financial Times 90SS HAFB	1163		14. 1.88	Financial Times Ltd	Newbury	5. 6.95A
					"Financial Times" (Cancelled 13.5.98 as WFU)		
					(On loan to British Balloon Museum & Library).		
G-FTIL	Robin DR.400/180 Regent	1825		10. 3.88	RAF Wyton Flying Club Ltd.	RAF Wyton	5.10.03T
G-FTIM	Robin DR.400/100 Cadet	1829		6. 5.88	M S Bird	Kemble	10. 5.04
G-FTIN	Robin DR.400/100 Cadet	1830		6. 5.88	G.D.Clark & M.J.D.Theobald	Blackpool	10.10.03
					t/a YP Flying Group		
G-FTSE	Fairey Britten-Norman BN-2A Mk.III-2 Trislander	1053	G-BEPI	23. 5.00	Aurigny Air Services Ltd	Guernsey	18.12.02T
					(Hambros Bank titles)		
G-FTUO	Van's RV-4	926	C-FTUQ	23.12.97	Euroclip 2000 Ltd	Hinton-in-the-Hedges	7. 3.02P
	(Lycoming IO-360-B4A)				*"Raven"*		
G-FTWO	Aérospatiale AS355F2 Twin Squirrel	5347	G-OJOR	27. 1.87	McAlpine Helicopters Ltd	Oxford	18. 3.02T
			G-FTWO/G-BMUS				
G-FUEL	Robin DR.400/180 Regent	1537		15. 5.81	R.Darch	East Chinnock, Yeovil	3. 8.03
G-FUJI*	Fuji FA.200-180 Aero Subaru	156	D-EMMI	14. 9.79	(M Colson)	(Redhill)	29. 6.92
	(Damaged Newton, Powys 5.5.92: cancelled 1.3.94 as WFU. sold & stored 7.95 for re-build: current status unknown)						
G-FULL	Piper PA-28R-200 Cherokee Arrow II	28R-7435248	G-HWAY	26.11.84	Stapleford Flying Club Ltd	Stapleford	13.12.02T
			G-JULI/(G-BKDC)/OY-POV/CS-AQF/N43128				
G-FUND	Thunder Ax7-65Z HAFB	376		3.11.81	Soft Sell Ltd *"Paddy Wagon"*	Wallingford	6.12.92A
G-FUNK	Yakovlev Yak-50	852908	RA-852908	27. 3.98	D.J.Gilmour	North Weald	1.11.02P
					t/a Intrepid Aviation Co		
G-FUNN	Plumb BGP-1 Biplane	PFA 083-12744		16.10.95	J.D.Anson	(Liskeard)	
G-FUZY	Cameron N-77 HAFB	1751		6. 5.88	Allan Industries Ltd	Chinnor	5.11.96A
					"Fuzzy Felt II"		
G-FUZZ	Piper PA-18 Super Cub 95	18-1016	(OO-HMY)	11. 9.80	G.W.Cline	Gipsy Wood, Yorkshire	8. 4.01P
	(L-18C-PI) *(Frame No.18-1086)*		ALAT-FMBIT/51-15319				
G-FVBF	Lindstrand LBL-210A HAFB	311		6.12.95	Virgin Balloon Flights Ltd	London SE16	26. 1.01T
					"Red November"		
G-FWPW	Piper PA-28-236 Dakota	2811018	N9145L	10.10.88	P.A. & F.C.Winters	Oxford	22.10.03
G-FWRP	Cessna 421C Golden Eagle III	421C0418	N3919C	9.12.82	Festival Property Co. Ltd	(London W1)	17.10.02
G-FXII	Supermarine 366 Spitfire F.XII	6S/197707	EN224	4.12.89	P.R.Arnold	(Newport Pagnell)	
					t/a Peter R.Arnold Collection		
					(On rebuild from components 3.00 as "EN224")		
G-FYAN	Williams Westwind MLB	MDW-1		6. 1.82	M.D.Williams	Dunstable	
G-FYAO	Williams Westwind MLB	MDW-001		6. 1.82	M.D.Williams	Dunstable	
G-FYAU	Williams Westwind Two MLB	MDW-002		6. 1.82	M.D.Williams	Dunstable	
G-FYAV	Osprey Mk.4E2 MLB	ASC-247		12. 1.82	C.D.Egan & C.Stiles	Hounslow	
G-FYBD	Osprey Mk.1E MLB	ASC-136		20. 1.82	M.Vincent	Jersey	
G-FYBE	Osprey Mk.4D MLB	ASC-128		20. 1.82	M.Vincent	Jersey	
G-FYBF	Osprey Mk.5 MLB	ASC-218		20. 1.82	M.Vincent	Jersey	
G-FYBG	Osprey Mk.4G2 MLB	ASC-204		20. 1.82	M.Vincent	Jersey	
G-FYBH	Osprey Mk.4G MLB	ASC-214		20. 1.82	M.Vincent	Jersey	
G-FYBI	Osprey Mk.4H MLB	ASC-234		20. 1.82	M.Vincent	Jersey	
G-FYCL	Osprey Mk.4G MLB	ASC-213		9. 2.82	P.J.Rogers	Banbury	
G-FYCV	Osprey Mk.4D MLB	ASK-276		19. 2.82	M.Thomson	London SW11	
G-FYCZ	Osprey Mk.4D2 MLB	ASC-244		24. 2.82	P.Middleton	Colchester	

G-FYDF	Osprey Mk.4D MLB	ASK-278		22. 3.82	K.A.Jones	Thornton Heath	
G-FYDI	Williams Westwind Two MLB	MDW-005		29. 3.82	M.D.Williams	Dunstable	
G-FYDN	European 8C MLB	DD34/S.22		5. 4.82	P.D.Ridout	Botley	
G-FYDO	Osprey Mk.4D MLB	ASK-262		15. 4.82	N.L.Scallan	Hayes	
G-FYDP	Williams Westwind Three MLB	MDW-006		29. 3.82	M.D.Williams	Dunstable	
G-FYDS	Osprey Mk.4D MLB	ASK-261		15. 4.82	M.E.Scallan	Hayes	
G-FYEK	Unicorn UE-1C MLB	82024		2. 7.82	D. & D.Eaves	Southampton	
G-FYEO	Scallan Eagle Mk.1A MLB	001		20. 7.82	M.E.Scallan	Hayes	
G-FYEV	Osprey Mk.1C MLB	ASK-294		10. 8.82	M.E.Scallan	Hayes	
G-FYEZ	Scallan Firefly Mk.1 MLB	MNS-748		22. 9.82	M.E. & N.L.Scallan	Hayes	
G-FYFI	European E.84PS MLB	S.29		1.12.82	M.A.Stelling	Barton-le-Clay	
G-FYFJ	Williams Westwind Two MLB	MDW-010		14.12.82	M.D.Williams	Dunstable	
G-FYFN	Osprey Saturn 2 DC3 MLB	ATC-250/MJS-11		17. 2.83	J.Woods & M.Woods	Bracknell	
G-FYFW	Rango NA-55 MLB *(Radio controlled)*	NHP-40		8.10.84	N.H.Ponsford & A.M.Lindsay t/a Rango Kite & Balloon Co *"Vaughan Williams"*	Leeds	
G-FYFY	Rango NA-55RC MLB *(Radio controlled)*	AL-43		28. 2.85	A.M.Lindsay *"Fifi"*	Leeds	
G-FYGI	Rango NA-55RC MLB *(Radio controlled)*	NHP-54		26. 6.90	D.K.Fish	Bedford	
G-FYGJ	Airspeed-300 MLB	001		8.10.91	N.Wells	Tunbridge Wells	
G-FYGM	Saffery/Smith Princess MLB	551		24.11.97	A. & N.Smith	Goole	
G-FZZA	General Avia F22-A	018		13. 8.98	APB Leasing Ltd	Welshpool	15.10.04T
G-FZZI	Cameron H-34 HAFB	2105		30.10.89	Magical Adventures Ltd	Chirk	30. 7.96A
G-FZZY*	Colt 69A HAFB	779		19. 2.86	Balloon Preservation Group *"Alka-Seltzer 2" (Cancelled 29.4.97 as WFU)*	Kirdford	16. 2.90A
G-FZZZ*	Colt 56A HAFB	507		23. 2.83	British Balloon Museum & Library *"Alka Seltzer 1" (Cancelled 29.4.97 as WFU)*	Newbury	

G-GAAA – G-GZZZ

G-GABD	Gulfstream GA-7 Cougar	GA7-0043	D-GABD	13. 4.82	C.B.Stewart *(Op Prestwick Flight Centre)*	Prestwick	5.12.02T
G-GACA	Hunting Percival P.57 Sea Prince T.1	P57/58	WP308	2. 9.80	P.G.Vallance Ltd *(Gatwick Aviation Museum: as "WP308/572")*	Charlwood, Surrey	4.11.80P
G-GAFA	Piper PA-34-200T Seneca II	34-7970218	D-GAFA N2247Z	12.10.99	SRC Contractors Ltd	Luton	6.12.02T
G-GAFX	Boeing 747-245F	20827	N641FE VP-BXP/N641FE/(N632FE)/N812FT/N702SW	28. 8.99	Airfreight Express Ltd *(Op Cargolux)*	Heathrow	9..9.02T
G-GAII	Hawker Hunter GA.11 *(Officially regd with c/n 41H-004038)*	HABL-003028	XE685	7.12.94	DAT Enterprises Ltd *(As "XE685/861/VL" in RN c/s)*	North Weald	24. 6.98P
G-GAJB	Gulfstream AA-5B Tiger	AA5B-1179	G-BHZN N37519	6. 4.87	G.A.J.Bowles	Elstree	7. 1.02T
G-GAJW	Bell 407	53186	N52245	15. 6.01	A.J.Walter (Aviation) Ltd	(Horsham)	15. 6.04T
G-GALA	Piper PA-28-180 Cherokee E	28-5794	G-AYAP N11C	31. 7.89	E.Alexander	(Braintree)	10. 5.02T
G-GALB	Piper PA-28-161 Warrior II	28-8616021	D-EHMP N9097E/(N157AV)/N9635N	1. 9.00	Goodair Leasing Ltd	Cardiff	14.12.03T
G-GALL	Piper PA-38-112 Tomahawk	38-78A0025	G-BTEV N9315T	1. 6.00	C.W.Good	Cardiff	15. 4.00T
G-GAME	Cessna T303 Crusader	T30300098	(F-GDFN) N2693C	25. 2.83	P.Heffron	Swansea	14. 6.04
G-GAND	Agusta-Bell 206B JetRanger II	8073	G-AWMK 9Y-TFC/G-AWMK/(VR-BCV)/G-AWMK	11. 1.00	Toms Helicopters Ltd.	Redhill	6. 6.03T
	(Airframe exchanged with 5N-AQJ during rebuild 1999 & became c/n 8051 by default, unofficially and ex 5N-AQJ/ G-BLPL/VR-BDY/I-EVBU. However, 5N-AQJ was cancelled 1.00 on export as VH-JEF with c/n 8051)						
G-GANE	Sequoia F.8L Falco (Lycoming IO-320)	906 & PFA 100-11100		25. 9.85	S.J.Gane	Kemble	13. 6.02P
G-GASC	Hughes 369HS (500)	110-0270S	G-WELD G-FROG/OO-KAR	11. 7.85	Crewhall Ltd	Effingham	21. 6.02
G-GASP	Piper PA-28-181 Cherokee Archer II	28-7790013	N4328F	15.10.90	D.J.Turner t/a G-GASP Flying Group	Fairoaks	21.12.02
G-GASS	Thunder Ax7-77 HAFB	1746		19. 4.90	M.W.Axon t/a Servowarm Balloon Syndicate *"Travel Gas III"*	London E9	5. 6.02A
G-GAWA	Cessna 140 (Continental C85)	9619	G-BRSM N72454/NC72454	17. 9.91	E.C.Murgatroyd	RAF Henlow	30. 5.02
G-GAZA	Aérospatiale SA.341G Gazelle 1	1187	G-RALE G-SFTG/N87712	19. 6.92	The Auster Aircraft Co Ltd	Waltham, Leics	23. 7.01
G-GAZI	Aérospatiale SA.341G Gazelle 1	1136	G-BKLU N32PA/N341VH/N90957	29. 6.90	Stratton Motor Co (Norfolk) Ltd & UCC International Group Ltd *(Stored 8.01)*	Stapleford	28. 6.00T

G-GAZZ	Aérospatiale SA.341G Gazelle 1	1271	F-GFHD	14. 3.90	Stratton Motor Co (Norfolk) Ltd		
			YV-242CP/HB-XGA/F-WMHC		& UCC International Group Ltd *(Op Cheqair)*		
						Long Stratton	22. 6.02T
G-GBAO	Robin R.1180TD Aiglon	277	F-GBAO	9. 9.81	J.Kay-Movat	Slinfold	10. 6.04
	(Rebuild of R.1180 prototype F-WVKU c/n 01)						
G-GBAY	Bell 206L-1 LongRanger II	45565	G-CSWL	29. 5.01	Helixair Ltd	Botany Bay, Chorley	20. 6.03T
			G-SIRI/G-CSWL/F-GDAD				
G-GBFF	Reims Cessna F172N	F17201565	F-GBFF	16. 6.99	E.J.Watts	(Wadebridge)	17 .6.02T
G-GBHI	SOCATA TB-10 Tobago	19	F-GBHI	12.11.97	A.B.S.Garden	Jersey	30.11.03
G-GBLP	Reims Cessna F172M Skyhawk II		G-GWEN	9.11.84	Aviate Scotland Ltd	Edinburgh	8.11.03T
		F17201042	G-GBLP/N14496		*(Op Edinburgh Air Centre)*		
G-GBLR	Reims Cessna F150L	F15001109	N961L	30. 4.85	G.Matthews	Coventry	7. 6.02T
			(D-EDJE)		t/a Blue Max Flying Group		
G-GBRB	Piper PA-28-180 Cherokee C	28-2583	N8381W	2. 2.00	G.Barker & R.Bradley	Carlisle	24. 2.03T
G-GBSL	Beechcraft 76 Duchess	ME-265	G-BGVG	27. 3.81	M.H.Cundey	Redhill/Alderney	12. 5.02
G-GBTA	Boeing 737-436	25859	G-BVHA	7. 2.94	British Airways plc	Gatwick	31.10.02T
			(G-GBTA)		*(Youm-Al-Suq t/s)*		
G-GBTB	Boeing 737-436	25860	OO-LTS	23.10.96	British Airways plc	Gatwick	28.10.02T
			G-BVHB/OO-LTS/G-BVHB/(G-GBTB)				
G-GBUE	Robin DR.400/120A Petit Prince	1354	G-BPXD	11. 5.89	J.A.Kane	Bagby	21. 6.04
			F-GBUE		t/a G-GBUE Group		
G-GBXS	Europa Aviation Europa Turbo XS	0005	"G-2000"	1. 4.98	Europa Aircraft Co Ltd	Wombleton	5. 6.02P
	(Mono-wheel u/c)		G-GBXS				
G-GCAT	Piper PA-28-140 Cherokee B	28-26032	G-BFRH	22.10.81	H.Skelton	Sturgate	18. 8.02
			OH-PCA		t/a Group CAT		
G-GCCL	Beechcraft 76 Duchess	ME-322	(G-BNRF)	5. 8.87	Aerolease Ltd	Conington	21.11.02T
			N6714U				
G-GCNZ*	Cessna 150M Commuter	15075933	C-GCNZ	8.11.88	Not known	Elstree	
					(Cancelled 8.6.99 as destroyed) (Wreck noted 2.01)		
G-GCJL	British Aerospace Jetstream Srs.4100			5. 2.91	BAE Systems (Operations) Ltd	Woodford	29. 4.95S
		41001			*(Stored 12.01)*		
G-GCKI	Mooney M.20K (231)	25-0401	N4062H	15. 8.80	B.Barr	Seething	15. 8.04
G-GCUB	Piper PA-18-150 Super Cub	18-7922	SE-GCO	11. 2.99	N.J.Morgan	Tatenhill	9 .6.02
			Swedish Army 51249/N10F				
G-GCYC	Reims Cessna F182Q Skylane	F18200157	F-GCYC	11. 2.00	G-GCYC Ltd	Barton	12..4.03
G-GDAM*	Piper PA-18-135 Super Cub	18-3535	PH-PVW	30. 6.81	Not known	Siege Cross Farm, Thatcham	11. 8.91
	(L-21B-PI) *(Frame No.18-3648)*		(PH-DKE)/R-107/54-2335		*(Cancelled by CAA 18.3.99: stored dismantled 10.01)*		
G-GDER	Robin R.1180TD	280	F-GDER	15. 5.97	Berkshire Aviation Services Ltd	Fairoaks	15. 5.03
G-GDEZ	British Aerospace BAe 125 Srs.1000B		N9026	30.10.95	Frewton Ltd	Jersey	9.11.01
		259026	G-5-743/ZS-ACT/ZS-CCT/G-5-743				
G-GDGR	SOCATA TB-20 Trinidad	378	F-GDGR	23. 7.97	Willwright Aviation Ltd	Liverpool	30. 8.03T
G-GDOG	Piper PA-28R-200 Cherokee Arrow II		G-BDXW	17. 4.89	R.K.& S.Perry	Thruxton	5. 8.02
		28R-7635227	N9235K				
G-GDRV	Van's RV-6	21367	C-GDRV	26.11.01	J.R.S.Heaton & R.Feather	Blackpool	
	(Built D.Piper)				*(Noted 11.01*		
G-GDTU	Avions Mudry CAP.10B	193	F-GDTU	27. 5.99	Sherburn Aero Club Ltd	Sherburn-in-Elmet	26 .5.02T
			(N....)/F-GDTK/F-WZCI				
G-GEDI	Dassault Falcon 2000	49	VP-BEF	23. 7.98	Victoria Aviation Ltd	(Guernsey)	22. 7.02T
			F-WWMD				
G-GEEE	Hughes 369HS	45-0738S	G-BDOY	2. 3.90	B.P.Stein	Denham	8.10.04
G-GEEP	Robin R.1180TD Aiglon	266		9. 4.80	Organic Concentrates Ltd	Booker	7. 8.04
G-GEES	Cameron N-77 HAFB	357		8.11.77	N.A.Carr *"Gee-Gees"*	Leicester	31. 5.00A
G-GEEZ	Cameron N-77 HAFB	1159		3. 5.85	Charnwood Forest Turf Accountants Ltd		
					"Tic Tac"	Leicester	7. 4.96A
G-GEGE*	Robinson R22 Beta-II	2994		19.10.99	C.& S.Hewgill	Gamston	28.10.02T
					t/a CSL Industrial *(Cancelled 2.7.01 by CAA)*		
G-GEHP	Piper PA-28RT-201 Arrow IV		F-GEHP	24. 4.98	Aeros Leasing Ltd	Gloucestershire	4. 7.04T
		28R-8218014	N82023				
G-GEMS	Thunder Ax8-90 Srs.2 HAFB	2287	G-BUNP	6.11.92	B.Sevenich, B.& S.Harren & W.Christoph		
					(Stolen 7.6.00)	Aachen, Germany	2. 4.01T
G-GENN	Gulfstream GA-7 Cougar	GA7-0114	G-BNAB	2.12.94	Abraxas Aviation Ltd	Elstree	15. 1.04T
			G-BGYP				
G-GEOF	Pereira Osprey 2	PFA 070-10384		7. 9.78	G.Crossley	(Blackpool)	
G-GERY	Stoddard-Hamilton GlaStar			6. 7.01	G.E.Collard	(Farnham)	
		PFA 295-13475					
G-GEUP*	Cameron N-77 HAFB	880		8.12.82	Balloon Preservation Group	Kirdford	19. 7.96
					"Gee-Up" (Cancelled 9.5.01 as wfu)		
G-GFAB	Cameron N-105 HAFB	2048		4. 8.89	The Andrew Brownsword Collection Ltd		
						Bath	8..6.02A
G-GFCA	Piper PA-28-161 Cadet	2841100	N9174X	24. 4.89	Aeros Leasing Ltd.	Gloucestershire	4.10.04T
G-GFCB	Piper PA-28-161 Cadet	2841101	N9175F	24. 4.89	AM & T Aviation Ltd	Bristol	11. 7.04T
G-GFCD	Piper PA-34-220T Seneca III		G-KIDS	31. 5.90	Stonehurst Aviation Ltd	Coventry	18.11.02T
		34-8133073	N83745				

G-GFCF	Piper PA-28-161 Cadet	2841259	G-RHBH N9193Z	28. 6.90	Aerohire Ltd	Wolverhampton	27. 1.02T
G-GFEY	Piper PA-34-200T Seneca II	34-7870343	D-GFEY D-IFEY/N36599	13. 5.98	Topa Panama Inc	Guernsey	28. 5.01
G-GFFA	Boeing 737-59D	25038	G-BVZF SE-DND/(SE-DNC)	10. 2.00	British Airways plc	Gatwick	2. 5.04T
G-GFFB	Boeing 737-505	25789	LN-BRT	15. 2.00	British Airways plc	Manchester	8. 5.03T
G-GFFC	Boeing 737-505	24272	LN-BRG	23. 3.00	British Airways plc	Gatwick	8. 6.03T
G-GFFD	Boeing 737-59D	26419	LY-BFV OY-SEG/G-OBMY/SE-DNI	3. 7.00	British Airways plc	Manchester	13. 8.03T
G-GFFE	Boeing 737-528	27424	LX-LGR (F-GJNP)	16. 6.00	British Airways plc	Manchester	10. 7.03T
G-GFFF	Boeing 737-53A	24754	G-OBMZ SE-DNC	2. 1.01	British Airways plc	Manchester	20. 9.02T
G-GFFG	Boeing 737-505	24650	LN-BRC N5573K	20. 9.00	British Airways plc	Manchester	29.10.03T
G-GFFH	Boeing 737-5H6	27354	VT-JAW 9M-MFG	24.10.00	British Airways plc	Manchester	23. 1.04T
G-GFFI	Boeing 737-528	27425	LX-LGS (F-GJNQ)	9.11.00	British Airways plc	Manchester	18.12.03T
G-GFFJ	Boeing 737-5H6	27335	VT-JAZ 9M-MFH	19. 1.01	British Airways plc	Manchester	12. 3.04T
G-GFKY	Zenair CH.250 (Lycoming O-235)	34	C-GFKY	23. 4.93	D.M.Edes	Inverness	6. 6.02P
G-GFLY	Reims Cessna F150L	F15000822	PH-CES	28. 8.80	Tindon Ltd	Little Snoring	1.12.04T
G-GFTA	Piper PA-28-161 Warrior III	2842047	N4132L <u>G-GFTA/N9525N</u>	1. 4.99	One Zero Three Ltd	Guernsey	31. 3.02T
G-GFTB	Piper PA-28-161 Warrior <u>III</u>	2842048	N4120V <u>G-GFTB/N4120V</u>	7. 5.99	One Zero Three Ltd	Guernsey	6..5.02T
G-GGGG	Thunder Ax7-77 HAFB	162		2. 8.78	T.A.Gilmour t/a Flying G Group *"Flying G"*	Stockbridge	17. 8.99A
G-GGLE	Piper PA-22-108 Colt	22-8914	N5234Z	13. 5.93	S.C.Hobden	(Hungerford)	25. 7.02T
	<u>(Frame No.108-915)</u> (Tail-wheel conversion incorporating parts from G-AROM c/n 22-8805)						
G-GGOW	Colt 77A HAFB	1542		19. 6.89	G.Everett *"Charles Rennie Mackintosh"*	Dartford	11. 3.02A
G-GGRR	Scottish Aviation Bulldog Srs.120/121	BH120/272	G-CBAM XX614	11. 7.01	F.P.Corbett	White Waltham	2. 9.04
G-GGTT	Agusta-Bell 47G-4A	2538	F-GGTT I-ANDO	21. 8.97	Face & Fragrance Ltd.	(Manchester)	8. 7.04
G-GHEE	Evektor-Aerotechnik EV-97 Eurostar	PFA 315-13840		14.12.01	C.J.Ball	(Cheltenham)	
G-GHIA	Cameron N-120 HAFB	2442		13.11.90	J.A.Marshall	Billingshurst	13. 8.02T
G-GHIN	Thunder Ax7-77 HAFB	1802		16. 7.90	N.T.Parry *"Pegasus"*	Binfield	4. 9.00A
G-GHOW	Reims Cessna F182Q Skylane	F18200151	OO-MCD F-BJCE	20. 2.01	G.How *(Noted 8.01)*	Top Farm, Croydon	3 .4.04T
G-GHRW	Piper PA-28RT-201 Arrow IV	28R-7918140	G-ONAB G-BHAK/N29555	8.12.83	Bonus Aviation Ltd	Cranfield	22.12.03T
G-GHSI	Piper PA-44-180T Turbo Seminole	44-8107026	SX-ATA N8278Z	2.12.94	M.G.Roberts	Bournemouth	1.12.97
				(Damaged late 1994: on rebuild 8.95: current status unknown)			
G-GHZJ	SOCATA TB-9 Tampico	941	F-GHZJ	4. 3.98	M.Haller	Little Snoring	30. 4.04
G-GIFT	Piper PA-28-181 Archer III	2843222	G-IMVA SE-KIH/N9524N/N4166F	13. 2.01	On Air Aviation Ltd	Sturgate	27. 9.02T
G-GIGI	SOCATA MS.893A Rallye Commodore 180	11637	G-AYVX F-BSFJ	28. 9.81	D.J.Moore	Aston Down	13. 4.00
G-GILT	Cessna 421C Golden Eagle III	421C0515	G-BMZC N555WV/N555WW/N885WW/N885EC/N88541	3. 7.97	Auto Corporation Ltd	Hawarden	9.10.03T
G-GINO	Auster V J/1 Autocrat				*<u>See entry for G-AJEM</u>*		
G-GIRA	British Aerospace HS.125 Srs.700B	257103	YL-VIR YL-VIP/VP-BOJ/VR-BOJ/G-LTEC/G-BHSU/G-5-12	16. 1.02	EAS Aeroserviza SAS	(Venice, Italy)	
G-GIRY	American General AG-5B Tiger	10146	F-GIRY	5. 2.99	Crestway Technologies Ltd	Denham	7..4.02T
G-GISO	Piper PA-44-180T Turbo Seminole	44-8107065	D-GISO N82112/N9602N	25.10.01	G.Cockerton	Coventry	26.11.04T
G-GIWT	Europa Aviation Europa XS	PFA 247-13623		29. 3.01	A.Twigg	(Wootton Bassett)	
G-GJCD	Robinson R22 Beta	0966		22. 2.89	J.C.Lane	Wolverhampton	21. 5.04T
G-GJKK	Mooney M.20K (252TSE)	25-1227	F-GJKK	26.11.93	Pergola Ltd	(Douglas, IoM)	15. 3.03
G-GKAT	Enstrom 280C Shark	1200	F-GKAT N5694Y	26. 8.97	Elham Valley Aviation Ltd	Lydd	8. 3.04
G-GKFC	Tiger Cub RL5A LW Sherwood Ranger (Jabiru 2200A)	PFA 237-12947	G-MYZI	24.11.98	K.F.Crumplin	Franklyn's Field, Chewton Mendip	26.11.01P
G-GLAD	Gloster Gladiator II	-	N5903	5. 1.95	Patina Ltd	Duxford	
				(Op The Fighter Collection) (On rebuild 1.01 as "N2276")			
G-GLAW	Cameron N-90 HAFB	1808		10.10.88	George Law Plant Ltd *"Law Civil Engineers"*	Kidderminster	17. 8.99A

G-GLED	Cessna 150M	15076673	C-GLED	6. 1.89	Firecrest Aviation Ltd	Elstree	26.11.04T
G-GLTT	Piper PA-31-350 Chieftain	31-8452004	N27JV	19. 9.97	Birchin International plc	Guernsey	18. 3.04T
			XA-SVW/XA-SGZ/N606SM/N4115D				
G-GLUC	Van's RV-6	20153	C-GLUC	15.10.99	Speedfreak Ltd	Crosland Moor	12 .6.02P
	(Built L De Sandeleer)						
G-GLUE	Cameron N-65 HAFB	390		17. 3.81	L.J.M.Muir & G.D.Hallett	East Molesey	17. 7.90A
					"Tacky Jack/Jack of Herts" (Mobile Windscreens titles)		
G-GLUG	Piper PA-31-350 Chieftain	31-8052077	N2287J	1. 9.94	Champagne-Air Ltd	Newcastle	23.11.02T
			G-BLOE/G-NITE/N3559A				
G-GMAB	British Aerospace BAe 125-1000B	259034	N81HH	21.11.01	Gama Aviation Ltd	Fairoaks	
			N290H/G-BUWX/G-5-761				
G-GMAX	SNCAN Stampe SV-4C	141	G-BXNW	19. 6.87	Glidegold Ltd	Booker	29. 8.93T
			F-BBPB				
			(Damaged in crash Booker 3.6.91: on rebuild 5.96: current status unknown)				
G-GMPA	Aérospatiale AS355F2 Twin Squirrel	5409	G-BPOI	26. 9.89	Police Aviation Services Ltd	Gloucestershire	9.11.01T
G-GMPS	MD Helicopters Explorer	900-00081	N7033K	8. 1.01	Greater Manchester Police Authority	Barton	12. 2.04T
G-GMSI	SOCATA TB-9 Tampico	145		18. 9.80	M.L.Rhodes	Wolverhampton	28. 5.03T
G-GNAT	Folland Gnat T.1	FL.595	8638M	14. 4.82	Brutus Holdings Ltd	Cranfield	17. 9.02P
			XS101		*(As "XS101" in CFS c/s)*		
G-GNJW	Comco Ikarus C42	PFA 322-13717		21. 8.01	I.R.Westrope	(Haverhill)	
G-GNTB	Saab-Scania SF.340A	340A-082	HB-AHL	30. 9.91	Swedish Aircraft Holdings AB	(Stockholm, Sweden)	10.10.01T
			OK-RGS/SE-E82				
G-GNTC	Saab-Fairchild SF.340A	340A-020	HB-AHE	25. 9.92	Aurigny Air Services Ltd	Guernsey	24. 9.02T
			SE-E20				
G-GNTE	Saab-Scania SF.340A	340A-133	SE-ISM	22. 1.93	Swedish Aircraft Holdings AB	(Stockholm, Sweden)	21. 1.02T
			SE-F33				
G-GNTF	Saab-Scania SF.340A	340A-113	HB-AHO	27.10.94	Swedish Aircraft Holdings AB	(Stockholm, Sweden)	27.10.01T
			SE-F13				
G-GNTG	Saab-Scania SF.340A	340A-126	HB-AHR	18.11.94	Aurigny Air Services Ltd	Guernsey	18.11.02T
			SE-F26				
G-GOBT	Colt 77A HAFB	1815		13. 2.91	British Telecommunications plc *"Sky Piper"*	Thatcham	18. 3.00A
G-GOCX	Cameron N-90 HAFB	2619		7. 8.91	R.D.Parry	Hong Kong, PRC	5. 1.02A
G-GOGW	Cameron N-90 HAFB	3304		31. 8.94	Great Western Trains Co Ltd	Swindon	19. 5.02A
G-GOLF	SOCATA TB-10 Tobago	250		21.12.81	E.H. & A.C.Scammell, G.J.Powell & B.Bain	Biggin Hill	6. 7.03
G-GOMM	Piper PA-32R-300 Lance	32R-7780030	(G-BHTR)	16. 5.80	L.Major	(Christchurch)	24..6.98
			N6571F		*(Damaged 15.8.95: valid CofR 3.01: current status unknown)*		
G-GONE	de Havilland DH.112 Venom FB.50 (FB.1)	752	J-1542	17. 9.84	D.G.Jones	Bournemouth	12.12.01P
	(Built F + W)						
	(Test flown 3.12.00 with Venom nose: made wheels-up landing Biggin Hill 2.6.01: damage to underside)						
G-GOOD	SOCATA TB-20 Trinidad	1657	F-GNHJ	4.11.94	N.J.Vetch	Goodwood	10. 1.04T
G-GORE	CFM Streak Shadow (Rotax 532)	K.138-SA & PFA 206-11646		12. 4.90	M.S.Clinton	Old Sarum	17. 4.02P
			(PFA c/n duplicates TEAM mini-MAX G-MWFD)				
G-GORF	Robin HR.200/120B	291	F-GORF	14. 1.00	J.A.Ingram	Nottingham	10. 2.03T
G-GOSL	Robin DR.400/180 Regent	1974	G-BSDG	14. 1.02	R.M.Gosling	Stones Farm, Wickham St Pauls, Essex	23. 5.02
G-GOSS	CEA Jodel DR-221 Dauphin	125	F-BPRA	4.12.80	D.Oddy t/a Avon Flying Group	Bidford	12. 5.03
G-GOTC	Gulfstream GA-7 Cougar	GA7-0074	G-BMDY	25. 6.97	Cambridge Aircraft Ltd	Elstree	9. 1.02T
			OO-LCR/OO-HRA				
G-GOTO	Piper PA-32R-301T Saratoga II TC	3257026	N92965	8. 1.98	J.A.Varndell	Blackbushe	21. 1.04
			G-GOTO/N92965				
G-GOUP	Robinson R22 Beta	1663	G-DIRE	9. 1.01	Heliair Ltd	Wellesbourne Mountford	27. 3.03T
G-GOZO	Cessna R182 Skylane RG II	R18201883	G-BJZO	9. 1.85	D.Pelling	Mount Airey, Hull	26. 6.04
			(G-BJYE)/N5521T				
G-GPAG	Van's RV-6	PFA 181-13306		18. 5.01	P.A.Green	(Romsey)	
G-GPAS	Jabiru Jabiru UL-450	PFA 274A-13823		15. 1.02	G.D.Allen	(Stowmarket)	
G-GPEG	Cameron Sky 90-24 HAFB	4849		31. 5.00	N.T.Parrry	Bracknell	24..6.02A
G-GPMW	Piper PA-28R-201T Turbo Arrow IV	28R-8031041	N3576V	3. 7.89	Calverton Flying Group Ltd	(Milton Keynes)	14. 5.04T
G-GPST	Phillips ST.1 Speedtwin (Continental O-200-A)	1 & PFA 207-11645		21. 6.90	Speedtwin Developments Ltd	Upper Cae Garw Farm, Trelleck, Monmouth	24.10.02P
	(PFA c/n duplicates Kolb Twinstar G-MWWM)						
G-GRID	Aérospatiale AS355F1 Twin Squirrel	5012	TG-BOS	28. 3.89	National Grid Co plc	Oxford	18. 6.04T
G-GRIF	Rockwell Commander 112TC-A	13258	G-BHXC	2.10.81	N.G.W.Cragg, E.T.N.Sutherland & C.Walker t/a Nicol Aviation	Gamston	28. 3.04
			N1005C				
G-GRAY*	Cessna 172N Skyhawk II	172-72375	N4859D	3.12.79	Not known	Nottingham	13. 2.95
			(Damaged ditching Firth of Forth, Mussleburgh 2.4.93: cancelled 27.9.00 as wfu: noted dismantled 4.01)				
G-GRIN	Van's RV-6	PFA 181-12409		8. 1.98	A.Phillips	Boarhunt Farm, Fareham	23. 5.02P
G-GRIP	Colt Bibendum 110SS HAFB	4224		5. 1.98	The Aerial Display Co Ltd *(Michelin titles)*	Looe	25. 1.02A

G-GROL	Maule MXT-7-180 Star Rocket	14091C		16. 6.98	D.C., C.& C.Croll	Southend	16.12.04
G-GRRC	Piper PA-28-161 Warrior II	2816076	G-BXJX	9. 3.98	Goodwood Road Racing Co Ltd	Goodwood	2.11.03T
			HB-POM/D-EJTB/N9149X				
G-GRRR	Scottish Aviation Bulldog Srs.120/122		G-BXGU	19.10.98	Horizons Europe Ltd	Old Sarum	25. 5.02T
		BH120/229	Ghana AF G-105				
G-GRYZ	Beechcraft F33A Bonanza	CE-1668	F-GRYZ	4.10.99	J.Kawadri & M.Kaveh	Booker	19.10.02
			D-ESNE/N80011/(OY-GEN)/N80011				
G-GSFC	Robinson R22 Beta	0569	N2425J	3. 7.86	Pegaso Team SRL	(Cagliari, Italy)	4.10.01T
G-GSFT	Piper PA-44-180 Seminole	44-7995202	EI-BYZ	12.10.98	Plane Talking Ltd	Elstree	19.12.04T
			N2193K				
G-GSSA	Boeing 747-47UF	29256	N495MC	23. 1.02	Global Supply Systems Ltd	Stansted	
			(N496MC)		*(British Airways c/s)*		
G-GGSB	Boeing 747-47UF	29255	N494MC	R	Global Supply Systems	Heathrow	
					(Op British Airways) (Atlas Air c/s)		
G-GTHM	Piper PA-38-112 Tomahawk II		C-GTHM	17.11.86	D.A.Whitmore	RAF Coltishall	15.11.04T
		38-81A0171	N91338				
G-GUAY	Enstrom 480	5036		1.12.98	Testactual Ltd	(Fareham)	30.12.04T
					t/a Heliway Aviation		
G-GUCK	Beechcraft C23 Sundowner 180	M-2221	G-BPYG	9. 4.92	J.T.Francis	Headcorn	25. 9.04
			N6638R				
G-GUFO	Cameron Saucer 80SS HAFB	1641	C-GUFO	10. 6.98	Magical Adventures Ltd	Chirk	2. 8.01A
			G-BOUB				
G-GULF	Lindstrand LBL-105A HAFB	320		3.11.95	M.A.Webb	Chard	17. 7.02A
G-GULP	III Sky Arrow 650T	PFA 298-13664		4.12.00	Lord Rotherwick	(Chipping Norton)	
G-GUNS	Cameron V-77 HAFB	2221		9. 5.90	Royal School of Artillery Hot Air Balloon Club		
					"Guns"	Larkhill	20. 9.01A
G-GURL*	Cameron A-210 HAFB	2387		3. 9.90	Balloon Preservation Group	(Austria)	29. 8.96T
					"Hot Airlines" (Cancelled 2.12.98 as WFU)		
G-GURN	Piper PA-31 Turbo Navajo C		G-BHGA	20. 6.01	Neric Ltd	(Guernsey)	5. 4.03
		31-7912117	N3539M				
G-GUSS	Piper PA-28-151 Cherokee Warrior		G-BJRY	16. 8.95	M.J.Cleaver & J.M.Newman	Southend	7. 6.03T
		28-7415497	N43453				
G-GUST	Agusta-Bell 206B JetRanger II	8192	G-CBHH	30. 8.96	Gatehouse Estates Ltd	Sywell	11. 1.03T
			F-GALU/G-AYBE				
G-GUYS	Piper PA-34-200T Seneca II		G-BMWT	14. 7.87	R.J.& J.M.Z.Keel	Sturgate	9. 5.02
		34-7870283	N31984				
G-GVBF	Lindstrand LBL-180A HAFB	250	PH-VBF	19. 5.95	Virgin Balloon Flights Ltd	London SE16	2. 4.00T
			G-GVBF				
G-GWIZ	Colt Clown SS HAFB	1369	(G-BPWU)	25. 4.89	Magical Adventures Ltd	(USA)	13. 4.99A
G-GWYN	Reims Cessna F172M Skyhawk II		PH-TWN	5. 3.81	D.J.Bruford	Exeter	27. 4.02
		F17201217					
G-GYAV	Cessna 172N Skyhawk II	17271362	C-GYAV	26. 8.87	Southport & Merseyside Aero Club (1979) Ltd		
						Liverpool	12. 3.03T
G-GYBO	Gardan GY-80-180 Horizon	228	OY-DTN	4. 8.98	M.J.Strother	Leeds-Bradford	23. 8.03T
			SE-FGL/OY-DTN				
G-GYMM	Piper PA-28R-200 Cherokee Arrow B		G-AYWW	22. 2.90	J.B.A.Ainsworth	Leicester	16.10.04
		28R-7135049	N11C		t/a Gymm Group		
G-GYRO	Campbell Cricket	PFA G/03-1046		26. 2.82	J.W.Pavitt	St.Merryn	2. 7.02P
	(Rotax 532) *(Originally registered as Bensen B.8 Gyrocopter (c/n 01 & PFA 0G-01-1046))*						
G-GYTO	Piper PA-28-161 Warrior III	2842082	N160FT	11. 5.00	Wellesbourne Flyers Ltd t/a Wellesbourne Aviation		
			N9511N			Wellesbourne Mountford	30. 5.03T
G-GZDO	Cessna 172N Skyhawk II	17271826	C-GZDO	11.10.88	G.Cambridge & G.W.J.Hall	Elstree	17. 5.04T
			(N5299E)		t/a Cambridge Hall Aviation *(Op Firecrest Aviation)*		
G-GZLE	Aérospatiale SA.341G Gazelle 1	1145	G-PYOB	8. 5.01	R.G.Fairall	Redhill	19.12.03
			G-IYOB/G-WELA/G-SFTD/G-RIFC/G-SFTD/N641HM/N341BB/F-WKQH				

G-HAAA – G-HZZZ

G-HACK	Piper PA-18-150 Super Cub	18-7168	SE-CSA	20.11.97	S.J.Harris	North Weald	2.12.03
			N10F				
G-HADA	Enstrom 480	5017		17. 9.96	W.B.Steele	Whitchurch, Shropshire	24. 9.02
G-HAEC	Commonwealth CAC-18 Mustang 22		VR-HIU	1. 5.85	R.W.Davies *"Big Beautiful Doll"*		
		CACM-192-1517	(RP-C651)/PI-C651/VH-FCB/A68-192		*(Op The Old Flying Machine Ltd)*		
						Little Robhurst Farm, Woodchurch	10. 6.02P
					(As "472218/WZ-I" in 78th FG USAAF c/s)		
	(Composite rebuilt 1974-76 using major components ex Philippine AF P-51D 44-72917)						
G-HAIG	Rutan LongEz 1983-L & PFA 074A-11149			20. 5.86	R.Casey & D.W.Parfrey	Coventry	9.12.02P
	(Lycoming 0-235)						
G-HAIR	Robin DR.400/180	2479		7.12.00	Arden Ridge Developments Ltd	(Southham)	25. 1.04T
					t/a Racoon International		
G-HAJJ	Glaser-Dirks DG-400	4-225		15. 2.88	P.W.Endean	Perranporth	21. 4.03
G-HALC	Piper PA-28R-200 Cherokee Arrow II		N91253	26.11.90	Halcyon Aviation Ltd	Barton	18. 7.03
		28R-7335042	C-FFQO/CF-FQO				

G-HALE	Robinson R44 Astro	0492		6. 8.98	Barhale Surveying Ltd	Elstree	19. 8.01T
G-HALJ	Cessna 140	8336	N89308	30. 4.96	H.A.Lloyd-Jennings	Old Sarum	24. 8.02
	(Continental C85)		NC89308				
G-HALL	Piper PA-22-160 Tri-Pacer	22-7423	G-ARAH	8.11.79	F.P.Hall	Maypole Farm, Chislet	29. 6.03
			N10F				
G-HALO	Elisport CH-7 Angel	A.031	I-2858	12.11.93	Taylor Woolhouse Ltd	(Rotherham)	30. 7.94P
					(Stored 6.97: valid CoR 3.01: current status unknown)		
G-HALP	SOCATA TB-10 Tobago	192	G-BITD	19. 8.81	D.Halpern	Booker	30. 5.97
G-HAMA	Beechcraft 200 Super King Air	BB-30	N244JB	16.11.84	Gama Aviation Ltd	Heathrow/Fairoaks	19.11.02T
			N211JB/N3090C/N3030C/N200CA				
	(Upgraded to B200 status with four blade propellers in 1999)						
G-HAMI	Fuji FA.200-180 Aero Subaru		G-OISF	31. 1.92	K.G.Cameron	Biggin Hill	31. 3.02T
		FA200-188	G-BAPT				
G-HAMP	Bellanca 7DCA Champ	30-72	N9173L	8. 8.88	K.Macdonald	Rushett Farm, Chessington	5. 8.02P
G-HANA	Westland Wessex HC.Mk.2	WA/624	XV729	9. 3.01	R.A.Fidler	Honeycrock Farm, Redhill	
	(C/n officially quoted as WA/513 but may be part of fuselage number)						
G-HAND*	Cameron Startac 105SS HAFB	3895		19. 8.96	Redmalt Ltd	Witham, Essex	6. 5.00A
					(Stolen 12.00: cancelled 29.11.01 by CAA)		
G-HANS	Robin DR.400 2 + 2	1384		2. 3.79	T.A.White t/a Bagby Aviation	Teesside	20. 6.03T
G-HANY	Agusta Bell 206B-3 JetRanger III		G-JEKP	5. 1.01	Swift Helicopters Ltd	(Macclesfield)	3. 4.03T
		8598	D-HMSF/G-ESAL/G-BHXW				
G-HAPI	Lindstrand LBL 105A HAFB	669		21. 3.00	Adventure Balloon Co Ltd	London W7	2. 7.02T
G-HAPR	Bristol 171 Sycamore HC.14	13387	8010M	15. 6.78	E.D.ap Rees	Weston-super-Mare	
			XG547		t/a The Helicopter Museum *(As "XG547/T-S" in CFS c/s)*		
G-HAPY	de Havilland DHC.1 Chipmunk 22		WP803	3. 7.96	G-HAPY Ltd	Booker	16. 9.02
		C1/0697			*(As "WP803")*		
G-HARE	Cameron N-77 HAFB	1467		12. 3.87	C.E. & J.Falkingham	Stevenage	25. 5.02A
G-HARF	Gulfstream Gulfstream IV	1117	N1761J	9.10.91	Fayair (Jersey) Co Ltd	Stansted/Jersey	20.12.02T
					(Op Harrods)		
G-HARH	Sikorsky S-76B	760391	N7600U	30. 9.91	Air Harrods Ltd	Stansted	17. 1.02T
G-HARI	Raj Hamsa X'Air 582 (2)			11. 6.99	E Joplin	Lower Mountpleasant, Chatteris	10 11.02P
	(Victor V2)	455 & BMAA/HB/103					
G-HARN	Piper PA-28-181 Archer II	28-8290108	G-DENK	3. 2.00	Harnett Air Services Ltd	Elstree	15. 2.04T
			G-BXRJ/HB-PGO				
G-HARP	Eurocopter EC 135T1	0115	VP-CAF	25. 4.01	Air Harrods Ltd	Stansted	25. 4.04T
			D-HECG				
G-HART	Cessna 152 II	15279734	(G-BPBF)	2. 2.89	Atlantic Air Transport Ltd	Coventry	25. 6.04T
	(Tail-wheel u/c conversion)		N757GS				
G-HARY	Alon A-2 Aircoupe	A.188	G-ATWP	15. 3.93	R.E.Dagless	Swanton Morley	22. 4.01
G-HASI	Cessna 421B Golden Eagle	421B0654	G-BTDK	17. 2.98	Hawarden Air Services Ltd	Hawarden	7. 3.02
			OY-BFA/N1558G				
G-HATF	Thorp T-18CW	PFA 076-11481		6.12.01	A.T.Fraser	(Crowthorne)	
G-HATZ	Hatz CB-1	17	N54623	11. 5.89	S.P.Rollason	Long Marston	23. 9.02P
	(Lycoming O-320)						
G-HAUL*	Westland WG.30-300	020	G-17-22	3. 7.86	The Helicopter Museum	Weston-super-Mare	27.10.86P
					(Cancelled 22.4.92 as WFU)		
G-HAUS	Hughes 369HM (500M)	52-0214M	G-KBOT	20. 7.99	J Pulford	Sywell	14.10.02
			G-RAMM/EI-AVN/N9037F		t/a Pulford Aviation		
G-HAZE	Thunder Ax8-90 HAFB	989		3. 8.88	T.G.Church	Blackburn	23. 6.97T
G-HBBC	de Havilland DH.104 Dove 8	04211	G-ALFM	24. 1.96	BBC Air Ltd	Compton Abbas	4. 7.04
			VP961/G-ALFM/VP961				
G-HBMW	Robinson R22	0170	G-BOFA	7. 7.94	Northumbria Helicopters Ltd	Newcastle	30. 9.03T
			N9068D				
G-HBOS	Scheibe SF-25C Rotax-Falke	44574	D-KTIN	26. 7.01	Coventry Gliding Club Ltd		
						Husbands Bosworth	29. 8.04
G-HBUG	Cameron N-90 HAFB	1991	G-BRCN	21. 6.89	R.T. & H.Revel *"Humbug"*	High Wycombe	4. 5.02A
G-HCFR	British Aerospace BAe 125 Srs.800B		HB-VLT	23. 7.98	Chauffair Ltd	Farnborough	26. 7.02T
		258240	G-SHEA/G-BUWC/G-5-772				
G-HCSL	Piper PA-34-220T Seneca III		N84375	9. 5.91	Shoreham Flight Centre Ltd	Shoreham	16.11.03T
		34-8133237					
G-HDEW	Piper PA-32R-301 Saratoga SP		G-BRGZ	4.12.89	R.J.F.Welsh, P.G.Foster & R.G.Gibbs		
		3213026	N91787		t/a Executors of the Estate of the late Lord Howard de Walden		
						(London EC4)	11. 3.04
G-HDGS	British Aerospace Jetstream Srs.3109		G-PLAM	5.12.01	Davis Air (Pty) Ltd	Cranfield	
		720	SE-LHV/G-BRGL/OK-SEK/G-OEDC/G-LOGU/G-BRGL/I-BLUA/G-31-720/G-BRGL/G-31-720				
G-HDIX	Enstrom 280FX	2076	N506DH	19. 2.98	J.Poupard	(King's Lynn)	3. 5.04T
			D-HDIX				
G-HEBE	Bell 206B-3 JetRanger III	3745	CS-HDN	5. 2.97	MGGR (UK) Ltd	Gloucestershire	8. 6.03T
			N3179A				
G-HELE	Bell 206B-3 JetRanger III	3789	G-OJFR	21. 2.91	B E E Smith	White Waltham	12. 5.03T
			N18095				
G-HELN	Piper PA-18 Super Cub 95	18-3365	G-BKDG	10. 1.86	J.J.Anziani	Booker	8. 5.02P
	(L-21B-PI) *(Frame No.18-3400)*		MM52-2392/EI-69/EI-141/I-EIWB/MM53-7765/53-7765				
	(Regd as c/n 18-1992 but frame exchanged in Italian AF service: c/n 18-3365 was officially regd as N9837Q)						

G-HELP*	Colt 17A Cloudhopper HAFB	902		16. 2.87	Balloon Preservation Group	Kirdford	7. 8.95A
					"Mondial Cloudhopper" (Cancelled 27.3.99 as PWFU)		
G-HELV	de Havilland DH.115 Vampire T.55	975	U-1215	17. 9.91	Hunter Wing Ltd	Bournemouth	28. 5.02P
	(Built F + W)				*(As "XJ771" in RAF c/s)*		
G-HEMH	Eurocopter AS 355N Twin Squirrel	5693	F-WQPV	18. 9.01	Hancocks Holdings Ltd	(Loughborough)	20.12.04T
G-HENS*	Cameron N-65 HAFB	740		8. 7.81	Balloon Preservation Group	Kirdford	N/E(A)
					"Free Range" (Cancelled 8.4.93 by CAA)		
G-HENT	SOCATA Rallye 110ST Galopin	3210	OO-MBV	28.11.01	R.J.Patton	Enniskillen, Co.Fermanagh	
G-HENY	Cameron V-77 HAFB	2486		9. 1.91	R.S.D'Alton *"Henny"*	Newbury	19. 8.02A
G-HEPY	Robinson R44 Astro	0695		11. 1.00	T.Everett	Thruxton	12..1.03T
G-HERA*	Robinson R22 Beta	1426		26. 6.90	G.R.Day	Wolverhampton	21. 8.99T
	(Crashed on landing Blackpool 24.2.99 & cancelled same date as Destroyed - cabin stored 8.00)						
G-HERB	Piper PA-28R-201 Arrow III	28R-7837118	ZS-LAG N3504M	5. 6.86	Consort Aviation Ltd	(Leeds)	18.10.04
G-HERC	Cessna 172S Skyhawk	172S8985	N5113P	10.12.01	The Cambridge Aero Club Ltd	Cambridge	
G-HERD	Lindstrand LBL 77B	707		31. 7.00	S.W.Herd	Mold	4.10.02A
G-HERO	Piper PA-32RT-300 Lance II	32R-7885086	G-BOGN N33LV/N30573	26. 4.88	Air Alize Communication Biarritz, France *(Noted 10.00)*		9. 7.97
G-HEWI	Piper J-3C-65 Cub (L-4J-PI) (Continental C90) *(Frame No.12396)*	12566	G-BLEN D-EBEN/HB-OFZ/44-80270	20. 7.84	R.Preston t/a Denham Grasshopper Flying Group	Denham	16. 3.03
G-HEYY	Cameron Bear 72SS HAFB *(Hofmeister Lager Bear)*	1244		21. 1.86	Magical Adventures Ltd *"George"*	Chirk	30.11.98A
G-HFBM	Curtiss Robin C-2 (Continental W-670)	352	LV-FBM NC9279	24. 4.90	D.M.Forshaw	High Cross, Ware	20. 8.02P
G-HFCA	Cessna A150L Aerobat *(Texas tail-wheel u/c conversion)*	A1500381	N6081J	30. 8.91	Horizon Flying Club Ltd	Earls Colne	4.10.04T
G-HFCB	Reims Cessna F150L	F15000798	G-AZVR	10. 2.87	Horizon Flying Club Ltd	Earls Colne	15. 3.03T
G-HFCI	Reims Cessna F150L	F15000823	PH-CET	11. 9.80	S O Smith	Earls Colne	27. 1.02T
G-HFCL	Reims Cessna F152 II	F15201663	G-BGLR	11.10.88	T.H.Hird	Earls Colne	24. 5.03T
G-HFCT	Reims Cessna F152 II	F15201861		27. 1.81	Stapleford Flying Club Ltd	Stapleford	17. 6.02T
G-HFLA	Schweizer Hughes 269C (300C)	S.1428		8.12.89	Sterling Helicopters Ltd	Norwich	4. 2.02T
G-HFTG	Piper PA-23-250 Aztec E	27-7405378	G-BSOB G-BCJR/N54040	30. 4.87	Widehawk Aviation Ltd t/a Hawkair *(Ordnance Survey titles)*	Cambridge	6. 4.02T
G-HGPI	SOCATA TB-20 Trinidad	851		4. 8.88	M.J.Jackson	Bournemouth	23. 4.04
G-HIBM	Cameron N-145 HAFB	3197		8. 2.94	P.M.Forster *(Op Alba Ballooning)*	Edinburgh	25. 2.02T
G-HIEL	Robinson R22 Beta	1120		28. 9.89	R.C.Hields t/a Hields Aviation	Sherburn-in-Elmet	27. 9.03T
G-HIJK	Cessna 421C Golden Eagle III	421C0218	G-OSAL OY-BEC/SE-GZI/N5471G	25. 2.00	Oxford Aviation Services Ltd	Oxford	14. 6.02T
G-HILO	Rockwell Commander 114	14224	N4894W	6. 2.98	F.H.Parkes	Stapleford	7. 4.04
G-HILS	Reims Cessna F172H	F172-0522	G-AWCH	20.12.88	B.F.W.Lowdon t/a Lowdon Aviation Group	Blackbushe	29. 2.04
G-HILT	SOCATA TB-10 Tobago	298	(G-BMYB) EI-BOF/G-HILT	13. 5.82	Cheshire Aircraft Leasing Ltd	Hawarden	7. 7.02T
G-HIND	Maule MT-7-235 Star Rocket	18037C		26. 3.98	R.G.Humphries	Bramshill Farm, Hatchgate	29. 4.04T
G-HINZ	Jabiru Jabiru SK	PFA 274-13441		1. 2.00	B.Faupel	Bourn	20.12.02P
G-HIPE	Sorrell SNS-7 Hyperbipe (Lycoming IO-360)	209	N18RS	6. 4.93	T.A.S.Rayner	Stapleford	30. 6.01P
G-HIPO	Robinson R22 Beta	1719	G-BTGB	11. 9.92	Fleet Street Travel Ltd	Sywell	19. 5.03T
G-HIRE	Gulfstream GA-7 Cougar	GA7-0091	G-BGSZ N704G	10.12.81	London Aerial Tours Ltd	Rochester	26. 5.03T
G-HISS	Aerotek Pitts S-2A Special (Lycoming AEIO-360)	2137	G-BLVU SE-GTX	17. 3.92	L.V.Adams & J.Maffia *"Always Dangerous"*	Panshanger	24. 8.02T
G-HITM	Raj Hamsa X'Air 582 (Jabiru)	455 & BMAA/HB/112		23. 2.00	J.A.C.Cockfield t/a G-HITM Flying Group *(F/f 29.1.01)*	RNAS Culdrose	
G-HITS	Piper PA-46-310P Malibu	46-8508063	G-BMBE N6908W	24.10.00	Law 2000 Ltd	(London NW11)	11. 4.04T
G-HIUP	Cameron A-250 HAFB	4464		16. 4.99	Bridges Van Hire Ltd	Nottingham	30. 8.01T
G-HIVA	Cessna 337A Super Skymaster	33700429	G-BAES SE-CWW/N5329S	28. 3.88	G.J.Banfield	Gloucestershire	28. 9.03
G-HIVE	Reims Cessna F150M	F15001186	G-BCXT	19. 4.85	M.P.Lynn	Fenland	10. 5.04T
G-HJSM	Schempp-Hirth Nimbus 4DM	22/32	G-ROAM	19. 2.01	R.Jones t/a 60 Group *"60"*	Aboyne	29. 4.03
G-HJSS	AIA Stampe SV-4C	1101	G-AZNF F-BGJM/Fr Mil	7. 9.92	H.J.Smith	Shoreham	16. 6.02
G-HKHM	Hughes 369D	711019D	B-HHM VR-HHM/N50605	8. 4.99	Heli Air Ltd	Denham	25 .5.02
G-HLAA	Airbus A300B4-203	047	EI-TLN G-HLAA/N740SC/F-BVGJ/F-WUAX	6.10.97	HC Airlines t/a Heavylift	Stansted	7. 7.04T
G-HLAB	Airbus A300B4-203F	045	N743SC F-BVGI/F-WNDA	20. 2.98	HC Airlines Ltd t/a Heavylift	Stansted	26. 2.04T
G-HLAC	Airbus A300B4-203	074	N829SC F-BVGL	23.11.98	HC Airlines Ltd t/a Heavylift	Stansted	3.12.04T

G-HLAD	Airbus A300B4-203	131	EI-TLQ 6Y-JMK/G-BIMB/F-WZEL	17. 5.01	HC Airlines Ltd t/a Heavylift	Stansted	5. 7.04T
G-HLCF	CFM Starstreak Shadow SA (Rotax 618)	K.256 & PFA 206-12796		10. 5.96	I.P.Hutchinson	(Heckmondwike)	14.11.02P
G-HLEN	Aérospatiale AS350B Ecureuil	1836	G-LOLY JA9897/N5805T/HP-…/N5805T	22. 4.93	Sloane Helicopters Ltd	Sywell	15.10.01T
G-HLFT	Short SC.5 Belfast C.1 *(Modified to Mk.2)*	SH.1819	XR365	11. 9.81	Heavylift Aviation Holdings Ltd t/a Heavylift Cargo Airlines *"St.George"*	Southend	20. 6.02T
G-HLIX*	Cameron Helix Oilcan 61SS HAFB *(Originally regd as 80SS)*	1192		20. 9.85	Balloon Preservation Group *"Shell Helix Oil Can" (Cancelled 29.4.97 as WFU)*	Kirdford	25. 4.90A
G-HMBJ	Commander Aircraft Commander 114B	14636	N6036F	30. 6.97	Bravo Juliet Aviation Ltd	Guernsey	24. 7.03
G-HMED	Piper PA-28-161 Warrior III	2842020	LX-III	21. 7.97	H.Faizal	Denham	12.12.03T
G-HMES	Piper PA-28-161 Warrior II	28-8216070	OY-CSN N8471N	21. 4.89	Cleveland Flying School Ltd *(Op Teesside Aero Club)*	Teesside	20. 8.01T
G-HMJB	Piper PA-34-220T Seneca III	34-8133040	N8356R	12. 7.89	Cross Atlantic Ventures Ltd	Blackpool	10.10.04
G-HMMV	Cessna 525 CitationJet	525-0358	N51564	16. 2.00	Gold Air International Ltd	Cambridge	5..3.02T
G-HMPF	Robinson R44 Astro	0730		8. 3.00	Mightycraft Ltd	White Waltham	20..3.03T
G-HMPH	Bell 206B JetRanger II	1232	G-BBUY N18090	20. 6.88	Sturmer Ltd	(Tring)	31. 3.02T
G-HMPT	Agusta-Bell 206B JetRanger II	8168	D-HARO	7.11.91	Helicopter Express Ltd	(London N21)	3. 5.04T
G-HNRY	Cessna 650 Citation VI	650-0219	N219CC N6829Z	23.10.92	Xjet Ltd	Farnborough	12. 1.03T
G-HNTR*	Hawker Hunter T.7	HABL-003311	8834M XL572	7. 7.89	Yorkshire Air Museum *(Cancelled 11.10.91 as WFU) (As "XL571/V" in "Blue Diamonds" c/s)*	Elvington	
G-HOBO	Denney Kitfox mk.4 (Rotax 582)	PFA 172A-12140		10. 9.92	E M Woods *"Navy Baby"*	Shobdon	29.10.02P
G-HOCK	Piper PA-28-180 Cherokee D	28-4395	G-AVSH N11C	15. 5.86	J.I.Simper t/a G-HOCK Flying Club	Goodwood	12. 8.04T
G-HOFC	Europa Aviation Europa (Rotax 912UL)	119 & PFA 247-12736		25. 9.95	W.R.Mills *(Resides in personal trailer)*	Upfield Farm, Whitson	7. 6.02P
G-HOFM	Cameron N-56 HAFB	1245		21. 1.86	Magical Adventures Ltd	Chirk	30.11.98A
G-HOGS	Cameron Pig 90SS HAFB	4121		7. 4.97	Flying Pictures Ltd *"Britannia Piggy Bank"*	Fairoaks	1. 7.99A
G-HOHO	Colt Santa Claus SS HAFB	1671		21.12.89	Oxford Promotions (UK) Ltd	Kentucky, USA	14. 4.99A
G-HOLY	SOCATA ST-10 Diplomate	108	F-BSCZ	31. 1.90	M.K.Barsham	Booker	14. 4.02
G-HOME	Colt 77A HAFB	032		26. 2.79	Anglia Balloon School Ltd *"Tardis" (On loan to British Balloon Museum & Library)*	Newbury	27. 5.86A
G-HONG	Slingsby T.67M-200 Firefly	2060	VR-HZR HKG-12/G-7-128	24. 3.94	Babcock Rosyth Defence Ltd t/a Hunting Contract Services	AAC Middle Wallop	18.10.03T
G-HONI	Robinson R22 Beta	0871	G-SEGO N9081N	27. 1.00	A.J.Da Costa-Greaves t/a Independent Aviation Services	Gloucestershire	14.12.03T
G-HONK	Cameron O-105 HAFB	1813		30. 9.88	T.F.W.Dixon & Son Ltd *"Dixons"*	Bromsgrove	14.9.971A
G-HONY	Lilliput Type 1 Srs.A MLB	L-01		31. 7.98	A.E. & D.E.Thomas	Honiton	
G-HOOD	SOCATA TB-20 Trinidad GT	2008	F-OILJ	25. 7.00	M.J.Hoodless	Blackbushe	31. 7.03
G-HOOV	Cameron N-56 HAFB	388		2. 3.78	Heather R.Evans *"Hoover"*	Ross-on-Wye	26. 5.89A
G-HOPE	Beechcraft F33A Bonanza	CE-805	N2024Z	27. 2.79	Hurn Aviation Ltd	Bournemouth	2. 4.04
G-HOPI	Cameron N-42 HAFB	2724		5.12.91	Ballonverbung Hamburg GmbH	Kiel, Germany	19. 7.02A
G-HOPS	Thunder Ax8-90 Srs.1 HAFB	1220		11. 3.88	A.C. & B.Munn	Hastings	2. 9.01T
G-HOPY	Van's RV-6A (Lycoming O-320-B2B)	PFA 181-12742		4.12.95	R.C.Hopkinson	Booker	3. 4.02P
G-HORN	Cameron V-77 HAFB	570		29.11.79	S.Herd	Mold	11.12.98A
G-HOST*	Cameron N-77 HAFB	434		4. 9.78	D.Grimshaw *"Suzanna"* *(Cancelled 13.11.01 as wfu: stored)*	Preston	18. 5.93A
G-HOTI	Colt 77A HAFB	750		13. 7.87	R.Ollier *"Horace Hot One"*	Northwich, Cheshire	30. 9.90A
G-HOTT	Cameron O-120 HAFB	2581		30. 4.91	D.L.Smith *"Floating Sensations"*	Newbury	17. 5.97T
G-HOTZ	Colt 77B HAFB	2218		16. 6.92	C.J. & S.M.Davies	Castleton, Sheffield	6. 7.02A
G-HOUS	Colt 31A Air Chair HAFB	099		7.10.80	Anglia Balloon School Ltd *"K9"* t/a Anglia Balloons *(Barratts titles)* *(On loan to British Balloon Museum & Library)*	Newbury	3. 5.90A
G-HOWE	Thunder Ax7-77 HAFB	1340		10. 4.89	M.F.Howe *"Howie/Howzat"*	Beverley	15. 8.95A
G-HOWL	Rotary Air Force RAF 2000 GTX-SE	H2-95-6-164	N4994U	2. 7.01	C.J.Watkinson	Charity Farm, Baxterley	22. 7.02P
G-HPOL	MD Helicopters Explorer	900-00082	N70082	24. 1.01	Humberside Police Authority	Leconfield	3. 9.04T
G-HPSB	Commander Aircraft Commander 114B	14678	N6118R	24.10.01	Guernsey Enterprises Ltd	Guernsey	23.10.04T
G-HPSE	Commander Aircraft Commander 114B	14638	N6038V	26. 8.97	Al Nisr Ltd	Guernsey	16. 9.03A
G-HPUX	Hawker Hunter T.Mk.7	41H-693455	8807M XL587	12. 3.99	Classic Aviation Ltd *(As "XL587/Z") (Stored 3.00)*	Duxford	

G-HPWH	Agusta A109E Power	11051	G-HWPH	9. 8.99	Lynton Corporate Jet Ltd & P.B.W.Hamlyn		
					t/a Aviation Partnership	Denham	23. 6.02T
G-HRHE	Robinson R22 Beta	1950	G-BTWP	24. 1.97	R.Whitear	(Hook)	18.12.03T
G-HRHI	Beagle B.206 Basset Srs.1	B.014	XS770	6. 7.89	Lawgra (No.386) Ltd	Cranfield	17.10.03
					t/a International Aerospace Engineering		
					(As "XS770" in Queens Flight c/s)		
G-HRHS	Robinson R.44 Astro	0323		15. 4.97	Stratus Aviation Ltd	Kemble	16. 4.03
G-HRIO	Robin HR.100/210 Safari	149	F-BTZR	22. 1.87	T.W.Evans	Southampton	17.12.04
G-HRLK	Saab 91D/2 Safir	91376	G-BRZY	6. 3.90	Sylmar Aviation & Services Ltd		
			PH-RLK			Lower Wasing Farm, Brimpton	12. 5.04
G-HRLM	Brugger MB.2 Colibri	PFA 043-10118		28.12.78	S.J.Perkins & D.Dobson		
	(VW 1834)				*"Titch"*	Roughay Farm, Bishops Waltham	21. 1.02P
G-HRNT	Cessna 182S Skylane	18280395	N2369H	29.1.99	Dingle Star Ltd	Denham	9. 2.02
G-HROI	Rockwell Commander 112A	326	N1326J	19. 6.89	Intereuropean Aviation Ltd	Jersey	28. 4.04
G-HRON	de Havilland DH.114 Heron 2B	14102	XR442	4. 4.91	M.E.R.Coghlan	Gloucestershire	
			G-AORH		*(Stored 4.01 unmarked)*		
G-HRVD	CCF Harvard 4	CCF4-548	G-BSBC	8.12.92	K.F.Mason & D.Featherby	Norwich	
	(T-6J-CCF Texan)		Moz PLAF 1741/FAP 1741/BF+055/AA+055/53-4629		t/a Anglia Flight		
	(Possibly a composite with rear fuselage of Moz PLAF/FAP 1780/AA+614/53-4622: on rebuild 1999) (New owners 10.01)						
G-HRZN	Colt 77A HAFB	536		14.12.83	A.J.Spindler *"Tequila Sunrise"*	Cleish	4. 5.88A
G-HSDW	Bell 206B JetRanger II	1789	ZS-HFC	16.12.85	Winfield Shoe Co Ltd & Stott Demolition Ltd		
						Rossendale	2. 2.02
G-HSFT	Piper PA-44-180 Seminole	44-7995179	EI-CCB	24. 9.99	Magenta Ltd	(Oxford)	27.10.02T
			N2093K		*(Op SFT Europe: ceased operations 12.01)*		
G-HSLA	Robinson R22 Beta	1130	G-BRTI	22.11.01	Helicopter Support Ltd		
			EI-CDW/(EI-CFJ)/G-BRTI/N8044U			(Ashleworth, Glos)	16. 4.03T
G-HSOO	Hughes 369HE	109-0208E	G-BFYJ	3.11.93	Edwards Aviation Ltd	(Wilmslow)	27. 9.03T
			F-BRSY				
G-HSTH	Lindstrand HS-110 Hot-Air Airship	546		20. 8.98	Ballonsport Helmet Seitz		
						Kisslegg, Germany	17.12.00A
G-HTEL	Robinson R44 Raven	1155	N70319	25. 1.02	Forestdale Hotels Ltd	(Ringwood)	
G-HTRL	Piper PA-34-220T Seneca III	34-8333061	G-BXXY	8. 2.00	Air Medical Ltd	Oxford	18. 2.04T
			PH-TLN/N4295X				
G-HUBB	Partenavia P.68B	194	OY-BJH	27. 5.83	G-HUBB Ltd	Denham	29. 7.04
			SE-GXL				
G-HUCH	Cameron Carrots 80SS HAFB	2258	G-BYPS	13. 3.91	Magical Adventures Ltd	Chirk	2. 8.01A
					"Magic Carrots"		
G-HUEY*	Bell UH-1H-BF Iroquois	13560	AE-413	23. 7.85	Bournemouth Aviation Museum	Bournemouth	12. 4.00P
			73-22077		*(Cancelled 25.2.00 by CAA)*		
G-HUFF	Cessna 182P Skylane II	18264076	PH-CAS	31.10.78	A.E.G.Cousins	Southend	31. 5.03T
	(Reims-assembled with c/n F18200033)		N6059F		*(Op Seawing Flying Club)*		
G-HUGG	Learjet Learjet 35A	35A-432	VR-CAD	9. 4.96	Northern Executive Aviation Ltd		
			N330BC/N4445Y/F-GDCN			Manchester	11. 4.03T
G-HUGO	Colt 260A HAFB	2559		20. 1.94	P.G.Hall t/a Adventure Ballooning	Chard	14. 5.02T
G-HULL	Reims Cessna F150M	F15001255	PH-TGR	19. 1.79	A.D.McLeod	Linley Hill, Leven	13. 9.04T
G-HUMF	Robinson R22 Beta	0534	N23743	18. 2.86	Plane Talking Ltd *(Op Cabair)*	Elstree	25. 6.01T
G-HUNI	Bellanca 7GCBC Scout	541-73	OO-IME	21.10.96	T.I.M.Paul	Denham	9. 7.04T
			D-EIME		*(Officially registered as "Scout" although 7GCBC = Citabria)*		
G-HUNK	Lindstrand LBL 77A HAFB	551		9. 9.98	Lindstrand Balloons Ltd	Oswestry	23. 9.00A
G-HUPW	Hawker Hurricane 1	G5-92301	R4118	21. 8.01	P.J. & P.M.A.Vacher	(Abingdon)	
	(Built Gloster Aircraft Co.Ltd)				t/a Minmere Farm Partnership		
G-HURI	Hawker Hurricane XIIA (IIB)	72036	RCAF5711	9. 6.83	Patina Ltd	Duxford	6. 5.02P
	(Built Canadian & Car Foundry Co)				*(Op The Fighter Collection) (As "Z7381/XR-T" in 71 Sqn RAF c/s)*		
	(Composite - probably includes parts from c/n 44019/RCAF 5424, RCAF 5625 and RCAF 5547)						
G-HURN	Robinson R22 Beta	1441		18. 7.90	R M Weyman	Coventry	3.12.03T
G-HURR	Hawker Hurricane XII (IIB)	52024	RCAF5589	30. 7.90	R.A.Fleming	Breighton	27. 4.02P
	(Built Canadian & Car Foundry Co)				*(As "AL-K")*		
G-HURY	Hawker Hurricane IV	-	(Israel)	31. 3.89	Patina Ltd	Duxford	
			Yugoslav AF/KZ321		*(Op B J S Grey/The Fighter Collection)*		
	(RAF p/i unlikely as KZ321 was written off 23.5.43: on rebuild 1.01 as "KZ321")						
G-HUTT	Denney Kitfox mk.2			24. 1.90	L.A.James	Wharf Farm, Market Bosworth	5. 5.01P
	(Rotax 582)	509 & PFA 172-11634					
G-HVAN	Tiger Cub RL5A LW Sherwood Ranger	PFA 237-13074		10.12.98	H.T.H.Van Neck	(Wirral)	
G-HVBF	Lindstrand LBL-210A HAFB	372		23. 5.96	Virgin Balloon Flights Ltd	London SE16	24. 6.02T
G-HVIP	Hawker Hunter T.68	HABL-003215	J-4208	7. 7.95	Golden Europe Jet De Luxe Club Ltd		
			G-9-415/Fv.34080/G-9-56		*(Op Dr.Karl Theurer)*	Bournemouth	16. 5.02P
G-HVRD	Piper PA-31-350 Navajo Chieftain	31-7305052	G-BEZU	11. 6.87	A Jahanfar	Biggin Hill	7.12.03T
			SE-GDP		*(Op London Executive Aviation)*		
G-HXTD	Robin DR.400/180	2510		24.10.01	Hayley Aviation Ltd	(Banstead)	
G-HYLT	Piper PA-32R-301 Saratoga SP	32R-8213001	N84588	23. 4.86	H.Young Transport Ltd	Old Sarum	31. 1.02
G-HYST	Enstrom 280FX Shark	2082		9. 7.98	Patten Helicopter Services Ltd	Barton	8. 10.04

G-IAAA – G-IZZZ

G-IAFT	Cessna 152 II	15285123	EI-BVW N6093Q	20. 6.95	Marham Investments Ltd *(Op Woodgate Executive Air Services)*	Newtownards, Co.of Down	14. 8.04T
G-IAGD	Robinson R22 Beta	0918	N2018Y G-DRAI/N8808V	16.11.99	M.Kenyon & A.Ingham t/a A & M Engineering	Blackpool	28.11.02T
G-IAMP*	Cameron H-34 HAFB	2541		11. 3.91	Balloon Preservation Group *"National Power" (Cancelled 6.11.01 as wfu)*	Kirdford	14. 6.97A
G-IANG	Bell 206L LongRanger	45132	SE-HSV PH-HMH/N16845	22. 1.98	Lothian Helicopters Ltd	(Pathhead, Oxenfoord Castle)	15. 2.04T
G-IANH	SOCATA TB-10 Tobago	1843	F-OILI	13. 3.00	XD Flight Management Ltd	(Horsham)	26..3.03T
G-IANI	Europa Aviation Europa XS T-G	PFA 247-13714		20. 4.01	I.F.Rickard & I.A.Watson	(Woking)	
G-IANJ	Reims Cessna F150K	F15000548	G-AXVW	19. 5.98	J.A.,G.M.,D.T.A. & J.A.Rees t/a Messrs Rees of Poyston West	Haverfordwest	19. 8.04T
G-IANW	Eurocopter AS 350B3 Ecureuil	3447	F-WQPU	18. 9.01	McAlpine Helicopters Ltd	Oxford	
G-IARC	Stoddard-Hamilton GlaStar	PFA 295-13261		9.11.99	A.A.Craig	Prestwick	9. 7.02P
G-IASL	Beechcraft 60 Duke	P-21	G-SING D-IDTA/SE-EXT	18. 4.97	Applied Sweepers Ltd	Perth	13. 4.04
G-IBBC	Cameron Sphere 105SS HAFB	4082		2. 4.97	Virgin Airship & Balloon Co Ltd	Telford	24. 7.02A
G-IBBO	Piper PA-28-181 Cherokee Archer II	28-7790107	D-EPCA N5389F	17.12.98	M.Gibbon	Panshanger	6. 1.02
G-IBBS	Europa Aviation Europa *(Mono-wheel u/c)* (Rotax 912-UL)	118 & PFA 247-12745		8. 9.94	R.H.Gibbs	Popham	14. 4.02P
G-IBED	Robinson R22 Alpha	0500	G-BMHN N50022	7. 9.93	B.C.Seedle t/a Brian Seedle Helicopters	Blackpool	30. 9.94
G-IBET	Cameron Can 70SS HAFB	1625		25. 1.88	M.R.Humphrey & J.R.Clifton *"Carling Black Label"*	Brackley	15. 8.97A
G-IBFC	BFC Quad City Challenger II	CH2-0898-UK-1774 & PFA 177B-13369		9.11.98	K.N.Dickinson	(Lytham St. Annes)	
G-IBFW	Piper PA-28R-201 Arrow III	28R-7837235	N31534	22. 1.79	A.W.Collett	Wolverhampton	25. 8.03T
G-IBHH	Hughes 269C	74-0327	G-BSCD PH-HSH/SE-HFG	20. 8.99	The Hughes Helicopter Co Ltd t/a Biggin Hill Helicopters	Biggin Hill	11. 7.03T
G-IBKA	Robinson R44 Astro	0315	G-USTE	17. 5.01	Bon Accord Glass Ltd	(Kintore)	6. 4.03T
G-IBLU	Cameron Z-90 HAFB	4913		4. 8.00	Blu SpA	Rome, Italy	14..6.02A
G-IBRO	Reims Cessna F152 II	F15201957	EI-BRO	11.10.95	Leicestershire Aero Club Ltd	Leicester	4. 3.02T
G-IBSF	Dassault Falcon 2000	151	F-WWVI	1.10.01	Marconda Services Ltd	Luton	4.10.02T
G-IBZS	Cessna 182S Skylane	18280529	N7269A	11.12.99	Patrick Eddery Ltd	Oxford	9.12.02
G-IBZT	Cessna 182T Skylane	18280967	N3536W	13. 8.01	Oxford Aviation Services Ltd	Oxford	25. 1.04
G-ICAB	Robinson R44 Astro	0086		28.11.94	JR Clark Ltd	Culverthorpe, Grantham	14.12.00
G-ICAS	Aviat Pitts S-2B Special	5344	N511P	19. 6.97	J.C.Smith	Sherburn-in-Elmet	10. 7.03T
G-ICBM	Stoddard-Hamilton Glasair III Turbine (Allison 250-B17B)	3337		18.12.00	G V Waters & D N Brown	Attleborough	
G-ICCL	Robinson R22 Beta	1608	G-ORZZ	25.11.93	JK Aviation Services Ltd	Headcorn	20. 2.03T
G-ICES	Thunder Ax6-56 SP.1 HAFB *(Ice Cream special shape)*	283		3. 7.80	British Balloon Museum & Library Ltd *"Ashfords"*	Newbury	3. 6.94A
G-ICEY	Lindstrand LBL-77A HAFB	043		11. 8.93	G.C.Elson t/a Lindstrand Balloon School	Ronda, Spain	22. 6.02A
G-ICFR	British Aerospace BAe 125 Srs.800B	258050	N9LR G-5-503/I-OSLO/G-5-503/G-BUCR/HZ-OFC/G-5-503	23.11.94	Chauffair Ltd	Farnborough	1.12.02T
G-ICKY	Lindstrand LBL-77A HAFB	029		19. 5.93	Blown Away UK Ltd	Shrewsbury	3. 5.00A
G-ICOI	Lindstrand LBL-105A HAFB	564		3.11.98	Virgin Airship & Balloon Co Ltd *(ICO titles)*	Telford	12.11.99A
G-ICOM	Reims Cessna F172M Skyhawk II	F17201212	G-BFXI PH-ABA/D-EEVC	25. 4.94	C G Elesmore	Manston	23. 6.03T
G-ICON	Rutan Long-EZ	PFA 074A-11104		29.11.00	S.J.& M.A.Carradice	(Sheffield)	
G-ICOZ	Lindstrand LBL-105A HAFB	565		3.11.98	Virgin Airship & Balloon Co Ltd *(ICO titles)*	Telford	12.11.99A
G-ICSG	Aérospatiale AS355F1 Twin Squirrel	5104	G-PAMI G-BUSA	6. 4.93	M W Helicopters Ltd	Stapleford	2. 5.00T
G-ICWT	Pegasus Quantum 15-912	7632		7. 4.00	C.W.Taylor *(Noted 9.01)*	Mill Farm, Shifnal	7. 4.02P
G-IDAY	Skyfox CA-25N Gazelle (Rotax 912)	CA25N-028	VH-RCR	29. 4.96	The Anglo-Pacific Aircraft Co (UK) Ltd & G.Horne	Perth	20. 6.03T
G-IDEA	Gulfstream AA-5A Cheetah	AA5A-0871	G-BGNO	7. 2.84	Plane Talking Ltd	Biggin Hill	16. 3.04T
G-IDII	Dan Rihn DR.107 One Design (Lycoming O-360)	PFA 264 12953		16. 6.99	C.Darlow	Sibson	11. 9.02P
G-IDUP	Enstrom 280C Shark	1163	G-BRZF N5687D	11. 5.92	Antique Buildings Ltd	Hunterswood Farm, Dunsfold	7. 6.04

G-IDWR	Hughes 369HS	69-0101S	G-AXEJ	26. 5.81	Ainderfield Ltd	Tadcaster	16.12.04
					t/a Copley Electrical Contractors		
G-IEJH	SAN Jodel 150A Mascaret	02	G-BPAM	28. 2.95	A.Turner & D.Worth	Crowfield	18. 4.02P
			F-BLDA/F-WLDA				
G-IEYE	Robin DR.400/180 Regent	2123		29. 1.92	E.Hopper	Sherburn-in-Elmet	28. 6.04
G-IFDM	Robinson R44 Astro	0707		24. 1.00	Bedgbury Aviation Ltd	Headcorn	3. 2.03T
G-IFFR	Piper PA-32-300 Cherokee Six	32-7340123	G-BWVO OO-JPC/N55520	1. 4.97	D.J.D & G.D.Ritchie & J.C.Gilbert	RAF Henlow	20. 3.03
G-IFIT	Piper PA-31-350 Chieftain	31-8052078	G-NABI G-MARG/N3580C	31.12.85	Dart Group plc *(Op Channel Express)*	Bournemouth	4.11.02T
G-IFLI	Gulfstream AA-5A Cheetah	AA5A-0831	N26948	7. 7.82	I-Fly Ltd	(Cottingham)	20.10.03T
G-IFLP	Piper PA-34-200T Seneca II	34-8070029	N81WS N81149	4. 1.88	Tayflite Ltd	Perth	25. 6.03T
G-IFTC	Hawker Siddeley HS.125 Srs.F3B/RA	25171	G-OPOL	21. 7.94	Albion Aviation Management Ltd	Gatwick	28. 7.02T
			G-BXPU/(N171AV)/G-BXPU/G-AXPU/G-IBIS/G-AXPU/HB-VBT/G-5-19				
G-IFTE	British Aerospace HS.125 Srs.700B	257037	G-BFVI G-5-18	16. 5.96	Albion Aviation Management Ltd	Gatwick	17. 8.02T
G-IFTS	Robinson R44 Astro	0366		16. 9.97	Context GB Ltd t/a Aviation In Context	Blackpool	24. 9.03T
G-IGEL*	Cameron N-90 HAFB	2726		7. 4.92	Balloon Preservation Group *"Computercentre II" (Cancelled 18.12.01 by CAA)*	Kirdford	12. 5.97A
G-IGGL	SOCATA TB-10 Tobago	146	G-BYDC F-GCOL	26. 3.99	M.P.Perkin t/a G-IGGL Flying Group	White Waltham	2.12.01
G-IGHH	Enstrom 480	5034		1.12.98	G.H.Harding	(Whitchurch)	17.12.01T
G-IGLA	Colt 240A HAFB	2228		3. 7.92	M.L. & S.M.Gabb t/a Heart of England Balloons *(Barclaycard titles)*	Alcester	10. 4.01T
G-IGLE	Cameron V-90 HAFB	2609		11. 6.91	A.A.Laing *"Giggle"*	Aberdeen	19. 8.01A
G-IGOA	Boeing 737-3Y0	24678	EI-BZK	16. 7.98	Orix Aviation Systems *(Op Go Fly Ltd) (Cyan c/s) "go again/let's go"*	Stansted	19. 7.04T
G-IGOB	Boeing 737-36Q	28660	EC-GNU	17.12.01	Go Fly Ltd *(Cyan c/s) "go fiesta/mi Amigo"*	Stansted	
G-IGOC	Boeing 737-3Y0	24546	EI-BZH	1. 5.98	Orix Aviation Systems *(Op Go Fly Ltd) (Purple c/s) "go today/just go"*	Stansted	7. 5.04T
G-IGOE	Boeing 737-3Y0	24547	EI-BZI	19. 5.98	Orix Aviation Systems *(Op Go Fly Ltd) (Pink c/s) "go together/ready to go"*	Stansted	20. 5.04T
G-IGOF	Boeing 737-3Q8	24698	PK-GWF	2. 4.98	Go Fly Ltd *(Aqua Green c/s) "go now/all go"*	Stansted	3. 6.0T
G-IGOG	Boeing 737-3Y0	23927	F-GLLE PT-TEK	3. 9.98	Go Fly Ltd *(Red c/s) "go often/come and go"*	Stansted	3. 9.04T
G-IGOH	Boeing 737-3Y0	23926	F-GLLD PT-TEJ	6.11.98	Go Fly Ltd *(Olive Green c/s) "go for it/don't wait go"*	Stansted	12.12.04T
G-IGOI	Boeing 737-33A	24092	G-OBMD	30.12.98	Go Fly Ltd *(Yellow c/s) "go enjoy/away we go"*	Stansted	13. 2.02T
G-IGOJ	Boeing 737-36N	28872	N1795B	11.11.98	Go Fly Ltd *(Medium Blue c/s) "go anytime/free to go"*	Stansted	20.11.04T
G-IGOK	Boeing 737-36N	28594		24. 4.99	Go Fly Ltd *(Purple Blue c/s) "go as you are/get set go"*	Bristol	23. 4.02T
G-IGOL	Boeing 737-36N	28596	N1015X	26. 6.99	Go Fly Ltd *(Terracota c/s) "go exploring/love to go"*	Stansted	25. 6.02T
G-IGOM	Boeing 737-36N	28599		13. 7.99	Go Fly Ltd *(Purple c/s) "go for a break/off we go"*	Stansted	12. 7.02T
G-IGOP	Boeing 737-36N	28602		12. 8.99	Go Fly Ltd *(Pink c/s) "go ahead/away we go"*	Bristol	11. 8.02T
G-IGOR	Boeing 737-36N	28606		22.10.99	Go Fly Ltd *(Cyan c/s) "go to work/off you go"*	Stansted	20.10.02T
G-IGOS	Boeing 737-3L9	27336	D-ADBH OY-MAO	21. 2 01	Go Fly Ltd *(Aqua Green c/s) "go-fly.com/click and go"*	Stansted	9. 3.04T
G-IGOT	Boeing 737-3L9	24571	N2393W TC-IAE/D-ADBF/OY-MMF	12. 7.01	Go Fly Ltd *(Terracota c/s) "go celebrate/here we go"*	Stansted	11. 7.04T
G-IGOU	Boeing 737-3L9	27337	D-ADBI OY-MAP	9. 5.01	Go Fly Ltd *(Red c/s) "go see/on the go"*	Stansted	14. 5.04T
G-IGOV	Boeing 737-3M8	25017	N250GE	13. 9.01	Go Fly Ltd	Stansted	13. 9.04T
			LZ-BOF/N250GE/9V-TRD/N760BE/N35030/(OO-LTH)		*(Medium Blue c/s) "go discover/got to go"*		
G-IGOW	Boeing 737-3Y0	23923	N923AP	24. 8.01	Go Fly Ltd	Stansted	23. 8.04T
			(G-OBWW)/N923AP/LZ-BOE/EC-FJZ/EC-898/EI-BZP/EI-CEE/G-TEAB/(N117AW)/ EI-BZP/(LN-AEQ)/EI-BZP/EC-EIA/EC-152		*(White c/s) "go escape/hasta lue go"*		
G-IGOX	Boeing 737-3L9	24219	PH-TSW OY-MMO/G-BOZB/OY-MMO/N1786B	R	Go Fly Ltd	Stansted	
G-IGPW	Eurocopter EC 120B	1027	G-CBRI	31. 7 99	Helihopper Ltd	Oxford	25. 5.02T
G-IHSB	Robinson R22 Beta	0982		16. 3.89	M.Walker *(Noted as "G-HISB" 12.01)*	Shobdon	6. 2.04T
G-IIAC	Aeronca 11AC Chief (Continental A65)	11AC-169	(G-BTPY) N86359/NC86359	2. 7.91	C.P.Whitwell	Fenland	4. 3.02P

G-IIAN	Aero Designs Pulsar	PFA 202-12123		10. 9.91	I.G.Harrison *(Under construction 2000)*	(Derby)	
G-IICM	Extra EA.300/L (Lycoming AEIO-540-L1B5)	100		19.11.99	Phonetiques Ltd	Denham	24.11.02T
G-IIDI	Extra EA.300/L (Lycoming AEIO-540) *(Tail-wheel u/c)*	047	G-XTRS D-EXJH	5.10.01	Power Aerobatics Ltd	Old Sarum	2. 9.01
G-IIFR	Robinson R22 Beta-II	2841		2. 9.98	R C Hields t/a Hields Aviation	Sherburn-in-Elmet	22.11.04T
G-IIID	Dan Rihn DR.107 One Design	PFA 264-12766		6. 7.00	A.J.& M.A.N.Newall	(Doncaster)	
G-IIIG	Boeing-Stearman A75N1 (PT-17) Kaydet (Continental W670)	75-4354	G-BSDR N61827/42-16191	25. 3.91	F.& S.Vormezeele *"Annie"*	(Brasschaat, Belgium)	11. 6.03T
G-IIII	Pitts S-2B Special (Lycoming AEIO-540)	5010	N5330G	6. 1.89	B.K.Lecomber *(Firebirds titles)*	Denham	5. 7.04T
G-IIIL	Pitts S-1T Special (Lycoming AEIO-360)	008	OH-XPT G-IIIL/N15JE	15. 2.89	The Sywell Boys Toy Box Ltd	Sywell	22. 8.02P
G-IIIR	Pitts S-1S Special (Lycoming IO-360)	604	N27M	21. 1.93	R.O.Rogers	Hulcote Farm, Salford, Bucks	20.12 01P
G-IIIT	Aerotek Pitts S-2A Special (Lycoming AEIO-360)	2222	N7YT	16. 1.89	Aerobatic Displays Ltd	Booker	9. 8.01A
G-IIIV	Pitts Super Stinker 11-260	PFA 273-13005		4. 2.97	G G Ferriman	Jericho Farm, Lambley	
G-IIIX	Pitts S-1S Special (Lycoming O-360)	AJT	G-LBAT G-UCCI/G-BIYN/N455T	22. 5.89	Jenks Air Ltd	RAF Halton	12. 3.02P
G-IILI	Extra EA.300/L	140	D-EXLB	23. 4.01	Firebird Aerobatics Ltd *(Microlease titles)*	Denham	3. 5.04T
G-IIMI	Extra EA.300/L	141	D-EXLE	2. 5.01	Firebird Aerobatics Ltd *(Microlease titles)*	Denham	17 .5.04T
G-IIPM	Aérospatiale AS350B Ecureuil	1790	G-GWIL	18.12.96	Kis Associates Ltd	(Bristol)	26.10.02T
G-IIPT	Robinson R22 Beta	2506	G-FUSI N83306	10. 5.01	P.R.Thorne	Aston Clinton	16. 5.04
G-IIRG	Stoddard-Hamilton Glasair IIS RG (Lycoming IO-360)	PFA 149-11937		29. 6.93	A.C.Lang	(Ottery St.Mary)	7. 6.02P
G-IISI	Extra EA.300/200	014	D-EXWE	5. 7.01	S.G.Jones	RAF Keevil	15. 7.04T
G-IITI	Extra EA.300 (Lycoming O-360)	018	D-EFRR	12. 5.92	Aerobatic Displays Ltd *(International Watch Company titles)*	Booker	13. 8.01A
G-IIXX	Montgomerie-Parsons Two Place (Rotax 912)	PFA G/08-1225		13.10.93	J.M.Montgomerie *(Noted 2.98 unmarked: current status unknown)*	(Crosshill)	14. 6.94*
G-IIZI	Extra EA.300 *(Rebuilt Southern Sailplanes Ltd)*	037	JY-RNB D-ETXA	12.12.96	P.J.Pengilly & S.G.Jones t/a 11-21 Flying Group	RAF Keevil	11. 2.04T
G-IJAC	Avid Speed Wing Mk.4	PFA 189-12095		31.12.92	I.J.A.Charlton	(Petworth)	
G-IJBB	Enstrom 480	5010	G-LIVA N900SA/G-PBTT/JA6169	17. 9.99	J.B.Booth	Barton	6.11.04
G-IJMC	VPM M-16 Tandem Trainer (Arrow GT1000R)	VPM16-UK-106	G-POSA G-BVJM	10. 6.98	I.J.McTear	Carlisle	3. 6.02P
G-IJOE	Piper PA-28RT-201T Turbo Arrow IV	28R-8031178	N8265X N9599N	14. 8.90	P.Randall	Sturgate	6. 7.02
G-IJYS	British Aerospace Jetstream Srs.3102	715	G-BTZT N416MX/G-31-715	5.10.92	Air Kilroe Ltd *(Op Eastern Airways) "Flying Scotsman"*	Humberside	18.11.03T
G-IKAP	Cessna T303 Crusader	T30300182	N63SA D-IKAP/N9518C	4. 3.99	T.M.Beresford	Cambridge	29..4.02T
G-IKBP	Piper PA-28-161 Warrior II	28-8216132	N81762	16. 7.90	K.B.Page	Shoreham	25. 8.02
G-IKIS	Cessna 210M Centurion II (Reims-assembled c/n F2100002)	21061754	N732TD	15. 5.78	R & H Trust Co Ltd t/a Chapple Investment Trust	(Jersey)	25.12.04
G-IKPS	Piper PA-31 Navajo C	31-7912098	D-IKPS (N444BK)/D-IKPS/N3539G	9. 8.96	Channel Aviation Ltd	Biggin Hill	23.11.03T
G-IKRS	Comco Ikarus C42	PFA 322-13719		1. 8.01	P.G. Walton *(Noted 11.01)*	Morgansfield, Fishburn	
G-ILEA	Piper PA-31 Navajo C	31-7812117	(8P-) G-ILEA/D-ILEA/N27775	7. 7.97	I.G.Fletcher	(London SW1)	7. 8.03
G-ILEE	Colt 56A Duo Chariot HAFB	2624		29. 7.94	G.I.Lindsay *"Gillie"*	Pulborough	6. 6.00A
G-ILLE	Boeing-Stearman E75 (PT-13D) Kaydet (Continental W670)	75-5028	N68979 42-16865/Bu.60906	7. 3.90	J.Griffin *(As "379" in USAAC c/s)*	Compton Abbas	7. 6.02T
G-ILLY	Piper PA-28-181 Cherokee Archer II	28-7690193	SE-GND	21. 2.80	A.G. & K.M.Spiers Ltd	Hinton-in-the-Hedges	19.12.93
G-ILSE	Corby CJ-1 Starlet (HAPI Magnum 1915cc)	PFA 134-10818		9. 1.84	S.Stride	Wolverhampton	6.11.01P
G-ILTS	Piper PA-32-300 Six	32-7940217	G-CVOK OE-DOH/N2941C	28. 3.90	Foremans Aviation Ltd	Full Sutton	6.10.01T
G-ILUM	Europa Aviation Europa XS	PFA 247-13565		15. 6.00	A.R.Haynes	(Stevenage)	
G-IMAB	Europa Aviation Europa XS	PFA 247-13128		1. 2.00	A.H.Brown	(Middlesbrough)	

G-IMAG*	Colt 77A HAFB	1718		9. 3.90	Balloon Preservation Group	Kirdford	19. 1.00A
	(Second envelope c/n 2254 as original dbf 6.92)				*"Agfa" (Cancelled 31.1.02 as wfu)*		
G-IMAN	Colt 31A Sky Chariot HAFB	2605		23. 6.94	Benedikt Haggeney GmbH	Ennigerloh, Germany	16. 2.00A
G-IMBY	Pietenpol Air Camper	PFA 047-12402		22.12.93	P.F.Bockh	(Horsham)	
G-IMGL	Beechcraft B200 Super King Air	BB-1564	VP-CMA N205JT	9. 8.99	IM Aviation Ltd	Coventry	6. 9.01T
G-IMLI	Cessna 310Q	310Q0491	G-AZYK N4182Q	3. 4.86	W.R.M.Beesley	Nottingham	5. 6.03T
G-IMOK	Hoffmann HK-36R Super Dimona	36317	I-NELI OE-9352	31. 7.97	A.L.Garfield	Dunstable	3. 8.03
G-IMPX	Rockwell Commander 112B	512	N1304J	25.10.90	T.L. & S.Hull	Aberdeen	27. 4.03
G-IMPY	Avid Flyer C	PFA 189-11439		10. 4.89	T.R.C.Griffin	Haverfordwest	26. 2.02P
G-INAV	Aviation Composites Europa	AC.001		23. 2.87	I.Shaw	(York)	
G-INCA	Glaser-Dirks DG-400	4-199		22. 1.87	K.D.Hook *"CA"*	Portmoak	31. 3.02
G-INDC	Cessna T303 Crusader	T30300122	G-BKFH N4766C	28. 6.83	Crusader Aviation Ltd	Oxford	19. 5.01
G-INDY	Robinson R44 Astro	0071		11. 7.94	M.B.Oastler t/a Lincoln Aviation	(Bicester)	19.10.03
G-INGA	Thunder Ax8-84 HAFB	2149		16. 6.92	M.L.J.Ritchie	Weybridge	14. 9.94A
G-INGE	Thruster T600N (Jabiru 2200A)	9039-T600N-033		23. 2.99	Thruster Air Services Ltd	Ginge Farm, Wantage	7. 4.02P
G-INIS	Robinson R22 Beta	1982	G-UPMW	31. 5.00	J.W.Lanchbury	Shobdon	13. 3.04T
G-INNI	Wassmer Jodel D.112	540	F-BHPU	30. 8.94	R.G.Andrews	Damyns Hall, Upminster	25.11.02P
G-INNY	Replica Plans SE.5A (Continental C90)	PFA 020-10439		18.12.78	K.S.Matcham *(As "F5459/Y" in RFC c/s)*	Roughay Farm, Bishops Waltham	15. 5.02P
G-INOW	ARV Monnett Moni 223 & (KEF 107)	PFA 142-10953		30. 3.84	W.C.Brown *(Stored 8.97: current status unknown)*	Fairoaks	20. 8.88P
G-INSR	Cameron N-90 HAFB	4320		23. 4.98	M.J.Betts & The Smith & Pinching Group Ltd	(Norwich)	8. 6.02A
G-INTL	Boeing 747-245F	20826	N640FE (N631FE)/N811FT/N701SW	8.12.00	Airfreight Express Ltd *(Op Cargolux)*	Heathrow	14. 3.04T
G-INVU	Agusta-Bell 206B JetRanger II	8530	G-XXII G-GGCC/G-BEHG	1. 3.95	Burman Aviation Ltd	Cranfield	21. 4.03T
G-IOCO	Beechcraft 58 Baron	TH-1783		6. 6.96	Arenberg Consultadoria E Servicos LDA	(Madeira, Portugal)	20. 6.02
G-IOIO	Bell 206B-3 JetRanger III	4359	N47EA	11. 4.96	Lynton Air Ltd	Denham	13. 5.02T
G-IOIT*	Lockheed L.1011-385-1 Tristar 200	193N-1145	G-CEAP SE-DPM/G-BEAL	6. 5.98	Classic Airways *(Cancelled 1.10.98 by CAA) (Stored 5.01)*	Stansted	
G-IOOI	Robin DR.400/160 Major 80	1700		31. 5.85	N.B.Mason & S.J.O'Rourke	Rendcomb	11.11.01
G-IOPT	Cessna 182P Skylane	18261731	N182EE D-ECVM/N21585	9. 6.98	M.J.Valentine & P.R.Davis	Elstree	26. 9.04
G-IORB	Bell 407	53375	N407RB N61161/C-GADP	24. 5.00	Robard Consulants Ltd	(Dukinfield)	29..5.03
G-IORG	Robinson R22 Beta	1679	OH-HRU G-ZAND	28. 1.00	G.M.Richardson t/a Commission-Air	(Market Deeping)	19..4.03T
G-IOSI	CEA Jodel DR.1050 Sicile	526	F-BLRS	6.10.80	G.A.Saxby t/a Sicile Flying Group	Bidford	25. 6.02
G-IOSO	CEA Jodel DR.1050 Ambassadeur	46	OO-VDV F-BJUE	13. 7.00	A.E.Jackson	Sibson	19.10.03
G-IOWE	Europa Aviation Europa XS	PFA 247-13303		30. 7.99	P.A.Lowe	Wolverhampton	4. 3.02P
G-IPSI(2)	Grob G-109B	6425	G-BMLO	29. 5.86	D.G.Margetts	Vaynor Farm, Llanidloes, Powys	31. 3.02
G-IPSY	Rutan VariEze (Continental PC60)	1512 & PFA 074-10284	(G-IPSI)	19. 6.78	R.A.Fairclough	Biggin Hill	8. 7.02P
G-IPUP	Beagle B.121 Pup 2	B121-036	HB-NAC G-35-036	17. 7.95	R.G.Hayes & S.Tvietan t/a Skyway Group	Elstree	18.10.04T
G-IRAF	Rotary Air Force RAF 2000 GTX-SE	PFA G/13-1278		17. 6.96	M.S.R.Allen	(Oakham)	20. 8.02P
G-IRAN	Cessna 152 II	15283907	OH-CKM C-GBJY/(N6150B)	19. 8.97	E.Alexander	Andrewsfield	23. 4.04T
G-IRIS	Gulfstream AA-5B Tiger	AA5B-1184	G-BIXU N4533N	14.12.87	A.H.McVicar *(Op Carlisle Flight Centre)*	Carlisle	17. 5.03T
G-IRJX	BAE Systems Avro 146-RJX100	E3378		24. 5.00	BAE Systems (Operations) Ltd *(Noted active 9.01)*	Woodford	
G-IRKB	Piper PA-28R-201 Cherokee Arrow III	28R-7737071	D-EJDS N5814V	7. 3.00	R.K.Brierley	Andrewsfield	31..5.03
G-IRLY	Colt 90A HAFB	1620		28.12.89	S.A.Burnett & L.P.Purfield *"Air Canada Cargo II"*	Leicester	6. 8.94A
G-IRPC	Cessna 182Q Skylane II	18266039	G-BSKM N559CT/N759JV	15. 5.91	J.W.Halfpenny	Cambridge	19. 7.02T
G-ISAX	Piper PA-28-181 Archer III	2843453	N5325G	28. 6.01	Anglo American Airmotive Ltd	Bournemouth	27. 6.04T

G-ISCA	Piper PA-28RT-201 Arrow IV		N8288Y	12. 2.91	D.J. & P.Pay	Exeter	25. 5.03
		28R-8118012	N9608N				
G-ISDB	Piper PA-28-161 Cherokee Warrior II		G-BWET	19. 2.96	Action Air Services Ltd	White Waltham	11. 4.04T
		28-7716074	SX-ALX/D-EFFQ/N9612N				
G-ISDN	Boeing-Stearman A75N1 (N2S-3) Kaydet		N4197X	6. 2.95	D.R.L.Jones	Rendcomb	12. 3.02
		75-1263	XB-WOV/Bu.3486		*(As "14" in US Army c/s)*		
G-ISEH	Cessna 182R Skylane II	18267843	G-BIWS	9.11.90	Hadsley Ltd	King's Farm, Thurrock	29. 5.03
			N6601N				
G-ISFC	Piper PA-31 Turbo Navajo B		G-BNEF	23. 3.94	G.R.E.Evans	Little Staughton	18.10.01
		31-7300970	N7574L				
G-ISIS	de Havilland DH.82A Tiger Moth	86251	G-AODR	20.12.83	D.R. & M.Wood	Tunbridge Wells	29. 3.62
			NL779	*(Crashed Nympsfield 18.9.61: on rebuild: current status unknown)*			
G-ISKA	WSK-PZL Mielec TS-11 Iskra	1H1018	1018	11. 5.00	P.C.Harper	Bruntingthorpe	
			Polish AF				
G-ISLA	Britten-Norman BN-2A-26 Islander	206	PH-PAR	7. 5.97	Hoe Leasing Ltd	Islay	21. 6.02T
			G-BNEA/SE-FTA/G-51-206 *(Op Macrins Hotel)*				
G-ISMO	Robinson R22 Beta	0870	OH-HOR	14.10.88	Moy Motorsport Ltd.	Sywell	3.12.04T
			G-ISMO/N8214T				
G-ISSY	Eurocopter EC 120B	1236	G-CBCG	11.10.01	D R Williams	(Brentwood)	3.12.04T
			F-WQPT				
G-ISTT	Thunder Ax8-84 HAFB	1787		12. 6.90	RAF Halton Hot Air Balloon Club		
					"RAF Halton"	RAF Halton	28.12.01A
G-ITEX	Fairey Britten-Norman BN-2A Mk.III-2 Trislander			21. 6.00	Aurigny Air Services Ltd	Guernsey	16 12.04T
		1008	G-OCTA/VR-CAA/DQ-FCF/G-BCXW				
G-ITII	Aerotek Pitts S-2A Special	2223	I-VLAT	5. 7.95	Aerobatic Displays Ltd	Booker	13. 8.01A
	(Lycoming AEIO-360)						
G-ITOI	Cameron N-90 HAFB	4785		14. 1.00	Flying Pictures Ltd	Fairoaks	27..3.02A
					(Vodaphone One To One titles)		
G-ITON	Maule MX-7-235 Star Rocket	10050C	N5670R	11. 9.96	J.R.S.Heaton	Hawksbridge Farm, Oxenhope	19.12.02
G-IUAN	Cessna 525 CitationJet	525-0324	N5163C	30. 6.99	RF Celada SpA	(Milan, Italy)	7. 7.02
			(N428PC)				
G-IVAC	Airtour AH-77B HAFB	012		28.11.89	T.D.Gibbs	Billingshurst	4. 9.01A
G-IVAN	Shaw Twin-Eze	39 & PFA 074-10502		11. 9.78	A.M.Aldridge	Ostend, Belgium	5.10.90P
	(Norton NR642 x 2)				*"Mistress" (Noted 2000)*		
G-IVAR	Yakovlev Yak-50	791504	D-EIVI	24. 2.89	R.A.L.Hubbard & S.Whitcombe	Meon	10. 3.02P
			(N5219K)/DDR-WQT/DM-WQT		t/a Foley Farm Flying Group		
G-IVEL	Sportavia Fournier RF4D	4029	G-AVNY	29. 6.95	V.S.E.Norman	Rendcomb	14. 4.01A
					(St.Ivel/Utterly Butterly titles)		
G-IVER	Europa Aviation Europa XS			14. 8.00	I.Phillips	(Orpington)	
		PFA 247-13632					
G-IVET	Europa Aviation Europa	PFA 247-12511		23. 5.97	K.J.Fraser	(Abingdon)	
G-IVIV	Robinson R44 Astro	0016	(N803EH)	2. 8.93	Rahtol Ltd	Redhill	16.10.02
G-IVOR	Aeronca 11AC Chief	11AC-1035	EI-BKB	18. 6.82	P.R.White & C.P.Matthews	Bodmin	16. 4.02P
			G-IVOR/EI-BKB/N9397E		t/a South Western Aeronca Group		
G-IVYS	Parsons Two Place Gyroplane			11. 1.00	R.M.Harris	(Nottingham)	
	(Mazda RX-7)	PFA G/08-1275					
G-IWON	Cameron V-90 HAFB	2504	G-BTCV	17. 2.92	D.P.P.Jenkinson *"Twenty One"*	Tring	21. 7.00A
G-IXIX	III Sky Arrow 650T	PFA 298-13257		24.10.00	W.J.De Gier	Old Sarum	22. 2.02P
G-IXTI	Extra EA.300/L	121		15. 9.00	Sundance Aviation Ltd	North Weald	29. 9.03T
G-IYAK	SPP Yakovlev Yak.C11	171103	OK-JIM	12. 1.94	E.K.Coventry	Earls Colne	25. 5.01P
			(Fr AF/Egypt AF)				
G-IYCO	Robin DR.500/200i President	0031		23. 2.01	L.M.Gould	Jersey	21. 3.04
	(Registered as DR.400/500)						
G-IZIT	Rans S-6-116 Coyote II			7. 3.96	Sport Air (UK) Ltd	Felixkirk	12. 7.01P
	(Rotax 912UL)	PFA 204A-12965					
G-IZOD	Jabiru Jabiru UL	PFA 274A-13541		26. 5.00	D.A.Izod	(Upminster)	4. 9.02P
G-IZZS	Cessna 172S Skyhawk	172S8152	N952SP	1. 7.99	Rankart Ltd	Hinton-in-the-Hedges	1. 7.02T
G-IZZY	Cessna 172R Skyhawk II	17280419	G-BXSF	7. 9.99	T.J.& P.S.Nicholson		
			N9967F			Maypole Farm, Chislet	30. 5.04T

G-JAAA – G-JZZZ

G-JABA	Jabiru Jabiru UL	189 & PFA 274-13297		14.12.99	A P Gornall	Booker	12 .6.02P
G-JABB	Jabiru Jabiru UL	PFA 274A-13555		27. 4.00	D.J.Royce	(Bestwood Village)	31. 7.01P
G-JABO	WAR Focke-Wulf FW190-A3 rep			23. 8.01	S.P. Taylor	(Crediton)	
		PFA 081-11786					
G-JABY	Jabiru Jabiru UL	PFA 274A-13672		2. 2.01	J.T.Grant	(Norwich)	
G-JACK	Cessna 421C Golden Eagle III		N421GQ	29. 4.97	JCT 600 Ltd	Leeds-Bradford	28. 4.04
		421C1411	N125RS/N12028				
G-JACO	Jabiru Jabiru UL	PFA 274A-13371		14. 4.99	R Hatton	(Douglas, IoM)	2.10.02P
	(Jabiru 2200A)						
G-JACS	Piper PA-28-181 Archer III	2843078	N9287J	15. 4.97	Vector Air Ltd	Fowlmere	17. 5.03T
			(G-JACS)				

G-JADJ	Piper PA-28-181 Archer III	2843009	N49TP	27. 7.99	S.J.Skilton	Southampton	28 .7.02T
	(Originally intended as c/n 2890240)		N92552		t/a Aviation Rentals *(Op Solent Flight Training)*		
G-JAGS	Reims Cessna FRA150L Aerobat		G-BAUY	24.10.01	P.A.Moslin	RAF Coltishall	7. 3.02T
		FRA1500167	N10633		t/a RAF Coltishall Flying Club		
G-JAHL	Bell 206B-3 JetRanger III	3565	N666ST	2. 1.98	D.T.Gittins	Shobdon	22. 2.04T
					t/a Jet Air Helicopters		
G-JAIR	Mainair Blade	1249-0500-7-W1042		11. 7.00	J.Loughran	(Stoke-on-Trent)	10. 7.01P
	(Rotax 582-2V)						
G-JAJK	Piper PA-31-350 Chieftain	31-8152014	G-OLDB	16.12.99	Keen Leasing (IOM) Ltd	Belfast	24. 7.03T
			OY-SKY/G-DIXI/N40717				
G-JAJP	Jabiru Jabiru UL	PFA 274A-13627		1.12.00	J W E Pearson & J Anderson *(Noted 1.02)*		
						Plaistows Farm, St Albans	26. 9.02P
G-JAKE	de Havilland DHC.1 Chipmunk 22		G-BBMY	21. 1.80	K.Ritter	(Bangor)	11.12.01
		C1/0584	WK565				
G-JAKI	Mooney M.20R Ovation	29-0030		7. 2.95	J.M.Moss & D.M.Abrahamson	(Dublin)	11. 4.04
G-JAKS	Piper PA-28-160 Cherokee	28-339	G-ARVS	2. 7.99	K.Harper	Stapleford	18. 1.04
G-JALC	Boeing 757-225	22194	N504EA	6. 3.95	Airtours International Airways Ltd		
						Manchester	22. 4.04T
G-JAMP	Piper PA-28-151 Cherokee Warrior		G-BRJU	3. 4.95	ANP Ltd	White Waltham	27. 6.04T
		28-7515026	N44762		*(Op West London Aero Club)*		
G-JAMY	Europa Aviation Europa XS			5. 1.01	J P Sharp	Rayne Hall Farm, Rayne	13. 6.02P
		PFA 247-13557					
G-JANA	Piper PA-28-181 Archer II	28-7990483	N2838X	12. 2.87	C.Dashfield	Stapleford	3. 6.02
					t/a Croaker Aviation		
G-JANB*	Colt Flying Bottle SS HAFB	1643		16. 2.90	Balloon Preservation Group	Kirdford	30. 9.96A
	(J & B Whisky Bottle shape)				*"J & B Whisky Too" (Cancelled 20.12.01 by CAA)*		
G-JANN	Piper PA-34-220T Seneca III	3433133	N9154W	23. 6.89	MBC Aviation Ltd	Fairoaks	30. 8.04T
G-JANO	Piper PA-28RT-201T Arrow IV		SE-IZR	14. 5.98	Abertawe Aviation Ltd	Swansea	24. 6.04T
		28R-7918091	N2146X				
G-JANS	Reims FR172J Rocket	FR17200414	PH-GJO	11. 8.78	I.G.Aizlewood	Rush Green	29.10.04
			D-EGJO				
G-JANT	Piper PA-28-181 Archer II	28-8390075	N4297J	23. 2.87	Janair Aviation Ltd	Denham	17. 3.02T
	(Originally built as c/n 28-8290117/N81992/YV-2234P: not delivered and re-manufactured as c/n stated)						
G-JARA	Robinson R22 Beta	1837		11. 6.91	S.G.Simpson t/a HJS Helicopters		
						Culter Helipad, Lower Baads Farm, Peterculter	18. 7.03T
G-JARV	Aérospatiale AS355F1 Twin Squirrel		G-OGHL	15.10.01	PLM Dollar Group Ltd	Inverness	27. 5.03T
		5164	N5796S				
G-JASE	Piper PA-28-161 Warrior II			13. 2.91	Mid-Anglia Flight Centre Ltd	Cambridge	24. 7.04T
		28-8216056	N8461R		t/a Mid-Anglia School of Flying		
G-JAVO	Piper PA-28-161 Warrior II		G-BSXW	17. 9.97	I.N.T.Thornhill	Wellesbourne Mountford	25. 6.03T
		28-8016130	N8119S				
G-JAWC	Pegasus Quantum 15-912	7692		21. 7.00	A.W.Chester	(Brentwood)	20. 7.02P
G-JAWZ	Pitts S-1S Special	PFA 09-12846		6.11.95	A.R.Harding	(Newton Farm, Sudbury)	15.11.01P
	(Lycoming AEIO-360)						
G-JAXS	Jabiru Jabiru UL	PFA 274A-13548		10.12.99	C A Palmer	Kemble	2. 5.02P
G-JAYI	Auster V J/1 Autocrat	2030	OY-ALU	5. 2.93	Bravo Aviation Ltd	Coventry	12. 8.02
			D-EGYK/OO-ABF		*(Op Air Atlantique)*		
G-JAZZ	Gulfstream AA-5A Cheetah	AA5A-0819	N26932	30. 3.82	R.W.Taylor t/a Jazz Club	Southend	28. 9.02
G-JBBS	Robinson R44 Raven	0784		14. 9.00	Fredat Ltd	Elstree	1.10.03T
G-JBDB	Agusta-Bell 206B JetRanger II	8238	G-OOPS	11. 4.96	Brad Helicopters Ltd	Denham	21.12.02T
			G-BNRD/Oman AF 602				
G-JBDH	Robin DR.400/180 Regent	1901		17. 3.89	W.A.Clark	Netherthorpe	23. 5.04
G-JBJB	Colt 69A HAFB	1274		26. 7.88	Justerini & Brooks Ltd	London SW1	19. 5.02A
					"J & B Jeremy"		
G-JBPR	Wittman W.10 Tailwind	PFA 031-11490		25. 5.89	P.A.Rose & J.P.Broadhurst	Walney Island	
G-JBRN	Cessna 182S Skylane	18280029	N432V	11. 6.99	Parallel Flooring Accessories Ltd		
			G-RITZ/N9872F			Wickenby	9. 3.04
G-JBSP	Jabiru Jabiru SP-470	PFA 274B-13486		12.10.99	C.R.James	Ludham	10. 6.02P
	(Jabiru 2200A)						
G-JCAR	Piper PA-46-350P Malibu Mirage		N4148N	17.12.99	J.A.Carr	Guernsey	21.12.02T
		4636223					
G-JCAS	Piper PA-28-181 Archer II	28-8690036	N9093N	12. 6.89	Charlie Alpha Ltd	Jersey	19. 6.04T
			(N170AV)/N9648N				
G-JCBA	Sikorsky S-76B	760352	N95UT	25.11.99	J C Bamford Excavators Ltd	East Midlands	10. 2.02
			N95LT/N120PP/N120PM				
G-JCBI	Dassault Falcon 2000	27	F-WWMM	13.11.96	J C Bamford Excavators Ltd	East Midlands	17.11.03
G-JCBJ	Sikorsky S-76C	760502		9. 7.99	J C Bamford Excavators Ltd	East Midlands	21. 7.02
G-JCFR	Cessna 550 Citation II	550-0282	G-JETC	14. 7.95	Chauffair Ltd	Farnborough	11. 4.02T
			N68644				
G-JCKT	Stemme S-10VT	11-004		8. 4.98	J.C.Taylor	(Castletown, IoM)	13. 5.04
G-JCMW	Rand Robinson KR-2	PFA 129-11064		3. 2.99	M.Wildish & J.Cook	(Gainsborough)	
G-JCUB	Piper PA-18-135 Super Cub	18-3531	PH-VCH	21. 1.82	N.Cummins & S.Bennett	(Dublin)	21. 7.02T
	(L-21B-PI) *(Frame No.18-3630)*		R-103 R.Neth AF/54-2331				

G-JDEE	SOCATA TB-20 Trinidad	333	G-BKLA F-BNGX	1. 5.84	A W Eldridge & J A Heard	Leicester	7. 9.02
G-JDEL	Jodel 150 Mascaret	112 & PFA 151-11276	G-JDLI	19. 9.95	K.F. & R.Richardson	(Solihull)	
G-JDIX	Mooney M.20B Mark 21	1866	G-ARTB	28.11.85	A.L.Hall-Carpenter	Shipdham	16. 1.00
G-JDJM	Piper PA-28-140 Cherokee C	28-26877	(G-HSJM) G-AYIF/N11C	11.10.00	R.Jackson-Moore & D.J.Street t/a The Hare Flying Group	Booker	17. 7.04
G-JEAD	Fokker F.27 Friendship 500	10627	VH-EWU PH-EXL	14.11.90	BAC Group Ltd *(Op BAC Express) "Midland Trader"*	(Horley)	21.11.02T
G-JEAE	Fokker F.27 Friendship 500 *(Freighter conversion)*	10633	VH-EWV PH-FSO	2. 1.91	BAC Leasing Ltd *(Op Channel Express)*	Exeter	15. 1.03T
G-JEAJ	British Aerospace BAe 146 Srs.200	E2099	G-OLCA G-5-099	20. 9.93	Jersey European Airways (UK) Ltd *"Pride of Guernsey"*	Exeter	17. 7.02T
G-JEAK	British Aerospace BAe 146 Srs.200	E2103	G-OLCB G-5-103	18. 3.93	Jersey European Airways (UK) Ltd *"Pride of Birmingham" (British European titles)*	Exeter	20. 6.02T
G-JEAM	British Aerospace BAe 146 Srs.300	E3128	G-BTJT HS-TBK/G-11-128	24. 5.93	Jersey European Airways (UK) Ltd *"Pride of Jersey"* *(Op Air France Express)*	Heathrow	23. 5.03T
G-JEAO	British Aerospace BAe 146 Srs.100	E1010	G-UKPC C-GNVX/N802RW/G-5-512/PT-LEP/G-BKXZ/PT-LEP	19. 9.94	Jersey European Airways (UK) Ltd *(Op Air France Express)*	Heathrow	29. 4.02T
G-JEAR	British Aerospace BAe 146 Srs.200	E2018	G-HWPB G-6-018/G-BSRU/G-OSKI/N603AW	14.11.95	Jersey European Airways (UK) Ltd *(Op Air France Express)*	Heathrow	7. 4.04T
G-JEAS	British Aerospace BAe 146 Srs.200	E2020	G-OLHB G-BSRV/G-OSUN/C-FEXN/N604AW	13. 2.96	Jersey European Airways (UK) Ltd *(Op Air France Express)*	Heathrow	13. 7.03T
G-JEAT	British Aerospace BAe 146 Srs.100	E1071	N171TR J8-VBB/G-BVUY/B-2706/G-5-071	11.10.96	Jersey European Airways (UK) Ltd *(Op Air France Express)*	Heathrow	23.10.02T
G-JEAU	British Aerospace BAe 146 Srs.100	E1035	N135TR J8-VBC/G-BVUW/B-584L/B-2704/G-5-035	30.12.96	Jersey European Airways (UK) Ltd *(Op Air France Express)*	Heathrow	24. 1.03T
G-JEAV	British Aerospace BAe 146 Srs.200	E2064	N764BA CC-CEN/N414XV/G-5-064/N404XV	17. 6.97	Jersey European Airways (UK) Ltd	Exeter	19. 6.03T
G-JEAW	British Aerospace BAe 146 Srs.200	E2059	(N759BA) CC-CEJ/N401XV/G-5-059/N401XV/G-5-059	21. 7.97	Jersey European Airways (UK) Ltd *(British European titles)*	Exeter	21. 8.03T
G-JEAX	British Aerospace BAe 146 Srs.200	E2136	N136JV C-FHAP/N136TR/N882DV/(N719TA)/N882DV/G-5-136	16. 2.98	Jersey European Airways (UK) Ltd *(Op Air France Express)*	Heathrow	19. 2.04T
G-JEAY	British Aerospace BAe 146 Srs.200	E2138	SE-DRL N138JV/C-FHAA/N138TR/(N719TA)/N883DV/G-5-138	27. 3.01	Jersey European Airways (UK) Ltd	Exeter	26. 3.04T
G-JEBA	British Aerospace BAe 146 Srs.300	E3181	HS-TBL G-6-181/G-BSYR/G-6-181	16. 6.98	Jersey European Airways (UK) Ltd *(Op Air France Express)*	Heathrow	27. 7.04T
G-JEBB	British Aerospace BAe 146 Srs.300	E3185	HS-TBK G-6-185	26. 6.98	Jersey European Airways (UK) Ltd *(Op Air France Express)*	Heathrow	1.11.04T
G-JEBC	British Aerospace BAe 146 Srs.300	E3189	HS-TBO G-6-189	4. 6.98	Jersey European Airways (UK) Ltd	Exeter	1. 7.04T
G-JEBD	British Aerospace BAe 146 Srs.300	E3191	HS-TBJ G-6-191	14. 7.98	Jersey European Airways (UK) Ltd	Exeter	17. 9.04T
G-JEBE	British Aerospace BAe 146 Srs.300	E3206	HS-TBM G-6-206	28. 5.98	Jersey European Airways (UK) Ltd	Exeter	25. 6.04T
G-JECA	Canadair CL600-2B19 Regional Jet *(CRJ 200)*	7345		29.10.99	Jersey European Airways (UK) Ltd *(Op Air France Express)*	Exeter	28.10.02T
G-JECB	Canadair CL600-2B19 Regional Jet *(CRJ 200)*	7393	C-GGKI C-FMNQ	2. 6.00	Jersey European Airways (UK) Ltd *(British European titles)*	Exeter	1 .6.03T
G-JECC	Canadair CL600-2B19 Regional Jet *(CRJ 200)*	7434	C-FMKV	13.10.00	Jersey European Airways (UK) Ltd	Exeter	26.10.03T
G-JECD	Canadair CL600-2B19 Regional Jet *(CRJ-200)*	7469	C-FMLI	19. 1.01	Jersey European Airways (UK) Ltd *(Stored 1.02)*	Exeter	31. 3.04T
G-JEDA	de Havilland DHC-8-311A	309	N394DC OE-LLW/C-GFHZ	23. 6.99	Jersey European Airways (UK) Ltd	Exeter	24. 6.02T
G-JEDB	de Havilland DHC-8-311A	323	N395DC OE-LLX/C-GFEN	29. 7.99	Jersey European Airways (UK) Ltd	Exeter	28. 7.02T
G-JEDC	de Havilland DHC-8-311A *(Q300)*	532	C-GEOA	1.10.99	Jersey European Airways (UK) Ltd	Exeter	30. 9.02T
G-JEDD	de Havilland DHC-8-311A *(Q300)*	533		21.10.99	Jersey European Airways (UK) Ltd	Exeter	25.10.02T
G-JEDE	de Havilland DHC-8-311A *(Q300)*	534	C-GERL	25.11.99	Jersey European Airways (UK) Ltd	Exeter	2.12.02T
G-JEDF	de Havilland DHC-8-311A *(Q300)*	548	C-GDIW	10. 7.00	Jersey European Airways (UK) Ltd	Exeter	9. 7.03T
G-JEDG	de Havilland DHC-8-402Q *(Q400)*			R	Jersey European Airways (UK) Ltd	Exeter	
G-JEDH	Robin DR.400/180	2343		3. 2.97	J.B.Hoolahan	Rochester	16. 5.03
G-JEDI	de Havilland DHC-8-402Q *(Q400)*	4052	C-GFOD	25.10.01	Jersey European Airways (UK) Ltd	Exeter	24.10.04T
G-JEDJ	de Havilland DHC-8-402Q *(Q400)*	4058	C-FDHZ	23. 1.02	Jersey European Airways (UK) Ltd	Exeter	
G-JEDK	de Havilland DHC-8-402Q *(Q400)*			R	Jersey European Airways (UK) Ltd	Exeter	
G-JEDL	de Havilland DHC-8-402Q *(Q400)*			R	Jersey European Airways (UK) Ltd	Exeter	

G-JEDX	de Havilland DHC-8-201B *(Q200)*	541	C-FDHV	16. 2.00	Jersey European Airways (UK) Ltd	Exeter	16. 2.03T
G-JEDY	de Havilland DHC-8-201B *(Q200)*	542	C-FNGB	27. 3.00	Jersey European Airways (UK) Ltd	Exeter	6..4.03T
G-JEDZ	de Havilland DHC-8-201B *(Q200)*	547	C-GDIU	7. 6.00	Jersey European Airways (UK) Ltd	Exeter	13. 6.03T
G-JEET	Reims Cessna FA152 Aerobat		G-BHMF	10.12.87	Willowair Flying Club (1996) Ltd		
		FA15200369				Southend	18.10.04T
G-JEFA	Robinson R44 Astro	0710		7. 2.00	Simlot Ltd	Denham	27. 4.03T
G-JEFF*	Piper PA-38-112 Tomahawk	38-79A0763		8. 3.79	(Skycraft Ltd)	(Spalding)	2. 2.01
					(Cancelled 18.4.01 as wfu: for spares 11.01)		
G-JEMY	Lindstrand LBL 90A HAFB	742		22.11.00	J.A.Lawton	(Godalming)	29.11.01A
G-JENA	Mooney M.20J (201)	24-1304	N1168D	5. 7.82	P.Leverkuehn	Antwerp-Deurne, Belgium	14.11.03
					t/a Mooney Partnership		
G-JENI	Cessna R182 Skylane RG II	R18200267	N3284C	17. 9.87	R.A.Bentley	Stapleford	23. 4.03
G-JENN	Gulfstream AA-5B Tiger	AA5B-1187	N4533T	7.12.81	M. Reed t/a Shadow Aviation	Elstree	23. 3.03T
G-JERL	Agusta A109E Power	11118		29. 5.01	Perment Ltd.	(Clitheroe)	6 .6.04T
G-JERS	Robinson R22 Beta	1610		21.12.90	Preveda Ltd	Bristol	7. 6.03T
G-JESS	Piper PA-28R-201T Turbo Arrow III		G-REIS	18. 9.95	N.E. & M.A.Bedggood	White Waltham	22. 5.03
		28R-7803334	N36689				
G-JETG	Learjet Learjet 35A	35A-324	G-JETN	5. 3.98	Gama Aviation Ltd	Fairoaks	31. 7.02T
			G-JJSG				
G-JETH	Armstrong-Whitworth Sea Hawk FGA.6		"XE364"	10. 8.83	P.G.Vallance Ltd	Charlwood, Surrey	
	(Composite with WM983/A2511)		XE489		*(Gatwick Aviation Museum as "XE489")*		
G-JETI	British Aerospace BAe 125 Srs.800B		G-5-509	9. 7.86	Ford Motor Co Ltd	Stansted	19.10.02T
		258056					
G-JETJ	Cessna 550 Citation II	550-0154	G-EJET	9. 2.93	Citation Flying Services Ltd	(Guernsey)	15. 8.02T
			G-DJBE/(N8887N)				
G-JETM	Gloster Meteor T.7	---	VZ638	10. 8.83	P.G.Vallance Ltd	Charlwood, Surrey	
					(Gatwick Aviation Museum: as "VZ638 in RN/FRU c/s)		
G-JETU	Aérospatiale AS355F2 Twin Squirrel		VR-CET	18. 4.96	Summit Aviation Ltd	Oxford	22. 5.02T
		5450	JA6623				
G-JETX	Bell 206B-3 JetRanger III	3208	N3898L	9. 2.88	Heli Charter Ltd	Manston	17. 5.03T
G-JETZ	MD Helicopters Hughes 369E (500E)		VR-HJI	26. 3.97	John Matchett Ltd	Sywell	15. 6.03
		0450E					
G-JFWI	Reims Cessna F172N Skyhawk II		PH-DPA	1. 9.80	Staryear Ltd	Barton	30. 1.03T
		F17201622	PH-AXY				
G-JGMN	CASA I-131E Jungmann Srs.2000	2011	E3B-407	17. 4.91	P.D.Scandrett	Rendcomb	25. 6.02P
	(Carries c/n plate 2104 in rear cockpit)						
G-JGBI	Bell 206L-4 LongRanger IV	52257	N91285	13. 8.01	Dorbcrest Homes Ltd	(Wigan)	16. 9.04
			C-GBUP				
G-JGSI	Pegasus Quantum 15-912	7515		19. 4.99	J.G.Spinks	Swinford, Rugby	16. 5.02P
G-JHEW	Robinson R22 Beta	0672	N23677	20. 7.87	Burbage Farms Ltd	Hinckley	2.11.02
G-JHYS	Europa Aviation Europa	PFA 247-13307		6. 3.01	J.D.Boyce & G.E.Walker		
					(Noted 11.01)	(Burnham-on-Crouch)	
G-JIGS	Lindstrand LBL 90A HAFB	656		9. 3.00	Jigsaw Connections Ltd	Reading	20..7.02A
G-JIII	Stolp SA.300 Starduster Too	2-3-12	N9043	27. 5.93	J.G.McTaggart	Cumbernauld	3. 5.02P
	(Lycoming IO-360)				t/a VTIO Company		
G-JILL	Rockwell Alpine Commander 112TC-A		(OO-HPB)	25. 7.80	P M & P A O'Hare	Humberside	6. 1.02T
		13304	G-JILL/N8070R/HB-NCW				
G-JILY	Robinson R44	0959		5. 1.01	N J Ferris	(Chipping Norton)	27. 2.04
					t/a Brilliant PR		
G-JIMB	Beagle B.121 Pup 1	B121-033	G-AWWF	7. 4.94	K.D.H.Gray & P.G.Fowler	Turweston	10. 5.04T
G-JIMW	Agusta-Bell 206B JetRanger II	8440	G-UNIK	4. 1.96	R.J.Watt	Phoenix Farm, Lower Upham	16. 4.04T
			G-TPPH/G-BCYP				
G-JIVE	MD Helicopters Hughes 369E (500E)		G-DRAR	24. 5.01	D.J.& J.B.Brown	Gloucestershire	8.11.04T
		0486E	N101LH/N1608Z		t/a First Flight		
G-JJAN	Piper PA-28-181 Archer II	2890007	N9105Z	28. 3.88	Redhill Aviation Ltd	Blackbushe	4. 5.03T
					t/a Redhill Flying Club		
G-JJEN	Piper PA-28-181 Archer III	2843370	N4190D	25. 8.00	J.E.Jenkins	Jersey	24. 8.03
G-JJWL	Robinson R44	0980		25. 1.01	Willbeth Ltd	Goodwod	8. 2.04T
G-JLCA	Piper PA-34-200T Seneca II		G-BOKE	3. 9.97	C.A.S.Atha	Teesside	25. 1.04T
		34-7870428	N21030				
G-JLEE	Agusta-Bell 206B-3 JetRanger III		G-JOKE	10. 2.88	Lee Aviation Ltd	Booker	5.10.03
		8588	G-CSKY/G-TALY				
G-JLHS	Beechcraft A36 Bonanza	E-2571	N8046U	30.11.90	I.G.Meredith	Lydd	21. 2.03
G-JLMW	Cameron V-77 HAFB	1768		23. 6.88	J.L.M.Watkins	Ivybridge	26. 2.99T
G-JLRW	Beechcraft 76 Duchess	ME-165	N60206	4.11.87	Magenta Ltd	Exeter	19. 1.03
					(Op Airways Flight Training)		
G-JMAA	Boeing 757-3CQ	32241		24. 4.01	JMC Airlines Ltd	Manchester	23 .4.04T
G-JMAB	Boeing 757-3CQ	32242		14. 5.01	JMC Airlines Ltd	Manchester	13. 5.04T
G-JMAC	British Aerospace Jetstream Srs.4100		G-JAMD	12. 6.92	BAE Systems (Operations) Ltd	Prestwick	6.10.97A
		41004	G-JXLI		*(Stored 7.97: current status unknown)*		
G-JMAN	Mainair Blade 912S	1290-0601-7-W1085		12. 7.01	J.Manuel	(Southport)	15. 7.02P
G-JMCD	Boeing 757-25F	30757		26. 5.00	JMC Airlines Ltd	Manchester	25. 5.03T
					(Op Ryan International)		
G-JMCE	Boeing 757-25F	30758		24. 6.00	JMC Airlines Ltd	Manchester	22. 6.03T

G-JMCF	Boeing 757-28A	24369	C-FOOE	20. 5.00	JMC Airlines Ltd	Manchester	26. 5.03T
G-JMCG	Boeing 757-2G5	26278	D-AMUQ	27. 4.00	JMC Airlines Ltd	Manchester	1. 6.03T
G-JMDI	Schweizer Hughes 269C (300C)	S.1398	G-FLAT	24. 9.91	J.J.Potter	Sherburn-in-Elmet	2.12.01
G-JMTS	Robin DR.400/180 Regent	2045		29.11.90	J.R.Whiting	Exeter	20 6.03
G-JMTT	Piper PA-28R-201T Turbo Arrow III		G-BMHM	8. 7.86	C.E.Passmore	Southend	25. 3.02
		28R-7803190	N3735M				
G-JNAS	Grumman American AA-5A Cheetah		SE-GEI	28.11.00	J.R.Nutter & A.L.Shore	Southampton	17. 1.04T
		AA5A-0604	LN-KLE				
G-JNET	Robinson R22 Beta	3195		6. 4.01	Park Head Helicopters Ltd	(Matlock)	25. 4.04T
G-JNNB	Colt 90A HAFB	2063		20.12.91	Justerini & Brooks Ltd *"J&B"*	London SW1	19. 5.02A
G-JODL	SAN Jodel DR.1050/M Excellence	99	F-BJJC	28. 4.86	D.Silsbury *(New owner 10.01)*	Dunkeswell	26.11.99
G-JOEL	Bensen B.8M	PFA G/03-1300		6. 7.99	G.C.Young	Swansea	
	(Converted from Air Command)						
G-JOEM	Airbus A320-231	0449	G-OUZO	17. 4.00	Airtours International Airways Ltd		
			EI-VIR/N449RX/SX-BSV/N449RX/F-WWIG			Manchester	7.11.04T
G-JOEY	Fairey Britten-Norman BN-2A Mk.III-2 Trislander			27.11.81	Aurigny Air Services Ltd	Guernsey	26. 8.02T
		1016	G-BDGG/C-GSAA/G-BDGG		*"Joey"*		
G-JOJO	Cameron A-210 HAFB	2674		20. 9.91	Joanna Barber	Ledbury	29. 3.01T
					t/a Worcester Balloons		
G-JOLY	Cessna 120	13872	OO-ACE	3. 9.81	B.V.Meade	Garston Farm, Marshfield	13. 6.02P
	(Continental C85)						
G-JONB	Robinson R22 Beta-II	2593		29. 4.96	J.Bignall	Mistletoe Farm, Pinner/Denham	27. 5.02
G-JONE	Cessna 172M Skyhawk II	17264490	N9724V	2.12.80	W.Bagnall	North Weald	13. 5.03
G-JONH	Robinson R22 Beta	2170		3. 6.93	Scotia Helicopters Ltd	Blackpool	22. 6.02T
G-JONI	Reims Cessna FA152 Aerobat		G-BFTU	6. 7.84	R.F.& J.S.Pooler	Sleap	28. 7.03
		FA15200346					
G-JONO	Colt 77A HAFB	1086		22. 6.87	The Sandcliffe Motor Group Ltd		
					"Sandcliffe Ford"	Stapleford, Notts	17. 9.95A
G-JONY	Cyclone AX2000 HKS	7503		12. 3.99	K.R.Matheson	Sandtoft	11. 3.02P
	(HKS 700E)				*(USAF c/s)*		
G-JONZ	Cessna 172P Skyhawk II	17276233	N97835	28. 9.89	Truman Aviation Ltd	Nottingham	26. 5.02T
G-JOOL	Mainair Blade 912			8.12.00	J R Gibson	Ince Blundell	13.12.02P
	(Rotax 912-UL)	1262-1000-7 & W1056					
G-JOON	Cessna 182D	18253067	(N)	9. 6.81	G.Jackson	Sibson	15. 7.01T
			G-JOON/OO-ACD/N9967T				
G-JOPF	Smyth Model S Sidewinder			19. 4.01	J.Furby	Nottingham	
		PFA 092-12313			*(Noted 9.01)*		
G-JOSS	Aérospatiale AS350B Ecureuil	1205	F-WQJY	31. 8.99	M.Burby	Jersey	26. 9.02T
			3A-…/G-WILX/G-RAHM/G-UNIC/G-COLN/G-BHIV				
G-JOST	Europa Aviation Europa	PFA 247-12916		17. 6.98	J.A.Austin	(Bangor)	
G-JOYT	Piper PA-28-181 Archer II	28-7990132	G-BOVO	13. 2.90	John K.Cathcart Ltd	St. Angelo	30. 3.03T
			N2239B				
G-JOYZ	Piper PA-28-181 Archer III	2843018	N9262R	19. 1.96	S.W. & Joy E.Taylor	Biggin Hill	23. 1.02
			(G-JOYZ)				
G-JPAL	Aérospatiale AS355N Twin Squirrel		F-GSJP	9.10.01	JPM Ltd	(Horsham)	6.11.04T
		5692					
G-JPAT	Robin HR.200/100 Club	76	G-BDJN	13. 9.00	J.C.F.Dalton	Bourn	29. 4.04
G-JPMA	Jabiru Jabiru UL	PFA 274A-13399		24. 5.99	J.P.Metcalfe	Lydd	12.11.02P
	(Jabiru 2200A)				*"Sheila"*		
G-JPOT	Piper PA-32R-301 Saratoga SP		G-BIYM	1. 8.94	S.W.Turley	Water Leisure Park, Skegness	22. 7.02T
		32R-8113065	N8385X				
G-JPRO	British Aircraft Corporation BAC.145 Jet Provost T.5A			10. 8.95	Edwalton Aviation Ltd	Humberside	5. 4.02P
		EEP/JP/1055	XW433		*(As "XW433 in CFS c/s)*		
G-JPSI	Dassault Falcon 50EX	313	F-WWHR	12. 9.01	Sorven Aviation Ltd	Gloucestershire	11. 9.04T
					(Noted 9.01)		
G-JPTV	British Aircraft Corporation BAC.145 Jet Provost T.5A			2. 5.96	Seagull Formation Ltd	North Weald	21. 8.02P
	(C/n '1002 reported)	EEP/JP/1005	XW355				
G-JPVA	British Aircraft Corporation BAC.145 Jet Provost T.5A			22. 2.95	T.J.Manna	Cranfield	17. 5.02P
		EEP/JP/953	G-BVXT/XW289		t/a Kennet Aviation *(As "XW289/73")*		
G-JREE	Maule MX-7-180 Star Rocket	11096C	N99MX	13. 4.01	J.M.P.Ree	(Newbury)	19. 4.04A
			N30051				
G-JRJR	Learjet LearJet 45	45-055	N45LR	24. 1.01	Richer Jet Ltd	(London SE1)	23. 1.02T
			N63MJ				
G-JSAK	Robinson R22 Beta-II	2959		30. 6.99	S.M.& J.W.F.Tuke	Headcorn	12. 7.02T
					t/a Tukair Aircraft Charter		
G-JSAT	Pilatus Britten-Norman BN-2T Islander		G-BVFK	5. 2.98	A.Wright	Weston-on-the-Green	5. 3.02A
		2277			t/a Rhine Army Parachute Centre		
G-JSCL*	Rans S-10 Sakota			12. 4.90	Not known	Emlyn's Field, Rhuallt	16. 5.92P
	(Rotax 532) 1289.075 & PFA 194-11781						
	(Damaged Emlyn's Field, Rhuallt 16.7.91: stored 9.96: cancelled 16.12.97 as WFU: current status unknown)						
G-JSFT	Piper PA-44-180 Seminole	44-7995084	D-GNFJ	21. 6.01	Plane Talking Ltd	Elstree	1. 8.04T
			PH-SYB/N2118A				
G-JSJX	Airbus A321-213	0808	(EC-)	3. 4.98	Airtours International Airways Ltd		
			D-AVZP			Manchester	27. 4.04T

G-JSON	Cameron N-105 HAFB	2933		21. 5.92	Up & Away Ballooning Ltd *"Jason"*	High Wycombe	17. 7.02A
G-JSPC	Pilatus Britten-Norman BN-2T Islander	2264	G-BUBG	21.12.94	A.Wright t/a Rhine Army Parachute Centre	Sennelager, Germany	13. 2.03A
G-JSPL	Jabiru Jabiru SPL-450	PFA 274A-13604		27.12.00	J A Lord	(Diss)	13. 5.02P
G-JSSD*	Handley Page HP.137 Jetstream 1	227	N510F N510E/N12227/G-AXJZ	14. 6.79	National Museums of Scotland/Museum of Flight	East Fortune	9.10.90S
	(Converted to BAe Jetsteam Srs.3001 prototype 1979/80: WFU Prestwick: cancelled 4.1.96 by CAA)						
G-JTCA	Piper PA-23-250 Aztec E	27-7305112	G-BBCU N40297	29.12.80	J.D.Tighe t/a Eastern Air Executive	Sturgate	8.11.03T
G-JTPC	Aeromot AMT-200 Super Ximango	200-067		28. 5.97	J.T.Potter & P.G.Cowling t/a G-JTPC Falcon 3 Group	Rufforth	22. 6.03
G-JTWO	Taylor J-2 Cub (Continental A65)	1754	G-BPZR N19554/NC19554	23.10.89	A.T.Hooper & C.C.Silk	Bericote Farm, Blackdown, Leamington Spa	3.10.00P
G-JTYE	Aeronca 7BM Champion (Continental C85) *(Mod ex 7AS standard)*	7AC-4185	N85445 NC85445	26. 9.91	G.D.Horn	Old Sarum	17. 6.99P
	(Damaged Longwood Farm, Southampton 2.8.98: current status unknown)						
G-JUDD	Jabiru Jabiru UL-450 (Jabiru 2200A)	PFA 274A-13570		9. 8.00	C.Judd	Lark Engine Farmhouse, Prickwillow, Ely	16. 1.02P
G-JUDE	Robin DR.400/180 Regent	1869		14.10.88	Bravo India Flying Group Ltd	Liverpool	15. 2.04
G-JUDI	North American AT-6D-NT Harvard III *(Regd with c/n "EX915-326165")*	88-14722	FAP 1502 SAAF7439/EX915/41-33888 *(As "FX301/FD-NQ")*	17.11.78	A.A.Hodgson	Bryngwyn Bach	13.12.00P
G-JUDY	Grumman-American AA-5A Cheetah	AA5A-0620	(G-BFWM) N26480	31. 8.78	Plane Talking Ltd	Biggin Hill	22.11.02T
G-JUIN	Cessna T303 Crusader	T30300014	OO-PEN N9401T	29. 2.88	M.J. & J M Newman	Denham	8. 5.03
G-JULL	Stemme S.10VT	11-039		10. 2.00	J.P.C.Fuchs	Rufforth	25. 4.03
G-JULU	Cameron V-90 HAFB	3611		7. 7.95	Datacentre Ltd	Bristol	12. 6.02A
G-JULZ	Europa Aviation Europa	PFA 247-13045		8.10.96	M.Parkin	(Doncaster)	
G-JUNG	CASA I-131E Jungmann	1121	E3B-143	23.11.88	K.H.Wilson	White Waltham	11. 6.02P
G-JURA	British Aerospace Jetstream Srs.3102	772	SE-LDH OY-SVK/C-FAMJ/G-31-772	21. 5.01	Highland Airways Ltd *"City of Inverness"*	Inverness	14. 6.04T
G-JURE	SOCATA TB-10 Tobago	597	N106U	6.11.92	P.M.Ireland	South Lodge Farm, Widmerpool	14. 1.05
G-JURG	Rockwell Commander 114A GT *(Laid-down as c/n 14449)*	14516	N4752W	19. 9.79	Oxford Aviation Services Ltd	Oxford	28. 8.04
G-JUST	Beechcraft F33A Bonanza	CE-1165	N334CW	11.10.00	Budge It Aviation Ltd	Elstree	14. 2.04
G-JVBF	Lindstrand LBL-210A HAFB	265		5. 6.95	Virgin Balloon Flights Ltd	London SE16	6. 4.01T
G-JVMD	Cessna 172N Skyhawk II	17267794	G-BNTV N75539	7. 2.92	C.A.Morris	Top Farm, Croydon	30.11.02T
G-JWBB	CEA Jodel DR.1050 Sicile	534	G-LAKI F-BLZD	17. 8.92	B.F.Baldock	Maypole Farm, Chislet	30. 6.02
G-JWBI	Agusta-Bell 206B JetRanger II	8435	G-RODS G-NOEL/G-BCWN	3. 4.96	J.W.Bonser (Walsall) Ltd	Walsall	13. 4.02T
G-JWCM	Scottish Aviation Bulldog Srs.120/1210	BH120/408	G-BHXB Botswana DF OD2/G-BHXB	19.10.99	M.L.J.Goff	Old Buckenham	16. 8.03T
G-JWDG	Grumman-American AA-5A Cheetah	AA5A-0662	G-OCML G-JAVA/N26705	9.10.91	Plane Talking Ltd *(Op Cabair)*	Blackbushe	20.11.03T
G-JWDS	Reims Cessna F150G	F150-0216	G-AVNB	15.12.88	C.R. & S.A.Hardiman *(Noted 4.01 unmarked)*	Gloucestershire	29. 9.94T
G-JWFT	Robinson R22 Beta	0989		16. 3.89	Leinster Warehousing & Distribution Ltd	(Dublin)	10. 5.04
G-JWIV	CEA Jodel DR.1051 Sicile	431	F-BLMD	6. 9.78	C.M.Fitton	Trenchard Farm, Eggsford	22.10.95
	(Damaged Hobbynoor Cross, Coldridge, Devon 23.9.95: noted 6.01)						
G-JWLS	Bell 206B JetRanger II	1114	G-BSXE N40EA/C-GMVM/N83150	8. 1.99	Autospeed Helicopters Ltd	(Sevenoaks)	20. 1.03T
G-JWXS	Europa Aviation Europa XS T-G	PFA 247-13743		5. 6.01	J.Wishart	(Carluke)	

G-KAAA – G-KZZZ

G-KAAT	MD Helicopters Explorer	900-00056	G-PASS N9234P	22. 2.00	Police Aviation Services Ltd *(Op Kent Air Ambulance Trust)*	Marden	19. 4.02T
G-KADY*	Rutan LongEz	PFA 074A-11094		3. 9.85	M.W.Caddy	(Mansfield)	
	(Reported as 60% complete by 1987: no longer shown on CAA database @ 12.01: cancellation details not known)						
G-KAFE	Cameron N-65 HAFB	1505		18. 5.87	J.R.Rivers-Scott	Loughborough	11. 5.02A
G-KAIR	Piper PA-28-181 Archer II	28-7990176	N3075D	28.12.78	Keen Leasing (IOM) Ltd	Belfast	2.10.03T
G-KAMM	Hawker Hurricane XIIA *(Built CCF)*	CCF/R32007	BW881	23. 2.95	Alpine Deer Group Ltd	Wananka, NZ	
	(On rebuild for American Flying Heritage Collection, Seattle, Washington 11.99)						
G-KAMP	Piper PA-18-135 Super Cub (L-18C)	18-3451	D-EDPM 96+27/NL+104/AC+502/AS+501/54-751	9. 5.97	A.P.Daines	Earls Colne	29. 7.04T
G-KAOM	Scheibe SF.25C Falke	4417	D-KAOM	3. 2.98	Cambridge Gliding Club Ltd	Gransden Lodge	18. 2.02

G-KAPW	Percival P.56 Provost T.1	PAC/F/311	XF603	22. 9.97	The Shuttleworth Trust	Old Warden	17. 3.02P
					(As "XF603/H")		
G-KARA	Brugger MB.2 Colibri	PFA 043-10980	G-BMUI	1. 6.95	Cara L.Reddish	Netherthorpe	27. 6.02P
	(VW 1834)						
G-KARI	Fuji FA.200-160 Aero Subaru	236	G-BBRE	19.12.84	The Scottish Civil Service Flying Club Ltd	Perth	10. 4.03T
G-KART	Piper PA-28-161 Warrior II	28-8016088	N8097B	10. 7.91	Newcastle upon Tyne Aero Club Ltd	Newcastle	24. 1.04T
G-KARY*	Fuji FA.200-180AO Aero Subaru	FA200-285	G-BEYP	28. 3.89	(Skycraft Ltd)	(Spalding)	11. 6.01
			(Force-landed 1m west Tibenham 23.7.01: cancelled as wfu 28.8.01: for spares 11.01)				
G-KATA	HOAC DV-20 Katana	20021	OE-CDV(1)	4. 2.94	E.Van Dun	(Barnstaple)	11. 5.03
G-KATE*	Westland WG.30 Srs.100	010		7. 7.83	Westland Helicopters Ltd	Yeovil	16. 9.88T
			(Cancelled 3.6.92 as WFU: dumped 12.99: Helicopter Hire c/s (orange & white)				
G-KATI	Rans S-7 Courier			5. 3.96	S.M. & K.E.Hall	Netherthorpe	29. 1.02P
	(Jabiru 2200A) 0795.151 & PFA 218-12917						
G-KATS	Piper PA-28-140 Cherokee Cruiser	28-7325022	G-BIRC	26. 8.83	A.G.Knight	Old Buckenham	17.11.02T
			OY-BGE		t/a Airlaunch		
G-KATT	Cessna 152 II	15285661	G-BMTK	10. 6.93	Aerohire Ltd	Wolverhampton	1. 7.02T
			N94387				
G-KAUR	Colt 315A HAFB	2536		1. 3.94	Balloon School (International) Ltd		
					t/a Balloon Safaris	Petworth	24. 7.02T
G-KAWA	Denney Kitfox mk.2	PFA 172-11822		11. 3.91	J.W.Barr	Long Marston	22.10.02P
	(Rotax 582)						
G-KAWW	Westland Wasp HAS Mk.1	F9663	NZ3907	29. 3.99	T.J.Manna	Cranfield	27. 7.02P
	(Correct p/i is NZ3908)		XT781		t/a Kennet Aviation *(As "XT781/426")*		
G-KAXF	Hawker Hunter F.6A	S4/U/3361	8830M	20.12.95	T.J.Manna	Cranfield	8. 9.02P
	(Built Armstrong-Whitworth Aircraft)		XF515		t/a Kennet Aviation *(As "XF515/R")*		
G-KAXL	Westland Scout AH.1	F.9715	XV140	16.11.95	T.J.Manna	Cranfield	12. 7.02P
	(Regd with c/n F8-7976)				t/a Kennet Aviation *(As "XV140/K")*		
G-KAZZ	Robinson R44	1135		21.12.00	Viking Office Supplies Ltd	(Lichfield)	
G-KBAC	Short SD.3-60 Var.100	SH.3758	VH-MJH	2. 1.98	BAC Leasing Ltd	Exeter	21. 1.02T
			G-BPXL				
G-KBKB	Thunder Ax8-90 Srs.2 HAFB	2089		30.10.91	G.Boulden *"KB Cars"*	Aldershot	20. 7.01A
G-KBPI	Piper PA-28-161 Cherokeee Warrior II	28-7816468	G-BFSZ	21. 5.81	Goodwood Road Racing Co Ltd	Goodwood	1. 9.02T
			N9556N				
G-KBWW	Comper CLA.7 Swift rep	PFA 103-13554		3. 2.00	Hurstgate Ltd	(London W4)	
G-KCIG	Sportavia Fournier RF5B Sperber	51005	D-KCIG	19. 6.80	J.R.Bisset	Aboyne	28. 8.01P
					t/a Deeside Fournier Group		
G-KDET	Piper PA-28-161 Cadet	2841158	(SE-KIR)	8. 8.89	Rapidspin Ltd	Biggin Hill	6.12.04T
			N9184Z		*(Op Biggin Hill School of Flying)*		
G-KDEY	Scheibe SF-25E Super Falke	4325	D-KDEY	8. 1.99	J.French	Aston Down	1. 3.02
					t/a Falke Syndicate		
G-KDFF	Scheibe SF-25E Super Falke	4330	D-KDFF	25. 4.83	Bowland Forest Gliding Club Ltd		
					Lower Cock Hill Farm, Chipping, Preston		25. 6.01
G-KDIX	Jodel D.9	PFA 054-10293		23.11.78	P.M.Bowden	(Stockport)	11. 6.02P
	(VW 1600)						
G-KDLN	LET Zlin Z.37A-2 Cmelak	19-05	OK-DLN	14. 8.95	J.Richards	Henstridge	27.10.02
G-KDMA	Cessna 560 Ultra	560-0553	N5145V	4. 4.01	Gamston Aviation Ltd	Gamston	3. 4.02T
G-KDOG	Scottish Aviation Bulldog Srs.120/121	BH120/289	XX624	18. 6.01	Gamit Ltd	North Weald	
					(Noted 7.01)		
G-KEAB*	Beechcraft 65-B80 Queen Air	LD-344	G-BSSL	3. 8.88	(N Franklin)	(Bruntingthorpe)	27. 9.87T
			G-BFEP/F-BRNR/OO-VDE		*(Cancelled 24.5.91 as WFU: noted 9.01)*		
G-KEAC*	Beechcraft 65-A80 Queen Air	LD-176	G-REXY	3. 8.88	(E.A.Prentice)	Little Gransden	18. 9.89T
			G-AVNG/D-ILBO		*(Cancelled by CAA 3.4.01) (Stored 11.01)*		
G-KEEN	Stolp SA.300 Starduster Too	800	PH-HAB	19. 7.78	H.Sharp	Belfast	15. 1.02P
	(Lycoming IO-540)		(PH-PET)/G-KEEN/N800RE		t/a Sharp Aerobatics		
G-KEES	Piper PA-28-180 Cherokee Archer	28-7505025	OO-AJV	29. 5.97	C.N.Ellerbrook	(Wymondham)	7. 9.03
			OO-HAC/N32102				
G-KELL	Van's RV-6	PFA 181-12845		16. 5.95	J.D.Kelsall	Netherthorpe	15. 2.02P
	(Lycoming O-320-B2C)						
G-KEMC	Grob G-109	6024	D-KEMC	19.10.84	D.L.H.Person, G.H.N.Chamberlain & R.S.Kiddy		
					t/a Eye-Fly	Rattlesden	11. 9.03
G-KEMI	Piper PA-28-181 Archer III	2843180	N41493	28.10.98	R.B. Kempster	Fowlmere	27.10.04T
G-KENB	Air Command 503 Commander	PFA G/04-1153		7.11.89	K.Brogden	Heywood, Lancs	24. 9.93P
	(Rotax 503)						
G-KENI	Rotorway Executive 152	3599		14. 3.89	A.J.Wheatley	Street Farm, Takeley	12 1 002
	(Rotorway RW 152)						
G-KENM	Luscombe 8EF Silvaire	2908	N21NK	9. 1.91	M.G.Waters	Compton Abbas	18.10.02P
	(Continental C90)		N71481/NC71481				
G-KENN*	Robinson R22 Beta	0715		10.12.87	The Hangar Nightclub	Stamford, Lincs	1. 1.97T
		(Damaged Sandtoft 31.10.94: cancelled 31.1.95 as WFU: rebuilt to static condition: current status unknown)					

G-KERY	Piper PA-28-180 Cherokee C	28-3049	G-ATWO	5.10.83	Seawing Flying Club Ltd & E.Alexander		
			N9021J		t/a General Aero Services		
	(Overshot landing King's Farm 14.4.00 & extensively damaged)					King's Farm, Thurrock	13. 4.01T
G-KEST	Steen Skybolt	1	G-BNKG	11. 6.91	B.Tempest	Leicester	16.10.02P
	(Lycoming IO-360)		G-RATS/G-RHFI/N443AT		t/a G-KEST Syndicate		
G-KEVB	Piper PA-28-181 Archer III	2843098	N9289E	29. 8.97	Palmair Ltd	Elstree	6. 9.03T
G-KEYS	Piper PA-23-250 Aztec F	27-7854052	N63909	6.10.78	T.M.Tuke & W.T.McCarter	City of Derry	1. 6.03T
G-KEYY	Cameron N-77 HAFB	1748	G-BORZ	14. 6.88	B.N.Trowbridge	Derby	4. 5.02A
G-KFAN	Scheibe SF-25B Falke	46301	D-KFAN	14. 5.96	R.G & J.A.Boyes	Eaglescott	29. 5.99
G-KFOX	Denney Kitfox mk.2			11.10.88	I.R.Lawrence	Eaglescott	25. 6.01P
	(Rotax 582)	298 & PFA 172-11447					
G-KFRA	Piper PA-32-300 Six	32-7840182	G-BGII	9. 9.97	M.Drake & W.Rankin	Weston, Co.Kildare	10.11.03
			N20879		t/a West India Flying Group		
G-KFZI	Williams KFZ-1 Tigerfalck			2. 2.89	L.R.Williams	(Aberdare)	
	(Continental C90)	PFA 153-11054	*(Originally laid-down as Kestrel Sport c/n PFA 1530)*				
G-KGAO	Scheibe SF-25C Falke 1700	44386	D-KGAG	30. 7.99	C.R.Ellis	(Bishops Castle)	8..8.02
					t/a Falke 2000 Group		
G-KHOM	Aeromot AMT-200 Super Ximango			5. 5.98	O.C.Masters & K.M.Haslet		
						Waterford, Co.Waterford	21. 5.04
G-KHRE	SOCATA Rallye 150SV Garnement	2931	F-GAYR	25. 3.82	D.M.Gale & K.F.Crumplin		
						Franklyn's Field, Chewton Mendip	28.12.03
G-KICK	Pegasus Quantum 15-912	7679		28. 6.00	G.D.Hall	Lower Mountpleasant, Chatteris	27. 6.02P
G-KIMB	Robin DR.300/140 Major	470	F-BPXX	23. 3.90	R.M.Kimbell	Sywell	8. 5.03
			F-WPXX				
G-KIMK	Partenavia P.68B	27	G-BCPO	23. 2.01	Kamair Ltd	North Weald	29. 6.01
G-KIMM	Europa Aviation Europa XS			20. 7.99	P.A.D.Clarke	(Bradford-on-Avon)	28.11.02P
		PFA 247-13404					
G-KIMY	Robin DR.400/140B Major	1401	PH-SRX	7. 6.00	P.W.& K.C.Johnson	Rochester	4. 7.03T
G-KINE	Gulfstream AA-5A Cheetah	AA5A-0896	N27173	20. 7.82	J.P.E.Walsh	Biggin Hill	27. 7.03T
					t/a Walsh Aviation *(Op London School of Flying)*		
G-KIRK	Piper J-3C-65 Cub	10536	F-BBQC	28. 2.79	M.J.Kirk	St.Donats	17. 5.01P
	(Frame No.12490)		Fr AF/43-29245				
G-KISS	Rand-Robinson KR.2	PFA 129-10899		2. 8.83	E.A.Rooney	(Whitstable)	
	(VW 1835)						
G-KITE	Piper PA-28-181 Archer II		N4338X	12. 4.88	L.G.Kennedy	Bournemouth	18. 4.03T
		28-8490053					
G-KITF	Denney Kitfox mk.1	156	N156BH	10. 5.89	P Smith	Long Marston	18. 4.02P
	(Rotax 532)						
G-KITI	Pitts S-2E Special	002	N36BM	21. 6.90	B.R.Cornes	Colerne	17. 4.01P
	(Lycoming IO-360)				*"Super Turkey II"*		
G-KITS	Europa Aviation Europa XS *(Tri-cycle u/c)*			13. 6.94	H E Perkins	Wombleton	29.10.02P
	(Midwest AE.100R)	003 & PFA 247-12844					
G-KITT	Curtiss TP-40M Kittyhawk	27490	F-AZPJ	4. 3.98	Patina Ltd	Duxford	31.10.02P
	(Officially c/n quoted as "31423")		N1009N/N1233N/RCAF 840/43-5802 *(Op The Fighter Collection)*				
	(C/n 31423 was P-40N 43-23484/RCAF 877/N1009N(1) which was scrapped in 1965 when identity adopted by RCAF 840)						
					(As "49/Bengal Tiger" in US Army c/s)		
G-KITY	Denney Kitfox mk.2			18. 8.89	T.Ringshaw	Nottingham	17.12.01P
	(IAME KFM112)	456 & PFA 172-11565			t/a Kitfox KFM Group		
G-KITZ	Europa Aviation Europa XS T-G			17. 2.00	Europa Aircraft Co Ltd	Kirkbymoorside	11. 7.02P
	(Tri-cycle u/c)	PFA 247-13578					
G-KKDL	SOCATA TB-20 Trinidad	1096	G-BSHU	3.12.90	M.S.Thompson	Biggin Hill	15. 8.02T
G-KKER	Jabiru Jabiru UL	PFA 274A-13474		1.10.99	W.K.Evans	(Llanelli)	1. 2.02P
	(Jabiru 2200A)						
G-KKES	SOCATA TB-20 Trinidad	1316	G-BTLH	2. 3.92	Knightsgate Ltd	(Douglas, IoM)	16. 5.04T
G-KKKK	Scottish Aviation Bulldog Srs.120/121		XX513	2.10.01	Drumforce Ltd	(London W1)	
		BH120/199			*(As "XX513/10")*		
G-KNAP	Piper PA-28-161 Warrior II		G-BIUX	15. 2.90	Keen Leasing (IOM) Ltd	Belfast	28. 4.02T
		28-8116129	N9507N				
	(Crashed on take off Stevensons Field, Letterkenny, Co Donegal 13.7.99: wreck stored 2.01)						
G-KNEK	Grob G.109B	6437	D-KNEK	22. 5.00	R.A.Winley	Currock Hill	7. 6.03
					t/a Syndicate 109		
G-KNIB	Robinson R22 Beta	3145		30.10.00	C.G.Knibb	Sywell	26.11.03T
G-KNOB	Lindstrand LBL-180A HAFB	065		20.12.93	Wye Valley Aviation Ltd	Ross-on-Wye	16. 4.01T
G-KNOT	Hunting Percival P.84 Jet Provost T.Mk.3A		G-BVEG	9. 6.99	R.S.Partridge-Hicks	North Weald	3. 8.02P
		PAC/W/13893	XN629		*(As "XN629/49" in RAF c/s)* (See entry for G-BVEG)		
G-KNOW	Piper PA-32-300 Six	32-7840111	N9694C	21. 9.88	Hi Fly Ltd	(London W1)	15. 6.04
G-KNYT	Robinson R44 Astro	0723		13. 3.00	C.Bootman t/a Aircol	(Bedford)	13. 3.03T
G-KODA	Cameron O-77 HAFB	1448		26. 3.87	N.J.Milton *"Kodasnap"*	Bristol	
G-KOFM	Glaser-Dirks DG-600/18M	6-66M16	D-KOFM	13. 7.99	A.Mossman	(Feshiebridge)	28..7.02
G-KOHF	Scheicher ASK-14	14033	D-KOHF	4. 9.01	J. Houlihan	(Hollywood, Co of Down)	6.11.04
G-KOKL	Hoffmann H-36 Dimona	36276	D-KOKL	4. 3.98	R.Smith & R.Stembrowicz	Rufforth	5. 4.04
G-KOLB	Kolb Twinstar mk.3A	PFA 205-12228		30. 6.93	J.L.Moar	Wick	26. 7.02P
	(Rotax 912UL)						
G-KOLI	PZL-110 Koliber 150	03900038		23. 7.90	J.R. Powell	Perth	1. 2.03

G-KONE	Rotorway Executive 162F	6432		15.10.99	G.Kresfelder	(Horsham)	
G-KONG	Slingsby T.67M-200 Firefly	2041	VR-HZP	24. 3.94	Babcock Rosyth Defence Ltd		
			HKG-10/G-7-119		t/a Hunting Contract Services *(Op JEFTS)*		
						RAF Barkston Heath	3. 8.03T
G-KOOL	de Havilland DH.104 Devon C.2/2	04220	"G-DOVE" VP967	12. 1.82	K.P.Hunt	(Reigate)	
					c/o 135 Sqdn (Reigate & Redhill) ATC		
					(Not converted: noted 8.00: new owner 12.01)		
G-KORN	Cameron Berentzen Bottle 70SS HAFB	1655		10. 5.88	A D & R.S.Kent, I M Martin & I Chadwick		
					t/a Balloon Preservation Flying Group		
					"Bottle Berentzen"	Kirdford	23. 6.00A
G-KOTA	Piper PA-28-236 Dakota	28-8011044	N8130R	23.12.88	D.J.Fravigar t/a JF Packaging		
						Clough Farm, Croft, Skegness	18. 8.01
G-KPAO	Robinson R44 Astro	0382	G-SSSS	19.11.98	Avonline Ltd	Bristol	20.11.03T
G-KPTT	SOCATA TB-20 Trinidad	1821	F-GRBI	13. 6.01	Chartfleet Ltd	Fenland	23. 8.04T
G-KRAY	Robinson R22HP	0266	EI-CEF	25. 5.95	G.P. Glibbery	(Chelmsford)	4. 7.04T
			G-BOBO/N712BH/N100GV/N90763		t/a Helisport		
G-KRES	Stoddard-Hamilton Glasair IIS RG	PFA 149-12984		12. 6.96	G.Kresfelder	Fairoaks	15. 1.02P
G-KRII	Rand Robinson KR-2	PFA 129-10934		4. 8.89	M.R.Cleveley	(Halesworth, Suffolk)	
G-KRIS	Maule M-5-235C Lunar Rocket	7357C	N56420	21. 4.81	A.C.Vermeer	(Antrim)	25. 1.04
G-KRNW	Eurocopter EC 135 T1	0175		9. 7.01	Bond Air Services Ltd	Aberdeen	11. 7.04T
G-KSIR	Stoddard-Hamilton Glasair IIS RG (Lycoming IO-360)	2151 & PFA 149-12137		15. 4.94	The Hon R.Cayzer	Oxford	19. 6.02
G-KSKS	Cameron N-54 HAFB	4963		21. 3.01	A.M Holly	Bristol	5. 2.02T
					t/a Exclusive Ballooning *(Kwik Save titles)*		
G-KSKY	Sky 77-24 HAFB	170		15.10.99	J.R.Howard	Poulton-le-Fylde	16.11.00A
G-KSVB	Piper PA-24-260 Comanche B	24-4657	G-ENIU	8.11.91	S.Juggler	Stapleford	28. 5.04
			G-AVJU/N9199P/N10F				
G-KTEE	Cameron V-77 HAFB	2177		28.12.89	D.C. & N.P.Bull *"Katie"*	Aylesbury	26. 5.01A
G-KTKT	Sky 260-24 HAFB	110		19. 5.98	T.M.Donnelly	Doncaster	25. 5.02T
G-KUBB	SOCATA TB-20 Trinidad GT	2026	F-OILS	1.12.00	Offshore Marine Consultants Ltd	Gamston	7.12.03
G-KUTU	QAC Quickie Q.2 (Limbach L2000)	PFA 94A-10758		8. 3.82	J.Parkinson & R.Nash	Booker	29. 4.86P
					(Damaged Cranfield 18.5.85: stored 4.99: current status unknown)		
G-KVBF	Cameron A-340HL HAFB	4313		6. 4.98	Virgin Balloon Flights Ltd	London SE16	6. 8.02T
G-KWAX	Cessna 182E Skylane	18253808	N9902 YV-T-PTS/N2808Y	18. 5.78	D.R.Graves	(Newton Abbot)	5. 1.03T
G-KWIK	Partenavia P.68B	152		27. 9.78	ACD Cidra NV	Wevelgem, Belgium	11. 6.03T
G-KWKI	QAC Quickie Q.200 (Continental O-200-A)	PFA 94-12158		22.10.91	B.M.Jackson	Enstone	17. 9.02P
G-KWLI	Cessna 421C Golden Eagle II	421C0168	G-DARR G-BNEZ/N87386	13.11.98	Langley Holdings plc	(Retford)	25. 1.02
G-KYAK	SPP Yakovlev Yak C-11	171101	F-AZQI	21.12.78	M.Gainza *"36"*	North Weald	12.11.02P
			G-KYAK/F-AZHQ/G-KYAK/Israeli DFAF/Egyptian AF 590/Czech AF				
G-KYDD	Robinson R.44 Astro	0106	N2123E D-HDLW	16. 9.99	EK Aviation Ltd	Cambridge	19. 9.02T
G-KYNG	Aviamilano F.8L Falco 1	105	I-KYNG HB-UOH/I-STRI	6. 8.97	A E Hutton	North Weald	19. 6.04

G-LAAA – G-LZZZ

G-LABS	Europa Aviation Europa	PFA 247-12595		1. 3.94	C.T.H.Pattinson	(Bicester)	
G-LACA	Piper PA-28-161 Cherokee Warrior II	28-7816036	N44883	22. 6.90	LAC (Enterprises) Ltd	Barton	21. 2.02T
G-LACB	Piper PA-28-161 Warrior II	28-8216035	N8450A	12. 6.90	LAC (Enterprises) Ltd	Barton	29. 7.02T
G-LACD	Piper PA-28-181 Archer III	2843157	G-BYBG N47BK	11.11.98	D.H.Brown	(Burnley)	22.11.04T
					t/a David Brown Aviation		
G-LACE	Europa Aviation Europa	PFA 247-12962		15. 4.96	J.H.Phillingham	(Wallingford)	
G-LACR	Denney Kitfox	PFA 172-11945		4.12.90	C.M.Rose	(Edinburgh)	
					(Under construction 6.00)		
G-LADD	Enstrom 480	5037		20. 5.99	Combi-Lift Ltd (Clontibret, Co.Monoghan)		10. 6.02T
G-LADE	Piper PA-32-300 Six	32-7940030	N3008L	21.11.80	B.E.Bergabo *"Harry O"*	Denham	21. 4.02T
G-LADI	Piper PA-30 Twin Comanche	30-334	G-ASOO N10F	8. 4.94	S.H.Eastwood	Blackbushe	7. 9.02T
G-LADS	Rockwell Commander 114	14314	N4994W (N114XT)/N4994W	6.12.90	D.F.Soul	Emberton, Olney	5. 1.03
G-LAGR	Cameron N-90 HAFB	1628		25. 1.88	J.R.Clifton	Brackley	19. 8.01A
G-LAIN	Robinson R22 Beta	1992		7. 2.92	Deadline Programming Ltd	Booker	4. 6.04T
G-LAIR	Stoddard-Hamilton Glasair IIS	2106		12. 9.91	D.L.Swallow	(Norwich)	
G-LAKE	Lake LA-250 Renegade	70	(EI-PJM) G-LAKE/N8415B	12. 7.88	P.J.McGoldrick	Lough Derg Marina, Killaloe	31. 8.01
G-LAMA	Aérospatiale SA.315B Lama	2348	SE-HET	17. 3.98	PLM Dollar Group Ltd	Cumbernauld	19. 3.04T
G-LAMM	Europa Aviation Europa	PFA 247-12941		20.11.95	S.A.Lamb	(Paddock Wood)	

G-LAMP	Cameron Lightbulb-110 SS HAFB	4899		21. 7.00	LE Electrical Ltd	Norwich	26..7.01A
G-LAMS	Reims Cessna F152 II	F15201431	N54558	23. 6.88	Jaxx Landing Ltd	Swansea	2.10.03T
G-LANC*	Avro 683 Lancaster B.X	-	KB889	31. 1.85	Imperial War Museum	Duxford	
	(Built Victory Aircraft, Canada)		RCAF		*(Cancelled 2.9.91 by CAA) (As "KB889/NA-I" in 428 Sqn c/s)*		
G-LAND	Robinson R22 Beta	0639		28. 4.87	Helicopter Training & Hire Ltd	Belfast	29. 3.02T
G-LANE	Reims Cessna F172N Skyhawk II	F17201853		27. 6.79	G.C.Bantin	Sproatley	4. 6.03
G-LAOL	Piper PA-28RT-201 Cherokee Arrow IV	28R-7918211	D-EAOL N2903Y	6.10.99	G.P.Aviation Ltd	Goodwood	13. 1.03T
G-LAPN	Avid Aerobat	PFA 189-12146		4. 3.93	R.M. & A.P.Shorter	White Waltham	20. 8.02P
G-LARA	Robin DR.400/180 Regent	2050		14. 2.91	K.D. & C.A.Brackwell	Goodwood	23. 4.03
G-LARE	Piper PA-39 Twin Comanche C/R	39-16	N8861Y	20. 2.91	Glareways (Neasden) Ltd	Biggin Hill	23. 4.03
G-LARK	Helton Lark 95	9517	N5017J	3.12.85	J.Fox	Booker	26. 3.02P
G-LASR	Stoddard-Hamilton Glasair II	2027		8. 1.90	G.Lewis	(Heswall, Wirral)	
G-LASS	Rutan VariEze (Continental O-200-A)	PFA 074-10209		20. 9.78	J.Mellor	(Neston, Cheshire)	10. 6.02P
G-LAST	Cessna 340 II	340-0305	G-UNDY G-BBNR/N69452	2. 9.96	Last Engineering Ltd	Cambridge	15. 8.03
G-LATK	Robinson R44 Astro	0064	G-BVMK	18. 7.94	Holly Aviation Ltd	Gloucestershire	27. 8.03T
G-LAVE	Cessna 172R Skyhawk	17280663	G-BYEV N2377J/N41297	10. 3.99	R.W.& A.M.Glaves	East Midlands	31. 3.02
G-LAWS	Sikorsky S-61N Mk.II	61-824	G-BHOF LN-ONK/G-BHOF/LN-ONK/G-BHOF	7. 7.99	Laws Helicopter Ltd	Aberdeen	9. 7.04T
G-LAZA	Lazer Z.200 (Lycoming AEIO-360)	PFA 123-12682		15. 6.95	M.Hammond	Hardwick	20. 9.02P
G-LAZL	Piper PA-28-161 Warrior II	28-8116216	D-EAZL N9536N	9. 6.99	S.Bagley & K.J.Amies t/a Hawk Aero Leasing	Coventry	19. 7.02T
G-LAZR	Cameron O-77 HAFB	2240		6. 3.90	Laser Civil Engineering Ltd *"Laser Engineering"*	Pershore	10. 6.97A
G-LAZY	Lindstrand LBL Armchair SS HAFB	129		18. 9.94	The Air Chair Co Ltd *"The Chair"*	Westville, Indiana, USA	9. 3.00A
G-LAZZ	Stoddard-Hamilton GlaStar	PFA 295-13059		31.10.96	A.N.Evans	(Congleton)	
G-LBLI	Lindstrand LBL-69A HAFB	010		4.11.92	N.M.Gabriel	Kimberley, Notts	4.11.01A
G-LBMM	Piper PA-28-161 Cherokee Warrior II	28-7816440	N6940C	28.11.89	Flexi-Soft Ltd	Wellesbourne Mountford	25. 4.02
G-LBNK	Cameron N-105 HAFB	3559		20. 3.95	Virgin Airship & Balloon Co Ltd *"Lloyds Bank"*	Telford	25. 3.99A
G-LBRC	Piper PA-28RT-201 Arrow IV	28R-7918051	N2245P	20. 7.88	D.J.V.Morgan	Wolverhampton	17. 1.04
G-LCGL	Comper CLA.7 Swift rep (Pobjoy Niagara 1A)	PFA 103-11089		1.7.92	J.M.Greenland	Blackacre Farm, Holt, Wilts	15.11.02P
G-LCIO*	Colt 240A HAFB	1381		23. 1.89	British Balloon Museum & Library *"Star Flyer 2"*	Newbury	
	(Damaged landing after first overflight of Mt Everest by hot air balloon 21.10.91: cancelled 25.5.94 as WFU)						
G-LCOC	Britten-Norman BN-2A mk.III-1 Trislander	366	G-BCCU 4X-CCK/G-BCCU/9L-LAR/G-BCCU/(LN-VIV)	30. 7.01	Airx Ltd t/a Lecocqs.com	Alderney	18.12.01T
G-LCON	Eurocopter AS 355N Twin Squirrel	5572		28. 6.94	Lancashire Constabulary *(Op Lancashire Air Support Unit)*	Warton	26.10.03T
G-LCRC	Boeing 757-23AER	24636	G-IEAB	27.10.93	Airtours International Airways Ltd	Manchester	9. 5.02T
G-LDYS	Thunder Ax6-56Z HAFB *(Regd as Colt 56A)*	347		18. 5.81	P.Glydon & M.J.Myddelton *"Gladys"*	Birmingham/Keynsham	27. 3.00A
G-LEAF	Reims Cessna F406 Caravan II	F406-0018	EI-CKY PH-ALN/OO-TIW/F-WZDX	7. 3.96	Atlantic Air Transport Ltd *(Op Highland Airways) (Atlantic Airlines c/s)*	Inverness	20. 5.03T
G-LEAM	Piper PA-28-236 Dakota	28-8011061	G-BHLS N35650	1. 7.80	C.S.Doherty	Gamston	8. 7.04
G-LEAP	Pilatus Britten-Norman BN-2T Islander	2183	G-BLND	19. 8.87	G Burton t/a Army Parachute Association	AAC Netheravon	18. 4.03A
G-LEAR	Learjet Learjet 35A	35A-265	G-ZEST N1462B	20. 8.79	Northern Executive Aviation Ltd	Manchester	10. 1.03T
G-LEAS	Sky 90-24 HAFB	158		4. 5.99	Leasing Group plc	Reading	17..7.02A
G-LEAU	Cameron N-31 HAFB	761		5. 8.81	P.L.Mossman *"Perrier"*	Bristol	24. 2.97A
G-LEBE	Europa Aviation Europa	PFA 247-12927		17. 5.01	P.Atkinson	(Carnforth)	
G-LECA	Aérospatiale AS355F1 Twin Squirrel	5043	G-BNBK C-GBKH	6. 2.87	South Western Electricity plc	Bristol	3. 6.02T
G-LEDA	Robinson R22 Beta	1938	G-IFOX	12.11.98	E.D.Obeng t/a Pentacle	Denham	13.11.00T
G-LEED	Denney Kitfox Mk.2 (Rotax 582)	450 & PFA 172-11577		24. 4.91	A.F.Stafford	Melrose Farm, Melbourne	20. 8.02P
G-LEEE	Jabiru Jabiru UL	PFA 274A-13516		18. 1.00	J.N.Fugl	(Uckfield)	2..8.02P
G-LEEN	Aero Designs Pulsar XP	PFA 202-12147	G-BZMP G-DESI	16. 7.01	R.B.Hemsworth	(Bideford)	
G-LEES	Glaser-Dirks DG-400	4-238		4.10.88	J Bradley	RAF Upavon	14. 3.04

G-LEEZ	Bell 206L-1 LongRanger II	45761	G-BPCT	22. 1.92	Pennine Helicopters Ltd	(Oldham)	7.12.03T
			D-HDBB/N3175G				
G-LEGG	Reims Cessna F182Q Skylane II		G-GOOS	26. 6.96	P.J.Clegg	Barton	19.12.02
		F18200145					
G-LEGO	Cameron O-77 HAFB	1975		14. 4.89	P.M.Traviss *"Jigsaw II"*	Yarm	4. 5.02A
G-LEIC	Reims Cessna FA152 Aerobat	F15200416		16. 9.86	Leicestershire Aero Club Ltd	Leicester	17. 6.02T
G-LELE	Lindstrand LBL 31A HAFB	806		16. 8.01	L.E.Electrical Ltd	Norwich	19. 8.02A
G-LEND*	Cameron N-77 HAFB	2012		25. 5.89	Southern Flight Co Ltd	Southampton	12. 9.96T
					"Southern Finance Co/Glenda" (Cancelled 8.10.01 as wfu)		
G-LENI	Aérospatiale AS355F1 Twin Squirrel		G-ZFDB	9. 8.95	Grid Aviation Ltd	Denham	21. 4.03T
		5311	G-BLEV				
G-LENN	Cameron V-56 HAFB	1833		29. 9.88	A.E.Austin	Naseby	13.11.01A
G-LENS	Thunder Ax7-77Z HAFB	168		3.11.78	R S Breakwell	(Bridgnorth)	13. 2.02A
					(Noted 2.97: official c/n change 2.01)		
G-LENY	Piper PA-34-220T Seneca III		N111PS	26. 7.00	Air Medical Ltd	Oxford	3. 8.03T
		34-8233205	(OK-MKN)/PH-SMS/(PH-CCC)/D-GAPN/N82396				
G-LEOS	Robin DR.400/120 Dauphin 2+2	1884		29.11.88	P.G.Newens	Fairoaks	3. 4.04
G-LESJ	Denney Kitfox mk.3	PFA 172-12001		4.10.94	P.Whittingham	Otherton, Cannock	21. 3.02P
	(Rotax 582)						
G-LEVI	Aeronca 7AC Champion	7AC-4001	N85266	17. 4.90	Jean P.A.Pumphrey	White Waltham	2.10.02P
			NC85266		t/a G-LEVI Group		
G-LEXI	Cameron N-77 HAFB	438		26.10.78	T.Gilbert	Weston-Super-Mare	16. 6.02A
G-LEZE	Rutan LongEz	PFA 074A-10702		31. 3.82	K.G.M.Loyal, A.J.Draper, J.R.J.Giesler & C.McGeachy		
	(Continental O-200-A)					Wombleton	5.11.01P
G-LEZZ	Stoddard-Hamilton GlaStar		G-BYCR	4.11.98	L.A.James	Wharf Farm, Market Bosworth	17. 6.02P
	(Lycoming O-320) *(Tri-cycle u/c)*	PFA 295-13241					
G-LFIX	Supermarine 509 Spitfire Trainer 9		IAC 162	1. 2.80	Carolyn S.Grace	Duxford	16. 4.02P
	(C/n is firewall plate no)	CBAF.8463	G-15-175/ML407		*"Nicholson Leslie"*		
			(As "ML407/OU-V" (stbd)" in 485 Sqn c/s & "ML407/"NL-D" (port) in 341 Sqn c/s)				
G-LFSA	Piper PA-38-112 Tomahawk	38-78A0430	G-BSFC	22.10.90	Liverpool Flying School Ltd	Liverpool	15. 3.03T
			N9739N				
G-LFSB	Piper PA-38-112 Tomahawk	38-78A0072	G-BLYC	20.10.94	Spencer Davies Engineering Ltd		
			D-ELID/N9715N			(Burry Port)	7.10.03T
G-LFSC	Piper PA-28-140 Cherokee Cruiser		G-BGTR	4. 9.95	M.B.North	(Beverley)	27.10.04T
		28-7425005	OY-BGO/SE-GDS				
G-LFSD	Piper PA-38-112 Tomahawk II		G-BNPT	21.10.96	Liverpool Flying School Ltd	Liverpool	1. 6.03T
		38-82A0046	N91522				
G-LFSF	Cessna 150M	15077651	G-BSRC	9. 7.99	Gems Europe SA	Charleroi, Belgium	27. 5.03T
			N6337K				
G-LFSG	Piper PA-28-180 Cherokee E	28-5799	G-AYAA	19. 6.00	Liverpool Flying School Ltd	Liverpool	3.11.04T
			N11C				
G-LFSH	Piper PA-38-112 Tomahawk	38-78A0352	G-BOZM	16. 7.01	Liverpool Flying School Ltd	Liverpool	19. 6.04T
			N6247A				
G-LFSI	Piper PA-28-140 Cherokee C	28-26850	G-AYKV	14. 7.89	P.S.Hoyle & S.Merriman	Humberside	15.11.01T
			N11C				
G-LFVB	Supermarine 349 Spitfire LF.V	8070M	5377M	9. 5.94	Patina Ltd	Duxford	31. 8.02P
		CBAF.2403	EP120		*"City of Winnipeg" (Op The Fighter Collection)*		
					(As "EP120/AE-A" in 402 Sqn c/s)		
G-LFVC	Supermarine 349 Spitfire L.Vc	--	ZK-MKV	28. 9.99	Historic Flying Ltd	(Duxford)	
			A58-178/JG891				
G-LGNA	Saab-Scania SF.340B	340B-199	N592MA	11. 6.99	Loganair Ltd	Glasgow	13. 6.02T
			SE-F99		*(Benyhone Tartan t/s)*		
G-LGNB	Saab-Scania SF.340B	340B-216	N595MA	8. 7.99	Loganair Ltd	Glasgow	8. 7.02T
			SE-G16		*(Waves of the City t/s)*		
G-LGNC	Saab-Scania SF.340B	340B-318	SE-KXC	9. 6.00	Loganair Ltd	Glasgow	11. 6.02T
			F-GTSF/EC-GMI/F-GMVZ/SE-KXC/SE-C18		*"Chatham Historic Dockyard"*		
G-LGND	Saab-Scania SF.340B	340B-169	G-GNTH	7. 9.01	Loganair Ltd	Glasgow	4. 2.02T
			N588MA/SE-F69				
G-LGNE	Saab-Scania SF.340B	340B-172	G-GNTI	31. 8.01	Loganair Ltd	Glasgow	5. 2.02T
			N589MA/SE-F72				
G-LGTD	Boeing 737-3..			R	British Airways plc	Gatwick	
G-LGTE	Boeing 737-3Y0	24908	TC-SUP	25. 1.01	British Airways plc	Gatwick	26. 3.04T
G-LGTF	Boeing 737-382	24450	N115GB	7. 3.01	British Airways plc	Gatwick	30. 4.04T
			TC-IAC/CS-TIE				
G-LGTG	Boeing 737-3Q8	24470	N696BJ	4. 4.01	British Airways plc	Gatwick	14. 6.04T
			SX-BFT/N470KB/PK-GWD				
G-LGTH	Boeing 737-3Y0	23924	OO-LTV	4. 4.01	British Airways plc	Gatwick	8. 6.04T
			XA-SEM/G-BNGL				
G-LGTI	Boeing 737-3Y0	23925	OO-LTY	2. 4.01	British Airways plc	Gatwick	25. 7.04T
			XA-SEO/G-BNGM				
G-LGTJ	Boeing 737-3..			R	British Airways plc	Gatwick	
G-LGTK	Boeing 737-3..			R	British Airways plc	Gatwick	
G-LGTL	Boeing 737-3..			R	British Airways plc	Gatwick	
					(For delivery 3.02)		

G-LHPL	Aérospatiale AS350 Ecureuil	2189	N612LH	11. 5.99	Lloyd Helicopters (Pte) Ltd		
			9M-BAZ/ZK-HJW/JA9808			(London SW10)	31. 5.02T
G-LIBB	Cameron V-77 HAFB	2463		21. 6.91	R.J.Mercer	Belfast	9. 6.01A
G-LIBS	Hughes 369HS (500C)	43-0469S	N9147F	20. 8.85	D.M.Stevens & A.R.Smith	(Cheltenham)	28. 6.01T
G-LIDA	Hoffman HK.36R Super Dimona	36355		15. 4.92	Bidford Airfield Ltd	Bidford	6.12.04
G-LIDE	Piper PA-31-350 Navajo Chieftain		(G-VIDE)	26.10.78	Woodgate Aviation (IOM) Ltd	Ronaldsway	17.10.04T
		31-7852156	N27800				
G-LIDR	Hoffmann H-36 Dimona	36208	G-BMSK	1. 4.96	B.Kerry	Bidford	16. 9.01
					t/a G-LIDR Flying Group		
G-LIDS	Robinson R22 Beta-II	2808		21. 4.98	Orange Aero Engine Supplies Ltd		
						(East Grinstead)	7. 5.04
G-LIFE	Thunder Ax6-56Z HAFB	135		11. 1.78	D.P.Hopkins *"Golden Delicious"*	Pidley	22. 4.01A
					t/a Lakeside Lodge Golf Centre		
G-LILY	Bell 206B-3 JetRanger III	4107	G-NTBI	14. 3.95	T.S.Brown	Goodwood	11. 4.02T
			C-FIJD				
G-LINC	Hughes 369HS	43-0467S	C-FDUZ	14. 5.87	Sleekform Ltd	(Sowerby Bridge)	13. 3.03T
			CF-DUZ				
G-LINE	Eurocopter AS 355N Twin Squirrel			22. 3.94	National Grid Co plc	Oxford	12. 5.03T
		5566					
G-LIOA	Lockheed 10A Electra	1037	N5171N	6. 5.83	The Science Museum *(As "NC5171N")*		
			NC243/NC14959			South Kensington, London SW7	
G-LION	Piper PA-18-135 Super Cub	18-3857	PH-KLB	29. 9.80	C.Moore	Kemble	18.11.02
	(L-21B-PI) *(Frame No.18-3841)*		(PH-DKG)		*(As "R-167" in R.Neth AF c/s) "Grin 'n Bare It"*		
			R.Neth AF R-167/54-2457				
G-LIOT	Cameron O-77 HAFB	2378		7. 8.90	N.D.Eliot	London SW19	.5. 6.02A
G-LIPE	Robinson R.22 Beta	1882	G-BTXJ	23. 1.92	F.C.Owen	Blackpool	4. 2.01T
G-LIPS	Cameron Lips-90 SS HAFB	4846	G-BZBV	15.11.00	Flying Pictures Ltd	Fairoaks	30. 7.02A
					(Polaroid JoyCam titles)		
G-LISE	Robin DR.500/200i President	0001		27. 7.98	J.Marks	Goodwood	26. 9.04
	(Registered as DR.400/500)						
G-LITE	Rockwell Commander 112A	291	OY-RPP	13. 6.80	J.E.Dixon	Norwich	19.10.03
G-LITZ	Pitts S-1E Special	PFA 09-11131		3. 3.92	G.G.Ferriman	Papplewick, Notts	2. 5.02P
	(Lycoming IO-360)				*"Glitz"*		
G-LIVH	Piper J-3C-65 Cub	11529	OO-JAN	31. 3.94	M.D.Cowburn	Barton	22. 5.03
	(L-4H-PI) *(Frame No.11354)*		OO-AAT/AO-PAX/43-30238		*(As "330238/A-24" in US Army c/s)*		
G-LIVR	Enstrom 480	5038		14. 7.99	Soil Tech BV	Meer, Belgium	22. 7.02T
G-LIZA	Cessna 340A II	340A1021	G-BMDM	15. 2.90	Tayflite Ltd	Perth	17. 2.02T
			ZS-KRH/N4620N				
G-LIZI	Piper PA-28-160 Cherokee	28-52	G-ARRP	26. 1.89	R.J.Walker & J.R.Lawson	Cranwell	19. 6.02
			N5050W				
G-LIZY*	Westland Lysander III	"504/39"	RCAF 1558	20. 6.86	Imperial War Museum	Duxford	
	(C/n also quoted as "Y1351")		V9300	*(Cancelled 18.4.89 as WFU)*	*(As "V9673/MA-J" in 161 Sqn c/s)*		
G-LIZZ	Piper PA-E23-250 Aztec E	27-7405268	G-BBWM	26. 7.93	T.J.Nathan	Fairoaks	28. 1.03
			N40532				
G-LJCC	Murphy Rebel	PFA 232-13355		8. 7.98	P.H.Hyde	(Biggleswade)	
G-LJET	Learjet Learjet 35A	35A-643	(N35NK)	2.12.88	Gama Aviation Ltd	Heathrow	19. 9.02T
			G-LJET/N39418				
G-LKTB	Piper PA-28-181 Archer III	2843496	N5339X	18.12.01	Top Cat Aviation Ltd	Manchester	
G-LLAI*	Colt 21A Cloudhopper HAFB	519	(G-BKTX)	18. 7.83	Balloon Preservation Group	Kirdford	
					"Lowndes Laing Insurance" (Cancelled 16.7.90 by CAA)		
G-LLEW	Aeromot AMT-200S Super Ximango			15.11.00	Lleweni Parc Ltd	Lleweni Parc	1. 3.04
		200126					
G-LLYD	Cameron N-31 HAFB	3558		20. 3.95	Virgin Airship & Balloon Co Ltd	Telford	17. 7.97A
					(Lloyds Bank titles)		
G-LMLV	Dyn'Aéro MCR-01 Club	PFA 301A-13524		25.10.99	L.& M.La Vecchia	Cambridge	18.10.02P
	(Rotax 912 ULS)						
G-LNAA	MD Helicopters Explorer	900-00074	G-76-074	26. 9.00	Police Aviation Services Ltd		
			G-LNAA/N7030B			RAF Waddington	27.11.03T
					(Op Lincs & Notts Air Ambulance)		
G-LNTI	Robinson R44 Astro	0457	G-TPTS	11. 4.00	LNT Aviation Ltd	Coney Park, Leeds	6. 5.04T
G-LNYS	Reims Cessna F177RG Cardinal		G-BDCM	30.11.92	J.W.Clarke	Tatenhill	28.12.02
		F177RG0120	OY-BIP				
G-LOAG*	Cameron N-77 HAFB	359		10.11.77	British Balloon Museum & Library	Newbury	6. 4.84A
					"Famous Grouse" (Cancelled as destroyed 31.3.93)		
G-LOAN	Cameron N-77 HAFB	1434		9. 1.87	P.Lawman	Northampton	8. 5.01A
					"Newbury Building Society"		
G-LOBL*	Bombardier BD-700 Global Express		C-GFJR	R	Not known	Cambridge	
		9038					
	(To Marshalls of Cambridge as "G-LOBL" by 30.10.01: flying under "B" Conditions as "G-52-24" by 1.11.01: not officially registered @ 4.1.02 & may now acquire VP-... registration)						
G-LOBO	Cameron O-120 HAFB	3389		3. 1.95	C.A.Butler	Newbury	1. 8.99A
					t/a Solo Aerostatics *(CofR restored 23.10.01)*		
G-LOCH	Piper J-3C-90 Cub	12687	HB-OCH	10.12.84	J.M.Greenland		
	(L-4J-PI) *(Frame No.12517)*		44-80391			Blackacre Farm, Holt, Wilts	5.11.02P

G-LOFA*	Lockheed L.188CF Electra	2002	N359Q	10. 2.94	Atlantic Air Transport Ltd	Coventry	9. 2.00T
			F-OGST/N359AC/TI-LRM/N359AC/HC-AVX/N359AC/VH-ECA				
			(Cancelled 29.7.98 as WFU: for spares 7.98: noted 11.99: current status unknown)				
G-LOFB	Lockheed L.188CF Electra	1131	N667F	28. 6.94	Atlantic Air Transport Ltd	Coventry	28. 6.03T
			N133AJ/CF-IJW/N131US				
G-LOFC	Lockheed L.188CF Electra	1100	N665F	15. 6.95	Atlantic Air Transport Ltd	Coventry	10. 7.04T
			N289AC/N6123A				
G-LOFD	Lockheed L-188CF Electra	1143	LN-FOG	12. 6.97	Atlantic Air Transport Ltd	Coventry	15. 6.03TC
			LN-MOD/N9745C/(CF-IJC)/N9745C				
G-LOFE	Lockheed L-188CF Electra	1144	EI-CET	5. 1.99	Atlantic Air Transport Ltd	Coventry	10..3.02T
			(G-FIGF)/N668Q/N668F/N24AF/N138US *(Interlink Ireland titles)*				
G-LOFF	Lockheed L-188C Electra	1128	LN-FON(2)	21. 6.00	Atlantic Air Transport Ltd	Coventry	
			N342HA/N417MA/OB-R-1138/HP-684/N417MA/CF-ZST/N7142C				
					(Open storage 12.01 as "LN-FON")		
G-LOFG	Lockheed L-188C Electra	1116	LN-FOL(2)	21. 6.00	Atlantic Air Transport Ltd	Coventry	
			N669F/N404GN/N6126A		*(WFU as "LN-FOL").*		
G-LOFM	Maule MX-7-180A Star Rocket	20027C	N31110	19. 7.95	Atlantic Air Transport Ltd	Coventry	10. 9.04T
G-LOFT	Cessna 500 Citation I	500-0331	LN-NAT	12. 1.95	Atlantic Air Transport Ltd	Jersey	25. 3.03T
			EC-FUM/EC-500/LN-NAT/N40AC/N96RE/N86RE/N331CC/(N5331J)				
					(Atlantic Executive Aviation c/s)		
G-LOGO	MD Helicopters Hughes 369E (500E)	0454E	G-BWLC	4.10.96	R.M.Briggs	Brough	11. 3.02T
			HB-XIJ/SE-JAM				
G-LOIS	Jabiru Jabiru UL	0144 & SAAC-68	EI-JAK	14. 9.00	D.A.Chamberlain	Plaistows Farm, St Albans	19. 4.02P
	(C/n officially quoted as 'PFA 274A-0144')						
G-LOKM	PZL-110 Koliber 160A	04990080	G-BYSH	26.11.99	PZL International Aviation Marketing & Sales plc	Earls Colne	16. 1.03T
			SP-WGH				
G-LOLL	Cameron V-77 HAFB	2964		4.12.92	C.N.Rawnson t/a Test Valley Balloon Group	Stockbridge	31. 8.03A
G-LOOK*	Reims Cessna F172M Skyhawk	F17201234	PH-MIG	4. 5.79	Not known	Fenland	
			(Damaged Laarbruch 11.8.85: cancelled 8.1.86 as WFU: mainplanes stored 8.98)				
G-LOOP	Pitts S-1C Special (Lycoming O-320)	850	5Y-AOX	11. 5.78	C.Butler	Netherthorpe	7. 6.02P
G-LOOS	Cameron Tissue Pack-100 SS HAFB	4767		17. 5.00	Flying Pictures Ltd	Fairoaks	14. 5.02A
G-LORA	Cameron A-250 HAFB	3828		22. 2.96	Global Ballooning Ltd	Uckfield	21. 3.02T
G-LORC	Piper PA-28-161 Cadet	2841339	D-ESTC	12. 1.99	Sherburn Aero Club Ltd	Sherburn-in-Elmet	25. 2.02T
			N9184W/(N620FT)/(SE-KMP)				
G-LORD	Piper PA-34-200T Seneca II	34-7970347	N2908W	6. 5.88	Carill Aviation Ltd, R.P.Thomas & P.J.Broome	Southampton	8. 5.03T
G-LORI*	Hawker Siddeley HS.125 Srs.403B	25246	G-AYOJ	19. 7.83	Not known	Lagos, Nigeria	26. 8.84
			9Q-COH/G-AYOJ/(G-5-16)				
			(Cancelled 21.4.93 by CAA: open storage 3.95: current status unknown)				
G-LORN	Avions Mudry CAP.10B	282		4. 3.99	AWE Aeronautics Ltd	Spilsted Farm, Sedlescombe	10. 5.02
G-LORR	Piper PA-28-181 Archer III	2843037	N9268X	19. 4.96	S.J.Sylvester	Wolverhampton	20. 5.02
			G-LORR				
G-LORT	Avid Speed Wing Mk.4	1124 & PFA 189-12219		12. 2.92	G.E.Laucht	Long Marston	7. 6.02P
G-LORY	Thunder Ax4-31Z HAFB	171		28.11.78	A.J.Moore *"Glory"*	Northwood, Middx	
G-LOSI	Cameron Z-105 HAFB	10011		5. 1.01	Aeropubblicita Vicenza SRL	(Caldogno, Italy)	11. 2.02A
G-LOSM	Armstrong-Whitworth Meteor NF.11	S4/U/2342	WM167	8. 6.84	Hunter Wing Ltd	Bournemouth	18. 5.02P
					(Op Jet Heritage Ltd) (As "WM167" in 141 Sqdn c/s)		
G-LOST	Denney Kitfox mk.3 Floatplane (Rotax 618)	PFA 172-12055		10. 8.95	J.H.S.Booth	Perth	6. 8.01P
G-LOTI	Bleriot Type XI rep (ABC Scorpion II)	PFA 088-10410		21.12.78	Brooklands Museum Trust Ltd	Brooklands	19. 7.82P
G-LOUN	Eurocopter AS 355N Twin Squirrel	5627		24. 1.97	Firstearl Ltd	Oxford	15. 6.03T
G-LOVB	British Aerospace Jetstream Srs.3102	622	VH-HSW	12. 8.99	London Flight Centre (Stansted) Ltd	Stansted	5.10.00T
			G-31-622/G-BLCB/G-31-622				
G-LOWA*	Colt 77A HAFB	1451		14. 4.89	K.D.Peirce	Cranbrook	7. 6.97A
					(Cancelled 25.9.01 by CAA)		
G-LOWE*	Monnett Sonerai I	367 & PFA 015-10344		16.11.78	Not known	Shennington	
					(Cancelled 16.9.97 as TWFU: on assembly 6.01)		
G-LOWS	Sky 77-24 HAFB	025		19. 3.96	A.J.Byrne & D.J.Bellinger *"Dawn Treader"*	Thatcham	30 6.01
G-LOYA	Reims FR172J Rocket	FR17200352	G-BLVT	4. 8.89	T.R.Scorer	Earls Colne	31. 5.03
			PH-EDI/D-EEDI				
G-LOYD	Aérospatiale SA.341G Gazelle 1	1289	G-SFTC	19. 6.85	Apollo Manufacturing (Derby) Ltd	Ripley, Derbys	7. 6.03
			N47298				
	(Rebuilt 1990 using major components of N6957 c/n 1060)						
G-LPAD	Lindstrand LBL 105A HAFB	632		5. 8.99	Line Packaging & Display Ltd	Gillingham	17. 5.02A
G-LPGI	Cameron A-210 HAFB	4196		13. 8.97	A.Derbyshire	Stretton	10. 9.01T
G-LRSN	Robinson R44 Raven	0984		28. 3.01	Larsen Manufacturing Ltd	Belfast	4. 4.04T

G-LSFI	Gulfstream AA-5A Cheetah	AA5A-0770	G-BGSK	13. 2.84	A.D.Prothero t/a G-LSFI Group	Mount Airey, Hull	20. 7.03
G-LSFT	Piper PA-28-161 Warrior II	28-8516008	G-BXTX PH-LEH/N130AV/N43682	10.11.99	Plane Talking Ltd	Elstree	2. 4.04T
G-LSHI	Colt 77A HAFB	1264		20. 7.88	J H Dobson *"Lambert Smith Hampton"*	Streatley, Berks	12. 7.95A
G-LSMI	Reims Cessna F152 II	F15201710		1. 2.80	A.S.Bamrah t/a Falcon Flying Services	(Blackbushe)	20. 3.02T
G-LSTR	Stoddard-Hamilton GlaStar *(Tail-wheel u/c)*	PFA 295-13093		20. 4.98	R.Y.Kendal	Brunton	27. 6.02P
G-LTFB	Piper PA-28-140 Cherokee	28-23343	G-AVLU N11C	28. 2.97	London Transport Flying Club Ltd	Fairoaks	11. 4.04T
G-LTFC	Piper PA-28-140 Cherokee B	28-26259	G-AXTI N11C	8. 6.94	London Transport Flying Club Ltd	Fairoaks	11. 9.03T
G-LTRF	Sportavia Fournier RF7	7001	G-EHAP (G-BGVC)/D-EHAP/F-WPXV	10.12.97	R G Trute	Dunkeswell	3. 7.02P
G-LTSB	Cameron LTSB-90SS HAFB	4483		15. 1.99	Virgin Airship & Balloon Co Ltd *(Lloyds TSB titles)*	Telford	30. 1.02A
G-LUBE*	Cameron N-77 HAFB	1127		25. 2.85	A.C.Rawson *"Lubey Loo"* *(Cancelled 23.10.01 by CAA)*	Stafford	6. 8.99A
G-LUCK	Reims Cessna F150M	F15001238	PH-LEO D-EHRA	13.12.79	Taylor Aviation Ltd	Sywell	23. 6.04T
G-LUED	Aero Designs Pulsar (Rotax 582)	PFA 202-12122		9. 3.92	J.C.Anderson	Sturgate	1. 8.02P
G-LUFF*	Rotorway Exec 90	6191		24. 4.97	D.C.Luffingham *(Cancelled 12.1.00 by CAA) (Noted 4.00)*	Street Farm, Takeley	
G-LUFT	Putzer Elster C	011	G-BOPY D-EDEZ	31. 3.92	A.& E.A.Wiseman *(On rebuild 1.01)*	(Rufforth)	
G-LUKE	Rutan LongEz (Lycoming O-235)	PFA 074A-10978		4. 7.84	S.G.Busby *(Nose wheel broke off landing Booker 15.7.01)*	Booker	30. 5.02P
G-LUKI	Robinson R44 Raven	0818	G-BZLN	20.10.00	Marcella Air Ltd	Panshanger	5.11.03T
G-LUKY	Robinson R44 Astro	0357		10. 7.97	English Braids Ltd	Gloucestershire	11. 9.03
G-LULU	Grob G-109	6137		6. 9.82	A.P.Bowden	Enstone	15. 5.04
G-LUMA	Jabiru Jabiru SP-430 (Jabiru 2200A)	PFA 274B-13458		11. 5.99	B.Luyckx	Keuheuvel, Belgium	2.10.01P
G-LUNA	Piper PA-32RT-300T Turbo Lance II	32R-7987108	N2246Q	19. 3.79	D.C.Settrington	Humberside	19. 4.03T
G-LUSC	Luscombe 8E Silvaire	3975	D-EFYR LN-PAT/(NC1248K)	1.11.84	M.Fowler *(On rebuild 9.97: current status unknown)*	Bruntingthorpe	
G-LUSH	Piper PA-28-151 Cherokee Warrior	28-7515201	OH-PAB	25. 7.01	J.Dunn *(Noted 10.01)*	Manor Farm, Glatton	
G-LUSI	Temco Luscombe 8F Silvaire (Continental C85)	6770	N838B	3.10.89	J.P.Hunt & D.M.Robinson	Bourne Park, Hurstbourne Tarrant	12. 5.02P
G-LUST	Luscombe 8E Silvaire (Continental C85)	6492	N2065B NC2065B	9.11.89	M.Griffiths	Gloucestershire	9. 7.98P
G-LUVY	Aérospatiale AS355F1 Twin Squirrel	5134	N358E ZS-HUA/(G-BPDP)/D-HOCH/N358E/N5792M	25. 2.00	Markoss Aviation Ltd	Biggin Hill	18. 6.03T
G-LUXE	British Aerospace BAe 146 Srs.300	E3001	G-5-300 G-SSSH/(G-BIAD)	9. 4.87	BAE Systems (Operations) Ltd	Woodford	8. 5.98S
G-LYDA	Hoffmann H-36 Dimona	3515	OE-9213	5. 4.94	M.A.Holmes & M.J.Philpott t/a G-LYDA Flying Group	Booker	9.10.03
G-LYDD*	Piper PA-31 Turbo Navajo	31-537	G-BBDU N6796L	8. 5.89	Not known *(Damaged Lydd 17.7.91: cancelled 30.3.93 as WFU: fuselage on fire dump 12.01)*	Blackpool	12. 5.89T
G-LYNC	Robinson R22 Beta	3069		5. 5.00	Whirlybirds Ltd	(Birmingham)	20. 7.03T
G-LYND	Piper PA-25-235 Pawnee D *(Rebuild of G-ASFZ [25-2246] with new frame)*	"25-6309"	SE-IXU G-BSFZ/N6672Z	8. 9.93	York Gliding Centre Ltd	Rufforth	23. 9.02
G-LYNK	CFM Shadow DD (Rotax 582)	303-DD		12.10.98	G.Linskey	(Douglas, IoM)	20. 5.02P
G-LYNX*	Westland WG.13 Lynx 800	WA/102	(ZA500) G-LYNX/ZB600	6.11.78	The Helicopter Museum *(Cancelled 27.2.98 as WFU) (As "ZB500" in Army c/s)*	Weston-super-Mare	13.12.83P
G-LYPG	Jabiru Jabiru UL-450 (Jabiru 2200A)	PFA 274A-13466		6. 7.99	P.G.Gale	Fitzroy Farms, Bratton, Wilts	10. 5.02P
G-LYTE	Thunder Ax7-77 HAFB	1113		29. 9.87	G.M.Bulmer *"Crispen"*	Hereford	19. 5.91A
G-LZZY	Piper PA-28RT-201T Turbo Arrow IV	28R-8031001	G-BMHZ ZS-KII/N8096D	8. 5.01	J.C.Lucas	Popham	25. 4.02

G-MAAA – G-MZZZ

G-MAAC*	Advanced Airship Corporation ANR-1			16. 1.89	Balloon Preservation Group *(Sold incomplete 12.93: cancelled 15.11.00 by CAA) (Dismantled 12.01)*	Malpas	
G-MAAH	British Aircraft Corporation One-Eleven 488GH	BAC.259	VP-CDA/G-MAAH/PK-TAL/G-BWES/PK-TAL/G-BWES/5N-UDE/LX-MAM/HZ-MAM	6.10.98	Aravco Ltd	Farnborough	27..4.03T

G-MABE	Reims Cessna F150L	F15001119	G-BLJP N962L	20. 6.97	Herefordshire Aero Club Ltd	Shobdon	18. 6.03T
G-MABR	British Aerospace BAe 146 Srs.100	E1015	G-DEBN EC-GEP/EC-971/N568BA/XA-RST/N461AP/G-5-01	13. 1.00	British Regional Airlines Ltd	Aberdeen	22.12.04T
G-MACH	SIAI-Marchetti SF.260	1-14	F-BUVY OO-AHR/OO-HAZ/(OO-RAB)	29.10.80	Cheyne Motors Ltd	Old Sarum	19. 5.02
G-MACK	Piper PA-28R-200 Cherokee Arrow II	28R-7635449	N5213F	18. 8.78	Haimoss Ltd	Old Sarum	18.12.04T
G-MAFA	Reims Cessna F406 Caravan II	F406-0036	G-DFLT F-WZDZ	2. 6.98	Directflight Ltd	Exeter	6. 6.04T
G-MAFB	Reims Cessna F406 Caravan II	F406-0080	F-WWSR	27. 5.98	Directflight Ltd	Prestwick	28. 9.04T
G-MAFE	Dornier 228-202K	8009	G-OALF G-MLDO/PH-SDO/D-IDON	21.12.92	FR Aviation Ltd *(Op Department for Environment, Food & Rural Affairs)*	Bournemouth	4.11.02T
G-MAFF	Pilatus Britten-Norman BN-2T Islander	2119	G-BJED	20. 4.82	Cobham Leasing Ltd *(Op Department for Environment, Food & Rural Affairs)*	Teesside	25. 9.02T
G-MAFI	Dornier 228-202K	8115	D-CAAE	16. 2.87	Cobham Leasing Ltd *(Op Department for Environment, Food & Rural Affairs)*	Bournemouth	15. 7.02T
G-MAGC	Cameron Grand Illusion SS HAFB	4000		19. 1.95	Magical Adventures Ltd	Chirk	2. 8.01A
G-MAGG	Pitts S-1SE Special (Lycoming O-360)	PFA 09-10873		17. 3.83	C.A.Boardman	Little Gransden	2. 4.02P
G-MAGL	Sky 77-24 HAFB	164		14. 7.99	RCM SARL	Stuppicht, Luxembourg	3..7.02
G-MAIE	Piper PA-32R-301T Saratoga IITC	3257046	N47BK N41283	1.12.00	B R Sennett	Jersey	30.11.03
G-MAIK	Piper PA-34-220T Seneca IV	3448078	N73BS	17.11.97	TEL (IOM) Ltd	Ronaldsway	7.12.03
G-MAIN	Mainair Blade 912 (Rotax 912-UL)	1202-0699-7 & W1005		16. 6.99	J.R.Moore	Baxby Manor, Husthwaite	4. 7.02P
G-MAIR	Piper PA-34-200T Seneca II	34-7970140	N3029R	15. 2.89	Barnes Olson Aeroleasing Ltd *(Op Bristol Flying Centre)*	Bristol	10. 4.04T
G-MAJA	British Aerospace Jetstream Srs.4100	41032	G-4-032	22. 4.94	British Regional Airlines Ltd *(Op Manx Airlines)*	Ronaldsway	24. 5.02T
G-MAJB	British Aerospace Jetstream Srs.4100	41018	G-BVKT N140MA/G-4-018	1. 6.94	British Regional Airlines Ltd *(Ndebele Martha t/s)*	Ronaldsway	8. 6.03T
G-MAJC	British Aerospace Jetstream Srs.4100	41005	G-LOGJ	12. 9.94	British Regional Airlines Ltd *(Colum t/s)*	Ronaldsway	20.12.03T
G-MAJD	British Aerospace Jetstream Srs.4100	41006	G-WAWR	27. 3.95	British Regional Airlines Ltd	Ronaldsway	2. 3.04T
G-MAJE	British Aerospace Jetstream Srs.4100	41007	G-LOGK	12. 9.94	British Regional Airlines Ltd	Ronaldsway	24. 2.03T
G-MAJF	British Aerospace Jetstream Srs.4100	41008	G-WAWL	6. 2.95	British Regional Airlines Ltd	Ronaldsway	18. 3.02T
G-MAJG	British Aerospace Jetstream Srs.4100	41009	G-LOGL	16. 8.94	British Regional Airlines Ltd	Ronaldsway	30. 3.02T
G-MAJH	British Aerospace Jetstream Srs.4100	41010	G-WAYR	4. 4.95	British Regional Airlines Ltd *"Viscount Tonypandy"*	Ronaldsway	13. 4.03T
G-MAJI	British Aerospace Jetstream Srs.4100	41011	G-WAND	20. 3.95	British Regional Airlines Ltd	Ronaldsway	27. 4.04T
G-MAJJ	British Aerospace Jetstream Srs.4100	41024	G-WAFT G-4-024	27. 2.95	British Regional Airlines Ltd *"Lord Louis Mountbatten"*	Ronaldsway	28.10.02T
G-MAJK	British Aerospace Jetstream Srs.4100	41070	G-4-070	27. 7.95	British Regional Airlines Ltd *(Wings t/s)*	Ronaldsway	2. 9.03T
G-MAJL	British Aerospace Jetstream Srs.4100		G-4-087	1. 4.96	British Regional Airlines Ltd *"R J Mitchell" (Op Eastern Airways)*	Humberside	16. 5.03T
G-MAJM	British Aerospace Jetstream Srs.4100		G-4-096	23. 9.96	British Regional Airlines Ltd	Ronaldsway	29.10.02T
G-MAJR	de Havilland DHC.1 Chipmunk 22	C1/0699	WP805	25. 9.96	C.Adams t/a Chipmunk Shareholders	(Gosport)	
G-MAJS	Airbus A300B4-605R	604	F-WWAX	26. 4.91	Monarch Airlines Ltd	Luton	25. 4.02T
G-MALA	Piper PA-28-181 Archer II	28-8190055	G-BIIU N82748	6. 3.81	D.C. & M.E.Dowell t/a M & D Aviation	Kemble	16. 4.02T
G-MALC	Grumman-American AA-5 Traveler	AA5-0664	G-BCPM N6170A	19.11.79	B.P.Hogan	Sywell	7. 6.03
G-MALK*	Reims Cessna F172N Skyhawk II	F17201886	PH-SVS PH-AXF(3)	1. 7.81	Edinburgh Airport Fire Service	Edinburgh	
	(Crashed near Lochgilphead 23.7.97: cancelled 23.12.97 as destroyed: fuselage for instructional use 2001)						
G-MALS	Mooney M.20K (231)	25-0573	N1061T	16. 8.84	J.Houlberg t/a G-MALS Group	Blackbushe	25. 4.02
G-MALT	Colt Flying Hop SS HAFB	1447		14. 4.89	P.J.Stapley *"Hoppie"* *(CofR restored 20.11.01)*	London Colney	11. 9.97A
G-MAMC	Rotorway Executive 90 (Rotorway RI 162)	5057		24. 5.94	J.R.Carmichael	(Inverary)	19. 2.99P
			(Damaged landing Cumbernauld 22.9.98 and removed: current status unknown				
G-MAMD	Beechcraft B200 Super King Air	BB-1549	N1069S	16. 7.99	Gamston Aviation Ltd	Gamston	15. 7.02T
G-MAMO	Cameron V-77 HAFB	1616		17.11.87	The Marble Mosaic Co Ltd *"Osprey"*	Portishead	6. 6.00A

G-MANA	British Aerospace ATP	2056	G-LOGH G-11-056	21. 2.94	British Regional Airlines Ltd *(Op Manx Airlines: Manx c/s)*	Ronaldsway	21. 3.04T
G-MANB	British Aerospace ATP	2055	G-LOGG G-JATP/G-11-055	14. 9.94	British Regional Airlines Ltd *(Op Manx Airlines: Manx c/s)*	Ronaldsway	26. 9.02T
G-MANC	British Aerospace ATP	2054	G-LOGF G-11-054	7.11.94	British Regional Airlines Ltd *(Op Manx Airlines: Manx c/s)*	Ronaldsway	20.10.03T
G-MAND*	Piper PA-28-161 Warrior II	28-8116284	G-BRKT N8082Z	8. 3.93	Halfpenny Green Flight Centre Ltd *(Cancelled 11.12.01 by CAA)*	Wolverhampton	3.12.01T
G-MANE	British Aerospace ATP	2045	G-LOGB G-11-045	7. 6.94	British Regional Airlines Ltd	Ronaldsway	26. 2.04T
G-MANF	British Aerospace ATP	2040	G-LOGA	19. 9.94	British Regional Airlines Ltd	Ronaldsway	5.11.04T
G-MANG	British Aerospace ATP	2018	G-LOGD	22. 8.94	British Regional Airlines Ltd	Ronaldsway	28. 9.04T
G-MANH	British Aerospace ATP	2017	G-LOGC	16.11.94	British Regional Airlines Ltd	Ronaldsway	14. 8.02T
G-MANI	Cameron V-90 HAFB	3038		8. 3.93	M.P.G.Papworth	Ilkley	3. 7.01A
G-MANJ	British Aerospace ATP	2004	G-LOGE	6. 9.94	British Regional Airlines Ltd	Ronaldsway	14. 4.04T
G-MANL	British Aerospace ATP	2003	G-ERIN G-BMYK	3.10.94	British Regional Airlines Ltd	East Midlands	25. 5.02T
G-MANM	British Aerospace ATP	2005	G-OATP G-BZWW/(N375AE)/G-BZWW	17.10.94	British Regional Airlines Ltd *"Elaine Griffiths"*	Ronaldsway	20. 3.02T
G-MANN	Aérospatiale SA.341G Gazelle 1	1295	G-BKLW N4DQ/N4QQ/N444JJ/N47316/F-WKQH	14. 4.86	First City Air (London) Ltd	Westland Heliport	31. 5.04T
G-MANO	British Aerospace ATP	2006	OK-TFN G-MANO/G-UIET/G-11-5/(N376AE)	28.11.94	Manx Airlines Ltd *(Rendezvous t/s)*	Ronaldsway	18. 1.05T
G-MANP	British Aerospace ATP	2023	OK-VFO G-MANP/G-PEEL	28.10.94	Manx Airlines Ltd	Ronaldsway	25.10.03T
G-MANT*	Cessna 210L Centurion II	21060970	G-MAXY N550SV	22. 5.85	Not known *(Damaged near Oxford 16.2.92: cancelled 3.4.92 by CAA: displayed Sea-front Crazy Golf course 2.99)*	Great Yarmouth	2.10.94
G-MANW	Tri-R Kis	PFA 239-12628		12. 9.96	M.T.Manwaring	(Barking)	
G-MANX	Clutton FRED Srs.II (Ardem 4C02)	PW.2 & PFA 029-10327		31. 5.78	S.Styles *(Crashed near Ronaldsway 30.10.81: on rebuild Wellesbourne Mountford 7.90)*	(Birmingham)	17. 8.82P
G-MAPP	Cessna 402B	402B0583	D-INRH N1445G	16. 4.99	Simmons Mapping (UK) Ltd	Cranfield	5.10.02T
G-MAPR	Beechcraft A36 Bonanza	E-2713	N55916	17. 9.92	Moderandum Ltd	(Guernsey)	2. 9.04
G-MAPS*	Sky Flying Map SS HAFB	105		20. 7.98	The Balloon Advertising Co Ltd *(Op Balloon Preservation Group) "Ordnance Survey"* *(Cancelled 31.7.01 as wfu)*	Kirdford	28. 2.01A
G-MARA	Airbus A321-231	0983	D-AVZB	31. 3.99	Monarch Airlines Ltd	Luton	30. 3.02T
G-MARE	Schweizer Hughes 269C	S-1320		12. 8.88	The Earl of Caledon	Caledon Castle, Co.Tyrone	17.12.03
G-MASC	SAN Jodel 150A Mascaret	37	F-BLDZ	1. 2.91	K.F. & R.Richardson	Wellesbourne Mountford	10. 7.02P
G-MASF	Piper PA-28-181 Cherokee Archer II	28-7790191	OY-EPT LN-NAP	24. 6.97	Mid-Anglia Flight Centre Ltd t/a Mid-Anglia School of Flying	Cambridge	6. 8.03T
G-MASH	Westland-Bell 47G-4A	WA/725	G-AXKU G-17-10	3.11.89	Defence Products Ltd *(US Army c/s)*	Redhill	4. 2.02
G-MASS	Cessna 152 II	15281605	G-BSHN N65541	6. 3.95	MK Aero Support Ltd *(Op The Pilot Centre)*	Denham	23. 7.02T
G-MASX	Masquito Masquito M.80	03		19. 6.98	Masquito Aircraft NV	(Roosdaal, Belgium)	
G-MASY	Masquito Masquito M.80	02		19. 6.98	Masquito Aircraft NV	(Roosdaal, Belgium)	
G-MASZ	Masquito Masquito M.58	01		29. 4.97	Masquito Aircraft NV	(Roosdaal, Belgium)	
G-MATE	Moravan Zlin Z.50LX	0068		26.10.90	J.H.Askew	Breighton	5. 7.04
G-MATS	Colt GA-42 Gas Airship	738	JA1009 G-MATS	11. 6.87	P.A.Lindstrand *(New owner 6.01)*	Oswestry	23. 5.90A
G-MATT	Robin R.2160	97	G-BKRC F-BZAC/F-WZAC	7. 5.85	D.J.Nicholson	East Midlands	27. 3.03
G-MATZ	Piper PA-28-140 Cherokee Cruiser	28-7325200	G-BASI N11C	11.12.90	R.B.Walker t/a Midland Air Training School	Coventry	19.10.03T
G-MAUD	British Aerospace ATP	2002	(G-MANK) G-MAUD/G-BMYM	14.12.93	British Regional Airlines Ltd *(Blue Poole t/s)*	East Midlands	13. 6.04T
G-MAUK	Colt 77A HAFB	901		16. 2.87	B.Meeson *"Mondial Assistance"*	Walsall	4. 6.92A
G-MAVI	Robinson R22 Beta	0960		7. 2.89	R.M.Weyman	Coventry	26. 4.04T
G-MAXG	Pitts S-1S Special	PFA 009-13233		27. 4.01	T.P.Jenkinson	(Radlett)	
G-MAXI	Piper PA-34-200T Seneca II	34-7670150	N8658C	11. 2.81	Draycott Seneca Syndicate Ltd	Kemble	15. 5.03T
G-MAXV	Van's RV-4	PFA 181-13266		20. 1.00	R.S.Partridge-Hicks	(Bury St. Edmunds)	15. 5.03P
G-MAYO	Piper PA-28-161 Cherokee Warrior II	28-7716278	G-BFBG N38848	20. 2.81	M.P.Catto t/a Jermyk Engineering	Fairoaks	11. 4.04T
G-MBAA	Hiway Skytrike Mk.II/Excalibur (Hiro 22)	01		23. 4.81	M.J.Aubrey	(Kington, Hereford)	
G-MBAB	Hovey WD-II Whing Ding II (Konig SC430)	MA-59 & PFA 116-10706		26. 5.81	M.J.Aubrey	(Kington, Hereford)	1. 2.98P
G-MBAD	Weedhopper JC-24A	0382		3. 6.81	M.Stott	(Prudhoe)	

G-MBAR	Wheeler Scout (Fuji-Robin EC-25-PS)	389W	8. 7.81	L.Chiappi	(Blackburn)	
G-MBAW	Pterodactyl Ptraveler (Cuyana 430R)	017	14. 7.81	J.C.K.Scardifield	(Lymington)	31. 8.86E
G-MBBB	Wheeler Scout II (Pixie 173)	0388W	3. 8.81	A.J.& B.Chalkley	(Pwllheli)	
G-MBBM	Eipper Quicksilver MX (Cuyana 430R)	10960	11. 9.81	J.Brown *(In storage)*	(Markfield, Leics)	9.12.84E
G-MBCJ	Mainair Tri-Flyer/Solar Wings Typhoon S JRN-1 & T881-225 *(May have replacement wing T382-390L)*		30. 9.81	R.A.Smith	(Doncaster)	30. 4.86E
G-MBCK	Eipper Quicksilver MX (Rotax 503)	GWR-10962	30. 9.81	P.Rowbotham	(Loughborough)	17.11.86E
G-MBCL	Hiway Skytrike 160/Solar Wings Typhoon 2332 & T1181-307		30. 9.81	P.J.Callis	(Kibworth, Leicester)	N/E
G-MBCU	American Aerolights Double Eagle (Amphibian) (Rotax 377)	3181	5.10.81	J.L.May	(Portsmouth)	21. 8.02P
G-MBCX	Hornet 250/Airwave Nimrod 165 (Fuji-Robin EC-25-PS) H090 & 0090 LJH		12.10.81	M.Maylor	(Louth)	31.12.87E
G-MBDE	Ultrasports Tripacer/Flexiform Solo Striker (Fuji-Robin EC-34-PM)	FS-1	15.10.81	A.R.Cantrill	(Kirkmichael, IoM)	3. 9.96P
G-MBDG	Eurowing Goldwing (Konig SC430)	E.20	19.10.81	B.Fussell	(Llanelli)	14.12.94P
G-MBDL*	Striplin (AES) Lone Ranger	109	21.10.81	North East Aircraft Museum *(Cancelled 13.6.90 by CAA)*	Sunderland	
G-MBDM	Southdown Sigma/Southdown trike (Fuji-Robin EC-25-PS)	SST/001	26.10.81	A.R.Prentice	(Dartford)	4.12.88E
G-MBEP*	American Aerolights Eagle 215B (Chrysler 820)	2877	9.11.81	Caernarfon Air Museum *(Cancelled 16.5.96 as WFU)*	Caernarfon	8. 4.96E
G-MBET	MEA Mistral Trainer (Fuji-Robin EC-44-PM)	MEA.103	10.11.81	B.H.Stephens	(Southampton)	27. 9.98P
G-MBEU	Chargus T.250/Hiway Demon (Fuji-Robin EC-25-PS)	T.250/06	10.11.81	R.C.Smith	(Clacton)	31. 5.86E
G-MBFK	Hiway Skytrike/Demon 175 (Fuji-Robin EC-25-PS)	LR17D	16.11.81	D.W.Stamp	(Kidderminster)	9. 3.89E
G-MBFO	Eipper Quicksilver MX (Cuyuna 430R)	MLD-01	17.11.81	J.C.Larkin	(Maryport, Cumbria)	20. 8.93P
G-MBFZ	MSS Eurowing Goldwing (Fuji-Robin EC-34-PM)	MSS-01	25.11.81	D.G.Palmer *(Under active rebuild 2001)*	Fetterangus	5. 9.00P
G-MBGA	Mainair Tri-Flyer/Flexiform Solo Sealander *(Originally regd as Mainair Tri-Flyer/Solar Wings Typhoon with same c/n)*	001	25.11.81	D.A.Caig	(Southport)	14. 9.97P
G-MBGF	Twamley Trike/Birdman Cherokee	RWT-01	26.11.81	T.B.Woolley	(Leicester)	
G-MBGL*	Flexiform Sealander	HF-1	1.12.81	Not known *(Cancelled as WFU 25.10.88) (Trike stored 2.01)*	Halwell, Totnes	
G-MBGS	Rotec Rally 2B	PCB-1	2.12.81	P.C.Bell	(Yalding, Kent)	
G-MBGX	Southdown Lightning DS (Sachs-Dolmar 340?) *(Believed fitted with UAS Storm Buggy trike ex G-MBKD)*	RBDB-1	7.12.81	T.Knight	(Newton Abbot)	7. 3.92E
G-MBHE	American Aerolights Eagle (Cuyuna 430R)	4210	18.12.81	R.J.Osborne	Long Marston	12.10.96P
G-MBHK	Mainair Tri-Flyer 330/Flexiform Solo Striker (Fuji-Robin EC-34-PM) EB-1 & 036-241181 *(Original Tri-Flyer 250 trike c/n 036 replaced by Tri-Flyer 330 c/n 060-382 in 1982)*		30.12.81	K.T.Vinning	(Stratford-upon-Avon)	11. 8.98P
G-MBHZ	Pterodactyl Ptraveler (Cuyuna 430R)	TD-01	6. 1.82	J.C.K.Scardifield	(Lymington)	28. 2.86E
G-MBIA	Hiway Skytrike/Flexiform Sealander (Fuji-Robin EC-34-PM)	6172349/336	6. 1.82	I.P.Cook	(Oldham)	9. 4.90E
G-MBIO	American Aerolights Eagle 215B (Zenoah G25B1)	E.4007-Z	12. 1.82	B.J.C.Hill	(Bridgnorth)	N/E
G-MBIT	Hiway Skytrike/Demon (Fuji-Robin EC-25-PS)	2501	18. 1.82	K.S.Hodgson *(Reported as taken to Canada 9.89 but new owner 6.00!)*	(Yarm)	5.12.87E
G-MBIY	Ultrasports Tripacer/Southdown Lightning Phase II (Fuji-Robin EC-34-PM)	330 *(Wing c/n L170-439)*	19. 1.82	J.W.Burton	(Morecambe)	18. 4.99P
G-MBIZ	Mainair Tri-Flyer 250/Hiway Vulcan (Fuji-Robin EC-25PS) 039-251181 & SD9V		20. 1.82	E.F.Clapham, W.B.S.Dobi, S.P.Slade & D.M.A.Templeman	(Bristol)	
G-MBJD	American Aerolights Eagle 215B (Zenoah G25B1)	4169	21. 1.82	R.W.F.Boarder	(Tring)	9. 7.88E
G-MBJF	Hiway Skytrike Mk.II/Vulcan (Fuji-Robin EC-25-PS) *(C/n is engine no)*	C 80-00099	22. 1.82	C.H.Bestwick	(Nottingham)	31. 1.87E
G-MBJG	Chargus T.250/Airwave Nimrod UP (Fuji-Robin EC-25-PS)	CMT165045	25. 1.82	D.H.George	Sandown	16.12.01P
G-MBJK	American Aerolights Eagle (Chrysler 820)	2742	16. 1.82	B.W.Olley *(In store 2000)*	(Ely)	

G-MBJL	Hornet/airwave Nimrod	JSRM-01		26. 1.82	A.G.Lowe	(Aberdeen)	20.10.96P
	(Fuji-Robin EC-25-PS)						
G-MBJM	Striplin Lone Ranger	LR-81-00138		26. 1.82	C.K.Brown	(Loughborough)	
	(Fuji-Robin) *(C/n 81-00138 is engine serial no)*						
G-MBJX*	Hiway Skytrike I/Hiway Super Scorpion			2. 2.82	National Museums of Scotland/Museum of Flight		
	(Valmet SM160 - no.15108) MM-01				*(Cancelled 13.6.90 by CAA)*	East Fortune	
G-MBKY	American Aerolights Eagle 215B	BF-01		12. 2.82	M.J.Aubrey	(Kington, Hereford)	
	(Zenoah G25B1 - no.15288)						
G-MBKZ	Hiway Skytrike/Super Scorpion			12. 2.82	S.I.Harding	(Camberley)	
	(Fuji-Robin EC-25-PS)	EC25P8-04 *(C/n is corruption of engine type)*					
G-MBLU	Ultrasports Tripacer/Southdown Lightning L195			26. 2.82	C.R.Franklin	(Barnstaple)	28.11.87E
	(Fuji-Robin EC-25-PS)	L195/191					
G-MBMG	Rotec Rally 2B	RJP-01		3. 3.82	J.R.Pyper	(Craigavon, Co Armagh)	
G-MBMT	Mainair Tri-Flyer/Southdown Lightning 195			8. 3.82	A.G.Rodenburg & T.Abro	(Tillicoultry)	25. 4.87E
	(Fuji-Robin EC-25-PS)	TRY-01 *(Wing c/n.L195-195?)*					
G-MBNK	American Aerolights Eagle	E.2398MJ		17. 3.82	R.Moss	(Manchester)	
G-MBNV	Sheffield Trident	816		24. 3.82	F.Elmore	(Sheffield)	
G-MBOF	Pakes Jackdaw	LGP-01		26. 3.82	L.G.Pakes	(Ryde, IoW)	
G-MBOH	MEA Mistral Trainer	008		29. 3.82	N.A.Bell	(Fordingbridge)	5. 9.88E
	(Fuji-Robin EC-44-PM)						
G-MBOK	Brooks Prone trike/Solar Wings Typhoon S4			1. 4.82	P.Huddleston	(Marlborough)	9. 5.93E
	(Sachs Dolmar 153)	153/042/6 *(C/n is engine no)*					
G-MBPB(2)	Pterodactyl Ptraveller	PEB-01		7. 4.82	N.A.Bell	(Fordingbridge)	
					(For rebuild 12.01)		
G-MBPG	Mainair Tri-Flyer/Solar Wings Typhoon			13. 4.82	S.D.Thorpe	Otherton, Cannock	14. 6.01P
	(Fuji-Robin EC-25-PS) 189-1983 & T381-105 *(Original trike was c/n 067-582 and may have been used for G-MMGT)*						
G-MBPJ	Centrair Moto-Delta G.11	001		14. 5.82	J.B.Jackson	(Chester)	
G-MBPM*	Eurowing Goldwing	EW-21		14. 4.82	National Museums of Scotland/Museum of Flight		
	(Fuji-Robin EC-34-PM)				*(Cancelled 30.8.00 as WFU)*	East Fortune	21. 8.98P
G-MBPX	Eurowing Goldwing SP	EW-42		21. 4.82	A.R.Channon	(Sawston, Cambridge)	6.11.96P
	(Konig SC430)						
G-MBPY	Ultrasports Tripacer 330/Wasp Gryphon II			21. 4.82	J.L.Thomas	(Bristol)	14. 5.00P
	(Fuji-Robin EC-34-PM)	RKP-01					
G-MBRB	Electraflyer Eagle Mk.I	E.2229		9.12.81	R.C.Bott	(Tywyn)	
G-MBRD	American Aerolights Eagle 215B			20. 4.82	R.J.Osborne	(Tiverton)	31. 8.85E
	(Fuji-Robin EC-25-PS)	E.2635					
G-MBRE	Wheeler Scout	73962		21. 4.82	C.A.Foster	(Leicester)	
G-MBRH	Ultraflight Mirage Mk.II			20. 4.82	R.W.F.Boarder	Oakley, Beds	8. 1.01P
	(Rotax 447)	83-009 & RALH-01					
G-MBRS	American Aerolights Eagle 215B	RWC.1		23. 4.82	W.J.Phillips	Haverfordwest	31. 8.85E
	(Zenoah G25B1)				*(Stored 6.90: current status unknown)*		
G-MBST	Mainair Gemini/Sprint	141-29383		10. 4.84	G.J.Bowen	(Llanelli)	30. 7.00P
	(Fuji-Robin EC-44-PM) *(Fitted with Trike from G-MJXA)*						
G-MBSX	Ultraflight Mirage II	240		14. 6.82	P.J.Careless & P.Samal	Sandy	9. 9.01P
	(Rotax 447)						
G-MBTF	Mainair Gemini/Sprint	168-30683		26. 4.82	J.R.Pyper	(Craigavon, Co Armagh)	26. 3.01P
	(Fuji-Robin EC-44-PM)						
G-MBTH	Whittaker MW4	001 & T1081-262L	(G-MBPB(1))	6. 4.82	L.Greenfield & M.Whittaker t/a The MW4 Flying Group		
	(Fuji-Robin EC-34-PM)					Otherton, Cannock	24. 7.01P
G-MBTJ	Ultrasports Tripacer/Solar Wings Typhoon			2. 4.82	H.A.Comber	(Poole)	13. 9.93P
	(Fuji-Robin EC-25-PS)	CSRS-01 *(Wing c/n may be T1081-286L)*					
G-MBTW	Aerodyne Vector 600	1188		10. 5.82	W.I.Fuller	Cambridge	5. 5.89E
	(Zenoah G25B1)						
G-MBUA	Hiway Skytrike/Hiway Demon	RJN-01		30. 4.82	R.J.Nicholson	(Lightwater)	
G-MBUS*	MEA Mistral Trainer	FGJ-01		7. 5.82	(N.A.Bell)	(Fordingbridge)	
					(Cancelled 25.10.88 as destroyed) (For spares 12.01)		
G-MBUZ	Wheeler (Skycraft) Scout II	0366		4. 5.82	A.C.Thorne	(Yelverton)	
G-MBVS	Hiway Skytrike II/Super Scorpion			14. 5.82	M.A.Brown	Swinford	
		25T3			*(Noted 7.01)*		
G-MBVW	Skyhook Cutlass/TR2	TR2/23		14. 5.82	M.Jobling	(Harrogate)	28. 5.87E
	(Solo 210 x 2)						
G-MBWG	Huntair Pathfinder 1	006		19. 5.82	H.R.Bell	(Perth)	14. 7.99P
	(Fuji-Robin EC-34-PM)						
G-MBWH	Jordan Duet 1	D82001		20. 5.82	Designability Ltd	Kemble	
G-MBWI*	Lafayette Hi-Nuski Mk.1	30680		8. 6.82	N H Ponsford	(Selby)	
					(Cancelled 13.6.90 by CAA). (Stored 12.01)		
G-MBXX	Ultraflight Mirage II	111		21. 1.82	E.J.Girling	St Just	14.11.88E
	(Kawasaki TA440)				*(Stored 5.94: current status unknown)*		
G-MBYD	American Aerolights Eagle 215B	3510		3. 6.82	J.A.Hambleton	(Market Drayton)	30. 1.92E
	(Fuji-Robin EC-25-PS) *(Sold together with G-MVSM early 1999 and parts probably used to support the latter)*						
G-MBYI	Ultraflight Lazair IIIE	A464/001		4. 6.82	M.Sumner	(Market Drayton)	5. 3.99P
	(Rotax 185 x 2) *(Built AMF Microflight Ltd from kit as c/n A522) (C/n amended during rebuild after accident 28.8.82)*						
G-MBYL	Huntair Pathfinder 1	009		4. 6.82	A.R.Hobbins	(Limavady, Co.Londonderry)	17. 2.02P
	(Fuji-Robin EC-44-PM)						

G-MBYM	Eipper Quicksilver MX	JW-01		4. 6.82	M.P.Harper & L.L.Perry		
	(Cuyuna 430R)					Priory Farm, Tibenham	21. 9.96P
G-MBZH	Eurowing Goldwing	EW-50		14. 6.82	J.Spavins	Long Acre Farm, Sandy	31. 3.02P
	(Fuji-Robin EC-34-PM)						
G-MBZJ	Southdown Puma/Lightning	L170-415		14. 6.82	A.K.Webster	(Wallingford)	1. 8.98P
	(Fuji-Robin EC-34-PM)				*(Stolen 24.8.97 from Chiltern Park: current status unknown)*		
G-MBZK	Ultrasports Tripacer 250/Solar Wings Typhoon			14. 6.82	J A Crofts	(Carmarthen)	14. 2.00P
	(Fuji-Robin EC-25-PS) AAL-01 & T381-104L						
G-MBZO	Mainair Tri-Flyer/Flexiform Medium Striker			15. 6.82	A.N.Burrows	(Kirkmichael, IoM)	15. 4.98P
	(Fuji-Robin EC-34-PM) GRH-01 & 021-101081						
G-MCEA	Boeing 757-225	22200	N510EA	6. 2.95	Airtours International Airways Ltd		
						Manchester	23. 3.04T
G-MCEL	Pegasus Quantum 15-912	7858		10.10.01	F.Hodgson	Sywell	9.10.02P
G-MCCF	Thruster T600N Sprint	0100-T600N-048		25. 4.01	C.C.F.Fuller	(Corsham)	24. 4.02P
	(Jabiru 2200)						
G-MCJL	Pegasus Quantum 15-912	7497		16. 3.99	M.C.J.Ludlow	(Sellindge, Ashford)	13. 5.02P
G-MCMS	Aero Designs Pulsar	PFA 202-11982		3. 2.93	B.R.Hunter	Easter Poldar Farm, Thornhill	19. 5.02P
	(Rotax 582)						
G-MCOX	Fuji FA.200-180AO Aero Subaru	296	(G-BIMS)	29.12.81	West Surrey Engineering Ltd	Fairoaks	7. 6.03
G-MCOY	Flight Design CT2K	01-04-01-12		25. 7.01	D.Young	Kemble	24. 7.02P
					t/a Pegasus Flight Training (Cotswolds)		
G-MCPI	Bell 206B-3 JetRanger III	3191	G-ONTB	4. 4.90	D.A.C.Pipe	Westbury-sub-Mendip	12. 3.03T
			N3896C				
G-MCXV	Colomban MC-15 Cri-Cri	371	F-PYVA	1. 3.00	H.A.Leek	(Melton Mowbray)	
	(Built J.P.Lorre)						
G-MDAC	Piper PA-28-181 Archer II	28-8290154	N8242T	6.11.87	B.R.McKay	Jersey/Compton Abbas	18. 5.03
					t/a Alpha Charlie Flying Club		
G-MDBC	Pegasus Quantum 15-912	7814		4. 5.01	D.B.Caiden	East Fortune	11. 6.02P
G-MDBD	Airbus A330-243	266	F-WWKG	24. 6.99	Airtours International Airways Ltd		
						Manchester	24..6.02T
G-MDKD	Robinson R22 Beta	1247		18. 4.90	B.C.Seedle	Blackpool	20. 5.02T
					t/a Brian Seedle Helicopters		
G-MEAH	Piper PA-28R-200 Cherokee Arrow II		G-BSNM	14. 6.91	Stapleford Flying Club Ltd	Stapleford	6. 4.03T
		28R-7435104	N46PR/G-BSNM/N46PR/N54439				
G-MEDA	Airbus A320-231	480	N480RX	12.10.94	British Mediterranean Airways Ltd		
			F-WWDU		*(Whale Rider t/s)*	Heathrow	11.10.03T
G-MEDB	Airbus A320-231	376	3B-RGY	19. 3.97	British Mediterranean Airways Ltd		
			F-OHMB/(XA-SGB)/F-WWIK		*(Rendezvous t/s)*	Heathrow	7. 4.03T
G-MEDD	Airbus A320-231	386	3B-RGZ	19. 3.97	British Mediterranean Airways Ltd		
			F-OHMC/(XA-SGC)/F-WWBI		*(Crossing Borders t/s)*	Heathrow	1. 4.03T
G-MEDE	Airbus A320-232	1194	F-WWDY	25. 4.00	British Mediterranean Airways Ltd		
						Heathrow	24..4.03T
G-MEDF	Airbus A321-231	1690	D-AVZX	R	British Mediterranean Airways Ltd		
					(For delivery 2.02)	Heathrow	
G-MEDG	Airbus A321-231	1711		R	British Mediterranean Airways Ltd		
					(For delivery 3.02)	Heathrow	
G-MEGA	Piper PA-28R-201T Turbo Arrow III		N999JG	13. 2.86	Multi Ltd	Breighton	14. 6.01T
		28R-7803303					
G-MEGG	Europa Aviation Europa XS			14. 6.00	M.E.Mavers	(Macclesfield)	
		PFA 247-13202					
G-MELT	Reims Cessna F172H	F172-0580	G-AWTI	23. 9.83	A.J.M.Shepherd	Goodwood	27. 2.03T
G-MELV	SOCATA Rallye 235E Gabier	13328	G-BIND	21. 5.86	J.W.Busby	Coventry	21.12.02
G-MEME	Piper PA-28R-201 Arrow	2837051	N9219N	17. 8.90	Henry J.Clare Ltd	Bodmin	20. 9.02
G-MEOW	CFM Streak Shadow			23. 4.93	G.J.Moor	Old Sarum	8. 5.02P
	(Rotax 582)	K.172 & PFA 206-12025					
G-MERC	Colt 56A HAFB	842		11. 6.86	A.F. & C.D.Selby	Loughborough	16. 6.00A
G-MERE	Lindstrand LBL-77A HAFB	092		7. 4.94	R.D.Baker	Canterbury	9. 5.96A
G-MERF	Grob G-115A	8091	EI-CAB	24. 7.95	G.Wylie t/a G-MERF Group	White Waltham	15. 4.02
G-MERI	Piper PA-28-181 Archer II	28-8090267	N8175J	17. 7.80	A H McVicar	Carlisle	30. 3.02T
G-MERL	Piper PA-28RT-201 Arrow IV		N2116N	27. 6.86	M.Giles	Cardiff	22. 8.04
		28R-7918036					
G-MEUP	Cameron A-120 HAFB	2117		5.10.89	Innovation Ballooning Ltd	Bath	15. 8.01T
G-MEYO	Enstrom 280FX	2059	SX-HCN	13. 1.95	J.N.Ainsworth	(West Drayton)	17. 5.04T
G-MFAC	Reims Cessna F172H	F172-0387	G-AVBZ	23. 8.01	Springbank Aviation Ltd		
						(Castletown, IoM)	16. 5.03T
G-MFEF	Reims FR172J Rocket	FR17200426	D-EGJQ	19.10.00	M.& E.N.Ford	Partridge Green	19.11.03
G-MFHI	Europa Aviation Europa	PFA 247-12841		14.11.97	M.F.Howe	Wombleton	26.10.02P
	(Rotax 912-UL)						
G-MFHT	Robinson R22 Beta-II	2601	N8334H	20. 6.96	MFH Helicopters Ltd	(London W1)	19. 6.02T
G-MFLI	Cameron V-90 HAFB	2650		14. 8.91	J.M.Percival *"Mayfly"*	Loughborough	8. 7.02A
					(Mouldform titles)		
G-MFMF	Bell 206B-3 JetRanger III	3569	G-BJNJ	4. 6.84	South Western Electricity plc	Bristol	16.11.03T
G-MFMM	Scheibe SF-25C Falke	4412	(G-MBMM)	20. 4.82	J.E.Selman	(Ardagh, Co.Limerick)	11. 1.03T
			D-KAEU				

G-MGAA	Quad City Challenger II			18. 8.97	P.Gibbs	Plaistows Farm, St Albans	22.12..02P
	(Rotax 582) CH2-0297-1568 & PFA 177A-13124						
G-MGAG	Aviasud Mistral 870545 & BMAA/HB/009			20. 6.89	M.Raj	Otherton, Cannock	27. 6.00P
	(Rotax 532)						
G-MGAN	Robinson R44 Astro	0588		10. 5.99	Meegan Motors Ltd		
						(Castleblayney, Co.Monoghan)	9. 5.02T
G-MGCA	Jabiru Jabiru UL	PFA 274A-13228		8. 5.98	P.A.James	Redhill	15. 3.02P
	(Jabiru 2200A)				t/a Cloudbase Aviation G-MGCA		
G-MGCB	Solar Wings Pegasus XL-Q			16.10.96	M.G.Gomez	Roddige, Fradley	25. 3.00P
	(Rotax 462) SW-TE-0344 & 7267 *(Trike ex G-MWUT)*						
G-MGDL	Pegasus Quantum 15	7400		17. 2.98	J.M.Huxham	Enstone	31. 3.02P
	(Rotax 582)						
G-MGDM*	Pegasus Quantum 15-912	7406		19. 3.98	R.Jeffes	(London SW13)	18. 4.00P
					(Cancelled 5.12.01 by CAA)		
G-MGEC	Rans S-6-ESD Coyote II XL *(Tri-cycle u/c)*			13.10.97	P.Crowhurst	Sywell	11. 9.02P
	(Rotax 503-2V)	PFA 204-13209					
G-MGEF	Pegasus Quantum 15-912	7261		18. 9.96	G.D.Castell	Long Acre Farm, Sandy	5.12.02P
G-MGFK	Pegasus Quantum 15-912	7396		2. 2.98	F.A.A.Kay	(Chorleywood)	10. 6.02P
G-MGGG	Pegasus Quantum 15-912	7377		3.11.97	R.A.Beauchamp	Shenstone	13. 5.02P
G-MGGT	CFM Streak Shadow SA-M			3. 6.94	R.K.& J.Hyatt	(Newquay)	16. 5.02P
	(Rotax 618) K.252 & PFA 206-12723						
G-MGGV	Pegasus Quantum 15-912	7484		12.10.98	R.W.Krake	Clench Common	18.12.02P
G-MGMC	Pegasus Quantum 15-912	7430		28. 4.98	M.Clare	Gayton, Northampton	10. 6.02P
G-MGND	Rans S-6-ESD Coyote II XL			27. 6.97	P.Vallis	(Alfreton)	14. 9.02P
	(Rotax 503)	PFA 204-13152					
G-MGOD	Medway Raven X	MRB110/106		6. 7.93	P.C.Collins & T A Hinton	(Bath)	1. 5.00P
	(Rotax 447)				*(New owners 1.02)*		
G-MGOM	Medway Hybred 44XLR	MR125/103		22.11.91	B.A.Showell	Stoke, Kent	3. 9.01P
	(Rotax 503)						
G-MGOO	Murphy Renegade Spirit UK			14.11.89	A.R.Max	White Waltham	23. 4.02P
	(Rotax 582) 301 & PFA 0188-11580						
G-MGPD	Solar Wings Pegasus XL-R	6905		9. 1.95	P.C.Davis	Weston Zoyland	15. 2.02P
	(Rotax 462)						
G-MGPH	CFM Streak Shadow SA-M		G-RSPH	27.11.97	R.S.Partridge-Hicks	(Bury St.Edmunds)	29. 7.00P
	(Rotax 582) K.286 & PFA 206-13166						
G-MGRH	Quad City Challenger II			20. 2.90	R.A. & B.M.Roberts		
	(Hirth 2705.R06)	CH2-1189-0482				Griffins Farm, Temple Bruer	16. 2.00P
G-MGRW	Cyclone AX3/S	BMAA/HB/024		8.11.93	K.G.W.Hicks	(Bembridge)	18. 5.02P
	(Rotax 503) *(Originally regd with c/n C.3093155/S)*						
G-MGTG	Pegasus Quantum 15-912	7369A	G-MZIO	19.12.97	R.B.Milton	Plaistows Farm, St Albans	21.10.02P
	(Orig c/n 7369 now amended after rebuild 11.98)						
G-MGTR	Hunt Wing/Experience	BMAA/HB/067		24. 7.97	A.C.Ryall	(Cardiff)	
	(Listed as "Huntwing Avon" in BMAA's records)						
G-MGTW	CFM Shadow DD	K.287 & 287-DD		23. 1.98	G.T.Webster	Glenrothes	29. 6.02P
	(Rotax 582)						
G-MGUN	Cyclone AX2000	7284		18.12.96	I.Lonsdale	(Burnley)	3. 5.02P
	(Rotax 582/48)						
G-MGUY	CFM Shadow CD	078		23.11.87	F.J.Luckhurst & R.G.M.Proost	(Old Sarum)	16. 8.91P
	(Rotax 447)				*(Crashed Home Farm, Pontisbury, Shrewsbury 20.7.91)*		
G-MGWH	Thruster T300	9013-T300-507		8.12.92	W.Corps & A.Bass	(Eastbourne)	9.10.01P
	(Rotax 582)						
G-MGWI	Robinson R44 Astro	0663	G-BZEF	4. 5.00	T.J.French	(Cronberry, Cumnock)	9. 5.03T
G-MHCB	Enstrom 280C Shark	1031	N892PT	11.10.95	Springbank Aviation Ltd		
						(Castletown, IoM)	14.10.02T
G-MHCD	Enstrom 280C-UK Shark	1112	G-SHGG	12. 7.96	S.J.Ellis	Bryngwyn Bach	25. 9.04T
G-MHCE	Enstrom F-28A	150	G-BBHD	22. 8.96	K.Bickley	Barton	3. 4.02T
G-MHCF	Enstrom 280C-UK Shark	1149	G-GSML	19. 9.96	K., H.K. & D.Collier	Barton	30. 7.04T
			G-BNNV/SE-HIY		t/a HKC Helicopter Services		
G-MHCG	Enstrom 280C-UK Shark	1155	G-HAYN	7. 3.97	E.Drinkwater	Barton	5. 9.03
			G-BPOX/N51776				
G-MHCH*	Enstrom 280C Shark	1043	N557H	19. 5.97	J.& S.Lewis Ltd	Barton	15.11.03T
					(Cancelled 15.1.02 as wfu)		
G-MHCI	Enstrom 280C Shark	1152	N100WZ	20. 5.97	B & B Helicopters Ltd	Barton	17. 9.03T
G-MHCJ	Enstrom F-28C-UK	453	G-CTRN	30. 3.98	P.E.Toleman	Hawarden	21. 6.04T
					t/a Paradise Helicopters		
G-MHCK	Enstrom 280FX	2006	G-BXXB	5. 6.98	N., C. & N.C. Bailey	Barton	16. 9.04T
			ZK-HHN/JA7702		t/a Manchester Helicopter Centre		
G-MHCL	Enstrom 280C Shark	1144	N51740	30. 6.98	Altolink Ltd	Hawarden	24.11.01T
G-MICH	Robinson R22 Beta	0647	G-BNKY	3. 9.87	Tiger Helicopters Ltd	Shobdon	4.10.02T
G-MICI	Cessna 182S Skylane	18280546	G-WARF	14. 6.01	M.J.Coleman	Rochester	30. 6.02T
			N7089F				
G-MICK	Reims Cessna F172N Skyhawk II		PH-JRA	9. 1.80	S.J.Gronow	Blackpool	23. 8.04
		F17201592	PH-AXB		t/a G-MICK Flying Group		

G-MICY	Everett Gyroplane Srs.1 (VW 1835)	018	(G-BOVF)	26. 2.90	D.M.Hughes	St.Merryn	2. 5.92P
G-MICZ	Piper PA-46-310P Malibu	46-8508096	N2494X	3. 7.95	M Linden	(Stockholm, Sweden)	16. 9.04T
G-MIDA	Airbus A321-231	806	D-AVZQ	31. 3.98	British Midland Airways Ltd *(Stored 1.02)*	East Midlands	30. 3.04T
G-MIDC	Airbus A321-231	835	D-AVZZ	12. 6.98	British Midland Airways Ltd *(Stored 1.02)*	East Midlands	11. 6.04T
G-MIDD	Piper PA-28-140 Cherokee Cruiser	28-7325444	G-BBDD N11C	20. 1.97	R.B.Walker t/a Midland Air Training School	Coventry	25. 5.04T
G-MIDE	Airbus A321-231	864	D-AVZB	14. 8.98	British Midland Airways Ltd *(Stored 1.02)*	East Midlands	13. 8.04T
G-MIDF	Airbus A321-231	810	D-AVZS	24. 4.98	British Midland Airways Ltd *(Stored 1.02)*	East Midlands	23. 4.04T
G-MIDG	Bushby-Long MM-1 Midget Mustang (Lycoming O-320)	385	N11DE	14. 3.90	C.E.Bellhouse	Headcorn	30. 4.02P
G-MIDH	Airbus A321-231	968	D-AVXZ	22. 3.99	British Midland Airways Ltd	East Midlands	21. 1.02T
G-MIDI	Airbus A321-231	974	D-AVZA	26. 3.99	British Midland Airways Ltd	East Midlands	25. 3.02T
G-MIDJ	Airbus A321-231	1045	D-AVZO	16. 7.99	British Midland Airways Ltd *(Stored 1.02)*	East Midlands	15. 7.02T
G-MIDK	Airbus A321-231	1153	D-AVZF	12. 1.00	British Midland Airways Ltd *(Star Alliance c/s)*	East Midlands	11. 1.03T
G-MIDL	Airbus A321-231	1174	D-AVZH	22. 2.00	British Midland Airways Ltd *(Star Alliance c/s)*	East Midlands	21. 2.03T
G-MIDM	Airbus A321-231	1207	D-AVZR	18. 4.00	British Midland Airways Ltd *(Stored 1.02)*	East Midlands	17. 4.03T
G-MIDN	Airbus A321-231			R	British Midland Airways Ltd *(For delivery 2.02)*	East Midlands	
G-MIDO	Airbus A321-231			R	British Midland Airways Ltd *(For delivery 3.02)*	East Midlands	
G-MIDP	Airbus A320-232	1732	F-WWBK	R	British Midland Airways Ltd *(For delivery 3.02)*	East Midlands	
G-MIDR	Airbus A320-232	1697	F-WWIQ	R	British Midland Airways Ltd *(For delivery 3.02)*	East Midlands	
G-MIDS	Airbus A320-232	1424	F-WWBO	21. 3.01	British Midland Airways Ltd	East Midlands	20. 3.04T
G-MIDT	Airbus A320-232	1418	F-WWBI	14. 3.01	British Midland Airways Ltd	East Midlands	13. 3.04T
G-MIDU	Airbus A320-232	1407	F-WWDC	27. 2.01	British Midland Airways Ltd	East Midlands	26. 2.04T
G-MIDV	Airbus A320-232	1383	F-WWIQ	30. 1.01	British Midland Airways Ltd	East Midlands	29. 1.04T
G-MIDW	Airbus A320-232	1183	F-WWDT	29. 3.00	British Midland Airways Ltd *(Star Alliance c/s)*	East Midlands	28. 3.03T
G-MIDX	Airbus A320-232	1177	F-WWDP	21. 3.00	British Midland Airways Ltd *(Star Alliance c/s)*	East Midlands	20. 3.03T
G-MIDY	Airbus A320-232	1014	F-WWDQ	28. 6.99	British Midland Airways Ltd	East Midlands	27. 6.02T
G-MIDZ	Airbus A320-232	934	F-WWII	19. 1.99	British Midland Airways Ltd	East Midlands	18. 1.05T
G-MIFF	Robin DR.400/180 Regent	2076		31. 5.91	G.E.Snushall	Leicester	16.10.03
G-MIII	Extra EA.300/L (Lycoming AEIO-540)	013	D-EXFI	5. 9.95	Firebird Aerobatics Ltd *(Firebirds titles)*	Denham	26. 9.04T
G-MIKE	Brookland Hornet (VW 1830)	MG.1		15. 5.78	M.H.J.Goldring	St.Merryn	25. 9.92P
G-MIKI	Rans S-6-ESA Coyote II *(Tri-cycle u/c)* (Rotax 912-UL)	0996.1040 & PFA 204-13094		28. 2.97	S.P.Slade	Kemble	16. 6.02P
G-MIKK	Robinson R22 Mariner	3262M		1.10.01	Direct Timber Ltd	(Coalville)	10.10.04T
G-MILA	Reims Cessna F172N Skyhawk II	F17201686	D-EGHC(2) PH-AYJ	9. 6.98	P.J.Miller	Cuckoo Tye Farm, Long Melford	28. 8.04A
G-MILE	Cameron N-77 HAFB	2411		26. 9.90	Miles Air Ltd *"Miles Architectural"*	Bristol	25. 7.02A
G-MILI	Bell 206B-3 JetRanger III	2275	C-GGAR 5H-MPV	5.10.94	Sirius Aviation Ltd	Liverpool	1.10.04T
G-MILN	Cessna 182Q Skylane	18265770	N735XQ	9. 7.99	Meon Hill Farms (Stockbridge) Ltd	Bournemouth	8. 7.02T
G-MILY	Grumman American AA-5A Cheetah	AA5A-0672	G-BFXY	2. 9.96	Plane Talking Ltd	Elstree	11.10.02T
G-MIMA	British Aerospace BAe 146 Srs.200	E2079	G-CNMF G-5-079	3. 3.93	Manx Airlines Ltd *(Op Manx Airlines: Manx c/s)*	Ronaldsway	25.11.04T
G-MIME	Europa Aviation Europa	PFA 247-12850		26. 9.97	N.W.Charles	Kemble	15.11.02P
G-MIND	Cessna 404 Titan II	404-0004	G-SKKC G-OHUB/SE-GMX/(N3932C)	27. 4.93	Atlantic Air Transport Ltd *(Op Highlands Airways Ltd)*	Inverness	13. 2.03T

G-MINS	Nicollier HN.700 Menestrel II PFA 217-12354		23.10.92	R.Fenion	West Freugh	8.11.02P
G-MINT	Pitts S-1S Special PFA 09-10292 (Lycoming AEIO-360)		7. 2.83	T.G.Sanderson	Leicester	12.11.01P
G-MINX	Bell 47G-4A 7604	N6242N G-FOOR/N6242N	16. 3.90	R.F.Warner *(Current status unknown)*	Elstree	22. 5.93T
G-MIOO	Miles M.100 Student 2 M1008 ..	G-APLK G-MIOO/G-APLK/XS941/G-APLK/G-35-4	26.10.84	Museum of Berkshire Aviation	Woodley	6. 5.86P
	(Damaged in forced landing Duxford 24.8.85: on rebuild as "G-APLK" 2.00)					
G-MISH	Cessna 182R Skylane II 18267888	G-RFAB G-BIXT/N6397H	16. 6.95	Kamair Ltd	(King's Farm, Thurrock)	1. 4.03
G-MISS	Taylor JT.2 Titch PFA 3234		18.12.78	P L.Brenen *(Noted 5.01)*	RAF Halton	
G-MITT	Jabiru Jabiru SK PFA 274-13427		29. 2.00	N.C.Mitton	Goodwood	15. 8.02P
G-MIWS	Cessna 310R II 310R1585	G-ODNP N19TP/N2DD/N1836E	1. 2.96	R.W.F.Warner	RAF Shawbury	9. 9.02P
G-MJAE	American Aerolights Eagle 1021 *(C/n not confirmed)*		12. 7.82	T.B.Woolley	(Leicester)	
G-MJAJ	Eurowing Goldwing EW-36 (Fuji-Robin EC-44-PM)		18. 6.82	J.S.R.Moodie	Rovie Farm, Rogart	6. 7.02P
G-MJAM	Eipper Quicksilver MX JCL-01 (Cuyuna 430)		18. 6.82	J.C.Larkin	Maryport, Cumbria	20. 8.93P
G-MJAN	Hiway Skytrike I/Flexiform Hilander (Valmet) RPFD-01 & 21U9		21. 6.82	G.M.Sutcliffe	(Stockport)	4. 3.92E
G-MJAV	Hiway Skytrike II/Hiway Demon 175 (Fuji-Robin 250) 817003		23. 6.82	J.N.J.Roberts	Long Acre Farm, Sandy	10. 5.90E
G-MJAY	Eurowing Goldwing EW-58 (Fuji-Robin EC-34-PM)		23. 6.82	M.Anthony	(Alfreton)	24. 7.90E
G-MJAZ	Vector 627SR Ultravector 1251 (Konig SC430)	PH-1J1 G-MJAZ	23. 6.82	B.Fussell *(Stored 1.97: current status unknown)*	(Swansea)	23. 9.93E
	(Orig regd as Aerodyne Vector 610 but converted 4.88 when PH-1J1)					
G-MJBK	Swallow AeroPlane Swallow B (Rotax 447) 582007-2		18.11.83	M.A.Newbould *(Current status unknown)*	(Harrogate)	N/E
G-MJBL	American Aerolights Eagle 2892		25. 6.82	B.W.Olley	(Ely)	16. 9.02P
G-MJBS	UAS Storm Buggy JL814S		29. 6.82	G.I.Sargeant *(BMAA records as damaged in 1982)*	(Bridgwater)	
G-MJBV	American Aerolights Eagle 215B (Fuji-Robin EC-25-PS) RSP-001		1. 7.82	B.H.Stephens	(Southampton)	11. 8.96P
G-MJBZ	Huntair Pathfinder 1 PK-17 (Fuji-Robin EC-34-PM)		2. 7.82	J.C.Rose	Eastbach Farm, English Bicknor	28.12.93P
G-MJCE	Ultrasports Puma/Southdown Sprint X (Fuji-Robin EC-44-PM) RGC-01 *(Designation amended by BMAA 1990)*		5. 7.82	L.I.Bateup & N.D.Dykes	Swinford, Rugby	25. 8.01P
G-MJCN	Southern Flyer Mk.1 005 (Fuji-Robin EC-44-PM)		5. 7.82	C.W.Merriam	(Billingshurst)	11. 6.99P
G-MJCU	Tarjani/Solar Wings Typhoon (Fuji-Robin EC-25-PS) SCG-01 & T982-610		7. 7.82	J.K.Ewing	Old Sarum	1. 9.94P
G-MJCW	Hiway Skytrike/Super Scorpion MGS-01		7. 7.82	M.G.Sheppard	(Bournemouth)	
G-MJCX	American Aerolights Eagle 215B 2759 (Chrysler 820?) *(May have Cuyana fitted)*		7. 7.82	J.Channer *(Current status unknown)*	(Nottingham)	11. 8.94P
G-MJDE	Huntair Pathfinder 1 020 (Fuji-Robin EC-34-PM)		9. 7.82	P.Rayson	(Swadlincote)	29. 5.02P
G-MJDH	Huntair Pathfinder 1 015 (Fuji-Robin EC-44-PM)		9. 7.82	T.Mahmood	Insch	12. 8.01P
G-MJDJ	Hiway Skytrike/Demon VW17D		9. 7.82	A.J.Cowan	(Billingham)	
G-MJDP	Eurowing Goldwing GW-001 (Fuji-Robin EC-34-PM)		12. 7.82	J.R.Ledbrook & F.C.James	(Camberley)	15.11.92P
G-MJDR	Hiway Skytrike/Demon PJB-01		14. 7.82	D.R.Redmile	(Leicester)	
G-MJDU	Eipper Quicksilver MXII 14002 (Rotax 503)		15. 7.82	J.Brown	Markfield, Leics	17.11.86E
G-MJDW	Eipper Quicksilver MXII RI-01 (Cuyuna 430) *(C/n noted as 3506)*		15. 7.82	J.A.Brumpton	(Horncastle)	17. 7.01P
G-MJEB	Southdown Puma Sprint SN1231/0041 (Rotax 447)		18. 4.85	R.J.Shelswell	(Warwick)	1. 5.96P
G-MJEE	Mainair Tri-Flyer 250/Solar Wings Typhoon (Fuji-Robin EC-25-PS) 038-251181		20. 7.82	M.F.Eddington	(Wincanton)	11.11.00P
G-MJEG	Eurowing Goldwing GJS-01 (Fuji-Robin EC-34-PM)		20. 7.82	G.J.Stamper *(Stored 9.01)*	Barton	23. 4.89E
G-MJEK	See G-MJGK below					
G-MJEO	American Aerolights Eagle 215B 4562 (Zenoah G25B1)		26. 7.82	A.M.Shaw	(Stoke-on-Trent)	25. 6.93E
G-MJER	Ultrasports Tripacer/Flexiform Solo Striker (Rotax 447) DSD-01		23. 7.82	D.S.Simpson	Radwell, Letchworth	26.12.00P
G-MJEY	Mainair Tri-Flyer 440/Southdown Lightning DS (Fuji-Robin EC-44-PM) 085-26782 & PMC-01		27. 7.82	M.McKenzie	Insch	7. 6.96P

G-MJFB	Ultrasports Tripacer/Flexiform Solo Striker		27. 7.82	B.Tetley	(Cowes)	2. 5.00P
	(Fuji-Robin EC-34-PM)	AJK-01				
G-MJFM	Huntair Pathfinder 1	ML-01	2. 9.82	R.Gillespie & S.P.Girr		
	(Fuji-Robin EC-34-PM)				Mullaghmore, Co.Antrim	23. 7.99P
G-MJFX	Skyhook TR1/Sabre	TR1/38	2. 8.82	M.R.Dean	(Hebden Bridge)	28. 2.87E
	(Hunting HS.525A)					
G-MJGK*	Eurowing Goldwing	040	3. 8.82	Not known	Rufforth	
	(Fuji-Robin EC-34-PM)		*(Cancelled 13.6.90 by CAA) (Noted in part built condition as "G-MJEK")*			
G-MJHC	Ultrasports Tripacer 330/Southdown Lightning Mk II		9. 8.82	E.J.Allen	(Cambridge)	12.12.89E
	(Fuji-Robin EC-34)	82-00044 *(C/n is engine serial no)*				
G-MJHM	Ultrasports Tripacer/Hiway Demon 175		11. 8.82	D.B.Markham	(Lincoln)	
	(Regd with c/n ME-170)	ME17D		*(Test flown 3.91)*		
G-MJHR	Mainair Dual Tri-Flyer/Southdown Lightning		12. 8.82	B.R.Barnes	(Bristol)	
		GNS-01				
G-MJHU	Eipper Quicksilver MX.II	10692	13. 8.82	P.J.Hawcock, J.W.Lupton & R.F.Hinton		
	(Cuyuna 430R)				(Hougham, Lincs)	30. 6.90E
				(Stored 9.96: current status unknown)		
G-MJHV	Hiway Skytrike II/Hiway Demon	AG-17	13. 8.82	A.G.Griffiths	(Avenchurch, Birmingham)	
G-MJHX	Eipper Quicksilver MXII	1033	13. 8.82	P.D.Lucas	(Needham, Harleston)	14. 5.95P
	(Rotax 503)			*(Stored 9.97: current status unknown)*		
G-MJIA	Ultrasports Tripacer/Flexiform Solo Striker		13. 8.82	D.G.Ellis	(Tamworth)	20. 9.96P
	(Rotax 377)	SE-007				
G-MJIC	Ultrasports Tripacer/Flexiform Solo Striker		13. 8.82	J.Curran	(Newry, Co.Down)	15.10.94P
	(Fuji-Robin EC-34-PM)	82-00043				
G-MJIF	Mainair Tri-Flyer/Flexiform Striker		16. 8.82	R.J.Payne	(Newmarket)	31.10.91E
	(Fuji-Robin EC-34-PL) "E-1 EC25PS-04" *(C/n was original engine type)*					
G-MJIR	Eipper Quicksilver MXII	1392	18. 8.82	H.Feeney	Long Marston	26. 1.95P
	(Rotax 503)			*(Stored 8.96: current status unknown)*		
G-MJIY	Ultrasports Puma/Southdown Sprint X		23. 8.82	M.I.McClelland	Old Sarum	10. 7.00P
	(Fuji-Robin EC-34-PM)	002 CSRS		t/a McClelland Aviation		
	(Originally regd as Ultrasports Tripacer/Flexiform Striker)					
G-MJIZ	Ultrasports Tripacer/Southdown Lightning		23. 8.82	Jacqueline J.Crudington	(Hockley, Essex)	
		JS-189				
G-MJJA	Huntair Pathfinder 1	031	23. 8.82	R.D.Bateman & J.M.Watkins		
					Davidstow Moor	25. 8.02P
G-MJJF	Ultrasports Tripacer/Solar Wings Large Typhoon		25. 8.82	G.Ravichandran	(London N13)	1. 4.01P
	(Fuji-Robin EC-34-PM) JGS-01 & 116-108 & T784-1152L					
G-MJJK	Eipper Quicksilver MXII	3397	25. 8.82	M.J.O'Malley	(Northolt)	13.10.02P
	(Rotax 503)					
G-MJJO	Mainair Tri-Flyer/Flexiform Dual Striker		26. 8.82	T.R.Marsh	(Frome)	5.11.96P
	(Fuji-Robin EC-44-PS)	JDH-01				
	(Mainair c/n originally shown as 073-31582 but this became G-MMII)					
G-MJKB	Striplin Sky Ranger	ST 161	2. 9.82	A.P.Booth	(Newbury)	
	(Officially quoted as c/n SRI-6-I)					
G-MJKF	Hiway Demon	WGR-01	2. 9.82	S.D.Hill	(Henley-on-Thames)	
G-MJKH*	Eipper Quicksilver MXII	1020	28. 1.83	D.O'Neill	Long Marston	23. 8.96P
	(Rotax 503)			*(Cancelled 6.11.00 by CAA) (Stored 8.01)*		
G-MJKO	Hiway Skytrike/Gold Marque Gyr 188		7. 9.82	M.J.Barry	(Bridgwater)	18.11.91E
	(Fuji-Robin EC-25-PS)	90030P *(Assembled from spares by Windsports)*				
G-MJKP*	Hiway Skystrike/Super Scorpion		7. 9.82	Aeroventure	Doncaster	
	(Fuji-Robin EC-25)	PEB-01		*(Cancelled 9.12.94 as WFU) (Noted 2001)*		
G-MJKX	Skyrider Airsports Phantom	PH.82005	14. 9.82	C.G.Johns	(Kidderminster)	1. 8.98P
	(Fuji-Robin EC-50)			*(New owner 5.01)*		
G-MJLK*	Dragon Dragonfly 250-II	D.105	10. 9.82	Not known	Breighton	
				(Cancelled 18.4.90 as WFU: reported dismantled 12.01)		
G-MJMD	Hiway Skytrike II/Demon 175	OE17D	27. 9.82	T.A.N.Brierley	Baxby Manor, Husthwaite	1. 8.97P
	(Fuji-Robin EC-34-PM)					
G-MJME*	Ultrasports Tripacer/Moyes Mega II		27. 9.82	Not known	Southwick, Trowbridge	
		WIA		*(Cancelled 29.1.88 as WFU) (Stored in workshop 2001)*		
G-MJMN	Mainair Tri-Flyer/Flexiform Striker		29. 9.82	E.D.Locke	Barton	2. 6.01P
	(Fuji-Robin EC-34-PM)	087-04882		*(Stored dismantled 1.02)*		
G-MJMR	Mainair Tri-Flyer 250/Solar Wings Typhoon		30. 9.82	J.C.S.Jones	Emlyn's Field, Rhuallt	
		DR-01 & 048-5182		*(Stored 12.97: current status unknown)*		
G-MJMS	Hiway Skytrike II/Demon 175	EEW-01	30. 9.82	D.E.Peace	(Rawdon, Leeds)	
G-MJMU	Hiway Skytrike II/Demon	817003	1.10.82	P.Hunt	(Bishop Auckland)	
	(Fuji-Robin EC-25-PS) *(C/n duplicates several a/c incl G-MJOI & PH-1B2 and is suspect!)*					
G-MJNK	Hiway Skytrike II/Demon 175	EA17D	14.10.82	S.W.Barker	Baxby Manor, Husthwaite	28.10.96P
	(Fuji-Robin EC-34-PM)			*(New owner 10.01)*		
G-MJNM	American Aerolights Double Eagle 430B		25.11.82	B.H.Stephens	(Southampton)	19. 9.93P
	(Cuyuna 430R)	702				
G-MJNO	American Aerolights Double Eagle Amphibian		24.11.82	R.S.Martin	(Gosport)	23. 6.02P
	(Rotax 447)	703				
G-MJNT	Hiway Skytrike II/Demon 175	RO17D	18.10.82	F.Tyreman	(Whitby)	25. 5.89E
	(Fuji-Robin EC-25-PS)					

G-MJNU	Skyhook TR1/Cutlass	TR1/17		19.10.82	R.W.Taylor	(Sheffield)	
G-MJNY	Skyhook TR1/Sabre	TR1/35		3.11.82	P.Ratcliffe	(Sheffield)	
G-MJOC	Huntair Pathfinder (Fuji-Robin EC-34-PM)	048		25.10.82	A.J.Glynn	Gerpins Lane, Upminster	31. 7.99P
G-MJOE	Eurowing Goldwing (Rotax 377)	EW-55		29.10.82	R.J.Osborne	(Tiverton)	19.11.88E
G-MJPA	Rotec Rally 2B	AT-01		5. 1.83	R.Boyd	(Armagh)	
G-MJPB*	Manuel Ladybird	WLM-14		9.11.82	Estate of W.L.Manuel *(Cancelled 13.6.90 by CAA: on loan to Museum)*	Brooklands	
G-MJPE	Mainair Tri-Flyer 330/Demon 175 (Fuji-Robin EC-34-PM)	117-151282 & 0G17D		10.11.82	E.G.Astin	(Whitby)	7. 8.96P
G-MJPO	Eurowing Goldwing	018		16.12.82	M.E.Merryman	(Dronfield)	
G-MJPV	Eipper Quicksilver MX (Cuyuna 430R)	JBW-01		30.11.82	F.W.Ellis	Water Leisure Park, Skegness	1. 2.95P
G-MJRL	Eurowing Goldwing (Rotax 377)	EW-79 & SWA-5K		30.12.82	M.Daniels	(Heanor)	15. 6.00P
G-MJRO	Eurowing Goldwing (Rotax 447)	EW-77 & SWA-04		31.12.82	H.P.Welch	(Taunton)	22. 9.99P
G-MJRR	Reece SkyRanger Srs.1	JR-3		26. 4.82	J.R.Reece	(Formby)	
G-MJRS	Eurowing Goldwing (Rotax 377)	EW-80 & SWA-6K		5. 1.83	G.B.Gratton & J.L.Macfarlane	Chilbolton	12.10.01P
G-MJRU	MBA Tiger Cub 440	SO.86		6. 1.83	D.J.Short	(Nailsea, Bristol)	31. 1.86E
G-MJSE	Skyrider Airsports Phantom (Fuji-Robin EC-40-PL)	SF-101		24. 1.83	C.L.Betts	(Hove)	20. 5.02P
G-MJSF	Skyrider Airsports Phantom (Rotax 462)	SF-105	SE- G-MJSF	24. 1.83	B.J.Towers *(On rebuild 5.00)*	(Pershore)	
G-MJSL	Dragon Light Aircraft Dragon 200 (Rotax 503)	0018		24. 2.83	G.Kingston *(New owner 1.02)*	Long Marston	22. 9.99P
G-MJSO	Hiway Skytrike III/Demon 175 (Hiro 22)	SA17D		1. 2.83	D.C.Read	(Ledbury)	N/E
G-MJSP	Romain MBA Super Tiger Cub Special 440 *(Tri-cycle u/c)*	SO.54		7. 2.83	A P Chapman *(Fuselage only 12.00)*	North Coates	31. 1.86E
G-MJST	MEA Pterodactyl Ptraveler (Fuji-Robin EC-34-PM)	GCS-01		2.12.81	C.H.J.Goodwin	(Bedford)	7. 5.99P
G-MJSU*	MBA Tiger Cub 440 *(Officialy regd with c/n SO.175)*	SO.75/1		2. 2.83	Not known *(Cancelled 23.6.93 by CAA: stored 7.01)*	Swanton Morley	31. 1.86E
G-MJSV*	MBA Tiger Cub 440 *(Officially regd with c/n SO.287)*	SO.87/2		2. 2.83	Not known *(Cancelled 9.11.89 by CAA) (Stored 2001)*	(Kinloss)	
G-MJSY	Eurowing Goldwing (Rotax 377)	EW-63		8. 2.83	A.J.Rex	(Wrexham)	5. 1.01P
G-MJSZ	Harker DH Wasp (Rotax 447)	HA.5		10. 2.83	J.J.Hill	Baxby Manor, Husthwaite	24. 3.01P
G-MJTC	Ultrasports Tri-Pacer/Typhoon	T1282-677		14. 2.83	V.C. Redhead	(Saxmundham)	
G-MJTD	Gardner T-M Scout *(Thomas-Morse S4 Scout 2/3rd rep)* *(Possibly c/n PFA 111-10664)*	83/001		14. 2.83	D.Gardner *(As "41386" in US Army Signal Corps c/s)*	(Rugby)	
G-MJTE	Skyrider Airsports Phantom (Fuji-Robin EC-44-PM)	SF-106		15. 2.83	S.R.Bradford	Haverfordwest	11. 6.02P
G-MJTM	Aerostructure Pipistrelle P2B (KFM-107ER)	019 & SAL/P2B/002		21. 2.83	K.S.Matcham	(Soberton, Southampton)	16. 2.02P
G-MJTP	Mainair Tri-Flyer/Flexiform Dual Sealander (Fuji-Robin EC-44-PM)	AJDH-01 & 139-7383		25. 2.83	P.Milton *(Possibly fitted with Dual Striker wing after accident 29.10.87)*	(Bedford)	22. 8.00P
G-MJTR	Southdown Puma DS Mk.1 (Fuji-Robin EC-44-PM)	H362		9. 3.83	A.G.Rodenburg & T.Abro	(Tillicoultry)	15. 7.96P
G-MJTX	Skyrider Airsports Phantom (Fuji-Robin EC-44-PM)	SF-110		1. 3.83	P.D.Coppin *(CofR restored 14.11.01)*	(Fareham)	22. 4.96P
G-MJTZ	Skyrider Airsports Phantom (Fuji-Robin EC-44-PM) *(Eng No.82-00119)*	MBS-01		29. 4.83	B.J.Towers	(Pershore)	N/E
G-MJUC	MBA Tiger Cub 440 (Fuji-Robin EC-44-PM)	RRH-01 & PFA 140-10908		7. 3.83	J.A.Harker *(Noted 9.01)*	Shipdham	20. 1.92E
G-MJUF*	MBA Super Tiger Cub 440 (Fuji-Robin EC-44)	MCT-01		8. 3.83	D G Palmer *(Cancelled 27.4.90 by CAA) (Stored 7.01)*	Fetterangus	
G-MJUH*	MBA Tiger Cub 440 (Fuji-Robin EC-44)	JEJ-01		9. 3.83	Not known *(Cancelled 2.7.96 as WFU: noted 6.00)*	Flix Public House, Girvan	
G-MJUO*	Eipper Quicksilver MX II	104C		22. 3.83	A Hamilton *(Cancelled 24.1.95 by CAA)*	Strathaven	
G-MJUT	Eurowing Goldwing	DLE-01		23. 3.83	D.L.Eite	(Newark)	
G-MJUU	Eurowing Goldwing (Fuji-Robin EC-344-PM)	EW-70		28. 3.83	E.F.Clapham	(Oldbury-on-Severn)	3. 5.97P
G-MJUV	Huntair Pathfinder mk.1 (Fuji-Robin EC-44-PM)	045		18. 5.83	S.J.Overton	(Colchester)	25. 7.00P
G-MJUW	MBA Tiger Cub 440 (Fuji-Robin EC-44-PM)	SO.69		29. 3.83	D.G.Palmer	Fetterangus	25. 7.00P

G-MJUX	Skyrider Airsports Phantom	RFF-01		29. 2.84	K.H.A.Negal	Sittles Farm, Alrewas	10. 3.02P
	(Fuji-Robin EC-44-PM)						
G-MJUY*	Eurowing Goldwing	EW-82		6. 4.83	Not known	(Hougham, Lincs)	30. 6.86E
				(Cancelled 24.1.95 by CAA: stored complete 9.96: current status unknown)			
G-MJUZ	Dragon 150	015		30. 3.83	G.S.Richardson	North Coates	28. 2.87E
	(Fuji-Robin EC-51)				*(Stored 8.00)*		
G-MJVE	Medway Hybred 44XL/Solar Wings Typhoon XLII			19. 4.83	T.A.Clark	(Manningtree)	5. 6.00P
	(Fuji-Robin EC-44-PM) 4483/1 & T483-761XL *(Orig wing c/n T283-703XL)*						
G-MJVF	CFM Shadow CD	002		12. 4.83	J.A.Cook	(Thorpeness)	12. 2.02P
	(Rotax 503)						
G-MJVN	Ultrasports Tripacer/Flexiform Striker			18. 4.83	R.McGookin	(West Kilbride)	5.10.93P
	(Fuji-Robin EC-44-PM) 82-00030-PR1 *(Orig Trike & engine fitted in G-MJRP)*						
G-MJVP	Eipper Quicksilver MXII	1149		19. 4.83	G.J.Ward	(Dorchester)	10. 7.96P
	(Rotax 503) *(Orig c/n 1124 became G-MTDO?)*						
G-MJVU	Eipper Quicksilver MX II	1118		3. 4.84	F.J.Griffith	(Denbigh)	23. 6.02P
	(Rotax 503)						
G-MJVX	Skyrider Airsports Phantom			27. 4.83	J.R.Harris	(Bewdley, Worcs)	6. 5.02P
	(Fuji-Robin EC-44-PM) JAG-01 & SF-102						
G-MJVY	Dragon 150	D.150/013		4. 5.83	J.C.Craddock	(Freshwater, IoW)	21. 9.02P
	(Rotax 503)						
G-MJWB	Eurowing Goldwing	EW-59		24. 5.83	D.G.Palmer	Fetterangus	25. 8.93P
	(Fuji-Robin EC-34-PM)				*(Noted 7.01)*		
G-MJWF	MBA Tiger Cub 440	BRH-001 & SO.79		4. 5.83	D.M.Stewart *(Op T Maycock)*	Glasgow	
G-MJWH*	Chargus Vortex 120			R	Midland Air Museum	Coventry	
	(Regn reserved in 1983 for a Chargus T.250 plus engine for F.Embleton but fitted to a 1974 Vortex hang glider: this was abandoned and only the wing is on display)						
G-MJWJ	MBA Tiger Cub 440	013/191		9. 5.83	J.W.Barratt	(Langport)	18. 3.96P
	(Fuji-Robin EC-44-PM)						
G-MJWK	Huntair Pathfinder 1	JWK-01		1.10.82	D.Young t/a Kemble Flying Club	Kemble	22. 4.01P
	(Rotax 447)						
G-MJWN	Hornet Single-Seat/Solo Striker			10. 5.83	G.de Clara	(Stoke-on-Trent)	26. 7.91E
	(Fuji-Robin EC-34-PM)	H430					
G-MJWS*	Eurowing Goldwing	EW-22		16. 5.83	Ulster Aviation Heritage	Langford Lodge	
	(Fuji-Robin EC-34-PM)			*(Stored 4.94: cancelled 23.6.97 by CAA: acquired 7.00)*			
G-MJWZ	Solar Wings Panther XL-S	T583-781XL		9. 9.85	C.P.Hughes	Emlyn's Field, Rhuallt	27. 1.01P
	(Fuji-Robin EC-44-2PM)						
G-MJXD	MBA Tiger Cub 440	011/061 & SO.179		16. 5.83	W.L.Rogers	(Totnes)	
					(Thought to have been re-registered as G-MJYD)		
G-MJXF*	MBA Tiger Cub 440	EJH-01		1. 6.83	Not known	(Southwater, Sussex)	
					(Cancelled 5.9.94 by CAA) (Stored 8.01)		
G-MJXS	Huntair Pathfinder II	134		25. 5.83	A.E.Sawyer	Melrose Farm Melbourn	
					(Stored 5.00)		
G-MJXY	Hiway Demon II/Skytrike 330	KQ17D		31. 5.83	H.C.Lowther	(Penrith)	25. 7.00P
	(Fuji-Robin EC-34-PM)						
G-MJYF	Mainair Gemini/Flash	305-585-3 & W45		18. 4.85	W.D.Crooks	Newtownards, Co.of Down	15. 6.01P
	(Fuji-Robin EC-44-PM)						
G-MJYJ*	MBA Tiger Cub	SO.177		6. 6.83	Not known	Spilsted Farm, Sedlescombe	
	(Regd as c/n OS.177)			*(Cancelled 23.6.93 by CAA) (Purchased for engine and dumped in barn 5.01)*			
G-MJYP	Mainair Gemini/Flexiform Dual Striker			7. 6.83	M.S.Whitehouse	(Solihull)	23. 7.02P
	(Fuji-Robin EC-44-PM)	167-13683					
G-MJYV	Mainair Rapier1 + 1/Flexiform Solo Striker			23.11.83	L.H.Phillips	(Solihull)	12.11.01P
	(Fuji-Robin EC-34-PM)	175-19783					
G-MJYW	Lancashire Micro-Trike Dual 330/Wasp Gryphon III	2/330PM/PGK/6.83/K		28. 6.83	P.D.Lawrence	(Munlochy, Ross-shire)	
				(Dismantled & Trike used on G-MMPL: parts noted 7.01)			
G-MJYX	Mainair Tri-Flyer/Hiway Demon			9. 6.83	K.A.Wright	North Coates	9. 9.01P
	(Fuji-Robin EC-33-PM)	108-251182					
G-MJYY	Hiway Skytrike II/Demon 175	ZD17D		9. 6.83	N.Smith	(Brunton)	1. 3.88E
	(Fuji-Robin EC-34-PM)						
G-MJZD	Mainair Gemini/Flash	311-585-3 & W50		18. 4.85	A.R.Gaivoto	Popham	11. 6.02P
	(Fuji-Robin EC-44-PM)						
G-MJZE	MBA Tiger Cub 440	SO.168		14. 6.83	J.E.D.Rogerson t/a Fishburn Flying Tigers	Morgansfield, Fishburn	31. 1.86E
G-MJZK(2)	Southdown Puma Sprint	SN1111/0081		3. 3.86	R.J.Osborne	(Tiverton)	18.10.91P
	(Fuji-Robin EC-44-PM)						
G-MJZL	Eipper Quicksilver MXII	EEW-01		15. 6.83	T.Scarborough	(Boston)	17. 7.01P
	(Rotax 503)						
G-MJZO	Lancashire Micro-Trike/Flexiform Solo Striker			24. 6.83	J.W.Coventry	Davidstow Moor	2.11.01P
	(Fuji-Robin EC-34-PM) 1/330PM/LM/683/2						
G-MJZU	Mainair Gemini/Flexiform Dual Striker			21. 6.83	M.J.J.Dunning & C.B.Godfray	(Baginton)	3. 6.99P
	(Fuji-Robin EC-44-PM) 214-41183 & JDR-02 *(Gemini trike from G-MMVX(1) fitted)*						
G-MJZX	Maxair Hummer TX	TX/16		21. 6.83	R.J.Folwell	(London W6)	
G-MKAK	Colt 77A HAFB	2039		15. 8.91	Virgin Airship & Balloon Co Ltd	Telford	21. 9.01T
G-MKAS	Piper PA-28-140 Cherokee Cruiser	28-7425338	G-BKVR OY-BGV	30. 4.98	MK Aero Support Ltd	Andrewsfield	14.11.04T

G-MKIA	Supermarine 300 Spitfire I	6S-30565	P9374	16.11.00	S.J.Marsh	(Castelcucco, Italy)	
G-MKIV*	Bristol 149 Bolingbroke IVT	-	(G-BLHM)	26. 3.82	G.A.Warner	Duxford	28. 5.88P
			RCAF 10038		*(As "V6028/GB-D" in 105 Sqdn c/s)*		
	(Crashed Denham 21.6.87: cancelled 1.11.88 as destroyed: on rebuild 3.00 for static exhibition)						
G-MKIX	Supermarine 361 Spitfire IXe		N238V	12.12.83	D.W.Arnold	(Bournemouth)	22. 5.93P
	(Firewall No.CBAF.8563)	CBAF.IX.2200	OO-ARE/Belg.AF SM-36/Fokker B-8/R.Neth AF H-60/H-103/NH238				
					t/a Warbirds of GB *(As "NH238/D-A": stored 1996)*		
G-MKSF	Agusta A.109A II	7275	N18SF	11.12.01	Markoss Aviation Ltd	Biggin Hill	
			F-GDPR				
G-MKSS	British Aerospace HS.125 Srs.700B		VP-BEK	29. 3.01	Markoss Aviation Ltd	Biggin Hill	4. 4.02T
		257175	VP-CEK/N770TJ/C9-TAC/(C9-TTA)				
G-MKVB	Supermarine 349 Spitfire LF.Vb		5718M	2. 5.89	Historic Aircraft Collection Ltd	Duxford	25. 3.02P
		CBAF.2461	BM597		*(As "BM597/JH-C" in 317 Sqdn c/s)*		
G-MKVI	de Havilland DH.100 Vampire FB.6	676	J-1167	2. 6.92	T.C.Topen	Swansea	14. 9.95P
	(Built FFW)	*(To De Havilland Aviation Ltd: as "WL505" in 614 Sqn c/s: stored 3.97: current status unknown)*					
G-MKXI	Supermarine 365 Spitfire PR.XII		PL965	13.11.89	R.A.Fleming & A.J.E.Smith		
	(Packard Merlin 266)	6S/504719	R Neth AF			Leeward Air Ranch, Florida, USA	10. 9.02P
		(Op Real Aeroplane Company) (As "PL965/R" in pink camouflage c/s with "Invasion" stripes)					
G-MLAS*	Cessna 182E	18253826	OO-HPE	2. 5.79	Not known	St.Merryn	2.10.82
			D-EGPE/N2826Y				
	(Crashed 14.12.80: cancelled 4.2.87 by CAA: cabin in use as para-trainer 5.98: current status unknown)						
G-MLFF	Piper PA-23-250 Aztec E	27-7305194	G-WEBB	31. 1.90	Channel Islands Aero Services Ltd	Jersey	28.11.02T
			G-BJBU/N40476		t/a Jersey Aero Club		
G-MLJL	Airbus A330-243	254	F-WWKT	15. 6.99	Airtours International Airways Ltd		
					"Ben Crossland"	Manchester	14 .5.02T
G-MLTI	Dassault Falcon 900B	164	F-WWFC	13. 6.97	Multiflight Ltd	Leeds-Bradford	12. 6.03T
G-MLTY	Aérospatiale AS365N2 Dauphin	6431	N365EL	4. 6.99	Multiflight Ltd	Leeds-Bradford	6..6.03
			JA6673				
G-MLWI	Thunder Ax7-77 HAFB	1000		3. 9.86	M.L. & L.P.Willoughby	Reading	12. 8.02A
					"Mr Blue Sky"		
G-MMAC	Dragon Srs.200	003	OY-...	14. 7.82	J.F.Ashton & J.Kirwan	(Liverpool)	14. 5.87E
	(Fuji-Robin EC-44-PM)		G-MMAC				
G-MMAE	Dragon Srs.200	005		7. 9.82	P.J.Sheehy & K.S.Matcham	(Southampton)	29. 7.96P
	(Fuji-Robin EC-44-PM)						
G-MMAG	MBA Tiger Cub 440	SO.47		22. 6.83	M.J.Aubrey	(Kington, Hereford)	14. 9.93P
	(Fuji-Robin EC-44-PM)						
G-MMAI	Dragon Srs.150	0032		1. 7.83	G.S.Richardson	(Cleethorpes)	13. 7.97P
	(Fuji-Robin EC-44-PM)	*(New CofR 6.01: dismantled & parts split between North Coates and owner's home)*					
G-MMAL*	Mainair Tri-Flyer/Flexiform Dual Striker			20. 9.83	Tina E.Simpson	(Bewdley, Worcs)	1. 4.94P
	(Fuji-Robin EC-44-PM)	DHM-01	*(On rebuild 10.97: cancelled 27.4.00 by CAA: current status unknown)*				
G-MMAN	Mainair Tri-Flyer 330/Flexiform Solo Striker			27. 9.83	K.F.Gittins	Rufforth	14.10.02P
		192-6983					
G-MMAO*	Southdown Puma Sprint X	HS.549		28.12.83	P A Kershaw	Ince Blundell	14. 3.00P
					(Cancelled 31.5.01 by CAA) (Stored 8.01)		
G-MMAP	Maxair Hummer TX	250TX-17		29. 9.83	P Williams	(Leicester)	5. 9.93E
	(Zenoah 250)						
G-MMAR	Mainair Gemini/Puma Sprint MS			23. 9.83	A.R. & J.Fawkes	(Newbury)	17. 9.98P
	(Fuji-Robin EC-44-PM)	195-11083-2					
G-MMAW	Mainair Rapier 1+1/Flexiform Solo Striker			18. 7.83	G.B.Hutchison	(Doncaster)	
	(Fuji-Robin EC-34-PM)	131/2-10283			*(New owner 8.01)*		
G-MMAX	Garland Trike/Flexiform Dual Striker			5. 8.93	M T Wells	(Newcastle, Staffs)	18. 2.02P
	(Fuji-Robin EC-44-PM)	0011					
G-MMAZ	Southdown Puma Sprint X	MAPB-01		5. 8.83	A.R.Smith	(Chelmsford)	22. 7.96P
	(Fuji-Robin EC-44-PM)						
G-MMBL	Ultrasports Puma/Southdown Lightning DS			4. 7.83	B.J.Farrell	(Preston)	7. 3.92E
	(Fuji-Robin EC-44-PM)	80-00083 *(C/n is engine serial no.)*					
G-MMBN	Eurowing Goldwing	EW-89		28. 6.83	E.H.Jenkins	(Newcastle upon Tyne)	27. 8.92E
	(Rotax 447)						
G-MMBT	MBA Tiger Cub 440	SO.131 & TA.01		19. 7.83	B.Chamberlain	(Otley, Ipswich)	31. 1.86E
	(Probably either c/n PFA 140-10924 or 10990)				*(Stored 1.91: current status unknown)*		
G-MMBU	Eipper Quicksilver MXII	CAL-222		8. 7.83	D.A.Norwood	Ash House Farm, Winsford	11. 6.02P
	(Rotax 503)						
G-MMBV	Huntair Pathfinder	044		8. 7.83	P.J.Bishop	Tarn Farm, Cockerham	17. 5.97P
	(Fuji-Robin EC-44-PM) *(New sailwing 1999)*						
G-MMBY	Solar Wings Panther XL	T483-759XL		20. 7.83	R.M.Sheppard & P.Huddleston		
	(Fuji-Robin EC-44-PM)					(Wantage/Marlborough)	7. 8.01P
G-MMBZ	Solar Wings Typhoon P	T981-5217		20. 7.83	S.C.Mann	(Kirbymoorside)	28. 4.96P
	(Fuji-Robin EC-34-PM) *(Originally believed to have had sailwing c/n T781-217 - 5217 almost certainly a corruption of S217 for Typhoon Small - and then rebuilt as c/n T981-228)*						
G-MMCB*	Huntair Pathfinder II	136		13. 7.83	Science Museum Air Transport Coln & Storage Facility		
					(Cancelled as WFU 23.11.88)	Wroughton	
G-MMCI	Ultrasports Puma Sprint X			28. 9.83	R.J.Webb	Long Marston	9. 9.01P
	(Fuji-Robin EC-44-PM)	DMP-01 & P.421					

G-MMCV	Hiway Skytrike II/Solar Wings Typhoon		27. 7.83	G.Addison	(Kinross)	8. 6.97P
	(Fuji-Robin EC-34-PM)	T583-783				
G-MMCX	MBA Super Tiger Cub 440	MU.002	8. 8.83	D.Harkin	(Johnstone, Renfrew)	
G-MMCZ	Mainair Tri-Flyer/Flexiform Dual Striker		10. 8.83	T.D.Adamson	Wombleton	10. 4.02P
	(Fuji-Robin EC-44-PM)	TE-01 *(Mainair Trike c/n 180-6883)*				
G-MMDE	Mainair Tri-Flyer 250/Solar Wings Typhoon S		12. 8.83	D.J.Moore	(Oakington)	11. 6.01P
		DES-1 & 025-211081-6				
G-MMDF	Southdown Wild Cat Mk.II/Lightning Phase II		24. 8.83	J.C.Haigh	(Tonbridge)	27. 1.99P
	(Fuji-Robin EC-34-PM)	007				
G-MMDK	Mainair Merlin/Striker	181-16883	7. 9.83	P.E.Blyth	(Rotherham)	30. 5.99P
	(Fuji-Robin EC-34-PM)					
G-MMDN	Mainair Tri-Flyer 330/Flexiform Dual Striker		30. 9.83	M.G.Griffiths	(Monmouth)	14. 9.89E
		197-983 & RPO.12 *(Mainair c/n not confirmed)*				
G-MMDP	Mainair Gemini/Sprint X	183-22883	20. 9.83	J.D.Bridgewater & C.H.Prince		
	(Fuji-Robin EC-44-PM)				(Kirkmichael, IoM)	25. 1.95P
G-MMDR	Huntair Pathfinder II	137	30. 8.83	C.Dolling	(United Arab Emirates)	
	(Rotax 377)			*(To UAE 11.84)*		
G-MMDX	Lloyd Trident/Solar Wings Typhoon		7. 9.83	E.J.Lloyd	(Caterham, Surrey)	
		EJL-01				
G-MMDY	Ultrasports Panther Sprint I	S.064	7. 9.83	C.Duffin	(Portlaoise, Co.Laois)	20.11.90E
	(Fuji-Robin EC-44-PM)					
G-MMEF	Hiway Skytrike I/Super Scorpion		13. 9.83	R.H.Evans	(Bury St.Edmunds)	
	(Valmet SM1608)	SM1608 10664 *(C/n is engine type)*				
G-MMEJ	Mainair Tri-Flyer/Flexiform Striker		15. 9.83	R.B.Tweedie	(Stoke-on-Trent)	9. 11.97P
		215-41183 & FF/LAI/83/JDR/03				
G-MMEK	Medway Hybred 44XL/Solar Wings Typhoon XL2		16. 9.83	M.G.J.Bridges	(Exeter)	28..8.00P
	(Fuji-Robin EC-44-PM)	12983/6				
	(Typhoon sailwing c/n either T883-884XL or '887XL - both originally supplied to Medway for G-MMEK & G-MMEN)					
G-MMFD	Mainair Tri-Flyer/Flexiform Dual Striker		20. 9.83	M.E. & W.L.Chapman	(Oldham)	6.12.93P
	(Fuji-Robin EC-44-PM)	210-31083-2 & FF/LAI/83/JDR/12				
G-MMFE	Mainair Tri-Flyer/Flexiform Striker		20. 9.83	W.Camm	(Barnsley)	16. 6.94P
	(Fuji-Robin EC-44-PM)	FF/LAI/83/JDR/13				
	(Trike unit replaced by c/n 256-784-2 & probably now podded to 440 Gemini standard)					
G-MMFG	Lancashire Micro-Trike/Flexiform Dual Striker		20. 9.83	M.G.Dean & M.J.Hadland		
	(Fuji-Robin EC-44-PM)	FF/LAI/83/JDR/15			Tarn Farm, Cockerham	18. 3.93E
G-MMFL	Ultrasports Tripacer/Flexiform Solo Sealander		25.10.83	T.C.Bradley	(Gloucester)	7. 9.89E
	(Fuji-Robin EC-34-PM)	JGM-01				
G-MMFN*	MBA Tiger Cub 440	SO.113	31.10.83	J.S.Skipp	(Bromyard, Hereford)	30.11.95P
	(Fuji-Robin EC-44-PM)			*(Cancelled 12.7.01 as temporarily wfu)*		
G-MMFS	MBA Tiger Cub 440	SO.64	1.11.83	G.S.Taylor	(Shrewsbury)	27. 7.01P
	(Fuji-Robin EC-44-PM)					
G-MMFT	MBA Tiger Cub 440	SO.56	2.11.83	E.N.Simmons	(Boston)	23. 1.95P
	(Fuji-Robin EC-44-PM)			*(Destroyed by fire on owner's driveway 12.01)*		
G-MMFY	Cliff Sims Aztec trike/Dual Striker		14.12.83	K.R.M.Adair & S.R.Browne	(Arundel)	10. 9.90E
		AZT001CS				
G-MMGF	MBA Tiger Cub 440	SO.124	18.11.83	J.G.Boxall	Pittrichie Farm, Whirerashes	22. 8.02P
G-MMGL	MBA Tiger Cub 440	SO.148 & BMAA/HB/050	23.11.83	H.E.Dunning	(Knaresborough)	18. 2.02P
	(Fuji-Robin EC-44-PM)					
G-MMGP	Ultrasports Puma Sprint X	RGC-01	24.11.83	J.Garcia	(Kilmarnock)	5. 2.92E
	(Fuji-Robin EC-44-PM)					
G-MMGS	Solar Wings Panther XL	T1283-939XL	28.12.83	D.W.Bock	(Saltash)	12. 8.98P
	(Fuji-Robin EC-44-PM)					
G-MMGT	Huntwing Pegasus Classic	JAH-7	28.11.83	H.Cook	(Newport)	17. 4.01P
	(Rotax 503) *(Currently with Trike c/n SW-TB-1228 ex G-MTOH)*					
G-MMGU	SMD Gazelle/Flexiform Sealander		1.12.83	A.D.Cranfield	(Wincanton)	19. 9.93E
	(Fuji-Robin EC-44-PM)	30-4883				
G-MMGV	Microknight Whittaker MW5 Sorcerer Srs.A		2.12.83	G.N.Haffey & M.W.J.Whittaker		
		001			(Chatham/Doncaster)	1. 9.02P
G-MMHL	Hiway Skytrike II/Super Scorpion		19.12.83	E.J.Blyth	(Pickering)	9.12.91E
	(Fuji-Robin EC-44)	KSC.84				
G-MMHN	MBA Tiger Cub 440	SO.136	19.12.83	M.J.Aubrey	(Kington, Hereford)	
	(Fuji-Robin EC-44)					
G-MMHP	Hiway Skytrike III/Demon 175		19.12.83	P.A.Bedford	(Tewkesbury)	26.10.86E
	(Hiro)	PCC-01 & OL17D *(Regd with c/n OL175)*				
G-MMHS	SMD Gazelle/Flexiform Dual Striker		21.12.83	C.J.Meadows	(Shepton Mallet)	
		104-11283				
G-MMHY	Hornet Invader 440/Flexiform Dual Striker		21.12.83	W.Finlay	(Leeds)	
	(Fuji-Robin EC-44)	RPO.17				
G-MMIB*	MEA Mistral Trainer	DH-01	3. 2.84	Not known	Old Sarum	
				(Cancelled 5.12.95 by CAA) (Stored 12.01)		
G-MMIE	MBA Tiger Cub 440	G7-7	3. 1.84	B.W.Olliver	(Telford)	31. 1.86E
	(Fuji-Robin EC-44)					
G-MMIH	MBA Tiger Cub 440	SO.130	25. 4.84	R.A.Davis	(Gloucester)	19. 8.93P
	(Fuji-Robin EC-44-PM)					

G-MMIL Eipper Quicksilver MXII 1046 6. 1.84 C.K.Brown (Loughborough) 24. 3.94P
(Rotax 503)

G-MMIM MBA Tiger Cub 440 SO.28 & BMAA/HB/060 11. 1.84 T.J.Bidwell (Newtown, Powys) 26. 3.00P
(Fuji-Robin EC-44-PM)

G-MMIR Mainair Gemini/Sprint 051-20182 25. 1.84 J.P.Wilson Long Marston 15. 8.97P
(Fuji-Robin EC-44-PM) *(Stored 10.00)*
(Regd with original Trike c/n ex G-MBKX then G-MJDO: now rebuilt with Trike 314-585-3 ex G-MMZK: wing ex G-MMTI: original Trike frame (c/n 051) gone by 10.00)

G-MMIW Southdown Puma Sprint 590 9. 2.84 J.Ryland (Swanley) 4.11.02P
(Fuji-Robin EC-44-PM)

G-MMIX MBA Tiger Cub 440 MBCB-01 14. 2.84 N.J.McKain (Dumfries) 11.11.90E
(Fuji-Robin EC-44-PM) *(To Dumfries & Galloway Museum)*

G-MMJD Southdown Puma Sprint SP/1001 28. 6.83 S.J.Hillyard (Felixstowe) 4. 8.01P
(Fuji-Robin EC-44-PM)

G-MMJF Solar Wings Panther Dual XL-S 27. 2.84 J.D.Nelson (Bushey) 28. 5.02P
(Fuji-Robin EC-44-PM) PXL842-150 & T284-988XL

G-MMJG Mainair Tri-Flyer/Flexiform Dual Striker 31. 9.83 A.Strang (Larkhall) 15. 7.02P
(Fuji-Robin EC-44-PM) 185-1983

G-MMJM Southdown Puma Sprint 440 27. 2.84 R.J.Sanger (Wickford) 31. 5.97P
PD.500 & SN1111/001

G-MMJT Mainair Gemini/Sprint X JBT-01 20.12.83 W.F.Murray Swinford, Rugby 29. 8.01P
(Fuji-Robin EC-44-PM) *(No Mainair identity & probably plans built by J B Tate)*

G-MMJV MBA Tiger Cub 440 SO.195 & PFA 140-1090 25. 3.84 D.G.Palmer Fetterangus 9. 5.93P
(Fuji-Robin EC-44-PM) *(Noted 7.01)*

G-MMJX Teman Mono-Fly 01 6. 3.84 M.Ingleton (Sheerness) 17. 7.02P
(Rotax 377)

G-MMKA Solar Wings Panther Dual XL 8. 3.84 R.S.Wood (Wallacestone, Falkirk) 30. 4.86E
(Fuji-Robin EC-44-PM) T284-986XL

G-MMKE Birdman WT-11 Chinook 01817 2. 4.84 D.M.Jackson (Belper) 31.12.87E
(Rotax 277)

G-MMKG Medway Hybred 44XL/Solar Wings Typhoon XL2 9. 3.84 G.P.Lane (Bristol) 18. 7.97P
(Fuji-Robin EC-44-PM) 22284/7 *(Reported with wing marked "G-MNYX" 8.96)*
(Typhoon sailwing c/n T-?84-1035XL - either '384 or '484)

G-MMKH Medway Hybred 44XL/Solar Wings Typhoon XL 9. 3.84 C.Richardson Baxby Manor, Husthwaite 16.10.01P
(Fuji-Robin EC-44-PM) 22284/8 *(Typhoon sailwing c/n T.?84-1047XL - either '384 or '484)*

G-MMKK Mainair Gemini/Flash 240-384-2 12. 3.84 M.Whittle Peterlee 20.12.02P
(Fuji-Robin EC-44)

G-MMKL Mainair Gemini/Flash 238-384-2-W11 12. 3.84 D.W.Cox (Kenilworth) 29 .9.93P
(Fuji-Robin EC-44-PM)

G-MMKM Mainair Gemini/Flexiform Dual Striker 12. 3.84 S.W.Hutchinson (Northallerton) 11. 6.99P
(Fuji-Robin EC-44-PM) 221-184-2 *(Regd/stamped with c/n 221-0184-0002)*
(Originally fitted with Mainair 440 Tri-Flyer trike c/n 210-1083 and then part-exchanged for the 440 Gemini now fitted. This is a rebuild of one originally exported to the USA and then returned to UK)

G-MMKP MBA Tiger Cub 440 SO.203 13. 3.84 J.W.Beaty (Kettering)

G-MMKR Mainair Tri-Flyer/Southdown Lightning DS 14. 3.84 C.R.Madden (Great Orton) 9. 8.01P
(Fuji-Robin EC-44-PM) 209-171083 & CM-01 *(Regd as G-MNDK in error and then restored as G-MMKR)*

G-MMKV Southdown Puma Sprint X P.521 24. 4.84 A.Turnbull (Clitheroe) 28. 8.02P
(Fuji-Robin EC-44-PM)

G-MMKX Skyrider Airsports Phantom 330 18. 3.85 C A James Doynton, S Gloucestershire 17. 6.01P
(Fuji-Robin EC-34-PL-02) PH-107R *(On rebuild 2001)*

G-MMKY* Jordan Duet Srs.1 CHS-01 19. 3.84 Not known Oakley, Beds
(Rotax 503) *(Cancelled by CAA 1.9.95: composite airframe being assembled 3.00 from this & G-MNIN)*

G-MMLB MBA Super Tiger Cub 440 SO.57 19. 3.84 A.Newton (Hull)
(Fuji-Robin EC-44)

G-MMLE Eurowing Goldwing SP EW-81 21. 3.84 B.K.Harrison (Glasgow)

G-MMLH Hiway Skytrike Mk.II 330/Demon 28. 3.84 P.M.Hendry & D.J.Lukey (Folkestone)
PMH-01 & DJL-01

G-MMLI* Mainair Tri-Flyer 250/Solar Wings Typhoon S 26. 3.84 National Museums of Scotland/Museum of Flight
RPAT-01 & T484-423L *(Cancelled 7.9.94 by CAA)* East Fortune
(Initially regd as Hiway Skytrike Mk.II 250)

G-MMLP Mainair Gemini/Sprint 242-484-2 & ACT-01 3. 4.84 K.D.Parnell Eaglescott 13. 9.00P
(Fuji-Robin EC-44-PM)

G-MMMB Mainair Tri-Flyer/Sprint 5. 4.84 K.Birkett (Southampton) 22. 9.02P
(Fuji-Robin EC-44-PM) CR-01/170 & 170-16583 *(Trike unit ex G-MJYU)*

G-MMMD Mainair Gemini/Sprint 224-184-2-P.504 30.12.83 R.J.Newsham (Fordingbridge) 14. 8.97P
(Fuji-Robin EC-44-PM)

G-MMMG Eipper Quicksilver MXL 1383 5. 6.84 J.G.Campbell (Barnsley) 19. 8.02P
(Rotax 447)

G-MMMH Hadland Willow/Flexiform Striker 9.12.83 M.J.Hadland (Wigan) 26. 8.02P
(BMW R80/7) MJH 383

G-MMML Dragon Srs.150 D150/002 OY-... 28. 6.83 R.G.Huntley South Wraxall, Wilts 6. 8.00P
(Fuji-Robin EC-44-PM) G-MMML *(Noted 12.01)*

G-MMMN Solar Wings Panther Dual XL-S 4. 4.84 C.Downton (Newton Abbot) 2. 6.02P
(Fuji-Robin EC-44-2PM) PXL 843-150 & T484-105?XL *(probably '1059)*

G-MMMR*	Ultrasports Tripacer/Flexiform Striker (Fuji-Robin EC-34-PM) MAR-01	14. 3.84	H.A.Lloyd-Jennings *(Cancelled 19.11.01 by CAA)*	(London SW6)	31. 3.00P
G-MMNB	Eipper Quicksilver MX 4286 (Cuyuna 430R)	30. 3.84	J.M Lindop *(New owner 6.01)*	Long Marston	12.10.97P
G-MMND	Eipper Quicksilver MXII Q2 1038 (Rotax 503)	30. 3.84	G.B.Burby *(Dismantled 8.96: current status unknown)*	(Burnley)	13.11.94P
G-MMNH	Dragon Srs.150 D150/42 (Fuji-Robin EC-44-PM)	27. 7.83	T.J.Barlow	Dromore	30. 3.93E
G-MMNN	Sherry Buzzard 1	6. 4.84	E.W.Sherry	(Stoke-on-Trent)	
G-MMNS	Mitchell Super Wing U-2 PFA 114-10690	11. 4.84	C.Baldwin & J.C.Lister	Valley Farm, Winwick	
G-MMNT	Flexiform trike/Flexiform Solo Striker (Rotax 277) SSL-1	16. 4.84	C.R.Thorne	(Lyndhurst, Hants)	8. 7.88E
G-MMOB	Mainair Gemini/Sprint 244-584-2(K) & EM-01 (Fuji-Robin EC-44-PM) *(C/n 'K' denotes Kit built)*	11. 5.84	D.Woolcock	(Preston)	3. 9.99P
G-MMOH	Solar Wings Pegasus XL-R SW-TB-1450 & T484-1054XL *(Trike fitted replacing one formerly on G-MBTT: new Trike now fitted ex G-MYGA)*	4. 5.84	T.H.Scott	Rayne Hall Farm, Rayne	
G-MMOI*	MBA Tiger Cub 440 SO.92 (Fuji-Ribin EC-44M) *(C/n reported as SO.59).*	8. 5.84	P Talbot *(Cancelled 13.7.93 by CAA) (Noted dismantled @ owner's home 6.01)*	(Cromer)	31. 1.86E
G-MMOK	Solar Wings Panther XL-S (Fuji-Robin EC-44-PM) PXL844-157 & T584-1066XL	9. 5.84	R.F. & A.J.Foster	(Woodbridge)	22. 8.02P
G-MMOW	Mainair Gemini/Flash 246-684-3 & W06 (Fuji-Robin EC-44-PM)	21. 5.84	J.Wakelin	Davidstow Moor	3. 6.02P
G-MMPG	Southdown Puma Sprint NEA-01 (Fuji-Robin EC-34-PM) *(Tripacer/Lightning Mk.II)*	8. 6.84	T.J.Hector	(Royston)	15. 4.01P
G-MMPH	Southdown Puma Sprint P.545 (Fuji-Robin EC-44-PM)	20. 6.84	S.Whittle	(Wigan)	26. 8.02P
G-MMPL	Lancashire Micro-Trike 440/Flexiform Dual Striker (Fuji-Robin EC-44-PM) PDL-02 & 2/330PM/PGK/683/K *(Trike unit from G-MJYW - possibly flown with exchangeable sailwings)*	5.12.83	P.D.Lawrence	Insch	20.11.01P
G-MMPO	Mainair Gemini/Flash 325-785-3 & W65 (Fuji-Robin EC-44-PM)	18. 4.85	F H Cook	(Whitchurch)	3. 8.01P
G-MMPT	SMD Gazelle/Flexiform Dual Striker ECP-01	5. 6.84	A.K.Buttle	(Sherborne)	1. 9.91E
G-MMPU	R J Heming trike/Typhoon S4 (Fuji-Robin EC-34-PM) RJH-01 & T782-553L	5. 6.84	J.T.Halford	(Holt, Norfolk)	22. 5.96P
G-MMPZ	Teman Mono-Fly JWH-01 (Rotax 447)	2. 7.84	P.B.Kylo	(Consett)	15. 6.02P
G-MMRH	Hiway Skytrike/Demon JSM-01 & 25R1	20. 6.84	J.S.McCaig	(North Berwick)	
G-MMRK	Ultrasports/Solar Wings Panther XL-S PXL846-175 & T684-1107XL	9. 7.84	J.A.Churchill	(Worthing)	28. 9.95P
G-MMRL	Ultrasports/Solar Wings Panther XL-S (Fuji-Robin EC-44-PM) PXL846-174 & T684-1102XL	17. 7.84	R.J.Hood	Plaistows Farm, St Albans	10. 7.02P
G-MMRN	Southdown Puma Sprint P.544 (Fuji-Robin EC-44-PM)	16. 7.84	D.C.Read	(Ledbury)	18. 4.01P
G-MMRP	Mainair Gemini/Sprint 259-884-2-P.561 (Fuji-Robin EC-44-PM)	7. 2.85	J.C.S.Jones	Emlyn's Field, Rhuallt	20. 5.02P
G-MMRW	Mainair Gemini 440/Flexiform Dual Striker LAI/DS/25 & 216-71283	5. 1.84	M.D.Hinge	Salisbury	N/E
G-MMRY	Chargus T.250/Hiway Vulcan EDG-01	17. 7.84	D.L.Edwards, I.R.Davis & R.J.Grantham	(Weston-super-Mare/Bath)	
G-MMRZ	Solar Wings Panther XL-S (Fuji-Robin EC-44-PM) PXL847-168 & T684-1099XL	16. 7.84	A.L.Lyall *(Stored 10.00)*	(Edinburgh)	20. 6.00P
G-MMSA	Solar Wings Panther XL-S (Fuji-Robin EC-44-2PM) PXL847-189 & T184-1142XL *(C/n probably T784-1142XL)*	9. 8.84	T.W.Thiele & G.Savage	(Baldock)	27. 5.98P
G-MMSE	Eipper Quicksilver MX 10021 *(C/n believed to relate to engine)*	23. 7.84	P.Rowbotham	(Loughborough)	31.10.85E
G-MMSG	Solar Wings Panther XL-S T884-1165XL (Fuji-Robin EC-44-2PM) *(Regd with c/n 8841/65XC which appears to be a corruption of the Typhoon sailwing c/n style: XC may indicate an exchange sailwing hence the apparent duplication with that known to be on G-MMTT)*	6. 9.85	R.W.McKee	(Deeside)	4. 6.01P
G-MMSH	Solar Wings Panther XL-S (Fuji-Robin EC-44-PM) PXL847-192 & T884-1163XL	28. 5.85	I.J.Drake	(Billericay)	7. 5.90P
G-MMSO	Mainair Gemini/Sprint 255-784-2-P.539 (Fuji-Robin EC-44-PM)	14. 1.86	K.A.Maughan	Sandtoft	26. 7.99P
G-MMSP	Mainair Gemini/Flash 265-984-2 (Fuji-Robin EC-44-PM) *(Original sailwing c/n W03 later sold to G-MNGF 1998: current sailwing identity not yet known)*	17. 8.84	J.Whiteford	East Fortune	24. 4.01P
G-MMSW	MBA Tiger Cub 440 SO.68 (Fuji-Robin EC-44)	8. 8.84	D.R.Hemmings *(Extant 1999)*	(Ringwood)	
G-MMSZ	Medway Half Pint/aerial Arts 130SX (JPL PUL425) 2/21385	27. 3.85	P.Sykes *(Current status unknown)*	(Bournemouth)	N/E
G-MMTA	Solar Wings Panther XL-R (Rotax 462HP) PXL848-194 & T884-1164XL	25.10.84	P.A.McMahon	(Dun Laoghaire, Co.Dublin)	29. 6.02P

G-MMTC Solar Wings Pegasus XL-R 28. 9.84 T.L.Moses Haverfordwest 8. 2.02P
(Rotax 447) SW-TB-1037 & T684-1101XL *(Orig Trike was Ultrasports c/n PXL847-170 & later fitted to G-MNHH)*

G-MMTD Mainair Tri-Flyer/Hiway Demon 175 16. 8.84 W.E.Teare (Ramsey, IoM) 2. 9.00P
(Fuji-Robin EC-34-PM) 150-30583 & EIA-01 *(Trike originally exported to Denmark)*

G-MMTH Southdown Puma Sprint P.538 4. 9.84 R.G.Tomlinson (Yeovil) 8.12.92P
(Fuji-Robin EC-44-PM)

G-MMTI Southdown Puma Sprint SN1221/0005 13. 9.84 S.A.Jackson (Polegate) 26. 5.02P
(Fuji-Robin EC-44-PM) *(C/n duplicates ZS-VLZ) (See G-MMIR - possibly fitted with new wing)*

G-MMTJ Southdown Puma Sprint SN1221/0006 17. 1.85 P J Kirwan (Geashill, Co.Offaly) 16. 4.00P
(Fuji-Robin EC-44-PM)

G-MMTL Mainair Gemini/Sprint 268-1084-2-P.576 3.10.84 T.W.Faragher Jurby, IoM 6. 7.02P
(Fuji-Robin EC-44-PM)

G-MMTR Solar Wings Pegasus XL-R KND-03 27. 9.84 P.M.Kelsey (Rufforth) 8. 9.01P
(Rotax 447) *(Orig fitted with Ultrasports trike/Typhoon wing c/n T984-1211XL: trike replaced by Solar Wings XL c/n SW-TB-1092 circa 8.86)*

G-MMTS Solar Wings Panther XL T784-1157XL 18. 9.84 A.S.Wason (Wootton Bassett) 23. 5.02P
(Fuji-Robin EC-44-PM)

G-MMTT Ultrasports/Solar Wings Panther XL-S 12.12.84 C.T.H.Tenison (Abergavenny) 7.11.97P
(Fuji-Robin EC-44-PM) T684-1165XL *(C/n possibly T884-1165XL but duplicates G-MMSG)*
(Solar Wings records show sailwing as G-MMTT when returned for repair: G-MMSG possibly had a replacement wing)

G-MMTV American Aerolights Eagle 215B Seaplane 25. 5.84 P.J.Scott (Seaview, IoW) 21.11.96P
(Fuji-Robin EC-25-PS) SGP-1

G-MMTX Mainair Gemini/Sprint 275-1284-2-P.590 25. 3.85 P.C.Askew Tarn Farm, Cockerham 6.11.00P
(Fuji-Robin EC-44-PM) *(Orig fitted wing wing P.577 fitted to G-MMTG)*

G-MMTY Fisher FP202U 2140 28. 9.84 B.E.Maggs *(Stored 4.96: current status unknown)*
Brickhouse Farm, Frogland Cross

G-MMTZ Eurowing Goldwing EW-60 & SWA-7 28. 9.84 R.B.D.Baker (Torquay) 11. 7.02P
(Rotax 447)

G-MMUA* Southdown Puma Sprint SN1221/0007 21.12.84 C.R.Gale (Kirk Michael, IoM) 21. 8.00P
(Fuji-Robin EC-44-PM) *(Cancelled 19.4.00 by CAA) (Stored 2001)*

G-MMUH Mainair Tri-Flyer/Sprint 8.11.84 J.P.Nicklin (Hayling Island) 16. 8.02P
(Fuji-Robin EC-44-PM) 270-1084-2-P.579

G-MMUK Ultrasports Tripacer II/Solar Wings Typhoon S4 15.10.84 K.T.Scholz Little Down Farm, Milson 18. 9.99P
(Rotax 447) BRK-01 & T782-532

G-MMUM MBA Tiger Cub 440 SO.019 8. 3.83 Coulson Flying Services Ltd (Skegness)
(Fuji-Robin EC-44) *(Current status unknown)*

G-MMUO Mainair Gemini/Flash 272-1084-2 & W08 29.10.84 B.D.Bastin & D.R.Howells Long Marston 13.10.02P
(Fuji-Robin EC-44-PM)

G-MMUR Hiway Skytrike II/Solar Wings Storm 28.12.84 R.J.Ripley (Oakley, Beds)
(Fuji-Robin EC-25) SLI.80180 *(Stored owner's house 1998)*

G-MMUT Mainair Gemini/Flash II 62-884-2 & W04 5.10.84 S.C.Briggs East Fortune 5. 7.01P
(Fuji-Robin EC-44-PM) *(Fitted 6.98 with Trike c/n 235-484-2-W04 first used on G-MMFC(3))*

G-MMUV Southdown Puma Sprint SN1121/0010 7.11.84 D.C.Read (Ledbury) 2.11.89P
(Fuji-Robin EC-44-PM)

G-MMUW Mainair Gemini/Flash II 17. 1.85 J.C.K.Scardifield (Lymington) 23. 3.87P
(Fuji-Robin EC-44-PM) 60-784-2 & W13
(Mainair Trike c/n 260 built as 440 Gemini with Sprint sailwing and regd G-MMSC. This sailwing sold and used on a Puma in 1985. Trike fitted with a Flash 1 sailwing and complete unit sold to Portugal in 1987)

G-MMVA Southdown Puma Sprint SN1121/0011 & P.588 7.11.84 C.H.Tomkins (Kettering) 26. 3.92P
(Fuji-Robin EC-44-PM)

G-MMVC Solar Wings Panther XL-S T684-1106XL 13.11.84 E.R.Holton (Lichfield) 18. 1.90P
(Fuji-Robin EC-44-PM)

G-MMVH Southdown Raven X SN2122/0015 10. 1.85 G.W. & K.M.Carwardine (Isle of Grain) 29. 4.01P
(Rotax 447)

G-MMVI Southdown Puma Sprint SN1121/0012 28.11.84 G.R.Williams (Haverfordwest) 2.11.97P
(Fuji-Robin EC-44-PM)

G-MMVO Southdown Puma Sprint SN1232/0017 20. 3.85 D.M.Pearson Chilton Park, Wallingford 28. 7.01P
(Rotax 447)

G-MMVP Mainair Gemini/Flash II 17.12.84 S.C.McGowan (Rufforth) 9.12.00P
(Fuji-Robin EC-44-PM) 76-1284-2 & W12

G-MMVS Skyhook Pixie/Zeus TR1/52 28. 2.85 B.W.Olley (Ely) 18.11.91E
(Solo 210)

G-MMVX Southdown Puma Sprint 41183 & P.452 29.11.83 M.P.Jones Haverfordwest 5. 4.02P
(Fuji-Robin EC-44-PM)
(Original Trike c/n quoted is corruption of Mainair 440 Tri-Flyer c/n 214-41183. Re-configured as a podded trike to become a Gemini. However, this was re-fitted to G-MJZU: current trike believed, therefore, to be a Southdown)

G-MMVZ Southdown Puma Sprint SN1121/0016 15. 1.85 M.J.Devane (Killarney, Co.Kerry) 2. 8.02P
(Fuji-Robin EC-44-PM)

G-MMWA Mainair Gemini/Flash II 22.11.84 D.Muir (Lancaster) 23. 7.02P
(Fuji-Robin EC-44-PM) 271-1184-1-W07

G-MMWC Eipper Quicksilver MXII 1041 22.10.84 T.J.Gayton-Polley (Billingshurst) 10. 6.02P
(Rotax 503)

G-MMWG P Greenslade trike/Flexiform Solo Striker 17.12.84 C.R.Green (Redruth) 26. 6.99P
(Rotax 377) FF/LAI/83/JDR/11 *(Trike originally fitted to G-MJGN: wing no. duplicates G-MMFC)*

G-MMWI	Southdown Puma/Lightning 190 (Fuji-Robin EC-34-PM) CAC-01	3. 1.85	A.W.Cove	(Wellingborough)	5. 9.93E
G-MMWL	Eurowing Goldwing SWA-09 & EW-91 (Rotax 447)	9. 4.85	P.J.Brookman	Knapthorpe Lodge, Caunton	14. 5.02P
G-MMWN	Mainair Tri-Flyer/Flexiform Striker (Rotax 377) 1283.NH *(Orig. fitted with Ultrasports Tripacer trike)*	21.11.84	D.H.George	(Sandown)	30. 3.97P
G-MMWS	Ultrasports Tripacer/Flexiform Solo Striker (Rotax 377) 983.SH *(Orig. fitted with Mainair trike)* *(Orig owners of G-MMWN & 'MMWS were Nigel & Sally Huxtable & believed the trikes were inter-changed)*	21.11.84	P.H.Risdale	Tower Farm, Woolaston	31. 5.02P
G-MMWT	CFM Shadow C B.009 (Rotax 503)	27. 3.85	J.A.C.du Plessis	(Brackley)	28. 6.02P
G-MMWX	Southdown Puma Sprint SN1121/0047 (Fuji-Robin EC-44-PM)	10. 4.85	D.M.Burgess	(Lockerbie)	10. 4.02P
G-MMXC	Mainair Gemini/Flash (Fuji-Robin EC-44-PM) 279-1284-2 & W17 *(Trike reported as c/n 292 9.96 - see G-MMXL) (Cancelled by CAA 26.4.00)*	28.12.84	M.P.Birks	St.Michaels	9. 6.94P
G-MMXD	Mainair Gemini/Flash II (Rotax 447) 282-185-3 & W20	28.12.84	W A Bibby	(Wirral)	14.10.01P
G-MMXG	Mainair Gemini/Flash II (Fuji-Robin EC-44-PM) 288-485-1 & W32 *(Damaged c6.00 - trike used to rebuilt G-MNBD & rest to store)*	17. 1.85	T.Birch	(Wolverhampton)	15. 6.01P
G-MMXJ	Mainair Gemini/Flash II (Rotax 447) 289-185-3 & W22	17. 1.85	R.Meredith-Hardy	Radwell, Letchworth	6. 8.96P
G-MMXK	Mainair Gemini/Flash II (Fuji-Robin EC-44-PM) 274-485-2 & W35	17. 1.85	G.K.Thornton	Higher Barn Farm, Houghton	12. 6.00P
G-MMXL	Mainair Gemini/Flash II (Fuji-Robin EC-44-PM) 292-385-3 & W36	17. 1.85	J.M.Marshall	(Urmston)	16. 5.97P
G-MMXN	Southdown Puma Sprint SN1121/0021 (Fuji-Robin EC-44-PM)	24. 1.85	N.Green	(Shrewsbury)	31. 7.00P
G-MMXO	Southdown Puma Sprint SN1121/0018 (Fuji-Robin EC-44-PM)	23. 1.85	D.J.Tasker	Swinford, Rugby	27.12.01P
G-MMXT*	Mainair Gemini/Flash 302-485-3 & W41 (Fuji-Robin EC-44-PM)	29. 1.85	L.R.Orriss *(Cancelled 5.12.01 by CAA)*	(Rotherham)	16. 4.00P
G-MMXU	Mainair Gemini/Flash II (Fuji-Robin EC-44-PM) 254-784-2 & W21	29. 1.85	T.J.Franklin	Graveley Farm, Herts	14. 7.01P
G-MMXV	Mainair Gemini/Flash II (Fuji-Robin EC-44-PM) 298-385-3 & W37	29. 1.85	A.Bishop	Ince Blundell	17. 3.02P
G-MMXW	Mainair Gemini/Sprint 286-185-3-P.597 (Fuji-Robin EC-44-PM)	23. 1.85	A.Hodgson	(Milton Keynes)	4. 6.02P
G-MMYA	Solar Wings Pegasus XL-R/Se (Rotax 447) XL-P Proto & T784-1151XL	30. 1.85	M.Harris	Redlands, Swindon	17. 5.02P
G-MMYF	Southdown Puma Sprint SN1121/0026 (Fuji-Robin EC-44-PM)	28. 3.85	E.Smith	Swinford, Rugby	12. 6.02P
G-MMYI	Southdown Puma Sprint SN1121/0036 (Fuji-Robin EC-44-PM)	6. 3.85	D.J.Brixton tr Shropshire Tow Group	Bishops Castle, Shropshire	20. 5.02P
G-MMYL	Cyclone 70/Aerial Arts 130SX CH.01 (Rotax 277)	8. 3.85	A.G.Smith & J.T.Halford	Holt, Norfolk	17. 1.02P
G-MMYN	Solar Wings Panther XL-R T784-1158XL (Rotax 447)	27. 2.85	B.& D.Bergin	(Athenry, Co.Galway)	16. 4.00P
G-MMYO	Southdown Puma Sprint SN1121/0037 (Fuji-Robin EC-44-PM) *(Fitted with new rainbow Medway sailwing c3.96 after accident 20.9.95)*	11. 4.85	P.R.Whitehouse	Otherton, Cannock	29. 8.00P
G-MMYR	Eipper Quicksilver MXII 3345 (Rotax 503)	27. 2.85	P.A.Pilkington	North Coates	17. 6.01P
G-MMYT	Southdown Puma Sprint (Fuji-Robin EC-44-PM) SN1121/0046 & T569/P621	15. 4.85	J.K.Divall	(Chichester)	25. 3.94P
G-MMYU	Southdown Puma Sprint SN1231/0045 (Rotax 447)	11. 6.85	P.W.Davidson & A.I.McPherson	Glenrothes	21. 4.02P
G-MMYV	John Webb trike/Flexiform Striker (Rotax 277) JW-2	22. 3.85	S.B.Herbert	(Presteigne)	20.12.95P
G-MMYY	Southdown Puma Sprint SN1231/0042 (Rotax 447)	18. 7.85	P.A.Tarplee	(Oldbury)	29. 4.02P
G-MMYZ*	Southdown Puma Sprint SN1231/0034 (Rotax 447) *(Damaged in gales Roddidge 1.98: trike, less sailwing, stored 10.00: cancelled 31.5.01 by CAA)*	28. 2.85	M.Bodill	Roddige, Fradley	19. 2.99P
G-MMZA	Mainair Gemini/Flash II (Fuji-Robin EC-44-PM) 266-984-3 & W60	4. 3.85	G.T.Johnston	(Craigavon, Co Armagh)	30. 6.00P
G-MMZB	Mainair Gemini/Flash 319-685-3 & W58 (Fuji-Robin EC-44-PM)	4. 3.85	M.A.Nolan	(Great Orton)	23. 5.02P
G-MMZE	Mainair Gemini/Flash 300-485-3 & W39 (Fuji-Robin EC-44-PM)	4. 3.85	I.P.Stubbins *(Badly damaged c7.00)*	Sandtoft	5. 4.01P
G-MMZF	Mainair Gemini/Flash II (Fuji-Robin EC-44-PM) 299-485-3 & W38	4. 3.85	A.R.Rhodes *(Flies from Kirkbride)*	(Annan)	13. 9.02P
G-MMZG	Solar Wings Panther XL-S (Fuji-Robin EC-44-PM) SW-TA-1008 & SW-WA-1022	12. 8.85	P.A.Jones	North Coates	2. 3.02P
G-MMZI	Medway Half Pint Srs.1/Aerial Arts 130SX (JPX PUL425) 2385/1 & 130SX-057	6. 3.85	J.Messenger	(Workington)	28. 3.93E

G-MMZJ	Mainair Gemini/Flash 312-585-3 & W51		18. 3.85	P.J.Glover	North Coates	22.12.01P
	(Rotax 462)					
G-MMZK	Mainair Gemini/Flash 326-785-3 & W53		18. 3.85	G.Jones & B.Lee	(Warrington)	3.11.99P
	(Fuji-Robin EC-44-PM) *(Trike ex G-MMEZ: originally regd with trike c/n 314-585-3: to G-MMIR)*					
G-MMZM	Mainair Gemini/Flash 304-585-3 & W44		18. 3.85	A.J.Hinks	(South Queensferry)	27.11.02P
	(Fuji-Robin EC-44-PM)					
G-MMZN	Mainair Gemini/Flash II		18. 3.85	W.K.Dalus	(Keyworth)	28. 9.93P
	(Fuji-Robin EC-44-PM) 283-185-3 & W23					
G-MMZP	Solar Wings Panther XL HP-01		14. 3.85	B.Richardson	(Sunderland)	12. 1.94P
	(Fuji-Robin EC-44-PM) *(Built H Phipps) (Possibly orig trike from G-MJWZ)*					
G-MMZR	Southdown Puma Sprint		4. 7.85	J.E.Hicks	Dunkeswell	6.12.93P
	(Fuji-Robin EC-44-PM) SN1121/0039 & T560/P622			t/a International Animal Rescue		
G-MMZV	Mainair Gemini/Flash 313-585-3 & W52		18. 4.85	P.R.M.Spengler	(Bracknell)	12. 5.02P
	(Rotax 447)					
G-MMZW	Southdown Puma Sprint		28. 3.85	M.G.Ashbee	(Cranbrook)	30. 9.00P
	(Fuji-Robin EC-44-PM) SN1121/0043 & T566/P620			*(Damaged c.8.00)*		
G-MMZX	Southdown Puma Sprint SN1231/0051		17. 4.85	J.V.Rozentals	(Sutton-in-Ashfield)	10. 4.95P
	(Rotax 447)					
G-MNAC	Mainair Gemini/Flash 335-885-3 & W72		18. 4.85.	L R Merrison	(Chard)	30. 7.02P
	(Rotax 503)					
G-MNAE	Mainair Gemini/Flash 343-885-3 & W77		18. 4.85	G.C.Luddington	(Bletsoe)	29. 7.00P
	(Rotax 447)					
G-MNAF	Solar Wings Pegasus XL-S		24. 4.85	G.Guy	(Telford)	28. 8.99P
	(Fuji-Robin EC-44-PM) SW-WA-1001 & SW-TA-1001					
G-MNAH	Solar Wings Panther XL-S		24. 4.85	J.H.Button & G.A.Harman	(Sandy)	18. 9.99P
	(Fuji-Robin EC-44-PM) SW-TA-1002 & SW-WA-1002					
G-MNAI	Solar Wings Panther XL-S		15. 5.85	R.G.Cameron	Muirhouses Farm, Errol	23. 6.98P
	(Fuji-Robin EC-44-PM) SW-TA-1003 SW-WA-1003					
G-MNAJ	Solar Wings Panther XL-S		17. 5.85	C.Lonsdale	Morgansfield, Fishburn	26. 1.02P
	(Fuji-Robin EC-44-PM) SW-TA-1004 & SW-WA-1004					
G-MNAK	Solar Wings Panther XL-S		15. 5.85	F.J.McVey	Insch	5. 5.02P
	(Fuji-Robin EC-44-PM) SW-TA-1005 & SW-WA-1005					
G-MNAO	Solar Wings Pegasus XL-R		2. 6.85	R.H.Cooke	(Southampton)	28. 8.00P
	(Rotax 447) SW-TB-0002 & SW-WA-1008			*(Damaged c11.00 @ Colemore Common)*		
G-MNAR	Solar Wings Pegasus XL-R		6. 8.85	B.Chantry	Plaistows Farm, St Albans	1. 3.02P
	(Rotax 447) SW-TB-0014 & SW-WA-1011					
G-MNAV	Southdown Puma Sprint SN1121/0033		28. 2.85	A.C.Shields	(Douglas, IoM)	16. 2.02P
	(Fuji-Robin EC-44-PM)					
G-MNAW	Solar Wings Pegasus XL-R		16. 8.85	D.J.Harber	(Henley-on-Thames)	3. 6.02P
	(Rotax 447) SW-TB-1010 & SW-WA-1014					
G-MNAX	Solar Wings Pegasus XL-R		16. 8.85	B.J.Phillips	(Newbury)	21. 7.96P
	(Rotax 447) SW-TB-1011 & SW-WA-1015					
G-MNAY	Solar Wings Pegasus XL-R		6. 8.85	S.J.Honeybourne	(Lowdham)	11. 9.99P
	(Rotax 447) SW-TB-1015 & SW-WA-1016					
G-MNAZ	Solar Wings Pegasus XL-R		6. 8.85	R.W.Houldsworth	(Rochford)	28. 8.01P
	(Rotax 447) SW-TB-1016 & SW-WA-1017					
G-MNBA	Solar Wings Pegasus XL-R		6. 9.85	K.D.Baldwin	Graveley Farm, Herts	20. 6.02P
	(Rotax 447) SW-TB-1024 & SW-WA-1018			*"Tigerfish"*		
G-MNBB	Solar Wings Pegasus XL-R		20. 9.85	M.Sims	(Brynmawr, Gwent)	1. 7.00P
	(Rotax 447) SW-TB-1020 & SW-WA-1019					
G-MNBC	Solar Wings Pegasus XL-R		11.10.85	I.Gordon	(Fleckney)	9. 9.02P
	(Rotax 447) SW-TB-1026 & SW-WA-1020					
G-MNBD	Mainair Gemini/Flash 162-683 & W42	G-MMSN	6. 1.86	P.Woodcock	Sittles Farm, Alrewas	2. 7.02P
	(Fuji-Robin EC-44-PM)					
	(Originally built as Mainair 440 Tri-Flyer c/n 341-585-3 & W42. Unsold &.reworked by Mainair as c/n 162-683 & fitted to G-MMSN. Later podded to become a Gemini &.used in the rebuild of G-MNBD after late 1996 accident)					
G-MNBE	Southdown Puma Sprint SN1121/0050		17. 5.85	J.Liversuch & C.Hershaw	(Almondbury)	5. 1.02P
	(Rotax 447)					
G-MNBF	Mainair Gemini/Flash 306-585-3 & W46		2. 5.85	H.G.Denton	Knapthorpe Lodge, Caunton	5. 5.01P
	(Fuji-Robin EC-44-PM)					
G-MNBG	Mainair Gemini/Flash 347-585-3 & W66		9. 5.85	T.Barnett	(Redcar)	28. 8.02P
	(Rotax 447)					
G-MNBI	Solar Wings Panther XL-S	G-MMVF?	3. 5.85	G.R.Cox	(Northampton)	29. 4.97P
	(Fuji-Robin EC-44-PM) PXL884-178 & T884-1161XL *(G-MNVF never permitted before cancellation in 1990)*					
G-MNBM	Southdown Puma Sprint SN1231/0058		25. 6.85	D.A.Hopewell	(Newcastle, Staffs)	7.10.01P
	(Rotax 447)					
G-MNBN	Mainair Gemini/Flash 303-485-3 & W43		11. 6.85	D.G.Knibbs	Long Marston	18. 5.02P
	(Fuji-Robin EC-44-PM)					
G-MNBP	Mainair Gemini/Flash 338-885-3 & W75		15. 5.85	A.S.Christodoulou & P.B.Watson		
	(Fuji-Robin EC-44-PM)				(Waltham Abbey)	30. 3.02P
G-MNBR*	Mainair Gemini/Flash 345-985-3 & W79		15. 5.85	N.A.P.Gregory	Long Marston	5. 2.94P
	(Rotax 447)			*(Cancelled 31.5.00 by CAA: stored 10.00)*		
G-MNBS	Mainair Gemini/Flash 308-585-3 & W48		15. 5.85	P.A.Comins	(Nottingham)	20. 6.94P
	(Fuji-Robin EC-44-PM)					

G-MNBT	Mainair Gemini/Flash 322-685-3 & W62 (Rotax 503)	15. 5.85	P.Brown	St.Michaels	6. 3.02P
G-MNBV	Mainair Gemini/Flash 333-685-3 & W70 (Rotax 447)	15. 5.85	J.Walshe	(Newtownards, Co.of Down)	17. 8.02P
G-MNBW	Mainair Gemini/Flash 332-685-3 & W69 (Rotax 447) *(C/n now SW-WF-0005 & W95 ex G-MNJI)*	15. 5.85	G.A.Brown & N.S.Brotherton	Weston Zoyland	25. 6.01P
G-MNCA	Hunt Avon/Hiway Demon 175 DA-01 (Fuji-Robin EC-34?)	28. 5.85	C.Kett	(Bridgwater)	26. 3.94E
G-MNCF	Mainair Gemini/Flash 321-685-3 & W61 (Rotax 447)	3. 6.85	D.J.Puxley	Stoke, Kent	2. 6.01P
G-MNCG	Mainair Gemini/Flash 320-685-3 & W59 (Rotax 503) *(Rebuilt c2000)*	3. 6.85	J E F Fletcher	Tarn Farm, Cockerham	24. 8.02P
G-MNCI	Southdown Puma Sprint SN1231/0059 (Rotax 447)	7. 6.85	R.M.Wait	(Stourbridge)	4. 3.02P
G-MNCJ	Mainair Gemini/Flash 351-785-3 & W83 (Fuji-Robin EC-44) *(Orig trike stolen & new one c/n 282-1284-2 ex G-MMXF fitted c.12.89)*	3. 6.85	R.S.McLeister	(Crington)	16.11.93P
G-MNCM	CFM Shadow C 006 (Rotax 503)	31. 5.85	K.G.D.Macrae	Drummiard Farm, Bonnybank	23. 5.02P
G-MNCO	Eipper Quicksilver MX II 1045	3. 6.85	S.Lawton	(Colne)	
G-MNCP	Southdown Puma Sprint SN1231/0071 (Rotax 447)	24. 6.85	R.A.Willetts & W.Atkinson	Long Marston	10. 4.00P
G-MNCS	Skyrider Airsports Phantom PH.00098 (Fuji-Robin EC-44-PM)	2. 1.86	C.G.Johns	(Bewdley, Worcs)	25. 5.02P
G-MNCU	Medway Hybred/Solar Wings Typhoon 44XL 26485/10 & SW-WA-1029	13. 6.85	A.Thornley	(Louth)	1. 5.02P
G-MNCV	Medway Hybred/Solar Wings Typhoon 44XL (Fuji-Robin EC-44-PM) 26485/11 & SW-WA-1030 *(Pegasus XL-R wing)*	13. 6.85	P.D.Mickleburgh	Swinford, Rugby	19.10.02P
G-MNDD	Mainair Scorcher 358-885-1 & W85 (Rotax 447)	12. 6.85	J.M.M.Bowles	Ince Blundell	24. 1.02P
G-MNDE	Medway Half Pint/Aerial Arts 130SX (JPL PUL425) 3/8685 *(Wing ex G-MNBZ)*	19. 6.85	C.D.Wills	(Andover)	7. 4.00P
G-MNDF	Mainair Gemini/Flash 327-785-3 & W67 (Rotax 447)	25. 6.85	M.Ellis	Sandtoft	6. 6.02P
G-MNDG	Southdown Puma Sprint SN1121/0057 (Fuji-Robin EC-44-PM)	18. 7.85	P.J.Kirwan	(Geashill, Co.Offaly)	14. 6.99P
G-MNDO	Solar Wings Pegasus/Flash SW-WF-0001 (Rotax 447) *(Trike is c/n SW-TB-1012 & Mainair sailwing c/n W86)*	2. 7.85	R.H.Cooke	(Southampton)	21. 7.02P
G-MNDU	Midland Ultralights Sirocco 377GB (Rotax 377) MU-011	22. 7.85	M.A.Collins	(St. Neots)	18. 8.01P
G-MNDV	Midland Ultralights Sirocco 377GB (Rotax 377) MU-012	1. 4.86	L.J.Dutch *(Stored 5.93 following suspension)*	(Wigan)	13. 7.92P
G-MNDW	Midland Ultralights Sirocco 377GB (Rotax 377) MU-014	30. 7.85	L.G.Horne	(Ashford)	24. 4.01P
G-MNDY	Southdown Puma Sprint DY-01 & P.536 (Fuji-Robin EC-44-PM) *(Trike rebuilt c4.99)*	2. 5.84	A.M.Marshall	(Oswestry)	25..5.02P
G-MNDZ*	Southdown Puma Sprint SN1121/0062 (Rotax 447) *(Fitted with trike from G-MNCK)*	28. 6.85	Wendy A.Guest *(Cancelled 5.7.01 by CAA)*	(Bridgnorth)	6. 1.01P
G-MNEF	Mainair Gemini/Flash 344-885-3 & W78 (Rotax 447)	8. 7.85	J.P.Faver	East Fortune	19.12.98P
G-MNEG	Mainair Gemini/Flash 360-885-3 & W92 (Rotax 447)	8. 7.85	T.McDowell	(Kells, Co.Meath)	18.10.99P
G-MNEH	Mainair Gemini/Flash 361-885-3 & W90 (Rotax 503)	8. 7.85	I.Rawson	St.Michaels	14. 7.02P
G-MNEI	Medway Hybred/Solar Wings Typhoon/XL-R (Fuji-Robin EC-44-PM) 8785/12 & SW-WA-1035	9. 7.85	L.G.Thompson *(Damaged 28.11.92 & stored 8.96: current status unknown)*	Long Marston	26. 7.93P
G-MNEK	Medway Half Pint/Aerial Arts 130SX (JPX PUL425) 4/8785	12. 7.85	M.I.Dougall *(Damaged Stoke 6.7.93: current status unknown)*	(Maidstone)	25. 9.94P
G-MNER	CFM Shadow CD 008 (Rotax 462)	15. 7.85	F.C.Claydon	Wickham Brook, Newmarket	6. 3.02P
G-MNET	Mainair Gemini/Flash 349-885-3 & W81 (Fuji-Robin EC-44-PM)	23. 7.85	I P Stubbins	North Coates	13. 7.02P
G-MNEV	Mainair Gemini/Flash (Rotax 447) 362-1085-3 & W108	23. 7.85	C.A.Denver	St.Michaels	27. 3.02P
G-MNEY	Mainair Gemini/Flash (Rotax 447) 365-1085-3 & W94	23. 7.85	D.A.Spiers	East Fortune	4. 8.02P
G-MNFB	Southdown Puma Sprint SN1231/0077 (Rotax 447)	22. 7.85	C.Lawrence	(Tiverton)	17. 7.00P
G-MNFE	Mainair Gemini/Flash 350-885-3 & W82 (Fuji-Robin EC-44-PM)	29. 7.85	D.R.Kennedy	East Fortune	20.10.01P
G-MNFF	Mainair Gemini/Flash (Rotax 447) 371-1185-3 & W110	29. 7.85	R.P.Cook & C.H.Spencer	St Michaels	24. 5.02P
G-MNFG	Southdown Puma Sprint SN1231/0078 (Rotax 447)	31. 7.85	A.C.Hing	Long Acre Farm, Sandy	12. 6.02P

G-MNFH	Mainair Gemini/Flash (Rotax 447) 364-1085-3 & W93	6. 8.85	K.Glynn	(Loughrea, Co.Galway)	30. 6.95P
G-MNFL	AMF Microflight Chevvron 2-32A (Konig SD570) CH.002	19. 8.85	P.W.Wright *(Noted 6.01)*	Saltby	13.12.00P
G-MNFM	Mainair Gemini/Flash (Rotax 447) 366-1085-3 & W98	10.10.85	P.M.Fidell	Wombleton	11. 3.02P
G-MNFN	Mainair Gemini/Flash (Rotax 447) 367-1085-3 & W99	6.11.85	J.R.Martin	(Bedale)	30. 4.94P
G-MNFP	Mainair Gemini/Flash (Rotax 447) 368-1085-3 & W100	23.10.85	S.Farnsworth & P.Howarth	(Clitheroe)	22. 5.02P
G-MNFW	Medway Hybred 44XL 10885/13 (Fuji-Robin EC-44-PM)	15. 8.85	A.T.Palmer	(Plymouth)	15. 8.99P
G-MNFX	Southdown Puma Sprint SN1231/0079 (Rotax 447)	14. 8.85	A.M.Shaw	(Stoke-on-Trent)	2. 9.02P
G-MNGD	Ultrasports Tripacer/Solar Wings Medium Typhoon (Fuji-Robin EC-34-PM) 012 & T681-171	13. 8.85	F.H.Cook	(Whitchurch)	3. 9.00P
G-MNGF	Solar Wings Pegasus/Flash (Rotax 447) W-TB-1022 & SW-WF-0003 *(Correct trike c/n is SW-TB-1022 plus Mainair sailwing c/n W87)*	21. 8.85	S.B.Williams	Headcorn	19. 6.02P
G-MNGG	Solar Wings Pegasus XL-R T784-1159XL (Rotax 447) (Trike c/n is US.TPR.0002)	21. 8.85	T.Peckham	(Faversham)	13. 5.02P
G-MNGH	Skyhook TR1 Pixie/Zeus TR1/61	24. 9.85	A.R.Smith	(Chelmsford)	
G-MNGK	Mainair Gemini/Flash (Rotax 447) 374-1085-3 & W112	5. 9.85	R.Paton	Old Sarum	15. 8.02P
G-MNGL	Mainair Gemini/Flash (Rotax 447) 376-1085-3 & W114	5. 9.85	G.Cusden	Davidstow Moor	15.11.02P
G-MNGM	Mainair Gemini/Flash (Rotax 447) 394-1285-3 & W109	5. 9.85	J.E.Caffull & D.R.Beale	Over Farm, Gloucester	10. 6.02P
	(Originally supplied with Mainair trike c/n 377. However, this & sailwing from G-MNIO, was stolen from Popham overnight 15/16.3.86. Consequently, the trike of G-MNIO was fitted with the sailwing of G-MNGM)				
G-MNGN	Mainair Gemini/Flash (Rotax 447) 378-1185-3 & W115	5. 9.85	T.B.Margetts	(Poole)	17. 6.99P
G-MNGS	Southdown Puma/Lightning 195 (Fuji-Robin EC-34-PM) GJS-02 *(Tripacer Trike from G-MJRF)*	8. 5.84	G.J.Sargent	(Weston Colville)	14. 8.02P
G-MNGT	Mainair Gemini/Flash (Rotax 447) 372-1085-3 & W106	30. 9.85	J.W.Biegus	Arclid Green, Sandbach	11. 3.01P
G-MNGU	Mainair Gemini/Flash (Rotax 503) 373-1085-3 & W111	30. 9.85	J.A.Ellis	(Dagenham)	4. 6.02P
G-MNGW	Mainair Gemini/Flash (Rotax 447) 386-1185-3 & W121	30. 9.85	D.G.Baker	Colemore Common, Hants	6.11.01P
G-MNGX	Southdown Puma Sprint SN1231/0088 (Rotax 447)	26. 9.85	R.J.Morris	(Ely)	19. 5.02P
G-MNHB	Solar Wings Pegasus XL-R/Se (Rotax 447) SW-TB-1031 & SW-WA-1045	1.11.85	P.J.Soukup	(Winkleigh)	3. 3.02P
G-MNHC	Solar Wings Pegasus XL-R (Rotax 447) SW-TB-1032 & SW-WA-1046/2	31.10.85	C.Thomas	Haverfordwest	12. 3.02P
	(Original sailwing [SW-WA-1046] damaged so planned rebuild as 'SW-WA-1058' for G-MNHO never came to fruition: replaced by SW-WA-1065, probably so marked on the sailwing, but re-numbered as SW-WA-1046/2)				
G-MNHD	Solar Wings Pegasus XL-R (Rotax 447) SW-TB-1033 & SW-WA-1047	5.11.85	P.D.Stiles	(Ashley Down, Bristol)	22. 6.02P
G-MNHE	Solar Wings Pegasus XL-R (Rotax 447) SW-TB-1036 & SW-WA-1048	11.12.85	J.R.Austin *(Noted 11.01)*	Davidstow Moor	2. 8.00P
G-MNHH	Solar Wings Pegasus XL-S SW-WA-1051 (Fuji-Robin EC-44-PM) *(Trike is an Ultrasports unit c/n PXL847-170)*	22. 1.86	F.J.Williams	(Shefford, Beds)	24. 6.01P
G-MNHI	Solar Wings Pegasus XL-R (Rotax 447) SW-TB-1042 & SW-WA-1052	8. 1.86	I.D.R.Hyde	Enstone	13. 7.95P
G-MNHJ	Solar Wings Pegasus XL-R (Rotax 447) SW-TB-1056 & SW-WA-1053	11. 3.86	S.J.Woodd	(Oxford)	26. 6.93P
G-MNHK	Solar Wings Pegasus XL-R (Rotax 462) SW-TE-0005 & SW-WA-1054	9. 7.86	R.D.Proctor	(Stamford)	13. 6.92P
G-MNHL	Solar Wings Pegasus XL-R (Rotax 447) SW-TB-1077 & SW-WA-1055	9. 7.86	S B Walters	(Sidcup)	14. 5.02P
G-MNHM	Solar Wings Pegasus XL-R (Rotax 447) SW-TB-1078 & SW-WA-1056	11. 7.86	J.Ellis	Baxby Manor, Husthwaite	28. 8.02P
G-MNHN	Solar Wings Pegasus XL-R (Rotax 447) SW-TB-1079 & SW-WA-1057	11. 8.86	J.L.Baker	Deenethorpe	27. 1.02P
G-MNHR	Solar Wings Pegasus XL-R (Rotax 447) SW-TB-1081 & SW-WA-1060	7. 8.86	B.D.Jackson	(Wincanton)	11.11.00P
G-MNHS	Solar Wings Pegasus XL-R (Rotax 447) SW-TB-1082 & SW-WA-1061	21. 8.86	M.Vearncombe	Weston Zoyland	12.10.02P
G-MNHT	Solar Wings Pegasus XL-R (Rotax 447) SW-TB-1084 & SW-WA-1062	4. 8.86	J.W.Coventry	Davidstow Moor	3.11.02P
G-MNHU*	Solar Wings Pegasus XL-R (Rotax 447) SW-TB-1085 & SW-WA-1063	4. 8.86	B.A.Wright & D.Lyon *(Cancelled 11.6.01 by CAA)*	Dunkeswell	16. 1.99P

G-MNHV	Solar Wings Pegasus XL-R (Rotax 447) SW-TB-1095 & SW-WA-1064		18. 8.86	E.Jenkins	(Crymych, Dyfed)	31. 7.99P
G-MNHZ	Mainair Gemini/Flash (Fuji-Robin EC-44-PM) 310-585-3 & W118		15.10.85	I.O.S.Ross	(Cowie)	26. 8.01P
G-MNIA	Mainair Gemini/Flash (Rotax 447) 370-1185-3 & W105		10.10.85	A.E.Dix *(Noted wrecked Long Marston 1990)*	(Bromsgrove)	10. 4.89P
G-MNIE	Mainair Gemini/Flash (Rotax 447) 388-1185-3 & W123		21.11.85	G.M.Hewer	(Cheltenham)	8. 7.02P
G-MNIF	Mainair Gemini/Flash (Rotax 447) 403-286-4 & W147		7. 1.86	K.Medd *(Stored 1.02)*	(Rochdale)	26. 7.02P
G-MNIG	Mainair Gemini/Flash (Rotax 447) 391-1285-3 & W129		9. 1.86	I.S.Everett	(Astwood)	22. 5.02P
G-MNIH	Mainair Gemini/Flash (Rotax 447) 379-1185-3 & W116		10.12.85	A.R.Richardson	(Barnsley)	8. 1.02P
G-MNII	Mainair Gemini/Flash (Rotax 447) 390-1285-3 & W128		6.11.85	R.F.Finnis *(Trike reported at St.Michaels 9.96: current status unknown)*	(Guildford)	6. 9.91P
G-MNIK	Solar Wings Pegasus Photon (Solo 210) SW-TP-0002 & SW-WP-0002		29.10.85	R.J.Garland	(Bristol)	14. 6.02P
G-MNIL	Southdown Puma Sprint SN1231/0094 (Rotax 447)		4.11.85	P.L.Speakman	(Prescot)	25. 1.02P
G-MNIM	Maxair Hummer PJB-01		29.10.85	K.Wood	(Leicester)	
G-MNIN*	Designability (Jordan) Duet 018 *(Cancelled by CAA 25.9.95: composite airframe being assembled 3.00 from this & G-MMKY qv)*		7.11.85	Not known	Oakley, Beds	
G-MNIP	Mainair Gemini/Flash (Rotax 447) 393-1285-3 & W134		6.11.85	G.S.Bulpitt	Chilbolton	18. 8.00P
G-MNIS	CFM Shadow C 014 (Rotax 503)		11.11.85	R.W.Payne	(Peterborough)	25. 4.92P
G-MNIT	Aerial Arts Alpha Mk.II/130SX (Rotax 277) 130SX-176		27. 2.86	M.J.Edmett	(London N3)	15. 8.99P
G-MNIU	Solar Wings Pegasus Photon (Fuji-Robin EC-34) SW-TP-0003 & SW-WP-0003		27.11.85	K.Roberts *(Damaged & stored 3.90: current status unknown)*	Tarn Farm, Cockerham	17. 1.90E
G-MNIW	Mainair Tri-Flyer/Airwave Nimrod 165 (Fuji-Robin EC-25-PS) 050/19181	EI-BOB	29.11.85	J.A.McIntosh & R.W.Mitchell	(Perth)	4. 9.00P
G-MNIX	Mainair Gemini/Flash (Rotax 447) 395-1285-3 & W136		29.11.85	S.Farnworth	(Kempston, Bedford)	11. 7.98P
G-MNIZ	Mainair Gemini/Flash (Rotax 447) 392-1285-3 & W130		26. 2.86	A.G.Power	(Darwen)	25. 4.02P
G-MNJB	Southdown Raven X SN2232/0098 (Rotax 447)		10.12.85	G.Elwes	Graveley Farm, Herts	25. 7.01P
G-MNJC	MBA Tiger Cub 440 SO.215 (Fuji-Robin EC-44)		8. 6.84	J.G.Carpenter	(Romsey)	20. 9.90E
G-MNJD	Mainair Tri-Flyer 440/Sprint (Fuji-Robin EC-44-PM) 243-10484-2-P.537		2. 4.84	M.E.Smith	(Verwood)	8. 8.00P
G-MNJF	Dragon Srs.150 0068 (Fuji-Robin EC-44-PM)	(OY)9-17	2. 1.86	B.W.Langley	South Wraxall, Wilts	14. 7.02P
G-MNJG	Mainair Gemini Sprint MS (Fuji-Robin EC-44-PM) SA.2030 & 251-684-2-P.593		29. 9.83	P.Batchelor	(Crawley)	19. 7.02P
G-MNJH	Solar Wings Pegasus/Flash (Rotax 447) SW-TB-1023 & SW-WF-0004 *(Mainair sailwing c/n W89)*		22.10.85	C.P.Course	Church Farm, Wellingborough	18. 8.02P
G-MNJJ	Solar Wings Pegasus/Flash (Rotax 447) SW-TB-1029 & SW-WF-0006 *(Mainair sailwing c/n W96)*		22.10.85	P.A.Shelley	Sutton Meadows, Ely	26.11.96P
G-MNJL	Solar Wings Pegasus/Flash (Rotax 447) SW-TB-1028 & SW-WF-0008 *(Mainair sailwing c/n W101)*		21.10.85	S.D.Thomas	(Bilston)	11.11.94P
G-MNJN	Solar Wings Pegasus/Flash (Rotax 447) SW-TB-1034 & SW-WF-0010 *(Mainair sailwing c/n W103)*		19.11.85	D.Thorn	(St. Austell)	7. 7.01P
G-MNJO	Solar Wings Pegasus/Flash (Rotax 447) SW-TB-1035 & SW-WF-0011 *(Mainair sailwing c/n W126)*		19.11.85	S.Clarke	Long Marston	13. 1.02P
G-MNJR	Solar Wings Pegasus/Flash (Rotax 447) SW-TB-1041 & SW-WF-0013 *(Mainair sailwing c/n W133)*		30.12.85	M.G.Ashbee	(Cranbrook)	16.11.00P
G-MNJS	Southdown Puma Sprint SN1231/0085 (Rotax 447)		18. 9.85	J.B.Mayes	(Newmarket)	17. 6.02P
G-MNJT	Southdown Raven X SN2232/0087 (Rotax 447)		20. 9.85	R.C.Hinkins	RAF Henlow	13. 3.02P
G-MNJU	Mainair Gemini/Flash (Rotax 447) 384-1185-3 & W119		20. 9.85	E.J.Wells	Over Farm, Gloucester	3. 6.02P
G-MNJV	Medway Half Pint/Aerial Arts 130SX 8/19985 *(Regd as c/n 9/19985)*		10.10.85	D.J.Lewis	(Cheltenham)	20. 8.92E
G-MNJX	Medway Hybred 44XL 15885/14 (Fuji-Robin EC-44-PM)		9.12.85	H.A.Stewart	(Sittingbourne)	23. 7.98P
G-MNKB	Solar Wings Pegasus/Photon (Solo 210) SW-TP-0005 & SW-WP-0005		14. 1.86	M.E.Gilbert	Drummard Farm, Bonnybank	29. 4.02P
G-MNKC	Solar Wings Pegasus/Photon (Solo 210) SW-TP-0006 & SW-WP-0006		14. 1.86	E.H.Jenkins	(Newcastle upon Tyne)	31. 8.97P

G-MNKD	Solar Wings Pegasus/Photon			14. 1.86	F.Walton	(Bishop Auckland)	28. 8.92P
	(Solo 210)	SW-WP-0007					
	(Originally allocated Trike c/n SW-TP-0007 but believed exported and current Trike is possibly c/n SW-TP-0016)						
G-MNKE	Solar Wings Pegasus/Photon			14. 1.86	M.J.Olsen	(Middlesbrough)	22. 9.01P
	(Solo 210)	SW-TP-0008 & SW-WP-0008					
G-MNKG	Solar Wings Pegasus/Photon			28. 1.86	T.W.Thompson	Eshott	11. 6.95P
	(Solo 210)	SW-TP-0010 & SW-WP-0010			*(Trike stored 9.97: current status unknown)*		
G-MNKI*	Solar Wings Pegasus/Photon		(EI-)	28. 1.86	T.Shivner	Salthill, Galway	24. 3.00P
	(Solo 210)	SW-TP-0012 & SW-WP-0012	G-MNKI		*(Cancelled 22.11.01 by CAA)*		
G-MNKK	Solar Wings Pegasus/Photon			28. 1.86	M.E.Gilbert	(Inverkeithing)	7. 5.95P
	(Fuji-Robin EC-34-PM)	SW-TP-0014 & SW-WP-0014 *(To be fitted with Zanzottera 340cc engine)*					
G-MNKM	MBA Tiger Cub	440 SO.213		30.12.85	R.Barcis	(Skelmersdale)	18. 2.02P
	(Fuji-Robin EC-44-PM)						
G-MNKO	Solar Wings Pegasus XL-Q			2. 1.86	G.Sharp	Eshott	28. 8.01P
	(Rotax 447)	SW-TB-1158 & SW-WX-0001					
G-MNKP	Solar Wings Pegasus/Flash			9. 1.86	C.Hasell	Graveley Farm, Herts	16. 2.02P
	(Rotax 447)	SW-TB-1043 & SW-WF-0014 *(Mainair sailwing c/n W131)*					
G-MNKS	Solar Wings Pegasus/Flash			9. 1.86	W.J.Walker	Drummiard Farm, Bonnybank	18. 4.02P
	(Rotax 447)	SW-TB-1044 & SW-WF-0016 *(Mainair sailwing c/n W132)*					
G-MNKU	Southdown Puma Sprint	SN1231/0100		29. 1.86	S.P.O'Hannrachain	Naas, Co.Kildare	25. 8.02P
	(Rotax 447)						
G-MNKV	Solar Wings Pegasus/Flash			15. 1.86	V.S.Rudham	Dunkeswell	15. 4.02P
	(Rotax 447)	SW-TB-1047 & SW-WF-0017 *(Mainair sailwing c/n W137)*			t/a G-MNKV Group		
G-MNKW	Solar Wings Pegasus/Flash			28. 1.86	S.Rumens	(Etchingham, E.Sussex)	11. 3.96P
	(Rotax 447)	SW-TB-1049 & SW-WF-0018 *(Mainair sailwing c/n W140)*					
G-MNKX	Solar Wings Pegasus/Flash			28. 2.86	P.Samal	(Sandy)	15.12.02P
	(Rotax 447)	SW-TB-1054 & SW-WF-0019 *(Mainair sailwing c/n W139)*					
G-MNKZ	Southdown Raven X	SN2232/0102		4. 2.86	G.B.Gratton	Chilbolton	13. 7.02P
	(Rotax 447)						
G-MNLB	Southdown Raven X	SN2232/0117		11. 4.86	D.A.Chamberlain	Long Marston	10. 6.00P
	(Rotax 447)						
G-MNLE	Southdown Raven X	SN2232/0128		30. 4.86	I.D. & P.G.Cresswell	(Rochester)	6.10.98P
	(Rotax 447)						
G-MNLH	Romain Cobra Biplane	001		23. 1.86	J.W.E.Romain	(Welwyn)	23. 7.02P
	(Midwest AE50R)						
G-MNLI	Mainair Gemini/Flash II			28. 1.86	C.E. & P.M.Fessi	(Bolton)	30. 7.02P
	(Rotax 503)	407-286-4 & W152					
G-MNLK	Southdown Raven X	SN2232/0108		4. 2.86	M.J.Robbins	(Tunbridge Wells)	27. 7.98P
	(Rotax 447)						
G-MNLM	Southdown Raven X	SN2232/0110		6. 2.86	A.P.White	(Exmouth)	9. 6.93P
	(Rotax 447)						
G-MNLN	Southdown Raven X	SN2232/0111		6. 2.86	A.S.Windley	(Matlock)	27.12.00P
	(Rotax 447)						
G-MNLT	Southdown Raven X	SN2232/0115		6. 2.86	J.L.Stachini	Stoke, Kent	12. 8.01P
	(Rotax 447)						
G-MNLU	Southdown Raven X	SN2232/0116		6. 2.86	D.J.Ainsworth	(Preston)	24. 7.00P
	(Rotax 447)						
G-MNLV	Southdown Raven X	SN2232/0118		6. 2.86	J.Murphy	(Tonbridge)	26. 5.02P
G-MNLY	Mainair Gemini/Flash			14. 2.86	A.McGlone	Ince Blundell	23.10.02P
	(Rotax 503)	406-386-4 & W151					
G-MNLZ	Southdown Raven X	SN2232/0123		6. 2.86	E.L.Jenkins	(Bexleyheath)	12. 6.02P
	(Rotax 447)						
G-MNMC	Mainair Gemini/Puma Sprint MS			20. 3.84	J.J.Milliken	(Winchester)	20. 9.96P
	(Fuji-Robin EC-44-PM)	222-284-2-P.524					
G-MNMD	Southdown Raven X	SN2000/0121		10. 2.86	P.G.Overall	(Crawley)	9. 5.02P
	(Rotax 447) *(Originally regd with c/n SN2232/0121)*						
	(SN2000 sailwing c/n prefix indicates sold without Trike which suggests that this may have changed also)						
G-MNMG	Mainair Gemini/Flash II			11. 2.86	N.A.M.Beyer-Kay	(Southport)	20. 8.94P
	(Rotax 447)	419-386-4 & W177					
G-MNMI	Mainair Gemini/Flash II			11. 2.86	A.D.Bales	(Norwich)	2. 8.02P
	(Fuji-Robin EC-44)	317-685-3 & W178 *(Trike & engine ex G-MMZL following accident 8.9.91)*					
G-MNMJ	Mainair Gemini/Flash II			11. 2.86	P.K.Appleton	Weston Zoyland	18. 9.99P
	(BMW R80)	387-1185-3 & W122					
G-MNMK	Solar Wings Pegasus XL-R			19. 8.85	A.F.Smallacombe	(Okehampton)	2. 7.00P
	(Rotax 447)	SW-TB-1021 & SW-WA-1038					
G-MNML	Southdown Puma Sprint	SN1111/0065		4. 8.83	R.C.Carr	(Launceston)	14. 7.97P
	(Fuji-Robin EC-44-PM)						
G-MNMM	Aerotech MW-5(K) Sorcerer	5K-0001-02		11. 2.86	G.R.Horner	(York)	17. 8.99P
	(Rotax 447) *(Orig regd with c/n SR101-R440B-01)*						
G-MNMN	Medway Hybred 44XLR	8286/16		7. 3.86	D.S Blofeld	Stoke, Kent	21. 5.02P
	(Rotax 447)						
G-MNMU	Southdown Puma Raven X	SN2232/0127		17. 2.86	M.J.Curley	(London Colney)	20. 5.01P
	(Fuji-Robin EC-44-PM)						

G-MNMV	Mainair Gemini/Flash (Rotax 447) 375-1085-3 & W113		3. 3.86	B.Light	(Lancaster)	2. 5.02P
G-MNMW	Whittaker MW6-1-1 Merlin (Rotax 582) PFA 164-11144		16. 4.86	E.F.Clapham t/a G-MNMW Flying Group	Otherton, Cannock	23. 7.02P
G-MNMY	Cyclone 70/Aerial Arts 110SX CH-02 (Rotax 277)		6. 3.86	N.R.Beale	(Leamington Spa)	23. 8.02P
G-MNNA	Southdown Raven X SN2232/0129 (Rotax 447)		4. 3.86	D. & G.D.Palfrey	(Tiverton)	20. 7.88P
G-MNNB	Southdown Raven SN2122/0130 (Fuji-Robin EC-44-PM)		4. 3.86	J.F.Horn	(Yelverton)	3. 6.02P
G-MNNC	Southdown Raven X SN2232/0131 (Rotax 447)		4. 3.86	S.A.Sacker	Deenethorpe	5. 8.00P
G-MNNF	Mainair Gemini/Flash II (Rotax 447) 402-286-4 & W148		28. 2.86	W.J.Gunn *(Stored 1.98: current status unknown)*	Long Marston	8. 4.97P
G-MNNG	Squires Lightfly/Solar Wings Photon (Rotax 277) SW-WP-0019 *(Trike may be Mainair Tri-Flyer c/n 032-221181 ex G-MJKY?)*		25. 2.86	C.C.Bilham	Huntingdon	4. 8.02P
G-MNNI	Mainair Gemini/Flash II (Rotax 503) 427-486-4 & W170		28. 2.86	J.C.Miller	(Burntisland)	2. 6.98P
G-MNNJ	Mainair Gemini/Flash II (Rotax 503) 405-286-4 & W150 *(ID Plate mis-marked as G-MNNZ)*		28. 2.86	R.Wilson & B.Skidmore	(Lancaster)	21. 6.02P
G-MNNK	Mainair Gemini/Flash II (Rotax 503) 428-486-4 & W185		28. 2.86	M.P.Shea *(Trike stolen 1.1.93: sailwing stored 10.00)*	Roddidge, Fradley	8. 4.93P
G-MNNL	Mainair Gemini/Flash II (Rotax 503) 429-486-4 & W186		28. 2.86	D.Wilson	(Nottingham)	19. 7.02P
G-MNNM	Mainair Scorcher Solo (Rotax 447) 424-486-1 & W182	(G-MNPE)	20. 3.86	D.A.Whiteside	(Ulverston)	8. 9.91P
G-MNNO	Southdown Raven X SN2232/0133 (Rotax 447)		26. 3.86	M.J.Robbins	(Tunbridge Wells)	16.12.01P
G-MNNP	Mainair Gemini/Flash II (Rotax 462) 409-386-4 & W155		5. 3.86	T.R.E.Brewster	(Brentwood)	28. 8.94P
G-MNNR	Mainair Gemini/Flash II (Rotax 503) 430-586-4 & W188 *(Wing originally quoted as c/n W157)*		6. 3.86	W.A.B.Hill	Davidstow Moor	9. 6.02P
G-MNNS	Eurowing Goldwing EW-74 (Rotax 377)		8. 4.86	J.S.R.Moodie	Rovie Farm, Rogart	
G-MNNV	Mainair Gemini/Flash II (Rotax 503) 431-586-4 & W187		10. 3.86	M.J.Lea	(Wigan)	11. 4.02P
G-MNNY	Solar Wings Pegasus/Flash (Rotax 447) SW-TB-1059 & SW-WF-0023 *(Mainair sailwing c/n W161)*		14. 3.86	S.W.Tallamy	Davidstow Moor	10. 9.02P
G-MNNZ	Solar Wings Pegasus/Flash II (Rotax 447) SW-TB-1060 & SW-WF-0101 *(Mainair sailwing c/n W162)*		24. 4.86	R.D.A.Henderson	(Exeter)	1. 4.98P
G-MNPA	Solar Wings Pegasus/Flash II (Rotax 462) SW-TB-1061 & SW-WF-0102 *(Originally Mainair sailwing c/n W174 but now acquired W210 from G-MNZA)*		18. 4.86	N.T.Murphy *(New owner 9.01)*	(Rathongon, Co.Kildare)	30. 5.98P
G-MNPC	Mainair Gemini/Flash II (Rotax 462) 423-586-4 & W181		17. 3.86	M.S.McGimpsey	Newtownards, Co of Down	29. 7.02P
G-MNPG	Mainair Gemini/Flash II (Rotax 447) 437-686-4 & W204		20. 3.86	P.Kirton	East Fortune	7. 7.02P
G-MNPV	Mainair Scorcher Solo (Rotax 447) 432-586-1 & W189		24. 3.86	D.Slassor *(New owner 7.01)*	(Washington)	17. 5.98P
G-MNPY	Mainair Scorcher Solo (Rotax 447) 452-886-1 & W229		25. 3.86	R.N.O.Kingsbury	(Tunbridge Wells)	31. 7.02P
G-MNPZ	Mainair Scorcher Solo 449-886-1 & W226 (Rotax 503) *(3-Blade Propeller Test a/c)*		25. 3.86	S.Stevens	(North Shields)	4. 9.93P
G-MNRE	Mainair Scorcher Solo (Rotax 447) 453-886-1 & W230		25. 3.86	A.P.Pearce	(Sudbury)	30. 7.97P
G-MNRF	Mainair Scorcher Solo (Rotax 447) 461-986-1 & W238		25. 3.86	Flylight Airsports Ltd	Sywell	3. 3.02P
G-MNRG	Mainair Scorcher Solo (Rotax 4447) 462-986-1 & W239		25. 3.86	C.Murphy	Ince Blundell	1. 8.02P
G-MNRI	Hornet Dual Trainer/Southdown Raven (Rotax 462) HRWA 0051 & SN2000/0119		26. 3.86	D.A.Robinson	Sandtoft	2. 8.02P
G-MNRK	Hornet Dual Trainer/Southdown Raven (Rotax 462?) HRWA 0053 & SN2000/0183		26. 3.86	R.K.Beynon	(Balmedie)	30. 7.95P
G-MNRL*	Hornet Dual Trainer/Southdown Raven (Rotax 462) HRWA 0054 & SN2000/0184		26. 3.86	A.G.Ward *(Cancelled 21.11.01 by CAA)*	Long Acre Farm, Sandy	18. 1.01P
G-MNRM	Hornet Dual Trainer/Southdown Raven (Rotax 462?) HRWA 0055 & SN2000/0214		26. 3.86	R.I.Cannan	(Ramsey, IoM)	26.12.02P
G-MNRP	Southdown Raven X SN2232/0135 (Rotax 447)		7. 4.86	C.Moore	(Egremont)	5. 7.95P
G-MNRS	Southdown Raven X SN2232/0137 (Rotax 447)		7. 4.86	D.Hamilton-Brown	(Pevensey)	12. 5.02P
G-MNRT	Midland Ultralights Sirocco 377GB (Rotax 377) MU-016		1. 4.86	R.F.Hinton	(Mansfield)	18. 8.01P

G-MNRW	Mainair Gemini/Flash II (Rotax 462) 411-486-4 & W156		7. 4.86	L.A.Maynard	Old Sarum	12.10.02P
G-MNRX	Mainair Gemini/Flash II (Rotax 503) 434-686-4 & W220		8. 4.86	J.H.Peet	(Preston)	8. 5.02P
G-MNRY	Mainair Gemini/Flash II (Rotax 462) 418-486-4 & W169		7. 4.86	M.Carolan	(Coalisland, Dungannon)	13. 8.01P
G-MNRZ	Mainair Scorcher Solo (Rotax 447) 426-586-1 & W184		4. 4.86	R Pattrick	Barton	27. 1.02P
G-MNSA	Mainair Gemini/Flash II (Rotax 503) 442-786-4 & W219		18. 4.86	R.E.Morris	(Kidwelly, Dyfed)	7. 8.01P
G-MNSB	Southdown Puma Sprint (Fuji-Robin EC-44-PM) 539 & SN1121/0066		15. 6.83	T.D.Gibson	(Ledbury)	17. 7.00P
G-MNSD	Ultrasports Tripacer 250/Solar Wings Typhoon S4 (Hunting HS.260A) T182-341L		23. 4.86	K.Shatford	(Northampton)	N/E
G-MNSH	Solar Wings Pegasus Flash II (Rotax 447) SW-TB-1063 & SW-WF-0104 *(Mainair sailwing c/n W163)*		14. 4.86	M.J.Aubrey	(Kington, Hereford)	15. 6.01P
G-MNSI	Mainair Gemini/Flash II (Rotax 462) 445-786-4 & W213		9. 4.86	A J Foster	Gravely Farm, Herts	12. 5.02P
G-MNSJ	Mainair Gemini/Flash II (Rotax 503) 443-886-4 & W223		11. 4.86	J.S.Dunlop	Newtownards, Co.of Down	15.12.02P
G-MNSL	Southdown Raven X SN2232/0145 (Rotax 447)		17. 4.86	P.B.Robinson	(Ely)	11. 8.00P
G-MNSN	Solar Wings Pegasus Flash II (Rotax 447) SW-TB-1066 & SW-WF-0105 *(Mainair sailwing c/n W173)*		25. 4.86	F.R. & V.L.Higgins *(Stored in wrecked condition 5.98: current status unknown)*	Weston Zoyland	19. 4.97P
G-MNSR	Mainair Gemini/Flash II (Rotax 503) 399-486-4 & W144	(G-MNLJ)	17. 4.86	A.M.Bell	(Rufforth)	22. 5.00P
G-MNSS	American Aerolights Eagle 215B 4131 (Zenoah G25B1)		24. 4.86	G.P.Jones	(Caernarfon)	16.10.86E
G-MNSV	CFM Shadow B 012 (Rotax 447)		24. 4.86	F.Lynch	Kildare	6. 4.02P
G-MNSX	Southdown Raven X SN2232/0148 (Rotax 447)		30. 4.86	S.F.Chave	(Honiton)	26. 6.02P
G-MNSY	Southdown Raven X SN2232/0149 (Rotax 447)		30. 4.86	J.B.Carter	Hatherton, Cannock	7. 7.99P
G-MNTC	Southdown Raven X SN2232/0150 (Rotax 447)		30. 4.86	D.S.Bancalari *(New owner 11.01)*	(Norwich)	12.10.92P
G-MNTD	Aerial Arts Chaser/110SX 110SX/255 *(C/n duplicates G-MTSF)*		24. 4.86	B.Richardson	(Sunderland)	
G-MNTE	Southdown Raven X SN2232/0151 (Rotax 447)		30. 4.86	E Foster	(Preston)	27. 6.02P
G-MNTI	Mainair Gemini/Flash II (Rotax 503) 447-886-4 & W231		8. 5.86	R.T.Strathie	(Melrose)	19. 8.01P
G-MNTK	CFM Shadow CD 024 (Rotax 503)		8. 5.86	T.A.R.Davies	(Brixham)	17. 8.02P
G-MNTM	Southdown Raven X SN2232/0154 (Rotax 447)		19. 5.86	D.M.Garland	(Atherstone)	24. 7.01P
G-MNTN	Southdown Raven X SN2232/0155 (Rotax 447)		2. 6.86	J.Hall	(Wolverhampton)	31.12.02P
G-MNTP	CFM Shadow C K.022 (Rotax 462)		19. 5.86	P.K.Hope-Lang	Milton Keynes	17. 6.02P
G-MNTS	Mainair Gemini/Flash II (Rotax 462) 450-886-4 & W227		3. 4.86	J.A.Colley	Over Farm, Gloucester	16. 1.02P
G-MNTT	Medway Half Pint/Aerial Arts 130SX (Rotax 462) 12/1486		7. 4.86	P.Sykes	(Bournemouth)	20. 6.02P
G-MNTU	Mainair Gemini/Flash II (Rotax 462?) 460-886-4 & W233		9. 7.86	S.Cogger	(Wickford)	3. 7.02P
G-MNTV	Mainair Gemini/Flash II (Rotax 462) 455-886-4 & W241		9. 7.86	P.Dunstan	Davidstow Moor	10.10.02P
G-MNTW	Mainair Gemini/Flash II (Rotax 503) 456-886-5 & W242		11. 9.86	J.E.Robinson	(Bootle)	21. 9.00P
G-MNTX	Mainair Gemini/Flash II (Rotax 503) 415-486-4 & W166		20. 5.86	D.Pearson	(Heywood)	19. 9.02P
G-MNTY	Southdown Raven X SN2232/0157 (Rotax 447)		29. 5.86	D.J.Puxley	Stoke, Kent	21. 5.02P
G-MNTZ	Mainair Gemini/Flash II (Rotax 503) 457-886-4 & W243		3. 6.86	R.W.Trenholm	Otherton, Cannock	30. 3.02P
G-MNUA	Mainair Gemini/Flash II (Rotax 462) 458-886-4 & W235		29. 5.86	J.McCullough	Castlewellan, Co.Down	14. 2.02P
G-MNUD	Solar Wings Pegasus Flash II (Rotax 462) SW-TE-0003 & SW-WF-0110 *(Mainair sailwing c/n W195)*		10. 6.86	P.G.H.Milbank	Sutton Meadows, Ely	20. 9.02P
G-MNUE	Solar Wings Pegasus Flash II (Rotax 462) SW-TE-0002 & SW-WF-0108 *(Orig Mainair sailwing c/n W193 buty fitted with W209 (ex original G-MNYA)*		10. 6.86	P.M.Rogers	(Rochdale)	15.11.02P

G-MNUF	Mainair Gemini/Flash II (Rotax 503) 472-786-4 & W252		13. 6.86	C.Hannaby *(Stored 12.97: current status unknown)*	Guy Lane Farm, Waverton	4. 2.96P
G-MNUG	Mainair Gemini/Flash II (Rotax 462) 465-986-4 & W245		13. 6.86	K.D.Adams	(Wirral)	22. 7.02P
G-MNUI	Mainair Tri-Flyer/Skyhook Cutlass (Fuji-Robin EC-44-PM) MH-01		21. 5.86	M.Holling	(Goole)	28. 2.87E
G-MNUM	Mainair Gemini Sprint MS (Fuji-Robin EC-44-PM) 226-184-2-P.508 *(Trike orig allocated to G-MNMC)*		12. 3.84	J.A.Sims	(Farnham)	31. 7.00P
G-MNUO	Mainair Gemini/Flash II (Rotax 462) 421-586-4 & W179		9. 7.86	P.S.Taylor	(Weybridge)	11. 5.02P
G-MNUR	Mainair Gemini/Flash II (Rotax 503) 470-986-4 & W250		14. 8.86	J.C.Greves	(Cobham)	30. 3.90P
G-MNUT	Southdown Raven X SN2232/0160 (Rotax 447)		10. 6.86	I A.De Groot *(Stored mid 1999: current status unknown)*	(Spalding)	15. 7.93P
G-MNUU	Southdown Raven X SN2232/0162 (Rotax 447)		26. 6.86	P.N.Jackson	Davidstow Moor	10. 9.02P
G-MNUX	Solar Wings Pegasus XL-R (Rotax 447) SW-TB-1072 & SW-WA-1076		24. 6.86	K.Jones	Peterlee	25. 9.00P
G-MNUY	Mainair Gemini/Flash II (Rotax 503) 422-586-4 & W180		23. 6.86	M.Nymark	Newtownards, Co.of Down	12.10.02P
G-MNVB	Solar Wings Pegasus XL-R (Rotax 447) SW-TB-1073 & SW-WA-1077		7. 7.86	M.J.Melvin	(Spalding)	4. 8.02P
G-MNVC	Solar Wings Pegasus XL-R (Rotax 447) SW-TB-1074 & SW-WA-1078		7. 7.86	M.N.C.Ward	Shobdon	11. 6.00P
G-MNVE	Solar Wings Pegasus XL-R (Rotax 447) SW-TB-1075 & SW-WA-1079		19. 6.86	M.P.Aris	(Welwyn)	11. 8.00P
G-MNVG	Solar Wings Pegasus Flash II (Rotax 447) SW-TB-1069 & SW-WF-0109 *(Mainair sailwing c/n W194)*		11. 6.86	D.J.Ward	Low Farm, South Walsham	7. 6.02P
G-MNVH	Solar Wings Pegasus Flash II (Rotax 462) SW-TE-0001 & SW-WF-0122 *(Mainair sailwing c/n W260)*		23. 6.86	J.A.Clarke & C.Hall	(London N22/E8)	9. 4.97P
G-MNVI	CFM Shadow C 026 (Rotax 503)		17. 6.86	D.R.C.Pugh	(Caersws, Powys)	13. 9.02P
G-MNVJ	CFM Shadow CD 028 (Rotax 503)		17. 6.86	V.C.Readhead	(Saxmundham)	4. 5.02P
G-MNVK	CFM Shadow CD 029 (Rotax 503)		17. 6.86	R.W.Hussey	Old Sarum	31. 7.02P
G-MNVL	Medway Half Pint/Aerial Arts 130SX 3/21585 & 130SX-100	G-MNBZ	22. 9.86	T.J.Gayton-Polley *(New owner 12.01)*	(Billingshurst)	
G-MNVN	Southdown Puma Raven SN2132/0165 (Fuji-Robin EC-44-PM)		27. 6.86	S.Hutchinson	(Scampton)	16.11.02P
G-MNVO	Hovey Whing-Ding II CW-01		14. 8.86	C.Wilson	(Basildon)	
G-MNVT	Mainair Gemini/Flash II (Rotax 503) 477-786-4 & W258		27. 6.86	A.C.Barker t/a ACB Hydraulics *(Stored 4.90: current status unknown)*	Hinton-in-the-Hedges	28. 7.87P
G-MNVU	Mainair Gemini/Flash II (Rotax 503) 468-986-4 & W248		26. 6.86	W.R.Marsh	Newhouse Farm, Hardwicke, Hereford	28. 6.99P
G-MNVV	Mainair Gemini/Flash II (Rotax 503) 467-986-4 & W247		26. 6.86	R.P.Hothersall *(Op Northern Microlight School)*	St.Michaels	1. 5.02P
G-MNVW	Mainair Gemini/Flash II (Rotax 503) 466-986-4 & W246		26. 6.86	J.C.Munro-Hunt	Little Down Farm, Milson	20. 9.98P
G-MNVZ	Solar Wings Pegasus Photon (Solo 210) SW-TP-0021 & SW-WP-0021		27. 6.86	J.J.Russ	Eshott	27. 6.94P
G-MNWA	Southdown Raven X SN2232/0167 (Rotax 447)		26. 6.86	P.R.Miller	(St. Neots)	9.11.02P
G-MNWD	Mainair Gemini/Flash II (Rotax 462) 474-986-4 & W254		27. 6.86	M.B.Rutherford	Swinford, Rugby	7. 7.01P
G-MNWG	Southdown Raven X SN2232/0170 (Rotax 447)		4. 8.86	A.J.McShane & M.J.Reeve	Sywell	28. 1.02P
G-MNWI	Mainair Gemini/Flash II (Rotax 503) 478-986-4 & W264		9. 7.86	W.H.Gilbertson	(Manchester)	10. 5.02P
G-MNWK	CFM Shadow C 030 (Rotax 503)		9. 7.86	J.E.Hunt	(Welling, Kent)	19. 8.98P
G-MNWL	Arbiter Services Trike/Aerial Arts 130S 130SX/333		23. 7.86	E.H.Snook	(Newport Pagnell)	
G-MNWP	Solar Wings Pegasus/Flash II (Rotax 447) SW-TB-1083 & SW-WF-0113 *(Mainair sailwing c/n W198)*		4. 8.86	D.Haynes	Swanton Morley	18. 3.02P
G-MNWU	Solar Wings Pegasus/Flash II (Rotax 462) SW-TE-0006 & SW-WF-0111 *(Mainair sailwing c/n W196)*		4. 8.86	F.J.E.Brownshill & W.Parkin	Oakley, Beds	26. 4.01P
G-MNWV	Solar Wings Pegasus/Flash II (Rotax 447) SW-TB-1090 & SW-WF-0121 *(Mainair sailwing c/n W206)*		4. 8.86	A.T.Palmer t/a Pegasus Group *(Noted 11.01)*	Davidstow Moor	4. 8.02P
G-MNWW	Solar Wings Pegasus XL Tug (Rotax 462) SW-TE-0008 & SW-WA-1085		8.10.86	N.P.Chitty t/a Chiltern Flyers Aero Tow Group	Ginge, Wantage	30. 6.00P
G-MNWY	CFM Shadow C (Rotax 503) K.021 & PFA 161-11130		28. 7.86	R.Savage t/a Air Photographic Ireland *(Noted 10.01)*	Newtownards, Co.of Down	1. 8.98P

G-MNWZ	Mainair Gemini/Flash II (Rotax 503) 436-686-4 & W203	(G-MNXV)	19. 8.86	W.T.Hume	(Newmilns)	16. 6.98P
G-MNXA	Southdown Raven X SN2232/0180 (Rotax 447)		5. 8.86	B.D.Acres	(Maidstone)	28. 6.02P
G-MNXB	Mainair Tri-Flyer/Solar Wings Photon (Fuji-Robin EC-34-PM) 016-29981 & SW-WP-0022		29. 7.86	G.W.Carwardine	(Uckfield)	16. 6.98P
G-MNXD	Southdown Puma Raven SN2132/0173 (Fuji-Robin EC-44-PM)		13. 8.86	P.Jephcott	(Solihull)	25.10.00P
G-MNXE	Southdown Raven X SN2232/0202 (Rotax 447)		7. 8.86	A.E.Silvey	Wilburton, Ely	30.11.02P
G-MNXF	Southdown Puma Raven SN2132/0176 (Fuji-Robin EC-44-PM)		2. 9.86	D.E.Gwenin	(Tring)	13. 5.99P
G-MNXG	Southdown Raven X SN2232/0181 (Rotax 447)		3. 9.86	M.A.Williams	(Tonbridge)	22. 7.02P
G-MNXI	Southdown Raven X SN2232/0179 (Rotax 447)		19. 8.86	A.M.Yates	(Wisbech)	13. 7.96P
G-MNXO	Medway Hybred 44XLR 29786/19 (Rotax 447)		3. 9.86	D.L.Turner	(Chatham)	6. 7.02P
G-MNXP	Solar Wings Pegasus Flash II (Rotax 447) SW-TB-1094 & SW-WF-0117 *(Mainair sailwing c/n W207)*		16. 9.86	D.Harrison	(Bewdley)	6. 8.96P
G-MNXS	Mainair Gemini/Flash II (Rotax 462) 480-986-4 & W267		8. 9.86	F.T.Rawlings *(Believed exported to Portugal c1988?: valid CofR 12.01)*	(Hereford)	16. 3.89P
G-MNXU	Mainair Gemini/Flash II (Rotax 503) 482-1086-4 & W272		18. 8.86	J.M.Hucker	(Abertillery)	10. 3.98P
G-MNXX	CFM Shadow CD K.027 (Rotax 503)		13. 8.86	P.G.Ward & N.J.C.Ray	Old Sarum	8. 2.02P
G-MNXZ	Whittaker MW5 Sorcerer (Fuji-Robin EC-34-PM) PFA 163-11156		13. 8.86	P.J.Cheyney	Newhouse Farm, Loughborough	3. 6.02P
G-MNYA	Solar Wings Pegasus Flash II (Rotax 447) SW-TB-1098 & SW-WF-0119 *(Orig laid down with Mainair sailwing c/n W209 but changed to W259 - see G-MNUE)*		3. 9.86	P.A.Banks	(Milton Keynes)	19. 1.02P
G-MNYB	Solar Wings Pegasus XL-R (Rotax 447) SW-TB-1096 & SW-WA-1089		8. 9.86	P.J.Conaghy	Drogheda, Co.Louth	26. 5.02P
G-MNYC	Solar Wings Pegasus XL-R (Rotax 447) SW-TB-1097 & SW-WA-1090		3. 9.86	A.N.Papworth	(Bury St. Edmunds)	14. 7.02P
G-MNYD	Aerial Arts Chaser/110SX 110SX/320 (Rotax 377)		19. 8.86	B.Richardson	(Sunderland)	25. 7.02P
G-MNYE	Aerial Arts Chaser/110SX 110SX/321 (Rotax 337)		19. 8.86	R.J.Ripley	Oakley, Beds	18.11.99P
G-MNYF	Aerial Arts Chaser/110SX 110SX/322 (Rotax 377)		19. 8.86	B.Richardson	(Sunderland)	25. 7.02P
G-MNYG	Southdown Puma Raven SN2122/0172 (Fuji-Robin EC-44-PM)		19. 8.86	K.Clifford	(Stanmore)	3. 7.00P
G-MNYI	Southdown Raven X SN2232/0211 (Rotax 447)		3. 9.86	N.Bowles *(Flies from Edzell)*	(Drumlithie)	26. 1.01P
G-MNYJ	Mainair Gemini/Flash II (Rotax 462) 485-1086-4 & W275		8. 9.86	M.A.Johnson	Otherton, Cannock	24. 6.02P
G-MNYK	Mainair Gemini/Flash II 494-1086-4 & W296		11. 9.86	J.J.Ryan	(Enniscorthy, Co.Wexford)	4.10.95P
G-MNYL	Southdown Raven X SN2232/0195 (Rotax 447)		2. 9.86	A.D.F.Clifford	Broadmeadow Farm, Hereford	9. 6.98P
G-MNYM	Southdown Raven X SN2232/0196 (Rotax 447)		2. 9.86	A.D.Montriou & C.E.Arter	Dunkeswell	13. 8.00P
G-MNYP	Southdown Raven X SN2232/0207 (Rotax 447)		3. 9.86	A.G.Davies	(Bristol)	14. 5.01P
G-MNYS	Southdown Raven X SN2232/0208 (Rotax 447)		8. 9.86	B.Ward	(Sheerness)	9. 1.99P
G-MNYV	Solar Wings Pegasus XL-R/Se (Rotax 447) SW-TB-1101 & SW-WA-1093		11. 9.86	B.J.Green	(Marlborough)	30.11.99P
G-MNYW	Solar Wings Pegasus XL-R (Rotax 447) SW-TB-1102 & SW-WA-1094		11. 9.86	M.P.Waldock	(Selsdon, Surrey)	7. 8.98P
G-MNYX	Solar Wings Pegasus XL-R (Rotax 462) SW-TE-0009 & SW-WA-1095		19. 9.86	P.Mayes & J.P.Widdowson *(See G-MMKG)*	(Bridgnorth)	15. 6.02P
G-MNYZ	Solar Wings Pegasus Flash II (Rotax 462) SW-TE-0010 & SW-WF-0114 *(Mainair sailwing c/n W199)*		11. 9.86	A.C.Bartolozzi	(Ely)	9. 3.00P
G-MNZB	Mainair Gemini/Flash II (Rotax 503) 483-1086-4 & W273		8. 9.86	P.A.Ryder	(Knebworth)	11. 3.00P
G-MNZC	Mainair Gemini/Flash II (Rotax 503) 484-1086-4 & W274		6. 9.86	C.J.Whittaker	(Ledbury)	19. 1.89P
G-MNZD	Mainair Gemini/Flash II (Rotax 503) 493-1086-4 & W295		8. 9.86	N.D.Carter *(Stored 9.96: current status unknown)*	Little Gransden	4. 4.96P
G-MNZE	Mainair Gemini/Flash II (Rotax 503) 495-1086-4 & W297 *(Wing regd as W279 - see G-MTEK)*		8. 9.86	K.J.Hughes	Tarn Farm, Cockerham	16. 7.01P
G-MNZF	Mainair Gemini/Flash II (Rotax 503) 496-1186-4 & W291		8. 9.86	A.L.Wright	Swinford, Rugby	13. 5.01P

G-MNZI	Prone Power Mk.2/Solar Wings Typhoon	PP-01		22. 9.86	R.J.Folwell	(London W6)	
G-MNZJ	CFM Shadow CD (Rotax 503)	033		19. 9.86	T.E.P.Eves t/a G-MNZJ Shadow Group	Baxby Manor, Husthwaite	11. 5.02P
G-MNZK	Solar Wings Pegasus XL-R/Se (Rotax 447)	SW-WA-1096		24. 9.86	J.G.Campbell & P.J.Perkins	Sandtoft	23. 7.02P
G-MNZO	Solar Wings Pegasus Flash II (Rotax 462)	SW-TE-0012 & SW-WF-0125 *(Mainair sailwing c/n W218)*		30. 9.86	K.B.Woods & D.Johnson	Newnham, Baldock	13.10.02P
G-MNZP	CFM Shadow BD (Rotax 447)	K.039 & PFA 161-11206		19. 9.86	J.G.Wakeford	Deanland, Hailsham	21. 6.02P
G-MNZR	CFM Shadow BD (Rotax 447)	040		19. 9.86	J.S.Wilson	Priory Farm, Tibenham	22. 4.02P
G-MNZS	Aerial Arts Alpha/130SX (Rotax 277)	130SX/376		23. 9.86	N.R.Beale	(Southam)	1. 8.00P
G-MNZU	Eurowing Goldwing (Fuji-Robin EC-34-PM)	EW-88		24. 9.86	H.B.Baker	Old Sarum	11.10.02P
G-MNZW	Southdown Raven X	SN2232/0220		17.10.86	C.A.James	(Bristol)	7. 7.02P
G-MNZX	Southdown Raven X (Rotax 447)	SN2232/0221		10.10.86	B.F.Hole	(East Grinstead)	5. 5.02P
G-MNZZ	CFM Shadow CD (Rotax 503)	036		19. 9.86	P.J.Lynch	(Farnborough)	26. 7.02P
G-MOAC	Beechcraft F33A Bonanza	CE-1349	N1563N	25. 5.89	R.L.Camrass	La Rochelle, France	30. 5.04
G-MOBI	Aérospatiale AS355F1 Twin Squirrel	5260	G-MUFF G-CORR	11.11.93	Faiman Aviation Ltd	(London SW3)	18. 4.03T
G-MOFB	Cameron O-120 HAFB	4275		13. 1.98	D.M.Moffat	Chateaux d'Oex, Switzerland	13. 1.02A
G-MOFF	Cameron O-77 HAFB	2040		27. 7.89	D.M.Moffat *"Moff"*	Alveston, Bristol	7. 9.95A
G-MOFZ	Cameron O-90 HAFB	3350		7. 9.94	D.M.Moffat	Alveston, Bristol	13. 1.02A
G-MOGI	Grumman-American AA-5A Cheetah	AA5A-0630	G-BFMU	1. 5.86	Icarus Aircraft Ltd	Fenland	24.10.02
G-MOGY	Robinson R22 Beta	0899		23.11.88	S.G.Simpson t/a HJS Helicopters	Culter, Lower Baads Farm, Peterculter	25. 1.04T
G-MOHS	Piper PA-31-350 Chieftain	31-8152115	G-BWOC N40898/CP-1665	29. 4.96	Sky Air Travel Ltd	Stapleford	28. 9.03T
G-MOJO	Airbus A330-243	301	F-WWYE	8.11.99	Premiair A/S	Copenhagen, Denmark	7.11 02T
G-MOKE	Cameron V-77 HAFB	3686		4.10.95	D.D.Owen	Wotton-under-Edge	5. 5.02A
G-MOLE	Taylor JT.2 Titch (Continental O-200-A)	PFA 060-10725		20. 1.87	S.R.Mowle *(Under construction 10.90: current status unknown)*	(Kenley)	
G-MOLI	Cameron A-250 HAFB	3429		26. 1.95	J.J.Rudoni *"Molly" (Op Balloon Preservation Group)*	Malpas	3. 7.02T
G-MOLL	Piper PA-32-301T Turbo Saratoga	32-8024040	N82535	25. 3.91	M.S.Bennett	Gamston	12. 5.03
G-MOLY	Piper PA-23-160 Apache	23-1686	EI-BAW G-APFV/EI-ALK/N10F	7. 6.79	R.R. & M.T.Thorogood	Henstridge	28. 2.02
G-MONB	Boeing 757-2T7ER	22780		7. 3.83	Monarch Airlines Ltd	Luton	1. 2.03T
G-MONC	Boeing 757-2T7ER	22781	PH-AHO D-ABNY/G-MONC/EC-211/G-MONC	15. 4.83	Monarch Airlines Ltd	Luton	29. 4.02T
G-MOND	Boeing 757-2T7	22960	D-ABNZ G-MOND	28. 4.83	Monarch Airlines Ltd	Luton	13. 5.02T
G-MONE	Boeing 757-2T7ER	23293		27. 2.85	Monarch Airlines Ltd *(Renaissance Cruise titles)*	Luton	25. 2.03T
G-MONI	Monnett Moni (IAME KFM.107)	PFA 142-10925		12. 1.84	R.M.Edworthy	(Littleover)	16. 4.02P
G-MONJ	Boeing 757-2T7ER	24104		26. 2.88	Monarch Airlines Ltd	Luton	23. 1.03T
G-MONK	Boeing 757-2T7ER	24105		26. 2.88	Monarch Airlines Ltd	Luton	31. 5.02T
G-MONR	Airbus A300B4-605R	540	VH-YMJ G-MONR/F-WWAT	15. 3.90	Monarch Airlines Ltd	Luton	2. 4.02T
G-MONS	Airbus A300B4-605R	556	VH-YMK G-MONS/F-WWAY	17. 4.90	Monarch Airlines Ltd	Luton	23. 3.03T
G-MONW	Airbus A320-212	391	F-WWDO	24. 2.93	Monarch Airlines Ltd	Luton	7. 3.03T
G-MONX	Airbus A320-212	392	F-WWDR	19. 3.93	Monarch Airlines Ltd	Luton	17. 3.03T
G-MONZ	Airbus A320-212	446	C-FTDI G-MONZ/C-FTDI/G-MONZ/C-FTDI/G-MONZ/F-WWDJ *(Stored 1.02)*	28.10.93	Monarch Airlines Ltd	Manchester	26. 4.03T
G-MOOR	SOCATA TB-10 Tobago	82	G-MILK	23. 7.91	M.Watkin	(Sheffield)	31.10.04
G-MOOS	Hunting-Percival P.56 Provost T.1	PAC/F/335	G-BGKA 8041M/XF690	5. 4.91	T.J.Manna t/a Kennet Aviation *(As "XF690" in RAF c/s)*	Cranfield	17. 6.02P
G-MOPB	Diamond DA40 Star	40067		19.11.01	Diamond Aircraft UK Ltd	Gamston	
G-MOSS	Beechcraft D55 Baron	TE-548	G-AWAD	12. 6.95	A.G.E.Camisa	Elstree	5. 6.03
G-MOSY	Cameron O-84 HAFB	2315	EI-CAO	17. 4.96	P.L.Mossman	Bristol	16. 6.02A
G-MOTA	Bell 206B-3 Jet Ranger III	4494	N81521	20.10.98	J W Sandle	Runcton Holme, King's Lynn	28.10.04T
G-MOTH	de Havilland DH.82A Tiger Moth *(CompositE rebuild to DH.82 standard)*	85340	7035M DE306	31. 1.78	M.C.Russell *(As "K2567")*	Top Farm, Croydon	4. 6.01
G-MOTI	Robin DR.500/200i President *(Registered as DR.400/500)*	0006		23.11.98	O.Graham-Flatebo & The Lord Saville of Newdigate t/a The Tango India Flying Group	Biggin Hill	2. 2.02

G-MOTO	Piper PA-24-180 Comanche	24-3239	G-EDHE	24. 3.87	L.T. & S.Evans	Sandown	4.10.02
			N51867/G-ASFH/EI-AMM/N7998P				
G-MOTT*	Avid Speed Wing	PFA 189-11738		29. 5.92	J.B.Ott	Cambridge	26. 2.99P
					(Cancelled 2 8.01 by CAA: current status unknown)		
G-MOUL	Maule M-6-235C Super Rocket	7518C		1. 5.90	M.Klinge	Prestwick	11. 5.03
G-MOUR	Folland Gnat T.1	FL.596	8624M	16. 5.90	D.J.Gilmour	North Weald	29. 4.99P
			XS102		t/a Intrepid Aviation Co *(As "XR991" in Yellowjacks c/s)*		
G-MOVE	Piper Aerostar 601P 61P-0593-7963263		OO-PKB	5. 1.79	A. Kazaz & A1 Hydraulics Ltd	Leicester	8. 7.02
			G-MOVE/N8144J				
G-MOVI	Piper PA-32R-301 Saratoga SP	32R-8313029	G-MARI	6. 2.89	G-BOON Ltd	Cranfield	22. 2.03T
			N8248H				
G-MOZZ	Avions Mudry CAP.10B	256		30.10.90	M.B.Smith & N.Skipworth	Booker	2. 5.03
G-MPAC	Pelican PL	PFA 165-12944		6. 4.00	M.J.Craven	Rayne Hall Farm, Rayne	11. 6.02P
G-MPBH	Reims Cessna FA152 Aerobat	FA15200374	G-FLIC	8.12.88	The Moray Flying Club (1990)	RAF Kinloss	18. 8.02T
			G-BILV				
G-MPBI	Cessna 310R II	310R0584	F-GEBB	21. 7.97	M.P.Bolshaw & Co Ltd	Elstree	15. 8.03
			HB-LMD/N87473				
G-MPCD	Airbus A320-212	379	C-GZCD	14. 3.94	Monarch Airlines Ltd	Luton	1. 5.04T
			G-MPCD/C-FTDU/G-MPCD/C-FTDU/G-MPCD/C-FTDU/G-MPCD/C-FTDU/G-MPCD/F-WWDY				
G-MPWH*	Rotorway Executive	3579		22. 6.90	Thistle Aviation Ltd	Henley-on-Thames	
		(Cancelled 28.3.00 by CAA - no Permit or CofA issued: believed stored incomplete)					
G-MPWI	Robin HR.100/210	163	F-GBTY	3. 3.80	Propwash Investments Ltd	Swansea	2. 3.02
			F-ODFA/F-BUPD				
G-MPWT	Piper PA-34-220T Seneca III	34-8333068	N4294X	26. 9.88	Modern Air (UK) Ltd *"Duke 2"*	Fowlmere	19. 5.04T
			N888DB/N4294X/N9539N/N8218K *(Originally built as c/n 34-8233163)*				
G-MRAJ	MD Helicopters Hughes 369E (500E)	0010E	N51946	19. 3.98	A.Jardine *"Duke 2"*	Sywell	5. 5.01T
G-MRAM	Mignet HM-1000 Balerit (Rotax 582)	134		15.11.99	R.A.Marven	Tower Hill Lane, Coleman Green, Herts	17.11.02P
G-MRED	Elmwood CA-05 Christavia mk.1	PFA 185-12935		2. 8.96	E.Hewett	(Fareham)	
G-MRKT	Lindstrand LBL-90A HAFB	037		7. 6.93	Marketplace Public Relations (London) Ltd *"Kaytee"*	Crowthorne, Berks	22. 3.01A
G-MRLN	Sky 240-24 HAFB	161		4. 8.99	M.Wady t/a Merlin Balloons	Hamstreet	30. 5.02T
G-MRMR	Piper PA-31-350 Navajo Chieftain	31-7952092	OH-PRE	21. 8.97	I.D. & P.J.Margetson-Rushmore	Stapleford	22.12.02T
			G-WROX/G-BNZI/N3517T		t/a MRMR Flight Services		
G-MROC	Pegasus Quantum 15-912	7498		22. 1.99	M.Convine	Tower Farm, Woolaston	27. 1.02P
G-MROY	Comco Ikarus C42	PFA 322-13755		9.10.01	R.Beckham	(Banbury)	
G-MRSI	Canadair CL600-2C10 Regional Jet *(CRJ 700)*	10034		R	Maersk Air Ltd *(For delivery 3.02)*	Birmingham	
G-MRSJ	Canadair CL600-2C10 Regional Jet *(CRJ 700)*	10029		20.11.01	Maersk Air Ltd	Birmingham	21.11.04T
G-MRSK	Canadair CL600-2C10 Regional Jet *(CRJ-700)*	10028	C-GIBG	16.10.01	Maersk Air Ltd	Birmingham	17.10.04T
G-MRSN	Robinson R22 Beta	1654		21. 1.91	M D Thorpe t/a Yorkshire Helicopters	Coney Park, Leeds	11. 6.03T
G-MRST	Piper PA-28RT-201 Arrow IV	28R-7918068	9H-AAU	27.11.86	Calverton Flying Group Ltd	(Milton Keynes)	13. 3.02T
			5B-CEC/N3019U				
G-MRTN	SOCATA TB-10 Tobago	62	G-BHET	9. 7.98	Underwood Kitchens Ltd	Turweston	30. 4.04
G-MRTY	Cameron N-77 HAFB	1008		24. 4.84	R.A, P.M.G. & N.T.M. Vale *"Marty" (New owners 7.01)*	Kidderminster	19. 5.96A
G-MSAL	Morane-Saulnier MS.733 Alcyon	143	F-BLXV	16. 6.93	North Weald Flying Services Ltd	North Weald	
			Fr.Mil		*(Stored 12.00: as "143" in Aeronavale c/s)*		
G-MSFC	Piper PA-38-112 Tomahawk II	38-81A0067	N25735	11. 5.90	Sherwood Flying Club Ltd	Nottingham	18. 7.02T
G-MSFT	Piper PA-28-161 Warrior II	28-8416093	G-MUMS	2. 4.97	M.J.Love	Bournemouth	1. 5.03T
			N118AV				
G-MSIX	Glaser Dirks DG-800B	8-156-B80		21. 4.99	E.Coles t/a G-MSIX Group	Dunstable	4. 5.02
G-MSKA	Boeing 737-5L9	24859	OY-MAC	18.10.96	Maersk Air Ltd	Birmingham	17.10.02T
			(OY-MMZ)				
G-MSKB	Boeing 737-5L9	24928	OY-MAD	12.11.96	Maersk Air Ltd	Birmingham	11.11.02T
			(OY-MMO)				
G-MSKC	Boeing 737-5L9	25066	OY-MAE	3.12.96	Maersk Air Ltd	Birmingham	2.12.02T
G-MSKO	Canadair CL600-2B19 Regional Jet *(CRJ 200)*	7299	C-FMOS	19. 3.99	Maersk Air Ltd *(Crossing Borders t/s)*	Birmingham	23. 3.02T
G-MSKP	Canadair CL600-2B19 Regional Jet *(CRJ 200)*	7329	C-FMOS	22. 7.99	Maersk Air Ltd	Birmingham	26. 7.02T
G-MSKR	Canadair CL600-2B19 Regional Jet *(CRJ 200)*	7373	C-FMNB	24. 2.00	Maersk Air Ltd	Birmingham	27. 3.03T
G-MSKS	Canadair CL600-2B19 Regional Jet *(CRJ 200)*	7386	C-FMNW	3. 4.00	Maersk Air Ltd	Birmingham	5. 4.03T
G-MSKT	Canadair CL600-2B19 Regional Jet *(CRJ 200)*	7436	C-FMKZ	23.10.00	Maersk Air Ltd	Birmingham	24.10.03T

G-MSKU	Canadair CL600-2B19 Regional Jet *(CRJ 200)*	7442	C-GHTK C-FMLU	10.11.00	Maersk Air Ltd	Birmingham	12.11.03T
G-MSKV	Canadair CL600-2B19 Regional Jet *(CRJ 200)*			R	Maersk Air Ltd	Birmingham	
G-MSKY	Comco Ikarus C42	PFA 322-13722		3.10.01	C.K.Jones	(Cogenhoe)	
G-MSOO	Revolution Helicopters Mini-500	0016		16.10.95	R.H.Ryan	(Sunderland)	
G-MSPY	Pegasus Quantum 15-912	7625		17. 3.00	J.Madhvani & R.K.Green	Plaistows Farm, St Albans	15..3.02P
G-MSTC	Gulfstream AA-5A Cheetah	AA5A-0833	G-BIJT N26950	30. 1.95	Plane Talking Ltd	Elstree	4. 2.02T
G-MSTG	North American P-51D-25-NT Mustang	124-48271	NZ2427 45-11518	2. 9.97	M.Hammond *(As "44-14419/LH-F" in USAAF c/s of 350th Fighter Squadron/353rd Fighter Group)*	Hardwick	19. 8.02P
G-MSTR	Cameron Monster-110SS HAFB	4957	G-OJOB	18. 7.01	Virgin Airship & Balloon Co Ltd	Telford	17. 1.02P
G-MTAA	Solar Wings Pegasus XL-R (Rotax 447)	SW-TB-1108 & SW-WA-1102		15.10.86	R.Scott	London Colney	30. 5.02P
G-MTAB	Mainair Gemini/Flash II (Rotax 503)	492-1086-4 & W290		8.10.86	G.S.Stokes	Pound Green, Buttonoak, Kidderminster	2. 6.02P
G-MTAC	Mainair Gemini/Flash II (Rotax 503)	486-1086-4 & W278		15.10.86	L.A.Le Roux	St.Michaels	13. 5.02P
G-MTAE	Mainair Gemini/Flash II (Rotax 503)	500-1186-4 & W302		15.10.86	M.Fowler	(Camborne)	26. 6.02P
G-MTAF	Mainair Gemini/Flash II (Rotax 503)	499-1186-4 & W301		5.10.86	P.A.Long *(Op North Lancs Micro School)*	St Michaels	10.11.02P
G-MTAG	Mainair Gemini/Flash II (Rotax 503)	487-1086-4 & W281		15.10.86	M.J.Cowie & J.P.Hardy	(Upton, Wirral)	23. 4.02P
G-MTAH	Mainair Gemini/Flash II (Rotax 503)	488-1086-4 & W282		16.10.86	T.G.Elmhirst	St.Michaels	15. 9.02P
G-MTAI	Solar Wings Pegasus XL-R (Rotax 503)	SW-TB-1109 & SW-WA-1103		14.10.86	D.Ruston	(Sheffield)	27. 1.02P
G-MTAJ	Solar Wings Pegasus XL-R (Rotax 447)	SW-TB-1110 & SW-WA-1104		16.10.86	G.A. & S.D.Batchelor	(Launceston)	31. 7.02P
G-MTAL	Solar Wings Pegasus Photon (Solo 210)	SW-TP-0023 & SW-WP-0023	*(Being converted to Rotax 277)*	15.10.86	R.P.Wilkinson	(Bath)	29.10.95P
G-MTAO	Solar Wings Pegasus XL-R (Rotax 447)	SW-TB-1107 & SW-WA-1107		21.10.86	S.P.Disney & R.Jones	Swinford, Rugby	26. 6.01P
G-MTAP	Southdown Raven X (Rotax 447)	SN2232/0225		15.10.86	D.B.McCalvey	(Hailsham)	13. 6.98P
G-MTAR	Mainair Gemini Flash II (Rotax 462)	504-1286-4-W307		16.10.86	J.B.Woolley	(Woodthorpe, Notts)	24. 5.02P
G-MTAS	Whittaker MW5 Sorcerer (Rotax 503-IV)	PFA 163-11166	*(May be Model MW5C?)*	14.10.86	J.T.Laity & F.W.Hubbard	Kemble	10. 6.02P
G-MTAT*	Solar Wings Pegasus XL-R (Rotax 447)	SW-TB-1113 & SW-WA-1108		28.10.86	J.Ryan *(Cancelled 15.8.01 by CAA)*	(Enniscorthy, Co.Wexford)	4. 7.01P
G-MTAV	Solar Wings Pegasus XL-R (Rotax 447)	SW-TB-1115 & SW-WA-1110		21.10.86	Susan Fairweather & Carolyn L.Harris	(Nottingham/Warrington)	19. 5.02P
G-MTAW	Solar Wings Pegasus XL-R (Rotax 447)	SW-TB-1116 & SW-WA-1111		21.10.86	M.G.Ralph	Weston Zoyland	13. 7.02P
G-MTAX	Solar Wings Pegasus XL-R (Rotax 447)	SW-TB-1117 & SW-WA-1112		27.10.86	G Hawes	Great Glen	21. 7.02P
G-MTAY	Solar Wings Pegasus XL-R (Rotax 447)	SW-TB-1118 & SW-WA-1113		27.10.86	S.A.McLatchie	Enstone	12. 2.01P
G-MTAZ	Solar Wings Pegasus XL-R (Rotax 447)	SW-TB-1119 & SW-WA-1114		28.10.86	J.P.Whitehead	Lower Mountpleasant, Chatteris	25. 3.01P
G-MTBA	Solar Wings Pegasus XL-R (Rotax 447)	SW-TB-1120 & SW-WA-1115		27.10.86	R.J.W.Franklin & M.C.Buffery *(Wrecked 5.97: current status unknown)*	(Cheltenham)	24. 6.93P
G-MTBB	Southdown Raven X (Rotax 447)	SN2232/0226		16.10.86	A.Miller	(Woking)	15.10.02P
G-MTBD	Mainair Gemini/Flash II (Rotax 503)	498-1186-4 & W299	*(Wing regd as W229)*	16.10.86	J.Williams	(Mansfield)	21. 7.02P
G-MTBE	CFM Shadow CD (Rotax 462HP)	K.035		16.10.86	S.K.Brown	Old Sarum	19.10.02P
G-MTBH	Mainair Gemini/Flash II (Rotax 462)	524-187-5 & W327		28.10.86	T.& P.Sludds	(Enniscorthy, Co.Wexford)	23. 6.02P
G-MTBI*	Mainair Gemini/Flash II (Rotax 462)	508-1286-4 & W311		27.10.86	A.Ormson *(Flood damage late 2000) (Cancelled 15.11.00 as wfu) (Stored 1.02)*	(Rochdale)	29. 5.01P
G-MTBJ	Mainair Gemini/Flash II (Rotax 503)	509-1286-4 & W312		27.10.86	R.M. & P.J.Perry *(Op Staffordshire Aero Club)*	Otherton, Cannock	6. 7.02P
G-MTBK	Southdown Raven X (Rotax 503)	SN2232/0230		28.10.86	R.J.Grimwood	Sywell	27. 6.99P
G-MTBL	Solar Wings Pegasus XL-R (Rotax 447)	SW-TB-1121 & SW-WA-1117		6.11.86	R.N.Whiting	Lower Mountpleasant, Chatteris	18. 1.02P

G-MTBN	Southdown Raven X (Rotax 447)	SN2232/0227	28.10.86	A.J. & S.E.Crosby-Jones	Hailsham	4. 9.02P
G-MTBO	Southdown Raven X (Rotax 447)	SN2232/0233	28.10.86	D.C.Britton	(Bristol)	27.10.02P
G-MTBP	Aerotech MW-5B Sorcerer (Fuji-Robin EC-44-PM)	SR102-R440B-02	28.10.86	G.Bennett	(Caister-on-Sea)	21. 9.94P
G-MTBR	Aerotech MW-5B Sorcerer (Fuji-Robin EC-44-PM)	SR102-R440B-03	20. 1.87	P.W.Hastings	(Stratford-upon-Avon)	31.10.02P
G-MTBS	Aerotech MW-5B Sorcerer (Fuji-Robin EC-44-PM)	SR102-R440B-04	27.10.86	T B Fowler	(Newent)	27. 9.02P
G-MTBU	Solar Wings Pegasus XL-R (Rotax 447)	SW-TB-1122 & SW-WA-1118	13.11.86	R.P.R.Staveley	(Alfreton)	27.12.01P
G-MTBW*	Mainair Gemini/Flash II	520-187-5 & W322	6.11.86	Not known *(Crashed Old Airfield, Aldridge 15.4.97 & cancelled by CAA 23.2.98) (Noted 4.01)*	Otherton, Cannock	
G-MTBX	Mainair Gemini/Flash II (Rotax 447)	510-1286-4 & W313	6.11.86	R.K.W.Moss	(Northwich)	21. 3.01P
G-MTBY	Mainair Gemini/Flash II	507-1286-4-W310	6.11.86	A.Worthington	(Chorley)	5. 4.97P
G-MTBZ	Southdown Raven X (Rotax 447)	SN2232/0232	10.11.86	C A M Anderton *(Noted badly damaged 8.01)*	Tarn Farm, Cockerham	15.10.01P
G-MTCA	CFM Shadow C (Rotax 503)	K.011	6.11.86	J.R.L.Murray	East Fortune	26. 7.02P
G-MTCC*	Mainair Gemini/Flash II (Rotax 503)	497-1186-4 & W298	13.11.86	J.Madhvani *(Damaged trike noted 9.00: cancelled 4.10.00 as wfu)*	Plaistows Farm, St.Albans	21.10.96P
G-MTCE	Mainair Gemini/Flash II (Rotax 462)	511-1286-4 & W314	2.12.86	R.S.Acreman	Hatherton, Cannock	23. 5.99P
G-MTCG	Solar Wings Pegasus XL-R/Se (Rotax 447)	SW-TB-1125 & SW-WA-1123	16.12.86	M K Nicholson	Eshott	11.12.02P
G-MTCH	Solar Wings Pegasus XL-R (Rotax 447)	SW-TB-1126 & SW-WA-1124	28.11.86	R.E.H.Harris	Davidstow Moor	29.11.95P
G-MTCK	Solar Wings Pegasus Flash II (Rotax 447)	SW-TB-1127 & SW-WF-0127 *(Mainair sailwing c/n W263)*	11.12.86	S.Suckling	(Worthing)	16. 9.01P
G-MTCM	Southdown Raven X (Rotax 447)	S N2232/0239	11.12.86	J.C Rose *(New owner 9.01)*	Oakley, Beds	2. 7.97P
G-MTCN	Solar Wings Pegasus XL-R (Rotax 447)	SW-TB-1128 & SW-WA-1126	16.12.86	N.Procopakis & C.Fullstone	(Birmingham)	12.12.00P
G-MTCO	Solar Wings Pegasus XL-R (Rotax 447)	SW-TB-1129 & SW-WA-1127	7. 1.87	A.J.Nesom	Baxby Manor, Husthwaite	6.11.00P
G-MTCP	Aerial Arts Chaser/110SX (Rotax 377)	110SX/476	16.12.86	B.Richardson	(Sunderland)	28. 6.00P
G-MTCR	Solar Wings Pegasus XL-R (Rotax 447)	SW-TB-1130 & SW-WA-1128	16.12.86	P.J.Bates	Rufforth	17. 7.02P
G-MTCT	CFM Shadow CD (Rotax 503)	042	16.12.86	F.W.McCann	Cumbernauld	25. 8.02P
G-MTCU	Mainair Gemini/Flash IIA (Rotax 503)	451-1286-4 & W228	5. 1.87	T.J.Philip	(Sale)	28. 5.02P
G-MTCW	Mainair Gemini/Flash II (Rotax 462)	502-1186-4 & W304	5. 1.87	R.A.Watering	(Bourne, Lincs)	20. 1.02P
G-MTCX	Solar Wings Pegasus XL-R (Rotax 447)	SW-TB-1131 & SW-WA-1129	9. 1.87	A.L.Davies	Emlyn's Field, Rhuallt	30. 6.99P
G-MTDD	Aerial Arts Chaser/110SX (Rotax 377)	110SX/437	26. 1.87	B.Richardson	(Sunderland)	4. 7.00P
G-MTDE	Aerial Arts Chaser/110SX (Rotax 377) *(May now have Rotax 330)*	110SX/438	5. 1.87	G.Firth	Sandtoft	19. 1.01P
G-MTDF	Mainair Gemini/Flash II (Rotax 503)	515-287-5 & W319	5. 1.87	S.R.Dalby	(Rossendale)	22. 4.02P
G-MTDG	Solar Wings Pegasus XL-R/Se (Rotax 447)	SW-TB-1132 & SW-WA-1130	20. 1.87	E.W.Laidlaw *(Noted 8.00)*	(Turriff)	7. 7.01P
G-MTDH	Solar Wings Pegasus XL-R (Rotax 447)	SW-TB-1133 & SW-WA-1131	22. 1.87	M.Shiner	Lamb Holm Farm, Orkney	30. 6.01P
G-MTDI	Solar Wings Pegasus XL-R/Se (Rotax 447)	SW-TB-1134 & SW-WA-1132	22. 1.87	W.Wood *(Stored 9.97: current status unknown)*	Eshott	13. 5.91P
G-MTDK	Aerotech MW-5B Sorcerer (Fuji-Robin EC-44-PM)	SR102-R440B-06 *(To be converted to Rotax 447)*	22. 1.87	R.R.Hadley	Dunkeswell	23. 6.00P
G-MTDN	Ultraflight Lazair IIIE (Rotax 185)	A465/002	22. 1.87	M.J.Broom *(New owner 6.01)*	Long Marston	27. 6.97P
G-MTDO	Eipper Quicksilver MXII (Rotax 503)	1124	27. 2.87	D.L.Ham *(Current status unknown)*	(Honiton)	5.11.87E
G-MTDR	Mainair Gemini/Flash II (Rotax 503)	516-287-5 & W276	26. 1.87	J.W. & C.Richardson	Baxby Manor, Husthwaite	25. 7.02P
G-MTDT	Solar Wings Pegasus XL-R (Rotax 447)	SW-TB-1137 & SW-WA-1135	2. 2.87	J.R.E.Gladstone t/a G-MTDT Syndicate	Enstone	7. 5.02P
G-MTDU	CFM Shadow CD (Rotax 503-2V)	K.037	26. 1.87	J.W.Taylor	(Ross-on-Wye)	31. 5.02P

G-MTDW	Mainair Gemini/Flash II		2. 2.87	S.R.Leeper	Priory Farm, Tibenham	21. 8.02P
	(Rotax 503)	517-387-5 & W212				
G-MTDX	CFM Shadow BD	K.043	10. 2.87	L.Fekete	(Ellesmere Port)	4. 6.00P
	(Rotax 503)					
G-MTDY	Mainair Gemini/Flash II		11. 2.87	S.Penoyre	(Windlesham)	13.10.00P
	(Rotax 462)	513-187-5 & W317				
G-MTEB	Solar Wings Pegasus XL-R		9. 2.87	F.Watt	(Insch)	10. 7.00P
	(Rotax 447)	SW-TB-1141 & SW-WA-1139				
G-MTEC	Solar Wings Pegasus XL-R		9. 2.87	R.W.Glover	Kemble	11. 6.94P
	(Rotax 447)	SW-TB-1142 & SW-WA-1140		*(Trike noted 2000)*		
G-MTED	Solar Wings Pegasus XL-R		9. 2.87	D.Marsh	Charminster, Bournemouth	31. 8.01P
	(Rotax 447)	SW-TB-1143 & SW-WA-1141				
G-MTEE	Solar Wings Pegasus XL-R		13. 2.87	S.M.Dewson		
	(Rotax 447)	SW-TB-1144 & SW-WA-1142			Shenstone Hall Farm, Shenstone	4. 8.99P
	(C/n plate incorrectly shows SW-WA-1144 & SW-WA-1142) (New wing ? - see G-MTLG) (Current status unknown)					
G-MTEJ	Mainair Gemini/Flash II		18. 2.87	G.J.Moore	Ince Blundell	2. 5.01P
	(Rotax 462)	522-387-5 & W277				
G-MTEK	Mainair Gemini/Flash II		3. 3.87	M.O'Hearne & G.M.Wrigley	Rufforth	3.10.94P
	(Rotax 503)	523-387-5 & W279				
G-MTEN	Mainair Gemini/Flash II		25. 2.87	B.Bennison	(Brough)	8. 1.02P
	(Rotax 503)	527-487-5 & W285				
G-MTER	Solar Wings Pegasus XL-R/Se		19. 2.87	I.Stratford	(Stoke-on-Trent)	7. 4.02P
	(Rotax 447)	SW-TB-1146 & SW-WA-1144				
G-MTES	Solar Wings Pegasus XL-R		19. 2.87	K.A.Lyons	Tregavethan, Truro	27.11.01P
	(Rotax 447)	SW-TB-1147 & SW-WA-1145				
G-MTET	Solar Wings Pegasus XL-R		19. 2.87	P.A.S.Talbot	(Camborne)	2. 5.00P
	(Rotax 447)	SW-TB-1148 & SW-WA-1146				
G-MTEU	Solar Wings Pegasus XL-R/Se		19. 2.87	B.Harris	(Northwich)	9. 4.01P
	(Rotax 447)	SW-TB-1149 & SW-WA-1147				
G-MTEW	Solar Wings Pegasus XL-R/Se		19. 2.87	R.W. & P.J.Holley	(Shifnal)	4. 5.02P
	(Rotax 447)	SW-TB-1151 & SW-WA-1149				
G-MTEX	Solar Wings Pegasus XL-R		19. 2.87	R.J.Coppin	(Hereford)	26. 8.02P
	(Rotax 447)	SW-TB-1152 & SW-WA-1150				
G-MTEY	Mainair Gemini/Flash II		20. 2.87	A.Wells	Baxby Manor, Husthwaite	4. 6.98P
	(Rotax 503)	518-387-5 & W217				
G-MTFB	Solar Wings Pegasus XL-R		24. 2.87	I.D.Stokes	(Camelford)	20. 3.00P
	(Rotax 462)	SW-TE-0015 & SW-WA-1157				
G-MTFC	Medway Hybred 44XLR	22087/24	23. 3.87	J.K.Masters	(Chigwell)	25. 7.97P
	(Rotax 447)					
G-MTFE	Solar Wings Pegasus XL-R		6. 3.87	D.A.Eastough	(Chellaston)	17. 5.02P
	(Rotax 447)	SW-TB-1157 & SW-WA-1155 *(New sailwing fitted 1999)*				
G-MTFF	Mainair Gemini/Flash II		12. 3.87	T.N.Taylor	(Sidcup)	19. 4.96P
	(Rotax 503)	528-487-5 & W286				
G-MTFG	AMF Chevvron 2-32C	CH.004	9. 3.87	R.Gardner	(Stratford-upon-Avon)	24. 7.02P
	(Konig SD570)					
G-MTFI	Mainair Gemini/Flash II		12. 3.87	M.Carolan	Annaghmore, Co.Tyrone	19. 5.02P
	(Rotax 503)	531-487-5 & W289				
G-MTFJ	Mainair Gemini/Flash II		12. 3.87	G.Souch & M.D.Peacock		
	(Rotax 503)	532-487-5 & W320			(Leatherhead/Guildford)	12. 5.02P
G-MTFK*	Moult Trike/Flexiform Striker	DIM-01	23. 3.87	The Norfolk & Suffolk Aviation Museum		
				(Cancelled 13.6.90 by CAA)	Flixton	
G-MTFL	Ultraflight Lazair IIIE	A466/003	12. 3.87	P.J.Turrell	(Halesowen)	26. 9.89P
	(Rotax 185 x 2)					
G-MTFM	Solar Wings Pegasus XL-R		13. 3.87	P.R.G.Morley	Newnham, Baldock	20. 4.02P
	(Rotax 462)	SW-TE-0016 & SW-WA-1158				
G-MTFN	Whittaker MW5 Sorcerer		13. 3.87	K.Southam	(Newcastle upon Tyne)	13. 2.02P
	(Fuji-Robin EC-44-PM)	PFA 163-11207 *(May be Model MW5B)*				
G-MTFO	Solar Wings Pegasus XL-R/Se		18. 3.87	A.Gonzalez & W.Highton	Carlisle	1. 5.02P
	(Rotax 447)	SW-TB-1159 & SW-WA-1159				
G-MTFP	Solar Wings Pegasus XL-R		18. 3.87	C.Rickards	(Swansea)	14.12.01P
	(Rotax 447)	SW-TB-1160 & SW-WA-1160				
G-MTFR	Solar Wings Pegasus XL-R/Se		18. 3.87	S.Ballantyne	(Blanefield)	19. 9.99P
	(Rotax 447)	SW-TB-1161 & SW-WA-1161				
G-MTFT	Solar Wings Pegasus XL-R		18. 3.87	A.T.Smith	Hughley, Much Wenlock	30. 7.00P
	(Rotax 447)	SW-TB-1163 & SW-WA-1163				
G-MTFU	CFM Shadow BD	K.034	18. 3.87	G.R.Eastwood	Full Sutton	13. 8.00P
	(Rotax 447)					
G-MTFZ	CFM Shadow CD	053	24. 3.87	R.P.Stonor	Long Marston	22. 3.02P
	(Rotax 503)					
G-MTGA	Mainair Gemini/Flash II		26. 3.87	B.E.Warburton	St Michaels	18. 7.01P
	(Rotax 503)	535-587-5 & W293		*(Op North Lancs Micro School)*		
G-MTGB	Thruster TST Mk.1	837-TST-011	10. 4.87	G.Arthur	Tarn Farm, Cockerham	11. 9.00P
	(Rotax 503)					

G-MTGC	Thruster TST Mk.1 (Rotax 503)	837-TST-012	10. 4.87	B.Foster & P.Smith	Gerpins Lane, Upminster	31. 5.02P
G-MTGD	Thruster TST Mk.1 (Rotax 503)	837-TST-013	10. 4.87	W.J.Lister	Fenland	31. 8.02P
G-MTGE	Thruster TST Mk.1 (Rotax 503)	837-TST-014	10. 4.87	G.W.R.Swift	(Hartfield)	17.10.99P
G-MTGF	Thruster TST Mk.1 (Rotax 503)	837-TST-015	10. 4.87	B.Swindon	(Chesham)	6. 6.02P
G-MTGH	Mainair Gemini/Flash II (Rotax 462)	536-587-5 & W294	31. 3.87	J.R.Gillies	(Hunsdon)	26. 5.02P
G-MTGJ	Solar Wings Pegasus XL-R (Rotax 447)	SW-TB-1165 & SW-WA-1165	1. 4.87	M.S.Taylor	(Gillingham)	17. 2.02P
G-MTGK	Solar Wings Pegasus XL-R (Rotax 447)	SW-TB-1166 & SW-WA-1166	1. 4.87	I.A.Smith	(Canterbury)	1. 8.91P
G-MTGL	Solar Wings Pegasus XL-R (Rotax 447)	SW-TB-1167 & SW-WA-1167	1. 4.87	P.J.& R.Openshaw	(Warrington)	15. 4.02P
G-MTGM	Solar Wings Pegasus XL-R (Rotax 447)	SW-TB-1168 & SW-WA-1168	1. 4.87	K.W.Olden	Roddige, Fradley	14. 5.01P
	(Original trike destroyed in gales 1.98 Roddige: fitted with trike from G-MNYT (c/n SW-TB-1099)					
G-MTGN	CFM Shadow BD (Rotax 447)	K.041	31. 3.87	N.G.Price	Bricket Wood, Radlett	9. 9.01P
G-MTGO	Mainair Gemini/Flash IIA (Rotax 462)	550-587-5 & W336	10. 4.87	J.Mumby	(Lilleshall)	29. 6.02P
G-MTGP	Thruster TST Mk.1 (Rotax 503)	847-TST-016	10. 4.87	J.H.Cooling	Fenland	16. 2.02P
G-MTGR	Thruster TST Mk.1 (Rotax 503)	847-TST-017	10. 4.87	M.R.Grunwell	(Brentwood)	30.11.02P
G-MTGS	Thruster TST Mk.1 (Rotax 503)	847-TST-018	10. 4.87	R.Dennett	Barton	31. 7.02P
G-MTGT	Thruster TST Mk.1 (Rotax 503)	847-TST-019	10. 4.87	R.T.Manderson	Strathaven	28.11.02P
G-MTGU	Thruster TST Mk.1 (Rotax 503)	847-TST-020	10. 4.87	W Doyle	Eshott	13. 9.02P
G-MTGV	CFM Shadow CD (Rotax 503)	052	8. 4.87	V.R.Riley	Tarn Farm, Cockerham	11. 3.01P
G-MTGW	CFM Shadow CD (Rotax 503)	054	8. 4.87	L.A.Gould	(Brighton)	9. 6.02P
G-MTGX	Hornet Dual Trainer/Southdown Raven (Rotax 462)	HRWA 0061 & SN2000/0270	13. 4.87	S.J.M.Morling	(Taunton)	11. 4.97P
G-MTHB	Aerotech MW-5B Sorcerer (Fuji-Robin EC-44-PM)	SR102-R440B-08	10. 4.87	P.A.Gasson	(Woking)	11. 7.02P
G-MTHC	Raven Aircraft Raven X (Rotax 447)	SN2232/0257	15. 4.87	J.Channer	(Nottingham)	18. 3.02P
G-MTHG	Solar Wings Pegasus XL-R (Rotax 447)	SW-TB-1170 & SW-WA-1171	13. 4.87	H.E.Paterson	(Poynton)	19. 2.99P
G-MTHH	Solar Wings Pegasus XL-R (Rotax 447)	SW-TB-1171 & SW-WA-1172	13. 4.87	J.Palmer	(Winkleigh)	28.12.98P
G-MTHI	Solar Wings Pegasus XL-R (Rotax 447)	SW-TB-1172 & SW-WA-1173	13. 4.87	J.R.Bowman	(Oxford)	27. 1.02P
G-MTHJ	Solar Wings Pegasus XL-R (Rotax 447)	SW-TB-1173 & SW-WA-1174	13. 4.87	S.A.Watson	Long Acre Farm, Sandy	13.10.02P
G-MTHN	Solar Wings Pegasus XL-R (Rotax 447)	SW-TB-1177 & SW-WA-1178	13. 4.87	G.E.Murphy	Haverfordwest	2. 9.01P
G-MTHS*	CFM Shadow CD (Rotax 582)	059	22. 4.87	A.J.McMenmamin *(Cancelled 11.6.99 by CAA: noted 5.00)*	Oakley, Beds	17. 5.97P
G-MTHT	CFM Shadow CD (Rotax 503)	058	22. 4.87	B.J.Topham	Old Sarum	23. 3.02P
G-MTHU	Hornet Dual Trainer/Southdown Raven (Rotax 462)	HRWA 0062 & SN2000/0269	30. 4.87	J.Barlow	(Castletown, IoM)	4. 9.93P
G-MTHV	CFM Shadow BD (Rotax 447)	K.049	7. 5.87	K.R.Bircher *(Noted 10.01)*	Over Farm, Gloucester	24. 7.00P
G-MTHW	Mainair Gemini/Flash II (Rotax 462)	540-587-5 & W325	14. 5.87	M.D.Kirby	Chase Farm, Billericay	31. 7.02P
G-MTHZ	Mainair Gemini/Flash IIA (Rotax 503)	541-587-5 & W329	14. 5.87	S.Bond & D.E.Lord	Crosland Moor	6.12.01P
G-MTIA	Mainair Gemini/Flash IIA (Rotax 503)	544-687-5 & W332	14. 5.87	R.M.Jarvis	(Welwyn Garden City)	4. 8.02P
G-MTIB	Mainair Gemini/Flash IIA (Rotax 503)	545-687-5 & W333	14. 5.87	M.A.Hope *(Op Northern Microlight School)*	St Michaels	15.11.02P
G-MTID	Raven Aircraft Raven X (Rotax 447)	SN2232/0276	18. 5.87	R.G.Featherby *(Cancelled 13.6.01 by CAA)*	(King's Lynn)	23. 2.99P
G-MTIE	Solar Wings Pegasus XL-R (Rotax 462)	SW-TE-0019 & SW-WA-1183	18. 5.87	A.H.Paterson & I.M.Vass	(Wick)	28. 6.02P

G-MTIH	Solar Wings Pegasus XL-R (Rotax 447) SW-TB-1183 & SW-WA-1186	18. 5.87	C.R.Cawley & B.Chapman	(Clemsford)	25. 3.02P
G-MTIJ	Solar Wings Pegasus XL-R/Se (Rotax 447) SW-TB-1185 & SW-WA-1188	18. 5.87	M.J.F.Gilbody	(Urmston, Manchester)	1. 4.98P
G-MTIK	Raven Aircraft Raven X SN2232/0272 (Rotax 447)	19. 5.87	G A Oldershaw	(Ely)	16.11.02P
G-MTIL	Mainair Gemini/Flash IIA (Rotax 462) 549-687-5 & W338	21. 5.87	S.Lunney	Ince Blundell	15. 8.02P
G-MTIM	Mainair Gemini/Flash IIA (Rotax 503) 553-687-5 & W341	21. 5.87	W.M.Swan	East Fortune	30. 4.02P
G-MTIN	Mainair Gemini/Flash IIA (Rotax 503) 547-687-5 & W335	1. 6.87	S.J.Firth	(Dallerie, Crieff)	29. 5.02P
G-MTIO	Solar Wings Pegasus XL-R (Rotax 447) SW-TB-1187 & SW-WA-1190	26. 5.87	M.A.Coe	(Kettering)	5. 7.02P
G-MTIP	Solar Wings Pegasus XL-R (Rotax 447) SW-TB-1188 & SW-WA-1191	26. 5.87	W.B.Cooper	Sutton Meadows, Ely	19.12.01P
G-MTIR	Solar Wings Pegasus XL-R/Se (Rotax 447) SW-TB-1189 & SW-WA-1192	26. 5.87	D.Raybould	(Chesterfield)	27. 6.01P
G-MTIS	Solar Wings Pegasus XL-R (Rotax 447) SW-TB-1190 & SW-WA-1193	26. 5.87	N.P.Power	(Eastbourne)	7. 4.02P
G-MTIU	Solar Wings Pegasus XL-R (Rotax 447) SW-TB-1191 & SW-WA-1194	26. 5.87	D.Burdett	(Chatteris)	8. 8.02P
G-MTIV	Solar Wings Pegasus XL-R (Rotax 447) SW-TB-1192 & SW-WA-1195	26. 5.87	P.J.Culverhouse t/a Syndicate IV	Sittles Farm, Alrewas	18.11.02P
G-MTIW	Solar Wings Pegasus XL-R (Rotax 447) SW-TB-1193 & SW-WA-1196	26. 5.87	G.S.Francis	(Bristol)	1. 9.02P
G-MTIX	Solar Wings Pegasus XL-R (Rotax 447) SW-TB-1194 & SW-WA-1197	26. 5.87	S.Pickering	Sutton Meadows, Ely	15. 1.01P
G-MTIY	Solar Wings Pegasus XL-R (Rotax 447) SW-TB-1195 & SW-WA-1198	26. 5.87	P.J.Tanner	Weston Zoyland	15. 2.02P
G-MTIZ	Solar Wings Pegasus XL-R (Rotax 447) SW-TB-1196 & SW-WA-1199	26. 5.87	S.L.Blount	Sutton Meadows, Ely	22.10.02P
G-MTJA	Mainair Gemini/Flash IIA (Rotax 503) 551-687-5 & W339	15. 6.87	A.W.Shellis & P.Davis	Otherton, Cannock	12.11.02P
G-MTJB	Mainair Gemini/Flash IIA (Rotax 462) 554-687-5 & W343	2. 6.87	A.Dixon	Tarn Farm, Cockerham	13. 1.02P
G-MTJC	Mainair Gemini/Flash IIA (Honda BF52 @ 808cc) 555-687-5 & W344	1. 6.87	T.A.Dockrell	Kingston Seymour	2. 7.02P
G-MTJD	Mainair Gemini/Flash IIA (Rotax 462) 552-687-5 & W340	5. 6.87	M.Bond	Shobdon	19.10.02P
G-MTJE	Mainair Gemini/Flash IIA (Rotax 503) 556-687-5 & W345	24. 6.87	C.J.Dyke	Redlands, Swindon	10. 8.02P
G-MTJG	Medway Hybred 44XLR 22587/25 (Rotax 447)	16. 6.87	Margaret A.Trodden	Tupton, Chesterfield	24. 2.99P
G-MTJH	Solar Wings Pegasus/Flash (Rotax 447) SW-TB-1050 & W342-687-3 *(Trike previously fitted to G-MMUF)*	17. 6.87	C.L.Parker	Ampthill	3. 7.02P
G-MTJK	Mainair Gemini/Flash IIA (Rotax 503) 559-787-5 & W348	17. 6.87	R.C.White	Aldermaston	16. 6.00P
G-MTJL	Mainair Gemini/Flash IIA (Rotax 503) 548-687-5 & W337	17. 6.87	D.J.Tuplin & B.G.M.Chapman	Sandtoft	27. 8.02P
G-MTJM	Mainair Gemini/Flash IIA (Rotax 462) 560-787-5 & W349	24. 6.87	K.J.Regan	(Teddington)	6. 8.00P
G-MTJN	Midland Ultralights Sirocco 377GB (Rotax 377) MU-020	23. 6.87	S.Armstrong *(New owner 7.01)*	(Canterbury)	19. 3.94P
G-MTJP	Medway Hybred 44XLR 25687/27 (Rotax 447)	6. 7.87	I.J.Alexander & P.Fitzsimmons	Plaistows Farm, St Albans	1. 7.02P
G-MTJS	Solar Wings Pegasus XL-Q (Rotax 462) SW-TE-0022 & SW-WX-0013	6. 7.87	R.J.H.Hayward	(Belmont)	22. 9.02P
G-MTJT	Mainair Gemini/Flash IIA (Rotax 462) 558-787-5 & W347	16. 7.87	D.T.A.Rees	Haverfordwest	2. 2.02P
G-MTJV	Mainair Gemini/Flash IIA (Rotax 503) 562-787-5 & W351	16. 7.87	N.Charles & J.Richards	Swinford, Rugby	5. 7.02P
G-MTJW	Mainair Gemini/Flash IIA (Rotax 503) 563-787-5 & W352	16. 7.87	J.F.Ashton	(Liverpool)	4.10.95P
G-MTJX	Hornet Dual Trainer/Southdown Raven (Rotax 462) HRWA 0063 & SN2000/0279	5. 8.87	J.P.Kirwan	(Liverpool)	31. 3.99P
G-MTJZ	Mainair Gemini/Flash IIA (Rotax 462) 561-787-5 & W350	16. 7.87	A.Robinson & J.Williams	Long Marston	19. 5.02P
G-MTKA	Thruster TST Mk.1 867-TST-021 (Rotax 503)	21. 7.87	M.R.Jones *(Under rebuild 12.01)*	Wing Farm, Longbridge Deverill	15. 7.00P
G-MTKB	Thruster TST Mk.1 867-TST-022 (Rotax 503)	21. 7.87	M.Hanna	Rathfriland, Co.Down	13. 3.01P
G-MTKD	Thruster TST Mk.1 867-TST-024 (Rotax 503)	21. 7.87	T.K.Duffy	Dunnyvadden, Co.Antrim	27.10.02P

G-MTKE	Thruster TST Mk.1 (Rotax 503)	867-TST-025		21. 7.87	W.Wells & D.F.Hughes	Stoke, Kent	31. 7.01P
G-MTKG	Solar Wings Pegasus XL-R/Se (Rotax 447)	SW-TB-1199 & SW-WA-1201		13. 7.87	W.J.Hodgins	Deenethorpe	9. 6.02P
G-MTKH	Solar Wings Pegasus XL-R (Rotax 447)	SW-TB-1200 & SW-WA-1202		13. 7.87	N.Harford	Horley	27. 4.01P
G-MTKI	Solar Wings Pegasus XL-R (Rotax 447)	SW-TB-1201 & SW-WA-1203		13. 7.87	I.D.A.Spanton	Malvern	24. 9.01P
G-MTKJ*	Solar Wings Pegasus XL-R/Se (Rotax 447)	SW-TB-1202 & SW-WA-1204		13. 7.87	S.W.Grainger *(Cancelled 2.10.01 as destroyed)*	(Wirral)	22. 7.01P
G-MTKM	Gardner T-M Scout S2	87/003		12. 8.87	D.Gardner *(As "38674" in USAS c/s)*	(Lutterworth)	
G-MTKN	Mainair Gemini/Flash IIA (Rotax 503)	566-887-5 & W355		15. 7.87	A.J.Taylor	(Colne)	9. 6.99P
G-MTKR	CFM Shadow CD (Rotax 503)	067	9H-ABL G-MTKR	20. 7.87	P.A.James t/a Cloudbase Aviation G-MTKR	Redhill	19. 5.02P
G-MTKV	Mainair Gemini/Flash IIA (Rotax 503)	565-887-5 & W354		26. 8.87	L.A.Davidson	Sandtoft	22. 5.02P
G-MTKW	Mainair Gemini/Flash IIA (Rotax 503)	569-887-5 & W358		13. 7.87	R.T.Henry	Newtownards, Co.of Down	3. 3.02P
G-MTKX	Mainair Gemini/Flash IIA (Rotax 503)	568-887-5 & W357		13. 7.87	A.S.Leach	(Warrington)	27. 8.00P
G-MTKZ	Mainair Gemini/Flash IIA (Rotax 503)	571-887-5 & W360		31. 7.87	J.A.Ewens	East Fortune	19. 9.02P
G-MTLB	Mainair Gemini/Flash IIA (Rotax 503)	573-887-5 & W362		31. 7.87	D.N.Bacon	Hucknall	16. 3.01P
G-MTLC	Mainair Gemini/Flash IIA (Rotax 503)	574-887-5 & W363		31. 7.87	R.J.Alston	(Cromer)	13. 7.02P
G-MTLD	Mainair Gemini/Flash IIA (Rotax 503)	575-887-5 & W364		31. 7.87	I.A.Forrest	East Fortune	28. 3.02P
G-MTLG	Solar Wings Pegasus XL-R (Rotax 447)	SW-TB-1207 & SW-WA-1211		31. 7.87	D.Young t/a Kemble Flying Club	Kemble	4.11.02P
G-MTLI	Solar Wings Pegasus XL-R (Rotax 447)	SW-TB-1209 & SW-WA-1213		31. 7.87	M.McKay	(Robertsbridge)	6. 6.97P
G-MTLJ	Solar Wings Pegasus XL-R/Se (Rotax 447)	SW-TB-1210 & SW-WA-1214		31. 7.87	R.E.Pratt	Sandtoft	27. 7.99P
G-MTLL	Mainair Gemini/Flash IIA (Rotax 503)	578-987-5 & W367		14. 8.87	M.S.Lawrence	Mill Farm, Shifnal	30. 6.02P
G-MTLM	Thruster TST Mk.1 (Rotax 503)	887-TST-027		5. 8.87	E.F.Howells t/a Chloe's Flying Group *"Chloe"*	Manor Farm, Croughton	4. 6.02P
G-MTLN	Thruster TST Mk.1 (Rotax 503)	887-TST-028		5. 8.87	A.G.E.Smith	Doynton, Gloucestershire	14. 7.02P
G-MTLR	Thruster TST Mk.1 (Rotax 503)	887-TST-031		5. 8.87	G.A.McKay	(Linlithgow)	17. 5.01P
G-MTLT	Solar Wings Pegasus XL-R (Rotax 447)	SW-TB-1212 & SW-WA-1216		12. 8.87	S.P.MacDonald	Crowland	11. 2.02P
G-MTLU	Solar Wings Pegasus XL-R/Se (Rotax 447)	SW-TB-1213 & SW-WA-1217		12. 8.87	M.W.Riley	(Morpeth)	22. 9.02P
G-MTLV	Solar Wings Pegasus XL-R (Rotax 447)	SW-TB-1214 & SW-WA-1218		12. 8.87	D.E.Watson	Long Marston	28. 8.02P
G-MTLX	Medway Hybred 44XLR (Rotax 447)	20687/26		14. 8.87	D.A.Coupland	RAF Wyton	31. 3.02P
G-MTLY	Solar Wings Pegasus XL-R (Rotax 462)	SW-TE-0026 & SW-WA-1220		12. 8.87	I.Johnston	(Bolton)	5. 7.92P
G-MTLZ	Whittaker MW5 Sorcerer (Rotax 377)	PFA 163-11241		13. 8.87	M.J.Davenport	Weston Zoyland	1. 8.02P
G-MTMA	Mainair Gemini/Flash IIA (Rotax 503)	579-987-5 & W368		14. 8.87	D.Bussell	St.Michaels	20. 6.02P
G-MTMC	Mainair Gemini/Flash IIA (Rotax 503)	581-987-5 & W370		14. 8.87	A.R.Johnson	Brenzett, Kent	25. 5.02P
G-MTME	Solar Wings Pegasus XL-R (Rotax 447)	SW-TB-1216 & SW-WA-1221		18. 8.87	M.T.Finch	Sutton Meadows, Ely	22.11.02P
G-MTMF	Solar Wings Pegasus XL-R (Rotax 447)	SW-TB-1217 & SW-WA-1222		18. 8.87	J.T.W.Smith	(Mallaig)	5. 5.02P
G-MTMG	Solar Wings Pegasus XL-R (Rotax 447)	SW-TB-1218 & SW-WA-1223		18. 8.87	C.W. & P.E.F.Suckling	(Rushden)	18. 8.00P
G-MTMI	Solar Wings Pegasus XL-R/Se (Rotax 447)	SW-TB-1220 & SW-WA-1225		18. 8.87	D.Crozier	Eshott	27. 1.02P
G-MTMK	Raven Aircraft Raven X (Rotax 447)	SN2000/0289		2. 9.87	D.W.Thomas	Long Marston	1. 8.02P
G-MTML	Mainair Gemini/Flash IIA (Rotax 462)	582-1087-5 & W371		27. 8.87	J.F.Ashton	(Liverpool)	30. 7.00P
G-MTMO	Raven Aircraft Raven X (Rotax 447)	SN2232/0278	(G-MTKL)	11. 9.87	H.Tuvey	(South Ockendon)	26. 7.02P

G-MTMP	Hornet Dual Trainer/Southdown Raven (Rotax 462)	HRWA 0064 & SN2000/0288	28. 8.87	P.G.Owen	Baxby Manor, Husthwaite	6. 8.99P
G-MTMR	Hornet Dual Trainer/Southdown Raven (Rotax 462)	HRWA 0065 & SN2000/0297	28. 8.87	D.J.Smith	Hucknall	10. 5.99P
G-MTMT	Mainair Gemini/Flash IIA (Rotax 462)	583-1087-5 & W372	3. 9.87	I.Howes	(Penrith)	3. 8.02P
G-MTMV	Mainair Gemini/Flash IIA (Rotax 503)	585-1087-5 & W374	3. 9.87	N.Hartley	(Bishop Auckland)	8. 4.02P
G-MTMW	Mainair Gemini/Flash IIA (Rotax 503)	587-1087-5 & W376	9. 9.87	J.C.Higham	(Willenhall)	8. 6.02P
G-MTMX	CFM Shadow CD (Rotax 503)	070	4. 9.87	I.M.Cross	Long Marston	27.11.01P
G-MTMY	CFM Shadow CD (Rotax 503)	071	4. 9.87	R.F.Learney t/a G-MTMY Syndicate	Redhill	1. 2.02P
G-MTNC	Mainair Gemini/Flash IIA (Rotax 503)	588-1087-5 & W377	15. 9.87	D.J.Kelly & M Titmus	Shobdon	27. 8.02P
G-MTNE	Medway Hybred 44XLR (Rotax 447) *(Fitted with new trike as original was transferred to G-MVDC in 1988)*	7987/32	12.10.87	A.G.Rodenburg	(Tillicoultry)	19. 7.02P
G-MTNF	Medway Hybred 44XLR (Rotax 447)	1987/31	12.10.87	P.A.Bedford	(Tewkesbury)	12. 2.00P
G-MTNG	Mainair Gemini/Flash IIA (Rotax 503)	590-1087-5 & W379	21. 9.87	G.M.Yule	Shobdon	25. 7.02P
G-MTNH	Mainair Gemini/Flash IIA (Rotax 462)	589-1087-5 & W378	17. 9.87	J.R.Smart	Over Farm, Gloucester	20. 5.02P
G-MTNI	Mainair Gemini/Flash IIA (Rotax 503)	595-1187-5 & W384	18. 9.87	D.Gatland	Rufforth	25.11.02P
G-MTNJ	Mainair Gemini/Flash IIA (Rotax 462)	593-1187-5 & W382	17. 9.87	S.F.Kennedy	(Market Harborough)	8.12.02P
G-MTNK	Weedhopper JC-24B (Fuji-Robin EC-34-PM) *(Test flown under "B" Conditions 29.6.00 as "G-???")*	1936	28. 9.87	P.Scott	Kemble	N/E
G-MTNL	Mainair Gemini/Flash IIA (Rotax 503)	591-1187-5 & W380	21. 9.87	A.K.Munro	Otherton, Cannock	4.11.01P
G-MTNM	Mainair Gemini/Flash IIA (Rotax 503)	592-1187-5 & W381	22. 9.87	C.J.Janson	Shobdon	25. 7.02P
G-MTNO	Solar Wings Pegasus XL-Q (Rotax 447)	SW-TB-1252 & SW-WQ-0001	23. 9.87	A.F.Batchelor	Rayne Hall Farm, Rayne	14. 6.02P
G-MTNP	Solar Wings Pegasus XL-Q (Rotax 447)	SW-TB-1253 & SW-WQ-0002	23. 9.87	G.G.Roberts	Rayne Hall Farm, Rayne	29. 6.02P
G-MTNR	Thruster TST Mk.1 (Rotax 503)	897-TST-032	1.10.87	S.J.David	Henstridge	28. 7.02P
G-MTNS	Thruster TST Mk.1 (Rotax 503)	897-TST-033	1.10.87	G.& B.W.Evan s	Archlid Green, Sandbach	25. 5.02P
G-MTNT	Thruster TST Mk.1 (Rotax 503)	897-TST-034	1.10.87	G.Bennett	(Yarmouth)	11. 3.01P
G-MTNU	Thruster TST Mk.1 (Rotax 503)	897-TST-035	1.10.87	T.Jackson	(Bristol)	15. 9.02P
G-MTNV	Thruster TST Mk.1 (Rotax 503)	897-TST-036	1.10.87	J.B.Russell	Larne, Co.Antrim	11.10.88P
G-MTNX	Mainair Gemini/Flash IIA (Rotax 503)	606-1187-5 & W393	29. 9.87	C.Evans	RAF Wyton	24. 6.02P
G-MTNY	Mainair Gemini/Flash IIA (Rotax 503)	594-1187-5 & W383	2.10.87	R.C.Granger	(Burnham-on-Crouch)	24. 7.02P
G-MTOA	Solar Wings Pegasus XL-R (Rotax 447)	SW-TB-1221 & SW-WA-1226	15. 9.87	R.A.Bird	East Hunsbury, Northampton	8. 8.01P
G-MTOB	Solar Wings Pegasus XL-R (Rotax 447)	SW-TB-1222 & SW-WA-1227	15. 9.87	P.S.Lemm	Hatherton, Cannock	1.10.97P
G-MTOD	Solar Wings Pegasus XL-R (Rotax 447)	SW-TB-1224 & SW-WA-1229	15. 9.87	T A Gordon	(Liskeard)	3. 9.00P
G-MTOE	Solar Wings Pegasus XL-R (Rotax 447)	SW-TB-1225 & SW-WA-1230	15. 9.87	K.J.Bright	Old Sarum	30. 5.02P
G-MTOG	Solar Wings Pegasus XL-R (Rotax 447)	SW-TB-1227 & SW-WA-1232	15. 9.87	C.R.M.Bannerman	(Balfron)	25. 4.02P
G-MTOH	Solar Wings Pegasus XL-R (Rotax 447)	SW-TB-1228 & SW-WA-1233	15. 9.87	H.Cook	(Pontypool)	2. 3.02P
G-MTOI	Solar Wings Pegasus XL-R (Rotax 447)	SW-TB-1229 & SW-WA-1234	15. 9.87	M.P.Kingston	(Attleborough)	15. 6.00P
G-MTOJ	Solar Wings Pegasus XL-R/Se (Rotax 447)	SW-TB-1230 & SW-WA-1235	15. 9.87	D.S.Main	Old Sarum	29. 9.01P
G-MTOK	Solar Wings Pegasus XL-R (Rotax 447)	SW-TB-1231 & SW-WA-1236	2.10.87	W.S. Davis	Oxton, Nottingham	13. 2.02P
G-MTOL	Solar Wings Pegasus XL-R (Rotax 447)	SW-TB-1232 & SW-WA-1237	2.10.87	H M Manning	Rochester	3. 6.00P
G-MTOM	Solar Wings Pegasus XL-R/Se (Rotax 447)	SW-TB-1233 & SW-WA-1238	2.10.87	R.J.Hood	Plaistows Farm, St Albans	27. 7.01P

G-MTON	Solar Wings Pegasus XL-R (Rotax 447) SW-TB-1234 & SW-WA-1239	2.10.87	D.J.Willett	(Malpas)	7. 8.02P
G-MTOO	Solar Wings Pegasus XL-R (Rotax 447) SW-TB-1235 & SW-WA-1240	2.10.87	G.W.Bulmer	(Bristol)	15. 7.02P
G-MTOP	Solar Wings Pegasus XL-R/Se (Rotax 447) SW-TB-1236 & SW-WA-1241	2.10.87	P.D.Larkin	Oakley, Beds	13.10.01P
G-MTOS	Solar Wings Pegasus XL-R (Rotax 447) SW-TB-1238 & SW-WA-1243	9.10.87	C.McKay	Strathaven	1. 9.02P
G-MTOT	Solar Wings Pegasus XL-R (Rotax 447) SW-TB-1239 & SW-WA-1244	9.10.87	G.J.Howley	(Coleford)	14. 1.02P
G-MTOU	Solar Wings Pegasus XL-R/Se (Rotax 447) SW-TB-1240 & SW-WA-1245	9.10.87	D.T.Smith	(Thornaby)	18.12.01P
G-MTOX	Solar Wings Pegasus XL-R (Rotax 447) SW-TB-1243 & SW-WA-1248	19.10.87	T.P.Wright	(Ilkeston)	6. 1.01P
G-MTOY	Solar Wings Pegasus XL-R (Rotax 447) SW-TB-1244 & SW-WA-1249	19.10.87	C.M.Bradford t/a G-MTOY Group	Yatesbury	7. 8.01P
G-MTOZ	Solar Wings Pegasus XL-R (Rotax 447) SW-TB-1245 & SW-WA-1250	19.10.87	P.J.McCool	Enstone	9. 6.02P
G-MTPA	Mainair Gemini/Flash IIA (Rotax 462) 598-1187-5 & W394	13.10.87	P.G.Eastlake	(Harlow)	24. 6.02P
G-MTPC	Raven Aircraft Raven X SN2232/0309 (Rotax 582) *(Modified to "Phillips Swphift" standard 1999 - awaiting BMAA approval)*	15.10.87	G.W.Carwardine	(Uckfield)	3.11.90P
G-MTPE	Solar Wings Pegasus XL-R (Rotax 447) SW-TB-1258 & SW-WA-1260	21.10.87	J.Bassett Brown Shutters Farm, Norton St Philips, Somerset		31. 3.01P
G-MTPF	Solar Wings Pegasus XL-R (Rotax 447) SW-TB-1259 & SW-WA-1261	21.10.87	P.J.C.Martins	Halwell, Totnes	4.10.00P
G-MTPG	Solar Wings Pegasus XL-R (Rotax 447) SW-TB-1260 & SW-WA-1262	21.10.87	J.Sullivan	Davidstow Moor	7. 7.01P
G-MTPH	Solar Wings Pegasus XL-R (Rotax 447) SW-TB-1261 & SW-WA-1263	30.10.87	L.M.Sams	Long Marston	9. 6.02P
G-MTPI	Solar Wings Pegasus XL-R/Se (Rotax 447) SW-TB-1262 & SW-WA-1264	30.10.87	R.J.Bullock	Long Marston	4. 8.02P
G-MTPJ	Solar Wings Pegasus XL-R (Rotax 447) SW-TB-1263 & SW-WA-1265	30.10.87	D.A.Whittaker	Roddige, Fradley	1. 7.02P
G-MTPK	Solar Wings Pegasus XL-R (Rotax 447) SW-TB-1264 & SW-WA-1266	30.10.87	S.H.James	Deenethorpe	21.10.01P
G-MTPL	Solar Wings Pegasus XL-R (Rotax 447) SW-TB-1265 & SW-WA-1267	30.10.87	I.R.F.King	(Tunbridge Wells)	2. 9.99P
G-MTPM	Solar Wings Pegasus XL-R (Rotax 447) SW-TB-1266 & SW-WA-1268	30.10.87	D.K.Seal	Roddige, Fradley	9. 9.01P
G-MTPN	Solar Wings Pegasus XL-Q (Rotax 447) SW-TB-1267 & SW-WQ-0004	21.10.87	B.& D.Bergin	Athenry, Co.Galway	23. 6.02P
G-MTPP	Solar Wings Pegasus XL-R (Rotax 447) SW-TB-1257 & SW-WA-1259	21.10.87	P Molyneux	(London NW8)	2.10.00P
G-MTPR	Solar Wings Pegasus XL-R (Rotax 447) SW-TB-1256 & SW-WA-1257	21.10.87	T.Kenny	(Ballygar)	16. 6.96P
G-MTPS	Solar Wings Pegasus XL-Q (Rotax 462) SW-TE-0021 & SW-WX-0011	23.10.87	G.Tyler	(Cambridge)	4. 6.02P
G-MTPT	Thruster TST Mk.1 8107-TST-038 (Rotax 503)	23.10.87	J.T.Kendrick	Popham	3.11.96P
G-MTPU	Thruster TST Mk.1 8107-TST-039 (Rotax 503)	23.10.87	M.R.Jones *"Poppy"*	Wing Farm, Longbridge Deverill	4. 8.02P
G-MTPV	Thruster TST Mk.1 8107-TST-040 (Rotax 503)	23.10.87	E.Bentley & A.Maxwell	Morgansfield, Fishburn	30. 5.01P
G-MTPW	Thruster TST Mk.1 8107-TST-041 (Rotax 503)	23.10.87	T.A.Jones	Sittles Farm, Alrewas	4. 5.01P
G-MTPX	Thruster TST Mk.1 8107-TST-042 (Rotax 503)	23.10.87	T.Snook	Long Marston	2. 5.93P
G-MTPY	Thruster TST Mk.1 8107-TST-043 (Rotax 503)	23.10.87	P.C.Appleton	(St.Blazey)	25. 7.02P
G-MTRA	Mainair Gemini/Flash IIA (Rotax 503) 605-1187-5 & W395	28.10.87	E.N.Alms *"Yellow Bird"*	Guy Lane Farm, Waverton	2. 2.02P
G-MTRC	Midland Ultralights Sirocco 377GB (Rotax 377) MU-021	2.11.87	D.Thorpe	Grantham	4. 8.01P
G-MTRL	Hornet Dual Trainer/Southdown Raven (Rotax 462) HRWA 0068 & SN2000/0326	4.11.87	J.McAlpine	(Largs)	10.12.02P
G-MTRM	Solar Wings Pegasus XL-R (Rotax 462) SW-TE-0030 & SW-WA-1276	10.11.87	D.B.Jones	Long Acre Farm, Sandy	26. 6.02P
G-MTRN	Solar Wings Pegasus XL-R (Rotax 447) SW-TB-1270 & SW-WA-1269	2.12.87	K.McCoubrey	(Stoke-on-Trent)	3. 8.01P
G-MTRO	Solar Wings Pegasus XL-R/Se (Rotax 447) SW-TB-1271 & SW-WA-1270	2.12.87	H.Lloyd-Hughes	Emlyn's Field, Rhuallt	5. 9.01P
G-MTRS	Solar Wings Pegasus XL-R (Rotax 447) SW-TB-1274 & SW-WA-1273	2.12.87	J.J.R.Tickle	Llanerchymedd, Gwynedd	13. 6.01P

G-MTRT	Raven Aircraft Raven X SN2232/0325 (Rotax 447)	12.11.87	D.Hines	Fordhall Villa Farm, Ternhill	25. 6.00P
G-MTRU	Solar Wings Pegasus XL-Q (Rotax 447) SW-TB-1275 & SW-WQ-0009	10.11.87	A.L.S.Routledge *(Noted wrecked 7.01)*	Rufforth	15.10.00P
G-MTRV	Solar Wings Pegasus XL-Q (Rotax 477) SW-TB-1276 & SW-WX-0010	10.11.87	R.P.Speight	Clench Common	10. 9.02P
G-MTRW	Raven Aircraft Raven X SN2232/0328 (Rotax 447)	12.11.87	P.K.J.Chun	Rochester	20. 9.02P
G-MTRX	Whittaker MW5 Sorcerer (Rotax 447) PFA 163-11202	11.11.87	W.Turner *(Stored 8.96: current status unknown)*	Otherton, Cannock	13. 2.95P
G-MTRZ	Mainair Gemini/Flash IIA (Rotax 503) 611-1287-5 & W400	17.11.87	D.F.G.Barlow	(Morecambe)	8. 7.02P
G-MTSC	Mainair Gemini/Flash IIA (Rotax 503) 618-188-5 & W407	17.11.87	M.Walker	(Chester)	4. 6.02P
G-MTSD	Raven Aircraft Raven X SN2232/0312 (Rotax 447)	24.11.87	D.Turner	Oakley, Beds	10. 3.01P
G-MTSG	CFM Shadow CD 079 (Rotax 503)	24.11.87	C.A.Purvis	Plaistows Farm, St Albans	22. 4.01P
G-MTSH	Thruster TST Mk.1 8117-TST-044 (Rotax 503)	3.12.87	R R Orr	Dromore, Co.of Down	13. 3.02P
G-MTSJ	Thruster TST Mk.1 8117-TST-046 (Rotax 503)	3.12.87	P.J.Mogg	Sturminster Newton	9. 6.02P
G-MTSK	Thruster TST Mk.1 8117-TST-047 (Rotax 503)	3.12.87	J.S.Pyke	Westfield Farm, Hailsham	15. 5.02P
G-MTSM	Thruster TST Mk.1 8117-TST-049 (Rotax 503)	3.12.87	Environment Agency, Thames Region	Oakley, Beds	14. 5.02P
G-MTSN	Solar Wings Pegasus XL-R (Rotax 447) SW-TB-1278 & SW-WA-1280	14.12.87	G.P.Lane	(Pucklechurch)	19. 2.02P
G-MTSO	Solar Wings Pegasus XL-R/Se (Rotax 447) SW-TB-1279 & SW-WA-1281	14.12.87	P.Wibberley	(Chesterfield)	24. 9.01P
G-MTSP	Solar Wings Pegasus XL-R (Rotax 447) SW-TB-1280 & SW-WA-1282	14.12.87	R.J.Nelson	Swinford, Rugby	19.10.02P
G-MTSR	Solar Wings Pegasus XL-R (Rotax 447) SW-TB-1281 & SW-WA-1283	14.12.87	J.Norman	Long Acre Farm, Sandy	13.10.02P
G-MTSS	Solar Wings Pegasus XL-R (Rotax 462) SW-TE-0031 & SW-WA-1284	14.12.87	T.M.Evans	(Haywards Heath)	31. 7.02P
G-MTST(2)	Thruster TST Mk.1 8128-TST-111 (Rotax 503)	12.12.88	D.J.Flower t/a Husthwaite Thruster Group	Baxby Manor, Husthwaite	4. 8.02P
G-MTSU	Solar Wings Pegasus XL-R (Rotax 447) SW-TB-1289 & SW-WA-1285	4. 1.88	J.McAldney	Newtownards, Co.of Down	23.11.02P
G-MTSV	Solar Wings Pegasus XL-R (Rotax 447) SW-TB-1290 & SW-WA-1286	4. 1.88	R.J.Bowden	Dunkeswell	20. 8.00P
G-MTSX	Solar Wings Pegasus XL-R (Rotax 447) SW-TB-1282 & SW-WA-1288	4. 1.88	F.J.Bridges	Sittles Farm, Alrewas	30. 5.01P
G-MTSY	Solar Wings Pegasus XL-R/Se (Rotax 447) SW-TB-1283 & SW-WA-1289	14. 1.88	N.F.Waldron	Swinford, Rugby	24. 5.99P
G-MTSZ	Solar Wings Pegasus XL-R/Se (Rotax 447) SW-TB-1284 & SW-WA-1290	14. 1.88	J.R.Appleton	(Colne)	17. 7.01P
G-MTTA	Solar Wings Pegasus XL-R (Rotax 462) SW-TE-0035 & SW-WA-1291	14. 1.88	J.J.McMennum *(Noted 12.01)*	Kemble	4. 9.00P
G-MTTB	Solar Wings Pegasus XL-R (Rotax 447) SW-TB-1285 & SW-WA-1292	14. 1.88	P.M.Golden	Siege Cross Farm, Thatcham	31.10.02P
G-MTTD	Solar Wings Pegasus XL-Q (Rotax 447) SW-TB-1286 & SW-WQ-0011	15. 1.88	R.S.Noremberg	(Clacton-on-Sea)	18. 5.02P
G-MTTE	Solar Wings Pegasus XL-Q (Rotax 462?) SW-TB-1287 & SW-WQ-0012	15. 1.88	T.R.Thomas	(Stroud)	31. 1.02P
G-MTTF	Whittaker MW6 Merlin PFA 164-11273 (Rotax 532)	14.12.87	P.Cotton	Long Marston	29. 3.95P
G-MTTH	CFM Shadow BD K.061 (Rotax 447)	15.12.87	G.F.Hill & A.Y-T.Leung	(Shenstone)	12. 5.02P
G-MTTI	Mainair Gemini/Flash IIA (Rotax 503) 620-188-5 & W409	14.12.87	S.M.Savage	(Guildford)	19. 7.96P
G-MTTM	Mainair Gemini/Flash IIA (Rotax 503) 609-1287-5 & W398	5. 1.88	R.K.Woods	(Sheffield)	8. 1.02P
G-MTTN	Skyrider Airsports Phantom PH.00100 *(Officially registered as Ultralight Flight Phantom)*	22. 1.88	K.H.A.Negal *(New owner 10.01)*	Sittles Farm, Alrewas	N/E
G-MTTP	Mainair Gemini/Flash IIA (Rotax 462) 612-188-5 & W401	18. 1.88	A.Ormson	Eshott	16. 6.02P
G-MTTR	Mainair Gemini/Flash IIA (Rotax 462) 614-188-5 & W403	27. 1.88	A.Westoby	Hucknall	22. 7.00P
G-MTTS	Mainair Gemini/Flash IIA (Rotax 503) 621-188-5 & W410	4. 1.88	J.B.Bailey	Shrewsbury	23. 4.91P
G-MTTU	Solar Wings Pegasus XL-R (Rotax 447) SW-TB-1332 & SW-WA-1294	25. 2.88	C.G.Jarvis	(Andover)	13. 7.02P

G-MTTW	Mainair Gemini/Flash IIA (Rotax 462) 622-188-5 & W411	15. 1.88	A.Worthington	Tarn Farm, Cockerham	22. 1.01P
G-MTTX	Solar Wings Pegasus XL-Q (Rotax 447) SW-TB-1293 & SW-WQ-0013	15. 2.88	P.G.Moss	Baxby Manor, Husthwaite	4. 5.02P
G-MTTZ	Solar Wings Pegasus XL-Q (Rotax 462) SW-TE-0039 & SW-WQ-0015	21. 1.88	J.Haskett	(King's Lynn)	6.10.01P
G-MTUA	Solar Wings Pegasus XL-R/Se (Rotax 447) SW-TB-1294 & SW-WA-1295	15. 1.88	P.A.Allwood	Rochester	5. 7.02P
G-MTUB	Thruster TST Mk.1 8018-TST-050 (Rotax 503)	15. 1.88	G.Millar	(Dungannon, Co.Tyrone)	18. 7.02P
G-MTUC	Thruster TST Mk.1 8018-TST-051 (Rotax 503)	15. 1.88	E.J.Girling	Davidstow Moor	22.12.01P
G-MTUD	Thruster TST Mk.1 8018-TST-052 (Rotax 503)	15. 1.88	A.J.Best	(Huby, York)	5.10.02P
G-MTUF	Thruster TST Mk.1 8018-TST-054 (Rotax 503)	15. 1.88	P.Stark	Strathaven	25.11.02P
G-MTUI	Solar Wings Pegasus XL-R/Se (Rotax 447) SW-TB-1296 & SW-WA-1296	21. 1.88	N.J.& C.S.Garrett	Enstone	28. 1.02P
G-MTUJ	Solar Wings Pegasus XL-R (Rotax 447) SW-TB-1297 & SW-WA-1297	21. 1.88	R.W.Pincombe	(Chumleigh, Devon)	31. 5.94P
G-MTUK	Solar Wings Pegasus XL-R (Rotax 447) SW-TB-1298 & SW-WA-1298	21. 1.88	D.L.Pickover	(Nelson, Lancs)	26. 8.04P
G-MTUL	Solar Wings Pegasus XL-R/Se (Rotax 447) SW-TB-1299 & SW-WA-1299	21. 1.88	A.G.Curtis	Deenethorpe	18. 2.02P
G-MTUN	Solar Wings Pegasus XL-Q SW-TB-1301 & SW-WQ-0016 *(Fitted with Wing from G-MVUK?)*	20. 1.88	C.D.Humphries	Long Marston	6. 9.95P
G-MTUP	Solar Wings Pegasus XL-Q (Rotax 447) SW-TB-1303 & SW-WA-0018	20. 1.88	S.J.Allen	Blisworth, Northampton	6. 6.01P
G-MTUR	Solar Wings Pegasus XL-Q (Rotax 447) SW-TB-1304 & SW-WQ-0019	20. 1.88	G.Ball	(Tewkesbury)	28. 1.02P
G-MTUS	Solar Wings Pegasus XL-Q (Rotax 447) SW-TB-1305 & SW-WQ-0020	20. 1.88	A.I.McPherson	Perth	4.11.02P
G-MTUT	Solar Wings Pegasus XL-Q (Rotax 462) SW-TE-0040 & SW-WQ-0021	21. 1.88	L.F.Tanner & D.D.Lock	Sutton Meadows, Ely	29. 5.02P
G-MTUU	Mainair Gemini/Flash IIA (Rotax 503) 623-288-5 & W412	10. 2.88	M.Harris	Eshott	27. 7.00P
G-MTUV	Mainair Gemini/Flash IIA (Rotax 462) 624-288-5 & W413	28. 1.88	J.F.Bolton	(Watford)	5. 4.02P
G-MTUX	Medway Hybred 44XLR 241287/33 (Rotax 503)	2. 2.88	P.A.R.Wilson	Baxby Manor, Husthwaite	29. 8.99P
G-MTUY	Solar Wings Pegasus XL-Q (Rotax 462) SW-TE-0041 & SW-WQ-0022	28. 1.88	H.C.Lowther	(Penrith)	1. 4.01P
G-MTVB	Solar Wings Pegasus XL-R (Rotax 447) SW-TB-1307 & SW-WA-1302	28. 1.88	M.Howland t/a Victor Bravo Group	Wickenby	21. 9.02P
G-MTVH	Mainair Gemini/Flash IIA (Rotax 503) 626-288-6 & W415	17. 2.88	K.Worthington	Tarn Farm, Cockerham	22. 5.02P
G-MTVI	Mainair Gemini/Flash IIA (Rotax 503) 629-388-6 & W416	12. 2.88	R.A.McDowell	(Slough)	10. 5.92P
G-MTVJ	Mainair Gemini/Flash IIA (Rotax 503) 627-388-6 & W418	12. 2.88	D.M.Waller	(Keighley)	3. 5.02P
G-MTVK	Solar Wings Pegasus XL-R (Rotax 447) SW-TB-1311 & SW-WA-1306	15. 2.88	J D MacNamara	(Crediton)	17. 3.98P
G-MTVL	Solar Wings Pegasus XL-R/Se (Rotax 447) SW-TB-1312 & SW-WA-1307	15. 2.88	J.K.Pattison	Weston Zoyland	6. 4.02P
G-MTVM	Solar Wings Pegasus XL-R (Rotax 447) SW-TB-1313 & SW-WA-1308	15. 2.88	C.Surman	(Cranleigh)	2. 6.02P
G-MTVN	Solar Wings Pegasus XL-R (Rotax 447) SW-TB-1314 & SW-WA-1309	15. 2.88	A.I.Crighton	Lower Mountpleasant, Chatteris	4. 4.98P
G-MTVO	Solar Wings Pegasus XL-R (Rotax 447) SW-TB-1315 & SW-WA-1310	15. 2.88	D A Payne	Long Marston	17. 4.02P
G-MTVP	Thruster TST Mk.1 8028-TST-056 (Rotax 503) *(C/n plate marked incorrectly as 8208-TST-056)*	10. 2.88	J.M.Evans	(Abingdon)	13. 3.02P
G-MTVR	Thruster TST Mk.1 8028-TST-057 (Rotax 503)	10. 2.88	D.B.Southworth	(York)	19. 7.02P
G-MTVS	Thruster TST Mk.1 8028-TST-058 (Rotax 503)	10. 2.88	W.J.Burrell	(Banbridge, Co.Down)	3. 4.02P
G-MTVT	Thruster TST Mk.1 8028-TST-059 (Rotax 503)	10. 2.88	M.L.Walsh & A.T.Farmer	Mill Farm, Shifnal	28. 3.02P
G-MTVV	Thruster TST Mk.1 8028-TST-061 (Rotax 503)	10. 2.88	W.A.Stephenson	(Newry, Co.Armagh)	22.10.02P
G-MTVX	Solar Wings Pegasus XL-Q (Rotax 462HP) SW-TE-0042 & SW-WQ-0025	3. 3.88	M.O.O'Brien	Rufforth	4. 8.02P
G-MTWA	Solar Wings Pegasus XL-R (Rotax 447) SW-TB-1317 & SW-WA-1311	25. 2.88	A.P.Watkins t/a G-MTWA Flying Group *(Noted 9.01)*	Roddidge, Fradley	18. 4.02P

G-MTWB	Solar Wings Pegasus XL-R (Rotax 447) SW-TB-1342 & SW-WA-1312 *(Originally fitted with Trike c/n SW-TB-1318: latter damaged, repaired & resold with Sailwing c/n SW-WA-1330 as SE-YOK. New trike is c/n SW-TB-1342)*	25. 2.88	M.W.A.Shemilt	(Henley-on-Thames)	13.11.98P
G-MTWC	Solar Wings Pegasus XL-R (Rotax 447) SW-TB-1321 & SW-WA-1313	25. 2.88	J.Clark	Davidstow Moor	8. 6.02P
G-MTWD	Solar Wings Pegasus XL-R (Rotax 447) SW-TB-1320 & SW-WA-1314	25. 2.88	D.M.Day	Sywell	14. 5.02P
G-MTWF	Mainair Gemini/Flash IIA (Rotax 503) 630-388-6 & W419	25. 2.88	W.Porter	Knapthorpe Lodge, Caunton	20. 4.02P
G-MTWG	Mainair Gemini/Flash IIA (Rotax 503) 631-288-6 & W420	25. 2.88	N.Mackenzie & P.S.Bunting	(Southport)	28. 7.00P
G-MTWH	CFM Shadow CD K.064 (Rotax 503)	25. 2.88	V.A.Hutchinson	(Nuneaton)	23. 6.02P
G-MTWK	CFM Shadow CD 073 (Rotax 503)	25. 2.88	R.C.Fendick	Westbury-sub-Mendip	25. 9.02P
G-MTWL	CFM Shadow BD 076 (Rotax 447)	25. 2.88	M.J.Gray	Manor Farm, Croughton	19.10.02P
G-MTWN	CFM Shadow CD 081 (Rotax 503)	25. 2.88	P.W.Heywood	Davidstow Moor	5. 7.01P
G-MTWR	Mainair Gemini/Flash IIA (Rotax 503) 632-388-6 & W421	3. 3.88	J.B.Hodson	Arclid Green, Sandbach	8. 4.02P
G-MTWS	Mainair Gemini/Flash IIA (Rotax 503) 633-388-6 & W422	3. 3.88	K W Roberts	Sandtoft	25. 8.02P
G-MTWX	Mainair Gemini/Flash IIA (Rotax 503) 634-488-6 & W423	11. 3.88	M.Warmerdam	(Leyland)	5. 6.02P
G-MTWY	Thruster TST Mk.1 8038-TST-062 (Rotax 503)	15. 3.88	M.F.Eddington	(Wincanton)	20. 4.02P
G-MTWZ	Thruster TST Mk.1 8038-TST-063 (Rotax 503)	15. 3.88	A.Makepeace	Walkeridge Farm, Hannington	21. 7.02P
G-MTXA	Thruster TST Mk.1 8038-TST-064 (Rotax 503)	15. 3.88	A.Maxwell	Morgansfield, Fishburn	21. 7.02P
G-MTXB	Thruster TST Mk.1 8038-TST-065 (Rotax 503)	15. 3.88	J.J.Hill	Baxby Manor, Husthwaite	29. 8.02P
G-MTXC	Thruster TST Mk.1 8038-TST-066 (Rotax 503)	15. 3.88	Joan A.Huntley	South Wraxall, Wilts	14. 7.02P
G-MTXD	Thruster TST Mk.1 8038-TST-067 (Rotax 503)	15. 3.88	B.E.Holloway	Baxby Manor, Husthwaite	1. 3.02P
G-MTXE	Hornet Dual Trainer/Southdown Raven (Rotax 462) HRWA 0070 & SN2000/0332	11. 3.88	F.J.Marton t/a Charter Systems	Long Marston	22. 5.00P
G-MTXH	Solar Wings Pegasus XL-Q (Rotax 447) SW-TB-1328 & SW-WQ-0030	11. 3.88	J.Rhodes	(Pontefract)	21. 7.97P
G-MTXI	Solar Wings Pegasus XL-Q (Rotax 447) SW-TB-1329 & SW-WQ-0031	11. 3.88	R.Lewis-Evans	(Poole)	20. 8.02P
G-MTXJ	Solar Wings Pegasus XL-Q (Rotax 447) SW-TB-1330 & SW-WQ-0032	11. 3.88	G.C.Weighell	Enstone	13.12.01P
G-MTXK	Solar Wings Pegasus XL-Q (Rotax 447) SW-TB-1331 & SW-WQ-0033	11. 3.88	M.J.McManamon	(Inverurie)	4. 8.02P
G-MTXL	Noble Hardman Snowbird Mk.IV SB-006 (Rotax 532)	4. 5.88	M.Fitch & D.Connolly	(Potters Bar)	12. 6.00P
G-MTXM	Mainair Gemini/Flash IIA (Rotax 503) 636-488-6 & W425	10. 5.88	K.Bradford	(Rayleigh)	30. 3.02P
G-MTXP	Mainair Gemini/Flash IIA (Rotax 503) 637-488-6 & W426	23. 3.88	M.B.Buttle	St.Michaels	26.12.01P
G-MTXR	CFM Shadow CD K.038 (Rotax 503)	23. 3.88	M.E.H.Quick	Old Sarum	9. 8.02P
G-MTXS*	Mainair Gemini/Flash IIA (Rotax 503) 638-488-6 & W427	23. 3.88	M.A.Sheehan t/a G-MTXS Group *(Cancelled 8.10.01 by CAA)*	Roddige, Fradley	27.10.00P
G-MTXU	Noble Hardman Snowbird Mk.IV SB-007	3. 5.88	J.A.Rees	Haverfordwest	16. 5.89P
G-MTXY	Hornet Dual Trainer/Southdown Raven (Rotax 462) HRWA 0073 & SN2000/0354	30. 3.88	J.McAvoy	(Bishopton)	17. 8.02P
G-MTXZ	Mainair Gemini/Flash IIA (Rotax 503) 641-588-6 & W430	10. 5.88	R.J.C.Hills	Shobdon	2. 5.02P
G-MTYA	Solar Wings Pegasus XL-Q (Rotax 462HP) SW-TE-0047 & SW-WQ-0037	29. 3.88	I.Clarkson	Long Marston	22. 9.02P
G-MTYC	Solar Wings Pegasus XL-Q (Rotax 462) SW-TE-0049 & SW-WQ-0039	30. 3.88	C.I.D.H.Garrison	Sutton Meadows, Ely	20. 9.02P
G-MTYD	Solar Wings Pegasus XL-Q (Rotax 462) SW-TE-0050 & SW-WQ-0040	29. 3.88	D.Young t/a Pegasus Flight Training (Cotswolds)	Kemble	19.10.01P
G-MTYE	Solar Wings Pegasus XL-Q (Rotax 462) SW-TE-0051 & SW-WQ-0041	29. 3.88	K.L.Chorley & A.Cook	Enstone	6. 4.02P
G-MTYF	Solar Wings Pegasus XL-Q (Rotax 462) SW-TE-0052 & SW-WQ-0042	29. 3.88	J.Hyde	(Spalding)	18. 5.02P
G-MTYI	Solar Wings Pegasus XL-Q (Rotax 462) SW-TE-0055 & SW-WQ-0045	30. 3.88	R.H.Stokes	(Warboys)	20. 9.02P

G-MTYL	Solar Wings Pegasus XL-Q			30. 3.88	E.T.H.Cox	(Church Stretton)	20.10.02P
	(Rotax 462) SW-TE-0058 & SW-WQ-0048 *(Original Sailwing c/n SW-WQ-0048 replaced by c/n 6412)*						
G-MTYP	Solar Wings Pegasus XL-Q			30. 3.88	J L Ker	Eshott	15.12.02P
	(Rotax 462) SW-TE-0062 & SW-WQ-0052						
G-MTYR	Solar Wings Pegasus XL-Q			30. 3.88	M.E.Grafton	(Hay-on-Wye)	30. 4.99P
	(Rotax 462) SW-TE-0063 & SW-WQ-0053				*(New owner 5.01)*		
G-MTYS	Solar Wings Pegasus XL-Q			30. 3.88	R.G.Wall	Caerleon	4. 9.00P
	(Rotax 462) SW-TE-0064 & SW-WQ-0054						
G-MTYT	Solar Wings Pegasus XL-Q			30. 3.88	M.G.Walsh	Rufforth	13. 9.99P
	(Rotax 462HP) SW-TE-0065 & SW-WQ-0055				*(CofR restored 2.11.01)*		
G-MTYU	Solar Wings Pegasus XL-Q			30. 3.88	N.I.Garland & M.Powell	Dunkeswell	14. 4.02P
	(Rotax 462HP) SW-TE-0066 & SW-WQ-0056						
G-MTYV	Raven Aircraft Raven X	SN2232/0341		8. 4.88	R.E.J.Pattenden	(Maidstone)	7. 5.02P
	(Rotax 447)						
G-MTYW	Raven Aircraft Raven X	SN2232/0344		8. 4.88	R.Solomans	Stoke, Kent	10. 6.02P
	(Rotax 447)						
G-MTYX	Raven Aircraft Raven X	SN2232/0345		8. 4.88	J.C.Hawkins	(Selsey)	15. 8.00P
	(Rotax 447)						
G-MTYY	Solar Wings Pegasus XL-R	SW-WA-1326		6. 5.88	G.J.Slater	Clench Common	3. 2.02P
	(Rotax 447)						
G-MTZA	Thruster TST Mk.1	8048-TST-068		13. 4.88	M.G.Davidson	(Craigavon, Co Armagh)	26. 1.02P
	(Rotax 503)						
G-MTZB	Thruster TST Mk.1	8048-TST-069		13. 4.88	S.J.O.Tinn	(Weymouth)	26. 2.02P
	(Rotax 503)						
G-MTZC	Thruster TST Mk.1	8048-TST-070		13. 4.88	R.W.Marshall	(Armagh)	6. 5.01P
	(Rotax 503)						
G-MTZD	Thruster TST Mk.1	8048-TST-071		13. 4.88	G.H.Hills	(Alton)	8.10.99P
	(Rotax 503)						
G-MTZE	Thruster TST Mk.1	8048-TST-072		13. 4.88	M R Jones	Wing Farm, Longbridge Deverill	26. 8.01P
	(Rotax 503)				*(Under rebuild 12.01)*		
G-MTZF	Thruster TST Mk.1	8048-TST-073		13. 4.88	D.Large	Long Marston	8. 9.00P
	(Rotax 503)				t/a Zulu Fox Group		
G-MTZG	Mainair Gemini/Flash IIA			10. 5.88	T.G.Greenhill	Swinford, Rugby	11. 6.02P
	(Rotax 503) 642-588-6 & W431						
G-MTZH	Mainair Gemini/Flash IIA			9. 6.88	D.C.Hughes	St.Michaels	17. 7.01P
	(Rotax 462) 643-588-6 & W433						
G-MTZK	Solar Wings Pegasus XL-R			6. 5.88	Sara J.Singlehurst	Long Acre Farm, Sandy	12.10.02P
	(Rotax 447) SW-TB-1336 & SW-WA-1329						
G-MTZL	Mainair Gemini/Flash IIA			10. 5.88	N.S.Brayn	Popham	31. 7.02P
	(Rotax 503) 645-588-6 & W435						
G-MTZM	Mainair Gemini/Flash IIA			3. 5.88	K.L.Smith	(Leicester)	1. 8.02P
	(Rotax 503) 646-588-6 & W436						
G-MTZO	Mainair Gemini/Flash IIA			6. 5.88	R.C.Hinds	(Newnham, Glos)	14. 6.02P
	(Rotax 462) 649-688-6 & W439						
G-MTZP	Solar Wings Pegasus XL-Q			6. 5.88	Island Micro Aviation Ltd	(Ventnor, IoW)	23. 6.02P
	(Rotax 447) SW-TB-1337 & SW-WQ-0059						
G-MTZR	Solar Wings Pegasus XL-Q			6. 5.88	P.J.Hatchett	Emlyn's Field, Rhuallt	19. 8.98P
	(Rotax 447) SW-TB-1338 & SW-WQ-0060						
G-MTZS	Solar Wings Pegasus XL-Q			6. 5.88	P.A.Darling	(Wilmslow)	15. 7.93P
	(Rotax 447) SW-TB-1339 & SW-WQ-0061						
G-MTZT	Solar Wings Pegasus XL-Q			6. 5.88	M.Y.Brown	Eshott	28. 6.02P
	(Rotax 447) SW-TB-1340 & SW-WQ-0062						
G-MTZV	Mainair Gemini/Flash IIA			6. 5.88	G.J.Donnellon	Barton	30. 8.01P
	(Rotax 503) 650-688-6 & W440						
G-MTZW	Mainair Gemini/Flash IIA			25. 5.88	L.McIntyre	Ince Blundell	11.10.02P
	(Rotax 503) 651-688-6 & W441						
G-MTZX	Mainair Gemini/Flash IIA			23. 6.88	J.G.Stancombe	Rufforth	11. 7.01P
	(Rotax 503) 652-688-6 & W442						
G-MTZY	Mainair Gemini/Flash IIA			24. 5.88	P.K.Dale	Bagby	8. 1.02P
	(Rotax 503) 653-688-6 & W443						
G-MTZZ	Mainair Gemini/Flash IIA			14. 6.88	P.J.Litchfield	Tarn Farm, Cockerham	14. 4.01P
	(Rotax 503) 654-688-6 & W444						
G-MUFY	Robinson R22 Beta	1248	D-HICH	13.12.96	Rotormurf Ltd	Caernarfon	22.12.02T
G-MUIR	Cameron V-65 HAFB	2037		23. 6.89	Lindsay J.M.Muir *"Muriel"*	East Molesey	20. 5.02A
G-MUNI	Mooney M.20J (201SE)	24-3118		12. 5.89	M.W.Fane	Fairoaks	15.10.04
G-MURI*	Learjet LearJet 35A	35A-646	N712JB	19. 2.98	Not known	Lyon/St Exupery, France	
			N717JB/N646EA/XA-UMA/N3812G				
	(Crashed Lyon/Satolas, France 2.5.00 & destroyed: cancelled 20.6.00 as destroyed) (Wreck dumped 7.01)						
G-MURR	Whittaker MW6 Merlin	PFA 164-12501		16. 4.99	D.Murray	Bristol	
G-MURY	Robinson R44 Astro	0201		19. 7.95	Simlot Ltd *(Op Jennifer Murray)*	Denham	17. 5.04T
G-MUSO	Rutan LongEz	PFA 074A-10590		11. 6.83	P.A.Willis	RAF Wyton	10. 7.02P
	(Lycoming O-235-C2A)						
G-MUTE	Colt 31A Air Chair HAFB	2099		2.12.91	K.Temple	Diss	11.11.99A

G-MUVG	Cessna 421C Golden Eagle III	421C1064	N421DD	13. 1.97	Air Montgomery Ltd	Leeds-Bradford	12. 3.02T
G-MVAA	Mainair Gemini/Flash IIA (Rotax 503)	655-688-6 & W445		8. 6.88	G.F.J.Field	(Hucknall)	7.12.02P
G-MVAB	Mainair Gemini/Flash IIA (Rotax 503)	656-688-6 & W446		10. 5.88	W.Anderson	Glenrothes	28. 1.02P
G-MVAC	CFM Shadow CD (Rotax 503)	K.077		12. 5.88	C.A.S.Powell	Insch	15. 9.02P
G-MVAD	Mainair Gemini/Flash IIA (Rotax 503)	657-688-6 & W447		10. 5.88	N.G.Woodall	Tarn Farm, Cockerham	10. 8.02P
G-MVAF	Southdown Puma Sprint (Fuji-Robin EC-44-2PM)	P.455	G-MBAF	24. 6.87	J.F.Horn	(Yelverton)	10. 5.02P
G-MVAG	Thruster TST Mk.1 (Rotax 503)	8058-TST-074		18. 5.88	N.S.Brown	Brook Farm, Pilling	17. 7.01P
G-MVAH	Thruster TST Mk.1 (Rotax 503)	8058-TST-075		18. 5.88	M.W.H.Henton *"Times Four"*	Popham	18. 8.02P
G-MVAI	Thruster TST Mk.1 (Rotax 503)	8058-TST-076		18. 5.88	D.J.Townsend	(Norwich)	25.10.01P
G-MVAJ	Thruster TST Mk.1 (Rotax 503)	8058-TST-077		18. 5.88	A.T.Harvey	Long Marston	16. 6.02P
G-MVAK	Thruster TST Mk.1 (Rotax 503)	8058-TST-078		18. 5.88	A.J.Dunlop & S.J.Pettitt	Long Acre Farm, Sandy	24. 8.02P
G-MVAL	Thruster TST Mk.1 (Rotax 503)	8058-TST-079		18. 5.88	G.C.Brooke	(Colchester)	7. 8.96P
G-MVAM	CFM Shadow CD (Rotax 503)	082		18. 5.88	C.P.Barber	(Preston)	12.10.02P
G-MVAN	CFM Shadow CD (Rotax 503)	K.048 & PFA 161-11219		18. 5.88	I.Brewster	Bourn	17.10.02P
G-MVAO	Mainair Gemini/Flash IIA (Rotax 503)	658-688-6 & W448		24. 5.88	S.J.Robson *(Op Mercury Microlight Club)*	Brook Farm, Pilling	24. 7.02P
G-MVAP	Mainair Gemini/Flash IIA (Rotax 503)	659-688-6 & W449		24. 5.88	R.J.Miller	Long Marston	31.10.02P
G-MVAR	Solar Wings Pegasus XL-R (Rotax 447)	SW-TB-1343 & SW-WA-1331		24. 5.88	M.L.Butlin	(Peterborough)	20. 9.02P
G-MVAT	Solar Wings Pegasus XL-R (Rotax 447)	SW-TB-1345 & SW-WA-1333		24. 5.88	P.Burtwistle	(Perth)	26. 2.02P
G-MVAV	Solar Wings Pegasus XL-R (Rotax 447)	SW-TB-1347 & SW-WA-1335		24. 5.88	D.J.Utting	(Bungay)	18. 1.02P
G-MVAW	Solar Wings Pegasus XL-Q (Rotax 447)	SW-TB-1348 & SW-WQ-0064		24. 5.88	G.Sharman	Sywell	20. 4.02P
G-MVAX	Solar Wings Pegasus XL-Q (Rotax 447)	SW-TB-1349 & SW-WQ-0065		24. 5.88	S.J.Rogers & D.W.Power	(Saundersfoot)	26. 8.02P
G-MVAY	Solar Wings Pegasus XL-Q (Rotax 447)	SW-TB-1350 & SW-WQ-0066		24. 5.88	V.O.Morris	(Swansea)	16. 4.97P
G-MVBB	CFM Shadow BD (Rotax 447)	K.051		24. 5.88	R.Garrod	(Mendlesham)	8.10.00P
G-MVBC	Mainair Tri-Flyer/Aerial Arts 130SX	130SX-616		24. 5.88	D.Beer *(Believed to be using Mainair Tri-Flyer 250 Trike from G-MJIX)*	(Ilfracombe)	
G-MVBD	Mainair Gemini/Flash IIA (Rotax 462)	660-688-6 & W450		8. 6.88	D.V.Batten	Barton	12. 6.02P
G-MVBF	Mainair Gemini/Flash IIA (Rotax 462)	662-688-6 & W452		14. 6.88	P.& C.Moore	(Corby)	19.10.02P
G-MVBG	Mainair Gemini/Flash IIA (Rotax 503)	663-688-6 & W453		25. 5.88	C.J.Walters	Shifnal	27. 7.02P
G-MVBH	Mainair Gemini/Flash IIA (Rotax 503)	664-688-6 & W454		25. 5.88	B.J.Egerton	(Bootle)	10. 7.98P
G-MVBI	Mainair Gemini/Flash IIA (Rotax 503)	665-788-6 & W455		7. 6.88	E.R.Wilson	(Barrow-in-Furness)	6. 9.92P
G-MVBJ	Solar Wings Pegasus XL-R (Rotax 462)	SW-TE-0033 & SW-WA-1338		7. 6.88	R.J.O.Page	Old Sarum	4. 8.02P
G-MVBK	Mainair Gemini/Flash IIA (Rotax 462)	666-788-6 & W456		7. 6.88	C.S.Bowen & M.D.Carruthers	Manor Farm, Inskip	11. 3.01P
G-MVBL	Mainair Gemini/Flash IIA (Rotax 503)	669-788-6 & W459		7. 6.88	P.M.Wright	Higher Barn Farm, Houghton	15.11.01P
G-MVBM	Mainair Gemini/Flash IIA (Rotax 503)	667-788-6 & W457		7. 6.88	A.M.Wood	(Chelmsford)	26. 7.02P
G-MVBN	Mainair Gemini/Flash IIA (Rotax 503)	668-788-6 & W458		8. 6.88	M.Frankcom	(Darwen)	2. 6.99P
G-MVBO	Mainair Gemini/Flash IIA (Rotax 503)	671-788-6 & W461		8. 6.88	R.Brasher	(Rugeley)	12.10.02P
G-MVBP	Thruster TST Mk.1 (Rotax 503)	8068-TST-080		14. 6.88	K.J.Crompton	Newtownards, Co.of Down	12. 3.02P
G-MVBT	Thruster TST Mk.1 (BMW R100)	8068-TST-083		14. 6.88	E.L.Everitt	Ley Farm, Chirk	23.11.02P

G-MVBY	Solar Wings Pegasus XL-R (Rotax 447) SW-TB-1357 & SW-WA-1344	17. 6.88	J.Catley	(Bristol)	6. 1.02P
G-MVBZ	Solar Wings Pegasus XL-R (Rotax 447) SW-TB-1358 & SW-WA-1345	17. 6.88	A.G.Butler	Shenstone Hall Farm, Shenstone	1. 8.01P
G-MVCA	Solar Wings Pegasus XL-R (Rotax 447) SW-TB-1359 & SW-WA-1346	17. 6.88	R.Walker	Sutton Meadows, Ely	6.10.01P
G-MVCB	Solar Wings Pegasus XL-R (Rotax 447) SW-TB-1360 & SW-WA-1347	17. 6.88	G.T.Clipstone	(Ipswich)	18. 6.00P
G-MVCC	CFM Shadow CD K.045 (Rotax 503)	17. 6.88	K.D.Mitchell	Shoreham	9. 5.02P
G-MVCD	Medway Hybred 44XLR MR001/34 (Rotax 447) *(Marked as "Raven") (Original sailwing transferred to G-MVOS: new wing c/n not yet known)*	14. 6.88	A.Cochrane	Long Acre Farm, Sandy	27. 7.02P
G-MVCE	Mainair Gemini/Flash IIA (Rotax 503) 672-788-6 & W462	23. 6.88	J.D.Berry	Ince Blundell	5. 4.99P
G-MVCF	Mainair Gemini/Flash IIA (Rotax 462) 673-788-6 & W463	14. 7.88	J.L.Hamer	(Hartpury, Glos)	23. 7.02P
G-MVCI	Noble Hardman Snowbird Mk.IV SB-011 (Rotax 532)	11.10.88	W.L.Chapman	Tarn Farm, Cockerham	13. 4.95P
G-MVCJ	Noble Hardman Snowbird Mk.IV SB-012 (Rotax 532)	11.10.88	J.P.Harris *"The Strumpet"*	Mill Farm, Shifnal	15. 8.02P
G-MVCK	Cosmos Trike/La Mouette Profil 19 SDA-01	19. 7.88	S.D.Alsop	(Bath)	
G-MVCL	Solar Wings Pegasus XL-Q (Rotax 462HP) SW-TE-0069 & SW-WQ-0075	27. 6.88	T.E.Robinson	(Insch)	22. 8.02P
G-MVCM	Solar Wings Pegasus XL-Q (Rotax 462) SW-TE-0070 & SW-WQ-0076	27. 6.88	M.M.Coggan	Sandtoft	7. 4.02P
G-MVCN	Solar Wings Pegasus XL-Q (Rotax 462) SW-TE-0071 & SW-WQ-0077	27. 6.88	S.R.S.Evans	(Chelmsford)	20. 3.01P
G-MVCP	Solar Wings Pegasus XL-Q (Rotax 462) SW-TE-0073 & SW-WQ-0079	27. 6.88	J.R.Fulcher	(Whittlesford)	27. 6.02P
G-MVCR	Solar Wings Pegasus XL-Q (Rotax 462) SW-TE-0069 & SW-WQ-0080	27. 6.88	A.V.Dunne	Plaistows Farm, St.Albans	29. 5.02P
G-MVCS	Solar Wings Pegasus XL-Q (Rotax 462) SW-TE-0075 & SW-WQ-0081	27. 6.88	J.J.Sparrow	Sywell	19. 7.02P
G-MVCT	Solar Wings Pegasus XL-Q (Rotax 462) SW-TE-0076 & SW-WQ-0082	27. 6.88	G.J.Lampitt	Pound Green, Buttonoak, Kidderminster	22. 8.02P
G-MVCV	Solar Wings Pegasus XL-Q SW-WQ-0084 (Rotax 462) *(Original Trike c/n SW-TE-0078 but damaged & replaced by SW-TE-0108. Original trike repaired & fitted with sailwing SW-WQ-0105 as G-MVHP)*	27. 6.88	G.E.& B.T.Nunn	Long Acre Farm, Sandy	20. 4.02P
G-MVCW	CFM Shadow BD 084 (Rotax 447)	28. 6.88	R.G.Calvert	Higher Barn Farm, Houghton	1. 8.02P
G-MVCY	Mainair Gemini/Flash IIA (Rotax 503) 674-788-6 & W464	14. 7.88	A.M.Smith	Otherton, Cannock	11. 4.02P
G-MVDA	Mainair Gemini/Flash IIA (Rotax 462) 676-788-6 & W466	13. 7.88	C.Tweedley	(Great Orton)	8. 5.02P
G-MVDB	Medway Hybred 44XLR MR005/36 (Rotax 447)	28. 7.88	G.P.Barnes & J.W.Davies	Sywell	2. 5.02P
G-MVDD	Thruster TST Mk.1 8078-TST-086 (Rotax 503)	12. 7.88	D.J.Love	(Witton, Norwich)	9.11.99P
G-MVDE	Thruster TST Mk.1 8078-TST-087 (Rotax 503)	12. 7.88	R.H.Davis *(Noted 12.01)*	Doynton, Gloucestershire	26. 8.99P
G-MVDF	Thruster TST Mk.1 8078-TST-088 (Rotax 503)	12. 7.88	J.Walsh & A.R.Sunley	Rayne Hall Farm, Rayne	2. 5.02P
G-MVDG	Thruster TST Mk.1 8078-TST-089 (Rotax 503)	12. 7.88	D.G.,P.M. & A.B.Smith	Popham	26. 7.00P
G-MVDH	Thruster TST Mk.1 8078-TST-090 (Rotax 503)	12. 7.88	P.E.Terrell	(Plymouth)	15. 8.02P
G-MVDJ	Medway Hybred 44XLR MR010/38 (Rotax 447)	20. 7.88	W.D.Hutchings	(Nottingham)	1. 4.02P
G-MVDK	Aerial Arts Chaser S CH.702 (Rotax 377)	5. 8.88	S.Adams *(Noted 9.01)*	Leicester	29.11.98P
G-MVDL	Aerial Arts Chaser S CH.701 (Rotax 462)	11. 8.88	J.M.Hucker	(Abertillery, Gwent)	18. 8.02P
G-MVDP	Aerial Arts Chaser S CH.706 (Rotax 447)	11. 8.88	P.Corke	Long Acre Farm, Sandy	9.11.02P
G-MVDR	Aerial Arts Chaser S CH.708 (Rotax 447)	11. 8.88	P.Jephcott	(Solihull)	27.12.01P
G-MVDT	Mainair Gemini/Flash IIA (Rotax 503) 670-788-6 & W460	20. 7.88	D.C.Stephens	(Coleford, Glos)	26. 5.00P
G-MVDU	Solar Wings Pegasus XL-R (Rotax 447) SW-TB-1361 & SW-WA-1348	13. 7.88	D.R.Western	Weston Zoyland	25. 5.02P
G-MVDV	Solar Wings Pegasus XL-R (Rotax 447) SW-TB-1362 & SW-WA-1349	13. 7.88	E.J.Blyth & L.D.Benson	(Pickering)	24. 8.97P

G-MVDW	Solar Wings Pegasus XL-R (Rotax 447) SW-TB-1363 * SW-WA-1350	13. 7.88	R.P.Brown	Long Acre Farm, Sandy	20. 7.97P
G-MVDX	Solar Wings Pegasus XL-R (Rotax 447) SW-TB-1364 & SW-WA-1351	13. 7.88	C.Kett	Weston Zoyland	8. 8.98P
G-MVDY	Solar Wings Pegasus XL-R (Rotax 447) SW-TB-1365 & SW-WA-1352	13. 7.88	C.G.Murphy	Biggin Hill	1. 6.92P
G-MVDZ	Solar Wings Pegasus XL-R (Rotax 447) SW-TB-1366 & SW-WA-1353	12. 7.88	A.K.Pickering	(Robertsbridge)	19. 5.00P
G-MVEC	Solar Wings Pegasus XL-R (Rotax 447) SW-TB-1369 & SW-WA-1356	20. 7.88	J.A.Jarvis	Chilbolton	25. 2.02P
G-MVED	Solar Wings Pegasus XL-R/Se (Rotax 447) SW-TB-1370 & SW-WA-1357	20. 7.88	P.A.Sleightholme	Baxby Manor, Husthwaite	24. 5.02P
G-MVEE	Medway Hybred 44XLR MR004/35 (Rotax 447) *(Trike c/n same as G-MYMJ and suggests this has a replacement unit)*	22. 7.88	D.S.L.Evans	(Gravesend)	8. 6.01P
G-MVEF	Solar Wings Pegasus XL-R (Rotax 462) SW-TE-0079 & SW-WA-1358	19. 7.88	E.J.Blyth	(Pickering)	15.11.93P
G-MVEG	Solar Wings Pegasus XL-R (Rotax 462) SW-TE-0080 & SW-WA-1359	19. 7.88	A.W.Leadley	(Strabane, Co.Tyrone)	15. 5.99P
G-MVEH	Mainair Gemini/Flash IIA (Rotax 503) 677-788-6 & W468	26. 8.88	D.L.Morris	(Dawlish)	31. 7.02P
G-MVEI	CFM Shadow CD 085 (Rotax 503)	26. 7.88	R.Hatton	Ronaldsway	29.12.02P
G-MVEJ	Mainair Gemini/Flash IIA (Rotax 462) 678-888-6 & W469	27. 7.88	M.Thornburn & S.Mair	(Moffat/Lockerbie)	22.11.01P
G-MVEK	Mainair Gemini/Flash IIA (Rotax 503) 679-888-6 & W470	27. 7.88	D.R.Gooby	Henstridge	20. 9.02P
G-MVEL	Mainair Gemini/Flash IIA (Rotax 503) 680-888-6 & W471	27. 7.88	M.R.Starling	Swanton Morley	30. 1.02P
G-MVEN	CFM Shadow CD K.047 (Rotax 503)	26. 7.88	D.J.Burton	(Brighton)	4. 8.02P
G-MVEO	Mainair Gemini/Flash IIA (Rotax 503) 682-888-6 & W472	28. 7.88	S.Macmillan	East Fortune	30. 1.02P
G-MVER	Mainair Gemini/Flash IIA (Rotax 503) 684-888-6 & W474	28. 7.88	J.R.Davis	(Cheltenham)	25. 4.02P
G-MVES	Mainair Gemini/Flash IIA (Rotax 503) 685-888-6 & W475	5. 8.88	R.H.Ferguson & F.W.McLean	East Fortune	4. 4.02P
G-MVET	Mainair Gemini/Flash IIA (Rotax 503) 686-888-6 & W476	19. 8.88	T.Bailey	Otherton, Cannock	3. 2.02P
G-MVEV	Mainair Gemini/Flash IIA (Rotax 503) 687-888-6 & W477	5. 8.88	C.Allen	(Alderley Edge)	8. 7.01P
G-MVEW	Mainair Gemini/Flash IIA (Rotax 503) 688-988-6 & W478	16. 9.88	N.A.Dye	Swanton Morley	27. 7.98P
G-MVEX	Solar Wings Pegasus XL-Q (Rotax 462) SW-TE-0082 & SW-WQ-0088	5. 8.88	R.Morelli	(Malahide, Co.Dublin)	26. 5.02P
G-MVEZ	Solar Wings Pegasus XL-Q (Rotax 462) SW-TE-0084 & SW-WQ-0090	9. 8.88	P.W.Millar	(Newnham)	13. 6.99P
G-MVFA	Solar Wings Pegasus XL-Q (Rotax 462HP) SW-TE-0085 & SW-WQ-0091	9. 8.88	A.Johnson	Deenethorpe	23. 6.02P
G-MVFB	Solar Wings Pegasus XL-Q (Rotax 462) SW-TE-0086 & SW-WQ-0092	9. 8.88	M.O.Bloy	(King's Lynn)	14. 4.02P
G-MVFC	Solar Wings Pegasus XL-Q (Rotax 462) SW-TE-0087 & SW-WQ-0093	9. 8.88	D.R.Joint	(Bournemouth)	25. 6.95P
G-MVFD	Solar Wings Pegasus XL-Q (Rotax 462) SW-TE-0088 & SW-WQ-0094	9. 8.88	C.D.Humphries	Long Marston	25. 5.01P
G-MVFE	Solar Wings Pegasus XL-Q (Rotax 462) SW-TE-0087 & SW-WQ-0095	9. 8.88	S.J.Weeks	Kemble	30. 4.00P
G-MVFF	Solar Wings Pegasus XL-Q (Rotax 462) SW-TE-0090 & SW-WQ-0096	9. 8.88	A.Makepeace	(Guildford)	13. 4.02P
G-MVFG	Solar Wings Pegasus XL-Q (Rotax 462) SW-TE-0091 & SW-WQ-0097	9. 8.88	R.J.Vaughan	(Northwich)	5.10.00P
G-MVFH	CFM Shadow CD 086 (Rotax 447)	9. 8.88	G.R.Read	(Mendlesham)	8. 1.00P
G-MVFJ	Thruster TST Mk.1 8088-TST-092 (Rotax 503)	11. 8.88	B.E.Renehan t/a Kestrel Flying Group	Popham	26. 1.02P
G-MVFK	Thruster TST Mk.1 8088-TST-093 (Rotax 503)	11. 8.88	A.M.Commons	(Newburgh, Fife)	10. 4.00P
G-MVFL	Thruster TST Mk.1 8088-TST-094 (Rotax 503)	11. 8.88	G.Hawkins	Otherton, Cannock	22. 5.02P
G-MVFM	Thruster TST Mk.1 8088-TST-095 (Rotax 503)	11. 8.88	W.J.H.Orr	(Blandford Forum)	24. 5.02P
G-MVFN	Thruster TST Mk.1 8088-TST-096 (Rotax 503-2V)	11. 8.88	A.G.Ward	Long Acre Farm, Sandy	29. 5.01P
G-MVFO	Thruster TST Mk.1 8088-TST-097 (Rotax 503-2V)	11. 8.88	A.L.Higgins & D.H.King t/a G-MVFO Group	(Newport Pagnell)	26. 1.02P

G-MVFP	Solar Wings Pegasus XL-R (Rotax 447) SW-TB-1371 & SW-WA-1365		9. 8.88	D J Brixton tr Shropshire Tow Group	Bishops Castle, Shropshire	13. 3.02P
G-MVFR	Solar Wings Pegasus XL-R (Rotax 447) SW-TB-1372 & SW-WA-1366		9. 8.88	P.Newton	(Macclesfield)	21.11.99P
G-MVFS	Solar Wings Pegasus XL-R/Se (Rotax 447) SW-TB-1373 & SW-WA-1367		9. 8.88	D.Sykes	(Dewsbury)	9. 5.02P
G-MVFT	Solar Wings Pegasus XL-R (Rotax 447) SW-TB-1374 & SW-WA-1368		9. 8.88	S.J.Whalley	Roddidge, Fradley	24.10.02P
G-MVFV	Solar Wings Pegasus XL-R (Rotax 447) SW-TB-1376 & SW-WA-1370		9. 8.88	N.Sullivan & C.J.Munton	(Corby)	18. 5.02P
G-MVFW	Solar Wings Pegasus XL-R (Rotax 447) SW-TB-1377 & SW-WA-1371		9. 8.88	S.F.Chaplin	Deenethorpe	28. 8.00P
G-MVFY	Solar Wings Pegasus XL-R (Rotax 447) SW-TB-1379 & SW-WA-1373		9. 8.88	L.Luscombe	Weston Zoyland	19. 1.02P
G-MVFZ	Solar Wings Pegasus XL-R (Rotax 447) SW-TB-1380 & SW-WA-1374		9. 8.88	R.K.Johnson	Popham	8. 5.01P
G-MVGA	Aerial Arts Chaser S CH.707 (Rotax 508) *(C/n now CH.859)*		11. 8.88	I.F.Bastin	(Liskeard)	29. 7.99P
G-MVGB	Medway Hybred 44XLR MR011/39 (Rotax 447)		1. 9.88	R.Graham	Rochester	28. 8.02P
G-MVGC	AMF Chevvron 2-32C 010 (Konig SD570)		2. 9.88	A.E.Dobson	Broadmeadow Farm, Hereford	8. 4.02P
G-MVGD	AMF Chevvron 2-32 011 (Konig SD570)		5. 9.88	T.R.James	(Southam)	19. 7.02P
G-MVGE	AMF Chevvron 2-32C 012 (Konig SD570)		26. 9.88	M.Lawley	(Blandford Forum)	15. 7.01P
G-MVGF	Aerial Arts Chaser S CH.720 (Rotax 377)		2. 9.88	J.H.Cooling *"The Dingbat" (Noted 10.01)*	Fenland	11.11.00P
G-MVGG	Aerial Arts Chaser S CH.721 (Rotax 377)		2. 9.88	J.B.Allan	Chase Farm, Billericay	28. 5.02P
G-MVGH	Aerial Arts Chaser S CH.722 (Rotax 447)		2. 9.88	J.E.Orbell *(Flies from Oban)*	(Spean Bridge)	4.11.02P
G-MVGI	Aerial Arts Chaser S CH.723 (Rotax 447?)		1. 9.88	J.Bagnall	(Congleton)	13. 7.97P
G-MVGM	Mainair Gemini/Flash IIA (Rotax 503) 691-988-6 & W481		25. 8.88	A.R.Pitcher	(Cranbrook, Kent)	27.10.02P
G-MVGN	Solar Wings Pegasus XL-R/Se (Rotax 447) SW-TB-1381 & SW-WA-1377		23. 8.88	M D Gregory	(Bideford)	20. 4.02P
G-MVGO	Solar Wings Pegasus XL-R (Rotax 447) SW-TB-1382 & SW-WA-1378		23. 8.88	J.B.Peacock	Lower Mountpleasant, Chatteris	2. 6.02P
G-MVGP	Solar Wings Pegasus XL-R (Rotax 447) SW-TB-1383 & SW-WA-1379	(EC-) G-MVGP	23. 8.88	J.P.Cox	(Kettering)	9. 6.00P
G-MVGS	Solar Wings Pegasus XL-R (Rotax 447) SW-TB-1385 & SW-WA-1381		23. 8.88	J.J.Featherstone	Long Marston	30. 6.01P
G-MVGT*	Solar Wings Pegasus XL-Q (Rotax 462) SW-TE-0092 & SW-WQ-0099		23. 8.88	R.Saunders *(Cancelled 5.10.01 as wfu)*	RAF Wyton	16. 7.00P
G-MVGU	Solar Wings Pegasus XL-Q (Rotax 462) SW-TB-0092 & SW-WQ-0100		23. 8.88	T.D.Turner	Redlands, Swindon	11. 6.02P
G-MVGW	Solar Wings Pegasus XL-Q (Rotax 462) SW-TE-0095 & SW-WQ-0102		23. 8.88	M.J.L.de Carvalho & V.V.P.Pedro t/a G-MVGW Group	Lagos, Algarve	8. 2.92P
G-MVGY	Medway Hybred 44XLR MR015/41 (Rotax 447)		31. 8.88	D.G.Baker	(Petersfield)	21. 8.02P
G-MVGZ	Ultraflight Lazair IIIE A.338 (Rotax 185 x 2)	(ex?)	21.10.88	M.F.Briggs	RAF Halton	24. 9.98P
G-MVHA	Aerial Arts Chaser S-1000 CH.729 (Mosler CB-38)		24. 8.88	R.Meredith-Hardy	Radwell Lodge, Baldock	24. 7.01P
G-MVHB	Powerchute Raider 80105 (Rotax 447)		26. 8.88	A.E.Askew	(Melton Mowbray)	14. 7.02P
G-MVHC	Powerchute Raider 80106 (Rotax 447)		26. 8.88	N.& S.A.Melrose	(Ripley)	19. 7.02P
G-MVHD	CFM Shadow CD 088 (Rotax 503)		8. 9.88	S R Groves	Plaistows Farm, St Albans	5. 5.01P
G-MVHE	Mainair Gemini/Flash IIA (Rotax 503) 692-988-6 & W482		4.10.88	D.C.Brotherton	East Fortune	31.10.02P
G-MVHF	Mainair Gemini/Flash IIA (Rotax 503) 693-988-6 & W483		4.10.88	M.G.Nicholson	(Kendal)	9. 5.02P
G-MVHG	Mainair Gemini/Flash IIA (Rotax 503) 694-988-6 & W484		14.10.88	C.A.J.Elder	(Bo'ness)	11. 3.01P
G-MVHH	Mainair Gemini/Flash IIA (Rotax 503) 607-1187-5 & W485 *(Originally Trike 695-...' replaced by 607-...' ex G-MTSA 1995)*		24.10.88	G.Addison	East Fortune	19. 9.02P
G-MVHI	Thruster TST Mk.1 8098-TST-100 (Rotax 503)		26. 9.88	C.P.Fox	(Frome)	14.10.00P
G-MVHJ	Thruster TST Mk.1 8098-TST-101 (Rotax 503)		26. 9.88	R.C.Barnett	Margaretting	10. 4.00P

G-MVHK	Thruster TST Mk.1	8098-TST-102		27. 9.88	D.J.Gordon	(St.Austell)	23. 6.02P
	(Rotax 503)						
G-MVHL	Thruster TST Mk.1	8098-TST-103		27. 9.88	G.Jones	(Llanfairfechan)	16. 7.02P
	(Rotax 532)						
G-MVHN	Aerial Arts Chaser S	CH.728		9. 9.88	J.E.Sweetingham	Benson's Farm, Laindon	10. 6.01P
	(Rotax 377)						
G-MVHO	Solar Wings Pegasus XL-Q			23. 9.88	S.J.Barkworth	Rufforth	29. 3.01P
	(Rotax 462HP) SW-TE-0097 & SW-WQ-0104						
G-MVHP	Solar Wings Pegasus XL-Q SW-WQ-0105			23. 9.88	J.B.Gasson		
	(Rotax 462)					Lower Mountpleasant, Chatteris	22. 7.02P
	(Original damaged trike c/n SW-TE-0078 from G-MVCV repaired and fitted with above sailwing)						
G-MVHR	Solar Wings Pegasus XL-Q			23. 9.88	J.M.Hucker	Full Sutton	26. 5.98P
	(Rotax 462) SW-TE-0099 & SW-WQ-0106						
G-MVHS	Solar Wings Pegasus XL-Q			23. 9.88	S.Sebastian	Long Acre Farm, Sandy	14. 6.02P
	(Rotax 462) SW-TE-0100 & SW-WQ-0107						
G-MVHT*	Solar Wings Pegasus XL-Q			23. 9.88	A.M.Gould	(Bristol)	15.12.01P
	(Rotax 462) SW-TE-0104 & SW-WQ-0108				(Cancelled 21.5.01 as wfu)		
G-MVHU*	Solar Wings Pegasus XL-Q			23. 9.88	A.McDermid	(Oakley, Beds)	30. 7.00P
	(Rotax 462HP) SW-TE-0182 & SW-WQ-0109				(Cancelled 20.7.01 by CAA)		
	(Originally allocated Trike c/n SW-TE-0102 but sale aborted & married with sailwing c/n SW-WQ-0115 as SE-YOP)						
G-MVHV	Solar Wings Pegasus XL-Q			23. 9.88	K.J.Tomlinson	(Mackworth, Derby)	1. 3.93P
	(Rotax 462) SW-TE-0103 & SW-WQ-0110						
G-MVHW	Solar Wings Pegasus XL-Q			23. 9.88	Ultralight Training Ltd		
	(Rotax 462) SW-TE-0101 & SW-WQ-0111					Roddige, Fradley	31. 8.02P
G-MVHX	Solar Wings Pegasus XL-Q			23. 9.88	D.F.Randall	Priory Farm, Tibengham	31. 5.02P
	(Rotax 462HP) SW-TE-0105 & SW-WQ-0112						
G-MVHY	Solar Wings Pegasus XL-Q			23. 9.88	R.P.Paine	(Mansfield)	25. 7.02P
	(Rotax 462HP) SW-TE-0106 & SW-WQ-0113						
G-MVHZ	Hornet Dual Trainer/Southdown Raven			26. 9.88	B.G.Colvin	(King's Lynn)	10.11.98P
	(Rotax 462) HRWA 0076 & MHR-101						
G-MVIA	Solar Wings Pegasus XL-R			4.10.88	K.Parkyn	St.Just	14. 6.01P
	(Rotax 462) SW-TE-0107 & SW-WA-1375						
G-MVIB	Mainair Gemini/Flash IIA			14.10.88	LSA Systems Ltd	Arclid Green, Sandbach	13. 5.02P
	(Rotax 503) 700-1088-4 & W490						
G-MVIC*	Mainair Gemini/Flash IIA			4.10.88	G.Tomlinson	Eshott	11. 4.00P
	(Rotax 503) 699-1188-4 & W489				(Cancelled 29.11.01 by CAA)		
G-MVIE	Aerial Arts Chaser S	CH.732		14.10.88	T.M.Stiles	(Heathfield)	6. 6.97P
	(Rotax 377)						
G-MVIF	Medway Raven X	MR020/43		4.10.88	J.R.Harrison	(Bolsover)	3. 6.02P
	(Rotax 447) (Originally regd as Hybred 44XLR)						
G-MVIG	CFM Shadow B	K.044		5.10.88	M.P.& P.A.G.Harper	Priory Farm, Tibenham	20. 1.94P
	(Rotax 447)				(Damaged 1993: stored 8.93: current status unknown)		
G-MVIH	Mainair Gemini/Flash IIA			14.10.88	T.M.Gilsenan	(Eaton Bray)	24. 5.02P
	(Rotax 503) 697-1088-6 & W487						
G-MVIL	Noble Hardman Snowbird Mk.IV SB-014			6. 2.89	G.R.Graham	Kirkbride	24.11.00P
	(Rotax 582)						
G-MVIM*	Noble Hardman Snowbird Mk.IV SB-015			6. 2.89	Yorkshire Air Museum	Elvington	28. 6.91P
					(Cancelled 15.5.00 by CAA: for restoration 12.00)		
G-MVIN	Noble Hardman Snowbird Mk.IV SB-016			6. 2.89	R.S.W.Jones	Haverfordwest	9. 4.02P
	(Rotax 582) (Rebuilt to Mk.V standard)						
G-MVIO	Noble Hardman Snowbird Mk.IV SB-017			12. 4.89	B.Mason-Baker	Shifnal	27. 7.01P
	(Rotax 532)				t/a Mobility Advice Line		
G-MVIP	AMF Chevvron 2-32	008		11. 5.88	C.D.Marsh	Chilbolton	21. 1.02P
	(Konig SD570)				t/a Chilbolton Chevvron Group		
G-MVIR	Thruster TST Mk.1	8108-TST-104		21.10.88	T D Gardner	Kingsclere, Hannington	14. 8.02P
	(Rotax 503) (C/n plate marked as 8118-TST-104)						
G-MVIT	Thruster TST Mk.1	8108-TST-106	(C-)	21.10.88	A.P.Trumper	(Grantham)	20. 9.02P
	(Rotax 503)		G-MVIT				
G-MVIU	Thruster TST Mk.1	8108-TST-107		21.10.88	R.J.Humphries	Popham	12. 4.02P
	(Rotax 503) (Rebuilt as T.300)						
G-MVIV	Thruster TST Mk.1	8108-TST-108		21.10.88	P.J.Sears	(Ivybridge)	24. 6.01P
	(Rotax 503)						
G-MVIW	Thruster TST Mk.1	8108-TST-109		21.10.88	J.M.Nicholson	(Denham)	4. 6.01P
	(Rotax 532)						
G-MVIX	Mainair Gemini/Flash IIA			14.10.88	R.S.T.MacEwen	East Fortune	3.10.02P
	(Rotax 503) 702-1088-6 & W492						
G-MVIY	Mainair Gemini/Flash IIA			14.10.88	J.J.Valentine	Ince Blundell	15. 7.02P
	(Rotax 503) 701-1088-6 & W491						
G-MVIZ	Mainair Gemini/Flash IIA			14.10.88	A.J.Geary	(Pickering)	7. 7.02P
	(Rotax 503) 703-1088-6 & W493						
G-MVJA	Mainair Gemini/Flash IIA			5.12.88	J.R.Harrison	(Wisbech)	25. 5.02P
	(Rotax 503) 696-988-6 & W486						
G-MVJC	Mainair Gemini/Flash IIA			24.10.88	B.Temple	Priory Farm, Tibenham	16.10.02P
	(Rotax 503) 705-1088-6 & W495

G-MVJD	Solar Wings Pegasus XL-R (Rotax 462) SW-TE-0109 & SW-WA-1386	24.10.88	R.S.Finlay	Perth	30. 4.02P
G-MVJE	Mainair Gemini/Flash IIA (Rotax 503) 706-1188-6 & W496	21.10.88	S.J.Whistance	(Bromyard)	19.11.02P
G-MVJF	Aerial Arts Chaser S CH.743 (Rotax 377)	21.11.88	N.R.Andrew	(Bristol)	17.10.99P
G-MVJG	Aerial Arts Chaser S CH.749	22.11.88	T.H.Scott *(New owner 12.01)*	Rayne Hall Farm, Rayne	24. 5.98P
G-MVJH	Aerial Arts Chaser S CH.751 (Rotax 377)	14.11.88	M.Van Rompaey	(Scunthorpe)	8. 8.02P
G-MVJJ	Aerial Arts Chaser S CH.753 (Rotax 508)	14.11.88	P.Brown	Eshott	28. 6.02P
G-MVJK	Aerial Arts Chaser S CH.754 (Rotax 377)	14.11.88	T.L.Travis	(Stafford)	7. 4.00P
G-MVJL	Mainair Gemini/Flash IIA (Rotax 503) 698-1188-6 & W488	21.10.88	F.Huxley	(Morpeth)	20. 5.01P
G-MVJM	Microflight Spectrum 007 (Rotax 503)	21.10.88	S.E.Matthews t/a Poppy Syndicate	Otherton, Cannock	11. 5.02P
G-MVJN	Solar Wings Pegasus XL-Q (Rotax 462) SW-TE-0110 & SW-WQ-0116	26.10.88	J.W.Wall *(Stored 6.96: current status unknown)*	Enstone	18. 2.96P
G-MVJO	Solar Wings Pegasus XL-Q (Rotax 462) SW-TE-0111 & SW-WQ-0117	26.10.88	J.D.Hoyland	(Winchester)	30. 5.02P
G-MVJP	Solar Wings Pegasus XL-Q (Rotax 462) SW-TE-0112 & SW-WQ-0118	26.10.88	S.H.Bakowski	Headcorn	18. 4.02P
G-MVJR	Solar Wings Pegasus XL-Q (Rotax 462) SW-TE-0113 & SW-WQ-0119	26.10.88	A.D.Woodroffe	(Henley-on-Thames)	30. 8.97P
G-MVJS	Solar Wings Pegasus XL-Q (Rotax 462) SW-TE-0114 & SW-WQ-0120	26.10.88	S.D.Morley	Rayne Hall Farm, Rayne	16.11.02P
G-MVJT	Solar Wings Pegasus XL-Q (Rotax 462HP) SW-TE-0115 & SW-WQ-0121	26.10.88	A.S.Johnson & T.M.Wakeley	(Poole)	15. 6.02P
G-MVJU	Solar Wings Pegasus XL-Q (Rotax 462) SW-TE-0116 & SW-WQ-0122	26.10.88	G.B.Hutchison	Sandtoft	11. 5.02P
G-MVJW	Solar Wings Pegasus XL-Q (Rotax 462) SE-TE-0118 & SW-WQ-0124	26.10.88	R.Dainty & D.W.Stamp	Pound Green, Buttonoak, Kidderminster	18.11.01P
G-MVKB	Medway Hybred 44XLR MR023/45 (Rotax 447)	11.11.88	J.Newby	Sandtoft	11. 9.00P
G-MVKC	Mainair Gemini/Flash IIA (Rotax 503) 709-1188-6 & W499	16.11.88	R.L.Bladon	(Burntwood)	25. 6.02P
G-MVKF	Solar Wings Pegasus XL-R (Rotax 447) SW-TB-1389 & SW-WA-1392	14.11.88	B.Shaw	(Northampton)	27. 1.02P
G-MVKH	Solar Wings Pegasus XL-R (Rotax 447) SW-TB-1393 & SW-WA-1396	14.11.88	K.M.Elson	Roddige, Fradley	14.11.02P
G-MVKJ	Solar Wings Pegasus XL-R (Rotax 462) SW-TE-0132 & SW-WA-1398	14.11.88	G.V.Warner	Croughton	7. 6.02P
G-MVKK	Solar Wings Pegasus XL-R (Rotax 462) SW-TE-0131 & SW-WA-1397	14.11.88	P.G.Sayers	Graveley Farm, Herts	29. 6.02P
G-MVKL	Solar Wings Pegasus XL-R (Rotax 447) SW-TB-1391 & SW-WA-1394 *(Although pod marked as "XL-Q" it remains a XL-R model)*	14.11.88	J.Powell-Tuck	(Pontypool)	6. 6.91P
G-MVKM	Solar Wings Pegasus XL-R (Rotax 462) SW-TE-0136 & SW-WA-1399 *(Trike originally ordered as c/n SW-TB-1396 with Rotax 447: fitted with Rotax 462, hence SW-TE-prefix: the data plate continues to record "SW-TB-0136")*	14.11.88	R J Coppin	Hereford	15. 8.01P
G-MVKN	Solar Wings Pegasus XL-Q (Rotax 462) SW-TE-0120 & SW-WQ-0126	14.11.88	T.A.Colman	(London NW8)	5. 5.02P
G-MVKO	Solar Wings Pegasus XL-Q (Rotax 462HP) SW-TE-0121 & SW-WQ-0127	14.11.88	B.J.Lyford	(Swanage)	19. 9.02P
G-MVKP	Solar Wings Pegasus XL-Q (Rotax 462) SW-TE-0122 & SW-WQ-0128	14.11.88	J.Urwin	Eshott	22. 9.02P
G-MVKS	Solar Wings Pegasus XL-Q (Rotax 462) SW-TE-0124 & SW-WQ-0130	14.11.88	K.S.Wright *(Stored 8.95: current status unknown)*	Long Marston	13. 5.94P
G-MVKT	Solar Wings Pegasus XL-Q (Rotax 462) SW-TE-0125 & SW-WQ-0131	14.11.88	N.C.Williams	Enstone	13.12.01P
G-MVKU	Solar Wings Pegasus XL-Q (Rotax 462) SW-TE-0126 & SW-WQ-0132	14.11.88	J.R.F.Shepherd	Long Acre Farm, Sandy	17. 7.02P
G-MVKV	Solar Wings Pegasus XL-Q (Rotax 462) SW-TE-0127 & SW-WQ-0152 *(Original sailwing c/n SW-WQ-0133 damaged 14.8.91 & replaced by '-0152)*	14.11.88	M D Callan	(Dundalk, Co.Louth)	8.12.02P
G-MVKW	Solar Wings Pegasus XL-Q (Rotax 462) SW-TE-0128 & SW-WQ-0134	14.11.88	A.T.Scott	(London SW17)	7. 5.02P
G-MVKX*	Solar Wings Pegasus XL-Q (Rotax 462) SW-TE-0129 & SW-WQ-0135	14.11.88	G.R.Soper *(Cancelled 20.11.01 as wfu)*	Popham	2. 5.00P
G-MVKY	Aerial Arts Chaser S CH.755 (Rotax 377)	5.12.88	R.W.Whitehead	Swinford, Rugby	3. 7.02P
G-MVKZ	Aerial Arts Chaser S CH.756 (Rotax 377)	5.12.88	J.Cresswell	Sittles Farm, Alrewas	23.10.02P

G-MVLA	Aerial Arts Chaser S (Rotax 377)	CH.762	12.12.88	T.Birch	(Wolverhampton)	12. 8.02P
G-MVLC	Aerial Arts Chaser S (Rotax 377)	CH.764	22.11.88	B.R.Barnes	(Bristol)	3. 4.01P
G-MVLD	Aerial Arts Chaser S (Rotax 377)	CH.765	22.11.88	G.F.Atkinson	Rufforth	7. 5.00P
G-MVLE	Aerial Arts Chaser S (Rotax 377)	CH.766	5.12.88	R.G.Hooker	Eshott	4. 9.00P
G-MVLF	Aerial Arts Chaser S (Rotax 508)	CH.767	11. 1.89	M.P.Hadden	Sittles Farm, Alrewas	23. 7.02P
G-MVLG	Aerial Arts Chaser S (Rotax 377)	CH.768	14.11.88	S.Bradie	East Fortune	25.11.96P
G-MVLH	Aerial Arts Chaser S (Rotax 377)	CH.769	22.11.88	A.W.Cove	(Wellingborough)	13.11.97P
G-MVLJ	CFM Shadow CD (Rotax 503)	092	11.11.88	B.E.Trinder	(Rushden)	11. 1.02P
G-MVLL	Mainair Gemini/Flash IIA (Rotax 503)	708-1188-6 & W498 *(Wing c/n now W396 ex G-MTSA)*	23.11.88	J.W.Peake	Otheron, Cannock	27.10.02P
G-MVLP	CFM Shadow C (Rotax 447)	095	22.11.88	D.Bridgland & D.T.Moran	Old Sarum	15.12.02P
G-MVLR	Mainair Gemini/Flash IIA (Rotax 503)	713-1288-6 & W503	30.11.88	K.B.A.Judson	(Colchester)	18.11.00P
G-MVLS	Aerial Arts Chaser S (Rotax 377)	CH.773	21. 2.89	E.W.P.Van Zeller	(Ashford, Kent)	1. 2.02P
G-MVLT	Aerial Arts Chaser S (Rotax 377)	CH.774	5.12.88	B.D.Searle	(Portsmouth)	6. 5.02P
G-MVLW	Aerial Arts Chaser S (Rotax 377)	CH.778	28.12.88	E.W.P.van Zeller	(Ashford)	5. 9.99P
G-MVLX	Solar Wings Pegasus XL-Q (Rotax 462)	SW-TE-0133 & SW-WQ-0114	30.11.88	J.F.Smith	(High Wycombe)	17. 6.02P
G-MVLY	Solar Wings Pegasus XL-Q (Rotax 462)	SW-TE-0137 & SW-WQ-0142	5.12.88	I.B.Osborn	Manston	28. 9.02P
G-MVMC	Solar Wings Pegasus XL-Q (Rotax 462HP)	SW-TE-0141 & SW-WQ-0146	5.12.88	P.G.Becker	Hougham, Lincs	10. 4.02P
G-MVMD	Powerchute Raider (Rotax 447)	80924	15.12.88	S.M.Paulin	(Reading)	13. 7.90P
G-MVME	Thruster TST Mk.1 (Rotax 503)	8128-TST-110	12.12.88	R.C.Whittall	Weston Zoyland	20. 4.02P
G-MVMG	Thruster TST Mk.1 (Rotax 503)	8128-TST-112	12.12.88	B.O.McCartan	(Banbridge, Co.Down)	23. 4.02P
G-MVMI	Thruster TST Mk.1 (Rotax 503)	8128-TST-114	12.12.88	G.J.Johnson	North Coates	6. 1.03P
G-MVML	Aerial Arts Chaser S (Rotax 377)	CH.781	28.12.88	G C Luddington	Wilden, Beds	29. 7.00P
G-MVMM	Aerial Arts Chaser S (Rotax 377)	CH.797	21. 2.89	D.Margereson	(Chesterfield)	10. 6.02P
G-MVMO	Mainair Gemini/Flash IIA (Rotax 503)	715-1288-6 & W507	12.12.88	M H Moulai	North Coates	31. 8.02P
G-MVMR	Mainair Gemini/Flash IIA (Rotax 503)	717-1288-6 & W509	9. 1.89	P.W.Ramage	(Rufforth)	20. 9.96P
G-MVMT	Mainair Gemini/Flash IIA (Rotax 503)	718-189-6 & W510	22.12.88	R.F.Sanders t/a Independent Financial Advisory Service	Hatherton, Cannock	25. 9.98P
G-MVMU	Mainair Gemini/Flash IIA (Rotax 503)	719-189-6 & W511	22.12.88	M.J.A.New & A.Clift *"Icarus"*	Mill Farm, Hughley, Much Wenlock	19. 8.02P
G-MVMV	Mainair Gemini/Flash IIA (Rotax 503)	720-189-6 & W512	22.12.88	R Nicklin	Otherton, Cannock	11.11.01P
G-MVMW	Mainair Gemini/Flash IIA (Rotax 503)	710-1188-6 & W500	11.11.88	K.Downes & B.Nock	(Wolverhampton)	31. 7.01P
G-MVMX	Mainair Gemini/Flash IIA (Rotax 462)	721-189-6 & W513 *(Trike stamped incorrectly as "W512")*	23.12.88	D.A.Johns	Tarn Farm, Cockerham	9. 6.02P
G-MVMY	Mainair Gemini/Flash IIA (Rotax 503)	722-189-6 & W514	22.12.88	N.G.Leteney	(Congleton)	4.10.01P
G-MVMZ	Mainair Gemini/Flash IIA (Rotax 503)	723-189-6 & W515	22.12.88	S A Unsworth	Otherton, Cannock	24. 5.02P
G-MVNA	Powerchute Raider (Rotax 447)	81230	12. 7.89	B.Gorvett	(Swansea)	24. 5.93P
G-MVNC	Powerchute Raider (Rotax 447)	81232	12. 7.89	W.R.Hanley	(Edinburgh)	25. 7.00P
G-MVNI	Powerchute Raider (Rotax 447)	90625	12. 7.89	N.J.Staib	Kemble	13. 7.02P
G-MVNK	Powerchute Raider (Rotax 447)	90623	12. 7.89	J.Cunliffe	(Stoke-on-Trent)	16. 7.95P
G-MVNL	Powerchute Raider (Rotax 447)	90624	12. 7.89	S.Penoyre	(Windlesham)	17. 3.01P

G-MVNM	Mainair Gemini/Flash IIA (Rotax 503)	725-189-6 & W517		6. 1.89	M.Castle & T.Hartwig	(Shrewsbury)	8. 6.00P
G-MVNN	Aerotech MW-5(K) Sorcerer (Rotax 447)	5K-0003-02 & BMAA/HB/022		28. 3.90	W S S Lubbock	(Callington)	21. 5.02P
G-MVNO	Aerotech MW-5(K) Sorcerer (Rotax 447)	5K-0004-02		4. 5.89	R.L.Wadley	Stoke, Kent	22. 5.02P
G-MVNP	Aerotech MW-5(K) Sorcerer (Rotax 447)	5K-0005-02		13. 7.89	A M Edwards	(Wokingham)	24. 9.96P
G-MVNR	Aerotech MW-5(K) Sorcerer (Rotax 447)	5K-0006-02		4. 5.89	F.Jones	Ley Farm, Chirk	23. 8.01P
G-MVNS	Aerotech MW-5(K) Sorcerer (Rotax 447)	5K-0007-02		19. 7.89	R.D.Chiles	Shenstone Hall Farm, Shenstone	15. 7.02P
G-MVNT	Aerotech MW-5(K) Sorcerer (Rotax 447)	5K-0008-02		28. 3.90	P.E.Blyth	Wombleton	21. 9.00P
G-MVNU	Aerotech MW-5(K) Sorcerer (Rotax 447)	5K-0009-02		4. 5.89	J.C.Rose	Oakley, Beds	2. 6.02P
G-MVNW	Mainair Gemini/Flash IIA (Rotax 503)	726-189-6 & W518		25. 1.89	A.Weatherall	(Preston)	14. 4.02P
G-MVNX	Mainair Gemini/Flash IIA (Rotax 503)	727-289-6 & W519		10. 1.89	I.Sidebotham	Barton	25. 1.02P
G-MVNY	Mainair Gemini/Flash IIA (Rotax 462)	724-189-6 & W516		11. 1.89	M.K.Buckland	(Daventry)	25. 7.02P
G-MVNZ	Mainair Gemini/Flash IIA (Rotax 503)	728-289-6 & W520		11. 1.89	B.Crouch	Oxton, Nottingham	22. 9.02P
G-MVOA	Aerial Arts Chaser S (Rotax 462) (Reported as Aerial Arts Alligator)	CH.780		16. 1.89	A.B.Potts	Eshott	7. 9.02P
G-MVOB	Mainair Gemini/Flash IIA (Rotax 503)	729-289-6 & W521		16. 1.89	B.J.Bader	(Taunton)	19. 4.02P
G-MVOD	Aerial Arts Chaser/110SX (Rotax 377)	110SX/653		16. 1.89	M.A.Hodgson	Baxby Manor, Husthwaite	29. 8.02P
G-MVOF	Mainair Gemini/Flash IIA (Rotax 503)	730-289-6 & W522		31. 1.89	C.Pearce	Beccles	27.11.02P
G-MVOH	CFM Shadow CD (Rotax 503)	K.090		23. 1.89	D.I.Farmer	Dunkeswell	2. 9.02P
G-MVOI	Noble Hardman Snowbird Mk.IV (Rotax 532)	SB-018		6. 2.89	K.W. & C.A.Warn	(Newbury/Uxbridge)	13. 6.02P
G-MVOJ	Noble Hardman Snowbird Mk.IV (Rotax 532)	SB-019		26. 7.89	T.D.Thwaites t/a The HFC Group	(Penrith)	28. 7.99P
G-MVOL	Noble Hardman Snowbird Mk.IV (Rotax 532)	SB-021		29. 8.89	E.J.Lewis t/a Swansea Snowbird Fliers	(Swansea)	26. 1.02P
G-MVON	Mainair Gemini/Flash IIA (Rotax 503)	731-289-6 & W523		30. 1.89	J.V.Bailey	(Leigh, Lancs)	14. 7.02P
G-MVOO	AMF Chevvron 2-32C (Konig SD570)	014		10. 1.89	I.R.F.Hammond	Lee-on-Solent	1. 8.02P
G-MVOP	Aerial Arts Chaser S (Rotax 377)	CH.787		21. 2.89	D.Thorpe *(Noted 7.01)*	Long Acre Farm, Sandy	28.10.96P
G-MVOR	Mainair Gemini/Flash IIA (Rotax 462)	732-289-6 & W524	(EC-) G-MVOR	6. 2.89	P.T. & R.M.Jenkins	Dunkeswell	24. 8.02P
G-MVOT	Thruster TST Mk.1 (Rotax 503)	8029-TST-116		17. 2.89	J.A.E.Bowen	Davidstow Moor	30. 7.02P
G-MVOU	Thruster TST Mk.1 (Rotax 503)	8029-TST-117		17. 2.89	A.T.Murray	(Great Orton)	28. 5.98P
G-MVOV	Thruster TST Mk.1 (Rotax 503)	8029-TST-118		17. 2.89	D.A.Duthie	Otherton, Cannock	26. 8.02P
G-MVOW	Thruster TST Mk.1 (Rotax 503)	8029-TST-119		17. 2.89	J.Short & B.J.Merret	Dunkeswell	17. 7.00P
G-MVOX	Thruster TST Mk.1 (Rotax 503)	8029-TST-120		17. 2.89	J.E.Davies	Haverfordwest	1. 6.02P
G-MVOY	Thruster TST Mk.1 (Rotax 503)	8029-TST-121		17. 2.89	G.R.Breaden	Tarn Farm, Cockerham	26. 8.02P
G-MVPA	Mainair Gemini/Flash IIA (Rotax 503)	735-289-7 & W527		29. 3.89	J.E.Milburn	Eshott	30. 8.95P
G-MVPB	Mainair Gemini/Flash IIA (Rotax 503)	736-389-7 & W528		29. 3.89	P Harrison	(Ripon)	15. 6.02P
G-MVPD	Mainair Gemini/Flash IIA (Rotax 503)	738-389-7 & W530		7. 2.89	A.S.Bates	(Ashton-under-Lyne)	7. 9.02P
G-MVPE	Mainair Gemini/Flash IIA (Rotax 503)	739-389-7 & W531		7. 2.89	E.A.Wrathall & H.N.Houghton	St.Michaels	10. 2.01P
G-MVPF	Medway Hybred 44XLR (Rotax 447)	MR036/52		27. 2.89	G H Crick	Plaistows Farm, St Albans	6. 6.02P
G-MVPG	Medway Hybred 44XLR (Rotax 447)	MR026/53		15. 2.89	M.A.Jones	(Wigan)	30.12.98P
G-MVPH	Whittaker MW6-S Fatboy Flyer (Rotax 503)	PFA 164-11404		7. 2.89	A.A.Rowson *(New owner 9.01)*	Emlyn's Field, Rhuallt	23. 8.99P

G-MVPI	Mainair Gemini/Flash IIA (Rotax 503) 740-389-7 & W532	9. 2.89	R.J.Bowden	Dunkeswell	26. 4.02P
G-MVPJ	Rans S-5 Coyote (Rotax 447) 88.083 & PFA 193-11470	15. 2.89	D.Harker	(Middlesbrough)	2. 8.99P
G-MVPK	CFM Shadow BD K.091 (Rotax 447)	15. 2.89	P.Sarfas *(Flies from Margaretting)*	(Billericay)	26. 7.02P
G-MVPL	Medway Hybred 44XLR MR034/50 (Rotax 447)	1. 3.89	J.N.J.Roberts	Long Acre Farm, Sandy	30. 4.98P
G-MVPM	Whittaker MW6 Merlin PFA 164-11272 (Rotax 503) *(Reported as MW6-T)*	21. 2.89	P.R.A. & S.Elliston	RAF Mona	25. 9.01P
G-MVPN	Whittaker MW6 Merlin PFA 164-11280 (Rotax 503)	21. 2.89	A.M.Field	(Glastonbury)	18. 5.93P
G-MVPO	Mainair Gemini/Flash IIA (Rotax 503) 741-389-7 & W533	3. 3.89	A.H. & C.I.King	(Rye)	9. 8.99P
G-MVPR	Solar Wings Pegasus XL-Q (Rotax 462) SW-TE-0149 & SW-WQ-0163	14. 3.89	R.S.Swift	Finmere	3. 6.02P
G-MVPS	Solar Wings Pegasus XL-Q (Rotax 462HP) SW-TE-0143 & SW-WQ-0140	14. 3.89	B.R.Chamberlain	(London Colney)	26. 7.02P
G-MVPU	Solar Wings Pegasus XL-Q (Rotax 462) SW-TE-0150 & SW-WQ-0164	29. 3.89	I.B.Smith	(Peterborough)	2. 9.02P
G-MVPW	Solar Wings Pegasus XL-R (Rotax 462) SW-TE-0177 & SW-WA-1411	28. 3.89	C.A.Mitchell	(Newport, Gwent)	24.10.98P
G-MVPX	Solar Wings Pegasus XL-Q (Rotax 462) SW-TE-0144 & SW-WQ-0158	28. 3.89	M.M.P.Evans	Plaistows Farm, St Albans	16. 3.02P
G-MVPY	Solar Wings Pegasus XL-Q (Rotax 462) SW-TE-0178 & SW-WQ-0188	28. 3.89	G.H.Dawson	(Swavesey, Cambridge)	6. 8.02P
G-MVRA	Mainair Gemini/Flash IIA (Rotax 503) 743-489-7 & W535	10. 4.89	A.J.Lowe-Jones	(Dukinfield)	7. 8.02P
G-MVRB*	Mainair Gemini/Flash (Rotax 503) 747-489-7 & W539	29. 3.89	M.J.Burns & P.A.McGivern *(Cancelled 5.12.01 by CAA)*	Newtownards, Co.of Down	17. 4.00P
G-MVRC	Mainair Gemini/Flash IIA (Rotax 503) 748-489-7 & W540	29. 3.89	M.O'Connell	Rufforth	11.12.01P
G-MVRD	Mainair Gemini/Flash IIA (Rotax 503) 749-489-7 & W541	9. 5.89	A.R.Helm	(Accrington)	4. 8.02P
G-MVRE	CFM Shadow CD K.087 (Rotax 503)	10. 4.89	J.Madhvani	Plaistows Farm, St Albans	6. 5.01P
G-MVRF	Rotec Rally 2B AIE-01	28. 4.89	A.I.Edwards	(Stafford)	
G-MVRG	Aerial Arts Chaser S CH.798 (Rotax 377)	14. 4.89	J.P.Kynaston	(Luton)	31. 8.99P
G-MVRH	Solar Wings Pegasus XL-Q (Rotax 462) SW-TE-0160 & SW-WQ-0177	10. 4.89	K.Farr	Swinford, Rugby	18. 8.02P
G-MVRI	Solar Wings Pegasus XL-Q (Rotax 462) SW-TE-0145 & SW-WQ-0159	10. 4.89	P.Martin	(Stevenage)	14.12.01P
G-MVRJ	Solar Wings Pegasus XL-Q (Rotax 462HP) SW-TE-0172 & SW-WQ-0165	10. 4.89	M.A.Potter & J.Goldsmith-Ryan	(Barnstaple)	27. 8.02P
G-MVRL	Aerial Arts Chaser S CH.801 (Rotax 447)	18. 4.89	C.N.Beale	Mill Farm, Shifnal	22. 7.02P
G-MVRM	Mainair Gemini/Flash IIA (Rotax 462) 752-489-7 & W545	12. 4.89	I.H.Barbour	East Fortune	25. 9.02P
G-MVRO	CFM Shadow BD K.105 (Rotax 447)	3. 4.89	J.R.Fairweather t/a G-MVRO Flying Group	Hougham, Lincs	28.11.02P
G-MVRP	CFM Shadow CD 097 (Rotax 503)	7. 4.89	D.R.G.Whitelaw	North Connel, Oban	27. 7.02P
G-MVRR	CFM Shadow CD 098 (Rotax 503)	7. 4.89	S.Fairweather & S.P.Christian	Hougham, Lincs	25. 8.02P
G-MVRT	CFM Shadow BD 104 (Rotax 447)	7. 4.89	S.C.Cornock	(Lichfield)	13.10.01P
G-MVRU	Solar Wings Pegasus XL-Q (Rotax 462) SW-TE-0166 & SW-WQ-0183	12. 4.89	P.J.Edwards	(Newmarket)	11.10.00P
G-MVRV	Powerchute Kestrel 90210 (Rotax 503)	28. 4.89	G.M.Fletcher	(Chesterfield)	3. 2.97P
G-MVRW	Solar Wings Pegasus XL-Q (Rotax 462) SW-TE-0161 & SW-WQ-0178 *(Rebuilt 1999 including new factory supplied sailwing)*	12. 4.89	L Harland	(Queenborough)	21. 8.02P
G-MVRX	Solar Wings Pegasus XL-Q (Rotax 462HP) SW-TE-0151 & SW-WQ-0165	12. 4.89	M.Everest	(Hailsham)	22. 5.02P
G-MVRY	Medway Hybred 44XLR MR049/56 (Rotax 447)	12. 4.89	K.Dodman	(Cambridge)	4. 3.99P
G-MVRZ	Medway Hybred 44XLR MR043/57 (Rotax 503)	9. 5.89	I.Oswald	(London SE9)	13.11.01P
G-MVSB	Solar Wings Pegasus XL-Q (Rotax 462) SW-TE-0184 & SW-WQ-0193	18. 4.89	M.J.Olsen	Wombleton	23.11.02P
G-MVSD	Solar Wings Pegasus XL-Q (Rotax 462) SW-TE-0186 & SW-WQ-0195	18. 4.89	M.T.Aplin t/a G-MVSD Group	Dunkeswell	22. 5.02P

G-MVSE	Solar Wings Pegasus XL-Q (Rotax 462) SW-TE-0187 & SW-WQ-0196		18. 4.89	A Gulliver	Thirsk	14. 8.02P
G-MVSG	Aerial Arts Chaser S CH.804 (Rotax 377)		24. 4.89	M.Roberts	(Melksham)	20. 8.00P
G-MVSJ	Aviasud Mistral 072 & BMAA/HB/013 (Rotax 532)		18. 4.89	A.J.Record	(Selby)	25. 9.02P
G-MVSK	Aerial Arts Chaser S CH.806 (Rotax 377)		27. 4.89	G.A.Inch	(Bristol)	8. 1.00P
G-MVSM	Midland Ultralights Sirocco 377GB (Rotax 377) MU-023		21. 4.89	J.S.Seddon-Harvey	(Ross-on-Wye)	23. 7.02P
G-MVSN	Mainair Gemini/Flash IIA (Rotax 503) 754-589-7 & W547		28. 4.89	D.Morrison	(Kelso)	16.11.02P
G-MVSO	Mainair Gemini/Flash IIA (Rotax 503) 755-589-7 & W548		27. 4.89	P.W.Taylor	Swanton Morley	24. 7.02P
G-MVSP	Mainair Gemini/Flash IIA (Rotax 503) 756-589-7 & W549		27. 4.89	D.R.Buchanan	Pulborough	28. 7.00P
G-MVSR*	Medway Hybred 44XLR MR038/59 (Rotax 447)		15. 5.89	G.Tate *(Cancelled 25.7.01 by CAA)*	Carlisle	4. 5.01P
G-MVST	Mainair Gemini/Flash IIA (Rotax 462) 750-589-7 & W543		12. 6.89	A.Raithby, A.Bower & N.McCusker	Rufforth	13. 5.02P
G-MVSU	Microflight Spectrum 008 (Rotax 503)		4. 5.89	G.Wilkinson	Otherton, Cannock	28. 1.01P
G-MVSV	Mainair Gemini/Flash IIA (Rotax 503) 757-589-7 & W550		11. 5.89	P.Shelton	St.Michaels	24. 8.02P
G-MVSW	Solar Wings Pegasus XL-Q (Rotax 462HP) SW-TE-0189 & SW-WQ-0198		17. 5.89	D.A.Ward	Enstone	31.12.02P
G-MVSX	Solar Wings Pegasus XL-Q (Rotax 462) SW-TE-0190 & SW-WQ-0199		11. 5.89	A.R.Law	(Plymouth)	14. 7.02P
G-MVSY	Solar Wings Pegasus XL-Q (Rotax 462) SW-TE-0191 & SW-WQ-0200		11. 5.89	C.M.Jones	(Yelverton)	30. 6.02P
G-MVSZ	Solar Wings Pegasus XL-Q (Rotax 462HP) SW-TE-0192 & SW-WQ-0201		11. 5.89	D.M.Goldsmith	Rufforth	11.11.01P
G-MVTA	Solar Wings Pegasus XL-Q (Rotax 462) SW-TE-0193 & SW-WQ-0202		11. 5.89	A.Garlick	Knapthorpe Lodge, Caunton	20. 9.02P
G-MVTC	Mainair Gemini/Flash IIA (Rotax 503) 759-689-7 & W552		30. 5.89	B.D.Bowen	Shobdon	8. 7.02P
G-MVTD	Whittaker MW6 Merlin PFA 164-11367 (Rotax 503)		11. 5.89	G.J.Green	(Matlock)	28. 4.97P
G-MVTI	Solar Wings Pegasus XL-Q SW-WQ-0206 (Rotax 462) SW-TE-0217 & SW-WQ-0206		25. 5.89	A.M.Prentice	(Great Shelford)	30. 8.01P
G-MVTJ	Solar Wings Pegasus XL-Q (Rotax 462) SW-TE-0197 & SW-WQ-0207		25. 5.89	P.D.Rowe	Dunkeswell	3.11.01P
G-MVTK	Solar Wings Pegasus XL-Q (Rotax 462) SW-TE-0198 & SW-WQ-0208		25. 5.89	S.Davis & S.E.Strangeway	(Hungerford/Reading)	18. 5.02P
G-MVTL	Aerial Arts Chaser S CH.809 (Rotax 337)		13. 6.89	R.J.Grainger	(Northampton)	20. 3.99P
G-MVTM	Aerial Arts Chaser S CH.810 (Rotax 447)		13. 6.89	C.C.W.Mates *(Noted 9.01)*	Margaretting	8. 8.99P
G-MVUA	Mainair Gemini/Flash IIA (Rotax 462) 760-689-7 & W553		14. 6.89	T.V.Almomd & K.Atherton	Ince Blundell	24. 4.02P
G-MVUB	Thruster T.300 089-T300-373 (Rotax 532)		13. 6.89	C J Badenhurst	(Steyning)	23. 7.02P
G-MVUD	Medway Hybred 44XLR MR037/55 (Rotax 503)		19. 6.89	B.H.Morton	(Great Orton)	19. 8.01P
G-MVUF	Solar Wings Pegasus XL-Q (Rotax 462) SW-TE-0203 & SW-WQ-0213		13. 6.89	G.& S.Simons	(Rustington)	24. 4.02P
G-MVUG	Solar Wings Pegasus XL-Q (Rotax 462) SW-TE-0204 & SW-WQ-0214		13. 6.89	E.D.Deed	Sywell	14. 6.02P
G-MVUH*	Solar Wings Pegasus XL-Q (Rotax 462) SW-TE-0205 & SW-WQ-0215		13. 6.89	A.Davis *(Temporary wfu 16.5.00) (Dismantled for spares?)*	(Macclesfield)	17. 8.99P
G-MVUI	Solar Wings Pegasus XL-Q (Rotax 462) SW-TE-0206 & SW-WQ-0216 *(Wing marked incorrectly as c/n SW-TE-0216)*		13. 6.89	J.K.Edgecombe	(Coalville)	10.11.02P
G-MVUJ	Solar Wings Pegasus XL-Q (Rotax 462) SW-TE-0207 & SW-WQ-0217		13. 6.89	J.H.Cooper	(Aylesbury)	17. 7.02P
G-MVUL	Solar Wings Pegasus XL-Q (Rotax 462HP) SW-TE-0209 & SW-WQ-0219		13. 6.89	P.J.Emery	(Waterlooville)	9. 6.01P
G-MVUM	Solar Wings Pegasus XL-Q (Rotax 462HP) SW-TE-0210 & SW-WQ-0220		13. 6.89	A.E.Ciantar *(New owner 8.00)*	(Bury St Edmunds)	5.11.95P
G-MVUO	AMF Chevvron 2-32C 015 (Konig SD570)		14. 6.89	D.Beevers	Melrose Farm, Melbourne	18. 7.01P
G-MVUP	Aviasud Mistral (Rotax 532) 1087-48 & BMAA/HB/003	83-CQ	10. 8.89	C.J.& B.W.Foulds	Ashbourne	1. 8.02P
G-MVUR	Hornet RS-ZA HRWA-0050 & ZA107 (Rotax 532) *(Originally regd as c/n HRWA-0076: HRWA-0050 was G-MVLK)*		3. 7.89	T.J.Gayton-Polley	(Billingshurst)	30.11.02P

G-MVUS	Aerial Arts Chaser S (Rotax 377)	CH.813		3. 7.89	H.Poyzer	Eshott	16.12.01P
G-MVUT	Aerial Arts Chaser S (Rotax 377)	CH.814		4. 7.89	A.J.Tyler	Beccles	21. 4.02P
G-MVUU	Hornet R-ZA (Rotax 462)	HRWB-0061 & ZA110		13. 7.89	M.J.Allen	(St.Helens)	17. 8.92P
G-MVVG	Medway Hybred 44XLR (Rotax 447)	MR045/62		12. 7.89	C.Smith t/a Avialite Southeast	(Hastings)	24. 6.94P
G-MVVH	Medway Hybred 44XLR (Rotax 447)	MR047/63		11. 7.89	M.S.Henson	(Portsmouth)	27. 7.02P
G-MVVI	Medway Hybred 44XLR (Rotax 503?)	MR050/64		12. 7.89	C.J.Newell	(Leigh, Surrey)	26.10.02P
G-MVVK	Solar Wings Pegasus XL-R (Rotax 447)	SW-TB-1414 & SW-WA-1423		11. 7.89	K.N.Cobb	(Bristol)	30. 6.02P
G-MVVM	Solar Wings Pegasus XL-R (Rotax 447)	SW-TB-1416 & SW-WA-1425		12. 7.89	N.B.Mehew	Oxton, Nottingham	7.10.01P
G-MVVN	Solar Wings Pegasus XL-Q (Rotax 462)	SW-TE-0214 & SW-WQ-0226		11. 7.89	M.J.Hall	(Rugeley)	21.10.02P
G-MVVO	Solar Wings Pegasus XL-Q (Rotax 462)	SW-TE-0215 & SW-WQ-0227		11. 7.89	A.L.Scarlett	Clench Common	3.11.01P
G-MVVP	Solar Wings Pegasus XL-Q (Rotax 462)	SW-TE-0216 & SW-WQ-0228		11. 7.89	M.P.Wimsey	(Louth)	2. 5.02P
G-MVVT	CFM Shadow CD (Rotax 503)	K.101 & PFA 161-11569		26. 7.89	R.R.Armstrong	(Headcorn)	23. 5.02P
G-MVVU	Aerial Arts Chaser S (Rotax 462)	CH.816		19. 7.89	S.Jackson	Broomhill Farm, West Calder	13. 5.01P
G-MVVV	AMF Chevvron 2-32C (Konig SD570)	016	PH-1W9 G-MVVV	11. 5.89	P.R.Turton	Old Sarum	27. 1.02P
G-MVVZ	Powerchute Raider (Rotax 447)	90628		25. 7.89	A.E.Askew	(Melton Mowbray)	13. 7.02P
G-MVWH	Powerchute Raider (Rotax 447)	90736		25. 7.89	M.H.Nice	(Taunton)	11. 8.00P
G-MVWJ	Powerchute Raider (Rotax 447)	90738		25. 7.89	N.J.Doubek	(Stanford-le-Hope)	30. 6.01P
G-MVWN	Thruster T300 (Rotax 503)	089-T300-374		26. 7.89	T.B.Reakes t/a Whisky November Group	Franklyns Field, Chewton Mendip	18. 5.02P
G-MVWR	Thruster T300 (Rotax 503)	089-T300-377		26. 7.89	A.Allan	North Connel, Oban	23 6.02P
G-MVWS	Thruster T300 (Rotax 503)	089-T300-378		26. 7.89	R.J.Humphries	(Southampton)	15. 8.95P
G-MVWV	Medway Hybred 44XLR (Rotax 447)	MR060/69		24. 7.89	K.Smith	(Rainham)	31. 7.02P
G-MVWW	Aviasud Mistral 532 (Rotax 532)	0389-81 & BMAA/HB/005		25. 7.89	P.S.Balmer & B.H.D.Minto	Tarn Farm, Cockerham	23. 9.02P
G-MVWX	Microflight Spectrum (Rotax 503)	009		24. 7.89	G.S.Taylor t/a Spectrum Otherton Syndicate	Otherton, Cannock	8. 2.02P
G-MVWZ	Aviasud Mistral (Rotax 532)	1288-70 & BMAA/HB/008		2. 8.89	B.R.Underwood	Little Battleflats Farm, Ellistown, Coalville	10. 5.02P
G-MVXA	Whittaker MW6 Merlin (Fuji-Robin EC-44-PM)	PFA 164-11337		17. 8.89	I.Brewster	Little Gransden	21. 4.02P
G-MVXB	Mainair Gemini/Flash IIA (Rotax 462)	762-789-7 & W555		3. 8.89	D.J.Cook	Northwich	19. 6.02P
G-MVXC	Mainair Gemini/Flash IIA (Rotax 503)	763-889-7 & W556		4. 8.89	D.Wood	Arclid Green, Sandbach	27.10.02P
G-MVXD	Medway Hybred 44XLR (Rotax 503)	MR061/70		3. 8.89	P.R.Millen	Clench Common	5. 5.02P
G-MVXE	Medway Hybred 44XLR (Rotax 447)	MR063/71		23. 8.89	A.M.Brittle	Sittles Farm, Alrewas	31. 7.00P
G-MVXI	Medway Hybred 44XLR (Rotax 447)	MR064/72		9. 8.89	G.R.Roach	Stoke, Kent	11. 5.02P
G-MVXJ	Medway Hybred 44XLR (Rotax 447)	MR065/73		25. 8.89	P.J.Wilks *(Current status unknown)*	(Edenbridge)	26..9.90P
G-MVXL	Thruster TST Mk.1 (Rotax 503)	8089-TST-122		18. 8.89	A.J.Smith	(Cardiff)	30. 8.00P
G-MVXM	Medway Hybred 44XLR (Rotax 503) *(Reported as Medway Raven)*	MR055/75		17. 8.89	T.Thomson	(Hereford)	2. 8.97P
G-MVXN	Aviasud Mistral (Rotax 532)	65 & BMAA/HB/002		18. 8.89	B.M.Roberts	(Lincoln)	25. 8.02P
G-MVXR	Mainair Gemini/Flash IIA (Rotax 462)	764-889-7 & W557		22. 8.89	D M Bayne	East Fortune	28. 7.02P
G-MVXS	Mainair Gemini/Flash IIA (Rotax 503)	766-889-7 & W559		22. 8.89	J.W.Wood	Tarn Farm, Cockerham	25. 7.02P
G-MVXV	Aviasud Mistral (Rotax 532)	92 & BMAA/HB/004		22. 8.89	P.H.Ronfell	Tarn Farm, Cockerham	19.12.01P

G-MVXW	Rans S-4 Coyote (Rotax 447) 89.098 & PFA 193-11545	22. 8.89	M.R.C.Sims & A.A.Castleton	Dunkeswell	9.12.02P
G-MVXX	AMF Chevvron 2-32 018 (Konig SD570)	27. 7.89	C.Dews & H.T.Boal	(Ely/Bottisham)	24. 3.02P
G-MVYC	Solar Wings Pegasus XL-Q (Rotax 462HP) SW-TE-0224 & SW-WQ-0239	8. 9.89	P.E.L.Street	(Lincoln)	3. 6.02P
G-MVYD	Solar Wings Pegasus XL-Q (Rotax 462) SW-TE-0225 & SW-WQ-0240	8. 9.89	S.A.Wright	(Tamworth)	15. 7.02P
G-MVYE	Thruster TST Mk.1 8089-TST-123 (BMW)	13. 9.89	S.J.Spavins	Plaistows Farm, St Albans	27. 5.02P
G-MVYI	Hornet R-ZA HRWB-0074 & ZA122 (Rotax 462) *(A trike unit with c/n HRWB-0074 amended to HRWB-0081 was noted @ Popham 4.96)*	22. 9.89	N.J.Warner	(Redditch)	21. 9.95P
G-MVYJ	Hornet R-ZA HRWB-0075 & ZA111 (Rotax 462) *(Trike unit shows deleted c/n HRWB-0070)*	22. 9.89	R.Williamson	(Great Orton)	26. 3.98P
G-MVYK	Hornet R-ZA HRWB-0076 & ZA117 (Rotax 462)	22. 9.89	P.Asbridge	Emlyn's Field, Rhuallt	22. 7.99P
G-MVYL	Hornet R-ZA HRWB-0077 & ZA115 (Rotax 462)	22. 9.89	J.L.Thomas *(Noted 10.01)*	Kingston Seymour	24. 6.00P
G-MVYN	Hornet R-ZA HRWB-0079 & ZA136 (Rotax 462)	22. 9.89	W.M.Studley	Weston Zoyland	26. 4.02P
G-MVYP	Medway Hybred 44XLR MR071/77 (Rotax 447)	19. 9.89	P.R.Chapman	(Swanley)	11. 8.01P
G-MVYR	Medway Hybred 44XLR MR068/76 (Rotax 447)	19. 9.89	T.Steward	(Portslade)	24. 9.01P
G-MVYS	Mainair Gemini/Flash IIA (Rotax 503) 770-989-7 & W563	19. 9.89	B Hall	Morecambe	9. 7.00P
G-MVYT	Noble Hardman Snowbird Mk.IV SB-022 (Rotax 532)	26. 9.89	D.T.A.Rees	Haverfordwest	7. 2.02P
G-MVYV	Noble Hardman Snowbird Mk.IV SB-024 (Rotax 532)	21. 8.90	D.W.Hayden t/a G-MVYV Group	(Swansea)	13. 4.02P
G-MVYW	Noble Hardman Snowbird Mk.IV SB-025 (Rotax 532)	22.10.90	T.J.Harrison	(Dalton-in-Furness)	15. 7.02P
G-MVYX	Noble Hardman Snowbird Mk.IV SB-026 (Rotax 532)	25.11.91	R.McBlain	Kilkerran	9. 7.01P
G-MVYY	Aerial Arts Chaser S CH.824 (Rotax 508)	26. 9.89	N.J.Rummery	Ince Blundell	5. 5.02P
G-MVYZ	CFM Shadow BD 121 (Rotax 447)	25. 9.89	K.W.Brunnenkant	(Lincoln)	2.10.02P
G-MVZA	Thruster T300 089-T300-379 (Rotax 503)	26. 9.89	C.C.Belcher	Popham	21. 9.02P
G-MVZB	Thruster T300 089-T300-380 (Rotax 503)	26. 9.89	J.F.Kenyon	(Holsworthy)	29. 6.00P
G-MVZC	Thruster T300 089-T300-381 (Rotax 532)	26. 9.89	R.A.Knight	Chilbolton	28. 5.02P
G-MVZD	Thruster T300 089-T300-382 (Rotax 532)	26. 9.89	T.Pearce t/a G-MVZD Syndicate	(Twickenham)	28. 8.02P
G-MVZE	Thruster T300 089-T300-383 (Rotax 532)	26. 9.89	T.L.Davis	(Graiguenamanagh, Co.Kilkenny)	9. 7.02P
G-MVZG	Thruster T300 089-T300-385 (Rotax 532)	26. 9.89	G.A.Clephane *(Stored 5.97: sold 11.00)*	(Tadley)	1. 7.95P
G-MVZI	Thruster T300 089-T300-387 (Rotax 503)	26. 9.89	R.R.R.Whittern	South Wraxall, Wilts	14. 7.02P
G-MVZJ	Solar Wings Pegasus XL-Q (Rotax 462) SW-TE-0226 & SW-WQ-0241	26. 8.89	M.Price	Shobdon	21. 8.02P
G-MVZK	Quad City Challenger II UK (BMW R.100) PFA 177-11498	28. 9.89	M.J.Downes	Breidden	6. 9.01P
G-MVZL	Solar Wings Pegasus XL-Q (Rotax 462) SW-TE-0227 & SW-WQ-0242	4.10.89	G.J.Pearce	Horsham	10. 5.02P
G-MVZM	Aerial Arts Chaser S CH.825 (Rotax 377)	2.11.89	P.S.Herbert	Godalming	21. 5.02P
G-MVZO	Medway Hybred 44XLR MR072/78 (Rotax 503)	25.10.89	D.L.Wright	(Northampton)	19. 1.02P
G-MVZP	Murphy Renegade Spirit UK (Rotax 582) 256 & PFA 188-11630	17.10.89	J W E Pearson *(New owner 1.02)*	(St Albans)	7. 8.95P
G-MVZR	Avidsud Mistral 90 & BMAA/HB/011 (Rotax 532)	9.10.89	S.E. & J.A.Robinson	Tarn Farm, Cockerham	7. 6.01P
G-MVZS	Mainair Gemini/Flash IIA (Rotax 503) 771-1089-7 & W564	17.10.89	R.L.Beese & A.M.Bettison	(Tarporley)	22. 5.02P
G-MVZT	Solar Wings Pegasus XL-Q (Rotax 462HP) SW-TE-0228 & SW-WQ-0243	6.10.89	C.J.Meadows	Franklyn's Field, Chewton Mendip	25. 8.02P
G-MVZU	Solar Wings Pegasus XL-Q (Rotax 462) SW-TE-0229 & SW-WQ-0244	6.10.89	R.D.Proctor	RAF Wittering	27.10.02P
G-MVZV	Solar Wings Pegasus XL-Q (Rotax 462HP) SW-TE-0230 & SW-WQ-0245	6.10.89	S.R.Bowsher	(Bristol)	9. 5.01P

G-MVZW	Hornet R-ZA (Rotax 462)	HRWB-0063 & ZA142	27.10.89	K.W.Warn	Popham	9. 8.02P
G-MVZX	Murphy Renegade Spirit UK (Rotax 582)	PFA 188-11590	18.10.89	G.Holmes	(Pickering)	29. 3.02P
G-MVZY	Aerial Arts Chaser S (Rotax 377)	CH.827	2.11.89	C.N.A.Batchelor-Wylam	(Doncaster)	12.10.02P
G-MVZZ	AMF Chevvron 2-32 (Konig SD570)	019	27. 7.89	D.Patrick	(Carlisle)	22. 5.02P
G-MWAB	Mainair Gemini/Flash IIA (Rotax 503)	772-1089-7 & W565	24.10.89	C.G.Deeley	(Lichfield)	3. 6.02P
G-MWAC	Solar Wings Pegasus XL-Q (Rotax 462)	SW-TE-0236 & SW-WQ-0260	25.10.89	P.A.Tabberer	Emlyn's Field, Rhuallt	17. 7.00P
G-MWAD	Solar Wings Pegasus XL-Q (Rotax 462)	SW-TE-0237 & SW-WQ-0261	25.10.89	R.S.Cochrane	Sutton Meadows, Ely	1. 4.02P
G-MWAE	CFM Shadow CD (Rotax 503)	130	24.10.89	D.J.Adams	North Coates	12. 5.02P
G-MWAF	Solar Wings Pegasus XL-R (Rotax 447)	SW-TB-1422 & SW-WA-1441	30.10.89	A.Butterworth	(Poynton)	10. 5.02P
G-MWAG	Solar Wings Pegasus XL-R (Rotax 447)	SW-TB-1423 & SW-WA-1442	30.10.89	D.Foster	(Leek)	24. 4.02P
G-MWAI	Solar Wings Pegasus XL-R (Rotax 462)	SW-TE-0238 & SW-WA-1443	1.11.89	A.G.Spurway	(Chard)	12.10.00P
G-MWAJ	Murphy Renegade Spirit UK (BMW R.100RS)	PFA 188-11438	1.11.89	J.G.McMinn *"Free Spirit"*	(Craigavon, Co Armagh)	28. 3.02P
G-MWAL	Solar Wings Pegasus XL-Q (Rotax 462)	SW-TE-0240 & SW-WQ-0263	2.11.89	A.W.Hill	Bluntisham	2.11.01P
G-MWAN	Thruster T300 (Rotax 532)	089-T300-389	14.11.89	S.Croydon-Fowler	(Bodmin)	25. 6.02P
G-MWAP	Thruster T300 (Rotax 503)	089-T300-391	14.11.89	S.F.Chave & A.G.Spurway *"Wanda"*	Honiton/Chard	21. 7.02P
G-MWAR	Thruster T300 (Rotax 532)	089-T300-392	14.11.89	S.M.Birbeck	Popham	8.12.02P
G-MWAT	Solar Wings Pegasus XL-Q (Rotax 462)	SW-TE-0241 & SW-WQ-0265	13.11.89	A.R.Hughes	Yatesbury	21. 6.02P
G-MWAU	Mainair Gemini/Flash IIA (Rotax 582)	773-1189-7 & W566	7.12.89	L.Roberts	(Ammanford)	5. 5.02P
G-MWAV	Solar Wings Pegasus XL-R (Rotax 447)	SW-TB-1424 & SW-WA-1444	13.11.89	S.P.Waine	(Fordingbridge)	25. 7.02P
G-MWAW	Whittaker MW6 Merlin (Rotax 503)	PFA 164-11460	10.11.89	J.A.Hindley	(Accrington)	19. 6.02P
G-MWBH	Hornet RS-ZA (Rotax 532)	HRWB-0071 & ZA120	14.11.89	J.Rossall	Tarn Farm, Cockerham	7. 7.02P
G-MWBI	Medway Hybred 44XLR (Rotax 503)	MR073/79	21.11.89	G.E.Coates	(Birmingham)	17. 5.02P
G-MWBJ	Medway Puma Sprint (Rotax 447)	MS003/1	21.11.89	C.C.Strong	(Buaes)	14. 7.00P
G-MWBK	Solar Wings Pegasus XL-Q (Rotax 462)	SW-TE-0248 & SW-WQ-0271	16.11.89	P.J.Harrison	Bracknell	23. 8.01P
G-MWBL	Solar Wings Pegasus XL-R/Se (Rotax 447)	SW-TB-1424 & SW-WA-1446 *(Trike c/n appears to have been duplicated with G-MWAV so two '1424s exist)*	16.11.89	C.J.Arthur	Eshott	17. 4.02P
G-MWBM	Hornet R-ZA (Rotax 462)	HRWB-0082 & ZA141	29.11.89	K.D.Shadforth	AAC Dishforth	2. 5.94P
G-MWBO	Rans S-4 Coyote (Rotax 447)	89.097 & PFA 193-11583	29.11.89	D.S.Coutts t/a G-MWBO Group	(Linlithgow)	30. 5.02P
G-MWBP	Hornet R-ZA (Rotax 462)	HRWB-0083 & ZA144	29.11.89	J.Rossall	Tarn Farm, Cockerham	1. 4.02P
G-MWBR	Hornet RS-ZA (Rotax 462)	HRWB-0084 & ZA145	29.11.89	I.A.Clark	(Grimsby)	1. 4.02P
G-MWBS	Hornet R-ZA (BMW R100)	HRWB-0085 & ZA146	29.11.89	P.D.Jaques	Sandtoft	23. 4.98P
G-MWBU	Hornet R-ZA (Rotax 462HP)	HRWB-0087 & ZA148	29.11.89	A R Mikolajczyk	(Mansfield)	2.11.02P
G-MWBW	Hornet R-ZA (Rotax 462)	HRWB-0089 & ZA150	29.11.89	C.G.Bentley	(Chesterfield)	15. 5.00P
G-MWBX	Hornet R-ZA (Rotax 462)	HRWB-0090 & ZA151	29.11.89	J.Johnson	(Bootle)	22.10.92P
G-MWBY	Hornet R-ZA (Rotax 462)	HRWB-0091 & ZA152	29.11.89	G.P.Austin	Mill Farm, Shifnal	19. 6.02P
G-MWCB	Solar Wings Pegasus XL-Q (Rotax 462)	SW-TE-0250 & SW-WQ-0273	1.12.89	I.P.Joyce	Long Acre Farm, Sandy	4. 8.02P
G-MWCC	Solar Wings Pegasus XL-R/Se (Rotax 447)	SW-TB-1387 & SW-WA-1447 *(Trike ex G-MVKD when latter's sailwing sold)*	1.12.89	C.King	(Ryton)	5. 9.00P
G-MWCE	Mainair Gemini/Flash IIA (Rotax 503)	775-1289-7 & W568	19.12.89	B.A.Tooze	Shobdon	28. 8.00P

G-MWCF	Solar Wings Pegasus XL-Q (Rotax 462) SW-TE-0252 & SW-WQ-0276		13.12.89	J.D.Amos t/a G-MWCF Group	(Marlborough)	20. 9.02P
G-MWCG	Microflight Spectrum (Rotax 503-2V)	011	15.12.89	P.E De-Ville & M W Shepherd	Otherton, Cannock	11. 4.02P
G-MWCH	Rans S-6-ESD Coyote II (Rotax 503) 0989.067 & PFA 204-11632 *(PFA c/n duplicates Kitfox G-BSFY)*		15.12.89	W.Lucy & J.Burns	Morgansfield, Fishburn	16. 8.02P
G-MWCI	Powerchute Kestrel (Rotax 503)	91245	3. 1.90	E.G.Bray	Clacton	17. 1.02P
G-MWCJ	Powerchute Kestrel (Rotax 503)	91246	3. 1.90	B.A.Dowland	(Thorney)	13. 7.02P
G-MWCK	Powerchute Kestrel (Rotax 503)	91247	3. 1.90	A.Evans	(Wolverhampton)	21.10.02P
G-MWCN	Powerchute Kestrel (Rotax 503)	91250	3. 1.90	H.J.Goddard	(Fleet)	22. 6.02P
G-MWCO	Powerchute Kestrel (Rotax 503)	91251	3. 1.90	T.F.Bakker	(Fairford)	17. 5.93P
G-MWCP	Powerchute Kestrel (Rotax 503)	91252	3. 1.90	I Fraser	(Corgarff, Strathdon)	20.10.01P
G-MWCR	Southdown Puma Sprint (Fuji-Robin EC-44-PM) P.516 & SN1121/0070		24. 2.84	S.R.Hall	(Stroud)	2. 8.02P
G-MWCS	Powerchute Kestrel (Rotax 503)	91253	3. 1.90	B.J.L.Clark t/a Fly High (KSPT)	(Maidstone)	25.10.98P
G-MWCU	Solar Wings Pegasus XL-R (Rotax 447) SW-TB-1412 & SW-WA-1449		27.12.89	J.M.Bales	(Stamford)	14.11.01P
G-MWCV	Solar Wings Pegasus XL-Q (Rotax 462HP) SW-TE-0256 & SW-WQ-0278		27.12.89	M.G.Taylor	(Stony Stratford)	20. 5.01P
G-MWCW	Mainair Gemini/Flash IIA (Rotax 462) 776-0190-7 & W569		29.12.89	A J Thomas	(Nottingham)	11. 5.02P
G-MWCX	Medway Hybred 44XLR (Rotax 503)	MR076/80	8. 1.90	P.A.Harris	(Petersfield)	31. 3.96P
G-MWCY	Medway Hybred 44XLR (Rotax 503)	MR077/81	15. 1.90	J.K.Masters	(Chigwell)	27. 6.02P
G-MWCZ	Medway Hybred 44XLR (Rotax 503)	MR078/82	10. 1.90	K.G.Meekcoms	Stoke, Kent	29. 5.02P
G-MWDB	CFM Shadow CD (Rotax 503)	100	3. 7.89	M.D.Meade	(St. Albans)	10. 8.01P
G-MWDC	Solar Wings Pegasus XL-R/Se (Rotax 462) SW-TE-0255 & SW-WA-1450		5. 1.90	A.N.Edwards	(Great Orton)	23. 4.01P
G-MWDD	Solar Wings Pegasus XL-Q (Rotax 462) SW-TE-0258 & SW-WQ-1450	SW-WQ-0280	15. 1.90	A.L.Brown	Long Marston	4. 5.02P
G-MWDE	Hornet RS-ZA (Rotax 532)	HRWB-0094 & ZA126	10. 1.90	H.G.Reid *(Trike unit noted 10.00)*	Roddige, Fradley	13. 6.98P
G-MWDI	Hornet RS-ZA (Rotax 532)	HRWB-0098 & ZA158	10. 1.90	R.J.Perrin	Brook Farm, Pilling	6.11.00P
G-MWDJ	Mainair Gemini/Flash IIA (Rotax 503) 777-0190-7 & W570		17. 1.90	M.Gardiner	Crosland Moor	9. 6.02P
G-MWDK	Solar Wings Pegasus XL-Q (Rotax 462) SW-TE-0259 & SW-WQ-0281		17. 1.90	T.Wicks	(Devizes)	14.12.01P
G-MWDL	Solar Wings Pegasus XL-Q (Rotax 462) SW-TE-0260 & SW-WQ-0282		17. 1.90	P.K.Dean	Sutton Meadow, Ely	31. 3.02P
G-MWDM	Murphy Renegade Spirit UK (Jabiru 2200A) 319 & PFA 188A-11628 *(PFA c/n duplicates Streak Shadow G-BRZZ)*		18. 1.90	P.A.Hill t/a Doctor & the Medics	Enstone	23. 9.00P
G-MWDN	CFM Shadow CD (Rotax 503)	K.102	17. 1.90	A.A.Duffus	(Unst, Shetland)	17. 7.02P
G-MWDP	Thruster TST Mk.1 (Rotax 503)	8129-TST-124	30. 1.90	J.Walker	(Ballymena)	5. 5.95P
G-MWDS	Thruster T300 (Rotax 532)	089-T300-395	30. 1.90	M.D.Tulloch	(Westhill, Aberdeeen)	14. 1.02P
G-MWDZ	Eipper Quicksilver MXL Sport II (Rotax 503)	022	29. 1.90	R.G.Cook	Cranfield	15. 5.02P
G-MWEE	Solar Wings Pegasus XL-Q (Rotax 462) SW-TE-0175 & SW-WQ-0147		12.12.88	R.J.Sharp	Rochester	2. 9.01P
G-MWEF	Solar Wings Pegasus XL-Q (Rotax 462HP) SE-TE-0261 & SW-WQ-0283		30. 1.90	N.R.Williams	Long Marston	13. 9.01P
G-MWEG	Solar Wings Pegasus XL-Q (Rotax 462) SW-TE-0262 & SW-WQ-0284		30. 1.90	D.Baker	(Worcester)	14. 7.02P
G-MWEH	Solar Wings Pegasus XL-Q (Rotax 462HP) SW-TE-0264 & SW-WQ-0286		7. 2.90	K.A.Davidson	(Leuchars)	27. 1.02P
G-MWEK	Whittaker MW5 Sorcerer (Rotax 447)	PFA 163-11284	20. 2.90	J.T.Francis	(Crowthorne)	15.10.00P
G-MWEL	Mainair Gemini/Flash IIA (Rotax 503) 780-0290-7 & W573		13. 2.90	B.L.Benson	(Malpas)	12.11.01P
G-MWEN	CFM Shadow CD (Rotax 503)	K.113	20. 2.90	P.Anning	(Torquay)	8. 8.01P

G-MWEO	Whittaker MW5 Sorcerer PFA 163-11263 (Fuji-Robin EC-34-PM)		21. 2.90	J Morton t/a Crazy Capers	(Ballymena, Co.Antrim)	1.12.00P
G-MWEP	Rans S-4 Coyote 89.096 & PFA 193-11616		21. 2.90	J.D.Webb	(Hereford)	1.10.02P
G-MWER	Solar Wings Pegasus XL-Q (Rotax 462) SW-TE-0265 & SW-WQ-0287		1. 3.90	S.V.Stojanovic	(Swansea)	21. 8.02P
G-MWES	Rans S-4 Coyote (Rotax 447) 89.099 & PFA 193-11737		1. 2.90	A P Worbey *(Wears "N89099" on tail: this matches c/n and is not a p/i)*	Lower Mount Pleasant, Chatteris	14. 1.02P
G-MWEU	Hornet RS-ZA HRWB-0100 & ZA160 (Rotax 532)		21. 2.90	K.H.Hicks	(March)	11.11.01P
G-MWEY	Hornet R-ZA HRWB0104 & ZA135 (Rotax 462)		21. 2.90	J.Kidd	Tarn Farm, Cockerham	24. 9.00P
G-MWEZ	CFM Shadow CD 136 (Rotax 503)		22. 2.90	M.Fitch	(Potters Bar)	9. 8.01P
G-MWFA	Solar Wings Pegasus XL-R SW-TB-1406 & SW-WA-1454		27. 2.90	A.W.Edwards	Davidstow Moor	23. 6.02P
G-MWFB	CFM Shadow CD K.119 (Rotax 503)		1. 3.90	K.Hopkinson	(West Bridgford)	5.10.01P
G-MWFC	TEAM mini-MAX 294 & PFA 186-11648 (Rotax 447)	G-BTXC G-MWFC	1. 3.90	A.E.Sellers	Fenland	17. 4.02P
G-MWFD	TEAM mini-MAX 293 & PFA 186-11646 (Rotax 447) *(PFA c/n duplicates Shadow G-GORE)*		1. 3.90	M.A.Bolshaw	Brook Farm, Pilling	25. 7.01P
G-MWFF	Rans S-5 Coyote (Rotax 447) 89.106 & PFA 193-11639		10. 1.90	T.S.Arnup	(Hexham)	21. 2.02P
G-MWFL	Powerchute Kestrel 00363 (Rotax 503)		20. 3.90	A.Vincent	Fenland	31. 3.02P
G-MWFS	Solar Wings Pegasus XL-Q (Rotax 462) SW-TE-0267 & SW-WQ-0289		14. 3.90	C.P.Hughes	(Holywell)	25.12.01P
G-MWFT	MBA Tiger Cub 440 WFT-02 (Fuji-Robin EC-44-PM)		24.11.83	J.R.Ravenhill	Kemble	20. 4.02P
G-MWFU	Quad City Challenger II UK (Rotax 503) PFA 177-11654		16. 3.90	M.E.Chamberlain	Higher Barn Farm, Houghton	29. 4.02P
G-MWFV	Quad City Challenger II UK (Rotax 503) PFA 177-11655		16. 3.90	W.D.Gordon	(Falgunzeon)	23. 8.02P
G-MWFW	Rans S-4 Coyote PFA 193-11662 (Rotax 447)		16. 3.90	C.C.B.Soden *(Noted 11.01)*	Dunkeswell	14. 9.99P
G-MWFX	Quad City Challenger II UK (Rotax 462) CH2-1189-UK-0485 & PFA 177-11706		20. 3.90	I.M.Walton	Wellesbourne Mountford	2.10.01P
G-MWFY	Quad City Challenger II UK (Rotax 503) PFA 177-11668		20. 3.90	P.J.Ladd	Craysmarsh Farm, Melksham	20. 7.01P
G-MWFZ	Quad City Challenger II UK CH2-0190-UK-0506 & PFA 177-11707		20. 3.90	A.Slade	(Enfield)	
G-MWGA	Rans S-5 Coyote (Rotax 447) 89.092 & PFA 193-11810		20. 3.90	D.B.Casley-Smith	(East Kirkby)	18. 9.02P
G-MWGC	Medway Hybred 44XLR MR087/85 (Rotax 503)		26. 3.90	I.Nicholls	Middle Stoke, Kent	12. 4.02P
G-MWGF	Murphy Renegade Spirit UK (Rotax 582) 220 & PFA 188-11771		21. 3.90	S.R.Monkcom	Long Acre Farm, Sandy	15. 3.02P
G-MWGG	Mainair Gemini/Flash IIA (Rotax 462) 785-0390-7 & W578		26. 3.90	B.E.Bell	(Stone-on-Trent)	1. 5.01P
G-MWGI	Aerotech MW5-K Sorcerer 5K-0012-02 (Rotax 447) *(Wings transferred to G-MTBT by 7.96)*		28. 3.90	B.Barrass	Sywell	3. 9.91P
G-MWGJ	Aerotech MW-5(K) Sorcerer 5K-0014-02 (Rotax 447)		6. 9.90	V.J.Morris	(Truro)	20. 5.02P
G-MWGK	Aerotech MW-5(K) Sorcerer 5K-0015-02 (Rotax 447)	(G-MWLV)	19. 9.90	R.M.Thomas	Wombleton	8. 1.01P
G-MWGL	Solar Wings Pegasus XL-Q (Rotax 462) SW-TE-0270 & SW-WQ-0293		28. 3.90	J.Walker	Deenethorpe	3. 6.02P
G-MWGM	Solar Wings Pegasus XL-Q (Rotax 462) SW-TE-0271 & SW-WQ-0294		28. 3.90	P.J. & L.S.Kirkpatrick	(Cambridge)	2. 5.00P
G-MWGN	Rans S-4 Coyote (Rotax 447) 89.113 & PFA 193-11709		26. 3.90	R.H.S.Cattle	Plaistows Farm, St Albans	31. 7.02P
G-MWGO	Aerial Arts 110SX/Chaser 110SX/566 (Rotax 377)		28. 3.90	B.Nicolson	(Middlesbrough)	28. 4.97P
G-MWGR	Solar Wings Pegasus XL-Q (Rotax 462) SW-TE-0272 & SW-WQ-0296		6. 4.90	K.Brown	(Kettering)	8. 7.02P
G-MWGS*	Powerchute Kestrel 00366 (Rotax 503)		26. 4.90	Not known *(Cancelled 4.1.91 on sale to Spain but noted 8.99: current status unknown)*	Dunkeswell	
G-MWGT	Powerchute Kestrel 00367 (Rotax 503)		26. 4.90	G.McAleer	Newtownards, Co.of Down	23. 6.01P
G-MWGU	Powerchute Kestrel 00368 (Rotax 503)	(9H-) G-MWGU	26. 4.90	M.Pandolfino	Luqa, Malta	19. 7.91P

G-MWGV*	Powerchute Kestrel (Rotax 503)	00369	26. 4.90	E.G.Bray *(Cancelled 6.6.01 by CAA)*	(Clacton)	20. 1.00P
G-MWGW	Powerchute Kestrel (Rotax 503)	00370	26. 4.90	S.P.Tomlinson	(Leominster)	13. 7.97P
G-MWGY	Powerchute Kestrel (Rotax 503)	00372	26. 4.90	C.N.Bond	RAF Manston	29. 7.00P
G-MWGZ	Powerchute Kestrel (Rotax 503)	00373	26. 4.90	L.J.Lynch	(Ventnor, IoW)	27. 5.97P
G-MWHC	Solar Wings Pegasus XL-Q (Rotax 462)	SW-TE-0274 & SW-WQ-0304	24. 4.90	P.J.Lowery	Long Acre Farm, Sandy	14. 5.99P
G-MWHD*	Microflight Spectrum (Rotax 503)	012	18. 4.90	P.B.& M.A.Howson *(Cancelled 15.2.01 by CAA)*	Arclid Green, Sandbach	14.12.00P
G-MWHF	Solar Wings Pegasus XL-Q (Rotax 462)	SW-TE-0275 & SW-WQ-0305	24. 4.90	N.J.Troke & S.Cox	Swinford, Rugby	10.11.02P
G-MWHG	Solar Wings Pegasus XL-Q (Rotax 462)	SW-TE-0276 & SW-WQ-0306	24. 4.90	I.A.Lumley	(Great Orton)	15. 9.01P
G-MWHH	TEAM mini-MAX (Rotax 447)	326 & PFA 186-11814	23. 4.90	B.F.Crick	(Desborough)	4. 8.00P
G-MWHL	Solar Wings Pegasus XL-Q (Rotax 462)	SW-TE-0278 & SW-WQ-0308	1. 5.90	T.G.Jackson	(London SW11)	12. 5.02P
G-MWHM	Whittaker MW6-S Fatboy Flyer (Rotax 532)	PFA 164-11463	18. 5.90	D.W. & M.L.Squire	Otherton, Cannock	19. 3.02P
G-MWHO	Mainair Gemini/Flash IIA (Rotax 503)	778-0190-5 & W571	10. 5.90	B.Epps	Arclid Green, Sandbach	9. 3.01P
G-MWHP	Rans S-6-ESD Coyote II *(Tri-cycle u/c)* (Rotax 532)	1089.093 & PFA 204-11768	8. 5.90	J.F.Bickerstaffe	Higher Barn Farm, Houghton	12. 6.01P
G-MWHR	Mainair Gemini/Flash IIA (Rotax 503)	787-0590-7 & W580	16. 5.90	B.Brazier	(Chorley)	31.10.01P
G-MWHT	Solar Wings Pegasus Quasar TC	SW-TQ-0005 & SW-WQQ-0314	15. 5.90	E.H.Gatehouse & D.M.Walters	Pound Green, Buttonoak, Kidderminster	13. 8.02P
G-MWHU	Solar Wings Pegasus Quasar	SW-TQ-0006 & SW-WQQ-0315	15. 5.90	A.F.Frost & S.J.Park	Sywell	13.11.02P
G-MWHV	Solar Wings Pegasus Quasar	SW-TQ-0007 & SW-WQQ-0316	15. 5.90	K.Wood	(Kingswinford)	23. 2.02P
G-MWHW	Solar Wings Pegasus XL-Q (Rotax 462)	SW-TE-0279 & SW-WQ-0317	15. 5.90	N C Leonard *(New owner 12.01)*	(Rowlands Gill)	20. 7.99P
G-MWHX	Solar Wings Pegasus XL-Q (Rotax 462)	SW-TE-0280 & SW-WQ-0318	15. 5.90	N.P.Kelly	(Navan, Co.Meath)	15. 7.02P
G-MWIA	Mainair Gemini/Flash IIA (Rotax 503)	789-0690-7 & W582	21. 5.90	M.Raj	Otherton, Cannock	27. 3.01P
G-MWIB	Aviasud Mistral (Rotax 532)	094 & BMAA/HB/010	16. 5.90	N.W.Finn-Kelcey *"Weston Belle"*	Weston Underwood, Olney	14. 6.02P
G-MWIC	Whittaker MW5-C Sorcerer (Rotax 447)	PFA 163-11224	20. 2.90	H.Lammers *"Freyja"*	(Liskeard)	24. 9.02P
G-MWIE	Solar Wings Pegasus XL-Q (Rotax 462)	SW-TE-0282 & SW-WQ-0325	30. 5.90	R.Mercer	Long Marston	21.10.01P
G-MWIF	Rans S-6-ESD Coyote II *(Tri-cycle u/c)* (Rotax 503)	1089.095 & PFA 204-11749	30. 5.90	S.P.Slade & R.Thorpe	Eshott	11. 5.01P
G-MWIG	Mainair Gemini/Flash IIA (Rotax 462)	790-0690-7 & W583	4. 6.90	D.R.Purslow	Shifnal	1. 8.02P
G-MWIH	Mainair Gemini/Flash IIA (Rotax 503)	791-0690-5 & W584	4. 6.90	G.Collins & K.Potter	(Melborne, York)	6. 9.01P
G-MWIK	Medway Hybred 44XLR (Rotax 503)	MR094/89	7. 6.90	J.L.Gowens	(Maidstone)	27. 8.99P
G-MWIL	Medway Hybred 44XLR (Rotax 447)	MR096/90	8. 6.90	J.W.Savage	(St Albans)	13. 9.95P
G-MWIM	Solar Wings Pegasus Quasar TC	SW-TQ-0008 & SW-WQQ-0326	11. 6.90	P.J.Bates & T.S.Smith	Long Marston	13. 9.01P
G-MWIO	Rans S-4 Coyote (Rotax 447)	90.117 & PFA 193-11774	11. 6.90	R.E.Harris	Leicester	29.10.02P
G-MWIP	Whittaker MW-6 Merlin (Rotax 582)	PFA 164-11360	7. 6.90	D.Beer & B.J.Merrett	(Ilfracombe)	12. 4.01P
G-MWIR	Solar Wings Pegasus XL-Q (Rotax 462HP)	SW-TE-0283 & SW-WQ-0330	8. 6.90	C.E.Dagless	(Dereham)	29. 5.02P
G-MWIS	Solar Wings Pegasus XL-Q (Rotax 462HP)	SW-TE-0284 & SW-WQ-0331	8. 6.90	M.Mazure	(Edgware)	17. 8.02P
G-MWIT	Solar Wings Pegasus XL-Q (Rotax 462)	SW-TE-0285 & SW-WQ-0332	8. 6.90	G.F.Ryland	Oxton, Nottingham	16. 2.02P
G-MWIU	Solar Wings Pegasus Quasar TC	SW-TQ-0010 & SW-WQQ-0333	8. 6.90	D.G.Bond	(Reading)	17. 3.02P
G-MWIV	Mainair Gemini/Flash (Rotax 503)	792-0690-5 & W585	15. 6.90	P.& J.Calvert	(Whitby)	14. 7.02P
G-MWIW	Solar Wings Pegasus Quasar	SW-TQ-0011 & SW-WQQ-0334	18. 6.90	T.Yates	(Alfreton)	24. 6.02P

G-MWIX	Solar Wings Pegasus Quasar TC	18. 6.90	T.D.Neal	Shobdon	26. 6.01P
	SW-TQ-0012 & SW-WQQ-0335				
G-MWIY	Solar Wings Pegasus Quasar TC	22. 6.90	C.J.Gordon	Perth	2. 1.03P
	SW-TQ-0014 & SW-WQQ-0336				
G-MWIZ	CFM Shadow CD 096	22.11.88	T.P.Ryan	Plaistows Farm, St Albans	13.10.02P
	(Rotax 462)				
G-MWJD	Solar Wings Pegasus Quasar	22. 6.90	A.J.Blackwell	Long Marston	30. 9.99P
	SW-TQ-0016 & SW-WQ-0339		*(Dismantled 7.01)*		
G-MWJF	CFM Shadow CD K.123	26. 6.90	R.H.Cooke	(Southampton)	24. 7.02P
	(Rotax 447)				
G-MWJG	Solar Wings Pegasus XL-R	26. 6.90	M.J.Piggott	Little Gransden	18. 6.02P
	(Rotax 447) SW-TB-1415 & SW-WA-1472 *(Uses trike unit ex G-MVVL)*				
G-MWJH	Solar Wings Pegasus Quasar	29. 6.90	N.J.Braund	(Bristol)	2.11.02P
	SW-TQ-0017 & SW-WQQ-0340				
G-MWJI	Solar Wings Pegasus Quasar	29. 6.90	L.Luscombe	Weston Zoyland	12. 2.02P
	SW-TQ-0018 & SW-WQQ-0341				
G-MWJJ	Solar Wings Pegasus Quasar	29. 6.90	R.Langham	Carlton Moor	14. 3.02P
	SW-TQ-0019 & SW-WQQ-0342				
G-MWJK	Solar Wings Pegasus Quasar	29. 6.90	M.Richardson	(Swansea)	10.10.01P
	SW-TQ-0020 & SW-WQQ-0343				
G-MWJN	Solar Wings Pegasus XL-Q	29. 6.90	J.C.Corrall		
	(Rotax 462) SW-TE-0288 & SW-WQ-0344			Lower Mount Pleasant, Chatteris	18. 8.02P
G-MWJO	Solar Wings Pegasus XL-Q	29. 6.90	C.Serra	Wareham, Dorset	23. 7.02P
	(Rotax 462HP) SW-TE-0289 & SW-WQ-0345				
G-MWJP	Medway Hybred 44XLR MR097/91	29. 6.90	D.W.Beach	Middle Stoke, Kent	13.12.02P
	(Rotax 503)				
G-MWJR	Medway Hybred 44XLR MR098/92	28. 6.90	J.Stokes	Stoke, Kent	7 .7.96P
	(Rotax 503)				
G-MWJS	Solar Wings Pegasus Quasar TC	6. 7.90	I.D.Midgeley	Sywell	4. 8.01P
	SW-TQ-0021 & SW-WQQ-0349				
G-MWJT	Solar Wings Pegasus Quasar TC	16. 7.90	K.V.Rands-Allen	Sywell	24. 1.02P
	SW-TQ-0022 & SW-WQQ-0350				
G-MWJU	Solar Wings Pegasus Quasar	6. 7.90	S.Baker	Long Marston	30. 7.02P
	SW-TQ-0023 & SW-WQQ-0351				
G-MWJV	Solar Wings Pegasus Quasar	6. 7.90	A.Davies	Halwell, Totnes	5. 6.00P
	SW-TQ-0024 & SW-WQQ-0352				
G-MWJW	Whittaker MW5 Sorcerer	11. 5.90	S.Badby	Tibenham	25. 9.02P
	(Fuji-Robin EC-44-PM) JDW-02 & PFA 163-11186				
G-MWJX	Medway Puma Sprint	17. 7.90	A.Tristram		
	(Rotax 447) MS009/3			Pound Green, Buttonoak, Kidderminster	19. 8.01P
G-MWJY	Mainair Gemini/Flash IIA	16. 7.90	M.D.Walton	(Ware)	5. 4.02P
	(Rotax 503) 797-0790-7 & W590				
G-MWKA	Murphy Renegade Spirit UK PFA 188-11864	26. 7.90	C.E.Neill	Deanland	8. 4.01P
	(Rotax 582) *(Incorporates project PFA 188-11690)*		t/a Downlands Flying Group *"Spirit of Lewes"*		
G-MWKE	Hornet RS-ZA HRWB-0108 & ZA167	30. 7.90	D.R.Stapleton	Tarn Farm, Cockerham	22.10.02P
	(Rotax 532) *(Trike c/n overstamped on HRWB-0107)*				
G-MWKO	Solar Wings Pegasus XL-Q	31. 7.90	D.D.Wardrope & G.W.Boyes	Carlisle	26. 7.01P
	(Rotax 462) SW-TE-0290 & SW-WQ-0357				
G-MWKP	Solar Wings Pegasus XL-Q	31. 7.90	G.N.Frost	Sywell	17. 6.02P
	(Rotax 462HP) SW-TE-0291 & SW-WQ-0358				
G-MWKW	Microflight Spectrum 015	3. 8.90	P.B. & M.Robinson	Sutton Meadows, Ely	29. 1.02P
	(Rotax 503)				
G-MWKX	Microflight Spectrum 016	3. 8.90	C.R.Ions	Eshott	20. 8.01P
	(Rotax 503)				
G-MWKY	Solar Wings Pegasus XL-Q	3. 8.90	C.R.Wright	Roddige, Fradley	16. 7.02P
	(Rotax 462HP) SW-TE-0292 & SW-WQ-0362				
G-MWKZ	Solar Wings Pegasus XL-Q	3. 8.90	T Bale & A Martin	(Barnstaple)	19. 1.02P
	(Rotax 462HP) SW-TE-0293 & SW-WQ-0363				
	(Another trike unit noted with same c/n almost certainly G-MWEG carrying manufacturer's incorrect I/D plate)				
G-MWLA	Rans S-4 Coyote	3. 8.90	B.J.Dowdle	(Middlesbrough)	1. 6.02P
	(Rotax 447) 89.114 & PFA 193-11787				
G-MWLB	Medway Hybred 44XLR MR104/93	15. 8.90	M.W.Harmer	Long Acre Farm, Sandy	11.10.02P
	(Rotax 503)				
G-MWLD	CFM Shadow CD 106	9. 5.89	P.C.Avery	Shipdham	1.11.01P
	(Rotax 503)				
G-MWLE	Solar Wings Pegasus XL-R	9. 8.90	D.Stevenson	Plaistows Farm, St Albans	13. 5.02P
	(Rotax 447) SW-TB-1425 & SW-WA-1474				
G-MWLF	Solar Wings Pegasus XL-R	9. 8.90	G.Rainey	Weston Zoyland	22. 8.01P
	(Rotax 447) SW-TB-1426 & SW-WA-1475				
G-MWLG	Solar Wings Pegasus XL-R	9. 8.90	M.Law	Perth	7. 8.02P
	(Rotax 447) SW-TB-1427 & SW-WA-1476				
G-MWLH	Solar Wings Pegasus Quasar	9. 8.90	R.A.Duncan	Drummaird Farm, Bonnybank	15. 6.02P
	SW-TQ-0030 & SW-WQQ-0364				

G-MWLI	Solar Wings Pegasus XL-Q (Rotax 503) SW-TB-1162 & SW-WQQ-0365	G-65-8 G-MWLI	9. 8.90	G.H.Betz & B.Cordi	(Royston)	7. 8.01P
	(Built as Quasar with trike c/n SW-TQ-0031 @ 8.90, modified to Quasar TC @ 10.91, to TL-Q (Rotax 447) @ 10.92 and rebuilt @ 4.99 with trike from G-MTFS following accident 5.4.96) (Trike '0081 to G-MWVM?)					
G-MWLJ	Solar Wings Pegasus Quasar SW-TQ-0032 & SW-WQQ-0366		9. 8.90	C.G.Rouse	Chandlers Ford	18. 9.02P
G-MWLK	Solar Wings Pegasus Quasar TC SW-TQ-0033 & SW-WQQ-0367		9. 8.90	R.P.Wilkinson	Charmy Down, Bath	29. 6.01P
G-MWLL	Solar Wings Pegasus XL-Q (Rotax 462) SW-TE-0287 & SW-WQ-0338		16. 8.90	J.Bacon	(Great Yarmouth)	22. 5.02P
G-MWLM	Solar Wings Pegasus XL-Q (Rotax 462) SW-TE-0286 & SW-WQ-0322		17. 8.90	P.J.Dale	(Chesham)	22. 5.02P
G-MWLN	Whittaker MW6-S Fatboy Flyer (Rotax 503) PFA 164-11844		16. 8.90	S.J.Field *"Red Lips"*	(Bridgwater)	5. 6.92P
G-MWLO	Whittaker MW6 Merlin PFA 164-11373 (Rotax 503)		21. 8.90	S.P.Ganecki & L.Prew	Otherton, Cannock	6. 6.02P
G-MWLP	Mainair Gemini/Flash (Rotax 503) 801-0990-5 & W594		24. 8.90	J.S.Potts	(Kilmarnock)	24. 8.99P
G-MWLS	Medway Hybred 44XLR MR081/95 (Rotax 503)		29. 8.90	J.Rochead	North Connel, Oban	28. 6.02P
G-MWLT	Mainair Gemini/Flash IIA (Rotax 503) 804-0990-7 & W597		31. 8.90	S.A.Sacker	Deenethorpe	31. 1.02P
G-MWLU	Solar Wings Pegasus XL-R/Se (Rotax 462) SW-TE-0294 & SW-WA-1478		6. 9.90	T.P.G.Ward *(Stored 9.97: current status unknown)*	(Great Orton)	14.10.91P
	(Trike c/n corrected from '0304 which is G-MWNC)					
G-MWLW	TEAM mini-MAX PFA 186-11717 (Rotax 377)		14. 9.90	R.Wheeler	(Kidlington)	24. 7.02P
G-MWLX	Mainair Gemini/Flash IIA (Rotax 503) 805-0990-7 & W598		5.10.90	G.Good & E.J.Robson	East Fortune	27. 1.01P
G-MWLZ	Rans S-4 Coyote (Rotax 447) 90.116 & PFA 193-11887		8.10.90	I.W.Critchley	(Stafford)	3. 6.00P
G-MWMB	Powerchute Kestrel 00399 (Rotax 503)		7.11.90	D.J.Whysall	Ripley, Derby	13. 7.02P
G-MWMC	Powerchute Kestrel 00400 (Rotax 503)		7.11.90	K.James	Kemble	30. 6.01P
G-MWMD	Powerchute Kestrel 00401 (Rotax 503)		7.11.90	D.J.Jackson	(Melton Constable)	20.11.91P
G-MWMG	Powerchute Kestrel 00404 (Rotax 503)		7.11.90	M.D.Walton	(Tregaron)	26.10.02P
G-MWMH	Powerchute Kestrel 00405 (Rotax 503)		7.11.90	E.W.Potts	(Crymych)	31. 3.02P
G-MWMI	Solar Wings Pegasus Quasar SW-TQ-0043 & SW-WQQ-0383		21. 9.90	M.A.Evans	Weston Zoyland	4. 5.02P
G-MWMJ	Solar Wings Pegasus Quasar SW-TQ-0044 & SW-WQQ-0384		21. 9.90	D.Webb	Kemble	15. 4.02P
G-MWMK	Solar Wings Pegasus Quasar SW-TQ-0045 & SW-WQQ-0385		21. 9.90	M.E.Lloyd	(Bath)	14. 5.02P
G-MWML	Solar Wings Pegasus Quasar SW-TQ-0046 & SW-WQQ-0386		21. 9.90	S.C.Key	(Norwich)	9. 9.02P
G-MWMM	Mainair Gemini/Flash IIA (Rotax 462) 800-0890-7 & W593		24. 8.90	R.H.Church	Croft Farm, Defford	6. 5.02P
G-MWMN	Solar Wings Pegasus XL-Q (Rotax 462HP) SW-TE-0297 & SW-WQ-0387		2.10.90	N.A.Rathbone & P.A.Arnold	Swinford, Rugby	23. 2.02P
G-MWMO	Solar Wings Pegasus XL-Q (Rotax 462) SW-TE-0298 & SW-WQ-0388		2.10.90	R.S.Wilson	Insch	8. 7.02P
G-MWMP	Solar Wings Pegasus XL-Q (Rotax 462HP) SW-TE-0299 & SW-WQ-0389		2.10.90	D.M.Orrock & F.E.Hall	(Rushden)	28. 7.02P
G-MWMR	Solar Wings Pegasus XL-R (Rotax 462) SW-TE-0300 & SW-WA-1483		2.10.90	J.A.Crofts	Meidrim, Carmarthen	13. 3.00P
G-MWMS	Mainair Gemini/Flash (Rotax 503) 807-1090-5 & W600		3.10.90	H N Barott	East Fortune	18.12.02P
G-MWMT	Mainair Gemini/Flash IIA (Rotax 503) 808-1090-7 & W601		3.10.90	K.Sene	(Warrington)	23. 8.02P
G-MWMU	CFM Shadow CD 150 (Rotax 503) *(Manufacturer's records show this a/c as c/n 142 - with c/n 150 sold to Namibia)*		2.10.90	A.J.Burton	Wickenby	12. 4.02P
G-MWMV	Solar Wings Pegasus XL-R (Rotax 462) SW-TE-0307 & SW-WA-1484		5.10.90	G.M.Stevens	Kemble	7. 5.02P
G-MWMW	Murphy Renegade Spirit UK (Rotax 532) 254 & PFA 188-11544		21. 8.89	H.Feeney *"Spirit of Cornwall"*	Long Marston	26. 7.02P
G-MWMX	Mainair Gemini/Flash IIA (Rotax 462) 810-1090-7 & W603		17.10.90	G.T.Snoddon	Newtownards, Co.of Down	28.11.02P
G-MWMY	Mainair Gemini/Flash IIA (Rotax 462) 809-1090-7 & W602		17.10.90	C.W.Lowe	Grove Farm, Raveningham	4. 6.02P

G-MWMZ	Solar Wings Pegasus XL-Q (Rotax 462) SW-TE-0301 & SW-WQ-0393	8.10.90	P.C.Ockwell	Redlands, Swindon	10. 8.02P
G-MWNA	Solar Wings Pegasus XL-Q SW-WQ-0394 (Rotax 462) SW-TE-0302 & SW-WQ-0394	8.10.90	R.Carr	(Alnwick)	17. 6.02P
G-MWNB	Solar Wings Pegasus XL-Q (Rotax 462) SW-TE-0303 & SW-WQ-0395	8.10.90	P.F.J.Rogers	(London SW17)	25. 6.02P
G-MWNC	Solar Wings Pegasus XL-Q (Rotax 462HP) SW-TE-0304 & SW-WQ-0396	8.10.90	G.S.Sage	(Sleaford)	9. 6.02P
G-MWND	Tiger Cub RL5A Sherwood Ranger (Rotax 532) 001 & PFA 237-12229	9.10.90	D.A.Pike	(Barmouth)	1. 5.96P
G-MWNE	Mainair Gemini/Flash IIA (Rotax 503) 803-1090-7 & W596	17.10.90	T.C.Edwards	(Ware)	10. 5.02P
G-MWNF	Murphy Renegade Spirit UK (Rotax 582) PFA 188-11853	15.10.90	D.J.White	Bodmin	6. 6.01P
G-MWNG	Solar Wings Pegasus XL-Q (Rotax 462HP) SW-TE-0305 & SW -WQ-0399	17.10.90	H.C.Thomson	Perth	6.10.02P
G-MWNK	Solar Wings Pegasus Quasar TC SW-TQA-0054 & SW-WQQ-0403	1.11.90	G.S.Lyon	RAF Wyton	1. 8.02P
G-MWNL	Solar Wings Pegasus Quasar SW-TQ-0055 & SW-WQQ-0404	1.11.90	Creation Company Films Ltd	Popham	30. 7.00P
G-MWNO	AMF Chevvron 2-32 025 (Konig SD570)	12.11.90	I.K.Hogg	Kirkbride	30. 4.02P
G-MWNP	AMF Chevvron 2-32C 026 (Konig SD570)	31.10.90	R.S.Tingle	(Burgess Hill)	17. 7.02P
G-MWNR	Murphy Renegade Spirit UK (Rotax 582) PFA 188-11926	12.11.90	J.J.Lancaster t/a RJR Flying Group	Cublington	21. 8.02P
G-MWNS	Mainair Gemini/Flash IIA (Rotax 503) 811-1190-7 & W604	6.11.90	S.R.Kerr	North Coates	24. 6.02P
G-MWNT	Mainair Gemini/Flash IIA (Rotax 582) 812-1190-7 & W605	6.11.90	C.G.Rodger	East Fortune	3. 6.02P
G-MWNU	Mainair Gemini/Flash IIA (Rotax 503) 813-1190-5 & W606	6.11.90	C.C.Muir	(Bristol)	20. 4.02P
G-MWNV	Powerchute Kestrel 00406	12.11.90	K.N.Byrne	(Colonsay)	13. 3.92P
G-MWNX	Powerchute Kestrel 00408 (Rotax 503)	12.11.90	J.H.Greenroyd	(Hebden Bridge)	24. 9.02P
G-MWOC	Powerchute Kestrel 00413	12.11.90	K.J.Foxall	(Tamworth)	10. 8.02P
G-MWOD	Powerchute Kestrel 00414 (Rotax 503)	12.11.90	T.Morgan	(Kidderminster)	4.10.00P
G-MWOE	Powerchute Kestrel 00415	12.11.90	E.G.Woolnough & P.K.Reason	(Halesworth)	21. 1.02P
G-MWOF	Microflight Spectrum 018 (Rotax 503)	13.11.90	P.Williams	Otherton, Cannock	7. 4.02P
G-MWOH	Solar Wings Pegasus XL-R/Se (Rotax 447) SW-TB-1429 & SW-WA-1485	28.11.90	L R Hodgson	(Haltwistle)	18. 3.02P
G-MWOI	Solar Wings Pegasus XL-R (Rotax 447) SW-TB-1430 & SW-WA-1486	29.11.90	P.Maller	Enstone	17. 6.02P
G-MWOJ	Mainair Gemini/Flash IIA (Rotax 503) 814-1290-7 & W608	6.12.90	J.K.Nicol	(Southport)	21. 8.00P
G-MWOK	Mainair Gemini/Flash IIA (Rotax 462) 815-1290-7 & W609	6.12.90	J.C.Miller	(Burnstisland)	19. 8.02P
G-MWOL	Mainair Gemini/Flash IIA (Rotax 503) 816-1290-7 & W610	6.12.90	I.V.Watters	(Swansea)	31. 1.94P
G-MWOM	Solar Wings Pegasus Quasar TC SW-TQ-0060 & SW-WQQ-0412	1. 3.91	T.J.Williams	(Tuam, Co.Galway)	18. 5.02P
G-MWON	CFM Shadow CD K.128 (Rotax 503)	18.12.90	R E M Gibson-Bevan	(Market Rasen)	14. 7.02P
G-MWOO	Murphy Renegade Spirit UK (Rotax 582) 318 & PFA 188-11811	14. 9.90	R.C.Wood	Lower Mountpleasant, Chatteris	12. 7.02P
G-MWOP	Solar Wings Pegasus Quasar TC SW-TQC-0059 & SW-WQQ-0410	31.12.90	A.Baynes	Sywell	2.10.02P
G-MWOR	Solar Wings Pegasus XL-Q (Rotax 462) SW-TE-0308 & SW-WQ-0411	21.12.90	I.D.Chantler	Long Acre Farm, Sandy	29. 7.02P
G-MWOV	Whittaker MW6 Merlin PFA 164-11301 (Rotax 503)	9. 1.91	D.J.Pennack	(Bridgwater)	13 8.02P
G-MWOX	Solar Wings Pegasus XL-Q (Rotax 462) SW-TE-0309 & SW-WQ-0413	7. 1.91	G.Milo	Popham	16. 6.99P
G-MWOY	Solar Wings Pegasus XL-Q (Rotax 462HP) SW-TE-0310 & SW-WQ-0414	7. 1.91	G.S.Beeby	Sutton Meadows, Ely	11.10.02P
G-MWPA	Mainair Gemini/Flash IIA (Rotax 462) 817-0191-7 & W611	9. 1.91	T.Beckham	Eshott	4. 7.00P
G-MWPB	Mainair Gemini/Flash IIA (Rotax 503) 823-0191-7 & W617	3. 1.91	J.Fenton	St.Michaels	27. 6.02P
G-MWPC	Mainair Gemini/Flash IIA (Rotax 503) 826-0191-7 & W620	3. 1.91	I.Shaw	Arclid Green, Sandbach	10. 9.01P

G-MWPD	Mainair Gemini/Flash IIA		9. 1.91	C S Mackenzie	East Fortune	1. 2.02P
	(Rotax 503) 824-0191-7 & W618					
G-MWPE	Solar Wings Pegasus XL-Q		9. 1.91	E.C.R.Hudson	Upper Stow, Weedon	25. 5.02P
	(Rotax 462HP) SW-TE-0096 & SW-WQ-0416 *(Trike ex G-MVGX)*					
G-MWPF	Mainair Gemini/Flash IIA		11. 1.91	Gemini Aviation Ltd	Mill Farm, Shifnal	30. 5.02P
	(Rotax 503) 825-0191-7 & W619					
G-MWPG	Microflight Spectrum 019		9. 1.91	P.Turnbull & B.Smith	(Whitley Bay)	4. 8.01P
	(Rotax 503)					
G-MWPH	Microflight Spectrum 020		9. 1.91	S.B.Mance & K.R.Wootton	Wombleton	29.10.00P
	(Rotax 503)					
G-MWPJ	Solar Wings Pegasus XL-Q		17. 1.91	D.S.Parker	Carlisle	30. 4.02P
	(Rotax 462) SW-TE-0312 & SW-WQ-0418					
G-MWPK	Solar Wings Pegasus XL-Q		17. 1.91	T.J.Gayton-Polley	(Billingshurst)	29. 4.02P
	(Rotax 462) SW-TE-0313 & SW-WQ-0419					
G-MWPN	CFM Shadow CD K.147		22. 1.91	W.R.H.Thomas	(Swansea)	11. 6.99P
	(Rotax 503)					
G-MWPP	CFM Streak Shadow M	G-BTEM	14. 2.91	W.C.Yates	Higher Barn Farm, Houghton	1. 8.02P
	(Rotax 582) K.166-SA & PFA 206-11992					
G-MWPR	Whittaker MW6 Merlin PFA 164-11260		16.10.90	S.F.N.Warnell	(Staines)	
				(New owner 10.01)		
G-MWPS	Murphy Renegade Spirit UK		18. 2.91	M.D.Stewart	(Leicester)	1. 7.98P
	(Rotax 582) PFA 188-11931			*(New owner 6.01)*		
G-MWPT	Hunt Avon/Hunt Wing	EI-CKF	18. 2.91	M.Leyden & S.Cronin	(Ennis, Co.Clare)	10. 5.97P
	(Fuji-Robin EC-44-PM) JAH-8 & BMAA/HB/015	G-MWPT				
G-MWPU	Solar Wings Pegasus Quasar TC		20. 2.91	N.J.Holt	Weston Zoyland	6. 7.02P
	SW-TQC-0062 & SW-WQQ-0426					
G-MWPW	AMF Chevvron 2-32C 027		26.11.90	E.L.T.Westman	Broadford, Isle of Skye	5.11.02P
	(Konig SD570)					
G-MWPX	Solar Wings Pegasus XL-R		27. 2.91	R.S.Amor	Weston Zoyland	20. 6.02P
	(Rotax 462) SW-TE-0315 & SW-WA-1488					
G-MWPZ	Murphy Renegade Spirit UK		18. 3.91	J.Ievers	Pains Castle	24. 2.99P
	PFA 188-11631					
G-MWRB	Mainair Gemini/Flash IIA		5. 2.91	A.S.Harvey	RAF Wyton	25. 4.01P
	(Rotax 503) 819-0191-7 & W613					
G-MWRC	Mainair Gemini/Flash IIA		5. 2.91	D.R.Talbot	Chilton Park, Wallingford	23. 8.02P
	(Rotax 503) 820-0191-7 & W614					
G-MWRD	Mainair Gemini/Flash IIA		5. 2.91	P.Hassett	Ince Blundell	15. 1.02P
	(Motavia) 821-0191-7 & W615					
G-MWRE	Mainair Gemini/Flash IIA		5. 2.91	A.Simon	(Dingwall)	7. 7.02P
	(Rotax 503) 822-0191-7 & W616					
G-MWRF	Mainair Gemini/Flash IIA		4. 2.91	R.D.Ballard	(Bexhill)	12. 5.02P
	(Rotax 503) 829-0191-7 & W623					
G-MWRG	Mainair Gemini/Flash IIA		5. 2.91	N.J.Hall	(Morpeth)	11. 4.00P
	(Rotax 503) 830-0191-7 & W624					
G-MWRH	Mainair Gemini/Flash IIA		5. 2.91	E.G.Astin	Eshott	19. 6.02P
	(Rotax 503) 831-0191-7 & W625					
G-MWRI	Mainair Gemini/Flash IIA		1. 3.91	R.N.Scarr	Clench Common	12.12.99P
	(Rotax 462) 828-0191-7 & W622					
G-MWRJ	Mainair Gemini/Flash IIA		28. 2.91	J.S.Walton	(Mold)	17.10.01P
	(Rotax 503) 832-0291-7 & W626					
G-MWRK*	Rans S-6 Coyote II *(Tri-cycle u/c)*		13. 2.91	R.H.Bambury	Breighton	10. 5.99P
	(Rotax 503) 0191.154 & PFA/204-11930		*(Damaged 7.99: cancelled 19.5.00 by CAA: remains noted 12.01)*			
G-MWRL	CFM Shadow CD K.152		13. 2.91	A.E.Southern	Clench Common	18. 8.01P
	(Rotax 503)			*"Shadow Hawk"*		
G-MWRM	Medway Hybred 44XLR MR086/94/91/S	G-MWLC	26. 2.91	M.A.Jones	(Wigan)	9.11.02P
	(Rotax 503)					
G-MWRN	Solar Wings Pegasus XL-R		5. 3.91	D.T.MacKenzie	(Glasgow)	10. 3.02P
	(Rotax 462) SW-TE-0316 & SW-WA-1489					
G-MWRO	Solar Wings Pegasus XL-R		5. 3.91	I.D.Stokes	Davidstow Moor	8. 6.99P
	(Rotax 462) SW-TE-0317 & SW-WA-1490					
G-MWRP	Solar Wings Pegasus XL-R		1. 3.91	J.Liddiard	(Didcot)	23. 7.01P
	(Rotax 462) SW-TE-0318 & SW-WA-1491					
G-MWRR	Mainair Gemini/Flash IIA		7. 3.91	G.P.Wiley	(Wolverhampton)	10. 4.02P
	(Rotax 503) 834-0391-7 & W628					
G-MWRS	Ultravia Super Pelican E001-201		9. 5.84	T.B.Woolley	(Narborough, Leics)	9. 9.87P
				(Current status unknown)		
G-MWRT	Solar Wings Pegasus XL-R		15. 3.91	G.L.Gunnell	Sywell	25. 7.02P
	(Rotax 447) SW-TB-1431 & SW-WA-1492					
G-MWRU	Solar Wings Pegasus XL-R		15. 3.91	J.McIver	(West Kilbride)	25. 8.96P
	(Rotax 447) SW-TB-1432 & SW-WA-1493					
G-MWRV	Solar Wings Pegasus XL-R		15. 3.91	M.S.Adams	Roddige, Fradley	23.10.01P
	(Rotax 447) SW-TB-1433 & SW-WA-1494					
G-MWRW	Solar Wings Pegasus XL-Q		25. 3.91	M Peters	Weston Zoyland	31. 8.02P
	(Rotax 462) SW-TE-0320 & SW-WQ-0431					

G-MWRX	Solar Wings Pegasus XL-Q (Rotax 462) SW-TE-0321 & SW-WQ-0432		25. 3.91	C.D.Humphries *(Noted 1.02)*	Long Marston	20. 4.02P
G-MWRY	CFM Shadow CD K.162 (Rotax 503) *(Initially reserved as c/n K.158 which became G-MWSZ)*		26. 3.91	A.W.Hodder	Belle Vue Farm, Yarnscombe	26.10.01P
G-MWRZ	AMF Chevvron 2-32C 028 (Konig SD570)		10. 4.91	M.J.Barrett	Davidstow Moor	4. 7.02P
G-MWSA	TEAM mini-MAX PFA 186-11855 (Rotax 377)		8. 4.91	G.R.Inston	(Birmingham)	13. 8.01P
G-MWSB	Mainair Gemini/Flash IIA (Rotax 582) 837-0591-7 & W631		30. 4.91	B.J Palfreyman	(Newthorpe)	18.10.02P
G-MWSC	Rans S-6-ESD Coyote II PFA 204-12019 (Rotax 503) (Tri-cycle u/c)		13. 5.91	E.M.Lear	(Langport)	30. 6.96P
G-MWSD	Solar Wings Pegasus XL-Q (Rotax 462) SW-TE-0319 & SW-WQ-0430		6. 3.91	A.M.Harley	Sutton Meadows, Ely	18. 7.02P
G-MWSE	Solar Wings Pegasus XL-R (Rotax 462) SW-TE-0323 & SW-WA-1496 *(Fitted with trike unit from G-MTJR)*		10. 4.91	Ultra Light Training Ltd	Roddige, Fradley	31. 5.02P
G-MWSF	Solar Wings Pegasus XL-R (Rotax 462) SW-TE-0324 & SW-WA-1497		10. 4.91	V.A.M.Bourne	Long Newnton, Malmesbury	18. 5.02P
G-MWSH	Solar Wings Pegasus Quasar TC SW-TQC-0064 & SW-WQ-0435		30. 4.91	B.Kirkland	Tarn Farm, Cockerham	11. 9.01P
G-MWSI	Solar Wings Pegasus Quasar TC SW-TQC-0065 & SW-WQ-0436		23. 5.91	J.A.Ganderton	Sywell	18.10.02P
G-MWSJ	Solar Wings Pegasus XL-Q (Rotax 462) SW-TE-0326 & SW-WQ-0437		12. 4.91	R.A.Barrett	Sutton Meadows, Ely	13. 6.02P
G-MWSK	Solar Wings Pegasus XL-Q (Rotax 462) SW-TE-0327 & SW-WQ-0438		12. 4.91	J.Doogan t/a Scottglass	(Galashiels)	26. 5.02P
G-MWSL	Mainair Gemini/Flash IIA (Rotax 503) 835-0491-7 & W629		16. 4.91	C.W.Frost	Rufforth	11. 6.98P
G-MWSM	Mainair Gemini/Flash IIA (Rotax 503) 836-0491-7 & W630		16. 4.91	R.M.Wall & P.A.Garside	St.Michaels	23. 8.01P
G-MWSO	Solar Wings Pegasus XL-R (Rotax 462) SW-TE-0329 & SW-WA-1503		25. 4.91	M.A.Clayton	(New Romney)	21. 5.02P
G-MWSP	Solar Wings Pegasus XL-R (Rotax 462) SW-TE-0330 & SW-WA-1504		25. 4.91	P.A.Ashton	Knapton Lodge, Caunton	21.10.02P
G-MWSR	Solar Wings Pegasus XL-R (Rotax 462) SW-TE-0331 & SW-WA-1505		25. 4.91	M.E.T.Taylor	(Lilleshall, Newport)	7. 8.02P
G-MWSS	Medway Hybred 44XLR MR117/97 (Rotax 503)		7. 5.91	F.S.Ogden	West Hoathly, Haywards Heath	6. 8.00P
G-MWST	Medway Hybred 44XLR MR118/98 (Rotax 503)		8. 5.91	A.Ferguson	(Sconser, Skye)	3. 9.01P
G-MWSU	Medway Hybred 44XLR MR119/99 (Rotax 503)		1. 5.92	T.D.Walker	Plaistows Farm, St Albans	26. 7.02P
G-MWSW	Whittaker MW6 Merlin PFA 164-11328		15. 2.91	S.N.F.Warnell	Staines	
G-MWSX	Aerotech MW5 Sorcerer PFA 163-11549 (Rotax 447)		3. 5.91	A.T.Armstrong	Yelverton	4. 6.02P
G-MWSY	Aerotech MW5 Sorcerer PFA 163-11218 (Rotax 447)		3. 5.91	J.E.Holloway	Saltash	4. 6.02P
G-MWSZ	CFM Shadow CD K.158 (Rotax 503)	(G-MWRY)	4. 4.91	P.G.Bibbey	Old Sarum	24. 9.02P
G-MWTA	Solar Wings Pegasus XL-Q (Rotax 462) SW-TE-0332 & SW-WQ-0444		8. 5.91	C D Arnold	(Trowbridge)	21. 5.02P
G-MWTB	Solar Wings Pegasus XL-Q (Rotax 462) SW-TE-0333 & SW-WQ-0445		8. 5.91	G.S.Highley	(Corby)	2. 9.02P
G-MWTC	Solar Wings Pegasus XL-Q (Rotax 462) SW-TE-0334 & SW-WQ-0446		8. 5.91	P.Nicholson	(London SE18)	23. 8.02P
G-MWTD	Microflight Spectrum 022 (Rotax 503)		13. 5.91	J.V.Harris t/a Group Delta	Ashbourne	18. 4.00P
G-MWTE	Microflight Spectrum 023 (Rotax 503)		13. 5.91	R.Kirkland	RAF Halton	28. 1.02P
G-MWTG	Mainair Gemini/Flash IIA (Rotax 582) 838-0591-7 & W632		16. 5.91	D.G.Emery & M.R.Smith	(Dudley)	29. 8.01P
G-MWTH	Mainair Gemini/Flash IIA 839-0591-7 & W633		21. 5.91	G.M.Hughes	(Edinburgh)	9. 6.95P
G-MWTI	Solar Wings Pegasus XL-Q (Rotax 462HP) SW-TE-0251 & SW-WQ-0274		23. 5.91	A.Crozier	Latch Farm, Kirknewton	15. 5.02P
G-MWTJ	CFM Shadow CD K.167 (Rotax 503)		16. 5.91	T.D.Wolstenholme	(Preston)	27.10.02P
G-MWTK	Solar Wings Pegasus XL-R/Se (Rotax 462) SW-TE-0335 & SW-WA-1507		28. 5.91	A.J.Thomas	(Nottingham)	23. 4.02P
G-MWTL	Solar Wings Pegasus XL-R (Rotax 462) SW-TE-0336 & SW-WA-1508		28. 5.91	B.Lindsay	(Chipping Sodbury)	19. 1.02P
G-MWTM	Solar Wings Pegasus XL-R SW-WA-1509 (Rotax 462) SW-TE-0337 & SW-WA-1509		28. 5.91	I.R.F.King	(Tunbridge Wells)	31. 3.02P

G-MWTN	CFM Shadow CD K.153 (Rotax 503)		23. 5.91	M.J.Broom	Long Marston	28. 7.99P
G-MWTO	Mainair Gemini/Flash IIA (Rotax 503) 840-0591-7 & W634		28. 5.91	J.Greenhalgh	St.Michaels	13. 6.02P
G-MWTP	CFM Shadow CD K.107 (Rotax 503)		23. 5.91	D.A.Crosbie	(Sudbury)	29. 4.02P
G-MWTR	Mainair Gemini/Flash IIA (Rotax 582) 842-0591-7 & W636		31. 5.91	A.A.Howland	(Battle)	26.11.02P
G-MWTT	Rans S-6-ESD Coyote II *(Tri-cycle u/c)* (Rotax 503) 20391.175 & PFA 204-12016		30. 4.91	L.E.Duffin *"Warrior 2"*	Insch	9. 2.02P
G-MWTU	Solar Wings Pegasus XL-R (Rotax 447) SW-TB-1435 & SW-WA-1501		21. 6.91	J.D.Doran	(Mullingar, Co.Westmeath)	2. 9.01P
G-MWTY	Mainair Gemini/Flash IIA (Rotax 503) 843-0691-7 & W637		12. 6.91	A.McGing & J.C.Townsend	(Bootle)	23. 9.02P
G-MWTZ	Mainair Gemini/Flash IIA (Rotax 503) 844-0691-7 & W638		12. 6.91	C.W.R.Felce	Riseley, Bedford	23. 6.02P
G-MWUA	CFM Shadow CD K.161 (Rotax 503)		10. 6.91	P.A.James t/a Cloudbase Aviation G-MWUA	Redhill	7. 6.02P
G-MWUB	Solar Wings Pegasus XL-R (Rotax 462) SW-TE-0338 & SW-WA-1510		12. 6.91	T.R.L.Bayley	(Edenbridge)	2. 6.02P
G-MWUC	Solar Wings Pegasus XL-R (Rotax 462) SW-TE-0339 & SW-WA-1511		12. 6.91	J.R.Hall	Halwell, Totnes	26.10.02P
G-MWUD	Solar Wings Pegasus XL Tug (Rotax 462) SW-TE-0340 & SW-WA-1512		12. 6.91	N.A.Martin	Clench Common	11. 6.02P
G-MWUE	Solar Wings Pegasus XL-R (Rotax 447) SW-TB-1438 & SW-WA-1513	EI-CGL G-MWUE	13. 6.91	O.Farrell	(Drogheda, Co.Louth)	11. 4.00P
G-MWUF	Solar Wings Pegasus XL-R (Rotax 447) SW-TB-1439 & SW-WA-1514		13. 6.91	J.G.Jackson	(Woodley)	26. 6.01P
G-MWUH	Murphy Renegade Spirit UK 343 (Rotax 582) *(Built Canada/Saudi Arabia)*		12. 6.91	Choicesource Ltd	Inverness	16. 9.00P
G-MWUI	AMF Chevvron 2-32C 029 (Konig SD570)		2. 7.91	N.D.A.Graham	(Lochgilphead)	26. 4.02P
G-MWUK	Rans S-6-ESD Coyote II *(Tri-cycle u/c)* (Rotax 503) 0491.187 & PFA 204-12090		1. 7.91	G.K.Hoult	Long Marston	18.10.02P
G-MWUL	Rans S-6-ESD Coyote II *(Tri-cycle u/c)* (Rotax 503) 0391.172 & PFA 204-12054		10. 6.91	C.K.Fry	(Lychett Minster)	21. 8.02P
G-MWUN	Rans S-6-ESD Coyote II *(Tri-cycle u/c)* (Rotax 503) 0695.841 & PFA 204-12075 *(Rebuilt with new Rans airframe as stated)*		10. 6.91	M.L.Robinson t/a Coyote Flying Group	Kirkbride	11. 4.02P
G-MWUO	Solar Wings Pegasus XL-Q (Rotax 462) SW-TE-0296 & SW-WQ-0379	(ZS-...?)	26. 6.91	A.P.Slade	High Wycombe	4. 8.02P
G-MWUP	Solar Wings Pegasus XL-R (Rotax 462) SW-TE-0341 & SW-WA-1517		21. 6.91	R.G.Mulford	Gillingham	22. 7.02P
G-MWUR	Solar Wings Pegasus XL Tug (Rotax 462) SW-TE-0342 & SW-WA-1518		21. 6.91	A.W.Buchan & C.D.Creasey t/a Nottingham Aerotow Club	Knapthorpe Lodge, Caunton	19. 8.02P
G-MWUS	Solar Wings Pegasus XL-R (Rotax 462) SW-TE-0343 & SW-WA-1519		21. 6.91	H.R.Loxton	Weston Zoyland	29. 8.01P
G-MWUU	Solar Wings Pegasus XL-R (Rotax 462) SW-TE-0346 & SW-WA-1521		28. 6.91	B.R.Underwood & P.E.Hadley	Swinford, Rugby	26. 6.02P
G-MWUV	Solar Wings Pegasus XL-R (Rotax 462) SW-TE-0347 & SW-WA-1522		28. 6.91	L.Birkett t/a Blast Clean	Carlisle	25. 6.01P
G-MWUX	Solar Wings Pegasus XL-Q SW-WQ-0454 (Rotax 462HP) *(Originally supplied as a sailwing only - Trike origin unknown)*		28. 6.91	B.D.Attwell	Caerphilly	25. 3.02P
G-MWUY	Solar Wings Pegasus XL-Q (Rotax 462) SW-TE-0345 & SW-WQ-0455		28. 6.91	S.Johnstone	(East Kilbride)	28. 7.01P
G-MWUZ	Solar Wings Pegasus XL-Q (Rotax 462) SW-TE-0350 & SW-WQ-0456		28. 6.91	K.J.Hoare	Plaistows Farm, St Albans	1.11.02P
G-MWVA	Solar Wings Pegasus XL-Q (Rotax 462) SW-TE-0351 & SW-WQ-0457		28. 6.91	P.C.Hancox	Croft Farm, Defford	15. 1.02P
G-MWVE	Solar Wings Pegasus XL-R (Rotax 447) SW-TB-1441 & SW-WA-1524		18. 7.91	W.A.Keel-Stocker	Long Marston	6. 5.02P
G-MWVF	Solar Wings Pegasus XL-R/Se (Rotax 447) SW-TB-1442 & SW-WA-1525		18. 7.91	T.Kendall	(Burntwood)	9. 4.00P
G-MWVG	CFM Shadow CD 151 (Rotax 503)		5. 8.91	Shadow Flight Centre Ltd	Old Sarum	16.10.02P
G-MWVH	CFM Shadow CD 181 (Rotax 503)		5. 8.91	D.J.Cross	(Glasgow)	18. 7.02P
G-MWVK	Mainair Mercury 849-0891-5 & W643 (Rotax 503)		13. 8.91	J.Northage	Baxby Manor, Husthwaite	12. 7.02P
G-MWVL	Rans S-6 ESD Coyote II *(Tri-cycle u/c)* (Rotax 503) 0892.341 & PFA 204-12118 *(Originally built with frame c/n 0491-186: this was damaged, repaired & fitted as a replacement frame to G-MZAH)*		13. 8.91	J.M.Keane	(Brighton)	19. 6.02P
G-MWVM	Solar Wings Pegasus Quasar IITC SW-TQ-0031 & SW-WX-0020 *(Trike c/n duplicates G-MWLI)*	G-65-8	2. 9.91	J.D.Jones & A.A.Edmonds	(Shrewsbury)	30. 9.01P

G-MWVN	Mainair Gemini/Flash IIA (Rotax 503) 850-0891-7 & W644		19. 8.91	J.McCafferty	Enstone	20.11.02P
G-MWVO	Mainair Gemini/Flash IIA (Rotax 582) 852-0891-7 & W646		27. 8.91	P.M.Knight	(Elm Farm, Wickford)	11 7.02P
G-MWVP	Murphy Renegade Spirit UK (Rotax 582) PFA 188-11735		22. 8.91	T.B.Woolley *"Spirit of Lancashire" (Damaged Redlands, Swindon 3.7.93)*	(Leicester)	29. 4.94P
G-MWVR	Mainair Gemini/Flash IIA (Rotax 503) 855-0991-7 & W650		30. 8.91	G.Cartwright	Northampton	20. 4.02P
G-MWVS	Mainair Gemini/Flash IIA (Rotax 503) 856-0991-7 & W651		30. 8.91	J.A.Brown	Otherton, Cannock	2. 1.02P
G-MWVT	Mainair Gemini/Flash IIA (Rotax 503) 860-1091-7 & W655		2. 9.91	J.Barlow & C.Osiejuk	Oxton, Nottingham	6.12.02P
G-MWVU	Medway Hybred 44XLR MR123/102 (Rotax 503)		18. 9.91	H.M.Manning	Rochester	24. 1.02P
G-MWVW	Mainair Gemini/Flash IIA (Rotax 503) 853-0891-7 & W647		9. 9.91	W.O'Brien	Arclid Green, Sandbach	29. 7.02P
G-MWVY	Mainair Gemini/Flash IIA (Rotax 503) 854-0991-7 & W649		4. 9.91	J.D.Hinton	(Tunbridge Wells)	4. 5.02P
G-MWVZ	Mainair Gemini/Flash IIA (Rotax 503) 863-1091-7 & W658		4. 9.91	K.T.Leach	(Skelmersdale)	1.11.02P
G-MWWB	Mainair Gemini/Flash IIA (Rotax 503) 864-1091-7 & W659		18. 9.91	J.H.Bradbury	Arclid Green, Sandbach	20. 6.02P
G-MWWC	Mainair Gemini/Flash IIA (Rotax 582) 868-1191-7 & W663		23. 9.91	A. & D.Margereson	(Chesterfield)	28. 6.02P
G-MWWD	Murphy Renegade Spirit UK (Rotax 582) 344 & PFA 188-11719		23. 9.91	F.Overall *"Winning Spirit"*	(Wethersfield)	31. 5.02P
G-MWWE	TEAM mini-MAX PFA 186-11925 (Rotax 447)		1.10.91	J.Entwistle *(Dismantled 8.01)*	Tarn Farm, Cockerham	23. 7.97P
G-MWWG	Solar Wings Pegasus XL-Q (Rotax 462HP) SW-TE-0355 & SW-WQ-0468		3.10.91	A.W.Guerri	Rufforth	2. 8.02P
G-MWWH	Solar Wings Pegasus XL-Q (Rotax 462) SW-TE-0356 & SW-WQ-0469		3.10.91	M.R.Dunnett	Ludham	21. 8.01P
G-MWWI	Mainair Gemini/Flash IIA (Rotax 503) 870-1291-7 & W665		11.10.91	R.J.Vaughan	(Northwich)	11. 9.01P
G-MWWJ	Mainair Gemini/Flash IIA (Rotax 503) 865-1191-7 & W660		22.10.91	J.Garcia	(Kilmarnock)	17. 8.98P
G-MWWK	Mainair Gemini/Flash IIA (Rotax 582) 866-1191-7 & W661		22.10.91	J.C.Boyd t/a JDS Group	Davidstow Moor	28. 4.02P
G-MWWL	Rans S-6-ESD Coyote II *(Tri-cycle u/c)* (Rotax 503) PFA 204-11849	(G-BTXD)	17.10.91	D.W.Lloyd	Long Acre Farm, Sandy	12. 6.02P
G-MWWM	Kolb Twinstar mk.2 PFA 205-11645 (Rotax 503) *(C/n duplicates G-GPST)*	(G-BTXC)	17.10.91	D.Jordan	RAF Brize Norton	21. 6.02P
G-MWWN	Mainair Gemini/Flash IIA (Rotax 503) 872-1291-7 & W667		22.10.91	G A J Edwards	Dunkeswell	15.10.01P
G-MWWP	Rans S-4 Coyote (Rotax 447) 90.115 & PFA 193-12073		21.10.91	R.McKinlay	Strathaven	1. 8.00P
G-MWWR	Microflight Spectrum 024 (Rotax 503)		23.10.91	B.Fukes	North Coates	20. 4.02P
G-MWWS	Thruster T300 089-T300-370 (Rotax 532)	EI-BYW	4.11.91	S.P.McCaffrey *(Stored 3.97: current status unknown)*	Ginge, Wantage	7. 7.95P
G-MWWV	Solar Wings Pegasus XL-Q (Rotax 462HP) SW-TE-0357 & SW-WQ-0470		30.10.91	R.W.Livingstone	Enniskillen, Co.Fermanagh	13. 1.02P
G-MWWX*	Microflight Spectrum 025 (Rotax 503)		25.10.91	P.Turnbull & B.Smith *(Accident 7.4.00) (Cancelled 21.9.00 as wfu)*	Eshott	13. 5.00P
G-MWWZ	Cyclone Chaser S CH.829 (Rotax 447)		29.10.91	D.J.Higham	Roddidge, Fradley	28. 6.02P
G-MWXB	Mainair Gemini/Flash IIA (Rotax 503) 869-1191-7 & W664		6.11.91	N.W.Barnett	Sittles Farm, Alrewas	11. 8.02P
G-MWXC	Mainair Gemini/Flash IIA (Rotax 503) 874-0192-7 & W669		6.11.91	G.Dufton-Kelly	(Wirral)	28. 1.02P
G-MWXF	Mainair Mercury 867-1191-5 & W662 (Rotax 503)		12.11.91	J.G.I.Muncey	(Witham)	1. 7.01P
G-MWXG	Solar Wings Pegasus Quasar IITC SW-TQC-0074 & SW-WQT-0471		7.11.91	J.E.Moseley	Saffron Walden	1. 7.02P
G-MWXH	Solar Wings Pegasus Quasar IITC SW-TQC-0075 & SW-WQT-0472		7.11.91	R.P.Wilkinson	Charmy Down, Bath	25. 5.02P
G-MWXJ	Mainair Mercury 861-1091-5 & W656 (Rotax 503)		15.11.91	P.J.Taylor	(Scunthorpe)	23. 2.02P
G-MWXK	Mainair Mercury 862-1191-5 & W657 (Rotax 503)		15.11.91	M.P.Wilkinson	Sandtoft	18. 7.96P
G-MWXL	Mainair Gemini/Flash IIA (Rotax 582) 859-1091-7 & W654		12.12.91	S.N.Catchpole	Beccles	16. 8.02P
G-MWXN	Mainair Gemini/Flash IIA (Rotax 582) 878-0192-7 & W673		20.11.91	P.I.Miles	(Chesterfield)	28. 5.02P

G-MWXO	Mainair Gemini/Flash IIA (Rotax 503) 880-0192-7 & W675			25.11.91	T.P.Wright	(Ilkeston)	19 9.02P
G-MWXP	Solar Wings Pegasus XL-Q (Rotax 462) SW-TE-0359 & SW-WQ-0475			26.11.91	A.P.Attfield	Sutton Meadows, Ely	18. 8.99P
G-MWXR	Solar Wings Pegasus XL-Q (Rotax 462) SW-TE-0360 & SW-WQ-0476			26.11.91	G.W.Craig	Insch	9. 6.02P
G-MWXU	Mainair Gemini/Flash IIA (Rotax 582) 882-0192-7 & W677			9.12.91	C.M.Mackinnon	Cumbernauld	13. 6.00P
G-MWXV	Mainair Gemini/Flash IIA (Rotax 582) 879-1291-7 & W674			9.12.91	Launch Link Systems Ltd	Sutton Meadows, Ely	21. 5.02P
G-MWXW	Cyclone Chaser S (Rotax 377)	CH.830		9.12.91	K.C.Dodd	Roddige, Fradley	22. 4.02P
G-MWXX	Cyclone Chaser S (Rotax 447)	CH.831	(G-MWEB) (G-MWCD)	9.12.91	R.E.J.Pattenden	Maidstone	5. 6.01P
G-MWXY	Cyclone Chaser S (Rotax 447)	CH.832	(G-MWEC)	19.12.91	C A Benjamin	(Bedford)	30. 6.02P
G-MWXZ	Cyclone Chaser S (Rotax 508)	CH.836		31.12.91	N.R.Beale *"Daedalus"*	(Southam)	27. 4.01P
G-MWYA	Mainair Gemini/Flash IIA (Rotax 462) 886-0292-7 & W681			3. 1.92	R.F.Hunt	St.Michaels	26. 7.02P
G-MWYB	Solar Wings Pegasus XL-Q (Rotax 462) SW-TE-0364 & SW-WQ-0485			15. 1.92	P.D.Myer	Kemble	3.11.02P
G-MWYC	Solar Wings Pegasus XL-Q (Rotax 462) SW-TE-0365 & SW-WQ-0486			15. 1.92	N.J.Duckworth	(Bovington)	27. 6.02P
G-MWYD	CFM Shadow C (Rotax 503)	K.179		8. 1.92	J.Anderson	Plaistows Farm, St Albans	28. 5.02P
G-MWYE	Rans S-6-ESD Coyote II *(Tri-cycle u/c)* (Rotax 503) 0591.189 & PFA 204-12223			10. 1.92	G A M Moffat	(Manchester)	5. 3.02P
G-MWYG	Mainair Gemini/Flash IIA (Rotax 582) 884-0292-7 & W679			15. 1.92	F.Tumelty & E.C.R.Brown	(Castlewellan, Co.of Down)	14. 7.02P
G-MWYH	Mainair Gemini/Flash IIA (Rotax 503) 887-0292-7 & W682			15. 1.92	D.C.Jackson	Nottingham	1. 6.02P
G-MWYI	Solar Wings Pegasus Quasar IITC SW-TQC-0083 & SW-WQT-0488			30. 1.92	T.S.Chadfield	Graveley Farm, Herts	1. 4.02P
G-MWYJ	Solar Wings Pegasus Quasar IITC SW-TQC-0084 & SW-WQT-0489			24. 1.92	L.C.Wellington-Graham	Baxby Manor, Husthwaite	13. 3.02P
G-MWYL	Mainair Gemini/Flash IIA (Rotax 503) 877-0192-7 & W672			17. 1.92	A.Gannon	East Fortune	22. 5.02P
G-MWYM	Cyclone Chaser S 1000 (Mosler MM-CB35) *(Reported as rebuild of G-MVJI - perhaps trike only?)*	CH.838		21. 1.92	C J Meadows	(Shepton Mallet)	16.12.01P
G-MWYN*	Rans S-6-ESD Coyote II *(Tri-cycle u/c)* (Rotax 503) 0491.185 & PFA 204-12168			22. 1.92	W.R.Tull *(Cancelled 22.11.01 by CAA)*	(Milton-under-Wychwood)	6. 5.00P
G-MWYS	CGS Hawk I Arrow (Rotax 447) H-T-470-R447 & BMAA/HB/020			17. 2.93	D.W.Hermiston-Hooper t/a Civilair	(Ryde, IoW)	
G-MWYT	Mainair Gemini/Flash IIA (Rotax 503) 881-0392-7 & W676			3. 2.92	M.A.Hodgson	Baxby Manor, Husthwaite	17. 9.02P
G-MWYU	Solar Wings Pegasus XL-Q (Rotax 462) SW-TE-0364 & SW-WQ-0491			30. 1.92	N.Hammerton	(Oxted)	12. 5.01P
G-MWYV	Mainair Gemini/Flash IIA (Rotax 582) 896-0392-7 & W691			3. 2.92	J.N.Whitworth	(Chesterfield)	4. 7.02P
G-MWYY	Solar Wings Pegasus XL-Q (Rotax 462) SW-TE-0365 & SW-WQ-0492			17. 2.92	R.D.Allard	Deenethorpe	24. 5.02P
G-MWYZ	Solar Wings Pegasus XL-Q (Rotax 462HP) SW-TE-0358 & SW-WQ-0474			20.11.91	P.V.Stevens	(Wantage)	19. 5.02P
G-MWZA	Mainair Mercury 888-0292-5 & W683 (Rotax 503)			7. 2.92	A.J.Malham	Rufforth	7. 2.012
G-MWZB	AMF Chevvron 2-32C (Konig SD570)	033		10. 2.92	A.J.Pickup	(Didcot)	23. 8.02P
G-MWZC	Mainair Gemini/Flash IIA (Rotax 503) 899-0492-7 & W694			7. 2.92	W.A.Kent	(Preston)	8. 4.02P
G-MWZD	Solar Wings Pegasus Quasar IITC SW-TQC-0086 & SW-WQT-0494			2. 3.92	B.Hamilton	Long Marston	3. 4.02P
G-MWZE	Solar Wings Pegasus Quasar IITC SW-TQC-0087 & SW-WQT-0495			17. 2.92	H.Lorimer	(Mauchline)	18. 7.01P
G-MWZF	Solar Wings Pegasus Quasar IITC (Rotax 582/40) SW-TQD-0108 & SW-WQT-0496 *(Trike c/n duplicates G-MYEK: although data plate is stamped as above G-MWZF was built & flown originally with trike c/n SW-TQC-0088 fitted with a Rotax 503. It was then used to prove the Rotax 582 with Trike c/n SW-TQD-108 but re-numbered in SW's build records as SW-TQD-0102)*			17. 2.92	R.G.T.Corney	Clench Common	30. 7.02P
G-MWZG	Mainair Gemini/Flash IIA (Rotax 582) 889-0392-7 & W684			7. 2.92	P.L.Braniff	Newtownards, Co.of Down	20. 7.02P
G-MWZH	Solar Wings Pegasus XL-R (Rotax 462) SW-TE-0366 & SW-WA-1532			17. 2.92	P.A.Ord	(Redcar)	17. 4.00P

G-MWZI	Solar Wings Pegasus XL-R (Rotax 462) SW-TE-0367 & SW-WA-1533		17. 2.92	S.A.Oerton	Roddige, Fradley	20. 9.02P
G-MWZJ	Solar Wings Pegasus XL-R/Se (Rotax 462) SW-TE-0368 & SW-WA-1534		17. 2.92	P.Kitchen	Peterlee	20. 2.02P
G-MWZL	Mainair Gemini/Flash IIA (Rotax 582) 900-0492-7 & W695		17. 2.92	D.Renton	East Fortune	24. 6.02P
G-MWZM	TEAM mini-MAX 91 PFA 186-12211 (Mosler MM-CB40)	G-BUDD G-MWZM	18. 2.92	C.Leighton-Thomas *"My Buddy"*	(Bath)	29. 7.02P
G-MWZN	Mainair Gemini/Flash IIA (Rotax 582) 902-0492-7 & W697		25. 2.92	A.G.Marsh	(Inverkip)	13. 2.02P
G-MWZO	Solar Wings Pegasus Quasar IITC SW-TQC-0089 & SW-WQT-0498		26. 2.92	R.Oseland	Roddige, Fradley	23. 3.02P
G-MWZP	Solar Wings Pegasus Quasar IITC SW-TQC-0090 & SW-WQT-0499		26. 2.92	M.G.Taylor	Long Acre Farm, Sandy	23. 8.02P
G-MWZR	Solar Wings Pegasus Quasar IITC SW-TQC-0091 & SW-WQT-0500		26. 2.92	J.A.Robinson	Tarn Farm, Cockerham	25. 7.02P
G-MWZS	Solar Wings Pegasus Quasar IITC SW-TQC-0092 & SW-WQT-0501	EI-CIP G-MWZS	26. 2.92	B.H.A.Van Duykeren	Grange Bannow, Co.Wexford	5. 7.02P
G-MWZT	Solar Wings Pegasus XL-R (Rotax 462) SW-TE-0370 & SW-WA-1535		26. 2.92	J.R.Lowman	Sutton Meadows, Ely	12. 8.02P
G-MWZU	Solar Wings Pegasus XL-R (Rotax 462) SW-TE-0371 & SW-WA-1536		26. 2.92	D.W.Palmer	(Bexhill)	8. 6.02P
G-MWZV	Solar Wings Pegasus XL-R (Rotax 462) SW-TE-0372 & SW-WA-1537		26. 2.92	D.J.Newby	Clench Common	3. 7.02P
G-MWZW	Solar Wings Pegasus XL-R (Rotax 462) SW-TE-0373 & SW-WA-1538		26. 2.92	V.Goddard	Yatesbury	16. 6.02P
G-MWZX	Solar Wings Pegasus XL-R (Rotax 462) SW-TE-0374 & SW-WA-1539		26. 2.92	N.M.S.Waters	(Arundel)	12. 8.01P
G-MWZY	Solar Wings Pegasus XL-R (Rotax 462) SW-TE-0375 & SW-WA-1540		26. 2.92	T.J.Birkbeck & P.G.Moss t/a Vale of York Hang Gliding Club	Rufforth	18. 3.02P
G-MWZZ	Solar Wings Pegasus XL-R (Rotax 503) SW-TE-0376 & SW-WA-1541		26. 2.92	M.P.Shea	Roddige, Fradley	18. 6.02P
G-MXVI	Supermarine 361 Spitfire LF.XVIe CBAF.IX.4394	6850M TE184	17. 2.89	De Cadenet Motor Racing Ltd *(As "TE184/D" in Free French & 328 Squadron RAF c/s)*	North Weald	30. 5.02P
G-MYAB	Solar Wings Pegasus XL-R/Se (Rotax 462) SW-TE-0377 & SW-WA-1542		26. 2.92	A.N.F.Stewart	Long Marston	17. 6.02P
G-MYAC	Solar Wings Pegasus XL-Q (Rotax 462) SW-TE-0378 & SW-WQ-0502		26. 2.92	M.A.Garner	Thetford	13. 7.02P
G-MYAD	Solar Wings Pegasus XL-Q (Rotax 462HP) SW-TE-0379 & SW-WQ-0503		26. 2.92	P.Byrne	Hacketstown, Co.Carlow	19. 6.02P
G-MYAE	Solar Wings Pegasus XL-Q (Rotax 462) SW-TE-0380 & SW-WQ-0504		26. 2.92	R.J.Waller	Redlands, Swindon	15. 1.03P
G-MYAF	Solar Wings Pegasus XL-Q (Rotax 462) SW-TE-0381 & SW-WQ-0505		26. 2.92	K.N.Rigley	(Newark)	30. 7.02P
G-MYAG	Quad City Challenger II (Rotax 503) PFA 177-12167		25. 2.92	J.W.G.Andrews	(Welwyn)	21.10.02P
G-MYAH	Whittaker MW5 Sorcerer (Rotax 447) PFA 163-11233		2. 3.92	W.G.Tait	Dunkeswell	31. 5.02P
G-MYAI	Mainair Mercury (Rotax 503) 892-0392-5 & W687		11. 3.92	E.M.Christoffersen	Baxby Manor, Husthwaite	6. 5.02P
G-MYAJ	Rans S-6-ESD Coyote II *(Tail-wheel u/c)* (Rotax 503) 1291.248 & PFA 204-12227		3. 3.92	A.J.Fraley	Kingston Seymour	16. 7.02P
G-MYAK	Solar Wings Pegasus Quasar IITC SW-TQC-0093 & SW-WQT-0506	D- G-MYAK	5. 3.92	R.S.McMaster	Sywell	1. 9.02P
G-MYAM	Murphy Renegade Spirit UK (Rotax 582) PFA 188-11907		6. 3.92	A.F.Reid	Newtownards, Co.of Down	14. 9.01P
G-MYAN	Aerotech MW-5(K) Sorcerer 5K-0017-02 (Rotax 447) *(Full Lotus floats)*	(G-MWNI)	24. 3.92	J.Hollings	Melbourne, Derby	24.11.01P
G-MYAO	Mainair Gemini/Flash IIA (Rotax 503) 894-0392-7 & W689		11. 3.92	L.Hogan	Glenrothes	25. 4.02P
G-MYAP	Thruster T300 9022-T300-501 (Rotax 582))		12. 3.92	W.Fletcher *(Noted 12.01)*	Clench Common	28.11.95P
G-MYAR	Thruster T300 9022-T300-502 (Rotax 503)		12. 3.92	H.G.Denton	Knapthorpe Lodge, Caunton	22. 8.02P
G-MYAS	Mainair Gemini/Flash IIA (Rotax 503) 895-0392-7 & W690		11. 3.92	A.N.Duncanson	Redlands, Swindon	11. 5.02P
G-MYAT	TEAM mini-MAX PFA 186-12017 (Rotax 447)		6. 3.92	M.A.Perry	Elm Farm, Wickford	6. 8.02P
G-MYAU	Mainair Gemini/Flash IIA (Rotax 462) 890-0392-7 & W685		25. 3.92	P.P.Allen	(Ely)	26. 8.01P
G-MYAV	Mainair Mercury 893-0392-5 & W688 (Rotax 503)		23. 3.92	J.Lynch	East Fortune	20. 5.02P
G-MYAY	Microflight Spectrum 027 (Rotax 503)		13. 3.92	S.A.Clarehugh	Eshott	21.12.00P

G-MYAZ	Murphy Renegade Spirit UK		16. 3.92	R.Smith	Kilkerran	2. 8.02P
	(Rotax 582) PFA 188-12027					
G-MYBA	Rans S-6-ESD Coyote II PFA 204-12210		12. 3.92	M.R.Cann	Dunkeswell	8. 5.02P
	(Rotax 503) *(Tail-wheel u/c)*			t/a Climsland Climber Society		
G-MYBB	Maxair Drifter MD.001 & BMAA/HB/014		10. 4.92	M.Ingleton	(Sheerness)	12. 6.92P
	(Rotax 503)	*(Owner seeking parts in 1999: BMAA still assessing design: current status unknown)*				
G-MYBC	CFM Shadow CD BMAA/HB/047		18. 3.92	M.E.Gilbert	Drummaird Farm, Bonnybank	24. 5.02P
	(Rotax 503) *(Originally regd with c/ns K.195 & PFA 206-12221 - PFA c/n indicates a Streak Shadow incorrectly)*					
G-MYBD	Solar Wings Pegasus Quasar IITC		26. 3.92	A.M.Brumpton	(Horncastle)	24. 6.02P
	SW-TQC-0094 & SW-WQT-0511					
G-MYBE	Solar Wings Pegasus Quasar IITC		26. 3.92	D.Lumsdon	(Sunderland)	14. 8.02P
	SW-TQC-0095 & SW-WQT-0512					
G-MYBF	Solar Wings Pegasus XL-Q		26. 3.92	K.H.Pead	(Ipswich)	7.12.02P
	(Rotax 462) SW-TE-0384 & SW-WQ-0513					
G-MYBG	Solar Wings Pegasus XL-Q		26. 3.92	P.A.Henretty & M.Aylett	(Northampton)	26. 5.02P
	(Rotax 462) SW-TE-0385 & SW-WQ-0514					
G-MYBI	Rans S-6-ESD Coyote II *(Tri-cycle u/c)*		26. 3.92	A Cook & S Richens	Clench Common	2. 7.02P
	(Rotax 503) 1291.249 & PFA 204-12186					
G-MYBJ	Mainair Gemini/Flash IIA		2. 4.92	C.Nicholson	Sandtoft	12. 9.00P
	(Rotax 462) 908-0593-7 & W706					
G-MYBL	CFM Shadow CD K.194		2. 4.92	I Jones	Weston Zoyland	19.10.02P
	(Rotax 503)			*(No external registration)*		
G-MYBM	TEAM mini-MAX 91 PFA 186-12212		3. 4.92	B Hunter	Wombleton	22.10.99P
	(Mosler MM-CB35)			*(New owner 12.01)*		
G-MYBN	Hiway Skytrike mkII/Demon 175 BRL-01		14. 4.92	B.R.Lamming	Seaton, Hull	
				(Current status unknown)		
G-MYBO	Solar Wings Pegasus XL-R		16. 4.92	D W Pearce	Enstone	27. 1.02P
	(Rotax 447) SW-TB-1445 & SW-WA-1545					
G-MYBP	Solar Wings Pegasus XL-R/Se		16. 4.92	N. & J.M.Hodgkinson	(Great Orton)	5. 7.01P
	(Rotax 447) SW-TB-1446 & SW-WA-1546					
G-MYBR	Solar Wings Pegasus XL-Q		16. 4.92	M.J.Larbey & G.T.Hunt	(Watford)	16. 6.00P
	(Rotax 462) SW-TE-0386 & SW-WQ-0517		*(Damaged in accident Radwell 21.8.99: current status unknown)*			
G-MYBS	Solar Wings Pegasus XL-Q		16. 4.92	J.L.Parker	(Maidstone)	17. 7.02P
	(Rotax 462) SW-TE-0387 & SW-WQ-0518					
G-MYBT	Solar Wings Pegasus Quasar IITC		16. 4.92	I.D.Rutherford	(High Wycombe)	4. 9.02P
	SW-TQC-0097 & SW-WQT-0519					
G-MYBU	Cyclone Chaser S CH.837	G-69-15	28. 4.92	R.L.Arscott	(Taunton)	21. 1.00P
	(Rotax 447)	G-MYBU				
G-MYBV	Solar Wings Pegasus XL-Q		5. 5.92	G.M.Balaam & F.A.Spiniello		
	(Rotax 462) SW-TE-0393 & SW-WQ-0522				Long Acre Farm, Sandy	26. 1.02P
G-MYBW	Solar Wings Pegasus XL-Q		5. 5.92	J.S.Chapman	Baxby Manor, Husthwaite	22. 8.02P
	(Rotax 462) SW-TE-0394 & SW-WQ-0523					
G-MYBY	Solar Wings Pegasus XL-Q		5. 5.92	P.R.Brooker	Smarden, Kent	12. 8.02P
	(Rotax 462) SW-TE-0396 & SW-WQ-0525					
G-MYBZ	Solar Wings Pegasus XL-Q		5. 5.92	J.M.Todd	Long Marston	27. 9.97P
	(Rotax 462) SW-TE-0397 & SW-WQ-0526					
G-MYCA	Whittaker MW6-T Merlin PFA 164-11821		14. 5.92	R.A.L.Harris	(Andover)	1. 8.02P
	(Rotax 532)					
G-MYCB	Cyclone Chaser S CH.839		18. 5.92	E.B.Jones	(Crickhowell)	6. 1.02P
	(Rotax 447)					
G-MYCE	Solar Wings Pegasus Quasar IITC		14. 5.92	J.G.Robinson	(Scarborough)	27. 6.02P
	SW-TQC-0098 & SW-WQT-0527					
G-MYCF*	Solar Wings Pegasus Quasar IITC		14. 5.92	I.J.Bratt	(Telford)	23. 1.01P
	SW-TQC-0099 & SW-WQT-0528			*(Cancelled 9.11.01 by CAA)*		
G-MYCJ	Mainair Mercury 906-0592-5 & W704		19. 5.92	W.Gray	East Fortune	28.11.02P
	(Rotax 503)					
G-MYCK	Mainair Gemini/Flash IIA		19. 5.92	J.P.Hanlon & A.C.McAllister		
	(Rotax 462) 909-0592-7 & W707				Ince Blundell	18.10.01P
G-MYCL	Mainair Mercury 910-0592-5 & W708		19. 5.92	Palladium Leisure Ltd	RAF Wyton	11. 5.02P
	(Rotax 503)					
G-MYCM	CFM Shadow CD 196		20. 5.92	T.Jones	Redhill	20. 5.99P
	(Rotax 503)					
G-MYCN	Mainair Mercury 901-0492-5 & W696		22. 5.92	P Lowham	Newtownards, Co.of Down	16. 6.02P
	(Rotax 503)					
G-MYCO	Murphy Renegade Spirit UK		28. 5.92	V.A. & C.V.Brierley	(Dover)	27. 7.00P
	(Rotax 582) PFA 188-12020					
G-MYCP	Whittaker MW6 Merlin PFA 164-11505		2. 6.92	A C Jones	(Bilston)	2. 8.02P
	(Rotax 532)					
G-MYCR	Mainair Gemini/Flash IIA		10. 6.92	I.G.Webster	(Stoke-on-Trent)	10. 2.02P
	(Rotax 503) 875-0192-7 & W670					
G-MYCS	Mainair Gemini/Flash IIA		12. 6.92	G.Penson	Baxby Manor, Husthwaite	25. 7.02P
	(Rotax 503) 911-0592-7 & W710			t/a Husthwaite Alpha Group		
G-MYCT	TEAM mini-MAX 91 PFA 186-12163		30. 3.92	S.R.Roberts	Priory Farm, Tibenham	5. 1.02P
	(Rotax 447)					

G-MYCU	Whittaker MW6 Merlin PFA 164-11627 (Rotax 532) *(PFA c/n duplicates Streak Shadow G-ORAF)*	9. 6.92	R.D.Thomasson	London Colney	3.12.02P
G-MYCV	Mainair Mercury 913-0792-5 & W712 (Rotax 503)	12. 6.92	D.P.Creedy	(Crewe)	29. 8.01P
G-MYCW	Powerchute Kestrel 00420 (Rotax 503)	15. 6.92	C.D.Treffers	(Basildon)	30. 4.02P
G-MYCX	Powerchute Kestrel 00421 (Rotax 503)	15. 6.92	D.Pedlow	(Oswestry)	19.10.02P
G-MYCY	Powerchute Kestrel 00422 (Rotax 503)	15. 6.92	R.S.McFadyen t/a British Powered Paragliding Association	(Tamworth)	26. 7.02P
G-MYDA	Powerchute Kestrel 00424 (Rotax 503)	15. 6.92	K.J.Greatrix	(Sleaford)	17.11.02P
G-MYDB	Powerchute Kestrel 00425 (Rotax 503)	15. 6.92	Coppard Plant Hire Ltd	(Crowborough)	28.10.93P
G-MYDC	Mainair Mercury 916-0792-5 & W715 (Rotax 503)	23. 6.92	D.J.Boylan & D.Gordon	Rufforth	12. 9.01P
G-MYDD	CFM Shadow CD K.197	22. 6.92	C.H.Gem	(Marbella, Spain)	22.11.95P
G-MYDE	CFM Shadow CD K.187 (Rotax 503)	24. 6.92	D.N.L.Howell	(Malvern)	6. 4.02P
G-MYDF	TEAM mini-MAX 91 PFA 186-12129 (Rotax 447)	24. 6.92	W.W.Vinton	(Westbury-on-Severn)	30. 8.02P
G-MYDI	Solar Wings Pegasus XL Tug (Rotax 462HP) SW-TE-0402 & SW-WA-1557	26. 6.92	W.Greenwood t/a Southern Hang Gliding Aerotow Group	Swanborough	17. 6.01P
G-MYDJ	Solar Wings Pegasus XL Tug (Rotax 462) SW-TE-0403 & SW-WA-1558	1. 7.92	E.A.Potter & P.Stevens t/a Cambridgeshire Aerotow Club	Sutton Meadows, Ely	24. 5.02P
G-MYDK	Rans S-6-ESD Coyote II *(Tri-cycle u/c)* (Rotax 503) 0392.276 & PFA 204-12239	21. 4.92	J.W.Caush	(Whitley Bay)	27. 6.02P
G-MYDL	Aerotech MW-5(K) Sorcerer PFA 163-12106	26. 6.92	S.J.Field	(Bridgwater)	
G-MYDM	Whittaker MW6-S Fatboy Flyer (Rotax 582) PFA 164-12105	26. 6.92	S.J.Miles	Rochester	19. 6.02P
G-MYDN	Quad City Challenger II UK (Rotax 462) CH2-1091-UK-0736 & PFA 177-12245	30. 6.92	T.C.& R.Hooks	Newtownards, Co.of Down	8.10.02P
G-MYDO	Rans S-5 Coyote (Rotax 447) 89.110 & PFA 193-12274	6. 7.92	B.J.Benton	Long Marston	24.10.02P
G-MYDP	Kolb Twinstar Mk.3 (Rotax 503) K0002-1291 & PFA 205-12231	15. 7.92	G.C.Reid	Deenethorpe	6. 8.02P
G-MYDR	Thruster T300 9072-T300-505 (Rotax 582)	21. 7.92	H.G.Soper	(Lewes)	19. 7.02P
G-MYDS	Quad City Challenger II UK (Rotax 503) CH2-1289-UK-0500 & PFA 177-11716	6. 3.90	A.C.Ryall	(Swansea)	4.11.02P
G-MYDU	Thruster T300 9072-T300-504 (Rotax 582)	21. 7.92	Euroflight Microlight Club Ltd	Dromore, Co.Down	9. 6.02P
G-MYDV	Mainair Gemini/Flash IIA (Rotax 462) 917-0892-7 & W716	29. 7.92	A.Gibson *(Op Northern Microlight School)*	St.Michaels	3.10.02P
G-MYDW	Whittaker MW6 Merlin PFA 164-12184 (Rotax 503)	27. 7.92	A.Chidlow	Mansfield	5. 8.02P
G-MYDX	Rans S-6-ESD Coyote II PFA 204-12238 (Rotax 503) *(Tri-cycle u/c)*	27. 7.92	R.J.Goodburn *"The Ruptured Duck"*	Spanhoe	19. 5.02P
G-MYDZ	Mignet HM-1000 Balerit 66 (Rotax 582)	3. 8.92	D S Simpson	(Luton)	27. 5.02P
G-MYEA	Solar Wings Pegasus XL-Q (Rotax 462HP) SW-TE-0404 & SW-WQ-0537	28. 7.92	A.M.Taylor	Long Marston	2.11.02P
G-MYEC	Solar Wings Pegasus XL-Q (Rotax 462HP) SW-TE-0406 & SW-WQ-0539	28. 7.92	D.Young t/a Pegasus Flight Training	Kemble	31. 8.02P
G-MYED	Solar Wings Pegasus XL-R (Rotax 462HP) SW-TE-0407 & SW-WA-1559	28. 7.92	A.J.Kentzer	(Sheffield)	28. 3.02P
G-MYEE*	Thruster TST Mk.1 8089-TST-206 *(Regd with c/n 087-TST-206) (Possibly ex ZK-FRW; imported 12.90)* *(Noted as wreck on 16.7.98; cancelled 16.10.98 as destroyed) (Wings, tail & fuselage parts remain 12.01)*	11. 8.92	(M Jones)	Westbury, Wilts	1.12.98P
G-MYEG	Solar Wings Pegasus XL-R (Rotax 447) SW-TB-1447 & SW-WA-1560	4. 8.92	D.G.Matthews	(London Colney)	15.10.01P
G-MYEH	Solar Wings Pegasus XL-R (Rotax 447) SW-TB-1448 & SW-WA-1561	4. 8.92	M.J.Hall t/a G-MYEH Flying Group	Roddidge, Fradley	18. 4.02P
G-MYEI	Cyclone Chaser S CH.841 (Rotax 447)	18. 8.92	T.J.Barley	(Sawbridgeworth)	26. 4.02P
G-MYEJ	Cyclone Chaser S CH.842 (Rotax 447)	18. 8.92	D.A.Cochrane	Newnham, Baldock	3. 4.00P
G-MYEK	Solar Wings Pegasus Quasar IITC (Rotax 582/40) SW-TQD-0108 & SW-WQT-0540	7. 8.92	B.A.McWilliams *(See G-MWZF)*	Long Marston	17. 7.00P
G-MYEM	Solar Wings Pegasus Quasar IITC (Rotax 582/40) SW-TQD-0101 & SW-WQT-0542	7. 8.92	D.J.Moore	Oakington, Cambs	26. 8.01P

G-MYEN	Solar Wings Pegasus Quasar IITC (Rotax 582/40) SW-TQD-0105 & SW-WQT-0543		7. 8.92	P.R.Jeffcoat & D.Johnson	Long Marston	11. 5.02P
G-MYEO	Solar Wings Pegasus Quasar IITC (Rotax 582/40) SW-TQD-0106 & SW-WQT-0544		7. 8.92	Avelec Ltd	Enstone	30. 8.01P
G-MYEP	CFM Shadow CD K.205 (Rotax 503)		13. 8.92	E.M.Middleton	(Hereford)	15. 4.02P
G-MYER	Cyclone AX2000 B.1052901 & CA.001 (Rotax 582/48)	G-69-27 G-MYER/G-69-5/59-GF	19. 8.92	W.J.Whyte	Insch	3. 7.02P
G-MYES	Rans S-6-ESD Coyote II *(Tri-cycle u/c)* (Rotax 503) 0392.283 & PFA 204-12254		3. 7.92	F.J.Percival t/a Dairy House Flyers	Dairy House Farm, Worleston	9. 7.02P
G-MYET	Whittaker MW6 Merlin PFA 164-12318 (Rotax 503)		19. 8.92	M.B.Haine	(Christchurch)	1.10.02P
G-MYEU	Mainair Gemini/Flash IIA (Rotax 503) 918-0892-7 & W718		1. 9.92	G.J.Webster & G.J.Williams	Mill Farm, Shifnal	11. 5.02P
G-MYEV	Whittaker MW6 Merlin PFA 164-11250		25. 8.92	M.J.Batchelor *(Valid CofR 4.01: current status unknown)*	(Thornbury, Bristol)	
G-MYEW	Powerchute Kestrel 00417 (Rotax 503) *(Fitted with Harley Ram-air parachute)*		28. 8.92	J.Weston	(Grantham)	13. 7.02P
G-MYEX	Powerchute Kestrel 00426 (Rotax 503)		28. 8.92	R.S.McFadyen	(Tamworth)	17.11.02P
G-MYFA	Powerchute Kestrel 00429 (Rotax 503)		28. 8.95	D.A.Gardner	(Balfron)	23. 3.98P
G-MYFE	Rans S-6-ESD Coyote II PFA 204-12232 (Rotax 503)		1. 9.92	K.A.Mitchell	(Henley-in-Arden)	22. 9.02P
G-MYFH	Quad City Challenger II UK (Rotax 503) CH2-0292-0798 & PFA 177-12282		9. 9.92	G.R.Inston	(Birmingham)	26. 7.02P
G-MYFI	Cyclone AX3 C.3093159 & CA.002 (Rotax 503)		9. 9.92	C.M.Bulmer & P.M.Voznick	Long Acre Farm, Sandy	5.12.00P
G-MYFK	Solar Wings Pegasus Quasar IITC SW-TQD-0113 & SW-WQT-0553		11. 9.92	L.M.Bassett	(Bedford)	24. 9.02P
G-MYFL	Solar Wings Pegasus Quasar IITC (Rotax 582/40) SW-TQD-0103 & SW-WQT-0541/A *(Originally regd as c/n SW-WQT-0554: replacement wing fitted to trike G-MYEL after wing stolen 1.1.93)*		11. 9.92	S.B.Wilkes	Roddige, Fradley	9. 6.02P
G-MYFM	Murphy Renegade Spirit UK (Rotax 582) PFA 188-12249		9. 9.92	A.C.Cale	Long Marston	20. 5.02P
G-MYFN	Rans S-5 Coyote (Rotax 447) 89.112 & PFA 193-12273		16. 9.92	D.J.Minary	Rufforth	20. 5.02P
G-MYFO	Cyclone Chaser S CH.843 (Rotax 377)		22. 9.92	A.P.Skipper	Sywell	29. 5.02P
G-MYFP	Mainair Gemini/Flash IIA (Rotax 503) 920-0992-7 & W719		2.10.92	J.S.Hill & G.H.S.Skilton	(Stone)	26.12.02P
G-MYFR	Mainair Gemini/Flash IIA (Rotax 503) 921-0992-7 & W720		30. 9.92	P.G.Bright	(Hull)	14 6.01P
G-MYFT	Mainair Scorcher 922-0992-3 & W234 (Rotax 503)		30. 9.92	N.Crowther-Wilton	Enstone	17. 1.02P
G-MYFU	Mainair Gemini/Flash IIA (Rotax 462) 924-1092-7 & W722		7.10.92	P.E.Hudson	Brook Farm, Pilling	24. 7.02P
G-MYFV	Cyclone AX3 C.2083050 (Rotax 503)		6.10.92	P.J.Barton	Long Acre Farm, Sandy	24. 3.01P
G-MYFW	Cyclone AX3 C.2083051 (Rotax 503)		13.10.92	T.W.Stewart & D.L.Frankland t/a G-MYFW Flying Group	Eshott	4. 8.02P
G-MYFX	Solar Wings Pegasus XL-Q (Rotax 462) SW-TE-0295 & SW-WQ-0378		25. 6.93	M.M.Danek	Redlands, Swindon	6. 8.01P
G-MYFY	Cyclone AX3 C.2083047 (Rotax 503)		1.10.92	T.A.Simpson	Long Acre Farm, Sandy	24. 4.02P
G-MYFZ	Cyclone AX3 C.2083048 (Rotax 503)		20.10.92	M.L.Smith t/a Buzzard Flying Group	Popham	6.12.02P
G-MYGD	Cyclone AX3 C.2083049 (Rotax 503)		21.10.92	D.Young t/a Kemble Flying Club	Kemble	3.12.02P
G-MYGE	Whittaker MW6 Merlin PFA 164-11650 (Rotax 532)		20.10.92	M.D. & S.M.North	Manor Farm, Croughton	24. 6.97P
G-MYGF	TEAM mini-MAX 91 PFA 186-12175 (Rotax 447)		22.10.92	R.D.Barnard	Ley Farm, Chirk	31. 7.01P
G-MYGH	Rans S-6-ESD Coyote II (Rotax 503) 0692.318 & PFA 204-12335		30.10.92	A.J.Alexander, K.G.Diamond & B.Knight	Redhill	16. 7.02P
G-MYGI	Cyclone Chaser S 447 CH.844 (Rotax 447)		2.11.92	B.Richardson	(Morpeth)	30.12.01P
G-MYGJ	Mainair Mercury 923-0992-7 & W721 (Rotax 503)		5.10.92	N.E.Parkinson	Arclid Green, Sandbach	9.12.01P
G-MYGK	Cyclone Chaser S CH.846 (Rotax 508)		3.11.92	P.C.Collins	(Bath)	14.11.95P
G-MYGM	Quad City Challenger II UK (Rotax 503) CH2-0391-UK-0662 & PFA 177-12261		6.11.92	J.White & G.J.Williams	Mill Farm, Shifnall	6. 8.01P

G-MYGO	CFM Shadow CD K.114 (Rotax 503)		28. 7.92	R.C.S.Mason	Sywell	28. 2.02P
G-MYGP	Rans S-6-ESD Coyote II *(Tail-wheel u/c)* (Rotax 503) 0992.349 & PFA 204-12368		10.11.92	J.H.Kempton	(Salcombe)	20. 5.02P
G-MYGR	Rans S-6-ESD Coyote II PFA 204-12378 (Rotax 503)		16.11.92	R.B.M.Etherington	(Totnes)	9. 8.02P
G-MYGT	Solar Wings Pegasus XL Tug (Rotax 462) SW-TE-0413 & SW-WA-1569		13.11.92	J.J.Hoer t/a Condors Aerotow Syndicate	Dunkeswell	29. 3.02P
G-MYGU	Solar Wings Pegasus XL-R (Rotax 462) SW-TE-0414 & SW-WA-1570		13.11.92	G.J.Boyer	(Highbridge)	26. 7.02P
G-MYGV	Solar Wings Pegasus XL Tug (Rotax 462HP) SW-TE-0415 & SW-WA-1571		13.11.92	D.J.Brixton tr Shropshire Tow Group	Bishops Castle, Shropshire	20. 5.02P
G-MYGZ	Mainair Gemini/Flash IIA (Rotax 582) 928-1192-7 & W726		18.11.92	M Ryall	(Stockport)	11. 4.02P
G-MYHF	Mainair Gemini/Flash IIA (Rotax 503) 929-1092-7 & W727		25.11.92	R.W.Thornborough	(Port Sunlight)	19. 7.02P
G-MYHG	Cyclone AX3 C.2103070 (Rotax 503)		27.11.92	I.McDiarmid t/a G-MYHG Flying Group	Strathaven	22. 8.02P
G-MYHH	Cyclone AX3 C.2103069 & CA.006 (Rotax 503)		30.11.92	M.L.Smith	Popham	23. 6.02P
G-MYHI	Rans S-6-ESD Coyote II *(Tailwheel u/c)* (Rotax 503) 0692.312 & PFA 204-12279		8.12.92	M.Mills	Otherton, Cannock	11.12.01P
G-MYHJ	Cyclone AX3 C.2103073 (Rotax 503) *(Reported as c/n C.3093157 - see G-MYME)*		11.12.92	B.Ireland	Clench Common	13. 5.02P
G-MYHK	Rans S-6-ESD Coyote II *(Tri-cycle u/c)* (Rotax 503) 0692.311 & PFA 204-12349		3.12.92	M.R.Williamson	Sutton Meadows, Ely	20. 5.02P
G-MYHL	Mainair Gemini/Flash IIA (Rotax 503) 932-0193-7 & W730		21.12.92	P.J.Lomax & J.A.Robinson	(Chorley)	3. 2.02P
G-MYHM	Cyclone AX3 C.2103068 & CA.007 (Rotax 503)		18.12.92	A.J.Bergman	Popham	14. 2.02P
G-MYHN	Mainair Gemini/Flash IIA (Rotax 582) 933-0193-7 & W731		29.12.92	D.M.Waddle	(Pontefract)	18. 5.02P
G-MYHP	Rans S-6-ESD Coyote II *(Tri-cycle u/c)* (Rotax 503) 0892.315 & PFA 204-12406		8. 1.93	S F Winter *"Grass Stripper"*	(Calne)	17. 7.02P
G-MYHR	Cyclone AX3 C.2103071 (Rotax 503)	G-68-8 G-MYHR	15. 1.93	G.Humphrey t/a G-MYHR Flying Group	Long Marston	7. 5.02P
G-MYHS	Powerchute Kestrel 00433 (Rotax 503) *(Frame No.00433/Parachute No.931013/Engine No.4104716)*		26. 1.93	R.Kent	(Newark)	6. 4.01P
G-MYHX	Mainair Gemini/Flash IIA (Rotax 582) 930-1292-7 & W728		2.12.92	C.P.Simmons	(London N10)	23. 4.01P
G-MYIA	Quad City Challenger II UK (Rotax 503) PFA 177-12400		21. 1.93	I.J.Arkieson	Ley Farm, Chirk	3.10.00P
G-MYIE	Whittaker MW6-S Fatboy Flyer (Rotax 532) PFA 164-11800		26. 1.93	T.C.Viner	(Coventry)	1. 6.02P
G-MYIF	CFM Shadow CD 217 (Rotax 503)		2. 2.93	A.Errington	(Market Drayton)	6. 6.01P
G-MYIH	Mainair Gemini/Flash IIA (Rotax 582) 937-0293-7 & W734		9. 3.93	C.A.Murray t/a G-MYIH Flying Group	(Loughton, Essex)	27. 5.02P
G-MYII	TEAM mini-MAX 91 PFA 186-12119 (Mosler CB40)		10.11.92	L.B.Roberts	Halwell, Totnes	5.11.02P
G-MYIJ	Cyclone AX3 C.2103072 (Rotax 503)		8. 2.93	G.A.Breen	(Lagos, Algarve)	22. 4.02P
G-MYIK	Kolb Twinstar mk.3 PFA 205-12220 (Rotax 582)		13. 1.93	J.Latimer	Barton	19. 6.02P
G-MYIL	Cyclone Chaser S CH.849 (Rotax 508)		3. 3.93	R.A.Rawes *"Fricky"*	Over Farm, Gloucester	2. 2.02P
G-MYIM	Solar Wings Pegasus Quasar IITC (Rotax 582) SW-TQD-0122 & SW-WQT-0579	(EI-) G-MYIM	22. 2.93	D.Forde	Clare Galway, Co.Galway	18. 5.02P
G-MYIN	Solar Wings Pegasus Quasar IITC (Rotax 582/40) SW-TQD-0123 & SW-WQT-0580		22. 2.93	W.P.Hughes	Long Acre Farm, Sandy	1. 8.02P
G-MYIO	Solar Wings Pegasus Quasar IITC (Rotax 582/40) SW-TQD-0124 & SW-WQT-0581		22. 2.93	K.W.Brock	(London SW19)	3.10.01P
G-MYIP	CFM Shadow CD K.198 (Rotax 503)		16. 3.93	S.Marshall & A.Halsall	(Southport)	18.11.02P
G-MYIR	Rans S-6-ESD Coyote II *(Tri-cycle u/c)* (Rotax 503) 0892.344 & PFA 204-12458		17. 3.93	P.Vergette	North Coates	29. 8.02P
G-MYIS	Rans S-6-ESD Coyote II PFA 204-12382 (Rotax 503) *(Tri-cycle u/c)*		31.12.92	I.R.Henderson	Moss Side Farm, Carluke	20. 8.02P
G-MYIT	Cyclone Chaser S CH.850 (Rotax 508)		19. 3.93	R.Barringer	Ravensthorpe, Northampton	28. 3.99P
G-MYIU	Cyclone AX3/503 C.3013084 (Zanzoterra Z-202)		22. 3.93	G.R.Hill	(Belfast)	17. 2.02P
G-MYIV	Mainair Gemini/Flash IIA (Rotax 582) 938-0393-7 & W735		30. 3.93	P.S.Nicholls	Finmere	2. 5.02P

G-MYIX	Quad City Challenger II UK (Rotax 503) CH2-0191-UK-0615 & PFA 177-12260	5. 1.93	A.Studley	(Crewkerne)	12. 3.02P
G-MYIY	Mainair Gemini/Flash IIA (Rotax 503) 942-0493-7 & W737	1. 4.93	I.C.Macbeth	Arclid Green, Sandbach	22. 6.00P
G-MYIZ	TEAM mini-MAX 91 PFA 186-12347 (Rotax 447)	31. 3.93	S.E.Richardson	Escrick, York	8.11.01P
G-MYJB	Mainair Gemini/Flash IIA (Rotax 503) 943-0593-7 & W738	7. 4.93	T.J.Dutton	RAF Wyton	5. 5.01P
G-MYJC	Mainair Gemini/Flash IIA (Rotax 462) 944-0593-7 & W739	7. 4.93	R G Hearsey	(Rye)	14. 4.02P
G-MYJD	Rans S-6-ESD Coyote II *(Tri-cycle u/c)* (Rotax 503) 0792.324 & PFA 204-12360	23. 4.93	D.M.Newbould *(Op Mercury Microlight Club)*	Brook Farm, Pilling	18.12.02P
G-MYJF	Thruster T.300 9013-T300-509 (Rotax 582)	14. 4.93	B.McConville	(Craigavon, Co Armagh)	1. 7.02P
G-MYJG	Thruster Super T.300 9043-ST300-510 (Rotax 582) *(Single-seat conversion)*	14. 4.93	J.E.L.Goodall	(Broadway)	5. 9.02P
G-MYJJ	Solar Wings Pegasus Quasar IITC (Rotax 582/40) SW-TQD-0131 & SW-WQT-0591	27. 4.93	J.H.Sparks	Franklyns Field, Chewton Mendip	15. 2.02P
G-MYJK	Solar Wings Pegasus Quasar IITC (Rotax 582/40) SW-TQD-0132 & SW-WQT-0592	27. 4.93	P.Kneeshaw	Insch	15. 6.02P
G-MYJL	Rans S-6-ESD Coyote II *(Tri-cycle u/c)* (Rotax 503) 0792.328 & PFA 204-12476	28. 4.93	C.R.Marriott	Sutton Meadows, Ely	14. 8.02P
G-MYJM	Mainair Gemini/Flash IIA (Rotax 582) 945-0593-7 & W740	29. 4.93	V.D.Carmichael	Newtownards, Co.of Down	27. 9.02P
G-MYJN	Mainair Mercury 946-0593-7 & W741 (Rotax 503)	29. 4.93	M T Jones	(Tullamore, Co.Offaly)	24. 5.95P
G-MYJO	Cyclone Chaser S CH.851 (Rotax 508)	30. 4.93	J.F.Phillips	(Liskeard)	24. 7.99P
G-MYJP	Murphy Renegade Spirit UK (Rotax 582) 357 & PFA 188-12045	3. 4.91	P.Bennett	Swinford, Rugby	6.11.01P
G-MYJR	Mainair Mercury 947-0593-7 & W742 (Rotax 503)	12. 5.93	C.J.Johnson	(Hornchurch)	7. 7.02P
G-MYJS	Solar Wings Pegasus Quasar IITC 6581 (Rotax 582)	19. 5.93	P.R.Saunders	Long Acre Farm, Sandy	1. 5.02P
G-MYJT	Solar Wings Pegasus Quasar IITC 6582 (Rotax 582/40)	19. 5.93	G.Stadler	Eshott	7. 4.01P
G-MYJU	Solar Wings Pegasus Quasar IITC 6573 (Rotax 582)	19. 5.93	P.G.Penhaligan	Brook Farm, Pilling	27. 6.02P
G-MYJW	Cyclone Chaser S CH.856 (Rotax 508)	19. 5.93	P.M.Coppola *(Noted 7.99: current status unknown)*	East Fortune	10. 9.94P
G-MYJY	Rans S-6-ESD Coyote II *(Tri-cycle u/c)* (Rotax 503) 0692.317 & PFA 204-12346	24. 5.93	F.N.Pearson	Baxby Manor, Husthwaite	18. 8.00P
G-MYJZ	Whittaker MW5-D Sorcerer (Rotax 447) PFA 163-12385	22. 4.93	P.A.Aston	(Newton Abbot)	2.12.99P
G-MYKA	Cyclone AX3 C.3013086 (Rotax 503)	25. 5.93	K.R.Haskell	(Blandford Forum)	27. 1.02P
G-MYKB	Kolb Twinstar mk.3 (Rotax 582) K0007-0193 & PFA 205-12398	31. 3.93	D.Young	Eastbach Farm, Coleford	1. 9.00P
G-MYKC	Mainair Gemini/Flash IIA (Rotax 582) 948-0593-7 & W743	26. 5.93	B.J.Egerton	(Bootle)	4. 6.01P
G-MYKD	Cyclone Chaser S CH.857 (Rotax 447)	26. 5.93	J.V.Clewer	(Ashford, Kent)	22. 8.02P
G-MYKE	CFM Shadow BD K.031 (Rotax 447)	14. 1.88	M.Hughes t/a MKH Engineering	Emlyn's Field, Rhuallt	26.10.96P
G-MYKF	Cyclone AX3 C.3013083 (Rotax 503)	8. 6.93	P.Jones	Brook Farm, Pilling	10. 7.01P
G-MYKG	Mainair Gemini/Flash IIA (Rotax 582) 950-0693-7 & W745	21. 6.93	P.G.Angus	Higher Barn Farm, Houghton	15.12.01P
G-MYKH	Mainair Gemini/Flash IIA (Rotax 582) 951-0693-7 & W746	21. 6.93	K.G. & G.F.Atkinson t/a F.Atkinson & Sons	Rufforth	9.11.02P
G-MYKI	Mainair Mercury 953-0693-7 & W748 (Rotax 503)	21. 6.93	M.Wilkinson	East Fortune	18.12.01P
G-MYKJ	TEAM mini-MAX PFA 186-12215 (Rotax 508)	10. 6.93	P.I.Frost	Guilsborough, Northampton	25. 2.02P
G-MYKL	Medway Raven X MRB116/104 (Rotax 447)	6. 7.93	S.Hutchinson	RAF Wyton	22.10.02P
G-MYKN	Rans S-6-ESD Coyote II *(Tri-cycle u/c)* (Rotax 503) 0892.338 & PFA 204-12361	23. 6.93	S.E. & L.Hartles *"Captain Airfix"*	Lower Mountpleasant, Chatteris	13.11.01P
G-MYKO	Whittaker MW6-S Fatboy Flyer (Hirth 2706) PFA 164-11919	25. 6.93	J.Glover	(Bristol)	30. 7.02P
G-MYKP	Solar Wings Pegasus Quasar IITC 6627 (Rotax 582/40)	7. 7.93	J.Mayer	(Stoke-on-Trent)	24.10.02P
G-MYKR	Solar Wings Pegasus Quasar IITC 6635 (Rotax 582/40)	7. 7.93	C.Stallard	Larkins Farm, Laindon	26. 8.02P

G-MYKS	Solar Wings Pegasus Quasar IITC (Rotax 582/40)	6636		7. 7.93	M.Hurn	Graveley Farm, Herts	26. 5.02P
G-MYKT	Cyclone AX3 (Rotax 503)	C.3013082		5. 7.93	P.J.Hepburn	Stoke, Kent	5. 8.02P
G-MYKV	Mainair Gemini/Flash IIA (Rotax 503)	954-0793-7 & W749		13. 7.93	J.White & P.Gulliver	Mill Farm, Shifnal	13. 2.02P
G-MYKW	Mainair Mercury (Rotax 503)	960-0893-7 & W755		9. 7.93	E.D.Bailey	(Cramlington)	4. 4.02P
G-MYKX	Mainair Mercury (Rotax 503)	961-0893-7 & W756		3. 9.93	N.P.Hurst	East Fortune	14. 5.02P
G-MYKY	Mainair Mercury (Rotax 503)	962-0893-7 & W757		6. 8.93	R.P.Jewitt	(York)	9.11.02P
G-MYKZ	TEAM mini-MAX 91 (Rotax 503)	PFA 186-11841	G-BVAV	26. 7.93	J.S.Harris	Old Sarum	21. 5.02P
G-MYLB	TEAM mini-MAX 91 (Rotax 532)	PFA 186-12419		2. 8.93	S.Stockill	RAF Halton	13.11.02P
G-MYLC	Pegasus Quantum 15 (Rotax 503)	6634		9. 8.93	D.M.Wood	(Banbury)	9. 6.02P
G-MYLD	Rans S-6-ESD Coyote II (Rotax 503) *(Tail-wheel u/c)*	PFA 204-12394		1. 3.93	J.White	(Ballymitty)	23. 8.02P
G-MYLE	Pegasus Quantum 15	6609		9. 8.93	Susan E.Powell	Enstone	29. 5.02P
G-MYLF	Rans S-6-ESD Coyote II *(Tri-cycle u/c)* (Rotax 503)	0493.483 & PFA 204-12544		4. 8.93	S J Honeybourne *"Low Flyer"*	(Grantham)	6. 1.03P
G-MYLG	Mainair Gemini/Flash IIA (Rotax 503)	959-0893-7 & W754		6. 8.93	B.A.Coombe	Corn Wood Farm, Adversane, Sussex	8. 5.02P
G-MYLH	Pegasus Quantum 15	6632		27. 8.93	A.R.Ashworth	(Radstock)	22. 6.02P
G-MYLI	Pegasus Quantum 15	6645		11. 8.93	A.M.Keyte	(West Wickham)	9. 5.02P
G-MYLJ	Cyclone Chaser S (Rotax 447)	CH.858		24. 8.93	B.W.Atkinson	North Coates	13. 7.02P
G-MYLK	Pegasus Quantum 15	6602		27. 8.93	C.L.Minter t/a G-MYLK Group	Deenethorpe	24. 9.02P
G-MYLL	Pegasus Quantum 15 (Rotax 462HP)	6650		31. 8.93	N.Demmar	(Warminster)	20. 4.02P
G-MYLM	Pegasus Quantum 15 (Rotax 582/40)	6651	(EC-) G-MYLM	31. 8.93	A.Young	Knapthorpe Lodge, Caunton	29. 7.02P
G-MYLN	Kolb Twinstar mk.3 (Rotax 582)	K0010-0193 & PFA 205-12430		3. 9.93	C.D.Hatcher	Deenethorpe	14. 6.02P
G-MYLO	Rans S-6-ESD Coyote II *(Tri-cycle u/c)* (Rotax 503)	0692.313 & PFA 204-12334		9. 9.93	A.Thornton	Ince Blundell	4.12.02P
G-MYLP	Kolb Twinstar mk.3 (Rotax 582)	K0005-0992 & PFA 205-12391	(G-BVCR)	9. 9.93	R.Thompson	(Bristol)	27. 5.99P
G-MYLR	Mainair Gemini/Flash IIA (Rotax 582)	964-0993-7 & W759		17. 9.93	L.Allen-McNaught & N.A.Angus	East Fortune	21. 8.02P
G-MYLS	Mainair Mercury (Rotax 503)	966-0993-7 & W761		5.10.93	D.Burnell-Higgs	Shobdon	6.11.96P
G-MYLT	Mainair Blade (Rotax 912)	967-1093-7 & W762		23. 9.93	A.R.Walsh	Ince Blundell	29. 5.02P
G-MYLV	CFM Shadow CD (Rotax 503)	220		24. 9.93	G.Gilhead & R.G.M.Proost t/a Aviation for Paraplegics & Tetraplegics Trust	Old Sarum	30. 3.02P
G-MYLW	Rans S-6-ESD Coyote II *(Tri-cycle u/c)* (Rotax 503)	1292.401 & PFA 204-12560		4. 8.93	M.J.Phillips	Priory Farm, Tibenham	15. 6.02P
G-MYLX	Medway Raven X (Rotax 447) *(Sailwing c/n also quoted for G-MYVV)*	MRB113/109		6.10.93	T.M.Knight	(Luton)	12. 2.00P
G-MYLY	Medway Raven X) (Rotax 447) *(Sailwing c/n also quoted for G-MYVU)*	MRB001/108		23. 9.93	C.R.Smith	(Stanford-le-Hope)	3.10.94P
G-MYLZ	Pegasus Quantum 15 (Rotax 462)	6672		6.10.93	J.L.Pollard & K.M.Walter	Knapthorpe Lodge, Caunton	21.11.02P
G-MYMB	Pegasus Quantum 15 (Rotax 582/40)	6674		6.10.93	C.A.Green *"Firebird"*	(Winterborne Earls)	27. 3.02P
G-MYMC	Pegasus Quantum 15 (Rotax 582/40)	6675		6.10.93	D.A.Smith & E.Robshaw	Rufforth	13. 1.02P
G-MYME	Cyclone AX3 (Rotax 503)	C.3093157		13.10.93	M.L.Smith *(See G-MYHJ)*	Popham	17.11.02P
G-MYMF	Cyclone AX3 (Rotax 503)	C.3093158		18.10.93	M.McClelland t/a McClelland Aviation	Old Sarum	8.11.02P
G-MYMH	Rans S-6-ESD Coyote II *(Tri-cycle u/c)* (Rotax 503)	0793.520 & PFA 204-12576		20.10.93	A P Armitage	(Blandford Forum)	19. 6.02P
G-MYMI	Kolb Twinstar mk.3 (Rotax 582)	K0016-0693 & PFA 205-12537		21.10.93	R.P.T.Harris	(High Wycombe)	27. 8.02P
G-MYMJ	Medway Raven X (Rotax 447) *(Sailwing c/n also quoted for G-MYVX)*	MRB004/110		28.10.93	N.Brigginshaw	RAF Wyton	26.10.02P
G-MYMK	Mainair Gemini/Flash IIA (Rotax 582)	968-1193-7 & W763		29.10.93	A.Britton	(Rickmansworth)	14.12.02P
G-MYML	Mainair Mercury (Rotax 503)	969-1193-7 & W765		29.10.93	D.J.Dalley	(Weymouth)	7. 6.01P

G-MYMM	Air Creation Ultraflight Fun 18S GT bis (Rotax 503) 93/001		30. 9.93	A.C.Parsons	Kingston Seymour	23. 8.01P
G-MYMN	Whittaker MW6 Merlin PFA 164-12124 (Rotax 582)		29.10.93	K.J.Cole	Over Farm, Gloucester	6. 6.02P
G-MYMO	Mainair Gemini/Flash IIA (Rotax 503) 955-0793-7 & W750		24. 6.93	T.Jones	(Nantwich)	16. 9.02P
G-MYMP	Rans S-6-ESD Coyote II *(Tri-cycle u/c)* (Rotax 503) 1291.250 & PFA 204-12436	(G-CHAZ)	5.11.93	J.B.Mayes	Sutton Meadows, Ely	22.12.01P
G-MYMR	Rans S-6-ESD Coyote II *(Tri-cycle u/c)* (Rotax 503) PFA 204-12580		17.11.93	J.Neilands	(Ballybofey, Co.Donegal)	11. 5.02P
G-MYMS	Rans S-6-ESD Coyote II *(Tri-cycle u/c)* (Rotax 503) 0893.526 & PFA 204-12581		17.11.93	M.R.Johnson & P.G.Briscoe	Long Marston	30.10.02P
G-MYMT	Mainair Mercury 970-1193-7 & W766 (Rotax 503)		19.11.93	W. & C.A.Bradshaw	St.Michaels	9.12.02P
G-MYMV	Mainair Gemini/Flash IIA (Rotax 503) 971-1193-7 & W767		26.11.93	A.Szczepanek	(Warrington)	8. 4.02P
G-MYMW	Cyclone AX3 C.3093156 (Rotax 503)		23.11.93	L.J.Perring	Oakley, Beds	21. 4.02P
G-MYMX	Pegasus Quantum 15 6705 (Rotax 582/40)		1.12.93	N.F.McKenzie	(Haddrington, Edinburgh)	23. 6.02P
G-MYMY	Cyclone Chaser S CH.860 (Rotax 508)		7. 9.93	D.L.Hadley	(Canterbury)	29. 5.02P
G-MYMZ	Cyclone AX3 C.3093154 (Rotax 503)		7.12.93	The Microlight School (Lichfield) Ltd	Roddige, Fradley	28. 9.01P
G-MYNA	CFM Shadow C K.023 (Rotax 503)		10. 2.88	D.D.Parry	(Ware)	4. 8.02P
G-MYNB	Pegasus Quantum 15 6719 (Rotax 582/40)		14.12.93	S.B.C.Wall	(Melton Mowbray)	14. 6.02P
G-MYNC	Mainair Mercury K973-1293-7 & W769 (Rotax 503) *(Supplied as Mainair Kit)*		17.12.93	A.Brotheridge	Redlands, Swindon	12. 5.01P
G-MYND	Mainair Gemini/Flash IIA (Rotax 503) 841-0591-7 & W635		28. 5.91	P.D.Daniel & C.O'Brian	Sandtoft	23. 4.02P
G-MYNE	Rans S-6-ESD Coyote II PFA 204-12497 (Rotax 503) *(Tail-wheel u/c)*		25. 6.93	J N W Moss	Sywell	4. 7.01P
G-MYNF	Mainair Mercury 974-1293-7 & W770 (Rotax 503)		17. 1.94	J.Wallis t/a G-MYNF Group	(Prudhoe)	24. 1.02P
G-MYNH	Rans S-6-ESD Coyote II *(Tail-wheel u/c)* (Rotax 912) 0493.487 & PFA 204-12616		30.12.93	E.F. & V.M.Clapham	Oldbury-on-Severn	29. 3.01P
G-MYNI	TEAM mini-MAX 91 PFA 186-12314 (Mosler MM-CB35)		22. 2.93	J.J.Penney	(Neath)	17.11.99P
G-MYNJ	Mainair Mercury K972-1293-7 & W768 (Rotax 503) *(Supplied as Mainair Kit)*		14. 1.94	S.M.Buchan	(Leamington Spa)	10. 8.02P
G-MYNK	Pegasus Quantum 15 6614 (Rotax 582/40)		17.11.93	N.D.Azevedo	(London N5)	3.10.02P
G-MYNL	Pegasus Quantum 15 6648 (Rotax 582/40)		17.11.93	R.J.Murphy	East Fortune	6.10.02P
G-MYNN	Pegasus Quantum 15 6679 (Rotax 582/40)		17.11.93	P.H.E.Woodliffe-Thomas	Oakley, Beds	22.12.01P
G-MYNO	Pegasus Quantum 15 6724 (Rotax 582/40)		10. 1.94	S.J.Baker	Sutton Meadows, Ely	20. 4.02P
G-MYNP	Pegasus Quantum 15 6688 (Rotax 582/40)		17.11.93	R.H.Braithwaite t/a RAF Microlight Flying Association	RAF Henlow	31. 3.02P
G-MYNR	Pegasus Quantum 15 6692 (Rotax 582/40)		17.11.93	P.R.Grady	Old Sarum	3. 4.02P
G-MYNS	Pegasus Quantum 15 6694 (Rotax 582/40)		17.11.93	D.E.Martin	Plaistows Farm, St Albans	18. 4.02P
G-MYNT	Pegasus Quantum 15 6693 (Rotax 582/40)		17.11.93	P.A.Vernon	Yatesbury	13.11.02P
G-MYNV	Pegasus Quantum 15 6725 (Rotax 582/40)		10. 1.94	H.M.Smith	(Witney)	28. 5.02P
G-MYNX	CFM Streak Shadow SA-M (Rotax 618) K.193-SA-M & PFA 206-12268		15. 6.92	T.J. & M.D.Palmer *(Flies from Oban)*	(Symington)	11. 9.02P
G-MYNY	Kolb Twinstar mk.3 (Rotax 582) K0014-0693 & PFA 205-12478		22.11.93	B.Alexander	Swinford, Rugby	25. 8.98P
G-MYNZ	Pegasus Quantum 15 6709 (Rotax 582/40)		18. 1.94	N.S.Lynall	Otherton, Cannock	14. 9.02P
G-MYOA	Rans S-6-ESD Coyote II *(Tri-cycle u/c)* (Rotax 503) 0793.523 & PFA 204-12578		23.11.93	M.D.Baylis t/a Orcas Syndicate	Otherton, Cannock	25. 1.02P
G-MYOB	Mainair Mercury 976-1293-7 & W772 (Rotax 503)		8.12.93	J.C. & B.E.Barnes	(Wisbech)	16.11.01P
G-MYOF	Mainair Mercury 975-1293-7 & W771 (Rotax 503)		3.12.93	P.S.Underwood	Over Farm, Gloucester	12. 4.02P
G-MYOG	Kolb Twinstar mk.3 (Hirth 2706) K0011-0193 & PFA 205-12449		19. 1.94	A.P. de Legh	Redhill	24. 7.02P

G-MYOH	CFM Shadow CD K.201 (Rotax 503)	27. 1.94	S.C.Smith & D.W.Bayliss	Popham	21. 5.02P
G-MYOI	Rans S-6-ESD Coyote II *(Tailwheel u/c)* (Rotax 503) 1292.409 & PFA 204-12503	3. 2.94	J.Meijerink	Coldharbour Farm, Willingham	14.10.02P
G-MYOL	Air Creation Ultraflight Fun 18S GT bis (Rotax 447) 94/001	7. 2.94	I.R.Scott	Roddidge, Fradley	7. 7.01P
G-MYOM	Mainair Gemini/Flash IIA (Rotax 582) 981-0294-7 & W777	14. 2.94	J.G.Callan	Newtownards, Co.of Down	3. 8.02P
G-MYON	CFM Shadow CD 240 (Rotax 503)	12. 1.94	D.W.& S.E.Suttill	Breighton	28. 2.02P
G-MYOO	Kolb Twinstar mk.3M (Rotax 582) K0004-0192 & PFA 205-12200	11. 5.92	P.D.Coppin	Colemore Common	24.10.02P
G-MYOR	Kolb Twinstar mk.3 PFA 205-12602 (Rotax 582)	16. 2.94	J.J.Littler	Chichester	13. 9.01P
G-MYOS	CFM Shadow CD 246 (Rotax 503)	18. 2.94	E.J. & C.A.Bowles	Old Sarum	6. 5.02P
G-MYOT	Rans S-6-ESD Coyote II *(Tail-wheel u/c)* (Rotax 503) 0893.525 & PFA 204-12668	21. 2.94	D.E.Wilson	(Wadebridge)	31. 5.02P
G-MYOU	Pegasus Quantum 15 6726 (Rotax 582/40)	1. 3.94	D.W.General Wood Machinists Ltd	(London Colney)	15. 7.02P
G-MYOV	Mainair Mercury K979-0294-7 & W775 (Rotax 503) *(Supplied as Mainair Kit)*	1. 3.94	A.Davis	(Macclesfield)	26. 8.02P
G-MYOW	Mainair Gemini/Flash IIA (Rotax 503) 983-0294-7 & W779	16. 3.94	A.J.A.Fowler	Corn Wood Farm, Adversane	16. 4.02P
G-MYOX	Mainair Mercury K984-0294-7 & W780 (Rotax 503) *(Supplied as Mainair Kit)*	23. 2.94	A.D.Dudding	Sandtoft	25. 5.02P
G-MYOY	Cyclone AX3 C.3123191 (Rotax 503)	23. 2.94	R.Nicklin	(Wolverhampton)	4. 5.02P
G-MYOZ	BFC Quad City Challenger II UK (Rotax 503) CH2-1093-1045 & PFA 177A-12640	24. 2.94	T.J.Wickham	(Bordon, Hants)	11. 3.02P
G-MYPA	Rans S-6-ESD Coyote II *(Tail-wheel u/c)* (Rotax 503) 0893.527 & PFA 204-12678	24. 2.94	L.J.Dutch	Tarn Farm, Cockerham	4.11.02P
G-MYPC	Kolb Twinstar mk.3 (Rotax 582) K0012-0199 & PFA 205-12437	2. 3.94	J.Young & S.Hussain	(Wolverhampton)	5. 9.01P
G-MYPD	Mainair Mercury 982-0294-7 & W778 (Rotax 462)	11. 3.94	A.Bennion	(Northwich)	7. 8.02P
G-MYPE	Mainair Gemini/Flash IIA (Rotax 582) 985-0394-7 & W781	11. 3.94	G.Kerr	East Fortune	18. 4.02P
G-MYPG	Solar Wings Pegasus XL-Q (Rotax 462) SW-TE-0159 & SW-WQ-0176	29. 3.89	D.W.Lunn	(Wallington)	26. 5.99P
G-MYPH	Pegasus Quantum 15 6764 (Rotax 582/40)	11. 3.94	P.M.J.White	Wombleton	4. 6.02P
G-MYPI	Pegasus Quantum 15 6767 (Rotax 582/40)	11. 3.94	P.L.Jarvis	(Ruislip)	2. 8.02P
G-MYPJ	Rans S-6-ESD Coyote II *(Tri-cycle u/c)* (Rotax 503) 1293.569 & PFA 204-12692	18. 3.94	G.P.Jones	(Stoke-on-Trent)	12. 5.02P
G-MYPL	CFM Shadow CD K.213 & BMAA/HB/080 (Rotax 503)	14. 2.94	G.I.Madden	(Milton Keynes)	6. 9.02P
G-MYPM	Cyclone AX3 C.3123188 (Rotax 503)	23. 3.94	Microflight Ireland Ltd	Mullaghmore, Co.Antrim	19. 4.02P
G-MYPN	Pegasus Quantum 15 6727 (Rotax 582/40)	12. 4.94	A.H.McBreen	(Rugby)	14. 6.02P
G-MYPO	Hunt Wing/Experience (Rotax 503) 9209011 & BMAA/HB/026 *(Engine No.3868983)*	28. 3.94	W.I.McMillan *(Stolen from Manchester area 11.4.00: current status unknown)*	(Conwy)	11.12.99P
G-MYPR	Cyclone AX3 C.3123190 (Rotax 503)	13. 4.94	N.E.Ashton	Ince Blundell	6. 6.00P
G-MYPS	Whittaker MW6 Merlin PFA 164-11585	19. 4.94	I.S.Bishop	Bicester	25. 3.02P
G-MYPT	CFM Shadow CD K.212 (Rotax 503)	22. 4.94	M.G. & S.A.Collins	(Oldbury-on-Severn)	25. 6.02P
G-MYPV	Mainair Mercury 986-0394-7 & W782 (Rotax 582)	18. 3.94	G.R.Bagnariol	Plaistows Farm, St Albans	9. 6.02P
G-MYPW	Mainair Gemini/Flash IIA (Rotax 582) 991-0494-7 & W787	3. 5.94	R.E.Parker	(Harlow)	1. 4.02P
G-MYPX	Pegasus Quantum 15 6785 (Rotax 582/40) *(Believed to have used "B Conditions" marks "G-69-29" during trials)*	28. 4.94	P.J.Callis & M.Aylett	Halwell, Totnes	3. 5.02P
G-MYPY	Pegasus Quantum 15 6786 (Rotax 582/40)	12. 5.94	G.& G.Trudgill	Peterlee	27. 4.02P
G-MYPZ	BFC Quad City Challenger II UK (Hirth 2706) CH2-1093-UK-1046 & PFA 177A-12689 *(Regd incorrectly as CH2-0194-UK-1046)*	2. 3.94	E.G.Astin t/a BFC	Whitby	30. 8.01P
G-MYRA	Kolb Twinstar mk.3 PFA 205-12434 (Rotax 503)	29. 3.94	S.J.Fox & A.P.Pickford	Popham	3. 5.02P
G-MYRB	Whittaker MW5 Sorcerer PFA 163-11543	14. 4.94	P.J.Careless *(Valid CofR 4.01: current status unknown)*	(Sandy)	

G-MYRC	Mainair Blade 988-0594-7 & W784 (Rotax 462)		1. 6.94	A.T.Hayward	Ince Blundell	11. 8.02P
G-MYRD	Mainair Blade 989-0594-7 & W785 (Rotax 582)		20. 5.94	T.W.Harrold	Croft Farm, Defford	21. 2.02P
G-MYRF	Pegasus Quantum 15 6795 (Rotax 462HP)		13. 5.94	I.Steele	Carlisle	23. 1.02P
G-MYRG	TEAM mini-MAX PFA 186-11891 (Rotax 447)		17. 5.94	D.G.Burrows	Shobdon	13. 5.02P
G-MYRH	BFC Quad City Challenger II UK (Rotax 582) CH2-1093-1044 & PFA 177A-12690		10. 3.94	R.T.Hall	Thorney Island	4. 3.02P
G-MYRI	Medway Hybred 44XLR MR180/841 (Rotax 503)		23. 5.94	B.D.Acres	(Maidstone)	1. 9.00P
G-MYRJ	BFC Quad City Challenger II UK (Rotax 582) CH2-1093-1042 & PFA 177A-12658		28. 3.94	H.F.Breakwell & P.Woodcock	Sittles Farm, Alrewas	9. 8.02P
G-MYRK	Murphy Renegade Spirit UK (Rotax 582) 215 & PFA 188-11425		3.10.89	P.Crowhurst	Sywell	28. 8.02P
G-MYRL	TEAM mini-MAX 91 PFA 186-11967 (Rotax 447)		17. 5.94	J.N.Hanson	Brook Farm, Pilling	15. 9.02P
G-MYRM	Pegasus Quantum 15 6800 (Rotax 582/40)		26. 5.94	T.Read	Old Sarum	2. 6.02P
G-MYRN	Pegasus Quantum 15 6801 (Rotax 582/40)		26. 5.94	M.K.Ashmore	Siege Cross Farm, Thatcham	23.11.02P
G-MYRO	Cyclone AX3 C.4043211 (Rotax 503)		6. 6.94	R.I.Simpson & R.Tarplee	(Broadstairs)	21. 8.02P
G-MYRP	Letov LK-2M Sluka (Rotax 447) 829409x09? & PFA 263-12725		6. 6.94	J.W.Hiestand	(Dereham)	4. 8.00P
G-MYRR	Letov LK-2M Sluka 829409x05? (Rotax 447)		10. 6.94	B.C.McCartan	(Banbridge)	24. 7.02P
G-MYRS	Pegasus Quantum 15 6803 (Rotax 582/40)		13. 6.94	R.M.Summers	Insch	8. 5.02P
G-MYRT	Pegasus Quantum 15 6732 (Rotax 582/40)		1. 3.94	M.C.Taylor	(Coleford)	29. 4.02P
G-MYRU	Cyclone AX3 C.4043210 (Rotax 503)		7. 6.94	S.Fraser	(Newcastle Upon Tyne)	3.11.01P
G-MYRV	Cyclone AX3 C.4043209 (Rotax 503)		8. 6.94	M.Gardiner	Rufforth	4. 7.02P
G-MYRW	Mainair Mercury 999-0694-7 & W795 (Rotax 503)		17. 6.94	G.C.Hobson *(Op Northern Microlight School)*	St.Michaels	5. 7.02P
G-MYRY	Pegasus Quantum 15 6813 (Rotax 582/40)		15. 6.94	S.D.J.Harvey	Shobdon	19. 8.02P
G-MYRZ	Pegasus Quantum 15 6812 (Rotax 582/40)		15. 6.94	C.Judd	Lark Engine Farmhouse, Prickwillow, Ely	27. 6.02P
G-MYSA	Cyclone Chaser S CH.864 (Rotax 508)		15. 6.94	P.Nicholls	(York)	3. 9.01P
G-MYSB	Pegasus Quantum 15 6809 (Rotax 582/40)		22. 6.94	N.Harford	(Horley)	9.11.02P
G-MYSC	Pegasus Quantum 15 6811 (Rotax 582/40)		22. 6.94	K.R.White	Dunkeswell	25. 7.02P
G-MYSD	BFC Quad City Challenger II CH2-1093-1043 & PFA 177A-12688		23. 6.94	C.E.Bell	(Oakham)	
G-MYSG	Mainair Mercury K993-0694-7 & W790 (Rotax 503) *(Supplied as Mainair Kit)*		12. 7.94	M.Donnelly	(Sale)	4. 6.02P
G-MYSI	Mignet HM.14/93 PFA 255-12700		18. 7.94	A.R.D.Seaman	Dagenham	
G-MYSJ	Mainair Gemini/Flash IIA (Rotax 503) 1001-0894-7 & W797		2. 8.94	E M Christoffersen	Baxby Manor, Husthwaite	19. 2.02P
G-MYSK	TEAM mini-MAX 91 PFA 186-12203 (Rotax 447)		25. 7.94	A.D.Bolshaw *(Op Mercury Microlight Club)*	Brook Farm, Pilling	1. 8.02P
G-MYSL	Aviasud Mistral 582GB (Rotax 582) 66 & BMAA/HB/007	83-DE	27. 2.92	P.C.Piggott & M.E.Hughes	Little Battleflats Farm, Ellistown, Coalville	21. 7.02P
G-MYSM	CFM Shadow CD K.243 & BMAA/HB/049 (Rotax 503)		22. 3.94	L.W.Stevens	(Grantham)	7. 5.02P
G-MYSN	Whittaker MW6-S Fatboy Flyer (Rotax 532) PFA 164-12285		27. 7.94	T.A.Dockrell	(Weston-super-Mare)	6. 1.01P
G-MYSO	Cyclone AX3 C.4043215 (Rotax 503)		1. 8.94	M.L.Smith	Popham	25. 3.02P
G-MYSP	Rans S-6-ESD Coyote II *(Tail-wheel u/c)* (Rotax 503) 0392.284 & PFA 204-12265		26. 5.92	G.C.Holmes	Sittle Farm, Alrewas	26. 7.02P
G-MYSR	Pegasus Quantum 15 6837 (Rotax 582)		3. 8.94	J.G.Watson	Perth	31. 3.02P
G-MYST	Aviasud Mistral (Rotax 532) 0489-83, GB.01 & BMAA/HB/012		11. 7.89	J.Willett *(Crashed Lower Hartall Farm, Nash, Ludlow 23.6.01 & badly damaged)*	Otherton, Cannock	6. 6.02P
G-MYSU	Rans S-6-ESD Coyote II PFA 204-12753 (Rotax 503)		5. 8.94	K.W.Allan	Drummaird Farm, Bonnybank	9. 2.02P

G-MYSV	Aerial Arts Chaser S	CH.812	(ex Korea)	24. 8.94	R J Sims & I G Reason	(Salisbury)	30. 4.02P
	(Rotax 377)						
G-MYSW	Pegasus Quantum 15	6834		13. 7.94	D.A.Southern	Tarn Farm, Cockerham	21. 8.01P
	(Rotax 582)						
G-MYSX	Pegasus Quantum 15	6832		13. 7.94	J.L.Treves	Long Acre Farm, Sandy	29. 7.02P
G-MYSY	Pegasus Quantum 15	6864		15. 8.94	F.Wilson	(Stone)	29. 3.02P
	(Rotax 582)						
G-MYSZ	Mainair Mercury	1006-0894-7 & W802		2. 9.94	N.Cox	Shobdon	23. 9.02P
	(Rotax 503) *(C/n confirmed but see G-MYYY)*						
G-MYTA	TEAM mini-MAX 91	PFA 186-12461		20. 5.94	A.R.Mikolajczyk	(Mansfield)	11. 2.02P
	(Rotax 447)						
G-MYTB	Mainair Mercury	1004-0894-7 & W800		19. 8.94	P.J.Higgins	Fenland	1. 8.02P
	(Rotax 582)						
G-MYTC	Solar Wings Pegasus XL-Q	SW-WQ-0246	(ex?)	28. 9.94	M.J.Edmett	(London N3)	
					(Sailwing only sold to France)		
G-MYTD	Mainair Blade	1002-0894-7 & W798		18. 8.94	D.M.Dunphy	Barton	5. 8.00P
	(Rotax 582)						
G-MYTE	Rans S-6-ESD Coyote II	PFA 204-12718		22. 7.94	J.A.Way	Lydd	9.11.02P
	(Rotax 503) *(Tail-wheel u/c)*				t/a The Rans Flying Group		
G-MYTG	Mainair Blade			16. 9.94	P.Lenk	Barton	1. 2.01P
	(Rotax 582)	1008-0994-7 & W804					
G-MYTH	CFM Shadow CD	089		7.11.88	J.E.Neil	Sheriff Hall, Balgone	22. 7.01P
	(Rotax 503)						
G-MYTI	Pegasus Quantum 15	6874		6.10.94	J.Madhvani	Plaistows Farm, St Albans	21. 2.02P
	(Rotax 582/40)						
G-MYTJ	Pegasus Quantum 15	6877		29. 9.94	K.Laud	Roddige, Fradley	4. 6.02P
	(Rotax 582/40)						
G-MYTK	Mainair Mercury	1009-1094-7 & W805		29. 9.94	D.A.Holroyd	(London W14)	13. 1.02P
	(Rotax 503)						
G-MYTL	Mainair Blade	1010-1094-7 & W807		4.10.94	S.Ostrowski	Davidstow Moor	28. 5.02P
	(Rotax 582)						
G-MYTM	Cyclone AX3	C.3123189		13. 4.94	J P Gardiner	(Farnworth)	17. 8.02P
	(Rotax 503)						
G-MYTN	Pegasus Quantum 15	6878		30. 9.94	R.Redman	(Grantham)	29. 4.02P
G-MYTO	Quad City Challenger II UK			22. 7.94	R.W.Sage	Priory Farm, Tibenham	16. 4.01P
	(Hirth 2705.R06)	PFA 177-12583					
G-MYTP	CGS Arrow Flight Hawk II	215		6.10.94	R.J.Turner	Otherton, Cannock	8. 5.97P
	(Rotax 503) H-CGS-489-P & PFA 266-12801 *(C/n 215 believed to relate to previous identity N215)*						
G-MYTR	Solar Wings Pegasus Quasar IITC	6880		11.10.94	M.E.Grafton	(Hay-on-Wye)	22. 5.02P
	(Rotax 582/40)						
G-MYTT	Quad City Challenger II			11.10.94	R.J.Shave	Dunkeswell	19. 4.02P
	(Rotax 503)	PFA 177-12761			t/a Challenger G-MYTT		
G-MYTU	Mainair Blade	1011-1094-7 & W808		21.10.94	C.J.Barker	(Bagthorpe, Notts)	19.11.01P
	(Rotax 582)						
G-MYTV	Hunt Wing/Avon	9204010 & BMAA/HB/029		13.10.94	P.J.Sutton	(Hereford)	27.10.02P
	(Rotax 503)						
G-MYTW	Mainair Blade	1012-1194-7 & W809		4.11.94	J.Parker	(Spalding)	27.11.97P
	(Rotax 582)				*(Current status unknown)*		
G-MYTX	Mainair Mercury	K1003-0894-7 & W799		23. 9.94	R.Steel	Rufforth	21. 6.02P
	(Rotax 503) *(Supplied as Mainair Kit)*						
G-MYTY	CFM Streak Shadow M			11. 7.94	K.H.A.Negal	Enstone	6. 6.02P
	(Rotax 912UL)	K.242 & PFA 206-12607					
G-MYTZ	Air Creation Ultraflight Fun 18S GT bis			7.11.94	J.K.Evans	Husbands Bosworth	5. 6.02P
	(Rotax 503)	94/003					
G-MYUA	Air Creation Ultraflight Fun 18S GT bis			8.11.94	J.Leden	(Buxton)	9 6.02P
	(Rotax 503)	94/002					
G-MYUB	Mainair Mercury	1014-1194-7 & W812		14.12.94	T.A. & C.M.Ross	Arclid Green, Sandbach	10.10.01P
	(Rotax 503)						
G-MYUC	Mainair Blade	1015-1294-7 & W813		16.11.94	A.D.Clayton	St.Michaels	4.11.02P
	(Rotax 462)						
G-MYUD	Mainair Mercury	1016-1294-7 & W814		24.11.94	S.A.Noble	(Audley End)	13. 2.01P
	(Rotax 582)						
G-MYUE	Mainair Mercury	1017-1294-7 & W815		22.11.94	R.J.Speight	(Amersham)	22. 7.01P
	(Rotax 582)						
G-MYUF	Murphy Renegade Spirit	PFA 188-12795		16.11.94	C.J.Dale	Rufforth	13. 7.02P
	(Jabiru 2200A)						
G-MYUH	Solar Wings Pegasus XL-Q	6810		28.11.94	K.S.Daniels	(London Colney)	30. 9.01P
	(Rotax 462)						
G-MYUI	Cyclone AX3	C.4043213		13.12.94	R. & M.Bailey	Plaistows Farm, St Albans	21. 4.02P
	(Rotax 503) *(C/n worn is C.102822 and probably results from a changed monopole)*						
G-MYUK	Mainair Mercury	1020-0195-7 & W818		12.12.94	S.Lear	(London N15)	12. 9.01P
	(Rotax 462)						
G-MYUL	Quad City Challenger II UK			10. 1.95	J C Miller	Cumbernauld	24. 5.02P
	(Rotax 503) CH2-1293-UK-1063 & PFA 177-12687						

G-MYUM	Mainair Blade 1018-1294-7 & W816 (Rotax 582)		24.11.94	M.E.Keefe	St.Michaels	10. 1.02P
G-MYUN	Mainair Blade 1019-0195-7 & W817 (Rotax 582)		5.12.94	G.A.Barratt	(Preston)	17. 1.02P
G-MYUO	Pegasus Quantum 15 6911 (Rotax 582)		23. 1.95	H.R.Bradwell	(Oxford)	15. 7.02P
G-MYUP	Letov LK-2M Sluka (Rotax 447) 829409x24, UK.2 & PFA 0263-12785		20.12.94	C J Meadows	(Shepton Mallet)	27. 2.02P
G-MYUR	Hunt Wing/Avon 9409030 & BMAA/HB/034 (Rotax 582)		24. 1.95	S.D.Pain	Rayne	16. 1.02P
G-MYUS	CFM Shadow CD 257 (Rotax 503)		26. 1.95	G.Gilhead & R.G.M.Proost t/a Aviation for Paraplegics & Tetraplegics Trust	Old Sarum	15. 7.02P
G-MYUU	Pegasus Quantum 15 6917 (Rotax 462)		30. 1.95	K.A.Wright	North Coates	15. 7.02P
G-MYUV	Pegasus Quantum 15 6918 (Rotax 582)		6. 2.95	D.Baillie	Carlisle	14. 7.02P
G-MYUW	Mainair Mercury 1024-0295-7 & W822 (Rotax 503)		7. 2.95	G.Suckling	(Saffron Walden)	11. 7.02P
G-MYUZ	Rans S-6-ESD Coyote II *(Tri-cycle u/c)* (Rotax 503) 1293.568 & PFA 204-12741		5. 1.95	B.Davies	Sittles Farm, Alrewas	29. 4.02P
G-MYVA	Kolb Twinstar mk.3 PFA 205-12756 (Rotax 582)		13. 2.95	M.A.Pantling	Henstridge	20. 6.01P
G-MYVB	Mainair Blade 1021-0195-7 & W819 (Rotax 582)		15.12.94	P.C.Watson	Arclid Green, Sandbach	24. 4.02P
G-MYVC	Pegasus Quantum 15 6904 (Rotax 582)		13. 2.95	G.Lace	(Liverpool)	19. 5.02P
G-MYVE	Mainair Blade 1027-0295-7 & W825 (Rotax 582)		8. 2.95	R.D.Serle & P.M.Jennings	Shobdon	15. 4.02P
G-MYVG	Letov LK-2M Sluka (Rotax 447) 829409x26 & PFA 0263-12786		15. 2.95	N.P.Sleigh	Ince Blundell	14. 6.02P
G-MYVH	Mainair Blade 1028-0295-7 & W826 (Rotax 582)		21. 2.95	J.Kennedy	Mill Farm, Shifnal	27. 3.02P
G-MYVI	Air Creation Ultraflight Fun 18S GT bis (Rotax 503) 94/004		17. 2.95	P.Osborne t/a Northampton Aerotow Club	(Northampton)	11. 9.01P
G-MYVJ	Pegasus Quantum 15 6974 (Rotax 582/40)		24. 2.95	G.R.Hall	(Canterbury)	27. 4.02P
G-MYVK	Pegasus Quantum 15 6970 (Rotax 582/40)		27. 2.95	C K Stow	(Market Rasen)	9. 4.02P
G-MYVM	Pegasus Quantum 15 6893 (Rotax 582/40)	G-69-17 G-MYVM	9. 3.95	A.F.A.Marreiros	Lisboa, Portugal	27. 4.97P
G-MYVN	Cyclone AX3 C.4043212 (Rotax 503)		16. 3.95	F.Watt	Insch	14. 8.02P
G-MYVO	Mainair Blade 1013-1194-7 & W811 (Rotax 582)		8.11.94	S.S.Raines	Shobdon	29. 3.02P
G-MYVP	Rans S-6-ESD Coyote II *(Tri-cycle u/c)* (Rotax 503) 0294.593 & PFA 204-12828		27. 3.95	C.E.Hormaeche	Eshott	23. 7.02P
G-MYVR	Pegasus Quantum 15 6980 (Rotax 582)		21. 3.95	I.W.Barlow	(Ilkeston)	1. 3.02P
G-MYVS	Mainair Mercury 1037-0495-7 & W835 (Rotax 462)		12. 4.95	P.S.Flynn	Sandtoft	25. 4.02P
G-MYVT	Letov LK-2M Sluka (Rotax 447) 829409x25 & PFA 263-12835		17. 3.95	J.Hannibal	(Kidderminster)	9.11.02P
G-MYVV	Medway Hybred 44XLR MR127/109 (Rotax 503) *(Sailwing c/n also quoted for G-MYLX)*		3. 4.95	S.Perity	(Wisbech)	21. 8.02P
G-MYVW	Medway Raven X MRB128/110 (Rotax 447) *(Sailwing c/n also quoted for G-MYMJ)*		15. 5.95	J.C.Woolgrove	(Beckenham)	5. 6.97P
G-MYVX	Medway Hybred 44XLR MR129/111 (Rotax 503)		3. 4.95	A.R.Fricker	(South Ockendon)	4. 6.02P
G-MYVY	Mainair Blade 1033-0495-7 & W831 (Rotax 582)		29. 3.95	N.Purdy	(Sutton-in-Ashfield)	12.10.02P
G-MYVZ	Mainair Blade 1034-0495-7 & W832 (Rotax 582)		31. 3.95	R.Llewellyn	(Chester)	27. 4.02P
G-MYWA	Mainair Mercury 1035-0495-7 & W833 (Rotax 503)		30. 3.95	D.James	(Neath)	12. 5.02P
G-MYWC	Hunt Wing/Avon 9409038 & BMAA/HB/043 (Rotax 503)		3. 4.95	F.J.C.Binks	Sutton Meadows, Ely	31. 7.02P
G-MYWD	Thruster T.600N 9035-T600-511 (Rotax 582)	(G-MYOJ)	18. 4.95	K.Draper	Stoke, Kent	16. 8.02P
G-MYWE	Thruster T.600T 9035-T600-512 (Rotax 503)	(G-MYOK)	18. 4.95	V.Goddard	Yatesbury	9. 1.02P
G-MYWF	CFM Shadow CD K.248 & BMAA/HB/068 (Rotax 503)		18. 4.95	M.A.Newman	(Saxmundham)	19. 1.02P
G-MYWG	Pegasus Quantum 15 6998 (Rotax 582/40)		20. 4.95	N.S.McNaughton	(Auchincruive)	1. 9.00P

G-MYWH	Hunt Wing/Experience 9409025 & BMAA/HB/037		20.12.94	G.N.Hatchett	North Connel, Oban	
G-MYWI	Pegasus Quantum 15 7006 (Rotax 582)		1. 5.95	J.R.Fulcher	(Whittlesford)	12. 6.01P
G-MYWJ	Pegasus Quantum 15 6919 (Rotax 582)		24. 1.95	P.A.Banks	Long Acre Farm, Sandy	25. 9.02P
G-MYWK	Pegasus Quantum 15 7011 (Rotax 582/40)		1. 5.95	M.S.McCrudden	Newtownards, Co.of Down	25. 9.02P
G-MYWL	Pegasus Quantum 15 6995 (Rotax 582)		2. 5.95	J.L.Richards	Plaistows Farm, St. Albans	19. 6.01P
G-MYWM	CFM Shadow CD K.227 & BMAA/HB/056 (Rotax 503)		9. 5.95	R.E.Peirse	Kingston, Royston	25. 7.02P
G-MYWN	Cyclone Chaser S CH.865 (Rotax 508)		9. 5.95	J.E.Borrill	North Connel, Oban	22. 8.02P
G-MYWO	Cyclone Pegasus Quantum 15 6932 (Rotax 582)		9. 5.95	J.W.Cope	Wickenby	12. 9.02P
G-MYWP	Kolb Twinstar mk.3 (Rotax 582/40) K0017-0993 & PFA 205-12561		7. 3.95	S.J.Spearey	(Bristol)	21. 9.01P
G-MYWR	Cyclone Pegasus Quantum 15 7002 (Rotax 582/40)		10. 5.95	A P Watkins & R Horton	Roddidge, Fradley	11. 8.02P
G-MYWS	Cyclone Chaser S 6946 & CH.866 (Rotax 447)		17. 5.95	M.H.Broadbent	(Bexhill-on-Sea)	25. 7.02P
G-MYWT	Pegasus Quantum 15 6997 (Rotax 582/40)		19. 5.95	B.J.Holloway & A.Gordon	Oakley, Beds	24. 7.02P
G-MYWU	Pegasus Quantum 15 7024 (Rotax 582)		25. 5.95	J.R.Buttle	Dunkeswell	23. 7.02P
G-MYWV	Rans S-4C Coyote (Rotax 447) 093.212 & PFA 193-12826		30. 5.95	A.H.Trapp	(Bewdley, Worcs)	7. 7.02P
G-MYWW	Pegasus Quantum 15 7021 (Rotax 503)		30. 5.95	C.W.Bailie	Newtownards, Co.of Down	10. 8.02P
G-MYWX	Pegasus Quantum 15 7019 (Rotax 582)		6. 6.95	D.J.Revell	Lower Mountpleasnt, Chatteris	26. 7.02P
G-MYWY	Pegasus Quantum 15 6982 (Rotax 582)		20. 3.95	D.Young	Kemble	29. 9.02P
G-MYWZ	Thruster TST mk.1 8128-TST-115 (Rotax 503)	G-MVMJ	22. 2.93	W.H.J.KNowles	Tiverton	8.10.01P
G-MYXA	TEAM mini-MAX 91 PFA 186-12266 (Rotax 447)		13. 6.95	L.H.S.Stephens	(Saltash)	14. 8.02P
G-MYXB	Rans S-6-ESD Coyote II *(Tri-cycle u/c)* (Rotax 503) 1293.567 & PFA 204-12787		20. 6.95	P.R.Day	(Southampton)	29. 3.02P
G-MYXC	BFC Quad City Challenger II UK (Hirth H2706) CH2-0294-UK-1099		16. 5.95	K.N.Dickinson	Higher Barn Farm, Houghton	
G-MYXD	Pegasus Quasar IITC 7029 (Rotax 582)		21. 6.95	A.Cochrane	Long Acre Farm, Sandy	30. 8.02P
G-MYXE	Pegasus Quantum 15 7061 (Rotax 582)		23. 6.95	D.Little	(Crawley)	7. 9.02P
G-MYXF	Air Creation Ultraflight Fun 18S GT bis (Rotax 503) 94/005		23. 6.95	T.A.Morgan	Popham	15. 1.01P
G-MYXG	Rans S-6-ESD Coyote II PFA 204-12879 (Rotax 503) *(Tri-cycle u/c)*		29. 6.95	G.H.Lee	Higher Barn Farm, Houghton	20. 6.01P
G-MYXH	Cyclone AX3 7028 (Rotax 503)		3. 7.95	E.G.White	(Wantage)	27. 9.02P
G-MYXI	Cook Aries 1 BMAA/HB/048 *(Design awaiting finalisation 10.01- planned engine fit is BMW R80)*		4. 7.95	H.Cook	(Newport, Gwent)	
G-MYXJ	Mainair Blade 1048-0795-7 & W846 (Rotax 582)		17. 7.95	L Seddon	(Cramlington)	22.11.02P
G-MYXK	BFC Quad City Challenger II (Rotax 503) CH2-1194-1254 & PFA 177A-12877		11. 7.95	V.Vaughan & N.O'Brien	(Mullinahone, Co.Tipperary)	24. 7.02P
G-MYXL	Mignet HM-1000 Balerit 112 (Rotax 582)		11. 7.95	R.W.Hollamby	Bardown, Wadhurst	17. 7.02P
G-MYXM	Mainair Blade 1047-0795-7 & W845 (Rotax 582)		19. 7.95	S.C.Hodgson	(Chesterfield)	3. 6.02P
G-MYXN	Mainair Blade 1046-0795-7 & W844 (Rotax 582)		27. 7.95	M.R.Sands	Peterlee	19. 7.02P
G-MYXO	Letov LK-2M Sluka (Rotax 447) 8295s001 & PFA 263-12873		27. 7.95	G.W.Allport	(Kingswinford)	1. 1.02P
G-MYXP	Rans S-6-ESD Coyote II *(Tail-wheel u/c)* (Rotax 503) PFA 204-12886		31. 7.95	R S Amor	Weston Zoyland	14. 8.02P
G-MYXR	Murphy Renegade Spirit UK PFA 188-12755		2. 8.95	S.Hooker *(Current status unknown)*	Ashford, Kent	
G-MYXS	Kolb Twinstar mk.3 (Rotax 582) K0015-0693 & PFA 205-12528		4. 5.94	R.Coar	Higher Barn Farm, Houghton	3.10.01P
G-MYXT	Pegasus Quantum 15 7073 (Rotax 582)		4. 8.95	W.A.Donnelly	Latch Farm, Kirknewton	3. 8.02P

G-MYXU	Thruster T.300	9024-T300-513	16. 8.95	D.W.Wilson	(Collone, Co.Armagh)	16. 3.01P
	(Rotax 582)					
G-MYXV	Quad City Challenger II UK		19. 7.95	S.G.Beeson	(Stoke-on-Trent)	8.11.02P
	(Rotax 503)	CH2-1194-UK-1243				
G-MYXW	Pegasus Quantum 15	7090	24. 8.95	D.Martin	Perth	17. 7.02P
	(Rotax 582)					
G-MYXX	Pegasus Quantum 15	7081	25. 8.95	J.H.Arnold	Milverton, Taunton	13.11.01P
	(Rotax 582)					
G-MYXY	CFM Shadow CD	K.245 & BMAA/HB/059	29. 8.95	N.H.Townsend	Old Sarum	21. 7.02P
	(Rotax 503)					
G-MYXZ	Pegasus Quantum 15	7023	21. 6.95	I.Fernihough	Ashbourne	24. 8.02P
	(Rotax 582)					
G-MYYA	Mainair Blade	1052-0995-7 & W850	1. 9.95	D.E.Bassett	(Marple Bridge)	18.10.02P
	(Rotax 462)					
G-MYYB	Pegasus Quantum 15	7079	4. 9.95	A.L.Johnson	Long Acre Farm, Sandy	17.10.01P
	(Rotax 582)					
G-MYYC	Pegasus Quantum 15	7094	12. 9.95	M.Wills & R.Jones	Tarn Farm, Cockerham	17. 8.02P
	(Rotax 582)					
G-MYYD	Cyclone Chaser S	CH.7099	15. 9.95	C Surman	(Cranleigh)	7.11.02P
	(Rotax 447)					
G-MYYE	Hunt Wing/Avon 462 (3)		21. 9.95	N.S.Payne	(Hereford)	18. 8.02P
	(Rotax 462)	9409035 & BMAA/HB/041				
G-MYYF	Quad City Challenger II UK		27. 9.95	G.Ferries	Insch	16.11.02P
	(Rotax 503)	PFA 177-12811				
G-MYYG	Mainair Blade	1054-0995-7 & W852	4.10.95	R.W.Smith	Beccles	23.10.02P
	(Rotax 462) *(Believed supplied as Mainair Kit, if so c/n K1054...)*					
G-MYYH	Mainair Blade	1056-1095-7 & W854	3.10.95	B.Hunter	Wombleton	29. 4.02P
	(Rotax 582)					
G-MYYI	Pegasus Quantum 15	7101	28. 9.95	S.Etches	Sandtoft	23. 7.99P
	(Rotax 582)					
G-MYYJ	Hunt Wing/Hunt Avon		29. 9.95	M.J.Slater	(Marlborough)	
	(Rotax 503)	9409033 & BMAA/HB/033		*(Completed 5.95 & stored 5.97: current status unknown)*		
G-MYYK	Pegasus Quantum 15	7100	2.10.95	L.Scarse	(Melksham)	1. 5.01P
	(Rotax 582)					
G-MYYL	Cyclone AX3	7110	4.10.95	P.M.Dewhurst & K.Meredith-Jones	Sywell	14.11.02P
	(Rotax 503)					
G-MYYN	Pegasus Quantum 15	7022	3.10.95	P.Richardson	(Newark)	28.12.01P
	(Rotax 582-40)					
G-MYYO	Medway Raven X	MRB134/114	5.10.95	J.R.Harrison	(Chesterfield)	30. 5.01P
	(Rotax 447)					
G-MYYP	AMF Chevvron 2-32C	036	31.10.95	G.A.Pentelow	Rothwell Lodge, Kettering	15.11.01P
	(Konig SD570)					
G-MYYR	TEAM mini-MAX 91	PFA 186-12724	31.10.95	J.J.James	East Kirby	7.11.01P
	(Rotax 447)			*(Noted 5.01)*		
G-MYYS	TEAM mini-MAX	PFA 186-11989	7.11.95	J.R.Hopkinson	(Chesterfield)	
G-MYYU	Mainair Mercury	1062-1295-7 & W862	17.11.95	G Firth	(Barnsley)	5. 4.02P
	(Rotax 503)					
G-MYYV	Rans S-6-ESD Coyote IIXL *(Tri-cycle u/c)*		17.11.95	B.W.Drake	(Gloucester)	16. 7.01P
	(Rotax 503) 0896.1026XL & PFA 204-12943					
G-MYYW	Mainair Blade	1051-0895-7 & W849	8. 8.95	M.J.Naylor	(Leicester)	12.10.01P
	(Rotax 582)					
G-MYYX	Pegasus Quantum 15	7126	17.11.95	M.L.Johnston	East Fortune	5. 4.02P
	(Rotax 582)					
G-MYYY	Mainair Blade	1031-0495-7 & W829	15. 3.95	E.D.Locke	Barton	30. 3.01P
	(Rotax 582)					
G-MYYZ	Medway Raven X	MRB135/116	10. 1.96	J W Leaper	(Lincoln)	7. 6.02P
	(Rotax 447)					
G-MYZA	Whittaker MW6 Merlin	PFA 164-11396	17. 7.95	D.C.Davies	Over Farm, Newent	13. 8.02P
	(Rotax 582)					
G-MYZB	Pegasus Quantum 15	7124	22.11.95	N G Barbour	(Sleaford)	11. 3.02P
	(Rotax 582)					
G-MYZC	Cyclone AX3	7125	5.12.95	A.B.Simpson	Brook Farm, Pilling	28. 5.02P
	(Rotax 503)			*(Op Mercury Microlight Club)*		
G-MYZE	TEAM mini-MAX 91	PFA 186-12570	28. 9.95	R.B.M.Etherington	Totnes	6. 6.02P
	(Global GMT-35)					
G-MYZF	Cyclone AX3	7133	11.12.95	R.L.H.Alexander	Holywood	6. 7.02P
	(Rotax 503)					
G-MYZG	Cyclone AX3/503	7137	11. 1.96	R.A.Johns	Weston Zoyland	9. 1.00P
G-MYZH	Chargus Titan 38	JPA-1	16. 1.96	P.A.James	(Crawley)	
G-MYZJ	Pegasus Quantum 15	7150	24. 1.96	P.Millar	Latch Farm, Kirknewton	28. 4.02P
	(Rotax 582)					
G-MYZK	Pegasus Quantum 15	7157	5. 2.96	J.Douglas	East Fortune	26. 5.02P
	(Rotax 582/40)					

G-MYZL	Pegasus Quantum 15	7158	5. 2.96	N.A.Harwood	(Littlehampton)	27. 7.02P
	(Rotax 582/40) *(Original sailwing believed sold, with trike c/n 7230, to Australia as T2-2906: the wing from G-MZHH was fitted to G-MYZL: previous marks noted underneath G-MYZL @ Shobdon 8.99: it is believed also that the only the trike of G-MZHH was sold to France 1.98 with another sailwing fitted)*					
G-MYZM	Pegasus Quantum 15	7159	5. 2.96	D.Hope	(Uckfield)	29. 4.02P
	(Rotax 582/40)					
G-MYZN	Whittaker MW6-S-LW Fatboy Flyer		31. 1.96	M.K.Shaw	RAF Halton	8. 5.02P
	(Rotax 582)	PFA 164-12431				
G-MYZO	Medway Raven X	MRB136/115	12. 2.96	B.C.Kealy	Rochester	24. 5.02P
	(Rotax 447)					
G-MYZP	CFM Shadow DD	249 & PFA 161-12914	7. 2.96	R.M.Davies & P.I.Hodgson	(Amersham)	19. 4.02P
	(Rotax 582)					
G-MYZR	Rans S-6-ESD Coyote II XL *(Tri-cycle u/c)*		9. 2.96	S.E.J.McLaughlin	Sutton Meadows, Ely	30. 5.02P
	(Rotax 503)	PFA 204-12958				
G-MYZV	Rans S-6-ESD Coyote II XL *(Tri-cycle u/c)*		26. 2.96	D.H.Robinson	(Pershore)	26. 6.02P
	(Rotax 503)	0795.849 & PFA 204-12946				
G-MYZW	Cyclone Chaser S	7165	27. 2.96	P.J.Sheehy	(Warsash, Southampton)	11. 5.02P
	(Rotax 508)					
G-MYZY	Pegasus Quantum 15	7156	8. 2.96	D.D.Appleford	Kemble	1. 6.02P
	(Rotax 582)					
G-MZAA	Mainair Blade	1059-1195-7 & W857	24.10.95	J.C.Kitchen	Plaistows Farm, St Albans	26. 2.02P
	(Rotax 462)					
G-MZAB	Mainair Blade	1043-0695-7 & W841	26. 5.95	A.Meadley	(Northallerton)	12.10.02P
	(Rotax 582)					
G-MZAC	BFC Quad City Challenger II		21. 7.95	M.N.Calhaem	Fradswell, Stafford	18. 6.02P
		CH2-0294-1100 & PFA 0177A-12716				
G-MZAE	Mainair Blade	1063-1295-7 & W863	4.12.95	A.C.Rowlands	Dalscote, Nether Heyford	2. 5.02P
	(Rotax 582)					
G-MZAF	Mainair Blade	1045-0795-7 & W843	1.12.95	G.C.Brown	Barton	3. 7.01P
	(Rotax 582)					
G-MZAG	Mainair Blade	1042-0695-7 & W840	26. 5.95	I.D.Milne	St.Michaels	23. 1.02P
	(Rotax 582)			*(Op Northern Microlight School)*		
G-MZAH	Rans S-6-ESD Coyote II *(Tri-cycle u/c)*		3. 9.93	C.J.Collett	Long Marston	5. 7.02P
	(Rotax 503)	0393.470 & PFA 204-12553 *(Orig built as tail-wheel u/c: repaired with frame 0491-186 [G-MWVL])*				
G-MZAI	Mainair Blade	1065-0196-7 & W867	4.12.95	P.& M.Boultby	Nottingham	8. 1.02P
	(Rotax 912UL)			*(Noted 9.01)*		
G-MZAJ	Mainair Blade	1067-0196-7 & W869	20.12.95	M.P.Daley	Arclid Green, Sandbach	24. 6.02P
	(Rotax 582)					
G-MZAK	Mainair Mercury	1070-0296-7 & W872	15. 1.96	S.J.Joseph	(Cheshunt)	11. 5.02P
	(Rotax 503)					
G-MZAL	Mainair Blade	1076-0396-7 & W878	21. 2.96	T.Dunn	(Nottingham)	4. 4.01P
	(Rotax 503)					
G-MZAM	Mainair Blade	1044-0695-7 & W842	31. 5.95	B.K.Robinson	Shobdon	9.11.01P
	(Rotax 582)					
G-MZAN	Pegasus Quantum 15	7188	7. 3.96	C.G.Veitch	Dunkeswell	7. 5.21P
	(Rotax 582/40)			t/a Zanco Syndicate		
G-MZAO	Mainair Blade	1069-0296-7 & W871	15. 3.96	S.W.Dow	(Cuffley)	7. 4.00P
	(Rotax 912UL)					
G-MZAP	Mainair Blade 912	1036-0495-7 & W834	31. 3.95	D.J.Baker	(Maldon)	2. 3.02P
	(Rotax 582) *(CAA's CofR is conflicting - type designation is shown as '912 with a Rotax 582)*					
G-MZAR	Mainair Blade	1072-0296-7 & W874	13. 2.96	T.R.Southall	Shobdon	4. 3.02P
	(Rotax 582)					
G-MZAS	Mainair Blade	1049-0895-7 & W847	15. 8.95	T.Carter		
	(Rotax 582)				Pound Green, Buttonoak, Kidderminster	25. 8.02P
G-MZAT	Mainair Blade	1060-1195-7 & W860	29.11.95	D.M.Newton	(Douglastown, Forfar)	5. 5.02P
	(Rotax 582)					
G-MZAV	Mainair Blade	1078-0396-7 & W881	11. 3.96	B.B.Boniface	St Michaels	8. 5.02P
	(Rotax 462)					
G-MZAW	Pegasus Quantum 15	7160	14. 2.96	S.Stone & R.Atkinson	(Dursley)	13. 3.02P
G-MZAX	Pegasus Quantum 15	7152	11. 3.96	T.A.E.McLaughlan Stewart	(Orpington)	30. 1.02P
	(Rotax 582)					
G-MZAY	Mainair Blade	1077-0396-7 & W880	15. 3.96	M.D.Harris	Earls Barton, Northampton	7. 4.02P
	(Rotax 462)					
G-MZAZ	Mainair Blade	1040-0595-7 & W838	26. 5.95	P.J.Kay	Barton	30. 6.02P
	(Rotax 462)					
G-MZBA	Mainair Blade	1068-0296-7 & W870	15. 3.96	D J Cross	Redlands, Swindon	23. 3.02P
	(Rotax 912UL)					
G-MZBB	Pegasus Quantum 15	7139	13. 3.96	C.D.C.Ashdown	Prestwick	23. 7.02P
	(Rotax 582/40)					
G-MZBC	Pegasus Quantum 15	7077	15. 8.95	B.M.Quinn	Barlow, Sheffield	3. 5.01P
	(Rotax 582)					
G-MZBD	Rans S-6-ESD Coyote II XL *(Tri-cycle u/c)*		15. 3.96	S P Yardley	Sittles Farm, Alrewas	19. 2.02P
	(Rotax 503)	0795.850XL & PFA 204-12957				

G-MZBE	CFM Streak Shadow SA-M	18. 3.96	N.J.Bushell	Old Sarum	11.12.02P
	(Rotax 618) K.271 & PFA 206-12905				
G-MZBF	Letov LK-2M Sluka	18. 3.96	B.Boylan	Mullaghmore, Co.Antrim	9. 5.02P
	(Rotax 447) PFA 263-12881				
G-MZBG	Whittaker MW6-S Fatboy Flyer	20. 3.96	M.W.Kilvert & I.Rowlands-Jones	(Newtown)	1. 6.01P
	(Rotax 503) PFA 164-12891				
G-MZBH	Rans S-6-ESD Coyote II PFA 204-12244	21. 3.96	D.Sutherland	Breighton	24. 5.02P
	(Rotax 503) *(Tri-cycle u/c)*				
G-MZBI	Pegasus Quantum 15 7189	21. 3.96	B.C.Blackburn	Perth	31. 5.02P
	(Rotax 582/40)				
G-MZBK	Letov LK-2M Sluka 8295s	26. 3.96	R.J.Porter	(Auchterless, Turriff)	26 .7.02P
	(Rotax 447) 8295s002 & PFA 263-12872				
G-MZBL	Mainair Blade	11. 4.96	J.R.Webster	(Ormskirk)	4. 7.02P
	(Rotax 582) 1080-0496-7 & W883				
G-MZBM	Pegasus Quantum 15 7196	12. 4.96	G.D.Ritchie	East Fortune	15. 6.02P
	(Rotax 582/40)				
G-MZBN	CFM Shadow CD 069 & BMAA/HB/073	22. 4.96	P.A.James	Redhill	19. 6.02P
	(Rotax 503) *(CFM c/n duplicates G-MTWP of which it is a rebuild)*		t/a Cloudbase Aviation G-MZBN		
G-MZBO	Pegasus Quantum 15 7218	3. 5.96	A.M.Dalgetty	Perth	24. 7.02P
	(Rotax 582)				
G-MZBR	Southdown Raven X SN2232/0082	24. 5.96	D.M.Lane	(Stourbridge)	
G-MZBS	CFM Shadow D K.274 & PFA 161-13008	14. 5.96	D.J.Abbott	Plaistows Farm, St Albans	25. 5.02P
	(Rotax 582/47)				
G-MZBT	Pegasus Quantum 15-912 7224	22. 5.96	T.M.Clark	(Guildford)	12. 5.02P
G-MZBU	Rans S-6-ESD Coyote II XL	30. 5.96	C.Clark & R.S.Marriott	(Scunthorpe)	11.11.02P
	(Rotax 503) PFA 204-12992				
G-MZBV	Rans S-6-ESD Coyote II XL *(Tri-cycle u/c)*	30. 5.96	L.C.Barham & R.I.Cannan	Jurby	18. 3.02P
	(Rotax 503) 0396.950XL & PFA 204-13009	*(Heavy landing Jurby 6.9.01, damaging nose, port undercarriage & propeller)*			
G-MZBW	Quad City Challenger II UK	19. 2.96	R.T.L.Chaloner	Dunkeswell	10. 5.02P
	(Rotax 582) PFA 177-12971				
G-MZBX	Whittaker MW6-S-LW Fatboy Flyer	16. 5.96	S.Rose & P.Tearall		
	(Rotax 503) PFA 164-12563			Gerpins Lane, Upminster	21. 1.02P
G-MZBY	Pegasus Quantum 15 7227	30. 5.96	S.E.Dancaster	(Warrington)	23. 6.02P
	(Rotax 582)				
G-MZBZ	Quad City Challenger II UK	11. 3.96	J.Flisher	Dunkeswell	17.10.02P
	(Hirth 2706) PFA 177-12928				
G-MZCA	Rans S-6-ESD Coyote II XL *(Tri-cycle u/c)*	31. 5.96	S.J.Everett, K.Kettles & F.Williams		
	(Rotax 503) 0396.953XL & PFA 204-12997			(Stratford-upon-Avon)	5. 8.02P
G-MZCB	Cyclone Chaser S 7220	4. 6.96	G.P.Hodgson	Rufforth	1. 8.02P
	(Rotax 447)				
G-MZCC	Mainair Blade 1086-0696-7 & W889	7. 6.96	D.E.McGauley	Ince Blundell	15. 5.02P
	(Rotax 912UL)				
G-MZCD	Mainair Blade 1087-0696-7 & W890	10. 6.96	J.R.Caylow	(Nottingham)	15. 9.02P
	(Rotax 582)				
G-MZCE	Mainair Blade K1088-0696-7 & W891	17. 6.96	P.Hayes	Ince Blundell	7. 4.02P
	(Rotax 462) *(Supplied as Mainair Kit)*				
G-MZCG	Mainair Blade 1090-0696-7 & W893	17. 6.96	M.J.Wilson	(Childwall)	22. 7.02P
	(Rotax 462)				
G-MZCH	Whittaker MW6-S Fatboy Flyer	7. 6.96	B.G.King & J.T.Moore	(Dartmouth)	5.11.02P
	(Rotax 503) PFA 164-12131				
G-MZCI	Pegasus Quantum 15 7231	10. 6.96	P.H.Risdale	(Wollaston)	26. 7.02P
G-MZCJ	Pegasus Quantum 15 7233	14. 6.96	A.W.Hay	Insch	19. 7.02P
	(Rotax 582/40)				
G-MZCM	Pegasus Quantum 15 7219	3. 5.96	A.J.Harper	Croughton	10. 6.01P
	(Rotax 582) *(Unfaired trike)*				
G-MZCN	Mainair Blade 1079-0396-7 & W882	27. 6.96	K.Cockersol & K.J.Ratcliffe		
				Ince Blundell	10.10.02P
G-MZCO	Mainair Mercury 1091-0796-7 & W894	26. 6.96	E.Rush	(Congleton)	25. 2.02P
	(Rotax 462)				
G-MZCP	Solar Wings Pegasus XL-Q	11. 2.93	C.Hamblin	Clench Common	31. 8.02P
	(Rotax 462) SW-TE-0434 & SW-WQ-0576				
G-MZCR	Pegasus Quantum 15 7234	28. 6.96	J.E.P.Stubberfield	(Kenley)	11. 5.02P
G-MZCS	TEAM mini-MAX 91 PFA 186-12646	20.12.95	D.T.J.Stanley	Kemble	3. 9.02P
	(Rotax 377)				
G-MZCT	CFM Shadow CD 277	11. 7.96	W.G.Gill	Plaistows Farm, St Albans	8. 6.02P
	(Rotax 503)				
G-MZCU	Mainair Blade 1082-0496-7 & W885	1. 5.96	C.E.Pearce	Beccles	15. 8.02P
	(Rotax 462)				
G-MZCV	Pegasus Quantum 15 7235	11. 7.96	B.S.Toole	Emlyn's Field, Rhuallt	24. 9.02P
G-MZCX	Hunt Wing/Avon Skytrike	17. 7.96	R.Harrison	Higher Barn Farm, Houghton	28. 4.00P
	(Rotax 503) 9510055 & BMAA/HB/072				
G-MZCY	Pegasus Quantum 15 7236	19. 7.96	M.H.Owen	Weston Zoyland	30. 8.02P
	(Rotax 582)				

G-MZCZ*	Hunt Wing/Experience		24. 7.96	C.Kiernan	(Mostrim, Co.Longford)	
	9409024 & BMAA/HB/039 *(BMAA records show as Hunt Wing/Avon 462)*					
				(Completed & taxi-trials undertaken but not flown) (Cancelled 1.8.01 by CAA)		
G-MZDA	Rans S-6-ESD Coyote II XL *(Tri-cycle u/c)*		29. 7.96	W.C.Lombard	Newby Wiske	16. 8.02P
	(Rotax 503) 0396.951 & PFA 204-13019					
G-MZDB	Pegasus Quantum 15-912 7237		31. 7.96	M.J.Reed & D.C.Sollom	Clench Common	13. 1.02P
G-MZDC	Pegasus Quantum 15 7246		2. 8.96	M.T.Jones	Long Marston	11.11.02P
	(Rotax 582)					
G-MZDD	Pegasus Quantum 15 7114	G-69-23	11. 7.96	I.K.Marshall	Weston Zoyland	16. 5.02P
G-MZDE	Pegasus Quantum 15 7238		12. 7.96	D.J.Taylor	(St.Neots)	6. 2.02P
	(Rotax 582)					
G-MZDF	Mainair Blade 1093-0896-7 & W896		15. 8.96	T.D.Thompson	(Knutsford)	24. 4.02P
	(Rotax 462)					
G-MZDG	Rans S-6-ESD Coyote II XL *(Tri-cycle u/c)*		7. 8.96	M.J.Rhodes	Barton	1. 5.02P
	(Rotax 503) 0696.1002.1100 & PFA 204-13030			t/a Barton Heritage Flying Group		
G-MZDH	Pegasus Quantum 15-912 7248		12. 8.96	R.Gill	Knapthorpe Lodge, Caunton	4.11.02P
G-MZDI	Whittaker MW6-S Fatboy Flyer Srs.A	G-BUNN	15. 8.96	J.M.Brooks	(Bromsgrove)	19. 2.02P
	(Rotax 503) PFA 164-11929					
G-MZDJ*	Medway Raven X MRB138/119		19. 8.96	R.Bryan & S.Digby	(Bristol)	1. 5.00P
	(Rotax 447)			*(Cancelled 28.12.01 by CAA)*		
G-MZDK	Mainair Blade 1084-0596-7 & W887		9. 5.96	K.J.Miles	St.Michaels	29. 5.02P
	(Rotax 582) *(C/n reported as 1084-0596-7)*					
G-MZDL	Whittaker MW6-S Fatboy Flyer		19. 8.96	C.D. & S.J.Wills	Chilbolton	27..6.02P
	(Hirth 2706) PFA 164-12412					
G-MZDM	Rans S-6-ESD Coyote II XL *(Tri-cycle u/c)*		2. 9.96	M.E.Nicholas	Chilbolton	11. 4.01P
	(Rotax 503) 0396.954XL & PFA 204-13022					
G-MZDN	Pegasus Quantum 15 7255		5. 9.96	P.G.Ford	(Ely)	31. 7.02P
	(Rotax 582)					
G-MZDO	Cyclone AX3 7252		11. 9.96	W.H.J.Knowles	Weston Zoyland	21. 9.02P
	(Rotax 503)					
G-MZDP	AMF Chevvron 2-32C 020		3. 4.90	A.S.Nicol & A.S.Gunn t/a G-MZDP Group		
	(Konig SD570)				Crowsheath Farm, Hanningfield	16. 3.96P
				(Damaged mid 1995: stored 2001)		
G-MZDR	Rans S-6-ESD Coyote II XL		8. 8.96	R.Pyper & P.McGil		
	(Rotax 503) PFA 204-13012				Newtownards, Co.of Down	22. 1.02P
G-MZDS	Cyclone AX3 7253		16. 9.96	D.S.Paton	Sywell	29.11.02P
	(Rotax 503)					
G-MZDT	Mainair Blade 1096-0996-7 & W899		19. 9.96	G.Sipson	Otherton, Cannock	20. 9.01P
	(Rotax 582)					
G-MZDU	Pegasus Quantum 15-912 7260		19. 9.96	G.A.Breen	(Lagos, Portugal)	26.10.02P
G-MZDV	Pegasus Quantum 15 7199		9. 4.96	P.M.Wilkinson	(Great Orton)	5. 6.01P
	(Rotax 582)					
G-MZDX	Letov LK-2M Sluka PFA 263-12882		30. 9.96	R.P.Stonor	(London W3)	7. 3.02P
	(Rotax 447 1-V)					
G-MZDY	Pegasus Quantum 15 7263		2.10.96	R.Bailey	Sutton Meadows, Ely	7.10.02P
	(Rotax 462HP)					
G-MZDZ	Hunt Avon/Wing 9501042 & BMAA/HB/045		23.10.96	E.W.Laidlaw	(Turriff)	
				(Under construction 2001)		
G-MZEA	BFC Quad City Challenger II		22. 4.96	G.S.Cridland	Thorney Island	28. 2.02P
	(Hirth 2706) CH2-0294-1101 & PFA 177A-12728					
G-MZEB	Mainair Blade		22. 7.96	G.R.Barker	(Epping)	21. 7.02P
	(Rotax 462) 1074-0396-7 & W876					
G-MZEC	Pegasus Quantum 15 7278		24.10.96	A.B.Godber	Bradley Ashbourne, Derby	19.11.02P
	(Rotax 582/40)					
G-MZED	Mainair Blade 1092-0796-7 & W895		3. 7.96	C.W.Potts	(Newcastle upon Tyne)	20.10.01P
	(Rotax 582)					
G-MZEE	Pegasus Quantum 15 7245		9. 8.96	B.J.Marsh	(Hemel Hempstead)	28. 8.01P
	(Rotax 582)					
G-MZEG	Mainair Blade 1095-0896-7 & W898		8. 8.96	J.Jasinczuk	Otherton, Cannock	5. 9.02P
	(Rotax 582)					
G-MZEH	Pegasus Quantum 15 7259		19. 9.96	P.S.Hall	Sywell	16.10.02P
	(Rotax 582/40)					
G-MZEI	Whittaker MW5-D Sorcerer		28.10.96	W.G.Reynolds	Overstrand	28. 8.02P
	(Rotax 447) PFA 163-12011			*(US Navy c/s)*		
G-MZEJ	Mainair Blade 1097-0996-7 & W900		8.10.96	A.D.R.Huddleston	(Liverpool)	27. 7.02P
	(Rotax 462)					
G-MZEK	Mainair Mercury 1098-1096-7 & W901		14.10.96	M.Whiteman-Heywood	(Bewdley)	15.11.02P
	(Rotax 462)					
G-MZEL	Cyclone AX3 7250		30.10.96	T.I.Bull	Tarn Farm, Cockerham	11. 5.02P
	(Rotax 503)					
G-MZEM	Pegasus Quantum 15-912 7277		8.11.96	M.Howland	Clench Common	8.11.02P
G-MZEN	Rans S-6-ESD Coyote II *(Tri-cycle u/c)*		9. 7.96	C.Slater	(Dronfield)	19. 7.02P
	(Rotax 503) 1294.705 & PFA 204-12823					

G-MZEO	Rans S-6-ESD Coyote II XL			19.11.96	J.R.Dobson	Eshott	10. 4.01P
	(Rotax 503)	PFA 204-13046			t/a G-MZEO Group		
G-MZEP	Mainair Rapier	1103-1296-7 & W906		13.12.96	M.J.Gerrish	Arclid Green, Sandbach	18. 5.02P
	(Rotax 503)						
G-MZER	Cyclone AX2000	7251	G-69-28	4.12.96	B.H.Stephens	Old Sarum	18. 3.02P
	(Rotax 582)		G-MZER		t/a Sarum AX2000 Group		
G-MZES	Letov LK-2M Sluka			5.12.96	J.L.Self	Lower Mountpleasant, Chatteris	15.10.02P
	(Rotax 447)	8296K10 & PFA 263-13064					
G-MZET	Cyclone Pegasus Quantum 15	7288		9.12.96	D.L.Walker	(Luxembourg)	12. 8.01P
G-MZEU	Rans S-6-ESD Coyote II XL *(Tri-cycle u/c)*			23.12.96	T.E.Owen & G.P.Gibson	(Holyhead)	4. 2.02P
	(Rotax 503)	PFA 204-13023					
G-MZEV	Mainair Rapier	1101-1296-7 & W904		7. 1.97	I.D.Woolley	Barton	11. 6.02P
	(Rotax 503)						
G-MZEW	Mainair Blade	1105-0197-7 & W908		13. 1.97	S.J.Meehan	Sittles Farm, Alrewas	6. 4.02P
	(Rotax 462)						
G-MZEX	Pegasus Quantum 15	7292		19.11.96	J.Wittering	(Uttoxeter)	7. 2.02P
	(Rotax 582/40)						
G-MZEY	Micro Aviation B.22S Bantam	96-002	ZK-TII	7. 1.97	F.D.Hatton	Pound Green, Kidderminster	11.10.02P
	(Rotax 582)				t/a Pound Green Syndicate		
G-MZEZ	Pegasus Quantum 15-912	7285		8.11.96	E.Daleki	Oakley, Beds	1. 5.02P
G-MZFA	Cyclone AX2000	7301		17.12.96	P.J.Howard & M.Kerrison		
	(Rotax 582/48)					(Ennis, Co.Clare)	2. 3.02P
G-MZFB	Mainair Blade	1108-0197-7 & W911		7. 1.97	S.Chapman	(Bootle)	30. 4.02P
	(Rotax 462)						
G-MZFC	Letov LK-2M Sluka			7. 1.97	P.B.Merritt	(Kingsclere)	24. 8.02P
	(Rotax 447)	8296K009 & PFA 263-13063					
G-MZFD	Mainair Rapier	1109-0197-7 & W912		24. 1.97	R.Gill	Knapthorpe Lodge, Caunton	4. 5.02P
	(Rotax 462)						
G-MZFE	Hunt Avon/Wing	9507049 & BMAA/HB/061		16. 1.97	G.J.Latham	Sittles Farm, Alrewas	15. 6.01P
	(Rotax 503)						
G-MZFF	Hunt Avon/Wing	9604058 & BMAA/HB/074		22. 1.97	B.J.Adamson	(Stockport)	
G-MZFG	Pegasus Quantum 15	7305		21. 1.97	P.Smith	(Ulverston)	6.12.01P
	(Rotax 582/40)						
G-MZFH*	AMF Chevvron 2-32C	039		27. 3.97	Finish Design Ltd t/a Air-Share	Membury	21. 4.98P
	(Konig SD570)		*(Cancelled by CAA 20.4.01) (Stored de-rigged with Aviation Enterprises 10.01)*				
G-MZFI	Lorimer Iolaire	BMAA/HB/035		30. 1.97	H.Lorimer	(Switzerland)	
	(BMW)				*"Iolaire"*		
G-MZFK	Whittaker MW6 Merlin	PFA 164-11626		10. 2.97	G.J.Chadwick	Tarn Farm, Cockerham	9. 2.02P
	(Rotax 532)				t/a G-MZFK Flying Group		
G-MZFL	Rans S-6-ESD Coyote II XL *(Tri-cycle u/c)*			12. 2.97	D.L.Robson & U.Y.S.O'Reilly	Eshott	19. 8.02P
	(Rotax 503)	0696.999XL & PFA 204-13041					
G-MZFM	Pegasus Quantum 15	7310		21. 2.97	T.Holford	(Cannock)	13. 7.01P
	(Rotax 582/40)						
G-MZFN	Rans S-6-ESD Coyote II	PFA 204-12977		26. 2.97	C.J. & W.R.Wallbank	Ley Farm, Chirk	27.11.02P
	(Rotax 503)						
G-MZFO	Thruster T.600N	9037-T600N-001		4. 3.97	J.Berry	Barton	10. 4.02P
	(Rotax 503)						
G-MZFP	Thruster T.600T	9047-T600T-002		4. 3.97	T.R.Villa	Priory Farm, Tibenham	12. 5.02P
	(Rotax 503) *(Noted with nosewheel configuration = T600N)*						
G-MZFR	Thruster T.600N	9047-T600N-003		4. 3.97	H.Larmour	Shobdon	14. 6.01P
	(Rotax 503)				t/a Blue Bird Syndicate		
G-MZFS	Mainair Blade	1110-0297-7 & W913		8. 1.97	M.H.Moulai	(Scunthorpe)	4. 8.02P
	(Rotax 582) *(Officially regd with trike c/n 1010-0297-7)*						
G-MZFT	Pegasus Quantum 15-912	7264		2.10.96	J.F.Woodham	(Buckenham)	25. 4.02P
G-MZFU	Thruster T.600N	9047-T600N-004		4. 3.97	G J Slater	Clench Common	30. 1.02P
	(Rotax 503)						
G-MZFV	Pegasus Quantum 15-912	7324		13. 3.97	G.J.Slater	Deenethorpe	22. 4.02P
	(Rotax 912)						
G-MZFX	Cyclone AX2000	7322		14. 3.97	Flylight Airsports Ltd	Sywell	27. 5.02P
	(Rotax 582/48)						
G-MZFY	Rans S-6-ESD Coyote II XL *(Tri-cycle u/c)*			17. 3.97	L.G.Tserkezos	(Reigate)	22. 6.02P
	(Rotax 503)	0696.1003 & PFA 204-13043					
G-MZFZ	Mainair Blade	1119-0497-7 & W922		2. 4.97	M J Day	(Bungay)	8.12.02P
	(Rotax 582/2V)				tr Blade G-MZFZ Flying Group		
G-MZGA	Cyclone AX2000	7303		17.12.96	Microflight Ireland Ltd		
	(Rotax 582/48)					Mullaghmore, Co.Antrim	11. 6.02P
G-MZGB	Cyclone AX2000	7302		28. 1.97	P.Hegarty	(Magherafelt, Co.Londonderry)	7. 5.02P
	(Rotax 582/48)						
G-MZGC	Cyclone AX2000	7304		20.12.96	Carol E.Walls	Mullaghmore, Co.Antrim	10. 4.02P
	(Rotax 582/2V)						
G-MZGD	Rans S-5 Coyote			1. 4.97	A.G.Headford	Barton	28 .6.02P
	(Rotax 447)	89.095 & PFA 193-13096					
G-MZGF	Letov LK-2M Sluka			8. 4.97	G.Lombardi	RAF Wyton	7.11.01P
	(Rotax 447)	8296K008 & PFA 263-13073					

G-MZGG	Pegasus Quantum 15	7327	10. 4.97	R.W.Partington	Sywell	17. 4.02P
G-MZGH	Hunt Wing/Avon 462(3)		20.10.96	G.C Horner	(Tyldesley, Manchester)	19. 6.02P
	(Rotax 462)	9406021 & BMAA/HB/070				
G-MZGI	Mainair Blade	1117-0397-7 & W920	11. 4.97	N.E.King	Rufforth	8. 6.02P
	(Rotax 912UL)					
G-MZGJ	Kolb Twinstar Mk.3		16. 4.97	P.Coppock	Kemble	5. 4.02P
	(Hirth 2705 R06)	K0008-0193 & PFA 205-12421				
G-MZGK	Pegasus Quantum 15	7331	30. 4.97	A.J.Wells	Sywell	24.10.01P
	(Rotax 582/40)					
G-MZGL	Mainair Rapier	1104-0197-7 & W907	18.12.96	L.R.Fox	(Aylesbury)	17. 5.02P
	(Rotax 503)					
G-MZGM	Cyclone AX2000	7334	1. 5.97	W.G.Dunn	Winkleigh, Devon	3. 8.02P
	(Rotax 582/48)					
G-MZGN	Pegasus Quantum 15	7332	2. 5.97	R.J.Townsend	Long Acre Farm, Sandy	16. 6.02P
G-MZGO	Pegasus Quantum 15	7320	20. 3.97	S.F.G.Allen	Barton	16. 5.02P
	(Rotax 582/40)					
G-MZGP	Cyclone AX2000	7333	7. 5.97	D.G.Palmer	Fetterangus	12. 6.02P
	(Rotax 582/48)			t/a Buchan Light Aeroplane Club		
G-MZGS	CFM Shadow DD	K.284 & PFA 161-13050	8. 5.97	J.Cresswell	Roddidge, Fradley	10. 5.02P
	(Rotax 447)					
G-MZGT	RH7B Tiger Light	PFA 230-13013	10. 3.97	J.B.McNab	(Coventry)	
	(5/8ths scale Tiger Moth)					
G-MZGU	Arrowflight Hawk II (UK)		8. 5.97	P.Duffin	Mullaghmore, Co.Antrim	3. 5.02P
	(Rotax 503)	PFA 266-13075				
G-MZGV	Pegasus Quantum 15	7339	12. 6.97	R.E.Kilby	Dunkeswell	22. 6.01P
	(Rotax 582/40)			t/a G-MZGV Syndicate		
G-MZGW	Mainair Blade	1112-0297-7 & W915	19. 2.97	R.Almond	(Bury St.Edmunds)	23. 7.02P
	(Rotax 462)					
G-MZGX	Thruster T.600N	9057-T600N-005	28. 4.97	R.L.Barton	Ginge Farm, Wantage	29. 7.02P
	(Rotax 503)					
G-MZGY	Thruster T.600N	9057-T600N-006	28. 4.97	M.J.& A.R.Wolldridge		
	(Rotax 503)				Siege Cross Farm, Thatcham	5. 9.02P
G-MZGZ	Thruster T.600N	9057-T600N-007	28. 4.97	K.Hanson	Dunkeswell	29. 9.02P
	(Rotax 503)			t/a G-MZGZ Group		
G-MZHA	Thruster T.600T	9057-T600T-008	28. 4.97	R.V.Buxton	Feshiebridge	17. 7.02P
	(Rotax 503)					
G-MZHB	Mainair Blade	1114-0297-7 & W917	19. 2.97	R.J.Butler	Guy Lane Farm, Waverton	30. 3.02P
	(Rotax 462)					
G-MZHC	Thruster T.600T	9067-T600T-009	13. 5.97	S.W.Tallamy	Davidstow Moor	12. 6.02P
	(HKS 700E)					
G-MZHD	Thruster T.600T	9067-T600T-010	13. 5.97	B.E.Foster	(Tain)	13. 7.02P
	(Rotax 503)					
G-MZHE	Thruster T.600N	9067-T600N-011	13. 5.97	C.Kemp & S.St.John	(Horsham)	3. 5.02P
	(Rotax 503)					
G-MZHF	Thruster T.600N	9067-T600N-012	13. 5.97	R.G.Noble	Enstone	22. 6.02P
	(Rotax 582)					
G-MZHG	Whittaker MW6-T	PFA 164-11420	16. 6.97	M.G.Speers	(Douglas, IoM)	26. 9.01P
	(Rotax 532 1-V)					
G-MZHI	Pegasus Quantum 15	7337	27. 5.97	P R Hope	Knapthorpe Lodge, Caunton	3. 7.02P
	(Rotax 582/40)			t/a Quantum HI Group		
				(Op Derbyshire & Nottingham Microlight Club)		
G-MZHJ	Mainair Rapier	1123-0697-7 & W926	17. 6.97	C.S.Povey & B.Hall	Tarn Farm, Cockerham	15. 6.02P
	(Rotax 462)					
G-MZHK	Pegasus Quantum Super Sport 15	7352	24. 6.97	A.D.S.Grant	Rufforth	19. 7.02P
	(Rotax 582/40)					
G-MZHL	Mainair Rapier	1126-0797-7 & W929	30. 6.97	K Mallin	(Halesowen)	6. 8.02P
	(Rotax 503)					
G-MZHM	TEAM hi-MAX 1700R	PFA 272-12912	8. 1.97	M.H.McKeown	(Gorey, Co.Wexford)	13. 5.02P
	(Robin 440)					
G-MZHN	Pegasus Quantum 15	7351	27. 6.97	T.G.Jones	Emlyn's Field, Rhuallt	17. 8.02P
	(Rotax 462HP)					
G-MZHO	Quad City Challenger II		15. 7.97	J.Pavelin	Barling, Essex	14. 6.02P
	(Rotax 503)	PFA 177-12936				
G-MZHP	Pegasus Quantum 15	7353	15. 7.97	A.S.Findley	Long Acre Farm, Sandy	20. 8.02P
	(Rotax 582/40)					
G-MZHR	Cyclone AX2000	7307	7. 3.97	A.M.Hemmings	Sandtoft	1. 5.02P
	(Rotax 582)					
G-MZHS	Thruster T.600T	9077-T600T-013	4. 7.97	D.Mahajan	Lower Mountpleasant, Chatteris	20.10.02P
	(Rotax 582)					
G-MZHT	Whittaker MW6 Merlin	PFA 164-11244	12. 6.97	S.J.Smith	Kemble	17. 6.02P
	(Rotax 503)					
G-MZHU	Thruster T.600T	9077-T600T-019	4. 7.97	M.S.Shelton		
	(Rotax 503-2V)				Stoneacre Farm, Farthing Corner	27. 8.02P

G-MZHV	Thruster T.600T	9077-T600T-018		4. 7.97	L G M Maddick	Leicester	17.12.02P
	(Rotax 503 UL) *(Officially regd as T.600N)*				t/a Hotel Victor Group		
G-MZHW	Thruster T.600N	9077-T600N-017		4. 7.97	K.N.Hopewell	Leicester	4. 6.01P
	(Rotax 503-2V)						
G-MZHX	Thruster T.600N	9077-T600N-016		4. 7.97	Thruster Air Services Ltd		
						Ginge Farm, Wantage	
G-MZHY	Thruster T.600N	9077-T600N-015		4. 7.97	J.R.North	Ince Blundell	11. 5.02P
	(Rotax 503)				t/a West Lancashire Microlight School		
G-MZHZ	Thruster T.600N	9077-T600N-014		4. 7.97	N.Jennings	Shobdon	29. 6.02P
	(Rotax 503 UL)				t/a The Red Arrow Syndicate		
G-MZIA	TEAM hi-Max 1700R	PFA 272-13020		25. 4.97	I.J.Arkieson	(Meols, Wirral)	
G-MZIB	Pegasus Quantum 15	7354		15. 7.97	S.Murphy	Trim, Co.Meath	2. 9.00P
	(Rotax 582/40)						
G-MZIC	Pegasus Quantum 15	7348		24. 6.97	Helen M.Squire & C.F.Two	(Swansea)	6. 8.02P
					t/a Swansea Airsports Services		
G-MZID	Whittaker MW6 Merlin	PFA 164-11383		15. 7.97	M.G.A.Wood	(Tadcaster)	27 .9.02P
G-MZIE	Pegasus Quantum 15	7359		6. 8.97	Flylight Airsports Ltd	Sywell	25. 8.02P
	(Rotax 582/40)						
G-MZIF	Pegasus Quantum 15	7355		16. 7.97	P.Simpson	Sywell	25. 8.02P
G-MZIH	Mainair Blade	1128-0797-7 & W931		16. 7.97	E.Scarisbrick	Brook Farm, Pilling	12. 9.01P
	(Rotax 462)				*(Op Mercury Microlight Club)*		
G-MZII	TEAM mini-MAX 88	PFA 186-11842		19. 3.97	G.F.M.Garner	Clench Common	13. 8.01P
	(Rotax 447)						
G-MZIJ	Pegasus Quantum 15	7362		14. 8.97	C.M.Saysell	Plaistows Farm, St Albans	19. 9.02P
	(Rotax 582/40)						
G-MZIK	Pegasus Quantum 15	7368		8. 9.97	D.Kiddy & P.Davies	(Torquay/Totnes)	10. 5.02P
	(Rotax 582/40)						
G-MZIL	Mainair Rapier	1132-0897-7 & W935		1. 9.97	A.J.Varga	Rufforth	8. 9.02P
	(Rotax 462)						
G-MZIM	Mainair Rapier	1124-0697-7 & W927		9. 6.97	M.J.McKegney	Newtownards, Co.of Down	21. 7.02P
	(Rotax 462)						
G-MZIP	Murphy Renegade Spirit UK			4. 7.89	C.G.Boulton	(Newbury)	8. 2.02P
	(Rotax 532)	216 & PFA 188-11426					
G-MZIR	Mainair Blade	1134-0997-7 & W937		18. 9.97	S.W.Tallamy	Davidstow Moor	29. 6.02P
	(Rotax 582)						
G-MZIS	Mainair Blade	1115-0397-7 & W918		17. 2.97	K.R.McCartney	Baxby Manor, Husthwaite	23. 4.02P
	(Rotax 462)						
G-MZIT	Mainair Blade	1129-0897-7 & W932		16. 7.97	P.M.Horn	Peterlee	25. 7.01P
	(Rotax 912UL)						
G-MZIU	Pegasus Quantum 15	7371		15.10.97	S.F.Winter	Redlands, Swindon	16.12.02P
	(Rotax 582/40)						
G-MZIV	Cyclone AX2000	7372		21.10.97	C.J.Tomlin	Knapthorpe Lodge, Caunton	6.12.02P
	(Rotax 582/48)						
G-MZIW	Mainair Blade	1127-0797-7 & W930		16. 7.97	N.E.J.Hayes	(Chorley)	11. 9.02P
	(Rotax 462)						
G-MZIX	Mignet HM-1000 Balerit	130		23. 9.97	P.E.H.Scott	(Stockbridge)	13. 2.01P
	(Rotax 582)						
G-MZIY	Rans S-6-ESD Coyote II XL *(Tri-cycle u/c)*			29. 9.97	P.A.Bell	Barton	10.12.02P
	(Rotax 503)	1096.1050XL & PFA 204-13184	*(Rebuilt with new fuselage frame c.1998)*				
G-MZIZ	Murphy Renegade Spirit UK		G-MWGP	21.10.92	G Long	Plaistows Farm, St Albans	4. 2.02P
	(Rotax 582)	257 & PFA 188-11701					
G-MZJA	Mainair Blade	1135-0997-7 & W938		30. 9.97	R.C.McArthur	Ince Blundell	7. 2.02P
	(Rotax 582)						
G-MZJB	Aviasud Mistral	047	(ex ?)	30. 9.97	D.M.Whitham	Crosland Moor	
G-MZJD	Mainair Blade	1130-0897-7 & W933		7. 8.97	R.J.Davey	(Sleaford)	20. 8.02P
	(Rotax 503)						
G-MZJE	Mainair Rapier	1136-1097-7 & W939		17.10.97	J.E.Davies	(Southport)	2. 8.02P
	(Rotax 503)						
G-MZJF	Cyclone AX2000	7378		2.12.97	A.J.Blackwell	Long Marston	21.12.02P
	(Rotax 582/48)						
G-MZJG	Pegasus Quantum 15	7335		2. 5.97	J.Gamlen	Oakley, Beds	28. 5.02P
	(Rotax 462)						
G-MZJH	Pegasus Quantum 15	7350		25. 6.97	J.Hardy	(Kettering)	19. 7.02P
G-MZJI	Rans S-6-ESD Coyote II XL *(Tri-cycle u/c)*			3.11.97	A.T.Morgan	Rayne Hall Farm, Rayne	24. 6.02P
	(Rotax 503)	1096.1046XL & PFA 204-13221					
G-MZJJ	Murphy Maverick	PFA 259-13016		5.11.97	N.B.Kirby	Dunkeswell	22. 3.02P
	(Jabiru 2200A)						
G-MZJK	Mainair Blade	1100-1196-7 & W903		19.11.96	A.H.Kershaw	(Bury)	15. 7.01P
	(Rotax 582)						
G-MZJL	Cyclone AX2000	7363		11. 8.97	A.J.Longbottom	Smeathorpe, Honiton	28.10.00P
	(Rotax 503)						
G-MZJM	Rans S-6-ESD Coyote II XL			19.11.97	R.J.Hopkins	Popham	17. 4.02P
	(Rotax 503-2V)	1096.1049XL & PFA 204-13215					

G-MZJN	Pegasus Quantum 15 (Rotax 582/40)	7376		11.11.97	J.Nelson *(Op Derbyshire & Nottingham Microlight Club)*	Knapthorpe Lodge, Caunton	16.11.02P
G-MZJO	Pegasus Quantum 15 (Rotax 582/40)	7338		17. 6.97	D.J.Cook	Eaglescott	30. 9.02P
G-MZJP	Whittaker MW6-S Fatboy Flyer	PFA 164-13049		21.10.97	D.J.Burton & C.A.J.Funnell	(Brighton)	
G-MZJR	Cyclone AX2000 (HKS 700E)	7385		11.11.97	Cyclone Airsports Ltd t/a Pegasus Aviation	(Manton, Marlborough)	16. 9.02P
G-MZJS	Murphy Maverick 430 (Jabiru 2200A)	PFA 259-13017		12.12.97	R.D.Barnard	(Stockport)	16. 4.02P
G-MZJT	Pegasus Quantum 15-912	7399		23.12.97	C.M.Theakstone	Sywell	23.12.02P
G-MZJV	Mainair Blade (Rotax 912)	1141-0198-7 & W944		7. 1.98	M.A.Roberts	West Malling	3. 2.99P
G-MZJW	Pegasus Quantum 15-912	7390		27. 1.98	W.H.J.Knowles	Weston Zoyland	8.10.02P
G-MZJX	Mainair Blade (Rotax 503-2V)	1139-0198-7 & W942		9. 1.98	R.H.H.Munro	(Sevenoaks)	30. 4.01P
G-MZJY	Pegasus Quantum 15-912	7394		23.12.97	S.G Payne t/a Yankee Syndicate	Long Acre Farm, Sandy	23.12.02P
G-MZJZ	Mainair Blade (Rotax 912UL)	1121-0597-7 & W924		23. 6.97	P.Crosby	Ince Blundell	22. 6.02P
G-MZKA	Pegasus Quantum 15	7380		1.12.97	A.S.R.McSherry	West Kilbride	11.12.02P
G-MZKC	Cyclone AX2000 (Rotax 582-48)	7398		22. 1.98	A.G. & G.L.Higgins	Bitteswell	20. 2.02P
G-MZKD	Pegasus Quantum 15	7404		19. 3.98	S.J.E.Smith	(Newcastle upon Tyne)	4. 7.02P
G-MZKE	Rans S-6-ESD Coyote II XL (Rotax 503-2V)	PFA 204-13248		19. 1.98	I.Findlay	Eshott	30. 5.02P
G-MZKF	Pegasus Quantum 15	7407		21. 1.98	T.A.Howe	(Margate)	5. 7.02P
G-MZKG	Mainair Blade (Rotax 582-2V)	1145-0198-7 & W948		23. 1.98	P.Olsson	(Ulverston)	17.12.00P
G-MZKH	CFM Shadow DD (Rotax 582)	292-DD		23. 1.98	K.D.Mitchell	Shoreham	5. 5.02P
G-MZKI	Mainair Rapier (Rotax 503-2V)	1147-0298-7 & W950		12. 2.98	C.K.Richardson	East Fortune	18. 5.02P
G-MZKJ	Mainair Blade (Rotax 582)	1039-0595-7 & W837		19. 5.95	L.G.M.Maddick	Leicester	27. 8.02P
G-MZKK	Mainair Blade (Rotax 912)	1140-0198-7 & W943		12. 2.98	D.L.Hadley	Lydd	1. 2.02P
G-MZKL	Pegasus Quantum 15 (Rotax 582/40)	7360		18. 8.97	C.W.Laskey	Shobdon	31. 8.02P
G-MZKM	Mainair Blade (Rotax 912UL)	1133-0897-7 & W936		15. 8.97	C.Bodill	(Nottingham)	25.10.01P
G-MZKN	Mainair Rapier (Rotax 503-2V)	1138-1297-7 & W941		12.12.97	G.Craig	Newtownards, Co.of Down	23. 1.02P
G-MZKO	Mainair Blade (Rotax 503)	1131-0897-7 & W934		5. 8.97	A.M.Durose	(Nottingham)	7.12.02P
G-MZKP	Thruster T.600N	9038-T600N-020		27. 1.98	Thruster Air Services Ltd	Ginge Farm, Wantage	
G-MZKR	Thruster T.600N (Rotax 582UL)	9038-T600N-021		27. 1.98	R.J.Arnett	(Albuferia, Portugal)	19 .6.00P
G-MZKS	Thruster T.600N (HKS 700E)	9038-T600N-022		27. 1.98	N.C.Harper t/a G-MZKS Group	(Norwich)	20. 8.02P
G-MZKT	Thruster T.600T (Rotax 582UL)	9038-T600T-023		27. 1.98	M.J.O'Connor	Margaretting	8. 7.02P
G-MZKU	Thruster T.600T (Rotax 503UL)	9038-T600T-024		27. 1.98	A.S.Day	RAF Wyton	24. 9.02P
G-MZKV	Mainair Blade (Rotax 912)	1144-0198-7 & W947		28. 1.98	M.P.J.Moore	(Stoke-on-Trent)	8. 5.02P
G-MZKW	Quad City Challenger II (Hirth 2705 R06)	PFA 177-12518		22. 3.94	K.W.Warn	Siege Cross Farm, Thatcham	10.12.02P
G-MZKX	Pegasus Quantum 15 (Rotax 582-40)	7395		15. 1.98	M.G.Evans	(Milton Keynes)	15. 1.02P
G-MZKY	Pegasus Quantum 15 (HKS 700E)	7403		16. 1.98	G.N.S.Farrant	RAF Benson	2. 5.02P
G-MZKZ	Mainair Blade (Rotax 582-2V) *(Supplied as Mainair Kit)*	K1137-0298-7 & W940		18. 2.98	R.P.Wolstenholme	(Warrington)	1. 9.01P
G-MZLA	Pegasus Quantum 15 (Rotax 582-40)	7415		27. 2.98	D.A.Morgan	Dunkeswell	24. 3.02P
G-MZLB	Hunt Wing/Experience	BMAA/HB/058		25. 2.98	M.Ffrench	(New Ross, Co.Wexford)	
G-MZLC	Mainair Blade (Rotax 912)	1146-0298-7 & W949		26. 2.98	M J Rummery	Ince Blundell	6. 4.02P
G-MZLD	Pegasus Quantum 15-912	7416		24. 3.98	B.Kirkland	Tarn Farm, Cockerham	14. 8.02P
G-MZLE	Murphy Maverick 430 (Jabiru 2200A)	PFA 259-12955	G-BXSZ	27. 2.98	A.A.Plumridge	Bodmin	15. 1.02P
G-MZLF	Pegasus Quantum 15	7417		30. 3.98	J.H.Tope & B J Harper	(Newton Abbot)	11. 5.01P

G-MZLG	Rans S-6-ESD Coyote II XL *(Tri-cycle u/c)*			3. 3.98	M.Rhodes	(Stoke-on-Trent)	20. 5.02P
	(Rotax 503-2V) 0897.1143XL & PFA 204-13192						
G-MZLH	Pegasus Quantum 15	7426		1. 4.98	R.J.Philpotts		
	(Rotax 582-40)					Pound Green, Buttonoak, Kidderminster	13. 8.02P
G-MZLI	Mignet HM-1000 Balerit	133		5. 3.98	B.W.Peacock	(Spalding)	5. 8.02P
	(Rotax 582)						
G-MZLJ	Pegasus Quantum 15	7421		20. 3.98	M.H.Colin	Otherton	29. 3.02P
G-MZLK	Ultrasports Tripacer/Solar Wings Typhoon			9. 3.98	J.A.Jones	(Winchester)	29. 9.02P
	(Fuji-Robin EC-34-PM)	T285-1471 *(Trike unit ex G-MJEC & Sailwing is Typhoon S4+ (ex-hanglider) s/n T785-1471M)*					
G-MZLL	Rans S-6-ESD Coyote II	PFA 204-13067		23. 9.97	J.A.Willats & G.W.Champion	(Crawley)	6. 9.02P
	(Rotax 503)						
G-MZLM	Cyclone AX2000	7425		22. 4.98	P.Bennett	Swinford, Rugby	11. 5.02P
	(Rotax 582-48) *(Modified to hang-glider tug version)*						
G-MZLN	Pegasus Quantum 15	7431		14. 4.98	P.Thomson	Deenethorpe	24. 4.02P
					t/a G-MZLN Flying Group		
G-MZLO	CFM Shadow D Srs.SS	K.298-D		1. 4.98	CFM Aircraft Ltd	Leiston	2.10.01P
	(Rotax 912-UL)						
G-MZLP	CFM Shadow D Srs.SS	K.299-D		1. 4.98	C.S.Robinson	Newtownards, Co.of Down	2.10.01P
	(Rotax 912-UL)						
G-MZLR	Solar Wings Pegasus XL-Q	7441		28. 5.98	T.I.Courtney	Jacksdale	31. 5.02P
	(Rotax 462HP) *(Trike c/n SW-TB-1040 ex G-MNJP fitted with new sailwing c/n 7441)*						
G-MZLS	Cyclone AX2000	7428		6. 7.98	G.Forster	North Coates	3. 8.02P
	(HKS 700E V3)						
G-MZLT	Pegasus Quantum 15-912	7438		24. 4.98	C.S.Bourne	(Stone)	28. 4.02P
G-MZLU	Cyclone AX2000	7439		28. 7.98	M.L.Smith	(Verwood)	20. 7.02P
	(HKS 700E V3)						
G-MZLV	Pegasus Quantum 15	7437		29. 4.98	M.W.Houghton	(Peterborough)	6. 7.02P
G-MZLW	Pegasus Quantam 15	7440		28. 4.98	I.A.Baker	Sywell	23. 5.02P
	(Rotax 582-40)						
G-MZLX	Micro Aviation B.22S Bantam	97-013	ZK-JIV	9.12.97	D.L.Howell	Long Acre Farm, Sandy	19. 8.02P
	(Rotax 582)						
G-MZLY	Letov LK-2M Sluka	PFA 263-13065		20. 4.98	W.McCarthy	Wick	12. 9.02P
	(Rotax 447 1V)						
G-MZLZ	Mainair Blade	1154-0498-7 & W957		21. 4.98	S.R.Winter	Hunsdon	14. 5.02P
	(Rotax 912)						
G-MZMA	Pegasus Quasar IITC	6611		1. 9.93	C.M.Addison	Knapthorpe Lodge, Caunton	7. 4.02P
	(Rotax 582/40)						
G-MZMB	Mainair Blade	1149-0398-7 & W952		5. 3.98	J T Hearle	(Blackburn)	11. 4.02P
	(Rotax 462)						
G-MZMC	Pegasus Quantum 15-912	7206		10. 5.96	J.J.Baker	Deenethorpe	20. 5.02P
G-MZMD	Mainair Blade	1148-0398-7 & W951		5. 3.98	T.Gate	(Clitheroe)	22. 4.02P
	(Rotax 912)						
G-MZME	Medway Hybred 44XLR EclipseR	151/129E	G-58	28. 4.98	T.Bowles	Ince Blundell	28. 9.02P
	(Jabiru 2200A) *(Test flown with "B" conditions marks but no suffix used)*						
G-MZMF	Pegasus Quantum 15(HKS)	7387		30. 4.98	A.Wales	Rufforth	11. 9.02P
	(HKS 700E V3)						
G-MZMG	Pegasus Quantum 15	7446		27. 5.98	J M Pattison	Weston Zoyland	27. 5.02P
G-MZMH	Pegasus Quantum 15-912	7402		27. 1.98	M.Hurtubise	(Leamington Spa)	19. 2.02P
G-MZMJ	Mainair Blade	1155-0598-7 & W958		8. 5.98	S.Miles	(Sutton-in-Ashfield)	1. 8.02P
	(Rotax 912)						
G-MZMK	AMF Chevvron 2-32C	040		19. 5.98	K.D.Calvert	Park Farm, Eaton Bray	17. 7.01P
	(Konig SD 570)						
G-MZML	Mainair Blade	1158-0698-7 & W961		19. 5.98	M.J.Allan	Latch Farm, Kirknewton	3. 7.02P
	(Rotax 912)						
G-MZMM	Mainair Blade	1162-0698-7 & W965		19. 5.98	J.F.Shaw	Baxby Manor, Husthwaite	12. 7.02P
	(Rotax 912) *(or Rotax 462?)*						
G-MZMN	Pegasus Quantum 15-912	7445		21. 5.98	L.A.Hosegood	Redlands, Swindon	16.12.01P
G-MZMO	TEAM mini-MAX 91	PFA 186-12951		20. 5.98	I.M.Ross	Insch	9 .5.02P
	(Rotax 447)						
G-MZMP	Mainair Blade	1160-0698-7 & W963		20. 5.98	A.Ambler	(Market Rasen)	28.11.02P
	(Rotax 582-2V)						
G-MZMS	Rans S-6-ES Coyote II *(Tri-cycle u/c)*			26. 5.98	D.G.Matthews	Long Marston	21.10.02P
	(Rotax 503) 1298.1203ES & PFA 204-13294						
G-MZMT	Pegasus Quantum 15	7449		18. 6.98	B.J.Kitson	Sutton Meadows, Ely	19. 7.02P
	(Rotax 582-40)						
G-MZMU	Rans S-6-ESD-XL Coyote II			5. 6.98	S.Cox	(Hinckley)	2.10.02P
	(Rotax 503-2V)	PFA 204-13242					
G-MZMV	Mainair Blade	1152-0496-7 & W955		30. 3.98	P.R.Whitehouse	Otherton, Cannock	13. 5.02P
	(Rotax 462)				t/a Blade Runners Syndicate		
G-MZMW	Mignet HM-1000 Balerit	125		2.10.96	M.E.Whapham	Corn Wood Farm, Adversane	8. 5.02P
	(Rotax 582)						
G-MZMX	Cyclone AX2000	7451		8. 9.98	R.H.Braithwaite	RAF Halton	10.10.02P
	(HKS 700E V3)				t/a RAF Microlight Flying Association		

G-MZMY	Mainair Blade	1153-0498-7 & W956		16. 3.98	C.J.Millership	Ince Blundell	18. 5.02P
	(Rotax 462)						
G-MZNA	Quad City Challenger II UK		EI-CLE	19. 3.98	S.Hennessy	(Dublin)	3. 9.02P
	(Rotax 503)	CH2-0894-UK-1193					
G-MZNB	Pegasus Quantum 15-912	7456		17. 7.98	F.Gorse	(Caernarfon)	7.12.02P
G-MZNC	Mainair Blade	1161-0698-7 & W964		22. 6.98	A.Costello	St Michaels	22. 6.02P
	(Rotax 912)				*(Op North Lancs Micro School)*		
G-MZND	Mainair Rapier	1170-0898-7 & W973		24. 6.98	S.D.Hutchinson	St Michaels	12. 7.02P
	(Rotax 912)						
G-MZNE	Whittaker MW6-S Fatboy Flyer			26. 6.98	K.Angel	Stoke, Kent	21 .6.02P
	(Rotax 582-47)	PFA 164-13120					
G-MZNG	Pegasus Quantum 15-912	7457		11. 8.98	G.G.Rowley	(Carlisle)	13. 8.01P
G-MZNH	CFM Shadow DD	K.297-DD		30. 6.98	P.A.James	Redhill	29. 7.02P
	(Rotax 582)						
G-MZNI	Mainair Blade	1163-0698-7 & W966		3. 7.98	D.Armstrong	(Ruislip)	12.12.02P
	(Rotax 912)						
G-MZNJ	Mainair Blade	1168-0798-7 & W971		6. 7.98	G.E.Cole	Over Farm, Gloucester	16. 8.02P
	(Rotax 462)						
G-MZNK	Mainair Blade	1164-0798-7 & W967		6. 7.98	D.S.Taylor & Taylor Refrigeration Ltd		
	(Rotax 912)					(Maidstone)	22. 6.02P
G-MZNL	Mainair Blade	1165-0798-7 & W968		6. 7.98	R.P.Taylor & Taylor Refrigeration Ltd		
	(Rotax 912)					Rochester	22. 6.02P
G-MZNM	TEAM mini-MAX 91	PFA 186-12304		10. 7.98	N.P.Thomson	Kirkbride	
	(Fuji-Robin EC-44) *(No built-up rear fuselage)*						
G-MZNN	TEAM mini-MAX 91	PFA 186-13125		10. 7.98	D.M.Dronsfield	Brook Farm, Pilling	17. 6.02P
	(Rotax 447)				*(Op Mercury Microlight Club)*		
G-MZNO	Mainair Blade	1167-0798-7 & W970		9. 6.98	R.C.Colclough	(Stoke-on-Trent)	24. 9.02P
	(Rotax 462)						
G-MZNP	Pegasus Quantum 15-912	7466		22. 7.98	O.W.Achurch	(Northampton)	30. 5.01P
G-MZNR	Pegasus Quantum 15	7465		17. 8.98	E.S.Wills	(Paignton)	2. 8.02P
G-MZNS	Pegasus Quantum 15-912	7473		31. 7.98	P.G.Leonard	(Luton)	14.12.01P
G-MZNT	Pegasus Quantum 15-912	7470		25. 9.98	M.P.Lewis	(Market Harborough)	27. 1.02P
G-MZNU	Mainair Rapier	174-0898-7 & W977		5. 8.98	D.N.Carnegie	(St. Bees)	21. 9.02P
	(Rotax 503-2V)						
G-MZNV	Rans S-6-ESD Coyote II *(Tri-cycle u/c)*			7. 8.98	D.E.Rubery & A.P.Thomas		
	(Rotax 503-2V)	1294.704 & PFA 204-12884				Lower Wasing Farm, Brimpton	22.10.02P
G-MZNW	Thruster T.600N	9098-T600N-025		10. 8.98	M.J.Lathe	Shobdon	7. 7.02P
	(Rotax 582UL)				t/a November Whiskey Syndicate		
G-MZNX	Thruster T.600N	9098-T600N-026		10. 8.98	M H Moulai	North Coates	4.11.02P
	(Rotax 503UL-2V)						
G-MZNY	Thruster T.600N	9098-T600N-027		10. 8.98	P.Young	Swanton Morley	26. 6.02P
	(Rotax 582)				t/a Thruster Group		
G-MZNZ	Letov LK-2M Sluka			21. 4.98	K.T.Vinning	(Stratford-upon-Avon)	20. 5.02P
	(Rotax 447)	8295s015 & PFA 0263-13274					
G-MZOA*	Thruster T.600T	9108-T600T-028		10. 8.98	Thruster Air Services Ltd		
						Ginge Farm, Wantage	
					(Cancelled 25.9.01 as wfu - no PtoF issued)		
G-MZOB*	Thruster T.600T	9098-T600T-029		10. 8.98	Thruster Air Services Ltd		
						Ginge Farm, Wantage	
					(Cancelled 25.9.01 as wfu - no PtoF issued)		
G-MZOC	Mainair Blade	1172-0898-7 & W975		10. 8.98	J D Sinclair-Day	(Ryton)	1. 9.01P
	(Rotax 912)						
G-MZOD	Pegasus Quantum 15-912	7435		28. 4.98	J.W.Mann	Enstone	26. 4.02P
G-MZOE	Cyclone AX2000	7472		17. 9.98	York Microlight Centre Ltd	Rufforth	2.10.01P
	(HKS 700E V3)						
G-MZOF	Mainair Blade	1122-0697-7 & W925		5. 6.97	A.P.S.John, T.D.Holland-Martin & P.J.Bossom		
	(Rotax 462)				t/a Overbury Farms	(Tewkesbury)	28. 7.01P
G-MZOG	Pegasus Quantum 15	7471		12.10.98	J.F.Leather	Weston Zoyland	6. 4.02P
	(Rotax 503)						
G-MZOH	Whittaker MW-5-D Sorcerer			14. 8.98	D.M.Precious	(Camelford)	16. 9.02P
	(Fuji-Robin EC-44)	PFA 163-13060 *(Officially recorded as Rotax 377)*					
G-MZOI	Letov LK-2M Sluka			17. 8.98	M.C.Reed	(Loughborough)	5. 9.02P
	(Rotax 447 1V)	8296s012 & PFA 263-13238					
G-MZOJ	Pegasus Quantum 15	7478		9.11.98	A.C. Lane	Long Acre Farm, Sandy	15.11.02P
	(Rotax 582-40)						
G-MZOK	Whittaker MW6 Merlin	PFA 164-11568		24. 8.97	T.A.Willcox	(Bristol)	6. 7.02P
	(Rotax 582)						
G-MZOM	CFM Shadow DD	302-DD		8. 9.98	P.S.Winteron & P.Tidd t/a Side-Stick Syndicate		
	(Rotax 582)					Lower Mountpleasant, Chatteris	10.11.01P
G-MZON	Mainair Rapier	1180-1098-7-W983		11. 9.98	K.A.Armstrong	Brough	5.10.01P
	(Rotax 503-2V)						
G-MZOP	Mainair Blade	1178-0998-7-W981		11. 9.98	P.Barrow	Arclid Green, Sandbach	15.10.02P
	(Rotax 912)						

G-MZOR	Mainair Blade (Rotax 912)	1173-0898-7-W976		21. 9.98	D.L.Foxley	Barton	7.10.01P
G-MZOS	Pegasus Quantum 15-912 (Rotax 912)	7458		6.10.98	Skyglobe Microlights Ltd	(London SE10)	13. 1.02P
G-MZOT	Letov LK-2M Sluka (Rotax 447 1V)	PFA 263-13346		21. 9.98	J.R.Walter	Quilkieston Farm, Stair	13 .8.02P
G-MZOV	Pegasus Quantum 15	7512		9. 3.99	J.C.Tunstall	Enstone	17. 3.02P
G-MZOW	Pegasus Quantum 15-912	7502		9. 3.99	W.P.Byrne	Newtownards, Co.of Down	30 .3.02P
G-MZOX	Letov LK-2M Sluka (Rotax 447)	PFA 263-13415		15. 2.99	C.M.James	(Canterbury)	
G-MZOY	TEAM mini-MAX 91	PFA 186-12526		29. 3.99	E.F.Smith	(Egremont)	
G-MZOZ	Rans S-6-ESD Coyote II XL *(Tri-cycle u/c)* (Rotax 582)	1096.1052XL & PFA 204-13168 *(Engine officially recorded as Rotax 503)*		20. 5.98	D.C.& S.G.Emmons	(Reading)	2. 9.02P
G-MZPB	Mignet HM-1000 Balerit (Rotax 582)	124		4.10.96	P.M.Baker	Corn Wood Farm, Adversane	4. 8.02P
G-MZPD	Pegasus Quantum 15 (Rotax 582)	7013		9. 5.95	P.M.Dewhurst	Sywell	5. 6.02P
G-MZPH	Mainair Blade (Rotax 582-2V)	1177-0998-7-W980		26. 8.98	C L G Innocent	(Worthing)	11.10.02P
G-MZPJ	TEAM mini-MAX 91 (Rotax 503)	PFA 186-12277		23.11.92	P.R.Jenson	Sittles Farm, Alrewas	21.11.02P
G-MZPW	Pegasus Quasar IITC (Rotax 582)	6892		26.10.94	D.R.Griffiths	Weston Zoyland	3. 6.02P
G-MZRC	Pegasus Quantum 15 (Rotax 582-40)	7482		25.11.98	M.Hopkins	Rufforth	26. 1.02P
G-MZRH	Pegasus Quantum 15 (Rotax 582/40)	7269		11.10.96	R.J.Ware	Sittles Farm, Alrewas	28.12.02P
G-MZRM	Pegasus Quantum 15-912	7455		10. 7.98	M.R.Mosley	(Retford)	2. 8.02P
G-MZRS	CFM Shadow CD (Rotax 503)	141		4. 4.90	M.R.Lovegrove	Croft Farm, Defford	29. 4.02P
G-MZSC	Pegasus Quantum 15	7370		3.10.97	R.J.Greaves	Sywell	11.10.02P
G-MZSD	Mainair Blade (Rotax 912)	1179-0998-7 & W978		21. 8.98	D.Sampson	East Fortune	5.12.02P
G-MZSM	Mainair Blade (Rotax 582)	1000-0794-7 & W796		15. 7.94	P.R.Anderson	Oxton, Nottingham	10. 9.02P
G-MZTA	Mignet HM-1000 Balerit (Rotax 582)	120		14. 5.96	A.Fusco t/a Sky Light Group	(Burwash)	8. 5.01P
G-MZTS	Aerial Arts Chaser S (Rotax 377)	CH703	G-MVDM	19. 3.96	D.G.Ellis	(Tamworth)	26.10.02P
G-MZUB	Rans S-6-ESD Coyote II XL *(Tri-cycle u/c)* (Rotax 503-2V)	PFA 204-13244		30. 4.98	B.O.Dowsett	(Astwood)	30. 7.02P
G-MZZT	Kolb Twinstar Mk.3 (Rotax 582)	K0006-0992 & PFA 205-12596		1. 5.98	P.I.Morgans	Haverfordwest	24. 5.02P
G-MZZY	Mainair Blade (Rotax 912UL)	1050-0895-7 & W848		13.11.95	A.Mucznik	Oxton, Nottingham	18. 1.02P

G-NAAA – G-NZZZ

G-NAAA	MBB Bö.105DBS-4	S.34/912	G-BUTN	6. 4.99	Bond Air Services	Blackpool	21. 2.02T
	(Rebuilt with new pod S.912 1993)		G-AZTI/EI-BTE/G-AZTI/EC-DRY/G-AZTI/D-HDAN *(Op Lancashire Air Ambulance/AA)*				
G-NAAB	MBB Bö.105DBS-4	S.416	D-HDMO	23. 3.99	Bond Air Services	Henstridge	8..4.02T
			D-HSTP/D-HDMO		*(Op Dorset & Somerset Air Ambulance/AA)*		
G-NAAS	Aérospatiale AS355F1 Twin Squirrel		G-BPRG	23. 3.90	Northumbria Ambulance Service NHS Trust		
		5203	G-NWPA/G-NAAS/G-BPRG/N370E			Blyth	18. 4.02T
					(Op North East Air Ambulance)		
G-NAAT*	Folland Gnat T.1	FL.507	XM697	27.11.89	Bournemouth Aviation Museum	Bournemouth	
					(Cancelled 10.4.95 as WFU)		
G-NABS*	Robinson R22 Beta	1564		29.10.90	Burman Aviation Ltd	Cranfield	
	(Crashed on approach Cumbernauld 30.6.91: cancelled 5.9.91 by CAA: sold as N5115C 11.92: reg cancelled 10.96: pod stored 9.99: current status unknown)						
G-NACA	Norman NAC-2 Freelance 180	2001		23.11.87	NDN Aircraft Ltd *(Stored 6.99)*	Coventry	
G-NACI	Norman NAC-1 Freelance 180	NAC.001	G-AXFB	20. 6.84	L.J.Martin *(Stored 6.01)*	Sandown	7. 4.94P
G-NACL*	Norman NAC-6 Fieldmaster	6001	G-BNEG	23. 4.87	EPA Aircraft Co Ltd	Sandown	5.12.90P
	(Aka Firemaster 65)	*(Fitted with rudder/marks of G-NACM: stored 8.00: cancelled 7.3.01 as temporarily wfu)*					
G-NACO*	Norman NAC-6 Fieldmaster	6004		2.12.87	EPA Aircraft Co Ltd	Bournemouth	27. 8.92A
	(Aka Firemaster 65)				*(Stored 8.00: cancelled 7.3.01 as temporarily wfu)*		
G-NACP*	Norman NAC-6 Fieldmaster	6005		2.12.87	EPA Aircraft Co Ltd	Bournemouth	6. 9.93A
	(Aka Firemaster 34)				*(Stored 8.00: cancelled 7.3.01 as temporarily wfu)*		
G-NADS	TEAM mini-MAX 91	PFA 186-12995		8. 2.99	G.Evans	Lower Mountpleasant, Chatteris	4. 2.02P
G-NAPO	Pegasus Quantum 15-912	7799		6. 4.01	D.Pick	Fenland	5. 4.02P
G-NARO	Cassutt Racer	M.14372	G-BTXR	14. 4.98	D.A.Wirdnam	Redhill	7.10.00P
	(Continental O-200-A) *(Aka Musso Racer Original)*		N68PM				
G-NATT	Rockwell Commander 114A	14538	N5921N	14. 1.80	Northgleam Ltd	Hawarden	3.10.04T
G-NATX	Cameron O-65 HAFB	1681		3. 3.88	A.G.E.Faulkner	Willenhall	5. 5.91T
					"National Express Rapide"		
G-NATY	Folland Gnat T.1	FL.548	8642M	19. 6.90	F.C.Hackett-Jones	Bournemouth	
			XR537		*(Displayed by Bournemouth Museum as "XR537/T")*		
G-NBAA	British Aerospace BAe 146 Srs.300			1. 8.01	BAE Systems (Operations) Ltd	Woodford	
	(Avro 146-RJ100)	E3386			*(F/f 28.8.01)*		
G-NBDD	Robin DR.400/180 Regent	1103	F-BXVN	26. 9.88	J.N.Binks	Sherburn-in-Elmet	11. 1.04
G-NCFC	Piper PA-38-112 Tomahawk	38-81A0107	N737V	14. 1.99	Light Aircraft Leasing (UK) Ltd	Norwich	21. 9.02T
			G-BNOA/N23272				
G-NCFE	Piper PA-38-112 Tomahawk	38-80A0081	G-BKMK	1. 7.99	R.M.Browes	(North Walsham)	19. 7.04T
			OO-GME/(OO-HKD)/N9676N				
G-NCFR	British Aerospace BAe 125 Srs.700B		G-BVJY	28. 4.97	Chauffair Ltd	Farnborough	27. 3.02T
		257054	RA-02802/G-BVJY/C6-BET				
G-NCUB	Piper J-3C-65 Cub	11599	G-BGXV	6. 7.84	R S Basinger	(Norwich)	2. 9.02P
	(L-4H-PI)		F-BFQT/AO-GAB/43-30308				
G-NDGC	Grob G-109	6150		7. 4.83	J.E.Bedford & M.Mathieson	Tibenham	24. 5.02
G-NDNI	Norman NDN-1 Firecracker	001		30. 3.77	N.W.G.Marsh *(Stored 5.00)*	Coventry	
G-NDOL	Europa Aviation Europa			30.11.93	S.Longstaff	(Sheffield)	5. 6.02P
	(Subaru EA81)	44 & PFA 247-12594					
G-NDRW*	Colt AS-80 mk.II Hot-Air Airship	2085		2.12.91	Huntair Ltd *"NDR"*	(Germany)	21. 1.00A
					(Cancelled 10.10.01 by CAA)		
G-NEAL	Piper PA-32-260 Cherokee Six	32-1048	G-BFPY	7.11.83	V.Walker	Wolverhampton	14. 9.03
			N5588J		t/a VSD Group		
G-NEAT	Europa Aviation Europa			28. 6.94	M.Burton	Nympsfield	29. 4.02P
	(Rotax 912UL)	65 & PFA 247-12642					
G-NEEL	Rotorway Executive 90	5002		7. 8.90	M.B.Sims	Street Farm, Takeley	17. 6.98P
	(Rotorway RW 162)				*(Noted 11.01)*		
G-NEGS	Thunder Ax7-77 HAFB	1059		18. 3.87	M.Rowlands	Ashton-in-Makerfield	2. 8.02A
					"Hot-Shot"		
G-NEIL	Thunder Ax3 Maxi Sky Chariot HAFB			2.12.81	N.A.Robertson	Combe Hay Manor, Bath	31. 5.01A
		379			*"Neil"*		
G-NELI	Piper PA-28R-180 Cherokee Arrow		OH-PWW	9. 2.01	European Light Aviation Ltd	Newcastle	8. 4.04T
		28R-31011	D-EMWE/N7693J				
G-NEON	Piper PA-32-300B Cherokee Six		D-EMKW	7. 4.00	S.C.A.Lever	Fairoaks	24. 5.03T
		32-40683	N4246R				
G-NERC	Piper PA-31-350 Navajo Chieftain		G-BBXX	26. 4.94	Natural Environment Research Council		
		31-7405402	N66869		*(Op Air Atlantique)*	Coventry	29. 5.04T
G-NERI*	Piper PA-28-181 Cherokee Archer II		G-BMKO	19. 3.93	Not Known	Bristol	10. 4.98T
		28-7890483	N31880		*(Cancelled 24.11.98 as destoyed) (Wreck stored 2.00)*		
G-NESA	Europa Avition Europa XS T-G			17. 4.01	K.G.& V.E.Summerhill	(Boston)	
		PFA 247-13544					
G-NESU	Pilatus Britten-Norman BN-2B-20 Islander			30. 5.95	Northumbria Police Authority	Teesside	20. 2.03T
		2260	G-BTVN		*(Op North East Air Support Unit)*		
G-NESV	Eurocopter EC 135 T1	0067		4. 2.99	Northumbria Police Authority	Newcastle	30. 3.02T
					(Op North East Air Support Unit)		

G-NESY	Piper PA-18 Super Cub 95	18-7482	N124SA	18. 8.00	V.Fisher	North Side, Thorney	28. 8.03
			SE-CUG				
G-NETY	Piper PA-18-150 Super Cub	1809108	N4159K	8. 9.95	N.B.Mason	Rendcomb	19. 1.02
G-NEUF	Bell 206L-1 LongRanger II	45548	G-BVVV	20.11.98	Yendle Roberts Ltd	Booker	13. 9.04T
			D-HUGO/OE-KXT/C-GLMM				
G-NEVS	Aero Designs Pulsar XP	PFA 202-12283		12.11.93	N.Warrener	(Stockport)	
G-NEWR	Piper PA-31-350 Navajo Chieftain	31-7952129	N35251	23. 8.79	Eastern Air Executive Ltd	Biggin Hill	8. 1.03T
G-NEWS	Bell 206B-3 JetRanger III	2547	N18098	29.11.78	Abington Aviation Ltd	Cambridge	3. 4.03T
G-NEWT	Beechcraft 35 Bonanza	D-1168	G-APVW	28. 2.90	F M.West	Sibson	8. 9.02
	(Continental E-185 = C35 status)		EI-BIL/G-APVW/N9866F/4X-ACI/IDFAF 0604/ZS-BTE				
G-NEWZ	Bell 206B-3 JetRanger III	4475	C-GBVZ	28. 1.98	Peter Press Ltd	Blackbushe	1. 4.04T
G-NFLC	HP.137 Jetstream 1	222	G-AXUI	12.12.95	Cranfield University	Cranfield	3. 6.03T
			G-8-9		*(Op National Flying Laboratory Centre)*		
G-NGBI*	American Aviation AA-5B Tiger	AA5B-1104	G-JAKK	5. 3.85	Not known	Elstree	
			G-BHWI/N3752E				
			(Crashed landing Thurrock 12.7.90: cancelled 7.11.96 as WFU: wreck noted 5.00)				
G-NGRM	Spezio DAL-1 Tuholer	134	N6RM	14. 8.90	S.H.Crook	Redhill	7. 2.00P
	(Lycoming O-290-G)				*(Crashed near Le Touquet 24.7.99 following engine failure)*		
G-NHRH	Piper PA-28-140 Cherokee	28-22807	OY-BIC	19. 5.82	J.E.Parkinson	Newcastle	22. 5.04
			SE-EZP				
G-NHRJ	Europa Aviation Europa XS	PFA 247-13112		30. 9.99	D.A.Lowe	(Telford)	
G-NHVH	Maule M-5-235C Lunar Rocket	7276C	N5634N	4. 7.80	Commercial Go-Karts Ltd	Exeter	21. 2.02
G-NICH	Robinson R22 Beta	0937		4. 1.89	Flightworks Sales & Leasing Ltd	Booker	6 .8.02T
G-NICK(2)*	Piper PA-18 Super Cub 95	18-2065	PH-CWA	17.10.79	I.Woolacott *"Jose"*	Headcorn	26. 6.85P
	(L-18C-PI) *(Frame No.18-2085)*		R.Neth AF R-79/8A-79/52-2465				
			(Cancelled 3.4.89 by CAA: on rebuild 2.96: current status unknown)				
G-NIDG	Evektor-Aerotechnik Model 99 Eurostar			29. 2.00	Skydrive Ltd	Shotteswell	6. 8.02P
	(Rotax 912-UL) c/n 990609 & PFA 315-13580		*(Regd as Aerotechnik EV-97 Eurostar)*				
G-NIGC	Jabiru Jabiru UL-450	PFA 274A-13703		3. 5.01	N.Creeney	Brook Farm, Pilling	9. 8.02P
G-NIGE	Luscombe 8E Silvaire	3525	G-BSHG	6. 6.90	Gardan Party Ltd	Popham	3.12.02P
	(Continental C85)		N72098/NC72098				
G-NIGL	Europa Aviation Europa	PFA 247-12775		6. 7.95	N.M.Graham	(Southampton)	
G-NIGS	Thunder Ax7-65 HAFB	1663		30. 1.90	A.N.F.Pertwee *"Bang Sai"*	Frinton-on-Sea	22. 9.00A
G-NIKE	Piper PA-28-181 Archer II	28-8390086	N4315N	4. 7.89	Key Properties Ltd	White Waltham	23. 9.04T
G-NIKO	Airbus A321-211	1250	D-AVZA	21. 6.00	Airtours International Airways Ltd	Manchester	20. 6.03T
G-NINA	Piper PA-28-161 Cherokee Warrior II	28-7716162	G-BEUC	29. 7.88	P.A.Layzell	Old Buckenham	28. 7.02T
			N35070				
G-NINB	Piper PA-28-180 Cherokee Challenger	28-7305234	SE-KHR	16. 7.99	P.A.Layzell	Old Buckenham	28. 7.02T
			OY-DLR/CS-AHY/N11C				
G-NINC	Piper PA-28-180 Cherokee G	28-7205016	SE-KVH	2. 2.00	P.A.Layzell	Old Buckenham	28. 3.03T
			N2166T				
G-NINE	Murphy Renegade 912			16. 6.93	R.F.Bond	Garston Farm, Marshfield	29. 5.02P
	(Rotax 912)	448 & PFA 188-12191					
G-NIOS	Piper PA-32R-301 Saratoga SP	32R-8513004	N4381Z	28. 9.90	L.A.Dingemans & D.J.Everett	Stapleford	13. 5.02
			N105DX/N4381Z		t/a Plant Aviaton		
G-NIPA	Slingsby Nipper T.66 RA.45 Srs.3	S.120/1627	G-AWDD	7. 6.96	R.J.O.Walker	(Lincoln)	3.11.93P
	(VW 1834(Acro))						
G-NIPP	Slingsby Nipper T.66 RA.45 Srs.3	S.103/1587	G-AVKJ	17. 1.00	T.Dale	(York)	21. 8.97P
	(VW 1834) *(Tipsy c/n 32)*				*(On rebuild 12.01)*		
G-NIPY	Hughes 369HS	124-0676S	OH-HMD	26.11.97	Jet Aviation (Northwest) Ltd	Blackpool	26. 4.04T
			SE-JAK/N65BL/N9232F				
G-NITA	Piper PA-28-180 Cherokee C	28-2909	G-AVVG	16. 1.84	T.Clifford	(Dunstable)	17.11.97T
	(Used spare Frame No.28-3807S)		N7517W		*(Current status unknown)*		
G-NJAG	Cessna 207 Skywagon	20700093	D-EMDN	2. 8.78	G.H.Nolan	Biggin Hill	17. 6.03T
			(N91152)				
G-NJIA	British Aerospace BAe 146 Srs.300	E3161	B-1775	.02R	National Jet Italia SpA	(Palermo, Italy)	
			G-BSOC/B-1775/G-6-161				
G-NJIC	British Aerospace BAe 146 Srs.300	E3202	B-17811	15. 6.00	National Jet Italia SpA	Exeter	25. 6.04T
			B-1781/G-BTUY/G-6-202		*(Stored 1.02)*		
G-NJIE	British Aerospace BAe 146 Srs.300	E3209	B-1778	15. 6.00	National Jet Italia SpA	Exeter	13. 7.04T
			G-BVCE/G-6-209		*(Stored 1.02)*		
G-NJSH	Robinson R22 Beta	0780		19. 4.88	A J.Hawes	Sywell	29. 6.03
G-NLEE	Cessna 182Q Skylane II	18265934	G-TLTD	1.12.93	J.S.Lee	Booker	27. 9.02
			N759EL				
G-NLYB	Cameron N-105 HAFB	10012		19. 4.01	P.H.E.Van Overwalle	Nazareth, Belgium	22. 4 02A
G-NMOS	Cameron C-80 HAFB	4966		5. 1.01	C J Thomas & M C East	Godalming/Alton	16.11.01A
G-NMHS	Eurocopter AS 355N Twin Squirrel	5502	G-DPPS	26. 3.98	North Midlands Helicopter Support Unit	Buttersley	28. 5.04T
			F-WYMM				
G-NNAC	Piper PA-18-135 Super Cub	18-3820	PH-PSW	19. 5.81	P.A.Wilde	Bagby	11. 4.04T
	(L-21B-PI) *(Frame No.18-3820)*		R.Neth AF R-130/54-2420		t/a PAW Flying Services		

G-NOBI	Spezio HES-1 Tuholer Sport	162	N1603	28.11.90	A.D.Pearce	(Lydney)	27. 7.00P
	(Continental C125)						
G-NOCK	Reims Cessna FR182 Skylane RG II	FR18200036	G-BGTK (D-EHZB)	18. 1.94	R.D.Masters	Blackbushe	6. 3.04
G-NODE	Gulfstream AA-5B Tiger	AA5B-1182	N4533L	22. 5.81	Strategic Telecom Networks Ltd	Blackbushe	5. 7.02T
G-NODY	American General AG-5B Tiger	10076	N1194C	3.10.91	Curd & Green Ltd *(Op Cabair)*	Elstree	12. 3.04T
G-NOIR	Bell 222	47031	G-OJLC	9. 8.91	Arlington Securities plc	Blackbushe	31. 5.02T
			G-OSEB/G-BNDA/A40-CG				
G-NOMO	Cameron O-31 HAFB	241		31.10.00	Balloon Promotion SAS	(Ceva, Italy)	
G-NONA	Westland SA.341G Gazelle 1	1108	G-FDAV	20.11.00	M.Persaud	Stapleford	10. 2.02
			G-RIFA/G-ORGE/G-BBHU		t/a Flytrue		
G-NONI	Grumman-American AA-5 Traveler	AA5-0383	G-BBDA (EI-AYL)/G-BBDA	1. 8.88	P.T.Harmsworth t/a November India Flying Group	Exeter	9. 5.04T
G-NOOK	Mainair Blade 912S	1281-0401-7-W1076		11. 6.01	P.J.Hughes	(Chelmsford)	10. 6 02P
G-NOOR	Commander Aircraft Commander 114B	14656		6. 2.98	As-Al Ltd	Zell-am-See, Austria	31. 5.04
G-NORD	SNCAC NC.854	7	F-BFIS	20.10.78	W.J.McCollum	Coagh, Co.Londonderry	27. 5.82P
					(Remains noted 11.01)		
G-NOSE	Cessna 402B	402B0823	N98AR	23. 4.96	Atlantic Air Transport Ltd	Coventry	11. 5.03T
			G-MPCU/SE-IRL/OO-TAT/(OO-SEL)/N3946C				
G-NOTE	Piper PA-28-181 Archer III	2843082	D-ESPI N9282N	19. 9.97	The General Aviation Trading Co Ltd	Elstree	27. 9.03T
G-NOTR	MD Helicopters MD 500N	LN018	N520MD	26. 2.01	S.G.Oliphant-Hope t/a Eastern Atlantic Helicopters	Shoreham	27. 3.04T
G-NOTT	Nott ULD/2 HAFB	06		11. 6.86	J.R.P.Nott	London NW3	
G-NOTY	Westland Scout AH.1	F.9630	XT624	5.11.97	R.P.Coplestone	Draycott Farm, Chiseldon	2. 3.02P
G-NOVO	Colt AS-56 Hot-Air Airship	1067		20. 5.87	J.R.Huggins	Dover	29. 4.97A
G-NOWW	Mainair Blade 912	1227-1299-7-W1020		10.12.99	C Bodill	Nottingham	9. 5.01P
	(Rotax 912S)						
G-NPKJ	Van's RV-6	PFA 181-13138		12. 2.98	K.Jones	Netherthorpe	21. 2.02P
G-NPNP*	Cameron N-105 HAFB	2959	G-BURX	18. 1.93	Balloon Preservation Group	Kirdford	18. 8.98A
					"National Power II" (Cancelled 6.11.01 as wfu)		
G-NPWR*	Cameron RX-100 HAFB	2849		13. 7.92	Balloon Preservation Group	Malpas	21.11.96A
					"Nuclear Electric 2" (Cancelled 15.7.98 as WFU)		
G-NRDC*	Norman NDN-6 Fieldmaster	004		8. 6.81	Not known	Sandown	17.10.87P
					(Cancelled 3.2.95 by CAA: stored 6.01)		
G-NROY	Piper PA-32RT-300 Lance II	32R-7985070	G-LYNN G-BGNY/N3024L	26.11.93	R.L.West t/a Roy West Cars	Norwich	6. 1.02
G-NRRA	SIAI-Marchetti SF.260W	116	F-GOBF BF8431/OO-SMB	29.11.00	G.N.Richardson	Shelsley Beauchamp, Worcester	
G-NRSC	Piper PA-23-250 Aztec E	27-7305142	N250MC	23. 6.00	Air Reconnaissance Ltd	(Leicester)	25. 6.03
			(N244AR)/N250MC/EI-BXP/G-BSFL/PH-NOA/9M-AUS/PH-NOA/N40378				
G-NSEW	Robinson R44 Astro	0615		6. 7.99	Pebblestar Ltd	Harefield	8..7.02T
G-NSOF	Robin HR.200-120B	334		4. 6.99	Northamptonshire School of Flying Ltd	Sywell	14 .6.02T
G-NSTG	Cessna F150F	F150-0058	G-ATNI	16. 8.89	N.S.Travers-Griffin	Blackpool	23. 8.04
	(Wichita c/n 15063499) (Tail-wheel conversion)				*"Iris"*		
G-NUDE	Robinson R44 Astro	0743	G-NSYT	16. 1.02	The Last Great Journey Ltd	(London SW3)	6. 4.03T
G-NUTS*	Cameron Mr Peanut 35SS HAFB	711		18. 2.81	British Balloon Museum & Library	Newbury	1. 4.84A
					"Mr Peanut II" (Cancelled 8.1.90 as WFU)		
G-NUTY	Aérospatiale AS350B Ecureuil	1490	G-BXKT	20. 7.98	Arena Aviation Ltd	Redhill	5.10.03T
			F-GXRT/N333FH/N5797V				
G-NVBF	Lindstrand LBL-210A HAFB	249		19. 5.95	Virgin Balloon Flights Ltd	London SE16	14. 5.00T
G-NVSA	de Havilland DHC-8-311A (Q300)	451	C-GDNG	20.11.98	Brymon Airways Ltd	Plymouth	20.11.04T
G-NVSB	de Havilland DHC-8-311A (Q300)	517	C-GHRI	14. 1.99	Brymon Airways Ltd	Plymouth	13. 1.02T
G-NVSC	de Havilland DHC-8-311A (Q300)	519	C-FDHO	R	Brymon Airways Ltd	Plymouth	
G-NWAC	Piper PA-31 Navajo C	31-7612040	G-BDUJ N59814	18. 2.94	North West Air Charters Ltd	Liverpool	5. 8.02
G-NWPB*	Thunder Ax7-77Z HAFB	278		13. 5.80	Balloon Preservation Group	Kirdford	
					"Royal Mail Postcode" (Cancelled 27.4.90 by CAA)		
G-NWPS	Eurocopter EC 135T 1	0063		15.10.98	North Wales Police Authority	Boddelwydden	11. 2.02T
G-NYTE	Reims Cessna F337G Skymaster	F33700056	G-BATH N10631	12. 5.86	I.M.Latiff	Little Staughton	9. 6.03T
	(Wichita c/n 33701465)						
G-NZGL	Cameron O-105 HAFB	1361		3. 9.86	R A, P M G & N T M Vale	Kidderminster	28. 5.00A
					"Nazgul"		
G-NZSS	Boeing-Stearman E75 (N2S-5) Kaydet	75-8611	N4325 Bu.43517/42-109578	31. 1.89	Anglian Aircraft Co Ltd	Swanton Morley	6. 1.02T
	(Lycoming R-680)				*(As "343251/27" in USAAC c/s)*		

G-OAAA – G-OZZZ

G-OAAA	Piper PA-28-161 Warrior II	2816107	N9142N	8. 9.93	Halfpenny Green Flight Centre Ltd	Wolverhampton	15. 9.02T
G-OAAC	Airtour AH-77B HAFB	010		13. 9.88	Army Air Corps, Historic A/c Board of Management *"Go AAC"*	AAC Middle Wallop	10. 1.00A
G-OABB	SAN Jodel D150 Mascaret	01	F-BJST F-WJST	21. 1.97	A.B.Bailey	Popham	19. 3.03
G-OABC	Colt 69A HAFB	1159		17.11.87	P.A.C.Stuart-Kregor	Newbury	26. 6.00A
G-OABO	Enstrom F-28A	097	G-BAIB	10. 7.98	ABO Ltd	Goodwood	13.11.04T
G-OABR	American General AG-5B Tiger	10124	C-GZLA N256ER	15. 4.98	Abraxas Aviation Ltd	Elstree	26. 4.04T
G-OACE	Valentin Taifun 17E	1017	D-KCBA	22. 1.87	J.E.Dallison	Enstone	27. 4.02
G-OACG	Piper PA-34-200T Seneca II	34-7870177	G-BUNR EI-CFI/N9245C	10. 3.94	Cega Aviation Ltd	Goodwood	26.11.04T
G-OACI	SOCATA MS.893E Rallye 180GT	13086	G-DOOR EI-BHD/F-GBCF	5. 5.98	A.M.Quayle	Alderney	6. 4.04
G-OACP	de Havilland DHC.1 Chipmunk 20 *(Built OGMA)* (Lycoming O-360)	35	(CS-DAO) FAP 1345	20. 8.96	Aeroclub de Portugal	(Lisbon)	14. 3.03
G-OADY	Beechcraft 76 Duchess	ME-56	N5022M	27.10.86	Multiflight Ltd	Leeds-Bradford	31. 1.02T
G-OAER	Lindstrand LBL-105A HAFB	359		4. 3.96	T.M.Donnelly *"Aero"*	Doncaster	25. 6.01A
G-OAFC*				15. 6.89	*Re-registered G-BWPL- see SECTION Part 2*		
G-OAFT	Cessna 152 II	15285177	G-BNKM N6161Q	19. 4.88	Evensport Ltd	Southend	18.11.02T
G-OAHC	Beechcraft F33C Bonanza	CJ-133	G-BTTF PH-BND	2. 9.91	V.D.Speck	Clacton	18. 7.04
G-OAJB	Cyclone AX2000 (Rotax 582-48)	7281	G-MZFJ	16. 2.99	G.K.R.Linney	Latch Farm, Kirknewton	29. 4.02P
G-OAJS	Piper PA-39 Twin Comanche C/R	39-15	G-BCIO N49JA/N57RG/G-BCIO/N8860Y	9. 3.94	Go-AJs Ltd	Sherburn-in-Elmet	16. 3.04
G-OAKJ	British Aerospace Jetstream Srs.3202	795	G-BOTJ G-OAKJ/G-BOTJ/G-31-795	20. 7.89	Air Kilroe Ltd *(Op Eastern Airways)*	Humberside	31. 8.03T
G-OALB	Aero L-39C Albatros	931523	ES-ZLD Soviet Air Force	27. 6.00	Rocket Seat Ltd *(Noted 9.01)*	North Weald	29.10.02P
G-OALD	SOCATA TB-20 Trinidad	490	N54TB F-GBLL	17. 3.88	D.A.Grief t/a Gold Aviation	Biggin Hill	24. 5.03
G-OALH	Tecnam P92-EM Echo	PFA 318-13675		12. 6.01	L.Hill	(Ulverston)	
G-OAMF	Pegasus Quantum 15-912	7764		20.12.00	W Rodham	Newtownards, Co.of Down	19.12.01P
G-OAMG	Bell 206B-3 JetRanger III	2901	G-COAL	25. 2.86	Alan Mann Helicopters Ltd	Fairoaks	31. 5.04T
G-OAMI	Bell 206B JetRanger II	464	G-BAUN 5N-BAY/G-BAUN/5N-AOU/VR-BIA/G-BAUN/N2261W	15. 3.01	Stephenson Marine Co Ltd	Goodwood	26. 1.02T
G-OAML	Cameron AML-105 HAFB	3881		4.12.96	Stratton Motor Co (Norfolk) Ltd	Long Stratton	25. 6.02A
G-OAMP	Reims Cessna F177RG Cardinal *(Wichita c/n 17700098)*	F177RG0006	G-AYPF	30.11.93	G.Hamilton & R.Sheldon t/a Vale Aero Group	Liverpool	2. 8.03
G-OAMS	Boeing 737-37Q	28548		9.12.97	British Regional Airlines Ltd *(Rendezvous t/s)*	Manchester	9. 1.04T
G-OAMT	Piper PA-31-350 Navajo Chieftain	31-7752105	G-BXKS N350RC/EC-EBN/N27230	23. 1.98	AM & T Solutions Ltd	Bristol	18.12.02T
G-OANI	Piper PA-28-161 Warrior II	28-8416091	N43570	8. 1.91	J.F.Mitchell *(Damaged Upton Farm, Dover 16.6.96: wreck noted 9.96: current status unknown)*	Oxford	8. 9.97
G-OANN	Zenair CH.601HDS Zodiac (Rotax 912-UL)	PFA 162-12932		2. 2.96	P.Noden	(Stoke-on-Trent)	8. 6.02P
G-OAPE	Cessna T303 Crusader	T30300245	N303MF D-INKA/N9960C/M303HW/N9960C	3. 2.99	C.Twiston-Davies & P L Drew	Jersey	8. 2.02
G-OAPR	Brantly B-2B	446	(G-BPST) N2280U	21. 4.89	E.D.ap Rees t/a Helicopter International Magazine	Weston-super-Mare	1. 7.04
G-OAPW	Glaser-Dirks DG-400	4-268		17. 4.90	J.R.Mousley *"434"*	Rufforth	10. 6.02
G-OARA	Piper PA-28R-201 Arrow	2837002	N802ND N9622N	28.10.98	S.Evans t/a Airsure	Denham	19.11.04T
G-OARG	Cameron C-80 HAFB	3379		20.10.94	G. & R.Madelin	Farnham/London SW15	3.11.02A
G-OARO	Piper PA-28R-201 Arrow	2837006	N171ND	30.10.01	Plane Talking Ltd	Elstree	5.11.04T
G-OART	Piper PA-23-250 Aztec D	27-4293	G-AXKD N6936Y	26.11.93	Levenmere Ltd *(Op Skydrift)*	Old Buckenham	20. 3.03T
G-OARV	ARV-1 Super 2 (Hewland AE75) *(Rebuilt with Kit No.008 1986)*	001 & PFA 152-11060		18. 6.84	N.R.Beale *(Stored Sproughton 1.91)*	(Leamington Spa)	12.10.87P
G-OASH	Robinson R22 Beta	0761	N2627Z	13. 6.88	J.C.Lane *(Op Heliflight)*	Wolverhampton	21. 6.03T
G-OASP	Aérospatiale AS355F2 Twin Squirrel	5479	F-GJAJ F-WYMH	3. 8.95	Avon & Somerset Constabulary *(Op Avon & Somerset Police)*	Filton	14.10.04T
G-OATS	Piper PA-38-112 Tomahawk	38-78A0007	N9659N	14. 3.78	Truman Aviation Ltd	Nottingham	28. 9.03T
G-OATG	Advanced Technologies AT-10	1001		29.11.01	Advanced Technologies Group Ltd	Cardington	

G-OATV	Cameron V-77 HAFB	2149		14. 2.90	W.G.Andrews	Plymouth	23.10.93A
G-OAWS	Cameron Colt 77A HAFB	4340		23. 4.98	Auto Windscreens Ltd	Chesterfield	11. 5.02A
G-OAXA	Cameron Cup-90 SS HAFB	4750		24.12.99	Flying Pictures Ltd	Fairoaks	25. 1.02A
G-OBAL	Mooney M.20J (201LM)	24-1601	N56569	27.11.86	Britannia Airways Ltd	Luton	24. 3.02T
					(Op Britannia Flying Club)		
G-OBAM	Bell 206B-3 JetRanger III	4511	N6379U	25. 5.99	Cherwell Tobacco Ltd	(Whitchurch)	4 .7.02T
G-OBAN	SAN Jodel D.140B Mousquetaire II	80	G-ATSU	20. 2.92	S.R.Cameron	North Connel, Oban	21. 5.04
			F-BKSA				
G-OBAX	Thruster T600N 450 Jab			12. 7.01	J.D.Smith	Baxby Manor, Husthwaite	13. 7.02P
		0051-T600N-053			t/a Baxby Airsports Club		
G-OBAY*	Bell 206B JetRanger II	276	G-BVWR	27. 7.98	Helixair Ltd	Botany Bay Village, Chorley	6. 3.03T
			C-GNXQ/N4714R				
	(Crashed into Lake Windermere 5.1.01: wreck recovered & noted 4.01 for sale: cancelled 7.6.01 as wfu)						
G-OBBC	Colt 90A HAFB	1358		11. 5.89	R.A. & M.A.Riley	Bromsgrove	16. 7.01A
					"Beeb" (BBC in the Midlands titles)		
G-OBBJ	Boeing 737-8DR	32777	N379BJ	29.11.01	Multiflight Ltd	Leeds-Bradford	28.11.04
G-OBBO	Cessna 182S Skylane	18280534	N7274Z	8. 6.99	F.Friedenberg	Denham	21. 6.02
G-OBBY	Robinson R44	0939		4.12.00	P.C.& J.A.Twigg	(Minsterworth, Glos)	
G-OBDA	Diamond DA-20-A1 Katana	10260		2. 7.98	Oscar Papa Ltd	Wolverhampton	2. 1.04T
G-OBEN	Cessna 152 II	15281856	G-NALI	16. 8.93	Airbase Aircraft Ltd	Shoreham	29. 3.03T
			G-BHVM/N67477				
G-OBET	Sky 77-24 HAFB	178		22. 2.00	Flying Pictures Ltd	Fairoaks	22. 2.01A
					(Victor Chandler titles)		
G-OBEV	Europa Aviation Europa	PFA 247-12813		3. 2.98	M.B.Hill & N.I.Wingfield	(Dursley)	
G-OBEY	Piper PA-23-250 Aztec C	27-2569	G-BAAJ	11. 5.79	Creaton Aircraft Services Ltd		
			SE-EIU		*(Stored 5.01)*	Wolverhampton	4. 8.86T
G-OBFC	Piper PA-28-161 Warrior III	2816118	N9252X	15. 7.96	Bflying Ltd	Bournemouth	27. 7.02T
					(Op Bournemouth Flying Club)		
G-OBFS	Piper PA-28-161 Warrior III	2842039	N41274	4.12.98	Plane Talking Ltd	Elstree	3.12.04T
G-OBGC	SOCATA TB-20 Trinidad	1898		13. 5.99	Bidford Airfield Ltd	Bidford	12 .5.02T
G-OBHD	Short SD.3-60 Var.100	SH.3714	G-BNDK	20. 1.87	Emerald Airways Ltd	Liverpool	5. 3.02T
			G-OBHD/G-BNDK/G-14-3714				
G-OBHL	Aérospatiale AS355F2 Twin Squirrel		G-HARO	7. 4.00	Brands Hatch Leisure Group Ltd		
		5364	G-DAFT/G-BNNN			Stapleford	16. 1.03T
G-OBIB	Colt 120A HAFB	4229		9. 1.98	The Aerial Display Co Ltd	Looe	25 .1.02A
					(Michelin titles)		
G-OBIL	Robinson R22 Beta	0792		10. 5.88	C.A.Rosenberg	Abergavenny	24. 8.03T
G-OBIO	Robinson R22 Beta	1402	N7724M	29. 6.98	A.E.Churchill	(Huntingdon)	7. 8.04
G-OBJB	Lindstrand LBL 90A HAFB	640		12.11.99	B.J.Bower	Andover	20. 1.02A
G-OBJH*	Colt 77A HAFB	2569		11. 3.94	UK Petroleum Products Ltd	Alcester	16. 7.00
					t/a Eurogas & Corralgas *(Cancelled 15.2.00 by CAA)*		
G-OBJP	Pegasus Quantum 15-912	7847		29. 8.01	B.J.Partridge	(Bar Hill, Cambridge)	28. 2.02P
G-OBJT	Europa Aviation Europa	PFA 247-12623	G-MUZO	16.11.00	B.J.Tarmar	(Fordingbridge)	
G-OBLC	Beechcraft 76 Duchess	ME-249	N6635R	3. 6.87	Pridenote Ltd	(Knaresborough)	31.10.02T
G-OBLK	Short SD.3-60 Var.100	SH.3712	G-BNDI	20. 1.87	BAC Express Airlines Ltd	(Horley)	11. 2.02T
			G-OBLK/G-BNDI/G-14-3712				
G-OBLN	de Havilland DH.115 Vampire T.11		XE956	14. 9.95	De Havilland Aviation Ltd		
		15664				(St Mary Hill, Bridgend)	
	(Regd with Nacelle No.DHP.48700)				*(As "XE956": on rebuild 1.01)*		
G-OBLU	Cameron H-34 HAFB	4914		4. 8.00	Blu SpA	Rome, Italy	14 .6.02A
G-OBMI	Mainair Blade	1289-0601-7-W1084		19. 6.01	P.Clark	(Crewe)	26. 7.02P
G-OBMM	Boeing 737-4Y0	25177		4.12.91	British Midland Airways Ltd		
						East Midlands	6. 4.02T
G-OBMP	Boeing 737-3Q8	24963		8. 1.92	British Midland Airways Ltd		
					(Op Air Europa)	East Midlands	19. 3.02T
G-OBMS	Reims Cessna F172N Skyhawk II		OO-BWA	16. 4.84	D.Beverley & A N Macdonald		
		F17201584	(OO-HWA)/D-EBYX			Sherburn-in-Elmet	10. 6.02
G-OBMW	Grumman-American AA-5 Traveler		G-BDFV	4. 7.79	Fretcourt Ltd	Sherburn-in-Elmet	3. 4.03
		AA5-0805					
G-OBNA	Piper PA-34-220T Seneca V	3449002	N9281D	25. 5.00	Anglo American Airmotive Ltd	Jersey	31. 5.03
			(N338DB)				
G-OBNF*	Cessna 310K	310K0109	F-BNFI	20. 7.94	P.H.Johnson	Boonhill, Fadmoor	20. 5.00T
			N7009L		t/a Fadmoor Flying Group		
					(Overran landing Fadmoor 21.8.00: cancelled 3.1.01 as wfu)		
G-OBPL	Embraer EMB-110P2 Bandeirante		PH-FVB	27.11.98	BAC Leasing Ltd	Southend	12.12.01T
		110.199	G-OEAB/G-BKWB/G-CHEV/(PT-GLR) *(Comed titles) (Open store w/o engines 1.02)*				
G-OBRI	Medway EclipseR	171/149		25.10.01	B.D.Campbell	(Maidstone)	
G-OBRY	Cameron N-180 HAFB	3010		1. 3.93	Bryant Group plc	Solihull	20. 4.00T
G-OBSF*	American Aviation AA-5A Cheetah		G-ODSF	21. 9.88	Not known	Elstree	
		AA5A-0374	G-BEUW/N6158A *(Crashed on landing Blackbushe 8.2.97: repaired & re-regd as G-ODAE 11.97: cancelled [no date]: wreck identified as G-OBSF 5.00 but see G-ODAE)*				
G-OBTS	Cameron C-80 HAFB	3589		18. 4.95	Bedford Tyre Service (Chichester) Ltd		
					"Hi-Q"	Chichester	24. 6.02A

G-OBUD*	Colt 69A HAFB	698		26. 6.85	British Balloon Museum & Library	Newbury	1. 2.90A
					"Budweiser" (Cancelled 29.4.97 as WFU)		
G-OBUN	Cameron A-250 HAFB	4711		29. 2.00	A.C.K.Rawson & J.J.Rudoni	(Stafford)	15 .2.02T
G-OBUS*	Piper PA-28-181 Archer II	28-7990242	G-BMTT	4. 8.86	Northbrook College	Shoreham	14. 8.89T
			N3002K				
	(Crashed Goodwood 18.4.89: cancelled 30.8.89 as destroyed: fuselage used as instructional airframe 3.00)						
G-OBUY	Colt 69A HAFB	2031		7. 8.91	Virgin Airship & Balloon Co Ltd	Telford	25. 8.00A
					"Virgin Megastore"		
G-OBWA	British Aircraft Corporation One-Eleven 518FG			1.12.92	British World Airlines Ltd	Southend	1. 5.03T
		BAC.232	G-BDAT/G-AYOR		*(Ceased trading 12.01: in open store 1.02)*		
G-OBWD	British Aircraft Corporation One-Eleven 518FG			14. 1.93	British World Airlines Ltd	Southend	14. 4.02T
		BAC.203	G-BDAE/G-AXMI		*(Ceased trading 12.01: in open store 1.02)*		
G-OBWE	British Aircraft Corporation One-Eleven 531FS			7. 4.93	British World Airlines Ltd	Southend	26. 5.02T
		BAC.242	G-BJYM/TI-LRI/TI-1095C		*(Ceased trading 12.01: in open store 1.02)*		
G-OBWL	British Aerospace ATP	2057	G-11-057	26. 9.97	British World Airlines Ltd	Aberdeen	25. 9.03T
					(CityJet c/s) (Ceased trading 12.01 & stored)		
G-OBWM	British Aerospace ATP	2058	G-11-058	22.12.97	British World Airlines Ltd	Aberdeen	21.12.03T
					(Ceased trading 12.01 & stored)		
G-OBWN	British Aerospace ATP	2059	G-BVEO	22.12.98	British World Airlines Ltd	Southend	21.12.02T
			G-11-059		*(Ceased trading 12.01 & stored)*		
G-OBWO	British Aerospace ATP	2060	(EI-COS)	6. 6.98	British World Airlines Ltd	Aberdeen	15. 6.04T
			G-11-060		*(Ceased trading 12.01 & stored)*		
G-OBWP	British Aerospace ATP	2051	G-BTPO	8.10.99	British World Airlines Ltd	Woodford	17.10.02T
			G-5-051		*(Ceased trading 12.01)*		
G-OBWR	British Aerospace ATP	2053	G-BUWP	8.10.99	British World Airlines Ltd	Aberdeen	20. 4.03T
			G-11-053		*(Ceased trading 12.01 & stored)*		
G-OBWS	Boeing 757-23A	24528	PH-AHP	12. 7.01	Tombo Aviation Netherlands BV		
			G-BXOL/SE-DSM/OO-ILI			Amsterdam, The Netherlands	12. 7.04T
G-OBWX	Boeing 737-3Y0	24255	SE-DUS	1. 6.00	British World Airlines Ltd	Lasham	13. 6.03T
			HB-IID/EI-CFQ/OO-IID/XA-RJP/G-MONL		*(Ceased trading 12.01 & stored)*		
G-OBWY	Boeing 737-3S3	24059	N202KG	24. 3.00	KG Aircraft Leasing Co Ltd	Dublin	9. 5.03T
			G-DEBZ/RP-C4006/EC-FGG/EC-711/G-BNPB/C-FGHT/G-BNPB				
G-OBWZ	Boeing 737-3Q8	24699	N699PU	28. 3.00	British World Airlines Ltd	Southend	27. 3.03T
			PK-GWG		*(Ceased trading 12.01)*		
G-OBYA	Boeing 767-304ER	28039	D-AGYA	15. 5.96	Britannia Airways Ltd	Luton	6. 4.03T
			G-OBYA/D-AGYA/G-OBYA				
G-OBYB	Boeing 767-304ER	28040		17. 5.96	Britannia Airways Ltd	Luton	16. 5.02T
G-OBYC	Boeing 767-304ER	28041	D-AGYC	21. 5.96	Britannia Airways Ltd	Luton	7.11.03T
			G-OBYC/D-AGYC/G-OBYC				
G-OBYD	Boeing 767-304ER	28042	SE-DZG	4. 3.97	Britannia Airways Ltd	Luton	2. 5.04T
			G-OBYD				
G-OBYE	Boeing 767-304ER	28979	D-AGYE	26. 2.98	Britannia Airways Ltd	Luton	28.10.02T
			G-OBYE				
G-OBYF	Boeing 767-304ER	28208	D-AGYF	8. 6.98	Britannia Airways Ltd.	Luton	30. 4.04T
			G-OBYF				
G-OBYG	Boeing 767-304ER	29137		13. 1.99	Britannia Airways Ltd	Luton	12. 1.05T
G-OBYI	Boeing 767-304ER	29138		1. 2.00	Britannia Airways Ltd	Luton	31. 1.03T
G-OBYJ	Boeing 767-304ER	29384		20. 2.00	Britannia Airways Ltd	Luton	18. 2.03T
G-OBYT	Agusta-Bell 206A JetRanger	8237	G-BNRC	30. 1.95	R.J.Everett	(Sproughton)	12. 7.03T
			Oman AF 601				
G-OCAA	Hawker Siddeley HS.125 Srs.700B		G-BHLF	22. 4.92	Magec Aviation Ltd	Luton	28. 4.02T
		257091			*(Op CAA)*		
G-OCAD	Sequoia Falco F8L	PFA 100-12114		8. 6.92	C.W.Garrard	Leicester	26.12.02P
	(Lycoming IO-320)				t/a Falco Flying Group		
G-OCAM	Gulfstream AA-5A Cheetah	AA5A-0741	G-BLHO	24. 3.94	Plane Talking Ltd	Cranfield	11.10.03T
			OO-RTJ/OO-HRN		*(Op Cabair)*		
G-OCAR	Colt 77A HAFB	1099		6. 8.87	S.C.J.Derham *"Toyota"*	(Bridgnorth)	25. 8.00A
G-OCAT	Eiri PIK.20E	20226	(D-KGAT)	19.11.79	D.Bonucchi	(Croxley Green)	3. 6.04
			G-OCAT				
G-OCAW	Lindstrand Bananas SS HAFB	388		22. 5.96	Flying Pictures Ltd	Fairoaks	16. 7.01A
G-OCBS	Lindstrand LBL 210A HAFB	602		21. 7.99	G.Binder	Sonnenbuhl, Germany	15. 7.02A
G-OCDB	Cessna 550 Citation II	550-0601	G-ELOT	20. 8.92	Paycourt Ltd	Birmingham	28. 2.02T
			(N1303M)		*(Op Eurojet)*		
G-OCDS	Aviamilano F.8L Falco Srs.II	114	G-VEGL	6. 9.85	C.O.P.Barth	(The Netherlands)	11. 8.02
			OO-MEN/I-VEGL				
G-OCEA	Short SD.3-60 Var.100	SH.3762	N162CN	26.10.95	BAC Express Airlines Ltd	(Horley)	26. 3.02T
			N162SB/G-BRMX				
G-OCFR	Learjet Learjet 35A	35A-614	G-VIPS	15. 6.92	Chauffair Ltd	Farnborough	12. 4.02T
			G-SOVN/HB-VJC/G-PJET/N3815G				
G-OCHM	Robinson R44 Raven	1055		4. 5.01	Westleigh Developments Ltd		
						Whetstone, Leics	30. 5.04T
G-OCJK	Schweizer Hughes 269C (300C)	S.1294	N69A	10.12.87	P.Crawley	Shipley	27. 5.00
G-OCJS*	Cameron V-90 HAFB	2805		24. 4.92	C.J.Sandell	Sevenoaks	29. 4.00T
					(Cancelled 18.10.01 by CAA)		

G-OCJW	Cessna 182R Skylane II	18268316	G-SJGM N357WC	18. 4.97	C.J.Ward	Wellesbourne Mountford	24.10.04
G-OCMJ	Aérospatiale SA.341G Gazelle 1	1301	G-HTPS G-BRNI/YU-HBI	5.10.01	Gazelle Investments Ltd	(Belize)	24. 7.03
G-OCMM	Agusta A109A II	7347	G-BXCB F-GJSH/G-ISEB/G-IADT/G-HBCA	20. 3.01	The Thomas Bolton Group Ltd	Ladyswood House, Sherston, Wilts	28. 4.03T
G-OCND*	Cameron O-77 HAFB	1020		6. 2.84	Balloon Preservation Group *"CND Airborne" (Cancelled 19.5.95 by CAA)*	Kirdford	N/E(A)
G-OCOV	Robinson R22 Beta	3217		23. 5.01	Flight Training Ltd	Coventry	14. 6.04T
G-OCPC	Reims Cessna FA152 Aerobat	FA15200343		20. 1.78	Westward Airways (Lands End) Ltd	St.Just	12. 8.02T
G-OCPF	Piper PA-32-300 Cherokee Six	32-7640082	G-BOCH N9292K	22. 9.97	Syndicate Clerical Services Ltd	Exeter	8. 9.03T
G-OCPS	Colt 120A HAFB	2047		27. 5.92	CPS Fuels Ltd *"CPS Gas"*	Norwich	19. 5.00T
G-OCRI	Colomban MC-15 Cri-Cri	524 & PFA 133-12288		24. 6.92	M.J.J.Dunning	(Coventry)	
G-OCST	Agusta-Bell 206B-3 JetRanger III	8694	N39AH VR-CDG/G-BMKM	14.12.94	Claygate Distribution Ltd	Paynetts Farm, Goudhurst	8. 1.04T
G-OCTI	Piper PA-32-260 Cherokee Six	32-288	G-BGZX 9XR-MP/5Y-ADH/N3427W	26. 7.88	D.G.Williams	Blackbushe	14. 5.04T
G-OCTU	Piper PA-28-161 Cadet	2841280	N91997	16.11.89	Plane Talking Ltd	Biggin Hill	13.12.04T
G-OCUB	Piper J-3C-90 Cub (L-4J-PI) *(Frame No.13078)*	13248	OO-JOZ PH-NKC/PH-UCH/45-4508	21. 4.81	C.A.Foss & P.A.Brook t/a Florence Flying Group *"Florence"*	Shoreham	12. 2.02P
	(Official c/n of 13215 is 45-4475/PH-UCW and was rebuilt as PH-UCH)						
G-ODAC	Reims Cessna F152 II	F15201824	G-BITG	19.12.96	T.M. & M.L.Jones *(Op Derby Aero Club)*	Derby	9. 8.04T
G-ODAD	Colt 77A HAFB	2001		20. 2.91	K.Meehan *"Odyssey"*	Much Wenlock	24. 6.01A
G-ODAE*	American Aviation AA-5A Cheetah	AA5A-0374	G-OBSF G-ODSF/G-BEUW/N6158A	17.11.97	Not known	Elstree	
	(Cancelled as WFU 14.9.98: wreck noted 5.00: appears that restoration as G-ODAE did not proceed as second fuselage abandoned alongside G-OBSF qv)						
G-ODAK	Piper PA-28-236 Dakota	28-7911162	D-EXMA OH-SMO/N386WT/N22328	29. 2.00	Airways Aero Associations Ltd	Booker	16. 3.03T
G-ODAM	Gulfstream AA-5A Cheetah	AA5A-0818	G-FOUX N8488H	16.11.88	Stop & Go Ltd *(Op London Aviation)*	Biggin Hill	22. 3.02T
G-ODAT	Aero L-29 Delfin	194227	ES-YLV Estonian AF/Soviet AF	28. 7.99	Graniteweb Ltd	North Weald	25.11.02P
G-ODBN	Lindstrand Flowers SS HAFB	389		22. 5.96	Flying Pictures Ltd *"Sainsbury's Flowers"*	Fairoaks	15. 6.00A
G-ODCS	Robinson R22 Beta-II	2828		19. 5.98	Heli Air Ltd	Panshanger	1. 6.04T
G-ODDY	Lindstrand LBL-105A HAFB	042		15. 7.93	P.& T.Huckle	Oakwood	7. 7.02A
G-ODEB	Cameron A-250 HAFB	4328		23. 4.98	A.Derbyshire	(Stafford)	31. 7.02T
G-ODEE	Van's RV-6	PFA 181-13173		14. 4.00	D.Powell	(Burntwood)	
G-ODEL*	Falconar F-11-3	PFA 032-10219		14. 8.78	G F Brummell *(Damaged Little Gransden 4.9.88: cancelled 15.11.00 by CAA: on rebuild 2000)*	Jubilee Farm, Bedford	17. 7.89P
G-ODEN	Piper PA-28-161 Cadet	2841282	N92004	22.11.89	J.Appleton t/a Holmes Rentals *(Op Denham School of Flying)*	Denham	18.12.04T
G-ODES	Robinson R44 Astro	0722		9. 2.00	Eagle Distribution Ltd	Bourn	2. 3.03
G-ODGS	Jabiru Jabiru UL	PFA 274A-13472		2. 8.99	D.G.Salt	(Ashbourne)	
G-ODHG	Robinson R44 Raven	1024		19. 4.01	Driver Hire Group Services Ltd	Leeds-Bradford	22. 4.04T
G-ODIN	Mudry CAARP CAP-10B	192	F-GDTH	16.12.93	T.W.Harris	(Hunstanton)	11. 4.04
G-ODIY	Colt 69A HAFB	1786		12. 6.90	P.Glydon	Barnt Green, Birmingham	18. 3.99A
G-ODJD	Raj Hamsa X'Air 582 (7)	559 & BMAA/HB/151		25. 4.01	D.J.Davis	(Bideford)	
G-ODJG	Europa Aviation Europa	PFA 247-12889		3. 5.96	D.J.Goldsmith	(Edenbridge)	
G-ODJH	Mooney M.20C Ranger	690083	G-BMLH N9293V	19. 1.93	R.M.Schweitzer	Hilversum, The Netherlands	13. 7.02
G-ODLY	Cessna 310J	310J0077	G-TUBY G-ASZZ/N3077L	21. 3.88	R.J.Huband	Top Farm, Croydon	18. 6.03
G-ODMC	Aérospatiale AS350B1 Ecureuil	2200	G-BPVF	17.10.89	D.M.Coombs t/a DM Leasing Co	Denham	25.10.04T
G-ODNH	Schweizer 269C-1 (300)	0112	N41S	5. 9.00	DNH Helicopters Ltd *(Op Kent Helicopters)*	Biggin Hill	14. 9.03T
G-ODOC	Robinson R44 Astro	0372		27. 8.97	Gas & Air Ltd	Booker	12.10.03T
G-ODOD	MD Helicopters MD 600N	RN052	N3204S	5.10.00	Sunseeker Sales (UK) Ltd	Poole Docks	12.10.03T
G-ODOG	Piper PA-28R-200 Cherokee Arrow II	28R-7235197	EI-BPB G-BAAR/N11C	2. 8.96	Advanced Investments Ltd	Sibson	22.10.02
G-ODOT	Robinson R22 Beta-II	2779		23. 1.98	Farm Aviation Ltd	Booker	8. 3.04T
G-ODSK	Boeing 737-37Q	28537		23. 7.97	British Midland Airways Ltd	East Midlands	27. 7.03T
G-ODTW	Europa Aviation Europa	PFA 247-12890		7. 9.95	D.T.Walters	(Longfield, Kent)	
G-ODUB	Embraer EMB-110 P1 Bandeirante	110.217	PH-FVC G-BNIX/N8536J	7. 2.00	Comed Aviation Ltd	Leeds-Bradford	6. 2.01T

G-ODUS	Boeing 737-36Q	28659	D-ADBX	17. 3.98	British Regional Airlines Ltd	Gatwick	15. 4.04T
					(Waves & Cranes t/s)		
G-ODVB	CFM Shadow DD	300-DD	G-MGDB	3.11.98	D.V.Brunt	Plaistows Farm, St Albans	24. 4.02P
	(Rotax 582)						
G-OEAC	Mooney M.20J (201)	24-1636	N57656	16. 6.88	D.Teece & R.Hodges	Nottingham	5. 4.03
					t/a DR Airgroup		
G-OEAT	Robinson R22 Beta	0650	G-RACH	8. 1.98	C.Y.O.Seeds Ltd	(Didcot)	21. 1.02T
G-OECH	Gulfstream AA-5A Cheetah	AA5A-0836	G-BKBE	24. 1.89	Plane Talking Ltd	Cranfield	10. 5.03T
			(G-BJVN)/N26952		*(Op London School of Flying)*		
G-OEDB	Piper PA-38-112 Tomahawk	38-79A0167	G-BGGJ	9. 5.89	Metropolitan Services Ltd	Hawarden	15. 6.03T
			N9694N				
G-OEDP	Cameron N-77 HAFB	2189		28.12.89	M.J.Betts	Norwich	12. 6.01A
					"Eastern Counties Press"		
G-OEGG	Cameron Egg 65SS HAFB	2140		4.12.89	Virgin Airship & Balloon Co Ltd	Telford	25. 3.00A
	(Cadbury's Creme Egg shape)				*"Cadburys Creme Egg"*		
G-OEGL	Christen Eagle II	001	N46JH	12. 1.98	R.Dauncey	Shoreham	11. 4.02P
	(Lycoming IO-360)				t/a The Eagle Flight Syndicate		
G-OEJA	Cessna 500 Citation	500-0264	G-BWFL	2. 8.96	Eurojet Aviation Ltd	Birmingham	20. 7.02T
			F-GLJA/N205FM/N5264J				
G-OELD	Pegasus Quantum 15-912	7765		20.12.00	T H Filmer	Newtownards, Co.of Down	19.12.01P
G-OERR	Lindstrand LBL-60A HAFB	469		30. 6.97	Lindstrand Balloons Ltd	Oswestry	22. 7.02
G-OERS	Cessna 172N Skyhawk II	17268856	G-SSRS	24. 5.94	E.R.Stevens	Leicester	29.10.99T
			N734HA				
G-OERX	Cameron O-65 HAFB	4004		23. 1.96	R.Roehsler	Vienna, Austria	27. 2.97A
G-OEST	British Aerospace Jetstream Srs.3202	836	OH-JAD	18. 6.99	Air Kilroe Ltd	Humberside	20 .6.02T
			N836JX/C-FGLH/G-31-836/N332QJ/G-31-836		*(Op Eastern Airways)*		
G-OESY	Flying K Enterprises Easy Raider J2.2(1)	BMAA/HB/193		16.11.01	Reality Aircraft Ltd	(Amesbury)	
G-OEWA	de Havilland DH.104 Dove 8	04528	G-DDCD	10. 6.98	D.C.Hunter	Kemble	
			G-ARUM		*(On rebuild 2001 for East West Airlines)*		
G-OEYE	Rans S-10 Sakota	PFA 194-11955		25. 4.91	I.M.J.Mitchell	Otherton, Cannock	26. 7.02P
	(Rotax 582-2V)						
G-OEZY	Europa Aviation Europa			8. 8.95	A.W.Wakefield	Conington	27. 6.02P
	(Rotax 912UL)	42 & PFA 247-12590					
G-OFAS	Robinson R22 Beta	0559		17. 6.86	J.L.Leonard	Shoreham	11. 4.02T
					t/a Findon Air Services		
G-OFBJ	Thunder Ax7-77A HAFB	2050		2. 9.91	N.D.Hicks *"Blue Horizon"*	Alton	25. 9.99A
G-OFBU	Ikarus C42 FB UK	PFA 322-13653		28. 8.01	Fly Buy Ultralights Ltd	(Cranfield)	
G-OFCH	Agusta-Bell 206B Jet Ranger II	8337	HB-XUI	15. 5.00	Fleet Coast Helicopters Ltd	Shoreham	11. 7.03T
			G-BKDA/LN-OQX				
G-OFCM	Reims Cessna F172L	F17200839	G-AZUN	21.10.81	FCM Aviation Ltd	Guernsey	24. 4.03
			(OO-FCB)				
G-OFER	Piper PA-18-150 Super Cub	18-7709058	N83509	29.12.89	Mary S.W.Meagher	Shenington	11. 5.03
G-OFFA	Pietenpol Aircamper	PFA 047-13181		3.11.98	D.J. Street t/a Offa Group	(Chinnor)	
G-OFHL	Aérospatiale AS350B Ecureuil	1805	C-GIQW	25. 6.93	Ford Helicopters Ltd	Brentwood	15. 7.02T
			G-OFHL/EI-BPM/G-BLSP				
G-OFIL	Robinson R44 Astro	0555		15. 1.99	W. & W.Potter Ltd	(Sowerby Bridge)	2. 2.02T
G-OFIT	SOCATA TB-10 Tobago	938	G-BRIU	11. 9.89	P.Hennessy	White Waltham	19. 1.02T
					t/a GFI Aviation Group		
G-OFIZ*	Cameron Can 80SS HAFB	2106		30.10.89	British Balloon Museum & Library	Newbury	2.12.91A
					"Andrews Can" (Cancelled 10.2.97 as temporary WFU)		
G-OFJC	Eiri Pik-20E	20291	OH-641	19. 3.93	M.J.Aldridge	Tibenham	3. 6.02
G-OFLG	SOCATA TB-10 Tobago	11	G-JMWT	11.12.91	Westward Airways (Lands End) Ltd	St.Just	2. 8.01T
			F-GBHF				
G-OFLI	Colt 105A HAFB	991		20. 1.87	Virgin Airship & Balloon Co Ltd	Telford	22.11.90A
					"Virgin Atlantic"		
G-OFLT	Embraer EMB-110P1 Bandeirante	110.211	G-MOBL	11.12.90	Flightline Ltd	Southend	1. 1.02T
			(G-BGCS)/PT-GMD				
G-OFLY	Cessna 210M Centurion II	21061600	(D-EBYM)	13.10.79	A.P.Mothew	Southend	3. 6.04
			N732LQ				
G-OFMB	Rand Robinson KR-2	7808	N5337X	29. 4.97	F M & S I Burden	(Gloucester)	
	(Built M.A.Shepard)						
G-OFOA	British Aerospace BAe 146 Srs.100	E1006	G-BKMN	3. 3.98	Formula One Adminstration Ltd		
			EI-COF/SE-DRH/G-BKMN/G-ODAN			Biggin Hill	14. 7.02
G-OFOM	British Aerospace BAe 146 Srs.100	E1144	N3206T	16. 3.00	Formula One Management Ltd	Biggin Hill	2.10.02
			PK-DTA/G-BSLP/(PK-DTA)/G-6-144/G-11-144/(G-BRLM)				
G-OFOX	Denney Kitfox	PFA 172-11523		1.11.89	P.R.Skeels	Barton	
G-OFRA	Boeing 737-36Q	29327		5. 5.98	British Regional Airlines Ltd	Manchester	17. 5.03T
					(Bauhaus t/s)		
G-OFRB*	Everett Gyroplane Srs.2	006	(G-BLSR)	7. 8.85	R.M.Savage	Carlisle	17. 6.92P
	(Rotax 503)				t/a Roger Savage (Photography) *"Little Patty"*		
					(Cancelled 9.6.99 by CAA: stored 11.01)		

G-OFRT	Lockheed L.188CF Electra	1075	N347HA N423MA/N23AF/N64405/SE-FGC/N5537	29.10.91	Dart Group plc t/a Channel Express *(Corrosion found and WFU by 3.01: still present 11.01)*	Coventry	28.10.01T
G-OFRY	Cessna 152 II	15281420	G-BPHS N49971	8. 2.93	Devon School of Flying Ltd	Dunkeswell	23. 8.01T
G-OFTI	Piper PA-28-140 Cherokee Cruiser	28-7325201	G-BRKU N15926	11. 6.90	P.E.Richardson	King's Farm, Thurrock	28. 9.02T
G-OGAN	Europa Aviation Europa (Rotax 912)	PFA 247-12734		28. 7.94	B.W.Rendall t/a G-OGAN Group	Wickenby	9. 4.02P
G-OGAR	PZL SZD-45A Ogar	B-601	SP-0004	29. 1.90	N.C.Grayson	Boscombe Down	9. 6.00
G-OGAS*	Westland WG.30 Srs.100	008	G-17-1 G-OGAS/G-BKNW	23. 3.83	Westland Helicopters Ltd *(Cancelled 3.6.92 as WFU: dumped 4.00 in BA Helicopters c/s (navy boom/tail, white cabin & red diagonal stripe))*	Yeovil	19. 5.88T
G-OGAV	Lindstrand LBL-240A HAFB	074		4. 2.94	Airborne Balloon Management Ltd	Tonbridge	12. 6.02T
G-OGAZ	Aérospatiale SA.341G Gazelle 1	1274	G-OCJR G-BRGS/F-GEQA/N341SG/(N341P)N341SG/N47295	12. 1.94	I.M.& S.M.Graham t/a Killochries Fold *(Op Forth Helicopters Ltd)*	Edinburgh	22. 2.04T
G-OGBA	Boeing 737-4S3	25596	G-OBMK	4. 4.97	GB Airways Ltd *(Waves & Cranes t/s)*	Gatwick	7. 5.02T
G-OGBB	Boeing 737-34S	29108		27. 1.98	GB Airways Ltd *(Colum t/s)*	Gatwick	26. 1.04T
G-OGBC	Boeing 737-34S	29109	N1787B	26. 2.98	GB Airways Ltd *(Koguty Lowickie t/s)*	Gatwick	25. 2.04T
G-OGBD	Boeing 737-3L9	27833	OY-MAR D-ADBJ/OY-MAR	16. 3.98	GB Airways Ltd *(Ndebele Martha t/s)*	Gatwick	12. 3.04T
G-OGBE	Boeing 737-3L9	27834	OY-MAS	24.11.98	GB Airways Ltd *(Crossing Borders t/s)*	Gatwick	17.12.04T
G-OGCA	Piper PA-28-161 Warrior II	28-8016262	N8154L	16. 8.90	Cardiff-Wales Aviation Services Ltd	Cardiff	7. 7.02T
G-OGEE	Christen Pitts S-2B Special (Lycoming AEIO-540)	5200	OH-SKY	1. 6.95	Display Aerobatics Ltd	Rochester	28. 6.04T
G-OGEM	Piper PA-28-181 Archer II	28-8190226	N83816	10. 3.88	GEM Rewinds Ltd	Coventry	24. 5.03T
G-OGEO	Aérospatiale SA.341G Gazelle 1	1417	G-BXJK F-GEHC/N341AT/N49536	28. 1.02	MW Helicopters Ltd	Stapleford	17. 8.03
G-OGET	Piper PA-39 Twin Comanche C/R	39-87	G-AYXY N8930Y	14. 3.83	P.G.Kitchingman	White Waltham	21.12.01
G-OGHH	Enstrom 480	5015		14. 2.96	Silver Lining Finance SA,	(Luxembourg)	12. 3.02T
G-OGIL*	Short SD.3-30 Var.100	SH.3068	G-BITV G-14-3068	23. 1.89	North East Aircraft Museum *(Damaged Newcastle 1.7.92: cancelled 12.11.92 as WFU)*	Sunderland	21. 4.93T
G-OGJM	Cameron C-80 HAFB	4869		21.11.00	G.J.Madelin	(Farnham)	10.11.01A
G-OGJP	Hughes 369E	0512E	N685F N5223X	23. 1.01	Motortrak Ltd	(Thames Ditton)	
G-OGJS	Rutan Puffer Cozy (Lycoming O-360)	PFA 159-11169		27. 1.89	G.J.Stamper	Carlisle	14. 9.98P
G-OGOA	Aérospatiale AS350B Ecureuil	1745	G-PLMD G-NIAL	16. 1.90	Lomas Helicopters Ltd	Lake, Bideford	23. 5.02T
G-OGOB	Schweizer Hughes 269C (300C)	S.1315	G-GLEE G-BRUW/N86G	2.10.90	Kingfisher Helicopters Ltd	Longdown	25. 3.02T
G-OGOG	Robinson R22 Beta	1475	G-TILL	2. 7.97	D.Thomas t/a Lake Services	Exeter	9.10.02T
G-OGOS	Everett Gyroplane (VW 1834)	004	7Q-YES G-OGOS	30. 7.84	N.A.Seymour	(Norwich)	12. 9.90
G-OGPN	Cassutt Special (Continental C90)	PFA 126-10778	G-OMFI G-BKCH	1. 5.01	S.Alexander	Bidford	28. 8.02P
G-OGRK	Aérospatiale AS355F1 Twin Squirrel	5185	G-BWZC (G-MOBZ)/N107KF/N5799R	26. 3.99	Kelwaiver Ltd	Stapleford	8. 2.03T
G-OGSA	Jabiru Jabiru UL (Jabiru 2200A)	PFA 274A-13540		10. 2.00	G.J.Slater & W.Moultrie	Clench Common	18. 9.01P
G-OGSS	Lindstrand LBL 120A HAFB	683		19. 5.00	R.Klarer	Erbach, Germany	15. 7.02A
G-OGTS	Air Command 532 Elite (Rotax 532)	0432 & PFA G/104-1125		19.12.88	GTS Engineering (Coventry) Ltd t/a GTS Cars	Coventry	1.10.90P
G-OGTX	Cessna T310R	310R1209	N37600	10.12.01	I.M.& S.M.Graham	(Kilmalcolm)	
G-OHAC	Reims Cessna F182Q Skylane	F18200048	D-ENCM	11. 7.01	The RAF Halton Aeroplane Club	RAF Halton	8. 8.04T
G-OHAJ	Boeing 737-36Q	29141		2. 6.98	British Regional Airlines Ltd *(Delftblue Daybreak t/s)*	Gatwick	30. 8.03T
G-OHAL	Pietenpol Aircamper	PFA 047-12840		25.11.96	H.C.Danby	(Sudbury)	
G-OHAT	Cessna 525 Citation Jet	525-0028	G-OICE N1330S	19. 2.01	Houston Air Taxis Ltd	Oxford	17.11.04T
G-OHCP	Aérospatiale AS355F1 Twin Squirrel	5249	G-BTVS G-STVE/G-TOFF/G-BKJX	14. 3.94	Plane Talking Ltd	Elstree	20. 2.04T
G-OHDC*	Colt Film Cassette SS HAFB *(Agfa Film shape)*	2633		8. 8.94	Balloon Preservation Group *"Agfa HDC" (Cancelled 31.1.02 as wfu)*	Kirdford	26. 8.99A

G-OHEA*	Hawker Siddeley HS.125 Srs.3B/RA		G-AVRG	25.11.86	Cranfield University	Cranfield	7. 8.92T
		25144	G-5-12				
	(WFU & dismantled 12.94: cancelled 23.6.94 as WFU: fuselage dumped 6.00 marked as "G-DHEA")						
G-OHFT	Robinson R22 Beta	1040	G-TYPO	18.12.01	Heliflight (UK) Ltd	Wolverhampton	19. 7.01T
			G-JBWI				
G-OHHI	Bell 206L-1 LongRanger II	45552	G-BWYJ	30. 4.98	I.R.Chisholm	Costock	6. 3.03T
			D-HOBD/D-HGAD		t/a Bradmore Helicopters		
G-OHIG*	Embraer EMB.110-P1 Bandeirante		G-OPPP	29..3 95	Air Tabernacle Ltd	Alton	26. 5.98T
		110.235	XC-DAI/PT-SAB		*(Cancelled 11.4.01 by CAA)*		
					(Fuselage @ Air Salvage International yard 11.01)		
G-OHKS(2)	Pegasus Quantum 15(HKS)	7505		7. 6.01	York Microlight Centre Ltd	Rufforth	8. 5.02T
	(HKS 700E s/n 99030A) *(G-OHKS (1) regd 24.3.99 & exported to Australia 1999/2000. CofR retained and orig reg re-issued by CAA @ 7.6.01 with same c/n!: the new airframe awaits identification)*						
G-OHLL	Robinson R22 Beta	1087	G-CHAL	2.12.97	Plane Talking Ltd	Elstree	9. 5.04T
G-OHMS	Aérospatiale AS355F1 Twin Squirrel		N367E	15. 6.90	South Western Electricity plc	Bristol	23. 6.02T
		5194					
G-OHRH	Lindstrand LBL 150A HAFB	754		12. 2.01	A.Holly t/a Exclusive Ballooning	Bristol	5. 2.02T
					(Prince's Trust titles)		
G-OHSA	Cameron N-77 HAFB	4269		2. 2.98	D.N. & L.J.Close	Andover	15. 4.01A
					(HSA Healthcare titles)		
G-OHSL	Robinson R22 Beta	0967	G-BPNF	4. 7.01	Helicopter Support Ltd		
			N8029Y			(Ashleworth, Glos)	24. 8.04T
G-OHVA	Mainair Blade 912	1189-0199-7-W992		6.11.98	M C Metatidj	(La Baule, France)	4 .3.02P
G-OHWV	Raj Hamsa X'Air 582 (5)			18.11.99	H.W.Vasey	(Newquay)	29. 5.02P
		474 & BMAA/HB/121	*(BMAA records show as '582 (4))*				
G-OIAN*	Morane Saulnier MS.880B Rallye Club		PH-MSB	17. 5.82	Not known	Sewell, Dunstable, Beds	
		5116	*(Did not aspire to a CofA & cancelled 2.9.91 by CAA) (Noted dumped 5.01)*				
G-OIBM	Rockwell Commander 114	14295	G-BLVZ	14.10.88	I.Rosewell	Blackbushe	4. 7.03
			SX-AJO/N4957W				
G-OIBO	Piper PA-28-180 Cherokee C	28-3794	G-AVAZ	21. 1.87	Britannia Airways Ltd		
			N11C			Wellesbourne Mountford	26. 3.03T
G-OICO	Lindstrand LBL-42A HAFB	566		3.11.98	Virgin Airship & Balloon Co Ltd	Telford	12.11.99A
G-OICV*	Robinson R22 Beta	0991	G-BPWH	11. 2.93	Helicentre Ltd	Blackpool	18. 3.01
			(Damaged Blackpool 18.7.99: cancelled 19.11.99 as wfu: wreck stored 12.01)				
G-OIDW	Cessna F150G	F150-0188	N70163	24. 4.90	K.J.Steele & D.J.Hewitt		
			D-EGTI			Wolverhampton	24. 5.03
G-OIFM	Cameron Dude 90SS HAFB	2841		18. 6.92	Magical Adventures Ltd	Chirk	29. 5.99A
	(Radio One FM DJ's Head & Earphones)				"Cool Dude"		
G-OIMC	Cessna 152 II	152-85506	N93521	15. 5.87	East Midlands Flying School Ltd		
						East Midlands	28. 6.02T
G-OINK	Piper J-3C-65 Cub	12613	G-BILD	22. 3.83	A.R.Harding	Newton Farm, Sudbury	19. 7.99P
	(L-4J-PI) *(Frame No.12443)*		G-KERK/F-BBQD/44-80317				
G-OINV	British Aerospace BAe 146 Srs.300		VH-EWI	17. 2.00	British Regional Airlines Ltd	Inverness	15. 5.03T
		E3171	G-6-171/VH-EWI/G-6-171		*"Chatham Historic Dockyard"*		
G-OIOZ	Thunder AX9-120 S2 HAFB	4434		17.11.98	The Flying Doctors Hot Air Balloon Co Ltd		
					(Spire FM titles)	Salisbury	14.11.01T
G-OISO	Reims Cessna FA150 Aerobat		G-BBJW	3. 4.90	V J Wilce & D A Miller		
	(Built as FRA150L)	FRA1500213			t/a Les Oiseaux	Poplar Hall Farm, Elmsett	26. 8.02T
G-OITN	Aérospatiale AS355F1 Twin Squirrel		N400HH	3.10.89	Independent Television News Ltd	Redhill	13.12.04T
		5088	N5788B				
G-OITV	Enstrom 280C Shark	1038	G-HRVY	9. 4.96	C.W.Brierley Jones	(Warrington)	24. 9.04T
			G-DUGY/G-BEEL				
G-OIZI	Europa Aviation Europa XS T-G			9.10.00	K.S.Duddy	(Malvern)	
		PFA 247-13615					
G-OJAB	Jabiru Jabiru SK	PFA 274-13031		19. 9.96	P.A.Brigstock	Leicester	10. 5.02P
	(Jabiru 2200A)						
G-OJAC	Mooney M.20J (201)	24-1490	N5767E	20. 8.90	Hornet Engineering Ltd	Biggin Hill	27. 1.03T
G-OJAE	Hughes 269C	90-0966	N1101W	12. 2.90	J.A. & C.M.Wilson		
						Slaithwaite, Huddersfield	17. 9.02
G-OJAN	Robinson R22 Beta	2012	G-SANS	22. 5.01	Heliflight (UK) Ltd	Wolverhampton	5. 9.04T
			G-BUHX				
G-OJAS	Auster J/1U Workmaster	3501	F-BJAS	21. 3.00	K.P.& D.S.Hunt	Shoreham	
			F-WJAS/(F-OBHT)		*(On rebuild 5.01)*		
G-OJAV	Fairey Britten-Norman BN-2A Mk.III-2 Trislander			6. 6.90	Atlantic Bridge Aviation Ltd	Lydd	25.11.00T
		1024	G-BDOS/(4X-CCI)/G-BDOS				
G-OJBB	Enstrom 280FX	2084		14. 6.99	Adenstar Developments Ltd	Shoreham	23. 6.02T
G-OJBM	Cameron N-90 HAFB	2899		28. 9.92	P.Spinlove	Chalfont St.Giles	23. 9.93A
G-OJBS	Cameron N-105 HAFB	4733		8. 3.00	Up and Away Ballooning Ltd	High Wycombe	4. 5.02T
G-OJBW	Lindstrand J & B Bottle SS HAFB	436		26. 8.97	Justerini & Brooks Ltd	London SW1	20. 5.02A
G-OJCM*	Rotorway Executive 90	5117		4. 8.92	Not known	Hawarden	28. 6.96P
	(Rotorway RI 162)		*(Damaged Whitchurch, Shropshire 25.9.95: cancelled 21.8.96 by CAA: stored 3.96)*				
G-OJCW	Piper PA-32RT-300 Lance II		N3016K	9. 1.80	P.G.Dobson	Blackbushe	6. 6.04
		32R-7985062			t/a CW Group		

G-OJDA	EAA Acrosport 2	PFA 072-11067		1. 4.98	D.B.Almey	Fenland	2. 6.02P
	(Lycoming O-360-A4A)						
G-OJDC	Thunder Ax7-77 HAFB	875		9. 1.89	Julia Crosby	Brighton	1. 8.02A
G-OJEG	Airbus A321-231	1015	D-AVZN	14. 5.99	Monarch Airlines Ltd	Luton	13. 5.02T
G-OJEN*	Cameron V-77 HAFB	3302		26. 5.94	Jensport Ltd	Bedale	18. 7.96A
					(Cancelled 25.10.01 by CAA)		
G-OJGT	Maule M-5-235C Lunar Rocket	7285C	LN-AEL	30. 6.98	J.G.Townsend	Draycott Farm, Chiseldon	8. 8.04
			(LN-BEK)/N5635V				
G-OJHB	Colt Flying Ice Cream Cone SS HAFB			23. 6.94	Benedikt Haggeney GmbH		
		2591				Ennigerloh, Germany	21. 2.02A
G-OJHL	Europa Aviation Europa	PFA 247-13039		12. 5.97	J.H.Lace	Prestwick	3. 9.02P
	(Rotax 912- UL) *(Mono-wheel u/c)*				*"Lady Lace"*		
G-OJIL	Piper PA-31-350 Navajo Chieftain		OY-BTP	28. 5.97	Redhill Aviation Ltd	Redhill/Southend	10.1.04T
		31-7625175			*(Op Redhill Charters)*		
G-OJIM	Piper PA-28R-201T Turbo Cherokee Arrow III		N38299	4. 8.86	B.J.Campbell & M.Arnell	Aberdeen	13.12.01
		28R-7703200			t/a Piper Arrow Group		
G-OJJB	Mooney M.20K (252TSE)	25-1161		12. 8.88	G Italiano	Roma-Urbe, Italy	4. 7.04
G-OJJF	Druine D.31 Turbulent	378 & 31	OO-30	6. 1.97	J.J.Ferguson	(Bideford)	
	(VW 1300)				*(Wings noted Eaglescott 10.00)*		
G-OJKM	Rans S-7 Courier	PFA 218-12982		5. 3.01	M.Jackson	Southend	
					(Under construction 1.02)		
G-OJLH	TEAM mini-MAX 91	PFA 186-12164	G-MYAW	12.12.01	J.L.Hamer	(Hartpury)	1. 4.01P
	(Rotax 447)						
G-OJMB	Airbus A330-243	427	F-WWYH	8.11.01	JMC Airlines Ltd	Jakarta, Indonesia	8.11.04T
					(Op Garuda Indonesia)		
G-OJMC	Airbus A330-243	456		R	JMC Airlines Ltd	Manchester	
					(For delivery 3.02)		
G-OJMF	Enstrom 280FX	2086	G-DDOD	12. 6.01	JMF Ltd	(Ballymoney)	9 .12.02
G-OJMR	Airbus A300B4-605R	605	F-WWAY	3. 5.91	Monarch Airlines Ltd	Luton	2. 5.02T
G-OJNB	Lindstrand LBL-21A HAFB	085		14. 2.94	Justerini & Brooks Ltd	London SW1	19. 5.02A
G-OJON	Taylor JT.2 Titch III	PFA 3208		6.10.78	J.H.Fell	(RAF Marham)	18. 5.01P
	(Continental C90)						
G-OJPB	Hawker Siddeley HS.125 Srs.F600B		VP-CJP	25. 9.97	Widehawk Aviation Ltd	Cambridge	9.11.01T
		25258	VR-CJP/G-BFAN/G-AZHS				
G-OJRH	Robinson R44 Astro	0321		11. 4.97	Holgate Construction Ltd		
						Emley Moor, Huddersfield	10. 4.03
G-OJRM	Cessna T.182T Turbo Skylane		N72778	19. 7.01	SPD Ltd	Old Sarum	31. 7.04T
		T18208007					
G-OJSH	Thruster T600N 450 Jab			29. 5.01	J.S.Holden	(Bradford-on-Avon)	23. 9.02P
		0061-T600N-052					
G-OJTA	Stemme S-10V	14-018	D-KGDA	18. 9.95	O.J.Truelove	RAF Halton	31. 3.02
					t/a OJT Associates		
G-OJTW	Boeing 737-36N	28558	(G-JTWF)	26. 4.97	British Midland Airways Ltd		
						East Midlands	1. 5.03T
G-OJVA	Van's RV-6	PFA 181-12292		6. 9.96	J.A.Village	Coal Aston	4.10.02P
G-OJVH	Cessna F150H	F150-0356	G-AWJZ	27. 3.81	A.W.Cairns	RAF Brize Norton	23. 5.04T
G-OJWS	Piper PA-28-161 Cherokee Warrior II		N6377C	13. 7.88	P.J.Ward	Denham	11. 7.03
		28-7816415					
G-OKAG	Piper PA-28R-180 Cherokee Arrow		N3764T	15. 4.88	N.F. & B.R.Green	Stapleford	13. 4.03T
		28R-30075					
G-OKAY	Pitts S-1E Special	12358	N35WH	27. 5.80	D S T Eggleton		
	(Lycoming IO-360)					Waits Farm, Belchamp Walter	10. 4.02P
G-OKBT	Colt 25A Sky Chariot mk.II HAFB	2301		10.11.92	British Telecommunications plc	Thatcham	10. 4.02A
					"Skypiper II"		
G-OKCC	Cameron N-90 HAFB	1741		6. 5.88	D.J.Head	Newbury	25. 7.00A
G-OKED	Cessna 150L	15074250	N19223	29. 1.93	L A Maynard	Old Sarum	31. 1.03T
					(Op Old Sarum Flying Club)		
G-OKEN	Piper PA-28R-201T Turbo Cherokee Arrow III		N47518	20.10.87	W.B.Bateson	Blackpool	25. 4.03T
		28R-7703390					
G-OKES	Robinson R44 Astro	0053		16. 3.94	Hecray Co Ltd	Southend	25. 5.03T
					t/a Direct Helicopters		
G-OKEV	Europa Aviation Europa	PFA 247-13091		11. 6.97	K.A.Pilcher	Wolverhampton	26 .9.02P
	(Rotax 912-UL) *(Tri-cycle u/c)*				*"Freedom"*		
G-OKEY	Robinson R22 Beta	2004		14. 1.92	Key Properties Ltd	Denham	12. 8.01
G-OKIS	Tri-R Kis	PFA 239-12248		15. 6.92	B.W.Davies	Fenland	30. 3.99P
	(CAM.100)				t/a Junipa Sales (Aviation) Ltd *(Stored 3.00)*		
G-OKJN	Boeing 727-225RE	21453	N8880Z	3. 5.00	Cougar Leasing Ltd	Stansted	8.10.04
	(Cnvtd to freighter configuration 2001)		N380KP/N8880Z				
G-OKMA	Tri-R Kis	PFA 239-12808		22.11.95	K.Miller	(Coventry)	
G-OKPW	Tri-R Kis	PFA 239-12359		17. 8.93	K.P.Wordsworth	Shoreham	15. 6.02P
	(Continental O-200-A)						
G-OKYA	Cameron V-77 HAFB	1259		4. 3.87	D.J.B.Woodd	BFPO.17, Germany	
	(Replacement envelope c/n 3331)				t/a Army Balloon Club *"Fly Army II"*		

G-OKYM	Piper PA-28-140 Cherokee	28-23303	G-AVLS N11C	10. 5.88	B.Marshall	Humberside	5.11.03
G-OLAU	Robinson R22 Beta	1119		5. 9.89	Thistle Aviation Ltd	Southend	25. 3.02
G-OLAW	Lindstrand LBL-25A Cloudhopper HAFB	170		9.12.94	George Law Plant Ltd *"Law Hopper"*	Kidderminster	24. 4.97A
G-OLDC	Learjet Learjet 45	45-156	N3017F	12.10.01	Gold Air International Ltd	Cambridge	11.10.02T
G-OLDD	British Aerospace BAe 125 Srs.800B	258106	PK-RGM PK-WSJ/G-5-580	11. 3.99	Gold Air International Ltd.	Cambridge	19..8.02T
G-OLDJ	Learjet Learjet 45	45-138	N5018G	24. 5.01	Gold Air International Ltd	Biggin Hill	23. 5.02T
G-OLDL	Learjet Learjet 45	45-124	N4003Q	19. 2.01	Gold Air International Ltd	Cambridge	18. 2.02T
G-OLDM	Pegasus Quantum 15-912	7589		10.12.99	P.Simpson	(Cuffley)	15.12.01P
G-OLDN	Bell 206L LongRanger	45077	G-TBCA G-BFAL/N64689/A6-BCL	2.10.84	Von Essen Aviation Ltd.	(Taunton)	26. 7.03T
G-OLDR	Learjet Learjet 45	45-161	N3000S	18. 1.02	Gold Air International Ltd	Cambridge	
G-OLDV*	Colt 90A HAFB	2592		5. 5.94	Balloon Preservation Group *"LDV" (Cancelled 29.6.99 as WFU)*	Kirdford	10.11.98A
G-OLEE	Reims Cessna F152 II	F15201797		11. 9.80	Redhill Air Services Ltd	Redhill	6. 4.03T
G-OLEL	American Blimp Corp A-60+ Airship	016	N606LG	9. 3.01	Lightship Europe Ltd ("www.mazda.de" titles)	(Rednal)	22. 3.02T
G-OLEO	Thunder Ax10-210 Srs.2 HAFB	3974		9. 1.97	P.J.Waller	Norwich	8. 7.02T
G-OLEZ	Piper J-3C-65 Cub	18432	G-BSAX N98260/NC98260	8. 8.01	L.Powell *(For restoration)*	(Canterbury)	
G-OLFB	Pegasus Quantum 15-912	7767		2. 3.01	A.J.Boyd	Newtownards, Co.of Down	1. 3.02P
G-OLFC	Piper PA-38-112 Tomahawk	38-79A0995	G-BGZG N9658N	6.12.85	M.W.Glencross	Luton	29. 5.04T
G-OLFT	Rockwell Commander 114	14274	G-WJMN N4954W	28. 3.85	D.A.Tubby	(Warrington)	14. 2.02
G-OLGA	CFM Starstreak Shadow SA.II (Rotax 618)	K.288 & PFA 206-13164		15.10.97	N.F.Smith	Halstead	17. 9.01P
G-OLIN*	Piper PA-30 Twin Comanche B	30-1716	OY-DLC G-AWMB/N8569Y	22.12.81	Not known	(Henstridge)	3. 3.88T
	(Crashed Stapleford 16.8.87: cancelled 11.4.88 as destroyed: stored 1992: current status unknown)						
G-OLIZ	Robinson R22 Beta	0779		29. 9.88	R S Forsyth & L T W Alderman	(Buntingford)	16. 8.04T
G-OLJT	Mainair Gemini/Flash 2A (Rotax 503)	570-887-5 & W359	G-MTKY	16. 9.98	A Wraith	(Huddersfield)	13. 3.02P
G-OLLE	Cameron O-84 HAFB	1520		15. 4.87	N.A.Robertson *"Golly IV"*	Combe Hay Manor, Bath	24. 8.01A
G-OLLI	Cameron O-31 HAFB *(Golly Special shape)*	196		11. 5.76	N.A.Robertson *"Golly III"*	Combe Hay Manor, Bath	17. 7.97A
G-OLMA	Partenavia P.68B	159	G-BGBT	15. 4.85	C.M.Evans	Bodmin	6. 7.02T
G-OLOW	Robinson R44 Astro	0100		3.10.94	J.E.Morris t/a Morris Transport	(Oswestry)	14. 6.04T
G-OLPG	Colt 77A HAFB	2568		11. 3.94	D.J.Farrar	Leeds	15. 6.01
G-OLRT	Robinson R22 Beta	1378	N4014R	21. 5.90	S.Farmer t/a First Degree Air	Tatenhill	29. 7.02T
G-OLSC*	Cessna 182A Skylane	34078	G-ATNU EI-ANC/N6078B	19. 8.87	Not known	St.Merryn	3. 7.93
	(Damaged landing Knettishall 6.6.93: cancelled 3.4.97 by CAA: fuselage stored 5.98: current status unknown)						
G-OLSF	Piper PA-28-161 Cadet	2841284	G-OTYJ G-OLSF/N92008	23.11.89	Bflying Ltd *(Op Bournemouth Flying Club)*	Bournemouth	22. 1.02T
G-OLVR*	Clutton FRED Srs.II (Continental A65)	PFA 029-10321		17.11.78	C.P.Whitwell *(Cancelled 23.12.99 by CAA: dismantled 1.00)*	Dunkeswell	2. 6.00P
G-OLYD	Beechcraft 58 Baron	TH-1427	N7255H ZS-LYC/N7255H	12. 9.97	I.G.Lloyd	Gamston	1.11.03
G-OLYN	Sky 260-24 HAFB	088		24. 4.98	Airborne Balloon Management Ltd	Tonbridge	20. 6.02T
G-OMAC	Reims FR172E Rocket	FR17200022	PH-HAI (PH-KRC)/D-EDDC	3. 7.84	S.G.Shilling	Manston	15.11.04T
G-OMAF	Dornier 228-200	8112	D-CAAD	16. 2.87	Cobham Leasing Ltd *(Op Department for Environment, Food & Rural Affairs/Fisheries Patrol)*	Bournemouth	22. 6.02T
G-OMAK	Airbus A319-132 CJ	913	F-WWIF G-OMAK/F-WWIF/G-OMAK/D-AVYL	7. 1.99	Twinjet Aircraft Sales Ltd	Luton	7. 1.03T
G-OMAL	Thruster T600N 450	0061-T600N-050		16. 5.01	M Howland	Wickenby	15.11.02P
G-OMAP	Rockwell Commander 685	12036	F-GIRX F-OCGX/F-ZBBU/N6525V	4.11.94	Cooper Aerial Surveys Ltd	Gamston	29. 4.02A
G-OMAT	Piper PA-28-140 Cherokee D	28-7125139	G-JIMY G-AYUG/N11C	27. 8.87	R.B.Walker t/a Midland Air Training School	Coventry	9.11.03T
G-OMAX	Brantly B.2B	473	G-AVJN	7. 8.87	P.D.Benmax	Denham	16.11.03
G-OMDD	Cameron Thunder AX8-90 S2 HAFB	4345		2. 4.98	M.D.Dickinson	(Bristol)	13. 4.01T
G-OMDG	Hoffmann H-36 Dimona	3510	OE-9215	19.11.98	P.Turner t/a Mendip Dimona Group	Halesland	7.12.01
G-OMDH	MD Helicopters Hughes 369E (500E)	0293E		14.11.88	Stiltgate Ltd	Booker	15. 5.04T

G-OMDR	Agusta-Bell 206B-3 JetRanger III	8610	G-HRAY G-VANG/G-BIZA	8.12.97	Aeromega Ltd *(Noted 11.01)*	Norwich	15.12.03T
G-OMEC	Agusta-Bell 206B-3 JetRanger III	8716	G-OBLD	16. 1.90	Kallas Ltd	(Monaco)	21.10.01
G-OMEL	Robinson R44 Astro	0073	G-BVPB	30. 9.96	Nedair Ltd	Blackpool	2.11.03T
G-OMEX	Zenair CH.701 STOL	PFA 187-13556		11.12.01	S.J.Perry	(Woodhall Spa)	
G-OMEZ	Zenair CH.601HDS Zodiac	PFA 162-13552		16. 7.01	C.J.Gow	Perth	6.11.02P
G-OMFG	Cameron A-120 HAFB	4965		7. 2.01	M.F.Glue	Hertford	5. 2.02T
G-OMGD	British Aerospace BAe 125 Srs.700B	257184	9K-AGA YI-AKG/9K-AGA/G-5-12	28.12.94	Magec Aviation Ltd	Luton	21. 2.02T
G-OMGE	British Aerospace BAe 125 Srs.800B	258197	G-5-696 G-BTMG	1. 7.91	Marconda Services Ltd	Luton	22. 5.01T
G-OMGG	British Aerospace BAe 125 Srs.800B	258058	N125JW G-5-637/N125JW/VH-NMR/ZK-EUI/(ZK-EUR)/G-5-510	21.11.94	Aviation One Co. Ltd	(George Town, Cayman Islands)	23.11.02T
G-OMHC	Piper PA-28RT-201 Arrow IV	28R-7918105	N3072Y	10. 2.81	M.R.Shelton t/a Tatenhill Aviation	Tatenhill	6. 5.02T
G-OMHI	Mills MH-1	MH.001		8.10.97	J.P.Mills	(Stockport)	
G-OMHP	Jabiru Jabiru UL	PFA 274A-13584		23. 5.00	M.H.Player	(Shepton Mallet)	
G-OMIA	SOCATA MS.893A Rallye Commodore 180	12074	D-ENME F-BUGE/(D-ENMH)	21. 7.98	P.W.Portelli	Elstree	19.12.04
G-OMIK	Europa Aviation Europa	PFA 247-12991		12. 1.98	M.J.Clews	White Waltham	15. 8.02P
G-OMJT	Rutan LongEz (Lycoming O-235)	968 & PFA 074A-10703		14.10.92	M.J.Timmons	Prestwick	6. 8.02P
G-OMKF	Aero Designs Pulsar (Rotax 582) *(Tri-cycle u/c)*	PFA 202-11866		15. 1.91	M.K.Faro	Henstridge	4. 9.01P
G-OMMG	Robinson R22 Beta	1041	G-BPYX	25. 2.94	R.D.Masters	Panshanger	27. 1.04T
G-OMMM	Colt 90A HAFB	2328		20. 1.93	V.Trimble	Henley-on-Thames	24. 5.02A
G-OMNH	Beechcraft 200 Super King Air	BB-108	N108BM RP-C1979/TR-LWC	19. 8.98	Maynard & Harris Holdings Ltd	Stapleford	20. 8.02T
G-OMNI	Piper PA-28R-200 Cherokee Arrow II	28R-7335130	G-BAWA N11C	3. 1.84	Avon Leasing Ltd t/a The Blue Book	Gloucestershire	16. 7.03T
G-OMOG*	Gulfstream AA-5A Cheetah	AA5A-0793	G-BHWR N26892	4. 3.88	Solent Flight Aircraft Ltd *(Cancelled 23.7.01 by CAA)*	Southampton	15. 4.02T
G-OMOL	Maule MX-7-180C Star Rocket	28012C		15. 8.00	Aeromarine Ltd	Owlesbury	2.10.03
G-OMRB	Cameron V-77 HAFB	2184		29. 8.90	M.R.Bayne *"Harlequin"*	Dunnington, Yorks	28. 7.02A
G-OMRG	Hoffmann H-36 Dimona	36132	G-BLHG	15.11.88	M.R.Grimwood	Gloucestershire	22. 2.03
G-OMSG	Robinson R22 Beta-II	2738		8.10.97	A.J.& P.D.Morgan t/a Morhire	(Usk)	15. 5.04T
G-OMST	Piper PA-28-161 Warrior III	2842121	G-BZUA N53363	1. 8.01	Mid-Sussex Timber Co. Ltd	Biggin Hill	11. 6.04T
G-OMUC	Boeing 737-36Q	29405		29. 6.98	British Regional Airlines Ltd *(Colum t/s)*	Gatwick	22.11.03T
G-OMUM	Rockwell Commander 114	14067	PH-JJJ (PH-MMM)/N4737W	24. 1.97	C.E.Campbell	Blackbushe	7. 3.03
G-OMWE	Zenair CH.601HD Zodiac (Mid-West AE.100R)	PFA 162-12740	G-BVXU	21. 3.97	Mid-West Engines Ltd	Egelsbach, Germany	14. 7.01P
G-OMXS	Lindstrand LBL-105A HAFB	172		7.12.94	Virgin Airship & Balloon Co Ltd *"Mazda"*	Telford	1. 4.97A
G-ONAF	Naval Aircraft Factory N3N-3 (Wright Whirlwind R.760)	--	N45192 Bu.4406	31. 1.89	R.P.W.Steele & J.D.Hutchinson	Sandown	30. 8.02
G-ONAV	Piper PA-31 Navajo C	31-7812004	G-IGAR D-IGAR/N27378	29. 1.93	Panther Aviation Ltd	Elstree	31. 5.03T
G-ONCB	Lindstrand LBL-31A HAFB	393		4. 6.96	Flying Pictures Ltd	Fairoaks	17. 9.02A
G-ONCL	Colt 77A HAFB	1637		4. 4.90	D.R.Pearce	Slimbridge	16. 6.02A
G-ONCM	Partenavia P.68C	217	I-CITT G-TELE/G-DORE/OY-CAD	5.12.01	Millair Ltd	Hawarden	1. 2.92T
G-ONEB	Westland Scout AH.1	F.9761	G-BXOE XW798	21. 1.98	N.E.Bailey & E M Smith	Draycott Farm, Chiseldon	24. 5.02P
G-ONES	Slingsby T.67M-200	2046	SE-LBB LN-TFB/G-7-122	12.11.01	L.J.Jones	(Martock)	
G-ONET	Piper PA-28-180 Cherokee E	28-5802	G-AYAU N11C	3. 6.98	J.Blackburn	Elstree	4. 8.02T
G-ONEW	Embraer EMB-110P1 Bandeirante	110.198	PH-FVA N522MW/PT-GLQ	18. 8.00	Sky Service NV	(Wevelgem, Belgium)	20. 9.01T
G-ONFL	Murphy Maverick (Rotax 503)	402 & PFA 259-12750	G-MYUJ	27.11 98	K.M.Dando	Shobdon	19. 3.02P
G-ONGC	Robin DR.400/180R Remorquer	1385	EI-CKA SE-GHM	11.11.98	Norfolk Gliding Club Ltd	Tibenham	3.12.01
G-ONHH	Forney F-1A Aircoupe	5725	G-ARHA N3030G	13.12.89	R.D.I.Tarry *"Easy Rider"*	(Kettering)	14. 3.04
G-ONIX	Cameron C-80 HAFB	4411		12. 8.98	Hillwalk Ltd	Weston-super-Mare	16. 6.02A
G-ONKA	Aeronca K (Lycoming O-145)	K283	N19780 NC19780	21.10.91	N.J.R.Minchin *"Aggnes"*	Manor Farm, Tongham	28. 6.02P

G-ONMT	Robinson R22 Beta-II	2963		20. 7.99	Redcourt Enterprises Ltd	Lanark	2 .8.02T
G-ONON	Rotary Air Force RAF 2000 GTX-SE	PFA G/13-1313		13. 8.99	M.S.R.Allen	(Oakham)	
G-ONOW	Bell 206A JetRanger	605	G-AYMX	8. 8.88	J.Lucketti	(Rochdale)	27. 4.00T
G-ONPA(2)	Piper PA-31-350 Navajo Chieftain	31-7952110	N89PA N35225	6. 5.98	Anglo American Airmotive Ltd	Bournemouth	15.10.04T
G-ONSF	Piper PA-28R-201 Cherokee Arrow III	28R-7737082	G-EMAK D-EMAK/N38180	17 .1.01	Northamptonshire School of Flying Ltd	Sywell	17. 4.04T
G-ONTV	Agusta-Bell 206B-3 JetRanger III	8733	D-HUNT TC-HKJ/(D-HSAV)/I-GPFP/I-PIEF	1. 4.98	Castle Air Charters Ltd	Liskeard	19. 4.04T
G-ONUN	Van's RV-6A	PFA 181-12976		20. 2.96	R.E.Nunn	Maypole Farm, Kent	14 .5.02P
G-ONUP	Enstrom F-28C	348	G-MHCA G-SHWW/G-SMUJ/G-BHTF	18. 1.00	R.E.Harvey	(West Deeping)	20. 6.02
G-ONYX	Bell 206B-3 JetRanger III	4160	G-BXPN N18EA/D-HOBA/(D-HOBE)	22. 1.98	N.C.Wheelwright	Gloucestershire	15. 3.04T
G-ONZO	Cameron N-77 HAFB *(Regd initially as "O-77")*	1089		13.11.84	K.Temple *"Gonzo"*	(Rickinghall)	19. 7.99A
G-OOAE	Airbus A321-211	852	(G-UNIF) D-AVZG	14. 7.98	Air 2000 Ltd	Manchester	13. 7.04T
G-OOAF	Airbus A321-211	677	G-UNID G-UKLO/D-AVZO	4.12.98	Air 2000 Ltd	Manchester	6. 5.03T
G-OOAH	Airbus A321-211	781	G-UNIE D-AVZK	4. 1.99	Air 2000 Ltd	Manchester	2. 3.04T
G-OOAI	Airbus A321-211	1006	D-AVZJ	30. 4.99	Air 2000 Ltd	Manchester	29. 4.02T
G-OOAJ	Airbus A321-211	1017	D-AVZM	12. 5.99	Air 2000 Ltd	Manchester	11. 5.02T
G-OOAL	Boeing 767-38AER	29617		29. 3.99	Air 2000 Ltd *"Sunrise"*	Manchester	29 .3.02T
G-OOAM	Boeing 767-38AER	29618		10. 5.00	Air 2000 Ltd	Manchester	8..5.03T
G-OOAN	Boeing 767-39HER	26256	G-UKLH	26. 1.99	Air 2000 Ltd *"Caribbean Star"* *(Stored 1.02)*	Filton	4 .4.03T
G-OOAP	Airbus A320-214	1306	F-WWBY	23.10.00	Air 2000 Ltd	Manchester	22.10.03T
G-OOAR	Airbus A320-214	1320	F-WWDT	3.11.00	Air 2000 Ltd	Manchester	2.11.03T
G-OOAS	Airbus A320-214	1571	F-WWBM	5.10.01	Air 2000 Ltd	Manchester	4.10.04T
G-OOAT	Airbus A320-214	1605	F-WWBV	26.11.01	Air 2000 Ltd	Manchester	26.11.04T
G-OOAU	Airbus A320-214	1637	F-WWDM	10. 1.02	Air 2000 Ltd	Manchester	9. 1.05T
G-OOBA	Boeing 757-28A	32446	N446GE (N558NA)	9. 2.01	Air 2000 Ltd *(Stored 1.02)*	Filton	4. 4.04T
G-OOBB	Boeing 757-28A	32447	N447GE (N559NA)	9. 2.01	Air 2000 Ltd *(Stored 1.02)*	Filton	11. 4.04T
G-OODE	SNCAN Stampe SV-4C (DH Gipsy Major 10)	500	G-AZNN F-BDGI	9. 5.77	A.R.Radford	Redhill	4. 7.02T
G-OODH	Schempp-Hirth Ventus 2CM	96		1. 3.01	D.J.M.Hill	(Norwich)	2 .5.04
G-OODI	Pitts S-1D Special (Lycoming IO-360)	KH.1	G-BBBU	23.12.80	R.M.Buchan	(Barnet)	5. 4.02P
G-OODW	Piper PA-28-181 Archer II	28-8490031	N4332C	14. 7.87	Goodwood Road Racing Co Ltd	Goodwood	18.11.02T
G-OOER	Lindstrand LBL-25A Cloudhopper HAFB	125		15. 8.94	Airborne Adventures Ltd	Skipton	18.10.95A
G-OOFT	Piper PA-28-161 Warrior III	2842083	N170FT	25. 5.00	Lyrical Computing Ltd *(Op Denham School of Flying)*	Denham	22. 6.03T
G-OOGA	Gulfstream GA-7 Cougar	GA7-0111	SE-IEA N758G	3. 2.86	Cougar Aviation Ltd	Elstree	25.11.04T
	(C/n confirmed correct but duplicates that for YV-1334P)						
G-OOGI	Gulfstream GA-7 Cougar	GA7-0077	G-PLAS G-BGHL/N789GA	16. 1.95	Plane Talking Ltd	Biggin Hill	23. 8.03T
	(Crashed on landing Denham 10.6.01: damage to port engine cowling, port wing & wing root fairing)						
G-OOGO	Grumman-American GA-7 Cougar	GA7-0049	N762GA	12.11.97	Leonard F.Jollye (Brookmans Park) Ltd	Elstree	7.12.03T
G-OOGS	Gulfstream American GA-7 Cougar	GA7-0105	G-BGJW N737G	19. 6.98	Bflying Ltd *(Op Bournemouth Flying Club)*	Bournemouth	23 .5.02T
G-OOHO	Bell 206B-3 JetRanger III	3370	G-OCHC G-KLEE/G-SIZL/G-BOSW/N2063T	4. 7.01	Into Space Ltd	Leicester	26. 6.04T
G-OOIO	Eurocopter AS 350B3 Ecureuil	3463		17.10.01	Hovering Ltd	(Douglas, IoM)	19.11.04
G-OOJC	Bensen B.8MR *(Converted ex Air Command)*	PFA G/101-1303		4.12.98	J.R.Cooper	Swansea	
G-OOJP	Commander Aircraft Commander 114B	14567	D-EYCA N92JT	24.12.99	Plato Management Ltd	Oxford	19..1.03
G-OOLE	Cessna 172M Skyhawk II	17266712	G-BOSI N80714	25. 8.89	P.S.Eccersley	Humberside	30. 1.04
G-OONE	Mooney M.20J (205)	24-3039		31. 7.87	J.H.Donald & K.B.Moore	Cumbernauld	11. 5.03
G-OONI	Thunder Ax7-77 HAFB	1534		9. 3.90	Fivedata Ltd *"Bridesnightie"*	Todmorden, Lancs	31. 3.01A
G-OONY	Piper PA-28-161 Warrior II	28-8316015	N83071	26. 7.89	D.A.Field & P.B.Jenkins	Compton Abbas	23.10.04T
G-OOOA	Boeing 757-28A	23767	C-FOOA G-OOOA (x3)/C-FOOA (x2)	6. 3.87	Air 2000 Ltd	Manchester	6. 4.04T

G-OOOB	Boeing 757-28A	23822	C-FOOB G-OOOB (x9)	19. 2.87	Air 2000 Ltd	Manchester	28. 4.04T
G-OOOC	Boeing 757-28AER	24017	C-FRYL C-FXOC/G-OOOC (x7)	19. 1.88	Air 2000 Ltd *(Alletiders titles)*	Manchester	27. 4.02T
G-OOOD	Boeing 757-28A	24235	C-GRYU G-OOOD (x4)/C-FXOD (x4)	28.10.99	Air 2000 Ltd	Manchester	27.10.02T
G-OOOG	Boeing 757-23AER	24292	C-FOOG G-OOOG (x5)	29. 3.89	Air 2000 Ltd *(TCS Expeditions/Air 2000 titles)*	Manchester	29.10.04T
G-OOOI	Boeing 757-23AER	24289	N510SK EC-EMV/EC-247	19.10.89	Air 2000 Ltd	Manchester	19.10.02T
G-OOOJ	Boeing 757-23AER	24290	N510FP EC-EMU/EC-248	19.10.89	Air 2000 Ltd	Manchester	1.11.02T
G-OOOM	Boeing 757-225	22612	SE-DUN G-OOOM/N523EA	19.10.89	Air 2000 Ltd	Manchester	13.12.02T
G-OOOO	Mooney M.20J (205)	24-3046	N205EE	25. 1.88	Pergola Ltd	Weston, Dublin	29.10.04
G-OOOS	Boeing 757-236ER	24397	G-BRJD EC-ESC/EC-349/G-BRJD	14. 5.91	Air 2000 Ltd	Manchester	18.10.02T
G-OOOU	Boeing 757-2Y0ER	25240		30. 8.91	Air 2000 Ltd	Manchester	24.10.02T
G-OOOV	Boeing 757-225	22211	N521EA	12. 2.92	Air 2000 Ltd *(Stored 1.02)*	Filton	17. 2.03T
G-OOOW	Boeing 757-225	22611	N522EA	20. 1.92	Air 2000 Ltd *(Stored 1.02)*	Filton	20. 1.03T
G-OOOX	Boeing 757-2Y0ER	26158		24. 2.93	Air 2000 Ltd *(TCS Expeditions/Air 2000 titles)*	Manchester	22. 3.03T
G-OOOY	Boeing 757-28AER	28203		21. 5.98	Air 2000 Ltd	Manchester	20. 5.04T
G-OOSE	Rutan VariEze	1536 & PFA 074-10326		7.12.78	B.O.Smith & J.A.Towers *(Stored dismantled 1.02)*	Yearby	
G-OOSY	de Havilland DH.82A Tiger Moth *(Composite rebuild)*	85831	F-BGFI Fr AF/DE971	6. 9.94	M.Goosey *(On rebuild 9.94: current status unknown)*	Eccleshall, Stafford	
G-OOTC	Piper PA-28R-201T Turbo Cherokee Arrow III	28R-7703086	G-CLIV N3011Q	18. 1.94	R.Noble Ltd	Seething	9. 1.03
G-OOUT	Colt Flying Shuttlecock SS HAFB	1938		16. 5.91	Shiplake Investments Ltd *"Shuttlecock"*	Guernsey	18.11.00A
G-OOXP	Aero Designs Pulsar XP (Rotax 912)	PFA 202-11915		25.10.90	T.D.Baker	Corby	18. 4.96P
G-OPAG	Piper PA-34-200 Seneca	34-7250348	N506DM G-BNGB/F-BTQT/F-BTMT	16.10.90	A.H.Lavender	Biggin Hill	10. 4.03
G-OPAL	Robinson R22 Beta	0535	N23750	11. 2.86	Heli Air Ltd *(Op The Leamington Hobby Centre Ltd)*	Leasowes Farm, Oxhill, Warks	20. 2.04T
G-OPAM	Reims Cessna F152 II	F15201536	G-BFZS	5. 9.86	PJC (Leasing) Ltd *"Little Red Rooster"*	Stapleford	17. 6.03T
G-OPAS*	Vickers V.806 Viscount	263	G-AOYN	5.10.94	Duxford Air Society	Duxford	
	(WFU 6.96 Southend & broken up: cancelled 28.7.97 as destroyed: nose noted with Parcelforce titles 2000)						
G-OPAT	Beechcraft 76 Duchess	ME-304	G-BHAO	6.12.82	R.D.J.Axford	Booker	7. 2.03
G-OPAZ	Pazmany PL-2	PFA 069-10673		20. 3.98	K.Morris *(Substantially complete mid 2001)*	Boscombe Down	18.12.02P
G-OPCS	Hughes 369E	0333E	CS-HBN N500AH	31. 1.01	Productivity Computer Solutions Ltd	(Ossett)	10. 4.04T
G-OPDM	Enstrom 280FX Shark	2021	N8627Q PH-GBL/N650PG	7. 1.98	Lamindene Ltd	Goodwood	15. 5.04T
G-OPDS	Denney Kitfox mk.4 (Rotax 582)	PFA 172A-12259		8. 1.93	P.D.Sparling	Popham	23. 7.02P
G-OPEP	Piper PA-28RT-201T Turbo Arrow IV	28R-7931070	OY-PEP N2217Q	3.12.97	Oxford Aviation Services Ltd	Oxford	5. 3.04T
G-OPET	Piper PA-28-181 Cherokee Archer II	28-7690067	OH-PET OY-BLC	3. 1.02	It's Just Plane Fun Ltd	(Wirral)	
G-OPFT	Cessna 172R Skyhawk II	17280316	N9491F	11. 3.98	Rankart Ltd	Lydd	19. 3.01T
G-OPFW	Hawker Siddeley HS.748 Srs 2A/266	1714	G-BMFT VP-BFT/VR-BFT/G-BMFT/5W-FAO/G11-10 *(Parcel Force titles)*	1. 7.98	Emerald Airways Ltd	Liverpool	16. 2.01T
G-OPHA	Robinson R44 Astro	0359	CS-HDW G-OPHA	17. 7.97	Simax Services Ltd *(Op Red Aviation)*	Bournemouth	2. 3.03T
G-OPHR	Diamond DA40 Star	40066		8.11.01	Diamond Aircraft UK Ltd	Gamston	
G-OPHT	Schleicher ASH 26E	26105		6. 2.97	Scheibler Filters Ltd *"T1"* *(Stored in trailer 4.01)*	Gloucestershire	21. 6.04
G-OPIC	Reims Cessna FRA150L Aerobat	FRA15000234	G-BGNZ PH-GAB/D-EIQE	20. 6.95	S.J.Burke t/a Peak Aviation Photography	Bodmin	4. 9.03T
G-OPIK	Eiri PIK-20E Srs.1	20233	PH-651	27. 1.82	A.J.McWilliam	Newtownards, Co.of Down	18.10.02
G-OPIT	CFM Streak Shadow (Rotax 532)	K.126-SA & PFA 161A-11624		22.11.89	I Sinnett	Bodmin	23. 6.00P
G-OPJC	Cessna 152 II	15282280	N68354	7. 6.88	PJC (Leasing) Ltd	RAF Henlow	17.10.03T
G-OPJD	Piper PA-28RT-201T Turbo Arrow IV	28R-8231028	N8097V	2.10.89	J M McMillan	(Hook)	16.12.04T
G-OPJH	Rollason Druine D.62B Condor	RAE/619	G-AVDW	15. 4.97	P.J.Hall	Oaksey Park	9.12.01
G-OPJK	Europa Aviation Europa *(Mono-wheel u/c)* (Rotax 912UL)	17 & PFA 247-12487		29. 4.93	P.J.Kember *"The First of the Many"*	Laddingford, Paddock Wood	24. 4.01P
G-OPJS	Pietenpol Aircamper	PFA 047-12834		10.11.00	P.J.Shenton	(Brackley)	

G-OPLB	Cessna 340A II	340A0486	G-FCHJ G-BJLS/(N6315X)	11. 7.95	Ridgewood Ltd	Jersey	19. 6.03
G-OPLC	de Havilland DH.104 Dove 8	04212	G-BLRB VP962	10. 1.91	W.G.T.Pritchard & I.D'Arcy-Bean *(Op Mayfair Dove)*	Redhill	9. 5.02T
G-OPME	Piper PA-23-250 Aztec D	27-4099	G-ODIR G-AZGB/N878SH/N10F	31. 3.94	S.G.Shilling	Manston	14. 4.04T
G-OPMN	Boeing 727-225RE	21578	N8881Z N381KP/N8881Z/(PP-ARR)/N8881Z	28. 4.00	Couga Leasing Ltd *(Op Cougar Airlines)*	Stansted	24. 5.03T
G-OPMT	Lindstrand LBL-105A HAFB	052		30. 9.93	Pace Micro Technology plc *"Pace"*	Shipley	31. 7.99A
G-OPNH	Stoddard-Hamilton Glasair IIRG	PFA 149-13011	G-CINY	14.10.98	P N Haigh	Crosland Moor	4. 7.02P
G-OPPL	Gulfstream AA-5A Cheetah	AA5A-0867	G-BGNN	11.10.85	J.P.E.Walsh t/a Walsh Aviation *(Op Cabair)*	Elstree	8. 8.03T
G-OPRC	Europa Aviation Europa XS	PFA 247-13281		22. 6.01	I.R.Chaplin *(Noted 2.02)*	Rayne Hall Farm, Rayne	
G-OPSF	Piper PA-38-112 Tomahawk	38-79A0998	EI-BLT G-BGZI/N9664N	13.10.82	Panshanger School of Flying Ltd	High Cross, Ware	17. 8.00T
G-OPSL	Piper PA-32R-301 Saratoga SP	32R-8013085	G-IMPW N8186A	4. 1.99	Photonic Science Ltd	Lydd	23. 3.03
G-OPST	Cessna 182R Skylane II	18267932	N9317H	16. 6.88	Lota Ltd	Shoreham	2. 6.03T
G-OPTS	Robinson R22 Beta-II	2712		16. 7.97	T.A.Knox (Shopfitters) Ltd	(Woodley, Stockport)	17. 8.03T
G-OPUB	Slingsby T.67M-160 Firefly	2002	G-DLTA G-SFTX	18.10.96	P.M.Barker	Kirkbymoorside	24. 7.04T
G-OPUP	Beagle B.121 Pup 2	B121-062	G-AXEU (5N-AJC)	31.10.84	A.Brinkley t/a Brinkley Light Aircraft Services	Standalone Farm, Meppershall	26. 4.04
G-OPUS	Jabiru Jabiru SK (Jabiru 2200A)	PFA 274-13343		16. 7.98	H.H.R.Lagache	Leicester	2. 5.02P
G-OPWK	Grumman-American AA-5A Cheetah	AA5A-0663	G-OAEL N26706	26. 5.92	A.H.McVicar *(Op Prestwick Flight Centre)*	Prestwick	6. 9.02T
G-OPWS	Mooney M.20K (231)	25-0663	N1162W	12. 4.91	A.R.Mills	Fowlmere	17. 7.03
G-OPYE	Cessna 172S Skyhawk	172S8059	N653SP	19. 2.99	Far North Aviation	Wick	25 .2.02T
G-ORAC	Cameron Van-110SS HAFB	4577		22. 6.99	Virgin Airship & Balloon Co Ltd *(RAC Titles)*	Telford	21 .5.02A
G-ORAF	CFM Streak Shadow (Rotax 532)	K.134-SA & PFA 161A-11627		18. 5.90	A.P.Hunn *(PFA c/n duplicates MW6 G-MYCU) (Dismantled 5.00)*	Swanton Morley	1.11.00P
G-ORAL	Hawker Siddeley HS.748 Srs.2A/334	1756	G-BPDA G-GLAS/9Y-TFS/G-11-8	13. 8.99	Emerald Airways Ltd *(Reed Aviation titles) "The Paper Plane"*	Liverpool	12.11.02T
G-ORAR	Piper PA-28-181 Archer II	2890224	N9255G	6. 6.95	P.N. & S.M.Thornton	Goodwood	26. 6.01T
G-ORAS	Clutton FRED Srs.2	PFA 029-11002		14. 6.01	A.I.Sutherland *(Under construction 2001)*	(Edderton)	
G-ORAY	Reims Cessna F182Q Skylane II	F18200132	G-BHDN	18. 3.94	G A Barret	Gamston	9.10.04
G-ORBD	Van's RV-6A (Lycoming O-320)	PFA 181-12677	G-BVRE	23. 7.01	C.M.Dixon	Barton	7. 3.02P
G-ORDN*	Piper PA-28R-200 Cherokee Arrow II	28R-7235294	G-BAJT N11C	21. 7.89	Not known *(Damaged Stapleford 27.5.96: cancelled 18.4.97 by CAA: open store 6.00)*	Stapleford	9. 4.99
G-ORDO	Piper PA-30 Twin Comanche B	30-1648	N8485Y	19. 4.91	C.A.Ringrose	Biggin Hill	31. 5.03
G-ORED	Pilatus Britten-Norman BN-2T Islander	2142	G-BJYW	10. 1.85	Red Devils Aviation Ltd	AAC Netheravon	25. 9.03A
G-OREV	Revolution Helicopters Mini 500	0112		8. 8.96	R.H.Everett	Thruxton	
G-ORFC	Jurca MJ.5 Sirocco (Lycoming O-290)	PFA 2210		16. 5.85	D.J.Phillips	Lasham	3. 7.02P
G-ORFE*	Cameron Golf 76SS HAFB	2474		2. 7.91	Not known *"Dimples"* *(Cancelled 2.12.98 on sale to USA: flying as "G-ORFE" Albuquerque, NM, USA 10.00)*	(USA)	
G-ORFH	ATR-42-300	346	F-WWEI	29.12.93	Gill Aviation Ltd *(Stored 10.01)*	Dinard, France	28.12.02T
G-ORHE	Cessna 500 Citation	500-0220	(N619EA) G-OBEL/G-BOGA/N932HA/N93WD/N5220J	25. 3.96	R.H.Everett	Thruxton	22. 5.03T
G-ORIG	Glaser-Dirks DG-800A	8-39-A29		5. 4.94	I.Godfrey *"386"*	Lasham	4. 2.04
G-ORIX	ARV K1 Super 2 (Norton AE.100R)	034 & PFA 152-12424	G-BUXH (G-BNVK)	16. 9.93	T.M.Lyons	(Newcastle-Under-Lyne)	17.12.01P
G-ORJB	Cessna 500 Citation	500-0364	G-OKSP N40DA/N20WP/(N221JB)/N221AC/HB-VFF/N36892	2. 7.92	L'Equipe Air Ltd	Gamston	20.10.04T
G-ORJW	Laverda F.8L Falco Srs.4	403	(PH-...) G-ORJW/D-ELDV/D-ELDY	2.12.85	W.R.M.Sutton	(Hilversum, The Netherlands)	1. 9.01
G-ORJX	BAE Systems Avro 146-RJX85	E2376		16. 2.00	BAE Systems (Operations) Ltd	Woodford	
G-ORMA	Aérospatiale AS355F1 Twin Squirrel	5192	G-SITE G-BPHC/N365E	9.11.98	Stratton Motor Co (Norfolk) Ltd	Stapleford	7. 6.04T
G-ORMB	Robinson R22 Beta	1607		14.12.90	R.M.Bailey	(Addison Mains, Edinburgh)	19. 4.03T
G-ORMG	Cessna 172R Skyhawk II	17280344	N9518F	25. 9.98	J.R.T.Royle	Andrewsfield	8.10.04

G-OROB	Robinson R22 Beta	0965	G-TBFC	11. 6.90	R.Culff	Redhill	25. 6.95T
			N80287		t/a Corniche Helicopters		
					(Spares use 9.97: current status unknown)		
G-OROD	Piper PA-18-150 Super Cub	18-7856	SE-CRD	27. 6.89	B.W.Faulkner	(Petersfield)	10. 3.02
G-ORON	Colt 77A HAFB	1149		8. 3.88	J.Charley	Wymeswold	1.10.00A
					t/a Orion Hot Air Balloon Group		
G-ORPR	Cameron O-77 HAFB	2341		26. 6.90	T.Strauss & A.Sheehan	London SW1	10. 8.01A
					"Batman"		
G-ORRR	Hughes H369HS	114-0673S	G-STEF	20. 6.01	The Lower Mill Estate Ltd	(Cirencester)	4. 3.04
			G-BKTK/OY-HCL/OO-JGR				
G-ORSP	Beechcraft A36 Bonanza	E-2723	N56037	26.10.92	C.W.Makin t/a Makins	Garforth	7. 1.02
G-ORTM	Glaser-Dirks DG-400	4-209		6. 3.87	M.A.Recht	Aboyne	29. 4.03
G-ORVB	McCulloch J.2	039	(G-BLGI)	2. 8.89	R.V.Bowles	(Rugby)	
			(G-BKKL)/Bahrain Public Security BPS-3/N4329G		*(Rebuilt 2000)*		
G-ORVG	Van's RV-6	PFA 181A-13509		2. 1.01	R J Fray	(Peterborough)	
G-ORVR	Partenavia P.68 Victor	115	G-BFBD	2.10.95	Cheshire Flying Services Ltd	Liverpool	17. 3.02T
	(Regd as "P.68B")				t/a Ravenair		
G-OSCC	Piper PA-32-300 Cherokee Six	32-7540020	G-BGFD	27.11.84	BG & G Airlines Ltd	Jersey	27. 6.02
			D-EOSH/N32186				
	(Made heavy landing Fairoaks 12.8.01: substantial damage to starboard wing spar)						
G-OSCH	Cessna 421C Golden Eagle III	421C0706	G-SALI	13. 9.95	Sureflight Aviation Ltd	(Birmingham)	8.11.02
			N26552				
G-OSCO	TEAM mini-MAX 91 (Rotax 447)	PFA 186-12878		24.12.96	P.J.Schofield	(Sproston, Crewe)	20. 8.02P
G-OSDI	Beechcraft 58 Baron	TH-1111	G-BHFY	27. 7.84	D.Darling	Wellesbourne Mountford	27. 4.02
G-OSEA	Pilatus Britten-Norman BN-2B-26 Islander	2175	G-BKOL	27. 8.85	W.T.Johnson & Sons (Huddersfield) Ltd	Crosland Moor	23. 3.04
G-OSEE	Robinson R22 Beta	0917		11. 1.89	Aero-Charter Ltd	(Canterbury)	13.10.02T
G-OSFA	Diamond HK.36TC Super Dimona	36-649		15. 6.99	Oxfordshire Sportflying Ltd	Enstone	19 .7.02T
G-OSFC	Reims Cessna F152 II	F15201872	G-BIVJ	31. 1.86	Stapleford Flying Club Ltd	Stapleford	12. 6.03T
G-OSGB	Piper PA-31-350 Navajo Chieftain	31-7952155	G-YSKY	25. 1.99	Gold Air International Ltd	Cambridge	1. 5.02T
			N3529D		*(Ordnance Survey titles)*		
G-OSHL	Robinson R22 Beta	1000		19. 4.89	Sloane Helicopters Ltd	Sywell	6. 9.04T
G-OSII	Cessna 172N Skyhawk II	17267768	G-BIVY	17.10.95	K.J.Abrams	Andrewsfield	14. 3.02T
			N73973				
G-OSIP	Robinson R22 Beta-II	2916		9. 2.99	Heli Air Ltd	Tatenhill	3 .3.02T
G-OSIS	Pitts S-1S Special	PFA 009-12043		19. 9.94	C.Butler	Netherthorpe	
G-OSIT	Pitts S-1T Special	1023	N96JD	7.12.01	G.C.J.Cooper	(Doncaster)	9.12.04
G-OSIX	Piper PA-32-260 Cherokee Six	32-499	G-AZMO	5. 8.86	A.E.Whittie	Blackpool	7. 4.02T
			SE-EYN				
G-OSKP	Enstrom 480	5002	F-GSOT	6. 6.94	Churchill Stairlifts Ltd	Hawarden	9. 8.04T
			G-OSKP/N480EN		*(Noted 6.01)*		
G-OSKY	Cessna 172M Skyhawk II	17267389	A6-KCB	27. 2.79	Skyhawk Leasing Ltd		
			N73343			Wellesbourne Mountford	8. 7.03T
G-OSLD	Europa Aviation Europa XS	PFA 247-13641		23. 8.00	Opus Software Ltd	(Grantham)	
G-OSLO	Schweizer Hughes 269C	S.1360	N7507L	15. 3.89	AH Helicopter Services Ltd	Newton Abbot	4. 3.04T
G-OSMD	Bell 206B JetRanger II	2034	G-LTEK	12. 2.99	Stuart Aviation Ltd	White Waltham	6. 2.04T
			G-BMIB/ZS-HGH				
G-OSMS	Robinson R22 Beta	1528	G-BXYW	22. 2.99	Heliflight (UK) Ltd	Wolverhampton	22. 9.01T
			HA-MIU/N528SH				
G-OSND	Reims Cessna FRA150M Aerobat	FRA1500272	G-BDOU	16.10.84	Wilkins & Wilkins (Special Auctions) Ltd		
					t/a Henlow Flying Club	RAF Henlow	30. 1.03T
G-OSNI	Piper PA-23-250 Aztec C	27-3852	G-AWER	2. 7.98	Marham Investments Ltd	Belfast	22. 5.04T
			N6556Y				
G-OSOE	Hawker Siddeley HS.748 Srs.2A/275	1697	G-AYYG	17.11.97	Emerald Airways Ltd	Liverpool	10.11.02T
			ZK-MCF/C-GRCU/ZK-MCF/G-AYYG/(x3)/G-11-9		*(Securicor Omega Express titles)*		
G-OSOO	MD Helicopters Hughes 369E (500E)	0298E		10. 5.89	Tyrone Fabrication Ltd	Dungannon, Co.Tyrone	16. 7.04T
G-OSPS	Piper PA-18 Super Cub 95 (L-18C-PI) *(Frame No.18-1527)*	18-1555	OO-SPS	9. 7.92	T.Gale, J.Morrissey, F.Keegan & D.Curtis	(Dublin)	17.11.02
			G-AWRH/OO-HMI/?ALAT 51-15555				
G-OSSF	Gulfstream AA-5A Cheetah	AA5A-0863	G-MELD	1. 2.00	Hecray Co Ltd	Southend	22. 1.04T
			G-BHCB		t/a Direct Helicopters *(Op Southend School of Flying)*		
G-OSST	Colt 77A HAFB	737		28.10.85	British Airways plc	Heathrow	10.10.96A
					"Concorde II"		
G-OSTA	Auster V J/1 Autocrat	1957	G-AXUJ	22. 7.99	D & M Nelson		
			PH-OTO			Coldharbour Farm, Willingham	1. 4.01
G-OSTC	Gulfstream AA-5A Cheetah	AA5A-0848	N26967	22. 4.91	5th Generation Designs Ltd	White Waltham	5.10.03T
G-OSTU	Gulfstream AA-5A Cheetah	AA5A-0807	G-BGCL	18. 4.95	Hecray Co Ltd	Southend	3. 7.03T
					t/a Direct Helicopters *(Op Southend School of Flying)*		
G-OSTY	Cessna F150G	F150-0129	G-AVCU	21. 3.97	C.R Guggenheim	Bournemouth	15.12.02T
G-OSUP	Lindstrand LBL-90A HAFB	098		17. 3.94	T.J.Orchard	Booker	19. 7.01T
					t/a British Airways Balloon Club *"Goes Up"*		

G-OSUS	Mooney M.20K (231)	25-0429	OY-SUS (N3597H)	7.11.94	J.B. & M.O.King	Goodwood	21. 1.04
G-OSVO*	Cameron Hopper Servo 30SS HAFB	3077		30. 4.93	Servo & Electronic Sales Ltd *"Twocon" (Cancelled 25.10.01 by CAA)*	Lydd	26. 6.97A
G-OSVY*	Sky 31-24 HAFB	104		28. 5.98	Balloon Preservation Group *"OS Hopper" (Cancelled 31.7.01 as wfu)*	Kirdford	11. 3.00A
G-OTAC	Robinson R22 Beta-II	2737		8.10.97	Hecray Co Ltd t/a Direct Helicopters	Southend	23.10.03T
G-OTAF	Aero L-39ZO Albatros	232337	N40VC N159JC/(N4321X)/Chad AF TT-ROB/Libyan Arab AF 2337 *(As "111") (Op OFMC)*	9. 2.95	C.P.B.Horsley	Duxford	24. 6.02P
G-OTAL	ARV1 Super 2 (Rotax 912)	024	G-BNGZ	10. 9.87	N.R.Beale	Shotteswell	20. 8.02P
G-OTAM	Cessna 172M Skyhawk II	17264098	N29060	13. 2.89	G.V.White	Swanton Morley	6.12.04T
G-OTAN	Piper PA-18-135 Super Cub (L-21B-PI) *(Frame No.18-3850)*	18-3845	OO-TAN (OO-DPD)/R.Neth AF R-155/54-2445	28.10.96	S.D.Turner	Andrewsfield	29. 5.03
G-OTBA	Hawker Siddeley HS.748 Srs.2A	1712	A3-MCA ZK-MCA/G-11-7	14. 3.01	Emerald Airways Ltd	Liverpool	3. 5.04T
G-OTBY	Piper PA-32-300 Six	32-7940219	N2932G	14. 2.91	GOTBY Ltd	Jersey	5. 4.03
G-OTCH	CFM Streak Shadow (Rotax 582)	K.207 & PFA 206-12401		28.10.93	H.E.Gotch	Redhill	3. 9.02P
G-OTDB	MD Helicopters Hughes 369E	0204E	G-BXUR HA-MSC	7. 4.98	D.E.McDowell	(Wantage)	9. 7.01T
G-OTED	Robinson R22HP	0209	G-BMYR ZS-HLG	17. 1.96	Andrews Heli-Lease Ltd	Denham	17. 2.02T
G-OTEL	Thunder Ax8-90 HAFB	1790		13. 6.90	D.N.Belton	Chard	2. 7.02A
G-OTFT	Piper PA-38-112 Tomahawk	38-78A0311	G-BNKW N9274T	14. 3.97	N.Papadroushotis	Panshanger	25. 4.03T
G-OTGA	Piper PA-28R-201 Cherokee Arrow III	28R-7837281	ZS-KFI	21. 2.01	TG Aviation Ltd	Manston	29. 3.04T
G-OTHE	Enstrom 280C-UK Shark	1226	G-OPJT G-BKCO	22. 9.87	GTS Engineering (Coventry) Ltd	Coventry	22. 7.02
G-OTHL*	Robinson R22 Beta	0738	G-DSGN	28.11.94	RAF Museum *(Cancelled 8.2.00 as WFU) (Displayed as fictitious "G-RAFM")*	Hendon	27. 4.03T
G-OTIB	Robin DR.400/180R Remorquer	1545	D-EGIA	26. 4.00	Norfolk Gliding Club Ltd	Tibenham	27. 4.03
G-OTIG	Gulfstream AA-5B Tiger	AA5B-0996	G-PENN (I-TIGR)/N3756L	28. 7.00	D H Green	Elstree	30. 9.04T
G-OTIM	Bensen B.8MV	PFA G/101-1084		5. 6.90	T.J.Deane	(Tilehurst, Reading)	
G-OTIS	Cessna 550 Citation II	550-0672	N550PF PT-OMB/N6763C	19. 4.00	The Streamline Partnership Ltd	(High Wycombe)	19. 4.03T
G-OTJB	Robinson R44 Raven	0813		4. 8.00	Heli Air Ltd	Wellesbourne Mountford	16. 8.03T
G-OTJH	Pegasus Quantum 15-912	7791		20. 3.01	T.J.Hector	(Royston)	19. 3.02P
G-OTNT*	Cameron Cider Bottle 120SS HAFB	3067		9. 7.93	A.J.Round *(Cancelled 25.10.01 by CAA)*	Wantage	24. 8.95A
G-OTOE	Aeronca 7AC Champion	7AC-4621	G-BRWW N1070E/NC1070E	2. 4.90	J.M.Gale Coombe Farm, Spreyton, Crediton *(Damaged Coombe Farm 31.5.95: new CofR 6.01)*		10. 5.95P
G-OTOO	Stolp SA.300 Starduster Too	PFA 035-13352		26. 8.98	I.M.Castle	(Market Harborough)	
G-OTOY	Robinson R22 Beta	0888	G-BPEW	5. 9.97	Tickstop Ltd	Kimpton Park, Hitchin	24. 9.03T
G-OTRG	Cessna TR182 Turbo-Skylane RG II	R18200766	(N736SU)	14. 3.79	Middleton Miniature Mouldings Ltd	Teesside	16.12.04
G-OTRV	Van's RV-6 (Lycomimg O-360-A1A)	PFA 181-13302		27. 5.98	W.R.C.Williams-Wynne	Talybont	2..6.02P
G-OTSP	Aérospatiale AS355F1 Twin Squirrel	5177	G-XPOL G-BPRF/N363E	31. 3.98	Aeromega Aviation plc *(Op Essex Police Air Support Unit)*	Boreham, Essex	20. 3.03T
G-OTTI	Cameron OTTI 34SS HAFB	3490		23. 3.95	Ballonverbung Hamburg GmbH	Kiel, Germany	19. 7.02A
G-OTTO	Cameron Katalog 82SS HAFB *(New envelope 1999 - c/n 4382)*	2843		15. 6.92	Ballonverbung Hamburg GmbH *"Otto Versand Katalog"*	Kiel, Germany	3. 7.02A
G-OTUG	Piper PA-18-150 Super Cub *(Frame No.18-5424)*	18-5352	(G-BKNM) PH-MBA/ALAT 18-5352/N10F	17. 2.83	B.F.Walker	Nympsfield	22. 7.04
G-OTUP	Lindstrand LBL-180A HAFB	111		28. 3.94	Airborne Adventures Ltd	Skipton	4. 5.01T
G-OTVS*	Britten-Norman BN-2T Islander	419	G-BPBN G-BCMY	14. 2.83	Headcorn Parachute Club Ltd *(Damaged Headcorn 11.3.89: open store 3.96)*	Headcorn	18. 5.90
G-OTWO	Rutan Defiant (Lycoming O-320)	114		24. 6.87	A.J.Baggarley	Shoreham	6. 9.01P
G-OUCH	Cameron N-105 HAFB	4830		3. 5.00	Flying Pictures Ltd *(Elastoplast titles)*	Fairoaks	18. 3.02A
G-OUHI	Europa Aviation Europa XS T-G	PFA 247-13684		7. 6.01	Europa Aircraft Co Ltd	(Kirkbymoorside)	
G-OUMC	Lindstrand LBL 105A HAFB	724		14. 9.00	A.Holly t/a Executive Ballooning *(Uphill Motor Company titles)*	Bristol	16. 9.02T
G-OURO	Europa Aviation Europa *(Tri-cyle u/c)* (NSI EA-81/100)	16 & PFA 0247-12522		13.12.93	D.Pitt	Lee-on-Solent	2. 4.02P
G-OURS	Sky 120-24 HAFB *(Bear's Head shape)*	168		22.12.99	M P A Sevrin *"Victor"*	Albuquerque, NM, USA	28. 7.02

G-OUVI	Cameron O-105 HAFB	1766		4. 5.89	P.Spellward *"Uvistat II"*	Bristol	31. 3.94A
					t/a Bristol University Hot Air Ballooning Society		
G-OVAA	Colt Jumbo SS HAFB	1426		11. 5.89	Virgin Airship & Balloon Co Ltd	Telford	21. 9.96A
	(Conventional shape with nose/wings/tail of Virgin 747)				*"Virgin Jumbo II"*		
G-OVAX	Colt AS-80 Mk II Hot-Air Airship	1501		3. 7.89	Gefa-Flug GmbH	Aachen, Germany	17. 5.02A
	(Reported as AS-105GD - new envelope?)				*"Vax Airship"*		
G-OVBF	Cameron A-250 HAFB	3494		1. 3.95	Virgin Balloon Flights Ltd	Northampton	27. 9.01T
					"Virgin Oscar"		
G-OVET	Cameron O-56 HAFB	3939		25. 6.96	E.J.A.Macholc	Saltburn-by-the-Sea	28. 7.02A
G-OVFM	Cessna 120	14720	N2119V	29. 4.88	R.B.& E.G.Woods	(Thatcham)	3.10.02P
	(Continental O-200-A)		NC2119V				
G-OVFR	Reims Cessna F172N Skyhawk II	F17201892		23. 5.79	Western Air (Thruxton) Ltd	Thruxton	11. 6.04T
G-OVID	Avid Flyer	NMFC.11760	N879UP	31. 5.91	L.G.Horne	(Ashford, Kent)	24. 5.02P
	(Rotax 532)						
G-OVMC	Reims Cessna F152 II	F15201667		29. 5.79	J.A.Lyons	Gloucestershire	19. 8.04T
					t/a Staverton Flying School		
G-OVNR	Robinson R22 Beta	1634		24.12.90	S.Lancaster & L.Clarke	Breighton	14. 5.03T
					t/a Rally Repaints		
G-OWAC	Reims Cessna F152 II	F15201678	G-BHEB	25. 2.80	K.McDonald	Compton Abbas	10. 4.04T
			(OO-HNW)				
G-OWAK	Reims Cessna F152 II	F15201677	G-BHEA	25. 2.80	A.S.Bamrah	Rochester	23.11.01T
					t/a Falcon Flying Services		
G-OWAL	Piper PA-34-220T Seneca III	3448030	D-GAPN	7. 7.98	R.G.& W.Allison	Gamston	25. 9.04
			N9163K				
G-OWAR	Piper PA-28-161 Warrior II	28-8616054	TF-OBO	18. 2.88	Bickertons Aerodromes Ltd	Denham	27. 3.03T
			N9521N		*(Op The Pilot Centre)*		
G-OWAX	Beechcraft Super King Air 200	BB-302	N86Y	4. 1.00	Context GB Ltd	Blackpool	10. 2.03T
			N300BW/N600CP				
G-OWAZ	Pitts S-1C Special	43JM	G-BRPI	22.11.94	P.E.S.Latham	RAF Shawbury	11. 2.02P
	(Lycoming O-320)		N199M		*"Tiny Dancer"*		
G-OWCG	Bell 222	47041	G-VERT	12. 8.94	Phoenix Helicopter Charters Ltd		
			G-JLBZ/G-BNDB/A40-CH		*(Op Air Hanson)*	Blackbushe	12. 3.02T
G-OWDB	Hawker Siddeley HS.125 Srs.700B	257040	G-BYFO	18. 2.99	Bizair Ltd.	Jersey	25 .4.02
			HB-VMD/VP-BPE/VR-BPE/N47TJ/EC-ETI/EC-375/G-OWEB/HZ-RC1				
G-OWEL	Colt 105A HAFB	1773		18. 5.90	S.R.Seager	Aylesbury	16. 3.98T
G-OWEN	K & S Jungster 1	PFA 044-10124		13.11.78	R.C.Owen	Danehill	
	(Continental C90)						
G-OWET	Thurston TSC-1A2 Teal	037	C-FNOR	28. 9.94	D.Nieman	Hinton-in-the-Hedges	10. 5.02
			(N1342W)				
G-OWGC	Slingsby T.61F Venture T.2	1875	XZ555	14. 8.91	Wolds Gliding Club Ltd	Pocklington	1.11.03
G-OWLC	Piper PA-31 Turbo Navajo	31-679	G-AYFZ	13. 6.91	Channel Airways Ltd	Guernsey	14. 8.03
			N6771L				
G-OWND	Robinson R44 Astro	0644		26. 8.99	W.N.Dore	Wellesbourne Mountford	7. 9.02T
G-OWOW	Cessna 152 II	15283199	G-BMSZ	10. 5.95	A.S.Bamrah	(Rochester)	15.11.04T
			N47254		t/a Falcon Flying Services		
G-OWRC	Cessna 525 Citation Jet	525-0177	G-OCSB	13.12.00	Softbreeze Ltd	Oxford	4 .2.02T
			N1280A/(RP-C717)/N1280A/N5163C				
G-OWRT	Cessna 182G Skylane	18255077	G-ASUL	24. 8.00	Blackpool & Fylde Aero Club Ltd		
			N3677U			Blackpool	17. 5.04
G-OWYE	Lindstand LBL 240A HAFB	645		27. 4.00	Wye Valley Aviation Ltd	Ross-on-Wye	17. 6.02T
G-OWYN	Aviamilano F.14 Nibbio	208	HB-EVZ	2. 2.87	D.Kynaston	Cambridge	31. 5.01P
			I-SERE				
G-OXBC	Cameron A-140 HAFB	4981		2. 2.01	J.E.Rose	(Abingdon)	15. 1.02T
G-OXBY	Cameron N-90 HAFB	1993	PH-DUM	9. 6.94	C.A.Oxby *"The Zit"*	Doncaster	
G-OXKB	Cameron Jaguar XK8 Sports Car 110SS HAFB	3941		9. 7.96	Flying Pictures Ltd	Fairoaks	17. 4.02A
					"Jaguar XK8"		
G-OXRG*	Colt Film Can SS HAFB	2138		17. 1.92	Balloon Preservation Group	Kirdford	
	(Agfacolor Film Can shape)				*"Agfa XRG" (Cancelled 29.4.97 as WFU)*		
G-OXTC	Piper PA-23-250 Aztec D	27-4344	G-AZOD	31. 5.89	A.S.Bamrah	Biggin Hill	15. 6.98T
			N697RC/N6976Y		t/a Falcon Flying Services		
G-OXVI	Supermarine 361 Spitfire LF.XVIe	CBAF.IX.4262	7246M	22. 8.89	Silver Victory BVBA	Duxford	14. 5.02P
			TD248		*(As "TD248/D" in 41 Sqn c/s)*		
	(Made heavy landing Duxford 11.5.01 with.damage to undercarriage, wings, fuselage & propeller)						
G-OYAK	SPP Yakovlev C.11	171205	EAF 705	25. 2.88	A.H.Soper	North Weald	3 5.02P
	(C/n quoted as 1701139 and/or 690120)		OK-KIH		*(As "27" in Soviet AF c/s)*		
G-OYES	Mainair Blade 912	1186-1198-7-W989		12.11.98	J.Crowe	East Fortune	9. 3.02P
	(Rotax 912-UL)						
G-OZAR	Enstrom 480	5007	G-BWFF	31. 7.95	Lancroft Air Ltd	RAF Shawbury	1.11.04T
G-OZBB	Airbus A320-212	389	C-GXBB	21. 3.94	Monarch Airlines Ltd	Luton	29. 4.04T
			G-OZBB x 6/C-FTDW x 5/F-WWDI				
G-OZBD	Airbus A321-231	1202	D-AVZN	19. 4.00	Monarch Airlines Ltd	Luton	18..4.03T
G-OZBE	Airbus A321-...	1707		R	Monarch Airlines Ltd	Luton	
					(For delivery 3.02)		

G-OZBF	Airbus A321-...	1763		R	Monarch Airlines Ltd *(For delivery 6.02)*	Luton	
G-OZEE	Avid Speed Wing Mk.4	PFA 189-12308		18. 4.94	S.C.Goozee	Bow, Totnes	11. 9.02P
G-OZEG	Cameron Egg-65 SS HAFB	4801		11. 2.00	Cameron Balloons Ltd	Bristol	23. 2.01A
G-OZLN	Moravan Zlin Z.242L	0651	OK-XNA (SE-KMM)	2.10.92	R.L.McDonald	(Edinburgh)	28. 3.02
G-OZOI	Cessna R182 Skylane RG II	R18201950	G-ROBK	31. 5.85	J.R. & F.L.Gibson Fleming t/a Ranston Farms	Ranston, Blandford Forum	28. 6.04
G-OZOO	Cessna 172N Skyhawk II	17267663	G-BWEI N73767	17.11.99	Atlantic Air Bridge Ltd	Lydd	27. 8.04T
G-OZRH	British Aerospace BAe 146 Srs.200	E2047	N188US N364PS	29. 1.96	Flightline Ltd *(Op Lufthansa Cityline)*	Cologne, Germany	1. 2.02T
G-OZZI	Jabiru Jabiru SK (Jabiru 2200A)	PFA 274-13176		15. 8.97	A.H.Godfrey	(Weston-Super-Mare)	22. 6.02P

G-PAAA – G-PZZZ

G-PACE	Robin R.1180T Aiglon	218		16.10.78	Millicron Instruments Ltd	Denham	21.11.03
G-PACL	Robinson R22 Beta	1893	N2314S	17.12.91	R.Wharam	(Rotherham)	14. 2.04
G-PADI	Cameron V-77 HAFB	1809		18. 8.88	R.F.Penney	Watford	23. 4.01A
G-PADS	Commander Aircraft Commander 114B	14637	N60987	15. 1.98	New Media Holdings Ltd	Guernsey	29. 1.04T
G-PAGS	Aérospatiale SA.341G Gazelle 1	1155	G-OAFY G-SFTH/G-BLAP/N62406	11. 3.96	P.A.G.Seers	Willingale	2.12.02T
G-PAIZ	Piper PA-12 Super Cruiser	12-2018	N3215M NC3215M	11. 4.94	B.R.Pearson *(Carries "NC3215M" on tail)*	Eaglescott	14. 6.04T
G-PALL	Piper PA-46-350P Malibu Mirage	4636091	G-RMST	4. 3.99	Pressurised Aircraft Leasing Ltd	Booker	4. 4.03
G-PALS	Enstrom 280C-UK-2 Shark	1191	N5688M	17. 7.80	G.Firbank	Eastwood End Farm, Adlington, Macclesfield	31. 1.03
G-PAPS	Piper PA-32R-301T Turbo Saratoga SP	32R-8529005	F-GELX N4385D	8. 7.97	W.J.Forrest	(New Mills)	25. 9.03
G-PARI	Cessna 172RG Cutlass II	172RG0010	N4685R	19.11.79	Applied Signs Ltd	Tatenhill	16. 2.02
G-PARR*	Colt Bottle 90SS HAFB *(Old Parr Whisky bottle shape)*	1953		15. 3.91	British Balloon Museum & Library *"Old Parr" (Cancelled 10.2.97 as temporary WFU)*	Newbury	29. 9.94A
G-PART	Partenavia P.68B Victor	62	F-GMPT G-PART/OY-CEY/D-GATE/PH-EEO/(N718R)	19.12.84	Springbank Aviation Ltd	(Castletown, IoM)	17. 8.95
G-PASB*	MBB Bö.105D	S.135	VH-LSA G-BDMC/D-HDEC	2. 3.89	The Helicopter Museum *(Original pod from 1994 rebuild: see G-WMAA: cancelled 9.8.94 as WFU)*	Weston-super-Mare	
G-PASF	Aérospatiale AS355F1 Twin Squirrel	5033	G-SCHU N915EG/N5777H	7. 3.91	Police Aviation Services Ltd *(Op Northumbria Police Air Support Unit)*	Newcastle	16.12.01T
G-PASG	MBB Bö.105DBS/4	S.819	G-MHSL D-HFCC	7.12.92	Police Aviation Services Ltd	Gloucestershire	12. 5.02T
G-PASH	Aérospatiale AS355F1 Twin Squirrel	5040	F-GHLI LX-HUG/F-GHLI/N356E	17. 5.96	Police Aviation Services Ltd *(Op Polo Aviation)*	Bristol	24. 3.04T
G-PASV	Pilatus Britten-Norman BN-2B-21 Islander	2157	G-BKJH HC-BNR/G-BKJH	26. 2.92	Police Aviation Services Ltd	Gloucestershire	18. 7.03T
G-PASX	MBB Bö.105DBS/4	S.814	D-HDZX	20.12.89	Police Aviation Services Ltd	Shoreham	10. 1.02T
G-PATF	Europa Aviation Europa	PFA 247-12757		5. 1.99	E P Farrell	(Beaconsfield)	
G-PATG	Cameron O-90 HAFB	3856		13. 3.96	P.A. & A.J.A.Bubb *"Purple Rain"*	Guildford	7. 5.02A
G-PATI	Reims Cessna F172M Skyhawk II	F17201311	G-WACZ G-BCUK	20. 4.00	Professional Air Training Ltd	Bournemouth	22. 4.02T
G-PATN	SOCATA TB-10 Tobago	307	G-LUAR	25. 3.97	N Robson	(Hessle)	23.11.03
G-PATP	Lindstrand LBL-77A HAFB	471		8. 7.97	P.Pruchnickyj	Weston Turville, Bucks	22. 7.01
G-PATS	Europa Aviation Europa	PFA 247-12888		19. 7.95	D.J.G.Kesterton	(Milton Keynes)	
G-PATX	Lindstrand LBL 90A HAFB	778		19. 6.01	P.A.Bubb	Guildford	22. 6.02A
G-PATZ	Europa Aviation Europa	PFA 247-12625		2. 6.98	H.P.H.Griffin	White Waltham	1. 8.02T
G-PAVL	Robin R.3000/120	170		22.11.96	Newcharter (UK) Ltd	Biggin Hill	10. 2.03T
G-PAWL	Piper PA-28-140 Cherokee	28-24456	G-AWEU N11C	8. 9.82	A.E.Davies t/a G-PAWL Group	Barton	14. 6.04
G-PAWN	Piper PA-25-260 Pawnee C	25-5207	G-BEHS	12. 3.01	A.P.Meredith *(On overhaul 2.95: new owner 3.01)*	Lasham	25. 6.93A
G-PAWS	Gulfstream AA-5A Cheetah	AA5A-0806	N26230	8. 2.82	Hecray Co Ltd t/a Direct Helicopters *(Op Southend School of Flying)* *(Damaged on landing Southend 2.11.01)*	Southend	24. 5.04T
G-PAZY	Pazmany PL-4A (Continental A65)	PFA 017-10378	G-BLAJ	20.11.89	C.R.Nash	(Fordingbridge)	3.10.95P
G-PBBT*	Cameron N-56 HAFB	1535		23. 6.87	E.C.Moore *"Little Book"* *(Cancelled 16.11.01 as wfu: current status unknown)*	Great Missenden	21. 9.96A
G-PBEE	Robinson R44 Raven	0829		11. 9.00	P.Barnard	Guernsey	21. 9.03T
G-PBEL	CFM Shadow DD	305-DD		27.10.98	P.C.Bell	(Maidstone)	

G-PBES	Robinson R22 Beta	1491	G-EXOR	17. 3.95	M.Horrell	Conington	14. 3.01T
			G-CMCM				
G-PBUS	Jabiru Jabiru SK	PFA 274-13269		18. 8.98	G.R.Pybus	Morgansfield, Fishburn	7. 5.02P
	(Jabiru 2200A)						
G-PBYY	Enstrom 280FX Shark	2077	G-BXKV	15. 8.97	J.J.Woodhouse	Sandown, IoW	9. 4.04T
			D-HHML				
G-PCAF	Pietenpol Aircamper	PFA 047-12433		1. 6.94	C.C. & F.M.Barley	(Farnborough)	
					(Under construction 2000)		
G-PCAM	Fairey Britten-Norman BN-2A Mk.III-2 Trislander			26. 9.01	Aurigny Air Services Ltd	Guernsey	14. 6.04T
		1052	G-BEPH/S7-AAG/G-BEPH		*(ABN AMRO Bank titles)*		
G-PCAR	Piper PA-46-500TP Malibu Meridian		N51151	30. 7.01	J.A.Carr	Guernsey	30. 7.04T
		4697078					
G-PCDP	Moravan Zlin Z.526F Trener Master		SP-CDP	24.10.94	R.A.Mills	Fairoaks	16. 7.01
		1163			t/a Zlin Group		
G-PCOM	Piper PA-30 Twin Comanche B	30-1053	HB-LDD	15.10.97	H. & P.Robinson	(Cheltenham)	2. 3.04
			N7957Y				
G-PDGE	Eurocopter EC 120B	1211	F-WQPD	20. 7.01	Cadenza Helicopters Ltd	(London W1)	10. 9.04
G-PDGG	Aeromere F.8L Falco Srs.3	208	OO-TOS	6. 1.98	P.D.G.Grist	Sibson	17. 5.04
			I-BLIZ				
G-PDGN	Aérospatiale SA.365N Dauphin 2	6074	PH-SSU	5. 4.01	PLM Dollar Group Ltd	Inverness	19. 7.04
			5N-ATX/PH-SSU/(G-BLDR)/G-TRAF/G-BLDR				
G-PDHJ	Cessna T182R Turbo Skylane II		N6888H	3. 1.85	P.G.Vallance Ltd	Redhill	28.12.03
		T18268092					
G-PDOC	Piper PA-44-180 Seminole	44-7995090	G-PVAF	17.12.85	T.White	Newcastle	8.10.04T
			N2242A		t/a Medicare		
G-PDOG	Cessna O-1E Bird Dog	24550	F-GKGP	25. 9.98	N.D.Needham	Old Manor Farm, Anwick	7. 4.02
	(Regd as Cessna 305C)		ALAT		*(As "24550/GP" in South Vietnamese AF c/s)*		
G-PDSI	Cessna 172N Skyhawk II	17270420	N739BU	4. 1.88	P.A.Hosey & A Clements	Blackbushe	26. 2.04T
					t/a DA Flying Group		
G-PDWI	Revolution Helicopters Mini-500	0248		14. 2.97	P.Waterhouse	(Stockport)	
G-PEAK	Agusta-Bell 206B JetRanger II	8242	G-BLJE	7. 3.94	Leisure Park Management Ltd	Goodwood	16. 5.03T
			SE-HBW				
G-PEAL	Aerotek Pitts S-2A Special	2048	N81LF	11. 5.88	Plymouth Executive Aviation Ltd	Plymouth	21. 2.92T
	(Lycoming AEIO-360)		N48KA		*(Damaged nr Kidderminster 28.6.91: uncovered airframe complete 2.01)*		
G-PEGA	Pegasus Quantum 15-912	7700		14. 8.00	J.J.Bowen	(Stockport)	9. 8.02P
G-PEGG	Colt 90A HAFB	1550		28. 6.89	Ballon Vole Association		
						Fontaine Les Dijon, France	20. 4.02A
G-PEGI	Piper PA-34-200T Seneca II		N2907A	27.11.89	Tayflite Ltd	Perth	20. 7.04T
		34-7970339					
G-PEGY	Europa Aviation Europa	PFA 247-12713		16. 5.00	M.T.Dawson	(Ilkley)	23. 1.02P
G-PEJM	Piper PA-28-181 Archer III	2843355	N41860	28. 6.00	E.J.Moorey	Bournemouth	29..6.03
G-PEKT	SOCATA TB-20 Trinidad	532	N24AS	28. 7.89	A.J.Dales	Mount Airey, Hull	24. 2.02
G-PELG	Mudry CAP.231	11	G-OPPS	6. 4.99	J.P.M.Groot		
			F-GGYN/F-WZCI/G-OPPS			Den Elder, The Netherlands	10. 6.03
G-PEPL	MD Helicopters MD 600N	RN047	N3047L	5. 2.01	Helidirect UK Ltd	Peplow Hall, Peplow	
					(Noted 5.01)		
G-PENT	Bell 206B-3 JetRanger III	3 958	G-IIRB	12. 7.99	Flying Tonight Ltd	Cranfield	29. 6.02
			N903CA				
G-PERC	Cameron N-90 HAFB	10127		29. 8.01	Stanton Marris Ltd	London W1	16. 7.02A
G-PERR*	Cameron Bottle 60SS HAFB	699		28. 1.81	British Balloon Museum & Library	Newbury	3. 6.84A
					"Perrier" *(Cancelled 24.1.92 as WFU)*		
G-PERZ	Bell 206B-3 JetRanger III	4411	N6272T	7. 1.97	C.P.Lockyer	Coventry	27. 2.03T
G-PEST	Hawker Tempest II	12202	HA604	9.10.89	Tempest Two Ltd	Hemswell	
	(Built Bristol) (Regd with c/n "1181")		Indian AF/MW401		*(Rebuild nearing completion 8.00)*		
G-PETR	Piper PA-28-140 Cherokee Cruiser		G-BCJL	23. 9.85	Marham Investments Ltd	(Castletown, IoM)	22. 1.03
		28-7425320	N9591N		*(Op Woodgate Executive Air Services)*		
G-PFAA	EAA Model P2 Biplane			19. 9.78	S.Alexander & M.Coffee	Bidford	15. 6.01P
	(Continental PC90)	PEB/03 & PFA 1338					
G-PFAF	Clutton FRED Srs.II	PFA 029-10310		30.10.78	M.S.Perkins	Stoke Golding	18. 6.02P
G-PFAG	Evans VP-1	PFA 7022		13.11.78	J.A.Hatch	Netherthorpe	30. 6.89P
	(VW 1600)						
G-PFAH	Evans VP-1	PFA 7004		23.11.78	J.A.Scott	Chestnut Farm, Tipps End	13. 8.01P
	(VW 1834)						
G-PFAL	Clutton FRED Srs.II	PFA 029-10243		7.12.78	J.M.Robinson	Bann Foot, Lough Neagh	27. 7.88P
	(VW 1600)				*(Stored 4.96)*		
G-PFAO	Evans VP-1	PFA 7008		12.12.78	P.W.Price	(Cheadle)	
G-PFAP	Phoenix Currie Wot	PFA 058-10315		12.12.78	J.H.Seed *(As "C1904/Z" in RFC c/s)*		
	(Continental O-200-A) *(Built as an SE-5A rep)*					Black Spring Farm, Castle Bytham	17.12.96P
G-PFAR	Isaacs Fury II	PFA 011-10220		18.12.78	J.W.Hale & R.Cooper	Netherthorpe	6. 6.02P
	(Continental O-200-A)				*(As "K2059" in 25 Sqdn RAF c/s)*		
G-PFAT	Monnett Sonerai II	PFA 015-10312		26.10.78	H.B.Carter	(St.Clement, Jersey)	24.10.92P
	(VW 1834)				*(Stored Newcastle 5.93: current status unknown)*		
G-PFAW	Evans VP-1	PFA 062-10183		18.12.78	R.F.Shingler	Forest Farm, Welshpool	13.11.01P
	(VW 1834)						

G-PFAY	EAA Biplane	PFA 1525		18.12.78	A.K.Lang & A.L.Young	(Stoke-sub-Hamdon)	
					(Project abandoned 5.98: valid CofR 4.01)		
G-PFFN	Beechcraft 200 Super King Air	BB-456	N456CD	7. 4.00	The Puffin Club Ltd	Carlisle	17. 4.04T
			N861D/N124BB/C6-BFP/C6-CAA/N80NF/N80NE/N100FB				
G-PFML	Robinson R44 Astro	0082		9. 9.94	Helicopter Training & Hire Ltd	Belfast	30.10.03T
G-PFSL	Reims Cessna F152	F15201746	PH-TWF	30. 8.00	P.A.Simon	Biggin Hill	17. 1.04T
			D-ENAX				
G-PGAC	Dyn'Aéro MCR-01 Ban-bi	PFA 301-13186		27. 1.99	D.T.S.Walsh & G.A.Coatesworth	Cambridge	2. 7.02P
G-PGFG	Tecnam P92-EM Echo	PFA 318-13772		30.10.01	P.G.Fitzgerald	(Bath)	
G-PGSA	Thruster T600N	0800-T600N-046		11. 8.00	G.J.Slater	Clench Common	20. 8.01T
G-PGSI	Robin R.2160 Alpha Sport	309	F-GSAF	9. 3.00	P.Spencer	Shoreham	17. 4.03
G-PGUY	Sky 70-16 HAFB	131	G-BXZJ	13.12.99	J L Guy	Skipton	19.12.00
					t/a Black Sheep Balloons		
G-PHAA	Reims Cessna F150M	F15001159	G-BCPE	19. 6.97	PHA Aviation Ltd	Elstree	11. 4.04T
G-PHEL	Robinson R22 Beta	1669	G-RUMP	15. 8.96	Focal Point Communications Ltd	Gamston	4. 5.03T
			N2405T				
G-PHIL	Brookland Hornet	17		7. 7.78	A.J.Philpotts	St.Merryn	11. 8.89P
	(VW 1600)				*(Stored 5.90: current status unknown)*		
G-PHON*	Cameron Phone SS HAFB	2505	G-BTEY	13.12.91	Redmalt Ltd	Witham, Essex	14. 7.97A
	(Motorola Microtac Mobile Phone)				*"Motorola Microtac" (Cancelled 29.11.01 as wfu)*		
G-PHOT	Thunder & Colt Film Cassette SS HAFB	4507		3. 2.99	Flying Pictures Ltd	Fairoaks	23. 3.02A
					(Agfa titles)		
G-PHSI	Colt 90A HAFB	2181		12. 5.92	P.H.Strickland & Simpson (Piccadilly) Ltd		
					"Daks"	Bedford/London W1	21. 7.01A
G-PHTG	SOCATA TB-10 Tobago	1008		15.11.89	A.J.Baggarley	Goodwood	14.10.02
G-PHYL	Denney Kitfox Mk.4	PFA 172A-12189		14. 9.98	J.Dunn	Siege Cross Farm, Thatcham	16. 4.02P
G-PIAF	Thunder Ax7-65 HAFB	1885		19.11.90	L.Battersey	Newbury	24. 3.94A
					"No Regrets/La Vie en Rose"		
G-PICT	Colt 180A HAFB	1723		22. 3.90	J.L.Guy	Skipton	9. 9.02T
G-PIDG	Robinson R44 Astro	0678		23.11.99	S.Farmer t/a First Degree Air	Tattenhill	9.12.02T
G-PIDS	Boeing 757-225	22195	N505EA	9. 1.95	Airtours International Airways Ltd		
						Manchester	23. 2.04T
G-PIEL	Menavia Piel CP.301A Emeraude	218	G-BARY	17.11.88	P.R.Thorne	Cublington	5. 3.02P
			F-BIJR				
G-PIES*	Thunder Ax7-77Z HAFB	263		13. 2.80	Not known	(Nottingham)	N/E(A)
					(Cancelled 23.8.89 by CAA) (Noted 2.97)		
G-PIET	Pietenpol Air Camper	PFA 047-12267		1. 4.93	N.D.Marshall	RAF Halton	14..5.02P
G-PIGG	Lindstrand Flying Pig SS HAFB	473		18. 8.97	Iris Heidenreich	Remscheid, Germany	19. 3.02A
G-PIGS	SOCATA Rallye 150ST	2696	G-BDWB	13. 6.88	D.Hodgson	Wombleton	17. 5.03
					t/a Boonhill Flying Group		
G-PIGY	Short SC.7 Skyvan 3A-100	SH.1943	LX-JUL	21.12.95	Babcock Rosyth Defence Ltd	Oxford	28. 1.01T
			5T-MAM/(G-14-111)		t/a Hunting Contract Services		
G-PIII	Pitts S-1D Special		G-BETI	11. 1.02	N.A.Scully	(Navenby)	9. 5.01P
	(Lycoming O-320)	7-0314 & PFA 09-10156			t/a On A Roll Aerobatics Group		
G-PIIX	Cessna P210N Pressurised Centurion II	P21000130	G-KATH	12. 6.95	J.R.Colthurst	(Hungerford)	17. 2.02
			(N4898P)				
G-PIKE	Robinson R22 Mariner	1718M		18. 3.91	Sloane Helicopters Ltd	Sywell	6.12.03T
G-PIKK	Piper PA-28-140 Cherokee	28-22932	G-AVLA	19. 8.88	O.D.Atkinson, N.Illman & M.Hill	(Keswick)	16. 9.04
			N11C/(N9509W)		t/a Executors of the Estate of the late W.D.Atkinson		
G-PILE	Rotorway Executive 90	5143		27. 7.93	J.B.Russell	Magheramorne, Co.Antrim	5.11.98P
	(Rotorway RI 162)						
G-PILL	Avid Flyer Mk.4	PFA 189-12333		12. 8.97	D.R.Meston	Old Sarum	16. 4.02P
	(Rotax 912-UL)						
G-PINE	Thunder Ax8-90 HAFB	1546		30. 5.89	J.A.Pine	London W4	15. 8.92A
G-PING	Gulfstream AA-5A Cheetah	AA5A-0878	G-OCWC	6.12.95	Plane Talking Ltd	Cranfield	4. 6.03T
			G-WULL/N27153		*(Op London School of Flying)*		
G-PINT	Cameron Barrel 60 SS HAFB	794		4. 1.82	D.K.Fish *"Charles Wells"*	Bedford	13. 2.98A
	(Wells Brewery Beer Barrel shape)						
G-PINX	Lindstrand Pink Panther SS HAFB	032		23. 4.93	Magical Adventures Ltd	Chirk	30. 5.99A
G-PIPR	Piper PA-18 Super Cub 95	18-826	G-BCDC	11.10.96	D.S.Sweet	Dunkeswell	29. 8.04T
	(Frame No.18-832)		4X-ANQ/IDF/AF/4X-ADE				
G-PIPS	Van's RV-4	PFA 181-11836		3. 8.90	C.J.Marsh	Sandown	11. 5.02P
	(Lycoming O-320-D1A)						
G-PIPY	Cameron Scottish Piper 105SS HAFB	3815		30. 1.96	Cameron Balloons Ltd	Almondsbury, Glos	4.11.01A
					"Pipy" (Op M Moffat)		
G-PITS	Pitts S-2AE Special	PFA 09-11001		4. 7.85	P.F.van Lonkhuyzen & E.Goggins		
	(Lycoming IO-360)				t/a The Eitlean Group	Weston, Dublin	20. 7.02P
G-PITZ	Pitts S-2A Special	100ER	N183ER	2.10.87	A.K.Halvorsen	Barton	22. 1.02P
	(Lycoming AEIO-360)						
G-PIXE	Colt 31A HAFB	4883		11. 7.00	N.D.Eliot	London SW19	21. 9.02A
G-PIXI	Pegasus Quantum 15-912	7557		27. 8.99	D.L.Goode	Enstone	6. 9.01P
G-PIXS	Cessna 336 Skymaster	336-0130	N86648	9. 9.88	Atlantic Bridge Aviation Ltd	Lydd	29. 1.95T
					(Stored 10.01)		
G-PIZZ	Lindstrand LBL 105A HAFB	629		27. 7.99	HD Bargain SRL	Firenze, Italy	27..8.02A

G-PJMT	Neico Lancair 320	PFA 191-12348		8. 5.98	M.T.Holland	Perth	17. 9.01P
	(Lycoming IO-320-D1B) *(Tri-cycle u/c)*						
G-PJTM	Reims Cessna FR172K Hawk II		EI-CHJ	13.10.98	P J McNamara	Haverfordwest	14.11.04T
		FR17200611	G-BFIF		t/a Jane Air		
G-PKPK	Schweizer Hughes 269C (300C)	S.1454	EI-CAR	3. 8.93	C.H.Dobson	(Louth)	14. 9.02T
			N69A				
G-PLAC	Piper PA-31-350 Chieftain	31-8052038	G-OLDA	23.12.98	D.B.Harper	Biggin Hill	12.12.01T
			G-BNDS/N131PP/N3550N				
G-PLAH	British Aerospace Jetstream Srs.3102		G-LOVA	1.11.99	Vale Aviation PLAH Ltd	Blackpool	26. 7.02T
		640	G-OAKA/G-BUFM/G-LAKH/G-BUFM/N410MX/G-31-640				
					(Ceased trading 11.01: impounded 12.01)		
G-PLAJ	British Aerospace Jetstream Srs.3102		N2274C	30. 3.00	Vale Aviation PLAJ Ltd	(London SW1)	18. 5.02T
		738	C-GJPH/N331QB/G-31-738		*(Ceased trading 11.01)*		
G-PLAN	Reims Cessna F150L	F15001066	PH-SPR	11. 8.78	D.A.Johnson	Barton	25.11.02
					t/a G-PLAN Flying Group		
G-PLAY	Robin R.2112	170	F-ODIT	1. 8.79	D.R.Austin	High Cross, Ware	28. 8.04
G-PLBI	Cessna 172S Skyhawk	172S8822	N35368	8. 5.01	Grandfort Properties Ltd	Booker	12. 6.04T
G-PLEE	Cessna 182Q Skylane II	18266570	N95538	4.12.87	Sunderland Parachute Centre Ltd	Peterlee	25. 4.03
					t/a Peterlee Parachute Centre		
G-PLIV	Pazmany PL-4A	PFA 017-10155		19.12.78	B.P.North	RAF Halton	15. 6.02P
	(Continental A65-8)						
G-PLMB	Aérospatiale AS350B Ecureuil	1207	G-BMMB	26. 3.86	PLM Dollar Group Ltd	Inverness	15. 2.04T
			C-GBEW/(N36033)				
G-PLMH	Eurocopter AS350B2 Ecureuil	2156	F-WQDJ	9. 1.95	PLM Dollar Group Ltd	Inverness	25. 2.04T
			G-PLMH/HB-XTE/F-WQPK/HB-XTE				
G-PLMI	Aérospatiale SA365C1 Dauphin 2	5001	F-GFYH	19. 6.95	PLM Dollar Group Ltd	Inverness	8. 7.04T
			F-WZAE				
G-PLOW	Hughes 269B	67-0317	G-AVUM	13. 9.83	Sulby Aerial Surveys Ltd	Sywell	29.11.92
					(Cockpit section only stored 12.01)		
G-PLPC	Schweizer Hughes 269C (300C)	S.1558	G-JMAT	14. 4.97	Power Lines, Piper & Cables Ltd		
						(Carluke)	3. 6.04
G-PLPM	Europa Aviation Europa XS			17. 5.00	P.L.P.Mansfield	(Hartley Wintney)	
		PFA 247-13287					
G-PLUG*	Colt 105A HAFB	1958		17. 4.91	British Balloon Museum & Library	Newbury	14. 8.95T
					(Cancelled 23.7.96 by CAA)		
G-PLXI	British Aerospace ATP	2001	G-MATP	26. 8.94	BAE Systems (Operations) Ltd	Woodford	2.12.92P
	(Development a/c with PW 127D engines)		(G-OATP)		*(Stored 12.01)*		
G-PMAM	Cameron V-65 HAFB	1155		29. 5.85	P.A.Meecham	Milton-under-Wychwood	31. 7.02A
					"Tempus Fugit"		
G-PMAX	Piper PA-31-350 Navajo Chieftain		G-GRAM	7. 7.99	AM & T Aviation Ltd	Bristol	9. 5.02T
		31-7305006	G-BRHF/N7679L				
G-PMNF	Supermarine 361 Spitfire HF.IX		SAAF??	29. 4.96	P.R.Monk	(Maidstone)	
		CBAF.10372	TA805		*(On rebuild 1995 as "TA805")*		
G-PNEU	Colt Bibendum 110SS HAFB	4223		5. 1.98	The Aerial Display Co Ltd	Lancing	26. 6.02A
					(Michelin titles) (Op Balloon Preservation Group)		
G-PNNI	Piper PA-28-181 Archer III	2843278	N41651	22.10.99	S.& J.Clumpas	Cumbernauld	21.10.02
					t/a Total Entertainments		
G-PNUT*	Cameron Mr.Peanut 35SS HAFB	643	N400AB	4. 2.80	British Balloon Museum & Library	Newbury	
			G-PNUT		*"Mr.Peanut" (Stored)*		
G-POAH	Sikorsky S-76B	760399		30. 3.92	Lynton Aviation Ltd	Blackbushe	17. 5.04T
					t/a Signature Aircraft Charter		
G-POAJ	Canadair CL604 Challenger	5442	N604PS	9. 6.00	P & O Containers (Assets) Ltd	Stansted	8..6.02T
			C-GLWR				
G-POGO	Flight Design CT2K	01-06-02-12		30. 7.01	P.A.& M.W.Aston *(Noted 9.01)*	Exeter	29. 7.02P
G-POLY	Cameron N-77 HAFB	428		13. 7.78	D.M.Barnes, N.F.Biggs, J.L.Hinton, M.A.C.Life &		
					D.J.Thornley *"Polywallets"*	Bristol	4. 8.00A
					t/a The Empty Wallets Balloon Group		
G-POND	Oldfield Baby Lakes	01	N87ED	2.10.90	C.Bellmer	Landshut, Germany	8. 6.02P
	(Continental A80)						
G-PONY*	Colt 31A Air Chair HAFB	434		23. 8.82	Balloon Preservation Group	Kirdford	
					"Neddie" (Cancelled 19.5.95 by CAA)		
G-POOH	Piper J-3C-65 Cub	6932	F-BEGY	17.10.79	P. & H.Robinson		
	(Frame No.7015)		NC38324		Upper Harford Farm, Bourton-on-the-Water		9. 8.04
G-POOL	ARV1 Super 2	025	G-BNHA	28. 8.87	P.A.Dawson	RAF Keevil	9. 9.90T
					(Fuselage stored 1.01)		
G-POOP	Dyn'Aéro MCR-01 Ban-bi	PFA 301-13190		5.11.97	K.& E.Nicholson	Leicester	26. 9.02P
	(Rotax 912 ULS)				t/a Eurodata Computer Supplies		
G-POPA	Beechcraft A36 Bonanza	E-2177	N7007F	20. 5.92	C.J.O'Sullivan	Southend	28. 1.05
			N7204R				
G-POPE	Eiri PIK.20E Srs.1	20257		5. 3.80	C.J.Hadley *"PE"*	Bidford	6. 6.04
G-POPI	SOCATA TB-10 Tobago	315	G-BKEN	20. 4.90	I.S.Hacon & C.J.Earle	Seething	27. 3.04
			(G-BKEL)				
G-POPP*	Colt 105A HAFB	1776		1. 3.91	Balloon Preservation Group	Kirdford	21.11.96A
					"Mercier" (Cancelled 5.2.99 as WFU)		

G-POPS	Piper PA-34-220T Seneca III	34-8133150	N8407H	11. 6.90	Alpine Ltd	Jersey	4. 5.02
G-POPW	Cessna 182S Skylane	18280204	N9451F	10. 7.98	D.L. Price	Little Staughton	19. 7.04
G-PORK	Grumman-American AA-5B Tiger	AA5B-0625	EI-BMT G-BFHS	28. 2.84	C.M.M.Grange & D.Thomas	Southampton	3. 2.05T
G-PORT	Bell 206B-3 JetRanger III	2784	N37AH N39TV/N397TV/N2774R	23. 8.89	Image Computer Systems Ltd *(Op Fast Helicopters)*	Thruxton	7. 8.04T
G-POSE	Sud SE.313B Alouette II	1430	G-BZGG EI-CTH/F-GKML/ALAT	3.12.01	Alouette Aviation Ltd	Booker	17. 9.04T
G-POSH	Colt 56A HAFB	822	G-BMPT	10. 6.86	B.K.Rippon	Didcot	18. 7.01A
G-POTT	Robinson R44 Astro	0383		21.11.97	Ranc Care Homes Ltd	Stapleford	10.12.03T
G-POWL	Cessna 182R Skylane II	18267813	N9070G D-EOMF/N6265N	11.11.82	Hillhouse Estates Ltd	Bowldown Farm, Tetbury	27. 4.04
G-PPAH	Enstrom 480	5032		9. 3.98	D.St.J.Tunnicliffe	(Guildford)	18. 5.04T
G-PPPP	Denney Kitfox mk.3 (Rotax 582)	771 & PFA 172-11830		9. 1.91	R.Powers	Otherton, Cannock	10. 7.02P
G-PPTS	Robinson R44 Clipper *(Float equipped)*	0664		14.10.99	Superstore Ltd	Cannes	2.11.02T
G-PRAG	Brugger MB.2 Colibri (VW 1835)	PFA 043-10362		29.11.78	D.Frankland t/a Colibri Flying Group	RAF Mona	28.11.02P
G-PRAH	Flight Design CT2K	01-06-01-12		31. 7.01	P.R.A.Hammond	London Colney	14. 8.02P
G-PRET	Robinson R44 Astro	0381		8.10.97	R.W.Raymond	Wolverhampton	26.10.03T
G-PREY	Pereira Osprey II (Lycoming IO-320)	88 & PFA 070-10193	G-BEPB	28. 9.99	D.W.Gibson	(Doseley)	8. 6.98P
G-PRII	Hawker Hunter PR.Mk.11	41H-670690	N723WT A2616/WT723	14. 7.99	Stick & Rudder Aviation Ltd *(As "WT723" in RN c/s)*	Ostend, Belgium	5. 9.02P
G-PRIM	Piper PA-38-112 Tomahawk	38-78A0669	N2398A	28. 1.87	Braddock Ltd	White Waltham	25.12.01T
G-PRIT	Cameron N-90 HAFB	1375	G-HTVI G-PRIT	6.11.86	B.J.Hammond	Chelmsford	9. 5.02A
G-PRNT	Cameron V-90 HAFB	2819		23. 3.92	E.K.Gray	Droitwich	16. 7.01A
G-PROB	Eurocopter AS 350B2 Ecureuil	2825	G-PROD	25. 6.01	Irvine Aviation Ltd.	Denham	29. 3.04T
G-PROF	Lindstrand LBL 90A HAFB	740		14. 2.01	S.J.Wardle	Thrapston	4 .1.02A
G-PROM	Aérospatiale AS350B Ecureuil	1486	G-MAGY G-BIYC	11.10.96	Peadar Hughes t/a General Cabins & Engineering	Dungannon, Co.Tyrone	23.10.02T
G-PROP	Gulfstream AA-5A Cheetah	AA5A-0845	G-BHKU (OO-HTF)	16. 2.84	Fortune Technology Ltd	Panshanger	28. 5.01T
G-PROV	Hunting P.84 Jet Provost T.52A (T.4)	PAC/W/23905	352 Sing AF/104 South Yemen AF/G-27-7/XS228	13.12.83	Hollytree Management Ltd t/a Provost Group	(Sutton)	25. 5.02P
G-PRSI	Pegasus Quantum 15-912	7492		17.12.98	M H Rollins	(Birmingham)	16.12.02P
G-PRTT	Cameron N-31 HAFB	1374		6.11.86	J.M.Albury *"Baby Pritt"*	Cirencester	13.11.00A
G-PRXI	Supermarine 365 Spitfire PR.XI *(Official c/n is HAI 6S-501431)*	6S/583003	PL983 G-15-109/N74138/PL983	6. 6.83	J.V.Fleming *(As "PL983/JV-F" in 4 Sqdn, 2 TAF c/s)* *(Crashed Vallee de Seine, nr Rouen, France 4.6.01)*	Goudhurst	11. 6.01P
G-PSIC	North American P-51C-10 Mustang *(Composite from major components P-51D IDF/AF 13)*	103-26778	N51PR 43-25147	16. 4.98	Patina Ltd *"Princess Elizabeth"* *(Op The Fighter Collection: under rebuild 6.00)*	Duxford	
G-PSON*	Colt Cylinder One SS HAFB *(Panasonic Battery shape)*	1780	PH-SON	14. 3.95	Balloon Preservation Group *"Panasonic Battery" (Cancelled 9.10.01 as wfu)*	Kirdford	7. 8.99A
G-PSRT	Piper PA-28-151 Cherokee Warrior	28-7615225	G-BSGN N9657K	18. 3.99	P.A.S.Dyke	Little Gransden	13. 6.99T
G-PSST	Hawker Hunter F.58A	HABL-003115	J-4104 G-9-317/A2568/XF947	12. 2.97	Heritage Aviation Developments Ltd *"Miss Demeanour"*	Kemble	30.10.02P
G-PSUE	CFM Shadow CD (Rotax 503)	K.139	G-MYAA	1. 4.99	P.F.Lorriman	Stoke, Kent	19. 5.02P
G-PTAG	Europa Aviation Europa (Jabiru 3300) *(Tri-cycle u/c)*	PFA 247-13121		14.12.98	R.C.Harrison	Wickenby	20. 2.02P
G-PTRE	SOCATA TB-20 Trinidad	762	G-BNKU	14. 6.88	Trantshore Ltd	Lydd	21. 4.04
G-PTWB	Cessna T303 Crusader	T30300306	G-BYNG G-PTWB/N6312V	6.12.84	F.Kratky t/a FK Global Aviation	Denham	3. 4.03
G-PTWO	Pilatus P.2-05	600-30	U-110 A-110	26. 2.81	Bulldog Aviation Ltd *(As "U-110" in Swiss AF c/s)*	Earls Colne	14. 9.01P
G-PTYE	Europa Aviation Europa (Rotax 912-UL)	1 & PFA 247-12496		22. 1.96	J.Tye *"Harriet"*	Holly Meadow Farm, Bradley	13. 8.02P
G-PUBS*	Colt Beer Glass 56SS HAFB	037		7. 6.79	British Balloon Museum & Library *(Cancelled 1.12.95 by CAA)*	Newbury	
G-PUDL	Piper PA-18-150 Super Cub	18-7292	SE-CSE	24. 2.98	R.A.Roberts	Sherburn-in-Elmet	22. 5.04
G-PUDS	Europa Aviation Europa (Rotax 914-UL) *(Tri-cycle u/c)*	PFA 247-12999		9.10.97	I.Milner	Carlisle	8. 2.02P
G-PUFF	Thunder Ax7-77 Bolt HAFB	165		17.11.78	C.A.Gould t/a Intervarsity Balloon Club *"Puffin II"*	Ipswich	20. 8.99A
G-PUFN	Cessna 340A II	340A0114	N532KG N532KC/N5477J	4.12.96	The Puffin Club Ltd	Leicester	15.12.02T
G-PUGS	Cessna 182H Skylane	18256480	SE-ESM N8380S	15. 5.00	N.C.& M.F.Shaw	Great Massingham	12. 6.03T

G-PULL*	Piper PA-18-150 Super Cub	18-5356	PH-MBB	17. 2.83	R.A.Yates	Sibsey	2. 4.89A
	(Frame No.18-5429)		ALAT 18-5356/N10F				
			(Crashed Eaglescott 13.6.86: cancelled 25.11.87 as WFU: stored 8.90: current status unknown)				
G-PUMA	Aérospatiale AS332L Super Puma	2038	F-WMHB	31. 1.83	CHC Scotia Ltd	Aberdeen	12. 4.03T
G-PUMB	Aérospatiale AS332L Super Puma	2075		31. 1.83	CHC Scotia Ltd	Aberdeen	15. 5.03T
G-PUMD	Aérospatiale AS332L Super Puma	2077	F-WXFD	31. 1.83	CHC Scotia Ltd	Aberdeen	23. 8.02T
G-PUME	Aérospatiale AS332L Super Puma	2091		3. 8.83	CHC Scotia Ltd	Aberdeen	6. 9.03T
G-PUMG(2)	Aérospatiale AS332L Super Puma	2018	F-ODOS	3. 8.83	CHC Scotia Ltd	Aberdeen	14. 5.02T
G-PUMH	Aérospatiale AS332L Super Puma	2101		3. 8.83	Bristow Helicopters Ltd	Aberdeen	22. 5.04T
G-PUMI	Aérospatiale AS332L Super Puma	2170		27. 1.86	Bristow Helicopters Ltd	Aberdeen	21. 5.02T
G-PUMK	Aérospatiale AS332L Super Puma	2067	LN-OMF	23. 3.90	CHC Scotia Ltd	Aberdeen	2. 8.03T
			G-PUMK/LN-OMF/F-WXFP				
G-PUML	Aérospatiale AS332L Super Puma	2073	LN-ODA	20. 7.90	CHC Scotia Ltd	Aberdeen	4. 7.03T
			G-PUML/LN-OMG				
G-PUMM	Eurocopter AS332L-2 Super Puma	2477		29. 7.98	CHC Scotia Ltd	Aberdeen	21. 9.02T
G-PUMN	Eurocopter AS332L-2 Super Puma	2484	LN-OHF	16. 7.99	CHC Scotia Ltd	Aberdeen	26. 7.03T
G-PUMO	Eurocopter AS332L-2 Super Puma	2467		30. 9.98	CHC Scotia Ltd	Aberdeen	25.10.02T
G-PUMS	Eurocopter AS332L-2 Super Puma	2504		18. 8.00	CHC Scotia Ltd	Aberdeen	30. 1.02T
G-PUPP	Beagle B.121 Pup 2	B121-174	G-BASD	23.11.93	P.A.Teichman		
			(SE-FOG)/G-BASD			Standalone Farm, Meppershall	16. 4.02
G-PURE*	Cameron Can 70SS HAFB	1913		18. 1.89	Balloon Preservation Group	Kirdford	
	(Guinness Can)				*"Guinness Can" (Cancelled 29.4.97 as WFU)*		
G-PURR	Gulfstream AA-5A Cheetah	AA5A-0794	G-BJDN	22. 2.82	N.Bass	Elstree	2. 9.02T
			N26893		t/a Nabco Retail Display		
G-PURS	Rotorway Executive	3827		19. 1.90	J.E.Houseman	Clitheroe	5. 6.96P
	(Rotorway RW 152)						
G-PUSH	Rutan LongEz	PFA 074A-10740		11. 7.83	E.G.Peterson	(Nottingham)	
G-PUSI	Cessna T303 Crusader	T30300273	N3479V	26. 7.88	Crusader Aviation Ltd	Oxford	18. 5.03T
G-PUSK	Piper PA-32R-301 Satatoga II HP	3246143	N237TB	24. 8.01	HN Consultancy (UK) Ltd	Panshanger	30. 8.04T
					(Noted 10.01)		
G-PUSS	Cameron N-77 HAFB	1577		6.10.87	L.D.Thurgar *"Dick Whittington"*	Bristol	18. 6.01A
G-PUSY	Tiger Cub RL-5ALW Sherwood Ranger		G-MZNF	25. 6.99	B.J.Chester-Master	Moccas	11.11.02P
	(Rotax 582)	PFA 237-12964					
G-PUTT	Cameron Golfball 76SS HAFB	2060	LX-KIK	8. 8.95	D.P.Hopkins	Pidley, Huntingdon	
					t/a Lakeside Lodge Golf Centre		
G-PVBF	Lindstrand LBL-260S HAFB	504		7. 4.98	Virgin Balloon Flights Ltd	London SE16	24. 6.02T
G-PVCU	Cameron N-77 HAFB	4376		22. 5.98	R.G.March & T.J.Maycock		
					(Coldseal titles)	Market Harborough	5. 5.01A
G-PVET	de Havilland DHC.1 Chipmunk 22	C1/0017	WB565	23. 5.97	Connect Properties Ltd	Kemble	12.11.03T
					(As "WB565/X" in Army c/s)		
G-PWBE	de Havilland DH.82A Tiger Moth	LES.1	VH-KRW	23. 7.99	P.W.Beales	(Bridgend)	
	(This ex-Australian Tiger Moth was one of 11 aircraft, with c/ns LES.1 to LES.11, constructed by Lawrence Engineering Services from ex-RAAF spares in the late 1950s) (On overhaul Berkshire 2001)						
G-PWEL	Robinson R22 Beta-II	2982		1. 9.99	DJP Ltd	Wolverhampton	19..9.02
G-PWER	Agusta A109E Power	11092		6.11.00	Powersense Ltd	Fairoaks	16. 1.04T
G-PWIT	Bell 206L-1 LongRanger II	45193	D-HHSW	18. 5.00	Formal Graphics Ltd	Gloucestershire	13. 7.03T
			G-DWMI/N18092				
G-PYLN*	Cameron Pylon 80SS HAFB	2958	G-BUSO	18. 1.93	Balloon Preservation Group	Kirdford	25. 4.97A
	(Electricity Pylon shape)				*"National Power Pylon" (Cancelled 6.11.01 as wfu)*		
G-PYRO	Cameron N-65 HAFB	567		8. 1.80	A.C.Booth *"Pyromania"*	Bristol	27. 6.02A
G-PZAZ	Piper PA-31-350 Navajo Chieftain	31-7405214	G-VTAX	18. 1.95	Air Medical Ltd	Oxford	22. 5.03T
			(G-UTAX)/N54266				
G-PZIZ	Piper PA-31-350 Navajo Chieftain	31-7405429	G-CAFZ	30.10.98	Air Medical Ltd	Oxford	22. 3.02T
			G-BPPT/N54297				

G-RAAA – G-RZZZ

G-RACA*	Hunting-Percival P.57 Sea Prince T.1	P57/49	WM735	2. 9.80	Not known	Long Marston	4.11.80P
					(Cancelled 28.11.95 by CAA: open storage 4.00)		
G-RACO	Piper PA-28R-200 Cherokee Arrow II	28R-7535300	N1498X	12. 9.91	Graco Group Ltd	Barton	12. 3.04
G-RACY	Cessna 182S Skylane	18280588	N7273Y	19.10.99	N.J.& P.D.Fuller	Cambridge	4.11.02
G-RADA	Soko P-2 Kraguj	024	30140	25. 9.96	Steerworld Ltd	Fairoaks	29. 6.01P
			Yugoslav AF				
G-RADI	Piper PA-28-181 Archer II	28-8690002	N2582X	6. 5.98	G.S. & D.V.Foster	Tatenhill	7. 6.04
			N9608N				
G-RAEM	Rutan LongEz	557 & PFA 074A-10638		15. 3.82	G.F.H.Singleton	(Matlock)	18. 6.93P
	(Lycoming O-235)				t/a Easy Group		
G-RAES	Boeing 777-236ER	27491	(G-ZZZN)	10. 6.97	British Airways plc	Heathrow	9. 6.03T
					(Delftblue Daybreak t/s)		
G-RAFA	Grob G-115A	8081	D-EGVV	2. 3.89	RAF College Flying Club Ltd	RAF Cranwell	30. 3.04T
G-RAFB	Grob G-115A	8079	D-EGVV	2. 3.89	RAF College Flying Club Ltd	RAF Cranwell	2. 4.04T

G-RAFC	Robin R.2112 Alpha	192		19. 5.80	J.E.Churchill	Conington	25. 6.04
					t/a RAF Charlie Group		
G-RAFE	Thunder Ax7-77 Bolt HAFB	176		18.12.78	L.P.Hooper	Bristol	7. 9.02A
					t/a Giraffe Balloon Syndicate *"Giraffe"*		
G-RAFF	Learjet Learjet 35A	35A-504	N8568B	12. 6.84	Graff Aviation Ltd	Coventry	26. 6.03T
			N10871		*(Op Aerocharter (Midlands) Ltd)*		
G-RAFG	Slingsby T.67C Firefly	2076		2.11.89	Arrow Flying Ltd	Denham	30. 3.02T
G-RAFI	Hunting-Percival P.84 Jet Provost T.4		8458M	18.12.92	R.J.Everett	North Weald	11. 3.00P
		PAC/W/17641	XP672		*(As "XP672/03")*		
G-RAFT	Rutan LongEz	PFA 074A-10734		9. 8.82	B.Wronski	Gloucestershire	19. 7.96P
	(Continental O-240-A)				*"A Craft of Graft" (For dismantling 9.99)*		
G-RAFW	Mooney M.20E Super 21	805	G-ATHW	14.11.84	Vinola (Knitwear) Manufacturing Co Ltd		
			N5881Q			Leicester	4.10.04
G-RAGG	Maule M-5-235C Lunar Rocket	7260C	N5632M	8. 9.95	P.Ragg	Innsbruck, Austria	12.10.01
					(Noted 7.01 in unairworthy state)		
G-RAGS	Pietenpol Aircamper	PFA 047-11551		8. 6.94	R.F.Billington	(Kenilworth)	
G-RAID	Douglas AD-4NA Skyraider	7722	F-AZED	7. 6.93	Patina Ltd	Duxford	22. 3.02P
	(SFERMA c/n 42)		TR-K../Fr AF 42/Bu.126922		*(Op B J S Grey/The Fighter Collection)*		
					(As "26922/AK/402" in VA-176 Sqn USN c/s)		
G-RAIL	Colt 105A HAFB	1434		31. 3.89	Ballooning World Ltd	London NW1	8. 1.01A
					"Railfreight"		
G-RAIN	Maule M-5-235C Lunar Rocket	7262C	N5632J	26. 7.79	D.S.McKay & J.A.Rayment		
						Hinton-in-the-Hedges	10.10.04
G-RAIX	CCF T-6J Texan (Harvard 4)	CCF4...	G-BIWX	16. 2.98	M.R.Paul & P.A.Shaw	Lee-on-Solent	3. 4.02P
	(Possibly c/n CCF4-409 ex 51-17227)		MM53846/RM-22/51-17		*(As "KF584")*		
G-RAJA	Raj Hamsa X'Air 582 (2)			13. 9.99	S.R.Roberts	Priory Farm, Stowmarket	11.10.02P
		456 & BMAA/HB/118			t/a Priory Flyers		
G-RALD	Robinson R22HP	0218	G-CHIL	25. 1.96	Heli Air Ltd		
			(G-BMXI)/N9074K			Wellesbourne Mountford/Denham	18. 2.02T
G-RAMI	Bell 206B-3 JetRanger III	2955	N1080N	18.10.90	M.D.Thorpe	Coney Park, Leeds	11. 9.03T
					t/a Yorkshire Helicopters		
G-RAMP	Piper J-3C-65 Cub	6658	N35941	5. 7.90	J.Whittall		
			NC35941			Brickhouse Farm, Frogland Cross	31. 8.01P
G-RAMS	Piper PA-32R-301 Saratoga SP		N8271Z	17.10.80	Air Tobago Ltd	Gamston	30. 5.02
		32R-8013134					
G-RAMY	Bell 206B JetRanger II	1401	N59554	22. 9.95	Lincair Ltd	(Brigg)	30.10.04T
G-RANS	Rans S-10 Sakota	PFA 194-11537		17. 8.89	J.D.Weller	Derby	23. 6.00P
	(Rotax 532)						
G-RANZ	Rans S-10 Sakota	PFA 194-11536		2.11.89	P.Whittingham	Otherton, Cannock	26. 6.02P
	(Rotax 532)						
G-RAPA	Pilatus Britten-Norman BN-2T-4R Defender 4000			11. 5.82	B-N Group Ltd	Bembridge	31. 7.91T
		115 & 4001	N360WT/G-RAPA/G-51-2115/G-BJBH		*(Stored 8.99)*		
G-RAPH	Cameron O-77 HAFB	1673		21. 3.88	P.B.D.Bird & M.E.Mason	Bristol	28. 5.00T
					"Walsal Litho"		
G-RAPP	Cameron H-34 HAFB	2380		16. 8.90	Cameron Balloons Ltd	St.Louis, USA	9. 2.01A
G-RARB	Cessna 172N Skyhawk II	17272334	G-BOII	4. 6.96	Richlyn Aviation Ltd	Rochester	27. 6.03T
			N4702D				
G-RARE	Thunder Ax5-42 SS HAFB	266		20. 2.80	Justerini & Brooks Ltd	Kirdford	7. 4.95A
	(J & B Rare Whisky Bottle shape)				*"J & B Hamish" (Op Balloon Preservation Group)*		
G-RASC*	Evans VP-2	V2-1178 & PFA 063-10422		14.12.78	E Phillips	(Soothill, Batley)	29. 5.94P
	(Continental C90)		*(Crashed Bagby 9.7.95: cancelled as TWFU: stored 4.97: current status unknown)*				
G-RATE	Gulfstream AA-5A Cheetah	AA5A-0781	G-BIFF	11. 6.84	J.Appleton	Blackbushe	14.11.04T
			(G-BIBR)/N26879		t/a Holmes Rentals		
G-RATZ	Europa Aviation Europa			16. 6.95	W.Goldsmith	Morgansfield, Fishburn	23. 8.02P
	(Rotax 912UL)	37 & PFA 247-12582					
G-RAVE	Southdown Raven X/Mercury Trike		G-MNZV	22.12.98	M.J.Robbins	Tunbridge Wells	7. 1.02P
		SN2232/0219					
	(Trike is a Mainair Gemini with Rotax 582 [538-0487]: sailwing is from G-MNCV [2000/0219] but not as officially registered. Original trike fitted with Rotax 462 & initially sold to Portugal but then sold to Swiss owner & attached to used Raven sailwing [T.15])						
G-RAVN	Robinson R44 Raven	1022		23. 3.01	Heli Air Ltd	Wellesbourne Mountford	5. 4.04T
G-RAWS	Rotorway Exec 162F	6492		14.11.00	Raw Sports Ltd	(Cinderford)	
G-RAYA	Denney Kitfox mk.4	PFA 172A-12403		14.12.92	A.K.Ray	(Stone)	
G-RAYC	Robinson R44 Raven	0771		5. 5.00	Whirlybirds Ltd	Birmingham	22. 6.03T
G-RAYE	Piper PA-32-260 Cherokee Six	32-460	G-ATTY	30. 5.96	G.R.Silver	Panshanger	8. 8.03
			N11C		t/a G-RAYE Group		
G-RAYS	Zenair CH.250	RED.001 & PFA 024-10460		26.10.78	M.J.Malbon	(Stafford)	
	(Lycoming O-235)				*(New owner 9.01)*		
G-RBBB	Europa Aviation Europa			6. 5.94	T.J.Hartwell	Sackville Lodge, Riseley	7. 5.99P
	(Rotax 912UL)	73 & PFA 247-12664					
G-RBIN*	Robin DR.400 2+2	1225	D-EEVT	25.10.78	(Southern Sailplanes)	Membury	
			(Crashed near Rochester 21.5.93: cancelled 7.9.93 by CAA: wreck noted 10.01)				
G-RBCI	Fairey Britten-Norman BN-2A Mk.III-2 Trislander			16. 3.01	Aurigny Air Services Ltd	Guernsey	15. 4.02T
		1035	G-BDWV/8P-ASF/G-BDWV		*(Royal Bank of Canada titles)*		

G-RBMV	Cameron O-31 HAFB	4658		27. 7.99	P.D.Griffiths	Romsey	29. 6.02
G-RBOS*	Colt AS-105 Hot-Air Airship	390		9. 2.82	Science Museum Air Transport Coln & Storage Facility	Wroughton	6. 3.87A
G-RBOW	Thunder Ax7-65 HAFB	1439		24. 4.89	A.C.Hall *"Rain-Beau-Lune"*	Melton Mowbray	10. 8.01A
G-RCED	Rockwell Commander 114	14241	VR-CED N4917W	19. 6.92	Echo Delta Ltd	Guernsey	13. 5.04
G-RCEJ	British Aerospace BAe 125 Srs.800B	258021	VR-CEJ G-GEIL/G-5-15	15. 6.95	Aravco Ltd	Farnborough	14. 6.02T
G-RCMC	Murphy Renegade 912 (Rotax 912)	485 & PFA 188-12483		1. 2.93	R.C.M.Collisson	Turweston	30. 6.02P
G-RCMF	Cameron V-77 HAFB	1618		23.11.87	Mouldform Ltd *"Mouldform I/Mayfly"*	Loughborough	19. 8.97A
G-RCML	Sky 77-24 HAFB	148		9. 3.99	R.C.M.Sarl	Luxembourg	10 .3.02
G-RDBS	Cessna 550 Citation II	550-0094	G-JETA (N26630)	7. 5.99	Albion Aviation Management Ltd	Biggin Hill	21. 6.02T
G-RDCI	Rockwell Commander 112A	345	G-BFWG ZS-JRX/N1345J	15. 5.85	P.Turner	Humberside	8. 3.04T
G-RDEL	Robinson R44 Raven	1071		5. 6.01	J A R Allwright t/a Jara Aviation	Clacton-on-Sea	27. 6.04T
G-RDVE	Airbus A320-231	0163	OY-CND F-WWDU	26. 2.97	Airtours International Airways Ltd	Manchester	2. 3.03T
G-READ	Colt 77A HAFB	1158	EI-BYI G-READ	16.11.87	J.Keena *(Flying as "EI-BYI" 9.98)*	Athlone, Co.Westmeath	1. 9.02A
G-REAH	Piper PA-32R-301 Saratoga SP	32R-8413017	G-CELL (G-BLRI)/N4361D	15. 8.94	M.Q.Tolbod & S.J.Rogers	Blackbushe	17. 8.03
G-REAP	Pitts S-1S Special (Lycoming O-360)	PFA 09-11557		7. 2.90	R.Dixon *"The Grim Reaper"*	Netherthorpe	30. 1.02P
G-REAS	Van's RV-6A (Lycoming O-320)	PFA 181-12188		16. 8.94	E.J.D.Proctor	Shobdon	17. 7.02P
G-REAT	Grumman-American GA-7 Cougar	GA7-0033	N29699	6.10.78	Goodtechnique Ltd	Leeds-Bradford	20. 7.03T
G-REBA	Rotary Air Force RAF 2000 GTX-SE	PFA G/13-1334		5.10.01	D.J.Pearce *(Noted 11.01)*	Henstridge	
G-REBK	Beechcraft B200 Super King Air	BB-1202	D-IHAP N44VM/N7207M	22. 5.97	Planstable Enterprises Ltd	Southend	17. 6.02T
G-REBL	Hughes 269B	67-0318	N9493F	25. 7.89	Farmax Ltd	(Maidstone)	9.10.95
G-RECK	Piper PA-28-140 Cherokee B	28-25656	G-AXJW N11C	17. 3.88	R.J.Grantham & D.Boatswain	Clutton Hill Farm, Clutton	12. 8.04
G-RECO	Jurca MJ-5L2 Sirocco	96	F-PYYD F-WYYD	30. 9.91	J D Tseliki *(Stored 6.93)*	Shoreham	
G-REDA	Robinson R22 Beta	3172		12. 2.01	Simax Services Ltd *(Op Red Aviation)*	Bournemouth	7. 3.04T
G-REDB	Cessna 310Q	310Q0811	G-BBIC N69600	17. 6.93	Red Baron Haulage Ltd	Full Sutton	9. 7.04T
G-REDC	Pegasus Quantum 15-912	7572		30. 9.99	Red Communications Ltd	Sutton Meadows, Ely	8.10.02P
G-REDD	Cessna 310R II	310R1833	G-BMGT ZS-KSY/(N2738X)	2.10.96	G.Wightman	Blackpool	17.12.01
G-REDI	Robinson R44 Raven	0817		2. 8.00	Redeye.com Ltd	Sheffield City	24. 8.03T
G-REDX	Experimental Aviation Berkut (Lycoming O-360-A1A)	002 & PFA 252-12481		27. 1.95	G.V.Waters	Norwich	23. 6.02P
G-REEC	Sequoia F.8L Falco (Lycoming IO-320)	654	LN-LCA	2. 7.96	J.D.Tseliki	Kittyhawk Farm, Deanland	17. 8.02P
G-REED	Mainair Blade 912S	1282-0501-7-W1077		11. 6.01	P.A.B.Morgan	(Cambridge)	10. 6.02P
G-REEF	Mainair Blade 912S	1285-0501-7-W1080		15. 6.01	G.B.Shaw	(Pwllheli)	4. 7.02P
G-REEK	Grumman-American AA-5A Cheetah	AA5A-0429		12. 9.77	J.& A.Pearson	Dundee	10.12.01
G-REEM	Aérospatiale AS355F1 Twin Squirrel	5175	G-EMAN G-WEKR/G-CHLA/N818RL/C-FLXH/N818RL/N818R/N5798U	9. 3.98	Heliking Ltd	Redhill	17.12.03T
G-REEN	Cessna 340	340-0063	G-AZYR N5893M	2. 2.84	E. & M.Green	Guernsey	5. 9.02
G-REES	SAN Jodel D.140C Mousquetaire III	156	F-BMFR	23. 4.80	W.H.Greenwood	Swanborough Farm, Lewes	20. 6.04
G-REFI*	Enstrom 280C-UK Shark	1090	N638H	2. 5.89	Not known	Coventry	15.10.95
			(DBF Dublin 22. 9.95: cancelled 21.11.96 by CAA:stored for rebuild 1.97: current status unknown)				
G-REKO	Solar Wings Pegasus Quasar IITC	SW-TQC-0073 & SW-WQT-0467	G-MWWA	14.11.01	G.S.Stokes	(Kingswinford)	26.10.02P
G-RENE	Murphy Renegade 912	PFA 188-12030		6.11.91	P.M.Whitaker	(Ilkley)	27. 7.00P
G-RENO	SOCATA TB-10 Tobago	249		10.12.81	Lamond Ltd	Birmingham	21. 5.04T
G-RENT	Robinson R22 Beta	0758	N2635M	17. 3.88	Rentatruck (Self Drive) Ltd	Newtownards, Co.of Down	12. 6.94T
			(Op Helicopter Training & Hire) (Damaged Newtownards 30.9.92: current status unknown)				
G-REPH	Pegasus Quantum 15-912	7785		6. 2.01	R.S.Partridge-Hicks	(Bury St. Edmunds)	5 .2.02P

G-REPM*	Piper PA-38-112 Tomahawk	38-79A0354	N2528D	8. 1.87	Nultree Ltd	Chilbolton	9.10.95T
			(Cancelled 16.3.01 as destroyed) (Forward fuselage & wings noted 10.01)				
G-REST	Beechcraft P35 Bonanza	D-7171	G-ASFJ	14.12.82	C.R.E.S.Taylor	Biggin Hill	8. 9.02
G-RETA	CASA I-131E Jungmann 2000	2197	E3B-305	24. 3.80	N.S.C.& G.English	North Weald	21. 4.02P
					(Noted 9.01)		
G-REXS	Piper PA-28-181 Archer II	28-8090102	N8093Y	14. 1.80	M.R.Shelton	Tatenhill	28. 6.04T
					t/a Tatenhill Aviation		
G-REYS	Canadair CL-604 Challenger	5467	N467RD	17. 9.01	Greyscape Ltd	Farnborough	16. 9.04T
			C-GLWX				
G-RFDS	Agusta A109A II	7411	N1YU	24. 5.99	Castle Air Charters Ltd	Liskeard	20. 7.02T
			VP-CLA/VR-CLA/G-BOLA/VR-CMP/G-BOLA				
G-RFIL	Thunder Colt 77A HAFB	1496		16. 4.98	G.Davis	(Reading)	1. 4.00T
G-RFIO	Aeromot AMT-200 Super Ximango	200-048		6. 3.95	M.D.Evens	Dunstable	30. 6.04
G-RFSB	Sportavia Fournier RF5B Sperber	51045	N55HC	2.12.88	S.W.Brown	Sibson	1. 4.04
G-RGDT	Dornier Do.228-201K	8070	TF-ELH	25. 5.00	Air Wales Ltd	Pembrey	3..8.03T
			SE-KVV/TF-ELH/SE-KVV/LN-NVG/D-CLIC				
G-RGEE	Extra EA.300/L	091	D-ESEW	25. 6.01	Skylane Aviation Ltd	Sherburn-in-Elmet	23. 7.04T
G-RGEN	Cessna T337D Turbo Super Skymaster	3371062	G-EDOT	24. 5.96	Legoprint SPA	(Lavis, Italy)	30.11.02
			G-BJIY/9Q-CPF/PH-JWL/N86056				
G-RGUS	Fairchild 24R-46A Argus III (UC-61K-FA)	1145	(PH-)	16. 9.86	Fenlands Ltd	Sturgate	3.11.01
			G-RGUS/ZS-UJZ/ZS-BAY/KK527/44-83184 *(As "44-83184/7" in USAAC c/s)*				
G-RHCB	Schweizer 269C-1	0036	N201WL	20. 3.98	S.J. Skilton	Bournemouth	9. 4.04T
					t/a Aviation Rentals *(Op Bournemouth Helicopters)*		
G-RHHT	Piper PA-32RT-300 Lance II	32R-7885190	N36476	3. 7.78	R.W. & M.Struth	Southend	19. 3.03
G-RHYS	Rotorway Executive 90 (Rotorway RI 162)	5140		8.11.93	A.K.Voase & K.Matthews	(Hornsea)	9. 1.02P
G-RIAN	Agusta-Bell 206A JetRanger	8056	G-SOOR	16. 9.87	Thorneygrove Ltd	Wardley	22.12.02
			G-FMAL/G-RIAN/G-BHSG/PH-FSW				
G-RIAT	Robinson R22 Beta-II	2684		27. 5.97	R.Cove & J.P.Gordon	Cranfield	29. 6.03T
					t/a RMJ Helicopters		
G-RIBS	Diamond DA.20-A1 Katana	10143	G-BWWM	7. 7.97	Phantom Air Ltd	Gamston	16.11.02T
G-RIBV	Cessna 560 Citation Ultra	560-0506	N50820	17. 3.99	Houston Air Taxis Ltd	Oxford	16. 3.02T
G-RICA	American General AG-5B	10164	N132U	7. 9.99	Gowad Aviation Ltd	Blackbushe	5.10.02T
G-RICC	Aérospatiale AS350B2 Ecureuil	2559	G-BTXA	30.10.91	Specialist Helicopters Ltd	Munlochy	8. 2.04T
G-RICE	Robinson R22 Beta	2509	N93MK	14. 3.97	Heli Air Ltd	Wellesbourne Mountford	3. 4.03T
G-RICK	Beechcraft 95-B55 Baron	TC-1472	G-BAAG	23. 5.84	James Jack (Invergordon) Ltd	Wick	7. 5.03T
G-RICO	American-General AG-5B Tiger	10162	N130U	14. 5.99	Dynasty Trading Ltd	(London SE10)	31. 5.02T
G-RICS	Europa Aviation Europa (Subaru EA81) *(Tail-wheel u/c)*	PFA 247-12747		19. 3.96	R.G.Allen	Kemble	26.10.01P
					t/a The Flying Property Doctor		
G-RIDE	Stephens Akro (Lycoming AIO-360)	111	N81AC	10. 8.78	R.Mitchell	RAF Cosford	13. 8.92P
			N55NM		t/a Mitchell Aviation *(PSA c/s) (Stored 3.95)*		
G-RIDL	Robinson R22 Beta	3194		30. 3.01	G.Riddell	Newcastle	23. 4.04T
G-RIFB	Hughes 269C	116-0562	N7428F	17. 5.90	J.C.McHugh & Son (Civil Eng) Contractors Ltd	Romford	6. 3.03
G-RIFN	Mudry CAP.10B	276		6. 6.96	S.A.W.Becker	Goodwood	30. 6.02T
G-RIGB	Thunder Ax7-77 HAFB	1201		16. 3.88	N.J.Bettin *(New owner 9.01)*	Farnham	15. 2.96A
G-RIGH	Piper PA-32R-301 Saratoga	3246123	N41272	23.12.98	G M R & I H L Graham	Fowlmere	22.12.04T
			G-RIGH/N41272		t/a Rentair		
G-RIGS	Piper Aerostar 601P	61P-0621-7963281	N8220J	18. 5.79	G G Caravatti & P G Penati	Monza, Italy	4.10.03
G-RIIN	WSK PZL-104M Wilga 2000	00010010	SP-WEI	27. 6.01	PZL International Aviation Marketing & Sales plc	North Weald	22.7.04T
G-RIKI	Mainair Blade 912	1280-0401-7 & W1075		29. 8.01	R.Cook	East Fortune	28.8.02P
G-RIKS	Europa Aviation Europa XS	PFA 247-13329		18.10.01	R.Morris	(Hertford)	
G-RILY*	Monnett Sonerai IIL (VW 1834)	PFA 015-10353		20.12.78	Not known	Hill Farm, Nayland	5.10.89P
					(Cancelled 26.3.97 by CAA: stored 5.00)		
G-RIMM	Westland Wasp HAS.Mk.1 *(Official records quote "ex NZ3907")*	F9605	NZ3908	11. 3.99	M.P.Grimshaw & T.Martin	RNAS Yeovilton	7. 8.02P
			XT435		*(As "NZ3907")*		
G-RINN	Mainair Blade (Rotax 582)	1261-1000-7-W1055		2 .1.01	J.P.Lang	(Chester)	1. 1.02P
G-RINO	Thunder Ax7-77 HAFB	975		24. 6.87	D.J.Head *"Cerous"*	Newbury	5. 3.94T
G-RINS	Rans S-6-ESD Coyote II (Rotax 582)	PFA 204-13361		15. 3.99	D.Watt	Ladthwaite Farm, Kirkby Steven	14. 5.02P
G-RINT	CFM Streak Shadow (Rotax 582)	K199-SA & PFA 206-12251		7.12.93	D. & J.S.Grint	Shoreham	3.11.02P
G-RIPE	Pitts S-1S Special	PFA 09-13485		16. 2.00	J.A.Harris	(Gillingham)	
G-RIPS	Cameron Action Man/Parachutist 110SS HAFB	4092		29. 4.97	Virgin Airship & Balloon Co Ltd *"Action Man"*		
					(Op Balloon Preservation Group)	Stockport	25. 5.00A
G-RISE	Cameron V-90 HAFB	2395		21. 9.90	D.L.Smith *"Rise N' Shine"*	Newbury	21.11.98T

G-RIST	Cessna 310R II	310R1294	G-DATS (N6128X)	28. 4.81	F B Spriggs	Bournemouth	22. 6.01
G-RIVR	Thruster T.600N (Hirth H2706)	9029-T600N-031		3.12.99	Thruster Air Services Ltd *(Noted 12.01)*	Ginge Farm, Wantage	7.12.00P
G-RIVT	Van's RV-6 (Lycoming O-320)	PFA 181-12743		31. 7.95	N.Reddish	Netherthorpe	26. 3.02P
G-RIZE	Cameron O-90 HAFB	3163		13.12.93	S.F.Burden	Noordwijk, The Netherlands	7. 5.02A
G-RIZI	Cameron N-90 HAFB	3080		12. 5.93	R.Wiles	Wadhurst	4. 5.01A
G-RIZZ	Piper PA-28-161 Cherokee Warrior II	28-7816494	D-EMFW N9563N	11. 2.99	Northamptonshire School of Flying Ltd	Sywell	21. 3.02T
G-RJAH	Boeing-Stearman D75N1 (PT-27BW) Kaydet (Continental W670)	75-4041	N75957 RCAF FJ991/42-15852	6. 4.90	R.J.Horne *(As "44" in US Army c/s)*	Kemble	11. 4.04
G-RJAM	Sequoia F.8L Falco	PFA 100-11665		26. 7.00	R.J.Marks	(Bridgwater)	
G-RJCP	Commander Aircraft Commander 114B	14606	N6001M	3. 7.96	Heltor Ltd	Exeter	30. 8.02
G-RJGR	Boeing 757-225	22197	N701MG N507EA	22.11.94	Airtours International Airways Ltd	Manchester	1. 2.04T
G-RJMS	Piper PA-28R-201 Arrow III	28R-7837059	N6223H	19. 1.88	M.G.Hill	Crosland Moor	21. 5.03
G-RJTT	Bell 206B-3 JetRanger III	4551	C-GJLE	28.11.01	J.A.Robson t/a Air Deluxe	Gloucestershire	
G-RJWW	Maule M-5-235C Lunar Rocket	7250C	G-BRWG N5632H	6.10.87	PAW Flying Services Ltd	Sandtoft	25. 9.03T
G-RJWX	Europa Aviation Europa XS	PFA 247-13197		11. 9.00	J.R.Jones	(Wrexham)	26. 9.02P
G-RJXA	Embraer EMB-145EP	145.136		18. 6.99	British Midland Airways Ltd *(Op bmi Regional)*	East Midlands	17. 6.02T
G-RJXB	Embraer EMB-145EP	145.142		23. 6.99	British Midland Airways Ltd *(Op bmi Regional)*	East Midlands	27. 6.02T
G-RJXC	Embraer EMB-145EP	145.153	PT-SEE	15. 7.99	British Midland Airways Ltd *(Op bmi Regional)*	East Midlands	14. 7.02T
G-RJXD	Embraer EMB-145EP	145.207		4. 2.00	British Midland Airways Ltd *(Op bmi Regional)*	East Midlands	3. 2.03T
G-RJXE	Embraer EMB-145EP	145.245		10. 4.00	British Midland Airways Ltd *(Op bmi Regional)*	East Midlands	9. 4.03T
G-RJXF	Embraer EMB-145EP	145.280		29. 6.00	British Midland Airways Ltd *(Op bmi Regional)*	East Midlands	28. 6.03T
G-RJXG	Embraer EMB-145EP	145.390		20. 2.01	British Midland Airways Ltd *(Op bmi Regional)*	East Midlands	19. 2.04T
G-RJXH	Embraer EMB-145EP	145.442	PT-SVD	1. 6.01	British Midland Airways Ltd *(Star Alliance c/s)*	East Midlands	31. 5.04T
G-RJXI	Embraer EMB-145EP	145.454	PT-SVD	22. 6.01	British Midland Airways Ltd *(Star Alliance c/s)*	East Midlands	21. 6.04T
G-RJXJ	Embraer EMB-145ER	145.473		23. 7.01	British Midland Airways Ltd *(bmi Regional titles)*	East Midlands	22. 7.04T
G-RJXK	Embraer EMB-135ER	145.494	PT-SXN	14. 9.01	British Midland Airways Ltd *(Star Alliance c/s)*	East Midlands	13. 9.04T
G-RKEL	Agusta-Bell 206B-3 Jet Ranger III	8617	HB-XPR F-GCVE	2. 8.01	Nunkeeling Ltd	(Brough)	
G-RKET	Taylor JT.2 Titch	PFA 3223	G-BIBK	25. 8.99	P.A.Dunley	RAF Valley	
G-RLFI	Reims Cessna FA152 Aerobat	FA15200340	G-DFTS	17. 1.90	Tayside Aviation Ltd	Dundee	18.11.01T
G-RLMC	Cessna 421C Golden Eagle II	421C0118	PH-SBI D-IMAZ/I-CCNN/N3849C	9. 3.88	R.D.Lygo	Farnborough	29. 4.02
G-RMAC	Europa Aviation Europa	PFA 247-12717		3. 7.97	P.J.Lawless	(Bath)	
G-RMAN	Aero Designs Pulsar	PFA 202-13071		6. 6.97	M.B.Redman *(Noted 4.01)*	Old Sarum	22. 5.02P
G-RMAX	Cameron C-80 HAFB	4705		6.12.99	M Quinn & D Curtain	Dublin	4. 9.02A
G-RMIE	Bell 206B-3 JetRanger III	2533	G-BPIE N327WM	6. 4.01	R & M International Engineering Ltd	North Creake	5.12.04T
G-RMIT	Van's RV-4 (Lycoming O-302-E3D)	PFA 181-12207		4. 9.96	J.P.Kloos	Truleigh Manor Farm, Edburton	21. 5.02P
G-RMUG	Cameron Nescafe Mug 90SS HAFB	3450		3. 5.95	Nestle UK Ltd *"Nescafe"*	Croydon	18. 7.02A
G-RNAS*	de Havilland DH.104 Sea Devon C.20	04473	XK896	16.11.82	Not known *(Cancelled 17.4.97 by CAA: for spares 9.01)*	Filton	3. 7.84
G-RNBW	Bell 206B JetRanger II	2270	F-GQFH F-WQFH/HB-XUF/F-GFBP/N900JJ/N16UC	9. 1.98	Rainbow Helicopters Ltd	Whimple	22. 2.04T
G-RNGO	Robinson R22 Beta	3035		19. 1.00	B.E.Llewellyn	Swansea	10. 2.03T
G-RNIE	Cameron Ball 70SS HAFB	2333		3. 8.90	N.J.Bland *"Schwarzenegger" (New owner 10.01)*	Didcot	16. 5.97A
G-RNLI	V-S.236 Walrus 1	S2/5591	W2718	13.12.90	R.E.Melton *(As "W2718/AA5Y" in 751 Sqn RN c/s: on rebuild 6.95: current status unknown)*	Great Yarmouth	
G-RNRM	Cessna A185F Skywagon	A18502541	N1826R	20. 1.87	Skydive St.Andrews Ltd *"Thunderchild"*	Sorbie Farm, Kingsmuir	20. 2.03

G-ROAR	Cessna 401	401-0166	G-BZFL G-AWSF/N4066Q	8. 3.82	Special Scope Ltd	Blackpool	16. 9.02
G-ROBD	Europa Aviation Europa	PFA 247-12671		23. 2.94	R.D.Davies	(Cowbridge)	
G-ROBN	Robin R.1180T Aiglon	220		16. 8.78	Bustard Flying Group Ltd	Boscombe Down	13. 8.03T
	(Port undercarriage caught fire on take off Boscombe Down 27.8.01 causing severe damage to underside & surface of port wing, probably including wing spar)						
G-ROBT	Hawker Hurricane I	--	P2902	19. 9.94	R.A.Roberts	Moat Farm, Milden	
	(Built Gloster Aircraft) (On rebuild by Hawker Restorations Ltd from remains salvaged in 1988 from wreck site at Dunkirk Beach: to be "P2902/DX-X")						
G-ROBY	Colt 17A Cloudhopper HAFB	483		7. 2.83	Virgin Airship & Balloon Co Ltd *"Cloudhopper"*	Telford	26. 9.92A
G-ROCH	Cessna T303 Crusader	T30300129	N4962C	29. 3.90	R.S.Bentley	Cambridge	7. 6.02
G-ROCK	Thunder Ax7-77 HAFB	781		25. 2.86	M.A.Green *"Rocky"*	Rednal	10. 6.02A
G-ROCR	Schweizer Hughes 269C	S.1336	N219MS	14. 6.90	Oxford Aviation Services Ltd	Oxford	14. 2.03T
G-RODD	Cessna 310R II	310R0544	G-TEDD G-MADI/N87396/G-MADI/N87396	2.10.89	R J Herbert Engineering Ltd	Cranfield	1. 8.02
G-RODG	Jabiru Jabiru XL (Jabiru 2200A)	PFA 274A-13379		14. 4.99	S.Jackson	Eshott	7. 8.01P
G-RODI	Isaacs Fury (Lycoming O-290)	PFA 011-10130		22.12.78	M.R.Baker	Westfield Farm, Hailsham	17. 8.95P
			(As "K3731" in 43 Sqdn c/s: stored 3.97: current status unknown)				
G-ROGY	Cameron Concept 60 HAFB	3055		11. 5.93	A.A.Laing	Aberdeen	8. 9.02A
G-ROLA	Piper PA-34-200T Seneca II	34-7670066	N4537X G-ROLA/N4537X	4.12.85	Deer Hill Aviation Ltd & Goss Challenges Ltd	Top Farm, Croydon	23.11.04T
G-ROLF	Piper PA-32R-301 Saratoga SP	32R-8113018	N83052	7. 1.81	P.F.Larkins	High Cross, Ware	29. 3.02
G-ROLL	Aerotek Pitts S-2A Special (Lycoming AEIO-360)	2175	N31444	20. 2.80	N.Lamb t/a Aerial & Aerobatic Services	Booker	13. 8.04A
G-ROLO	Robinson R22 Beta	1226		24. 1.90	Plane Talking Ltd *(Op Cabair Helicopters)*	Elstree	22.12.04T
G-ROME	III Sky Arrow 650TCC	011		26. 5.99	Sky Arrow (Kits) UK Ltd	Old Sarum	16. 6.02T
G-ROMS	Lindstrand LBL-105G HAFB	401		13. 9.96	T D Donnelly *"Gromit"* t/a Gromit Balloon Group	Doncaster	13. 9.00A
G-ROMW	Cyclone AX2000 (HKS 700E V3)	7486		4. 2.99	Financial Planning (Wells) Ltd	Wells	14. 5.02P
G-RONA	Europa Aviation Europa *(Mono-wheel u/c)* (Rotax 912UL)	43 & PFA 247-12588		17. 1.95	C.M.Noakes *"Mr Jake"*	Shenstone	17. 6.02P
G-ROND	Short SD.3-60 Var.100	SH.3604	EI-CWG G-OLAH/G-BPCO/G-RMSS/G-BKKU	1.11.01	Emerald Airways Ltd	Liverpool	26.11.02T
G-RONG	Piper PA-28R-200 Cherokee Arrow II	28R-7335148	N16451	14. 6.90	E.Tang	Elstree	22. 9.02
G-RONI	Cameron V-77 HAFB	2349		27. 7.90	R.E.Simpson t/a Elbow Beach Balloon Club *"Roni"*	Great Missenden	15. 8.02A
G-RONN	Robinson R44 Astro	0267	N770SC G-RONN/D-HIRR	8. 1.98	R Hallam & S E Watts	Leicester	15. 2.04
G-RONS	Robin DR.400/180 Regent	2088		17. 7.91	R. & K.Baker	Newcastle	10. 8.03
G-RONW	Clutton FRED Srs.II (VW 1834)	PFA 029-10121		18.12.78	K.Atkinson	Haverfordwest	29. 3.02P
G-ROOK	Reims Cessna F172P Skyhawk II	F17202081	PH-TGY G-ROOK	12. 1.81	Rolim Ltd *(Op Bon Accord Flying Group)*	Aberdeen	7.11.02
G-ROOV	Europa Aviation Europa XS *(Tri-cycle u/c)* (Rotax 914-UL)	PFA 247-13204 *(C/n could be PFA 247-13214)*		16. 7.98	E.Sheridan & P.W.Hawkins	Biggin Hill	18. 3.02P
G-RORI	Folland Gnat T.1	FL.549	8621M XR538	18.10.93	D.S.Milne	(Banchory)	16. 3.02P
G-RORO	Cessna 337B Super Skymaster	33700554	G-AVIX N5454S	8. 1.80	H.D.Hezlett	(Andreas)	15. 7.00
				(Damaged landing Castlerock, Co.Londonderry 25.6.99: noted 6.00)			
G-RORY	Focke-Wulf Piaggio FWP.149D *(Piaggio c/n 338)*	014	G-TOWN D-EFFY/90+06/BB+394	2. 8.88	Bushfire Investments Ltd	Booker	6.10.02
G-ROSE	Evans VP-1	PFA 7031		22. 1.79	A.P.M.Long	(Leighton Buzzard)	
G-ROSI	Thunder Ax7-77 HAFB	1284		29. 6.88	J.E.Rose *"Rosi"*	Abingdon	21. 9.96A
G-ROTI	Luscombe 8A (Continental A65)	2117	N45590 NC45590	18. 4.89	R.Ludgate & A.L.Chapman	Old Hay, Paddock Wood	9.10.97P
G-ROTR	Brantly B.2B	403	N2192U	9.12.91	P.G.R.Brown	Trenchard Farm, Eggesford	17.11.02
G-ROTS	CFM Streak Shadow (Rotax 582)	K.120-SA & PFA 161A-11603		21.12.89	G.K.Kenealy	Warrington	18. 2.02P
G-ROUP	Reims Cessna F172M Skyhawk II	F17201451	G-BDPH	23. 5.84	Stapleford Flying Club Ltd	Stapleford	23. 4.03T
G-ROUS	Piper PA-34-200T Seneca II	34-7870187	(G-BFTB) N9412C	26. 4.78	Oxford Aviation Services Ltd	Oxford	10. 2.03T
G-ROUT	Robinson R22 Beta	1241	N8068U	23. 1.90	Preston Associates Ltd	(Saltburn-by-the-Sea)	16.10.03T
G-ROVE	Piper PA-18-135 Super Cub (L-21B-PI) *(Frame No.18-3853)*	18-3846	PH-VLO (PH-DKF)/R-156/54-2446	6. 5.82	S.J.Gaveston	Headcorn	13. 8.04T
			(As "54-2446/R-156")				
G-ROVY	Robinson R22 Beta-II	2957		9. 7.99	R.Rice	Wellesbourne Mountford	15. 7.02T

G-ROWE	Reims Cessna F182P Skylane II	F18200007	OO-CNG	18.12.95	D.Rowe	Liverpool	15. 2.02
G-ROWI	Europa Aviation Europa XS	PFA 247-13482		16. 6.99	R.M.Carson	(Cheltenham)	
G-ROWL	Grumman-American AA-5B Tiger	AA5B-0595	(N28410)	26.10.77	Airhouse Corporation Ltd	Elstree	10. 5.04T
G-ROWN	Beechcraft 200 Super King Air	BB-684	G-BHLC N27L/N8511L/G-BHLC	13.10.87	Valentia Air Ltd.	Oxford	10. 4.02T
G-ROWR	Robinson R44 Raven	1036		17. 4.01	R.A.Oldworth	(Petworth)	
G-ROWS	Piper PA-28-151 Cherokee Warrior	28-7715296	N8949F	15. 9.78	Mustarrow Ltd	Manchester	9. 3.03
G-ROZI	Robinson R44 Astro	0252		26. 3.96	Milford Garage Ltd	(Sheffield)	29. 4.02T
G-ROZY	Cameron R-36 Gas/HAFB	1141		20. 5.85	Jacques W.Soukup Enterprises Ltd	Florida, USA	18. 9.96A
G-RPEZ	Rutan LongEz	PFA 074A-10746		3. 4.84	B.A.Fairston & D.Richardson *(Stored uncomplete 5.00)*	Booker	
G-RRCU	CEA DR221B Dauphin	129	F-BRCU	9.12.99	Merlin Flying Club Ltd	Hucknall	4..9.03T
G-RRGN	Supermarine 390 Spitfire PR.XIX	6S/594677	G-MXIX PS853	23.12.96	Rolls-Royce plc *(As "PS853/C" in 2nd TAF/PRU c/s)*	Filton	2. 9.02P
G-RRFC	SOCATA TB-20 Trinidad GT	2053	F-OILV	9. 5.01	A.T.Paton	Blackbushe	15. 5.04
G-RROD	Piper PA-30 Twin Comanche B	30-1221	G-SHAW LN-BWS/N10F	20. 6.00	R.P.Coplestone	Thruxton	2. 9.02P
G-RSCJ	Cessna 525 Citation Jet	525-0298		15. 1.99	SMD Investments Ltd	Jersey	15. 2.02T
G-RSFT	Piper PA-28-161 Warrior II	28-8616038	G-WARI N9276Y	15.12.95	J E Howe	Compton Abbas	26. 2.04T
G-RSKR	Piper PA-28-161 Warrior II	28-7916181	G-BOJY N3030G	27. 4.95	R.Sherwin-Smith t/a Krown Group	Slinfold	26.10.03T
G-RSSF	Denney Kitfox mk.2 (Rotax 582)	PFA 172-12125		9.10.92	R.W.Somerville *(Current status unknown)*	Comber, Co.of Down	15. 5.97P
G-RSVP	Robinson R22 Beta-II	2788		5. 2.98	Pearce Enterprise Ltd	Brands Hatch	8. 3.04T
G-RSWO	Cessna 172R Skyhawk II	17280206	N9401F	25. 2.98	AC Management Associates Ltd	Kemble	11. 3.04T
G-RSWW	Robinson R22 Beta	1775	N40815	16. 5.91	R.S.Weston-Woods t/a Woodstock Enterprises	Brands Hatch, Dartford	6. 7.03T
G-RTBI	Thunder Ax6-56 HAFB	2584		19. 4.94	P.J.Waller	Norwich	8. 7.02A
G-RTWW	Robinson R44 Astro	0438		20. 3.98	R.Woods t/a Rotorvation	(Longfield)	7. 5.04T
G-RUBB	Gulfstream AA-5B Tiger	AA5B-0928	(G-BKVI) OO-NAS/(OO-HRC)	20. 9.83	D.E.Gee	Blackbushe	23.11.04
G-RUBI	Thunder Ax7-77 HAFB	1051		27. 2.87	G.Warren t/a Warren & Johnson *"Rubicon Computer Systems"*	Norwich	20.11.93A
G-RUBY	Piper PA-28RT-201T Turbo Arrow IV	28R-8331037	G-BROU N4306K	5. 1.90	R.Harman t/a Arrow Aircraft Group	Tatenhill	16. 6.02
G-RUDD	Cameron V-65 HAFB	844		19. 5.82	N.A.Apsey *"Smilie" (Kodak titles)*	High Wycombe	20. 5.00A
G-RUFF	Mainair Blade 912 (Rotax 912-UL)	1203-0799-7-W1006		18. 6.99	C.G.P.Holden	(Chesterfield)	17 .6.02P
G-RUFS	Jabiru Jabiru UL	PFA 274A-13359		19.11.99	J.W.Holland	Kemble	14. 3.02
G-RUGB*	Cameron Egg 89SS HAFB *(Rugby Ball shape)*	1936		9. 2.89	Not known *(Cancelled 14.7.98 by CAA: stolen from beach in Cornwall 12.8.99: current status unknown)*	NK	
G-RUGS	Campbell Cricket Mk.4	PFA G/103-1307		11. 2.99	J.L.G.Mclane	(York)	
G-RUIA	Reims Cessna F172N Skyhawk II	F17201856	PH-AXA(3)	4.10.79	Knockin Flying Club Ltd	Knockin, Shropshire	13. 7.04
G-RUMM	Grumman F8F-2P Bearcat	D.1088	NX700HL NX700H/N1YY/N4995V/Bu.121714	20. 3.98	Patina Ltd *(Op The Fighter Collection) (As "21714/201B" in USN c/s)*	Duxford	5. 7.02P
G-RUMN	Grumman-American AA-1A Trainer	AA1A-0086	N87599 D-EAFB/(N9386L)	30. 5.80	T.J.White	Stapleford	17. 3.03
G-RUMT	Grumman F7F-3P Tigercat	C.167	N7235C BuA.80425	6. 4.98	Patina Ltd *(Op The Fighter Collection) (As "80425/WT-4" in US Marines c/s)*	Duxford	5. 7.02P
G-RUMW	Grumman FM-2 Wildcat	5765	N4845V BuA.86711	15. 4.98	Patina Ltd *(Op The Fighter Collection) (As "F" in FAA c/s)*	Duxford	28. 6.02P
G-RUNG	SAAB-Scania SF.340A	340A-086	F-GGBV SE-E86	3. 6.97	Aurigny Air Services Ltd	Guernsey	5. 6.02T
G-RUNT	Cassutt Racer IIIM (Lycoming O-235)	161149 & PFA 034-10860		12. 4.83	N.A.Scully	(Navenby)	12. 9.02P
G-RUSA	Pegasus Quantum 15-912	7517		7. 4.99	A.D.Stewart	Perth	14..4.02P
G-RUSL	Van's RV-6A	PFA 181-13522		22.10.01	G.R.Russell	(Crewkerne)	
G-RUSO*	Robinson R22 Beta	1387		25. 5.90	R.M.Barnes-Gorell *(Damaged Thruxton 27.3.00: cancelled 8.6.00 as wfu)*	Thruxton	6. 4.02T
G-RUVY	Van's RV-9A	PFA 320-13807		4. 1.02	R Taylor	(Wincanton)	
G-RVAL	Van's RV-8	PFA 303-13532		23. 7.01	R.N.York	(Pulborough)	
G-RVAN	Van's RV-6 (Lycoming IO-320)	PFA 181-12657		25. 4.97	D.Broom	Benington	22. 4.02P
G-RVAW	Van's RV-6	PFA 181-13234		24.11.97	A.A.Wordsworth	Netherthorpe	16. 5.02P

G-RVBA	Van's RV-8A	PFA 303-13309		26.10.99	S.Hawksworth	(Nuneaton)	
					(Under construction 2000)		
G-RVBC	Van's RV-6A	PFA 181-12618		16. 2.00	B.J.Clifford	(Bristol)	
G-RVCE	Van's RV-6A	PFA 181-13372		28. 6.01	M.D.Barnard & C.Voelger	(Welwyn)	
G-RVCG	Van's RV-6A	PFA 181A-13602		26. 4.01	C.J.Griffin	(Stratford-upon-Avon)	
G-RVCL	Van's RV-6	PFA 181A-13439		18. 2.99	C.T.Lamb	(Stamford)	
G-RVDJ	Van's RV-6	PFA 181-12938		8. 2.99	J.D.Jewitt	(Selby)	3.10.02P
	(Lycoming 0-360-A4A)						
G-RVDP	Van's RV-4	PFA 181-13416		10. 5.00	D.H.Pattison	Upham Farm, Chiseldon	
G-RVDR	Van's RV-6A	PFA 181-13098		15. 5.00	T M Norman	Nottingham	25 .4.02P
G-RVEE	Van's RV-6	PFA 181-12262		16. 2.93	J.C.A.Wheeler	Perth	30. 1.02P
	(Lycoming 0-360-A1AD)						
G-RVET	Van's RV-6	PFA 181-12852		9. 3.98	D.R.Coleman	Rochester	22. 1.02P
	(Lycoming 0-300-D2A)						
G-RVGA	Van's RV-6A	PFA 181-13079		11. 5.98	D.P.Dawson	Rush Green	2. 5.02P
	(Lycoming IO-320-D2A)						
G-RVHT	Cessna 550 Citation II	550-0441	N221GA	17.11.99	Ravenheat Manufacturing Ltd		
			HB-VKS/VR-CCE/N56PC/N50LM/N1220J			Leeds-Bradford	22.11.03T
G-RVIA	Van's RV-6A	PFA 181-12289		13. 8.97	A.N.Tyers	Cumbernauld	26.10.02P
	(Lycoming 0-320-E2A))						
G-RVIB	Van's RV-6	PFA 181-13220		22. 6.99	I.M.Belmore	(Horsham)	
					(Under construction 2000)		
G-RVII	Van's RV-7	PFA 181A-13576		13. 9.01	P.H.C.Hall	(Swindon)	
	(Project was originally conceived as a RV-6, hence the '181A prefix)						
G-RVIN	Van's RV-6	PFA 181-13236		28.11.97	N.Reddish	Netherthorpe	9. 6.02P
	(Lycoming 0-320-D1A)						
G-RVIT	Van's RV-6	PFA 181-12422		1. 5.95	P.J.Shotbolt	Ingthorpe	28. 8.02P
	(Lycoming 0-360-A1D)						
G-RVIV	Van's RV-4	PFA 181-12366		31.12.97	G.S.Scott	Truleigh Manor Farm, Edburton	20 .5.02P
	(Lycoming 0-320-D3G)						
G-RVIX	Van's RV-9A	PFA 320-13779		11. 9.01	R.E.Garforth	(Hockley)	
G-RVMJ	Van's RV-4	PFA 181-13433		16. 2.99	M.J.de Ruiter	(Craigavon)	
G-RVMT	Van's RV-6	PFA 181A-13644		30. 1.01	M R Tingle	(Norwich)	
G-RVMZ	Van's RV-8	PFA 303-13395		12.11.99	M.W.Zipfell	(Bury St.Edmunds)	
G-RVRA	Piper PA-28-140 Cherokee Cruiser		G-OWVA	14. 1.97	Cheshire Flying Services Ltd	Liverpool	19. 4.03T
		28-7625038	N4459X		t/a Ravenair		
			(Made heavy landing Welshpool 10.9.01, damaging nose undercarriage & propeller)				
G-RVRB	Piper PA-34-200T Seneca II		G-BTAJ	24. 2.97	Cheshire Flying Services Ltd	Manchester	11. 7.04T
		34-7970440	N22MJ/N45113		t/a Ravenair		
G-RVRC	Piper PA-23-250 Aztec E	27-7405336	G-BNPD	14.10.97	Cheshire Flying Services Ltd	Manchester	23. 1.04T
			N101VH/N40591		t/a Ravenair		
G-RVRD	Piper PA-23-250 Aztec E	27-4634	G-BRAV	16. 3.98	Cheshire Flying Services Ltd	Manchester	9.11.02T
			G-BBCM/N14021		t/a Ravenair		
G-RVRF	Piper PA-38-112 Tomahawk	38-78A0714	G-BGEL	21.11.97	Cheshire Flying Services Ltd	Liverpool	24. 5.03T
			N9723N		t/a Ravenair		
G-RVRG	Piper PA-38-112 Tomahawk	38-79A1092	G-BHAF	3. 8.98	Cheshire Flying Services Ltd	Manchester	4. 7.02T
			N9703N		t/a Ravenair		
G-RVRS	Robinson R22 Beta	1478	G-XTEC	31. 1.01	Holly Aviation Ltd	Duxford	11.11.01T
			G-BYCK/N101EJ		*(Damaged in heavy landing Duxford 26.10.01)*		
G-RVRV	Van's RV-4	PFA 181-13024		29. 9.98	P Jenkins	(Nairn)	
					(Under construction 2001)		
G-RVSA	Van's RV-6A	PFA 181-12574		19. 5.99	W.H.Knott	(Inverness)	
					(Under construction 2001)		
G-RVSX	Van's RV-6	PFA 181-13090		18. 9.97	R.L. & V.A.West	(Worthing)	
G-RVVI	Van's RV-6	PFA 181-12418		26. 1.93	J.E.Alsford & J.N.Parr	Sibson	17.10.01P
G-RWHC	Cameron A-180 HAFB	2700		16. 4.92	J.J.Rudoni & A.C.K.Rawson	Stafford	13. 4.00T
					t/a Wickers World Hot Air Balloon Co		
G-RWIN	Rearwin 175 Skyranger	1522	N32391	12. 9.90	G.Kay	Yew Tree Farm, Lymm Dam	15. 7.02P
	(Continental A75)		NC32391				
G-RWLY	Europa Aviation Europa XS			22. 3.01	C.R.Arkle	(Ascot)	
		PFA 247-13701					
G-RWSS	Denney Kitfox mk.2	PFA 172-12008		16. 4.91	R.W.Somerville *(Current status unknown)*		
	(Rotax 582)					Comber, Newtownards, Co.of Down	14. 6.93P
G-RWWW*	Westland WS-55 Whirlwind HCC.12		8727M	21. 6.90	The Helicopter Museum	Weston-super-Mare	25. 8.96P
		WA/418	XR486		*(As "XR486" in Queens Flight c/s) (Cancelled 10.7.00 as wfu)*		
G-RXUK	Lindstrand LBL-105A HAFB	232		29. 3.95	P.A.Hames *"Rank Xerox"*	Reading	19. 5.02A
G-RYAL	Jabiru Jabiru UL	PFA 274A-13365		6. 7.99	A.C.Ryall	Cardiff	3.10.02P
G-RYPH	Mainair Blade 912	1248-0500-7-W1041		8. 6.00	R.J.Griffiths	Rush Green	3. 8.02P
	(Rotax 912-UL)						
G-RZPH	CFM Streak Shadow SLA	PFA 206-13776		1. 5.01	CFM Aircraft Ltd	Framlingham	

G-SAAA – G-SZZZ

G-SAAB	Rockwell Commander 112TC	13002	G-BEFS N1502J	5.12.79	M.R.J.Hill	Old Sarum	13. 7.03
G-SAAM	Cessna T182R Turbo Skylane II	18268200	G-TAGL G-SAAM/N2399E	23. 5.84	M.D.Harvey, M.A.Tokley & J.R.Partner	Earls Colne	22.11.04
G-SABA	Piper PA-28R-201T Turbo Cherokee Arrow III	28R-7703268	G-BFEN N38745	22. 8.79	D.Booth	Sherburn-in-Elmet	3. 5.04
G-SABR	North American F-86A-5NA Sabre *(Regd with c/n 151-083)*	151-43547	N178 N68388/48-178	6.11.91	Golden Apple Operations Ltd *(Op The Old Flying Machine Co)* *(As "8178/FU-178" in 4th Fighter Wing USAF c/s)*	Duxford	10. 6.99P
G-SACB	Reims Cessna F152 II	F15201501	G-BFRB	7. 3.84	Flight Ltd	Crowfield	12. 4.03T
G-SACD	Cessna F172H	F172-0385	G-AVCD	13. 6.83	Northbrook College of Design & Technology *(Op Sky Leisure Aviation)*	Shoreham	27. 7.00T
G-SACF*	Cessna 152 II	15283175	G-BHSZ N47125	21. 3.85	T M & A L Jones	Derby	8. 6.95T
	(Damaged Egginton 21.3.97: cancelled 11.8.97 by CAA: fuselage noted 8.99: current status unknown)						
G-SACH	Stoddard-Hamilton Glastar	PFA 0295-13088		27. 8.99	R.S.Holt	(Evesham)	
G-SACI	Piper PA-28-161 Warrior II	28-8216123	N81535	26. 7.89	PJC (Leasing) Ltd	Stapleford	28. 4.02T
G-SACK	Robin R.2160	316		2. 5.97	Sherburn Aero Club Ltd	Sherburn-in-Elmet	6. 6.03T
G-SACO	Piper PA-28-161 Warrior II	28-8416085	N4358Z	1. 6.89	D.C.& M.Brooks t/a The Barn Gallery	Oxford	16. 7.04
G-SACR	Piper PA-28-161 Cadet	2841046	N91618	6. 2.89	Sherburn Aero Club Ltd	Sherburn-in-Elmet	20. 2.04T
G-SACS	Piper PA-28-161 Cadet	2841047	N91619	6. 2.89	Sherburn Aero Club Ltd	Sherburn-in-Elmet	20. 2.04T
G-SACT	Piper PA-28-161 Cadet	2841048	N9162D	6. 2.89	Sherburn Aero Club Ltd	Sherburn-in-Elmet	25. 2.04T
G-SACU*	Piper PA-28-161 Cadet	2841049	N9162X	6. 2.89	Sherburn Aero Club Ltd	Sherburn-in-Elmet	19. 2.98T
	(Damaged landing Sherburn-in-Elmet 29.6.96: wrecked fuselage stored 2.00: cancelled 7.6.01 as wfu)						
G-SACZ	Piper PA-28-161 Warrior II	28-7916258	N2098N	26. 7.89	Lima Delta Aviation Ltd	Shoreham	15. 4.02T
G-SADE	Reims Cessna F150L	F15000752	G-AZJW	28. 5.91	N.E.Sams *(Op Billins Air Services)*	Cranfield	21. 9.97T
G-SAFE	Cameron N-77 HAFB	511		14. 2.79	P.J.Waller *"The High Flyer"*	Norwich	21. 4.91A
G-SAFI	Piel CP.1320	PFA 183-12103		23. 7.01	C.S.Carleton-Smith	(Great Missenden)	
G-SAFR	Saab 91D Safir	91-382	PH-RLR	10.10.95	Sylmar Aviation & Services Ltd	Lower Wasing Farm, Brimpton	
G-SAGA	Grob G-109B	6364	OE-9254	28. 6.90	G-GROB Ltd	Booker	16. 7.02
G-SAGE	Luscombe 8A Silvaire (Continental A65)	2581	G-AKTL N71154/NC71154	15. 8.90	R.J.P.Herivel	Alderney	21. 1.02P
G-SAHI	FLS Sprint 160 (Lycoming O-235) *(Design known originally as Trago Mills SAH-1)*	001		21.10.80	Sunhawk Ltd	North Weald	30. 4.94P
G-SAIR	Cessna 421C Golden Eagle III	421C0471	G-OBCA N6812C	1. 4.86	Air Support Aviation Services Ltd	Aberdeen	21. 4.03
G-SAIX	Cameron N-77 HAFB	626	N386CB	14. 1.99	C.Walther, B.Sevenich, B. & S.Harren	Aachen, Germany	21. 2.00A
G-SALA	Piper PA-32-300 Six	32-7940106	(G-BHEJ) N2184Z	17.10.79	Stonebold Ltd	Elstree	16. 3.04
G-SALL	Reims Cessna F150L	F15000682	PH-LTY D-ECPH	19. 1.79	D.& P.A.Hailey	Thruxton	7. 8.03
G-SAMG	Grob G-109B	6278		16. 5.84	T.Holloway t/a RAFGSA	RAF Bicester	20. 4.02
G-SAMI	Cameron N-90 Sainsbury Strawberry SS HAFB	3907	G-BWSE	21. 8.96	Flying Pictures Ltd	Fairoaks	15. 7.02A
G-SAMJ	Partenavia P.68 Victor *(Regd as "P.68B")*	101	D-GERA CS-AYB/D-GERA	27. 4.01	S.M.Jack t/a G-SAMJ Group *(Noted 7.01)*	Sherburn-in-Elmet	4. 6.04T
G-SAMM	Cessna 340A II *(RAM-conversion)*	340A0742	N37TJ N2671A	7. 3.88	M.R.Cross	Exeter	5. 7.03
G-SAMY	Europa Aviation Europa	PFA 247-12901		17. 8.95	K.R.Tallent *(Owner abandoned project as a partially finished kit 4.01)*	(Farnborough)	
G-SAMZ*	Cessna 150D	15060536	G-ASSO N4536U	19. 4.84	N.E.Sams *(Cancelled 10.10.01 by CAA)*	Cranfield	9. 2.01T
G-SAND	Schweizer Hughes 269C (300C)	S.1399		17. 8.89	R.C.Hields t/a Hields Aviation	Sherburn-in-Elmet	7.11.04T
G-SARA	Piper PA-28-181 Archer II	28-7990039	N21270	6. 4.81	R.P.Lewis	Full Sutton	2. 5.04T
G-SARH	Piper PA-28-161 Warrior II	28-8216173	N8232Q	18. 2.91	Sussex Flying Club Ltd	Shoreham	18. 2.04T
G-SARK	British Aircraft Corpn BAC.167 Strikemaster mk.84	EEP/JP/1931	N2146S/Sing.AF 311/G-27-140	13. 1.95	Sark International Airways Ltd *(Op A.Gjertsen Classic Jets Aircraft) (Noted 8.01)*	North Weald	
G-SARO	Saro Skeeter AOP.12	S2/5097	XL812	17. 7.78	B.Chamberlain *(As "XL812")*	Otley, Ipswich	1. 8.01P
G-SARV	Van's RV-4	PFA 181-12606		2.10.00	S.N.Aston	(Bicester)	

G-SASA	Eurocopter EC 135 T1	0147		12.10.00	Bond Air Services Ltd *(Op Scottish Ambulance Service)*	Inverness/Glasgow City Heliport	22.10.03T
G-SASB	Eurocopter EC 135 T1	0151		29. 9.00	Bond Air Services Ltd *(Op Scottish Ambulance Service)*	Inverness/Glasgow City Heliport	5.10.03T
G-SASK	Piper PA-31P Pressurised Navajo	31P-39	G-BFAM SE-GLV/OH-PNF/N6834L	30.10.97	Middle East Business Club Ltd *(Noted as "G-BFAM" 12.00 qv)*	(Guernsey)	30. 8.91T
G-SATL	Cameron Sphere 105SS HAFB	2696		5.12.91	Ballonverbung Hamburg GmbH	Kiel, Germany	29. 4.97A
G-SAUF	Colt 90A HAFB *(New envelope c/n 2492 1990/1)*	1497		25. 5.89	K.H.Medau	Baden, Germany	11. 5.02A
G-SAWI	Piper PA-32RT-300T Turbo Lance II	32R-7887069	OY-CJJ N36719	23. 6.99	S.A.& K.J.Williams	Wellesbourne Mountford	6 .7.02
G-SAXO	Cameron N-105 HAFB	3864		1. 4.96	Flying Pictures Ltd *(Citroen Saxo titles)*	Fairoaks	25. 5.00A
G-SAYS	Rotary Air Force RAF 2000 GTX-SE	PFA G/13-1322		4. 9.00	The Aziz Corporation Ltd	(Winchester)	9. 7.02P
G-SAZZ	Piel CP.328 Super Emeraude	PFA 216-11940		4. 7.01	D.J.Long	(Wotton-Under-Edge)	
G-SBAE	Reims Cessna F172P Skyhawk	F17202200	D-EOCD(3)	3. 6.98	BAE Systems (Operations) Ltd	Blackpool	25. 7.04T
G-SBAS	Beechcraft B200 Super King Air	BB-1007	SE-IVZ N777GA/G-BJJV	16.11.90	Gama Aviation Ltd	Aberdeen/Fairoaks	20.12.03T
G-SBLT	Steen Skybolt	MH-01		14. 4.92	S.D.Arnold t/a Skybolt Group	Coventry	
G-SBMO	Robin R.2160I	116	EI-BMO SE-GSZ	12. 2.99	D.Henderson, U.Simpson & M.Mannion	Waterford	26. 4.02T
G-SBUS	Britten-Norman BN-2A-26 Islander *(Built PADC)*	3013	G-BMMH RP-C578	31.10.86	Isles of Scilly Skybus Ltd	St.Just	17. 4.03T
G-SBUT	Robinson R22 Beta-II	2739	G-BXMT	18. 5.98	Princepro Ltd	(Alfreton)	12.11.03T
G-SCAH*	Cameron V-77 HAFB	788		18. 1.82	Balloon Preservation Group "Orpheus" *(Cancelled 30.11.01 by CAA)*	Southampton	24. 7.87A
G-SCAN	Vinten Wallis WA-116 Srs.100/R (Rotax 532)	001		5. 7.82	K.H.Wallis *(Stored 8.01)*	Reymerston Hall, Norfolk	10. 7.91P
G-SCAT	Cessna F150F *(Wichita c/n 15063455) (Tail-wheel u/c)*	F150-0054	G-ATRN (G-ATMN)	15. 9.86	G.D.Cooper	Rochester	26. 3.02T
G-SCBI	SOCATA TB-20 Trinidad	1908	F-OIGV	10. 8.99	S.C.Brown t/a Ace Services	Enstone	17. 8.02T
G-SCFO	Cameron O-77 HAFB	1131		3. 5.85	M.K.Grigson "Southern Counties" *(Op Balloon Preservation Group)*	Kirdford	24. 5.95A
G-SCHI	Eurocopter AS 350B2 Ecureuil	3337	F-WQOQ	5. 2.01	Patriot Aviation Ltd	(Birmingham)	22. 3.04T
G-SCIP	SOCATA TB-20 Trinidad GT	2014	F-OILO	19. 9.00	J.C.White	Oxford	24..9.03
G-SCLX	FLS Aerospace Sprint 160	002	G-PLYM	14. 7.94	Sunhawk Ltd	North Weald	16. 7.03T
G-SCOO	Bell 206B JetRanger II	1129	G-CORC G-CJHI/G-BBFB/N18094	23. 6.00	Hughes Helicopter Co Ltd t/a Biggin Hill Helicopters	Biggin Hill	12. 7.03T
G-SCOW	Aérospatiale AS355F2 Twin Squirrel	5346	ZS-HSW G-POON/G-MCAL	19. 5.99	B.K.Scowcroft *(Railtrack titles)*	Belle Isle, Lake Windermere	14 .9.02T
G-SCPL	Piper PA-28-140 Cherokee Cruiser	28-7725160	G-BPVL N1785H	4. 5.89	Aeros Leasing Ltd	Gloucestershire	19. 8.04T
G-SCRU	Cameron A-250 HAFB	3935	G-BWWO	30. 9.96	Societe Bombard SARL	Meursanges, France	10.10.02A
G-SCTA	Westland Scout AH.1	F.9701	XV126	18.12.95	G.R.Harrison *(As "XV126/X" in AAC c/s)*	(Guildford)	3. 7.02P
G-SCUB	Piper PA-18-135 Super Cub (L-21B-PI) *(Frame No.18-3849)*	18-3847	PH-GAX R.Neth AF R-157/54-2447	13.12.78	N.D. & Mrs.C.L.Needham t/a N.D.Needham (Farms) *(As "54-2447" in US Army c/s)*	Old Manor Farm, Anwick	23. 8.03
G-SCUD	Montgomerie-Bensen B.8MR	PFA G/101-1294		18. 8.97	D.Taylor	Belper	
G-SCUL	Rutan Cozy	PFA 159-13212		28. 5.98	K.R.W.Scull	(Usk)	
G-SCUR	Eurocopter EC 120B	1090		1. 3.00	JS Aviation Ltd	Luton	18..5.03T
G-SDCI	Bell 206B JetRanger II	925	G-GHCL G-SHVV/N72GM/N83106	24. 2.00	S.D.Coomes	(Auldhouse, East Kilbride)	3. 6.02T
G-SDEV	de Havilland DH.104 Sea Devon C.20	04472	XK895	29. 3.90	Wyndeham Press Group plc *(As "XK895/CU19" in 771 Sqn RN c/s)*	Kemble	17. 9.01
G-SDLW	Cameron O-105 HAFB	2460		11. 3.91	P.J.Smart	Bath	15 .5.99a
G-SEAI	Cessna U206G Stationair 6	U20604059	N756FQ	20. 3.92	Aerofloat Ltd	Prestwick/Belfast	8. 3.03T
G-SEAT	Colt 42A HAFB	817		28. 5.86	Virgin Airship & Balloon Co Ltd *"Virgin Atlantic"*	Telford	7. 4.95A
G-SEED	Piper J-3C-90 Cub (L-4H-PI) *(Frame No.10932)* *(Official identity is c/n 12499/44-80203 & probably rebuilt 1945)*	11098	EI-BAP F-BFBZ/44-80203/43-29807	28. 1.80	J.H.Seed	Black Spring Farm, Castle Bytham	20. 3.02P
G-SEEK	Cessna T210N Turbo-Centurion II	21064579	N9721Y	14.10.83	A.Hopper	Little Shelford	15. 2.02
G-SEGA*	Cameron Sonic 90SS HAFB *(Sonic The Hedgehog shape)*	2896		16. 9.92	Balloon Preservation Group "Sonic" *(Cancelled 26.6.00 as WFU)*	Kirdford	29. 6.00A
G-SEJW	Piper PA-28-161 Cherokee Warrior II	28-7816469	N9557N	19. 4.78	Keen Leasing Ltd	Belfast	26. 4.03T

G-SELF	Europa Aviation Europa PFA 247-12996			10. 8.01	N.D.Crisp, A.H.Lames & E.J.Hatcher	(Leigh-on-Sea)	
G-SELL	Robin DR.400/180 Regent	1153	D-EEMT	7. 3.85	C.Morris t/a G-SELL Regent Group	Bidford	10. 4.03
G-SELY	Agusta-Bell 206B-3 JetRanger III	8740		26. 7.96	GR8 Developments Ltd *(Op G Riddel)*	Glenrothes	15. 9.02T
G-SEMI	Piper PA-44-180 Seminole	44-7995052	G-DENW N21439	23. 2.99	T.Hiscox	Wolverhampton	22.12.02T
G-SENA	Rutan LongEz	1325	F-PZSQ F-WZSQ	11.11.96	G.Bennett	(Great Yarmouth)	
G-SEND	Colt 90A HAFB	2100		2.12.91	B.Nigrowsky	Bouzille, France	21. 1.02T
G-SENX	Piper PA-34-200T Seneca II	34-7870356	G-DARE G-WOTS/G-SEVL/N36742	15. 5.95	Katotech Ltd	Cardiff	2. 7.04T
G-SEPA	Eurocopter AS 355N Twin Squirrel	5525	G-METD G-BUJF/F-WYMF	25. 7.96	Metropolitan Police Authority	Fairoaks/Lippitts Hill, Loughton	4. 8.02T
G-SEPB	Eurocopter AS 355N Twin Squirrel	5574	G-BVSE	1. 2.95	Metropolitan Police Authority	Fairoaks/Lippitts Hill, Loughton	1. 3.04T
G-SEPC	Eurocopter AS 355N Twin Squirrel	5596	G-BWGV	29.11.95	Metropolitan Police Authority	Fairoaks/Lippitts Hill, Loughton	20. 3.02T
G-SEPT	Cameron N-105 HAFB	1880		22.11.88	P.Gooch *"Septodont"*	Alresford	5. 5.02A
G-SERA	Enstrom F-28A-UK	103	G-BAHU EI-BDF/G-BAHU	14. 3.91	W.R.Pitcher t/a Enstrom Associates	Leatherhead	1. 5.03T
G-SERL	SOCATA TB-10 Tobago	109	G-LANA EI-BIH	28. 5.92	R.J.Searle	Rochester	19. 4.03
G-SETI	Cameron Sky 80-16 HAFB	4853		25. 9.00	R.P.Allan	Chinnor	28..9.01A
G-SEUK*	Cameron TV 80SS HAFB *(Samsung Computer shape)*	3810		12. 4.96	Balloon Preservation Group *"Samsung" (Cancelled 31.1.02 as wfu)*	Kirdford	24. 3.00A
G-SEVA	Replica Plans SE.5A PFA 020-10955 (Continental C90)			19. 6.85	I.D.Gregory *(As "F-141/G" in 141 Sqn RFC c/s)*	Boscombe Down	20.12.01P
G-SEVE	Cessna 172N Skyhawk II	17269970	N738GR	10. 1.90	MK Aero Support Ltd	Andrewsfield	28. 1.02T
G-SEVN	Van's RV-7 PFA 323-13795			13. 9.01	N.Reddish	(Kirkby-in-Ashfield)	
G-SEWP	Aérospatiale AS355F2 Twin Squirrel	5480	G-OFIN G-DANS/G-BTNM	14. 8.00	Veritair Ltd	Cardiff Heliport	14. 6.02T
G-SEXI	Cessna 172M Skyhawk II	17263806	N1964V	21. 4.92	Willowair Flying Club (1996) Ltd	Southend	5. 9.04T
G-SEXY*	American American AA-1 Yankee *(Regd incorrectly as c/n 0042)*	AA1-0442	G-AYLM	30. 6.81	Not known *(Damaged landing Burscough, Lancs 11.2.94: stored 1.01)*	Liverpool	17. 3.95
G-SFBH	Boeing 737-46N	28723		28. 5.97	British Midland Airways Ltd	East Midlands	5. 6.03T
G-SFHR	Piper PA-23-250 Aztec F	27-8054041	G-BHSO N2527Z	24. 6.82	Comed Aviation Ltd	Blackpool	22.11.01T
G-SFOX	Rotorway Executive 90 (Rotorway RI 162)	5059	G-BUAH	11.10.93	Magpie Computer Services Ltd	Crabtree Farm, Crowborough	29.10.02P
G-SFPA	Reims Cessna F406 Caravan II	F406-0064		11.11.91	Sec of State for Scotland/Dept of Agriculture & Fisheries *(Op Direct Flight for Fisheries Protection Agency)*	Prestwick	12. 3.03T
G-SFPB	Reims Cessna F406 Caravan II	F406-0065		11.11.91	Sec of State for Scotland/Dept of Agriculture & Fisheries *(Op Direct Flight for Fisheries Protection Agency)*	Prestwick	26. 4.03T
G-SFRY	Thunder Ax7-77 HAFB	1667		23. 1.90	K.J.Baxter & P.Szczepanski	Birmingham	6. 2.02A
G-SFTA*	Westland SA.341G Gazelle 1	1039	"G-BAGJ" G-SFTA/HB-XIL/G-BAGJ/(XW858)	10. 9.82	North East Aircraft Museum	Sunderland	24. 2.86
	(Crashed near Alston, Cumbria 7.3.84: cancelled 21.5.86 as WFU: rebuilt to static condition in Army c/s)						
G-SFTZ	Slingsby T.67M-160 Firefly	2000		7. 2.83	Western Air (Thruxton) Ltd	Thruxton	24. 1.02T
G-SGAS*	Colt 77A HAFB	2073		31.10.91	SGL Ltd t/a Shellgas South West Area *"Shell Gas"* *(Cancelled 9.11.01 by CAA: stored)*	Barton	26. 4.01A
G-SGSE	Piper PA-28-181 Archer II	28-7890332	G-BOJX N3774M	2.12.96	Mountune Racing Ltd *(Op Southend School of Flying)*	Andrewsfield	12. 9.03
G-SHAA	Enstrom 280-UK Shark	1011	N280Q	8. 7.88	C.J.& D.Whitehead t/a ELT Radio Telephones	(Burnley)	17.11.01T
G-SHAH	Reims Cessna F152 II	F15201839	OH-IHA SE-IHA	7. 2.97	E.Alexander	Andrewsfield	17. 5.03T
G-SHAM	Beechcraft C90 King Air	LJ-819	N2063A	12. 4.99	Aerospeed Ltd	Southend	3. 7.02T
G-SHAY	Piper PA-28R-201T Turbo Arrow III	28R-7703365	G-JEFS G-BFDG/N47381	17. 9.01	R.J.Shay	Andrewsfield	2.10.04
G-SHCB	Schweizer Hughes 269C-1	0038	N41S	28. 6.96	Oxford Aviation Services Ltd	Oxford	7.10.02T
G-SHED	Piper PA-28-181 Cherokee Archer II	28-7890068	G-BRAU N47411	12. 6.89	R B Kay	Gloucestershire	16. 8.04
G-SHEP	SOCATA TB-20 Trindad GT	2061	F-OILU F-WWRB	16. 7.01	L.W.Shepherd	(Heathfield)	31. 7.04T
G-SHIM	CFM Streak Shadow (Rotax 582) K.228-SA & PFA 206-12501			19. 5.93	K.R.Anderson	Shobdon	25. 8.01P

G-SHIP*	Piper PA-23-250 Aztec F	27-7654015	N62490	18. 1.77	Not known	Hockley Heath, Solihull	1. 7.85T
	(Crashed Keystone 4.12.83: cancelled 13.2.89 as WFU: in "Paint-Ball" woodland 11.92: current status unknown)						
G-SHIV	Gulfstream GA-7 Cougar	GA7-0092	N713G	22.11.84	Westley Aircraft Ltd	Cranfield	18. 1.98T
G-SHNN	Enstrom 280C Shark	1119	N51685	22. 5.89	W.R.Pitcher	(Leatherhead)	10. 1.04T
G-SHOG	Colomban MC-15 Cri-Cri	001	G-PFAB	3.10.96	V.S.E.Norman	Rendcomb	24. 6.02P
	(JPX PUL-212)		F-PYPU		*(Mitsubishi Shogun titles - see SECTION 9, Part 2)*		
G-SHOT*	Cameron V-77 HAFB	972		14.12.83	E.C.Moore *"Buckshot"*	Great Missenden	20. 5.97A
					(Cancelled 25.9.01 as wfu)		
G-SHOW*	Morane-Saulnier MS.733 Alcyon	125	F-BMQJ	1.10.80	Not known	NK	24. 5.83P
			Fr.AF 125/MZ				
	(Sold to US buyer at Duxford auction in 4.83 but never delivered: cancelled 4.12.84 by CAA: current status unknown)						
G-SHPP	Hughes 269A (TH-55A)	36-0481	N80559	24. 7.89	R.P.Bateman	White Waltham	15.12.02T
			64-18169				
G-SHRK	Enstrom 280C-UK Shark	1173	N373SA	6. 1.97	D.R.Kenyon t/a Aviation Bureau	Redhill	26. 9.02T
			G-SHRK/G-BGMX/EI-CCS/G-SHXX/G-BGMX/EI-BHR/G-BGMX/(F-GBOS)				
G-SHSH	Europa Aviation Europa	PFA 247-12722		7. 4.98	D.G.Hillam	(Birkenhead)	
G-SHSP	Cessna 172S	172S8079	N6535P	25. 3.99	Shropshire Aero Club Ltd	Sleap	25. 3.02T
			N9552Q				
G-SHSS	Enstrom 280C-UK Shark	1060	N6892X	11.10.89	R.J.Patten	Enniskillen, Co.Fermanagh	11.11.03T
			G-SHSS/EI-CHG/G-SHSS/G-BENO t/a St Angelo Helicopters				
G-SHUF	Mainair Blade	1241-0200-7-W1034		10. 3.00	J.A.Shufflebotham	Macclesfield	24. 3.02P
G-SHUG	Piper PA-28R-201T Turbo Cherokee Arrow III	28R-7703048	N1026Q	17. 5.88	Nicola E.Rennie	Booker	10. 7.03T
G-SHUU	Enstrom 280C-UK-2 Shark	1221	G-OMCP	16.10.89	D.Ellis	Hawarden	23. 6.01
			G-KENY/G-BJFG/N8617N				
G-SIAI	SIAI-Marchetti SF.260W	361/31-005	F-GVAB(2)	15. 1.01	D Gage	Booker	20. 3.02P
			OO-XCP/FAB-184		*(As "FA Boliviana FAB-184" 7.00)*		
G-SIAL	Hawker Hunter F.58	41H-697457	J-4090	2.10.95	Classic Aviation Ltd	Duxford	21. 3.01P
					(Op The Old flying Machine Co as "J4090")		
G-SIAM	Cameron V-90 HAFB	4096	G-BXBS	7. 3.01	D Tuck *"Warners"*	London NW1	6. 4.02A
G-SIGN	Piper PA-39 Twin Comanche C/R	39-8	OY-TOO	9. 2.78	D.Buttle	Blackbushe	20. 1.03
			N8853Y				
G-SIIA	Aerotek Pitts S-2A	2127	D-ECKC	14.11.01	B.Brown	Breighton	9.12.04
			N8073				
G-SIIB	Aviat Pitts S-2B Special	5218	G-BUVY	24. 3.93	G.Ferriman	Felthorpe	30. 4.02
	(Lyc AEIO-540)		N6073U				
G-SIIC	Aviat Pitts S-2C	6021	N16JV	7. 4.00	Technoforce Ltd	Biggin Hill	26. 4.03
					(Goldair titles)		
G-SIII	Extra EA.300	058	D-ETYE	10. 1.95	Callmast Ltd	Hawarden	1. 8.03T
G-SIJW	Scottish Aviation.Bulldog Srs.120/121	BH120/295	XX630	31. 3.00	M.Miles	(Milton Keynes)	2..9.04
					(As "XX630/5")		
G-SILS	Pietenpol Air Camper	PFA 047-13331		29. 6.98	D.Silsbury	Ivybridge	
G-SIMI	Cameron A-315 HAFB	3391		10. 3.95	Balloon School (International) Ltd		
					t/a Balloon Safaris	Petworth	23. 7.02T
G-SIMN	Robinson R22 Beta-II	2769		10.12.97	Flight Training Ltd	Coventry	18. 1.04T
G-SIMP	Jabiru Jabiru SP	PFA 274B-13794		4. 1.02	J C Simpson	(Pulborough)	
G-SION	Piper PA-38-112 Tomahawk II	38-81A0146	N23661	30. 1.91	F.N.Dunstan	Hinton-in-the-Hedges	28.12.00T
					t/a Naiad Air Services *(Op Avon Flying School)*		
G-SIPA	SIPA 903	63	G-BGBM	31. 5.83	G.K.Brothwood & P.R.Tonks	Liverpool	14. 2.89P
			F-BGBM		t/a Mersey SIPA Group		
G-SIRR	North American P-51D-25NA Mustang	122-39798	N51RR	3. 2.97	D.J.Gilmour	Duxford	10. 6.02P
			(N151MC)/TNI-AU F-3../44-73339 t/a Intrepid Aviation Co				
					(As "474008/VF-R" in 4th FG/1336th FS USAAF c/s)		
	(Adopted identity of c/n 122-40548/44-74008/RCAF 9274/N8676E/N76AF/(N151MC) during 1982-84 rebuild)						
G-SIRS	Cessna 560XL Citation Excel	560-5185	N51042	1. 8.01	Amsail Ltd	Stansted	1. 8.04T
G-SITA	Pegasus Quantum 15-912	7797		18. 6.01	A.R.Oliver	Dunkeswell	17. 6.02P
G-SIVC	Agusta A109E Power	11115		10. 5.01	Mandarin Aviation Ltd	Redhill	14. 5.04T
G-SIVX	Robinson R22 Beta	3241		23. 7.01	Mandarin Aviation Ltd	Redhill	30. 7.04T
G-SIXC	Douglas DC-6A/B	45550	N93459	20. 3.87	Atlantic Air Transport Ltd	Coventry	4. 4.02T
			N90645/B-1006/XW-PFZ/B-1006				
G-SIXD	Piper PA-32-300 Cherokee Six D	32-7140007	HB-OMH	25. 3.98	M.B.Payne & I.Gordon		
			N8615N			King's Farm, Thurrock	9.10.04
G-SIXX	Colt 77A HAFB	1327		21.10.88	M.Dear & M.Taylor	Marlow	19. 5.02A
G-SIXY	Van's RV-6	PFA 181-13368		9. 3.99	C.J.Hall & C.R.P.Hamlett	(Cambridge)	
G-SJCH	Pilatus Britten-Norman BN-2T-4S Islander	4006	G-BWPK	18.11.99	Hampshire Police Authority	Lee-on-Solent	26. 2.02T
					"Sir John Charles Hoddinott"		
G-SJDI	Robinson R44 Astro	0626		16. 7.99	R.Kibble	(Burntwood)	2. 8.00T
G-SJKR	Lindstrand LBL 90A HAFB	756		26..1.01	S J Roake	(Camberley)	12. 3.02A
G-SJMC	Boeing 767-31KER	27205	N6038E	16. 3.94	Airtours International Airways Ltd		
						Manchester	15. 3.03T
G-SKAN	Reims Cessna F172M Skyhawk II	F17201120	G-BFKT	8. 7.85	Bustard Flying Club Ltd	Boscombe Down	5. 4.04T
			F-BVBJ				
G-SKCI	Rutan VariEze	PFA 074-12081		30. 3.01	S.K.Cockburn *(Noted 3.01)*	Southend	

G-SKID	Lake LA-4-200 Buccaneer	680	G-BMGY	4.11.99	D.J.Lindsey Wood	Bournemouth	20. 9.03T
			N39RG/G-BWKS/G-BDDI/N1087L				
G-SKIE	Steen Skybolt	AACA/357	ZK-DEN	29. 8.97	S.Gray	Redhill	12. 9.02P
G-SKIL	Cameron N-77 HAFB	2264		19. 3.90	S.P.Johnston *"Skillball"*	Longfield	30. 4.01T
G-SKOT	Cameron V-42 HAFB	4813		27. 6.00	A.A.Laing	Aberdeen	8. 9.02A
G-SKYC	Slingsby T.67M Firefly	2009	G-BLDP	13. 6.97	T.W.Cassells	Bagby	7.10.02T
G-SKYD	Christen Pitts S-2B Special	5057	N5331N	15.10.92	S.D.Harris	Redhill	6. 3.02
	(Lycoming AEIO-540)				t/a G-SKYD Syndicate		
G-SKYE	Cessna TU206G Turbo Stationair 6 II		(G-DROP)	1. 8.79	P.M.Hall	RAF Weston-on-the-Green	5. 7.04
		U20604568	N9783M		t/a RAF Sport Parachute Association		
G-SKYF	SOCATA TB-10 Tobago	1589	VH-YHG	1. 5.01	Air Touring Ltd	Goodwood	24. 5.04T
G-SKYG	III Sky Arrow 650 TC	C008		15.12.98	G.F.Smith	(Milton Keynes)	13. 1.02
G-SKYH*	Cessna 172N Skyhawk 100	17268098	A6-GRM	20. 2.79	Not known	Abbeyshrule, Co.Longford	9. 8.91T
			N76034				
	(Crashed Connaught, Co.Cork 21.7.91: cancelled 6.2.92 by CAA: stored 4.96: current status unknown)						
G-SKYK	Cameron A-275 HAFB	4879		31. 7.00	Cameron Flights Southern Ltd	Pewsey	17. 7.02T
G-SKYL	Cessna 182S Skylane	18280176	N4104D	19. 6.98	Skylane Aviation Ltd	Sherburn-in-Elmet	12. 6.04
G-SKYO	Slingsby T.67M-200 Firefly	2264		20. 9.00	T.W.Cassells	Bagby	28. 9.03T
G-SKYR	Cameron A-180 HAFB	2826		31. 3.92	Cameron Flights Southern Ltd	Pewsey	29. 4.00T
					"Candy Floss"		
G-SKYT	III Sky Arrow 650TC	C.004		6. 9.96	I.R.Malby	Thruxton	7. 3.03
	(Rotax 912)						
G-SKYU	Cameron A-210 HAFB	10129		28. 8.01	PSH Skypower Ltd	Pewsey	27. 8.02T
G-SKYX	Cameron A-210 HAFB	4613		22. 6.99	PSH Skypower Ltd	Pewsey	5. 6.02T
					(Whitely Village titles)		
G-SKYY	Cameron A-250 HAFB	3402		9. 3.95	Cameron Flights Southern Ltd	Pewsey	9. 3.01T
					"City of Southampton"		
G-SLCE	Cameron C-80 HAFB	4022		24. 2.97	Z.Bayat	Bristol	9.11.01T
G-SLEA	Mudry/CAARP CAP.10B	124		19.12.80	P.D.Southerington	Cranwell North	28. 6.03
G-SLII	Cameron O-90 HAFB	2388		20. 9.90	R.B. & A.M.Harris *"Mad Dash"*	Huntingdon	17. 8.01A
G-SLOW	Pietenpol Aircamper	PFA 047-13488		8.10.99	C.Newton	(Brackley)	
G-SLTN	SOCATA TB-20 Trinidad	763	HB-KBR	6. 8.99	S.N.Adamson	Biggin Hill	15. 9.02T
G-SLYN	Piper PA-28-161 Warrior II		N161WA	12. 4.89	G.E.Layton	Dunkeswell	31. 5.04
		28-8116204	N8373K				
G-SMAF	Sikorsky S-76A	760149	N130TL	6. 9.88	Air Harrods Ltd	Stansted	3.10.02T
			N5425U				
G-SMAN	Airbus A330-243	261	F-WWKR	26. 3.99	Monarch Airlines Ltd	Luton	25. 3.02T
G-SMBM	Pegasus Quantum 15-912	7602		24. 1.00	B.J.Mould	(Oswestry)	3. 2.02P
G-SMDB	Boeing 737-36N	28557		15. 3.97	British Midland Airways Ltd		
						East Midlands	20. 3.03T
G-SMDH	Europa Aviation Europa XS			8.10.98	S.W.Pitt	(Petersfield)	
		PFA 247-13367					
G-SMDJ	Eurocopter AS 350B2 Ecureuil	3187		21. 4.99	Denis Ferranti Hoverknights Ltd	(Bangor)	12. 8.02
G-SMIG	Cameron O-65 HAFB	922		6. 6.83	R D Parry *(New owner 12.01)*	Stroud	28. 7.87A
G-SMJH	Robinson R44 Astro	0024	G-NTEE	22.11.01	M.J.Hayward	Sywell	4. 5.03T
G-SMJJ	Cessna 414A Chancellor II	414A0425	N2694H	24. 3.81	Gull Air Ltd	Guernsey	31. 5.03
G-SMTC	Colt Flying Hut SS HAFB	1828		7. 1.91	Shiplake Investments Ltd	(Switzerland)	18.11.00A
G-SMTH	Piper PA-28-140 Cherokee C	28-26916	G-AYJS	28. 9.90	Rangecycle Ltd	Kemble	14. 1.02
			N11C		t/a Masonair		
G-SNAK	Lindstrand LBL-105A HAFB	404		23. 9.96	Ballooning Adventures Ltd	Hexham	30. 5.02T
G-SNAP	Cameron V-77 HAFB	1217		29.11.85	C.J.S.Limon *"Snapshot"*	Great Missenden	26. 6.97A
G-SNAZ	Enstrom F-28F	761	G-BRCP	31.10.94	Thornhill Aviation Ltd	Barton	5. 1.02T
G-SNEV	CFM Streak Shadow SA			17. 9.96	N.G.Smart	(Feltham)	23. 2.02P
	(Rotax 582) K.283 & PFA 206-13042						
G-SNOW	Cameron V-77 HAFB	541	(G-BGWA)	21. 6.79	M.J.Ball	Clitheroe	9. 6.01A
	(Fitted with replacement envelope 1989 - c/n 2050 which was the original G-BSDX)						
G-SNUZ	Piper PA-28-161 Warrior II		G-PSFT	19.12.01	J.C.O.& C.A.Adams	(Walton-on-Thames)	6.11.03T
		28-8416021	G-BPDS/N4328P				
G-SOAR	Eiri PIK-20E	20214		21. 6.79	F.W.Fay *"AR"*	Bidford	7. 6.02
G-SOAY	Cessna T303 Crusader	T30300060	OH-AIL	5. 9.00	Bulldog Aviation Ltd	Jersey	18.10.03
			EC-ETD/N1426C				
G-SOBI	Piper PA-28-181 Archer II	28-7690212	D-EAQL	3. 5.00	Alliance Aerolink Ltd	Biggin Hill	8. 8.03T
			N9542N				
G-SOEI	Hawker Siddeley HS.748 Srs.2A/242		ZK-DES	25. 2.98	Emerald Airways Ltd	Liverpool	17. 4.04T
		1689			*(Securicor Omega Express titles)*		
G-SOFA*	Cameron N-65 HAFB	968		30. 8.83	M.J.Axtell	Todmorden	10. 6.90A
					(Cancelled 25.10.01 by CAA)		
G-SOFT	Thunder Ax7-77 HAFB	1339		5.12.88	A.J.Bowen	Edinburgh	11. 9.99A
					"Enterprise Software"		
G-SOHI	Agusta A109E Power	11045		23. 4.99	Tri-Ventures Group Ltd	Elstree	28. 4.02T
G-SOKO	Soko P-2 Kraguj	003	G-BRXK	6. 1.94	J A Keen	Liverpool	22. 2.02P
			Yugoslav Army 30149				
G-SOLA	Star-Lite SL-1 203TG & PFA 175-11311			9. 6.88	J.P.Roberts-Lethaby	(Lynton)	31. 3.93P
	(Rotax 447)				*"A Star Is Born" (Stored 6.93: current status unknown)*		

G-SOLD	Robinson R22 Alpha	0471	N8559X	16. 5.85	J.F.H.James	Banbury	15. 6.03
G-SOLH	Bell 47G-5	2639	G-AZMB	5. 3.97	Sol Helicopters Ltd	Elstree	9. 3.03T
			CF-NJW				
G-SOLO	Anvil-Pitts S-2S Special	AA/1/1980		30. 5.80	Landitfast Ltd	Denham	6. 4.96P
	(Lycoming AEIO-540)				*(Current status unknown)*		
G-SONA	SOCATA TB-10 Tobago	151	G-BIBI	24.10.80	M.Kelly	Sherburn-in-Elmet	17. 5.02
G-SONY	Aero Commander 200D	358	G-BGPS	24.11.88	General Airline Ltd	(Blackbushe)	29. 7.01
			5Y-AFT/N2985T		t/a European Flyers *(Ceased trading 10.01)*		
G-SOOC	Hughes 369HS (500C)	111-0354S	G-BRRX	6.10.93	J.Rawding	(Lincoln)	14.10.02
			N9083F		t/a Helicopter Experience		
G-SOOE	Hughes 369E (500E)	0227E		27. 4.87	R.W.Nash	Rochester	26. 5.02
G-SOOS	Colt 21A Cloudhopper HAFB	1263		7. 6.88	P.J.Stapley	Redcar	25. 3.95A
G-SOOT	Piper PA-28-180 Cherokee C	28-4033	G-AVNM	19. 8.88	J.A.Bridger	Exeter	22. 8.04T
			N11C				
G-SOOZ	Rans S-6-ES Coyote II	PFA 204-13543		27. 4.01	A.Batters	(Ilkley)	29. 7.02P
G-SOPP	Enstrom 280FX	2024	G-OSAB	23.10.97	F.P. & M.Sopp & L.A.Moore		
			N86259			Jefferies Farm, Billingshurst	5.11.04T
G-SORT	Cameron N-90 HAFB	2878		13. 7.92	A.Brown *"Streamline"*	Bristol	4. 8.02A
G-SOUL	Cessna 310R II	310R0140	N5020J	27. 6.88	Atlantic Air Transport Ltd	Coventry	10. 6.04T
G-SOUP*	Cameron C-80 HAFB	3387		24.10.94	M.G.Barlow	(Skipton)	
					(Cancelled 16.10.01 as wfu: possibly not built))		
G-SPAM	Avid Aerobat	829 & PFA 189-12074		9. 5.91	J.Lee	(Full Sutton)	19. 7.02P
G-SPAU	Eurocopter EC 135T1	0142	D-HECF	27. 6.00	Bond Air Services Ltd *(Op Strathclyde Police)*		
						Glasgow City Heliport	22 .8.03T
G-SPDR	de Havilland DH.115 Sea Vampire T.Mk.35		VH-RAN	19. 5.00	M.J.Cobb	Swansea	
		15641	RAN N6-766/XG766		*(Noted 9.99: current status unknown)*		
G-SPEE	Robinson R22 Beta	0939	G-BPJC	20. 7.94	Verve Systems Ltd	Shobdon	21. 9.03T
G-SPEL	Sky 220-24 HAFB	045		26. 7.96	T.G.Church	Blackburn	5.10.01T
					t/a Pendle Balloon Co		
G-SPEY	Agusta-Bell 206B-3 JetRanger III		G-BIGO	1. 4.81	Castle Air Charters Ltd	Liskeard	13. 5.02T
		8608					
G-SPFX	Rutan Cozy	PFA 159-13113		30. 4.97	B.D.Tutty	(Gillingham, Kent)	
G-SPIN	Aerotek Pitts S-2A Special	2110	N5CQ	13. 3.80	N.M.R.Richards	(London W1)	22. 4.02T
	(Lycoming AEIO-360)						
G-SPIT	Supermarine 379 Spitfire FR.XIVe		(G-BGHB)	2. 3.79	Patina Ltd	Duxford	6. 5.02P
		6S/649205	Indian AF T-20/MV293		*(Op The Fighter Collection: as "MV268/JE-J")*		
G-SPOG	San Jodel DR.1050 Ambassadeur	155	G-AXVS	25. 9.95	A.C.Frost	(Ware)	13. 6.77S
			F-BJNL		*(Damaged Stonacre Farm, Bredhurst 17.2.91: on rebuild 1995)*		
G-SPOL	MBB Bö.105DBS-4	S-392	VR-BGV	23. 3.90	Bond Air Services Ltd	Glasgow Heliport	5. 6.02T
					(Op Strathclyde Police)		
G-SPOR	Beechcraft B200 Super King Air		N57TL	3. 9.99	Select Plant Hire Co Ltd	Southend	19 .9.02T
		BB-1557	N57TS		*(Op Platinum Airways)*		
G-SPUR	Cessna 550 Citation II	550-0714	N593EM	27.10.98	Banecorp Ltd	Stansted	15.11.04T
			N12035				
G-SPYI	Bell 206B-3 Jet Ranger III	3689	G-BVRC	9. 5.96	K.H.Bott	Blackpool	29. 6.02T
			G-BSJC/N3175S				
G-SRII	Flying K Enterprises Easy Raider II 503			2. 3.01	Reality Aircraft Ltd	(Amesbury)	14. 8.02P
		BMAA/HB/163					
	(Orig regd as Sky Raider II 503(1) until 8.01) (Trailered to Old Sarum for operation)						
G-SROE	Westland Scout AH.1	F.9508	XP907	26.10.95	Bolenda Engineering Ltd	Ipswich	31.10.01P
					(As "XP907")		
G-SRVO	Cameron N-90 HAFB	3551		10. 4.95	Servo & Electronic Sales Ltd	Lydd	23. 7.02A
					"Connect One"		
G-SSAS	Airbus A320-231	0338	D-AFTI	R	Airtours International Airways Ltd		
			N302ML/N338RX/F-WWIM			Manchester	
G-SSCL	MD Helicopters Hughes 369E (500E)		N684F	25. 4.98	Shaun Stevens Contractors Ltd		
		0491E				(Maidstone)	30. 5.04
G-SSFC	Piper PA-34-200 Seneca	34-7450016	G-BBXG	28. 4.94	Air Consul SL	Seville, Spain	26. 3.04T
			N56647				
G-SSFT	Piper PA-28-161 Warrior II		G-BHIL	16. 7.86	Plane Talking Ltd	Elstree	15. 3.04T
		28-8016069	N80821				
G-SSGS	Europa Aviation Europa	082		25. 1.94	G.Szurovy	Old Sarum	24. 7.02P
	(Rotax 912UL)				*"Fledermaus" (Noted 10.01)*		
G-SSIX	Rans S-6-116 Coyote II *(Tailwheel u/c)*			5. 9.94	T.J.Bax	Henstridge	25. 5.02P
	(Rotax 582)	PFA 204A-12749					
G-SSKY	Pilatus Britten-Norman BN-2B-26 Islander		G-BSWT	11. 5.92	Isles of Scilly Skybus Ltd	St.Just	29. 4.03T
		2247					
G-SSLF	Lindstrand LBL 210A HAFB	649		29. 2.00	A.M.Holly	Berkeley	30. 7.02T
					t/a Exclusive Ballooning		
G-SSPP	Sky Science Powerhawk L70/500	SS001		18. 7.00	Sky Science Powered Parachutes Ltd		
						(Tidworth)	
G-SSSC	Sikorsky S-76C	760408		26.10.93	CHC Scotia Ltd	Aberdeen	13. 1.04T
G-SSSD	Sikorsky S-76C	760415		26.10.93	CHC Scotia Ltd	Humberside	22.12.02T
G-SSSE	Sikorsky S-76C	760417		23.11.93	CHC Scotia Ltd	Humberside	2. 2.03T

G-SSTI	Cameron N-105 HAFB	3238		30. 3.94	British Airways plc *"Concorde"*	Heathrow	17.12.01T
G-SSWA	Short SD.3-30 Var.100	SH.3042	D-CTAG	15.10.99	Streamline Aviation (SW) Ltd	Southend	14.12.02TC
			G-BHHU/OY-MUC/G-BHHU/N181AP/N332MV/G-BHHU/G-14-3042 *(Stored 12.01)*				
G-SSWB	Short SD.3-60 Var.100	SH.3690	C6-BFT	17. 8.00	Freshleave Ltd	Exeter	25. 9.02T
			N690PC/G-BMLE/G-14-3690 *(Op Streamline Aviation)*				
G-SSWC	Short SD.3-60 Var.100	SH.3686	SE-LGE	2.11.00	Streamline Aviation (SW) Ltd	Exeter	14.11.02TC
			G-BMHX/G-14-3686				
G-SSWM	Short SD.3-60 Var.100	SH.3648	SE-KCI	28. 9.01	Freshleave Ltd	Exeter	14.10.02T
			G-OOAS/G-BLIL/OY-MMB/G-BLIL/G-14-3648				
G-SSWO	Short SD.3-60 Var.100	SH.3609	SE-KLO	8.10.01	Streamline Aviation (SW) Ltd	Exeter	4.12.02T
			N343MV/(G-BKMY)/G-14-3609				
G-SSWP	Short SD.3-30 Var.100	SH.3030	CS-DBY	21. 6.00	Freshleave Ltd	Exeter	3. 8.02T
			(5N-OJU)/G-BGNB/N330MV/G-BGNB/G-14-3030				
G-SSWR	Short SD.3-60 Var.100	SH.3670	SE-KGV	2.10.01	Freshleave Ltd	Exeter	13.11.02T
			HR-IAT/N108PS/B-3603/G-BLWJ/G-14-3670				
G-SSWT	Short SD.3-30 Var.100	SH.3095	4X-CSQ	2. 6.98	Freshleave Ltd	Southend	18. 6.01T
			G-BNYA/G-BKSU/G-14-3095 *(Broken up 8.01)*				
G-SSWU*	Short SD.3-30 Var.100	SH.3076	C-FYXF	24. 2.99	Streamline Aviation (SW) Ltd		
			G-BIYH/N181AP/N338MV/G-BIYH/G-14-3076				
						Valley Farm Nurseries, Alton	7. 3.00TC
	(Ground collision with AA-5B Tiger G-BDLR Luton 18.9.99 & declared a write-off: fuselage noted 3.00: cancelled 3.5.00 as destroyed)						
G-SSWV	Sportavia Fournier RF5B Sperber	51032	N55WV	31. 5.90	E.C.Neighbour & J.A.Melville t/a Skylark Flying Group	Camphill	20. 8.02P
G-SSWX	Short SD.3-60 Var.200	SH.3715	N711PM	19.10.99	Streamline Aviation (SW) Ltd	Southend	2.12.02T
			G-BNDL/G-14-3715		*(Stored 12.01)*		
G-STAT	Cessna U206F Stationair II	U20603485	A6-MAM N8732Q	20. 2.79	Wingglider Ltd	Hibaldstow	11. 9.98
G-STAV*	Cameron O-84 HAFB	2913		29. 9.92	F.Horsfall *(Cancelled 21.9.01 by CAA)*	Moreton-in-Marsh	27. 3.00A
G-STAY	Reims Cessna FR172K Hawk XP	FR17200620	D-EOVX OE-DVX	15.12.00	Staywhite UK Ltd	Rochester	20. 2.04
G-STEM	Stemme S-10V	14-027		2. 7.97	Warwickshire Aerocentre Ltd	Husbands Bosworth	26.10.03
G-STEN	Stemme S-10	10-32	D-KGCH	9. 1.92	J P Lyell tr G-STEN Syndicate	(Winchester)	24. 5.04
G-STEP	Schweizer Hughes 269C	S.1494		1.10.90	M.Johnson	Neath	29.10.03T
G-STER	Bell 206B-3 JetRanger III	4116	OO-EGA	23. 3.94	P.J.Brown t/a P.J.Brown Civil Engineer & Haulage Contractors	Redhill	18. 4.03T
G-STEV	CEA Jodel DR-221 Dauphin	61	F-BOZD	9. 3.82	S.W.Talbot	Long Marston	25. 2.02
G-STMP	SNCAN Stampe SV-4A	241	F-BCKB	11. 3.83	A.C.Thorne	(Yelverton)	
					(On overhaul Ivybridge 5.93: current status unknown)		
G-STOK	Cameron Colt 77B HAFB	4791		4. 5.00	Christows Ltd	Bournemouth	27..6.02A
G-STOW	Cameron Wine Box-90 SS HAFB	4420		2.10.98	I.Martin & D.Groombridge t/a Flying Enterprises Partnership *(Stowells of Chelsea titles)*	Bristol	19. 8.99A
G-STOX	Bell 206B JetRanger II	1513	G-BNIR N59615	27. 4.89	Burman Aviation Ltd	Cranfield	7. 6.02T
G-STOY*	Robinson R22 Beta	0700		10.11.87	Burman Aviation Ltd *(Cancelled 4.10.01 by CAA)*	Cranfield	29.11.99T
G-STPI	Cameron A-250 HAFB	4102		26. 2.97	A.D.Pinner *(Central Auto Supplies titles)*	Northampton	27. 7.02T
G-STRG	Cyclone AX2000 (HKS 700E)	7837		24. 7.01	D.Young t/a Pegasus Flight Training (Cotswolds)	Kemble	23. 7.02P
G-STRK	CFM Streak Shadow SA (Rotax 582)	K.143-SA & PFA 161-11762		4. 4.90	E.J.Hadley	(Arch, Switzerland)	17. 7.01P
G-STRM	Cameron N-90 HAFB	3568		3. 7.95	B.G.Jones t/a High Profile Balloons	Devizes	19. 7.02T
G-STUA	Aerotek Pitts S-2A Special (Lycoming AEIO-360)	2164	N13GT	6. 3.91	Rollquick Ltd	White Waltham	21. 3.03T
G-STUB	Christen Pitts S-2B Special (Lycoming AEIO-540)	5163	N260Y	5. 5.94	P.A.Greenhalgh	Manston	13. 8.03
G-STWO	ARV1 Super 2 (Hewland AE75)	002 & PFA 152-11048		24. 4.85	G.E.Morris	Dunkeswell	24. 9.01P
G-STYL	Pitts S-1S Special (Lycoming-O-320)	GJSN-1P	N665JG	26. 1.88	C.A.Wills	(Ely)	19. 6.02P
G-SUCH	Cameron N-77 HAFB *(Orig regd as V-77)*	676	G-BIGD	3. 9.01	D.G.Such	Redditch	4. 1.84A
G-SUEB	Piper PA-28-181 Archer III	2843466	N5330M	18. 7.01	GYTO Ltd	(Bury St.Edmunds)	18. 7.04T
G-SUEE	Airbus A320-231	0363	G-IEAG F-WWBX	23. 9.93	Airtours International Airways Ltd	Manchester	18. 3.03T
G-SUEZ	Agusta-Bell 206B JetRanger II	8319	SU-YAE YU-HAZ	16. 9.98	Aerospeed Ltd	Manston	16. 5.02T
G-SUFF	Eurocopter EC 135T1	0118		1. 2.00	Suffolk Constabulary Air Support Unit	Beccles	23. 8.03T

G-SUKI	Piper PA-38-112 Tomahawk	38-79A0260	G-BPNV	22. 5.91	Western Air (Thruxton) Ltd	Thruxton	20. 5.02T
			N2313D				
G-SULL*	Piper PA-32R-301 Saratoga SP		N82818	19. 6.86	Home Office Fire & Emergency Training Centre		
		32R-8113002				Moreton-in-Marsh	27. 7.95T
			(Crashed Crowfield 1.2.95: cancelled 17.5.95 as WFU: in Fire Service use 8.98)				
G-SUMT	Robinson R22 Beta	2147	G-BUKD	24. 9.92	EK Aviation Ltd	(Bury St.Edmunds)	23. 9.04T
			N23381				
G-SUMX	Robinson R22 Beta	3274		1.11.01	Frankham Brothers Ltd	Leicester	28.11.04
G-SUNY*	Robinson R44 Astro	0540		8.12.98	PS Helicopter Ltd	Denham	13.12.01T
					(Cancelled 19.4.01 by CAA)		
G-SUPA	Piper PA-18-150 Super Cub	18-5395	PH-BAJ	13.12.78	D.Sutton	(Maidstone)	2.12.04
	(Frame No.18-5512)		PH-MBF/ALAT 18-5395/N10F		t/a G-SUPA Owners Group		
G-SURG	Piper PA-30 Twin Comanche B	30-1424	G-VIST	18. 6.90	A.R.Taylor	Turweston	20. 1.02T
			G-AVHZ/N8287Y				
G-SURV	Pilatus Britten-Norman BN-2T-4S Defender 4000			14. 4.94	Atlantic Air Transport Ltd	Coventry	7. 7.02T
		4005	G-BVHZ				
G-SUSI	Cameron V-77 HAFB	1133		22. 7.85	J.H.Dyden *"Susi"*	Okehampton	10. 8.02A
G-SUSX	MD Helicopters Explorer	900-00065	N3065W	19. 1.00	Sussex Police Authority	Shoreham	18. 2.04T
G-SUSY	North American P-51D-25NA Mustang		N12066	23. 7.87	P.J.Morgan *"Susy"*	Sywell	20. 5.01P
		122-39232	FAN GN120/44-72773		*(As "472773/AJ-C" in 354th FG USAF c/s)*		
G-SUTN	III Sky Arrow 650TC	C007		27. 8.98	G.C.Sutton	Headcorn	4.11.04
G-SUZI	Beechcraft 95-B55 Baron	TC-1574	G-BAXR	11. 3.84	Bebecar (UK) Ltd	Elstree	25. 7.04
G-SUZN	Piper PA-28-161 Warrior II		N3573C	16. 1.91	E.Reed	Teesside	29. 3.03T
		28-8016187	N9540N		t/a The St.George Flying Club		
G-SUZY	Taylor JT.1 Monoplane	PFA 055-10395		1.12.78	N.C.Stone	Brunton	24. 9.02P
	(VW 1600)						
G-SVBF	Cameron A-180 HAFB	3587		2. 6.95	Virgin Balloon Flights Ltd	London SE16	1. 6.01T
					"Virgin Sierra"		
G-SVEA	Piper PA-28-161 Warrior II		N30299	16.12.98	A.Hastings & E.Lowery	Coventry	15.12.01T
		28-7916082			t/a Avion Aviation		
G-SVIP	Cessna 421B Golden Eagle II	421B0820	G-BNYJ	12. 3.97	Stephenson Marine Co Ltd	Southampton	26.12.03T
			N4686Q/D-IMVB/N1590G				
G-SVIV	SNCAN Stampe SV-4C	475	N65214	7. 8.90	R.Taylor	Vendee Air Park, France	12. 6.02
	(DH Gipsy Major)		F-BDBL				
G-SWEB	Cameron N-90 HAFB	2413		1.10.90	South Western Electricity plc	Bristol	1. 8.01T
					"SWEB"		
G-SWEL	Hughes 369HS	61-0328S	G-RBUT	18. 7.96	M A Crook & A E Wright	Barton	27. 3.03
			C-FTXZ/CF-TXZ				
G-SWIF	Supermarine 552 Swift F.7	VA.9597	XF114	1. 6.90	Heritage Aviation Developments Ltd		
					(Stored 9.98)	Scampton	
G-SWIS*	de Havilland DH.100 Vampire FB.6	658	J-1149	21. 5.91	Bournemouth Aviation Museum	Bournemouth	
	(Built FFW)		*(No CofA issued: cancelled by CAA 3.4.97 as PWFU) (As "J-1149" in Swiss AF c/s)*				
G-SWJW	Airbus A300B4-203	302	OH-LAB	19. 5.98	OY Air Scandic International Aviation AB		
			F-WZMY			Manchester	18. 5.04T
G-SWOT	Phoenix Currie Super Wot	PFA 3011		10. 9.80	D.Watt	Sibson	2. 5.02P
	(Continental O-200-A)				*(As "C3011/S" in SE.5A guise)*		
G-SWPR	Cameron N-56 HAFB	829		16. 3.82	A.Brown *"Post Code"*	Bristol	5. 7.95A
G-SWUN	Pitts S-1M Special	338-H	G-BSXH	18. 4.95	T.G.Lloyd	Little Gransden	5. 9.02P
	(Lycoming O-320)		N14RM				
G-SYCO	Europa Aviation Europa *(Mono-wheel u/c)*			27.11.95	R Oliver	(Colchester)	8. 6.02P
	(NSI EA-81/118)	31 & PFA 247-12540					
G-SYFW	WAR Focke-Wulf 190 rep			28. 2.83	M.R.Parr	Guernsey	29. 6.87P
	(Continental O-200-A)	269 & PFA 081-10584			*(As "WNo.7334/2+1" in Luftwaffe c/s: stored 12.01)*		
G-SYPA	Aérospatiale AS355F2 Twin Squirrel		LV-WHC	25. 9.96	South Yorkshire Police Authority		
		5193	F-WYMS/G-BPRE/N366E			Sheffield City	2. 4.03T

G-TAAA – G-TZZZ

G-TAAL	Cessna 172R Skyhawk	17280733	N9535G	11. 8.99	Eagle Cruise Aviation. Ltd	Booker	6. 9.02T
G-TABS	Embraer EMB.110P1 Bandeirante		G-PBAC	18. 8.98	Skydrift Ltd	Norwich	21.10.02T
		110.212	F-GCLA/F-OGME/F-GCLA/PT-GME				
G-TACE*	Hawker Siddeley HS.125 Srs.403B		G-AYIZ	23. 1.81	British Airways Aircraft Recovery Unit		
		25223	F-BSSL/PJ-SLB/G-AYIZ/G-5-15			Dunsfold	16. 7.86F
					(Cancelled 9.1.90 as WFU: dumped 3.00)		
G-TACK	Grob G-109B	6279		30. 5.84	A.P.Mayne	Exeter	4. 5.02
G-TAFF	CASA I-131E Jungmann	1129	G-BFNE	7. 9.84	A.Horsfall	Breighton	15. 5.02P
			E3B-148				
G-TAFI	Dornier Bücker Bü.133C Jungmeister		N2210	27. 1.93	R.J.Lamplough	North Weald	5. 7.01P
		24	HB-MIF/SwAF U-77				
G-TAGS	Piper PA-28-161 Warrior II		N4329D	6. 5.88	Oxford Aviation Services Ltd	Oxford	12.10.03T
		28-8416026					
G-TAIL	Cessna 150J	15070152	N60220	21. 4.89	L.I.D.Denham-Brown	Blackpool	15. 1.98T
					(New owner 10.01: on rebuild 12.01)		

G-TAIR	Piper PA-34-200T Seneca II	34-7970055	N3059H	17.11.87	D.I.G. & J.de Souza t/a Branksome Dene Garage	Bournemouth	12. 3.03T
G-TAMS	Beech A23-24 Musketeer Super	MA-190	OY-DKF	30. 6.00	Aerograde Ltd	Old Buckenham	23.11.03T
G-TAMR	Cessna 172S Skyhawk	172S8480	N2458J	7. 6.00	C.Durbidge t/a Tamair Leasing	Oxford	11. 7.03T
G-TAMY	Cessna 421B Golden Eagle	421B0512	SE-FNS N2BH/N69865	14.11.77	Malcolm Enamellers (Midlands) Ltd	Wolverhampton	15.11.03
G-TAND	Robinson R44 Astro	0478		12. 6.98	Global Air Charter Ltd	(Ascot)	23.11.03T
G-TANI	Gulfstream GA-7 Cougar	GA7-0107	G-VJAI G-OCAB/G-BICF/N8500H/N29707	18. 5.95	S.Spier	Elstree	15.11.03T
G-TANJ	Raj Hamsa X'Air 582 (5)	629 & BMAA/HB/171		21. 6.01	R.Thorman	(Abernethy)	
G-TANK	Cameron N-90 HAFB	3625		20. 6.95	Hoyers (UK) Ltd *(DFDS/Hoyer titles)*	Huddersfield	30. 3.02A
G-TANS	SOCATA TB-20 Trinidad	1870	F-GRBX	25. 9.98	K.& G.Threfall t/a Tettenhall Leisure	Wolverhampton	30.10.04
G-TAOS	McDonnell Douglas DC-10-10	47832	OY-CNU SE-DHU//N914WA	30. 8.00	Airtours International Airways Ltd	Manchester	21..9.03T
G-TAPE	Piper PA-23-250 Aztec D	27-4054	G-AWVW OY-RPF/G-AWVW/N6799Y	7.10.83	D.J.Hare *(Op Merlix Air)*	Fairoaks	5. 4.03T
G-TARN	Pietenpol Air Camper	PFA 047-13349		3. 8.98	P.J.Heilbron	(Guildford)	
G-TART	Piper PA-28-236 Dakota	28-7911261	N2945C	18.12.90	Prescot Planes Ltd	(Godalming)	18. 6.03T
G-TARV	ARV.1 Super 2	PFA 152-12627		1. 6.94	M.F.Filer	Dunkeswell	29. 5.02P
G-TASH	Cessna 172N	17270531	PH-KOS N739GL	4.11.98	A.Ashpitel	Popham	30.11.04T
G-TASK	Cessna 404 Titan II	404-0829	PH-MPC SE-IHL/N6806Q	10. 3.93	Bravo Aviation Ltd *(Op Department of Transport)*	Coventry	8. 7.03T
G-TATS	Aérospatiale AS350BA Ecureuil	1905	F-GHSN N37AW	14. 5.01	Air Medina Ltd	(London SW1)	7..6.04T
G-TATT	Gardan GY-20 Minicab	PFA 056-10347		30.11.78	P.W.Tattershall t/a Tatt's Group	(Clitheroe)	
G-TATY	Robinson R44 Astro	0627		27. 7.99	W.R.Walker	Denham	2. 8.02T
G-TAXI	Piper PA-23-250 Aztec E	27-7305085	N40270	6. 4.78	M.L.D.Levi & S.Waite t/a SWL Leasing	Blackpool	17.12.04T
G-TAYI	Grob G.115	8008	(D-ENFT) G-TAYI/G-DODO/D-ENFT	12. 9.90	K.P.Widdowson	Sandtoft	8. 2.04
G-TAYS	Reims Cessna F152 II	F15201697	G-LFCA	28.10.91	Tayside Aviation Ltd	Dundee	28. 5.01T
G-TBAG	Murphy Renegade 912 (Rotax 912)	PFA 188-11912		11.12.90	M.R.Tetley	Newton-on-Rawcliffe, Yorks	12.10.02P
G-TBAH	Bell 206B Jet Ranger II	2051	G-OMJB N315JP/N712WG/N712WC/N9989K	10.12.01	Murray Galloway Ltd	(Ascot)	20.11.04T
G-TBBC	Pegasus Quantum 15-912	7583		6.12.99	Big Bamboo Co Ltd	Eshott	8. 5.02P
G-TBEE	Dyn'Aéro MCR-01 Ban-bi	PFA 301-13514		30.11.99	A.D.S.Baker	Shoreham	24.10.01P
G-TBGL	Agusta A109A II	7412	G-VJCB G-BOUA	6. 1.99	Bulford Holdings Ltd	(Jersey)	22. 3.04T
G-TBGT	SOCATA TB-20 Trinidad GT	2027	F-OILF	1.12.00	A J Maitland-Robinson	(Jersey)	7.12.03T
G-TBIC	British Aerospace BAe 146 Srs.200	E2025	N167US N349PS	15. 1.97	Flightline Ltd	Southend	16. 1.03T
G-TBIO	SOCATA TB-10 Tobago	340	F-BNGZ	10. 2.83	Kilo Aviation Ltd	Liverpool	20. 4.02T
G-TBLY	Eurocopter EC 120B	1192	F-WQOV	12. 3.01	A.D.Bly Aircraft Leasing Ltd	(Knebworth)	28. 6.04T
G-TBMW	Murphy Renegade Spirit	PFA 118-11725	(G-MYIG)	20.10.98	S J & M J Spavins	(St Albans)	
G-TBRD	Canadair CL-30 (T-33AN) Silver Star mk.3	T33-261	N33VC G-JETT/G-OAHB/CF-IHB/133261 CAF/21261 RCAF	18.12.96	Golden Apple Operations Ltd.	Duxford	10.10.01P
	(Op The Old Flying Machine Co) (As "21261" in RCAF c/s)						
G-TBXX	SOCATA TB-20 Trinidad	276		16. 3.82	D.A.Phillips & C.S.Swaine	Headcorn	12. 6.03
G-TBZI	SOCATA TB-21 Trinidad TC	871	N21HR	25. 7.96	M D Bond	(Rugby)	14.11.02
G-TBZO	SOCATA TB-20 Trinidad	444		8. 8.84	D.L.Clarke & M.J.M.Hopper	Shoreham	24. 4.03
G-TCAN	Colt 69A HAFB	1996		19. 7.91	H.C.J.Williams *"Toucan"*	Bristol	7. 4.97A
G-TCAP	British Aerospace BAe 125 Srs.800B	258115	G-5-599 104 RSAF/G-5-665/104 RSAF/G-BPGR/G-5-599	24. 4.96	BAE Systems (Operations) Ltd.	Warton	28. 8.03
G-TCDI	Hawker Siddeley HS.125 Srs.F400B	25248	N792A G-5-707/G-SHOP/G-BTUF/G-5-707/D-CFCF	10.10.96	Aravco Ltd	Farnborough	16. 1.03T
G-TCMP*	Robinson R22 Beta	0890		3.11.88	Not known	Thruxton	19. 2.01T
	(Crashed on take-off Thruxton 30.6.00 & severely damaged: cancelled 6.12.00 as wfu) (Wreck stored 5.01)						
G-TCOM	Piper PA-30 Twin Comanche C	30-1967	N555JC N8810Y	29. 1.96	C.A.C.Burrough	Jersey	9. 4.02
G-TCSL*	Rockwell Commander 112A	322	N506CA	17. 9.92	The Works Night Club	(Corby)	7.10.95
	(Damaged on take off from Spanhoe 5.12.94: cancelled 2.3.95 as destroyed: on display 12.95: current status unknown)						
G-TCTC	Piper PA-28RT-201T Turbo Arrow IV *(Built as N9524N [28R-8631006]*	2831001	N9130B	1.12.89	T.Haigh	Wellesbourne Mountford	26. 3.02
G-TCUB	Piper J-3C-65 Cub *(Frame No.13805)*	13970	N90390 N67666/NC67666/Bu.29684/45-55204	31. 7.87	C.Kirk	(Lincoln)	28. 5.04
G-TDFS	IMCO Callair A.9	1200	G-AVZA SE-EUA/N26D	8.10.86	Dollarhigh Ltd t/a TD Flight Services	Sturgate	11.12.00A

G-TDOG	Scottish Aviation Bulldog Srs.120/121	BH120/230	XX538	17. 9.01	G.S Taylor	(Kidderminster)	
G-TDTW	McDonnell Douglas DC-10-10	46983	OY-CNY SE-DHY/N909WA	25.10.00	Airtours International Airways Ltd	Manchester	29.11.03T
G-TEAL	Thurston TSC-1A1 Teal	15	C-GDQD	8.12.92	K.Heeley	Crosland Moor	
					(Damaged Crosland Moor 3.93: on rebuild 4.00)		
G-TEBZ	Piper PA-28R-201 Cherokee Arrow III	28R-7737050	N105CC	7. 1.00	R.W.Tebby	Bristol	7. 6.03T
					t/a S.F.Tebby & Son *(Op Bristol Flying Centre)*		
G-TECC	Aeronca 7AC Champion	7AC-5269	N1704E NC1704E	26. 6.91	G.S.Claybourn	Walton Wood, Doncaster	20.11.02P
G-TECH	Rockwell Commander 114	14074	G-BEDH N4744W	8. 8.85	P.A.Reed	Elstree	7. 8.03
G-TECK	Cameron V-77 HAFB	625		21. 3.86	G.M.N.Spencer *"Spring Fever"*	Watford	5. 8.02A
G-TECM	Tecnam P92-EM Echo	PFA 318-13667		1.12.00	D A Lawrence	(Swindon)	
G-TEDF	Cameron N-90 HAFB	2634		8. 8.91	Fort Vale Engineering Ltd	Nelson	14. 7.02A
G-TEDS	SOCATA TB-10 Tobago	57	G-BHCO	29. 3.83	E.W.Lyon	Wolverhampton	11. 3.02
G-TEDY	Evans VP-1 (VW 1834)	PFA 062-10383	G-BHGN	4.10.90	N.K.Marston	(Harrow)	1. 7.97P
					"The Plank" (Current CofR @ 6.01)		
G-TEEZ	Cameron N-90 HAFB	4005		27.11.96	Fresh Air Ltd	London NW2	13. 3.00T
	(New c/n 1005 allocated after stolen Slapton, Bucks 11.00)						
G-TEFC	Piper PA-28-140 Cherokee F	28-7325088	OY-PRC N15530	18. 6.80	P.M.Havard	Andrewsfield	14. 4.02
G-TEHL	CFM Streak Shadow M (Rotax 503)	185	G-MYJE	20.11.98	A.K. Paterson	Sleaford	13. 8.02P
G-TELY	Agusta A109A II	7326	N1HQ N200SH	10. 3.89	Castle Air Charters Ltd	Liskeard	23. 7.02T
G-TEMP	Piper PA-28-180 Cherokee E	28-5806	G-AYBK N11C	15. 5.89	M.J.Groome t/a Bev Piper Group	Andrewsfield	23. 8.04T
G-TEMT	Hawker Tempest II	420	HA586 (RIAF)/MW763	9.10.89	Tempest Two Ltd	(Hemswell)	
					(On rebuild 11.96: to be "MW763/HF-A" in 183 Sqn c/s)		
G-TENS	HOAC DV20 Katana 100	20148	G-BXBW D-ESHM	28. 2.01	Ewan Ltd	Gloucestershire	18. 6.03T
G-TENT	Auster J/1N Alpha	2058	G-AKJU TW513	1. 2.90	R.C.Callaway-Lewis	Goodwood	26. 8.02
G-TERN	Europa Aviation Europa (NSI EA81/100)	PFA 247-12780		18. 7.97	J.E.G.Lundesjo	White Waltham	25.10.02P
G-TERY	Piper PA-28-181 Archer II	28-7990078	G-BOXZ N22402	13. 1.89	T.Barlow *(Noted 5.01)*	Barton	26. 6.98T
G-TEST	Piper PA-34-200 Seneca	34-7450116	OO-RPW G-BLCD/PH-PLZ/N41409	28. 7.89	Stapleford Flying Club Ltd	Stapleford	23.12.04T
G-TETI	Cameron N-90 HAFB	2877	D-OBMW	9. 2.00	Teti SpA	(Florence, Italy)	
G-TEWS	Piper PA-28-140 Cherokee B	28-25128	G-KEAN G-AWTM/N11C	23. 5.88	M.J.Tew t/a G-TEWS Flying Group	Liverpool	30. 9.04T
G-TFCI	Reims Cessna FA152 Aerobat	FA15200358		25.10.79	Tayside Aviation Ltd	Dundee	21. 6.04T
G-TFOX	Denney Kitfox mk.2 (Rotax 582)	PFA 172-11817		3. 6.91	F.A.Bakir	Barton	25. 9.01P
G-TFRB*	Air Command 532 Elite Sport	0628 & G/04-1167		26. 4.90	Yorkshire Air Museum *(Cancelled 7.6.01 by CAA)*	Elvington	6. 8.98P
G-TFUN	Valentin Taifun 17E	1011	D-KIHP	28.12.83	G.F.Wynn & D.H.Evans t/a North West Taifun Group	Blackpool	10. 5.04
G-TFYN	Piper PA-32RT-300 Lance II	32R-7885128	N5HG D-ELAE/N31740	28. 4.00	Premiair Engineering Ltd *(Premiair titles)*	Shoreham	5. 7.03T
G-TGAS	Cameron O-160 HAFB	1315		12. 8.87	Zebedee Balloon Service Ltd	Hungerford	26. 5.00T
G-TGER	Gulfstream AA-5B Tiger	AA5B-0952	G-BFZP	20. 2.86	P.J.Haldenby	(Maidstone)	5.11.03T
G-TGRA	Agusta A109A	7201	D-HEED N3983N/HB-XNF/I-PATZ	15. 2.01	Tiger Helicopters Ltd	Shobdon	8. 2.04T
G-TGRS	Robinson R22 Beta	1069	G-DELL N80466	5.11.97	Tiger Helicopters Ltd	Shobdon	9. 8.04T
					(Rolled over on landing Duxford 18.11.01 & damaged)		
G-TGRZ	Bell 206B JetRanger II	2288	G-BXZX N27EA/N286CA/N93AT/N16873	15. 6.00	Tiger Helicopters Ltd	Shobdon	21.11.04T
G-THEA	Boeing-Stearman E75 (N2S-5) Kaydet (Lycoming R-680)	75-5736A	(EI-RYR) N1733B/USN Bu.38122	18. 3.81	C.M.Ryan *(As "33" in Navy c/s)*	Weston, Co.of Down	4.11.02
G-THEL	Robinson R44 Astro	0159	G-OCCB G-STMM	2. 9.98	N.Parkhouse	Elstree	3. 5.04T
G-THEO	TEAM mini-MAX 91 (Rotax 447) *(Built up rear fuselage)*	PFA 186-13099		9. 2.99	T.Willford	Blandford Forum	22. 5.02P
G-THLS	MBB Bö.105DBS-4 *(Rebuilt with new pod c/n S.859 1992)*	S.80/859	G-BCXO D-HDCE	20. 2.92	Bond Air Services *(Op Trinity House Lighthouse Service)*	RAF St.Mawgan	27. 2.04T
G-THOM	Thunder Ax6-56 HAFB	366		14. 7.81	T.H.Wilson *"Macavity"*	Diss	19. 2.02A
G-THOS	Thunder Ax7-77 HAFB	769		20. 2.86	C.E.A.Breton	Bristol	14. 3.01A
G-THOT	Jabiru Jabiru SK (Jabiru 2200A)	PFA 274-13159		16. 9.97	D J & S C Reed	Booker	5. 5.02P
G-THRE	Cessna 182S Skylane	18280454	N2391A	6. 5.99	S.J.G.Mole	Wolverhampton	5. 5.02

G-THSL	Piper PA-28R-201 Arrow III	28R-7837278	N36396	11. 9.78	D.M.Markscheffel	Elstree	28. 4.03
G-THUN	Republic P-47D Thunderbolt	-	N47DD	18. 6.99	Patina Ltd *(Op The Fighter Collection) (As "226671/MH-X/LH-X")*	Duxford	7. 7.02P
	(Note 1: Composite re-build from wreck of original N47DD plus new P-47N fuselage identification unknown)						
	(Note 2: "Original" N47DD is c/n 399-55731 ex Peruvian AF 119/Peruvian AF 545/45-49192 and is also exhibited statically at Duxford in the American Air Museum.						
G-THZL	SOCATA TB-20 Trinidad	534	F-GJDR N65TB	9. 5.96	Ewan Ltd	Gloucestershire	1. 8.02T
G-TICH	Taylor JT.2 Titch	PFA 060-3213		12. 2.01	A.J.House, C.J.Wheeler & R.Davitt *(40% complete in 1973! : current status unknown)*	(Reading)	
G-TICL	Airbus A320-231	0169	OY-CNG F-WWIH	10.12.96	Airtours International Airways Ltd	Manchester	11.12.02T
G-TIDS	SAN Jodel 150 Mascaret	44	OO-GAN	15. 4.86	J.B.Dovey	Crowfield	20.11.02P
G-TIGA	de Havilland DH.82A Tiger Moth	83547	G-AOEG T7120	5. 6.85	D.E.Leatherland	Nottingham	20. 8.04T
G-TIGB	Aérospatiale AS332L Super Puma	2023	G-BJXC F-WTNM	31. 3.82	Bristow Helicopters Ltd *"City of Aberdeen"*	Aberdeen	27. 4.04T
G-TIGC	Aérospatiale AS332L Super Puma	2024	G-BJYH F-WTNJ	14. 4.82	Bristow Helicopters Ltd *"Royal Burgh of Montrose"*	Aberdeen	17. 5.02T
G-TIGE	Aérospatiale AS332L Super Puma	2028	G-BJYJ F-WTNM	15. 4.82	Bristow Helicopters Ltd *"City of Dundee"*	Aberdeen	7. 6.04T
G-TIGF	Aérospatiale AS332L Super Puma	2030	F-WKQJ	15. 4.82	Bristow Helicopters Ltd *"Peterhead"*	Aberdeen	27. 6.03T
G-TIGG	Aérospatiale AS332L Super Puma	2032	F-WXFT	15. 4.82	Bristow Helicopters Ltd *"Macduff"*	Aberdeen	1. 8.04T
G-TIGH*	Aérospatiale AS332L Super Puma	2034	F-WXFL	15. 4.82	Bristow Helicopters Ltd *(Damaged 100m NE of Shetland Isles 14.3.92: cancelled 3.8.92 as destroyed) (Instruction use 2001)*	Aberdeen	24. 8.92T
G-TIGI	Aérospatiale AS332L Super Puma	2036	F-WTNP	15. 4.82	Bristow Helicopters Ltd *"Fraserburgh"*	Shenzhen, China	5. 9.02T
G-TIGJ	Aérospatiale AS332L Super Puma	2042	VH-BHT *G-TIGJ*	15. 4.82	Bristow Helicopters Ltd *"Rosehearty"*	Aberdeen	29. 6.02T
G-TIGL	Aérospatiale AS332L Super Puma	2050		15. 4.82	Bristow Helicopters Ltd *"Portsoy"*	Aberdeen	9.12.02T
G-TIGM	Aérospatiale AS332L Super Puma	2045		15. 4.82	Bristow Helicopters Ltd *"Banff"*	Shenzhen, China	1. 8.03T
G-TIGO	Aérospatiale AS332L Super Puma	2061	PP-MIM G-TIGO/F-WMHH	18. 2.83	Bristow Helicopters Ltd. *"Royal Burgh of Arbroath"*	Aberdeen	22. 8.04T
G-TIGP	Aérospatiale AS332L Super Puma	2064		11. 3.83	Bristow Helicopters Ltd *"Carnoustie"*	Shenzhen, China	8. 5.03T
G-TIGR	Aérospatiale AS332L Super Puma	2071	F-WTNW	11. 3.83	Bristow Helicopters Ltd *"Stonehaven"*	Shenzhen, China	19. 5.02T
G-TIGS	Aérospatiale AS332L Super Puma	2086		6. 5.83	Bristow Helicopters Ltd *"Findochty"*	Aberdeen	27. 6.02T
G-TIGT	Aérospatiale AS332L Super Puma	2078		6. 5.83	Bristow Helicopters Ltd *"Portknockie"*	Aberdeen	2. 5.04T
G-TIGV	Aérospatiale AS332L Super Puma	2099	LN-ONC G-TIGV/LN-ONC/G-TIGV/LN-OPF/G-TIGV	12. 1.84	Bristow Helicopters Ltd.	Aberdeen	25. 6.04T
G-TIGZ	Aérospatiale AS332L Super Puma	2115	C-GQKK G-TIGZ	8. 8.84	CHC Scotia Ltd	Aberdeen	14.10.03T
G-TIII	Aerotek Pitts S-2A Special (Lycoming AEIO-360)	2196	G-BGSE N947	27. 2.89	D.G.Cowden	Redhill	14. 7.04
G-TIKO	Hatz CB-1	PFA 143-13396		9. 7.99	K.Robb t/a Tiko Architecture	(Yeovil)	
G-TILE	Robinson R22 Beta	1100		4. 8.89	M.J.Webb & C.R.Woodwiss	Coventry	16. 2.02T
G-TILI	Bell 206B JetRanger II	2061	F-GHFN N7037A/XC-BOQ	6. 3.96	C.I.Threlfall t/a CIM Helicopters	Ream Hill Farm, Weeton, Preston	22. 4.02
G-TIMB	Rutan VariEze (Continental O-200-A)	PFA 074-10795	G-BKXJ	11. 6.85	T.M.Bailey "Kitty"	Shoreham	14. 6.02P
G-TIME	Piper PA-61P Aerostar 601P	61P-0541-230	N8058J	21. 7.78	T & G Engineering Co Ltd	(West Byfleet)	21.12.02
G-TIMG	Beagle Terrier 3	'PFA 00-318'		7. 3.01	T.J.Goodwin	(Manningtree)	
G-TIMK	Piper PA-28-181 Archer II	28-8090214	OO-TRT PH-EAS/OO-HLN/N8142H	25. 8.81	T.Baker	Wolverhampton	5. 6.03
G-TIMM	Folland Gnat T.1	FL.519	8618M XP504	19. 2.92	T.J.Manna t/a Kennet Aviation *(As "XM693")*	Cranfield	23. 2.02P
G-TIMP	Aeronca 7BCM Champion (Continental C85)	7AC-3392	N84681 NC84681	14. 8.92	M G Rumney *"Nancy"*	(Chichester)	5. 8.02P
G-TIMS	Falconar F-12A	PFA 022-12134		1.10.91	T.Sheridan	Wellingborough	
G-TIMW*	Piper PA-28-140 Cherokee C	28-26404	G-AXSH N11C	22. 3.85	Taylor Aircraft Servics Ltd *(Crashed near Netherthorpe 25.3.90: cancelled 3.9.90 by CAA: stored 3.91: current status unknown)*	Sywell	15. 5.91T
G-TIMY	Gardan GY-80-160 Horizon	36	I-TIKI	17. 1.00	R.G.Whyte	Dunstable	
G-TINA	SOCATA TB-10 Tobago	67		30.10.79	A.Lister	Shipdham	13. 9.04
G-TING	Cameron O-120 HAFB	4007		4.10.96	Floating Sensations Ltd	Thatcham, Berks	30.10.01T

G-TINK	Robinson R22 Beta	0937	G-NICH	22. 5.01	N.T.Burton	Costock	5. 5.04T
G-TINS	Cameron N-90 HAFB	1626		27. 1.88	J.R.Clifton	Brackley	10. 3.01A
					(Carling Black Label titles)		
G-TINY	Moravan Zlin Z.526F Trener Master		OK-CMD	10. 5.95	D.Evans	Little Gransden	17. 8.98
		1257	G-TINY/YR-ZAD				
G-TIPS	Tipsy Nipper T.66 Srs.5 PFA 025-12696		OO-VAL	27. 3.95	R.F.L.Cuypers	Grimbergen, Belgium	27. 6.02P
	(Jabiru 2200A) *(Rebuild of Fairey c/n 50)*		9Q-CYJ/9O-CYJ/(OO-CYJ)/(OO-CCD)				
G-TJAY	Piper PA-22-135 Tri-Pacer	22-730	N730TJ	11. 5.93	D.D.Saint	Garston Farm, Marshfield	22. 7.02
			N2353A				
G-TKAY	Europa Aviation Europa PFA 247-12804			2. 6.99	A.M.Kay	Nuthampstead	1. 8.02P
G-TKGR	Lindstrand Racing Car SS HAFB	380		28. 8.96	Brown & Williamson Tobacco Corporation (Export) Ltd		
					"Team Green"	Louisville, KY, USA	20. 8.99A
G-TKIS	Tri-R Kis 029 & PFA 239-12358			23.12.93	J.L.Bone	Biggin Hill	15.12.02P
	(Lycoming O-290-D2) *(Tail-wheel variant)*						
G-TKPZ	Cessna 310R II	310R1225	G-BRAH	19. 3.90	Air Charter Scotland Ltd	Edinburgh	1. 4.02T
			N1909G				
G-TLDK	Piper PA-22-150 Tri-Pacer	22-4726	N6072D	27. 1.97	A.M.Thomson	Phoenix Farm, Lower Upham	
					(Noted 12.99)		
G-TMCC	Cameron N-90 HAFB	4327		30. 3.98	Prudential Assurance Co Ltd	Bristol	7. 6.02A
					"The Mall/Cribbs Causeway"		
G-TMDP	Airbus A320-231	0168	OY-CNF	19.11.96	Airtours International Airways Ltd		
			(D-ADSL)/OY-CNF/F-WWIF			Manchester	19.11.02T
G-TMKI	Percival P.56 Provost T.1	PAC/F/268	WW453	1. 7.92	B.L.Robinson,	(Clevedon)	
					(As "WW453/W-S" in RAF c/s)		
G-TMOL	SOCATA TB-20 Trinidad	2103	F-OJBQ	24.12.01	West Wales Airport Ltd	Gloucestershire	
G-TNTN	Thunder Ax6-56 HAFB	1991		25. 4.91	H.M.Savage & J.F.Trehern	Edinburgh	8 9.02A
G-TOAD	SAN Jodel D.140 Mousquetaire	27	F-BIZG	27. 9.88	J.H.Stevens	Headcorn	25. 6.03
G-TOAK	SOCATA TB-20 Trinidad	468	N83AV	5.12.89	C.Wade & A.Young t/a Phoenix Grp	Belfast	11. 1.05
G-TOBA	SOCATA TB-10 Tobago	625	N600N	4. 4.91	E.J.Downing	Farley Farm, Winchester	17. 9.03
G-TOBE*	Piper PA-28R-200 Cherokee Arrow II		G-BNRO	25.11.87	Not known	Headcorn	6. 3.94
		28R-7435148	N40979				
			(Damaged near Cranbrook, Kent 6.3.92: cancelled 6.5.92 as WFU: stored 7.00)				
G-TOBI	Reims Cessna F172K	F17200792	G-AYVB	5. 1.84	G.Hall	Henstridge	14. 7.02
G-TOBY*	Cessna 172B	47852	G-ARCM	8. 4.81	Northbrook College	Shoreham	28. 4.85
			N6952X				
			(Damaged Sandown 15.10.83: cancelled 27.2.90 by CAA: instructional airframe 1.99)				
G-TODD	ICA IS-28M2A	59		18. 4.86	C.I.Roberts & C.D.King	Shobdon	7. 9.01
G-TODE	Ruschmeyer R90-230RG	016	D-EEAX	20. 6.94	A.I.D.Rich	Elstree	6. 8.03
G-TOFT	Colt 90A HAFB	1693		8. 3.90	C.S.Perceval *"Bumble"*	Great Missenden	17. 6.00A
G-TOGA*	Piper PA-32-301 Saratoga	32-8006028	G-BIEG	15.11.82	Not known	(Blackpool)	1. 2.95
			N81852				
	(Damaged Belmont, Lancs 29.8.93: cancelled 24.9.93 as WFU: wreck stored 9.95: current status unknown)						
G-TOGO	Van's RV-6	PFA 181A-13447		6. 4.99	G.Schwetz	(Southampton)	
G-TOLL	Piper PA-28R-201 Arrow III		N52HV	12.10.00	Plymouth School of Flying Ltd	Plymouth	16.11.03T
		28R-7837025	D-ECIW/N9007K				
G-TOLY	Robinson R22 Beta-II	2809	G-NSHR	8. 2.01	K.N.Tolley	(Bromyard)	27. 6.04T
G-TOMS	Piper PA-38-112 Tomahawk	38-79A0453	N9658N	22. 1.79	Juno Estates Ltd	Wellesbourne Mountford	11. 7.04T
G-TOMZ	Denney Kitfox Mk.2	PFA 172-11977		15.11.00	P.T.Knight	Leicester	17. 6.02P
G-TOOL	Thunder Ax8-105 HAFB	1670		29. 3.90	W.J.Honey *"Trademaster"*	Bristol	13. 5.02A
G-TOOT	Dyn'Aéro MCR-01	PFA 301-13542		1. 3.01	E.K.Griffin	(Bicester)	
G-TOPC	Aérospatiale AS355F1 Twin Squirrel		I-LGOG	29. 7.97	Bridge Street Nominees Ltd	Stapleford	6.11.03T
		5313	3A-MCS/D-HOSY/OE-BXV/D-HOSY				
G-TOPS	Aérospatiale AS355F1 Twin Squirrel		G-BPRH	7. 5.91	Sterling Helicopters Ltd	Norwich	7.12.01T
		5151	N360E/N5794F				
G-TORE*	Hunting-Percival P.84 Jet Provost T.3A		XM405	14. 6.91	R.J.Everett	Sproughton	5. 5.95P
		PAC/W/9212			*(As "42": cancelled 25.2.00 by CAA: noted 10.01)*		
G-TORS	Robinson R22 Beta	3021		4. 1.00	GT Investigations (International) Ltd		
						Galway, Co.Galway	12. 1.03T
G-TOSH	Robinson R22 Beta	0933	N2629S	14. 3.97	Heli Air Ltd	Leicester	20. 3.03T
			LV-RBD/N8012T				
G-TOTO	Reims Cessna F177RG Cardinal		G-OADE	29. 8.89	W.G.Walton	Cranfield	11. 7.04
		F177RG0049	G-AZKH				
G-TOUR	Robin R.2112	187		9.10.79	Mardenair Ltd	Goodwood	12. 3.04T
G-TOWS	Piper PA-25-260 Pawnee C	25-4853	PH-VBT	17. 7.91	Lasham Gliding Society Ltd	Lasham	23.12.03
	(Hoffman 4 blade propellor)		D-EAVI/N4370Y/N10F				
G-TOYS	Enstrom 280C-UK-2 Shark	1218	G-BISE	17. 6.82	Stephenson Aviation Ltd	Goodwood	26. 2.94T
					(Stored 4.96: current status unknown)		
G-TOYZ	Bell 206B-3 JetRanger III	3949	G-RGER	21.11.96	P.B.Ellis	Blackpool	24.10.03T
			N75EA/JA9452/N32018				
G-TPSL	Cessna 182S	18280398	N23700	11.12.98	A.N.Purslow	Blackbushe	17.12.01T
G-TRAC	Robinson R44 Astro	0598		10. 5.99	C.Sharples	Newbury	9. 6.02T
G-TRAM	Pegasus Quantum 15-912	7552		29. 7.99	T.F.J.Roach	Knapthorpe Lodge, Caunton	28. 7.02P
G-TRAN	Beechcraft 76 Duchess	ME-408	G-NIFR	15. 3.93	Multiflight Ltd	Leeds-Bradford	25. 9.04T
			N1808A				

G-TRCY	Robinson R44 Astro	0668		22.10.99	T.Fletcher	Collingham, Newark	18.11.02T
G-TRDM	SOCATA TB-20 Trinidad GT	2032	F-OILX	2. 1.01	The Mann Organ'tion Ltd	Gloucestershire	8. 1.04T
G-TREC	Cessna 421C Golden Eagle III	421C0838	G-TLOL (N2659K)	2. 7.96	C.P.Lockyer	Coventry	6 3.02
G-TRED	Cameron Colt Bibendum 110SS HAFB	4222		12.12.97	The Aerial Display Co Ltd	Looe	11. 2.02A
G-TREE	Bell 206B-3 JetRanger III	2826	N2779U	15. 6.87	LGH Aviation Ltd *(Op Alan Mann Helicopters)*	Fairoaks	9.12.02T
G-TREK	Jodel D.18 (Limbach L.2000)	182 & PFA 169-11265		1. 5.92	R.H.Mole	Leicester	7. 8.02P
G-TREN	Boeing 737-4S3	24796	G-BRKG	3. 4.91	GB Airways Ltd *(Blue Poole t/s)*	Gatwick	11. 7.02T
G-TRIB	Lindstrand HS-110 Hot Air Airship (Rotax 582)	174	(N...)	23. 1.95	J Addison	Melton Mowbray	13. 5.02A
G-TRIC	de Havilland DHC.1 Chipmunk 22A	C1/0080	G-AOSZ WB635	18.12.89	D.M.Barnett *(As "18013" in RCAF c/s)*	High Cross, Ware	26.10.03
G-TRIM	Monnett Moni	00258T & PFA 142-11012		16. 2.84	J.E.Bennell	(High Wycombe)	
G-TRIN	SOCATA TB-20 Trinidad	1131		25. 6.90	TL Aviation Ltd	Jersey	9. 3.03
G-TRIO	Cessna 172M Skyhawk II	17266271	G-BNXY N9621H	30. 7.91	C.M.B.Reid	Rochester	17. 1.03T
G-TROP	Cessna T310R II	T310R1381	N4250C	31.12.86	D E Carpenter	Shoreham	29. 4.02T
G-TROY	North American T-28A Fennec	142/174-545	F-AZFV FrAF No 142/51-7692	21. 4.99	S.G.Howell & S.Tilling *(As "51-7692")*	Duxford	22. 3.02P
G-TRUD	Enstrom 480	5022	XT-BOK	27. 2.01	Sussex Aviation Ltd	Shoreham	1. 3.04T
G-TRUE	MD Helicopters Hughes 369E	0490E	N6TK ZK-HFP	12. 9.94	Bailey Employment Services Ltd	(Melksham)	20. 3.04T
G-TRUK	Stoddard-Hamilton Glasair IIRG (Lycoming O-320)	575R & PFA 149-11015		23. 7.84	M.P.Jackson	Fairoaks	22. 5.04P
G-TRUX	Colt 77A HAFB	1860		13.11.90	Highway Truck Rental Ltd	Gateshead	2.12.99A
G-TRYG	Robinson R44	0960		4. 1.01	Productive Investments Ltd	(Guildford)	17. 1.04t
G-TRYK	Air Creation Kiss 400-582(1) *(Other c/ns: Import Kit No FL004..Air Creation wing c/n A01157-1163 & Trike T01098)*	BMAA/HB/191		31.10.01	S.Elsbury	(Brentwood)	
G-TSAM	British Aerospace BAe 125 Srs.800B	258028	G-5-12	31. 1.85	BAE System (Operations) Ltd	Warton	5. 9.03
G-TSFT	Piper PA-28-161 Warrior II	28-8216117	G-BLDJ N9632N	5. 4.89	Plane Talking Ltd	Elstree	7. 2.02T
G-TSGJ	Piper PA-28-181 Archer II	28-8090109	N8097W	12. 9.88	A.Dove & A.D.S.Peat t/a Golf Juliet Flying Club	Teesside	7. 1.04
G-TSIX	North American AT-6C-1NT Harvard IIA	88-9725	FAP1535 SAAF7183/EX289/41-33262	19. 3.79	J.M.& B.E.Adams *(As "111836/JZ/6" in USN c/s)*	Tatenhill	24. 5.02P
G-TSKD	Raj Hamsa X'Air Jabiru (1)	633 & BMAA/HB/165		8. 5.01	T.Sexton & K.B.Dupuy	(Westcliff-on-Sea)	
G-TSKY	Beagle B.121 Pup Srs.2	B121-010	OE-CFM HB-NAA/G-AWDY/HB-NAA/G-AWDY	6. 4.98	R.G.Hayes	Elstree	7. 5.04T
G-TSOL	EAA Acrosport 1 (Lycoming O-320)	PFA 072-11391		18. 7.00	T.G.Solomon	(Kittyhawk Farm, Ripe)	31. 3.00P
G-TTDD	Zenair CH.701 STOL (Jabiru 2200A)	PFA 187-13106		1. 9.97	D.B.Dainton & V.D.Asque *(Blown over and damaged at strip "18 months ago" and to Sibsey for repair 7.01)*	Sackville Farm, Riseley	9. 2.00T
G-TTFN	Cessna 560 Citation V	560-0537	N5181V	19.11.99	Corporate Administration Management Ltd	Shoreham	18.11.02T
G-TTHC	Robinson R22 Beta	1196		21.12.89	Multiflight Ltd	Leeds-Bradford	27. 5.02T
G-TTIA	Airbus A321-231	1428	D-AVZA	19. 2.01	GB Airways Ltd	Gatwick	18. 2.04t
G-TTIB	Airbus A321-231	1433	D-AVZC	27. 2.01	GB Airways Ltd	Gatwick	26. 2.04t
G-TTIM*	Cassutt Racer IIIM	PFA 034-13116		10. 7.98	J.D.Llewellyn *(Cancelled 7.9.01 by CAA - no Permit to Fly issued)*	(Coalville)	
G-TTMC	Airbus A300B4-203	299	OH-LAA (LX-LGP)/F-WZMX	25. 4.98	OY Air Scandic International Aviation AB	Manchester	29. 4.04T
G-TTOA	Airbus A320-232	1215	F-WWDB	18. 5.00	GB Airways Ltd	Gatwick	17. 5.03T
G-TTOB	Airbus A320-232	1687	F-WWIM	R	GB Airways Ltd *(For delivery 2.02)*	Gatwick	
G-TTOC	Airbus A320-232	1715	F-WWDB	R	GB Airways Ltd *(For delivery 3.02)*	Gatwick	
G-TTOD	Airbus A320-232	1723	F-WWBH	R	GB Airways Ltd *(For delivery 3.02)*	Gatwick	
G-TTOE	Airbus A320-232	1754		R	GB Airways Ltd *(For delivery 4.02)*	Gatwick	
G-TTOY	CFM Streak Shadow SA (Rotax 618)	K.233 & PFA 206-12805		15. 4.96	S.Marriott	Old Sarum	1. 8.02P
G-TTWO*	Colt 56A HAFB	087		14. 5.80	Balloon Preservation Group *"Tea 4 Two" (Cancelled 14.11.95 as WFU)*	Kirdford	1. 9.87A
G-TUBB	Jabiru Jabiru UL-450 (Jabiru 2200A)	PFA 274A-13484		1.10.99	A.H.Bower	Kemble	20.11.02P

G-TUCH	Bell 206B JetRanger II	969	G-OCBB G-BASE/N18093	4. 4.01	P.Dobson t/a Touchdown	Redhill	30.10.03T
G-TUDR	Cameron V-77 HAFB	1135		20. 5.85	Jacques W.Soukup Enterprises Ltd *"Tudor Rose/HVIIIR"*	(USA)	21. 3.99A
G-TUGG	Piper PA-18-150 Super Cub (Lycoming O-360-A3) *(Frame No.18-8497)*	18-8274	PH-MAH N5451Y	10. 1.83	Ulster Gliding Club Ltd	Bellarena	9. 4.04
G-TUGY	Robin DR.400/180 Regent	2052	D-EPAR	27. 4.98	J.M.Airey	Saltby	19. 5.04T
G-TULL	Jabiru Jabiru UL-450	PFA 274A-13535		29.10.99	W.R.Tull	(Chipping Norton)	1. 1.03P
G-TULP	Lindstrand LBL Tulips SS HAFB	662	(PH-AJT) (PH-TLP)/PH-ORA)	16.10.00	Oxford Promotions (UK) Ltd *(Op F Prell)*	Kentucky, USA	8. 3.02A
G-TUNE	Robinson R22 Beta	0818	N60661 G-OJVI/(G-OJVJ)	12. 1.99	Ecurie Ecosse (Scotland) Ltd *(Op Scotia Helicopters)*	Cumbernauld	7. 2.02T
G-TURF	Reims Cessna F406 Caravan II	F406-0020	PH-FWF (EI-CND)/PH-FWF/F-WZDS	17.10.96	Atlantic Air Transport Ltd *(Op HM Coast Guard) "Lord of the Isles"*	Inverness	21.11.00T
G-TURK	Cameron Sultan 80SS HAFB	1711		12. 4.88	Forbes Europe Inc *"Suliman"*	Balleroy, Normandy	18. 6.00A
G-TURN	Steen Skybolt (Lycoming IO-360)	003 & PFA 064-11349		14. 7.88	R.Bentley	(Congleton)	24. 2.01P
G-TURP*	Aérospatiale SA.341G Gazelle 1	1445	G-BKLS N17MT/N14MT/N49549	21. 1.88	See G-BKLS		
G-TURV	Robinson R44 Clipper	0819		21. 7.00	C.Coult	(Gilmerton, Edinburgh)	14. 8.03T
G-TUSA	Pegasus Quantum 15-912	7841		9. 8.01	C.J.Cullen	Dunkeswell	16. 8.02P
G-TUSK	Bell 206B-3 JetRanger III	4406	G-BWZH N53114	13. 1.97	Heli Aviation Ltd	Blackbushe	23. 2.03T
G-TVAA	Agusta A109E Power	11052		24. 9.99	Agusta SpA	(Cascina, Italy)	7.11.02T
G-TVAC	Agusta A109E Power	11090		26.10.00	Sloane Helicopters Ltd *(Op Thames Valley Air Ambulance)*	White Waltham	12.11.03T
G-TVBF	Lindstrand LBL-310A HAFB	439		2. 4.97	Virgin Balloon Flights Ltd	London SE16	6. 4.01T
G-TVII	Hawker Hunter T.7	41H-693834	XX467 RJordAF 836/RSAF 70-617/G-9-214/XL605	8.12.97	G.R.Montgomery *(As "XX467" in TWU c/s)*	Kemble	
G-TVIJ	CCF Harvard 4 (T-6J-CCF Texan)	CCF4-442	G-BSBE Moz PLAF 1730 FAP 1730/AA+652/52-8521	10.12.93	R.W.Davies *(As "28521/TA-521" in USAF c/s)*	Little Robhurst Farm, Woodchurch	28. 5.02P
G-TVIP	Cessna 404 Titan Courier II	404-0644	G-KIWI G-BHNI/LN-LGM/SE-IFV/G-BHNI/(N5302J)	16. 8.00	Capital Trading (Aviation) Ltd	Filton	5. 2.03T
G-TVSI	Campbell Cricket (Rotax 503)	CA/340	G-AYHH	8. 4.82	C.Smith	(Hastings)	16. 4.98P
G-TVTV	Cameron TV 90SS HAFB	2357		14. 9.90	J.Krebs	Erfstadt, Germany	2. 6.99A
G-TWEL	Piper PA-28-181 Archer II	28-8090290	N81963	12. 6.80	International Aerospace Engineering Ltd	Cranfield	22. 4.02T
G-TWEY	Colt 69A HAFB	700		24. 7.85	N.Bland	Didcot	12. 1.02A
G-TWIG	Reims Cessna F406 Caravan II	F406-0014	PH-FWD F-WZDS	21.10.98	Highland Airways Ltd *"Wee Dram"*	Inverness	22.10.04T
G-TWIN	Piper PA-44-180 Seminole	44-7995072	N30267	6.11.78	Bonus Aviation Ltd	Cranfield	22. 5.03T
G-TWIZ	Rockwell Commander 114	14375	SE-GSP N5808N	9. 5.90	B.C.& P M Cox	Redhill	5. 7.02
G-TXSE	Rotary Air Force RAF 2000 GTX-SE	PFA G/113-1271		1. 3.96	M.H.J.Goldring *(New owner 10.01)*	Newton Abbot	1. 1.98P
G-TYER	Robin DR.400/500	0021	F-GTZB	25. 4.00	Alfred Graham Ltd	Southend	14. 5.03
G-TYGA	Gulfstream AA-5B Tiger	AA5B-1161	G-BHNZ (D-EGDS)/N4547L	22. 2.82	D H & R J Carman	Rochester	29. 1.04T
G-TYKE	Jabiru Jabiru UL	PFA 274A-13739		8. 6.01	A.Parker	(Bingley)	
G-TYNE	SOCATA TB-20 Trindad	1523	F-GRBM F-WWRW/CS-AZH/F-OHDE	6.11.97	D.T.Watkins	Newcastle	26.11.03
G-TYRE	Reims Cessna F172M Skyhawk II	F17201222	OY-BIA	16. 2.79	J.A.Lyons t/a Staverton Flying School	Gloucestershire	2. 9.03T
G-TZII	Thorp T.211B	PFA 305-13285		2. 6.99	AD Aviation Ltd	Barton	

G-UAAA – G-UZZZ

G-UAPA	Robin DR.400/140B Major	2213	F-GMXC	11. 1.95	Carlos Saraiva Lda	(Alges, Portugal)	3.10.04
G-UAPO	Ruschmeyer R90-230RG	019	D-EECT	2. 3.95	S.J.Green	Lagoa, Portugal	2. 7.04
G-UCCC	Cameron Sign 90SS HAFB	3918		5. 7.96	Flying Pictures Ltd *(Unipart Car Care Centres titles)*	Fairoaks	6. 9.99A
G-UDAY	Robinson R22 Beta	1101		4. 8.89	Newmarket Plant Hire Ltd	Cambridge	11. 5.02T
G-UDGE	Thruster T.600N (Rotax 503UL)	9099-T600N-037	G-BYPI	17. 9.99	L.J.Appleby	Leicester	17.10.02P
G-UDOG	Scottish Aviation.Bulldog Srs.120/121	BH.120/204	XX518	24. 1.02	Gamit Ltd	(Stansted)	
G-UEST	Bell 206B JetRanger II	1484	G-RYOB G-BLWU/ZS-PAW	8. 9.89	Summit Aviation Ltd	Oxford	1. 2.03T
G-UESY	Robinson R22 Beta-II	2801		13. 3.98	EW Guess (Holdings) Ltd	(Stamford)	2. 4.04

G-UFAW	Raj Hamsa X'Air 582 (5) 582 & BMAA/HB/167		24. 7.01	J.H.Goddard	(Taunton)	
G-UFCA	Cessna 172S Skyhawk 172S8313	N2461P	26. 1.00	Ulster Flying Club (1961) Ltd	Newtownards, Co.of Down	9..2.03T
G-UFCB	Cessna 172S Skyhawk 172S8318	N455SP	25. 1.00	Ulster Flying Club (1961) Ltd	Newtownards, Co.of Down	3 .2.03T
G-UFCC	Cessna 172S Skyhawk 172S8611	N2466X	8. 1.01	Ulster Flying Club (1961) Ltd	Newtownards, Co.of Down	8. 1.04T
G-UFCD	Cessna 172S Skyhawk 172S8443	G-OYZK	4. 1.01	Ulster Flying Club (1961) Ltd	Newtownards, Co.of Down	12. 7.03T
	(Swung on landing Newtownards 22.8.01, damaging propeller & starboard wing tip)					
G-UFLY	Cessna F150H F150-0264	G-AVVY	29. 9.89	Westair Flying Services Ltd	Blackpool	16.11.01T
G-UGLY	Sud SE.313B Alouette II 1500	G-BSFN XP967	7. 6.00	S.Cox	(Barnsley)	16. 7.04
G-UILD	Grob G-109B 6419		28. 1.86	Runnymede Consultants Ltd	Blackbushe	30. 4.04
G-UILE	Neico Lancair 320 PFA 191-12538		17. 1.94	R.J.Martin	(Alresford, Hants)	
G-UILT	Cessna T303 Crusader T30300280	G-EDRY N4817V	3. 7.00	Rock Seat Ltd	Lydd	3. 4.02
G-UINN	Stolp SA.300 Starduster Too (Lycoming O-360) HB.1980-1	EI-CDQ C-GTLJ	16. 3.98	J.D.H.Gordon *(Also carries "EI-CDQ")*	Charterhall	28.11.02P
G-UJAB	Jabiru Jabiru UL PFA 274A-13373		27. 1.99	C.A.Thomas	Top Farm, Croydon	23. 8.02P
G-UJGK	Jabiru Jabiru UL PFA 274A-13558		17. 4.00	W.G.Upton & J.G.Kosak	RNAS Culdrose	22. 4.02P
G-UKAC	British Aerospace BAe 146 Srs.300 E3142	G-5-142	25.10.89	KLM UK Ltd *(Op Buzz)*	Stansted	19.11.04T
G-UKAG	British Aerospace BAe 146 Srs.300 E3162	G-6-162	28.11.90	Air UK Ltd *(Op Buzz)*	Stansted	11.12.04T
G-UKFA	Fokker F.28 Mk.0100 11246 *(Fokker 100)*	N602RP C-FICY/PH-EZB	1. 7.92	KLM UK Ltd	Norwich	12.10.02T
G-UKFB	Fokker F.28 Mk.0100 11247 *(Fokker 100)*	N602TR C-FICW/PH-EZC	1. 7.92	KLM UK Ltd	Norwich	12. 8.02T
G-UKFC	Fokker F.28 Mk.0100 11263 *(Fokker 100)*	N602DG C-FICL/PH-EZF	1. 7.92	KLM UK Ltd	Norwich	27. 7.02T
G-UKFD	Fokker F.28 Mk.0100 11259 *(Fokker 100)*	C-FICP PH-EZJ	22. 7.92	KLM UK Ltd	Norwich	9.11.02T
G-UKFE	Fokker F.28 Mk.0100 11260 *(Fokker 100)*	C-FICQ PH-EZK	22. 7.92	Air UK Ltd	Norwich	30.11.02T
G-UKFF	Fokker F.28 Mk.0100 11274 *(Fokker 100)*	PH-ZCK (G-FIOB)/PH-ZCK/PH-EZB/(PH-KLK)	9.11.93	Air UK Ltd	Norwich	8.11.03T
G-UKFG	Fokker F.28 Mk.0100 11275 *(Fokker 100)*	PH-ZCL (G-FIOC)/PH-ZCL/PH-EZV/(PH-KLL)	19.11.93	KLM UK Ltd	Norwich	18.11.03T
G-UKFH	Fokker F.28 Mk.0100 11277 *(Fokker 100)*	PH-ZCM (G-FIOD)/PH-ZCM/PH-EZW/(PH-KLN)	29. 9.93	KLM UK Ltd	Norwich	28. 9.03T
G-UKFI	Fokker F.28 Mk.0100 11279 *(Fokker 100)*	PH-ZCN (G-FIOE)/PH-ZCN/PH-EZX/(PH-KLO)	12.10.93	KLM UK Ltd	Norwich	11.10.03T
G-UKFJ	Fokker F.28 Mk.0100 11248 *(Fokker 100)*	F-GIOV C-FICB/PH-INC/PH-EZD	30. 1.96	KLM UK Ltd	Norwich	22. 2.02T
G-UKFK	Fokker F.28 Mk.0100 11249 *(Fokker 100)*	F-GIOX C-FICO/PH-INA/PH-EZE	19. 2.96	KLM UK Ltd	Norwich	1. 4.02T
G-UKFM	Fokker F.28 Mk.0100 11269 *(Fokker 100)*	PH-KLD F-GIDQ/PH-KLD	27.10.98	KLM UK Ltd.	Stansted	25.11.04T
G-UKFN	Fokker F.28 Mk.0100 11270 *(Fokker 100)*	PH-KLE F-GIDP/PH-KLE	16. 6.97	KLM UK Ltd	Norwich	21. 7.03T
G-UKFO	Fokker F.28 Mk.0100 11271 *(Fokker 100)*	PH-KLG F-GIDO/PH-KLG	20.10.97	KLM UK Ltd	Norwich	20.10.03T
G-UKFR	Fokker F.28 Mk.0100 11273 *(Fokker 100)*	PH-KLI F-GIDM/F-OGQB/PH-KLI	21. 3.97	KLM UK Ltd	Norwich	26. 3.03T
G-UKHP	British Aerospace BAe 146 Srs.300 E3123	G-5-123	26.10.88	KLM UK Ltd *(Op Buzz)*	Stansted	26. 2.02T
G-UKID	British Aerospace BAe 146 Srs.300 E3157	G-6-157	28. 2.90	KLM UK Ltd *(Op Buzz)*	Stansted	6. 3.02T
G-UKOZ	Jabiru Jabiru SK PFA 274-13310		16. 6.99	D.J.Burnett	(Wallingford)	15. 8.02P
G-UKRB	Colt 105A HAFB 1769		10.12.90	Virgin Airship & Balloon Co Ltd *"Lloyds Bank II"*	Telford	16. 5.97A
G-UKRC	British Aerospace BAe 146 Srs.300 E3158	G-BSMR G-6-158	14. 2.91	KLM UK Ltd *(Op Buzz)*	Stansted	24. 2.02T
G-UKSC	British Aerospace BAe 146 Srs.300 E3125	G-5-125	26.10.88	KLM UK Ltd *(Op Buzz)*	Stansted	9. 3.02T
G-UKTA	Fokker F.27 Mk 050 *(Fokker 50)* 20246	PH-KXF	22. 2.95	KLM UK Ltd *"City of Norwich"*	Norwich	21. 2.04T
G-UKTB	Fokker F.27 Mk.050 *(Fokker 50)* 20247	PH-KXG	21. 3.95	KLM UK Ltd *"City of Aberdeen"*	Norwich	21. 3.04T
G-UKTC	Fokker F.27 Mk.050 *(Fokker 50)* 20249	PH-KXH	25. 1.95	KLM UK Ltd *"City of Bradford"*	Norwich	25. 1.04T
G-UKTD	Fokker F.27 Mk.050 *(Fokker 50)* 20256	PH-KXT	20. 1.95	KLM UK Ltd *"City of Leeds"*	Norwich	19. 1.04T
G-UKTE	Fokker F.27 Mk.050 *(Fokker 50)* 20270	PH-LXJ	14. 2.95	KLM UK Ltd *"City of Hull"*	Norwich	14. 2.04T
G-UKTF	Fokker F.27 Mk.050 *(Fokker 50)* 20271	PH-LXK	31. 1.95	KLM UK Ltd *"City of York"*	Norwich	31. 1.04T
G-UKTG	Fokker F.27 Mk.050 *(Fokker 50)* 20276	PH-LXP	28. 2.95	KLM UK Ltd *"City of Durham"*	Norwich	28. 2.04T

G-UKTH	Fokker F.27 Mk.050 *(Fokker 50)*	20277	PH-LXR	28. 3.95	KLM UK Ltd *"City of Amsterdam"*	Norwich	28. 3.04T
G-UKTI	Fokker F.27 Mk.050 *(Fokker 50)*	20279	PH-LXT	17. 3.95	Air UK Ltd *"City of Stavanger"*	Norwich	16. 3.04T
G-UKTK	ATR 72-202	519	F-WWLQ	30. 1.98	KLM UK Ltd	Norwich	29. 1.04T
G-UKTM	ATR 72-202	508	F-WWLU	23. 4.98	KLM UK Ltd	Jersey	22. 4.04T
					(Op British Regional)		
G-UKTN	ATR 72-202	496	F-WWLT	4. 6.98	KLM UK Ltd	Norwich	3. 6.04T
G-UKUK	Head Ax8-105 HAFB	248	N8303U	1. 9.97	P.A.George	Princes Risborough	14. 7.02A
G-ULAB	Robinson R22 Beta	2444	N8311Z	18. 8.94	D.J.Parker	(Machynlleth)	21. 9.03T
					t/a Skyscraper Aviation		
G-ULAS	de Havilland DHC.1 Chipmunk 22	C1/0554	WK517	14. 6.96	Search & Management Services Ltd	Booker	12. 8.02
					(As "WK517")		
G-ULIA	Cameron V-77 HAFB	2860		20. 5.92	J.M.Dean	Oswestry	15 .7.01A
G-ULLS	Lindstrand LBL-90A HAFB	434		18. 2.97	J R Clifton	Brackley	19.12.01A
G-ULPS	Everett Gyroplane Srs.1 (VW 1835)	007	G-BMNY	13. 7.93	C.J.Watkinson	(Goole)	10. 7.01P
G-ULTR	Cameron A-105 HAFB	4100		24. 2.97	P.Glydon	Birmingham	6. 4.02T
					(Ultrafilter titles)		
G-UMBO	Colt Jumbo SS HAFB	747		2. 4.86	Virgin Airship & Balloon Co Ltd	Telford	21. 5.96A
	(Special shape with nose/tail/wings of Virgin 747)				*"Virgin Jumbo"*		
	(Built as c/n 816 but amended: replacement envelope c/n 1645 fitted 1990)						
G-UMMI	Piper PA-31 Navajo C	31-7912060	G-BGSO N3519F	11. 8.92	J.A, G.M, D.T.A.& J.A.Rees t/a Messrs Rees of Poynston West	Haverfordwest	1. 8.03T
G-UNDD	Piper PA-23-250 Aztec E	27-4832	G-BATX N14271	22. 3.00	G.J.& D.P.Deadman	Goodwood	13. 5.04T
G-UNGE	Lindstrand LBL-90A HAFB	122	G-BVPJ	6.12.96	M.T.Stevens	Solihull	10. 6.02A
					t/a Silver Ghost Balloon Club		
G-UNIP*	Cameron Oil Container SS HAFB	2532		15. 3.91	Balloon Preservation Group	Kirdford	7.11.96A
	(Unipart Sureflow Oil Can)				*"Unipart Oil" (Cancelled 31.1.02 as wfu)*		
G-UNIT	Partenavia P.68B	23	G-BCNT	21.10.93	Aliservice SRL	(Pordenone, Italy)	16.12.01T
G-UNIV	Montgomerie-Parsons Two-Place Gyroplane	PFA G/08-1276	G-BWTP	3. 8.99	Dept of Aerospace Eng, University of Glasgow	(Glasgow)	1. 3.00P
G-UNNY	British Aircraft Corpn BAC.167 Strikemaster mk.87	EEP/JP/2872 & PS.164 *(or PS.170?)*	G-AYHR/Botswana DF OJ4/Kenya AF 601/G-27-141/G-AYHR/G-27-191	19. 3.98	Transair (UK) Ltd	Duxford	27. 4.02P
					(As "OJ4/Z-2" in Botswana c/s)		
G-UNRL	Lindstrand RR-21 HAFB	260		25. 5.95	Virgin Airship & Balloon Co Ltd	Telford	23. 7.99A
					"Virgin Cola"		
G-UNYT	Robinson R22 Beta	0985	G-BWZV G-LIAN	17.11.97	Heli Air Ltd	Wellesbourne Mountford	16.11.03T
G-UPHL	Cameron Concept 80 HAFB	3002		23. 2.93	CSM (Weston) Ltd	Weston-super-Mare	8. 9.00T
					t/a Uphill Motor Co *(Uphill Motors titles)*		
G-UPPP	Colt 77A HAFB	852		4. 8.86	M.Williams *"Nugget"*	Wadhurst	25. 3.95A
G-UPPY	Cameron DP-80 Hot-Air Airship	2274		29. 3.90	Jacques W.Soukup Enterprises Ltd *"Jacques Soukup"*	Beaulieu Court, Wilts/Great Missenden	27. 8.94A
G-UPUP	Cameron V-77 HAFB	1828		21. 7.89	S.R.Burden	Noordwijk, The Netherlands	23. 5.02T
					"Fantasia"		
G-URCH	Rotorway Executive 162F (Rotorway RI 162F)	6414		1.10.99	D.L.Urch	(Winscombe)	
G-UROP	Beechcraft B55 Baron	TC-2452	N64311	17. 9.90	Pooler International Ltd	Sleap	15. 3.03
G-URRR	Air Command 582 Sport	0630 & PFA G/104-1200		13. 6.90	L.Armes	(Basildon)	
G-URUH	Robinson R44 Astro	0354		3. 7.97	Heli Air Ltd	(Wellesbourne Mountford)	10. 8.03T
G-USAM	Cameron Uncle Sam SS HAFB	1120		20. 5.85	Corn Palace Balloon Club Ltd	Bristol	27. 6.00A
	(Uncle Sam head shape) (New envelope c/n 4526 c.3.99)						
G-USFT	Piper PA-23-250 Aztec F	27-7654174	G-BEGV N62720	8. 5.97	Plane Talking Ltd	Elstree	2. 1.04T
G-USGB*	Colt 105A HAFB	1130		26. 8.87	Virgin Airship & Balloon Co Ltd	Telford	22.11.92A
					"Virgin Replica" (Cancelled 4.10.01 as wfu)		
G-USIL	Thunder Ax7-77 HAFB	1587		22. 8.89	Window on the World Ltd	London SE1	27. 5.99A
					"Mantis"		
G-USMC	Cameron Chestie 90SS HAFB	1251		24. 4.86	Jacques W.Soukup Enterprises Ltd	South Dakota, USA	15. 6.00A
	(US Marine Corps Bulldog shape)						
G-USSR	Cameron Doll 90SS HAFB	2273		29. 3.90	Corn Palace Balloon Club Ltd	Bristol	9. 6.00A
	(Russian Doll shape)				*"Matrioshka"*		
G-USSY	Piper PA-28-181 Archer II	28-8290011	N8439R	7.11.88	Western Air (Thruxton) Ltd	Thruxton	18. 2.04T
G-USTA*	Agusta A109A	7170	G-MEAN G-BRYL/G-ROPE/G-OAMH	3.12.96	Markoss Aviation Ltd	Biggin Hill	21. 4.00T
			(Damaged Bedlam Street, Hurstpierpoint 27.3.99: cancelled 5.8.99 as wfu: stored w/o boom 12.00)				
G-USTB	Agusta A109A	7163	D-HEEG (D-HEEF)/VR-CKN/HB-XKM	9. 6.97	Newton Aviation Ltd.	Redhill	19. 7.03T
G-USTV*	Messerschmitt Bf.109G-2/Trop	10639	8478M RN228/Luftwaffe	26.10.90	RAF Museum	Hendon	30. 5.98P
	(Built Erla Maschinenwerk GmbH)				*(As "10639/6" in Luftwaffe III/JG77 c/s)*		
			(Cancelled as PWFU 24.9.98) (Rebuilt Duxford during 2001 and resprayed during 10.01)				
G-USTY	Clutton FRED Srs.III (VW 1834)	PFA 029-10390		11.10.78	R.T.Mosforth	Netherthorpe	17. 6.02P
					t/a GUSTY Group		

G-USUK*	Colt 2500A HAFB	1100		1. 6.87	Virgin Atlantic Airways Ltd	Duxford	19. 8.87P
					"Virgin Atlantic Flyer"		
				(Cancelled 21.8.90 as WFU: gondola displayed - remainder stored)			
G-UTSI	Rand Robinson KR-2	KBG-01		2.10.89	K.B.Gutridge *(Stored 12.00)*	Biggin Hill	
G-UTSY	Piper PA-28R-201 Cherokee Arrow III	28R-7737052	N3346Q	29. 8.86	Arrow Aviation Ltd	Southend	8. 2.02
G-UTTS	Robinson R44 Raven	0865	G-ROAP	20.10.00	Heli Hire Ltd	Gamston	12.10.03T
G-UTZY	Aérospatiale SA.341G Gazelle 1	1307	G-BKLV N341SC	21.12.87	Animal Air Ambulance Rescue Service Ltd	Broxbourne	4. 3.01T
G-UVIP	Cessna 421C Golden Eagle III	421C0603	G-BSKH N88600	23.11.98	Capital Trading Aviation Ltd	Filton	2.11.04T
G-UVNR	British Aircraft Corpn BAC.167 Strikemaster mk.87 *(Or PS.174?)*	EEP/JP/2876 & PS.168	G-BXFS/ OJ10 Botswana DF/605 Kenyan AF/G-27-195 *(As "OJ-10")*	4. 5.01	Global Aviation Services Ltd	Humberside	23.12.02P
G-UZEL	Aérospatiale SA.341G Gazelle 1	1413	G-BRNH YU-HBO	21.11.89	MCC Ltd	(Kirk Michael, IoM)	3. 7.04
G-UZLE	Colt 77A HAFB	2021		1. 8.91	Flying Pictures Ltd *"John Courage"*	Fairoaks	25. 5.00A

G-VAAA – G-VZZZ

G-VAEL	Airbus A340-311	015	F-WWJG	15.12.93	Virgin Atlantic Airways Ltd *"Maiden Toulouse"*	Gatwick	14.12.02T
G-VAGA	Piper PA-15 Vagabond (Lycoming O-145-B2)	15-248	N4458H NC4458H	14.11.80	I.M.Callier	(Windsor)	29. 8.98P
G-VAIR	Airbus A340-313	164	F-WWJA	21. 4.97	Virgin Atlantic Airways Ltd *"Maiden Tokyo"*	Gatwick	20. 4.03T
G-VAJT	SOCATA MS.894E Rallye 220GT	12195	EI-BAB (S9-NAF)/EI-BAB/(G-BLPN)/EI-BAB	25. 7.89	W.M.Patterson	City of Derry	29. 9.04
G-VALS	Pietenpol Aircamper	PFA 047-13157		30. 7.97	I.G.& V.A.Price	(Liphook)	
G-VALZ	Cameron N-120 HAFB	4998		9..1.01	D Ling	(Nottingham)	4. 1.02T
G-VANS	Van's RV-4 (Lycoming O-320)	355	N16TS	7. 9.92	M.Swanborough & D.Jones	Breighton	14. 2.02P
G-VANZ	Van's RV-6A	PFA 181-12531		15. 7.93	S.J.Baxter *(Under constructiom 2000)*	(Macclesfield)	
G-VARG	Varga 2150A Kachina	VAC 157-80	OO-RTY N80716	14. 5.84	A.C.Fletcher	Sherburn-in-Elmet	19. 6.02
G-VASA	Piper PA-34-200 Seneca	34-7350080	G-BNNB (N...)/G-BNNB/N15625	29. 3.96	V.Babic	Bournemouth	5. 7.03T
G-VAST	Boeing 747-41R	28757		17. 6.97	Virgin Atlantic Airways Ltd *"Ladybird"*	Heathrow	16. 6.03T
G-VATH	Airbus A321-211	1219	D-AVZB	12. 5.00	Virgin Atlantic Airways Ltd *"Hellenic Beauty" (Virgin Sun titles) (Stored 1.02)*	Filton	11. 5.03T
G-VATL	Airbus A340-642	376	F-WWCC	R	Virgin Atlantic Airways Ltd *"Atlantic Angel" (For delivery 9.03)*		
G-VAUN	Cessna 340 II	340-0538	D-IOWS N5148J	25.11.77	K.L.Burnett	Humberside	25.11.04
G-VBAC	Short SD.3-60 Var.100	SH.3736	VH-MJU G-BOEJ/G-14-3736	15. 9.97	BAC Leasing Ltd *(Op BAC Express) "City of Norwich"*	Exeter	15. 9.02T
G-VBIG	Boeing 747-4Q8	26255		10. 6.96	Virgin Atlantic Airways Ltd *"Tinker Belle"*	Gatwick	9. 6.02T
G-VBUS	Airbus A340-311	013	F-WWJE	26.11.93	Virgin Atlantic Airways Ltd *"Lady in Red"*	Gatwick	25.11.03T
G-VCED	Airbus A320-231	0193	OY-CNI F-WWIX	21. 1.97	Airtours International Airways Ltd	Manchester	30. 1.03T
G-VCIO	EAA Acrosport 2	PFA 072-12388		9.10.97	V Millard *(Under construction 1999)*	(Ipswich)	
G-VCML	Beechcraft 58 Baron	TH-1346	N2289R	31.10.97	St.Angelo Aviation Ltd *(Noted 11.01)*	Dunkeswell	10. 1.04T
G-VCSI*	Rotorway Executive	3660		25.10.90	Not known	Ley Farm, Chirk	
				(Stored 5.94: cancelled 3.4.97 by CAA: current status unknown)			
G-VDIR	Cessna 310R II	310R0211	N5091J	31. 1.91	J.Driver	(Pinner)	13. 6.04T
G-VECA	Robin HR.200/120B	344		1. 3.00	S.J.Skilton t/a Aviation Rentals	Bournemouth	9. 3.03T
G-VECB	Robin R.2160 Alpha Sport	300	G-BYMZ F-GOVZ/F-WZZX	16. 3.00	Mistral Aviation Ltd *(Crashed Goodwood 28.12.01 & substantially damaged)*	Goodwood	10. 2.03T
G-VECD	Robin R.1180T Aiglon II	234	F-GCAD	22. 6.00	Mistral Aviation Ltd	Goodwood	21. 9.03T
G-VECE	Robin R.2120U	355		11. 5.01	Mistral Aviation Ltd	Goodwood	8 .7.04T
G-VEIL	Airbus A340-642	460		R	Virgin Atlantic Airways Ltd *"Dancing Girl" (For delivery 11.02)*		
G-VELA	SIAI-Marchetti S.205-22R *(Confirmed as S.208A Waco Vela)*	4-149	N949W	30.10.89	K.R.Allen t/a G-VELA Partnership	Gamston	29. 4.02
G-VELD	Airbus A340-313	214	F-WWJY	16. 3.98	Virgin Atlantic Airways Ltd *"African Queen"*	Gatwick	15. 3.04T

G-VENI	de Havilland DH.112 Venom FB.50 (FB.1) *(Built F + W)*	733	J-1523	8. 6.84	Lindsay Wood Promotions Ltd *(Op Source Classic Jet Flight) (As "VV612" in silver RAF c/s)*	Bournemouth	25. 7.01P
G-VENM	de Havilland DH.112 Venom FB.50 (FB.1) *(Built F + W)*	824	G-BLIE J-1614	16. 6.99	T.J.Manna *(First post-restoration flight Cranfield 23.11.01)* *(Fitted with original DH-type nose as "WK436" in 11 Sqdn c/s)*	Cranfield	
G-VENT	Schempp-Hirth Ventus 2CM	3/17	D-KBTL	25. 9.01	D.Rance	(Kemberton)	5.11.04
G-VERA	Garden GY-201 Minicab	PFA 056-12236		7. 6.94	D.K.Shipton	(Peterborough)	
G-VETA	Hawker Hunter T.7	41H-693751	G-BVWN XL600	2. 7.96	Veta Ltd	Kemble	18. 4.02P
G-VETS	Enstrom 280C-UK Shark	1015	G-FSDC G-BKTG/OY-HBP	11. 9.95	C.Upton	Barton	28. 7.02
G-VEYE	Robinson R22	0140	G-BPTP N9056H	8. 2.00	J.B.Errington *(Hangared less rotors 8.01)*	Shobdon	2. 6.01T
G-VEZE	Rutan Varieze	PFA 074-10285		2. 9.77	S.D.Brown, S.Evans & M.Roper	(West Wickham/Haywards Heath)	
G-VFAB	Boeing 747-4Q8	24958		28. 4.94	Virgin Atlantic Airways Ltd *"Lady Penelope"*	Gatwick	27. 4.03T
G-VFAR	Airbus A340-313X	225	(G-VPOW) F-WWJZ	12. 6.98	Virgin Atlantic Airways Ltd *"Diana"*	Gatwick	11. 6.04T
G-VFLY	Airbus A340-311	058	F-WWJE	24.10.94	Virgin Atlantic Airways Ltd *"Dragon Lady"*	Gatwick	23.10.03T
G-VFOX	Airbus A340-642	449		R	Virgin Atlantic Airways Ltd *"Silver Lady" (For delivery 10.02)*		
G-VFSI	Robinson R22 Beta	1785	N4081L	19.12.96	Survey & Construction (Roofing) Ltd	Redhill	14. 6.03T
G-VGAL	Boeing 747-443	32337	(EI-CVH)	26. 4.01	Virgin Atlantic Ltd *"Jersey Girl"*	Gatwick	25. 4.04T
G-VGOA	Airbus A340-642	371		R	Virgin Atlantic Airways Ltd *"Indian Princess" (For delivery 7.03)*		
G-VHOL	Airbus A340-311	002	F-WWAS	30. 5.97	Virgin Atlantic Airways Ltd *"Jetstreamer"*	Gatwick	29. 5.03T
G-VHOT	Boeing 747-4Q8	26326		12.10.94	Virgin Atlantic Airways Ltd *"Tubular Belle"*	Gatwick	11.10.03T
G-VIBA	Cameron DP-80 Hot Air Airship	1729		28. 5.91	Jacques W.Soukup Enterprises Ltd	Beaulieu Court, Wilts/Great Missenden	3. 2.99A
G-VIBE	Boeing 747-219B	22791	ZK-NZZ 9M-MHH/ZK-NZZ/N6108N	24. 9.99	Virgin Atlantic Airways Ltd *"Spirit of New York"*	Gatwick	23. 9.02T
G-VICC	Piper PA-28-161 Warrior II	28-7916317	G-JFHL N2249U	3. 3.92	J.R.Green t/a Charlie Charlie Syndicate	Hinton-in-the-Hedges	4. 8.01T
G-VICE	MD Helicopters Hughes 369E (500E)	0365E	D-HLIS	16. 5.95	Bramington Properties Ltd	Wolverhampton	21. 8.04
G-VICI	de Havilland DH.112 Venom FB.50 (FB.1) *(Built F + W)*	783	HB-RVB (G-BMOB)/J-1573	6. 2.95	Lindsay Wood Promotions Ltd *(Op Source Classic Jet Flight)* *(Noted 7.01 as "J-1573" in Swiss AF c/s)*	Bournemouth	24.11.99P
G-VICM	Beechcraft F33C Bonanza	CJ-136	PH-BNG	3. 7.91	Velocity Engineering Ltd	Booker	20. 5.03
G-VICS	Commander Aircraft Commander 114B	14655	N655V	3. 2.98	Millennium Aviation Ltd	Guernsey	17. 4.04
G-VICT	Piper PA-31 Turbo Navajo B	31-7401211	G-BBZI N7590L	10. 9.99	ILS Air Ltd	Cambridge	9. 8.02T
G-VIEW	Vinten Wallis WA-116/L (Limbach L2000)	002		5. 7.82	K.H.Wallis *(Stored 8.01)*	Reymerston Hall, Norfolk	6.10.85P
G-VIIA	Boeing 777-236ER	27483	N5022E (G-ZZZF)	3. 7.97	British Airways plc *(Waves of the City t/s)*	Gatwick	2. 7.03T
G-VIIB	Boeing 777-236ER	27484	N5023Q (G-ZZZG)	23. 5.97	British Airways plc	Heathrow	22. 5.03T
G-VIIC	Boeing 777-236ER	27485	N5016R (G-ZZZH)	6. 2.97	British Airways plc	Heathrow	20. 8.02T
G-VIID	Boeing 777-236ER	27486	(G-ZZZI)	18. 2.97	British Airways plc	Heathrow	15. 9.02T
G-VIIE	Boeing 777-236ER	27487	(G-ZZZJ)	27. 2.97	British Airways plc	Heathrow	23. 9.02T
G-VIIF	Boeing 777-236ER	27488	(G-ZZZK)	19. 3.97	British Airways plc *(Landor c/s)*	Heathrow	1.11.02T
G-VIIG	Boeing 777-236ER	27489	(G-ZZZL)	9. 4.97	British Airways plc *(Landor c/s)*	Heathrow	8. 4.03T
G-VIIH	Boeing 777-236ER	27490	(G-ZZZM)	7. 5.97	British Airways plc *(Landor c/s)*	Heathrow	6. 5.03T
G-VIIJ	Boeing 777-236ER	27492	(G-ZZZP)	29.12.97	British Airways plc *(Benyhone Tartan t/s)*	Gatwick	21.12.03T
G-VIIK	Boeing 777-236ER	28840		3. 2.98	British Airways plc *(Animals & Trees t/s)*	Gatwick	2. 2.04T
G-VIIL	Boeing 777-236ER	27493		13. 3.98	British Airways plc *(Wings t/s)*	Heathrow	12. 3.04T
G-VIIM	Boeing 777-236ER	28841		26. 3.98	British Airways plc *(Waves & Cranes t/s)*	Gatwick	13. 9.03T
G-VIIN	Boeing 777-236ER	29319		21. 8.98	British Airways plc *(Whale Rider t/s)*	Heathrow	20. 8.04T

G-VIIO	Boeing 777-236ER	29320		26. 1.99	British Airways plc *(Chelsea Rose t/s)*	Gatwick	25. 1.02T
G-VIIP	Boeing 777-236ER	29321		9. 2.99	British Airways plc *(Colum t/s)*	Heathrow	8. 2.02T
G-VIIR	Boeing 777-236ER	29322		18. 3.99	British Airways plc *(Benyhone Tartan t/s)*	Gatwick	17. 3.02T
G-VIIS	Boeing 777-236ER	29323		1. 4.99	British Airways plc *(Chelsea Rose t/s)*	Heathrow	31. 3.02T
G-VIIT	Boeing 777-236ER	29962		26. 5.99	British Airways plc *(Rendezvous t/s)*	Heathrow	25. 5.02T
G-VIIU	Boeing 777-236ER	29963		28. 5.99	British Airways plc *(Delftblue Daybreak t/s)*	Heathrow	27. 5.02T
G-VIIV	Boeing 777-236ER	29964		29. 6.99	British Airways plc	Gatwick	28. 6.02T
G-VIIW	Boeing 777-236ER	29965		30. 7.99	British Airways plc	Heathrow	29. 7.02T
G-VIIX	Boeing 777-236ER	29966		11. 8.99	British Airways plc	Gatwick	10 .8.02T
G-VIIY	Boeing 777-236ER	29967		22.10.99	British Airways plc	Heathrow	21.10.02T
G-VIKE	Bellanca 17-30A Super Viking 300A	79-30911	N302CB	8. 7.80	W.G.Prout	(Fareham)	27. 6.02
G-VIKY	Cameron A-120 HAFB	3068		27. 4.93	D.W.Pennell	Broadway	31. 8.02A
G-VILL	Carmichael Lazer Z.200 (Lycoming AEIO-360)	10	G-BOYZ	10. 6.96	M.G.Jefferies *(Global Village titles)*	Little Gransden	12. 7.02P
G-VINO	Sky 90-24 HAFB	102		25. 2.98	Fivedata Ltd *(Lambrini titles)*	Todmorden	8 7.02A
G-VINS	Cameron N-90 HAFB	4731		12. 1.00	PSH Skypower Ltd *(Cotes du Rhone titles)*	Pewsey	18. 1.02A
G-VIPA	Cessna 182S Skylane	18280720	N148ME	13. 9.00	Stallingborough Aviation Ltd	Biggin Hill	19.10.03T
G-VIPH	Agusta A109C	7643	EI-CUV G-BVNH/G-LAXO	21. 9.01	Sloane Helicopters Ltd	Sywell	23. 9.04T
G-VIPI	British Aerospace BAe 125 Srs.800B	258222	G-5-745	27. 7.92	Yeates of Leicester Ltd	Southampton	16. 9.03T
G-VIPP	Piper PA-31-350 Navajo Chieftain	31-7952244	G-OGRV G-BMPX/N3543D	6. 8.93	Capital Trading Aviation Ltd	Filton	26. 8.02T
G-VIPY	Piper PA-31-350 Navajo Chieftain	31-7852143	EI-JTC G-POLO/(EI-...)/G-POLO/N27750	10.10.97	Capital Trading Aviation Ltd	Filton	12.10.02T
G-VITE	Robin R.1180T Aiglon	219		16.10.78	D.C.Perrett & D.T.Scrutton t/a G-VITE Flying Group	Stapleford	14. 9.03
G-VITL	Lindstrand LBL 105A HAFB	720		24. 8.00	Actionstrength Ltd t/a Vital Resources	Manchester	22..8.01A
G-VIVA	Thunder Ax7-65 Bolt HAFB	190		28.11.78	R.J.Mitchener	Andover	18. 3.99A
G-VIVI	Taylor JT.2 Titch	PFA 060-12405		4.11.96	D.G.Tucker	Hill Farm, Nayland	12.11.02P
G-VIVM	British Aircraft Corporation P.84 Jet Provost T.5	PAC/W/23907	G-BVWF/XS230	25. 3.96	K.Lyndon-Dykes	North Weald	1.11.02P
G-VIXN	de Havilland DH.110 Sea Vixen FAW.2 (TT)	10145	8828M XS587	5. 8.85	P.G.Vallance Ltd *(Gatwick Aviation Museum: as "XS587 in RN c/s)*	Charlwood, Surrey	
G-VIZZ	Sportavia RS.180 Sportsman	6018	D-EFBK	25.10.79	J.D.Howard & S.J.Morris t/a Exeter Fournier Group	Exeter	23. 7.04
G-VJAB	Jabiru Jabiru UL (Jabiru 2200A)	PFA 274-13322		25. 6.98	ST Aviation Ltd	Southery	31.10.01P
G-VJET	Avro 698 Vulcan B.2	--	XL426	7. 7.87	R.J.Clarkson t/a The Vulcan Restoration Trust *(As "XL426/G-VJET"))*	Southend	
G-VJIM	Colt Jumbo 77SS HAFB *(Registered as "Jumbo-2")*	1298	(G-BPJI)	7. 8.89	Magical Adventures Ltd. *"Jumbo Jim" (Virgin Atlantic titles)*	Chirk	2. 8.01A
G-VKID	Airbus A320-214	1130	F-WWIR	16.12.99	Virgin Atlantic Airways Ltd *"Sundance Kid" (Virgin Sun titles) (Stored 1.02)*	Filton	15.12.02T
G-VKIS	Airbus A321-211	1233	D-AVZD	31. 5.00	Virgin Atlantic Airways Ltd *"Sunkissed Girl (Virgin Sun titles)*	Gatwick	30. 5.03T
G-VKIT	Europa Aviation Europa	PFA 247-12783		11. 6.01	T.H.Crow	(Bicester)	
G-VLAD	Yakovlev Yak-50	791502	D-EIVR N51980/DDR-WQR/DM-WQR	14.11.88	M.B.Smith	Top Farm, Croydon	11. 9.02P
G-VLCN	Avro 698 Vulcan B.2		XH558	6. 2.95	C.Walton Ltd *(As "XH558")*	Bruntingthorpe	
G-VLIP	Boeing 747-443	32338	(EI-CVI)	15. 5.01	Virgin Atlantic Airways Ltd *"Hot Lips"*	Gatwick	14. 5.04T
G-VMCO	Agusta A109E Power	11123		31. 7.01	Unique Aviation Group Ltd	Jacobstowe, Devon	30. 7.04T
G-VMDE(2)	Cessna P210N Pressurised Centurion II	P21000088	(N4717P)	20. 7.78	Royton Express Deliveries (Welwyn) Ltd	North Weald	4. 4.04
G-VMED	Airbus A320-214	0978	F-WWDC	16. 4.99	Virgin Atlantic Airways Ltd *"Mediteranean Maiden" (Virgin Sun titles) (Stored 1.02)*	Filton	15 .4.02T
G-VMEG	Airbus A340-642	391		R	Virgin Atlantic Airways Ltd *"Mystic Maiden" (For delivery 6.02)*		
G-VMJM	SOCATA TB-10 Tobago	1361	G-BTOK	21. 4.92	S.C.Brown	Enstone	2. 5.04T
G-VMPR	de Havilland DH.115 Vampire T.11	15621	8196M XE920	13. 3.95	J.N.Kerr *(As "XE920/A" in 603 (County of Edinburgh) Sqdn c/s)*	Bournemouth	3. 4.01P
G-VMSL	Robinson R22 Alpha	0483	G-KILY N8561M	5. 2.98	L.L.F.Smith *(Force landed & rolled over near Turweston 4.6.01)*	Booker	26.12.03T

G-VNOM	de Havilland DH.112 Venom FB.50 (FB.1) *(Built F + W)*	842	J-1632	13. 7.84	T.J.Mann *(As "J-1632" in Swiss AF c/s 3.00)*	Cranfield	
G-VNUS	Hughes 269C (300)	122-0175	G-BATT	20. 9.00	Heli Air Ltd	Wellesbourne Mountford	21.11.03T
G-VOAR	Piper PA-28-181 Archer III	2843011	N9256Q	3.11.95	S.J.Skilton t/a Aviation Rentals *(Op Solent Flight Training)*	Bournemouth	15.12.01T
G-VODA	Cameron N-77 HAFB *(New envelope c/n 4164 @ 12.97)*	2208		8. 2.90	Vodafone Group plc *(Vodafone titles)*	Newbury	14. 6.01A
G-VOGE	Airbus A340-642	416		R	Virgin Atlantic Airways Ltd *"Cover Girl" (For delivery 7.02)*		
G-VOID	Piper PA-28RT-201 Arrow IV	28R-8118049	ZS-KTM (G-GCAA)/ZS-KTM/N83232	17. 8.87	Newbus Aviation Ltd	Shoreham	13. 1.03T
G-VOLH	Airbus A321-211	0823	(EC-) D-AVZX	15. 5.98	Airtours International Airways Ltd	Manchester	27. 6.04T
G-VOLT*	Cameron N-77 HAFB	2157		8.11.89	Balloon Preservation Group *"National Power" (Cancelled 23.10.01 as wfu)*	Kirdford	25. 4.97A
G-VOTE*	Ultramagic M-77 HAFB	77-164		10. 3.99	Window on the World Ltd *(Cancelled 6.4.01 by CAA)*	London SE1	28. 4.01A
G-VPSJ	Europa Aviation Europa	PFA 247-12520		29. 7.93	J.D.Bean	(Oxford)	
G-VPUF	Boeing 747-219B	22725	ZK-NZY N6005C	21. 3.00	Virgin Atlantic Airways Ltd *"High as a Kite"*	Gatwick	21 .3.03T
G-VROE	Avro 652A Anson T.21	3634	G-BFIR 7881M/WD413	3. 3.98	Air Atlantique Ltd	Coventry	28. 6.02P
G-VROC	Boeing 747-41R			R	Virgin Atlantic Airways Ltd *"Mustang Sally" (For delivery 2003)*	Gatwick	
G-VROM	Boeing 747-443	32339	(EI-CVJ)	29. 5.01	Virgin Atlantic Airways Ltd *"Barbarella"*	Gatwick	28. 5.04T
G-VROS	Boeing 747-443	30885	(EI-CVG)	22. 3.01	Virgin Atlantic Airways Ltd *"English Rose"*	Heathrow	21. 3.04T
G-VROY	Boeing 747-443	32340	(EI-CVK)	18. 6.01	Virgin Atlantic Airways Ltd *"Pretty Woman"*	Gatwick	17. 6.04T
G-VRST	Piper PA-46-350P Malibu Mirage	4636189		7.12.98	Winchfield Development Ltd	Fairoaks	11. 2.02
G-VRVI	Cameron O-90 HAFB	2522		27. 2.91	Cooling Services Ltd *"Daikin"*	Portishead	1. 8.00A
G-VSBC	Beechcraft B200 Super King Air	BB-1290	N3185C JA8859/N3185C	17. 6.93	Vickers Shipbuilding & Engineering Ltd	Walney Island	21. 6.03
G-VSEA	Airbus A340-311	003	F-WWDA	7. 7.97	Virgin Atlantic Airways Ltd *"Plain Sailing"*	Gatwick	6. 7.03T
G-VSHY	Airbus A340-642	383		R	Virgin Atlantic Airways Ltd *"Madam Butterfly" (For delivery 6.02)*		
G-VSKY	Airbus A340-311	016	F-WWJH	21. 1.94	Virgin Atlantic Airways Ltd *"China Girl"*	Gatwick	20. 1.03T
G-VSSH	Airbus A340-642	468		R	Virgin Atlantic Airways Ltd *"Sweet Dreamer" (For delivery 12.02)*		
G-VSUN	Airbus A340-313	114	F-WWJI (F-GLZJ)	30. 4.96	Virgin Atlantic Airways Ltd *"Rainbow Lady"*	Gatwick	29. 4.02T
G-VTAN	Airbus A320-214	0764	G-BXTA F-WWDF	29. 4.99	Virgin Atlantic Airways Ltd *"Sunshine Girl" (Virgin Sun titles) (Stored Filton 1.02)*	Gatwick	29. 4.01T
G-VTEN*	Vinten-Wallis WA.117 Venom (Continental O-200-B)	UMA-01 & 003		22. 4.85	K.H.Wallis *(Cancelled 12.6.89 as WFU: stored unmarked 8.01)*	Reymerston Hall, Norfolk	3.12.85P
G-VTII	de Havilland DH.115 Vampire T.11 *(Fuselage No.DHP40273)*	15127	WZ507	9. 1.80	De Havilland Aviation Ltd *(As "WZ507")*	Swansea	13. 8.95P
G-VTOL*	Hawker Siddeley Harrier T.52	B3/41H/735795	ZA250 G-VTOL/(XW273)	27. 7.70	Brooklands Museum *(Cancelled 3.90 by CAA)*	Brooklands	2.11.86S
G-VTOP	Boeing 747-4Q8	28194		28. 1.97	Virgin Atlantic Airways Ltd *"Virginia Plain"*	Gatwick	17. 3.03T
G-VULC	Avro 698 Vulcan B.2A		N655AV G-VULC/XM655	27. 2.84	Radarmoor Ltd *(As "XM655") (Noted 2000)*	Wellesbourne Mountford	
G-VVBF	Colt 315A HAFB	4058		3. 3.97	Virgin Balloon Flights Ltd	London SE16	18. 7.02T
G-VVBK	Piper PA-34-200T Seneca II	34-7570303	G-BSBS G-BDRI/SE-GLG	26. 1.89	The Mann Organisation Ltd	Gloucestershire	15. 8.04T
G-VVIP	Cessna 421C Golden Eagle III	421C0699	G-BMWB N2655L	7. 7.92	Capital Trading Aviation Ltd	Filton	30. 4.04T
G-VWOW	Boeing 747-41R	32745		31.10.01	Virgin Atlantic Airways Ltd *"Cosmic Girl"*	Heathrow	12.12.04T
G-VXLG	Boeing 747-41R	29406		30. 9.98	Virgin Atlantic Airways Ltd *"Ruby Tuesday"*	Heathrow	29. 9.04T
G-VYGR	Colt 120A HAFB	2479		24. 9.93	A.van Wyk	Caxton	27. 5.02T
G-VZZZ	Boeing 747-219B	22722	ZK-NZV	7. 7.99	Virgin Atlantic Airways Ltd *"Morning Glory"*	Gatwick	6 .7.02T

G-WAAA – G-WZZZ

G-WAAC	Cameron N-56 HAFB	492		14. 2.79	N.P.Hemsley t/a Whacko Balloon Group *"Whacko"*	Crawley	26. 6.97A
G-WACB	Reims Cessna F152 II	F15201972		16. 9.86	Wycombe Air Centre Ltd	Booker	24. 2.02T
G-WACE	Reims Cessna F152 II	F15201978		16. 9.86	Wycombe Air Centre Ltd	Booker	23. 4.02T
G-WACF	Cessna 152 II	15284852	N628GH (LV-PMB)/N628GH	20. 1.87	Wycombe Air Centre Ltd	Booker	24.11.03T
G-WACG	Cessna 152 II	15285536	ZS-KXY (N93699)	4.11.86	Wycombe Air Centre Ltd	Booker	3. 4.03T
G-WACH	Reims Cessna FA.152 Aerobat	0425		18. 6.87	Wycombe Air Centre Ltd	Booker	4. 8.02T
G-WACI	Beechcraft 76 Duchess	ME-289	N6703Y	26. 7.88	Wycombe Air Centre Ltd	Booker	14.11.03T
G-WACJ	Beechcraft 76 Duchess	ME-278	N6700Y	3. 1.89	Wycombe Air Centre Ltd	Booker	6. 5.02T
G-WACL	Reims Cessna F172N Skyhawk II	F17201912	G-BHGG	19. 6.89	The Exeter Flying Club Ltd	Exeter	21. 4.04T
G-WACM	Cessna 172S Skyhawk	172S9005	N35526	21.12.01	Wycombe Air Centre Ltd	Booker	
G-WACO	Waco UPF-7	5400	N29903 NC29903	28. 1.87	R.G.Vincent t/a RGV (Aircraft Services) & Co *(Damaged Liverpool 15.4.89: stored 4.01)*	Gloucestershire	13. 5.90
G-WACP	Piper PA-28-180 Cherokee Archer	28-7405007	G-BBPP N9559N	5. 4.89	Wycombe Air Centre Ltd	Booker	10. 7.04T
G-WACR	Piper PA-28-180 Cherokee Archer	28-7505090	G-BCZF N9517N	18.12.86	Wycombe Air Centre Ltd	Booker	9. 7.03T
G-WACT	Reims Cessna F152 II	F15201908	G-BKFT	24. 6.86	The Exeter Flying Club Ltd	Exeter	5.10.03T
G-WACU	Reims Cessna FA152 Aerobat	FA1520380	G-BJZU	10. 7.86	Wycombe Air Centre Ltd	Booker	9. 6.03T
G-WACW	Cessna 172P Skyhawk II	17274057	N5307K	16. 5.88	Wycombe Air Centre Ltd	Booker	16. 6.03T
G-WACY	Reims Cessna F172P Skyhawk II	F17202217	F-GDOZ	3.10.86	Wycombe Air Centre Ltd	Booker	14. 1.02T
G-WADI	Piper PA-46-350P Malibu Mirage	4636205		8. 5.99	H.J.D.S.Baioes	Cranfield	2. 6.02T
G-WADS	Robinson R22 Beta	1224	G-NICO	25. 4.96	Helicentre Ltd	Blackpool	3. 3.02T
G-WAGG	Robinson R22 Beta-II	2960		7. 7.99	J.B.Wagstaff t/a N.J.Wagstaff Leasing	Costock	15 .7.02T
G-WAHL	QAC Quickie	PFA 094-10619		20. 9.00	A.A.M.Wahlberg	Lee-on-Solent	
G-WAIR	Piper PA-32-301 Saratoga	32-8506010	N2607X N9577N	14. 1.91	P.H.Burtwhistle t/a Thorne Aviation	Thorne, Doncaster	13. 5.03
G-WAIT	Cameron V-77 HAFB	2390		20.11.90	C.P.Brown	Ely	24. 7.99A
G-WAKE	Mainair Blade 912	1244-0300-7-W1037		6. 3.00	J.G.Lloyd	(Harlow)	6. 3.02P
G-WALS	Cessna A152 Aerobat	A1520843	N4614A	27. 9.88	Redhill Aviation Ltd t/a Redhill Flying Club	Redhill	5. 2.01T
G-WARB	Piper PA-28-161 Warrior III	2842034	N41286 (G-WARB)/N41286	4. 9.98	Muller Aircraft Leasing Ltd	Biggin Hill	7. 9.04T
G-WARC	Piper PA-28-161 Warrior III	2842035	N41244 (G-WARC)/N41244	11. 9.98	Plane Talking Ltd	Elstree	13. 9.04T
G-WARD	Taylor JT.1 Monoplane (VW 1834)	WB.VI & PFA 1407		1.12.80	R.P.J.Hunter *(Damaged Redhill 17.9.99)*	Redhill	22. 2.00P
G-WARE	Piper PA-28-161 Warrior II	28-8416080	N4357L ("N4354Z")	21. 7.89	W.B.Ware	Filton	17.11.01
G-WARH	Piper PA-28-161 Warrior III	2842063	N4177Y G-WARH	4. 2.00	Newcastle Upon Tyne Aero Club Ltd	Newcastle	10. 2.03T
G-WARK	Schweizer Hughes 269C (300C)	S.1354		13.11.89	K.Sutcliffe	(Halifax)	15. 4.02
G-WARP	Cessna 182F	18254633	G-ASHB N3233U	6. 6.95	G.Burton t/a Army Parachute Association	AAC Netheravon	16. 8.04
G-WARR	Piper PA-28-161 Warrior II	28-7916321	N3074U	15. 9.88	T.J. & G.M.Laundy *(Op RAF Halton Aeroplane Club)*	RAF Halton	5. 2.04T
G-WARS	Piper PA-28-161 Warrior III	2842022	N9281X (G-WARS)/N9281X	7.11.97	Blaneby Ltd	Biggin Hill	6.11.03T
G-WARV	Piper PA-28-161 Warrior III	2842036	N41247 (G-WARV), N41247	9.10.98	Plane Talking Ltd	Elstree	13.10.04T
G-WARW	Piper PA-28-161 Warrior III	2842037	N41254 (G-WARW)/N41254	17.11.98	C.J.Simmonds	St.Just	19.11.01T
G-WARX	Piper PA-28-161 Warrior III	2842038	N4126D (G-WARX)/N4126D	15.12.98	C.M.A.Clark	Wellesbourne Mountford	20.12.01
G-WARY	Piper PA-28-161 Warrior III	2842024	N9287X (G-WARY)/N9287X	13.11.97	Armstrong Aviation Ltd	Blackpool	29.11.03T
G-WASP	Brantly B-2B	445	G-ASXE	7. 2.77	N.J.R.Minchin	Hill Top Farm, Godalming	9. 9.02
G-WATS	Piper PA-34-220T Seneca III	34-8333058	G-BOVJ N8202J	3. 2.89	Oxford Aviation Services Ltd	Gloucestershire	10. 7.04T
G-WATT*	Cameron Cooling Tower SS HAFB	2158		8.11.89	Balloon Preservation Group *"Enterprise" (Cancelled 23.10.01 as wfu)*	Kirdford	22. 8.96A
G-WAVA	Robin HR.200/120B	352		10. 7.00	Wellesbourne Flyers Ltd t/a Wellesbourne Aviation	Wellesbourne Mountford	3. 8.03T

G-WAVE(2)	Grob G-109B	6381		1. 8.85	M.L.Murdoch	Park Farm, Eaton Bray	11. 3.04
G-WAVI	Robin HR.200/120B	346	G-BZDG	8. 5.01	Wellesbourne Flyers Ltd	Wellesbourne Mountford	12. 4.03T
G-WAZZ	Pitts S-1S Special (Lycoming 0-360)	7-0332	G-BRRP N3TD	17. 6.94	D.T.Knight	White Waltham	13. 7.00P
G-WBAT	Wombat Gyrocopter (Rotax 532)	CJ-001	G-BSID	31. 5.90	M.R.Harrison	(Guernsey)	
G-WBMG	Cameron N Ele 90SS HAFB	3086	G-BUYV	5. 7.93	M.Sevrin	Court St.Etienne, Belgium	22. 6.02A
G-WBPR	British Aerospace BAe 125 Srs.800B	258085	G-5-551	29. 9.87	Granada Group plc	RAF Northolt	13.11.02
G-WBTS	Falconar F-11W-200 (Continental 0-200-A)	PFA 032-10070	G-BDPL	22.10.90	W.C.Brown	White Waltham	15. 7.02P
G-WCAT	Colt Flying Mitt SS HAFB	1744		30. 5.90	I.Chadwick *"Washcat"* t/a Balloon Preservation Flying Group	Kirdford	19..8.00A
G-WCEI	SOCATA MS.894E Rallye 220GT	12141	G-BAOC	28. 5.85	R.A.L.Lucas	Walney Island	23. 7.04
G-WCUB	Piper PA-18-150 Super Cub	18-8278	HB-OLR N5514Y	11. 5.01	P.A.Walley	(Bushey)	6. 8.04T
G-WDEB	Thunder Ax7-77 HAFB	1606		26. 9.89	W.de Bock "Landplan"	Peterborough	2. 8.01A
G-WDEV	Westland SA.341G Gazelle 1	1098	G-IZEL G-BBHW	30. 9.98	M W Helicopters Ltd	Stapleford	9. 3.03T
G-WEAC	Fairey Britten-Norman BN-2A mk.III-2 Trislander	1042	5H-AZD/ G-BEFP/(4X-CCL)/G-BEFP/N30WA/JA6401/G-BEFP	16.12.94	Keen Leasing Ltd *(Op Woodgate Executive Air Services)*	Belfast	12.12.02T
G-WELI	Cameron N-77 HAFB	1078		26. 9.84	M.A.Shannon *"Wellie"*	Southampton	18. 8.01A
G-WELL	Beechcraft E90 King Air	LW-198	N202CC (N7PB)/N202CC	18. 7.85	Colt Transport Ltd	Goodwood	5. 6.03T
G-WELS	Cameron N-65 HAFB	1297		7. 4.86	K.J.Vickery *"Talisman"*	Billingshurst	26. 6.92A
G-WEND	Piper PA-28RT-201 Arrow IV	28R-8118026	PH-SYL N8296L	8.11.82	Tayside Aviation Ltd	Perth	20. 5.02T
G-WERY	SOCATA TB-20 Trinidad	305		2. 4.82	Fastour Aviation Ltd	(Tadcaster)	11. 5.03
G-WEST	Agusta A109A	7213		21. 1.81	Westland Helicopters Ltd	Yeovil	28. 3.02
G-WESX	CFM Streak Shadow (Rotax 582)	K.116-SA & PFA 161A-11561		2. 2.90	K.Kerr	(Wirral)	16.12.02P
G-WETI	Cameron N-31 HAFB	449		27.11.78	C.A.Butter & J.J.T.Cooke *"Puddleduck"*	Marsh Benham	11 9.00A
G-WFFW	Piper PA-28-161 Warrior II	28-8116161	N8342A	26.10.93	N.F.Duke	Bournemouth	27. 1.03
G-WFOX	Robinson R22 Beta-II	2826		2. 6.98	Heli-Air Ltd	Wolverhampton	27. 6.04T
G-WGAL	Bell 206B-3 JetRanger III	3165	G-OICS N678TM	22. 3.93	Watkiss Group Aviation Ltd	Keysoe	27. 3.04T
G-WGCS	Piper PA-18 Super Cub 95 (L-18C-PI) *(Frame No.18-1500)*	18-1528	(G-BLSV) ALAT F-MBCH/51-15528	21.12.84	S.C.Thompson	Newells Farm, Bolney	6. 7.02P
G-WGHB	Canadair (CL-30) T-33AN Silver Star mk.3	T33-640	CF-EHB CAF 133640/RCAF 21640	9. 5.74	R.H.& G.C Cooper *(Stored 5.00)*	Hibaldstow	13. 6.77P
G-WGSC	Pilatus PC-6/B2-H4 Turbo-Porter	848	OE-ECS	2. 1.90	D.M.Penny *(Op Wild Geese Parachute Centre)*	Movenis, Co.Londonderry	23. 3.04
G-WHAM	Eurocopter AS350B3 Ecureuil	3494		18. 1.02	McAlpine Helicopters Ltd	Oxford	
G-WHAT	Colt 77A HAFB	1911		15. 3.91	M.A.Scholes *"Chad"*	London SE25	10.10.02T
G-WHAZ	Agusta-Bell 206A Jet Ranger	8112	OH-HRE G-WHAZ/OH-HRE	26. 6.97	Heli Charter Ltd	Manston	31.10.03
G-WHEE	Pegasus Quantum 15-912	7510		26. 3.99	D.Young t/a PFT (Cotswolds)	Kemble	9 .4.02P
G-WHEN	Tecnam P92-EM Echo	PFA 318-13679		7. 2.01	C.D.Marsh	(Camberley)	
G-WHIM	Colt 77A HAFB	1476		10. 4.89	D.L.Morgan	Ilford	14. 8.01A
G-WHOG	CFM Streak Shadow (Rotax 618)	K.253-SA & PFA 206-12776		21. 9.94	B.R.Cannell *"Wart Hog"*	Old Sarum	4. 9.02P
G-WHOO	Rotorway Exec 162F	6495		5. 6.01	C.A.Saul	(Canvey Island)	
G-WHRL	Schweizer 269C	S 1453	EC-GGX CS-HDG/G-WHRL/N41S	19. 4.90	G.Wood t/a Graham Wood Decorators	(York)	26 .8.02T
G-WHST	Eurocopter AS 350B2 Ecureuil	2915	G-BWYA	9. 8.96	Hawkrise Ltd	Sutton Coldfield	26. 9.02T
G-WIBB	Jodel D.18 (Subaru EA81)	PFA 169-11640		18. 6.96	J.& D.Wibberley	Priory Farm, Tibenham	1. 6.02P
G-WIBS	CASA I-131E Srs.2000	2005	E3B-401	25. 3.99	C Willoughby	(Ashford)	
G-WIFE	Cessna R182 Skylane RG II	R18200244	G-BGVT N3162C	11.12.01	J.Brennan t/a Wife Group	(Sligo, Co.Sligo)	9.11.00
G-WILD	Aerotek Pitts S-1T Special (Lycoming AEIO-360)	1017	ZS-LMM	6.12.85	A McClean	White Waltham	12. 1.04
G-WILG	WSK PZL-104 Wilga 35A	62153	G-AZYJ	15. 4.97	M.H.Bletsoe-Brown	Sywell	4. 4.04
G-WILS	Piper PA-28RT-201T Turbo Arrow IV	28R-8431005	PH-DPD N4330W	16. 1.96	B. Walker & Co (Dursley) Ltd	Gloucestershire	22. 3.02T
G-WILY	Rutan LongEz (Lycoming 0-320)	1200 & PFA 074A-10724		8. 6.83	W.S.Allen *"Time Flies"*	Gloucestershire	28. 3.00P
G-WIMP	Colt 56A HAFB	755		13. 2.86	T.& B.Chamberlain	York	3. 9.01A

G-WINE	Thunder AX7-77Z HAFB	472		25.11.82	S.M.Miles *"Gemini"*	Mitcham	17. 6.97A
					(Op Balloon Preservation Group)		
G-WINK	Grumman-American AA-5B Tiger	AA5B-0327	N74658	14.12.90	B.S.Cooke	Elstree	19. 3.03
G-WINS	Piper PA-32-300 Cherokee Six	32-7640065	N8476C	24. 4.91	Cheyenne Ltd	Jersey	14. 3.03
G-WIRE	Aérospatiale AS355F1 Twin Squirrel	5312	G-CEGB G-BLJL	22. 1.90	National Grid Co plc	Oxford	12. 6.03T
G-WIRL	Robinson R22 Beta	0671		27. 7.87	T.W.Finlay	(Dungannon)	12. 8.02T
G-WISH	Lindstrand Cake SS HAFB	006		14.12.92	Oxford Promotions (UK) Ltd	Kentucky, USA	23. 4.01A
	(Birthday Cake shape)				*(Op F Prell)*		
G-WIXI	Avions Mudry CAP.10B	279		27. 1.98	J.M. & E.M.Wicks		
					Boones Farm, High Garrett, Braintree		2. 8.04
G-WIZA	Robinson R22 Beta	0861	G-PERL N90815	16.11.94	Burman Aviation Ltd	Cranfield	12. 1.01T
					(Op Burman Helicopters)		
G-WIZB	Grob G.115A	8104	EI-CAD	2. 9.98	A.G.Wisbey	Sywell	22.10.04T
G-WIZD	Lindstrand LBL-180A HAFB	066		12.11.93	T.H.Wilson	Diss	29. 8.01T
G-WIZO	Piper PA-34-220T Seneca III	34-8133171	N8413U	16.12.86	B.J.Booty	Bristol	26. 4.04T
G-WIZR	Robinson R22 Beta-II	2799		9. 3.98	J.D.Forbes-Nixon & N.H.Taylor	Bristol	5. 4.04T
					t/a Clifton Helicopter Hire		
G-WIZY	Robinson R22 Beta	0566	G-BMWX N24196	26. 8.97	B.J.North	Redhill	18. 6.03T
G-WIZZ	Agusta-Bell 206B JetRanger II	8540		7.12.77	Rivermead Aviation Ltd	(Reading)	3.10.02T
G-WJAN	Boeing 757-21KER	28674		18. 3.97	Airtours International Airways Ltd		
						Manchester	3.11.02T
G-WKRD	Eurocopter AS 350B2 Ecureuil	2668	G-BUJG G-HEAR/G-BUJG	16. 3.99	Wickford Development Co	Wickford	22. 9.04T
G-WLAC	Piper PA-18-150 Super Cub	18-8899	G-HAHA G-BSWE/N9194P	2. 6.98	White Waltham Airfield Ltd		
						White Waltham	11. 7.04T
G-WLGA	WSK PZL-104 Wilga 80	CF21910932	EC-FYY F-GMLR	8.11.96	A.J.Renham	Teesside	10. 4.03
G-WLLY	Bell 206B JetRanger II	405	G-OBHH G-WLLY/G-RODY/G-ROGR/G-AXMM/N1469W	24. 3.93	Blue Five Aviation Ltd	Redhill	13. 7.02T
G-WLMS	Mainair Blade 912	1223-0999-7-W1016		23. 9.99	J.R.North	Ince Blundell	10 10.02P
G-WMAA	MBB Bö.105DBS-4	S.135/914	G-PASB VH-LSA/G-BDMC/D-HDEC	8. 9.94	Bond Air Services	RAF Cosford	29. 9.03T
					(Op West Midlands Air Ambulance)		
	(Rebuilt with new airframe S.914 1994 - see G-PASB)						
G-WMAN	Aérospatiale SA.341G Gazelle 1	1277	ZS-HUR N4491R/YV-54CP	4. 8.99	J.Wightman	(Ballynahinch)	4..7.03
G-WMAS	Eurocopter EC 135 T1	0174		18. 6.01	Bond Air Services Ltd	RAF Cosford	26 .7.04T
G-WMCC*	British Aerospace Jetstream Srs.3102-01	601	G-31-601 (N....)/G-TALL/G-31-601	22. 9.83	Not known	Birmingham	
	(Stored engineless 8.96: cancelled 26.11.97 on sale to USA: derelict Fire Station 3.98: current status unknown)						
G-WMID	MD Helicopters Explorer	900-00062	N3063T	12.10.99	West Midlands Police Authority		
					"Miss Molly Collins"	Birmingham	13 .1.03T
G-WMPA	Aérospatiale AS355F2 Twin Squirrel	5401		7. 2.89	Police Aviation Services Ltd		
						Gloucestershire	25. 6.04T
G-WMTM	Gulfstream AA-5B Tiger	AA5B-1035	N4517V	8. 1.91	A.Allen	(Scunthorpe)	10. 8.02T
					(Carries "4517V" on fin)		
G-WMWM	Robinson R44 Raven	0767		27. 4.00	K.Cummins	Cambridge	1. 6.03T
G-WNGS	Cameron N-105 HAFB	4385		15. 7.98	R M Horn	Chelmsford	15. 8.02A
					(Motorola Wings titles)		
G-WOLF	Piper PA-28-140 Cherokee Cruiser	28-7425439	OY-TOD	20. 3.80	Aircraft Management Services Ltd		
						(Uckfield)	4. 2.02T
G-WOOD	Beechcraft 95-B55A Baron	TC-1283	SE-GRC G-AYID/SE-EXK	17. 9.79	T.D.Broadhurst	Sleap	10.12.01
					t/a Baron Aviation		
G-WOOF	Enstrom 480	5027		3. 3.98	Netcopter.co.uk Ltd	(Knutsford)	9. 5.04T
G-WOOL	Colt 77A HAFB	2044		23. 2.93	T.G.& C.L.Pembrey & N.P.Helmsley		
					t/a Whacko Balloon Group	Steyning	20. 6.02
G-WORK*	Thunder Ax10-180 Srs.2 HAFB	2396	DQ-PBF G-WORK	12. 5.93	(Balloon Preservation Group)	Malpas	
					(Paradise Balloon Flights titles)		
			(Sold as DQ-HBF 11.97 & cancelled 3.11.97: returned to UK 2000 as "DQ-PBF")				
G-WORM	Thruster T600N	9109-T600N-039		5.10.99	R.& J.Gibson	Ince Blundell	4. 3.02P
	(Rotax 582 UL-DCDI)						
G-WOSY	MBB Bö.105DBS/4	S.656	G-PASD G-BNRS/N14ES/N4572Q/D-HDTZ	28.11.01	Redwood Aviation Ltd	(Newport, IoW)	26. 9.03T
G-WOTG	Pilatus Britten-Norman BN-2T Islander	2139	(ZF444) G-WOTG/G-BJYT	10.11.83	P.M.Hall	Weston-on-the-Green	16. 2.03
					t/a RAF Sport Parachute Association		
G-WPAS	MD Helicopters Explorer	900-00053		1. 7.98	Police Aviation Services Ltd	Devizes	7.11.04T
					(Op Wiltshire Police/Ambulance Authority)		
G-WREN	Aerotek Pitts S-2A Special	2229	N947	28. 1.81	Northamptonshire School of Flying Ltd		
	(Lycoming AEIO-360)					Sywell	31. 3.02T

G-WRFM	Enstrom 280C-UK Shark	1202	G-CTSI	21. 4.89	A.J.MacFarlane	Goodwood	6. 6.04
			G-BKIO/(G-BKHN)/SE-HLB		t/a Skywalker Enterprises		
G-WRIT	Colt 77A HAFB	1328		15. 9.88	G.Pusey *"Legal Eagle"*	Seville, France	15. 6.02A
G-WRLY	Robinson R22 Beta	0699	G-OFJS	22.11.00	Burman Aviation Ltd	Gloucestershire	26.10.02T
			G-BNXJ				
G-WRWR	Robinson R22 Beta-II	2964		20. 7.99	Air Foyle Ltd	Luton	2..8.02T
G-WSEC	Enstrom F-28C	398	G-BONF	19.12.88	AJD Engineering Ltd	Moat Farm, Milden	10.12.01
			N51661				
G-WSFT	Piper PA-23-250 Aztec F	27-7754059	G-BTHS	18. 6.86	Plane Talking Ltd	Elstree	15. 6.01T
			N62824				
G-WSKY	Enstrom 280C-UK-2 Shark	1037	G-BEEK	25. 7.83	M.I.Edwards	Brandon, Suffolk	6.12.03
G-WUFF	Europa Aviation Europa	PFA 247-12942		19. 1.99	M.A.Barker *(Noted 9.01)*	Gamston	
G-WULF	WAR Focke-Wulf 190 204 &	PFA 081-10328		24. 2.78	A.Howe	(Birmingham)	22. 6.01P
	(Continental 0-200-A)				*(As "8+-" in Luftwaffe c/s)*		
G-WVBF	Lindstrand LBL-210A HAFB	312		6.12.95	Virgin Balloon Flights Ltd	(London SE16)	21. 6.01T
G-WWAL	Piper PA-28R-180 Cherokee Arrow		G-AZSH	23.10.98	C.& G.Clarke	White Waltham	23. 8.02T
		28R-30461	N4612J				
G-WWAS	Piper PA-34-220T Seneca III		G-BPPB	2. 3.95	D.Intzevidis	Athens, Greece	10. 9.01
		34-8133222	N83270/(N707WF)/N83270/N9579N				
G-WWBB	Airbus A330-243	404	F-WWKP	30. 5.01	British Midland Airways Ltd	Manchester	29. 5.04T
					(Star Alliance c/s)		
G-WWBC	Airbus A330-243	455		R	British Midland Airways Ltd	Manchester	
G-WWBD	Airbus A330-243	401	F-WWKN	9. 5.01	British Midland Airways Ltd	Manchester	8. 5.04T
					(Stored 1.02)		
G-WWBM	Airbus A330-243	398	F-WWKL	27. 4.01	British Midland Airways Ltd	Manchester	26. 4.04T
G-WWIZ	Beechcraft 58 Baron	TH-429	G-GAMA	18.10.96	Chase Aviation Ltd	Bournemouth	16. 6.02T
			G-BBSD				
G-WWWG	Europa Aviation Europa *(Mono-wheel u/c)*		"G-DSEL"	31. 7.95	Chloe F.Williams-Wynne	Talybont, Gwynedd	10.11.98P
	(Wilksch-Airmotive WAM120) 40 &	PFA 247-12597					
G-WYAT	CFM Streak Shadow SA	PFA 206-12993		9. 6.97	M.G.Whyatt	(High Peak, Derbyshire)	20. 6.02P
G-WYCH	Cameron Witch 90SS HAFB	1330		30. 9.86	Corn Palace Balloon Club Ltd	Bristol	13. 7.99A
					"Hilda"		
G-WYMP	Cessna F150J	F150-0521	G-BAGW	26. 2.82	R.Hall	Full Sutton	18. 8.99T
			SE-FKM				
G-WYMR	Robinson R44 Astro	0439		15. 4.98	Heli Air Ltd	(Wellesbourne)	3. 5.04T
					(Heli-Air Flying Training Schools titles)		
G-WYND	Wittman W.8 Tailwind	PFA 031-12407		2. 8.99	R.S.Marriott & C.Clark	(Scunthorpe)	
					t/a Forge Group		
G-WYNN	Rand Robinson KR-2	PFA 129-11141		28. 8.85	W.Thomas	(Wrexham)	
	(Originally regd as c/n PFA 129-11093: probably composite of both projects)						
G-WYNS	Aero Designs Pulsar XP	PFA 202-11976		22. 2.91	S.L.Bauza	(Palma de Mallorca)	27. 4.98P
	(Rotax 912)						
G-WYNT	Cameron N-56 HAFB	1038		3. 4.84	S.L.G.Williams	Bristol	21. 3.98A
					"Gwyntoedd Dros Cymru/Winds over Wales"		
G-WYPA	MBB Bö.105DBS/4	S.815	D-HDZY	27.10.89	Police Aviation Services Ltd		
						Gloucestershire	19.12.01T
G-WYSP	Robinson R44 Astro	0657		17. 9.99	Calderbrook Estates Ltd	(Sowerby Bridge)	28 .9.02T
G-WZOL	Tiger Cub RL5B LWS Sherwood Ranger		G-MZOL	20. 1.99	G.W.F.Webb	Coldharbour Farm, Willingham	13.12.02P
	(Jabiru 2200A)	PFA 237-12887					
G-WZZZ	Colt AS-42 Hot Air Airship	459		10.12.82	Lindstrand Balloons Ltd	Oswestry	4. 9.01A
	(Rebuilt 1984/85 using new AS-56 envelope c/n 607)				*"Kit Kat"*		

G-XAAA – G-XZZZ

G-XALP	Schweizer Hughes 269C (300C)	S.1314		27. 6.88	J.Rawding	Wickenby	8.12.03T
					t/a Helicopter Experience		
G-XANT	Cameron N-105 HAFB	3003		4. 3.93	Flying Pictures Ltd	Fairoaks	21.11.96A
					"Citroen Xantia"		
G-XARV	ARV1 Super 2	010	G-OPIG	8.11.95	N.R.Beale	Shotteswell	3.10.01P
			G-BMSJ				
G-XATS	Aerotek Pitts S-2A	2147	CS-AZE	29. 3.01	Air Training Services Ltd	Booker	8.11.04T
			N338BD				
G-XAXA	Fairey Britten-Norman BN-2A-26 Islander		G-LOTO	22. 8.00	Airx Ltd	Bournemouth	28.11.03A
		530	G-BDWG/(N90255)/(C-GYUF)/G-BDWG		*(Op Le Cocq)*		
G-XAYR	Raj Hamsa X'Air 582 (2)			4. 1.00	D.L.Connolly & R.Barber	(Bedford)	4. 4.02P
		471 & BMAA/HB/122					
G-XBAT	Aeroprakt A22 Foxbat	PFA 317-13786		21. 9.01	P.J.Harlow	(London W4)	
G-XBHX	Boeing 737-36N	28572		21. 5.98	British Regional Airlines Ltd	Gatwick	5. 9.03T
					(Grand Union t/s)		
G-XCCC	Extra EA.300/L	142		20. 8.01	P.T.Fellows	Rochester	20. 9.04T
	(Force landing Rochester 21.9.01 due to engine failure: engine, propeller, undercarriage & wing damaged)						
G-XCEL	Aérospatiale AS355F1 Twin Squirrel		G-HBAC	16. 5.95	Von Essen Aviation Ltd	Taunton	5. 6.03T
		5324	G-HJET/F-GEOX/F-WYMC/OY-HDL				

G-XCUB	Piper PA-18-150 Super Cub	18-8109036	N9348T	1. 5.81	M.C.Barraclough	(Selborne, Alton)	26. 4.04
G-XENA	Piper PA-28-161 Cherokee Warrior II	28-7716158	N3486Q	29. 6.98	Braddock Ltd	Blackbushe	10. 5.02T
G-XFLY	Lambert Aircraft Mission M212-100	PFA 306-13380		3. 2.00	Lambert Aircraft Engineering BVBA	(Kortrijk, Belgium)	
G-XITD*	Cessna 310G	310G0048	G-ASYV HB-LBY/N8948Z	15.10.87	Cambridge Regional College	Arbury College, Cambridge	14. 9.86
	(Damaged Leavesden 14.7.88: cancelled 10.1.89 as WFU: instructional airframe 2.97: current status unknown)						
G-XKEN	Piper PA-34-200T Seneca III	34-7970003	N3036A	5. 9.01	Choicecircle Ltd	(Rugby)	16. 9.04T
G-XLAA	Boeing 737-8Q8	28226	G-OKDN	13. 3.01	Excel Airways Ltd *(Leased Miami Air International 2001/02)*	Miami, Florida, USA	26. 7.04T
G-XLAB	Boeing 737-8Q8	28218	G-OJSW	14. 5.01	Excel Airways Ltd	Gatwick	10.12.04T
G-XLAC	Boeing 737-81Q	29051	G-LFJB N8254G/N1786B	26. 4.01	Excel Airways Ltd	Gatwick	17. 2.03P
G-XLAD	Boeing 737-81Q	29052	G-ODMW N8254Q	27. 2.01	Excel Airways Ltd *(Op Miami Air International @ Winter 2001/2002)*	Miami, Florida, USA	23. 5.03T
G-XLAE	Boeing 737-8Q8	30637	D-ABAA G-OKJW/N1787B	9.11.01	Excel Airways Ltd	Gatwick	8.11.04T
G-XLAF	Boeing 737-			R	Excel Airways Ltd	Gatwick	
G-XLAG	Boeing 737-86N	33003		R	Excel Airways Ltd	Gatwick	
G-XLAH	Boeing 737-86N	29833		R	Excel Airways Ltd	Gatwick	
G-XLIV	Robinson R44 Raven	0810		11. 7.00	Defence Products Ltd	Redhill	25. 7.03T
G-XLTG	Cessna 182S Skylane	18280234	N9571L	17. 7.98	GX Aviation Ltd	Denham	30. 7.01
G-XLXL	Robin DR.400/160 Knight	813	G-BAUD	3. 1.92	R.Pykett & D.Shutter t/a 40-40 Aero Group	Gamston	5. 5.03
G-XMAN	Boeing 737-36N	28573		18. 6.98	British Regional Airlines Ltd *(Golden Khokhloma t/s)*	Manchester	16.10.03T
G-XMGO	Aeromot AMT-200S Super Ximango	200127		18. 4.01	R.P.Beck & G.McLean	Rufforth	3. 5.04
G-XPBI	Letov LK-2M Sluka	PFA 263-13341		4.12.98	B.G.M.Chapman	North Coates	29. 3.02P
G-XPSS	Short SD.3-60 Var.100	SH.3713	EI-CPR G-OBOH/G-BNDJ/G-14-3713	2. 5.01	BAC Express Airlines Ltd	Gatwick	7. 5.02T
G-XPTS	Robinson R44 Astro	0433		11. 3.98	Heli Air Ltd	Wellesbourne Mountford	12. 7.04T
G-XPXP	Aero Designs Pulsar XP *(Tail-wheel u/c)* (Rotax 912)	218 & PFA 202-11958		30. 3.92	B.J.Edwards	Belle Vue Farm, Yarnscombe	18. 6.02P
G-XRAF	Raj Hamsa X'Air 582 (2)	513 & BMAA/HB/132		7. 4.00	M.E.Howard t/a X'Air Syndicate	RAF Halton	2. 7.02P
G-XRAY	Rand Robinson KR-2	PFA 129-11227		30. 4.87	R.S.Smith *(Under construction 2001)*	Barthol Chapel	
G-XRLD	Cameron A-250 HAFB	4820		25. 4.00	Red Letter Days Ltd	London N12	7 11.01T
G-XRXR	Raj Hamsa X-Air 582 (1)	429 & BMAA/HB/102		13. 9.99	I.S.Walsh	(Ivybridge)	
G-XSDJ	Europa Aviation Europa XS	PFA 0247-13378		3. 2.99	D.N.Joyce *(Completed 12.01)*	(Berkeley)	
G-XSFT	Piper PA-23-250 Aztec F	27-7754103	G-CPPC G-BGBH/N63773	18. 6.86	T.L.B.Dykes *(Op SFT Europe: ceased operations 12.01)*	Bournemouth	1. 6.03T
G-XSKY	Cameron N-77 HAFB	2508		26. 3.91	T.D.Gibbs *(Op D Hempleman-Adams)*	Corsham	11. 8.00A
G-XTEK	Robinson R44 Astro	0647		11. 8.99	PLM Properties plc	(Burton-on-Trent)	31. 8.02T
G-XTOR	Fairey Britten-Norman BN-2A Mk.III-2 Trislander	359	G-BAXD	1. 4.96	Aurigny Air Services Ltd *(Fuselage ex N3266G [1065] (NTU) fitted 2.96)*	Guernsey	5. 7.03T
G-XTRR	Extra EA.300/200	018	D-EVNO	25.10.00	P.N.Davis & H.Wilebore t/a Taildragger Classics	Leicester	19.12.03
G-XTUN	Westland-Bell 47G-3B1 *(Line No.WAP/81)*	WA/382	G-BGZK XT223	11. 5.99	R.C.Hields t/a Hields Aviation *(As "XT223" in Army Air Corps c/s)*	Sherburn-in-Elmet	29. 5.03T
G-XVIE*	Supermarine 361 Spitfire LF.XVIe	CBAF.IX.3807	8073M 7281M/7257M/TB252	3. 7.92	Historic Flying Ltd	Audley End	
	(Stored 7.97 awaiting rebuild as "TB252/GW-H": cancelled 28.3.01 by CAA)						
G-XVOM	Van's RV-6	PFA 181-12894		6. 4.01	A.Baker-Munton	(Leicester)	
G-XWWF	Lindstrand LBL-56A HAFB	595		25. 2.99	D.D.Maimone *"WWF"*	Guildford	4 12.00A
G-XXEA	Sikorsky S-76C	760492		21.12.98	T.C.Hewlett, Director of Royal Travel *(Op Queen's Flight)*	Blackbushe	4. 1.03T
G-XXIV	Agusta-Bell 206B-3 JetRanger III	8717		27. 4.89	A.N.Onn	Headcorn	4. 7.04T
G-XXVI	Sukhoi Su-26M	04-10	RA-0410	2. 4.93	A.N.Onn *(As "39"*	Headcorn	30. 4.02P

G-YAAA – G-YZZZ

G-YACB	Robinson R22 Beta	3092	G-VOSL	24. 1.02	A.C.Barker t/a ACB Hydraulic Services	(Stoke-on-Trent)	27 .6.03A
G-YAKA	Yakovlev Yak-50	822303	LY-ANJ DOSAAF 80	10.11.94	R.C.Berger	Turweston	29. 4.02P
G-YAKI	IAV-Bacau Yakovlev Yak-52	866904	LY-ANM DOSAAF 100	20. 9.94	Yak One Ltd *"100"* *(DOSAAF c/s)*	Popham	31. 1.02P
G-YAKM	Yakovlev Yak-55M	820506	RA-01333 DOSAAF 40	R	Mrs B.Abela *(See SECTION 5, Part 1)*	White Waltham	
G-YAKO	Yakovlev Yak-52	822203	RA-01493(1)	8. 5.99	M.K.Shaw	Norwich	14 .6.02P
G-YAKS	Aerostar Yakovlev Yak-52	9311708		16.12.93	Two Bees Associates Ltd *"2"*	Little Gransden	23. 4.02P
G-YANK	Piper PA-28-181 Archer II	28-8090163	N81314	19. 3.93	Janet A.Millar-Craig t/a G-YANK Flying Group	Tatenhill	2. 5.02
G-YARR	Mainair Rapier	1255-0700-7-W1049		14. 8.00	D.Yarr	(Stockport)	20..7.02P
G-YARV	ARV1 Super 2 (Hewland AE75) *(Built Hornet Aviation Ltd)*	K.004 & PFA 152-11127	G-BMDO	15.10.01	P.R.Snowden *(Current status unknown)*	(Bury St.Edmunds)	12. 6.97P
G-YAWW	Piper PA-28RT-201T Turbo Arrow IV	28R-8031024	N2929Y	15.11.90	Barton Aviation Ltd	Barton	9. 7.03
G-YBAA	Reims FR172J Rocket	FR17200579	5Y-BAA	15.11.84	A.Evans	Bourn	21. 6.03
G-YCII	LET Yakovlev C.11	2511108	F-AZPA Egyptian AF	13. 1.00	R.W.Davies	(Woodchuch, Kent)	3..8.01
G-YCUB	Piper PA-18-150 Super Cub	1809077	N4993X N4157T	23. 8.96	F.W.Rogers Garage (Saltash) Ltd	Bodmin	9. 3.03
G-YEAR	Revolution Helicopters Mini-500 (Rotax 582)	0050		6.10.95	D.J.Waddington	(Preston)	
G-YELL	Murphy Rebel	PFA 232-12381		1. 5.95	A.D.Keen	(Totnes)	
G-YEOM	Piper PA-31-350 Chieftain	31-8352022	N41108	3. 1.89	Foster Yeoman Ltd	Bristol	21. 3.02
G-YEWS	Rotorway Exec 152	DGP-1 & 3850		22. 6.89	R.Turrell & P.Mason	(Wickford)	17. 6.93P
G-YFLY	VPM M-16 Tandem Trainer (Arrow GT1000R)	VPM16-UK114	G-BWGI	14.10.96	A.J.Unwin	Kemble	13. 8.02P
G-YIII	Reims Cessna F150L	F15000827	PH-CEX	5. 6.80	Sherburn Aero Club Ltd	Sherburn-in-Elmet	31. 8.03T
G-YIIK	Robinson R44 Astro	0640		9. 8.99	The Websiteshop (UK) Ltd	Denham	15 .8.02T
G-YJBM	Airbus A320-231	362	G-IEAF F-WWIN	28. 9.93	Airtours International Airways Ltd	Manchester	26. 1.03T
G-YJET	Montgomerie-Bensen B.8MR (Rotax 582)	PFA G/101-1072	G-BMUH	25. 9.96	A.Shuttleworth	Barton	12. 6.01P
G-YKEN	Robinson R22 Beta-II	2875		22.10.98	R.L.Moody *(Crashed 12 miles near Beaune, France 5.5.01)*	Bennett's Field, Denham	5.11.01
G-YKSZ	Aerostar Yakovlev Yak-52	9311709		16.12.93	J.N. & C.J.Carter *(As "01" in Soviet AF c/s)*	Poplar Hall Farm, Elmsett	23. 9.02P
G-YLYB	Cameron N-105 HAFB	4482		15. 1.99	Virgin Airship & Balloon Co Ltd *(Lloyds TSB titles)*	Telford	30. 1.02A
G-YMBO	Robinson R22 Mariner	2054M	OY-HFR	21. 8.95	J.Robinson	(Bridlington)	20. 9.04T
G-YMMA	Boeing 777-236ER	30302	N5017Q	7. 1.00	British Airways plc	Heathrow	6. 1.03T
G-YMMB	Boeing 777-236ER	30303		18. 1.00	British Airways plc	Heathrow	17. 1.03T
G-YMMC	Boeing 777-236ER	30304		4. 2.00	British Airways plc	Heathrow	3. 2.03T
G-YMMD	Boeing 777-236ER	30305		19. 2.00	British Airways plc	Heathrow	17. 2.03T
G-YMME	Boeing 777-236ER	30306		16. 4.00	British Airways plc	Heathrow	14. 4.03T
G-YMMF	Boeing 777-236ER	30307		17. 5.00	British Airways plc	Heathrow	16. 5.03T
G-YMMG	Boeing 777-236ER	30308		28. 9.00	British Airways plc	Heathrow	26..9.03T
G-YMMH	Boeing 777-236ER	30309		14.10.00	British Airways plc	Heathrow	13.10.03T
G-YMMI	Boeing 777-236ER	30310		2.11.00	British Airways plc	Heathrow	1.11.03T
G-YMMJ	Boeing 777-236ER	30311		8.12.00	British Airways plc	Heathrow	7.12.03T
G-YMMK	Boeing 777-236ER	30312		8.12.00	British Airways plc	Heathrow	7.12.03T
G-YMML	Boeing 777-236ER	30313		10. 4.01	British Airways plc	Heathrow	13. 4.04T
G-YMMM	Boeing 777-236ER	30314		31. 5.01	British Airways plc	Heathrow	30 .4.04T
G-YMMN	Boeing 777-236ER	30316		15. 6.01	British Airways plc	Heathrow	14. 6.04T
G-YMMO	Boeing 777-236ER	30317		17. 9.01	British Airways plc	Heathrow	13. 9.04T
G-YMMP	Boeing 777-236ER	30315		30.10.01	British Airways plc	Heathrow	29.10.04T
G-YNOT	Rollason Druine D.62B Condor	RAE/649	G-AYFH	10.11.83	A.Littlefair	Lymington	12. 8.02P
G-YOGI	Robin DR.400/140B Major	1090	G-BDME	1.10.86	A Titmus	(Huntingdon)	19. 4.04
G-YORK	Reims Cessna F172M Skyhawk II	F17201354	PH-LUY F-WLIT	14.12.78	H-R.A.E.Waetjen	(Athboy, Co.Meath)	10.10.03
G-YOYO	Pitts S-1E Special (Lycoming O-360)	PFA 09-10885	G-OTSW G-BLHE	22. 5.96	J.D.L.Richardson	Exeter	21. 7.02P
G-YPOL	MD Helicopters Explorer	900-00078	N7038S	4.10.00	West Yorkshire Police Authority	(Wakefield)	25. 1.04T
G-YPSY	Andreasson BA.4B (Continental O-200-A)	PFA 038-10352		7. 6.78	R.W.Hinton	(Bury St. Edmunds)	29.11.01P
G-YRAF	Rotary Air Force RAF 2000 GTX-SE	PFA G13/1289		1. 6.01	C.V.King	(Swansea)	23. 8.02P

G-YRAT*	VPM M-16 Tandem Trainer	VPM16-UK104		16.11.92	A.J.Unwin	Kemble	31. 8.96P
	(Arrow GT1000R)	*(Damaged near Kemble 23. 2.96: cancelled 18.6.96 by CAA: stored 6.97: current status unknown)*					
G-YRIL	Luscombe 8E Silvaire	5945	N1318B	3. 2.92	C.Potter	North Weald	12.10.02P
	(Continental O-200-A)		NC1318B				
G-YROI	Air Command 532 Elite	0002	N532CG	3. 9.87	W.B.Lumb	Melrose Farm, Melbourne	17.12.90P
	(Rotax 532)						
G-YROO	Rotary Air Force RAF 2000 GTX-SE			27.11.01	K.D.Rhodes & C.S.Oakes	(Wimborne)	
		PFA G/13-1341					
G-YROS	Montgomerie-Bensen B.8M			29. 1.81	N.B.Gray	(Wardley, Manchester)	6. 6.97P
	(HAPI 60-6M)	PFA G/101-1004			*(Current status unknown)*		
G-YROY	Montgomerie-Bensen B.8MR			12. 9.89	S.Brennan	Carlisle	22. 3.02P
	(Rotax 532)	PFA G/101A-1145					
G-YSON	Eurocopter EC 120B	1068		14. 1.00	Heli-Express Ltd	Elstree	2. 3.03T
G-YSTT	Piper PA-32R-301 Saratoga IIHP		N848T	4. 8.97	A.W.Kendrick	Wolverhampton	5. 8.00
		3246056	N9282D				
G-YTUK	Cameron A-210 HAFB	4640		30. 9.99	Societe Bombard SRL	Beaune, France	10.10.02A
G-YUGO*	Hawker Siddeley HS.125 Srs.1B/R-522		G-ATWH	25. 8.88	British Airways Aircraft Recovery Unit		
		25094	HZ-BO1/G-ATWH			Biggin Hill	19. 4.91
					(Cancelled 29.3.93 as WFU: fuselage noted 3.01)		
G-YULL	Piper PA-28-180 Cherokee E	28-5603	G-BEAJ	30. 3.79	Fortescue Investments & Consulting Ltd		
			9H-AAC/N2390R			Guernsey	2.10.03
G-YUMM	Cameron N-90 HAFB	2723		12.12.91	Wunderbar Ltd *"Boulevard"*	York	18. 3.01A
G-YUPI	Cameron N-90 HAFB	1602		12. 1.88	MCVH SA	Brussels, Belgium	22.11.98A
G-YURO*	Europa Aviation Europa			6. 4.92	Yorkshire Air Museum	Elvington	9. 6.95P
	(Rotax 912UL)	001 & PFA 220-11981			*(Cancelled 22.4.98 as WFU)*		
G-YVBF	Lindstrand LBL-317S HAFB	505		2. 4.98	Virgin Balloon Flights Ltd	London SE16	17.11.01T
					"Virgin Yankee"		
G-YVET	Cameron V-90 HAFB	3182		11.10.93	K.J.Foster	Coleshill, Birmingham	16. 4.02A
G-YYYY	Max Holste MH.1521 C1 Broussard	208	F-GDPZ	10. 3.00	Aerosuperbatics Ltd	Rendcomb	29..3.03
			French Air Force		*(Shape titles)*		

G-ZAAA – G-ZZZZ

G-ZABC	Sky 90-24 HAFB	062		10. 4.97	J.A.Lister *"Bart"*	Aldershot	12. 8.02A
G-ZACH	Robin DR.400/100 Cadet	1831	G-FTIO	20.10.92	A.P.Wellings	Sandown	5. 9.04
G-ZAIR	Zenair CH.601HD Zodiac	PFA 162-12194		21. 2.92	Speedfreak Ltd	Crosland Moor	29. 6.02P
	(Rotax 912UL)						
G-ZAPH	Bell 206B-3 JetRanger III	4401	G-DBMW	6. 2.01	Titan Airways Ltd	Stansted	9. 6.02T
			C-GAJH				
G-ZAPJ	ATR-42-312	113	EI-CIQ	17. 5.96	Titan Airways Ltd	Stansted	19. 5.02T
			DQ-FEQ/F-WWEJ				
G-ZAPK	British Aerospace BAe 146 Srs.200QC		G-BTIA	25. 4.96	Titan Airways Ltd	Stansted	17. 4.03T
		E2148	ZS-NCB/G-BTIA/G-6-148/G-PRIN				
G-ZAPM	Boeing 737-33A	27285	DQ-FJD	2. 6.99	Titan Airways Ltd	Stansted	2 .6.02T
			N102AN/CS-TKG				
G-ZAPN	British Aerospace BAe 146 Srs.200QC		ZK-NZC	20. 9.99	Titan Airways Ltd	Stansted	15.11.02T
		E2119	G-BPBT				
G-ZAPO	British Aerospace BAe 146 Srs.200QC		F-GMMP	28. 7.00	Titan Airways Ltd	Stansted	3. 8.03T
		E2176	G-BWLG/VH-NJQ/G-PRCS				
G-ZAPT	Beechcraft B200C Super King Air		N200KA	24. 9.01	Titan Airways plc	Stansted	23. 9.02T
		BL-141	N5141Y				
G-ZAPY	Robinson R22 Beta	0788	G-INGB	8. 7.98	Heli Air Ltd	Wellesbourne Mountford	9. 8.04T
G-ZARI	Grumman-American AA-5B Tiger		G-BHVY	7. 3.86	ZARI Aviation Ltd	Biggin Hill	23. 2.04
		AA5B-0845	N28835				
G-ZARV	ARV1 Super 2	PFA 152-13035		26. 2.97	P.R.Snowden	Cambridge	21. 6.02P
G-ZAZA	Piper PA-18 Super Cub 95	18-2041	D-ENAS	1. 5.84	Airborne Taxi Services Ltd	Wantage	11. 4.02P
	(L-18C-PI)		R.Neth AF R-66/52-2441 *(Op Adrian Swire)*				
G-ZBED	Robinson R22 Beta	1684	N63993	18.11.99	P.D.Spinks		
			F-GHHM			Stream Farm, Sherburn-in-Elmet	17.11.02T
G-ZBHH	Hughes 269C	129-0869	G-GINZ	20. 8.99	The Hughes Helicopter Co Ltd	Biggin Hill	9. 8.04T
			F-GINZ/SE-HMX/PH-HAN/C-GFKF/N1091N		t/a Biggin Hill Helicopters		
					(Made heavy landing & bounced Redhill 6.9.01: severely damaged)		
G-ZBLT	Cessna 182S Skylane	18280910	N72764	6. 7.01	N.P., R.D.& S.R.Spencer	Fenland	17. 7.04T
					t/a Blue Line Trailers		
G-ZEBO	Thunder Ax8-105 Srs.2 HAFB	2197		22. 5.92	S.M.Waterton *"Gazebo"*	Borehamwood	5. 5.02T
G-ZEIN	Slingsby T.67M-260 Firefly	2234		19. 7.95	RV Aviation Ltd	Blackbushe	25. 3.02T
G-ZENA	Zenair CH.701UL	PFA 187-13637		16.10.00	A.N.Aston	(Wolverhampton)	
G-ZEPI	Colt GA-42 Gas Airship	878	G-ISPY	9. 4.92	P A Lindstran	Oswestry	12. 5.93A
	(RR Continental O-200B)		(G-BPRB)				
G-ZERO	Grumman-American AA-5B Tiger		OO-PEC	3. 9.80	D.M.Ashford	Southampton	6. 2.02T
		AA5B-0051			t/a G-ZERO Syndicate		
G-ZHWH	Rotorway Exec 162F	6596		19.11.01	B.Alexander	(Canterbury)	
G-ZIGI	Robin DR.400/180 Regent	2107		19.11.91	R.J.Dix	Bodmin	8. 3.04

G-ZIPA	Rockwell Commander 114A *(Laid down as c/n 14436)*	14505	G-BHRA N5891N	3. 9.98	M.F.Luke	Goodwood	15. 2.04T
G-ZIPI	Robin DR.400/180 Regent	1557		22. 2.82	H.U. & D.C.Stahlberg	Rochester	14. 5.04
G-ZIPY	Wittman W.8 Tailwind (Lycoming O-235)	PFA 031-11339		29. 5.91	M.J.Butler	Ranksborough Farm, Langham	23. 5.02P
G-ZIZI	Cessna 525 Citationjet	525-0345	N5185V	10.11.99	Ortac Air Ltd	Guernsey	17.11.02T
G-ZLIN	Moravan Zlin Z.326 Trener Master *(Modified to Z.526 standard)*	916	G-BBCR OH-TZF	30. 6.81	N.J.Arthur *(C/n confirmed but duplicates I-ETRM)*	Finmere	6.10.01
G-ZLLE	Aérospatiale SA.341G Gazelle 1	1012	N504KH JA9098	4.10.01	G-ZZLE Ltd	Stapleford	8.11.04T
G-ZLOJ	Beechcraft A36 Bonanza	E-1677	ZS-LOJ N6748J	11. 9.98	W.D.Gray	Bournemouth	20.12.04
G-ZLYN	Moravan Zlin Z.526F Trener Master	1255	OK-CMC YR-ZAB	4. 8.95	H.G.Philippart	(London N1)	24.10.03
G-ZMAM	Piper PA-28-181 Archer II	28-7890059	G-BNPN N47379	3.11.00	Z.Mahmood	Elstree	6. 2.03T
G-ZODI	Zenair CH.601UL Zodiac (Rotax 912UL)	PFA 162A-13585		13. 3.00	B.McFadden	Sturgate	18. 1.02P
G-ZONK	Robinson R44 Astro	0179	G-EDIE	16. 7.97	CCB Aviation Ltd	Thruxton	25. 6.04T
G-ZOOL	Reims Cessna FA152 Aerobat	FA15200357	G-BGXZ	11.11.94	A.S.Bamrah t/a Falcon Flying Service	(Blackbushe)	9. 5.04T
G-ZORO	Europa Aviation Europa	PFA 247-12672		20. 6.95	N.T.Read	(Gillingham, Kent)	
G-ZTED	Europa Aviation Europa	PFA 247-12492		30. 4.96	J.J.Kennedy & E.W.Gladstone *(Part built 7.01)*	(Edinburgh)	
G-ZULU	Piper PA-28-161 Warrior II	28-8316043	N4292X	25. 2.88	R.W.Tebby t/a S.F.Tebby & Son *(Op Bristol Flying Centre)*	Bristol	29. 6.03T
G-ZUMP*	Cameron N-77 HAFB *(Rebuilt with new canopy c/n 1107 in 1985)*	377		18. 1.78	British Balloon Museum & Library *"Gazump" (Cancelled 8.4.98 as WFU)*	Newbury	
G-ZVBF	Cameron A-400 HAFB	4280		21. 1.98	Virgin Balloon Flights Ltd	London SE16	22. 2.02T
G-ZWAR	Eurocopter EC 120B	1024	D-HVIP	14. 4.00	Hedgeton Trading Ltd	Marbella, Spain	22. 5.03
G-ZWRC	Eurocopter AS 350B3 Ecureuil	3362	F-GPNE	14. 5.01	Proflight Ltd	(Banbury)	5. 7.04
G-ZZAG	Cameron Z-77 HAFB	4588		6. 4.99	T.Charlwood *"Zig Zag"*	Chichester	27 12.01A
G-ZZIP	Mooney M.20J (205)	24-3167	N1086N	14. 6.91	H.T.El-Kasaby	Southend	3. 7.04T
G-ZZOE	Eurocopter EC 120B	1196	F-WQOX	21. 3.01	McAlpine Helicopters Ltd	Oxford	9. 7.04T
G-ZZWW	Enstrom 280FX	2052	G-BSIE HA-MIN/G-BSIE	22. 2.00	Loune Ltd	Oxford	27. 3.04T
G-ZZZA	Boeing 777-236	27105	N77779	20. 5.96	British Airways plc	Heathrow	19. 5.02T
G-ZZZB	Boeing 777-236	27106	N77771	28. 3.97	British Airways plc	Heathrow	3.12.02T
G-ZZZC	Boeing 777-236	27107	N5014K	11.11.95	British Airways plc	Heathrow	10.11.04T
G-ZZZD	Boeing 777-236	27108		28.12.95	British Airways plc	Heathrow	2. 8.04T
G-ZZZE	Boeing 777-236	27109		12. 1.96	British Airways plc	Heathrow	28. 9.04T

SECTION 2 – IRELAND

I am very grateful that once again the Irish Register has been compiled by Peter Hornfeck and appreciate his contribution. The details have been supplemented by further specific information from Richard Cawsey, Paul Cunniffe, Ken Parfitt, Tony Pither, Colin Smith and as noted below, with many thanks.

No official C of A data is available and it remains difficult to determine the status of many aircraft so we are grateful to Paul Cunniffe and those reports which appear in the "Round and About" section of Air-Britain News. This information is used to update the notation system which indicates if an aircraft has been seen as either active (A) or noted (N) throughout the year. But, as will be observed, many aircraft escape this net and are not reported. We invite members to update these records and report back during 2002. I exclude the notation system from commercial airline aircraft as most will expect to be active in normal trading conditions. Details relating to other preserved or non-currently registered Irish civil aircraft are shown and marked with an asterisk.

Regn	Type	C/n	P/I	Date	Owner/operator	Probable Base	Remarks
EI-ABI(2)	de Havilland DH.84 Dragon 2	6105	EI-AFK	12. 8.85	Aer Lingus plc	Dublin	A 6.00
			G-AECZ/AV982/G-AECZ		*"Iolar"*		
EI-ADV	Piper PA-12 Super Cruiser	12-3459	NC4031H	11. 5.48	R.E.Levis	Weston	N 7.99
	(Lycoming 0-235)			*(Badly*	*damaged in force landing Maynooth, Weston 8.7.99)*		
EI-AFE	Piper J-3C-90 Cub	16687	OO-COR	11. 3.49	J.Conlon	Kildare	N 4.96
			D-ELAB/N9954F/EI-AFE/NC79076 *(On rebuild)*				
EI-AFF	BA L.25C Swallow II	406	G-ADMF	18. 5.49	J.Molloy, J.J.Sullivan & B.Donoghue		
	(Pobjoy Cataract II)			*(Damaged*	*Coonagh 24.10.61: on rebuild)*	Ashbourne	N 4.96
EI-AGD	Taylorcraft Plus D	108	G-AFUB	26. 5.53	B. & K.O'Sullivan	Abbeyshrule	N 4.96
			HL534/G-AFUB		*(On rebuild)*		
EI-AGJ	Auster V J/1 Autocrat	2208	G-AIPZ	3.11.53	T.G.Rafter	Ballyboughal, Co.Dublin	
					(On rebuild)		
EI-AHI(2)	de Havilland DH.82A Tiger Moth	85347	G-APRA	17. 9.93	High Fidelity Flyers	Birr	A 8.00
			DE313				
EI-AKM	Piper J-3C-65 Cub	15810	N88194	17.11.58	Setanta Flying Group	Kilmoon	
			NC88194		*(Stored)*		
EI-ALH	Taylorcraft Plus D	106	G-AHLJ	5. 5.60	N.Reilly	Ballyjamesduff	
			HH987/G-AFTZ				
EI-ALP	Avro 643 Cadet	848	G-ADIE	12. 9.60	J.C.O'Loughlin	Weston	N11.00
	(Genet Major)		*(Engine seizure 12.6.77:*		*awaiting spares & stored in poor condition)*		
EI-ALU*	Avro 631 Cadet	657	G-ACIH	14. 3.61	M P Cahill	Brittas Bay	N 4.99
					(Under restoration)		
EI-AMF*	Taylorcraft Plus D	157	G-ARRK	26. 4.62	Not known	Carr Farm, Newark	N 4.98
			G-AHUM/LB286		*(Fuselage partly restored)*		
EI-AMK	Auster V J/1 Autocrat	1838	G-AGTV	19. 9.62	Irish Aero Club	Newcastle,Dublin	N1998
			(Wfu after engine failure 5.79:		*sold 4.95: stored for Air Corps Museum)*		
EI-AMY	Auster J/1N Alpha	2634	G-AJUW	9. 4.63	T.Lennon	Maynooth, Co.Kildare	N 4.92
					(For rebuild)		
EI-ANA*	Taylorcraft Plus D	206	G-AHCG	29. 8.63	N.Reilly	Ballyjamesduff, Co.Cavan	N 4.92
			LB347		*(Stored as "G-AHCG")*		
EI-AND	Cessna 175A	56444	G-APYA	29. 8.63	M. & A.Cooke	Ronaldsway	
			N6944E		*(Crashed Irish Sea nr Formby Point, Lancs 30.10.94)*		
EI-ANN*	de Havilland DH.82A Tiger Moth	83161	G-ANEE	6.10.64	Not known	Abbeyshrule	N 4.96
			T5418 *(Damaged Culmullen 18.10.64:*		*for restoration using parts of EI-AOP)*		
EI-ANT	Champion 7ECA Citabria	7ECA-38		13. 1.65	T.Croke, H.Sydner, D.Foley & E.Lennon		
						Gorey	A 6.01
EI-ANY	Piper PA-18 Super Cub 95	18-7152	G-AREU	18.11.64	The Bogavia Group	Waterford	A10.00
			N3096Z				
EI-AOB	Piper PA-28-140 Cherokee	28-20667		28. 4.65	J.Surdival, L.Moran, J.Kilcoyne & J.Cowell		
						Waterford	A 5.01
EI-AOK(2)	Reims Cessna F172G	F172-0208		14. 3.66	D.Bruton	Abbeyshrule	N 7.01
					(Stripped hulk noted)		
EI-AOP*	de Havilland DH.82A Tiger Moth	84320	G-AIBN	24. 9.65	Not known	Abbeyshrule	N 5.96
			T7967		*(Stored)*		
EI-AOS	Cessna 310B	35578	G-ARIG	1.11.65	Joyce Aviation Ltd	Kildimo	
			EI-AOS/G-ARIG/N5378A		*(Wfu and to scrapyard)*		
EI-APF	Reims Cessna F150G	F150-0112		6. 3.66	Sligo Aero Club Ltd	Strandhill	A 8.98
EI-APS(2)	Schleicher ASK 14	14008	(EI-114)	24.11.69	SLG Group	Gowran Grange	
			G-AWVV/D-KOBB				
EI-ARH(2)	Slingsby T.56 SE5 rep	1590	G-AVOT	22. 6.67	L.Garrison	Flabob, CA, USA	N 5.96
	(Lycoming 0-235)						
EI-ARM	Slingsby T.56 SE5 rep	1594	G-AVOX	22. 6.67	M L Putman	Sanger, Texas, USA	N10.99
	(Lycoming 0-235) *(Regd with c/n 1595, ex G-AVOY)*				*(Registered in USA as N912AC)*		
EI-ARW	SAN Jodel DR.1050 Ambassadeur	118	F-BJJH	14. 8.67	P.Walsh & P.Ryan	Abbeyshrule	N 4.96

					(Damaged nr Carnmore 28.7.86: stored)		
EI-ASR(2)	McCandless M.4 Gyroplane (VW) *(C/n M4/4 quoted also)*	M.4/5	G-AXHZ	29. 9.69	G.J.J.Fasenfeld *(Sold to R.McGregor: stored)*	Sion Mills, Strabane	N 4.96
EI-AST	Reims Cessna F150H	F150-0273		30. 1.68	S.Coughlan *(New owner 2.01)*	Waterford	A12.01
EI-ASU*	Beagle A.61 Terrier 2	B.633	G-ASRG WE599	10. 1.68	C Lebroda & Pntrs *(Stored)*	Trim	N 4.96
EI-ATJ	Beagle B.121 Pup 2	B121-029	G-35-029	10. 2.69	L.O'Leary	Waterford	N 1.02
EI-ATK*	Piper PA-28-140 Cherokee	28-24120	G-AVUP N11C	18.10.68	Mayo Flying Club *(Damaged Connaught 14.2.87: stripped hulk noted)*	Abbeyshrule	N 7.01
EI-ATL	Aeronca 7AC Champion	7AC-4674	N1119E	22. 9.69	Kildare Flying Club	Abbeyshrule	
					(Damaged Weston 26.11.75: used for spares in restoration of EI-AVB)		
EI-ATP*	Phoenix Luton LA-4A Minor	PAL/1124	G-ASCY	29. 8.69	E Batchelor *(Displayed in Concourse as EI-ATP/N924GB)*	Miami Int, Florida, USA	N10.94
EI-ATS	SOCATA MS.880B Rallye Club	1582		20. 4.70	ATS Group *(Stored)*	Abbeyshrule	N 4.96
EI-AUC	Reims Cessna FA150K Aerobat	FA1500040		10. 4.70	Garda Aviation Club Ltd	Weston	
					(Badly damaged in force landing north of Weston 15.7.99)		
EI-AUE	SOCATA MS.880B Rallye Club	1359	G-AXHU	1. 4.70	Kilkenny Flying Club Ltd	Waterford	A12.01
EI-AUG	SOCATA MS.894A Rallye Minerva 220	11080		17. 6.70	K.O'Leary	Rathcoole	N10.00
EI-AUJ	SOCATA MS.880B Rallye Club	1370	G-AXHF F-BNGV	12. 6.70	Ormond Flying Club Ltd *(Stored)*	Abbeyshrule	N 8.98
EI-AUM	Auster V J/1 Autocrat	2612	G-AJRN	11. 9.70	T.G.Rafter *(On rebuild)*	Ballyboughal, Co.Dublin	N 6.96
EI-AUO	Reims Cessna FA150K Aerobat	FA1500074		2. 3.70	Kerry Aero Club Ltd	Waterford	A12.01
EI-AUP*	SOCATA MS.880B Rallye Club	1143	G-AVVK	30. 9.70	Not known *(Damaged Coonagh 1.9.83: stored for spares use)*	Abbeyshrule	N 5.99
EI-AUS	Auster J/5F Aiglet Trainer	2779	G-AMRL	17.11.70	T.Stevens & T.Lennon *(On rebuild)*	Powerscourt	N 4.95
EI-AUT	Forney F-1A Aircoupe	5731	G-ARXS D-EBSA/N3037G	21.12.70	Joyce Aviation Ltd (To N.Glass & A.Richardson?) *(Stored)*	Bann Foot, Lough Neagh, NI	N 8.97
EI-AUY*	Morane-Saulnier MS.502 Criquet (Argus AS.10)	338	F-BCDG Fr.Mil	30.11.70	G Warner *(As "CF+HF" in Luftwaffe c/s)*	Duxford	
EI-AVB	Aeronca 7AC Champion (Continental A65)	7AC-1790	7P-AXK ZS-AXK	14. 6.71	J D Cooper *(Registered in USA as N151JC [7AC-71790]*	Thonotosassa, Florida, USA	N10.99
EI-AVC	Reims Cessna F337F Super Skymaster *(Wichita c/n 337001355)*	F33700032	N4757	26. 8.71	Christy Keane (Saggart) Ltd *(Stored Abbeyshrule & used as spares source)*	Castlerock	N10.01
EI-AVM	Reims Cessna F150L	F15000745		3. 3.72	T.Carter & Partners	Abbeyshrule	A 7.01
EI-AWD	Piper PA-22-160 Tri-Pacer	22-6411	G-APXV N9437D	17. 1.73	J.P.Montcalm *(Blown over in gales Cork 12.81: stored)*	Carrigtwo hil, Co.Cork	N 1989
EI-AWE	Reims Cessna F150L	F15000877		22. 2.73	D.Bruton *(Fuselage stored)*	(Dublin)	N 4.01
EI-AWH	Cessna 210J Centurion	21059067	G-AZCC	19. 1.73	Rathcoole Flying Club Ltd	Rathcoole	
			(EI-AWH)/G-AZCC/5N-AIE/N1734C/(N6167F)				
EI-AWP	de Havilland DH.82A Tiger Moth *(Regd with c/n 19577)*	85931	F-BGCL Fr.AF/DF195	4. 7.72	Anne.P.Bruton	Abbeyshrule	N 5.00
EI-AWR	Malmo MFI-9 Junior	010	LN-HAG (SE-EBW)	12. 6.73	M.Whyte & J.Brennen *(New owners 7.01)*	Galway	N12.00
EI-AWU	SOCATA MS.880B Rallye Club	880	G-AVIM	12. 1.74	Longford Aviation Ltd	Rosnakil	N 8.98
EI-AYA	SOCATA MS.880B Rallye Club	2256	G-BAON	27. 7.73	Limerick Flying Club (Coonagh) Ltd	Coonagh	A 8.99
EI-AYB	Gardan GY-80-180 Horizon	156	F-BNQP	5.10.73	J.B.Smith	Abbeyshrule	A11.00
EI-AYD	Grumman-American AA-5 Traveler	0380	G-BAZE N5480L	9. 7.73	P.Howick, H.Martini & V.O'Rourke	Powerscourt	
EI-AYF	Reims Cessna FRA150L Aerobat	FRA1500218		26. 3.74	Limerick Flying Club (Coonagh) Ltd *(New owner 5.01)*	Coonagh	N 5.00
EI-AYI	Morane MS.880B Rallye Club	189	F-OBXE	21.11.73	J.McNamara	Trim	
EI-AYK	Reims Cessna F172M Skyhawk II	F17201092		25. 3.74	D.Gallagher	Waterford	A 8.01
EI-AYN	IRMA BN-2A-8 Islander	704	G-BBFJ	26. 3.74	Aer Arann *"Inis-Mor"* t/a Galway Aviation Services Ltd	Connemara	A 9.00
EI-AYO(2)	Douglas DC-3A-197	1911	N655GP	5. 3.76	Science Museum Air Transport Coln & Storage Facility	Wroughton	N2000
			N65556/N255JB/N8695E/N333H/NC16071				
EI-AYR	Schleicher ASK 16	16022	(EI-119)	5. 4.74	Brian O'Broin	Kilrush	A 9.00
EI-AYS*	Piper PA-22-108 Colt	22-8448	G-ARKT	28. 6.74	M.F.Skelly *(Cancelled.21.12.00 pending possible ownership change)*	Abbeyshrule	N 5.00
EI-AYT(2)	SOCATA MS.894A Rallye Minerva 220	*11065*	G-AXIU	6. 8.74	K.A.O'Connor *(Damaged Palklasmore 12.11.89: wreck only)*	Abbeyshrule	N 5.00
EI-AYV	SEEMS MS.892A Rallye Commodore 150	10482	F-BLSP	27. 8.74	P.Murtagh	Strandhill	
					(Open stored 2.84 - wind damaged 1.85 & scrapped 1986)		
EI-AYY	Evans VP-1 (VW 1500)	MD-01 & SAAC-03		18. 8.75	M.Donoghue	Newcastle	A10.98
EI-BAG*	Cessna 172A	172-47571	G-ARAV N9771T	7. 8.74	Cork Parachute Club *(Damaged 3.10.76: on rebuild Langford Lodge)*	Portadown, Belfast	N 4.96

EI-BAJ	SNCAN Stampe SV-4C	171	F-BBPN	17.10.74	Dublin Tiger Group	Trim	
					(Reported badly damaged in force landing in 8.99)		
EI-BAL*	Beagle A.109 Airedale	B.515	G-ARZS	17.10.74	S.Bruton	Abbeyshrule	N 9.99
					(Cancelled - details not known)		
EI-BAO	Reims Cessna F172G	F172-0278	G-ATNH	11. 2.75	D.Bruton	Abbeyshrule	N 7.01
EI-BAR	Thunder Ax8-105 HAFB	014	G-BCAM	26. 2.75	J.Burke & V.Hourihane	Cahir	
					"Rockwell" (WFU)		
EI-BAS	Reims Cessna F172M Skyhawk II	F17201262		2. 5.75	Falcon Aviation Ltd	Waterford	A12.01
EI-BAT	Reims Cessna F150M	F15001196		2. 5.75	K.A.O'Connor	Weston	A 5.00
EI-BAV	Piper PA-22-108 Colt	22-8347	G-ARKO	30. 4.75	J.Davy	Moyne	A 9.00
EI-BAY*	Cameron O-84 HAFB	16	G-AYJZ	28. 5.75	British Balloon Museum & Library	Newbury	
	(Original canopy replaced by c/n 433)				*"Godolphin"*		
EI-BBC	Piper PA-28-180 Cherokee B	28-1049	G-ASEJ	18. 6.75	Vero Beach Ltd	Strandhill	N 8.01
					(New owner 11.01)		
EI-BBD	Evans VP-1	VP-1-No.2 & SAAC-02		13. 8.76	The Volksplane Group	Celbridge	N 1999
	(VW 1600)				*(Damaged 12.9.81: on rebuild)*		
EI-BBE	Champion 7FC Tri-Traveler	7FC-393	G-APZW	7. 9.75	P.Forde & D.Connaire	Galway	A 8.00
	(Tail-wheel conversion to 7EC Traveler status)						
EI-BBG	SOCATA Rallye 100ST	2592		27.10.75	Weston Ltd	Weston	N 4.01
					(Dismantled fuselage hangared)		
EI-BBI	SOCATA Rallye 150ST	2663		13.10.75	Kilkenny Airport Ltd	Kilkenny	A12.01
EI-BBJ	SOCATA MS.880B Rallye 100S	2361	F-BUVX	7.11.75	Weston Ltd	Weston	A 5.98
EI-BBN*	Reims Cessna F150M	F15001281		27. 2.76	Sligo North West Aero Club Ltd	Strandhill	N 8.99
					(Cancelled as destroyed 23.6.98: fuselage in Club hangar)		
EI-BBO	SOCATA MS.893E Rallye 180GT	12522	F-BVNM	8. 3.76	G.P.Moorhead	Hacketstown	
EI-BBV	Piper J-3C-65 Cub	13058	D-ELWY	14. 6.76	F.Cronin	Weston	N 5.97
	(L-4J-PI) *(Frame No.12888)*		F-BEGB/44-80762		*(Stored)*		
EI-BCE	BN-2A-26 Islander	519	G-BDUV	14. 9.76	Aer Arann *"Inis-Meain"*	Connemara	A 8.00
					t/a Galway Aviation Services Ltd		
EI-BCF	Bensen B-8M Gyrocopter	47941	N....	24. 8.76	P.Flanagan	(Kilrush)	N1997
	(McC.O-100)				*(Stored)*		
EI-BCH	GEMS MS.892A Rallye Commodore 150	10561	G-ATIW	17. 9.76	Limerick Flying Club (Coonagh) Ltd	Coonagh	A 9.01
EI-BCJ(2)	Aeromere F.8L Falco 3	204	G-ATAK	19. 1.77	D.Kelly	Abbeyshrule	N 5.00
			D-ENYB		*(On rebuild)*		
EI-BCK	Reims Cessna F172N Skyhawk II	F17201543		22.11.76	K.A.O'Connor	Abbeyshrule	A 8.01
EI-BCL	Cessna 182P Skylane II	18264300	N1366M	22.11.76	L.Burke	Newcastle	A12.01
	(Reims assembled with c/n F1820045)						
EI-BCM	Piper J-3C-65 Cub	11983	F-BNAV	26.11.76	Kilmoon Flying Group	Trim	A 8.00
	(L-4H-PI)		N9857F/44-79687				
EI-BCN	Piper J-3C-65 Cub	12335	F-BFQE	26.11.76	Snowflake Flying Group	Trim	A 1.00
	(L-4H-PI)		OO-PIE/44-80039				
EI-BCO	Piper J-3C-65 Cub	"1"	F-BBIV	26.11.76	J.Molloy	Kilmoon	
					(Not converted and remains stored)		
EI-BCP	Rollason Druine D.62B Condor	RAE/618	G-AVCZ	27. 1.77	A.Delaney	Dolla	
EI-BCS	SOCATA MS.880B Rallye 100T	2550	F-BVZV	4. 2.77	Organic Fruit & Vegetables of Ireland Ltd	Kilkenny	A 5.00
EI-BCU	SOCATA MS.880B Rallye 100T	2595	F-BXTH	10. 2.77	Weston Ltd *(Derelict)*	Weston	N 4.01
EI-BCW	SOCATA MS.880B Rallye Club	1783	G-AYKE	18. 4.77	Kilkenny Flying Club	Abbeyshrule	N 6.97
					(Stored)		
EI-BDH	SOCATA MS.880B Rallye Club	1270	G-AWOB	18. 7.77	Munster Wings Ltd	Abbeyshrule	
					(Damaged Cork 5.12.78: status uncertain - believed scrapped)		
EI-BDK	SOCATA MS.880B Rallye 100T	2561	F-BXMZ	10. 8.77	Limerick Flying Club (Coonagh) Ltd		
					(Airframe stored)	Abbeyshrule	N 9.99
EI-BDL	Evans VP-2			7. 9.77	P.Buggle	Kildare	N 5.00
	(VW) V2-2101/PFA 7213 & SAAC-04						
EI-BDM	Piper PA-23-250 Aztec D	27-4166	G-AXIV	10.10.77	G.A.Costello	Waterford	N 4.96
			N6826Y		t/a Executive Air Services		
			(WFU & scrapped Shannon 4.85: fuselage to SE Aviation Enthusiasts' Museum & stored				
EI-BDP*	Cessna 182P Skylane	18260867	G-AZLC	14.11.77	O.Bruton	Abbeyshrule	N 8.99
			N9327G		*(Damaged 1988: cancelled 27.11.98 as WFU: wings only)*		
EI-BDR	Piper PA-28-180 Cherokee C	28-3980	G-BAAO	8.12.77	Cherokee Group	Farranfore	A12.01
			LN-AEL/<u>SE-FAG</u>				
EI-BEA	SOCATA Rallye 100ST	3007		28. 2.78	Weston Ltd	Weston	N 4.01
					(Dismantled fuselage hangared)		
EI-BEN	Piper J-3C-65 Cub	12546	G-BCUC	28. 4.78	J.J.O'Sullivan	Weston	A 8.00
	(L-4J-PI) *(Frame No.12376)*		F-BFMN/44-80250				
EI-BEP	SOCATA MS.892A Rallye Commodore 150	11947	F-BTJT	14. 4.78	H.Lynch & J.O'Leary	Abbeyshrule	N 7.01
					(Stripped hulk noted)		
EI-BFB*	SOCATA Rallye 100ST	3044		12. 6.78	Weston Ltd	Weston	N 2.95
					(Crashed nr Weston 18.10.87: wreck stored)		

EI-BFE	Reims Cessna F150G	F150-0158	G-AVGM	3. 8.78	Joyce Aviation Ltd *(Stored dismantled)*	Waterford	N 1.02
EI-BFF	Beechcraft A23-24 Musketeer Super III	MA-352	G-AXCJ	20. 8.78	P.McCoole *(New owner 9.01)*	Coonagh	A10.01
EI-BFI	SOCATA Rallye 100ST	2618		10. 8.78	J O'Neill *(Crashed 14.12.85: stripped hulk noted)*	Abbeyshrule	N 7.01
EI-BFM	SOCATA MS.893E Rallye 180GT	12958	F-GARN	12.10.78	Limerick Flying Group (Coonagh) Ltd *(Stripped hulk noted)*	Abbeyshrule	N 7.01
EI-BFO	Piper J-3C-90 Cub (L-4J-PI) *(Frame No.12531) (Regd as c/n 8911)*	12701	F-BFQJ N79856/NC79856/44-80405	11. 9.78	D.Gordon	Weston	
EI-BFP	SOCATA Rallye 100ST	2942	F-GARR	6.10.78	Weston Ltd	Weston	A12.98
EI-BFR	SOCATA Rallye 100ST	2429	F-OCVK	9.11.78	J.Power	Waterford	A 1.02
EI-BFV	SOCATA MS.880B Rallye 100T	2415	F-BVAH	2. 2.79	Ormond Flying Club Ltd *(Stored 8.94: status unknown,but believed scrapped 1976)*	NK	
EI-BGA	SOCATA Rallye 100ST	2549	G-BCXC F-OCZQ	23.11.78	J.J.Frew	Mullaghmore, NI	N 7.01
EI-BGB	SOCATA MS.880B Rallye Club	1913	G-AZKB	22. 1.79	Limerick Flying Club (Coonagh) Ltd *(Stored)*	Abbeyshrule	N 3.98
EI-BGC	SOCATA MS.880B Rallye Club	1265	F-BRDC	22.12.78	P.Moran *(WFU & cannibalised)*	Roscommon	
EI-BGD	SOCATA MS.880B Rallye Club	2287	F-BUJI (D-EKHD)	18.12.78	N.Kavanagh *(Stored)*	Abbeyshrule	N 3.98
EI-BGF	Piper PA-28R-180 Cherokee Arrow	28R-30121	SE-FAS	30. 1.79	Arrow Group *(Crashed Mynydd Prescelly near Haverfordwest, Dyfed 6.10.83)*	NK	
EI-BGG	SOCATA MS.892E Rallye 150GT	12824	F-GAFS	30. 1.79	J.Dowling & M.Martin	Abbeyshrule	A 8.01
EI-BGJ	Reims Cessna F152 II	F15201664		14. 5.79	Sligo Aero Club Ltd	Strandhill	N 8.01
EI-BGS	SOCATA MS.893E Rallye 180GT	12675	F-BXTY	25. 4.79	M.Farrelly *(Damaged Claive 3.91: wreck stored)*	Abbeyshrule	N 4.96
EI-BGT	Colt 77A HAFB *(New envelope c/n 1092 - original to EI-BBM)*	041		14. 5.79	M.J.Mills *(New owner 9.01)* *"Spirit of Ireland" (Ryan Air titles)*	Navan	
EI-BGU	SOCATA MS.880B Rallye Club	875	F-BONM	9. 5.79	M.F.Neary) *(Wreck stored)*	Abbeyshrule	N 9.99
EI-BHB*	SOCATA MS.887 Rallye	2162	F-BUCH	7. 6.79	Hotel Bravo Flying Club Ltd *(Open store: cancelled 29.11.99)*	Abbeyshrule	N 5.99
EI-BHC	Reims Cessna F177RG Cardinal *(Wichita c/n 17700117)*	F177RG0010	G-AYTG	11. 7.79	B.J.Palfrey & Partners *"Hot Chocolate/90"*	Dublin	A 5.01
EI-BHF	SOCATA MS.892A Rallye Commodore 150	10742	F-BPBP	10. 7.79	B.Mullen *(Wfu Strandhill '87: engine to EI-BYL: scrapped c.1989)*	Strandhill	
EI-BHI	Bell 206B JetRanger II	906	G-BAKX	14. 8.79	H.S.S.Ltd *(New owner 9.01)*	Rathcoole	
EI-BHM	Reims Cessna F337E Super Skymaster (Wichita c/n 33701217)	F33700004	OO-PDC OO-PDG	1.11.79	Ross Flying Group *(With Dublin College of Technology: instructional airframe 1993)*	Bolton St, Dublin	
EI-BHN	SOCATA MS.893A Rallye Commodore 180	11422	F-BRRO	11.10.79	T.Garvan *(On overhaul)*	Hacketstown	N 6.96
EI-BHP	SOCATA MS.893A Rallye Commodore 180	11459	F-BSAA	12.10.79	Spanish Point Flying Club	Spanish Point	
EI-BHT	Beechcraft 77 Skipper	WA-77		17.10.79	Waterford Aero Club Ltd	Waterford	A 1.02
EI-BHV	Aeronca 7EC Traveler	7EC-739	G-AVDU N9837Y	30.10.79	E.P.O'Donnell & Partners	Clonmel	N 9.99
EI-BHW	Reims Cessna F150F *(Wichita c/n 15062671)*	F150-0013	G-ATMK	22.11.79	R.Sharpe	Weston	
EI-BHY	SOCATA Rallye 150ST	2929	F-GARL	19.11.79	Limerick Flying Club (Coonagh) Ltd	Coonagh	A12.01
EI-BIB	Reims Cessna F152 II	F15201724		30.11.79	Galway Flying Club Ltd	Abbeyshrule	A 7.01
EI-BIC	Reims Cessna F172N Skyhawk II	F17201965	(OO-HNZ)	15. 2.80	Oriel Flying Group Ltd *(Damaged Castlebar 13.4.95: open store)*	Abbeyshrule	N 9.99
EI-BID	Piper PA-18 Super Cub 95 (L-18C-PI)	18-1524	D-EAES ALAT 18-1524/51-15524	30.11.79	S.Coghlan & P.Ryan	Galway	N12.00
EI-BIG	Moravan Zlin 526 Trener Master	1086	D-EBUP OO-BUT	7.12.79	P.von Lonkhuyzen *(Damaged 9.91: stored)*	Rushett Farm, Chessington	N10.97
EI-BIJ	Agusta-Bell 206B JetRanger II	8432	G-BCVZ	29. 1.80	Medavia Properties Ltd *(Op Celtic Helicopters Ltd)*	Dublin Heliport	A12.01
EI-BIK	Piper PA-18-150 Super Cub *(Modified to 180hp)*	18-7909088	N82276	1. 2.80	Dublin Gliding Club Ltd	Gowran Grange	N10.01
EI-BIM	Morane MS.880B Rallye Club	305	F-BKYJ	28. 3.80	D.Millar *(Stored)*	Abbeyshrule	N 6.97
EI-BIO	Piper J-3C-65 Cub (L-4J-PI)	12657	F-BGXP OO-GAE/44-80361	27. 5.80	Monasterevin Flying Group	Harristown Nurney, Monasterevin	A 8.00
EI-BIR	Reims Cessna F172M Skyhawk II	F17201225	F-BVXI	24. 3.80	B.Harrison, K.Brereton, P.Rogers & F.Maher	Clonbullogue	A11.00
EI-BIS	Robin R.1180TD Aiglon	268		14. 5.80	The Robin Aiglon Group	Abbeyshrule	N 5.00
EI-BIT	SOCATA MS.887 Rallye 125	2169	F-BULQ	18. 3.80	Spanish Point Flying Club	Spanish Point, Co.Clare	A 1.00
EI-BIV	Bellanca 8KCAB Super Decathlon	464-79	N5032Q	3. 6.80	Aerocrats Flying Group Ltd	Abbeyshrule	N 7.01

EI-BIW	SOCATA MS.880B Rallye Club	1144	F-BPGB	19. 5.80	E.J.Barr	Buncrana	
					(Crashed on take off Rosnakil 10.8.86 & scrapped 1990)		
EI-BJB	Aeronca 7DC Champion	7AC-925	G-BKKM	16. 4.80	W.Kennedy	Killenaule	N 12.00
	(Continental C85)		EI-BJB/N82296/NC82296		*(Stored incomplete)*		
EI-BJC	Aeronca 7AC Champion	7AC-4927	N1366E	2. 4.80	E.Griffin	Blackwater	
	(Continental A65)		NC1366E				
EI-BJI	Reims FR172E Rocket	FR17200040	G-BAAS	23. 5.80	Irish Parachute Club Ltd	Dublin	
			SE-FBW/OY-DKN		*(Crashed Edenderry 9.82: probably scrapped pre 1990)*		
EI-BJJ	Aeronca 15AC Sedan	15AC-226	(G-BHXP)	6. 6.80	O.Bruton	Abbeyshrule	N 3.98
			EI-BJJ/N1214H		*(Stored)*		
EI-BJK	SOCATA Rallye 110ST	3226	F-GBKY	8. 7.80	Malachy Keenan	Weston	A 5.01
EI-BJM	Cessna A152 Aerobat	A1520936	N761CC	18. 9.80	Leinster Aero Club Ltd	Abbeyshrule	A 9.01
EI-BJO	Cessna R172K Hawk XP II	R1723340	N758TD	6. 8.80	P.Hogan & G.Ryder	Galway	A 9.01
EI-BJS	Gulfstream AA-5B Tiger	AA5B-0979	G-BFZR	3. 9.80	P.Morrissey	Newcastle	A 6.01
EI-BJT	Piper PA-38-112 Tomahawk	38-78A0818	G-BGEU	16.10.80	S.Corrigan & W.Lennon	Abbeyshrule	A 9.00
			N9650N				
EI-BJW*	de Havilland DH.104 Dove 6	04485	G-ASNG	7.11.80	Waterford Airport Fire Service	Waterford	N 3.99
			HB-LFF/G-ASNG/HB-LFF/G-ASNG/PH-IOM		*(No external marks)*		
EI-BKC	Aeronca 15AC Sedan	15AC-467	N1394H	5.11.80	G.Hendrick, M.Farrell & J.Keating	Birr	A 8.00
					(New owners 11.01)		
EI-BKE*	Morane MS.885 Super Rallye	278	F-BKUN	9. 2.81	Not known	Abbeyshrule	N 7.01
			F-WKUN		*(Crashed Ballyclumack, Wexford 5.4.81: stripped hulk noted)*		
EI-BKF	Reims Cessna F172H	F172-0476	G-AVUX	4.12.80	E.McEllin	Abbeyshrule	N 7.01
EI-BKK	Taylor JT.1 Monoplane	PFA 1421	G-AYYC	2. 2.81	Waterford Aero Club	Waterford	N 1.02
	(VW 1500)				*(Stored dismantled)*		
EI-BKN	SOCATA Rallye 100ST	3035	F-GBCK	18. 2.81	Weston Ltd	Weston	A 5.98
EI-BKS	Eipper Quicksilver	IMA-001		15. 4.81	Irish Microlight Aircraft Ltd	Shannon	
	(Yamaha KT100SD)				*(Believed scrapped)*		
EI-BKT	Agusta-Bell 206B-3 JetRanger III	8562	D-HAFD	6. 4.81	Irish Helicopters Ltd	Dublin	A 6.01
			HB-XIC				
EI-BKU	SOCATA MS.892A Rallye Commodore 150	10990	F-BRLG	21. 5.81	Limerick Flying Club (Coonagh) Ltd		
					(Open stored)	Abbeyshrule	N 5.99
EI-BLB	SNCAN Stampe SV-4C	323	F-BCTE	27. 7.81	J.E.Hutchinson & R.A.Stafford		
					(Crashed Drumsna, Carrick-on-Shannon 1.6.97)	Abbeyshrule	
EI-BLD	MBB Bö.105DB	S.381	D-HDLQ	21. 7.81	Irish Helicopters Ltd	Dublin	A 9.01
EI-BLE	Eipper Quicksilver	IMA-003		20. 8.81	R.P.St.George-Smith	Kilkenny	
	(Yamaha KT100SP)				*(Believed scrapped following accident date unknown)*		
EI-BLN	Eipper Quicksilver MX	MX.01		26. 8.81	O.J.Conway & B.Daffy	Ennis	
	(Cuyana 340)				*(Believed scrapped)*		
EI-BLU	Evans VP-1	SAAC-05		13.10.81	S.Pallister	(Ballymore Eustace)	N2000
	(VW)				*(Stored dismantled at owner's home)*		
EI-BLW*	Piper PA-23-250 Aztec C	27-3173	G-BBAV	16.11.81	Shannon Executive Aviation	Shannon	N 9.99
			PH-KNV/LN-NPD/SE-EPW				
					(Dismantled 1995: extant Engineering School, Airport Industrial Estate)		
EI-BMA	SOCATA MS.880B Rallye Club	1965	F-BTJR	26. 1.82	W.Rankin & M.Kelleher	Abbeyshrule	N 5.00
					(Wings only noted)		
EI-BMB	SOCATA MS.880B Rallye 100T	2505	G-BJCO	5. 1.82	Glyde Court Developments Ltd	Weston	N 4.01
			F-BVLB		*(WFU?)*		
EI-BMF	Laverda F.8L Super Falco Srs.IV	416	G-AWSU	28. 1.82	M.Slazenger & H.McCann	Powerscourt	A 5.99
EI-BMH	SOCATA MS.880B Rallye Club	1277	(G-BIDS)	19. 2.82	N.S.Bracken	Donegal	
			F-BSTJ		*(Scrapped near Lifford, Co.Donegal c.1990)*		
EI-BMI	SOCATA TB-9 Tampico	203	F-GCOV	12. 5.82	Ashford Flying Group	Weston	N 7.01
EI-BMJ	SOCATA MS.880B Rallye 100T	2594	F-BXTG	10. 3.82	Weston Ltd	Weston	N 5.98
EI-BMM	Reims Cessna F152 II	F15201899		10. 3.82	P.Redmond	Weston	
EI-BMN	Reims Cessna F152 II	F15201912		10. 3.82	BMN Group	Abbeyshrule	N12.01
EI-BMU	Monnett Sonerai IIL	01224		19. 5.82	A.Fenton	Ballyshannon	N 7.01
	(VW 2100)						
EI-BMV	American Aviation AA-5 Traveler	AA5-0200	G-BAEJ	28. 7.82	E.Tierney & K.A.Harold	Abbeyshrule	N 7.01
					(Damaged Brittas Bay 3.93: stripped hulk noted)		
EI-BMW	Maddock Skytrike/Hiway Vulcan	LM-100		1. 6.82	L.Maddock	Carlow	
	(Fuji-Robin)						
EI-BNA	McDonnell-Douglas DC-8-63CF	45989	LX-ACV	15. 4.83	Aer Turas Teoranta	Marana, USA	N11.99
			(CX-BOU)/TF-ACV/LX-ACV/N779FT		t/a Irish Cargo Airlines		
					"City of Dublin" (For storage/scrapping)		
EI-BNF	Eurowing Goldwing	-		22. 9.82	N Irwin	Cork	
	(Fuji-Robin)				*(WFU & scrapped 1985)*		
EI-BNH	Hiway Skytrike	AS.09		18.10.82	M.Martin	Tullamore	
	(Fuji-Robin EC-25-PS)						
EI-BNJ	Evans VP-2	-		24. 1.83	G.A.Cashman	Bartlemy	
	(VW 2000)				*(WFU & believed scrapped 1996)*		
EI-BNK	Cessna U206F Stationair	U20601706	G-HILL	23.12.82	Irish Parachute Club Ltd	Clonbulloge	A11.00
			PH-ADN/D-EEXY/N9506G				
EI-BNL	Rand Robinson KR-2	-		13. 1.83	K.Hayes	Birr	N 1.01
	(VW 2000)				*(Under construction)*		

EI-BNP	Rotorway Executive 145	-		1. 3.83	R.L.Renfroe	Letterkenny	
					(Not completed 1989)		
EI-BNR*	American Avn AA-5 Traveler	AA5-0203	N9992Q	12. 4.83	Victor Mike Flying Group Ltd	Abbeyshrule	N 5.99
			CS-AHM		*(Crashed 21.2.88: open store for spares)*		
EI-BNT	Cvjetkovic CA-65	-		23. 3.83	B.Tobin & P.G.Ryan	(Tallaght)	
EI-BNU	SOCATA MS.880B Rallye Club	1204	F-BPQV	7. 4.83	P.A.Doyle	Coonagh	A 8.00
EI-BOA	Pterodactyl	-		3. 5.83	A.Murphy	Athenry	
EI-BOE	SOCATA TB-10 Tobago	301	F-GDBL	12. 9.83	P.Byron, K.Lawford, L.Naye, E.Murtagh, G.Haughey,		
					M.Verling & J.Byron	Weston	A10.01
EI-BOH	Eipper Quicksilver	-		8. 9.83	J.Leech	Waterford	
	(Yamaha 970cc)				*(Status unknown - thought dismantled)*		
EI-BOP*	SOCATA MS.892A Rallye Commodore 150		G-BKGS	13. 3.84	Not known	Abbeyshrule	N 5.99
		11748	F-BSXS		*(Crashed Coonagh 29.3.86: open store for spares)*		
EI-BOV	Rand Robinson KR-2	SAAC-11		7. 5.84	G.O'Hara & G.Callan *"Kitty Hawk"*	NK	
	(VW 1835)				*(Damaged Carnmore 3.91 on re-build 1999)*		
EI-BOX	Box Duet	-		12.10.84	Dr.K.Riccius	(Newcastle)	
	(Rotax 503)				*(Status unknown - thought still under construction)*		
EI-BPE	Viking Dragonfly	SAAC-16		15.10.84	G.G.Bracken	Castlebar	N 1.01
	(VW 1835)				*(Not completed & stored)*		
EI-BPJ	Cessna 182A Skylane	18234949	G-BAGA	4.12.84	Falcon Parachute Club Ltd	Abbeyshrule	N 9.99
			N4849D		*(Damaged pre 7.95: fuselage open store)*		
EI-BPL	Reims Cessna F172K	F17200758	G-AYSG	28. 3.85	Phoenix Flying Ltd	Shannon	A12.01
EI-BPN	Flexiform Striker	-		12. 3.85	P.H.Collins	Dunlaoghaire	
	(Fuji Robin)						
EI-BPO	Southdown Puma	1923		12. 3.85	A.Channing	Clane	
	(Fuji-Robin EC-44-PM - E/No.82-00108) *(Also quoted as Southdown Sailwing c/n 1924)*						
EI-BPP	Eipper Quicksilver MX	3207		12. 3.85	J.A.Smith	Abbeyshrule	N 8.93
	(Cuyana 430)				*(Stored)*		
EI-BPT	Skyhook Sabre	-		26. 3.85	T.McGrath	Glounthane	
	(Solo 210)				*(Status unknown: thought dismantled)*		
EI-BPU	Hiway Demon	-		26. 3.85	A.Channing	Abbeyshrule	N 5.00
	(Fuji-Robin EC-25-PS)						
EI-BRK	Flexiform Trike	LM.102		17. 6.85	L.Maddock	Hacketstown	
	(Fuji Robin)				*(WFU & scrapped 1994)*		
EI-BRS	Cessna P172D	P17257173	G-WPUI	2. 9.85	D.& M.Hillary	Weston	A 5.98
			G-AXPI/9M-AMR/N11B/(N8573X)				
EI-BRT*	Flexwing M17727	990059		5.11.85	Not known	Ballymore Eustace	N 8.97
	(Fuji-Robin EC-44-PM)				*(Stored)*		
EI-BRU	Evans VP-1	V-12-84-CQ & SAAC-18		5.11.85	Home Bru Flying Group	Weston	N12.00
	(VW 1600)						
EI-BRV	Hiway Demon/Skytrike	NK		5.11.85	M.Garvey & C.Tully	Kells	
	(Fuji-Robin EC-25-PS)						
EI-BRW	Hovey Delta Bird	NK		5.11.85	A & E Aerosport	Curraglass	
	(VW 1300) *(Originally regd as Ultra-Lite Deltabird but is a Bimax Osprey: was built to re-enact a scene nr Fermoy 1986 from the "Blue Max" film: dismantled and scrapped)*						
EI-BRX	Reims Cessna FRA150L Aerobat		G-BACM	9. 1.86	Auburn Air Ltd	Abbeyshrule	A 8.01
		FRA1500160			*(New owner 11.01)*		
EI-BSB	Wassmer Jodel D.112	1067	G-AWIG	23. 6.87	Estartit Ltd	Kilrush	A 5.01
			F-BKAA				
EI-BSC	Reims Cessna F172N Skyhawk II		G-NIUS	10.12.85	S.Phelan	Weston	A 4.00
		F17201651					
EI-BSF*	Avro 748 Srs.1/105	1544	EC-DTP	28. 5.86	Ryanair Ltd	Dublin	N 9.99
			G-BEKD/LV-HHF/LV-PUM		*"Spirit of Tipperary"*		
	(Wings, tail removed & scrapped 10.92: remainder used as cabin trainer: for fire training in all-white c/s)						
EI-BSG	Bensen B-80 Gyrocopter	HB		30. 1.86	J.Todd	(Riverstick)	N 3.90
	(McC.4318)				*(Stored)*		
EI-BSK	SOCATA TB-9 Tampico	618		9. 4.86	Weston Ltd	Weston	A12.01
EI-BSL	Piper PA-34-220T Seneca III		N8468X	27. 6.86	P Greenan	Weston	A11.00
		34-8233041					
EI-BSN	Cameron O-65 HAFB	1278		14. 4.86	Carol O'Neill & Tracy Hooper	Cavan	
					"Erin-Go-Bragh" (New owners 5.01)		
EI-BSO	Piper PA-28-140 Cherokee B	28-25449	C-GOBL	16. 4.86	H.M.Hanley	Waterford	A 1 02
			N8241N				
EI-BSV	SOCATA TB-20 Trinidad	579	G-BMIX	15. 8.86	J.Condron	Abbeyshrule	A10.01
EI-BSW	Solar Wings Pegasus XL-R			22. 6.87	E.Fitzgerald	Waterford	N 8.95
	(Rotax 447)	SW-TB-1124&SW-WA-1122					
EI-BSX	Piper J-3C-65 Cub	8912	G-ICUB	25. 3.86	J. & T.O'Dwyer	Gowran Grange	
	(Frame No.8999)		F-BEGT/NC79805/45-4515/42-36788				
	(Official c/n 13255 is incorrect as a/c probably rebuilt c.1945)						
EI-BTX	McDonnell Douglas DC9-82	49660	(N59842)	23. 3.88	Airplanes Holdings Ltd		
	(MD-82)				*(Leased Aeromexico)*	Mexico City, Mexico	
EI-BTY(2)	McDonnell Douglas DC9-82	49667	N12844	6. 5.88	Airplanes Holdings Ltd		
	(MD-82)				*(Leased Aeromexico)*	Mexico City, Mexico	
EI-BUA	Cessna 172M Skyhawk II	17265451	N5458H	8. 8.86	Skyhawks Flying Club	Abbeyshrule	A 8.01

EI-BUC	Jodel D.9 Bebe (VW 1500)	PFA 929	G-BASY	20. 1.87	D.Lyons	Abbeyshrule	A 7.01
EI-BUF	Cessna 210N Centurion II	21063070	G-MCDS G-BHNB/N6496N	18.12.86	210 Group	Abbeyshrule	A10.01
EI-BUG	SOCATA ST-10 Diplomate	125	G-STIO OH-SAB	4. 2.87	J.Cooke *(WFU)*	Weston	A 5.01
EI-BUH	Lake LA-4-200 Buccaneer	543	G-PARK G-BBGK/N39779	27. 5.87	T.Henderson	Lough Derg Marina, Killaloe	A 9.01
EI-BUJ	SOCATA MS.892A Rallye Commodore 150	10737	G-FOAM G-AVPL	27. 2.87	T.Cunniffe *(Damaged pre 1992: stored)*	Abbeyshrule	N 3.98
EI-BUL	Whittaker MW.5 Sorcerer (Citroen 602cc)	1		4. 3.87	J.Culleton	Mountmellick, Co.Laois	
EI-BUN	Beechcraft 76 Duchess	ME-371	(EI-BUO) N37001	26. 6.87	K.A.O'Connor	Weston	A10.01
EI-BUO	Aero Composites Sea Hawker (Lycoming O-320) *(Now regd as Glass S.005E)*	80		25. 8.87	C.Donaldson & C.Lavery *(Displayed Ulster Aviation Society Museum)*	Langford Lodge	N 9.99
EI-BUR	Piper PA-38-112 Tomahawk	38-79A0363	G-BNDE N2541D	10. 7.87	Westair Aviation Ltd	Shannon	A 4.01
EI-BUS	Piper PA-38-112 Tomahawk	38-79A0186	G-BNDF N2439C	10. 7.87	Westair Aviation Ltd	Shannon	A 3.01
EI-BUT	GEMS MS.893A Rallye Commodore 180	10559	SE-IMV F-BNBU	30. 7.87	T.Keating *(Galerien c/s)*	Weston	A 5.00
EI-BUW	Noble-Hardman Snowbird IIIA (Rotax 532)	SB-F001	77-DS (French)	8. 9.87	TIFC & IS Ltd *(Damaged Dromiskin, Co.Louth 1.6.92: status unknown)*	Dundalk	
EI-BUX	Agusta A109A	7147	N790SC (N466MP)/N790SC/N72521	10. 6.88	Orring Ltd *(Stored dismantled)*	Kilcock	N 9.99
EI-BVB	Whittaker MW.6 Merlin (Rotax)	1		14. 9.87	R.England	Watergrasshill	N 9.00
EI-BVJ(2)	AMF Chevvron 2-32 (Konig SD570)	009		16. 2.88	S.J.Dunne	Bolybeg, Ballymore Eustace	
EI-BVK	Piper PA-38-112 Tomahawk	38-79A0966	OO-FLG OO-HLG/N9705N	2. 3.88	Pegasus Flying Group Ltd	Weston	A 5.98
EI-BVT	Evans VP-2 (VW 1834)	V2-2129/PFA 7221 & SAAC-20	G-BEIE	29. 4.88	P.Morrison *(Under construction)*	(Cork)	N 1.01
EI-BVY	Heintz Zenith CH.200AA-RW (Lycoming O-320)	2-582		7. 6.88	J.Matthews, M.Skelly & T.Coleman	Abbeyshrule	A 7.01
EI-BWH	Partenavia P.68C	212	G-BHJP	11.12.87	K.Buckley	Cork	A 9.01
EI-BXB	Boeing 737-448	24521		27.10.89	Aer Lingus Ltd *"St.Gall"*	Dublin	
EI-BXC	Boeing 737-448	24773		26. 4.90	Aer Lingus Ltd *"St.Brendan/Breandan"*	Dublin	
EI-BXD	Boeing 737-448	24866		1. 6.90	Aer Lingus Ltd *"St.Colman"*	Dublin	
EI-BXI	Boeing 737-448	25052		29. 4.91	Aer Lingus Ltd *"St.Finnian"* *(Leased Ryan International 2001/2002)*	Dublin	
EI-BXK	Boeing 737-448	25736		14. 4.92	Aer Lingus Ltd *"St.Calmin"* *(Leased Ryan International 2001/2002)*	Dublin	
EI-BXL	Polaris FIB OK350 (Rotax 503)	M.561628		27. 6.91	M.McKeon	Lough Gowna	
EI-BXO	Fouga (Valmet) CM-170 Magister *(C/n FM-28 quoted)*	213	N18FM FM-28	21.11.88	G.W.Connolly *(Stored)*	Swords, Dublin	N 4.96
EI-BXT	Rollason Druine D.62B Condor	RAE/626	G-AVZE	24. 8.88	S.Bruton	Abbeyshrule	A12.00
EI-BXX	Agusta-Bell 206B-3 JetRanger III	8560	G-JMVB G-OIML	15.11.88	Westair Aviation Ltd	Shannon	A 8.01
EI-BYA	Thruster TST Mk.1	8504	G-MNDA	1. 2.89	E.Fagan *(Scrapped following storm damage at Abbeyshrule 1992)*	Ballyheelan	
EI-BYF	Cessna 150M Commuter	15076654	N3924V	20.11.89	Twentieth Air Training Group Ltd	Dublin	A12.01
EI-BYG	SOCATA TB-9 Tampico Club	928		23. 8.89	Weston Ltd	Weston	A 8.01
EI-BYJ	Bell 206B JetRanger II	1897	N49725	23. 6.89	Medeva Properties Ltd	Dublin Heliport	A12.01
EI-BYL	Heintz Zenith CH-250 (Lycoming O-320) *(C/n quoted as c/n A2-866)*	MS/FAS 2866	(EI-BYD)	14. 6.89	M.McLoughlin *(Noted 8.01)*	Kilrush	A12.01
EI-BYR	Bell 206L-3 LongRanger III	51284	(EI-LMG) EI-BYR/D-HBAD	15. 8.89	H.S.S.Ltd *(New owner 9.01)*	Rathcoole	A 8.01
EI-BYX	Champion 7GCAA Citabria	7GCAA-40	N546DS	4. 4.90	P.J.Gallagher	Abbeyshrule	A 7.01
EI-BYY	Piper J-3C-85 Cub *(Frame No.12322)* *(Regd with c/n 22288 and officially ex G-AKTJ/N3595K/NC3595K therefore)*	12494	EC-AQZ HB-OSG/44-80198	12. 4.90	V.Murphy	Thurles	A12.01
EI-BZE	Boeing 737-3Y0	24464		2. 8.89	Paloma Developments (PAL) *(Leased Philippine Airlines)*	Manila, Philippines	
EI-BZF	Boeing 737-3Y0	24465		7. 8.89	Pergola Ltd	NK	
EI-BZJ	Boeing 737-3Y0	24677		29. 3.90	Pergola Ltd *(Leased Philippine Airlines)*	Manila, Philippines	
EI-BZL	Boeing 737-3Y0	24680		4.10.90	GECAS Technical Services Ltd	NK	
EI-BZM	Boeing 737-3Y0	24681		15.10.90	GECAS Technical Services Ltd *(Leased Philippine Airlines)*	Manila, Philippines	

EI-BZN	Boeing 737-3Y0	24770		30.10.90	Airplanes Finance Ltd *(Leased Philippine Airlines)* Manila, Philippines		
EI-CAA*	Reims FR172J Rocket	FR17200486	G-BHTW 5Y-ATO	17. 8.89	O.Bruton *(Damaged 1993/94: cancelled 27.11.98 as WFU: open store)*	Abbeysrule	N 9.00
EI-CAC	Grob G-115A	8092		22.10.89	G.Tracey	Weston	A 5.01
EI-CAE	Grob G-115A	8105		5. 4.90	D.Kehoe	Waterford	A 1.02
EI-CAN	Aerotech MW.5(K) Sorcerer (Rotax 447)	5K-0011-02	(G-MWGH)	15. 6.90	V.Vaughan	Mulinahone	
EI-CAP	Cessna R182 Skylane RGII	R18200056	G-BMUF N7342W	27. 4.90	M.J.Hanlon	Weston	A 9.01
EI-CAQ	*Allocated to Aer Lingus 2.3.91 for Flight Simulator testing using "c/n" 1.666 (1666 also quoted)*						
EI-CAU	AMF Chevvron 2-32 (Konig SD32)	022		14.11.90	J.Farrant	Rathcoole	
EI-CAW	Bell 206B JetRanger II	780	N2947W	11. 7.90	Celtic Helicopters (Maintenance Services) Ltd *(Dismantled)*	Dublin Heliport	N 5.00
EI-CAX	Cessna P210N Pressurized Centurion II	P21000215	(EI-CAS) G-OPMB/N4553K	9. 7.90	J.Rafter	Abbeyshrule	A 7.01
EI-CAY	Mooney M.20C Ranger	690074	N9272V	14.11.90	Ranger Flights Ltd	Dublin	
EI-CAZ*	Fairchild-Hiller FH-227D	519	SE-KBR C-FNAK/CF-NAK/(N701U)/N2735R	23. 9.91	Norwich Airport Fire Service	Norwich	
EI-CBJ	de Havilland DHC-8-102 Dash Eight	215	C-GFCF	25. 5.90	Debis Airfinance Jetprop Ltd *(Leased Allegheny Commuter)*	Harrisburg, PA, USA	
EI-CBK	ATR 42-312	199	F-WWEM	25. 7.90	GPA-ATR Ltd *(Op Aer Arran)*	Naples, Italy	
EI-CBR	McDonnell Douglas DC-9-83 (MD-83)	49939		3.12.90	Airplanes 111 Ltd *(Leased Avianca) "Ciudad de Bucaramanga"*	Bogota, Columbia	
EI-CBS	McDonnell Douglas DC-9-83 (MD-83)	49942		10.12.90	GECAS Technical Services Ltd *(Leased Avianca) "Ciudad de Cucuta"*	Bogota, Columbia	
EI-CBY	McDonnell Douglas DC-9-83 (MD-83)	49944		30. 7.91	GECAS Technical Services Ltd *(Leased Avianca) "Ciudad de Barranquilla"*	Bogota, Columbia	
EI-CBZ	McDonnell Douglas DC-9-83 (MD-83)	49945		13. 8.91	GECAS Technical Services Ltd *(Leased Avianca) "Ciudad de Santiago de Cali"*	Bogota, Columbia	
EI-CCA*	Beechcraft 19A Musketeer Sport	MB-411	G-AWTR N2758B	18. 7.90	P.F.McCoole *(Cancelled 4.9.01 after accident damage at unknown location)*	Coonagh	N 5.00
EI-CCC	McDonnell Douglas DC-9-83 (MD-83)	49946		27. 9.91	Airplanes 111 Ltd *(Leased Avianca) "Ciudad de Pereira"*	Bogota, Columbia	
EI-CCD	Grob G-115A	8108	D-EIUD or D-EIWD ?	15. 8.90	MOD Aviation Ltd	Weston	A 4.01
EI-CCE(2)	McDonnell Douglas DC-9-83 (MD-83)	49947		19. 9.91	GECAS Technical Services Ltd *(Leased Avianca)"Ciudad de Medelin"*	Bogota, Columbia	
EI-CCF	Aeronca 11AC Chief (Continental A65)	11AC-S-40	N3826E NC3826E	10. 1.91	L.Murray & Partners	Trim	A11.00
EI-CCH	Piper J-3C-65 Cub	7278	N38801 NC38801	24. 1.91	J.Matthews & Partners	Trim	N11.00
EI-CCJ	Cessna 152 II	15280174	N24251	9.10.90	M.P.Cahill *(Stored)*	Dublin	N 2.95
EI-CCK	Cessna 152 II	15279610	N757BM	9.10.90	M.P.Cahill *(Damaged pre 1995)*	Newcastle	
EI-CCL	Cessna 152 II	15280382	N24791	9.10.90	M.P.Cahill *(Damaged Bray Head, Co.Wicklow 4.5.93: status uncertain)*	Dublin	
EI-CCM	Cessna 152 II	15282320	N68679	9.10.90	E Hopkins	Newcastle	
EI-CCV	Cessna R172K Hawk XPII	R1723039	N758EP	2. 3.91	Kerry Aero Club Ltd	Farranfore	
EI-CCY	Grumman-American AA-1B Trainer	AA1B-0617	G-BDYC	19. 3.91	N.F. & C.Whisler *(Crashed Galway/Carnmore 5.11.94: wreck stored)*	Galway	N 4.96
EI-CDA	Boeing 737-548	24878	YR-BGZ EI-CDA/EI-BXE	31.5.01R	Aer Lingus Ltd	Dublin	
EI-CDB	Boeing 737-548	24919	EI-BXF	27. 5.91	Aer Lingus Ltd *"St.Albert/Ailbhe"*	Dublin	
EI-CDC	Boeing 737-548	24968	EI-BXG	19. 6.91	Aer Lingus Ltd *"St.Munchen/Maincin"*	Dublin	
EI-CDD	Boeing 737-548	24989	EI-BXH	3. 7.91	Aer Lingus Ltd *"St.Macartan/Macarthain"*	Dublin	
EI-CDE	Boeing 737-548	25115	PT-SLM EI-CDE/(EI-BXJ)	21. 5.91	Aer Lingus Ltd *"St.Jarlath/Iarflaith"*	Dublin	
EI-CDF	Boeing 737-548	25737		23. 3.92	Aer Lingus Ltd *"St.Cronan"*	Dublin	
EI-CDG	Boeing 737-548	25738		7. 4.92	Aer Lingus Ltd *"St.Moling"*	Dublin	
EI-CDH	Boeing 737-548	25739		14. 4.92	Aer Lingus Ltd "St.Ronan"	Dublin	
EI-CDP	Cessna 182L	18258955	G-FALL OY-AHS/N4230S	20. 5.91	Irish Parachute Club Ltd	Clonbulloge	A11.00
EI-CDV	Cessna 150G	15066677	N2777S	17. 7.91	K.A.O'Connor	Weston	N 5.98
EI-CDX	Cessna 210K Centurion	21059329	G-AYGN N9429M	14. 8.91	Falcon Aviation Ltd	Waterford	A 1.02

EI-CDY	McDonnell Douglas DC-9-83 (MD-83)	49948		27. 9.91	GECAS Technical Services Ltd *(Leased Avianca) "Ciudad de Santa Maria"*	Bogota, Columbia	
EI-CEG	SOCATA MS.893E Rallye 180GT	13083	SE-GTS	31.10.91	M.Farrelly	Powerscourt	
EI-CEK	McDonnell Douglas DC-9-83 (MD-83)	49631	EC-FMY EC-113/EI-CEK/EC-EPM/EC-261	13.12.91	Airplanes IAL Finance Ltd *(Leased Eurofly)*	Turin, Italy	
EI-CEN	Thruster T.300 (Rotax 582)	9012-T300-500		2. 3.92	P.J.Murphy	Macroom	
EI-CEP	McDonnell Douglas DC-9-83 (MD-83)	53122		14. 4.92	GECAS Technical Services Ltd *(Leased Avianca) "San Andres Isla"*	Bogota, Columbia	
EI-CEQ	McDonnell Douglas DC-9-83 (MD-83)	53123		14. 4.92	GECAS Technical Services Ltd *(Leased Avianca) "Ciudad de Leticia"*	Bogota, Columbia	
EI-CER	McDonnell Douglas DC-9-83 (MD-83)	53125	N9017P	20. 5.92	Airplanes 111 Ltd *(Leased Avianca) "Ciudad de Monteria"*	Bogota, Columbia	
EI-CES	Taylorcraft BC-65	2231	G-BTEG N27590/NC27590	25. 3.92	N.O'Brien	Kilkenny	N 9.00
EI-CEX	Lake LA-4-200 Buccaneer	1115	N8VG N3VC/N8544Z	18. 5.92	Derg Developments Ltd	Lough Derg Marina, Killaloe	A10.01
EI-CEY	Boeing 757-2Y0	26152		10. 8.92	Pergola Ltd *(Leased Avianca)*	Bogota, Columbia	
EI-CEZ	Boeing 757-2Y0	26154		18. 9.92	Airplanes Holdings Ltd *(Leased Avianca)*	Bogota, Columbia	
EI-CFE	Robinson R22 Beta	1709	G-BTHG	15. 5.91	Premier Aviation Services Ltd *(New owner 6.01)*	Weston	A 3.00
EI-CFF	Piper PA-12 Super Cruiser (Lycoming O-235)	12-3928	N78544 NC78544	23. 5.91	J.O'Dwyer & J.Molloy	Gowran Grange	A 5.99
EI-CFG	Rousseau Piel CP.301B Emeraude	112	G-ARIW F-BIRQ	1. 6.91	Southlink Ltd *(Stored complete)*	Waterford	N 1.02
EI-CFH	Piper PA-12 Super Cruiser (Lycoming O-320)	12-3110	(EI-CCE) N4214M/NC4214M	1. 6.91	G.Treacy	Shinrone	A10.99
EI-CFN	Cessna 172P Skyhawk II	17274113	N5446K JA4172/N5446K	10. 5.92	B.Fitzmaurice & G.O'Connell	Weston	A 8.01
EI-CFO	Piper J-3C-65 Cub (L-4H-PI)	11947	OO-RAZ OO-RAF/44-79651	13. 5.92	J.Mathews & Partners *(USAAF c/s)*	Trim	N 8.98
EI-CFP	Cessna 172P Skyhawk II	17274428	N52178	15. 7.91	K A O'Connor	Abbeyshrule	A 8.01
EI-CFV*	SOCATA MS.880B Rallye Club	1850	G-OLFS G-AYYZ	13. 5.92	Not known *(Cancelled 15.11.00 as scrapped) (Stripped hulk noted)*	Abbeyshrule	N.7.01
EI-CFX	Robinson R22 Beta	0793	G-OSPI	16. 6.92	Helicopter Aviation Sales Ltd	Weston	A 8.01
EI-CFY	Cessna 172N Skyhawk II	17268902	N734JZ	18. 6.92	K.A.O'Connor	Weston	A 8.01
EI-CFZ	McDonnell Douglas DC-9-83 (MD-83)	53120	N6206F	29. 7.92	Airplanes 111 Ltd *(Leased Avianca) "Ciudad de San Juan de Pasto"*	Bogota, Columbia	
EI-CGB	TEAM miniMAX	SAAC-36		20. 8.92	M.Garvey	Abbeyshrule	
EI-CGC	Stinson 108-3 Station Wagon	108-5243	OO-IAC OO-JAC/N3B	17. 7.92	Anne P.Bruton	Kildare	N12.00
EI-CGD	Cessna 172M Skyhawk II	17262309	OO-BMT N12846	30. 7.92	J Murray	Weston	A12.01
EI-CGE*	Hiway Demon/Skytrike (Fuji-Robin EC-25PS-04) *(C/n is engine type)*	EC-25PS-04K		19. 8.92	T Carr *(Temp unregd 11.2.97)*	Kilpedder	
EI-CGF	Phoenix Luton LA-5 Major	PAL-1124/PFA 1208 & SAAC-19	G-BENH	31. 7.92	F.Doyle & J.Duggan	(Newlands)	A 4.01
EI-CGG	Ercoupe 415C (Continental C75)	3147	N2522H NC2522H	10. 9.92	Irish Ercoupe Group *(WFU)*	Weston	N10.00
EI-CGH	Cessna 210N Centurion II	21063524	N6374A	16.11.92	J.J.Spollen	Abbeyshrule	A 9.01
EI-CGJ	Solar Wings Pegasus XL-R (Rotax 447)	SW-WA-1506	G-MWTV	5. 4.93	P.Hearty *(Crashed Portarlington late 1995: status unknown)*	Portarlington	
EI-CGM	Solar Wings Pegasus XL-R (Rotax 447)	SW-WA-1502	G-MWVC	14.11.92	Microflight Ltd	Ballyfore	
EI-CGN	Solar Wings Pegasus XL-R (Rotax 447)	SW-WA-1529	G-MWXM	14.11.92	V.Power	Donamore, New Ross	A 8.00
EI-CGO	McDonnell Douglas DC-8-63AF	45924	N353AS (N791AL)/SE-DBH/OY-SBM/HS-TGZ/SE-DBH	25. 4.89	Aer Turas Teoranta *(Stored 1.02)* t/a Irish Cargo Airlines	Manston	
EI-CGP	Piper PA-28-140 Cherokee C	28-26928	G-MLUA G-AYJT/N11C	25.11.92	G.Cashman *(Op Euroair Training)*	Cork	A12.01
EI-CGQ	Aérospatiale AS350B Ecureuil	2076	G-BUPK JA9740	21. 1.93	Caulstown Air Ltd	Dublin Heliport	A10.01
EI-CGT	Cessna 152 II	15282331	G-BPBL N16SU/N68715	10.12.92	J.J.Dunne	Stamullen	
EI-CGV	Piper J-5A Cub Cruiser	5-624	G-BPKT N35372/NC35372	11.12.92	J5 Grp	Trim	N12.00
EI-CGX	Cessna 340	340-0106	(EI-CHH) N51388/G-BALM/N4553L	27. 3.93	Meckfield Construction Co Ltd *(Crashed nr Knock 19.8.94: stored)*	Galway	N 1.95

EI-CHK	Piper J-3C-65 Cub Special	23019	C-FHNS CF-HNS/N1492N/NC1492N	10. 3.93	N.Higgins	Longwood	A 7.99
EI-CHM	Cessna 150M Commuter	15079288	G-BSZX N714MU	2. 3.93	K.A.O'Connor	Abbeyshrule	N 5.00
EI-CHN	SOCATA MS.880B Rallye Club	901	G-AVIO	22. 2.93	Limerick Flying Club (Coonagh) Ltd	Coonagh	N 7.01
EI-CHP	de Havilland DHC-8-103 Dash Eight	258	VH-FNQ C-GFRP	7. 4.93	Airplanes Jetprop Finance Ltd *(Leased US Airways Express/Allegheny Airlines)*	Harrisburg, PA, USA	
EI-CHR	CFM Shadow BD (Rotax 447)	063	G-MTKT	20. 5.93	J.Smith	Laytown	
EI-CHS	Cessna 172M Skyhawk II	17266742	G-BREZ N80775	26. 4.93	Kerry Aero Club Ltd	Farranfore	A 9.01
EI-CHV	Agusta A109A II	7149	VR-BMM HB-XTJ/D-HASV	10. 6.93	Celtic Helicopters Ltd	Dublin Heliport	A10.01
EI-CIA	SOCATA MS.880B Rallye Club	1218	G-MONA G-AWJK	26. 4.93	G.Hackett & C.Mason	Thurles	A 8.01
EI-CIF	Piper PA-28-180 Cherokee C	28-2853	G-AVVV N8880J	12. 6.93	AA Flying Group *(Rebuilt 1967 with spare frame c/n 28-3808S)*	Weston	A12.01
EI-CIG	Piper PA-18-150 Super Cub *(Frame No.18-7360)*	18-7203	G-BGWF ST-AFJ/ST-ABN	12. 6.93	K.A.O'Connor	Weston	A 8.00
EI-CIJ	Cessna 340	3400304	G-BBVE N69451	2. 7.93	Airlink Airways Ltd	Sligo	A11.01
EI-CIK	Mooney M.20C Mk 21	2620	G-BFXC 9H-ABD/G-BFXC/OH-MOA/N1349W	2. 7.93	T.G.Gordon	Connemara	N 5.00
EI-CIM	Avid Flyer mk.IV	1125D		17. 8.93	P.Swan	Weston	A10.98
EI-CIN	Cessna 150K	15071728	G-OCIN EI-CIN/G-BSXG/N6228G	6. 9.93	K.O'Connor	Weston	A 7.01
EI-CIR(2)	Cessna 551 Citation II *(Built as Cessna 550 EI-CIR(1) c/n 550-0128)*	551-0174	N60AR EI-CIR(1)/F-WLEF/9A-BPU/RC-BPU/YU-BPU/N220LA/N536M/N2631V	29.11.93	Air Group Finance Ltd	Dinard, France	A12.01
EI-CIV	Piper PA-28-140 Cherokee Cruiser	28-7725232	G-BEXY N9648N	20.11.93	G.Cashman & E.Callanan	Cork	A12.01
EI-CIW	McDonnell Douglas DC-9-83 (MD-83)	49785	HL-7271	30.12.93	Carotene Ltd *(Leased Meridiana)*	Olbia, Italy	
EI-CIZ	Steen Skybolt (Lycoming IO-360)	001	G-BSAO N303BC	12.12.93	J.Keane	Coonagh	N12.00
EI-CJC	Boeing 737-204ADV	22640	G-BJCV CS-TMA/G-BJCV/C-GCAU/G-BJCV/C-GXCP/G-BJCV	25. 1.94	Ryanair Ltd *(Hertz Car Rental titles)*	Dublin	
EI-CJD	Boeing 737-204ADV	22966	G-BKHE (G-BKGU)	18. 2.94	Ryanair Ltd *(Eirecell titles)*	Dublin	
EI-CJE	Boeing 737-204ADV	22639	G-BJCU EC-DVE/G-BJCU	10. 3.94	Ryanair Ltd *(Jaguar titles)*	Dublin	
EI-CJF	Boeing 737-204ADV	22967	G-BTZF G-BKHF/(G-BKGV)	24. 3.94	Ryanair Ltd	Dublin	
EI-CJG	Boeing 737-204ADV	22058	G-BGYK PP-SRW/G-BGYK/(G-BGRV)	25. 3.94	Ryanair Ltd	Dublin	
EI-CJH	Boeing 737-204ADV	22057	G-BGYJ (G-BGRU)/N8278V	30. 3.94	Ryanair Ltd	Dublin	
EI-CJI	Boeing 737-2E7	22875	G-BMDF (PK-RI.)/G-BMDF/4X-BAB/N4570B	8. 7.94	Ryanair Ltd	Dublin	
EI-CJK*	Airbus A300B4-103	020	F-BUAR D-AMAY/(F-WGLB)	13. 1.94	Channel Express *(Cancelled 19.5.00 as "removed from service")*	Bournemouth	N 7.01
EI-CJR	SNCAN Stampe SV-4A	318	G-BKBK OO-CLR/F-BCLR	28. 2.94	C.Scully, P.Ryan & P.McKenna - *(New owners 11.01)*	Carnmore	N12.00
EI-CJS	Jodel Wassmer D.120A Paris-Nice	339	F-BOYF	28. 2.94	K.Houlihan	Kilrush	N12.00
EI-CJT	Slingsby Cadet III (VW 1835)	830 & PCW-001	G-BPCW XA288	25. 2.94	J.Tarrant	Rathcoole	
EI-CJV	Moskito 2 (Rotax 582)	004	D-MBGM	12. 3.94	Peril, Kingston, Hanly & Fitzgerald	Coonagh	A 8.01
EI-CJZ	Whittaker MW-6S Fatboy Flyer (Rotax 503)	PFA 164-11493	G-MWTW	24. 3.94	M.McCarthy	Watergrasshill	N 9.00
EI-CKG	Hunt Avon (Rotax 447)	92009013		2. 7.94	B.Kenny	Clara	
EI-CKH	Piper PA-18 Super Cub 95	18-7248	G-APZK N10F	3. 6.94	G.Brady & C.Keenan	Weston	A 8.00
EI-CKI	Thruster TST mk.1 (Rotax 503)	8078-TST-091	G-MVDI	3. 6.94	S.Pallister	Brannockstown	
EI-CKJ	Cameron N-77 HAFB	3305		6. 7.94	F.Meldon *"Goodfellas"*	Blackrock	
EI-CKM	McDonnell Douglas DC-9-83 (MD-83)	49792	TC-INC EI-CKM/(D-ALLW)/EI-CKM/XA-RPH/EC-FFP/EC-733/XA-RPH	10. 8.94	Airplanes Finance Ltd *(Leased Meridiana)*	Olbia, Italy	
EI-CKN	Whittaker MW-6S Fatboy Flyer (Rotax 462)	BCA.8942		29. 7.94	F.Byrne & M.O'Carroll	Kilrush	

EI-CKP	Boeing 737-2K2ADV	22296	PH-TVS	7.10.94	Ryanair Ltd	Dublin	
			PP-SRV/PH-TVS/LV-RBH/PH-TVS/LV-RAO/PH-TVS/EC-DVN/PH-TVS				
EI-CKQ	Boeing 737-2K2ADV	22906	PH-TVU	20. 2.95	Ryanair Ltd	Dublin	
			G-BPLA/PH-TVU/C-FCAV/PH-TVU				
EI-CKR	Boeing 737-2K2ADV	22025	PH-TVR	4. 5.95	Ryanair Ltd	Dublin	
			C-FICP/PH-TVR/(D-AJAA)/PH-TVR				
EI-CKS	Boeing 737-2T5ADV	22023	PH-TVX	1. 6.95	Ryanair Ltd	Dublin	
			OE-ILE/PH-TVX/G-BGTW				
EI-CKT	Mainair Gemini/Flash 307-585-3 & W47		G-MNCB	27. 9.94	C.Burke	Bartlemy	
	(EC-44-PM)						
EI-CKU	Solar Wings Pegasus XL-R		G-MWVB	14.10.94	M.O'Regan	Edenderry	
	(Rotax 447) SW-TB-1434 & SW-WA-1500						
EI-CKX	Wassmer Jodel D.112	1166	G-ASIS	7.12.94	W.R.Prescott	Riverstown, Co.Louth	A 6.00
			F-BKNR				
EI-CKZ	Jodel D.18	229		5. 4.95	J.O'Brien	Glen of Imal	
	(VW 1834)						
EI-CLA	HOAC DV-20 Katana	20106		24. 3.95	Weston Ltd	Weston	A 9.01
EI-CLB	ATR 72-212	423	F-WWEB	23. 2.95	Tarquin Ltd	Olbia, Italy	
					(Leased Alitalia Express) "Lago di Bracciano"		
EI-CLC	ATR 72-212	428	F-WWEF	24. 2.95	Tarquin Ltd	Olbia, Italy	
					(Leased Alitalia Express) "Fiume Simeto"		
EI-CLD	ATR 72-212	432	F-WWEL	3. 3.95	Tarquin Ltd	Olbia, Italy	
					(Leased Alitalia Express) "Fiume Piave"		
EI-CLF*	Fairchild-Hiller FH-227E	505	SE-KBP	12. 7.95	Ireland Airways Holdings Ltd		
			C-FNAI/CF-NAI/PP-BUK/N7802M			Dinard, France	N 8.99
					(Stored: cancelled 16.8.01)		
EI-CLG	British Aerospace BAe 146 Srs.300		G-BRAB	7. 6.95	Aer Lingus Ltd	Dublin	
		E3131	HS-TBL/G-BRAB/G-11-131 *"St.Finbarr/Fionnbar"*				
EI-CLH	British Aerospace BAe 146 Srs.300		G-BOJJ	2. 6.95	Aer Lingus Ltd	Dublin	
		E3146	I-ATSC/G-BOJJ/G-6-146 *"St.Aoife"*				
EI-CLI	British Aerospace BAe 146 Srs.300		G-BVSA	19. 4.95	Aer Lingus Ltd	Dublin	
		E3159	I-ATSD/G-6-159/G-5-159 *"St.Eithne"*				
EI-CLJ	British Aerospace BAe 146 Srs.300		G-BTNU	1. 3.96	Aer Lingus Ltd	Dublin	
		E3155	(G-BSLS)/G-6-155		*"St.Senan/Seanen"*		
EI-CLL	Whittaker MW-6S Fatboy Flyer	1069		2. 4.95	F.Stack	Midleton, Co Cork	
	(Rotax 503)						
EI-CLQ	Reims Cessna F172N Skyhawk II		G-BFLV	26. 5.95	K.Dardis & Partners	Abbeyshrule	N 7.01
		F17201653					
EI-CLW	Boeing 737-3Y0	25187	XA-SAB	10. 6.95	Airplanes Finance Ltd	Pescara, Italy	
					(Leased Air One)		
EI-CLY	British Aerospace BAe 146 Srs.300		G-BTZN	16. 4.97	Aer Lingus Ltd	Dublin	
		E-3149	N146PZ/ZP-CCY/N146PZ/G-BTZN/HS-TBN/G-11-149 *"St.Eugene/Eoghan"*				
EI-CLZ	Boeing 737-3Y0	25179	XA-RJR	27. 7.95	Airplanes Finance Ltd	Pescara, Italy	
			N3521N		*(Leased Air One)*		
EI-CMB	Piper PA-28-140 Cherokee Cruiser		G-BELR	5. 9.95	Kestrel Flying Group Ltd	Dublin	A12.01
		28-7725094	N9541N				
EI-CMF	CFM Streak Shadow K.260 & SAAC 50		G-MTFY	13. 9.95	O.Williams	Galway	
	(Rotax 582) *(Possible re-build as G-MTFY has c/n 50)*						
EI-CMI	Robinson R.22 Beta	1129	G-BRRZ	30.11.95	Santail Ltd	Leeds-Bradford	A 7.00
			N8050N				
EI-CMJ	ATR 72-210	467	F-WWLU	21.12.95	Tarquin Ltd	Olbia, Italy	
					(Leased Alitalia Express) "Fiume Volturno"		
EI-CMK	Eurowing Goldwing ST 76 & SAAC-57			22.12.95	M.Garrigan	Clondara, Longford	
	(Fuji-Robin EC-PM-34)						
EI-CML	Cessna 150M	15076786	G-BNSS	5. 1.96	K.A.O'Connor	Weston	A 8.99
			N45207				
EI-CMM	McDonnell Douglas DC-9-83	49937	G-COES	1. 2.96	Irish Aerospace Ltd	Turin, Italy	
	(MD-83)		N30010		*(Leased Eurofly)*		
EI-CMN	Piper PA-12 Super Cruiser	12-1617	N2363M	26. 1.96	D.Graham & Partners	Birr	A10.01
	(Lycoming O-235)		NC2363M				
EI-CMR	Rutan LongEz	1716		2. 5.96	F. & C.O'Caoimh	Waterford	A 1.02
	(Lycoming O-235)						
EI-CMS	British Aerospace BAe 146 Srs.200A		N184US	24. 4.96	Cityjet Ltd	Paris, France	
		E2044	N361PS		*(Op Air France)*		
EI-CMT	Piper PA-34-200T Seneca II		G-BNER	23. 4.96	Atlantic Flight Training Ltd	Cork	A12.01
		34-7870088	N2590M				
EI-CMU	Mainair Mercury 1071-0296-7 & W873			3. 5.96	L.Langan & L.Laffan -	Wexford/Waterford	
	(Rotax 462)				*(Restored 8.01)*		
EI-CMV	Cessna 150L	150-72747	G-MSES	17. 5.96	K.A.O'Connor	Weston	A12.00
			N1447Q				
EI-CMW	Rotorway Executive	3550		13. 5.96	B.McNamee	Dunboyne	
	(Rotorway RW 162D)						
EI-CMY	British Aerospace BAe 146 Srs.200A		N177US	19. 6.96	Cityjet Ltd	Paris, France	
		E2039	N356PS		*(Op Air France)*		

EI-CMZ	McDonnell Douglas DC-9-83 (MD-83)	49390	9Y-THN	20. 7.96	Airplanes Finance Ltd *(Leased Eurofly)*	Turin, Italy	
EI-CNA	Letov LK-2M Sluka (Rotax 447)	8295S005		28. 6.96	G.Doody	Portlaoise	A 7.00
EI-CNB	British Aerospace BAe 146 Srs.200A	E2046	(EI-CMZ) N187US/N363PS	3. 8.96	Cityjet Ltd *(Op Air France)*	Paris, France	
EI-CNC	Team miniMax 1600 (Rotax 447)	514		10. 9.96	A.M.S.Allen	Enniskillen	A 7.01
EI-CNG	Air & Space 18-A Gyroplane	18-75	G-BALB N6170S	10. 9.96	P.Joyce	Waterford	A 1.02
EI-CNI	British Aerospace BAe 146 Srs.200 (Avro RJ85)	E-2299	G-6-299	26.11.96	Peregrine Aviation Leasing Co Ltd *"Lombardia"* *(Leased Azzurra Air)*	Bergamo, Italy	
EI-CNJ	British Aerospace BAe 146 Srs.200 (Avro RJ85)	E-2300	G-6-300	2.12.96	Peregrine Aviation Leasing Co Ltd *"Piemonte"* *(Leased Azzurra Air)*	Bergamo, Italy	
EI-CNK	British Aerospace BAe 146 Srs.200 (Avro RJ85)	E-2306	G-6-306	8. 5.97	Peregrine Aviation Leasing Co Ltd *"Lazio"* *(Leased Azzurra Air)*	Bergamo, Italy	
EI-CNL	Sikorsky S-61N Mk.II	61746	G-BDDA ZS-RBU/G-BDDA/N91201/G-BDDA	19.12.96	CHC Ireland Ltd *(Op Irish Marine Emergency Service)*	Cork	A12.98
EI-CNM	Piper PA-31-350 Navajo Chieftain	31-7305107	N1201H G-BBNT/N74958	16.12.96	M.Goss *(Op Air Atlantic)*	Dublin	A12.01
EI-CNN	Lockheed L.1011-385-1 Tristar	1024	VR-HHV G-BAAA	30. 1.97	Aer Turas Teoranta t/a Irish Cargo Airlines	Dublin	
EI-CNO	McDonnell Douglas DC-9-83 (MD-83)	49672	EC-FTU EC-487/EC-EJQ/EC-150	19. 2.97	Airplanes Finance Ltd *(Leased Nouvelair)*	Tunis, Tunisia	
EI-CNQ	British Aerospace BAe 146 Srs.200	E2031	G-OWLD N173US/N353PS	2. 7.97	Cityjet Ltd *(Op Air France)*	Paris, France	
EI-CNR	McDonnell Douglas DC-9-83 (MD-83)	53199	SE-DLU N13627	10. 4.97	Aircraft Finance Trust Ireland Ltd *(Leased Eurofly)*	Turin, Italy	
EI-CNT	Boeing 737-230ADV	22115	D-ABFC	5.12.96	Ryanair Ltd *(Vodaphone titles)*	Dublin	
EI-CNU	Pegasus Quantum 15-912	7326		10. 4.97	M.Ffrench	Donamore, New Ross	A 6.01
EI-CNV	Boeing 737-230ADV	22128	D-ABFX (D-ABFW)	26. 3.97	Ryanair Ltd	Dublin	
EI-CNW	Boeing 737-230ADV	22133	D-ABHC (B-)/D-ABHC/(D-ABHB)	31. 5.97	Ryanair Ltd	Dublin	
EI-CNX	Boeing 737-230ADV	22127	D-ABFW N5573K/(D-ABFU)	4. 7.97	Ryanair Ltd	Dublin	
EI-CNY	Boeing 737-230ADV	22113	D-ABFB N5573K	10.10.97	Ryanair Ltd *(Kilkenny - Cream of Irish Beer titles)*	Dublin	
EI-CNZ	Boeing 737-230ADV	22126	D-ABFU (D-ABFT)	5.11.97	Ryanair Ltd	Dublin	
EI-COA	Boeing 737-230ADV	22637	CS-TES D-ABHX	16.12.97	Ryanair Ltd	Dublin	
EI-COB	Boeing 737-230ADV	22124	D-ABFR	16. 1.98	Ryanair Ltd	Dublin	
EI-COE	Europa Aviation Europa (Jabiru 2200)	286		29. 5.97	F.Flynn *(Under construction)*	(Urlanmore)	N 1.01
EI-COG	Gyroscopic Gyroplane *(Imported from Australia during 1996 and flown without marks in 8.97: design is 2-seat side by side open cockpit gyro and the quoted c/n G.120 may be the type designation)*	G.120		11. 3.98	R.C.Fidler & D.Bracken	Letterkenny	A 8.98
EI-COH	Boeing 737-430	27001	D-ABKB (VT-S)/D-ABKB	6. 6.97	Flightlease (Ireland) Ltd *(Leased Air One)*	Pescara, Italy	
EI-COI	Boeing 737-430	27002	D-ABKC	13.11.97	Challey Ltd *(Leased Air One)*	Pescara, Italy	
EI-COJ	Boeing 737-430	27005	D-ABKK (D-ABKF)	13.11.97	Challey Ltd *(Leased Air One)*	Pescara, Italy	
EI-COM	Whittaker MW-6S Fatboy Flyer (Rotax 582)	1		10.10.97	M.Watson *(Under construction)*	Clonbullogue	N 1.01
EI-CON	Boeing 737-2T5	22396	PK-RIW EI-CON/PK-RIW/VT-EWF/A40-BM/C-GVRE/(EI-B)/G-BHVH	21. 7.97	Ryanair Ltd	Dublin	
EI-COO	Carlson Sparrow II (Rotax 532)	302		13. 8.97	D.Logue	Weston	
EI-COP	Reims Cessna F150L	F15001058	G-BCBY PH-TGI/(G-BCBY)	26. 6.97	High Kings Flying Group Ltd	Greigs, Navan	A 5.01
EI-COQ	British Aerospace BAe 146 Srs.100 (Avro RJ70)	E-1254	9H-ACM (9H-ABW)/G-BVRJ/G-6-254	17.10.97	Peregrine Aviation Leasing Co Ltd *"Puglia"* *(Leased Azzurra Air)*	Bergamo, Italy	
EI-COT	Reims Cessna F172N Skyhawk II	F17201884	D-EIEF	24.11.97	Kawasaki Distributors (Ireland) Ltd	Newcastle	A 9.00
EI-COV	British Aerospace 125 Srs.700B	257178	N621S N700CJ/G-5-747/VH-LMP/G-5-570/G-BMYX/G-5-530/4W-ACM/G-5-14	28. 5.98	Wilton Bridge Ltd	Farnborough	A 9.0
EI-COX	Boeing 737-230ADV	22123	D-ABFP	9. 1.98	Ryanair Ltd	Dublin	
EI-COY	Piper J-3C-65 Cub Special	22519	N3319N NC3319N	5.11.97	P.McWade	Abbeyshrule	N 9.00

EI-COZ	Piper PA-28-140 Cherokee C	28-26796	G-AYMZ N11C	5.11.97	G Cashman	Cork	A12.01
EI-CPB	McDonnell Douglas DC-9-83 (MD-83)	49940	TC-IND G-TTPT/N30016	27.11.97	Irish Aerospace Ltd *(Leased Eurofly)*	Turin, Italy	
EI-CPC	Airbus A321-211	815	D-AVZT	8. 5.98	ILFC *"St.Fergus/Faergus"* *(Leased Aer Lingus)*	Dublin	
EI-CPD	Airbus A321-211	841	D-AVZA	19. 6.98	ILFC *"St.Davnet/Damhnat"* *(Leased Aer Lingus)*	Dublin	
EI-CPE	Airbus A321-211	926	D-AVZQ	11.12.98	ILFC *"St.Enda/Eanna"* *(Leased Aer Lingus)*	Dublin	
EI-CPF	Airbus A321-211	991	D-AVZE	9. 4.99	Aer Lingus Ltd *"St Ida/Ide"*	Dublin	
EI-CPG	Airbus A321-211	1023	D-AVZR	28. 5.99	Aer Lingus Ltd *"St.Aidan/Aodhan"*	Dublin	
EI-CPH	Airbus A321-211	1094	F-WWDD D-AVZA	22.11.99	Aer Lingus Ltd *"St.Dervilla/Derbhile"*	Dublin	
EI-CPI	Rutan LongEz (Lycoming O-235)	17		18.12.97	D.J.Ryan *"Lady Elizabeth"*	Waterford	A 1.02
EI-CPJ	British Aerospace BAe 146 Srs.100 *(Avro RJ70)*	E1258	9H-CAN/(9H-ABX)/G-6-258	27. 3.98	Peregrine Aviation Leasing Co Ltd *"Calabria"* *(Leased Azzura Air)*	Bergamo, Italy	
EI-CPK	British Aerospace BAe 146 Srs.100 *(Avro RJ70)*	E1260	9H-ACO/(9H-ABY)/G-6-261	27. 3.98	Peregrine Aviation Leasing Co Ltd *(Leased Azzura Air)*	Bergamo, Italy	
EI-CPL	British Aerospace BAe 146 Srs.100 *(Avro RJ70)*	E1267	9H-ACP/(9H-ABZ)/G-6-267	31. 3.98	Peregrine Aviation Leasing Co Ltd *(Leased Azzura Air)*	Bergamo, Italy	
EI-CPN	Auster J/4	2073	G-AIJR	1. 4.98	E.Fagan	Abbeyshrule	N12.00
EI-CPO	Robinson R.22B2 Beta	2775	G-BXUJ	23. 9.98	Santail Ltd	Weston	A 4.01
EI-CPP	Piper J-3C-65 Cub (L-4H-PI) *(Rebuilt Glasthule, Dublin 1994/1998)*	12052	G-BIGH F-BFQV/OO-GAS/OO-GAZ/44-79756	23. 3.98	E.Fitzgerald	Newcastle	A12.01
EI-CPS	Beechcraft 58 Baron	TH-862	G-BEUL	21. 5.98	F.Doherty	Carrickfinn	A10.01
EI-CPT	ATR-42-312	191	C-GIQS (ZS-NYP)/C-GIQS/F-WWEA	12. 6.98	GPA-ATR Ltd *(Op Aer Arran) (Stored 12.00))*	Dinard, France	
EI-CPX	III Sky Arrow 650T	K.122 & SAAC-67		24. 6.98	N.Irwin	Watergrasshill	N.8.00
EI-CRB	Lindstrand LBL-90A HAFB	550		23. 9.98	J.& C.Concannon	Tuam	
EI-CRC	Boeing 737-46B	24124	PT-TDH EC-HME/EI-CRC/EC-HCP/EI-CRC/EC-GNC/SU-SAB/EC-GHF/EC-309/SU-SAA/EC-FYG/EC-655/N689MA/G-BOPK	6. 4.01	Aer Lingus Ltd *(Lease Ryan International for 2001/2002)*	Wichita, USA	
EI-CRD	Boeing 767-31BER	26259	B-2565	29.10.98	ILFC Ireland Ltd *(Leased EuroFly: op Alitalia)*	Rome, Italy	
EI-CRE	McDonnell Douglas DC-9-83 (MD-83)	49854	D-ALLL	11.12.98	AAR Ireland Ltd *(Leased Meridiana)*	Olbia, Italy	
EI-CRF	Boeing 767-31B	25170	B-2566	4.12.98	ILFC Ireland Ltd *(Leased Eurofly: op Alitalia)*	Rome, Italy	
EI-CRG	Robin DR.400-180R	2021	D-EHEC	11.12.98	D & B Lodge	Waterford	A 1.02
EI-CRH	McDonnell Douglas DC-9-83 (MD-83)	49935	HB-IKM G-DCAC/N3004C	10. 2.99	Airplanes 111 Ltd *(Leased Meridiana)*	Olbia, Italy	
EI-CRJ	McDonnell Douglas DC-9-83 (MD-83)	53013	D-ALLP	27. 1.99	C A Aviation Ltd *(Leased Meridiana)*	Olbia, Italy	
EI-CRK	Airbus A330-301	070	(EI-NYC) F-WWKV	18.11.94	Aer Lingus Ltd *"St Patrick/Padraig"*	Dublin	
EI-CRL	Boeing 767-343ER	30008	(I-DEIB)	22. 3.99	GECAS Technical Services Ltd *(Leased Alitalia TEAM) "Leonardo da Vinci"*	Rome, Italy	
EI-CRM	Boeing 767-343	30009		8. 4.99	GECAS Technical Services Ltd *(Leased Alitalia TEAM) "Amerigo Vespucci"*	Rome, Italy	
EI-CRO	Boeing 767-3Q8ER	29383		16. 4.99	ILFC Ireland Ltd *(Leased Alitalia TEAM) "Francesco Agelio"*	Rome, Italy	
EI-CRP	Boeing 737-73S	29078	N1014S N60436/N1787B	15. 4.99	Pembroke B737-7006 Leasing Ltd *(Leased Azzurra Air)*	Bergamo, Italy	
EI-CRQ	Boeing 737-73S	29080	N1782B N1786B.	14. 4.99	Pembroke B737-7006 Leasing Ltd "Lavalette" *(Leased Azzurra Air)*	Bergamo, Italy	
EI-CRR	Aeronca 11AC Chief	11AC-1605	OO-ESM (OO-DEL)/OO-ESM	13. 4.99	L.Maddock & Partners	Killamaster	
EI-CRS	Boeing 777-2Q8	29908		15. 7.99	ILFC (Ireland) Ltd *(Leased Air Europe Italy)*	Milan, Italy	
EI-CRT	Boeing 777-2Q8	28676		8.10.99	ILFC (Ireland) Ltd *(Leased Air Europe Italy)*	Milan, Italy	
EI-CRU	Cessna 152	15285621	G-BNSW N94213	21. 9.99	W.Reilly	Inis Mor	
EI-CRV	Hoffman H.36 Dimona	3674	OE-9319 HB-2081	2. 6.99	Falcon Aviation Ltd	Waterford	A 1.02
EI-CRW	McDonnell Douglas DC-9-83 (MD-83)	49951	HB-IKN G-GMJM/N13627	8. 4.99	Airplanes IAL Ltd *(Leased Meridiana)*	Olbia, Italy	
EI-CRX	SOCATA TB-9 Tampico	1170	F-GKUL	21. 5.99	Hotel Bravo Flying Club Ltd	Weston	A 8.99
EI-CRY	Medway EclipseR	160/138		2. 6.99	G.A.Murphy	Rathcoole	
EI-CRZ	Boeing 737-36E	26322	EC-GGE EC-798	14. 4.99	ILFC Ireland Ltd *(Leased Air One)*	Pescara, Italy	

EI-CSA	Boeing 737-8AS	29916	N5537L	12. 3.99	Ryanair Ltd	Dublin	
			N1786B				
EI-CSB	Boeing 737-8AS	29917	N1786B	16. 6.99	Ryanair Ltd	Dublin	
EI-CSC	Boeing 737-8AS	29918	N1786B	25. 6.99-	Ryanair Ltd	Dublin	
EI-CSD	Boeing 737-8AS	29919	N1786B	9. 8.99	Ryanair Ltd	Dublin	
EI-CSE	Boeing 737-8AS	29920	N1786B	31. 8.99	Ryanair Ltd	Dublin	
EI-CSF	Boeing 737-8AS	29921	N1786B	24. 5.00	Ryanair Ltd	Dublin	
EI-CSG	Boeing 737-8AS	29922	N1786B	31. 5.00	Ryanair Ltd	Dublin	
EI-CSH	Boeing 737-8AS	29923	N1787B	9. 6.00	Ryanair Ltd	Dublin	
EI-CSI	Boeing 737-8AS	29924	N1796B	12. 6.00	Ryanair Ltd	Dublin	
EI-CSJ	Boeing 737-8AS	29925	N1786B	20. 6.00	Ryanair Ltd	Dublin	
EI-CSK	British Aerospace BAe 146 Srs.200A		N810AS	3. 4.98	Cityjet Ltd *"St.Ciara/Ciara"*	Dublin	
		E2062	N880DV/G-5-062/N406XV/(G-BNDR)/G-5-062		*(Air France c/s)*		
EI-CSL	British Aerospace BAe 146 Srs.200A		N812AS	8. 5.98	Cityjet Ltd *"St.Cormac/Cormac"*	Dublin	
		E2074	N881DV/G-5-074/G-BNND/HS-TBQ/G-BNND/N146SB/N192US/N368PS/(G-BNND)/G-5-074				
EI-CSM	Boeing 737-8AS	29926	N...	7.12.00	Ryanair Ltd	Dublin	
EI-CSN	Boeing 737-8AS	29927	N...	11.12.00	Ryanair Ltd	Dublin	
EI-CSO	Boeing 737-8AS	29928	N...	11. 1.01	Ryanair Ltd	Dublin	
EI-CSP	Boeing 737-8AS	29929	N...	25. 1.01	Ryanair Ltd	Dublin	
EI-CSQ	Boeing 737-8AS	29930	N...	26..1.01	Ryanair Ltd	Dublin	
EI-CSR	Boeing 737-8AS	29931	N	5.12.01	Ryanair Ltd	Dublin	
EI-CSS	Boeing 737-8AS	29932	N	14.12.01	Ryanair Ltd	Dublin	
EI-CST	Boeing 737-8AS	29933	N	19.12.01	Ryanair Ltd	Dublin	
EI-CSU	Boeing 737-36E	27626	EC-GGZ	14. 4.99	ILFC Ireland Ltd	Pescara, Italy	
			EC-799		*(Leased Air One)*		
EI-CSV	Boeing 737-8AS			18. 1.02	Ryanair Ltd	Dublin	
EI-CSW	Boeing 737-8AS			R	Ryanair Ltd	Dublin	
EI-CSX	Boeing 737-8AS			R	Ryanair Ltd	Dublin	
					(For delivery 7.02)		
EI-CSY	Boeing 737-8AS			R	Ryanair Ltd	Dublin	
					(For delivery 7.02)		
EI-CSZ	Boeing 737-8AS			R	Ryanair Ltd	Dublin	
					(For delivery 2002)		
EI-CTA	Boeing 737-8AS			R	Ryanair Ltd	Dublin	
					(For delivery 2002)		
EI-CTB	Boeing 737-8AS			R	Ryanair Ltd	Dublin	
					(For delivery 2002)		
EI-CTC	Medway EclipseR	158/137		2. 6.99	C.Brogan	Kilrush	A 5.01
EI-CTD	Airbus A320-211	085	F-GJVZ	6. 5.99	Aerco Ireland Ltd	Milan, Italy	
			F-WWDF		*(Leased Air Europe Italy)*		
EI-CTG	Stoddard-Hamilton SH-2R Glasair RG		N721WR	3. 6.99	K.Higgins	Galway	A 8.01
EI-CTI	Reims Cessna FRA150L	FRA1500261	G-BCRN	29. 4.99	D.Bruton	Abbeyshrule	N12.00
EI-CTJ	McDonnell-Douglas DC-9-82	53147	HL7547	11. 6.99	Lift Ireland Leasing Ltd	Tunis, Tunisia	
	(MD-82)		HL7203		*(Leased Nouvelair)*		
EI-CTL	Aerotech MW-5B Sorcerer		G-MTFH	21. 5.99	M.Wade	Kilrush	
	(Fuji-Robin EC-44-PM)	SR102-R440B-07					
EI-CTM	British Aerospace BAe 146 Srs.300		G-JEAL	23. 3.99	Trident Aviation Leasing Services (Jersey) Ltd		
		E3129	G-BTXN/HS-TBM/G-5-129		*"St.Fiacre/Fiacra"*	Dublin	
					(Leased Aer Lingus Ltd)		
EI-CTN	British Aerospace BAe 146 Srs.300		G-BSNS	4. 7.00	Trident Aviation Leasing Services (Jersey) Ltd		
		E3169	EC-FHU/EC-839/G-6-169/G-BSNS/N887DV/G-BSNS/(N887DV)/G-6-169		*"St Cormac"*		
					(Leased Aer Lingus Ltd)	Dublin	
EI-CTO	British Aerospace BAe 146 Srs.300		G-BUHC	30. 5.00	Aer Lingus Ltd	Dublin	
		E3193	G-BTMI/(N883DV)/G-6-193		*"St.Ciara/Ciara"*		
EI-CTT	Piper PA-28-161 Cherokee Warrior II		N38974	14. 7.99	M.Farrell	Connaught	A12.01
		28-7716305					
EI-CTW	Boeing 767-341ER	30342		8.12.99	GECAS Technical Services Ltd	Rome, Italy	
					(Leased Eurofly: op Alitalia)		
EI-CUA	Boeing 737-4K5	24901	D-AHLR	29. 9.99	Gustav Leasing XI Ltd	Rome, Italy	
					(Leased Blue Panorama Airlines)		
EI-CUB	Piper J-3C-65 Cub	16010	G-BPPV	17. 7.91	J.Connelly & Partners	Galway	N 5.00
			N88392/NC88392		*(Crashed on t/o Galway 26.3.00 & wrecked)*		
EI-CUC	Airbus A320-214	1152	F-WWBS	3. 2.00	Lift Ireland Leasing Ltd	Verona, Italy	
					(Leased Volare Airlines)		
EI-CUD	Boeing 737-4Q8	26298	TC-JEI	13. 3.00	ILFC Ireland Ltd	Rome, Italy	
					(Leased Blue Panorama)		
EI-CUE	Cameron N-105 HAFB	4683		16. 9.99	Bord Telecom Eireann *"EIRCOM"*	Dublin	A 9.01
EI-CUG	Bell 206B JetRanger II	4177	N248BC	21.10.99	J.O'Reilly & B.McNamara	Dublin	A 6.01
			N118GC				
EI-CUI	Robinson R44 Astro	0110	G-JANI	3. 3.00	Santail Ltd	Weston	A11.01
			D-HIMM		*(New owner 10.01)*		
EI-CUJ*	Cessna 172N Slyhawk II	17271985	G-BJGO	19.11.99	M.Casey & Partners	Cork	A12.00
			N6038E		*(Cancelled 3.5.01)*		

EI-CUK	Airbus A320-214	1198	F-WWIE	17. 4.00	GECAS Technical Services Ltd *(Leased Volare Airlines)*	Verona, Italy	
EI-CUL	Boeing 737-36N	28559	PH-OZC	16. 2.00	Aircraft Finance Trust (Ireland) Ltd *(Leased Philippine Airlines)*	Manila, Philippines	
EI-CUN	Boeing 737-4K5	27074	D-AHLS (D-AHLG)	13. 4.00	Gustav Leasing XI Ltd *(Leased Blue Panorama Airlines)*	Rome, Italy	
EI-CUP	Cessna 335	335-0018	N2706X	5. 5.00	J.Greany	Kerry	A12.01
EI-CUQ	Airbus A320-214	1259	F-WWIZ	24. 7.00	Lumehavi Finance Ltd (Flightlease (Ireland) Ltd) *(Leased Volare Airlines)*	Verona, Italy	
EI-CUS	Agusta-Bell 206B-3 JetRanger III	8721	G-BZKA (EI-...)/G-OONS/G-LIND/G-OONS	24. 8.00	Emerald Helicopter Consultants	Castleknock	A 7.01
EI-CUT	Maule MX 7-180A	21080C		6. 4.01	Cosair Ltd	Trim	
EI-CUW	Pilatus BN-2B-20 Islander	2293	G-BWYW	8.11.00	Galway Aviation Services Ltd. t/a Aer Arann	Inverin	A 7.01
EI-CVA	Airbus A320-214	1242	F-WWIT	22. 6.00	Aer Lingus Ltd *"St Schiri/Scire"*	Dublin	
EI-CVB	Airbus A320-214	1394	F-WWIV	8. 2.01	Aer Lingus Ltd *"St Mobhi"*	Dublin	
EI-CVC	Airbus A320-214	1443	F-WWBG	6. 4.01	Aer Lingus Ltd *"St Kealin/Caoilfhionn"*	Dublin	
EI-CVD	Airbus A320-214	1467	F-WWDK	10. 5.01	Aer Lingus Ltd *"St Kevin/Caoimhin"*	Dublin	
EI-CVE	Airbus A320-214	1665		R	Aer Lingus Ltd *(For delivery 2.02 but now cancelled)*	Dublin	
EI-CVF	Airbus A320-214	1708		R	Aer Lingus Ltd *(For delivery 7.02 but now cancelled)*	Dublin	
EI-CVL	Ercoupe 415CD	4754	G-ASNF PH-NCF/NC94647	??	D Lyons *(New owner 3.01)*	Thurles	N10.10
EI-CVM	Schweizer Hughes 269C	S1328	G-GIRO N41S	7.11.00	W.Moloney	Tralee, Co.Kerry	A 4.01
EI-CVN	Boeing 737-4Y0	24684	TC-AFK	21.11.00	Airplanes Finance Ltd *(Leased Philippine Airlines)*	Manila, Philippines	
EI-CVO	Boeing 737-4S3	25594	SP-LLH TC-AVA/9M-MLJ	28.10.00	Aerco Ireland Ltd *(Leased Philippine Airlines)*	Manila, Philippines	
EI-CVP	Boeing 737-4Y0	26081	TC-AFU	22.12.00	Airplanes Finance Ltd *(Leased Philippine Airlines)*	Manila, Philippines	
EI-CVR	ATR 42-310	022	F-GGLK OH-LTB/F-WWEI	17. 1.01	Comhfhorbairt (Gaiiimh) Teo *(Op Aer Arran Express)*	Dublin	
EI-CVS	ATR 42-310	033	F-GIRC F-WIAF/OH-LTC/F-WWEO	16. 3.01	Comhfhorbairt (Gaiiimh) Teo *(Op Aer Arann Express)*	Dublin	
EI-CVT	Gulfstream IV-SP	1419	N419GA	5. 4.01	AC Executive Aircraft Leasing. *(Op International Jet Club)*	Farnborough	A 9.01
EI-CWA	British Aerospace BAe 146 Srs.200	E2022	G-DEBE N163US/N346PS	2.01R	Cityjet Ltd	Dublin	
EI-CWB	British Aerospace BAe 146 Srs.200	E2051	SE-DRE N694AA/N141AC/G-5-003/N141AC/G-5-003	29. 3.01	Cityjet Ltd	Dublin	
EI-CWC	British Aerospace BAe 146 Srs.200	E2053	SE-DRC N695AA/N142AC/G-5-053/N142AC/G-5-053	27. 4.01	Cityjet Ltd *(Op Air France)*	Dublin	
EI-CWD	British Aerospace BAe 146 Srs.200	E2108	SE-DRK N295UE/G-5-108	13. 6.01	Cityjet Ltd *(Op Air France)*	Dublin	
EI-CWE	Boeing 737-42C	24232	PH-BPE G-UKLD	18. 5.01	Rockshaw Ltd *(Op Air One)*	Milan, Italy	
EI-CWF	Boeing 737-42C	24814	PH-BPG G-UKLG	16. 5.01	Rockshaw Ltd *(Op Air One)*	Milan, Italy	
EI-CWH	Agusta A109E	11106		17. 7.01	Lochbrea Aircraft Ltd	Cork	A12.01
EI-CWJ	Boeing 717-23S	55068	N6204C	R	Pembroke Capital *(Op Vuelamex)*	Mexico	
EI-CWK	Boeing 717-23S			R	Pembroke Capital *(Op Vuelamex)*	Mexico	
EI-CWL	Robinson R22 Beta	0885	G-BXCX G-MFHL	19. 9.01	J.McLoughlin	Dunboyne	
EI-CWM	Boeing 717-23S			R	Pembroke Capital *(Op Vuelamex)*	Mexico	
EI-CWN	Boeing 717-23S			R	Pembroke Capital *(Op Vuelamex)*	Mexico	
EI-CWP	Robinson R22 Beta	3233	G-CBBK	23.10.01	Santail Ltd	Weston	
EI-CWR	Robinson R22 Beta	3234	G-CBDB	2.11.01	Inflight Aviation Ltd	Weston	
EI-CWS	Schweizer 269C-1	0129	G-CBCN	27.11.01	Bob Scanlon (European Helicopter Academy)	Dunboyne	
EI-CWT	Airbus A320-214	1413	OO-SNH F-WWDI	30.11.01	Singapore Aircraft Leasing Enterprise S.A.L.E.	Bordeaux-Merignac, France	
EI-CWU	Airbus A320-214	1439	OO-SNI F-WWBM	30.11.01	Singapore A/C Leasing Enterprise S.A.L.E.	Bordeaux-Merignac, France	
EI-CWV	Airbus A320-214	1450	OO-SNJ F-WWBX	30.11.01	S.A.L.E Ireland Ltd (Caladborg Leasing Ltd)	Bordeaux-Merignac, France	

EI-CWW	Boeing 737-4Y0	24906	EC-GAZ	19.12.01	Airplanes Holdings Ltd	Milan, Italy	
			EC-850/9M-MJO		*(Op Air One Italy)*		
EI-CWX	Boeing 737-4Y0	24912	EC-GBN	6.12.01	Airplanes Holdings Ltd	Milan, Italy	
			EC-851/9M-MJQ		*(Op Air One Italy)*		
EI-CWY	Airbus A319-112	1429	OO-SSN	30.11.01	S.A.L.E.Ireland Ltd (Bellevue Aircraft Holding)		
			D-AVYH			Bordeaux-Merignac, France	
EI-CWZ	Airbus A319-112	1494	OO-SSO	30.11.01	S.A.L.E.Ireland Ltd		
			D-AVYB		(Singapore Aircraft Leasing Enterprise)		
						Bordeaux-Merignac, France	
EI-CXA	Airbus A319-112	1612	(C-GKZB)	13.12.01	EFG Aircraft (Ireland)Ltd		
			D-AVWC				
EI-DAA	Airbus A330-202	397	F-WWKX	17. 4.01	Aer Lingus Ltd *"St Keeva/Caoimhe"*	Dublin	
EI-DAB	Cessna 550 Citation Bravo	550-0917	N5100V	4. 4.00	D.Colgan/Eurojet	Biggin Hill	A11.01
					(New owner 8.01)		
EI-DHL	Airbus A300B4-203F	274	PH-SFM	21. 6.01	Air Contractors (Ireland)Ltd	Dublin	
			N227KW/N14977/N235EA/F-GDVC		*(Op DHL)*		
EI-DLA	McDonnell Douglas DC-10-30	46958	N883LA	22. 6.94	GECAS Technical Services Ltd *(Stored)*		
			EI-DLA/RP-C2003/(RP-C2000)/(PH-DTM)			Mojave, Colorado, USA	N10.00
EI-DLP	Agusta A109			.01R			
EI-DMG	Cessna 441 Conquest	441-0165	N140MP	4. 7.01	Dawn Meats Group	Waterford	A 1.02
			N27214				
EI-DUB	Airbus A330-301ER	055	F-WWKP	6. 5.94	Aer Lingus Ltd	Dublin	
					"St.Brigid/Brighid"		
EI-EAA	Airbus A300B4-203F	150	F-WQGT	2. 4.98	Air Contractors (Ireland) Ltd		
			SU-BCC/F-WZMD		*(Op DHL)*	Brussels, Belgium	
EI-EAB	Airbus A300B4-203F	199	F-WQFO	4. 6.98	Air Contractors (Ireland) Ltd		
			SU-BDF/(SU-BCD)/F-WZMF		*(Op DHL)*	Brussels, Belgium	
EI-EAC	Airbus A300B4-203F	250	N10970	20.11.98	Air Contractors (Ireland) Ltd		
			N970C/F-WZMU			Brussels, Belgium	
					(Leased Household Commercial Services) ((Op DHL)		
EI-EAD	Airbus A300B4-203F	289	N13972	18. 5.99	Air Contractors (Ireland) Ltd	Dublin	
			N972C/F-WZMM		*(Leased Household Financial Services) ((Op DHL)*		
EI-EAE	Airbus A300B4-203F	095	N226KW	23.11.00	Air Contractors (Ireland) Ltd		
			9M-MHC/F-WZEM		*(Op DHL)*	Brussels, Belgium	
EI-EAF	Airbus A300B4-203F	259	N865PA	R	Air Contractors (Ireland) Ltd		
			OB-1634/AP-BFG/SE-DSG/N72990/N232EA/F-GBNZ				
EI-EAT	Airbus A300B4-203F	116	F-WQFR	16.12.97	Air Contractors (Ireland) Ltd		
			D-ASAY/SU-BCB/F-WZES		*(Op DHL)*	Brussels, Belgium	
EI-ECA	Agusta A109A II	7387	N109RP	28. 2.97	Backdrive Ltd	Drogheda	A12.01
			JA9662		*(Op Ace Helicopters Ltd)*		
EI-EDR	Piper PA-28R-200 Cherokee Arrow II		G-BCGD	19.11.87	Kestrel Flying Group Ltd	Dublin	A12.01
		28R-7435265	N9628N		*(New owner 10.01)*		
EI-EEC	Piper PA-23-250 Aztec E	27-7554045	G-SATO	6. 2.92	Westair Aviation Ltd	Shannon	A 9.01
			G-BCXP/N54257				
EI-EIO	Piper PA-34-200T Seneca II		N6257J	1.10.91	K.A.O'Connor	Weston	A 5.00
		34-7670274					
EI-ELL	Medway EclipseR	157/136		2. 6.99	Microflex Ltd	Kilrush	A 5.01
EI-EUR	Eurocopter EC 120B	1138	G-BZMK	14.12.00	Atlantic Helicopters Ltd.	Dublin	A 7.01
			F-WQOE				
EI-EWR	Airbus A330-202	330	F-WWKV	9. 5.00	Aer Lingus Ltd	Dublin	
					"Laurence O'Toole/Lorcan O'Tuathail"		
EI-EXP*	Short SD.3-30 Var.100	SH.3092	G-BKMU	23. 7.92	Ireland Airways Holdings Ltd		N 4.00
			SE-IYO/G-BKMU/G-14-3092/EI-BEH/EI-BEG/G-BKMU/G-14-3092				
					(Noted Valley Nurseries, Alton, Hants: cancelled as scrapped 22.8.00)		
EI-FBG	Reims Cessna F182Q Skylane	F18200032	D-EFBG	4. 7.00	Messrs Tunney, Helly & Spelman	Weston	A12.01
			(F-GAGU)				
EI-FKC	Fokker F.27 Mk 050	20177	PH-EXC	23. 2.90	Aer Lingus Ltd *"St.Fidelma (Stored 2.01)*		
	(Fokker 50)					Woensdrecht, The Netherlands	
EI-FKD	Fokker F.27 Mk 050	20181	PH-EXG	12. 4.90	Aer Lingus Ltd *"St.Mel" (Stored 2.01)*		
	(Fokker 50)					Woensdrecht, The Netherlands	
EI-FKE	Fokker F.27 Mk 050	20208	PH-EXA	28. 1.91	Aer Lingus Ltd *"St.Pappin (Stored 2.01)*		
	(Fokker 50)					Woensdrecht, The Netherlands	
EI-FKF	Fokker F.27 Mk 050	20209	PH-EXE	8. 2.91	Aer Lingus Ltd *"St.Ultan" (Stored 4.01)*		
	(Fokker 50)					Woensdrecht, The Netherlands	
EI-GER	Maule MX-7-180A Star Rocket	20006C		7. 1.94	P.J.L.Ryan	Trim	A 9.01
	(Tail-wheel u/c)						
EI-GFC	SOCATA TB-9 Tampico	141	G-BIAA	9.10.93	B.McGrath, J.Ryan & D.O'Neill	Waterford	A 1.02
EI-GHP	Cessna 550 Citation	550-0897	N5079V	4. 1.00	Goldair International (Ireland) Ltd		
						Biggin Hill	A 1.02
EI-GSM	Cessna 182S	18280188	N9541Q	17. 6.98	Westpoint Flying Group	Dublin	A12.01
EI-GWY	Cessna 172R Skyhawk	17280162	N9497F	31.12.97	Galway Flying Club Ltd	Galway	A 9.01
EI-HAM	Light-Aero Avid Flyer	1072-90		18.11.96	H.Goulding	Bray	
	(Rotax 582)						
EI-HCA	Boeing 727-225F	20382	N8839E	15. 4.94	Air Contractors (Ireland) Ltd	Dublin	

EI-HCB	Boeing 727-223F	19492	N6817	2. 9.95	Air Contractors (Ireland) Ltd	Dublin	
			EI-HCB/N6817				
EI-HCC	Boeing 727-223F	19480	N6805	26. 9.95	Air Contractors (Ireland) Ltd	Dublin	
EI-HCD	Boeing 727-223F	20185	N6832	8.11.95	Air Contractors (Ireland) Ltd	Dublin	
EI-HCI	Boeing 727-223F	20183	N6830	23. 5.95	Air Contractors (Ireland) Ltd	Dublin	
EI-HCS	Grob G-109B	6414	G-BMHR	18. 8.95	H.Sydner	Boleybeg, Ballymore Castle	A 9.01
EI-HER	Bell 206B-3 JetRanger III	3408	G-HIER	1. 7.94	SELC Ireland Ltd & Partners	Belmullet	A10.00
			G-BRFD/N2069N				
EI-HXM	Bell 206B JetRanger II	4105	ZS-HXM	28. 7.00	Euprepia Enterprises Ltd		
			N7131J			Celtic/Knocksedan	A 6.01
EI-IAU	Learjet Learjet 60	190	N190LJ	11.12.00	Irish Air Transport	Prestwick	A 5.01
			N5012K				
EI-IAW	Learjet Learjet 60	218	N8084J	14. 6.01	Irish Air Transport	Prestwick	A11.01
			N50157				
EI-IPC	Fairey Britten-Norman BN-2A-26 Islander		G-CHES	R	Irish Parachute Club		
		2011	G-PASY/G-BPCB/G-BEXA/G-MALI/(ZB503)/G-DIVE/G-BEXA				
EI-IRV	Aérospatiale AS350B Ecureuil	1713	D-HENY	7.10.96	Rathalope Ltd	Barberston House	A12.01
EI-IZO	Eurocopter EC 120B	1191	G-BZUS	26. 7.01	Cloud Nine Helicopters Ltd	Carlow	A12.01
			F-WQOU				
EI-JBC	Agusta A109A	7126	F-GATN	24. 7.97	Medeva Properties Ltd	Dublin Heliport	N 5.00
EI-JFD	Robinson R44	0969		R	New World Plant Ltd	Galway	A 9.01
EI-JFK	Airbus A330-301	086	F-GMDE	11. 7.95	Aer Lingus Ltd *"St.Colmcille"*	Dublin	
EI-JWM	Robinson R.22 Beta	1386	G-BSLB	21.11.92	C.Shiel	Weston	A10.00
EI-LAX	Airbus A330-202	269	F-WWKV	29. 4.99	Aer Lingus Ltd *"St.Mella/Mella"*	Dublin	
EI-LCH	Boeing 727-281F	20466	N903PG	6. 2.95	Air Contractors (Ireland) Ltd	Dublin	
			N527MD/HL7355/JA8332				
EI-LIT	MBB Bö.105S	S.434	A6-DBH	20. 2.96	Irish Helicopters Ltd	Cork	A 9.01
			Dubai 105/D-HDMH				
EI-LRS	Schweizer Hughes 269C	S.1701	N41S	6. 3.95	Lynch Roofing Systems Ltd	Galway	
EI-MAG	Robinson R22 Beta	2592	G-DHGS	3. 8.01	Airo Helicopters Ltd	Bagnelstown, Carlow	
EI-MCF	Cessna 172R	172080799	N2469D	20. 1.00	Galway Flying Club	Galway	A 7.01
EI-MEL	Agusta A109C	7672	LV-WXA	20. 6.00	Mercury Engineering Ltd	Dublin Heliport	A 9.01
			N27ET/LV-WXA/N4NM				
EI-MER	Bell 206B	4513	N60507	28. 9.99	Gaelic Helicopters Ltd	Westpoint	A12.01
EI-MES	Sikorsky S-61N	61776	G-BXAE	27. 3.97	CHC Ireland Ltd	Cork	A12.01
			LN-OQO		*(Op Irish Marine Emergency Service)*		
EI-MIK	Eurocopter EC 120B	1104	G-BZIU	22. 6.01	Bachir Ltd	Oranmore	A 8.01
EI-MIP	Aérospatiale SA.365N Dauphin 2	6119	G-BLEY	20. 3.96	CHC Ireland Ltd	Cork	A 4.01
			F-WTNM				
EI-MUL	Robinson R44 Raven	1074		29. 8.01	Cotton Box Design Group Ltd	Galway	
EI-ONE	Bell 206B JetRanger II	1761	EI-CJM	30. 5.96	Helicopter Sales Leasing Ltd	Weston	A 3.01
			N281C/N49582				
EI-OPM	Cessna 525A	054		R	Atron *(For delivery 2.02)*		
EI-ORD	Airbus A330-301	059	(EI-USA)	6. 6.97	Aer Lingus plc	Dublin	
			F-GMDD		*"St.Maeve/Maedh"*		
EI-PAL	Cessna 550 Citation Bravo	550-0935	N5264A	31. 8.00	Pacific Aviation Ltd	Dublin	A12.01
					(Op Eurojet Aviation Ltd)		
EI-PAM	Boeing 737-4Q8	24069	G-BNNK	21.12.01	IAI Marichan Ltd	Palermo Italy	
					(Op Panair)		
EI-PAR	Boeing 737-308	24300	N737FA	13. 7.01	IAI Bailey Ltd	Palermo, Italy	
			XA-AMH/N737FA/B-1980/G-OBML/SE-DLA/G-KKUH *(Op Panair)*				
EI-PAT	British Aerospace BAe.146 Srs.200		G-ZAPL	11.10.99	Brimstage Ltd	Dublin	
		E2030	G-WLCY/N172US/N352US		*(Leased Cityjet)*		
EI-PAX	Cessna 560XL	5228		.01R	Pacific Aviation Ltd	Dublin	
					(Op Eurojet Ireland Ltd) (For delivery 1.02)		
EI-PMI	Agusta-Bell 206B-3 JetRanger III		EI-BLG	19. 9.96	Ping Golf Equipment Ltd	Dublin	A 8.99
		8614	G-BIGS				
EI-POD	Cessna 177B Cardinal	177B02729	N1444C	3. 8.95	Trim Flying Club Ltd	Trim	A10.01
EI-PRE	Robinson R44			.01R			
EI-PRI	Bell 206B Jet Ranger	4523	N6389V	29. 2.00	Brentwood Properties Ltd	Castleknock	A12.01
			C-GLZM				
EI-RCG	Sikorsky S.61N	61807	G-BZSN	25. 9.01	CHC Ireland Ltd	Shannon	N 9.01
			LN-OQB				
EI-RMC	Bell 206B Jet Ranger	488	G-BWLO	16.12.99	Westair Aviation Ltd	Shannon	A 7.01
			N2290W				
EI-RRR	Hawker Siddeley HS.125 Srs.700A		N80CL	11.10.99	Star Air (Ireland) Ltd	Dublin	A10.00
		257170/NA0318	N819M/G-5-14				
EI-SAC	Cessna 172P Skyhawk	17276263	N98149	22. 9.00	Sligo Aero Club	Strandhill	N 8.01
EI-SAF	Airbus A300B4-203	220	PH-SFL	26. 7.01	Air Contractors (Ireland)Ltd	Dublin	
			N860PA/SE-DSF/N74989/N231EA/F-GBNY *(Op DHL)*				
EI-SAM	Extra EA.300/200	031	(D-EDGE(5))	19. 7.01	S & D Bruton	Abbeyshrule	A 8.01
EI-SAR	Sikorsky S-61N	61-143	G-AYOM	26. 6.98	CHC Ireland Ltd	Cork	A12.01
	(Mitsubishi c/n M61-001)		N4585/JA9506/N94565		*(Op Irish Marine Emergency Service)*		
EI-SAT	Steen Skybolt	1	N52DH	22.10.99	Capt B.O'Sullivan	- Trim	A 6.00

EI-SBP	Cessna T.206H	T20608159	N2354M	16. 8.00	P.Morrissey	Dublin	A 6.01
			N4234H				
EI-SHN	Airbus A330-301	054	F-WWKJ	27. 4.94	Aer Lingus Ltd *"St.Flannan"*	Dublin	
EI-SKT	Piper PA-44-180 Seminole	44-7995004	G-BGSG	01R	Skytrace		
			N36538				
EI-SQG	Agusta A109E Power	11084		1. 8.00	Quinn Group Ltd	Dublin	A12.01
					(Slieve Russel Hotel titles)		
EI-STR	Bell 407	53282	N44504	19. 5.00	S.Ryan	Dublin Heliport	A12.01
EI-STT	Cessna 172M	17266228	D-EVBB	30 .8.00	Garda Aviation Club Ltd	Weston	A 5.01
			N9557H				
EI-TAA	Airbus A320-233	912	N458TA	20.9.01	Rockshaw Ltd	San Salvador, El Salvador	
			F-WWDU		*(Op TACA)*		
EI-TAI	Airbus A320-233	916	N459TA	19.9.01	Rockshaw Ltd	San Salvador, El Salvador	
			F-WWDX		*(Op TACA)*		
EI-TKI	Robinson R.22 Beta	1195	G-OBIP	22. 8.91	J.McDaid	Weston	A10.00
EI-TVD	Boeing 737-			R	Virgin Express (Ireland) Ltd	Shannon	
EI-TVE	Boeing 737-			R	Virgin Express (Ireland) Ltd	Shannon	
EI-TVF	Boeing 737-			R	Virgin Express (Ireland) Ltd	Shannon	
EI-TVG	Boeing 737-			R	Virgin Express (Ireland) Ltd	Shannon	
EI-TVH	Boeing 737-			R	Virgin Express (Ireland) Ltd	Shannon	
EI-TVH	Boeing 737-			R	Virgin Express (Ireland) Ltd	Shannon	
EI-TVJ	Boeing 737-			R	Virgin Express (Ireland) Ltd	Shannon	
EI-TVK	Boeing 737-			R	Virgin Express (Ireland) Ltd	Shannon	
EI-TVL	Boeing 737-			R	Virgin Express (Ireland) Ltd	Shannon	
EI-TVM	Boeing 737-			R	Virgin Express (Ireland) Ltd	Shannon	
EI-TVT				R	Virgin Express (Ireland) Ltd	Shannon	
EI-TVU				R	Virgin Express (Ireland) Ltd	Shannon	
EI-TVV				R	Virgin Express (Ireland) Ltd	Shannon	
EI-TVW				R	Virgin Express (Ireland) Ltd	Shannon	
EI-TVX				R	Virgin Express (Ireland) Ltd	Shannon	
EI-TVY				R	Virgin Express (Ireland) Ltd	Shannon	
EI-TVZ				R	Virgin Express (Ireland) Ltd	Shannon	
EI-UCD	Rotorway Executive	SAAC-29		R	Brendan McNamee	Clonee	
	(Construction started in 1987 by Jim Lacey, University College, Dublin)						
EI-UFO	Piper PA-22-150 Tri-Pacer	22-4942	G-BRZR	12. 2.94	W.Treacy	Trim	N 9.00
	(Tail-wheel conversion)		N7045D				
EI-WAC	Piper PA-23-250 Aztec E	27-4683	G-AZBK	26. 5.95	Westair Aviation Ltd	Shannon	A 7.01
			N14077				
EI-WAV	Bell 430	49028	N4213V	24.12.97	Westair Aviation Ltd	Shannon	A12.01
EI-WBC	Bell 222A	47021	EI-BOR	?	Westair Aviation Ltd	Shannon	
			LN-OSB				
EI-WDC	Hawker Siddeley HS.125 Srs.3B	25132	G-OCBA	2. 7.94	Westair Aviation Ltd	Shannon	A11.01
			EI-WDC/G-OCBA/G-MRFB/G-AZVS/OY-DKP				
EI-WGV	Gulfstream G.1159 Gulfstream V	505	N505GV	21.11.97	Westair Aviation Ltd *"Born Free"*	Shannon	A12.01
EI-WHE	Beechcraft B200 Super King Air		VP-CHE	7. 5.98	Westair Aviation Ltd	Shannon	A 8.01
		BB-1569	N20505				
EI-WJN	Hawker Siddeley HS.125 Srs.700A		N416RD	30. 5.00	Westair Aviation Ltd	Shannon	A12.01
		257062	RA-02809/G-5-708/RA-02809/(G-BWJX)/G-5-708/N7062B/HB-VGF/G-5-708/HB-VGF/G-5-16				
EI-WMN	Piper PA-23-250 Aztec F	27-7954063	G-ZSFT	12.10.00	Westair Aviation Ltd	Shannon	A 9.01
			G-SALT/G-BGTH/N2551M/N9731N				
EI-WRC	Bell 222A	47029	EI-TAR	4. 5.00	Westair Aviation Ltd -	Shannon	A 8.00
			N121NN/N121NC/N120NC				
EI-WRN	Piper PA-28-151 Cherokee Warrior		G-BDZX	5.10.99	B.A.Carpenter	Shannon	A 6.01
		28-7615212	N9559N		*(Op Westair Aviation Ltd)*		
EI-WSN	Bell 206B JetRanger II	1669	G-CHGL	24. 3.00	Westair Aviation Ltd	Shannon	A 9.01
			G-BPNG/G-ORTC/G-BPNG/N20EA/C-GHVB				
EI-WYO	Piper PA-31 Navajo C	31-7912022	G-BIYO	15. 9.00	Westair Aviation Ltd	Ronaldsway	A11.01
			PH-ECG/N27845				
EI-XMC	Robinson R.22 Beta	1655		17. 5.91	McAuliffe Photographic Laboratories Ltd		
			(Crashed Dingle Harbour, Co.Kerry 31.5.92: wreck to store)			Dublin	

<u>Registrations awaited:</u>

EI-...	Bensen B8MV	PFA G/01-1044	G-BKZJ	.99R	Not known *(Cancelled by UK CAA 22.12.98)*
EI-...	Hornet RS-ZA	HRWB-0052 & ZA137	G-MWAH	12.99	Not known
	(Rotax 532)				*(Cancelled by UK CAA 17.12.99)*
EI-...	Robin HR.100/200D	112	F-BTBP	11.01R	Not known
EI-	Southdown Raven X	SN2232/0166	G-MNVP	12.01R	Not known
	(Rotax 447)				*(Cancelled by UK CAA 7.12.01)*
EI-	Airbus A300B4-203F	158	N158GE		Air Contractors (Ireland) *(For delivery 2002)*
EI-	Airbus A300B4-203F	161	N161GE		Air Contractors (Ireland) *(For delivery 2002)*

SECTION 3

UNITED KINGDOM & IRELAND REGISTRATIONS ADDED & REMOVED DURING 2001

Regn	Type	C/n	P/I	Date	Owner/operator	Cancellation Details	
G-BZOY	Beechcraft 76 Duchess	ME-144	F-GFFH 5T-AOH/F-ODJQ/F-GBLO	3. 1.01	S.J.Skilton t/a Aviation Rentals	Sold as EC-...	15.10.01
G-BZRK	SOCATA TB-10 Tobago	1586	VH-YHD	25. 1.01	Air Touring Ltd	Sold as PH-DFC	27. 2.01
G-BZRL	SOCATA TB-10 Tobago	1588	VH-YHF	25. 1 01	Air Touring Ltd	Sold as PH-DFJ	27. 2.01
G-BZRT	Beechcraft 76 Duchess	ME-89	F-GHBL N2074G	21. 3.01	S.J.Skilton	Sold as EC-HYO	6. 7.01
G-BZSN	Sikorsky S-61N	61-807	LN-OQB	11. 4.01	CHC Scotia Ltd	Sold as EI-RCG	25. 9.01
G-BZUA	Piper PA-28-161 Warrior III	2842121	N53363	7. 6.01	Plane Talking Ltd	Re-regd G-OMST	1. 8.01
G-BZUS	Eurocopter EC 120B	1191	F-WQOU	6. 4.01	McAlpine Helicopters Ltd	Sold as EI-IZO	26. 7.01
G-BZWA	SOCATA TB-10 Tobago	1585	VH-YHC	1. 5.01	Air Touring Ltd	Sold as PH-DFW	15. 6.01
G-BZWL	BAC.167 Strikemaster Mk.80	EEP/JP/144 & PS.114	1102 R.Saudi AF/G-27-21	22. 5.01	R.J.Everett	Sold as N399WH	7. 6.01
G-BZWP	British Aerospace 146-200	E-2054	SE-DRG N696AA/N144AC/G-5-024/N144AC/G-5-024	18. 6.01	BAE Systems (Operations) Ltd	Sold as ZA-MAL	9. 7.01
G-CBAA	Piper PA-34-220T Seneca V	3449217	N53445	23. 7.01	Technical Flight Services Ltd	Sold as N61HB(2)	27. 7.01
G-CBAM	Scottish Aviation Bulldog Srs.120/121	BH120/272	XX614	6. 7.01	F.P.Corbett	Re-regd G-GGRR	11. 7.01
G-CBBE	Robinson R44 Clipper	1085		16. 7.01	Heli Air Ltd	Sold as OY-HLN	24. 9.01
G-CBBJ	Eurocopter AS350B3 Ecureuil	3417	F-WQDT	20. 7.01	McAlpine Helicopters Ltd	Sold as HB-ZCB	19.11.01
G-CBBK	Robinson R.22 Beta	3233		26. 7.01	Heli Air Ltd	Sold as EI-CWP	17.10.01
G-CBCG	Eurocopter EC 120B	1236		7. 8.01	McAlpine Helicopters Ltd	Re-regd G-ISSY	11.10.01
G-CBCN	Schweizer 269C-1	0129		17. 9.01	Oxford Aviation Services Ltd	Sold as EI-CWS	19.11.01
G-CBDB	Robinson R22 Beta	3234		20. 8.01	Heli Air Ltd	Sold as EI-CWR	17.10.01
G-CBDE	Cameron Thunder AX10-210 S2 HAFB	10146		31. 8.01	Cameron Balloons Ltd	Sold as OO-BOI	11. 9.01
G-OKJW	Boeing 737-8Q8	30637		27. 3.01	Excel Airways Ltd	Sold as D-...	28. 3.01
G-OJOB	Cameron Monster-110SS HAFB	4957		15. 1.01	Virgin Airship & Balloon Co Ltd	Re-regd G-MSTR	18. 7.01
EI-CVV	Airbus A321-211	1451	D-AVXC	2.01R	GECAS	NTU to I-PEKM	19. 3.01
EI-CWG	Short SD.3-60 Var.100	SH.3604	G-OLAH G-BPCO/G-RMSS/G-BKKU/G-14-3604	14. 6.01	Comhfhorbairt (Gaillimh) Teo	To G-ROND	1.11.01
(EI-...)	Solar Wings Pegasus XL-Q (Rotax 462)	SW-TE-0127 & SW-WQ-0152	G-MVKV	29. 1.01	M D Callan	Sold as G-MVKV	31. 1.01

SECTION 4

PART 1 - BRITISH AVIATION PRESERVATION COUNCIL

The British Aviation Preservation Council (BAPC) was formed in 1967 and is the national body for the preservation of aviation related items. It is a voluntary staffed body which undertakes a representation, co-ordination and enabling role. BAPC membership includes national, local authority, independent and service museums, private collections, voluntary groups and other organisations involved in the advancement of aviation preservation in the UK. A number of overseas aircraft preservation organisations have affiliated membership. The Secretary is Nick Foster c/o Museum of Science & Industry, Liverpool Road, Castlefield, Manchester M3 4FP (tel: 0161 8322244), email: curatorial@mussci.u-net.com

The BAPC register of historic aircraft was started in the 1980s to identify and record the many aircraft which were never allocated an official military or civil identity. These include hang gliders, RAF "plastic replicas", film replicas, German & Japanese aircraft and homebuilts. Most exhibits held in Museums are usually on display and the identities shown in the second column are carried. To co-incide with the 18th edition of Ken Ellis' "Wrecks & Relics" I have taken the opportunity to update the information. We are very grateful to Ken for this. Further information about many of these aircraft, their various locations and the availabilty of Museums can be found in "Wrecks & Relics". I would remind you that the London collections of the Imperial War, Science, and RAF Museums can now be viewed free of charge.

Thanks also to Mark Collington, Howard Curtis and Alistair Ness for providing information this year. If any reader can provide further updates on some of the more elderly entries then we would be pleased to hear from you.

BAPC No.	Identity	Type	C/n	P/I	Owner/operator	Location
1		Roe Triplane rep			*See G-ARSG in SECTION 1*	
2		Bristol Boxkite rep			*See G-ASPP in SECTION 1*	
3		Bleriot XI			*See G-AANG(2) in SECTION 1*	
4		Deperdussin			*See G-AANH(2) in SECTION 1*	
5		Blackburn monoplane			*See G-AANI(2) in SECTION 1*	
6	14	Roe Triplane Type IV rep			Museum of Science & Industry	Manchester
		(JAP 9hp)			*"Bullseye Avroplane"*	
7		SUMPAC			Hall of Aviation	Southampton
		(Southampton University Manpowered Aircraft)				
8		Dixon Ornithopter			The Shuttleworth Collection	Old Warden
9		Bleriot XI Monoplane rep			Midland Air Museum	Coventry
		(Humber) *(Converted to 1911 Humber Bleriot Monoplane: assembled from some original parts Old Warden 1959)*				
10		Hafner R.II Revoplane			The Helicopter Museum	Weston-super-Mare
		(Salmson 45hp)				
11		English Electric Wren			*See G-EBNV in SECTION 1*	
12		Mignet HM.14 Pou-Du-Ciel			Museum of Science & Industry	Manchester
		(Scott A2S)				
13		Mignet HM.14 Pou-Du-Ciel			Brimpex Metal Treatments Ltd	Sheffield
		(Douglas 600cc)			*(Under restoration 3.98)*	
14		Addyman Standard Training Glider			A.Lindsay & N.H.Ponsford	Selby
					(Stored 2.00)	
15		Addyman Standard Training Glider			N.H.Ponsford	Wigan
		(Yorkshire Aeroplanes rebuild)	YA2		*(Stored 2.00)*	
16		Addyman Ultralight			A.Lindsay & N.H.Ponsford	Selby
					(Stored incomplete 2.00)	
17		Woodhams Sprite			BB Aviation	Canterbury
					(Stored incomplete 2.00)	
18		Killick Gyroplane			A.Lindsay & N.H.Ponsford	Selby
		(Stored 2.00)				
19	B4	Bristol F2b			Musee Royal De L'Armee	Brussels, Belgium
		(Rebuilt to static condition by Skysport Engineering 6.89 with parts from J8264) (As "66" in Belgian AF c/s)				
20		Lee-Richards Annular Biplane rep			The Archive Visitor Centre	Shoreham
		("Those Magnificent Men in Their Flying Machines" film)				
21		Thruxton Jackaroo			M.J.Brett	Not known
		(Used as spares in rebuild of G-APAL: current status unknown)				
22	"G-AEOF"	Mignet HM.14 Pou-Du-Ciel	WM.1		R.R.Mitchell	Schiphol
		(Scott A2S)			*(Loaned Aviodome and stored 1992)*	The Netherlands
23		*Allocation cancelled - originally used by ½ scale SE.5 rep at Newark Air Museum*				
24		*Allocation cancelled - originally used by 2/3rd scale Currie Wot rep at Newark Air Museum*				
25		Nyborg TGN.III Sailplane			P Williams *(Stored 1.92)*	Warwick
26		Auster AOP.6			*(Fuselage frame only since scrapped*	*Swansea)*
27		Mignet HM.14 Pou-Du-Ciel			M J Abbey *(Under construction 1988)*	Not known
28		Wright Flyer rep			Yorkshire Air Museum	Elvington
29	"G-ADRY"	Mignet HM.14 Pou-Du-Ciel			Brooklands Museum	Brooklands
		(Anzani "V") *(Built P.D.Roberts, Swansea 1960/78)*				

30		DFS Grunau Baby			Not known *(Destroyed by fire Swansea 1969)*	
31		Slingsby T.7 Tutor			Not known *(Believed scrapped Swansea)*	
32		Crossley Tom Thumb			Midland Air Museum	Coventry
					(Not completed Banbury 1937: stored 4.96)	
33		DFS 10849 Grunau Baby IIB		VN148	Russavia Collection	Bishops Stortford
				LN+ST	*(On rebuild as BGA.2400 1978: status unknown)*	
34		DFS 10849 Grunau Baby IIB	030892	RAFGSA281	D.Elsdon	Hazlemere, Bucks
				RAFGGA GK.4/LZ+AR		
			(Originally on rebuild as BGA.2362: status unknown but possibly used for spares)			
35		EoN AP.7 Primary	EoN/P/063		Not known *(ex Russavia Collection)*	Pocklington
					(On rebuild as BGA.2493 8.89)	
36		Fieseler Fi 103 V1 model			Kent Battle of Britain Museum	Hawkinge
		("Operation Crossbow" film)				
37		Blake Bluetit			<u>*See G-BXIY in SECTION 1*</u>	
38	"A1742"	Bristol Scout D rep			K Williams & M Thorn	Solihull
		(80 hp Gnome)			*(On rebuild 11.99)*	
39		Addyman Zephyr Sailplane			A Lindsay & N.H Ponsford	Selby
					(Parts held for eventual rebuild 2.00)	
40		Bristol Boxkite rep	BM.7281		City Museum & Art Gallery	Clifton, Bristol
		(Gnome) *("Those Magnificent Men in Their Flying Machines" film)*				
41		RAF BE.2C rep		"6232"	Yorkshire Air Museum	Elvington
42	"H1968"	Avro 504K rep			Yorkshire Air Museum	Elvington
43		Mignet HM.14 Pou-Du-Ciel			Newark Air Museum	Winthorpe
		(Scott A2S)			*(Stored 3.96)*	
44	"L6906"	Miles M.14A Magister			<u>*See G-AKKY in SECTION 1*</u>	
45		Pilcher Hawk glider rep			Percy Pilcher Museum	Stanford Hall Rugby
		(Built AWA apprentices 1957/58)				
46		Mignet HM.14 Pou-Du-Ciel			Not known	Tump Farm, Coleford
		(Status unknown: probably scrapped)				
47		Watkins CHW Monoplane			National Museum of Wales	Cardiff
		(Watkins 40hp)				
48		Pilcher Hawk glider rep			National Museums of Scotland/Museum of Transport	Kelvin Hall, Glasgow
		(Built No.2175 Sqdn ATC, Glasgow 1966)				
49		Pilcher Hawk glider *(1896 original)*			National Museums of Scotland/Museum of Flight	East Fortune
		(Rebuilt after fatal crash Stanford Hall, Leics 30.9.<u>1899</u>)				
50		Roe Triplane Type I			The Science Museum	South Kensington London W7
		(JAP 9hp) *(1909 original)*				
51		Vickers FB.27 Vimy IV	13		The Science Museum	South Kensington London W7
		(RR Eagle VIII 360hp)				
52		Lilienthal Glider Type XI			The Science Museum	Wroughton
		(1895 original)				
53		Wright Flyer rep			The Science Museum	South Kensington London W7
54		JAP/Harding Monoplane			The Science Museum	South Kensington London W7
		(JAP Anzani 45hp) *(Modified Bleriot XI built J.A.Prestwich & Co 1910)*				
55		Levasseur-Antoinette Developed Type VII Monoplane			The Science Museum	South Kensington London W7
		(Antoinette V8 50hp) *(1910 original)*				
56	210/16	Fokker E.III			The Science Museum	South Kensington London W7
		(Oberusal 100hp) *(Captured in Somme 1916: reported as ex XG4 of RFC: skeletal airframe)*				
57		Pilcher Hawk Glider rep			The Science Museum	Wroughton
		(Built Martin & Miller, Edinburgh 1930)				
58	15-1585	Yokosuka MXY7 Ohka 11			Fleet Air Arm Museum	RNAS Yeovilton
59	"B5577"	Sopwith F1 Camel rep		"D3419" "F1921"	RAF Museum Cosford	RAF Cosford
60		Murray M.1 Helicopter			The Helicopter Museum	Weston-super-Mare
		(JAPJ99 36hp)				
61		Stewart Ornithopter			North Coates Flyng Club	North Coates
					"Bellbird II" (Stored 12.00)	
62	304	Cody Type V Bi-plane			The Science Museum	South Kensington London W7
		(Austro-Daimler 120hp) *(1912 original)*				
63	"P3208"	Hawker Hurricane fsm		"L1592"	Kent Battle of Britain Museum	Hawkinge
		("Battle of Britain" film)			*(As "SD-T" in 501 Sqdn c/s)*	
64	"P3059"	Hawker Hurricane fsm			Kent Battle of Britain Museum	Hawkinge
		("Battle of Britain" film)			*(As "SD-N" in 501 Sqdn c/s)*	
65	"N3289"	Supermarine Spitfire fsm			Kent Battle of Britain Museum	Hawkinge
		("Battle of Britain" film)			*(As "DW-K" in 610 Sqdn c/s)*	
66	"6"	Messerschmitt Bf109 fsm	1480		Kent Battle of Britain Museum	Hawkinge
		(Hispano HA.1112) *("Battle of Britain" film)*				
67	"14"	Messerschmitt Bf109 fsm			Kent Battle of Britain Museum	Hawkinge
		(Hispano HA.1112) *("Battle of Britain" film)*			*(In JG52 c/s)*	
68	"H3426"	Hawker Hurricane fsm			Hooton Park Trust	Hooton Park
		("Battle of Britain" film)				
69	"N3313"	Supermarine Spitfire fsm			Kent Battle of Britain Museum	Hawkinge
		("Battle of Britain" film)			*(As "KL-B" in 54 Sqn c/s)*	

70	"TJ398"	Auster AOP.5	TAY/33153	"GALES"	National Museums of Scotland/Museum of Flight	
			(On loan from Aircraft Preservation Society of Scotland)			East Fortune
71	"P8140"	Supermarine Spitfire fsm		"P9390"	Norfolk & Suffolk Aviation Museum	Flixton
		("Battle of Britain" film)		"N3317"	"Nuflier" *(As "ZP-K" in 74 Sqn c/s)*	
72	"V6779"	Hawker Hurricane fsm			Jet Age Museum	(Gloucester)
			(Gloucestershire Aviation Collection) (As "SD-X" of 501 RAAF Sqdn)			
73		Hawker Hurricane rep			Not known	Bishops Stortford
			(Displayed "Queens Head" Public House: current status unconfirmed)			
74	"6"	Messerschmitt Bf109 fsm	6357		Kent Battle of Britain Museum	Hawkinge
		(Hispano HA.1112) *("Battle of Britain" film)*				
75		Mignet HM.14 Pou-Du-Ciel			*See G-AEFG in SECTION 1*	
76	"G-AFFI"	Mignet HM.14 Pou-Du-Ciel			Yorkshire Air Museum	Elvington
		(Scott) *(Modern reproduction)*				
77	"G-ADRG"	Mignet HM.14 Pou-Du-Ciel			Stondon Transport Museum	Lower Stondon
		(Citroen 425cc) *(Modern reproduction)*				
78					*See G-AENP in SECTION 1*	
79	"ZI-4"	Fiat G.46-4b	71	FHE	T P Luscombe/British Air Reserve	
				MM53211	*(Not constructed)*	
80	"KJ351"	Airspeed AS.58 Horsa II			Museum of Army Flying	AAC Middle Wallop
		(Composite from LH208, TL659 & 8569M)				
81		RFD (Hawkridge) Dagling	10471	BGA.493	Russavia Collection	Hemel Hempstead
					(On rebuild)	
82		Hawker Afghan Hind	41H/81899		RAF Museum	Hendon
		(RR Kestrel)			*(R.Afghan AF c/s)*	
83	"24"	Kawasaki Ki 1001b		8476M	RAF Cosford Museum	RAF Cosford
84		Mitsubishi Ki 46III (Dinah)	5439	8484M	RAF Cosford Museum	RAF Cosford
			(ATAIU/SEA)/Jap Army AF/81st Sentai)			
85	W-2	Weir W-2			National Museums of Scotland/Museum of Flight	
		(Weir Dryad II 50hp)			*(On loan)*	East Fortune
86		DH.82A Tiger Moth			Yorkshire Aircraft Preservation Society	
					(Current status unknown)	Acaster Malbis
87	"G-EASQ"	Bristol 30/46 Babe III rep	1		Bristol Aero Collection	Kemble
		(Built W.Sneesby)				
88	"102/17"	Fokker DR.1 5/8th rep			Fleet Air Arm Museum	RNAS Yeovilton
		(Modified Lawrence Parasol airframe)				
89		Cayley Glider rep			Yorkshire Air Museum	Elvington
90		Colditz Cock rep			Lincolnshire Aviation Heritage Centre	
		(BBC "The Colditz Story" film)				East Kirkby
91		Fieseler Fi 103R-IV			Lashenden Air Warfare Museum	Headcorn
		(Believed to be a genuine piloted version)				
92		Fieseler Fi 103 (V1)			RAF Museum	Hendon
93		Fieseler Fi 103 (V1)			Imperial War Museum	Duxford
94		Fieseler Fi 103 (V1)		8483M	RAF Cosford Museum	Cosford
95		Gizmer Autogyro			F.Fewsdale	Darlington
					(Current status unknown)	
96		Brown Helicopter			North East Aircraft Museum	Sunderland
97	"G-AFUG"	Luton LA.4 Minor			North East Aircraft Museum	Sunderland
		(JAP J99)				
98	997	Yokosuka MXY7 Ohka 11		8485M	Museum of Science & Industry	Manchester
99		Yokosuka MXY7 Ohka 11		8486M	RAF Cosford Museum	RAF Cosford
100		Clarke Chanute biplane glider			The Science Museum	Hendon
					(On loan to RAF Museum)	
101		Mignet HM.14 Pou-Du-Ciel			Newark Air Museum	Winthorpe
102		Mignet HM.14 Pou-Du-Ciel			Not constructed - parts to BAPC.75	
103		Hulton Hang-glider			Personal Plane Services Ltd	Booker
		(Built E.A.S.Hulton, London 1969)			*("Blue Max" Movie Aircraft Museum)*	
104		Bleriot XI		G-AVXV	Sold as F-AZIN 1992	
105		Bleriot XI	54		Arango Collection	Los Angeles
		(Anzani "V" 25hp)				California, USA
		(Composite from original components including c/n 54: built by L.D.Goldsmith in 1976 @ RAF Colerne)				
106	164	Bleriot XI		9209M	RAF Cosford Museum	RAF Cosford
		(Anzani 40hp) (1910 original)				
107	433	Bleriot XXVII		9202M	Royal Aeronautical Society	Hendon
		(1911 original)			(On loan to RAF Museum)	
108		Fairey Swordfish IV		HS503	RAF Museum Reserve Collection & Restoration Centre	
						RAF Wyton
109		Slingsby T.7 Cadet	28	8599M	RAF Museum	RAF Henlow
				BGA.679	*(Current status unknown: presumed stored)*	
110	"5125/18"	Fokker D.VII rep			Not known (ex Leisure Sport)	Not known
					(Current status unknown: sold 10.87)	
111	"N5492"	Sopwith Triplane rep			Fleet Air Arm Museum	RNAS Yeovilton
		("Black Maria")				
112	"5964"	De Havilland DH.2 rep			Museum of Army Flying	AAC Middle Wallop
					(See G-BFVH/5964 in SECTION 1)	

113	"B4863"	RAF SE.5A rep		Not known (ex Leisure Sport)	Not known
				(Current status unknown: sold 10.87)	
114	"G-EBED"	Vickers 60 Viking IV rep	"R4"	Brooklands Museum	Brooklands
		("The Land Time Forgot" film)			
115		Mignet HM.14 Pou-Du-Ciel		I Hancock	Flixton
		(Douglas 500cc)		(On loan to Norfolk & Suffolk Aviation Museum)	
116		Santos-Dumont Demoiselle XX rep		Flambards Triple Theme Park	Helston
		(JAP J99)		(Status unknown: sold 1993)	
117	"1701"	RAF BE.2C rep		RAF Manston History Museum	Manston
		(Gipsy Major) *(Built Ackland & Shaw for BBC TV "Wings" 1976)*			
		(Two similar aircraft were built but only one appears in the BAPC listing)			
118	"C19/15"	Albatros D.V static rep		North Weald Aircraft Restoration Flight	North Weald
119		Bensen B.7 Gyroglider		North East Aircraft Museum	Sunderland
120				<u>See G-AEJZ in SECTION 1</u>	
121				<u>See G-AEKR in SECTION 1</u>	
122	"1881"	Avro 504 rep		Not known	Not known
		(Ford 1300) *(Built PPS for BBC TV "Wings" 1976)*		*(Current status unknown)*	
123	"P641"	Vickers FB.5 Gunbus rep	1186/2 ZS-UHN	A.Topen	Cranfield
		(Built IES Projects Ltd 1975 for "Shout at the Devil" film: small components only remain & stored 3.90)			
124		Lilienthal Glider Type XI rep		The Science Museum	South Kensington London W7
		(Display reproduction of BAPC.52)			
125		Clay Cherub ground trainer			(Coventry)
126		Rollason-Druine D.31 Turbulent		Midland Air Museum	Coventry
		(Static airframe)			
127		Halton Jupiter MPA		C.Roper	Filching Manor
				(On loan Foulkes-Halbard Collection)	Wannock
128		Watkinson CG-4 rotorcraft		The Helicopter Museum	Weston-super-Mare
129		Blackburn 1911 Monoplane rep		Not known	NK
		(Built for TV series "The Flambards")		*"Mercury" (Sold 1993: current status unknown)*	
130		Blackburn 1911 Monoplane rep		Yorkshire Air Museum	Elvington
		(Built for TV series "The Flambards")		*"Mercury"*	
131		Pilcher Hawk glider rep		C.Paton	London E
		(Built C.Paton for film 1972)		*(Current status unknown: probably stored)*	
132		Bleriot XI	EMK010 & PFA/8810864	Not known	
		(Anzani 25hp) *(L.D.Goldsmith 1976 rebuild from original components: rebuilt again by EMK in 1982 & initially allotted G-BLXI: reported as sold to unidentified Musee de l'Automobile, France in 1986: possibly the same a/c as BAPC.189)*			
133	"425/17"	Fokker DR.1 model		Kent Battle of Britain Museum	Hawkinge
134		Pitts S.2A	"G-RKSF"	Toyota	Northampton
				(See "G-CARS" in SECTION 4)	
135	"C4912"	Bristol M.1C Monoplane rep		Not known	Not known
		(Status unknown: sold 10.87)		*(ex Leisure Sport)*	
136	"619"	Deperdussin 1913 floatplane rep		National Air Race Museum	Sparks, NV, USA
137	"8151"	Sopwith Baby floatplane rep		Not known *(ex Leisure Sport)*	Not known
		(Built FEM Displays Ltd 1978)		*(Current status unknown: sold 10.87)*	
138	"2292"	Hansa Brandenberg W.29 rep		Not known *(ex Leisure Sport)*	Not known
		(Ford 1300)		*(Current status unknown: sold prior to 10.87)*	
139	"DR1/17"	Fokker DR.1 Triplane rep		Not known *(ex Leisure Sport)*	Not known
				(Current status unknown: sold 10.87)	
140	"3"	Curtiss 42A R3C2 rep		National Air Race Museum	Sparks,
				<u>(US Army c/s)</u>	
141	"5"	Macchi M.39 rep		National Air Race Museum	Sparks, Nevada, USA
		(Gipsy Queen)			
142	"F5459"	RAF SE.5A rep		Not known	Switzerland
				(As "Y") (Current status unknown: sold 1.5.93)	
143		Paxton MPA		R.A.Paxton	Gloucestershire
				(Current status unknown: presumed stored)	
144		Weybridge MPA		Not known "Mercury"	Cranwell
		(Previously "Dumbo" rebuilt)		*(Current status unknown)*	
145		Oliver MPA		Not known	Warton
				(Current status unconfirmed, possibly scrapped)	
146		Pedal Aeronauts MPA		Not known *"Toucan"*	Not known
		(Current status uncertain: centre section/power train only departed London Colney 1995)			
147	"LHS-1"	Bensen B7 Gyroglider		Norfolk & Suffolk Aviation Museum	Flixton
148	"K7271"	Hawker Fury II rep		High Ercall Aviation Museum	High Ercall
				(In 1 Sqdn c/s) (Noted 5.01 @ Sleap))	
149		Short S.27 rep		Fleet Air Arm Museum	RNAS Yeovilton
150	"XX725"	BAC/Sepecat Jaguar GR.1 fsm	"XX718"	RAF Marketing & Recruitment Unit	RAF St.Athan
			"XX732"	*(As "GU" in 54 Sqdn c/s)*	
151	"XZ363"	BAC/Sepecat Jaguar GR.1A fsm	"XX824"	RAF Marketing & Recruitment Unit	RAF St.Athan
				(As "A")	
152	"XX226"	BAe Hawk T.1A fsm	"XX262"	RAF Marketing & Recruitment Unit	RAF St.Athan
			"XX162"	*(As "74 in 74 Sqdn c/s)*	

153		Westland WG-33			The Helicopter Museum	Weston-super-Mare
		(Engineering mock-up)				
154		Druine D.31 Turbulent	PFA/1654		Lincolnshire Aviation Society	East Kirkby
					(Unfinished: stored 3.96)	
155	"ZA368"	Panavia Tornado GR.1 model		"ZA446"	RAF Marketing & Recruitment Unit	RAF St.Athan
				"ZA600/ZA322"	(As "AJ-P")	
156	"S1595"	Supermarine S.6B rep			National Air Race Museum	Sparks, Nevada, USA
157	"237123"	WACO CG-4A Hadrian			Yorkshire Air Museum	Elvington
					(Fuselage frame section only & tail pieces ex 456476)	
158		Fieseler Fi 103 (V1)			Defence Explosives Ordnance Disposal School	Chattenden
159		Yokosuka MXY7 Ohka 11			Defence Explosives Ordnance Disposal School	Chattenden
160		Chargus 18/50 Hang-Glider			National Museums of Scotland/Museum of Flight	East Fortune
161		Stewart MP Ornithopter			A Stewart *"Coppelia" (Stored 8.98)*	Louth
162		Goodhart MPA			The Science Museum	Wroughton
					"Newbury Manflier" (Parts only stored)	
163	"B-415"	Hafner AFEE 10/42 Rotabuggy rep			Wessex Aviation Society	AAC Middle Wallop
					(On loan to Museum of Army Flying)	
164	"N546"	Wight Quadruplane Type 1 rep			Hall of Aviation	Southampton
165	E2466	Bristol F.2b			RAF Museum	Hendon
		(RR Falcon rep)			*(22 Sqdn c/s)*	
166	"D7889"	Bristol F.2b			*See G-AANM in SECTION 1*	
167		RAF SE.5A rep			TDL Replicas Ltd *(Exported 12.97)*	USA
168	"G-AAAH"	DH.60G Moth rep	8058		Gatwick Hilton Hotel *"Jason"*	Gatwick
		(Another reproduction DH.60 Moth exists as "G-AAAH" -see SECTION 8 (ii))				
169	"XX110"	BAC/Sepecat Jaguar GR.1			RAF/No.1 School of Technical Training	RAF Cosford
		(Engine systems static demonstration airframe)				
170		Pilcher Hawk glider rep			A Gourlay	Strathallan
		(Built A.Gourlay 1983) ("Kings Royal" BBC film)			*(Current status unknown: stored 3.93)*	
171	"XX253"	BAe Hawk T.1 fsm		"XX297" "XX262"	RAF Marketing & Recruitment Unit	RAF St.Athan
172		Chargus Midas Super E Hang-Glider			The Science Museum	Wroughton
173		Birdman Grasshopper Hang-Gglider			The Science Museum	Wroughton
174		Bensen B.7 Gyro-glider			The Science Museum	Wroughton
175		Volmer VJ-23 Swing-wing			Museum of Science & Industry	Manchester
		(McCulloch 9hp)				
176	"A4850"	RAF SE.5A scale rep			Botany Bay Village	Chorley
		(Currie Wot basic airframe) (Built Slingsby for "The Blue Max" film)				
177	"G-AACA"	Avro 504K rep		"G1381"	Brooklands Museum	Brooklands
		(Clerget 130hp)			*(Brooklands School of Flying c/s)*	
178		Avro 504K rep		"E373"	By-gone Times Antique Warehouse	Eccleston, Lancs
					(German c/s)	
179	"A7317"	Sopwith Pup rep			Midland Air Museum	Coventry
180		McCurdy Silver Dart rep			Reynolds Pioneer Museum	Wetaskiwin
					(Delivered 4.94)	Alberta, Canada
181	"687"	RAF BE.2b rep			RAF Museum	Hendon
		(Renault V8) *(Restoration from original components)*				
182		Wood Ornithopter			Museum of Science & Industry	Manchester
183		Zurowski ZP.1			Newark Air Museum	Winthorpe
		(Panhard 850cc)			*(Polish AF c/s)*	
184	"EN398"	Supermarine Spitfire IX fsm			R.J.Lamplough/Fighter Wing Display Team	North Weald
		(Built Specialised Mouldings Ltd 1985)			*(As "WO-A")*	
185	"243809"	WACO CG-4A Hadrian			Museum of Army Flying	AAC Middle Wallop
					(Fuselage only)	
186	"LF789"	DH.82B Queen Bee		"K3584"	De Havilland Heritage Museum	London Colney
		(Correct identity not known)			*(As "R2-K")*	
187		Roe Type I Biplane rep			Brooklands Museum	Brooklands
		(ABC 24hp) *(Built M.L.Beach)*				
188		McBroom Cobra 88 Hang-Glider			The Science Museum	Wroughton
189		Bleriot XI rep			Not known *(Current status uncertain: see BAPC.132)*	
		(Anzani) *(Some original parts ex Goldsmith Trust)*			*(Sold Christies 31.10.86, probably to France)*	
190		Supermarine Spitfire prototype fsm		"K5054"	P.Smith	Hawkinge
191	"ZH139"	BAe Harrier GR.7 fsm		"ZD472"	RAF Marketing & Recruitment Unit	RAF St.Athan
					(As "01")	
192		Weedhopper JC24			N.Dykes	Bacup, Lancs
193		Hovey WDII Whing Ding			N.Dykes	Bacup, Lancs
194		Santos Dumont Type 20 Demoiselle rep	PPS/DEM/1	24 bis	RAF Museum Reserve Collection & Restoration Centre	RAF Wyton
		(ABC Scorpion 30hp)				
		("Those Magnificent Men in Their Flying Machines" film)				
195		Birdman Sports Moonraker 77 Hang-Glider			National Museums of Scotland/Museum of Flight	East Fortune
		(Built c.1977)				

196		Southdown Sailwings Sigma 2m Hang-Glider *(Built c.1980)*		National Museums of Scotland/Museum of Flight	East Fortune
197		Scotkites Cirrus III Hang-Glider *(Built 1977)*		National Museums of Scotland/Museum of Flight	East Fortune
198		Fieseler Fi 103 (V1)	477663	Imperial War Museum	South Lambeth London W7
199	442795	Fieseler Fi 103 (V1)		The Science Museum	South Kensington London W7
200		Bensen B.7 Gyroglider *(Composite three airframes)*		Not known *(Last noted stored 11.93)*	Leeds
201		Mignet HM.14 Pou-Du-Ciel		Caernarfon Airworld	Caernarfon
202	"MAV467"	Supermarine Spitfire V fsm *("A Piece of Cake" film)*		Not known *(As "RO")*	Llanbedr
203	"G-AFIN"	Chrislea LC.1 Airguard rep		The Aeroplane Collection *(Current status unknown: burnt 1998?)*	Wigan
204		McBroom Hang-Glider		Newark Air Museum	Winthorpe
205	"BE421"	Hawker Hurricane IIc fsm		RAF Museum *(As "XP-G" in 174 Sqn c/s)*	Hendon
206	"MH486"	Supermarine Spitfire IX fsm		RAF Museum *(As"FF-A" in 132 Sqn c/s)*	Hendon
207	"K.158"	Austin Whippet rep *(Built Ken Fern/Vintage & Rotary Wing Collection c.1993)*	"G-EAGS"	South Yorkshire Aviation Museum	Doncaster
208	"D276"	RAF SE.5A rep *(Built AJD Engineering)*		Prince's Mead Shopping Centre *(As "A")*	Farnborough, Hants
209	"MJ751"	Supermarine Spitfire LF.IXC fsm *("Piece of Cake" film)*		Museum of D-Day Aviation *(As "DU-V" in 321 Sqn c/s)*	Shoreham
210	"C4451"	Avro 504J rep (Gnome Monosoupape 100hp) *(Built AJD Engineering)*		Hall of Aviation	Southampton
211	"G-ADVU"	Mignet HM.14 Pou-Du-Ciel *(Built Ken Fern/Vintage & Rotary Wing Collection 1993)*		North East Aircraft Museum	Sunderland
212		Bensen B.6 Gyrocopter		The Helicopter Museum	Weston-super-Mare
213		Cranfield Vertigo MP Helicopter		The Helicopter Museum	Weston-super-Mare
214	"K5054"	Supermarine Spitfire prototype fsm		Tangmere Military Aviation Museum	Tangmere
215		Airwave Hang Glider prototype		Hall of Aviation	Southampton
216	"G-ACSS"	DH.88 Comet fsm		Not known *(For Mosquito Museum 2001)*	St Albans
217	"N9926"	Supermarine Spitfire I fsm	"K9926"	Royal Air Force HQ 11/18 Groups *(As "JH-C" in 317 Sqn c/s)*	RAF Bentley Priory
218	"P3386"	Hawker Hurricane IIc fsm		Royal Air Force *(As "FT-I"in 43 Sqn c/s)*	RAF Bentley Priory
219	"L1710"	Hawker Hurricane I fsm		Royal Air Force *(As "AL-D" in 79 Sqn c/s)*	Memorial Chapel Biggin Hill
220	"N3194"	Supermarine Spitfire I fsm		Royal Air Force *(As "GR-Z" in 92 Sqn c/s)*	Memorial Chapel Biggin Hill
221	"MH777"	Supermarine Spitfire LF.IX fsm		Royal Air Force *(As "RF-N" in 303 Sqn c/s)*	RAF Northolt
222	"BR600"	Supermarine Spitfire IX fsm		RAF Museum *(As "SH-V in 64 Sqn c/s)*	RAF Uxbridge
223	"V7467"	Hawker Hurricane I fsm		Royal Air Force *(As "LE-D"in 242 Sqn c/s)*	RAF Coltishall
224	"BR600"	Supermarine Spitfire V fsm *(Built TDL Replicas)*		AJD Engineering/Hawker Restorations Ltd	Sudbury
225	"P8448"	Supermarine Spitfire IX fsm		Royal Air Force *(As "UM-D" in 52 Sqn c/s)*	RAF Cranwell
226	"EN343"	Supermarine Spitfire XI fsm		Royal Air Force *(PRU c/s)*	RAF Benson
227	"L1070"	Supermarine Spitfire IA fsm		Cit of Edinburgh Council *(As "XT-A" in 603 Sqn c/s)*	Edinburgh
228		Olympus Hang Glider		North East Aircraft Museum	Sunderland
229	"MJ832"	Supermarine Spitfire IX fsm	"L1096"	Royal Air Force *(As "DN-Y" in 416 Sqn c/s) "City of Oshawa"*	RAF Digby
230	"AD550"	Supermarine Spitfire fsm *(Built TDL Replicas 1993)*	"AA908"	Eden Camp Modern History Theme Museum *(As "GE-P" in 152 Sqn c/s)*	Malton, N.Yorks
231	"G-ADRX"	Mignet HM.14 Pou-Du-Ciel *(Thought originally built Ulverston 1936 with Anzani engine: on rebuild with modern DAF engine from remains acquired from Torver, Cumbria)*		South Copeland Aviation Group *(Op RAF Millom Museum Project)*	Haverigg, Millom
232		Airspeed AS.58 Horsa I/II *(Composite airframe from unidentified components)*		De Havilland Heritage Museum	London Colney
233		Broburn Wanderlust Sailplane *(Built 1946)*		Museum of Berkshire Aviation	Woodley
234	"2882"	Vickers FB.5 Gunbus fsm *(Built 1985 for "Gunbus" film)*		Not known *(Noted 7.98)*	Manston
235		Fieseler Fi 103 (V1 fsm) *(Built TDL Replicas 1993)*		Eden Camp Modern History Theme Museum	Malton, N.Yorks

236	"P2793"	Hawker Hurricane fsm		Eden Camp Modern History Theme Museum	
		(Built TDL Replicas 7.93)		(As "SD-M" in 501 Sqn c/s)	Malton, N.Yorks
237		Fieseler Fi 103 (V1)		RAF Museum Reserve Collection & Restoration Centre	
					RAF Wyton
238		Waxflatter Ornithopter rep		Personal Plane Services Ltd	Booker
		(Built PPS for "Young Sherlock Holmes")		*("Blue Max" Movie Aircraft Museum)*	
239		Fokker D.VIII 5/8th scale rep		Norfolk & Suffolk Aviation Museum	Flixton
240		Messerschmitt Bf.109G fsm		Yorkshire Air Museum	Elvington
		(Built D.Thorton 1994)			
241	"L1679"	Hawker Hurricane I fsm		Tangmere Military Aviation Museum	Tangmere
		(Built Aerofab 1994)		*(As "JX-G" in 1 Sqn c/s)*	
242	"BL924"	Supermarine Spitfire VB rep		Tangmere Military Aviation Museum	Tangmere
		(Built TDL Reps 1994)		*(As "AZ-G" in 234 Sqn c/s) "Valde Maar Atterdag"*	
243	"G-ADYV"	Mignet HM.14 Pou-Du-Ciel	"A-FLEA"	P.Ward	Malvern Wells
		(Scott A2S) *(Built Bill Francis)*		*(Stored 8.95)*	
244		Solar Wings Typhoon Hang-Glider		National Museums of Scotland/Museum of Flight	
		(Built 1981)		*(Wing only)*	East Fortune
245		Electraflyer Floater Hang-Glider		National Museums of Scotland/Museum of Flight	
		(Built 1979)		*(Wing only)*	East Fortune
246		Hiway Cloudbase Hang-Glider		National Museums of Scotland/Museum of Flight	
		(Built 1978)			East Fortune
247		Albatros ASG.21 Hang-Glider		National Museums of Scotland/Museum of Flight	
		(Built 1977)			East Fortune
248		McBroom Hang-Glider		Museum of Berkshire Aviation	Woodley
		(Built 1974)			
249	"K5673"	Hawker Fury I fsm		Brooklands Museum	Brooklands
				(1 Sqn 'A' Flight c/s)	
250	"F5475"	RAF SE.5A rep		Brooklands Museum	Brooklands
				(As "A") "1st Battalion Honourable Artillery Company"	
251		Hiway Spectrum Hang-Glider		Museum of Science & Industry	Manchester
		(Built 1980)			
252		Flexiform Wing Hang-Glider		Museum of Science & Industry	Manchester
		(Built 1982)			
253	"G-ADZW"	Mignet HM.14 Pou-Du-Ciel rep		H.Shore	Sandown
		(Built 1990s)		*(On loan Front Line Aviation Museum)*	
254	"P3873"	Hawker Hurricane fsm		Yorkshire Air Museum	Elvington
				(As "YO-H" in 609 Sqdn c/s)	
255	"463209"	NA P-51D Mustang fsm	"88"	American Air Museum	Duxford
		(Built Rialto, Ca, USA 1990?)		*(As "WZ-S" in 78th FS c/s)*	
256		Santos Dumont Type 20 Demoiselle rep		Brooklands Museum	Brooklands
		(Built J Aubot 1996/97)			
257	"G-ACSS	DH.88 Comet fsm		Galleria Mall	Hatfield
				"Grosvenor House"	
258		Adams Balloon (14,000 cu.ft)		British Balloon Museum & Library	Newbury
		(Built GQ Parachutes)			
259		Gloster Gamecock fsrep		Jet Age Museum	(Gloucester)
		(Under construction by Gloucestershire Aviation Collection 2.00)			
260		Not known			
261	"HH379"	GA Hotspur rep		Museum of Army Flying	AAC Middle Wallop
		(Comprises anonymous cockpit of Mk.1 ex Airborne Forces Museum, Aldershot & rear of Mk.II, HH379 ex RAF Hendon - under rebuild 2.00)			
262		Catto CP-16		National Museums of Scotland/Museum of Flight	
					East Fortune
263		Chargus Cyclone		Ulster Aviation Heritage	Langford Lodge
		(Built 1979)			
264		Bensen B8M		The Helicopter Museum	Weston-super-Mare
		(Built 1984)			
265	"P3873"	Supermarine Spitfire 1 fsm		Yorkshire Air Museum	Elvington
				(Coded "YO-H" in 609 Sqdn c/s)	

PART 2- IRISH AVIATION HISTORICAL COUNCIL

The IAHC Register came into existence with similar objectives to the BAPC. Thanks to Mark Shortman for a liitle new information this year.

IAHC No.	Identity	Type	C/n	P/I	Owner/operator	Location
1		Mignet HM.14 Pou-Du-Ciel			South East Aviation Enthusiasts Group *"Patrick" (Stored 4.00)*	New Ross
2		Aldritt Monoplane			Foulkes-Halbard Collection *(Under restoration 4.98)*	Filching Manor Wannock
3		Mignet HM.14 Pou-Du-Ciel *(Built 1937 but unflown)*			M.Donohoe *(Last noted 4.96)*	Delgany
4		Hawker Hector		IAAC....	D.McCarthy *(Believed components on rebuild Florida, USA)*	NK
5		Not known			Not known	
6		Ferguson Monoplane rep *(Built Capt J.Kelly Rogers 1974: original engine)*			Ulster Folk & Transport Museum *(Noted 2.01)*	Belfast
7		Sligo Concept			G.O'Hara *(Current status unknown - was stored incomplete 8.91)*	Sligo
8		O'Hara Autogyro			G.O'Hara *(Current status unknown - was stored unflown 8.91)*	Sligo
9		Ferguson Monoplane rep *(Built L.Hannah 1980)*			Ulster Folk & Transport Museum	Belfast

SECTION 5

PART 1 - FOREIGN CIVIL REGISTERED AIRCRAFT LOCATED IN UK & IRELAND

I am indepted to Paul Hewins for his substantial work on this section Other valuable contributions have come from Peter Budden, Mike Cain, Russell Carter, Richard Cawsey, Mark Collington, Peter Gerhardt, Paul Jackson, Bob Kent, Richard Kerr, Bernard Martin, Alistair Ness, Trevor Sexton, Colin Smith & Ken Tilley. My thanks to you all.

An asterisk relates to registrations which no longer appear on the relevant Registers. United States entries have been checked against the FAA register. Underlining denotes a substantial change to type designations. Dates are provided for the latest sightings except in the case of Museum aircraft which are known to be "in (permanent) situ".

Regn	Type	C/n	P/I	Owner/operator	Probable Base
UNITED ARAB EMIRATES					
A6-ALG	MBB Bö.105	S-94		Bond Air Services Ltd *(On rebuild 2.00)*	Bourn
A6-ESH(2)	Airbus A319-133X	910		Ruler of Sharjah *(Noted 7.01)*	Farnborough/Sharjah
A6-HHH	Gulfstream Gulfstream IV	1011	(A6-DLF) N17581	Government of Dubai *(Noted 4.01)*	Farnborough/Dubai
A6-HRS	Boeing 737-7E0	29251		Dubai Royal Flight *(Noted 10.01)*	Farnborough/Dubai
A6-SHK	British Aerospace BAe 146 Srs.100	E1091	G-BOMA G-5-091	Not known *(Stored dismantled 2.01 @ Valley Nurseries)*	Alton
MUSCAT & OMAN					
A40-AB	Vickers VC-10-1103	820	G-ASIX	Brooklands Museum	Brooklands
A40-CT(1)	Britten Norman BN-2T Islander	2201	G-51-2201 G-BOMC	Britten-Norman Group *(Original fuselage derelict 1.00)*	Bembridge
CANADA					
CF-BXO*	Supermarine 304 Stranraer	CV-209	RCAF 920	RAF Museum *(As "920/QN-" in RCAF c/s)*	Hendon
CF-EPV*	Aviation Traders ATL.98 Carvair	10448/8	EI-AMR N88819/42-72343	Old Airfield Estate *(Cockpit section only 12.99)*	Halesworth
CF-EQS*	Boeing-Stearman A75N1 (PT-17-BW) Kaydet	75-1728	41-8169	Imperial War Musem Collection/American Air Museum *(As "217786/25" in USAAF c/s)*	Duxford
CF-KCG*	Grumman TBM-3E Avenger AS.3	2066	RCN326 Bu.69327	Imperial War Musem Collection/American Air Museum *(As "46214/X-3" in USN c/s)*	Duxford
C-FQIP	Lake LA-4-200 Buccaneer	679	N1068L	P J Molloy *(Noted 11.01)*	Elstree
C-GYZI	Cameron O-77 HAFB	269		(Balloon Preservation Group) *"Aeolus"*	Southampton
PORTUGAL					
CS-AZS	de Havilland DHC.1 Chipmunk T.20 *(Built OGMA)*	55	FAP1365	Windmill Aviation *(Noted 11.01)*	Spanhoe
CS-AZT	de Havilland DHC.1 Chipmunk T.20 *(Built OGMA)*	63	FAP1373	Windmill Aviation *(Noted 11.01)*	Spanhoe
CS-AZY	de Havilland DHC.1 Chipmunk T.20 *(Built OGMA)*	40	FAP1350	Not known *(Noted 6.00)*	Bourn
CS-HBK	Hughes 369E	0165E	N5233N	March Helicopters *(Noted 3.01)*	Sywell
CS-HBL	Hughes 369E	0377E		March Helicopters *(Wreck noted 12.01)*	Sywell
CS-HBN	Hughes 369E	0333E		March Helicopters *(Wreck noted 12.01)*	Sywell
CS-HCE	Hughes 369D	120-0856D	G-JIMI N1109T	March Helicopters *(Noted dismantled 12.01)*	Sywell
GERMANY					
D-CATA*	Hawker Sea Fury T.20S	ES.8503	D-FATA G-9-30/VZ345	Royal Naval Historic Flight *(As "VZ345": crashed 19.4.85: stored 11.97)*	RNAS Yeovilton
D-CFLX	Short SD.3-60 Var.300	SH3735	VP-BKL VR-BKL/G-BOEI/G-14-3735	Fortis Aviation *(Stored 5.01)*	Guernsey
D-EALX(2)	Cessna F150L	F15000766	OE-ALX	S A Young *(Noted 9.01)*	Hill Farm, Nayland
D-EAWD*	Reims Cessna F150M	F15001259		Not known *(Noted w/o engine, damaged fin, wings & rear fuselage 2.02)*	Andrewsfield

D-EAXX*	SEEMS MS.885 Super Rallye	260	F-BKUI	P Garcia (Noted 2.00)	King's Farm, Thurrock
D-EBLI	Bölkow Bö.207	223		Not known *(Noted 1.02)*	Crowfield
D-EBLO	Bölkow Bö.207	224		Not known *(Noted 4.01)*	Popham
D-ECDU(1)*	Reims Cessna F172E	F172-0068		M Dunn *(Carries fictitious marks "G-ASOK" 6.00)*	Longside, Peterhead
D-ECLY	Reims Cessna FR172E Rocket	FR17200046		R Ross & A Simmers *(Damaged in gales Southend 30.10.00: on rebuild 2001)*	Lower Wasing Farm Brimpton
D-EEAH	Bölkow Bö.208C Junior	658	(D-EJMH)	J Webb *(Stored 10.01)*	Bourne Park, Hurstbourne Tarrant
D-EELY	Piper PA-28-161 Warrior II	28-8216121	N9636N	Small World Aviation Inc *(Noted 8.01)*	North Weald
D-EEPC	Reims/Cessna F182P Skylane	F18200005		Small World Aviation Inc *(Noted 8.01)*	North Weald
D-EEPI	Wassmer WA.54 Atlantic	151		E S Davison *(Noted 1.02)*	Shoreham
D-EFFA(4)	Ruschmeyer RG90-230RG	018	D-ELVY(2) (D-EEBY(2))	H-J Krebs *(Noted 11.01)*	Old Buckenham
D-EFJD	Bölkow Bö.209 Monsun 160RV	126		W Williams-Wynne *(Noted 7.01)*	Old Sarum
D-EFNO*	Bölkow Bö.208A-1 Junior	604		Aero Engines & Airframes *(For composite rebuild with G-ASFR 2.00)*	Yearby
D-EFTI	Bölkow Bö.207	219		Mark Hayles *(Noted 5.01)*	Turweston
D-EFZO	Reims Cessna F172F	F172-0156		Not known *(Noted 11.01)*	Fenland
D-EGEU	Piper PA-22-108 Colt	22-9055	EL-AEU 5N-AEH	Not known *(Noted 10.01)*	Sibson
D-EGJD	Reims FR172J Rocket	FR17200420		Small World Aviation Inc *(Noted 8.01)*	North Weald
D-EHBH	Piper PA-28-180 Cherokee Challenger	28-7305466	N55782	Small World Aviation Inc *(Noted 8.01)*	North Weald
D-EHJL	Piaggio FWP.149	045	90+31 AC+441/AS+441/GA+394/D-EGEW/GA+394	C A Tyers/Windmill Aviation *(Noted 8.01)*	Spanhoe
D-EHLA	Bölkow Bö.207	273		J Webb *(Noted 11.01)*	Popham
D-EHUQ	Bölkow Bö.207	207		Not known *(Noted 8.01)*	Nuthampstead
D-EHYX	Bölkow Bö.207	209		Not known *(Noted 4.01)*	Haverfordwest
D-EIAL	Piper PA-28-161 Warrior II	28-8116076	N8291D	Not known *(Noted 2.01)*	Alderney
D-EIAR	CEA DR.250/160 Capitaine	98		D G Holmann *(Noted 11.01)*	Leicester
D-EJBI	Bölkow Bö.207	242		E J Jonker *(Noted 7.01)*	Rochester
D-EMIX(2)	Piper PA-32R-300 Lance	32R-7780225	N1137Q	Not known *(Noted 1.02)*	Gloucestershire
D-EMUH	Bölkow Bö.208 Junior	623		Not known *(Noted 5.01)*	Rayne Hall Farm Rayne
D-EMZC	Reims FR.172G Rocket	FR17200154		Small World Aviation Inc *(Noted 8.01)*	North Weald
D-EPUD	Bölkow Bö.209 Monsun 160FV	196	HB-UED D-EAIL	Not known *(Noted 9.01)*	Lydd
D-EQQQ	Cessna 172N	17273670		Small World Aviation Inc *(Noted 8.01)*	North Weald
D-ERAC	Piper PA-28-161 Warrior II	28-8116103	N83079	Small World Aviation Inc *(Noted 8.01)*	North Weald
D-ERCH*	Mooney M.20M TLS	27-0210		J W Davey *(Noted 6.01)*	Biggin Hill
D-EXGC	Extra EA.200	027		Not known *(Noted 8.01)*	Meppershall
D-EXLH	Extra EA.400	06		Not known *(Noted 7.01)*	Seething
D-EZAP	Cessna 152	15283078	N46598	Not known *(Noted 11.01)*	Stapleford
D-FKMA	Antonov An-2T	117411	LSK440	Not known *(Noted 11.01)*	Wellesbourne Mntfrd
D-FLOH	Cessna 208B Grand Caravan	208B0576	N1041F	Not known *(Noted 8.01)*	Langar
D-GDCO	Piper PA-23-160 Apache	23-1800	SE-EDG D-GABA/N4369P	Small World Aviation Inc *(Noted 8.01)*	North Weald
D-GIFR	Partenavia P.68B	57	LN-LMS	L Bax *(Noted 7.01)*	Old Sarum
D-HCKV	Agusta A109A-11	7345	N109C N2GN	The Global Travel Group plc *(Damaged near Newby Bridge, Cumbria 2.1.00: wreck stored)*	Sywell
D-HMED*	MBB Bö.105S	S.341		Bond Air Services Ltd *(Pod stored 12.99 - white/green & carries "Polizei" titles)*	Bourn
D-HMQV*	Bolkow Bö.102 Helitrainer	6216		The Helicopter Museum *(Development a/c)*	Weston-super-Mare
D-HMUR*	MBB Bö.105C	S.91		Bond Air Services Ltd *(Pod stored 5.00)*	Bourn
D-HOAY*	Kamov Ka.26	7001309	DDR-SPY DM-SPY	The Helicopter Museum	Weston-super-Mare
D-IFSB(1)*	de Havilland DH.104 Dove 6	04379	D-CFSB G-AMXR/N4280V	De Havilland Heritage Museum	London Colney
D-NFBA	Hang-glider *(Type?)*	NK		Not known *(Noted 3.00)*	Edburton
D-Opha*	Fire Balloons 3000 HAFB	057	D-TALCID	(Balloon Preservation Group) "Talcid"	Kirdford
D-Pamgas*	Cameron N-90 HAFB	1288		(Balloon Preservation Group) "Pamgas"	Kirdford
D-0369	Glasflugel H201 Standard Libelle	289		Not known "J" *(Noted 8.99)*	Dunstable

FIJI

DQ-PBF — *See G-WORK in SECTION 1, Part 2*

SPAIN

EC-AOY*	Aero-Difusion Jodel D.1190-S Compostela	E.56		G.Janney *(Water damaged remains 2001- thought very little useable)*	Sibsey
EC-AXZ*	Bell 47J	2079		M Masters *(Boom only - used for spares 5.99)*	Lower Upham
EC-GSI	British Aerospace BAe ATP	2044	EC-GNJ G-BTPN	Air Europa Express *(Stored 12.01)*	Southend
EC-HFM	British Aerospace BAe ATP	2015	G-BTPH (N385AE)	Air Europa Express *(Stored 12.01)*	Southend
EC-HND	Airbus A300B4-203F	101	N59101 I-BUSB/F-WZEA	Euro First Air/Iberia *(Stored 10.01)*	Filton

LIBERIA

EL-AKJ	Boeing 707-321C	19375	(N2NF) EL-AKJ/(PP-BRR)/EL-AKJ/9Q-CSW/5N-TAS/N864BX/OB-R-1243/HK-2473/HK-2473X/N473RN/N473PA	Omega Air *(Open store 1.02)*	Southend
EL-AKU	Boeing 707-347C	19964	ZS-NLJ 9J-AFT/HR-AMA/TT-EAP/TT-WAB/B-2425/N707PD/EI-BLC/N1502W/TF-VLG/N1502W	Not known *(Stored 5.01)*	Manston
EL-WXA	Bristol 175 Britannia 253F	13508	9Q-CJH CU-T120/G-BDUP/XM496	Britannia Aircraft Preservation Trust *(As "XM496" in RAF c/s)*	Kemble

ESTONIA

ES-NOB	Antonov An-72	35672070695	CCCP72931	Enimex *(Op Channel Express) (Noted 12.01)*	Bournemouth
ES-YLB	Aero L-39 Albatros	730932		Ou Musket "55" *(Noted 8.01)*	North Weald
ES-YLK	Aero L-29A Delfin	194521	Est.AF Sov AF	R Patton *(Noted 8.01)*	Cork, Co.Cork

FRANCE

F-BBGH*	Brochet MB.100	01		Not known *(Frame stored 2001)*	Sibsey
F-BBSO*	Auster 5	1792	G-AMJM TW452	C.J.Baker *(Frame dismantled 4.98)*	Carr Farm, Newark
F-BDRS*	Boeing B-17G-95DL Flying Fortress	---	N68269 32376/NL68269/44-83735	Imperial War Museum Collection/American Air Museum *"Mary Alice"* *(As "231983/IY-G" in 401st BG/615th BS USAAF c/s)*	Duxford
F-BGEQ*	de Havilland DH.82A Tiger Moth	86305	Fr.AF NL846	Brooklands Museum *(For restoration 2001)*	Denford Manor, Hungerford
F-BGNR*	Vickers V.708 Viscount	35	(OY-AFO) (OY-AFN)/F-BGNR	Skysport Engineering *(Stored 10.99)*	Rotary Farm, Hatch
F-BGNX*	de Havilland DH.106 Comet 1XB	6020	G-AOJT	*See entry for G-AOJT in SECTION 1, Part 2*	
F-BMCY*	Potez 840	02	N840HP F-BJSU/F-WJSU	Highlands & Islands Airports Ltd *(Damaged Sumburgh 29.3.81: Fire Service use 2001)*	Sumburgh
F-BOXQ*				*See entry for N2209P below*	
F-BTGV*	Aero Spacelines 377SGT Super Guppy 201	001	N211AS	British Aviation Heritage-Cold War Jets Collection *(As "1") (Stored 2.00)*	Bruntingthorpe
F-BTMM	Piper PA-31 Turbo Navajo	31-480	N449TA	Alarm Service France SA *(Noted 11.01)*	Elstree
F-BTRP*	Sud SA.321F Super Frelon *(Converted from SA.321 c/n 116)*	01	F-WMHC F-BTRP/F-WKQC/F-OCZV/F-RAFR/F-OCMF/F-BMHC/F-WMHC	The Helicopter Museum *(As "F-OCMF" in Olympic Airways c/s)*	Weston-super-Mare
F-CCHG	Wassmer WA.21 Javelot II	19		E Monnier *(Noted 6.99)*	Yeatsall Farm, Abbotts Bromley
F-GCCZ	Aérospatiale SA.342J Gazelle	1393	(KAF-401)	MW Helicopters Ltd *(Noted 7.01)*	Stapleford
F-GDPA*	Cessna 172RG Cutlass	172RG1091	N9945B	Not known *(Fuselage stored 8.98: current status unknown)*	Shobdon
F-GEHA	Aérospatiale SA.341G Gazelle	1064	N7721Y N6952/F-WMHG	MW Helicopters Ltd *(Spares use 8.01)*	(Stapleford)
F-GEHD	Aérospatiale SA.341G Gazelle	1390	N6KT N49527	MW Helicopters Ltd *(Noted 9.01)*	Stapleford
F-GFDG	Aérospatiale SA.342 Gazelle	1204	TG-KOV	P Holder *(Op MW Helicopters) (Noted 12.01)*	Blackpool
F-GFLD*	Beechcraft C90 King Air	LJ-741	HB-GGW I-AZIO	RFS Aircraft Engineering *(Stored unmarked 1.02)*	Southend
F-GFNO	Robin ATL	16	F-WFNO	B Walker *(Noted 11.01)*	Kemble
F-GFOR	Robin ATL	42		M Godsell *(Noted 6.01)*	Haverfordwest
F-GFRO	Robin ATL	64		B Sharpen *(Noted 8.01)*	North Weald
F-GFVE	Cessna 305C (L-19E) Bird Dog	24541	F-WFVE ALAT	T Mould *(Noted 12.01)* *(As "24541" in US Marines c/s) (Noted 11.01)*	Redhill

F-GGGG	Cessna T310R	310R1805	N310AF	Est Aff'Air SNC	Nottingham
			N2642B		
	(Bought from French insurers 3.00 by Eric Bannister (Donnington Aviation) & on rebuild 11.01)				
F-GGHZ	Robin ATL	123		D.R.G.Whielaw *(Noted 7.01)*	North Connel, Oban
F-GGKR	Holste MH.1521M Broussard	316	F-WGKR	S.Brugnolo	NK
			Fr.AF	*(As "316/315-SN" 11.99: current status unknown)*	
F-GGTJ	Aérospatiale SA.342J Gazelle	1473	C-GVWC	M W Helicopters Ltd	Bristol
	(Converted from SA.341G to SA.342J @ 3.92)		F-WXFX	*(Noted 9.01)*	
F-WGTX	Heli Atlas	01		Intora Firebird plc *(Noted 2001)*	Southend
F-WGTY	Heli Atlas	02		Intora Firebird plc *(Noted 2001)*	Southend
F-GHOB*	Chaize CS.2200-F12 HAFB	30		M.Hammond	Lindfield, W.Sussex
				"Hobicat" (Last noted 6.97: current status unknown)	
F-GIBU	Aérospatiale SA.342J Gazelle	1470	HB-XMU	Global Aviation Services Ltd	Hawarden
			N9000A	*(Noted 9.01)*	
F-GJGM	Mudry CAP.232	07		P Williams	White Waltham
				(Breitling titles) (Noted 5.01)	
F-GJQI	Robin ATL L	133		C Fox *(Noted 12.00)*	Longbridge Deverill
F-GJSL	Aérospatiale SA.342J Gazelle	1052	C-GPGO	MW Helicopters Ltd	Stapleford
	(Converted from SA.341G to SA.342J)		N8350	*(Noted 5.01)*	
F-GKKI	Avions Mudry CAP.231EX	02	(G-BVXL)	Not known	Barton
			F-GKKF/F-WGZC	*(Noted 11.01)*	
F-GMPA	Aerospatiale AS350B Ecureuil	1749	D-HSAN	MW Helicopters Ltd	Stapleford
			SE-HUV/D-HCHL	*(Noted 11.01)*	
F-GNGH	Schweizer 269C	S-1535	D-HLIL	March Helicopters	Sywell
			N86G	*(Noted dismantled 11.00)*	
F-GNVB	Sud-Est SE.3130 Alouette II	1920	V-66	G Snook	Barnsley
			Swiss AF	t/a G S Helicopters *(Noted 7.00)*	
F-GOTC	Mudrey CAP.232	15		T Cassells *(Noted 5.01)*	Bagby
F-GPYV	Beech 1900C-1	UC-121	N121ZR	Air Littoral Express	Hawarden
			N528LX	*(Stored 8.01)*	
F-GPYX	Beech 1900C-1	UC-111	N111YV	Air Littoral Express *(Stored 8.01)*	Hawarden
F-WQKF	Eurocopter AS365N2 Twin Squirrel	6219	N29EH	Multiflight Ltd *(Noted 6.00)*	Leeds-Bradford
F-WWGM*	Thunder & Colt AS-261 HA Airship	1380	(F-GHRI)	British Balloon Museum & Library	Newbury
			G-BPLD	*"Budweiser"*	
F-WWMX	Aerotech Europe CAP.222	C03		(A Cassidy) *(Noted 6.01)*	White Waltham
F-GXDB	Mudry CAP.232	33		Diane Britten *(Noted 6.01)*	Fairoaks
F-GYRO	Mudry CAP.232	25		A Cassidy	White Waltham
				(Securicor titles) (Noted 5.01)	
F-HMFI*	Farman F.40	6799	9204M	RAF Museum	RAF Cosford
	(Modified to F141 Status)				
F-PAGD	Auster V J/1 Autocrat	2218	G-AJID	J Guerin *(Noted 7.01)*	Eggesford
F-PFUG*	Adam RA-14	11		Not known *(Stored 2001)*	Sibsey
F-PYOY	Heintz Zenith 100	52		B L Featherstone *(Noted 1.02)*	Southend
F-PYYV (2)	Rutan LongEz	1046		N W Ruston *(Noted 6.01)*	Shipdham
50-BH	Fisher FP-202 Super Koala	--		K.Riches t/a MUL International	(Guernsey)
				(Stored 12.01)	

HUNGARY

HA-ABP	WSK-PZL Antonov An-2R	1G-185-52	RA-54885	Not known	Hinton-in-the Hedges
			CCCP54885	*(Noted 7.01)*	
HA-ACL	Dornier Do.28G-92 Skyservant	4125		Not known	Sherburn-in-Elmet
				(Crashed 1.00: stored 8.00)	
HA-ACO	Dornier Do.28D-2 Skyservant	4335	G-BWCN	Not known	Hibaldstow
			5N-AYE/D-ILID/9V-BKL/D-ILID	*(Op Wingglider Ltd) (Noted 5.01)*	
HA-MKE	WSK-PZL Antonov An-2R	1G-158-34	UR-07714	Air Foyle	White Waltham
			CCCP-07714	*(Noted 6.01)*	
HA-MKF	WSK-PZL Antonov An-2TP	1G-233-43	OM-248	Transair	White Waltham
			OM-UIN/OK-UIN	*(Noted 11.01)*	
HA-PPY	SOKO SO341 Gazelle	021	HA-LFR	J R Saul	Brierley, S Yorks
	(Aérospatiale c/n 1118)		HA-VLA/YU-HDN/JRV	*(Noted 5.00)*	
HA-YDF	Technoavia SMG-92 Finist	01-0005		G-92 Kereskedelmi.Kft	Hibaldstow
				(Op Wingglider Ltd) (Noted 6.01)	
HA-YFC	Letovlev Let 410-FG	851528		Farnair Hungary	Cark
				(Farner Air/Farnair titles) (Noted 11.01)	

SWITZERLAND

HB-BOU(1)*	Brighton MAB-65 HAFB	MAB-3	G-AWJB	British Balloon Museum & Library	Newbury
HB-CAZ*	Cessna 170A	19674	N5720C	Not known *(Fuselage stored 7.01)*	Perth
HB-EZR	SOCATA TB-10 Tobago	129		Not known *(Noted 7.01)*	Cambridge
HB-FOU	Pilatus PC-12/45	334		Not known *(Noted 7.01)*	Fairoaks
HB-IBX	Gulfstream Gulfstream IV/SP	1183	VR-BDC	Jet Club SA	Farnborough
			N476GA	*(Noted 5.01)*	

HB-IVR	Canadair CL604 Challenger	5318	HB-IKQ	Sintec SA	Luton
			(TC-DHE)/C-FYYH/C-GLXO *(Noted 7.01)*		
HB-LTG	de Havilland DHC-6 Twin Otter 300	628	D-IFLY	Zimex Aviation	Weston on the Green
			LN-BNT	*(Noted 4.01)*	
HB-NAV*	Beagle B.121 Pup Srs.2	B121-155	G-AZCM	RAF Manston History Museum	Manston
				(As "A") (Front fuselage stored 3.00)	
HB-UXL	Bölkow Bö.207	208	(D-EHUM)	Not known *(Noted 10.01)*	Bideford
HB-XFH*	Bell 206 Jet Ranger	1051		Not known *(Gutted pod stored 8.01)*	North Weald
HB-XMO	Enstrom F280C Shark	1213	N5697N	Eastern Atlantic Helicopters	Shoreham
				(Tail boom noted 5.00)	
HB-XOV	Bell 214ST	28129	N13158	Not known *(Stored 2.01)*	Redhill
HB-ZCD	Agusta A109C	7663	N109JN	Not known	Fairoaks
			OO-AAI	*(Op Jet Club) (Noted 12.00)*	

THAILAND

HS-TFS	Boeing 707-321C	19372	9G-SGF	Thai Flying *(Believed sold 1.02)*	Southend
			9G-EBK/9G-ESI/5N-AWO/TF-IUE/HL7427/N462PA		

SAUDI ARABIA

HZ-123	Boeing 707-138B	17696	"17696"	Not known *(Open store 1.02)*	Southend
			HZ-123/N138MJ/N220M/N138TA/(N112TA)/C-FPWV/CF-PWV/VH-EBA/N31239		
HZ-KAA	Gulfstream Gulfstream IV/SP	1294	N416GA	Mawarid Ltd	Farnborough
			HZ-MAL/N416GA	*(Noted 9.01)*	
HZ-SJP3	Canadair CL604 Challenger	5346	N604JP	Jouannou & Parskevaides	Farnborough
			C-GLXS	*(Noted 4.01)*	

ITALY

I-EIXM*	Piper PA-18-<u>135</u> Super Cub	18-3572	MM54-2372	Not known	Kesgrave, Ipswich
			54-2372	*(As "EI-184") (Open store 2.00)*	
I-JULI	Beech 95-B55 Baron	TC-629	HB-GBH	Not known *(Noted 6.01)*	Elstree
I-LELF	SIAI-Marchetti SF.260C	568/41-004		Not known *(Noted 10.01)*	Elstree
I-TOMI*	Nardi FN.305D	--	I-UEBI	Kermit Weeks	Booker
				(Last noted 7.99 - current status unknown)	
I-6052	Jabiru Jabiru UL	--		Not known	Lower Mountpleasant
				(Noted 1.02)	Chatteris

NORWAY

LN-BNM*	Noorduyn AT-16-ND Harvard IIB	14-639	31-329	RAF Museum	Hendon
			R.Dan AF/FE905/42-12392 *(As "FE905" in RAF/RCAF c/s)*		
LN-FOI(3)*	Lockheed L-188C Electra	2005	(LN-MOF)	Air Atlantique Ltd	Coventry
			N31231/ZK-TEA/(ZK-BMP)/N9724C *(DHL c/s: stored 7.00)*		

ARGENTINA

LQ-BLT	MBB Bö.105/CBS	S.863		North East Aircraft Museum	(Sunderland)
	(Non-airworthy pod is original airframe which crashed 13.6.96: shipped to UK and rebuilt with airframe c/n S.915)				
LV-RIE	Nord 1002 Pingouin	240		R.J.Lamplough *(Stored 8.01)*	North Weald

LITHUANIA

LY-ABV	Yakovlev Yak-52	8910004	DOSAAF 106	Not known *(Noted 10.01)*	Sibson
LY-ABW	Antonov An-2	1G-195-26	DOSAAF	Not known	Kemble
			CCCP-68121	*(Noted 7.01)*	
LY-ABZ	Yakovlev Yak-52	9611914		Not known *(Noted 5.01)*	Panshanger
LY-AFA	Yakovlev Yak-52	822608	DOSAAF 110	Not known *"110" (Noted 10.01)*	Barton
LY-AFB	Yakovlev Yak-52	822610	DOSAAF 112	Termikas Co *"112"*	Little Gransden
				(Last noted 11.01)	
LY-AFK	Yakovlev Yak-52	877415	DOSAAF 27	Not known *(Noted 1.01)*	Dunkeswell
LY-AFO	Antonov An-2R	1G-211-42	LY-ADL	Not known	Cork
			CCCP-32683	*(Noted 9.01)*	
LY-AFV	Yakovlev Yak-52	899915	DOSAAF 102	A Fraser *(Noted 11.01)*	RAF Halton
LY-AFZ	Yakovlev Yak-50	842706	DOSAAF 24	Not known *(Noted 7.00)*	(Hampshire?)
LY-AGL*	Yakovlev Yak-55	---		Yak-UK	Little Gransden
	(Built 1987)			*(Noted 10.00)*	
LY-AGN	Yakovlev Yak-52	---	DOSAAF	Not known	Popham
				(Poke Software titles) (Noted 9.01)	
LY-AHB	Yakovlev Yak-52	9812106	DOSAAF	Not known *(Noted 8.01)*	North Weald
LY-AHD	Yakovlev Yak-12	30119	SP-CXW	Not known	Little Gransden
			PLW....	*(Noted 8.01)*	
LY-AHE	Yakovlev Yak-52	822710	DOSAAF 100	Not known *"10"*	Little Gransden
				(Last noted 10.99: current status unknown)	
LY-AHF	Yakovlev Yak-52	---	DOSAAF	Not known	Galway
				(Last noted 5.99: current status unknown)	
LY-AID	Yakovlev Yak-52	822603	DOSAAF 105 (red)	Not known *"105" (Noted 11.01)*	Gloucestershire

LY-AIE	Yakovlev Yak-52	899907	DOSAAF 94	Not known *(Noted 12.01)*	Breighton
LY-AIG	Yakovlev Yak-52	8910106	UkrAF 23 (yellow)	Not known *(Noted 4.01)*	Weston
LY-AIJ*	Yakovlev Yak-52	---	DOSAAF	Not known *(Noted 7.01)*	White Waltham
LY-AJR	Yakovlev Yak-52	9812108		Not known *(Noted 2001)*	Little Gransden
LY-AKC	Yakovlev Yak-52	867212	DOSAAF	Not known *(Noted 12.01)*	Andrewsfield
LY-AKW	Yakovlev Yak-52	855601	DOSAAF 56	A.Harris *"56" (Noted 7.01)*	Exeter
LY-ALJ*	Yakovlev Yak-52	8910115	DOSAAF 132	D.Hawkins *(Noted 11.01)*	Little Gransden
LY-ALO	Yakovlev YAK-52	844815	DOSAAF 135	Sky Associates (UK) Ltd	Little Gransden
				(Noted 2.01)	
LY-ALS	Yakovlev Yak-52	855509	DOSAAF 69	M.Jefferies *"69"*	North Weald
			DOSAAF 49	*"Once a Knight" (Noted 8.01)*	
LY-ALT	Yakovlev Yak-52	822704	DOSAAF 121	Titan Airways Ltd *(Noted 11.01)*	North Weald
LY-ALU	Yakovlev Yak-52	9011107	DOSAAF 124	S.Goodridge *(Noted 7.01)*	Exeter
LY-AMJ	Yakovlev Yak-18T	22202047812	DOSAAF	Not known *(Noted 7.01)*	Earls Colne
LY-AMP	Yakovlev Yak-52	800708	DOSAAF 52	B Brown *"52" (Noted 5.01)*	Sherburn-in-Elmet
	(Offically registered as c/n 800708 but carries c/n plate 856103 - but see LY-ALN above)				
LY-AMS	Yakovlev Yak-52	844306	DOSAAF 51(red)	Willowair Flying Club	Southend
				(Noted 1.02)	
LY-AMU	Yakovlev Yak-52	833901	DOSAAF 42(red)	G.Sharp *"42" (Noted 12.01)*	North Weald
LY-ANG	Yakovlev Yak-50	832409	DOSAAF 81	Not known	North Weald
		(c/n 822409 also quoted)		*(Noted 8.01)*	
LY-ANI	Yakovlev Yak-52	9411812	DOSAAF	Not known	Little Gransden
				(Last noted 7.98: current status unknown)	
LY-ANU*	Yakovlev Yak-52	---		Not known *(Noted 8.01)*	North Weald
LY-AOB	Yakovlev Yak-52	9211517	DOSAAF	M.Schwarz	Kemble
				(Polydron c/s) (Noted 8.01)	
LY-AOC	Yakovlev Yak-52	811308	DOSAAF 30	T Boxhall *(Noted 5.01)*	Headcorn
LY-AOK	Yakovlev Yak-52	877404	DOSAAF 16	I.Vaughan *"IV62" (Noted 8.01)*	Humberside
LY-AOM	Yakovlev Yak-52	878101	DOSAAF 118	Yak UK *(Noted 12.01)*	Teesside
LY-AOO	Yakovlev Yak-18T	22202040425	LY-AOG	Not known *(Damaged 5.01)*	Wickenby
LY-AOT	Yakovlev Yak-50	853101		Not known *(Noted 5.01)*	White Waltham
LY-AOV	Yakovlev Yak-52	NK		Not known *(Noted 9.01)*	North Weald
LY-AOX	Yakovlev Yak-52	833708	DOSAAF 122	J & J Van der Luit	Biggin Hill
	(Previously reported as c/n 877604 - correct c/n not confirmed) (Noted 9.01)				
LY-AOZ*	Yakovlev Yak-52	856907		Not known	Elstree
	(Built 1985)			*(ETPS c/s) (Noted 11.01)*	
LY-APP	Yakovlev Yak-18T	01-03	LY-AOG	Alan Hyatt *(Noted 7.01)*	Leicester
LY-APT	Yakovlev Yak-50	NK		N K Geddes, S Cleary & D Munro	Perth
				(Noted 8.01)	
LY-ASG	Yakovlev Yak-50	812101	DOSAAF	Not known *"50" (Noted 8.01)*	North Weald
LY-FKD	Yakovlev Yak-12M	210999	SP-FKD	M Jefferies	Lee-on-Solent
			SP-AAD(3)/PLW…	*(Noted 7.01)*	
LY-FUT	Yakovlev Yak-52	NK		Not Known *(Noted 2001)*	Haverfordwest
LY-IOO	Yakovlev Yak-50	NK		Not known *(Noted 11.01)*	NK
LY-JDR	Yakovlev Yak-50	792006	DOSAAF	J D Rooney *"Oh Rats"*	White Waltham
				(As "JD-R/J-DR" in US c/s) (Noted 5.01)	

Note: Lithuania is applying for membership of the European Community and is in the process of adopting JAA standards. The Yak-12A&M, -18T, -50, -52 & -56 and Sukhoi Su-26, -29, & -31 aircraft are certified to Russian type certificates. The JAA do not recognise these and they do not meet JAR requirements. Therefore, it is likely that several Yak & Sukhoi aircraft currently with Lithuanian registrations may be cancelled and placed on the Russian civil register".

UNITED STATES OF AMERICA

N1FD	SOCATA TB-200 XL Tobago	1614		Siek Aviation Inc *(Noted 11.01)*	Elstree
N1FY	Cessna 421C Golden Eagle II	421C1067	N345TG	Southern Aircraft Consultancy Inc	Guernsey
				(Noted 12.01)	
N2CL	Piper PA-28RT-201T Turbo Arrow IV		N8333S	Southern Aircraft Consultancy Inc	Elstree
		28R-8131054	N9649N	*(Noted 7.01)*	
N2FU	Learjet Learjet 31	31-027	N30LJ	Wilmington Trust Company	Biggin Hill
			N91201	*(Op Formula One Administration) (Noted 6.01)*	
N2MD	Piper J3C-65 Cub	17521	N70515	Merlin Aire Limited *(Noted 3.00)*	Rendcomb
			NC70515	*(Op V.S.E.Norman) (Kia Cars titles)*	
N3TQ	Cessna 310Q	310Q0752	N1534T	American Aviation Ltd	(Blackbushe)
				(Noted 5.00: cuurent status unknown)	
N4H	Eurocopter AS365N2	6450	ZS-RLI	Otter Corp	Oxford
			G-BUTR	*(Noted 10.00)*	
N5LL	Piper PA-31 Navajo C	31-7812041	N27495	Southern Aircraft Consultancy Inc	Guernsey
				(Noted 12.01)	
N6FL	Latulip LM-3X	LM-3X-1001		J.Parkins	Bidford
	(Rotax 377) *(Aeronca 7AC scale rep)*			*(USAAF c/s) (Stored 9.95 - current status unknown)*	
N6NE	Lockheed Jetstar 731	5006/40	(VR-CCC)	Aerospace Finance Leasing Inc	Southampton
			N6NE/N222Y/N731JS/N227K/N12R/N9280R		
				(Damaged Southampton 27.11.92: on fire dump 7.01)	

N7SY*	Hunting Percival P.57 Sea Prince	P57/71	G-BRFC WP321	Bournemouth Aviation Museum	Bournemouth
N9AY	Cessna 421C Golden Eagle III	421C0844	G-NSGI	Sooty Aviation Inc	Jersey
			N421EL/XA-RAE/N421EB/(N21MW)/N421EB/N2659Z *(Noted 12.01)*		
N11EV(2)	Cessna T303 Crusader	T30300133	G-BXRI HB-LNI/(N5143C)	Auster Aviation *(Noted 12.01)*	Guernsey
N12FU	Learjet Learjet 60	60-027	N4230S XA-ICA/N4027S	Wilmington Trust Company Owner *(Noted 6.01)*	Biggin Hill
N12NM	Cessna 501 Citation I	501-0257	OE-FLY	Pektron Aviation Inc	Gamston
			N500NW/(N992NW)/N2631V *(Op L'Equipe Air) (Noted 10.01)*		
N12ZP	American Lightship A-60	012		Virgin Lightships Inc *"Spirit of Europe 2"(Goodyear titles) (Noted 3.01)*	(Rednal)
N15FH	Cessna 340A II	340A0722	G-CMAC	Kestrelair Inc	Liverpool
			G-JIMS/G-PETE/N2667N *(Op F.R.Foran & D.Hanley)*	*(Last noted 8.99: current status unknown)*	
N18E*	Boeing 247D	1722	NC18E NC18/NC13340	Science Museum Air Transport Coln &	Storage Facility Wroughton
N18SF	Agusta A109A Mk.II	7275	F-GDPR	Markoss Aviation Inc *(Op Castle Air Charters) (Noted 9.01)*	Liskeard
N18V	Beechcraft UC-43-BH Traveler	6869	NC18	R.J.Lamplough	North Weald
			Bu 32898/FT507/44-67761 *(As "DR828/PB1") (Noted 8.01)*		
N19F	Cessna 337A Super Skymaster *(Robertson STOL conversion)*	33700289	N6289F	Southern Aircraft Consultancy Inc *(Noted 4.01)*	Fakenham
N19GL	Brantly B.2B	2004		Southern Aircraft Consultancy Inc *(Noted 1.01)*	Fairoaks
N20RJ	Beechcraft H35 Bonanza	D-5193	N7945D	Tickton Inc *(Noted 7.01)*	Shobdon
N20UK	Mooney M.20F Executive	22-1380	N9155J G-BDVU	R D Garretson *(Noted 10.01)*	Biggin Hill
N21PM	SNCAN Stampe SV-4C	556		J T Meyers *(On rebuild 6.01)*	Roughay Farm Bishops Waltham
N22CG	Cessna 441 Conquest II	441-0119		Jubilee Airways Inc *(Op M.Klinge) (Noted 7.01)*	Prestwick
N25PJ	Cessna 340A II	340A0912	HB-LNM LN-TEA/N27026	Southern Aircraft Consultancy Inc *(Noted 12.01)*	Guernsey
N25PR	Piper PA-30-160 Twin Comanche B	30-1511	G-AVPR N8395Y	PSL Aviation *(Noted 3.01)*	Gloucestershire
N26HE	Cessna 421C Golden Eagle II	421C0687		Uniphase Corp *(Noted 5.01)*	Fairoaks
N26PJ	Piper PA-30-160 Twin Comache B	30-1477	G-BAWU(2)	Southern Aircraft Consultancy Inc	Guernsey
			(G-BAWV)(1)/9J-RFW/ZS-FAM/N8332Y *(Noted 12.01)*		
N27BG	Cessna 340A	340A0656		Traca Inc *(Op B Gregory) (Noted 11.00)*	Cardiff
N27MW	Beechcraft B58 Baron	TH-995		B58 Aviation Inc *(Noted 5.01)*	Fairoaks
N29KF	SOCATA TB-20 Trinidad	2003		Southern Aircraft Consultancy Inc *(Noted 12.01)*	Jersey
N30NW	Piper PA-30-160 Twin Comanche	30-312	G-ASON N7273Y	R S Barnett *(Noted 10.01)*	Norwich
N31NB	Piper PA-31 Turbo Navajo B	31-7401239	G-OSFT	Navajo Aviation Inc	Old Buckenham
			G-MDAS/5N-AEP/G-BJCZ/N61427 *(Op N.Brown) (Noted 6.00)*		
N31RB	Grumman-American AA-5B Tiger	AA5B-0156		Southern Aircraft Consultancy Inc *(Op Forest Aviation Ltd) (Noted 8.01)*	Bournemouth
N32LE	Piper PA-32R-301T Turbo Saratoga SP	32R-8329016		Southern Aircraft Consultancy Inc *(Noted 9.01)*	Southend
N33CJ	Cessna 525 CitationJet	525-0245	N5214J	William Aviation Inc *(Noted 12.01)*	Blackpool
N33EW	Mitsubishi MU-2B-60	1519SA	N331W N33TW/N434MA	Florida Express Corp *(Op King Aviation) (Noted 11.01)*	Southend
N34FA	SOCATA TB-20 Trinidad	866	G-BPFG	Southern Aircraft Consultancy Inc *(Noted 11.01)*	Elstree
N35AL	Piper PA-34-220T Seneca IV	3447014	D-GLPE	Able Liston Aviation *(Noted 12.01)*	Jersey
N36NB	Beechcraft A36 Bonanza	E-2274	F-GKTZ N7249H	Air Bickerton Inc *(Noted 1.02)*	Biggin Hill
N37US	Piper PA-34-200T Seneca II	34-8070111	G-PLUS	Southern Aircraft Consultancy Inc *(Noted 12.01)*	Jersey
N37WC	Cessna 401	401-0183	N917WS N4083Q	Flywest Inc *(Op Durston Air Service) (Noted 9.01)*	Blackpool
N39N	Cessna 560 Citation V	560-0243	N12890	Longborough Aviation *(Noted 7.01)*	Gloucestershire
N40D	Stolp SA-100 Starduster 1	4258549		Cesna Inc *(Noted 5.01)*	Rochester
N41AK	Beechcraft F90 King Air	LA-188	N41CK N6429M	Southern Aircraft Consultancy Inc *(Noted 12.01: reserved as N46BA?)*	Guernsey
N41FT	PiperPA-39 Twin Comanche C/R	39-59	G-BZLW	Southern Aircraft Consultancy Inc	Biggin Hill
			ZS-NLF/ZS-MRH/ZS-IKG/N8904Y *(Noted 9.01)*		
N42FW	Beech E33 Bonanza	CD-1199	N7682N	Southern Aircraft Consultancy Inc *(Op Feroz Wadia) (Noted 8.01)*	Kirknewton
N45AW	Piper PA-28RT-201T Turbo Arrow IV	28R-8431003	N43230 N9548N	Andair Inc *(Op Powersway Aviation) (Noted 7.01)*	Turweston

N45CD(2)	Piper PA-28-161 Warrior II	28-7916467	PH-AND N2841J	Hill Air Inc *(Noted 9.01)*	Sigwells, Somerset
N46BA				<u>*See N41AK above*</u>	
N46EA*	Percival P.66 Pembroke C.1 *(Regd with c/n K66-046)*	P66/83	8452M XK885	P.G.Vallance Ltd *(Gatwick Aviation Museum)*	Charlwood, Surrey
N47DD(2)*	Republic P47D-30-RA Thunderbolt	399-55731	N47DD Peru AF FAP119/45-49192 *"Oregon's Britannia"*	Imperial War Museum Collection/American Air Museum *(As "226413/UN-Z")*	Duxford
N47DG*	Republic P-47G Thunderbolt	21962	N42354 42-25068	Flying A Services *(Stored in container 8.01)*	North Weald
N47FK	Douglas C-47A-35-DL Dakota III	9700	EC-FNS EC-187/N2669A/C-FEEX/CF-EEX/N308FN/N3PG/N3W/N7V/NC49538/42-23838	Kilo Aviation Inc *(Op The Dakota Club) (As "292912/LN-F") (Noted 8.01)*	North Weald
N47SA	Brantly B.2B	451	N199BB(1) G-ATGH	W F Chmura *(Current status unknown)*	St Just
N52NW	Gulfstream G1159 Gulfstream II	52	N211MT N711MT/(N52TJ)/(N52NE)/N5SJ/N38KM/N69SF/C-FFNM/CF-FNM	Northwestern Aircraft Capital Corp *(Op Global Trading Ltd) (Noted 1.01)*	Bristol
N55AE	Beechcraft 95-C55 Baron	TE-84		Avcorp Inc *(Noted 1.02)*	Jersey
N55BN	Beechcraft 95-B55 Baron	TC-1572	G-KCAS G-KCEA/N2840W	Snowadam Inc *(Op C.Butler) (Noted 12.00)*	White Waltham
N55EN	Beechcraft 95-E55 Baron	TE-942		Monckton Byng Inc *(Noted 11.01)*	Elstree
N58GT	Beech B58 Baron *(winglets)*	TH-1090	HB-GIK	Swiftair Inc *(Noted 10.01)*	Elstree
N59SD	MDH MD 369E	0019E	SE-JBH	Sky Dock Helicopter Holdings Inc *(Op Nunkeeling Ltd)* *(Current status unknown)*	Elloughton, Humberside
N59VT	Beechcraft K35 Bonanza	D-5897	D-EMEF	Southern Aircraft Consultancy Inc *(Noted 10.01)*	Kemble
N60GM	Cessna 421C Golden Eagle III	421C0828		Southern Aircraft Consultancy Inc *(Noted 10.01)*	Ronaldsway
N60NB	Mitsubishi MU-2B-60 Marquise	1528SA	5Y-VIZ	Dogfox Airways Inc *(Noted 12.01)*	Dublin
N60VB	Ted Smith Aerostar 600A *(Machen Superstar conversion)*	60-0182-080	N7513S	Southern Aircraft Consultancy Inc *(Noted 12.00)*	Henstridge
N61AN	Reims Cessna F182Q Skylane	F18200127	G-IFAB OO-ELM/(OO-HNU)	Southern Aircraft Consultancy Inc *(Noted 8.01)*	Stapleford
N61HB(2)	Piper PA-34-220T Seneca <u>V</u>	3449217	G-CBAA N53445	HBC Aviation Inc *(Noted 12.01)*	Jersey
N64MS	Piper PA-28-180 Cherokee Challenger	28-7305466		M.Swan *(Noted 2.02)*	Andrewsfield
N64GA	Beech 200 Super King Air	BB-790	D-IAMB F-GIAX/N3814B	Imperial Consolidated Holdings Inc *(Op JJB Sports) (Noted 10.01)*	Blackpool
N65JF	Piper PA-28-181 Archer <u>II</u>	28-7990140	N2087C	Southern Aircraft Consultancy Inc *(Noted 8.01)*	Nottingham
N65TD	IAI 1125A Astra-SPX	093		Helios Ltd *(Noted 8.01)*	North Weald
N66SG	Learjet Learjet 45	45-073	N65U	C E Rodriguez *(Op Sagesoft) (Noted 7.01)*	Luton
N66SW	Cessna 340	340-0011	N5035Q	Cabledraw Inc *(Noted 10.01)*	Elstree
N70AA	Beechcraft 70 Queen Air	LB-35	G-KEAA G-REXP/G-AYPC	Metals & Alloys International *(Op Trygon Ltd) (Noted 12.01)*	Sleap
N70VB	Ted Smith Aerostar 600A	60-0446-150	C-GVHQ N9805Q	Southern Aircraft Consultancy Inc *(Noted 7.01)*	Thruxton
NX71MY	Vickers Vimy rep *(Op Greenco (UK) Ltd/K.Snell) (Active 8.01)*	01		Aviation Adventures LLC *(As "G-EAOU")* <u>*(See SECTION 8, Part 2 (iii))*</u>	Kemble
N71VE	Rockwell Commander 690A	11043	N71VT N2VQ/N2VA	Airbourne Inc *(Noted 7.01)*	Gamston
N74BF	Stoddard-Hamilton Glasair	2274		Netkonect Communications *(Noted 7.01)*	Bournemouth
N74DC	Pitts S-2A Special	2228	I-ALAT	H J Seery *(Op D.Cockburn) (Noted 11.01)*	Norwich
N74PM	Agusta A109C	7636	I-SEIN	Ortac Inc *(Op Huktra UK Ltd) (Noted 5.01)*	Hawarden
N75*	Hanriot HD.1	75	G-AFDX OO-APJ/H-1/75	RAF Museum *(As "HD-75" in Belgian AF c/s)*	Hendon
N75TL	Boeing-Stearman A75N1 (N2S-4) Kaydet	75-3616	N5148N Bu.37869	Pluto Inc *(As "669" in US Army c/s: noted 5.00)*	Headcorn
N76TH	Sikorsky S-76A	76-0373	VR-CWH I-DVRM	Turbine Helicopters Inc *(Noted 7.01)*	Leeds-Bradford
N77XB	Piper PA-31-310 Navajo	31-583	G-AXXB N7XB/N6645L/G-AXXB/N6645L	Spacetronics Inc *(Noted 9.01)*	Denham
N77YY	Piper PA-32R-301T Saratoga II TC	3257120	G-LLYY N4165C	Flying Start Aviation Inc *(Op M J Start) (Noted 12.01)*	Guernsey
N78HB	Aviat A-1B Huskey	2066	N115BB G-FOFF/N115BB	HBC Aviation Inc *(Op T Holding) (Noted 10.01)*	King's Farm, Thurrock

N79AP	Beechcraft 58P Baron	TJ-206	VH-ORP ZK-TML/N6648Z	Aircraft Guaranty LLC *(Op R & B Services Ltd) (Noted 5.01)*	Southend
N79EL	Beechcraft 400A Beechjet	RK-214		Edra Lauren Leasing Corp *(Op DFS Furniture) (Noted 10.01)*	East Midlands
N79GW	Cessna 340A	340A-0680	D-IKOM	Bee Bee Aviation Inc *(Noted 6.01)*	Elstree
N80BA	Pitts S-1A Special	648-4		T.D.Stronge *(Crashed 11.7.99: stored 12.99: current status unknown)*	Newtownards
N80JN	Mitsubishi MU-2J	626	EC-GLU OY-ATZ/SE-GHY/N476MA	Aircraft Guaranty Title Group *(Noted 9.01)*	Waterford
N80RF	Beechcraft 60 Duke	P-17	(G-BMSO) I-DUKA/F-BRAX/HB-GDO	Goldwing Aviation Inc *(Op MLP Aviation/E.Lundquist) (Noted 10.00)*	Fairoaks
N83WA	Gulfstream 695B	96063	N61508 VH-LTI	Wal-Mart Stores Inc *(Noted 7.01)*	Leeds-Bradford
N88PL	Piper PA-46-310P Malibu	46-8508099	N9605N	Clarkco Ltd *(Op D.Clark) (Noted 7.00)*	Grove Fields Farm, Wellesbourne Mntfrd
N90SA	Reims Cessna F172M	F17201402	PH-TWS OY-BUL	W F Chmura *(Noted 8.01)*	St Just
N90U	Piper PA-46-350P Malibu Mirage	4622106		Speedair Inc *(Noted 4.01)*	Gloucestershire
N93GS	Grumman G.21A Goose (Pratt & Whitney R-985)	B-76	C-FBAE CF-BAE/CF-FEM/RCAF 392/Bu.37823	Caribbean Clipper Inc *(Op T.Friedrich) (Noted 7.01)* *"Caribbean Clipper"*	(Isle of Islay)
N94SA	Citabria 7ECA Champion	227	OY-AUG D-EFLO	Southern Aircraft Consultancy Inc *(Noted 8.01)*	Kilkeel
N95D	Piper PA-34-220T Seneca V	3449060	N9506N	Zeta Aviation Inc *(Noted 7.01)*	Welshpool
N97RJ	Piper PA-31 Turbo Navajo	31-7300956	G-SKKB G-BBDS/N7565L	Transair Aviation Inc *(Noted 7.01)*	Earls Colne
N99ET	SOCATA TB-10 Tobago	226	G-BJDG F-BNGR	E.A.Terris *(Noted 6.00)*	Oxford
N100UP	Dassault Falcon 900B	44	HB-IVY	UPC Aviation Services Inc *(Noted 1.01)*	RAF Northolt
N101AP	Beechcraft B200 King Air	BB-1004		Pacific Diversified Investments Inc *(Op Nigel Webb) (Last noted 10.99: current status unknown)*	Cranfield
N104WF	Cessna P210N Centurion	P21000033		D O Miller *(Noted 7.01)*	Exeter
N109AB	Agusta A109E Power	11015		Monument Aircraft Services Inc *(Noted 8.01)*	Rhyader
N109AR	Agusta A109A	7390		Adrian Raymond Aviation Inc *(Op Castle Air Charters) (Noted 8.01)*	Liskeard
N109GR	Agusta A109E Power	11043		Castle Helicopters Inc *(Op Castle Air Charters) (Noted 8.01)*	Liskeard
N109TW	Agusta A109C	7650	D-HCKM	TWR Aviation Inc *(Op Tom Walkinshaw Racing) (Noted 9.01)*	Oxford
N109UK	Agusta A109A-II	7304	F-GKGV N109PS/(N109FS)/N109FM	M W Helicopters Inc *(Noted 7.01)*	Stapleford
N109WF	Agusta A109A MK.II	7298		Agusta 109 LLC *(Op Lenham Racing) (Noted 11.01)*	Elstree
N112WG	Westland WG-30-100	012		The Helicopter Museum	Weston-super-Mare
N114WG	Westland WG-30-100	014	G-EFIS G-17-18	The Helicopter Museum	Weston-super-Mare
N116WG	Westland WG-30-100	016	(G-BLLG)	Oil Petroleum Training Industry Board *(Instruction use 2001)*	(Montrose)
N118WG	Westland WG-30-100	018		The Helicopter Museum	Weston-super-Mare
N123AX	Piper PA-32R-301 Saratoga IIHP	3246060	G-LLTT N9283P	Axis Aircraft Leasing Inc *(Noted 4.01)*	Gloucestershire
N123SA	Piper PA-18-150 Super Cub	18-1372		Southern Aircraft Consultancy Inc *(Noted 8.01)*	North Weald
N124CD	Cirrus Design SR-20	1011		Southern Aircraft Consultancy Inc *(Noted 6.01)*	Denham
N125GP	Learjet Learjet 31A	31A-162	N162LJ N525GP	TR Airways Inc *(Op Damon Hill) (Noted 11.00)*	Dublin
N125XX	British Aerospace HS.125-700A	NA0254 & 257075	N124AR N125TR/N125AM/(G-BHKF)/G-5-13	Surewings Inc *(Op Aviation/Ambrion Aviation)* *(Last noted 6.99: current status unknown)*	Luton
N128M	Dassault Falcon 50EX	276	N159M F-WWHB	Motorola Inc *(Noted 11.00)*	Farnborough
N132CK	Cessna 421A	421A0038	EI-TCK G-AXAW/(EI-TCK)/G-AXAW/N2238Q	Southern Aircraft Consultancy Inc *(Noted 4.01)*	Weston
N133H	Agusta A109C	7609	N1NQ	Thames Aviation Inc *(Op Graff Aviation Ltd) (Noted 5.01)*	Fairoaks
N135XX	Piper PA-20-135 Pacer	20-1107	G-PAXX (G-ARCE)/F-BLLA/CN-TDJ/F-DADR	D.W. & M.R.Grace *(Noted 5.01)*	Wellcross Grange, Slinfold
N139DB	Piper PA-23-250 Aztec E	27-4611	G-AYUL N13992	Pyramis Inc *(Op Earlsfield Investments) (Noted 11.01)*	White Waltham
N139JV	Commander Acft Commander 114TC	20034		LCM Airways *(Noted 8.01)*	St Just
N141CA	Piper Aerostar 601P	61P-0711-7963343		R V Richter *(Noted 7.01)*	Fairoaks

N142TW	Beech 58 Baron	TH-1841		Specialized Aircraft Services Inc	Fairoaks
				(Noted 11.00)	
N145DF(2)	Cessna S550 Citation II	S550-0018	N1AF	Star Aviation Ltd	Luton
			N814CC/N501NB/(N1259K) *(Noted 2.01)*		
N145DR	Piper PA-34-220T Seneca	3449240		Cleevewood Aviation Inc	Gloucestershire
				(Noted 1.02)	
N146FL	Beech F90 King Air	LA-59	G-FLTI	Keep Holdings	Guernsey
			N7P	*(Operated Flightline) (Noted 1.02)*	
N147BK	Piper PA-46-350P Malibu Mirage	4636236		Brenkmaps Ltd *(Noted 12.01)*	Guernsey
N147DC	Douglas C-47A-75-DL Dakota	19347	G-DAKS	Aces High US Inc	North Weald
			TS423/"108841/"KG374"/"G-AGHY"/TS423/42-100884 *(As "07") (Noted 8.01)*		
N150JC	Beechcraft A35 Bonanza	D-2084	N8674A	R.M.Hornblower	Southend
				(Substantially complete & stored mid 2001)	
N154CD	Cirrus Design SR20	1053		Blue Morning Aviation *(Noted 1.02)*	Biggin Hill
N156LG	American Blimp A-1-50	106		American Blimp Corp *(Noted 4.01)*	Cardington
N158JC	Aero Vodochody L-39ZO	831201	F-ZVLS	Avstar Inc	Hawarden
			N4312E/Libyan AF 8201 *(Stored 2.00)*		
N167B	Douglas A-26B Invader	27881	44-34602	Joda LLC	North Weald
				(Op Scandinavian Historic Flight Ltd) (Noted 8.01)	
N167F	North American P-51D Mustang	122-40417	CF-PCZ	Joda LLC *"Detroit Miss"*	North Weald
			N6320T/RCAF 9279/44-73877 *(Op Scandinavian Historic Flight Ltd)*		
				(As "473877") (Noted 8.01)	
N172AM	Cessna 172M Skyhawk II	17264993	G-BXHG	R S Barnett *(Noted 11.01)*	Norwich
N176AF	Cessna 650 Citation III	650-0176		General Electric Capital Corp	Coventry
				(Op Ilmor Engineering) (Noted 2001)	
N180BB	Cessna 180K	18053103		Southern Aircraft Consultancy Inc	Humberside
				(Noted 9.01)	
N180FN	Cessna 180K	18053201		Noise Abroad Inc (Noted 10.01)	(Ronaldsway)
N181WW	Beagle B.206 Srs.1	B.018	G-BCJF	Southern Aircraft Consultancy Inc	Biggin Hill
			N181WW/G-BCJF/XS773 *(Noted 7.01)*		
N182VV	Cessna 182P	18264973		Eastern Atlantic Helicopters Inc	Southend
				(Noted 1.02)	
N184CD	Cirrus Design SR20	1087		Plane Holdings Inc *(Noted 5.01)*	Turweston
N187SA	Piper PA-28R Cherokee Arrow II	28R-7235139	G-BOJH	Southern Aircraft Consultancy Inc	Glasgow
			N2821T	*"Knight of the Thistle" (Noted 8.01)*	
N189SA	Piper PA-31-325 Navajo C/R	31-7512045	G-BMGH	Southern Aircraft Consultancy Inc	Southend
			ZS-LEU/N8493/A2-CAT *(Stored 8.01)*		
N191ME	Cessna T206H	T20608188		Anglo Irish Air Services	Weston
				(Noted 6.01)	
N195AL	Beech 300 Super King Air	FA-102	C-FPCC	Woosie Aviation Inc *(Noted 12.01)*	Jersey
N196B*	North American F-86A-5-NA Sabre	151-43611	48-0242	Imperial War Museum Collection/American Air Museum	
				(As "8242/FU-242" in USAF c/s)	Duxford
N198SL	Cessna 550 Citation Bravo	550-0835	N835CB	Sealpoint Aviation (USA) Inc	Jersey
				(Op Aviation Beauport) (Noted 1.01)	
N200UP	Dassault Falcon 50	55	N96UH	UIH Turkey c/o Streamline Partnership Ltd	
			N300CR/N625CR/N332MQ/N332MC/N1CN/(N30NO/N839F/N73FJ/F-WZHU		
				(Op UPC Aviation) (Noted 1.01)	RAF Northolt
N201XJ	Mooney M.20J	24-0494		M E Irvin *(Noted 2.01)*	Shoreham
N201YK	Mooney M.20J	24-0518		Conmacair Inc	Cumbernauld
				(Op W Fraser) (Noted 5.01)	
N202AA	Cessna 421C Golden Eagle	421C1015		Simply Living Ltd *(Noted 11.01)*	Elstree
N206NS	Bell 206B-3 JetRanger III	4474		Biztech International Inc	(Swindon)
				(Noted 6.01)	
N210MP	Cessna T210N Turbo Centurion II	21063193	(G-BPGO)	Southern Aircraft Consultancy Inc	(Denham)
			N210MP	*(Op Welback Estates Ltd) (Noted 8.00)*	
N210SA	Maule M.7-235B	23062C			
N213CT	Beechcraft C90-1 King Air	LJ-1028	VP-CCT	Southern Aircraft Consultancy Inc	Oxford
			VR-CCT/N6420H/G-BKFY *(Op Corgi Toys) (Noted 5.01)*		
N220SC	Piper PA-31T Cheyenne II	31T-8120041	N79CA	Entrechato Inc *(Noted 12.01)*	Guernsey
			N8361T/N816SW/N818SW/N2604X *(Op Sark International Airways)*		
N220TW(2)	Canadair CL601-3A Challenger	5067	9A-CRT	TWR Aero Inc	Oxford
			9A-CRO/N603CC/C-GLXF *(Noted 9.01)*		
N228CX	SOCATA TBM-700	084		Turbine Aviation Inc	Southend
				(Op B.Holmes) (Noted 1.02)	
N228TM	Raytheon Hawker 800XP	258458		Wells Fargo Bank Northwest NA	Cork
				(Noted 6.00)	
N235PF	Piper PA-28-235 Charger	28-7410083	OO-DDC	Southern Aircraft Consultancy Inc	Southend
				(Noted 8.01)	
N237TD*	Beech 95 Travelair	TD-237	HB-GOC	Aerodynamics Worldwide Inc	Cardiff
				(Cancelled by FAA 6.01 as sold in UK: noted 9.01)	
N240JS	ATR 42-320	240	5Y-JNT	Jet Systems	Exeter
			XA-RUC/N240JS/XA-RUC/F-WWEG *(Stored 7.01)*		
N240SA	Cessna 337D Super Skymaster	337-1070	G-AXFG	Southern Aircraft Consultancy Inc	Gloucestershire
			OY-BVP/G-AXFG/N86081 *(Noted 6.01)*		

N243SA	Piper PA-22-108 Colt	22-8376	G-ARKR	Southern Aircraft Consultancy Inc *(Noted 10.01)*	Booker
N250SM	Cessna 560XL Citation Excel	560-5167	N5188N	Pilot International *(Noted 12.01)*	Jersey
N250TB	Piper PA-23-250 Aztec D	27-4577	G-VHFA	Motor City Aviation LLC c/o Computaplane *(Stored 5.01)*	Prestwick
N250TP	Beechcraft A36TP Bonanza *(Allison 250-B17)*	E-2408	N416HC N600TT/N3107K	Minster Enterprises Inc *(Noted 7.01)*	Tatenhill
N251JS	Gulfstream G1159 Gulfstream II	251	N36GS N567A/N9PY/N9PG/N944H	Eurolynx Corporation *(Noted 2.01)*	Stansted
N260QB	Aerotek Pitts S-2S Special	3002		Western Aviation Leasing Inc *(Op Baker Petroleum) (Noted 12.99) (Current status unknown)*	Exeter
N273TB	Beech 58 Baron	TH-305		Rogers Aviation Inc *(Noted 6.01)*	Welshpool
N277CD	Cessna 210L Centurion	21059663	SE-IGY N1163Q	Bonner-Davies Aviation Inc *(Noted 2.01)*	White Waltham
N280SA	Maule MX-7-180 Star Rocket	11070C	G-BSKT	Southern Aircraft Consultancy Inc	NK
N281Q	Enstrom F.28A	266		M A Crook *(Wreck stored for spares 1999: current status unknown)*	Goodwood
N285RA	Consolidated PBY-6A Catalina	2087	N212DM G-BPFY/N212DM/G-BPFY/N212DM/C-FHNH/CF-HNH/F-ZBAV/N5555H/N2864D/Bu.64017	Randsburg Corporation *(Noted 8.01)*	North Weald
NC285RS*	North American Navion	NK		South East Aviation Enthusiasts Group *"My Way" (Crashed 11.6.79: fuselage only 4.00)*	New Ross, Co.Wexford
N287AB	Cessna 500 Citation I	500-0287	PT-WHZ N31LH/OY-CGO/N57MB/N73LL/N287CC/(N5287J)	Wrangler Aviation Corp *(Noted 9.01)*	Filton
N295SS	Piper PA-46-350P Malibu Mirage	4636174		Speedbird Aviation Inc *(Noted 8.01)*	Bournemouth
N300GB	Beechjet 400A	RK-262		Wells Fargo Bank Northwest NA *(Op Liberty Aviation) (Noted 10.00)*	Leeds-Bradford
N310QQ	Cessna 310Q	310Q0695	G-BAUE N8048Q	Veryord Inc *(Op H Gold) (Noted 11.01)*	Elstree
N312CJ	Cessna 525A CitationJet	525A0031		JCT Inc *(Noted 9.01)*	Ronaldsway
N314BG	North American P-51D-20NA Mustang *(Regd with c/n 122-39599 ex C-FBAU/44-73140: this crashed & dbf 7.7.84: possibly a composite rebuild: stored 8.01)*	--	C-GZQX	Ice Strike Corporation *(Op Flying A Services/David Arnold)*	North Weald
N320MR	Piper PA-30 Twin Comanche C *(Mod.to PA-39 C/R status)*	30-1917	G-CALV(2) G-AZFO/N8761Y	N320MR Inc *(Noted 2.01)*	Elstree
N322MC	MDH MD 369E	0224E		AAA Flight Inc *(Op Jepar Rotorcraft) (Noted 8.01)*	Blackpool/ Gloucestershire
N322RJ	Beech 60 Duke	P-322		Aircraft Guaranty Title Corp *(Noted 5.01)*	Waterford
N338DB	Piper PA-46-500TP Meridian	4697111		Anglo-American Airmotive Inc *(Noted 12.01)*	Jersey
N340SC	Cessna 340	340-0363		E C Rodriguez *(Noted 12.01)*	North Weald
N340YP	Cessna 340A II	340A0990	VR-CHR G-OCAN/D-ICIC/(N3970C)	ILEA Inc *(Noted 9.01)*	Biggin Hill
N341D	Beech 60 Duke	P-397		Mentor Adi Recruitment *(Noted 12.01)*	Teesside
N350UK	Aérospatiale AS350B Ecureuil	1244	F-GJYG	Starbuc Ltd *(Noted 3.01)*	Stapleford
N359DW	Piper PA-30 Twin Comanche C	30-770	G-ATET N230ET	L W Durrell *(Noted 12.01)*	Jersey
N363DG	SOCATA TB-10 Tobago	1901	G-GINS	Ginsberg Aviation *(Noted 7.01)*	Ronaldsway
N369AN	Cessna 182S	18280696		Air View Ltd *(Noted 12.01)*	Jersey
N370SA	Piper PA-23-250 Aztec F	27-8054005	G-BKVN N6959A	Southern Aircraft Consultancy Inc *(Op B K Pugh) (Noted 1.02)*	Guernsey/Southend
N372SA	Cessna 172RG Cutlass II	172RG0550	G-BHVC N5515V	Southern Aircraft Consultancy Inc *(Noted 5.01)*	High Cross
N375SA	Piper PA-34-200T Seneca II	34-7670002	G-BMWP N3946X	Southern Aircraft Consultancy Inc *(Noted 7.01)*	Gamston
N385AT	Cessna T303	T303-00195	G-BKXG N9616C	Nitor Aviation Inc *(Noted 7.01)*	Denham
N395TC	Commander Acft Commander 114TC	20003		BNZ Aviation Inc *(Noted 7.01)*	Denham
N402R	Cessna 402B II	402B1364	G-BTVY N402R/N888EE/(N4609A)	Not known *(Last noted 1.97: current status unknown)*	Cardiff
N413JB	Cameron O-84 HAFB	723		Balloon Preservation Group *"Autumn Fall"*	Kirdford
N414FZ	Cessna 414RAM	414-0175	G-AZFZ N8245Q	Lizard Aviation Inc *(Noted 12.01)*	Jersey
N417RK	Piper PA-46-350P Malibu Mirage	4636249	G-BYSO N9533N	K-Air Aviation Inc *(Noted 12.01)*	Jersey
N418WS	Beech 58 Baron	TH-1967	N4467N	Millburn World Travel Services Two Inc *(Noted 11.01)*	Edinburgh
N421CA	Cessna 421C Golden Eagle III	421C0153		USA Marine Inc *(Noted 10.00)*	Gamston
N421N	Cessna 421C Golden Eagle III	421C1235		IMVA Aviation Inc *(Noted 5.01)*	Humberside

N423RS	Consolidated-Vultee PBY-5A Catalina	1785	C-FJJG CF-JJG/N4002A/BuAer48423	Southern Aircraft Consultancy Inc *(Op Super Catalina Restoration)* *(As "JV828" of 210 Sqdn in RAF c/s) (Noted 11.01)*	Lee-on-Solent
N425DR	Cessna 425 Conquest I	425-0199	VP-BDR	Intercity Co Inc *(Noted 6.01)*	Booker
N425RR	Rockwell Commander 690A	11259	VP-BRR SE-KYY/OY-BEO/SE-IYX/OY-BEO/N57090	Rami Aviation Inc *(Op Mann Aviation) (Noted 5.01)*	Fairoaks
N425TV	Cessna 425 Corsair	425-0176	ZS-LDR N6873T	Intersection Inc *(Op Apex Tubulars Ltd) (Noted 1.02)*	Aberdeen
N429PK	Cessna 525 CitationJet	525-0429		E C Rodriguez *(Noted 4.01)*	Oxford
N431WH	Bell 430	49066		Southern Aircraft Services *(Op Westair) (Noted 7.01)*	Shannon
N448JC	Cessna 525 CitationJet	525-0448		Jet-Care Aviation *(Noted10.01)*	Bournemouth
N454CC	Bell UH-1E *(C/n 6199 quoted also)*	6200	Bu155344	S W Firczak *(Op Independent Helicopters Ltd) (Noted 7.00)*	Howth, Co Dublin
N473BS	Piper PA-28RT-201T Turbo Arrow IV	28R-8631003	G-BNYY N25WA/N77860/G-BNYY/N9129X/N9517N	Sales Force Management Inc *(Op B.Strickland) (Noted 1.02)*	Southend
N480DS	Enstrom 480	5045		Eastern Atlantic Helicopters *(Noted 7.01)*	Gloucestershire
N480E	Enstrom F480	5001	HB-XUX	S W Freeborn *(Noted 9.01)*	Jersey
N485A	Enstrom F480	5029		Eastern Atlantic Helicopters *(Noted 9.01)*	Tadcaster
N485ED	Piper PA-23-250 Aztec C	27-3864	G-BAED N6567Y	Southern Aircraft Consultancy Inc *(Noted 9.01)*	Waterford
N492PA	Beech B90 KingAir	LJ492		Incat Aviation Inc *(Noted 12.01)*	Jersey
N494AT	British Aerospace BAe 125-800XP	258103/NA0404		Vodaphone Americas Asia Inc *(Noted 4.01)*	Farnborough
N499MS	Piper PA-28-181 Archer III	2843166	G-EPJM N41268	MS Aviation *(Noted 12.01)*	Jersey
N500AV	Piper PA-24-260 Comanche	24-4805	OO-SAP	Southern Aircraft Consultancy Inc *(Noted 6.01)*	Blackbushe
N500LN	Howard 500 *(Lockheed PV-1 Ventura [5560] conversion)*	500-113	N381RD N206G/N200G/N539N/SAAF 6417/FP579/Bu.34670	Western Aviation Leasing Inc *(Noted 7.01)* *(Op Baker Petroleum)*	Exeter
N500UD	PA-31 Turbo Navajo	31-761	G-EEAC G-SKKA/G-FOAL/G-RMAE/G-BAEG/N7239L	Universal Direct Inc *(Noted 7.01)* t/a Universal Consumer Products	Sleap
N501VH	Cessna 500 Citation I	500-0044	N501WW PH-CTY/OO-ATS/N501WW/VR-CWW/N892CA/N712US/N942B/N544CC	Personal Airliner Ltd *(Noted 4.01)*	Biggin Hill
N502TC	Piper PA-30-160 Twin Comanche	30-881	G-BMSX N502TC/N7802Y	Southern Aircraft Consultancy Inc *(Noted 7.01)*	Blackbushe
N508MV	Beech B200 Super King Air	BB-877	N711BU N4CQ/N4C/N877AJ/N3837S	Ziff Air Services Inc *(Noted 4.01)*	Farnborough
N510PS	Cessna 310N	310N0054	G-AWTA EI-ATB/N4154Q	Island Seaplane Inc *(Op Heliscott Ltd) (Noted 6.01)*	Walton Wood, Pontefract
N511VA	MD Helicopters MD 600N	RN023	G-SIVB	Marks Parks Inc *(Noted 8.01)*	Shoreham
N519MC	Piper PA-28-140 Cherokee Cruiser	28-7325519	G-BBID	R Lobell *(Noted 10.01)*	Elstree
N521JS	ATR 42-320	205	5Y-LNT XA-RME/N521JS/XA-RME/F-WWET	Jet Systems *(Stored 7.01)*	Exeter
N525AD	Cessna 525 CitationJet	525-0435		Aircraft Guaranty Corp *(Op A Davies) (Noted 6.01)*	Edinburgh
N525CM	Cessna 525 CitationJet	525-0093	I-IDAG N5151S	Wells Fargo Bank Northwest NA *(Op Airmac Ltd) (Noted 6.01)*	Edinburgh
N527EW	Cessna 501 Citation 1	501-0322	(N769EW) (N669DM)/N314GS/N374GS/N2663J	Rockville Aero Inc *(Noted 12.01)*	Jersey
N554RB	Beech E55 Baron	TE-1141		Rodney Badham Inc *(Noted 8.01)*	Coventry
N585D	Gulfstream Gulfstream IV/SP	1258	N400UP N416GA	E I Dupont de Nemours & Co *(Noted 12.01)*	Teesside
N560S	Cessna 560XL Citation Excel	560-5190		Tim Leacock Aircraft Sales *(Noted 12.01)*	Jersey
N600MG	MD Helicopters MD 600N	RN049	N3266A	Paul Bundy Aviation Inc *(Op Metafin Group) (Noted 9.01)*	Wolverhampton
N600HV	MD Helicopters MD 600N	RN058		Cumbrian SeafoodsInc *(Noted 9.01)*	(Maryport, Cumbria)
N600PV	MD Helicopters MD 600N	RN048		Southern Aircraft Consultancy Inc *(Noted 7.01)*	(Maryport, Cumbria)
N600SY	MD Helicopters MD 600N	RN031	N9211F	Wells Fargo Bank Northwest NA *(Op Westover Park Ltd) (Noted 8.01)*	Gloucestershire
N601UK	Ted Smith Aerostar 601P	61P-0183-012		Southern Aircraft Consultancy Inc *(Op Airwing 2000) (Noted 10.01)*	Coventry
N605LG	American Lightship A-60	015		Lightship Group *(Noted 2.00)*	(Rednal)
N611VA	Agusta A109C	7657	N97CN	Eilean Inc *(Op Alan Mann Helicopters) (Noted 7.01)*	Fairoaks
N620LH	Aérospatiale AS355F Twin Squirrel 2	5463		MJD Aviation Inc *(Noted 11.01)*	Redhill

N620PL	Piper PA-32R-301 Saratoga SP	3213078		Marcella Thiel *(Noted 7.01)*	Booker
N625LH	Eurocopter AS355N Twinstar	5577	RP-C3688	Lloyd Helicopters US Inc *(Noted 9.01)*	Redhill
N637CG	Agusta A109C	7619	D-HARI	Castle Air Services Inc *(Noted 4.01)*	Denham
N646JR	Piper PA-32RT-300T Turbo Lance II	32R-7987019	PH-LFD N3032A	Southern Aircraft Consultancy Inc *(Noted 12.01)*	Jersey
N656AG	Piper PA-34-220T Seneca III	34-8333087	F-GLMB N42996	Southern Aircraft Consultancy Inc *(Noted 8.01)*	Popham
N656JM	Reims Cessna FR182 Skylane RGII	FR1820049	G-BHEO	JM Aviation Inc *(Noted 11.01)*	Old Sarum
N666AW	Piper PA-31 Navajo C	31-7612061		Atlantic International Air Charter Inc *(Noted 4.01)*	Biggin Hill
N666EX	Piper PA-32R-301T	3257241		Wells Fargo Bank Northwest NA *(Op Redbus Ltd) (Noted 8.01)*	Southend
N666GA	Gulfstream AA-5B Tiger	AA5B-1136		Southern Aircraft Consultancy Inc *(Op Mr.Fasano) (Noted 7.01)*	Enniskillen
N666JH	Cessna 182T	18281025		Hoggair Inc *(Noted 9.01)*	Rochester
N669MM	Bellanca 8KCAB-180 Super Decathlon	825-99		American Champion Aircraft Corporation *(Noted 8.01)*	Rendcomb
N670AT	Beech B90 King Air	LJ-481	G-BVRS G-KJET/G-AXFE	Sherman Aircraft Sales *(Noted 4.01)*	Biggin Hill
N685TT	Rockwell 685 Commander	12043		RPM Family Limited Partnership *(Op Coopers Aerial Surveys) (Noted 1.01)*	Gamston
N700AR	SOCATA TBM-700	23	F-GLBF F-WNGO/N700XL	Isnet Aviation Inc *(Noted 7.01)*	Biggin Hill
N700PK	SOCATA TBM-700	52	F-OHEV VH-PTG/(VH-FIS)/F-OHBH	Sky High Aviation Inc *(Noted 6.01)*	Ronaldsway
N700S	SOCATA TBM-700	193		Speedbird Aviation *(Noted 4.01)*	Fairoaks
N703JS	Dassault Falcon 10	157		Wickhaven Aviation Inc *(Op Medusa International) (Noted 10.01) (N450ST reserved)*	Farnborough
N707LD	Piper PA-E23-250 Aztec C	27-2754	G-JANK EI-BOO/G-ATCY/N5640Y	Southern Aircraft Consultancy Inc *(Op I A Qureshi) (Keenair titles/fin) (Noted 1.02)*	Southend
N707TJ	Boeing-Stearman A75N1 (N2S-1) Kaydet (Pratt & Whitney R-985 450hp)	75-950	N9PK N50057/Bu.3173	M G Plaskett *"Honey"* *(Op V.S.E.Norman t/a Aerosuperatics Ltd) (Utterly Butterly titles) (Noted 9.01)*	Rendcomb
N708SP	Learjet Learjet 45	45-014		E C Rodriguez *(Op Hamlin Jet) (Noted 4.00)*	Luton
N709AT	Agusta A109E Power	11017	HB-XQM	Associated Technologies *(Noted 7.01)*	(Turweston)
N709EL	Beechcraft 400A Beechjet	RK-52	(N709EW) N709JB	GAL Air Inc *(Op DFS Furniture) (Noted 4.00)*	East Midlands
N711TL	Piper PA-60 Aerostar 700P	60-8423017	N700SX N15GK/XB-EXQ/N6906Y	Southern Aircraft Consultancy Inc *(Noted 12.01)*	Biggin Hill
N719CD	Cirrus Design SR22	0051		Southern Aircraft Consultancy Inc *(Noted 8.01)*	Exeter
N719CS	Piper PA-18S-135 Super Cub (L-21C)	18-3569	G-BWUC SX-ASM/EI-181/I-EIYB/MM54-2369/54-2369	W F Chmura *(Under restoration 1.02) (Op Caledonian Seaplanes Ltd)*	Cumbernauld
N720B	Bell 206L-1 LongRanger II	45452	G-DALE G-HBUS	Omega Air Inc *(Last noted 12.99: current status unknown)*	Dublin
N735CX	Cessna 182Q Skylane II *(Mod to Advanced Lift 260 STOL)*	18265329		Wilmington Trust Company *(Op B.Holmes) (Noted 1.02)*	Barnard Farm, Thurrock
N736GX	Cessna R172K Hawk XP *(Tail-wheel)*	R1722526		Project Air Inc *(Noted 10.00)*	Headcorn
N741CD	Cirrus Design SR22	0137		Southern Aircraft Consultancy Inc *(Noted 1.02)*	Cambridge
N747MM	Piper PA-28R-200 Arrow II	28R-7335445	PH-MLP N56489	Rivers Air Inc *(Noted 8.01)*	Coventry
N747SD	Cessna 414	4140934		N747SD Inc *(Noted 1.02)*	Southend
N754AM	Agusta A109A	7154	I-CELB	Capital Helicopters London Inc *(Op Biggin Hill Helicopters Ltd) (Noted 12.01)*	Biggin Hill
N758BK	Cessna R172K Hawk XP	R1722963		Eros Inc *(Noted 8.01)*	Jersey
N766AM	Aérospatiale AS355N Twin Sqirrel	5601		E C Rodriguez *(Op Beacon Energy (Aviation) Ltd) (Noted 7.00)*	Beacon Farm, Leics
N767CW	SOCATA TBM-700	96		High Sierra Inc *(Noted 4.01)*	Biggin Hill
N773DC	Beechcraft 58 Baron	TH-755	G-BDWK (G-BEET)	DC Aviation Inc *(Op DC Energy Ltd) (Noted 7.01)*	Gamston
N777NG	Cessna 550 Citation Bravo	550-0992		Tazio Aviation Inc *(Noted 10.01)*	Hawarden
N797HG	Piper PA-46-310P Malibu	46-8408064		Rocol Aviation *(Noted 1.02)*	Guernsey
N799JH	Piper PA-28RT-201T Turbo Arrow IV	28R-8231051	HB-PNE PH-HJM/N8206B	Southern Aircraft Consultancy Inc *(Op J Havers) (Carries Swiss Cross on tail) (Noted 1.02)*	King's Farm, Thurrock

N800HL	Bell 222	47054		Yorkshire Helicopters USA Inc *(Noted 10.01)*	(Coney Park, Leeds)
N800VM	Beech 76 Duchess	ME-318	G-BHGM	Southern Aircraft Consultancy Inc *(Noted 4.01)*	Gloucestershire
N800VP	Beechcraft 95-B55 Baron	TC-1805	OY-POB	Southern Aircraft Consultancy Inc *(Op Shipping & Airlines) (Noted 11.01)*	Biggin Hill
N808NC	Gulfstream 695B Commander 1200	96085		Wilmington Trust Co *(Op Coopers Aerial Surveys) (Noted 1.01)*	Gamston
N816RL	Beechcraft E90 King Air	LW-187	N66BP N816EP/N900MH/N2187L	Springair Inc *(Op English Braids Ltd) (Noted 111.01)*	Gloucestershire
N818MJ	Piper PA-23-250 Aztec	27-2486	G-ASNH	Retail Management Associates *(Noted 8.01)*	Charlton Park, Malmesbury
N818Y	Piper PA-30 Twin Comanche B	30-1458	ZS-CAO ZS-EYB/A2-ZFE/ZS-EYB/VQ-ZIY/ZS-EYB/N8318Y	One Eight Yankee Aviation Inc *(Noted 12.01)*	Guernsey
N829CB	Cessna 550 Citation Bravo	550-0829	N5096S	Wells Fargo Bank Northwest NA *(Op JJB Sports) (Noted 12.01)*	Blackpool
N836TP	Beechcraft A36TP Bonanza	E-2124	N6770M	Hastingwood Aviation Inc *(Op Velcourt East plc) (Noted 7.01)*	Anwick
N840LE	Rockwell Commander 690C	11709	N690BA ZS-KZM/N5961K	Wells Fargo Bank Northwest NA *(Op O.Henriksen) (Noted 12.01)*	Guernsey
N841WS	Cessna 550 Citation Bravo	550-0841	N5086W	Millburn World Travel Services Inc *(Op Walter Scott & Ptnrs) (Noted 10.00)*	Edinburgh
N844F	Dassault Falcon 100	201		RTAF LLC *(Op Avionicare) (Noted 11.01)*	Cambridge.
N864AE	British Aerospace Jetstream Srs.3201	864	Z3-ASA Z3-MCA/N864AC/G-31-864	Wells Fargo Bank Northwest NA *(Air Service titles) (Noted 8.01)*	Southampton
N866LP	Piper PA-46-350P Malibu Mirage	4636130	N666LP N92928	TLP Aviation Inc *(Noted 12.01)*	Guernsey
N874RA	Gulfstream G1159A Gulfstream III	361	(N875E)	Banc of America Leasing & Capital LLC *(Noted as N874RA 2000: N874RR reserved)*	Stansted
N882JH	Maule M.7-235B	23056C		Everbright Aviation Inc *(Noted 8.01)*	Henstridge
N900CB	Cessna 421C Golden Eagle III	421C0837	VP-CPR VR-CPR/N2659F	Southern Aircraft Consultancy Inc *(Op Fifty North) (Noted 12.01)*	Guernsey
N909RM	Mooney M.20J (201)	24-0636		D.Christoffersen *(Crashed Thurrock 14.5.01: wreck noted 1.02)*	Southed
N909WJ	Grumman FM-2 Wildcat	--	BuAer 16203	Iron Baron Corp *(Noted 8.01)* *(Op Flying A Service/Wizzard Investments Ltd)*	North Weald
N913PM*	Lockheed L-1011 Tristar 200	1223	A40-TT	Interlease Aviation Investors V LLC *(Being scrappd 4.01)*	Cambridge
N915TC	Aeronca 15AC Sedan	15AC-429	EI-ETC G-CETC/HB-ETC	Southern Aircraft Consultancy Inc *(Op H.Moreau) (Noted 6.00)*	Athboy, Co.Meath
N920RP	Cessna T310R	310R0877		Avalon Air Services *(Noted 8.01)*	Biggin Hill
N950H	Dassault Falcon 50EX	307		Island Aviation Inc *(Noted 8.01)*	Farnborough
N951SF	Beechcraft 56TC Baron	TG-83	N23PB	Timcar Inc *(Noted 11.01)*	Elstree
N971RJ	Piper PA-39 Twin Comanche C/R	39-111	G-AZBC N8951Y	Simply Living Ltd *(Noted 11.01)*	Wellcross Grange, Slinfold
N973BB	Mitsubishi MU-2B-60 Marquise	1509SA		Romeo Aviation Inc *(Noted 12.01)*	Jersey
N980HB	Rockwell Commander 695	95006		HBC Aviation Inc *(Noted 12.01)*	Guernsey
N991RV	Dassault Falcon 10	24	N301JJ F-GBTI/N1924V/N116FJ/F-WJML	E I Aviation Inc *(Op Eddie Irvine) (Noted 7.01)*	Dublin
N997JB	Partenavia P.68C-TC	288-20-TC	F-GROG HB-LSB/F-GEQD/N60CH/YV-2318P	Pangaea Air Service *(Noted 2.01)*	Little Staughton
N999BE	Dassault Falcon 2000	147	F-WWVB	Formula One Management *(Op Bernie Ecclestone) (Noted 7.01)*	Biggin Hill
N999MH	Cessna 195B	7168	OH-CSE	E Detiger *(Noted 7.01)*	Compton Abbas
N999PJ	Morane-Saulnier MS.760 Paris	2	F-BJLY 89	R.J.Lamplough *(Noted 8.01)*	North Weald
N1024L	Beechcraft 60 Duke	P-78	C-FOPH CF-OPH/N1024L/CF-OPH	Flytru Aviation Inc *(Op R.Ogden) (Noted 8.01)*	North Weald
N1027G	Maule M.7-235B	23032C		Southern Aircraft Consultancy Inc *(Last noted 5.99: current status unknown)*	Exeter
N1061Y	Navion Rangemaster H	NAV-4-2531	D-EBBP (N2531T)	R D Garretson *(Noted 1.02)*	Southend
N1062U	Piper PA-32-300 Cherokee Six	32-40070	OE-DPC N4042W	R D Garretson *(Noted 8.01)*	Biggin Hill
N1089D	Hughes 369D	51-0966D		Sky Dock Helicopter Holdings *(Op Nunkeeling Ltd) (Noted 6.01)*	Elloughton, Humberside
N1092H	Beechcraft C90A King Air	LJ-1454		Park Close Aviation Inc *(Noted 1.02)*	Blackbushe
N1120Z	Raytheon B200 Super King Air	BB-1570		Air Direct Inc *(Noted 12.01)*	Guernsey
N1158V	Cessna 310J	310J0172		Southern Aircraft Consultancy Inc *(Noted 7.01)*	Gamston

N1172X	Piper PA-34-200T Seneca II	34-7570228		Southern Aircraft Consultancy Inc *(Noted 1.02)*	Shoreham
N1325M	Boeing-Stearman E75 (N2S-5) Kaydet	--	Bu.43390 75-8484	Eastern Stearman Inc *(Op Blackbarn Aviation) (Noted 6.99: current status unknown)*	Priory Farm, Tibenham
NC1328	Fairchild F24R-46KS Argus	3310		Eastern Stearman Inc *(Op Blackbarn Aviation) (Noted 6.99: current status unknown)*	Priory Farm, Tibenham
N1344	Ryan PT-22-RY Recruit	2086	41-20877	Flying Heritage Inc *(Op Mrs.H.Mitchell t/a PT Flight) (Noted 8.99: current status unknown)*	RAF Cosford
N1350J	Rockwell Commander 112B	516		Southern Aircraft Consultancy Inc *(Op G.Richards) (Noted 5.99: current status unknown)*	Cardiff
N1364V	Boeing E75	75-8672		Tranzair Inc *(Noted 8.01)*	North Weald
N1407J	Rockwell Commander 112A	407		Blue Lake Aviation Inc *(Noted 5.01)*	Blackbushe
N1551D	Cessna 190	7773		Southern Aircraft Consultancy Inc *(Noted 8.01)*	Old Buckenham
N1565B	Beechcraft 400 Beechjet	RJ-65		International Aviation Leasing Inc *(Op A.Ogden & Sons plc) (Noted 11.00)*	Leeds-Bradford
N1731B	Boeing A75N-1 Stearman	75-5716		Eastern Stearman Inc *(Noted 5.00)*	Priory Farm, Tibenham
N1745M	Cessna 182P Skylane II	18264424		D Thomas *(Noted 3.99: current status unknown)*	Cardiff
N1778X	Cessna 210L Centurion	21060798		Central Investment Corporation *(Noted 9.01)*	Denham
N1937Z	Cessna 172RG Cutlass RG	172RG0908	EI-BVS	Virginia Aircraft Trust Corp *(Noted 8.00)*	Ronaldsway
N1944A	Douglas C-47A	19677	(N5211A) N3239W/RDanAF K-683/RnorAF/43-15211	Wings Venture Ltd *(Noted 9.01) (As "315211/JB-Z")*	Kemble
N2000M	Cessna 560 Citation V	560-0146	(N6877Q)	Wells Fargo Bank Northwest NA *(Op Invensys plc) (Noted 4.01)*	Farnborough
N2099L	Beechcraft 95B55 Baron	TC-1983		A M McPherson *(Noted 12.98: current status unknown)*	Blackbushe
N2121T	Gulfstream AA-5B Tiger	AA5B-1031		J.Siebols *(Noted 1.02)*	Southend
N2138J	English Electric Canberra TT.18 *(Built Avro)*	EEA/R3/EA3/6640	WK126	S D Picatti *(Loaned to Gloucestershire Aviation Collection as "WK126/843")*	Gloucestershire
N2209P	Piper PA-23-250 Aztec C	27-3788	G-BYRW F-BOXQ/N6500Y	E Walsh *(Noted as "F-BOXQ" 12.00 - not allocated 3.01)*	Elstree
N2273Q	Piper PA-28-181 Cherokee Archer II	28-7790389		Minwriston Inc *(Noted 8.01)*	Marley Hall
N2326Y	Beechcraft 58P Baron	TJ-83	F-GALL	Southern Aircraft Consultancy Inc *(Noted 4.01)*	Gamston
N2341S	Raytheon B300 Super King Air	FL-241		Specsavers Aviation Inc *(Noted 12.01)*	Guernsey
N2366D	Cessna 170B	20518		Southern Aircraft Consultancy Inc *(Noted 8.01)*	Turweston
N2379C	Cessna R182 Skylane RG	R18200170		West Country Aviation Inc *(Noted 7.01)*	Ledbury
N2401Z	Piper PA-23-250 Aztec B	27-8054034		Pan Maritime Inc *(Noted 9.01)*	Filton
N2423C	Piper PA-38-112 Tomahawk	38-79A0177		Phoenix East Aviation Inc *(Stored 2.00)*	Bristol
N2480X	Piper PA-31T1 Cheyenne I	31T-8104026		Jane Air *(Noted 6.01)*	Southampton
N2495Q	Piper PA-34-200T Seneca II	34-7770188		Southern Aircraft Consultancy Inc *(Noted 8.01)*	Alderney
N2548T	Navion Model H Rangemaster	NAV-4-2548		Navion Airways Inc *(Noted 12.01)*	Guernsey
N2612	Stinson Junior R	8754	NC2612	A.L.Young *(As "NC2612") (Stored 3.00)*	Henstridge
N2652P	Piper PA-22-135 Tri-Pacer	22-2992		J L Morris *"Jeff Jeff" (Op Anne Lait) (Noted 8.01)*	Weston
N2700*	Fairchild C-119G-FA	10689	3C-ABA Belg AF CP-9/51-2700	Aces High Flying Museum *(Nose only noted 8.01)*	North Weald
N2923N	Piper PA-32-300 Cherokee Six	32-7940207		S W Freeborn *(Noted 9.01)*	Buttermilk Hall Farm, Blisworth
N2929W	Piper PA-28-151 Cherokee Warrior	28-7415457	OO-GPE N9619N	Funair Inc *(Op R.Lobell) (Noted 1.02)*	Elstree
N2937A	Cessna 180	30137		Southern Aircraft Consultancy Inc *(Op A Gregori) (Noted 8.01)*	Inverness
N2943D	Piper PA-28RT-201 Arrow IV	28R-7918231	G-BSLD N2943D	Southern Aircraft Consultancy Inc *(Op E.Gawronek) (Noted 1.01)*	Barton
N2967N	Piper PA-32-300 Six	32-7940242		Aerotechnics Aviation Inc *(Stored 12.01)*	Guernsey
N2975K*	Luscombe 8E	5702		Not known *(Noted 10.01 for UK restoration)*	Westland Zoyland

N3023W	Beechcraft V35B Bonanza	D-9517		M A Sargent *(Noted 12.01)*	Guernsey
N3044B	Piper PA-34-200T Seneca II	34-7970012		Aerotechnics Aviation Inc	Alderney
				(Noted 9.01)	
N3188H*	ERCO 415C Ercoupe	3813	NC3188H	Not known	Maypole Farm,
				(Damaged c 7.92: stored for spares 5.98)	Chislet
N3536N	Mooney M.20F	68-0088		J E M Williams *(Noted 7.01)*	North Weald
N3839H	Piper Aerostar 601P	61P-0569-7963247	F-GKCL	Wellsprings Aviation Inc	Jersey/Southend
			N3839H/G-RACE/N8083J *(Noted 1.02)*		
N3922B	Boeing-Stearman E75 (PT-17) Kaydet		42-17642	Eastern Stearman Inc	Priory Farm,
	(Continental W670)	75-5805		*(Noted 8.01)*	Tibenham
N3995W	Piper PA-32-260 Cherokee Six	32-963		E W Wells	Bournemouth
				(Crashed Le Rignolent, France 31.5.98: fuselage stored 5.00)	
N4085E	Piper PA-18-150 Super Cub	18-7809059		R N Hall *(Noted 5.00)*	Goodwood
N4168D	Piper <u>PA-34-220T Seneca V</u>	3449158		AAL Inc *(Noted 9.01)*	Plymouth
N4173T	Cessna 320D Skyknight	320D0073		N4173T Inc	Cranfield
				(Op J.Irwin) (Noted 8.01)	
N4178W	Piper PA-32R-301T Saratoga II TC	3257178		Anglo American Airmotive	Jersey
				(Noted 8.01)	
N4232Y	Reima Cessna F150G	F1500098	D-EBYW	F Acevedo *(Noted 5.01)*	Stapleford
N4306Z	Piper PA-28-161 Warrior II	28-8316073		Thomas Stuer Aviation Inc	Stapleford
				(Op USAF Flying Club) (Noted 8.01)	
N4337K	Cessna 150K	15071583	G-BTSA	T L Crook	Branscombe
			N6083G	*(Noted 5.01)*	
N4422P	Piper PA-23-160 Geronimo	23-1936		W J Armstrong Inc *(Noted 7.01)*	Thruxton
N4519U	Head AX9-118 HAFB	184		Northern Light Balloon Expeditions	Kirdford
				<u>"Ground Hog"</u> (Op Balloon Preservation Group)	
N4545	Learjet Learjet 45	45-045		P N C Leasing *(Noted 1.01)*	Jersey
N4565L	Douglas DC-3-201A	2108	(N3TV)	390th BG Memorial Air Museum	Framlingham
			LV-GYP/LV-PCV/N129H/N512/N51D/N80C/NC21744		
				(Damaged in gales 10.87 & 25.1.90: on rebuild 2.00)	
N4575C	Grumman G.21A Goose	B-120		Aerofloat G21A Inc *(Noted 10.01)*	Belfast
N4596N	Boeing-Stearman E75 (PT-13D) Kaydet		42-17782	Phil Dacy Aviation *(US Mail c/s)*	North Weald
	(Lycoming R680-7)	75-5945		*(Op N.Mason & D.Gilmour t/a Intrepid Aviation Co) (Noted 8.01)*	
N4599W	Rockwell Commander 112TC	13089		Skyfast Inc *(Noted 3.00)*	Haverfordwest
N4647J	Piper PA-28R-180 Cherokee Arrow			Southern Aircraft Consultancy Inc	Blackbushe
		28R-30541		(Op R.Breckell) *(Noted 8.01)*	
N4698W	Rockwell Commander 112TC-A	13274		Syston Aviation Inc	Denham
				(Op W.Haynes) (Noted 9.01)	
N4770B	Cessna 152	15283626		Walkwitz Aviation *(Noted 6.01)*	Panshanger
N4990T*	Thunder Ax7-65B HAFB	123		British Balloon Museum & Library	Newbury
				<u>"Tumbleweed"</u>	
N5023U*	Avian Magnum IX HAFB	169		Balloon Preservation Group	Kirdford
N5057V	Boeing-Stearman PT-13D Kaydet	75-5598	42-17435	Merin Aire Ltd *"Charlie Brown"*	Rendcomb
				(Op V.S.E.Norman) (Utterly Butterly titles) (Noted 9.01)	
N5107N	Boeing B75N1 Stearman	75-7166		A F Farhat	Swanton Morley
				(Last noted 2.99: current status unknown)	
NC5171N*	Lockheed 10A Electra	1037		*<u>See G-LIOA in SECTION 1, Part 2</u>*	
N5180Y	Piper PA-23-250 Aztec B	27-2226		Southern Aircraft Consultancy Inc	Glasgow
				(Noted 4.01)	
N5237V*	Boeing B-17G-95-DL Flying Fortress	32509	(N6466D)	RAF Museum	Hendon
			N5237V/Bu.77233/44-83868 *(As "44-83868/N" in 94th BG USAAF c/s)*		
N5240H	Piper PA-16 Clipper	16-44		Southern Aircraft Consultancy Inc	Wellcross Grange,
				(Op D.Hillier) (Noted 1.01)	Slinfold
N5277T	Piper PA-32-260 Cherokee Six	32-7200031		K R Denman *(Noted 9.01)*	Goodwood
N5315V	Hiller UH-12C	757		W F Chmura *(Noted 5.01)*	Sancreed, Cornwall
N5345N	Boeing Stearman PT-13D Kaydet	75-5718	42-17555	Eastern Stearman Inc	Priory Farm,
				(On rebuild 8.01)	Tibenham
N5346S	Piper PA-32R-301T Saratoga II TC			Anglo American Airmotive Inc	Elstree
		3257257		*(Noted 11.01)*	
N5360H	Piper PA-16 Clipper	16-167		Not known *(Noted 1.01)*	White Waltham
N5419*	Bristol Scout D rep	01		Bristol Aero Collection	RNAS Yeovilton
	(Built Leo Opdycke 1983)			*(Frame displayed @ FAA Museum)*	
N5428C	Cessna 170A	19462		28 Charlie Inc	Audley End
				(Op P.Norman) (Noted 8.00)	
N5632R	Maule M-5-235C Lunar Rocket	7244C		Southern Aircraft Consultancy Inc	Stowes Farm,
				(Op RD.Group) (Noted 8.01)	Tillingham
N5644L	American AA-1 Yankee	AA1-0044		Southern Aircraft Consultancy Inc	Biggin Hill
				(Noted 4.01)	
N5647S	Maule M-5-235C Rocket	7345C		Virginia Aircraft Trust Corp	Yeatsall Farm,
				(Noted 8.00)	Abbotts Bromley
N5668H	Maule MX-7-180 Star Rocket	11028C		T D Beck *(Noted 8.01)*	Headcorn
N5675Z*	Piper PA-22-108 Colt	22-9501		Not known *(Noted 5.00)*	Kilrush

N5730H	Piper PA-16 Clipper	16-342		Southern Aircraft Consultancy Inc *(Noted 8.01)*	Cork Farm, Streethay
N5736	Raytheon Hawker 800XP	258471	N43642	Wilmington Trust Co *(Noted 7.00)*	Luton
N5820T	Westland WG-30-100	004	G-BKFD G-17-28	Airspur Helicopters Inc *(Op The Helicopter Museum)*	Weston-super-Mare
N5824H	Piper PA-38-112 Tomahawk II	38-81A0118	D-EFFX N23138	J E Martin *(Op Lakenheath Flying Club) (Noted 7.99)*	RAF Lakenheath
N5840T	Westland WG-30-100	006	G-BKFF G-17-30	Airspur Helicopters Inc *(Op The Helicopter Museum)*	Weston-super-Mare
N5880T	Westland WG-30-100	009	G-17-31	Westland Inc *(Op The Helicopter Museum)*	Weston-super-Mare
N5900H	Piper PA-16 Clipper	16-520		Southern Aircraft Consultancy Inc *(Noted 6.00)*	Shenstone
N5966D	Zenair CH-801	8-4152		D A Defelici *(Noted 9.01)*	Shoreham
N6003F	Commander Aircraft 114B Commander	14590		Deskey Aviation Inc *(Noted 8.01)*	Exeter
N6010Y	Commander Aircraft 114B Commander	14589		Camrose Inc *(Noted 11.01)*	Biggin Hill
N6095A	Commander Aircraft 114B Commander	14635		Bonbois Aviation *(Noted 12.01)*	Guernsey
N6107Y	Commander Aircraft 114B Commander	14627		Tamboti Aviation Inc *(Op IPP Aviation) (Noted 12.01)*	Guernsey
N6182G	Cessna 172N Skyhawk II	17273576		Southern Aircraft Consultancy Inc *(Noted 11.01)*	Cambridge
N6268	Travelair 2000	707	NC6268	"Blue Max" Movie Aircraft Collection *(As Fokker D.VII "626/8" in Ernst Udet c/s)*	Booker
N6302W	Government Aircraft Factory N22B Nomad	F-159	VH-HWB	Chatteris Aviation Inc *(Noted 9.01)* *(Op London Parachute Centre)*	Lower Mt.Pleasant Chatteris
N6315X	Cessna 421C	421C-1003		Transatlantic Flyers Ltd *(Noted 7.01)*	Oxford
N6339U	Piper PA-28-236 Dakota	28-8011089	OO-JFD F-GCMU or V?/OO-HLM/N8152S	Thistle Aviation Inc *(Noted 5.01)*	Pittrichie Farm, Whiterashes
N6498V	Cessna T303 Crusader	T30300313	G-CRUS N6498V	Southern Aircraft Consultancy Inc *(Noted 12.01)*	Guernsey
N6526D*	North American P-51D-25NA Mustang *(Composite)*	122-39874	9289 RCAF 44-73415	RAF Museum *"Little Friend"* *(As "413573/B6-K" in 361st FS/357th FG USAAF c/s)*	Hendon
N6593W	Cessna P210N	P210-00801		R S Barnett *(Noted 7.00)*	Stapleford
N6601Y	Piper PA-23-250 Aztec C	27-3905	XA-DAZ N6601Y	Aerospace Financial Services Ltd *(Noted 11.01)*	Norwich
N6602Y	Piper PA-28-140 Cherokee	28-21943	G-ATTG N11C	T.P.Hughston *(Noted 1.02)*	Little Staughton
N6632L	Beechcraft C23 Musketeer	M-2188		W J Forrest *(Noted 6.01)*	White Waltham
N6690D	Piper PA-18-135 Super Cub	18-3848	PH-KNK	6688 Delta Inc *(Op S Gruver) (Noted 6.00)*	Netherley
N6699D	Piasecki HUP-3 Retriever	51	622 RCN USN/51-16622	The Helicopter Museum *(As "622" in RCN c/s)*	Weston-super-Mare
N6819F	Cessna 150F	15063419		W J Davies *(Dumped 12.99)*	Shoreham
N6830B	Piper PA-22-150 Tri-pacer	22-4128		Vintage Aircraft Lelystad Inc *(Noted 1.02)*	Leicester
N6834L	Cessna T310R II	310R2137		NL Aviation Inc *(Op P.Basch/Tropair Engineering Ltd) (Noted 5.01)*	Leeds-Bradford
N6907E	Cessna 175A Skylark	56407		Southern Aircraft Consultancy Inc *(Noted 9.01)*	White Waltham
N6954J	Piper PA-32R-300 Cherokee Lance	32R-7680394		Matrix Aviation Inc *(Noted 8.01)*	Norwich
N7027E	Hawker Tempest V	---	EJ693	K Weeks *(On rebuild 6.01)*	Booker
N7070A	Cessna S550 Citation II	S550-0068	N4049 N404G/N1272Z	Omega Air Inc *(Noted 6.01)*	Dublin
N7133J	Mooney M.20C Mk 21	3116	G-BJAK OO-CAB/OO-VLB/N5814Q	G Albin *(Damaged fuselage noted 6.99)*	Bodmin
N7148R	Beechcraft B55 Baron	TC-2028	N2198L C-GWFD/N2198L/D-IGRW/N2198L	Air Services Holdings Corp *(Noted 7.01)*	Guernsey
N7214Y	Beechcraft A36 Bonanza	E-2169		Southern Aircraft Consultancy Inc *(Noted 9.01)*	(St Just)
N7219L	Beechcraft B55 Baron	TC-717		Southern Aircraft Consultancy Inc *(Noted 8.01)*	Kemble
N7263S	Cessna 150H	15067963		Cesna Inc *(On rebuild 3.01)*	Plaistows Farm, St Albans
N7348P	Piper PA-24-250 Comanche	24-2526		Southern Aircraft Consultancy Inc *(Op J.Bown) (Noted 8.01)*	Netherthorpe
N7374A	Cessna A150M Aerobat 135 *(Tail-wheel conversion)*	A1500726		J A Thomas *"Turnin' Tricks" (Noted 8.01)*	Branscombe
N7423V	Mooney M.20E Chapparal	21-1163		Southern Aircraft Consultancy Inc *(Noted 7.01)*	Hinton-in-the Hedges
N7564J*	Piper PA-28R-180 Cherokee Arrow	28R-30942		Southern Aircraft Consultancy Inc *(Cancelled by FAA 10.00) (Noted as "N7564J" 2.01)*	Thruxton

N7614C*	North American B-25J/PBJ-1J Mitchell	108-37246	44-31171	Imperial War Museum/American Air Museum *(As "31171" in US Marines c/s)*	Duxford
N7777G*	Lockheed L.749A-79 Constellation	2553		*See G-CONI in SECTION 1, Part 2*	
N7801R	Bell 47G-5	7801		Skyman Logistics *(Op W C Evans) (Noted 12.99)*	Launton, Oxon
N7813M	Piper PA-28-180 Cherokee D	28-5227	G-AZYF 5Y-AJK/N7813N	Southern Aircraft Consultancy Inc *(Noted 1.02)*	Leicester
N7832P	Piper PA-24-250 Comanche	24-3052		Three Two Papa Inc *(Noted 10.01)*	White Waltham
N7976Y	Piper PA-30 Twin Comanche B	30-1075		Southern Aircraft Consultancy Inc *(Noted 12.01)*	Guernsey
N8075U	Cessna 150G	15065381	N4081J	J P Morgan *(Last noted as "N4081J" 7.97: cancelled by FAA 8.98 as sold to UK: current status unknown)*	NK
N8153E	Piper PA-28RT-201T Turbo Arrow IV	28R-8131185	N9561N N84205	P B Payne *(Noted 7.01)*	Caernarfon
N8241Z	Piper PA-28-161 Warrior II	28-8316079		Pett Air Inc *(Noted 5.01)*	Goodwood
N8258F	Beech B36TC Bonanza	EA-513		Millfore Aviation Inc *(Noted 2.01)*	Elstree
N8360Y	Piper PA-28-181 Archer II	28-8190195		N G Kelman *(Noted 10.00)*	Booker
N8471Y	Piper PA-28-236 Dakota	28-8211019		Turbo Arrow Inc *(Noted 12.01)*	Panshanger
N8754J	Aviat A-1 Husky *(Built Christen)*	1160		Southern Aircraft Consultancy Inc *(Op A.Febrache) (Noted 12.01)*	Guernsey
N8829P	Piper PA-24-260 Comanche	24-4285		Southern Aircraft Consultancy Inc *(Noted 9.01)*	Filton
N8862V	Bellanca 17-31ATC Turbo Viking	31022		Southern Aircraft Consultancy Inc *(Op M Hales) (Noted 9.99)*	Wickenby
N8911Y	Piper PA-39 Twin Comanche C/R	39-66	G-AYFT N8911Y	S B Barber *(Noted 10.01)*	Blackbushe
N9045C	Barnes SS Condom HAFB	FS7-001		Balloon Preservation Group *"The Big One"*	Kirdford
N9050T*	Douglas C-47A-10DK Dakota	312472	5N-ATA PH-MAG/G-AGYX/KG437/42-9264	J.Woodhouse/Dakota's American Bistro *(Parts displayed in restaurant 3.96: current status unknown)*	Fleet
N9089Z	North American TB-25J-25NC Mitchell	108-34136	"HD368" N9089Z/(G-BKXW)/N9089Z/44-30861	Aero Asociates Inc *(Op Aces High Flying Museum) "Bedsheet Bomber" (As "430861" in USAAF c/s)*	North Weald
N9115Z*	North American TB-25N-20NC Mitchell	108-32641	44-29366	RAF Museum *"Hanover Street/Catch 22" (As "34037" in USAAF c/s: allotted 8838M)*	Hendon
N9122N	Piper PA-46-310P Malibu	4608097		Libra Air Inc *(Noted 10.00)*	Oxford
N9123X	Piper PA-32R-301 Saratoga	3229003		Vector Sky Service Inc *(Noted 1.02)*	Shoreham
N9143C	Aero Commander 685	12040	G-BWEK CS-APB/N9132N	Cooper Aerial Surveys Ltd Corp *(Fuselage noted 11.99)*	Sandtoft
N9146N	Cessna 401B *(RAM conversion)*	401B0010		A J Air Ltd Inc *(Noted 9.00)*	Weston
N9201U	MD Helicopters MD Explorer	900-00042		MD Helicopters Inc *(Noted 9.01)*	Shoreham
N9232Y	Piper PA-31P-350 Mojave	31P-8414018		Saratoga Air Club Inc *(Op Anglo American Airmotive) (Noted 8.00)*	Bournemouth
N9239Y	Piper PA-31P-350 Mojave	31P-8414040		Castle Aviation Inc *(Noted 12.01)*	Guernsey
N9303W	Piper PA-28-235 Cherokee B	28-10981		R.K.Spence (Noted 3.99)	Cardiff
N9308V	Mooney M.20F	69-0086		Southern Aircraft Consultancy Inc *(Noted 9.01)*	Biggin Hill
N9325N	Piper PA-28R-200 Cherokee Arrow *(Lopresti version)*	28R-35025		Southern Aircraft Consultancy Inc *(Op Hiam Mercado) (Noted 7.01)*	Panshanger
N9381P	Piper PA-24-260 Comanche C	24-4882		Southern Aircraft Consultancy Inc *(Noted 11.01)*	Elstree
N9469P	Piper PA-24-260 Comanche C	24-4979		Southern Aircraft Consultancy Inc *(Noted 12.01)*	Guernsey
N9521C	Consolidated 28-5ACF (PBY-5A) Catalina	1656	Bu48294	Weavair Inc *(Noted 8.01) (Temporarily as "AH545/WQ-Z" of 209 Squadron 2001)*	North Weald
N9606H*	Fairchild M.62A-4 Cornell (PT-26-FA) *(Quoted p/i thought unlikely: true c/n may be T43-3642 ?)*	T43-4361	FH768 42-14361	Rebel Air Museum *(Last noted 7.99: current status unknown)*	Martham, Norfolk
N9727G	Cessna 180H	18052227	G-FESC N9727G	Simply Living Ltd *(Op B Richardson) (Noted 12.01)*	Wellcross Grange, Slinfold
N9861M	Maule M.4-210C	1058C		Southern Aircraft Consultancy Inc *(Noted 11.01)*	Headcorn
N9950	Curtiss P-40N Warhawk	33723	44-7983	Ice Strike Corp *(Stored in container 8.01)*	North Weald
N11824	Cessna 150L	15075652		R R Powers *(Noted 10.01)*	Manor Farm, Glatton
N12006	Raven S.50A HAFB	111		R Higbie *"Cheers" (On loan to British Balloon Museum & Library)*	Newbury
N12739(3)	de Havilland DH.83 Fox Moth	4026(2)		J M Hirtle *(Airframe noted 1.02)*	Denford Manor Hungerford
N13253	Cessna 172M	17262613		Anglia Aviation Inc *(On rebuild 3.01)*	Plaistows Farm, St Albans

N14113	North American T-28B Trojan	174-398	1236 HaitiAF	Radial Revelations Ltd	Duxford/Guernsey
			N14113/FrAF 119/51-7545 *"Little Rascal" (Noted 12.01)*		
				(As "119" in French AF/AdlA c/s)	
N14152	Piper PA-23-250 Aztec E	27-4715	G-AZMK	Western Aviation Leasing Inc	Exeter
			OY-AJA/G-AZMK/N14152 *(Noted 7.01)*		
N14234*	Handley Page HP.137 Jetstream	234	N102SC	Barron Thomas Aviation Inc	East Fortune
	(Fuselage used by BAe as Jetsteam 31 mock-up)		N1BE/(N200SE)/G-BBBV/G-8-12		
				(Loaned to National Museums of Scotland/Museum of Flight)	
NC16403*	Cessna C.34 Airmaster	322		Alan House	Lower Wasing Farm,
				(Stored 2001)	Brimpton
N16676	Fairchild F.24CR-C8F Argus	3101	NC16676	A Langendal *(Frame stored 2001)*	Priory Farm,
				(Op Blackbarn Aviation)	Tibenham
N18028	Beechcraft D17S Staggerwing	147	NC18028	P.H.McConnell *(Noted 7.01)*	Popham
N21381	Piper PA-34-200 Seneca	34-7350274	F-BUTM	Tickton Inc	Dunkeswell
			F-ETAL	*(Noted 11.99: current status unknown)*	
N23659	Beechcraft B58 Baron	TH-893		S W Freeborn *(Noted 12.01)*	Guernsey
N24136	Beechcraft A36 Bonanza	E-1233		Dickens Aviation Inc *(Noted 1.02)*	Panshanger
N24730*	Piper PA-38-112 Tomahawk	38-80A0004		Not known	Eaglescott
				(Cancelled by FAA as sold to UK 3.91: stored 9.98)	
N26634	Piper PA-24-250 Comanche	24-3551	G-BFKR	J A McMahon	Ronaldsway
			PH-BUS/D-ELPY/N8306P *(Noted 8.00)*		
N27597	Piper PA-31-350 Navajo Chieftain			Matthew Airlines Inc	Guernsey/Southend
		31-7852073		*(Noted 1.02)*	
N32625*	Piper PA-34-200T Seneca II	34-7570039		Guernsey Airport Fire Service	Guernsey
				(Hulk only 12.01)	
N33600*	Cessna L-19A-CE Bird Dog	22303	51-11989	Museum of Army Flying	AAC Middle Wallop
				(As "111989" in US Army c/s)	
N33870	Fairchild M62A (PT-19-FA) Cornell		G-BTNY	Ice Strike Corp *(Noted 8.01)*	North Weald
		T40-237	N33870/US Army	*(Op R.M Lamplough) (As "02538" in US Army c/s)*	
N33884	Aeronca 65CA Chief	CA.14101	NC33884	N.A.Evans *(Noted 7.01)*	Branscombe
N36362	Cessna 180 Skywagon	31691	G-BHVZ	Southern Aircraft Consultancy Inc	Sibson
			F-BHMU/N4739B	*(Op W Burgess) (Noted 8.01)*	
N37600	Cessna T310R	310R1209		Southern Aircraft Consultancy Inc	Perth
				(Op I M Graham) (Noted 2.01)	
N38049	Beechcraft A36TC Bonanza	EA-178		T B Ellison Inc *(Noted 8.01)*	Old Sarum
N38273	Piper PA-28R-201 Cherokee Arrow III			S W Freeborn	Blackbushe
		28R-7737086		*(Op L.Slater) (Noted 8.01)*	
N38940	Boeing-Stearman A75N1 (PT-17) Kaydet		(G-BSNK)	Eastern Stearman Inc *(Noted 7.01)*	Priory Farm,
	(Continental R670)	75-1822	N38940/N55300/41-8263 *(As "18263/822" in US Army c/s)*		Tibenham
				(Op R.W.Sage t/a Blackbarn Aviation)	
N39132*	Piper PA-38-112 Tomahawk	38-82A0065	(G-NCFD)	Not known	Swanton Morley
			D-EIIS/N2477V	*(Noted derelict 7.01)*	
N39605	Piper PA-34-200T Seneca	34-7870397		Heliquick Aviation *(Noted 11.01)*	Biggin Hill
N41098	Cessna 421B Golden Eagle	421B0448		Universal Aviation Corp Inc	Elstree
				(Noted 10.01)	
N41762	Raytheon Hawker 800XP	258456		Wells Fargo Bank Northwest NA	Blackpool
				(Noted 12.01)	
N46294	Steen Skybolt	SB-1990		A26 Europe Inc	King's Farm,
				(Noted 9.99: current status unknown)	Thurrock
N47914	Piper PA-32-300 Six	32-7840018		Southern Aircraft Consultancy Inc	Alderney
				(Noted 12.01)	
N49272	Fairchild M.62/PT-23-HO Cornell		42-.....	Flying Heritage Inc *(Noted 8.99)*	RAF Cosford
	(Continental W670)	HO-437		*(Op R.E.Mitchell t/a PT Flight) (As "23" in USAAC c/s)*	
N50029	Cessna 172	28807	LX-AIB	Southern Aircraft Consultancy Inc	Exeter
			N6707A	*(Op E.Byrd) (Noted 7.01)*	
N52485	Boeing-Stearman A75N1 (PT-17) Kaydet			V S E Norman *(As "169" US Navy)*	Rendcomb
		75-4494		*(Noted 2001)*	
N53091	Boeing-Stearman A75N1 (PT-17) Kaydet		41-25306	R C Vajdos Jr	NK
		75-2795		*(On rebuild 5.99: current status unknown)*	
N54211	Piper PA-23-250 Aztec E	27-7554006	G-ITTU	Southern Aircraft Consultancy Inc	Elstree
			D-IKLW/G-BCSW/N54211 *(Noted 11.01)*		
N54922	Boeing-Stearman A75N1 (N2S-4) Kaydet		Bu.30054	M G Plaskett *"Sweetie"*	Rendcomb
	(Pratt & Whitney 985-14B)	75-3491		*(Op V.S.E.Norman) (Utterly Butterly titles) (Noted 8.01)*	
N56421	Ryan PT-22-RY Recruit	1539	41-15510	Flying Heritage Inc *(Noted 8.99)*	RAF Cosford
				(Op R.E.Mitchell t/a PT Flight) (As "855" in US Army c/s)	
N56462	Maule M.6-235 Rocket	7409C		Avocet (US) Inc *(Noted 8.01)*	Old Buckenham
N56643	Maule M.5-180C	8086C		Southern Aircraft Consultancy Inc	Duxford
				(Noted 9.01)	
N58093	Mooney M.20K Srs 231	25-0877		Aircraft Sales International Inc	Coventry
				(Noted 6.01)	
N58566	Consolidated-Vultee BT-15-VN Valiant		42-41882	Flying Heritage Inc *(Noted 8.99)*	RAF Cosford
		10670		*(Op R.E.Mitchell t/a PT Flight) (US Army c/s)*	
N60256	Beechcraft C35 Bonanza	D-3346	OO-DOL	R.M.Hornblower	Southend
			OO-JAN	*(Noted 11.01)*	

N60526	Beechcraft E55 Baron	TE-1159		E Walsh *(Noted 11.01)*	Elstree
N61422	Piper PA-31 Turbo Navajo B/Panther	31-7401236		Swiftair Inc *(Noted 11.01)*	Elstree
N61787	Piper J3C-65 Cub	13624	NC61787 45-4884	Gypsy Fliers Ltd *(Noted 8.99)*	Rendcomb
N61970	Piper PA-24-250 Comanche	24-3364	OO-GOE F-OCBM/5R-MVA/N8198P/N10F	Southern Aircraft Consultancy Inc *(Noted 5.01)*	Gamston
N62840*	Boeing-Stearman PT-17 Kaydet	---	??	(Blackbarn Aviation) *(Stored 7.98: current status unknown)*	Priory Farm, Tibenham
N63560	Piper PA-31 Turbo Navajo	31-188	HB-LFW N9141Y	Southern Aircraft Consultancy Inc *(Noted 11.01)*	Norwich
N63590	Boeing-Stearman N2S-3 Kaydet	75-7143	Bu.07539	(Eastern Stearman Inc) *(Stored 8.01)*	North Weald
N65200	Boeing-Stearman D75N1 Kaydet	75-3817	FJ767	(Eastern Stearman Inc) *(Stored 7.01)*	Swanton Morley
N66630	Schweizer TG-3A	63 *(P/i not confirmed)*	42-52983	Imperial War Museum *(As "252983" in USAAC c/s)*	Duxford
N67501	Beechcraft A36 Bonanza	E-2116		S N Mermagen *(Noted 9.01)*	Elstree
N67548	Cessna 152	15281906		Southern Aircraft Consultancy Inc *(Noted 11.01)*	Norwich
N68427	Boeing-Stearman A75N1 (N2S-4) Kaydet	75-5008	Bu.55771	(Eastern Stearman Inc) *(Op Blackbarn Aviation)* *(Stored 7.98: current status unknown)*	Priory Farm, Tibenham
N70154	Piper J-3C-65 Cub	17139		R Long *(Noted 7.01)*	Rendcomb
N72127	Cessna U206D Skywagon *(Robertson STOL conversion)*	U2061368	G-AXJY N72326	R Herron *(Noted 5.01)*	Hill Farm, Nayland
N73410	Boeing-Stearman B75N1 (N2S-3) Kaydet	75-7761	Bu.38140	(Eastern Stearman Inc) *(As "N73410/29") (Noted 10.01)*	Kemble
N76402*	Cessna 140	10828	NC76402	C.Murgatroyd *(Cancelled by FAA 3.96) (Wreck noted 12.01)*	Blackpool
N80388	Beech D18S	A-288		Kingfisher Aviation *(Noted 5.01)*	North Weald
N80533	Cessna 172M Skyhawk	17266640		Southern Aircraft Consultancy Inc *(Noted 10.01)*	Popham
N82507	Piper PA-28RT-201 Arrow IV	28R-8018100		Ronair Inc *(Noted 5.01)*	Stapleford
N83196	Piper PA-28RT-201 Arrow IV	28R-8118045	N9646N	P C Laine *(Noted 1.02)*	Southend
N90724	Hiller UH-12C	810		W F Chmura *(Noted 5.01)*	Sancreed, Cornwall
N91384	Rockwell Commander 690A	11118	SE-FLN	Airbourne Data Inc *(Noted 10.01)*	Gamston
N92001	MD Helicopters MD Explorer	900-00040		Wells Fargo Bank NA Northwest *(Op Eastern Atlantic Helicopters) (Noted 1.02)*	Blackbushe
NC92782	Piper PA-12 Super Cruiser	12-228		Southern Aircraft Consultancy Inc *(Noted 10.01)*	(Somerset)
N93938	Erco 415C	1261		Merkado Holdings *(Noted 6.01)*	Panshangar
N96240	Beechcraft D18S (3TM)	CA-159	G-AYAH N6123/RCAF 1559	Euroworld Miami Inc *(Op Aces High Flying Museum)*	North Weald
N97121*	Embraer EMB-110P1 Bandeirante	110.334	PT-SDK	Guernsey Airport Fire Service *(Hulk only 12.01)*	Guernsey
N99153	North American T-28C Trojan *(FAA quote c/n 226-93)*	252-52	FG-289 Zaire AF FA-289 Congo AF/Bu.146289	W R Montague *(Op Norfolk & Suffolk Aviation Museum)* *(Crashed Limoges, France 14.12.77: fuselage only as "146289/2W")*	Flixton

AUSTRIA

OE-DPC	Piper PA-32-300 Cherokee Six	32-40070	N4042W	Not known *(Noted 5.01)*	Hill Farm, Nayland

FINLAND

OH-LBS	Boeing 757-2Q8	27623	N5573K	Finnair *(Op Air Scandic) (Noted 2001)*	Manchester

CZECH REPUBLIC

OK-DUU-15	Urban Air UFM-13 Lambada	3/11		M.Tormey *(Noted 7.01)*	Abbeyshrule
OK-EUU-55	Urban Air UFM-13 Lambada	NK		M.Tormey *(Noted 7.01)*	Abbeyshrule
OK-EUU-56	Urban Air UFM-13 Lambada	12/11		M.Tormey *(Noted 7.01)*	Abbeyshrule
OK-FUA-05	Urban Air UFM-10 Samba	NK	OK-EUU-02	Not known *(Noted 9.01)*	Waterford
OK-FUU-31	Urban Air UFM-10 Samba			Not known *(Noted 7.01)*	Abbeyshrule
OK-GUA-19	Urban Air UFM-13 Lambada			Not known *(Noted 7.01)*	Abbeyshrule
OK-JIY*	Yakovlev C.11	172673 *(C/n not confirmed)*	(Egypt AF)	Personal Plane Services Ltd *(Stored 3.96 for rebuild: current status unknown)*	(Booker)
OK-PDO	Letovlev LET L-410UVP Turbolet	851411	UR-67507 CCCP67507	Not known *(Noted 6.01)*	Hinton-in-the Hedges
OK-XTA	Extra EA.300/S	004	D-EBEW	Not known *(Noted 11.01)*	White Waltham

BELGIUM

OO-BDO(2)*	Cameron N-90 HAFB	1960	(LX-PRO)	Balloon Preservation Group *"Profi 2" (Spares use)*	Lancing
OO-BFH*	Piccard Gas Balloon	---		The Science Museum *(Gondola 3.00)*	South Kensington London SW.7
OO-FAN*	Beechcraft 56TC Baron	TG-10	G-AZOJ N5443U	Not known *(Stored 10.97 : current status unknown)*	Shoreham
OO-JAT*	Cameron Zero 25 Airship	1407		Balloon Preservation Group *(On loan to Farnbrough Air Sciences Trust)*	Farnborough
OO-MHB*	Piper PA-28-236 Dakota	28-8011143	G-BMHB D6-PAD/N81321/N9593N	R W H Watson *(Damaged Southend 20.10.90: wreck stored 12.01)*	Blackpool
OO-NAT	SOCATA MS.880B Rallye Club	2253	G-BAOK	R W H Watson *(Fuselage stored 2001)*	Grimmet Farm, Maybole
OO-RTC	Reims FR172H Rocket *(Damaged Brussels 5.99 & exported to the UK: noted road running on M25, Surrey 6.4.01 in damaged state)*	FR17200265	F-BSHK	Not known	(Surrey)
OO-VPC	Cessna 182P Skylane II *(Reims-assembled c/n F18200019)*	18263928	D-EHTW N9859E	Not known *(Damaged Maasbree, Holland 26.7.94: wreck stored 1.96)*	Farley Farm, Winchester
OO-WIO	Reims Cessna FRA150L Aerobat	FRA1500183	F-BUMG	Department of Engineering *(Instructional Airframe 2001)*	Salford University

DENMARK

OY-ALW	Miles M.28 Mercury 6	6268	D-EHAB G-AHAA	Not known *(Noted 2.01)*	Turweston
OY-ANZ*	Maule M.5-210C Strata Rocket	6027C	D-EMKK N15B	Not known *(Noted 2.99)*	East Winch
OY-BOB*	Omega O-80 HAFB	01	G-AWWO	British Balloon Museum & Library *"Blue Strike"*	Newbury
OY-BOW(2)*	Colting 77A HAFB	77A-014	SE-ZVB	British Balloon Museum & Library *"Circus"*	Newbury
OY-JRR	de Havilland DHC.2 Turbo Beaver III	1632/TB-18	N911CC C-FUKK/CF-UKK	Not known *(Noted 10.01)*	Headcorn
OY-PBA	Pilatus PC-6/B-4-H2 Turbo-Porter	678	LN-VIT HB-FEY/I-ALPJ/HB-FEY	Not known *(Noted 7.00)*	Langar

ARUBA

P4-ESP	Boeing 707-328C	19292	9XR-VO 9XR-JA/F-BLCF	Not known *(Stored 10.00)*	Manston

THE NETHERLANDS

PH-DUC	Stoddard-Hamilton Glasair IIRG-S	2069		R Sivandijk *(Noted 11.01)*	RAF Wyton
PH-NLH*	Hawker Hunter T.7	41H-695342		Not known *(Forward fuselage noted 10.00: wings Long Marston as part of "XJ714")*	Eaglescott
PH-NLK*	Piper PA-23-160 Apache	23-1694	OY-DCG SE-CKW/N10F	Not known *(Wreck stored for spares 6.01)*	Water Leisure Park, Skegness
PH-PAB	Neico Lancair 360	766		D C Ratcliffe *(Noted 1.02)*	Shoreham

RUSSIA

RA-1765	Piper PA-28-181 Archer II	2890093	G-BTAM N9153D	Not known *(Noted 10.01)*	Ronaldsway
RA-4147	Reims Cessna FA.337G Super Skymaster *(Cessna c/n 33701589)*	F33700070	G-BOYR PH-RPE	Not known *(Noted 6.01)*	Newtownards
RA-01096	Yakovlev Yak-50	NK		Not known *"Sasha"* *(Noted 10.01)*	Bourne Park, Hurstbourne Tarrant
RA-01153	Yakovlev Yak-18T	22202047817		Not known *(Noted 6.01)*	Haverfordwest
RA-01193	Yakovlev Yak-50	NK		Not known *(Noted 1.02)*	Leicester
RA-01274	Yakovlev Yak-55	910103	DOSAAF 03	Not known *(Noted 8.00)*	Wolverhampton
RA-01277	Sukhoi Su-29	80-02	RA8002	Mr Shann *(Noted 10.00)*	Bagby
RA-01293	Yakovlev Yak-50	NK		P N A Whitehead *(Noted 8.01)*	Leicester
RA-01294	Yakovlev Yak-50	853104		Not known *(Noted 8.01)*	North Weald
RA-01333	Yakovlev Yak-55M	920506	DOSAAF 40	Mrs B.Abela *(Noted 5.01) (G-YAKM reserved)*	White Waltham
RA-01370	Yakovlev Yak-18T	NK		F.M.Govern *(Crashed 5.01: wrecked stored 7.01)*	NK
RA-01378	Yakovlev Yak-52 *(Composite with c/n 833805/DOSAAF 134 which is now N54GT)*	833004	DOSAAF 14	T.Evans *(Open storage - unflyable 2.00)*	Wellesbourne Mntfrd
RA-01491	Yakovlev Yak-50	NK		Not known *(Noted 9.01)*	Thruxton
RA-01493(2)	Yakovlev Yak-50	853001		Not known *"R93" (Noted 8.01)*	North Weald
RA-01555	Yakovlev Yak-18T	NK		Not known *(Noted 8.01)*	Old Sarum
RA-01564	Yakovlev Yak-52	8910302	DOSAAF 149	Not known *(Noted 10.01)*	White Waltham
RA-01596	Yakovlev Yak-52			Not known *(Noted 1.02)*	Popham
RA-01607	Sukhoi Su-29	77-02	RA-7702	S Jones *(Noted 6.01)*	White Waltham
RA-01609	Sukhoi Su-29	75-03	RA-7503	Mr Moshe *(Noted 9.01)*	White Waltham

RA-01610	Sukhoi Su-29	78-02	RA-7802	P.Williams *(Noted 8.01)*	White Waltham
RA-01641	Antonov An-2R	1G-190-47		Black Country Aircraft Collection *(As "3"):(Crashed Milton 2.11.99: fuselage extant 2.00)*	Madeley
RA-01813	Yakovlev Yak-52	NK		Not known *(As "13") (Noted 6.01)*	(Peplow)
RA-02042	Yakovlev Yak-52	888911	DOSAAF 98(yellow)	S Jackson *"98" (Noted 8.01)*	Rochester
RA-02075	Yakovlev Yak-52	888914	DOSAAF 101(yellow)	Not known "101" *(Noted 9.00)*	White Waltham
RA-02080	Yakovlev Yak-52	9010508	DOSAAF 35 (yellow)	Not known "35" *(Noted 1.01)*	White Waltham
RA-02090	Yakovlev Yak-52	9111205	DOSAAF 10 (grey)	O Hutcheon "10" *(Noted 12.01)*	Guernsey
RA-02135	Aeropract A-21M Solo	01		Not known *(Last noted 3.97: current status unknown)*	Newcastle, Co.Wicklow
RA-02149	Yakovlev Yak-52	8910001		D Munroe *(Noted 8.01)*	Booker
RA-02209	Yakovlev Yak-52	9111311	DOSAAF 31	P.Scandrett *"31" (Noted 6.00)*	Rendcomb
RA-02246	Yakovlev Yak-50	8425905		Not known *"46" (Noted 8.01)*	North Weald
RA-02293	Yakovlev Yak-52	9011013	DOSAAF 115	A.Tyler *(Noted 2.00)*	Wolverhampton
RA-02622	Yakovlev Yak-52	9612001	LY-AFH	Not known *(Noted 9.01)*	White Waltham
RA-02705	Yakovlev Yak-52	866915	LY-ABQ	Not known *"101" (Noted 7.01)*	Rochester
RA-22521	Yakovlev Yak-52	9211612	DOSAAF 04	D.Squires *"04" (Noted 6.00)*	Wellesbourne Mntfrd
RA-44400	Yakovlev Yak-18T	11-35		Richard Goode Aerobatics *(Noted 6.01)*	White Waltham
RA-44435	Yakovlev Yak-52	NK		Not known *(Noted 8.00)*	Wolverhampton
RA-44444	Sukhoi Su-26	04-05		Not known *(Noted 11.01)*	White Waltham
RA-44445	Yakovlev Yak-55	911209		D Samuels *(Noted 10.01)*	White Waltham
RA-44449	Yakovlev Yak-50	822210	LY-AGG DOSAAF 107	Not known *"107" "Svetlana" (Noted 8.01)*	Compton Abbas
RA-44454	Yakovlev Yak-52	822807		Not known *(Noted 10.01)*	White Waltham
RA-44455	Yakovlev Yak-52	877902		Not known *(Noted 9.01)*	Southend
RA-44461	Yakovlev Yak-50	NK		Not known *(Noted 9.01)*	White Waltham
RA-44463	Yakovlev Yak-52	888912	DOSAAF 99	Not known *(As "N/123" in FAA Sea Fury c/s) (Noted 6.01)*	RNAS Yeovilton
RA-44464	Yakovlev Yak-52	9111415	DOSAAF 50	Not known *"50" (Noted 7.01)*	White Waltham
RA-44465(2)	Yakovlev Yak-18T	NK	LY-AOL(?)	Yak UK *(Noted 12.01)*	Leicester
RA-44466(2)	Yakovlev Yak-52S	855905		Not known *(Noted 10.01)*	White Waltham
RA-44469(2)	Yakovlev Yak-52	899413	LY-AFX	D Noble *(As DOSAAF 69) (Noted 10.01)*	Compton Abbas
RA-44470	Technoavia Yak-18T	18-33		B.Austen *(Noted 7.01)*	Spanhoe
RA-44473	Yakovlev Yak-52	9111307	G-YAKX RA9111307/DOSAAF 27	Not known *(Noted 9.01)*	White Waltham
RA-44480	Technoavia Yak-18T	08-34	CCCP-44480	Not known *(Noted 9.01)*	White Waltham
RA-44484	Technoavia SM-92 Finist	NK		Not known *(Noted 9.01)*	RAF Benson
RA-44502(3)	Aerostar Yak-52	9411711		Not known *(Noted 6.01)*	White Waltham
(RA-44502(2) also reported as c/n 941171 and noted White Waltham 5.01 - now believed returned to France)					
RA-44506	Yakovlev Yak-18T	22202034139	HA-JAC FLA-02159	Not known *(Noted 9.01)*	Tilstock
RA-44508(2)	Sukhoi Su-31	03-01		Not known *(Noted 9.01)*	(Jersey)
RA-44510	Yakovlev Yak-55M	930707	DOSAAF 59	T Shears *"59" (Noted 3.01)*	White Waltham
RA-44514	Yakovlev Yak-52	9111413	DOSAAF 48	Not known *"48" (Noted 5.00)*	Manston
RA-44515	Yakovlev Yak-52	9111515	DOSAAF 56	M.Stebbing *"65" (Noted 6.00)*	Poplar Hall Farm, Elmsett
RA-44518	Yakovlev Yak-50	832601	RA-44418	Not known *(Noted 9.01)*	White Waltham
RA-44525	Yakovlev Yak-55M	901103	DOSAAF 96	Not known *(Noted 5.01)*	Headcorn
RA-44527	Yakovlev Yak-18T	15-35		Not known *(Noted 10.01)*	White Waltham
RA-44531	Sukhoi Su-26	01-04	PK-SDM	Not known *(Noted 12.01)*	White Waltham
RA-44533	Yakovlev Yak 50	853206		Not known *(Noted 8.01)*	Compton Abbas
RA-44534	Yakovlev Yak-52	822013		Not known *(Noted 5.01)*	Compton Abbas
RA-44536	Yakovlev Yak-18T	22202034143	LY-AMI DOSAAF	M Webb *(Noted 2.01)*	Popham
RA-44537	Yakovlev Yak-55M	910104	HA-JAM	Not known *(Noted 5.01)*	White Waltham
RA-44538	Yakovlev Yak-18T	22202052122		Not known *(Noted 6.01)*	White Waltham
RA-44544	Yakovlev Yak-18T	11-33		Not known *(Noted 8.01)*	Benson's Farm, Laindon
RA-44545	Yakovlev Yak-18T	22202034023	LY-AIH ES-FYE	Not known *(Noted 10.01)*	White Waltham
RA-44546	Yakovlev Yak-52	889012	LY-ALM DOSAAF 114	Not known *"114" "Tatiyana II" (Destroyed 11.8.01)*	Compton Abbas
RA-44547	Technoavia SP-55M	0101-0007		Not known *(Noted 10.01)*	White Waltham
RA-44549	Yakovlev Yak-50	822305	G-BXNO LY-ASD/DOSAAF 82	Not known *(Noted 8.01)*	Compton Abbas
RA-44550	Yakovlev Yak-52	877409	LY-AKF	Not known *(Noted 7.01)*	White Waltham
RA-44553	Yakovlev Yak-50			Not known *(Noted 9.01)*	NK
RA-44777	Yakovlev Yak-18T	12-35		V Norman *(Noted 8.00)*	Rendcomb
RA-81584	Yakovlev Yak-18T	22202054812		Mr Newman *(Noted 5.00)*	Henstridge

SWEDEN

SE-AZB*	Avro 671 Cierva C.30A Autogiro	R3/CA.954	K4232	RAF Museum *(As "K4232")*	Hendon
SE-BNN	Saab 91A Safir	91130	OY-DBT OO-MUG/OO-HUG/PH-UEB/SE-BNN	L.de Jonge *(Stored 10.97: current status unknown)*	Luxters Farm, Hambledon
SE-BZP	Stinson V-77 Reliant	6375	OO-NUT FB536	M Hales *(Noted 6.00)*	Little Staughton
SE-DXA	Hawker Hunter F.Mk.58 *(C/n 41H-697456 quoted in ERH 2001)*	41H-679995	(OY-SKP) J-4089	Scandinavian Historic Flight *(Noted 8.01)*	North Weald
SE-DXY	de Havilland DH.100 Vampire FB.Mk.6 *(Built FFW)*	693	J-1184	Scandinavian Historic Flight *(Noted 8.01)*	North Weald
SE-GVH	Piper PA-38-112 Tomahawk	38-78A0053		Not known *(Fuselage noted 2.00)*	Little Staughton
SE-IIV	Piper PA-24-260 Comanche C	24-4970	HB-OHZ N9462P	Not known *(Noted 11.00)*	Gamston
SE-KBU	Christen A-1 Husky	038		A Allen *(Noted 2001)*	Perth
SE-LBR*	Yakovlev Yak-50	791602	DOSAAF	Not known *(Noted 7.01)*	Rochester
SE-RAB(2)	Embraer EMB-135ER	145453		SEB Finans AB *(Op British Midland/Eastern Airways)*	Edinburgh *(Noted 8.01)*

POLAND

SP-CHD*	PZL-101A Gawron	74134		Not known *(On rebuild 8.01)*	North Weald
SP-FBO(2)*	Antonov An-2T	1G-108-55	PLW-0855	Not known *(Noted 7.01)*	Swanton Morley
SP-SAY*	Mil Mi-2	529538125		The Helicopter Museum	Weston-super-Mare

SUDAN

ST-AHZ	Piper PA-31 Turbo Navajo	31-473	G-AXMR N6558L	Not known *(Fire practice: burnt-out fuselage remains 6.00)*	Elstree

GREECE

SX-BFM	Piper PA-31-350 Chieftain	31-8052204	N4504J	(Bouremouth Aviation Museum) *(Fuselage stored unmarked 7.01)*	Bournemouth
SX-HCF	Agusta A109A-II	7207	N71PT N4263A	Castle Air Charters Ltd *(Spares use 10.00)*	Liskeard

SEYCHELLE ISLANDS

S7-AAW	Airbus A300C4-103	033	HS-THH HS-TAX/HS-TGH/F-WNDC	Not known *(Stored 9.01)*	Filton
VQ-SAC	Britten Norman BN-2A Islander	287		Frank Matthews *(Crashed 4.9.76: front fuselage 3.94: current status unknown)*	Littlehampton

ICELAND

TF-ABP*	Lockheed L.1011-385-100 Tristar	1045	VR-HOG N323EA	British Aviation Heritage Cold War Jets Collection *(Stored 2.00)*	Bruntingthorpe
TF-ELL	Boeing 737-210C	20138	N41026 F-GGFI/N4906	Islandsflug *(Noted 8.00/6.01)*	Stansted
TF-ELP	Boeing 737-330QC	23522	D-ABXA N1786B	Islandsflug *(Channel Express lease) (Noted 6.01)*	Stansted
TF-ELR	Boeing 737-330QC	23523	D-ABXB	Islandsflug *(Channel Express lease) (Noted 8.01)*	Stansted
TF-SHC*	Miles M.25 Martinet TT.1	--	MS902	Museum of Berkshire Aviation *(Crashed 18.7.51: on rebuild with Master components 2.00)*	Woodley
TF-TOA	Piper PA-28R-200 Cherokee Arrow III	28R-7635029	TF-GLK SE-GLK	Not known *(Noted 8.99: current status unknown)*	Elstree

UKRAINE

UR-67199	Letovlev Let L410UVP Turbolet	790305	CCCP-67199	Air Ukraine *(Noted 6.01)* *(Quoted in error in UKI2001 as becoming HA-LAK)*	Langar
UR-67439	Letovlev LET L-410UVP Turbolet	841204		Not known *(Universal Avia c/s) (Noted 8.01)*	Headcorn
UR-67477	Letovlev LET L-410UVP Turbolet	841302	CCCP-67477	Not known *(Universal Avia c/s) (Noted 11.01)*	Sibson

AUSTRALIA

VH-ALB*	Supermarine 228 Seagull V	---	A2-4	RAF Museum *(As "A2-4")*	Hendon
VH-ASM*	Avro 652A Anson I	72960	W2068	RAF Museum *(As "W2068/68" in RAF c/s)*	Hendon
VH-AYY	Kavanagh D-77 HAFB	KB136		Balloon Preservation Group *"Carlsberg"*	Kirdford
VH-BRC*	Short S.24 Sandringham IV	SH.55C	N158C	The Science Museum VP-LVE/N158C/VH-BRC/ZK-AMH/JM715 *"Beachcomber"* *(On loan to Hall of Aviation) (Ansett c/s)*	Southampton

VH-DHS	Beech 58 Baron	TH-1386	VH-NSN	Global Aviation	Filton
			N6921Y	*(Noted 9.01)*	
VH-SNB*	de Havilland DH.84A Dragon	2002	VH-ASK	National Museums of Scotland/Museum of Flight	
			A34-13		East Fortune
VH-UQB*	de Havilland DH.80A Puss Moth	2051	(G-ABDW)	National Museums of Scotland/Museum of Flight	
			VH-UQB/G-ABDW		East Fortune
VH-UTH*	General Aircraft Monospar ST-12	ST12/36		Newark Air Museum	Innsworth
				(On rebuild by Cotswold Aircraft Restoration Group 2.00)	
VH-UUP*	Short S.16 Scion 1	S.776	G-ACUX	<ins>*See G-ACUX in SECTION 1, Part 2*</ins>	
			VH-UUP/G-ACUX		
VH-YOT	Skyfox Gazelle CA25N	CA25N030		Not known	Dunkirk, Canterbury
	(Rotax 912)			*(Last noted 8.97: current status unknown)*	

BERMUDA (1)

VP-BAT	Boeing 747SP-21	21648	VR-BAT	Worldwide Aircraft Holding (Bermuda)	
			N148UA/N539PA	*(Noted 12.01)*	Bournemouth
VP-BBG	Piaggio P.180 Avanti	1037	F-GUAE	Not known *(Noted 9.01)*	Fairoaks
VP-BCE	Eurocopter AS355N Twin Squirrel	5663		Sioux Corporation *(Noted 12.01)*	Jersey
VP-BCI	Canadair CL601 Challenger	5193	VR-BCI	Consolidated Contractors (UK) Ltd	Farnborough
			N604D/C-GLYK	*(Noted 5.00)*	
VP-BCN	British Aerospace BAe 125-600B	256035		ICN Pharaceuticals *(Noted 2000)*	Glasgow
VP-BCO	Canadair CL604 Challenger	5420	N603CC	Consolidated Contractors (UK) Ltd	Farnborough/Athens
			C-GLWR	*(Noted 4.01)*	
VP-BDB	Cessna 560 Citation V	560-0503	(ZS-FCB)	Fegotila Ltd	Gloucestershire
			N52059	*(Noted 7.01)*	
VP-BDF	Boeing 707-312	18085	N435MA	South East Enthusiasts Group	New Ross,
			G-14-372/G-AYAG/N759PA *(Nose only 4.00)*		Co.Wexford
VP-BDL	Dassault Falcon 2000	111	F-WWVF	Sioux Corporation *(Noted 5.01)*	Luton
VP-BFE	Boeing 737-7CP	30753	N329K	Ford Air Services LLC *(Noted 5.01)*	Stansted
VP-BFO	Boeing 737-7CP	30755	N330K	Ford Air Services LLC *(Noted 5.01)*	Stansted
VP-BIE	Canadair CL601 Challenger 1A	3016	N601CL	Inflite Aviation	Stansted
			N1107Z/N4562Q/C-GLWV *(Noted 10.01)*		
VP-BIS	Gulfstream Gulfstream IV	1150	N151G	ISPAT Group Ltd	Luton
			V8-SRI/V8-009/V8-ALI/N433GA *(Noted 7.01)*		
VP-BJT	Cessna 425 Corsair	425-0027	VP-BNM	Rig Design Services Group Ltd	Booker
			VR-BNM/N181AA/HI-598SP/N97DA/(N711EF)/N97DA/N67720 *(Noted 11.01)*		
VP-BJV	Gulfstream G1159 Gulfstream II	186	VR-BJV	Uniexpress Jet Services	NK
			(D-AAMD)/5N-AML/D-AFKG/(D-ACVG)/N17582		
				(Last noted 3.98: current status unknown)	
VP-BKH	Gulfstream Gulfstream IV	1029	VP-BKI	Specialised Transportation	Ronaldsway
			VR-BKI/N429GA	*(Noted 10.01)*	
VP-BKK	Hawker Siddely HS.125-400A/731	25238	VR-BKK	Air 125 Ltd/Business Real Estates	Southampton
			N808V/N125GC/G-TOPF/G-AYER/9K-ACR/G-AYER *(Noted 7.01)*		
VP-BKQ	Bell 430	49008	N62833	Jud Investments Co Ltd *(Noted 6.01)*	Blackbushe
VP-BLK	Rockwell 690C Turbo Commander	11672	VR-BLK	Control Techniques (Bermuda) Ltd	Welshpool
	(Built Gulfstream American)		OE-FIT/D-IKOM/(N5924K) *(Noted 7.01)*		
VP-BLS	Pilatus PC-XII	176	N176BS	B.L.Schroeder	Fairoaks
			VP-BLS/HB-FSL	*(Noted 7.01)*	
VP-BMF	Dassault Falcon 50	206	F-WWHB	Sally Navigation *(Noted 4.01)*	Farnborough
VP-BMZ	Rockwell 690D Turbo Commander		VR-BMZ	Aviatica Trading Co Ltd/Marlborough Fine Art Ltd	
	(Built Gulfstream Aerospace)	15033	G-MFAL/N49GA/(N5925N) *(Noted 6.01)*		Fairoaks
VP-BNS	Cessna 550 Citation Bravo	550-0939	(N939BB)	Tower House Consultants	Jersey
			N5076K	*(Noted 12.01)*	
VP-BNU	Robin DR400/180 Regent	2047	VR-BNU	N.French	Biggin Hill
			G-BTDU	*(Noted 4.01)*	
VP-BNZ(3)	Gulfstream Gulfstream V	509	N5GA	Dennis Vanguard International (Switchgear)	
			N509GA/V8-001/N509GA *(Noted 7.01)*		Birmingham
VP-BPS	Consolidated 28-5ACF (PBY-5A) Catalina		VR-BPS	Not known *(On rebuild 2002)*	Lee-on-Solent
		1997	G-BLSC/C-FMIR/N608FF/CF-MIR/N10023/Bu.46633		
				(Op Super Catalina Restoration)	
VP-BPW	Dassault Falcon 900B	135	VR-BPW	Tower House Consultants Ltd	Jersey
			F-WWFJ	*(Noted 8.99)*	
VP-BRD	Eurocopter EC.120B	1155		Not known *(Noted 7.01)*	Redhill
VP-BUS	Gulfstream Gulfstream IV	1127	VR-BUS	U Schwarzenbach	Farnborough
			VR-BLR/N427GA	*(Noted 10.01)*	

CAYMAN ISLANDS

VP-CAD	Cessna 525 CitationJet	525-0297	N316MJ	Reynard Motorsport *(Noted 9.01)*	Oxford
VP-CAM	Canadair CL601 Challenger	5090	N400KC	Qamar Ltd	Jersey
			N818TH/N818LS/N404CB/N601CB/C-GLXF *(Noted 4.01)*		
VP-CAS	British Aerospace BAe 125-800A	258167	VR-CAS	Cavalier Air Corporation	Southampton
			N125AS/G-5-662/N125AS/G-5-662 *(Noted 6.01)*		

VP-CAT	Cessna 501 Citation 1	501-0232	VR-CAT	Kestrel Aviation/Aviation Jet	Guernsey
			VR-CHF/N35TL/N853KB/N2616C/(N2616G) *(Noted 6.01)*		
VP-CBM	Cessna 550 Citation II	550-0729	VR-CBM	Bernard Matthews plc	Norwich
			N1210V	*(Noted 7.01)*	
VP-CBW	Gulfstream Gulfstream IV	1096	VR-CDW	Rolls-Royce plc	Farnborough
			(G-....)/N17589	*(Noted 4.01)*	
VP-CBX	Gulfstream Gulfstream V	511	N511GA	Aravco *(Noted 7.01)*	Farnborough
VP-CCO	Cessna 550 Citation II	550-0321	N321GN	Not known	Biggin Hill
			TC-COY/N321SE/N5430G *(Noted 4.01)*		
VP-CCP	Cessna 550 Citation Bravo	550-0857	VP-CNM(1)	Not known	Blackpool
			N51246	*(Op Trustair) (Noted 9.01)*	
VP-CCW	MD Helicopters MD 600N	RN030		Weetabix plc *(Noted 5.01)*	Sywell
VP-CED	Cessna 550 Citation Bravo	550-0870	N50612	Iceland Foods *(Noted 9.01)*	Hawarden
VP-CEO	Eurocopter EC.135	0031		Not known *(Noted 2.01)*	Redhill
VP-CFG	Cessna 501 Citation I/SP	501-0176	VR-CFG	Alpha Golf Aviation Ltd	Gloucestershire
			(VR-CIA)/N49LC/N44LC/N6779L *(Noted 11.01)*		
VP-CGE	Cessna 650 Citation VII	650-7077	(N582JF)	Not known *(Op Grosvenor Estates)*	Hawarden
			N532JF/N877CM/N5203J *(Noted 12.01)*		
VP-CGP	Dassault Falcon 900	163	VP-BEH	Williams Grand Prix Engineering Ltd *(Noted 7.01)*	Oxford
VP-CHJ	Agusta A109C	7634	VR-CHJ	Estate of F.Hackett-Jones	Guernsey
			VR-CEC/3A-MSG	*(Stored 12.01)*	
VP-CIC	Canadair CL601 Challenger	5011	VR-CIC	TGC Aviation Ltd/Fakhar Ltd	Stansted
			N602UK/N611MH/JA8283/N603CC/C-GLXD	*(Last noted 8.98: current status unknown)*	
VP-CIS	Cessna 525 CitationJet	525-0252	N740JV	Flightline Ltd	Southend/Guernsey
			(N5223P)	*(Noted 1.02)*	
VP-CJR	Cessna 550 Citation II	550-0354	VR-CJR	Broome & Wellington (Aviation) Ltd	Manchester
			N121C/N121CG	*(Noted 8.01)*	
VP-CLA	Beech F90	LA-231	N27PA	Claessons International Ltd	Farnborough
			N7220T	*(Noted 10.01)*	
VP-CLD	Cessna 550 Citation II	550-0323	N323AM	Not known *(Op Dovey Aviation)*	Filton
			TC-YZB/TC-FMB/TC-FAL/OE-GCP/(N5703C) *(Noted 9.01)*		
VP-CMF	Gulfstream Gulfstream IV	1062	VR-CMF	Aravco Ltd/Sheikh Mohammed Fakhry	Luton
			N688H/N462GA/N17583 *(Noted 9.01)*		
VP-CMS	Cessna 560 Citation Ultra	560-0457	N59HA	Redbus Group	Luton
			N51564	*(Op Redbus Charter) (Noted 10.01)*	
VP-CNF	Cessna 525 CitationJet	525-0153	(N525EF)	Foster Aviation	Biggin Hill
			N551Q/N551G/N5090V *(Noted 4.01)*		
VP-CNM(2)	Cessna 560XL Citation Excel	560-5070	N5207A	Not known *(Op Nigel Mansell) (Noted 12.01)*	Jersey
VP-CNP	Gulfstream G1159A Gulfstream III	496	N843HS	Fitzwilton plc	Dublin
			(N99SU)/N99SC/N89AB/N89AE/N21NY/N310SL/N327GA *(Noted 12.00)*		
VP-COM	Cessna 500 Citation I	500-318	VR-COM	Rapid 3864 Ltd	Biggin Hill
			N944B/N518CC/N5318J *(Noted 4.01)*		
VP-CPC	Cessna 560 XL Citation Excel	560-5215	N560TH	Trustair Ltd (Noted 12.01)	Blackpool
			N5091J		
VP-CPT	British Aerospace BAe 125 Srs.1000B	259004	VR-CPT	Reno Investments Inc	Biggin Hill
			G-LRBJ/G-5-779	*(Noted 7.01)*	
VP-CRB	Learjet Learjet 60	60-125	N60LR	Lisane Ltd *(Noted 12.01)*	Guernsey
VP-CRY	Gulfstream Gulfstream IV	1176	N176G	Avia Carriers	Luton
			V8-008/N468GA	*(Current status unknown)*	
VP-CSC	Cessna 560 Citation Ultra	560-0439	(N39LX)	Stadium City Ltd	Humberside
			N50612	*(Noted 7.01)*	
VP-CSN	Cessna 560 Citation Ultra	560-0401	N401CV	Scottish & Newcastle Breweries Ltd	Edinburgh
			N5197A	*(Noted 9.01)*	
VP-CTJ	Cessna 550 Citation II	F550-0073	F-GBTL	Flight Consultancy Services	Biggin Hill
			N4621G	*(Noted 4.01)*	
VP-CWA	Agusta A109C	7628	JA6610	Williams Grand Prix Engineering Ltd *(Op Alan Mann Helicopters) (Noted 8.01)*	Oxford

FALKLAND ISLANDS & DEPENDENCIES

VP-FAZ	de Havilland DHC.6-310 Twin Otter	748	C-GEOA	British Antarctic Survey	Oxford
			(FAP-2029)/C-GEOA	*(Noted 8.01)*	
VP-FBB	de Havilland DHC.6-310 Twin Otter	783	C-GDKL	British Antarctic Survey	Oxford
				(Noted 9.01)	
VP-FBC	de Havilland DHC.6-310 Twin Otter	787	C-GDIU	British Antarctic Survey	Oxford
				(Noted 9.01)	
VP-FBL	de Havilland DHC.6-310 Twin Otter	839	C-GDCZ	British Antarctic Survey	Oxford
				(Noted 9.01)	
VP-FBQ	de Havilland DHC-7-110	111	G-BOAX	British Antarctic Survey	Coventry
			C-GDNG	*(Noted 5.01)*	

SOUTHERN RHODESIA – now ZIMBABWE

VP-YKF	de Havilland DH.104 Dove 6	04292	3D-AAI VQ-ZJC/G-AMDD	South East Aviation Enthusiasts Group *(Damaged 9.8.82: stored 4.00 :as "IAC 176")*	New Ross Co.Wexford

BERMUDA (2)

VR-BEB	BAC One-Eleven 527FK	BAC.226	RP-C1181 PI-C1181	European Aviation Ltd *(Fire Compound 5.01 - all white & no marks)*	Bournemouth
VR-BEP	Westland WS-55 Whirlwind 3	WA.83	G-BAMH XG588	East Midlands Aeropark *(As "XG588 in SAR c/s) "Cormorant"*	East Midlands
VR-BEU	Westland WS-55 Whirlwind 3	WA.493	G-ATKV EP-HAN/G-ATKV	The Helicopter Museum	Weston-super-Mare
VR-BMB	Hawker Siddley HS.125-400B	25240	VR-BKN I-GJBO/G-AYLI/G-5-11	Not known *(Open storage 5.01)*	Stansted

INDIA

VT-EKE	Westland WG.30-160	021	G-BLPR G-17-17	Turbine World *(Current status unknown)*	Honeycrock Farm, Redhill
VT-EKK	Westland WG.30-160	025	G-17-13	Turbine World *(Current status unknown)*	Honeycrock Farm, Redhill
VT-EKL	Westland WG.30-160	028	G-17-14	Turbine World *(Current status unknown)*	Honeycrock Farm, Redhill
VT-EKM	Westland WG.30-160	027	G-17-15	Turbine World *(Current status unknown)*	Honeycrock Farm, Redhill
VT-EKT	Westland WG.30-160	035	G-17-23	Turbine World *(Current status unknown)*	Honeycrock Farm, Redhill
VT-EKW	Westland WG.30-160	038	G-17-26	Turbine World *(Current status unknown)*	Honeycrock Farm, Redhill
VT-EKX	Westland WG.30-160	039	G-17-27	Turbine World *(Current status unknown)*	Honeycrock Farm, Redhill

MEXICO

XA-NAA	MBB Bö.105CBS/4	S-759		Bond Air Services Ltd *(Noted 5.00)* *(Non-airworthy pod with "Pegasus" logo as operated by Transportes Aereos Pegaso)*	Bourn
XA-NAN	MBB Bö.105CBS/4	S-761		Bond Air Services *(Stored 6.00)*	Peterhead
XA-PBA	Boeing 737-2H6	20631	XA-APB PK-IJD/9M-MBG/9M-ARG	European Aviation *(Stored for spares 12.01)*	Bournemouth
XA-RIY	Boeing PT-17 Stearman	75-7275		Not known *(Stored 6.97: current status unknown)*	Rendcomb
XA-TLJ	Boeing 737-2H6	20926	PK-IJE 9M-MBH/9M-ASR	European Aviation *(Stored for spares 12.01)*	Bournemouth

LATVIA

YL-CBH*	Yakovlev Yak-50 *(C/n conflicts with YL-YAK)*	832507	DOSAAF 05	Hawarden Air Services *(As "05" blue) (Last noted 11.97: current status unknown)*	Hawarden
YL-CBI*	Yakovlev Yak-52	811202	DOSAAF 09	Hawarden Air Services *(As "09" green) (Last noted 11.96: current status unknown)*	Hawarden
YL-CBJ*	Yakovlev Yak-52	790404	DOSAAF 20	Hawarden Air Services *(As "20" black) (Last noted 11.97: current status unknown)*	Hawarden
YL-LEU*	WSK-PZL Antonov An-2R	1G-165-45	CCCP19731 SP-ZFP/CCCP19731	Hooton Park Trust *(As "CCCP-19731" 7.00)*	Hooton Park
YL-LEV*	WSK-PZL Antonov An-2R	1G-148-29	CCCP07268	Hawarden Air Services *(As "CCCP07268" 5.00)*	Hawarden
YL-LEW*	WSK-PZL Antonov An-2R	1G-182-28	CCCP56471	Hawarden Air Services *(As "CCCP56471" 5.00)*	Hawarden
YL-LEX*	WSK-PZL Antonov An-2R	1G-187-58	CCCP54949	Hawarden Air Services *(As "CCCP54949" 5.00)*	Hawarden
YL-LEY*	WSK-PZL Antonov An-2R	1G-173-11	CCCP40784	Hawarden Air Services *(As "CCCP40784" 5.00)*	Hawarden
YL-LEZ*	WSK-PZL Antonov An-2R	1G-165-47	CCCP19733	Hawarden Air Services *(As "CCCP19733" 2.00)*	Hawarden
YL-LFA*	WSK-PZL Antonov An-2R	1G-172-20	CCCP40748	Hawarden Air Services *(As "CCCP40748" 5.00)*	Hawarden
YL-LFB*	WSK-PZL Antonov An-2R	1G-173-12	CCCP40785	Hawarden Air Services *(As "CCCP40785" 5.00)*	Hawarden
YL-LFC*	WSK-PZL Antonov An-2R	1G-206-44	CCCP17939	Hawarden Air Services *(As "CCCP17939" 5.00)*	Hawarden
YL-LFD*	WSK-PZL Antonov An-2R	1G-172-21	CCCP40749	Hawarden Air Services *(As "CCCP40749" 5.00)*	Hawarden
YL-LHN*	Mil Mi-2	524006025	CCCP20320	Hawarden Air Services *(As "CCCP20320" 2.00)*	Hawarden
YL-LHO*	Mil Mi-2	535025126	CCCP20619	Hawarden Air Services *(As "CCCP20619" 2.00)*	Hawarden

YL-VIP(2)	British Aerospace BAe 125-800B	258078	OE-GHS	Viking International Group	Southampton
			ZS-FSI/G-BNEH/G-5-713/G-BNEH/G-5-544 *(Noted 7.01)*		
YL-YAK*	Yakovlev Yak-50	832507		Hawarden Air Services	Hawarden
		(C/n conflicts with YL-CBH)		*(As "05" red) (Last noted 11.95: current status unknown)*	

NICARAGUA

YN-CCN	Boeing 707-123B	18054	5B-DAO	Omega Air	Shannon
			G-BGCT/N7526A	*(Aeronica c/s) (Stored 5.99)*	

SERBIA

YU-DMN(2)	UTVA-66	---	JRV51182	M Roberts t/a F C S	Biggin Hill
				(As "51182" in Serbia AF c/s) (Noted 7.01 @ Oshkosh)	
YU-DMT	UTVA-66	---	JRV51...	M Roberts t/a F C S	Biggin Hill
				(Stored 11.97: current status unknown)	
YU-HCE	Agusta-Bell 212	5713		Serbian Police	Redhill
				(On rebuild 12.99: current status unknown)	
YU-HEH	SOKO SO341 Gazelle	011	JRV12619	Kestrel Shipping *(Noted 6.01)*	Redhill
YU-HEI	SOKO SO341 Gazelle	008	JRV126..	M Roberts t/a F C S	Biggin Hill
				(Noted 11.99: current status unknown)	
YU-HEK	SOKO SO341 Gazelle	012	JRV12620	Not known	Stapleford
				(Noted 1999: current status unknown)	
YU-YAB	SOKO G-2A Galeb (Seagull)	NK	JRV23170	Shuttle Air *(Noted 6.01)*	Biggin Hill
YU-YAG	SOKO G-2A Galeb	NK	JRV23194	Shuttle Air *(Noted 4.01)*	Biggin Hill

NEW ZEALAND

ZK-MKV	Supermarine Spitfire Vc	---	A-58-178	Historic Flying Ltd	Audley End
			JG891	*(On rebuild 3.00 as "JG891"/79)*	
ZK-RMH	Curtiss P-40E-CU Kittyhawk	19669	NZ3009	The Old Flying Machine Co	Duxford
			ET482/41-25158	*(Breitling Fighter Team titles) (Noted 11.01)*	
				(As "663/P11151/88" in Chinese AF c/s)	

REPUBLIC of SOUTH AFRICA

ZS-JVL	Lockheed L-100-30 Hercules	4676	PH-RMH	Safair *(Op Air Contractors)*	Dublin
			ZS-JVL/(PH-...)/ZS-JVL/D2-TAA/ZS-JVL *(Noted 7.01)*		
ZS-KCT	Beechcraft A36 Bonanza	E-1280		Not known *(Noted 8.01)*	Shobdon
ZS-LWI	Piper PA-34-220T Seneca	34-8533024		SWJ Beleggings Pty *(Noted 7.01)*	Fairoaks
ZS-OGX	Piper PA-32R-300	32R-7780069		Wild Aviation *(Noted 8.01)*	Wellesbourne Mntfrd
ZS-SDA	Airbus A300B2K-3C	032	F-WLGA	Channel Express	Bournemouth
				(Stored for spares 12.01))	
ZS-SDD	Airbus A300B2K-3C	040	F-WUAX	Channel Express	Bournemouth
				(Stored for spares 12.01)	

EQUATORIAL GUINEA

3C-GIG	Boeing 707-373C	19179	3D-CSB	Koda Air Cargo	Southend
			9Q-CSB/CS-TBJ/N372WA *(Impounded 12.01)*		

SWAZILAND

3D-HVW	Westland Gazelle HT.3	WA/1906	G-BZDW	MW Helicopters Ltd	Stapleford
			ZB626	*(Noted 10.01)*	
3D-HXL	Westland Gazelle HT.2	WA/1150	G-BZDV	MW Helicopters Ltd	Stapleford
			XW884	*(Noted 11.01)*	

AZERBAIJAN

4K-AZ3*	Boeing 707-341C	19321	(N8190U)	Southend Airport*(For scrap 2.02)*	Southend
			N107BW/PP-VJS/(FAB2405)/PP-VJS *(Azerbaijan Airlines c/s)*		

ISRAEL

4X-AVY	Piper PA-30-160B Twin Comanche	30-1552	N8403Y	Not known *(Noted 9.01)*	Elstree

CYPRUS

5B-DBE	Boeing 727-30	18371	9M-SAS	Aimes Co *(Noted 7.01)*	Luton
			V8-BG2/V8-BG1/V8-UHM/N727CH/VS-UHM/VR-UHM/VR-BHP/N727CH/D-ABIQ		

NIGERIA

5N-AAN	British Aerospace BAe.125-F3B/RA	25125	F-GFMP	Air Atlantic Nigeria Ltd	Biggin Hill
			G-AVAI/LN-NPA/G-AVAI *(Stored 4.01)*		
5N-ABJ	Boeing 707-3F9C	20474		Not known	Shannon
				(Being broken up 1.98: current status unknown)	
5N-AJW	Bell 212	30601	G-BGML	Bristow Helicopters Ltd	Redhill
			EP-HBL/VR-BEX	*(Stored as hulk 9.01)*	

5N-ALQ	Bell 212	30670	G-BGMF EP-HBQ/VR-BFN/N18091	Bristow Helicopters Ltd *(Crashed 11.9.95: stored 3.00)*	Redhill
5N-AQW	Bell 212	30600	G-BGLL P2-PHJ/VR-BGB/PK-HCI/VR-BGB/G-BGLL/EP-HBW/VR-BGB/9M-ATB	Bristow Helicopters Ltd *(Crashed 14.1.93: stored 3.00)*	Redhill
5N-ATU	Beechcraft A90 King Air	LJ-136	F-BFRE HB-GDF	Not known *(On fire dump 3.99)*	Gamston
5N-BHM	Bell 212	32134	G-BJJO	Bristow Helicopters Ltd *(Stored as hulk 9.01)*	Redhill
5N-HHH	British Aircraft Corporation One-Eleven 401AK	064	HZ-NB2/N5024	Kabo Air *(Open store 1.02)*	Southend

KENYA

VP-KJL*	Miles M.38 Messenger 4A	---	G-ALAR RH371	The Miles Aircraft Collection *(For rebuild off-site 2.00)*	(Woodley)
5Y-SIL	Cameron A-140 HAFB	138	F-BTVO F-WTVO/G-AZUW	British Balloon Museum & Library *"Cumulonimbus" (Stored 1998)*	Newbury

SENEGAL

6W-SAE	Douglas C-47A-25-DK	13430	F-GEFY Senegal AF/FrAF/OK-WAR/42-93510	Kew Trucking *(Cockpit section 8.94 as "42-93510/CM": current status unknown)*	(Kew)
6W-SAF	Douglas C-47A-65-DL	19074	F-GEFU 42-100611	Not known *"Lilly Belle"* *(Nose section only as "42-100766" 1.00)*	Hatfield

MALAWI

7Q-YDF	Piper J3C-65 Cub	18711	5Y-KEV VP-KEV/VP-NAE/ZS-AZT	Not known *(Stored 2000)*	(Folkestone)

GHANA

G-108	Scottish Aviation Bulldog Srs.120/122	BH120-372	G-BCUP	Aerofab Restorations *(Stored 11.01)*	Bourne Park Hurstbourne Tarrant

THE GAMBIA

9L-LCD	Letovlev LET L-410UVP Turbolet	810611	C5-LES "010"/UR-67010/CCCP67010	Sierra National Airways *(Noted 4.01)*	Bruntingthorpe
9L-LCI	Letovlev LET L-410UVP Turbolet	831036	C5-LET "67408"/UR-67408/CCCP67408	Sierra National Airways *(Stored 5.01)*	Bruntingthorpe

DEMOCRATIC REPUBLIC of CONGO

9Q-CBW	Boeing 707-329C	20200	9Q-CBS OO-SJO	Not known *(Believed sold 2.02)*	Southend

PART 2 - FOREIGN ENTRIES REMOVED DURING 2001

Many thanks to Paul Hewins for providing the bulk of this section and for spotting some elderly departures!

Regn	Type	C/n	Reason for Change
TONGA			
A3-MCA	Hawker Siddeley HS.748 Srs.2A/242	1712	To G-OTBA 3.01
CANADA			
C-FLNP	Cessna 172M Skyhawk II	17261809	To Canada 3.01
C-GCYL	Piper PA-31 Turbo Navajo	31-688	Sold in Canada
C-GFCK	Bell 427	56006	To N7561A
PORTUGAL			
CS-TML	Convair CV-440-54	484	To G-CONV 7.01
GERMANY			
D-EHEP(2)	CASA 1-131E Jungmann	2013	To G-BZVS 5.01
D-EMEF(2)	Beechcraft K35 Bonanza	D-5897	To N59VT - see SECTION 5, Part 1
D-ESEW(3)	Extra EA.300/L	091	To G-RGEE 6.01
D-HEED	Agusta A109A	7201	To G-TGRA 2.01
FRANCE			
F-AZJD	Dewoitine D.26	SA-290 & 322	To France 8.01
F-GLFB	SOCATA TB-200 Tobago XL	1375	To N156BB
HUNGARY			
HA-MEP	WSK-PZL Antonov An-2R	1G-190-25	To France 11.00
HA-MKA	WSK-PZL Antonov An-2R	1G-186-29	No longer UK based
SWITZERLAND			
HB-XPR	Agusta-Bell 206B-3 JetRanger III	8617	To G-RKEL 8.01
HB-XQM	Agusta A109E Power	11017	To N709AT - see SECTION 5, Part 1
SAUDI ARABIA			
HZ-DG1	Boeing 727-51	19124	No longer UK based
ITALY			
I-AXLE	Agusta A109A Mk.II	7436	To N7AG
I-FARB	de Havilland DHC-7-102 Dash Seven	22	Scrapped Guernsey 3.01
NORWAY			
LN-AMY	North American AT-6D Harvard	88-16849	To Norway 10.01
LITHUANIA			
LY-AFJ	Yakovlev Yak-52	9712003	To Italy
LY-AFX	Yakovlev Yak-52	899413	To RA-44469 - see SECTION 5, Part 1
LY-AGG	Yakovlev Yak-50	822210	To RA-44449 - see SECTION 5, Part 1
LY-AKF	Yakovlev Yak-52	877409	To RA-44550 - see SECTION 5, Part 1
LY-ALM	Yakovlev Yak-52	889012	To RA-44546 - see SECTION 5, Part 1
LY-ALN	Yakovlev Yak-52	800708	Sold in France 2001
LY-ASA	Antonov An-2T	1G-139-49	Damaged Cornwall 23.6.99 & scrapped
UNITED STATES OF AMERICA			
N11ZP	American Blimp Co Lightship A-60	011	Operating in Germany 2001
N33PV	Partenavia P.68TC	347-33TC	Crashed near Tatenhill 3.6.01
N36SF	Hawker Iraqi Fury FB.11	37539	To G-CBEL 8.01
N43SV	Boeing PT-13D Kaydet	75-5541	No reports since 1997
N58MS	Beechcraft A36 Bonanza	E-2889	Returned to USA 5.01
N61HB (1)	Piper PA-34-220T Seneca	3449091	To G-CBOB 9.01
N99BA	Beechcraft 65-80 Queenair	LD-80	Left UK 10.00
N99MX	Maule MX-7-180	11096C	To G-JREE 4.01
N107GM	Cessna 501 Citation 1	501-0221	To N106GM
N115BB	Aviat Aircraft A-1B Husky	2066	To N78HB - see SECTION 5, Part 1
N139DP	Bell P-39Q-5BE Airacobra	---	No recent sighting
N140MP	Cessna 441	441-0165	To EI-DMG

N146GA	Cessna 425 Corsair	425-0074	Returned to USA 4.01
N185UK	Cessna A185F Skywagon	18504367	Returned to Sweden 8.01
N190LJ	Learjet Learjet 60	60-190	To EI-IAU
N198M	Dassault Falcon 50EX	277	Returned to USA
N220TW	Cessna 650 Citation III	650-0060	To N220TV
N237TB	Piper PA-32R-301 Saratoga II HP	3246163	To G-PUSK 8.01
N252JP	Hughes 369E	0346E	To Spain 2001
N310KZ	Cessna 310R Srs III	310R1861	To USA 1.02
N311DG	Cessna 560 Citation V	560-0167	Sold in USA 3.01
N331SJ	Learjet Learjet 31A	31A-113	Returned to USA 1.01
N338DB	Piper PA-46-350P Malibu Mirage	4636248	To N638DB
N345TG	Cessna 421C Golden Eagle II	421C1067	To N1FY - see SECTION 5, Part 1
N407FD	SIAI-Marchetti SF-260D	772	To USA 7.01
N504KH	Aérospatiale SA.341G Gazelle	1012	To G-ZZLE 10.01
N523B	Beechcraft 95-58 Baron	TH-1933	Crashed off Isle of Man, Irish Sea 6.6.01
N606LG	American Lightship A-60	016	To G-OLEL 3.01
N624TC	Cessna T303 Crusader	T30300130	Scrapped 12.98
N650J	Cessna 650 Citation III	650-0022	Returned to USA 3.01
N700E	Hispano HA-1112-MIL	577	Returned to USA 2001
N768WM	Boeing-Stearman B75N-1 Kaydet (N2S-3)	75-7394	Sold in USA 7.01
N824SC	Airbus A300B4-203	271	To N505TA 2001
N838DB	Piper PA-46-350P Malibu Mirage	4636168	To G-BZSD 2.01
N904RE	Rotec Rally III	25513	Last known stored 8.95
N971JX	BAe Jetstream 3201	971	Sold as YR-KAA ??
N973JX	BAe Jetstream 3201	973	Sold as YR-KAB ??
N1065B	Beechcraft 58 Baron	TH-1765	To USA 10.01
N1134K	Luscombe 8A Silvaire	3861	Believed used for spares
N1351H	Piper PA-32-300 Cherokee Six	32-7740034	To USA 7.01
N1553N	Beech C90A King Air	LJ-1238	Sold in USA 8.01
N2187V	Cessna 140	14416	Sold in USA 5.01
N2469F	Cessna 182S	80696	To N369AN - see SECTION 5, Part 1
N2668Z	Cessna 340A II	340A0731	Last noted 6.97
N3036A	Piper PA-34-200T Seneca II	34-7970003	To G-XKEN 9.01
N3455	Douglas C-47B-25DK Dakota	16631/33379	See entry for G-AMSN in SECTION 1, Part 2
N4806E	Douglas A-26B-45DL Invader	27451	Last known stored 12.96
N5025J	Hiller UH-12B	726	No sighting for sevarl years
N5052P	Piper PA-24-180 Comanche	24-56	No sighting since 2.97
N5115C	Robinson R.22 Beta	1564	See entry for G-NABS in SECTION 1, Part 2
N5718H	Piper PA-16 Clipper	16-323	Cancelled by FAA 4.01 as exported to UK
N5832M	Aero Dynamics Sparrowhawk	8411-2	No sighting since 6.96
N6191K	Republic RC-3 Seabee	382	No sighting since 5.96
N8162G	Boeing-Stearman PT-17 Kaydet	75-323	Sold to Luxembourg 10.01
N8190U	Boeing 707-341C		NTU - see 4K-AZ3
N8713Z	Cessna P.206C Super Skylane	P206-0513	Sold in USA 7.01
N8728A	Aero Dynamics Sparrow Hawk II	87005-26	No sighting since 10.95
N9677N	Hughes 369HS	102-0422S	Sold in USA 6.01
N12426	SNCAN Stampe SV-4C	677	To G-BZSY 3.01
N14485	Rearwin 7000 Sportster	403	No sighting since 8.94
N15750	Beechcraft D.18S	A-850	No sighting since 2.97
N23840	Beechcraft C24R Sierra 200	MC-556	To G-BZPG 3.01
N50755	Boeing-Stearman D75N1 (PT-27) Kaydet	75-4020	No sighting since 4.94 - thought cannibalised
N52245	Bell 407	53186	To G-GAJW 6.01
N55904	North American NA-64 Yale	64-2171	To G-BYNF 1.00
N62734	Bell 412EP	36133	To OY-HSR 5.01
N79863	Grumman F6F-5K Hellcat	A-11008	Sold in USA 7.01

CZECH REPUBLIC

"OK-RGM"	Cessna 182P Skylane	18263117	Mis-report of OO-RGM which is now G-BWMC

BELGIUM

OO-ARK	Cameron N-56 HAFB	276	Reduced to spares
OO-MCD	Reims Cessna F.182Q Skylane	F1820151	To G-GHOW 2.01

ARUBA

P4-FDH	Boeing 707-351B	18586	To N707CA 6.01

RUSSIA

RA-01276	Sukhoi Su-26MX	90-02	No reported since 8.99
RA-01278	Sukhoi Su-29	80-05	To EC-HPX
RA-01358	Yakovlev Yak-50	832509	To USA 8.01
RA-02694	Sukhoi Su-31	04-05	To Italy 11.99
RA-02050	Yakovlev Yak-52	855907	Damaged 1998 and believed disposed

RA-44438	Technoavia Yak-18T	NK	Not confirmed - believed misread registration
RA-44450	Sukhoi Su-26	03-10	To Slovakia 7.00
RA-44460	Yakovlev Yak-52	NK	Not confirmed - believed misread registration
RA-44462	Yakovlev Yak-52	NK	Not confirmed - believed misread registration
RA-44467	Technoavia Yak-18T	15-33	To Germany by 5.00
RA-44477	Technoavia Yak-18T	NK	Not confirmed - misread of RA-44777
RA-44485	Technoavia SMG-92 Finist *(C/ns "03" & "00-004" also reported)*	01-007	To HA-YDG 10.01
RA-44508(2)	Sukhoi Su-31	03-01	Returned to France 2001
RA-44516	Yakovlev Yak-52	9111506	Exported 1999
RA-44523	Yakovlev Yak-52	822012	Sold in France 2001
RA-44528	Sukhoi Su-26	03-05	Exported 2000?
RA-44532	Yakovlev Yak-18T	14-35	Returned to France 2001
RA-44540	Sukhoi Su-29	80-01	To Italy 5.00
RA-44541	Yakovlev Yak-50	832703	Returned to France by 9.01
RA-76758	Ilyushin Il-76TD	0073474203	Marketing Agreement terminated 2.01
RA-82042	Antonov An-124-100 Ruslan	9773054055093	Marketing Agreement terminated 2.01
RA-82043	Antonov An-124-100 Ruslan	9773054155101	Marketing Agreement terminated 2.01
RA-82044	Antonov An-124-100 Ruslan	9773054155109	Marketing Agreement terminated 2.01
RA-82045	Antonov An-124-100 Ruslan	9773052255113	Marketing Agreement terminated 2.01
RA-82046	Antonov An-124-100 Ruslan	9773052255117	Marketing Agreement terminated 2.01
RA-82047	Antonov An-124-100 Ruslan	9773053259121	Marketing Agreement terminated 2.01

SWEDEN

SE-EXL	Beechcraft 95-B55 Baron	TC-1287	Sold in Spain 6.01
SE-IYL	Piper PA-30-160 Comanche C	30-1923	To G-BZRO 3.01
SE-KGV	Short SD.3-60 Var.100	SH.3670	To G-SSWR 10.01
SE-KOC	Cessna A185F Skywagon	18504367	To N185UK - see SECTION 5, Part 1

GABON

TR-LBV	Lockheed L385G-65C-100-30 Hercules	5024	To 1215 UAE Air Force

AUSTRALIA

VH-FHJ	Cessna 560 Citation Ultra	560-0278	To USA 4.01

BERMUDA (1)

VP-BHJ	Dassault Falcon 900B	138	To VH-FHR
VP-BIF	Boeing 727-1H2	20533	No longer UK based
VP-BIV	Gulfstream Gulfstream IV	1103	Returned to USA
VP-BNJ	Dassault Falcon 900B	120	To F-GRAX 3.01
VP-BNZ(2)	Gulfstream Gulfstream IV/SP	1406	To N404GA

CAYMAN ISLANDS

VP-CAF	Eurocopter EC.135T1	0115	To G-HARP 4.01
VP-CFI	Dassault Falcon 50EX	278	Sold to USA (N623QW reserved)
VP-CMD	Cessna 550 Citation II	550-0726	To N726BM
VP-CRX	Canadair CL600-Challenger	3052	To N425WN
VP-CTF	Cessna 550 Citation II	550-0716	To N550TL
VP-CYM	Gulfstream Gulfstream IV	1090	To N9999M

BERMUDA (2)

VR-BPS	Consolidated (PBY-5A) Catalina	1997	To VP-BPS - see SECTION 5, Part 1

SERBIA

YU-YAC	SOKO G-2A Galeb	NK	Left UK 4.01
YU-YAD	SOKO G-2A Galeb	NK	Left UK 7.01
JRV30137	SOKO P-2 Kraguj (Sparrowhawk)	NK	No foreign registry provenance
JRV30139	SOKO P-2 Kraguj	NK	No foreign registry provenance
JRV30142	SOKO P-2 Kraguj	NK	No foreign registry provenance

REPUBLIC of SOUTH AFRICA

ZS-RSI	Lockheed L.100-30 Hercules	4600	Returned to RSA
ZS-VFW	SNCAN Stampe SV-4C	186	Restored to G-AXCZ 2.01
ZU-BVB	Jabiru Jabiru	232	To G-BZDZ 5.01

EQUATORIAL GUINEA

3C-QQA	Fairchild F.27F	84	To HR-ASR

ISRAEL

4X-DZH	Beech A36 Bonanza	E-2189	To N728S

NIGERIA

5N-BAB	BAC One-Eleven 414EG	BAC.127	Broken up Bournemouth 2001
5N-BBD	Boeing 707-338C	19625	Broken up Bournemouth 2001
5N-HTC	BAC One-Eleven 208AL	BAC.049	Broken up Bournemouth 8.01
5N-MXX	Boeing 707-323C	18940	To 9G-LAD 11.00

GHANA

9G-DAN	Westland S-58 Wessex 60 Srs.1	WA/739	To New Zealand by 10.00

HONG KONG

HKG-11	Slingsby T-67	2042	To G-BYRY 9.99
HKG-13	Slingsby T-67	2061	To G-BXKW 8.97

SECTION 6

PART 1 – BRITISH GLIDING ASSOCIATION

The Register includes the Certificate of Airworthiness reference number as issued by the British Gliding Association (BGA). This is usually found below the tailplane in small characters. We include, as a primary reference, the corresponding three-letter coding (or trigraph (TG) system) frequently marked on the tails. If gliders are known to be wearing their respective trigraphs then we have indicated this and/or any other identity in the first composite column, for example BGA Competition Numbers are shown if carried with further details contained in SECTION 7, Parts 1 & 2. The official BGA list is extended by including non-current gliders and those with recently lapsed Certificates of Airworthiness (CA) for which no cancellation details are known but which may survive. These are identified by * in the CA expiry column. In this edition, to be consistent with the presentation used in the powered aircraft sections, we have shown the complete expiry dates for Certiificates of Airworthiness, and the complete date for the first issue of a CofA where this information is known. Where the latter information is not readily available, efforts will be made to add the missing data in future editions. Where a BGA CofA number has been reserved for future use, the reservation date is now shown, prefixed by the letter 'R'. The non-current gliders include many examples known to be in storage or under restoration in the ownership of members of the Vintage Glider Club (VGC); for this data we are once again very grateful to Peter Chamberlain.

Many thanks, once again, to Phil Butler for updating the BGA register and to Richard Cawsey, Wal Gandy, Barry Taylor and Tony Morris. Special thanks are given to the BGA's Secretary, Barry Rolfe, for his valued assistance. The information is current to 30th January 2002.

TG/BGA/Code	Type	C/n	P/I	Date	Owner/operator	Probable Base	CA Expy
162	Manuel Willow Wren			9.34	Brooklands Museum	Brooklands	*
					"The Willow Wren" (Stored)		
AAA 231	Abbott-Baynes Scud II	215B	G-ALOT	8.35	*(Under repair)*	Dunstable	22. 4.01
	(Built Slingsby)		BGA.231		*(On display 3.96)*		
AAF 236	Slingsby T.6 Kite 1	27A	G-ALUD	14.11.35	Not known	Dunstable	*
			BGA.236/(BGA.222)		*(Stored pending rebuild 12.95)*		
AAX 251	Slingsby T.6 Kite 1	227A	(ex RAF)	30. 3.36	R.Boyd	Rivar Hill	7.12.02
			BGA.251				
ABG 260	Schleicher Rhonsperber	32-16		4. 5.36	F.K.Russell	Dunstable	22. 7.02
					t/a Rhonsperber Syndicate		
(ABN) 266	Slingsby T.1 Falcon 1 Waterglider			29. 5.36	Windermere Steamboat Museum		
		237A			*(On display 5.95)*	Windermere	*
ABZ 277	Grunau Baby 2	?	RAFGSA.270	25. 8.36	J.L.Smoker & Ptnrs		
	(Built F.Coleman)		BGA.277/G-ALKU/BGA.277			Hinton in the Hedges	22. 7.95*
ACF 283	Abbott-Baynes Scud III	2	G-ALJR	18.12.36	L.P.Woodage	Dunstable	11. 4.00
			BGA.283				
ACH 285 E	Slingsby T.6 Kite 1	247A	G-ALNH	30.12.36	E.B.Scott	AAC Middle Wallop	5.99*
			BGA.285		*(On loan to The Museum of Army Flying)*		
					(As "G285/E" in 1 GTS RAF c/s)		
ADJ 310	Slingsby T.6 Kite 1	258B	RAFGSA182	9. 2.37	A.M.Maufe	Tibenham	17. 7.01
			VD218/BGA.400				
	(Rebuilt 1982 with components from BGA.327 c/n 285A)						
AEM 337	Schleicher Rhonbussard	620	G-ALME	25. 4.38	C.Wills & S.White	Booker	31. 5.02
			BGA.337				
(AFW) 370	Grunau Baby 2	1		11.10.38	Not known	Saltby	
	(Built J.Hobson)				*(Under restoration 2000)*		
AGE 378 900	Slingsby T.12 Gull I	312A	G-ALPJ	14. 9.38	T.Smallwood & Ptnrs	Bidford	11. 6.02
			BGA.378				
AHC 400 F	Slingsby T.6 Kite 1	336A	VD165	6. 5.39	R.Hadlow & Ptnrs	Thame	27. 4.97
	(Wings from Special T.6 c/n 355A)		BGA.400		*(In 1 GTS RAF c/s)*		
AHU 416 G-ALRD	Scott Viking 1	114	G-ALRD	19. 6.39	M.L.Beach	Dunstable	16. 6.02
			BGA.416				
AHW 418	Slingsby T.13 Petrel 1	348A	G-ALNP	30. 4.46	R.I.Davidson	Husbands Bosworth	5.97
			BGA.418		*(To N39UK and cancelled 01.10.01)*		
AJW 442 AJW	Slingsby T.8 Tutor	MHL/RC/8	G-ALMX	8.46	M.Hodgson	Dunstable	14. 8.98
			BGA.442				
AKC 448	DFS 108-68 Weihe	000348	G-ALJW	6.47	D.Philips	Snitterfield	*
			BGA.448/LO+WQ		*(Damaged Thun, Switzerland 20.7.79: on rebuild 1994)*		
AKD 449	DFS/70 Olympia-Meise	227	LF+VO	7.47	L.S.Phillips	Perranporth	5.85*
					(Stored and for sale)		
AKW 466	Slingsby T.8 Tutor	MHL/RT/7		11.46	D.Kitchen	Tibenham	6. 7.96
ALA 470	Short Nimbus	S.1312		.47	Ulster Folk & Transport Museum		
					(Stored 6.97)	Holywood, Belfast	8.75*
ALR 485	Slingsby T.8 Tutor	513	G-ALPE	11.46	M.H.Birch	Booker	14. 6.97
			BGA.485		*(Stored)*		

ALW 490	G-ALRK	Hutter H-17A *(Built D.Campbell)*		G-ALRK BGA.490	8.48	N.I.Newton	Booker	30. 6.02
ALX 491		Hawkridge Dagling	08471		2.47	N.H.Ponsford *(Stored 1.98)*	(Breighton)	*
(ALZ) 493		Hawkridge Nacelle Dagling	10471		7.47	P. & D.Underwood *(Also allotted BAPC.81: on rebuild 2000)*	Eaton Bray	*
AMK 503	AMK	EoN AP.5 Olympia 2	EoN/O/003	G-ALJP BGA.503	5.47	D.T.Staff *(Under restoration)*	Booker	28. 5.95*
AMM 505		EoN AP.5 Olympia 2	EoN/O/006	G-ALJV BGA.505	5.47	I.Hodge	RAF Marham	21. 6.01
AMP 507		EoN AP.5 Olympia 2	EoN/O/008	G-ALJO BGA.507	6.47	M.Briggs	Cranfield	25. 6.95*
AMR 509	AMR	EoN AP.5 Olympia 2	EoN/O/011	G-ALLA BGA.509	5.47	P.Nurcombe	Husbands Bosworth	3.10.97
AMT 511	AMT	EoN AP.5 Olympia 2	EoN/O/005	G-ALLM BGA.511	5.47	E.W.Burgess	Lyveden	25. 7.97
AMU 512		EoN AP.5 Olympia 2	EoN/O/012			Not known *(Under rebuild 2000)*	Challock	
AMV 513		EoN AP.5 Olympia 2	EoN/O/014	G-ALNB BGA.513		Not known *(Under refurbishment 2000)*	Camphill	
AMW 514	AMW	EoN AP.5 Olympia 2	EoN/O/015	G-ALKM BGA.514	6.47	M.R.Fox	Pocklington	30.10.00
AND 521		Slingsby T.26 Kite II	MHL/RK.5			Not known *(Stored)*	Chalfont St.Giles	
ANW 538	AMW	EoN AP.5 Olympia 2B	EoN/O/040	G-ALNE BGA.538	7.47	E.A.Barnacle	Snitterfield	9. 7.02
ANZ 541		EoN AP.5 Olympia 2	EoN/O/043		9.47	Not known *(Under restoration)*	RAF Halton	
APC 544	APC	EoN AP.5 Olympia 2	EoN/O/046	G-ALMJ BGA.544	9.47	N.G.Oultram	Seighford	24. 8.01
APV 561		EoN AP.5 Olympia 2B	EoN/O/032	G-ALKN BGA.561	6.47	A.Kepley *(Stored 8.97)* t/a Fenland & West Norfolk Aviation Museum	Crowland	8.78*
APZ 565		Slingsby T.25 Gull 4	505	G-ALPB (BGA.565)		E.A.Arthur	Lasham	12. 8.01
AQE 570		Slingsby T.21B	538	G-ALNJ BGA.570		Not known *(Stored pending rebuild 10.97)*	Camphill	*
AQG 572		Slingsby T.21B Sedbergh TX.1	539	8884M VX275/BGA.572		RAF Museum *(Stored 5.93)*	RAF Wyton	*
AQH 573		Slingsby T.21B	540	G-ALJU BGA.573		Not known	(Zimbabwe)	9.90*
AQN 578	AQN	Hawkridge Grunau Baby 2B	G.3348	G-ALSO BGA.578	.48	R G Hood	Lasham	18. 6.02
AQQ 580		EoN AP.7 Primary	EoN/P/003	G-ALPS BGA.580		Imperial War Museum *(Stored)*	Duxford	*
AQY 588		EoN AP.7 Primary	EoN/P/011			N.H.Ponsford *(Stored 1.98)*	(Breighton)	*
AQZ 589		EoN AP.7 Primary	EoN/P/012	G-ALMN BGA.589		Not known *(Stored 1992)*	(Farnborough)	4.51*
ARK 599	ARK	Slingsby T.30A Prefect	548	PH-1 BGA.599/G-ALLF/BGA.599		K.M.Fresson	RNAS Yeovilton	15. 7.02
ARM 601	ARM	Slingsby T.21B	543	G-ALKX BGA.601	8.48	South London Gliding Centre	Kenley	31. 5.02
ASB 614	T42	Slingsby T.21B	549	RNGSA G-ALLT/BGA.614	9.48	J.L.Rolls & Ptnrs	Talgarth	26. 7.02
ASC 615		Grunau Baby 2B *(Built Hawkridge)*	G-4848	G-ALMM BGA.615	2.49	C.D.Stainer & Ptnrs *(Stored 8.95 - sold in Germany)*	Rufforth	8.94*
ASN 625		Slingsby T.30B Prefect	567	G-ALPC BGA.625	1.49	G.Martin	Rhigos	5.99
ASR 628		EoN AP.8 Baby	EoN/B/004	G-ALRU BGA.628	3.49	Not known *(Crashed Bardney 28.5.71; stored 8.01)*	Aston Down	*
AST 629		G-ALRH EoN AP.8 Baby	EoN/B/005	G-ALRH BGA.629	3.49	EoN Baby Syndicate "Liver Bird" *(Extant 2000)*	Chipping	9.96
ATH 643		Slingsby T.15 Gull III	364A	TJ711	11.49	Brooklands Museum	Brooklands	9.94*
ATL 646		Slingsby T.21B	536	G-ALKS	6.50	G.Markham *(Stored 2.01)*	Enstone	7.96
ATR 651		Slingsby T.13 Petrel 1	361A	EI-101 IGA.101/IAC.101/BGA.651/G-ALPP	7.50	G.Saw	Booker	20. 4.02
ATV 655	OK-8592	Zlin 24 Krajanek	101	G-ALMP OK-8592	4.50	N.Barr	Booker	9. 5.02
AUD 663	663	Slingsby T.26 Kite 2B	727		1.52	R.S.Hooper	Lasham	19. 5.02
AUG 666		Slingsby T.21B	643		6.51	Cambridge University GC	Gransden Lodge	9. 5.02
AUJ 668		Slingsby T.21B *(Built Aero & Engineering)*	639		6.51	Not known *(Damaged Feshiebridge 16.7.85: stored 7.97)*	Rufforth	6.86*
AUP 673	N21	Slingsby T.21B	636		7.51	The Solent T21 Group	Lee-on-Solent	14. 4.01
AUU 678	AUU	EoN AP.5 Olympia	EoN/O/076		4.52	J.M.Lee	Parham Park	19. 8.00

AUW	680		Avia 40P	117		8.52	F.Ragot	(St.Auban, France)	27. 7.98
AVA	684		Abbott-Baynes Scud III	3		1.53	E.A.Hull	Dunstable	24. 5.02
AVB	685	AVB	Slingsby T.34 Sky	644	G-644	2.53	R.Moyse	Lasham	9. 4.01
AVC	686	AVC	Slingsby T.34 Sky	670		3.53	P.J.Teagle	Camphill	1. 9.02
							"Kinder Scout II"		
AVD	687	AVD	Eon AP.5 Olympia 2	EoN/0/092		3.53	A.C.Jarvis	Parham Park	26. 7.98
AVF	689	AVF	Slingsby T.26 Kite 2A	728	RAFGSA.294	4.53	C.P.Raine	Dunstable	21. 7.02
					BGA.689				
AVG	690		Slingsby T.31B	717		4.53	A.R.Worters	North Connel	
							(Refurbishing: previously reported as becoming G-BMDD)		
AVL	694		Slingsby T.34 Sky	671	G-671	5.53	M.P.Wakem	Long Mynd	12. 5.02
AVQ	698	AVQ G46	Slingsby T.34 Sky	645	G-645	8.53	Miss A.G.Veitch & B.Middleton		
							"Gertie"	Easterton	19. 6.02
AVT	701		Slingsby T.30B Prefect	857	AGA...	1.53	Booker GC	Booker	14. 5.00
					BGA.701				
AWD	711	AWD	Slingsby T.21B	950		30. 9.54	D.B.Brown	Chipping	25. 6.01
							t/a T.21 Syndicate		
AWS	724	AWS	Slingsby T.41 Skylark 2	997		6.55	D.M.Cornelius	Dunstable	14. 7.01
AWU	726		EoN AP.5 Olympia 2	EoN/0/082		5.55	M J Riley	Sackville Farm, Riseley	25. 4.02
AWX	729	AWX	Slingsby T.41 Skylark 2	946		1.56	A.G.Leach	Cranfield	14. 7.01
AWZ	731	AWZ	Slingsby T.7 Cadet	SSK/FF/169	RA847	8. 1.57	R.Moyse	Lasham	10. 6.02
AXB	733	AXB	Slingsby T.41 Skylark 2	926		2.55	A.L.Shaw	Lyveden	30. 6.02
AXD	735		Slingsby T.43 Skylark 3	1014		.55	F.G.T.Birlison	Aston Down	20. 5.02
AXE	736	AXE	Slingsby T.43 Skylark 3	1029		24. 3.57	C.J.Bushell	Snitterfield	21. 8.01
AXJ	740	AXJ	Slingsby T.42A Eagle 2	994		.55	P.C.Horn	Parham Park	4. 4.02
							t/a The Eagle Syndicate		
AXL	742		Slingsby T.43 Skylark 3	1030		6.56	M.Chalmers & Ptnrs	Kingston Deverill	14. 4.02
AXP	745	AXP	Slingsby T.41 Skylark 2	949		4.55	M.Sanderson	Milfield	16. 3.99
AXR	747	AXR	Slingsby T.41 Skylark 2	945		.56	Kilham	Crowland 31.3.00	
AXU	750	AXU	Slingsby T.41 Skylark 2	944		3.55	M.A.Langhurst	Halesland	24. 6.95*
AXV	751		Slingsby T.26 Kite 2A			4.56	Not known *(Refurbishing)*	Booker	
AYD	759	AYD	Slingsby T.41 Skylark 2	1048		.56	B.Milburn	Currock Hill	17. 6.01
AYF	761	AYF	Slingsby T.43 Skylark 3B	1058		9.56	A.A.Jenkins	Hinton in the Hedges	19. 6.02
AYH	763	AYH	Slingsby T.43 Skylark 3B	1066		.56	A.Griffiths	Lyveden	16. 6.02
AYN	768		Slingsby T.41 Skylark 2	996			Not known (*Stored*)	NK	
AYY	778	33	Slingsby T.41 Skylark 2C	1073		.56	H.Johnson	Long Mynd	12. 6.96*
AZA	780	AZA	Slingsby T.42 Eagle 3	1085	RNGSA 2-08		J.M.Crewe	Hinton-in-the-Hedges	23. 7.01
					BGA.780				
AZC	782	782	Slingsby T.21B	1096		5.57	C.Stachulla	(Augsberg)	31. 7.02
AZF	785		Slingsby T.30B Prefect	1100		.56	L.J.Smith	RNAS Culdrose	26. 3.96*
							t/a The Prefect Syndicate		
AZK	789		Slingsby T.8 Tutor		VM650	6.57	Not known	Croft, Skegness	7.90*
							(Stored 5.93)		
AZP	793	136	Slingsby T.41 Skylark 2		999	1.57	G.Dixon & Ptnr	Currock Hill	13. 8.97
AZQ	794	VM687	Slingsby T.8 Tutor		VM687	.57	J.M.Brookes	Strubby	7. 6.02
AZR	795	AZR	EoN AP.5 Olympia 2	EoN/0/101		7.58	Not known	Syerston	28. 7.95*
							(Under restoration)		
AZT	797	AZT	EoN AP.5 Olympia 2	EoN/0/063	ZS-GCM	3.57	N.C.Kerr	Winthorpe	10. 8.02
AZX	801	AZX	Slingsby T.41 Skylark 2	995	BGA.1909	4.57	B.Griffin	Saltby	
					AGA.4/BGA.801		*(Under rebuild)*		
AZY	802	AZY	Slingsby T.41 Skylark 2	963		16. 4.57	A.J.Jackson	Burn	29. 6.97*
BAA	804		Slingsby T.8 Tutor	931	XE761	5.57	A.Chadwick	Rufforth	9. 3.97*
					VM589				
			(A Cadet TX.1 identified as "BGA.804 ex VM589" is stored by Midland Air Museum, Coventry)						
BAC	806		Slingsby T.43 Skylark 3B	1101	RNGSA CU19	6.58	M.Stokeld	Carlton Moor	27. 5.97
					BGA.806				
BAH	810	BAH	Slingsby T.41 Skylark 2	1104		7.58	B.Jackson	Cranfield	7. 9.97
BAM	814	BAM	Slingsby T.41 Skylark 2	1108		1.58	B.H.Thwaites	Wormingford	2. 6.02
BAN	815		Slingsby T.30B Prefect	1120		1.58	J.S.Allison	RAF Halton	15. 5.00
BAV	822	BAV	Slingsby T.41 Skylark 2B	1113		2.58	M.H.Simms	Rattlesden	16. 4.02
BAW	823	BAW	Slingsby T.43 Skylark 3B	1126		2.58	G.E.Sarjeant	Halesland	21. 8.02
BAY	825	BAY	Slingsby T.42B Eagle 3	1116		3.58	M.Lodge	Bidford	15. 8.00
BAZ	826	BAZ	Slingsby T.41 Skylark 2	1112		3.58	W.Fuller	Currock Hill	22. 5.99
BBA	827	BBA	Slingsby T.41 Skylark 2	1128		3.58	M.Bosher	Winthorpe	1. 5.99
BBB	828	BBB	Slingsby T.42B Eagle 3	1118		4.58	I.K.Mitchell	North Hill	21. 9.01
BBG	833		Slingsby T.8 Tutor	-	VW535	3. 9.57	R.H.Short	Husbands Bosworth	7. 7.02
BBH	834	BBH	EoN Olympia 2	EoN/0/041	BGA.539	8.57	J.W.Bonham	Cranfield	17. 6.99
BBP	840		Slingsby T.43 Skylark 3	1125		6.58	*(Under repair 2000)*		
BBQ	841	BBQ	Slingsby T.42B Eagle 3	1115		5.58	Eagle Syndicate	Milfield	6. 7.02
BBT	844	BBT	Slingsby T.43 Skylark 3B	1134	RAFGSA.234	.58	J.P.Gilbert	Wormingford	11. 5.02
					BGA.844				
BBU	845	BBU	Slingsby T.41 Skylark 2B	1135		.58	J.A.Timpany	Bicester	17. 5.00
BCB	852	TS291	Slingsby T.8 Tutor	-	TS291	2. 7.58	National Museums of Scotland/Museum of Flight		
								East Fortune	*

BCF 856		Slingsby T.21B	1		10.58	P.Underwood	Eaton Bray	*
		(Built Leighton Park School)				*(Stored during 2000)*		
BCH 858	BCH	Slingsby T.8 Tutor	SSK/FF/489	VM547	9.58	N.James	Lyveden	13. 8.02
BCL 861	BCL	Slingsby T.43 Skylark 3B	1139		9.58	R.Aylett	Bidford	18. 5.96*
BCP 864	BCP	Slingsby T.43 Skylark 3B	1140		11.58	K.I.Latty	Milfield	13. 4.02
BCS 867	549	Slingsby T.43 Skylark 3B	1144		12.58	M.Wright & Ptnrs	Rattlesden	24. 3.01
BCU 869	2	Slingsby T.21B	1148		1.59	Not known *(Stored 2001)*	North Connel	*
BCV 870	BCV&155	Slingsby T.43 Skylark 3B	1195		4.59	W R Davis	Challock	15. 6.02
BCW 871	BCW	Slingsby T.43 Skylark 3B	1147		3.59	I.Tittensor	Bidford	8.10.01
BCX 872		Slingsby T.41 Skylark 2B	1197		4.59	G W Haworth	Tibenham	20. 5.00
BCY 873	T45	Slingsby T.45 Swallow	1198		4.59	D.C.Unwin	Talgarth	16. 7.00
BDA 875		Slingsby T.21B	1205	AGA.7	6.59	W Grobkinsky	Dahlemer Binz, Germany	4. 7.02
				BGA.875				
BDF 880	BDF	Slingsby T.42B Eagle 3	1213		9.59	D.C.Phillips	Snitterfield	18. 7.00
BDM 886		Slingsby T.21B	1216		11.59	D.G.Cooper	Wormingford	15. 7.98
BDR 890	BDR	Slingsby T.45 Swallow	1243		6.60	R.J.Shallcrass	Challock	27. 8.01
BDW 895		Slingsby T.8 Tutor TX.2		VM637	4.59	R.Patrick & Ptnrs	Winthorpe	6.93*
						(On rebuild 1.96: probably to be VM637)		
BDX 896	BDX	Slingsby T.41 Skylark 2	CH.095/1		6.59	H D Maddams	Wormingford	11. 6.02
		(Built C Hurst)						
BEA 899	BEA	Slingsby T.41 Skylark 2	1194		7.59	M.L.Ryan	RAF Keevil	25.12.01
BED 902		Slingsby T.12 Gull I	-	-	15. 5.59	National Museums of Scotland/Museum of Flight	East Fortune	
BEF 904	BEF	Slingsby T.8 Tutor	-	(ex RAF)	10.59	D.Chaplin	Sutton Bank	2. 5.96*
		(Frame No.SSK/FF 934)				(Tutor Syndicate)		
BEL 909	BEL	EoN AP.5 Olympia 2B	EoN/O/126		12.59	J.G.Gilbert & Ptnrs	Wormingford	13. 4.02
BEM 910		Slingsby T.45 Swallow	1221		5. 2.60	T.J.Linee	Kingston Deverill	29. 6.02
BER 914	BER	Slingsby T.43 Skylark 3B	1225		3.60	K.V.Payne	Llantisilio	3. 2.99
BET 916	600	Slingsby T.43 Skylark 3B	1227		3.60	A.C.Robertson & Ptnrs	Feshiebridge	31. 5.98
BEX 920	BEX	Slingsby T.43 Skylark 3F	1229		4.60	P.J.Mortimer	Rivar Hill	4. 2.01
BEY 921	BEY	Slingsby T.45 Swallow	1230		4.60	G.P.Hayes	Kenley	6. 5.02
BEZ 922	BEZ	Slingsby T.43 Skylark 3F	1232		4.60	R.G.Gillow	Perranporth	4. 8.01
BFB 924		Slingsby T.45 Swallow	1235		5.60	Essex & Suffolk GC	North Weald	16. 6.01
						(Crashed at Ridgewell 18.6.00)		
BFC 925	BFC	Slingsby T.43 Skylark 3F	1239		20. 5.60	Strathclyde GC	Strathaven	31. 8.99
BFD 926		Slingsby T.21B	1240	RAFGSA	5.60	B.Jaessing	(Hamburg)	26. 7.96*
				BGA.926				
BFE 927	BFE	Slingsby T.43 Skylark 3F	1244		6.60	Essex Skylark Gliding Syndicate (I.F.Barnes)	North Weald	29. 5.02
BFG 929	BFG	Slingsby T.43 Skylark 3F	1245		8. 7.60	T.J.Wilkinson	Sackville Lodge, Riseley	15. 6.02
BFL 933	BFL	Slingsby T.41 Skylark 2B	1220		5.60	D G Coats	Milfield	31. 8.99
BFN 935		EoN AP.5 Olympia 2B	EoN/O/125		2. 3.60	Not known	NK	
						(Being refurbished during 2000)		
BFP 936		Schleicher Ka7 Rhonadler	702/60		5.60	Dartmoor GC	Brent Tor	28. 4.96*
						(Damaged Brent Tor 15.11.95)		
BFS 939		SZD-8ter-ZO Jaskolka	235		3.60	Not known	NK	
						(Stored during 2000; damaged by fire)		
BFY 945	BFY	Slingsby T.21B	1251	RAFGGA.515	9.60	D.M.Hayes & Ptnrs	Sutton Bank	4. 5.02
				RAFGSA.286/BGA.945				
BGB 948		Slingsby T.21B	1274	RAFGSA.282	11.60	Shenington GC	Edgehill	9.12.97
		(Robin EC-33)		BGA.948		*(Stored 6.00)*		
BGD 950	BGD	Slingsby T.43 Skylark 3F	1276		26.11.60	Essex University GC	Wormingford	9. 8.99
BGG 953		Slingsby T.21B	1294		12.60	West Wales Gliding Trust	Templeton	31. 3.98
BGH 954	BGH	Slingsby T.43 Skylark 3F	1295		12.60	Denbigh GC	Lleweni Parc	23. 5.00
		(Written-off Denbigh 8.1.00)						
BGL 957	BGL	Slingsby T.43 Skylark 3F	1296		3.61	C.Willey & Ptnrs	Perranporth	11. 7.02
BGP 960	BGP	Slingsby T.21B	1297	RAFGSA.283	1.61	Bannerdown GC	RAF Keevil	29. 6.02
				BGA.960				
BGR 962	BGR	EoN AP.5 Olympia 2B	EoN/O/124		6.60	M.H.Gagg	RAF Cosford	5. 1.00
BGS 963		Grunau Baby II		RAFGSA	19. 6.60	Not known	NK	
				RNGSA 1-14		*(Stored during 2000 - previously reported sold as N20GB)*		
BGT 964		DFS/30 Kranich II	087	SE-STF	29.10.6	C.Wills	Booker	29. 6.02
		(Built AB Flygplan)		Fv.8226				
BGX 968		EoN AP.5 Olympia 2	EoN/O/123	(BGA.892)	8.60	C.Kaminski	Eaglescott	7. 7.97*
BHC 973	BHC	EoN AP.5 Olympia 2B	EoN/O/138		1.61	M.Pedwell	Bidford	15. 5.01
						(Damaged beyond repair in hangar)		
BHQ 985	760	Slingsby T.43 Skylark 3F	1304		4.61	R.Furness	Cranfield	1. 5.96*
BHS 987		Slingsby T.43 Skylark 3F	1305	RAFGSA293		Not known	NK	
				BGA.987		*(Under repair during 2000)*		
BHT 988	BHT	Slingsby T.43 Skylark 3F	1306		4.61	K.Chichester & Ptnrs	Hinton-in-the-Hedges	13. 5.02
BHV 990	BHV	Slingsby T.45 Swallow	1308	NEJSGSA.4	4.61	M.G.Dawson	Spilsby	27. 3.01
				BGA.990				
BHY 993		Slingsby T.31B	1292		5.61	*(Stored during 2000 ; ex Pakistan Air Force)*		

BJB 996 BJB	Slingsby T.43 Skylark 3F	SSK/JPS/1		4.61	R.A.Mills	Turweston	7. 7.02
	(Built Jones, Pentelow & Saint)						
BJC 997 BJC	EoN AP.5 Olympia 2B	EoN/0/135		4.61	A.Videon & Ptnrs	Lyveden	23. 9.01
BJD 998	SZD-9 bis Bocian 1D	P-391		5.61	D.L.Martlew	Lasham	17. 5.02
					(Bocian Syndicate)		
BJF 1000 BJF	Slingsby T.21B	1309		6.61	Sedbergh Syndicate	Wormingford	7. 7.02
BJK 1004	Slingsby T.43 Skylark 3F	1311		7.61	D.A.Wiseman & Ptnrs	Wormingford	28. 7.02
BJP 1008 BJP	Slingsby T.45 Swallow	1316		9.61	S R Grant	Stow Maries	30. 3.01
BJQ 1009 BJQ	Slingsby T.49A Capstan	1314			L.Glover & Ptnrs	Husbands Bosworth	12. 5.02
BJV 1014	Slingsby T.21B	556	SE-SHK	1.62	National Museums of Scotland/ Museum of Flight	East Fortune	*
BJW 1015 198	Slingsby T.43 Skylark 3G	1321		3.62	J.B.Strzebrakowski	Lyveden	31. 3.01
					(Written-off Melton Mowbray 16.04.00)		
BJY 1017 BJY	Slingsby T.45 Swallow	1324		3.62	C.Devine	Portmoak	19. 9.99
BJZ 1018	Slingsby T.45 Swallow	1325		3.62	J.P.Marshall	North Connel	20.11.96*
BKA 1019 BKA	Slingsby T.50 Skylark 4	1326	EI-117 BGA.1019	28. 5.62	Staffordshire GC	Seighford	22. 6.02
BKC 1021 BKC	DFS 108-68 Weihe	231	SE-SNE Fv.8312	4.61	B.Briggs	RAF Cranwell	9. 9.96*
	(Built AB Flygindustri)						
BKE 1023 BKE	Slingsby T.43 Skylark 3F			13. 7.61	D.H.Clack	Kingston Deverill	21. 5.02
	(Built C Ross)	1715/CR/1					
BKJ 1027	BKJ Schleicher Ka6CR	565/59	9G-AAR	7.61	P.M.Hogan	Sandhill Farm, Shrivenham	15. 4.02
BKK 1028	EoN AP.5 Olympia 2	EoN/0/139	RNGSA.CU11 BGA.1028	7.61	J.Bradley	Thruxton	24. 7.99
BKL 1029 BKL	EoN AP.5 Olympia 2B	EoN/0/134		6.61	J.S.Orr	Lasham	20. 5.02
BKN 1031 BKN	Schleicher Ka7 Rhonadler	1091/61		9.61	East Sussex GC	Ringmer	11. 8.01
BKP 1032 BKP	Slingsby T.45 Swallow	1203		10.61	E.Traynor	Easterton	9. 5.02
BKS 1035 BKS	EoN AP.5 Olympia 2B	EoN/0/144		11.61	N W Woodward	Booker	27. 4.02
BKU 1037 BKU	EoN AP.5 Olympia 2B	EoN/0/153		1.62	D.N.MacKay	Aboyne	4. 5.02
BKW 1039 BKW	Schleicher Ka6 Rhonsegler	295	OH-RSA	10.62	I.M.Hembling	Rattlesden	2. 5.01
BKX 1040 BKX	EoN AP.5 Olympia 2B	EoN/0/148		3.62	D.J.Allibone	Gallows Hill	1. 7.02
BLA 1043 327	Slingsby T.50 Skylark 4	1331		5.62	I.A.Masterton	Portmoak	15. 5.00
BLE 1047 BLE	Slingsby T.50 Skylark 4	1335	RNGSA 1-228 BGA.1047	6.62	S.Frank	Easterton	5. 3.02
BLH 1050 BLH	Slingsby T.50 Skylark 4	1338	RAFGSA BGA.1050	7.62	M.D.Cohler	Rufforth	25. 9.02
BLJ 1051 BLJ	EoN AP.6 Olympia 419X	EoN/4/009		3.62	G.Balshaw & Ptnrs	Lleweni Parc	10.10.96*
					"Big Bird"		
BLK 1052 67	EoN AP.6 Olympia 419X	EoN/4/007	G-APSX	4.62	C.J.Abbott & Ptnrs	Long Mynd	14. 1.02
BLN 1055 BLN	EoN AP.5 Olympia 2B	EoN/0/152		5.62	M.R.Derwent	RAF Cranwell	31. 3.02
BLP 1056	EoN AP.5 Olympia 2B	EoN/0/149		3.62	D.Birtwhistle & Ptnrs	Chipping	25. 5.95*
					(Being refurbished during 2000)		
BLQ 1057	EoN AP.5 Olympia 2 Special	EoN/0/042	RAFGSA 145 BGA.540	7.62	R.J.McAdam	Winthorpe	22. 5.02
BLS 1059	EoN AP.5 Olympia 2B	EoN/0/151		7.62	D.J.Wilson	Seighford	30. 5.01
	(EoN rebuild of BGA.897 [EoN/0/128])						
BLU 1061	Slingsby T.45 Swallow	1340		7.62	Not known	Strubby	9. 7.94*
					(Under repair 2000)		
BLW 1063 BLW	Slingsby T.50 Skylark 4	1342		8.62	S.R.A.Trusler	Weston-on-the-Green	2. 6.02
BLZ 1066	Slingsby T.50 Skylark 4	1346		11.62	R.M Lambert	Easterton	19. 5.02
BML 1077	Slingsby T.45 Swallow	1328		6.62	Dartmoor GS	Burnford Common	9. 7.97*
BMM 1078	SZD-9bis Bocian 1	P-397		8.99	D.R.Wilcox	Crowland	14. 7.02
BMQ 1081 BMQ	Slingsby T.21B	1351		11.62	W.Masterton	(Jamaica)	16.12.02
BMU 1085	Slingsby T.21B (T)	1355	9G-ABD BGA.1085	12.62	D.Woolerton & Ptnrs	East Kirkby	27. 9.97
	(Rotax 503)				*"Spruce Goose"*		
BMW 1087 BMW	Slingsby T.50 Skylark 4	1357		12.62	M.Williams	RAF Halton	13.11.02
BMX 1088 789	Slingsby T.50 Skylark 4	1358	RAFGSA.308 BGA.1088	1.63	R.O.Linee	Kingston Deverill	20. 4.02
					(789 Syndicate)		
BMY 1089 163	Slingsby T.50 Skylark 4	1361		1.63	N.Dickenson	Chipping	7. 4.98
BNA 1091	Shenstone Harbinger Mk.2	1		12.62	A.C.Wood	Crowland	28. 7.01
BNC 1093	DFS 108-68 Weihe	1	SE-SHU	3.63	K.S.Green	Lasham	22. 9.02
	(Built AB Kockums Flygindustri)						
BND 1094 BND	Schleicher Ka6CR	1157		3.63	S.A.Doran	Tibenham	30. 4.01
BNE 1095 BNE	Slingsby T.50 Skylark 4	1375		4.63	T.Davies	Usk	28. 4.01
	(C/n now believed to be 1375 rather than 1343 or 1433)						
BNH 1098 BNH	Schleicher Ka6CR	6115		3.63	Bath, Wilts & North Dorset GC	Kingston Deverill	16. 4.02
BNK 1100 BNK	Slingsby T.50 Skylark 4	1362		2.63	E.D.Weekes & Ptnrs	Weston-on-the-Green	22. 5.02
BNM 1102	Slingsby T.50 Skylark 4	1367		3.63	D.Hertzburg	North Weald	11. 7.02
	(Reported as BMN)						
BNN 1103 BNN	Slingsby T.50 Skylark 4	1366		3.63	J R Robinson	Pocklington	6.12.98
BNP 1104 653	Slingsby T.50 Skylark 4	1368		3.63	A.R.Worters	North Connel	22. 7.01
BNQ 1105 BNQ	Slingsby T.50 Skylark 4	1369		3.63	R Pye	Chipping	29. 4.00
BNR 1106 BNR	Slingsby T.49B Capstan	1370		8.63	C.M.Hurst	Gransden Lodge	14. 7.02

BNS 1107 XS652	Slingsby T.45 Swallow	1373	XS652 BGA.1107	20. 3.63	York GC Swallow Syndicate	Rufforth	30. 6.02
BNU 1109	Slingsby T.45 Swallow	1377		5.63	P.Cammish	Sutton Bank	15. 6.02
BPA 1115 BPA	Slingsby T.50 Skylark 4	1383		5.63	D.Penney	Lasham	17. 2.02
BPB 1116 255	Slingsby T.50 Skylark 4	1384	RNGSA BGA.1116	6.63	A.J.Hall	Lasham	14. 7.00
BPC 1117 BPC	Slingsby T.50 Skylark 4	1389		7.63	J.L.Grayer & Ptnr	Ringmer	11. 5.02
BPD 1118 N55	Slingsby T.49B Capstan	1390		22. 7.63	Culdrose GC	RNAS Culdrose	14. 3.02
BPE 1119 BPE	Slingsby T.50 Skylark 4	1391		6.63	D.H.Scales	Currock Hill	22. 5.02
BPG 1121 741	Slingsby T.50 Skylark 4	1393		7.63	R.M.Neill & Ptnrs	Long Mynd	4. 3.02
BPJ 1123 809	Slingsby T.50 Skylark 4	1360		4.63	M.Cooper *(Damaged Challock 26.3.97)*	Challock	6. 3.98*
BPK 1124 BPK	Slingsby T.50 Skylark 4	1381		6.63	D.Crowhurst	Crowland	14. 8.02
BPL 1125 BPL	EoN AP.5 Olympia 2B	EoN/O/136	G-APXC	6.63	D.Harris & Ptnrs (Stored)	(Essex)	19. 5.97*
BPN 1127 571	Oberlerchner Standard Austria	003	OE-0496	6.63	R.K.Avery & Ptnrs	Eaglescott	21. 7.98
BPS 1131	Slingsby T.49B Capstan	1399		9.63	Capstan Gliding Group	Aboyne	7. 4.02
BPT 1132	Slingsby T.49B Capstan	1400		10.63	J.E.Neville *(Stored 2001)*	Laurencekirk	11. 2.95*
BPU 1133	Slingsby T.49B Capstan	1402		11.63	I.T.Godfrey *(Under repair)* t/a Capstan Syndicate	Dunstable	17. 3.98
BPV 1134 BPV	Slingsby T.49B Capstan	1404		20.12.63	G.L.Barrett	Weston on the Green	27. 9.02
BPW 1135	Slingsby T.49B Capstan	1408		1.64	Ulster GC	Bellarena	18. 5.02
BPX 1136 859	Slingsby T.45 Swallow	1397	XS859 BGA.1136	1. 1.64	F.Pape & Ptnrs	Rufforth	5. 7.98
BPZ 1138 BPZ	Slingsby T.50 Skylark	41406		3.64	A.Pattermore & Ptnrs	Old Sarum	10. 7.00
BQA 1139	Slingsby T.51 Dart 15	1421		4.64	*(Stored at RAF Odiham during 2000; being refurbished)*		
BQE 1143 RA905	Slingsby T.7 Cadet	RAFGSA.273	RA905	8.63	M.L.Beach	Aston Down	14. 3.00
BQF 1144 1	Slingsby T.21B	1168	XN189	10.63	Connel GC	North Connel	13. 4.02
BQJ 1147	DFS/30 Kranich II *(Built Schleicher)*	821	RAFGSA.215	11.63	M.C.Russell *(As "D-11-3224": stored 3.96)*	Bishops Stortford	*
BQK 1148 BQK	Schleicher Ka7 Rhonadler	7120		12.63	R.B Armitage *(Damaged Waldershare Park 21.8.95)*	Waldershare Park	21. 6.96*
BQL 1149	Schleicher Ka6CR	725/60	D-7117	12.63	R.O.Toop	Eaglescott	15. 7.00
BQM 1150 BQM	EoN AP.10 460 Srs.1B	EoN/S/002	RAFGSA.276	12.63	A.Duncan	Portmoak	5. 6.01
BQP 1152 BQP	Slingsby T.30B Prefect	646	RAFGSA.159	9.99	A.Downie	Dunstable	9. 9.00
BQQ 1153	EoN AP.5 Olympia 2B *(Rebuilt 1993 using wings from BGA.678)*	EoN/O/121	RAFGSA.244	2.64	P.R.Brinson *"Dopey"*	Nympsfield	17. 4.02
BQS 1155 BQS	EoN AP.10 460 Srs.1	EoN/S/008		3.64	P.Williams	Bidford	6. 4.97*
BQT 1156 BQT	EoN AP.10 460 Srs.1	EoN/S/007	BGA.2666 AGA.6/BGA.1156	26. 1.64	J.H.May *(On display at Museum of Science & Industry 3.01)*	Manchester	18. 4.97*
BQU 1157 BQU	Schleicher Ka7 Rhonadler	7141	RNGSA AR66 BGA.1157	4.64	A.J.Pellatt	Llantisilio	9. 4.02
BQZ 1162 BQZ	Slingsby T.50 Skylark 4	1416		4.64	G.Colledge	Edgehill	3. 8.02
BRA 1163 BRA	Slingsby T.49B Capstan	1417		4.64	K.R.Brown	Nympsfield	16. 6.02
BRB 1164 T51	Slingsby T.51 Dart 15	1423	RAFGSA.334 BGA.1164	4.64	M.Sansom	North Hill	29. 1.02
BRC 1165 BRC	Slingsby T.45 Swallow 1	1407		5.64	J.R.Smalley	Kirton-in-Lindsey	6. 4.02
BRD 1166 BRD	Slingsby T.51 Dart 15	1425	RAFGSA.335 BGA.1166	5.64	V.Day	Lyveden	6. 5.02
BRE 1167	Slingsby T.45 Swallow 2	1415		5.64	A.Swannock & Ptnrs	Gamston	19. 5.01
BRG 1169	Slingsby T.45 Swallow	1410		5.64	A.W.F.Edwards	Gransden Lodge	19. 5.02
BRH 1170	EoN AP.5 Olympia 2B	EoN/O/154		3.64	A.Shallcrass *(For refurbishment)*	Challock	
BRK 1172 243/G-APWL	EoN AP.10 460	EoN/S/001	G-APWL BGA.1172/G-APWL/RAFGSA.268/G-APWL	4.99	D.G.Andrew	Eaglescott	26. 4.00
BRL 1173	EoN AP.5 Olympia 2B	EoN/O/132			A.Cutts & Ptnrs	Ridgewell	27. 3.99
BRM 1174 BRM	Schleicher Ka7 Rhonadler	776/60	D-4635	5.64	D.S.Driver	Currock Hill	15. 4.02
BRQ 1177 BRQ	EoN AP.10 460 Srs.1C	EoN/S/003	G-ARFU	6.64	J.Steel & Ptnrs *(Stored 2001)*	Falgunzeon	4. 8.96*
BRT 1180	Slingsby T.51 Dart 15	1430		6.64	H.E.Birch & Ptnrs	AAC Dishforth	5. 5.01
BRU 1181 BRU	Slingsby T.51 Dart 15	1429		6.64	K.M.Charlton	Currock Hill	23. 3.02
BRW 1183 BRW	Slingsby T.49B Capstan	1413		6.64	A.West & Ptnrs	Lasham	21.11.02
BRY 1185 BRY	Slingsby T.51 Dart 15	1434		7.64	S.R.Wilkinson & Ptnrs	Kirton-in-Lindsey	13. 5.02
BSA 1187 BSA	Slingsby T.51 Dart 15	1405		7.64	N G Oultram	Seighford	12. 7.01
BSC 1189 H23	Slingsby T.50 Skylark 4	1422		8.64	A.Etchells	Bidford	19.10.01
BSE 1191 BSE	Slingsby T.49B Capstan	1414		9.64	D.A Bullock	Bicester	26. 2.02
BSG 1193 BSG	Slingsby T.50 Skylark 4	1436		9.64	Denbigh GC	Llantisilio	22. 7.01
BSH 1194 BSH	Slingsby T.50 Skylark 4	1444		11.64	M Mathieson	Wormingford	14. 7.99
BSK 1196 BSK	Slingsby T.49B Capstan	1418		10.64	Kermit Syndicate	Lleweni Parc	17. 4.00
BSL 1197 BSL	Slingsby T.51 Dart 17	1445		10.64	C.J.Owles	Tibenham	27. 7.02
BSM 1198 597	Slingsby T.51 Dart 15	1439		10.64	M.Robertson	Strathaven	21. 5.02
BSQ 1201 463	EoN AP.10 460 Srs.1	EoN/S/014		5.64	K.G.Ashford	Husbands Bosworth	5. 8.02
BSR 1202 BSR	Slingsby T.50 Skylark 4	1443		12.64	D.Johnstone	Rattlesden	6. 4.02

BSS 1203 T49	Slingsby T.49B Capstan	1449		12.64	J.F.Rogers	Talgarth	26. 7.02
BST 1204	Slingsby T.49 Capstan	1451		1.65	P H Pickett	Snitterfield	11. 5.02
BSV 1206 BSV	Slingsby T.51 Dart 15	1454		7.65	G.G.Butler	Snitterfield	11. 2.97*
BSW 1207 BSW	Slingsby T.51 Dart 15	1459		2.65	B.L.Owen	Tibenham	19. 8.01
BSX 1208 BSX	Slingsby T.45 Swallow	1461	OO-ZWC	4.65	P.Brownlow & Ptnrs	Sackville Lodge, Riseley	30. 5.01
			F-OTAN-C5/BGA.1208				
BSY 1209 BSY	Slingsby T.50 Skylark 4	1448		4.65	G B Dennis	Nympsfield	9. 2.00
BSZ 1210 BSZ	Slingsby T.50 Skylark 4	1460		4.65	J.Farley	Lleweni Parc	18. 5.02
BTA 1211 BTA	Slingsby T.45 Swallow	1473		6.65	M.Morley	RAF Odiham	12. 8.01
BTD 1214 BTD	DFS/49 Grunau Baby 2C	?	(ex RAFGSA)	8.64	Bidford Gliding Centre	Bidford	14. 5.97*
BTE 1215	Slingsby T.21B	557	OH-KSA	1.65	Not known	NK	
			SE-SHL		*(Stored)*		
BTG 1217 BTG	EoN AP.10 460 Srs.1	EoN/S/024		2.65	J.Libell	Strubby	19. 3.02
BTH 1218 WB981/BTH	Slingsby T.21B	JHB/2		3.65	P.Gilmore	Aston Down	19. 8.02
	(Built J.Hulme: restored 1995 with wings from BGA.3238/WB981)						
BTJ 1219 BTJ	Schleicher Ka6CR	6367		3.65	D.Keith	Kingston Deverill	18. 8.02
BTK 1220 BTK	Slingsby T.50 Skylark 4	1364	SE-SZW	3.65	J.A.Lewis & Syndicate	Lasham	30. 4.01
BTM 1222 211	Schleicher Ka6CR	6174		3.65	P.D.Maller	Aston Down	6. 1.03
BTN 1223 BTN	EoN AP.10 460 Srs.1	EoN/S/022	AGA.15	4.65	S.C.Thompson	Parham Park	11. 5.02
			BGA.1223				
BTQ 1225 BTQ	EoN AP.10 460 Srs.1	EoN/S/029		4.65	P.L.Storey	Burn	14. 7.02
BTV 1230	DFS/68 Weihe	000358	RAFGGA	7. 5.65	B.Briggs	RAF Cranwell	23. 5.93*
					(Being refurbished)		
BUC 1237 BUC	Slingsby T.49B Capstan	1472		6.65	Lakes GC	Walney Island	27. 1.02
BUE 1239 BUE	Slingsby T.50 Skylark 4	1468		7.65	D.Craven	Seighford	5. 5.01
BUF 1240 366	Slingsby T.51 Dart 17R	1469		7.65	C.H.Brown & Ptnrs	Chipping	9. 3.02
BUG 1241 BUG	EoN AP.10 460 Srs.1	EoN/S/028		5.65	A.Rowson & Ptnrs	Long Mynd	5. 3.97*
BUH 1242 EoN	AP.10 460 Srs.1	EoN/S/021	G-ASMP	.65	A.E.Lawrence	Sackville Lodge, Riseley	19. 5.96*
					(Damaged Gransden Lodge 29. 6.95)		
BUK 1244 EoN	AP.10 460 Srs.1	EoN/S/027		5.65	M.Hodgson	Booker	28. 6.97*
BUL 1245 BUL	Slingsby T.51 Dart 17R	1470		7.65	A.Parrish & Ptnr	Lyveden	17.12.02
BUP 1247 837	Slingsby T.51 Dart 17R	1478		9.65	D.S.Carter	Enstone	10. 6.99
BUR 1249 BUR	Slingsby T.49B Capstan	1482		11.65	Denbigh GC	Llantisilio	8. 7.00
BUT 1251 BUT	Slingsby T.43 Skylark 3F	VRT.1		7.65	I.Bannister	Chipping	24. 5.02
	(Built V.R.Tull & Ptnrs)				t/a Sky Syndicate		
BUV 1253	EoN AP.10 460 Srs.1	EoN/S/030		7.65	S.H.Gibson	Gransden Lodge	8. 6.02
BUW 1254 BUW	Slingsby T.21B	?	RAFGSA.242	8.65	J.N.Wardle *"Lucy"*	Lasham	19. 9.00
BUZ 1257 BUZ	Schleicher Ka6CR	6418		8.65	R.Leacroft	Lyveden	29.12.02
BVB 1259 BVB	Schleicher Ka7 Rhonadler	7230	RAFGSA R75	9.65	York Gliding Centre	Rufforth	21. 6.02
	(Modified to ASK 13 standard)		BGA1259				
BVC 1260	Slingsby T.51 Dart 17R	1479		3.66	R.M.Hitchin & Ptnrs	Kingston Deverill	2.01
					(Sold in the USA in 2001 as N531F, and de-registered 24.04.01)		
BVE 1262 61	Slingsby T.51 Dart 17R	1483		11.65	P.Leach & Ptnr	Sandhill Farm, Shrivenham	2. 9.01
BVF 1263 BVF	Slingsby T.45 Swallow	1481		11.65	Pershore F/C	Bidford	20. 8.02
BVH 1265 BVH	Slingsby T.51 Dart 17R	1485		12.65	D.J.Simpson	Halesland	30. 6.02
BVJ 1266 BVJ	Slingsby T.51 Dart 17R	1486		1.66	R.& M.Weaver	Usk	14.12.01
BVL 1268 404	Slingsby T.51 Dart 15	1487		1.66	D.Stabler & Ptnrs	Tibenham	16. 8.99
BVM 1269 150	Slingsby T.51 Dart 17R	1492		1.66	N.H.Ponsford	(Breighton)	5.89*
					(Stored 12.99)		
BVN 1270	EoN AP.10 460 Srs.1	EoN/S/023		3.65	F J Clarke & Ptnrs	North Hill	25. 9.02
BVR 1273 BVR	Schleicher Ka6CR	6441		5.10.65	R.C Cannon & Ptnrs	Lasham	12. 3.02
BVS 1274	SZD-9 bis Bocian 1D	F-831			Spilsby Soaring	Spilsby	28. 7.01
BVW 1278	EoN AP.6 Olympia 403	EoN/4/001	RAFGSA.306	8.65	J.B. & K.D.Dumville	Camphill	29. 5.01
			G-APEW				
BVX 1279 BVX	Schleicher Ka6CR	6439		10.65	C.G.Stoves	Burn	9. 9.02
BVY 1280 BVY	LET L-13 Blanik	173121		17.10.65	Strathclyde GC	Strathaven	14. 7.01
BVZ 1281	Schleicher Ka6CR	6446		10.65	L.Blair	Bellarena	11. 5.02
BWB 1283 B96	EoN AP.10 460 Srs.1	EoN/S/036		12.65	S Metcalfe	Tibenham	27. 4.02
BWC 1284 BWC	Schleicher Ka6CR	6449		12.65	M.E.Hazlewood	Lasham	3. 5.02
BWE 1286 BWE	EoN AP.10 460 Srs.2	EoN/S/035		12.65	C.Hughes	Nympsfield	8. 8.02
BWG 1288 465	EoN AP.10 465 Srs.2	EoN/S/038		7.12.65	K.S.Green & Ptnr	Lasham	27. 4.97*
					(Being refurbished)		
BWJ 1290 377	Slingsby T.51 Dart 17R	1495		2.66	D.Godfrey & Ptnrs	Edgehill	8.10.02
BWK 1291	Slingsby T.45 Swallow	1493		2.66	K.Hubbard & Ptnrs	North Hill	14. 5.00
BWM 1293 182	Slingsby T.51 Dart 17R	1500		4.66	P.L. & L.E.Poole	Lasham	6. 5.02
BWP 1295 861	Slingsby T.51 Dart 17R	1501		3.66	D Champion	Parham Park	2. 3.02
BWQ 1296 BWQ	Slingsby T.51 Dart 15	1505		3.66	C.Uncles	Halesland	4. 6.02
BWS 1298 517	Slingsby T.51 Dart 17R	1502		4.66	R.D.Broom & E.A.Chalk	Hinton-in-the-Hedges	13. 5.02
BWT 1299 163	Slingsby T.51 Dart 15R	1508		4.66	R.Parker (Stored)	AAC Dishforth	29. 8.96*
BWU 1300	EoN AP.10 460 Srs.1	EoN/S/034		1.66	P.Berridge	Ridgewell	29. 6.02
BWX 1303	EoN AP.5 Olympia 2B	101		2.66	P.Kent	Seighford	5. 9.02
					(Built from spares)		
BXB 1307	EoN AP.10 460 Srs.1	EoN/S/040		3.66	J.M.Lee	Parham Park	30.10.02
BXC 1308 BXC/781	EoN AP.10 460 Srs.1	EoN/S/006		4.66	D.D.Copeland	Dunstable	15. 4.96*

BXE 1310 BXE	Slingsby T.51 Dart 15R	1509		5.66	M.P.Holburn	Currock Hill	23.10.02
BXG 1312 686	Slingsby T.51 Dart 17R	1512		5.66	B.W.Compton	Usk	14. 3.02
BXH 1313	Slingsby T.51 Dart 17R	1516		6.66	S.A.Stokes	Usk	17. 3.02
BXK 1315	Slingsby T.21B	1510		6.66	Not known	Rufforth	*
					(Damaged Falgunzeon 18.5.80; being refurbished 2000)		
BXL 1316 121	Slingsby T.51 Dart 17R	1517		6.66	W.R.Longstaff & Ptnr	Feshiebridge	24. 5.98
BXM 1317 9	Slingsby T.51 Dart 17R	1521		7.66	P.R.Davie	Dunstable	18. 5.02
BXP 1319	Slingsby T.45 Swallow 2	1522		7.66	Carlton Moor GC	Carlton Moor	25.10.02
BXR 1321	LET L-13 Blanik	173301	G-ATPX	5.66	Not known	Cranfield	12.92*
					(Stored 7.98)		
BXT 1323 BXT	Schleicher Ka6CR	6492		4.66	J.& A.Briggs	Tibenham	18. 2.02
BXV 1325 G-ATRA	LET L-13 Blanik	173304	G-ATRA	12. 5.66	Blanik Syndicate	Husbands Bosworth	6. 7.01
BXW 1326 BXW	LET L-13 Blanik	173305	G-ATRB	16. 6.66	R Chapman	Bidford	22. 8.01
BXY 1328 BXY	EoN AP.10 460 Srs.1	EoN/S/042		6.66	G.K.Stanford	Brent Tor	23. 8.00
BYA 1330 BYA	Slingsby T.51 Dart 17R	1518		7.66	G.A.Chalmers	Easterton	19. 3.02
BYB 1331 352	Slingsby T.45 Swallow	1525		7.66	Surrey Hills GC	Kenley	8. 7.97*
BYC 1332 BYC	Slingsby T.51 Dart 17R	1526		8.66	G.Woodman	Sandhill Farm, Shrivenham	15. 5.02
BYE 1334 BYE	EoN AP.10 463 Srs.1	EoN/S/044		9.66	C.J.Bushell	Snitterfield	29. 4.01
BYG 1336 225	Slingsby T.51 Dart 17R	1535	RAFGSA BGA.1336	11.66	W.T.Emery	Rufforth	25. 4.02
BYJ 1338	Slingsby T.45 Swallow	1568		2.67	D.I.Johnstone t/a Swallow Soaring Group	Strathaven	18.11.96*
BYK 1339	Slingsby T.45 Swallow	1566		1.67	G.E.Williams	Seighford	19. 9.02
BYL 1340	Schleicher Ka6CR	6517		7.66	D.Heaton	Llantisilio	3.10.02
BYM 1341 558	Schleicher Ka6CR	6518	RAFGSA.381 BGA.1341	7.66	K.S.Smith	Wormingford	13. 9.02
BYU 1348 350	Schleicher Ka6CR	6525	XW640 BGA.1348	9.66	R.N.John	Haylesland	15. 2.02
BYX 1351 BYX	Schleicher Ka6E	4055		12.66	J.Dent & D.B.Andrews	Chipping	5. 5.02
BYY 1352 BYY	Slingsby T.21B	628	RAFGSA.338 BGA.1352/WB967	11.66	T.Akerman	Bicester	28. 6.02
BZA 1354 BZA	Slingsby T.21B	1162	RAFGSA.318 XN183	11.66	A Hill	RAF Wattisham	26. 6.02
BZB 1355 BZB	EoN AP.10 460 Srs.1	EoN/S/047		10.66	D.C.Ratcliffe Syndicate	Parham Park	24. 4.02
BZC 1356 BZC	Slingsby T.51 Dart 17R	1563		2.67	A.N.Ely	Strubby	23. 9.02
BZF 1359 311	Slingsby T.51 Dart 17R	1570		3.67	P.C.Gill & Ptnrs	Ridgewell	1.10.02
BZG 1360 N54	Slingsby T.49B Capstan	1581		28. 4.67	Culdrose GC	RNAS Culdrose	14. 3.02
BZH 1361 406	Slingsby T.51 Dart 17R	1580		4.67	C.Long	Bidford	19.12.00
BZJ 1362 362	Slingsby T.51 Dart 17R	1567		4.67	D.M.Steed "*Anastasia*"	Enstone	13. 8.98
BZL 1364 BZL	Slingsby T.45 Swallow	1596		7.67	Cairngorm Swallow Syndicate	Feshiebridge	14. 8.00
BZM 1365	Slingsby T.45 Swallow	1597		7.67	F.Webster	Drumshade	22. 5.97*
BZP 1367 F4	SZD-24-4A Foka 4	W-301		1.67	I.K.Mitchell	North Hill	17. 2.02
BZQ 1368 453	Schleicher Ka6CR	6551		2.67	A.Holland	North Hill	24. 8.99
BZR 1369 471	EoN AP.10 460 Srs.1	EoN/S/049		2.67	G.Wardell	Camphill	6. 7.02
BZS 1370 BZS	EoN AP.10 460 Srs.1	EoN/S/052		2.67	R.Hutchinson	Carlton Moor	25. 4.97*
BZV 1373 BZV	EoN AP.10 460 Srs.1	EoN/S/046		2.67	I.F.Smith	Lasham	15. 7.02
BZW 1374 Z11	EoN AP.10 460 Srs.1	EoN/S/053		3.67	J.Bradley & Ptnrs	Lleweni Parc	12. 4.97*
BZX 1375	Schleicher Ka6CR	6571		3.67	Leeds University GC	Rufforth	19. 5.01
BZY 1376	Slingsby T.31B *(Rebuild of BGA.1175)*	SSK/FF1817	BGA.1175	3.67	A.L.Higgins t/a The Blue Brick Syndicate	Dunstable	19. 7.01
BZZ 1377 77	SZD-24-4A Foka 4	W-308		3.67	M.Hudson & Ptnrs	Lasham	3. 5.02
CAB 1379 CAB	EoN AP.10 460 Srs.1	EoN/S/033	RAFGSA.344	3.67	P.Green & Ptnr	Enstone	21.10.98
CAC 1380 994	Schleicher Ka6E	4054		3.67	L.I.Rigby	Crowland	9. 3.02
CAE 1381 575	Schleicher Ka6E	4076		8. 4.67	D.Craven	Long Mynd	29. 3.02
CAF 1382	EoN AP.5 Olympia 2B	EoN/O/131	RAFGSA.254	5. 4.67	G.D.Griffiths	Brent Tor	3. 3.01
CAG 1383 715	Schleicher Ka6E	4080		4.67	S.L.Beaumont	Crowland	9. 6.02
CAK 1386 117	EoN AP.5 Olympia 2B	EoN/O/122	RAFGSA.246	3.67	P.Hatfield t/a Olympia 2B Syndicate	Rufforth	4. 5.02
CAN 1389	EoN AP.10 460 Srs.1	EoN/S/050		3.67	R.Gibson	Bidford	14. 4.01
CAQ 1391 812	Schempp-Hirth SHK	37		3.67	M.A.Thorne	Old Sarum	14. 7.02
CAR 1392 422	Schempp-Hirth SHK-1	40		4.67	P.Gentil & M.Gresty	Aston Down	24. 3.01
CAS 1393 372	Schleicher Ka6E	4029	RAFGSA.372	5.67	R.F.Tindall	Gransden Lodge	22. 8.02
CAT 1394 CAT	EoN AP.10 460 Srs.1	EoN/S/051		5.67	D.C.Phillips & Ptnrs	Snitterfield	13. 7.02
CAV 1396 CAV	Schleicher ASK13	13015		5.67	M.Cuming	Edgehill	3. 8.00
CAW 1397 357	LET L-13 Blanik	173202	RAFGSA.357 G-ASZK	5.67	Not known *(Stored - spares use 6.96)*	Enstone	2.83*
CAX 1398 CAX	Slingsby T.45 Swallow	1598		7.67	R.B Armitage	Waldershare Park	17. 8.02
CAZ 1400 702	Slingsby T.51 Dart 17WR	1611		7.68	J.M.Young & Ptnrs	Easterton	31. 5.98
CBA 1401 679	Slingsby T.51 Dart 17WR	1612		7.68	D.R.Bennett & P.H.Pickett	Snitterfield	27. 5.02
CBK 1410	Grunau Baby III *(Built Sfg.Schaffin)*	-	RAFGSA.378 D-4676	5. 9.67	N.H.Ponsford (Op Real Aeroplane Club) *(Stored 1.98)*	Breighton	4.83*
CBM 1412 343	Schleicher Ka6CR	6607		7.67	R.H.Moss	Nympsfield	15. 3.01
CBN 1413 CBN	SZD-30 Pirat	W-320		5.67	B.C.Cooper	Portmoak	12.11.01
CBP 1414 CBP	SZD-24C Foka	W-198	OY-BXR	7.67	G.Sutton	Sutton Bank	18. 6.01

CBR 1416 CBR	Aeromere M.100S	044		7.67	G.Viglione	Rattlesden	21. 9.02
CBS 1417 EoN	AP.5 Olympia 2B	EoN/0/143	RAFGSA.291	7.67	G.Moden & Ptnrs	Edgehill	4. 9.94*
	(Possibly kit-built - c/n incorrect - EoN/0/143 became BGA.1034 & sold to Zambia) (Stored 6.95)						
CBU 1419 905	Schempp-Hirth SHK-1	53	D-8441	17.10.67	M.Dodd	Shobdon	26.12.99
CBV 1420 362	EoN AP.10 460 Srs.1	EoN/S/055		6.67	J.Sharples & Ptnr	Burn	13.10.96*
CBW 1421 CBW	Schleicher ASK13	13034		8.67	Stratford-upon-Avon GC	Snitterfield	4. 5.02
CBY 1423 475	Schleicher Ka6CR	960	RAFGSA.322	10.67	G.Martin	Talgarth	13. 6.02
			D-3222				
CCA 1425 CCA	Schleicher Ka6E	4126		10.67	R.K.Forrest	Feshiebridge	16.12.02
CCB 1426 CCB	Schempp-Hirth SHK-1	52		7.67	R.M.Johnson	Milfield	15. 9.02
CCC 1427	Schleicher ASK13	13035	RAFGSA.R83	6.99	RAFGSA Centre	Bicester	4. 6.01
			BGA.1427				
CCD 1428 373	Schleicher Ka6E	4127		12.67	M.H.Phelps	Husbands Bosworth	8. 3.02
CCE 1429 CCE	Schleicher ASK13	13047		12.67	Oxford GC	Weston-on-the-Green	29. 3.02
CCF 1430 CCF	Schleicher ASK13	13042		12.67	Norfolk GC	Tibenham	28. 5.02
CCG 1431	Schleicher Ka6E	4125		12.67	G.A.Fudge	Thame	21. 6.02
CCJ 1433 878	Schleicher Ka6CR	6145	RAFGSA.323	10.67	P.Green	Weston-on-the-Green	8. 4.99
CCL 1435 47	Schleicher Ka6E	4129		3.68	M.T.Stanley	Sutton Bank	10. 1.02
CCM 1436 CCM	Schleicher ASK13	13053		2.68	Burn GC	Burn	29. 5.02
CCN 1437 CCN	SZD-9 bis Bocian 1E	P-431		3.68	South London Gliding Centre	Kenley	26. 4.00
CCP 1438 L99	Schleicher ASK13	13052		2.68	DRA GC	RAF Odiham	26. 1.02
CCR 1440 CCR	Schleicher Ka6E	4149		2.68	A E Burgess	Enstone	27. 9.01
CCS 1441 CCS	Slingsby T.41 Skylark	21008	PH-230	3.68	S.L.Benn	Cranwell	31.10.97*
CCT 1442 CCT	Schleicher ASK13	13057		3.68	Stratford-upon-Avon GC	Snitterfield	17.12.02
CCU 1443	Schleicher Ka6E	4122		3.68	D.C.Findlay	RAF Keevil	16. 2.02
CCV 1444	Schleicher Ka6E	4160		3.68	C.J.Nicholas	Ridgewell	25. 7.02
CCW 1445 CCW	Schleicher ASK13	13051		3.68	J E.Hart & Ptnrs	Sutton Bank	17. 2.02
CCX 1446 CCX	Schleicher ASK13	13054		3.68	Trent Valley GC	Kirton-in-Lindsey	15. 4.02
CCY 1447 CCY	Schleicher ASK13	13050		3.68	D.L.Woolf & Ptnrs	Long Mynd	6. 4.02
CCZ 1448 CCZ	Schleicher ASK13	13070		3.68	Trent Valley GC	Kirton-in-Lindsey	29. 7.02
CDA 1449	Schleicher Ka6E	4136		3.68	F.T.Bick & Ptnrs	Aboyne	7 .4.02
CDB 1450	Schleicher Ka6E	4137		3.68	K.L.Holburn	Currock Hill	23.10.02
CDC 1451 CDC	Schleicher K8B	8743		3.68	Enstone Eagle GC	Rivar Hill	15. 3.99
					(Stored 7.01)		
CDD 1452	Schleicher Ka6E	4165		3.68	D.T.Staff	Booker	29. 3.99
CDF 1454 683	Schleicher Ka6E	4162		3.68	J.Reid & Ptnrs	Rivar Hill	8. 4.02
CDG 1455	FFA Diamant 18	35		3.68	J.A.Luck	Cranfield	7. 4.02
CDH 1456 619	Schempp-Hirth HS.2 Cirrus	10		4.68	A.A.Jenkins	Enstone	15. 1.02
CDJ 1457	Schleicher ASK13	13077		4.68	Southdown GC	Parham Park	4.01
					(Crashed Parham 3.12.00 and remains sold as scrap)		
CDK 1458	Schleicher K8B	8747		5.68	Burn GC	Burn	25.10.01
CDN 1461	EoN AP.7 Primary				Norfolk & Suffolk Aviation Museum		
						Flixton	7.00
CDQ 1463	Grunau Baby III	R161		6.68	Not known *(Under repair 2000)*		
CDR 1464 CDR	Scheibe Bergfalke III	5625		8.68	N.M Neil	Hinton-in-the-Hedges	24. 4.01
CDV 1468 CDV	Schleicher Ka6E	4159		5.68	Not known	Cranfield	4.87*
					(Wreck stored 7.97)		
CDW 1469	FFA Diamant 18	033		8.68	J.L.McIver	Falgunzeon	8.11.02
CDX 1470 303	SZD-30 Pirat	W-392		5.68	S.Cynalski	Rufforth	19. 6.00
CDZ 1472 CDZ	Schleicher Ka6E	4177		5.68	J R Minnis	North Weald	15. 5.02
CEA 1473 CEA	Schempp-Hirth HS.2 Cirrus	21	XZ405	8.68	M.S.Whitton	Long Mynd	12. 5.02
			BGA.1473/D-8437				
CEB 1474 CEB	SZD-9 bis Bocian 1E	P-433		5.68	Bath, Wilts & North Dorset GC		
						Kingston Deverill	24. 6.02
CEC 1475 18	Schempp-Hirth HS.2 Cirrus	22		7.68	C.R.Ellis	Long Mynd	15. 1.02
CED 1476 814	Schleicher Ka6E	4196		6.68	H.G.Williams & Ptnrs	Snitterfield	1. 5.02
CEG 1479	Schleicher Ka6E	4203		6.68	J.C.Boley	Halesland	21. 3.96*
CEH 1480 CEH	Wassmer WA.22 Super Javelot	68	F-OTAN-C6	7.68	N.A.Mills	Lasham	25. 4.02
			F-CCLU				
CEJ 1481 CEJ	Schleicher ASK13	13102		8.68	Devon & Somerset GC	North Hill	16. 5.02
CEK 1482	Slingsby T.21B (T)	1151	RAFGSA.369	7.68	D.Woolerton	North Coates	26. 1.02
	(Fuji-Robin EC34PM s/n 82-00391)		XN147				
CEL 1483 JD	Schleicher Ka6E	4174		8.68	Essex & Suffolk GC	Wormingford	19.12.02
CEM 1484 CEM	Schleicher Ka6E	4212		8.68	G.D.Bowes	Pocklington	17. 6.02
CEN 1485 CEN	SZD-30 Pirat	W-393	SP-2520	7.68	A.Bogan	Kirton-in-Lindsey	2.12.01
CEQ 1487 458	Schleicher Ka6E	4230		8.68	C.L.Lagden & Ptnrs	Ridgewell	31. 7.02
CEV 1492	Scheibe Bergfalke II	184	???	8.68	A.Lewis *(Stored 10.96)*	Jurby, IoM	17.12.93*
CEW 1493 CEW	Schleicher Ka6E	4209		8.68	J.W.Richardson	Dunstable	11. 5.02
CEX 1494 CEX	Schleicher ASK13	13108		9.68	Newcastle & Teesside GC	Carlton Moor	25.10.02
CEY 1495 CEY	Schleicher Ka6E	4222		8.68	S.N.Longland & Ptnrs	Gransden Lodge	7. 7.02
CFA 1497 CFA	Schleicher ASK13	13113		10.68	Booker GC	Booker	25. 3.02
CFB 1498	Schleicher ASK13	13110		10.68	Not known *(Wrecked)*	Burn	*
CFC 1499 CFC	Schleicher Ka7 Rhonadler	470	RAFGSA.387	11.68	K.F.Marchant	Edgehill	17. 8.02
			F-OTAN-C1				

CFD 1500 B1	LET L-13 Blanik	173214	G-ATCG	10.68	M D White	Burn	19. 3.01
CFF 1502 CFF	Schleicher K8B	8765		10.68	Norfolk GC	Tibenham	14. 5.02
CFG 1503 CFG	Schleicher ASK13	13115		10.68	Staffordshire GC	Seighford	21. 5.02
CFK 1506	Schempp-Hirth HS.2 Cirrus	38		11.68	C.V Webb & Ptnrs	Sleap	16.12.02
CFL 1507 CFL	Schleicher Ka6E	4215		10.68	Bath, Wilts & North Dorset GC	Kingston Deverill	1. 7.02
CFM 1508 CFM	Schleicher ASK13	13121		7.12.68	Vale of The White Horse GC	Sandhill Farm Shrivenham	21.11.02
CFS 1513 CFS	Glasflugel H.201 Standard Libelle	83		4.70	J.L.H.Pegman	Milfield	7. 6.02
CFT 1514 62	Slingsby T.59A Kestrel 17	1729		3.73	J.A.Kane	Carlton Moor	30. 6.01
CFX 1518 CFX	Glasflugel H.201 Standard Libelle	274		2.72	D.F.Porter	Seighford	24. 4.01
CFY 1519 862	Glasflugel H.201 Standard Libelle	270		3.72	C.W.Stevens	Camphill	3. 5.02
CGB 1522 CGB	Schleicher Ka6E	4247		12.68	M.S Colebrook & Ptnrs	Bembridge	24. 4.01
CGD 1524 418	Schleicher Ka6E	4202		1.69	I F Smith	Lasham	29. 9.02
CGE 1525	Schleicher Ka6E	4246		1.69	C.Weir	Bellarena	19. 5.02
CGH 1528 153	Schleicher K8B	8772		23. 2.69	I.G.Brice	Lasham	13. 4.02
CGJ 1529 CGJ	Schleicher K8B	8773		2.69	Nene Valley GC	Upwood	6. 4.02
CGK 1530 124	Schleicher Ka6E	4261		3.69	J.A.F.Barnes & Ptnrs	Wormingford	24. 9.02
CGM 1532 CGM	FFA Diamant 18	053		4. 4.69	J.G.Batch	Hinton-in-the Hedges	22. 5.02
CGN 1533 309	Schleicher Ka6E	4173		3.69	K.R Brown & Ptnr	Nympsfield	18. 4.01
CGQ 1535 CGQ	Schleicher ASK13	13153		7. 4.69	Oxford GC	Weston-on-the-Green	14. 5.02
CGR 1536 913	Schleicher ASK13	13142		31. 3.69	Bristol & Glos GC	Nympsfield	1. 12.96*
					(Damaged near Nympsfield 2.6.96)		
CGS 1537 CGS	FFA Diamant 18	055		7.69	C.J.Wimbury	Ringmer	14. 5.02
CGT 1538 449	Schempp-Hirth SHK-1	38	D-1966	4.69	B.W.Svenson	Pocklington	21. 2.02
CGU 1539 CGU	EoN AP.5 Olympia 2B	EoN/O/115	RAFGSA.228	4.69	M.Skinner & Ptnrs	Pocklington	30. 8.97*
CGV 1540 CGV	PIK-16C Vasama	48		4.69	D.J.Osborne & Ptnrs	Currock Hill	23. 8.02
CGX 1542 CGX	Bolkow Phoebus C	869		4.69	W.N.Smith & Ptnrs	Sackville Lodge, Riseley	19. 5.02
CGY 1543 CGY	Schempp-Hirth HS.2 Cirrus	51		18. 4.69	R.Munday & Ptnrs	Eaglescott	31. 5.02
CGZ 1544 CGZ	Schempp-Hirth SHK	39		5.69	M.C.Ridger	Saltby	23. 1.02
CHB 1546 577	Schleicher Ka6E	4235		5.69	D.L.Jones	Weston-on-the-Green	16. 5.01
CHC 1547	Bolkow Phoebus C	858		5.69	D.Garner Syndicate	Rhigos	7. 9.00
CHE 1549 CHE	Slingsby T.41 Skylark 2	DSS.002		6.69	M.S.Howey	Burn	28. 3.02
	(Built Doncaster Sailplane Services)						
CHF 1550 CHF	SZD-9 bis Bocian 1E	P-432		5.69	T.J.Wilkinson	Sackville Lodge, Riseley	2. 8.96*
					(Damaged Sackville Lodge 27. 8.95)		
CHG 1551 N52	SZD-30 Pirat	B-294		27. 6.69	Culdrose GC	RNAS Culdrose	6 .4.02
CHJ 1553 CHJ	Bolkow Phoebus 17C	879		6.69	D.C.Austin	Sutton Bank	30. 4.02
CHK 1554 CHK	EoN AP.5 Olympia 2B	?	RAFGSA	6.69	Oly Gliding Syndicate	Halesland	30. 6.02
CHL 1555 CHL	SZD-30 Pirat	B-295		6.69	W.Sage & Syndicate	Rufforth	11. 5.02
CHQ 1559	Slingsby T.31B	1186	XN247	6.69	N.H.Ponsford (*Stored 1.98*)	Wigan	7.82*
CHT 1562 846	Schleicher ASW15	15013		8.69	N.A.Kelly & Ptnrs	Lasham	30. 4.02
CHU 1563 CHU	Schleicher K8B	8794		10. 8.69	H B Chalmers (Highland GC Syndicate)	Easterton	26. 4.02
CHW 1565 CHW	Schleicher ASK13	13187		8.69	Dorset GC	Gallows Hill	26. 4.02
CHY 1567 CHY	Slingsby T.45 Swallow	RG.103		9.69	J.L.H.Pegman & Ptnrs	Currock Hill	27. 6.02
	(Built R.Greenslade from kit)						
CHZ 1568 857	Schleicher Ka6E	4153	N6916	9.69	M.Uphill	Usk	17. 2.02
CJB 1570 764	Bolkow Phoebus C	919		12.69	T.J.Wilkinson	Sackville Lodge, Riseley	1. 6.01
CJC 1571	Ginn-Lesniak Kestrel	1		10.69	P.G.Fairness & K Burns	Milfield	25. 3.02
CJD 1572 S14	Schleicher ASK13	13182		19.10.69	Shenington GC	Edgehill	7. 1.03
CJF 1574 474	Schleicher K8B	8803		29.11.69	Surrey & Hants GC	Lasham	18. 6.01
CJG 1575 CJG	Wassmer WA.21 Javelot II	38	F-OTAN-C4 F-CCEZ	1.70	R S Hanslip	Burn	9. 4.02
CJJ 1577 CJJ	Bolkow Phoebus C	913		15. 1.70	P Maddocks	Falgunzeon	22. 8.01
CJK 1578 CJK	Schempp-Hirth SHK	35	RAFGSA.	25 2.70	R.H.Short	Lyveden	21. 8.02
CJL 1579 222	Schempp-Hirth SHK-1	42	OO-ZLG	2.70	M.F.Brook	Camphill	27. 5.01
CJM 1580 CJM	Schleicher K8B	8814		8. 3.70	Surrey & Hants GC	Lasham	18. 2.02
CJN 1581 CJN	Schempp-Hirth SHK-1	55		3.70	G.Kench	Dunstable	21. 8.02
CJP 1582	Schleicher ASW15	15041		3.70	C.Pain	Cranfield	22. 5.02
CJR 1584 83	Schempp-Hirth HS.2 Cirrus	87		3.70	J.H.Stanley	Lasham	11. 1.03
CJY 1591 CJY	Schleicher Ka6CR	555	(RAFGSA)	4.70	Bristol & Glos GC	Nympsfield	4. 5.02
CKC 1595 CKC	Bolkow Phoebus C	936	(BGA.1590)	21. 4.70	S.J.Bennett	Bidford	18. 7.02
CKD 1596 CKD	SZD-30 Pirat	B-327		4.70	L.D.Crisp	Bidford	2. 1.02
CKF 1598 961	Glasflugel H.201 Standard Libelle	101		4.70	S.M.Turner	Crowland	25. 5.02
CKJ 1601	Slingsby T.30B Prefect	740	PH-197	4.71	Not known (*Stored*)	Crosshill	14. 4.90*
CKL 1603 CKL	Schleicher Ka6E	4336		4.70	I.Lowes & Ptnrs	Milfield	7. 8.02
CKN 1605 CKN	SZD-9 bis Bocian 1E	P-496		5.70	Strubby GC "Enola Gay"	Strubby	3. 7.02
CKP 1606 CKP	Schleicher ASW15	15058		7.70	M.G.Shaw & Ptnrs	Portmoak	26.10.01
CKR 1608	Schleicher ASK13	13247		7.70	Essex GC	North Weald	11. 5.02

CKT 1610	Scheibe Bergfalke II	E.03	D-9208	7.70	Not known *(Being restored)*	Thame	
CKU 1611 CKU	Schleicher ASK13	13243		11. 8.70	Essex GC	North Weald	18. 5.02
CKV 1612 T10	Schleicher ASK13	13253		8.70	Black Mountain GC	Talgarth	23. 7.02
CKW 1613 CKW	Schleicher K8B	8836		9.70	D.R Crompton	Bidford	14. 6.98
CKY 1615 743	Glasflugel H.201 Standard Libelle	139		22. 8.70	P G Mullis	Edgehill	23. 4.01
CKZ 1616 724	Schempp-Hirth HS.4 Standard Cirrus	52	RAFGSA BGA.1616	8.70	M.E.Kingston	Dunstable	5. 5.02
CLA 1617 CLA	Schempp-Hirth HS.4 Standard Cirrus	63		11.70	J.A.Wight & D.Dye	Nympsfield	21.10.02
CLC 1619	Slingsby T.21B	1200	RNGSA 2-07	11.70	Not known *(Stored 2000)*		
CLF 1622 CLF	Schleicher Ka7 Rhonadler	931	D-5062	5. 1.71	P.Morgan & Ptnrs	Tibenham	9. 4.02
CLG 1623 CLG	Schempp-Hirth SHK-1	36	RAFGSA.27	9. 1.71	J.E.Kenny	Bembridge	6. 4.02
CLH 1624 252	Schempp-Hirth HS.4 Standard Cirrus	77		??	P.C.Bray & Ptnrs	Nympsfield	26. 1.02
CLJ 1625	EoN AP.7 Primary	EoN/P/035	WP267	8. 2.71	T Ackerman *(On rebuild 2000)*	Bicester	2.72*
CLK 1626 CLK	Schleicher Ka7 Rhonadler *(Partly modified to ASK-13 standard)*	607	D-5714	2.71	Cornish GC	Perranporth	21. 4.02
CLM 1628 535	Glasflugel H.201 Standard Libelle	178		2.71	J.N.Cochrane	North Hill	4. 3.02
CLN 1629 142	Glasflugel H.201 Standard Libelle	175		4.71	J.N.Wardle	Lasham	14. 4.02
CLP 1630 948	Glasflugel H.201B Standard Libelle	176		2.71	A.Jelden	Booker	28. 3.02
CLQ 1631 CLQ	Schempp-Hirth HS.2 Cirrus	99		29. 1.71	K.Bastenfield	Brent Tor	9. 1.03
CLR 1632 284	Glasflugel H.201B Standard Libelle	173		4.71	D G.Shepherd	Easterton	5. 3.02
CLT 1634	Schleicher Ka7 Rhonadler	251	D-5529	4.71	R.Spencer t/a The Syndicate	Rhigos	18.10.99
CLV 1636	Glasflugel H.201 Standard Libelle	180		3.71	G.B.Monslow	Bidford	7. 6.02
CLW 1637 937	Glasflugel H.201 Standard Libelle	174		12. 3.71	N.A.Dean & Ptnrs	Kirton-in-Lindsey	11.10.02
CLX 1638 CLX	Schleicher K8B	8851		12. 3.71	Midland GC	Long Mynd	9. 1.03
CLY 1639	Hirth Go.III Minimoa	378	PH-390 D-5076	20. 3.72	Not known *(On rebuild 2000)*	Dunstable	1.79*
CLZ 1640 799	Schleicher Ka6E	4056	AGA.2	2. 4.71	H.N.Craven	Pocklington	18. 8.02
CMF 1646 CMF	SZD-32A Foka 5	W-534		7.71	D J Linford	Lasham	5. 6.02
CMG 1647 CMG	Schleicher Ka7 Rhonadler	462	D-8116	7.71	P.M.Williams *"Fledermaus"*	Lasham	24. 2.02
CMH 1648 165	Glasflugel H.201B Standard Libelle	224		12. 7.71	D.N Greig	North Hill	18. 3.02
CMK 1650	Schleicher ASK13	13305		8.71	South Wales GC	Usk	17. 2.02
CML 1651 CML	Schleicher K8B	8862		8.71	Vectis GC	Bembridge	13. 3.01
					(Collided with Super Cub G-BAFS at Bembridge 8.10.00)		
CMN 1653 CMN	Schleicher K8B	8870		23. 8.71	Bristol & Glos GC	Nympsfield	5. 6.02
CMQ 1655 CF	Glasflugel H.201 Standard Libelle	233		13. 8.71	I.H.Molesworth	Ridgewell	14. 3.02
CMR 1656 CMR	Glasflugel H.201 Standard Libelle	225		15. 8.71	J.A.Dandie & Ptnrs	Portmoak	24. 8.02
CMS 1657 602	Glasflugel H.201 Standard Libelle	234		8.71	D.Manser & Ptnrs	Challock	25. 4.02
CMT 1658	Scheibe Bergfalke II	124	D-6012	22. 8.71	Not known *(Stored 2000)*		
CMV 1660 184	Glasflugel H.201 Standard Libelle	235		11. 8.71	S.E.Evans & Ptnrs	Weston on the Green	7. 4.02
CMW 1661 CMW	Glasflugel H.201B Standard Libelle	242		9.71	A M Dalton	Dunstable	20. 1.02
CMX 1662 226	Glasflugel H.201 Standard Libelle	232		9.71	W D Johnson	Burn	20. 3.02
CMY 1663	Grunau Baby IIIC *(Built LSV Fussen)*	1	RAFGSA.373 D-1090	22. 1.72	Not known *(Stored for rebuild 7.95)*	Manor Farm, Glatton	*
CMZ 1664 CMZ	Schleicher Ka7 Rhonadler	323	D-5589	11. 6.72	Cornish GC	Perranporth	25. 5.02
CND 1668 CND	SZD-9 bis Bocian 1	EP-428	RAFGSA.392	1.72	Angus GC	Drumshade	10. 4.02
CNE 1669 525	Glasflugel H.201 Standard Libelle	266		1.72	E.T.Melville	Portmoak	8.12.01
CNF 1670 709	Glasflugel H.201B Standard Libelle	271		1.72	D.F.Mazingham	Pocklington	4. 4.02
CNG 1671 622	Glasflugel H.201 Standard Libelle	265		2.72	C.F.Smith & Ptnr	Nympsfield	7.11.02
CNH 1672 442	Glasflugel H.201 Standard Libelle	269		2.72	A.D'Otreppe	Lasham	22. 7.02
CNJ 1673 CNJ	Glasflugel H.201 Standard Libelle	272		9. 2.72	R.E.Gretton	Crowland	28. 8.01
CNK 1674 CNK	SZD-30 Pirat	B-459		3.72	H.Forshaw & Ptnrs	Rufforth	19. 9.01

CNM 1676 CNM	SZD-9 bis Bocian 1	EP-551		2.72	M.Williamson & Ptnrs	Crowland	22. 6.02
CNN 1677	Schempp-Hirth HS.4 Standard Cirrus	173		2.72	R.W.Asplin	Camphill	18. 4.02
CNP 1678 CNP	Glasflugel H.201 Standard Libelle	264		3.72	S. & J.McKenzie	Camphill	15. 7.01
CNS 1681	Slingsby T.59A Kestrel 17	1724		4.72	J.R.Greenwell	Carlton Moor	1. 5.02
CNV 1683 229	Slingsby T.59F Kestrel 19	1790		6.72	P.H.Fanshawe & E.A.Smith	Snitterfield	4. 1.03
CNW 1684 625	Slingsby T.59F Kestrel 19	1791		7.72	S.R.Watson	Camphill	24. 3.02
CNX 1685 818	Slingsby T.59F Kestrel 20	1792		27. 7.72	D.Starer	Dunstable	13. 2.02
CNY 1686 151	Glasflugel H.201 Standard Libelle	322		9.72	S.B.Marshall & Ptnrs	Portmoak	17. 9.02
CPA 1688 466	Glasflugel H.201B Standard Libelle	328		9.72	K.Hampson	Kenley	5. 3.02
CPB 1689 858	Slingsby T.59D Kestrel 19	1796		10.72	A.T.Videon	North Weald	8. 4.02
CPC 1690 CPC	SZD-32A Foka 5	W-546		3.72	J.Davidson *(Sold in Poland as SP-3645 and de-registered 15.02.00)*	Parham Park	5.00
CPD 1691 292	Schleicher ASW17	17026		3.74	E.F.Allsop	Long Mynd	8. 6.02
CPE 1692 CPE	EoN AP.5 Olympia 2B	EoN/O/120	RAFGSA.233	3.72	Not known *(W/O Arbroath 10. 9.94; stored 5.97)*	Edgehill	9. 8.95*
CPF 1693 T15	Glasflugel H.201 Standard Libelle	267		3.72	J.M.Norman & P.Elvidge	Pocklington	8. 3.02
CPG 1694 CPG	Schleicher Ka7 Rhonadler	7036	D-4029	15. 4.72	Queens University GC	Bellarena	7.12.02
CPJ 1696 CPJ	Schleicher Ka6E	4059	OO-ZDA	9. 4.72	J.Herd & Ptnrs	Pocklington	4. 5.02
CPL 1698	Slingsby T.8 Tutor	FF477	RAFGSA183	26. 4.72	Not knoqwn *(Being refurbished 2001)*	Lasham	
CPM 1699 CPM	Glasflugel H.201 Standard Libelle	179		4.72	M.J.Wilson	Dunstable	3. 4.02
CPU 1706 761	Schempp-Hirth HS.4 Standard Cirrus	194		4.72	J.P.J.Ketelaar	Feshiebridge	6.11.02
CPV 1707 CPV	SZD-30 Pirat	B-470		3.72	D.Hale & Ptnrs	Bidford	7. 2.98
CPX 1709 CPX	SZD-30 Pirat	B-460		4.72	J.Murphy	Usk	8. 6.02
CQC 1714 601	SZD-30 Pirat	B-472		15. 4.72	A.White	Winthorpe	4. 5.02
CQD 1715 CQD	Schleicher K8B	419/58	D-5625	4.72	E.McCaig	Challock	19. 4.01
CQG 1718 CQG	EoN AP.5 Olympia 2B	EoN/O/044	RAFGSA.206 BGA.542	4.72	L.McKenzie	Sutton Bank	15. 2.02
CQJ 1720 K17	Slingsby T.59A Kestrel 17	1727		5.72	A.Shelton	Portmoak	27. 7.02
CQL 1722 339	Schempp-Hirth HS.5 Nimbus 2	11		5.72	M N Erlund	East Kirkby	3. 3.02
CQM 1723 234	Slingsby T.59F Kestrel 19	1765		22. 5.72	J.A.Knowles	RAF Odiham	2. 6.02
CQN 1724 CQN	Schempp-Hirth HS.4 Standard Cirrus	204G		19. 5.72	M.G.Sankey & Ptnrs	Lasham	29. 3.02
CQP 1725 918	Schempp-Hirth HS.5 Nimbus 2	4		4.72	D.Caunt & Ptnrs	Booker	2. 2.02
CQQ 1726 139	Schempp-Hirth HS.5 Nimbus 2	5		4.72	D.J.White	Camphill	28. 3.02
CQR 1727 703	Schempp-Hirth HS.4 Standard Cirrus	220G		28. 5.72	B.E.Richards	Sandhill Farm Shrivenham	25. 6.02
CQT 1729 CQT	Schleicher Ka7 Rhonadler	603	D-5712	6.72	Shenington GC *(Stored Kemble 7.97: current status unknown)*	Edgehill	6. 7.96*
CQW 1732 342	SZD-36A Cobra 15	W-572		6.72	W.Alexander	Portmoak	6.10.02
CQX 1733 789	SZD-30 Pirat	B-483		9. 6.72	The B Syndicate	Lleweni Parc	6. 7.01
CQY 1734 D49	Schempp-Hirth HS.4 Standard Cirrus	214		16. 6.72	S.R.Blackmore	Edgehill	17. 3.02
CRA 1736 CRA	Schleicher Ka7 Rhonadler	7009	???	7. 7.72	Welland GC	Lyveden	19. 5.02
CRB 1737 242	Glasflugel H.201 Standard Libelle	243		6.72	A.I.Mawer	Winthorpe	23. 5.02
CRD 1739	SZD-36A Cobra 15	W-578		8. 7.72	J.Durman	Pocklington	13. 6.94*
CRF 1741	Birmingham Guild BG-135	001		2.72	C D Stevens	Lee-on-Solent	6. 4.02
CRH 1743 650	Schempp-Hirth HS.4 Standard Cirrus	233G		8.72	E MacDonald	Portmoak	11. 4.02
CRJ 1744	Slingsby T59A Kestrel 17		1728	7.72	W.Hand-Gerd	Nordhorn, Germany	5. 3.02
CRK 1745	Slingsby T.8 Tutor	930	XE760 VM539	25. 7.72	I.D.Smith *(Stored 8.01)*	Nympsfield	8.82*
CRL 1746 CRL	Schleicher ASK13	13013	???	4. 8.72	Midland GC	Long Mynd	16. 2.02
CRM 1747	Grunau Baby III	1	RAFGSA.361 D-8061	27. 7.72	R.Wasey & Ptnrs *"Grumpy"*	Sandown	26. 11.96*
CRN 1748 566	Schempp-Hirth HS.4 Standard Cirrus	234G		4. 8.72	M.G.Woollard	Dunstable	7. 3.02
CRQ 1750 CRQ	Glasflugel H.201B Standard Libelle	326		10. 8.72	K.Counsell & Ptnrs	Usk	31. 3.02
CRS 1752	Glasflugel H.201B Standard Libelle	325		13. 8.72	S.Biggs	Husbands Bosworth	9. 7.02
CRT 1753 CRT	Schleicher ASK13	13396		1. 8.72	Bowland Forest GC	Chipping	3. 5.02
CRV 1755	Glasflugel H.201B Standard Libelle	329		22. 8.72	P.Arthur & Ptnr	Perranporth	25. 5.02
CRW 1756 417	Glasflugel H.201 Standard Libelle	324		10.72	M.Buick	Nympsfield	18. 4.02

CRZ	1759		Slingsby T.8 Tutor	-	RAFGSA.178	10.72	Boulton Paul Museum	Wolverhampton	
CSA	1760	182	Slingsby T.59F Kestrel 20	1797		11.72	P.L Poole	Parham Park	30. 5.01
CSB	1761	CSB	Slingsby T.59F Kestrel 19	1798		17.11.72	N.D.Paveley	Pocklington	12. 1.01
CSD	1763	53	Slingsby T.59D Kestrel 19	1800		1.12.72	M.J.Silver	Pocklington	7. 6.01
CSF	1765	347	Slingsby T.59F Kestrel 19	1802		1.73	G.R.Glazebrook	Dunstable	17. 1.02
CSG	1766	217	Slingsby T.59D Kestrel 19	1804		3.73	A.Swann & D.Williams	Lasham	5. 6.99
							(Mid-air collision with BGA.1943 Bidford 27.7.98)		
CSJ	1768	CSJ	Glasflugel H.201B Standard Libelle	372		26. 1.73	S.N.Croner	Challock	21. 4.02
CSK	1769	387	Slingsby T.59D Kestrel 20	1806		3.73	H.A. & J.E.Torode	RAF Odiham	8. 4.99
CSL	1770		Slingsby T.8 Tutor	928	XE758 VF181	15.10.72	W.D.Baars	(The Netherlands)	19. 9.00
CSN	1772	CSN	Pilatus B4 PC-11	021		12.72	M.Hine	North Hill	23. 9.02
CSP	1773	CSP	Pilatus B4 PC-11	027		3.73	I.T.Ashton	Chipping	9. 6.02
CSR	1775	808	Glasflugel H.201 Standard Libelle	368		14. 1.73	W.G.Miller & Ptnrs	North Connel	18. 5.02
CSU	1778		Manuel Hawk	1		11.72	Not known *(Stored)*	Sackville Lodge Riseley	
CSV	1779	CSV	SZD-30 Pirat	B-515		3.12.72	P.Uden & Ptnrs	Gamston	31. 8.02
CSW	1780	CSW	Pilatus B4 PC-11	022		12.72	I.H.Keyser	Waldershare Park	2. 4.02
CTA	1784	CTA	EoN AP.5 Olympia 2B	EoN/O/146	RAFGSA.285	12.72	P.N.Tolson	Wormingford	30. 9.00
CTB	1785	579	Schempp-Hirth HS.4 Standard Cirrus	264G		1.73	M.J.Gibbons & Ptnrs	Weston-on-the-Green	21. 2.02
CTD	1787		Yorkshire Saiplanes YS-53	1721		4.74	P.Older	Andreas, IoM	
							(Under restoration in 2000 after heavy landing)		
CTE	1788	40	Schleicher ASW17	17012		1.73	D.Edwards & S.Blackmore	Lasham	17. 2.02
CTF	1789		Schleicher Ka4 Rhonlerche	01	D-3574	1.73	M.Goodman	Winthorpe	9. 2.02
			(Owner quotes p/i D-4346, but unconfirmed)						
CTJ	1792	CTJ	Slingsby T.59D Kestrel 19	1810		14. 3.73	H.B.Walrond & Ptnrs	Rattlesden	2. 3.02
CTL	1794	CTL	Slingsby T.59D Kestrel 19	1812		28. 3.73	P.G.Codd	Wormingford	18. 4.02
CTM	1795	254	Slingsby T.59D Kestrel 19	1813		3.73	G.P.Emsden	Dunstable	9. 2.02
CTN	1796	CTN	Slingsby T.59D Kestrel 19	1814		4.73	J.T Goodall	Sutton Bank	28. 3.02
							(Written-off in landing accident, Elkington, Northants, 23.6.01)		
CTP	1797	49	Slingsby T.59D Kestrel 19	1815		14. 4.73	D.C.Austin	Sutton Bank	31. 5.02
CTQ	1798	924	Slingsby T.59D Kestrel 20	1816		27. 4.73	K.A.Moules	Bicester	24. 2.02
CTR	1799	402	Slingsby T.59D Kestrel 19	1817		5.73	D.J.Marpole	Kingston Deverill	26. 3.02
CTS	1800	CTS	EoN AP.5 Olympia 2B	EoN/O/157	RNGSA	13. 1.73	M.D.Smith	Parham	6. 9.02
CTT	1801	873	Schempp-Hirth HS.4 Standard Cirrus	277G		17. 2.73	S.M.L.Young	Nympsfield	13. 3.02
CTU	1802	502	Glasflugel H.201 Standard Libelle	371		2.73	J.R.Humpherson	Camphill	15. 4.02
CTV	1803		SZD-30 Pirat	B-528		2.73	B.Fantham	Rhigos	30.10.02
CTW	1804	1	SZD-9 bis Bocian 1	EP-598		2.73	Mendip GC	Halesland	1. 9.01
CTX	1805	CTX	SZD-30 Pirat	B-527		2.73	P.Goulding	Crowland	9. 7.02
CTZ	1807	CTZ	Schleicher K8B	8035/B5	D-KOCU D-5203	3. 4.73	Scottish Gliding Union Ltd	Portmoak	13. 6.02
CUB	1809	CUB	Pilatus B4 PC-11	047		31. 3.73	P.Noonan & D.Wardell	Enstone	14. 7.02
CUC	1810		Pilatus B4 PC-11	003	HB-1102	5.73	H.M.Pantin & Ptnrs	AAC Dishforth	14. 4.02
CUD	1811	CUD	Yorkshire Sailplanes YS-53 Sovereign	02		7.72	D R Bricknell	Saltby	20. 5.01
					(Built from Slingsby T.53B XV951 [1574] w/o 11.4.72)				
CUF	1813	331	Yorkshire Sailplanes YS-55 Consort	04		9.11.73	C.G.Taylor & Ptnrs	Sutton Bank	21. 7.00
CUJ	1816	706	Glasflugel H.201B Standard Libelle	370		13. 2.73	T.G.B.Hobbis & Ptnrs	Lasham	2. 4.02
CUK	1817	380	Glasflugel H.201 Standard Libelle	367		3.73	G.R.Brown	Dunstable	9. 8.01
CUL	1818	550/10	Schempp-Hirth HS.4 Standard Cirrus	265G		7. 4.73	L.G.Watts	Husbands Bosworth	20. 7.98
CUM	1819	CUM	SZD-30 Pirat	B-534		24. 2.73	E.Hughes	Pocklington	10. 2.02
CUQ	1821	633	Pilatus B4 PC-11	040		2.73	A.E.Hayes & Ptnrs	Aston Down	3. 6.02
CUS	1822	842	Schempp-Hirth HS.2 Cirrus VTC	126Y		3.73	G.F.Wearing	Chipping	2. 6.02
CUT	1823		Pilatus B4 PC-11	041		3.73	N.R.Cawte	Gamston	11.10.95*
							(On repair 1997: current status unknown))		
CUZ	1829	CUZ	LET L-13 Blanik	025409		4.73	East Sussex GC	Andreas, IoM	11.98
							(Damaged 7.7.98, to Andreas GC as spares)		
CVA	1830	CVA	LET L-13 Blanik	025418		3.73	D.Wiseman *"Boggles the Blanik"*	Andreas, IoM	7. 4.02
CVB	1831	CVB	LET L-13 Blanik	025419		3.73	W.N.Smith	Sackville Lodge Riseley	4 .5.02
CVC	1832	CVC	SZD-30 Pirat	B-535		3.73	J.P.Batty	Dunstable	12. 5.00
CVE	1834	BZ	Schempp-Hirth HS.2 Cirrus VTC	127Y		15. 3.73	B.Roberts	Gransden Lodge	7. 3.02

CVF	1835	CVF	Schempp-Hirth HS.2 Cirrus VTC	128Y		16. 3.73	I.Hamilton	Chipping	7. 5.00
							(Damaged at Chipping 4.9.99)		
CVG	1836	656	Pilatus B4 PC-11	045		19. 3.73	I H Keyser	Waldershare Park	23. 4.99
CVH	1837	CVH	Schempp-Hirth SHK	34	N6524A	30. 3.73	J.C.Fletcher	Dunstable	29. 7.02
CVJ	1838	CVJ	Breguet Br.905S Fauvette	37	F-CCJH	29. 6.73	I.Gutsell	Burn	22. 5.02
CVK	1839	92	Pilatus B4 PC-11	048		22. 3.73	T.M.Perkins	Dunstable	28. 6.99
CVL	1840	253	Glasflugel H.201B Standard Libelle	369		2.73	N.A.Dean	Kirton-in-Lindsey	1. 4.02
CVM	1841		Pilatus B4 PC-11 (powered)	036		23. 3.73	J.A.Mace	Old Sarum	27. 3.02
CVN	1842		SZD-36A Cobra 15	W-608		3.73	N.Bickham	Dunkeswell	21. 9.96*
CVP	1843	CVP	SZD-9 bis Bocian 1E	P-597		17. 3.73	M.Boyle	Rufforth	22. 5.02
CVQ	1844	428	Glasflugel H.201 Standard Libelle	374		23. 3.73	C.J.Taunton & Ptnrs	Dunstable	13. 4.02
CVR	1845	CVR	SZD-30 Pirat	B-538		27. 3.73	M.Langford	Weston-on-the-Green	13. 4.02
CVS	1846	CVS	SZD-36A Cobra 15	W-610		3.73	E.W.Room	Pocklington	15. 8.01
CVT	1847		SZD-36A Cobra 15	W-609		27. 3.73	J.Amor	Ridgewell	1.95*
CVV	1849	CVV	Pilatus B4 PC-11	028		27. 3.73	F.R.Wolff & Ptnrs	Brent Tor	17. 2.02
CVW	1850	423	Slingsby T.59D Kestrel 19	1818		29. 5.73	P.B.Hogarth	Halesland	23. 5.02
CVX	1851	3	Slingsby T.59D Kestrel 19	1823		7.73	Not known	Aston Down	*
							(Crashed Portmoak 6.9.80: wreck stored 7.99)		
CVY	1852	355	Slingsby T.59D Kestrel 19	1821		4. 7.73	J.Ainsworth	Sleap	19. 6.98*
							(Damaged Upavon 15.6.97)		
CVZ	1853	269	Slingsby T.59D Kestrel 19	1824		3. 8.73	T.R.F.Gaunt & Ptnrs	Kingston Deverill	22. 3.02
CWA	1854	539	Slingsby T.59D Kestrel 19	1825		9.73	I.B.Kennedy	Usk	13.12.01
CWB	1855		Slingsby T.59D Kestrel 19	1833		9. 1.74	K.Fairness	Milfield	23. 6.02
CWD	1857		Slingsby T.59D Kestrel 19	1835		1.74	J.R.Dransfield	Aboyne	4. 3.02
CWE	1858	468	Glasflugel H.201 Standard Libelle	482		31. 1.74	T.W.S.Stoker	Rufforth	9. 4.02
CWF	1859	CWF	Slingsby T.59D Kestrel 19	1838		2.74	P.F.Nicholson	Thame	11. 4.02
CWG	1860	322	Glasflugel H.201 Standard Libelle	391		7. 4.73	G.Pledger	Currock Hill	16. 8.02
CWH	1861	CWH	Schleicher ASK13	13424		12. 4.73	York Gliding Centre	Rufforth	25. 3.02
CWJ	1862	CWJ	Schleicher Ka7 Rhonadler	630	D-6057 D-5723	27. 4.73	Wolds GC	Pocklington	30. 7.02
CWL	1864		Schempp-Hirth HS.2 Cirrus VTC	125Y		4.73	J.Richardson	Chipping	26. 1.98*
							(Damaged Horningnsea 15.8.97)		
CWN	1866	CWN	Glasflugel H.201B Standard Libelle	386		4.73	R.B.Petrie	Portmoak	1. 4.02
CWR	1869	917	Schempp-Hirth HS.2 Cirrus VTC	133Y		4.73	S.T.Bonser	Dunstable	25. 1.02
CWS	1870	CWS	Schempp-Hirth HS.2 Cirrus VTC	129Y		19. 4.73	R.W.Cassels & Ptnrs	Ridgewell	11. 5.02
CWT	1871	978	Glasflugel H.201B Standard Libelle	384		4.73	B.Harvey	Camphill	13. 4.02
CWU	1872		Schleicher Rhonlerche II	390	D-5627	22.4.73	*(Under restoration, 2001; West Sussex)*		
CWV	1873	Z	Schleicher Rhonlerche II	123	D-8226	22. 4.73	11th Bristol (Headley Park) Scout Troop		
							(Stored 8.01)	Aston Down	5.94*
CWX	1875	832	Glasflugel H.201 Standard Libelle	36	RAFGSA.132	4.73	C.A.Weyman & Ptnrs	Gallows Hill	15. 4.02
CWY	1876	146	Glasflugel H.201 Standard Libelle	387		14. 4.73	J Dixon	Portmoak	2. 2.02
CWZ	1877	CWZ	Glasflugel H.201 Standard Libelle	392		30. 4.73	Derby & Lancs GC	Camphill	21. 9.02
CXH	1885	CXH	SZD-36A Cobra 15	W-619		10. 6.73	C D Street	Parham Park	26. 9.02
CXJ	1886	791	SZD-36A Cobra 15	W-618		6.73	S R Bruce	Feshiebridge	18. 7.00
CXK	1887		Glasflugel H.201 Standard Libelle	383		6.73	C.A Turner	Cross Hayes	10. 1.03
CXL	1888	CXL	SZD-30 Pirat B-	548		6.73	R.T.Page & Ptnrs	Wormingford	10. 8.02
CXM	1889	532	Slingsby T.59D Kestrel 19	1820		7.73	R.P.Beck & Ptnrs	AAC Dishforth	15. 4.02
CXN	1890	508	Yorkshire Sailplanes YS-55 Consort	05		21.12.73	A.A.Priestley & Ptnrs	Sutton Bank	13. 3.02
CXP	1891		Yorkshire Sailplanes YS-55 Consort	07	BGA.1892	5.76	A.D.Coles	North Hill	14.12.01
CXV	1897	CXV	Yorkshire Sailplanes YS-53 Sovereign	03		7.74	C.Wright	Chipping	18. 8.01
CXW	1898		Yorkshire Sailplanes YS-53 Sovereign	1654		7. 3.74	The Tin Bird Syndicate	Aboyne	7.93*
							(Wreck stored 5.94)		
CYA	1902	503	Pilatus B4 PC-11	072		7.73	E.J.Bromwell & Ptnrs	North Hill	5.10.02
CYC	1904	CYC	Pilatus B4 PC-11	029	N47247	7.73	B.Gent & Ptnrs	Ringmer	22. 7.02
CYD	1905		SZD-30 Pirat	B-559		25. 7.73	I.Johnstone	Portmoak	11. 7.00
CYG	1908	CYG	Glasflugel H.201 Standard Libelle	441		8.73	M.J Guard	Husbands Bosworth	23. 1.02

CYH	1909	CYH	Slingsby T.41 Skylark 2	995	AGA.4 BGA.801	8.73	B.J.Griffin *(Under rebuild to be restored as BGA.801)*	Kirton-in-Lindsey	8.99
CYJ	1910	CYJ	DFS/49 Grunau Baby 2B *(Built Petera 1943)*	031000	D-6021	11. 8.73	C.Bird *(Under restoration during 2000)*	Dunstable	1.90*
CYK	1911	248	Pilatus B4 PC-11	078		8.73	I.M.Trotter t/a Pilatus Soaring Syndicate	Portmoak	19.10.02
CYM	1913	299	Schempp-Hirth HS.4 Standard Cirrus	48	RAFGSA D-0578	9.73	L.J.Hartfield	Lasham	7. 4.02
CYN	1914	N4	Slingsby T.59D Kestrel 19 *(Built D Jones & T Pentelow)*	JP.054		10.74	S.J.Cooke & Ptnrs	Gransden Lodge	22.12.02
CYP	1915	982	Schempp-Hirth HS.4 Standard Cirrus	369		9.73	O.Stuart-Menteth	Cranfield	25. 3.00
CYQ	1916	477	Schempp-Hirth HS.4 Standard Cirrus	364		27.9.73	B.M.Reeves	Nympsfield	1. 3.02
CYR	1917	CYR	LET L-13 Blanik *(Damaged near Bidford 8.7.90; rebuilt using fuselage of BGA.2958 c/n 025817) (Stored 7.97)*	025610		9.10.73	Not known	Cranfield	12.90*
CYT	1919	CYT	Schempp-Hirth HS.4 Standard Cirrus	357G		9.73	R.Francis	Llantisilio	9. 4.02
CYW	1922		Birmingham Guild BG-135	6		1.10.73	Not known	*(Stored 2000)*	
CYY	1924		Schleicher Rhonlerche		AGA.19	4.11.73	Not known	*(Stored 2000)*	
CYZ	1925	CYZ	Schleicher K8B	8882	RAFGSA	8. 9.74	Oxford GC	Weston-on-the-Green	28. 1.01
CZD	1929	CZD	Pilatus B4 PC-11	081		12.73	G.A.Furness	Walney Island	14. 7.02
CZE	1930	CZE	SZD-30 Pirat	S-0114		23.12.73	M.Pedwell	Bidford	26. 4.02
CZG	1932	CZG	SZD-30 Pirat	S-0116		31.12.73	J.T.Pajdak	Kenley	10. 5.02
CZJ	1934	CZJ	SZD-30 Pirat	S-0115		29.12.73	C.L Groves & Ptnrs	Husbands Bosworth	20. 5.02
CZL	1936	504	Glasflugel H.201 Standard Libelle	483		31. 1.74	L P Woodage	Dunstable	29.11.02
CZM	1937	CZM	Munchen Mu-13D-III	10/52	D-1488	9.74	H.Chapple	Bicester	6. 4.02
CZN	1938	CZN	Schleicher ASW15B	15329		13. 3.74	P.C.Tuppen & Ptnrs	Bembridge	29. 4.02
CZQ	1940	CZQ	Slingsby T.59D Kestrel 19	1840		5. 4.74	J.P.Walker & Ptnrs	Husbands Bosworth	19. 5.02
CZR	1941	CZR	Slingsby T.59D Kestrel 19	1842		4.74	R.P.Brisbourne	Rufforth	10. 1.02
CZS	1942	CZS	Slingsby T.59D Kestrel 22	1844		3. 5.74	P.Glennie	Portmoak	22. 3.97*
CZT	1943	A3	Slingsby T.59D Kestrel 19	1848		30. 5.74	G.W.Camp	Enstone	1. 3.99
CZU	1944	826	Slingsby T.59D Kestrel 19	1849		14. 6.74	K.R.Merrett & P.F.Croote	Halesland	11. 5.02
CZV	1945	415	Slingsby T.59D Kestrel 19	1850		16. 7.74	V.F.G.Tull	Dunstable	21. 7.01
CZW	1946	CZW	Slingsby T.59D Kestrel 20	1846		17.10.76	C.D Berry	Cranfield	25. 2.02
CZZ	1949		Slingsby T.59D Kestrel 19	1739		6.74	R.M.Grant	Lasham	19.11.96*
DAA	1950	DAA	SZD-9 bis Bocian 1	EP-639		10. 3.74	Highland GC	Easterton	24. 9.01
DAC	1952		SZD-36A Cobra 15	W-656		3.74	C.D.Peacock	Husbands Bosworth	23. 7.02
DAF	1955		LET L-13 Blanik	025825		4.74	*(Stored 2000)*		
DAJ	1958	14	Schempp-Hirth HS.5 Nimbus 2	50		21. 3.74	J.D.Jones	Nympsfield	1. 4.02
DAL	1960	DAL	EoN AP.6 Olympia 419	EoN/4/010	RAFGSA.301	4.74	D.M.Judd & Ptnrs	Snitterfield	5. 9.99
DAM	1961	675	ICA IS-29D	27		4.74	W.T.Barnard	Strathaven	24. 9.00
DAN	1962		SZD-30 Pirat	S-0145		23. 3.74	W.Pottinger & Ptnrs	Ridgewell	1. 7.02
DAP	1963	DAP	SZD-30 Pirat	S-0147		4.74	N.Crawford	Currock Hill	1. 5.02
DAQ	1964	DAQ	SZD-36A Cobra 15	W-657		4.74	C.Bigwood & Ptnrs	Lyveden	3. 7.97*
DAR	1965	DAR	Slingsby T.21B	?	RAFGSA.404	1. 6.74	D.Bourne	Upwood	16. 6.02
DAS	1966	DAS	Schempp-Hirth HS.4 Standard Cirrus	378	(BGA.1925)	4.74	G.Goodenough	Burn	9. 4.02
DAT	1967		SZD-30 Pirat	S-0149		27. 4.74	The Borders GC *(Crashed Milfield 1.8.99)*	Milfield	3. 5.00
DAU	1968		SZD-30 Pirat	S-0150		4.74	W.Fisher	Winthorpe	6. 5.02
DAV	1969	240	SZD-38A Jantar-1	B-608		4.74	R.M.Roberts	Brent Tor	2. 9.01
DAW	1970	DAW	Schleicher Ka6CR	951	RAFGSA D-2025	8. 6.74	P.S.Holmes	Bellarena	7. 4.02
DBA	1974	207	EoN AP.5 Olympia 2B	EoN/O/156	RNGSA.208	25. 5.74	W.R.Williams	RAF Halton	11. 7.01
DBB	1975	DBB	Slingsby T.51 Dart 17R *(Built Greenfly Aviation)*	DG/51/01		5. 2.76	S.D.Codd	Crowland	16. 6.02
DBC	1976	DBC	Pilatus B4 PC-11	135		6.74	J.H.France & Ptnrs	Shobdon	24. 3.02
DBD	1977	DBD	SZD-30 Pirat	S-0202		6.74	E W Burgess	Cranfield	30. 6.02
DBF	1979	DBF	Schleicher Ka7 Rhonadler	179	RAFGS RAFGGA.552/D-5473	6.74	Welland GC *(Crashed at Lyveden 10.9.00)*	Lyveden	3. 3.01
DBG	1980	DBG	ICA IS-29D	31		6.74	N.D Hughes	Lasham	8. 6.02
DBJ	1982	691	Slingsby T.59D Kestrel 22	1856	BGA.1892 BGA.1982	19.10.74	P L Sanderson	RAF Syerston	5. 5.01
DBK	1983	523	Slingsby T.59D Kestrel 22	1861		2.12.74	R.E.Perry & C.Crabb	North Hill	9. 8.02
DBN	1986	617	Slingsby T.59D Kestrel 19	1857		25. 3.75	A.C.Wright	Sutton Bank	10. 2.02
DBP	1987	551	Glasflugel H.205 Club Libelle	51		1. 5.75	N.A.White	Rattlesden	10. 4.02
DBQ	1988	101	Slingsby T.59D Kestrel 22	1863		17. 4.75	P.Ramsden	Rufforth	15. 5.02
DBR	1989	95	Slingsby T.59D Kestrel 19	1858		22. 4.75	J.G.Bell	Parham Park	30.10.00
DBS	1990	DBS	Slingsby T.59D Kestrel 22	1864		24. 4.75	J.W.Rice	Kirton-in-Lindsey	10. 6.02
DBT	1991	11	Schempp-Hirth Standard Austria S	35	F-CCPQ	7.74	F.J.Tucker	Parham Park	20. 8.00

DBU 1992	Hirth Go IV Goevier 3	557	D-5233	13. 7.74	Boulton & Paul Museum	Norwich	19. 7.87*
DBV 1993 DBV	SZD-30 Pirat	S-0227		1. 7.74	M.H.Bryan & Ptnrs	Usk	12. 2.02
DBW 1994 DBW	SZD-9 bis Bocian 1E	P-641		12. 7.74	Sackville GC	Sackville Lodge Riseley	3. 4.99
DBX 1995 DBX	SZD-9 bis Bocian 1E	P-642		20. 7.74	Miss A.G.Veitch t/a Highland Bocian Syndicate	Easterton	3. 1.02
DCA 1998 DCA	SZD-36A Cobra 15	W-686		18. 9.74	M.J.North	Husbands Bosworth	15. 8.01
DCC 2000 324	Glasflugel H.201B Standard Libelle	585		11.74	J.Warbey & M.Hutchinson	Shobdon	24. 1.02
DCE 2002	Slingsby T.41 Skylark 2B	1003 PH-225	RAFGGA.540	11.74	C.P.Race	Winthorpe	25. 8.02
DCF 2003	Schleicher Ka6CR	6520	RAFGSA.356	11.74	R.Spencer	Burn	17. 7.95*
DCG 2004	Schleicher Ka2B	2	D-7064	12.74	Not known (Stored)	Falgunzeon	*
DCH 2005 DCH	SZD-30 Pirat	S-0315		11.74	Spilsby Soaring	Spilsby	31. 8.96*
DCJ 2006	SZD-30 Pirat	S-0316		11.74	N.Jones *(Crashed near North Hill 29.3.97)*	North Hill	25. 3.98*
DCL 2008	LET L-13 Blanik	026154		12.74	Not known *(Wreck noted 2001)*	Strathaven	7. 8.92*
DCN 2010	Slingsby T.21B	1250	RAFGGA.501 RAFGSA.287/BGA.943	31.12.74	A.R.Worters	North Connel	16. 7.95*
DCR 2013 DCR	SZD-9 bis Bocian 1	EP-670		1.75	Mendip GC *(Crashed Halesland 13.6.96)*	Halesland	23.10.96*
DCS 2014 DCS	Slingsby T.45 Swallow	1538	RAFGGA.544	4.74	A.B.Dickenson	Chipping	23. 8.01
DCW 2018 DCW	Schleicher Ka6CR	1076	D-5228	2.75	Trent Valley GC	Kirton-in-Lindsey	11. 7.01
DCY 2020 DCY	Swales SD.3-15V *(Rebuild of incomplete Yorkshire Sailplanes YS-55 Consort c/n 09)*	01		2.75	T.R.Edwards	Chipping	16. 5.97*
DCZ 2021 DCZ	King-Elliott-Street Osprey *(Believed to be converted Slingsby T.51 Dart but c/n conflicts with BGA.1245)*	1470		10.75	G.R.Burkert	Lasham	28. 5.00
DDA 2022 DDA	Schempp-Hirth HS.4 Standard Cirrus	532G		2.75	R.G.Johnson	Parham Park	26. 3.02
DDB 2023 DDB	Schleicher ASK13	13493		2.75	Norfolk GC	Tibenham	28. 9.02
DDC 2024	Slingsby T.21B	1157	RAFGSA.313 XN153	3.75	J.S.Shaw & Ptnrs	Perranporth	25. 3.02
DDD 2025 695	Schempp-Hirth HS.5 Nimbus 2	84	G-BKPM BGA.2025	3.75	D.D.Copeland	Dunstable	24. 2.02
DDE 2026 DDE	SZD-38A Jantar-1	B-641		4.75	B.Jones	Bidford	19. 3.98
DDJ 2030 DDJ	ICA IS-29D	37		3.75	P.Andrews	Lyveden	7.98*
	(Written-off Lyveden 8.97 : to East Surrey College, Redhill as instructional airframe 10.97)						
DDK 2031	SZD-30 Pirat	S-0408		4.75	T.A.Buckley	Bembridge	23. 5.02
DDL 2032 DDL	Schleicher K8B	218/61	D-5156	4.75	Ouse GC	Rufforth	24. 5.02
DDM 2033 959	Schempp-Hirth HS.2 Cirrus VTC	164Y		3.75	J.J.Smith	Wormingford	13. 3 02
DDN 2034 DDN	SZD-9 bis Bocian 1	EP-429	RAFGSA.393	3.75	Bath, Wilts & North Dorset GC	Kingston Deverill	16. 5.02
DDR 2037 680	Schempp-Hirth HS.4 Standard Cirrus	531G		3.75	J.Smith	Pocklington	20. 2.02
DDS 2038 647	Schleicher ASW15	15009	D-0256	4.75	C.Skeate & Ptnrs *(Sold as scrap following mid-air collision)*	Lasham	11.01
DDV 2041 536	SZD-38A Jantar	1	B-664	4.75	G.V.McKirdy	Edgehill	11. 5.98*
DDW 2042 DDW	SZD-30 Pirat	S-0433		4.75	C.P.Offen	Parham Park	13. 5.02
DDY 2044 DDY	Schleicher Ka6CR	678	D-8841	4.75	Needwood Forest GC	Cross Hayes	5. 5.02
DEB 2047 DEB	Slingsby T.59D Kestrel 19	1866		24.10.75	T.Moss	Weston-on-the-Green	27. 9.01
DEG 2051 DEG	ICA IS-28B2	48			P.S. & H.Whitehead	Sutton Bank	23. 5.02
DEN 2057 588	ICA IS-29D	41		4.75	S.E.Marples	Feshiebridge	13. 3.01
DEP 2058 DEP	Schleicher Ka6CR	6452	AGA... BGA.2058/RAFGSA.350	4.75	S.J.Aldridge	Saltby	30. 3.02
DEQ 2059 716	Glasflugel H.205 Club Libelle	97		4.75	J.A.Holland & Ptnrs	Kingston Deverill	2. 3.01
DEV 2064 DEV	Schleicher Ka6CR	6453	RAFGSA.354	5.75	P.J.Groves & Ptnrs	Long Mynd	16. 7.02
DEW 2065 DEW	ICA IS-29D	40		12. 6.75	M.D.Smith	Lee on Solent	19.10.02
DEX 2066 DEX	LET L-13 Blanik	026348	RAFGSA.R4 BGA.2066	1. 7.75	L.Wright	Talgarth	14. 2.02
DEY 2067 DEY	LET L-13 Blanik	026352	RAFGSA.R12 BGA.2067	10. 7.75	Bath, Wilts & North Dorset GC	Kingston Deverill	2. 8.01
DEZ 2068 977	ICA IS-29D	43		6.75	R.J.Everett *(Damaged Lewknor 7.3.90: stored 12.95)*	Sproughton	19. 4.91*
DFC 2071 128	Schempp-Hirth HS.4 Standard Cirrus	592G		7.75	R.J.Marriott & A.Weatherhead	Cranfield	18. 2.02
DFE 2073 DFE	Molino PIK-20	20052		7.75	M.Roff-Jarrett	Parham Park	19.12.02
DFK 2078 DFK	Molino PIK-20	20039	OH-500	14. 9.75	M.J Fairclough	North Hill	24. 2.02
DFL 2079 DFL	SZD-38A Jantar-1	B-682		9.75	J.Howlett	Crowland 25.5.02	
DFN 2081	Glaser-Dirks DG-100	30		9.75	D.J.Clarke	Wormingford	28. 7.02
DFP 2082 DFP	Aeromere M.100S	029	I-LSUO	9.75	D. & J.Lee	Pocklington	16. 6.98
DFR 2084 906	Grob G.102 Astir CS	1038		10.75	P.Gee	Lasham	7. 1.03
DFU 2087 30	SZD-38A Jantar-1	B-685		3.12.75	J.E.New & Ptnrs	Lasham	12. 3.96*

DFV 2088 164	SZD-38A Jantar-1	B-684		7.12.75	R.R.Rodwell	Bellarena	15.12.01
DFW 2089 DFW	SZD-30 Pirat	S-0545		26.11.75	R.G.Skerry	Strubby	10. 2.02
DFX 2090 767	SZD-41A Jantar Standard	B-691		10.75	J.C.Tait & Ptnrs	Easterton	19. 3.00
DFY 2091	Schempp-Hirth HS.4 Standard Cirrus	396	AGA...	5.11.75	M.H.Challans	Booker	9. 5.02
DFZ 2092 774	Molino PIK-20	20080		27.11.75	M.J.Leach & J.P.Ashcroft	Sandhill Far Shrivenham	14. 4.02
DGA 2093 DGA	Schleicher K8B	8587	RAFGSA BGA.1926/D-...	11.75	Welland GC	Lyveden	31. 8.02
DGB 2094 DGB	LET L-13 Blanik *(Rebuilt with fuselage from BGA.2061 pre 1995)*	026459		27.11.75	Black Mountains GC *(Damaged Bidford 21.10.95; stored 5.98)*	Bidford	2.96*
DGE 2097	Schempp-Hirth HS.4 Standard Cirrus 75	606		12.75	T.E.Snoddy	Bellarena	17. 7.02
DGG 2099 DGG	Schleicher Ka6E	4061	RAFGSA.263	15.12.75	N.F.Holmes & Ptnrs	Long Mynd	2. 5.01
DGH 2100 DGH	SZD-30 Pirat	B-533	RNGSA BGA.2100	12.75	E.Lowne	Snitterfield	13. 6.02
DGK 2102 DGK	Schleicher Ka6CR	6287	D-3224	21.12.75	IBM GC *"Betty Blue"*	Lasham	25. 4.02
DGM 2104	Slingsby T.45 Swallow	1506	RAFGGA	12.75	*(Being refurbished 2000)*	North Hill	8.11.93
DGP 2106 DGP	LET L-13 Blanik	026560		26. 5.76	J.M.Purves	Rufforth	16. 7.01
DGT 2110	Schleicher Ka2B	181	D-5469	5.76	Not known *(Stored 2001)*	Falgunzeon	23.10.93*
DGV 2112 DGV	Brequet Br.905S Fauvette	2	HB-632	5.76	R.M.Cust & Ptnrs	Burn	18.10.01
DGX 2114 610	Schempp-Hirth HS.4 Standard Cirrus 75	619	AGA.3 BGA.2114	11. 5.76	G.R.Seaman & Ptnrs	Lasham	10. 5.02
DGY 2115 195	Schempp-Hirth HS.5 Nimbus 2	105		11. 5.76	J.H.Taylor	Nympsfield	28. 2.02
DHA 2117 DHA	Schleicher K8B *(C/n conflicts with D-8616)*	1055	D-8848 D-5148	23. 6.76	Booker GC	Booker	6. 1.03
DHB 2118 DHB	SZD-30 Pirat	S-0643		9. 6.76	J.T.Winsworth	Tibenham	11. 4.00
DHC 2119 811	SZD-41A Jantar Standard	B-710	(BGA.2109)	9. 6.76	M.C.Burlock	Aston Down	5. 2.02
DHG 2123 DHG	Schleicher Ka6CR	1131	D-5170	23. 6.76	Angus GC	Drumshade	24. 7.02
DHH 2124 116	Molino PIK-20B	20124		5.76	R.A.Holroyd	Pocklington	28.11.01
DHJ 2125 DHJ	Glaser-Dirks DG-100	48		1.76	H.D.Armitage	Usk	13. 4.02
DHK 2126 A30	Glaser-Dirks DG-100	50		1.76	R.Dell & B.J.Griffin	Kirton-in-Lindsey	11. 4.02
DHL 2127 DHL	Glaser-Dirks DG-100	52		1.76	K.J.Adam	Aboyne	30. 7.01
DHM 2128 DHM	Schleicher Ka6E	4124	RAFGSA.26	6. 2.76	J.G.Heard	Seighford	29. 3.02
DHN 2129 824	Molino PIK-20B	20082		1.76	G J Bass	Challock	13. 6.02
DHP 2130	Slingsby T.45 Swallow *(Components ex BGA.1041 [1329]: c/n = type/year)*	45176		5. 2.76	Dumfries & Galloway GC *(W/o 3.4.64 with parts from BGA.1032; on rebuild 5.95)*	Falgunzeon	10.89*
DHR 2132 DHR	Slingsby T.53B	1718		2.76	E.MacDonald	Portmoak	29. 9.00
DHT 2134 DHT	Schleicher Ka6E	4065	???	2.76	D.Wilkinson	Nympsfield	13. 1.03
DHV 2136 DHV	Molino PIK-20B	20111		3.76	J.D. & G.J.Walker	Booker	30. 6.02
DHW 2137 951	Schempp-Hirth HS.5 Nimbus 2	106		23. 4.76	A.J.Bauld	Portmoak	15. 4.02
DHY 2139 DHY	Schleicher Ka7 Rhonadler	1137	RAFGSA.266 D-5162	14. 4.76	G.Whittaker	Chipping	25. 5.02
DHZ 2140 DHZ	SZD-30 Pirat	S-0641		23. 4.76	Peterborough & Spalding GC	Crowland	14. 4.02
DJA 2141 DJA	SZD-30 Pirat	S-0642		23. 4.76	A.Latty	Milfield	11.11.01
DJB 2142 N11	Schleicher K8B	8879	(RAFGSA.N11) AGA.17/BGA.2142/RAFGSA.R97(1)/RAFGSA.198(2)/RAFGSA.397(1)	7. 4.76	Portsmouth Naval GC	Lee-on-Solent	19.12.99
DJD 2144 DJD	Grob G.102 Astir CS	1226		5. 8.76	P.Gascoigne & Ptnrs	Kingston Deverill	16. 4.02
DJE 2145 DJE	Schleicher Ka6CR	6412	D-3682	15. 7.76	M.Burton	Shobdon	29. 3.02
DJF 2146 500	Halford JSH Scorpion	001		7.77	R.G.Greenslade *(Previously at South Yorkshire Air Museum - for restoration)*	(Doncaster)	
DJG 2147 K2	Schleicher Ka2B Rhonschwalbe	231	D-6179	6.76	J.Harmer	Lasham	10. 6.01
DJJ 2149 176	Schleicher ASK18	18029		16. 7.76	Mendip GC	Halesland	14. 7.02
DJK 2150 DJK	Schleicher ASK18	18030		15. 7.76	Booker GC	Booker	20. 5.02
DJL 2151 DJL	SZD-41A Jantar Standard	B-714		16. 7.76	A.M.Cooper	Llantisilio	17. 1.02
DJM 2152 DJM	SZD-41A Jantar Standard	B-715		17. 8.76	T.E.Betts	Cross Hayes	11. 7.99
DJN 2153 407	Molino PIK-20B	20140C		16. 7.76	S.L.Cambourne	Lasham	15. 3.02
DJP 2154 DJP	Schleicher K8B	8588	RAFGSA.335	21. 7.76	Sackville GC	Sackville Lodge Riseley	15. 6.02
DJQ 2155 214	Grob G.102 Astir CS	1258		17.10.76	H.Evans & D.J.Jeffries	Usk	17. 2.02
DJR 2156	Schleicher Ka6CR6	80	D-8423	4. 8.76	J.A.Walker	Thruxton	21.11.96*
DJS 2157 608	Schempp-Hirth SHK-1	51	SE-TNF OY-MFX/HB-898	16. 7.76	S.J.Collins	Nympsfield	23.11.01
DJT 2158 DJT	Schleicher Ka7 Rhonadler *(BGA.4271 is marked "DJT" also)*	?	RAFGSA	7.76	Enstone Eagles GC	Enstone	23.11.02
DJU 2159	Scheibe Bergfalke II/55	204	D-....	7.76	Not known	*(Stored 2000)*	
DJW 2161	Manuel Condor	1		7.76	C.V. & R.C.Inwood	Booker	18. 5.98
DJX 2162 614	Grob G.102 Astir CS	1259		17.11.76	R.Duke	Lyveden	26. 4.02
DJZ 2164 989	Eiri PIK-20B20	144		4. 8.76	D.S.Puttock	Halesland	26. 8.02
DKB 2166 DKB	Schempp-Hirth Standard Austria S	32	F-CCPR	4. 8.76	J R Parr	Burn	24. 9.02
DKC 2167 DKC	Schleicher K8B	8261	D-1431	8.76	Yorkshire GC	Sutton Bank	6.12.01
DKD 2168 759	Glasflugel H.206 Hornet	67	(BGA.2165)	8.76	I.M.Evans	Usk	14. 6.02
DKE 2169 DKE	Schleicher ASK13	13548		28. 9.76	South Wales GC	Usk	19. 1.02

DKG 2171 DKG	Schleicher Ka6CR	6233	D-4327	8.76	C.Nunn & Ptnrs	Wormingford	10. 3.02
DKH 2172 769	LET L-13 Blanik	026644		8. 9.76	H.E.Birch	Rufforth	12. 6.00
DKK 2174 884	Schempp-Hirth SHK-1	32	HB-864	8. 9.76	C.Buzzard & D.J.Deacon	Husbands Bosworth	29. 5.95*
DKL 2175 444	Schempp-Hirth HS.5 Nimbus 2	086	D-2111	8. 9.76	G.J.Croll	Snitterfield	14. 4.02
DKM 2176 DKM	Glasflugel H.206 Hornet	49	(BGA2213) BGA2176/D-7816	9.76	M.Lee	Rattlesden	2. 4.01
DKN 2177 DKN	Schleicher Ka6CR	6456	D-9358	12 .3.77	D.Lees & Ptnrs	Wormingford	8. 6.02
DKQ 2179 DKQ	Glaser-Dirks DG-100G	91G11		9.76	G.Peters	North Hill	27. 2.02
DKR 2180 360	Grob G.102 Astir CS	1327		9.76	Oxford GC	Weston-on-the-Green	28.11.02
DKS 2181 788	Grob G.102 Astir CS	1330		23.12.76	C.K.Lewis	Lasham	14. 8.02
DKT 2182 DKT	Eiri PIK-20B	20155		4.11.76	G.Barnham	Rufforth	13. 3.02
DKU 2183 DKU	Grob G.102 Astir CS	1326		11.76	G.Jennings	Lasham	11. 2.02
DKV 2184 391	Grob G.102 Astir CS	1328		9.76	T.J.Ireson	Sandhill Farm Shrivenham	31. 1.99
DKW 2185 DKW	Grob G.102 Astir CS	1329		9.76	J.H.C.Friend	Llantisilio	6. 5.02
DKX 2186 353	Grob G.102 Astir CS	1331		9.76	L.R. & J.M.Bennett	Usk	12. 2.02
DKY 2187 DKY	Schleicher Ka7 Rhonadler	7187	RAFGSA.342	4.11.76	Defford Aero Club	Bidford	14. 8.02
DKZ 2188 DKZ	Glasflugel H.205 Club Libelle	111	RAFGSA.774	4.11.76	P.Jackson & C.Parsons	Bidford	17. 5.02
DLA 2189 DLA	Pilatus B4 PC-11	149	RAFGSA	17.10.76	P.R.Seddon	Chipping	31. 3.02
DLB 2190 DLB	Schleicher ASK18	18040		17.10.76	Vale of The White Horse GC	Sandhill Farm Shrivenham	2.11.02
DLC 2191 C	Schleicher ASK13	13549		4.11.76	Lasham Gliding Society	Lasham	5. 7.02
DLD 2192 DLD	Schleicher K8B	8766	RAFGSA.383	17.11.76	Shalbourne SG	Rivar Hill	5. 1.02
DLE 2193 433	Schleicher Ka6E	4074	AGA.8 RAFGSA	10.76	D.C.Unwin	Snitterfield	29. 6.02
DLG 2195 596	Schempp-Hirth HS.4 Standard Cirrus	579	AGA.2	17.10.76	S.Naylor	Burn	13. 4.02
DLH 2196 378	Grob G.102 Astir CS77	1646		2.77	B.Bamber & R.Smith	Lasham	28. 2.02
DLJ 2197 DLJ	Molino PIK-20B	20157		16.12.76	M.S Parkes	Milfield	27. 7.02
DLM 2200 266	Grob G.102 Astir CS	1260	(BGA.2163)	1.12.76	Highland GC	Easterton	9. 4.02
DLP 2202 DLP	Schleicher Ka6CR	6519	RAFGSA.355	11.76	J.R Crosse	Crowland	27. 4.02
DLR 2204 DLR	Scheibe L-Spatz 55	647	BGA.2654	17.11.76	Dumfries & District GC	Falgunzeon	30. 8.99
	(Quoted as ex D-3659 but unconfirmed)		BGA.2204/D-5638		*(Crashed near Falgunzeon 3.1.99)*		
DLS 2205 DLS	Schleicher K8B	8650	D-5718	1.12.76	D.B.Rich	Eaglescott	15. 4.02
DLT 2206 DLT	ICA IS-28B2	32		12.76	A.Woodrow	Tibenham	23. 5.02
DLU 2207 R93	ICA IS-28B2	33	RAFGSA.R93 NEJSGSA.3/EI-141/BGA.2207	12.76	Crusaders GC	Kingsfield Dhekelia	24.11.02
DLW 2209 DLW	SZD-30 Pirat	B-467	PH-433	12.76	G.Bryce & Ptnrs	North Connel	29. 4.96*
DLX 2210	Slingsby T.45 Swallow	1494	RAFGGA.539	12.76	M.Sanderson	Milfield	29. 5.95*
DLY 2211	Eiri PIK-20D	20509		5. 1.77	D.C.Adlam & Ptnrs	Dunstable	14. 1.02
DLZ 2212	Swales SW.3-15T	03		12.76	R.Harris	Thruxton	27. 6.01
DMB 2214	Schleicher K8B	8209	D-4331	18. 1.77	DRA GC *"Kate"*	RAF Odiham	16. 7.02
DMD 2216 251	Glaser-Dirks DG-100	75		12.76	B.T.Payne & A.Jenkins	Weston-on-the-Green	8.12.01
DMF 2218 DMF	Schleicher Ka7 Rhonadler	7073	D-4313	2. 3.77	Staffordshire GC	Seighford	22. 8.02
DMG 2219 DMG	Schleicher K8B	8763	RAFGSA.382	19. 3.77	Dorset GC	Gallows Hill	2. 6.02
DMH 2220 DMH	Grob G.102 Astir CS	1511		23. 4.77	Oxford GC	Weston-on-the-Green	4. 6.02
DMJ 2221 DMJ	Schleicher K8B	8077	PH-290	19. 3.77	Not known *(Stored)*	Strathaven	23. 9.93*
DMK 2222 593	Schempp-Hirth SHK	25	D-5401	5. 4.77	M.Oliver	Aston Down	22. 2.02
DML 2223 DML	Schleicher Ka7 Rhonadler	929	D-6194 D-5005	4. 2.77	Newark & Notts GC	Winthorpe	17. 2.02
DMM 2224 74	Schempp-Hirth HS.5 Nimbus 2	125		4. 2.77	T.E.Linee	Gallows Hill	20. 4.02
DMN 2225 DMN	Glasflugel H.303 Mosquito	20		2.77	R.P.Brecknock	Booker	11. 4.02
DMP 2226 233	Grob G.102 Astir CS	1239	ZS-GKF	28. 2.77	D.G.Nisbet	Dunstable	19. 1.01
DMQ 2227 DMQ	Schleicher Ka6E	4062	RAFGSA.264	12. 3.77	A.R.Bushnell & Ptnr	Crowland	31. 5.02
DMR 2228 511	Grob G.102 Astir CS	1435		19. 3.77	L.A.Beale & Ptnrs	Parham Park	11. 4.02
DMS 2229 259	Glasflugel H.201B Standard Libelle	385	RNGSA	19. 3.77	M.D.White & Ptnrs	Burn	7. 4 02
DMU 2231 392	Eiri PIK-20D	20524		3.77	A.C.Walford & Ptnrs	Gransden Lodge	10. 3.02
	(C/n confirmed: C-GOPN reported as duplicate is c/n 20525)						
DMV 2232 DMY	Eiri PIK-20D	20526		12. 4.77	F.S.Parkhill	Crowland	17.11.02
DMX 2234 DMX	Schleicher ASK13	13567		5. 4.77	Kent GC	Challock	1. 3.02
	(Incorrectly marked as BGA.2294)						
DMY 2235 371	Eiri PIK-20D	20532		3.77	G.A.Piper	Parham Park	9. 4.00
DNB 2238	DFS/49 Grunau Baby 2B	2	RAFGSA.380	2.77	P.Underwood	Eaton Bray	*
	(Built Flg.u.Arbeitsg.Hall)		D-803		*(On rebuild 2000; to be in Luftwaffe c/s)*		
DNC 2239 588	Grob G.102 Astir CS	1428		13. 4.77	A.J.Carpenter "*Natural High*"	Edgehill	27. 6.99
DND 2240 DND	Pilatus B4 PC-11AF	136		19. 3.77	R J Happs	Lasham	19. 4.02
DNE 2241 DNE	Grob G.102 Astir CS77	1631		3.77	S P Woolcock	Cranfield	4. 3.02
DNF 2242 DNF	SZD-9 bis Bocian 1D	P-354	HB-657	23. 4.77	M.G.Shaw	Portmoak	17. 5.02
DNG 2243 265	Schempp-Hirth HS.5 Nimbus 2	126		5. 4.77	A.O.Harkins & A Brown	Gallows Hill	8. 6.02
DNJ 2245 DNJ	Schleicher ASK18	18042		13. 4.77	Derby & Lancs GC	Camphill	27.11.02
DNK 2246 745	Grob G.102 Astir CS	1434		3. 5.77	745 Syndicate	Wormingford	24. 3.02

DNL	2247	DNL	Glasflugel H.201 Standard Libelle	82	RAFGSA.742 RAFGSA 16/G-AXZH	23. 4.77	P.J.Luckhurst	Tibenham	6. 4.02
			(Owner reports c/n as 82, not 382 as previously recorded)						
DNQ	2251	307	Rolladen-Schneider LS-3	3035		1.77	M.Cooper	Challock	16. 2.02
DNT	2254	DNT	SZD-30 Pirat	S-0712		25. 5.77	M.Davidson & Ptnrs	Drumshade	11. 5.00
DNU	2255	U2	SZD-42-1 Jantar 2	B-783		4.77	C.D.Rowland & Ptnrs	Booker	6. 7.02
DNV	2256	DNV	Schleicher ASK13	13568		4.77	Buckminster GC	Saltby	25. 7.02
DNW	2257	DNW	Schleicher Ka6CR 829	???		5.77	F.G.Broom	Rhigos	2. 2.02
DNX	2258		Schleicher Ka6CR	6094Si	D-5107	14. 6.77	C.J.Riley	Burn	15.11.02
DNZ	2260	DNZ	Schleicher K8B	8095	???	5.77	North Wales GC	Llantisilio	17. 5.00
DPA	2261	DPA	Schleicher ASK18	18044		25. 5.77	Vectis GC	Bembridge	15. 7.02
DPD	2264	DPD	LET L-13 Blanik	026860		14. 6.77	E.McCaig	Challock	27. 8.01
			(Incorporates major portions of BGA2121)						
DPG	2267	DPG	Munchen Mu-13D III	005	D-1327	14. 6.77	G.J.Moore	Dunstable	15. 2.02
DPH	2268	287	Schempp-Hirth HS.7 Mini Nimbus	009		5.77	J.W.Murdoch	Strathaven	21. 5.02
DPJ	2269	DPJ	Grob G.102 Astir CS77	1641		8. 7.77	J.Liddiard & Ptnrs	Lasham	18. 3.02
DPK	2270		Glasflugel H.303 Mosquito	27		6.77	G.Lawley	Cross Hayes	21. 5.02
DPL	2271	437	Eiri PIK-20D	20549		26. 6.77	D.W.Standen	Dunstable	20. 8.02
DPP	2274	DPP	Schleicher Ka2B Rhonschwalbe	105	D-1880	1. 7.77	B.G.Hoekstra	Breda, The Netherlands	8. 7.02
DPQ	2275	DPQ	Grob G.102 Astir CS77	1632		8. 7.77	J.Bone	Wormingford	2.10.02
DPR	2276	D-1265	Scheibe L-Spatz	05	D-1265	8. 7.77	V.W.Jennings *"Sparrowfahrt"*	Thame	25. 7.01
DPT	2278		Scheibe L-Spatz 55	01	???	25. 8.77	B.V.Smith	AAC Dishforth	12. 7.98
DPU	2279	DPU	EoN AP.5 Olympia 2B	EoN/O/142	RAFGSA.274	6. 9.77	C.H.Thompson	RAF Marham	12. 4.02
DPX	2282	440	Schleicher ASW19	19126		7.77	S.L.Morecraft	Nympsfield	29. 3.02
DPY	2283	375	Grob G.192 Astir CS77	1652		8.77	D S Burton	Lasham	19. 5.02
DPZ	2284	DPZ	Slingsby T.34A Sky	822	HB-561	9. 8.77	N McLaughlin	Saltby	3. 7.00
DQA	2285	DQA	Schleicher ASK13	13582		8.77	Essex & Suffolk GC	Wormingford	28. 2.02
DQB	2286	844	Grob G.102 Astir CS77	1653		8.77	G.R.Davey	Kirton-in-Lindsey	24. 3.02
DQC	2287	572	Schleicher Ka6CR	6373Si	D-5725	26. 9.77	I.F.Smith	Lasham	20. 2.02
DQD	2288	DQD	Slingsby T.8 Tutor	-		25. 8.77	K.J.Nurcombe	Husbands Bosworth	30. 7.02
			(Built from parts by F.Breeze)						
DQE	2289	480	Grob G.102 Astir CS77	1636		8.77	Heron GC	RNAS Yeovilton	14. 4.02
DQF	2290	DQF	Schleicher Ka6CR	6417	D-5827	9.77	P.James	Saltby	9. 2.02
DQG	2291	770	Grob G.102 Astir CS77	1649		6. 9.77	Miss A.G.Veitch	Easterton	1. 7.02
DQH	2292		Schmetz Condor IV	2	D-8538	7. 7.78	M.H.Birch	Utersen, Germany	21. 6.02
DQJ	2293	DQJ	Schleicher Ka6CR	228	D-5467	7.10.77	K.Whitworth	Kenley	27. 1.02
DQK	2294	542	Schleicher Ka6E	4341	D-0541	15.10.77	S.Y.Duxbury & R.S.Hawley *(See BGA.2234)*	Camphill	7. 3.01
DQL	2295	DQL	Schleicher Ka8	509	D-5675	15.11.77	Lakes GC	Walney Island	13. 1.02
DQM	2296		Pilatus B4 PC-11	138	RAFGSA	15.10.77	A.R.Dearden	Ringmer	4. 9.02
DQP	2298	DQP	Schleicher K8B	1181	???	15.11.77	Soaring Centre	Husbands Bosworth	9. 4.02
DQR	2300	556	Grob G.102 Astir CS77	1667		10.77	N.R.Warren & Ptnrs	Kingston Deverill	6. 1.03
DQS	2301	DQS	Schleicher Ka6CR	1065	D-5144	23.11.77	L.Hill	North Hill	17. 3.02
DQU	2303	DQU	Eiri PIK-20D	20579		10.77	A.Duncan	Portmoak	28. 6.02
DQX	2306	DQX	Schleicher Ka7 Rhonadler	743	D-9127	15.11.77	Scottish Gliding Union Ltd	Portmoak	3. 4.02
DQY	2307		Schleicher K8B	647	D-4375	11.77	Mendip GC	Halesland	28. 8.01
DRA	2309		Schleicher Ka6CR	1118	D-9041	11.77	P Davis	Bidford	22.11.02
DRB	2310	86	Glaser-Dirks DG-100	31	PH-532	11.77	J.D.Peck	Bicester	5. 3.02
DRD	2312	DRD	Schleicher Ka6CR	6377Si	D-9080	11.77	Essex & Suffolk GC	Wormingford	27. 3.02
DRE	2313	DRE	Schleicher Ka6CR	6197	D-8558	25. 1.78	J.H.Jowett	North Hill	12. 3.02
DRF	2314	DRF	Schleicher Ka6CR	943	D-8600	11.77	Devon & Somerset GC *(Damaged North Hill 14.7.97)*	North Hill	11. 4.98*
DRG	2315	DRG	Schleicher Ka6CR	6157	D-4090	11.77	W.E.Smith t/a Summer Wine Syndicate	Gallows Hill	14. 8.01
DRJ	2317	D	Schleicher ASK13	13583		11. 1.78	Lasham Gliding Society	Lasham	1. 8.02
DRK	2318	DRK	Grob G.102 Astir CS77	1686		12.77	N.Toogood	Lasham	24. 5.02
DRL	2319	DRL	Scheibe SF-26 Standard	5040	D-7073	15.12.77	T McKinley	Kirton-in-Lindsey	16. 2.02
DRM	2320	DRM	Schleicher Ka7 Rhonadler	7017	D-4666	1. 2.78	L.G.Cross & Syndicate	Dunstable	11. 5.02
DRN	2321	821	Glasflugel H.303 Mosquito	082		11. 2.78	A.Roberts	North Hill	14. 4.02
DRP	2322	DRP	Pilatus B4 PC-11	080	RAFGSA BGA.1927	5. 1.78	M.C.Moxon	Weston-on-the-Green	2. 2.02
DRQ	2323	258	Grob G.103 Twin Astir	3027		25. 1.78	V.C.Carr & Ptnrs	Sleap	19. 5.02
DRR	2324	DRR	Schleicher Ka2B Rhonschwalbe	49	D-8108	11. 1.78	Dumfries & District GC	Falgunzeon	21. 6.02
DRS	2325	DRS	SZD-9 bis Bocian 1E	P-783		1. 2.78	Mendip GC	Halesland	30. 5.02
DRT	2326	688	Eiri PIK-20D	20587		5. 1.78	P F Fowler	Sleap	5. 4.02
DRU	2327	334	Grob G.102 Astir CS77	1685		5. 1.78	J.R.Goodenough	Wormingford	2. 5.02
DRV	2328	DRV	Schleicher K8b	8026	D-6169	1.78	P.G.Clayton	Portmoak	28. 4.02
DRW	2329	798	Grob G.102 Astir CS	1081	D-3311	23. 2.78	P.A.Brooks	Lasham	3. 5.02
DRY	2331		Schleicher Ka6BR	370	D-5533	11. 2.78	A.May	RAF Marham	25. 7.99
DRZ	2332	DRZ	Schleicher K8B	668	D-4622 D-KANB/D-4622	1. 2.78	East Sussex GC	Ringmer	14. 6.02

DSA 2333	Slingsby T.30 Prefect	575	WE985	11. 2.78	R.J.Sharman	Crowland	15. 6.02
DSB 2334 DSB	Schleicher Ka6E	4300	D-0263	15. 3.78	M H Yates	Ridgewell	5. 5.01
DSE 2337 227	Schempp-Hirth HS.7 Mini Nimbus	36		2.78	G Binnie	Portmoak	11. 1.97*
DSF 2338 DSF	Schleicher K8B	8220	D-7114	2.78	Edinburgh University GC *"Snoopy"*	Portmoak	4. 1.03
DSG 2339	Schleicher Ka6CR	6395	D-5696	13. 4.78	R P Maddocks	Booker	11. 8.00
DSH 2340 648	Grob G.102 Astir CS77	1696		13. 4.78	R B Petrie	Portmoak	9. 4.02
DSJ 2341	Grob G.103 Twin Astir	3050		8. 3.78	L J Kaye	Shobdon	5. 7.02
DSL 2343 447	Grob G.103 Twin Astir	3041		2. 3.78	J.G.Hampson	Enstone	1. 4.01
DSM 2344	Fauvel AV.22S	3	F-CCGM	4.78	I.Dunkley	Camphill	1. 8.95*
DSN 2345 893	Grob G.102 Astir CS77	1698		23. 3.78	J.J.M.Riach	Feshiebridge	11. 6.02
DSP 2346 270	Schempp-Hirth HS.7 Mini Nimbus	33		9. 3.78	R.I.Hey & Ptnrs	Nympsfield	5. 3.02
DSR 2348 DSR	Schleicher Ka6CR	970	D-5040	31. 5.78	Cornish GC	Perranporth	21. 4.02
DST 2350 972	Schleicher ASW20L	20059		24. 8.78	J.G.Haines	Dunstable	17. 1.02
DSU 2351 DSU	Grob G.102 Astir CS77	1663		19. 4.78	Bowland Forest GC	Chipping 25.2.02	
DSV 2352 718	Pilatus B4 PC-11	134	RAFGSA.718 RAFGGA.518	23.3.78	Staffordshire GC	Seighford	11.95*
DSW 2353 533	Schempp-Hirth HS.7 Mini Nimbus	37	RNGSA.N33	3.78	S.C.Fear	Crowland	9 .3.02
DSX 2354 877	Schleicher ASW19	19188		13. 4.78	R.Grundy	Kingston Deverill	2. 3.02
DSY 2355 DSY	Schleicher Ka6CR	561	D-5702	28. 4.78	D.J.L.Smith	Chipping	30.11.02
DTA 2357 699	Glaser-Dirks DG-2002-	27		9. 5.78	R P Hardcastle	Camphill	9. 5.02
DTC 2359	Schempp-Hirth HS.6 Janus B	63	RAFGSA.R9 RAFGSA 16/BGA.2359	4.78	Dukeries GC	Gamston	29. 6.02
DTD 2360 DTD	Schleicher ASW19	19187		4.78	R.K.Warren	Cross Hayes	18. 3.02
DTE 2361 DTE	Schleicher ASW19	19185		28. 4.78	G.R.Purcell	Lasham	1. 2.02
DTG 2363 DTG	Schempp-Hirth SHK-1	012	D-2034	9. 5.78	M.A.T.Jones & F.A.W.Elliott	Rattlesden	26. 5.02
DTK 2366 760	Glasflugel H.303 Mosquito B	109		4.78	P.France	Usk	15. 5.02
DTM 2368	Glaser-Dirks DG-200	2-34		31. 5.78	Miss J.Walker & Ptnrs	Lasham	17. 3.01
DTN 2369 DTN	Schleicher K8B	117/58	NK	1. 6.78	F.McKeegan	RAF Keevil	7.11.01
DTP 2370 915	Schleicher ASW20	20078		5.78	T.S.Hills & Ptnrs	Lasham	15. 1.02
DTQ 2371 DTQ	Schleicher ASW20	20054		31. 7.78	D.H.Garrard	Cranfield	26. 4.00
DTR 2372 DTR	EoN AP.6 Olympia 401	EoN/4/005	NEJSGSA.7 RAFGSA.252/G-APSI	31. 5.78	B.D.Clarke	Ringmer	15. 5.02
DTS 2373 DTS	CARMAM M.100S Mesange	031	F-CCST	18. 5.78	R.C.Holmes	Llantisilio	20. 9.01
DTU 2375 DTU	Schempp-Hirth HS.5 Nimbus 2B	167		9. 5.78	R.E.Wooler	Chipping	28. 3.02
DTV 2376 704	Glasflugel H.303 Mosquito B	110		7. 6.78	A.J.Watson	Lasham	20. 5.02
DTW 2377 DTW	SZD-30 Pirat	S-0711		7. 6.78	C Kaminski	North Hill	8. 6.02
DTX 2378 320	Glasflugel H.303 Mosquito B	111		18. 5.78	K.D.Hook	Portmoak	23 .1.02
DTY 2379 766	Glasflugel H.303 Mosquito B	112		18. 5.78	R.Ward	Gransden Lodge	13. 4.02
DTZ 2380 S30	Slingsby T.30 Prefect	573	WE983	21. 6.78	C.Hughes	Nympsfield	18.12.02
DUB 2382 911	Glasflugel H.303 Mosquito B	113		31. 5.78	A.G.Reid & Ptnrs	Kenley	5. 5.02
DUC 2383	CARMAM M.100S Mesange	012	F-CCSA	7. 6.78	Not known *(Stored 5.94)*	Carlton Moor	5.88*
DUD 2384	Grunau Baby III		BGA.2074 RAFGSA.374/D-9142	7. 6.78	Not known *(Under restoration 2001)*	(West Sussex)	
DUE 2385 A11	Schleicher ASK-13	13591	AGA.15 BGA.2385	4. 7.78	Kestrel GC	RAF Odiham	23.5.02
DUF 2386	Schleicher K8B	8296A	D-5294	11. 7.78	Essex GC	Ridgewell	1. 6.02
DUH 2388 DUH	Scheibe L-Spatz 55	760	NK	28. 7.78	R J Aylesbury	Upwood	16. 6.02
DUK 2390 DUK	Schleicher K8B	752	D-4048	21. 6.78	Bristol & Glos GC	Nympsfield	5. 3.02
DUL 2391 642	Grob G.102 Astir CS77	1720		21. 6.78	C.Warren	Long Mynd	2. 3.02
DUQ 2394 DUQ	Glaser-Dirks DG-200	2-43		4. 7.78	D.M.Cottingham	North Hill	9.12.02
DUR 2395 DUR	Schleicher Ka6CR	6273	OY-DLX	15. 8.78	Rattlesden GC	Rattlesden	25. 6.02
DUS 2396 638	Schleicher Ka6E	4263	OY-XCB HB-948	8.78	M.Toon & C.S.Crocker	Tibenham	15. 9.02
DUT 2397 T34	Schleicher ASW20	20089		24. 8.78	T.J.Murphy	Portmoak	4. 5.02
DUW 2400	DFS 108/49 Grunau Baby 2B *(Also allocated BAPC.33)*	-	VN148 LN+ST	12.77	C.Tonks *(On rebuild 2000)*	(North Wales)	*
DUX 2401 885	Grob G.102 Club Astir	2140		7.78	B.T.Spreckley	Le Blanc, France	15.10.02
DUY 2402 652	Glaser-Dirks DG-100	24	PH-525	13.10.78	A.C.Saxton & Ptnrs	Carlton Moor	14. 7.02
DVB 2405	Schleicher ASK13	13596		8.78	Essex & Suffolk GC	Wormingford	17. 3.02
	(Components, incl c/n plate, donated to BGA.3493 & possibly discarded parts from crash Dunstable 5.6.82)						
DVC 2406 DVC	Schleicher ASK13	13597		31. 8.78	Southdown GC	Parham Park	6. 2.02
DVD 2407 DVD	LET L-13 Blanik	027021	RNGSA.N22	9. 9.78	Vectis GC	Bembridge	15. 4.02
DVE 2408 879	Schleicher Ka6E	4226	RAFGSA.379	15. 8.78	H.F.Young	Sandhill Farm, Shrivenham	25.11.02
DVG 2410 DVG	Schleicher Ka6CR *(Built Holzmann-Drespack)*	003	D-1916	22.11.78	R.F.Warren	Ringmer	28. 6.02
DVH 2411 615	Schleicher Ka6E	4117	RAFGSA	31. 8.78	P.Brett	Perranporth	15. 8.02
DVJ 2412 869	Eiri PIK-20D	20638		9. 9.78	M.C.Hayes	Bidford	3. 5.02
DVK 2413 732	SZD-48 Jantar Standard 2	W-868		22. 9.78	K.J.Mellor	Gransden Lodge	20. 4.01
DVL 2414 X96	Schleicher ASW19	19222		10.10.78	P.T Healy & Ptnrs	Lasham	29. 6.02

DVM 2415 DVM	Glasflugel H.205 Club Libelle	52	RAFGGA.581	12. 9.78	M.J.Gooch	Rattlesden	15. 4.02
DVN 2416 DVN	Eiri PIK-20D	20641		22.11.78	P.J.Goulthoorpe	Husbands Bosworth	21. 4.02
DVP 2417 971	Schleicher ASW19	19220		23. 9.78	E.F.Davies	Booker	18. 7.02
DVQ 2418 DVQ	Schleicher K8B	8134	D-0288	16. 9.78	Staffordshire GC	Seighford	6. 6.99
			D-KICE/D5235				
DVR 2419	Scheibe L-Spatz 55	663	D-1565	23. 9.78	J.Young	Lyveden	6.96*
DVS 2420 VS	Schempp-Hirth HS.4 Standard Cirrus			26. 9.78	D.S.Hands & Ptnr	Parham Park	7. 3.02
	(C/n duplicates VH-GGC)	380	RAFGSA.824				
DVV 2423 810	Schleicher ASW20L	20100		9.78	Mrs A.F.Coppen	Lasham	27. 4.02
DVW 2424 590	Schleicher ASW20	20099		9.78	Not known	Aston Down	2.85*
			(Damaged in collision with BGA.2618 Lasham 17.8.84; wreck stored 7.99)				
DVX 2425 S13	Schleicher ASK13	13598		5.10.78	Shenington GC	Edgehill	15. 2.02
DVY 2426 272	Schempp-Hirth HS.2 Cirrus	52	OO-ZIR	10.78	M.G.Ashton	Perranporth	27. 7.02
DVZ 2427 Z25	Glasflugel H.303 Mosquito B	133		31.10.78	B.H.Shaw	Husbands Bosworth	30. 4.00
DWB 2429 733	Glasflugel H.303 Mosquito B	135		10.11.78	C.G.Salt & Ptnrs	Lasham	2. 4.02
	(Marked as BGA.2924)						
DWC 2430 DWC	Schleicher Ka6E	4111	AGA.11	24.10.78	D.Jones	Wormingford	2. 5.02
DWE 2432 DWE	Schleicher Ka7 Rhonadler	7132	D-5427	3.11.78	N.T.Large	Llantisilio	24.10.02
DWF 2433 DWF	DFS/49 Grunau Baby 2B	-	AGA.16	11.78	L.P.Woodage	Dunstable	9. 1.02
	(Built RNAY Fleetlands)		RNGSA 1-13/VW743				
DWG 2434	Schleicher K8B	165/60	D-5750	11.78	Newark & Notts GC	Winthorpe	18. 3.02
DWH 2435 DWH	Schleicher K8B	1	D-8614	11.78	Essex GC	Ridgewell	9.96*
	(Built by Gebr.Huber)		D-8331				
DWJ 2436 191	Glaser-Dirks DG-200	2-59		11.78	P.R.Desmond	Chipping	19. 4.02
DWL 2438 755	Glasflugel H.303 Mosquito B	141		2.12.78	A.Stanford & Ptnrs	Husbands Bosworth	6. 6.02
DWN 2440 DWN	Schleicher Ka7 Rhonadler	7101	D-5360	12.78	L.R.Merritt	Edgehill	8. 5.02
DWP 2441 DWP	Glasflugel H.303 Mosquito B	136		15.12.78	N.Whiteman	Lasham	27. 9.02
DWQ 2442 DWQ	Grob G.102 Astir CS77	1758		9. 1.79	F.Prime	Gransden Lodge	24. 2.02
DWR 2443 P9	Glasflugel H.303 Mosquito B	134	(BGA.2428)	23. 1.79	C.D.Lovell	Lasham	15. 2.02
DWS 2444 728	Eiri PIK-20D	20652		7. 3.79	R. & B.Madelin	Lasham	30. 4.02
DWT 2445 886	Slingsby T.65A Vega	1898		28. 3.79	A.P.Grimley	Husbands Bosworth	28. 9.00
DWU 2446 DWU	Grob G.102 Astir CS	1201	D-7269	30. 1.79	G.V.McKirdy	Parham Park	9. 5.98
DWW 2448 DWW	Slingsby T.65A Vega	1896		2. 3.79	J.Sorrell	Usk	16. 5.02
DWZ 2451 DWZ	Schleicher ASW19	19243		14. 2.79	J.A.Stirk & Ptnrs	Burn	4. 5.02
DXA 2452 483	Glasflugel H.303 Mosquito B		137	14. 2.79	S H Gibson	Dunstable	13. 4.02
DXB 2453 81	Schleicher ASW20	20142		.	J.A.Timpany & Ptnrs	Nympsfield	22. 2.02
DXD 2455 132	Slingsby T.65A Vega	1901		20. 4.79	T.C.Harrington & Ptnrs	Bicester	28. 4.02
DXE 2456	Slingsby T.65A Vega	1902		16. 5.79	L.M.Astle	Husbands Bosworth	10. 3.02
DXF 2457 815	Slingsby T.65A Vega	1903		16. 5.79	P.Goulding	Crowland	23. 2.02
DXG 2458 46	Slingsby T.65A Vega 17L	1906		2. 6.79	M.H.Pope	Bidford	29. 4.00
DXH 2459 DXH	Schleicher Ka6E	4198	RAFGSA.489	28. 3.79	B.Hughes	Bicester	21. 2.02
			D-4093				
DXJ 2460 DXJ	Grob G.102 Astir CS77	1762		2. 3.79	B.Meech	Gransden Lodge	11. 2.02
DXK 2461 160	Centrair ASW20F	20108		15. 5.79	A.Townsend	Booker	20. 6.02
DXL 2462 DXL	Schempp-Hirth HS.4 Standard Cirrus		AGA.1	6. 3.79	P. & A.Gelsthorpe	Lasham	29. 3.02
		203G					
DXM 2463 DXM	Schleicher Ka7 Rhonadler	626	RAFGGA.551	20. 3.79	Vale of Neath GC	Rhigos	13. 7.02
			D-5707				
DXN 2464 267	Glaser-Dirks DG-200	2-63		17. 3.79	J.A.Johnston	Gransden Lodge	3. 3.02
DXP 2465 DXP	Schleicher K8B	8646A	D-8537	24. 3.79	Stratford-upon-Avon GC	Snitterfield	24. 2.02
DXQ 2466 147	Schempp-Hirth HS.7 Mini Nimbus C			13. 3.79	T.Lamb & P.Hawkins	Weston-on-the-Green	22. 5.02
	(Build No.MN97)	96					
DXR 2467	Slingsby T.65A Vega	1905		21. 6.79	D.R.Sutton	Sutton Bank	29. 8.94*
DXT 2469 286	Schempp-Hirth HS.7 Mini Nimbus C			14. 3.79	C.Chapman	Booker	17.12.02
		97					
DXU 2470 DXU	Slingsby T.59J Kestrel 22	1867	G-BDWZ	11. 4.79	P.L.Bisgood & Ptnrs	Cranfield	9. 4.02
DXV 2471 DXV	Schleicher ASK13	13602		16. 3.79	Cambridge University GC	Gransden Lodge	22. 2.99
DXW 2472 354	Glasflugel H.303 Mosquito B	142		7. 4.79	P.Newmark & Ptnrs	Burn	12. 2.02
DXX 2473 580	Schleicher ASW19B	19245		17. 3.79	P.F.Whitehead	Bicester	6. 1.03
DXY 2474 HB-474	Muller Moswey III	?	HB-474	20. 4.79	G.M.Bacon & Ptnrs	Gransden Lodge	22. 7.01
DYB 2477	Schleicher Ka7 Rhonadler		D-5775	29. 3.79	South London Gliding Centre		
		167/59			"6" *(Reported as "DYN")*	Kenley	7. 5.02
DYC 2478 DYC	Schleicher Ka6CR	6390	D-1545	20. 3.79	F.J.Smith	Burn	4. 5.02
DYE 2479 828	Schleicher ASW20L	20143		27. 3.79	T.A.Sage	Dunstable	4. 1.02
DYF 2480 850	Grob G.102 Astir CS77	1805		7. 4.79	York Gliding Centre	Rufforth	3. 4.02
DYG 2481 592	Slingsby T.59H Kestrel 22	1868	G-BDZG	31. 3.79	R.E.Gretton & R.L.Darby	Crowland	19. 7.02
DYH 2482 DYH	Glaser-Dirks DG-200	2-75		5. 4.79	W.A.Urwin	Milfield	26. 5.96*
DYJ 2483 DYJ	Schleicher Ka6CR	6583	D-5838	15. 5.79	R.M.Morris	Dunstable	9 .6.02
DYL 2485 DYL	CARMAM JP/15-36A Aiglon	37		4.79	M.P.Edwards	Crowland	6. 5.02
DYN 2486	Schleicher Ka6CR	6129Si	D-8458	1. 5.79	C.N.Harder	Lasham	19. 5.01
	(See BGA.2477)						
DYP 2487 BR	Schleicher Ka6BR	191	OO-ZXL	15. 5.79	D.S.Ling	Ridgewell	23. 3.98*
			D-5482		*(Crashed Ridgewell 31.5.97)*		
DYQ 2488 DYQ	Schleicher Ka6CR	6178	D-5328	9. 5.79	Dorset GC	Gallows Hill	20. 8.00

DYR	2489	DYR	Schleicher Ka7 Rhonadler	766	D-5220	12. 4.79	Avon Soaring Centre	Bidford	30.11.02
DYT	2490	537	Eiri PIK-20D	20657		18. 5.79	P.J.Hampshire	Parham Park	9. 3.98*
							(Damaged near Parham 12.4.97)		
DYU	2491	531	Schempp-Hirth HS.5 Nimbus 2C	181		18. 4.79	A.Pickles	Lasham	7. 7.01
DYX	2494	102	Schleicher ASW20	20135		23. 6.79	R.Cousins	Challock	4. 5.02
DYZ	2495	943	Schempp-Hirth HS.5 Nimbus 2C	180		24. 4.79	N.A.Britton	Bidford	25. 3.02
DZA	2496	DZA	Slingsby T.65A Vega 17L	1907		26. 6.79	M.P.Garrod	Lasham	27. 2.02
DZB	2497	DZB	Slingsby T.65A Vega	1908		10. 7.79	A.N.Christie	Drumshade	29. 8.02
DZC	2498	DZC	Scheibe L-Spatz 55	642	RAFGGA	4. 5.79	G.A.Ford	Nympsfield	23.10.98
					D-5629				
DZD	2499	573	Schleicher ASW19B	19268		30. 5.79	J.Anderson	Llantisilio	18. 8.02
DZF	2501	152	Schempp-Hirth HS.4 Standard Cirrus	421G	RAFGSA.27	15. 5.79	L.S.Hood	Bicester	29. 4.02
DZG	2502	909	Schleicher ASW19B	19267		10. 5.79	S.P.Wareham	Gallows Hill	11. 2.02
DZJ	2504	576	Grob G.102 Club Astir	2230		11. 5.79	J. & R.Acreman	Halesland	11. 5.02
DZK	2505	957	Schempp-Hirth HS.5 Nimbus 2C			10. 5.79	R Hudson	Sutton Bank	3.12.02
			(Fuselage No.195)	198					
DZM	2507	DZM	Slingsby T.65A Vega	1909		10. 7.79	D.G.MacArthur	Long Mynd	17. 4.02
DZN	2508	990	Slingsby T.65A Vega 17L	1910		13. 7.79	D.A.White	Aboyne	17.12.02
DZP	2509	DZP	Slingsby T.65A Vega	1911		17.11.79	M.T.Crews	Currock Hill	10. 5.02
DZR	2511	DZR	ICA IS-28B	287		13. 6.79	Lakes GC	Walney Island	20. 1.02
DZS	2512	DZS	SZD-8bis-0 Jaskolka	183	HB-583	30. 5.79	N.A Clark	Parham Park	18. 8.01
DZT	2513	106	Eiri PIK-20D	20661		9. 6.79	A.C.Garside	Challock	13. 3.02
DZU	2514	DZU	Grob G.102 Astir CS	1076	D-3308	6. 6.79	P.F.Clarke	Booker	27. 2.02
DZV	2515	839	Scheibe SF-27A Zugvogel V	6065	D-5839	17. 7.79	A.P.Montague	Nympsfield	24. 4.02
DZW	2516	DZW	Schleicher Ka6CR	6628	D-1045	11. 7.79	A.Wildman	Husbands Bosworth	6. 5.02
DZY	2518	757	Schleicher ASW19B	19275		13. 6.79	M.C.Fairman & T.Marlow	Dunstable	4. 4.02
EAC	2522	367	Grob G.102 Astir CS77	1803		14. 6.79	B.T.Pratt	Husbands Bosworth	11. 5.02
EAD	2523	EAD	Slingsby T.65A Vega	1912		30.11.79	I.McCague	Pocklington	15. 8.02
EAE	2524	107	Schleicher ASW20L	20224		20. 6.79	L.Clayton	Challock	1. 4.02
EAF	2525	EAF	Grob G.102 Astir CS77	1830		12. 7.79	J.Bell	Milfield	15. 9.02
EAG	2526		Slingsby T.65A Vega	1913		4. 9.79	D.R.Moore	Gransden Lodge	13. 5.02
EAH	2527	EAH	Schleicher Ka6E	4085	D-7542	12. 7.79	M.Lodge	Lasham	9. 5.02
					D-7142				
EAJ	2528	79	Schempp-Hirth HS.5 Nimbus 2	7	D-0699	28.6.79	G.Harvey	Currock Hill	29.10.02
EAK	2529	594	Glasflugel H.303 Mosquito B	155		29.6.79	A.R.L.Parker & Ptnrs	Aston Down	25. 4.02
EAL	2530		Schleicher Rhonlerche II	3051/BR	PH-331	7.79	Newcastle & Teesside GC	Carlton Moor	13. 9.91*
							(Stored 2000)		
EAM	2531	EAM	Schempp-Hirth HS.5 Nimbus 2B	93	D-2787	10. 7.79	C.H.Brown	Chipping	28. 4.02
EAP	2533	R31	Schleicher ASK-13	13609	RAFGSA.R31	19. 7.79	RAFGSA Centre	Bicester	9. 2.02
					BGA.2533				
EAR	2535	EAR	Eiri PIK-20D	?		28. 7.79	D.Coker	RAF Syerston	20.12.02
EAT	2537	786	Eiri PIK-20D	20664		22. 8.79	P.T.Reading & Ptnrs	Lasham	17. 9.01
EAU	2538	EAU	Schleicher Ka7 Rhonadler	7092	PH-304	7.79	Welland GC	Upwood	23. 3.02
			(Part modified to ASK13)						
EAV	2539		Schempp-Hirth HS.7 Mini Nimbus C	136		31. 7.79	W.Cook & K.Porter	Lasham	5. 8.00
EAW	2540	EAW	Grob G.102 Astir CS77	1831		21. 7.79	W.Severn	Cross Hayes	5. 7.02
EBA	2544	EBA	Slingsby T.65A Vega 17L	1914		1.11.79	F.T.Bick	Aboyne	11. 6.02
EBB	2545	881	Grob G.102 Speed Astir IIB	4040		28. 7.79	M.Malcolm & A.F.Grinter	Pocklington	10. 5.02
EBC	2546	EBC	Slingsby T.30B Prefect	583	RAFGSA.33	1. 8.79	K.R.Reeves	RAF Syerston	10. 4.00
					WE993		*"Jonathan Livingstone Prefect"*		
			(Rebuilt with components ex BGA.808 & BGA.1618?)						
EBD	2547		Scheibe Bergfalke IV	5822	D-1005	4. 9.79	D.Clarke	Burn	28. 4.02
EBE	2548	EBE	Issoire E78 Silene	07		20.11.79	B.A.Burgess	Husbands Bosworth	11. 4.02
EBF	2549	EBF	Schempp-Hirth HS.7 Mini Nimbus C	138		17. 8.79	M.J.Gooch	Rattlesden	12. 4.02
EBG	2550		Eiri PiK-20D	20662		4. 9.79	P.F.Woodcock	Camphill	19. 5.00
			(Assembled from BGA.2550 [fuselage] & BGA.2490 [wings])						
EBJ	2552	h11	Schleicher ASW19B	19282		21. 8.79	J.D.Hill	Sutton Bank	7.11.02
EBK	2553	552	Schempp-Hirth HS.7 Mini Nimbus C	139	AGA.2	17. 8.79	J.B.Burgoyne	Lyveden	20. 6.02
					BGA.2553				
EBL	2554	EBL	Schleicher ASK13	13610		7. 9.79	Bristol & Glos GC	Nympsfield	25.10.02
EBM	2555	807	Grob G.102 Astir CS77	1843		8.79	D.O.Sephton	Ringmer	10. 4.02
EBN	2556	37	Centrair ASW20F	20118		22. 8.79	K.W.Blake & Ptnrs	Camphill	15. 6.02
EBP	2557	EBP	Allgaier Geier I	3/4	D-9025	4. 9.79	D.P.Raffan	RAF Marham	21. 7.01
EBQ	2558		Schleicher Ka6CR	6051Si	D-5237	3.10.79	Not known	Tibenham	
							(Under repair 2000)		
EBR	2559	EBR	Glaser-Dirks DG-200/17	2-89/1706	D-6893	6. 9.79	M.D.Parsons	Lee-on-Solent	26. 5.02
EBS	2560	EBS	Scheibe Zugvogel IIIA	1054	LX-CAF	21.11.79	I.D.McLeod	Challock	2. 6.02
					D-8363		*"Schwarzhornfalke"*		
EBX	2565	644	Schleicher ASW20	20058	D-7973	21. 9.79	J P Davies	Gransden Lodge	7. 3.02
EBZ	2567	EBZ	Schleicher ASK13	13614		9.79	Booker GC	Booker	10.12.02
ECA	2568		Wright Falcon	1		9.79	P.W.Wright	Saltby	22. 8.98

ECC	2570	ECC	Schleicher Ka6CR	60/01	D-5080	10.10.79	A.Allison & Ptnrs	Burn	7. 4.02
ECF	2573	ECF	Schleicher Ka6CR	856	D-5808	10.79	D.Goldup	Aston Down	31. 5.02
ECG	2574		Schempp-Hirth SHK	19	D-5359	10.10.79	M.F.Hardy	AAC Upavon	24. 3.02
					D-1329				
ECH	2575	ECH	Glasflugel H.303 Mosquito B	173		24. 1.80	A.Walker & Ptnrs	Rattlesden	2. 4.02
ECJ	2576	ECJ	Slingsby T.65A Vega	1916		21.12.79	J.E.B.Hart & Ptnrs	Sutton Bank	19. 4.02
ECK	2577	ECK	Slingsby T.65A Vega	1917		13.12.79	L.Gibson	Milfield	6. 4.97*
ECL	2578		Slingsby T.65A Vega 17L	1918		2. 2.80	J.B.Strzebrakowski	Gransden Lodge	19. 6.02
ECM	2579	ECM	Slingsby T.65A Vega	1919		15. 1.80	F.L.Wilson	Aston Down	22. 5.02
ECN	2580	645	Slingsby T.65A Vega 17L	1920		20.11.79	C.Claxton Syndicate	Booker	29. 3.01
ECP	2581	ECP	Rolladen-Schneider LS-3-17	3426		26. 3.80	D.Crowhurst	Lyveden	26. 1.02
ECQ	2582	ECQ	Grob G.102 Astir CS77	1837		25.10.79	N.Harrison	Tibenham	3. 6.02
ECS	2584	955	Glasflugel H.303 Mosquito B	166		26.10.79	R.C.Adams & P.Robinson	Wormingford	17. 3.02
ECT	2585	604	Glasflugel H.604	2	I-FEVG	4.10.79	F.K.Russell	Dunstable	9.11.01
					D-0279				
ECW	2588	ECW	Schleicher ASK21	21008		2. 3.80	Norfolk GC	Tibenham	18. 2.02
ECX	2589	600	Schleicher ASW20L	20315		10. 6.80	A.C.Robertson	Feshiebridge	17. 5.02
ECY	2590	ECY	Glasflugel H.201B Standard Libelle	530	RAFGGA.557	13.11.79	E.W.Fry	Bidford	17.5.02
ECZ	2591	ECZ	Schleicher ASK21	21009		26. 4.80	Booker GC	Booker	19. 4.02
EDA	2592	647	Slingsby T.65A Vega 17L	1888	G-BFYW	30.11.79	A.R.Worters	North Connel	17. 9.01
EDB	2593	EDB	CARMAM JP-15-36AR Aiglon	40		1. 2.80	P.J.Martin & Ptnrs	Crowland	20. 2.02
EDC	2594		Schleicher Ka7 Rhonadler	244	D-8527	13. 2.80	J.C.Shipley	Camphill	23. 6.02
EDD	2595	EDD	Schleicher ASW17	17043	D-6865	12.79	C.Curtiss	Crowland	6. 5.02
EDE	2596	750	Centrair ASW20F	20128		27. 2.80	G.M.Cumner	Aston Down	17. 5.00
EDF	2597	530	Schempp-Hirth HS.7 Mini Nimbus C	149		8. 1.80	C.W.Boutcher	Snitterfield	27. 9.02
EDG	2598	EDG	Schleicher Ka6CR	6512	RAFGSA	9. 1.80	M.Wood	Saltby	27. 8.01
EDH	2599		Glasflugel H.303 Mosquito B	184		25. 3.80	D.G.Cooper	Tibenham	21. 7.02
EDJ	2600	EDJ	Glasflugel H.303 Mosquito B	185		4. 4.80	A.J.Leigh & Ptnrs	Camphill	30. 3.02
EDK	2601	EDK	Schleicher Ka7	7791	D-1633	13. 2.80	York Gliding Centre	Rufforth	1. 4.02
EDL	2602		Focke-Wulf Weihe 50	4	D-0893	26. 1.80	F.K.Russell	Dunstable	14.10.96*
					HB-555		*(Being restored during 2000)*		
EDM	2603	EDM	Glaser-Dirks DG-2002-	98		17. 2.80	A.H.St Pierre	Sutton Bank	9. 4.02
EDN	2604	820	Glaser-Dirks DG-100G Elan	E12G6		14. 2.80	A.P.Scott & Ptnrs	Currock Hill	30. 6.02
EDP	2605	448	Glaser-Dirks DG-100G Elan	E19G7		12. 2.80	B.Jenkinson	Nympsfield	1. 3.02
EDS	2608	EDS	Scheibe SF-26 Standard	5038	RAFGGA.???	1. 2.80	I.Davidson	Long Mynd	28. 3.96*
			(Probably ex RAFGGA.548)		D-8454				
EDU	2610	EDU	Schleicher ASK13	13613		22. 3.80	Kent GC	Challock	19. 1.02
EDV	2611	541	Slingsby T.65A Vega 17L	1893	G-BGCU	8. 2.80	J.L.Clegg	Aston Down	11. 4.02
EDW	2612	EDW	Schleicher ASK21	21010		5. 4.80	UCLU GC	RAF Halton	3. 8.02
EDX	2613	EDX	Slingsby T.65D Vega	1928		20. 5.80	A.James	Usk	17. 5.02
EDY	2614	EDY	Slingsby T.65D Vega	1929		23. 5.80	C.J.Steadman	Husbands Bosworth	24. 4.02
EDZ	2615	EDZ	Slingsby T.65C Sport Vega	1931		18. 6.80	R.C.Copley	Chipping	4.12.02
EEA	2616	EEA	Slingsby T.65C Sport Vega	1932		27. 6.80	Peterborough & Spalding GC	Crowland	5. 7.02
EEC	2618	EEC	Schleicher ASW20L	20311	(G-BSTS)	27. 6.80	D.M.Cushway	Challock	24. 2.02
EED	2619	R91	Schleicher K8B	590	RAFGSA.R91	1. 3.80	R.D.Welsh	Bicester	9. 2.02
					NEJSGSA/BGA.2619/D-5703				
EEE	2620	EEE	Schleicher ASW20L	20312		4. 4.80	T E MacFadyen	Nympsfield	10. 5.02
EEF	2621	EEF	Rolladen-Schneider LS-3-17	3441		13. 6.80	G.J.Nicholas	Rivar Hill	22.10.02
EEG	2622	EEG	Slingsby T.65C Sport Vega	1922	EI-129	3.80	G.Harris	Rufforth	20. 3.02
					BGA.2622				
EEH	2623	166	Schleicher ASW19	19042	RAFGSA	27. 2.80	K Kiely	AAC Dishforth	17. 6.02
EEJ	2624	EEJ	Schleicher ASW20L	20314		20. 9.80	R.R.Stoward	Dunstable	4. 9.02
EEK	2625	141	Schempp-Hirth HS.5 Nimbus 2C	201		23. 2.80	R.E.Cross	Lasham	22.11.02
EEM	2627	EEM	Schleicher K8B	8688AB	D-0254	28. 2.80	South Wales GC	Usk	19. 5.02
EEN	2628		Schempp-Hirth HS.4 Standard Cirrus	75		1. 3.80	J.Hanlon	Weston-on-the-Green	16. 4.02
				621	RAFGSA 87/(BGA.2609)				
EEP	2629	EEP	Wassmer WA.26P Squale	36	F-CDSX	3.80	R.H.Parker	Aston Down	1. 7.02
EEQ	2630	EEQ	Grob G.102 Standard Astir II	5015S	RNGSA.N12	3.80	S.W.Bradford	Dunstable	24. 4.02
EER	2631		Schempp-Hirth HS.7 Mini Nimbus	150		14. 3.80	D.J.Uren	Perranporth	20. 4.02
EES	2632	50	Rolladen-Schneider LS-3-17	3248		26. 3.80	J.Illidge & Ptnrs	Camphill	18.10.02
EEU	2634	456	Issoire E78 Silene	08		3.80	M.B.Jefferyes & Ptnrs	Ridgewell	8. 8.98
EEV	2635	129	Centrair ASW20FL	20145		15. 5.80	J.P.Lyell & Ptnr	Lasham	14. 8.02
EEW	2636	EEW	Schleicher Ka6CR	6188	RAFGGA	26. 3.80	P.E.Lowden	Winthorpe	4. 6.02
					D-6151				
EEX	2637	EEX	Rolladen-Schneider LS-3-17	3442		5. 7.80	W A.Dallimer & Ptnr	Aston Down	27. 5.02
EEZ	2639	157	Rolladen-Schneider LS-3A	3458		10. 6.80	P.Holland	Sutton Bank	29.11.02
EFA	2640	470	Schleicher ASW20L	20326		2. 7.80	B.Middleton	Dunstable	21. 3.02
EFB	2641	EFB	Schempp-Hirth HS.5 Nimbus 2C	216		3. 4.80	N.Revell & Ptnrs	Gamston	13. 3.02
EFC	2642	EFC	Siebert Sie-3	3018	D-0811	3.4.80	M.S.A.Skinner	Cross Hayes	29. 6.02
EFD	2643	EFD	Schleicher Ka7 Rhonadler	7007	PH-277	15.7.80	South London Gliding Centre	Kenley	19. 1.99

EFE	2644	586	Centrair ASW20F	20139		1. 5.80	J.A.Quartermaine & Ptnrs	Sutton Bank	29. 1.02
EFF	2645	737	Schempp-Hirth HS.5 Nimbus 2C	208		10. 4.80	E.R.Duffin & D.L.Jobbins	Rhigos	6. 5.02
EFG	2646	EFG	Schleicher K8B	?	RAFGGA	10. 4.80	Rattlesden GC	Rattlesden	7. 2.98
EFH	2647	939	Schleicher ASW20	20308		18. 4.80	M B Judkins	Lasham	4. 2.02
EFJ	2648	CW	Centrair ASW20F	20127		12. 4.80	D.E.Ball	Booker	14. 8.02
EFK	2649	543	Centrair ASW20FL	20140		15. 5.80	G.B.Mounslow	Long Mynd	15. 3.02
EFL	2650	297	Centrair ASW20FL	20133		15. 5.80	D.J.Connolly	Kingston Deverill	16. 4.99
							(Believed w/o North Hill 15.5.98)		
EFM	2651	GAZ	Schleicher Ka6E	4103	RAFGSA	4. 6.80	G.S.Foster	Parham Park	3. 8.02
EFN	2652	EFN	Scheibe L-Spatz 55	635	D-1617	17. 5.80	I.L.Pattingdale	RAF Odiham	27. 5.02
EFP	2653		Schleicher K8B	E.01	D-8859	13. 5.80	Not known *(Stored 3.95)*	Portmoak	7.88*
EFR	2655	EFR	Scheibe L-Spatz	320	RAFGGA	4.80	H. & A.Purser	Cranfield	25. 9.98
EFS	2656	636	Rolladen-Schneider LS-3	3022	HB-1356	14. 5.80	G.I Boswell	Dunstable	11. 6.99
EFT	2657	J45	Schempp-Hirth HS.5 Nimbus 2B	26	HB-1160	23. 4.80	N.L.Jennings	Lleweni Parc	26. 5.02
EFV	2659		Schleicher ASW20	20041	OE-5162	12. 6.80	A.R McKillen	Bellarena	9. 9.02
EFW	2660	EFW	Slingsby T.65C Sport Vega	1938		18. 7.80	Dukeries GC	Gamston	8. 6.02
EFX	2661		LET L-13 Blanik	026460	AGA.21	24. 2.80	Enstone Eagles GC	Edgehill	10.11.94*
					RAFGSA.R7/BGA.2095				
							(Crashed Enstone 25.6.94; parts to BGA.3666; wreck stored 6.95)		
EFZ	2663	EFZ	Rolladen-Schneider LS-3A	3273		21.7.80	D.H.Gardner & J.Higgins	Aston Down	22. 3.02
EGD	2667	D3	Schleicher ASW17	17028	D-2343	25. 6.80	W.J.Dean	Booker	9. 1.01
EGE	2668	EGE	Rolladen-Schneider LS-3A	3465		31. 7.80	D.Barker	Nympsfield	11. 1.02
EGF	2669	EGF	Slingsby T.65C Sport Vega	1936		28. 6.80	B.Snook	Old Sarum	14. 2.02
EGG	2670	JH	Slingsby T.65C Sport Vega	1939		23. 9.80	J.Milson	Usk	20. 2.02
EGH	2671	EGH	Slingsby T.65C Sport Vega	1943		28.11.80	M.J Davies & Ptnrs	Winthorpe	23. 3.02
EGJ	2672	672	Slingsby T.65C Sport Vega	1944		12.12.80	K.J.Towell & Ptnrs	Lasham	22.11.02
EGK	2673	569	Schempp-Hirth HS.4 Standard Cirrus	542G	RAFGGA.569	1. 7.80	I.M.Deans & Ptnrs	Lasham	24. 2.02
					RAFGSA.R2(2)				
EGL	2674	EGL	Schleicher Ka6CR	6330	D-6037	6.80	G.B.Dennis	Halesland	24.11.97*
							t/a Mendip K6 Syndicate *(Damaged North Hill 9.7.97)*		
EGN	2676	EGN	Grob G.103 Twin II	3542		19. 8.80	Enstone Eagles GC	Enstone	15. 4.02
EGP	2677	172	Schleicher ASW20L	20336		17. 9.80	A.W.Gillett & Ptnrs	Nympsfield	5. 3.02
EGR	2679	EGR	Breguet Br.905SA Fauvette	18	F-CCGT	22. 8.80	P.Parker	Dunstable	18. 7.01
EGS	2680	2	Schempp-Hirth HS.5 Nimbus 2CS	192	D-2111	21. 7.80	P.G.Myers	Chipping 27.5.01	
EGT	2681	EGT	Slingsby T.65D Vega	1933		28. 7.80	D.M.Badley & Ptnrs	Sleap	26. 2.02
EGU	2682	EGU	Slingsby T.65A Vega	1921		28. 7.80	M.N.Bishop	Challock	27. 4.02
EGW	2684	844	Schempp-Hirth HS.7 Mini Nimbus B		HB-1447	1. 8.80	I F Barnes	Ridgewell	24. 8.02
			(Modified to Mini Nimbus C?)	78					
EGX	2685	EGX	Slingsby T.65C Sport Vega	1937	RAFGSA.R23	15.10.80	M.D.Organ	Weston-on-the-Green	21. 2.02
					BGA.2685				
EGZ	2687	EGZ	Schleicher ASK21	21030		28.10.80	Needwood Forest GC	Cross Hayes	24. 3.02
EHA	2688		Schleicher K8B	136/59	D-5084	6. 9.80	Not known	Fairwood Common	*
							(Stored as "D-5084" 1.97)		
EHB	2689	K3	Schleicher Ka3	3	????	23.10.80	L.S.Hood	Cranwell	30. 5.02
EHC	2690	EHC	Eichelsdorfer SB-5B	5017	D-9310	14. 8.80	R.I.Davidson	Husbands Bosworth	8. 8.02
EHD	2691	891	Schleicher ASW20L	20386		10.80	B.Lumb	Burn	16. 2.02
EHE	2692	WE992	Slingsby T.30B Prefect	582	WE992	29. 9.80	A.P.Stacey	RAF Keevil	5. 3.98
							t/a A.T.C.Syndicate		
EHF	2693		Caudron C.801	320/4	F-CBTE	11. 5.89	Dutch Aircastle Society	Loosdrecht	
								The Netherlands	5. 4.99
EHG	2694	453	Slingsby T.65C Sport Vega	1940		21.10.80	M.J.Vickery & Ptnrs	Lasham	7 .2.01
EHH	2695	95	Schempp-Hirth Ventus A	07		5.11.80	P.G.Sheard & A.Stone	Lasham	15. 1.02
EHK	2697	490	Rolladen-Schneider LS-4	4068		15. 3.81	S.J.C.Parker	Nympsfield	28. 1.02
EHL	2698	138	Rolladen-Schneider LS-440	24		24. 4.81	C.J.Evans	Booker	9. 3.02
EHM	2699	EHM	Schleicher Ka6E	4118	RAFGSA.318	28. 3.81	D.J.Pengilly	Kingston Deverill	15. 8.02
EHN	2700	EHN	Slingsby T.65C Sport Vega	1942	G-BILH	17.12.80	G.D.Hayter	Challock	21. 5.02
					BGA.2700				
EHP	2701	EHP	Schempp-Hirth HS.5 Nimbus 2C	234		11.80	L.Kirkham	Seighford	11. 3.02
EHQ	2702	431	Schleicher ASK21	21035		21.11.80	University of Surrey GC	Lasham	25. 1.02
EHS	2704	EHS	ICA IS-28B	289		3.12.80	B.Crowhurst	Crowland	12. 8.02
EHT	2705	EHT	Schempp-Hirth HS.5 Nimbus 2C	235		12.80	P.M.Kirschner	Cranfield	14. 4.02
EHU	2706	849	Glasflugel H.304	209		5.11.80	F. & J.M.Townsend	Camphill	27.11.02
EHV	2707	481	Schleicher ASW20L	20385		6. 1.81	G.S.Neumann & Ptnrs	Booker	18. 2.02
EHW	2708	EHW	ICA IS-28B	286		9. 1.81	M Sanderson	Milfield	7.12.00
EHX	2709	1128	DFS/49 Grunau Baby 2B	134	D-1128	21.12.80	J.A.Knowles	RAF Odiham	10. 3.98
EHY	2710		Slingsby T.65D Vega	1941		8. 1.81	R.Spear	Ringmer	19.12.01
EHZ	2711	413	Schleicher ASW20L	20388		29. 1.81	D.Hoolahan	Challock	9. 6.02
EJA	2712		ICA IS-28B	288		16. 1.81	DRA GC	RAF Odiham	15.12.00
EJB	2713	EJB	Slingsby T.65C Sport Vega	1945		23. 1.81	I.G.Walker & Ptnrs	Camphill	15. 4.02
EJC	2714	EJC	Slingsby T.65C Sport Vega	1946		9. 2.81	A M.Raper & Ptnrs	Rattlesden	27. 5.02
EJD	2715	261	Slingsby T.65D Vega 17L	1930		29. 6.81	A.J.French	Rufforth	28. 5.97*
							(Damaged Dunstable 28.3.97: wreck noted 5.99)		
EJE	2716	EJE	Slingsby T.65C Sport Vega	1947		16. 2.81	DRA GC	RAF Odiham	21. 5.01

EJF	2717	EJF	Schleicher K8B	8966	D-2328	15. 1.81	Cambridge University GC	Gransden Lodge	24.11.02
EJG	2718		Schleicher K8B	01	D-5679	30. 1.81	Kent GC	Challock	28. 2.99
EJH	2719	EJH	Eichelsdorfer SB-5E	5041A	D-5430	14. 1.81	H.J.McEvaddy	Husbands Bosworth	11. 6.01
					D-0087				
EJJ	2720	EJJ	Slingsby T.21B	618	RAFGSA.120	1. 3.81	N.P.Marriott	Parham Park	13. 4.02
					BGA.662/WB957				
EJK	2721	76	Centrair ASW20FLP	20172		15. 4.81	A.M.Blackburn	Camphill	4. 5.01
							(Crashed Camphill 21.7.00)		
EJL	2722	904	Centrair ASW20FL	20183		27. 4.81	S.R.Jarvis	Bidford	3. 5.02
EJP	2725		Slingsby T.21B	1131	RAFGSA.238	5. 2.81	Upward Bound Trust	Thame	29. 6.96*
					BGA.846		*(To Zimbabwe 1997)*		
EJQ	2726	EJQ	Centrair ASW20FL	20184		20. 4.81	G.Falcke & Ptnrs	Gransden Lodge	26. 1.02
EJR	2727	193	Schleicher ASW19B	19334		12. 4.81	Bristol & Glos GC	Nympsfield	6. 9.01
EJS	2728	319	Slingsby T.65C Sport Vega	1948		20. 3.81	A.D.McLeman	Portmoak	9. 9.02
EJT	2729	890	Slingsby T.65A Vega	1889	G-VEGA	5. 3.81	W.A.Sanderson	Rattlesden	8. 2.02
					(G-BFZN)				
EJW	2732		Issoire D77 Iris	04		30. 4.81	T.Hurley	Husbands Bosworth	27. 2.95*
EJY	2734	EJY	SZD-9 bis Bocian 1D	P-351	D-1587	13. 4.81	The Borders GC	Milfield	1. 9.02
EKA	2736	EKA	Glaser-Dirks DG-200/17			3. 8.81	M J Lindsey	Tibenham	19. 5.02
				2-128/1730					
EKB	2737	710	Schempp-Hirth HS.6 Janus C	129		16. 4.81	D.A.Head	Bicester	21. 2.99
							(Reported damaged RAF Halton 1.3.98)		
EKC	2738	EKC	Schleicher Ka6E	4079	OO-ZDV	18. 6.81	S L Benn	RAF Cranwell	22. 3.02
					OE-0813				
EKD	2739	EKD	Schleicher ASK13	13539	OH-494	21. 4.81	Devon & Somerset GC	North Hill	21. 2.02
							(Crashed at North Hill 23.6.01)		
EKE	2740	20L	Schleicher ASW20L	20387		15. 4.81	A.G.Mackenzie	Ringmer	3. 5.02
EKF	2741	EKF	Grob G.102 Club Astir III	5519C		14. 6.81	Bristol & Glos GC	Nympsfield	9. 3.02
EKG	2742	EKG	Schleicher ASK21	21067	AGA.8	11.99	Wyvern GC	AAC Upavon	1.12.01
					BGA.2742				
EKH	2743	714	Schempp-Hirth Ventus B	32		1. 5.81	R Bottomley	Lasham	11. 3.02
EKJ	2744	186	Schempp-Hirth Ventus B	36		7. 5.81	I.J.Metcalfe	Nympsfield	6. 6.02
EKK	2745	EKK	SZD-48 Jantar Standard 2	W-853		9. 5.81	S.Nutley	Portmoak	31. 8.02
EKM	2747	EKM	Schleicher K8B	647	PH-258	28. 5.81	Not known	Aston Down	
							(Wreck stored 8.01)		
EKP	2749	EKP	Glaser-Dirks DG-100G Elan	E71G46		3.10.81	P.J.Masson	Lasham	13. 5.01
EKR	2751	117	Schempp-Hirth HS.5 Nimbus 2C	195	D-4904	25. 6.81	J.W.Evans	Bidford	9. 2.02
EKS	2752	EKS	Scheibe SF-27A Zugvogel V	6096	D-8166	28. 4.81	A.B.Pemberton	Parham Park	14. 3.02
EKT	2753		Wassmer WA30 Bijave	241	F-CDML	11. 5.81	D.C.Austin	Dishforth	1.10.02
EKU	2754	408	Schleicher ASW20L	20384		19. 5.81	A.Gilson	Sleap	5. 1.03
EKV	2755	EKV	Rolladen-Schneider LS-4	4102		12. 7.81	M.Ray	Lasham	15.11.02
EKW	2756	430	Schempp-Hirth HS.5 Nimbus 2B	111	D-7245	7. 6.81	R.S.Jobar	Lasham	14. 5.02
EKX	2757	D1221	Schleicher Ka6E	4027	D-1221	20. 6.81	A.Coatsworth	Gallows Hill	10. 8.02
EKY	2758	EKY	Slingsby T.65C Sport Vega	1949		17. 6.81	Essex & Suffolk GC	Wormingford	23. 2.02
ELA	2760	ELA	Schleicher ASW19B	19346		28. 7.81	A.G.Stark	Portmoak 2.4.02	
ELC	2762	ELC	Slingsby T.45 Swallow	1474	AGA	25. 5.81	J.Povall	AAC Dishforth	19. 4.01
					RAFGSA.346				
ELD	2763	ELD	Slingsby T.65C Sport Vega	1950		17. 8.81	D.J Clark & Ptnrs	Challock	26. 1.02
ELE	2764	797	Schleicher ASK21	21065		1. 7.81	Midland GC	Long Mynd	23. 3.02
ELG	2766	ELG	Schempp-Hirth Ventus B	46		19. 8.81	H.Forshaw	Burn	31. 3.02
ELH	2767		Slingsby T.21B	?	RAFGSA.314	16. 9.81	Not known	Enstone	7.91*
			(Possibly ex WB966 [627])		(RAF)		*(Stored 3.97)*		
ELJ	2768	ELJ	Breguet Br.905SA Fauvette	21	F-CCGU	20. 8.81	E.A.Hull	Dunstable	3.12.01
ELK	2769		Slingsby T.9 King Kite rep.			8.83	D.G.Jones	Husbands Bosworth	26. 5.99
ELL	2770	L01	Vogt Lo-100 Zwergreiher	25	HB-591	27. 7.81	I.E.Tunstall	RAF Syerston	14. 5.01
ELN	2772	ELN	Grob G.102 Astir CS Jeans	2024	???	12. 8.81	J.M.Hughes	Dunstable	9. 3.02
ELQ	2774	ELQ	Slingsby T.65D Vega	1934		3. 9.81	J.Bell	Milfield	15. 9.02
ELR	2775	188	Schempp-Hirth Ventus B	45		19. 8.81	I.D.Smith	Nympsfield	7. 4.02
ELS	2776		EoN AP.10 460 Srs.1	EoN/S/020	RAFGGA.530	8.81	D.G.Shepherd	Easterton	6.11.02
ELT	2777	ELT	Rolladen-Schneider LS-4	4186		9.81	P.D.MaCarthy	Lasham	24. 3.02
ELU	2778	696	Schleicher ASW20L	20462		9.81	D.W.Lilburn	Aston Down	19. 3.02
ELV	2779	ELV	Scheibe Zugvogel IIIB	1088	F-CCPX	5. 9.81	C.R.W.Hill	Crowland	27. 4.02
ELX	2781		Schleicher Ka7 Rhonadler	928	D-4023	18. 9.81	Rattlesden GC	Rattlesden	6.00
ELY	2782	ELY	Schleicher Ka6CR	6485Si	D-5172	28. 9.81	P.F.Richardson & Ptnrs	Bellarena	11. 5.02
ELZ	2783	719	Schleicher ASW20L	20310		4.10.81	D.A.Fogden	Booker	16. 2.02
EMB	2785	L11	Rolladen-Schneider LS-4	4185		10.81	M.E.Lee	Winthorpe	11. 2.02
EME	2788	515	Glaser-Dirks DG-202/17C			11.81	E.D.Casagrande	Usk	2. 1.02
				2-176CL18					
EMF	2789	452	Rolladen-Schneider LS-4	4187		11.81	E.R.Smith & Ptnrs	Thruxton	16. 3.02
EMG	2790	EMG	Rolladen-Schneider LS-4	4242		8. 5.82	R C Bowsfield	Nympsfield	12. 2.02
EMH	2791		Schleicher ASK18	18009	D-6872	13.12.81	Staffordshire GC	Seighford	1.99*
			(Officially regd with c/n 18096)				*(W/O in mid-air collision Seighford 2.5.98)*		
EMJ	2792	EMJ	Slingsby T.65C Sport Vega	1951		1. 2.82	Staffordshire GC	Seighford	7. 6.02
EMK	2793		Slingsby T.45 Swallow	1514	RAFGGA.545	12.81	A.Povey & Ptnrs	RAF Syerston	5.00

EML	2794	218	Slingsby T.65A Vega	1892	G-BGCB	8.12.81	P.W.Williams	North Hill	28. 4.03
EMN	2796	EMN	Slingsby T.65D Vega	1935		25. 1.82	C.D.Sword & Ptnrs	Currock Hill	23. 7.02
EMP	2797		Slingsby T.65C Sport Vega	1952		2. 2.82	D.R Freehold	Kenley	25. 2.02
EMR	2799		Slingsby T.65C Sport Vega	1954		10. 2.82	P.Greenway & Ptnrs	Shobdon	15. 8.02
EMS	2800	T65	Slingsby T.65A Vega 17L	1890	G-BGBV	26. 1.82	M.P.Day	Kenley	12.10.02
EMT	2801	55	Rolladen-Schneider LS-4	4243		12.81	D.B.Eastell	Challock	7. 2.02
EMU	2802	606	Glaser-Dirks DG-202/17			1.82	P.B.Gray & Ptnrs	Camphill	17. 4.02
				2-162/1753					
EMV	2803	EMV	Schleicher Ka7 Rhonadler	?	AGA.13	1. 1.82	Shalbourne Soaring Group	Rivar Hill	20. 6.02
					BGA.2803				
EMW	2804	17	Grunau Baby III	?	D-1373	5. 7.89	M.T.A.Sands	(France)	27. 9.99
EMY	2806	264	Rolladen-Schneider LS-4	4189		15. 4.82	N.V.Parry	Nympsfield	6. 3.02
EMZ	2807	EMZ	Slingsby T.65A Vega	1891	G-BGCA	5. 2.82	F.S.Smith	Portmoak	6. 3.02
ENA	2808	288	Rolladen-Schneider LS-4	4191		31. 5.82	J.D.Collins & Ptnr	Bidford	3. 4.02
ENC	2810	ENC	Schleicher Ka7 Rhonadler	384	D-8111	2. 3.82	I.H.Keyser	Waldershare Park	23. 4.02
			(Modified to ASK13 status)						
ENE	2812	281	Rolladen-Schneider LS-4	4271		1. 6.82	D.M.Abbey	Husbands Bosworth	25. 2.02
ENG	2814	ENG	Focke-Wulf Kranich III	9	D-5420	8. 3.82	P.R.Davie & Ptnrs	Dunstable	5. 5.01
ENJ	2816	771	Schempp-Hirth Ventus B	62		25. 3.82	S.J.Boyden	Lasham	17. 6.00
ENK	2817	ENK	Schleicher ASK21	21106		12. 4.82	H Jakeman	Aston Down	25 .2.02
ENN	2820	345	Schempp-Hirth Nimbus 3	9		5. 4.83	R.Kalin & Ptnrs	Gransden Lodge	1. 1.03
ENP	2821	626	Schempp-Hirth Nimbus 3	10		12.11.82	L.Bleaken	Aston Down	15. 6.02
ENT	2825	902	Glasflugel H.304	210		13. 5.82	P.D.Light	Dunstable	8. 4.02
ENU	2826	435	Glaser-Dirks DG-100G Elan			8. 8.82	R.D.Platt	Camphill	4. 5.02
				E108G78					
ENV	2827	181	Schleicher ASW20L	20554		27. 5.82	R.D.Hone	Booker	7. 7.02
ENW	2828	ENW	Schleicher ASW20L	20567		28. 5.82	A.Hunter	Pocklington	12. 3.02
ENY	2830	ENY	Schleicher ASK13	13606	RAFGSA.R17	22. 7.82	Aquila GC	Hinton-in-the-Hedges	2. 5.02
ENZ	2831		Schleicher ASW19B	19366		29. 6.82	O.Pugh	Booker	27. 4.00
EPD	2835	EPD	Schleicher ASK21	21119		29. 8.82	J.E.Ashcroft	Chipping	5. 4.02
EPE	2836	EPE	Schleicher ASW19B	19335	RAFGSA.R18	29. 6.82	J.Horner	Pocklington	27. 4.02
					BGA.2836				
EPF	2837	323	Centrair ASW20FLP	20515		1. 7.82	D.J.Howse	Gransden Lodge	13. 6.01
EPG	2838		CARMAM M.100S Mesange	3	F-CCPB	7.82	P.Shanahan	Templeton	24. 2.95*
EPJ	2840		Nord 2000 (Olympia)	10399/69	F-CACX	8.82	B.V.Smith	Sutton Bank	1. 5.02
EPK	2841	742	Centrair 101A Pegase	101-012		16. 1.83	742 Syndicate	Bicester	14. 3.02
EPM	2843	EPM	Scheibe SFH-34 Delphin	5115		22.10.82	Angus GC	Drumshade	2. 6.02
EPN	2844		Breguet Br.905SA Fauvette	11	F-CCIO	18. 7.82	P.F.Woodcock	Camphill	31. 7.95*
EPP	2845	EPP	Schleicher ASK13	1609		28.12.82	Black Mountains GC	Talgarth	6. 7.02
			(Rebuild of PH-368 c/n 13064: c/n is spare fuselage no.)						
EPR	2847		Hutter H-17	-	(Kenya)	30. 9.82	D.Shrimpton	Halesland	29. 6.97
					PH-269				
EPS	2848	765	Schleicher ASW20L	20245	RAFGSA.87	5. 7.85	D.Richardson	Booker	30. 4.98
EPT	2849	EPT	Schleicher K8B	?	RAFGGA.504	14. 9.82	Trent Valley GC	Kirton-in-Lindsey	18.10.01
EPU	2850		Glaser-Dirks DG-100G Elan		(BGA.2833)	31.10.82	J.F.Rogers	Booker	20. 4.02
				E116G85					
EPV	2851	EPV	Schleicher Ka7 Rhonadler	7148	D-5468	8.10.82	Surrey Hills GC	Kenley	24. 6.02
EPW	2852	EPW	Schleicher Ka6CR	6537	(Kenya)	21. 3.83	J.Kitchen	Strubby	16. 2.02
EPX	2853	906	Schempp-Hirth Ventus B/16.6	107		20.10.82	W.T.Craig	Saltby	8. 4.02
EPZ	2855		Scheibe Bergfalke II/55	370	D-4012	15. 1.83	G.W.Sturgess	Upavon	11. 8.96*
							(Being refurbished 2000)		
EQA	2856	275	Rolladen-Schneider LS-4	4259		24. 6.83	R.L.Smith	Booker	4. 3.02
EQB	2857		SZD-30 Pirat	S-0648	D-2702	31.10.82	R.Firman	Booker	19. 6.02
EQD	2859	EQD	Grob G.102 Astir CS77	1614	PH-570	14. 1.83	D.S.Fenton & Ptnrs	Rhigos	20. 4.02
EQE	2860	EQE	Schleicher ASK13	13627		14. 4.83	Essex GC	Ridgewell	17. 2.02
EQF	2861		Schleicher ASK13	13626		8. 3.85	Essex GC	Ridgewell	28. 8.01
EQG	2862	239	Schleicher ASW19B	19265	PH-665	16.12.82	C.M.Whittington & Ptnrs	Challock	27. 4.02
EQJ	2864	968	Centrair ASW20FL	20512		21. 1.83	R.Grey	Lasham	25. 3.02
EQK	2865	EQK	Centrair 101A Pegase	101-054		30. 5.83	F.G.Irving & Ptnrs	Lasham	9. 3.02
EQL	2866		Avialsa (Rocheteau) CRA-60 Fauconnet		F-CDNR	18. 1.86	J.James	Saltby	30. 6.01
				03K					
EQM	2867		CARMAM M.100S Mesange	81	F-CDKQ	20. 3.83	R.Boyd	Rivar Hill	29. 6.02
EQN	2868	340	Schempp-Hirth Nimbus 3	31		21. 2.83	A.D.Purnell	Lasham	28. 1.02
EQQ	2870	451	Schleicher Ka6CR	6541	AGA.24	6. 3.83	G.H.Costin & Ptnrs	Challock	22. 2.02
					BGA.1353				
EQR	2871	EQR	Schleicher ASK21	21157		25. 4.83	London GC	Dunstable	7.11.02
EQT	2873	R58	Grob G.103A Twin II Acro		RAFGSA.R58	15. 4.83	R.Tyrell	Bidford	28.10.02
				3787-K-65	BGA.2873				
EQU	2874	EQU	Pilatus B4 PC-11	201	PH-535	2. 4.83	P.I.Punt	Chipping	31. 3.02
EQV	2875		Schempp-Hirth Janus C	169	ZD974	8. 3.83	Burn GC	Burn	3. 2.02
					BGA.2875				
EQW	2876	383	Schempp-Hirth Janus C	171	ZD975	24. 4.83	J.N.Mills	Lasham	14. 4.02
					BGA.2876				
EQX	2877	EQX	CARMAM M.200 Foehn	54	F-CDKR	11.4.83	C.A.McLay & Ptnrs	Chipping	23. 4.02

EQY 2878	BAC.VII rep	01		8. 9.91	M.H.Maufe	Sutton Bank	21. 5.96P*
	(Rebuild of BAC Drone using wings of G-AEJR & new fuselage; being refurbished)						
EQZ 2879 EQZ	Schleicher K8B	8113A	D-8763	13. 4.83	Cotswold GC	Aston Down	3. 5.02
ERA 2880 283	Centrair ASW20FL	20526		4.83	C.C.Pike	Booker	12. 4.02
ERB 2881	Slingsby T.50 Skylark 4 Special (*Built C.Almack*)	001		25. 4.83	B.V.Smith	Sutton Bank	15. 5.02
ERH 2887 ERH	Schleicher ASK21	21147	ZD647 BGA.2887	28. 4.83	Burn GC	Burn	11. 4.02
ERJ 2888 R35	Schleicher ASK21	21148	RAFGSA.R35 ZD648/BGA.2888	28.4.83	Cranwell GC	RAF Cranwell	2. 2.02
ERP 2893 SH5	Schleicher ASW-19B	19348	ZD657 BGA.2893	28. 4.83	Surrey & Hants GC	Lasham	18. 1.02
ERQ 2894	Schleicher ASW-19B	19381	ZD658 BGA.2894	28. 4.83	G.Lane	Riseley	7. 3.02
ERS 2896 ERS	Schleicher ASW-19B	19383	ZD660 BGA.2896	28. 4.83	J.C.Marshall	Kingston Deverill	15. 1.02
ERU 2898 ERU	Schempp-Hirth Nimbus 3	13	RAFGSA.R26 D-6330	4. 5.83	L.Urbani	Rieti, Italy	30. 6.02
ERV 2899 854	Rolladen-Schneider LS-4	4257		19. 5.83	R E Francis	Nympsfield	1.11.02
ERW 2900	Slingsby T.21B	1130	RAFGSA.237 BGA.842	24. 5.83	High Moor GC "*The Spruce Goose*"	Hafotty Bennett	10.11.02
ERX 2901 180	Centrair 101A Pegase	101-058		3. 8.83	C.N.Harder	Lasham	23. 4.02
ERY 2902 983	Slingsby T.59D Kestrel 19	1839	EI-125 D-9253	14. 6.83	R.J.Hart & Ptnr	Crowland	31. 3.02
ERZ 2903	Oberlerchner Mg19a Steinadler	015	OE-0324	1. 6.83	C.Wills	Booker	4. 5.02
ESA 2904 ESA	SZD-9 bis Bocian 1E	P-750		21. 6.83	The Soaring Centre	Husbands Bosworth	27. 9.02
ESB 2905 ESB	Schleicher ASK21	21176		2. 9.83	A.L.Garfield	Dunstable	2. 3.02
ESC 2906 379	Rolladen-Schneider LS-4	4261		25. 6.83	J.M.Staley	Bicester	21. 8.02
ESD 2907 640	Centrair 101A Pegase	101-065		2. 7.83	R.I.Cowderoy	Lasham	4. 3.97*
	(Destroyed in mid-air collision with SNC-34C Alliance F-CIHA, La Motte du Caire, France, 23.8.96)						
ESE 2908 LS4	Rolladen-Schneider LS-4	4260		26. 6.83	P.C.Fritche	Parham Park	21.12.01
ESH 2911 118	Centrair 101A Pegase	101-069		2. 7.83	D.M.Byass	Booker	3. 2.02
ESJ 2912 ESJ	Schleicher K8B	8730	D-5010	13. 7.83	Bowland Forest GC	Chipping	12. 1.03
ESK 2913	Schleicher Ka2B	697	RAFGGA.594 D-5947	23. 7.83	W.R.Williams	RAF Halton	20. 5.00
ESM 2915 ESM	Breguet Br.905SA Fauvette	30	F-CCJA	14.10.83	A C Jarvis	Parham Park	26.10.02
ESP 2917 ESP	SZD-48-3 Jantar Standard 3	B-1294		19. 4.84	J.Durman	Pocklington	18. 3.02
ESQ 2918 231	Glaser-Dirks DG-300 Elan	3E10		4.84	G.R.Brown	Sandhill Farm Shrivenham	24. 6.02
ESU 2922 ESU	Schleicher ASK21 (*Composite with RAFGSA.R28 c/n 21154*)	21180	RAFGSA.R40 BGA.2922	12.11.83	Aquila GC	Hinton-in-the-Hedges	22. 5.02
ESV 2923	LET L-13 Blanik	173328	EI-110 G-ATWW	22. 5.84	Herefordshire GC *(Noted as wreck 8.99)*	Shobdon	17. 4.98
ESW 2924 590	Centrair 101A Pegase	101-068		20. 3.84	D.A.Brown	Usk	23. 1.02
ESX 2925 ESX	Schleicher K8B	8805	RAFGGA.553	10. 9.83	Wolds GC *(W/o Pocklington 2. 2.96 ; stored 7.01)*	Aston Down	13.12.96*
ESY 2926 ESY	Rolladen-Schneider LS-4	4334		4. 2.84	K.Jenkins & Ptnrs	North Hill	7. 3.02
ETA 2928 ETA	Schleicher ASK21	21181		19.11.83	R W Collings	Husbands Bosworth	5. 7.02
ETB 2929 ETB	Schleicher Ka6E	4365	HB-1021	20.11.83	A.J.Padgett	Tibenham	18. 5.01
ETD 2931 R44	Schleicher K8B	8918	RAFGSA.R44 BGA2931	30.12.83	RAFGSA Centre	RAF Keevil	5.12.02
ETE 2932	Fauvel AV.36C	214	RAFGSA.R53 D-5353/D-8259	25. 8.87	J.F.Beringer "The Budgie"	Wormingford	7. 6.98
ETG 2934 ETG	Rolladen-Schneider LS-4	4349		7. 2.84	M.W.Rebbeck & Ptnrs	Rattlesden	23. 5.02
ETH 2935 ETH	Schleicher K8B	120	D-5755	23. 3.84	North Wales GC	Llantisilio	3. 8.02
ETJ 2936 223	Centrair 101A Pegase	101A-0110		8. 8.84	K.J.Bye	Wormingford	6. 2.02
ETK 2937 215	SZD-48 Jantar Standard 2	W-876	OY-XJO	14. 2.84	J.A.Cowie	Portmoak 3.6.02	
ETL 2938	Jansson BJ-1B Duster	01		1.85	I.Beckett	North Hill	28. 3.96*
ETM 2939 312	Centrair 101 Pegase	101-111		11. 4.84	Booker GC	Booker	24. 6.02
ETN 2940	CARMAM M.100S Mesange	23	F-CCSL	24. 2.84	T.E.Betts	Seighford	27. 8.96*
ETP 2941 WB943	Slingsby T.21B	610	WB943	7.84	P.Hepworth t/a Ouse T.21 Syndicate	Rufforth	4. 7.02
ETQ 2942	Centrair 101A Pegase	101A-0123		11. 5.84	A R Jennings *(Crashed Great Saxham, Norfolk, 19.8.98)*	Gransden Lodge	4.99
ETR 2943 S7	Schleicher Ka7 Rhonadler	3	D-8339	21. 2.84	Shenington GC	Edgehill	26. 3.02
ETS 2944	Schleicher ASK13	13635AB		3. 3.84	Upward Bound Trust	Thame	11.11.02
ETU 2946 ETU	Schleicher Ka7 Rhonadler	?	RAFGSA R.8	24. 3.84	R.Cullum	Strubby	26. 3.01
ETV 2947 ETV	Rolladen-Schneider LS-4	4314	(BGA.2919)	23. 3.84	T.A.Meaker	Kirton-in-Lindsey	27. 6.02
ETY 2950 249	Rolladen-Schneider LS-4	4368		16. 4.84	R.Harris	Booker	3. 1.02
ETZ 2951 20	Schleicher ASW20CL	20730		20. 3.84	N.L.Clowes	Lasham	30. 3.02
EUC 2954 EUC	Schleicher ASK13	13104	AGA.12	15. 4.84	Bristol & Glos GC	Nympsfield	1. 3.02
EUD 2955 56	Schleicher ASW20C	20734		3. 6.84	J.E.Gilbert	Lasham	25. 2.02

EUE 2956 EUE	Scheibe SF-27A Zugvogel V	6106	D-5342	6. 4.84	Newark & Notts GC	Winthorpe	18. 3.02
EUF 2957	SZD-50-3 Puchacz	B-1090		30. 5.84	D.B.Meeks t/a Bidford Gliding Centre	Bidford	31. 3.00
EUG 2958	LET L-13 Blanik	025817	RAFGSA.R56 RAFGSA.426/BGA.1953	14. 5.84	Avon Soaring Centre *(Wreck stored 8.94)*	Bidford	31. 5.93*
	(Composite rebuild - fuselage/tail: BGA.1917 [025610], port [025817] & starboard wings (BGA.2028 [026257])						
EUH 2959 446	Rolladen-Schneider LS-4	4382		14. 4.84	A.Turner Nympsfield	23.4.02	
EUJ 2960 210	Schempp-Hirth Ventus B/16.6	162		9. 4.84	T.Paterson & Ptnrs	Portmoak	5. 3.02
EUK 2961 992	Centrair ASW20FL	20530		20. 5.84	J.L.Caton	Lasham	6. 3.02
EUM 2963	Scheibe SF-26A Standard	5039	RAFGSA	20. 4.84	Vale of Neath GC	Rhigos	14. 7.97*
EUN 2964	Slingsby T.21B	588	RAFGSA.R92 RAFGSA.212/WB925	20. 4.84	Booker GC	Booker	28. 5.02
EUQ 2966 EUQ	Schleicher Ka7 Rhonadler	863	D-4639	8. 5.84	Kent GC	Challock	24. 4.02
EUS 2968 443	Schempp-Hirth Ventus B/16.6	192		19. 5.84	J.C.Bastin	Rivar Hill	11. 4.02
EUT 2969	Schleicher Rhonlerche *(Both p/is need confirmation)*	?	RAFGSA.R89 D-1789	4. 5.84	G.DeOrfe & Ptnrs	Gransden Lodge	30.11.99
EUV 2971	SZD-42-2 Jantar 2BB-	934		29. 5.84	G.V.McKirdy	Edgehill	9. 5.98
EUX 2973 EUX	Schleicher ASK18	18005	D-3988	28. 5.84	Southdown GC	Parham Park	7.11.02
EUY 2974 88	Schleicher ASW20BL	20645		8. 6.84	D.G.Roberts & Ptnrs	Aston Down	24.11.02
EUZ 2975	Slingsby T.21B	620	WB959	24. 6.84	Dartmoor Gliding Association	Brent Tor	13. 9.00
EVA 2976	Slingsby T.31B	683	WT873	1. 9.84	T.Bull *(To G-BZLK 8.00 - <u>see SECTION 1</u>)*	Parham Park	15. 6.99
EVB 2977 EVB	Schleicher Ka7 Rhonadler	7004	D-5109	12. 6.84	R.Armitage t/a Channel GC	Waldershare Park	19. 1.02
EVC 2978 EVC	CARMAM M.200 Foehn	55	F-CDKT	20. 6.84	W.Young & Ptnrs	Pocklington	11. 6.02
EVD 2979 382	Rolladen-Schneider LS-3	3024	N63LS D-7914	11. 8.84	C.R.Appleyard	Lasham	6. 4.02
EVE 2980 491	Centrair 101A Pegase	101A-0141		19. 6.84	B.M.Chaplin	Lasham	12. 4.02
EVF 2981 90	Schempp-Hirth Nimbus 3T	15/76	D-KHIJ	19. 3.85	R.A.Foot & Ptnrs	Lasham	3. 4.02
EVG 2982 EVG	Schleicher Ka7 Rhonadler	396	D-0018	17. 7.84	Derby & Lancs GC	Camphill	13.12.01
EVH 2983 EVH	Schleicher Ka10	10008	HB-791	26. 5.86	J.W Bolt	Brent Tor	20. 7.02
EVJ 2984 H	Schleicher ASK13	13637AB		14. 7.84	Lasham Gliding Society	Lasham	5.12.01
EVK 2985 EVK	Grob G.102 Astir CS	1397	PH-546	20.12.86	Peterborough & Spalding GC	Crowland	22.12.02
EVL 2986 SA1	Grob G.102 Astir CS77	1638	PH-575	26. 7.84	Southdown Aero Service	Lasham	26. 7.02
EVM 2987 N51	Centrair 101A Pegase	101A-0157		17. 8.84	Culdrose GC	RNAS Culdrose	14. 3.02
EVP 2989 K	Schleicher ASK13	13638AB		23. 8.84	Lasham Gliding Society	Lasham	17. 1.02
EVQ 2990 682	Centrair 101A Pegase	101A-0149		19. 8.84	R.J.Dann & Ptnr	Rivar Hill	8. 6.02
EVR 2991 EVR	LET L-13 Blanik	172604	G-ASVS OK-3840	30. 8.84	D.Latimer	Hinton-in-the-Hedges	6. 9.02
EVS 2992	SZD-50-3 Puchacz	B-1091		6. 9.84	Connel GC	North Connel	25. 5.02
EVT 2993 EVT	Scheibe Bergfalke IV	5807	D-0730	24. 9.84	J.Selman	(Limerick)	18.11.01
EVU 2994	Raab Doppelraab *(Built Wolf Hirth 1952)*	515	RAFGSA.666 D-5223	R	Not known *(Frame stored 9.94)*	Bicester	*
EVV 2995 EVV	Schleicher ASK23	23004		21.11.84	Midland GC	Long Mynd	4. 2.02
EVW 2996 EVW	Schleicher ASK23	23006		4. 1.85	London GC	Dunstable	25.10.02
EVX 2997 EVX	Schleicher ASK23	23007		7. 1.85	London GC	Dunstable	29. 3.02
EVY 2998 EVY	Schleicher ASK23	23008		31. 1.85	London GC	Dunstable	9.10.02
EWP 3013	Grob G.103A Twin II Acro	33892-K-130	ZE523 BGA.3013	3.11.84	Cambridge University GC	Gransden Lodge	19. 4.02
EWR 3015 R70	Grob G.103A Twin II Acro	33894-K-132	RAFGSA.R70 ZE525/BGA.3015	9.11.84	Anglia GC	RAF Wattisham	27. 4.02
EYS 3064 R71	Grob G.103A Twin II Acro	33961-K-194	RAFGSA.R71 ZE612/BGA.3064	3.99	Fenland GC	RAF Marham	6. 3.02
EZE 3076	Grob G.103A Twin II Acro	33981-K-214	ZE634 BGA.3076	3. 5.85	Oxford GC	Weston-on-the-Green	25. 1.00
FAF 3101 271	Schleicher ASW20	20214	RAFGSA.271 RAFGSA.R27	5.10.84	M.S.Armstrong	Gallows Hill	14. 6.02
FAJ 3103 FAJ	Glaser-Dirks DG-300 Elan	3E50		3.10.84	B.A.Brown	Lyveden	9. 4.02
FAK 3104 FAK	Avialsa A.60 Fauconnet	104K	F-CDFG	12. 5.85	I.D.Gumbrell	Kingston Deverill	9. 5.01
FAM 3106 J15	Schempp-Hirth Nimbus 3/24.5	79		16. 3.85	I.M.Stromberg	Camphill	18. 5.02
FAN 3107 202	Centrair 101A Pegase	101A-0161		25.10.84	M Heslop	Parham Park	18. 2.02
FAP 3108	Monnett Monerai	123		1. 5.87	D.B Rich	Eaglescott	29. 5.99
FAQ 3109 646	Rolladen-Schneider LS-4	4465		9. 3.85	C.H.Meir	Camphill	24.11.02
FAR 3110 FAR	Glasflugel H.205 Club Libelle	58	HB-1262	5. 6.85	G.A.Gair	Kenley	27. 4.02
FAT 3112 FAT	Schleicher ASK13	13528	PH-456	22. 1.85	Dorset GC	Gallows Hill	17. 2.02
FAV 3114 FAV	ICA IS-32A	05		27.12.84	Black Mountains GC	Talgarth	21. 4.02
FAW 3115 333	Schempp-Hirth Ventus B/16.6	26	D-6768	23. 3.85	P.Stafford-Allen	Crowland	5. 1.02
FAZ 3118 FAZ	Schleicher K8B	8558	D-1043	2. 3.85	Southdown GC "Katie" *(Crashed Parham 19.7.00)*	Parham Park	3. 3.01
FBA 3119 178	Schleicher ASW20BL	20665		23. 1.85	R.W.Prestwich	Sleap	3.12.02
FBB 3120 822	Schempp-Hirth HS.4 Standard Cirrus	327G	RAFGGA.312	1.85	M.Andrewartha	Bidford	16. 1.02

FBC	3121	FBC	Schleicher ASW15B	15356	OH-439	19. 5.85	C.Knock	Sandhill Farm	
								Shrivenham	20. 4.02
FBD	3122		Schleicher ASW15B	15407	OH-445	19. 5.85	R.Pettifer & C.A.McLay	Chipping	8. 9.02
FBE	3123	1	Rolladen-Schneider LS-6	6028	D-9384	2. 6.85	T.J.Wills	New Zealand/Booker	3. 8.02
FBF	3124	175	Glaser-Dirks DG-300 Elan	3E9	BGA.2952	16. 1.85	A.L.Garfield	Dunstable	21. 3.02
FBG	3125		SZD-50-3 Puchacz	B-1081		14. 2.85	Not known	NK	27. 3.90*
					(Wrecked in gales Booker 25.1.90; stored Rivar Hill 5.94: removed by 5.99)				
FBH	3126	177	Glaser-Dirks DG-100G Elan			1. 4.85	IBM (S.Hants) GC	Lasham	24. 4.02
				E156G123					
FBJ	3127	FBJ	Schleicher K8B	8221	D-6340	18. 2.85	Bidford GC	Bidford	28. 5.02
FBL	3129		Schleicher Ka2B Rhonschwalbe	373	HB-606	17. 2.85	J.D.Melling	Andreas	2. 5.96*
FBM	3130	727	Schempp-Hirth Nimbus 3/24.5	73		28. 2.85	D.K.Gardiner	Portmoak	14. 6.02
FBN	3131	FBN	Glasflugel H.303 Mosquito B	167	D-6364	1. 5.85	D.R Andrews & Ptnrs	Sleap	10. 2.02
FBQ	3133	464	Schleicher ASW20BL	20669		16. 4.85	D.W.Gosden	Usk	23. 2.02
FBR	3134	773	Grob G.102 Astir CS77	1701	SE-TSV	5. 3.89	G.Smith & Ptnrs	Pocklington	9. 4.02
FBT	3136	488	Schempp-Hirth Ventus BT	218/35		12. 3.85	S.M.Young	Easterton	11.10.02
FBV	3138	FBV	Schleicher ASK21	21223		2. 5.85	London GC	Dunstable	29. 3.02
FBW	3139	395	Glaser-Dirks DG-101G Elan			11. 4.85	Surrey & Hants GC	Lasham	19.11.02
				E174G140					
FBY	3141	780	Schempp-Hirth Discus B	20		12. 4.85	D Latimer	Dunstable	11. 8.02
FBZ	3142	D4667	Schleicher Ka6CR	6016	D-4667	12. 5.85	R.Martin & Ptnrs	Booker	16. 2.02
					D-KIMN/D-4667				
FCB	3144	FCB	Centrair 101 Pegase	101-0178	F-CGEA	15. 4.85	N.Stratton	Portmoak	2. 1.03
FCC	3145	XN243	Slingsby T.31B	1182	XN243	6. 5.85	D.A.Head & Ptnrs	Bicester	6. 7.02
FCD	3146	841	Centrair 101A Pegase B	101A-0207		1. 5.85	G.K.Drury	Challock	16. 3.02
FCF	3148	993	Slingsby T.21B	MHL.017	WB990	12. 5.85	N.Worrell	Lasham	13. 2.02
FCG	3149	WT871	Slingsby T.31B	681	WT871	5.85	J.Desmond	RAF Marham	11. 1.99
FCH	3150	FCH	CARMAM M.100S Mesange	72	F-CDKD	29. 5.85	P A Pickering	Upwood	29. 1.02
FCJ	3151	571	Grob G.102 Astir CS	1231	D-4205	19. 5.85	M.Levitt & G.Fellows	Aston Down	5. 2.02
FCK	3152	671	Schempp-Hirth Ventus B/16.6	241		6. 5.85	L.J.Scott	Llantisilio	24. 5.02
FCL	3153		Schleicher K8B	8045E	D-5225	20. 5.85	M.Jackson	Challock	20. 4.98
							(Reported damaged Lasham 14.2.98)		
FCM	3154	411	Glaser-Dirks DG-300 Elan	3E94		17. 5.85	R.B.Coote	Parham Park	8.12.02
FCN	3155	920	Schempp-Hirth HS.4 Standard Cirrus	131		18. 6.85	P.Burniss & Syndicate	Nympsfield	2. 3.01
				131G	D-0191				
FCP	3156	721	Rolladen-Schneider LS-6	6030		2. 7.85	E.W.Johnston	Aston Down	6. 3.02
FCQ	3157		Schleicher K8B	1	RAFGGA..	27. 4.85	M.W.Meagher	Edgehill	28. 3.98
			(Built Bayer)		D-8322 or D-0322?				
FCR	3158	113	Schleicher Ka6E	4223	OH-375	10. 6.85	R.F.Whitaker & Ptnrs	Lasham	24. 2.02
					OH-REC				
FCS	3159	2R	Schempp-Hirth HS.5 Nimbus 2C		D-5993	7. 7.85	R.W.Hawkins	Parham Park	10. 5.02
				233/81					
FCT	3160	FCT	Slingsby T.21B	611	WB944	16.12.86	A.Dyer	Haddenham/Thame	2. 6.01
FCV	3162		Schleicher ASW20	20076	RAFGSA.R24	7. 6.85	M.J.Davis & Ptnrs	RAF Cosford	17. 4.02
FCW	3163	L	Schleicher ASK13	13642AB		27. 6.85	Lasham Gliding Society	Lasham	14.12.02
FCX	3164		Schleicher ASK23	23011		7. 7.85	Midland GC	Long Mynd	29. 1.98*
							(Damaged Long Mynd 26.7.97 & w/o)		
FCY	3165	FCY	Schleicher ASW15	15122	D-0748	29. 6.85	M.D.Evershed & Ptnrs	Dunstable	26. 2.01
FCZ	3166		Slingsby T.1 Falcon 1 rep	-		7.85	D.D.Knight & J.Harber	RAF Halton	N/E(P)
			(Built Southdown Aero Services)						
FDA	3167	7D	Schleicher ASW15	15050	D-0511	2. 7.85	N W Woodward	Booker	2. 3.02
FDB	3168		ICA IS-30	07		23. 9.85	Black Mountains GC	Talgarth	19. 6.00
FDC	3169	FDC	CARMAM JP-15/34 Kit Club			10. 3.87	T.A.Hollins	Rufforth	6. 8.02
				TAH.50/60					
FDD	3170	FDD	Schleicher K8B	8972	AGA.5	11. 7.85	Shalbourne Soaring Society	Rivar Hill	17. 2.02
FDE	3171	510	Schempp-Hirth Ventus BT	256/53		8.85	P.L.Roberts	Cross Hayes	17. 4.02
FDF	3172	FDF	Grob G.102 Astir CS	1321	D-7338	2. 9.85	R.H.Davies	Aston Down	10. 5.02
FDG	3173	FDG	ICA IS-29D2 Club	02		23. 8.85	D.Mole	Sackville Lodge	
								Riseley	1. 6.02
FDL	3177		Schleicher Ka8	Liz.105/58	D-4650	9. 9.85	G.F.Millar & Ptnrs	Cranfield	25.11.95*
FDP	3180	996	ICA IS-30	08		24. 5.86	C.H.Bolton	Llantisilio	14. 7.02
FDQ	3181		Slingsby T.31B	710	WT915	19. 9.85	J.F.J.M.Forster	RAF Bruggen	3. 8.01
							"Chris Wills"		
FDR	3182	FDR	Schleicher Ka6CR	6119	D-8456	18.11.85	P.Hill & R.J.Grayling	Burnford Common	26. 2.02
FDT	3184	W22	Schleicher ASW22	22025	D-7709	28.10.85	O.Riccius	(Switzerland)	13. 4.02
FDU	3185	H20	Schempp-Hirth Discus B	87		23. 5.86	J.L.Whiting	Long Mynd	1. 2.02
FDV	3186		LET L-13 Blanik	173333	D-5826	8. 4.86	T.Wiltshire	East Kirkby	4. 7.98
					D-KOEB/D-5826				
FDW	3187	FDW	Glaser-Dirks DG-300 Elan	3E143		26.1.86	N Kelly	Enstone	19. 6.02
FDX	3188	FDX	SZD-48-1 Jantar Standard 2		(BGA.2916)	22.12.85	A.P.Twort	Ringmer	4. 9.02
					B-1251				
FDY	3189		Slingsby T21B	MHL.005	WB978	26. 1.86	R.B.Armitage	Waldershare Park	15. 5.02
FEA	3191	FEA	Grob G.103 Twin Astir	3151	RAFGSA.R83	6.12.85	G.M.Brightman	Edgehill	11. 5.02
					RAFGSA 833				

FEB	3192	398	Grob G.102 Club Astir III	5643C		15.11.85	Surrey & Hants GC	Lasham	18. 1.02
FEE	3195		Slingsby T.21B	MHL.016	WB989	20. 1.86	K.Schickling	Aschaffenburg, Germany	28. 7.02
FEF	3196	FEF	Grob G.102 Astir CS	1164	OY-XGC	9. 2.86	Oxford University GC	Bicester	23. 3.02
FEG	3197	120	Schempp-Hirth Ventus B/16.6	279		12. 2.86	K.Moorhouse & Ptnr	Rivar Hill	10. 3.02
FEH	3198	318	Centrair 101A Pegase Club	101A-0268		1. 5.86	Booker GC	Booker	10. 2.02
					(Rebuilt with new fuselage c/n 01304: original fuselage rebuilt as BGA.3560)				
FEJ	3199	538	Schempp-Hirth Discus B	76		22. 2.86	D.Geddes	Lasham	25. 1.02
FEL	3201	FEL	Schleicher Ka7 Rhonadler	7231	RAFGGA..	22. 9.86	Burn GC	Burn	23. 5.02
			(See BGA.3231)		D-???				
FEN	3203	FEN	SZD-50-3 Puchacz	B-1326		24. 3.86	Northumbria GC	Currock Hill	25. 5.02
FEP	3204	209	Schempp-Hirth Ventus BT	284/69		1. 4.86	R.J.Nicholls	Husbands Bosworth	9. 5.02
FEQ	3205	M	Schleicher ASK13	13650AB		7. 4.86	Lasham Gliding Society	Lasham	18. 1.02
FER	3206	FER/370	Schempp-Hirth Discus B	75		27. 3.86	D.R.Campbell & Ptnr	Booker	3. 4.02
FES	3207	564	Schempp-Hirth Discus B	88		4. 4.86	N.G.Storer	Lasham	2. 2.02
FEW	3209	499	Schleicher ASW22	22030	D-8888	12. 4.86	D.P.Taylor	Sutton Bank	24. 5.01
							(Crashed, Sierra de Guadarrama, Spain, 4.8.00)		
FEX	3210	ZS-GFZ	Glasflugel H.301B Libelle	100	ZS-GFZ	5.86	T.J.Wills	(New Zealand)	29.10.02
FEX	3212	FEX	Grob G.102 Astir CS77	1660	D-7492	6. 4.86	J.Taylor	Upwood	19. 5.02
FEZ	3214	FEZ	EoN AP.7 Primary	EoN/P/037	RAFGSA.R13	19. 9.86	G.J.Moore	Dunstable	3. 6.01
					RAFGSA 113/WP269				
FFA	3215	FFA	Schleicher ASK13	13651AB		15. 5.86	Staffordshire GC	Seighford	13. 4.02
FFB	3216	R9	Grob G.102 Astir CS	1123	RAFGSA.R9	10. 6.86	RAF GSA Centre	Bicester	7. 3.02
					RAFGSA.R97/BGA.3216/D-6977				
FFC	3217	FFC	Centrair 101A Pegase	101A-0255		30. 5.86	C.A Hitchin	Kingston Deverill	20. 6.02
FFG	3221	WB920	Slingsby T.21B	559	WB920	2. 6.86	J.H.Wisselink	Roosendaal The Netherlands	8. 6.02
FFH	3222	FFH	Schleicher ASW20	20037	D-7947	4. 4.87	J.Hayes	AAC Dishforth	4. 7.02
FFJ	3223	623	Grob G.103A Twin II Acro	34075-K-305		6. 6.86	Derby & Lancs GC	Camphill	24.11.99
							(Mid-air collision Camphill, 31.5.99)		
FFK	3224	7	Schempp-Hirth Nimbus 3	87		11. 4.87	Dr.Brennig-James	Booker	11. 4.02
FFL	3225	FFL	Slingsby T.21B	MHL.020	WB993	28. 6.87	J.P.Visser	Zwolle, The Netherlands	23. 5.02
FFM	3226		Grob G.102 Club Astir IIIb	5609CB	PH-730	15. 7.86	Imperial College GC	Lasham	3.99
							(Cancelled 21.10.99 - exported as PH-730)		
FFN	3227	987	ICA IS-29D	21	D-9223	13. 8.86	A.Sutton & Ptnrs	Snitterfield	11. 6.00
FFP	3228	93	Schleicher ASW19B	19317	RAFGSA.R19	12. 6.86	K.A.Ford	Lasham	2. 3.02
FFQ	3229		Slingsby T.31B	913	XE800	18. 8.86	I.F.Smith	Lasham	26. 9.99
FFS	3231	FFS	Centrair 101A Pegase	101A-0265		27. 6.86	W Murray	Gransden Lodge	18. 2.02
							(Carries BGA.3201)		
FFT	3232		Schempp-Hirth Discus B	110		30. 6.86	R.Maskell & Ptnrs	Ridgewell	6. 4.02
FFU	3233	FFU	Glaser-Dirks DG-100G Elan	E200G166		11. 1.87	S.Robinson	Chipping	3. 3.02
FFV	3234		SZD-51-1 Junior	B-1616	F-WGJA	26. 8.86	Herefordshire GC	Shobdon	28.11.02
FFW	3235		Slingsby T21B	1155	XN151	2.10.87	S.C.Luck	Cranfield	25. 6.00
							(Sold in Germany during 2000)		
FFX	3236	627	Schempp-Hirth Discus B	109		12. 7.86	P.J.Tiller	Crowland	26. 4.02
FFY	3237	FFY	SZD-51-1 Junior	W-938		24.11.86	Cornish GC	Perranporth	1. 5.02
FFZ	3238		Slingsby T.21B	MHL.008	WB981	21. 8.86	M.Lake	Aston Down	5. 6.95*
							(Wfu: wings to BGA.1218 1995; fuselage stored 8.98: as "WB981")		
FGA	3239	WT913	Slingsby T.31B	708	WT913	26.10.86	J.M.Brookes & Ptnrs	Strubby	21. 7.96*
							(Being refurbished)		
FGB	3240		Slingsby T.21B	654	WJ306	23. 8.86	Oxford GC	Weston-on-the-Green	10. 7.02
FGC	3241		Slingsby T.31B	713	WT918	24. 8.86	E.Woefeel	(Jena, Germany)	7. 4.02
FGF	3244	110	Schempp-Hirth Nimbus 3T	25/91		16. 8.86	R.E.Cross	Lasham	2. 5.02
FGG	3245	WG498	Slingsby T.21B	665	WG498	29. 9.86	G.A.Ford & Ptnrs	Aston Down	23. 7.01
FGJ	3247	FGJ	Schleicher Ka6CR	6634	D-1041	22. 9.86	JCB Syndicate	Lleweni Parc	24. 9.02
FGK	3248	FGK	Grob G.102 Astir CS	1323	RAFGSA.R61	9.86	E.Sparrow	Rivar Hill	13. 3.02
					RAFGSA.316				
FGM	3250	FGM	Slingsby T.21B	1160	XN156	19. 7.87	R.B.Petrie	Strathaven	14. 9.01
			(Modified with 330cc engine)						
FGP	3252	FGP	Schleicher ASW19	19121	C-GJXG	1.11.86	C.I.Sullivan	Gransden Lodge	30. 4.02
FGR	3254	N29	Schleicher ASK13	13655AB		24.10.86	Portsmouth Naval GC	Lee-on-Solent	10. 4.02
			(Built Jubi)						
FGS	3255	XN157	Slingsby T.21B	1161	XN157	11.10.86	D.W.Cole & Ptnrs	Long Mynd	30. 7.95*
			(Fuselage No.SSK/FF/1745)						
FGT	3256	FGT	Glaser-Dirks DG-300 Elan	3E217		6. 3.87	S.C.Williams	Booker	18.10.02
FGU	3257	806	Schempp-Hirth HS.4 Standard Cirrus	147	D-0193	27. 4.87	L.E.Ingram	Snitterfield	9. 3.02
FGV	3258	FGV	Schleicher Ka7 Rhonadler	?	OO-Z..	15.12.86	Nene Valley GC	Upwood	14. 4.02
			(Hybrid using ex Belgian Ka7 fuselage & wings from Ka2 BGA.2662)						
FGW	3259	701	Centrair 101A Pegase	101A-0275		23. 6.87	L.P.Smith	Nympsfield	7 .2.02
FGY	3261	527	Schleicher ASW22	22027	D-3527	3.12.86	M.J.Bird	Dunstable	4 .5.02
FGZ	3262	D2	Schleicher Ka7 Rhonadler	7238	D-5376	17. 1.87	Dartmoor GC	Brent Tor	9.10.99

FHB	3264		Slingsby T.21B(T)	MHL.018	WB991	17. 2.87	G.Traves	East Kirkby	7. 8.02
			(Fuji-Robin EC-34PM)						
FHC	3265		Slingsby T.21B	MHL.013	WB986	7. 6.87	G.Traves	East Kirkby	5. 7.97
FHD	3266	196	Schleicher ASW20BL	20694	RAFGGA...	15. 2.87	K.J.Hartley	Bicester	14. 6.02
FHE	3267		Scheibe L-Spatz III	817	LX-CLM	3.87	C.W.Matten & Ptnrs	RNAS Culdrose	23. 3.98
FHF	3268		SZD-51-1 Junior	W-952		20. 3.87	Black Mountains GC	Talgarth	15. 4.02
FHG	3269	187	Schempp-Hirth HS.7 Mini Nimbus C	140	(BGA.3213) ZS-GNI	22. 3.87	R.W.Weaver	Usk	14. 2.02
FHJ	3271	987	Centrair 101A Pegase	101A-0278		13. 5.87	Booker GC	Booker	15. 2.02
FHK	3272	FHK	Slingsby T.31B	695	WT900	22. 4.87	N.A.Scully & Ptnrs *"Tweety"*	Saltby	9. 6.01
FHL	3273	136	Rolladen-Schneider LS-4	4633		17. 4.87	I.P.Hicks	Cranfield	
FHM	3274	P	Schleicher ASK13	13662AB		7. 6.87	Lasham Gliding Society	Lasham	14. 5.02
FHN	3275	FHN	Schleicher K8B	?	RAFGSA.R85 RAFGSA.385/RAFGSA.360	5. 6.87	B.F.Cracknell	Crowland	14. 4.02
FHQ	3277		Hols-der-Teufel Replica			6.87	M.L.Beach	Brooklands	N/E
			(Built M.L.Beach)				*(Sold to Germany in 1998)*		
FHR	3278	Q5	Schempp-Hirth Discus B	152		8. 6.87	P.Tratt & Syndicate	Parham Park	19.12.02
FHS	3279	154	Schempp-Hirth Ventus CT	326/82		11. 6.87	R.Andrews	Long Mynd	16. 7.02
FHT	3280	FHT	Grob G.102 Astir CS	1234	D-4208	12. 6.87	A.C.Howells	Rattlesden	16. 3.02
FHU	3281	FHU	Schleicher Ka7 Rhonadler	629	RAFGSA.R15	17. 6.87	Dartmoor GC	Brent Tor	27. 6.02
			(Modified to ASK13 standard)		RAFGGA/D-5722				
FHV	3282	FHV	SZD-48-1 Jantar Standard 2	B-1036	D-4516	25. 6.87	R.A.Williams & Ptnrs	Long Mynd	14. 4.02
FHW	3283	698	Grob G.102 Astir CS	1087	D-6987	30. 6.87	P.R.J.Halliday	Lasham	25. 2.02
FHY	3285	H5	Scheibe SF-27A Zugvogel V	6045	D-1868	28. 6.87	J.M.Pursey	North Hill	3.10.02
FHZ	3286	FHZ	Schleicher Ka6CR	949	D-4661	20. 8.87	J.Hiley	Husbands Bosworth	16. 4.02
FJA	3287	FJA	Slingsby T.21B	1152	XN148	8. 7.87	M.Steiner	Sembach, Germany	12. 5.02
FJB	3288	FJB	Slingsby T.21B	MHL.002	WB975	8. 7.87	Angus GC	Drumshade	2. 5.02
FJD	3290	FJD	Slingsby T.21B	MHL.007	WB980	29. 8.87	R.H.Short & Ptnrs	Lyveden	10.12.02
FJE	3291	744	Schleicher ASW20BL	20953		1. 8.87	B.Pridal	Booker	4.12.02
FJF	3292	FJF	Slingsby T.21B	586	WB923	7. 9.87	R.L.Hill	Snitterfield	29. 3.02
			(Frame No.SSK/FF 1085)						
FJH	3294	FJH	Grob G.102 Astir CS77	1763	AGA.7	11. 7.87	Shalborne Soaring Society	Rivar Hill	15. 2.02
FJJ	3295	134	Schempp-Hirth Ventus BT	344.93		20. 8.87	A.D.Purnell	Lasham	13. 1.02
FJK	3296	FJK	Centrair 101A Pegase	101-070	N4429W	30. 4.88	D.J.Ingledew	Lee on Solent	11. 5 02
FJM	3298	143	Rolladen-Schneider LS-4A	4665	D-1431	4.12.87	G.C.Beardsley & Ptnr	Dunstable	28. 1.02
FJN	3299	903	Slingsby T.31B	698	WT903	17. 2.88	R.R.Beazer	Husbands Bosworth	27. 3.02
FJQ	3301	FJQ	Schempp-Hirth Ventus CT	104/365		24. 3.88	B.Rood	Hinton-in-the-Hedges	16. 8.00
FJR	3302	950	Glaser-Dirks DG-300 Club Elan	3E270C2		12. 2.88	G Smith	(France)	13. 3.02
FJS	3303	257	Glaser-Dirks DG-300 Club Elan	3E271C3		28. 5.88	Yorkshire GC	Sutton Bank	2. 1.02
FJT	3304	997	Centrair 101A Pegase	101A-0284		20. 2.88	D.M.Smith & A.Marlow	Booker	28. 5.02
FJU	3305	FJT	Schleicher K8B	976	OH-240 OH-RTC	1.11.87	Northumbria GC	Currock Hill	24. 6.02
FJV	3306	713	Schleicher ASW15	15109	D-0710	3.11.87	G.N.Turner & Ptnr	Sandhill Farm, Shrivenham	14. 5.01
FJW	3307	FJW	Schleicher Ka7	980	OH-241 OH-KKF	15.11.88	A.J.Pettitt & Syndicate	Rivar Hill	12. 8.02
FJX	3308	728	Glaser-Dirks DG-300 Elan	3E261		6. 2.88	D.S Jones	North Hill	22. 7.02
FJZ	3310	FJZ	Schempp-Hirth SHK	14	D-9330	2. 4.88	R H.Hanna & A.& R.Willis	Bellarena	14.12.02
FKA	3311	FKA	Schleicher Ka6CR	6239	D-7037 D-5435	21. 2.88	S.T.Dry & B.Davies	Kingston Deverill	23. 6.01
FKB	3312	FKB	Glaser-Dirks DG-600	6-08		10.88	J.A.Watt	Dunstable	29. 1.02
FKE	3315	G2	Schleicher ASW15	15146	D-0794	6. 3.88	D.G.Lloyd & Syndicate	Bidford	7. 2.02
FKG	3317	125	Rolladen-Schneider LS-4A	4673		18. 5.88	B.A.Pocock	Kingston Deverill	13. 5.02
FKH	3318	FKH	Schleicher Ka6CR	6343	EI-109 IGA.106	3.88	F.McGuigan	Bellarena	11. 7.02
FKJ	3319	FKJ	Schleicher K8B	8032	OH-264 OH-RTE	4. 4.88	Aquila GC	Hinton-in-the Hedges	5. 7.02
FKK	3320	406	Schempp-Hirth Discus B	219		12. 3.88	D.J.Eade	Lasham	25. 1.02
FKL	3321	152	Schleicher ASW20BL	20954		21. 3.88	J.M.Ley & J.Rollason	Ridgewell	20. 5.02
FKM	3322	399	Schempp-Hirth Discus B	212		19. 3.88	Surrey & Hants GC	Lasham	4.10.01
FKN	3323	13	Schleicher ASH25	25042	(BGA.3491) BGA.3323	19. 7.88	M Bird	Dunstable	13. 4.02
FKP	3324	WB971	Slingsby T.21B	632	WB971	28. 2.88	M.Powell	Tibenham	25. 4.01
FKQ	3325	FKQ	Scheibe SFH-34 Delphin	5119	D-1412	22. 4.88	Bristol & Glos GC	Nympsfield	30. 3.01
FKT	3328	FKT	Schleicher K8B	8382	D-5366	8. 5.88	P.Willock	Shobdon	19. 5.02
FKU	3329	FKY	Schleicher Ka6CR	822	D-0025	6. 4.88	J.A.Timmis	Camphill	23. 6.02
FKV	3330		CARMAM M.100S Mesange	60	F-CDDV	3. 5.88	G.G Hunt	Bidford	29. 7.97*
FKW	3331	FKW	Schleicher Ka7 Rhonadler	7145	OH-302 OH-KKJ	2. 4.88	Welland GC	Lyveden	20. 5.02
FKX	3332	FKX	Schleicher Ka6CR	6433	D-4316	30. 4.88	D Bowtell & Ptnrs	Lasham	30. 4.02
FLB	3336		Slingsby T.31B	837	XA295	23 .8.88	Not Known	*(Stored 2000)*	
FLC	3337	368	Glaser-Dirks DG-300 Elan	3E310		26. 9.88	A.R.Milne	Gallows Hill	26. 2.02

FLE	3339	314	Schempp-Hirth Discus B	207		7. 5.88	Booker GC	Booker	8. 2.02
FLF	3340	Z4	Rolladen-Schneider LS-4A	4694		20. 3.88	D.E.Lamb	Booker	18. 3.02
FLG	3341	A25	Schleicher ASH25E (Turbo)	25044		6.88	D.S.McKay	Enstone	27. 4.02
FLH	3342	FLH	Schleicher K8B *(Built KK Lehtovaara O/Y)*	22	OH-361 OH-RTW	12. 5.88	Aquila GC	Hinton-in-the-Hedges	16. 6.02
FLK	3344		Schleicher Ka7 Rhonadler	985	D-5047	12. 1.89	Dukeries GC	Gamston	30. 3.02
FLL	3345		SZD-9 bis Bocian 1D	F-877	OH-336 OH-KBP	30. 7.88	R.G.Wardell-Yerburgh	Kingston Deverill	4. 2.02
FLP	3348	FLN	Schleicher K8B *(Built KK Lehtovaara O/Y)*	07	OH-316 OH-RTP	7. 5.88	Bath, Wilts & North Dorset GC	Kingston Deverill	4. 5.02
FLQ	3349	FLQ	Schleicher K8B	8195A	D-8887	15. 8.88	F.J.Glanville	Long Mynd	27. 3.02
FLS	3351	FLS	Schleicher Ka6CR	6180	D-4001	16.11.88	P.B.Arms	RAF Halton	27. 6.02
FLT	3352		Glasflugel H.201B Standard Libelle	41	D-0211	11.12.88	C.Glover	Husbands Bosworth	20. 8.00
FLU	3353	DJ2	Glasflugel H.201B Standard Libelle	52	D-0298	22. 6.88	C.D.Duthy-James	Talgarth	26. 5.02
FLV	3354	3354	LET L-13 Blanik	173312	D-1335	30. 7.88	North Devon GC *"Jenny"*	Eaglescott	10. 5.96*
FLW	3355	127	Schempp-Hirth HS.4 Standard Cirrus 75	656	F-CEMT	3. 7.88	J.R.Taylor	Perranporth	17.12.02
FLX	3356		Glaser-Dirks DG-300 Club Elan	3E304C19		19.10.88	S.R.Walker	Rufforth	30. 3.01
FLY	3357	B21	Schleicher ASW24	24012		7.88	I.J.Lewis *(De-registered 6.8.01, sold in the USA)*	North Weald	4.01
FLZ	3358	FLZ	Scheibe SF-27A Zugvogel V	6061	D-5378	14. 7.88	R Russon	Long Mynd	15. 4.02
FMA	3359		Slingsby T.38 Grasshopper	793	WZ797	8. 8.88	Not known *(On rebuild 8.98)*	Edgehill	7. 8.89
FMC	3361	68	Rolladen-Schneider LS-6B	6184		27. 7.88	B.L.Cooper	Booker	2. 2.02
FMD	3362	FMD	Schleicher Ka7 Rhonadler	343	D-2877 HB-603	23. 7.88	Not known *(Damaged Ringmer 6.5.92: stored at Aston Down 8.01)*	Aston Down	1.12.92*
FME	3363	927	Schleicher ASW15	15164	D-0825	1. 8.88	T.J.Stanley	Rufforth	9. 2.02
FMG	3365	969	Schempp-Hirth Discus B	242		3. 8.88	J.Melvin	Nympsfield	29. 3.02
FMH	3366	B	Schleicher ASK13	13673AB		22. 8.88	Lasham Gliding Society	Lasham	21. 2.02
FMK	3368	FMK	Centrair 101 Pegase *(Model 101B?)*	101-0293		20. 1.90	A.Bailey	Bidford	25. 3.02
FML	3369	FML	Schleicher ASW15B	15294	F-CEGR	21.11.89	A.D.Duke & Ptnrs	Nympsfield	17. 5.02
FMM	3370	FMM	Schleicher Ka6CR	6328	D-1260	20.10.88	K.E Hebdon	Gamston	3. 8.02
FMN	3371	CKF	Schempp-Hirth Ventus CT	123/397		12. 9.88	S.C.Kovac	Lasham	4. 3.02
FMP	3372	328	Schleicher ASW24	24023		21. 1.89	D.S.Pitman	Booker	28.2.02
FMQ	3373	158	Schempp-Hirth Discus B	243		1.10.88	A.L Harris	Nympsfield	3. 4.02
FMR	3374	FMR	Neukom Standard Elfe	S-2 05	HB-801	8.11.88	M.Powell & Ptnrs	Camphill	9. 5.02
FMS	3375	519	Schleicher ASW15	15061	N111SP	11.88	A.J.Pettit	Lasham	27. 3.02
FMT	3376	FMT	Schempp-Hirth HS.4 Standard Cirrus	249	N2HM	10.89	S.R.Westlake	Nympsfield	22. 6.02
FMU	3377		Schempp-Hirth HS.4 Standard Cirrus	236	N3LB	14. 7.90	S.A Manktelow	Aston Down	25. 2.02
FMW	3379	XA229	Slingsby T.38 Grasshopper	862	XA229	R	NTU (Stored)	Burn	
FMX	3380	FMX	Schleicher ASW24	24014		5. 3.90	D.T.Reilly	North Hill	21. 3.02
FMY	3381	371	Rolladen-Schneider LS-77	004	D-1256	18.12.88	M.Newman	Camphill	28. 6.02
FMZ	3382	FMZ	Schleicher Ka7 Rhonadler	7018	D-6035	22.11.88	Nene Valley GC	Upwood	27. 4.02
FNA	3383	FNA	Schleicher K8B	8499	D-5670	13.11.88	Bowland Forest GC	Chipping	4. 5.02
FNC	3385		Slingsby T.21B	601	WB934	5.11.88	P.Hoffmann	(The Netherlands)	8. 6.02
FND	3386	FND	Schleicher Ka6E	4069	PH-366	14.11.88	J.M.Smith	North Hill	30. 3.00
FNE	3387	FNE	SZD-38A Jantar-1	B-612	HB-1215	20.12.88	D.A Salmon & Ptnrs	Camphill	15. 6.02
FNF	3388	461	Schleicher ASW22B	22053		20.12.88	T.J.Parker	Dunstable	31. 1.02
FNG	3389	104	Schleicher ASW24	24015		10. 5.89	P.H.Pickett	Snitterfield	27. 1.02
FNH	3390	A19	Schleicher ASW19	19174	D-7969	9. 2.89	P.W.Roberts	Lasham	25. 1.02
FNK	3392	FNK	Slingsby T.65A Vega	1897	N9023H	10.12.88	A.P.Brown	Kenley	28. 4.02
FNL	3393	705	Schempp-Hirth Discus B	253		28.11.88	P.A.Holland	Kirton-in-Lindsey	1. 4.02
FNM	3394	FNM	Centrair 101B Pegase	101B-0289	F-CGSE	30. 3.89	R.Harrison	Sleap	20. 2.02
FNN	3395	109	Schempp-Hirth Ventus CT	130/407		8.12.88	C.A.Marren	Aston Down	20. 1.03
FNP	3396	FNP	Schleicher Ka6CR	567	D-4657	16. 1.89	Notts University GC	RAF Syerston	21. 6.02
FNQ	3397	282	Schempp-Hirth Discus B	259		18.12.88	P.J.Hart	Tibenham	4. 1.03
FNR	3398	130	Schempp-Hirth Discus B	255		20. 3.89	R.Lemin	Nympsfield	11 .2.02
FNS	3399		Glaser-Dirks DG-300 Club Elan	3E314C23		2. 4.89	P.E.Williams	Portmoak	6 .6.02
FNT	3400	674	Glaser-Dirks DG-600	6-12		12.88	D.M.Hayes	Rufforth	9. 4.02
FNU	3401	190	Rolladen-Schneider LS-4A	4732	D-1376	9. 4.89	R J Simpson	Nympsfield	18 .2.02
FNW	3403	FNW	Schleicher Ka6CR	598	HB-634	20. 3.89	Cotswold GC	Aston Down	17. 1.99
FNX	3404	FNX	Wassmer WA.30 Bijave	84	F-CCTJ	2. 1.89	The Borders GC	Milfield	12. 1.03
FPB	3408	FPB	Schleicher ASW15B	15243	D-2068	18.12.88	R C Tatlow	Winthorpe	10. 6.02
FPD	3410	973	Rolladen-Schneider LS-77	033	D-5178	14. 1.89	P.H.Rackham	Dunstable	27.11.02
FPE	3411	238	Schempp-Hirth Ventus CT	131/408		14. 1.89	P.Whitt & N.Francis	Shobdon	27. 3.02
FPF	3412	FPF	Scheibe L-Spatz 55	2720	RAFGGA...	11. 2.89	P.Saunders	Usk	18. 5.01
FPG	3413		Scheibe Bergfalke II/55	.	C-....	18. 1.89	Not known	*(Stored 2000)*	

FPH	3414	FPH	Centrair ASW 20F	20132	F-CFFX	29. 1.89	R.Gibson & Ptnrs	Bidford	23. 3.01
FPJ	3415	459	Schleicher ASW19	19001	D-1909	29. 1.89	F.W.Pinkerton	Lyveden	30. 4.01
FPK	3416	Y1	Glaser-Dirks DG-300 Elan	3E6	D-1233	21. 1.89	G.C.Keall & Ptnrs	Husbands Bosworth	4. 2.02
FPL	3417	242	Schempp-Hirth Ventus C	409		27. 1.89	R.V Barrett	Nympsfield	22. 3.02
FPM	3418	FPM	SZD-51-1 Junior	B-1788		6. 3.89	Kent GC	Challock	2. 1.02
FPN	3419	69	Schleicher ASW20	20376	RAFGGA.545	5. 3.89	E C Wright	RAF Syerston	5. 7.02
					D-8780				
FPP	3420	N2	Schempp-Hirth HS.5 Nimbus 2B	142	D-6779	26. 3.89	R.Jones	Walney Island	31. 3.02
					D-2111				
FPQ	3421	FPQ	Schleicher Ka7 Rhonadler		D-5184	15. 2.89	East Sussex GC	Ringmer	24. 9.01
				EB180/61					
FPT	3424	574	Schleicher ASW20	20007	D-7574	18. 2.89	L.Hornsey & Ptnrs	RAF Halton	27. 3.02
FPU	3425	FPU	Schleicher Ka2B Rhonschwalbe -		HB-698	17. 2.89	T.J.Wilkinson	Sackville Lodge	
			(Built Segelfluggruppe Zwingen)					Riseley	27. 3.02
FPV	3426	FPV	Schleicher Ka6E	4123	N29JG	10. 3.89	J.E.Stewart	Bembridge	13. 4.02
					G-AWTP				
FPW	3427	39	Glaser-Dirks DG-600	6-17		13. 4.89	W.S.Stephen	Aboyne	23. 2.02
FPX	3428		Schleicher ASK13	13325	F-CDYR	21. 6.89	M.Breen	Booker	1. 8.02
FQB	3432	FQB	Schleicher ASW15B	15340	D-2345	10. 8.89	P.Usborne	Dunstable	31.10.02
FQC	3433	201	Glaser-Dirks DG-202/17c		HB-1645	8. 3.89	A.T.MacDonald	Ridgewell	16. 2.02
				2-178CL19					
FQD	3434	FQD	Schleicher K8B	8289	D-1908	6. 3.89	Kent GC	Challock	9. 2.02
FQE	3435	FQE	Schleicher K8	3	D-6329	3. 4.89	Cotswold GC	Aston Down	9. 4.01
FQF	3436		Scheibe SF-27A Zugvogel V	6025	D-0009	19. 2.89	S.Maddox	Winthorpe	23. 3.02
FQG	3437	952	Rolladen-Schneider LS-7	7050	D-1712	4. 6.89	R.W.Spiller	Sutton Bank	9. 6.02
FQH	3438	A98	Rolladen-Schneider LS-7	7029	D-1316	15. 4.89	P.J.Lazenby	Rufforth	17. 4.02
FQK	3440	FQK	Grob G.103C Twin III Acro	34123		15. 8.89	P.O'Donald	Gransden Lodge	7. 3.02
FQL	3441	772	Schleicher Ka6CR	6235	HB-772	18. 3.89	C. & N.Worrell	Lasham	27. 1.02
FQM	3442	FQM	Scheibe SF-27A Zugvogel V	6098	D-9421	19. 2.89	R.D.Noon	Winthorpe	7. 4.02
FQN	3443	479	Schempp-Hirth Ventus B/16.6	141	D-8772	26. 3.89	R.Parsons & Ptnrs	Challock	9. 1.02
					D-KHIB	*(Composite rebuild of D-8772 - ex Ventus BT D-KHIB (10/141): w/o 27.5.85 & possibly HB-1626 (91) as 3443 holds Build plate V91)*			
FQQ	3445	656	Glaser-Dirks DG-600	6-11		3.89	M.B.Jefferyes & Ptnr	Ridgewell	2. 6.02
FQR	3446	B	Schleicher K8B	8537	PH-349	9. 3.89	Dorset GC	Gallows Hill	17. 2.02
FQT	3448	484	SZD-48-3 Jantar Standard 3		(BGA.3409)	28. 3.90	T H Greenwood	Sandhill Farm	
					B-1891			Shrivenham	16. 4.02
FQU	3449	FQU	Schleicher Ka7 Rhonadler	1139	D-8614	13. 3.89	J.E.Harber	RAF Halton	26. 4.02
					HB-709				
FQV	3450	P	CARMAM JP-15/36AR Aiglon	28	F-CETX	20. 3.89	K.H.Withey	Perranporth	11. 4.98
FQX	3452		Schleicher K8B	8037	D-5205	5. 4.89	Burn GC	Burn	6. 1.96*
FQY	3453	785	Schempp-Hirth Discus B	274		16. 4.89	P.Studer	Nympsfield	1. 4.02
FQZ	3454		Rolladen-Schneider LS-1F	391	F-CEKH	12. 6.89	G.P.Hibberd	Sleap	5. 7.01
FRA	3455	321	Rolladen-Schneider LS-6B	6151	D-8081	20. 4.89	M.Randle	Enstone	6. 2.02
FRB	3456	758	Schempp-Hirth Ventus C	404		4 .3.89	C.J.Ratcliffe	Cross Hayes	31. 3.02
FRC	3457	988	Schempp-Hirth HS.5 Nimbus 2B	151	D-4980	15. 5.89	C.F.Whitbread	Challock	20 .3.02
FRD	3458	JPB	Centrair 101A Pegase	101A-0311		15. 4.89	A.Kangars	Husbands Bosworth	31 .5.02
FRE	3459	FRE	Schleicher Ka6E	4349	F-CDTL	13. 4.89	D.J.Stewart	Parham Park	12 .6.02
FRF	3460	FRF	Schleicher Ka7 Rhonadler	450/58	D-5653	7. 4.89	P.Roberts & Co	Dunstable	6. 9.01
FRG	3461		Siebert Sie-3	3009	D-0739	7. 4.89	I.R.Taylor & Co	Cross Hayes	1. 5.02
FRH	3462	634	Schleicher ASW20CL	20740	D-9229	2. 4.89	J.N.Wilton & Ptnr	Husbands Bosworth	3. 6.02
FRJ	3463	FRJ	Schempp-Hirth HS.4 Standard Cirrus		HB-1041	23. 4.89	P.D.Oswald & Ptnrs	Portmoak	28. 2.02
				103					
FRK	3464	FRK	Schleicher ASW15B	15214	D-0941	21. 3.89	A.D.Smith	Booker	9.11.02
FRL	3465	609	Grob G.102 Astir CS	1373	D-7402	22. 4.89	South Wales GC	Usk	17. 6.02
FRM	3466		Scheibe SF-27A Zugvogel V	6040	D-3644	22. 4.89	Burn GC	Burn	14. 5.98
FRP	3468	995	Schempp-Hirth Nimbus 3/24.5	43	N697L	28. 7.89	T.R.Gardner & J.Mardon	Aston Down	9.10.95*
					D-2518				
FRQ	3469		Slingsby T.45 Swallow	1420	XT653	27. 4.89	D.Shrimpton	Halesland	8. 6.98
FRR	3470	495	Centrair 101A Pegase	101A-0034	(BGA.3451)	16. 4.89	P.A.Lewis	Walney Island	2. 5.02
					F-CFQA		*"Scoundrel"*		
FRS	3471	FRS	Scheibe Zugvogel IIIB	1097	D-2171	27. 4.89	S.W.Vallei	Rivar Hill	11. 6.02
					HB-749				
FRT	3472	S9	Schempp-Hirth Ventus CT	137/421		26. 4.89	S.Edwards	Dunstable	21. 3.02
FRV	3474	FRV	Centrair 101A Pegase	101A-0325		28.10.89	C.Colton	Gransden Lodge	7. 4.02
FRW	3475	268	Schleicher ASW20L	20202	D-5981	5. 5.89	D.Cooper	Booker	19. 4.02
FRX	3476	FRX	Centrair 101A Pegase	101A-0315		30. 5.89	BBC Gliding Group	Booker	15. 2.02
FRZ	3478	H6	Schempp-Hirth HS.4 Standard Cirrus		HB-1194	15. 5.89	N.A.Maclean	Lasham	11. 4.02
				348G	D-2172				
FSA	3479	498	Grob G.102 Astir CS	1277	D-7371	9. 4.89	J.Claxton	Dunstable	4. 5.02
FSC	3481		Slingsby T.38 Grasshopper	751	WZ755	27. 4.90	Not known	Gallows Hill	30. 4.93
							(Stored 5.98)		
FSD	3482	N28	Schleicher ASK13	13367	D-0863	24. 5.89	Portsmouth Naval GC	Lee-on-Solent	28. 3.02
FSE	3483		Schleicher Ka6CR	6021	D-1946	19. 8.89	G.W.Lobb	North Hill	15 .8.02
FSF	3484	FSF	Schleicher Ka2	120	D-1688	31. 5.89	B.T.Spreckley	Le Blanc, France	1.10.99

FSH	3486	FSH	Grob G.102 Astir CS Jeans	2090	D-7532	9. 5.89	Buckminster GC	Saltby	28.12.01
FSJ	3487	WT908	Slingsby T.31B	703	WT908	22. 5.89	R.J.Abraham	Dunstable	8. 1.99
FSL	3489	F11	Schempp-Hirth HS.7 Mini Nimbus	52	HB-1413	9. 6.89	S.C.Waddell	Booker	13. 3.02
FSP	3492		Slingsby T.21B	660	WB992	11. 6.89	*(To VH-GCV 12.93)*		
FSQ	3493		Schleicher ASK13	13596		13. 6.89	London GC	Dunstable	12. 1.99
			(Composite containing c/n plate from BGA.2405; crashed at Dunstable 9.7.98)						
FSR	3494	FSR	Glaser-Dirks DG-300 Elan	3E343		24. 8.89	E.J.Dent	Nympsfield	1.11.02
FSS	3495	FSS	Schleicher Ka6E	4019	D-5260	19. 8.89	C.Davies	Lasham	1. 7.02
FST	3496	FST	Schleicher ASH25E	25073	(BGA.3530) (BGA.3496)	12.10.89	K.H.Lloyd & Ptnrs	Aston Down	15. 4.02
FSU	3497	FSU/55	Scheibe Zugvogel IIIA	1060	D-9055	30. 6.89	P.W.Williams	Brent Tor	31. 5.02
FSV	3498	WZ819	Slingsby T.38 Grasshopper	800	WZ819	26. 6.89	P.D.Mann	RAF Halton	18. 6.02
FSX	3500	405	Glaser-Dirks DG-300 Elan	3E344		11. 7.89	C.Hyett	Lasham	11. 1.02
FSY	3501	162	Schleicher ASH25	25064	D-1578	14. 7.89	B.T.Spreckley	Le Blanc, France	14.10.02
FSZ	3502	FSZ	Grob G.102 Astir CS77	1841	D-2908	29. 7.89	D.Gardiner & Ptnr	Aston Down	25. 2.02
FTA	3503	FTA	Schleicher K8B	8702	D-0048	15. 7.89	Lincolnshire GC	Strubby	29. 3.97*
							(Crashed Strubby 1996)		
FTB	3504	FTB	Schleicher Ka6CR	019	D-8900	22. 7.89	P.J.Blair	Bidford	31. 3.02
			(Built Bitz)						
FTC	3505	N56	SZD-51-1 Junior	B-1860		23. 7.89	Culdrose GC	RNAS Culdrose	14. 3.02
FTD	3506	205	Schleicher ASW15B	15191	D-0872	23. 8.89	L.G.Callow	Dunstable	7. 4.02
FTF	3508	FTF	Schleicher Ka6CR	6294	D-6081	5. 9.89	A.Sparrow	Parham Park	25. 2.02
FTG	3509	FTG	Schleicher Ka7 Rhonadler	535	D-8321	18.10.89	Angus GC	Drumshade	26. 3.00
FTH	3510	FTH	SZD-50-3 Puchacz	B-1881		24. 8.89	Buckminster GC	Saltby	15. 4.02
FTJ	3511	FTI	SZD-48 Jantar Standard 2	W-889	HB-1472	25. 8.89	G.J.Burton & Ptnrs	Enstone	3. 4.02
FTK	3512	518	Grob G.102 Astir CS Jeans	2059	OE-5152	10.89	R.Lapsley	Bellarena	17. 5.02
FTL	3513	FTL	Schleicher ASW20CL	20751	D-3564	2. 9.89	J.S.Shaw	Dunstable	8. 3.02
FTM	3514		Schleicher K8B	513	D-5708	30. 8.89	West Wales GC	Usk	10. 8.02
FTN	3515	853	Schleicher K8B	996	D-8539 D-KAEL/D-8539	11. 3.89	Vale of The White Horse GC	Sandhill Farm Shrivenham	28. 4.02
FTP	3516	332	Schleicher ASW20CL	20733	D-3640	4. 1.90	A J Mainwaring	Dunstable	22. 3.02
FTQ	3517	FTQ	Centrair ASW20FL	20123	F-CFFR	12. 8.89	C.Wilby	Camphill	13.11.99
FTR	3518	FTR	Grob G.102 Astir CS77	1606	D-4807	6.10.89	Lakes GC	Walney Island	6. 1.02
FTS	3519	FTS	Glaser-Dirks DG-300 Club Elan	3E349C38		12.10.89	Southdown GC	Parham Park	20. 2.02
FTT	3520	WB926	Slingsby T.21B	589	WB926	14. 9.89	R.Acreman	Gallows Hill	7.01
							(De-registered 9.3.01 - sold in Switzerland as HB-1367)		
FTU	3521	FTU	Schleicher Ka7 Rhonadler	302	HB-599	25. 9.89	Dartmoor GS *"Fondue"*	Brent Tor	27. 6.02
FTV	3522	944	Rolladen-Schneider LS-7	7073		9.10.89	D.Hilton & S.White	Booker	10. 3.02
FTW	3523	230	Schempp-Hirth Discus B	292		4.10.89	N.H.Wall & Ptnrs	Nympsfield	23. 2.02
			(Rebuilt with new fuselage after accident 21.6.91; original fuselage rebuilt as BGA.3879)						
FTY	3525	753	Rolladen-Schneider LS-7	7075		8.10.89	A.M.Burgess	Easterton	19. 3.02
FUB	3528		Schleicher Ka6CR	6007	D-8573	6.11.89	D.E.Hooper	Brent Tor	23. 7.99
FUD	3529	2	SZD-9 bis Bocian 1E	P-689	SP-2807	2.11.89	Mendip GC	Halesland	3. 8.02
FUF	3531	FUF	Scheibe SF-27A Zugvogel V	6089	D-6068	30. 9.89	East Sussex GC	Ringmer	25. 5.02
FUG	3532	BB	Schleicher ASH25	25074	(BGA.3526)	20.10.89	J.P.Gorringe & D.S.Hill	Lasham	11. 2.02
FUH	3533	192	Schempp-Hirth Ventus C	438		12.10.89	M.A.Gale & Ptnrs	Gallows Hill	24. 3.02
FUJ	3534	FUJ	Glaser-Dirks DG-300 Elan	3E353		5.12.89	J.D.Cook & Ptnrs	Portmoak	25. 2.02
FUL	3535	803	Schempp-Hirth Discus B	293		14. 3.90	R.Banks	Dunstable	12.12.02
FUM	3536	FUM	Schleicher Ka6CR	808	D-6289	25. 3.90	A.C.Marvin	Rufforth	19. 5.01
FUN	3537	FUN	Schleicher ASW20CL	20813	D-3432	5. 4.91	W.H.Parker	Dunstable	23. 2.02
FUP	3538	397	Schempp-Hirth Discus B	291		18.10.89	Surrey & Hants GC	Lasham	20.12.02
FUQ	3539	FUQ	Scheibe SF-27A Zugvogel V	6090	D-5196	1. 4.90	G.Elliott & Ptnrs	Ringmer	2. 5.02
FUR	3540	256	Schempp-Hirth Ventus CT	145/446		15. 3.90	D.S.Towson	Shobdon	24. 3.02
FUS	3541	FUS	SZD-51-1 Junior	B-1912		20.11.89	Scottish Gliding Union Ltd	Portmoak	13. 4.02
FUT	3542	612	Glaser-Dirks DG-300 Club Elan	3E350C39		11. 3.90	A.Eltis	Gransden Lodge	14. 6.02
FUU	3543	FUU	Glaser-Dirks DG-300 Club Elan	3E360C45		4. 3.90	P.J.Dixon-Clarke	Lasham	8. 3.02
FUV	3544	194	Rolladen-Schneider LS-7	7068		4.11.89	E.Alston	Brent Tor	18.12.02
FUW	3545	XE807	Slingsby T.31B Cadet TX.3	920	XE807	20.11.89	D.Shrimpton	Halesland	19. 2.02
FUY	3546	FUY	SZD-50-3 Puchacz	B-1983		30.11.89	M.G.Ashton	Eaglescott	20. 5.02
FVA	3548	N15	Schleicher K8B	1051	D-5117	13. 4.90	Portsmouth Naval GC	Lee-on-Solent	27. 9.02
FVB	3549	228	Schempp-Hirth Ventus CT	144/445		13. 1.90	M.J.Sesemann	Challock	2. 5.02
FVC	3550	FVC	Schleicher ASK13	13682AB		11.12.89	Devon & Somerset GC	North Hill	28. 1.02
			(Built Jubi)						
FVD	3551	FVD	Scheibe Bergfalke IV	5806	D-0729	9.12.89	North Wales GC	Llantisilio	28. 4.01
FVE	3552	FVE	Rolladen-Schneider LS-4	4190	RAFGSA232 RAFGSA R30/D-4542	12. 1.90	R.J.Rebbeck	Edgehill	3. 6.02
FVF	3553	FVF	Schempp-Hirth HS.5 Nimbus 2C	202	D-2880	3. 3.90	L.C.Mitchell & J.Wood	Chipping	2. 4.02
FVG	3554	660	Glaser-Dirks DG-600	6-41		17.12.89	R.G.Tomlinson	Winthorpe	22. 4.02
FVH	3555	246	Rolladen-Schneider LS-7	7067	(BGA.3527)	18.12.89	B.R.Forrest & A.Hallum	Booker	3. 4.02
FVL	3558	FVL	Scheibe Zugvogel IIIB	1082	D-5224	29.12.89	F.Hunt	Kirton-in-Lindsey	10. 8.02

FVM	3559	369	Centrair 101A Pegase	101A-0345		15. 3.90	S.H.North	RNAS Yeovilton	10. 5.02
FVN	3560	FVN	Centrair 101A Pegase	101A-0268/2		16. 1.90	G.G.Butler	Snitterfield	9. 2.02
			(Rebuild of BGA.3198 and carries c/n 10100268)						
FVP	3561	FVP	Centrair 101A Pegase	101A-0350		22. 4.90	J.R.Parry & Ptnr	Long Mynd	12. 5.02
FVQ	3562	FVQ	Rolladen-Schneider LS-7	7079		18. 1.90	P.Harvey	Gransden Lodge	19. 4.02
FVS	3564	FVS	Schempp-Hirth HS.4 Standard Cirrus	359G	D-2168	25. 3.90	P.A Clark	Lasham	25. 2.02
FVT	3565	760	Schempp-Hirth HS.5 Nimbus 2	18	N795	17. 5.90	I.Dunkley	Camphill	29. 7.98
FVU	3566	FVU	Schleicher ASK13	13062	D-1348	17. 4.90	Edinburgh University GC	Portmoak	15. 6.02
FVV	3567	FVV	Centrair 101A Pegase	101A-0353		27. 4.90	Cambridge University GC	Gransden Lodge	19. 3.02
FVW	3568	FVW	Schempp-Hirth Ventus BT	252/51	D-KORN	26. 1.90	I.Champness	Lasham	13. 2.02
FVY	3570	FVY	Scheibe Zugvogel IIIA	1046	D-8323	21. 2.90	S.C.Ottner & Ptnrs	Rivar Hill	16. 5.99
FVZ	3571	PS	Schleicher Ka6E	4007	D-4104	27. 2.90	R.P.Filipkiewicz	Booker	14. 4.02
FWA	3572	FWA	Schleicher Ka6CR	6227	D-1062	26. 3.90	D.Cousins	Usk	3. 8.02
FWB	3573	FWB	Schleicher ASK13	13224	HB-989	2. 4.90	Cotswold GC	Aston Down	4.10.02
FWC	3574	45	Grob G.103C Twin III Acro	34154		5. 4.90	Lasham Gliding Society Ltd	Lasham	8.11.02
FWD	3575	888	Schempp-Hirth Ventus CT	148/468		10. 5.90	R.S.Maxwell-Fendt	Lasham	31. 3.02
FWE	3576		SZD-50-3 Puchacz	B-1984	(BGA.3547)	5. 2.90	Deeside GC	Aboyne	27. 2.02
FWF	3577	L57	Rolladen-Schneider LS-7	7097		28. 2.90	G.P.Hibberd	Sleap	19. 4.02
FWG	3578	FWG	Centrair 101A Pegase	101A-0252	PH-793	22. 2.90	Devon & Somerset GC	North Hill	16. 4.02
FWH	3579	FWH	Scheibe SF-27A Zugvogel V	6024	D-4733	10. 2.90	R.Sampson	Husbands Bosworth	16. 4.02
FWJ	3580	S3	Rolladen-Schneider LS-7WL	7078		22. 3.90	J.P.Popika	Gransden Lodge	7. 4.01
FWK	3581	29	Schempp-Hirth Nimbus 3DT	32		22. 3.90	J.D.Glossop	Gransden Lodge	19. 6.02
FWL	3582		Schleicher K8B	106/58	D-7151	24. 2.90	Dukeries GC	Gamston	13.10.02
FWM	3583	FWM	Glaser-Dirks DG-300 Club Elan	3E373C50		15. 6.90	N.Clements	Snitterfield	11. 3.02
FWN	3584	FWN	Schleicher ASK13	13285	HB-1023	20. 4.90	Booker GC	Booker	5. 4.02
FWP	3585	980	Schleicher ASW19B	19262	D-5980	4. 4.90	K.Harris & Ptnrs	Dunstable	17. 4.02
FWQ	3586	FWQ	Schleicher ASK21	21460		15. 5.90	Midland GC	Long Mynd	19.12.01
FWR	3587	277	Glasflugel H.303 Mosquito	34	N77RL	26. 3.90	S.J.Ferguson	Aston Down	27. 5.02
FWS	3588	662	Schleicher ASW20C	20765	D-6623	18. 2.90	P.C.Gill	North Weald	27. 3.02
FWT	3589	FWT	SZD-50-3 Puchacz	B-1988		24. 3.90	The Soaring Centre	Husbands Bosworth	11. 3.02
FWU	3590	768	Rolladen-Schneider LS-7	7080		19. 3.90	C.Brown	Husbands Bosworth	26. 4.02
FWW	3592	FWW	Schleicher ASH25E	25093		19. 6.90	A.T.Farmer	Weston-on-the-Green	4. 5.02
FWX	3593	B38	Centrair 101A Pegase	101A-033	F-CFRZ	27. 3.90	I.R.Stanley	Booker	22. 6.02
FWY	3594	FWY	Centrair 101A Pegase	101A-071	F-CFXE	23. 3.90	Cheeseman & Ptnrs	Lasham	17. 4.02
FWZ	3595	FWZ	Schleicher ASW19B	19342	D-2603	14. 4.90	C.Fowler	Camphill	16.12.02
FXA	3596	567	Grob G.102 Speed Astir IIB	4083	D-2671	16. 4.90	A.D.Duke	Nympsfield	25.10.02
FXB	3597		Schleicher K8B	8193/A	D-5597	29. 3.90	R.J.Morris	Brent Tor	15. 7.02
FXC	3598	FXC	Schleicher Ka6E	4268	D-0150	9. 8.90	B.Laverick-Smith	Challock	17. 8.02
FXD	3599	285	Centrair 101A Pegase	101A-0346	(BGA.3563)	31. 3.90	The Soaring Centre	Husbands Bosworth	29.10.02
FXE	3600	35	Rolladen-Schneider LS-7	7090		23. 3.90	J.C.Kingerlee	Weston-on-the-Green	28. 9.01
FXF	3601	FXF	Slingsby T.50 Skylark 4	1455	HB-812	7. 5.90	S.White	Booker	13. 5.02
FXG	3602	FXG	Schempp-Hirth HS.2 Cirrus	23	N1216	23. 8.90	G.F.King	Kingston Deverill	15. 2.00
						(Crashed North Hill 15.9.99; at Rufforth 5.01 for potential rebuild)			
FXH	3603		Schleicher Ka7 Rhonadler	353	D-4040	10. 4.90	Vale of Neath GC	Rhigos	19.12.00
FXJ	3604	247	Schleicher ASW24	24086		4. 5.90	A.K.Laylee	Booker	24. 5.02
FXL	3606	108	Schleicher ASH25	25088		11. 4.90	R.H.Blackmore	Husbands Bosworth	15.11.02
FXM	3607	173	Schempp-Hirth Discus BT	16/301	D-KHIA	12. 4.90	R.J.H.Fack	Shobdon	4. 7.02
FXN	3608	FXN	CARMAM M.200 Foehn	4	OO-ZNI	14. 4.90	I.C.Gutsell & Ptnrs	Burn	9. 9.01
					(OO-ZXS)/F-CCXS				
FXP	3609	FXP	LET L-23 Super Blanik	907609		17. 7.90	Dill Faulke Education Trust	Sutton Bank	28. 5.02
FXQ	3610	954	Schempp-Hirth Nimbus 3DT	31		21. 4.90	D.G.Tanner	Kingston Deverill	14. 3.02
							(See BGA.3658)		
FXR	3611	L12	LAK-12 Lietuva	6162		9.90	S R Blackmore	Enstone	7. 5.01
FXS	3612	FXS	Schleicher Ka6E	4228	D-0073	7. 5.90	R.Woodhouse & B.C.Wade	Tibenham	31. 5.02
FXT	3613		Centrair 101A Pegase	101A-0056	F-CFQV	4.90	K.Ludlow	Viterbo, Italy	4. 8.02
FXU	3614	FXU	Schleicher Ka6E	4071	OH-343	8. 6.90	M E Mann Syndicate	Lasham	9. 3.02
					OH-RSY				
FXW	3616	FXW	Schleicher K8B	8651	D-7203	5. 4.90	South Wales GC	Usk	23. 4.01
					D-KOLA/D-7203				
FXX	3617		Scheibe L-Spatz 55	756	D-3598	1. 9.91	P.Brown	Ridgewell	19. 6.00
FXY	3618	723	Schleicher ASW15B	15348	F-CEJL	21. 5.90	C.I.Willey	Dunstable	29.11.02
FYA	3620	FYA	SZD-50-3 Puchacz	B-2022		9. 5.90	Cairngorm GC	Feshiebridge	15. 4.02
FYB	3621	779	Rolladen-Schneider LS-7	7102		2. 5.90	J.T.Hitchcock	Sandhill Farm Shrivenham	8. 2.02
FYC	3622	A10	Schempp-Hirth Ventus B	83		2. 5.90	D.B.Meeks	Sutton Bank	13. 9.02
					F-CEDR/F-WEDR				
FYD	3623	942	Schleicher ASH25	25095		19. 5.90	C.C.Lyttleton	Challock	8. 2.02
FYE	3624	FYE	Scheibe Zugvogel IIIB	1067	OY-MHX	20. 5.90	R.J.Hawley	Brent Tor	4. 7.02
					SE-TCE/OY-EFX/D-1814				
FYF	3625	FYF	Schleicher ASK21	21470		4. 8.90	London GC	Dunstable	8. 2.02
FYG	3626	FYG	Glasflugel H.205 Club Libelle	22	OH-545	13. 5.90	I.H Shattock	Usk	25. 7.02
FYH	3627	224	Rolladen-Schneider LS-4A	4804		4. 7.90	G.W.Craig	Weston-on-the-Green	7. 8.02

FYJ	3628		Schempp-Hirth HS.4 Standard Cirrus	581G	D-8931	12. 7.90	T.D.Winn	Pocklington	15. 5.02
FYK	3629	34	Rolladen-Schneider LS-7	7108		1. 6.90	J.C.Ferguson	Portmoak	25. 2.02
FYL	3630		SZD-50-3 Puchacz	B-1990		6.90	Deeside GC	Aboyne	29. 5.02
FYM	3631	326	Schempp-Hirth Discus BT	31/328		1. 6.90	J.A.Denne	Enstone	4. 4.02
FYN	3632	J3	Schempp-Hirth Discus B	179	N75J	14. 7.90	P.Foulger	Wormingford	27. 3.02
FYP	3633		LET L-23 Super Blanik	907620		4. 8.90	Needwood Forest GC	Cross Hayes	14. 4.02
FYR	3635	FYR	LET L-23 Super Blanik	917816		2. 7.92	North Wales GC	Llantisilio	24. 6.00
FYU	3638	M5	Glaser-Dirks DG-100 Elan	E111	OY-XMR SE-TYO	28. 6.90	J.L Bugbee	North Hill	16. 5.02
FYV	3639	FYV	Schleicher ASK21	21468		25. 7.90	Booker GC	Booker	13. 4.02
FYW	3640	Z7	Rolladen-Schneider LS-7	7111		6. 6.90	J.D.Williams	Saltby	18. 1.02
FYX	3641	208	Schempp-Hirth Discus bT	32/333		3. 7.90	M.P.Brockington	Talgarth	29. 4.02
FYY	3642	S	Schleicher ASK13	13685AB		9. 7.90	Lasham Gliding Society	Lasham	14. 6.02
FYZ	3643	171	Schleicher ASH25	25097		18. 7.90	M.G.Thick	Sutton Bank	17. 8.02
FZA	3644	FZA	SZD-51-1 Junior	B-1913		23. 7.90	Booker GC	Booker	20. 2.02
FZB	3645	669	Glasflugel H.201B Standard Libelle	112	OH-388 OH-GLA	31. 7.90	C.Thomas & J.E.Herring	Lasham	19. 3.02
FZC	3646	FZC	Schempp-Hirth SHK-1	58	OH-357 OH-SHA	30. 8.91	J.F Mills	RAF Cranwell	20. 7.02
FZF	3649	FZF	SZD-51-1 Junior	B-1861		21. 7.90	Devon & Somerset GC	North Hill	9. 5.02
FZG	3650	FZG	SZD-9 bis Bocian 1D	F-859	SP-2450	24. 9.90	The Borders GC	Milfield	16. 6.02
FZH	3651	FZH	Schempp-Hirth Ventus C	455		26. 7.90	G.D.Clack	Rivar Hill	27. 2.02
FZK	3653	FZK	Schempp-Hirth HS.4 Standard Cirrus	81	HB-967	2. 9.90	J.L.Rodgers & Syndicate	Aston Down	26. 8.02
FZL	3654	Z6	Schleicher ASW20CL	20764	D-5937	12. 7.90	R.M.Housden	Aston Down	25. 8.01
FZM	3655	FZM	Scheibe SF-27A Zugvogel V	6103	D-1772	7. 8.90	N.Dickenson	Camphill	17. 4.02
FZN	3656	K13	Schleicher ASK13	13045	D-5759	9. 8.90	Black Mountains GC	Talgarth	21. 8.01
FZP	3657	N16	SZD-51-1 Junior	B-1926		9. 8.90	Portsmouth Naval GC	Lee-on-Solent	2. 3.02
FZQ	3658	FXQ	SZD-50-3 Puchacz	B-2024	(BGA.3637)	9. 8.90	Coventry GC	Husbands Bosworth	18.12.02
FZR	3659	FZR	Schleicher Ka6CR	6136	D-8459	17.12.90	P.S.Huggins	North Hill	24.11.02
FZS	3660	L13	LET L-13 Blanik	025609	NEJSGSA.8	28. 8.90	B.J.Shackell & A.Pattemore	Gallows Hill	7. 4.99
			(Rebuild with parts from BGA.2661)						
FZU	3662		Slingsby T.38 Grasshopper	761	WZ765	8.8.91	H.Chapple	Berlin	26.12.96*
			(Probably composite wings ex WZ765 & spare fuselage c/n SSK/FF2069: as "WZ765": to Luftwaffen Museum 1996)						
FZV	3663	480	Rolladen-Schneider LS-7	7116		16.12.90	R.N.Boddy	Booker	1.10.02
FZW	3664	FZW	Glaser-Dirks DG-300 Club Elan	3E378C53		23. 9.90	Mr & Mrs S.L.Barter	Ringmer	6. 2.02
FZX	3665	FZX	SZD-51-1 Junior	B-1925		18. 9.90	Nene Valley GC	Upwood	6. 4.02
FZY	3666		LET L-33 Solo	940206		19. 3.94	A.W.Cox	Bicester	18. 3.95*
FZZ	3667	FZZ	LET L-33 Solo	940220		28. 4.95	D.A Wiseman	Andreas	6. 4.02
GAB	3669		LAK-12 Lietuva	6170		12. 1.91	M.Wilshere	RAF Halton	5. 4.02
GAC	3670	GAC	Schleicher Ka6CR	6301	(BGA.3647) RAFGGA.557(2)/D-5572	17.11.90	York Gliding Centre	Rufforth	2. 2.99
							(Crashed Rufforth 25.11.98)		
GAD	3671	L5	Rolladen-Schneider LS-3	3032	HB-1363	19.11.90	M.J.Towler	Bidford	7. 3.02
GAF	3673	778	Schleicher ASK21	21152	ZD652 BGA.2892	8.11.90	Lasham Gliding Society	Lasham	2. 4.02
GAG	3674	GAG	Schleicher ASK21	21143	ZD645 BGA.2885	24. 1.91	Stratford-upon-Avon GC	Snitterfield	7.12.02
GAH	3675	GAH	Schempp-Hirth HS.4 Standard Cirrus	572	HB-1240	3.12.90	M.G.Harris	Nympsfield	18.11.02
GAJ	3676	GAJ	Glaser-Dirks DG-300 Club Elan	3E385C56		10.12.90	M.R Wooley & Ptnrs	Long Mynd	16. 7.02
GAK	3677	GAK	LET L-13 Blanik	174522	2-84 (Lithuania)	7.97	North Wales GC	Llantisilio	26.10.02
GAL	3678	GAL	Schempp-Hirth HS.4 Standard Cirrus	335	HB-1150	3. 4.91	D.Reynolds & S.Cooke	Aston Down	8. 2.02
							(Collided with Pawnee G-ASLK Aston Down 14.9.01)		
GAM	3679	GAM	Schleicher ASK21	21144	ZD646 BGA.2886	21.11.90	Oxford University GC	Bicester	13. 2.02
GAN	3680	83	Glasflugel H.301 Libelle	8	D-4111	12.12.90	W.J.Dean	Long Mynd	16. 3.01
GAP	3681	GAP	Schempp-Hirth Ventus bT	14/150	OH-774 N416DP	28. 4.91	J.R.Greenwell	Currock Hill	23.7.00
GAQ	3682	GAQ/K7	Schleicher Ka7 Rhonadler	3	PH-788 D-5550	19. 4.91	York Gliding Centre	Rufforth	23. 6.01
GAR	3683	148	Rolladen-Schneider LS-6C	6205		2.11.90	A.J.Burton	Shobdon	3. 5.02
GAS	3684	GAS	Schempp-Hirth Ventus CT	157/509		30. 5.91	M W Edwards	Kingston Deverill	12. 4.02
GAT	3685	GAT	Grob G.102 Astir CS	1130	D-4176	23.11.90	R.S.Scott	Lasham	7. 2.02
GAU	3686	725	Glasflugel H.201B Standard Libelle	498	F-CELA	11. 6.93	D.R.Pickett	Crowland	17. 4.02
GAV	3687	GAV	Scheibe SF-27A Zugvogel V	6073	D-5287	18.11.90	W.Waite	Lleweni Parc	20. 1.02
GAW	3688	GAW	Schleicher Ka6CR	61/08	D-6320	30.12.90	B.D.Floyd	Saltby	18. 2.02
GAX	3689	302	SZD-55-1	551190008		30. 4.91	Rattlesden GC	Rattlesden	16. 2.02
GBA	3692	GBA	Schleicher ASK13	13417	D-2114	4.12.90	Burn GC	Burn	24. 5.02
GBB	3693		Schleicher ASK21	21073	D-3239	11.12.90	B.T.Spreckley	Le Blanc, France	21. 2.02

GBD	3695	GBD	SZD-50-3 Puchacz	B-2028		27. 4.91	Northumbria GC	Currock Hill	13. 5.01
GBE	3696		Schleicher Ka6CR (Pe)	6133A	D-4085	23.12.90	J.Swannock	Gamston	7. 9.02
GBF	3697	GBF	Schleicher ASK21	21142	ZD644	3. 2.91	BBC Gliding Group	Booker	10. 1.02
					BGA.2883				
GBG	3698	S21	Rolladen-Schneider LS-6c	6214		12.12.90	C.M.Greaves	Rufforth	9. 1.02
GBJ	3700	GBJ	Grob G.102 Astir CS	1107	D-4167	5. 1.91	J.D.Banham	Lasham	2. 1.02
GBK	3701	GBK	Grob G.102 Astir CS	1461	D-7451	5. 1.91	R.J.Thacker	Cross Hayes	4. 4.02
							"Mountain Man"		
GBL	3702	720	Rolladen-Schneider LS-7	7119		12.11.90	A.N.Redington	North Hill	10. 3.02
GBM	3703	GBM	Scheibe SF-27A Zugvogel V	6060	RAFGGA	2. 1.91	G.Cook	North Hill	7. 6.02
					D-5409		t/a BFMT Syndicate		
GBN	3704	843/MD	Schleicher ASK21	21141	ZD643	14.3.91	Essex & Suffolk GC	Wormingford	6.10.02
					BGA.2884				
GBP	3705	GBP	Schleicher ASK21	21150	ZD650	29. 1.91	London GC	Dunstable	30.11.99
					BGA.2890		*(Destroyed by mid-air lightning strike 4.99)*		
GBQ	3706	630	Rolladen-Schneider LS-6	6082	D-3725	6. 2.91	A. & P.R.Pentecost	Kingston Deverill	15. 5.02
GBR	3707	218	Rolladen-Schneider LS-6C	6196	D-3482	25.11.90	S.Hurd	Dunstable	6. 3.02
GBS	3708	206	Glaser-Dirks DG-300 Club Elan			15. 3.91	Yorkshire GC	Sutton Bank	31. 1.02
				3E389C58					
GBT	3709	IV	Rolladen-Schneider LS-4A	4355	N220BB	8. 4.91	S.A.Adlard	Long Mynd	15. 2.02
GBU	3710	922	Centrair 101A Pegase	101A-0394		3. 4.91	S.I.Ross	Parham Park	24. 6.02
GBV	3711	649	Schleicher ASK21	21149	ZD649	23. 4.91	Wolds GC	Pocklington	8. 4.02
					BGA.2889				
GBX	3713	290	Schleicher ASW22	22029	D-4325	27. 2.91	E.J.Rogers & Ptnrs	Gransden Lodge	9. 5.02
GBY	3714	425	Rolladen-Schneider LS-7	121		21. 1.91	W.J.Morecraft & Ptnrs	Saltby	9. 2.02
GBZ	3715	GBZ	Glaser-Dirks DG-500 Elan Trainer			10. 8.91	Needwood Forest GC	Cross Hayes	11. 4.02
				5E34T10					
GCA	3716		Schleicher ASW19B	19281	D-3179	2. 3.91	Deeside GC	Aboyne	31. 3.02
GCB	3717	637	LAK-12 Lietuva	647		29. 3.91	B.Middleton	Dunstable	10. 7.01
GCC	3718	GCC	SZD-51-1 Junior	B-1928		10. 3.91	The Soaring Centre	Husbands Bosworth	17. 2.02
GCD	3719	507	Schempp-Hirth HS.4 Standard Cirrus		PH-507	21. 2.91	B.Van Woerd	Chipping	1. 4.02
				476					
GCE	3720	8	Schleicher ASH25	25105		19. 2.91	C.L.Withall	Dunstable	21. 2.02
GCF	3721	GCF	Schleicher ASK23	23010	AGA.9	8. 2.91	Needwood Forest GC	Cross Hayes	9. 2.02
GCG	3722	S81	Schleicher K8B	8186	D-5227	5. 2.91	Shenington GC	Edgehill	8. 8.02
GCH	3723	438	Schleicher ASW15B	15212	PH-438	17. 4.91	M.D.Woodman-Smith & Ptnr	Dunstable	24. 4.99
				D-0950					
GCJ	3724	GCJ	LAK-12 Lietuva	626		30. 3.91	P.Crowhurst	Crowland	10.10.01
			(New wings with reconditioned 1982-built fuselage)						
GCK	3725	GCK	SZD-50-3 Puchacz	B-2025	(G-BTJV)	8. 3.91	Kent GC	Challock	20. 4.02
					BGA.3725				
GCL	3726	GCL	Grob G.102 Astir CS	1194	D-7311	10. 3.91	D.Draper	Rivar Hill	22. 2.02
GCM	3727	Z29	Rolladen-Schneider LS-6C	6216		12. 3.91	M.H.Hardwick	Enstone	21.11.02
GCN	3728	B35	Centrair 101A Pegase	101A-0035	(BGA.3694)	12. 3.91	B.T.Spreckley	Le Blanc, France	14. 3.96*
					F-CFQB		(Damaged Nympsfield 18.6.95)		
GCP	3729	GCP	Schleicher Ka6CR	6416	D-6369	3. 5.91	D.Clarke	Burn	21. 4.01
GCQ	3730	GCQ/845	Schempp-Hirth HS.2 Cirrus VTC		D-2945	2. 4.91	Dumfries & Galloway GC	Falgunzeon	20. 6.02
				135Y					
GCR	3731	748	Schleicher ASW15B	15447	D-6887	23. 3.91	K.A.Harrison	Dunstable	27. 2.02
GCS	3732	H12	Glasflugel H.205 Club Libelle		F-CEQL	7. 7.91	N.Stainton	Bidford	24. 6.02
				159					
GCT	3733	GCT	Schempp-Hirth Discus B	360		22. 3.91	J.C.Leonard	Bembridge	14. 5.02
GCU	3734	GCU	SZD-50-3 Puchacz	B-2023	(BGA.3619)	19. 3.91	Buckminster GC	Saltby	22. 5.02
GCX	3736	N6	Schleicher ASW15	15034	D-0420	21. 5.91	A.S.Edlin	Husbands Bosworth	26. 4.02
GCY	3737	908	Centrair 101A Pegase	101A-0392		22. 4.91	London GC	Dunstable	23.11.00
GCZ	3738		Rolladen-Schneider LS-7WL	7130		23. 3.91	*(De-registered 18.9.00 - sold as EC-...)*		
GDA	3739	546	Rolladen-Schneider LS-3-17M	3448	RAFGGA.546	20. 5.91	D.J.Moore	Aston Down	1. 6.02
GDB	3740	GDB	Schleicher K8B	8152	HB-738	23. 3.91	Welland GC	Lyveden	24. 3.02
GDC	3741	GDC	Slingsby T.38 Grasshopper	FF.1795		11. 5.91	F.K.Russell & Ptnrs	Dunstable	2. 5.97*
			(Built from spare frame - also carries marking SSK/RF.3107)						
GDD	3742	GDD	Bolkow Phoebus 17C	836	D-0060	18. 4.91	I.D.McLeod	Challock	2. 6.02
GDE	3743	GDE	Schleicher Ka6CR	6570Si	D-5306	26. 4.91	D.N.Jones	North Hill	25. 5.02
GDF	3744		Schleicher Ka6BR	389	D-8544	17. 4.91	A.D.Chapman	Burn	22. 6.02
GDJ	3747	450	Rolladen-Schneider LS-4A	4832		27. 4.91	A Clark	Aboyne	18. 5.02
GDK	3748	GDK	Schleicher K8B	8240	D-5381	15. 4.91	East Sussex GC	Ringmer	3. 5.02
					D-KANU/D-5381				
GDM	3750	668	Glasflugel H.201B Standard Libelle		D-6666	29. 4.91	K.Fear & Syndicate	Crowland	6. 3.02
				597					
GDN	3751	294	Rolladen-Schneider LS-3-17M	3291	D-6932	28. 4.91	S.J Peppler	Sandhill Farm	
								Shrivenham	9. 6.02
GDP	3752	GDP	Schleicher ASW19B	19285	D-3160	2. 5.91	W.M.Leutfeld	Cranfield	6. 5.02
GDQ	3753	GDQ	Grob G.102 Astir CS	1145	D-7229	11. 5.91	J.T.Harrison	Camphill	30. 6.02
GDR	3754		Schempp-Hirth Discus CS	016CS		5. 5.91	R.H.Wright	Husbands Bosworth	14. 7.02
			(Built Orlican)						

GDS	3755	GDS	Schleicher ASW15B	15205	D-0902	20. 6.91	J.Edwards	Dunstable	21. 8.02
							(See BGA.3751)		
GDT	3756	T54	Schleicher ASW24	24120		10. 5.91	A.Ditchfield	Camphill	4. 4.02
GDU	3757	801	Schleicher ASW24	24118		8. 6.91	G.J.Moore	Dunstable	5. 4.02
GDV	3758	GDV	Schleicher Ka6E	4099	OO-ZWQ	20. 6.91	L.D.Howell	Snitterfield	26. 4.02
					I-NEST/OE-0807				
GDW	3759		Scheibe SF-27A Zugvogel V	6116	D-1997	16. 5.91	M.W.Hands	Camphill	11. 6.02
GDX	3760	896	Schempp-Hirth Discus CS	023CS		2. 7.91	The Soaring Centre	Husbands Bosworth	22. 2.02
GDY	3761	GDY	Schleicher ASW15B	15220	D-0947	6. 5.91	J Archer	Bidford	29.11.01
GDZ	3762	524	Schleicher ASW24	24116		17. 5.91	I.C.Lees	Pocklington	5. 4.02
GEA	3763	GEA	Schleicher Ka6CR	849	(BGA.3605)	7. 6.91	M Wood	Rufforth	19. 5.02
					D-5801				
GEB	3764	GEB	Grob G.102 Astir CS77	1628	PH-576	7. 6.91	J.O.Lavery	Bellarena	30. 6.02
GEE	3767	928	Glasflugel H.201B Standard Libelle		D-0928	6. 6.91	C.Metcalfe	Gamston	13. 5.02
				94					
GEF	3768	GEF	Schleicher Ka6CR	6459	D-1068	24. 5.91	J.B Christie	Nympsfield	4. 7.98
GEG	3769		Schleicher K8B	689	HB-639	27. 4.91	Newark & Notts GC	Winthorpe	17. 2.02
GEH	3770	219	Schleicher ASW15B	15276	D-2124	9. 7.91	K.G.Vincent & Ptnrs	Challock	16. 5.02
GEL	3772	N23	SZD-50-3 Puchacz	B-2030		29. 5.91	Portsmouth Naval GC	Lee-on-Solent	10. 3.02
GEM	3773	GEM	Schleicher Ka6CR	6249	D-8486	4. 6.91	E.R.V.Nash	Rivar Hill	5. 5.02
GEN	3774	GEN	Slingsby T.21B	1154	RAFGGA.550	16. 5.92	A.Harris	RAF Bruggen	23. 5.02
					XN150				
GEP	3775	GEP	Schempp-Hirth HS.4 Standard Cirrus		D-0917	10. 6.91	G.S.Wadforth	Pocklington	9. 5.02
				205G					
GEQ	3776	2001	SZD-12A Mucha 100A	462	SP-2001	6. 6.91	T.Slater (*Stored 11.01*)	(Bury St.Edmunds)	
HAA	3777	263	Glasflugel H.201B Standard Libelle		HB-1090	20. 6.91	T.J.Mormin & Ptnrs	Gransden Lodge	30. 4.02
				356					
HAB	3778	HAB	Schleicher Ka6CR	6596	D-1596	1.92	M Greenwood	Rhigos	4. 2.02
HAC	3779		SZD-50-3 Puchacz	B-2035		29. 6.91	Peterborough & Spalding GC	Crowland	9. 2.02
HAD	3780	429	Glasflugel H.201 Standard Libelle		D-8914	5. 7.91	G.S Roe & Ptnrs	Lasham	14. 2.02
				3					
HAE	3781	HAE	Glasflugel H.205 Club Libelle	75	D-8687	5. 7.91	J.P.Kirby	Lee on Solent	30. 4.02
HAF	3782	N53	SZD-50-3 Puchacz	B-2031		4. 7.91	Culdrose GC	RNAS Culdrose	14. 3.02
HAG	3783	HAG	Schleicher Ka7 Rhonadler	834	D-5795	21. 5.92	Denbigh GC	Lleweni Parc	17. 4.02
HAJ	3785	391	Schempp-Hirth Ventus C	517		19. 7.91	Surrey & Hants GC	Lasham	11. 1.02
HAK	3786	XA302	Slingsby T.31B	844	XA302	17. 8.91	W.Walker	RAF Syerston	24. 5.96*
HAL	3787	HAL	Schleicher ASK1313	690AB		7. 9.91	Cotswold GC	Aston Down	13.12.02
HAN	3789	278	Schempp-Hirth HS.4 Standard Cirrus		D-0326	14. 8.91	M.Hastings & Syndicate	Weston-on-the-Green	26. 5.00
				130					
HAP	3790	HAP	Schleicher Ka6E	4335	HB-985	29. 8.91	T.Turner	Dunstable	30. 8.02
HAQ	3791	114	Rolladen-Schneider LS-6B	6150	D-8079	2. 9.91	A R Hughes	Gransden Lodge	27. 4.02
HAR	3792	HAR	Schleicher K8B	8151	D-8453	4. 9.91	G.Weale	Brent Tor	4. 7.97*
HAS	3793	HAS	SZD-50-3 Puchacz	B-2043		17. 8.91	The Soaring Centre	Husbands Bosworth	5. 2.02
HAT	3794	HAT	Glaser-Dirks DG-200/17	2-93/1709	D-6843	26. 8.91	D.Simon	Carlton Moor	15.12.02
HAU	3795	HAU	Grob G.102 Astir CS Jeans	2043	D-3887	11. 9.91	Yorkshire GC	Sutton Bank	4. 3.02
HAV	3796	HAV	Glasflugel H.201B Standard Libelle		HB-950	25. 8.91	P.W.Andrews	Husbands Bosworth	6. 5.02
				40					
HAX	3798	HAX	Schempp-Hirth HS.4 Standard Cirrus		ZS-GHZ	10.10.91	P.J.Mortimer	Rivar Hill	28. 3.02
				02	ZS-TIM/ZS-GGR/D-0302				
HAY	3799		Rolladen-Schneider LS-77	154		15.10.91	N.Leaton & Ptnrs	Challock	14. 7.96*
HBA	3801	729	Rolladen-Schneider LS-77	156	D-6041	12.10.91	P.O'Donald	Gransden Lodge	23.11.02
HBB	3802	S1	Schleicher ASW24	24132		19. 9.91	S.D.Steinberg	Gransden Lodge	31.10.02
HBC	3803	HBC	Rolladen-Schneider LS-6C	6209	D-....	20. 9.91	J.Burry	Lasham	8. 4.02
HBD	3804	HBD	Glaser-Dirks DG-2002-	12	HB-1384	5.10.91	L.Marshall & Ptnrs	Rattlesden	31. 5.02
HBE	3805	356	Glaser-Dirks DG-300 Elan	3E237	SE-UFB	21. 5.92	A.W.Cox & Ptnrs	Enstone	24.10.02
HBF	3806	HBF	Schempp-Hirth HS.5 Nimbus 2C		D-3369	5.10.91	T.Cauldwell	Sackville Lodge	
				191				Riseley	21. 7.00
HBG	3807	96	Schleicher ASW24	24133		10.12.91	Imperial College GC	Lasham	30. 3.02
HBH	3808	496	Grob G.103C Twin III	36006		14.10.91	Imperial College GC	Lasham	27.12.01
HBJ	3809	949	Rolladen-Schneider LS-6C-	186230		26. 9.91	D.J.Hill	Tibenham	8. 3.02
HBK	3810	HBK	Grob G.103 Twin Astir	3254-T-31	RAFGGA..	29. 9.91	R.W.Idle	Burn	19. 9.02
					D-2389				
HBL	3811	HBL	Grob G.102 Astir CS77	1626	RAFGSA R78	17.10.91	J.McCormick	Bidford	4. 6.02
					RAFGSA.778				
HBM	3812	HBM	Grob G.102 Astir CS77	1633	RAFGSA R65	3.12.91	M.Wood	RAF Syerston	9. 6.02
					RAFGSA.R66/RAFGSA.546				
HBP	3814	522	Glaser-Dirks DG-500/22 Elan			10.91	A.Taverna	Florence, Italy	17. 6.02
				5E36S8					
HBQ	3815		Schleicher Ka6CR	6611	D-5616	22.11.91	P.N.Jones	Dunstable	28. 4.02
HBR	3816	PM	Schempp-Hirth Nimbus 4T	3/6	(BGA.3784)	1. 8.92	P S Hawkins	(Australia)	19. 4.02
HBS	3817	HBS	SZD-41A Jantar Standard	B-852	D-4160	2.12.91	A.Henderson	Milfield	29. 7.02
HBT	3819		Grob G.102 Club Astir	2235	PH-675	9. 2.92	M.D.Evans	Winthorpe	23. 3.02
HBU	3820	605	Centrair ASW20F	20527	F-CFSI	22.11.91	R.Palmer & R.Mann	Bidford	10. 1.02
HBV	3821	667	Schempp-Hirth HS.5 Nimbus 2B	143	D-7850	11.91	C.J.Teagle	Sutton Bank	15.12.01

HBW	3822	829	Glaser-Dirks DG-300 Club Elan	3E405C64		15.12.91	P.C.Cannon	Lasham	19. 4.00
HBX	3823	HBX	Slingsby T.45 Swallow	1386	8801M XS650	16. 5.93	C.D.Street & Ptnrs	Lasham	26. 9.02
HBY	3824	664	Rolladen-Schneider LS-77	148		7.11.91	K.W.Payne	Husbands Bosworth	17. 7.02
HBZ	3825	HBZ	Slingsby T.15 Gull III rep			28. 6.92	P.R.Philpot	Chipping	21. 6.02
HCA	3826	HCA	Grob G.103 Twin Astir	3289	D-0094 OO-ZOH/D-3063	24.12.91	M.Wright	Rattlesden	6. 9.02
HCB	3827	754	Schempp-Hirth Nimbus 3DT	47		24.12.91	P.A.Green	Lasham	14. 5.02
HCC	3829		SZD-50-3 Puchacz	B-2048		4. 1.92	Heron GC	RNAS Yeovilton	4. 2.02
HCD	3830	HCD	SZD-50-3 Puchacz	B-2049		7. 1.92	The Soaring Centre	Husbands Bosworth	6. 4.02
HCE	3831	346	Schleicher ASW19B	19305	D-6527	6. 1.92	N.J.Morgan	Dunstable	17. 2.02
HCF	3832	HCF	SZD-50-3 Puchacz	B-2047		20.12.91	Shalbourne Soaring Society	Rivar Hill	28. 1.02
HCG	3833	HCG	Maupin Woodstock One *(Built R.Harvey)*	-		10.92	R.Harvey	Swanton Morley	8.11.02
HCH	3834	355	Centrair ASW20FP	20178	F-CEUL	20. 3.92	A.Henderson	Saltby	1. 9.02
HCJ	3835	HCJ	Grob G.103 Twin II	3709	D-2611	24. 1.92	Peterborough & Spalding GC	Crowland	18. 5.02
HCK	3836	WB962	Slingsby T.21B	623	RAFGGA5.. WB962	2. 1.92	V.Mallon	Laarbruch Germany	24. 8.02
HCL	3837	144	Schempp-Hirth Discus B	136	D-4682	13. 3.92	M.A.Powell-Brett	Snitterfield	3. 4.02
HCM	3838	HCM	Schleicher Ka7 Rhonadler	498	D-5669	4. 3.92	M.Barnard	Dunstable	29. 8.02
HCN	3839	HCN	CARMAM M.200 Foehn	24	F-CDDR	21.12.92	J S Shaw	Perranporth	19. 7.99
HCP	3840	HCP	Avialsa A.60 Fauconnet	123K	F-CDLA	3.93	C.Kaminski *(Being refurbished)*	Eaglescott	31. 7.95*
HCQ	3841	HCQ	Glasflugel H.201B Standard Libelle	197	HB-999	28. 1.92	E.K.Harris	Dunstable	23. 2.02
HCR	3842	394	SZD-51-1 Junior	B-2003		28. 4.92	Surrey & Hants GC	Lasham	7.12.02
HCS	3843	HCS	Grob G.102 Astir CS77	1727	RAFGSA.R84 RAFGSA.884	5. 2.92	Buckminster GC	Saltby	26. 4.97*
HCU	3845	78	Glaser-Dirks DG-300 Club Elan	3E407C66		7. 2.92	M.S Smith & Ptnrs	Aston Down	6. 5.02
HCV	3846	HCV	Schleicher ASW19B	19084	D-4486	14. 5.93	Miss W.J.Palmer	Dunstable	17. 5.00
HCW	3847	HCN	SZD-51-1 Junior	B-2002	(BGA.3844)	1. 2.92	Deeside GC	Aboyne	11. 3.02
HCX	3848	HCX	Schleicher ASK21	21541		16. 5.92	Devon & Somerset GC	North Hill	20. 6.02
HCY	3849	HCY	Glaser-Dirks DG-300 Club Elan	3E413C67		10. 5.94	S.T.Dry	RAF Keevil	9. 8.02
HCZ	3850	HCZ	Schleicher K8B	8114A	D-4675	21. 2.92	South London Gliding Centre	Kenley	25. 2.02
HDA	3851	HDA	Pilatus B4 PC-11AF	017	D-0964	18. 3.92	P.Bois	(Jersey)	24. 7.02
HDB	3852	HDB	SZD-51-1 Junior	B-1997		4. 3.92	Stratford-upon-Avon GC	Snitterfield	22.12.02
HDC	3853	HDC	Schleicher ASK13	13308	D-0750	19. 3.93	Bowland Forest GC	Chipping	5.12.02
HDD	3854	591	Centrair 101B Pegase	101B-0425		5. 4.92	Scottish Gliding Union	Portmoak	10.12.02
HDE	3855		Pilatus B4 PC-11AF	223	VH-XOZ VH-WQP	12. 4.92	A.J.Hamilton	Shobdon	4. 7.01
HDF	3856	910	Schempp-Hirth Discus B	404		21. 2.92	T.M.Lipscombe	Lasham	6. 3.02
HDH	3858	991	Glaser-Dirks DG-202-15	2-197	???	24. 5.92	R.J.Pirie	Parham Park	16. 4.02
HDJ	3859	HDJ	Schleicher ASW20CL	20828	D-8442	4. 3.92	G.E.Lambert	Booker	2. 3.02
HDL	3861	137	Schleicher ASW20	20082	D-1617 OH-495	13. 4.92	S.Thackray	Booker	5. 6.02
HDM	3862	HDH	SZD-12A Mucha 100A	448	SP-1987	15. 4.92	T.J.Wilkinson	Sackville Lodge Riseley	22. 4.02
HDN	3863	HDN	Schleicher K8B	2	D-8017	17. 3.92	Upward Bound Trust	Thame	4. 7.02
HDP	3864	N36	SZD-50-3 Puchacz	B-2050		3.92	Heron GC	RNAS Yeovilton	28. 5.02
HDR	3866	467	Glaser-Dirks DG-300 Elan	3E95	RAFGSA R30	14. 3.92	C.J.Cornish	Booker	16. 5.02
HDT	3868	291	Schempp-Hirth Discus BT	76/405		18. 3.92	J.D.J.Glossop & Ptnrs	Gransden Lodge	28. 2.02
HDU	3869	HDU	SZD-51-1 Junior	B-1996		25. 3.92	Cambridge University GC	Gransden Lodge	9. 1.02
HDV	3870	882	Schleicher ASW19B	19345	D-2876	20. 4.92	R.J.Hinley	Long Mynd	14. 6.02
HDW	3871	HDW	Centrair 101A Pegase	101A-0179	F-CGEE	21. 3.92	T.Head	Husbands Bosworth	9. 6.02
HDX	3872	A2	Rolladen-Schneider LS-7	7161		27. 3.92	P.W.Rodwell	Crowland	9. 3.02
HDY	3873		Schleicher K8B	8277	D-4094	24. 3.92	M.A Everett	Crowland	21. 4.01
HDZ	3874	W1	Schempp-Hirth Discus CS	078CS		7. 7.92	J.P.Wright & G.Bennett	Challock	13. 2.02
HEA	3875	HEA	Slingsby T.38 Grasshopper	'SSK/FF529'	(ex RAF)	4. 7.92	R.L.McLean	Rufforth	19.11.01
HEB	3876	HEB	Schleicher Ka6CR	6289	HB-773	6. 5.92	J.W.Watt	North Hill	22. 6.02
HEC	3877	308	SZD-55-1	551191019		10. 5.92	G.P Davis	Nympsfield	1. 3.02
HED	3878	840	Schempp-Hirth Ventus A	17	D-2524	18. 4.92	M.R.Dawson	RAF Keevil	3. 5.02
HEE	3879	316	Schempp-Hirth Discus B *(Rebuild of BGA.3523 after accident 21.6.91 but see BGA.4047)*	292		19. 4.92	Booker GC	Booker	9. 2.02
HEF	3880	HEF	Glaser-Dirks DG-500 Elan Trainer	5E53T20		24. 5.92	Yorkshire GC	Sutton Bank	13. 4.02
HEG	3881	HEG	LAK-12 Lietuva	6206		27. 6.92	R.Kmita & Ptnrs	Kirton-in-Lindsey	3. 3.02
HEH	3882	795	Rolladen-Schneider LS-7WL	7163	D-6078	24. 6.92	P.D.Candler	Gransden Lodge	4. 1.02
HEJ	3883	687	Schleicher ASW15B	15441	D-6871	5.92	R.Bickerton	Weston on the Green	12. 1.02
HEK	3884	HEK	SZD-51-1 Junior	B-2009	BGA.3893 (BGA.3884)	29. 5.94	Cambridge University GC	Gransden Lodge	9. 1.02

HEL	3885 A9	Rolladen-Schneider LS-4	4027	(BGA.3896)	26. 5.92	G.C.Alison	Dunstable	7. 2.02
				BGA.3885/D-6431				
HEM	3886 473	Schempp-Hirth Discus CS	073CS		22. 5.92	J.H.Nunnerley	Booker	16. 3.02
HEN	3887 735	Schempp-Hirth Discus B	422		5. 6.92	A.R.Verity & Ptnrs	Challock	6. 3.01
HEP	3888	SZD-50-3 Puchacz	B-2057		30. 5.92	Peterborough & Spalding GC	Crowland	13. 1.02
HEQ	3889 611	Schleicher ASW20L	20410	D-6747	6. 6.92	M.Chant	Brent Tor	16. 3.02
HER	3890 HER	Schleicher ASW19	19240	F-CERR	1. 4.93	B.T.Spreckley	Le Blanc, France	25. 4.02
HES	3891 B39	Centrair 101A Pegase	101A-039	F-CFQF	13. 2.93	B.T.Spreckley	Le Blanc, France	23. 2.02
HET	3892 335	Rolladen-Schneider LS-6C	6263		26. 5.92	M.P.Brooks	Lasham	4. 3.02
HEV	3894 HEV	Schempp-Hirth HS.2 Cirrus	41	OO-ZXY	26. 5.92	D.A Clempson	Portmoak	14. 4.02
				(OO-ZOZ)/D-0104				
HEW	3895 486	Rolladen-Schneider LS-6C	6250		29. 4.92	R.M.Underhill	Bicester	30. 1.02
HEY	3897	Hutter H-17A	02		6.92	J.M.Lee	Parham Park	17. 5.00
		(Built J.M.Lee - possibly ex BGA.3661)						
HEZ	3898 607	Rolladen-Schneider LS-6C	6264		16. 7.92	J.E.Cruttenden	Lasham	24. 6.02
HFA	3899 495	Schempp-Hirth Ventus B/16.6	251	RAFGSA.R24	26. 6.92	D.R.Stewart	Winthorpe	25. 6.95*
HFB	3900 HFB	Schleicher Ka6CR	6344Si	D-5825	13. 7.92	S.Tomlinson	Templeton	25.10.02
HFC	3901 WB924	Slingsby T.21B	587	WB924	7.92	M.G.Stringer	Dunstable	25.11.02
HFD	3902 289	Grob G.102 Astir CS Jeans	2229	D-5912	29. 6.92	East Sussex GC	Ringmer	26. 8.97*
						(Damaged Kitson Field 15.6.97 & w/o)		
HFE	3903 XN187	Slingsby T.21B	1166	XN187	23. 6.92	A.J.Oultram	Seighford	11. 1.03
HFF	3904 870	Schempp-Hirth Standard Cirrus		D-8916	14. 2.93	R.S.Morrisroe	Upwood	7. 3.02
			539					
HFG	3905 HFG	Slingsby T.21B	1165	XN186	28. 6.92	A.M.Thompson	RAF Marham	2. 5.00
HFH	3906 HFH	SZD-50-3 Puchacz	B-2059		4. 8.92	Trent Valley GC	Kirton-in-Lindsey	7. 4.02
HFJ	3907	SZD-42-1 Jantar 2A	B-792	RAFGGA..	5. 4.92	P.Stein	RAF Bruggen	9. 3.02
				OO-ZDE				
HFL	3909 925/SSC	Schleicher ASH25	25147		18. 7.92	T.W.Slater	Portmoak	1. 3.02
HFM	3910 747	Rolladen-Schneider LS-6C	6266		8. 7.92	F.J.Sheppard	Booker	1. 7.02
HFN	3911	Wassmer WA-26P Squale	18	F-CDQP	24. 6.92	C.Duthy-James	Talgarth	22. 8.96*
HFP	3912	CARMAM M.100S Mesange	87K	F-CDPQ	24. 6.92	D.Patrick & Ptnr	Falgunzeon	28. 9.96*
HFQ	3913 126	Rolladen-Schneider LS-6C	6260	(BGA.3908)	23. 6.92	M.E.Baker	Gamston	31. 3.02
HFU	3917 HFU	SZD-9 bis Bocian 1D	P-334	SP-2038	22. 6.94	T.Wiltshere	(Spilsby)	15. 8.96*
HFV	3918 F2	Schempp-Hirth Ventus B 16.6	204	D-5235	1.10.92	A.Cliffe	Camphill	24. 3.02
HFW	3919 HFW	Schleicher K8B	8108	HB-705	24. 9.92	Oxford GC	Weston-on-the-Green	8. 2.02
HFX	3920 82	Schempp-Hirth Nimbus 4T	12		3. 7.92	R.Jones	Lasham	19.12.02
HFY	3921 940	Schempp-Hirth Ventus CT	168/554	(BGA.3916)	21. 7.92	M.T.Day & D.J.Ellis	Lasham	28. 2.02
				(BGA.3867)				
HFZ	3922	Abbott-Baynes Scud I rep.	001		R	Brooklands Museum	Brooklands *(Noted 4.99)*	
HGA	3923 HGA	Wassmer WA-26P Squale	43	F-CDUH	30. 3.93	E.C.Murgatroyd	Sackville Lodge	
							Riseley	29. 5.02
HGB	3924 509	Grob G.102 Astir CS	1356	D-7386	16.11.92	P.J.Hollamby & Ptnrs	Lee-on-Solent	8. 5.02
		(Rebuilt with wings & components from RAFGGA.507)						
HGC	3925 HGC	Schleicher Ka7 Rhonadler	540	D-5689	6. 3.94	T.A.Joint	Lasham	27. 8.00
HGF	3928 HGF	Schleicher ASW15B	15264	D-2128	25. 8.92	I.Thompson	Camphill	25. 4.02
HGG	3929	Schempp-Hirth HS.4 Standard Cirrus		HB-1172	31.12.92	P.Hodgetts	Seighford	23. 2.02
			362					
HGH	3930 HGH	Schleicher ASW19B	19351	D-1199	26. 8.92	A.Wood	Brent Tor	19. 4.01
HGJ	3931	CARMAM M.200 Foehn	33	F-CDHG	28. 9.92	M.Skinner	Cross Hayes	11.95*
HGK	3932 HGK	Schempp-Hirth Discus BT	96/435		30.10.92	C.T.Skeate	Parham Park	3. 1.02
HGL	3933 183	Schempp-Hirth Discus B	431		30. 7.92	P.J.Ward	Aston Down	28. 2.02
HGM	3934 HGM	Scheibe SF-27A Zugvogel V	6017	D-9351	26. 9.92	S.R.Algeo	Lyveden	6. 9.02
HGN	3935 808	Schempp-Hirth Ventus CT	172/562		18. 9.92	A.R.Milne	North Hill	26 .8.02
HGP	3936 HGP	Rolladen-Schneider LS-6C	6270		3.11.92	D.Elrington	Camphill	25 .2.02
HGQ	3937 637	LAK-12 Lietuva	6208		1.12.92	R.A.M.Lovegrove	Dunstable	7. 9.02
HGR	3938 HGR	LAK-12 Lietuva	6186		22. 3.93	R.G.Stevens	Husbands Bosworth	23. 4.02
HGS	3939 730	Schempp-Hirth Discus B	439		6.11.92	P.J.Bramley	Challock	15. 1.02
HGT	3940	FFA Diamant 16.5	40	HB-929	12. 4.94	R.W.Collins	Burn	30. 3.02
HGU	3941 HGU	Avionautica Rio M.100S	048	HB-1038	3. 6.93	R.D.Colman	Old Sarum	7. 5.98
				I-RIKI				
HGV	3942 HGV	Glaser-Dirks DG-500/22 Elan			26. 2.93	B.H.Bryce-Smith	Gransden Lodge	24. 2.02
			5E70S11					
HGW	3943 HGW	Centrair ASW20F	20102	F-CFFB	1. 1.93	C.Smith	Husbands Bosworth	29. 5.02
HGX	3944 783	LAK-12 Lietuva	6201		3. 5.93	K.Pickering	Parham Park	19. 6.02
HGY	3945	SZD-24C Foka	W-180	SP-2385	16.12.92	Peterborough & Spalding GC	Crowland	3. 6.02
HGZ	3946 502	Schempp-Hirth Discus BT	95/434		18.12.92	R.F.Aldous & Ptnrs	Booker	18. 4.02
HHA	3947 HHA	SZD-50-3 Puchacz	B-2058		18. 2.93	Derby & Lancs GC	Camphill	13. 4.02
HHC	3949 HHC	SZD-50-3 Puchacz	B-2080		16. 4.93	Derby & Lancs GC	Camphill	31. 5.02
HHD	3950 HHD	SZD-51-1 Junior	B-2010		19. 3.93	Derby & Lancs GC	Camphill	19. 3.02
HHE	3951 HHE	SZD-51-1 Junior	B-2008		30. 6.93	Derby & Lancs GC	Camphill	19. 3.02
HHG	3953 WT910	Slingsby T.31B	705	WT910	9. 1.93	P.Wickwar & Ptnr	Challock	30. 5.97*
HHH	3954 963	Rolladen-Schneider LS-6C	6289		11.12.92	B.R.Wise	Booker	21. 2.02
HHJ	3955 97	Glaser-Dirks DG-500/22 Elan			9. 2.93	British Gliding Association		
			5E71S12				Bicester	12. 1.02

HHK	3956	838	Schleicher ASW19B	19384	ZD661	14. 3.93	A.J.Peters Syndicate	Lasham	31. 3.02
					BGA.2897				
HHL	3957	HHL	Schleicher Ka7 Rhonadler	446	OY-XCK	30. 7.93	Lincolnshire GC	Strubby	29. 5.02
					D-5619		*"Buttercup"*		
HHM	3958	HHM	LAK-12 Lietuva	6195		9. 8.93	R.Parayre	(France)	21. 4.02
HHN	3959	979	Schempp-Hirth Ventus B/16.6	205	RAFGSA.R27	6. 2.93	N.A.C.Norman	Feshiebridge	28. 4.02
			(Build No. V-204)						
HHP	3960	KL	Schempp-Hirth Discus B	399	SE-UKL	12. 2.93	D.J.Knowles	Camphill	25.10.02
HHQ	3961	977	Schempp-Hirth Discus BT	106/453		12. 2.93	J.P.Galloway	Portmoak	11. 4.02
HHR	3962	100	SZD-55-15	51191020		18. 4.93	R.T.Starling	Nympsfield	24. 2.02
HHS	3963	746	Schleicher ASW20	20008	SE-TTU	3. 3.93	P.J.Rocks	Kirton-in-Lindsey	18. 8.02
HHT	3964	855	Rolladen-Schneider LS-6C	6292		18. 7.93	R.C.Bromwich	Kingston Deverill	15. 5.02
HHU	3965	23	Rolladen-Schneider LS-6C	6296		15. 2.93	J.S.Weston	Bellarena	25. 1.02
HHW	3967	237	LAK-12 Lietuva	6212		19. 3.93	A.J.Dibdin	Dunstable	22. 2.02
HHX	3968	HHX	Wassmer WA-26P Squale	14	F-CDQJ	27. 2.93	M.H.Gagg	Chauvigny, France	25. 2.02
HHY	3969	HHY	Glasflugel H.201B Standard Libelle	119	SE-TIU	1. 5.93	R.Tietma & M.Ainsworth	Husbands Bosworth	28. 2.02
HJA	3971	HJA	VFW-Fokker FK-3	0008	D-0409	9. 8.93	M.A Johnson & Ptnrs	Sackville Lodge Riseley	27. 6.02
HJC	3973	25	Rolladen-Schneider LS-6C	6290		17. 3.93	F.J Davies & I.C.Woodhouse	Enstone	28.11.02
HJD	3974	HJD	Schleicher Ka6E	4141	D-....	4. 2.94	D.Weitzel	Edgehill	23. 5.02
					OH-505/SE-TFM				
HJE	3975	505	Schleicher K8B	8259	(BGA.3926)	16. 4.93	Denbigh GC	Lleweni Parc	2. 8.01
					RAFGGA.505 (&/or RAFGGA.981?)				
HJF	3976	245	Rolladen-Schneider LS-6C	6291		29. 4.93	J.L.Bridge	Gransden Lodge	4. 2.02
HJH	3978	HJH	Schempp-Hirth Discus BT	65/391	N224WT	22. 4.93	P.J.Goulthorpe	Crowland	25. 2.02
HJJ	3979		Slingsby T.38 Grasshopper	797	WZ816	R	J.Wilkins *(On rebuild 2000)*	Redhill	
HJK	3980	HJK	Schleicher Ka7 Rhonadler	795	RAFGSA.R5	14. 6.93	Leeds University GC	Rufforth	5. 2.01
					D-5791				
HJL	3981	306	Schempp-Hirth Discus BT	105/451		3. 5.93	A.R.MacGregor	Kingston Deverill	2. 1.02
HJM	3982	HJM	Hutter H.28-III rep	ED.02		25. 5.93	E.R.Duffin	Nympsfield	12. 6.99
			(Built E.R.Duffin; being refurbished)						
HJN	3983	HJN	Grob Standard Cirrus	440G	HB-1206	2. 6.93	D.F Marlow	Aston Down	4. 6.02
HJR	3986	HJR	Glasflugel H.201B Standard Libelle	102	SE-TIO	26. 5.95	B.Magnani	Wormingford	10. 5.02
HJT	3988	292	Centrair ASW20F	20115	F-CFFL	3. 6.93	C.I Roberts & Ptnrs	Snitterfield	3. 4.01
HJU	3989	HJU	Schempp-Hirth Standard Cirrus		EC-DNE	8. 7.93	A M Cooper	Usk	7. 7.01
					D-0327		*(Crashed Usk 15.7.01 on take-off)*		
HJV	3990	HJV	Grob G.102 Astir CS	1007	D-7000	7. 6.93	Cotswold GC	Aston Down	13.12.02
HJX	3991	203	Rolladen-Schneider LS-6C	6271		28. 5.93	R.S.Hatwell & M.Haynes	Swanton Morley	19. 3.02
HJY	3992	HJY	Schempp-Hirth Standard Cirrus	459	HB-1207	23. 6.93	W.W Turnbull & Ptnrs	Currock Hill	23. 7.02
HJZ	3993	865	Schleicher ASW15B	15190	OH-408	15. 5.94	R.R.Beezer	Camphill	21. 8.02
HKA	3994	135	Schempp-Hirth Discus CS	120CS		20. 5.93	The Soaring Centre	Husbands Bosworth	25. 2.02
HKB	3995	HKB	Grob G.102 Astir CS77	1658	D-7491	26.10.93	K.J.McPhee	RAF Keevil	17. 2.02
HKC	3996	HKC	Grob Standard Cirrus	520G	D-3268	28. 8.93	L.White	Dunstable	11. 5.02
HKD	3997	C34	Grob Standard Cirrus	576G	F-CEMF	7. 7.93	J.A.Clark	Edgehill	14. 5.02
HKE	3998		CARMAN JP-15/36AR Aiglon	6	F-CETD	9. 7.93	M.F.Cuming	Bidford	
							(W/o Bidford 9.7.95: wreck stored 8.99 as "CETD")		
HKF	3999	HKF	CARMAM JP-15/36AR Aiglon	23	F-CETU	31. 7.93	K. & C.Vincent	Bidford	26. 7.00
HKJ	4002		Penrose Pegasus 2	001		7.93	J.M.Lee	Parham Park	15. 9.98
			(Built J.M.Lee)						
HKK	4003	HKK	Schleicher K8B	8886	D-0866	16. 1.94	R.K.Lashly	Easterton	18. 4.02
HKL	4004	919	Schempp-Hirth Discus bT	120/476		2.94	M.A.Thorne	Rivar Hill	25. 1.02
HKM	4005	HKM	Grob G.102 Astir CS Jeans	2108	D-7636	3.94	D.Simpson	Ridgewell	9. 3.02
HKN	4006	HKN	Centrair 101C Pegase	101-902	N101CR	23. 7.93	J.A.Sutton	Currock Hill	19. 2.99
					F-WFXB		*(Crashed at Milfield 23.1.99)*		
HKP	4007	HKP	Schleicher ASK23B	23100	D-2935	9. 8.93	Midland GC	Long Mynd	23. 2.02
					HB-1935				
HKQ	4008	970	Schempp-Hirth Nimbus 3DT	63		7. 8.93	R.I.Hey & Syndicate	Nympsfield	8.11.02
HKR	4009	985	Jastreb Standard Cirrus G/81	276	OH-663	15.10.93	J.Evans	Lyveden	14. 8.02
HKS	4010	HKS	Jastreb Standard Cirrus G/81	361	SE-TZS	11.11.93	E.W.Richards	Booker	29. 4.02
HKT	4011	HKT	Schleicher ASW19	19168	D-7958	4.10.93	A.Birkenshaw & Ptnr	Burn	7. 9.02
			(C/n conflicts with OE-5174 but believed correct)						
HKU	4012	C29	Grob Standard Cirrus	513G	F-CEMA	5.12.93	T.J Wheeler & Ptnr	Lyveden	1. 3.02
HKV	4013		Scheibe Zugvogel IIIA	1034	D-8294	6.10.93	Dartmoor GC	Brent Tor	21.10.02
HKW	4014	HKW	Marco J-5	009	G-BSBO	2. 6.94	G.K Owen	Seighford	18. 2.02
			(Built D.Austin - regd with c/n 001; "Flying Penguin II")						
HKX	4015	HKX	Rolladen-Schneider LS-4B	4933		18.12.93	D.J Hughes	Long Mynd	2. 2.02
HKY	4016	JA	Schempp-Hirth Discus B	461		14.10.93	J.G Arnold	RAF Keevil	6. 4.02
HKZ	4017	P31	CARMAM JP-15/36AR Aiglon	31	F-CFGA	27. 9.93	R.Borthwick	Milfield	16. 7.02
HLB	4019	365	Rolladen-Schneider LS-4	4935		27. 4.94	E.G.Leach	Gransden Lodge	4. 8.02
HLC	4020	HLC	Pilatus B4 PC-11	177	SE-UFX	10. 3.94	E.A.Lockhart	Wormingford	1. 2.02
					OH-455				

HLD	4021	462	Schempp-Hirth Discus BT	122/479		30.10.93	C.M.Robinson & Ptnrs	Kenley	21.10.95*
							(Damaged Parham 7.5.95 & w/o)		
HLG	4024	HLG	Schleicher ASK21	21596		1. 4.95	London GC	Dunstable	26. 4.02
HLH	4025	HLH	Schleicher K8B	8637	RAFGGA.569	26. 2.94	R.Das	Usk	1. 8.02
			(See BGA.4162)		D-5691				
HLK	4027	HLK	Glasflugel H.301 Libelle	85	SE-TFS	11. 4.95	E.Sweetland	Dunstable	8. 8.02
HLM	4029	819	Schleicher ASW19B	19269	OH-538	10. 2.94	R.A.Colbeck	Booker	16. 5.02
HLN	4030	805	Schempp-Hirth Discus CS	143CS		18. 1.94	Portsmouth Naval GC	Lee-on-Solent	29.11.02
HLP	4031	HLP	Schleicher ASK21	21597		24. 3.94	Yorkshire GC	Sutton Bank	16. 3.02
HLQ	4032	381	Schempp-Hirth Discus bT	128/490		22.12.93	J.F.Goudie	Portmoak	1. 3.02
HLR	4033		Slingsby T31B	899	XE786	18.12.93	D.Thomson	Arbroath	30.11.00
HLS	4034	V5	Schempp-Hirth Discus B	114	RAFGSA.R11	28. 1.94	R.A.Lennard	Dunstable	16. 1.02
HLT	4035		LAK-12 Lietuva	6190		8. 2.94	Baltic Sailplanes Ltd	Rufforth	7 .2.95*
							(Damaged Rufforth 16.7.94; stored 7.97)		
HLU	4036	HLU	Scheibe SF-27A Zugvogel V	6101	SE-TGP	22. 2.94	T.R.Bainbridge	Booker	19. 7.02
HLV	4037	UIM	Schleicher K8B	8760	SE-UIM	24. 2.94	M.Cuming	Edgehill	12. 1.97*
					D-5005		*(Damaged Chedworth 18.7.96: wreck stored)*		
HLW	4038	HLW	Schleicher ASW19B	19325	D-8799	3. 4.94	F.J.Hayden	Gransden Lodge	9. 1.02
HLX	4039	260	Schleicher ASH25	25124	D-3988	27. 2.94	P.Pozerskis	Husbands Bosworth	5. 4.02
HLY	4040	565	Schempp-Hirth Discus CS	161CS		15. 6.94	F.G.Birlison	Aston Down	28.11.02
HLZ	4041	359	Schleicher ASW20BL	20951	D-8188	19. 3.94	T Vines	Dunstable	27. 4.02
HMA	4042		SZD-51-1 Junior	B-2132		30. 3.94	The Soaring Centre	Husbands Bosworth	30.11.02
HMB	4043	445	Glaser-Dirks DG-300 Elan	3E105	D-4676	31. 3.94	A.D.Langlands	Thame	1. 3.02
HMG	4044	HMG	ICA IS-28B2	353	HA-....	20. 4.94	J.W.Courchee	Tibenham	8. 4.02
HMH	4045	S82	Schleicher K8B	5	D-5735	15. 4.94	Shenington GC	Edgehill	17.6.02
			(Officially regd as c/n 2330)						
HMK	4046	941	Rolladen-Schneider LS-6-18W	6324	D-1245	18. 3.94	A.S.Decloux	Gransden Lodge	4. 2.02
HML	4047	38	Schempp-Hirth Discus CS	114CS	OO-ZTU	16. 3.94	M.E.Hahnefeld	Parham Park	17. 2.02
			(Composite with wings from BGA.3879)						
HMM	4048	D19	Glasflugel H.304B	322	SE-UGZ	31. 3.94	I.P.Freestone	Husbands Bosworth	1. 6.01
					D-1005				
HMP	4050	297	Schempp-Hirth Discus B	497		13. 3.94	D.J.Connolly	North Hill	26. 4.02
HMQ	4051	364	Schempp-Hirth Discus CS	099CS	D-7160	8. 3.94	S.A.Hindley	Edgehill	2.12.01
HMR	4052	CCZV	Wassmer WA.30 Bijave	140	F-CCZV	4. 4.94	Bidford GC	NK	3. 4.95*
							(Wreck stored 9.97 Bidford but gone by 8.99)		
HMS	4053	HMS	Glaser-Dirks DG-100	40	D-2579	8. 4.94	B.Walton-Knight	Cross Hayes	2. 7.02
HMT	4054	380	Glasflugel H.303 Mosquito B	153	F-CEDY	20. 3.94	B.T.Spreckley	Le Blanc, France	1. 3.02
HMU	4055		CARMAM JP-15/36AR Aiglon	22	F-CETT	7. 5.94	J.R.Holmes	Kingston Deverill	13. 2.02
HMV	4056	N26	Schleicher ASK13	13177	D-0268	9. 5.94	Portsmouth Naval GC	Lee-on-Solent	6. 7.02
HMW	4057		Scheibe SF-27A Zugvogel V		D-0289	9. 5.94	Surrey Hills GC	Kenley	8.98
				AB.6111			*(W/o Cerdanya, Spain 14.4.98)*		
HMX	4058	V19	Rolladen-Schneider LS.4B	4230	OO-ZNN	14. 5.94	D.Robson	Currock Hill	24. 3.02
					F-CEIO				
HMY	4059	HMY	Schempp-Hirth HS.4 Standard Cirrus		HB-1034	29. 4.94	C.P.Woodcock & B.J.Thomas	Weston-on-the-Green	20. 2.02
				121					
HMZ	4060	469	Federov Me-7 Mechta	M.004		4.94	R.Ellis	Rufforth	12. 2.96*
							(Crashed Camphill 12.6.96 & major components stored 7.97)		
HNA	4061	HNA	Glaser-Dirks DG-500/20 Elan			14. 7.94	J.P.Boneham	Winthorpe	17.12.01
				5E128W3					
HNB	4062	563	Schempp-Hirth HS.6 Janus	C215	D-4149	16. 4.94	C.M.Fox	Lleweni Parc	10. 3.02
HNC	4063		Schleicher ASW19B	19297	OH-515	18. 4.94	K.C.Morgan	Tibenham	22. 6.02
HND	4064	HND	Scheibe Zugvogel IIIA	1044	HB-735	23. 5.94	D.Spillane	Lyveden	11. 5.02
					D-9119				
HNE	4065	708	Schempp-Hirth HS.5 Nimbus 2B	91	D-2786	10. 5.94	S.Noad & Ptnrs	Challock	4. 1.03
HNF	4066	315	Schempp-Hirth Duo Discus	11		11. 5.94	Booker GC	Booker	13 .4.02
HNG	4067	HNG	Schleicher K8B	132/59	D-8378	5. 5.94	Bidford GC	Bidford	1. 8.02
HNH	4068	599	Schempp-Hirth HS.5 Nimbus 2C	187	D-2830	31. 3.94	A.P.Hatton	Winthorpe	7. 3.02
HNJ	4069	HNJ	Schleicher Ka7 Rhonadler	7031	D-1667	6. 5.94	N.J.Orchard-Armitage	Waldershare Park	18. 1.02
					RAFGGA??/D-6233				
HNK	4070	HNK	SZD-51-1 Junior	B-1496	SP-3299	20. 5.94	Booker GC	Booker	9. 2.02
					(SP-3290)				
HNM	4072	167	Jastreb Standard Cirrus G/81	360	SE-TZT	2. 7.94	V.L.Brown & Ptnr	Snitterfield	1. 3.02
HNN	4073	HNN	Schempp-Hirth Duo Discus	21		15. 9.94	M.R.Smith	Aboyne	26. 1.02
HNS	4077	XN185	Slingsby T.21B	1164	8942M	21. 6.94	B.Walker	RAF Syerston	17. 7.02
					XN185				
HNT	4078	105	Schleicher ASW15	15167	F-CEAQ	27. 4.94	A.P.Moulang	Challock	16. 6.02
HNU	4079	48	Schempp-Hirth Nimbus 4DT	3/5	D-KHIA	25. 5.94	D.E.Findon	Bidford	26. 3.02
HNV	4080	692	Rolladen-Schneider LS-4B	4960		11.12.94	P.W.Armstrong	Kirton-in-Lindsey	3. 6.02
HNW	4081	2UP	Schempp-Hirth Duo Discus	25		21.11.94	J.L.Birch	Dunstable	19. 4.02
HNX	4082	585	Rolladen-Schneider LS-4B	4937		6. 7.94	C.S.Crocker	Long Mynd	23. 3.01
HNY	4083	HNY	Centrair 101A Pegase	101A-020	F-CFRP	12.10.95	M.Breen	Booker	13.10.98
HNZ	4084	RY	Centrair 101A Pegase	101A-032	F-CFRY	14. 7.94	R.H.Partington	Kirton-in-Lindsey	6.12.02
HPA	4085		Issoire E78 Silene	4	F-CFEA	R	T.M.Perkins	Dunstable	
HPB	4086		Hutter H.28 II replica	-		24. 8.94	D.G.Jones	Husbands Bosworth	8.95P*

HPC	4087	HPC	Schleicher ASW20CL	20787	D-3424	20 .7.94	D.R.Sutton	Pocklington	17. 4.02
HPD	4088	717	Rolladen-Schneider LS-6C-18	6331	D-1054	24.10.94	S.G.Sampson	Lasham	20.11.01
HPE	4089	HPE	Schleicher ASK13	13510	D-3992	2.10.94	Nottingham University GC	RAF Syerston	31.12.01
HPF	4090	HPH	SZD-9 bis Bocian 1E	P-740	OH-508	3. 8.94	Bath, Wilts & North Dorset GC		
								Kingston Deverill	23. 2.01
HPG	4091	HPG	Maupin Woodstock	551	VR-HKI	8.94	J.M.Stockwell	Perranporth	3. 4.02
			(Built J.M.Stockwell)						
HPH	4092	73	Schempp-Hirth Discus CS	174CS		21. 9.94	M.T.Burton	Ridgewell	12. 9.02
HPJ	4093	HPJ	Edgley EA9 Optimist	EA9/001		5.94	Edgley Aeronautics Ltd	Lasham	11. 8.01
			(C/n reported by John Edgely as '004')						
HPK	4094		Bibby G.1	1		R	K.Bibby		
HPL	4095	655	Rolladen-Schneider LS-4B	4959	(BGA.4071)	28. 7.94	P.G.Mellor	Booker	10. 4.02
HPM	4096	HPM	Grob G.102 Astir CS	1072	D-3304	21.11.94	S.K.Moeller	Lasham	22. 1.02
HPP	4098		Slingsby T.38 Grasshopper	863	XA230	5. 2.95	S.Butler	Gransden Lodge	12. 8.02
HPQ	4099	HPQ	Schleicher Ka6CR	6200	D-1933	5.10.94	M.Ewer	Crowland	5. 3.02
HPR	4100	127	Schempp-Hirth Discus B	532		20. 2.95	J.S.McCullagh	Dunstable	11.10.02
HPS	4101	HPS	Federov Me-7 Mechta	M.005		30. 5.95	R.Ellis	(Bellarena?)	16. 6.98
							(W/o Tibenham 23.5.98)		
HPT	4102	HPT	Federov Me-7 Mechta	M.006		29. 3.96	A E.Griffiths	Long Mynd	1. 1.02
HPU	4103	848	Glaser-Dirks DG-800S	8-38S9	(BGA.4074)	20.11.94	R.J.Middleton	Portmoak	17. 2.01
HPV	4104	HPV	Schleicher ASK21	21608		13.10.94	Scottish Gliding Union Ltd	Portmoak	24.11.01
HPW	4105	HPW	Schleicher ASK21	21609		25.11.94	Scottish Gliding Union Ltd	Portmoak	9. 3.02
HPX	4106	693	Schempp-Hirth Discus CS	177CS		12. 4.95	P.C.Whitmore & M.A.Whitehead		
								Gransden Lodge	24. 2.02
HPY	4107		ASC Spirit	EUR.001		5.95	Repclif Aviation Ltd	(Crewe)	2. 6.98
HPZ	4108		ASC Falcon	EUR.002		1.96	Repclif Aviation Ltd	(Crewe)	26.11.97
HQB	4110	HQB	Slingsby T.21B	602	WB935	1.10.94	C.E.Anson	(Germany)	23.11.02
			(Officially regd with c/n 1099 which is a corruption of fuselage no.SSK/FF/1099)						
HQC	4111	HQC	Scheibe Bergfalke II/55	322	D-9004	20.12.94	S.H.Gibson	Gransden Lodge	1. 5.99
							(Being refurbished)		
HQD	4112	A20	Schleicher ASW20	20288	SE-ULA	1.11.94	D.G.Brain & Ptnrs	Dunstable	25. 5.02
					OH-548				
HQE	4113	BD	Schempp-Hirth Duo Discus	29		19. 2.95	3D Syndicate	Aboyne	20. 3.02
HQF	4114	HQF	CARMAM M.100S Mesange	26	F-CCSO	3.11.94	R.E.Stokes	Rhigos	9. 6.01
HQG	4115	HQG	LAK-12 Lietuva	6222		30. 4.95	M.Boyle & Ptnrs	Rufforth	18. 4.02
HQH	4116	HQH	Schleicher Ka4 Rhonlerche II		(BGA.4097)	5.95	D.Fulchiron	Bellechasse	
				3072/Br	HB-877			France	31. 7.02
HQJ	4117	762	Schempp-Hirth Discus B	336	D-1762	10. 2.95	D.G.Lingafelter	Dunstable	4. 3.02
HQK	4118	S2	Schleicher ASW20CL	20854	D-3366	18. 1.95	S.D.Minson	Halesland	27. 3.02
HQL	4119	LS6	Rolladen-Schneider LS-6C-18W		D-0794	3. 3.95	D.P.Masson	Lasham	1. 6.02
				6352					
HQM	4120	HQM	Schempp-Hirth Discus B	44	RAFGSA.R10	23. 1.95	Cambridge University GC	Gransden Lodge	9. 1.02
HQN	4121	D64	Schempp-Hirth HS.5 Nimbus 2B	139	D-6494	29. 1.95	D.Peters	Burn	25. 3.02
HQR	4123	19	Schempp-Hirth Discus B	531		26. 4.95	British Gliding Association		
								Bicester	17.12.02
HQS	4124	HQS	Grob G.103 Twin Astir	3155	OO-ZEG	26. 2.95	Essex & Suffolk GC	Wormingford	24. 4.02
HQT	4125	A77	Grob G.102 Astir CS77	1678	RAFGGA.561	12. 2.95	D.F.Bailey	Kenley	6. 6.02
HQU	4126		SZD-9 bis Bocian 1D	F-848	SP-2439	9. 7.97	T.Wiltshere	(Spilsby)	8. 7.98
HQV	4127		SZD-51-1 Junior	B-2139		20. 3.95	The Soaring Centre	Husbands Bosworth	18. 4.02
HQW	4128	329	Schempp-Hirth Discus B	538		9. 3.95	J.E.May	Nympsfield	7.11.02
HQX	4129	HQX	Schleicher ASW15B	15326	D-2315	13. 3.95	R.Emms	Crowland	23. 3.02
HQY	4130	487	Schempp-Hirth HS.7 Mini Nimbus C		D-....	14. 3.95	D.S.Hill	Lasham	8. 4.02
				328					
HQZ	4131	U2	Rolladen-Schneider LS-6C-18W		D-1486	6. 3.95	N.P.Marriott	Lasham	15. 4.02
				6353					
HRA	4132	N19	Grob G.102 Astir CS	1109	D-4169	21. 4.95	Portsmouth Naval GC	Lee-on-Solent	7. 8.02
HRB	4133		LAK-12 Lietuva	6223		3.95	J.E.Neville	Aboyne	11. 1.03
HRC	4134	390	Glaser-Dirks DG-500-20 Elan Trainer			15. 5.95	N.J.Allcoat	Portmoak	4. 3.01
				5E136W5					
HRD	4135		Slingsby T.21B	634	WB973	18. 3.95	U.Seegers	(Germany)	8. 6.02
HRE	4136	HRE	Schleicher Ka6CR	572	D-9326	26. 4.96	R.J.Playle	Edgehill	11. 5.02
HRF	4137	JM	Schleicher Ka6E	4272	OO-ZJR	12. 5.95	J.F.Morris	Gransden Lodge	14. 9.02
					D-0165				
HRG	4138	HRG	SZD-51-1 Junior	B-2013		25. 4.95	Scottish Gliding Union Ltd	Portmoak	17. 1.02
HRJ	4139	504	Schleicher K8B	8093Ei	D-5048	26. 4.95	M.Barnard	Turweston	5. 6.01
HRK	4140	HRK	Centrair 101A Pegase	101A-048	F-CFQJ	16. 5.95	I.P Bramley	Dunstable	8. 5.02
HRL	4141	HRL	Schempp-Hirth HS.4 Standard Cirrus		D-3099	26. 4.95	M.Harbour	Camphill	3. 4.02
				525					
HRN	4143	HRN	Schleicher ASK18	18026	HB-1308	7. 4.95	Stratford-upon-Avon GC	Snitterfield	4. 5.02
HRP	4144	HRP	SZD-51-1 Junior	B-1807	SP-3442	19. 5.95	Wolds GC	Pocklington	2. 2.02
HRQ	4145	169	Schempp-Hirth HS.7 Mini Nimbus C		(BGA.4122)	17.4.95	C.Buzzard	Husbands Bosworth	19. 4.02
				123	SE-TVB				
HRR	4146	D70	Schleicher ASK21	21033	D-7083	2. 2.95	Lakes GC	Walney Island	6. 1.02
HRS	4147	B33	Schempp-Hirth Discus CS	100CS	D-5100	1. 5.95	M.E.Hughes	Husbands Bosworth	22. 5.02

HRT	4148		Schleicher K8B	8390A	D-5599	9. 3.96	Heron GC	RNAS Yeovilton	6. 4.02
HRU	4149	FK	Centrair ASW20F	20114	F-CFFK	27. 7.95	European Soaring Club	Le Blanc, France	14.10.02
HRV	4150		SZD-55-1	551195076		2.11.95	R.W.Southworth	Warsaw, Poland	24.11.01
HRW	4151	802	Schempp-Hirth Duo Discus	43	(BGA.4160) BGA.4151	22. 6.95	A.J.Davis	Nympsfield	5.12.02
HRX	4152	P5	Schempp-Hirth Discus A	545		24. 5.95	P.G.Sheard	Dunstable	24.11.02
HRY	4153	L8	Rolladen-Schneider LS-6C-18W	6362		2. 6.95	F.K.Russell	Dunstable	5. 2.02
HSA	4155	A1	Rolladen-Schneider LS-6C-18W	6361		8. 8.95	D.A.Benton	Long Mynd	1. 6.01
HSB	4156	HSB	Glaser-Dirks DG-300 Elan3E	461		20. 7.95	J.S.Forster	Parham Park	16. 4.02
HSC	4157	99	SZD-50-3 Puchacz	B-2079		15. 8.95	British Gliding Association	Bicester	25. 1.02
HSD	4158	D15	Schempp-Hirth Discus B *(Rebuild of BGA.3406 c/n 258 w/o 26.8.94)*	258/1	(BGA.4142)	19. 6.95	J.R.Reed	Dunstable	21. 2.02
HSE	4159	HSE	Grob G.102 Astir CS77	1635	RAFGSA.R68 RAFGSA.548	2. 9.95	R.G.Tait	Easterton	19. 3.02
HSG	4161	7827	Scheibe SF-27A Zugvogel V	1705/E	D-7827 OE-0827	11. 7.95	Welland GC	Lyveden	6. 9.02
HSH	4162	HSH	Scheibe Zugvogel IIIB	7/1041	D-6558	12. 7.95	J.E.Harman *"Brigitta"*	Bidford	22. 7.02
HSJ	4163	D54	Schempp-Hirth Discus	B546		3. 7.95	K.L.Rowley	Pocklington	11. 7.02
HSK	4164	933	Schleicher ASW20CL	20827	D-3499	18. 7.95	T.M.World *(Damaged in accident near Bicester 16.8.99)*	Lasham	14. 5.00
HSL	4165	213	Schempp-Hirth Ventus 2C *(Incomplete airframe assembled by Southern Sailplanes)*	1/2	(BGA.4154)	4. 7.95	H.G.Woodsend	Weston-on-the-Green	14. 3.02
HSM	4166	HSM	Schleicher ASK13	13145	D-0168	18. 7.95	Stratford-upon-Avon GC	Snitterfield	29. 3.02
HSN	4167		Schleicher Ka6CR	6218	OO-ZZF D-8546	1. 8.95	M.Brennan	Enstone	9. 8.02
HSP	4168	385	Schempp-Hirth HS.6 Janus C	112	RAFGSA.R1 BGA.2723/D-7013	R	D.H.Garrard *(Active)*	Gransden Lodge	
HSQ	4169	493	Schempp-Hirth Discus B	99	D-2943	8. 8.95	Midland GC	Long Mynd	26. 1.02
HSR	4170	313	LAK-12 Lietuva	6178		3. 8.95	J.F.Morris & Ptnr	Gransden Lodge	14. 8.01
HSS	4171		Schleicher Ka7 Rhonadler	7015	RAFGSA.R29 D-5241	29. 8.95	M.Cuming	Edgehill	28. 8.96*
HSU	4173	K18	Schleicher ASK18	18025	AGA.16	R	R.C.Martin *(Being refurbished)*		
HSV	4174		Schempp-Hirth HS.4 Standard Cirrus	195	D-0785	14. 3.96	J.Harman	Edgehill	26. 4.02
HSW	4175	895	Schempp-Hirth Duo Discus	48		25. 8.95	C.R.Simpson	Husbands Bosworth	23. 2.02
HSX	4176	HSX	Scheibe SF-27A Zugvogel	V6031	SE-TDT	26. 9.95	S.D.Jones	Wormingford	14. 6.01
HSY	4177	A15	Pilatus B4 PC-11	050	SE-UFF OH-431	22. 9.95	A.L.Dennis	Walney Island	19. 9.00
HSZ	4178	V8	Rolladen-Schneider LS-8a	8030		9.95	C.L.Withall	Dunstable	3. 1.03
HTA	4179		Centrair C-201B1 Marianne	201-014	F-CGMM	21.10.95	E.Crooks	Kirton-in-Lindsey	31.10.00
HTB	4180	TE	Schempp-Hirth HS.6 Janus A	007	D-3114	27. 7.95	P.J.Gibbs & Ptnrs	Edgehill	23.12.01
HTC	4181	HTC	Schleicher ASW15B	15188	OE-0930	26.10.95	N.A.Page	Camphill	25. 3.01
HTD	4182	VMC	Grob G.102 Astir CS	1012	D-6508	20. 5.96	G.V.McKirdy	Edgehill	15. 4.00
HTE	4183	HTE	Grob G.102 Astir CS77	1716	RAFGSA.R82 RAFGSA.882	23.11.95	J.R.Whittington	Challock	16. 3.02
HTF	4184	HTF	LAK-12 Lietuva	6180		1. 6.96	D.Stidwell	Cross Hayes	22. 5.02
HTG	4185	HTG	Grob G.102 Astir CS	1510	RAFGSA.R59(2) RAFGSA.R69(2)/RAFGSA.519	30.10.95	Trent Valley GC	Kirton-in-Lindsey	29. 7.02
HTH	4186	C4	Schempp-Hirth Janus CT	185/2	N137DB D-KHIE	13.11.95	S.A.Adlard *(Cambridge Aero Instruments research vehicle)*	Long Mynd	13. 6.02
HTJ	4187	HTJ	Schleicher ASK13	13125	D-6048	2.12.95	Ulster GC	Bellarena	10. 5.02
HTL	4189	LS	Rolladen-Schneider LS-8-18	8038	D-3156	10.95	A. & L.Wells	RAF Keevil	6.12.02
HTM	4190	Z8	Rolladen-Schneider LS-8-18	8036		10.95	W.Payton	Sutton Bank	13. 4.02
HTN	4191	S22	Schleicher ASW22	22013	ZS-GLN	16. 4.96	J.B.Giddins	Edgehill	28.10.02
HTP	4192	L58	Rolladen-Schneider LS-8-18	8039	D-3175	11.95	R.A.Browne	Crowland	14. 4.02
HTQ	4193	C64	Rolladen-Schneider LS-8-18	8037	D-2993	11.95	P.G. & S.J.Crabb	Sandhill Farm Shrivenham	20. 9.02
HTR	4194	HTR	Grob G.102 Astir CS	1190	D-7307	20.11.95	I.Wright	Kingston Deverill	26. 2.02
HTS	4195	H8	Rolladen-Schneider LS-8-18	8040		22.11.95	D.J.Howse	Gransden Lodge	29.11.02
HTT	4196	HTT	Schleicher ASW20CL	20627	D-2410	24.11.95	J.Potter	Camphill	8. 3.02
HTU	4197	HTU	Schempp-Hirth HS.2 Cirrus	88	D-0478	29.12.95	S.Kochanowski	Lasham	13. 5.02
HTV	4198	HTV	Schleicher ASK21	21624	D-8355	3. 3.96	Cambridge University GC	Gransden Lodge	7. 3.02
HTW	4199		Pottier JP15-34 Kit Club	50-39	F-CFGF	4.12.95	R.P Halton	Bidford	16. 3.99
HTX	4200	900	Schleicher ASW20	20239	D-3180	3. 3.96	C.Ramshorn	Gransden Lodge	18. 2.02
HTY	4201		LET L-13 Blanik	026318	LY-GDT DOSAAF	1. 4.96	North Devon GC	Brent Tor	31. 5.02
HTZ	4202	833	Bolkow Phoebus 17C	908	OO-ZDJ BGA.1573	9.12.95	A.de Tourtoulon	Wormingford	3 .8.02
HUA	4203		Schleicher ASW19	19091	D-3840	29.12.95	M.T Davenport	Lasham	20. 8.02
HUB	4204		SZD-48-3 Jantar Standard	B-1527	DOSAAF	17. 3.96	C.F.Sermanni	Strathaven	7. 1.03

HUC	4205	HUC	Schempp-Hirth Janus CE	170	(BGA.4188)	24. 2.96	C.W.Price	Wormingford	14.11.02
					D-3189				
HUD	4206	HUD	Schleicher ASK13	13018	D-9203	21. 2.96	Welland GC	Lyveden	1.11.02
HUE	4207	N5	Schleicher ASW27	27022		10.96	E.H.Downham	Dunstable	10. 6.02
HUF	4208	HUF	Schleicher ASK13	13109	OO-ZWE	10. 3.96	London GC	Dunstable	20. 4.02
HUH	4210	D31	Schempp-Hirth HS.6 Janus	15	D-3116	9. 5.96	B.A.Fairston	Husbands Bosworth	16. 7.02
HUJ	4211	HUJ	Centrair ASW20F	20170	F-CFLY	5. 3.96	R.S.Lee	Rattlesden	18. 5.02
HUK	4212	HUK	Schleicher Ka6CR	6385	SE-TCN	15. 4.96	T.J Donovan & Ptnr	Lyveden	3. 4.02
HUL	4213	624	Schempp-Hirth HS.2 Cirrus	V3	HB-900	26. 2.96	I.Ashton & Ptnrs	Chipping	18. 5.02
HUM	4214	241	Rolladen-Schneider LS-6C	6267	OO-ZXS	25. 3.96	A.Hall	Lasham	3. 4.02
					D-4350				
HUN	4215	HUN	Grob G.102 Astir CS Jeans	2089	D-7531	27. 2.96	D P.Manchett	Lleweni Parc	4.11.02
HUP	4216	170	Schempp-Hirth Ventus 2CT	4/11		16. 2.96	C G Corbett	Tibenham	14. 2.02
HUQ	4217		Federov Me-7 Mechta	007		21. 6.96	J S Fielden	Brent Tor	2. 5.02
HUR	4218	HUR	Schempp-Hirth HS.2 Cirrus	12	HB-927	20. 4.96	D G Slocombe	Burn	20. 5.02
HUS	4219	HUS	Scheibe SF-27A Zugvogel	V6010	D-1035	6. 8.97	C J Palmer	Booker	30.12.01
HUT	4220	HUT	Centrair ASW20F	20187	F-CEUQ	14. 4.96	G.A MacFadyen	Nympsfield	16. 5.02
HUU	4221		Schleicher ASK13	13527AB	D-7506	15. 4.96	Upward Bound Trust	Thame	15.11.01
					D-8945				
HUV	4222	64	Rolladen-Schneider LS-8A-18	8056	D-3823	4.96	C.P.Jeffery	Gransden Lodge	14. 3.02
HUW	4223	S8	Rolladen-Schneider LS-8A	8058		3.96	S.E.Bort	Kenley	5.12.01
HUX	4224	58	Schempp-Hirth Ventus 2C	7/12		17. 3.96	E.R.Lysakowski	Lasham	16. 3.99
		(Crashed	Cavenham 11.7.98 after midair collision)						
HUY	4225	HUY	Schempp-Hirth Ventus CT	84/329	D-KILZ	3. 4.96	M A Challans	Lasham	19. 2.02
HUZ	4226	200	Schempp-Hirth Discus BT	158/559		2. 3.96	J.Lynchenhaun	Lleweni Parc	5. 4.02
HVA	4227	HVA	SZD-59 Acro	B-2169		2. 5.96	T.Williams	Lasham	20. 9.01
HVB	4228	HVB	Slingsby T.31B	850	(BGA.3249)	27. 4.96	M.Hoogenbosch	Hilversum	
					XA308		*"Top Less"*	The Netherlands	1. 6.02
HVC	4229		Slingsby T.38 Grasshopper	766	WZ770	4. 5.01	J.Forster	Hilversum	
								The Netherlands	3. 5.02
HVD	4230	304	SZD-55-1	551193052		23. 4.96	Anglo-Polish Sailplanes Ltd	Booker	8. 4.02
HVE	4231	W54	Schempp-Hirth Ventus 2CT	8/19	D-KHIA	28. 3.96	Glyndwr Soaring Club	Lleweni Parc	26. 2.02
HVF	4232	321	Rolladen-Schneider LS-8-18	8059	D-1683	4.96	M.D.Wells	Bidford	29. 4.02
HVG	4233	RP1	Schleicher ASK21	21062	D-2606	17. 4.96	Rattlesden GC	Rattlesden	21. 2.02
HVH	4234	HVH	Pilatus B4 PC-11	067	D-2156	21. 5.96	C.Cain	Lasham	6. 6.00
HVJ	4235	962	Scheibe SF-27A Zugvogel V	6012	OE-0762	1. 6.96	C.P.Bleaden	Kirton-in-Lindsey	7.00
HVK	4236	HVK	Grob G.102 Astir CS	1161	D-4182	26. 4.96	F.R.Panter	Tibenham	22. 3.02
HVL	4237	LS8	Rolladen-Schneider LS-8-18	8060		4.96	J. Allison	Bidford	2. 1.02
HVM	4238	393	Glaser-Dirks DG-300 Elan	3E177	D-4314	17. 5.96	Surrey & Hants GC	Lasham	31. 1.02
HVP	4240	930	Schleicher ASW20	20374	D-1961	3. 5.96	E.J.Smallbone	Lasham	6.11.01
					BGA.4076/EC-DLN				
HVQ	4241	HVQ	Schleicher ASK13	13251	D-0605	27. 4.96	R.B.Brown	Edgehill	24. 4.02
HVR	4242	HVR	Schempp-Hirth Discus B	560		3. 5.96	Yorkshire Gliding Club (Pty) Ltd	Sutton Bank	3. 4.02
HVT	4244	210	Schempp-Hirth Ventus 2B	37		10. 5.96	P.R.Jones	Booker	30. 4.02
HVU	4245	C65	Rolladen-Schneider LS-8A	8066		4.96	S.J.Crabb	Sandhill Farm	
								Shrivenham	24.11.01
HVV	4246	HVV	Rolladen-Schneider LS-4B	41009		5. 1.97	A.Bardgett	Currock Hill	13. 1.02
HVW	4247	HVW	Schleicher ASK13	13431	D-2140	14. 4.96	Rattlesden GC	Rattlesden	25. 5.02
HVX	4248		Centrair ASW20F	20528	F-CFSJ	13. 6.96	A.S Goldsmith	Camphill	24. 6.99
HVY	4249	584	Schempp-Hirth Ventus 2C	9/21		17. 5.96	R.Ashurst	Lasham	15. 2.02
HVZ	4250	HVZ	Schempp-Hirth HS.4 Standard Cirrus	567G	HB-1269	5. 6.96	J.Bennett	Gransden Lodge	24. 2.02
HWA	4251	31	Schempp-Hirth Ventus 2C	8/20		7. 6.96	C.Garton	Lasham	6. 9.02
HWB	4252	775	Schempp-Hirth Duo Discus	84		25. 5.96	Lasham Gliding Society	Lasham	15. 1.02
HWC	4253	L18	Glasflugel H.201B Standard Libelle	310	HB-1076	7. 7.96	J.C.Rogers	Winthorpe	3. 3.02
HWD	4254	HWD	Schempp-Hirth HS.4 Standard Cirrus	97	HB-987	3. 6.96	A.J.Pettitt	Rivar Hill	21. 6.02
HWE	4255	HWE	Schleicher K8B	1151	HB-700	31. 5.96	J.P.Brady	Brent Tor	27. 6.02
HWF	4256	ZC	Jastreb Standard Cirrus G/81	281	SE-TZC	12. 6.96	M.Langford	Booker	29. 6.02
HWG	4257	HWG	Glasflugel H.201B Standard Libelle	259	HB-1051	19. 6.96	S.C.J.Barker	Pocklington	27. 9.02
HWH	4258	712	Schempp-Hirth Ventus CT	182/599	RAFGGA.506	7. 7.96	H.R.Browning	Lasham	6.11.02
HWK	4260		Grob G.104 Speed Astir IIB	4070	OO-ZVQ	14.7.96	P.Gilbert	Tours, France	13. 7.97*
					LX-CRT				
HWL	4261	84	Rolladen-Schneider LS-8A	8076		15. 6.96	M.Coffee	Bidford	25. 3.02
HWM	4262	D7	Rolladen-Schneider LS-8A	8079		7.96	C.D.Marsh	Bidford	20. 3.02
HWN	4263	598	Schempp-Hirth Nimbus 3T	8/60	D-KHIF	5. 7.96	H.Hampel	(Germany)	18. 6.02
HWP	4264	HWP	Glaser-Dirks DG-100G Elan	E24G13	D-3772	12. 7.96	C.A.Sheldon	Pocklington	25. 7.01
HWQ	4265	HWQ	Scheibe L-Spatz 55	607	D-6195	7.96	A.Gruber	Usk	28. 8.00
HWR	4266	M1	Rolladen-Schneider LS-3A	3098	D-3902	19. 7.96	G.L.Askew & Ptnr	Seighford	7.97
							(Collided with BGA.2791	*Seighford 2.5.98)*	
HWS	4267	75	Rolladen-Schneider LS-8-18	8080		14. 2.97	E.A.Coles	Dunstable	15. 3.02

HWT	4268	S83	Schleicher K8B	8780	HB-958	13. 7.96	Shenington GC	Edgehill	2. 8.02
HWV	4270	526	Schempp-Hirth Discus B	561		12. 8.96	J.R.Martindale	Walney Island	2. 4.02
			(Rebuild of fuselage from AGA.4 c/n 206 with new wings c/n 561)						
HWW	4271	DJT	Grob G.103 Twin II Acro	3658-K-27	OE-5285	23. 8.96	T.Gage	Lasham	7. 2.02
HWX	4272	HWX	SZD-59 Acro	B-2170		3. 9.96	D.W.Gosden	Usk	9. 8.02
HWY	4273	168	Jastreb Standard Cirrus VTC	G/81 359	LN-GAL	6. 9.96	D.D.Copeland	Booker	23. 9.02
HWZ	4274	HWZ	Schleicher ASW19B	19316	HB-1524	6. 9.96	K.Commins	Dublin	29. 5.02
HXA	4275	HXA	Scheibe Zugvogel IIIB	1107	D-2005	17. 3.97	B W Millar	North Connel	21. 4.01
HXB	4276	HXB	Grob G.102 Astir CS77	1819	D-6755	29. 9.96	K.S.Wells	Crowland	1. 9.02
HXC	4278	M8	Rolladen-Schneider LS-8A	8094		24. 2.97	S.M.Smith	Gransden Lodge	24. 2.02
HXD	4279	HXD	Schleicher ASW27	27030		8. 3.97	M.Jerman	Wormingford	22. 1.02
HXE	4280	Y4	Schleicher ASW19B	19053	D-6699	25. 9.96	M.Lloyd-Owen	Lasham	9. 1.02
HXH	4283	HXH	Schempp-Hirth Discus B	573	BGA.4375 (BGA.4283)	6.98	Deesside GC	Aboyne	15.11.02
			(Originally NTU then re-allotted as BGA.4375 and finally reverted to BGA.4283)						
HXJ	4284	HXJ	Schleicher ASK13	13216	D-0417	29.11.96	Cotswold GC	Aston Down	25.10.02
HXL	4286	OK-0927	Letov LF-107 Lunak	39	OK-0927 OK-0827	1.11.96	G.P.Saw	Booker	5. 1.02
HXM	4287	HXM	Grob G.102 Astir CS	1272	D-7367	15.11.96	C.Fretwell	Challock	1. 6.02
HXN	4288	57	Rolladen-Schneider LS-8-18	8095		28. 1.97	J.L Birch	Dunstable	13. 2.02
HXP	4289	HXP	Schleicher ASK13	13023	D-3656	19.11.96	K.E.Ballington	Cross Hayes	28. 4.02
HXQ	4290	156	Schleicher ASH25B	25187	OH-874	23.11.96	M.Chant	Brent Tor	23.11.01
HXR	4291	560	Schempp-Hirth Ventus CT	88/333	D-KESH	20. 2.97	J.W.A'Court	Lasham	20.12.02
HXS	4292	V11	Schempp-Hirth Ventus 2CT	10/41		27.11.96	I.R.Cook	Rivar Hill	5. 3.02
HXT	4293	LS4	Rolladen-Schneider LS-4A	4325	ZS-GNV	21. 3.97	B.T.Spreckley	Le Blanc, France	28. 3.01
HXU	4294	HXU	Schleicher ASW19B	19359	SE-TXN	14. 4.97	G.A.Chalmers	Easterton	17. 3.02
HXV	4295	HXV	Schleicher ASK13	13080	D-5462	5.12.96	Aquila GC	Hinton-in-the-Hedges	31.12.01
HXW	4296	325	Rolladen-Schneider LS-8-18	8097		7. 3.97	W.Aspland	Dunstable	8. 3.02
HXX	4297	HXX	Schempp-Hirth HS.4 Standard Cirrus (*Built Grob*)	154G	D-0363	29. 1.97	E J Winning	Usk	22. 2.02
HXY	4298	HXY	Grob G.102 Astir Jeans	1781	D-7689	8.12.96	I.D.Worten	Bidford	9. 3.02
HXZ	4299	S5	Rolladen-Schneider LS-4	4249	SE-TXF	30. 3.97	E.J.Foggin	Sandhill Farm Shrivenham	17. 4.02
HYA	4300	DD	Rolladen-Schneider LS-6	634B		28. 2.97	R.H.Dixon	Parham Park	15. 2.02
			(Probably c/n 6349 ex D-2162)						
HYB	4301	T5	Schempp-Hirth Discus B	140	D-4684	19. 4.97	K.A.Boost	Lasham	2. 3.02
HYD	4303	HYD	Schleicher ASW24	24039	OE-5460	13. 2.97	M.Makari	Lasham	25. 1.02
HYE	4304	913	Glaser-Dirks DG-505 Elan Orion	5E167X22		22.12.96	Bristol & Glos GC	Nympsfield	29.11.02
HYF	4305	KM	Rolladen-Schneider LS-8-18	8106		15. 3.97	A.T.Johnstone	Dunstable	28. 9.02
HYH	4307	HYH	Rolladen-Schneider LS-3-17	3186	D-6650	18. 1.97	J.Lamb	Bellarena	18. 5.02
HYJ	4308	HYJ	Schleicher ASK21	21066	D-2724	17. 1.97	Highland GC	Easterton	6. 4.02
HYK	4309		Centrair ASW20FLP	20176	F-CEUN	25. 9.97	J.C.Riddell	Rufforth	14. 6.01
HYL	4310	K4	Schempp-Hirth Ventus 2A	44		31. 5.97	A J Stone	Booker	31. 1.02
HYM	4311	PW5	DWLKK PW-5 Smyk	17.06.020		28. 2.97	T.A.Joint "Iceman"	Lasham	11. 5.02
			(C/n is officially recorded as "100")						
HYN	4312	HYN	Schleicher K8B	8310A	D-1018	11.97	G.Brook	Crowland	27. 1.02
HYP	4313	HYP	SZD-50-3 Puchacz	B-2082		22. 2.97	Rattlesden GC	Rattlesden	9. 2.02
HYR	4315	432	Schleicher ASW27	27013	D-8733	11. 3.97	A.R.Hutchings	Dunstable	21. 3.02
HYS	4316	A14	Schleicher ASK21	21519	RAFGGA.514	6.99	RAFGSA	Bicester	12.10.01
HYT	4317	HYT	Schleicher ASK21	21568	AGA.20 RAFGGA.515	1.99	Wyvern GC	AAC Upavon	26. 1.02
HYU	4318	A61	Schempp-Hirth Discus CS	192CS	RAFGSA.R61 RAFGGA.561	6.99	Anglia GC	Wattisham	20. 7.02
HYW	4320	HYW	Schleicher K8B	8163A	D-5316 D-3202	13. 3.97	Lincs GC	Strubby	29. 5.02
HYX	4321	HYX	Schleicher K8B	686	D-5742	???	Oxford University GC	Bicester	12. 5.02
HYY	4322	A26	Schempp-Hirth Nimbus 3DT	21	RAFGSA.R26 D-KAFA	1. 3.97	N.J.Wright	Bidford	9. 4.02
HYZ	4323	L88	Rolladen-Schneider LS-8-18	8104		12. 4.97	P J Coward	Crowland	1.12.02
HZA	4324	376	Schempp-Hirth Nimbus 3/24.5	94	SE-UFO	27. 4.97	C.J.Short	Lasham	18. 5.02
HZB	4325	HZB	DWLKK PW-5 Smyk	17.06.021		28. 2.97	J.D.Scott	Gransden Lodge	16. 5.02
HZC	4326	216	Grob G.102 Astir CS	1092	D-6991	24. 3.97	K.G.Laws	Lasham	1. 2.02
HZD	4327	HZD	Schleicher ASW15B	15327	D-2191	20. 3.97	C.P.Ellison	Booker	6. 4.02
HZE	4328	T3	Schempp-Hirth Discus CS	121CS	D-6946	24. 3.97	A.D.Irving	Kenley	16. 9.02
HZF	4329	G7	Centrair 101A Pegase	101A-0262	PH-796	6. 5.97	B.R.George	Gransden Lodge	7. 3.02
HZG	4330	X7	Rolladen-Schneider LS-8-18	8118		10. 3.97	N.G.Hackett	Husbands Bosworth	18. 6.02
HZH	4331	HZH	Schleicher Ka6CR	6461	HB-836	1. 6.97	M.E.de Torre	Gamston	22. 6.02
HZJ	4332	HZJ	Schempp-Hirth HS.4 Standard Cirrus	23	HB-981	18. 3.97	A.B.Stokes	Enstone	16. 1.02
HZL	4334	HZL	Schempp-Hirth HS.4 Standard Cirrus	304	D-2060	5. 4.97	P.Conran	Lasham	14. 4.01

HZM 4335 U1	Rolladen-Schneider LS-4A	4762	D-1394	14. 4.97	J.M.Bevan	Crowland	13. 3.02
HZN 4336 D6173	Schleicher Ka2B Rhonschwalbe	195	D-6173	28. 3.97	R.A.Willgoss	Booker	22. 5.02
HZP 4337 56	Rolladen-Schneider LS-8-18	8117		12. 3.97	S.J.Redman	Gransden Lodge	7. 6.02
HZQ 4338 K5	Schleicher ASW27	27018	D-4499	10. 3.97	M.D.Rogers	Dunstable	21. 2.02
HZR 4339 HZR	Schleicher ASK21	21079	D-4491	1. 5.97	A.Roseberry	Aston Down	9. 3.02
HZS 4340 K1	Schempp-Hirth Ventus 2A	43		3.97	A.E.Kay	Weston-on-the-Green	2. 5.02
HZT 4341 X50	Centrair ASW20F	20150	F-CFLL	19. 8.97	T.J.Banks	Ringmer	14.10.02
HZU 4342 B11	Schempp-Hirth HS.4 Standard Cirrus	366	HB-1258 N71KW	30. 4.97	D.R.Piercy	Winthorpe	22 .1.02
HZV 4343 P61	Schempp-Hirth HS.4 Standard Cirrus	305	HB-1457 D-2061	30. 4.97	P.Cox *(De-registered 19.10.00 - sold to Australia as VH-..)*	Enstone	2.00
HZW 4344 112	Schempp-Hirth Nimbus 3T	22/88	D-KILO	1. 6.97	J.Ellis	Sutton Bank	9. 4.02
HZX 4345 476	Schleicher K8B	8257	D-8476	12.4.97	G.E.W.Woodward	Upwood	22. 6.02
HZY 4346 EN	Rolladen-Schneider LS-4A	4479	D-3458	19.4.97	N.P.Wedi	Booker	4. 2.02
HZZ 4347 LD	Schleicher ASW20L	20273	N727AM	27.4.97	P.E.Rice	Wormingford	22. 5.02
JAA 4348 JAA	Schempp-Hirth HS.6 Janus B	163	D-3147	18. 4.97	A.A.Baker	Lasham	31.12.02
JAB 4349 TC	Glaser-Dirks DG-300 Elan	3E320	OY-XTC	24. 4.97	P.B.Jones	Lasham	11. 4.02
JAC 4350 98	Schempp-Hirth Duo Discus	128		24. 5.97	British Gliding Association	Bicester	27. 3.02
JAD 4351	Schleicher ASK21	21659		10.97	Borders GC	Milfield	8.10.02
JAE 4352 N8	Glaser-Dirks DG-200/17C	2-62	HB-1443	21. 4.97	S.A.White	Hinton-in-the-Hedges	19. 2.02
JAF 4353 620	Schempp-Hirth Ventus 2B	33	(BGA.4306)	24. 4.97	D.K.McCarthy	Gransden Lodge	11. 1.02
JAG 4354 JAG	Schleicher ASW20L	20136	HB-1474	15. 7.97	654 Syndicate	Currock Hill	9. 5.02
JAH 4355 921	Schempp-Hirth Discus	B572		30. 5.97	K.Neave	Nympsfield	6. 6.02
JAJ 4356 916	Glaser-Dirks DG-202/17	2-150/1744	D-4154	8. 5.97	T.R Dews	Kingston Deverill	8. 2.02
JAK 4357	Schleicher Ka6E	4301	F-CDRJ	R			
JAL 4358 JAL	Schleicher Ka6E	4360	F-CDTX	19. 6.97	N.Gilkes	Lasham	6. 4.02
JAM 4359 777	Schleicher ASW15B	15353	D-2360	5.97	T.J.Beckwith	Sackville Lodge Riseley	20. 1.00
JAN 4360 JAN	Schempp-Hirth Discus B	575		10.97	Wolds GC	Pocklington	14.12.02
JAP 4361	Slingsby T.38 Grasshopper *(Thought to be ex WZ818 [799]*	779	WZ783	R	R.H.Targett	Nympsfield	
JAQ 4362 823	Schempp-Hirth Discus B	190	D-0960	2. 6.97	P.D.Duffin	Wormingford	21. 4.02
JAR 4363 P3	Schempp-Hirth Discus BT	83/417	D-KHEI	16. 5.97	C.J.Partridge	Lasham	19. 4.02
JAS 4364 7Q	Glasflugel H.201 Standard Libelle	109	SE-TIS	29. 5.97	M.D.Wells	Enstone	28. 5.98
JAT 4365 JAT	Schleicher K8B	8150	D-4390	6. 6.97	Wolds GC	Pocklington	4. 3.02
JAU 4366 WB922	Slingsby T.21B	585	WB922	27. 5.97	J.Priddle	Kingston Deverill	1. 7.02
JAV 4367 JAV	Schleicher ASK21	21662		1.97	Wolds GC	Pocklington	17.11.02
JAW 4368 M4	Glaser-Dirks DG-200/17	2-180/1759	D-5618	12. 6.97	C.J.Walker	Lasham	19. 2.02
JAX 4369 JAX	Schleicher ASK21	21665		1.98	Wolds GC	Pocklington	20.10.02
JAY 4370 123	Schleicher ASW20	20034	D-7941	19. 6.97	D.A.Smith	Kingston Deverill	19. 4.02
JAZ 4371 JAZ	Grob G.102 Astir Jeans	2073	D-7586	28. 8.97	Bath, Wilts & North Dorset GC	Kingston Deverill	13. 9.02
JBA 4372 JBA	Slingsby T.38 Grasshopper *(Assembled from components; p/i is starboard wing only)*	1262	XP463	6.98	J A Northen & Pntr	Challock	5. 8.00
JBB 4373 B3	Rolladen-Schneider LS-8	8003	D-8023	22. 8.97	R F Thirkell	Lasham	16.12.02
JBC 4374 2B	Schempp-Hirth Ventus 2CT	15/61		20. 6.97	B.A.Bateson	Ringmer	7. 5.01
JBE 4376 LX	ISF Mistral C	MC.020/79	OY-XLX PH-667	4. 7.97	H.H.Crowther	Aston Down	10. 6.02
JBF 4377	Glasfugel H.201 Standard Libelle	246	F-CDPV	22. 7.97	L.Coles	Booker	2. 5.02
JBG 4378 U9	Schempp-Hirth Ventus B	135	OE-5315	20. 7.97	W.R.Longstaff	Feshiebridge	1. 9.02
JBH 4379 537	Eiri PIK-20D	20621	OH-529	6. 7.97	537 Syndicate (P.J.Holloway)	Parham Park	27. 4.02
JBJ 4380 G81	Jastreb Standard Cirrus G/81	280	SE-TZD	8. 7.97	T.Rendell	Lasham	9. 5.02
JBK 4381 L3	Schleicher ASW19B	19204	D-4099 PH-602	11.97	R.E.Robertson	Dunstable	20.12.01
JBM 4383 S21	Schleicher ASK21	21089	D-6391	26. 7.97	Staffs GC	Seighford	2. 7.02
JBN 4384	Schempp-Hirth Discus B	94	D-7175	R			
JBP 4385 B2	Rolladen-Schneider LS-6-18W	6378		25. 7.97	I.C.Baker	Nympsfield	11. 8.01
JBQ 4386 LH7	Rolladen-Schneider LS-8-18	8148		24. 9.97	L.Hill	North Hill	24. 9.02
JBR 4387 AB	Schempp-Hirth Discus B	90	F-CGGD F-WGGD	8. 8.97	A.A.Baker	RAF Odiham	14. 2.02
JBS 4388 JBS	LAK-12 Lietuva	6115	???	10. 8.97	I.G.Smith & Ptnrs	Ringmer	20. 3.01
JBT 4389 JBT	Schleicher ASW19	19075	D-4477	2. 8.97	Aquila GC	Hinton-in-the-Hedges	23. 3.02
JBU 4390 HL	Rolladen-Schneider LS-6-18W	6350	D-0462	23. 9.97	J.Gorringe	Lasham	23. 1.02
JBV 4391	Monnett Monerai *(Built J.Foxson/B.Niblett)*	-		7.97	W.B.Niblett	Kingston Deverill	19. 7.98
JBW 4392 710	Schempp-Hirth Discus BT	34/337	D-KBJR	8.97	N.C.Pringle	Lasham	28. 1.02
JBX 4393 JBX	Rolladen-Schneider LS-4A	4293	D-9111	4.98	P.W.Lee & Ptnr	Aston Down	10. 4.02
JBY 4394 960	LAK-12 Lietuva	6185		12. 8.97	C.J.Nicholas	Gransden Lodge	26. 6.01
JBZ 4395 JBZ	Grob G.102 Astir CS	1492	D-4794	30. 8.97	K.R.Bryer	RAF Keevil	31.10.01

JCA	4396	JCA	Schleicher ASW15B	15202	(BGA.4049) OH-410	11. 9.97	R.H. & A.Moss	Nympsfield	28. 9.02
JCB	4397	JCB	Rolladen-Schneider LS-6C-18WL	6234	D-6116	4.98	A.Binks	Dunstable	11.12.01
JCD	4399	H5	Schleicher ASW24	24101	D-6091	10.97	M.D.Evershed	Crowland	4. 2.02
JCE	4400	911	Schempp-Hirth Ventus BT	46/240	D-KFMS	15. 9.97	A.G.Reid	Kenley	14.11.01
JCF	4401	JCF	Grob G.102 Astir CS77	1705	PH-1012 D-7634	23. 9.97	Northumbria GC	Currock Hill	9.12.02
JCG	4402	JCG	DWLKK PW-5 Smyk	17.09.003		9.97	V.H.Spencer	Dunstable	6. 7.02
JCH	4403	FOX	MDM-1 Fox	218		.97	C.Cain	Lasham	24. 8.01
							(De-registered 18.12.01 - sold in the USA)		
JCJ	4404	C7	Grob Standard Cirrus	434G	SE-TNC	5.98	M R Garwood	Crowland	10. 6.02
JCK	4405	DC	Schempp-Hirth Discus BT	92/430	D-KIDE	10.97	D.Coppin	Lasham	24. 2.02
JCL	4406	T2	Rolladen-Schneider LS-8-18	8147		10.97	T.W.Slater	Aboyne	11. 4.02
JCM	4407	JCM	Schleicher ASW27	27064		12.97	M.J.Clayton	Bidford	31. 5.01
JCN	4408	JCN	Schempp-Hirth HS.4 Standard Cirrus	646	D-7247	10.97	P.W.Reavill	Camphill	25. 9.02
JCP	4409	36	Rolladen-Schneider LS-8-18	8146		10.97	A.J.Emck	Lasham	19. 1.02
JCQ	4410	W19	Schleicher ASW19B	19086	PH-562	12.97	A.J.Preston	Dunstable	17. 2.02
JCR	4411	JCR	Grob G.102 Astir CS	1181	OE-5188	10.97	B Harrison	Kingston Deverill	21.11.02
JCS	4412	WT898	Slingsby T.31B	693	BGA.3284 WT898	10.97	M.Steiner	(Germany)	29.10.01
JCT	4413	176	Schempp-Hirth Nimbus 4T	21	D-KKKL	10.97	D S Innes	Lasham	6. 5.02
JCU	4414	616	Schempp-Hirth HS.4 Standard Cirrus 75	688	D-6604	10.97	N.Swinton	RAF Halton	14.12.02
JCV	4415	IM	Schleicher ASH25E	25069	D-KAIM	11.97	B.R.George	Gransden Lodge	16. 3.02
JCW	4416	JCW	Grob G.102 Astir CS77	1612	PH-573	10.97	C.R.Phipps	Llantisilio	12. 4.01
JCX	4417	JCX	Schempp-Hirth Discus BT	93/432	D-KJOB	10.97	J.E.Bowman	Bidford	1.11.02
JCY	4418	F3	Rolladen-Schneider LS-8-18	8171		12.97	R.Starey	Lasham	4.12.02
JCZ	4419	JCZ	Schleicher Ka6CR	6108	D-7152	11.97	N.W.Hanney	Kingston Deverill	3. 3.02
JDA	4420	GR	Schempp-Hirth Nimbus 3/24.5	8	D-1788	11.97	G.R.Ross	Lasham	1. 7.02
JDB	4421	WZ828	Slingsby T.38 Grasshopper	809	WZ828	11.97	H.Chapple	Bicester	6. 4.02
JDC	4422	A27	Schleicher ASW27	27010	D-6209	12.97	P.J.Henderson	Challock	6. 2.02
JDD	4423	JDD	Glaser-Dirks DG-200/17C	2-171/CL17	PH-717	12.97	J.Richardson	Chipping	9. 2.02
JDE	4424	543	Rolladen-Schneider LS-8-18	8151		5.98	M.N.Davies	Snitterfield	17. 5.02
JDF	4425	907	Schleicher ASH25E	25150	D-KPAS	11.97	J.E.Cruttenden	Lasham	27. 1.02
JDG	4426	KW	Rolladen-Schneider LS-6B	6145	D-5675	2.98	A.Moss	Nympsfield	9. 1.03
JDH	4427	2F	Rolladen-Schneider LS-6C-18W	6287	D-9128	2.98	F.Schlafke	(Germany)	9.11.02
JDJ	4428	434	Rolladen-Schneider LS-3	3010	D-7729	11.97	J.C.Burdett	Chipping	30.12.02
JDK	4429	SK1	Rolladen-Schneider LS-8-18	8153		3.98	Acro Enterprises	Challock	14. 4.02
JDL	4430	JDL	Schempp-Hirth Discus BT	165/578		4.98	S Robinson	Chipping	19. 5.02
JDM	4431	JDM	Schleicher ASW15B	15280	F-CEGL	1.98	D C Blyth	Tibenham	9. 3.02
JDN	4432	JDN	Glaser-Dirks DG-505 Elan Orion	5E180X31		3.98	Devon & Somerset GC	North Hill	19. 3.01
JDP	4433	JDP	Glaser-Dirks DG-200/17	2-136/1734	D-0152	12.97	J.J.Benton	Camphill	8. 1.03
JDQ	4434	JDQ	Schleicher ASW19	19106	D-3862	2.99	Surrey & Hants. GC	Lasham	20. 3.02
							(Written-off in take-off accident at Lasham. 25.5.01)		
JDR	4435	JDR	Schleicher ASW15A	15053	D-6910	2.98	L Whitaker	Booker	12.11.02
JDS	4436	JDS	Schempp-Hirth HS.4 Standard Cirrus 75	638	D-4057/OY-XCZ	3.98	Burn GC	Burn	25. 6.01
JDT	4437	232	Rolladen-Schneider LS-8a	8172		1.98	R.J.Rebbeck	Dunstable	14. 6.02
JDU	4438		LET L-13 Blanik	026303	D-8919	12.97	Herefordshire GC	Shobdon	9. 2.02
JDV	4439	JDV	Glaser-Dirks DG-303	3E481A24		3.98	I.N.Busby	Booker	20. 3.02
JDW	4440	JDW	DWLKK PW-5 Smyk	17.09.018		12.97	G.Pledger	Currock Hill	14.12.00
							(Damaged Charterhall 11.8.00)		
JDX	4441		Wassmer WA-28F Espadon	101	F-CDZU	12.97	S.S.Turner	Upwood	26. 2.01
JDY	4442	P2	Rolladen-Schneider LS-8-18	8173		2.98	P.O.Paterson	Booker	30. 4.02
JDZ	4443	N1	Schempp-Hirth Nimbus 4T	18	D-KOLF	1.98	A.J.French	Lasham	20. 3.02
JEA	4444	D4	Rolladen-Schneider LS-8-18	8159	D-2411	3.98	R.I.Davidson	Husbands Bosworth	24. 4.02
JEB	4445	JEB	Schleicher ASW24	24172	D-9344	2.98	M.A.& J.Taylor	Rattlesden	30.10.02
JEC	4446	JEC	SZD-50-3 Puchacz	B-2197		4.98	Cambridge University GC	Gransden Lodge	16. 3.02
JED	4447		Schleicher ASW15B	15427	D-3976	1.98	P.R.Williams	Lyveden	25. 2.02
JEE	4448	787	Schleicher ASW20L	20073	(BGA.4456) D-7666	2.98	C.J.Bailey	Wormingford	28. 9.01
JEF	4449	M2	Schempp-Hirth Ventus CT	126/400	D-KFWH	1.98	M.R.Emmett	Booker	26.11.02
JEG	4450	685	Rolladen-Schneider LS-8-18	8150		1.98	J.R.Luxton	Booker	11.12.02
JEH	4451	KE	Glasflugel H.303 Mosquito B	172	OY-XKE	2.98	C.L.Kidd	Booker	13. 3.02
JEJ	4452	F1	Rolladen-Schneider LS-7WL	7074	OE-5477	3.98	I.Mountain	Dunstable	23. 3.02
JEK	4453		Grob G.102 Astir CS	1374	(BGA.4398) D-7403	8.99	S.R.Allen	Thame	5. 8.00
JEL	4454	W2	Schleicher ASW24	24044	PH-866	2.98	D.Robson	Currock Hill	15. 4.02
JEM	4455	570	Schempp-Hirth Duo Discus	146	-	3.98	H.Kindell	Lasham	9. 1.03

JEP	4457	JEP	Rolladen-Schneider LS-4B	41021		3.99	C.F.Carter	Long Mynd	31. 3.02
JEQ	4458	OZ	Schempp-Hirth Nimbus 3D	1/6	OO-ZOZ HB-1921/D-7695	2.98	M.Pocock	Kingston Deverill	15. 4.02
JER	4459	JH	Schempp-Hirth Standard Cirrus 75	654	D-6475 OO-ZBM	4.98	J.H.Hoskins	AAC Upavon	21. 1.02
JES	4460	V4	Schleicher ASW19	19119	SE-TTV	3.98	D.Crosby	Sutton Bank	6. 3.02
JET	4461	JET	Schempp-Hirth Ventus cT	161/521	RAFGSA.R38	2.98	B.H.Bryce-Smith	Gransden Lodge	19. 3.01
JEU	4462	JEU	Glasflugel H201 Standard Libelle	55	SE-TIC	4.98	D.Johns	Bidford	27. 3.02
JEV	4463	JEV	Schempp-Hirth Standard Cirrus B	650	OE-5072	2.98	G.F.King	Brent Tor	18.12.02
JEW	4464	D41	Schleicher Ka6CR	6493	D-4116	2.98	J.McLaughlan	Sleap	18. 3.02
JEX	4465	DW	Schempp-Hirth Ventus 2A	64	-	3.98	D.S.Watt	Bicester	14. 1.02
JEY	4466	T7	Schempp-Hirth Standard Cirrus	456G	D-3255	3.98	R.Lockett	North Weald	3. 3.02
JEZ	4467	274	Glaser-Dirks DG-100	3	PH-792 D-3721	3.98	S.Parramore	Booker	2. 5.02
JFA	4468	JFA	Schempp-Hirth Standard Cirrus	225	D-0974	4.98	P.M.Sheahan	Lasham	21. 3.02
JFB	4469	S6	Rolladen-Schneider LS-8-18	8152		3.98	J.A.Clark	Lyveden	13. 3.02
JFC	4470	R55	Schempp-Hirth Discus CS	054CS	RAFGSA.R55	3.98	RAFGSA Fenland GC	RAF Marham	18. 1.02
JFD	4471	R8	Grob G.102 Astir CS	1379	RAFGSA.R8 OY-XGE	3.98	RAFGSA Centre	Bicester	18.10.02
JFE	4472	16	Schempp-Hirth Janus C	21/299	RAFGSA.R16	3.98	RAFGSA Bannerdown GC	RAF Keevil	29. 3.02
JFF	4473	26	Schempp-Hirth Duo Discus	131	RAFGSA.R26	3.98	RAFGSA Centre	Bicester	9.12.02
JFH	4475	R1	Schempp-Hirth Duo Discus	118	RAFGSA R1	3.98	Four Counties GC	RAF Syerston	18. 3.02
JFJ	4476	JFJ	Schleicher ASW20CL	20830	D-8307 F-CGCS	4.98	W.R.Mills	Usk	2. 3.02
JFK	4477	JFK	Schleicher ASW20L	20201	D-5979	4.98	M.K.Field	Sleap	12. 5.02
JFL	4478	42	Rolladen-Schneider LS-8-18	8178		3.98	G.N.Smith	Dunstable	3.12.02
JFM	4479	JFM	Schleicher ASK13	13222	D-0396	3.98	Newark & Notts GC	Winthorpe	23. 2.02
JFN	4480	M25	Schleicher ASH25E	25060	D-KCOH	6.98	R.J.Baker	Cranfield	31. 3.02
JFP	4481	HB	Schempp-Hirth Ventus A	19	PH-707	3.98	S.J.Harris	Dunstable	10. 2.01
JFQ	4482	66	Schempp-Hirth Nimbus 4DT	9/40		5.98	P.Whitt	Camphill	22. 3.02
JFR	4483	221	Schempp-Hirth Ventus cT	170/560	RAFGSA.R24	12.97	J.G.Allen	Bicester	21. 3.02
JFS	4484	528	Schempp-Hirth Ventus cT	147/456	RAFGSA.R28	7.98	M.J.Towler	Snitterfield	28. 7.00
JFT	4485	JFT	Schleicher K8B	8451	D-1883	3.98	South London Gliding Centre	Kenley	7. 5.02
JFU	4486	JFU	Schleicher ASW19	19038	D-4531	3.98	East Sussex GC	Ringmer	2. 2.00
JFV	4487	WA1	Schleicher ASK21	21675		6.98	Scottish GU	Portmoak	24. 6.02
JFW	4488	JFW	LAK-12 Lietuva	6192	LX-CDM	4.98	A.M.Hatfield	Crowland	23. 6.02
JFX	4489	144	Rolladen-Schneider LS-8A	8174		3.98	P.E.Baker	Gransden Lodge	24. 2.02
JFY	4490		Federov Me-7b	8		10.98	D.S.Adams	Booker	22.10.02
JFZ	4491		Federov Me-7b	9		10.98	M.Powell-Brett	Long Mynd	16.11.00
JGA	4492		Federov Me-7b	10		10.98	N.Wilkinson	Challock	13. 3.02
JGB	4493	CU	Schleicher K8B	AB.02	D-8868	5.98	Cambridge UGC	Gransden Lodge	28. 2.02
JGC	4494	CC	Rolladen-Schneider LS-6A	6031	D-6699 PH-763	4.98	Gliding Expeditions Ltd	Les Ages, France	25. 4.02
JGD	4495	JGD	Schleicher K8B	8214A-SH	D-??..	4.98	R.E.Pettifer	Chipping	21. 4.02
JGE	4496	K21	Schleicher ASK21	21068	RAFGSA.R21	2.98	N.Wall	Long Mynd	20. 6.02
JGF	4497	JGF	Neukom Elfe S4D	416	D-4820 BGA.3316	5.98	C.V.Inwood	Lasham	14. 5.02
JGG	4498	JGG	Schleicher ASW15B	15332	D-2325	4.98	L.R.Groves	Ringmer	20. 4.02
JGH	4499		Schempp-Hirth Nimbus 2c	188	OO-ZZM D-2834	4.98	J.Swannack	Gamston	23. 6.02
JGJ	4500	JGJ	Schleicher ASK21	21039	RAFGSA.R22	4.98	Midland GC	Long Mynd	4. 2.02
JGK	4501	JGK	Molino Pik-20D	20571	OO-ZDL D-6707	4.98	R.Cassidy	Milfield	22. 4.02
JGL	4502	27	Schempp-Hirth Discus CS	148CS	RAFGSA.R27	4.98	Chilterns GC	RAF Halton	1. 3.02
JGM	4503	R53	Schempp-Hirth Discus CS	036CS	RAFGSA.R53	4.98	Chilterns GC	RAF Halton	26. 3.02
JGN	4504		Schempp-Hirth Standard Cirrus	554	D-8674	4.98	F.G.Wilson	Pocklington	11. 5.02
JGP	4505	E8	Schempp-Hirth Ventus 2cT	3/10	N200EE D-KHIA	4.98	C.Morris	Bidford	8. 3.02
JGQ	4506	JGQ	LET L-13 Blanik	026224	HB-1282	6.98	Joint Aviation Services	Lasham	19. 3.02
JGR	4507	BT	Schempp-Hirth Discus bT	10/275	D-KGPS D-5461	5.98	J.A.Horne	Wormingford	16. 3.02
JGS	4508	L2	Rolladen-Schneider LS-8-18	8180		5.98	M.D.Allan	Shobdon	7. 1.03
JGT	4509	JGT	Scheibe SF27	6021	D-1126	4.98	South London Gliding Centre	Kenley	28. 4.99
JGU	4510	JGU	Schempp-Hirth Mini Nimbus	69	HB-1427	5.98	P.Etherington	Husbands Bosworth	23. 3.01
JGV	4511	LGC	Schempp-Hirth Duo Discus	173	D-4020	4.00	London GC	Dunstable	2.12.02
JGW	4512		Schleicher ASK13	13146	D-0169	5.98	Newark & Notts GC	Winthorpe	17. 2.02
JGX	4513	JGX	Schleicher K8B	753	D-1878	5.98	J.Fisher	Andreas	6. 4.02
JGY	4514	C3	Schempp-Hirth Standard Cirrus	333	SE-TMU	5.98	P.A.Chapman	Husbands Bosworth	2. 4.02

JGZ	4515	JGZ	Glasflugel H-201 Standard Libelle	193	D-0697	5.98	J.Edwards	Pocklington	26. 5.02
JHA	4516	EU	Schempp-Hirth Standard Cirrus	645	D-4240	5.98	J.Lee	Pocklington	13. 4.02
JHB	4517	JHB	Scheibe L-Spatz 55	552	D-1618	8.98	A.Gruber	Rhigos	24. 7.00
JHC	4518	JHC	Schleicher ASW19B	19304	OO-ZBN	8.98	Scottish GU *(Written-off Portmoak 25.9.99)*	Portmoak	17. 8.00
JHD	4519	JHD	Schleicher Ka6E	4307	OY-XGS D-0272	5.98	T.Kendall	Lyveden	2. 6.02
JHE	4520	JHE	Grob G.102 Astir CS Jeans	2189	CS-PBI BGA3977/D-7764	5.98	AC de Portugal	Lisbon	23. 2.02
JHF	4521	VW	Schempp-Hirth Nimbus 4T	30		5.98	P.S.Kurstjens-Hawkins	(Australia)	1. 5.02
JHG	4522	51	Grob G.102 Astir CS	1084	D-6984	5.98	J.K.G.Pack	Kingston Deverill	14. 2.02
JHH	4523	JHH	Schempp-Hirth Standard Cirrus	349G	D-3006	5.98	R.J.Lodge	Rufforth	10. 5.02
JHJ	4524		Glasflugel H-201 Standard Libelle	495	HB-1187	30. 6.01	A.C.Jarvis	Parham	29. 6.02
JHK	4525	JHK	Schleicher K8B	558	(BGA4319) AGA.21/RAFGGA.558	8.98	AGA Kestrel GC	RAF Odiham	20. 4.02
JHL	4526	JHL	Schleicher Ka6E	4073	SE-TFB	6.98	N.J.Banks	Tibenham	1.11.02
JHM	4527	JHM	Schempp-Hirth Discus b	373	???	6.98	J.H.May	Camphill	16. 6.02
JHN	4528	JHN	Grob G.102 Astir Jeans CS	2110	D-7638	5.98	B.Niblett	Kingston Deverill	31. 1.02
JHP	4529	JHP	Valentin Mistral C	MC048-82	D-4948	6.98	R.H.Targett	Nympsfield	13. 2.01
JHQ	4530	R43	Schleicher ASK18	18021	RAFGSA.R43 RAFGSA.713/RAFGSA.113	9.98	RAFGSA Centre	Bicester	2.11.02
JHR	4531	JHR/A34	Centrair Alliance SNC-34c	34026		6.98	Borders GC	Milfield	19. 6.02
JHS	4532	JHS	Schleicher ASW19B	19047	D-6716	3.99	B.Crow	Usk	14. 3.02
JHT	4533	D2	Schempp-Hirth Discus 2A	2	- ? -	5.98	R.Jones	Membury	26. 4.02
JHU	4534	OP8	Rolladen-Schneider LS-8-18	8197		7.98	J.H.Russell	Sutton Bank	14. 5.02
JHW	4536	JHW	Glaser-Dirks DG-200	2-19	HB-1400	6.98	P.I.Fenner	Lasham	19. 9.02
JHX	4537	JHX	Bolkow Phoebus C	930	OO-ZYN F-CDON	6.98	M.Dunlop	Usk	28. 2.02
JHY	4538	LT	Rolladen-Schneider LS-8a-18	8181	D-9988	7.98	L.E.N.Tanner	Aboyne	3.12.01
JHZ	4539	G41	Schleicher ASW20	20313	D-6532	6.98	S.A.Hughes	Camphill	14.10.02
JJA	4540	JJA	Schempp-Hirth Cirrus	13	D-8114	7.98	P.Tolson *(Crashed Falgunzeon 29.5.99)*	Saltby	3. 7.99
JJB	4541	615	Rolladen-Schneider LS-4	4542	D-2397	6.98	M.Tomlinson	Rhigos	25. 4.02
JJC	4542	JJC	Schleicher ASK13	13661AB	D-1503	7.98	East Sussex GC *(Written-off Ringmer 12.8.00)*	Ringmer	9. 7.01
JJD	4543	K11/SUF	Schempp-Hirth Discus bT	5/262	D-KIHS	7.98	D.Wilson	Burn	3. 7.02
JJE	4544	J01	Schempp-Hirth Discus a	379	OE-5530 VH-XQT	7.98	N.Braithwaite	Walney Island	14. 7.02
JJF	4545	G1	Schleicher ASW27	27086-		6.98	G.F.Read	Booker	15.12.02
JJG	4546	V1	Schempp-Hirth Nimbus 4T	3	D-KIXL	7.98	P.G.Sheard	Dunstable	19. 5.02
JJH	4547	899	Glaser-Dirks DG-800S	8-137S30		4.99	W.R.Brown	Husbands Bosworth	19. 4.02
JJJ	4548	JJJ	Schempp-Hirth Standard Cirrus	284	D-2946	7.98	F.R.Stevens	Bidford	26. 3.02
JJK	4549	K8	Rolladen-Schneider LS-8-18	8199		8.98	J.E.C.White	Dunstable	27. 2.02
JJL	4550	JJL	Schleicher ASW19B	19302	D-4227	4.99	Newark & Notts GC	Winthorpe	27. 4.02
JJM	4551	JJM	Schempp-Hirth Standard Cirrus	403G	D-2933	7.98	S.A.Young	Husbands Bosworth	27. 6.02
JJN	4552	JJN	Slingsby T.38 *(Registered as '2067', from Frame no.SSK/FF/2067)*	1267	XP490	7.98	Swanton Morley Collection	Swanton Morley	21. 7.99
JJP	4553	494	Schempp-Hirth Duo Discus	180		7.98	R.J.Fack	Long Mynd	19. 3.02
JJQ	4554	JJQ	SZD-51-1 Junior	B-2191		9.98	Norfolk GC	Tibenham	22. 9.01
JJR	4555	R73	Schleicher ASK21	21054	RAFGSA.R73 RAFGGA.513	8.98	RAFGSA Centre	Bicester	10. 5.02
JJS	4556		Slingsby T.38	873	XA240	R	*(Believed damaged Booker 24.8.00)*		
JJT	4557	933	Schleicher ASW27	27070	D-6209	8.98	T.M.World	Booker	3. 5.02
JJU	4558	H2	Rolladen-Schneider LS-8a	8200		8.98	P.Harvey	Cranfield	25. 2.02
JJV	4559	JJV	Schleicher Ka6CR	1001	D-1719	8.98	Cotswold GC	Aston Down	29.12.01
JJX	4561	T9	Schleicher ASW15B	15323	D-2312	9.98	T.J.Davies	Portmoak	18.11.01
JJY	4562	JJY	Schempp-Hirth Ventus bT	273/61	PH-981 D-KMIH	9.98	I.H.Molesworth	Challock	28. 3.02
JJZ	4563	BW	Schempp-Hirth Discus bT	156/556	OO-ZQX	9.98	S.Walker	Nympsfield	19. 1.02
JKA	4564	JKA	Schleicher ASK21	21059	D-8835	10.98	E Sussex GC	Ringmer	14. 3.02
JKB	4565	JKB	DWLKK PW-5	17.10.08		9.98	J.C.Gibson	Chipping	3. 9.02
JKC	4566	FOX	MDM-1 Fox	224	SP-P632	9.98	G.C.Westgate & Ptnr	Ringmer	10.10.02
JKD	4567	P1	Rolladen-Schneider LS-8-18	8215		10.98	R.J.Large	Lyveden	3. 1.03
JKE	4568	JKE	DWLKK PW-5	17.11.025		10.98	Burn GC	Burn	11. 4.02
JKF	4569		Glaser-Dirks DG-200	2-35	D-6069	10.98	R.Hutchinson	Sutton Bank	20.10.02
JKG	4570	R48	Schleicher ASK18	18036	RAFGSA.R48 RAFGSA.448	3.99	RAFGSA Centre	Bicester	7. 2.02
JKH	4571	P30	Schempp-Hirth Ventus cT	174/566	RAFGSA.R30	10.98	E.Fitzgerald	Usk	29.11.02

JKJ 4572 R21	Schleicher ASK21	21679	RAFGSA.R21	10.98	RAFGSA Centre	Bicester	20.11.02
JKK 4573 A7	Schleicher ASK21	21182	AGA.11	10.98	AGA Kestrel GC	RAF Odiham	12. 5.02
JKL 4574 W8	Rolladen-Schneider LS-8-18	8218		4.99	R.J.Welford	Gransden Lodge	25. 4.02
JKM 4575 Z10	Glaser-Dirks DG-202-17M	2-148/1746	D-4155	10.98	A.H.Brown	Portmoak	4.12.01
JKN 4576 790	Rolladen-Schneider LS-8-18	8214		10.98	D.A.Booth	Crowland	4.12.02
JKP 4577 PH1	Rolladen-Schneider LS-4B	41000	PH-1089	12.98	D.M.Hope	Booker	23. 2.02
JKQ 4578 R20	Schleicher ASK21	21098	RAFGSA.R20	1.99	RAFGSA Bannerdown GC	RAF Keevil	24. 1.02
JKR 4579 P12	Schempp-Hirth Discus b	151	RAFGSA.R12	11.98	RAFGSA Wrekin GC	RAF Cosford	10. 5.02
JKS 4580 S19	Schleicher ASW19B	19362	D-1273	11.98	P.R.Taverner	Tibenham	28.11.02
JKT 4581 R7	Schleicher ASK13	13615	RAFGSA.R7	8.99	Clevelands GC	AAC Dishforth	11. 8.02
JKU 4582 R33	Schleicher ASK18	18022	RAFGSA.R33 RAFGSA.223	6.99	Clevelands GC	AAC Dishforth	2. 6.02
JKV 4583 R52	Grob G103A Twin II Acro	34042-K-273	RAFGSA.R52	5.99	Clevelands GC	AAC Dishforth	2. 6.02
JKW 4584 R60	Grob G.102 Astir CS 77	1666	RAFGSA.R60 RAFGSA.560	1.99	Clevelands GC	AAC Dishforth	18. 5.02
JKX 4585 R17	Schempp-Hirth Discus B	247	RAFGSA.R17	8.99	Clevelands GC	AAC Dishforth	4. 8.02
JKY 4586 24	Schempp-Hirth Ventus cT	181/597	RAFGSA.R24 RAFGGA.557	11.98	Clevelands GC	AAC Dishforth	27.12.02
JKZ 4587 R25	Schleicher ASK21	21123	RAFGSA.R25	12.98	RAFGSA Centre	Bicester	27.11.02
JLA 4588 JLA	Schempp-Hirth Ventus 2cT	26/94	PH-1129	11.98	E.C.Neighbour	Camphill	23. 9.02
JLB 4589 70	Schempp-Hirth Ventus 2A	74		11.98	R.J.Knight	Usk	30. 8.01
JLC 4590 R10	Schempp-Hirth Discus CS	193CS	RAFGSA.R10	11.98	RAFGSA Four Counties GC	RAF Syerston	19. 1.02
JLE 4592 R90	Schleicher ASK13	13245	RAFGSA.R90 NEJSGSA.1	10.98	RAFGSA Crusaders GC	Dhekelia	19.10.00
JLF 4593 JLF	Schleicher ASK13	13150	AGA.14	12.98	Wyvern GC	AAC Upavon	23.11.02
JLG 4594 JLG	SZD-51-1 Junior	B.1933	AGA.5 BGA.3699	2.99	Wyvern GC	AAC Upavon	2. 2.02
JLH 4595 JLH	Rolladen-Schneider LS-4	4256	AGA.1	3.99	Wyvern GC	AAC Upavon	4. 1.03
JLJ 4596 A8	Rolladen-Schneider LS-4B	4997	AGA.2	12.98	Wyvern GC	AAC Upavon	24. 3.02
JLK 4597 12	Rolladen-Schneider LS-7	7112	AGA.3	4.99	Wyvern GC	AAC Upavon	17. 3.02
JLL 4598 N25	Schleicher ASK13	13144	HB-952	11.98	Portsmouth Naval GC	Lee-on-Solent	1.12.02
JLM 4599 R2	Schempp-Hirth HS.6 Janus C	210	RAFGSA.R2	5.99	Cranwell GC	RAF Cranwell	5.11.02
JLN 4600 R4	Rolladen-Schneider LS-8-18	8169	RAFGSA.R4	3.99	Buckminster GC	Saltby	4. 1.03
JLP 4601 R39	Schempp-Hirth Discus CS	034CS	RAFGSA.R39	4.99	Cranwell GC	RAF Cranwell	2. 2.02
JLQ 4602 R40	Schleicher ASK13	13608	RAFGSA.R40 RAFGSA.R4	4.99	Cranwell GC	RAF Cranwell	2. 3.02
JLR 4603 R57	Grob G.102 Astir CS	1509	RAFGSA.R57 RAFGSA.507	2.99	Cranwell GC	RAF Cranwell	23.11.02
JLS 4604 R75	Schleicher K8B8	950	RAFGSA.R75(2) RAFGSA.285(2)	3.99	Cranwell GC	RAF Cranwell	11.12.02
JLT 4605 JLT	Schleicher Ka6E	4115	D-6082	11.98	M.Thompson	Husbands Bosworth	29.11.02
JLU 4606 11	Schempp-Hirth Ventus 2cT	37/126		3.99	J.C.Mitchell	Chipping	23. 2.02
JLV 4607 JLV	Schleicher Ka6E	4192	OY-XEU D-4424	1.99	M.S.Neal	Crowland	28. 2.02
JLW 4608 87	Schempp-Hirth Discus CS	033CS	RAFGSA.R87	12.98	RAFGSA Centre	Bicester	13. 2.02
JLX 4609 JLX	Grob Standard Cirrus	279G	OO-ZGL D-1985	11.98	M.W..Fisher	Edgehill	3. 2.02
JLY 4610 JLY	Schleicher ASW27	27111		6.99	P.C.Piggott	Husbands Bosworth	31. 5.02
JLZ 4611 21	Grob G.103A Twin II Acro	3633-K-15	D-7912	12.98	R.A.Walker	Kingston Deverill	14. 1.02
JMA 4612 R36	Schleicher ASK18	18038	RAFGSA.R36 RAFGSA.236	6.99	RAFGSA Centre	Bicester	9. 4.02
JMB 4613 R5	Rolladen-Schneider LS-8-18	8130	RAFGSA.R5	2.99	RAFGSA Centre	Bicester	10. 2.02
JMC 4614 R22	Schleicher ASK21	21681	(RAFGSA.R22)	12.98	RAFGSA Wrekin GC	RAF Cosford	14.12.02
JMD 4615 P23	Schempp-Hirth Discus b	241	RAFGSA.R23	4.99	R.C.Oliver	Kenley	24. 4.02
JME 4616 JME	Schleicher Ka7	5	D-8867	12.98	W.Masterson	Kingston, Jamaica	13.11.01
JMG 4618 JMG	SZD-51-1 Junior	B.2192		4.99	Kent GC	Challock	4. 5.02
JMH 4619 JMH	Schempp-Hirth Standard Cirrus	571	HB-1263	12.98	F.Davidson	Rufforth	6.12.02
JMJ 4620 R46	Schleicher ASK13	13616	RAFGSA.R46(2) RAFGSA.R16	9.99	RAFGSA Fenland GC	RAF Marham	4. 9.02
JMK 4621 R49	Schleicher ASK18	18023	RAFGSA.R49 RAFGSA.318(2)	1.99	RAFGSA Fenland GC	RAF Marham	15. 2.02
JML 4622 R63	Grob G.102 Astir CS 77	1718	RAFGSA.R63 RAFGSA.883	1.99	Fenland GC	RAF Marham	27. 4.02
JMM 4623 JMM	Schempp-Hirth Discus b	254	BGA.4474 RAFGSA.R15	12.98	M.R.Fox	Pocklington	24. 3.02
JMN 4624 636	Schempp-Hirth Nimbus 2	38	D-1129 HB-1159	12.98	R.A.Holroyd	Pocklington	15.12.02
JMO 4625 781	Rolladen-Schneider LS-8-18	8225		12.98	D.J.Langrick	Husbands Bosworth	9. 3.02
JMP 4626 JMP	Schleicher ASK13	13436	D-2984	1.99	East Sussex GC	Ringmer	16. 4.02

JMQ	4627	KR	Schleicher ASW20L	20499	F-CADB	1.99	S.G.Back	Crowland	14.12.02
					D-2026				
JMR	4628	628	Rolladen-Schneider LS-8-18	8198	D-0280	12.98	D.Williams	Lasham	12. 4.02
JMS	4629	521	Schleicher ASK21	21212	RAFGGA.521	11.98	Phoenix GC	RAF Bruggen	15. 4.02
JMT	4630	301	Rolladen-Schneider LS-8-18	8223		2.99	J.Burry	Lasham	4.12.02
JMU	4631	140	Rolladen-Schneider LS-8-18	8246		3.99	R.D.Payne	Nympsfield	2. 3.02
JMV	4632	EW	Schempp-Hirth HS.5 Nimbus 2C	179	D-6738	1.99	K.R.Walton	Lasham	15. 2.02
JMW	4633	R61	Schleicher ASK13	13688AB	RAFGSA.R59(3)	1.99	RAFGSA Bannerdown GC	RAF Keevil	30.11.02
					RAFGGA.567				
JMX	4634	JMX	Schleicher ASK13	13107	RAFGSA.R86	2.99	Shalbourne SG	Rivar Hill	30. 3.02
					RAFGSA.R46/RAFGSA.386				
JMY	4635	JMY	SZD-51-1 Junior	W-959	OO-ZRH	3.99	Highland GC	Easterton	26. 4.02
JMZ	4636	R37	Schleicher ASK13	13099	RAFGSA.R37(2)	1.99	RAFGSA Wrekin GC	RAF Cosford	9. 3.02
					RAFGSA.378(2)				
JNA	4637	JNA	Grob G.102 Astir CS Jeans	2160	D-4556	2.99	Shenington GC	Edgehill	18. 3.02
JNB	4638	D1	Rolladen-Schneider LS-8-18	8227		2.99	Tatenhall Aviation	Cross Hayes	17. 2.02
JNC	4639	Z22	Schempp-Hirth Standard Cirrus	322	HB-1157	2.99	S.M.Veness	Bicester	1. 5.02
JND	4640		Slingsby T38 Grasshopper		.(ex ?)	R	S.Williams	NK	
			(C/n given as 'SSK/OW2987', which is a part number)						
JNE	4641	561	Schempp-Hirth Discus 2A	18	D-4499	2.99	J.R.W.Kronfeld	Lasham	2.12.02
JNF	4642	80	Schempp-Hirth Discus 2A	12		2.99	A.J.Davis	Nympsfield	12. 2.02
JNG	4643	JNG	Glasflugel H.201B Standard Libelle	6	SE-TFU	3.99	P.K.Spencer	Edgehill	14. 3.00
JNH	4644	E3	Schleicher ASW27	27102		3.99	E.Drew	Crowland	23. 6.02
							(De-registered 12.12.01 - sold in the USA)		
JNJ	4645	601	Rolladen-Schneider LS-8-	188226		2.99	J.D.Spencer	Dunstable	19. 4.02
JNK	4646	676	Rolladen-Schneider LS-8-	188244		2.99	M.J.Jordy	Enstone	20. 2.02
JNL	4647	DR7	Schempp-Hirth HS.6 Janus	25	HB-1313	2.99	D.M.Ruttle	Saltby	15. 2.02
JNM	4648	P4	Rolladen-Schneider LS-8-18	8232	(BGA.4617)	3.99	P.Onn	Dunstable	23. 2.02
					D-8217				
JNN	4649	JNN	Schleicher K-8B	8744	D-8583	3.99	Buckminster GC	Saltby	26.10.02
JNP	4650		Rolladen-Schneider LS-6B	6109	D-5853	R	P.Fink		
JNQ	4651	441	Glaser-Dirks DG-300 Elan	3E-341	SE-UHO	4.99	F.C.Roles	Camphill	3. 4.02
JNR	4652	JNR	Glasflugel H.303 Mosquito B	159	D-5908	3.99	I.Agutter	Wormingford	25. 1.02
JNS	4653	Z2	Schleicher ASW27	27103		3.99	B.H.Owen	Lasham	3. 1.03
JNT	4654	SC	Schleicher ASW19B	19371	D-2233	4.99	S.Cheshire	Booker	31. 3.01
JNU	4655	R69	Rolladen-Schneider LS-6-18W	6345	RAFGSA.R69(3)	3.99	RAFGSA Chilterns GC	RAF Halton	22. 2.02
					RAFGGA.553/D-8037				
JNV	4656	E2	Schleicher ASW22BL	22079		4.99	R.A.Cheetham	Husbands Bosworth	13. 6.02
JNW	4657	L4	Rolladen-Schneider LS-8	8217		3.99	A.J.Limb	Husbands Bosworth	26. 3.02
JNX	4658	JNX	LET L-13 Blanik	027408	OK-2712	5.99	Vectis GC	Bembridge	6. 5.02
JNY	4659	CZ	Schempp-Hirth Discus 2B	17	D-4498	3.99	D.H.Conway	RAF Keevil	14. 4.02
JNZ	4660	813	Glaser-Dirks DG-100	70	(D-7324)	3.99	R.C.Martin	RAF Odiham	18. 4.02
					HB-1324				
JPA	4661	HB1	Schempp-Hirth Duo Discus	201		3.99	The Soaring Centre	Husbands Bosworth	31. 1.02
JPB	4662	A5	Schleicher ASK23	23005	AGA.18	4.99	Kestrel GC	RAF Odiham	5.01
							(De-registered 05.09.01 - sold in The Netherlands)		
JPC	4663	R51	Schleicher ASK13	13256	RAFGSA.R51	3.99	Anglia GC	RAF Wattisham	8. 2.02
JPD	4664	V2T	Schempp-Hirth Ventus 2cT	39/129		3.99	P.A.Hearne	Challock	22. 3.02
JPE	4665	L77	Rolladen-Schneider LS-1f	488	F-CESC	5.99	A.A.Darlington	Lasham	1. 2.02
JPF	4666	JPF	Glaser-Dirks DG-100	22	D-3735	5.99	H.G.Burkert	Rivar Hill	5. 6.02
JPG	4667	520	Schempp-Hirth Ventus 2cT	2/3	D-KLYC	4.99	P.Naegeli	Rivar Hill	14.11.02
							(De-registered 14.12.01 - sold in Denmark)		
JPH	4668	CB	Rolladen-Schneider LS-8-18	8259		7.99	J.P.Ben-David	Lasham	22. 9.02
JPJ	4669	SA	Grob G.104 Speed Astir IIB	4089	OE-5352	4.99	R.J.Maisonpierre	Rattlesden	17. 5.02
JPK	4670		Slingsby T34 Sky	672	RAFGSA.876	5.99	J.Tournier	Booker	18. 5.02
					XA876/G-672				
JPL	4671	RW	Rolladen-Schneider LS-8-18	8249	D-2562	4.99	I.Reekie	Thame	31. 1.02
JPM	4672	JPM	Grob G.102 Astir CS Jeans	2209	D-3825	5.99	J.Thorpe	Cross Hayes	8. 5.02
JPN	4673	280	Schleicher ASW27	27117		6.99	M.Strathern	Nympsfield	3. 8.02
JPP	4674	388	Schempp-Hirth Discus B	206	AGA.4	4.99	Kestrel GC	RAF Odiham	13. 4.02
JPQ	4675	R32	Schleicher ASK18	18002	RAFGSA.R32	5.99	RAFGSA Fulmar GC	Easterton	26.12.02
					RAFGSA.213/D-3978				
JPR	4676	161	Rolladen-Schneider LS-8-18	8245		4.99	D.M.Byass	Dunstable	29. 4.02
JPS	4677	CL	Schleicher ASW27	27108		5.99	C.C.Lyttleton	Dunstable	15. 2.02
JPT	4678	JPT	Schleicher ASW27	27113		10.99	R & W Willis-Fleming	North Hill	19. 9.02
JPU	4679	TL2	Schempp-Hirth Discus CS	257CS4.99			K.Armitage	Camphill	22.11.02
JPV	4680	R88	Schleicher ASK13	13312	RAFGSA.R88	5.99	RAFGSA Centre	Bicester	7. 5.00
					RAFGSA.186				
JPW	4681	JPW	Glaser-Dirks DG-200	2-48	D-2201	5.99	J.P.Goodison	Burn	20. 5.02
JPX	4682	JPX	Schleicher ASW15	15160	D-0823	5.99	P.Seymour	Cranfield	13. 2.02
JPY	4683	R59	Schleicher ASK13	13653AB	RAFGGA.509	5.99	Phoenix GC	RAF Bruggen	25. 6.01

JPZ 4684	R56	Schleicher ASK18	18027	RAFGGA.563	4.99	Phoenix GC	RAF Bruggen	17. 5.01
JQA 4685	547	Schempp-Hirth Discus b	265	BGA.4535 RAFGGA.547/RAFGGA.500	4.99	Phoenix GC	RAF Bruggen	22. 5.02
JQB 4686	JQB	Schleicher K8B	8880	RAFGSA.R98 RAFGSA.398	5.99	A.J.Taylor & Ptnrs	Lee on Solent	4. 6.02
JQC 4687	JT	Schempp-Hirth Discus bT	127/488	D-KITT(3)	5.99	J.C.Taggart	Bellarena	18. 5.02
JQD 4688	R3	Rolladen-Schneider LS-8A	8224		5.99	Bannerdown GC	RAF Keevil	31.12.02
JQE 4689	JQE	Schempp-Hirth HS4 Standard Cirrus	7525	OO-ZRS D-0483	6.99	C.Nunn	Rattlesden	13. 7.02
JQF 4690	5GC	Glaser-Dirks DG-505 Elan Orion	5E194X38	S5-7516	6.99	Scottish Gliding Union	Portmoak	1. 5.02
JQG 4691	R50	Grob G.103A Twin II Acro	33964-K-197	RAFGSA.R50	5.99	Fulmar GC	Easterton	14. 4.02
JQH 4692		LAK-12 Lietuva	6188		5.99	S.R.Brown	Snitterfield	30. 4.02
JQJ 4693	JQJ	Schleicher K8B	8795	RAFGSA.R47 BGA.1564	5.99	Staffordshire GC	Seighford	27. 9.02
JQK 4694	506	Schempp-Hirth Discus CS	075CS	RAFGGA.501	5.99	Phoenix GC	RAF Bruggen	15. 3.02
JQL 4695	W2	Schempp-Hirth Ventus 2A	79		5.99	M.L.Dawson	Nympsfield	15. 2.02
JQM 4696	Z9	Schleicher ASW-27	27114		6.99	A.Haynor	Weston-on-the-Green	19.12.02
JQN 4697	R67	Grob G.102 Astir CS 77	1634	RAFGSA.R67 RAFGSA.547	6.99	RAFGSA Centre	Bicester	9. 6.02
JQP 4698	JQP	Centrair 101A Pegase	101-066	F-CFQY	6.99	J.Rees	Usk	15. 6.02
JQQ 4699	185	Schempp-Hirth Duo Discus	227		3.00	K.G.Reid & Ptnrs.	RAF Keevil	24. 2.02
JQR 4700	JQR	Schempp-Hirth Ventus 2cT	49/152		10.99	M.C.Costin	Crowland	14.12.02
JQS 4701	JQS	Schempp-Hirth (Grob) Standard Cirrus	251G	D-1147	6.99	M.Charlton	Currock Hill	30. 6.02
JQT 4702	JQT	Grob G.102 Astir CS Jeans	2076	D-7589	6.99	Southdown GC	Parham Park	25. 6.02
JQU 4703	L17	LAK-17A	102		6.99	A Pozerskis	Husbands Bosworth	22. 5.02
JQV 4704	Z12	Schleicher ASW27	27112		7.99	I.N.Lingham	Booker	22.11.02
JQW 4705	JQW	Schempp-Hirth HS.2 Cirrus	18 47	D-0186	7.99	G.E.Smith	Parham Park	16. 2.02
JQX 4706	JQX	Schleicher ASK21	21702		9.99	Southdown GC	Parham Park	18.10.02
JQY 4707	R92	Slingsby T21 Sedbergh	666	RAFGSA.R92 NEJSGSA.4/WG499	6.99	Crusaders GC	Kingsfield Dhekelia	2. 6.02
JQZ 4708	JQZ	Schleicher K8B	8854	RAFGSA.R42 RAFGSA.323	7.99	Bowland Forest GC	Chipping	5. 7.02
JRA 4709	E11	Rolladen-Schneider LS-8-18	8263		7.99	S.R.Ell	Sutton Bank	5. 2.02
JRB 4710	S33	Schleicher ASW19B	19227	D-2713	7.99	K.F.Bell	Lasham	6.12.01
JRC 4711	JRC	Glaser-Dirks DG300 Club Elan	3E-20	HB-1718	8.99	D.P.Sillett	Rattlesden	27. 7.02
JRD 4712	R18	Grob G102 Astir CS	1487	RAFGSA.R18 RAFGGA.540/D-4791	6.99	RAFGSA Centre	Bicester	8. 2.02
JRE 4713	JP	Schleicher ASW-15	15048	LN-GGL OH-391/OH-RWA/D-4391	8.99	J.D.Pride	Long Mynd	14. 8.02
JRF 4714	JRF	SZD-50-3 Puchacz	B-1395	OO-ZTX D-8213/SP-3285	8.99	Derby & Lancs GC	Camphill	29. 4.02
JRG 4715	JRG	Schempp-Hirth Standard Cirrus	146	D-0297	8.99	D.Draper	Rivar Hill	6. 2.02
JRH 4716	T27	Schleicher ASW27	27118		8.99	P.C.Jarvis	Booker	14.12.02
JRJ 4717	JRJ	SZD-50-3 Puchacz	503199327		8.99	Bidford GC	Bidford	22. 8.02
JRK 4718	618	Rolladen-Schneider LS-8-18	8267		9.99	D.King	Snitterfield	18. 9.02
JRL 4719	F84	Glaser-Dirks DG-100G Elan	E185G151	D-1246	2.00	A.McKay	Sleap	28. 2.02
JRM 4720	212	Grob G102 Astir CS	1332	AGA.6 BGA.4314	9.99	Kestrel GC	RAF Odiham	23.11.02
JRN 4721	PT	Glaser-Dirks DG-202/17C *(C/n 2-118CL04?)*	2-118CL01	D-7267	9.99	T.G.Roberts	Lasham	3. 4.02
JRP 4722	JRP	Grob G102 Astir CS Jeans	2244	D-5951	9.99	Borders GC	Milfield	23. 9.02
JRQ 4723	PM3	Neukom Elfe PM3	001	N6351U N63514/HB-526	11.99	G.Mclean	Lleweni Parc	23. 3.02
JRR 4724	LA	Schempp-Hirth Discus bT	50/367	PH-1087 D-KBHM	3.00	C.R.Lear	RAF Keevil	12. 4.02
JRS 4725	AT	Valentin Mistral C	MC021/79	D-4921	3.00	A.Towse	RAF Wattisham	17. 7.02
JRT 4726		Schempp-Hirth Standard Cirrus	99	D-0734	10.99	S.Hutchinson	Husbands Bosworth	14.10.02
JRU 4727	MB	Schleicher ASW-24	24168	D-7085	1.00	M.Bull	Lasham	9. 3.02
JRV 4728	B19	Schleicher ASW19B	19233	D-2644	10.99	M.Roome	Lasham	14.12.02
JRW 4729	R95	Grob G103A Twin II Acro	34040-K-271	RAFGGA.556	10.99	RAFGSA Centre	Bicester	6.12.02
JRX 4730	R41	Schleicher ASK13	13375	RAFGSA.R41 RAFGSA.241(2)	10.99	Chilterns GC	RAF Halton	22.11.01
JRY 4731		Edgely EA9	008		R	*(To BGA.4917)*		
JRZ 4732		Colditz Cock rep *(Under construction by M.Francis)*	-			R M.Francis	Camphill	

JSA	4733		Scheibe SF-27MB	6303	(G-BSUM)	R	M.Davies		
					D-KIBE				
JSB	4734	JSB	Rolladen-Schneider LS-4	4424	D-4541	2.00	H.Vare	Speyer, Germany	22. 2.02
JSC	4735	827	Schempp-Hirth Nimbus 3dT	10	F-CFUE	11.99	D.P.Taylor & P.J.Teagle	Sutton Bank	18.12.01
					F-WFUE/D-KFUE				
JSD	4736	R77	Grob G102 Astir CS	1133	RAFGSA.R77	2.00	RAFGSA Wrekin GC	RAF Cosford	19. 4.02
					D-4177				
JSE	4737	296	Schempp-Hirth Discus b	365	PH-918	3.00	Imperial College GC	Lasham	25. 2.02
JSF	4738	514	Rolladen-Schneider LS-1f	383	LN-GGE	3.00	R.Johnson & Ptnrs	Husbands Bosworth	10. 6.02
					SE-TOU				
JSG	4739	500	Schleicher K-6E	4248	D-0090	2.00	J.S.Halford	Kingston Deverill	17. 2.02
JSH	4740	396	Grob G102 Astir IIIB	5504CB	D-6470	11.99	Surrey & Hants GC	Lasham	29. 1.02
JSJ	4741	7X	Rolladen-Schneider LS-7WL	7058	D-5774	10.99	T.Moyes	Camphill	15.12.01
JSK	4742	JSK	Grob G102 Astir CS	1521	D-7455	11.99	J.W.Bolt	North Hill	19. 2.02
JSL	4743	JSL	Schempp-Hirth Ventus cT	121/395	D-KIFL	11.99	B.Ingles	Bidford	28.11.02
JSN	4745	R45	Schleicher K8B	8916	RAFGSA.R45	11.99	Chilterns GC	RAF Halton	29.11.02
					RAFGSA.245				
JSP	4746		Slingsby T31B	909	XE796	R			
JSQ	4747		Rolladen-Schneider LS-8T	8301	D-KKAF	5.00	Strong Words Ltd	Gransden Lodge	24. 9.01
JSR	4748	JSR	SZD-50-3 Puchacz	B-1386	OY-XRV	3.00	Bidford GC	Bidford	25. 3.02
					SP-3283				
JSS	4749	JB	Schleicher ASW27B	27121		12.99	J.H.Belk	Dunstable	12.12.02
JST	4750	X5	Rolladen-Schneider LS-1c	86	OO-ZPA	1.00	L.Gerrard	Husbands Bosworth	16. 2.02
					D-0766				
JSU	4751	95	Rolladen-Schneider LS-8-18	8297	D-0543	3.00	J.G.Bell	(Chichester)	25. 3.02
JSV	4752	R80	Schleicher ASK13	13127	RAFGSA.R80	1.00	RAFGSA Centre	Bicester	11.11.02
					BGA.1509				
JSW	4753	H4	Rolladen-Schneider LS-4	4262	ZS-GOP	10.00	B.Spreckley	(France)	28.10.01
JSX	4754	JSX	Glaser-Dirks DG-505 Elan Orion	5E200X44		5.00	Oxford GC	Weston on the Green	7. 5.02
JSY	4755		Pilatus B4 PC-11	127	D-3055	1.00	A.de Tourboulon & ptnr.	Wormingford	20. 2.02
					D-5787/PH-578				
JSZ	4756	JSZ	Schleicher ASK-18	18012	D-6878	4.00	C.J.N.Weston	Challock	25. 6.02
JTA	4757	-	Colditz Cock rep	-		1.00	Southdown Aero Services	Lasham	*
			(Built Southdown Aero Services & J.Lee)						
JTB	4758	V17	Schleicher ASW-24	24017	D-3465	2.00	P.Shaw	Halesland	3. 2.02
JTC	4759	JTC	Glaser-Dirks DG-100G	84G5	(BGA.4744)	5.00	A.Burger	Nunstadt, Germany	20. 5.02
					HB-1335				
JTD	4760	103	Rolladen-Schneider LS-6-18W	6371	D-2571	2.00	C.J.Mayhew	Lasham	27. 8.02
JTE	4761	JTE	Schempp-Hirth Standard Cirrus	470G	D-3718	2.00	G.Reeves	Parham Park	22. 5.02
JTF	4762	Z3	Schleicher ASW-27B	27125		3.00	P.M.Wells		4. 3.02
JTG	4763	D55	SZD-55	551197100	N4364R	3.00	N.A.McLean	Booker	14. 3.02
JTH	4764	H3	Schleicher ASW-24	24218	D-7681	3.00	R.H.Yarney	Lasham	13. 3.02
JTJ	4765	.	Schempp-Hirth Mini Nimbus b	73	D-7620	3.00	A.Richards	North Hill	2. 3.02
JTK	4766	JTK	Glaser-Dirks DG-303 Elan	3E487A28		5.00	B.J.Edwards	Booker	4. 1.03
JTL	4767	352	Rolladen-Schneider LS-8-18	8317		3.00	L.S.Hood	Cranwell	27. 3.02
JTM	4768	205	Rolladen-Schneider LS-8-18	8268		2.00	M.Young & Ptnr	Dunstable	11. 2.02
JTN	4769	E5	Glaser-Dirks DG-300	3E19	HB-1717	3.00	M.J.Chapman	Seighford	13. 3.02
JTP	4770	JTP	Schleicher ASW-20L	20569	D-4688	3.00	C.A.Sheldon	Rufforth	8. 4.02
JTQ	4771	JTQ	Glasflugel H303 Mosquito	88	OO-ZYL	4.00	I.Hamilton	Chipping	3. 4.02
JTR	4772		Rolladen-Schneider LS-7	7104	D-5309	3.00	B.L.Anson	Booker	26. 4.02
JTS	4773	JTS	Schempp-Hirth Cirrus VTC	108	S5-3059	3.00	S.Smith	(Sutton)	1. 3.02
					SL-3059/YU-4200				
JTU	4775	377	Schempp-Hirth Duo Discus	234		3.00	R.Starmer Syndicate	Burn	17. 5.02
JTV	4776	666	Schempp-Hirth Ventus 2cT	52/173		3.00	A.P.Moulang	Challock	15. 1.02
JTW	4777	AV8	Glasflugel H303 Mosquito	199	F-CELX	4.00	M.Wright	AAC Wattisham	7. 4.02
JTX	4778	JTX	Start+Flug H101 Salto	47	D-9260	3.00	C.Schneeberger	Maxdorf, Germany	15. 3.02
JTY	4779	JTY	Rolladen-Schneider LS-8A	8102	SE-USA	4.00	BBC Club	Booker	19. 1.02
JTZ	4780	GC	Schempp-Hirth Ventus 2B	23	OO-ZQS	2.00	G.Costacurta	Asiago, Italy	27. 2.01
JUA	4781	Y2K	Schempp-Hirth Discus 2B	48		2.00	C.Costa	(Italy)	8. 7.02
JUB	4782	894	Schempp-Hirth Discus CS	268CS		4.00	D.F.Wass	Lasham	15. 2.02
JUC	4783	X1	Rolladen-Schneider LS-8-18	8305		4.00	G.P.Stingemore	Winthorpe	10. 9.02
JUD	4784	Z19	Rolladen-Schneider LS-8-18	8309		3.00	D.S.Haughton	Camphill	7. 3.02
JUE	4785	X15	Rolladen-Schneider LS-8-18	8295		3.00	R.Arkle	Aboyne	28. 8.02
JUF	4786	46	Schempp-Hirth Ventus 2cT	53		4.00	M.H.Pope	Aston Down	18. 4.02
JUG	4787	FE	Issoire E78 Silene	9	F-CFED	7.00	Essex & Suffolk GC	Wormingford	31.10.02
JUH	4788	R6	Schleicher ASW-27B	27129		4.00	RAFGSA Centre	Bicester	25. 2.02
JUJ	4789	370	Schleicher ASW-27B	27127		4.00	D.R.Campbell	Booker	7. 5.02
JUK	4790	554	Grob G102 Astir CS	1430	PH-552	6.00	C.Shepherd	Booker	8. 3.02
JUL	4791	621	Schleicher ASW-27B	27132		4.00	T.Stuart	Nympsfield	3. 5.02
JUM	4792	2UP	Schempp-Hirth Duo Discus	243		4.00	B.A.Bateson	Parham Park	11. 6.02
JUN	4793	M19	Schleicher ASW-19B	19096	D-3844	5.00	M.P.Roberts	Gransden Lodge	4. 5.02

JUP	4794	183	Schempp-Hirth Discus 2b	60		5.00	P.J.Ward	Aston Down	22. 5.02
JUQ	4795	250 .	Schempp-Hirth Ventus 2cT	55/179		5.00	W.J.Murray	Rivar Hill	10. 5.02
JUR	4796	JUR	Valentin Mistral C	MC042/81	HB-1596	5.00	Essex & Suffolk GC	Wormingford	8. 6.02
JUS	4797	JUS	Grob G102 Astir CS	1403	(BGA.4774)	5.00	Rattlesden GC	Rattlesden	5. 4.02
					D-4269				
JUT	4798		Schempp-Hirth Nimbus 4DT	10/56			*(See JVD/BGA.4808)*		
JUU	4799	JUU	Schempp-Hirth Standard Cirrus		PH-500	5.00	J.Simpson	Rufforth	11. 6.02
				450					
JUV	4800	SH2	Schempp-Hirth Discus b	551	D-8257	6.00	Surrey & Hants GC	Lasham	21. 1.02
JUW	4801	4T	Schleicher ASW-19B	19074	D-4476	5.00	E.Cole	Halesland	30. 5.02
JUX	4802	CD1	Avia Stroitel AC-4c	051		5.00	C.J.Davison	Winthorpe	15. 2.02
			(Formerly known as Federov Me-7)						
JUY	4803	JUY	Valentin Mistral C	MC041/81	D-4941	5.00	C.A.Pennifold	Lee-on-Solent	10. 5.02
JUZ	4804	SH6	Schleicher ASW-19B	19146	D-7932	6.00	Surrey & Hants GC	Lasham	5. 6.02
JVA	4805		Schempp-Hirth Ventus 2cT	66		8. 1.02	N.A.Leigh	Camphill	7. 2.02
JVB	4806	DF	Schempp-Hirth Discus bT	111/462	D-KUNK	5.00	D.J.Fawcett	Lasham	3. 5.02
JVC	4807	JVC	SZD-51-1 Junior	B-1799	SP-3434	6.00	Yorkshire Gliding Centre	Rufforth	3. 5.02
JVD	4808	929	Schempp-Hirth Nimbus 4DT	10/56	(BGA4798)	5.00	Southern Sailplanes	Membury	27. 5.01
							(Crashed Montes de Toledo, Spain, 31.7.00)		
JVE	4809	JVE	Eiri PiK-20D	20631	OY-XJC	6.00	S.R.Wilkinson	Kirton-in-Lindsey	17. 6.02
JVF	4810	JH1	Schempp-Hirth Discus CS	271CS		6.00	J.Hodgson	Wormingford	14. 5.02
JVG	4811	420	Schempp-Hirth Discus bT	121/477	D-KSOP	6.00	P.J.Charnell	Lasham	13. 6.02
JVH	4812	AC4	Avia Stroitel AC-4c	052		6.00	R.Hurley Shobdon		29. 7.02
JVJ	4813	JS	LAK-17A	108		6.00	J.A.Sutton	Currock Hill	25. 2.02
JVK	4814	CP	Rolladen-Schneider LS-6c-15/18		D-6417	7.00	M.F.Collins	Lasham	25. 6.02
				6236					
JVL	4815	400	Glaser-Dirks DG-300	3E158	HB-1833	7.00	A.M.Blackburn	Camphill	16. 7.02
JVM	4816	GP	Schleicher ASW-27B	27138		6.00	G.K.Payne	Booker	20.12.02
JVN	4817	T4	Schleicher ASW-27B	27134		6.00	N & R Tillett	Dunstable	3. 1.02
JVP	4818	JVP	Glaser-Dirks DG-200	2-1	D-8200	7.00	M.P.Ellis & Ptnrs	Rufforth	3. 7.02
JVQ	4819	275	Schleicher ASW-27B	27136		7.00	M.R.Fountain	Booker	4. 7.02
JVR	4820	540	Schempp-Hirth Discus 2b	72		7.00	P.Davis	Lasham	8. 7.02
JVS	4821	Z1	Schleicher ASW-28	28003	D-4008	9.00	S.J.Steinberg	Gransden Lodge	30.11.02
JVT	4822	JE	Schempp-Hirth Nimbus 3-25	5 37	D-3176	7.00	J.R.Edyvean	Winthorpe	25. 7.02
JVU	4823		Lanverre Cirrus CS11-75L	28	F-CEVT	7.12.00	C.R.Coates	Snitterfield	6.12.01
JVV	4824	J50	Sch-Hirth Janus Ce	176	D-4150	8.00	G.R.Jenkins	Lasham	27. 2.02
JVW	4825		Schleicher ASW-15A	15042	HB-992	20. 2.01	G.J.Armes	Rattlesden	19. 2.02
JVX	4826	163	Schempp-Hirth Discus CS	087CS	D-0263	8.00	L.Marks	Lasham	10. 8.02
JVY	4827	F6	Schempp-Hirth Discus b	175	RAFGSA.R6	8.00	M.R.Garwood	Crowland	9. 8.01
JVZ	4828	JVZ	Schleicher ASK-21	21721		12.00	Yorkshire GC	Sutton Bank	10.01
							"Sharpe's Classique"		
JWA	4829	E1	Schleicher ASW-28	28005		10.00	R.A.Cheetham	Winthorpe	2.11.02
JWB	4830	JWB	Schleicher ASK-13	13671	D-1066	12.00	East Sussex GC	Ringmer	23.12.01
JWC	4831	900	Schleicher ASW-27B	27142		10.00	C.Starkey	Lasham	27.11.02
JWD	4832	GWD	Schleicher ASK-21	21724		16. 2.00	London GC	Dunstable	15. 2.01
			(Reported marked as "GWD")						
JWE	4833		Slingsby T.21B	1159	XN155	1. 7.00	M.Selss	Munich	30. 6.01
JWF	4834	S27	Schleicher ASW-27B	27144		11.00	B.A.Fairston	Husbands Bosworth	1.11.02
JWG	4835	111	Schempp-Hirth Nimbus 3DT	11	D-KMGD	11. 2.01	T.P.Browning	Lasham	10. 2.02
JWH	4836		Schempp-Hirth Standard Cirrus		SE-TMZ	14. 6.01	M.F.Cuming	Edgehill	13. 6.02
				256					
JWJ	4837	R38	Schleicher ASK-13	13599	RAFGSA R3	11.00	RAFGSA	Bicester	2.11.02
JWK	4838	722	Schempp-Hirth Discus bT	106	HB-1860	11.00	D.E.Barker	Aston Down	14.11.01
JWL	4839	D4	Schempp-Hirth Ventus B	125	D-6667	11.00	S Weber	(Germany)	28.10.02
JWM	4840		Grob G.103 Twin II	3536	D-8730	11.00	Norfolk GC	Tibenham	15.11.01
JWN	4841		Rolladen-Schneider LS.4	4728	D-7008	24. 2.01	B.Dieter	Speyer, Germany	23. 2.02
JWP	4842		Bolkow Phoebus B1	875	D-0128	R22.11.00	P.A.Hearne	*(See BGA.4858 below)*	
JWQ	4843	310	Schempp-Hirth Discus 2A	82		11.00	P.S.Sheard	Dunstable	13.11.02
JWR	4844	NJ1	Grob G.102 Astir CS	1271	D-7366	1.01	N.J.Irving	Portmoak	23. 1.02
JWS	4845		Schleicher ASW-15B	15098	D-4656	14. 4.01	P Lyons		13. 4.02
JWT	4846	JWT	Glaser-Dirks DG-200	2-42	D-6560	11.00	A Farr	Kingston Deverill	11.01
					D-6660				
JWU	4847		Schempp-Hirth Ventus bT	19/159	ZS-GOW	10.00	G Tabbner	Gransden Lodge	9.10.02
JWV	4848		Glasflugel Standard Libelle	411	OY-XBG	14. 3.01	G.K.Drury	Challock	13. 3.02
JWW	4849		Schleicher ASW-19	19381	ZD658	R8.12.00	G Lane		
					BGA.2894				
JWX	4850	63	Schempp-Hirth Ventus 2cT	66		20.12.00	S.G.Olender	(Spain)	19.12.01
JWY	4851	JWY	Schleicher ASK-13	13504	D-3977	12. 1.01	Southdown GC	Parham Park	11. 1.02
							(Written-off in crash at Parham 23.5.01)		
JWZ	4852		Schleicher ASW-22	22037	D-3422	22. 1.01	D.Prosolek	Gamston	22. 1.02
JXA	4853	Y44	Schempp-Hirth Nimbus 3dT	9	D-KKYY	3. 2.01	B.C.Morris	Booker	2. 2.02
					D-4444				
JXB	4854		Centrair 201 Marianne	201-015	F-CGMN	27. 1.01	M.J.Thompson	Rufforth	26. 1.02
JXC	4855		Wassmer WA.28F	102	F-CDZV	27. 3.01	A.Montague	Nympsfield	26. 3.02

JXD 4856		Slingsby T.21B	?	?	20. 1.01	F.Brune	(Germany)	19. 1.02
JXE 4857		SZD-22C Mucha Standard	F-717	SP-2330	12. 8.01	C.E.Harwood	Challock	11. 8.02
JXF 4858		Bolkow Phoebus B	875	(BGA.4842) D-0128	R18. 1.01	P.A.Hearne		
JXG 4859	W5	Eiri PIK-20D	20660	PH-670	23. 2.01	T.J.Clubb	Lasham	22. 2.02
JXH 4860	W20	Schleicher ASW-20L	20067	D-7657	17. 2.01	G.M.Brightman	Dunstable	16. 2.02
JXJ 4861	W7	Schleicher ASW-28	28012		29. 1.01	E.W.Johnston	Dunstable	28. 1.02
JXK 4862		Schempp-Hirth Ventus bT	49	D-KLOE	25. 1.01	P.L.Manley	Wormingford	24. 1.02
JXL 4863	SG1	Schempp-Hirth Discus CS	278CS		5. 4.01	Southdown GC	Parham Park	4. 4.02
JXM 4864	R34	Schleicher ASK-13	13542	RAFGSA.R34 F-CERF	25. 2.01	Chilterns GC	RAF Halton	24. 2.02
JXN 4865	JXN	Centrair 201B Marianne	201B-035	F-CBLI	21. 2.01	E.Crookes	Kirton-in-Lindsey	20. 2.02
JXP 4866	H52	Glaser-Dirks DG-100	18	PH-520	16. 5.01	P.Butcher	Husbands Bosworth	15. 5.02
JXQ 4867		Wassmer WA.26P	19	F-CDQQ	26. 9.01	J.A.French	Nympsfield	25. 9.02
JXR 4868	DM	Schempp-Hirth Discus B	540	D-9152	8. 4.01	Cambridge GC	Gransden Lodge	7. 4.02
JXS 4869		Schleicher K8B	8778	RAFGSA.R95 RAFGSA.395	R6. 3.01	Stratford GC	Snitterfield	
JXT 4870	CT	Schleicher ASW-24B	24233	D-6706	9. 3.01	C.Thwaites	Rufforth	5.12.02
JXU 4871	646	Rolladen-Schneider LS-8	8354		10. 3.01	C.Alldis	Long Mynd	9. 3.02
JXV 4872	JXV	Glaser-Dirks DG-100	63	PH-543	24. 3.01	R.Voss	Challock	23. 3.02
JXW 4873	871	Schempp-Hirth Duo Discus T	7		11. 5.01	C.Bainbridge	NK	10. 5.02
JXX 4874	JXX	Pilatus PC-11 B4	13	HB-1112	28. 5.01	K.J.Sleigh	Rattlesden	27. 5.02
JXY 4875	JXY	Neukom Standard Elfe	68	HB-1267	29. 5.01	K.J.Sleigh	Rattlesden	28. 5.02
JXZ 4876	27B	Schleicher ASW-27B	27152		16. 3.01	M.Fryer	Rufforth	15. 3.02
JYA 4877	JYA	Slingsby T.21B	MHL015	WB988	31. 3.01	C.Bravo	Madrid, Spain	30. 3.02
JYB 4878	IZ	Glaser-Dirks DG-202/17	2-143/1738	D-1086	1. 5.01	N.Wood	Rufforth	30. 4.02
4879						Not allotted		
JYC 4880	T6	Schleicher ASW-27B	27155		25. 3.01	J.Garfield	Booker	24. 3.02
JYD 4881	R19	Grob G102 Astir CS	1429	RAFGSA.R19 D-7425	9. 4.01	Phoenix GC	Bruggen	8. 4.02
JYE 4882		Schleicher ASK-13	13191	D-0347	11. 4.01	Ulster GC	Bellarena	10. 4.02
JYF 4883	N55	Schempp-Hirth Discus CS	281CS		11. 4.01	D.Bradley	Rufforth	10. 4.02
JYG 4884		Letov LF107 Lunak	49	OK-0833	R17. 4.01	M.Laurner	(Germany)	
JYH 4885		Schempp-Hirth Ventus 2B	114			*(See BGA.4895)*		
JYJ 4886	JYJ	Schempp-Hirth Ventus 2cT	64		1. 5.01	A.Evans	Chipping	30. 4.02
JYK 4887	115	Glaser-Dirks DG-800B	8-194B116	(G-BZEM)	2. 5.01	I.Stromberg	Camphill	1. 5.02
JYL 4888		LAK-12 Lietuva	6197	(Slovenia)	9. 5.01	C.Arrigo	Udine, Italy	8. 5.02
JYM 4889	LR	Schempp-Hirth Discus 2A	86		9. 5.01	S.Meriziola	Rome, Italy	8. 5.02
JYN 4890		Schempp-Hirth Discus 2B	94		9. 5.01	G.Aliman	Briauzo, Italy	8. 5.02
JYP 4891	B12	Grob G102 Astir IIB	5018C	D-8743	19. 5.01	Norfolk GC	Tibenham	18. 5.02
JYQ 4892		Glaser-Dirks DG-100G	E181G147	D-1485	R17. 5.01	A.Booth		
JYR 4893	B20	Schempp-Hirth Duo Discus T	16		3. 7.01	B.Walker	Nympsfield	2. 7.02
JYS 4894	878	Schempp-Hirth Mini Nimbus C	106	HB-1437	6. 6.01	A.Jenkins	Shobdon	5. 6.02
JYT 4895	E4	Schempp-Hirth Ventus 2B	114	(BGA.4884)	15. 6.01	J.Bastin	Booker	14. 6.02
JYU 4896	R11	Schempp-Hirth Ventus 2cT	70/216		15. 6.01	RAFGSA Clevelands GC	Dishforth	14. 6.02
JYV 4897	JYV	Schleicher K8B	133	D-8395	18. 6.01	European Soaring Club	Le Blanc, France	17. 6.02
JYW 4898	JYW	Schleicher K8B	8432A	D-5682	18. 6.01	European Soaring Club	Le Blanc, France	17. 6.02
JYX 4899	JYX	Rolladen-Schneider LS-3-17	3289	D-3517	18. 6.01	European Soaring Club	Le Blanc, France	17. 6.02
JYY 4900	PB	Schleicher ASW-28	28029		21. 6.01	P.Brice	Dunstable	20. 6.02
JYZ 4901		Bolkow Phoebus B	855	OE-0872	7.01	K.Sleigh	Rattlesden	. 7.02
JZA 4902	JZA	Start+Flug H101 Salto	27	D-2997	10. 7.01	C.Pollard	Rattlesden	9. 7.02
JZB 4903	JZB	Glaser-Dirks DG-505 Orion	5E223X61		28. 7.01	Faulkes Flying Foundation		27. 7.02
JZC 4904		Rolladen-Schneider LS-8-18	"40708"		R27. 6.01	M.H.Patel		
JZD 4905		Dittmar Condor IV	018	(D-0125) LV-DHV	R4. 7.01	P.Underwood		
JZE 4906	SG2	Schleicher ASK-13	13423	OY-XPJ D-2125	11.11.01	Southdown GC	Parham Park	10.11.02
JZF 4907	SOOM	Glaser-Dirks DG-500-22	5E42M20	G-SOOM	9. 7.01	G.W.Kirton	Husbands Bosworth	8. 7.02
JZG 4908	SM	Schempp-Hirth Discus bT	9	D-KISM	9. 7.01	R.J.Middleditch	Nympsfield	8. 7.02
JZH 4909	JZH	Schleicher ASW-20CL	20745	F-CBDJ F-WBDJ	10. 7.01	C.Hunt	Lasham	9. 7.02
JZJ 4910		Schleicher ASW-15	15147	D-0791	R12. 7.01	K.Sleigh	Rattlesden	
JZK 4911	JZK	Glaser-Dirks DG-505 Orion	5E225X63		1. 9.01	Faulkes Flying Foundation		31. 8.02
JZL 4912	BS	Schempp-Hirth Mini Nimbus B	92	HB-1453	25. 8.01	S.Ware & Ptnr.	Kirton-in-Lindsey	24. 8.02
JZM 4913	110	Schempp-Hirth Ventus 2A	117		24. 8.01	Southern Sailplanes	Membury	23. 8.02
JZN 4914		Schleicher ASW-28	"2G2808"		R24 .8.01	C.Lees		
JZP 4915	JZP	Marganski Swift S1	119	F-CIAB	26. 9.01	I.Tunstall	Winthorpe	25. 9.02
JZQ 4916		Edgely EA9 Optimist	006		R3. 9.01	T.Henderson		
JZR 4917		Edgely EA9 Optimist	008	(BGA.4731)	R3. 9.01	University of London		
JZS 4918		Schempp-Hirth Ventus	3	?	R3. 9.01			

JZT 4919 L30	Schleicher ASW-27	27163	D-4115	22. 8.01	L.Brigliadori	Sirtori, Italy	21. 8.02
JZU 4920	Glaser-Dirks DG-101G	E64G39	HB-1579	R12. 9.01	M.Robinson		
JZV 4921 V2C	Schempp-Hirth Ventus 2cT	72/225		14. 9.01	P.McLean	Tibenham	13. 9.02
JZW 4922 JZW	Grob G102 Astir CS	1208	D-7281	27. 9.01	R.Theil	Cranwell	26. 9.02
JZX 4923	Schleicher ASW-27	27166		22. 9.01	P.R.Barley	Bicester	21. 9.02
JZY 4924	Grob G104 Astir III	5600	D-6951	2.10.01	T.R.Dews	Kingston Deverill	1.10.02
JZZ 4925	Rolladen-Schneider LS-7	7128		R25. 9.01	J.Tucker		
KAA 4926	Slingsby T31B	903	XE790	R26. 9.01	N.Stalpers	Alkmaar, The Netherlands	
KAB 4927	Slingsby T59 Kestrel 19	1832	G-BBVC BGA.3176	R27. 9.01	T.Gauder		
KAC 4928	Glaser-Dirks DG-200	2-159	HB-1611	3.10.01	C.Morton-Fincham	Kirton-in-Lindsey	2.10.02
KAD 4929	Glaser-Dirks DG-300 Elan	3E259	D-8411 OE-5420	5.10.01	N.G.Maxey	Challock	4.10.02
KAE 4930	Centrair Pegase	101-0152	F-CGBN	R8.10.01	M.Robinson		
KAF 4931	Schempp-Hirth Duo Discus T	49		R10.10.01	M.Smith		
KAG 4932	Schempp-Hirth Nimbus 3T	23	D-KMHF	R29.10.01	K.Engelhardt		
KAH 4933 KAH	Schempp-Hirth Discus Bt	464/112	D-KNZZ	13.11.01	R.Brown	Bicester	12.11.02
KAJ 4934	Schempp-Hirth Ventus 2cT	86		R29.10.01	A.Reddington		
KAK 4935 J1	Schleicher ASW-28	28032		1.11.01	R.A.Johnson	Husbands Bosworth	31.10.02
KAL 4936 A28	Schleicher ASW-28	28031		13.11.01	A.Smith	Nympsfield	12.11.02
KAM 4937 TS2	Glasflugel H205 Club Libelle	83	D-8928	R5.11.01	T.Slater		
KAN 4938 KAN	SZD-50-3 Puchacz	B2106	PH-1104	10.12.01	Bath, Wilts & North Dorset GC	Kingston Deverill	9.12.02
KAP 4939	Schempp-Hirth Discus CS		290CS	R21.11.01	A.Stewart		
KAQ 4940 BG	LAK-17A	125		8.12.01	LAK Deutschland	Musbach, Germany	
KAR 4941	Schempp-Hirth Duo Discus T	35	D-KHAF	3.12.01	J.Galloway	Portmoak	2.12.02
KAS 4942	Schempp-Hirth Ventus cT	93/582	D-KREB	R11.12.01	J.E.Bowman		
KAT 4943	Schempp-Hirth Ventus 2cT	82		R9. 1.02	P.Naegeli		
KAU 4944	Glaser-Dirks DG-303 Elan	3E500A35		R16. 1.02	E.Greville		
KAV 4945	Rolladen-Schneider LS-4A	4996	D-2975	R18. 1.02	G.Ware		
KAW 4946	Glaser-Dirks DG-505 Orion	5E228X66		R18. 1.02	Faulkes Flying Foundation		
KAX 4947	Glaser-Dirks DG-505 Orion	5E229X67		R18. 1.02	Faulkes Flying Foundation		
KAY 4948	Grob G102 Astir CS	1452	D-7433	R21. 1.02	P.Pickering		
KAZ 4949	Glaser-Dirks DG-600			R23. 1.02	M.Geiser		
KBA 4950	Centrair 101 Pegase	101-435	HB-3096	R30. 1.02	Go Soaring		

PART 2 – IRISH GLIDING & SOARING ASSOCIATION

The system is similar to the British Glider Association with the register maintained by the, now renamed, Irish Gliding & Soaring Association. The IGSA listing is updated from Air-Britain sources although little has happened during the year. Any help in filling the gaps would be appreciated. The last known CofA status, as at 31 January 1997, is also in need of some substantial updating. Thanks to Lloyd Robinson for additional information this year.

No/Code		Type	C/n	P/I	Date	Owner/operator	Probable Base	CA Expy
IGA.6		Slingsby T.8 Tutor	-	IAC.6	.56	Meath Aero Museum	Ashbourne, Co.Meath	
				VM657		*(Noted 3.01)*		
EI-100		SZD-12A Mucha 100A	494	OY-XAN	.95	J.Finnan & M.O'Reilly	Gowran Grange	1. 7.97
EI-102		Slingsby T.26 Kite 2	?	IGA.102	.54	Dublin GC	Gowran Grange	
				IAC.102/BGA...		*(Stored 5.99)*		
EI-105		Schleicher Ka7 Rhonadler	775	IGA.7	.60	Dublin GC	Gowran Grange	14. 6.97
						(Noted 5.99)		
EI-108	08	Schleicher K8B	8486		.65	Dublin GC	Gowran Grange	13. 4.97
		(Logbook shows c/n 8468)				*(Active 10.01)*		
EI-111	11	Schleicher Ka6CR	6565		.67	Not known	Gowran Grange	30. 3.97
						(Noted 5.99)		
EI-112		Schleicher ASK13	13131		.69	Dublin GC	Gowran Grange	9. 3.97
						(Noted 5.99)		
EI-113		Schleicher ASK13	13189		.69	Clonmel GC	Kilkenny	17. 7.97
EI-114		Schleicher ASK14	14008	EI-APS	.69	SLG Group	Gowran Grange	
				G-AWVV/D-KOBB		*(Not used: see EI-APS in SECTION 2)*		
EI-115		EoN AP.5 Olympia 2B	EoN/O/155	BGA.1097		Dublin GC	Gowran Grange	
						(Active 5.99)		
EI-118		EoN AP.8 Baby	EoN/B/001	BGA.608	.73	B.Douglas	Gowran Grange	
				RAFGSA.217/BGA.608/G-ALLU/BGA.608		*(Stored 6.95)*		
EI-119		Schleicher ASK16	16022	EI-AYR		*(Not used)*		
EI-120		LET L-13 Blanik	175205	RAFGSA	.75	Private Syndiate	Gowran Grange	
				BGA.1730		*(Active 10.01)*		
EI-121		Pilatus B4 PC11AF	199		.77	Clonmel GC *(Stored 6.95)*	Kilkenny	
EI-124		Grob G.102 Astir Standard CS 77	1761	D-...	.80	Nutgrove Shopping Centre	Churchtown, Dublin	
						(Noted 5.99)		
EI-127		Schleicher Ka6CR	662	PH-259		Not known *(Current 1993)*		
EI-128		Schleicher Ka6CR	6649	???		Dublin GC	Gowran Grange	
						(On rebuild 4.96)		
EI-130		Scheibe L-Spatz	200	BGA.2199		J.J.Sullivan	Gowran Grange	
				D-4707		*"White Cloud"*		
EI-132	TK	Schleicher ASW17	17031	D-2365		Not known	Gowran Grange	17. 6.97
EI-133	33	Schleicher K8B	8557	D-8517	.91	Dublin GC	Gowran Grange	14. 6.97
				D-9367		*(Active 10.01)*		
EI-134	34	Schleicher ASW15B	15249	D-1087	.91	Not known	Gowran Grange	7. 5.97
EI-135		Slingsby T.38 Grasshopper	758	WZ762	.91	(Syndicate)	Gowran Grange	
		(Wings from WZ756 or WZ768)				*(Stored as "WZ762" 5.99)*		
EI-136		Schleicher ASK18	18007	BGA.2945	.91	Dublin GC	Gowran Grange	30. 7.97
				D-6868		*(Noted 5.99)*		
EI-137		Rolladen-Schneider LS3-17	3308	D-3521	.92	Not known	Gowran Grange	1. 3.97
EI-138	BR	Schempp-Hirth Discus CS	089CS		.92	B.Ramseyer	Gowran Grange	
						(Sold as N189HH 12.00)		
EI-139		Slingsby T.31B	902	BGA.3485	.93	P.Bedford Syndicate	Gowran Grange	2. 8.97
				G-BOKG/XE789				
EI-140		SZD-12A Mucha 100A	491	HB-647	.93	D.Mongey	Gowran Grange	
EI-142		Scheibe SF-27A Zugvogel V	6049	(EI-144)	.94	Not known	Gowran Grange	19. 7.97
				D-1444		*(Active 5.99)*		
EI-143		Schleicher ASK13	13112	BGA.1501	.94	Dublin GC	Gowran Grange	
EI-144		Scheibe SF-27A Zugvogel V	6049	(EI-142)	.94R	*(NTU - to EI-142)*		
				D-1444				
EI-145		Glaser-Dirks DG-200	2-88	PH-930	.95	Not known	Gowran Grange	
				D-7610		*(Noted 5.99)*		
EI-146	TK	Scheibe Zugvogel IIIB	1085	D-4096	.96	N Short & T Daly	Gowran Grange	
						(Active 10.01)		
EI-147		Glaser-Dirks DG-200	2-22	D-6760	.97	Not known	Gowran Grange	
						(Active 6.00)		
EI-157		Slingsby T.21B	1158	BGA.1465		Dublin GC	Gowran Grange	
				RAFGSA.333/XN154		*(Active 10.01)*		

SECTION 7- GLIDER INDICES

PART 1 - ALPHABETICAL TYPE INDEX (UK & IRELAND)

Herewith a summary of BGA No/Tri-graph tie-ups but note the letters I and O are not used except in the case of JMO.

BGA No.	Tri-graph	BGA No.	Tri-graph
101- 230	None	3535-3545	FUL-FUW
231- 246	AAA-AAR	3546-3735	FUY-GCV
247- 605	AAT-ARR	3736-3770	GCX-GEQ
606- 628	ART-ASR	3771-3776	GEK-GEQ
629- 806	AST-BAC	3777-3817	HAA-HBS
807- 1245	BAE-BUL	3818	Not used
1246-1380	BUN-CAC	3819-3827	HBT-HCB
1381-1681	CAG-CNS	3828	Not used
1682-1819	CNU-CUM	3829-3990	HCC-HJV
1820-1821	CUP-CUQ	3991-4043	HJX-HMB
1822-2048	CUS-DEC	4044-4045	HMG-HMH
2049-2391	DEE-DUL	4046-4122	HMK-HQP
2392-2478	DUN-DYC	4123-4138	HQR-HRG
2479-2485	DYE-DYL	4139-4276	HRJ-HXB
2486-2489	DYN-DYR	4277	Not used
2490-2494	DYT-DYX	4278-4624	HXC-JMN
2495-3101	DYZ-FAF	4625	JMO
3102-3528	FAH-FUB	4626-4878	JMP-JYB
3529-3534	FUD-FUJ	4880-4950	JYC-KBA

ABBOTT-BAYNES SAILPLANES LTD

SCUD I
HFZ
SCUD II
AAA
SCUD III
ACF AVA

AEROMERE - see CARMAM

ALLGAIER

GEIER
EBP

ASC

FALCON
HPZ
SPIRIT
HPY

AVIA

40P
AUW

AVIASTROiTEL - see FEDEROV

AC-4
JUX JVH

AVIALSA - see SCHEIBE

AVIONAUTICA RIO - see CARMAM

BAC

VII rep
EQY

BIBBY

G.1
HPK

BIRMINGHAM GUILD LTD - see SWALES & YORKSHIRE SAILPLANES

BG.135
CRF CUF CYW CXN CXP DCY DLZ

BOLKOW

PHOEBUS C
CGX CHC CHJ CJB CJJ CKC GDD HTZ JHX JVH JWP JYZ

BREGUET

905 FAUVETTE
CVJ DGV EGR ELJ EPN ESM

CARMAM (SOCIÉTÉ CARMAM) - see AEROMERE/AVIONAUTICA RIO

M.100S MESANGE
CBR CLU DFP DTS DUC EPG EQM ETN FCH FKV HFP HGU HQF
M.200 FOEHN
EQX EVC FXN HCN HGJ
JP.15/34 KIT-CLUB/15/36A AIGLON
DYL EDB FDC FQV HKE HKF HKZ HMU HTW

CAUDRON
C.801
EHF

(SA) CENTRAIR - see SCHLEICHER
101 PEGASE
EPK EQK ERX ESD ESH ESW ETJ ETM ETQ EVE EVM EVQ FAN FCB FCD FEH FFC FFS FGW FHJ FJK FJT FMK FNM FRD FRR FRV FRX FVM FVN FVP FVV FWG FWX FWY FXD FXT GBU GCN GCY HDD HDW HES HKN HNY HNZ HRK HZF JQP KAE KBA
201 MARIANNE
HTA JXB JXN
ALLIANCE SNC-34
JHR

CHARD - see KING-ELLIOTT-STREET

COLDITZ
COCK REP
JRZ JTA --*Both designs are unrelated*

DFS -see GRUNAU/EoN/NORD &
Incl FOCKE-WULF/WEIHE/SCHLEICHER production
KRANICH
BGT BQJ
OLYMPIA-MEIS
AKD
108-68 WEIHE
AKC BKC BNC BTV BWR EDL

DITTMAR
CONDOR IV
JZD

DWLKK
PW-5 SMYK
HYM HZB JCG JDW JKB JKE

EDGLEY
EA.9
HPJ JRY JZQ JZR

EICHELSDORFER
SB.5
EHC EJH

EIRI
PIK-20
DFE DFK DFZ DHH DHN DHV DJN DJZ DKT DLJ DLY DMU DMV DMY DPL DQU DRT DVJ DVN DWS DYT DZT EAR EAT EBG JBH JGK JVE JXG

EoN - see DFS/NORD
AP.5 OLYMPIA
AMK AMM AMP AMR AMT AMU AMV AMW ANW ANZ APC APV AUU AVD AWU AZR AZT BBH BEL BFN BGR BGX BHC BJC BKK BKL BKS BKU BKX BLN BLP BLQ BLS BNG BPL BQQ BRH BRL BWX CAF CAK CBS CGU CHK CPE CQG CTA CTS DBA DPU EI-115
AP.6 OLYMPIA 401/403/419
BLJ BLK BVW CDW DAL DTR
AP.7 PRIMARY/ETON TX.1
AQQ AQY AQZ CLJ FEZ
AP.8 BABY
ASS AST G-ALRH EI-118
AP.10 460/463/465
BQM BQS BQT BRK BRQ BSQ BTG BTN BTQ BUG BUH BUK BUV BVN BWB BWE BWG BWU BXB BXC BXY BYE BZB BZR BZS BZV BZW CAB CAN CAT CBV ELS

FAUVEL
AV.22S
DSM
AV.36C
ETE

FEDEROV - see AVIA STROITEL
Me-7 MECHTA
HMZ HPS HPT HUQ JFY JFZ JGA

FFA FLUGZEUGWERKE AG
DIAMANT
CDG CDW CGM CGS HGT

FOCKE-WULF - see DFS WEIHE
KRANICH III
ENG

GINN-LESNIAK
KESTREL
CJC

GLASER-DIRKS
DG-100/DG-101
DFN DHJ DHK DHL DKQ DMD DRB DUY EDN EDP EKP ENU EPU FBH FBW FFU FYU HMS HWP JEZ JNZ JPF JRL JSM JTC JXP JXV JYQ JZU
DG.200/DG.202
DTA DTM DUQ DWJ DXN DYH EBR EDM EKA EME EMU EQP FQC HAT HBD HDH JAE JAJ JAW JDD JDP JHW JKF JKM JPW JRN JVP JXG JYB KAC EI-145 EI-147
DG.300/DG.303 ELAN
ESQ FAJ FBF FCM FDW FGT FJR FJS FJX FLC FLX FNS FPK FSR FSX FTS FUJ FUT FUU FWM FZW GAJ GBS HBE HBW HCU HCY HDR HMB HSB HVM JAB JDV JNQ JRC JTK JTN JVL KAD KAU
DG-500/DG-505 ELAN
GBZ HBP HEF HGV HHJ HNA HRC HYE JDN JQF JSX JZB JZF JZK KAW KAX
DG-600
FKB FNT FPW FQQ FVG KAZ
DG-800
HPU JBL JJH JYK

GLASFLUGEL

H.201 STANDARD LIBELLE

CFS CFX CFY CKF CKY CLM CLN CLP CLR CLV CLW CMH CMQ CMR CMS CMV CMW CMX CNE CNF CNG CNH CNJ CNP CNY CPA CPF CPM CRB CRQ CRS CRV CRW CSJ CSR CTU CUJ CUK CVL CVQ CWE CWG CWN CWT CWX CWY CWZ CXK CYG CZL DCC DMS DNL ECY FLT FLU GAU GDM GEE HAA HAD HAV HCQ HHY HJR HWC HWG JAS JBF JEU JGZ JHJ JNG JVW

H.205 CLUB LIBELLE

DBP DEQ DKZ DVM FAR FYG GCS HAE KAM

H.206 HORNET

DKD DKM

H.301 LIBELLE

FEV GAN HLK

H.303 MOSQUITO

DMN DPK DRN DTK DTV DTX DTY DUB DVZ DWB DWL DWO DWR DXA DXW EAK ECH ECS EDH EDJ FBN FWR HMT JEH JNR JTQ JTW

H.304

EHU ENT HMM

H.604

ECT

GROB (BURKHART GROB LUFT-und RAUMFAHRT GmbH) - see SCHEMPP-HIRTH

G.102/G.104 SPEED ASTIR

DFR DJD DJQ DJX DKR DKS DKU DKV DKW DKX DLH DLM DMH DMP DMR DNC DNE DNK DPJ DPQ DPY DQB DQE DQG DQR DRK DRU DRW DSH DSN DSU DUL DUX DWQ DWU DXJ DYF DZJ DZU EAC EAF EAW EBB EBM ECQ EEQ EKF ELN EQD EVK EVL FBR FCJ FDF FEB FEF FEX FFB FGK FHT FHW FJH FRL FSA FSH FSZ FTK FTR FXA GAT GBJ GBK GCL GDQ GEB HAU HBL HBM HBT HCS HFD HGB HJV HKB HKM HPM HQT HRA HSE HTD HTE HTG HTR HUN HVK HWK HXB HXM HXY HYQ HZC JAZ JBZ JCF JCR JCW JEK JFD JHE JHG JHN JKW JLR JML JNA JPJ JPM JQN JQT JRD JRM JRP JSD JSH JSK JTT JUK JUS JWR JYC JYP JZW JZY KAY EI-124

G.103 TWIN ASTIR/ACRO

DRQ DSJ DSL EGN EQT EWP EWR EYS EZE FEA FFJ FQK FWC HBH HBK HCA HCJ HQS HWW JKV JLZ JQG JRW

GRUNAU - incl DFS/FOKKER/HAWKRIDGE production

BABY

ABZ AFY AQN ASC BGS BTD CBK CDQ CMY CRM CYJ DNA DNB DUD DUW DWF EHX EMW HJB

HALFORD

JSH SCORPION

DJF

HAWKRIDGE

DAGLING

ALX ALZ

HIRTH

Go.III MINIMOA

CLY

GOEVIER

DBU

HOLS-DER-TEUFEL

REP

FHQ

HUTTER

H.17

ALW EPR HEY

H.28

HJM HPB

ICA (INTREPRINDERA DE CONSTRUCTII AERONAUTICE OF CIAR 1968)

IS-28B2

DEG DLT DLU DZR EHS EHW EJA HMG R93

IS-29D

DAM DBG DDJ DEN DEW DEZ FDG FFN

IS-30

FDB FDP

IS-32A

FAV

ISF

MISTRAL C

JBE JRS

ISSOIRE (SOCIÉTÉ ISSOIRE-AVIATION)

D77 IRIS

EET EJW

E78 SILENE

EBE EEU HPA JUG

JANSSON

BJ-1B: DUSTER

ETL

JASTREB - see SCHEMPP-HIRTH

KING-ELLIOTT-STREET

OSPREY

DCZ

LAK

LAK-12 LIETUVA

FXR GAB GCB GCJ HEG HGQ HGR HGX HHM HHW HLT HQG HRB HSR HTF JBS JBY JFW JQH JYL

LAK-17

JQU JVJ KAQ

LANAVERRE - see SCHEMPP-HIRTH

LET

L-13 BLANIK
BVY BXR BXV BXW CAW CFD CUZ CVA CVB CYR DAF DCL DEX DEY DGB DGP DKH DPD DVD EFX ESV EUG EVR FDV FLV FZS GAK HTY JDU JGQ JNX EI-120
L-23 SUPER BLANIK
FXP FYP FYR
L-33 SOLO
FZY FZZ

LETOV (VOJENSKÁ továrna na letadla LETOV)

LF-107 LUNAK
HXL JYF

MANUEL

CONDOR
DJW
HAWK
CSU
WILLOW WREN
BGA.162

MARCO

J-5: HKW

MARGANSKI

SWIFT S1
JZP

MAUPIN

WOODSTOCK
HCG HPG

MDM

MDM-1 FOX
JCH JKC

MOLINO - see EIRI

MONNETT

MONERAI
FAP JBV

MULLER

MOSWEY III
DXY

MUNCHEN

MU-13D
CZM DPG

NEUKOM

STANDARD ELFE S-2
FMR JGF JXY
ELFE PM3
JRQ

NORD - see EoN

2000
EPJ

OBERLERCHNER - see SCHEMPP-HIRTH

Mg19a STEINADLER
ERZ

PENROSE

PEGASUS
HKJ

PIK - see EIRI

PIK-16C VASAMA
CGV

PILATUS FLUGZEUGWERKE

B4 PC-11
CSN CSP CSW CUB CUC CUQ CUT CVG CVK CVM CVV CYA CYC CYK CZD DBC DLA DND DQM DRP DSV EQU HDA HDE HLC HSY HVH JSY JXX EI-121

POTTIER - see CARMAM

RAAB

DOPPELRAAB
EVU

ROLLADEN-SCHNEIDER

LS1F
FQZ JPE JSF JST
LS3
DNQ ECP EEF EES EEX EEZ EFS EFZ EGE EVD GAD GDA GDN HWR HYH JDJ JYX EI-137
LS4
EHK EHL EKV ELT EMB EMF EMG EMT EMY ENA ENE EQA ERV ESC ESE ESY ETG ETV ETY EUH FAQ FHL FJM FKG FLF FNU FVE FYH GBT GDJ HEL HKX HLB HMX HNV HNX HPL HVV HXF HXT HXZ HZM HZY JBX JEP JJB JKP JLH JLJ JSB JSW JWN KAV
LS6
FBE FCP FMC FRA GAR GBG GBQ GBR GCM HAQ HBC HBJ HET HEW HEZ HFM HFQ HGP HHH HHT HHU HJC HJF HJX HMK HPD HQL HQZ HRY HSA HUM HYA JBP JBQ JBU JCB JDG JDH JGC JNP JNU JTD JVK
LS7
FMY FPD FQG FQH FTV FTY FUV FVH FVQ FWF FWJ FWU FXE FYB FYK FYW FZV GBL GBY GCZ HAY HBA HBY HDX HEH JEJ JLK JSJ JTR JZZ

LS8

HSZ HTL HTM HTP HTQ HTS HUG HUV HUW HVF HVL HVU HWL HWM HWS HXC HXN HXW HYF HYZ HZG HZP JBB JCL JCP JCY JDE JDK JDT JDY JEA JEG JFB JFL JFX JGS JHU JHY JJK JJU JKD JKL JKN JLN JMB JMO JMR JMT JMU JMW JNB JNJ JNK JNM JNW JPH JPL JPR JQD JRA JRK JSQ JSU JTL JTM JTY JUC JUD JUE JXU JZC

SCHEIBE-FLUGZEUGBAU – incl AVIALSA/ROCHETEAU production

BERGFALKE

CDR CEV CKT CMT DJU EBD EPZ EVT FPG FVD HQC

L-SPATZ

DLR DPR DPT DUH DVR DZC EFN EFR EQL FAK FHE FPF FXX HCP HWQ JHB GGA.502 EI-130

ZUGVOGEL III

EBS ELV FRS FSU FVL FVY FYE HKV HND HSH HXA EI-146

SF-26 STANDARD

DRL EDS EUM

SF-27A ZUGVOGEL V

DZV EKS EUE FHY FLZ FQF FQM FRM FUF FUQ FWH FZM GAV GBM GDW HGM HLU HMW HSG HSX HUS HVJ JSA EI-142

SFH-34 DELPHIN

EPM FKQ

SCHEMPP-HIRTH OHG incl GROB/JASTREB/OBERLERCHNER production

STANDARD AUSTRIA

BPN DBT DKB

SHK/SHK-1

CAQ CAR CBU CCB CGT CGZ CJK CJL CJN CLG CVH DJS DKK DMK DTG ECG FJZ FZC

HS.2 CIRRUS/CIRRUS VTC

CDH CEA CEC CFK CGY CJR CLQ CUS CVE CVF CWL CWR CWS DDM DVY FXG GCQ HEV HTU HUL HUR JJA JQW JTS

HS.4 STANDARD CIRRUS

CKZ CLA CLH CNN CPU CQN CQR CQY CRH CRN CTB CTT CUL CYM CYP CYQ CYT DAS DDA DDR DFC DFY DGE DGX DLG DVS DXL DZF EEN EGK FBB FCN FGU FLW FMT FMU FRJ FRZ FVS FYJ FZK GAH GAL GCD GEP HAN HAX HFF HGG HJN HJU HJY HKC HKD HKR HKS HKU HMY HNM HRL HSV HVZ HWD HWF HWY HXX HZJ HZL HZU HZV JBJ JCJ JCN JCU JDS JER JEV JEY JFA JGN JGY JHA JHH JJJ JJM JLX JMH JNC JQS JRG JRT JTE JUU JVU JWH

HS.5 NIMBUS 2

CQL CQP CQQ DAJ DDD DGY DHW DKL DMM DNG DTU DYU DYZ DZK EAJ EAM EEK EFB EFF EFT EGS EHP EHT EKR EKW FCS FPP FRC FVF FVT HBF HBV HNE HNH HQN JGH JMN JMV JQE

HS.6 JANUS

DTC EKB EQV EQW HNB HSP HTB HTH HUC HUH JAA JFE JLM JNL JVV

HS.7 MINI NIMBUS

DPH DSE DSP DSW DXQ DXT EAV EBF EBK EDF EER EGW FHG FSL HQY HRQ JGU JTJ JYS JZL

NIMBUS ¾

ENN ENP EQN ERU EVF FAM FBM FFK FGF FRP FWK FXQ HBR HCB HFX HKQ HNU HWN HYY HZA HZW JCT JDA JDZ JEQ JFQ JHF JJG JSC JUT JVD JVT JWG JXA KAG

DISCUS A/B/CS

FBY FDU FEJ FER FES FFT FFX FHR FKK FKM FLE FMG FMQ FNL FNQ FNR FQY FTW FUL FUP FXM FYM FYN FYX GCT GDR GDX HCL HDF HDT HDZ HEE HEM HEN HGK HGL HGS HGZ HHP HHQ HJH HJL HKA HKL HKY HLD HLN HLQ HLS HLY HML HMP HMQ HPH HPR HPX HQJ HQM HQR HQW HRS HRX HSD HSJ HSQ HUZ HVR HWV HXH HYB HYU HZE JAH JAN JAQ JAR JBD JBN JBR JBW JCK JCX JDL JFC JFG JGL JGM JGR JHM JHT JHV JJD JJE JJZ JKR JKX JLC JLP JLW JMD JMM JPP JPU JQA JQC JQK JRR JSE JUB JUV JVB JVF JVG JVX JVY JWK JXL JXR JYE JZG KAH KAP EI-138

DISCUS 2

JNE JNF JNY JUA JUP JVR JWQ JYM JYN

DUO DISCUS

HNF HNN HNW HQE HRW HSW HWB JAC JEM JFF JFH JGV JJP JPA JQQ JTU JUM JXW JYR KAF KAR

VENTUS A/B/C

EHH EKH EKJ ELG ELR ENJ EPX EUJ EUS FAW FBT FCK FDE FEG FEP FHS FJJ FJQ FMN FNN FPE FPL FQN FRB FRT FUH FUR FVB FVW FWD FYC FZH GAP GAS HAJ HED HFA HFV HFY HGN HHN HUY HVE HWH HXR HYG JBG JCE JEF JET JFP JFR JFS JJY JKH JKY JLA JLU JSL JWL JWU JXK JZS KAS

VENTUS 2

HSL HUP HUX HVE HVT HVY HWA HXS HYL HZS JAF JBC JEX JGP JLB JLU JPD JPG JQL JQR JTV JTZ JUF JUQ JVA JWX JYH JYJ JYT JYU JZM JZV KAJ KAT

SCHLEICHER - including CENTRAIR production

RHONBUSSARD

AEM

RHONSPERBER

ABG

Ka2B RHONSCHWALBE

DCG DGT DJG DPP DRR ESK FBL FPU FSF HZN

Ka3

EHB

Ka4 RHONLERCHE II

CTF CVY CWU CWV EAL EUT HQH GGA.591

Ka6/BR/CR RHONSEGLER

BKJ BKW BND BNH BQL BTJ BTM BUZ BVR BVX BVZ BWC BXT BYL BYM BYU BZQ BZX CBM CBY CCJ CJY DAW DCF DCW DDY DEP DEV DGK DHG DJE DJR DKG DKN DLP DNW DNX DQC DQF DQJ DQS DRA DRD DRE DRF DRG DRY DSG DSR DSY DUR DVG DYC DYJ DYN DYP DYQ DZW EBQ ECC ECF EDG EEW EGL ELY EPW EQQ FBZ FDR FGJ FHZ FKA FKH FKU FKX FLS FMM FNP FNW FQL FSE FTB FTF FUB FUM FWA FZR GAC GAW GBE GCP GDE GDF GEA GEF GEM HAB HBQ HEB HFB HPQ HRE HSN HUK HZH JCZ JEW JJV EI-111 EI-127 EI-128

Ka6E

BYX CAC CAE CAG CAS CCA CCD CCG CCL CCR CCU CCV CDA CDB CDD CDF CDV CDZ CED CEG CEL CEM CEQ CEW CEY CFL CGB CGD CGE CGK CGN CHB CHZ CKL CLZ CPJ DGG DHM DHT DLE DMQ DQK DSB DUS DVE DVH DWC DXH EAH EFM EHM EKC EKX ETB FCR FND FPV FRE FSS FVZ FXC FXS FXU GDV HAP HJD HRF JAK JAL JHD JHL JLT JLV JSG

Ka7 RHONADLER

BFP BKN BQK BQU BRM BVB CFC CLF CLK CLT CMG CMZ CPG CQT CRA CWJ DBF DHY DJT DKY DMF DML DQX DRM DWE DWN DXM DYB DYR EAU EDC EDK EFD ELX EMV ENC EPV ETR ETU EUQ EVB EVG FEL FGV FGZ FHU FJW FKW FLK FMD FMZ FPQ FQU FRF FTG FTU FXH GAQ HAG HCM HGC HHL HJK HNJ HSS JME EI-105

K8B

CDC CDK CFF CGH CGJ CHU CJF CJM CKW CLX CML CMN CQD CTZ CYZ DDL DFQ DGA DHA DJB DJP DKC DLD DLS DMB DMG DMJ DNZ DQL DQP DQY DRV DRZ DSF DTN DUF DUK DVQ DWG DWH DXP EAZ EED EEM EFG EFP EHA EJF EJG EKM EPT EQZ ESJ ESX ETD FAZ FBJ FCL FCQ FDD FDL FHN FJU FKJ FKT FLH FLP FLQ FNA FQD FQE FQR FQX FTA FTM FTN FVA FWL FXB FXW GCG GDB GDK GEG HAR HCZ HDN HDY HFW HJE HKK HLH HLV HMH HNG HRJ HRT HWE HWT HYN HYV HYW HYX HZX JAT JFT JGB JGD JGX JHK JLS JNN JQB JQJ JQZ JSN JXS JYV JYW EI-108 EI-133

Ka10

EVH

ASK13

CAV CBW CCC CCE CCF CCM CCP CCT CCW CCX CCY CCZ CDJ CEJ CEX CFA CFB CFG CFM CGQ CGR CHW CJD CKR CKU CKV CMK CRL CRT CWH DDB DKE DLC DMX DNV DQA DRJ DUE DVB DVC DVX DXV EAP EBL EBZ EDU EKD ENY EPP EQE EQF ETS EUC EVJ EVP FAT FCW FEQ FFA FGR FHM FHU FMH FPX FSD FSQ FVC FVU FWB FWN FYY FZN GBA HAL HDC HMV HPE HSM HTJ HUD HUF HUU HVQ HVW HXJ HXP HXV JFM JGW JJC JKT JLE JLF JLL JLQ JMJ JMP JMW JMX JMZ JPC JPV JPY JRX JSV JWB JWJ JWY JXM JYD JZE EI-112 EI-113 EI-143

ASW15
CHT CJP CKP CZN DDS FBC FBD FCY FDA FJV FKE FME FML FMS FPB FQB FRK FTD FXY GCH GCR GCX GDS GDY GEH HEJ HGF HJZ HNT HQX HTC HZD JAM JCA JDM JDR JED JGG JJX JPX JRE JVW JWS JZJ EI-134
ASW17
CPD CTE EDD EGD EI-132
ASK18
DJJ DJK DLB DNJ DPA EMH EUX HRN HSU JHQ JKG JKU JMA JMK JPQ JPZ JSZ EI-136
ASW19
DPX DSX DTD DTE DVL DVP DWZ DXX DZD DZG DZY EBJ EEH EJR ELA ENZ EPE EQG ERP ERQ ERS FFP FGP FNH FPJ FWP FWZ GCA GDP HCE HCV HDV HER HGH HHK HKT HLM HLW HNC HUA HWZ HXE HXU JBK JBT JCQ JDQ JES JFU JHC JHS JJL JKS JNT JRB JRV
ASW20
DST DTP DTQ DUT DVV DVW DXB DXK DYE DYX EAE EBN EBX ECX EDE EEC EEE EEJ EEV EFA EFE EFH EFJ EFK EFL EFV EGP EHD EHV EHZ EJK EJL EJQ EKE EKU ELU ELZ ENV ENW EPF EPS EQJ ERA ETZ EUD EUK EUY FAF FBA FBQ FCV FFH FHD FJE FKL FPH FPN FPT FRH FRW FTL FTP FTQ FUN FWS FZL HBU HCH HDJ HDL HEQ HGW HHS HJT HLZ HPC HQD HQK HRU HSK HTT HTX HUJ HUT HVP HVX HYK HZT HZZ JAG JAY JEE JEN JFJ JFK JHZ JMQ JTP JXH JZH
ASK21
ECW ECZ EDW EGZ EHQ EKG ELE ENK EPD EQR ERH ERJ ESB ESU ETA FBV FWQ FYF FYV GAF GAG GAM GBB GBF GBN GBP GBV HCX HLG HLP HPV HPW HRR HTV HVG HYJ HYS HYT HZR JAD JAV JAX JBM JFV JGE JGJ JJR JKA JKJ JKQ JKZ JMC JMS JQX JVZ JWD
ASW22
FDT FEU FGY FNF GBX HTN JNV JWZ
ASK23
EVV EVW EVX EVY FCX GCF HKP JPB
ASW24/E
FLY FMP FMX FNG FXJ GDT GDU GDZ HBB HBG HYD JCD JEB JEL JRU JTC JXT
ASH25
FKN FLG FST FSY FUG FWW FXL FYD FYZ GCE HFL HLX HXQ JCV JDF JFN
ASW27
HUE HXD HYR HZQ JCM JDC JJF JJT JLY JNH JNS JPN JPS JPT JQM JQV JRH JSS JTF JUH JUJ JUL JVM JVN JVQ JWC JWF JXZ JYD JZT JZX
ASW28
JVS JWA JXJ JYY JZN KAK KAL

SCHMETZ
CONDOR
DQH

SCOTT
VIKING
AHU

SHENSTONE
HARBINGER
BNA

SHORT
NIMBUS
ALA

SIEBERT
SIE 3
EFC FRG

SLINGSBY SAILPLANES LTD
incl YORKSHIRE SAILPLANES production
T.1 FALCON 1
ABN FCZ
T.6 KITE 1
AAF AAX ACH ADJ AHC
T.7 CADET
AWZ BQE
T.8 TUTOR
AJW AKW ALR AZK AZQ BAA BBG BCB BCH BDW BEF CPL CRK CRZ CSL DQD IGA.6
T.9 KING KITE REP
ELK
T.12 GULL I
AGE BED
T.13 PETREL
AHW ATR
T.15 GULL III
ATH HBZ
T.21
AQE AQG AQH ARM ASB ATK AUG AUJ AUP AWD AZC BCF BCU BDA BDM BFD BFY BGB BGG BGP BJF BJV BMQ BMU BQF BTH BUW BXK BYY BZA CEK CLC DAR DCN DDC EJJ EJP ELH ERW ETP EUN EUZ FCF FCT FDY FEE FFG FFL FFW FFZ FGB FGG FGM FGS FHB FHC FJA FJB FJD FJF FKP FNC FSP FTT GEN HCK HFC HFE HFG HNS HQB HRD JAU JQY JXD JYA
T.25 GULL 4
APZ
T.26 KITE 2
AND AUD AVF EI-102
T.30B PREFECT
ARK ASN AVT AZF BAN BQP CKJ DSA DTZ EBC EHE
T.31B
AVG BHY BZY CHQ EVA FCC FCG FDQ FFQ FGA FGC FHK FJN FLB FSJ FUW HAK HHG HLR HVB JCS JSP JWE KAA EI-139
T.34 SKY
AVB AVC AVL AVQ DPZ JPK
T.38 GRASSHOPPER
FMA FMW FSV GDC HEA HJJ HPP HVC JAP JBA JDB JJN JJS JND EI-135
T.41 SKYLARK 2
AWS AWX AXB AXP AXR AXU AYD AYY AZP AZX AZY BAH BAM BAV BAZ BBA BBU BCX BDY BEA BFL CCS CHE DCE
T.42 EAGLE
AXJ AZA BAY BBB BBQ BDF
T.43 SKYLARK 3
AXD AXE AXL AYF AYH BAC BAW BBP BBT BCM BCP BCS BCV BCW BER BET BEX BEZ BFC BFE BFG BGD BGH BGL BHQ BHS BHT BJB BJK BJW BKE BUT
T.45 SWALLOW
BCY BDR BEM BEY BFB BHV BJP BJY BJZ BKP BLU BML BNS BNU BPX BRC BRE BRG BSX BTA BVF BWK BXP BYB BYJ BYK BZL BZM CAX CHY DCS DGM DHP DLX ELC EMK FRQ HBX
T.49 CAPSTAN
BJQ BNR BPD BPS BPT BPU BPV BPW BRA BRW BSE BSK BSS BST BUC BUR BZG
T.50 SKYLARK 4
BKA BLA BLE BLH BLW BLZ BMW BMX BMY BNE BNK BNM BNN BNP BNQ BPA BPB BPC BPE BPG BPJ BPK BPZ BQZ BSC BSG BSH BSR BSY BSZ BTK BUE ERB FXF
T.51 DART
BQA BRB BRD BRT BRU BRY BSA BSL BSM BSV BSW BUF BUL BUP BVC BVE BVH BVJ BVL BVM BWJ BWM BWP BWQ BWS BWT BXE BXG BXH BXL BXM BYA BYC BYG BZC BZF BZH BZJ CAZ CBA DBB
T.53
CUD CXV CXW DHR
T.59 KESTREL
CFT CNS CNV CNW CNX CPB CQJ CQM CRJ CSA CSB CSD CSF CSG CSK CTJ CTL CTM CTN CTP CTQ CTR CVW CVX CVY CVZ CWA CWB CWD CWF CXM CYN CZQ CZR CZS CZT CZU CZV CZW CZZ DBJ DBK DBN DBQ DBR DBS DEB DXU DYG ERY KAB

T.65 VEGA
DWT DWW DXD DXE DXF DXG DXR DZA DZB DZM DZN DZP EAD EAG
EBA ECJ ECK ECL ECM ECN EDA EDV EDX EDY EDZ EEA EEG EFW
EGF EGG EGH EGJ EGT EGU EGX EHG EHN EHY EJB EJC EJD EJE
EJS EJT EKY ELD ELQ EMJ EML EMN EMP EMR EMS EMZ FNK

STANDARD AUSTRIA - see SCHEMPP-HIRTH

START + FLUG
H101 SALTO
JTX JZA

SWALES - see BIRMINGHAM GUILD

SZD
SZD-8 JASKOLKA
BFS DZS
SZD-9 BOCIAN
BJD BMM BVS CCN CEB CHF CKN CND CNM CTW CVP DAA DBW DBX
DCR DDN DNF DRS EJY ESA FLL FUD FZG HFU HPF HQU
SZD-12A MUCHA
GEQ HDM EI-100 EI-140
SZD-22C MUCHA STANDARD
JXE
SZD-24/SZD-32 FOKA
BZP BZZ CBP CMF CPC HGY
SZD-30 PIRAT
CBN CDX CEN CHG CHL CKD CNK CPV CPX CQC CQX CSV CTV CTX
CUM CVC CVR CXL CYD CZE CZG CZJ DAN DAP DAT DAU DBD DBV
DCH DCJ DDK DDW DFW DGH DHB DHZ DJA DLW DNT DTW EQB FKD
SZD-36A COBRA 15
CQW CRD CVN CVS CVT CXH CXJ DAC DAQ DCA
SZD-38A JANTAR-1
DAV DDE DDV DFL DFU DFV FNE
SZD-41A/SZD-48 JANTAR-STANDARD
DFX DHC DJL DJM DVK EKK ESP ETK FDX FHV FQT FTJ HBS HUB
SZD-42 JANTAR-2
DNU EUV HFJ
SZD-50-3 PUCHACZ
EUF EVS FBG FEN FTH FUY FWE FWT FYA FYL FZQ GBD GCK GCU
GEL HAC HAF HAS HCC HCD HCF HDP HEP HFH HHA HHC HSC HYP
JEC JRF JRJ JSR KAN
SZD-51-1 JUNIOR
FFV FFY FHF FPM FTC FUS FZA FZF FZP FZX GCC HCR HCW HDB
HDU HEK HHD HHE HMA HNK HQV HRG HRP JJQ JLG JMG JMY
SZD-55
GAX HEC HHR HRV HVD JTG
SZD-59 ACCRO
HVA HWX

VFW-FOKKER GmbH
FK-3
HJA

VALENTIN
MISTRAL
JHP JUR JUY

VOGT
LO-100 ZWERGREIHER
ELL

WASSMER (SOCIÉTÉ DES ETABLISSEMENTS BENJAMIN WASSMER)
WA21 JAVELOT II
CJG
WA22 SUPER JAVELOT
CEH
WA26P SQUALE
EEP HFN HGA HHX JXQ
WA28F ESPADON
JDX JXC
WA30 BIJAVE
EKT FNX HMR

WRIGHT
FALCON
ECA

YORKSHIRE SAILPLANES - see BIRMINGHAM GUILD/SLINGSBY

ZLIN (ZLINSKÁ LETECKNÁ AKCIOVÁ)
24 KRAJANEK
ATV

PART 2 - BGA COMPETITION NUMBERS & (TAIL) CODES

BGA Competition Numbers are issued to members/pilots and not to individual gliders but, beware, they change frequently. There is no formal list of Competition Numbers and little control over other gliders wearing similar or past numbers, or other (tail) codes- see below. The listing is a composite based on BGA information and reported sightings. The missing numbers are not allocated. Competition Numbers marked with an asterisk indicate where gliders have been noted with the numbers shown, although not listed in the current BGA record. In some cases because joint (syndicate) ownership is common this means that the Competition Number belongs to a member of a syndicate other than the one whose name appears as owner in the BGA's records. The member's name/glider type is shown where the glider concerned is not identified. This sub-section now includes the separate Alpha-Numeric (tail)-code listing.

No.	BGA No.	No.	BGA No.	No.	BGA No.	No.	BGA No.
1	1144*/1804*/3123	2	869*/2680/3529*	3	(JD Bally)/1861*	4	(WA Kahn)
5	(G.D.Green)	7	3224	8	3720	9	1317*
10	1818	11	1991*/4606*	12	4597	13	3323*
14	1958	15	(S.J.Parker)	16	4472	17	2804
18	1475	19	4123	20	2951*	21	(MI Gee) 4611*
22	TS Zealley	23	(PR Redshaw)/3965*	24	4586	25	3973
26	4473	27	4502	28	3341	29	3581*
30	2087	31	4251	33	778	34	3629*
35	3600	36	4409	37	(S MacArthur)/2556*	38	4047*
39	3427	40	1788*	41	3946	42	4478
43	1949	44	(TB Sarjeant)	45	3574	46	2458/4786
47	1435	48	4079	49	1797	50	2632
51	4522	52	(CP Jeffery)	53	1763	54	(R Jones)
55	2801/3497*	56	4337/2955*	57	4288*	58	4224
59	(BT Spreckley)	60	(SH Marriott)	61	1262	62	1514
63	4850	64	4222	65	(AK Lincoln)	66	(J Delafield)/4482
67	1052	68	3361	69	3419	70	4589
71	(JF D'Arcy)	73	4092*	74	2224	75	4267*
76	2721*	77	1377	78	3845	79	(J Randle)/2528*
80	4642	81	2453*	82	3920	83	3680/1584*
84	4261	85	(DJ Robertson)	86	2310	87	4608
88	2974	89	(JA Millar)	90	2981	91	4783
92	1839	93	3228/2667	94	3964	95	1989/2695*/4751
96	3807	97	3955	98	4350	99	4157
100	3962	101	1988	102	(JC Bailey)/2494*	103	4760
104	(GC Metcalfe)/3389	105	4478	106	2513	107	(GO Avis)/2524*
108	3606	109	3395	110	4913/3244*/4695*	111	4835
112	4344	113	3158	114	3791		
115	4887	116	2124	117	1386*/2751*	118	2911
119	4010	120	3197	121	1316	122	4046
123	4370	124	(JE Hampson)/1530*	125	3317	126	3913
127	(J Richards)/3355*/4100*	128	2071	129	2635	130	3398
131	(WJ Dean)/2667/3680	132	2455	134	3295	135	3994
136	793*/3273	137	(SJ Parsonage)/3861*	138	2698	139	1726
140	4631	141	2625	142	1629	143	3298
144	3837*/4489	145	(NL Jennings)	146	1876	147	2466
148	3683	150	4100/1269*	151	1686	152	2501/3321*
153	1528*	154	3279	155	(JM Turner)/870*	156	4290*
157	(P Clay)/2639*	158	3373	160	2461	161	(JA McCoshim)/4676*
162	(BH Owen)/3501*	163	1089*/1299*/4826	164	2088	165	1648
166	2623	167	4072	168	4273	169	4145
170	4216	171	3643	172	2677	173	3607
175	3124	176	2149*/4413	177	3126	178	3119
180	2901	181	2827	182	1293/1760	183	3933/4794
184	1660	185	4699	186	2744	187	3269
188	2775	190	3401	191	2436	192	3533
193	2727	194	3544	195	2115	196	3266
198	1015	199	(J Fuchs)	200	4226	201	3433*
202	3107	203	3991	205	3506*/4768	206	3708
207	1974	208	3641	209	3204	210	2960*/4244
211	(GA Childs)/1222*	212	4720	213	4165	214	2155*
215	2937*	216	4326	217	(RJ Clement)/1766*	218	2794*/3707
219	(CJ Ireland)/3770	221	4483	222	1579	223	2936
224	3627	225	1336	226	(DM Bellamy)/1662	227	2337*
228	3549	229	1683	230	3523	231	2918*
232	4437	233	2226*	234	1723	236	(HB Middleton)
237	3967	238	3411	239	2862	240	1969
241	4214	242	1737*/3417	243	1172*	244	(SG Olender)
245	3976	246	3555	247	3604*	248	1911
249	2950*	250	4795	251	(NM Hill)/2216*	252	1624
253	1840	254	1795	255	1116*	256	3540

257	3303	258	2323	259	2229	260	4039
261	2715*	262	(DW Allison)	263	(RN Turner)/3777*	264	2806
265	2243	266	(IA Davidson)/2200*	267	2464	268	3475
269	1853	270	2346	271	3101	272	(G Martin)/2426*
274	4467	275	4819/2856*	277	3587	278	3789
280	4673	281	2812	282	3397	28	(DJ Maynard)/2880
284	1632	285	3599/2880	286	(JM Beattie)/2469	287	2268
288	2808	289	3902*	290	3713	291	3868
292	3988*/1691*	294	(SC Foggin)/3751	296	4737	297	4050/2650
298	2898	299	1913	301	(KM Draper)/4630*	302	3689
303	(SG Olender)/1470*	304	4230	306	3981	307	2251
308	3877	309	(GF Fisher)/ 1533	310	4843	311	1359
312	2939	313	4170	314	3339	315	4066
316	3879	317	(P Bell)	318	3198	319	2728
320	2378	321	4232/3455*	322	1860*	323	2837
324	2000	325	4296	326	3631	327	1043*
328	3372*	329	4128	331	1813	332	3516
333	3115	334	2327	335	3892	337	(PE Kettle)
339	1722	340	2868	342	1732*	343	(IR Starfield)/1412
345	2820	346	(GG Pursey)/3831	347	1765	350	1348
351	1741	352	1331*/4767	353	2186	354	2472
355	1852*/3834	356	3805	357	(MP Brooks)/1397*	359	(CC Watt)/4041*
360	2180*	362	1362*/1420*	364	4051	365	4019
366	1240	367	2522	368	(JL Hey)/3337	369	3559
370	3206/4789	371	2235*/3381	372	1393	373	1428*
374	(PJ Kite)	375	2283	376	4324	377	1290*/4775
378	2196	379	2906	380	(PJ Kite)/1817*/4054*	381	4032
382	2979*	383	2880/2876*	385	4168*	386	G-ORIG
387	1769	388	4674	390	4134	391	2184*/3785
392	2231	393	4238	394	3842	395	3139
396	4740	397	3538	398	3192	399	3322
400	4815	402	1799	404	1268	405	3500
406	3320	407	2153	408	2754*	410	(R Jones)
411	3154	413	2711	415	1945	417	(PM Dunster)/1756*
418	1524*	419	(ML Boxall)	420	4811	422	1392
423	1850	425	3714	428	1844	429	(SM Sagun)/3780
430	2756	431	2702*	432	4315	433	2193
434	4428/G-OAPW*	435	2826	437	2271	438	3723*
440	2282*	441	4651	442	1672	443	(RJ Whitaker)/2968*
444	2175	445	(JS Weston)/4043	446	2959	447	(N Whiteman)/2343*
448	2605*	449	1538	450	3747	451	(CR Reese)/2870*
452	2789	453	1368* 2694	456	2634	458	1487
459	3415	461	3388	462	4021*	463	1201
464	(RA Robertson)/3133	465	1288	466	1688	467	3866*
468	1858	469	4060*	470	2640*	471	1369
473	3886	474	1574	475	(RA Robertson)1423*	476	4345
477	1916*	479	3443	480	3663/2289*	481	2707
483	(KS Whiteley)/2452	484	3448	486	3895	487	(AH Sparrow)/4130*
488	3136	490	(RT Starling)/2697	491	(JW North)/2980	492	G-BRRG*
493	4169	494	4553	495	3470/3899*	496	3808
497	(AL Green)	498	3479	499	3209	500	2146*/4739
502	1802*/3946	503	1902	504	(NM Claiden)/1936/4139	505	3975*
506	4694	507	3719	508	1890*	509	3924
510	3171	511	(BG Cooper)/2228*	512	(AK Mitchell)	514	4738*
515	2228*/2788	517	1298	518	3512*	519	(AF Brind)/3375
520	4667	521	(CM Greaves)/4629	522	3814*	523	1983*
524	3762	525	1669	526	4270	527	3261*
528	4484	529	(JA Tanner)	530	(AA Maitland)/2597*	531	2491*
532	1889	533	2353	535	1628*	536	2041*
537	(SR Domoney)/2490*/4379	538	3199	539	1854	540	(MF Evans)/4820*
541	2611	542	2294	543	2649/4424	545	3739*
546	3739*	547	4685	549	867*/4725	550	1818
551	1987	552	2553	554	4790	556	(RG Wardell)/2300*
558	1341	560	4291	561	4641*	563	4062
564	3207	565	4040	566	1748	567	3596
569	2673	570	4455	571	3151/1127*	572	2287
573	2499	574	3424	575	1381*	576	2504*
577	1546	579	(B.T.Payne)/1785	580	2473	581	(PT Worth)
584	4249	585	4082	586	2644	588	2057*/2239*
590	2424*/2924	591	3854	592	2481	593	2222
594	2529	596	2195	597	1198	598	4263*
599	4068	600	916*/2589	601	4645/1714*	602	1657
604	2585/3585	605	3820	606	2802	607	3898
608	2157*	609	3465	610	2114	611	3889

612	3542*	614	2162*	615	2411*/4541	616	4414
617	1986	618	4718	619	1456	620	4353
621	4791	622	1671	623	3223*	624	4213
625	1684	626	2821	627	3236	628	4628
630	3706	631	(CH Meir)	633	1821*	634	3462
636	2656*/4624	637	3717*/3937*	638	2396	640	2907*
642	2391*	643	(GB Monslow)	644	2565	645	2580*
646	3109*/4871	647	2038*/2592*	648	2340	649	3711
650	1743	651	3411 4482	652	2402*	653	1104*
655	4095	656	1836*/3445	660	3554		
662	3588	663	663*	664	3824	665	(JB Dalton)
666	4776	667	(RJ Strarup)/3821	668	3750	669	3645
671	3152	672	(MJ Henegan)/2672	674	3400	675	1961
676	4646	677	1855	678	1810	679	1401
680	2037	682	2990	683	1454	685	4450
686	(SJ Jenkins)/1312*	687	3883	688	(L Dent)/2326	691	1982
692	4080	693	4106	695	2025	696	(ER Walker)/2778*
698	3283	699	2357	700	(AR Head)	701	3259
702	1400	703	1727	704	(SR Evans)/2376	705	3393
706	1816	707	1752	708	4065*	709	1670
710	(M Dowding)/2737*/4392	712	4258	713	3306	71	(RG Johnson)/2743*
715	1383	716	2059*	717	4088	718	2352*
719	2783	720	(C Sutton)/3702*	721	3156	722	4838
723	(N Climpson)/3618	724	(RN Johnston)/1616*	725	3686	727	3130*
728	2444*/3308	729	3801	730	3939	732	2413*
733	2429	735	3887	737	2645	739	(SR Stanwix)
741	1121	742	2841	743	(GR Herbert)/1615	744	3291
745	2246	746	(DP Holdcroft)/3963*	747	3910	748	3731
750	2596	753	3525	754	3827	755	2438*
757	2518	758	(J Nash)/3456*	759	2168*	760	985*/2366/3565*
761	1706	762	4117	764	1570*	765	2848*
766	2379	767	2090	768	3590*	769	2172*
770	2291	771	(GE Wick)/2816*	772	3441	773	3134
774	2092	775	4252	777	4359*	778	3673
779	3621	780	3141	781	4625/1308*	782	782
783	3944	785	3453	786	(MJ Crawley)/2537	787	4448
788	2181	789	1088/1733	790	4576	791	1886
795	3882	797	2764	798	2329	799	(M Pagram)/1640
800	3395	801	3757	802	4151	803	3535
805	4030	806	3257	807	2555	808	1775*/3935
809	1123*	810	2423*	811	2119	812	1391
813	4660	814	1476	815	2457*	818	1685
819	4029	820	(SM Hall)/2604*	821	2321	822	3120
823	4362	824	2129	826	1944	827	4735
828	2479	829	3822	830	916/2589	832	1875
833	4202	837	1247	838	3956	839	2515
840	3878*	841	3146	842	1822	843	3704
844	2286/2684*	845	3730*	846	1562	848	4103
849	2706	850	2480	853	3515	854	2899
855	3964	856	4289	857	(PD Everett)/1568*	858	(P Ryland)/1689
859	1136*	861	1295	862	1519	865	3993
868	4534	869	2412	870	3904	871	4873
873	(C Osgood)/1801*	877	2354	878	1433*/4894	879	2408
881	2545	882	3870	884	2174*	885	2401
886	2445	888	3575	890	2729	891	2691
893	2345	894	4782	895	4175	896	3760
899	4547	900	378*/4200*/4831	902	2825	903	3299*
904	2722	905	1419*	906	2084*	907	2853/4425*
908	3737*	909	2502	910	3856	911	2382/4400
912	(FB Reilly)	913	1536/4304	915	2370	916	(PI Fenner)/4356*
917	(AI Galbraith)/1869*	918	1725	919	4004	920	3155*
921	4355	922	3710*	924	1798	925	3909
927	3363	928	3767	929	4808*	930	4240
933	4164/4557	937	(J Williams)/1637*	939	(RJ Williams)/2647*	940	3921
941	(RJ Smith)/4046	942	3623	943	2495	944	3522
948	1630*	949	(GJ Lyons)/3809*	950	3302*	951	2137*
952	(DW Smith)/3437*	954	3610*	955	2584	957	2505
959	2033	960	4394	961	1598	962	4235*
963	3954	968	2864	969	3365	970	(P Harper)/4008
971	2417	972	2350*	973	3410	977	2068*/3961
978	1871	979	3959	980	(AG Kefford)/3585*	982	1915
983	(SW Bradford)/2902*	985	4009*	987	3227*/3271	988	3457
989	2164	990	2508	991	3858*	992	2961
993	3148*	994	1380	995	3468*	996	3180

997	3304	B	3366/3446*	C	2191	D	2317
H	2984	K	2989	L	3163	M	3205
P	3274	S	3642				

Alpha/Numeric Tail Codes

2B	4374*	2CS	2680	2F	4427*	2R	3159	2UP	4081*/4792
3D	4113	4T	4801	5GC	4690	5U	(SK Armstrong)	7D	3167*
7H	4377	7Q	4364*	7X	4741	17K	4720	20L	2740
27B	4876	97Z	(PJ Tratt)						
A1	4155	A2	3872	A3	1943*	A7	4573*	A8	4596
A9	3885	A10	3622	A11	2385*	A14	4316	A15	4177
A19	3390	A20	4112	A23	(PR Redshaw)	A25	3341	A26	4322
A27	4422	A28	4936	A29	3581*	A30	2126	A34	4531
A61	4318*	A71	4540	A77	4125	A98	3438	AB	4387
AC4	4812	AC5	(S Kotomin)	AL	2868/3295	AT	4725	AV8	4777
B	3366/3446*	B1	1500*	B2	4385	B3	4373	B4	3272
B9	(BO Marcham)	B11	4342	B12	4891	B19	4728	B20	4893
B21	3357	B33	4147	B35	3728*	B38	3593	B39	3891*
B96	1283	BA	4929	BB	(MJ Wells)/3532	BD	4113*	BG	4940
BIT	4522	BR	2487*	BS	4912	BT	4507	BW	4563*
BZ	1834	C	2191	C3	4514	C4	4186	C7	4404
C8	(C Bradley)	C29	4012	C34	3997	C64	4193	C65	4245
CB	4668	CC	4494	CD1	4802	CF	(JA Murdock)/1655		
CL	4677	CP	(LG Blows)/4814*	CT	4870	CU	4493	CW	2648
CZ	4659	D	2317	D1	4638	D2	3262/4533	D3	2667*/4544*
D4	4444	D5	(DH Smith)	D7	4262	D10	1804*	D15	4158
D19	4048*	D31	(M Costin)/4210*	D41	4464	D49	1734	D53	4772
D54	4163	D55	4763	D64	4121	D70	4146	DC	4405
DD	4300	DD2	(MR Smith)	DF	4806	DH	3809	DJ2	3352*
R7	4647	DV8	(P Thelwall)	DW	4465	E	285*	E1	4829
E2	4656	E4	4895	E5	4769	E8	4505	E11	4709
EN	4336	EO	4862	EU	4516	EW	4632	EZ	2168
F	400*	F1	(AJ Clarke)/4452	F2	(DP Francis)/3918*	F3	4418		
F4	(JH Mare)/1367	F6	4827	F11	3489	F84	4719*	FE	4787
FK	4149	FOX	4566	FTI	3511	G1	4545	G2	3315
G7	4329	G41	(TJ Stanley) 4539	G46	698	G81	4380	GA	4847
GC	4780	GG	(G Goudie)	GP	4816	GR	4420	H	2984
H2	4558	H3	4764	H4	4753	H5	3285/4399	H6	3478
H8	(DJ Howse)/4195	H11	2552	H12	3732	H20	3185	H23	(LBlick)/1189*
H52	4866	HB	4481	HB1	4461	HL	4390	IH4	(BTSpreckley)
IM	4415	IV	3709	IZ	4878*	J1	4935	J3	3632
J15	3106	J45	2657*	J50	4824	JA	4016	JB	4749
JD	1483	JE	4822	JH	4459	JH1	4810	JJ	4562
JM	4137	JO1	4544	JP	4713	JS	4813	JT	4687
JW	4853	K	2989	K1	4340	K2	2147	K3	2689*
K4	431	K5	(RA King)/4338*	K7	3682*	K8	4549	K11	4543
K13	3656	K17	1720*	K18	4173	K21	4496	KE	4451
KL	3960	KM	4305*	KR	4627	KW	4426	L	3163
L1	2770	L2	4508	L3	4381	L4	4657	L5	3671
L8	4153	L11	2785	L12	3611	L13	3660	L17	4703
L18	4253	L30	4919*	L55	2652	L57	3577	L58	4192
L77	4665	L88	4323	L99	1438	L01	2770	LA	4724
LD	4347	LH7	4386	LR	4889*	LS	4189	LS4	2908/4293
LS6	4119	LS8	4237	LT	4538	LX	4376	M	3205
M1	4266*	M2	4449	M4	4368	M5	3638	M6	(P Richer)
M7	(MD Evens)	M8	4278	M9	4904	M19	4793	M25	4480
MB	4727	MD	4704*	N1	4443	N2	(R Murfitt)/3420*	N4	1914
N5	4207	N6	3736*	N8	4352	N11	2142	N15	3548
N16	3657	N19	4132	N21	673	N23	3772	N25	4598
N26	4056*	N28	3482	N29	3254	N36	3864*	N51	2987
N52	1551*	N53	3782*	N54	1360*	N55	1118*/4883	N56	3505
NJ1	4844	OP8	4534	OZ	(R Lynch)/4458	P	3274	P1	4567
P2	4442	P3	4363	P4	4648	P5	4152	P9	2443
P12	4579*	P23	4615	P30	4571	P31	4017	P61	4343
PB	4900	PH1	4577	PM	3816	PM3	4723	PN	4943
PS	3571	PT	4721	PW5	4311	PZ	(IM Evans)	Q5	3278
R1	4475	R2	4599	R3	4688	R4	4600	R5	4613
R6	4788	R7	4581	R8	4471	R9	3216	R10	4590
R11	4896	R12	4579	R17	4585	R18	4712	R19	4881
R20	4578*	R21	4572	R22	4614	R25	4587	R31	2533*
R32	4675*	R33	4582*	R35	2888*	R36	4612*	R37	4636
R38	4837	R39	4601	R40	4602*	R41	4730*	R43	4530*

R44	2931*	R45	4745*	R46	4620*	R48	4570	R49	4621*
R50	4691*	R51	4663*	R52	4583*	R53	4503	R55	4470
R56	4684*	R57	4603	R58	2873*	R59	4683	R60	4584
R61	4633	R63	4622	R67	4697	R69	4655	R70	3015*
R71	3064	R73	4555	R75	4604*	R77	4736	R80	4752*
R88	4680*	R90	4592	R91	2619*	R92	4707*	R93	2207*
R95	4729*	RA	3946	RP1	4233	RW	4671	RY	4084
S	3642	S1	3802	S2	4118	S3	3580	S4	(BT Spreckley)
S5	4299	S6	4469	S7	2943	S8	4223	S9	3472
S10	(BC Marsh)	S13	2425	S14	1572	S19	4580	S21	3698*/4383*
S22	4191	S27	4834	S30	2380	S33	4710	S60	(SR Drury)
S81	3722	S82	4045	S83	4268	SA	4669	SA1	2986
SC	4654	SG1	4863	SG2	4906	SH2	4800	SH5	2893
SH6	4804	SK1	4429	SM	4908	SSC	3909	T2	4406
T3	4328	T4	4817	T5	4301	T7	4466	T8	(PG Wright)
T9	4561	T10	1612	T15	1693	T27	4716	T34	2397
T42	614	T45	873	T49	1203	T51	1164	T54	3756
T65	2800	T99	(TN McGee)	TC	4349*	TE	4180*	TF	4541
TL2	4679	TS2	4937	U1	4335	U2	4131/2255*	U9	4378
UIM	4037	V1	4546	V2	(R Jones)	V2T	4664	V4	4460
V5	4034	V7	2695	V8	4178	V11	4292	V17	4758
V19	4058	V26	(FB Jeynes)	V2C	4921	V2T	4664	VMC	4182*
VS	2420*	VW	4521*	W1	3874	W2	4695	W5	4859
W7	4861	W8	4574	W19	4410	W20	4860	W22	3184*/4852
W54	4231	WA1	4487	X1	4783	X5	4750	X7	4330
X15	4785	X19	(AB Laws)	X50	4341	X96	2414	XL5	4709
Y1	(MA Edmonds)/3416	Y2K	4781	Y4	4280	Y44	4853	Z	1873
Z1	4821	Z2	4653	Z3	4762	Z4	3340	Z6	3654*
Z7	3640	Z8	(W Payton)/4190*	Z9	4696	Z10	4575	Z11	1374
Z12	4704	Z19	4784	Z22	4639	Z25	2427	Z29	3727
Z35	(RG Parker)	ZC	4256*						

Notes:

(i) Codes "SY" to "ZZ" are allocated to the Air Cadets Central Gliding School

(ii) A few gliders wear foreign identities but without any nationality mark, namely: CCZV = BGA.4052, 1128 = BGA.2709 & 7827 = BGA.4161.

(iii) Some imported, or ex British civil and military, gliders still carry their previous marks. Known examples include:

G-ALRD = BGA.416	RA809 = BGA.1143	WT908 = BGA.3487	G-ALRH = BGA.629
TS291 = BGA.852	WT910 = BGA.3953	G-ALRK = BGA.490	VM687 = BGA.794
WT913 = BGA.3239	G-ATRA = BGA.1325	WB920 = BGA.3221	WZ819 = BGA.3498
D-1221 = BGA.2757	WB922 = BGA.4366	WZ828 = BGA.4421	D-1265 = BGA.2276
WB924 = BGA.3901	XA240 = BGA.4556	D-4667 = BGA.3142	WB926 = BGA.3520
XA302 = BGA.3786	D-5084 = BGA.2688	WB943 = BGA.2941	XE807 = BGA.3545
D-6173 = BGA.4336	WB962 = BGA.3836	XN157 = BGA.3255	D-8538 = BGA.2292
WB971 = BGA.3324	XN185 = BGA.4077	G285 = BGA.285	WB981 = BGA.1218
XN187 = BGA.3903	HB-474 = BGA.2474	WE992 = BGA.2692	XN243 = BGA.3145
OK-0927 = BGA.4286	WG498 = BGA.3245	XA229 =BGA.3379	XS652 = BGA.1107
OK-8592 = BGA.655	WT871 = BGA.3149	ZS-GFZ = BGA.3210	WT898 = BGA.4412

SECTION 8

PART 1 - ALPHABETICAL TYPE INDEX- (UNITED KINGDOM)

ABINGDON

GAS BALLOON
G-ATXR

ACRO

ADVANCED
G-BPAA

ADAM

RA.14 LOISIRS
G-BHIK

ADVANCED AIRSHIP CORPORATION

ANR-1
G-MAAC

ADVANCED TECHNOLOGIES INC

FIREBIRD CH1 ATI
G-BXZN
AT-10
G-OATG

AERIAL ARTS LTD including CYCLONE

110/130SX (wing)/ALPHA/AVENGER (combi)
G-MMSZ MMYL MMZI MNDE MNEK MNEL MNIT MNJV MNMY MNTT MNWL MNZS MVBC
CHASER
G-MNTD MNYD MNYE MNYF MTCP MTDD MTDE MVDK MVDL MVDP MVDR MVGA MVGF MVGG MVGH MVGI-MMGJ MVHA MVHN MVID MVIE MVJF MVJG MVJH MVJJ MVJK MVKY MVKZ MVLA MMLB MVLC MVLD MVLE MVLF MVLG MVLH MVLS MVLT MVLW MVML MVMM MVOA MVOD MVOP MVRG MVRL MVSG MVSK MVTL MVTM MVUS MVUT MVVU MVYY MVZM MVZY MWGO MWWZ MWXW MWXX MWXY MWXZ MWYM MYBU MYCB MYEI MYEJ MYFO MYGI MYGK MYIL MYIT MYJO MYJW MYKD MYLJ MYMY MYSA MYSV MYWN MYWS MYYD MYZW MYZX MZCB MZTS

AERO COMMANDER INC incl ROCKWELL/GULFSTREAM production

200
G-SONY
500S SHRIKE
G-BDAL
680/685/690
G-AWOE OMAP

AERO DESIGNS

PULSAR
G-BSFA BTDR BTRF BTWY BUDI BUJL BULM BUOW BUSR BUYB BUZB BVJH BVSF BVTW BXDU BYJL EPOX IIAN LEEN LUED MCMS NEVS OMKF OOXP RMAN WYNS XPXP

AERO DIFUSIÓN - see JODEL

AERO DYNAMICS LTD

SPARROWHAWK
G-BOZU

AERO VODOCHODY - see CZL/LET

L-29 DELFIN
G-BYCT BZNT DELF DLFN ODAT
L-39 ALBATROS
G-BZDI OALB OTAF
SB LIM-2
G-OMIG

AEROCAR including TAYLOR

MINI IMP
G-BLWW
SOOPER COOT
G-COOT

AERODYNE - see RAVEN

AEROMERE -see AVIAMILANO

AEROMOT INDUSTRIA MECANICO

AMT-200 SUPER XIMANGO
G-BWNY JTPC KHOM LLEW RFIO XMGO

AERONCA - see CHAMPION

C-3/100
G-ADRR ADYS AEFT AESB AETG AEVS AEXD
K
G-ONKA
11AC CHIEF/11CC SUPER CHIEF
G-AKTK AKUO AKVN BJEV BJNY BPRA BPRX BPXY BRCW BRFJ BRWR BRXF BRXL BSTC BTFL BTRI BTSR BUAB BUTF IIAC IVOR
15AC SEDAN
G-AREX
A65TAC/65C SUPER CHIEF/O-58B/L-3 GRASSHOPPER
G-BRHP BRPR BTRG BTUV

AEROPRAKT

A22 FOXBAT
G-CBGJ CBJH FBAT XBAT

AEROSPACE DEVELOPMENTS

AD.500/Skyship 50
G-BECE BIHN

AÉROSPATIALE - see AÉROSPATIALE/ALENIA ATR/SOCATA/SUD AVIATION & incl EUROCOPTER production

AS332 SUPER PUMA
G-BKZE BKZG BKZH BLPM BLRY BLXR BMCW BMCX BOZK BRXU BSOI BUZD BWMG BWWI BWZX CHCF PUMA PUMB PUMD PUME PUMG PUMH PUMI PUMK PUML PUMM PUMN PUMO PUMS TIGB TIGC TIGE TIGF TIGG TIGH TIGI TIGJ TIGL TIGM TIGO TIGP TIGR TIGS TIGT TIGV TIGZ
AS350B ECUREUIL
G-BMAV BRVO BVJE BVXM BWFY BXGA BXNE BXNJ BXNY BXOG BXOK BXPG BXPJ BYYH BYZE BZVG CBHL COPT CWIZ DOIT DRHL EJOC FIBS FROH HLEN IANW IIPM JOSS LHPL ODMC OFHL OGOA OOIO NUTY PLMB PLMH PROB RICC SCHI SMDJ TATS WHAM WHST WKRD ZWRC

AS355 TWIN SQUIRREL
G-BOOV BPRI BPRJ BPRL BSTE BSYI BTIS BVLG BXBT BYPA BYZA BZGC BZVZ CAMB CCAO CLIP CPOL DANZ DOOZ ECOS EMAN EMHH EPOL FFRI FTWO GMPA GRID HARO HEMH ICSG JARV JETU JPAL LCON LECA LENI LINE LOUN LUVY MOBI NAAS NMHS OASP OGRK OHCP OHMS OITN OROM ORMA OTSP PASF PASH REEM SASU SCOW SEPA SEPB SEPC SEWP SYPA TOPC TOPS WIRE WMPA XCEL
SA365 DAUPHIN 2
G-MLTY PLMI

AEROSPORT
SCAMP
G-BKFL BKPB BOOW
WOODY PUSHER
G-AWWP AYVP BSFV

AEROSTAR SA - see TED SMITH & YAKOVELEV

AEROSTRUCTURE including SOUTHDOWN
PIPISTRELLE
G-MJTM

AEROTEC/AEROTEK INC - see PITTS

AEROTECH - see WHITTAKER

AESL - see VICTA

AGUSTA S.p.A - see BELL HELICOPTER
A109
G-BVCJ BWNZ BWZI BXIV BXWD BZEI CBDR DATE DPPH EXEK HPWH JERL MKSF OCMM PWER RFDS SIVC SOHI TBGL TELY TGRA TVAA TVAC USTA USTB VIPH VMCO WEST

AHERNE
BARRACUDA
G-BZSV

AIR & SPACE
18A
G-BVWK BVWL

AIR COMMAND MANUFACTURING
503 COMMANDER
G-BMZA BOAS BOIK
532 ELITE/582 SPORT
G-BOGV BOHG BOJF BOKF BOOJ BPAO BPGC BPPR BPPU BPRS BPTH BPUE BPUG BPUI BREM BRGO BRKX BRLB BRLK BRSP BSCB BSND BSRZ BTCB KENB OGTS TFRB URRR YROI

AIR CREATION
KISS 400-582
G-BZXP CBEB CBJA CBKS CHKN TRYK
ULTRAFLIGHT FUN 18 GT
G-MYMM MYOL MYTZ MYUA MYVI MYXF

AIRBUS INDUSTRIE
A300
G-CEAA CEAB CEXH CEXI CEXJ HLAA HLAB HLAC HLAB MAJS MONR MONS OJMR SWJW TTMC
A310
G-BZTB
A319
G-EUOA EUOB EUOC EUOD EUOE EUOF EUOG EUOH EUOI EUOJ EUPA EUPB EUPC EUPB EUPC EUPD EUPE EUPF EUPG EUPH EUPJ EUPK EUPL EUPM EUPN EUPO EUPP EUPR EUPS EUPT EUPU EUPV EUPW EUPX EUPY EUPZ OMAK
A320
G-BXKA BXKB BUSB BUSC BUSD BUSE BUSF BUSG BUSH BUSI BUSJ BUSK BVYA BVYB BVYC BXKC BXKD BYFS COEZ CRPH CVYD CVYE CVYG DJAR EPFR EUOK EUOL EUOM EUON EUOO EUOP EUOR EUOS EUOT EUOU EUOV EUOW EUOX EUOY EUOZ EUUA EUUB EUUC EUUD EUUE EUUF EUUG EUUH EUUI EUUJ EUUK EUUL EUUM EUUN EUUO EUUP EUUR EUUS EUUT EUUU EUUV FHAJ MEDA MEDB MEDD MEDE MIDK MIDP MIDR MIDS MIDT MIDU MIDV MIDW MIDX MIDY MIDZ MONW MONX MONZ MPCD OOAI OOAJ OOAP OOAR OOAS OOAT OOAU OUZO OZBB RDVE SSAS SUEE TICL TMDP TTOA TTOB TTOC TTOD TTOE UNIH VCED VKID VMED VTAN
A321
G-DHJH JSJX MEDF MEDG MIDA MIDC MIDE MIDF MIDH MIDI MIDJ MIDK MIDL MIDM MIDN MIDO MIDT MIDU NIKO OOAE OOAF OOAH OZBD OZBE OZBF TTIA TTIB VATH VOLH VKIS YJBM
A330
G-EOMA MDBD MLJL MOJO OJMB SMAN WWBB WWBC WWBD WWBM
A340
G-VAEL VAIR VATL VBUS VEIL VELD VFAR VFLY VFOX VGOA VHOL VMEG VOGE VSEA VSHY VSKY VSSH VSUN

AIRCO
DH.2
G-BFVH
DH.6
G-EAML
DH.9
G-EAQM

AIRMARK - see CASSUTT
TSR.3
G-AWIV

AIRSHIP INDUSTRIES - see AEROSPACE DEVELOPMENTS

AIRSPEED LTD
AS.40 OXFORD
G-AHTW AITB AITF
AS.57 AMBASSADOR
G-ALZO

AIRSPEED
300 MLB
G-FYGJ

AIRTOUR BALLOONS
HAFB
AH-31
G-BKVY
AH-56
G-BKVW BKVX BLVA BLVB BSGH BWPL OAFC
AH-77
G-BLYT BOBH IVAC OAAC

AIRWAVE GLIDERS LTD
MERLIN (wing)
G-MMIJ
NIMROD (wing)
G-MBCX MBJG MBJL MNIW MNZY

ALON INC - see ERCOUPE

ALLPORT
MLB variants
G-BJIA BJSS

AMD-BA - SEE DASSAULT

AMERICAN AEROLIGHTS including ELECTRAFLYER
EAGLE/DOUBLE EAGLE
G-MBCU MBEP MBHE MBIO MBJD MBJK MBKY MBNK MBRB MBRD MBRS MBYD MJAE MJBL MJBV MJCX MJEO MJNM MJNO MMTV MNSS

AMERICAN BLIMP CORP
A-60+ AIRSHIP
G-OLEL

AMERICAN AVIATION CORPN - see GRUMMAN-AMERICAN

AMETHYST BALLOONS
AX6 series
G-BFLP

AMF MICROFLIGHT LTD
CHEVVRON
G-MNFL MTFG MVGC MVGD MVGE MVIP MVOO MVUO MVVV MVXX MVZZ MWNO MWNP MWPW MWRZ MWUI MWZB MYYP MZDP MZFH

ANDERSON
EA-1 KINGFISHER AMPHIBIAN
G-BUTE BXBC

ANDREASSON including CROSBY
BA.4B
G-AWPZ AYFV BEBS BEBT BFXF YPSY

ANEC
II
G-EBJO
IV MISSEL THRUSH
G-FBPI

ARBITER SERVICES
TRIKE
G-MNWL

ARKLE - see MITCHELL

ARMSTRONG-WHITWORTH AIRCRAFT see GLOSTER
SEAHAWK
G-JETH
AW.650 ARGOSY
G-APRL BEOZ

ARROW AIRCRAFT (LEEDS) LTD
ACTIVE
G-ABVE

ARROWFLIGHT LTD - see CGS

ARV AVIATION LTD
ARV1 SUPER 2
G-BMOK BMWE BMWF BMWM BNGV BNGW BNGY BNHB BNHD BNHE BNVI BOGK BPMX BSRK BWBZ COWS DEXP ERMO OARV ORIX OTAL POOL STWO TARV XARV YARV ZARV

AUSTER AIRCRAFT LTD incl TAYLORCRAFT production
PLUS C/D
G-AHCR AHGW AHGZ AHSD AHUG AHWJ AHXE AIXA
Model E III
G-AHLK AREI BUDL
Model G/H 4/5/5D/ALPHA 5
G-AGLK AIKE AJGJ AJHJ AJVT AJXC AJXV AJXY AKOW AKSY AKSZ AKWS AKWT AKXP ALBJ ALBK ALFA ALNV ALXZ ALYB ALYG AMVD ANFU ANHR ANHS ANHU ANHW ANHX ANIE ANIJ ANIS ANLU ANRP AOCP AOCR AOCU AOFJ AOVW APAF APAH APBE APBW APRF APTU BDFX BICD BXKX
J/1 AUTOCRAT/J/1N ALPHA & KINGSLAND/CROFTON SPECIAL
G-AGTO AGTT AGVN AGXN AGXU AGXV AGYD AGYH AGYK AGYT AHAL AHAM AHAP AHAT AHAU AHAV AHCK AHCL AHHH AHHP AHHT AHHU AHSO AHSP AHSS AHST AIBH AIBM AIBR AIBW AIBX AIBY AIFZ AIGD AIGF AIGP AIGR AIGT AIGU AIJI AIJZ AIPV AIRC AIZU AIZY AJAE AJAJ AJAS AJDW AJEB AJEE AJEH AJEI AJEM AJIH AJIS AJIT AJIU AJIW AJPZ AJRB AJRC AJRE AJUD AJUE AJUL AJYB AMTM APIK APJZ APKM APKN APTR APUK ARRL ARUY ASEE BLPG BRKC BVGT [GINO] JAYI OJAS OSTA TENT
J/1B AIGLET
G-AMKU ARBM
J/1U WORKMASTER
G-AGVG APMH APSR
J/2 ARROW
G-AJAM AWLX BEAH
J/4
G-AIJK BIJM BIJS BIJT BIPR
J/5B/G/P/V AUTOCAR
G-AOBV AOFM AOHZ AOIY APUW ARKG ARNB ARUG ASFK AXMN
J/5F/K/L AIGLET TRAINER
G-AMMS AMRF AMTA AMUI G-AMYD AMZI AMZT AMZU ANWX AOFS APVG BGKZ
J/5Q/R ALPINE
G-ANXC AOGV AOZL APCB
6A/AOP.6/TUGMASTER
G-ARDX ARGB ARGI ARHM ARIH ARRX ARXU ARYD ASEF ASIP ASNB ASOC ASTI BKXP BNGE
AOP.9/11/BEAGLE E.3
G-ASCC AVHT AVXY AXRR AXWA AYUA AZBU BDFH BGBU BGKT BGTC BJXR BKVK BUCI BURR BWKK BXON
B.4
G-AMKL

AUTOMOBILOVE ZAVODY MRAZ
M.1 SOKOL
G-AIXN

AVENGER
MLB variants
G-BHMJ BHMK BIGR BIPW BIRL

AVIA
FL.3
G-AGFT

AVIAMILANO SRL incl AEROMERE/LAVERDA/SEQUOIA production)
F.8L FALCO
G-BVDP BWYO BYLL CWAG FALC GANE KYNG OCAD OCDS ORJW PDGG REEC RJAM
F.14 NIBBIO
G-OWYN

AVIASUD ENGINEERING SA
MISTRAL
G-MGAG MVSJ MVUP MVWW MVWZ MVXN MVXV MVZR MWIB MYSL MYST MZJB

AVID AIRCRAFT INC
AVID FLYER/SPEEDWING/AEROBAT
G-BSPW BTGL BTHU BTKG BTMS BTNP BTRC BUFV BUIR BUJJ BUJV BULC BULY BUON BUSZ BUZE BUZM-BVAA BVBR BVBV BVFO BVHT BVIV BVLW BVSN BVYX BWLW BWRC BWZD BXNA CURV EFRY ELKS FOLD IJAC IMPY LAPN LORT MOTT OVID OZEE PILL SPAM

AVIONS DE TRANSPORT REGIONAL
ATR-42
G-BUPS BVEF BVJP BXEH ORFH ZAPJ
ATR-72
G-BVTJ BVTK BWDA BWDB BXTN BXYV BYTO BYTP UKTK UKTM UKTN

AVIONS MAURICE BROCHET - see BROCHET

AVIONS MAX HOLSTE – see MAX HOLSTE

AVIONS MUDRY ET CIE - see CAARP/MUDRY

AVIONS PIERRE ROBIN – see ROBIN

AVRO AIRCRAFT LTD - see ENGLISH ELECTRIC/HAWKER

A V ROE & CO LTD incl HSA & BAe production)
TRIPLANE - see ROE
504K/L
G-EASD EBJE ECKE
G-ABAA ADEV BYKV
534 BABY
G-EACQ
581/594 AVIAN
G-EBOV, EBZM
G-ACGT
621 TUTOR
G-AHSA
652A ANSON/NINETEEN
G-AGPG AGWE AHKX AMDA APHV AVVO AWRS AWSA AYWA BFIR VROE
683 LANCASTER
G-ASXX BVBP LANC
685 YORK
G-AGNV ANTK
694 LINCOLN
G-APRJ
698 VULCAN
G-BLMC VJET VLCN VULC
748
G-ARAY ARMX ATMI ATMJ AVXI AVXJ AYIM BEJD BGMN BGMO BIUV BORM BVOU BVOV OPFW ORAL OSOE OTBA SOEI

AVRO (CANADA)
CF-100 CANUCK
G-BCYK

B

BA- see BRITISH KLEMM & KLEMM
EAGLE 2
G-AFAX
SWALLOW 2
G-ADPS AFCL AFGC AFGD AFGE AFHC

BAC incl KRONFELD & PROCTOR
DRONE
G-ADPJ AEDB
L.25 SWALLOW
G-ACXE

BAC-SUD - see BRITISH AIRCRAFT CORPORATION/AÈROSPATIALE

BAE SYSTEMS (OPERATIONS) LTD including BRITISH AEROSPACE plc/BRITISH AEROSPACE (REGIONAL AIRCRAFT LTD)/HANDLEY-PAGE & SCOTTISH AVIATION production)
JETSTREAM variants to Srs.32
G-ATXJ AXUM BBYM BKUY BLKP BRGN BTXG BUIO BURU BUTW BUUZ BUVC BUVD BWWW BXLM BYMA BYRA BYRM BYYI BZYP CBCS CBDA CBEA CBEP EEST HDGS IJYS JSSD JURA LOVB NFLC OAKJ OEST PLAH PLAJ WMCC

JETSTREAM Srs.41 variants
G-BWUI GCJL JMAC MAJA MAJB MAJC MAJD MAJE MAJF MAJG MAJH MAJI MAJJ MAJK MAJL MAJM MSKJ
ATP/JETSTREAM 61
G-BTNI BTPA BTPC BTPD BTPF BTPG BTPJ BTPK BTPL BTPM BTPN BTTO BTUE BTZG BTZH BTZK BUKJ BUUP BUUR BUWM BUWP CORP MANA MANB MANC MANE MANF MANG MANH MANJ MANL MANM MANO MANP MANU MAUD OBWL OBWM OBWN OBWO OBWP OBWR OEDJ PLXI WISS
146 (including AVRO variants)
G-BKMN BLRA BPNT BSNR BSXZ BTTP BTVO BXAR BXAS BZAT BZAU BZAV BZAW BZAX CBFL CFAA CFAB CFAC CFAD CFAE CFAF CFAH CLHA CHLB CLHC CLHD CLHE DEBE DEFK DEFL DEFM FLTA IRJX JEAJ JEAK JEAM JEAO JEAR JEAS JEAT JEAU JEAV JEAW JEAX JEAY JEBA JEBB JEBC JEBD JEBE LUXE MABR MIMA NBAA NJIA NJIC NJIE OFOA OFOM OINV ORJX OZRH TBIC UKAC UKAG UKHP UKID UKRC UKSC ZAPK ZAPL ZAPN ZAPO

BARNES
AVON (Trike)
G-MJGO

BARNETT ROTORCRAFT
BARNETT J4B
G-BRVR BRVS BWCW

BAT
FK-23 BANTAM
G-EACN

BEAGLE AIRCRAFT LTD
A.109 AIREDALE
G-ARNP AROJ ARRO ARXB ARXC ARXD ARYZ ARZS ASAI ASBH ASBY ASRK ASWB ATCC AVKP
B.121 PUP
G-AVDF AVLM AVLN AVZN AVZP AWKM AWKO AWVC AWWE AWYJ AWYO AXCX AXDU AXDV AXDW AXEV AXHO AXIA AXIE AXIF AXJH AXJI AXJJ AXJO AXMW AXMX AXNL AXNM AXNN AXNP AXNR AXNS AXOJ AXOZ AXPA AXPB AXPC AXPM AXPN AXSC AXSD AXTZ AXUA AZCK AZCL AZCN AZCP AZCT AZCU AZCV AZCY AZCZ AZDA AZDG AZEU AZEV AZEW AZEY AZFA AZGF AZSW BAKW BASP BDCO IPUP JIMB OPUP PUPP TSKY
B.206
G-ARRM ASWJ ATDD BSET HRHI FLYP

BEAGLE-AUSTER AIRCRAFT LTD
A.61 TERRIER
G-ARLO ARLP ARLR ARNO ARSL ARTM ARUI ASAJ ASAK ASAN ASAX ASBU ASCD ASDK ASDL ASEG ASKJ ASMZ ASOI ASOM ASUI ASYG ASYN ASZE ASZX ATBU ATDN ATHU AVCS AVYK AYDW AYDX TIMG
D.4
G-ARLG
D.5 HUSKEY
G-ASNC ATCD ATMH AVOD AVSR AWSW AXBF
D.6
G-ARCS ARDJ

BEDE - see BROOKMOOR BEDE AIRCRAFT

BEECH AIRCRAFT CORPORATION
17 TRAVELER/UC-43
G-BRVE BUXU
18/3NM. 3TM & C-45
G-ASUG BKGL BKGM BKRN BSZC
23/24 MUSKETEER/SUNDOWNER/SIERRA
G-ASJO ASWP ATBI AWFZ AWTS AWTV AYYU BAHO BARH BARI BASN BBSB BBSC BBTX BBTY BBVJ BBXU BUXN BYDG CBCY BZPG DJHB GUCK TAMS
33 DEBONAIR/33 BONANZA
G-BGSW BTHW BTZA BYRT COLA ENSI GRYZ HOPE JUST MOAC OAHC VICM
35 BONANZA/("V" tail)
G-APTY ARKJ ARZN ASJL ATSR BBTS BONZ EHMJ NEWT REST
36 BONANZA
G-BMYD BSEY JLHS MAPR ORSP POPA ZLOJ
55/56/58 BARON
G-ASDO ASOH AWAH AWAJ AYKA AYPD AZDK AZXA BFLZ BLJM BLKY BMLM BNBY BNUN BNVZ BRTN BTFT BWRP BXDF BXNG BXPM BYDY BZIT DAFY FABM FLAK FLTZ FRBY IOCO MOSS OLYD OSDI RICK SUZI UROP VCML WOOD WWIZ
60 DUKE
G-IASL
65/70/80 QUEEN AIR
G-ASDA AVDR AVDS AWKX KEAB KEAC TUBS WJPN
76 DUCHESS
G-BGHP BGRG BGVH BIMZ BMJT BNTT BNUO BNYO BODX BOFC BRPU BXHD BXMH BXWA BXXT BYNY BZNN BZPJ CBBF GBSL GCCL JLRW OADY OBLC OPAT TRAN WACI WACJ
90 KING AIR
G-BMKD DEXY ERAD SHAM WELL
95 TRAVEL AIR
G-ASMF ASYJ ATRC
200/300/350 SUPER KING AIR
G-BGRE BPPM BVMA BYCK BYCP BZNE CBFS CEGP CEGR CLOW FPLA FPLB FPLD FRYI HAMA IMGL KMCD MAMD OMNH OWAX REBK ROWN SBAS SPOR VSBC WRCF ZAPT

BELL
MLB
G-BITY

BELL AIRCRAFT CORPORATION
P-63 KINGCOBRA
G-BTWR

BELL HELICOPTER TEXTRON INC including AGUSTA/BELL HELICOPTER CO/BELL HELICOPTER TEXTRON CANADA & WESTLAND production
47D/G (**WESTLAND**)
G-ARXH ASOL AXKO AXKS AXKW AXKX AXKY BAXS BBRI BBVP BFEF BFVM BFYI BGID BGMU BGZK BHAR BHBE BHNV BLGR BPAI BPDY CHOP CIGY GGTT MASH MINX SOLH XTUN
47H/J (**AGUSTA**)
G-ATFV AZYB BFPP EURA
206A/B JET RANGER I/II/III
G-AVII AVSZ AYMW BAML BARP BBCA BBNG BBOR BODH BEWY BIZB BKEW BKZI BLCA BLGV BLZN BNYD BOLO BORV-BOTM BPWI BSBW BTFX BTFY BTHY BUZZ BVGA BWZW BXAY BXDS BXKL BXLI BXNS BXNT BXRY BXUF BYBA BYBC BYBI BYSE BZEE BZNI CCLY CBDF CITZ CODE COIN CORN CORT CPTS CTPW DENN DNCN DOFY DORB ELLI FINS FOXM GAND GUST HANY HEBE HELE HMPH HMPT HSDW INVU IOIO JAHL JBDB JETX JIMW JLEE JWBI JWLS LILY MCPI MFMF MILI MOTA NEWS NEWZ OAMG OAMI OBAM OBAY OBYT OCST OFCH OMDR OMEC ONOW OOHO OOOW ONTV ONYX OSMD PEAK PENT PORT RAMI RAMY RIAN RJTT RKEL RMIE RNBW SCOO SDCI SELY SPEY SPYI STER STOX SUEZ TBAH TGRZ TILI TOYZ TREE TUCH UEST WGAL WHAZ WIZZ WLLY XXIV ZAPH
206L LONG RANGER
G-ELIT EYLE EYRE GBAY IANG JGBI LEEZ NEUF OHHI OLDN PWIT
212
G-BCMC BFER BIXV
214ST SUPER TRANSPORT
G-BKFN

222
G-NOIR OWCG
407
G-DCDB GAJW IORB
UH-1H IROQUOIS
G-HUEY

BELLANCA-AIRCRAFT CORPORATION - see CHAMPION
17-30 SUPER VIKING
G-VIKE

BENSEN AIRCRAFT CORPORATION including CAMPBELL-BENSEN, & MONTGOMERIE-BENSEN
B.7/B.8 GYROCOPTER
G-APSY APUD ARTJ ASCT ASME ASNY ASWN ASYP ATLP ATOZ AVXB AWDW AWLM AWPY AXBG AXCI AZAZ BCGB BDJF BGIO BHEM BHKE BIFN BIGP BIGU BIHX BIPY BIVK BIVL BIZT BJAO BJSU BKBS BKUS BLGO BLLA BLLB BMBW BMOT BMYF BMZW BNBU BNJL BOTZ BOUV BOWZ BOZW BPBA BPCV BPIF BPNN BPOO BPSK BPTV BRBS BRCF BREA BREU BRFW BRHL BRXN BSBX BSJB BSMG BSMX BSNL BSNY BSPJ BSZM BTAH BTBL BTFW BTIG BTJN BTJS BTST BTTD BUJK BUPF BVAZ BVIF BVJF BVKJ BVMG BVPX BWAH BWEY BWJN BWSZ BXCL BYTS BZID BZJR CBFW HAGS JOEL OOJC OTIM SCUD YJET YROS YROY

BEST OFF
SKYRANGER 912(1)
G-CBIV

BETTS
TB.1
G-BVUG

BINDER AVIATIK GmbH - see PIEL

BIRDMAN ENTERPRISES LTD
WT-11 CHINOOK
G-MMKE

BLACKBURN AEROPLANE & MOTOR CO LTD
B.2
G-ACBH ADFV AEBJ
MONOPLANE
G-AANI

BLAKE
BLUETIT
G-BXIY

BLERIOT
XI
G-AANG BPVE BWRH LOTI

BOEING AIRCRAFT CO/BOEING COMPANY
B-17G FLYING FORTRESS
G-BEDF
B-29 SUPERFORTRESS
G-BHDK
707-400 series
G-APFG APFJ
727-200 series
G-BNNI BPND OKJN
737-200 series
G-BYYF BYYK BZKP CEAC CEAD CEAE CEAF CEAG CEAH CEAI CEAJ
-300 series
G-BYZJ BZZA BZZB ECAS EZYB EZYC EZYD EZYF EZYG EZYH EZYI EZYJ EZYK EZYL EZYO EZYP EZYR EZYT IGOA IGOB IGOC IGOE IGOF IGOG IGOH IGOI IGOJ IGOK IGOL IGOM IGOP IGOR IGOS IGOT IGOU IGOV IGOW IGOX LGTD LGTE LGTF LGTG LGTH LGTI LGTJ LGTK LGTL OAMS OBWX OBWY OBWZ ODSK ODUS OFRA OGBB OGBC OGBD OGBE OHAJ OJTW OMUC SMDB XBHX XMAN ZAPM
-400 series
G-BNNL BSNV BSNW BUHJ BUHK BUHL BVNM BVNN BVNO DOCA DOCB DOCD DOCE DOCF DOCG DOCH DOCI DOCJ DOCK DOCL DOCM DOCN DOCO DOCP DOCR DOCS DOCT DOCU DOCV DOCW DOCX DOCY DOCZ GBTA GBTB OBMM OGBA SFBH TREN
-500 series
G-BVKA BVKB BVKC BVKD BVZE BVZG BVZH BVZI GFFA GFFB GFFC GFFD GFFE GFFF GFFG GFFH GFFI GFFJ MSKA MSKB MSKC
-700 series
G-EZJA EZJB EZJC EZJD EZJE EZJF EZJG EZJH EZJI EZJJ EZJK EZJL
-800 series
G-OBBJ OBMP XLAA XLAB XLAC XLAD XLAE XLAF XLAG XLAH
747-200 series
G-BDXA BDXB BDXC BDXE BDXF BDXG BDXH BDXI BDXJ BDXK BDXL BDXN BDXO GAFX INTL VIBE VPUF VZZZ
-400 series
G-BNLA BNLB BNLC BNLD BNLE BNLF BNLG BNLI BNLJ BNLK BNLL BNLM BNLN BNLO BNLP BNLR BNLS BNLT BNLU BNLV BNLW BNLX BNLY BNLZ BYGA BYGB BYGC BYGD BYGE BYGF BYGG CIVA CIVB CIVC CIVD CIVE CIVF CIVG CIVH CIVI CIVJ CIVK CIVL CIVM CIVN CIVO CIVP CIVR CIVS CIVT CIVU CIVV CIVW CIVX CIVY CIVZ GSSA GSSB VAST VBIG VFAB VGAL VHOT VLIP VROM VROS VROY VTOP VWOW VXLG
757-200 series
G-BIKB BIKC BIKD BIKF BIKG BIKJ BIKK BIKL BIKM BIKN BIKO BIKR BIKS BIKT BIKU BIKV BIKW BIKX BIKY BIKZ BMRA BMRB BMRC BMRD BMRE BMRF BMRG BMRH BMRI BMRJ BPEC BPED BPEE BPEF BPEI BPEJ BYAD BYAE BYAF BYAH BYAI BYAJ BYAK BYAL BYAN BYAO BYAP BYAR BYAS BYAT BYAU BYAW BYAX BYAY CDUO CDUP CPEL CPEL CPEM CPEN CPEO CPEP CPER CPES CPET CPEU CPEV DAJB FCLA FCLB FCLC FCLD FCLE FCLF FCLG FCLH FCLI FCLJ FCLK JALC JMAA JMAB JMCD JMCE JMCF LCRC MCEA MONB MONC MOND MONE MONJ MONK OBWS OOBA OOBB OOOA OOOB OOOC OOOD OOOG OOOI OOOJ OOOM OOOS OOOU OOOV OOOW OOOX OOOY PIDS RJGR WJAN
767-200 series
G-BYAA BYAB
-300 series
G-BNWA BNWB BNWC BNWD BNWH BNWI BNWM BNWN BNWO BNWR BNWS BNWT BNWU BNWV BNWW BNWX BNWY BNWZ BRIF BRIG BZHA BZHB BZHC DAJC DIMB OBYB OBYC OBYE OBYG OBYH OBYI OBYJ OOAM OOAN SJMC UKLI
777-200 series
G-RAES VIIA VIIB VIIC VIID VIIE VIIF VIIG VIIH VIIJ VIIK VIIL VIIM VIIN VIIO VIIP VIIR VIIS VIIT VIIU VIIV VIIX VIIY VIIZ YMMA YMMB YMMC YMMD YMME YMMF YMMG YMMH YMMI YMMJ YMMK YMML YMMM YMMN YMMO YMMP ZZZA ZZZB ZZZC ZZZD ZZZE

BOEING AIRPLANE CO
75 KAYDET/N2S/PT-13/PT-17 STEARMAN:
G-AROY AWLO AZLE BAVO BIXN BNIW BRHB BRSK BRTK BRUJ BSDS BSGR BSWC BTFG BTGA ERIX IIIG ILLE ISDN NZSS RJAH

BOLAND
52 HAFB
G-BYMW

BÖLKOW including MALMO & MBB production
Bö.207
G-EFTE
Bö.208 JUNIOR
G-ASFR ASZD ATDO ATRI ATSI ATSX ATTR ATUI ATVX ATXZ AVKR AVLO AVZI BIJD BSME CLEM ECGO
Bö.209 MONSUN
G-AYPE AZBB AZDD AZOA AZOB AZRA AZTA AZVA AZVB BLRD

BOMBARDIER INC - see CANADAIR/DE HAVILLAND CANADA
BD-700 GLOBAL EXPRESS
G-LOBL

BOND
SKY DANCER
G-BLUK

BONSALL
DB-1 MUSTANG
G-BDWM

BOWERS
FLY BABY
G-BFRD BNPV BUYU

BRADSHAW
HAB-76
G-AXXP

BRANDLI
BX-2 CHERRY
G-BXUX

BRANTLY HELICOPTER CORPORATION
B.2
G-ASHD ASXD ATFG AVIP AWDU AXSR BPIJ OAPR OMAX ROTR WASP
305
G-ASXF

BREMNER - see MITCHELL WING

BRIGHTON
AX7-65 HAFB
G-AVTL

BRISTOL AEROPLANE CO LTD
BOXKITE
G-ASPP
BABE
G-EASQ
F.2B FIGHTER
G-AANM ACAA AEPH
M.1C REP
G-BLWM BWJM
105 BULLDOG
G-ABBB
149 BOLINGBROKE (BLENHEIM)
G-BPIV MKIV
156 BEAUFIGHTER
G-DINT
171 SYCAMORE
G-ALSX HAPR
173
G-ALBN
175 BRITANNIA
G-ANCF AOVF AOVS AOVT
192 BELVEDERE
G-BRMB

BRITISH AIRCRAFT CORPN/AÈROSPATIALE
CONCORDE
G-AXDN BBDG BOAA BOAB BOAC BOAD BOAE BOAF BOAG SSST

BRITISH AIRCRAFT CORPORATION (BAC) - see HUNTING
ONE-ELEVEN
G-ASYD AVMH AVMI AVMJ AVMK AVMN AVMO AVMP AVMS AVMT AVMU AVMW AVMY AVMZ AWYV AZMF MAAH OBWA OBWD OBWE

BRITTEN
SHERIFF
G-FRJB

BRITTEN-NORMAN LTD including FAIREY BRITTEN-NORMAN LTD/IRMA/PILATUS (BN-2) production
BN.1F
G-ALZE
BN.2A/B/T ISLANDER/DEFENDER
G-AWNT AXHE AXUB AXZK AYRU BCEN BEEG BELF BFNU BIIP BJOP BJWO BLDV BLNJ BLNL BOMG BPCA BPLR BSWR BUBN BVFK BVHX BVHY BVSJ BVSL BWPM BWPR BWPU BWPV BWPW BWPX BWYZ BWZF CHES CHEZ CIAS ISLA ITEX JSAT JSPC LEAP MAFF NESU ORED OSEA OTVS PASV RAPA SBUS SJCH SSKY SURV WOTG XAXA
BN.2A/III TRISLANDER
G-AZLJ BBYO BDOT BDTN BDTO BEDP BEFO BEVR BEVT BEVV FTSE JOEY LCOC OJAV PCAM RBCI WEAC XTOR

BROCHET
MB.50 PIPISTRELLE
G-AVKB BADV
MB.84
G-AYVT

BROOKLAND
HORNET
G-BRPP MIKE PHIL

MOSQUITO
G-AWIF BGEX

BROOKLANDS AIRCRAFT CO- see OPTICA

BROOKMOOR BEDE AIRCRAFT
BD.4
G-BEKL BKZV BOPD BYLS
BD.5
G-BCLV BCOX BDTT BGLB BJPI BYFB

BROOKS
PULSAR
G-MBOK

BRÜGGER
MB.2/MB.3 COLIBRI
G-BKCI BKRH BNDP BNDT BOBF BPBP BRWV BSUJ BUDW BUTY BVIS BVVN BXVS HRLM KARA PRAG

BÜCKER including CASA & DORNIER production
Bü.131 JUNGMANN (CASA 1.131)
G-BECT BECW BEDA BHPL BHSL BIRI BJAL BPDM BPTS BPVW BRSH BSAJ BSFB BSLH BTDT BTDZ BUCC BUCK BUOR BUTA BUVN BUVP BVPD BWHP BXBD BYIJ BZJV BZVS CBCE CDRU DUDS EHBJ EMJA JGMN JUNG RETA TAFF WIBS
Bü.133 JUNGMEISTER
G-AEZX AXMT AYSJ BSZN BUKK BUTX BVXJ BZTJ TAFI
Bü 181 BESTMANN
G-CBKB

BUSHBY-LONG - see LOEHLE
MIDGET MUSTANG
G-AWIR BDGA MIDG

CAARP - incl AVIONS MUDRY, CAP AVIATION & PIEL production

CAP.10

G-BECZ BKCX BLVK BRDD BXBK BXBU BXFE BXRA BXRB BXRC BYFY CAPI CAPX CPZC CZCZ GDTU LORN MOZZ ODIN RIFN SLEA WIXI

CAP.20/21

G-BIPO BPPS

CAP.231

G-PELG

CAB - see GARDAN

CALL AIRCRAFT CO - see IMCO

CAMBRIDGE HOT-AIR BALLOONING ASSOCIATION

HAFB

G-BBGZ

CAMERON BALLOONS LTD - see CAMERON-COLT & CAMERON-THUNDER

Gas Airship

DG-19: G-BKIK BPWT

DP-50: G-BMEZ

DP-70: G-BRDT

DP-80: G-BTBR UPPY VIBA

D-96: G-BAMK

Gas/HAFB

R-15: G-CICI

R-36: G-ROZY

R-42: G-BLIO

R-77: G-BUFA BUFC BUFE

R-150: G-BVUO

HAFB

20 variants

G-BIBS BJUV BOYO BPRU BRCJ BRCO

24 series

G-BSCK BVCY

31 variants

G-BAGI BEJK BEUY BGHS BMST BKIX BPUB BRMT BVFB BZYR CBIH COOP LEAU LLYD NOMO PRTT RBMV WETI

34 HOPPER series

G-BRKL BRWY BUCB BVZX BXYI BYNW BZBT FZZI IAMP OBLU RAPP

42 variants

G-AZER BCDL BCEU BISH BKNB BMWU BPHD BUPP BVLC BWEE BWGX BXJH BXTG BYRK HOPI SKOT

54 series

G-KSKS

56 variants

G-AZKK BBYU BCAP BCOJ BCXZ BDPK BDSF BDUI BDUZ BDYH BECK BEEH BELX BEND BENN BERT BEXX BEXZ BFAB BFFT BFKL BFME BGLX BGOI BGUY BHGF BHSN BICU BKRS BKZF BLWX BMOJ BNIF BOWM BRIR BRSA BTHZ BUVG BYSL BZKK HOFM HOOV LENN OVET PBBT SWPR WAAC WYNT

65 variants

G-AZIP AZUP AZUV AZXB BAOW BAYC BBGR BBYR BCFN BCRI BDFG BDGP BDRK BDSK BEIF BETP BGJU BHKH BHNC BHND BHOT BHOU BIBO BIGL BIGY BISW BIWK BIWU BIYI BJAW BJWJ BJZA BKGR BKJT BKWR BKXX BLEP BLJF BLZB BMCD BMJN BMKY BMPD BMVW BMYJ BNAN BNAU BNAW BOAL BOOB BOWV BPGD BPPA BPXF BREH BRMI BROE BROG BSAS BSGP BTUH BWBA BWHB BWHG BXGY BXUU BYZL GLUE HENS KAFE MUIR NATX OERX PMAM PYRO RUDD SMIG SOFA WELS

77 variants

G-BAXF BBCK BBOC BBYL BCNP BCRE BCZO BDAC BDBI BDCU BDNZ BDSE BEEI BEPO BFUG BFYK BGAZ BGHV BHDV BHHB BHHK BHHN BHII BHYO BIDU BIEF BIET BIRY BJGK BKNP BKPN BKTR BKWW BKZB BLFY BLIP BLJH BLLD BLPP BLSH BLVN BLXF BLZS BMAD BMCK BMKJ BMKP BMKW BMLJ BMLW BMOH BMPP BMTN BMTX BMVO BMZB BNCB BNCH BNCJ BNCK BNDN BNDV BNEO BNES BNFG BNFO BNGJ BNGN BNHI BNIN BNIU BNJG BNKT BNMA BNMG BNNC BNNE BNPE BNTW BNTZ BNUC BOAU BOBR BOEK BOFF BOGP BOJB BOJD BOJU BOOZ BORB BORN BOSV BOTW BOVV BOWB BOWL BOXG BOYS BOZN BPBU BPBV BPBY BPDF BPDG BPHH BPHJ BPLF BPLV BPPP BPSH BPSR BPTD BPVC BPVM BPWC BPYI BPYS BPYT BPYV BRAJ BRBO BRFE BRFO BRHC BRIE BRKW BRLX BRMU BRMV BRNW BROB BRRF BRRO BRRR BRRW BRTV BRUV BRZA BRZT BSBI BSBM BSBR BSDX BSEV BSGY BSHO BSHT BSIC BSIJ BSKD BSLI BSMS BSUV BSWV BSWY BSXM BTAG BTIX BTJH BTKZ BTOI BTOP BTPT BTWJ BTWM BTXW BTZV BUAF BUAM BUDU BUEV BUGD BUGP BUGS BUHM BUNG BUOX BUPI BUTJ BUWU BUWY BUZK BVBS BVBU BVDR BVFF BVHK BVIM BVLI BVMF BVUK BVXB BWAJ BWAN BWHC BWKV BWPB BWPC BWTJ BWYN BXAX BXSX BXTJ BXVT BYBN BYHY BYLY BYNJ BYRF BZPU BZPW CBHX CCAR CCSC CEJA CGOD CHOK CHUK CRAK CTGR CXHK DASU DRYI EIIR ENNY EPDI ERIK FABB FELT FUZY GEES GEEZ GEUP GUNS HARE HENY HORN HOST JLMW KEYY KODA KTEE LAZR LEGO LEND LEXI LIDD LIOT LOAG LOAN LOLL LUBE MAMO MILE MOFF MOKE MRTY OATH OCND OEDP OHSA OJEN OKYA OMRB ONZO ORPR PADI POLY PUSS PVCU RAPH RCMF RONI SAFE SAIX SCAH SCFO SHOT SKIL SNOW SUCH SUSI TECK TUDR UPUP ULIA VODA VOLT WAIT WELI XSKY ZUMP ZZAG

84 series

G-AYAJ AYVA AZBH AZDF AZNT AZRN AZSP BZVT BAGY BAKO BALD BAND BAST BBLL BCEZ BNET BNFP BNXR BOWU BOYM BRGD BSKE BSKU BSMK BUYN BVXD BWLN KEYB MOSY OLLE STAV

90 variants

G-BMFU BMJZ BNII BOOP BOWK BPSO BPUJ BRGE BROH BROY BRPJ BRZC BSCA BSNJ BSSO BSWX BTBP BTCM BTFU BTHF BTJU BTTB BTTL BTWV BTXF BUAJ BUFJ BUFX BUGY BUIE BUIU BUIZ BUOE BUUO BUVW BVBX BVDX BVEJ BVFP BVHO BVHR BVKV BVMR BVOC BVOP BVPK BVTN BWAU BWBC BWDU BWIP BWJI BWNO BWNS BWPT BWUU BWVU BWYC BXAM BXCS BXJO BXVV BYDT BYHC BYIU BYJC BYKX BYMY BYNN BYOK BYOX BYTW BYZX BZFD BZIX BZJH BZKX BZLJ BZMX BZOX BZRU BZTK BZUU BZXR BZYW BZYY CBAT CBCW CBED CHAA COMP CONC CPSF CTEL CXCX DHLB DIAL DRYS ELLE ENUS FBNW FOGG GLAW GOCX GOGW HBUG IBLU IGEL IGLE INSR ITOI IWON JULU LAGR LTSB MANI MFLI MOFZ OJBM OJBW OXBY PATG PERC PKCC PRIT PRNT RISE RIZE RIZI SIAM SLII SORT SRVO STRM SWEB TANK TEDF TEEL TETI TINS TMCC VINS VRVI YUMM YUPI YVET

100 series

G-NPWR

105 variants

G-BAVU BMEE BMOV BMVI BNFN BOTD BOTK BOYY BPBW BPJE BRFR BRLL BRZB BSNZ BTEA BTFM BTIZ BTKW BTPB BTRL BTOU BUHU BULD BUPT BUWF BVCA BVEU BVHV BVNR BVUA BVXA BWDH BWEW BWKF BWOW BWPZ BWRY BWSU BXBM BXBR BXBY BXEN BXGC BXWY BXXG BXXL BXYG BYFB BYFJ BYHU BYIL BYMX BYNX BYPD BZDJ BZKU BZVU BZXO CAMP CBEC CBHW CLIC DRGN ELEE ENRY FOWS GFAB HONK JSON LBNK LOSI NPNP NYLB NZGL OAML OJBS OUCH OUVI SAXO SDLW SEPT SSTI ULTR WNGS XANT YLYB

120 variants

G-BNEX BOBB BOHL BOZY BPSS BPTX BPZK BRXA BSYB BTEE BTKN BTUU BTXS BUDV BUFT BURN BVSO BVXF BWAG BWKD BWLD BWYS BXNL BXVJ BXWI BYSV CBFF FLOA GHIA HOTT LOBO MEUP MOFB OMFG TING VIKY VALZ

133 series

G-BWAA BZVE

140 variants

G-BVPU BVYU BWTE BYLU FLTG OXBC

145 series

G-DENT HIBM

160 variants

G-BNIE BOBD BPCN BPLE BRIM BYHW TGAS

165 series

G-BIAZ

180 variants

G-BPPJ BPYY BRTH BRVC BRZI BSWD BSWZ BSYD BSZY BTCW BTYE BUAU BUJR BUKC BVKL BWBR BWHW BXMM OBRY RWHC SKYR SVBF

200 series

G-BXOS BZJU

210 series
G-BRVX BTXV BUAY BUEE BUHY BUOC BUVK BVBN BWZK BXBA BXJC BXNM BXRM BXZG BXZH BYDI BYJV BYMG BYSM BZBE CBFY CVBF FLYE JOJO LPGI SKYU SKYX YTUK

250 series
G-BUBR BUXE BUXR BUZY BVIG BVYR BWKU BWKX BWZJ BXPK BYHX BYYD BZIK HIUP LORA MOLI OBUN ODEB OVBF SCRU SKYY STPI

275 series
G-BWML BXIC BXKJ BXMW BXTE BXYL BYSK BYZG BZTE BZTT SKYK

300 series
G-BZSU SIMI

315 series
G-BZNU

340 series
G-BWPA BZUO KVBF KYBF RANG

375 series
G-BWNH

400 series
G-BZJG ZVBF

CONCEPT series

C-60
G-BTZU BVDM BVDY BWRT BXJZ ROGY

C-70
G-BXOT BYJX BZEK

C-80
G-BUYC BVEK BVEN BVGJ BVSV BVSW BVUU BVWE BVZN BWAO BWGP BXJP BXLG BXSC BXSJ BYER BYJJ BYTJ BZMV BZPK CBEY EVET NMOS OARG OBTS OGJM ONIX RMAX SLCE SOUP UPHL

SPECIAL SHAPES

SHAPE	REGISTRATION(S)	SHAPE	REGISTRATION(S)
ACTION MAN PARACHUTIST	G-RIPS	APPLE	G-BWSO
BALL	G-RNIE	BEER BARREL	G-PINT
BEER CAN	G-IBET	BEETHOVEN BUST	G-BNJU
BELLS WHISKY BOTTLE	G-BUUU	BENIHANA	G-BMVS
BERENTZEN BOTTLE	G-KERN KORN	BERTIE BASSETT	G-BXAL BZTS
BRADFORD AND BINGLEY	G-BWMY	BUDWEISER CAN	G-BPFJ
BULB	G-BVWI	BULL	G-BZOH
BUS	G-BUSS	CADBURY'S CARAMEL BUNNY	G-BUNI
CADBURY'S CRÈME EGG	G-OEGG	CAN	G-OFIZ
CARROTS	G-BWSP HUCH	CART	G-BYDU
CHAMPION SPARK PLUG	G-BETF	CHATEAU DE BALLEROY	G-BKBR BTCZ
CHICK	G-BYEI	CIDER BOTTLE	G-OTNT
CLUB	G-BWNP	COCA COLA BOTTLE	G-BXSA BYIV BYIW BYIX
COOLING TOWER	G-WATT	COTTAGE	G-COTT
CUP	G-OAXA	DOLL	G-BVDF
DUDE	G-OIFM	EAGLE	G-BVMJ
EGG	G-OZEG	ELEPHANT	G-BLRW BMKX BPRC
EXPANSION JOINT	G-BIUL	FABERGE EGG	G-BNFK
FIRE EXTINGUISHER	G-BZJA	FORBES' MAGAZINE	G-BPOV
FURNESS BUILDING	G-BSIO	GOLFBALL	G-ORFE PUTT
GOLLY	G-OLLI	GRAND ILLUSION	G-MAGC
HOFMEISTER LAGER BEAR	G-HEYY	HOME SPECIAL	G-BWZP
HOPPER SERVO	G-OSVO	ICE CREAM CONE	G-BZTL
KATALOG	G-OTTO	KOOKABURRA	G-CHKL
KP CHOC DIPS TUB	G-DIPI	LIGHTBULB	G-BVWH LAMP
LIPS	G-LIPS	MACAW	G-BRWZ
MICKEY MOUSE	G-MOUS	MOBILE PHONE	G-PHON
MONSTER TRUCK	G-BWMU	MR.PEANUTNUTS	G-PNUT
MUG	G-RMUG	N ELE	G-WBMG
OIL CAN	G-UNIP	OTTI	G-OTTI
PERRIER BOTTLE	G-PERR	PIG	G-HOGS
POT	G-CHAM	PRINTER	G-BYFK
ROBINSON'S BARLEY WATER	G-BKES	RUGBY BALL	G-RUGB
RUPERT BEAR	G-BTML	RUSSIAN DOLL	G-USSR
SAMSUNG COMPUTER	G-SEUK	SANTA MARIA SHIP	G-BPSP
SATURN	G-DREX	SAUCER	G-GUFO
SCOTTISH PIPER	G-PIPY	SIGN	G-UCCC
SONIC THE HEDGEHOG	G-SEGA	SPHERE	G-BVFU BYJW IBBC SATL
STARTAC	G-HAND	STRAWBERRY	G-BXTF SAMI
SULTAN	G-TURK	TEMPLE	G-BMWN
TENNENT'S LAGER GLASS	G-BTSL	THOMAS	G-BXND
TISSUE PACK	G-LOOS	TRAINER'S SHOE	G-BUDN
TRUCK	G-BLDL DERV	TV	G-TVTV
UFO	G-BUFO	UNCLE SAM	G-USAM
VAN	G-ORAC	WITCH	G-WYCH
WINE BOX	G-STOW		

CAMPBELL AIRCRAFT including BENSEN & EVERETT production

COUGAR
G-BAPS

CRICKET
G-AXPZ AXRC AXVM AYCC AYPZ BHBA BKVS BORG BRLF BSRL BTEI BTMP BUIG BULT BVDJ BVIT BVLD BVOH BWSD BWUA BWUZ BXCJ BXHU BXUA BYMO BYMP BZKN GYRO RUGS TVSI

CANADAIR LTD

CL604 CHALLENGER

G-DAAC POAJ REYS

CRJ 200 REGIONAL JET

G-JECA JECB JECC JECD MSKO MSKP MSKR MSKS MSKT MSKU MSKV

CRJ 700 REGIONAL JET

G-MRSI MRSJ MRSK

CARLSON

SPARROW: G-BSUX BVVB

CASA - see BUCKER (*1.131*), & JUNKERS (*C.352L*)

CASSUTT including MUSSO/SPECIAL

RACER

G-BDTW BEUN BNJZ BOMB BOXW BPVO BUFK BWEC BXMF FRAY NARO OGPN RUNT TTIM

CAUDRON

G.III

G-AETA

CCF see HAWKER & NORTH AMERICAN

CEA see JODEL/ROBIN

CENTRAIR

MOTO-DELTA

G-MBPJ

CESSNA AIRCRAFT COMPANY including REIMS (F.prefix) production

C.165 AIRMASTER

G-BTDE

120/140

G-AHRO AJJS AJJT AKTS AKUR AKVM ALOD ALTO ANGK BHLW BJML BOCI BPHW BPHX BPKO BPUU BPWD BPZB BRJC BRPE BRPF BRPG BRPH BRUN BRXH BSUH BTBV BTBW BTEW BTOS BTVG BTYW BUHO BUHZ BUJM BVUZ BYCD GAWA HALJ JOLY OVFM

150

G-APXY APZR ARAU ARFI ARFO ARSB ARTY ASMS ASMU ASMW ASST ASUE ASYP ASZB ASZU ATAT ATEF ATHV ATHZ ATIE ATKF ATMC ATML ATMM ATMN ATMY ATNE ATNL ATOE ATRK ATRM ATUF ATYM ATZY AVAR AVCT AVCU AVEM AVEN AVER AVGU AVHM AVHN AVIA AVIB AVIT AVJE AVMD AVMF AVNC AVPH AVUG AVUH AVVL AVVW AVVX AVZU AWAV AWAW AWAX AWBX AWCK AWCM AWCO AWCP AWEO AWES AWFF AWFH AWGK AWGY AWLA AWLJ AWMT AWOT AWPJ AWPP AWPU AWRK AWSD AWTJ AWTX AWUG AWUH AWUJ AWUK AWUL AWUN AWUO AWUT AWUU AXGG AXPF AYBD AYEY AYGC AYKL AYRF AYRK AZLH AZLY AZLZ AZXC BABB BABC BABH BAEU BAHI BAIK BAIP BAMC BAXU BAXV BAYO BAYP BAZS BBBC BBCI BBDT BBJX BBKA BBKB BBKE BBKY BBNJ BBTT BBTZ BCBX BCCC BCRT BCTW BCUH BCUJ BCZN BDBU BDFJ BDFZ BDOD BDSL BDTX BDUM BDUO BDZC BEIG BELT BEOK BEWP BFFY BFGW BFIY BFLM BFOG BFSR BFVU BFWL BGBI BGEA BHIY BIFY BIOC BJOV BLVS BMBB BMLX BMXJ BNFI BOBV BOIV BOMN BORY BOTP BOUJ BOUZ BOVS BOVT BOWC BPAB BPAW BPAX BPCJ BPEM BPGB BPGY BPGZ BPNA BPOS BPRP BPUX BPWG BPWM BPWN BRBH BRJT BRLR BRNC BRTJ BSBZ BSEJ BSJU BSJZ BSKA BSSB BSYV BSYW BSZU BSZV BTES BTGP BTHE BTIN BTSN BTTE BTYC BUCS BUCT BUGG BUNS BURH BWGU BWII BWVL BZTE CSBM CSFC DENA DENB DENC DEND ECBH EJMG FAYE FFEN FINA GBLR GCNZ GFLY GLED HFCB HFCI HIVE HULL IANJ JWDS LFSF LUCK MABE NSTG OIDW OJVH OKED OSTY PHAA PLAN SADE SALL SAMZ SCAT TAIL UFLY WYMP YIII

A150 AEROBAT

G-AXRT AXRU AXSW AXUF AYCF AYOZ AYRO AYRP AZID AZJY AZKV AZLL AZOZ AZUZ BACC BACN BABD BACO BACP BAEP BAEV BAEZ BAII BAIN BAOP BAPH BAPI BAPJ BBCF BBEO BBKF BBKU BBNX BBNY BBTB BBTK BBXB BCDY BCFR BCKU BCKV BCTU BCUY BCVG BCVH BDAI BDEX BDNR BDOW BDRD BEIA BEKN BEMY BEOE BEOY BFGG BFGX BFGZ BFIE BFRR BHRH BIBN BJTB BLPH BMEX BOFW BOFX BOYU BPJW BTFS BUCA BUTT CLUB FMSG HFCA JAGS OISO OPIC OSND

152

G-BFEK BFFC BFFE BFFW BFHT BFHU BFHV BFKG BFKH BFLU BFOE BFOF BFRL BFSB BGAA BGAB BGAD BGAE BGFX BGGO BGGP BGHI BGIB BGLG BGNT BHAA BHAI BHAV BHCP BHCX BHDM BHDR BHDS BHDU BHDW BHEC BHFC BHFI BHHG BHIN BHNA BHPY BHRB BHRM BHRN BHSA BHUI BHWA BHWB BHYX BHZH BICG BIDH BIJV BIJW BIJX BILR BILS BIOK BIOM BITF BITH BIUM BIXH BIZG BJKX BJKY BJNF BJVJ BJVT BJWH BJYD BKAZ BKFC BKGW BKTV BKWY BLJO BLWV BLZE BLZH BLZP BMCN BMCV BMFZ BMGG BMJB BMJC BMJD BMMM BMSU BMTA BMTB BMTJ BMVB BMXA BMXB BMXC BMXX BNAJ BNDO BNFR BNFS BNHJ BNHK BNID BNIV BNJB BNJC BNJD BNJH BNJJ BNJV BNKC BNKI BNKP BNKR BNKS BNKV BNMC BNMD BNME BNMF BNNR BNOZ BNPY BNPZ BNRK BNRL BNSI BNSM BNSN BNSU BNSV BNUL BNUS BNUT BNXC BNYL BNYN BOAI BODO BOFL BOFM BOGC BOGG BOHI BOHJ BOIO BOIP BOIR BOIW BOKY BOLV BOLW BONW BOOI BORI BORJ BORO BOTB BOTG BOYL BOZR BPBG BPBJ BPBK BPEO BPFZ BPGM BPHT BPIO BPJL BPME BPTF BPTU BRBP BRND BRNE BRNK BRNN BRPV BRTD BRTP BRUA BSCP BSCZ BSDO BSDP BSFP BSFR BSRC BSTO BSTP BSWH BSZI BSZO BSZW BTAL BTCE BTDW BTFC BTGH BTGR BTGW BTGX BTIK BTVW BTVX BTYT BUEF BUEG BVTM BWEU BWEV BWNB BWNC BWND BXGE BXJM BXRN BXTB BXUZ BXVB BXVY BXWC BYFA BYMH BYMJ BZAD BZAE BZEB BZEC BZWH CHIK CPFC CWFY DACF DESY DRAG ENTT ENTW FIGA FIGB HART HFCL HFCT IAFT IBRO IRAN KATT LAMS LSMI MASS OAFT OBEN ODAC OFRY OIMC OLEE OPAM OPJC OSFC OVMC OWAC OWAK OWOW PFSL RICH SACB SACF SHAH TAYS WACB WACE WACF WACG WACT

A152 AEROBAT

G-BFGL BFKF BFMK BFRV BFZN BFZT BFZU BGAF BGLN BHAC BHAD BHED BHEN BHJA BHJB BHMG BHMH BIHE BILJ BIMT BLAC BLAX BMUO BMYG BOPX BOSO BOYB BRCD BRUM BZEA FIFE FLIP JEET JONI LEIC MPBH OCPC RLFI TFCI WACH WACU WALS ZOOL

170

G-AORB APVS AWOU BCLS

172/SKYHAWK

G-APSZ ARID ARLU ARMO ARMR AROA ARWH ARWO ARWR ARYI ARYK ARYS ARZE ASFA ASIB ASMJ ASNW ASOK ASPI ASSS ASUH ASUP ASVM ASWL ATAF ATFY ATGO ATKT ATKU ATLM ATSL ATWJ AVCC AVEC AVHH AVIC AVIS AVJF AVJI AVKG AVPI AVTP AVVC AVZV AWBW AWGD AWGR AWLF AWMP AWMZ AWUX AWUZ AWVA AXBH AXBJ AXDI AXSI AXVB AXWF AYCT AYRG AYRT AYUV AZDZ AZJV AZKW AZKZ AZLM AZLV AZTK AZTS AZUM AZXD AZZV BAAL BAEO BAEW BAEY BAIW BAIX BANX BAOB BAOS BAVB BAXY BAZT BBDH BBJD BBJY BBJZ BBKI BBKZ BBNZ BBOA BBTG BBTH BCCD BCEC BCHK BCOL BCPK BCRB BCUF BCVJ BCYR BCZM BDCE BDNU BDZD BEBI BEHV BEMB BENK BEUX BEWR BEZK BEZO BEZR BEZV BFGD BFKB BFMX BFOV BFPH BFPM BFRS BFTH BFTX BFZV BGAG BGBR BGHJ BGIU BGIY BGLO BGMP BGND BGNS BGRO BGSV BHAW BHCC BHCM BHDX BHDZ BHIH BHMI BHPZ BHSB BHUG BHUJ BHVR BHYP BHYR BIBW BIDF BIGJ BIHI BIIB BIIE BING BIOB BITM BIZF BJDE BJDW BJGY BJVM BJWI BJWW BJXZ BKCE BKEP BKEV BKHZ BKII BKIJ BKKO BKLP BKRB BLHJ BLVW BMCI BMHS BMIG BMTS BMVJ BNKD BNKE BNRR BNST BNTP BNXD BNYM BOEN BOHH BOIL BOIX BOIY BOJR BOJS BOLI BOLX BOLY BOMS BOMT BONO BONR BONS BOOL BORW BOUE BOUF BOVG BOYP BPML BPRM BPTL BPVA BPVY BPWS BRAK BRBI BRBJ BRCM BRWX BRZS BSCR BSEP BSHR BSNG BSOG BSOO BSPE BSTM BTMA BTMR BTRE BUAN BUJN BULH BUOJ BURD BUZN BWJP BXGV BXHG BXOI BXSD BXSE BXSM BXSR BXXD BXXK BYBD BYEA BYEB BYES BYET BYNA BZBF BZKB BZZD BZGH BZPM CBFO CBOR CCCC CFLY CLUX COCO CSCS CURR DCKK DEMH DENR DODD DRAM DRBG DREY DUVL ECGC EGEG ENII ENNK ENOA EOFM ETDC EWUD FNLD FNLY GBFF GBLP GRAY GWYN GYAV GZDO HERC HILS ICOM IZSS IZZY JFWI-JONE JONZ JVMD LANE LAVE LOOK MALK MELT MFAC MICK MILA OBMS OERS OFCM OOLE OPFT OPYE ORMG OSII OSKY OTAM OVFR OZOO PDSI PLBI RARB ROOK ROUP RSWO RUIA SACD SBAE SEVE SEXI SHSP SKAN SKYH TAAL TASH TOBI TOBY TRIO TYRE UFCA UFCB UFCC UFCD WACL WACM WACW WACY WACZ YORK

172RG CUTLASS

G-BHYC BILU BIXI PARI

FR172 HAWK/REIMS ROCKET
G-AWCN AWDR AWWU AWYB AXBU AYGX AYJW BARC BBKG BBXH BCTK BDOE BEZS BFFZ BFIG BFIU BFSS BHYD BLPF BPCI BPWR BTMK BXYY BZVB DAVD DIVA EDTO FANL JANS LOYA MFEF OMAC PJTM STAY YBAA
175/SKYLARK
G-ARCV ARFG ARFL ARML ARMN AROC ARRG ARRI ARUZ ARWS OTOW
177(RG) CARDINAL
G-AYPG AYPH AYPI AYSX AYSY AZTF AZTW AZVP BAGN BAIS BAJA BAJB BAJE BBHI BBJV BCUW BEBN BFIV BFMH BPSL BRDO BRPS BTSZ BUJE FIJJ LNYS OAMP TOTO
180/SKYWAGON
G-ARAT ASIT AXZO BEOD BETG BNCS BOIA BTSM BUPG DAPH
182/SKYLANE variants
G-ARAW ASNN ASRR ASSF ASXZ ATCX ATLA ATPT ATTD AVCV AVDA AVGY AVID AXNX AXZU AYOW AYWD AZNO BAAT BAFL BAHD BAHX BAMJ BBGX BBYH BBYS BCWB BDBJ BDIG BEKO BFOD BFSA BFZD BGAJ BGFH BGPA BHDP BHIB BHIC BHVP BHYA BIRS BJDI BJVH BKHJ BKKN BKKO BLEW BMMK BMUD BNMO BNOX BNRY BOPG BOPH BOTH BOWO BPUM BRKR BRRK BSDW BSRR BTHA BUVO BWMC BWRR BXEZ BXZM BYEM BZVF BZVO CBIL DATG DOVE DRGS EEZS EIRE EIWT ELIE EOHL GCYC GHOW GOZO HRNT HUFF IBZS IBZT IOPT IRPC ISEH JBRN JENI JOON KWAX LEGG LSKW MICI MILN MISH MLAS NLEE NOCK OBBO OCJW OHAC OJRM OKOS OLSC OPST ORAY OTRG OWRT OZOI PDHJ PLEE POWL POWR PUGS RACY ROWE SAAM SKYL THRE TPSL VIPA WARP WIFE XLTG ZBLT
185 SKYWAGON/AG CARRYALL
G-AYNN BBEX BDKC BKPC BLOS BWWF BXRH BYBP RNRM
(T)188 AG WAGON/AG TRUCK/AG HUSKY
G-AZZG BHTD
190/195
G-BSPK BTBJ
205
G-ASNK ASOX
206 SUPER SKYLANE/SUPER SKYWAGON/STATIONAIR
G-ASVN ATCE ATLT AWUA AYCJ AZRZ BAGV BATD BFCT BGED BGWR BMHC BMOF BNRI BOFD BPGE BRID BSMB BSUE BXDB BXRO BYIC CTFF DROP EESE SEAI SKYE STAT
207 SKYWAGON/STATIONAIR 8
G-NJAG PARA
208/B (GRAND) CARAVAN
G-BZAH EELS ETHY
210 CENTURION
G-ASXR BBRY BENF BEYV BNZM BSGT BVZM DECK IKIS MANT OFLY PIIX SEEK VMDE
T303 CRUSADER
G-BSPF CRUZ CYLS DOLY GAME IKAP INDC JUIN OAPE PTWB PUSI ROCH SOAY UILT
305 BIRD DOG (L-19)
G-PDOG
310
G-APNJ ARCI AVDB AXLG AYGB AYND AZRR AZUY AZYM BALN BARG BARV BBBX BBXL BCTJ BGTT BHEH BIFA BJMR BKSB BMMC BODY BPIL BRIA BTFF BTGN BTYK BWYE BWYG BWYH BXUY BXYF EGEE EGLT FFWD FISH IMLI MIWS MPBI OBNF ODLY OGTX REDB REDD RIST RODD SOUL TKPZ TROP VDIR XITD
320 SKYKNIGHT
G-AZCI BKRD
335
G-FITZ
336 SKYMASTER
G-ASLL ATAH PIXS
337 SUPER SKYMASTER
G-ATCU ATID ATSM AXHA AZKO AZLO BARD BBBL BCBZ BFGH BFJR BMJR BOWD BTVV HIVA NYTE RGEN RORO
340
G-BISJ BVES FEBE LAST LIZA OPLB PUFN REEN SAMM VAUN
401/402
G-AVKN AWWW AZFR AZRD BXJA DACC DOBN EYES MAPP NOSE ROAR
404 TITAN/AMBASSADOR/COURIER
G-BWLF BYLR EXEX MIND TASK TVIP
406 CARAVAN II
G-BVJT DFLT FLYN LEAF MAFA MAFB SFPA SFPB SURF TWIG
414/CHANCELLOR
G-DYNE SMJJ
421/GOLDEN EAGLE
G-BAGO BBUJ BDYF BDZU BFTT BHKJ BKNA BLST BTDK CSNA CJEA FTAX FWRP GILT HASI HIJK JACK KWLI MUVG OSCH RLMC SAIR TAMY TREC UVIP VVIP
425/441 CONQUEST I/II
G-BNDY FCAL FPLC FRAX FRAZ
500/501 CITATION 1
G-CITI DJAE LOFT OEJA ORHE ORJB
525 CITATIONJET
G-BVCM HMMV IUAN OHAT OWRC RSCJ ZIZI
550/CITATION BRAVO/551 CITATION II:
G-BJIR BWOM EJEL ESTA FIRM FCDB FJET FLVU JCFR JETJ OCDB RDBS RVHT SPUR
560 CITATION/EXCEL/ULTRA
G-CFRA CZAR KDMA RIBV SIRS TTFN
650 CITATION III
G-HNRY

CFM METAL-FAX

(STREAK) SHADOW
G-BONP BROI BRSO BRWP BRZZ BSMN BSOR BSPL BSRX BSSV BTDD BTEL BTGT BTKP BTZZ BUGM BUIL BULJ BUOB BUTB BUVX BUWR BUXC BVDT BVFR BVLF BVOR BVPY BVTD BWAI BWCA BWOZ BWPS BXFK BXVD BXWR BXXZ BXZV BXZY BYAZ BYCI BYFI BYOO BZDF BZEZ BZLF BZMZ BZWJ BZWY CAIN CBCZ CBGI DARK DMWW ENEE FAME GORE HLCF LYNK MEOW MGGT MGPH MGTW MGUY MJVF MMWT MNCM MNER MNIS MNSV MNTK MNTP MNVJ MNVK MNWK MNWY MNXX MNZJ MNZP MNZR MNZZ MTBE MTCA MTCT MTDU MTDX MTFU MTFZ MTGN MTGV MTGW MTHS MTHT MTHV MTKR MTMX MTMY MTSG MTTH MTWH MTWK MTWL MTWN MTXR MVAC MVAM MVAN MVBB MVCC MVCW MVEI MVEN MVFH MVHD MVIG MVLJ MVLP MVOH MVPK MVRE MVRO MVRP MVRR MVRT MVVT MVYZ MWAE MWDB MWDN MWEN MWEZ MWFB MWIZ MWJF MWLD MWMU MWON MWPN MWPP MWRL MWRY MWSZ MWTJ MWTN MWTP MWUA MWVG MWVH MWYD MYBC MYBL MYCM MYDD MYDE MYEP MYGO MYIF MYIP MYKE MYLV MYNA MYNX MYOH MYON MYOS MYPL MYPT MYSM MYTH MYTY MYUS MYWF MYWM MYXY MYZP MZBE MZBN MZBS MZCT MZGS MZKH MZRS MZLO MZLP MZNH MZOM ODVB OLGA OPIT ORAF OTCH PBEL PSUE RINT ROTS RZPH SHIM SNEV STRK TEHL TTOY WESX WHOG WYAT

CGS (including ARROWFLIGHT)

HAWK
G-MWYS MYTP MZGU

CHAMPION/AERONCA including BELLANCA production

7AC/7DC CHAMPION
G-AJON AKTO AKTR AOEH ATHK AVDT AWVN BGWV BPFM BPGK BRAR BRCV BRER BRFI BRWA BRXG BTGM BTNO BTRH BUYE BVCS CHMP HAMP JTYE LEVI OTOE TECC
7BCM (L-16)
G-BFAF TIMP
7EC TRAVELER
G-ARAP
7FC TRI-TRAVELER
G-APYT APYU ARAS
CITABRIA/DECATHLON/SCOUT
G-AYXU BBEN BBXY BDBH BFHP BGGA BGGB BGGC BGGD BITA BIZW BKBP BOID BOIN BOLG BOTO BPMM BRJW BSLW BTXX BUGE BVLT CIDD EXPL HUNI

CHANCE-VOUGHT - see VOUGHT

CHARGUS

T.225/T.250 (Trike)
G-MBEU MBJG MMRY

CHICHESTER-MILES

LEOPARD
G-BRNM

CHILTON AIRCRAFT

DW.1/1A/1B/2
G-AESZ AFGH AFGI AFSV AFSW BWGJ DWIA DWIB

CHRISLEA AIRCRAFT CO LTD

LC.1 AIRGUARD
G-AFIN
CH.3 SUPER ACE
G-AKUW AKVF
CH.3 SRS.4 SKYJEEP
G-AKVR

CHRISTEN INDUSTRIES INC - see PITTS

EAGLE
G-BPZI EEGL EGAL EGLE EGUL ELKA OEGL
A-1 HUSKY
G-BUVR

CHRIS TENA

MINI COUPE
G-BPDJ

CIERVA

C.24
G-ABLM
C.30A AUTOGIRO (AVRO 671)
G-ACUU ACWM ACWP

CIVILIAN AIRCRAFT CO.

CAC.1 COUPE
G-ABNT

CLUTTON-TABENOR

FRED
G-BBBW BDBF BDSA BGAH BGFF BGHZ BISG BITK BKAF BKDP BKEY BKVF BKZT BLNO BMAX BMMF BMOO BMSL BNZR BOLS BPAV BVCO BWAP BYLA FRED MANX OLVR ORAS PFAF PFAL RONW USTY

COLT BALLOONS LTD see COLTING & including CAMERON production

Gas Airship
GA-42
G-MATS ZEPI
Hot Air Airship
AS-42
G-WZZZ
AS-56
G-BNKF BTXH NOVO
AS-80
G-BPCF BPGT BPKN BROL BTSW NDRW OVAX
AS-105
G-BNAO BROL BTFD BUKV BWKE BWMV BXEY BXNV BXYF RBOS
AS-120
G-BXKU BZWF
Gas Balloon
AA-1050
G-BWVM
Hot Air Balloon
12A Cloudhopper
G-BHOJ
14A Cloudhopper
G-BHKN BHKR BHPN BVKX
17A Cloudhopper
G-BIDV IYT BJWV BKBO BKIU BKXM BLHI BONV BOSG BPXH BRBU HELP ROBY
21A Cloudhopper
G-BKIV BKSH BLXG BMKI BNFM BNPI BNZJ BOLN BOLP BOLR BPFX BSAK BSIG BTNN BTXM BUEU BWBJ LLAI SOOS
H-24
G-BZUV
25A Sky Chariot
G-BSOF BVAO OKBT
31A Air Chair
G-BHIG BLOB BROJ BSDV BSMM BVTL BXXU DNGR DHLZ DOWN HOUS IMAN MUTE PIXE PONY
42 variants
G-BJZR BVHP SEAT
56 variants
G-BGIP BHEX BHGX BHRY BICM BISX BIXW BJXP BJYF BKSD BLCH BLLW BLOT BMNX BMYA BPWV BTZY BUGO BVCN BVOZ BVUC BVYL CFBI ILEE FZZZ MERC POSH TTWO WIMP
69 series
G-BOSF BOVW BPAH BSHC BSHD BTMO BVDD COLR FZZY JBJB OABC OBUD OBUY ODIY TCAN TWEY
77 variants
G-BGOD BIGT BKOW BLSK BLTA BMYN BNGP BOCF BOGT BOHD BORA BORE BORT BPEZ BPFB BPJK BRLT BRVF BRVU BSCI BSUB BSUK BTDS BTTS BTVH BTXB BTZR BTZS BUJH BUKS BULF BURG BUVB BUVE BUVS BUVT BUYO BUZF BVAX BXFN BXIE BYFX CHEL CURE DING DRAW DURX FLAG GGOW GOBT HOME HOTI HOTZ HRZN IMAG JONO LOWA LSHI MAUK MKAK OAWS OBJH OCAR ODAD OLPG ONCL ORON OSST READ RFIL SGAS SIXX STOK TRUX UPPP UZLE WHAT WHIM WOOL WRIT
90 series
G-BLWE BMLU BOBU BPUW BRFH BRHG BRRU BSIU BTCS BTMH BTPV BVEI BXUW EXPR FOWL IRLY JNNB OBBC OLDV OMMM PEGG PHSI SAUF SEND TOFT
105 series
G-BGAS BLHK BLMZ BMBS BNAG BPZS BRUH BSBK BSCC BSHS BSNU BTHX BURL BUSV BWMA BWRM BXOV BXOW BYIO DYNG HSHS OFLI PLUG RAIL TIKI USGB
120 series
G-BXAI BXCO BYDJ BYPV BZIL BZNF CBEJ OBIB OCPS VYGR
180 series
G-BOGR BONK BSUU CUCU PICT
210 series
G-BTYZ BUGN BULN BUXA BVFY BZYO
240 series
G-BNAP BVVT IGLA LCIO

SPECIAL SHAPES:
260 series
G-HUGO
300 series
G-RAPE
315 series
G-KAUR VVBF
2500 series
G-USUK

SHAPE	REGISTRATION(S)	SHAPE	REGISTRATION(S)
AGFA FILM CASSETTE	G-OHDC	APPLE	G-BRZV
ARIEL BOTTLE	G-BNHN	BEER GLASS	G-BNHL PUBS
BIBENDUM	G-GRIP PNEU TRED	BLACK KNIGHT	G-BNMI
BOTTLE	G-BOTL BUEL BVHU	BUDWEISER CAN	G-BUET BVIO
CAN	G-BXPR	CHEESE	G-BRZU
DRACHENFISCH	G-BMUJ	EGG	G-BWWL
FINANCIAL TIMES	G-ETFT FTFT	FIRE EXTINGUISHER	G-CHUB
FLAME	G-BLKU	FLYING MITT	G-WCAT
FLYING YACHT	G-AXXJ	GAS FLAME	G-BGOO
GOLF BALL	G-BJUY	GORDON'S GIN BOTTLE	G-BUYG
HAND	G-BUDM	HOP	G-MALT
HOT DOG	G-BVKG	HUT	G-SMTC
ICE CREAM CONE	G-BWBE BWBF OJHB	J & B WHISKY BOTTLE	G-JANB
JUMBO JET	G-BRDP OVAA UMBO VJIM	KINDERMOND	G-BMUL
MAXWELL HOUSE COFFEE JARS	G-BVBJ BVBK	MICKEY MOUSE	G-BTRB
MONTGOLFIERE	G-BPHV	OLD PARR WHISKY BOTTLE	G-PARR
PANASONIC BATTERY	G-PSON	PAPER BAG	G-BNAH
PIG	G-BUZS	PIGGY BANK	G-BWBV BXVW
SANTA CLAUS	G-HOHO	SATZENBRAU BOTTLE	G-BIRE
SHUTTLECOCK	G-OOUT	SKOL LAGER CAN	G-BTUN
SNOWFLAKE	G-BNBP	SPARKASSE BOX	G-BXKH
STORK	G-BRGP	SUGAR BOX	G-BZDX BZDY BZKR
UFO	G-BMUK	WORLD	G-DHLI

COLTING
AX7-77 HAFB
G-BHBB BLUE

COLOMBAN including ZENAIR
MC.12/15 CRI-CRI
G-BOUT BWFO CRIC MCXV OCRI SHOG

COMCO IKARUS
IKARUS C42
G-CBFV CBGP CBIJ GNJW IKRS MROY MSKY OFBU

COMMANDER AIRCRAFT COMPANY
- see ROCKWELL

COMMONWEALTH - see NORTH AMERICAN

COMPER AIRCRAFT CO.
CLA.7 SWIFT
G-ABTC ABUS ACTF KBWW LCGL

CONSOLIDATED-VULTEE - see STINSON
L-13A
G-BGHE

CONVAIR
CV-440-54
G-CONV

COSTRUZIONI AERONAUTICHE GIOVANNI AGUSTA S.p.A - see AGUSTA

COOK
ARIES P
G-MYXI

COPE
BUG
G-BXTV

CORBEN
BABY ACE
G-BTSB BUAA

JUNIOR ACE
G-BSDI

CORBY
CJ-1 STARLET
G-BVVZ CBHP ILSE

COSMOS
TRIKE
G-MVCK

COUGAR
(Wing)
G-MMUJ

CRANFIELD
A.1-400 EAGLE
G-COAI

CREMER
MLB variants
G-BJLX BJLY BJRP BJRR BJRV BJVB

CROSBY - see ANDREASSON

CUB PROSPECTOR - see PIPER

CULVER
LCA CADET
G-CDET

CURRIE including TURNER
WOT
G-APNT ARZW ASBA AVEY AYMP AYNA BANV BDFB BEBO BFAH BFWD BKCN BLPB BXMX CWBM CWOT PFAP SWOT

CURTISS AEROPLANE & MOTOR CO
JN-4D
G-ECAB

CURTISS-WRIGHT CORPORATION
TRAVEL AIR 12Q
G-AAOK
P-40 KITTYHAWK/TOMAHAWK
G-KITT TOMA

CURTISS ROBERTSON
ROBIN C.2
G-BTYY HFBM

CUTLASS - see SKYHOOK

CVJETKOVIC
CA-65 SKYFLY HAFB
G-BWBG

CYCLONE AIRSPORTS LTD - see AERIAL ARTS/CHARGUS/PEGASUS AVIATION/SOLAR WINGS (AVIATION)
70 (Trike)
G-MMYL MNMY
AX3
G-BVJG BVRY MGRW MYFI MYFV MYFW MYFY MYFZ MYGD MYHG MYHH MYHJ MYHM MYHR MYIJ MYIU MYKA MYKF MYKT MYME MYMF MYMW MYMZ MYOY MYPM MYPR MYRO MYRU MYRV MYSO MYTM MYUI MYVN MYXH MYYL MYZC MYZF MYZG MZDO MZDS ZELE
AX 2000
G-BYJM CBHC CBIT ONY MGUN MYER MZER MZFA MZFX MZGA MZGB MZGC MZGM MZGP MZHR MZIV MZJF MZJL MZJR MZKC MZLS MZLU MZMX MZOE OAJB ROMW STRG YROO
Cyclone (Wing)
G-MBOK
TS.440 (Wing)
G-MBDU
Vortex (Wing)
G-MJWH
Titan 38 (Trike)
G-MBDU MYZH

CZAL
AERO 45/145
G-APRR ATBH AYLZ

D

DALOTEL
DM-165 VIKING
G-BILA

DAN RIHN
DR.107 ONE DESIGN
G-IDDI IIID

DART AIRCRAFT LTD.
KITTEN
G-AEXT

DASSAULT
FALCON 20/200
G-DAEX FFRA FRAE FRAF FRAH FRAI FRAJ FRAK FRAL FRAM FRAO FRAP FRAR FRAS FRAT FRAU FRAW FRBA
FALCON 50
G-JPSI
FALCON 900
G-EVES CBHT MLTI JCBG OPWH
FALCON 2000
G-GEDI IBSF JCBI

DAVIS
DA-2
G-BPFL

DE HAVILLAND AIRCRAFT CO LTD - see AIRCO/HAWKER SIDDELEY AVIATION & including F + W/MORANE/MORRIS MOTORS/MOTH CORPORATION/OGMA production
DH.51
G-EBIR
DH.53 HUMMING BIRD
G-EBHX EBQP
DH.60/60G/60M/60X MOTH
G-EBLV EBWD EBZN
G-AAAH AACD AADR AAEG AAHI AAHY AAMX AALY AAMY AANF AANL AANO AANV AAOR AAWO AAZG ABAG ABDX ABEV ABSD ABYA ATBL
DH.60GIII MOTH MAJOR
G-ABZB ACGZ ACNS ACXB ADHD BVNG
DH.71 TIGER MOTH
G-ECDX
DH.80A PUSS MOTH
G-AAZP ABLS AEOA
DH.82A TIGER MOTH
G-ABUL ACDA ACDC ACDI ACDJ ACMD ADGT ADGV ADIA ADJJ ADNZ ADPC ADWJ ADWO ADXT AFGZ AFVE AFWI AGEG AGHY AGNJ AGPK AGYU AGZZ AHAN AHIZ AHLT AHMM AHMN AHOO AHPZ AHUF AHUV AHVU AHVV AIDS AIRI AIRK AIXJ AJHS AJHU AJOA AJTW AJVE AKUE AKXS ALBD ALIW ALJL ALNA ALND ALRI ALTW ALUC ALVP ALWS ALWW AMBB AMCK AMCM AMHF AMIU AMIV AMNN AMTF AMTK AMTV AMVS ANCS ANCX ANDE ANDM ANDP ANEH ANEL ANEM ANEN ANEW ANEZ ANFC ANFI ANFL ANFM ANFP ANFV ANFW ANHK ANJA ANJD ANJK ANKK ANKT ANKV ANKZ ANLD ANLH ANLS ANMO ANMV ANMY ANNB ANNE ANNG ANNI ANNK ANOD ANOH ANOM ANON ANOO ANOR ANPC ANPE ANPK ANRF ANRM ANRN ANRX ANSM ANTE ANZU ANZZ AOAA AOBH AOBO AOBX AODT AOEI AOEL AOES AOET AOGI AOGR AOHY AOIL AOIM AOIS AOJJ AOJK AOUR AOZH APAL APAM APAO APAP APBI APCC APFU APGL APIH APJO APLU APMX APPN ARAZ AREH ARTL ASKP ASPV AVPJ AXAN AXBW AXBZ AXXV AYDI AYIT AZDY AZGZ AZZZ BAFG BBRB BEWN BFHH BHLT BHUM BJAP BJZF BMPY BNDW BPAJ BPHR BRHW BTOG BUJY BWIK BWMK BWMS BWVT BXMN BYLB BYTN DHTM DHZF EMSY ERDS ISIS MOTH OOSY PWBE TIGA

DH.82B QUEEN BEE
G-BLUZ
DH.83/C FOX MOTH
G-ACCB ACEJ AOJH
DH.84 DRAGON
G-ACET ACIT ECAN
DH.85 LEOPARD MOTH
G-ACLL ACMA ACMN ACOJ ACUS AIYS APKH
DH.87B HORNET MOTH
G-ADKC ADKK ADKL ADKM ADLY ADMT ADND ADNE ADOT ADRH ADUR AELO AESE AHBL AHBM
DH.88 COMET
G-ACSP ACSS
DH.89A DRAGON RAPIDE
G-ACZE ADAH AEML AGJG AGSH AGTM AHAG AHED AHGD AIDL AIUL AIYR AJBJ AJCL AKDW AKIF AKOE AKRP ALAX ALXT
DH.90 DRAGONFLY
G-AEDU
DH.94 MOTH MINOR
G-AFNG AFNI AFOB AFOJ AFPN
DH.98 MOSQUITO
G-ASKC AWJV
DH.100 VAMPIRE
G-DHXX FBIX MKVI SWIS
DH.104 DOVE/DEVON
G-AHRI ALCU ALFT ALFU AMXT ANAP ANOV ANUW APSO ARBE ARDE AREA ARHW ARHX ARJB AVVF BLRN BVXR DHDV DVON HBBC KOOL OEWA OPLC RNAS SDEV
DH.106 COMET
G-ALYW AOJT APAS APDB APDF APMB APYD BDIX BEEX CPDA
DH.110 SEA VIXEN
G-CVIX VIXN
DH.112 VENOM
G-BLID BLKA BLSD DHSS DHTT DHUU GONE VENI VENM VICI VNOM
DH.114 HERON
G-ANUO ANXB AORG AOTI HRON
DH.115 VAMPIRE TRAINER
G-BZRC BZRD DHVV DHWW DHYY DHZZ DUSK HELV OBLN SPDR VMPR VTII
DH.121 TRIDENT - **see HAWKER SIDDELEY**
DH.125 - **see HAWKER SIDDELEY**

DE HAVILLAND (AUSTRALIA)
DHA.3 DROVER
G-APXX

DE HAVILLAND (CANADA) incl BOMBARDIER/OGMA production
DHC-1 CHIPMUNK
G-AKDN ALWB AMUF ANWB AOFE AOJR AOJZ AORW AOSF AOSK AOSO AOSU AOSY AOTD AOTF AOTR AOTY AOUO AOUP AOZP APLO APPA APPM APYG ARGG ARMB ARMC ARMD ARMF ARMG ARWB ATHD ATVF BAPB BARS BAVH BBMN BBMO BBMR BBMT BBMV BBMW BBMX BBMZ BBNA BBNC BBND BBRV BBSS BBWN BCAH BCCX BCEY BCGC BCHL BCHV BCIH BCIW BCKN BCOI BCOO BCOU BCOY BCPU BCRX BCSA BCSL BCXN BCYJ BCYM BCZH BDCC BDDD BDEU BDRJ BFAW BFAX BFDC BHRD BNZC BPAL BTWF BVBT BVTX BVWP BVZZ BWHI BWJY BWMX BWNK BWNT BWOX BWTG BWTO BWUN BWUT BWUV BWVY BWVZ BXCP BXCT BXCV BXDA BXDG BXDH BXDI BXDM BXDP BXEC BXGL BXGM BXGO BXGP BXGX BXHA BXHF BXIA BXIM BXNN BYHL BYSJ BYYW BZDU BZGA BZGB BZXE CBAJ CHPY CPMK DHCC DHCI HAPY JAKE MAJR OACP PVET TRIC ULAS
DHC-2 BEAVER
G-BUCJ BVER
DHC-6 TWIN OTTER
G-BIHO BVVK BZFP
DHC-8 DASH EIGHT variants
G-BRYH BRYI BRYJ BRYM BRYO BRYP BRYS BRYT BRYU BRYV BRYW BRYY BRYX BRYZ JEDA JEDB JEDC JEDD JEDE JEDF JEDG JEDI JEDJ JEDK JEDL JEDX JEDY JEDZ NVSA NVSB NVSC

DEMON - see HIWAY

DENNEY AEROCRAFT COMPANY
KITFOX
G-BNYX BONY BPII BPKK BRCT BSAZ BSCG BSCH BSCM BSFX BSFY BSGG BSHK BSIF BSIK BSMO BSNO BSRT BSSF BSUZ BSVK BTAT BTBG BTBN BTDC BTDN BTFA BTIF BTIR BTKD BTMT BTMX BTNR BTOL BTSV BTTY BTVC BTWB BUDR BUIC BUIP BUKF BUKP BULZ BUNM BUOL BUPW BUWS BUYK BUZA BVAH BVCT BVEY BVGO BWAR BWHV BWSJ BWSN BWWZ BWYI BXCW BXWH BZAR BZLO CBDI CJUD CRES CTOY DJNH ELIZ EYAS FOXC FOXD FOXE FOXF FOXG FOXI FOXS FOXZ FSHA HOBO HUTT KAWA KFOX KITF KITY LACR LEED LESJ LOST OFOX OPDS PHYL PPPP RAYA RWSS RSSF RWSS TFOX TOMZ

DEPERDUSSIN
MONOPLANE
G-AANH

DESIGNABILITY - see JORDAN

DESOUTTER
DESOUTTER 1
G-AAPZ

DIAMOND AIRCRAFT INDUSTRIES GMBH - see HOAC

DORNIER-WERKE AG - see BUCKER
EKW C-3605
G-DORN
DO.27
G-BMFG BNMK
DO.28/SKYSERVANT
G-ASUR BWCO BXTK
228
G-BUXT MAFE MAFI OMAF RGDT
328
G-BWIR BWWT BYHG BYMK BYML BYTY BZIF BZOG

DOUGLAS AIRCRAFT COMPANY INC/AIRCRAFT CORPN - also see McDONNELL DOUGLAS
AD-4 SKYRAIDER
G-RAID
DC-3/C-47 DAKOTA/SKYTRAIN
G-ALWC AMCA AMHJ AMPO AMPP AMPY AMPZ AMRA AMSM AMSN AMSV AMYJ ANAF APML BGCG BHUB DAKK DAKS
DC-6
G-APSA SIXC

DRAGON BALLOONS
DRAGON G77 HAFB
G-BKRZ

DRAGON LIGHT AIRCRAFT CO LTD
DRAGON Srs 150/200/250
G-MJLK MJSL MJUZ MJVY MMAC MMAE MMAI MMML MMNH MNJF

DRAYTON BALLOONS
DRAYTON B-56 HAFB
G-BITS

DRUINE including ROLLASON production

D.5 TURBI

G-AOTK APBO APFA

D.31 TURBULENT

G-AJCP APIZ APNZ APOL APTZ APUY APVN APVZ APWP ARBZ AREZ ARGZ ARIM ARJZ ARLZ ARMZ ARNZ ARRZ ARZM ASAM ASDB ASFX ASHT ASMM ASPU ASSY ASTA ATBS AVPC AWBM AWDO AWFR AWMR AWWT BFXG BGBF EGMA BKXR BLTC BUKH BVLU BWID OJJF

D.62 CONDOR

G-ARHZ ARVZ ASEU ASRB ASRC ATAU ATAV ATOH ATUG ATVW AVAW AVEX AVJH AVKM AVMB AVOH AVXW AWAT AWEI AWFN AWFO AWFP AWSN AWSP AWSS AWST AXGS AXGU AXGV AXGZ AYFC AYFD AYFE AYFF AYFG AYZS BADM BUOF OPJH YNOT

(SOCIÉTÉ) DYN'AÉRO

CR100

G-BZGY

MCR-01 BAN-BI/CLUB

G-BYEZ BYTM BZXG CUTE LMLV PGAC POOP TBEE TOOT

E

AA

ACROSPORT

G-BJHK BKCV BLCI BPGH BSHY BTAK BTWI BVVL OJDA TSOL VCIO

BIPLANE

G-ATEP AVZW BBMH BPUA BRUU PFAA PFAY

EAGLE - see AMERICAN AEROLIGHTS

EAVES (EUROPEAN)

MLB variants

G-BJDK BJFB BJFC BJIC FYDN FYFI

ECLIPSE

SUPER EAGLE

G-BGWZ

EDGAR PERCIVAL including LANCASHIRE AIRCRAFT COMPANY production

EP.9 PROSPECTOR

G-APWZ APXW ARDG

EDGLEY including BROOKLANDS/OPTICA production

OPTICA

G-BMPF BMPL BOPM BOPN BOPO BOPR TRAK

EDWARDS

HELICOPTER

G-ASDF

EH INDUSTRIES

EH-101

G-EHIL

EIPPER AIRCRAFT INC

QUICKSILVER

G-MBBM MBCK MBFO MBYM MJAM MJDU MJDW MJHU MJHX MJIR MJJK MJKH MJPV MJUO MJVP MJVU MJZL MMBU MMIL MMMG MMNB MMND MMSE MMWC MMYR MNCO MTDO MWDZ

EIRI.EINO RHIELA KY

PIK-20E

G-BGZL BHFR BHNP OCAT OFJC OPIK POPE SOAR

ELECTRAFLYER - see AMERICAN AEROLIGHTS

ELISPORT

CH-7 ANGEL

G-HALO

ELMWOOD

CA-05 CHRISTAVIA

G-MRED

EMBRAER

EMB-110 BANDEIRANTE

G-BGYT FLTY OBPL ODUB OFLT ONEW TABS

EMB-145 variants

G-EMBA EMBB EMBC EMBD EMBE EMBF EMBG EMBH EMBI EMBJ EMBK EMBL EMBM EMBN EMBO EMBP EMBS EMBT EMBU EMBV EMBW EMBX EMBY ERJA ERJB ERJC ERJD ERJE ERJF ERJG RJXA RJXB RJXC RJXD RJXE RJXF RJXG RJXH RJXI RJXJ RJXK

EMB-312 TUCANO

G-BTUC

ENGLISH ELECTRIC CO LTD including AVRO production

WREN

G-EBNV

CANBERRA

G-BURM BVIC BVWC BVXC

LIGHTNING

G-BTSY

ENSIGN

CROSSLEY RACER

G-BKRU

ENSTROM HELICOPTER CORPORATION

F-28

G-BAAU BAWI BBHE BBIH BBPN BBPO BBXO BDKD BHAX BPPL BRZG BSHX BSHZ BURI BWOV BXLV BXLW BXXB BXXW BYKF BZHI DICE MHCE MHCJ OABO SERA SNAZ WSEC

280 SHARK

G-BEYA BGWS BIBJ BPXE BRPO BSDZ BSLV BWSK BXEE BXFD BXRD BYSW CKCK COLL ECHO GKAT HDIX HYST IDUP MEYO MHCB MHCD MHCF MHCG MHCH MHCI MHCK MHCL OITV OJBB OJMF ONUP OPDM OTHE PALS PBYY REFI SHAA SHNN SHRK SHSS SHUU SOPP TOYS VETS WRFM WSKY ZZWW

480

G-BWMD GUAY HADA IGHH IJBB LADD LIVR OGHH OSKP OZAR PBTT PPAH TRUD WOOF

EoN

EoN AP.10 460 Srs.1A: G-APWL

ERCO incl ALON/FORNEY production

ERCOUPE 415: G-ARHB ARHC ARHF AROO AVIL AVTT BKIN BZKS BZNO COUP EGHB ERCO HARY ONHH

EUROCOPTER - see AÉROSPATIALE/SUD AVIATION/MBB
EC 120
G-BXYD BZHH CBHS CBJF CBNB ECZZ EMCM FEDA IGPW ISSY PDGE SCUR TBLY YSON ZZOE
EC 135
G-BZRM BZRS CCAU CHSU EMAS ETHU HARP KRNW NESV NWPS SASA SASB SPAU SUFF WMAS

EUROPA AVIATION
EUROPA
G-BVGF BVIZ BVJN BVKF BVLH BVLV BVOS BVOW BVRA BVUV BVVH BVVP BVWM BWCV BWDP BWDX BWEG BWFH BWFX BWGH BWIJ BWIV BWJH BWKG BWON BWRO BWUP BWVS BWWB BWYD BWRA BWZT BXCH BXDY BXEF BXFG BXGG BXHY BXII BXIJ BXLK BXLZ BXNC BXOB BXTD BXUM BYFG BYIK BYPM BYJI BYSA BZAM BZNY BZTH BZTI BZTN CBES CBHI CHAV CHEB CHET CHUG COPY CROY CUTY DAMY DAYI DAYS DEBR DLCB DONZ DRMM EENI EESA EIKY EMIN EMSI EOFS EORJ EURX FELL FIZY FLOR FLOX FLYT GIWT GBXS HOFC IANI IBBS ILUM IMAB INAV IOWE IVER IVET JAMY JHYS JOST JULZ JXWS KIMM KITS KITZ LABS LACE LAMM LEBE MFHI MIME MEGG NDOL NEAT NESA NHRJ NIGL OBEV OBJT ODJG ODTW OEZY OGAN OIZI OJHL OKEV OMIK OPJK OPRC OSLD OUHI OURO PATF PATS PATZ PEGY PLPM PTAG PTYE PUDS RATZ RBBB RICS RIKS RJWX RMAC ROBD RONA ROOV ROWI RWLY SAMY SELF SHSH SMDH SSGS SYCO TERN TKAY VKIT VPSJ WUFF WWWG XSDJ YURO ZORO ZTED

EUROWING LTD
GOLDWING
G-MBDG MBFZ MBPM MBPX MBZH MJAJ MJAY MJDP MJEG MJGK MJOE MJPO MJRL MJRO MJRS MJSY MJUT MJUU MJUY MJWB MJWS MMBN MMLE MMTZ MMWL MNNS MNZU

EVANS
VP-1
G-AYUJ AYXW BAAD BAFH BAJC BBXZ BCTT BDAH BDAR BDTB BDTL BDUL BEIS BEKM BFAS BFHX BFJJ BGEE BGFK BGLF BHMT BHYV BICT BIDD BIFO BKFI BLCW BLKK BLWT BMJM BVAM BVEL BVJU BVUT BWFJ PFAG PFAH PFAO PFAW ROSE TEDY
VP-2
G-BCVE BEFV BEHX BEVP BEYN BFFB BFYL BGFC BGPM BHXL BJVC BJZB BMSC BPBB BTAZ BTHJ BTSC BUGI BUKZ BVPM BXOC RASC

EVEKTOR-AEROTECHNIK
EV-97 EUROSTAR
G-CBIY CBJR CSMK GHEE NIDG

EVERETT ENGINEERING - see CAMPBELL
GYROPLANE
G-BIPI BKPK BMZN BMZP BMZS BOUU BOUX BSJW BTMV BTVB BUAI BUZC BWCK MICY OFRB OGOS ULPS

EXPERIENCE
TRIKE
G-MYLU

EXPERIMENTAL AVIATION
BERKUT
G-REDX

EXTRA FLUGZEUGBAU GMBH
EA.230/260
G-EXTR
EA.300
G-BZFR BZII DUKK ECCC EIII EXEA IICM IIDI IILI IIMI IISI IITI IIZI IXTI MIII RGEE SIII XCCC XTRR

EXTREME SARL
EXTREME/SILEX
G-BZKG

F

FAIRCHILD
24/ARGUS
G-AIZE AJOZ AJPI AJSN BCBH BCBL FANC RGUS

FAIREY AVIATION
FLYCATCHER
G-BEYB
FIREFLY
G-ASTL
FULMAR
G-AIBE
GANNET
G-BMYP
SWORDFISH
G-AJVH BMGC
ULTRA-LIGHT HELICOPTER
G-AOUJ OPJJ

FAIRTRAVEL - see PIEL

FALCONAR
F-9/F-11/F-12
G-AWHY AXDY AYEG BGHT ODEL TIMS WBTS

FARNELL
TRIKE
G-MJKO

FEWSDALE TIGERCRAFT
GYROPLANE
G-ATLH

F + W - see DE HAVILLAND

FIAT
G.46
G-BBII

FISHER
FP202U KOALA/SUPER KOALA
G-BTBF BUVL MMTY

FLAGLOR
SKY SCOOTER
G-BDWE

FLEET
80 CANUCK
G-FLCA

FLEXIFORM - see MAINAIR
HILANDER (Wing)
G-MJAN
SEALANDER (Wing)
G-MBBY MBGA MBIA MMFL MMGU
STRIKER (Wing)/SOLO & DUAL STRIKER
G-MBDE MBHK MBWF MBZO MJER MJFB MJFI MJIA MJIC MJIF MJJO MJMN MJMX MJTP MJVN MJWN MJYP MJZO MJZU MMAL MMAN MMAW MMAX MMCZ MMDK MMDN MMEJ MMFD MMFE MMFG MMFH MMFV MMFY MMGH MMGI MMHY MMJG MMKM MMMR MMNT MMPL MMPT MMRW MMWG MMWN MMWS MMYV MTFK
TRIKE
G-MBGL

FLIGHT DESIGN GmbH
CT2K
G-CBAI CBDH CBDJ CBEW CBEX CBIB CBIE CTCT DMCT MCOY POGO PRAH

FLYING K ENTERPRISES
EASY RAIDER
G-CBKF OESY SRII

FLYLIGHT AIRPORTS LTD
DOODLE BUG/TARGET
G-BZKH BZKI BZKJ

FLS
SPRINT
G-BVNU BXWU BXWV FLSI SAHI SCLX

FOCKE WULF - see PIAGGIO
FW 189
G-BZKY

FOKKER AIRCRAFT BV/FOKKER VFW NV --incl FAIRCHILD-HILLER production
D.VII
G-BFPL
D.VIII
G-BHCA
DR.1
G-ATJM BVGZ
E.III
G-AVJO
S.11 INSTRUCTOR
G-BEPV BIYU
F-27 FRIENDSHIP/FH-227
G-BAUR BCDN BCDO BHMW BHMY BMXD BNCY BNIZ BVOB CEXA CEXB CEXD CEXE CEXF CEXG JEAD JEAE JEAH JEAI
F.27-050 (Fokker 50)
G-UKTA UKTB UKTC UKTD UKTE UKTF UKTG UKTH UKTI
F.28-0070 (Fokker 70)
G-BVTE BVTF BVTG
F.28-100 (Fokker 100)
G-BVJA BVJB BVJC BVJD BXWE BXWF BYDN BYDO BYDP UKFA UKFB UKFC UKFD UKFE UKFF UKFG UKFH UKFI UKFJ UKFK UKFM UKFN UKFO UKFR

FOLLAND
GNAT
G-BVPP FRCE GNAT MOUR NAAT NATY RORI TIMM

FORNEY - see ERCOUPE

FOSTER-WIKNER
GM.1 WICKO
G-AFJB

(AVIONS) FOURNIER
RF3
G-ATBP AYJD BCWK BFZA BHLU BIIA BIPN BLXH BNHT
RF4D
G-AVHY AVKD AVLW AVNX AVNZ AVWY AWBJ AWEL AWEM AWGN AWLZ AYHY BHJN IIF BUPJ BXLN IVEL
RF5/RF5B SPERBER
G-AYME AZJC AZPF AZRK AZRM BACE BEVO BJXK BLAA BPWK KCIG RFSB SSWV
RF6B
G-BKIF BLWH BOLC
RF7
G-LTRF

FRED - see CLUTTON

FUJI
FA.200
G-BAPM BBGI BBNV BBRC BBZN BBZO BCFF BCKS BCKT BCNZ BDFR BDFS BEUK BFGO FUJI HAMI KARI KARY MCOX

GADFLY
HDW-1
G-AVKE

GAERTNER
AX4 SKYRANGER HAFB
G-BSGB

GARDAN including CAB & BARRITAULT production
GY-20 MINICAB
G-ATPV AVRW AWEP AWUB AWWM AZJE BANC BBFL BCER BCNC BCPD BDGB BGKO BGMJ BGMR BRGW TATT VERA
GY-80 HORIZON
G-ASJY ASZS ATGY ATJT AVMA AVRS AWAC AZAW AZRX AZYA BFAA BJAV BKNI BYBL BYME BYPE GYBO TIMY

GARDNER
T-M SCOUT
G-MJTD MTKM

GARLAND-BIANCHI - see PIEL

GAZEBO
AX6-65 HAFB
G-BCGP

GAZELLE - see SOUTHERN MICROLIGHT

GEMINI - see MAINAIR

GENERAL AIRCRAFT
GAL.42 CYGNET
G-AGBN

GENERAL AVIA
F22
G-FZZA

GLASER-DIRKS
DG-400
G-BLJD BLRM BNCN BNXL BPIN BPXB BRTW BYTG SBOM DGDG DGLM DIRK HAJJ INCA LEES OAPW ORTM
DG-500M/MB
G-BRRG BZYG
DG-600
G-KOFM
DG-800
G-BVJK BXSH BXUI BYEC DGCL DGIV MSIX ORIG

GLOBE
GC-1B SWIFT
G-AHUN ARNN

GLOSTER AIRCRAFT CO LTD including ARMSTRONG-WHITWORTH production
GLADIATOR
G-AMRK CBHO GLAD
METEOR variants
G-ARCX BPOA BWMF JETM LOSM

GOLD MARQUE SPORTS
GYR (Wing)
G-MJKO

GOULD-TAYLORCRAFT - see TAYLORCRAFT

GRANGER
ARCHEOPTERYX
G-ABXL

GRASSHOPPER including SERVOTEC
GRASSHOPPER: G-ARVN AWRP AXFM AZAU

GREAT LAKES - see OLDFIELD
2T-1A SPORT TRAINER
G-BIIZ BUPV

GREEN
S-25 HAFB
G-BSON

GREGA - see PIETENPOL

GRIFFITHS
GH.4
G-ATGZ

GROB-WERKE GMB & CO KG
G.109
:G-BIXZ BJVK BJZX BLMG BLUV BMCG BMFY BMGR BMLK BMLL BMMP BRCG BXSP BXXG BYJH CHAR DEWS DKDP IPSI KEMC KNEK LULU NDGC SAGA SAMG TACK UILD WAVE
G.115/HERON/TUTOR
G-BOPT BOPU BPKF BVHC BVHD BVHE BVHF BVHG BYDB BYFD BYUA BYUB BYUC BYUD BYUE BYUF BYUG BYUH BYUI BYUJ BYUK BYUL BYUM BYUN BYUO BYUP BYUR BYUS BYUT BYUU BYUV BYUW BYUX BYUY BYUZ BYVA BYVB BYVC BYVD BYVE BYVF BYVG BYVH BYVI BYVJ BYVK BYVL BYVM BYVN BYVO BYVP BYVR BYVS BYVT BYVU BYVV BYVW BYVX BYVY BYVZ BYWA BYWA BYWB BYWC BYWD BYWE BYWF BYWG BYWH BYWI BYWJ BYWK BYWL BYWM BYWN BYWO BYWP BYWR BYWS BYWT BYWU BYWV BYWW BYWX BYWY BYWZ BYXA BYXB BYXC BYXD BYXE BYXF BYXG BYXH BYXI BYXJ BYXK BYXL BYXM BYXN BYXO BYXR BYXS BYXT BYXX BYXY BYXZ BYYA BYYB MERF RAFA RAFB TAYI WIZB

GRUMMAN AIRCRAFT ENGINEERING
F-6F HELLCAT
G-BTCC
F-7F TIGERCA
G-RUMT
F-8F BEARCAT
G-RUMM
FM-2 WILDCAT
G-RUMW
TBM-3 AVENGER
G-BTDP

GRUMMAN-AMERICAN AVIATION CORPN including AMERICAN AVIATION, AMERICAN-GENERAL & GULFSTREAM-AMERICAN production
AA-1 YANKEE/TRAINER/LYNX:
G-AYHA AYLP AZKS BBFC BBWZ BCIL BCLW BDLS BDNW BDNX BERY BEXN BFOJ BTLP RUMN SEXY
AA-5/AG-5 TRAVELER/CHEETAH/TIGER
G-AZMJ AZVG BAFA BAJN BAJO BAOU BASG BASH BAVR BAVS BBBI BBCZ BBDL BBDM BBLS BBRZ BBSA BBUE BBUF BCCJ BCCK BCEE BCEF BCEO BCEP BCIJ BCIK BCLI BCLJ BCPN BCRR BDCL BDFY BDLO BEBE BEZC BEZF BEZG BEZH BEZI BFIJ BFIN BFLW BFLX BFPB BFTF BFTG BFVS BFXW BFXX BFZO BGCM BGFG BGFI BGPH BGVV BGVW BGVY BHKV BHLX BHZK BHZO BIAY BIBT BIPA BIPV BIVV BIWW BJAJ BJDO BKPS BLFW BLSF BMYI BNVB BOXU BOZO BOZZ BPIZ BSTR BTII BTUZ BXHH BXOO BXOX BXTT BYDX CCAT CHTA DAVO DINA DOEA DONI ERRY ESTE GAJB GIRY IDEA IFLI IRIS JAZZ JENN JNAS JUDY JWDG KINE LSFI MALC MILY MOGI MSTC NGBI NODE NODY NONI OABR OBMW OBSF OCAM ODAE ODAM OECH OMOG OPPL OPWK OSSF OSTC OSTU OTIG PAWS PING PORK PROP PURR RATE REEK RICA RICO ROWL RUBB TGER TYGA WINK WMTM ZARI ZERO
GA-7 COUGAR
G-BGNV BGON BGSY BLHR BOGS BOOE BOXR CYMA EENY FLII GABD GENN GOTC HIRE OOGA OOGI OOGO REAT SHIV TANI

GRYPHON SAILWINGS - see WASP/WILLGRESS
GRYPHON
G-MMYC

GULFSTREAM AEROSPACE CORPORATION
G159 GULFSTREAM I
G-BNCE
GULFSTREAM IV/V
G-DNVT HARF

GULFSTREAM-AMERICAN CORPORATION
- see GRUMMAN-AMERICAN

GYROFLIGHT - see BROOKLAND

HADLAND

WILLOW
G-MMMH

HALLAM

FLECHE
G-FLCT

HANDLEY PAGE LTD

O/400 Rep
G-BKMG
HP.39 GUGNUNC
G-AACN
HP.81 HERMES
G-ALDG
HP.137 JETSTREAM **-see BAe**

HANDLEY PAGE (READING) LTD

HPR.7 DART HERALD
G-APWA APWJ ASKK ASVO ATDS ATIG AVEZ AVPN BAZJ BBXJ BEYF BEYK CEAS CEXP

HAPI

CYGNET SF-2A
G-BRZD BWFN BXCA BXHJ BYYC CYGI

HARKER

DH/WASP
G-MJSZ

HATZ

CB-1
G-BRSY BXXH HATZ TIKO

HAWKER AIRCRAFT LTD -see W.A.R & including AVRO/CCF production

CYGNET
G-CAMM EBJI EBMB
AUDAX
G-BVVI
DEMON
G-BTVE
FURY (Biplane)
G-BKBB
TOMTIT
G-AFTA
HART
G-ABMR
HIND
G-AENP
NIMROD
G-BURZ BWWK
HURRICANE
G-AMAU BKTH BWHA BYDL HUPW HURI HURR HURY KAMM ROBT
TEMPEST
G-PEST TEMT
FURY/SEA FURY
G-AGHB BUCM BWOL CBEL
HUNTER
G-BNCX BUEZ BVGH BVMB BVVC BWAF BWFR BWFS BWFT BWGK BWGL BWGM BWGN BWIU BWKB BWOU BXFI BXKF BXNZ BZPB BZPC BZRH BZRI BZSE BZSF BZSR EGHH FFOX GAII HNTR HPUX HVIP KAXF PRII PSST SIAL TVII VETA

HAWKER SIDDELEY AVIATION incl DE HAVILLAND/BAe/RAYTHEON HAWKER production

HS.121 TRIDENT
G-ARPH ARPK ARPL ARPO ARPP ARPZ AVFB AVFE AVFG AVFH AVFJ AVFK AVFM AVYE AWZI AWZJ AWZK AWZM AWZO AWZP AWZR AWZS AWZU AWZX
HS.125
G-ARYB ARYC ASSM ATPD AWYE AXDM BGYR BLSM BLTP BOCB BTAB BWSY BYHM BZNR DBAL DEZC ETOM FANN GDEZ GIRA GMAB HCFR ICFR IFTC IFTE JETI LORI MKSS NCFR OCAA OHEA OJPB OLDD OMGD OMGE OWDB RCEJ SUFC SVLB TACE TCAP TCDI TSAM VIPI WBPR YUGO
HARRIER
G-CBCU CBGK VTOL

HEAD

Ax8-105 HAFB
G-UKUK

HEATH

PARASOL
G-AFZE

HEINTZ - see ZENAIR

HELIO

SUPER COURIER
G-BAGT BGIX

HELTON

LARK 95:
G-LARK

HILL - see MAXAIR

HILLER

UH-12 (360)
G-ASAZ ASTP ATKG BBAZ BEDK

HINDUSTAN

PUSHPAK
G-AVPO BXTO

HISPANO - see MESSERSCHMITT

HIWAY HANG GLIDERS LTD

DEMON (Wing)
G-MBEU MBFK MBIT MBUA MJAV MJDJ MJDR MJHM MJHV MJKF MJMD MJNK MJNT MJRP MJSO MJXY MJYX MJYY MMHD MMHP MMLH MMNW MMRH MMTD MNCA MTHD MWXE MYBN
EXCALIBUR (Wing)
G-MBAA
SKYTRIKE
G-MBAA MBCL MBDD MBFK MBIA MBIT MBJF MBKZ MBLM MBPU MBTE MBVS MBVV MBXF MBXJ MJAN MJAV MJCW MJDJ MJDR JMHV MJMA MJMD MJMS MJMT MJMU MJNK MJNT MJOU MJPE MJPP MJSO MJUM MJXY MJYY MMBS MMCV MMEF MMEI MMHL MMHP MMLH MMOO MMRH MMUR MNME MYBN
SUPER SCORPION (Wing)
G-MBGW MBJX MBVS MJCW MJKP MMEF MMHK MMHL
VULCAN (Wing)
G-MBIZ MJAP MMRY

HOAC FLUGZEUGWERKE incl DIAMOND production

DV-20 KATANA
G-BWEH BWFD BWFE BWFI BWFV BWGY BWGZ BWIO BWLP BWLS BWLT BWLV BWPY BWTA BWYM BXGH BXJV BXJW BXMZ BXOF BXPB BXPC BXPD BXPE BXTP BXTR BXTS BYFL BYMB KATA OBDA OSFA RIBS TENS
DA-40 STAR
G-CBFA CBFC MOPB OPHR

HOFFMANN FLUGZEUGBAU FRIESACH

H-36 DIMONA/HK-36 SUPER DIMONA
G-BKPA BLCV BNUX IMOK KOKL LIDA LIDR LYDA OMDG OMRG

HORNET MICROLIGHTS LTD

TRIKE
G-MBCX MBJL MJDA MJWN MMHD MMNM
INVADER (Trike)
G-MMHY
DUAL TRAINER/RAVEN (Combi)
G-MNRI MNRK MNRL MNRM MTGX MTHU MTJX MTMP MTMR MTRL MTXE MTXY MVHZ
R/RS (Combi)
G-MVUR MVUU MVYI MVYJ MVYK MVYL MVYN MVZW MWBH MWBM MWBN MWBP MWBR MWBS MWBU MWBW MWBX MWBY- MWDE MWDI MWEU MWEY MWKE

HOVEY

WD-II/III WHING DING
G-MBAB MNVO

HOWARD

SPECIAL T-MINUS
G-BRXS

HOWES

AX6 HAFB
G-BDWO

HUGHES TOOL CO/HELICOPTERS INC incl SCHWEIZER AIRCRAFT CORPORATION (269 wef 1986) & McDONNELL DOUGLAS (369) production

269 (Srs 300)
G-BAUK BAXE BMWA BOVX BOXT BPJB BPPY BRTT BSML BSVR BUEX BWAV BWDV BWNJ BWWJ BWZJ BXMY BXRP BXTL BXUP BZXJ DRKJ ECLI GINZ HFLA IBHH JMDI MARE OCJK ODNH OGJP OGOB OJAE OPCS OSLO OZAP PKPK PLOW PLPC REBL RHCB RIFB ROCR SAND SHCB SHPP STEP VNUS WARK WHRL XALP ZBHH
369 (Srs 500)
G-AYIA AZVM BIOA BPLZ BRTL BTRP CSPJ DADS DIZZ ERIS GASC GEEE HAUS HKHM HSOO IDWR JETZ JIVE LIBS LINC LOGO MRAJ NIPY OMDH ORRR OSOO OTDB SOOC SOOE SSCL SWEL TRUE VICE

HUNT

WING/AVON/EXPERIENCE/PEGASUS
G-BZRG BZTW BZUZ MGTR MMGT MNCA MWPT MYPO MYTV MYUR MYWE MYWH MYYE MYYJ MZCX MZCZ MZDZ-MZFE MZFF MZGH MZLB MZLK

HUNTAIR LTD

PATHFINDER
G-MBWG MBYL MJBZ MJDE MJDH MJFM MJJA MJOC MJTY MJUV MJWK MJXS MMBV MMCB MMDR

HUNTING PERCIVAL AIRCRAFT LTD - see PERCIVAL & including BRITISH AIRCRAFT CORPORATION (BAC) production

P.84 JET PROVOST/BAC.145/167 STRIKEMASTER
G-AOBU AYHR BESY BKOU BVEZ BVSP BVTC BWBS BWCS BWDR BWEB BWGF BWGS BWGT BWOF BWOT BWSG BWSH BWUW BWZZ BXBH BXBI BXDL BXFP BXFU BXFV BXFW BZRE BZRF FLYY JPRO JPTV JPVA KNOT PROV RAFI SARK TORE-UNNY UNVR VIVM

HYBRED - see MEDWAY

I

IAV-BACHAU - see YAKOVLEV

ICA

IS.28B2/M2
G-BKAB BKXN BMMV BMOM BROM TODD

I.C.P srl

MXP-740 SAVANNAH J(1)
G-CBBM

III

SKY ARROW
G-BXGT BYCY BYZR BZVT CIAO GULP IXIX ROME SKYG SKYT SUTN

ILYUSHIN

Il-2
G-BZVW BZVX

IMCO

CALLAIR A.9
G-TDFS

INTERAVIA

HAFB
70TA
G-BUUT
80TA
G-BZYT

ISAACS
FURY
G-ASCM AYJY BBVO BCMT BEER BIYK BKFK BKZM BMEU BTPZ BWWN BZAS BZNW PFAR RODI
SPITFIRE
G-BBJI BXOM

JABIRU AIRCRAFT (PTY) LTD
JABIRU SK/SPL/UL
G-BXAO BXNU BXSI BYBM BYBZ BYCZ BYFC BYIA BYIF BYIM BYJD BYJF BYKY BYNL BYNR BYNS BYSF BYTK BYTV BYYL BYYT BYZS BZAP BZDZ BZEN BZFI BZGT BZHR BZIV BZLV BZMC BZST BZSZ BZTY BZUL BZWK BZXN BZYK CBFZ CBGR CBIF CBJM CNAB COVE CSDJ DJAY DMAC DWMS ENRE EWBC GPAS HINZ IZDD JABA JABY JACO JAJP JAXS JBSP JPMA JSPL JUDD KKER LEEE LOIS LUMA LYPG MGCA MITT NIGC ODGS OGSA OJAB OMHP OPUS OZZI PBUS RODG RUFS RYAL SIMP THOT TUBB TULL UKOZ UJAB VJAB

JACKAROO AIRCRAFT - SEE THRUXTON

JODEL - see FALCONAR/ROBIN & incl CEA/SAN/WASSMER production
D.9 BEBE (including D.92 variants)
G-AVPD AWFT AXYU AZBL BAGF BDEI BDNT BGFJ BURE BZBZ KDIX
D.11 (including D.112/D.117/D.119 & AERO D.1190S variants)
G-ARDO ARNY ASJZ ASXY ATIN ATIZ ATJN ATWB AVPM AWFW AWMD AWVB AWVZ AWWI AXAT AXCG AXCY AXFN AXHV AXWT AXXW AXZT AYBP AYBR AYCP AYEB AYGA AYHX AYKJ AYKK AYKT AYMU AYWH AYXP AZFF AZHC AZII AZKP AZVL BAAW BAKR BAPR BARF BATJ BAUH BAZM BBPS BCGL BCGW BCLU BDBV BDDG BDIH BDJD BDMM BEDD BEZZ BFEH BFGK BFNG BFXR BGEF BGTX BGWO BHCE BHEL BHFF BHHX BHKT BHNL BHNX BIAH BIDX BIEO BIOU BIPT BITO BIVB BIVC BIWN BIYW BIZY BJOT BKAO BKIR BMIP BOOH BPFD BRCA BRVZ BVEH BVPS BVVE BWMB DAVE
D.18
G-BODT BRZO BSBP BSYA BTRZ BUAG BUPR BWVC BWVV BXFC TREK WIBB
D.120 PARIS-NICE
G-ASPF ASXU ATLV AVLY AVYV AXNJ AYGG AYLV AYRS AZEF AZGA AZLF BACJ BANU BCGM BDDF BDEH BDWX BFOP BGZY BHGJ BHNK BHPS BHXD BHXS BHZV BICR BIEN BJFM BJOE BJYK BKAE BKCW BKCZ BKGB BKJS BKPX BMDS BMID BMLB BMYU BOWP BYBE DIZO
D.140 MOUSQUETAIRE
G-ARDZ ARLX AROW ARRY ATKX AYFP BJOB BSPC BWAB DCXL OBAN REES TOAD
150 variants
G-ASKL ASRT AVEF AZBI BACL BFEB BHEG BHEZ BHVF BIDG BKSS BLAT BLXO BMEH BVSS BVST BZXH DISO EDGE FARR IEJH JDLI MASC OABB TIDS
DR.100/105/1050/1051 variants
G-ARFT ARRD ARRE ARXT ASXS ATAG ATEV ATFD ATGE ATHX ATIC ATJA ATLB ATWA AVGJ AVGZ AVHL AVJK AVOA AWEN AWUE AWVE AWWN AWWO AXLS AXSM AXUE AXUK AXUY AYEH AYEJ AYEV AYEW AYGD AYJA AYKD AYLC AYLF AYLL AYUT AYYO AYYT AYZK AZOU AZWF BAEE BDMW BEAB BEYZ BFBA BGBE BGRI BHHE BHOL BHSY BHTC BHUE BIOI BKDX BLKM BLRJ BLUL BOBG BPLH BTHH BTIW BXIO BXYJ BYCS BYFM DAST IOSI IOSO JODL JWBB JWIV SPOG
DR.200/220/221 variants
G-AVOM AYDZ BANA BFHR BHRW BLCT BLLH BMKF BUTH CPCD GOSS RRCU STEV
DR.250/253 variants
G-ATTM AWKP AWYL AXWV AYUB BJBO BKPE BOSM BSZF BUVM BXCG BYEH BYHP
DR.315/340/360 variants
G-AXDK AYCO AZIJ AZJN BGVB BICP BLAM BLGH BLHH BOEH BOZV BVYG BVYM BXOU DRSV DRZF KIMB

JORDAN AVIATION
DUET
G-MBWH MMKY MNIN

JURCA
MJ.2 TEMPETE
G-ASUS AYTV
MJ.5 SIROCCO
G-AZOS CLAX ORFC RECO

K & S
SA.102.5 CAVALIER
G-AZHH BCMJ BCKF BCRK BDKJ BDLY

KAY
GYROPLANE
G-ACVA

KEN BROCK
KB-2
G-BSEG BUYT BUZV BVMN BVUJ

KENSINGER
KF
G-ASSV

KIRK
SKYRIDER MLB
G-BJTF

KLEMM - see BA & BRITISH KLEMM
L.25
G-AAUP AAXK
KL.35
G-BWRD

KNIGHT - see PAYNE

KOLB
TWINSTAR
G-BUZT KOLB BYTA MWWM MYDP MYIK MYKB MYLN MYLP MYMI MYNY MYOG MYOO MYOR MYPC MYRA MYVA MYWP MYXS MZGJ MZZT

KRONFELD - see BAC

LA MOUETTE
PROFIL (Wing)
G-MVCK

LAFAYETTE
HI-NUSKI Mk.1
G-MBWI

LAKE AIRCRAFT CORPORATION
LA-4/LA-250/BUCCANEER RENEGADE/SKIMMER
G-BASO BOLL LAKE SKID

LAMBERT AIRCRAFT ENGINEERING
MISSION M212-100
G-XFLY

LANCAIR - see NEICO

LANCASHIRE AIRCRAFT - see EDGAR PERCIVAL

LANCASHIRE
MICRO-TRIKE
G-MJXX MJYW MJZO MMFG MMPL

LAVERDA - see AVIAMILANO

LAZAIR - see ULTRAFLIGHT

LAZER - see STEPHENS

LEARJET CORPORATION INC
LEARJET 35A
G-HUGG JETG LEAR LJET MURI OCFR RAFF
LEARJET 45
G-JRJR OLDC OLDJ OLDL OLDR

LEDERLIN
380L LADYBUG
G-AYMR

LEOPOLDOFF
L-6
G-BYKS
L-7
G-AYKS

LET - see YAKOVLEV
L-200A/D MORAVA
G-ASFD BNBZ
Z-37 CMELAK
G-AVZB KDLN

LETOV AIR
LK-2M SLUKA
G-MYRP MYRR MYUP MYVG MYVT MYXO MZBF MZBK MZDX MZES MZFC MZGF MZLY MZNZ MZOI MZOT MZOX XPBI

LE VIER
COSMIC WIND
G-ARUL BAER

LIGHTNING - see SOUTHDOWN

LILLIPUT BALLOONS UK
TYPE 1 MLB
G-HONY

LINDSTRAND BALLOONS LTD
Gas Balloon
AS-2
G-BYPC
HA Airship
HS-110
G-HSTH TRIB
HAB
LBL-9
G-BVRP
LBL-14
G-BWBB BWEO BWER BXAJ BXEP
LBL-21/RR-21
G-BVRL BYEY OJNB UNRL
LBL-25 CLOUDHOPPER
G-BVUI BXHM BYYJ BZKZ EECO OLAW OOER
LBL-31 AIR CHAIR
G-BVOJ BWHD BXIZ BXUH BZIH BZNV BZUK ELLE FFFT ONCB
LBL-42
G-BWCG
LBL-56
G-COSY XWWF
LBL-60
G-OERR
LBL-69
G-BVDS BVGG BVIR BWLA BYKA BZJY CBBX LBLI
LBL-77
G-BUBS BUWI BUZR BVPV BVRR BWAW BWBO BWEP BWFK BWKZ BWMH BWTU BXDR BYJG BYKW BYLW BYRZ BYYE BYYR BZBJ BZKE HERD HUNK ICEY ICKY G-MERE PATP
LBL-90
G-BVAG BVWW BVXG BVZT BWBT BWRV BWTN BWWE BWZU BXLF BXXO BXZF BXZI BYEP BZLU BZNA CBIM DUGI FLEW JEMY JIGS MRKT OBJB OSUP PATX PROF SJKR ULLS UNGE
LBL-105
G-BUUN BUYJ BUZJ BVDO BVON BVOO BVRU BWGA BWOK BWRZ BWSB BWTB BWWY BXHE BXHP BXJG BXSO BXUO BYFU BYIY BYJN BYJZ BYLX BZAG BZPV BZUD ENRI GULF HAPI ICOI ICOZ LPAD OAER ODDY OICO OMXS OPMT OUMC PIZZ ROMS RXUK SNAK VITL
LBL-120/A
G-BVLZ BWDM BWEA BZBL OGSS
LBL-150
G-BVEW BXCM BZTO OHRH
LBL-180
G-BVBM BVIX EVNT GVBF KNOB OTUP WIZD
LBL-203
G-BXGK
LBL-210
G-BVLL BVML BXNX BZDE FVBF HVBF JVBF NVBF OCBS SSLF WVBF
LBL-240
G-BXBL OGAV
LBL-260
G-PVBF
LBL-310
G-BZPE CBIW TVBF
LBL-317
G-YVBF
LBL-330
G-BXVE

SPECIAL SHAPES

SHAPE	REGISTRATION	SHAPE	REGISTRATION
BABY BEL	G-BXUG	BANANAS	G-OCAW
BIRTHDAY CAKE	G-WISH	BUDWEISER CAN	G-BXHN
BUNNY	G-FLUF	CAKE	G-BZNZ
DIET PEPSI CAN	G-DIET	FLOWERS	G-ODBN
NEWSPAPER	G-FFTT	PIG	G-PIGG
PINK PANTHER	G-PINX	RACING CAR	G-TKGR
SUN	G-BZIC	SYRUP BOTTLE	G-BXUB
TELEWEST SPHERE	G-BXHO	TULIPS	G-TULP

LOCKHEED AIRCRAFT CORPN/LOCKHEED-CALIFORNIA CO including CANADAIR production

10 ELECTRA
G-LIOA

414 HUDSON
G-BEOX

L.188 ELECTRA
G-BYEF CEXS CHNX FIJR FIJV FIZU LOFB LOFC LOFD LOFE LOFF LOFG OFRT

L.749 CONSTELLATION
G-CONI

L.1011 TRISTAR
G-IOIT

T-33A
G-BYOY TBRD WGHB

LORIMER

IOLAIRE: G-MZFI

LOVEGROVE - see BENSEN

AV-8 GYROPLANE
G-BXXR

LVG

C.VI
G-AANJ

LUSCOMBE AIRPLANE CORPORATION

8 SILVAIRE/MASTER/RATTLER
G-AFUP AFYD AFZK AFZN AGMI AHEC AICX AJAP AJJU AJKB AKPG AKTI AKTM AKTN AKTT AKUF AKUG AKUH AKUI AKUJ AKUK AKUL AKUM AKUP AKVP BNIO BNIP BPOU BPPO BPVZ BPZA BPZC BPZE BRDJ BRGF BRGG BRHX BRHY BRJA BRJK BRKA BROO BRPZ BRRB BRSW BRUG BSHH BSHI BSNE BSNT BSOE BSOX BSSA BSTX BSUD BSYF BSYH BTCH BTCJ BTDF BTIJ BTJA BTJB BTJC BUAO BUKT BUKU BULO BVEP BVGW BVGY BVMD BWOB DAIR EITE KENM LUSC LUSI LUST NIGE ROTI SAGE YRIL

M

MACAIR

MERLIN
G-BWEN

McCANDLESS

M.4 GYROPLANE
G-ARTZ ATXX AXVN BVLE

McCULLOGH

J.2
G-ORVB

McDONNELL DOUGLAS CORPORATION

DC-10
G-BYDA DMCA DPSP TAOS TDTW

McDONNELL-DOUGLAS HELICOPTERS - see MD HELICOPTERS

MAINAIR SPORTS LTD -see PEGASUS/FLASH

BLADE
G-BYHN BYHO BYHS BYJB BYKC BYKD BYLK BYNM BYON BYOS BYOW BYRO BYRP BYRR BYTL BYTU BYZB BZAA BZAL BZDC BZDD BZEG BZEL BZHY BZFO BZFS BZIR BZJL BZJN BZLM BZMS BZNS BZPA BZPN BZPZ BZRB BZRW BZTM BZTR BZTU BZTV BZTX BZUB BZUM BZUN BZWB BZXM BZXT CBAD CBBG CBDD CBDL CBDN CBDP CBEM CBET CBGM CBGT CBHG CBHJ CBHM CBJT CBKM ENVY JAIR JMAN JOOL MAIN MYRC MYRD MYTD MYTG MYTL MYTU MYTW MYUC MYUM MYUN MYVB MYVE MYVH MYVO MYVY MYVZ MYXJ MYXM MYXN MYYA MYYG MYYH MYYW MYYY MZAA MZAB MZAE MZAF MZAG MZAI MZAJ MZAL MZAM MZAP MZAR MZAS MZAT MZAY MZAZ MZBA MZBL MZCC MZCD MZCE MZCG MZCN MZCU MZDF MZDK MZDT MZEB MZED MZEG MZEJ MZEW MZFB MZFS MZFZ MZGI MZGW MZIH MZIR MZIS MZIT MZIW MZJA MZJD MZJK MZJV MZJX MZJZ MZKG MZKJ MZKK MZKM MZKO MZKV MZKZ MZLC MZLZ MZMB MZMD MZMJ MZML MZMM MZMP MZMV MZMY MZNC MZNI MZNJ MZNK MZNL MZNO MZOC MZOF MZOP MZOR MZPH MZSD MZSM MZZY NOOK OBMI OHVA OYES REED REEF RIKI RINN RUFF RYPH SHUF WAKE WLMS

GEMINI/FLASH (Combi)
G-MJYF MJZD MMDP MMKL MMOW MMPO MMSP MMUO MMUT MMUW MMVP MMWA MMXC MMXD MMXG MMXJ MMXK MMXL MMXT MMXU MMXV MMZA MMZB MMZC MMZE MMZF MMZJ MMZK MMZM MMZV MNAC MNAE MNBD MNBF MNBG MNBN MNBP MNBR MNBS MNBT MNBV MNBW MNCF MNCG MNCJ MNDF MNEF MNEG MNEH MNET MNEV MNEY MNFE MNFF MNFH MNFM MNFN MNFP MNGK MNGL MNGM MNGN MNGT MNGU MNGW MNHZ MNIA MNIE MNIF MNIG MNIH MNII MNIP MNIX MNIZ MNJU MNLI MNLX MNLY MNMG MNMI MNMJ MNMV MNNF MNNI MNNJ MNNK MNNL MNNR MNNV MNPC MNPG MNRW MNRX MNRY MNSA MNSI MNSJ MNSR MNTI MNTS MNTU MNTV MNTW MNTX MNTZ MNUA MNUF MNUG MNUO MNUR MNUY MNVT MNVU MNVV MNVW MNWD MNWI MNWZ MNXS MNXU MNYJ MNZB MNZC MNZD MNZE MNZF MTAB MTAC MTAE MTAF MTAG MTAH MTAR MTBD MTBH MTBI MTBJ MTBW MTBX MTBY MTCC MTCE MTCU MTCW MTDF MTDR MTDW MTDY MTEJ MTEK MTEN MTEY MTFF MTFI MTFJ MTGA MTGH MTGO MTHW MTHZ MTIA MTIB MTIL MTIM MTIN MTJA MTJB MTJC MTJD MTJE MTJK MTJL MTJM MTJT MTJV MTJW MTJZ MTKN MTKV MTKW MTKX MTKZ MTLB MTLC MTLD MTLL MTMA MTMC MTML MTMT MTMV MTMW MTNC MTNG MTNH MTNI MTNJ MTNL MTNM MTNX MTNY MTPA MTRA MTRZ MTSC MTTI MTTM MTTP MTTR MTTS MTTW MTUU MTUV MTVH MTVI MTVJ MTWF MTWG MTWR MTWS MTWX MTXM MTXP MTXS MTXZ MTZG MTZH MTZL MTZM MTZO MTZV MTZW MTZX MTZY MTZZ MVAA MVAB MVAD MVAO MVAP MVBD MVBF MVBG MVBH MVBI MVBK MVBL MVBM MVBN MVBO MVCE MVCF MVCY MVDA MVDT MVEH MVEJ MVEK MVEL MVEO MVEP MVER MVES MVET MVEV MVEW MVGM MVHE MVHF MVHG MVHH MVIB MVIC MVLH MVIX MVIY MVIZ MVJA MVJC MVJE MVJL MVKC MVLL MVLR MVMO MVMR MVMT MVMU MVMV MVMX MVMY MVMZ MVNM MVNW MVNX MVNY MVNZ MVOB MVOF MVON MVOR MVPA MVPB MVPD MVPE MVPI MVPO MVRA MVRB MVRC MVRD MVRM MVSN MVSO MVSP MVST MVSV MVTC MVUA MVXB MVXC MVXR MVXS MVYS MVZS MWAB MWAU MWCE MWCW MWDJ MWEL MWGG MWHO MWHR MWIA MWIG MWIH MWIV MWJY MWLP MWLT MWLX MWMM MWMS MWMT MWMX

MWMY MWNE MWNS MWNT MWNU MWOJ MWOK MWOL MWPA MWPB MWPC MWPD MWPF MWRB MWRC MWRD MWRE MWRF MWRG MWRH MWRI MWRJ MWRR MWSL MWSM MWTG MWTH MWTO MWTR MWTY MWTZ MWVN MWVO MWVR MWVS MWVT MWVW MWVY MWVZ MWWB MWWC MWWI MWWJ MWWK MWWN MWXB MWXC MWXL MWXN MWXN MWXO MWXU MWXV MWYA MWYG MWYH MWYL MWYT MWYV MWZC MWZG MWZL MWZN MYAO MYAS MYAU MYBJ MYCK MYCR MYCS MYDV MYEU MYFP MYFR MYFU MYGZ MYHF MYHL MYHN MYHX MYIH MYIV MYIY MYJB MYJC MYJM MYKC MYKG MYKH MYKV MYLG MYLR MYMK MYMO MYMV MYND MYOM MYOW MYPE MYPW MYSJ OLJT

GEMINI (Trike)

G-MBST MBTF MJYP MMAJ MMAR MMIR MMIV MMJT MMKM MMLP MMMD MMOB MMRP MMRW MMSC MMSO MMTL MMTX MMXW MNGB MNMC MNUM MTBY

MERCURY

G-MWVK MWXF MWXJ MWXK MWZA MYAI MYAV MYCJ MYCL MYCN MYCV MYDC MYGJ MYJN MYJR MYKI MYKW MYKX MYKY MYLS MYML MYMT MYNC MYNF MYNJ MYOB MYOF MYOV MYOX MYPD MYPV MYRW MYSG MYSZ MYTB MYTK MYTX MYUB MYUD MYUE MYUK MYUW MYVS MYWA MYYU MZAK MZCO

RAPIER

G-BYBV BYOZ BZAB BZUF BZWR MZEP MZEV MZFD MZGL MZHJ MZHL MZIL MZIM MZJE MZKN MZND MZNU MZON YARR

SCORCHER SOLO

G-MNDD MNNM MNPV MNPY MNPZ MNRE MNRF MNRG MNRZ MYFT MZKI MZKN

STARLET

G-MYLT

TRI-FLYER (Trike)

G-MBCJ MBGA MBHK MBIZ MBPG MBPZ MBUK MBZA MBZO MJEE MJEY MJFK MJHR MJIF MJJO MJMN MJMR MJPE MJTP MJXE MJYV MJYX MJZU MMAL MMAN MMCZ MMDK MMDN MMDT MMEJ MMFD MMFE MMFK MMJG MMKR MMLI MMMB MMNW MMTD MMUH MMWG MMWN MMYV MNIW MNJD MNJG MNUI MNXB MVBC

MAINAIR/FLEXIFORM

RAPIER 1+1 (Combi)

G-MJYV

MALMO - see BÖLKOW

MANNING-FLANDERS

MF.1

G-BAAF

MANTA

PFLEDGE (Wing)

G-MBNY

MANUEL

LADYBIRD

G-MJPB

MARQUART

MA.5 CHARGER

G-BHBT BVJX

MARTIN

MONOPLANE

G-AEYY

MASQUITO

MASQUITO M.58

G-MASX MASY MASZ

MAULE AIRCRAFT CORPORATION

M-5 LUNAR ROCKET

G-BHJK BICX BIES BPMB BVFT BVFZ KRIS NHVH OJGT RAGG RAIN RJWW

M-6 SUPER ROCKET

G-BKGC MOUL

M(XT)-7 SUPER/STAR ROCKET/STARCRAFT

G-BSKG BSKO BTMJ BTWN BTXT BUEP BUXD BVIK BVIL BZDT CROL GROL HIND ITON JREE LOFM OMOL

MAX HOLSTE

MH.1521M BROUSSARD

G-BWGG BWLR CBGL YYYY

MAXAIR

DRIFTER

G-MYBB

HUMMER

G-MJZX MMAP MNIM

MBB

Bö.105

G-AZOR BAMF BATC BCXO BFYA BGKJ BTHV BTKL BUXS CDBS DNLB ESAM EYNL NAAA NAAB PASB PASG PASX SPOL THLS WMAA WOSY WYPA

BK.117

G-DCPA

MD HELICOPTERS INC

MD 500N

G-NOTR

MD 600N

G-BZTZ ODOD PEPL

MD EXPLORER

G-BXZK EHMS GMPS HPOL KAAT LNAA SUSX WMID WPAS YPOL

MCDONNELL DOUGLAS HELICOPTER CO - see HUGHES

MEA

MISTRAL TRAINER

G-MBET MBOH MBUS MMIB

MEDWAY MICROLIGHTS LTD - see RAVEN/SOUTHDOWN

ECLIPSE R

G-BYBO BYXV BYXW BZGE BZWI OBRI

HALF PINT (Trike)

G-MMSZ MMZI MNDE MNEK MNJV MNLW MNTT MNVL

HYBRED (Trike/Combi/R44XLR)

G-BYBJ BYRH MGOM MJVE MMEK MMKG MMKH MNCU MNCV MNEI MNFW MNJK MNMN MNXO MTFC MTJG MTJP MTLX MTNE MTNF MTUX MVCD MVDB MVDJ MVEE MVGB MVGY MVKB MVPF MVPG MVPL MVRY MVRZ MVSR MVUD MVVG MVVH MVVI MVWV MVXD MVXE MVXI MVXJ MVXM MVYP MVYR MVZO MWBJ MWCX MWCY MWCZ MWGC MWIK MWIL MWJP-MWJR MWJX MWLB MWLS MWRM MWSS MWST MWSU MWVU MYRI MYVV MYVX MZME

PUMA SPRINT

G-MMJM MWBI

RAVEN

G-MVIF

REBEL

G-BYPP BYSS

(SOCIÉTÉ) MENAVIA - see PIEL

MESSERSCHMITT - see NORD & incl HISPANO production

Bf.109
G-BWUE BYDS

MICKLEBURGH

L107
G-BZVC

MICRO AVIATION

B-22 BANTAM
G-BXZU BZYS MZEY MZLX

MICRO BIPLANE AVIATION (MBA)

TIGER CUB
G-MJRU MJSP MJSU MJSV MJUC MJUF MJUH MJUW MJWF MJWJ MJXD MJXF MJYJ MJZE MMAG MMBH MMBT MMCX MMFN MMFS MMFT MMGF MMGL MMHN MMIE MMIH MMIM MMIX MMJV MMKP MMLB MMOI MMSW MMUM MNJC MNKM MWFT

MICROFLIGHT AIRCRAFT LTD

SPECTRUM
G-MVJM MVSU MVWX MWCG MWHD MWKW MWKX MWOF MWPG MWPH MWTD MWTE MWWR MWWX MYAY

MIDLAND ULTRALIGHTS LTD

SIROCCO
G-MNDU MNDV MNDW MNRT MTJN MTRC MVSM

MIGNET

HM.14/HM.19 POU-DU-CIEL
G-ADRG ADRX ADRY ADVU ADXS ADYV ADZW AEBB AEEH AEFG AEGV AEHM AEJZ AEKR AEMY AEOH AFFI BWRI MYSI
HM.293
G-AXPG
HM-1000 BALERIT
G-MRAM MYDZ MYXL MZIX MZLI MZMW MZPB MZTA

MIKOYAN AVIATION including WSK-PZL

MiG-15 (Lim-2)
G-BMZF
MiG-17 (Lim 5)
G-BWUF
MiG-21
G-BRAM

MILES AIRCRAFT LTD

M.2H HAWK MAJOR
G-ADMW
M.2L HAWK SPEED SIX
G-ADGP
M.3 FALCON
G-AEEG
M.5 SPARROWHAWK
G-ADNL
M.11A WHITNEY STRAIGHT
G-AERV AEUJ
M.12 MOHAWK
G-AEKW
M.14A HAWK TRAINER 3
G-AFBS AHUJ AIUA AJRS AKAT AKKR AKKY AKPF ANWO
M.17 MONARCH
G-AFJU AFLW AFRZ
M.18
G-AHKY
M.38/48 MESSENGER
G-AGOY AHUI AIEK AILL AJOC AJOE AJWB AKBO AKEZ AKIN AKIS AKVZ ALAH
M.65 GEMINI
G-AKDK AKEK AKEL AKER AKGD AKGE AKHP AKHW AKHZ AKKB AKKH
M.75 ARIES
G-AOGA
M.100 STUDENT
G-APLK MIOO

MILLS

MH-1
G-OMHI

MIRAGE - see ULTRAFLIGHT

MITCHELL

WING B-10
G-MMJA
WING U-2
G-MMNS

MITCHELL-PROCTER - see PROCTER

KITTIWAKE
G-ATXN AWGM BBRN BBUL

MONG

SPORT
G-BTOA

MONNETT

MONI
G-BMVU INOW MONI TRIM
SONERAI
G-BGEH BGLK BICJ BJBM BJLC BKDC BKNO BLAI BMIS BOBY BSGJ BVCC CCOZ LOWE PFAT RILY

MONOCOUPE

90A
G-AFEL

MONTGOMERIE-BENSEN - see BENSEN & PARSONS

MOONEY AIRCRAFT CORPORATION

M.20/M.252
G-APVV ASTH ASUB ATOU AWLP BCJH BDTV BHBI BHJI BIBB BIWR BJHB BKMA BKMB BPCR BPFC BSXI BVZY BWJG BWTW BXML BYDD BYEE CERT DBYE DESS DEST DPUK FLYA GCKI GJKK JAKI JDIX JENA MALS MUNI OBAL ODJH OEAC OJAC OJJB OONE OOOO OPWS OSUS RAFW ZZIP

MORANE-SAULNIER - see DE HAVILLAND/FIESELER & including GEMS/MORANE/SEEMS & SOCATA production

TYPE N
G-AWBU

MS.315
G-BZNK

MS.502/505
G-BIRW BPHZ
MS.733 ALCYON
G-MSAL SHOW
MS.880/885/887/892/894 RALLYE/GALERIEN/GALOPIN
G-ARXW ASAT ASAU AVIN AVPK AVTV AVVJ AVZX AWAA AWKT AWOA AWYX AXCL AXCM AXCN AXGC AXGE AXHS AXHT AXOH AXOS AXOT AYDG AYET AYRH AYTA AYYX AZEE AZGI AZGL AZKC AZKE AZMZ AZUT AZVF AZVH AZVI AZYD BAAI BAOG BAOH BAOJ BAOM BBAK BBED BBGC BBHX BBLM BCAC BCLT BCOR BCST BCUL BCVC BCXB BDEC BDWH BECA BECB BECC BEIL BERA BERC BETO BEVB BEVC BEVW BFAK BFDF BFGS BFTZ BGKC BGMT BGPZ BGSA BGZO BHWK BIAC BIIK BIOR BIRB BJDF BKBF BKGA BKGT BKJF BKOA BKUT BKVA BKVB BLGS BLIY BOJL BPJD BRDN BTIU BTOW BTUG BUGX BUKR BVAN BVWA BWWG BXZT BYPN BZNX EISO EXIT FARM FOSY GIGI HENT KHRE MELV OACI OIAN OMIA PIGS VAJT WCEI

MORRIS MOTORS LTD - see DE HAVILLAND

MOSSCRAFT
MA.1/MA.2
G-AFHA AFJV

MOTH CORPORATION - see DE HAVILLAND

MOTO-DELTA - see CENTRAIR

MOULT
(Trike)
G-MTFK

MOYES ULTRASPORTS LTD
MEGA (Wing)
G-MZCL

MSS - see EUROWING

MUDRY - see CAARP

MURPHY AIRCRAFT MANUFACTURING LTD
MAVERICK
G-BYCV MZJJ MZJS MZLE ONFL
REBEL
G-BUTK BVHS BWCY BWFZ BWLL BYBK BZFT CBFK DIKY LJCC YELL
RENEGADE/SPIRI
G-BTHN BTKB BWPE BYBU FIRZ MGOO MVZP MVZX MWAJ MWDM MWGF MWKA MWMW MWNF MWNR MWOO MWPS MWPZ MWUH MWVP MWWD MYAM MYAZ MYCO MYFM MYJP MYRK MYUF MYXR MZIP MZIZ NINE RCMC RENE TBAG TBMW

N

NANCHANG - see YAKOVLEV

NASH - see PROCTER

NAVAL AIRCRAFT FACTORY
N3N-3
G-ONAF

NEICO
LANCAIR 235/320/IV
G-BSPX BSRI BUNO BUST CBAF FOPP PJMT UILE

NICOLLIER
HN.700 MENESTREL
G-BVHL MINS

NIEUPORT
SCOUT 17/23: G-BWMJ

NIMROD - see AIRWAVE

NOBLE HARDMAN AVIATION LTD
SNOWBIRD
G-BZYV MTXL MTXU MVCI MVCJ MVIL MVIM MVIN MVIO MVOI MVOJ MVOL MVYT MVYV MVYW MVYX

NOORDUYN - see NORTH AMERICAN

NORD - see SNCAC
1002 PINGOUIN
G-ASTG ASUA ATBG
1101 NORALPHA
G-ATDB ATHN BAYV SMD
1203 NORECRIN
G-BAYL BEDB BHXJ
3202
G-BIZK BIZM BPMU
3400
G-BOSJ

NORMAN
NAC-1 FREELANCE
G-NACA NACI
NDN-1 FIRECRACKER/TURBO FIRECRACKER
G-NDNI
NAC-6 FIELDMASTER/FIREMASTER
G-NACL NACO NACP NRDC

NORTH AMERICAN - see LOEHLE & including CCF/FENNEC production)
B-25 MITCHELL
G-BWGR BYDR
F-86 SABRE
G-SABR
P-51 MUSTANG
G-BIXL BTCD HAEC MSTG PSIC SIRR SUSY
NA-64 YALE
G-BYNF
OV-10B BRONCO
G-BZGK BZGL
T-6/AT-16 HARVARD/TEXAN
G-AZBN AZSC BBHK BDAM BGHU BGOR BGPB BICE BIWX BJST BKRA BMJW BRBC BRLV BRVG BSBG BTXI BWUL BZHL CTKL DDMV ELMH HRVD JUDI RAIX TSIX TVIJ

T-28/A TROJAN/FENNEC
G-TROY

NOSTALGAIR
N.3 PUP
G-BVEA

NOTT-CAMERON
ULD-1/2/3 HAFB
G-BLJN BNXK NOTT

NOVA
VERTEX
G-BYLI BYZT BZVI
PHOCUS
G-BZYI
PHILOU
G-BZXI
X LARGE 37
G-BZJI

OLDFIELD
BABY LAKES
G-BBGL BGEI BGLS BKCJ BKHD BMIY BRKO BTZL BWMO POND

OMEGA BALLOONS
HAFB
0-20
G-AXMD
56
G-AYAL
84
G-AXJB AXVU

OPTICA - see EDGLEY

ORD-HUME - see LUTON

ORIENTAL
MLB
G-BINY

ORLICAN
L-40 META-SOKOL
G-APUE APVU AROF

OSPREY (CHOWN)
MLB variants
G-BJID BJLE BJND BJNH BJPL BJRA BJRG BJTN BJTY BJUE BJUU FYAV FYBD FYBE FYBF FYBG FYBH FYBI FYBJ FYCL FYCV FYCZ FYDF FYDO FYDS FYEV FYFN

PAKES
JACKDAW
G-MBOF

PANTHER - see MAINAIR/SOLAR WINGS/ULTRASPORTS

PARKER
CA-4
G-AFIU

PARNALL
ELF
G-AAIN

PIXIE
G-EBJG

PARSONS including MONTGOMERIE production
GYROCOPTER/GYROPLANE
G-BPIF BTFE BUWH IIXX IVYS UNIV

PARTENAVIA COSTRUZIONI AERONAUTICHE S.p.A
P.64B OSCAR
G-BMDP
P.68B/C VICTOR
G-BCDK BFBU BGXJ BHBZ BHJS BIFZ BMOI ENCE FJMS HUBB KIMK KWIK OLMA ONCM ORVR PART SAMJ UNIT

PAYNE
AX6-62 HAFB
G-AZRI BFMZ

PAYNE KNIGHT
TWISTER
G-APXZ BRAX

PAZMANY
PL-2
G-OPAZ
PL-4/A
G-BMMI BRFX FISK PAZY PLIV

PEARSON
MLB
G-BIXX

PEGASUS AVIATION - see CYCLONE AIRSPORTS
QUANTUM 15 variants
G-BYEU BYDM BYDZ BYEW BYFF BYFG BYIS BYIZ BYJK BYKT BYLC BYMF BYMI BYMT BYND BYNO BYOG BYOV BYPB BYPJ BYPL BYRJ BYRU BYSR BYSX BYTC BYYN BYYP BYYY BZAI BZBR BZED BZGZ BZHN BZHO BZIM BZIW BZJF BZJO BZJZ BZKT BZLL BZLX BZLZ BZMI BZMW BZNB BZNC BZNM BZOC BZOD BZOE BZOO BZOU BZOV BZRJ BZRP BZSA BZSG BZSI BZSM BZSS BZSX BZUC BZUE BZUI BZUX BZVJ BZVV BZWS BZWU BZXV BZXX BZYN CBAY CBBB CBBD CBBN CBBP CBBZ CBCD CBCF CBCX CBDX CBDZ CBEN CBEU CBEV CBGG CBHK CBHN CBHY CBIZ CBJO DINO DSLL EDMC EMLY EOFW FFUN JAWC JGSI KICK MCEL MCJL MDBC MGDL MGDM MGEF MGFK MGGG MGGV MGMC MGTG MROC MSPY MYLC MYLE MYLH MYLI MYLK MYLL MYLM MYLZ MYMB MYMC MYMD MYMX MYNB MYNK MYNL MYNN MYNO MYNP MYNR MYNS MYNT MYNV MYNZ MYOU MYPH MYPI MYPN MYPX MYPY MYRF MYRM MYRN MYRS MYRT MYRY MYRZ MYSB MYSC MYSR MYSW MYSX MYSY MYTI MYTJ MYTN MYUO MYUU MYUV MYVC MYVJ MYVK MYVM MYVR MYWG MYWI MYWJ MYWK MYWL MYWO MYWR MYWT MYWU MYWW MYWX MYWY MYXE MYXT MYXW MYXX MYXZ MYYB MYYC MYYI MYYK MYYN

MYYX MYZB MYZJ MYZK MYZL MYZM MYZY MZAN MZAW MZAX MZBB MZBC MZBI MZBM MZBO MZBT MZBY MZCI MZCJ MZCM MZCR MZCV MZCY MZDB MZDC MZDD MZDE MZDH MZDN MZDU MZDV MZDY MZEC MZEE MZEH MZEM MZET MZEX MZEZ MZFG MZFM MZFV MZGG MZGK MZGN MZGO MZGV MZHI MZHK MZHN MZHP MZIB MZIC MZIE MZIF MZIJ MZIK MZIU MZJG MZJH MZJN MZJO MZJT MZJW MZJY MZKA MZKD MZKF MZKL MZKX MZKY MZLA MZLD MZLF MZLH MZLJ MZLN MZLT MZLV MZLW MZMC MZMF MZMG MZMH MZNP MZMN MZMT MZNB MZNG MZNR MZNS MZNT MZOD MZOG MZOJ MZOS MZOV MZOW MZPD MZRC MZRH MZRM MZSC NAPO OAKS OAMF OBJP OELD OLDM OLFB OTJH PEGA PIXI PRSI REDC REPH RUSA SITA SMBM TBBC TRAM TUSA WHEE

QUASAR variants

G-MWHT MWHU MWHV MWIM MWIU MWIW MWIX MWIY MWJD MWJH MWJI MWJJ MWJK MWJS MWJT MWJU MWJV MWLH MWLI MWLJ MWLK MWMI MWMJ MWMK MWML MWNK MWNL MWOM MWOP MWPU MWSH MWSI MWTK MWTL MWVM MWXG MWXH MWYI MWYJ MWZD MWZE MWZF MWZO MWZP MWZR MWZS MYAK MYBD MYBE MYBT MYCE MYCF MYEK MYEM MYEN MYEO MYFK MYFL MYIM MYIN MYIO MYJJ MYJK MYJS MYJT MYJU MYKP MYKR MYKS MYTR MYXD MZMA MZPW REKO

PENN-SMITH

GYROPLANE

G-AXOM

PERCIVAL AIRCRAFT CO/LTD - see HUNTING

P.1 GULL

G-ACGR ADPR

P.6 MEW GULL

G-AEXF

P.10 VEGA GULL

G-AEZJ

P.16 Q SIX

G-AFFD

P.28/31/34/44 PROCTOR

G-AHTE AHWO AKIU AKZN ALCK ALJF ANPP ANXR

P.40 PRENTICE

G-AOKH AOKL AOKO AOKZ AOLK AOLU APIT APIU APIY APJB APPL

P.56 PROVOST

G-ASMC AWPH AWRY AWVF BDYG BKFW BLIW KAPW MOOS TMKI

P.57/66 PRINCE/SEA PRINCE/PEMBROKE

G-AMLZ BNPH BNPU BXES DACA GACA RACA

PEREIRA

OSPREY

G-BEPB BVGI GEOF PREY

PHANTOM - see SKYRIDER

PHILLIPS

ST.1 SPEEDTWIN

G-DPST EMNI GPST

PHOENIX - see CURRIE WOT/ROLLASON

LUTON LA-4/A MINOR/PARKER CA-4/PHOENIX DUET

G-AFIR AMAW ARIF ARXP ASAA ASEA ASEB ASML ASXJ ATCJ ATCN ATFW ATKH ATWS AVDY AVUO AWIP AWMN AXGR AXKH AYDY AYSK AYTT AZHU AZPV BANF BBCY BBEA BCFY BDJG BIJS BKHR BRWU

LA-5A MAJOR

G-ARAD

PIAGGIO including FOCKE WULF production

P.149

G-BPWW RKD RORY

P.166

G-APWY

PICCARD

HAFB:

G-ATTN

AX6

G-AWCR AZHR

PIEL incl COOPAVIA, MENAVIA, ROUSSEAU, SCINTEX production & BINDER, FAIRTRAVEL variants

CP.301/328 EMERAUDE

G-APNS ARDD ARRS ARUV ASCZ ASLX ASMT ASVG ASZR AXXC AYCE AYEC AYTR AZGY AZYS BBKL BCCR BDCI BDDZ BDKH BHRR BIDO BIJU BIVF BKFR BKNZ BKUR BLHL BLRL BPRT BSVE BXAH BXYE DENS PIEL SAZZ

CP.1310/1315/1320 SUPER EMERAUDE

G-ASMV ASNI BANW BCHP BGVE BHEK BJCF BJVS BLXI BXRF SAFI

PIETENPOL including GREGA

AIR CAMPER

G-ADRA BBSW BKVO BMDE BMLT BNMH BPOL BRXY BSVZ BUCO BUXK BUZO BVYY BWAT BWVB BXZO BYFT BYKG BYLD BYZY DAYZ ECOX EDFS IMBY OFFA OHAL OPJS PCAF PIET RAGS SILS SLOW TARN VALS

PIK -- see EIRI/SIREN

PILATUS AIRCRAFT LTD

P.2

G-BLKZ BONE CJCI PTWO

P.3

G-BTLL

PC.6 PORTER

G-BYNE WGSC

PIPER AIRCRAFT CORPORATION - see TED SMITH & including TAYLOR AIRCRAFT CO.LTD & THE NEW PIPER AIRCRAFT INC production

J-2 CUB

G-AEXZ AFFH JTWO

J-3C CUB (L-4/O-59)

G-AFDO AGAT AGIV AGVV AHIP AIIH AISS AISX AJAD AJES AKAZ AKIB AKRA AKTH AKUN ASPS ATKI ATZM AXGP AXHP AXHR AYCN AYEN BAET BBHJ BBLH BBUU BBXS BCNX BCOB BCOM BCPH BCPJ BCUB BCXJ BDCD BDEY BDEZ BDHK BDJP BDMS BDOL BECN BEDJ BEUI BFBY BFDL BFHI BFZB BGPD BGSJ BGTI BGXA BHPK BHVV BHXY BHZU BIJE BILI BJAF BJAY BJSZ BJTO BKHG BLPA BMKC BOTU BOXJ BPCF BPUR BPVH BPYN BREB BROR BSBT BSFD BSNF BSTI BSVH BSYO BTBX BTET BTSP BTUM BTZX BVAF BVPN BWEZ CCUB COPS CUBS CUBY FRAN HEWI KIRK LIVH LOCH NCUB OCUB OINK OLEZ POOH RAMP SEED TCUB

J-4A CUB COUPE

G-AFGM AFWH AFZA BSDJ

J-5A CUB CRUISER

G-BRIL BRLI BSDK BSXT BTKA

PA-12 SUPER CRUISER

G-AMPG ARTH AWPW AXUC BCAZ BOWN BSYG PAIZ

PA-15/PA-17 VAGABOND

G-AKTP ALEH ALGA ALIJ AMYL ASHU AWKD AWOF AWOH BCVB BDVA BDVB BDVC BIHT BLMP BOVB BRJL BRPY BRSX BSFW BSMV BSWG BTBY BTCI BTFJ BTOT BUKN BUXX FKNH VAGA

PA-16 CLIPPER

G-BAMR BBUG BIAP BSVI BSWF

PA-18/A SUPER CUB (L-18/L-21)

G-AMEN APZJ ARAN ARAO ARCT AREO ARGV ARVO ASCU ATRG AVOO AWMF AXGA AXLZ AYPM AYPO AYPP AYPR AYPS AYPT AZRL BAFT BAFV BAKV BAVA BBOL BBYB BCFO BCMD BEOI BEUA BEUU BFFP BGPN BGWH

BGYN BHGC BHOM BHPM BIDJ BIDK BIID BIJB BIMM BIRH BITA BIYJ
BIYR BIYY BIZV BJBK BJCI BJEI BJFE BJIV BJLH BJTP BJWX BJWZ
BKET BKJB BKRF BKTA BKVM BLGT BLHM BLIH BLLN BLLO BLMI BLMR
BLMT BLPE BLRC BMAY BMEA BMKB BNXM BOOC BPJG BPJH BPUL BROZ
BRRL BSGC BSHV BTBU BTDX BTUR BUBA BVIE BVIW BVMI BVRZ BWHH
BWOR BWUB BZHT CBFI CUBB CUBI CUBJ CUBP FUZZ GCUB GDAM HACK
HELN JCUB KAMP LION NESY NETY NICK NNAC OFER OROD OSPS OTAN
OTUG PIPR PUDL PULL ROVE SCUB SUPA TUGG WCUB WGCS WLAC XCUB
YCUB ZAZA

PA-20 PACER/PA-22 conversions

G-APTP APYI ARBS ARGY ARNK ATBX AVDV ATXA BFMR BIYP BSED
BTLM BUDE BUOI BUXV BWWU BXBB GGLE

PA-22 TRI-PACER/CARIBBEAN/COLT

G-APUR APXR APXT APXU APYN APZL APZX ARAI ARAX ARBV ARCC
ARCF ARDS ARDT ARDV AREL ARET AREV ARFB ARFD ARGO ARHN ARHP
ARHR ARHU ARIK ARIL ARJE ARJF ARJH ARKK ARKM ARKN ARKP ARKS
ARND ARNE ARNG ARNH ARNI ARNJ ARNL ARON ARSU ARSW ARSX ARYH
ASSE AWLI AZRS BMCS BNED BRNX BTKV BTWU BUVA HALL TJAY TLDK

PA-23/PA-27 APACHE/AZTEC

G-APMY ARBN ARCW ARHL ARJR ARJS ARJT ARJU ARJV ARYF ASEP
ASER ASHH ASHV ASMO ASMY ASND ASRI ATFF ATHA ATJR ATMU ATOA
AXDC AXZP AYBO AYMO AYSA AYWY AZRG AZSZ AZXG AZYU BADI BADJ
BAPL BATN BAUI BAUJ BAUW BAVL BAVZ BBCC BBCW BBDO BBEW BBEY
BBGB BBGE BBHF BBIF BBMJ BBRA BBTJ BBTL BBVG BCBG BCBM BCCE
BCEX BCRP BEXO BDAX BFBB BFVP BFWE BGTG BGWW BHNG BICY BJNZ
BJXX BKJW BKVT BLLM BMFD BNUV BRAV BSVP BXPS BYRW CALL CSFT
ESKU ESKY FOTO HFTG JTCA KEYS LIZZ MLFF MOLY NRSC OART OBEY
OPME OSNI OXTC RVRC RVRD SFHR SHIP TAPE TAXI UNDO USFT WSFT
XSFT

PA-24/PA-26 COMANCHE

G-APUZ APXJ ARBO ARDB ARFH ARHI ARIN ARLK ARUO ARXG ARYV
ASCJ ASEO ATIA ATJL ATNV ATOY AVCM AVGA AXMA AXTO AYED AZKR
AZWY BAHG BAHJ BRDW BRXW BUTL BWNI BYTI DISK KSVB MOTO

PA-25 PAWNEE

G-ASIY ASKV ASLK ASVP ATFR AVPY AVXA AXED AZPA BAUC BCBJ
BDDS BDDT BDPJ BDWL BEII BENL BEPN BETL BETM BFEV BFEW BFPS
BFRX BFRY BFSC BFSD BHUU BILL BLDG BNZV BPWL BSTH BUXY BVYP
BXST CMGC DSGC LYND PAWN TOWS

PA-28-140/160 CHEROKEE/CHALLENGER/CRUISER/FLITE-LINER

G-ARUR ARVT ARVU ARVV ASLV ASPK ASSW ASVZ ATDA ATEZ ATIS
ATJF ATJG ATMW ATOI ATOJ ATOK ATOL ATOM ATON ATOO ATOP ATOR
ATOS ATPN ATRO ATRP ATRR ATTF ATTI ATTK ATTV ATUB ATUD ATVK
ATVL ATVO AVFP AVFR AVFX AVFZ AVGC AVGD AVGE AVGG AVGH AVGI
AVLB AVLC AVLD AVLE AVLF AVLG AVLH AVLI AVLJ AVLR AVLT AVSI
AVUS AVUT AVUU AVUT AVUU AVWA AVWD AVWE AVWG AVWI AVWJ AVWL
AVWM AVYP AVYR AWBE AWBG AWBH AWBS AWEV AWEX AWPS AWSM AWTM
AXAB AXIO AXJV AXJX AXSZ AXTA AXTC AXTJ AXTL AYAT AYIG AYJP
AYJR AYKW AYKX AYMK AYNF AYNJ AYPV AYRM AYWE AZEG AZFC AZMX
AZRH AZWB AZWD AZWE AZZO BAFU BAFW BAGX BAHE BAHF BAKH BAMM
BASL BATW BAWK BAXZ BBBK BBBY BBDC BBEF BBEV BBHY BBIL BBIX
BBYP BBZF BCDJ BCGI BCGJ BCGN BCGT BCJM BCJN BCJP BDGY BDSH
BDWY BEAC BEEU BEEV BEFF BEYO BEYT BFBF BFXK BGAX BGPU BGRC
BHXK BIFB BIHG BIYX BOFY BOSR BOSU BRBW BRPK BRPL BRWO BSER
BSLM BSLU BSSE BSTZ BTEX BTGO BTON BTVR BULR BWYB BXPL BXVU
BXYM BYCA BZWG CGHM COLH DAKS DENE DIAT FIAT GCAT JAKS JDJM
KATS LFSC LFSI LIZI LTFC MATZ MIDD MKAS NHRH OFTI OKYM OMAT
PAWL PETR PIKK RECK SCPL SMTH TEFC TEWS TIMW WOLF

PA-28-151/161 CHEROKEE WARRIOR/CADET

G-BCIE BCIR BCRL BCTF BDGM BDPA BEBZ BEFA BELP BFBR BFDK
BFMG BFNI BFNJ BFNK BFWB BFWK BGKS BGOG BGPJ BGPL BGVK BHFK
BHJO BHOR BHRC BHVB BICW BIEY BIIT BIUW BJBW BJBX BJBY BJCA
BJSV BJYG BLEJ BLVL BMFP BMKR BMTR BMUZ BNCR BNEL BNJM BNJT
BNMB BNNO BNNS BNNT BNNY BNNZ BNOE BNOF BNOG BNOH BNOI BNOJ
BNOK BNOL BNOM BNON BNOO BNOP BNOR BNOS BNOT BNOU BNOV BNOW
BNRG BNSY BNSZ BNTD BNXE BNXT BNXU BNZB BNZZ BOAH BODA BODB
BODC BODD BODE BODF BODR BOER BOFZ BOHA BOHO BOHR BOIG BOJW
BOJZ BOKB BOKK BOKL BOKM BOKN BOKO BOKP BOKR BOKS BOKT BOKU
BOKX BOMY BOPC BORK BORL BOSP BOTF BOTI BOTN BOUP BOUR BOVK
BOXA BOXB BOXC BOYH BOYI BOZI BPAC BPAF BPAU BPBM BPCK BPDT
BPDU BPEL BPFH BPHB BPHE BPHL BPID BPIU BPJO BPJP BPJR BPJT
BPJU BPKM BPKR BPMF BPMR BPOM BPPK BPRN BPRY BPWA BPWE BRBA
BRBB BRBD BRBE BRDF BRDG BRDM BRFM BRJV BRRN BRSE BRSG BRTM
BRTX BRUB BRXC BSAW BSBA BSCV BSCY BSFK BSGL BSJX BSLE BSLK
BSLT BSMZ BSOK BSOZ BSPI BSPM BSSC BSSW BSSX BSVG BSVM BSXA
BSXB BSXC BSYZ BSZT BTAW BTBC BTDV BTFO BTGY BTID BTIM BTIV
BTKT BTNE BTNT BTNV BTRK BTRS BTRY BTSJ BTUW BUFH BUFY BUIF
BUIJ BUIK BUJO BUJP BUKX BURT BVBF BVIH BVJZ BVTO BXAB BXJJ
BXJX BXLY BXNH BXTX BXTY BXTZ BYHH BYHI BYKN BYKO BYKR BYXU
BYZM BZBS BZDA BZLH BZMT CBAL CDON CLAC CLEA CPTM CWFZ DENH
DOME EDGI EGLD EGTR EKKL ELZY EOLD ESFT ESSX ETDA FIZZ FLAV
FLEN FMAM FOXA FPIG GALB GBRB GFCA GFCB GFCF GFTA GFTB GRRC
GUSS GYTO HMED HMES IKBP ISDB JAMP JASE JAVO KART KBPI KDET
KNAP LACA LACB LAZL LBMM LORC LSFT LUSH MAND MAYO MSFT NINA
NSFT OAAA OANI OBFC OCTU ODEN OGCA OJWS OMST OOFT OONY OTYJ
OWAR PSRT RIZZ RSFT RSKR ROWS SACI SACO SACR SACS SACT SACU
SACZ SARH SEJW SLYN SNUZ SSFT SUZN TAGS TSFT VICC WARB WARC
WARE WARH WARR WARS WARV WARW WARX WARY WFFW XENA ZULU

PA-28-180/181 CHEROKEE/CHALLENGER/ARCHER

G-ARYR ASFL ASHX ASII ASIJ ASIL ASKT ASRW ASUD ASWX ATAA
ATAS ATEM ATHI ATHR ATNB ATOT ATTX ATUL ATVS ATXM ATYS ATZK
AVAX AVBG AVBH AVBS AVBT AVGK AVNN AVNO AVNP AVNR AVNS AVNU
AVNW AVOZ AVPV AVRK AVRU AVRY AVRZ AVSA AVSB AVSC AVSD AVSE
AVSF AVSP AVYL AVYM AVZR AWDP AWET AWIT AWSL AWTL AWXR AWXS
AXOR AXSG AXTP AXZD AXZF AYAB AYAR AYAS AYAW AYEE AYEF AYPJ
AYUH AYUI AZDX AZLN BABG BAJR BASJ BATV BBBN BBDB BBEC BBNY
BBKX BBPY BCCF BCLL BDSB BEIP BEMW BEXW BEYL BFDI BFMM BFSY
BFVG BGBG BGTJ BGVZ BGWM BHNO BHWZ BHYS BHZE BIIV BIUY BJAG
BJOA BKCC BLFI BMIW BMPC BMSD BNGT BNPO BNRP BNVE BNYP BOBZ
BODM BOEE BOHM BOJM BOMP BOMU BOOF BOPA BORS BOSE BOXY BPAY
BPFI BPGU BPOT BPTE BPXA BPYO BRBG BRBX BRGI BRME BRNV BRUD
BRXD BSCS BSEF BSEU BSGD BSIM BSIZ BSKW BSNX BSVB BSXS BSZJ
BTGZ BTKX BTYI BUMP BUTZ BUUX BUYY BVNS BVOA BWPH BWUH BXEX
BXIF BXJD BXOZ BXRG BXRJ BXTW BXWO BYFP BYHK BYKL BYSP BZHK
BZHV CHAS CHIP CIFR CJBC DEVS DIXY DJJA DLTR EFIR EGLS EHGF
EHLX EMAZ ERNI FBRN GALA GASP GBRB GIFT HARN HOCK IBBO ILLY
ISAX JACS JADJ JANA JANT JCAS JJAN JJEN JOYT JOYZ KAIR KEES
KEMI KERY KEVB KITE LACD LFSG LKTB LORR MALA MASF MDAC MERI
NERI NIKE NINB NINC NITA NOTE OBFS OBUS OGEM OIBO ONET OODW
OPET ORAR PEJM PIPA PNNI RADI REXS SARA SGSE SHED SOBI SOOT
SUEB SVEA TEMP TERY TIMK TSGJ TWEL USSY VOAR WACP WACR YANK
YULL ZMAM

PA-28-235/236 CHEROKEE/DAKOTA

G-BGXS BHTA BNYB BOKA BPCX BRKH BWSX BXCC BZEH DAKO FRGN
FWPW KOTA LEAM ODAK TART

PA-28R/28RT CHEROKEE ARROW

G-AVWN AVWO AVWR AVWT AVWU AVWV AVXF AVYS AVYT AWAZ AWBA
AWBB AWBC AWEZ AWFB AWFC AWFD AWFJ AXCA AXWZ AYAC AYII AYPU
AYRI AZAJ AZDE AZFI AZFM AZNL AZOG AZSF AZSH AZRV AZWS BAHS
BAIH BAMY BAPW BAWG BAZU BBDE BBEB BBEL BBFD BBIA BBZH BBZV
BCGS BCJO BCOP BCPG BEOH BEWX BFDO BFLI BFTC BFZH BGKU BGKV
BGOL BGVN BHAY BHEV BHFJ BHGY BHIR BHWY BIDI BIKE BIZO BKFZ
BKXF BLXP BMGB BMHT BMIV BMJG BMKK BMLS BMNL BMOE BMPR BNEE
BNJR BNNX BNSG BNTC BNTS BNVT BNZG BOBA BOET BOGM BOIC BOJI
BONC BOOG BOWY BOYV BPBO BPXJ BPZM BRLG BRMS BRRJ BSNP BSPN
BTLG BTRT BUND BUNH-BUUM BVDH BWMI BWNM BXVC BXYO BXYP BXYR
BXYS BXYT BYHJ BYKP BZDH BZKL CBEE DAAH DDAY DIZY DMCS DNCS
DONS DORA DSFT ECJM EDVL EPTR FBWH FULL GDOG GEHP GHRW GPMW
GYMM HALC HERB IBFW IJOE IRKB ISCA JANO JESS JMTT LAOL LBRC
LZZY MACK MEAH MEGA MEME MERL MRST NELI OARO ODOG OJIM OKAG
OKEN OMHC OMNI ONSF OOTC OPEP OPJD ORDN OTGA RACO RJMS RONG
RUBY SABA SHAY SHUG TCTC TEBZ THSL TOBE TOLL UTSY VOID WEND
WILS WWAL-YAWW

PA-30/39 TWIN COMANCHE

G-ASMA ASON ASRO ASSB ASSP ASWW ATEW ATMT ATSZ ATWR ATXD
AVAU AVCX AVCY AVJJ AVKL AVPS AVUD AWBN AWBT AXAU AYSB AYZE
AZAB BAKJ BAWN BFUF BKCL BLOR BZRO COMB LADI LARE OAJS OGET
OLIN ORDO PCOM RROD SIGN SURG TCOM

PA-31/31T NAVAJO/CHIEFTAIN/CHEYENNE

G-AYEI BBDS BBZI BEZL BFAM BFIB BFOM BJLO BLFZ BPYR BTLE
BVYF BWDE BWHF BXKS CBGF CITY EEJE EHJM EMAX EPED FILL GLTT
GLUG GURN HVRD IFIT IKPS ILEA ISFC JAJK LIDE LYDD MOHS MRMR
NERC NEWR NWAC OAMT OJIL ONAV ONPA OSGB OWLC PLAC PMAX PZAZ
PZIZ SASK UMMI VICT VIPP YEOM

PA-32/32R CHEROKEE SIX/LANCE/SARATOGA

G-ATES ATJV ATRW ATRX AVFU AVTK AVUZ AZDJ AZTD BAGG BAXJ
BBFV BBSM BDWP BEHH BEZP BFUB BFYC BGUB BHBG BHGO BIWL BJCW
BKEK BKMT BMDC BMEV BMJA BNJF BOGO BOON BOTV BPVI BPVN BRGT

BRHA BRNZ BSTV BSUF BSYC BTCA BVBG BVWZ BXWP BYFR BYPU CBCA CCST CCSW CSIX CTCP DCAV DENI DIGI DIWY EENA ELLA ETAV ETBY FLJA FRAG GOMM GOTO HDEW HERO HYLT IFFR ILTS IMPW JPOT KFRA KNOW LADE LUNA MAIE MOLL MOVI NIOS NROY NEAL OCPF OCTI OJCW OSCC OSIX OTBY PAPS PUSK RAMS RAYE REAH RHHT RIGH ROLF SALA SAWU SIXD SULL TOGA WAIR WINS WYST

PA-34 SENECA

G-AZIK AZOL AZOT AZVJ BABK BACB BAIG BAKD BASM BASX BATR BBLU BBNH BBNI BBPX BBXK BBZJ BCGA BCID BCVY BDEF BDUN BEAG BEHU BEJV BETT BEVG BFKY BFLH BGFT BGLW BHFH BHYE BHYF BHYG BLWD BLYK BMDK BMJO BMUT BNEI BNEN BNRX BOCG BOCP BOCR BOCS BOCT BOCU BOCV BOCW BOCX BOCY BOFE BOIZ BOJK BOPV BORH BOSD BOUK BOUL BOUM BOWE BPAD BPON BPXX BRHO BRXO BSDN BSGK BSHA BSII BSOY BSPG BSUW BTGU BTGV BUBU BVDN BVEV BWDT BXPV BXPW BYBH BYKM BZTG CAHA CBOB CDAV CEGA CHEM CLOS CLUE CTWW DARA DCEA DSID ELBC EMER EXEC EZYU FILE FLYI GAFA GFEY GFCD GUYS HCSL HMJB HTRL IFLP JANN JLCA LENY LORD MAIK MAIR MAXI MPWT OACG OBNA OPAG OWAL PEGI POPS ROLA ROUS RVRB SENX SSFC TAIR TEST VASA VVBK WATS WIZO WWAS XKEN

PA-38 TOMAHAWK

G-BFVF BGBN BGBW BGBY BGEK BGGE BGGF BGGG BGGI BGGL BGGM BGGN BGIG BGKY BGLA BGRL BGRM BGRN BGRR BGRX BGSH BGSI BGVL BGWN BGWU BGXB BGXN BGXO BGZF BGZJ BGZW BHCZ BJNN BJUR BJUS BJYN BKAS BKCY BLWP BMKG BMML BMNP BMSF BMTO BMTP BMVL BMVM BMXL BNCO BNEK BNGR BNGS NBHG BNIM BNKH BNNU BNPL BNPM BNSL BNUY BNVD BNXV BNYK BNYV BOBJ BOBL BOCC BODP BODS BOHN BOHS BOHT BOHU BOLD BOLE BOLF BOMO BOMZ BOUD BPER BPES BPHI BPIK BPJF BPPD BPPE BPPF BRFL BRFN BRHR BRHT BRJR BRLO BRLP BRMJ BRML BRNJ BRSJ BSFE BSKC BSKK BSKL BSOT BSOU BSVV BSVW BSVX BSYK BSYL BSYM BTAP-BTAR BTAS BTFP BTIL BTJK BTJL BTND BTOD BTOM BVHM BVLP BWNR BWNU BWSC BXET BXZA BYLE BYMC BYMD CHER CWFA CWFB CWFC CWFD CWFE DFLY-DTOO DYOU EDNA EMMS EORG EGNR GALL GTHM JEFF LFSA LFSB LFSD LFSH MSFC NCFC NCFE OATS OEDB OLFC OPSF OTFT PRIM REPM PVRF PVRG SION SUKI TOMS

PA-44 SEMINOLE

G-BGCO BGJB BGSG BGTF BHFE BHRP BOHX BRUI BRUX DENZ FRST FSFT GSFT GHSI GISO HSFT PDOC SEMI TWIN

PA-46 MALIBU/MERIDIAN

G-BXER BYLM BZJE BZSD BZTP CREW CUPN DNOP DODI HITS JCAR JSFT MICZ PALL PCAR VRST WADI

PIPER

CP.1 METISSE: G-BVCP

PITTS including AEROTEK/CHRISTEN INDUSTRIES INC

S.1/2 SPECIAL

G-AXNZ AZCE AZPH BADW BADZ BBOH BHSS BIRD BKDR BKPZ BKVP BLAG BMTU BOEM BOXH BOXV BOZS BPDV BPLY BPRD BPVP BPZY BRAW BRBN BRCE BRCI BRJN BRRS BRVL BRVT BRZL BRZX BSDB BSRH BTEF BTOO BTTR BTUK BTUL BUAW BUWJ BVSZ BXAF BXAU BXFB BXTI BYIP BYIR BYJP BZSB EWIZ FLIK FOLY HISS ICAS IIII IIIL IIIR IIIT IIIX ITII JAWZ KITI LITZ LOOP MAGG MAXG MINT OGEE OKAY OODI OSIS OSIT OWAZ PEAL PIII PITS PITZ REAP RIPE ROLL SIIA SIIB SKYD SOLO SPIN STUA STUB STYL SWUN TIII WAZZ WILD WREN XATS YOYO

PIXIE - see SKYHOOK

PLUMB

BGP.1 BIPLANE

G-BGPI FUNN

PMPS DRAGONFLY

MPA Mk 1

G-BDFU

POBER

P-9 PIXIE

G-BUXO

PORTERFIELD

CP-50

G-AFZL

CP-65

G-BVWY

PORTSWOOD

HAFB

G-FYBS FYBX

(AVIONS) POTTIER

P.80S

G-BTYH

POWERCHUTE SYSTEMS INTERNATIONAL LTD

KESTREL

G-MVRV MWCI MWCJ MWCK MWCN MWCO MWCP MWCS MWFL MWGS MWGT MWGU MWGW MWGY MWGZ MWMB MWMC MWMD MWMG MWMH MWNV MWNX MWOC MWOD MWOE MYCW MYCX MYCY MYDA MYDB MYEW MYEX MYFA MYHS

RAIDER

G-MVHB MVHC MVMD MVNA MVNC MVNI MVNK MVNL MVNM MVVZ MVWH MVWJ

PRACTAVIA

PILOT SPRITE

G-AXRK AZZH BALY BCVF BCWH

PRICE

AX7-77 HAFB

G-BMDJ

TPB.2 HAFB

G-BULE

PRIVATEER - see SLINGSBY

PROCTER - see MITCHELL

PETREL

G-AXSF

PROTECH

PT-2C SASSY

G-EWAN

PTERODACTYL LTD- see SOLEAIR

PFLEDGLING/PTRAVELER

G-MBAW MBHZ MBPB MJST

(ALFONS) PUTZER KG

ELSTER B

G-APVF BMWV LUFT

PZL

PZL-104 WILGA variants

G-BTNS BUNC BWDF BXBZ BXMU RIIN WILG WLGA

PZL SZD-45A OGAR
G-BEBG BKTM BMFI OGAR

QAC

QUICKIE/TRI-Q
G-BKFM BKSE BMFN BMVG BMZG BNCG BNJO-BOBS BPMW BPNL BPUC BSPA BSSK BUBC BUXM BVYT BWIT BXOY KUTU KWKI WAHL

QUAD CITY

CHALLENGER
G-BYKU CAMR CBDU IBFC MGAA MGRH MVZK MWFU MWFV MWFX MWFY MWFZ MYAG MYDN MYDS MYFH MYGM MYIA MYIX MYOZ MYPZ MYRH MYRJ MYSD MYTO MYTT MYUL MYXC MYXK MYXV MYYF MZAC MZBW MZBZ MZEA MZHO MZKW MZNA

RAF - see REPLICA PLANS & SLINGSBY

BE.2E
G-BVGR
SE-5
G-EBIA EBIB EBIC
G-BKDT

RAJ HAMSA

X'AIR variants
G-BYCL BYHV BYJU BYLN BYLT BYMM BYMR BYNT BYOH BYOJ BYOR BYPO BYPW BYRV BYSY BYTW BYTT BYTZ BYYM BYYR BYZF BYZW BZAF BZAK BZBP BZDK BZEJ BZER BZEX BZFF BZGX BZIA BZIS BZIY BZKC BZLD BZLT BZMR BZNG BZUP BZVH BZVK BZVR BZWC BZXA BZYM BZYX CBAH CBAV CBBH CBCI CBCM CBDO CBDV CBDW CBDY CBFE CBFT CBHB CBHV CBIC CBII CBIS HARI HITM ODJD OHWV RAJA TANJ TKSD UFAW XAYR XRXR

RAND-ROBINSON

KR-2
G-BEKR BETW BFKC BLDN BMFL BMMD BNAD BNML BOLZ BOUN BPIH BPRR BRJY BRSN BTGD BUDF BUDS BURF BUWT BVIA BVZJ BXXE BYLP CBAU DGWW JCMW KISS KRII OFMB UTSI WYNN XRAY

RANGO - including RANGO-SAFFERY

MLB variants
G-BJAS BJRH FYEU FYFW FYFY FYGI FYGK

RANS

S-4/S-5 COYOTE
G-MVPJ MVXW MWBO MWEP MWES MWFF MWFW MWGA MWGN MWIO MWLA MWLZ MWWP MYDO MYWV MZGD
S-6 variants
G-BSMU BSSI BSTT BSUA BSUT BTNW BTXD BUEW BUOK BUTM BUWK BVCL BVFM BVIN BVOI BVPW BVRK BVUM BVZO BVZV BWHK BWWP BWYR BXCU BXRZ BXWK BYBR BYCM BYCN BYCO BYIB BYID BYJO BYKE BYMN BYMU BYMV BYNP BYOT BYOU BYPZ BYRG BYRS BYSN BYZO BZBC BZBX BZEW BZKD BZKO BZLE BZMJ BZNH BZNJ BZRA BZRY BZUH BZVM BZYA BZYL CBAS CBAZ CBFX CLEE IZIT MGEC MGND MWCH MWHP MWIF MWRK MWSC MWTT MWUK MWUL MWUN MWVL MWWL MWYE MWYN MYAJ MYBA MYBI MYDK MYDX MYES MYFE MYFN MYGH MYGP MYGR MYHI MYHK MYHP MYIR MYIS MYJD MYJL MYJY MYKN MYLD MYLF MYLO MYLW MYMH MYMP MYMR MYMS MYNE MYNH MYOA MYOI MYOT MYPA MYPJ MYSP MYSU MYTE MYUZ MYVP MYXB MYXG MYXP MYYV MYZR MZAH MZBD MZBH MZBU MZBV MZCA MZDA MZDG MZDM MZDR MZEN MZEO MZEU MZFL MZFN MZFY MZIY MZJI MZJM MZKE MZLG MZLL MZMP MZMS MZMU MZNV MZOZ MZUB RINS SOOZ SSIH
S-7 COURIER
G-BVNY BWKJ BWMN KATI OJKM
S-9 CHAOS
G-BPUS BSEE
S-10 SAKOTA
G-BRPT BRSC BRZW BSBV BSGS BSMT BSNN BSWB BSWI BTCR BTGG BTJX BTWZ BUAX BUGH BUKB BULW BVCB BVFA BVHI BWIA BWIL BYRE JSCL OEYE RANS RANZ
S-12
G-BZAO

RAVEN AIRCRAFT INTERNATIONAL - see MEDWAY/SOUTHDOWN

VECTOR
G-MBTW MJAZ

RAYTHEON HAWKER - see HAWKER SIDDELEY AVIATION

REARWIN

175 SKYRANGER
G-BTGI RWIN
8125 CLOUDSTER
G-BVLK
8500 SPORTSTER
G-AEOF
9000L SPORTSTER
G-BGAU

REECE

SKY RANGER
G-MJRR

REID & SIGRIST

RS.4 DESFORD
G-AGOS

REIMS AVIATION SA - see CESSNA

RENEGADE - see MURPHY

REPLICA PLANS

SE-5A
G-BDWJ BIHF BKER BMDB BUOD BUWE INNY SEVA

REPUBLIC

P-47 THUNDERBOLT
G-THUN

REVOLUTION HELICOPTERS

MINI-500
G-BWCZ MSOO OREV PDWI YEAR

RH7B

TIGER LIGHT
G-MZGT

RIDOUT
MLB variants
G-BIRP BIWF BIWG BJMX BJMZ BJNA

RIGG
MLB variants
G-BHLJ BIAR

(AVION PIERRE) ROBIN
DR.400/500 variants
G-BAEB BAEM BAEN BAFP BAFX BAGC BAGR BAGS BAHL BAJY BAJZ BAKM BALF BALG BALH BALI BALJ BAMS BAMT BAMU BAMV BANB BAPV BAPX BAZC BBAX BBAY BBCH BBCS BBDP BBJU BBMB BCXE BDUY BEUP BFJZ BGRH BGWC BHAJ BHFS-BHJU BHLE BHLH BHOA BIHD BIZI BJUD BKDH BKDI BKDJ BKVL BNFV BNXI BOGI BPHG BPZP BRBK BRBL BRBM BRNT BRNU BSDH BSFF BSLA BSSP BSVS BSYU BSZD BTRU BUGJ BUYS BXRT BYHT BYIT BZIJ BZMM CBBA CHIX CONB DUDZ EGGS EHMM ELEN ETIV EYCO FCSP FTIL FTIM FTIN FUEL GBUE GOSL HAIR HANS-HXTD IEYE IOOI IYCO JBDH JEDH JMTS JUDE KIMY LARA LEOS LISE MIFF MOTI NBDD ONGC RBIN RONS SELL TUGY UAPA XLXL YOGI ZACH ZIGI ZIPI
HR.100 ROYALE/SAFARI/TIARA
G-AZHB AZHK AZKN BAEC BAPY BAWR BAYR BBAW BBCN BBIO BBPW BEUD BGTP BLHN BLWF BVMZ BWPG BXWB HRIO MPWI
HR.200/CLUB
G-BBOE BCCB BCCY BETD BFBE BGXR BLTM BNIK BUWZ BVMM BWFG BWPG BXDT BXGW BXOR BXVK BYLG BYLH BYNK BYSG BZLG BZXK GORF JPAT NSOF VECA WAVA WAVI
R.1180T AIGLON
G-BGHM BIRT BJVV GBAO GDER GEEP PACE ROBN VECD VITE
R.2100/2112/2120/2160 variants
G-BGBA BICS BIVA BKXA BLWY BVYO BWZG BYBF BYOF BZFB BZYZ MATT PGSI PLAY RAFC SACK SBMO TOUR VECB VECE
R.3000
G-BLYP BOLU BZOL ENNI PAVL

ROBINSON AIRCRAFT CO.
REDWING
G-ABNX

ROBINSON HELICOPTER CO INC
R22 ALPHA/BETA/MARINER
G-BJUC BLDK BLME BLTF BOAM BOCN BODZ BOEW BOEX BOEZ BOVR BOXX BOYC BOYX BPGV BPIT BPNI BPTZ BRBY BRKN BROX BRRY BRVI BRWD BRXV BSCE BSCL BSEK BSGF BSIN BSXN BSZS BTBA BTHI BTNA BTNB BTOC BTVU BUBW BVGS BVPR BWHY BWTH BXLA BXOA BXRK BXSG BXSY BXTU BXUC BXXN BXYK BYCF BYCK BYCU BYHD BYHE BYTD BYTE BYZP BYZZ BZBU BZJJ BZJK BZMO BZYE CHIS CHYL CHZN CNDY CRAY DAAM DABS DEER DELT DERB DLDL DMCD DODB DODR EFGH EIBM EPAR ERBL ETIN FAGN FEBY FIRS FOGY FOLI GEGE GJCD GOUP GSFC HBMW HERA HIEL HIPO HONI HRHE HSLA HUMF HURN IAGD IBED ICCL IHSB IIFR IIPT INIS IORG ISMO JARA JERS JHEW JNET JONH JSAK JWFT KENN KNIB KRAY LAIN LAND LEDA LIDS LIPE LYNC MAVI MDKD MFHT MICH MIKK MOGY MRSN MUFY NABS NJSH OASH OBIL OBIO OCOV ODCS ODOT OEAT OFAS OGOG OHFT OHLL OHSL OICV OJAN OKEY OLAU OLIZ OLRT OMMG OMSG ONMT OPAL OPTS ORMB OROB OSEE OSHL OSIP OSMS OTAC OTED OTHL OTOY OVNR PACL PBES PHEL PIKE PWEL RALD REDA RENT RIAT RICE RIDL RNGO ROLO ROUT ROVY RSVP RSWW RUSO RVRS SBUT SIMN SIVX SOLD SPEE STOY SUMT SUMX TCMP TGRS TINK TILE TOLY TORS TOSH TTHC TUNE UDAY UESY ULAB UNYT VEYE VFSI VMSL WADS WAGG WFOX WIRL WIZA WIZR WIZY WRLY WRWR YACB YKEN YMBO ZAPY
R44 ASTRO/CLIPPER/RAVEN
G-BVMC BWVH BXPY BXUK BYCE BYKK BZIN BZLP BZMG BZOP BZPL BZRN BZTA BZVP BZXY CBAK CBEG CBFJ CHAP CHUM CLKE DCOM DCSE DSPI EKKO EUGN EYET FABI FODI HALE HEPY HMPF HRHS HTEL IBKA ICAB IFDM IFTS INDY IVIV JBBS JEFA JILY JJWL KAZZ KPAO KYDD KYNT LATK LRSN LUKI LUKY MGAN MGWI MURY NSEW NUDE OBBY OCHM ODES ODHG ODOC OFIL OJRH OKES OLOW OMEL OPAO OPHA OTJB OWND PBEE PFML PIDG POTT PPTS PRET RAVN RAYC RDEL REDI RONN ROZI RTWW SJDI SMJH SUNY TAND TATY THEL TPTS TRAC TRCY TRYG TURV URUH UTSS WYMR WYSP XLIV XPTS XTEK YIIK YKDD ZONK

ROCKWELL INTERNATIONAL CORPORATION - see AERO COMMANDER & including COMMANDER AIRCRAFT CORPN (114)
COMMANDER 112/114
G-BDAK BDFW BDIE BDKW BDLT BDYD BEBU BEDG BENJ BEPY BERI BERW BFAI BFPO BFRA BFXS BFZM BGBZ BHRO BHSE BIOJ BIUO BKAY BLTK BMJL BMWR BOLT BPTG BUSW BVNL BYKB CRIL DANT DASH DIME EHXP ERIC FATB FLPI GRIF HILO HMBJ HPSB HPSE HROI IMPX JILL JURG LADS LITE NATT NOOR OIBM OLFT OMUM OOJP PADS RCED RDCI RJCP SAAB TCSL TECH TWIZ VICS ZIPA

ROE
TRIPLANE
G-ARSG

ROGERSON
HORIZON 1
G-DOGZ

ROLLASON - see DRUINE
BETA
G-AWHX BADC BETE BUPC

ROMAIN
COBRA BIPLANE
G-MNLH

ROOSTER - see LIGHTWING

ROTARY AIR FORCE INC
RAF 2000
G-BUYL BVSM BWAD BWAE BWHS BWTK BWWS BXAC BXEA BXEB BXGS BXKM BXMG BYDW BYIN BYJA CBAG CBCJ CBHZ CBIT CBJE CBJN HOWL IRAF ONON REBA SAYS YRAF

ROTEC
RALLY 2B
G-MBAZ MBGS MBMG MJPA MVRF

ROTORWAY
SCORPION/EXEC
G-BHHZ BNZL BNZO BPCM BRGX BSGV BSRP BSUR BTVF BUJZ BURP BUSN BVOY BVTV BWJK BWLY BWUJ BYNI BYNJ BZBW BZOM BZXD CHTG CBIK ESUS FLIT KENI KONE LUFF MAMC NEEL OJCM PILE PURS RAWS RHYS SFOX URCH VCSI WHOO YEWS ZHWH

ROUSSEAU - see PIEL

RUSCHMEYER LUFTFAHRTTECHNIK GMBH
RUSHMEYER R90
G-EERH TODE UAPO

RUTAN
COZY
G-BXDO BXVX COZI OGJS SCUL SPFX
DEFIANT
G-OTWO
LONG-EZ/VARIEZE
G-BEZE BEZY BIMX BKST BKVE BKXO BLLZ BLMN BLTS BMHA BMIM BMUG BNCZ BNUI BOOX BPWP BRFB BSIH BUPA BVAY BVKM BZMF EMMY EZOS HAIG ICON IPSY LASS LEZE LUKE MUSO OMJT OOSE PUSH RAEM RAFT RPEZ SENA SKCI TIMB VEZE WILY

RYAN
ST3KR/PT-22
G-AGYY BPUD BTBH BYPY

SAAB-SCANIA AB
32 LANSEN
G-BMSG
91 SAFIR
G-ANOK BCFW BKPY HRLK SAFR
SF.340
G-GNTB GNTC GNTE GNTF GNTG LGNA LGNB LGNC LGND LGNE RUNG

SABRE - see SKYHOOK
(Wing)
G-MJFX MJIB MJNY

SAFFERY
MLB variants
G-BERN BFBM BIHU FYGM

SAI
KZ.VIII
G-AYKZ

SAN - see JODEL

SAUNDERS-ROE (SARO)
SKEETER
G-APOI AWSV BJWC BKSC BLIX SARO

SCALLAN
MLB variants
G-FYEO FYEZ

SCHEIBE-FLUGZEUGBAU GmbH
SF.23 SPERLING
G-BCHX
SF.24 MOTORSPATZ
G-BBKR BZPF
SF.25 & SLINGSBY T.61 variants
G-AVIZ AXEO AXIW AXJR AYBG AYSD AYUM AYUN AYUP AYUR AYYL AYZU AYZW AZHD AZHE AZIL AZMC AZMD AZPC AZYY BADH BAIZ BAKY BAMB BDZA BECF BEGG BFPA BFUD BGMV BHSD BIGZ BKVG BLCU BLTR BLZA BMBZ BMVA BODU BPIR BPZU BRRD BRWT BSEL BSUO BSWL BSWM BTDA BTRW BTTZ BTUA BTWC BTWD BTWE BUDA BUDB BUDC BUDT BUED BUEK BUFG BUFN BUFR BUGL BUGT BUGV BUGW BUGZ BUHA BUHR BUIH BUJA BUJB BUJI BUJX BUNB BUXJ BVKK BVKU BVLX BWTR BXAN BXMV BXXC FEFE FHAS FLKE FLKS HBOS KAOM KDEY KDFF KFAN KGAO MFMM OWGC
SF.28 TANDEM FALKE
G-BARZ BYEJ

SCHEMPP-HIRTH FLUGZEUBAU GmbH
3DM/4DM
G-BPMH HJSM
JANUS CM
G-BMBJ BXJS
VENTUS 2CM
G-OODH VENT

(ALEXANDER) SCHLEICHER GmbH & CO
ASK-14
G-BKSP BSIY KOHF
ASK-16
G-BCHT BCTI
ASH-26E
G-BWBY DAVT OPHT

SCHWEIZER AIRCRAFT CORPN - see HUGHES

SCOBLE - see SOUTHERN MICROLIGHT

SCINTEX - see PIEL

SCOTTISH AVIATION
BULLDOG
G-ASAL AXEH AXIG BCUO BCUS BCUV BDOG BHXA BHZR BHZS BHZT BPCL BULL BWIB BZDP BZEP BZLB BZND BZME BZMH BZML BZON BZPS BZXC BZXS BZXZ CBAB CBAN CBBC CBBL CBBR CBBS CBBT CBBU CBBW CBCB CBCO CBCR CBCT CBCV CBDK CBDS CBEF CBEH CBEK CBFP CBGX CBID CBJJ CBJK CCOA DDOG DOGG EDAV GGRR GRRR JWCM KDOG KKKK SIJW TDOG UDOG
TWIN PIONEER
G-APRS AYFA AZHJ BBVF

SCRUGGS
MLB variants
G-BILE BILG BINI BINL BINM BINX BIPH BISL BISM BISS BIST BIWB BIWC

SE - see R.A.F./SLINGSBY/REPLICA PLANS

SEEMS - see MORANE-SAULNIER

SEQUOIA - see AVIAMILANO

SERVOTEC - see CIERVA

SHARP & SONS
TARTAN (Trike)
G-MBDE

SHAW
TWIN-EZE
G-IVAN

SHEFFIELD
TRIDENT
G-MBNV

SHERRY
BUZZARD
G-MMNN

SHERWOOD RANGER - see TIGER CUB

SHIELD
XYLA
G-AWPN

SHORT BROTHERS LTD - see EMBRAER
S.16 SCION
G-ACUX AEZF
SA.6 SEALAND
G-AKLW
SC.5 BELFAST
G-BEPS HLFT
SC.7 SKYVAN
G-BEOL BVXW PIGY
SD.3-30
G-BDBS BGNH BJLK BKIE BKMW BNTX DACS OGIL ROND SSWA SSWP SSWT SSWU XPSS
SD.3-60
G-BKMX BLZT BMLC BNMT BNMU BNYI BPFN BPFR CBAC CEAL CLAS DASI EXPS KBAC OBHD OBLK SSWB SSWC SSWM SSWO SSWR SSWX UBAC VBAC

SIAI-MARCHETTI S.p.A
S.205
G-AVEH AYXS BBRX BFAP VELA
SF.260
G-BAGB MACH NRRA SIAI

SIGMA - see SOUTHDOWN

SIKORSKY AIRCRAFT - see WESTLAND
S-52 - **see VERTICAL AVIATION TECHNOLOGIES**
S-61
G-ATBJ ATFM AYOY BBHL BBHM BBVA BCEA BCEB BCLC BCLD BDIJ BDOC BEJL BFFJ BFFK BFRI BGWJ BGWK BHOH BIMU BPWB LAWS
S-76
G-BHBF BHGK BIEJ BISZ BITR BJFL BJGX BJVX BMAL BOYF BURS BUXB BVKR BWDO BXZS BYDF BYOM CBJB CHCD CHCE DRNT EWEL HARH JCBA JCBJ POAH SMAF SSSC SSSD SSSE UKLS XXEA

SIPA
901/903/91
G-AMSG ASXC ATXO AWLG BBBO BBDV BDAO BDKM BGME BHMA SIPA

SKY BALLOONS LTD including CAMERON
HAFB:
21
G-BYCB
25
G-BXWX BZSL
31
G-BWOY BXVP OSVY
56
G-BWYP
65
G-BWLM BWUS BXFZ BXKO BXUS DUNG
70
G-PONY
77
G-BWSL BXHL BXVG BXXP BZLS CLRK KSKY LOWS MAGL OBET RCML
80
G-BYBS BYOI SETI
90
G-BWKR BXGD BXJT BXJU BXLP BXPP BXVR BXWL BYZV BZKV CLOE CZAG GPEG LEAS VINO ZABC
105
G-BWDZ BWOA BWPP BWUM BXCN BXDV BXIW BXVN BXXS BYNV DONG
120
G-BWIX BWJR BWPF BWYU BXDW BXLC BXWG BYEX OURS
140
G-BWHM BYKZ
160
G-BWUK BXZZ BYHZ
180
G-BWIW BXVL
200
G-BWEL BWST BXIH
220
G-BWRW BXDH EGUY SPEL
240
G-BXUE MRLN
260
G-KTKT OLYN
SPECIAL SHAPE FLYING MAP
G-MAPS

SKYCRAFT - see WHEELER

SKYFOX
CA-25N GAZELLE
G-IDAY

SKYHOOK
SAILWINGS TR1 (Trike)/PIXIE
G-MJFX MJNU MJNY MMVS MNGH
SAILWINGS CUTLASS (Wing
G-MBHJ MBVW MJNU MNUI
SAILWINGS ZEUS (Wing
G-MMVS MNGH

SKYRAIDER
GYROCOPTER
G-BUUS

SKYRIDER
AIRSPORTS PHANTOM
G-MJKX MJSE MJSF MJTE MJTX MJTZ MJUX MJVX MMKX MNCS MTTN

SKY SCIENCE POWERED PARACHUTES LTD
POWERHAWK L70/500
G-SSPP

SKYTRIKE - see HIWAY

SLEPCEV
STORCH
G-BZOB

SLINGSBY AIRCRAFT CO LTD - see TIPSY

SLINGSBY SAILPLANES LTD - see FOURNIER/SCHEIBE/SOPWITH
T.21/T.29/T.31 MOTOR CADET/TUTOR
G-AYAN AZSD BCYH BDSM G-BDUX BEMM BMDD BNPF BODG BODH BOKG BOOD BPIP BRTZ BRVJ BUAC BVFS BZLK
T.67/T.67M FIREFLY
G-BIOW BJIG BJNG BJXA BJXB BJZN BKAM BKTZ BLLP BLLR BLLS BLLV BLPI BLRF BLRG BLTT BLTU BLTV BLTW BLUX BLVI BNSO BNSP BNSR BOCL BOCM BONT BONU BUUA BUUB BUUC BUUD BUUE BUUF BUUG BUUI BUUJ BUUK BUUL BWGO BWXA BWXB BWXC BWXD BWXE BWXF BWXG BWXH BWXI BWXJ BWXK BWXL BWXM BWXN BWXO BWXP BWXR BWXS BWXT BWXU BWXV BWXW BWXX BWXY BWXZ BXKW BYBX BYOA BYOB BYOD BYRY BYYG CBHE DLTA EFSM FORS HONG KONG ONES OPUB RAFG SFTZ SKYC SKYO ZEIN

SMD - see SOUTHERN MICROLIGHT

SMITH
DSA-1 MINIPLANE
G-BTGJ

SMYTH
SIDEWINDER
G-BRVH JOPF

SNCAC including NORD production
NC854/858
G-BCGH BDJR BDXX BGEW BIUP BJEL BJLB BPZD NORD

SNCAN/STAMPE including AIA production
SV-4A/B/C
G-AIYG AMPI ASHS ATIR AWEF AWIW AWXZ AXCZ AXHC AXNW AXRP AYCG AYCK AYDR AYGE AYIJ AYJB AYWT AYZI AZCB AZGC AZGE AZNK AZSA AZTR BAKN BALK BEPC BEPF BHFG BHYI BIMO BKRK BKSX BMNV BNYZ BPLM BRXP BTIO BWEF BWRS BYDK BZSY EEUP FORC FORD GMAX HJSS OODE STMP SVIV

SNIAS - see SUD/AËROSPATIALE

SOCATA - see MORANE-SAULNIER
ST-10 DIPLOMATE
G-AZIB BBTU HOLY
TB-9 TAMPICO/TB-10 TOBAGO
G-BGXC BGXD BGXT BHDE BHER BHGP BHIT BHJF BHOZ BIAK BIBA BITE BIXA BIXB BIZE BIZR BJDT BJKF BJUG BKBN BKBV BKBW BKCR BKIA BKIB BKIS BKIT BKUE BKVC BLCG BLCM BLYE BMEG BMYC BMZE BNDR BNIJ BNRA BOIT BOIU BPGX BRIV BSDL BTHR BTIE BTWX BTZP CBGC CBHA CFME CMED COCL CONL DAND EDEN GBHI GHZJ GMSI GOLF HALP HILT IANH IGGL JURE MOOR MRTN OFIT OFLG PATN PHTG POPI RENO SERL SONA SKYF TBIO TEDS TINA TOBA VMJM
TB-20/TB-21 TRINIDAD & TB.200 TOBAGO GT/XL
G-BLXA BLYD BNXX BPAS BPFG BPTI BSCN BTEK BTZO BXLT BXVA BYJS BYTB BZLI BZPI CBFM CORB CPMS DLOM DMAH EGHR EGJA EWFN FITI FIFI GDGR GOOD HGPI HOOD JDEE KKDL KKES KPTT KUBB OALD OBGC PEKT PTRE RRFC SCBI SCIP SHEP SLTN TANS TBGT TBXX TBZI TBZO THZL TMOL TOAK TRDM TRIN TYNE WERY

SOKO
P-2 KRAGUJ
G-BSXD RADA SOKO

SOLAR WINGS LTD/SOLAR WINGS AVIATION LTD – incl HOLDCONTOL plc & see CYCLONE/PEGASUS
XL-P
G-MMYA
XL-Q
G-BZWM DEAN MGCB MNKO MTNO MTNP MTPN MTPS MTRU MTRV MTTD MTTE MTTX MTTZ MTUP MTUR MTUS MTUT MTUY MTVX MTXH MTXI MTXJ MTXK MTYA MTYC MTYD MTYE MTYF MTYI MTYL MTYP MTYR MTYS MTYT MTYU MTZP MTZR MTZS MTZT MVAW MVAX MVAY MVCL MVCM MVCN MVCP MVCR MVCS MVCT MVCV MVEX MVEZ MVFA MVFB MVFC MVFD MVFE MVFF MVFG MVGT MVGU MVGW MVHO MVHP MVHR MVHS MVHT MVHU MVHV MVHW MVHX MVHY MVIA MVJD MVJN MVJO MVJP MVJR MVJS MVJT MVJU MVJW MVKF MVKG MVKL MVKN MVKO MVKP MVKS MVKT MVKU MVKV MVKW MVKX MVLX MVLY MVMC MVPR MVPS MVPU MVPW MVPX MVPY MVRH MVRI MVRJ MVRU MVRW MVRX MVSB MVSD MVSE MVSW MVSX MVSY MVSZ MVTA MVTI MVTJ MVTK MVUF MVUG MVUH MVUI MVUJ MVUL MVUM MVVN MVVO MVVP MVYC MVYD MVZJ MVZL MVZT MVZU MVZV MWAC MWAD MWAL MWAT MWBK MWCB MWCF MWCV MWDD MWDK MWDL MWEE MWEF MWEG MWEH MWER MWFS MWGL MWGM MWGR MWHC MWHF MWHG MWHL MWHW MWHX MWIE MWIR MWIS MWIT MWJN MWJO MWKO MWKP MWKY MWKZ MWLL MWLM MWMN MWMO MWMP MWMZ MWNA MWNB MWNC MWNG MWOR MWOX MWOY MWPE MYPG MWPJ MWPK MWRV MWRW MWRX MWSD MWSJ MWSK MWTA MWTB MWTC MWTI MWUO MWUX MWUY MWUZ MWVA MWWG MWWH MWWV MWXP MWXR MWYB MWYC MWYU MWYY MYAC MYAD MYAE MYAF MYBF MYBG MYBR MYBS MYBV MYBW MYBY MYBZ MYEA MYEC MYED MYFX MYTC MYUH MZCP MZLR
XL-R
G-BZXU MGPD MMOH MMTA MMTC MMTR MNAO MNAR MNAW MNAX MNAY MNAZ MNBA MNBB MNBC MNGG MNHB MNHC MNHD MNHE MNHI MNHJ MNHK MNHL MNHM MNHN MNHR MNHS MNHT MNHU MNHV MNMK MNUX MNVB MNVC MNVE MNWW MNYB MNYC MNYV MNYW MNYX MNZK MTAA MTAI MTAJ MTAO MTAT MTAV MTAW MTAX MTAY MTAZ MTBA MTBL MTBU MTCG MTCH MTCN MTCO MTCR MTCX MTDG MTDH MTDI MTDS MTDT MTEB MTEC MTED MTEE MTER MTES MTET MTEU MTEW MTEX MTFB MTFE MTFM MTFO MTFP MTFR MTFT MTGJ MTGK MTGL MTGM MTHG MTHH MTHI MTHJ MTHN MTIE MTIH MTIJ MTIO MTIP MTIR MTIS MTIU MTIV MTIW MTIX MTIY MTIZ MTJH MTJS MTKG MTKH MTKI MTKJ MTLG MTLI MTLJ MTLT MTLU MTLV MTLY MTME MTMF MTMG MTMH MTMI MTOA MTOB MTOD MTOE MTOG MTOH MTOI MTOJ MTOK MTOL MTOM MTON MTOO MTOP MTOS MTOT MTOU MTOX MTOY MTOZ MTPP MTPR MTRM MTRN MTRO MTRS MTSN MTSO MTSP MTSR MTSS MTSU MTSV MTSX MTSY MTSZ MTTA MTTB MTTU MTUA MTUI MTUJ MTUK MTUL MTVB MTVK MTVL MTVM MTVN MTVO MTWA MTWB MTWC MTWD MTYY MTZK MVAR MVAT MVAV MVBJ MVBY MVBZ MVCA MVCB MVDU MVDV MVDW MVDX MVDY MVDZ MVEC MVED MVEF MVEG MVFP MVFR MVFS MVFT MVFV MVFW MVGN MVGO MVGP MVGS MVKH MVKJ MVKK MVKM MVVK MVVM MWAF MWAG MWAI MWAV MWBL MWCC MWCU MWDC MWFA MWJG MWLE MWLF MWLG MWLU MWMR MWMV MWOH MWOI MWPX MWRN MWRO MWRP MWRT MWRU MWSE MWSF MWSO MWSP MWSR MWTM MWTU MWUB MWUC MWUD MWUE MWUF MWUP MWUR MWUS MWUU MWUV MWVE MWVF MWZH MWZI MWZJ MWZT MWZU MWZV MWZW MWZX MWZY MWZZ MYAB MYBO MYBP MYDI MYDJ MYEG MYEH MYGT MYGU MYGV
XL-S
G-MNAF MNAH MNAI MNAJ MNAK MNBI MNHH MJWZ MMJF MMMN MMOK MMRK MMRL MMRZ MMSA MMSG MMSH MMTT MMVC MMZG
FLASH
G-MNDO MNGF MNJH MNJJ MNJL MNJN MNJO MNJR MNKP MNKS MNKV MNKW MNKX MNNY MNNZ MNPA MNPB MNSH MNSN MNUD MNUE MNVG MNVH MNWP MNWU MNWV MNXP MNYA MNYK MNYZ MNZO MTCK

PHOTON
G-MNIK MNIU MNKB MNKC MNKD MNKE MNKG MNKI MNKK MNNG MNVZ MNXB MTAL
STORM (Wing)
G-MMUR
TYPHOON (Wing)
G-MBCI MBCJ MBCL MBGP MBJS MBOK MBPG MBTJ MJCU MJEE MJMR MJPP MJVE MMBJ MMBZ MMCV MMDX MMKG MMKH MMLI MMPU MMTK MMUG MMUK MNCU MNCV MNEI MNFA MNFR MNGD MNSD MNZI MZLK

SOMERS-KENDAL
SK.1
G-AOBG

SOPWITH AVIATION CO.
CAMEL
G-AWYY BFCZ BPOB BZSC
PUP/DOVE
G EAGA EAVX EBKY
G-ABOX APUP BIAU BZND
TABLOID SCOUT
G-BFDE
TRIPLANE
G-BOCK BWRA
"1 ½" STRUTTER REP
G-BIDW

SORRELL
SNS-7 HYPERBIPE
G-BPDK HIPE

SOUTHDOWN SAILWINGS LTD - see MEDWAY & including SOUTHDOWN INTERNATIONAL LTD
LIGHTNING (Wing)
G-MBGX MBLU MBMT MJEY MJHC MJHR MJIZ MJZH MMAS MMDF MMKR MMKZ MMMI
PIPISTRELLE - **see AEROSTRUCTURE**
PUMA/PUMA SPRINT (Combi-unit)
G-MBZJ MJCE MJEB MJHZ MJRT MJTR MJVN MJYT MMAO MMAR MMAZ MMBL MMCI MMCM MMGP MMIR MMIW MMJD MMJT MMKV MMMD MMPG MMPH MMRN MMTH MMTI MMTM MMTZ MMUA MMUV MMVI MMVO MMVX MMVZ MMWI MMWX MMXN MMXO MMYF MMYI MMYO MMYT MMYU MMYY MMYZ MMZR MMZW MMZX MNAV MNBE MNBM MNCI MNCP MNDG MNDY MNDZ MNFB MNFG MNFX MNGS MNGX MNHL MNJD MNJG MNJS MNKU MNMC MNSB MNUM MVAF MWCR
RAVEN/HORNET DUAL TRAINER
G-MGOD MMVH MNFD MNJB MNJT MNKZ MNLB MNLE MNLK MNLM MNLN MNLT MNLU MNLV MNLZ MNMD MNMU MNNA MNNB MNNC MNNO MNRP MNRS MNSL MNSX MNSY MNTC MNTE MNTM MNTN MNTY MNUT MNUU MNVN MNWA MNWG MNXA MNXD MNXE MNXF MNXI MNYG MNYI MNYL MNYM MNYP MNYS MNZW MNZX MTAP MTBB MTBK MTBN MTBO MTBZ MTCM MTHC MTID MTIK MTMK MTMO MTPC MTRT MTRW MTSD MTYV MTYW MTYX MVOS MYKL MYLX MYLY MYMJ MYVW MYYZ MYZO MZBR MZDJ RAVE
SIGMA (Wing)
G-MBDM
SPRINT (Wing)/PUMA
G-MBST MBTF MBTG MMDP MMHR MMKU MMLP MMMB MMOB MMRO MMRP MMSO MMTB MMTG MMTL MMTO MMTX MMUH MMXW MWTF
WILD CAT (Trike)
G-MJUE MMDF

SOUTHERN
FLYER
G-MJCN
MICROLIGHT (SMD) GAZELLE (Trike)
G-MMGU MMPT
MICROLIGHT (SMD) VIPER
G-MMHS

SOUTHERN
MARTLET
G-AAYX

SPAD
XIII
G-BFYO

SPARTAN AIRCRAFT LTD
ARROW
G-ABWP
CRUISER
G-ACYK
THREE-SEATER
G-ABYN

SPEZIO
DAL-1 TUHOLER/SPORT
G-NGRM NOBI

SPORTAVIA - see FOURNIER
RS.180 SPORTSMAN
G-VIZZ

SPP - see YAKOVLEV

SQUIRES
LIGHTFLY
G-MNNG

STAAKEN
Z-1/Z-21A FLITZER
G-BVAW BYYZ FLIZ FLZR

STARCK
AS.80
G-BJAE

STAR-LITE
SL-1
G-BUZH FARO SOLA

STEARMAN - see BOEING-STEARMAN

STEEN AERO LAB.INC
SKYBOLT
G-BGRT BIMN BRIS BUXI BVXE BZWV ENGO BWPJ KEST SBLT SKIE TURN

STEMME GmbH & Co.KG
S-10
G-BVYZ BXGZ BXHR BZSP CHLT EXPD JCKT JULL OJTA STEM STEN

STEPHENS
AKRO/LAZER 200
G-BRHZ BWKT CBHR LAZA RIDE VILL

STERN
ST.80 BALADE
G-BWVI

STEVENDON
SKYREACHER MLB
G-BIWA

STINSON AIRCRAFT CORPORATION
RELIANT
G-BUCH
HW-75/105 VOYAGER
G-AFYO BMSA
108 STATION WAGON
G-BHMR BPTA BRZK

STITS
SA.3A PLAYBOY
G-BDRL BGLZ BVVR

STODDARD-HAMILTON
GLASAIR
G-BMIO BODI BOVU BSAI BUBT BUHS BZBO CINY ICBM IIRG KRES KSIR LAIR LASR OPNH TRUK
GLASTAR
G-BYEK BZDM CBAR CBCL CBJD CTEC ETCW GERY IARC LAZZ LEZZ LSTR SACH

STOLP
SA.100 STARDUSTER
G-BSZG
SA.300 STARDUSTER TOO
G-BNNA BOBT BPCE BRVB BSZB BTGS BUPB BZKD DUST JIII KEEN OTOO UINN
SA.500 STARLET
G-AZTV
SA.750 ACRODUSTER TOO
G-BLES BUGB
SA.900 V-STAR
G-BLAF

STRIKER - see FLEXIFORM

STRIPLIN
LONE RANGER
G-MBDL MBJM
SKY RANGER
G-MJKB

STROJNIK
S-2A
G-BMPS

SUD AVIATION - see GARDAN/SOCATA & including AËROSPATIALE/SOKO/WESTLAND production
SE.3130 ALOUETTE II/SA.315 LAMA
G-BSFU BVSD LAMA POSE UGLY
SA.341 GAZELLE
G-BAGL BCHM BKLS BXTH BXZD BXZE BZLA BZOS BZOT BZYB BZYC BZYD CBBV CBBY CBFD CBGZ DMSS EHUP EZEL GAZA GAZI GAZZ GZLE LOYD MANN NONA OCMJ OGAZ OGEO PAGS SFTA TURP UTZY UZEL WDEV WMAN ZLLE
SA.365 DAUPHIN 2
G-BKXD BLEZ BLUM BLUN BTEU BTNC BTUX BXLL BXPA MLTY PDGN PLMI

SUKHOI
Su-26M
G-XXVI

SUPER SCORPION - see HIWAY

SUPERMARINE
WALRUS/SEAGULL
G-AIZG RNLI
SPITFIRE/SEAFIRE
G-AIST AISU AWII AWIJ BKMI BMSB BRAF BRDV BRMG BRRA BRSF BSKP BUAR BUOS BWEM BXHZ BXVI BYDE CCIX CCVV CTIX FXII LFIX LFVB LFVC MKIA MKIX MKVB MKXI MXVI OXVI PMNF PRXI RRGN SPIT XVIE
SWIFT
G-SWIF

SURREY FLYING SERVICES
AL-1
G-AALP

SUSSEX
GAS BALLOON
G-AWOK

SWALLOW AEROPLANE CO
SWALLOW B
G-MJBK

SWEARINGEN
SA-227 METRO III
G-BUKA

SZD - see PZL

T

TARJANI
(Trike)
G-MJCU

TAYLOR
JT.1 MONOPLANE
G-APRT AWGZ AXYK AYSH AYUS BBBB BDAD BDAG BDJB BDKU BDNC BDNG BDNO BEHM BEUM BEVS BEYW BFBC BFDZ BFOU BFRF BGCY BGHY BILZ BJMO BKEU BKHY BLDB BMAO BMET BNAR BRUO BUXL BVDE BXTC BYAV CDGA CJIM CRIS DIPS DRAY SUZY WARD
JT.2 TITCH
G-BABE BARN BCSY BDRG BFID BGMS BIAX BKWD BVNI BZJS MISS MOLE OJON RKET TICH VIVI

TAYLOR - see AEROCAR

TAYLOR-WATKINSON

DINGBAT
G-AFJA

TAYLOR AIRCRAFT CO. INC - see PIPER

TAYLORCRAFT – see AUSTER

TAYLORCRAFT AIRCRAFT CORPN

BC-12D/BL-65/DF-65/DCO-65
G-AHNR AKVO BIGK BOLB BPHO BPHP BPPZ BREY BRIH BRIY BRPX BRXE BSCW BSDA BTFK BVDZ BVRH-BVXS BWLJ
F-19/F-21/F-22
G-BPJV BRIJ BVOX BWBI

TEAM

HI-MAX
G-MZHM MZIA
MINI-MAX
G-BVSB BVSX BVYK BXCD BXSU BYBW BYFV BYII BYJE BYYX BZDR BZTC CBIN MWFC MWFD MWHH MWLW MWSA MWWE MWZM MYAT MYBM MYCT MYDF MYGF MYGL MYII MYIZ MYKJ MYKZ MYLB MYNI MYRG MYRL MYSK MYTA MYXA MYYR MYYS MYZE MZCS MZII MZMO MZNM MZNN MZOY MZPJ NADS OJLH OSCO THEO

TECNAM (CONSTRUZIONI AERONAUTICHE TECNAM SRL)

P92 ECHO
G-BZHG BZWT CBAX CBDM CBGE CBUG OALH PGFG TECM WHEN

TED SMITH including PIPER production

AEROSTAR 601
G-MOVE RIGS TIME

TEMAN

MONO-FLY
G-MMJX MMPZ

TEVERSON

BISPORT
G-CBGH

THORN

COAL GAS BALLOON
G-ATGN

THORP including VENTURE

T-18
G-BLIT BSVN BYBY HATF
T-211
G-BTHP BXPF BXPO BYJF TZII

THRUSTER AIR SERVICES LTD inc THRUSTER AIRCRAFT (UK) LTD

TST
G-CBBC DRUM MCCF MTGB MTGC MTGD MTGE MTGF MTGP MTGR MTGS MTGT MTGU MTKA MTKB MTKD MTKE MTLM MTLN MTLR MTNR MTNS MTNT MTNU MTNV MTPT MTPU MTPV MTPW MTPX MTPY MTSH MTSJ MTSK MTSM MTST MTUB MTUC MTUD MTUF MTVP MTVR MTVS MTVT MTVV MTWY MTWZ MTXA MTXB MTXC MTXD MTZA MTZB MTZC MTZD MTZE MTZF MVAG MVAH MVAI MVAJ MVAK MVAL MVBP MVBT MVDD MVDE MVDF MVDG MVDH MVFJ MVFK MVFL MVFM MVFN MVFO MVHI MVHJ MVHK MVHL MVIR MVIT MVIU MVIV MVIW MVME MVMG MVMH MVMI MVOT MVOU MVOV MVOW MVOX MVOY MVXL-MVYE MWDP MYWZ MYEE OBAX OJSH OMAL
T.300/SUPER T300
G-MGWH MVUB MVWN MVWR MVWS MVZA MVZB MVZC MVZD MVZG MVZI MWAN MWAP MWAR MWDS MWWS MYAP MYAR MYDR MYDU MYJF MYJG MYXU
T.600
G-BYFN BYPF BYPG BYPH BYPI BZBG BZDB BZJC BZJD BZNP BZTD CBGU CBGV CBGW CBIO CBIP CBIR EVEY FJCE INGE MYWD MYWE MZFO MZFP MZFR MZFU MZGX MZGY MZGZ MZHA MZHC MZHD MZHE MZHF MZHS MZHU MZHV MZHW MZHX MZHY MZHZ MZKP MZKR MZKS MZKT MZKU MZNW MZNX MZNY MZOA MZOB PGSA RIVR UDGE WORM

THRUXTON - see JACKAROO AIRCRAFT

JACKAROO
G-ANFY ANZT AOEX AOIR

THUNDER BALLOONS LTD incl THUNDER & COLT LTD

Airship
AS-33
G-ERMS
AS-120
G-BZWF
Gas FB
AA-1050
G-BSRJ
HAFB
AX3 SKY CHARIOT
G-BHUR BJGE BJVF BKBD BKFG BKIY BKMR NEIL
AX4 series
G-LORY
AX5 series
G-BDAY BEEP BEMU BLOV
AX6 series
G-BBCP BBOO BBOY BCCH BCFU BEEE BEJB BERD BECS BETH BFIT BFOS BFOZ BGPF BGWY BGZZ BHAM BHTG BHXT BIIG BIIL BJVU BKUJ BLWB BPSJ BPUF BUSY BVRI BVUH DICK LDYS LIFE RTBI THOM TNTN
AX7 series
G-BAIR BAWW BAXK BBDJ BBOX BCAN BCAR BCAS BCCG BCIN BCNR BCSX BCZI BDGH BDGO BDMO BDON BEVI BFIX BGRS BGST BHAT BHEU BHHH BHIS BHOO BHSP BHZX BIGF BJHT BJSW BJZC BKDK BKUU BLAD BLAH BLCY BLET BLGX BLKJ BLTN BLUI BLZF BMCC BMHJ BMJS BMMU BMMW BMMY BMOG BMUU BMVT BMYS BNBL BNBV BNBW BNCC BNCU BNGO BNHO BNMX BNXZ BNZK BOAO BOIJ BORD BOSB BPBZ BPGF BPHU BPNU BPVU BPYK BPYZ BRDC BRDE BRLS BROA BRVN BRWF BRXB BRZE BSAV BSBN BSCF BSCO BSOJ BSZH BTAN BTAU BTHK BTRR BTTW BTVA BTXK BUDK BUIN BUKI BULB BUNV BUPU BUYI BVDB BWED BYNU BZBH FUND GASS GGGG GHIN HOWE LENS LYTE MLWI NEGS NIGS NWPB OFBJ OJDC OONI ORDY PIAF PIES PUFF RAFE RBOW RIGB RINO ROCK ROSI RUBI SFRY SOFT THOS USIL VIVA WDEB WINE
AX8 series
G-BJMW BOHF BORR BOTE BPZZ BRTT BRVY BSCX BSKI BSPB BSTK BSTY BTBB BTHM BTJD BTPX BTRO BTTK BUBL BUBY BUEI BUJW BUXW BUYD BVDW BVGB BVKH BVLS BVPA BVWB BWKW BYLV CBFG CBFH GEMS HAZE HOPS INGA ISTT KBKB OMDD OTEL PINE THOR TOOL ZEBO
AX9 series
G-BGHW BTOZ BTRN BTUJ BUAT BULK BVKZ BVSY BZBL IOAZ

AX10 series
G-BPSI G-BTJF BTNL BTYF BUNZ BUOZ BUVZ BWNX BWUR OLEO WORK
AX11 series
G-BXAD BXVF BZHX BZRZ
MLB
SPECIAL SHAPES

0.5
G-BBOD

	REGISTRATION	SHAPE	REGISTRATION
FILM CASSETTE	G-PHOT	FORK LIFT TRUCK	G-BWBH
ICE CREAM	G-ICES	JUMBO JET	G-UMBO
WHISKY BOTTLE	G-RARE		

THURSTON
TEAL
G-OWET TEAL

TIGER
T.200 MLB
G-BIMK

TIGER CUB - see MBA
RL5A SHERWOOD RANGER
G-BZUG CBHU GKFC HVAN MWND WZOL PUSY

TIPSY - including COBELAVIA/SLINGSBY production
TRAINER/B/BELFAIR
G-AFJR AFSC AFVN AFWT AISA AISC APIE APOD
JUNIOR
G-AMVP
T.66 NIPPER
G-APYB ARBG ARBP ARDY ARFV ARXN ASXI ASZV ATBW ATKZ ATUH AVKI AVKK AVKT AVXC AVXD AWDA BWHR AWJE AWJF AWLR AWLS AXLI AXZM AZBA BLMW BRIK BRPM BWCT BYLO CBCK CORD ENIE NIPA NIPP TIPS

TRAGO MILLS - see FLS

TREKKING - see AIRWAVE

TRI-FLYER - see MAINAIR

TRI-R TECHNOLOGIES
KIS
G-BVTA BVZD BXJI BZDR MANW OKIS OKMA OKPW TKIS
KIS CRUISER
G-BYZD

TRIDENT - see SHEFFIELD

TRIPACER - see ULTRASPORTS

TROTTER
AX3-90 HAFB
G-BRBT

TURLEY - see RAVEN

TURNER
SUPER T-40A
G-BRIO

TURNER - see CURRIE

TWAMLEY
TRIKE
G-MBGF MJWI

U AS

SOLAR/STORM BUGGY (Trike)
G-MJBS

ULTIMATE AIRCRAFT
10 DASH 200
G-BOFO

ULTRAFLIGHT
LAZAIR
G-MBYI MTDN MTFL MVGZ
MIRAGE
G-MBRH MBSX MBXX

ULTRAMAGIC SA
H-31
G-BZIZ BZPY
77 Variants
G-BXPT BZKW BZSH DAIV DWPH VOTE
105 Variants
G-BZPX BZRX
M-145: G-BZGI
N-210: G-BZPR BZPT
N-250: G-BZJX

ULTRASPORTS - see SOUTHDOWN
TRIPACER
G-MBAL MBFU MBLU MBPY MBTJ MBZA MJER MJFB MJFI MJHC MJHM MJHZ MJIA MJIC MJIZ MJTC MMEO MMFL MMMR MMPU MMUK MNGD MNSD

(combi PANTHER/TRIPACER/TYPHOON)
G-MBZK MJIY MMBY MMDE MMGS MMKA MMRR MMTC MMTS MMTT MMVF MMYN MMZP

ULTRAVIA

SUPER PELICAN
G-MWRS
PELICAN CLUB
G-BWWA

UNICORN

MLB variants
G-BINR BINS BINT BIWJ BJGM BJLF BJLG FYEK

V

VAHDAT

SEMICOPTER GYROPLANE
G-BZEV

VALENTIN

TAIFUN 17E
G-BMSE CEOA TFUN

VAN'S

RV-3
G-BVDC
RV-4/RV-4A
G-BOHW BROP BULG BVDI BVLR BVRV BVUN BVVS BXPI BXRV BZPH CBGN FTUO MAXV PIPS RMIT RVMJ RVDP RVRV SARV VANS
RV-6/RV-6A
G-BUEC BUTD BVCG BXJY BXVM BXVO BXWT BXYN BXYX BYDV BYEL BZOZ BZRV BZUY BZVN BZWZ BZXB CBCP EDRV EERV ESTR EYOR GDRV GLUC GPAG GRIN HOPY KELL NPKJ OJVA ONUN ORBD ORVG OTRV REAS RIVT RUSL RVAN RVAW RVBC RVCE RVCG RVCL RVDJ RVDR RVEE RVET RVGA RVIA RVIB RVIN RVIT RVIV RVMT RVSA RVSX RVVI SIXY TOGO VANZ XVOM
RV-7
G-RVII SEVN
RV-8
G-BZWN DUDE RVAL RVBA RVMX
RV-9A
G-RUVY RVIX

VAN DEN BEMDEN

GAS BALLOON
G-BBFS BDTU BIHP BWCC

VARGA

2150A KACHINA
G-BLHW BPVK CHTT DJCR VARG

VENTURE - see THORP

VERTICAL AVIATION TECHNOLOGIES

S-52-3 HUMMINGBIRD
G-BVBD BVBO

VICKERS

FB-5 GUNBUS
G-ATVP
FB.27 VIMY (incl rep)
G-EAOU
G-AWAU
V.600 VIKING
G-AGRU AGRW AIVG
V.668 VARSITY
G-BEDV BHDD
V.700/800 VISCOUNT
G-ALWF AMOG AOHL AOJD APIM AZLP AZLS AZNC BAPF OPAS
V.953 VANGUARD MERCHANTMAN
G-APEK APEP APES
(SUPER) VC-10
G-ARVM ASGC

VICKERS SUPERMARINE LTD – see SUPERMARINE

VICTA - including AESL production

AIRTOURER
G-ATCL ATEX ATHT ATJC AWMI AWVG AXIX AYLA AYMF AYWM AZBE AZHI AZHT AZMN AZOE AZOF AZRP AZTN BANY

VIKING

DRAGONFLY
G-BKPD BNEV BRKY DKGF

VOISIN

REP
G-BJHV

VOLMER

VJ.22 SPORTSMAN
G-BAHP

VOUGHT

F4U CORSAIR
G-BXUL CCMV FGID

VPM SNC

M-14 SCOUT
G-BUEN
M-16 TANDEM TRAINER
G-BUPM BUZL BVWX BXEJ BXIX BZJM BZXW CVPM DBDB POSA YFLY YRAT

W

WACO

UPF-7
G-WACO
YKS-7
G-BWAC

WAG-AERO INC

CUBY ACROTRAINER
G-BLDD BTWL
CUBY SPORT TRAINER
G-BVMH BZHU
WAG-A-BOND
G-BNJA

WALLBRO

MONOPLANE
G-BFIP

WALLINGFORD (WMB)
MLB variants
G-BIAI BIBX BILB

WALLIS including BEAGLE-WALLIS/VINTEN production
WA.116/WA.122
G-ARRT ARZB ASDY ATHM ATTB AVJV AVJW AXAS AYVO BAHH BGGU BGGV BGGW BLIK BMJX SCAN VIEW VTEN
WA.201
G-BNDG

W.A.R.
FOCKE-WULF FW190
G-BSLX JABO SYFW WULF
REPUBLIC P-47 THUNDERBOLT
G-BTBI
VOUGHT F-4U CORSAIR
G-BJNB

WARD
P45 GNOME
G-AXEI

WASP
GRYPHON (Wing)
G-MBPY MJYW

(SOCIETE) WASSMER - see JODEL
WA.41 SUPER BALADOU
G-ATSY ATZS AVEU
WA.52 PACIFIC/EUROPA
G-AZYZ BTLB
WA.81 PIRANHA
G-BKOT

WATKINSON - see TAYLOR-WATKINSON

WEEDHOPPER OF UTAH INC
JC-24
G-BHWH MBAD MTNK

WEST
AX3-15 HAFB:
G-BCFD

WESTERN
HAFB:
20
G-AYMV
O-31
G-AZPX
O-56
G-AZUX
O-65
G-AZBT AZJI AZOO BBCB BBUT

WESTLAND AIRCRAFT LTD & WESTLAND HELICOPTERS) LTD see SUD AVIATION & including SIKORSKY production)
LYSANDER
G-AZWT LIZY
WS.51 DRAGONFLY
G-BRMA
WS.51/2 WIDGEON
G-ANLW AOZE APTW
WS.55 WHIRLWIND
G-ANFH ANJV AODA APWN AYXT AYZJ BDBZ BEBC BJWY BVGE RWWW
WS.58 WESSEX
G-ATBZ AVNE AWOX AZBY BYRC HANA
WG.13 LYNX
G-BEAD BFDV LYNX
WG.30
G-BGHF BIWY BKGD BKKI BKXY BLLF HAUL KATE OGAS
SCOUT
G-BKLJ BWHU BWJW BWLX BXOE BXRR BXRS BXSL BYKJ BYRX BZBO CRUM KAXL NOTY ONEB SCTA SROE
WASP
G-BMIR BZPP KAWW RIMM

WESTLAND-AGUSTA - see EH INDUSTRIES

WESTLAND-BELL - see BELL

WHE
AIRBUGGY
G-AXYZ AXZA

WHEELER - see FLYLITE
SCOUT/SKYCRAFT
G-MBAR MBBB MBRE MBUZ

WHEELER
SLYMPH
G-ABOI

WHITTAKER - including AEROTECH
MW2B EXCALIBUR
G-BDDX
MW4/5/SORCERER
G-BZWX BZXL CBBO MBTH MMGV MNMM MNXZ MTAS MTBP MTBR MTBS MTDK MTFN MTHB MTLZ MTRX MVNN MVNO MVNP MVNR MVNS MVNT MVNU MWEK MWEO MWGI MWGJ MWGK MWIC MWJW MWLN MWSX MWSY MYAH MYAN MYDL MYDW MYJZ MYRB MZEI MZOH
MW6 MERLIN/MW6-S FATBOY FLYER/MW6-T
G-BUOA BYTX BZYU MNMW MTTF MURR MVPH MVPM MVPN MVTD MVXA MWAW MWHM MWIP MWLO MWOV MWPR MWSW MYCA MYCP MYCU MYDM MYET MYEV MYGE MYIE MYKO MYMN MYPS MYSN MYZA MYZN MZBG MZBX MZCH MZDI MZDL MZFK MZFS MZHG MZHT MZID MZJP MZNE MZOK
MW7
G-BOKH BOKJ BPUP BREE BRMW BSXX BTFV BTUS BWVN BZOW

WILD
BVS SPECIAL MLB
G-BJUB

WILLGRESS - see GRYPHON
GRYPHON
G-MBPS

WILLIAMS
KFZ-1 TIGERFALCK
G-KFZI

WILLIAMS (WESTWIND)
MLB variants
G-FYAN FYAO FYAU FYDI FYDP FYFJ

WILLS
AERA 2
G-BJKW

WINDSOR
MLB
G-BJGD

WITTMAN
TAILWIND
G-BCBR BDAP BDBD BDJC BJWT BMHL BNOB BOHV BOIB BPYJ CIPI JBPR WYND ZIPY

WITTY
SPHINX HAFB
G-BJLV

WOLF
W-II BOREDOM FIGHTER
G-BMZX BNAI

WOMBAT
GYROCOPTER
G-BFYP BWLZ WBAT

WOOD
DUET
G-DUET

WOODS - see AEROSPORT

WSK-PZL - see MIKOYAN
PZL-110 KOLIBER 150A/160A
G-BUDO BVAI BXLR BXLS BYSI BZAJ BZLC CBGA KOLI LOKM
MIELEC TS-11 ISKRA
G-BXVZ ISKA

YAKOVLEV - including ACROSTAR/IAV-BACHAU/LET/NANCHANG/SPP production
Yak-1
G-BTZD
Yak-3
G-BTHD BWOE
Yak-11
G-BTUB BTZE BZMY IYAK KYAK OYAK YCII
Yak-18
G-BMJY BVVG BVVX BXZB
Yak-50
G-BTZB BVVO BWFM BWJT BWWH BWWX BWYK FUNK IVAR VLAD YAKA
Yak-52
G-BVMU BVOK BVVA BVVW BVXK BWFP BWOD BWSV BWVR BXAK BXAV BXID BXJB BZJB BZTF CCCP YAKI YAKS YAKO YKSZ
Yak-55
G-YAKM

ZEBEDEE
V-31 HAFB
G-BXIT

ZENAIR - see HEINTZ/COLOMBAN
CH.200/250 ZENITH variants
G-BIRZ BPTO BTXZ DUNN GFKY RAYS
CH.600/601 ZODIAC variants
G-BRII BRJB BUTG BUZG BVAB BVAC BVPL BVVM BVZR BYEO BYJT BYLF BYPR BZFV CBAP CBCH CBDG CBDT CBGB CBIX CBJP CLEO OANN OMEZ OMWE ZAIR ZODI
CH.701 STOL/UL variants
G-BRDB BTMW BXIG BZJP BZVA CBGD EOIN FAMH OMEX TTDD ZENA

ZLIN
226/326/526 TRENER/TRENER MASTER/AKROBAT
G-AWJX AWJY AWSH BEWO BEZA BKOB BLMA BPNO BUPO EJGO TINY ZLIN ZLYN
Z.242
G-BWTC BWTD EKMN OZLN
Z.50L
G-MATE

SECTION 8

PART 2 - ALPHABETICAL TYPE INDEX-(IRELAND)

AERO COMPOSITES TECHNOLOGY INC

SEA HAWKER
EI-BUO

AERONCA

11AC CHIEF
EI-CCF CRR
15AC SEDAN
EI-BJJ BKC

AÉROSPATIALE

AS.350B ECUREUIL
EI-CGQ IRV
SA.365 DAUPHIN 2
EI-MIP

AGUSTA S.p.A

A109
EI-BUX CHV DLP ECA JBC MEL SQG

AIR & SPACE

18A
EI-CNG

AIRBUS INDUSTRIE

A.300
EI-CEB CJK CPC CPD CPE CPF DHL EAA EAB EAC EAD EAE EAF EAT SAF
A.319
EI-CWY CWZ CXA
A.320
EI-CTD CUC CUK CUQ CVA CVB CVC CVD CVE CVF CWT CWU CWV TAA TAI
A.321
EI-CPC CPD CPE CPF CPG CPH CUM
A.330
EI-CRK EI-DAA DUB EWR JFK LAX ORD SHN

AMF MICROFLIGHT LTD

CHEVVRON
EI-BVJ CAU

AUSTER AIRCRAFT LTD incl TAYLORCRAFT production

PLUS C/D
EI-AGD ALH AMF ANA
J/1 AUTOCRAT/J/1N ALPHA:
EI-AGJ AMK AMY AUM
J/4
EI-CPN
J/5F AIGLET TRAINER
EI-AUS

AVIAMILANO SRL

F.8L FALCO
EI-BCJ BMF

AVID AIRCRAFT INC

AVID SPEEDWING
EI-CIM

AVIONS DE TRANSPORT REGIONAL

ATR-42
EI-CBK CPT CVR CVS
ATR-72
EI-CBD CLB CLC CLD CMJ

A V ROE & CO LTD

631/643 CADET
EI-ALP ALU
748
EI-BSF

BA

SWALLOW 2
EI-AFF

BAE SYSTEMS (OPERATIONS) LTD

BAe 146 (including Avro variants)
EI-CLG CLH CLI CLJ CLY CMS CMY CNB CNI CNJ CNK CNQ COF COQ CPJ CPK CPL-CPY CSK CSL CTM CTN CTO CWA CWB CWC CWD PAT

BEAGLE AIRCRAFT LTD

A.109 AIREDALE
EI-BAL
B.121 PUP
EI-ATJ

BEAGLE-AUSTER AIRCRAFT LTD

A.61 TERRIER
EI-ASU

BEECH AIRCRAFT CORPORATION

23 MUSKETEER
EI-BFF
58 BARON
EI-CPS
76 DUCHESS
EI-BUN CMX
77 SKIPPER
EI-BHT
200 SUPER KING AIR:
EI-WHE

BELL HELICOPTER TEXTRON INC

206A/B JET RANGER I/II
EI-BHI BIJ BKT BXX BYJ CAW CLT CUG CUS HER HXM MER ONE PMI PRI RMC WSH WSN
206L LONG RANGER
EI-BYR CHL CIO
222
EI-WBC-WRC

407
EI-STR
430
EI-WAV

BENSEN AIRCRAFT CORPORATION

B.8 GYROCOPTER
EI-BCF BSG

BOEING AIRCRAFT CO/BOEING COMPANY

717-200 series
EI-CWJ CWK CWM CWN
727-200 series
EI-HCA HCB HCC HCD HCI LCH SKY
737-200 series
EI-CJC CJD CJE CJF CJG CJH CJI CKP CKQ CKR CKS CNT CNV CNW CNX CNY CNZ COA COB CON COX
-300 series
EI-BZE BZF BZJ BZL BZM BZN CLW CLZ CRZ CUL
-400 series
EI-BXB BXC BXD BXI BXK COH COI COJ CUA CUD CUN CVN CVO CVP CWE CWF CWW CWX PAM PAR
-500 series
EI-CDB CDC CDD CDE CDF CDH CHH
-700 series
EI-CRP CRQ
-800 series
EI-CSA CSB CSC CSD CSE CSF CSG CSH CSI-CSJ CSM CSN CSO CSP CSR CSS CST CSU CSV CSW CSX CSY CSZ CTA CTB
-XXX series
EI-TVD TVE TVF TVG TVH TVI TVJ TVK TVL TVM
757-200 series
EI-CEY CEZ
767-300 series
: EI-CRD CRF CRL CRO CRM CTW
777-200 series
EI-CRS CRT

BRITTEN-NORMAN LTD

BN.2A ISLANDER
EI-AYN BCE CUW IPC

CAMERON BALLOONS LTD

65 variants
EI-BBM BSN BVC
77 variant
EI-CKJ
84 variant
EI-BAY
105 variant
EI-CUE

CARLSON

SPARROW
EI-COO

CESSNA AIRCRAFT COMPANY including REIMS (F.prefix) production

150
EI-APF AST AVM AWE BAT BFE BHW BYF CDV CHM CIN CML CMV COP
A150 AEROBAT
EI-AUC AUO AYF BRX CTI
152
EI-BGJ BIB BMM BMN CCJ CCK CCL CCM CGT CRU
A152 AEROBAT
EI-BJM
172/SKYHAWK
EI-AOK AYK BAG BAO BAS BCK BIC BIR BKF BPL BRM BRS BSC CFN CFP CFY CGD CHS CLQ COT GWY MCF EI-SAC STT
172RG CUTLASS
EI-BPC
R172 HAWK XP/FR172 ROCKET
EI-BJI BJO CCV
175
EI-AND
177(RG) CARDINAL
EI-BHC POD
(R)182/SKYLANE (RG)
EI-AOD BCL BPJ CAP CDP GSM
206 SUPER SKYLANE/STATIONAIR
EI-BGK BNK SBP
210 CENTURION
EI-AWH BUF CAX CDX CGH
310
EI-AOS
335
EI-CUP
337 SUPER SKYMASTER
EI-AVC BHM
340
EI-CGX CIJ
441
EI-DMG
525A CITATIONJET
EI-OPM
550 CITATION BRAVO/551 CITATION II
EI-CIR DAB GHP PAL
560XL CITATION EXCEL
EI-PAX

CFM METAL-FAX

(STREAK) SHADOW
EI-CHR CMF

CHAMPION/AERONCA including BELLANCA production

7AC/7DC CHAMPION
EI-ATL AVB BJB BJC
7EC TRAVELER
EI-BBE BHV
CITABRIA
EI-ANT BYX
SUPER DECATHLON
EI-BIV

COLT BALLOONS LTD

77A HAFB
EI-BGT

DE HAVILLAND AIRCRAFT CO LTD

DH.82A TIGER MOTH
EI-AHI ANN AOP AWP
DH.84 DRAGON
EI-ABI
DH.104 DOVE
EI-BJW

DE HAVILLAND (CANADA)
DHC-8 DASH EIGHT
EI-CBJ CHP

DOUGLAS AIRCRAFT COMPANY INC - also see McDONNELL DOUGLAS
DC-3
EI-AYO

DRUINE
D.62 CONDOR
EI-BCP BXT

EIPPER
QUICKSILVER
EI-BKS BLE BLN BOH BPP

ERCO
ERCOUPE 415
EI-AUT CGG CVL

EUROCOPTER
EC 120
EI-EUR IZO MIK

EUROPA AVIATION
EUROPA
EI-COE

EUROWING LTD
GOLDWING
EI-BNF CMK

EVANS
VP-1
EI-AYY BBD BLU BRU
VP-2
EI-BNJ BVT

EXTRA
EA.300/200
EI-SAM

FLEXIFORM - see MAINAIR
STRIKER
EI-BPN
TRIKE
EI-BRK

FLEXWING
M.17727
EI-BRT

FOKKER AIRCRAFT BV/FOKKER VFW NV including FAIRCHILD-HILLER production
F.27-050
EI-FKC FKD FKE FKF
FH-227
EI-CAZ CLF

FOUGA
CM-170 MAGISTER
EI-BXO

GARDAN
GY-80 HORIZON
EI-AYB

GROB-WERKE GMB & CO KG
G-109
EI-HCS
G-115
EI-CAC CAE CCD

GRUMMAN-AMERICAN AVIATION CORPN
AA-1 TRAINER:
EI-CCY
AA-5 TRAVELER/TIGER
EI-AYD BJS BMV BNR

GULFSTREAM AEROSPACE CORPORATION
GULFSTREAM IV/V
EI-CVT WGV

GYROSCOPIC
GYROPLANE
EI-COG

HAWKER SIDDELEY AVIATION
HS.125
EI-COV RRR WDC WJN

HIWAY HANG GLIDERS LTD
DEMON (Wing)SKYTRIKE
EI-BNH BPU BRV CGE
VULCAN (Wing)
EI-BMW

HOAC FLUGZEUGWERKE incl DIAMOND production
DV-20 KATANA
EI-CLA

HOFFMANN FLUGZEUGBAU FRIESACH
H-36 DIMONA
EI-CRV

HOVEY
DELTA BIRD
EI-BRW

HUGHES TOOL CO/HELICOPTERS INC incl SCHWEIZER AIRCRAFT CORPORATION
269 (Srs 300)
EI-CVM CWS LRS

HUNT
AVON
EI-CKG

III
SKY ARROW
EI-CPX

JABIRU AIRCRAFT (PTY) LTD
JABIRU UL
EI-JAK

JODEL incl CEA/SAN/WASSMER production
D.9 BEBE
EI-BUC
D.112
EI-BSB CKX
D.18
EI-CKZ
D.120 PARIS-NICE
EI-CJS
DR.1050 AMBASSADEUR
EI-ARW

LAKE AIRCRAFT CORPORATION
LA-4 BUCCANEER
EI-BUH CEX

LEARJET CORPORATION INC
LEARJET 60
EI-IAU IAW

LETOV AIR
LK-2M SLUKA
EI-CAN

LINDSTRAND BALLOONS LTD
LBL-90A
EI-CRB

LOCKHEED-CALIFORNIA CO
L.1011 TRISTAR
EI-CNN

McCANDLESS
M.4 GYROPLANE
EI-ASR

McDONNELL DOUGLAS CORPORATION
DC-8
EI-BNA CGO
DC-9-82/83
EI-BTX BTY BWD CBR CBS CBY CBZ CCC CCE CDY CEK CEP CEQ CFZ CIW CKM CMM CMZ CNR CPB CRE CRH CRJ CRW CTJ
DC-10
EI-DLA

MAINAIR SPORTS LTD
GEMINI/FLASH (Combi)
EI-CKT
MERCURY
EI-CMU

MALMO
Bo.208 JUNIOR
EI-AWR

MAULE AIRCRAFT CORPORATION
MX-7
EI-CUT GER

MBB
Bo.105
EI-BLD LIT

MEDWAY MICROLIGHTS LTD
ECLIPSE R
EI-CRY CTC ELL

MONNETT
MONI
EI-BMU

MOONEY AIRCRAFT CORPORATION
M.20
EI-CAY CIK

MORANE-SAULNIER
MS.502
EI-AUY
MS.880/885/887/892/894 RALLYE variants
EI-ATS AUE AUG AUJ AUP AWU AYA AYI AYT AYV BBG BBI BBJ BBO BCH BCS BCU BCW BDH BDK BEA BEP BFB BFI BFM BFP BFR BFV BGA BGB BGC BGD BGG BGS BGU BHB BHF BHN BHP BHY BIM BIT BIW BJK BKE BKN BKU BMA BMB BMH BMJ BNG BNU BOP BUJ BUT CEG CHN CIA

MOSKITO
MOSKITO 2
EI-CJV

NOBLE HARDMAN AVIATION LTD
SNOWBIRD
EI-BUW

PARTENAVIA COSTRUZIONI AERONAUTICHE S.p.A
P.68
EI-BWH

PEGASUS AVIATION
QUANTUM
EI-CNU

PHOENIX
LUTON LA-4A MINOR:
EI-ATP
LUTON LA-5A MAJOR
EI-CGF

PIEL
CP.301 EMERAUDE
EI-CFG

PIPER AIRCRAFT CORPORATION
J-3C CUB
EI-AFE AKM BBV BCM BCN BCO BEN BFO BIO BSX BYY CCH CFO CHK COY CPP CUB
J-5A CUB CRUISER
EI-CGV
PA-12 SUPER CRUISER
EI-ADV CFF CFH
PA-18 SUPER CUB
EI-ANY BID BIK CIG CKH
PA-22 TRI-PACER/COLT
EI-AWD AYS BAV UFO
PA-23 AZTEC
EI-BDM BLW EEC WAC WMN
PA-28-140/160 CHEROKEE/CRUISER
EI-AOB ATK BSO CGP CIV CMB COZ
PA-28-151/161 CHEROKEE/WARRIOR
EI-CTT WRN
PA-28-180/181 CHEROKEE
EI-BBC BDR CIF
PA-28R CHEROKEE ARROW
EI-BGF EDR
PA-31 NAVAJO CHIEFTAIN
EI-CNM WYO
PA-34 SENECA
EI-BSL CMT EIO
PA-38 TOMAHAWK
EI-BJT BUR BUS BVK
PA-44 SEMINOLE
EI-SKT

POLARIS MOTOR SRL
FIB OK350
EI-BXL

PTERODACTYL LTD
Microlight
EI-BOA

RAND-ROBINSON
KR-2
EI-BNL BOV

(AVION PIERRE) ROBIN
DR.400/180R REMORQUER
EI-CRG
R.1180T AIGLON
EI-BIS

ROBINSON HELICOPTER CO INC
R22 BETA
EI-CFE CFX CMI CPO CWL CWR JWM MAG TKI XMC
R44 ASTRO
EI-CUI JFD MUL

ROTORWAY
EXECUTIVE
EI-CMW UCD

RUTAN
LONG-EZE
EI-CMR CPI

SCHLEICHER
ASK14
EI-APS
ASK16
EI-AYR

SHORT BROTHERS LTD
SD.3-30
EI-EXP

SIKORSKY AIRCRAFT
S-61
EI-BLY CNL MES RCG SAR

SKYHOOK
SAILWINGS SABRE (Wing)
EI-BPT

SLINGSBY SAILPLANES LTD
T.21 CADET
EI-CJT
T.56 SE.5 rep
EI-ARH ARM

SNCAN STAMPE including AIA production
STAMPE SV.4A/C
EI-BAJ BLB CJR

SOCATA
ST.10 DIPLOMATE
EI-BUG
TB.9 TAMPICO
EI-BMI BSK BYG CRX GFC
TB.10 TOBAGO
EI-BOE
TB.20 TRINIDAD
EI-BSV

SOLAR WINGS LTD
XL-R
EI-BSW CGJ CGM CGN CKU

SOUTHDOWN SAILWINGS LTD
PUMA
EI-BPO

STEEN AERO LAB.INC
SKYBOLT
EI-CIZ SAT

STINSON AIRCRAFT CORPORATION
108 STATION WAGON
EI-CGC

STODDARD-HAMILTON
GLASAIR
EI-CTG

STOLP
SA.300 STARDUSTER TOO
EI-CDQ

TAYLOR
JT.1 MONOPLANE
EI-BKK

TAYLORCRAFT AIRCRAFT CORPN
BC-65
EI-CES

TEAM
MINIMAX
EI-CGB CNC

THRUSTER AIR SERVICES LTD
T.300
EI-CEN
TST
EI-BYA CKI

THUNDER BALLOONS LTD
AX8 variant
EI-BAR

VIKING
DRAGONFLY
EI-BPE

WHITTAKER
MW5
EI-BUL CAN CTL
MW6 MERLIN/MW6-S FATBOY FLYER:
EI-BVB CJZ CKN CLL COM

ZENAIR - see HEINTZ/COLOMBAN
CH.200/250 ZENITH variants
EI-BVY BYL

ZLIN
526 TRENER MASTER
EI-BIG

SECTION 8

PART 3 - AIRCRAFT WEARING MILITARY MARKINGS

In certain circumstances the Civil Aviation Authority may permit the operation of an aircraft without the need to carry regulation size national registration letters. These conditions are referred to as "exemptions". The CAA will issue to each operator an Exemption Certificate which is usually valid for two years. The basic requirements are that the owner undertakes to notify the CAA of the markings carried and may not, without specific permission of the overseas country, fly overseas.

In the case of aircraft wearing military marks the authority of the relevant department at the Ministry of Defence is required for UK markings whilst an equivalent establishment must sanction any overseas markings to be carried. Below are current details of all aircraft and gliders which are known to be wearing military or, in a very few cases, Class B marks. The information is compiled from member's observations and includes any BAPC & "B" Conditions identitites and overseas registered aircraft known to be based in the UK & Ireland. Full details of BAPC markings are carried in SECTION 4 and c/ns for all can be found in their respective Sections. We should point out that some of the serials used below are spurious - these are annotated with asterisks.

Country	Serial		Code	Regn	Type
UNITED KINGDOM - (RAF unless otherwise shown)					
	168			G-BFDE	Sopwith Tabloid Scout rep (RNAS)
	304	*		BAPC.62	Cody Biplane (RFC)
	687	*		BAPC.181	RAF BE.2b (RFC)
	1701	*		BAPC.117	RAF BE.2c rep (RFC)
	2345			G-ATVP	Vickers FB.5 Gunbus rep (RFC)
	2882	*		BAPC.234	Vickers FB.5 Gunbus rep (RFC)
	3066			G-AETA	Caudron G.III (RNAS)
	5964	*		BAPC.112	DH.2 rep (RFC)
	5964			G-BFVH	DH.2 rep
	6232	*		BAPC.41	RAF BE.2c rep (RFC)
	A1742	*		BAPC.38	Bristol Scout D rep (RFC)
	A4850	*		BAPC.176	SE.5A rep (RFC)
	A7317	*		BAPC.179	Sopwith Pup rep (RFC)
	A8226			G-BIDW	Sopwith "1 ½" Strutter rep (RFC)
	B415	*		BAPC.163	AFEE 10/45 Rotabuggy rep
	B595		W	G-BUOD	SE.5A rep (RFC)
	B1807		A7	G-EAVX	Sopwith Pup (RFC) - intended marks
	B2458		R	G-BPOB	Sopwith Camel rep (RFC)
	B3459		2	G-BWMJ	Nieuport Scout 17/23 rep (RFC)
	B5577	*		BAPC.59	Sopwith F1 Camel rep
	B6401			G-AWYY	Sopwith Camel rep (RFC)
	B7270			G-BFCZ	Sopwith Camel rep (RFC)
	C1904		Z	G-PFAP	SE.5A (Currie Wot) (RFC)
	C3011		S	G-SWOT	SE.5A (Currie Wot) (RFC)
	C4451	*		BAPC.210	Avro 504J rep (RFC)
	C4918			G-BWJM	Bristol M.1C rep
	C4994			G-BLWM	Bristol M.1C rep (RFC)
	C9533		M	G-BUWE	SE.5A rep (RFC)
	D276	*	A	BAPC.208	SE.5A rep (RFC)
	B5577	*		BAPC.59	Sopwith Camel rep (RFC)
	D7889			G-AANM	Bristol F.2b
	D8084	*	S	G-ACAA	Bristol F.2b
	D8096			G-AEPH	Bristol F.2b
	D8781			G-ECKE	Avro 504K rep (RFC)
	E449			G-EBJE	Avro 504K
	E2466	*		BAPC.165	Bristol F2b
	F141		G	G-SEVA	SE.5A rep (RFC)
	F235		B	G-BMDB	SE.5A rep (RFC)
	F904		H	G-EBIA	SE.5A (RFC)
	F938			G-EBIC	SE.5A (RFC)
	F943			G-BIHF	SE.5A rep (RFC)
	F5447		N	G-BKER	SE.5A rep (RFC)
	F5459		Y	G-INNY	SE.5A rep (RFC)
	F5459	*	Y	BAPC.142	SE.5A rep (RFC)
	F5475	*		BAPC.250	SE.5A rep (RFC)
	F8010		Z	G-BDWJ	SE.5A rep (RFC)
	F8614			G-AWAU	Vickers FB.27A Vimy rep
	H1968	*		BAPC.42	Avro 504K rep
	H3426	*		BAPC.68	Hawker Hurricane rep

H5199			G-ADEV	Avro 504K
J7326			G-EBQP	DH.53 Humming Bird - intended marks
J9941			G-ABMR	Hawker Hart II
K1786			G-AFTA	Hawker Tomtit
K1930			G-BKBB	Hawker Fury II
K2050			G-ASCM	Hawker (Isaacs) Fury
K2059			G-PFAR	Hawker (Isaacs) Fury
K2060			G-BKZM	Hawker (Isaacs) Fury
K2075			G-BEER	Hawker (Isaacs) Fury
K2227			G-ABBB	Bristol Bulldog IIA
K2567			G-MOTH	DH.82 Tiger Moth
K2572			G-AOZH	DH.82A Tiger Moth
K2587			G-BJAP	DH.82A Tiger Moth
K3215			G-AHSA	Avro Tutor
K3731			G-RODI	Hawker (Isaacs) Fury
K4232			SE-AZB	Cierva C.30A (Avro Rota)
K4259		71	G-ANMO	DH.82A Tiger Moth
K5054			G-BRDV	V-S Spitfire Prototype rep
K5054	*		BAPC.190	V-S Spitfire rep
K5054	*		BAPC.214	V-S Spitfire rep
K5414		XV	G-AENP	Hawker Hind
K5600			G-BVVI	Hawker Audax
K5673	*		BAPC.249	Hawker Fury I rep
K5673			G-BZAS	Hawker Fury I rep
K7271	*		BAPC.148	Hawker Fury rep
K8203			G-BTVE	Hawker Demon I
K8303		D	G-BWWN	Hawker (Isaacs) Fury
L1070	*	XT-A	BAPC.227	V-S Spitfire rep
L1679	*	JX-G	BAPC.241	Hawker Hurricane 1 rep
L1710	*	AL-D	BAPC.219	Hawker Hurricane rep
L2301			G-AIZG	V-S Walrus 1 (RN)
L6906			G-AKKY	Miles Magister
N500			G-BWRA	Sopwith Triplane rep (RNAS)
N546	*		BAPC.164	Wight Quadruplane rep
N1854			G-AIBE	Fairey Fulmar 2 (RN)
N2276	*		G-GLAD	Gloster Gladiator II
N3194	*	GR-Z	BAPC.220	V-S Spitfire rep
N3289	*	QV-K	BAPC.65	V-S Spitfire rep
N3313	*	KL-B	BAPC.69	V-S Spitfire rep
N4877			G-AMDA	Avro 652A Anson 1
N5182			G-APUP	Sopwith Pup (RNAS)
N5195			G-ABOX	Sopwith Pup (RNAS)
N5492	*	B	BAPC.111	Sopwith Triplane rep (RNAS)
N6181			G-EBKY	Sopwith Pup (RNAS)
N6290			G-BOCK	Sopwith Triplane rep (RNAS)
N6452			G-BIAU	Sopwith Pup rep (RNAS)
N6466			G-ANKZ	DH.82A Tiger Moth
N6740			G-AISY	DH.82A Tiger Moth
N6797			G-ANEH	DH.82A Tiger Moth
N6847			G-APAL	DH.82A Tiger Moth
N6965		FL-J	G-AJTW	DH.82A Tiger Moth
N6985			G-AHMN	DH.82A Tiger Moth
N9191			G-ALND	DH.82A Tiger Moth (RN)
N9192		RCO-N	G-DHZF	DH.82A Tiger Moth
N9389			G-ANJA	DH.82A Tiger Moth
N9926	*	JH-C	BAPC.217	V-S Spitfire rep
P2793	*	SD-M	BAPC.236	Hawker Hurricane rep
P2902		DX-X	G-ROBT	Hawker Hurricane I
P3059	*	SD-N	BAPC.64	Hawker Hurricane rep
P3208	*	SD-T	BAPC.63	Hawker Hurricane rep
P3386	*	FT-I	BAPC.218	Hawker Hurricane rep
P6382		C	G-AJRS	Miles Magister
P7350		BA-Y	G-AWIJ	V-S 329 Spitfire F.IIA
P8140	*	ZF-K	BAPC.71	V-S Spitfire rep
P8448	*	UM-D	BAPC.225	V-S Spitfire rep
R1914			G-AHUJ	Miles Magister
R3821		UX-N	G-BPIV	Bristol Blenheim IV
R4897			G-ERTY	DH.82A Tiger Moth
R4959		59	G-ARAZ	DH.82A Tiger Moth
R5136			G-APAP	DH.82A Tiger Moth
S1287		5	G-BEYB	Fairey Flycatcher rep (FAA)
S1579		571	G-BBVO	Hawker Nimrod (Isaacs Fury) (RN)
S1581		573	G-BWWK	Hawker Nimrod 1 (FAA)
T5424			G-AJOA	DH.82A Tiger Moth

T5672			G-ALRI	DH.82A Tiger Moth
T5854			G-ANKK	DH.82A Tiger Moth
T5879		RUC-W	G-AXBW	DH.82A Tiger Moth
T6313			G-AHVU	DH.82A Tiger Moth
T6562			G-ANTE	DH.82A Tiger Moth
T6818			G-ANKT	DH.82A Tiger Moth
T6953			G-ANNI	DH.82A Tiger Moth
T6991			G-ANOR	DH.82A Tiger Moth
T7230			G-AFVE	DH.82A Tiger Moth
T7281			G-ARTL	DH.82A Tiger Moth
T7328			G-APPN	DH.82A Tiger Moth
T7404		04	G-ANMV	DH.82A Tiger Moth
T7471			G-AJHU	DH.82A Tiger Moth
T7842			G-AMTF	DH.82A Tiger Moth
T7909			G-ANON	DH.82A Tiger Moth
T7997			G-AHUF	DH.82A Tiger Moth
T8191			G-BWMK	DH.82A Tiger Moth
T9707			G-AKKR	Miles M.14A Hawk Trainer
T9738			G-AKAT	Miles M.14A Hawk Trainer
V1075			G-AKPF	Miles M.14A Hawk Trainer
V3388			G-AHTW	Airspeed Oxford 1
V6028		GB-D	G-MKIV	Bristol Blenheim IV
V6799	*	SD-X	BAPC.72	Hawker Hurricane rep
V7476	*	LE-D	BAPC.223	Hawker Hurricane rep
V9367		MA-B	G-AZWT	Westland Lysander IIIA
V9545		BA-C	G-BCWL	Westland Lysander IIIA
V9673		MA-J	G-LIZY	Westland Lysander III
W2718		AA5Y	G-RNLI	V-S Walrus (RN)
W5856		A2A	G-BMGC	Fairey Swordfish II
W9385		YG-L	G-ADND	DH.87B Hornet Moth
Z2033		N/275	G-ASTL	Fairey Firefly TT.1
Z5053			G-BWHA	Hawker Hurricane IIB
Z5252		GO-B	G-BWHA	Hawker Hurricane IIB
Z7015		7-L	G-BKTH	Hawker Sea Hurricane IB (RN)
Z7197			G-AKZN	Percival Proctor III
Z7381		XR-T	G-HURI	Hawker Hurricane IIB
AA908	*	UM-W	BAPC.230	V-S Spitfire rep
AB910		ZD-C	G-AISU	V-S Spitfire LF.Vb
AH545		WQ-Z	N9521C	Consolidated 28-5ACF (PBY-5A) Catalina
AP507		KX-P	G-ACWP	Cierva C.30A (Avro Rota)
AR213		PR-D	G-AIST	V-S Spitfire IA
AR352	*	RF-C	G-MKVB	V-S Spitfire Vb - see BM597
AR501		NN-A	G-AWII	V-S Spitfire Vc
AR614		DU-Z	G-BUWA	V-S Spitfire Vc
AR654	*	RF-T	G-BKMI	V-S Spitfire VIIIc - see MT928
AR3185	*	RF-M	G-LFVB	V-S Spitfire V - see EP120
AR4474	*	RF-Y	G-AWII	V-S Spitfire Vc - see AR501
BB807			G-ADWO	DH.82A Tiger Moth
BE417		AE-K	G-HURR	Hawker Hurricane IIB
BE421	*	XP-G	BAPC.205	Hawker Hurricane rep
BL924	*	AZ-G	BAPC.242	V-S Spitfire Vb rep
BM597		JH-C	G-MKVB	V-S Spitfire Vb
BR600		SH-V	BAPC.222	V-S Spitfire rep
BR600		JP-A	BAPC.224	V-S Spitfire rep
BW881			G-KAMM	Hawker Hurricane XIIA
CB733			G-BCUV	SA Bulldog
DE208			G-AGYU	DH.82A Tiger Moth
DE470		16	G-ANMY	DH.82A Tiger Moth
DE623			G-ANFI	DH.82A Tiger Moth
DE673			G-ADNZ	DH.82A Tiger Moth
DE970			G-AOBJ	DH.82A Tiger Moth
DE992			G-AXXV	DH.82A Tiger Moth
DF112			G-ANRM	DH.82A Tiger Moth
DF128		RCO-U	G-AOJJ	DH.82A Tiger Moth
DF155			G-ANFV	DH.82A Tiger Moth
DG590			G-ADMW	Miles Hawk Major
DR628		PB-1	N18V	Beechcraft Traveler
EM720			G-AXAN	DH.82A Tiger Moth
EN224			G-FXII	V-S Spitfire XII - intended marks
EN343			BAPC.226	V-S Spitfire rep
EN398		WO-A	BAPC.184	V-S Spitfire IX rep
EP120		AE-A	G-LFVB	V-S Spitfire Vb
FB226		MT-A	G-BDWM	N-A Mustang (Bonsall Mustang)
FE695		94	G-BTXI	N-A Harvard IIB

FE905			LN-BNM	N-A Harvard IIB
FE992		K-T	G-BDAM	N-A Harvard IIB
FJ777			G-BIXN	Boeing-Stearman Kaydet
FR886	*		G-BDMS	Piper Cub
FR887	*		G-BWEZ	Piper L-4 Cub (US Army)
FS628	*		G-AIZE	Fairchild Argus
FT323		GN	FAP 1513	N-A Harvard III
FT375			G-BWUL	N-A Harvard IIB
FT391			G-AZBN	N-A Harvard IIB
FX301	*	FD-NQ	G-JUDI	N-A Harvard III
HB275			G-BKGM	Beechcraft Expeditor
HB751			G-BCBL	Fairchild Argus III
HM580		KX-K	G-ACUU	Cierva C.30A (Avro Rota)
JV828			N423RS	Consolidated-Vultee PBY-5A Catalina
KB889		NA-I	G-LANC	Avro Lancaster X
KD345		A-130	G-FGID	Vought FG-1D Corsair (RN)
KF584			G-RAIX	N-A Harvard IV
KJ351			BAPC.80	Airspeed Horsa II
KZ321			G-HURY	Hawker Hurricane IV
LB312			G-AHXE	Taylorcraft Plus D (Auster I)
LB367			G-AHGZ	Taylorcraft Plus D (Auster I)
LB375			G-AHGW	Taylorcraft Plus D (Auster I)
LF789			BAPC.186	DH.82B Queen Bee
LF858			G-BLUZ	DH.82B Queen Bee
LS326		L/2	G-AJVH	Fairey Swordfish II
LZ766			G-ALCK	Percival Proctor III
MAV467		R-O	BAPC.202	V-S Spitfire V rep
MH434		ZD-B	G-ASJV	V-S Spitfire IXB
MH486		FF-A	BAPC.206	V-S Spitfire rep
MH777		RF-N	BAPC.221	V-S Spitfire rep
MJ627		9G-P	G-BMSB	V-S Spitfire IX
MJ730		GZ-?	G-HFIX	V-S Spitfire IXe
MJ751		DU-V	BAPC.209	V-S Spitfire rep
MJ832		DN-Y	BAPC.229	V-S Spitfire rep
MK732		3W-17	G-HVDM	V-S Spitfire IXc
MK805	*	SH-B	*	V-S Spitfire IX rep
* Built by TDL Rep Aircraft, in 64 Sqn c/s, as SH-B/"Peter John III"				
MK912		SH-L	G-BRRA	V-S Spitfire IX
ML407		OU-V/NL-D	G-LFIX	V-S Spitfire IX
ML417		2I-T	G-BJSG	V-S Spitfire IXe
MP425			G-AITB	Airspeed Oxford I
MT438			G-AREI	Auster III
MT928		ZX-M	G-BKMI	V-S Spitfire VIIIc
MV262			G-CCVV	V-S Spitfire XIV - intended marks
MV268		JE-J	G-SPIT	V-S Spitfire XIVe
MV370		EB-Q	G-FXIV	V-S Spitfire XIV
MW763		HF-A	G-TEMT	Hawker Tempest II
MW800		HF-V	G-BSHW	Hawker Tempest II
NH238		D-A	G-MKIX	V-S Spitfire IX
NJ673			G-AOCR	Auster 5
NJ695			G-AJXV	Auster 4
NJ703			G-AKPI	Auster 5
NJ719			G-ANFU	Auster 5 - intended marks
NL750			G-AOBH	DH.82A Tiger Moth
NL772			G-BXMN	DH.82A Tiger Moth
NL985			G-BWIK	DH.82A Tiger Moth
NM181			G-AZGZ	DH.82A Tiger Moth
NS519	*		G-MOSI	DH.98 Mosquito 35 (RAF/USAAF)
NX534			G-BUDL	Auster III
NX611		LE-C/DX-C	G-ASXX	Avro Lancaster B.VII
PL344		Y2-B	G-IXCC	V-S Spitfire IXe
PL965		R	G-MKXI	V-S Spitfire PR.XI
PL983		JV-F	G-PRXI	V-S Spitfire XI
PP972			G-BUAR	V-S Seafire III
PR772			G-BTTA	Hawker Iraqi Fury FB.11
PS853		C	G-RRGN	V-S Spitfire PR.XIX
PT462		SW-A	G-CTIX	V-S Spitfire IX
PV202		5R-Q	G-TRIX	V-S Spitfire IX
PZ865		Q	G-AMAU	Hawker Hurricane IIc
RG333	*		G-AIEK	Miles Messenger
RM221			G-ANXR	Percival Proctor IV
RN201			G-BSKP	V-S Spitfire XIV - intended marks
RN218		N	G-BBJI	Isaacs Spitfire
RR232			G-BRSF	V-S Spitfire IXc

RT486	PF-A	G-AJGJ	Auster 5
RT610		G-AKWS	Auster 5A
RX168		G-BWEM	V-S Seafire L.III - intended marks
SM520		G-BXHZ	V-S Spitfire HF.IX
SM845		G-BUOS	V-S Spitfire XVIIIe
SM969	D-A	G-BRAF	V-S Spitfire XVIII
SX336		G-BRMG	V-S Seafire XVII
TA634	8K-K	G-AWJV	DH.98 Mosquito TT.35
TA719		G-ASKC	DH.98 Mosquito TT.35
TA805		G-PMNF	V-S Spitfire IX
TB252	GW-H	G-XVIE	V-S Spitfire XVIe
TD248	D	G-OXVI	V-S Spitfire XVIe
TE184	D	G-MXVI	V-S Spitfire XVIe
TE517		G-CCIX	V-S Spitfire IXe - intended marks
TJ398 *		BAPC.70	Auster 5
TJ534		G-AKSY	Auster 5
TJ565		G-AMVD	Auster 5
TJ569		G-AKOW	Auster 5
TJ672		G-ANIJ	Auster 5
TS291 *		BGA.852	Slingsby T.8 Tutor
TS423	YS-L	G-DAKS	Douglas Dakota III
TS798		G-AGNV	Avro 685 York C.1
TW439		G-ANRP	Auster 5
TW467	ROD-F	G-ANIE	Auster 5
TW511		G-APAF	Auster 5 (Army)
TW536	TS-V	G-BNGE	Auster AOP.6
TW591		G-ARIH	Auster AOP.6 (Army)
TW641		G-ATDN	Auster AOP.6
TX183		G-BSMF	Avro Anson C.19
VF512	PF-M	G-ARRX	Auster AOP.6
VF516		G-ASMZ	Auster AOP.6
VF526	T	G-ARXU	Auster AOP.6 (Army)
VF581		G-ARSL	Auster AOP.6
VL348		G-AVVO	Avro Anson C.19/2
VL349		G-AWSA	Avro Anson C.19/2
VM360		G-APHV	Avro Anson C.19/2
VP955		G-DVON	DH.104 Devon C.2/2
VR192		G-APIT	Percival Prentice T.1
VR249	FA-EL	G-APIY	Percival Prentice T.1
VR259	M	G-APJB	Percival Prentice T.1
VS356		G-AOLU	Percival Prentice T.1
VS610	K-L	G-AOKL	Percival Prentice T.1
VS623		G-AOKZ	Percival Prentice T.1
VT871		G-DHXX	DH.100 Vampire FB.6
VV612		G-VENI	DH.112 Venom FB.1
VX118		G-ASNB	Auster AOP.6
VX147*		G-AVIL	Ercoupe 415
VX653		G-BUCM	Hawker Sea Fury FB.11
VX926		G-ASKJ	Auster AOP.6
VZ345		D-CATA	Hawker Sea Fury T.20 (RN)
VZ467	A	G-METE	Gloster Meteor F.8
VZ638		G-JETM	Gloster Meteor T.7 (RN/FRU)
VZ728		G-AGOS	Reid & Sigrist Bobsleigh
WA591		G-BWMF	Gloster Meteor T.7 - intended marks
WB188		G-BZPB	Hawker Hunter GA.Mk.11
WB188		G-BZPC	Hawker Hunter GA.Mk.11
WB531		G-BLRN	DH.104 Devon C.2/2
WB533		G-DEVN	DH.104 Devon C.2/2
WB565	X	G-PVET	DHC.1 Chipmunk T.10 (Army)
WB569		G-BYSJ	DHC-1 Chipmunk T.10
WB571	34	G-AOSF	DHC.1 Chipmunk T.10
WB585	M	G-AOSY	DHC.1 Chipmunk T.10
WB588	D	G-AOTD	DHC.1 Chipmunk T.10
WB615	E	G-BXIA	DHC.1 Chipmunk T.10
WB652		G-CHPY	DHC.1 Chipmunk T.10
WB654	U	G-BXGO	DHC.1 Chipmunk T.10
WB660		G-ARMB	DHC.1 Chipmunk T.10
WB671	910	G-BWTG	DHC.1 Chipmunk T.10
WB697		G-BXCT	DHC.1 Chipmunk T.10
WB702		G-AOFE	DHC.1 Chipmunk T.10
WB703		G-ARMC	DHC.1 Chipmunk T.10
WB711		G-APPM	DHC.1 Chipmunk T.10
WB726	E	G-AOSK	DHC.1 Chipmunk T.10
WB763		G-BBMR	DHC.1 Chipmunk T.10

WD286		J	G-BBND	DHC.1 Chipmunk T.10
WD288			G-AOSO	DHC.1 Chipmunk T.10
WD292			G-BCRX	DHC.1 Chipmunk T.10
WD305			G-ARGG	DHC.1 Chipmunk T.10
WD310			G-BWUN	DHC.1 Chipmunk T.10
WD331			G-BXDH	DHC.1 Chipmunk T.10
WD347			G-BBRV	DHC-1 Chipmunk T.10
WD363			G-BCIH	DHC.1 Chipmunk T.10
WD373		12	G-BXDI	DHC.1 Chipmunk T.10
WD379	*	K	G-APLO	DHC.1 Chipmunk T.10
WD390			G-BWNK	DHC.1 Chipmunk T.10
WE569			G-ASAJ	Beagle Terrier (Auster T.7)
WE591		Y	G-ASAK	Beagle Terrier (Auster T.7)
WF118			G-DACA	Percival P.57 Sea Prince T.1
WF877			G-BPOA	Gloster Meteor T.7
WG307			G-BCYJ	DHC.1 Chipmunk T.10
WG316			G-BCAH	DHC.1 Chipmunk T.10
WG321			G-DHCC	DHC.1 Chipmunk T.10
WG348			G-BBMV	DHC.1 Chipmunk T.10
WG350			G-BPAL	DHC.1 Chipmunk T.10
WG407		67	G-BWMX	DHC.1 Chipmunk T.10
WG422			G-BFAX	DHC.1 Chipmunk T.10
WG465			G-BCEY	DHC.1 Chipmunk T.10
WG469			G-BWJY	DHC.1 Chipmunk T.10
WG472			G-AOTY	DHC.1 Chipmunk T.10
WG719			G-BRMA	Westland Dragonfly HR.5
WJ358			G-ARYD	Auster AOP.6
WJ680		CT	G-BURM	EE Canberra TT.18
WJ945		21	G-BEDV	Vickers Varsity T.1
WK126		843	N2138J	EE Canberra TT.18
WK163			G-BVWC	EE Canberra B.2(mod)
WK436	*		G-VENM	DH.112 Venom FB.50 (FB.1)
WK511		901	G-BVBT	DHC.1 Chipmunk T.10 (RN)
WK512		A	G-BXIM	DHC.1 Chipmunk T.10 (Army)
WK517			G-ULAS	DHC.1 Chipmunk T.10
WK522			G-BCOU	DHC.1 Chipmunk T.10
WK549			G-BTWF	DHC.1 Chipmunk T.10
WK585			G-BZGA	DHC.1 Chipmunk T.10
WK586		V	G-BXGX	DHC.1 Chipmunk T.10 (Army)
WK590		69	G-BWVZ	DHC.1 Chipmunk T.10
WK609		93	G-BXDN	DHC.1 Chipmunk T.10
WK611			G-ARWB	DHC.1 Chipmunk T.10
WK622			G-BCZH	DHC.1 Chipmunk T.10
WK624		M	G-BWHI	DHC.1 Chipmunk T.10
WK628			G-BBMW	DHC.1 Chipmunk T.10
WK630			G-BXDG	DHC.1 Chipmunk T.10
WK633		B	G-BXEC	DHC.1 Chipmunk T.10
WK640		C	G-BWUV	DHC.1 Chipmunk T.10
WK642			G-BXDP	DHC.1 Chipmunk T.10
WL505			G-FBIX	DH.100 Vampire FB.9
WL505			G-MKVI	DH.100 Vampire FB.6
WL626		P	G-BHDD	Vickers Varsity T.1
WM167			G-LOSM	AW Meteor NF.11
WP308		572	G-GACA	Hunting Percival P.57 Sea Prince T.1
WP788			G-BCHL	DHC.1 Chipmunk T.10
WP790		T	G-BBNC	DHC.1 Chipmunk T.10
WP795		901	G-BVZZ	DHC.1 Chipmunk T.10 (RN)
WP800		2	G-BCXN	DHC.1 Chipmunk T.10
WP803			G-HAPY	DHC.1 Chipmunk T.10
WP808			G-BDEU	DHC.1 Chipmunk T.10
WP809		778	G-BVTX	DHC.1 Chipmunk T.10 (RN)
WP840		9	G-BXDM	DHC.1 Chipmunk T.10
WP844			G-BWOX	DHC.1 Chipmunk T.10
WP856		904	G-BVWP	DHC.1 Chipmunk T.10 (RN)
WP857		24	G-BDRJ	DHC.1 Chipmunk T.10
WP859			G-BXCP	DHC.1 Chipmunk T.10
WP860		6	G-BXDA	DHC.1 Chipmunk T.10
WP896		M	G-BWVY	DHC.1 Chipmunk T.10
WP901			G-BWNT	DHC.1 Chipmunk T.10
WP903			G-BCGC	DHC.1 Chipmunk T.10 (Queens Flight)
WP920			G-BXCR	DHC.1 Chipmunk T.10
WP925		C	G-BXHA	DHC.1 Chipmunk T.10
WP928		D	G-BXGM	DHC.1 Chipmunk T.10
WP929		F	G-BXCV	DHC.1 Chipmunk T.10

WP930		J	G-BXHF	DHC.1 Chipmunk T.10
WP971			G-ATHD	DHC.1 Chipmunk T.10
WP977			G-BHRD	DHC.1 Chipmunk T.10
WP983		B	G-BXNN	DHC.1 Chipmunk T.10
WP984		H	G-BWTO	DHC.1 Chipmunk T.10
WR360			G-DHSS	DH.112 Venom FB.1
WR410		N	G-BLKA	DH.112 Venom FB.4
WR410			G-DHUU	DH.112 Venom FB.1
WR421			G-DHTT	DH.112 Venom FB.1
WT327			G-BXMO	EE Canberra B.6
WT333			G-BVXC	EE Canberra B(I).8
WT722		878/VL	G-BWGN	Hawker Hunter T.8C (RN)
WT723			G-PRII	Hawker Hunter PR.11 (RN)
WV198		K	G-BJWY	Sikorsky Whirlwind HAR.21
WV318			G-FFOX	Hawker Hunter T.7B
WV372		R	G-BXFI	Hawker Hunter T.7
WV493		29/A-P	G-BDYG	Percival Provost T.1
WV666		O-D	G-BTDH	Percival Provost T.1
WV740			G-BNPH	Hunting Percival Pembroke C.1
WW453		W-S	G-TMKI	Percival Provost T.1
WZ507			G-VTII	DH.115 Vampire T.11
WZ553		40	G-DHYY	DH.115 Vampire T.11
WZ589			G-DHZZ	DH.115 Vampire T.55
WZ662			G-BKVK	Auster AOP.9 (Army)
WZ706			G-BURR	Auster AOP.9 (Army)
WZ711			G-AVHT	Auster AOP.9 (Army)
WZ729			G-BXON	Auster AOP.9
WZ819			BGA.3498	Slingsby T.38 Grasshopper
WZ847			G-CPMK	DHC.1 Chipmunk T.10
WZ868	*	H	G-ARMF	DHC.1 Chipmunk T.10
WZ868		H	G-BCIW	DHC.1 Chipmunk T.10 (wreck)
WZ876			G-BBWN	DHC.1 Chipmunk T.10
WZ879		73	G-BWUT	DHC.1 Chipmunk T.10
WZ882		K	G-BXGP	DHC.1 Chipmunk T.10
XA880			G-BVXR	DH.104 Devon C.2 (RAE)
XD693		Z-Q	G-AOBU	Percival Jet Provost T.1
XE489			G-JETH	Armstrong-Whitworth Sea Hawk FGA.6
XE665		876/VL	G-BWGM	Hawker Hunter T.8C (RN)
XE685		861/VL	G-GAII	Hawker Hunter GA.11 (RN)
XE689		864/VL	G-BWGK	Hawker Hunter GA.11 (RN)
XE897			G-DHVV	DH.115 Vampire T.55
XE920		A	G-VMPR	DH.115 Vampire T.11
XE956			G-OBLN	DH.115 Vampire T.11
XF114			G-SWIF	V-S Swift F.7
XF515		R	G-KAXF	Hawker Hunter F.6A
XF516		19	G-BVVC	Hawker Hunter F.6A
XF597		AH	G-BKFW	Percival Provost T.1
XF603		H	G-KAPW	Percival Provost T.1
XF690			G-MOOS	Percival Provost T.1
XF836			G-AWRY	Percival Provost T.1
XF877		J-X	G-AWVF	Percival Provost T.1
XG232			G-BWIU	Hawker Hunter F.6
XG452			G-BRMB	Bristol Belvedere HC.1
XG547		T-S/S-T	G-HAPR	Bristol Sycamore HR.14
XG775			G-DHWW	DH.115 Vampire T.11 (RN)
XH558			G-VLCN	Avro Vulcan B.2
XH568			G-BVIC	English Electric Canberra B.2/B.6
XJ615			G-BWGL	Hawker Hunter T.8C (representing T.7 prototype)
XJ729			G-BVGE	Westland Whirlwind HAR.10
XJ763		P	G-BKHA	Westland Whirlwind HAR.10
XJ771			G-HELV	DH.115 Vampire T.55
XK416			G-AYUA	Auster AOP.9
XK417			G-AVXY	Auster AOP.9
XK895		CU-19	G-SDEV	DH.104 Sea Devon C.20 (RN)
XK940			G-AYXT	Westland Whirlwind HAS.7
XL426			G-VJET	Avro Vulcan B.2
XL502			G-BMYP	Fairey Gannet AEW.3 (RN)
XL571		V	G-HNTR	Hawker Hunter T.7 (Blue Diamonds)
XL573			G-BVGH	Hawker Hunter T.7
XL587		Z	G-HPUX	Hawker Hunter T.Mk.7
XL602			G-BWFT	Hawker Hunter T.8M
XL613			G-BVMB	Hawker Hunter T.7A
XL616		D	G-BWIE	Hawker Hunter T.7A
XL621			G-BNCX	Hawker Hunter T.7

XL714		G-AOGR	DH.82A Tiger Moth
XL809		G-BLIX	Saro Skeeter AOP.12 (Army)
XL812		G-SARO	Saro Skeeter AOP.12
XL929		G-BNPU	Hunting Percival Pembroke C.1
XL954		G-BXES	Hunting Percival Pembroke C.1
XM223		G-BWWC	DH.104 Devon C.2
XM365		G-BXBH	Hunting Jet Provost T.3A
XM376	27	G-BWDR	Hunting Jet Provost T.3A
XM424		G-BWDS	Hunting Jet Provost T.3A
XM470		G-BWZZ	Hunting Jet Provost T.3
XM478		G-BXDL	Hunting Jet Provost T.3A
XM479	54	G-BVEZ	Hunting Jet Provost T.3A
XM553		G-AWSV	Saro Skeeter AOP.12
XM575		G-BLMC	Avro Vulcan B.2A
XM655		G-VULC	Avro Vulcan B.2A
XM685	PO/513	G-AYZJ	Westland Whirlwind HAS.7
XM693		G-TIMM	Folland Gnat T.1
XM819		G-APXW	Lancashire Aircraft EP.9 (Army)
XN351		G-BKSC	Saro Skeeter AOP.12 (Army)
XN437		G-AXWA	Auster AOP.9
XN441		G-BGKT	Auster AOP.9
XN459		G-BWOT	Hunting Jet Provost T.3A
XN470		G-BXBJ	Hunting Jet Provost T.3A
XN498	16	G-BWSH	Hunting Jet Provost T.3A
XN510		G-BXBI	Hunting Jet Provost T.3A
XN629	49	G-KNOT	Hunting Jet Provost T.3A
XN637	03	G-BKOU	Hunting Jet Provost T.3
XP242		G-BUCI	Auster AOP.9 (Army)
XP254		G-ASCC	Auster AOP.11
XP279		G-BWKK	Auster AOP.9 (Army)
XP282		G-BGTC	Auster AOP.9
XP355	A	G-BEBC	Westland Whirlwind HAR.10
XP672	03	G-RAFI	Hunting Jet Provost T.4
XP772		G-BUCJ	DHC.2 Beaver AL.1 (Army)
XP907		G-SROE	Westland Scout AH.1
XP924		G-CVIX	DH.110 Sea Vixen D.3
XR240		G-BDFH	Auster AOP.9 (Army)
XR246		G-AZBU	Auster AOP.9
XR267		G-BJXR	Auster AOP.9
XR486		G-RWWW	Westland Whirlwind HCC.12 (Queens Flight c/s)
XR537	T	G-NATY	Folland Gnat T.1
XR595	M	G-BWHU	Westland Scout AH.1 (Army)
XR673		G-BXLO	Hunting Jet Provost T.4
XR724		G-BTSY	EE Lightning F.6
XR944		G-ATTB	Wallis WA.116
XR991		G-MOUR	Folland Gnat T.1 (Yellowjacks c/s)
XR993		G-BVPP	Folland Gnat T.1 (Red Arrows c/s)
XS101	1	G-GNAT	Folland Gnat T.1 (Red Arrows c/s)
XS587		G-VIXN	DH.110 Sea Vixen FAW.2 (RN
XS765		G-BSET	Beagle Basset CC.1
XS770		G-HRHI	Beagle Basset CC.1 (Queens Flight c/s)
XT223		G-XTUN	Westland Sioux AH.1 (Army)
XT634		G-BYRX	Westland Scout AH.1 (Army)
XT653		BGA.3469	Slingsby T.45 Swallow
XT781	426	G-KAWW	Westland Wasp HAS.1 (RN)
XT788		G-BMIR	Westland Wasp HAS.1 (RN)
XV121		G-BYKJ	Westland Scout AH.1 (Army)
XV126	X	G-SCTA	Westland Scout AH.1 (Army)
XV130	R	G-BWJW	Westland Scout AH.1 (Army)
XV134		G-BWLX	Westland Scout AH.1 (Army)
XV137		G-CRUM	Westland Scout AH.1
XV140	K	G-KAXL	Westland Scout AH.1 (Army)
XV268		G-BVER	DHC.2 Beaver (Army)
XW281	U	G-BYNZ	Westland Scout AH.1 (Royal Marines)
XW289	73	G-JPVA	BAC Jet Provost T.5A
XW293	Z	G-BWCS	BAC Jet Provost T.5
XW310	37	G-BWGS	BAC Jet Provost T.5A
XW324		G-BWSG	BAC Jet Provost T.5
XW325	E	G-BWGF	BAC Jet Provost T.5A
XW333		G-BVTC	BAC Jet Provost T.5A
XW423	14	G-BWUW	BAC Jet Provost T.5A
XW431	A	G-BWBS	BAC Jet Provost T.5A
XW433		G-JPRO	BAC Jet Provost T.5A (CFS)
XW613	T	G-BXRS	Westland Scout AH.1 (Army)

XW635		G-AWSW	Beagle Husky
XW784	VL	G-BBRN	Mitchell-Procter Kittiwake (RN)
XW858		G-DMSS	Westland Gazelle HT.3
XX110		BAPC.169	BAC/Sepecat Jaguar GR.1
XX263	263	BAPC.152	BAe Hawk T.1A
XX297		BAPC.171	BAe Hawk T.1 (Red Arrows)
XX467	86	G-TVII	Hawker Hunter T.7 (TWU)
XX513	10	G-KKKK	SA Bulldog
XX514 *		G-BWIB	SA Bulldog
XX528	D	G-BZON	SA Bulldog
XX537	C	G-CBCB	SA Bulldog
XX543	F	G-CBAB	SA Bulldog
XX551	E	G-BZDP	SA Bulldog
XX619	T	G-CBBW	SA Bulldog
XX630	5	G-SIJW	SA Bulldog
XX698		G-BZME	SA Bulldog
XX725	GU	BAPC.150	BAC/Sepecat Jaguar GR.1
XZ363	A	BAPC.151	BAC/Sepecat Jaguar GR.1A
ZA368	AJ-P	BAPC.155	Panavia Tornado GR.1
ZA634	C	G-BUHA	Slingsby T-61F Venture T.2
ZB500		G-LYNX	Westland WG.13 Lynx 800 (Army)
ZD472	01	BAPC.191	BAe Harrier GR.5
	42	G-TORE	Hunting Jet Provost T.3A
	AL-K	G-HURR	Hawker Hurricane XII
	F	G-RUMW	Grumman FM-2 Wildcat (RN/FAA)
	VO-B	G-BYDR	N-A B-25D Mitchell II
G-17-3		G-AVNE	Westland Wessex 60
G-29-1		G-APRJ	Avro Lincoln
G-48/1		G-ALSX	Bristol Sycamore
U-0247		G-AGOY	Miles Messenger - intended marks
W-2		BAPC.85	Weir W-2

OTHER ARMED FORCES

AUSTRALIA

A2-4		VH-ALB	V-S Seagull
A16-199	SF-R	G-BEOX	Lockheed Hudson IIIA
A17-48		G-BPHR	DH.82A Tiger Moth

BELGIUM

HD-75	N75	G-AFDX	Hanriot HD.1

BOLIVIA

FAB-184		G-SIAI	SIAI-Marchetti SF.260W (FA Boliviana)

BOTSWANA

OJ-1		G-BXFU	BAC.167 Strikemaster 83
OJ-4	Z-2	G-UNNY	BAC.167 Strikemaster 87
OJ-7	Z-28	G-BXFX	BAC.167 Strikemaster 83
OJ-8		G-BXFV	BAC.167 Strikemaster 83
OJ10		G-UNVR	BAC.167 Strikemaster 87

CANADA

622		N6699D	Piasecki HUP-3 Retreiver (RCN)
920	QN-	CF-BXO	V-S Stranraer
3349		G-BYNF	NA Yale
16693 *	693	G-BLPG	Auster J/1N (In AOP.6 c/s)
18013		G-BNZC	DHC.1 Chipmunk
18013		G-TRIC	DHC.1 Chipmunk
18393		G-BCYK	Avro Canada CF.100 Canuck IV
20310	310	G-BSBG	N.A. Harvard IV
21261		G-TBRD	Lockheed T-33A

PEOPLES' REPUBLIC OF CHINA (inc HONG KONG)

663/P11151	88	ZK-RMH	Curtiss P-40E Kittyhawk
2028	69	G-BVVF	Nanchang CJ-6A
1532008	08	G-BVFX	Nanchang CJ-6A
HKG-5		G-BULL	SA Bulldog
HKG-6		G-BPCL	SA Bulldog
HKG-11		G-BYRY	Slingsby T.67M-200 Firefly
HKG-13		G-BXKW	Slingsby T.67M-200 Firefly

FRANCE

120	3	G-AZGC	Stampe SV-4C
124		G-BOSJ	Nord 3400
143		G-MSAL	Morane-Saulnier MS.733 (Aeronavale)
185	44-CA	G-BWLR	Max Holste Broussard
316	315-SN	F-GGKR	Max Holste Broussard
394		G-BIMO	Stampe SV-4C
MS.824		G-AWBU	Morane-Saulnier N rep
1/4513		G-BFYO	SPAD XII rep
(F-GGKG)	315-SQ	G-BWGG	Max Holste Broussard
-	CDG	G-CUBJ	Piper L-18C Super Cub (ALAT)

GERMANY

1+4		G-BSLX	WAR FW190 scale rep
2+1	7334	G-SYFW	WAR FW190 Scale rep
3		G-BAYV	Nord 1101 (Messerschmitt guise)
8+-		G-WULF	WAR FW190 scale rep
10	KG+EM	G-ETME	Nord 1002 Pingouin
14		BAPC.67	Messerschmitt Bf.109 rep
+14		G-BSMD	Nord 1101 (Messerschmitt guise)
28+10		G-BWTT	Aero L-39ZO Albatros
50	CW+BG	G-BXBD	CASA I-131 Jungmann
97+04		G-APVF	Putzer Elster B
124		G-BHCA	Fokker D.VIII rep
152/17		G-ATJM	Fokker DR.1 rep
422/15		G-AVJO	Fokker E-III rep
425/17		BAPC.133	Fokker DR.1 rep
626/8		N6268	Fokker D.VII (Travel Air 2000)
1227	DG+HO	G-FOKW	Focke-Wulfe FW190A-5
1480	6	BAPC.66	Messerschmitt Bf.109 rep
6357	6	BAPC.74	Messerschmitt Bf.109 rep
7198/18		G-AANJ	LVG C.VI
10639	6 (Black)	G-USTV	Messerschmitt Bf.109G-2
D604		G-FLIZ	Staaken Flitzer
D692		G-BVAW	Staaken Flitzer
D5397/17		G-BFXL	Albatros D.VA rep
	6J+PR	G-AWHB	Heinkel (CASA) He.111H-16
	BU+CC	G-BUCC	CASA I-131E Jungmann
	BU+CK	G-BUCK	CASA I-131E Jungmann
	CC+43	G-CJCI	Pilatus P.2 (Arado Ar.96B guise)
	CF+HF	EI-AUY	Fieseler Storch (MS.502)
	F+IS	G-BIRW	Fieseler Storch (MS.505)
	LG+01	G-AYSJ	Bucker 133 Jungmeister
	LG+03	G-AEZX	Bucker 133 Jungmeister
	NJ+C11	G-ATBG	Messerschmitt Bf.108 (Nord 1002)
	RJ+NP	G-BFHF	Junkers (CASA) Ju52/3m
	S4+A07	G-BWHP	CASA I-131E Jungmann
	S5+B06	G-BSFB	CASA I-131E Jungmann
	TA+RC	G-BPHZ	Fieseler Storch (MS.505)

HUNGARY

503		G-BRAM	MiG 21PF (Russian c/s)

IRELAND

177		G-BLIW	Percival Provost T.51

ITALY

	W7	G-AGFT	Avia FL.3

JAPAN

24		BAPC.83	Kawasaki Ki 100-1b

THE NETHERLANDS

BI-005		G-BUVN	CASA I-131E Jungmann
E-15		G-BIYU	Fokker S.11 Instructor
R-151		G-BIYR	Piper L-21B Super Cub
R-163		G-BIRH	Piper L-21B Super Cub
R-156		G-ROVE	Piper L-21B Super Cub
R-167		G-LION	Piper L-21B Super Cub

NEW ZEALAND

NZ3907		G-RIMM	Westland Wasp HAS.Mk.1
NZ5648		G-BXUL	Vought FG-1D Corsair
NZ6361		G-BXFP	BAC.167 Strikemaster 87

NORTH KOREA

01420		G-BMZF	MiG-15
1211		G-BWUF	WSK PZL-Mielec Lim-5 (MiG-17F)

NORWAY

321		G-BKPY	Saab Safir
423 & 427		G-AMRK	Gloster Gladiator

PORTUGAL

85		G-BTPZ	Hawker (Isaacs) Fury
1377		G-BARS	DHC.1 Chipmunk
1747		G-BGPB	CCF Harvard 4

RUSSIA

01		G-YKSZ	Yak 52
07 (Yellow)		G-BMJY	Yak 18
09		G-BVMU	Yak 52 (DOSAAF)
11 (White)		G-BZMY	SPP Yakovlev Yak C-11
12 (Red)		G-DELF	Aero L-29A Delfin
26		G-BVXK	Yak 52 (DOSAAF)
27		G-OYAK	Yak 11
39		G-XXVI	Sukhoi Su-26M
52		LY-AMP	Yak-52 (DOSAAF)
55		G-BVOK	Yak 52 (DOSAAF)
69		G-BTZB	Yak 50 (DOSAAF)
69	*	RA-44469(2)	Yakovlev Yak-52
72		G-BXAV	Yak 52 (DOSAAF)
139		G-BWOD	Yak 52 (DOSAAF)
6247		G-OMIG	MiG-15 (Korean War c/s)
853007		G-BVVO	Yak 50

REPUBLIC OF SOUTH AFRICA

92		G-BYCX	Westland Wasp HAS.Mk.1 (Navy)

SAUDI ARABIA

1133		G-BESY	BAC 167 Strikemaster Mk.80A

SPAIN

E3B-153	781-75	G-BPTS	CASA I.131 Jungmann
E3B-350	05-97	G-BHPL	CASA I.131 Jungmann
E3B-369	781-32	G-BPDM	CASA I.131 Jungmann
-	781-25	G-BRSH	CASA I.131 Jungmann

SWITZERLAND

A-10		G-BECW	CASA I-131E Jungmann
A-57		G-BECT	CASA I-131E Jungmann
A-125		G-BLKZ	Pilatus P.2-05
A-806		G-BTLL	Pilatus P.3
C-552		G-DORN	EKW C-3605
J-1149		G-SWIS	DH.100 Vampire FB.6
J-1573		G-VICI	DH.112 Venom FB.50
J-1605		G-BLID	DH.112 Venom FB.50
J-1611		G-DHTT	DH.112 Venom FB.50
J-1632		G-VNOM	DH.112 Venom FB.50
J-1758		G-BLSD	DH.112 Venom FB.50
J-4031		G-BWFR	Hawker Hunter F.58
J-4058		G-BWFS	Hawker Hunter F.58
J-4066		G-BXNZ	Hawker Hunter F.58
J-4083		G-EGHH	Hawker Hunter F.58
J-4090		G-SIAL	Hawker Hunter F.58
U-80		G-BUKK	Bucker Jungmeister
U-95		G-BVGP	Bucker Jungmeister
U-99		G-AXMT	Bucker Jungmeister
U-110		G-PTWO	Pilatus P.2
U-1234		G-DHAV	DH.115 Vampire T.11

V-54		G-BVSD	SE.3130 Alouette II

UNITED NATIONS

001		G-BFRI	Sikorsky S-61N Mk.II

UNITED STATES OF AMERICA

2		G-AZLE	Boeing-Stearman Kaydet (US Army)
5		G-BEEW	Taylor Monoplane (Boeing P-26A) (US Army)
14		G-ISDN	Boeing-Stearman Kaydet (US Army)
23		N49272	Fairchild PT-23 Cornell (USAAC)
26		G-BAVO	Boeing-Stearman Kaydet (US Army)
27		G-AGYY	Ryan PT-21 (USAAC)
27		G-BRVG	NA SNJ-7 Texan (US Navy)
28		N8162G	Boeing-Stearman Kaydet (US Army)
33		G-THEA	Boeing-Stearman Kaydet (US Navy)
43	SC	G-AZSC	NA AT-16 Texan (USAAF)
44		G-BWHH	Piper L-21B Super Cub (US Army)
44		G-RJAH	Boeing-Stearman Kaydet (US Army)
49		G-KITT	Curtiss TP-40M Kittyhawk (US Army)
54		G-BCNX	Piper L-4H (USAF)
85		G-BTBI	Republic P-47 Thunderbolt Scale rep (USAF)
112		G-BSWC	Boeing-Stearman Kaydet (US Army)
118		G-BSDS	Boeing-Stearman Kaydet (US Army)
379		G-ILLE	Boeing-Stearman Kaydet (US Army)
441		G-BTFG	Boeing-Stearman Kaydet (US Navy)
526		G-BRWB	NA T-6G Texan (USAF)
624	D-39	G-BVMH	Piper L-4 (Wag-Aero Cuby) (USAAC)
669		N75TL	Boeing-Stearman Kaydet (US Army)
854		G-BTBH	Ryan PT-22 (US Army)
855		N56421	Ryan PT-22 (US Army)
897E		G-BJEV	Aeronca Chief (US Navy)
985		G-ERIX	Boeing-Stearman Kaydet (US Navy)
1164		G-BKGL	Beechcraft C-45 (US Army)
2807	V-103	G-BHTH	NA T-6G Texan (US Navy)
7797		G-BFAF	Aeronca L-16A (US Army)
8178	FU-178	G-SABR	NA F-86A Sabre (USAF)
8242	FU-242	N196B	NA F-86A Sabre (USAF)
02538		N33870	Fairchild PT-19 Cornell (USAAC)
14863	TA-863	G-BGOR	NA AT-6D Texan (USAAF)
16136	205	G-BRUJ	Boeing-Stearman Kaydet (US Navy)
18263	822	N38940	Boeing-Stearman Kaydet (USAAC)
21714	201B	G-RUMM	Grumman F8F-2P Bearcat (USN)
28521	TA-521	G-TVIJ	NA T-6J Harvard (USAF)
26922	AK-402	G-RAID	Douglas AD-4NA Skyraider (US Navy)
29261		G-CDET	Culver Cadet (USAAF)
31145	G-26	G-BBLH	Piper L-4B (US Army)
31171		N7614C	NA B-25J Mitchell (US Marines)
31952		G-BRPR	Aeronca L-3C Grasshopper (US Army)
34037		N9115Z	NA B-25N Mitchell (USAAF)
38674		G-MTKM	Thomas-Morse S4 Scout Scale rep (USASC)
40467	19	G-BTCC	Grumman F6F Hellcat (US Navy)
41386		G-MJTD	Thomas-Morse S4 Scout Scale rep (USASC)
46214	X-3	CF-KCG	Grumman TBM-3E Avenger (USN)
53319	RB/319	G-BTDP	Grumman TBM-3R Avenger (US Navy)
54137	69	G-CTKL	Noorduyn Harvard IIB (US Navy)
80425	WT-4	G-RUMT	Grumman F7F-3P Tigercat (USN)
80480	E-44	G-BECN	Piper L-4J (USAAC)
91007	TR-007	G-NASA	Lockheed T-33A (USAF)
92399	17	G-CCMV	Chance Vought FG-1D Corsair (US Navy)
93542	LTA-542	G-BRLV	NA T-6 Texan (USAF)
111836	JZ/6	G-TSIX	NA AT-6C Texan (US Navy)
111989		N33600	Cessna L-19A Bird Dog (US Army)
115042	TA-042	G-BGHU	NA T-6G Texan (USAF)
115302	TP	G-BJTP	Piper L-18C Super Cub (US Marines)
115684	VM	G-BKVM	Piper L-21A Super Cub (US Army)
124485	DF-A	G-BEDF	Boeing B-17G Flying Fortress (USAAC)
122351		G-BKRG	Beechcraft C-45G
126603		G-BHWH	Weedhopper JC-24C (US Navy)
151632		G-BWGR	NA TB-25N Mitchell (USAF)
217786	25	CF-EQS	Boeing-Stearman Kaydet (USAAF)
224319	L4-D	N147DC	Douglas C-47A-75-DL Dakota (USAAF)
226413	ZU-N	N47DD	Republic P-47D Thunderbolt (USAAF)
226671	MX-X/LH-X	G-THUN	Republic P-47D Thunderbolt (USAAF)

231983	IY-G	F-BDRS	Boeing B-17G Flying Fortress (USAAF)
236800	A-44	G-BHPK	Piper L-4A (USAAF)
237123		BAPC.157	Waco CG-4A Hadrian
243809		BAPC.185	Waco CG-4A Hadrian
252983		N66630	Schweizer TG-3A
269097		G-BTWR	Bell P-63A Kingcobra (USAAF)
292912	LN-F	N47FK	Douglas C-47A-35-DL Dakota III (USAAF)
314887		G-AJPI	Fairchild UC-61 Forwarder (USAAF)
315509	W7-S	G-BHUB	Douglas C-47A Dakota (USAAF)
329405	A-23	G-BCOB	Piper L-4H (USAAC)
329417		G-BDHK	Piper L-4A Cub (USAAC)
329471	F-44	G-BGXA	Piper L-4H (USAAC)
329601	D-44	G-AXHR	Piper L-4H (USAAC)
329854	R-44	G-BMKC	Piper L-4H (USAAC)
329934	B-72	G-BCPH	Piper L-4H (USAAC/French)
330238	A-24	G-LIVH	Piper L-4H (USAAC)
330485	C-44	G-AJES	Piper L-4H (USAAC)
343251	27	G-NZSS	Boeing-Stearman Kaydet (USAAC)
413573	B6-V	N6526D	NA P-51D Mustang (USAAC)
454467	J-44	G-BILI	Piper L-4J (US Army)
454537	J-04	G-BFDL	Piper L-4J (US Army)
461748	Y	G-BHDK	Boeing B-29A Superfortress (USAF)
463209 *	WZ-S	BAPC.255	NA P-51D Mustang (USAAF)
463221	E2-Z	G-BTCD	NA P-51D Mustang (USAAF)
472216	HO-M	G-BIXL	NA P-51D Mustang (USAAF)
472218	WZ-I	G-HAEC	NA P-51D Mustang (USAAF)
472773	AJ-C	G-SUSY	NA P-51D Mustang (USAAF)
473877		N167F	NA P-51D Mustang (USAAF)
479609	PR-L4	G-BHXY	Piper L-4H (USAAC)
479744	M-49	G-BGPD	Piper L-4H (USAAC)
479766	D-63	G-BKHG	Piper L-4H (USAAC)
480015	M-44	G-AKIB	Piper L-4H (USAAC)
480133	B-44	G-BDCD	Piper L-4J (USAAC)
480321	H-44	G-FRAN	Piper L-4J (USAAC)
480636	A-58	G-AXHP	Piper L-4J (USAAC)
480752	E-39	G-BCXJ	Piper L-4J (USAAC)
483868	N	N5237V	Boeing B-17G Flying Fortress (USAF)
493209		G-DDMV	NA T-6G Texan (Calif ANG)
517962		G-TROY	NA T-28B Trojan
607327	L-09	G-ARAO	Piper (L-21B) Super Cub (US Army)
3-1923		G-BRHP	Aeronca O-58B Grasshopper (US Army)
18-2001		G-BIZV	Piper L-18C Super Cub (US Army)
41-33275	CE	G-BICE	NA AT-6C Texan (USAAC)
42-58678	IY	G-BRIY	Taylorcraft L-2A (USAAC)
42-78044		G-BRXL	Aeronca L-3F (US Army)
42-84555	EP-H	G-ELMH	NA AT-6D Harvard (USAAC)
44-14419	LH-F	G-MSTG	NA P-51D Mustang (USAF)
44-30861		N9089Z	NA B-25J Mitchell (USAAC)
44-63507		NL51EA	NA P-51D Mustang
44-80594		G-BEDJ	Piper L-4J (USAAC)
44-83184	7	G-RGUS	Fairchild UC-61K Forwarder (USAAC)
51-7545		N14113	NA T-28B Trojan
51-11701A	AF258	G-BSZC	Beechcraft C-45H (USAF)
51-15227	10	G-BKRA	NA T-6G Texan (US Navy)
54-2446		G-ROVE	Piper L-21B Super Cub (US Army)
54-2447		G-SCUB	Piper L-21B Super Cub (US Army)
146-11042	7	G-BMZX	SPAD rep (Wolf W.II) (US Army/AEF)
146-11083	5	G-BNAI	SPAD rep (Wolf W.II) (US Army/AEF)
	H-57	G-AKAZ	Piper L-4A (USAAF)
	K-33 44	G-BJLH	Piper L-18C Super Cub (US Army)
	R-55	G-BLMI	Piper L-18C Super Cub

YUGOSLAVIA

30140	G-RADA	Soko Kraguj
30146	G-BSXD	Soko Kraguj
30149	G-SOKO	Soko Kraguj

UNATTRIBUTED

001	G-BYPY	Ryan ST3-KR
111	G-OTAF	Aero L-39ZO Albatros

SECTION 8

PART 4 - AIRCRAFT WEARING FICTITIOUS CIVIL MARKINGS INCLUDING AUTHENTIC, REPRODUCTION & MOCK-UP (STATIC) SPECIMENS.

The majority of the aicraft listed below have originated from with the BAPC ranks. We welcome any amendments.

Regn	Type	Comments
"K.158"	Austin Whippet rep	See BAPC.207 in SECTION 4
"EI-ABH"	HM.14 Pou-du-Ciel rep (1)	Under construction @ Meath Aero Museum 2001
"F-OCMF"		See F-BTRP in SECTION 5, Part 1
"G-EAOU"	Vickers Vimy rep	See NX71MY in SECTION 5, Part 1
"G-EASQ"	Bristol 30/46 Babe III rep	See BAPC.87 in SECTION 4
"G-EBED"	Vickers 60 Viking IV rep	See BAPC.114 in SECTION 4
"G-AAAH"	DH.60 Moth rep	Located at Yorkshire Aircraft Museum, Elvington
"G-AAAH"	DH.60G Moth rep	See BAPC.168 in SECTION 4
"G-AACA"	Avro 504K rep	See BAPC.177 in SECTION 4
"G-ABUL"	DH.82A Tiger Moth	See G-AOXG in SECTION 1, Part 2
"G-ACDR"	DH.82A Tiger Moth	US regd as N9295 [c/n 86536]
"G-ACSS"	DH.88 Comet model	See BAPC.216 in SECTION 4
"G-ACSS"	DH.88 model	See BAPC.257 in SECTION 4
"G-ADRG"	Mignet HM.14 Pou-Du-Ciel	See BAPC.77 in SECTION 4
"G-ADRX"	Mignet HM.14 Pou-Du-Ciel	See BAPC.231 in SECTION 4
"G-ADRY"	Mignet HM.14 Pou-Du-Ciel	See BAPC.29 in SECTION 4
"G-ADVU"	Mignet HM.14 Pou-Du-Ciel	See BAPC.211 in SECTION 4
"G-ADYV"	Mignet HM.14 Pou-Du-Ciel	See BAPC.243 in SECTION 4
"G-ADZW"	Mignet HM.14 Pou-Du-Ciel	See BAPC.253 in SECTION 4
"G-AEAJ"	DH.89 Dragon Rapide rep	Marriott Hotel South, Liverpool Airport (Railway Air Services titles) (Static FSM)
"G-AEOF"	Mignet HM.14 Pou-Du-Ciel	See BAPC.22 in SECTION 4
"G-AFAP"	CASA 352L (Junkers Ju52/3m)	ex Sp AF T2B-272 (c/n 163) @ RAF Museum, Cosford (Original British Airways titles)
"G-AFFI"	Mignet HM.14 Pou-Du-Ciel	See BAPC.76 in SECTION 4
"G-AFUG"	Luton LA.4 Minor	See BAPC 97 in SECTION 4
"G-AJOV"	Westland WS-51 Dragonfly HR.3	ex WP495 (c/n WA/H/80) @ RAF Museum, Cosford (BEA titles)
"G-AJOZ"	Fairchild F.24W-41A Argus 1	The Thorpe Camp Preservation Group Woodhall Spa (Full-scale replica)
"G-AMAF"	Cessna 150J	See G-BOWC in SECTION 1, Part 2
"G-AMSU"	Douglas C-47A Dakota 3	See G-AMPP in SECTION 1, Part 2
"G-AOXL"	DH.114 Heron 2	See G-ANUO in SECTION 1, Part 2
"G-ASOK"	Cessna F172E Rocket	See (D-ECDU) in SECTION 5, Part 1
"G-ATCX"	Cessna 182A Skylane	Is G-OLSC (qv) - used mid 1990s for film work -
"G-CARS"	Pitts S-2A Special	See BAPC.134 in SECTION 4
"G-CDBS"	MBB Bo.105D	See G-BCXO in SECTION 1, Part 2
"G-DRNT"	Sikorsky S-76A	Petak Offshore Industry Training Centre, Norwich
"G-ESKY"	Piper PA-23-250 Aztec	Is G-BADI (qv)- used 1999 for TV work as "G-BADF"
"G-MAZY"	DH.82A Tiger Moth	H.Hodgson, Winthorpe "Maisie" (Cotswold Aircraft Restoration Group) (Composite ex Newark components & G-AMBB/T6801; also reported ex DE561 lost at sea 1942; rebuilt for static display & loaned Newark Air Museum 3.97)
"G-RAFM"	Robinson R22 Beta	See G-OTHL in SECTION 1, Part 2
"G-SHOG"	Colomban MC-15 Cri-Cri	V.S.E.Norman, Rendcomb (Static model 1999)

SECTION 8

PART 5 - AIRCRAFT WITH NO EXTERNAL MARKINGS CARRIED.

These are listed by Type to ease identification! Amendments and alterations are always welcome.

Type	Regn	Comments
Blackburn Monoplane	G-AANI	See SECTION 1
Bleriot XI	G-AANG	See SECTION 1
Bristol M.1C rep	G-BWJM	See SECTION 1
Bristol Boxkite rep	G-ASPP	See SECTION 1
CFM Shadow CD	G-MYBL	See SECTION 1
Deperdussin Monoplane	G-AANH	See SECTION 1
English Electric Wren	G-EBNV	See SECTION 1
Manning-Flanders MF.1	G-BAAF	See SECTION 1
Roe Triplane IV rep	G-ARSG	See SECTION 1
Wallbro Monoplane	G-BFIP	See SECTION 1

SECTION 8

PART 6 (i) – "B CONDITIONS" ORIGINAL SERIES MARKINGS

The latest Air Navigation Order (ANO2000) continues to promulgate the specific circumstances under which aerospace maufacturers can pursue the conduct of aircraft trials without the need for valid Certificates of Airworthiness. ANO2000 establishes both "A" & "B" conditions but we are only concerned here with the latter requirements which stipulate the use of identity marks as approved by the CAA for the purposes of "B Conditions" flight.

In brief, under "B Conditions" an aircraft must fly only for the purpose of:

(a) experimenting with or testing the aircraft (including any engines installed thereon) or any equipment installed or carried in the aircraft;
(b) enabling it to qualify for the issue of a certificate of airworthiness or the validation thereof or the approval of a modification of the aircraft or the issue of a permit to fly;
(c) demonstrating and displaying the aircraft, any engines installed thereon or any equipment installed or carried in the aircraft with a view to the sale thereof or of other similar aircraft, engines or equipment;
(d) demonstrating and displaying the aircraft to employees of the operator;
(e) the giving of flying training to or the testing of flight crew employed by the operator or the training or testing of other persons employed by the operator; or
(f) proceeding to or from a place at which any experiment, inspection, repair, modification, maintenance, approval, test or weighing of the aircraft, the installation of equipment in the aircraft, demonstration, display or training is to take place or at which installation of furnishings in, or the painting of, the aircraft is to be undertaken.

The flight must be operated by a person approved by the CAA for the purposes of these Conditions and subject to any additional conditions which may be specified in such an approval. If not registered in the United Kingdom the aircraft must be marked in a manner approved by the CAA for the purposes of these Conditions. The aircraft must carry such flight crew as may be necessary to ensure the safety of the aircraft. No person can act as pilot in command of the aircraft except a person approved for the purpose by the CAA.

In May 1978 the former Merseyside Aviation Society published an excellent booklet "Under B Conditions" by D S Revell and edited by Phil Butler. The book set out to detail the background to "B Conditions" flights and to delineate every known aircraft which had carried "B Conditions" identities from 1929 up to that time. Readers who wish to know more should seek out this publication. At that time the latest manufacturer identity was "G-53", that is to NDN Aircraft as at May 1977 although there was no record of any usage. The listing in Section 8, Part 6 (ii) below attempts to bring such "G-" identities up to date.
I look forward to your amendments!

Prefix	Company	Period	Remarks
A	Armstrong Whitworth	1929-1948	
B	Blackburn	1929-1948	
C	Boulton Paul	1929-1948	
D	Bristol Aeroplane Co.		Not taken up
D	Cunliffe Owen Aircraft		Not taken up
D	Portsmouth Aviation	1947-1948	
E	de Havilland	1929-1948	
F	Fairey	1929-1948	
G	Gloster	1929-1948	
H	Handley Page	1929-1948	
I	Hawker Aircraft	1929-1948	
J	George Parnall & Co	1929-1946	
J	Reid & Sigrist Ltd	1947-1948	
K	A V Roe & Co Ltd	1929-1948	
L	Saunders Roe Ltd	1929-1948	
M	Short Bros.	1929-1948	
N	Supermarine	1929-1948	
O	Vickers (Aviation)	1929-1948	
P	Westland Aircraft	1929-1948	
R	Bristol Aeroplane Co.	1929-1948	
S	Spartan Aircraft	1930-1936	
S	Heston Aircraft Ltd	1936-1948	
T	General Aircraft Ltd	1933-1948	
U	Phillips & Powis (Miles)	1934-1948	
V	Airspeed Ltd	1934-1948	
W	G & J Weir Ltd	1933-1948	
X	Percival Aircraft	1936-1948	
Y	British Aircraft Manufacturing Ltd	1936-1948	
Y	Cunliffe Owen Aircraft	1940-1948	
Z	Auster Aircraft	1946-1948	
AA	Slingsby Sailplanes	1947-1948	

SECTION 8

PART 6 (ii) - "B CONDITIONS" CURRENT SERIES MARKINGS

Whilst deemed "current" many of the companies shown below have long merged with each other or ceased to trade. However, one of the more recent "B Conditions" identities, G-86-01 a scale version of ATG's Stratsat, was noted late last year.

The current list was based on member Roger House's web-site and expanded with thanks to the contributions of Phil Butler, Nigel Burch and Pete Webber via the Air-Britain Information Exchange (ABIX) web -site which is available, exclusively, to all Air-Britain members.

Prefix	Company	Period	Remarks
G-1-	Armstrong-Whitworth	1948-1967	
G-1-	Rolls-Royce (Bristol Engines)	1949-	
G-2-	Blackburn	1949-	
G-3-	Boulton Paul	1948-1973	
G-4-	Miles Aviation and Transport	1969-	
G-4-	Portsmouth Aviation	1948-1949	
G-5-	De Havilland	1948-	
G-6-	Fairey	1948-1969	
G-7-	Gloster	1948-1961	
G-7-	Slingsby Sailplanes	1971-	
G-8-	Handley Page	1948-1970	
G-9-	Hawker Aircraft	1948-	
G-10-	Reid and Sigrist Ltd	1948-1953	
G-11-	A.V. Roe and Company	1948-	
G-12-	Saunders Roe Ltd	1948-1967	
G-13-	Not allocated		
G-14-	Short Brothers	1948-	
G-15-	Supermarine	1948-1968	
G-16-	Vickers (Aviation)	1948-	
G-17-	Westland Aircraft	1948-	
G-18-	Bristol Aeroplane Company	1948-1975	
G-19-	Heston Aircraft Ltd.	1948-1960	
G-20-	General Aircraft Ltd	1948-1949	
G-21-	Phillips and Powis (Miles)	1948-1963	
G-22-	Airspeed Ltd.	1948-1952	
G-23-	Percival Aircraft	1948-1966	
G-24-	Cunliffe Owen Aircraft	1948-1949	
G-25-	Auster Aircraft	1948-1962	
G-26-	Slingsby Sailplanes	1948-1949	
G-27-	English Electric	1948-	
G-28-	BEA Helicopter Unit	1948-	
G-29-	D Napier and Son Ltd	1948-1962	
G-30-	Pest Control Ltd	1952-1957	
G-31-	Scottish Aviation Ltd.	1948-	
G-32-	Cierva Autogiro Company	1948-1951	
G-33-	Flight Refuelling	1948-1972	
G-34-	Chrislea Aircraft Ltd.	1948-1952	
G-35-	F.G.Miles Ltd/Beagle Aircraft	1951-1970	
G-36-	College of Aeronautics	1954-	
G-37-	Rolls-Royce	1954-1971	
G-38-	D.H.Propellers Ltd.	1954-1975	
G-39-	Folland Aircraft Company	1954-1965	
G-40-	Wiltshire School of Flying		Not taken up
G-41-	Aviation Traders	1956-1976	
G-42-	Armstrong Siddeley Motors Ltd.	1956-1959	
G-43-	Edgar Percival Ltd.	1956-1959	
G-44-	Agricultural Aviation Ltd.	1959-1959	
G-45-	Bristol Siddeley Engines Ltd	1959-1969	
G-46-	Saunders Roe Ltd (Helicopter Division)	1959-1962	
G-47-	Lancashire Aircraft Company	1960	
G-48-	Westland Aircraft Ltd (Bristol Division)	1960-1969	
G-49-	F.G.Miles Engineering	1965-1969	
G-50-	Alvis Ltd.	1967-1975	
G-51-	Britten-Norman Ltd	1967-	
G-52-	Marshall of Cambridge Ltd	1968-	
G-53-	NDN Aircraft	1977-	
G-54-	Cameron Balloons Ltd		
G-55-	W.Vinten Ltd		

G-56-	Edgley Aircraft Ltd.	
G-57-	Airship Industries	
G-58-	ARV Aviation	
G-59-	Mainair Sports	
G-60-	Flight Refuelling	
G-61-	Aviation Enterprises	
G-62-	Not known	
G-63-	Thunder & Colt Balloons	1994?-
G-64-	Not known	
G-65-	Not known	
G-66-	Not known	
G-67-	Atlantic Aerengineering	
G-68-	Medway Microlights	
G-69-	Cyclone Airsports	
G-70-	FLS	
G-71-	Flight Refuelling	
G-72-	Lindstrand Balloons	
G-73-	Not known	
G-74-	Not known	
G-75-	Chichester Miles	
G-76-	Police Aviation Services	
G-77-	Thruster Air Services	
G-78-	Bristow Helicopters	
G-79-	McAlpine Helicopters	
G-80-	Not known	
G-81-	Not known	
G-82-	Not known	
G-83-	Alan Mann Group	
G-84-	Not known	
G-85-	CFM	
G-86-	Advanced Technologies Group	

SECTION 8

PART 7 (i) -ICAO HISTORICAL AIRCRAFT NATIONALITY AND REGISTRATION MARKS

To help the discerning reader decipher the many and varied origins of UK & Irish registered aircraft, we have decided to include a list of foreign aircraft markings. Both lists are based on member Roger House's web-site and expanded with reference to Tony Pither's "Airline Fleets" and Ian Burnett's Overseas Registers section in "Air-Britain News". Any amendments will be welcomed.

Regn Prefix	Prev Prefix	Country	Period	Remarks
A-		Austria	1929-1939	Changed to OE-
AN-		Nicaragua	1936-	Changed to YN-
BR-		Burundi	1962-1965	Changed to 9U-
C-		Colombia	1929-1946	Changed to HK-
CB-		Bolivia	1929-1954	Changed to CP-
CCCP-		Soviet Union	1929-	Changed to RA-
CF-		Canada	1929-1974	Changed to C-
CH-		Switzerland	1929-1936	Changed to HB-
CR-A		Mozambique	1929-1975	Changed to C9-
CR-B		Mozambique	1971-1975	Changed to C9-
CR-C		Cape Verde Islands	1929-	Changed to D4-
CR-G		Portuguese Guinea /Guinea Bissau	1929-1975	Changed to J5-
CR-I		Portuguese India	1929-1961	Changed to VT-
CR-L		Angola	1929-1975	Changed to D2-
CR-S		Sao Tome and Principe	1929-	Changed to S9-
CR-T		Timor	1929-1975	Changed to PK-
CV-		Romania	1929-1936	Changed to YR-
CY-	VP-C	Ceylon	1948-1954	Changed to 4R-
CZ		Monaco	1929-1949	Changed to MC-
DDR-		East Germany	1945-1956	Changed to DM-
DM-		East Germany	1956-	Changed to D-
ES-		Estonia	1929-1939	Merged into Soviet Union CCCP-
EZ-		Saar Territory	1929-1933	Changed to SL-
FC-		Free French	1940-1944	Changed to F-
F-D		French Morocco	1929-1952	Changed to CN-
F-KH		Cambodia	1945-1954	Changed to XU-
F-L		Laos	1945-1954	Changed to XW-
F-O		Dahomey / Benin	1929-1960	Changed to TY-
F-O		Algeria	1929-1962	Changed to 7T-
F-O		Upper Volta	1929-1960	Changed to XT-
F-O		Ubangi-Shari	1929-1960	Changed to TL-
F-O		Tunisia	1929-1956	Changed to TS-
F-O		Cameroon	1929-1960	Changed to TJ-
F-O		Chad	1929-1960	Changed to TT-
F-O		Senegal	1929-1960	Changed to 6V-
F-O		Congo	1929-1960	Changed to TN-
F-O		Mauritania	1929-1960	Changed to 5T-
F-O		Gabon	1929-1960	Changed to TR-
F-O		Guinea	1929-1958	Changed to 3X-
F-O		Ivory Coast	1929-1960	Changed to TU-
F-O		Madagascar	1929-1960	Changed to 5R-
F-O		Niger	1929-1960	Changed to 5U-
F-O		Mali	1929-1960	Changed to TZ-
F-VN		French Indochina (Vietnam)	1929-1954	Changed to XV-
J		Japan	1929-1945	
JZ-		Dutch East Indies	1945-	
K-		Kuwait	1967-1968	Interim - Changed to 9K-
KA-		Katanga	1961-1963	Unofficial - Changed to 9O-
KW-		Cambodia	1954	Changed to XU-
LG-		Guatemala	1936-1948	Changed to TG
LI-		Liberia	1929-1952	Changed to EL-
LR-		Lebanon	1944-1954	Changed to OD-
LY-		Lithuania	1929-1939	Merged into Soviet Union CCCP-
M-		Spain	1929-1933	Changed to EC-
MC-		Monaco	1949-1959	Changed to 3A-
OA-		Peru	1929-1950	Changed to OB-
OO-C		Belgian Congo	1929-1960	Changed to 9O-
PI-		Philippines	1941-1975	Changed to RP-
R-		Argentina (thre digits)	1929-1932	Changed to LV-
R-		Panama (two digits)	1929-1943	Changed to RX-
RV-		Persia (Iran)	1929-1944	Changed to EP-

RX-		Panama	1943-1952	Changed to HP-
RY-		Lithuania	1929-1939	Merged into Soviet Union CCCP-
SL-	EZ-	Saar Territory	1947-1959	Changed to D-
SN-		Sudan	1929-1959	Changed to ST-
TJ-		Transjordan	1946-1954	Changed to JY-
TS-		Saar Territory	1930-1931	Unofficial - Changed to EZ-
UH-		Saudi Arabia	1945	Interim - Changed to HZ-
UL-		Luxembourg	1929-1939	Changed to LX-
UN-		Yugoslavia	1929-1935	Changed to YU-
VO-		Newfoundland	1929-1939	Merged into Canada CF-
VP-A		Gold Coast (Ghana)	1929-1957	Changed to 9G-
VP-B		Bahamas	1929-1975	Changed to C6-
VP-C		Ceylon	1929-1948	Changed to CY-
VP-G		British Guiana	1929-1967	Changed to 8R-
VP-H		British Honduras (Belize)	1947-	Changed to V3-
VP-J		Jamaica	1930-1964	Changed to 6Y-
VP-K		Kenya	1929-1963	Changed to 5Y-
VP-L		Leeward and Windward Islands	1929-	Now Antigua V2-
VP-LKA-LLZ		St. Kitts and Nevis		Changed to V4-
VP-M		Malta	1929-1968	Changed to 9H-
VP-N		Nyasaland	1929-1953	Changed to VP-Y
VP-P		Western Pacific Islands	1929-	Now Solomon Islands H4-
VP-R		Northern Rhodesia	1929-1953	Changed to VP-Y
VP-S		Somaliland	1929-1960	Changes to 6OS-
VP-T		Trinidad and Tobago	1931-1965	Changed to 9Y-
VP-U		Uganda	1929-1962	Changed to 5X-
VP-V		St. Vincent and Grenadines	1959-	Changed to J8-
VP-W		Rhodesia	1971-	Changed to Z-
VP-W		China (Wei-Hai-Wei)	1929-1939	
VP-X		Gambia	1929-1945	
VP-Y		Southern Rhodesia, Rhodesia & Nyasaland	1929-1964	Changed to 7Q-, 9J-
VP-Z		Zanzibar	1929-1964	Changed to 5H-
VQ-B		Barbados	1952-1968	Changed to 8P-
VQ-C		Cyprus	1952-1960	Changed to 5B-
VQ-F		Fiji/Tonga/Friendly Isles	1929-1971	Changed to DQ-
VQ-G		Grenada	1962-	Changed to J3-
VQ-L		St. Lucia	1965-	Changed to VQ-L
VQ-M		Mauritius	1929-1968	Changed to 3B-
VQ-P		Palestine	1930-1948	Changed to either TJ- or 4X-
VQ-S		Seychelles	1929-1977	Changed to S7-
VQ-ZA, -ZD		Basutoland	1929-1967	Changed to 7P-
VQ-ZE, -ZH		Bechuanaland	1929-1968	Changed to A2-
VQ-ZI		Swaziland	1929-1975	Changed to 3D-
VR-A		Aden	1939	
VR-B		Bermuda	1931-	Changed to VP-B
VR-C		Cayman Islands	1968-	Changed to VP-C
VR-G		Gibraltar	1929-1939	Changed to G-
VR-H		Hong Kong	1929-	Changed to B-H
VR-J		Johore	1929-1963	Changed to 9M-
VR-L		Sierra Leone	1929-1961	Changed to 9L-
VR-N		British Cameroons	1929-1958	Changed to either TJ- or 5N-
VR-O		Sabah (North Borneo)	1929-1963	Changed to 9M-
VR-R		Malaya	1929-1963	Changed to 9M-
VR-S		Singapore	1929-1965	Changed to 9V-
VR-U		Brunei	1929-	Changed to V8-
VR-W		Sarawak	1929-	
XH-		Honduras	1929-1960	Changed to HR-
XT-		China	1929-1949	
XV-	3W-	South Vietnam	1959-1975	
XW-		Laos	1954-	Changed to RDPL-
YE-		Yemen	1955-1969	Changed to 4W-
YL-		Latvia	1929-1939	Merged in Soviet Union CCCP-
YM-		Danzig Free State	1929-1939	Changed to D-
YN-		Nicaragua	1929-1936	Changed to AN-
ZM-		New Zealand	1929-1939	
3W-		Vietnam	1954-1959	Interim - Changed to XV-
4W-		Yemen	1969-	Merged into 7O-
6OS-		Somalia	1960-1969	Changed to 6O-
9O-		Zaire	1960-1966	Changed to 9Q-

SECTION 8

PART 7 (ii) - ICAO CURRENT AIRCRAFT NATIONALITY AND REGISTRATION MARKS

Regn Prefix	Prev Prefix	Country	Period	Remarks
AP-		Pakistan	1947-	
A2-	VQ-ZE, -ZH	Botswana	1972-	
A3-		Tonga		
A40-		Oman	1974-	
A5-		Bhutan		
A6-		United Arab Emirates	1977-	
A7-		Qatar	1975-	
A9C-		Bahrain	1977-	
B-	XT-	China, Republic of	1975-	
B-		Taiwan	1949-	
B-H	VR-H	Hong Kong, China		
C-	CF-	Canada	1974-	
CC-		Chile	1929-	
CN-		Morocco	1952-	
CP-	CB-	Bolivia	1954-	
CS-	CR-	Portugal	1929-	
CU-		Cuba	1945-	
CX		Christmas Islands		
CX-		Uruguay	1929-	
C2-		Nauru	1971-	
C3-		Andorra		
C5-	VP-X	The Gambia	1978-	
C6-	VP-B	Bahamas	1975-	
C9-	CR-A, CR-B	Mozambique	1975-	
D-	DM-, DDR-	Germany	1929-	
D2-	CR-L	Angola	1975-	
D4-	CR-C	Cape Verde Islands		
D6-		Comoro Islands	1977-	
DQ-	VQ-F	Fiji	1971-	
EC-	M	Spain	1929	
EI-		Ireland	1929	Also EJ- but not used
EK-	CCCP-	Armenia		
EL-	LI-	Liberia	1952-	
EP-	RV-	Iran	1944-	
ER-	CCCP-	Moldova, Republic of		
ES-	CCCP-	Estonia		
ET-		Ethiopia	1929-	
EW-	CCCP-	Belarus		
EX-	CCCP-	Kyrgyzstan		
EY-	CCCP-	Tajikistan		
EZ-	CCCP-	Turkmenistan		
E3-		Eritrea		
F-		France	1929-	
F-O		Frech Overseas Territories		
G-		United Kingdom	1929-	
GL-		Greenland		
HA-		Hungary	1935-	
HB-	CH-	Switzerland	1935-	
HC-		Ecuador	1929-	
HH-		Haiti	1929-	
HI-		Dominican Republic	1929-	
HK-	C-	Colombia	1946-	
HL		Korea, Republic of	1948-	
HP-	RX-	Panama	1952-	
HR-	XH-	Honduras	1961-	
HS-		Thailand	1929-	
HV-		Vatican City		
HZ-	UH-	Saudi Arabia	1945-	
H4-	VP-P	Solomon Islands		
I-		Italy	1929-	
JA	J	Japan	1948-	
JU-	MT	Mongolia		
JY-		Jordan	1954-	
J2-		Djibouti		
J3-	VQ-G	Grenada		
J5-	CR-G	Guinea Bissau		

J5-	CR-G	Guinea Bissau	
J6-	VQ-L	St. Lucia	
J7-		Dominica	
J8-	VP-V	St. Vincent and Grenadines	
LN-		Norway	1931-
LQ-		Argentina (Government)	1932-
LV-	R-	Argentina	1932-
LX-	UL-	Luxembourg	1946-
LY-		Lithuania	
LZ-		Bulgaria	1929-
N	NC,NL,NR,NS,NX	United States of America	1929-
OB-	OA-	Peru	1950-
OD-	LR-	Lebanon	1954-
OE-	A-	Austria	1945-
OH-		Finland	1931-
OK-		Czech Republic	1929-
OM-	OK-	Slovakia	
OO-		Belgium	1929-
OY-		Denmark	1929-
P-		Korea, Democratic Peoples Rep.of	
PJ-		Netherlands Antilles	1945-
PK-		Indonesia	1929-
PP-		Brazil	1932-
PR-		Brazil	
PT-		Brazil	1950-
PZ-		Suriname	1929-
P2-		Papua New Guinea	1974-
P4-		Aruba	
RA-	CCCP-	Russian Federation	
RDPL-	F-L, XW-	Laos	1975-
RP-	PI-	Philippines	1975-
SE-		Sweden	1929-
SP-		Poland	1929-
ST-	SN-	Sudan	1959-
SU-		Egypt	1931-
SX-		Greece	1929-
S2-		Bangladesh	1972-
S3-		Bangladesh	1976
S5-	SL-	Slovenia	
S7-	VQ-S	Seychelles	1977-
S9-	CR-S	Sao Tome Island	
TC-		Turkey	1929-
TF-		Iceland	1937-
TG-	LG-	Guatemala	1948-
TI-		Costa Rica	1931-
TJ-	F-O, VR-N	Cameroon	1960-
TL-	F-O	Central African Republic	1960-
TN-	F-O	Congo Brazzaville	1960-
TR-	F-O	Gabon	1960-
TS-	F-O	Tunisia	1956-
TT-	F-O	Chad	1960-
TU-	F-O	Ivory Coast	1960-
TY-	F-O	Benin	1960-
TZ-	F-O	Mali	1960-
T3-		Kiribati	
T7-		San Marino	
T9-	YU-	Bosnia Herzegovina	
UK-	CCCP-	Uzbekistan	
UN-	CCCP-	Kazakstan	
UR-	CCCP-	Ukraine	
V8-	VR-U	Brunei	
VH-		Australia	1929-
VN-	XV-	Vietnam	
VP-A		Anguilla	
VP-B	VR-B	Bermuda	
VP-C	VR-C	Cayman Islands	
VP-F		Falkland Islands	1929-
VP-L-		British Virgin Islands	1971-
VQ-H		St. Helena	1929-
VQ-T		Turks & Caicos Islands	
VT-		India	1930-
V2-	VP-L	Antigua	
V3-	VP-H	Belize	
V4-	VP-LKA-LLZ	St.Kitts & Nevis	

V6-		Micronesia		
V7-		Marshall Islands		
XA-		Mexico	1929-	Commercial
XB-		Mexico	1929-	Private
XC-		Mexico	1929-	Government
XT-	F-O	Burkina Faso		
XU-	F-KH, KW-	Kampuchea	1954-	
XY-		Myanmar	1948-	
XZ-		Myanmar		
YA-		Afghanistan	1929-	
YI-		Iraq	1931-	
YJ-		Vanuatu	1929-	
YK-		Syria	1952-	
YL-		Latvia		
YN-	AN-	Nicaragua		
YR-	CV-	Romania	1936-	
YS-		El Salvador	1939-	
YU-	UN-	Yugoslavia (Serbia & Montenegro)	1935-	
YV-		Venezuela	1931-	
Z-	VP-W, VP-Y	Zimbabwe		
Z3-		Macedonia		
ZA-		Albania	1946-	
ZK-		New Zealand	1929-	
ZL-		New Zealand		
ZP-		Paraguay	1929-	
ZS-		South Africa	1929-	
ZT-		South Africa		
ZU-		South Africa		
3A-	CZ, MC	Monaco	1959-	
3B-	VQ-M	Mauritius	1968-	
3C-	VQ-ZI	Equatorial Guinea	1975-	
3D-		Swaziland	1975-	
3X-	F-O	Guinea	1958-	
4K-		Azerbaijan		
4L-		Georgia		
4R-	VP-C, CY-	Sri Lanka	1954-	
4X-		Israel	1948	
5A-		Libya	1951-	
5B-	VQ-C	Cyprus	1960-	
5H-	VP-Z	Tanzania	1964-	
5N-	VR-N	Nigeria	1961-	
5R-	F-O	Malagasy Republic	1960-	
5T-	F-O	Mauritania	1960-	
5U-	F-O	Niger	1960-	
5V-		Togo	1976-	
5W-		Samoa	1962-	
5X-	VP-U	Uganda	1962-	
5Y-	VP-K	Kenya	1963-	
6O-	6OS-	Somalia	1969-	
6V-	F-O	Senegal	1960-	
6W-		Senegal		
6Y-	VP-J	Jamaica	1964-	
7O-	YE-, 4W-	Yemen	1974-	
7P-	VQ-ZA, -ZD	Lesotho	1967-	
7Q-	VP-Y	Malawi	1964-	
7T-	F-O	Algeria	1962-	
8P-	VQ-B	Barbados	1968-	
8Q-		Maldives	1976-	
8R-	VP-G	Guyana	1967-	
9A-	RC-	Croatia		
9G-	VP-A	Ghana	1957-	
9H-	VP-M	Malta	1968-	
9J-	VP-Y	Zambia	1964-	
9K-	K-	Kuwait	1961-	
9L-	VR-L	Sierra Leone	1961	
9M-	VR-J, VR-O, VR-R	Malaysia	1963-	
9N-		Nepal	1961-	
9Q-	9O-	Democratic Republic of Congo	1966-	Formerly Zaire
9U-	BR-	Burundi	1962-	
9V-	VR-S	Singapore	1970-	
9XR-		Rwanda	1962	
9Y-	VP-T	Trinidad and Tobago	1965-	

NOTES

NOTES

NOTES

NOTES

AIR-BRITAIN SALES

Companion publications to this UNITED KINGDOM & IRELAND CIVIL AIRCRAFT REGISTERS 2002 are also available by post-free mail order from

Air-Britain Sales Department (Dept WMTF02)
41 Penshurst Road, Leigh,
Tonbridge, Kent TN11 8HL

For a full list of current titles and details of how to order, visit our e-commerce site at www.air-britain.com
Visa / Mastercard / Delta / Switch accepted - please give full details of card number and expiry date.

ANNUAL PUBLICATIONS - AVAILABLE EARLY 2002:

UK & IRELAND QUICK REFERENCE 2002 £6.00 (Members) £6.95 (Non-members)
New, basic easy-to-carry registration and type listing, UK-based foreign aircraft, current military serials and base index. A5 size.
Buy this together with Airline Fleets Quick Reference for special price: £10.00 (Members) £12.00 (Non-members)

AIRLINE FLEETS 2002 £18.00 (Members) £22.50 (Non-members)
Almost 3000 fleets listed by country plus numerous appendices including airliners in non-airline service, IATA and ICAO airline and base codes, operator index, short-lived airlines, etc. Over 750 pages A5 size hardback.

AIRLINE FLEETS QUICK REFERENCE 2002 £6.00 (Members) £6.95 (Non-members)
New pocket guide now expanded to airliners of over 19 seats of major operators likely to be seen worldwide; regn, type, c/n, fleet nos.
Buy BOTH the above Airline Fleets titles together for considerable saving: £23.00 (Members) £28.50 (Non-members)

EUROPEAN REGISTERS HANDBOOK 2002 £20.00 (Members) £25.00 (Non-members)
Current civil registers of 36 European countries, all powered aircraft, balloons, gliders, microlights. Full previous identities and many extra permit and reservation details. Now in new A4 softback format.

BUSINESS JETS INTERNATIONAL 2002 Hardback: £15.00 (Members) £18.50 (Non-members)
Complete production lists of all purpose-built business jets with 48,000+ entry registration and c/n cross-reference. Approx 400 pages. *Also available in softback:* £14.00 (Members) £17.50 (Non-members)

OTHER PUBLICATIONS AVAILABLE NOW:

JET AIRLINERS OF THE WORLD 1949-2001 £16.00 (Members) £20.00 (Non-members)
Detailed production lists of over 70 jet airliner types with expanded coverage of Russian-built types and purely military jet transports. Full cross-reference index containing over 56,000 registrations and serials.

BUSINESS TURBOPROPS INTERNATIONAL 2000 £15.00 (Members) £19.00 (Non-members)
Complete production lists of over 75 types including all B-N Islanders, with 42,000+ cross-reference index. 360 pages, hardback.

TURBOPROP AIRLINERS AND MILITARY TRANSPORTS OF THE WORLD 1948-2000
£16.00 (Members) £20.00 (Non-members) 528 pages
Detailed production lists of 112 turboprop airliner types including Eastern European and military transports with full cross-reference master index containing over 47,000 entries.

And don't forget the 'Big Book': **BRITISH CIVIL AIRCRAFT REGISTERS 1919-1999**
£30.00 (Members) £37.50 (Non-members) 912 pages A4 hardback, listing all known UK and Commonwealth G-registrations and EI- registrations with c/ns, dates, identities and fates. Invaluable reference guide.

Air-Britain also publishes a comprehensive range of military titles, please check for latest details of RAF Serial Registers, detailed RAF aircraft type "Files", Squadron Histories and Royal Navy Aircraft Histories.

IMPORTANT NOTE - Members receive substantial discounts on prices of all the above Air-Britain publications. For details of membership - see page 660 or visit our website at http://www.air-britain.com

AIR-BRITAIN MEMBERSHIP

If you are not currently a member of Air-Britain, the publishers of this book, you may be interested in what we have on offer to provide for your interest in aviation.

About Air-Britain

Formed over 50 years ago, we are the world's most progressive aviation society, and exist to bring together aviation enthusiasts with every type of interest. Our members include aircraft historians, aviation writers, spotters and pilots – and those who just have a fascination with aircraft and aviation. Air-Britain is a non-profit organisation, which is independently audited, and any financial surpluses are used to provide services to the ever-growing membership. In each of the last 7 or more years, our membership has increased annually, and our current membership now stands at over 4,000.

Membership of Air-Britain

Membership is open to all. A basic membership fee is charged and every member receives a copy of the quarterly house magazine, Air-Britain Digest, and is entitled to use all the Air-Britain specialist services and buy Air-Britain publications at discounted prices. A membership subscription includes the choice to add any or all of our other 3 magazines, News &/or Archive &/or Aeromilitaria. Air-Britain publishes 15-20 books per annum (around 70 titles in stock at any one time).

Air-Britain Digest is the quarterly 40-page house magazine containing not only news of Air-Britain activities, but also a wealth of features, often illustrated in colour, on many different aviation subjects, contemporary and historical, contributed by our 4,000 members.

Air-Britain News is the world aviation news monthly, containing data on aircraft registrations worldwide, and news of Airlines, Business Jets, Air Shows and Military Intelligence. 160 pages of lavishly–illustrated information for the dedicated enthusiast

Air-Britain Archive is the quarterly 36-page specialist journal of civil aviation history. Packed with the results of historical research by Air-Britain specialists into aircraft types, overseas registers and previously unpublished photographs and facts about the rich past of civil aircraft.

Air-Britain Aeromilitaria is the unique source for meticulously researched details of military aviation history edited by the acclaimed authors of Air-Britain's military monographs. Quarterly, illustrated in colour and black & white.

Other Benefits

Additional to the above, members have access to the Air-Britain e-mail Information Exchange Service (ab-ix) where members can exchange information, or ask others for information they may have at their fingertips; access to Branches and the Specialists' Information Service; Air-Britain trips; slide and photograph sales libraries. During the summer we also host our own popular FLY-IN. Each autumn, we host an aircraft recognition contest.

Membership Subscription Rates – from £10 per annum.

Membership subscription rates start from as little as £10 per annum, and this amount provides a copy of 'Digest' quarterly as well as all the other benefits covered above. Subscriptions to include any or all of our other three magazines vary between £18 and £48 per annum (slightly higher to overseas).

Join on-line at www.air-britain.co.uk.
or, write to 'Air-Britain' at 1 Rose Cottages, 179 Penn Road, Hazlemere, High Wycombe, Bucks HP15 7NE, UK, or telephone/fax on 01394 450767 (+44 1394 450767) and ask for a membership pack containing the full details of subscription rates, samples of our magazines and a book list.